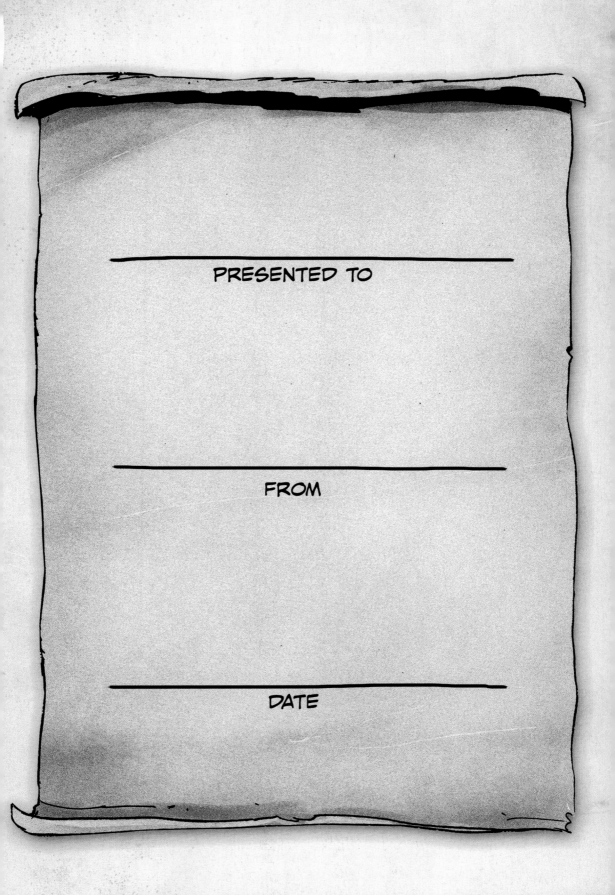

PRESENTED TO

FROM

DATE

THE ACTION BIBLE

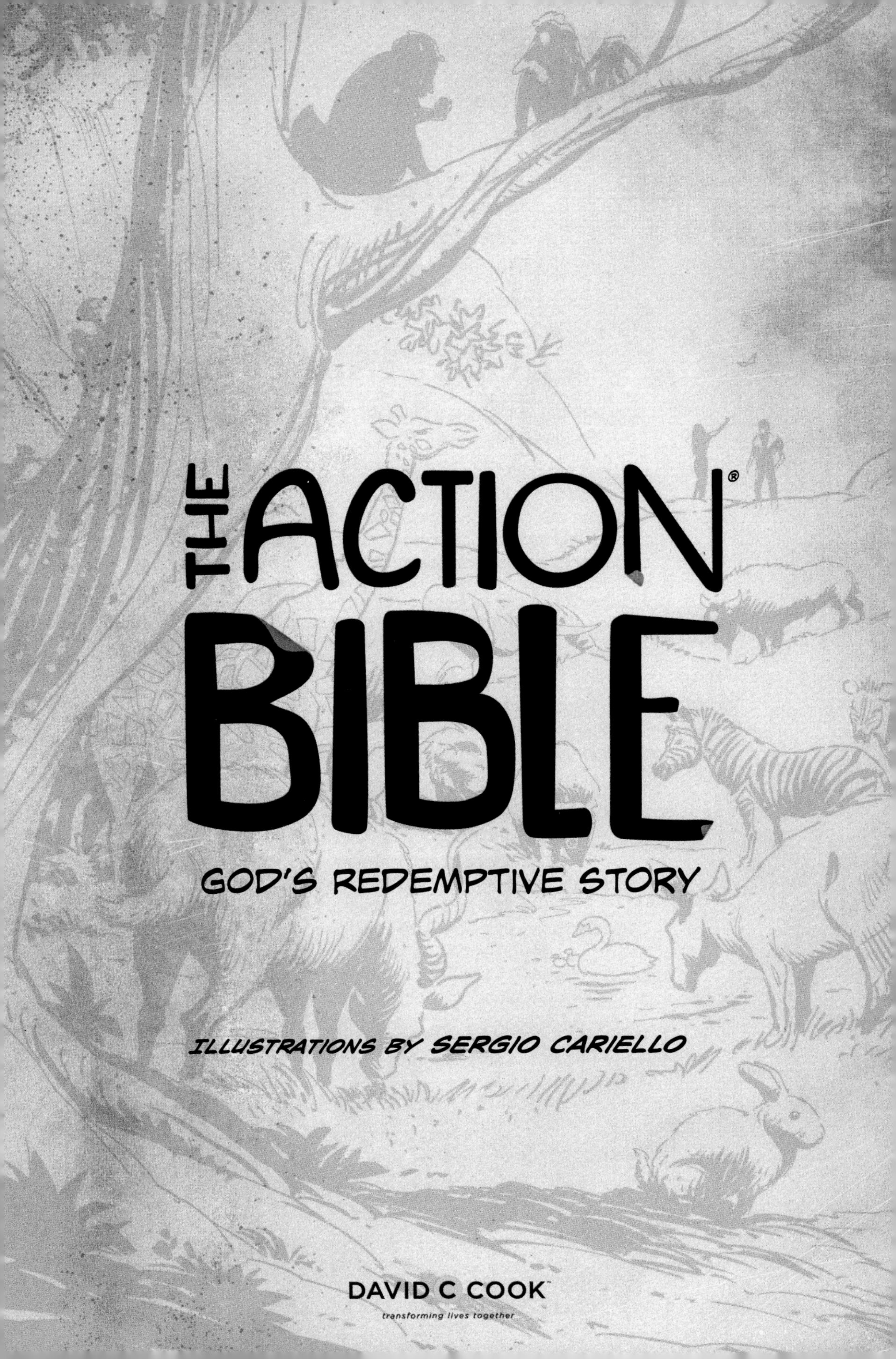

THE ACTION® BIBLE

GOD'S REDEMPTIVE STORY

ILLUSTRATIONS BY SERGIO CARIELLO

DAVID C COOK™
transforming lives together

THE ACTION BIBLE®
Published by David C Cook
4050 Lee Vance Drive
Colorado Springs, CO 80918 U.S.A.

Integrity Music Limited, a Division of David C Cook
Brighton, East Sussex BN1 2RE, England

The graphic circle C logo is a registered trademark of David C Cook.

Library of Congress Control Number 2020933834
ISBN 978-0-8307-7744-0
eISBN 978-0-8307-7745-7

The Team: Amy Konyndyk, Stephanie Bennett,
Judy Gillispie, James Hershberger, and Susan Murdock.
General Editor: Doug Mauss
Art Director: Kevin Mullins
Bible Editors: Shawn Yost, MDiv; Ed Stucky, MDiv
Cover Design: James Hershberger
Letterers: Sergio Cariello, Dave Lanphear, Dave Rothe
Colorists: Patrick Gama, and
Wellington Marçal, Priscila Ribeiro, Fabrício Sampaio Guerra,
MaxFlan Araujo, Alex Guim of Impacto Studio

Printed in the United States
First Edition 2020

2 3 4 5 6 7 8 9 10 11

110620

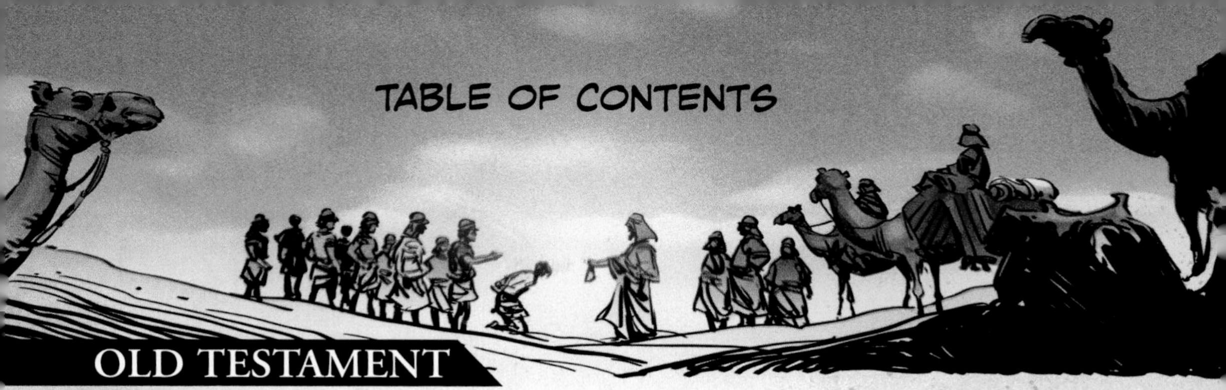

TABLE OF CONTENTS

OLD TESTAMENT

CREATION

FATHERS OF THE FAITH

THE LIFE OF JOSEPH

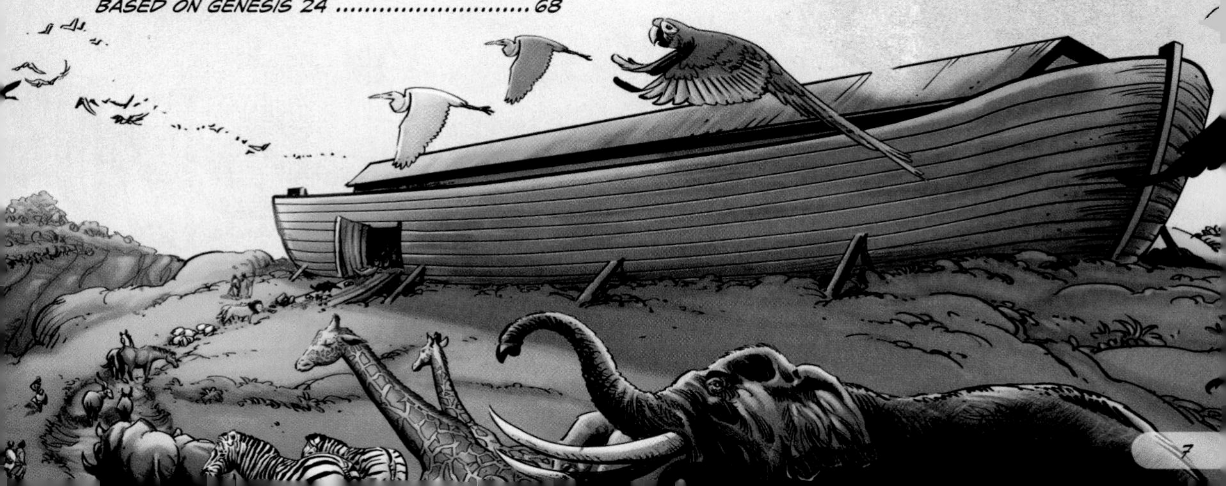

MOSES

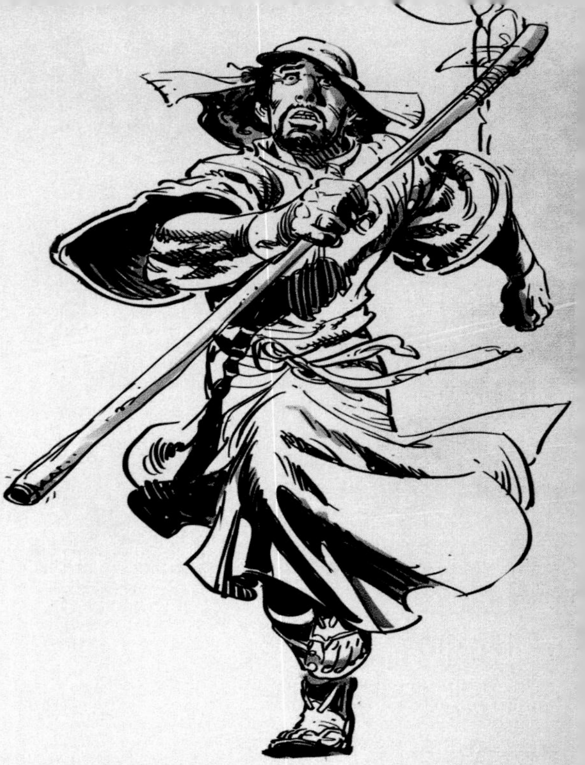

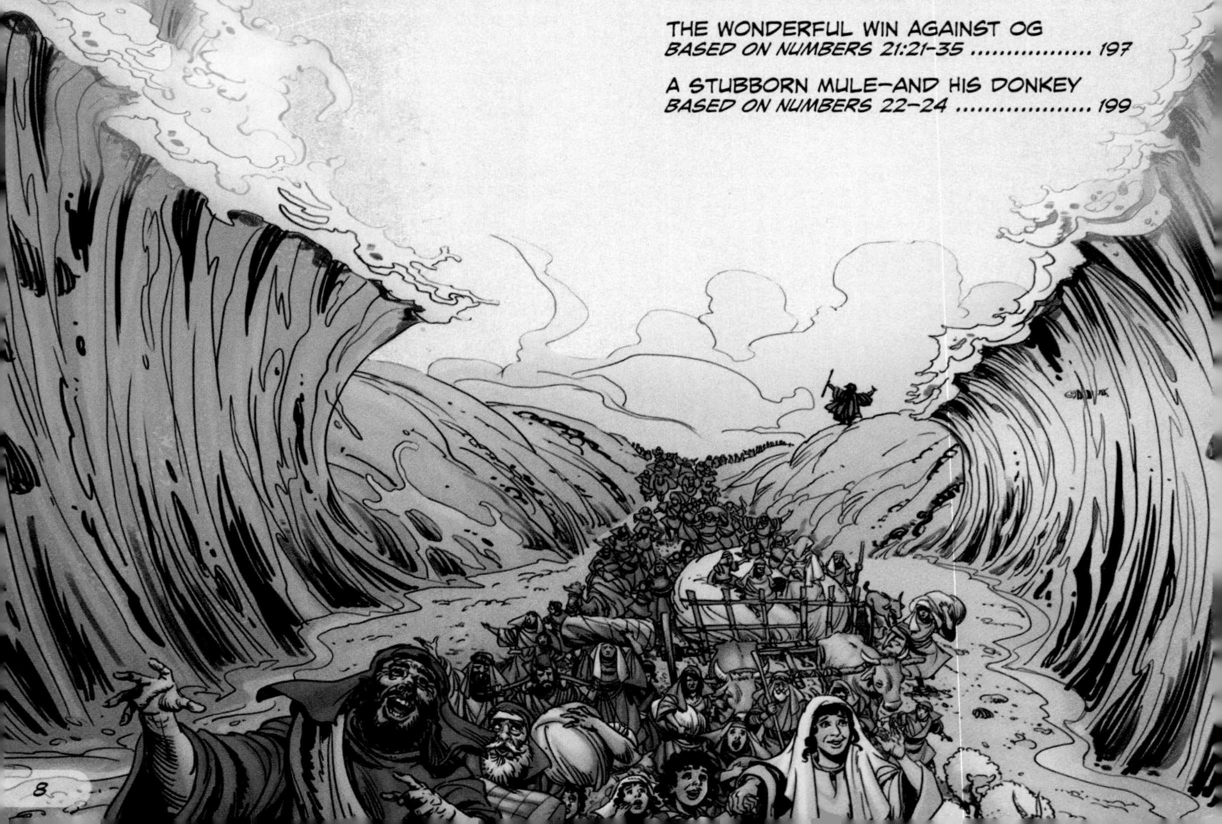

JOSHUA

GOD'S JUDGES

THE KINGS

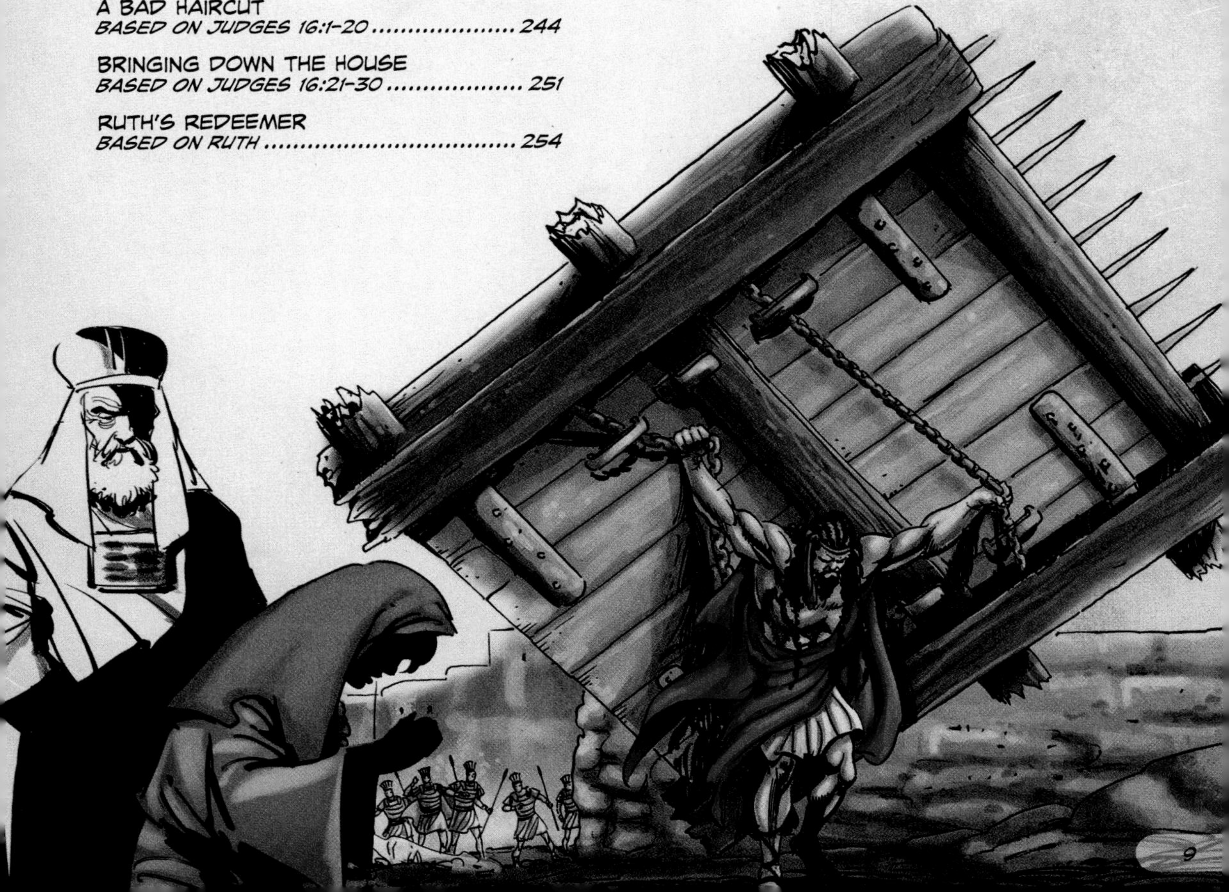

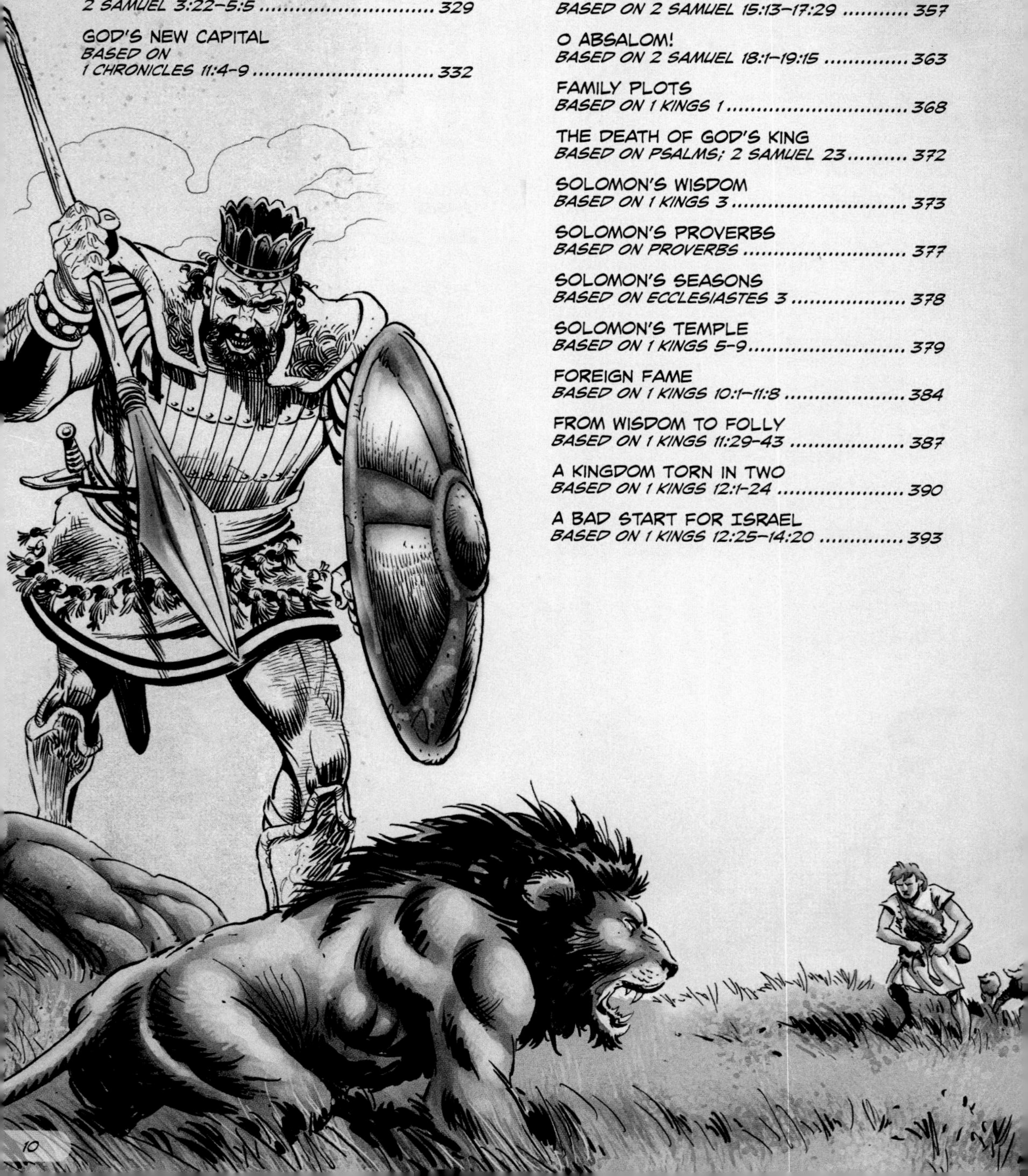

THE PROPHETS

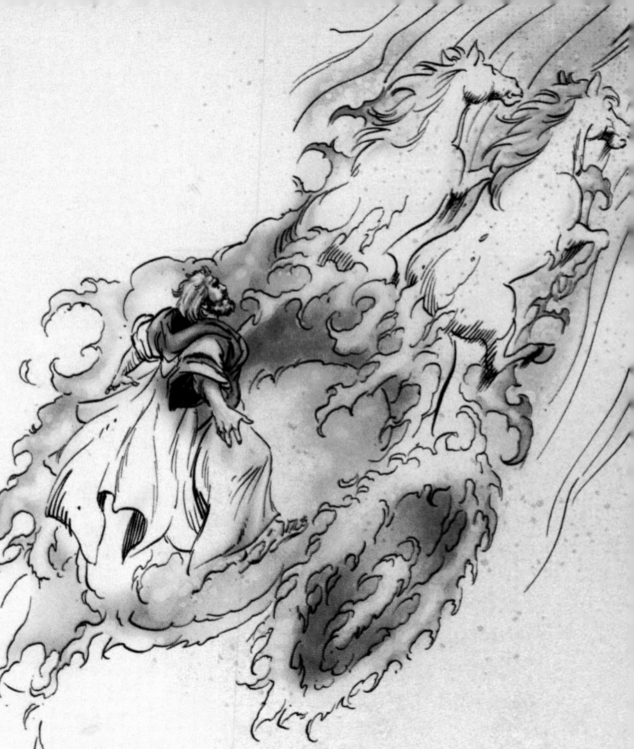

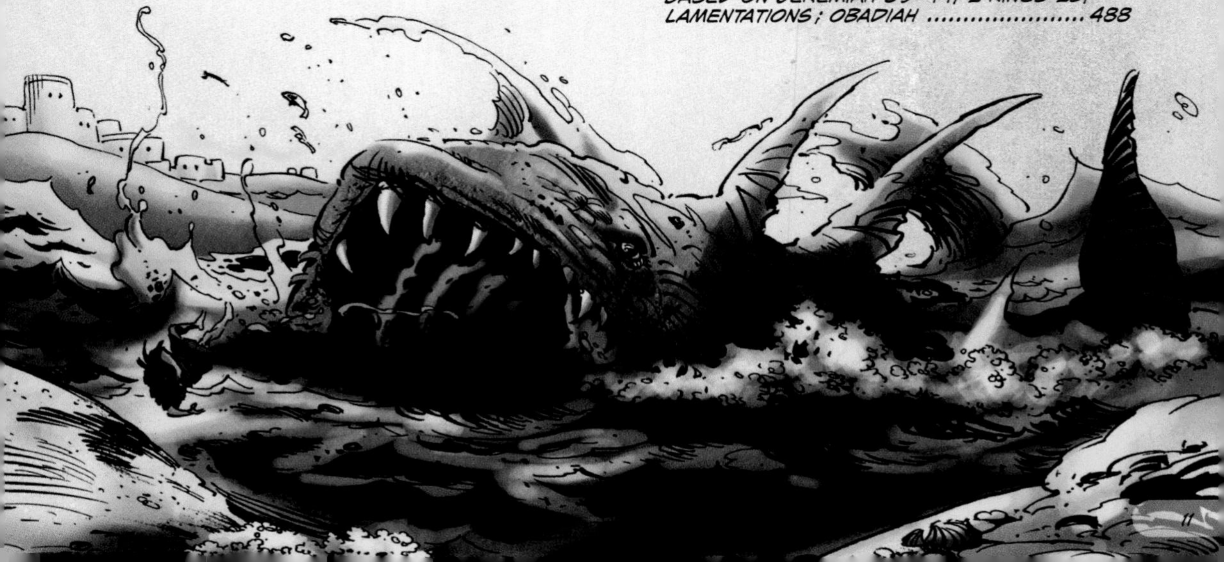

THE EXILES

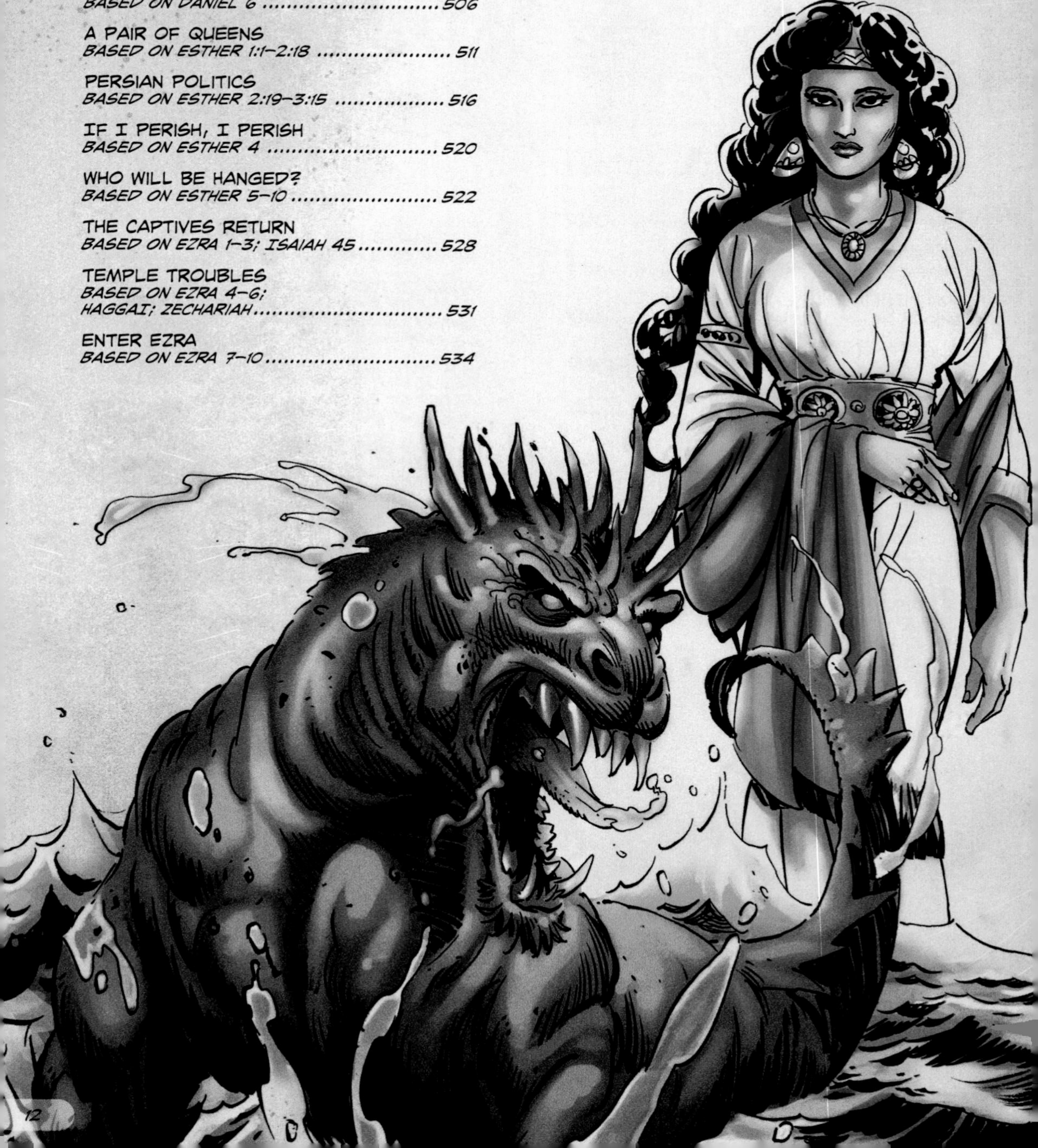

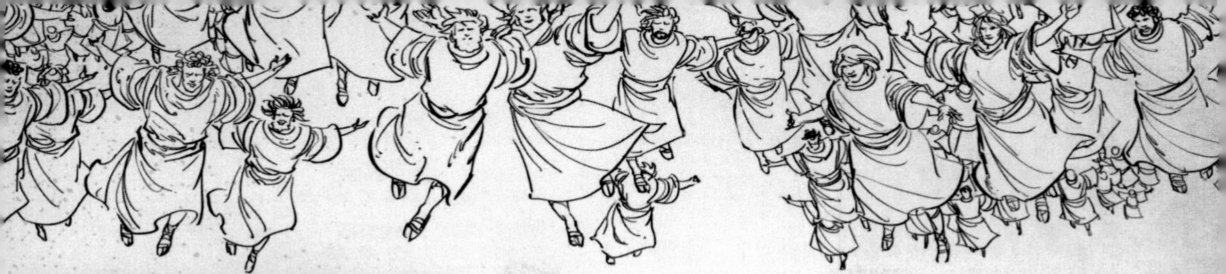

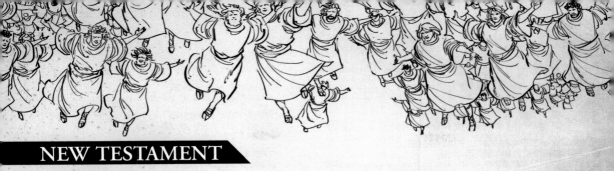

NEW TESTAMENT

JESUS' BIRTH AND MINISTRY

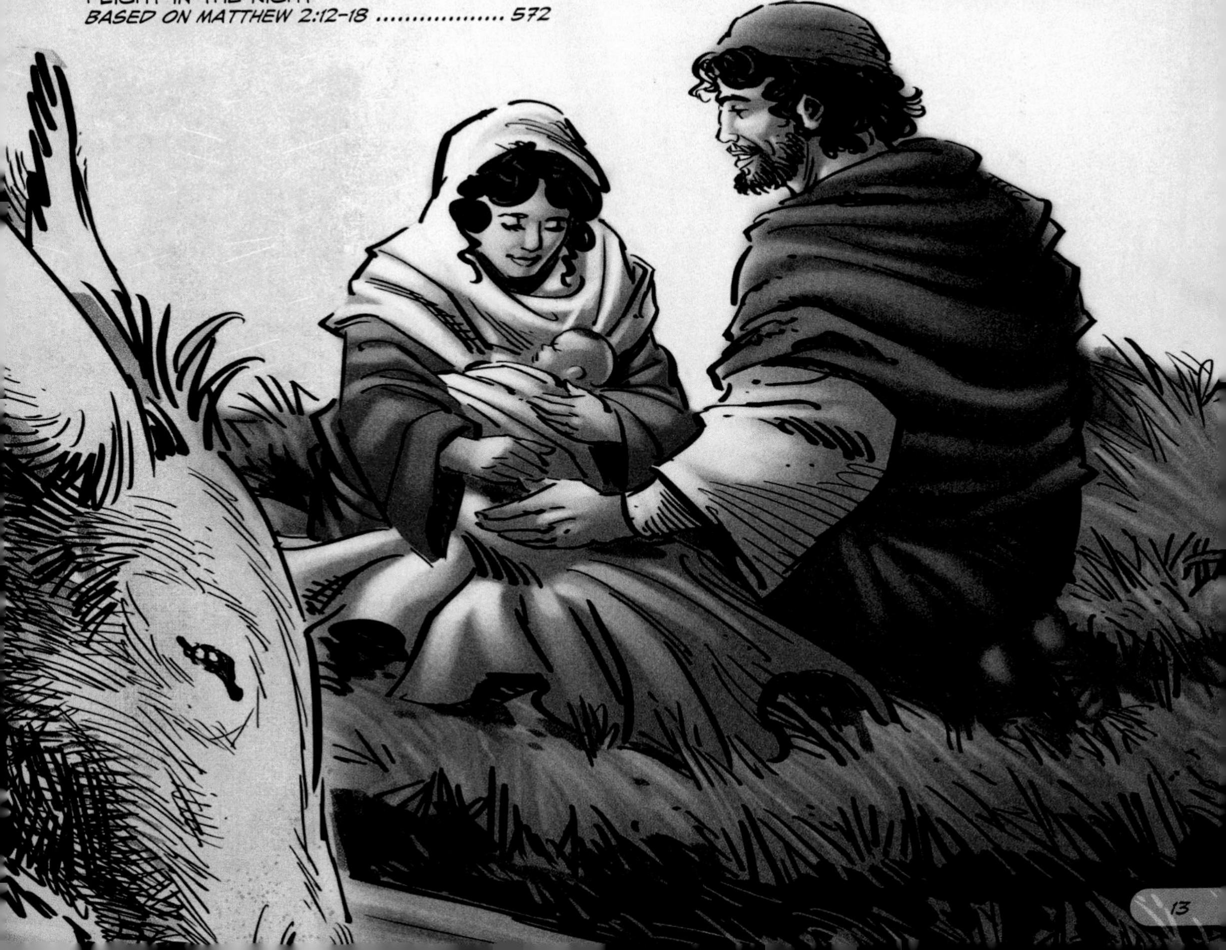

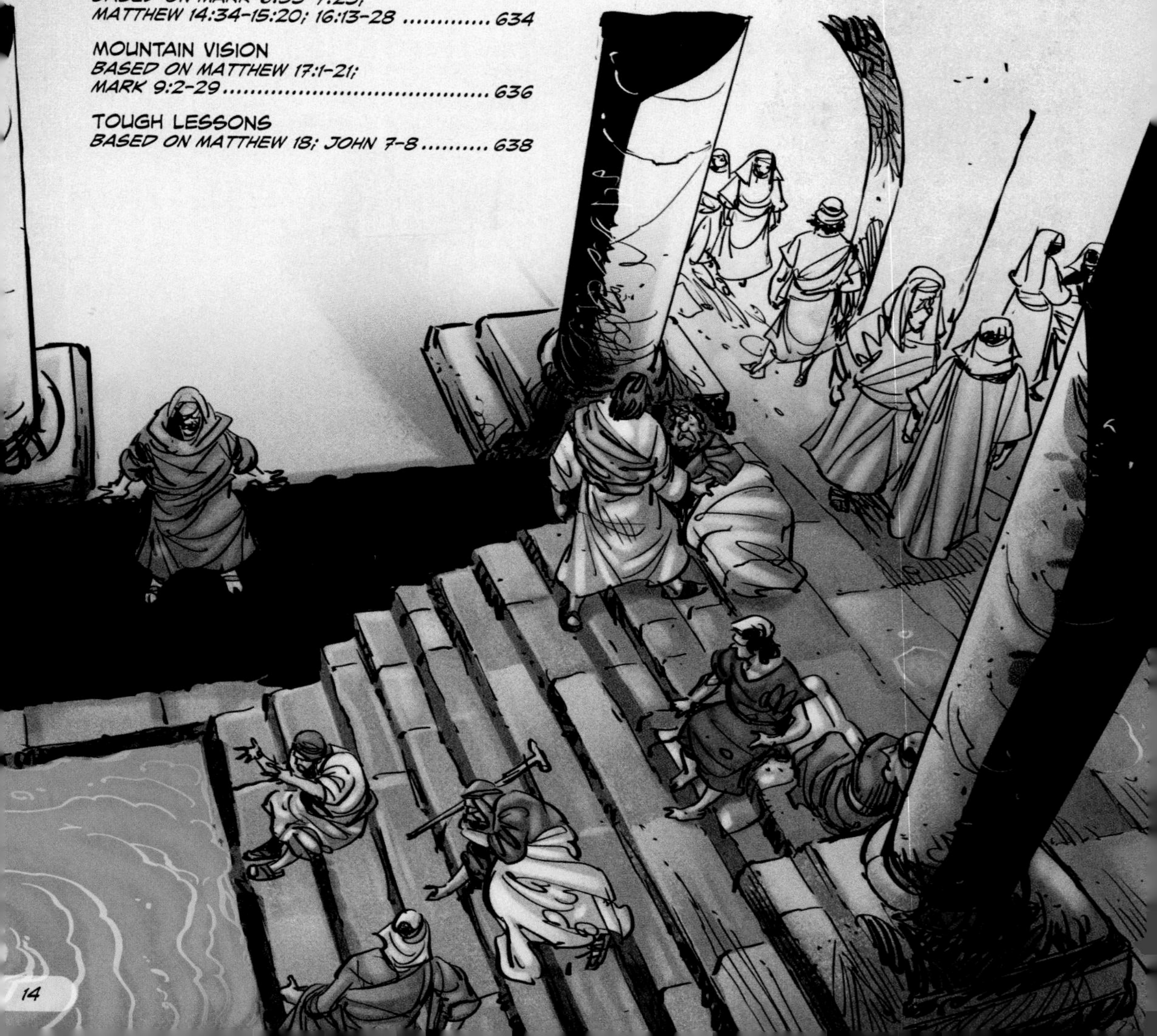

JESUS' FINAL DAYS

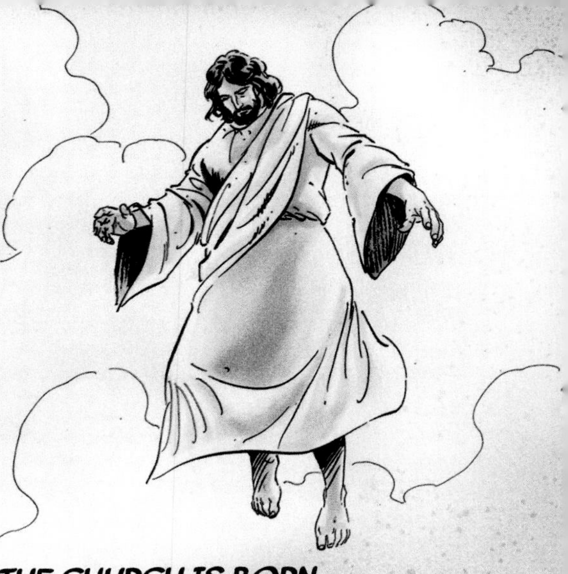

THE CHURCH IS BORN

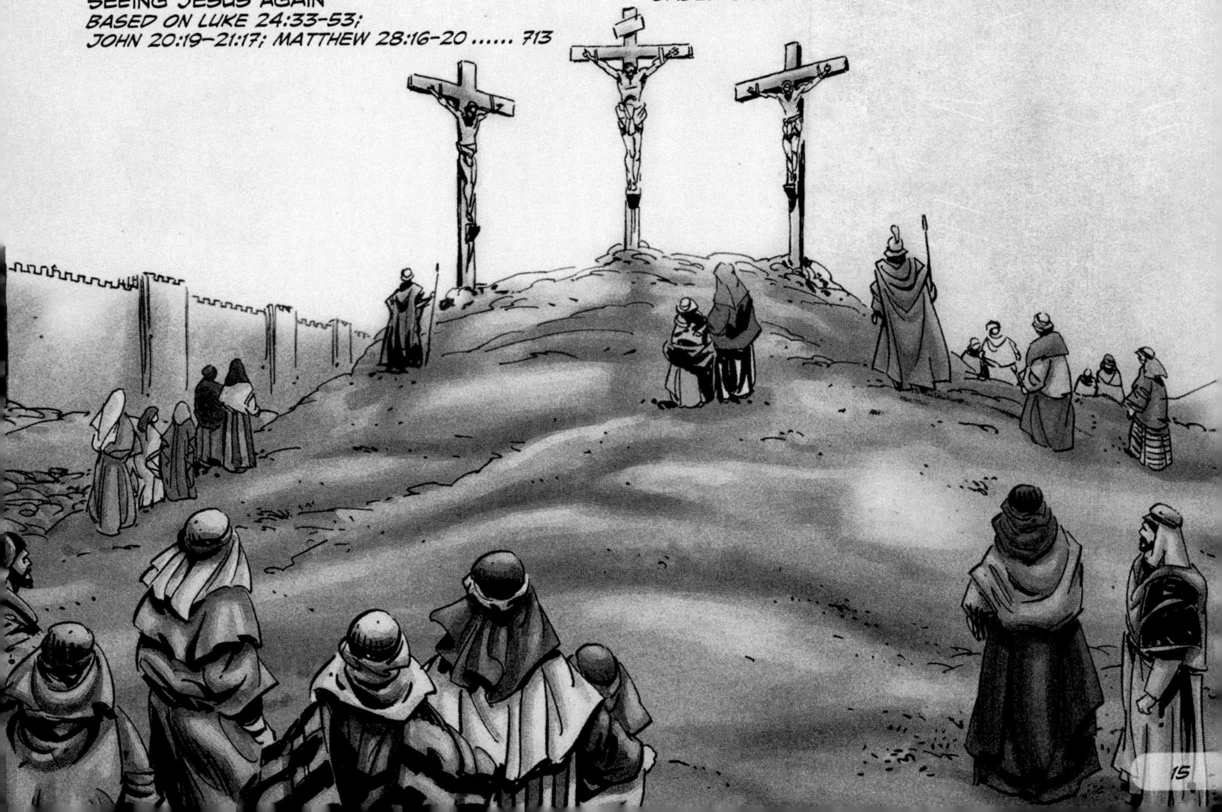

WORDS TO THE CHURCH

BIBLE BOOK INDEX

In the Beginning ...

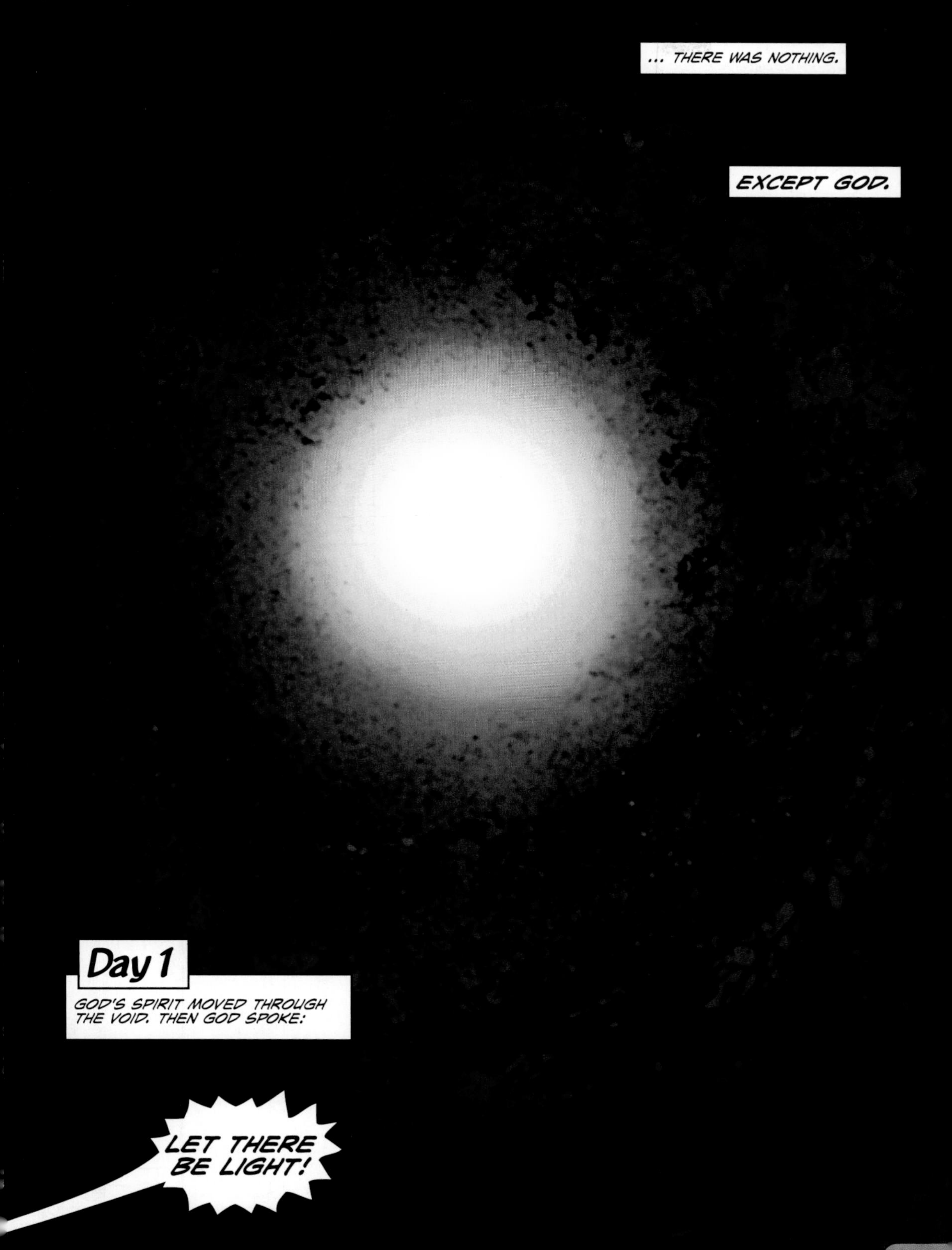

... THERE WAS NOTHING.
EXCEPT GOD.
Day 1
GOD'S SPIRIT MOVED THROUGH THE VOID. THEN GOD SPOKE:
LET THERE BE LIGHT!

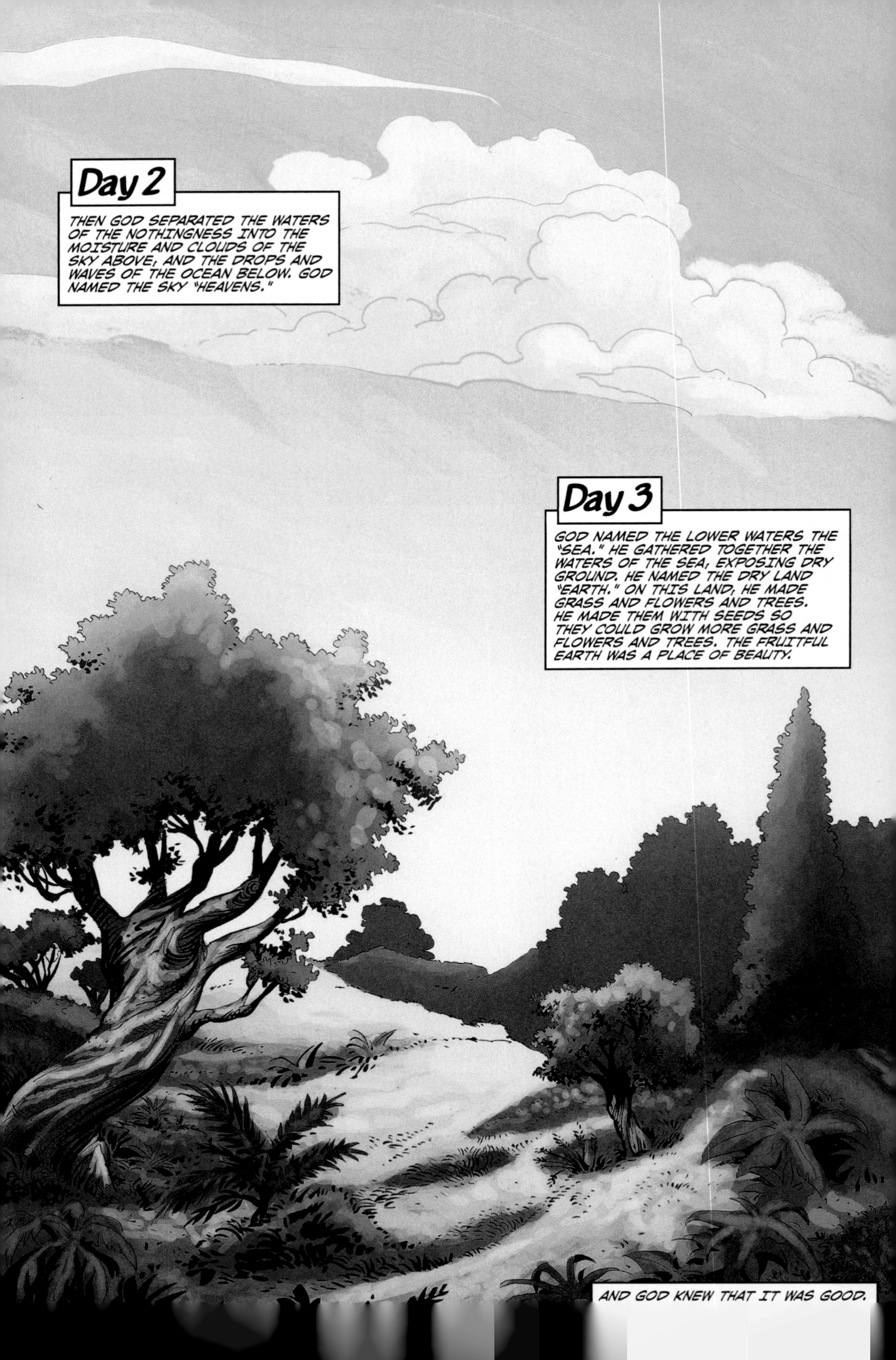
Day 2
THEN GOD SEPARATED THE WATERS OF THE NOTHINGNESS INTO THE MOISTURE AND CLOUDS OF THE SKY ABOVE, AND THE DROPS AND WAVES OF THE OCEAN BELOW. GOD NAMED THE SKY "HEAVENS."
Day 3
GOD NAMED THE LOWER WATERS THE "SEA." HE GATHERED TOGETHER THE WATERS OF THE SEA, EXPOSING DRY GROUND. HE NAMED THE DRY LAND "EARTH." ON THIS LAND, HE MADE GRASS AND FLOWERS AND TREES. HE MADE THEM WITH SEEDS SO THEY COULD GROW MORE GRASS AND FLOWERS AND TREES. THE FRUITFUL EARTH WAS A PLACE OF BEAUTY.
AND GOD KNEW THAT IT WAS GOOD.

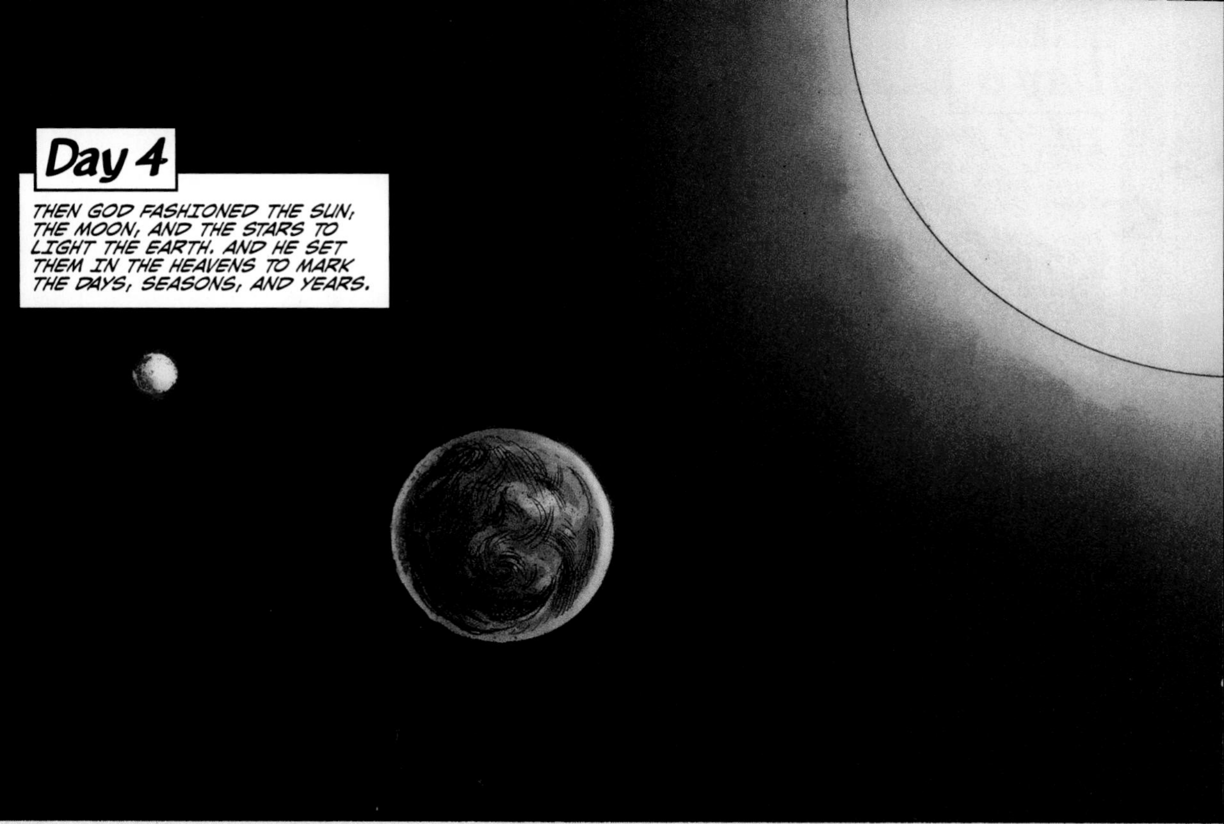
Day 4
THEN GOD FASHIONED THE SUN, THE MOON, AND THE STARS TO LIGHT THE EARTH. AND HE SET THEM IN THE HEAVENS TO MARK THE DAYS, SEASONS, AND YEARS.

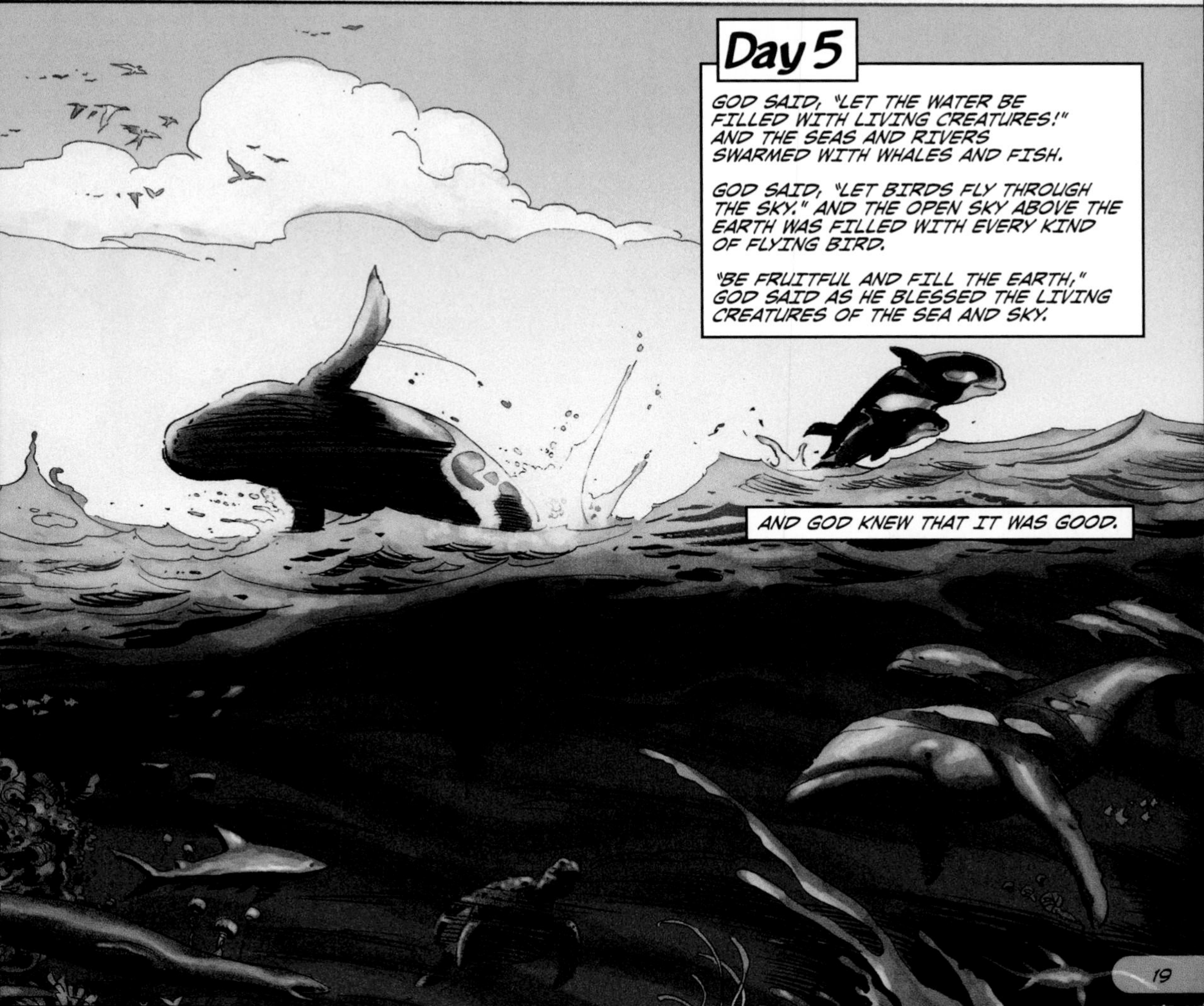
Day 5
GOD SAID, "LET THE WATER BE FILLED WITH LIVING CREATURES!" AND THE SEAS AND RIVERS SWARMED WITH WHALES AND FISH.
GOD SAID, "LET BIRDS FLY THROUGH THE SKY." AND THE OPEN SKY ABOVE THE EARTH WAS FILLED WITH EVERY KIND OF FLYING BIRD.
"BE FRUITFUL AND FILL THE EARTH," GOD SAID AS HE BLESSED THE LIVING CREATURES OF THE SEA AND SKY.
AND GOD KNEW THAT IT WAS GOOD.

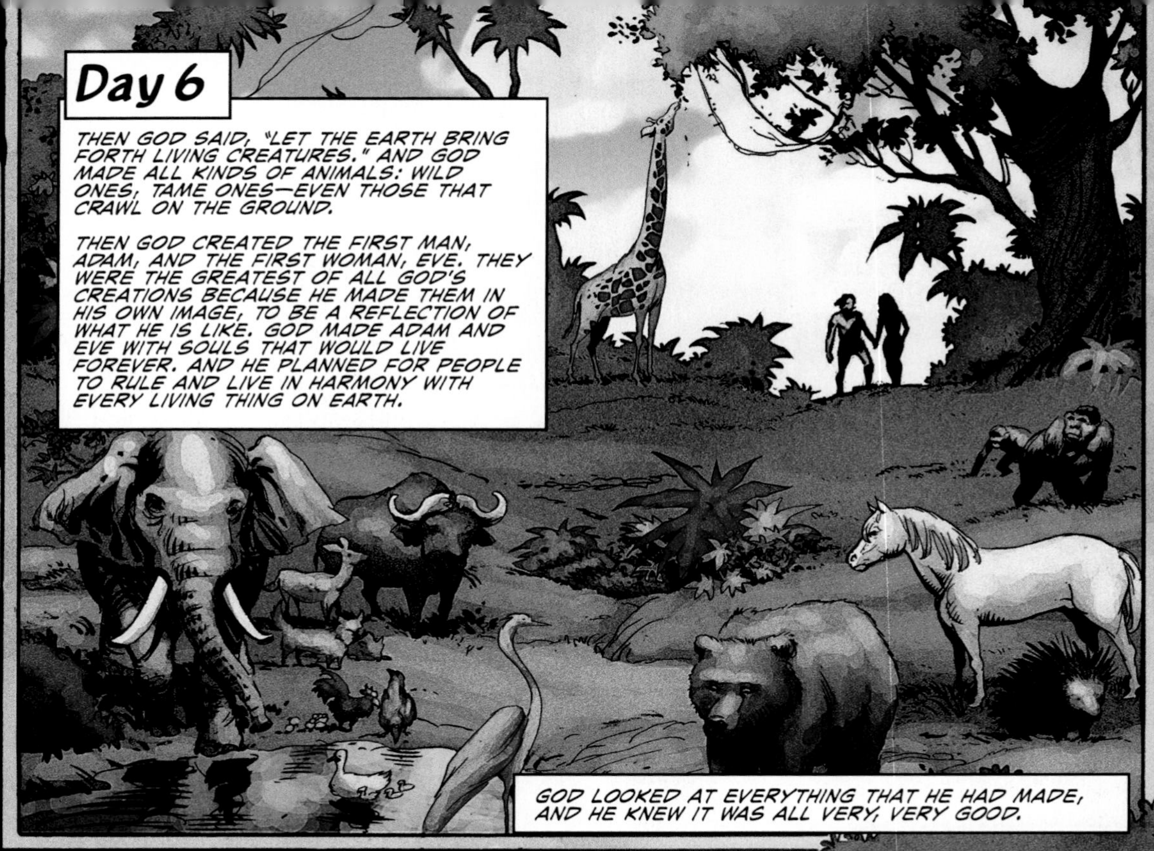
Day 6
THEN GOD SAID, "LET THE EARTH BRING FORTH LIVING CREATURES." AND GOD MADE ALL KINDS OF ANIMALS: WILD ONES, TAME ONES—EVEN THOSE THAT CRAWL ON THE GROUND.
THEN GOD CREATED THE FIRST MAN, ADAM, AND THE FIRST WOMAN, EVE. THEY WERE THE GREATEST OF ALL GOD'S CREATIONS BECAUSE HE MADE THEM IN HIS OWN IMAGE, TO BE A REFLECTION OF WHAT HE IS LIKE. GOD MADE ADAM AND EVE WITH SOULS THAT WOULD LIVE FOREVER. AND HE PLANNED FOR PEOPLE TO RULE AND LIVE IN HARMONY WITH EVERY LIVING THING ON EARTH.
GOD LOOKED AT EVERYTHING THAT HE HAD MADE, AND HE KNEW IT WAS ALL VERY, VERY GOOD.

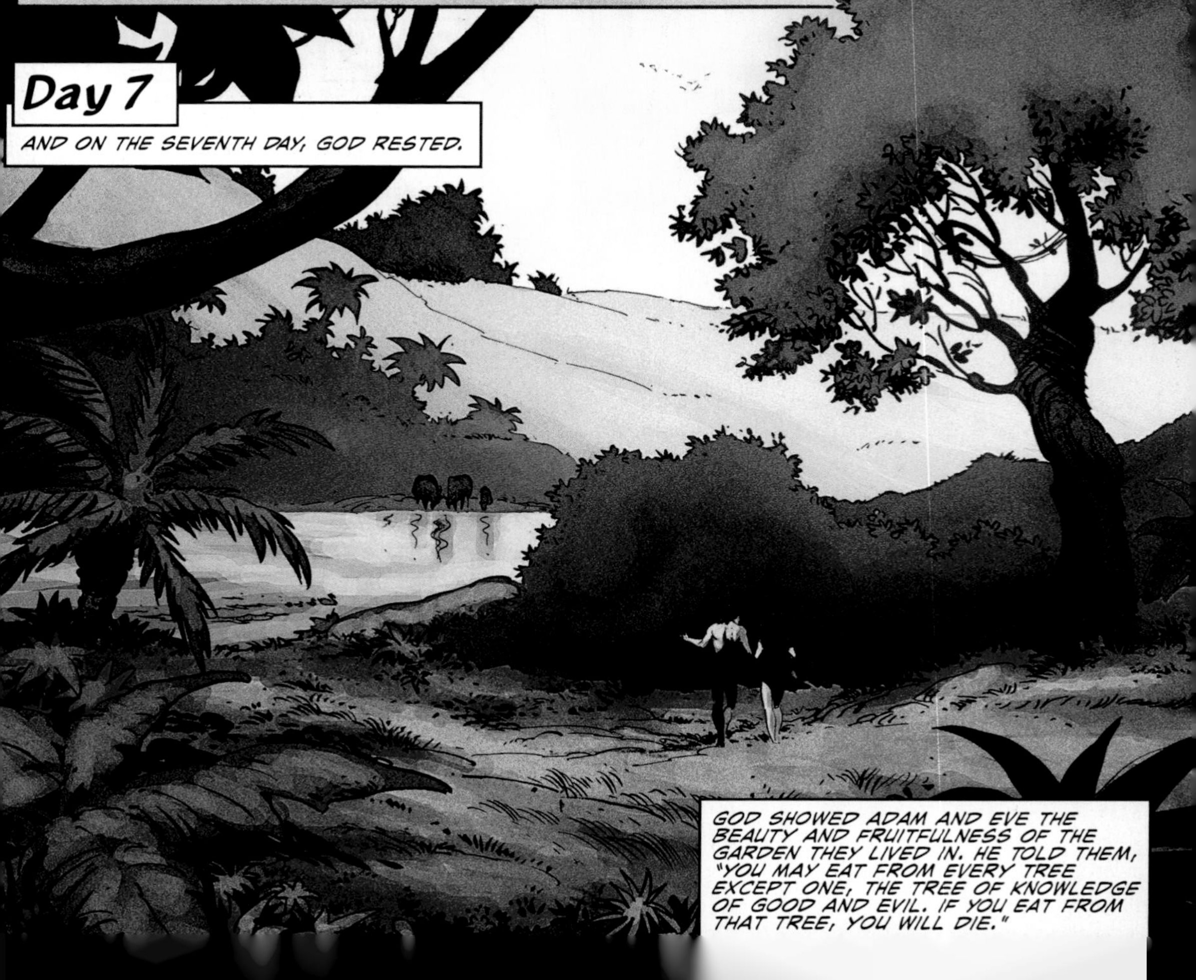
Day 7
AND ON THE SEVENTH DAY, GOD RESTED.
GOD SHOWED ADAM AND EVE THE BEAUTY AND FRUITFULNESS OF THE GARDEN THEY LIVED IN. HE TOLD THEM, "YOU MAY EAT FROM EVERY TREE EXCEPT ONE, THE TREE OF KNOWLEDGE OF GOOD AND EVIL. IF YOU EAT FROM THAT TREE, YOU WILL DIE."

Tempted in the Garden

BASED ON GENESIS 3

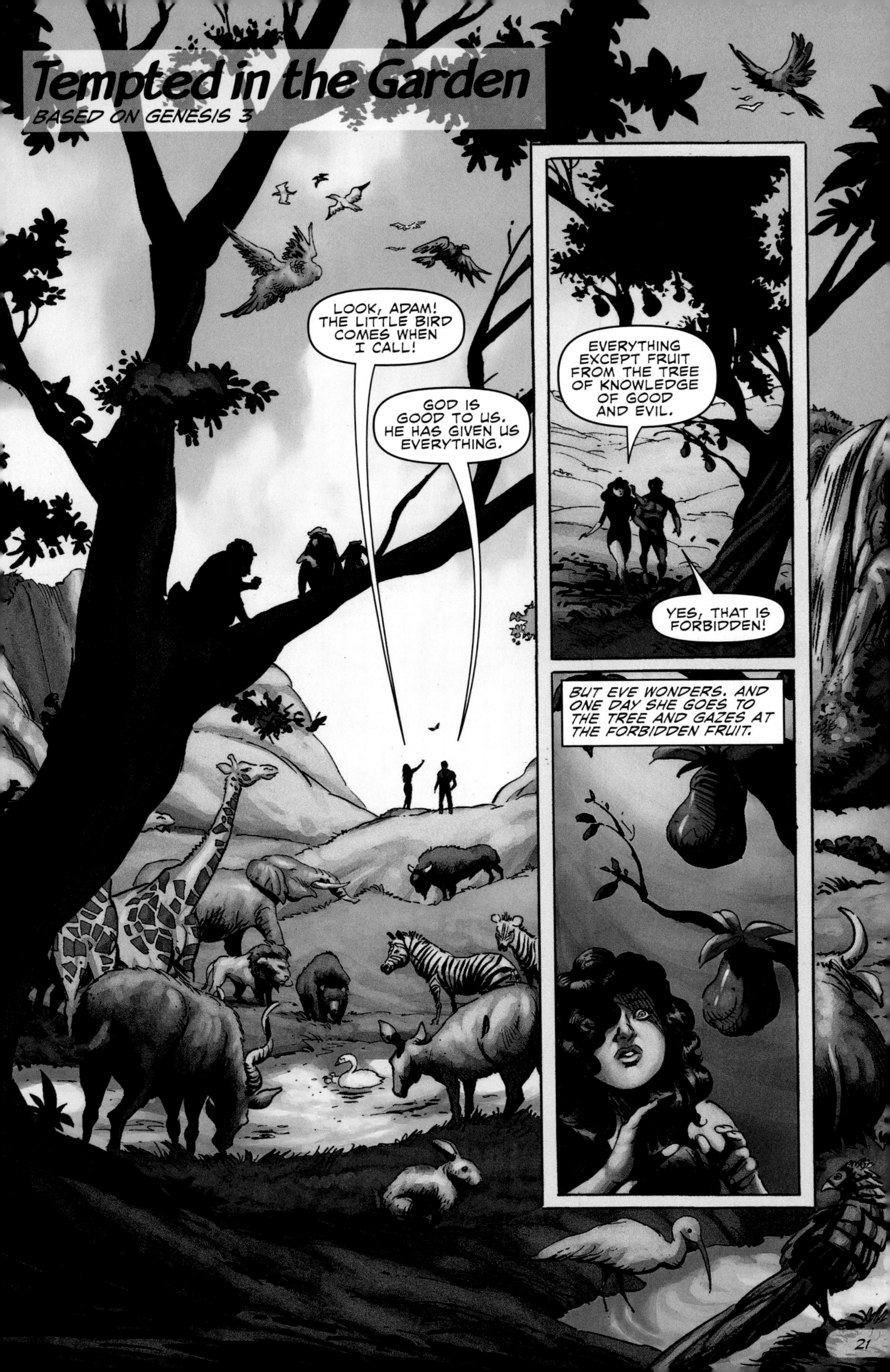
LOOK, ADAM! THE LITTLE BIRD COMES WHEN I CALL!
GOD IS GOOD TO US. HE HAS GIVEN US EVERYTHING.
EVERYTHING EXCEPT FRUIT FROM THE TREE OF KNOWLEDGE OF GOOD AND EVIL.
YES, THAT IS FORBIDDEN!
BUT EVE WONDERS. AND ONE DAY SHE GOES TO THE TREE AND GAZES AT THE FORBIDDEN FRUIT.

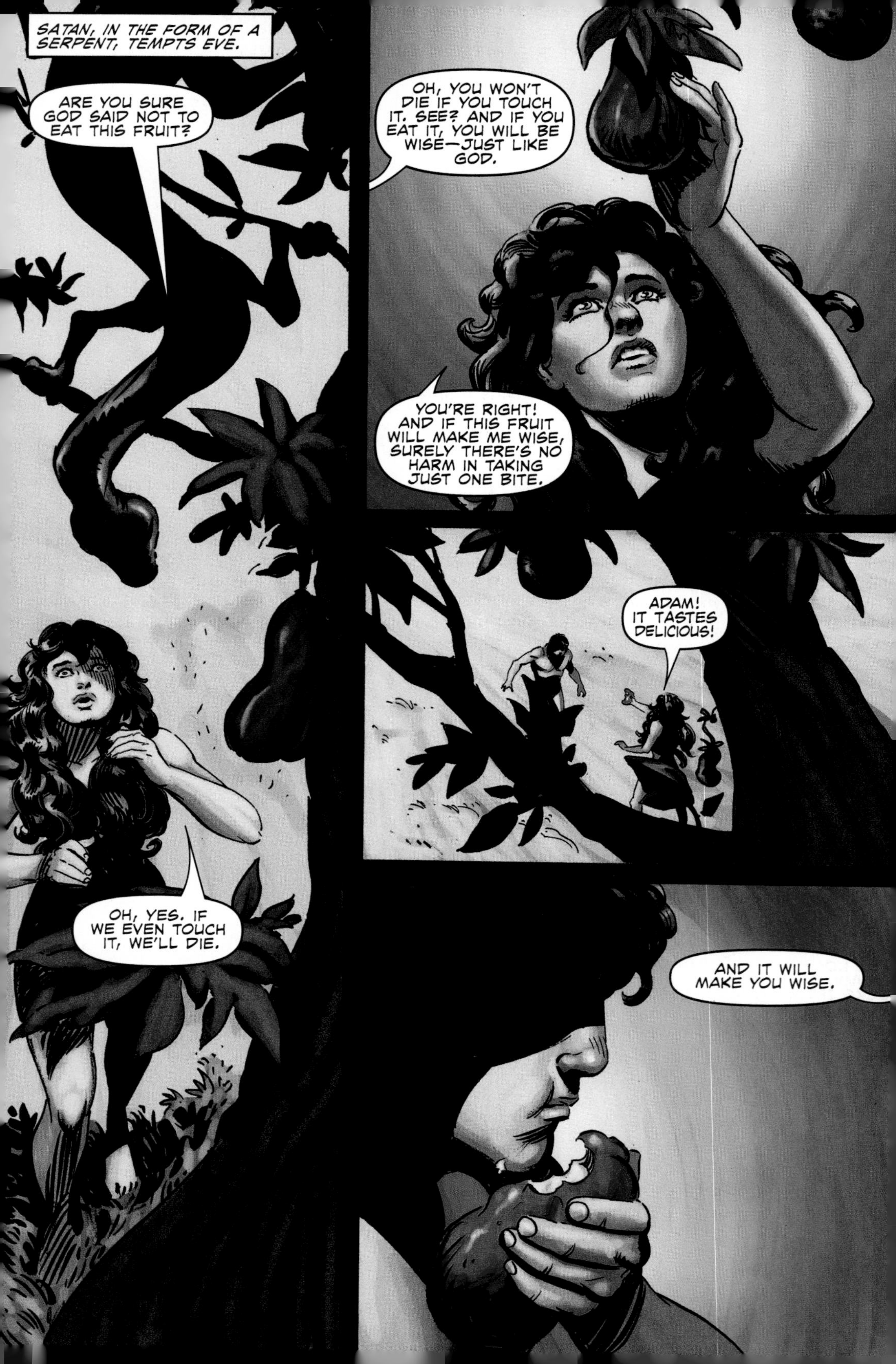
SATAN, IN THE FORM OF A SERPENT, TEMPTS EVE.
ARE YOU SURE GOD SAID NOT TO EAT THIS FRUIT?
OH, YES. IF WE EVEN TOUCH IT, WE'LL DIE.
OH, YOU WON'T DIE IF YOU TOUCH IT. SEE? AND IF YOU EAT IT, YOU WILL BE WISE—JUST LIKE GOD.
YOU'RE RIGHT! AND IF THIS FRUIT WILL MAKE ME WISE, SURELY THERE'S NO HARM IN TAKING JUST ONE BITE.
ADAM! IT TASTES DELICIOUS!
AND IT WILL MAKE YOU WISE.

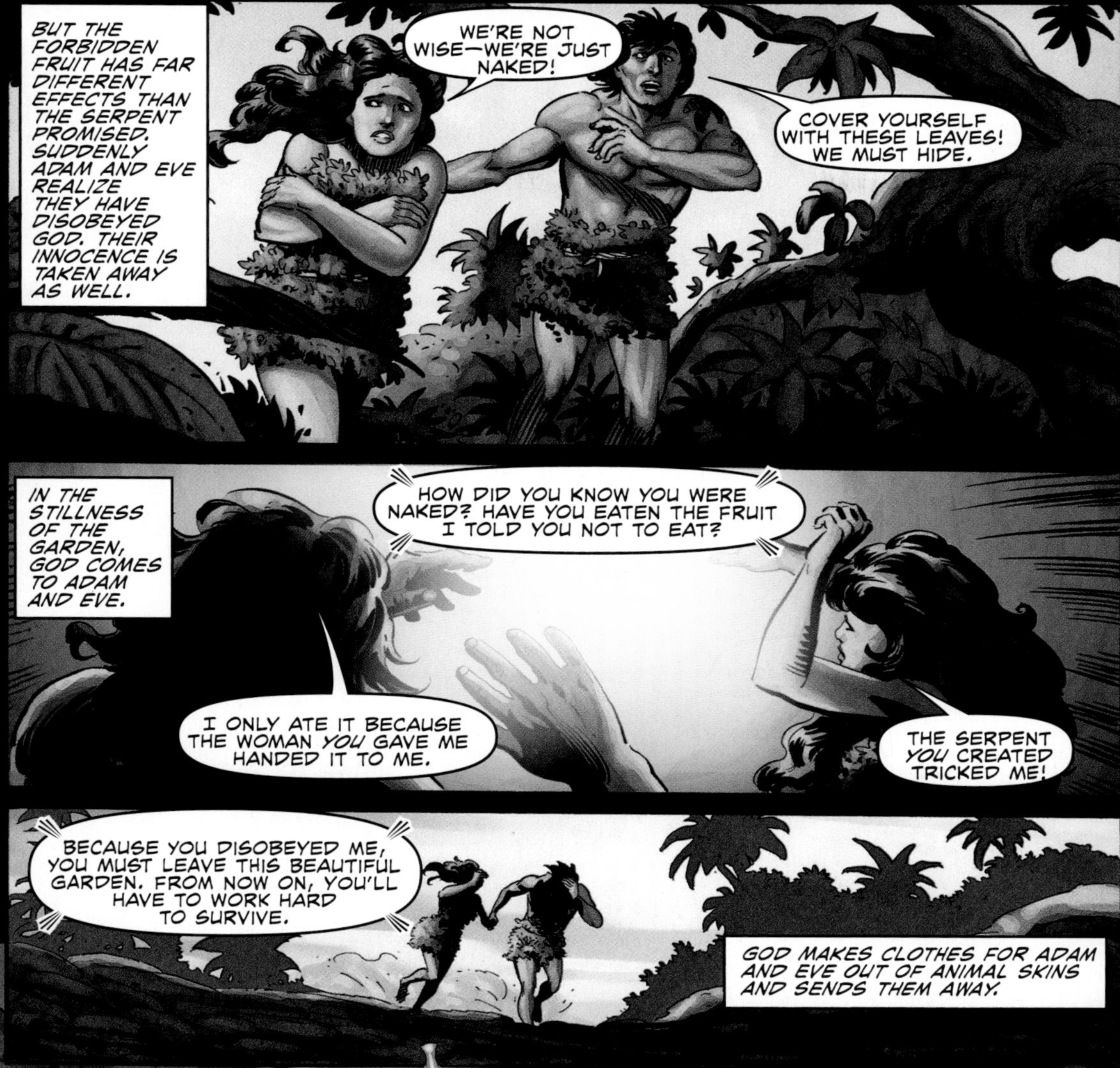
BUT THE FORBIDDEN FRUIT HAS FAR DIFFERENT EFFECTS THAN THE SERPENT PROMISED. SUDDENLY ADAM AND EVE REALIZE THEY HAVE DISOBEYED GOD. THEIR INNOCENCE IS TAKEN AWAY AS WELL.
WE'RE NOT WISE—WE'RE JUST NAKED!
COVER YOURSELF WITH THESE LEAVES! WE MUST HIDE.
IN THE STILLNESS OF THE GARDEN, GOD COMES TO ADAM AND EVE.
HOW DID YOU KNOW YOU WERE NAKED? HAVE YOU EATEN THE FRUIT I TOLD YOU NOT TO EAT?
I ONLY ATE IT BECAUSE THE WOMAN *YOU* GAVE ME HANDED IT TO ME.
THE SERPENT *YOU* CREATED TRICKED ME!
BECAUSE YOU DISOBEYED ME, YOU MUST LEAVE THIS BEAUTIFUL GARDEN. FROM NOW ON, YOU'LL HAVE TO WORK HARD TO SURVIVE.
GOD MAKES CLOTHES FOR ADAM AND EVE OUT OF ANIMAL SKINS AND SENDS THEM AWAY.

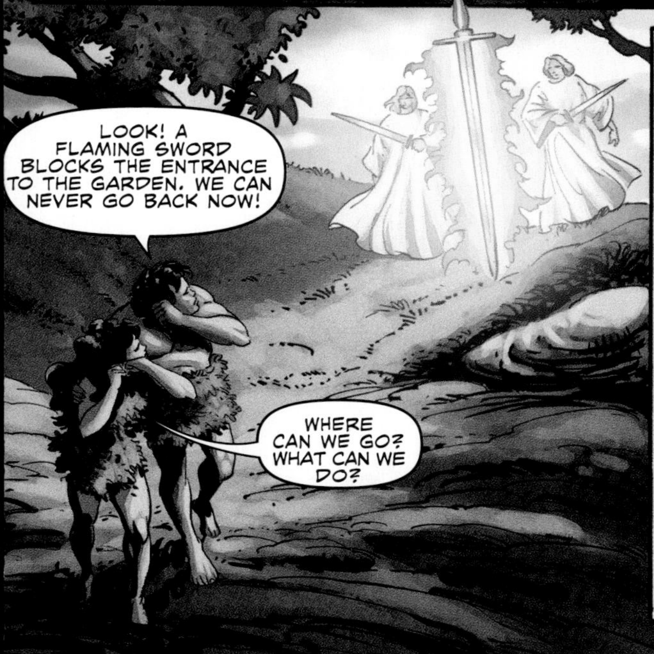
LOOK! A FLAMING SWORD BLOCKS THE ENTRANCE TO THE GARDEN. WE CAN NEVER GO BACK NOW!
WHERE CAN WE GO? WHAT CAN WE DO?

GOD'S PROMISE OF SALVATION

THE PERFECT UNITY BETWEEN GOD AND HIS BELOVED CREATION IS NOW BROKEN FOR ALL TIME. ADAM AND EVE ARE FORCED TO CREATE A NEW LIFE OUT OF THEIR KNOWLEDGE AND SHAME.

BUT ALREADY, GOD HAS A PLAN TO REDEEM HIS CREATION. GOD PROMISES THAT ONE DAY HE WILL SEND A SAVIOR FOR HIS PEOPLE.

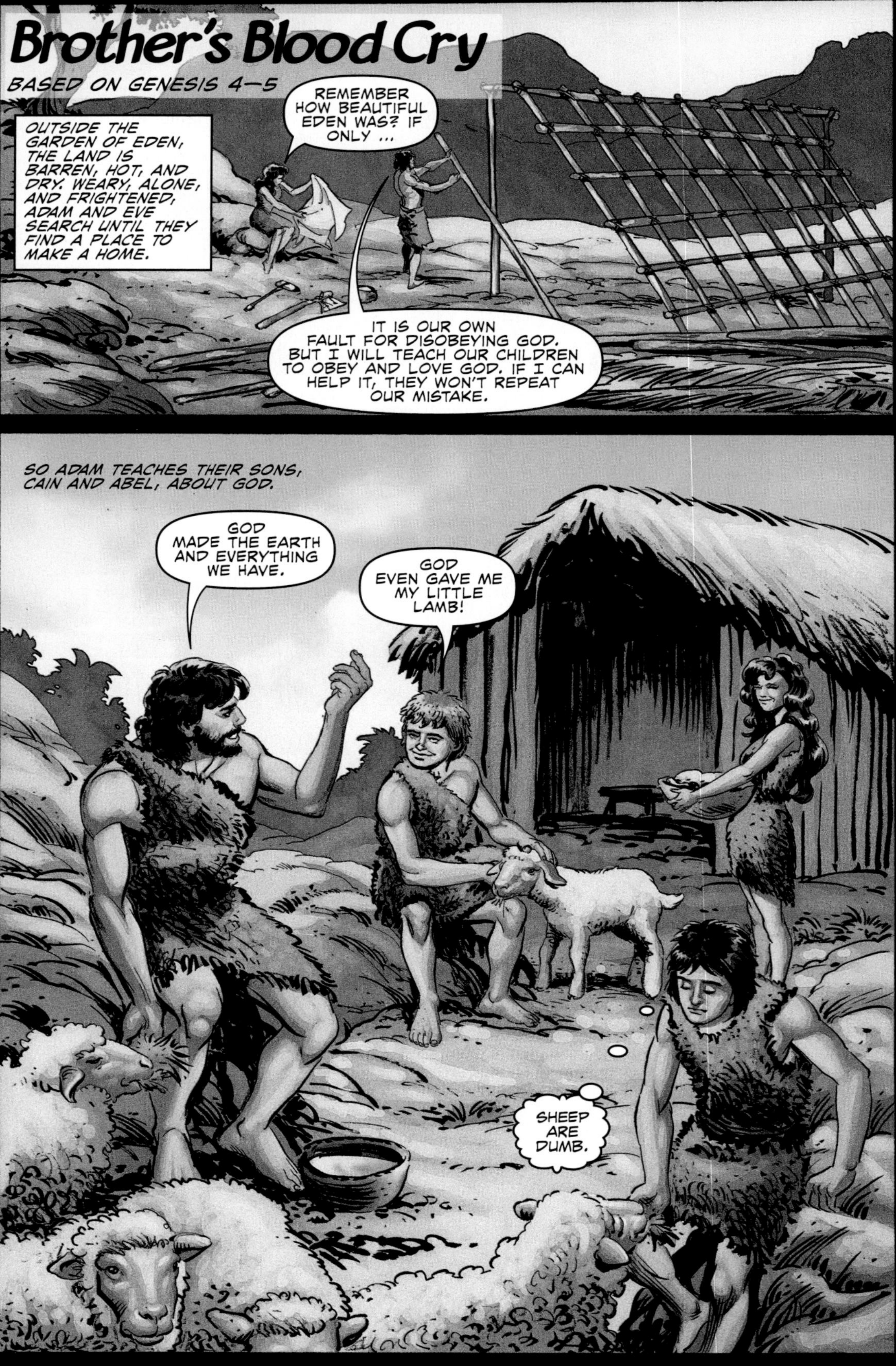
Brother's Blood Cry
BASED ON GENESIS 4—5
OUTSIDE THE GARDEN OF EDEN, THE LAND IS BARREN, HOT, AND DRY. WEARY, ALONE, AND FRIGHTENED, ADAM AND EVE SEARCH UNTIL THEY FIND A PLACE TO MAKE A HOME.
REMEMBER HOW BEAUTIFUL EDEN WAS? IF ONLY ...
IT IS OUR OWN FAULT FOR DISOBEYING GOD. BUT I WILL TEACH OUR CHILDREN TO OBEY AND LOVE GOD. IF I CAN HELP IT, THEY WON'T REPEAT OUR MISTAKE.
SO ADAM TEACHES THEIR SONS, CAIN AND ABEL, ABOUT GOD.
GOD MADE THE EARTH AND EVERYTHING WE HAVE.
GOD EVEN GAVE ME MY LITTLE LAMB!
SHEEP ARE DUMB.

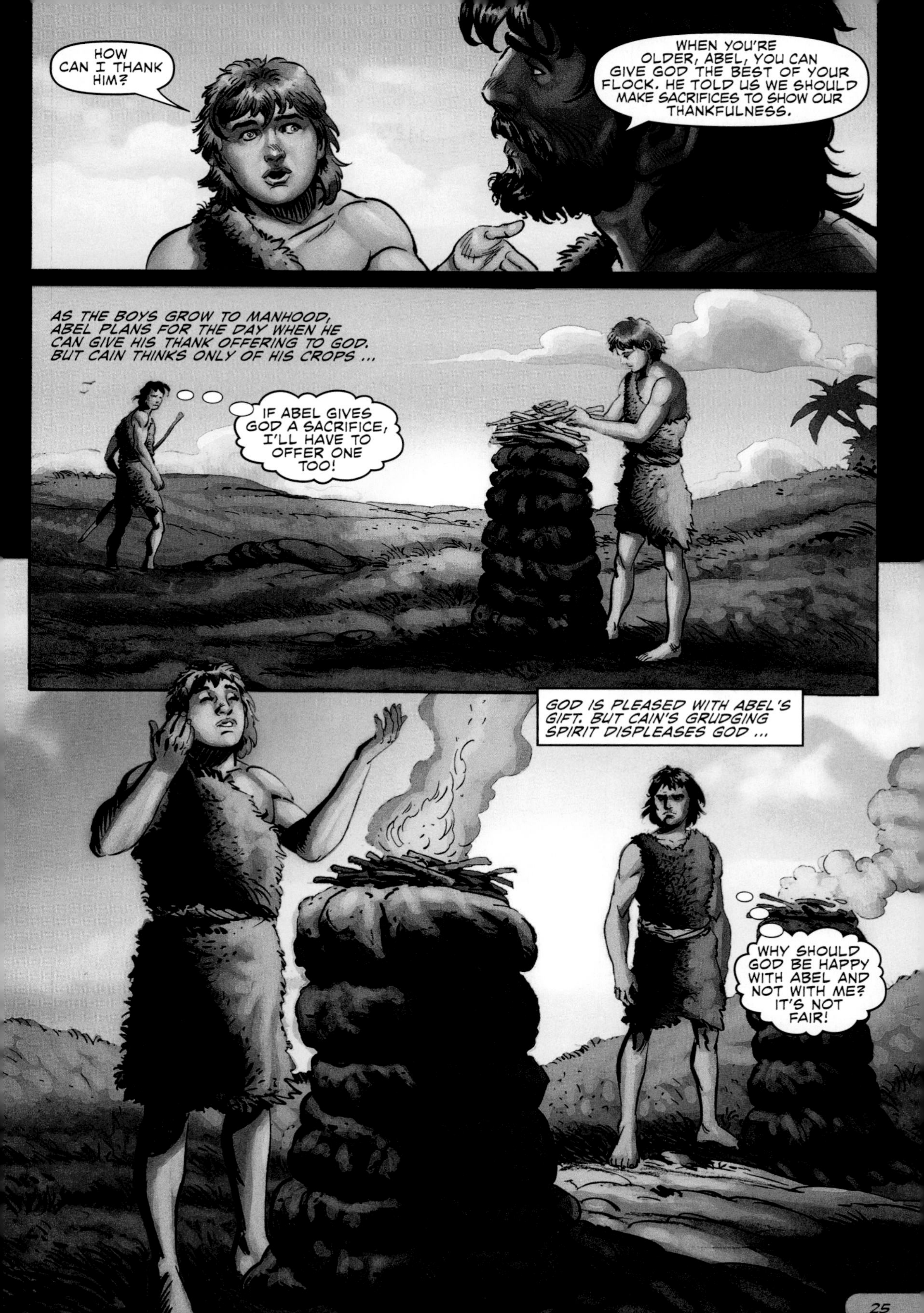

HOW CAN I THANK HIM?
WHEN YOU'RE OLDER, ABEL, YOU CAN GIVE GOD THE BEST OF YOUR FLOCK. HE TOLD US WE SHOULD MAKE SACRIFICES TO SHOW OUR THANKFULNESS.
AS THE BOYS GROW TO MANHOOD, ABEL PLANS FOR THE DAY WHEN HE CAN GIVE HIS THANK OFFERING TO GOD. BUT CAIN THINKS ONLY OF HIS CROPS ...
IF ABEL GIVES GOD A SACRIFICE, I'LL HAVE TO OFFER ONE TOO!
GOD IS PLEASED WITH ABEL'S GIFT. BUT CAIN'S GRUDGING SPIRIT DISPLEASES GOD ...
WHY SHOULD GOD BE HAPPY WITH ABEL AND NOT WITH ME? IT'S NOT FAIR!

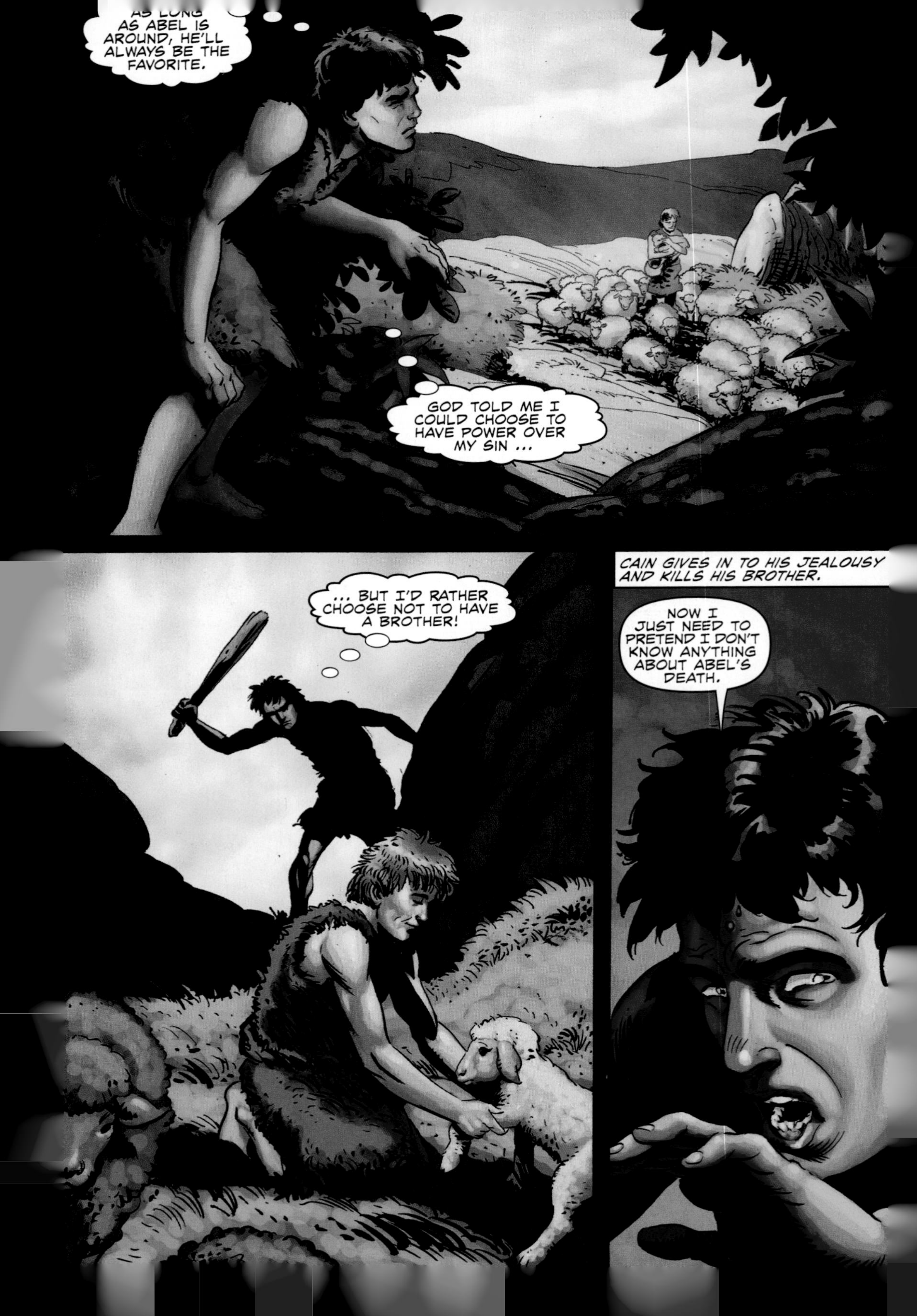
AS LONG AS ABEL IS AROUND, HE'LL ALWAYS BE THE FAVORITE.
GOD TOLD ME I COULD CHOOSE TO HAVE POWER OVER MY SIN ...
... BUT I'D RATHER CHOOSE NOT TO HAVE A BROTHER!
CAIN GIVES IN TO HIS JEALOUSY AND KILLS HIS BROTHER.
NOW I JUST NEED TO PRETEND I DON'T KNOW ANYTHING ABOUT ABEL'S DEATH.

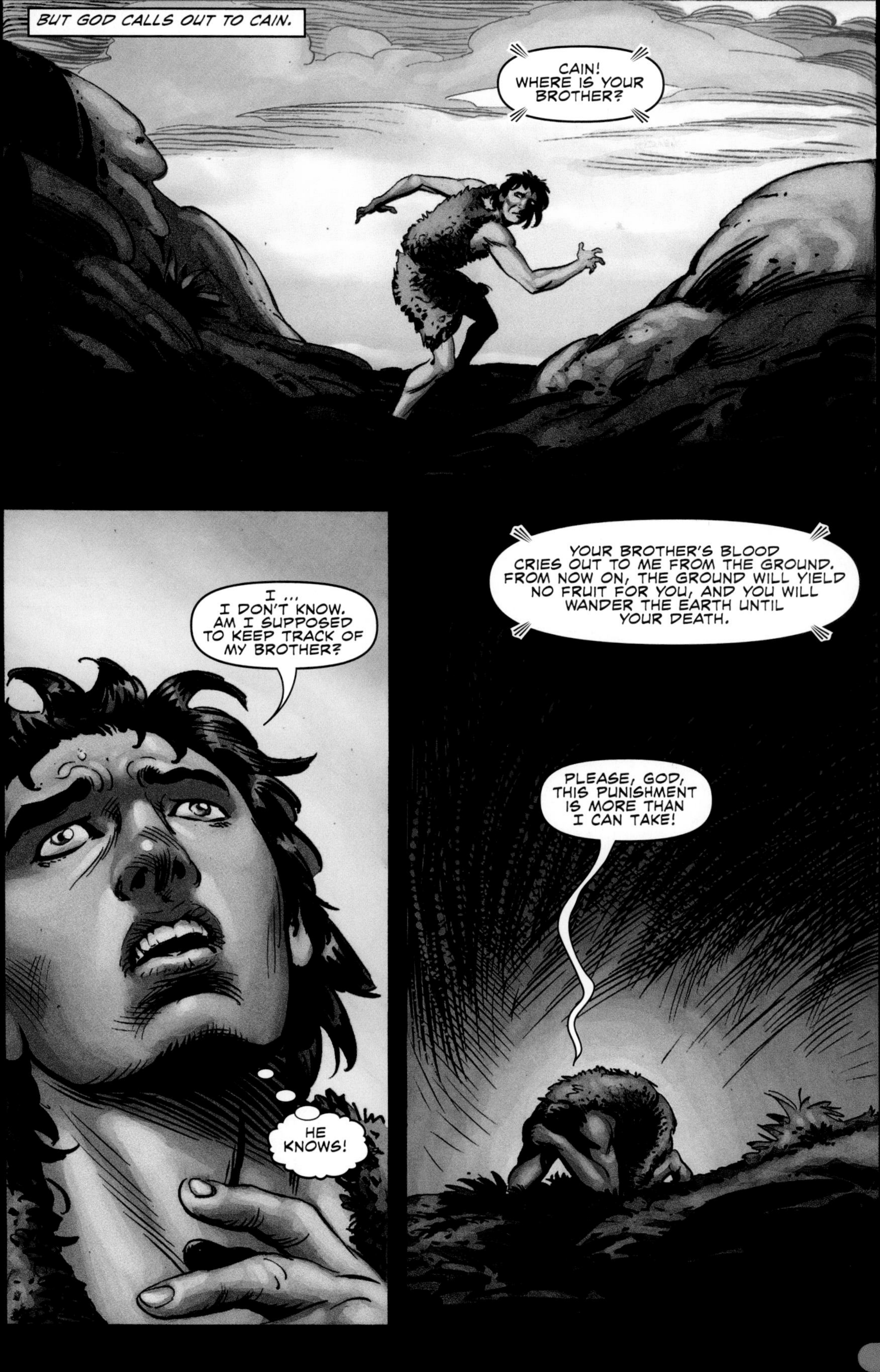
BUT GOD CALLS OUT TO CAIN.
CAIN! WHERE IS YOUR BROTHER?
I ... I DON'T KNOW. AM I SUPPOSED TO KEEP TRACK OF MY BROTHER?
HE KNOWS!
YOUR BROTHER'S BLOOD CRIES OUT TO ME FROM THE GROUND. FROM NOW ON, THE GROUND WILL YIELD NO FRUIT FOR YOU, AND YOU WILL WANDER THE EARTH UNTIL YOUR DEATH.
PLEASE, GOD, THIS PUNISHMENT IS MORE THAN I CAN TAKE!

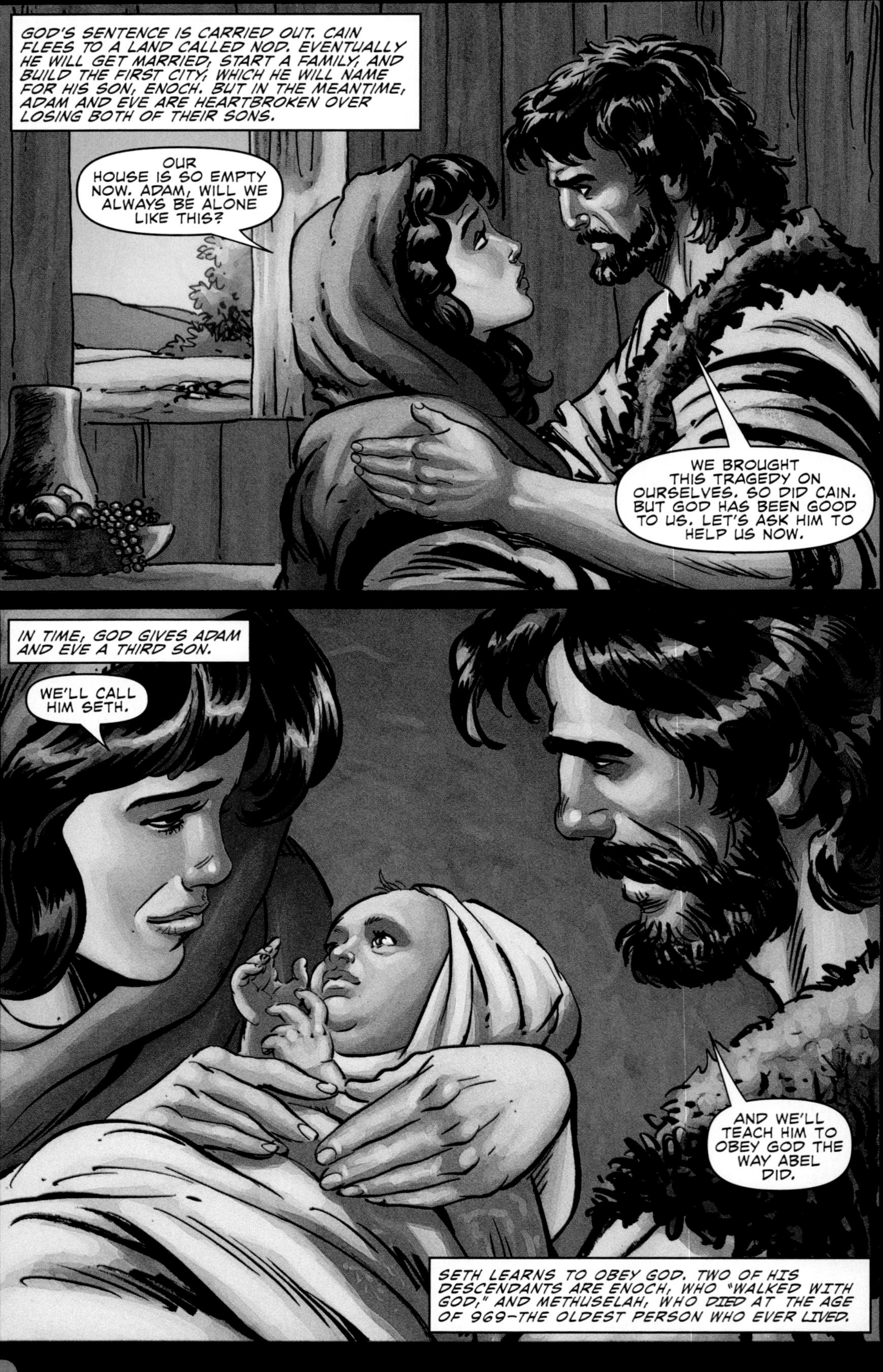
GOD'S SENTENCE IS CARRIED OUT. CAIN FLEES TO A LAND CALLED NOD. EVENTUALLY HE WILL GET MARRIED, START A FAMILY, AND BUILD THE FIRST CITY, WHICH HE WILL NAME FOR HIS SON, ENOCH. BUT IN THE MEANTIME, ADAM AND EVE ARE HEARTBROKEN OVER LOSING BOTH OF THEIR SONS.
OUR HOUSE IS SO EMPTY NOW. ADAM, WILL WE ALWAYS BE ALONE LIKE THIS?
WE BROUGHT THIS TRAGEDY ON OURSELVES. SO DID CAIN. BUT GOD HAS BEEN GOOD TO US. LET'S ASK HIM TO HELP US NOW.
IN TIME, GOD GIVES ADAM AND EVE A THIRD SON.
WE'LL CALL HIM SETH.
AND WE'LL TEACH HIM TO OBEY GOD THE WAY ABEL DID.
SETH LEARNS TO OBEY GOD. TWO OF HIS DESCENDANTS ARE ENOCH, WHO "WALKED WITH GOD," AND METHUSELAH, WHO DIED AT THE AGE OF 969—THE OLDEST PERSON WHO EVER LIVED.

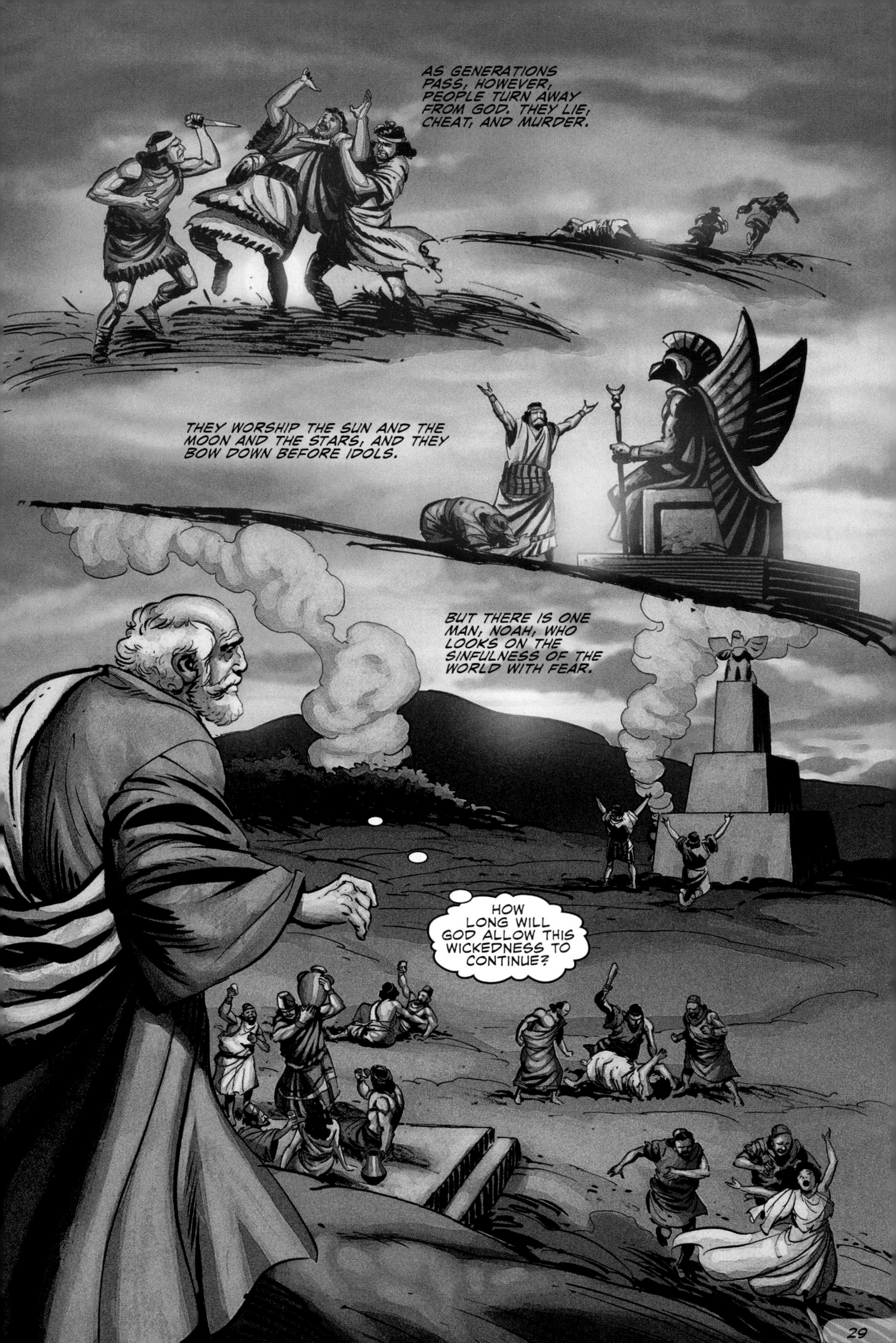
AS GENERATIONS PASS, HOWEVER, PEOPLE TURN AWAY FROM GOD. THEY LIE, CHEAT, AND MURDER.
THEY WORSHIP THE SUN AND THE MOON AND THE STARS, AND THEY BOW DOWN BEFORE IDOLS.
BUT THERE IS ONE MAN, NOAH, WHO LOOKS ON THE SINFULNESS OF THE WORLD WITH FEAR.
HOW LONG WILL GOD ALLOW THIS WICKEDNESS TO CONTINUE?

Rainy Days

BASED ON GENESIS 6–7

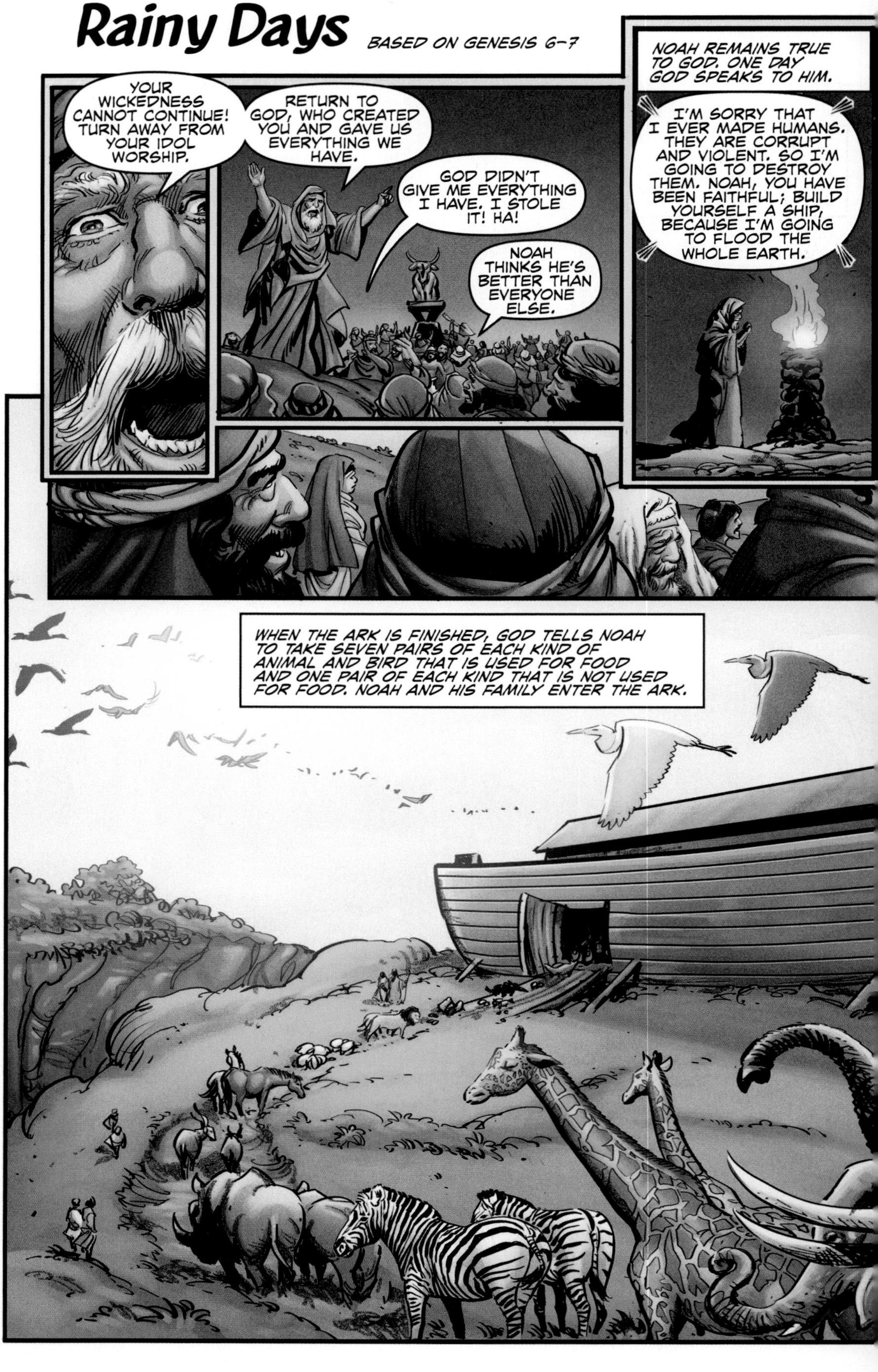
YOUR WICKEDNESS CANNOT CONTINUE! TURN AWAY FROM YOUR IDOL WORSHIP.
RETURN TO GOD, WHO CREATED YOU AND GAVE US EVERYTHING WE HAVE.
GOD DIDN'T GIVE ME EVERYTHING I HAVE. I STOLE IT! HA!
NOAH THINKS HE'S BETTER THAN EVERYONE ELSE.
NOAH REMAINS TRUE TO GOD. ONE DAY GOD SPEAKS TO HIM.
I'M SORRY THAT I EVER MADE HUMANS. THEY ARE CORRUPT AND VIOLENT. SO I'M GOING TO DESTROY THEM. NOAH, YOU HAVE BEEN FAITHFUL; BUILD YOURSELF A SHIP, BECAUSE I'M GOING TO FLOOD THE WHOLE EARTH.
WHEN THE ARK IS FINISHED, GOD TELLS NOAH TO TAKE SEVEN PAIRS OF EACH KIND OF ANIMAL AND BIRD THAT IS USED FOR FOOD AND ONE PAIR OF EACH KIND THAT IS NOT USED FOR FOOD. NOAH AND HIS FAMILY ENTER THE ARK.

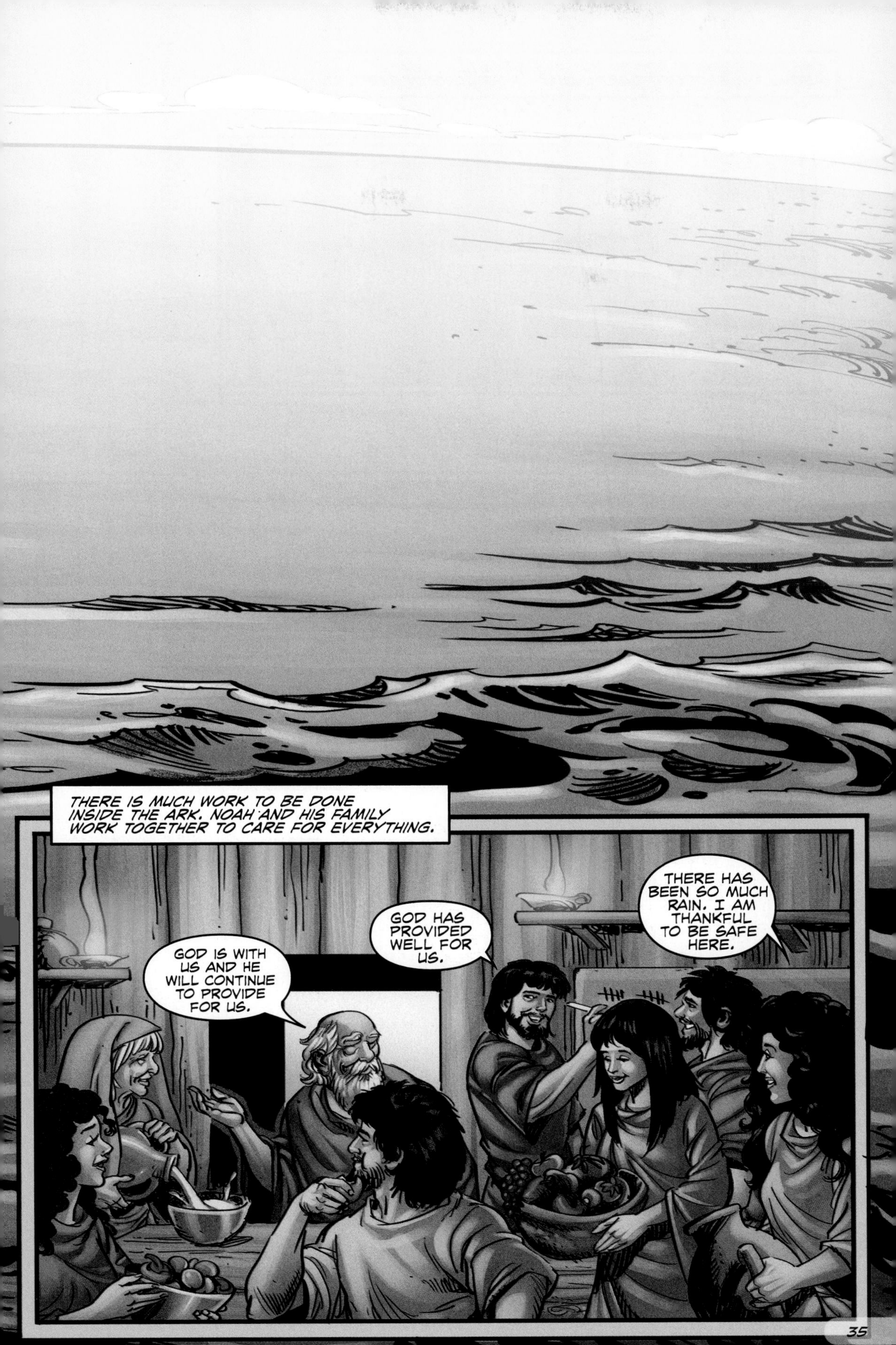
THERE IS MUCH WORK TO BE DONE INSIDE THE ARK. NOAH AND HIS FAMILY WORK TOGETHER TO CARE FOR EVERYTHING.
GOD IS WITH US AND HE WILL CONTINUE TO PROVIDE FOR US.
GOD HAS PROVIDED WELL FOR US.
THERE HAS BEEN SO MUCH RAIN. I AM THANKFUL TO BE SAFE HERE.

ONE DAY THE RAIN STOPS! BUT THE ARK STILL FLOATS ABOVE THE FLOODED EARTH. LAND IS NOWHERE IN SIGHT.

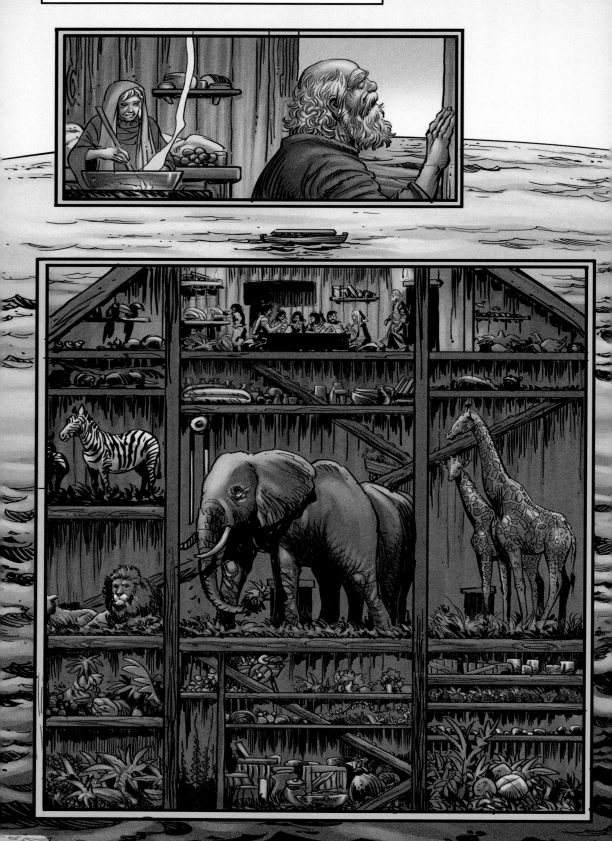

A Rainbow Promise

BASED ON GENESIS 8—10

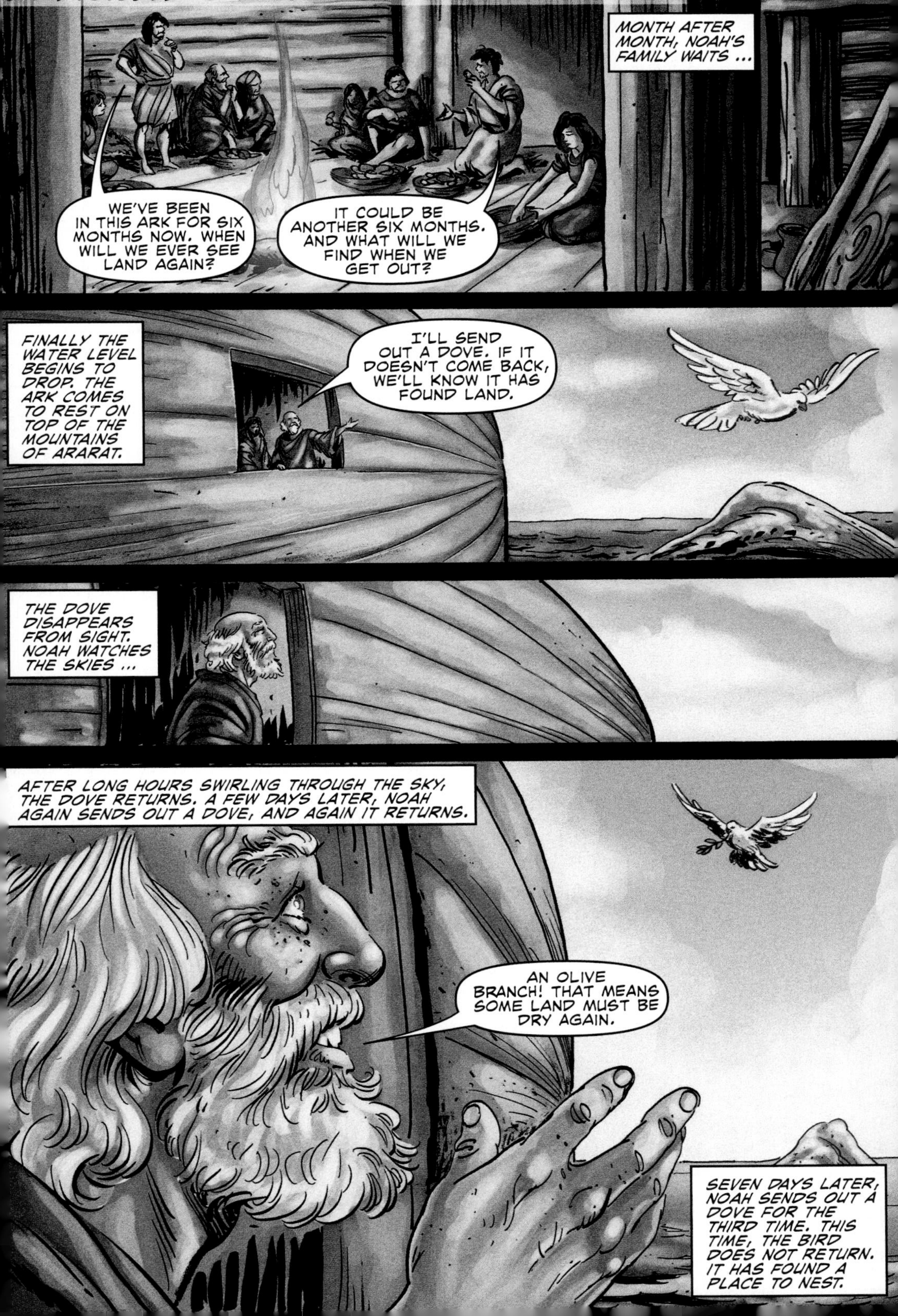
MONTH AFTER MONTH, NOAH'S FAMILY WAITS ...
WE'VE BEEN IN THIS ARK FOR SIX MONTHS NOW. WHEN WILL WE EVER SEE LAND AGAIN?
IT COULD BE ANOTHER SIX MONTHS. AND WHAT WILL WE FIND WHEN WE GET OUT?
FINALLY THE WATER LEVEL BEGINS TO DROP. THE ARK COMES TO REST ON TOP OF THE MOUNTAINS OF ARARAT.
I'LL SEND OUT A DOVE. IF IT DOESN'T COME BACK, WE'LL KNOW IT HAS FOUND LAND.
THE DOVE DISAPPEARS FROM SIGHT. NOAH WATCHES THE SKIES ...
AFTER LONG HOURS SWIRLING THROUGH THE SKY, THE DOVE RETURNS. A FEW DAYS LATER, NOAH AGAIN SENDS OUT A DOVE, AND AGAIN IT RETURNS.
AN OLIVE BRANCH! THAT MEANS SOME LAND MUST BE DRY AGAIN.
SEVEN DAYS LATER, NOAH SENDS OUT A DOVE FOR THE THIRD TIME. THIS TIME, THE BIRD DOES NOT RETURN. IT HAS FOUND A PLACE TO NEST.

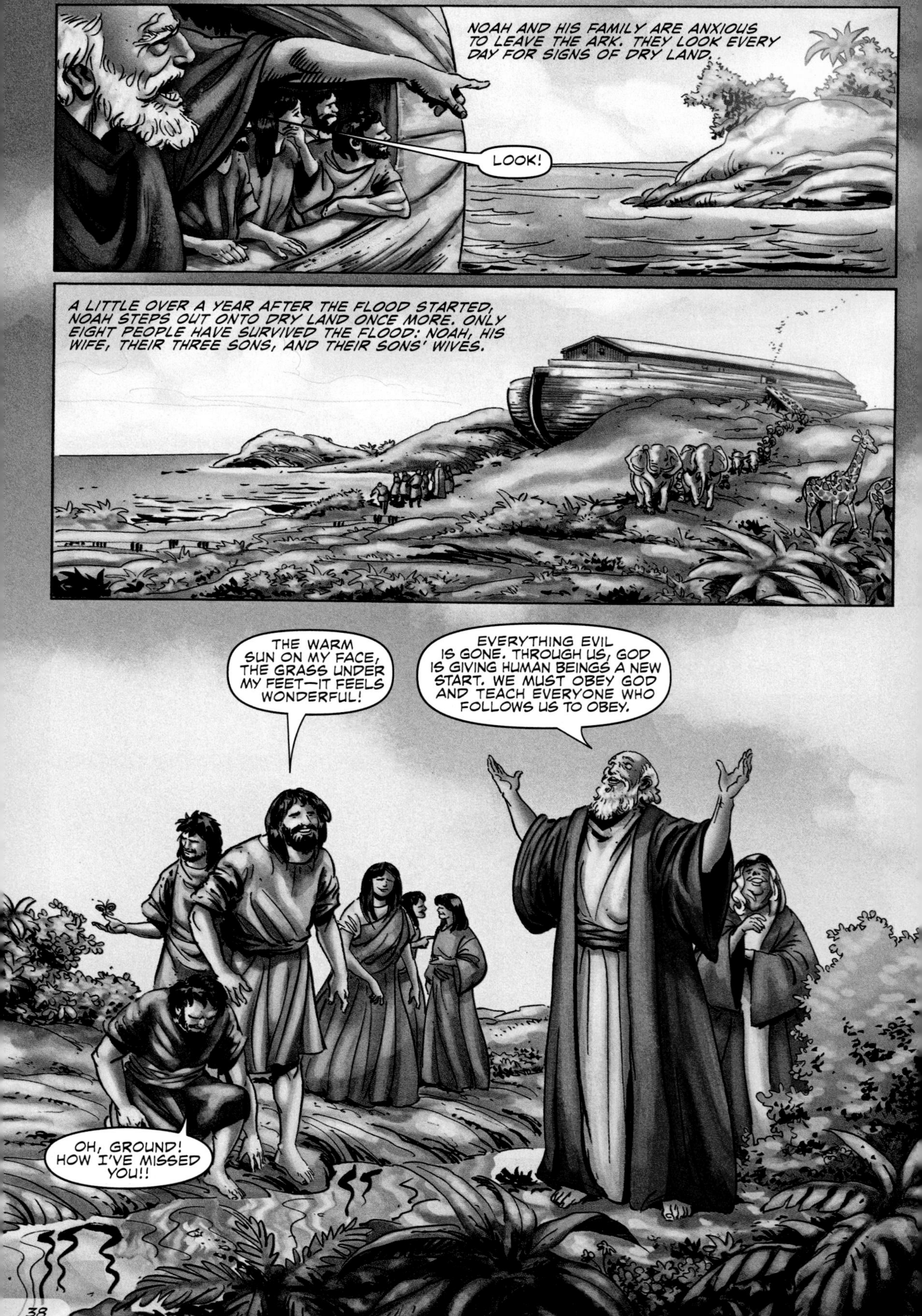

NOAH AND HIS FAMILY ARE ANXIOUS TO LEAVE THE ARK. THEY LOOK EVERY DAY FOR SIGNS OF DRY LAND.
LOOK!
A LITTLE OVER A YEAR AFTER THE FLOOD STARTED, NOAH STEPS OUT ONTO DRY LAND ONCE MORE. ONLY EIGHT PEOPLE HAVE SURVIVED THE FLOOD: NOAH, HIS WIFE, THEIR THREE SONS, AND THEIR SONS' WIVES.
THE WARM SUN ON MY FACE, THE GRASS UNDER MY FEET—IT FEELS WONDERFUL!
EVERYTHING EVIL IS GONE. THROUGH US, GOD IS GIVING HUMAN BEINGS A NEW START. WE MUST OBEY GOD AND TEACH EVERYONE WHO FOLLOWS US TO OBEY.
OH, GROUND! HOW I'VE MISSED YOU!!

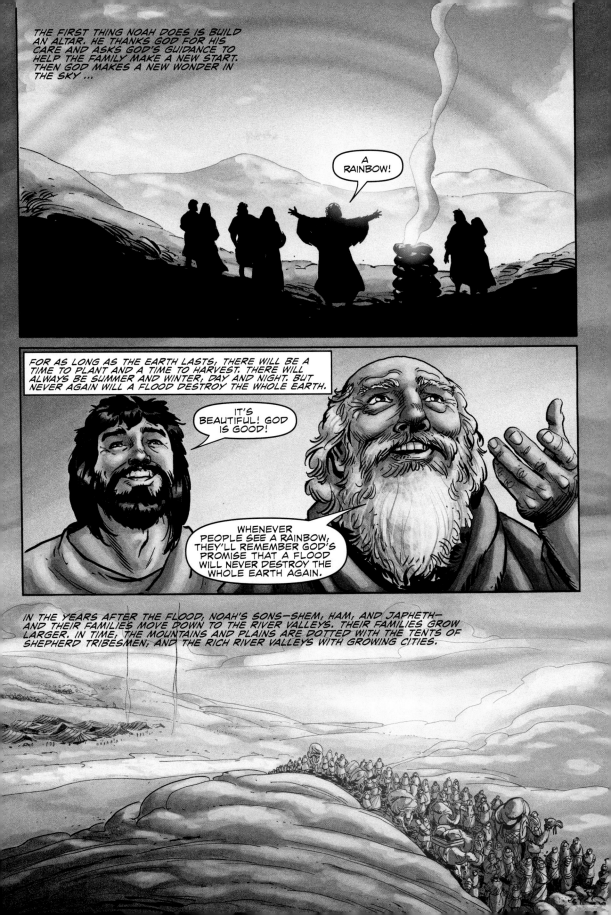

THE FIRST THING NOAH DOES IS BUILD AN ALTAR. HE THANKS GOD FOR HIS CARE AND ASKS GOD'S GUIDANCE TO HELP THE FAMILY MAKE A NEW START. THEN GOD MAKES A NEW WONDER IN THE SKY ...

A RAINBOW!

FOR AS LONG AS THE EARTH LASTS, THERE WILL BE A TIME TO PLANT AND A TIME TO HARVEST. THERE WILL ALWAYS BE SUMMER AND WINTER, DAY AND NIGHT. BUT NEVER AGAIN WILL A FLOOD DESTROY THE WHOLE EARTH.

IT'S BEAUTIFUL! GOD IS GOOD!

WHENEVER PEOPLE SEE A RAINBOW, THEY'LL REMEMBER GOD'S PROMISE THAT A FLOOD WILL NEVER DESTROY THE WHOLE EARTH AGAIN.

IN THE YEARS AFTER THE FLOOD, NOAH'S SONS—SHEM, HAM, AND JAPHETH—AND THEIR FAMILIES MOVE DOWN TO THE RIVER VALLEYS. THEIR FAMILIES GROW LARGER. IN TIME, THE MOUNTAINS AND PLAINS ARE DOTTED WITH THE TENTS OF SHEPHERD TRIBESMEN, AND THE RICH RIVER VALLEYS WITH GROWING CITIES.

A Babbling Tower

BASED ON GENESIS 11:1–9

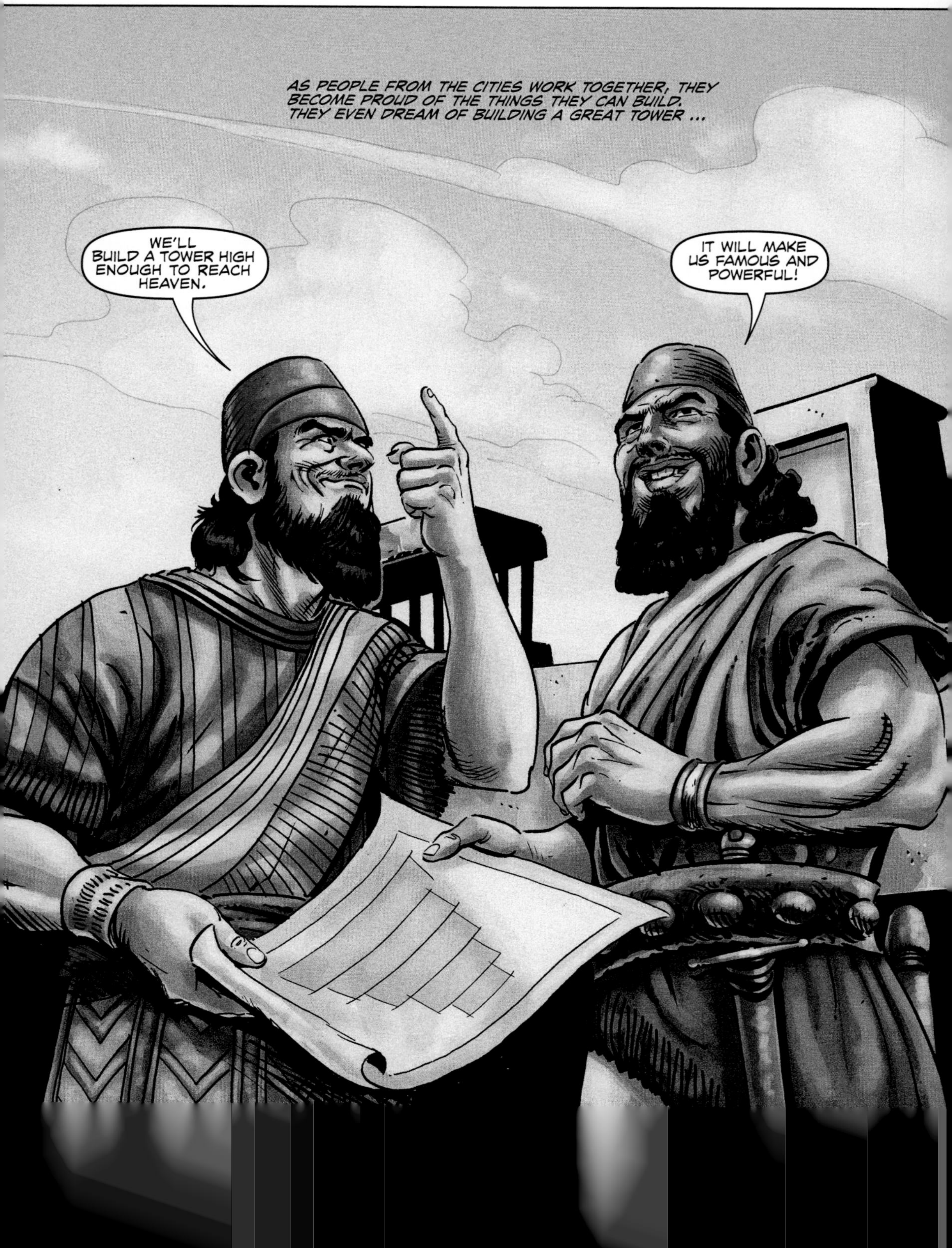
AS PEOPLE FROM THE CITIES WORK TOGETHER, THEY BECOME PROUD OF THE THINGS THEY CAN BUILD. THEY EVEN DREAM OF BUILDING A GREAT TOWER ...
WE'LL BUILD A TOWER HIGH ENOUGH TO REACH HEAVEN.
IT WILL MAKE US FAMOUS AND POWERFUL!

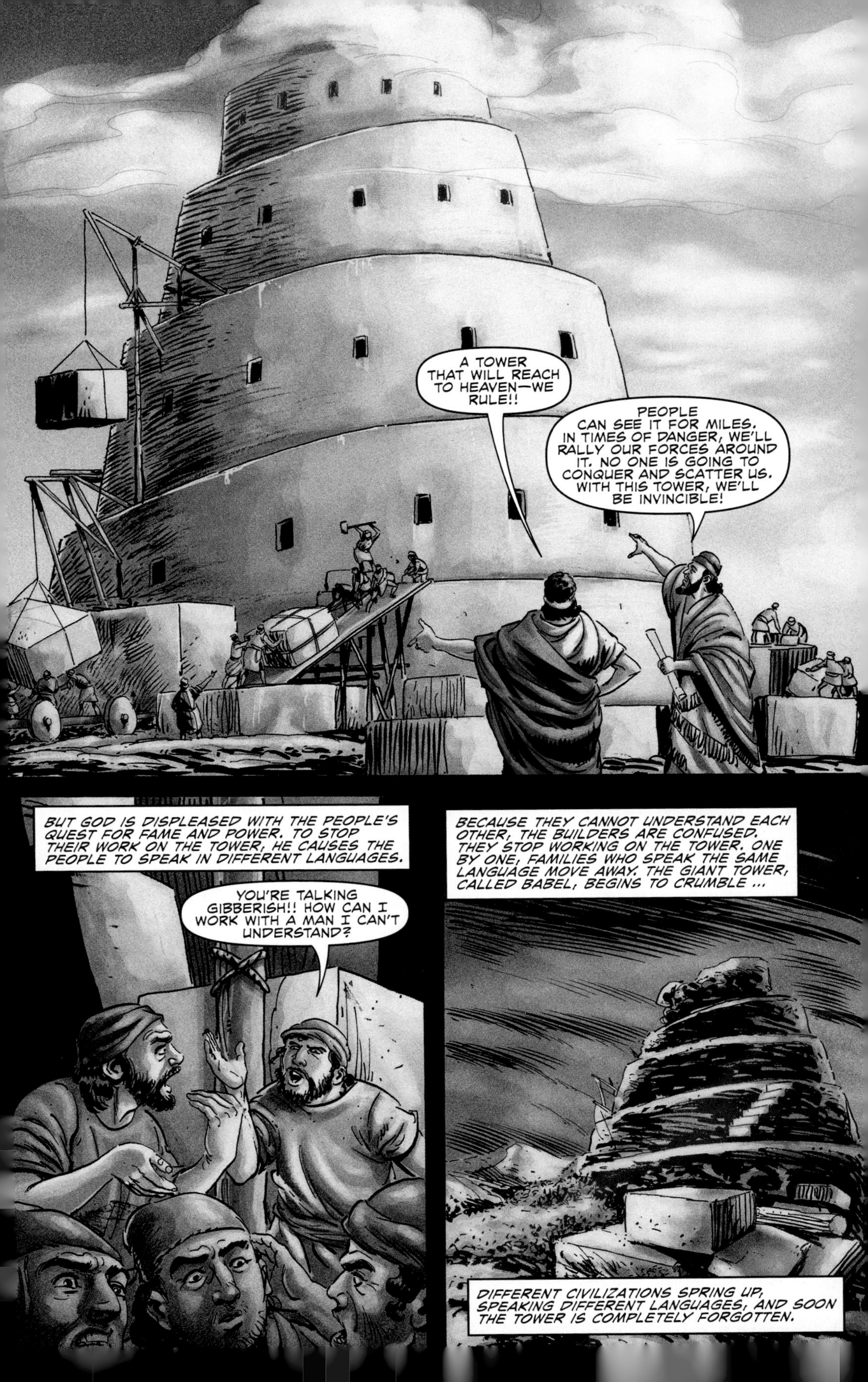
A TOWER THAT WILL REACH TO HEAVEN—WE RULE!!
PEOPLE CAN SEE IT FOR MILES. IN TIMES OF DANGER, WE'LL RALLY OUR FORCES AROUND IT. NO ONE IS GOING TO CONQUER AND SCATTER US. WITH THIS TOWER, WE'LL BE INVINCIBLE!
BUT GOD IS DISPLEASED WITH THE PEOPLE'S QUEST FOR FAME AND POWER. TO STOP THEIR WORK ON THE TOWER, HE CAUSES THE PEOPLE TO SPEAK IN DIFFERENT LANGUAGES.
YOU'RE TALKING GIBBERISH!! HOW CAN I WORK WITH A MAN I CAN'T UNDERSTAND?
BECAUSE THEY CANNOT UNDERSTAND EACH OTHER, THE BUILDERS ARE CONFUSED. THEY STOP WORKING ON THE TOWER. ONE BY ONE, FAMILIES WHO SPEAK THE SAME LANGUAGE MOVE AWAY. THE GIANT TOWER, CALLED BABEL, BEGINS TO CRUMBLE ...
DIFFERENT CIVILIZATIONS SPRING UP, SPEAKING DIFFERENT LANGUAGES, AND SOON THE TOWER IS COMPLETELY FORGOTTEN.

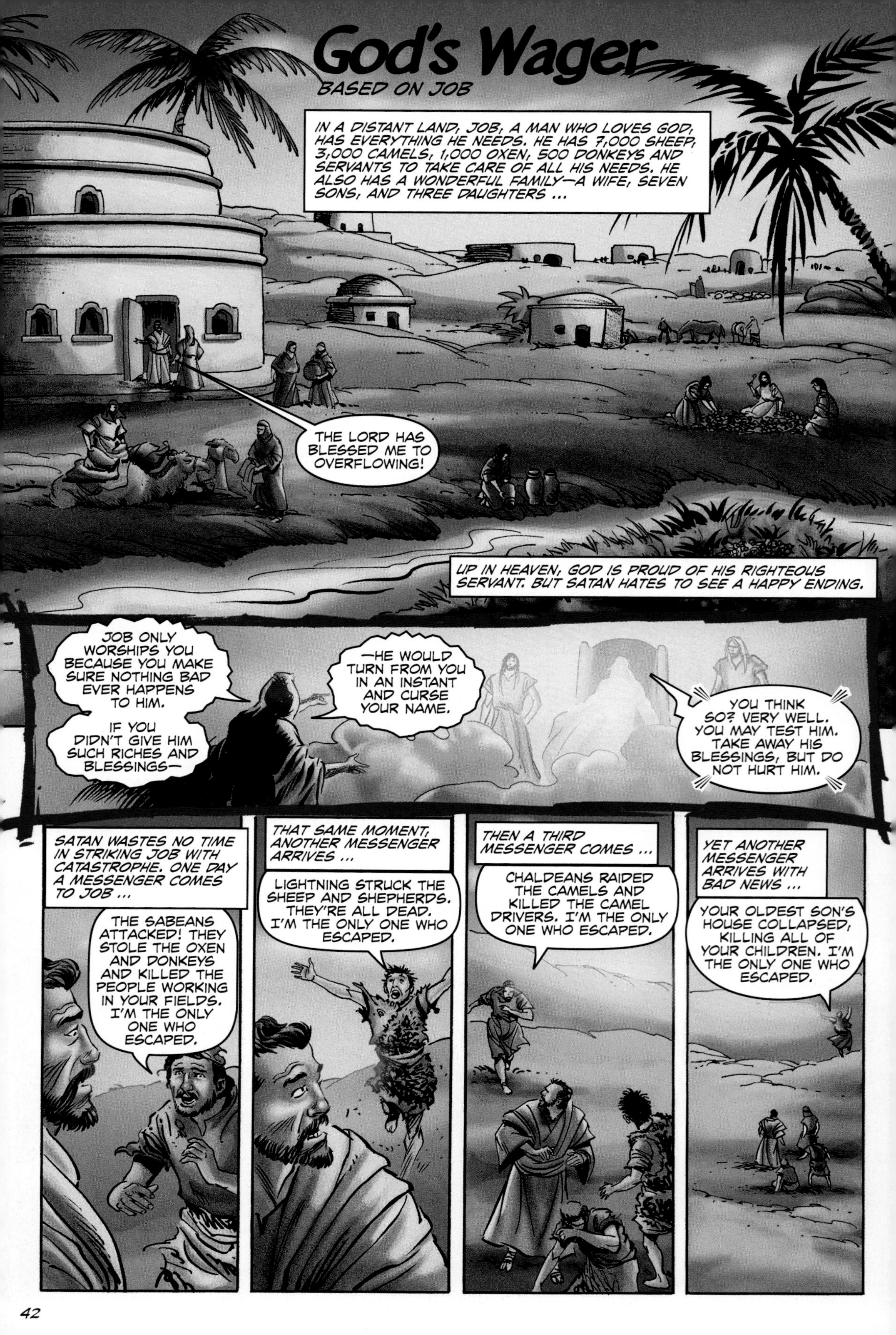

God's Wager
BASED ON JOB
IN A DISTANT LAND, JOB, A MAN WHO LOVES GOD, HAS EVERYTHING HE NEEDS. HE HAS 7,000 SHEEP, 3,000 CAMELS, 1,000 OXEN, 500 DONKEYS AND SERVANTS TO TAKE CARE OF ALL HIS NEEDS. HE ALSO HAS A WONDERFUL FAMILY—A WIFE, SEVEN SONS, AND THREE DAUGHTERS ...
THE LORD HAS BLESSED ME TO OVERFLOWING!
UP IN HEAVEN, GOD IS PROUD OF HIS RIGHTEOUS SERVANT. BUT SATAN HATES TO SEE A HAPPY ENDING.
JOB ONLY WORSHIPS YOU BECAUSE YOU MAKE SURE NOTHING BAD EVER HAPPENS TO HIM.
IF YOU DIDN'T GIVE HIM SUCH RICHES AND BLESSINGS—
—HE WOULD TURN FROM YOU IN AN INSTANT AND CURSE YOUR NAME.
YOU THINK SO? VERY WELL. YOU MAY TEST HIM. TAKE AWAY HIS BLESSINGS, BUT DO NOT HURT HIM.
SATAN WASTES NO TIME IN STRIKING JOB WITH CATASTROPHE. ONE DAY A MESSENGER COMES TO JOB ...
THE SABEANS ATTACKED! THEY STOLE THE OXEN AND DONKEYS AND KILLED THE PEOPLE WORKING IN YOUR FIELDS. I'M THE ONLY ONE WHO ESCAPED.
THAT SAME MOMENT, ANOTHER MESSENGER ARRIVES ...
LIGHTNING STRUCK THE SHEEP AND SHEPHERDS. THEY'RE ALL DEAD. I'M THE ONLY ONE WHO ESCAPED.
THEN A THIRD MESSENGER COMES ...
CHALDEANS RAIDED THE CAMELS AND KILLED THE CAMEL DRIVERS. I'M THE ONLY ONE WHO ESCAPED.
YET ANOTHER MESSENGER ARRIVES WITH BAD NEWS ...
YOUR OLDEST SON'S HOUSE COLLAPSED, KILLING ALL OF YOUR CHILDREN. I'M THE ONLY ONE WHO ESCAPED.

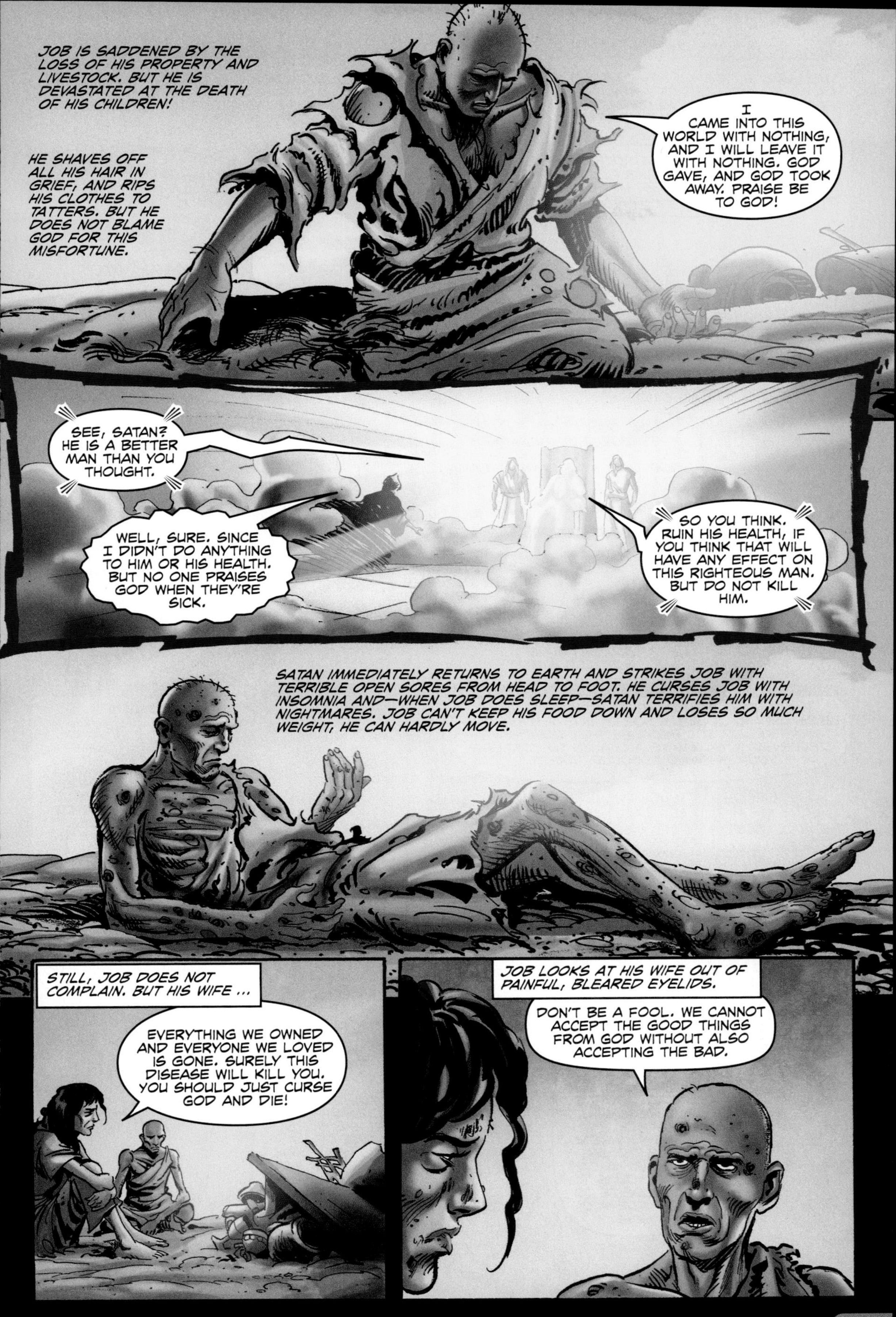
JOB IS SADDENED BY THE LOSS OF HIS PROPERTY AND LIVESTOCK. BUT HE IS DEVASTATED AT THE DEATH OF HIS CHILDREN!
HE SHAVES OFF ALL HIS HAIR IN GRIEF, AND RIPS HIS CLOTHES TO TATTERS. BUT HE DOES NOT BLAME GOD FOR THIS MISFORTUNE.
I CAME INTO THIS WORLD WITH NOTHING, AND I WILL LEAVE IT WITH NOTHING. GOD GAVE, AND GOD TOOK AWAY. PRAISE BE TO GOD!
SEE, SATAN? HE IS A BETTER MAN THAN YOU THOUGHT.
WELL, SURE. SINCE I DIDN'T DO ANYTHING TO HIM OR HIS HEALTH. BUT NO ONE PRAISES GOD WHEN THEY'RE SICK.
SO YOU THINK. RUIN HIS HEALTH, IF YOU THINK THAT WILL HAVE ANY EFFECT ON THIS RIGHTEOUS MAN. BUT DO NOT KILL HIM.
SATAN IMMEDIATELY RETURNS TO EARTH AND STRIKES JOB WITH TERRIBLE OPEN SORES FROM HEAD TO FOOT. HE CURSES JOB WITH INSOMNIA AND—WHEN JOB DOES SLEEP—SATAN TERRIFIES HIM WITH NIGHTMARES. JOB CAN'T KEEP HIS FOOD DOWN AND LOSES SO MUCH WEIGHT, HE CAN HARDLY MOVE.
STILL, JOB DOES NOT COMPLAIN. BUT HIS WIFE ...
EVERYTHING WE OWNED AND EVERYONE WE LOVED IS GONE. SURELY THIS DISEASE WILL KILL YOU. YOU SHOULD JUST CURSE GOD AND DIE!
JOB LOOKS AT HIS WIFE OUT OF PAINFUL, BLEARED EYELIDS.
DON'T BE A FOOL. WE CANNOT ACCEPT THE GOOD THINGS FROM GOD WITHOUT ALSO ACCEPTING THE BAD.

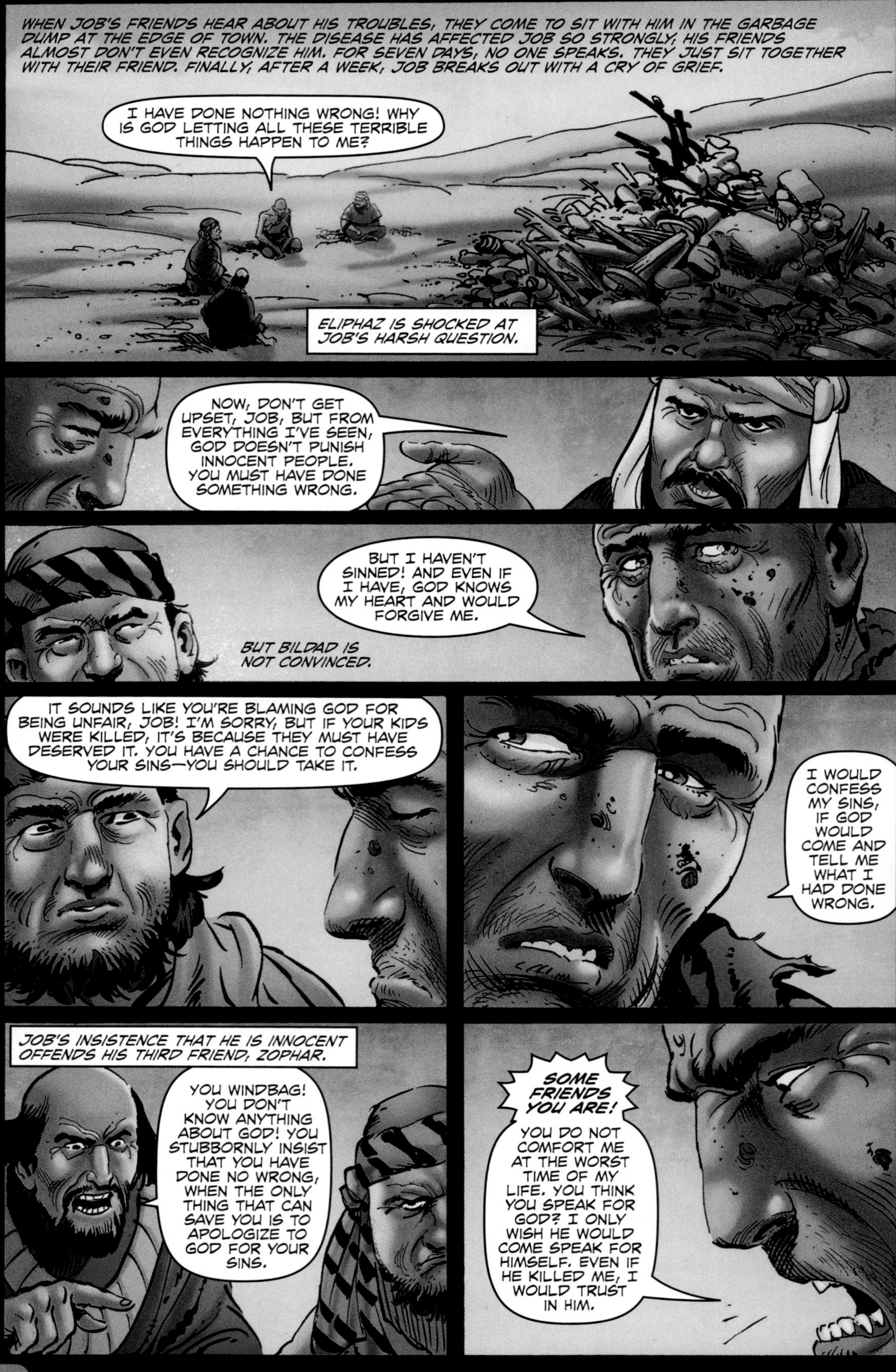
WHEN JOB'S FRIENDS HEAR ABOUT HIS TROUBLES, THEY COME TO SIT WITH HIM IN THE GARBAGE DUMP AT THE EDGE OF TOWN. THE DISEASE HAS AFFECTED JOB SO STRONGLY, HIS FRIENDS ALMOST DON'T EVEN RECOGNIZE HIM. FOR SEVEN DAYS, NO ONE SPEAKS. THEY JUST SIT TOGETHER WITH THEIR FRIEND. FINALLY, AFTER A WEEK, JOB BREAKS OUT WITH A CRY OF GRIEF.
I HAVE DONE NOTHING WRONG! WHY IS GOD LETTING ALL THESE TERRIBLE THINGS HAPPEN TO ME?
ELIPHAZ IS SHOCKED AT JOB'S HARSH QUESTION.
NOW, DON'T GET UPSET, JOB, BUT FROM EVERYTHING I'VE SEEN, GOD DOESN'T PUNISH INNOCENT PEOPLE. YOU MUST HAVE DONE SOMETHING WRONG.
BUT I HAVEN'T SINNED! AND EVEN IF I HAVE, GOD KNOWS MY HEART AND WOULD FORGIVE ME.
BUT BILDAD IS NOT CONVINCED.
IT SOUNDS LIKE YOU'RE BLAMING GOD FOR BEING UNFAIR, JOB! I'M SORRY, BUT IF YOUR KIDS WERE KILLED, IT'S BECAUSE THEY MUST HAVE DESERVED IT. YOU HAVE A CHANCE TO CONFESS YOUR SINS—YOU SHOULD TAKE IT.
I WOULD CONFESS MY SINS, IF GOD WOULD COME AND TELL ME WHAT I HAD DONE WRONG.
JOB'S INSISTENCE THAT HE IS INNOCENT OFFENDS HIS THIRD FRIEND, ZOPHAR.
YOU WINDBAG! YOU DON'T KNOW ANYTHING ABOUT GOD! YOU STUBBORNLY INSIST THAT YOU HAVE DONE NO WRONG, WHEN THE ONLY THING THAT CAN SAVE YOU IS TO APOLOGIZE TO GOD FOR YOUR SINS.
SOME FRIENDS YOU ARE!
YOU DO NOT COMFORT ME AT THE WORST TIME OF MY LIFE. YOU THINK YOU SPEAK FOR GOD? I ONLY WISH HE WOULD COME SPEAK FOR HIMSELF. EVEN IF HE KILLED ME, I WOULD TRUST IN HIM.

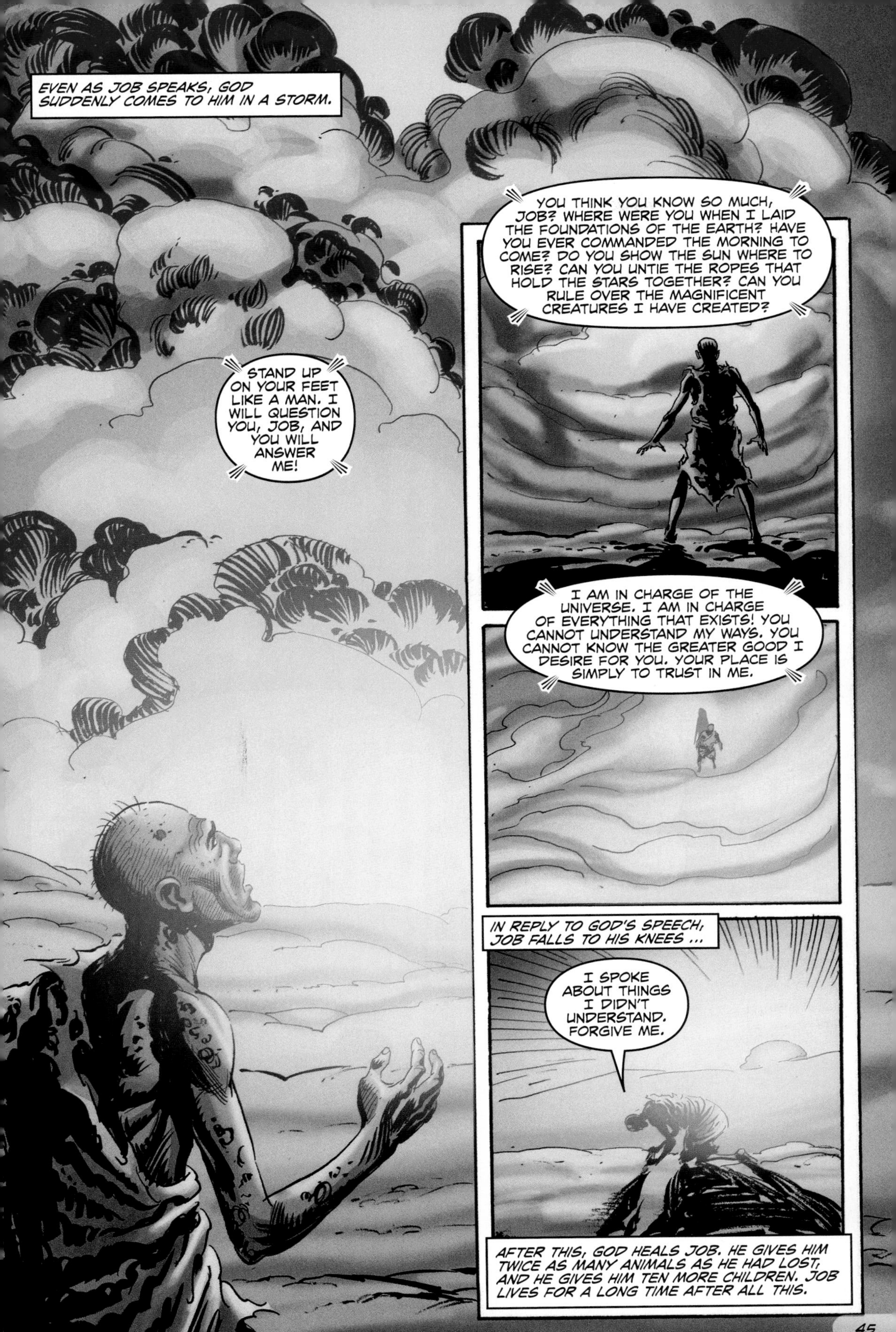
EVEN AS JOB SPEAKS, GOD SUDDENLY COMES TO HIM IN A STORM.
STAND UP ON YOUR FEET LIKE A MAN. I WILL QUESTION YOU, JOB, AND YOU WILL ANSWER ME!
YOU THINK YOU KNOW SO MUCH, JOB? WHERE WERE YOU WHEN I LAID THE FOUNDATIONS OF THE EARTH? HAVE YOU EVER COMMANDED THE MORNING TO COME? DO YOU SHOW THE SUN WHERE TO RISE? CAN YOU UNTIE THE ROPES THAT HOLD THE STARS TOGETHER? CAN YOU RULE OVER THE MAGNIFICENT CREATURES I HAVE CREATED?
I AM IN CHARGE OF THE UNIVERSE. I AM IN CHARGE OF EVERYTHING THAT EXISTS! YOU CANNOT UNDERSTAND MY WAYS. YOU CANNOT KNOW THE GREATER GOOD I DESIRE FOR YOU. YOUR PLACE IS SIMPLY TO TRUST IN ME.
IN REPLY TO GOD'S SPEECH, JOB FALLS TO HIS KNEES ...
I SPOKE ABOUT THINGS I DIDN'T UNDERSTAND. FORGIVE ME.
AFTER THIS, GOD HEALS JOB. HE GIVES HIM TWICE AS MANY ANIMALS AS HE HAD LOST, AND HE GIVES HIM TEN MORE CHILDREN. JOB LIVES FOR A LONG TIME AFTER ALL THIS.

God Calls Abram

BASED ON GENESIS 11—12

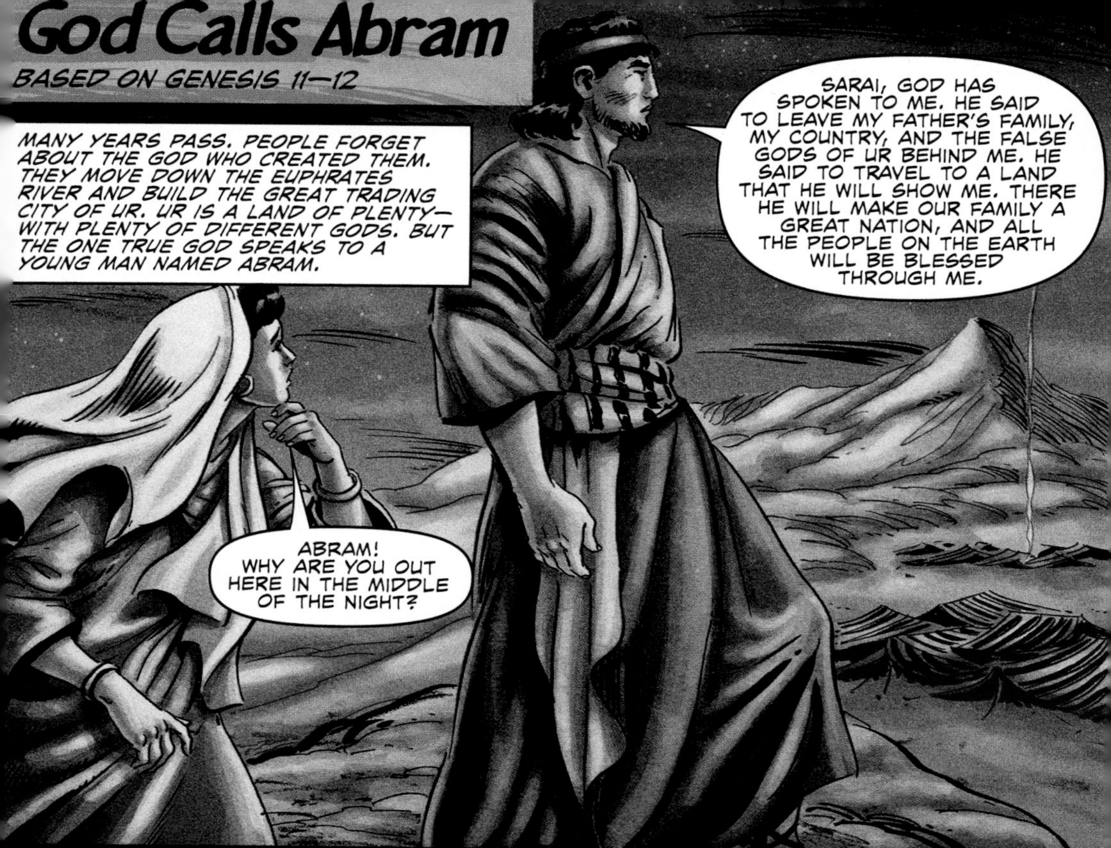
MANY YEARS PASS. PEOPLE FORGET ABOUT THE GOD WHO CREATED THEM. THEY MOVE DOWN THE EUPHRATES RIVER AND BUILD THE GREAT TRADING CITY OF UR. UR IS A LAND OF PLENTY—WITH PLENTY OF DIFFERENT GODS. BUT THE ONE TRUE GOD SPEAKS TO A YOUNG MAN NAMED ABRAM.
ABRAM! WHY ARE YOU OUT HERE IN THE MIDDLE OF THE NIGHT?
SARAI, GOD HAS SPOKEN TO ME. HE SAID TO LEAVE MY FATHER'S FAMILY, MY COUNTRY, AND THE FALSE GODS OF UR BEHIND ME. HE SAID TO TRAVEL TO A LAND THAT HE WILL SHOW ME. THERE HE WILL MAKE OUR FAMILY A GREAT NATION, AND ALL THE PEOPLE ON THE EARTH WILL BE BLESSED THROUGH ME.

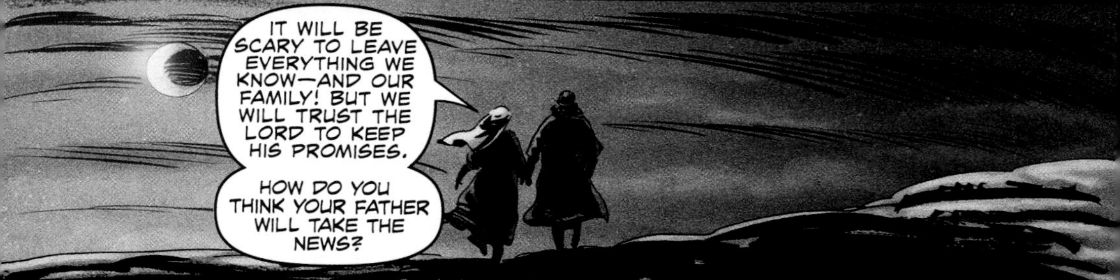
IT WILL BE SCARY TO LEAVE EVERYTHING WE KNOW—AND OUR FAMILY! BUT WE WILL TRUST THE LORD TO KEEP HIS PROMISES.
HOW DO YOU THINK YOUR FATHER WILL TAKE THE NEWS?

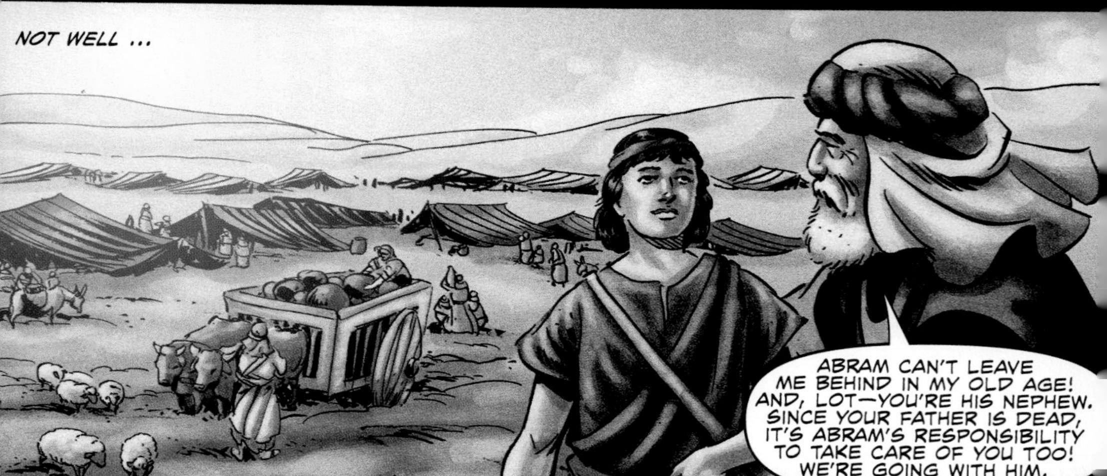
NOT WELL ...
ABRAM CAN'T LEAVE ME BEHIND IN MY OLD AGE! AND, LOT—YOU'RE HIS NEPHEW. SINCE YOUR FATHER IS DEAD, IT'S ABRAM'S RESPONSIBILITY TO TAKE CARE OF YOU TOO! WE'RE GOING WITH HIM.

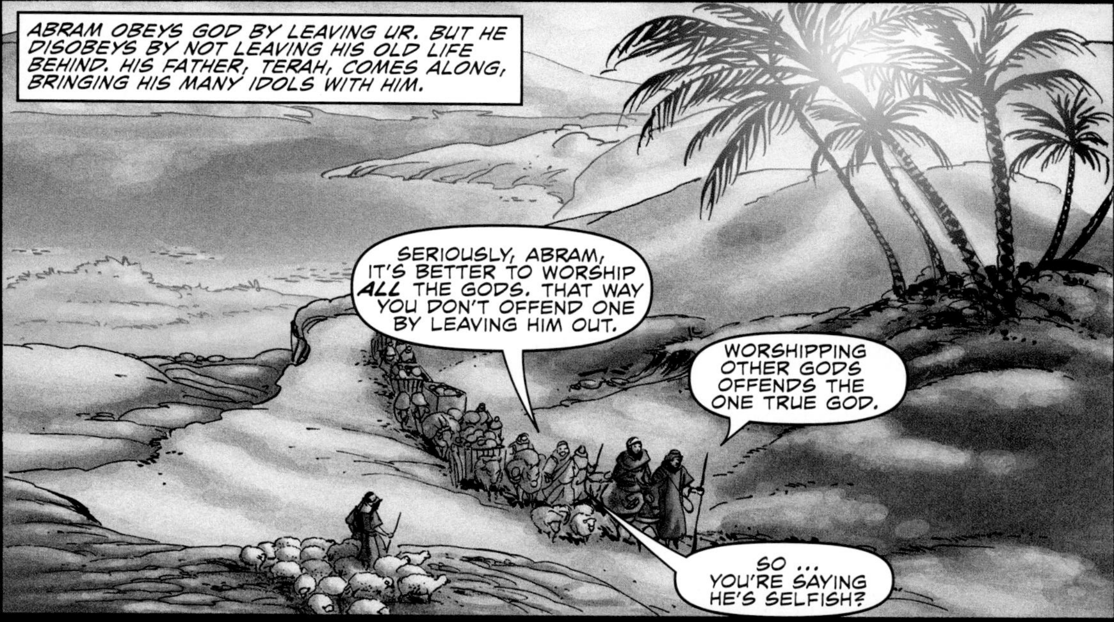
ABRAM OBEYS GOD BY LEAVING UR. BUT HE DISOBEYS BY NOT LEAVING HIS OLD LIFE BEHIND. HIS FATHER, TERAH, COMES ALONG, BRINGING HIS MANY IDOLS WITH HIM.
SERIOUSLY, ABRAM, IT'S BETTER TO WORSHIP **ALL** THE GODS. THAT WAY YOU DON'T OFFEND ONE BY LEAVING HIM OUT.
WORSHIPPING OTHER GODS OFFENDS THE ONE TRUE GOD.
SO ... YOU'RE SAYING HE'S SELFISH?

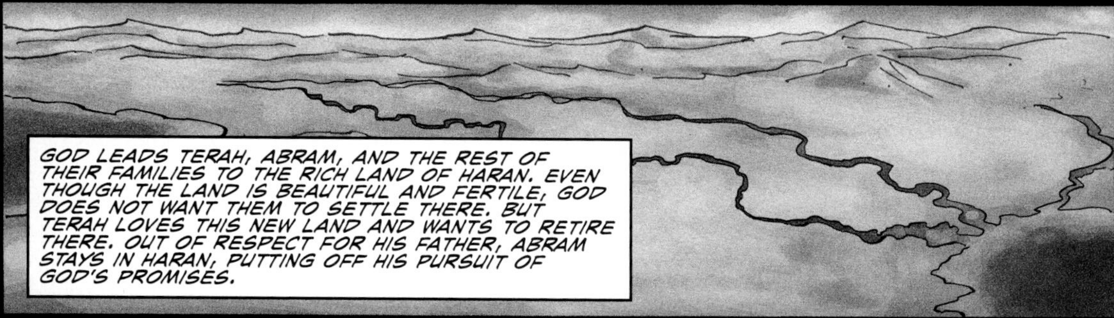
GOD LEADS TERAH, ABRAM, AND THE REST OF THEIR FAMILIES TO THE RICH LAND OF HARAN. EVEN THOUGH THE LAND IS BEAUTIFUL AND FERTILE, GOD DOES NOT WANT THEM TO SETTLE THERE. BUT TERAH LOVES THIS NEW LAND AND WANTS TO RETIRE THERE. OUT OF RESPECT FOR HIS FATHER, ABRAM STAYS IN HARAN, PUTTING OFF HIS PURSUIT OF GOD'S PROMISES.

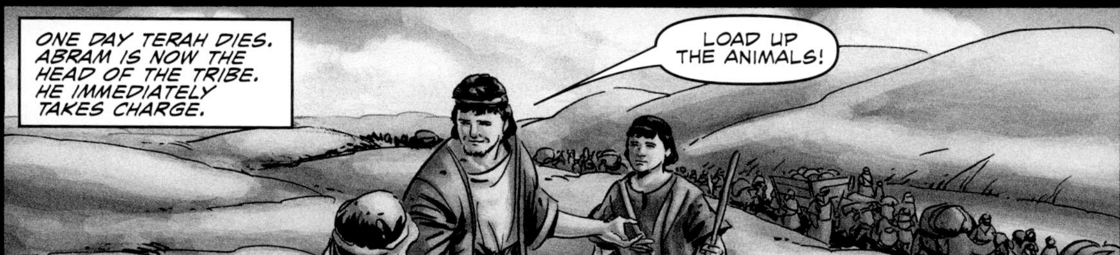
ONE DAY TERAH DIES. ABRAM IS NOW THE HEAD OF THE TRIBE. HE IMMEDIATELY TAKES CHARGE.
LOAD UP THE ANIMALS!

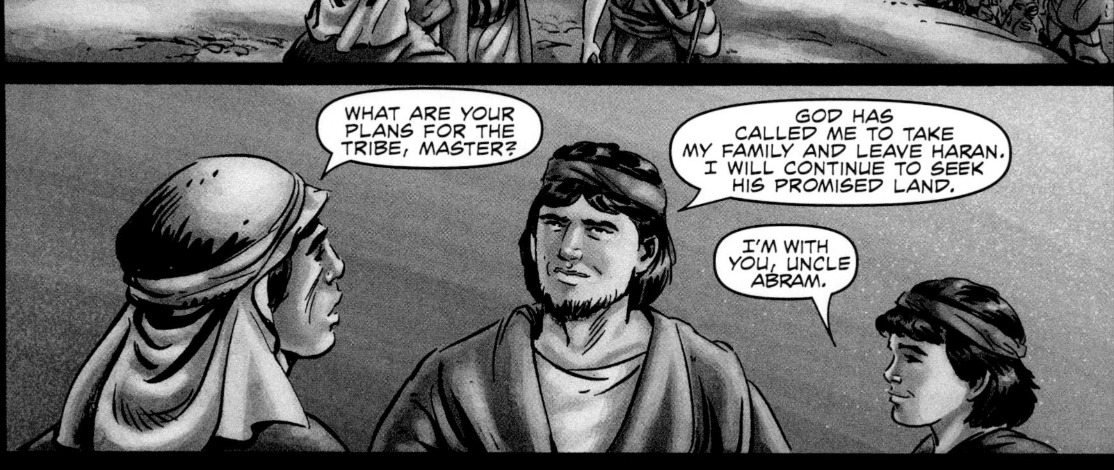
WHAT ARE YOUR PLANS FOR THE TRIBE, MASTER?
GOD HAS CALLED ME TO TAKE MY FAMILY AND LEAVE HARAN. I WILL CONTINUE TO SEEK HIS PROMISED LAND.
I'M WITH YOU, UNCLE ABRAM.

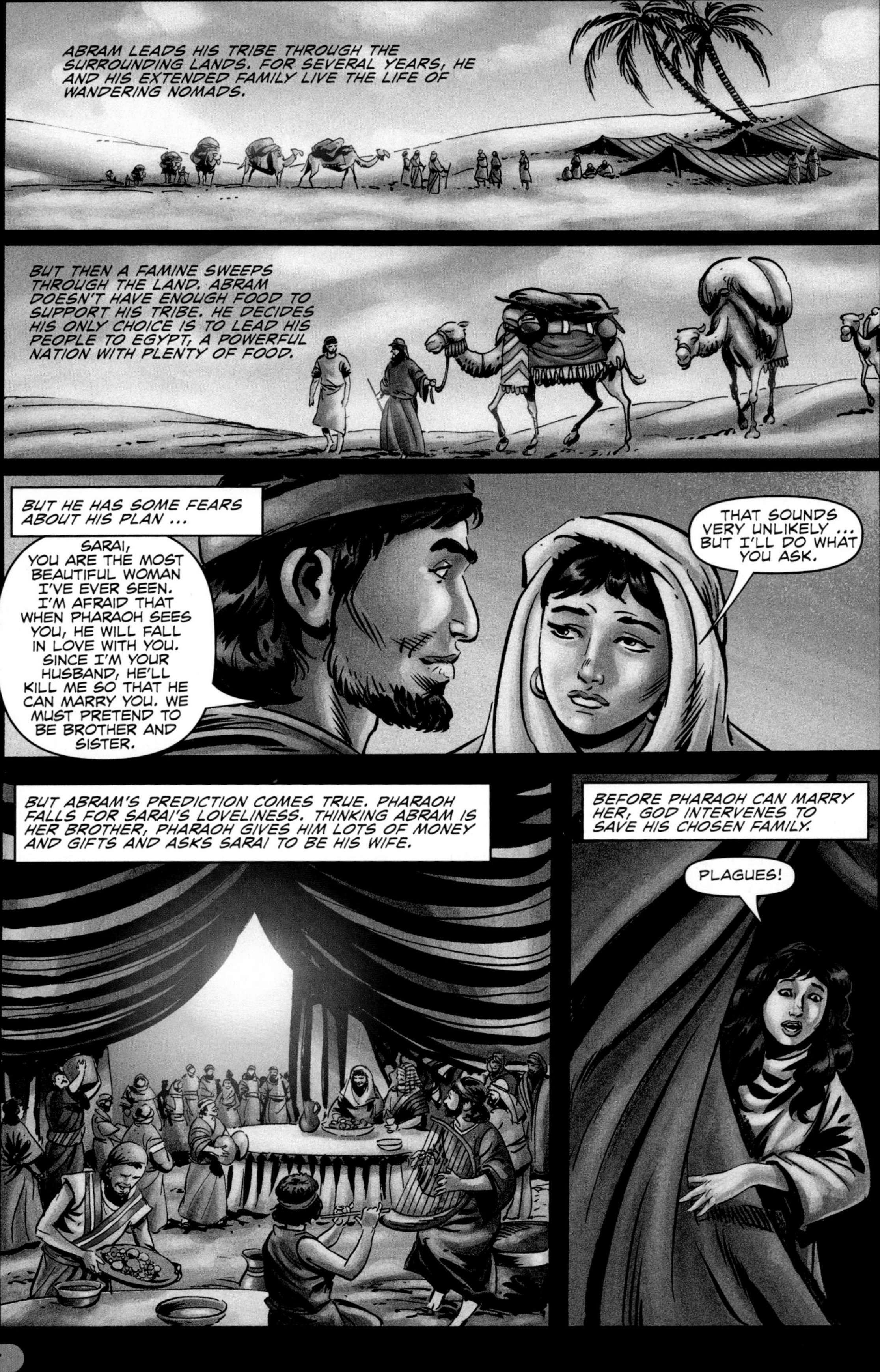
ABRAM LEADS HIS TRIBE THROUGH THE SURROUNDING LANDS. FOR SEVERAL YEARS, HE AND HIS EXTENDED FAMILY LIVE THE LIFE OF WANDERING NOMADS.
BUT THEN A FAMINE SWEEPS THROUGH THE LAND. ABRAM DOESN'T HAVE ENOUGH FOOD TO SUPPORT HIS TRIBE. HE DECIDES HIS ONLY CHOICE IS TO LEAD HIS PEOPLE TO EGYPT, A POWERFUL NATION WITH PLENTY OF FOOD.
BUT HE HAS SOME FEARS ABOUT HIS PLAN ...
SARAI, YOU ARE THE MOST BEAUTIFUL WOMAN I'VE EVER SEEN. I'M AFRAID THAT WHEN PHARAOH SEES YOU, HE WILL FALL IN LOVE WITH YOU. SINCE I'M YOUR HUSBAND, HE'LL KILL ME SO THAT HE CAN MARRY YOU. WE MUST PRETEND TO BE BROTHER AND SISTER.
THAT SOUNDS VERY UNLIKELY ... BUT I'LL DO WHAT YOU ASK.
BUT ABRAM'S PREDICTION COMES TRUE. PHARAOH FALLS FOR SARAI'S LOVELINESS. THINKING ABRAM IS HER BROTHER, PHARAOH GIVES HIM LOTS OF MONEY AND GIFTS AND ASKS SARAI TO BE HIS WIFE.
BEFORE PHARAOH CAN MARRY HER, GOD INTERVENES TO SAVE HIS CHOSEN FAMILY.
PLAGUES!

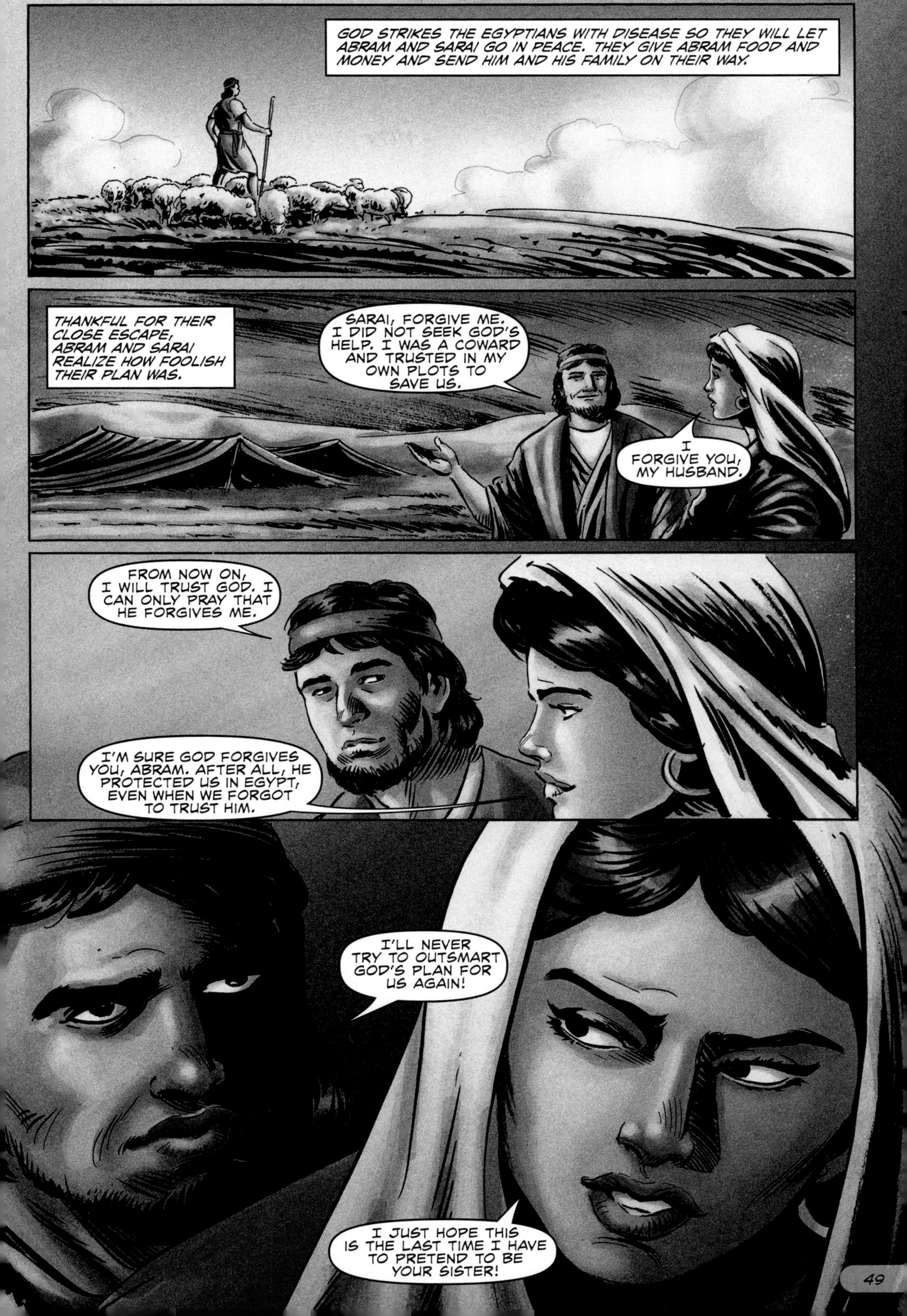

GOD STRIKES THE EGYPTIANS WITH DISEASE SO THEY WILL LET ABRAM AND SARAI GO IN PEACE. THEY GIVE ABRAM FOOD AND MONEY AND SEND HIM AND HIS FAMILY ON THEIR WAY.
THANKFUL FOR THEIR CLOSE ESCAPE, ABRAM AND SARAI REALIZE HOW FOOLISH THEIR PLAN WAS.
SARAI, FORGIVE ME. I DID NOT SEEK GOD'S HELP. I WAS A COWARD AND TRUSTED IN MY OWN PLOTS TO SAVE US.
I FORGIVE YOU, MY HUSBAND.
FROM NOW ON, I WILL TRUST GOD. I CAN ONLY PRAY THAT HE FORGIVES ME.
I'M SURE GOD FORGIVES YOU, ABRAM. AFTER ALL, HE PROTECTED US IN EGYPT, EVEN WHEN WE FORGOT TO TRUST HIM.
I'LL NEVER TRY TO OUTSMART GOD'S PLAN FOR US AGAIN!
I JUST HOPE THIS IS THE LAST TIME I HAVE TO PRETEND TO BE YOUR SISTER!

A Lot Is Too Much

BASED ON GENESIS 13

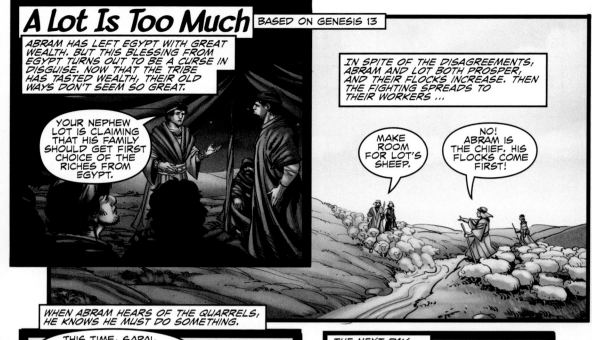

ABRAM HAS LEFT EGYPT WITH GREAT WEALTH. BUT THIS BLESSING FROM EGYPT TURNS OUT TO BE A CURSE IN DISGUISE. NOW THAT THE TRIBE HAS TASTED WEALTH, THEIR OLD WAYS DON'T SEEM SO GREAT.

YOUR NEPHEW LOT IS CLAIMING THAT HIS FAMILY SHOULD GET FIRST CHOICE OF THE RICHES FROM EGYPT.

IN SPITE OF THE DISAGREEMENTS, ABRAM AND LOT BOTH PROSPER, AND THEIR FLOCKS INCREASE. THEN THE FIGHTING SPREADS TO THEIR WORKERS ...

MAKE ROOM FOR LOT'S SHEEP.

NO! ABRAM IS THE CHIEF. HIS FLOCKS COME FIRST!

WHEN ABRAM HEARS OF THE QUARRELS, HE KNOWS HE MUST DO SOMETHING.

THIS TIME, SARAI, I'LL HANDLE THIS THE WAY I THINK GOD WOULD WANT ME TO. I AM AFRAID THAT WE MUST LET LOT GO HIS OWN WAY.

IF YOU ARE TRUSTING THE LORD, THEN YOUR PLAN CANNOT FAIL.

THE NEXT DAY, ABRAM SEEKS OUT HIS NEPHEW.

COME WITH ME, LOT. I HAVE A SOLUTION TO OUR PROBLEM.

LOOK! GOD'S PROMISED LAND IS HUGE! CHOOSE WHERE YOU WOULD LIKE TO LIVE AND I'LL TAKE WHAT IS LEFT.

THAT'S VERY GENEROUS OF YOU, UNCLE. I'LL TAKE THE VALLEY—NEAR THE CITY OF SODOM.

Rescue Mission

BASED ON GENESIS 14; HEBREWS 7:1-3

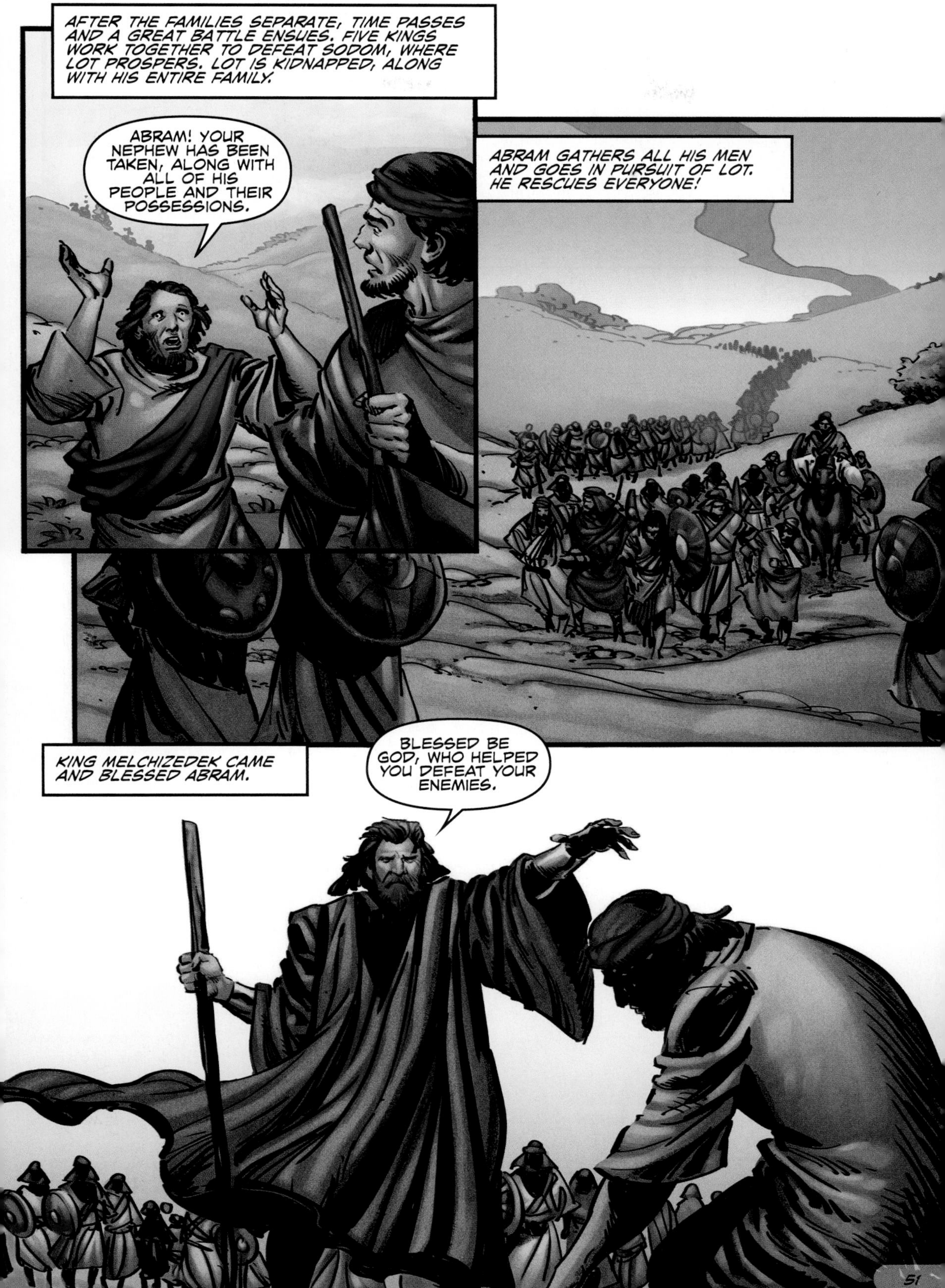
AFTER THE FAMILIES SEPARATE, TIME PASSES AND A GREAT BATTLE ENSUES. FIVE KINGS WORK TOGETHER TO DEFEAT SODOM, WHERE LOT PROSPERS. LOT IS KIDNAPPED, ALONG WITH HIS ENTIRE FAMILY.
ABRAM! YOUR NEPHEW HAS BEEN TAKEN, ALONG WITH ALL OF HIS PEOPLE AND THEIR POSSESSIONS.
ABRAM GATHERS ALL HIS MEN AND GOES IN PURSUIT OF LOT. HE RESCUES EVERYONE!
KING MELCHIZEDEK CAME AND BLESSED ABRAM.
BLESSED BE GOD, WHO HELPED YOU DEFEAT YOUR ENEMIES.

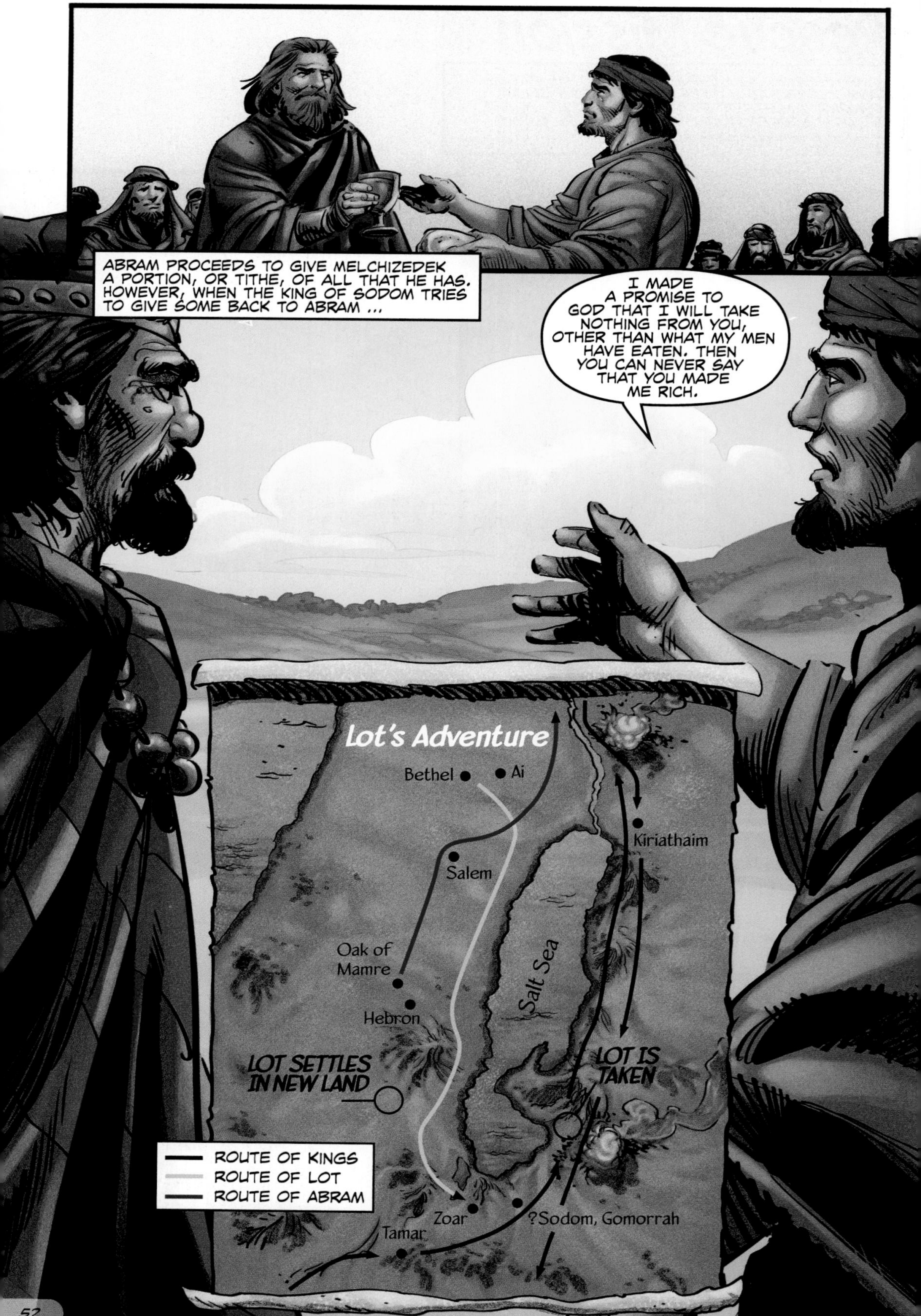
ABRAM PROCEEDS TO GIVE MELCHIZEDEK A PORTION, OR TITHE, OF ALL THAT HE HAS. HOWEVER, WHEN THE KING OF SODOM TRIES TO GIVE SOME BACK TO ABRAM ...
I MADE A PROMISE TO GOD THAT I WILL TAKE NOTHING FROM YOU, OTHER THAN WHAT MY MEN HAVE EATEN. THEN YOU CAN NEVER SAY THAT YOU MADE ME RICH.
Lot's Adventure
Bethel
Ai
Salem
Kiriathaim
Oak of Mamre
Hebron
Salt Sea
LOT SETTLES IN NEW LAND
LOT IS TAKEN
ROUTE OF KINGS
ROUTE OF LOT
ROUTE OF ABRAM
Zoar
?Sodom, Gomorrah
Tamar

Insufficient Sons

BASED ON GENESIS 15—18

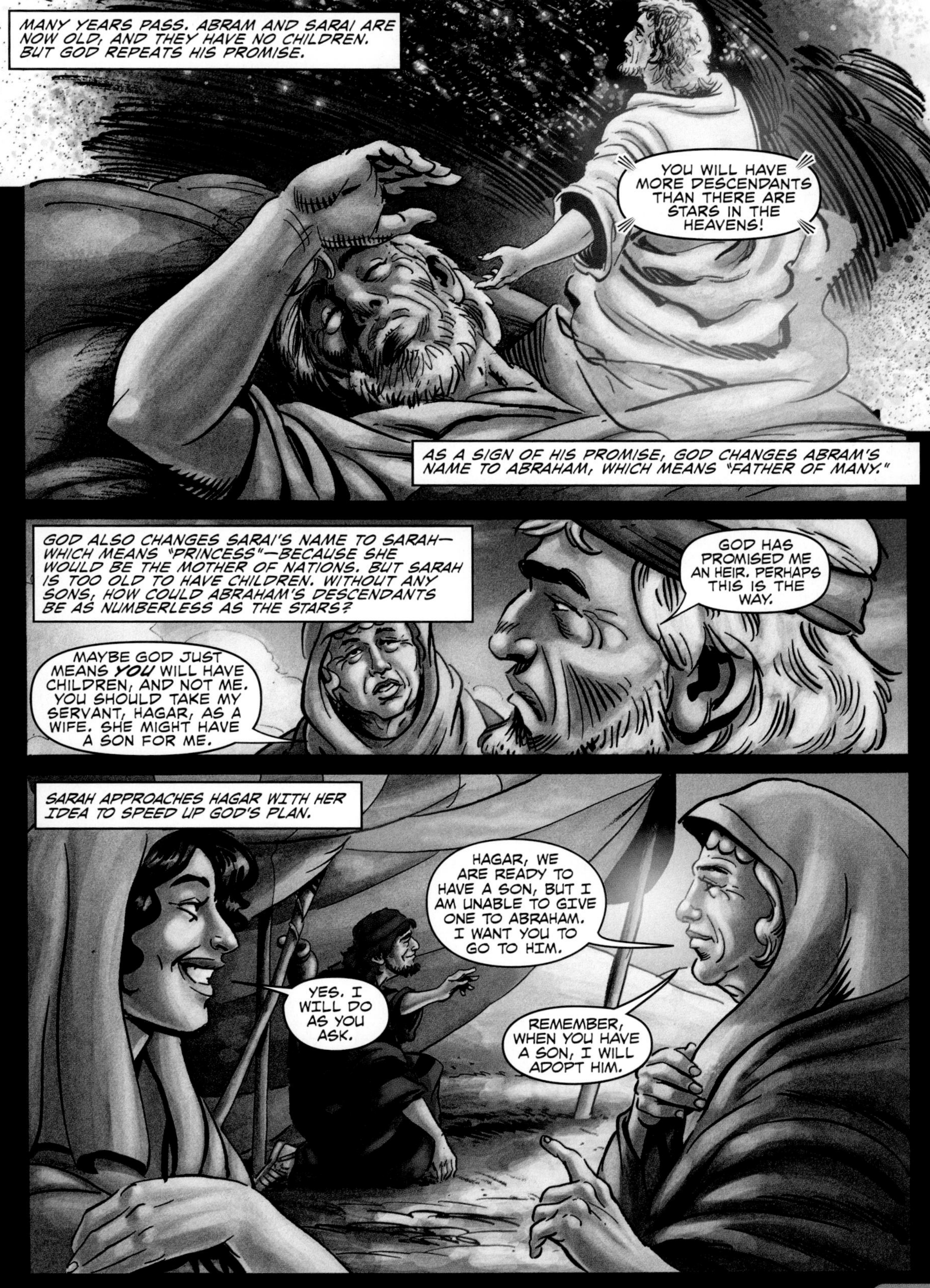
MANY YEARS PASS. ABRAM AND SARAI ARE NOW OLD, AND THEY HAVE NO CHILDREN. BUT GOD REPEATS HIS PROMISE.
YOU WILL HAVE MORE DESCENDANTS THAN THERE ARE STARS IN THE HEAVENS!
AS A SIGN OF HIS PROMISE, GOD CHANGES ABRAM'S NAME TO ABRAHAM, WHICH MEANS "FATHER OF MANY."
GOD ALSO CHANGES SARAI'S NAME TO SARAH—WHICH MEANS "PRINCESS"—BECAUSE SHE WOULD BE THE MOTHER OF NATIONS. BUT SARAH IS TOO OLD TO HAVE CHILDREN. WITHOUT ANY SONS, HOW COULD ABRAHAM'S DESCENDANTS BE AS NUMBERLESS AS THE STARS?
MAYBE GOD JUST MEANS YOU WILL HAVE CHILDREN, AND NOT ME. YOU SHOULD TAKE MY SERVANT, HAGAR, AS A WIFE. SHE MIGHT HAVE A SON FOR ME.
GOD HAS PROMISED ME AN HEIR. PERHAPS THIS IS THE WAY.
SARAH APPROACHES HAGAR WITH HER IDEA TO SPEED UP GOD'S PLAN.
HAGAR, WE ARE READY TO HAVE A SON, BUT I AM UNABLE TO GIVE ONE TO ABRAHAM. I WANT YOU TO GO TO HIM.
YES. I WILL DO AS YOU ASK.
REMEMBER, WHEN YOU HAVE A SON, I WILL ADOPT HIM.

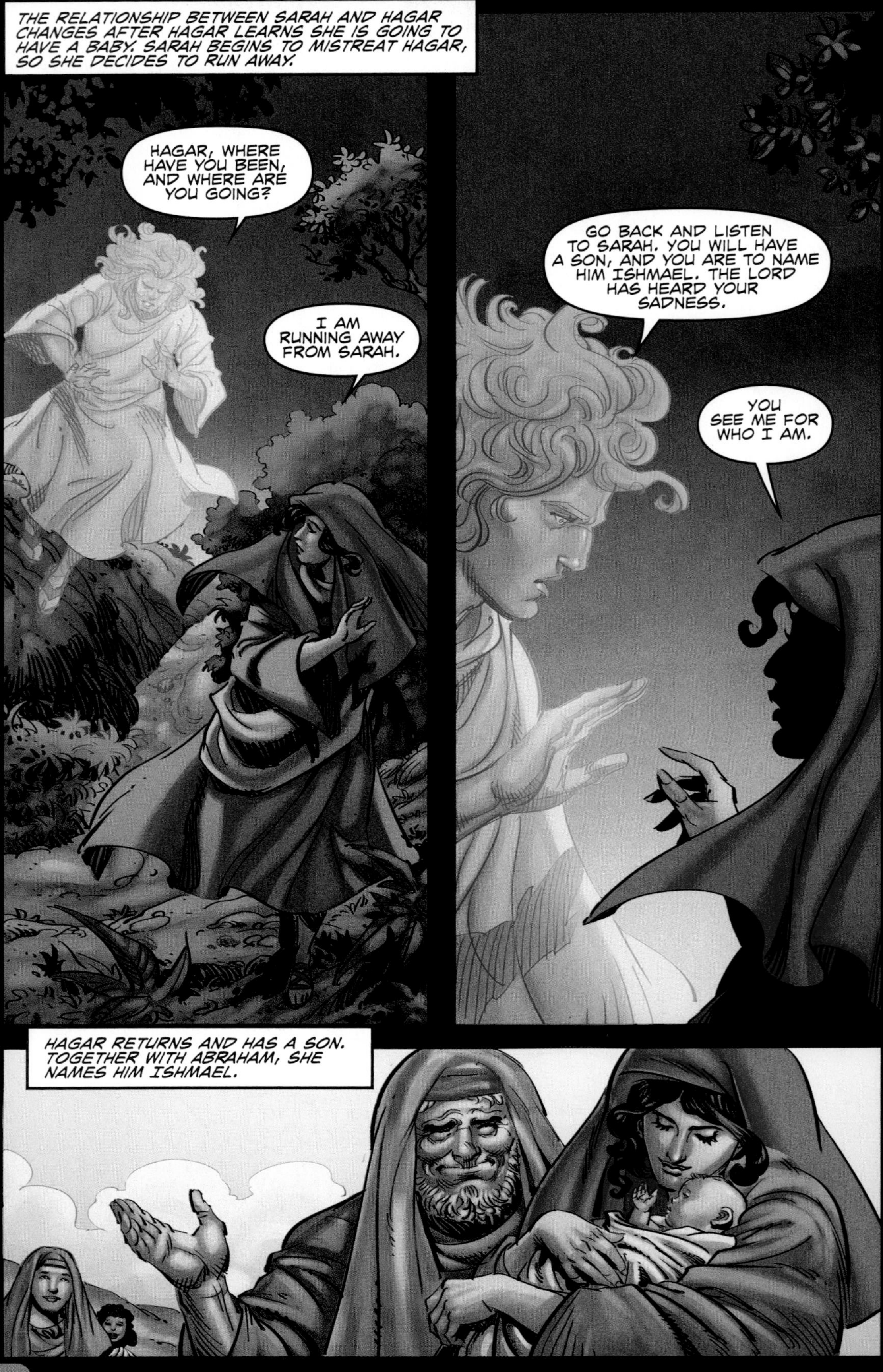
THE RELATIONSHIP BETWEEN SARAH AND HAGAR CHANGES AFTER HAGAR LEARNS SHE IS GOING TO HAVE A BABY. SARAH BEGINS TO MISTREAT HAGAR, SO SHE DECIDES TO RUN AWAY.
HAGAR, WHERE HAVE YOU BEEN, AND WHERE ARE YOU GOING?
I AM RUNNING AWAY FROM SARAH.
GO BACK AND LISTEN TO SARAH. YOU WILL HAVE A SON, AND YOU ARE TO NAME HIM ISHMAEL. THE LORD HAS HEARD YOUR SADNESS.
YOU SEE ME FOR WHO I AM.
HAGAR RETURNS AND HAS A SON. TOGETHER WITH ABRAHAM, SHE NAMES HIM ISHMAEL.

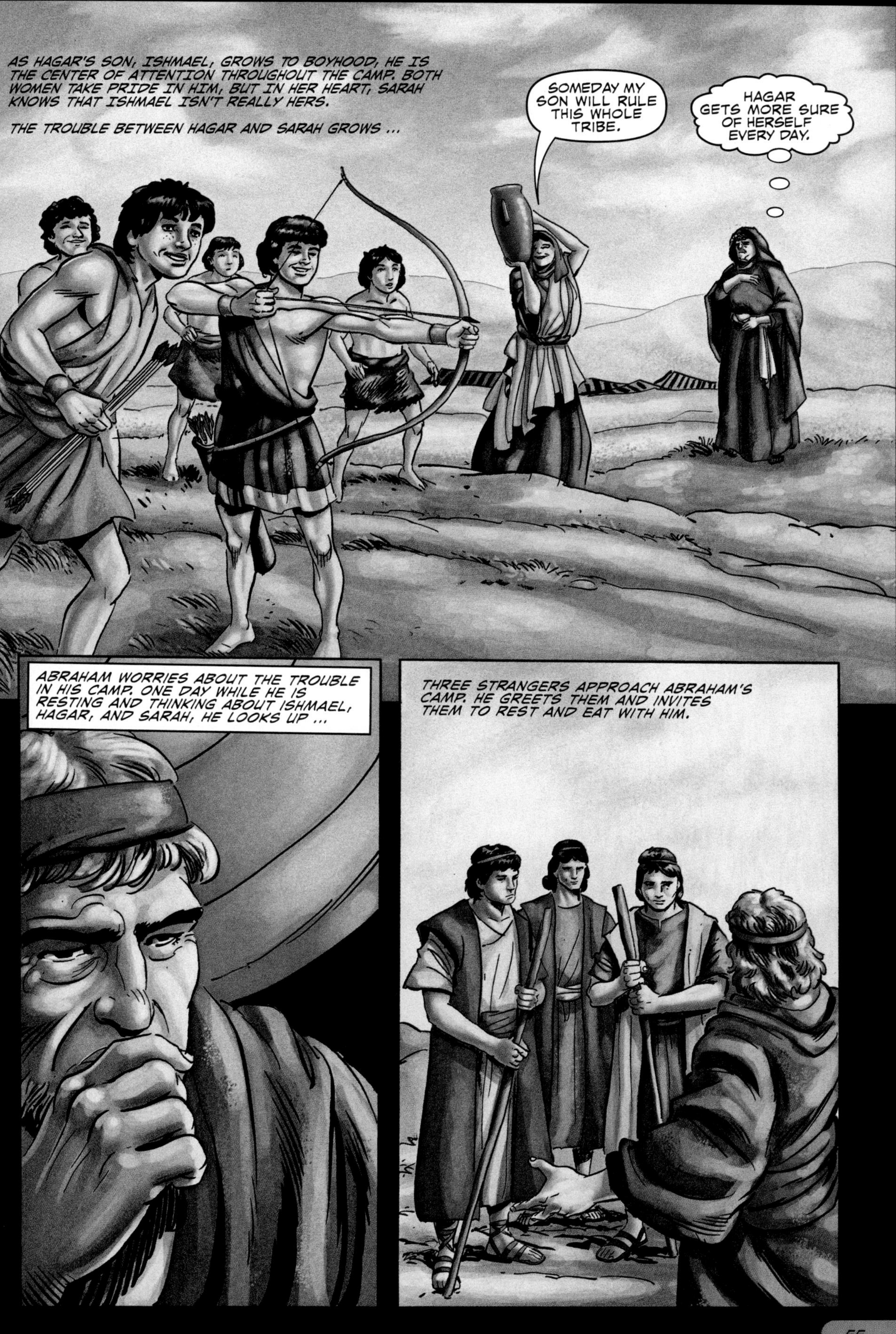
AS HAGAR'S SON, ISHMAEL, GROWS TO BOYHOOD, HE IS THE CENTER OF ATTENTION THROUGHOUT THE CAMP. BOTH WOMEN TAKE PRIDE IN HIM, BUT IN HER HEART, SARAH KNOWS THAT ISHMAEL ISN'T REALLY HERS.
THE TROUBLE BETWEEN HAGAR AND SARAH GROWS ...
SOMEDAY MY SON WILL RULE THIS WHOLE TRIBE.
HAGAR GETS MORE SURE OF HERSELF EVERY DAY.
ABRAHAM WORRIES ABOUT THE TROUBLE IN HIS CAMP. ONE DAY WHILE HE IS RESTING AND THINKING ABOUT ISHMAEL, HAGAR, AND SARAH, HE LOOKS UP ...
THREE STRANGERS APPROACH ABRAHAM'S CAMP. HE GREETS THEM AND INVITES THEM TO REST AND EAT WITH HIM.

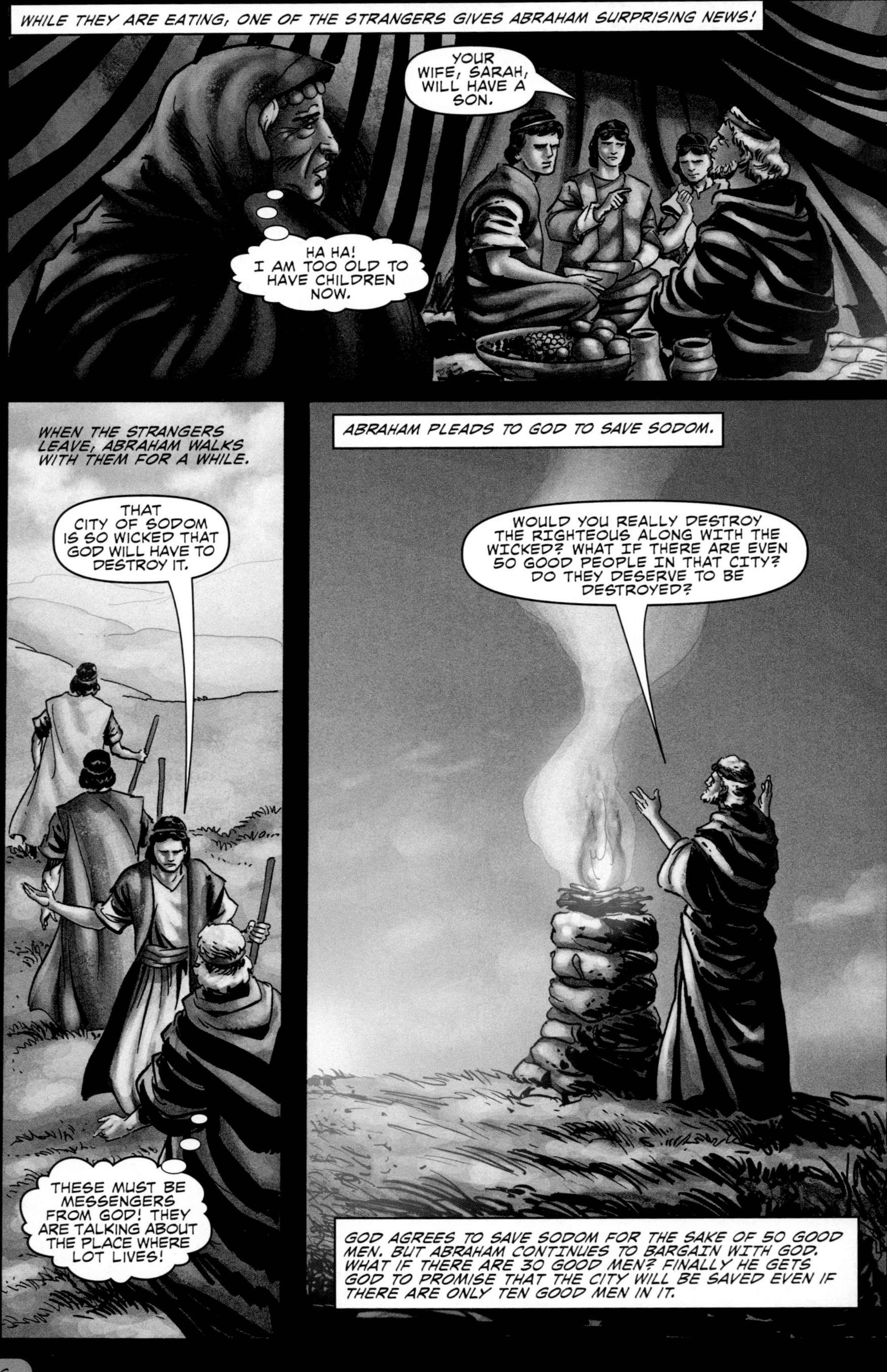
WHILE THEY ARE EATING, ONE OF THE STRANGERS GIVES ABRAHAM SURPRISING NEWS!
YOUR WIFE, SARAH, WILL HAVE A SON.
HA HA! I AM TOO OLD TO HAVE CHILDREN NOW.
WHEN THE STRANGERS LEAVE, ABRAHAM WALKS WITH THEM FOR A WHILE.
THAT CITY OF SODOM IS SO WICKED THAT GOD WILL HAVE TO DESTROY IT.
THESE MUST BE MESSENGERS FROM GOD! THEY ARE TALKING ABOUT THE PLACE WHERE LOT LIVES!
ABRAHAM PLEADS TO GOD TO SAVE SODOM.
WOULD YOU REALLY DESTROY THE RIGHTEOUS ALONG WITH THE WICKED? WHAT IF THERE ARE EVEN 50 GOOD PEOPLE IN THAT CITY? DO THEY DESERVE TO BE DESTROYED?
GOD AGREES TO SAVE SODOM FOR THE SAKE OF 50 GOOD MEN. BUT ABRAHAM CONTINUES TO BARGAIN WITH GOD. WHAT IF THERE ARE 30 GOOD MEN? FINALLY HE GETS GOD TO PROMISE THAT THE CITY WILL BE SAVED EVEN IF THERE ARE ONLY TEN GOOD MEN IN IT.

Destruction of Sodom

BASED ON GENESIS 19

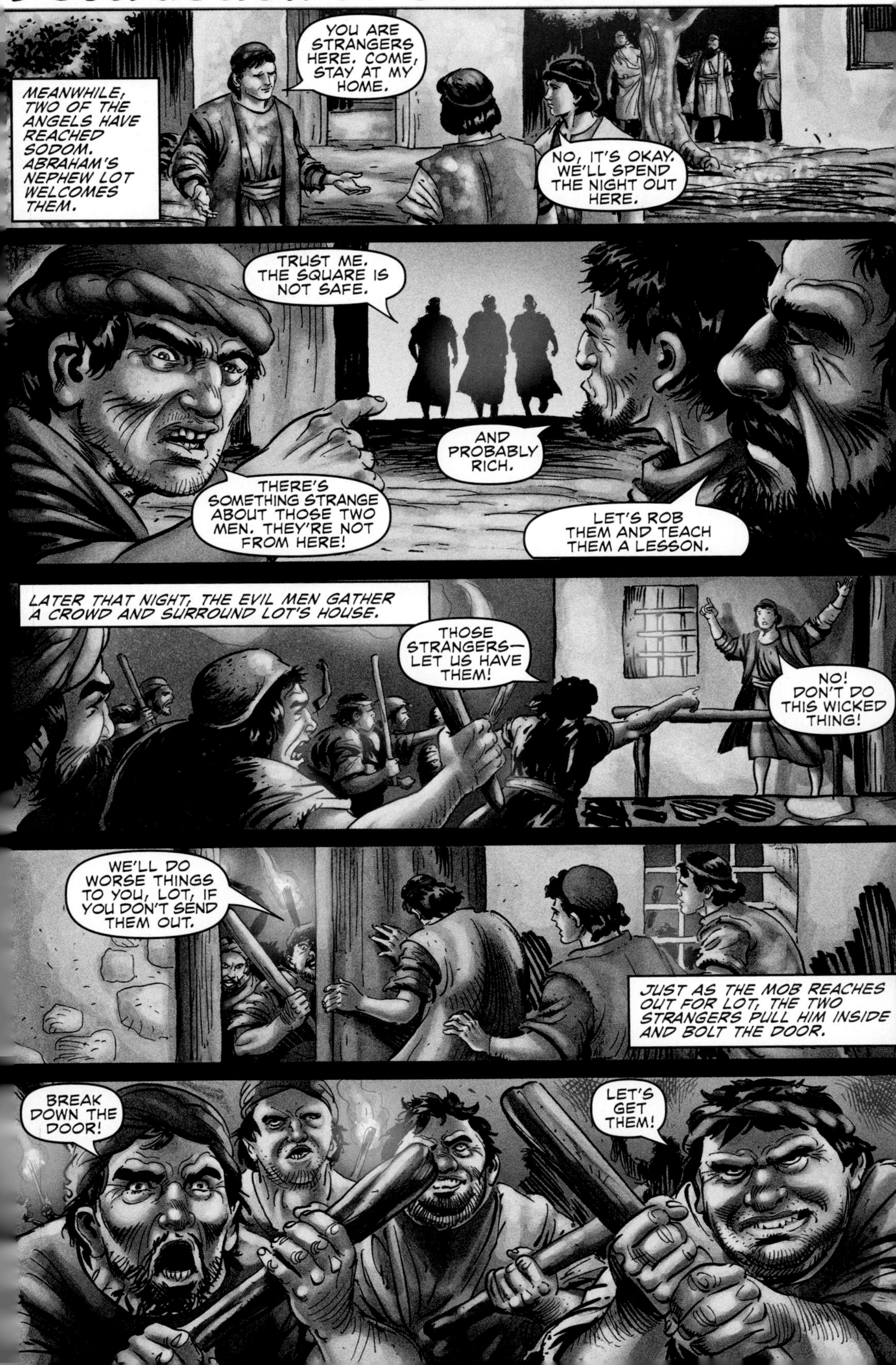
MEANWHILE, TWO OF THE ANGELS HAVE REACHED SODOM. ABRAHAM'S NEPHEW LOT WELCOMES THEM.
YOU ARE STRANGERS HERE. COME, STAY AT MY HOME.
NO, IT'S OKAY. WE'LL SPEND THE NIGHT OUT HERE.
TRUST ME. THE SQUARE IS NOT SAFE.
THERE'S SOMETHING STRANGE ABOUT THOSE TWO MEN. THEY'RE NOT FROM HERE!
AND PROBABLY RICH.
LET'S ROB THEM AND TEACH THEM A LESSON.
LATER THAT NIGHT, THE EVIL MEN GATHER A CROWD AND SURROUND LOT'S HOUSE.
THOSE STRANGERS— LET US HAVE THEM!
NO! DON'T DO THIS WICKED THING!
WE'LL DO WORSE THINGS TO YOU, LOT, IF YOU DON'T SEND THEM OUT.
JUST AS THE MOB REACHES OUT FOR LOT, THE TWO STRANGERS PULL HIM INSIDE AND BOLT THE DOOR.
BREAK DOWN THE DOOR!
LET'S GET THEM!

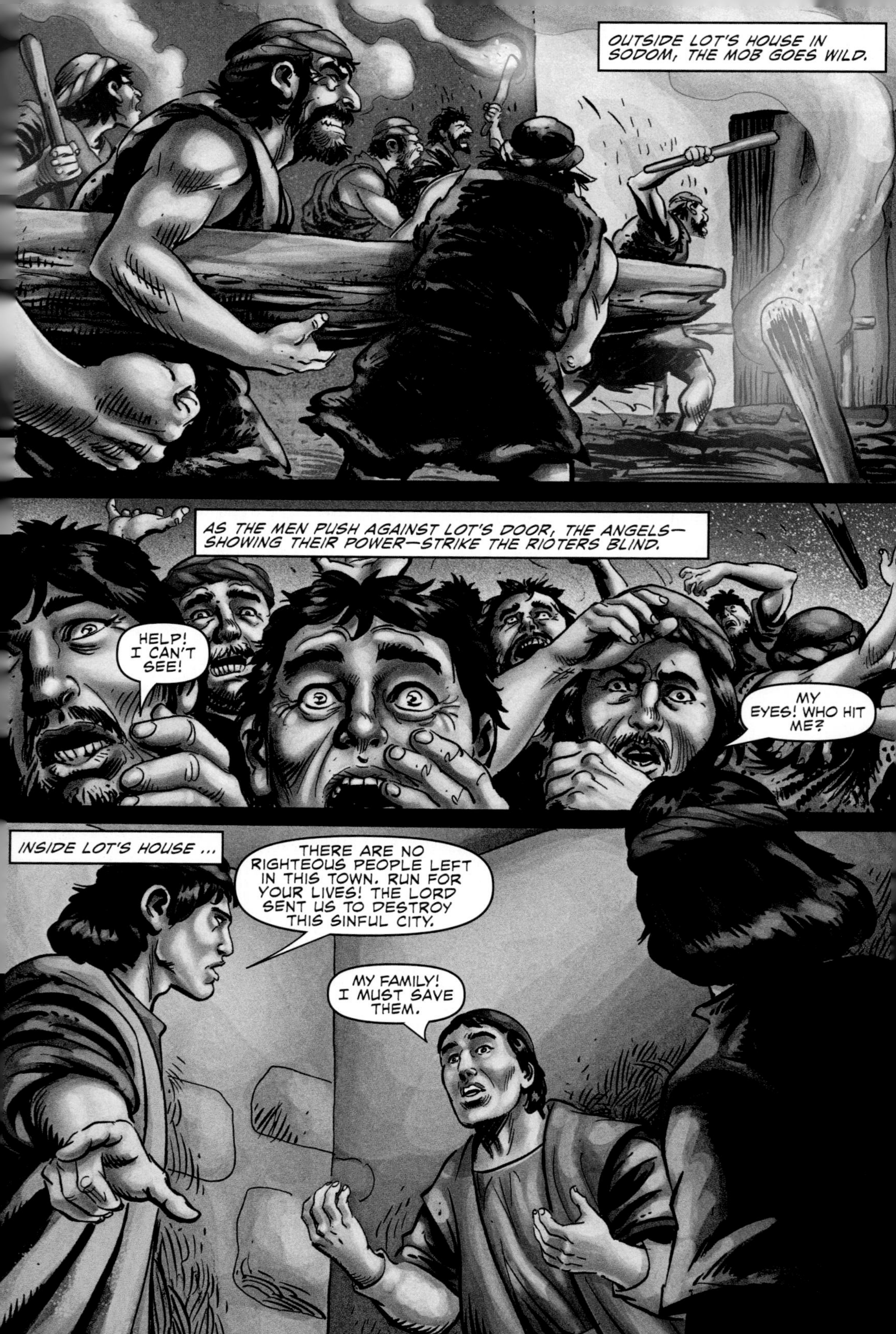
OUTSIDE LOT'S HOUSE IN SODOM, THE MOB GOES WILD.
AS THE MEN PUSH AGAINST LOT'S DOOR, THE ANGELS—SHOWING THEIR POWER—STRIKE THE RIOTERS BLIND.
HELP! I CAN'T SEE!
MY EYES! WHO HIT ME?
INSIDE LOT'S HOUSE ...
THERE ARE NO RIGHTEOUS PEOPLE LEFT IN THIS TOWN. RUN FOR YOUR LIVES! THE LORD SENT US TO DESTROY THIS SINFUL CITY.
MY FAMILY! I MUST SAVE THEM.

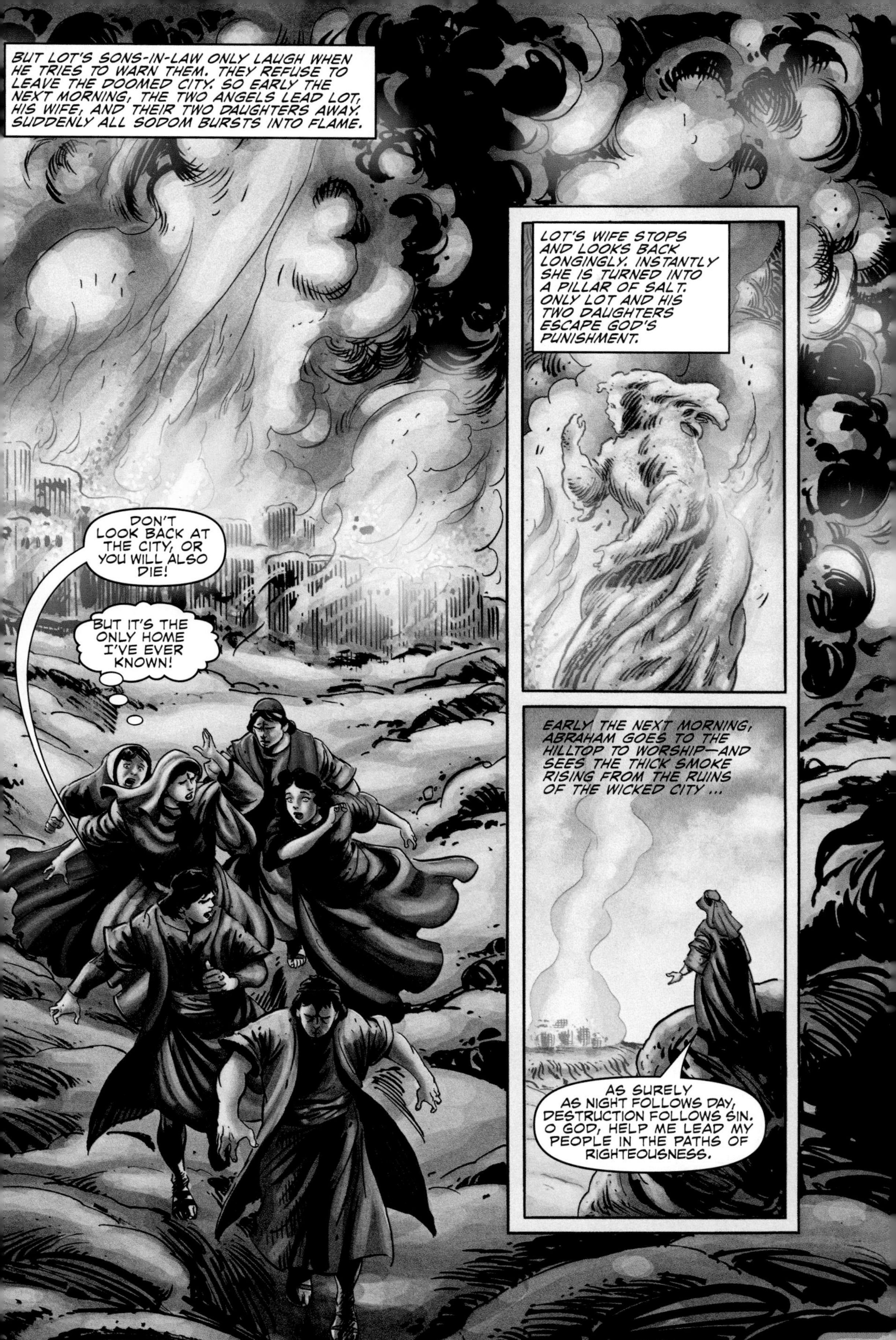
BUT LOT'S SONS-IN-LAW ONLY LAUGH WHEN HE TRIES TO WARN THEM. THEY REFUSE TO LEAVE THE DOOMED CITY. SO EARLY THE NEXT MORNING, THE TWO ANGELS LEAD LOT, HIS WIFE, AND THEIR TWO DAUGHTERS AWAY. SUDDENLY ALL SODOM BURSTS INTO FLAME.
DON'T LOOK BACK AT THE CITY, OR YOU WILL ALSO DIE!
BUT IT'S THE ONLY HOME I'VE EVER KNOWN!
LOT'S WIFE STOPS AND LOOKS BACK LONGINGLY. INSTANTLY SHE IS TURNED INTO A PILLAR OF SALT. ONLY LOT AND HIS TWO DAUGHTERS ESCAPE GOD'S PUNISHMENT.
EARLY THE NEXT MORNING, ABRAHAM GOES TO THE HILLTOP TO WORSHIP—AND SEES THE THICK SMOKE RISING FROM THE RUINS OF THE WICKED CITY ...
AS SURELY AS NIGHT FOLLOWS DAY, DESTRUCTION FOLLOWS SIN. O GOD, HELP ME LEAD MY PEOPLE IN THE PATHS OF RIGHTEOUSNESS.

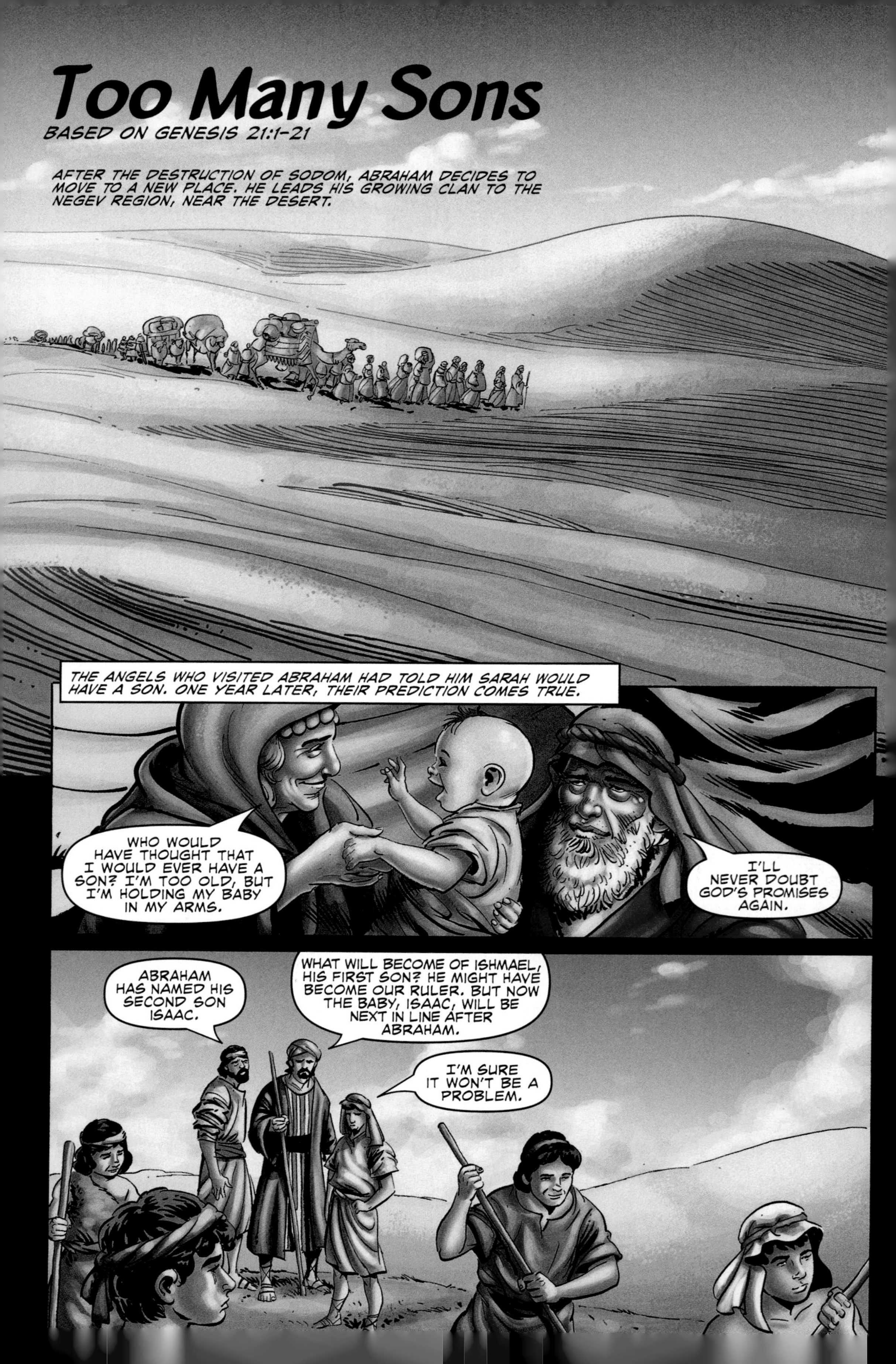
Too Many Sons
BASED ON GENESIS 21:1–21
AFTER THE DESTRUCTION OF SODOM, ABRAHAM DECIDES TO MOVE TO A NEW PLACE. HE LEADS HIS GROWING CLAN TO THE NEGEV REGION, NEAR THE DESERT.
THE ANGELS WHO VISITED ABRAHAM HAD TOLD HIM SARAH WOULD HAVE A SON. ONE YEAR LATER, THEIR PREDICTION COMES TRUE.
WHO WOULD HAVE THOUGHT THAT I WOULD EVER HAVE A SON? I'M TOO OLD, BUT I'M HOLDING MY BABY IN MY ARMS.
I'LL NEVER DOUBT GOD'S PROMISES AGAIN.
ABRAHAM HAS NAMED HIS SECOND SON ISAAC.
WHAT WILL BECOME OF ISHMAEL, HIS FIRST SON? HE MIGHT HAVE BECOME OUR RULER. BUT NOW THE BABY, ISAAC, WILL BE NEXT IN LINE AFTER ABRAHAM.
I'M SURE IT WON'T BE A PROBLEM.

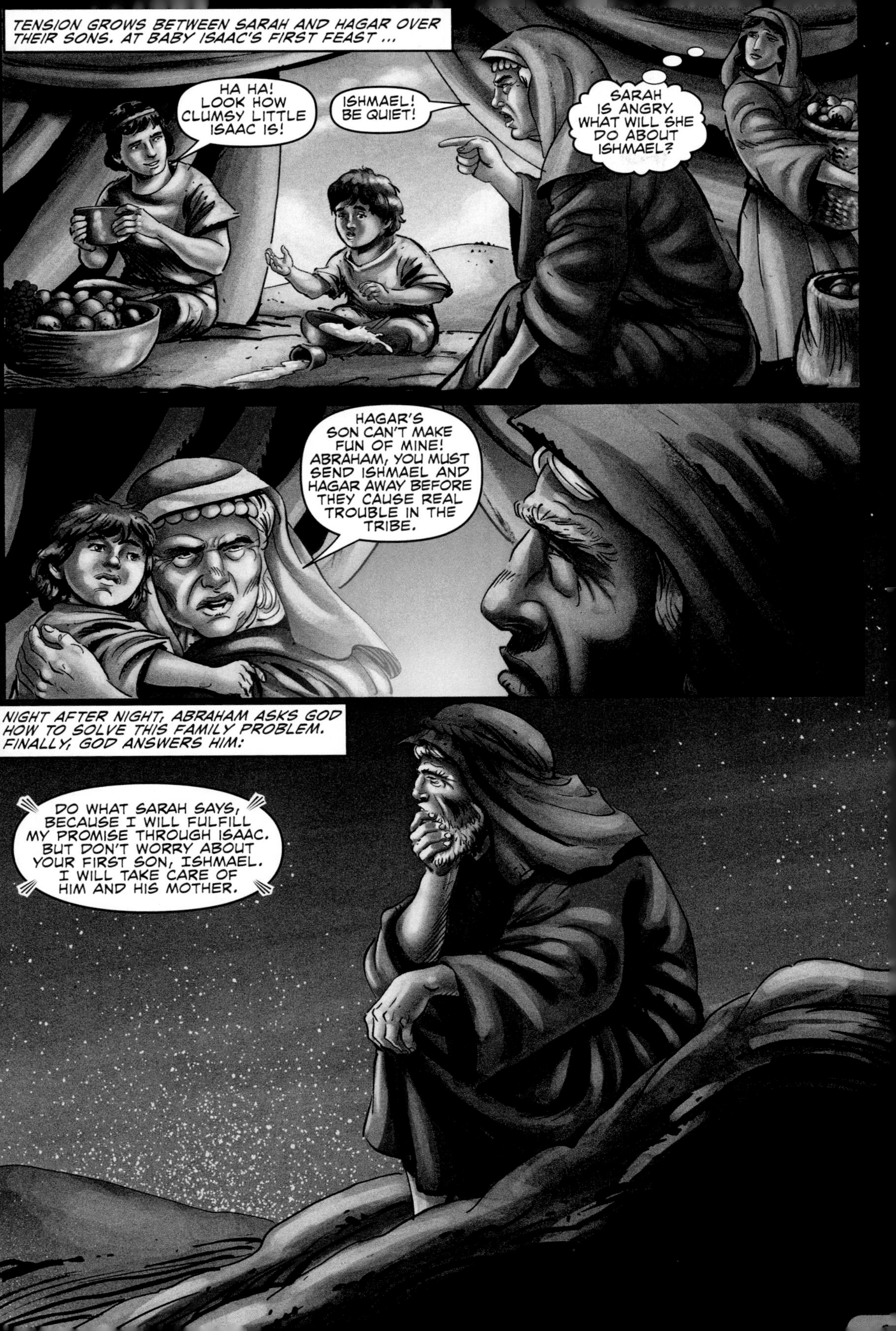
TENSION GROWS BETWEEN SARAH AND HAGAR OVER THEIR SONS. AT BABY ISAAC'S FIRST FEAST ...
HA HA! LOOK HOW CLUMSY LITTLE ISAAC IS!
ISHMAEL! BE QUIET!
SARAH IS ANGRY. WHAT WILL SHE DO ABOUT ISHMAEL?
HAGAR'S SON CAN'T MAKE FUN OF MINE! ABRAHAM, YOU MUST SEND ISHMAEL AND HAGAR AWAY BEFORE THEY CAUSE REAL TROUBLE IN THE TRIBE.
NIGHT AFTER NIGHT, ABRAHAM ASKS GOD HOW TO SOLVE THIS FAMILY PROBLEM. FINALLY, GOD ANSWERS HIM:
DO WHAT SARAH SAYS, BECAUSE I WILL FULFILL MY PROMISE THROUGH ISAAC. BUT DON'T WORRY ABOUT YOUR FIRST SON, ISHMAEL. I WILL TAKE CARE OF HIM AND HIS MOTHER.

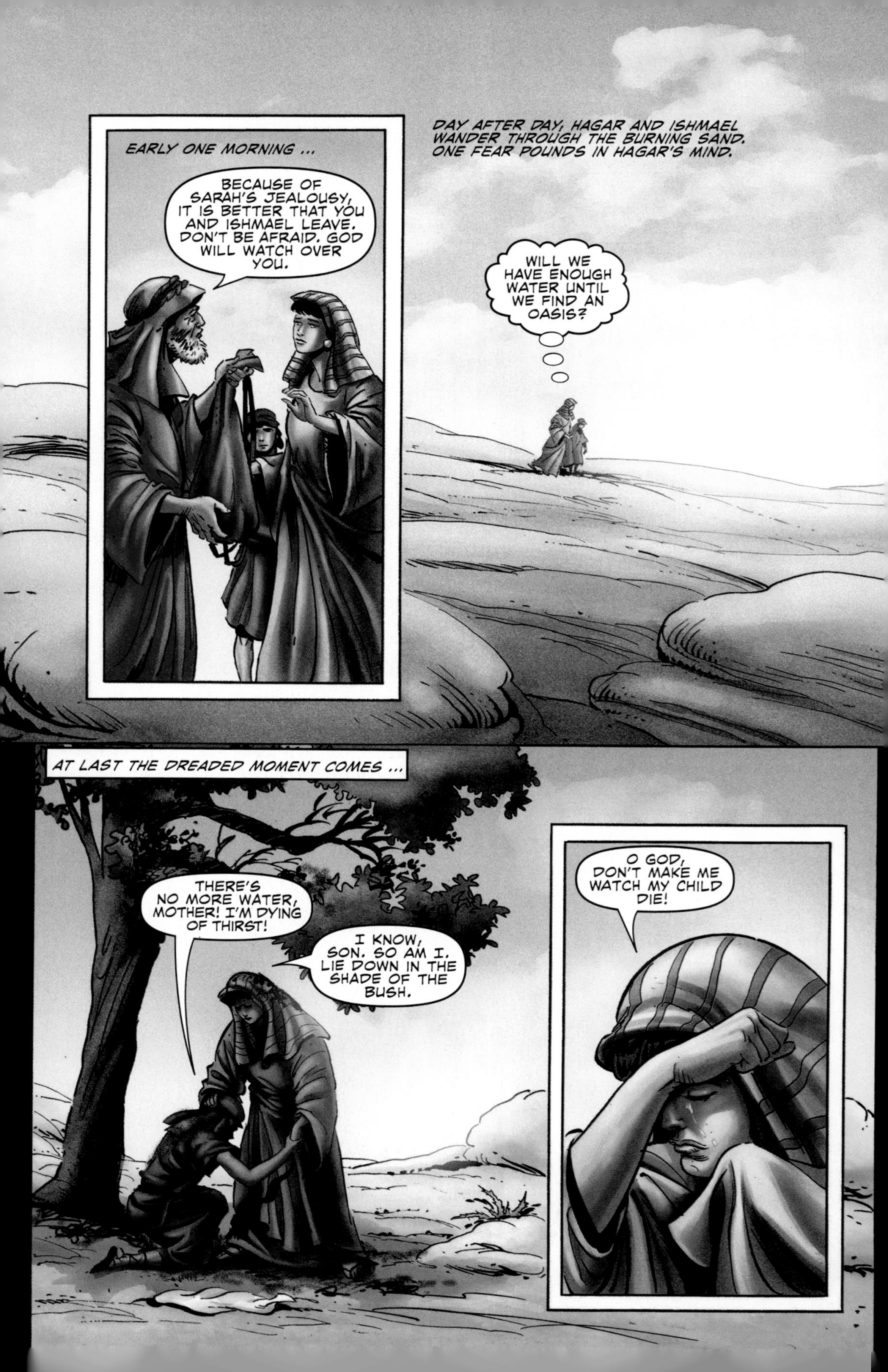
EARLY ONE MORNING ...
BECAUSE OF SARAH'S JEALOUSY, IT IS BETTER THAT YOU AND ISHMAEL LEAVE. DON'T BE AFRAID. GOD WILL WATCH OVER YOU.
DAY AFTER DAY, HAGAR AND ISHMAEL WANDER THROUGH THE BURNING SAND. ONE FEAR POUNDS IN HAGAR'S MIND.
WILL WE HAVE ENOUGH WATER UNTIL WE FIND AN OASIS?
AT LAST THE DREADED MOMENT COMES ...
THERE'S NO MORE WATER, MOTHER! I'M DYING OF THIRST!
I KNOW, SON. SO AM I. LIE DOWN IN THE SHADE OF THE BUSH.
O GOD, DON'T MAKE ME WATCH MY CHILD DIE!

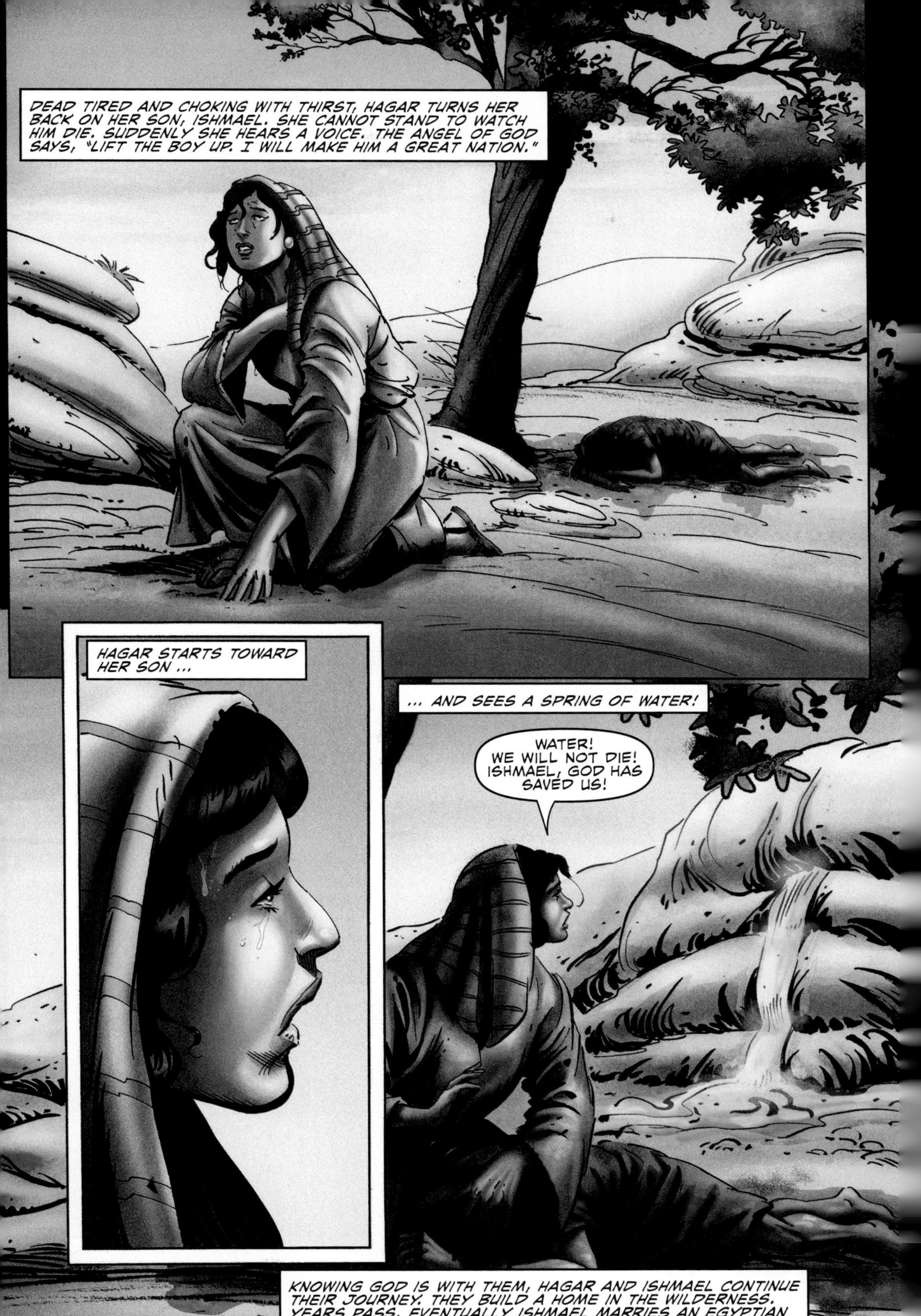

DEAD TIRED AND CHOKING WITH THIRST, HAGAR TURNS HER BACK ON HER SON, ISHMAEL. SHE CANNOT STAND TO WATCH HIM DIE. SUDDENLY SHE HEARS A VOICE. THE ANGEL OF GOD SAYS, "LIFT THE BOY UP. I WILL MAKE HIM A GREAT NATION."
HAGAR STARTS TOWARD HER SON ...
... AND SEES A SPRING OF WATER!
WATER! WE WILL NOT DIE! ISHMAEL, GOD HAS SAVED US!
KNOWING GOD IS WITH THEM, HAGAR AND ISHMAEL CONTINUE THEIR JOURNEY. THEY BUILD A HOME IN THE WILDERNESS. YEARS PASS. EVENTUALLY ISHMAEL MARRIES AN EGYPTIAN GIRL AND BECOMES THE HEAD OF A GREAT DESERT TRIBE.

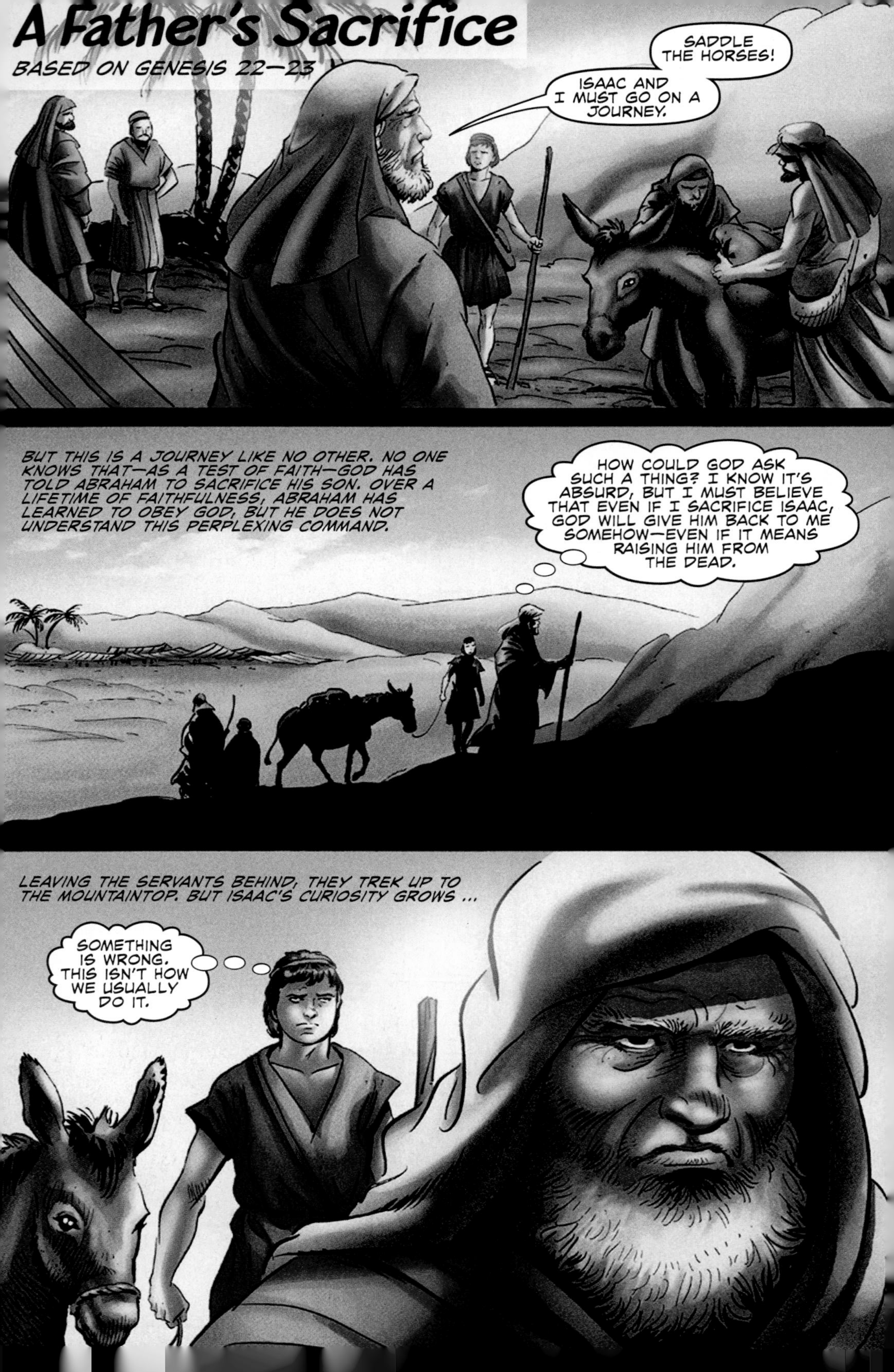
A Father's Sacrifice
BASED ON GENESIS 22—23
SADDLE THE HORSES!
ISAAC AND I MUST GO ON A JOURNEY.
BUT THIS IS A JOURNEY LIKE NO OTHER. NO ONE KNOWS THAT—AS A TEST OF FAITH—GOD HAS TOLD ABRAHAM TO SACRIFICE HIS SON. OVER A LIFETIME OF FAITHFULNESS, ABRAHAM HAS LEARNED TO OBEY GOD, BUT HE DOES NOT UNDERSTAND THIS PERPLEXING COMMAND.
HOW COULD GOD ASK SUCH A THING? I KNOW IT'S ABSURD, BUT I MUST BELIEVE THAT EVEN IF I SACRIFICE ISAAC, GOD WILL GIVE HIM BACK TO ME SOMEHOW—EVEN IF IT MEANS RAISING HIM FROM THE DEAD.
LEAVING THE SERVANTS BEHIND, THEY TREK UP TO THE MOUNTAINTOP. BUT ISAAC'S CURIOSITY GROWS ...
SOMETHING IS WRONG. THIS ISN'T HOW WE USUALLY DO IT.

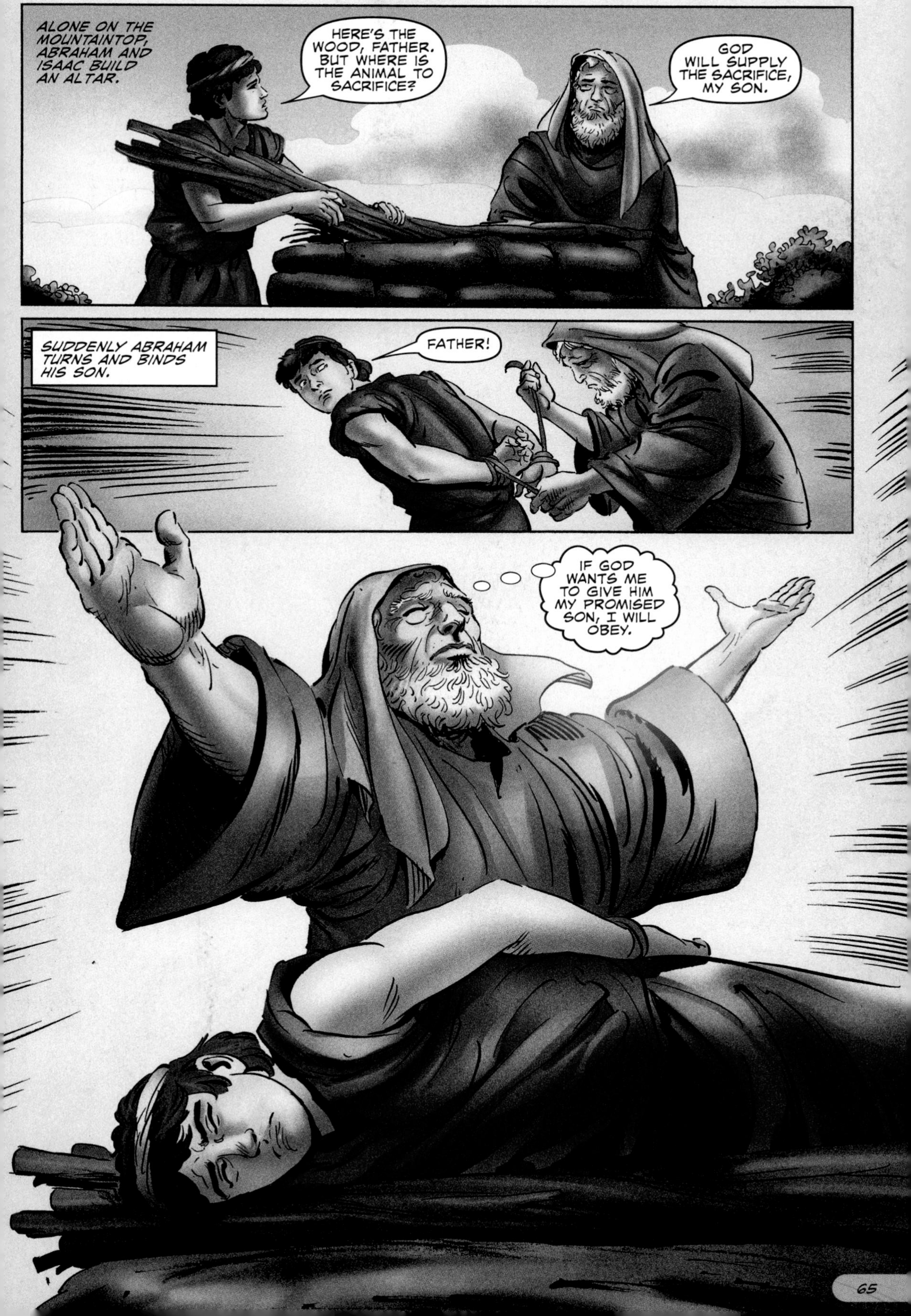
ALONE ON THE MOUNTAINTOP, ABRAHAM AND ISAAC BUILD AN ALTAR.
HERE'S THE WOOD, FATHER. BUT WHERE IS THE ANIMAL TO SACRIFICE?
GOD WILL SUPPLY THE SACRIFICE, MY SON.
SUDDENLY ABRAHAM TURNS AND BINDS HIS SON.
FATHER!
IF GOD WANTS ME TO GIVE HIM MY PROMISED SON, I WILL OBEY.

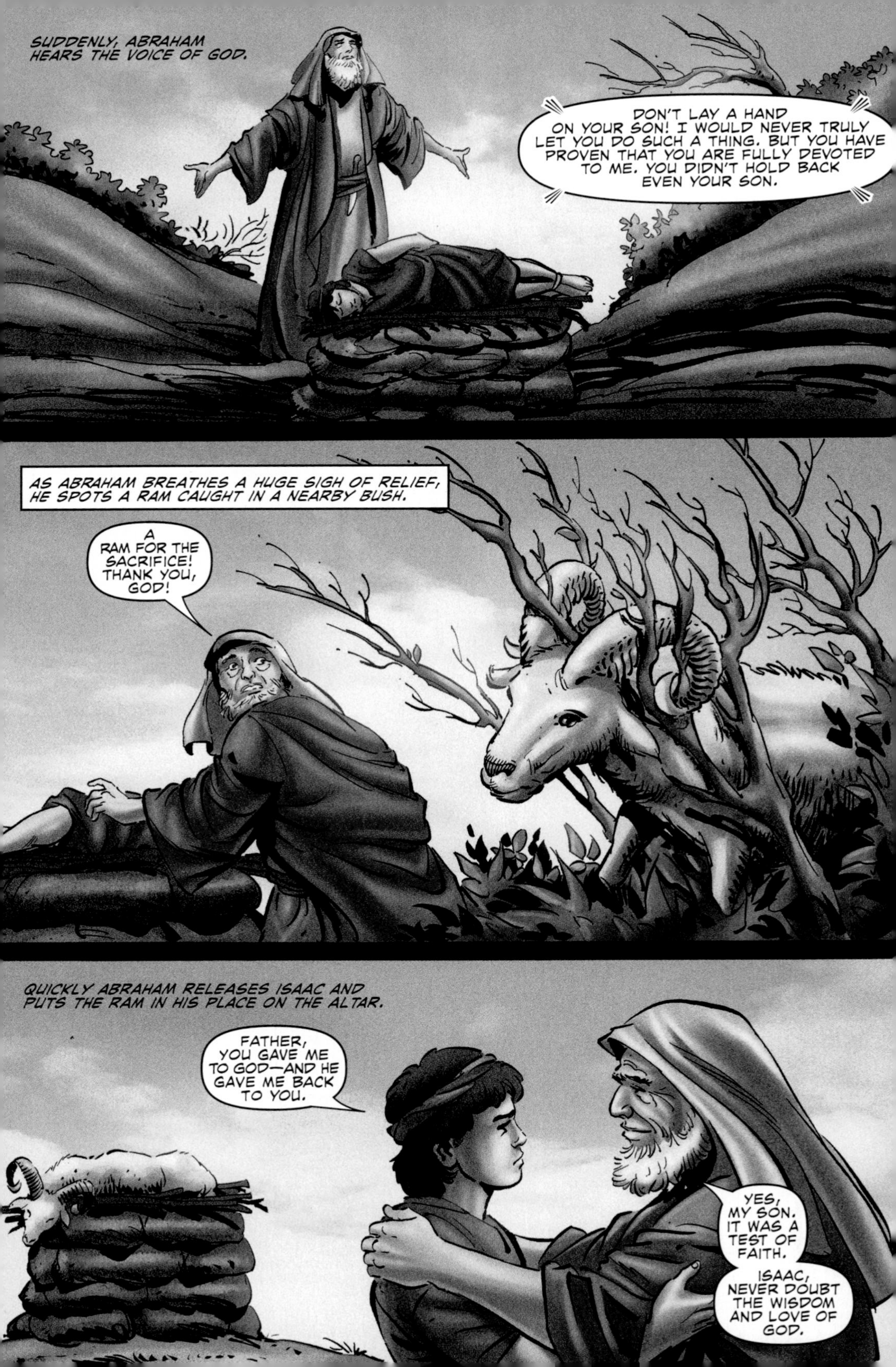
SUDDENLY, ABRAHAM HEARS THE VOICE OF GOD.
DON'T LAY A HAND ON YOUR SON! I WOULD NEVER TRULY LET YOU DO SUCH A THING. BUT YOU HAVE PROVEN THAT YOU ARE FULLY DEVOTED TO ME. YOU DIDN'T HOLD BACK EVEN YOUR SON.
AS ABRAHAM BREATHES A HUGE SIGH OF RELIEF, HE SPOTS A RAM CAUGHT IN A NEARBY BUSH.
A RAM FOR THE SACRIFICE! THANK YOU, GOD!
QUICKLY ABRAHAM RELEASES ISAAC AND PUTS THE RAM IN HIS PLACE ON THE ALTAR.
FATHER, YOU GAVE ME TO GOD—AND HE GAVE ME BACK TO YOU.
YES, MY SON. IT WAS A TEST OF FAITH.
ISAAC, NEVER DOUBT THE WISDOM AND LOVE OF GOD.

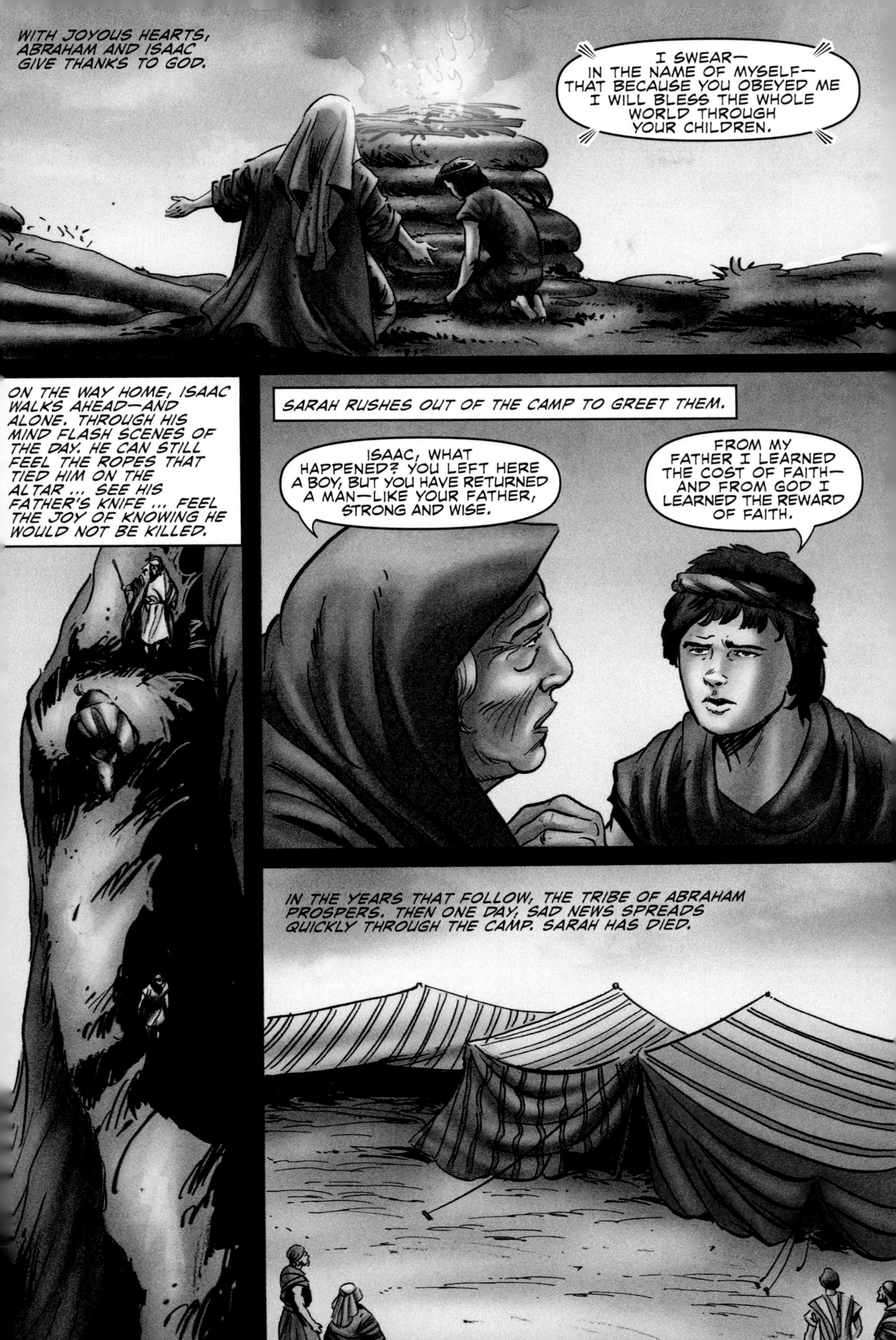
WITH JOYOUS HEARTS, ABRAHAM AND ISAAC GIVE THANKS TO GOD.
I SWEAR— IN THE NAME OF MYSELF— THAT BECAUSE YOU OBEYED ME I WILL BLESS THE WHOLE WORLD THROUGH YOUR CHILDREN.
ON THE WAY HOME, ISAAC WALKS AHEAD—AND ALONE. THROUGH HIS MIND FLASH SCENES OF THE DAY. HE CAN STILL FEEL THE ROPES THAT TIED HIM ON THE ALTAR ... SEE HIS FATHER'S KNIFE ... FEEL THE JOY OF KNOWING HE WOULD NOT BE KILLED.
SARAH RUSHES OUT OF THE CAMP TO GREET THEM.
ISAAC, WHAT HAPPENED? YOU LEFT HERE A BOY, BUT YOU HAVE RETURNED A MAN—LIKE YOUR FATHER, STRONG AND WISE.
FROM MY FATHER I LEARNED THE COST OF FAITH— AND FROM GOD I LEARNED THE REWARD OF FAITH.
IN THE YEARS THAT FOLLOW, THE TRIBE OF ABRAHAM PROSPERS. THEN ONE DAY, SAD NEWS SPREADS QUICKLY THROUGH THE CAMP. SARAH HAS DIED.

A Wife for Isaac
BASED ON GENESIS 24

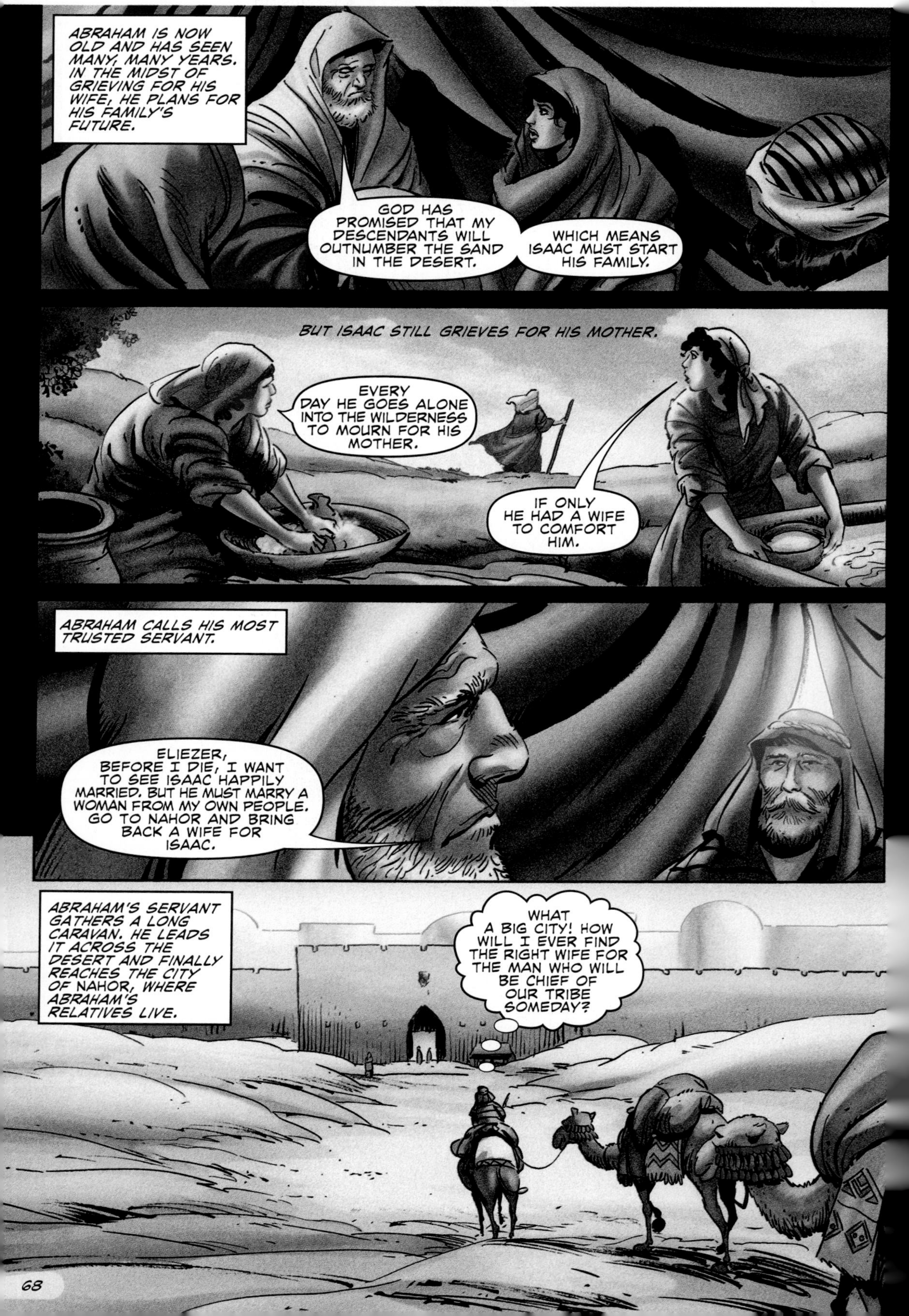

ABRAHAM IS NOW OLD AND HAS SEEN MANY, MANY YEARS. IN THE MIDST OF GRIEVING FOR HIS WIFE, HE PLANS FOR HIS FAMILY'S FUTURE.
GOD HAS PROMISED THAT MY DESCENDANTS WILL OUTNUMBER THE SAND IN THE DESERT.
WHICH MEANS ISAAC MUST START HIS FAMILY.
BUT ISAAC STILL GRIEVES FOR HIS MOTHER.
EVERY DAY HE GOES ALONE INTO THE WILDERNESS TO MOURN FOR HIS MOTHER.
IF ONLY HE HAD A WIFE TO COMFORT HIM.
ABRAHAM CALLS HIS MOST TRUSTED SERVANT.
ELIEZER, BEFORE I DIE, I WANT TO SEE ISAAC HAPPILY MARRIED. BUT HE MUST MARRY A WOMAN FROM MY OWN PEOPLE. GO TO NAHOR AND BRING BACK A WIFE FOR ISAAC.
ABRAHAM'S SERVANT GATHERS A LONG CARAVAN. HE LEADS IT ACROSS THE DESERT AND FINALLY REACHES THE CITY OF NAHOR, WHERE ABRAHAM'S RELATIVES LIVE.
WHAT A BIG CITY! HOW WILL I EVER FIND THE RIGHT WIFE FOR THE MAN WHO WILL BE CHIEF OF OUR TRIBE SOMEDAY?

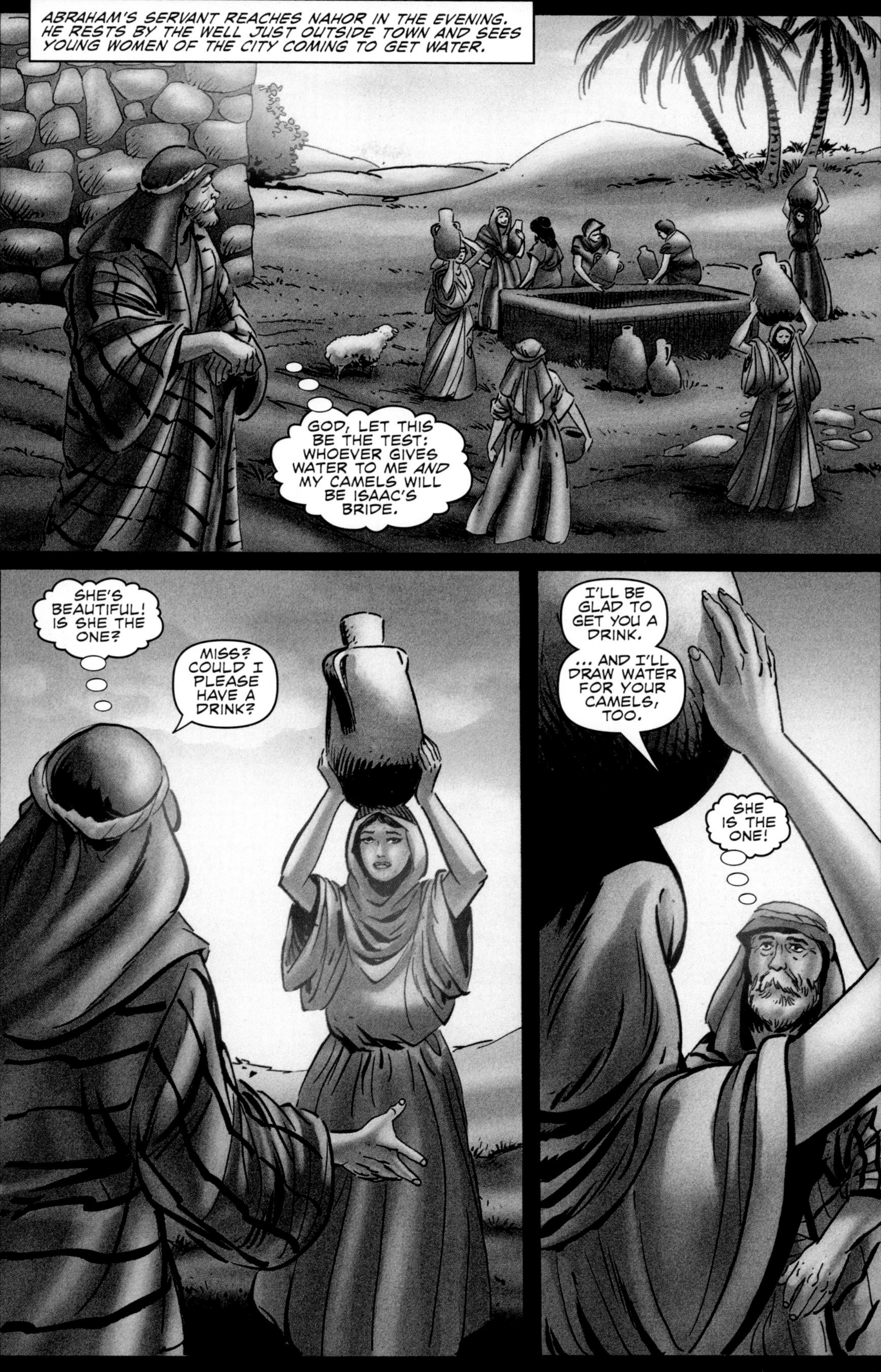
ABRAHAM'S SERVANT REACHES NAHOR IN THE EVENING. HE RESTS BY THE WELL JUST OUTSIDE TOWN AND SEES YOUNG WOMEN OF THE CITY COMING TO GET WATER.
GOD, LET THIS BE THE TEST: WHOEVER GIVES WATER TO ME *AND* MY CAMELS WILL BE ISAAC'S BRIDE.
SHE'S BEAUTIFUL! IS SHE THE ONE?
MISS? COULD I PLEASE HAVE A DRINK?
I'LL BE GLAD TO GET YOU A DRINK.
... AND I'LL DRAW WATER FOR YOUR CAMELS, TOO.
SHE IS THE ONE!

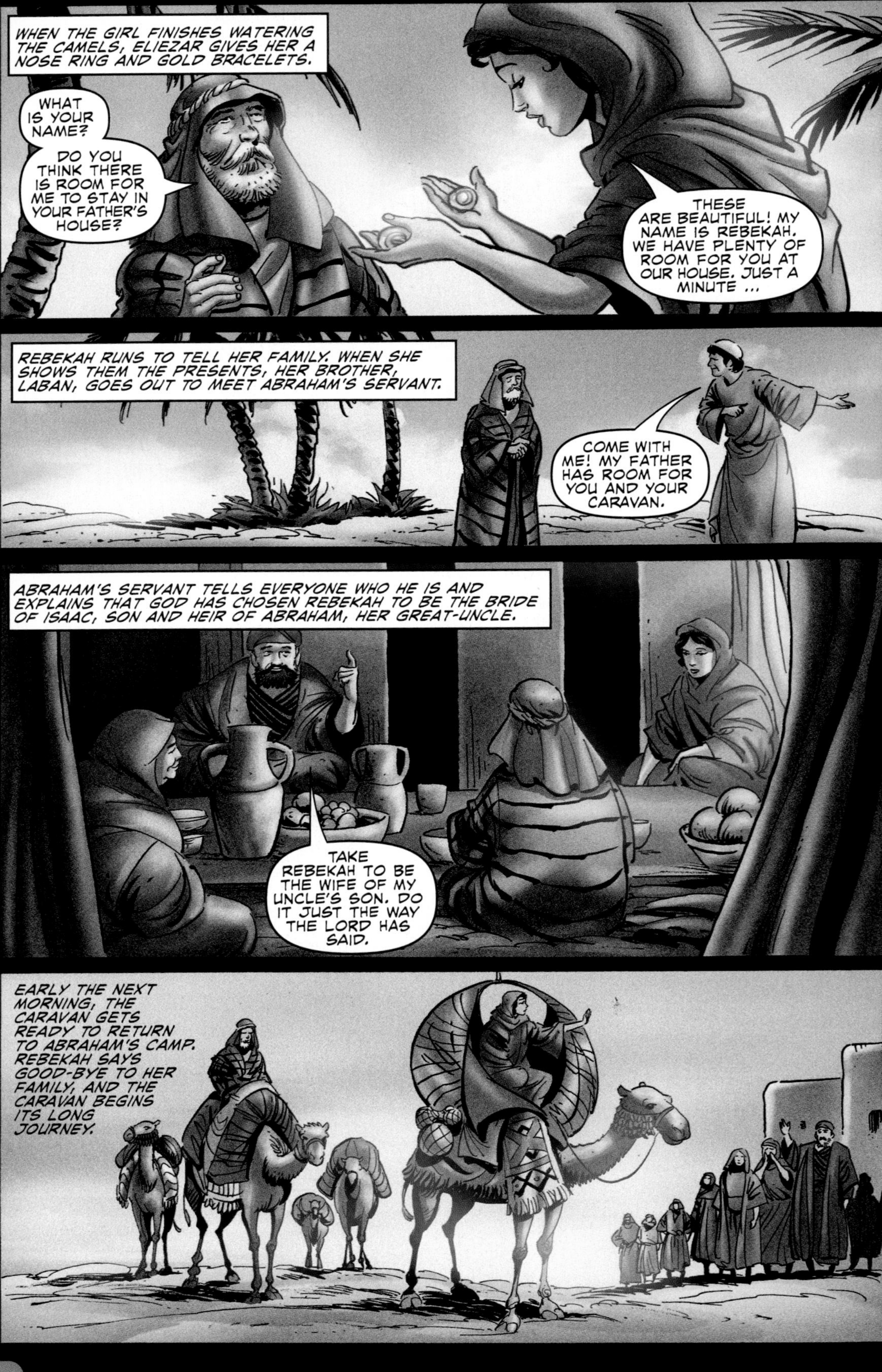

WHEN THE GIRL FINISHES WATERING THE CAMELS, ELIEZAR GIVES HER A NOSE RING AND GOLD BRACELETS.
WHAT IS YOUR NAME?
DO YOU THINK THERE IS ROOM FOR ME TO STAY IN YOUR FATHER'S HOUSE?
THESE ARE BEAUTIFUL! MY NAME IS REBEKAH. WE HAVE PLENTY OF ROOM FOR YOU AT OUR HOUSE. JUST A MINUTE ...
REBEKAH RUNS TO TELL HER FAMILY. WHEN SHE SHOWS THEM THE PRESENTS, HER BROTHER, LABAN, GOES OUT TO MEET ABRAHAM'S SERVANT.
COME WITH ME! MY FATHER HAS ROOM FOR YOU AND YOUR CARAVAN.
ABRAHAM'S SERVANT TELLS EVERYONE WHO HE IS AND EXPLAINS THAT GOD HAS CHOSEN REBEKAH TO BE THE BRIDE OF ISAAC, SON AND HEIR OF ABRAHAM, HER GREAT-UNCLE.
TAKE REBEKAH TO BE THE WIFE OF MY UNCLE'S SON. DO IT JUST THE WAY THE LORD HAS SAID.
EARLY THE NEXT MORNING, THE CARAVAN GETS READY TO RETURN TO ABRAHAM'S CAMP. REBEKAH SAYS GOOD-BYE TO HER FAMILY, AND THE CARAVAN BEGINS ITS LONG JOURNEY.

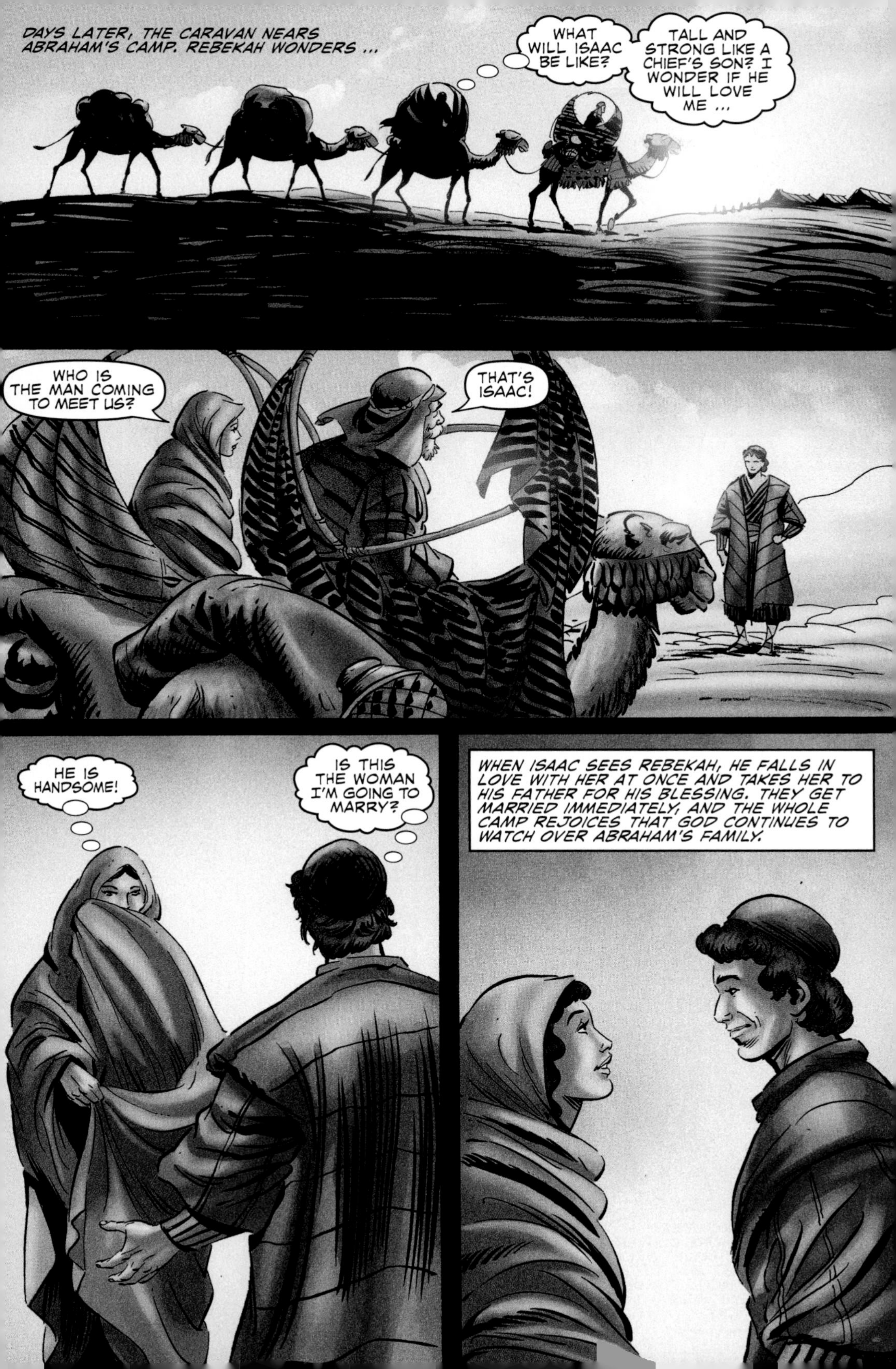
DAYS LATER, THE CARAVAN NEARS ABRAHAM'S CAMP. REBEKAH WONDERS ...
WHAT WILL ISAAC BE LIKE?
TALL AND STRONG LIKE A CHIEF'S SON? I WONDER IF HE WILL LOVE ME ...
WHO IS THE MAN COMING TO MEET US?
THAT'S ISAAC!
HE IS HANDSOME!
IS THIS THE WOMAN I'M GOING TO MARRY?
WHEN ISAAC SEES REBEKAH, HE FALLS IN LOVE WITH HER AT ONCE AND TAKES HER TO HIS FATHER FOR HIS BLESSING. THEY GET MARRIED IMMEDIATELY, AND THE WHOLE CAMP REJOICES THAT GOD CONTINUES TO WATCH OVER ABRAHAM'S FAMILY.

Birthright Stew

BASED ON GENESIS 25—26

AFTER A LONG AND HAPPY LIFE, ABRAHAM FINALLY JOINS HIS WIFE IN DEATH. ISAAC LEADS ABRAHAM'S TRIBE TO THE BURIAL CAVE OF MACHPELAH TO PLACE THE BODY OF ITS GREAT CHIEFTAIN BESIDE HIS WIFE, SARAH.

BUT ISAAC, LIKE HIS FATHER, HAS GONE A LONG TIME WITHOUT HAVING ANY CHILDREN.

REBEKAH IS BARREN. WE'VE TRIED EVERY REMEDY KNOWN TO MAN. NOTHING HAS WORKED. NOW I MUST PRAY TO GOD AND TRUST HIS PROMISE.

THE LORD ANSWERS ISAAC'S PRAYERS, AND REBEKAH BECOMES PREGNANT. BUT HER PREGNANCY SEEMS UNUSUAL. WHEN THEY INQUIRE OF THE LORD, HE TELLS REBEKAH THAT SHE IS PREGNANT WITH TWINS! "YOU WILL GIVE BIRTH TO TWO NATIONS. ONE WILL BE STRONGER THAN THE OTHER, AND THE YOUNGER WILL RULE THE OLDER."

WHEN REBEKAH GIVES BIRTH, HER FIRST SON IS REDDISH AND HAIRY. THEY NAME HIM ESAU. BUT CLUTCHING ESAU'S HEEL IS JACOB, WHO DOES NOT WANT TO BE LEFT BEHIND. AS THE BOYS GROW UP, ISAAC EARNS A REPUTATION AS A MAN WHO AVOIDS CONFLICT. BUT ISAAC FAILS TO SEE THE CONFLICT GROWING BETWEEN HIS OWN TWIN SONS.

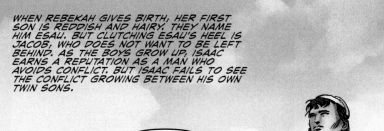

WHICH ONE WILL BE OUR RULER AFTER ISAAC?

ESAU IS STRONGER— BUT JACOB IS MORE CLEVER. ESAU HAS THE BIRTHRIGHT BECAUSE HE IS THE OLDEST. BUT I'D BE SURPRISED IF JACOB DOESN'T DO SOMETHING TRICKY.

IF I WERE ISAAC, I'D PAY MORE ATTENTION TO THE COMPETITION BETWEEN THOSE TWO BOYS.

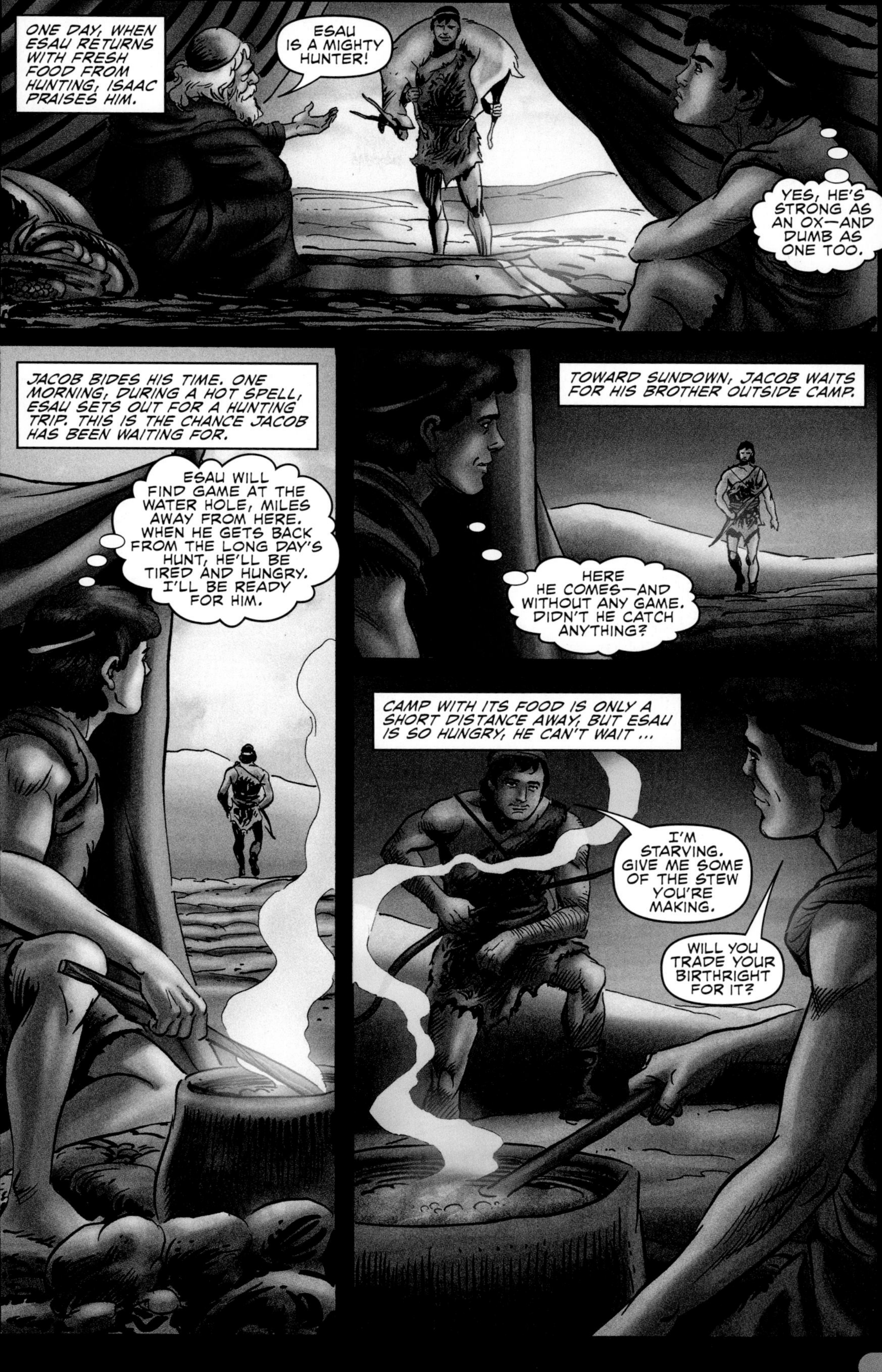
ONE DAY, WHEN ESAU RETURNS WITH FRESH FOOD FROM HUNTING, ISAAC PRAISES HIM.
ESAU IS A MIGHTY HUNTER!
YES, HE'S STRONG AS AN OX—AND DUMB AS ONE TOO.
JACOB BIDES HIS TIME. ONE MORNING, DURING A HOT SPELL, ESAU SETS OUT FOR A HUNTING TRIP. THIS IS THE CHANCE JACOB HAS BEEN WAITING FOR.
ESAU WILL FIND GAME AT THE WATER HOLE, MILES AWAY FROM HERE. WHEN HE GETS BACK FROM THE LONG DAY'S HUNT, HE'LL BE TIRED AND HUNGRY. I'LL BE READY FOR HIM.
TOWARD SUNDOWN, JACOB WAITS FOR HIS BROTHER OUTSIDE CAMP.
HERE HE COMES—AND WITHOUT ANY GAME. DIDN'T HE CATCH ANYTHING?
CAMP WITH ITS FOOD IS ONLY A SHORT DISTANCE AWAY, BUT ESAU IS SO HUNGRY, HE CAN'T WAIT ...
I'M STARVING. GIVE ME SOME OF THE STEW YOU'RE MAKING.
WILL YOU TRADE YOUR BIRTHRIGHT FOR IT?

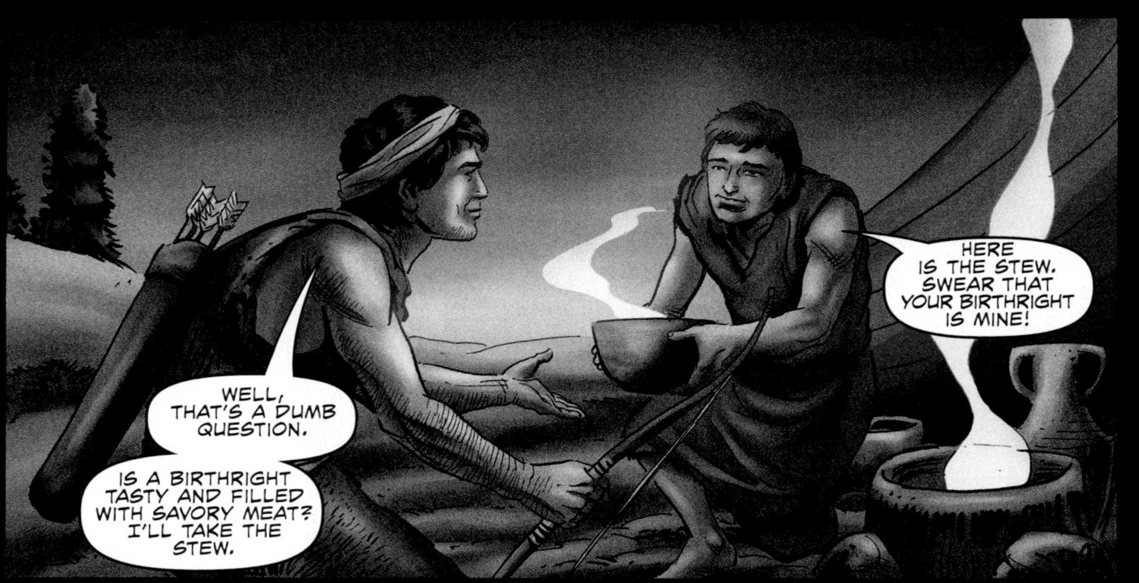
HERE IS THE STEW. SWEAR THAT YOUR BIRTHRIGHT IS MINE!
WELL, THAT'S A DUMB QUESTION.
IS A BIRTHRIGHT TASTY AND FILLED WITH SAVORY MEAT? I'LL TAKE THE STEW.

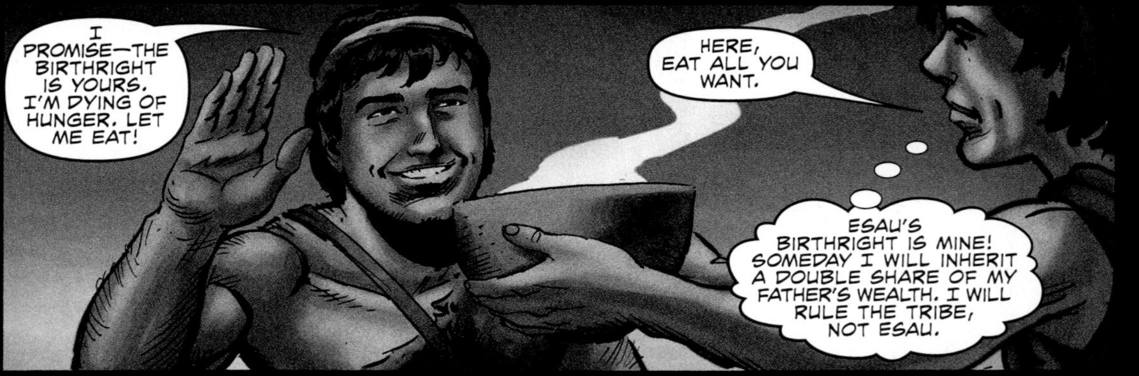
I PROMISE—THE BIRTHRIGHT IS YOURS. I'M DYING OF HUNGER. LET ME EAT!
HERE, EAT ALL YOU WANT.
ESAU'S BIRTHRIGHT IS MINE! SOMEDAY I WILL INHERIT A DOUBLE SHARE OF MY FATHER'S WEALTH. I WILL RULE THE TRIBE, NOT ESAU.

BUT JACOB HAS A LONG TIME TO WAIT. HIS FATHER IS STILL STRONG AND POWERFUL. AND AS ISAAC GROWS OLDER, IT BECOMES CLEAR THAT ESAU IS HIS FAVORITE SON. JACOB REALIZES THAT TRICKING ESAU INTO GIVING HIM THE BIRTHRIGHT IS NOT ENOUGH. SOMEHOW HE MUST CONVINCE HIS FATHER TO GIVE HIM THE FAMILY BLESSING AS WELL. FOR ALL HIS TRICKY PLOTS, JACOB CAN'T DISOBEY HIS FATHER. HIS FATHER, ISAAC, IS THE HEAD OF THE FAMILY; HIS MOTHER, REBEKAH, HOWEVER, IS THE BRAINS ...

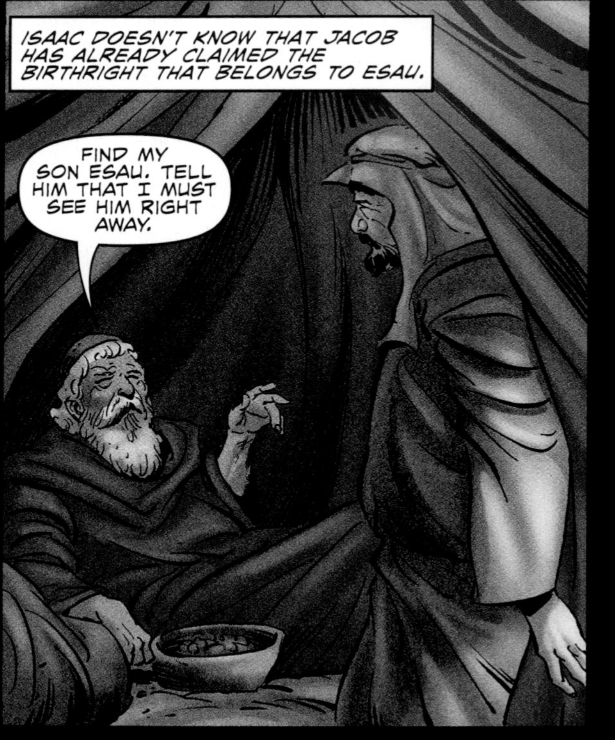
ISAAC DOESN'T KNOW THAT JACOB HAS ALREADY CLAIMED THE BIRTHRIGHT THAT BELONGS TO ESAU.
FIND MY SON ESAU. TELL HIM THAT I MUST SEE HIM RIGHT AWAY.

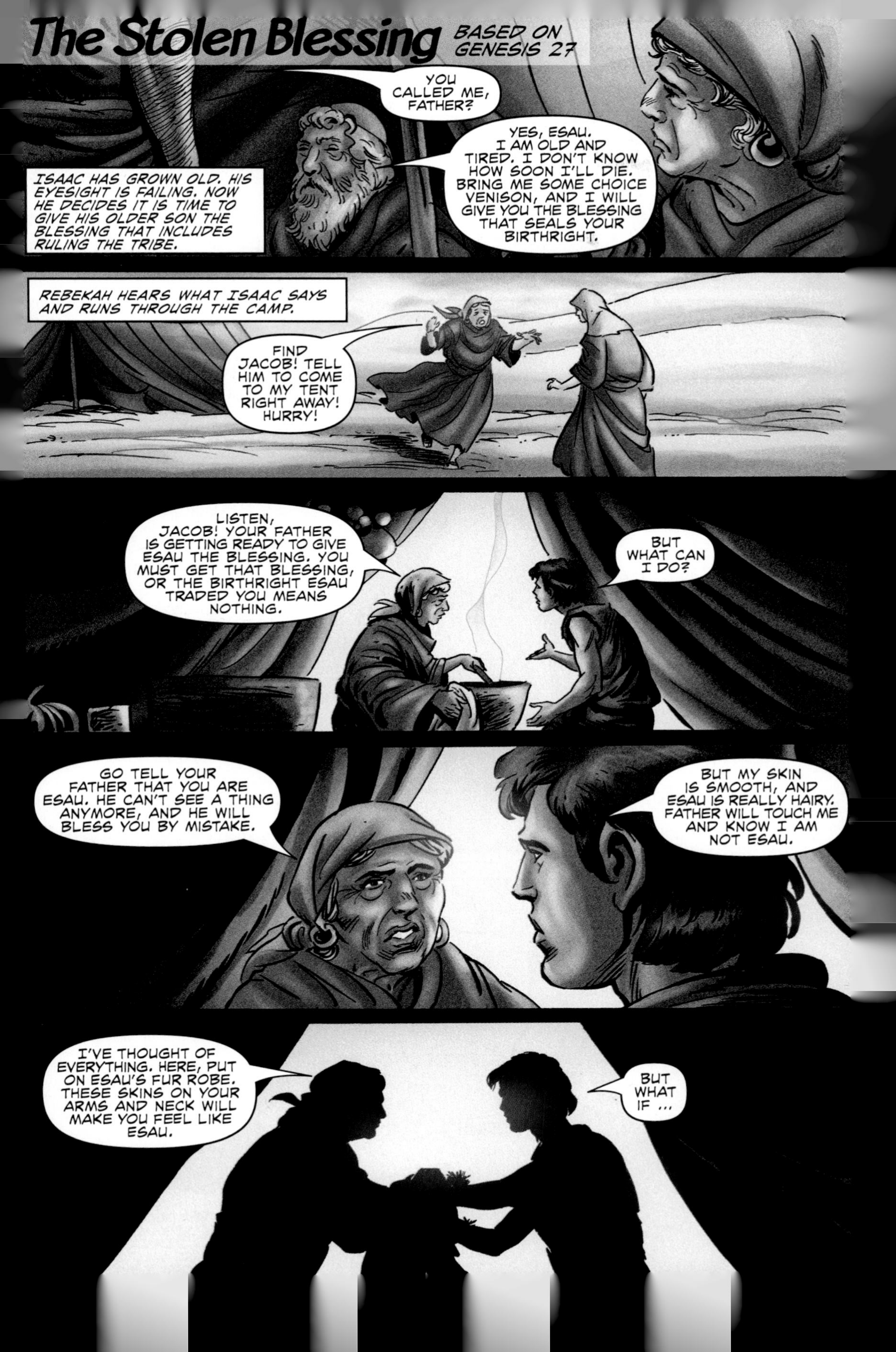
The Stolen Blessing
BASED ON GENESIS 27
ISAAC HAS GROWN OLD. HIS EYESIGHT IS FAILING. NOW HE DECIDES IT IS TIME TO GIVE HIS OLDER SON THE BLESSING THAT INCLUDES RULING THE TRIBE.
YOU CALLED ME, FATHER?
YES, ESAU. I AM OLD AND TIRED. I DON'T KNOW HOW SOON I'LL DIE. BRING ME SOME CHOICE VENISON, AND I WILL GIVE YOU THE BLESSING THAT SEALS YOUR BIRTHRIGHT.
REBEKAH HEARS WHAT ISAAC SAYS AND RUNS THROUGH THE CAMP.
FIND JACOB! TELL HIM TO COME TO MY TENT RIGHT AWAY! HURRY!
LISTEN, JACOB! YOUR FATHER IS GETTING READY TO GIVE ESAU THE BLESSING. YOU MUST GET THAT BLESSING, OR THE BIRTHRIGHT ESAU TRADED YOU MEANS NOTHING.
BUT WHAT CAN I DO?
GO TELL YOUR FATHER THAT YOU ARE ESAU. HE CAN'T SEE A THING ANYMORE, AND HE WILL BLESS YOU BY MISTAKE.
BUT MY SKIN IS SMOOTH, AND ESAU IS REALLY HAIRY. FATHER WILL TOUCH ME AND KNOW I AM NOT ESAU.
I'VE THOUGHT OF EVERYTHING. HERE, PUT ON ESAU'S FUR ROBE. THESE SKINS ON YOUR ARMS AND NECK WILL MAKE YOU FEEL LIKE ESAU.
BUT WHAT IF ...

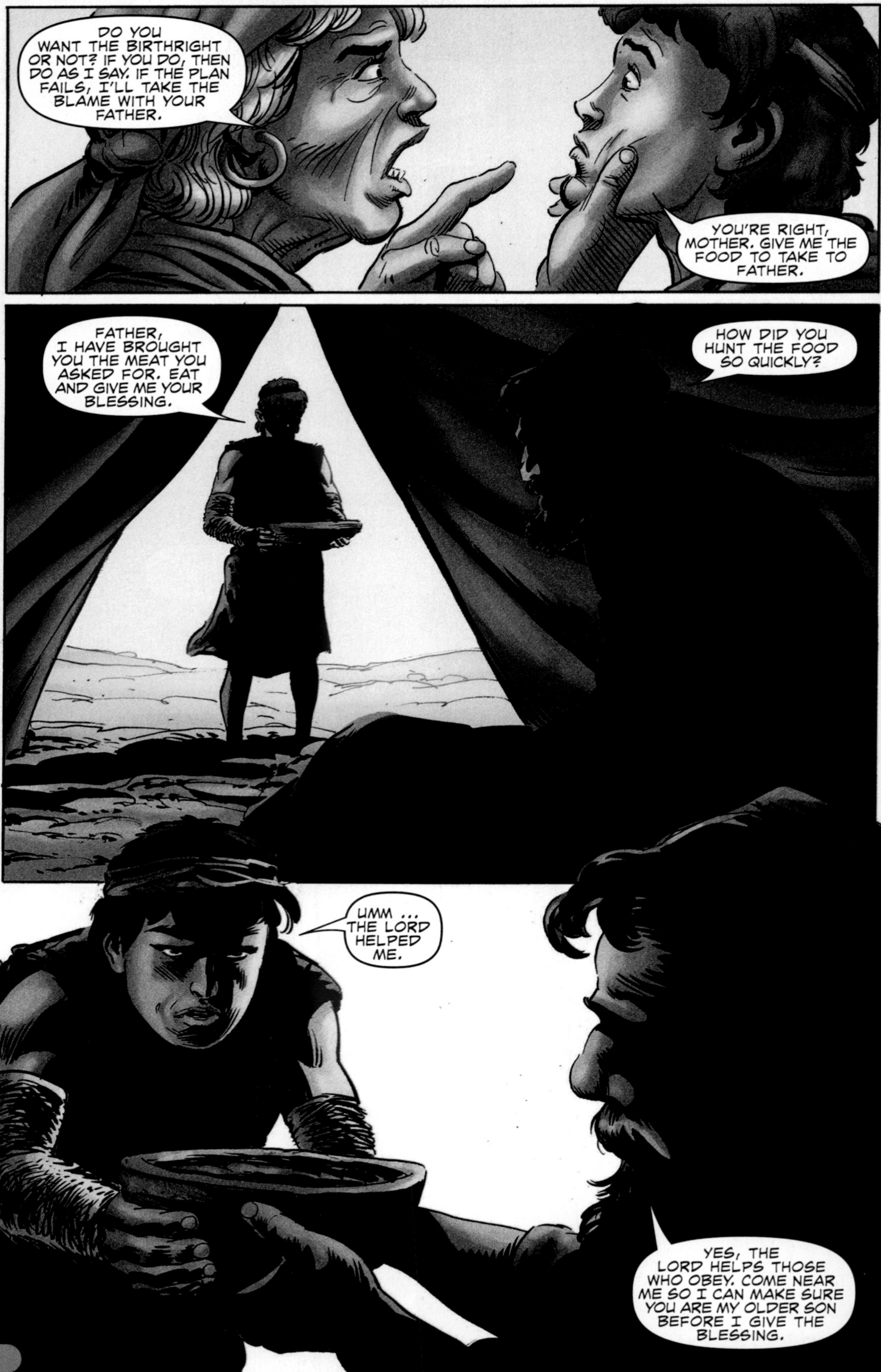
DO YOU WANT THE BIRTHRIGHT OR NOT? IF YOU DO, THEN DO AS I SAY. IF THE PLAN FAILS, I'LL TAKE THE BLAME WITH YOUR FATHER.
YOU'RE RIGHT, MOTHER. GIVE ME THE FOOD TO TAKE TO FATHER.
FATHER, I HAVE BROUGHT YOU THE MEAT YOU ASKED FOR. EAT AND GIVE ME YOUR BLESSING.
HOW DID YOU HUNT THE FOOD SO QUICKLY?
UMM ... THE LORD HELPED ME.
YES, THE LORD HELPS THOSE WHO OBEY. COME NEAR ME SO I CAN MAKE SURE YOU ARE MY OLDER SON BEFORE I GIVE THE BLESSING.

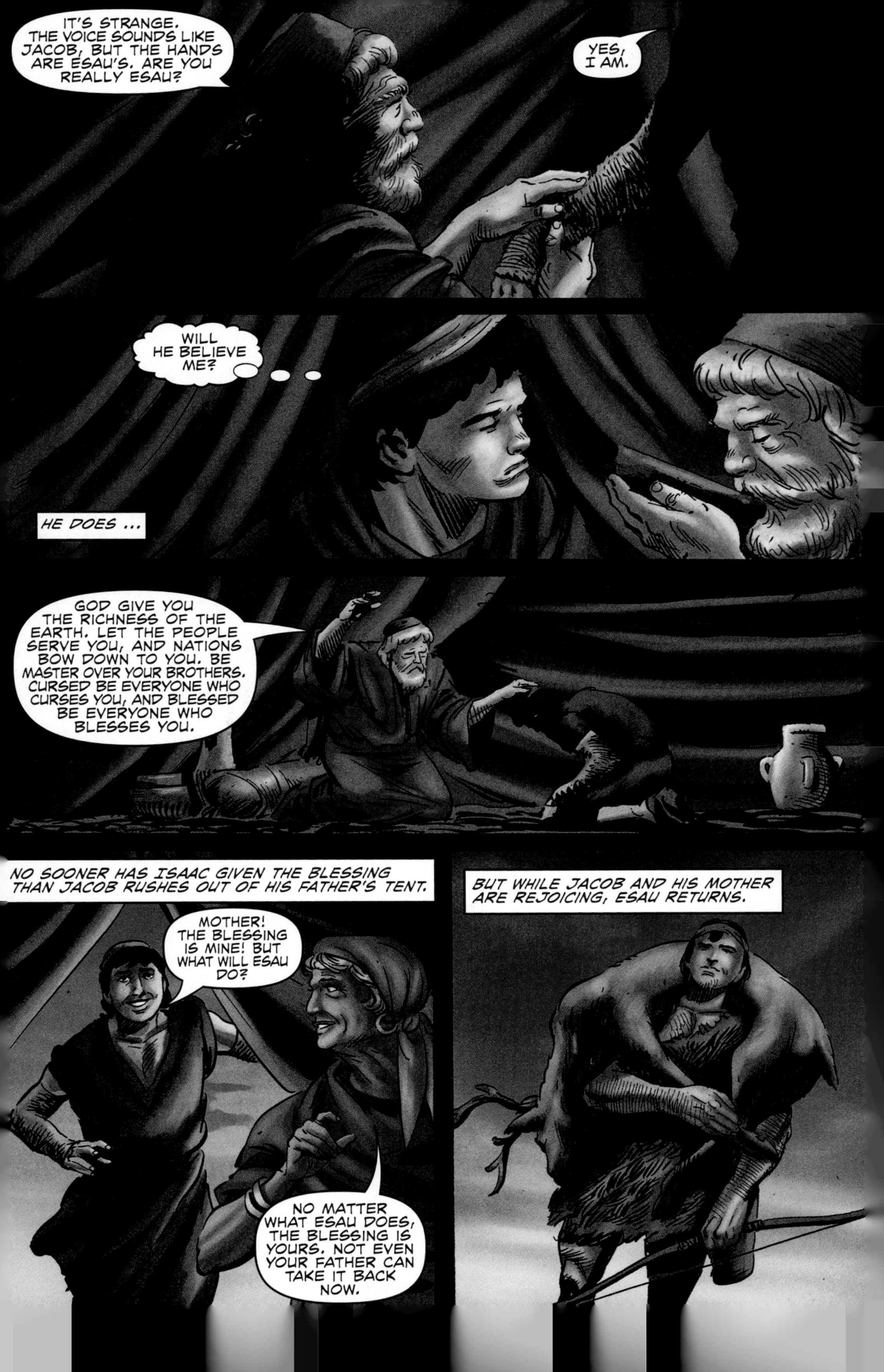
IT'S STRANGE. THE VOICE SOUNDS LIKE JACOB, BUT THE HANDS ARE ESAU'S. ARE YOU REALLY ESAU?
YES, I AM.
WILL HE BELIEVE ME?
HE DOES ...
GOD GIVE YOU THE RICHNESS OF THE EARTH. LET THE PEOPLE SERVE YOU, AND NATIONS BOW DOWN TO YOU. BE MASTER OVER YOUR BROTHERS. CURSED BE EVERYONE WHO CURSES YOU, AND BLESSED BE EVERYONE WHO BLESSES YOU.
NO SOONER HAS ISAAC GIVEN THE BLESSING THAN JACOB RUSHES OUT OF HIS FATHER'S TENT.
MOTHER! THE BLESSING IS MINE! BUT WHAT WILL ESAU DO?
NO MATTER WHAT ESAU DOES, THE BLESSING IS YOURS. NOT EVEN YOUR FATHER CAN TAKE IT BACK NOW.
BUT WHILE JACOB AND HIS MOTHER ARE REJOICING, ESAU RETURNS.

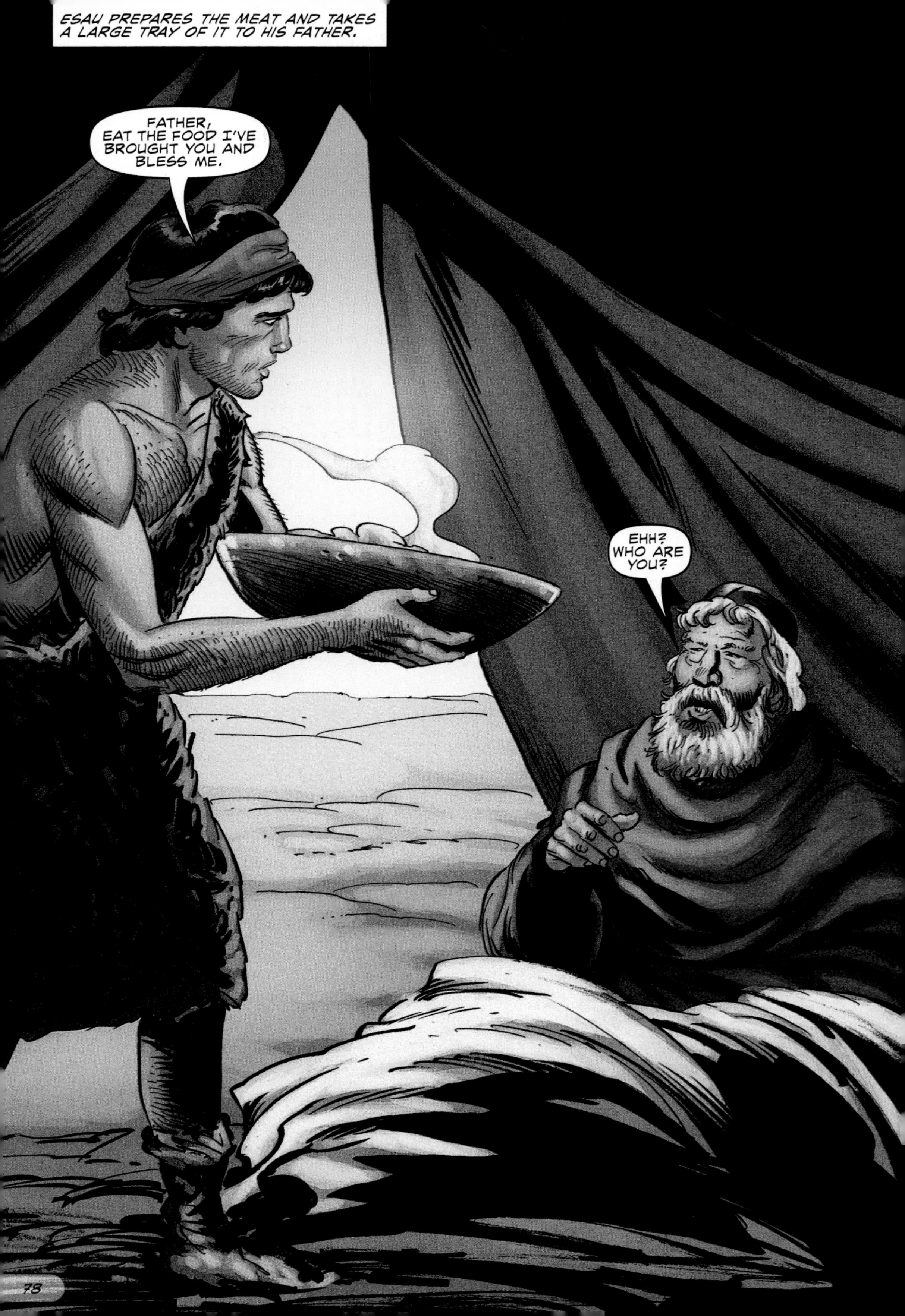
ESAU PREPARES THE MEAT AND TAKES A LARGE TRAY OF IT TO HIS FATHER.
FATHER, EAT THE FOOD I'VE BROUGHT YOU AND BLESS ME.
EHH? WHO ARE YOU?

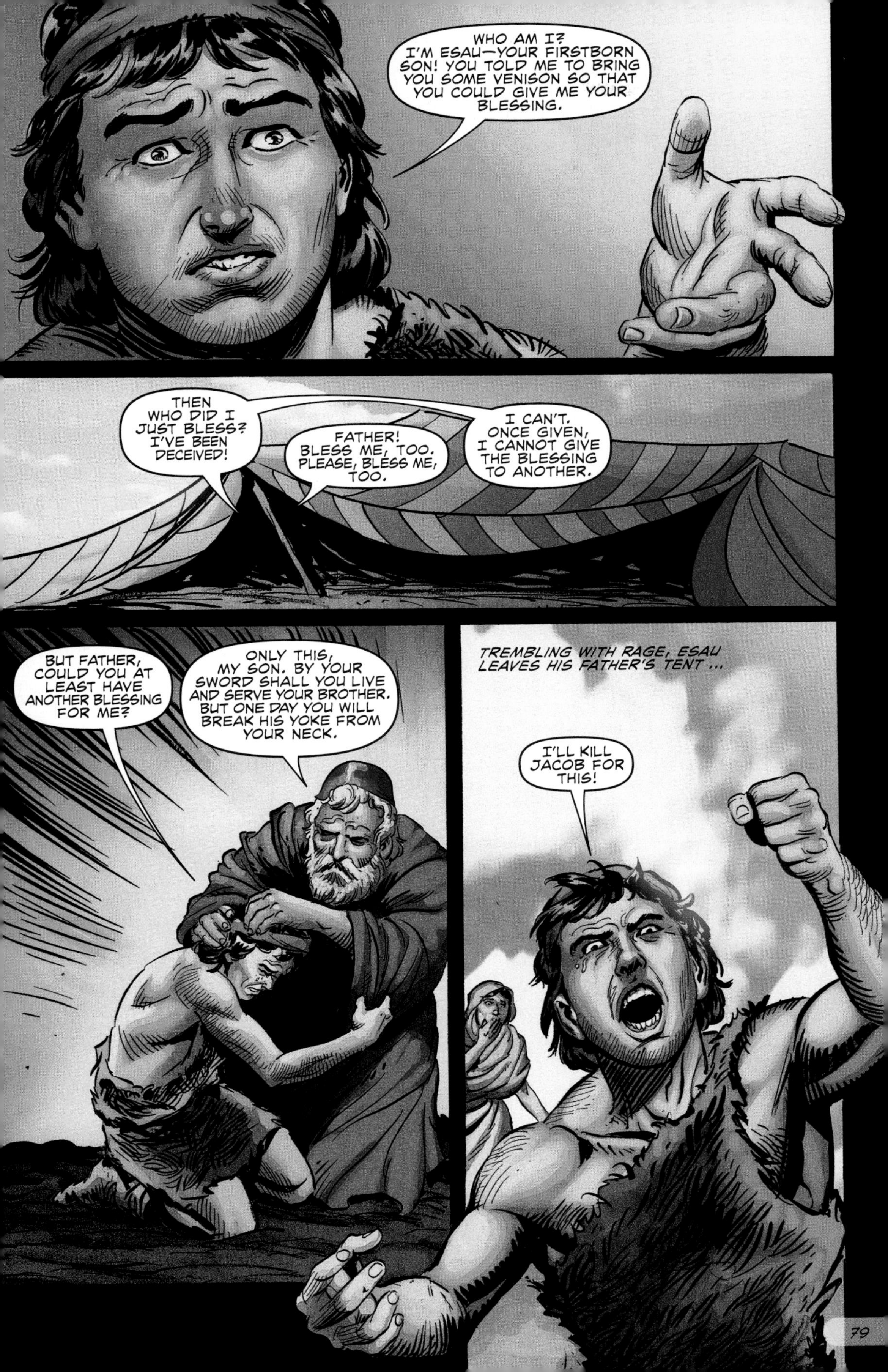
WHO AM I? I'M ESAU—YOUR FIRSTBORN SON! YOU TOLD ME TO BRING YOU SOME VENISON SO THAT YOU COULD GIVE ME YOUR BLESSING.
THEN WHO DID I JUST BLESS? I'VE BEEN DECEIVED!
FATHER! BLESS ME, TOO. PLEASE, BLESS ME, TOO.
I CAN'T. ONCE GIVEN, I CANNOT GIVE THE BLESSING TO ANOTHER.
BUT FATHER, COULD YOU AT LEAST HAVE ANOTHER BLESSING FOR ME?
ONLY THIS, MY SON. BY YOUR SWORD SHALL YOU LIVE AND SERVE YOUR BROTHER. BUT ONE DAY YOU WILL BREAK HIS YOKE FROM YOUR NECK.
TREMBLING WITH RAGE, ESAU LEAVES HIS FATHER'S TENT ...
I'LL KILL JACOB FOR THIS!

Stairway to Heaven

BASED ON GENESIS 27:41—28:22

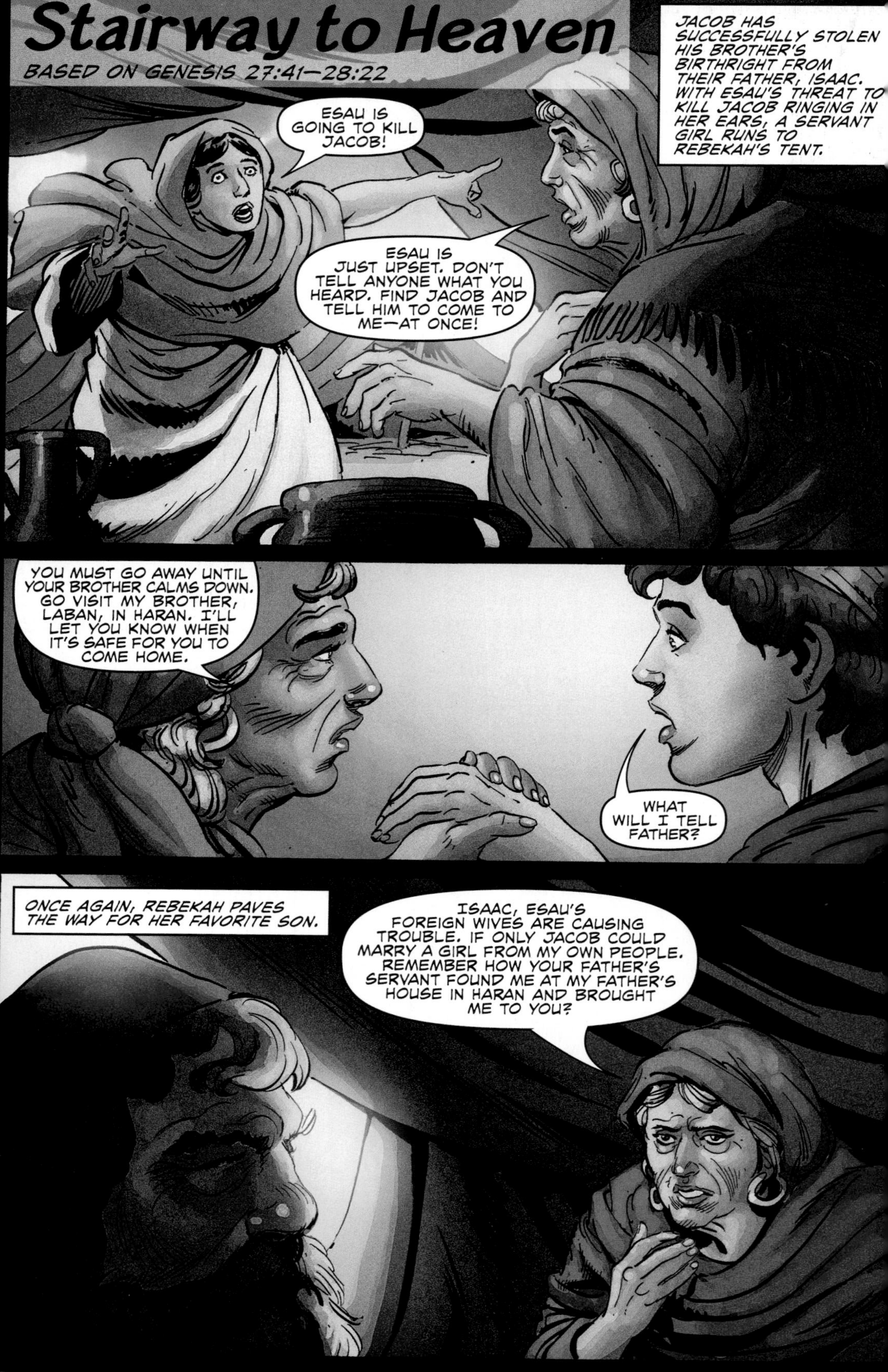

JACOB HAS SUCCESSFULLY STOLEN HIS BROTHER'S BIRTHRIGHT FROM THEIR FATHER, ISAAC. WITH ESAU'S THREAT TO KILL JACOB RINGING IN HER EARS, A SERVANT GIRL RUNS TO REBEKAH'S TENT.
ESAU IS GOING TO KILL JACOB!
ESAU IS JUST UPSET. DON'T TELL ANYONE WHAT YOU HEARD. FIND JACOB AND TELL HIM TO COME TO ME—AT ONCE!
YOU MUST GO AWAY UNTIL YOUR BROTHER CALMS DOWN. GO VISIT MY BROTHER, LABAN, IN HARAN. I'LL LET YOU KNOW WHEN IT'S SAFE FOR YOU TO COME HOME.
WHAT WILL I TELL FATHER?
ONCE AGAIN, REBEKAH PAVES THE WAY FOR HER FAVORITE SON.
ISAAC, ESAU'S FOREIGN WIVES ARE CAUSING TROUBLE. IF ONLY JACOB COULD MARRY A GIRL FROM MY OWN PEOPLE. REMEMBER HOW YOUR FATHER'S SERVANT FOUND ME AT MY FATHER'S HOUSE IN HARAN AND BROUGHT ME TO YOU?

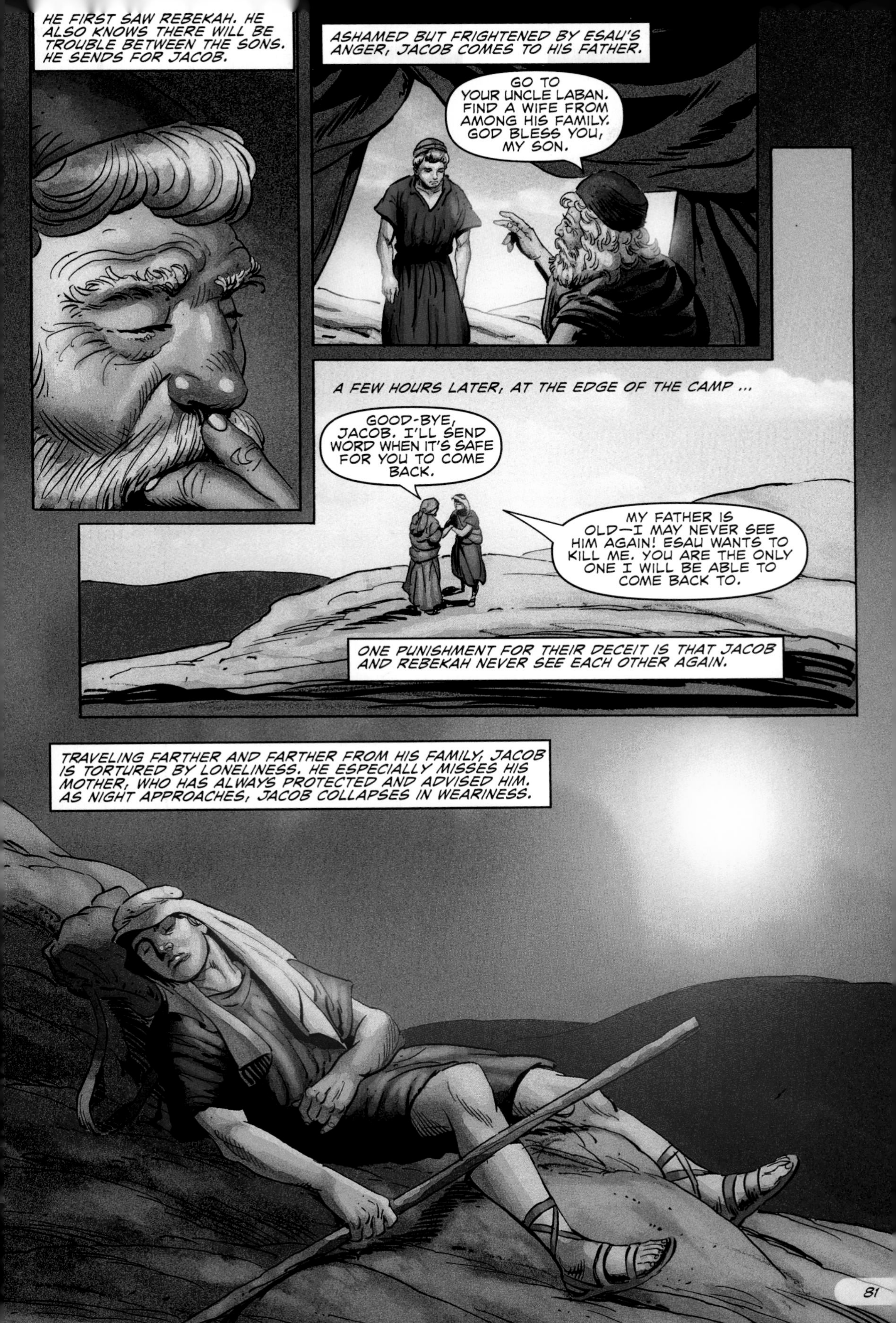

HE FIRST SAW REBEKAH. HE ALSO KNOWS THERE WILL BE TROUBLE BETWEEN THE SONS. HE SENDS FOR JACOB.
ASHAMED BUT FRIGHTENED BY ESAU'S ANGER, JACOB COMES TO HIS FATHER.
GO TO YOUR UNCLE LABAN. FIND A WIFE FROM AMONG HIS FAMILY. GOD BLESS YOU, MY SON.
A FEW HOURS LATER, AT THE EDGE OF THE CAMP ...
GOOD-BYE, JACOB. I'LL SEND WORD WHEN IT'S SAFE FOR YOU TO COME BACK.
MY FATHER IS OLD—I MAY NEVER SEE HIM AGAIN! ESAU WANTS TO KILL ME. YOU ARE THE ONLY ONE I WILL BE ABLE TO COME BACK TO.
ONE PUNISHMENT FOR THEIR DECEIT IS THAT JACOB AND REBEKAH NEVER SEE EACH OTHER AGAIN.
TRAVELING FARTHER AND FARTHER FROM HIS FAMILY, JACOB IS TORTURED BY LONELINESS. HE ESPECIALLY MISSES HIS MOTHER, WHO HAS ALWAYS PROTECTED AND ADVISED HIM. AS NIGHT APPROACHES, JACOB COLLAPSES IN WEARINESS.

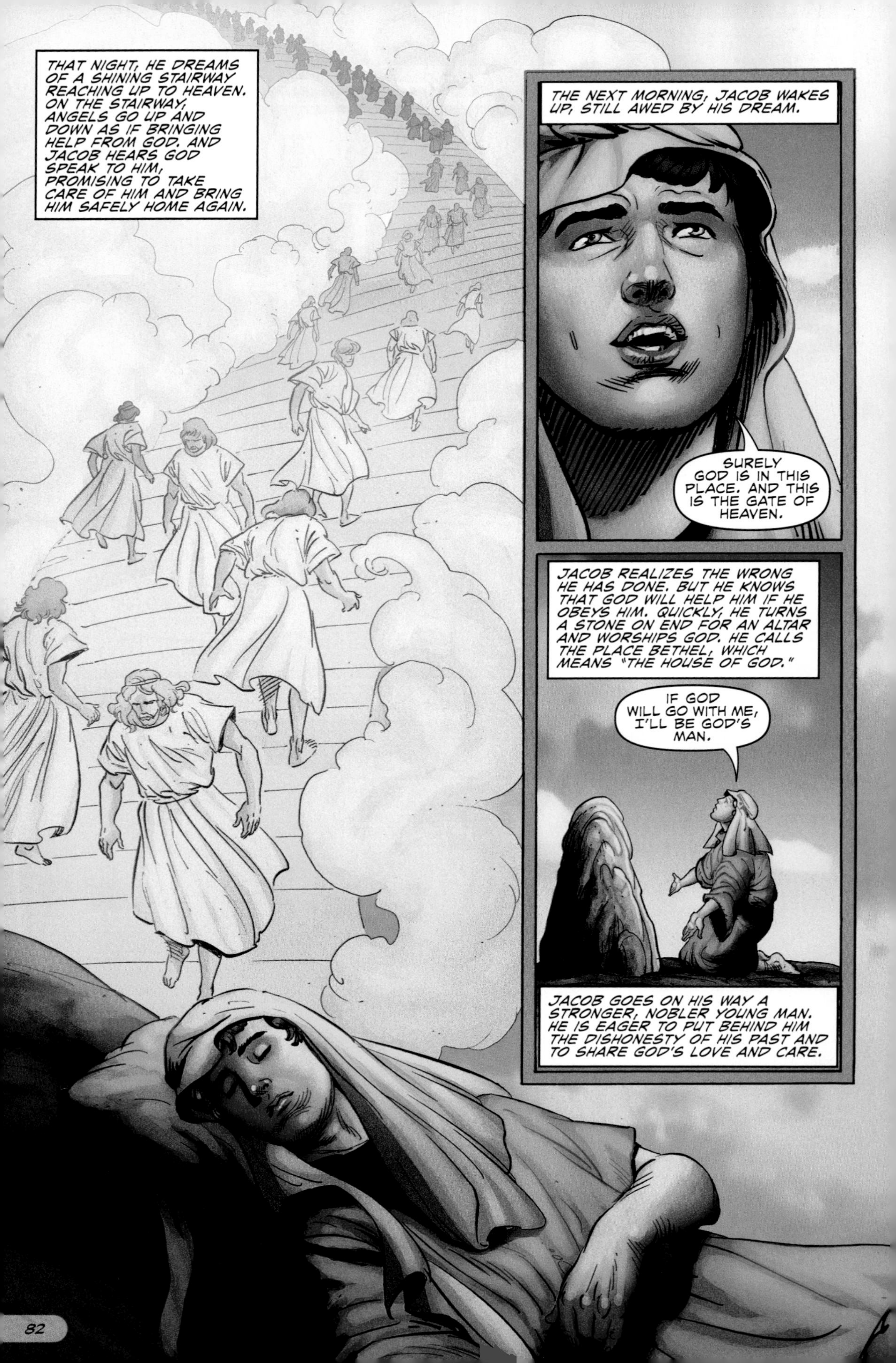
THAT NIGHT, HE DREAMS OF A SHINING STAIRWAY REACHING UP TO HEAVEN. ON THE STAIRWAY, ANGELS GO UP AND DOWN AS IF BRINGING HELP FROM GOD. AND JACOB HEARS GOD SPEAK TO HIM, PROMISING TO TAKE CARE OF HIM AND BRING HIM SAFELY HOME AGAIN.
THE NEXT MORNING, JACOB WAKES UP, STILL AWED BY HIS DREAM.
SURELY GOD IS IN THIS PLACE. AND THIS IS THE GATE OF HEAVEN.
JACOB REALIZES THE WRONG HE HAS DONE. BUT HE KNOWS THAT GOD WILL HELP HIM IF HE OBEYS HIM. QUICKLY, HE TURNS A STONE ON END FOR AN ALTAR AND WORSHIPS GOD. HE CALLS THE PLACE BETHEL, WHICH MEANS "THE HOUSE OF GOD."
IF GOD WILL GO WITH ME, I'LL BE GOD'S MAN.
JACOB GOES ON HIS WAY A STRONGER, NOBLER YOUNG MAN. HE IS EAGER TO PUT BEHIND HIM THE DISHONESTY OF HIS PAST AND TO SHARE GOD'S LOVE AND CARE.

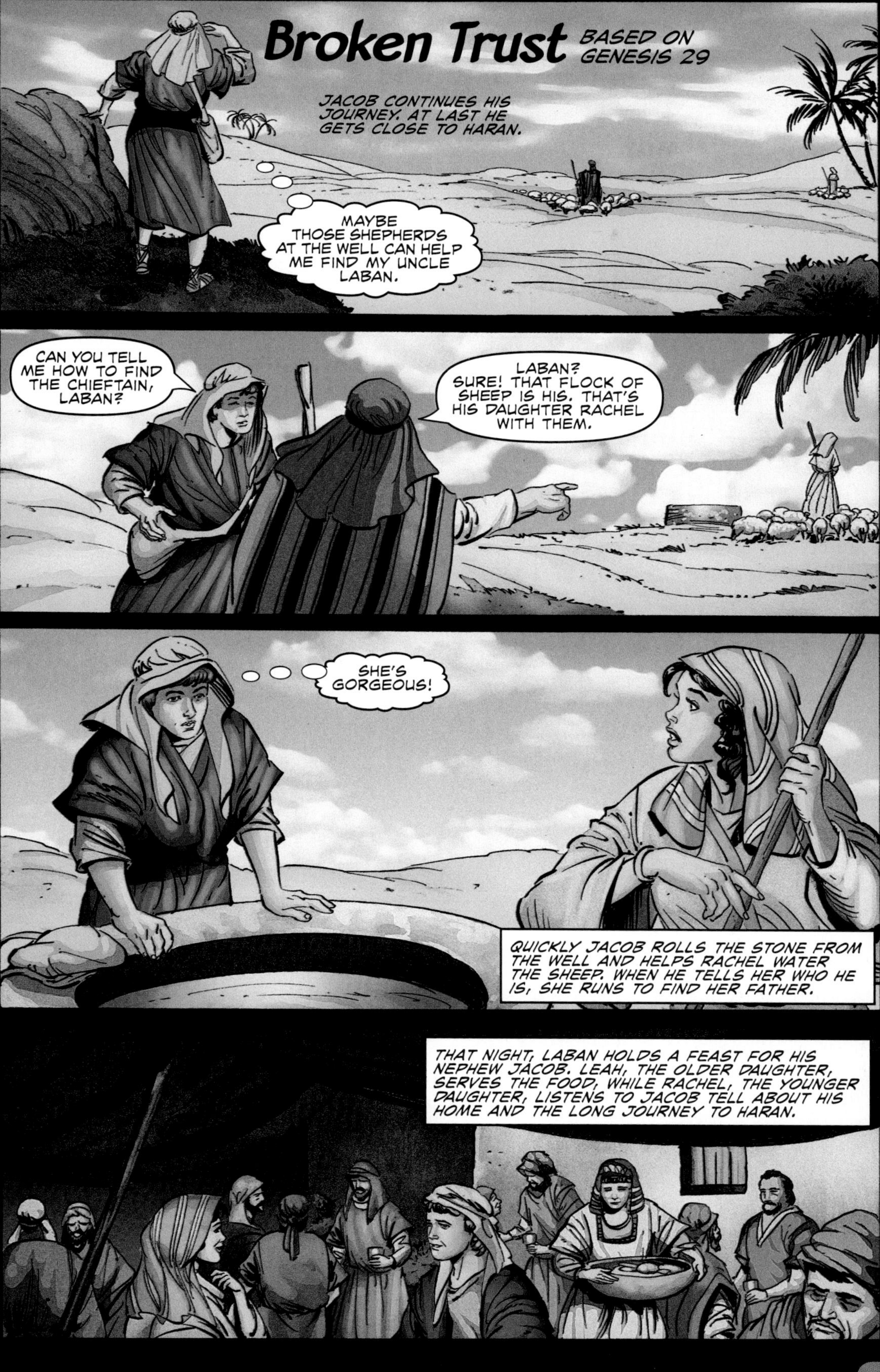
Broken Trust
BASED ON GENESIS 29
JACOB CONTINUES HIS JOURNEY. AT LAST HE GETS CLOSE TO HARAN.
MAYBE THOSE SHEPHERDS AT THE WELL CAN HELP ME FIND MY UNCLE LABAN.
CAN YOU TELL ME HOW TO FIND THE CHIEFTAIN, LABAN?
LABAN? SURE! THAT FLOCK OF SHEEP IS HIS. THAT'S HIS DAUGHTER RACHEL WITH THEM.
SHE'S GORGEOUS!
QUICKLY JACOB ROLLS THE STONE FROM THE WELL AND HELPS RACHEL WATER THE SHEEP. WHEN HE TELLS HER WHO HE IS, SHE RUNS TO FIND HER FATHER.
THAT NIGHT, LABAN HOLDS A FEAST FOR HIS NEPHEW JACOB. LEAH, THE OLDER DAUGHTER, SERVES THE FOOD, WHILE RACHEL, THE YOUNGER DAUGHTER, LISTENS TO JACOB TELL ABOUT HIS HOME AND THE LONG JOURNEY TO HARAN.

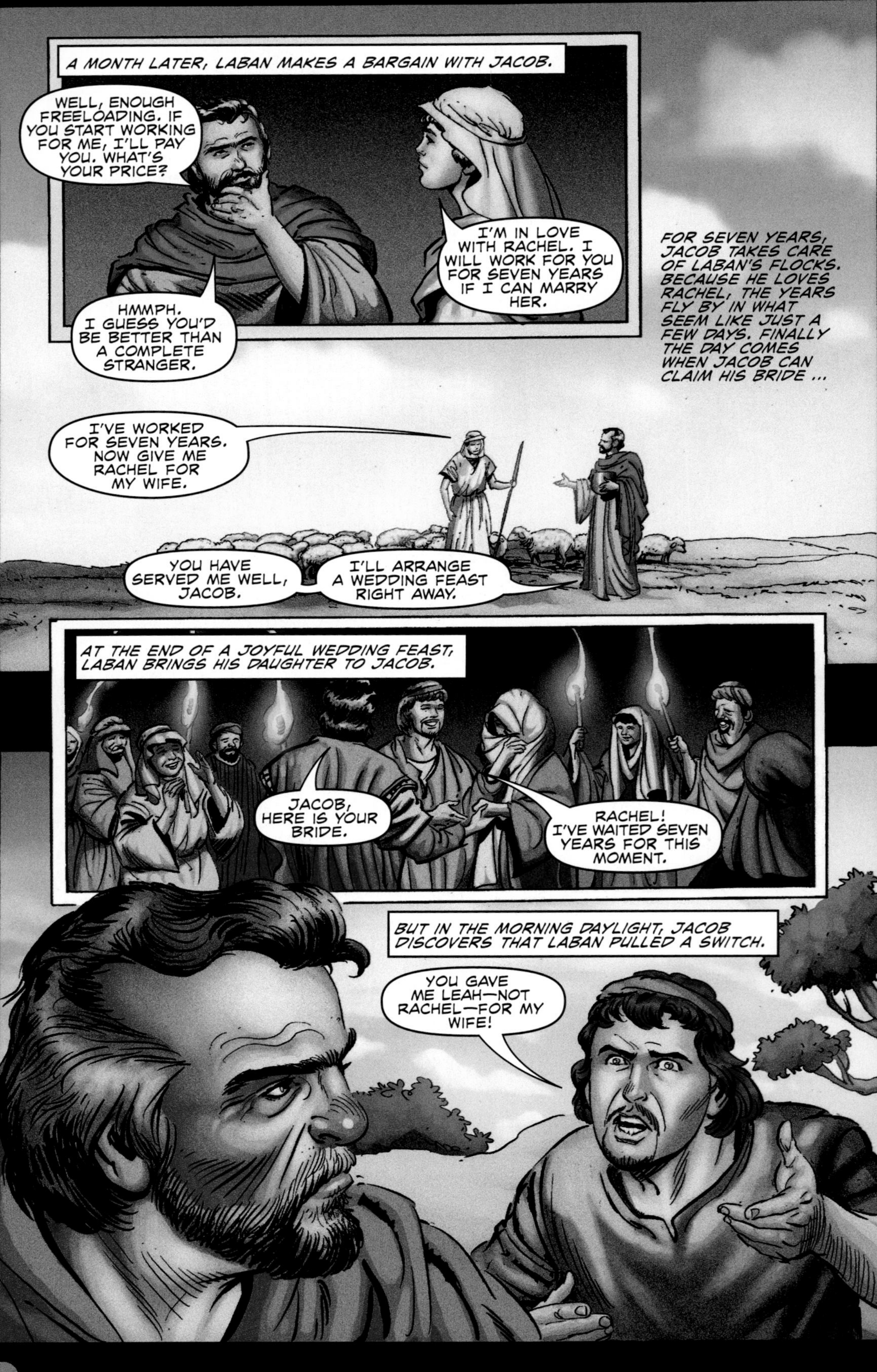

A MONTH LATER, LABAN MAKES A BARGAIN WITH JACOB.
WELL, ENOUGH FREELOADING. IF YOU START WORKING FOR ME, I'LL PAY YOU. WHAT'S YOUR PRICE?
I'M IN LOVE WITH RACHEL. I WILL WORK FOR YOU FOR SEVEN YEARS IF I CAN MARRY HER.
HMMPH. I GUESS YOU'D BE BETTER THAN A COMPLETE STRANGER.
FOR SEVEN YEARS, JACOB TAKES CARE OF LABAN'S FLOCKS. BECAUSE HE LOVES RACHEL, THE YEARS FLY BY IN WHAT SEEM LIKE JUST A FEW DAYS. FINALLY THE DAY COMES WHEN JACOB CAN CLAIM HIS BRIDE ...
I'VE WORKED FOR SEVEN YEARS. NOW GIVE ME RACHEL FOR MY WIFE.
YOU HAVE SERVED ME WELL, JACOB.
I'LL ARRANGE A WEDDING FEAST RIGHT AWAY.
AT THE END OF A JOYFUL WEDDING FEAST, LABAN BRINGS HIS DAUGHTER TO JACOB.
JACOB, HERE IS YOUR BRIDE.
RACHEL! I'VE WAITED SEVEN YEARS FOR THIS MOMENT.
BUT IN THE MORNING DAYLIGHT, JACOB DISCOVERS THAT LABAN PULLED A SWITCH.
YOU GAVE ME LEAH—NOT RACHEL—FOR MY WIFE!

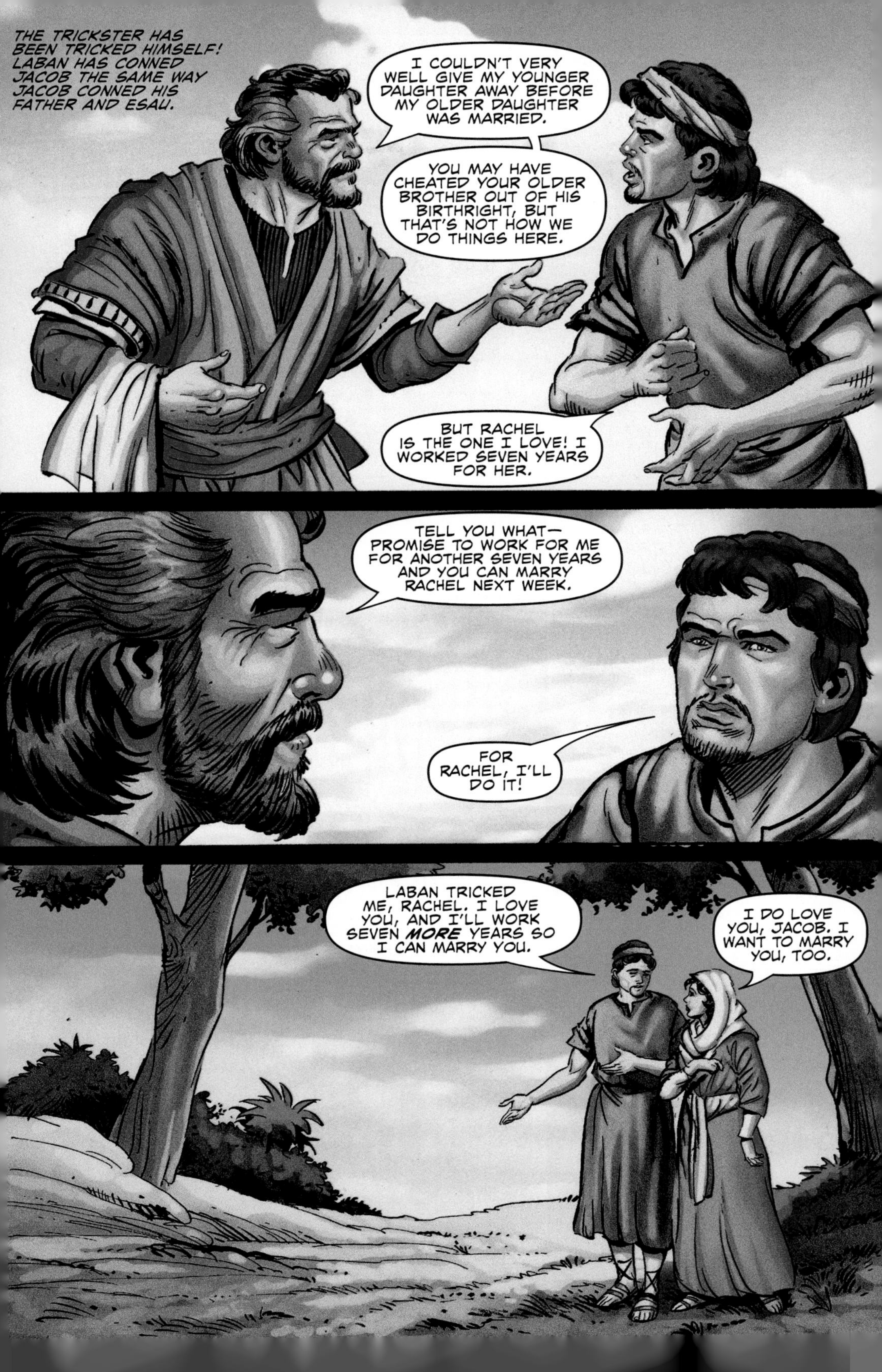
THE TRICKSTER HAS BEEN TRICKED HIMSELF! LABAN HAS CONNED JACOB THE SAME WAY JACOB CONNED HIS FATHER AND ESAU.
I COULDN'T VERY WELL GIVE MY YOUNGER DAUGHTER AWAY BEFORE MY OLDER DAUGHTER WAS MARRIED.
YOU MAY HAVE CHEATED YOUR OLDER BROTHER OUT OF HIS BIRTHRIGHT, BUT THAT'S NOT HOW WE DO THINGS HERE.
BUT RACHEL IS THE ONE I LOVE! I WORKED SEVEN YEARS FOR HER.
TELL YOU WHAT—PROMISE TO WORK FOR ME FOR ANOTHER SEVEN YEARS AND YOU CAN MARRY RACHEL NEXT WEEK.
FOR RACHEL, I'LL DO IT!
LABAN TRICKED ME, RACHEL. I LOVE YOU, AND I'LL WORK SEVEN *MORE* YEARS SO I CAN MARRY YOU.
I DO LOVE YOU, JACOB. I WANT TO MARRY YOU, TOO.

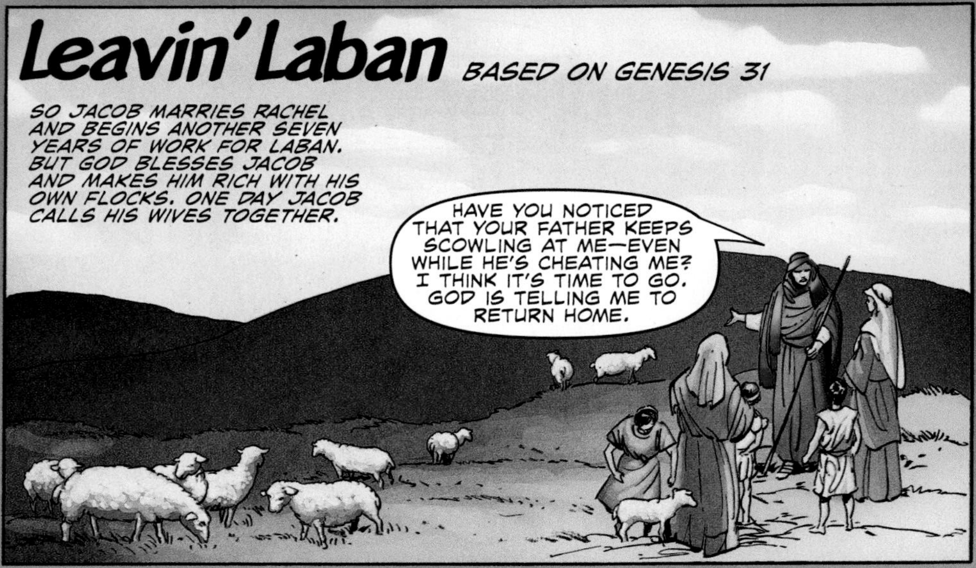
Leavin' Laban
BASED ON GENESIS 31
SO JACOB MARRIES RACHEL AND BEGINS ANOTHER SEVEN YEARS OF WORK FOR LABAN. BUT GOD BLESSES JACOB AND MAKES HIM RICH WITH HIS OWN FLOCKS. ONE DAY JACOB CALLS HIS WIVES TOGETHER.
HAVE YOU NOTICED THAT YOUR FATHER KEEPS SCOWLING AT ME—EVEN WHILE HE'S CHEATING ME? I THINK IT'S TIME TO GO. GOD IS TELLING ME TO RETURN HOME.

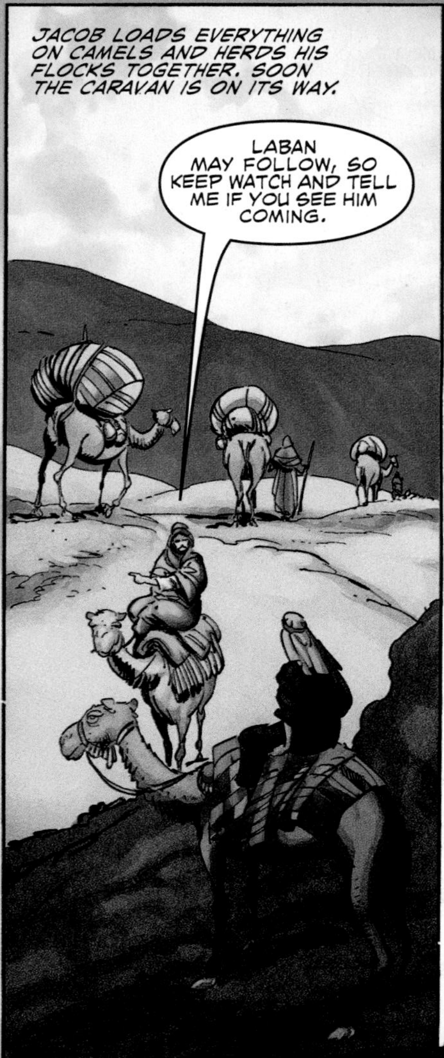
JACOB LOADS EVERYTHING ON CAMELS AND HERDS HIS FLOCKS TOGETHER. SOON THE CARAVAN IS ON ITS WAY.
LABAN MAY FOLLOW, SO KEEP WATCH AND TELL ME IF YOU SEE HIM COMING.

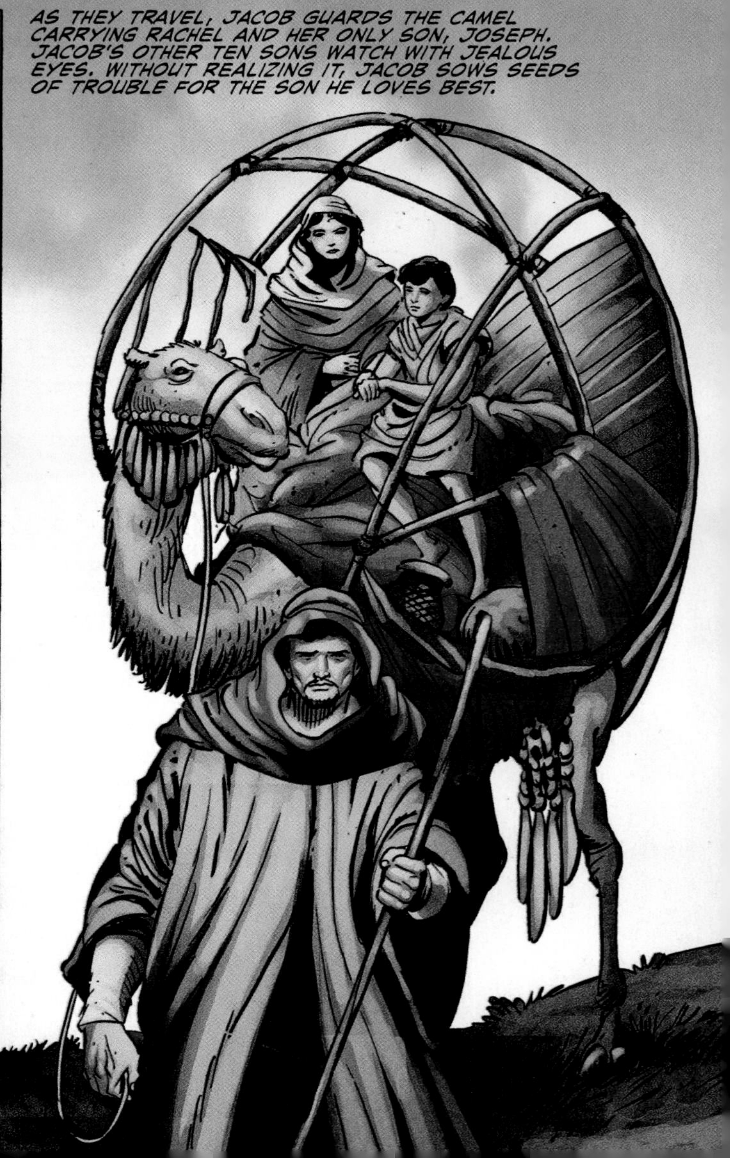
AS THEY TRAVEL, JACOB GUARDS THE CAMEL CARRYING RACHEL AND HER ONLY SON, JOSEPH. JACOB'S OTHER TEN SONS WATCH WITH JEALOUS EYES. WITHOUT REALIZING IT, JACOB SOWS SEEDS OF TROUBLE FOR THE SON HE LOVES BEST.

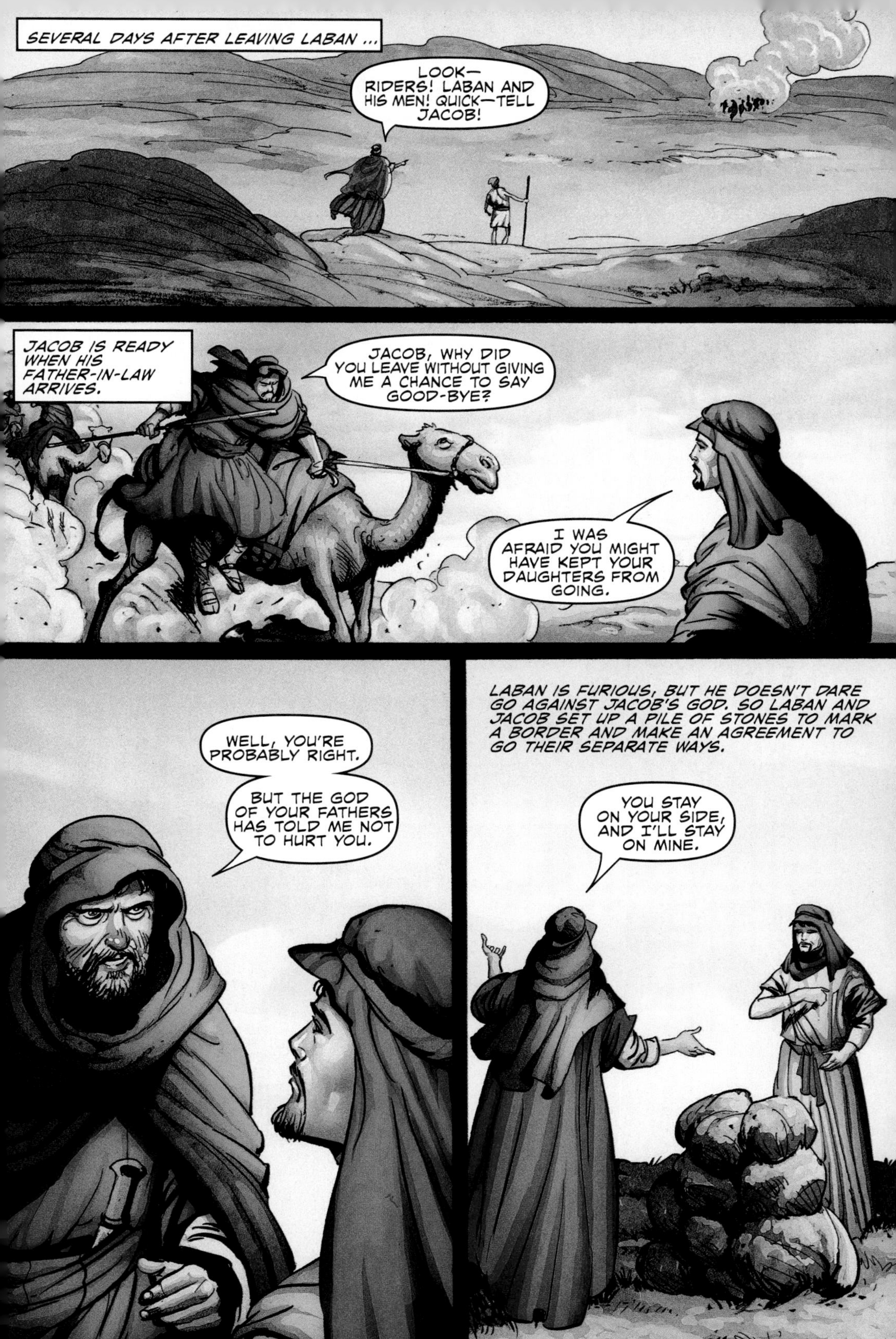
SEVERAL DAYS AFTER LEAVING LABAN ...
LOOK— RIDERS! LABAN AND HIS MEN! QUICK—TELL JACOB!
JACOB IS READY WHEN HIS FATHER-IN-LAW ARRIVES.
JACOB, WHY DID YOU LEAVE WITHOUT GIVING ME A CHANCE TO SAY GOOD-BYE?
I WAS AFRAID YOU MIGHT HAVE KEPT YOUR DAUGHTERS FROM GOING.
WELL, YOU'RE PROBABLY RIGHT.
BUT THE GOD OF YOUR FATHERS HAS TOLD ME NOT TO HURT YOU.
LABAN IS FURIOUS, BUT HE DOESN'T DARE GO AGAINST JACOB'S GOD. SO LABAN AND JACOB SET UP A PILE OF STONES TO MARK A BORDER AND MAKE AN AGREEMENT TO GO THEIR SEPARATE WAYS.
YOU STAY ON YOUR SIDE, AND I'LL STAY ON MINE.

Touched by an Angel

BASED ON GENESIS 32—33

EAGERLY, JACOB CONTINUES HIS JOURNEY HOME. ON THE WAY, HE HAS A WONDERFUL VISION ...

AN ARMY OF ANGELS! THE ARMY OF GOD IS CAMPED BESIDE ME!

THE ANGELS COMFORT JACOB, BUT AS HE GETS CLOSER TO HOME, HE BEGINS TO WORRY ABOUT HIS BROTHER, ESAU, WHO ONCE PLANNED TO MURDER HIM.

RIDE AHEAD OF ME AND LOOK FOR ESAU. TELL HIM I'M COMING HOME WITH MY FAMILY AND FLOCKS. TELL HIM I HOPE HE WILL FORGIVE ME.

JACOB WAITS ANXIOUSLY FOR THE RIDERS TO COME BACK. HE REMEMBERS THE TIME HE LIED TO HIS FATHER AND STOLE HIS BROTHER'S BLESSING—AND WHEN ESAU THREATENED TO KILL HIM.

FINALLY, THE SCOUTS RETURN ...

WE SAW ESAU! HE'S COMING TO MEET YOU—WITH 400 MEN!

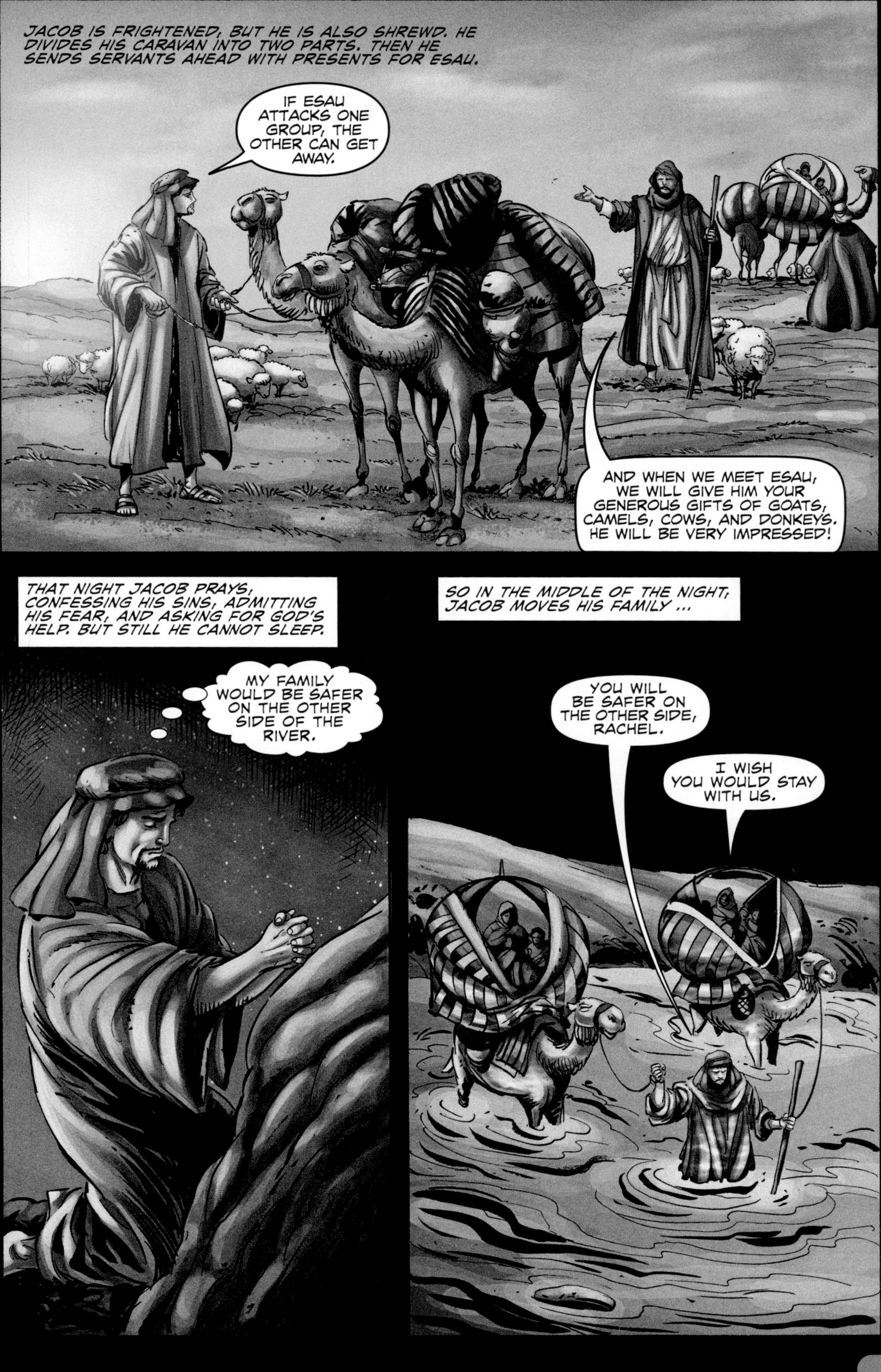
JACOB IS FRIGHTENED, BUT HE IS ALSO SHREWD. HE DIVIDES HIS CARAVAN INTO TWO PARTS. THEN HE SENDS SERVANTS AHEAD WITH PRESENTS FOR ESAU.
IF ESAU ATTACKS ONE GROUP, THE OTHER CAN GET AWAY.
AND WHEN WE MEET ESAU, WE WILL GIVE HIM YOUR GENEROUS GIFTS OF GOATS, CAMELS, COWS, AND DONKEYS. HE WILL BE VERY IMPRESSED!
THAT NIGHT JACOB PRAYS, CONFESSING HIS SINS, ADMITTING HIS FEAR, AND ASKING FOR GOD'S HELP. BUT STILL HE CANNOT SLEEP.
MY FAMILY WOULD BE SAFER ON THE OTHER SIDE OF THE RIVER.
SO IN THE MIDDLE OF THE NIGHT, JACOB MOVES HIS FAMILY ...
YOU WILL BE SAFER ON THE OTHER SIDE, RACHEL.
I WISH YOU WOULD STAY WITH US.

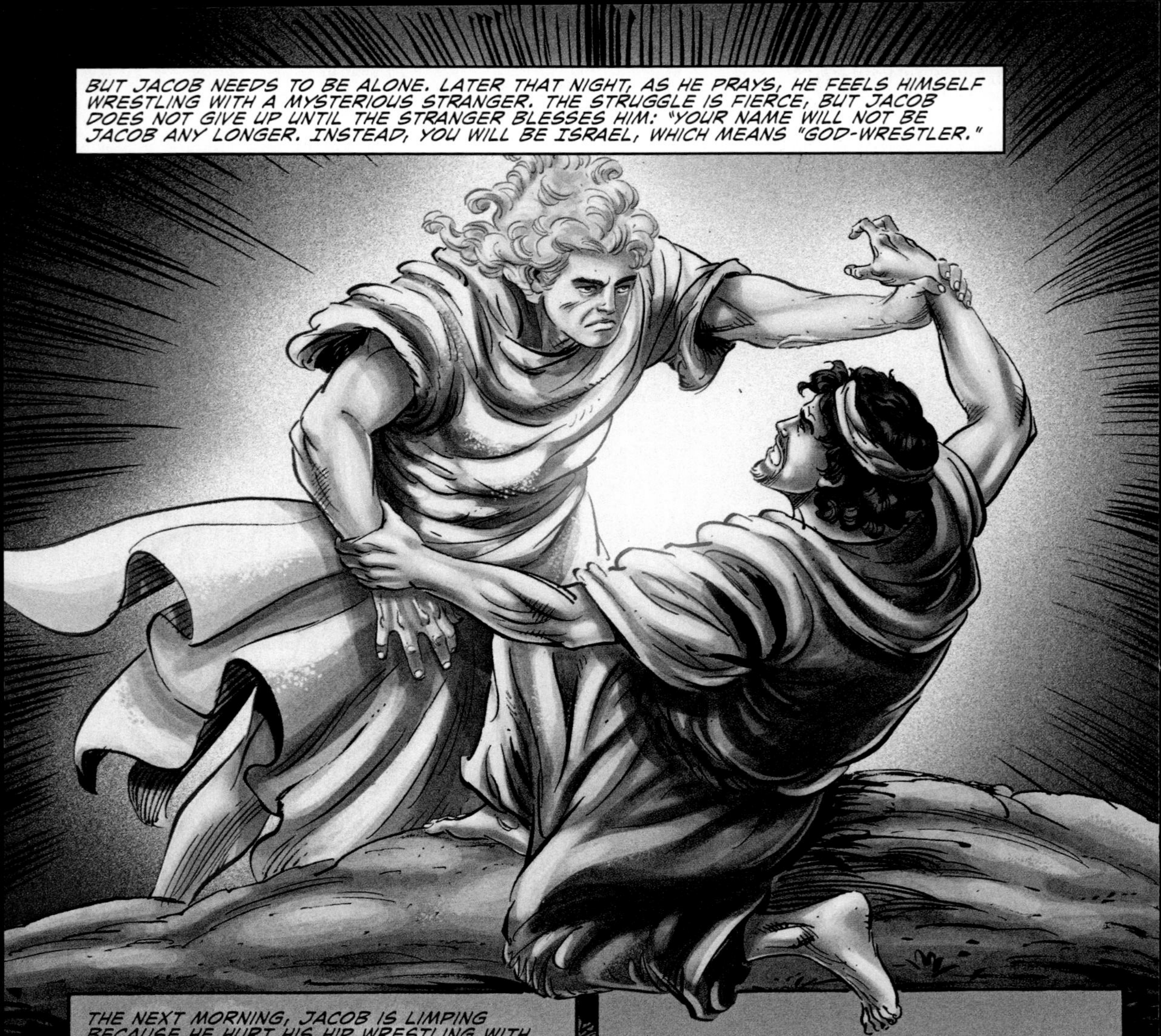
BUT JACOB NEEDS TO BE ALONE. LATER THAT NIGHT, AS HE PRAYS, HE FEELS HIMSELF WRESTLING WITH A MYSTERIOUS STRANGER. THE STRUGGLE IS FIERCE, BUT JACOB DOES NOT GIVE UP UNTIL THE STRANGER BLESSES HIM: "YOUR NAME WILL NOT BE JACOB ANY LONGER. INSTEAD, YOU WILL BE ISRAEL, WHICH MEANS "GOD-WRESTLER."

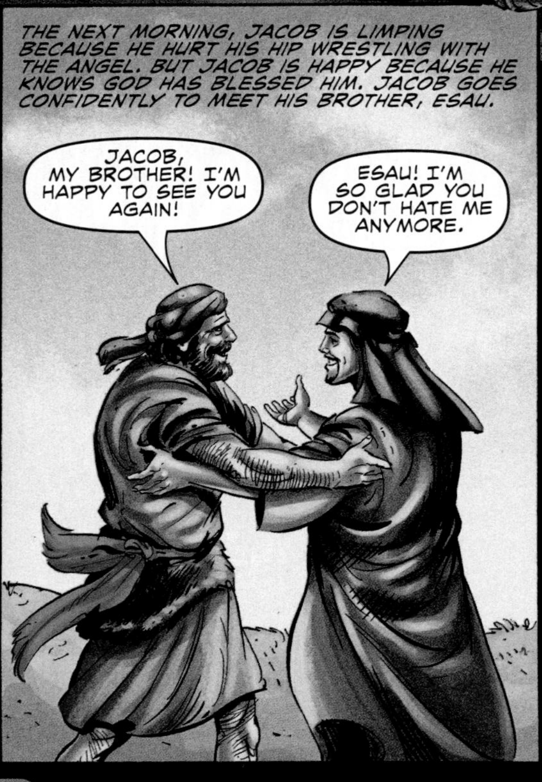
THE NEXT MORNING, JACOB IS LIMPING BECAUSE HE HURT HIS HIP WRESTLING WITH THE ANGEL. BUT JACOB IS HAPPY BECAUSE HE KNOWS GOD HAS BLESSED HIM. JACOB GOES CONFIDENTLY TO MEET HIS BROTHER, ESAU.
JACOB, MY BROTHER! I'M HAPPY TO SEE YOU AGAIN!
ESAU! I'M SO GLAD YOU DON'T HATE ME ANYMORE.

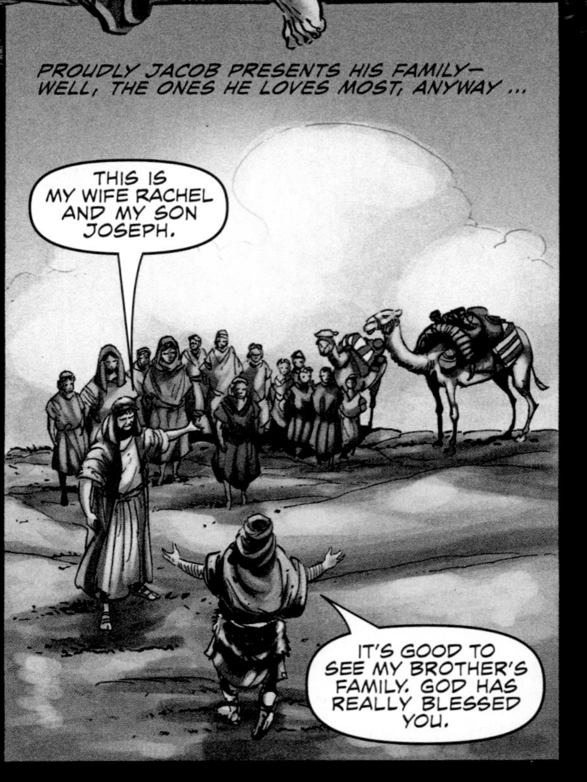
PROUDLY JACOB PRESENTS HIS FAMILY— WELL, THE ONES HE LOVES MOST, ANYWAY ...
THIS IS MY WIFE RACHEL AND MY SON JOSEPH.
IT'S GOOD TO SEE MY BROTHER'S FAMILY. GOD HAS REALLY BLESSED YOU.

Homecoming BASED ON GENESIS 35

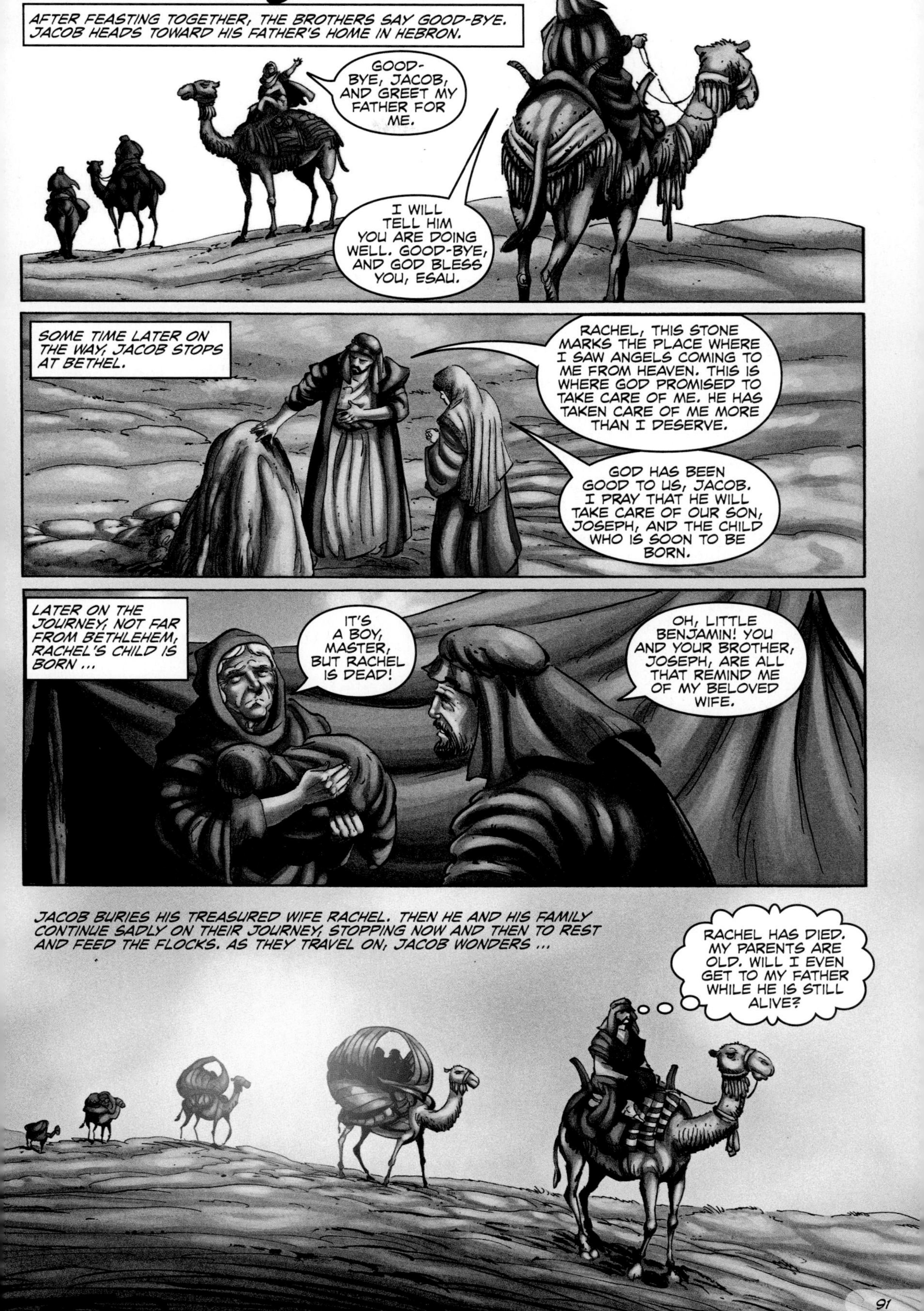
AFTER FEASTING TOGETHER, THE BROTHERS SAY GOOD-BYE. JACOB HEADS TOWARD HIS FATHER'S HOME IN HEBRON.
GOOD-BYE, JACOB, AND GREET MY FATHER FOR ME.
I WILL TELL HIM YOU ARE DOING WELL. GOOD-BYE, AND GOD BLESS YOU, ESAU.
SOME TIME LATER ON THE WAY, JACOB STOPS AT BETHEL.
RACHEL, THIS STONE MARKS THE PLACE WHERE I SAW ANGELS COMING TO ME FROM HEAVEN. THIS IS WHERE GOD PROMISED TO TAKE CARE OF ME. HE HAS TAKEN CARE OF ME MORE THAN I DESERVE.
GOD HAS BEEN GOOD TO US, JACOB. I PRAY THAT HE WILL TAKE CARE OF OUR SON, JOSEPH, AND THE CHILD WHO IS SOON TO BE BORN.
LATER ON THE JOURNEY, NOT FAR FROM BETHLEHEM, RACHEL'S CHILD IS BORN ...
IT'S A BOY, MASTER, BUT RACHEL IS DEAD!
OH, LITTLE BENJAMIN! YOU AND YOUR BROTHER, JOSEPH, ARE ALL THAT REMIND ME OF MY BELOVED WIFE.
JACOB BURIES HIS TREASURED WIFE RACHEL. THEN HE AND HIS FAMILY CONTINUE SADLY ON THEIR JOURNEY, STOPPING NOW AND THEN TO REST AND FEED THE FLOCKS. AS THEY TRAVEL ON, JACOB WONDERS ...
RACHEL HAS DIED. MY PARENTS ARE OLD. WILL I EVEN GET TO MY FATHER WHILE HE IS STILL ALIVE?

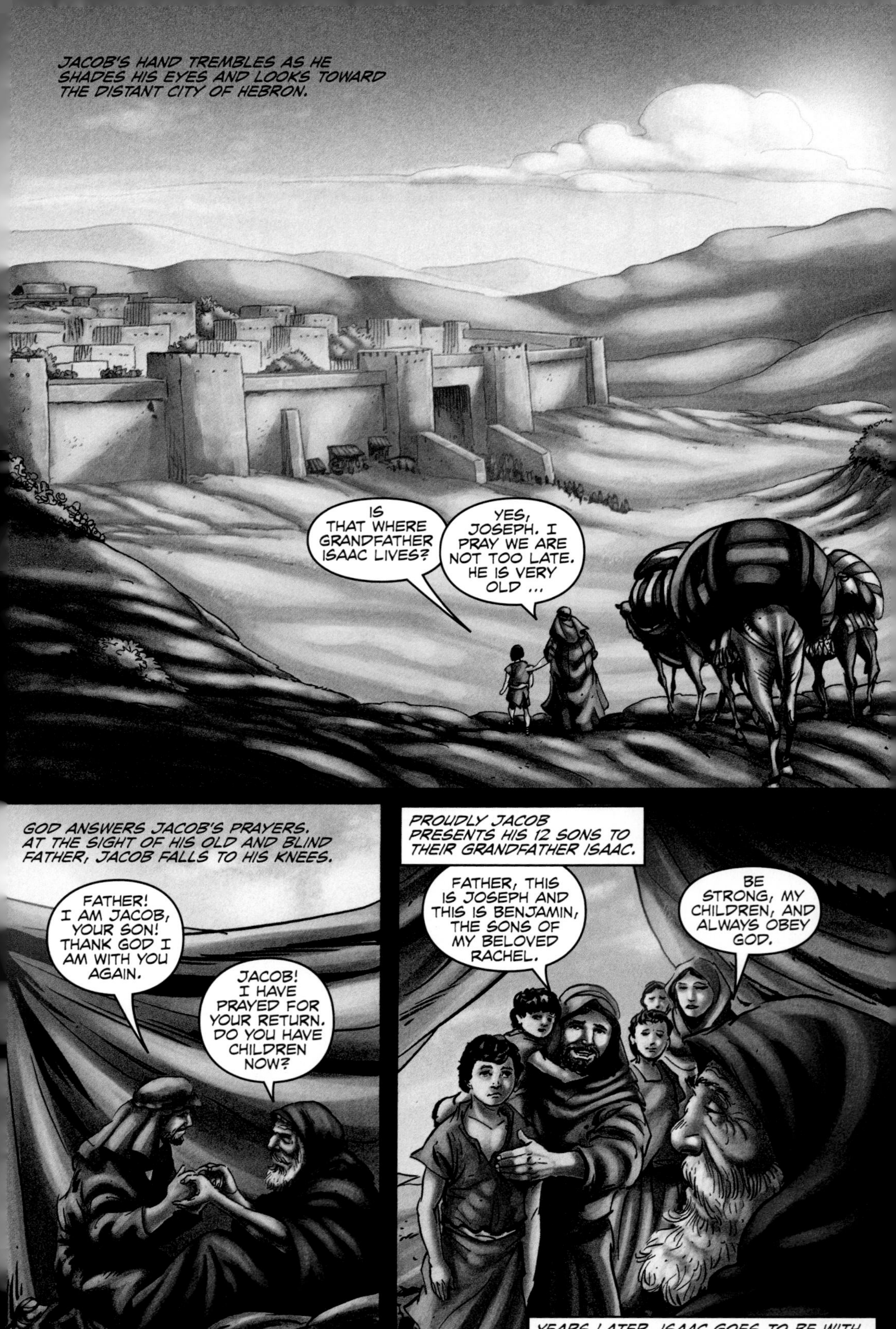
JACOB'S HAND TREMBLES AS HE SHADES HIS EYES AND LOOKS TOWARD THE DISTANT CITY OF HEBRON.
IS THAT WHERE GRANDFATHER ISAAC LIVES?
YES, JOSEPH. I PRAY WE ARE NOT TOO LATE. HE IS VERY OLD ...
GOD ANSWERS JACOB'S PRAYERS. AT THE SIGHT OF HIS OLD AND BLIND FATHER, JACOB FALLS TO HIS KNEES.
FATHER! I AM JACOB, YOUR SON! THANK GOD I AM WITH YOU AGAIN.
JACOB! I HAVE PRAYED FOR YOUR RETURN. DO YOU HAVE CHILDREN NOW?
PROUDLY JACOB PRESENTS HIS 12 SONS TO THEIR GRANDFATHER ISAAC.
FATHER, THIS IS JOSEPH AND THIS IS BENJAMIN, THE SONS OF MY BELOVED RACHEL.
BE STRONG, MY CHILDREN, AND ALWAYS OBEY GOD.
YEARS LATER, ISAAC GOES TO BE WITH HIS GOD, THE GOD OF HIS FATHERS.

Big Dreams

BASED ON GENESIS 37:1–11

WHEN ISAAC DIES, JACOB TAKES OVER AS HEAD OF THE TRIBE. HE SETTLES HIS FAMILY IN HIS FATHER'S LAND OF CANAAN. HIS SONS TAKE CARE OF HIS FLOCKS OF SHEEP. JOSEPH IS A YOUNGER SON, AND HE HAS SOME NEWS FOR HIS FATHER ...

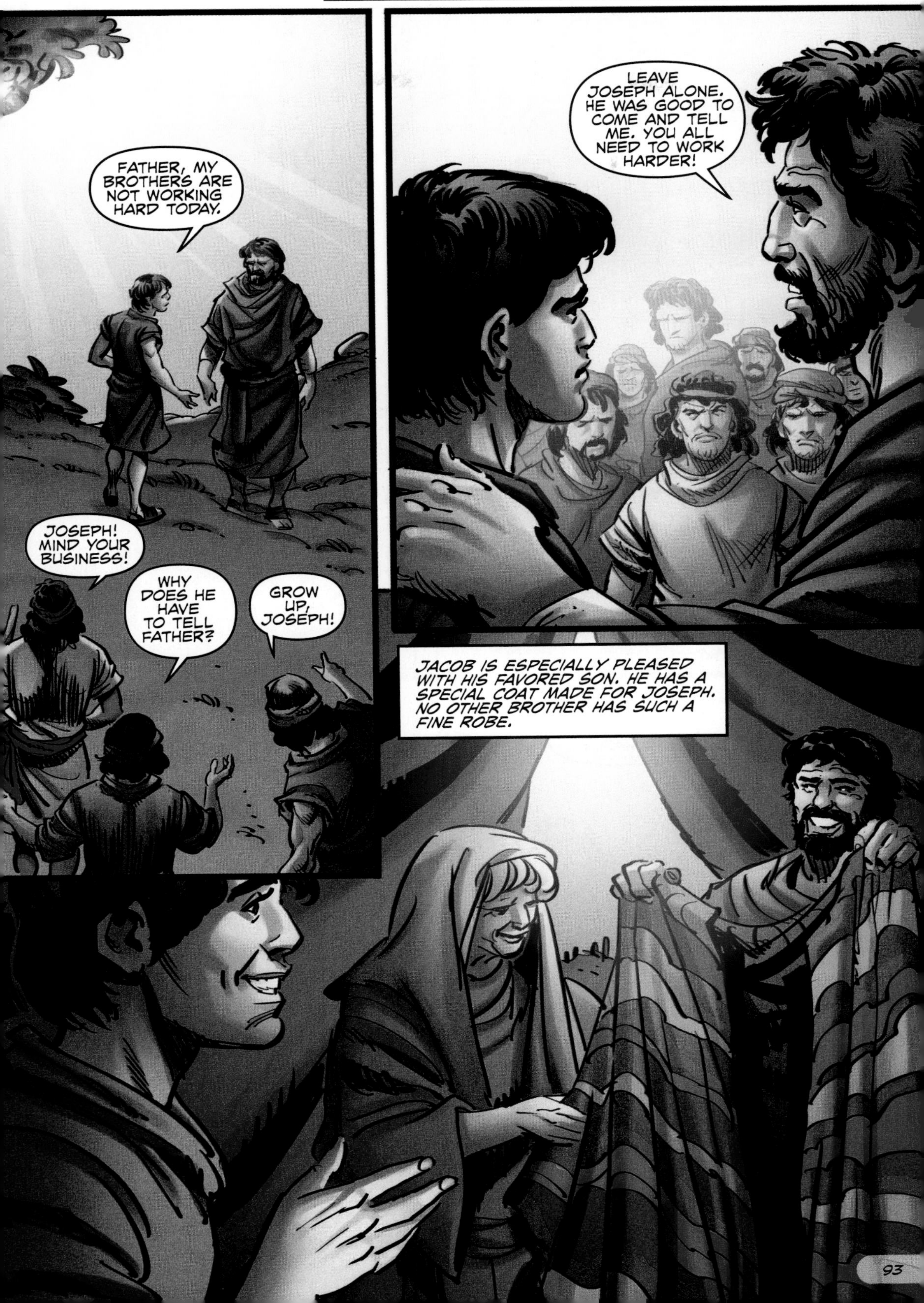

FATHER, MY BROTHERS ARE NOT WORKING HARD TODAY.
JOSEPH! MIND YOUR BUSINESS!
WHY DOES HE HAVE TO TELL FATHER?
GROW UP, JOSEPH!
LEAVE JOSEPH ALONE. HE WAS GOOD TO COME AND TELL ME. YOU ALL NEED TO WORK HARDER!
JACOB IS ESPECIALLY PLEASED WITH HIS FAVORED SON. HE HAS A SPECIAL COAT MADE FOR JOSEPH. NO OTHER BROTHER HAS SUCH A FINE ROBE.

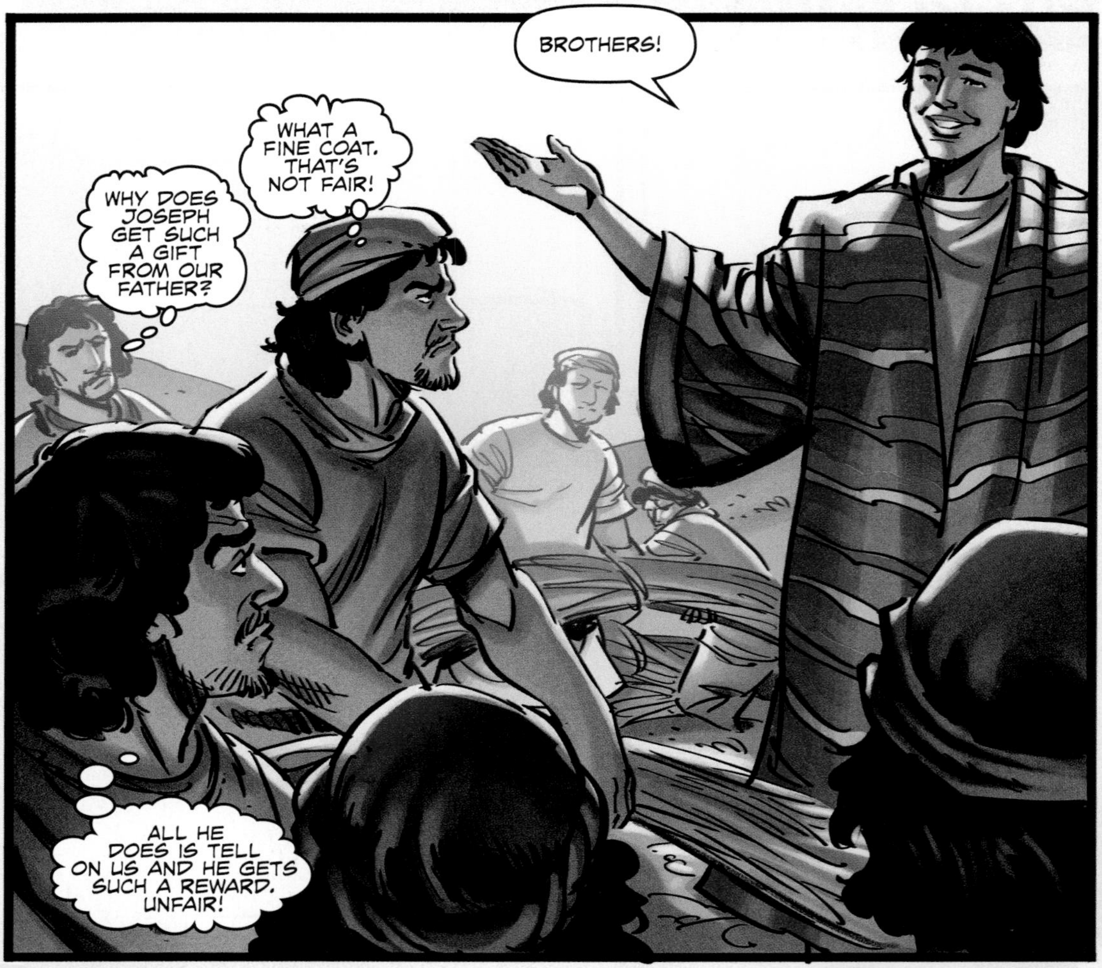
BROTHERS!
WHAT A FINE COAT. THAT'S NOT FAIR!
WHY DOES JOSEPH GET SUCH A GIFT FROM OUR FATHER?
ALL HE DOES IS TELL ON US AND HE GETS SUCH A REWARD. UNFAIR!

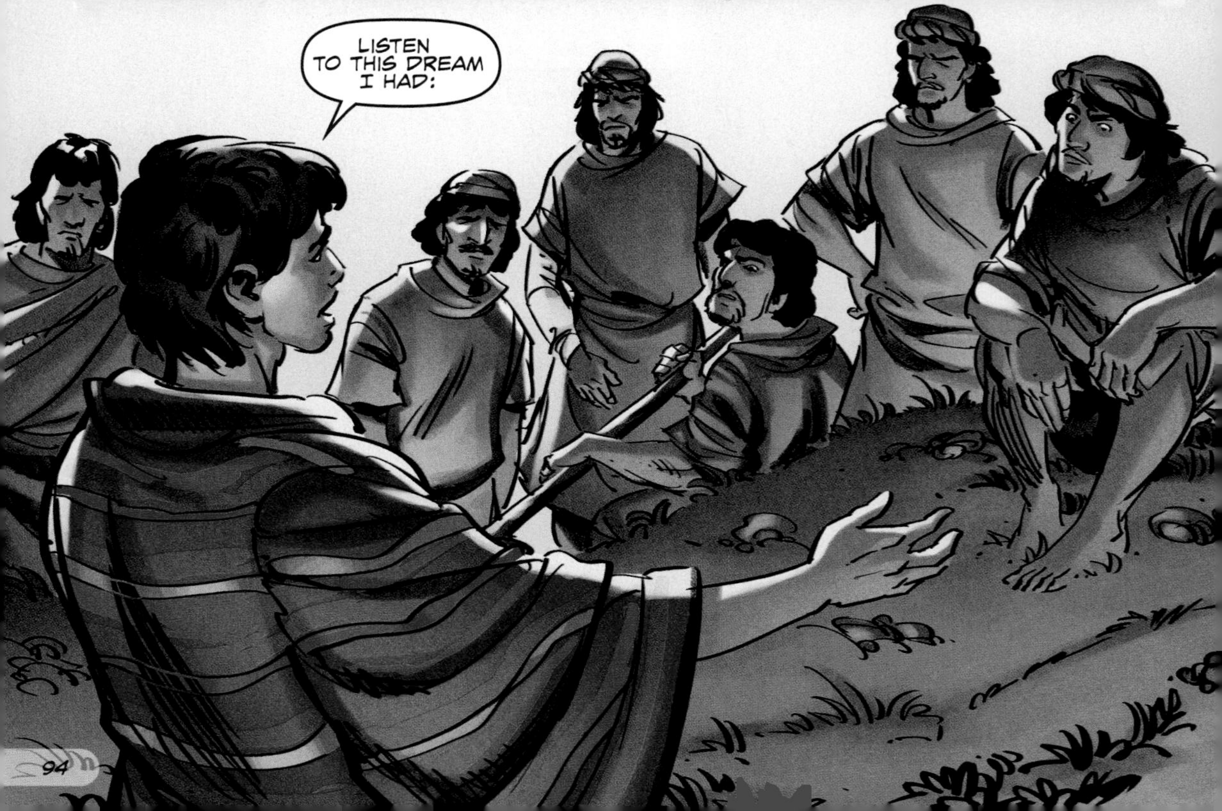
LISTEN TO THIS DREAM I HAD:

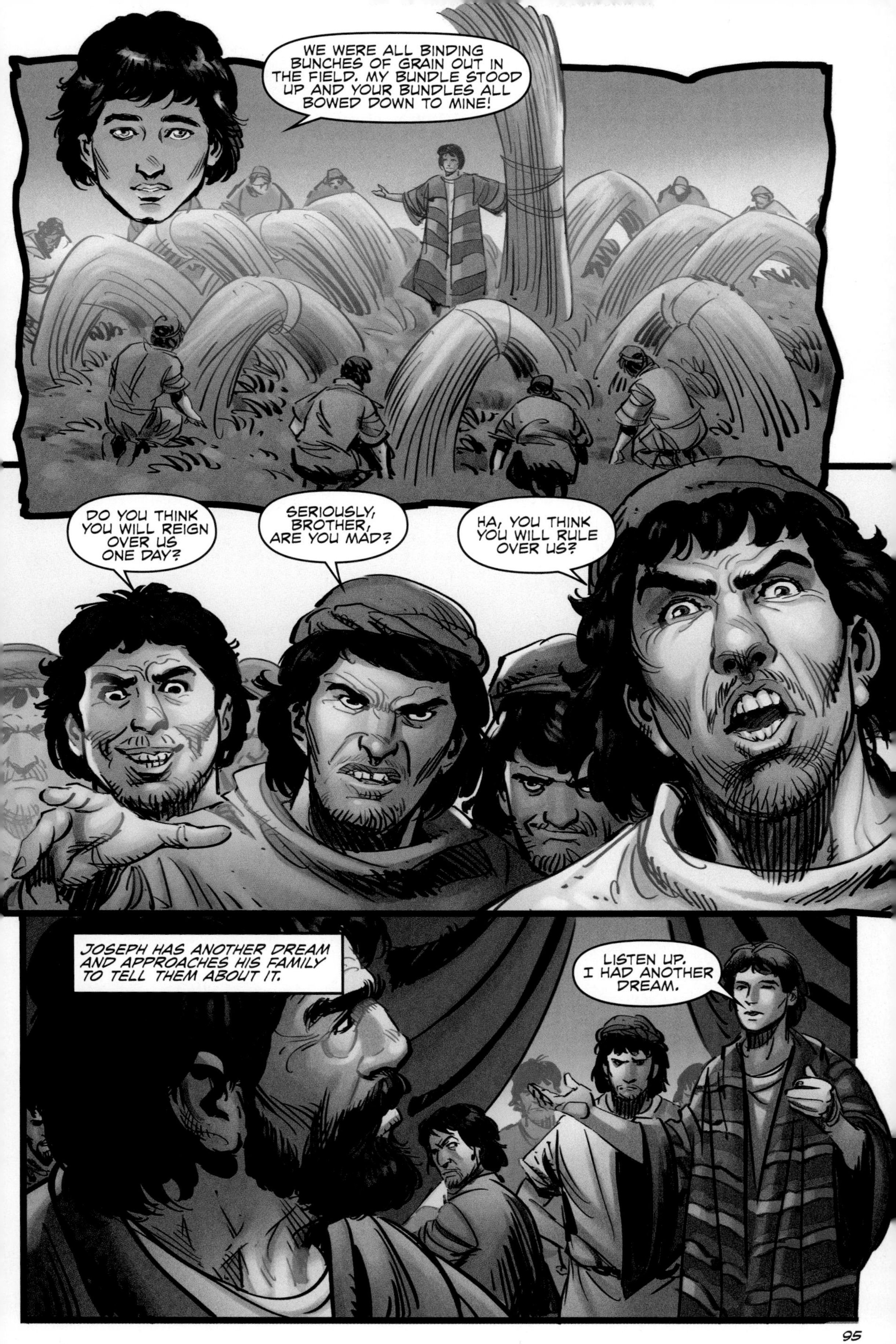
WE WERE ALL BINDING BUNCHES OF GRAIN OUT IN THE FIELD. MY BUNDLE STOOD UP AND YOUR BUNDLES ALL BOWED DOWN TO MINE!
DO YOU THINK YOU WILL REIGN OVER US ONE DAY?
SERIOUSLY, BROTHER, ARE YOU MAD?
HA, YOU THINK YOU WILL RULE OVER US?
JOSEPH HAS ANOTHER DREAM AND APPROACHES HIS FAMILY TO TELL THEM ABOUT IT.
LISTEN UP. I HAD ANOTHER DREAM.

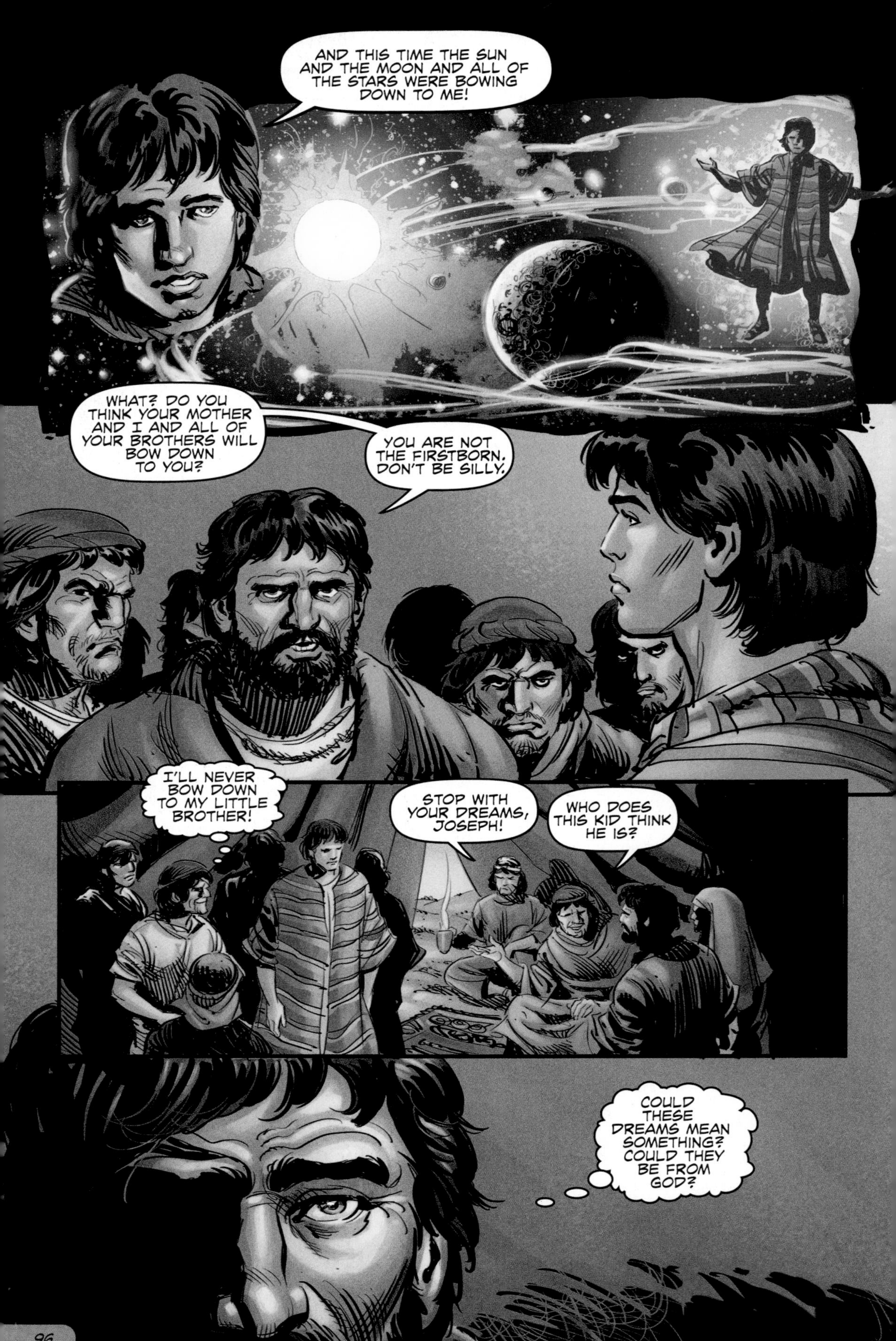
AND THIS TIME THE SUN AND THE MOON AND ALL OF THE STARS WERE BOWING DOWN TO ME!
WHAT? DO YOU THINK YOUR MOTHER AND I AND ALL OF YOUR BROTHERS WILL BOW DOWN TO YOU?
YOU ARE NOT THE FIRSTBORN. DON'T BE SILLY.
I'LL NEVER BOW DOWN TO MY LITTLE BROTHER!
STOP WITH YOUR DREAMS, JOSEPH!
WHO DOES THIS KID THINK HE IS?
COULD THESE DREAMS MEAN SOMETHING? COULD THEY BE FROM GOD?

Dreamer for Sale *GENESIS 37:12-36*

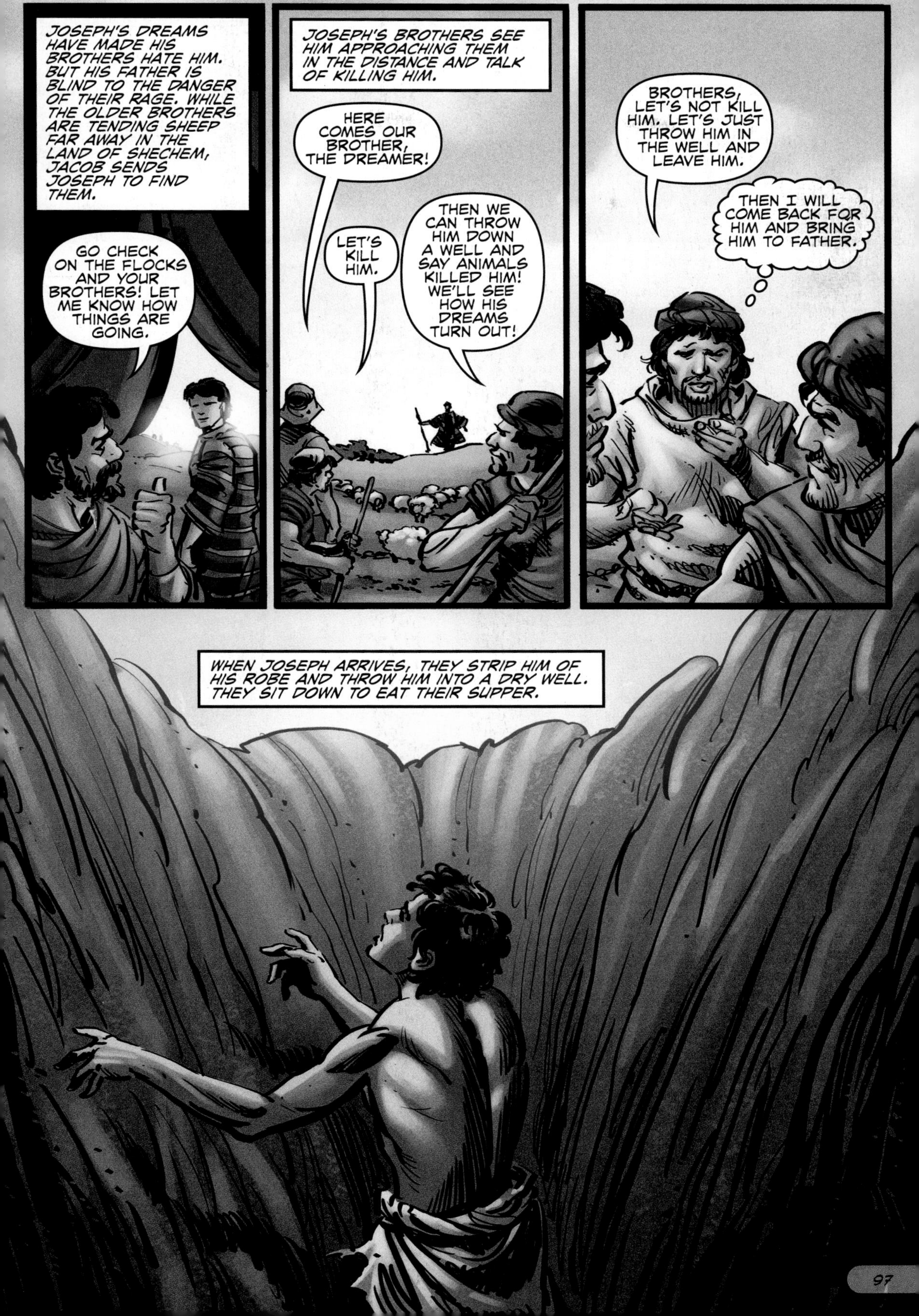
JOSEPH'S DREAMS HAVE MADE HIS BROTHERS HATE HIM. BUT HIS FATHER IS BLIND TO THE DANGER OF THEIR RAGE. WHILE THE OLDER BROTHERS ARE TENDING SHEEP FAR AWAY IN THE LAND OF SHECHEM, JACOB SENDS JOSEPH TO FIND THEM.
GO CHECK ON THE FLOCKS AND YOUR BROTHERS! LET ME KNOW HOW THINGS ARE GOING.
JOSEPH'S BROTHERS SEE HIM APPROACHING THEM IN THE DISTANCE AND TALK OF KILLING HIM.
HERE COMES OUR BROTHER, THE DREAMER!
LET'S KILL HIM.
THEN WE CAN THROW HIM DOWN A WELL AND SAY ANIMALS KILLED HIM! WE'LL SEE HOW HIS DREAMS TURN OUT!
BROTHERS, LET'S NOT KILL HIM. LET'S JUST THROW HIM IN THE WELL AND LEAVE HIM.
THEN I WILL COME BACK FOR HIM AND BRING HIM TO FATHER.
WHEN JOSEPH ARRIVES, THEY STRIP HIM OF HIS ROBE AND THROW HIM INTO A DRY WELL. THEY SIT DOWN TO EAT THEIR SUPPER.

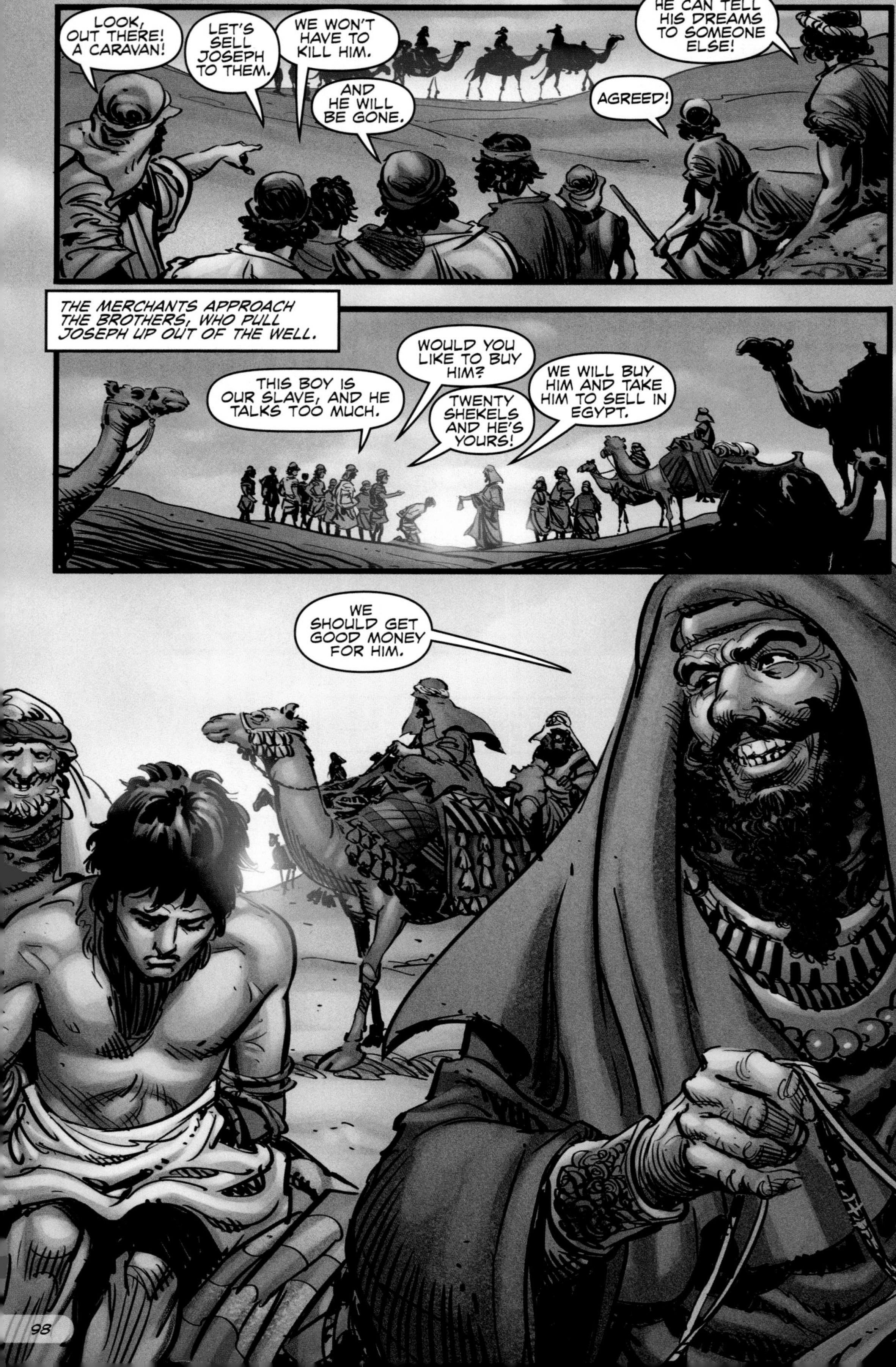

LOOK, OUT THERE! A CARAVAN!
LET'S SELL JOSEPH TO THEM.
WE WON'T HAVE TO KILL HIM.
AND HE WILL BE GONE.
HE CAN TELL HIS DREAMS TO SOMEONE ELSE!
AGREED!
THE MERCHANTS APPROACH THE BROTHERS, WHO PULL JOSEPH UP OUT OF THE WELL.
THIS BOY IS OUR SLAVE, AND HE TALKS TOO MUCH.
WOULD YOU LIKE TO BUY HIM?
TWENTY SHEKELS AND HE'S YOURS!
WE WILL BUY HIM AND TAKE HIM TO SELL IN EGYPT.
WE SHOULD GET GOOD MONEY FOR HIM.

REUBEN WAS BUSY TENDING TO THE SHEEP AND WASN'T PART OF THE PLAN TO SELL JOSEPH.

WHERE IS JOSEPH? WHAT HAVE YOU DONE?

HE IS GONE TO EGYPT WHERE HE CAN'T BRAG OF HIS DREAMS TO US ANYMORE. WE SOLD HIM! HERE IS YOUR SHARE OF THE MONEY.

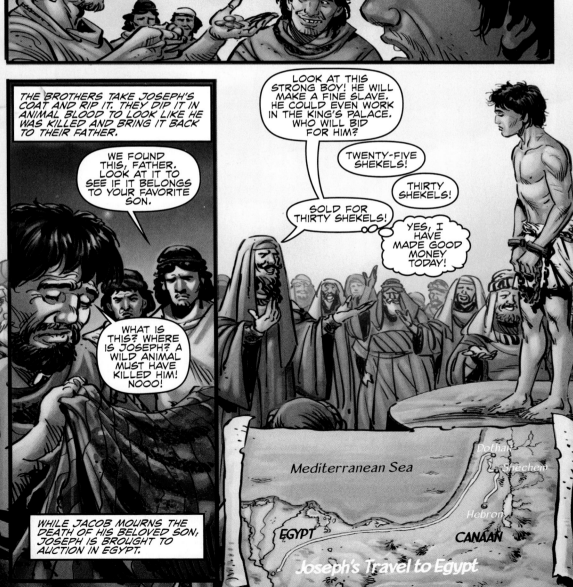

THE BROTHERS TAKE JOSEPH'S COAT AND RIP IT. THEY DIP IT IN ANIMAL BLOOD TO LOOK LIKE HE WAS KILLED AND BRING IT BACK TO THEIR FATHER.

WE FOUND THIS, FATHER. LOOK AT IT TO SEE IF IT BELONGS TO YOUR FAVORITE SON.

WHAT IS THIS? WHERE IS JOSEPH? A WILD ANIMAL MUST HAVE KILLED HIM! NOOO!

LOOK AT THIS STRONG BOY! HE WILL MAKE A FINE SLAVE. HE COULD EVEN WORK IN THE KING'S PALACE. WHO WILL BID FOR HIM?

TWENTY-FIVE SHEKELS!

THIRTY SHEKELS!

SOLD FOR THIRTY SHEKELS!

YES, I HAVE MADE GOOD MONEY TODAY!

WHILE JACOB MOURNS THE DEATH OF HIS BELOVED SON, JOSEPH IS BROUGHT TO AUCTION IN EGYPT.

Mediterranean Sea

Dothan

Shechem

Hebron

EGYPT

CANAAN

Joseph's Travel to Egypt

Management Crisis

BASED ON GENESIS 39:1-20

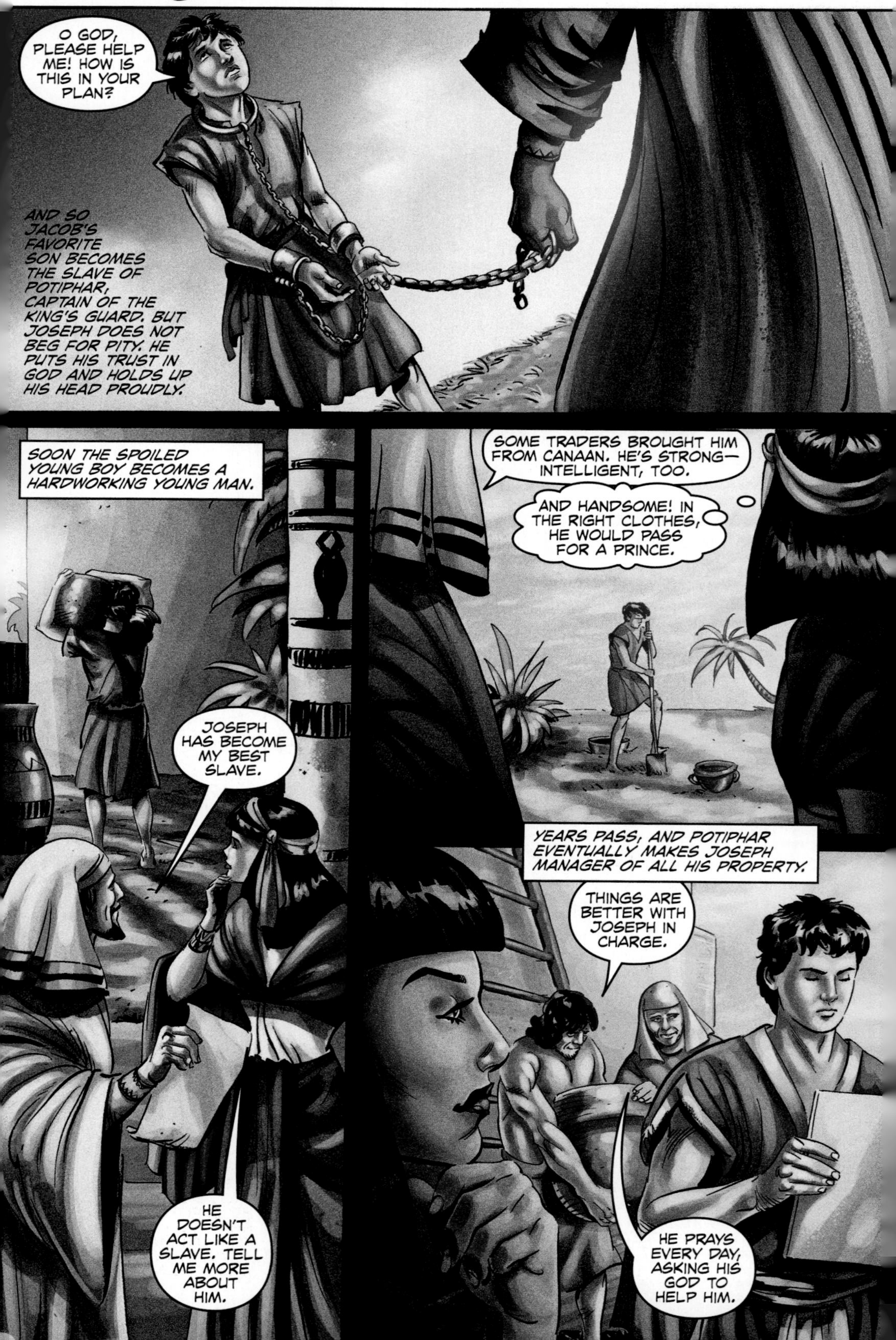
O GOD, PLEASE HELP ME! HOW IS THIS IN YOUR PLAN?
AND SO JACOB'S FAVORITE SON BECOMES THE SLAVE OF POTIPHAR, CAPTAIN OF THE KING'S GUARD. BUT JOSEPH DOES NOT BEG FOR PITY. HE PUTS HIS TRUST IN GOD AND HOLDS UP HIS HEAD PROUDLY.
SOON THE SPOILED YOUNG BOY BECOMES A HARDWORKING YOUNG MAN.
JOSEPH HAS BECOME MY BEST SLAVE.
HE DOESN'T ACT LIKE A SLAVE. TELL ME MORE ABOUT HIM.
SOME TRADERS BROUGHT HIM FROM CANAAN. HE'S STRONG—INTELLIGENT, TOO.
AND HANDSOME! IN THE RIGHT CLOTHES, HE WOULD PASS FOR A PRINCE.
YEARS PASS, AND POTIPHAR EVENTUALLY MAKES JOSEPH MANAGER OF ALL HIS PROPERTY.
THINGS ARE BETTER WITH JOSEPH IN CHARGE.
HE PRAYS EVERY DAY, ASKING HIS GOD TO HELP HIM.

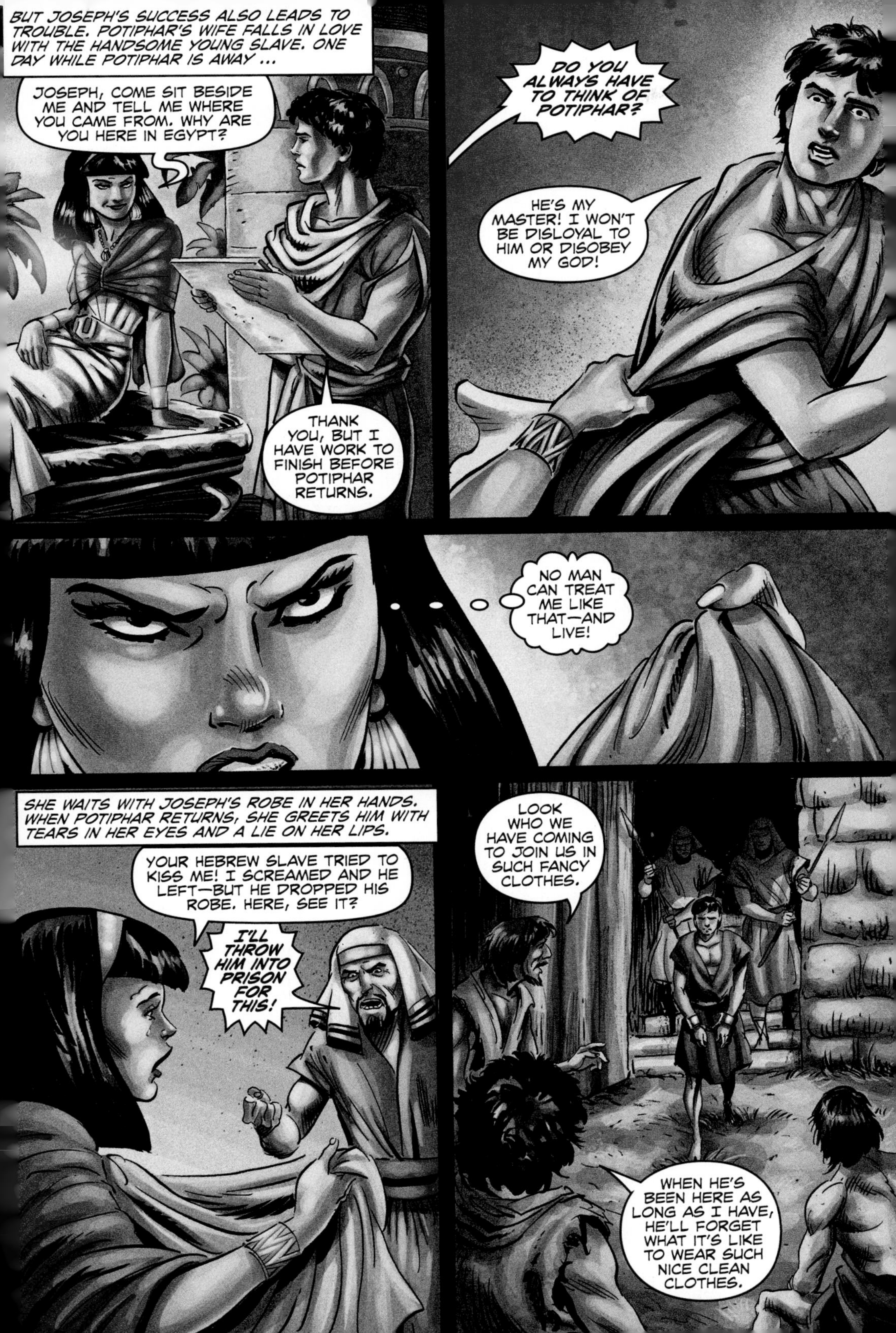
BUT JOSEPH'S SUCCESS ALSO LEADS TO TROUBLE. POTIPHAR'S WIFE FALLS IN LOVE WITH THE HANDSOME YOUNG SLAVE. ONE DAY WHILE POTIPHAR IS AWAY ...
JOSEPH, COME SIT BESIDE ME AND TELL ME WHERE YOU CAME FROM. WHY ARE YOU HERE IN EGYPT?
THANK YOU, BUT I HAVE WORK TO FINISH BEFORE POTIPHAR RETURNS.
DO YOU ALWAYS HAVE TO THINK OF POTIPHAR?
HE'S MY MASTER! I WON'T BE DISLOYAL TO HIM OR DISOBEY MY GOD!
NO MAN CAN TREAT ME LIKE THAT—AND LIVE!
SHE WAITS WITH JOSEPH'S ROBE IN HER HANDS. WHEN POTIPHAR RETURNS, SHE GREETS HIM WITH TEARS IN HER EYES AND A LIE ON HER LIPS.
YOUR HEBREW SLAVE TRIED TO KISS ME! I SCREAMED AND HE LEFT—BUT HE DROPPED HIS ROBE. HERE, SEE IT?
I'LL THROW HIM INTO PRISON FOR THIS!
LOOK WHO WE HAVE COMING TO JOIN US IN SUCH FANCY CLOTHES.
WHEN HE'S BEEN HERE AS LONG AS I HAVE, HE'LL FORGET WHAT IT'S LIKE TO WEAR SUCH NICE CLEAN CLOTHES.

Jailhouse Shock

BASED ON GENESIS 39:20—41:43

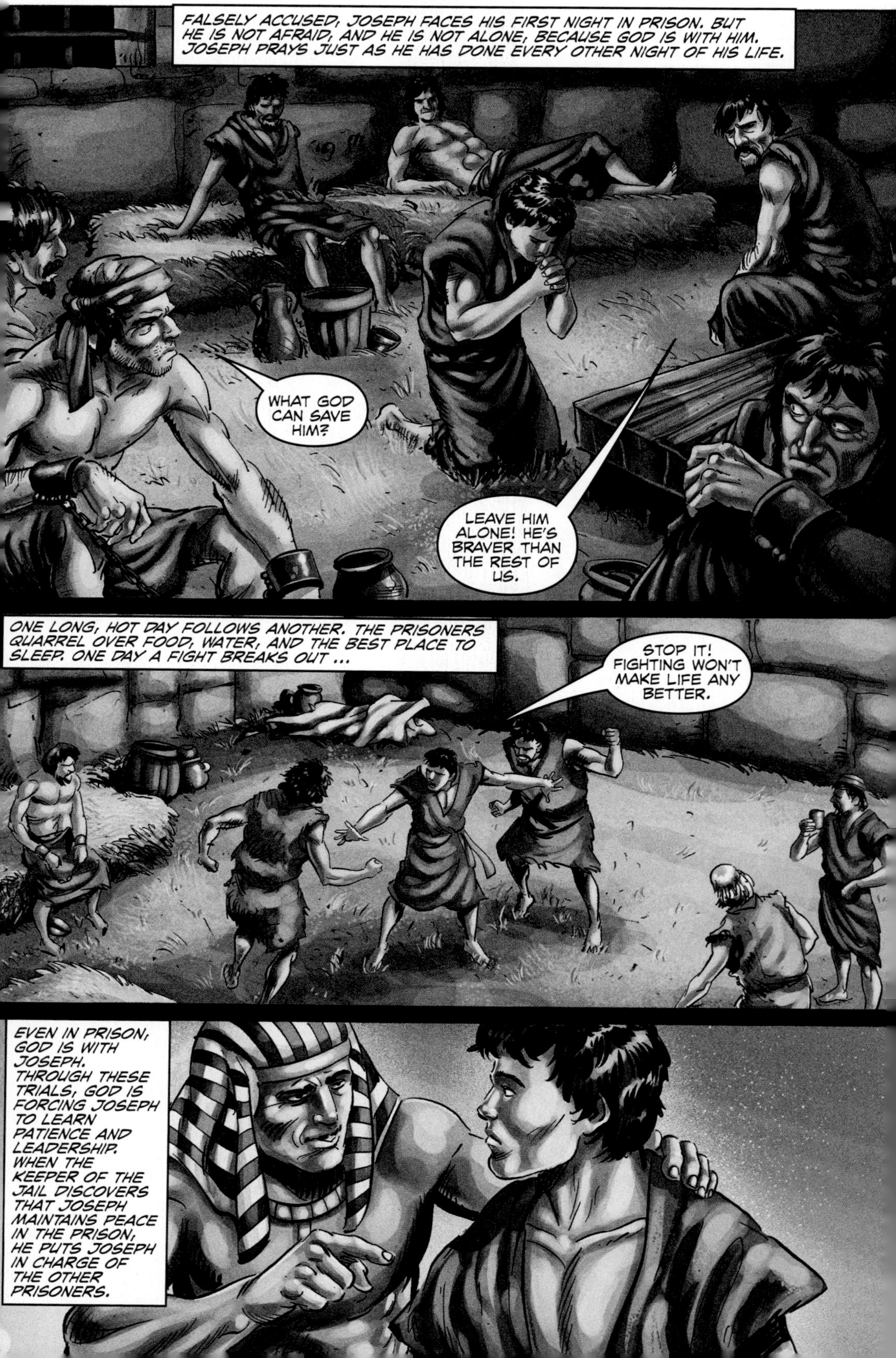
FALSELY ACCUSED, JOSEPH FACES HIS FIRST NIGHT IN PRISON. BUT HE IS NOT AFRAID, AND HE IS NOT ALONE, BECAUSE GOD IS WITH HIM. JOSEPH PRAYS JUST AS HE HAS DONE EVERY OTHER NIGHT OF HIS LIFE.
WHAT GOD CAN SAVE HIM?
LEAVE HIM ALONE! HE'S BRAVER THAN THE REST OF US.
ONE LONG, HOT DAY FOLLOWS ANOTHER. THE PRISONERS QUARREL OVER FOOD, WATER, AND THE BEST PLACE TO SLEEP. ONE DAY A FIGHT BREAKS OUT ...
STOP IT! FIGHTING WON'T MAKE LIFE ANY BETTER.
EVEN IN PRISON, GOD IS WITH JOSEPH. THROUGH THESE TRIALS, GOD IS FORCING JOSEPH TO LEARN PATIENCE AND LEADERSHIP. WHEN THE KEEPER OF THE JAIL DISCOVERS THAT JOSEPH MAINTAINS PEACE IN THE PRISON, HE PUTS JOSEPH IN CHARGE OF THE OTHER PRISONERS.

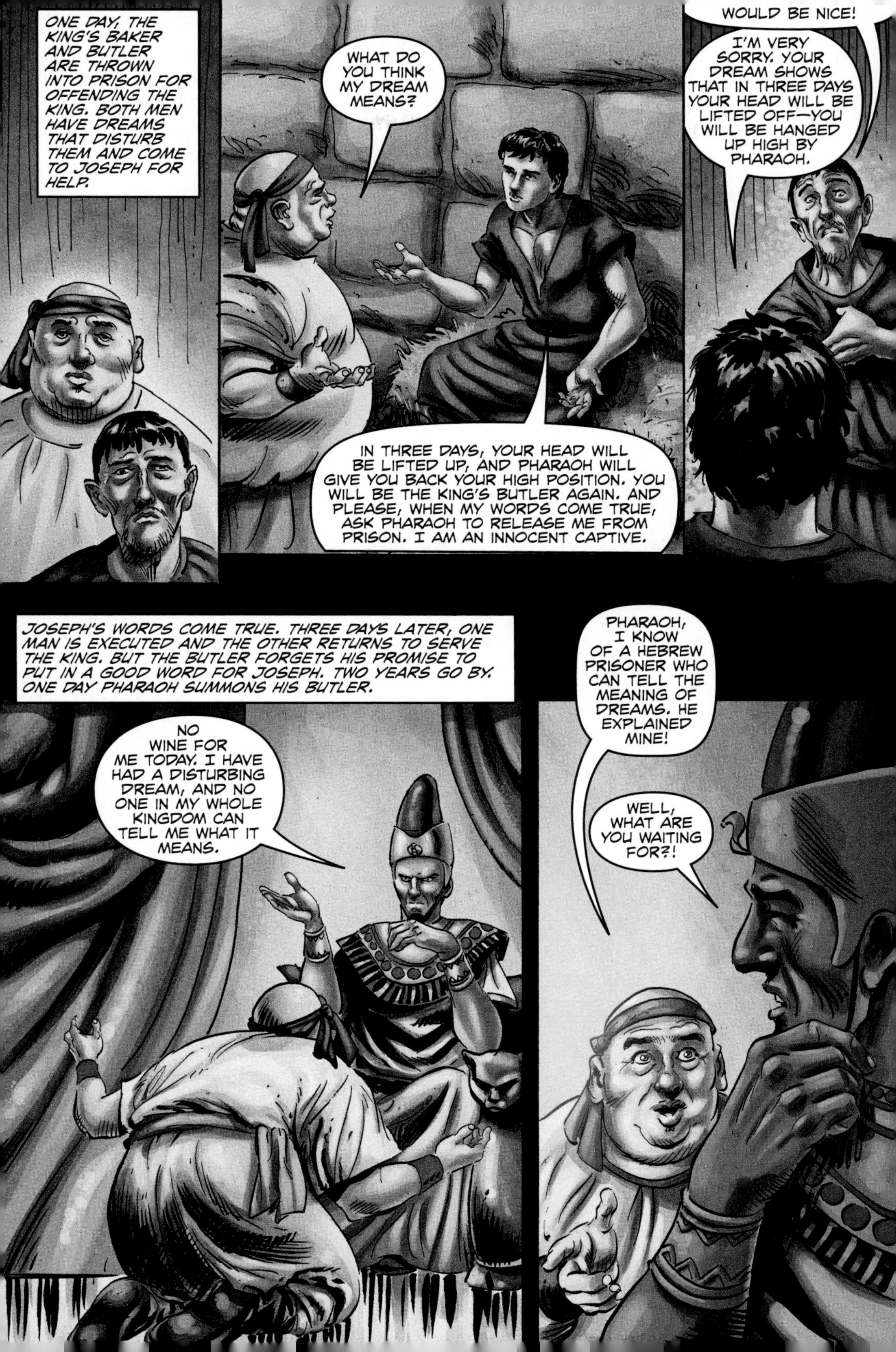
ONE DAY, THE KING'S BAKER AND BUTLER ARE THROWN INTO PRISON FOR OFFENDING THE KING. BOTH MEN HAVE DREAMS THAT DISTURB THEM AND COME TO JOSEPH FOR HELP.
WHAT DO YOU THINK MY DREAM MEANS?
IN THREE DAYS, YOUR HEAD WILL BE LIFTED UP, AND PHARAOH WILL GIVE YOU BACK YOUR HIGH POSITION. YOU WILL BE THE KING'S BUTLER AGAIN. AND PLEASE, WHEN MY WORDS COME TRUE, ASK PHARAOH TO RELEASE ME FROM PRISON. I AM AN INNOCENT CAPTIVE.
WOULD BE NICE!
I'M VERY SORRY. YOUR DREAM SHOWS THAT IN THREE DAYS YOUR HEAD WILL BE LIFTED OFF—YOU WILL BE HANGED UP HIGH BY PHARAOH.
JOSEPH'S WORDS COME TRUE. THREE DAYS LATER, ONE MAN IS EXECUTED AND THE OTHER RETURNS TO SERVE THE KING. BUT THE BUTLER FORGETS HIS PROMISE TO PUT IN A GOOD WORD FOR JOSEPH. TWO YEARS GO BY. ONE DAY PHARAOH SUMMONS HIS BUTLER.
NO WINE FOR ME TODAY. I HAVE HAD A DISTURBING DREAM, AND NO ONE IN MY WHOLE KINGDOM CAN TELL ME WHAT IT MEANS.
PHARAOH, I KNOW OF A HEBREW PRISONER WHO CAN TELL THE MEANING OF DREAMS. HE EXPLAINED MINE!
WELL, WHAT ARE YOU WAITING FOR?!

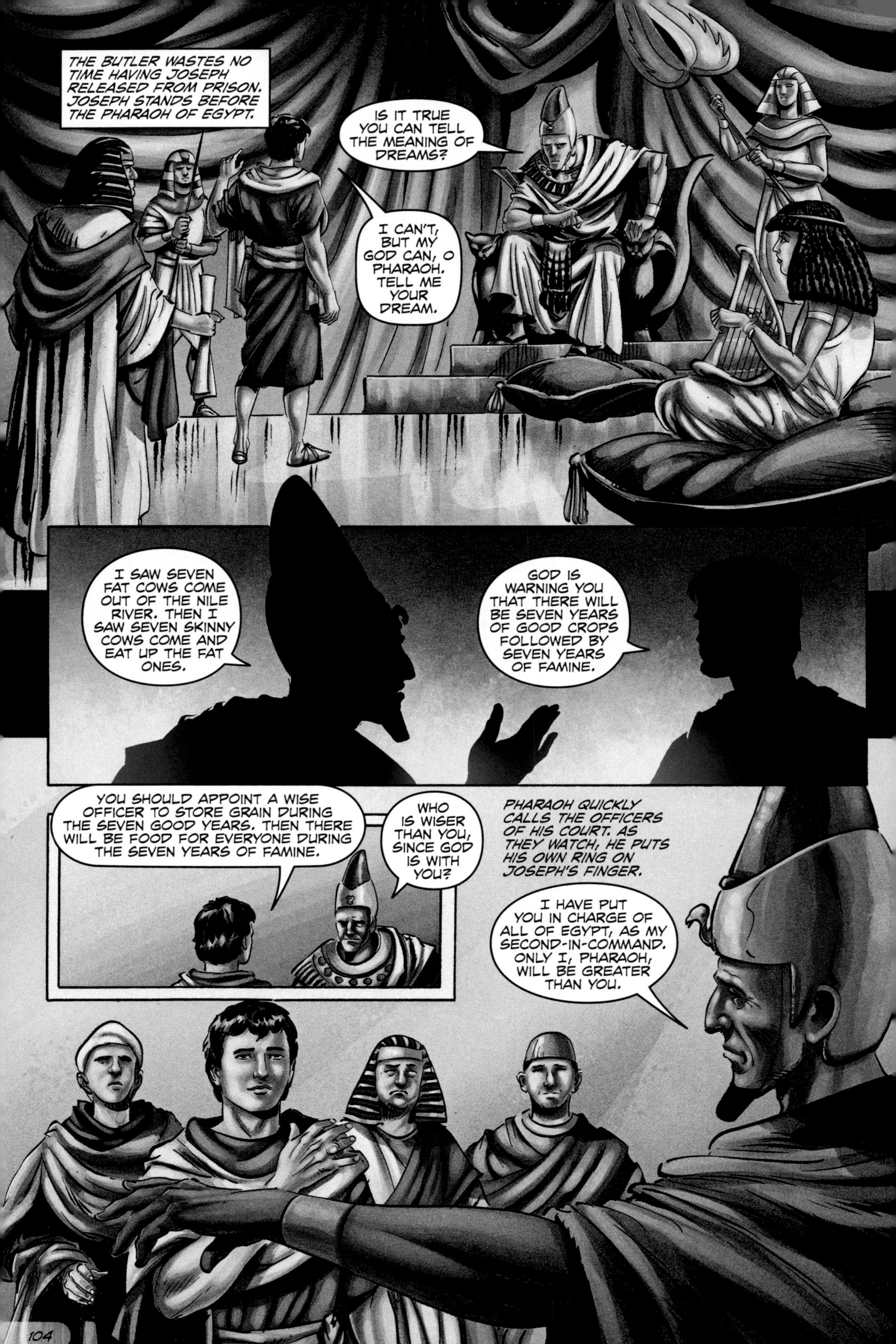
THE BUTLER WASTES NO TIME HAVING JOSEPH RELEASED FROM PRISON. JOSEPH STANDS BEFORE THE PHARAOH OF EGYPT.
IS IT TRUE YOU CAN TELL THE MEANING OF DREAMS?
I CAN'T, BUT MY GOD CAN, O PHARAOH. TELL ME YOUR DREAM.
I SAW SEVEN FAT COWS COME OUT OF THE NILE RIVER. THEN I SAW SEVEN SKINNY COWS COME AND EAT UP THE FAT ONES.
GOD IS WARNING YOU THAT THERE WILL BE SEVEN YEARS OF GOOD CROPS FOLLOWED BY SEVEN YEARS OF FAMINE.
YOU SHOULD APPOINT A WISE OFFICER TO STORE GRAIN DURING THE SEVEN GOOD YEARS. THEN THERE WILL BE FOOD FOR EVERYONE DURING THE SEVEN YEARS OF FAMINE.
WHO IS WISER THAN YOU, SINCE GOD IS WITH YOU?
PHARAOH QUICKLY CALLS THE OFFICERS OF HIS COURT. AS THEY WATCH, HE PUTS HIS OWN RING ON JOSEPH'S FINGER.
I HAVE PUT YOU IN CHARGE OF ALL OF EGYPT, AS MY SECOND-IN-COMMAND. ONLY I, PHARAOH, WILL BE GREATER THAN YOU.

Pharaoh's Man

BASED ON GENESIS 41:44–42:38

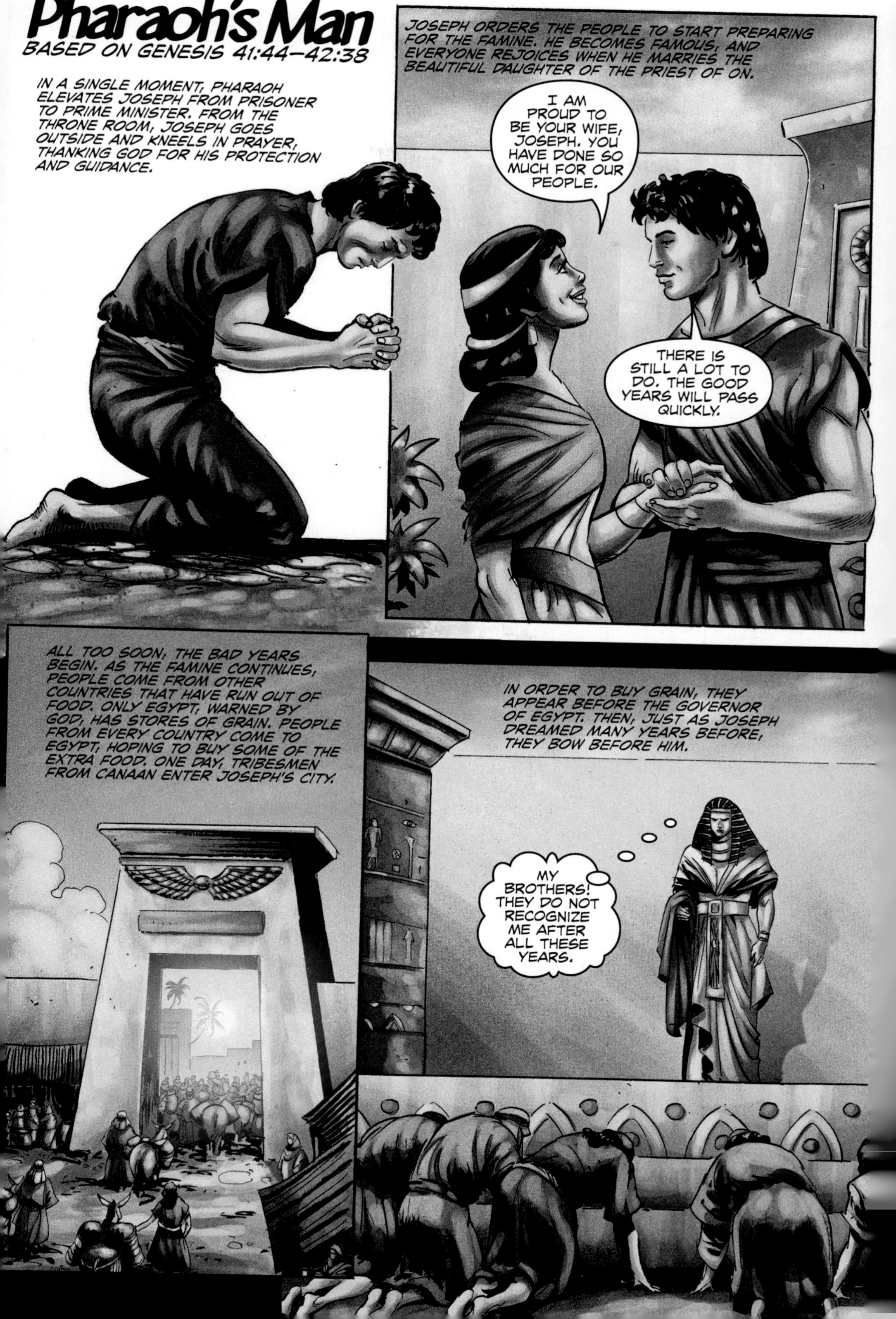

IN A SINGLE MOMENT, PHARAOH ELEVATES JOSEPH FROM PRISONER TO PRIME MINISTER. FROM THE THRONE ROOM, JOSEPH GOES OUTSIDE AND KNEELS IN PRAYER, THANKING GOD FOR HIS PROTECTION AND GUIDANCE.
JOSEPH ORDERS THE PEOPLE TO START PREPARING FOR THE FAMINE. HE BECOMES FAMOUS, AND EVERYONE REJOICES WHEN HE MARRIES THE BEAUTIFUL DAUGHTER OF THE PRIEST OF ON.
I AM PROUD TO BE YOUR WIFE, JOSEPH. YOU HAVE DONE SO MUCH FOR OUR PEOPLE.
THERE IS STILL A LOT TO DO. THE GOOD YEARS WILL PASS QUICKLY.
ALL TOO SOON, THE BAD YEARS BEGIN. AS THE FAMINE CONTINUES, PEOPLE COME FROM OTHER COUNTRIES THAT HAVE RUN OUT OF FOOD. ONLY EGYPT, WARNED BY GOD, HAS STORES OF GRAIN. PEOPLE FROM EVERY COUNTRY COME TO EGYPT, HOPING TO BUY SOME OF THE EXTRA FOOD. ONE DAY, TRIBESMEN FROM CANAAN ENTER JOSEPH'S CITY.
IN ORDER TO BUY GRAIN, THEY APPEAR BEFORE THE GOVERNOR OF EGYPT. THEN, JUST AS JOSEPH DREAMED MANY YEARS BEFORE, THEY BOW BEFORE HIM.
MY BROTHERS! THEY DO NOT RECOGNIZE ME AFTER ALL THESE YEARS.

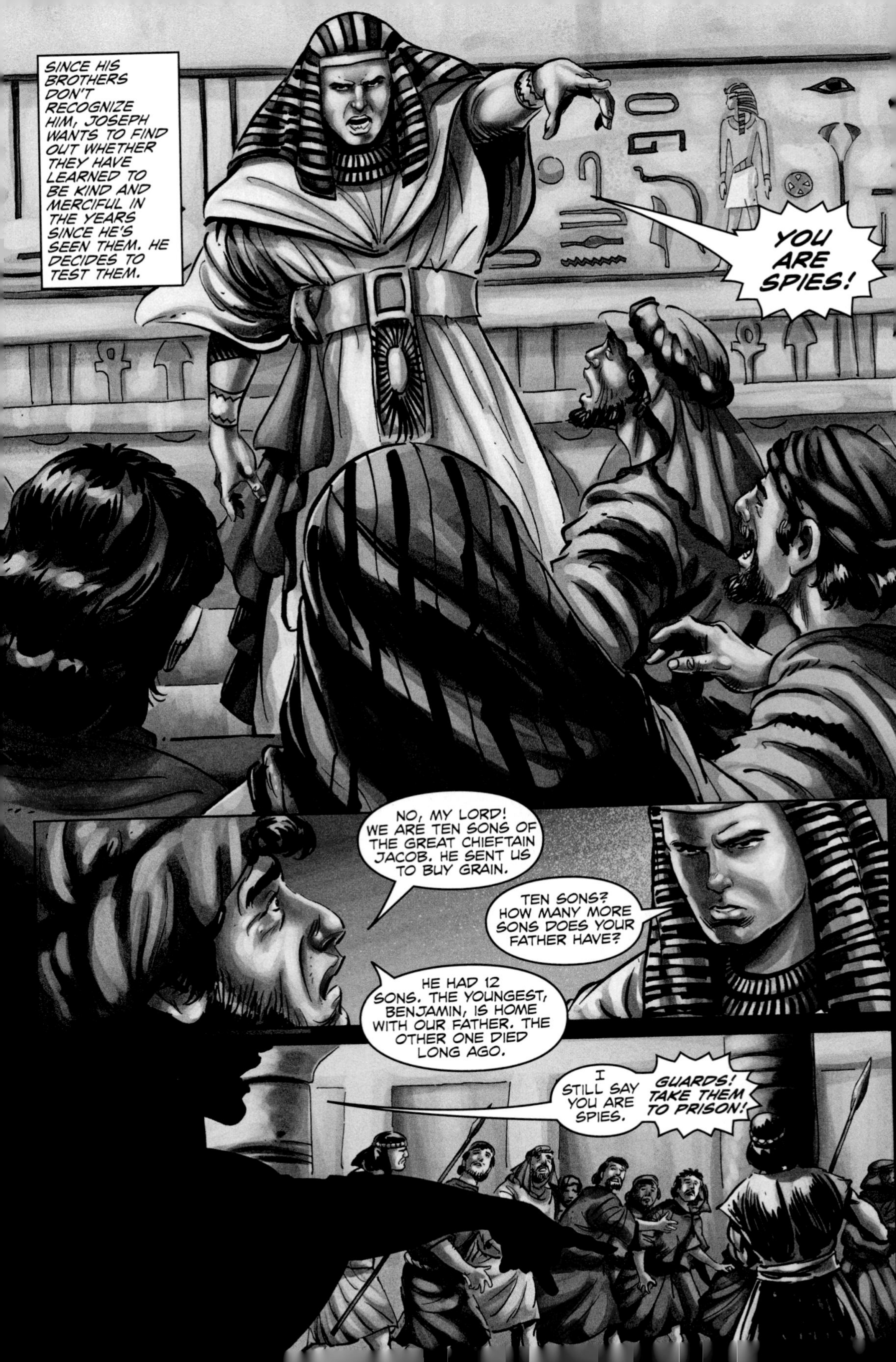
SINCE HIS BROTHERS DON'T RECOGNIZE HIM, JOSEPH WANTS TO FIND OUT WHETHER THEY HAVE LEARNED TO BE KIND AND MERCIFUL IN THE YEARS SINCE HE'S SEEN THEM. HE DECIDES TO TEST THEM.
YOU ARE SPIES!
NO, MY LORD! WE ARE TEN SONS OF THE GREAT CHIEFTAIN JACOB. HE SENT US TO BUY GRAIN.
TEN SONS? HOW MANY MORE SONS DOES YOUR FATHER HAVE?
HE HAD 12 SONS. THE YOUNGEST, BENJAMIN, IS HOME WITH OUR FATHER. THE OTHER ONE DIED LONG AGO.
I STILL SAY YOU ARE SPIES.
GUARDS! TAKE THEM TO PRISON!

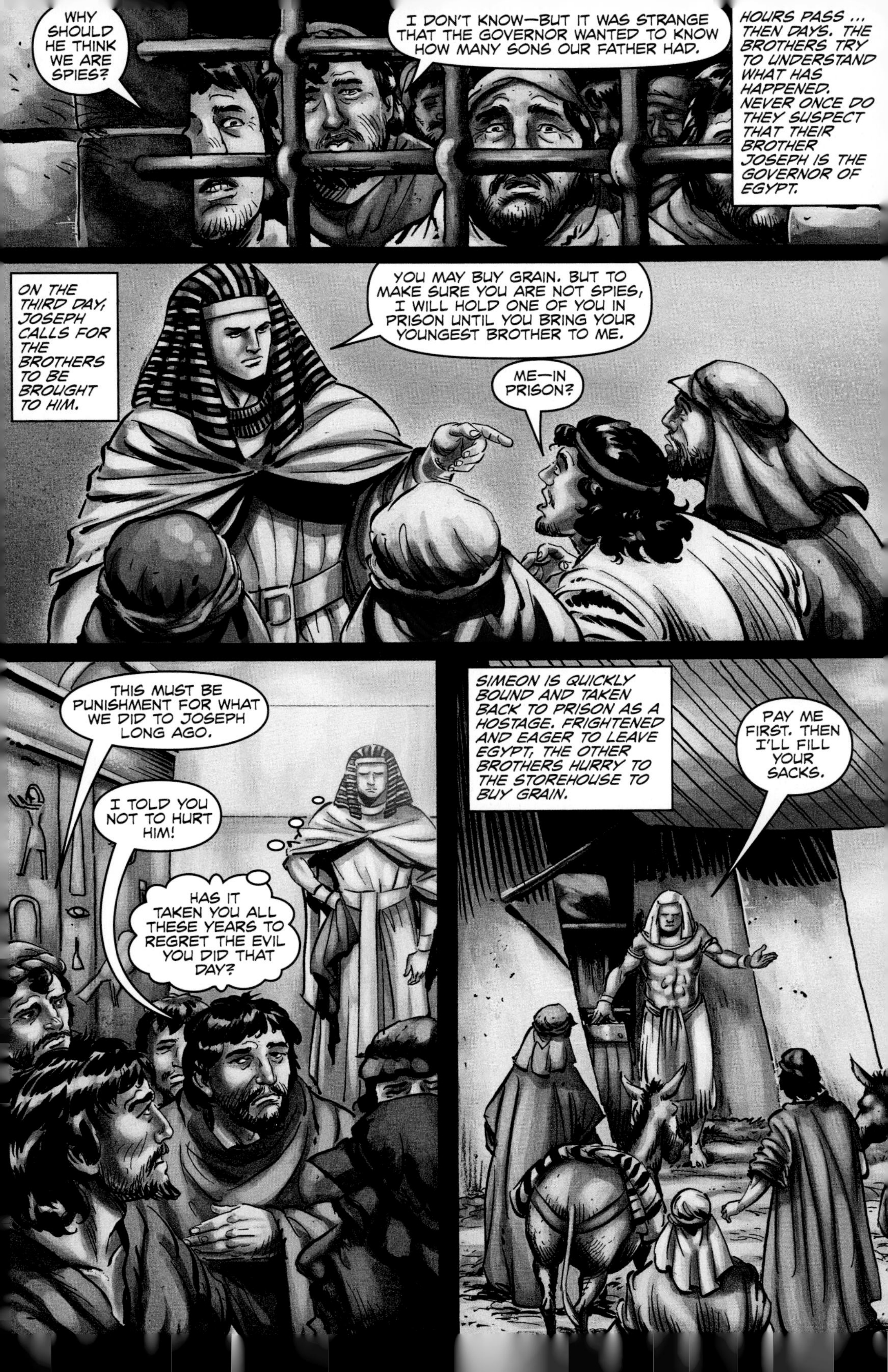
WHY SHOULD HE THINK WE ARE SPIES?
I DON'T KNOW—BUT IT WAS STRANGE THAT THE GOVERNOR WANTED TO KNOW HOW MANY SONS OUR FATHER HAD.
HOURS PASS ... THEN DAYS. THE BROTHERS TRY TO UNDERSTAND WHAT HAS HAPPENED. NEVER ONCE DO THEY SUSPECT THAT THEIR BROTHER JOSEPH IS THE GOVERNOR OF EGYPT.
ON THE THIRD DAY, JOSEPH CALLS FOR THE BROTHERS TO BE BROUGHT TO HIM.
YOU MAY BUY GRAIN. BUT TO MAKE SURE YOU ARE NOT SPIES, I WILL HOLD ONE OF YOU IN PRISON UNTIL YOU BRING YOUR YOUNGEST BROTHER TO ME.
ME—IN PRISON?
THIS MUST BE PUNISHMENT FOR WHAT WE DID TO JOSEPH LONG AGO.
I TOLD YOU NOT TO HURT HIM!
HAS IT TAKEN YOU ALL THESE YEARS TO REGRET THE EVIL YOU DID THAT DAY?
SIMEON IS QUICKLY BOUND AND TAKEN BACK TO PRISON AS A HOSTAGE. FRIGHTENED AND EAGER TO LEAVE EGYPT, THE OTHER BROTHERS HURRY TO THE STOREHOUSE TO BUY GRAIN.
PAY ME FIRST. THEN I'LL FILL YOUR SACKS.

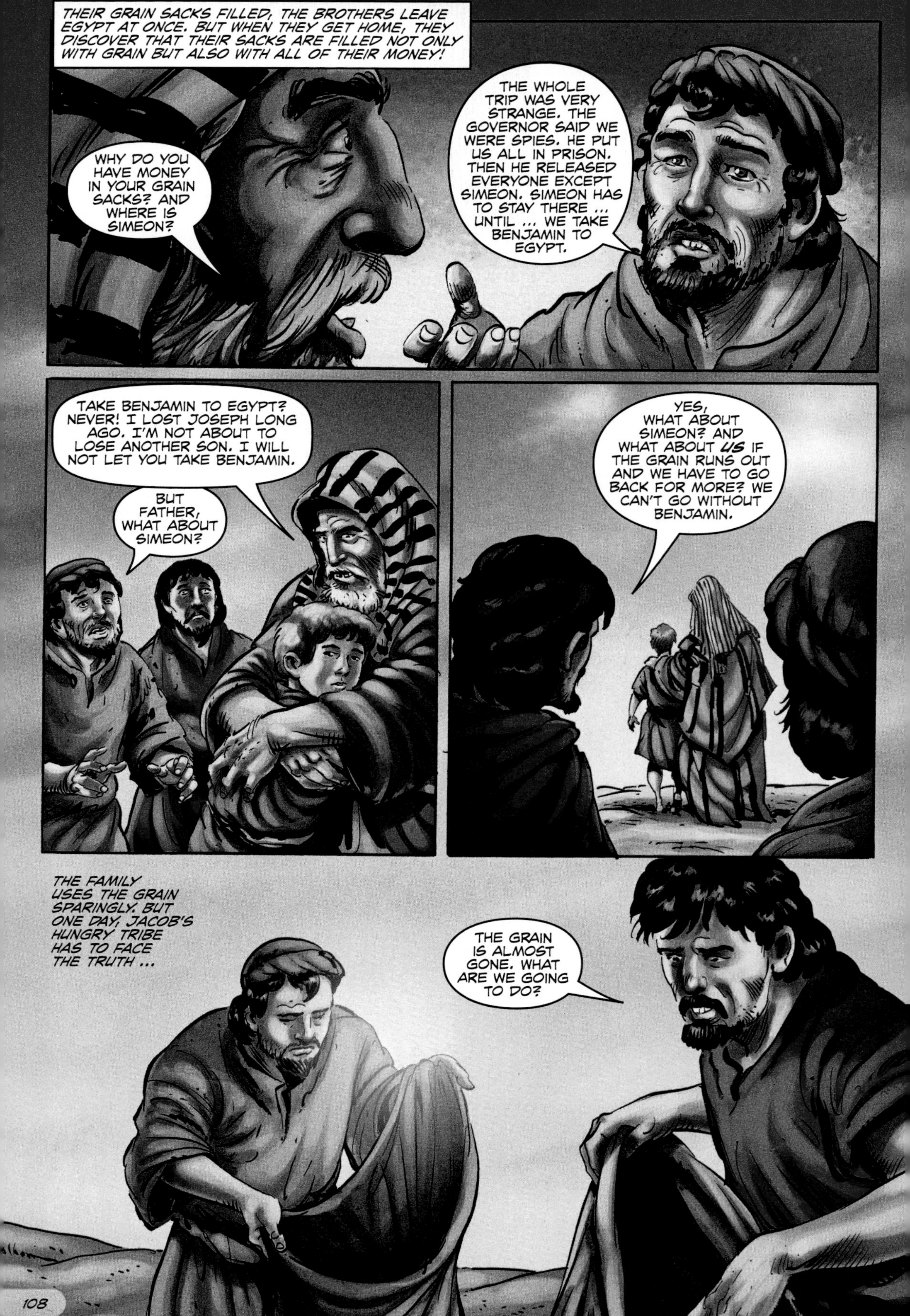
THEIR GRAIN SACKS FILLED, THE BROTHERS LEAVE EGYPT AT ONCE. BUT WHEN THEY GET HOME, THEY DISCOVER THAT THEIR SACKS ARE FILLED NOT ONLY WITH GRAIN BUT ALSO WITH ALL OF THEIR MONEY!
WHY DO YOU HAVE MONEY IN YOUR GRAIN SACKS? AND WHERE IS SIMEON?
THE WHOLE TRIP WAS VERY STRANGE. THE GOVERNOR SAID WE WERE SPIES. HE PUT US ALL IN PRISON. THEN HE RELEASED EVERYONE EXCEPT SIMEON. SIMEON HAS TO STAY THERE ... UNTIL ... WE TAKE BENJAMIN TO EGYPT.
TAKE BENJAMIN TO EGYPT? NEVER! I LOST JOSEPH LONG AGO. I'M NOT ABOUT TO LOSE ANOTHER SON. I WILL NOT LET YOU TAKE BENJAMIN.
BUT FATHER, WHAT ABOUT SIMEON?
YES, WHAT ABOUT SIMEON? AND WHAT ABOUT US IF THE GRAIN RUNS OUT AND WE HAVE TO GO BACK FOR MORE? WE CAN'T GO WITHOUT BENJAMIN.
THE FAMILY USES THE GRAIN SPARINGLY. BUT ONE DAY, JACOB'S HUNGRY TRIBE HAS TO FACE THE TRUTH ...
THE GRAIN IS ALMOST GONE. WHAT ARE WE GOING TO DO?

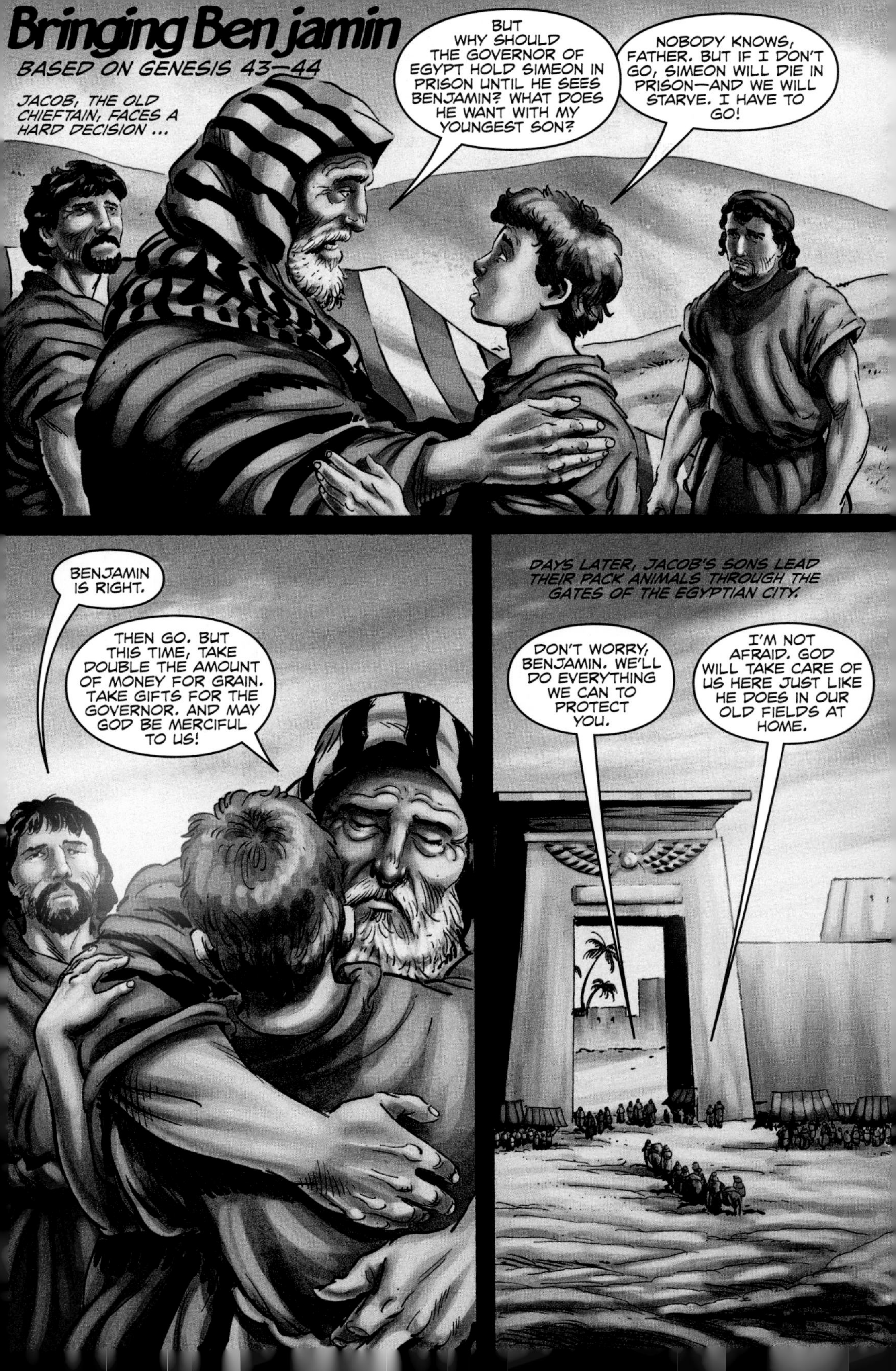

Bringing Benjamin
BASED ON GENESIS 43—44
JACOB, THE OLD CHIEFTAIN, FACES A HARD DECISION ...
BUT WHY SHOULD THE GOVERNOR OF EGYPT HOLD SIMEON IN PRISON UNTIL HE SEES BENJAMIN? WHAT DOES HE WANT WITH MY YOUNGEST SON?
NOBODY KNOWS, FATHER. BUT IF I DON'T GO, SIMEON WILL DIE IN PRISON—AND WE WILL STARVE. I HAVE TO GO!
BENJAMIN IS RIGHT.
THEN GO. BUT THIS TIME, TAKE DOUBLE THE AMOUNT OF MONEY FOR GRAIN. TAKE GIFTS FOR THE GOVERNOR. AND MAY GOD BE MERCIFUL TO US!
DAYS LATER, JACOB'S SONS LEAD THEIR PACK ANIMALS THROUGH THE GATES OF THE EGYPTIAN CITY.
DON'T WORRY, BENJAMIN. WE'LL DO EVERYTHING WE CAN TO PROTECT YOU.
I'M NOT AFRAID. GOD WILL TAKE CARE OF US HERE JUST LIKE HE DOES IN OUR OLD FIELDS AT HOME.

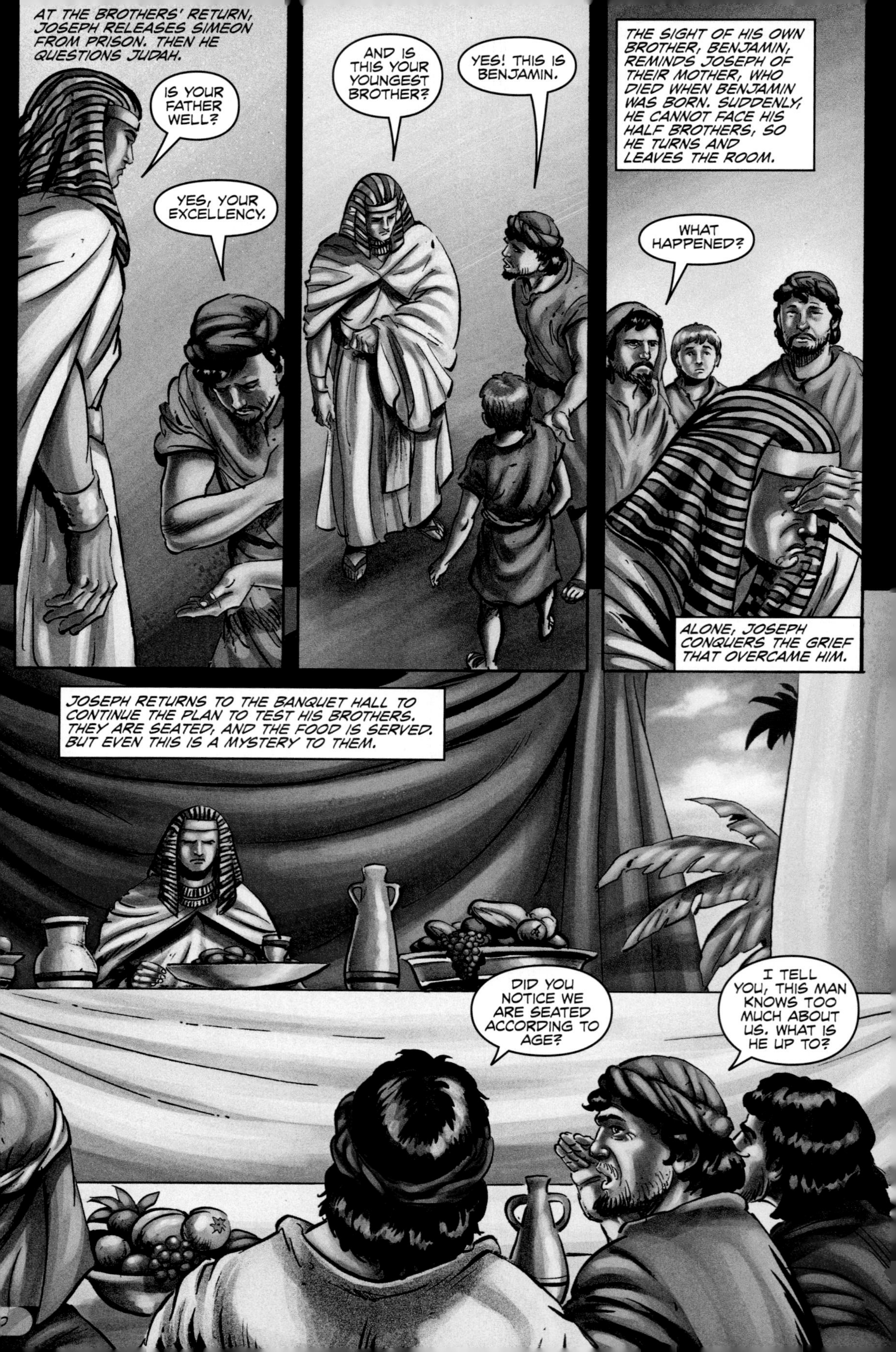
AT THE BROTHERS' RETURN, JOSEPH RELEASES SIMEON FROM PRISON. THEN HE QUESTIONS JUDAH.
IS YOUR FATHER WELL?
YES, YOUR EXCELLENCY.
AND IS THIS YOUR YOUNGEST BROTHER?
YES! THIS IS BENJAMIN.
THE SIGHT OF HIS OWN BROTHER, BENJAMIN, REMINDS JOSEPH OF THEIR MOTHER, WHO DIED WHEN BENJAMIN WAS BORN. SUDDENLY, HE CANNOT FACE HIS HALF BROTHERS, SO HE TURNS AND LEAVES THE ROOM.
WHAT HAPPENED?
ALONE, JOSEPH CONQUERS THE GRIEF THAT OVERCAME HIM.
JOSEPH RETURNS TO THE BANQUET HALL TO CONTINUE THE PLAN TO TEST HIS BROTHERS. THEY ARE SEATED, AND THE FOOD IS SERVED. BUT EVEN THIS IS A MYSTERY TO THEM.
DID YOU NOTICE WE ARE SEATED ACCORDING TO AGE?
I TELL YOU, THIS MAN KNOWS TOO MUCH ABOUT US. WHAT IS HE UP TO?

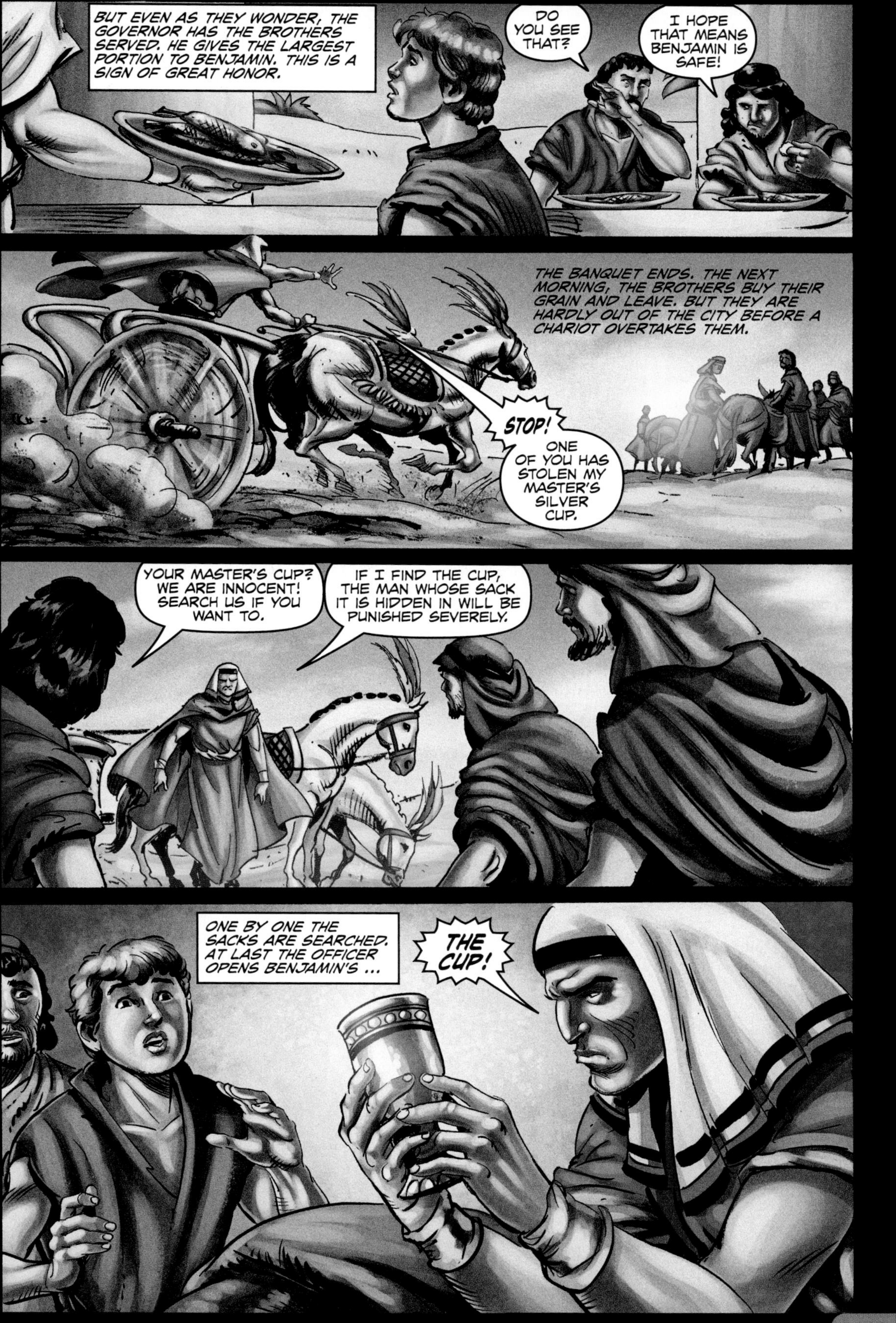
BUT EVEN AS THEY WONDER, THE GOVERNOR HAS THE BROTHERS SERVED. HE GIVES THE LARGEST PORTION TO BENJAMIN. THIS IS A SIGN OF GREAT HONOR.
DO YOU SEE THAT?
I HOPE THAT MEANS BENJAMIN IS SAFE!
THE BANQUET ENDS. THE NEXT MORNING, THE BROTHERS BUY THEIR GRAIN AND LEAVE. BUT THEY ARE HARDLY OUT OF THE CITY BEFORE A CHARIOT OVERTAKES THEM.
STOP! ONE OF YOU HAS STOLEN MY MASTER'S SILVER CUP.
YOUR MASTER'S CUP? WE ARE INNOCENT! SEARCH US IF YOU WANT TO.
IF I FIND THE CUP, THE MAN WHOSE SACK IT IS HIDDEN IN WILL BE PUNISHED SEVERELY.
ONE BY ONE THE SACKS ARE SEARCHED. AT LAST THE OFFICER OPENS BENJAMIN'S ...
THE CUP!

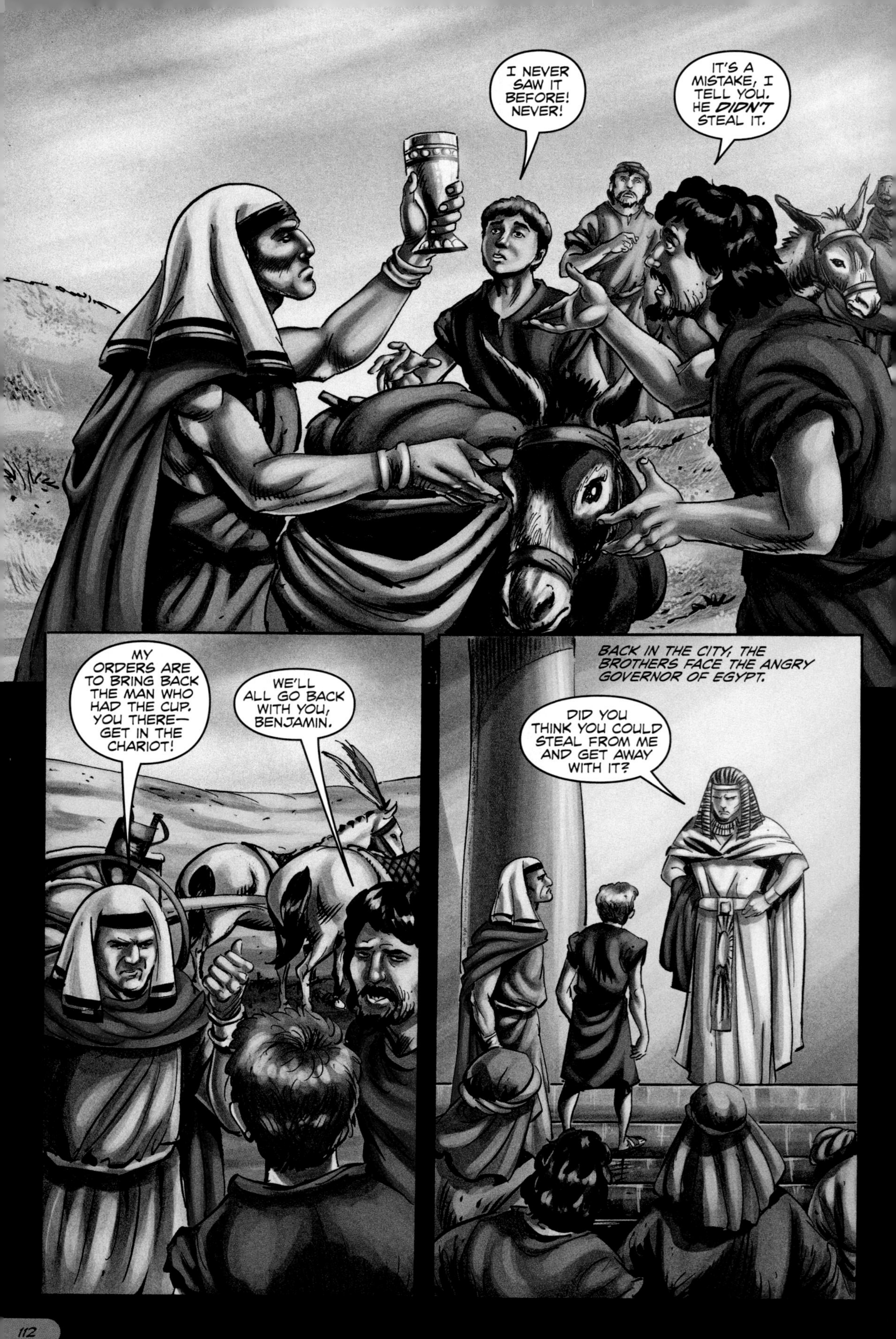

I NEVER SAW IT BEFORE! NEVER!
IT'S A MISTAKE, I TELL YOU. HE *DIDN'T* STEAL IT.
MY ORDERS ARE TO BRING BACK THE MAN WHO HAD THE CUP. YOU THERE—GET IN THE CHARIOT!
WE'LL ALL GO BACK WITH YOU, BENJAMIN.
BACK IN THE CITY, THE BROTHERS FACE THE ANGRY GOVERNOR OF EGYPT.
DID YOU THINK YOU COULD STEAL FROM ME AND GET AWAY WITH IT?

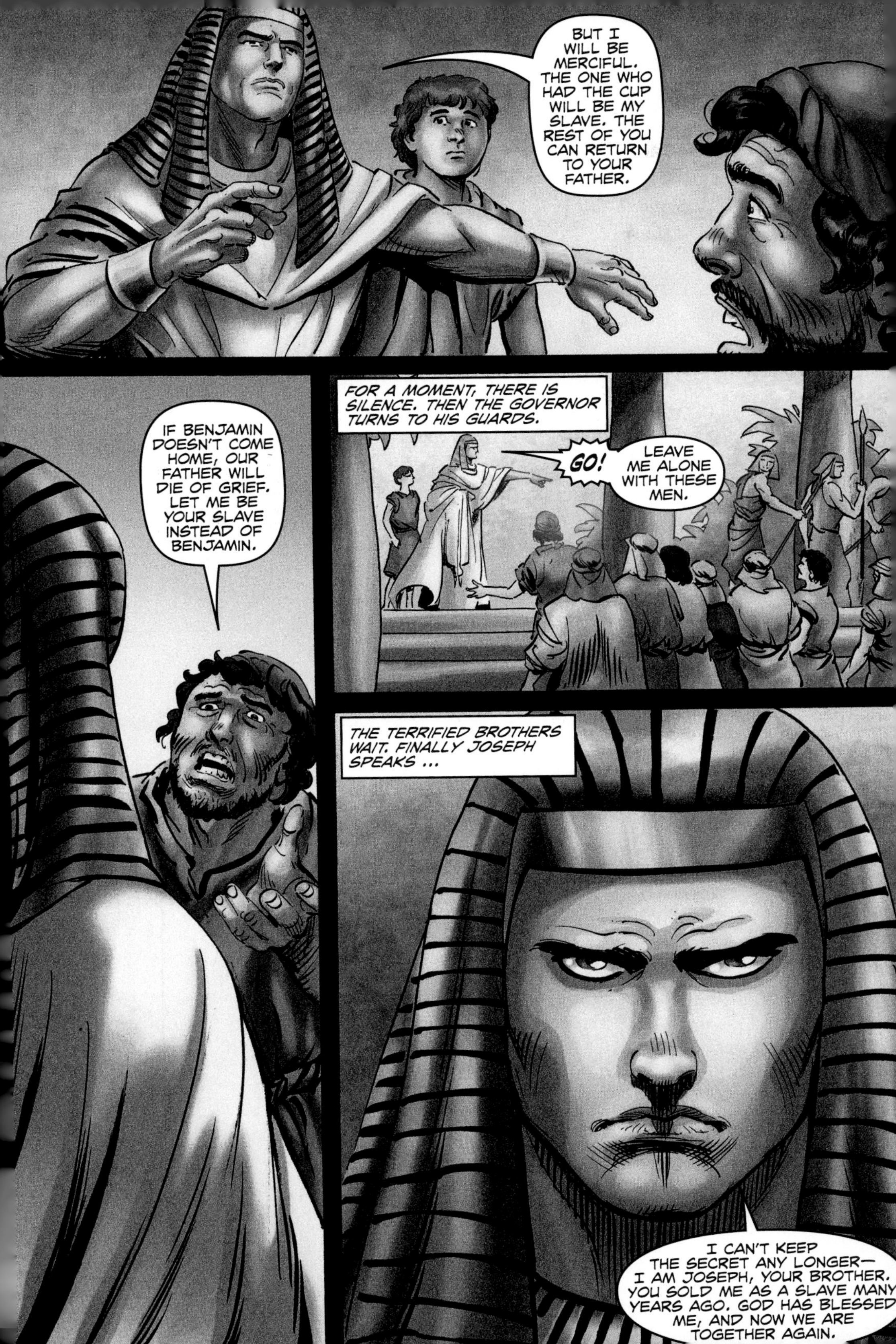
BUT I WILL BE MERCIFUL. THE ONE WHO HAD THE CUP WILL BE MY SLAVE. THE REST OF YOU CAN RETURN TO YOUR FATHER.
IF BENJAMIN DOESN'T COME HOME, OUR FATHER WILL DIE OF GRIEF. LET ME BE YOUR SLAVE INSTEAD OF BENJAMIN.
FOR A MOMENT, THERE IS SILENCE. THEN THE GOVERNOR TURNS TO HIS GUARDS.
GO!
LEAVE ME ALONE WITH THESE MEN.
THE TERRIFIED BROTHERS WAIT. FINALLY JOSEPH SPEAKS ...
I CAN'T KEEP THE SECRET ANY LONGER— I AM JOSEPH, YOUR BROTHER. YOU SOLD ME AS A SLAVE MANY YEARS AGO. GOD HAS BLESSED ME, AND NOW WE ARE TOGETHER AGAIN.

Family Reunion

BASED ON GENESIS 45—47

JACOB'S SONS ARE SHOCKED TO REALIZE THAT THE GOVERNOR OF ALL EGYPT IS ACTUALLY THEIR LONG-LOST BROTHER. THEN THEY REMEMBER HOW THEY LAST TREATED HIM ...

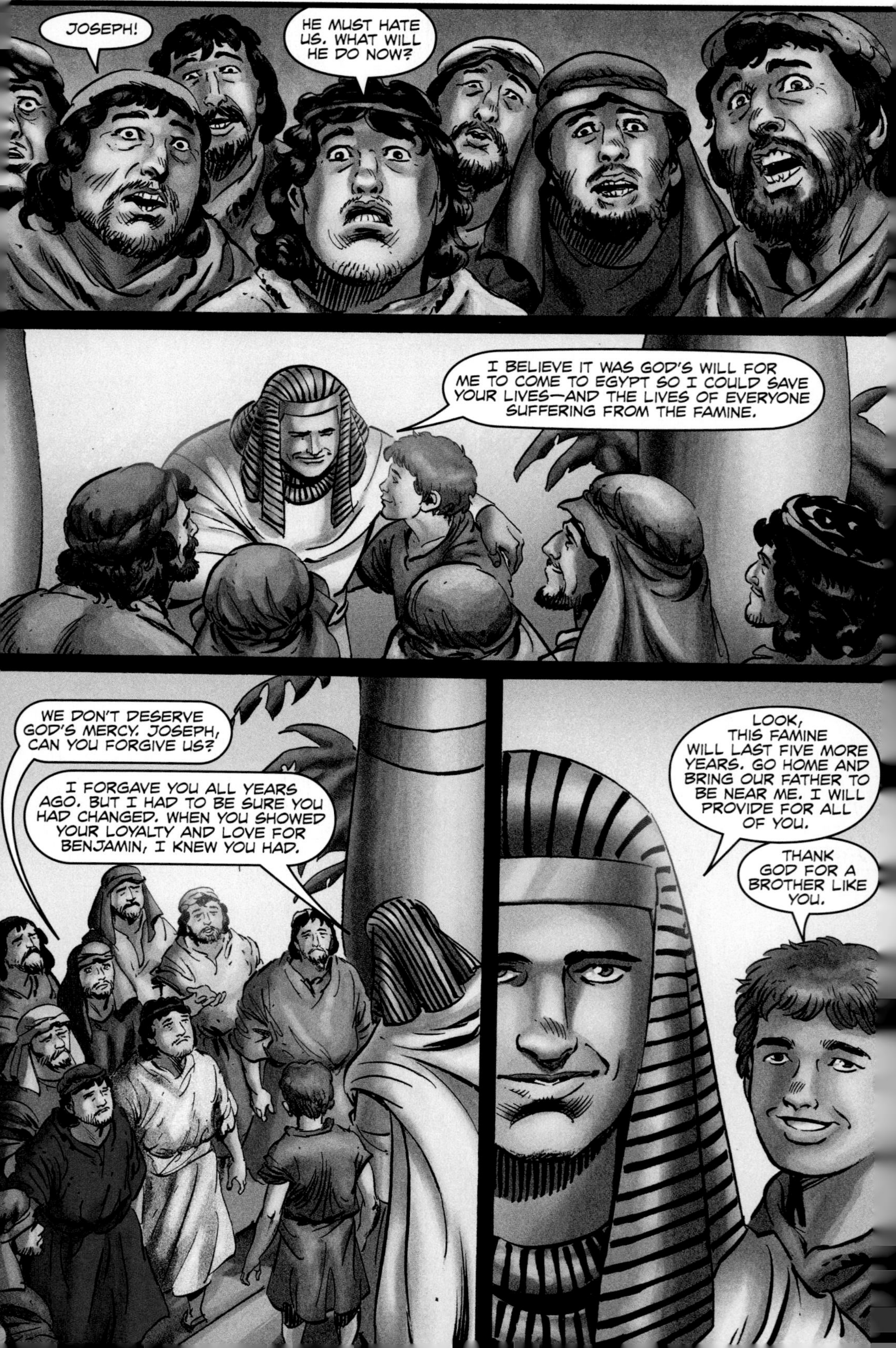

JOSEPH!
HE MUST HATE US. WHAT WILL HE DO NOW?
I BELIEVE IT WAS GOD'S WILL FOR ME TO COME TO EGYPT SO I COULD SAVE YOUR LIVES—AND THE LIVES OF EVERYONE SUFFERING FROM THE FAMINE.
WE DON'T DESERVE GOD'S MERCY. JOSEPH, CAN YOU FORGIVE US?
I FORGAVE YOU ALL YEARS AGO. BUT I HAD TO BE SURE YOU HAD CHANGED. WHEN YOU SHOWED YOUR LOYALTY AND LOVE FOR BENJAMIN, I KNEW YOU HAD.
LOOK, THIS FAMINE WILL LAST FIVE MORE YEARS. GO HOME AND BRING OUR FATHER TO BE NEAR ME. I WILL PROVIDE FOR ALL OF YOU.
THANK GOD FOR A BROTHER LIKE YOU.

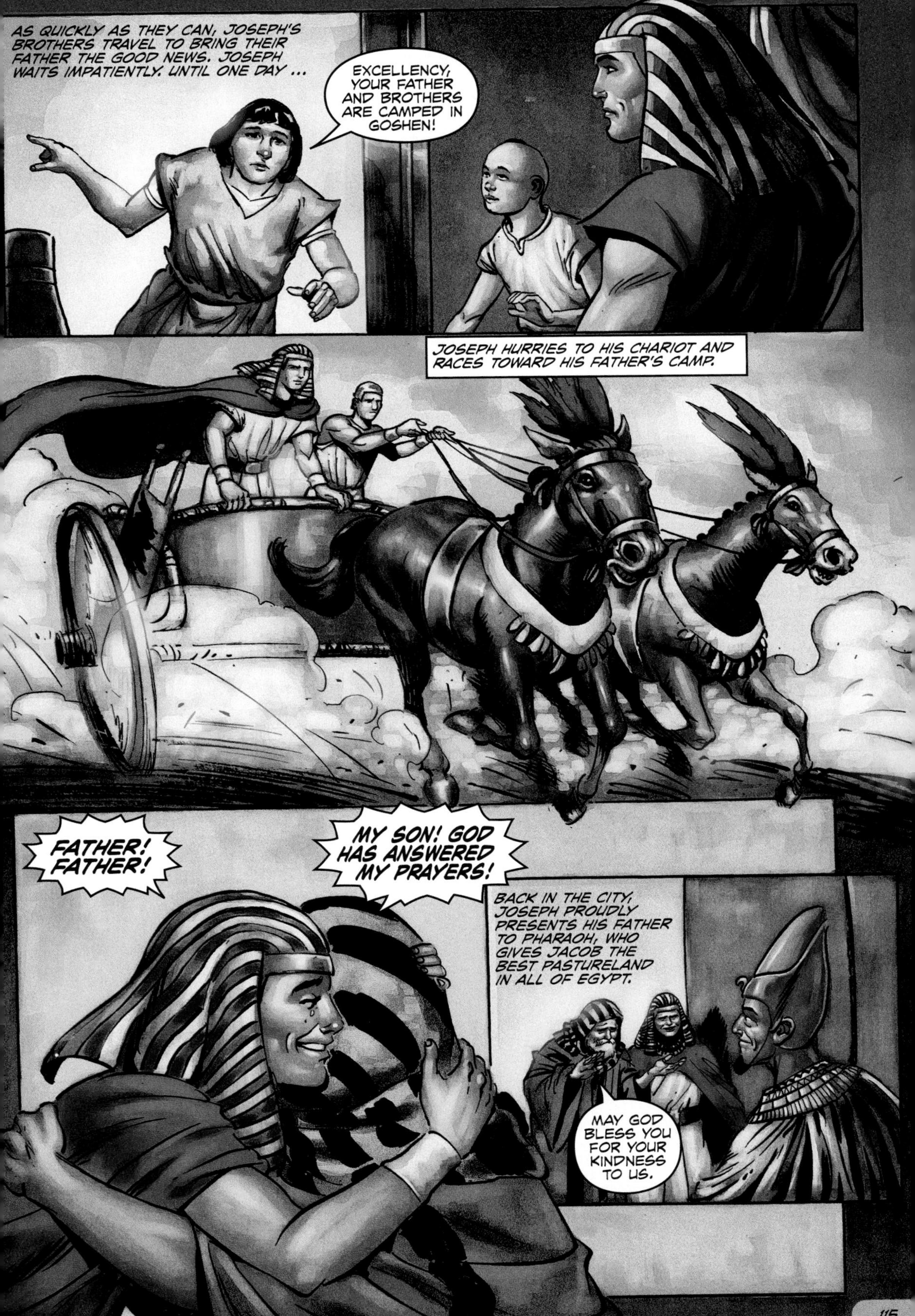
AS QUICKLY AS THEY CAN, JOSEPH'S BROTHERS TRAVEL TO BRING THEIR FATHER THE GOOD NEWS. JOSEPH WAITS IMPATIENTLY. UNTIL ONE DAY ...
EXCELLENCY, YOUR FATHER AND BROTHERS ARE CAMPED IN GOSHEN!
JOSEPH HURRIES TO HIS CHARIOT AND RACES TOWARD HIS FATHER'S CAMP.
FATHER! FATHER!
MY SON! GOD HAS ANSWERED MY PRAYERS!
BACK IN THE CITY, JOSEPH PROUDLY PRESENTS HIS FATHER TO PHARAOH, WHO GIVES JACOB THE BEST PASTURELAND IN ALL OF EGYPT.
MAY GOD BLESS YOU FOR YOUR KINDNESS TO US.

The End of an Era

FOR 17 YEARS, JACOB AND HIS SONS LIVE HAPPILY IN EGYPT. THEN ONE DAY A MESSENGER BRINGS SAD NEWS TO JOSEPH ...

SIR, YOUR FATHER IS VERY ILL. HE WANTS YOU AND YOUR SONS TO COME RIGHT AWAY!

THEY HURRY TO JACOB'S BEDSIDE.

BRING YOUR SONS TO ME SO I CAN BLESS THEM BEFORE I DIE.

MAY GOD, WHO HAS GUIDED ME ALL OF MY LIFE, BLESS MY GRANDSONS.

BECAUSE OF THE WICKEDNESS OF HIS OLDER SONS, JACOB GIVES THE FAMILY BIRTHRIGHT TO JOSEPH AND HIS SONS. REMEMBERING HOW HE WAS THE YOUNGEST, JACOB CROSSES HIS ARMS WHEN HE BLESSES MANASSEH AND EPHRAIM. THIS GIVES THE LARGER SHARE OF THE BIRTHRIGHT TO THE YOUNGER EPHRAIM.

THEN JACOB CALLS ALL OF HIS SONS TO HIM AND BLESSES THEM. JACOB DIES AND HIS SONS CARRY THE OLD CHIEFTAIN'S BODY BACK TO HIS HOMELAND OF CANAAN.

AFTER JACOB'S FUNERAL, JOSEPH WALKS AWAY FROM THE CAMP ALONE. HIS BROTHERS WATCH HIM IN HIS GRIEF.

EVEN AFTER ALL THESE YEARS, JOSEPH WAS CLOSEST WITH OUR FATHER.

AND WE HAVE NO WAY TO COMFORT HIM.

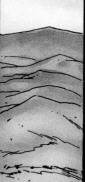

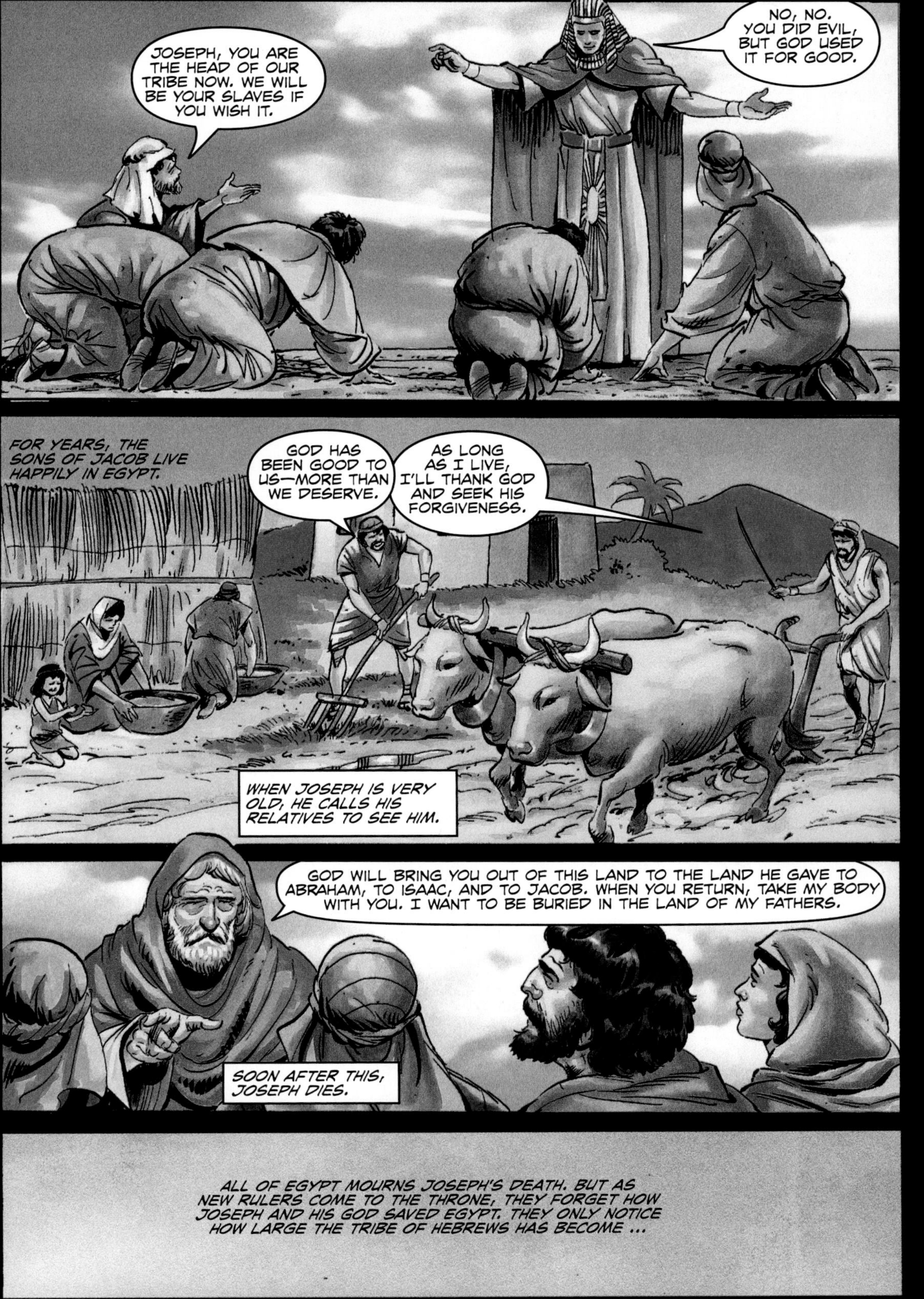
JOSEPH, YOU ARE THE HEAD OF OUR TRIBE NOW. WE WILL BE YOUR SLAVES IF YOU WISH IT.
NO, NO. YOU DID EVIL, BUT GOD USED IT FOR GOOD.
FOR YEARS, THE SONS OF JACOB LIVE HAPPILY IN EGYPT.
GOD HAS BEEN GOOD TO US—MORE THAN WE DESERVE.
AS LONG AS I LIVE, I'LL THANK GOD AND SEEK HIS FORGIVENESS.
WHEN JOSEPH IS VERY OLD, HE CALLS HIS RELATIVES TO SEE HIM.
GOD WILL BRING YOU OUT OF THIS LAND TO THE LAND HE GAVE TO ABRAHAM, TO ISAAC, AND TO JACOB. WHEN YOU RETURN, TAKE MY BODY WITH YOU. I WANT TO BE BURIED IN THE LAND OF MY FATHERS.
SOON AFTER THIS, JOSEPH DIES.
ALL OF EGYPT MOURNS JOSEPH'S DEATH. BUT AS NEW RULERS COME TO THE THRONE, THEY FORGET HOW JOSEPH AND HIS GOD SAVED EGYPT. THEY ONLY NOTICE HOW LARGE THE TRIBE OF HEBREWS HAS BECOME ...

Baby in a Basket

BASED ON EXODUS 1:1–2:10

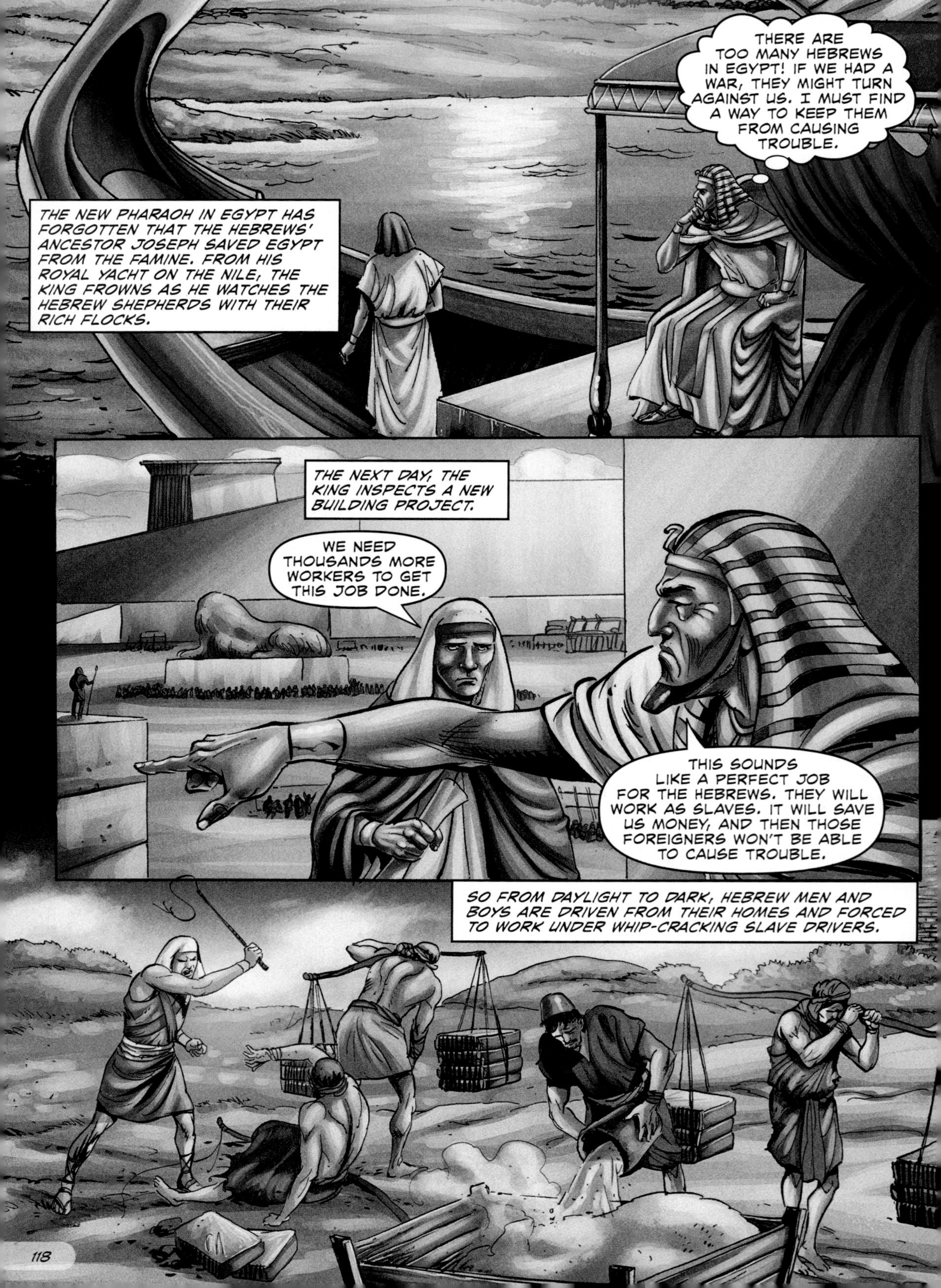
THE NEW PHARAOH IN EGYPT HAS FORGOTTEN THAT THE HEBREWS' ANCESTOR JOSEPH SAVED EGYPT FROM THE FAMINE. FROM HIS ROYAL YACHT ON THE NILE, THE KING FROWNS AS HE WATCHES THE HEBREW SHEPHERDS WITH THEIR RICH FLOCKS.
THERE ARE TOO MANY HEBREWS IN EGYPT! IF WE HAD A WAR, THEY MIGHT TURN AGAINST US. I MUST FIND A WAY TO KEEP THEM FROM CAUSING TROUBLE.
THE NEXT DAY, THE KING INSPECTS A NEW BUILDING PROJECT.
WE NEED THOUSANDS MORE WORKERS TO GET THIS JOB DONE.
THIS SOUNDS LIKE A PERFECT JOB FOR THE HEBREWS. THEY WILL WORK AS SLAVES. IT WILL SAVE US MONEY, AND THEN THOSE FOREIGNERS WON'T BE ABLE TO CAUSE TROUBLE.
SO FROM DAYLIGHT TO DARK, HEBREW MEN AND BOYS ARE DRIVEN FROM THEIR HOMES AND FORCED TO WORK UNDER WHIP-CRACKING SLAVE DRIVERS.

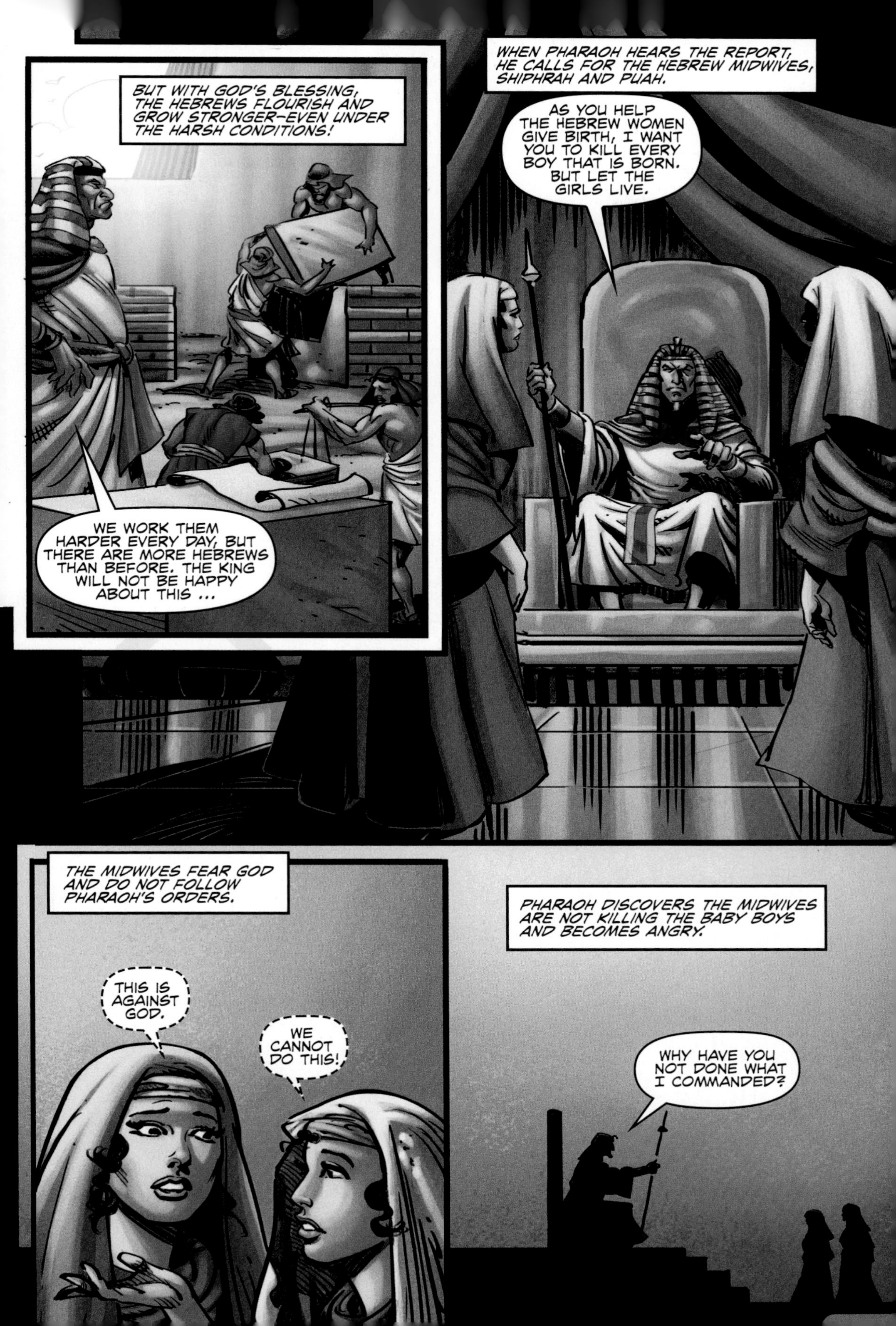
BUT WITH GOD'S BLESSING, THE HEBREWS FLOURISH AND GROW STRONGER—EVEN UNDER THE HARSH CONDITIONS!
WE WORK THEM HARDER EVERY DAY, BUT THERE ARE MORE HEBREWS THAN BEFORE. THE KING WILL NOT BE HAPPY ABOUT THIS ...
WHEN PHARAOH HEARS THE REPORT, HE CALLS FOR THE HEBREW MIDWIVES, SHIPHRAH AND PUAH.
AS YOU HELP THE HEBREW WOMEN GIVE BIRTH, I WANT YOU TO KILL EVERY BOY THAT IS BORN. BUT LET THE GIRLS LIVE.
THE MIDWIVES FEAR GOD AND DO NOT FOLLOW PHARAOH'S ORDERS.
THIS IS AGAINST GOD.
WE CANNOT DO THIS!
PHARAOH DISCOVERS THE MIDWIVES ARE NOT KILLING THE BABY BOYS AND BECOMES ANGRY.
WHY HAVE YOU NOT DONE WHAT I COMMANDED?

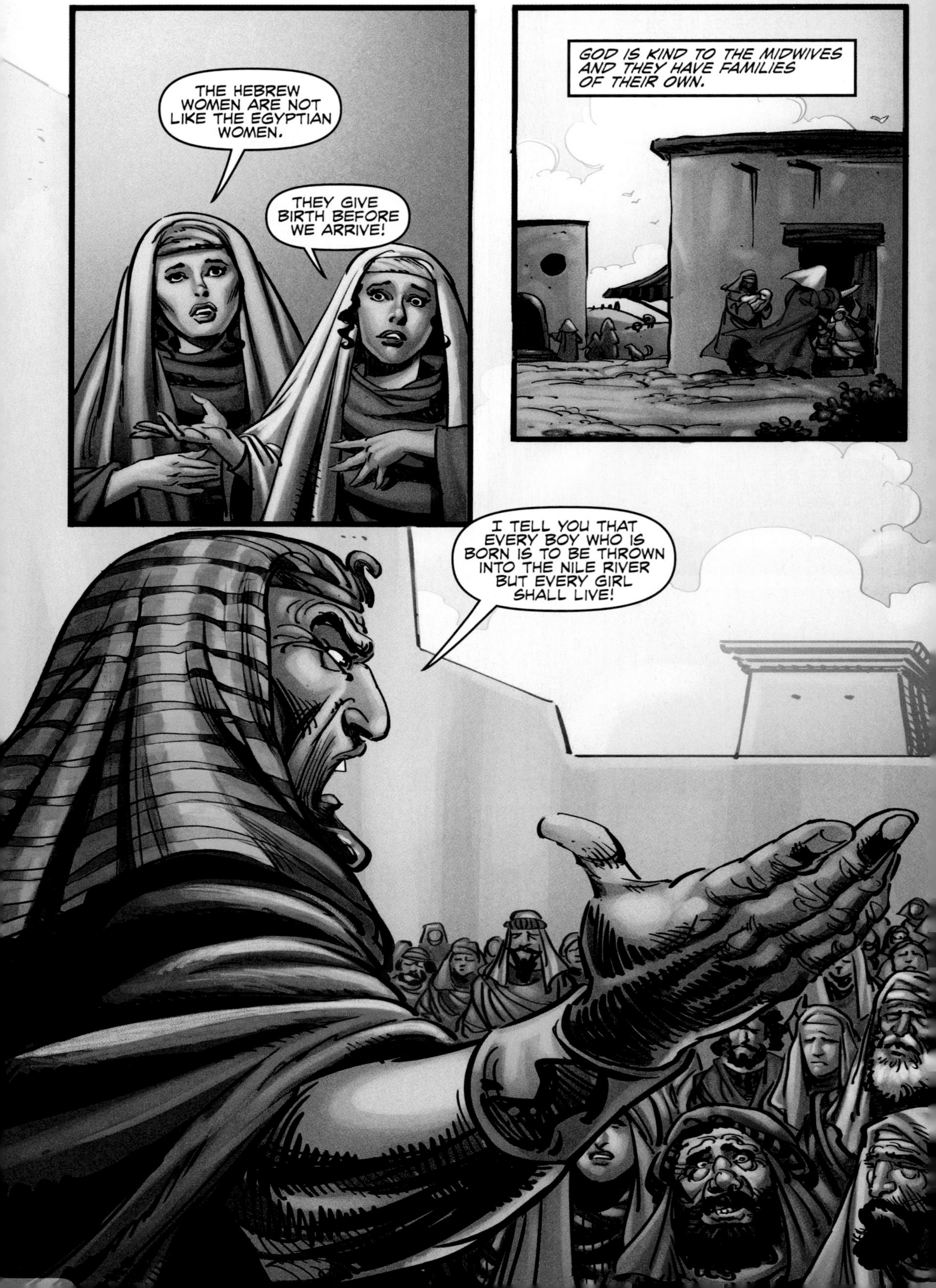
THE HEBREW WOMEN ARE NOT LIKE THE EGYPTIAN WOMEN.
THEY GIVE BIRTH BEFORE WE ARRIVE!
GOD IS KIND TO THE MIDWIVES AND THEY HAVE FAMILIES OF THEIR OWN.
I TELL YOU THAT EVERY BOY WHO IS BORN IS TO BE THROWN INTO THE NILE RIVER BUT EVERY GIRL SHALL LIVE!

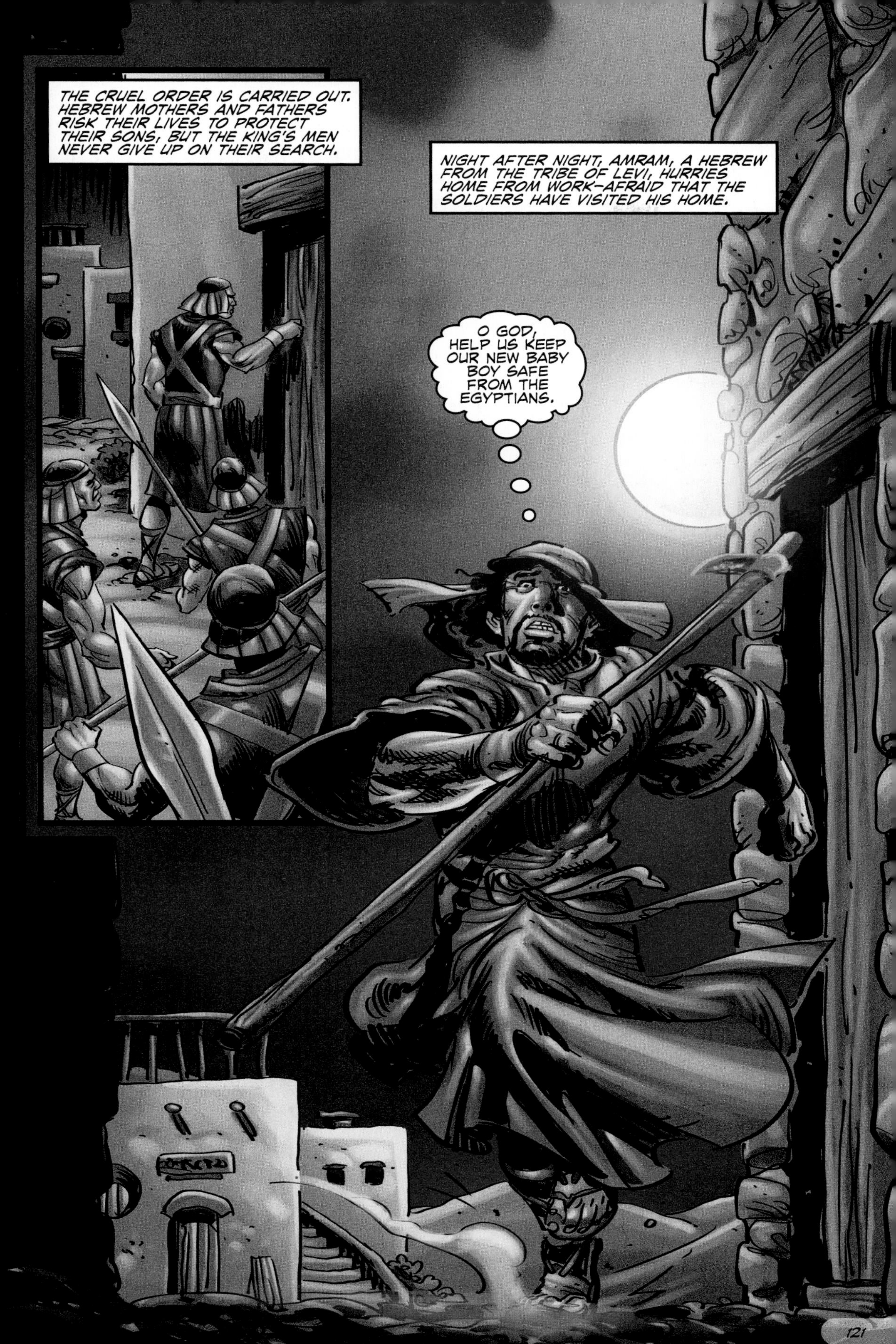

THE CRUEL ORDER IS CARRIED OUT. HEBREW MOTHERS AND FATHERS RISK THEIR LIVES TO PROTECT THEIR SONS, BUT THE KING'S MEN NEVER GIVE UP ON THEIR SEARCH.
NIGHT AFTER NIGHT, AMRAM, A HEBREW FROM THE TRIBE OF LEVI, HURRIES HOME FROM WORK—AFRAID THAT THE SOLDIERS HAVE VISITED HIS HOME.
O GOD, HELP US KEEP OUR NEW BABY BOY SAFE FROM THE EGYPTIANS.

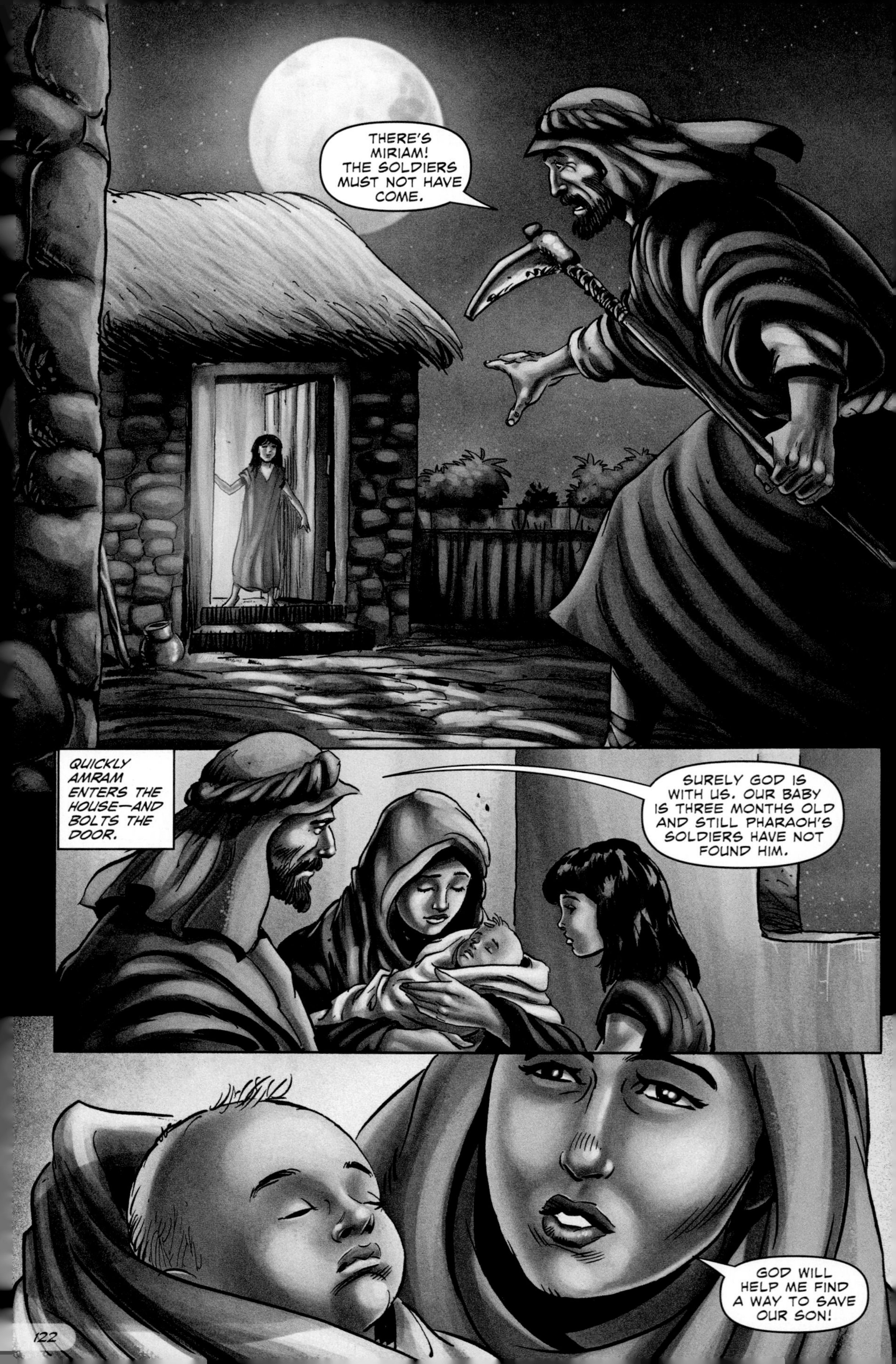
THERE'S MIRIAM! THE SOLDIERS MUST NOT HAVE COME.
QUICKLY AMRAM ENTERS THE HOUSE—AND BOLTS THE DOOR.
SURELY GOD IS WITH US. OUR BABY IS THREE MONTHS OLD AND STILL PHARAOH'S SOLDIERS HAVE NOT FOUND HIM.
GOD WILL HELP ME FIND A WAY TO SAVE OUR SON!

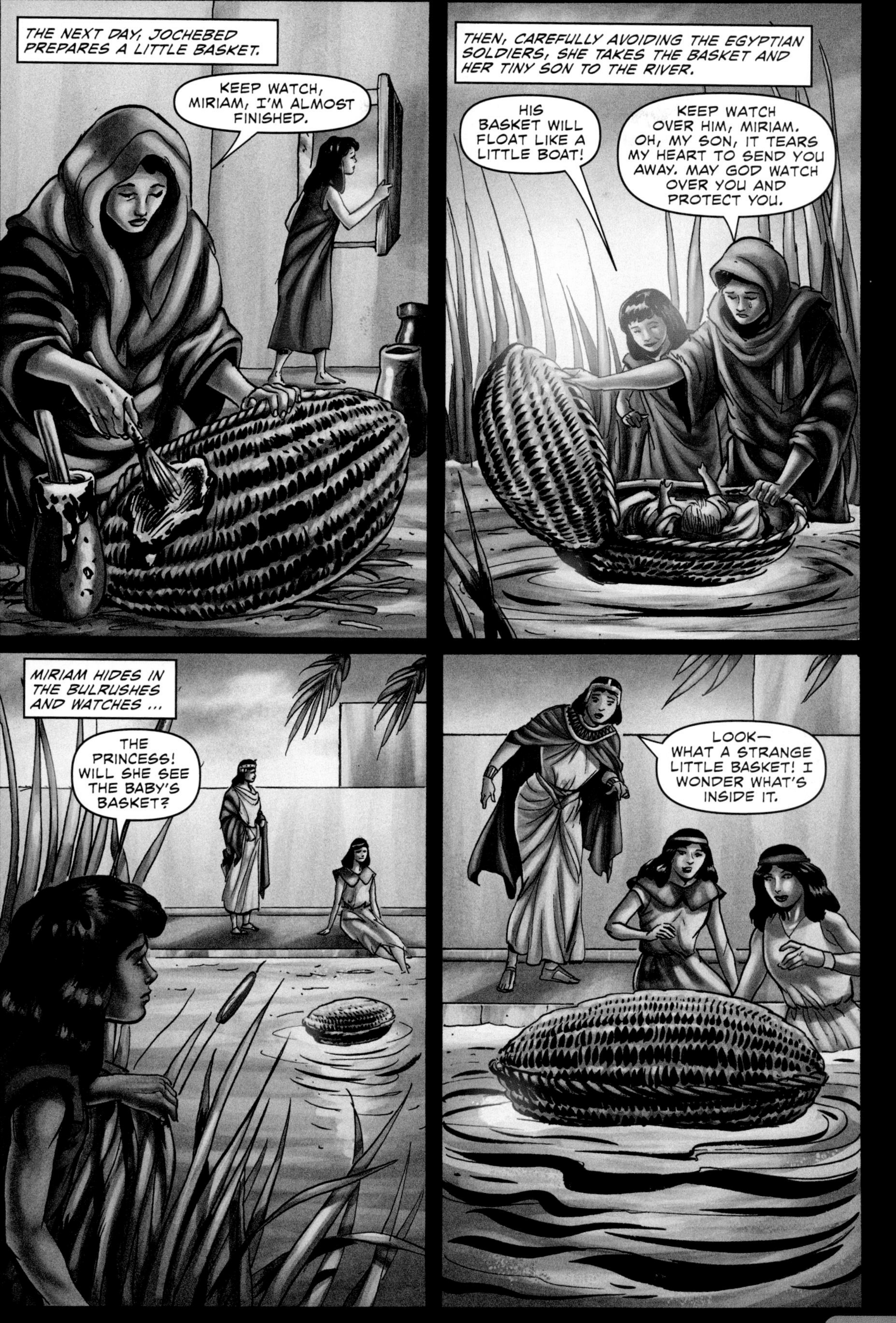
THE NEXT DAY, JOCHEBED PREPARES A LITTLE BASKET.
KEEP WATCH, MIRIAM, I'M ALMOST FINISHED.
THEN, CAREFULLY AVOIDING THE EGYPTIAN SOLDIERS, SHE TAKES THE BASKET AND HER TINY SON TO THE RIVER.
HIS BASKET WILL FLOAT LIKE A LITTLE BOAT!
KEEP WATCH OVER HIM, MIRIAM. OH, MY SON, IT TEARS MY HEART TO SEND YOU AWAY. MAY GOD WATCH OVER YOU AND PROTECT YOU.
MIRIAM HIDES IN THE BULRUSHES AND WATCHES ...
THE PRINCESS! WILL SHE SEE THE BABY'S BASKET?
LOOK— WHAT A STRANGE LITTLE BASKET! I WONDER WHAT'S INSIDE IT.

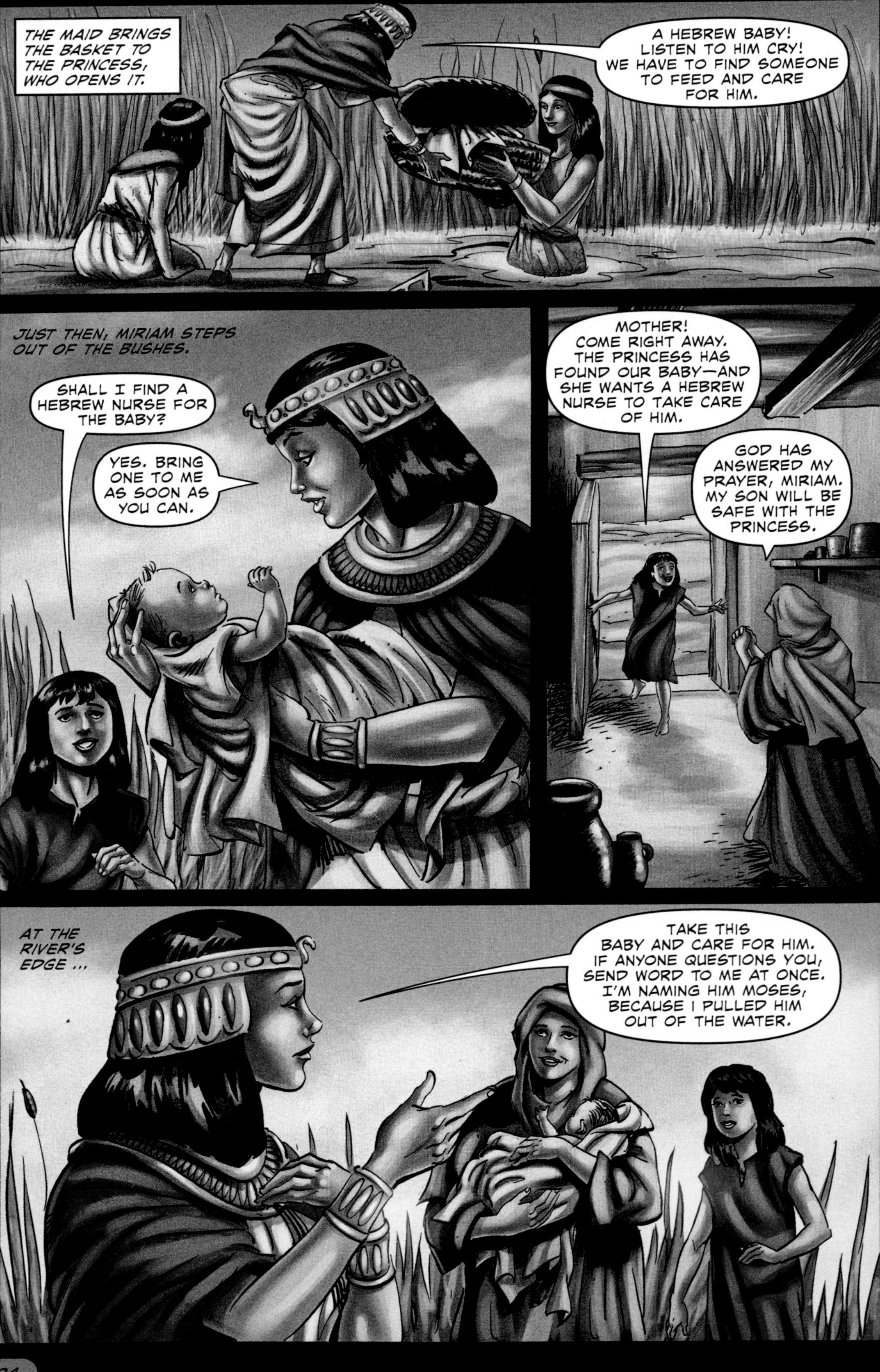
THE MAID BRINGS THE BASKET TO THE PRINCESS, WHO OPENS IT.
A HEBREW BABY! LISTEN TO HIM CRY! WE HAVE TO FIND SOMEONE TO FEED AND CARE FOR HIM.
JUST THEN, MIRIAM STEPS OUT OF THE BUSHES.
SHALL I FIND A HEBREW NURSE FOR THE BABY?
YES. BRING ONE TO ME AS SOON AS YOU CAN.
MOTHER! COME RIGHT AWAY. THE PRINCESS HAS FOUND OUR BABY—AND SHE WANTS A HEBREW NURSE TO TAKE CARE OF HIM.
GOD HAS ANSWERED MY PRAYER, MIRIAM. MY SON WILL BE SAFE WITH THE PRINCESS.
AT THE RIVER'S EDGE ...
TAKE THIS BABY AND CARE FOR HIM. IF ANYONE QUESTIONS YOU, SEND WORD TO ME AT ONCE. I'M NAMING HIM MOSES, BECAUSE I PULLED HIM OUT OF THE WATER.

Prince on the Run

BASED ON EXODUS 2

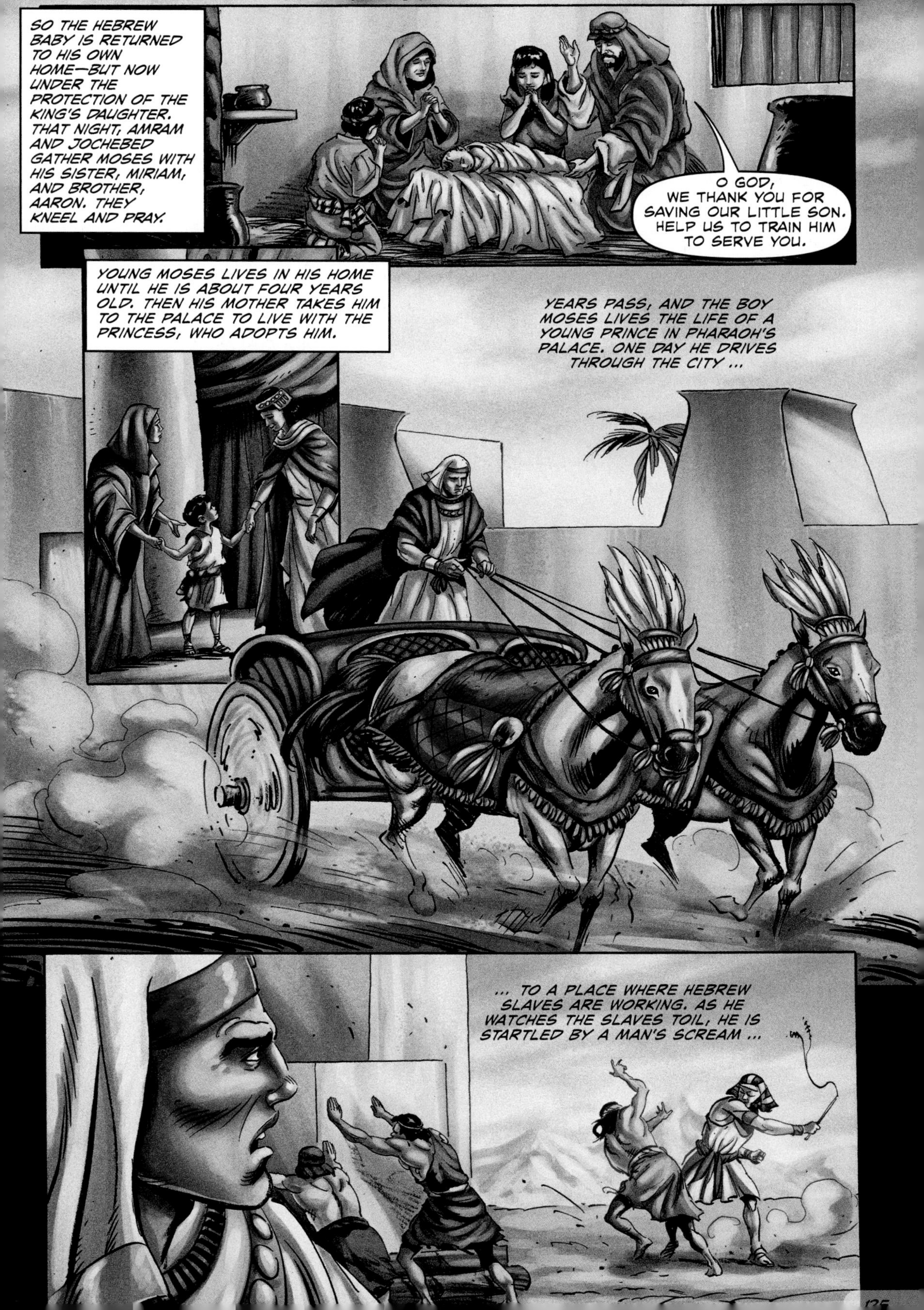

SO THE HEBREW BABY IS RETURNED TO HIS OWN HOME—BUT NOW UNDER THE PROTECTION OF THE KING'S DAUGHTER. THAT NIGHT, AMRAM AND JOCHEBED GATHER MOSES WITH HIS SISTER, MIRIAM, AND BROTHER, AARON. THEY KNEEL AND PRAY.
O GOD, WE THANK YOU FOR SAVING OUR LITTLE SON. HELP US TO TRAIN HIM TO SERVE YOU.
YOUNG MOSES LIVES IN HIS HOME UNTIL HE IS ABOUT FOUR YEARS OLD. THEN HIS MOTHER TAKES HIM TO THE PALACE TO LIVE WITH THE PRINCESS, WHO ADOPTS HIM.
YEARS PASS, AND THE BOY MOSES LIVES THE LIFE OF A YOUNG PRINCE IN PHARAOH'S PALACE. ONE DAY HE DRIVES THROUGH THE CITY ...
... TO A PLACE WHERE HEBREW SLAVES ARE WORKING. AS HE WATCHES THE SLAVES TOIL, HE IS STARTLED BY A MAN'S SCREAM ...

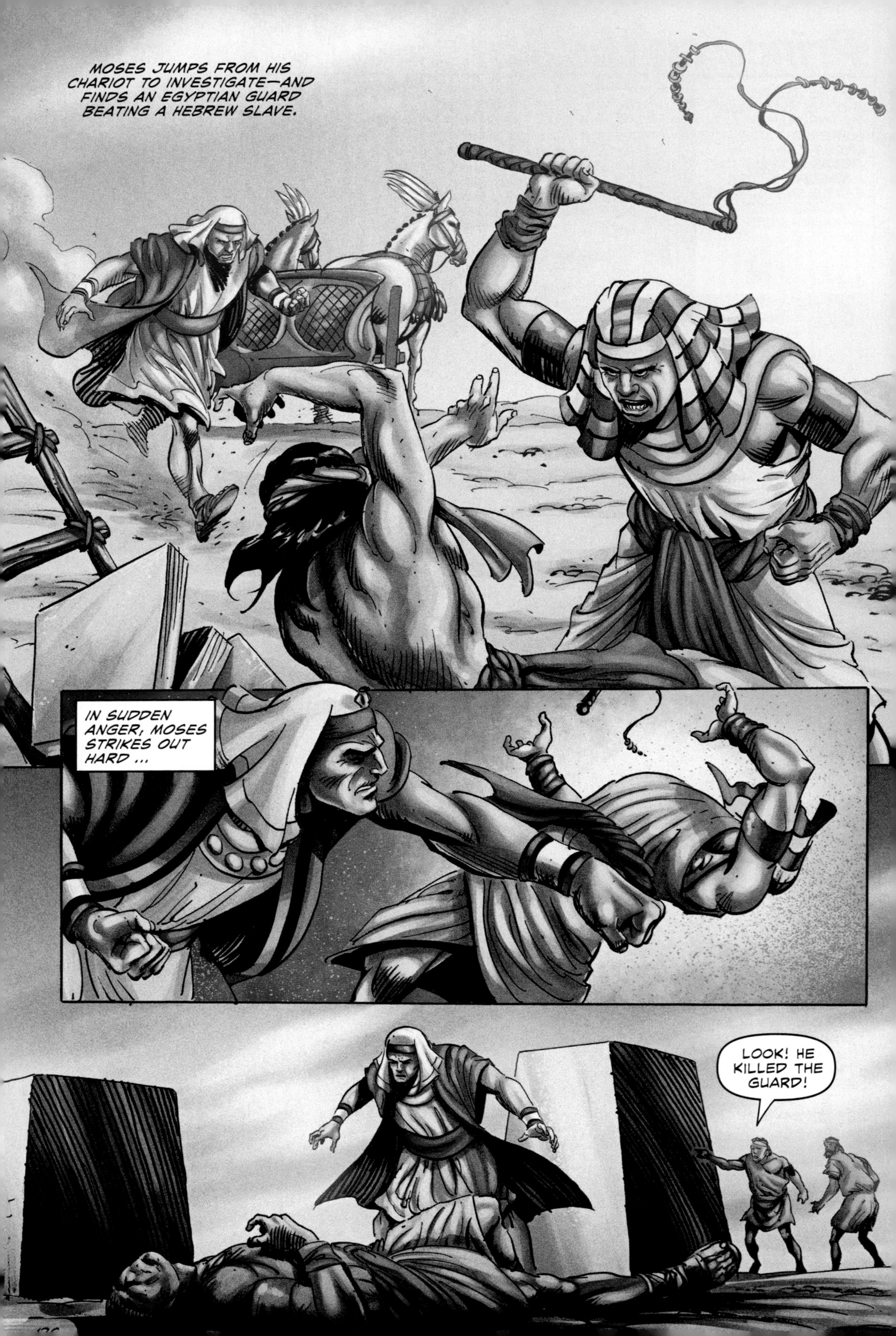
MOSES JUMPS FROM HIS CHARIOT TO INVESTIGATE—AND FINDS AN EGYPTIAN GUARD BEATING A HEBREW SLAVE.
IN SUDDEN ANGER, MOSES STRIKES OUT HARD ...
LOOK! HE KILLED THE GUARD!

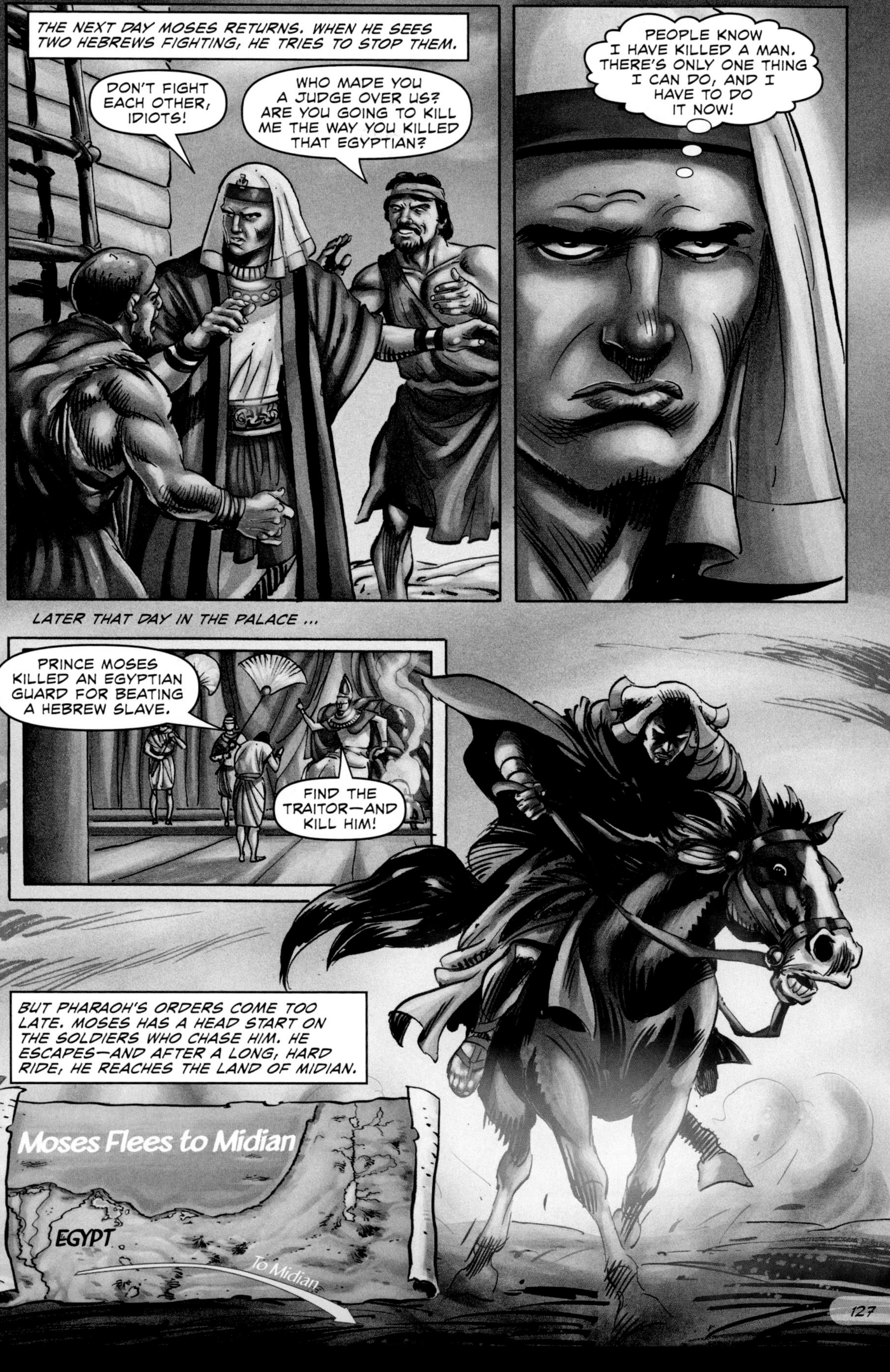
THE NEXT DAY MOSES RETURNS. WHEN HE SEES TWO HEBREWS FIGHTING, HE TRIES TO STOP THEM.
DON'T FIGHT EACH OTHER, IDIOTS!
WHO MADE YOU A JUDGE OVER US? ARE YOU GOING TO KILL ME THE WAY YOU KILLED THAT EGYPTIAN?
PEOPLE KNOW I HAVE KILLED A MAN. THERE'S ONLY ONE THING I CAN DO, AND I HAVE TO DO IT NOW!
LATER THAT DAY IN THE PALACE ...
PRINCE MOSES KILLED AN EGYPTIAN GUARD FOR BEATING A HEBREW SLAVE.
FIND THE TRAITOR—AND KILL HIM!
BUT PHARAOH'S ORDERS COME TOO LATE. MOSES HAS A HEAD START ON THE SOLDIERS WHO CHASE HIM. HE ESCAPES—AND AFTER A LONG, HARD RIDE, HE REACHES THE LAND OF MIDIAN.
Moses Flees to Midian
EGYPT
To Midian

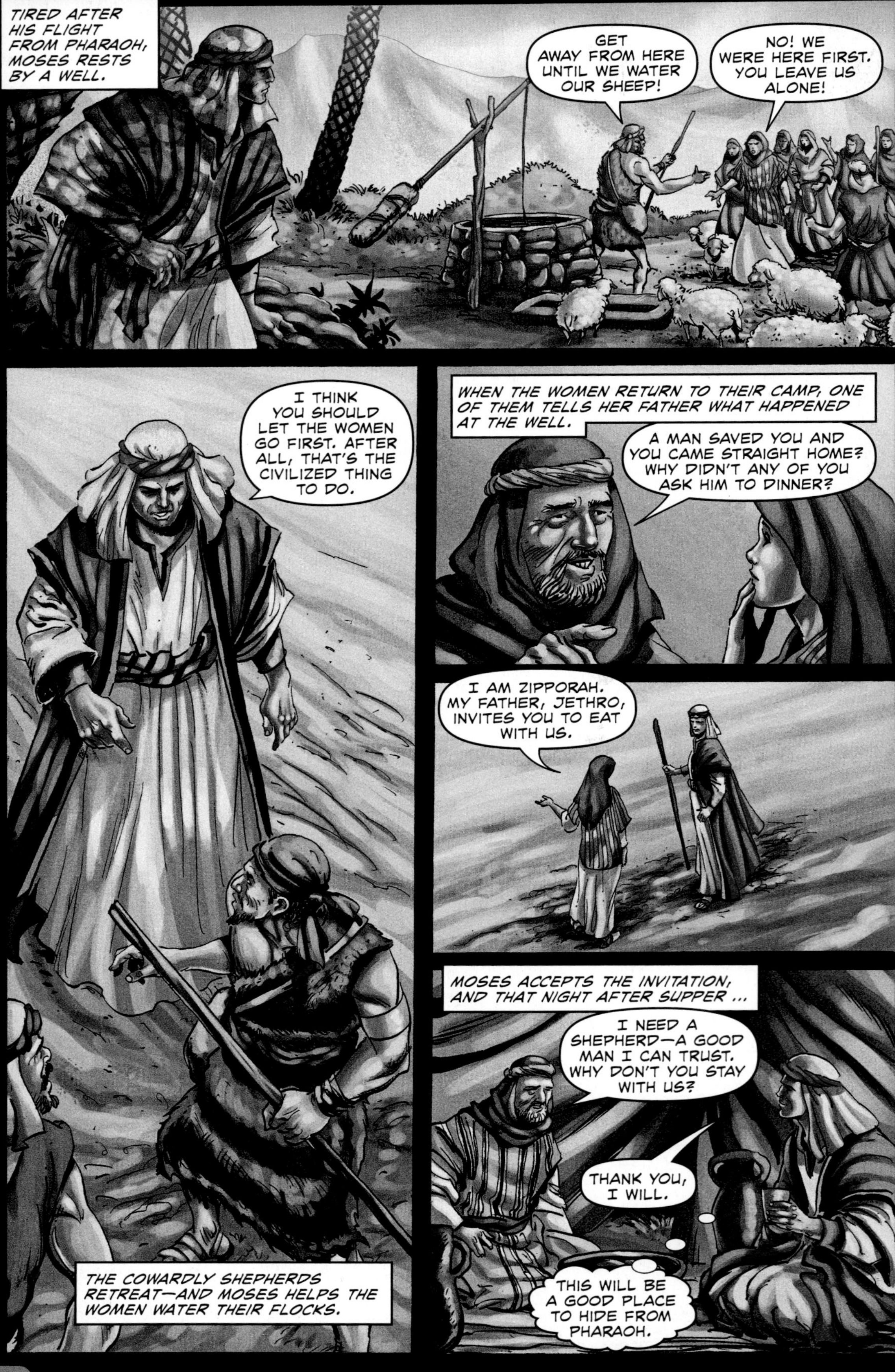
TIRED AFTER HIS FLIGHT FROM PHARAOH, MOSES RESTS BY A WELL.
GET AWAY FROM HERE UNTIL WE WATER OUR SHEEP!
NO! WE WERE HERE FIRST. YOU LEAVE US ALONE!
I THINK YOU SHOULD LET THE WOMEN GO FIRST. AFTER ALL, THAT'S THE CIVILIZED THING TO DO.
THE COWARDLY SHEPHERDS RETREAT—AND MOSES HELPS THE WOMEN WATER THEIR FLOCKS.
WHEN THE WOMEN RETURN TO THEIR CAMP, ONE OF THEM TELLS HER FATHER WHAT HAPPENED AT THE WELL.
A MAN SAVED YOU AND YOU CAME STRAIGHT HOME? WHY DIDN'T ANY OF YOU ASK HIM TO DINNER?
I AM ZIPPORAH. MY FATHER, JETHRO, INVITES YOU TO EAT WITH US.
MOSES ACCEPTS THE INVITATION, AND THAT NIGHT AFTER SUPPER ...
I NEED A SHEPHERD—A GOOD MAN I CAN TRUST. WHY DON'T YOU STAY WITH US?
THANK YOU, I WILL.
THIS WILL BE A GOOD PLACE TO HIDE FROM PHARAOH.

A Burning Bush! BASED ON EXODUS 2:21—4:17

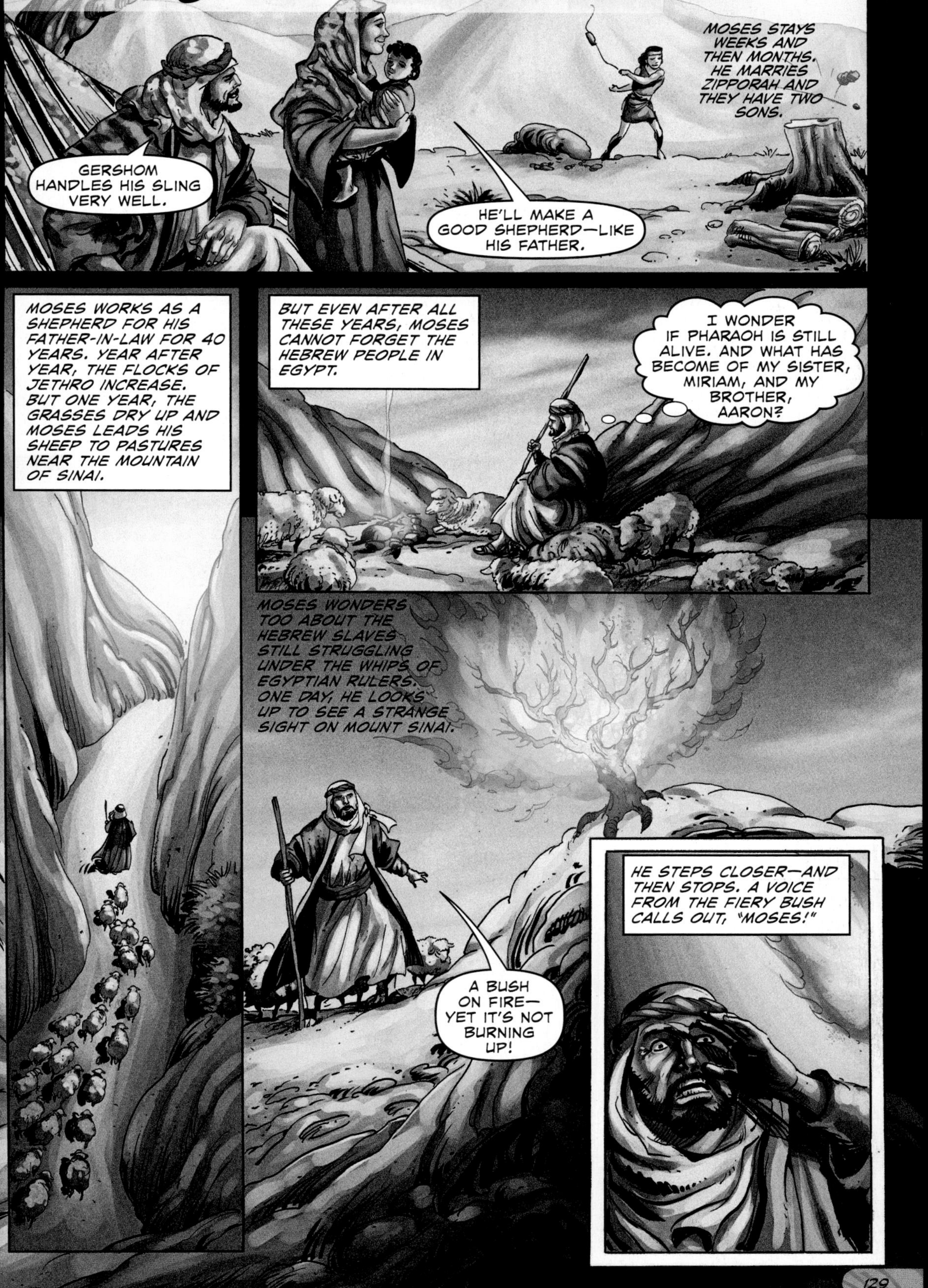
MOSES STAYS WEEKS AND THEN MONTHS. HE MARRIES ZIPPORAH AND THEY HAVE TWO SONS.
GERSHOM HANDLES HIS SLING VERY WELL.
HE'LL MAKE A GOOD SHEPHERD—LIKE HIS FATHER.
MOSES WORKS AS A SHEPHERD FOR HIS FATHER-IN-LAW FOR 40 YEARS. YEAR AFTER YEAR, THE FLOCKS OF JETHRO INCREASE. BUT ONE YEAR, THE GRASSES DRY UP AND MOSES LEADS HIS SHEEP TO PASTURES NEAR THE MOUNTAIN OF SINAI.
BUT EVEN AFTER ALL THESE YEARS, MOSES CANNOT FORGET THE HEBREW PEOPLE IN EGYPT.
I WONDER IF PHARAOH IS STILL ALIVE. AND WHAT HAS BECOME OF MY SISTER, MIRIAM, AND MY BROTHER, AARON?
MOSES WONDERS TOO ABOUT THE HEBREW SLAVES STILL STRUGGLING UNDER THE WHIPS OF EGYPTIAN RULERS. ONE DAY, HE LOOKS UP TO SEE A STRANGE SIGHT ON MOUNT SINAI.
A BUSH ON FIRE—YET IT'S NOT BURNING UP!
HE STEPS CLOSER—AND THEN STOPS. A VOICE FROM THE FIERY BUSH CALLS OUT, "MOSES!"

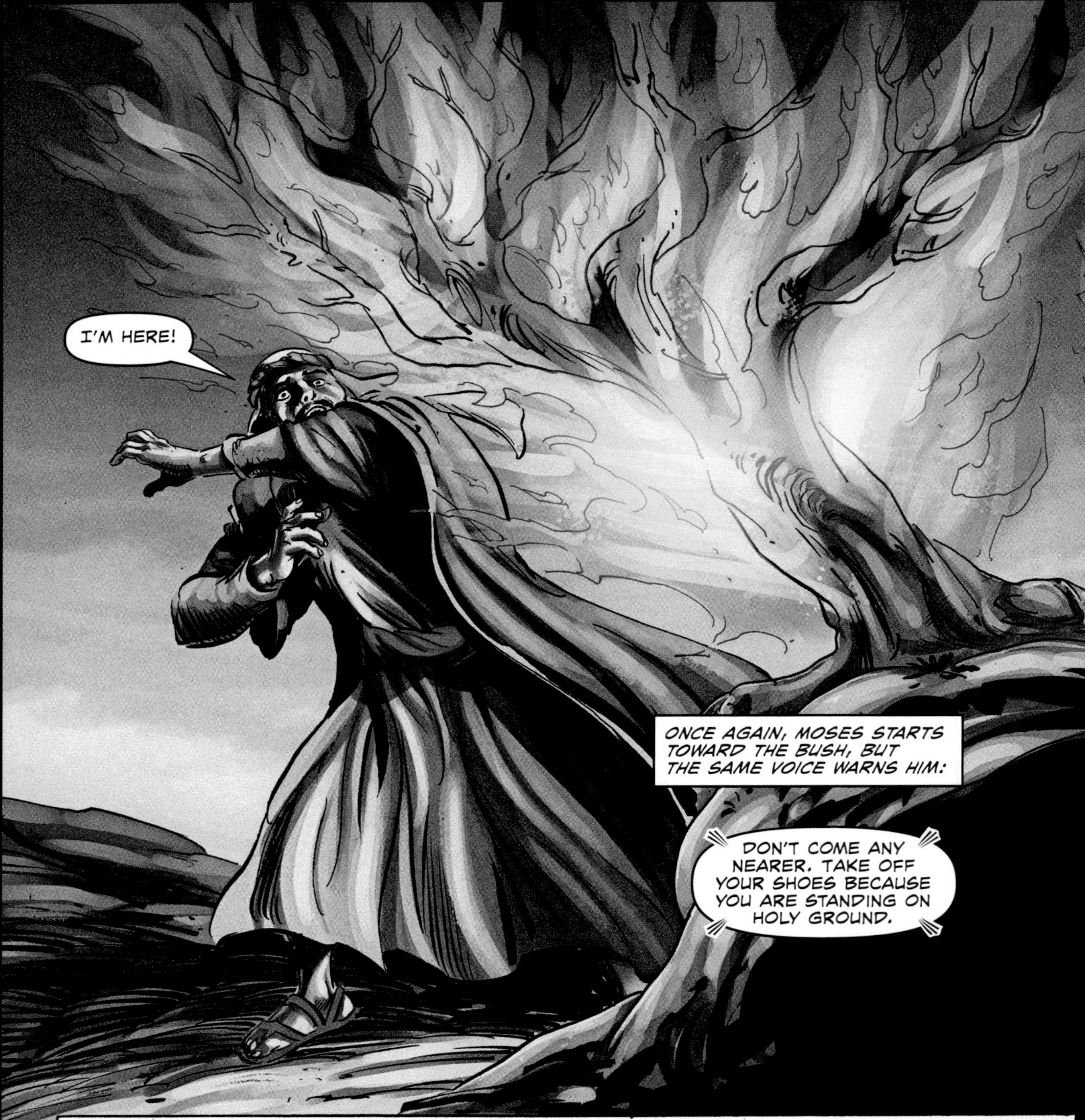
I'M HERE!
ONCE AGAIN, MOSES STARTS TOWARD THE BUSH, BUT THE SAME VOICE WARNS HIM:
DON'T COME ANY NEARER. TAKE OFF YOUR SHOES BECAUSE YOU ARE STANDING ON HOLY GROUND.

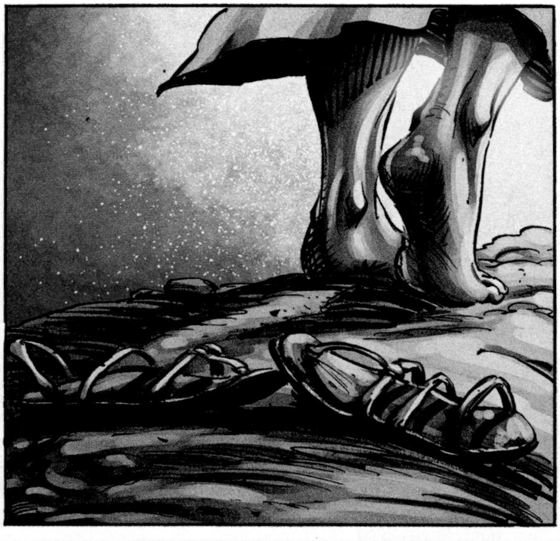

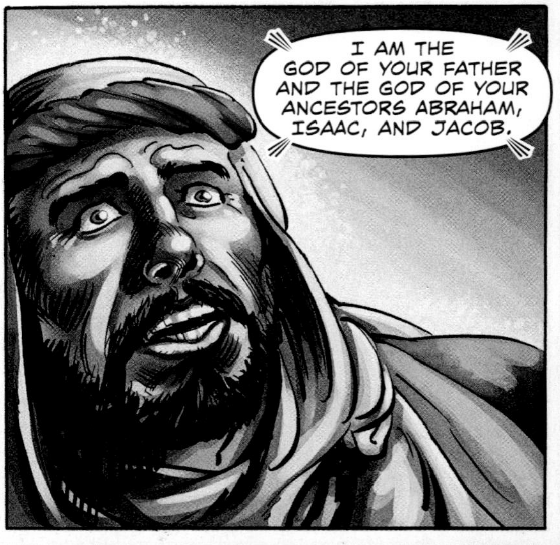
I AM THE GOD OF YOUR FATHER AND THE GOD OF YOUR ANCESTORS ABRAHAM, ISAAC, AND JACOB.

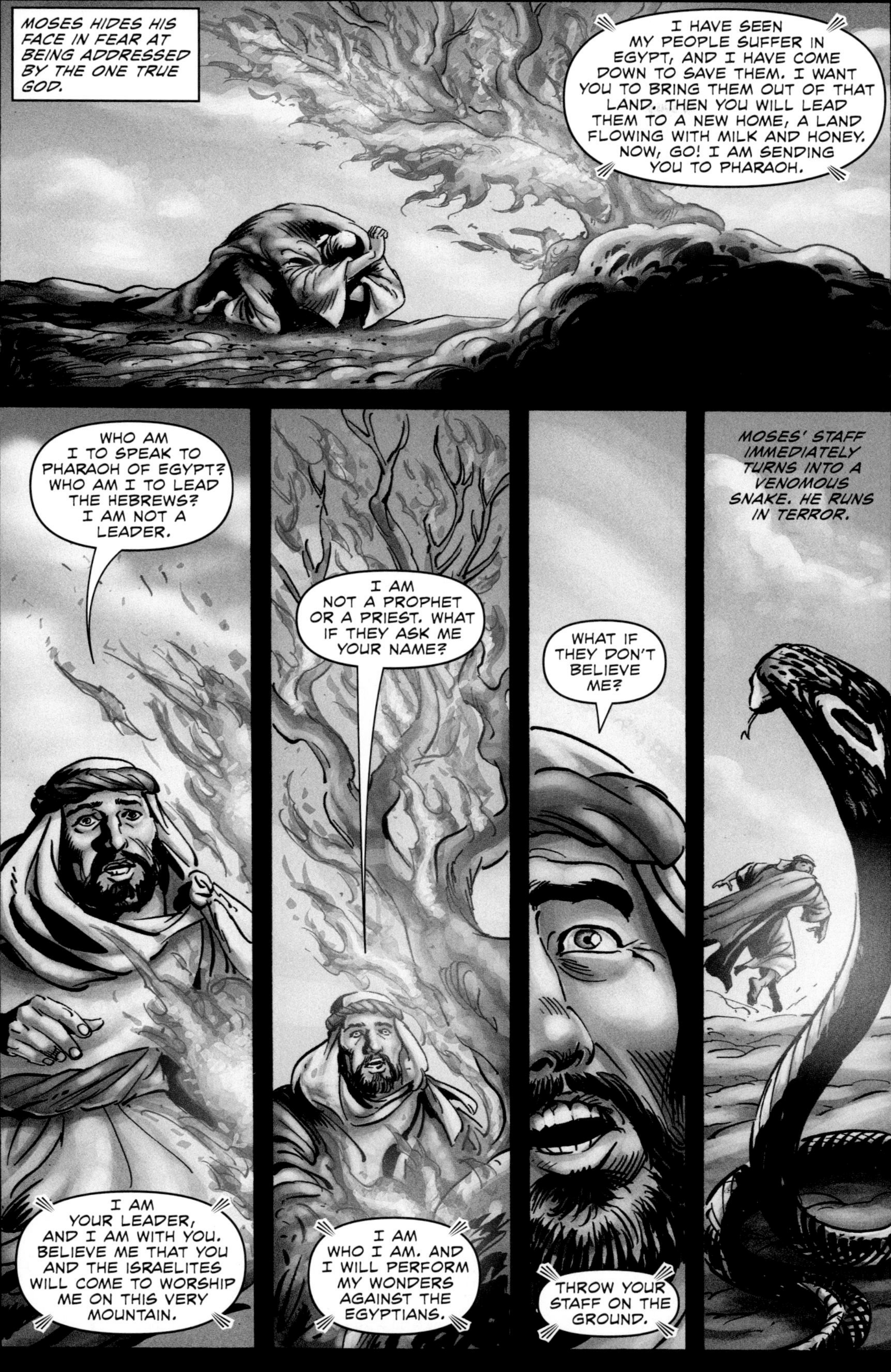
MOSES HIDES HIS FACE IN FEAR AT BEING ADDRESSED BY THE ONE TRUE GOD.
I HAVE SEEN MY PEOPLE SUFFER IN EGYPT, AND I HAVE COME DOWN TO SAVE THEM. I WANT YOU TO BRING THEM OUT OF THAT LAND. THEN YOU WILL LEAD THEM TO A NEW HOME, A LAND FLOWING WITH MILK AND HONEY. NOW, GO! I AM SENDING YOU TO PHARAOH.
WHO AM I TO SPEAK TO PHARAOH OF EGYPT? WHO AM I TO LEAD THE HEBREWS? I AM NOT A LEADER.
I AM YOUR LEADER, AND I AM WITH YOU. BELIEVE ME THAT YOU AND THE ISRAELITES WILL COME TO WORSHIP ME ON THIS VERY MOUNTAIN.
I AM NOT A PROPHET OR A PRIEST. WHAT IF THEY ASK ME YOUR NAME?
I AM WHO I AM. AND I WILL PERFORM MY WONDERS AGAINST THE EGYPTIANS.
WHAT IF THEY DON'T BELIEVE ME?
THROW YOUR STAFF ON THE GROUND.
MOSES' STAFF IMMEDIATELY TURNS INTO A VENOMOUS SNAKE. HE RUNS IN TERROR.

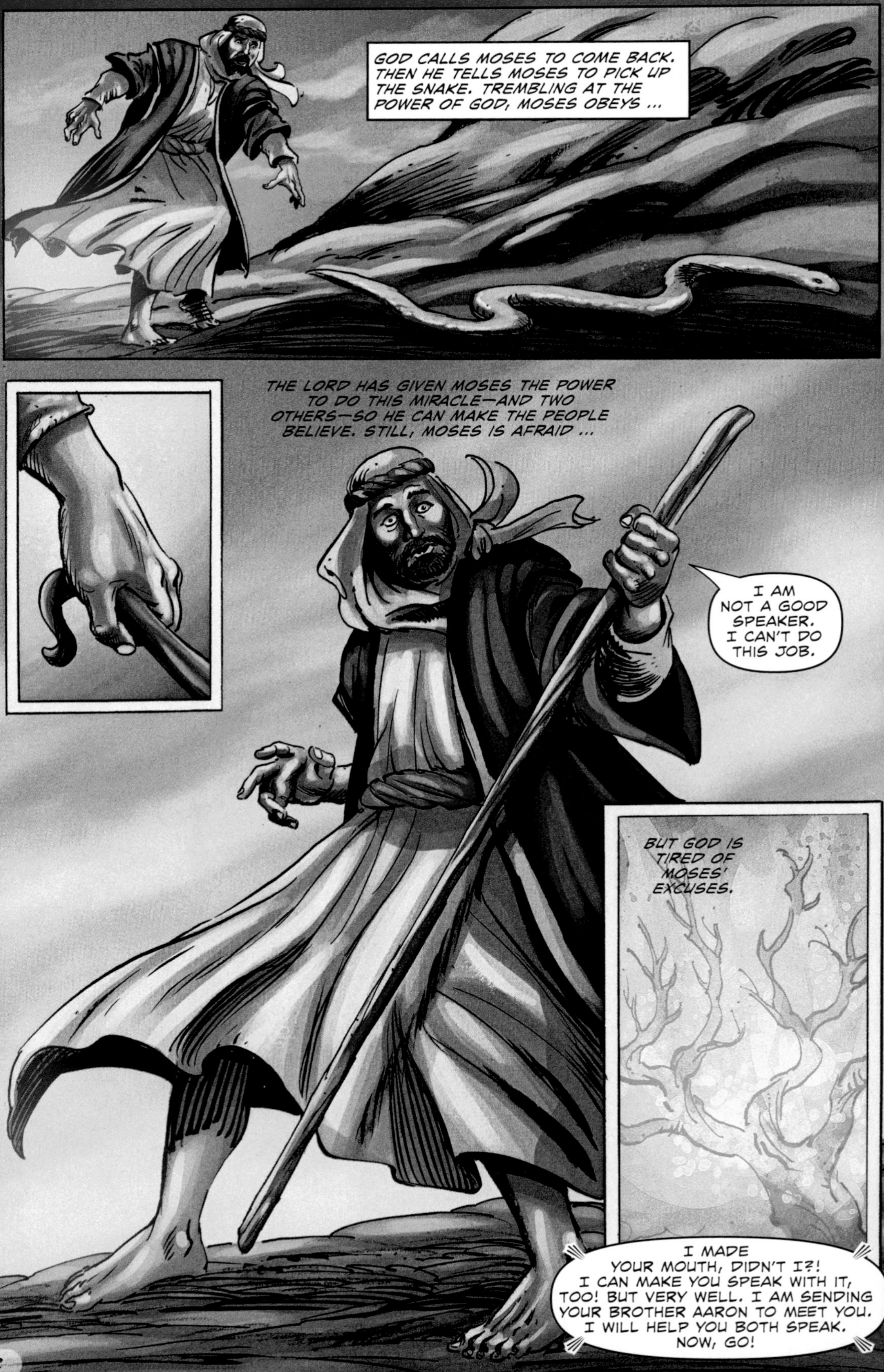
GOD CALLS MOSES TO COME BACK. THEN HE TELLS MOSES TO PICK UP THE SNAKE. TREMBLING AT THE POWER OF GOD, MOSES OBEYS ...
THE LORD HAS GIVEN MOSES THE POWER TO DO THIS MIRACLE—AND TWO OTHERS—SO HE CAN MAKE THE PEOPLE BELIEVE. STILL, MOSES IS AFRAID ...
I AM NOT A GOOD SPEAKER. I CAN'T DO THIS JOB.
BUT GOD IS TIRED OF MOSES' EXCUSES.
I MADE YOUR MOUTH, DIDN'T I?! I CAN MAKE YOU SPEAK WITH IT, TOO! BUT VERY WELL. I AM SENDING YOUR BROTHER AARON TO MEET YOU. I WILL HELP YOU BOTH SPEAK. NOW, GO!

Spokesmen for God

BASED ON EXODUS 4:27—7:11

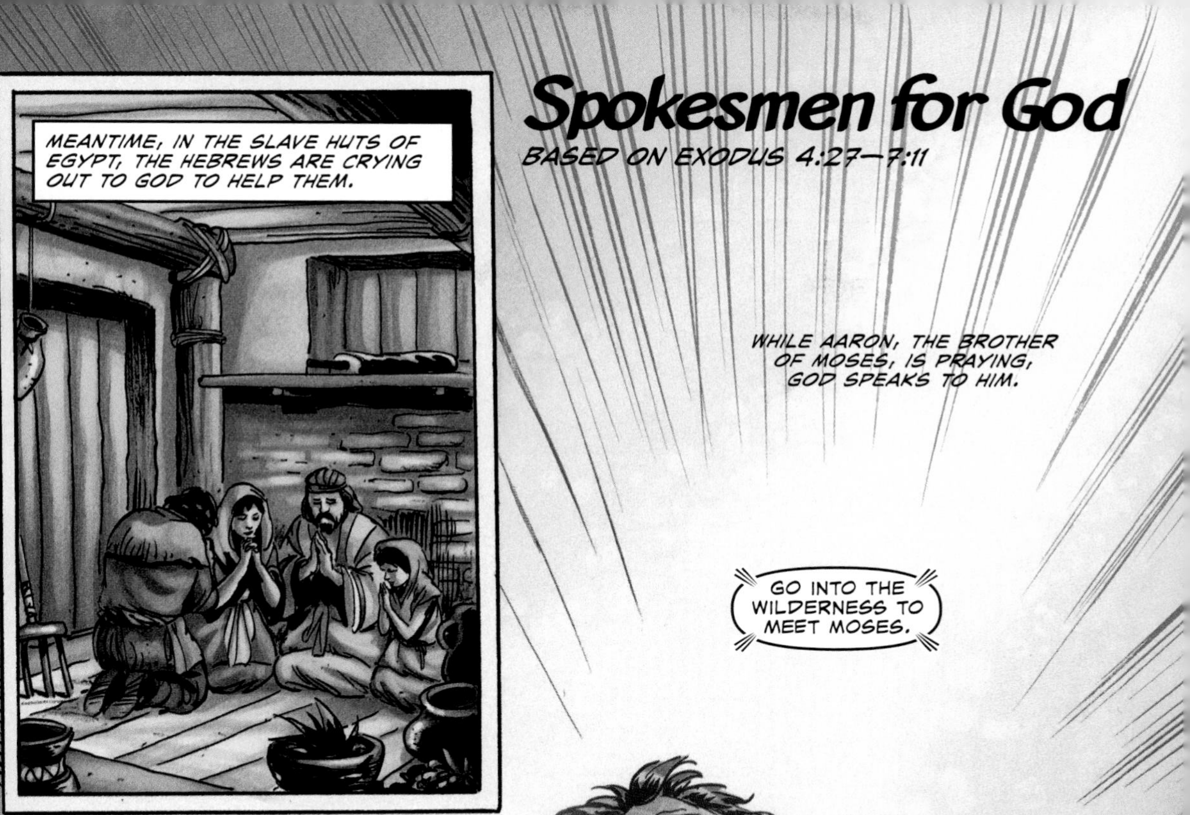
MEANTIME, IN THE SLAVE HUTS OF EGYPT, THE HEBREWS ARE CRYING OUT TO GOD TO HELP THEM.

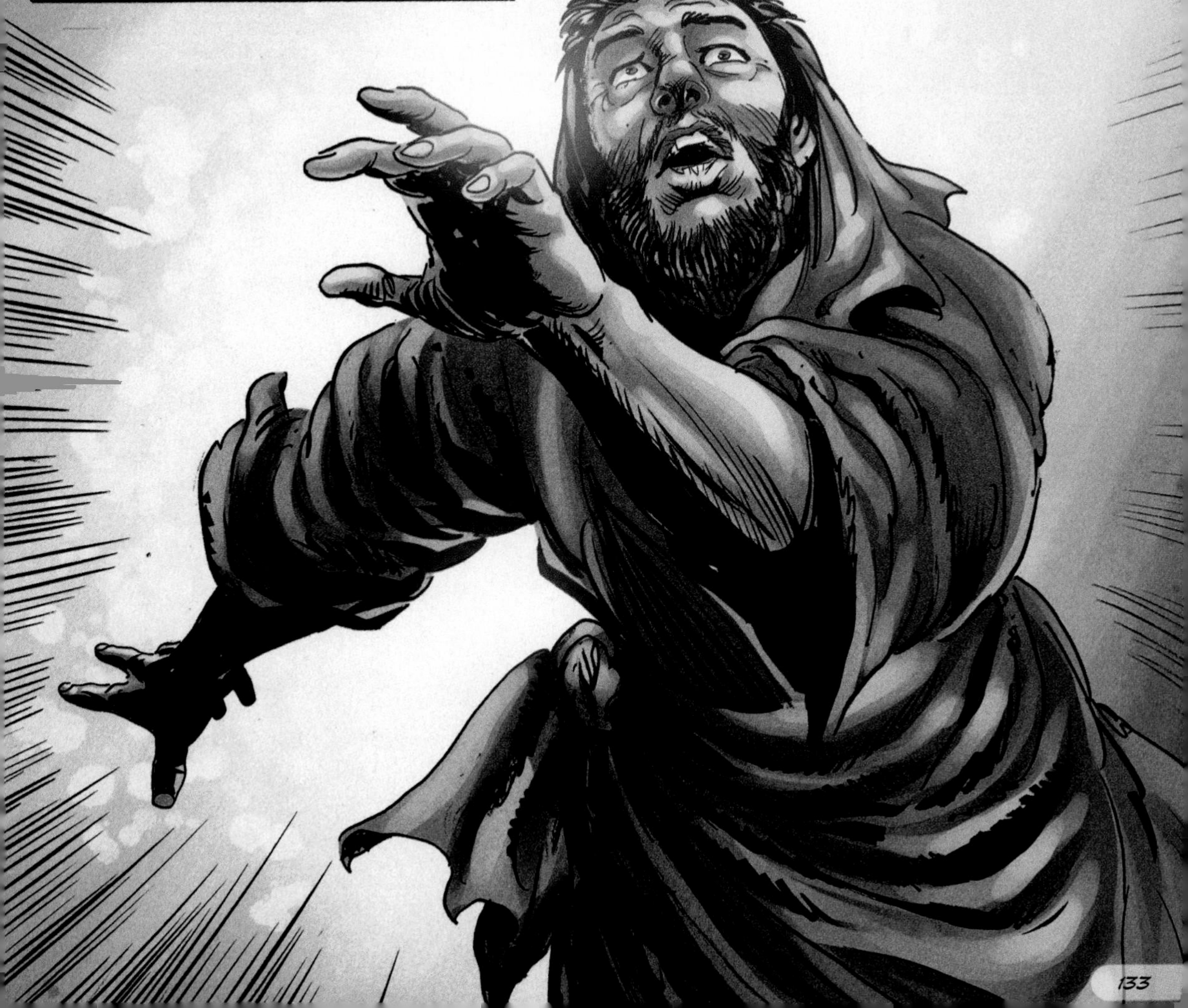
WHILE AARON, THE BROTHER OF MOSES, IS PRAYING, GOD SPEAKS TO HIM.
GO INTO THE WILDERNESS TO MEET MOSES.

AARON IS SURPRISED AT THE STRANGE COMMAND. BUT, UNLIKE MOSES, HE OBEYS WITHOUT COMPLAINT. HE HEADS OUT ALONE INTO THE WILDERNESS.

I DON'T EVEN KNOW WHERE IN THE WILDERNESS MOSES *IS.* I HOPE I'M GOING THE RIGHT WAY.

AARON EVENTUALLY WINDS UP AT MOUNT SINAI. MOSES IS WAITING FOR HIM.

BROTHER?

BROTHER! I'VE BEEN WATCHING FOR YOU. GOD TOLD ME YOU WOULD COME.

QUICKLY, MOSES EXPLAINS THAT GOD HAS CALLED THEM TO LEAD THE HEBREWS OUT OF SLAVERY IN EGYPT. THEY TRAVEL TOGETHER TO TALK TO THE ELDERS OF ISRAEL IN EGYPT. MOSES PERFORMS THE MIRACLES GOD GAVE HIM, AND THE ELDERS BELIEVE.

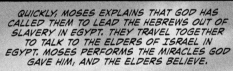

TOMORROW, WE'LL TAKE GOD'S MESSAGE TO PHARAOH.

THE NEXT DAY ...

YOU'LL DO ALL THE TALKING, RIGHT, AARON?

I'M JUST HERE FOR MORAL SUPPORT. YOU'RE THE ONE WHO KNOWS EGYPTIAN POLITICS.

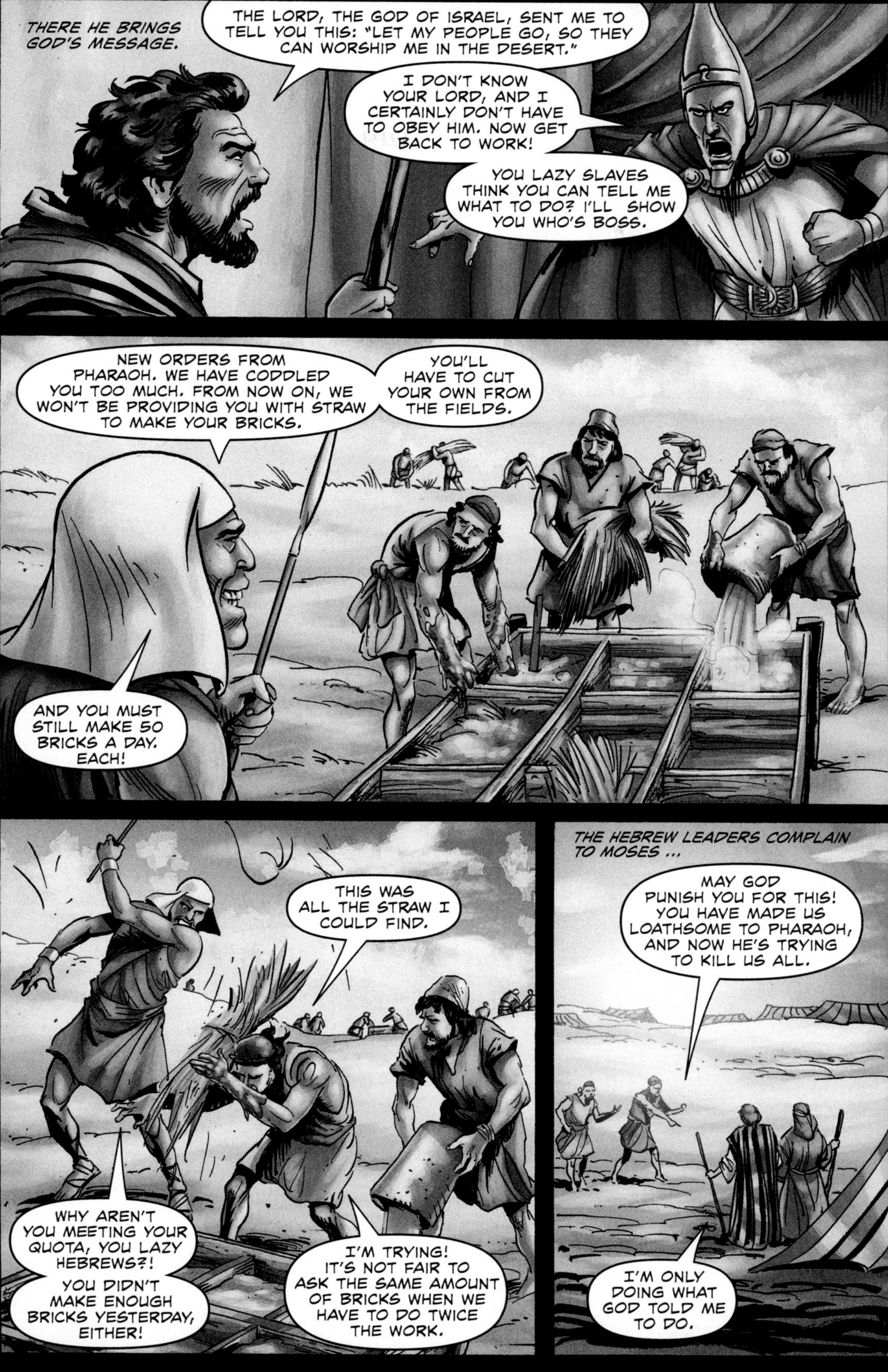
THERE HE BRINGS GOD'S MESSAGE.
THE LORD, THE GOD OF ISRAEL, SENT ME TO TELL YOU THIS: "LET MY PEOPLE GO, SO THEY CAN WORSHIP ME IN THE DESERT."
I DON'T KNOW YOUR LORD, AND I CERTAINLY DON'T HAVE TO OBEY HIM. NOW GET BACK TO WORK!
YOU LAZY SLAVES THINK YOU CAN TELL ME WHAT TO DO? I'LL SHOW YOU WHO'S BOSS.
NEW ORDERS FROM PHARAOH. WE HAVE CODDLED YOU TOO MUCH. FROM NOW ON, WE WON'T BE PROVIDING YOU WITH STRAW TO MAKE YOUR BRICKS.
YOU'LL HAVE TO CUT YOUR OWN FROM THE FIELDS.
AND YOU MUST STILL MAKE 50 BRICKS A DAY. EACH!
THIS WAS ALL THE STRAW I COULD FIND.
WHY AREN'T YOU MEETING YOUR QUOTA, YOU LAZY HEBREWS?!
YOU DIDN'T MAKE ENOUGH BRICKS YESTERDAY, EITHER!
I'M TRYING! IT'S NOT FAIR TO ASK THE SAME AMOUNT OF BRICKS WHEN WE HAVE TO DO TWICE THE WORK.
THE HEBREW LEADERS COMPLAIN TO MOSES ...
MAY GOD PUNISH YOU FOR THIS! YOU HAVE MADE US LOATHSOME TO PHARAOH, AND NOW HE'S TRYING TO KILL US ALL.
I'M ONLY DOING WHAT GOD TOLD ME TO DO.

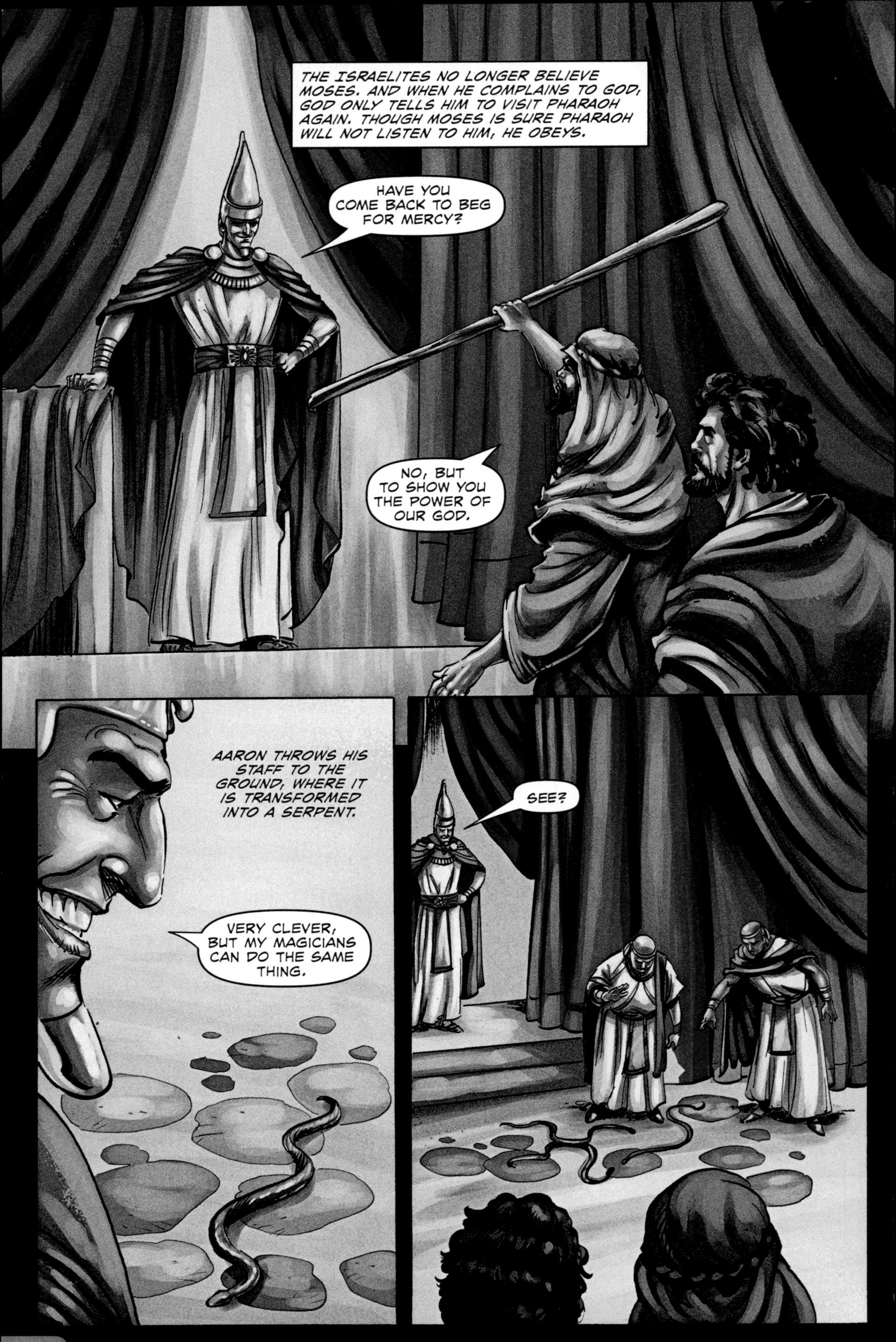

THE ISRAELITES NO LONGER BELIEVE MOSES. AND WHEN HE COMPLAINS TO GOD, GOD ONLY TELLS HIM TO VISIT PHARAOH AGAIN. THOUGH MOSES IS SURE PHARAOH WILL NOT LISTEN TO HIM, HE OBEYS.
HAVE YOU COME BACK TO BEG FOR MERCY?
NO, BUT TO SHOW YOU THE POWER OF OUR GOD.
AARON THROWS HIS STAFF TO THE GROUND, WHERE IT IS TRANSFORMED INTO A SERPENT.
VERY CLEVER, BUT MY MAGICIANS CAN DO THE SAME THING.
SEE?

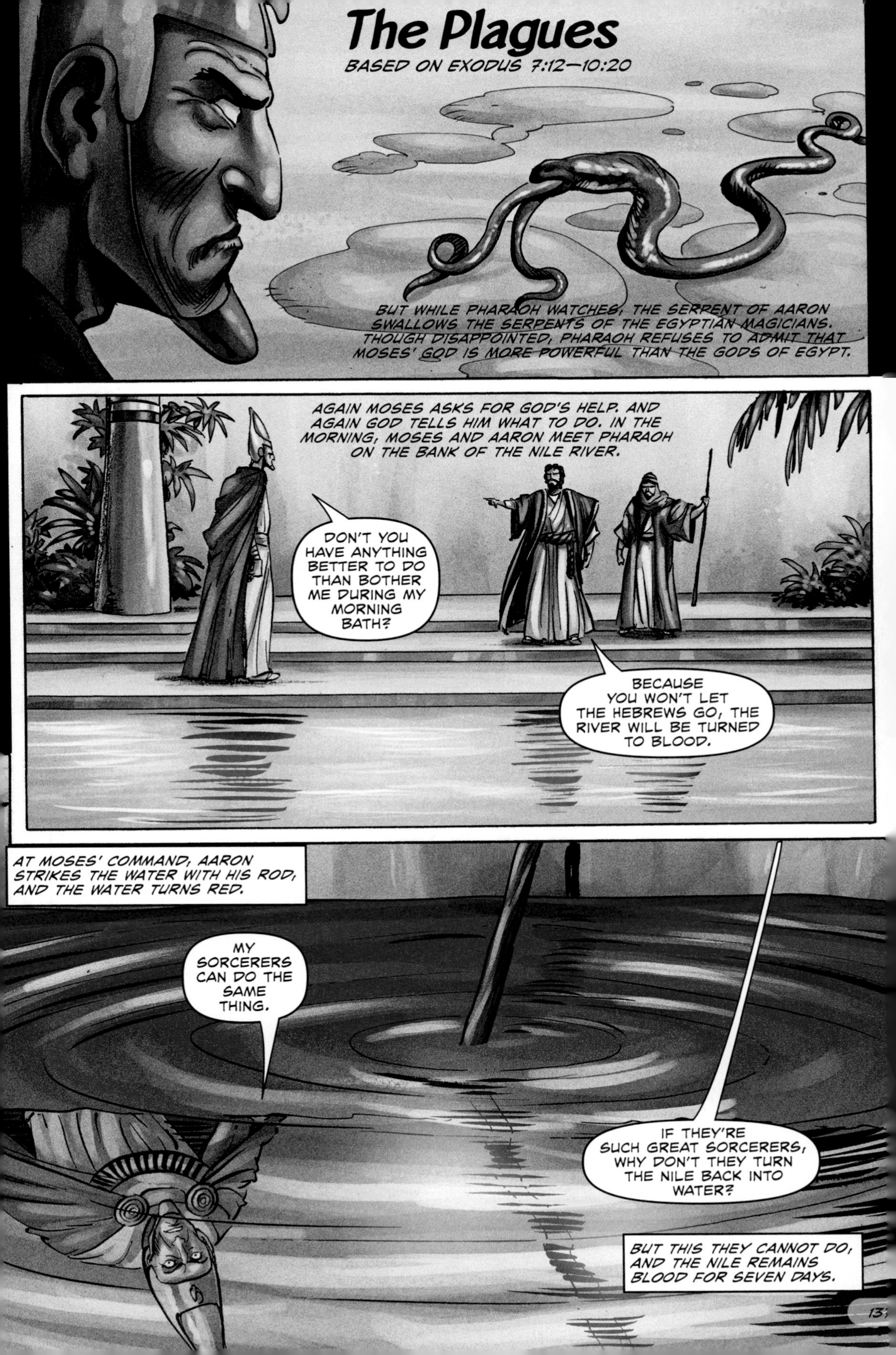
The Plagues
BASED ON EXODUS 7:12—10:20
BUT WHILE PHARAOH WATCHES, THE SERPENT OF AARON SWALLOWS THE SERPENTS OF THE EGYPTIAN MAGICIANS. THOUGH DISAPPOINTED, PHARAOH REFUSES TO ADMIT THAT MOSES' GOD IS MORE POWERFUL THAN THE GODS OF EGYPT.
AGAIN MOSES ASKS FOR GOD'S HELP. AND AGAIN GOD TELLS HIM WHAT TO DO. IN THE MORNING, MOSES AND AARON MEET PHARAOH ON THE BANK OF THE NILE RIVER.
DON'T YOU HAVE ANYTHING BETTER TO DO THAN BOTHER ME DURING MY MORNING BATH?
BECAUSE YOU WON'T LET THE HEBREWS GO, THE RIVER WILL BE TURNED TO BLOOD.
AT MOSES' COMMAND, AARON STRIKES THE WATER WITH HIS ROD, AND THE WATER TURNS RED.
MY SORCERERS CAN DO THE SAME THING.
IF THEY'RE SUCH GREAT SORCERERS, WHY DON'T THEY TURN THE NILE BACK INTO WATER?
BUT THIS THEY CANNOT DO, AND THE NILE REMAINS BLOOD FOR SEVEN DAYS.

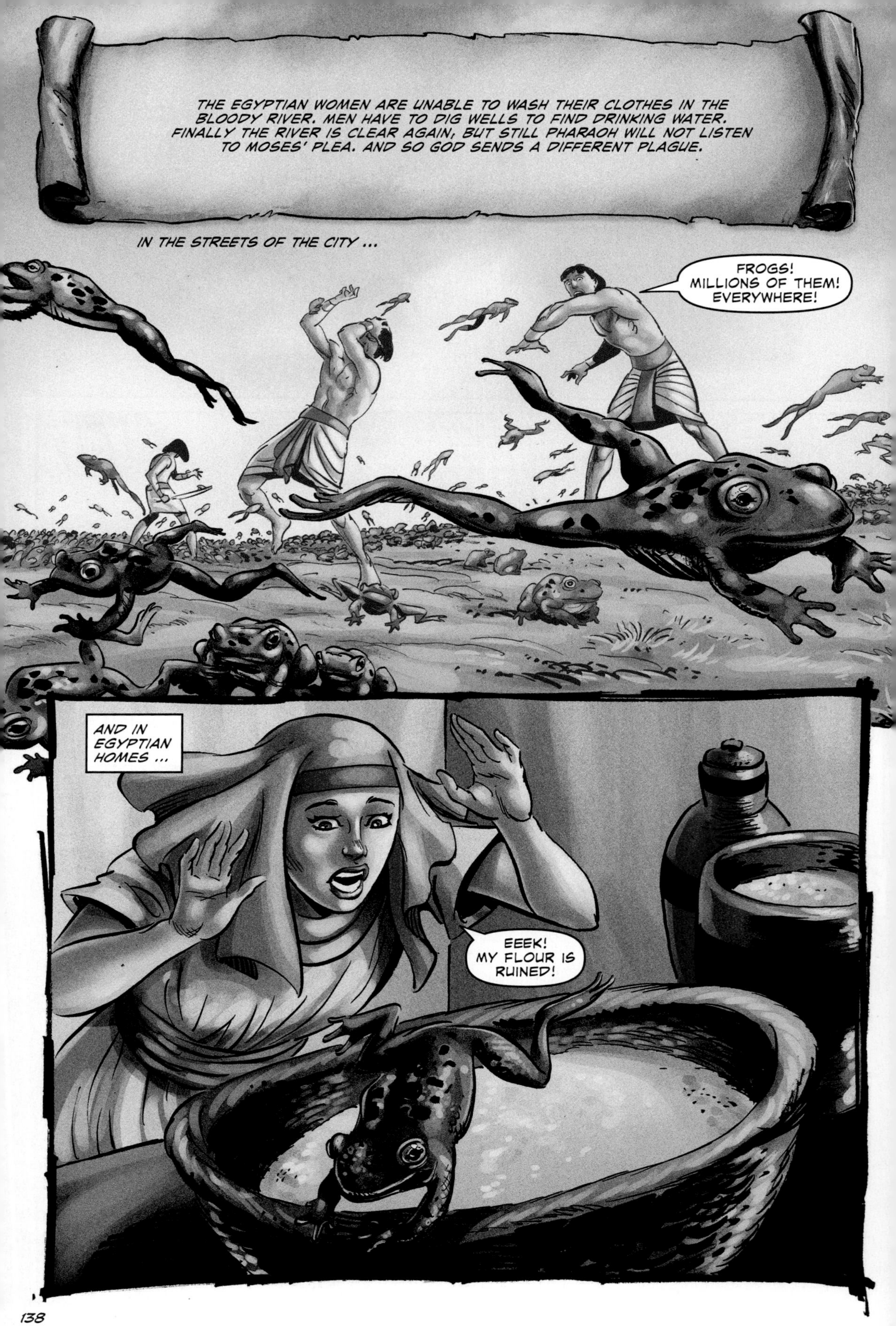
THE EGYPTIAN WOMEN ARE UNABLE TO WASH THEIR CLOTHES IN THE BLOODY RIVER. MEN HAVE TO DIG WELLS TO FIND DRINKING WATER. FINALLY THE RIVER IS CLEAR AGAIN, BUT STILL PHARAOH WILL NOT LISTEN TO MOSES' PLEA. AND SO GOD SENDS A DIFFERENT PLAGUE.
IN THE STREETS OF THE CITY ...
FROGS! MILLIONS OF THEM! EVERYWHERE!
AND IN EGYPTIAN HOMES ...
EEEK! MY FLOUR IS RUINED!

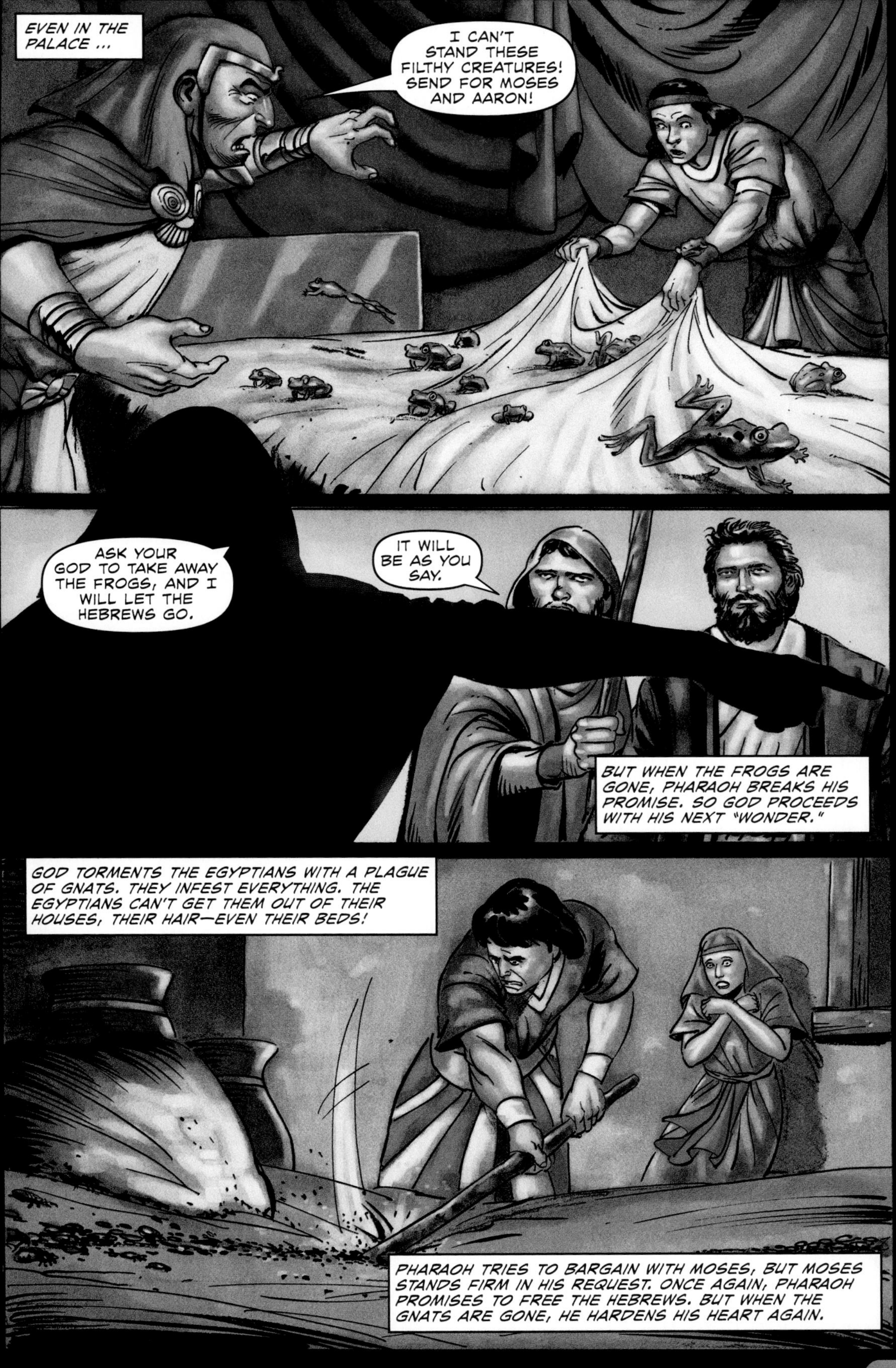
EVEN IN THE PALACE ...
I CAN'T STAND THESE FILTHY CREATURES! SEND FOR MOSES AND AARON!
ASK YOUR GOD TO TAKE AWAY THE FROGS, AND I WILL LET THE HEBREWS GO.
IT WILL BE AS YOU SAY.
BUT WHEN THE FROGS ARE GONE, PHARAOH BREAKS HIS PROMISE. SO GOD PROCEEDS WITH HIS NEXT "WONDER."
GOD TORMENTS THE EGYPTIANS WITH A PLAGUE OF GNATS. THEY INFEST EVERYTHING. THE EGYPTIANS CAN'T GET THEM OUT OF THEIR HOUSES, THEIR HAIR—EVEN THEIR BEDS!
PHARAOH TRIES TO BARGAIN WITH MOSES, BUT MOSES STANDS FIRM IN HIS REQUEST. ONCE AGAIN, PHARAOH PROMISES TO FREE THE HEBREWS. BUT WHEN THE GNATS ARE GONE, HE HARDENS HIS HEART AGAIN.

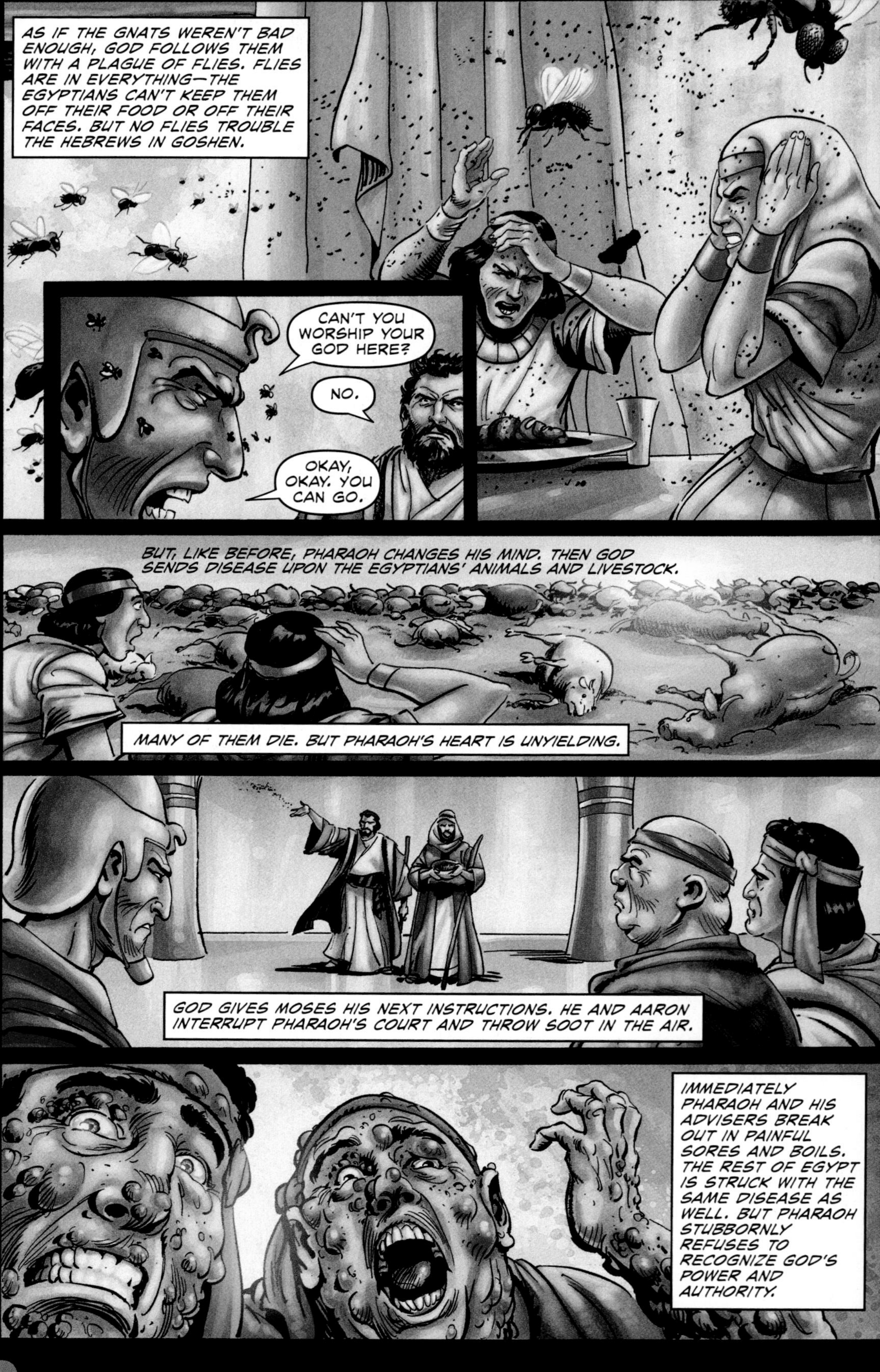

AS IF THE GNATS WEREN'T BAD ENOUGH, GOD FOLLOWS THEM WITH A PLAGUE OF FLIES. FLIES ARE IN EVERYTHING—THE EGYPTIANS CAN'T KEEP THEM OFF THEIR FOOD OR OFF THEIR FACES. BUT NO FLIES TROUBLE THE HEBREWS IN GOSHEN.
CAN'T YOU WORSHIP YOUR GOD HERE?
NO.
OKAY, OKAY. YOU CAN GO.
BUT, LIKE BEFORE, PHARAOH CHANGES HIS MIND. THEN GOD SENDS DISEASE UPON THE EGYPTIANS' ANIMALS AND LIVESTOCK.
MANY OF THEM DIE. BUT PHARAOH'S HEART IS UNYIELDING.
GOD GIVES MOSES HIS NEXT INSTRUCTIONS. HE AND AARON INTERRUPT PHARAOH'S COURT AND THROW SOOT IN THE AIR.
IMMEDIATELY PHARAOH AND HIS ADVISERS BREAK OUT IN PAINFUL SORES AND BOILS. THE REST OF EGYPT IS STRUCK WITH THE SAME DISEASE AS WELL. BUT PHARAOH STUBBORNLY REFUSES TO RECOGNIZE GOD'S POWER AND AUTHORITY.

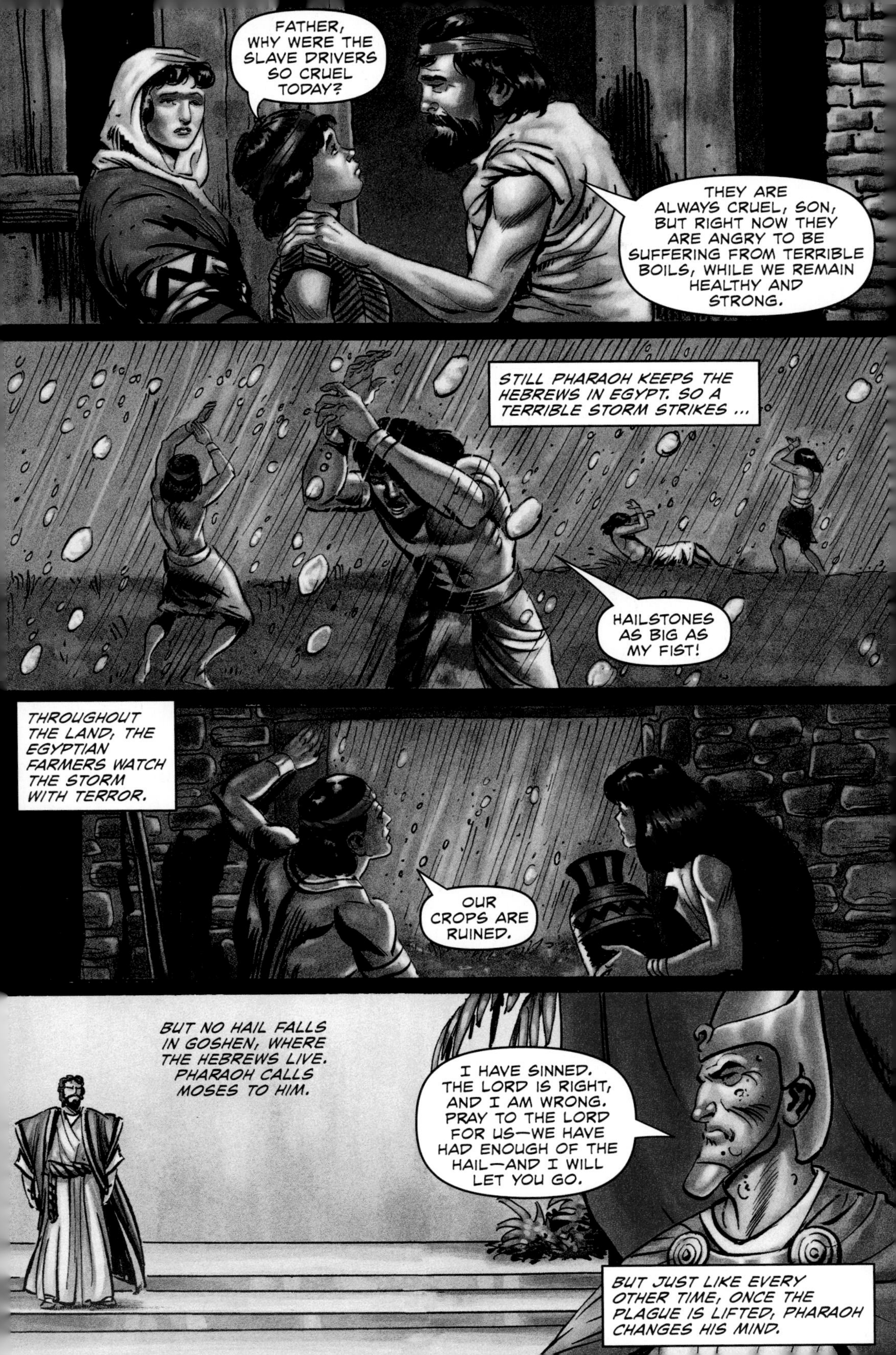
FATHER, WHY WERE THE SLAVE DRIVERS SO CRUEL TODAY?
THEY ARE ALWAYS CRUEL, SON, BUT RIGHT NOW THEY ARE ANGRY TO BE SUFFERING FROM TERRIBLE BOILS, WHILE WE REMAIN HEALTHY AND STRONG.
STILL PHARAOH KEEPS THE HEBREWS IN EGYPT. SO A TERRIBLE STORM STRIKES ...
HAILSTONES AS BIG AS MY FIST!
THROUGHOUT THE LAND, THE EGYPTIAN FARMERS WATCH THE STORM WITH TERROR.
OUR CROPS ARE RUINED.
BUT NO HAIL FALLS IN GOSHEN, WHERE THE HEBREWS LIVE. PHARAOH CALLS MOSES TO HIM.
I HAVE SINNED. THE LORD IS RIGHT, AND I AM WRONG. PRAY TO THE LORD FOR US—WE HAVE HAD ENOUGH OF THE HAIL—AND I WILL LET YOU GO.
BUT JUST LIKE EVERY OTHER TIME, ONCE THE PLAGUE IS LIFTED, PHARAOH CHANGES HIS MIND.

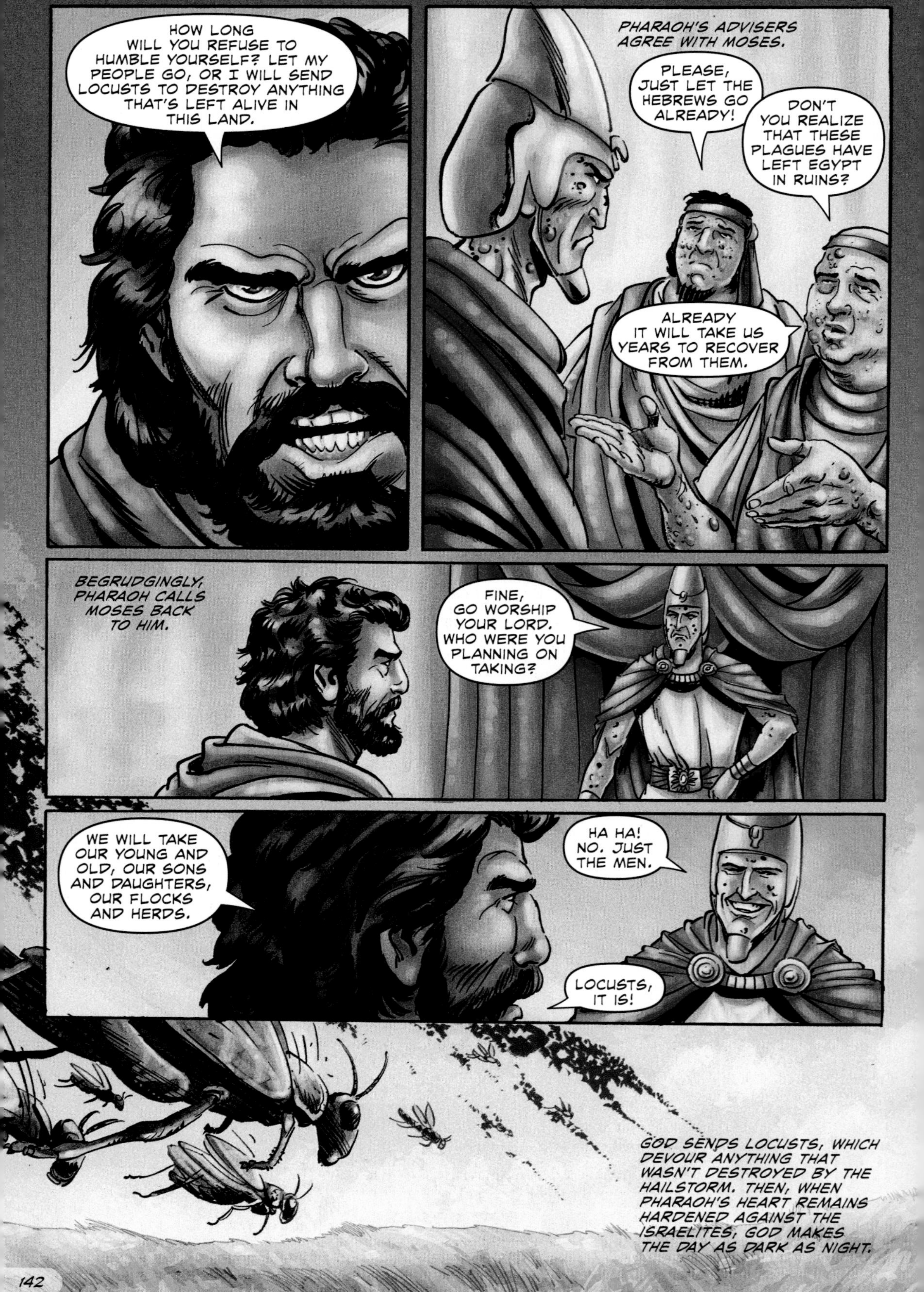

HOW LONG WILL YOU REFUSE TO HUMBLE YOURSELF? LET MY PEOPLE GO, OR I WILL SEND LOCUSTS TO DESTROY ANYTHING THAT'S LEFT ALIVE IN THIS LAND.
PHARAOH'S ADVISERS AGREE WITH MOSES.
PLEASE, JUST LET THE HEBREWS GO ALREADY!
DON'T YOU REALIZE THAT THESE PLAGUES HAVE LEFT EGYPT IN RUINS?
ALREADY IT WILL TAKE US YEARS TO RECOVER FROM THEM.
BEGRUDGINGLY, PHARAOH CALLS MOSES BACK TO HIM.
FINE, GO WORSHIP YOUR LORD. WHO WERE YOU PLANNING ON TAKING?
WE WILL TAKE OUR YOUNG AND OLD, OUR SONS AND DAUGHTERS, OUR FLOCKS AND HERDS.
HA HA! NO. JUST THE MEN.
LOCUSTS, IT IS!
GOD SENDS LOCUSTS, WHICH DEVOUR ANYTHING THAT WASN'T DESTROYED BY THE HAILSTORM. THEN, WHEN PHARAOH'S HEART REMAINS HARDENED AGAINST THE ISRAELITES, GOD MAKES THE DAY AS DARK AS NIGHT.

The Final Plague

BASED ON EXODUS 10:21–12:51

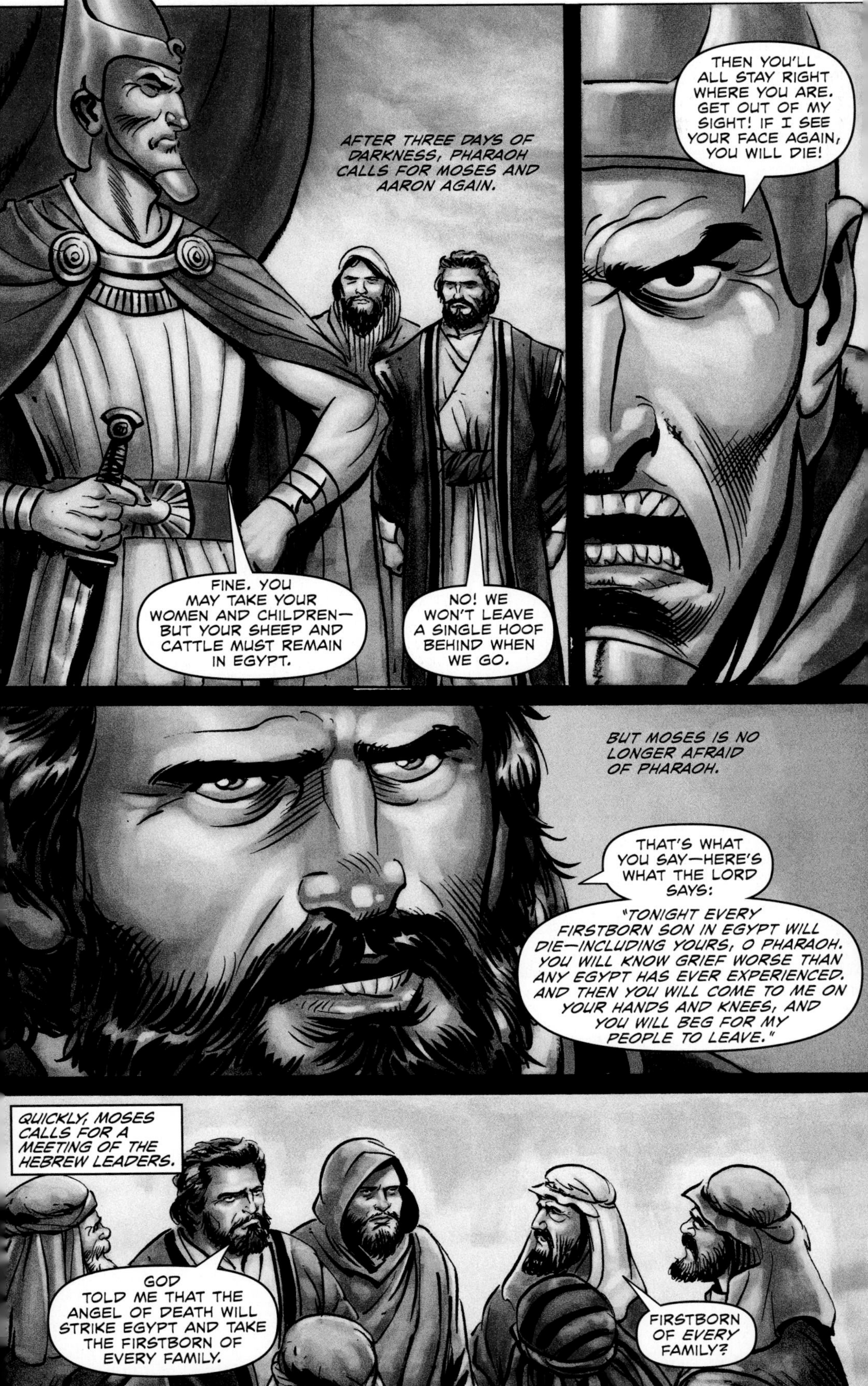
AFTER THREE DAYS OF DARKNESS, PHARAOH CALLS FOR MOSES AND AARON AGAIN.
FINE. YOU MAY TAKE YOUR WOMEN AND CHILDREN—BUT YOUR SHEEP AND CATTLE MUST REMAIN IN EGYPT.
NO! WE WON'T LEAVE A SINGLE HOOF BEHIND WHEN WE GO.
THEN YOU'LL ALL STAY RIGHT WHERE YOU ARE. GET OUT OF MY SIGHT! IF I SEE YOUR FACE AGAIN, YOU WILL DIE!
BUT MOSES IS NO LONGER AFRAID OF PHARAOH.
THAT'S WHAT YOU SAY—HERE'S WHAT THE LORD SAYS:
"TONIGHT EVERY FIRSTBORN SON IN EGYPT WILL DIE—INCLUDING YOURS, O PHARAOH. YOU WILL KNOW GRIEF WORSE THAN ANY EGYPT HAS EVER EXPERIENCED. AND THEN YOU WILL COME TO ME ON YOUR HANDS AND KNEES, AND YOU WILL BEG FOR MY PEOPLE TO LEAVE."
QUICKLY, MOSES CALLS FOR A MEETING OF THE HEBREW LEADERS.
GOD TOLD ME THAT THE ANGEL OF DEATH WILL STRIKE EGYPT AND TAKE THE FIRSTBORN OF EVERY FAMILY.
FIRSTBORN OF EVERY FAMILY?

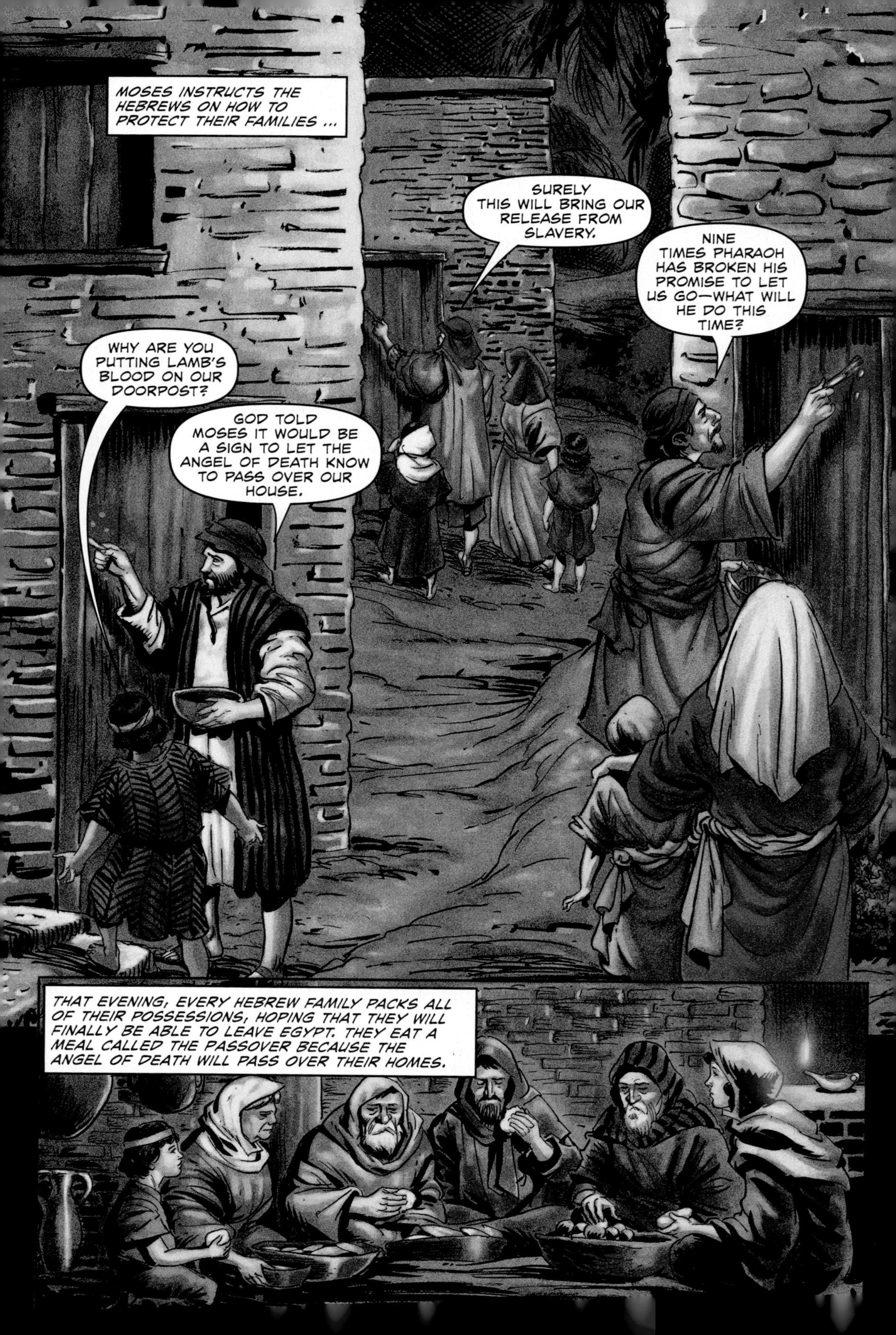
MOSES INSTRUCTS THE HEBREWS ON HOW TO PROTECT THEIR FAMILIES ...
SURELY THIS WILL BRING OUR RELEASE FROM SLAVERY.
NINE TIMES PHARAOH HAS BROKEN HIS PROMISE TO LET US GO—WHAT WILL HE DO THIS TIME?
WHY ARE YOU PUTTING LAMB'S BLOOD ON OUR DOORPOST?
GOD TOLD MOSES IT WOULD BE A SIGN TO LET THE ANGEL OF DEATH KNOW TO PASS OVER OUR HOUSE.
THAT EVENING, EVERY HEBREW FAMILY PACKS ALL OF THEIR POSSESSIONS, HOPING THAT THEY WILL FINALLY BE ABLE TO LEAVE EGYPT. THEY EAT A MEAL CALLED THE PASSOVER BECAUSE THE ANGEL OF DEATH WILL PASS OVER THEIR HOMES.

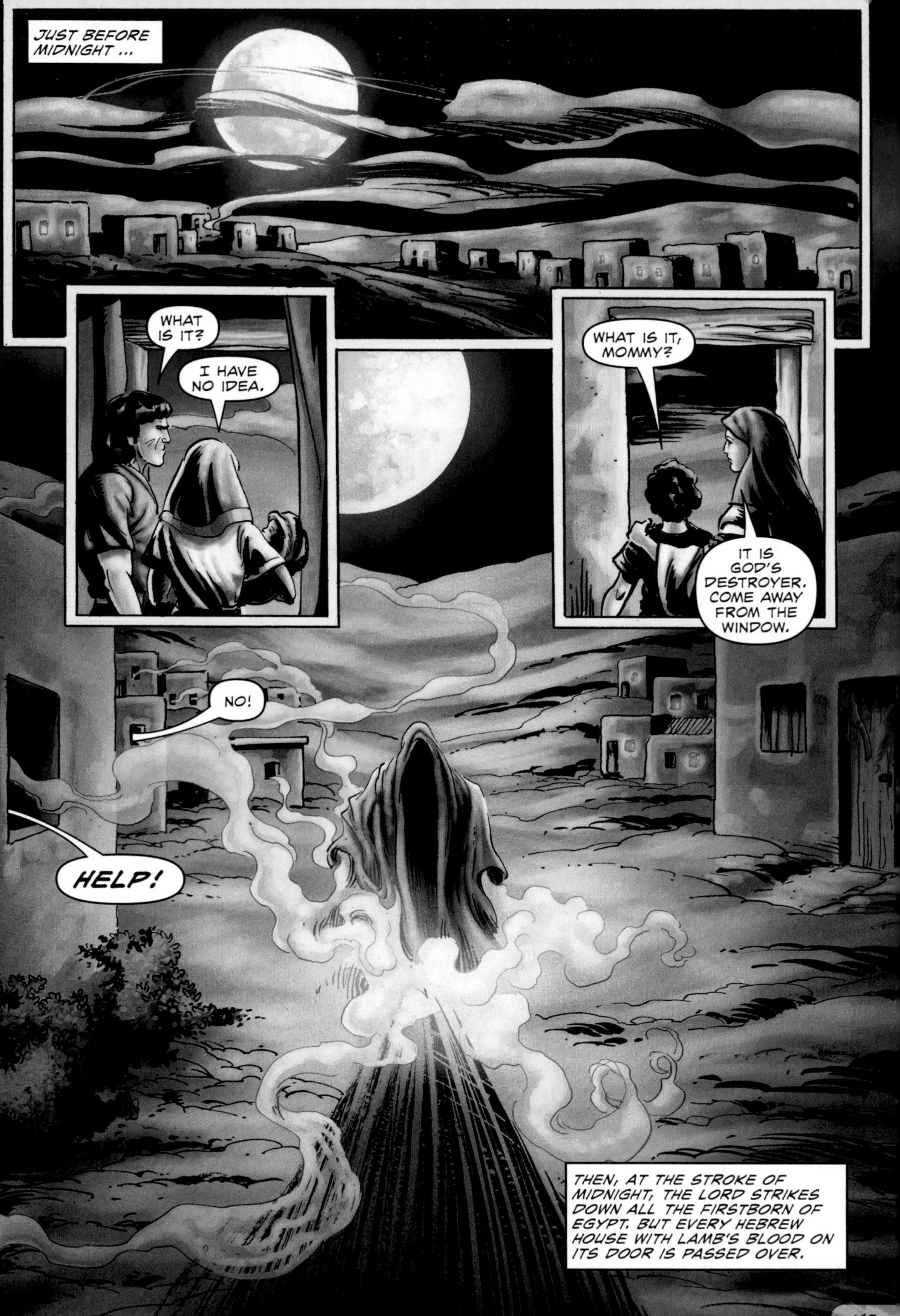
JUST BEFORE MIDNIGHT ...
WHAT IS IT?
I HAVE NO IDEA.
WHAT IS IT, MOMMY?
IT IS GOD'S DESTROYER. COME AWAY FROM THE WINDOW.
NO!
HELP!
THEN, AT THE STROKE OF MIDNIGHT, THE LORD STRIKES DOWN ALL THE FIRSTBORN OF EGYPT. BUT EVERY HEBREW HOUSE WITH LAMB'S BLOOD ON ITS DOOR IS PASSED OVER.

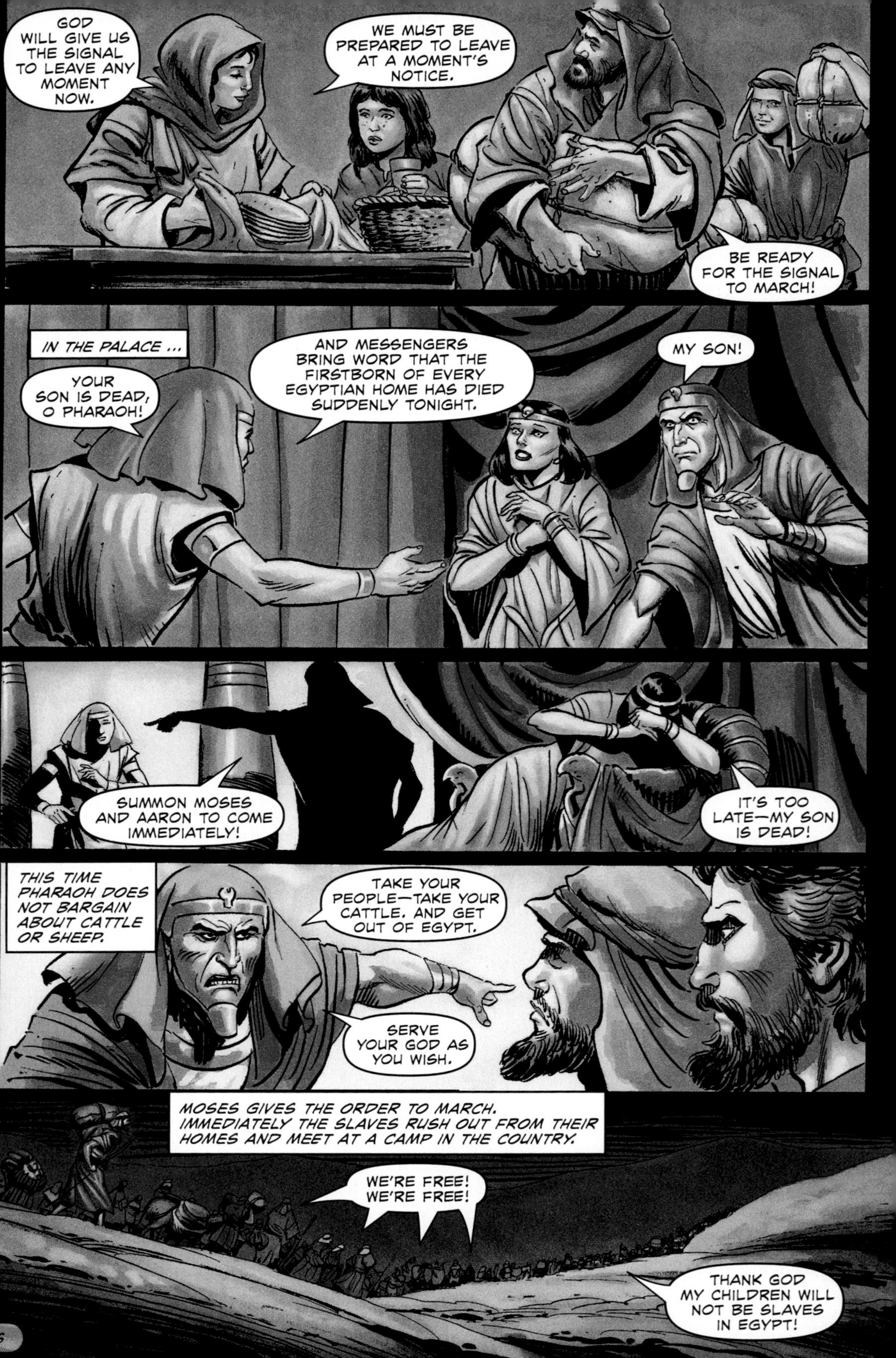

GOD WILL GIVE US THE SIGNAL TO LEAVE ANY MOMENT NOW.
WE MUST BE PREPARED TO LEAVE AT A MOMENT'S NOTICE.
BE READY FOR THE SIGNAL TO MARCH!
IN THE PALACE ...
YOUR SON IS DEAD, O PHARAOH!
AND MESSENGERS BRING WORD THAT THE FIRSTBORN OF EVERY EGYPTIAN HOME HAS DIED SUDDENLY TONIGHT.
MY SON!
SUMMON MOSES AND AARON TO COME IMMEDIATELY!
IT'S TOO LATE—MY SON IS DEAD!
THIS TIME PHARAOH DOES NOT BARGAIN ABOUT CATTLE OR SHEEP.
TAKE YOUR PEOPLE—TAKE YOUR CATTLE. AND GET OUT OF EGYPT.
SERVE YOUR GOD AS YOU WISH.
MOSES GIVES THE ORDER TO MARCH. IMMEDIATELY THE SLAVES RUSH OUT FROM THEIR HOMES AND MEET AT A CAMP IN THE COUNTRY.
WE'RE FREE! WE'RE FREE!
THANK GOD MY CHILDREN WILL NOT BE SLAVES IN EGYPT!

20,000 Egyptians Under the Sea

BASED ON EXODUS 13:17–15:21

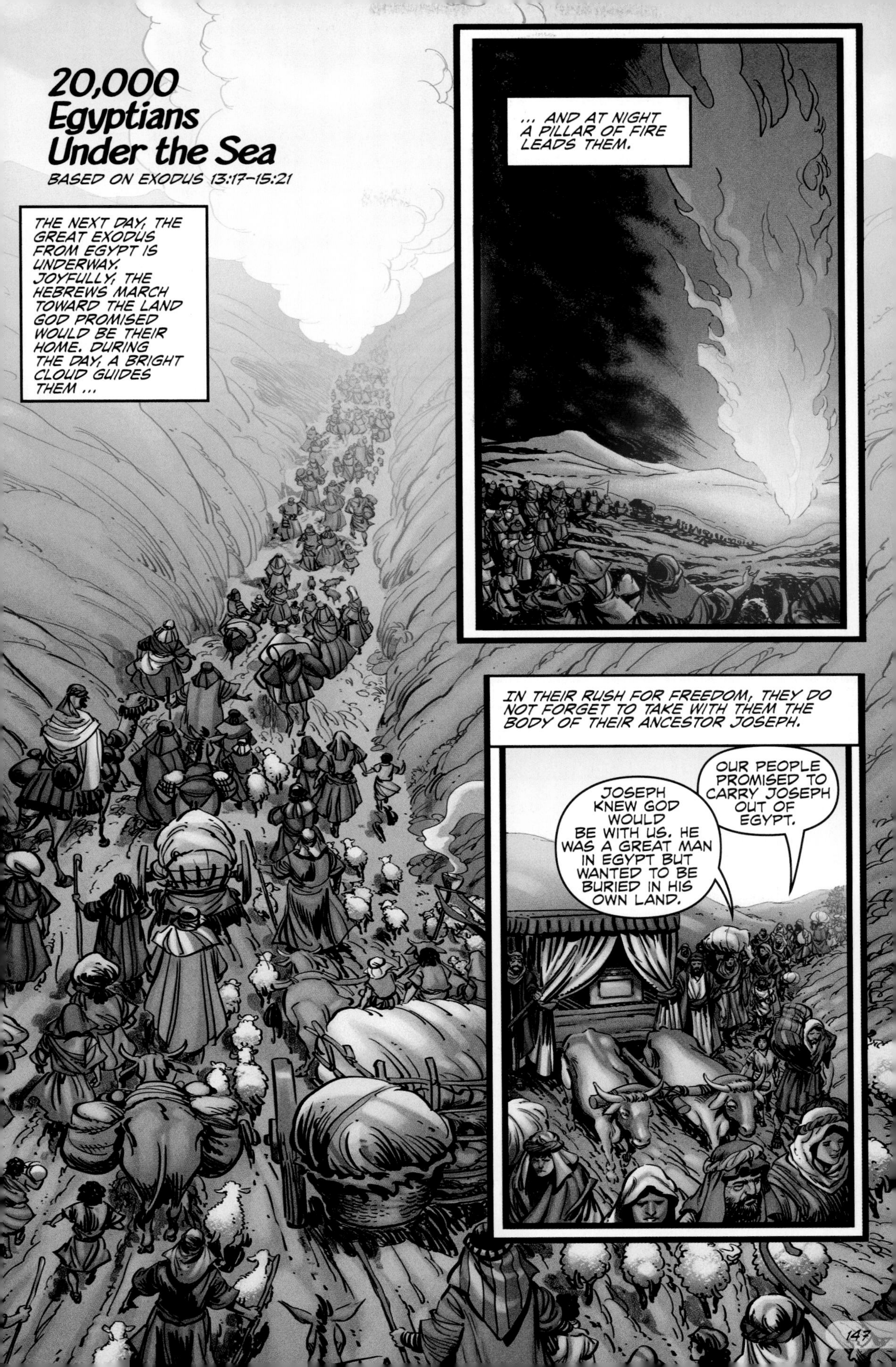
THE NEXT DAY, THE GREAT EXODUS FROM EGYPT IS UNDERWAY. JOYFULLY, THE HEBREWS MARCH TOWARD THE LAND GOD PROMISED WOULD BE THEIR HOME. DURING THE DAY, A BRIGHT CLOUD GUIDES THEM ...
... AND AT NIGHT A PILLAR OF FIRE LEADS THEM.
IN THEIR RUSH FOR FREEDOM, THEY DO NOT FORGET TO TAKE WITH THEM THE BODY OF THEIR ANCESTOR JOSEPH.
OUR PEOPLE PROMISED TO CARRY JOSEPH OUT OF EGYPT.
JOSEPH KNEW GOD WOULD BE WITH US. HE WAS A GREAT MAN IN EGYPT BUT WANTED TO BE BURIED IN HIS OWN LAND.

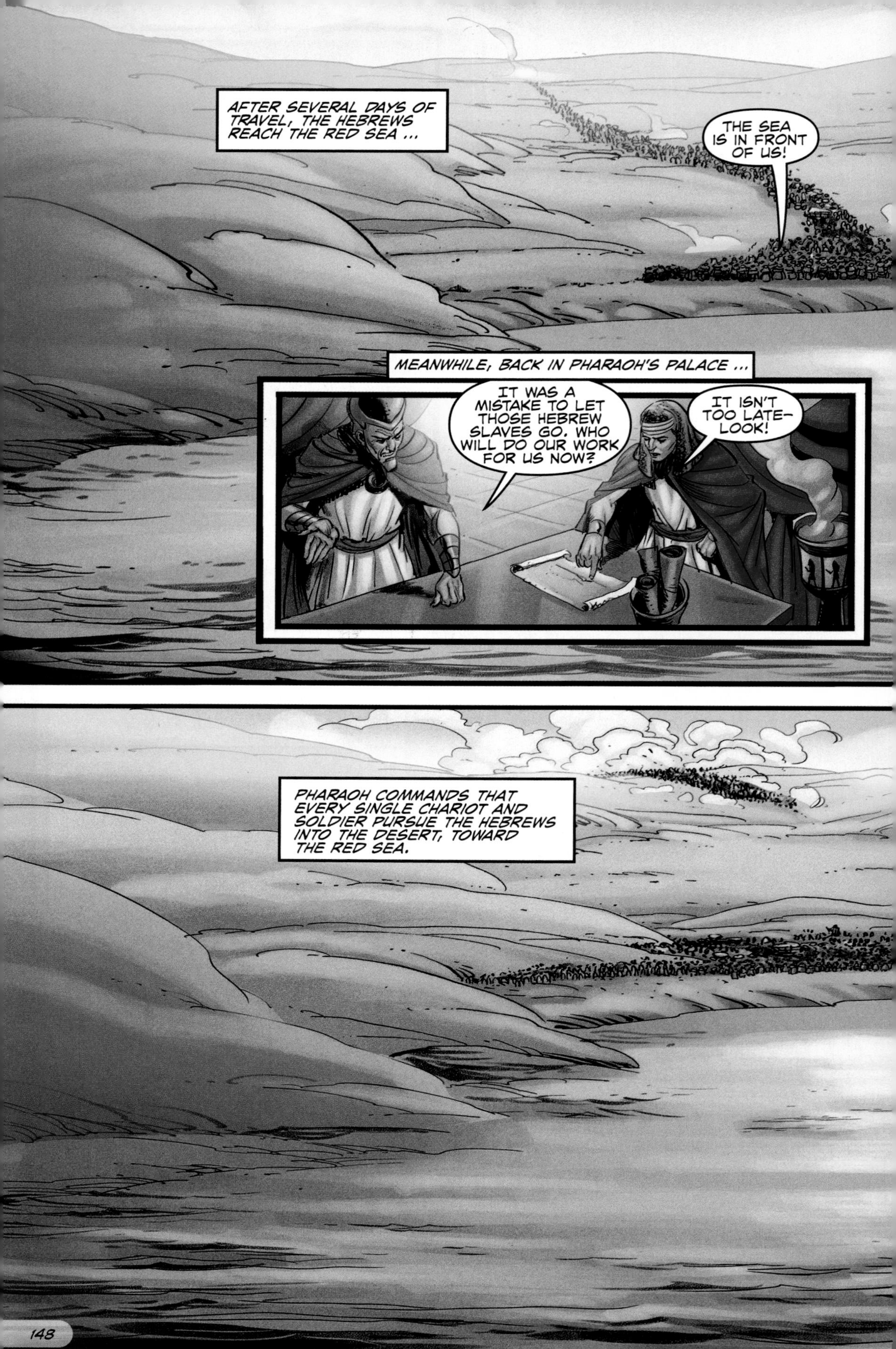
AFTER SEVERAL DAYS OF TRAVEL, THE HEBREWS REACH THE RED SEA ...
THE SEA IS IN FRONT OF US!
MEANWHILE, BACK IN PHARAOH'S PALACE ...
IT WAS A MISTAKE TO LET THOSE HEBREW SLAVES GO. WHO WILL DO OUR WORK FOR US NOW?
IT ISN'T TOO LATE— LOOK!
PHARAOH COMMANDS THAT EVERY SINGLE CHARIOT AND SOLDIER PURSUE THE HEBREWS INTO THE DESERT, TOWARD THE RED SEA.

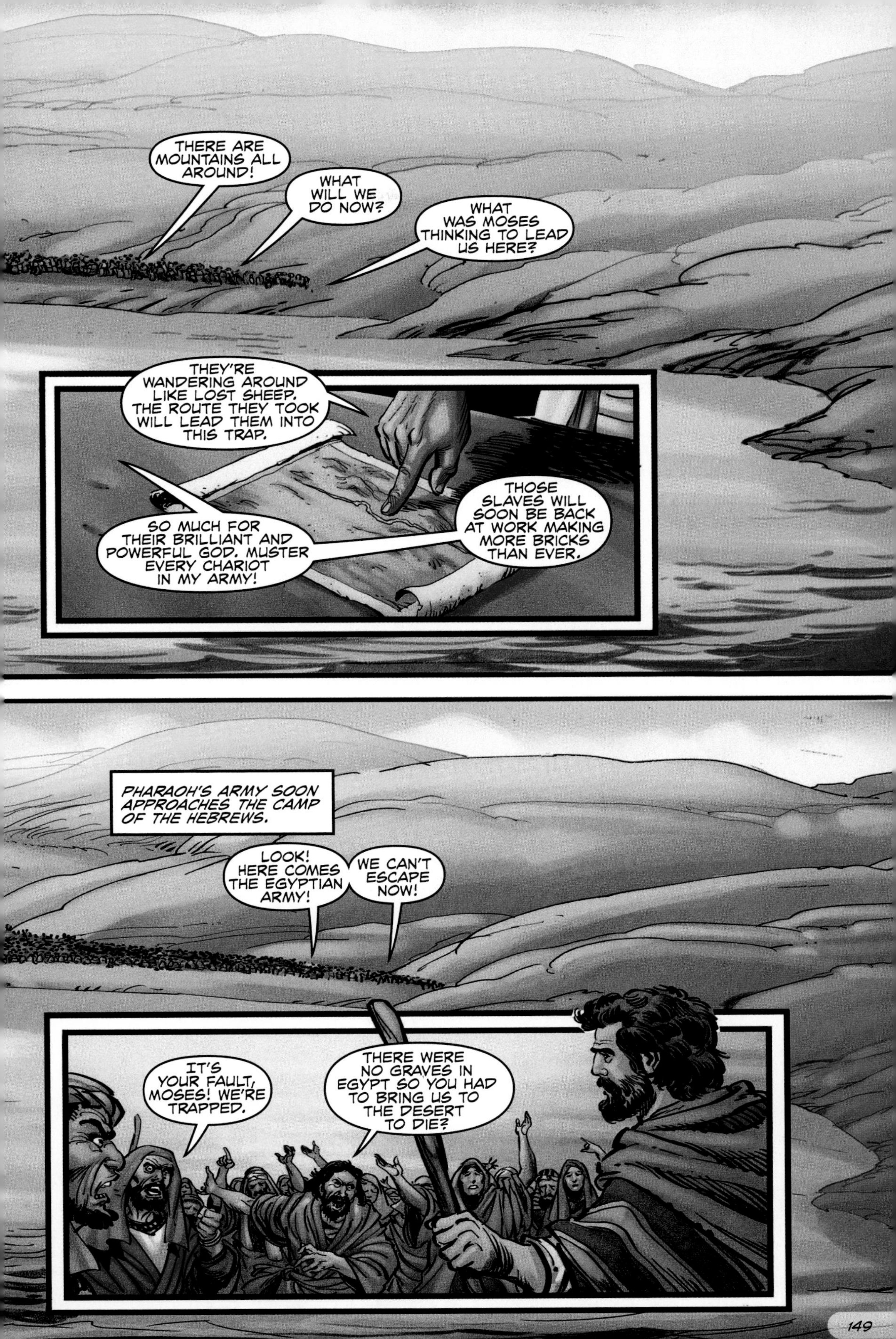
THERE ARE MOUNTAINS ALL AROUND!
WHAT WILL WE DO NOW?
WHAT WAS MOSES THINKING TO LEAD US HERE?
THEY'RE WANDERING AROUND LIKE LOST SHEEP. THE ROUTE THEY TOOK WILL LEAD THEM INTO THIS TRAP.
SO MUCH FOR THEIR BRILLIANT AND POWERFUL GOD. MUSTER EVERY CHARIOT IN MY ARMY!
THOSE SLAVES WILL SOON BE BACK AT WORK MAKING MORE BRICKS THAN EVER.
PHARAOH'S ARMY SOON APPROACHES THE CAMP OF THE HEBREWS.
LOOK! HERE COMES THE EGYPTIAN ARMY!
WE CAN'T ESCAPE NOW!
IT'S YOUR FAULT, MOSES! WE'RE TRAPPED.
THERE WERE NO GRAVES IN EGYPT SO YOU HAD TO BRING US TO THE DESERT TO DIE?

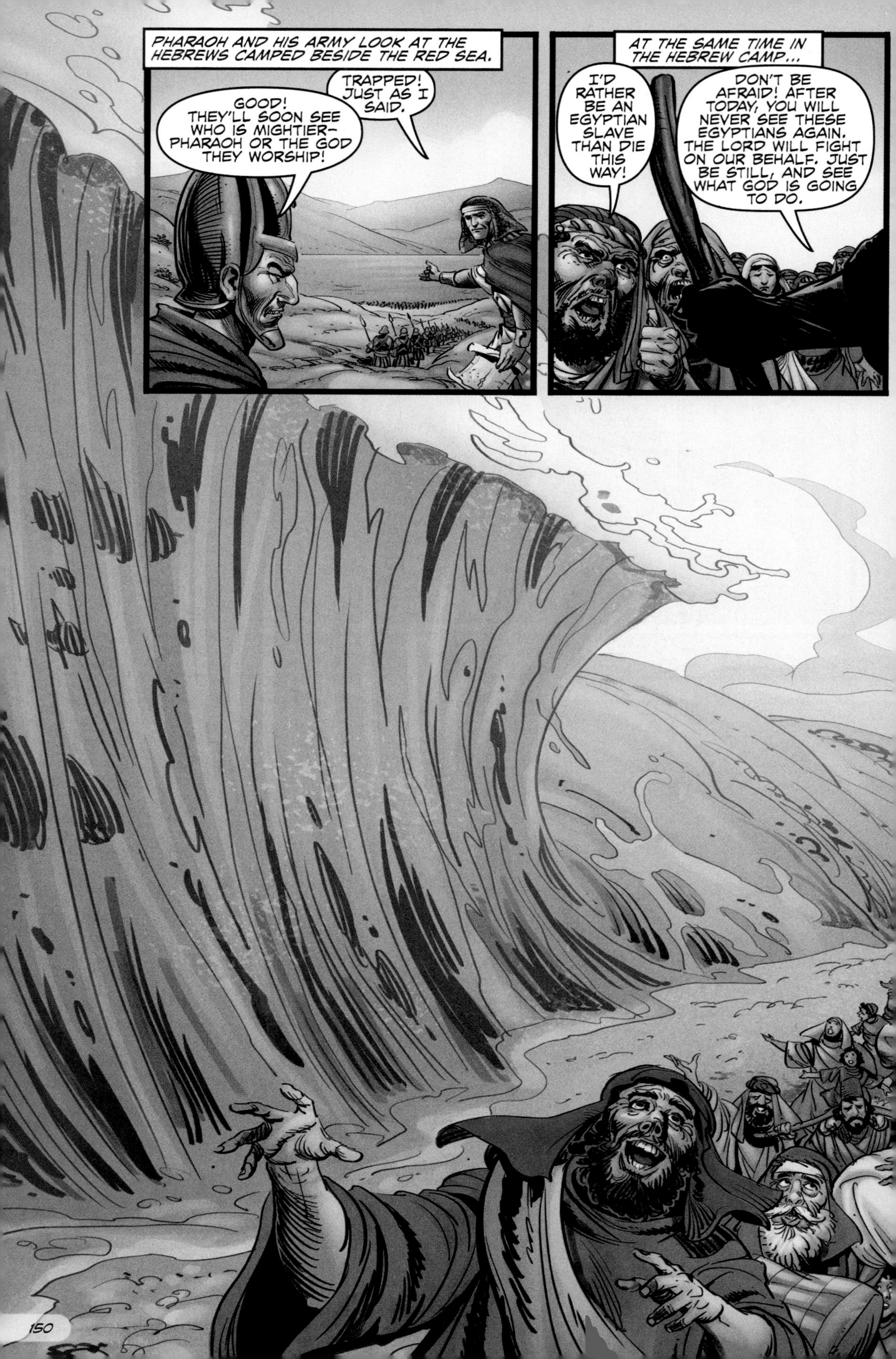
PHARAOH AND HIS ARMY LOOK AT THE HEBREWS CAMPED BESIDE THE RED SEA.
TRAPPED! JUST AS I SAID.
GOOD! THEY'LL SOON SEE WHO IS MIGHTIER—PHARAOH OR THE GOD THEY WORSHIP!
AT THE SAME TIME IN THE HEBREW CAMP...
I'D RATHER BE AN EGYPTIAN SLAVE THAN DIE THIS WAY!
DON'T BE AFRAID! AFTER TODAY, YOU WILL NEVER SEE THESE EGYPTIANS AGAIN. THE LORD WILL FIGHT ON OUR BEHALF. JUST BE STILL, AND SEE WHAT GOD IS GOING TO DO.

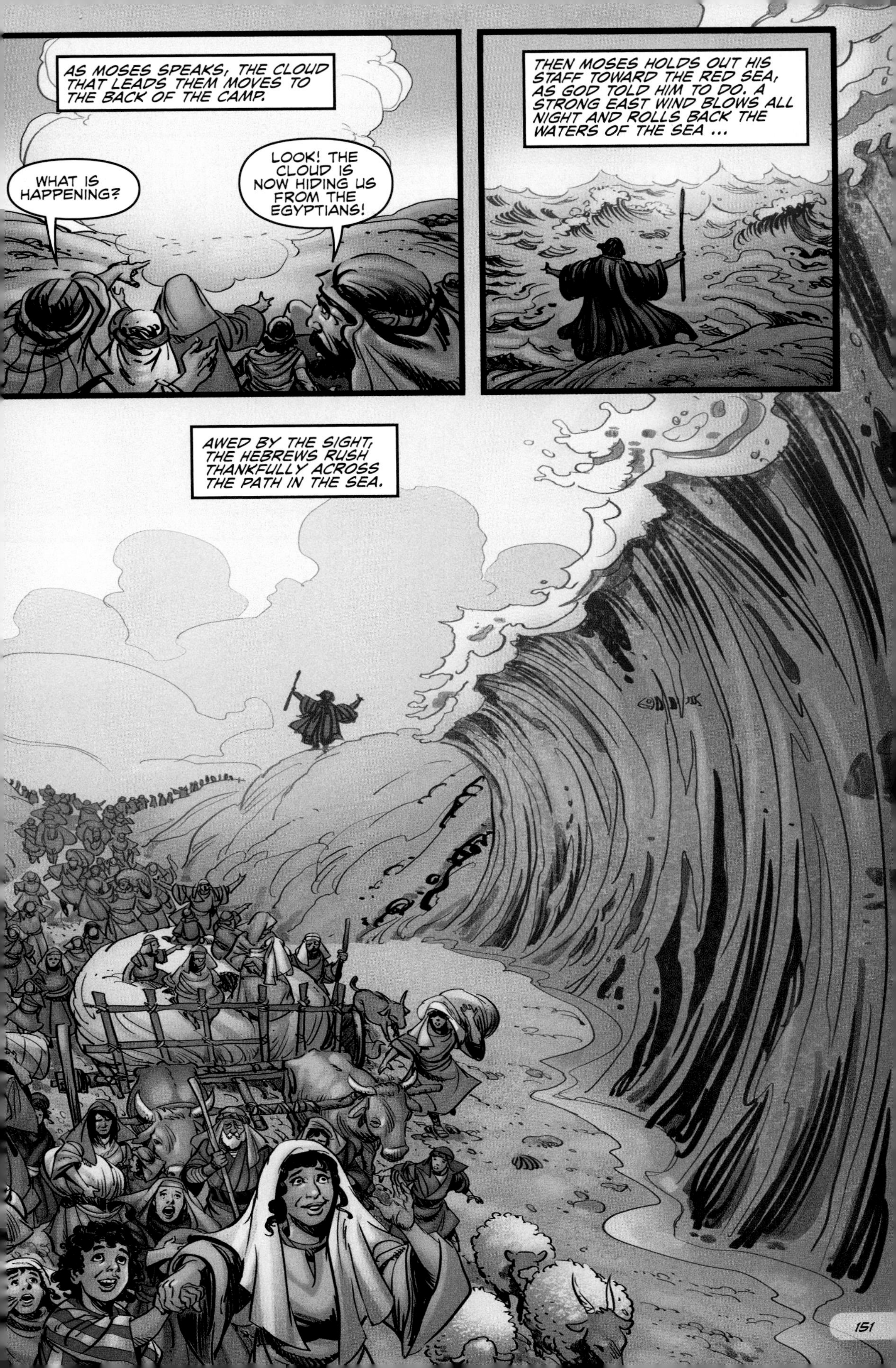
AS MOSES SPEAKS, THE CLOUD THAT LEADS THEM MOVES TO THE BACK OF THE CAMP.
WHAT IS HAPPENING?
LOOK! THE CLOUD IS NOW HIDING US FROM THE EGYPTIANS!
THEN MOSES HOLDS OUT HIS STAFF TOWARD THE RED SEA, AS GOD TOLD HIM TO DO. A STRONG EAST WIND BLOWS ALL NIGHT AND ROLLS BACK THE WATERS OF THE SEA ...
AWED BY THE SIGHT, THE HEBREWS RUSH THANKFULLY ACROSS THE PATH IN THE SEA.

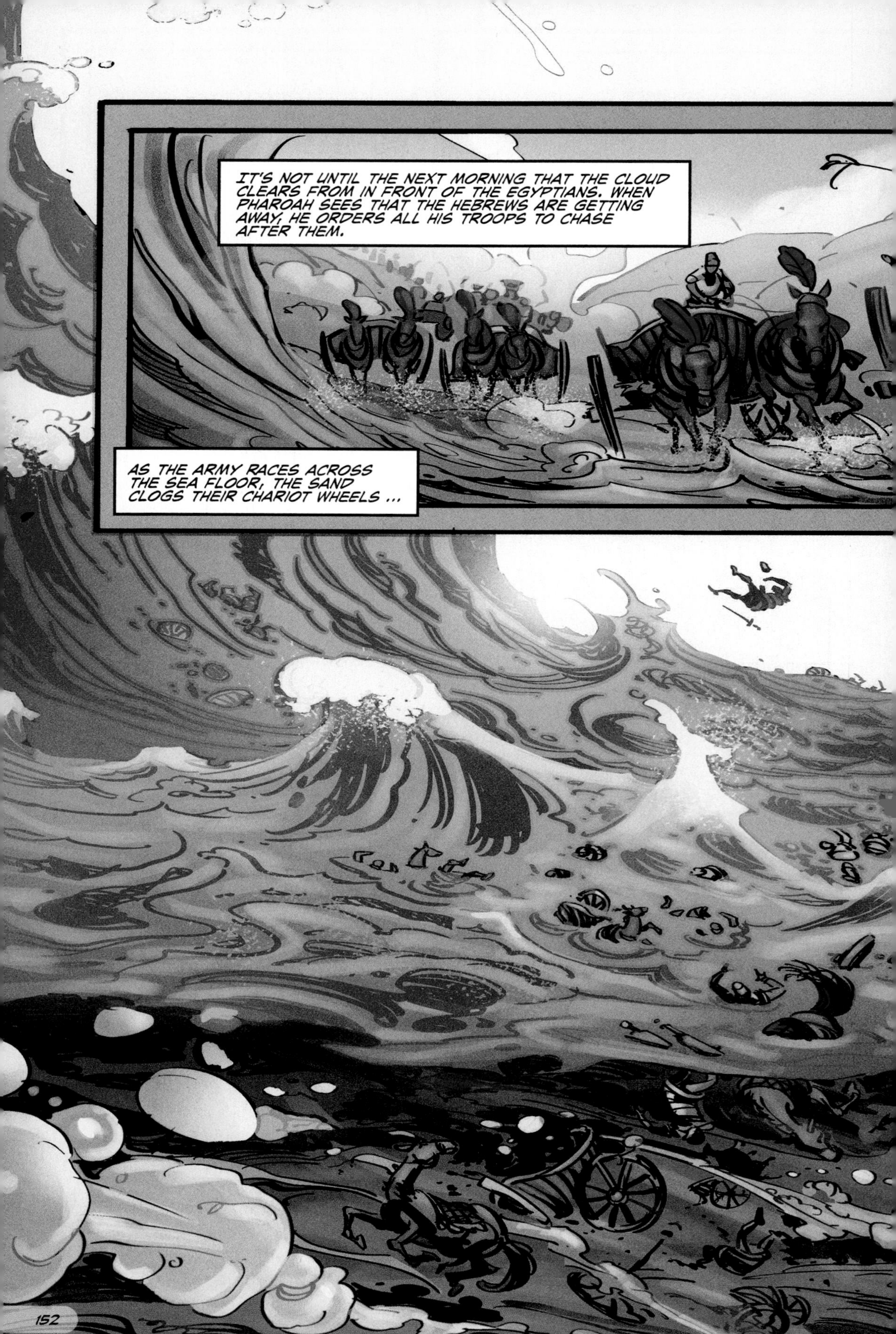
IT'S NOT UNTIL THE NEXT MORNING THAT THE CLOUD CLEARS FROM IN FRONT OF THE EGYPTIANS. WHEN PHAROAH SEES THAT THE HEBREWS ARE GETTING AWAY, HE ORDERS ALL HIS TROOPS TO CHASE AFTER THEM.
AS THE ARMY RACES ACROSS THE SEA FLOOR, THE SAND CLOGS THEIR CHARIOT WHEELS ...

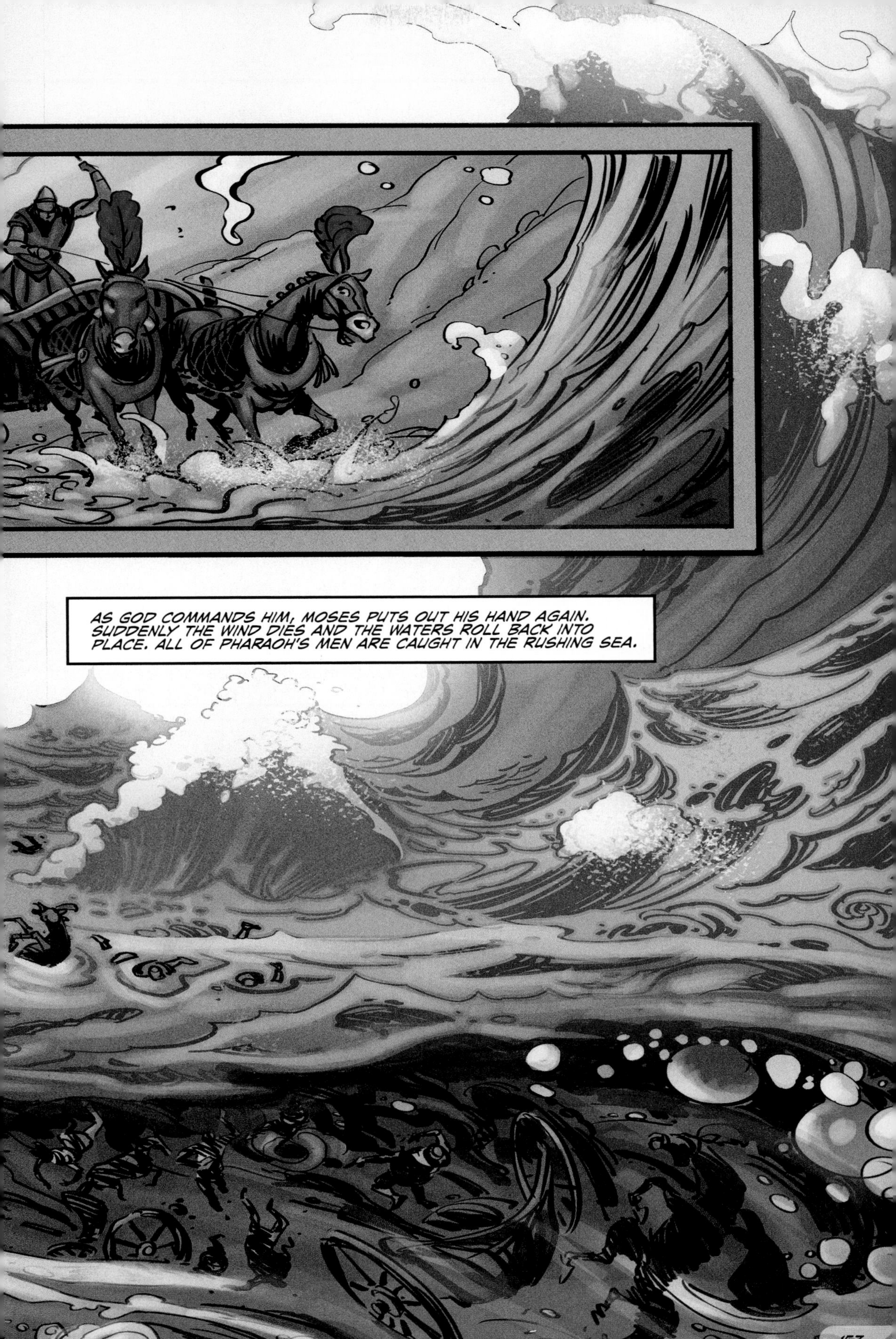
AS GOD COMMANDS HIM, MOSES PUTS OUT HIS HAND AGAIN. SUDDENLY THE WIND DIES AND THE WATERS ROLL BACK INTO PLACE. ALL OF PHARAOH'S MEN ARE CAUGHT IN THE RUSHING SEA.

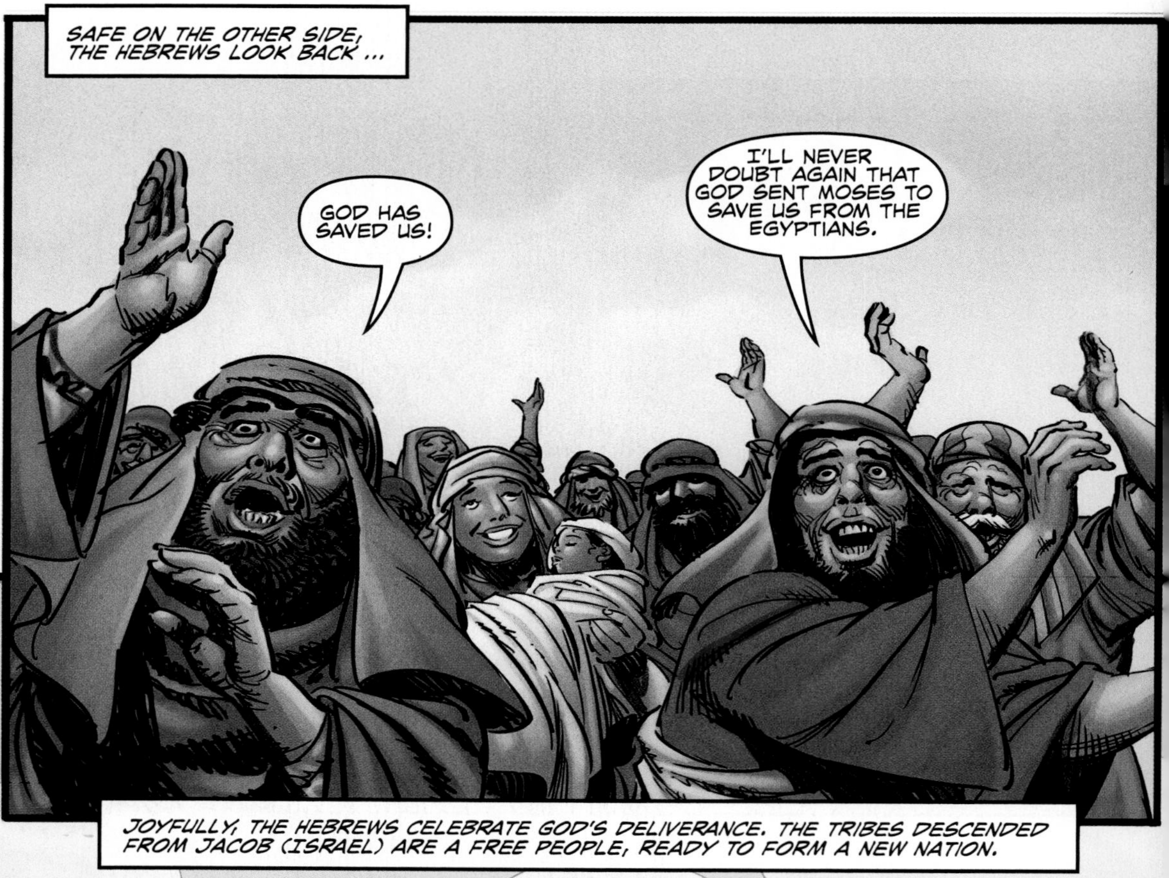
SAFE ON THE OTHER SIDE, THE HEBREWS LOOK BACK ...
GOD HAS SAVED US!
I'LL NEVER DOUBT AGAIN THAT GOD SENT MOSES TO SAVE US FROM THE EGYPTIANS.
JOYFULLY, THE HEBREWS CELEBRATE GOD'S DELIVERANCE. THE TRIBES DESCENDED FROM JACOB (ISRAEL) ARE A FREE PEOPLE, READY TO FORM A NEW NATION.

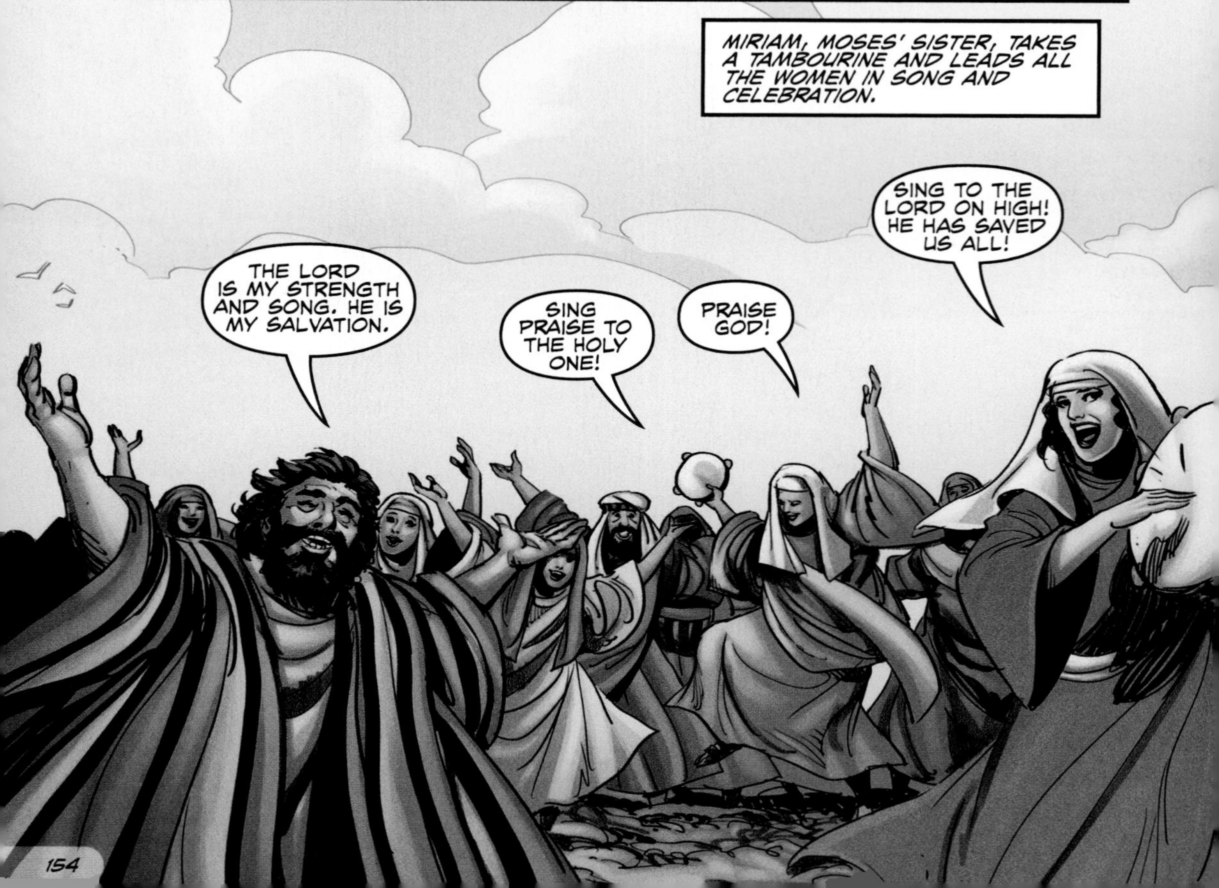
MIRIAM, MOSES' SISTER, TAKES A TAMBOURINE AND LEADS ALL THE WOMEN IN SONG AND CELEBRATION.
THE LORD IS MY STRENGTH AND SONG. HE IS MY SALVATION.
SING PRAISE TO THE HOLY ONE!
PRAISE GOD!
SING TO THE LORD ON HIGH! HE HAS SAVED US ALL!

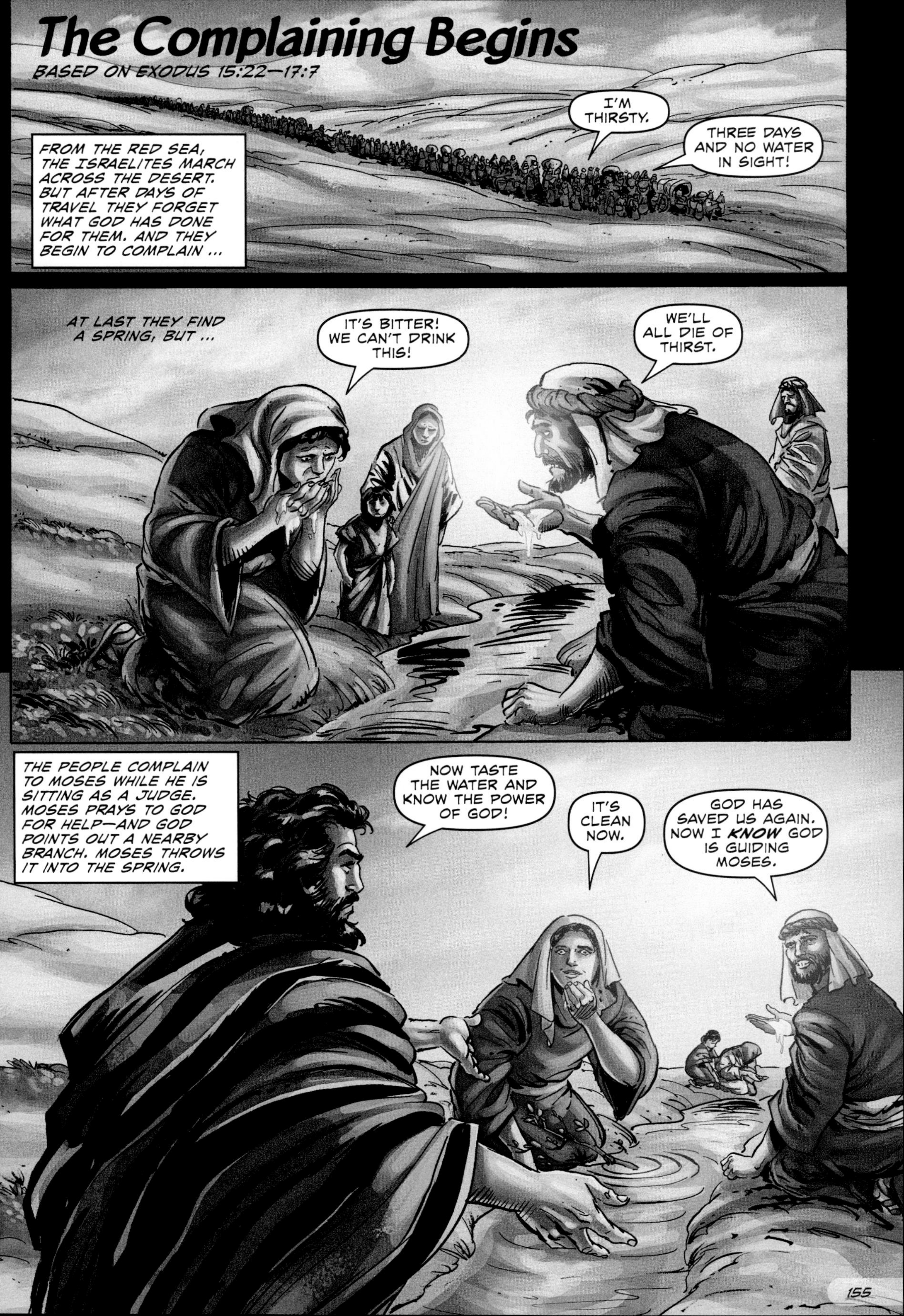
The Complaining Begins
BASED ON EXODUS 15:22—17:7
FROM THE RED SEA, THE ISRAELITES MARCH ACROSS THE DESERT. BUT AFTER DAYS OF TRAVEL THEY FORGET WHAT GOD HAS DONE FOR THEM. AND THEY BEGIN TO COMPLAIN ...
I'M THIRSTY.
THREE DAYS AND NO WATER IN SIGHT!
AT LAST THEY FIND A SPRING, BUT ...
IT'S BITTER! WE CAN'T DRINK THIS!
WE'LL ALL DIE OF THIRST.
THE PEOPLE COMPLAIN TO MOSES WHILE HE IS SITTING AS A JUDGE. MOSES PRAYS TO GOD FOR HELP—AND GOD POINTS OUT A NEARBY BRANCH. MOSES THROWS IT INTO THE SPRING.
NOW TASTE THE WATER AND KNOW THE POWER OF GOD!
IT'S CLEAN NOW.
GOD HAS SAVED US AGAIN. NOW I KNOW GOD IS GUIDING MOSES.

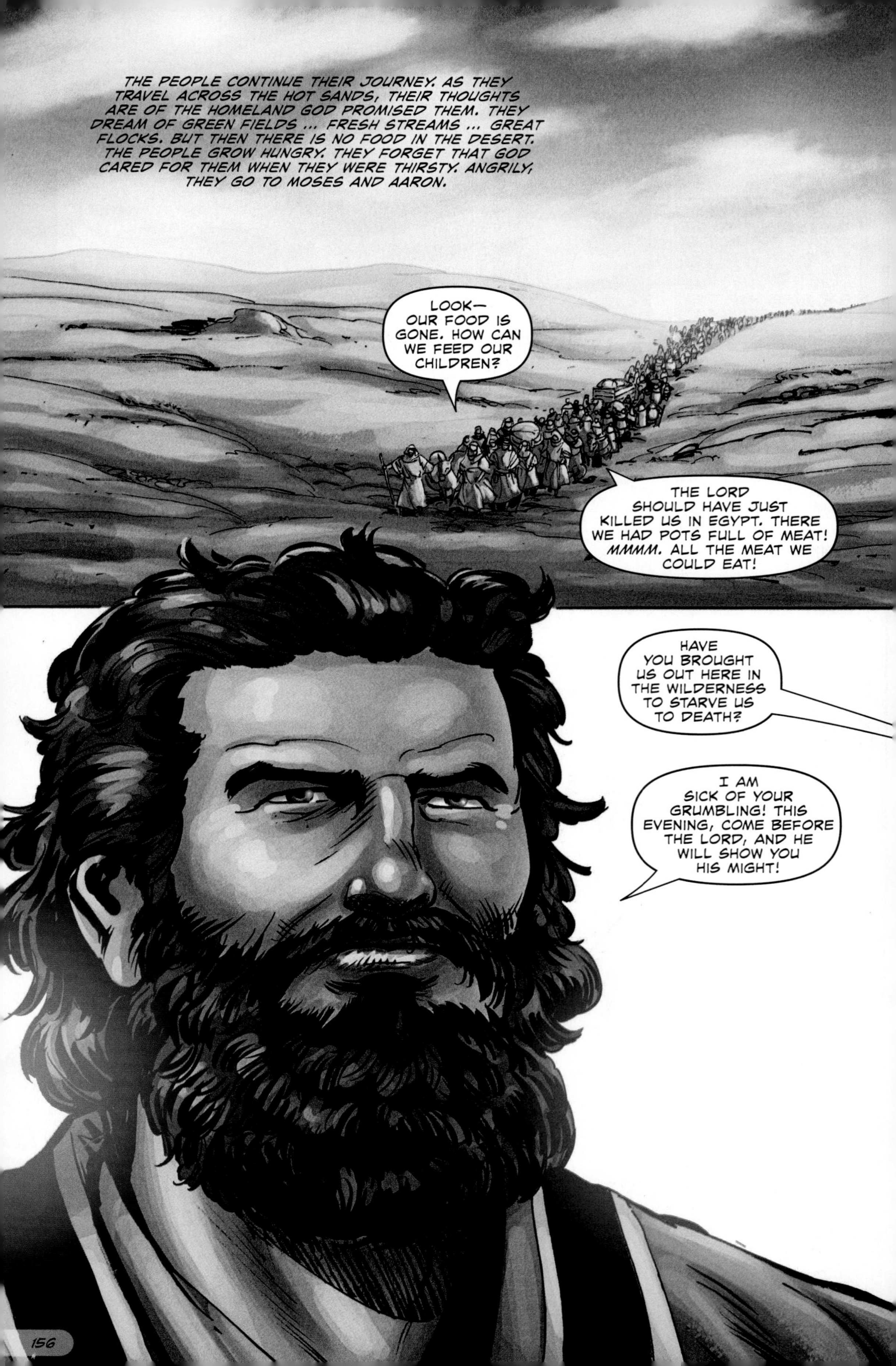
THE PEOPLE CONTINUE THEIR JOURNEY. AS THEY TRAVEL ACROSS THE HOT SANDS, THEIR THOUGHTS ARE OF THE HOMELAND GOD PROMISED THEM. THEY DREAM OF GREEN FIELDS ... FRESH STREAMS ... GREAT FLOCKS. BUT THEN THERE IS NO FOOD IN THE DESERT. THE PEOPLE GROW HUNGRY. THEY FORGET THAT GOD CARED FOR THEM WHEN THEY WERE THIRSTY. ANGRILY, THEY GO TO MOSES AND AARON.
LOOK— OUR FOOD IS GONE. HOW CAN WE FEED OUR CHILDREN?
THE LORD SHOULD HAVE JUST KILLED US IN EGYPT. THERE WE HAD POTS FULL OF MEAT! MMMM. ALL THE MEAT WE COULD EAT!
HAVE YOU BROUGHT US OUT HERE IN THE WILDERNESS TO STARVE US TO DEATH?
I AM SICK OF YOUR GRUMBLING! THIS EVENING, COME BEFORE THE LORD, AND HE WILL SHOW YOU HIS MIGHT!

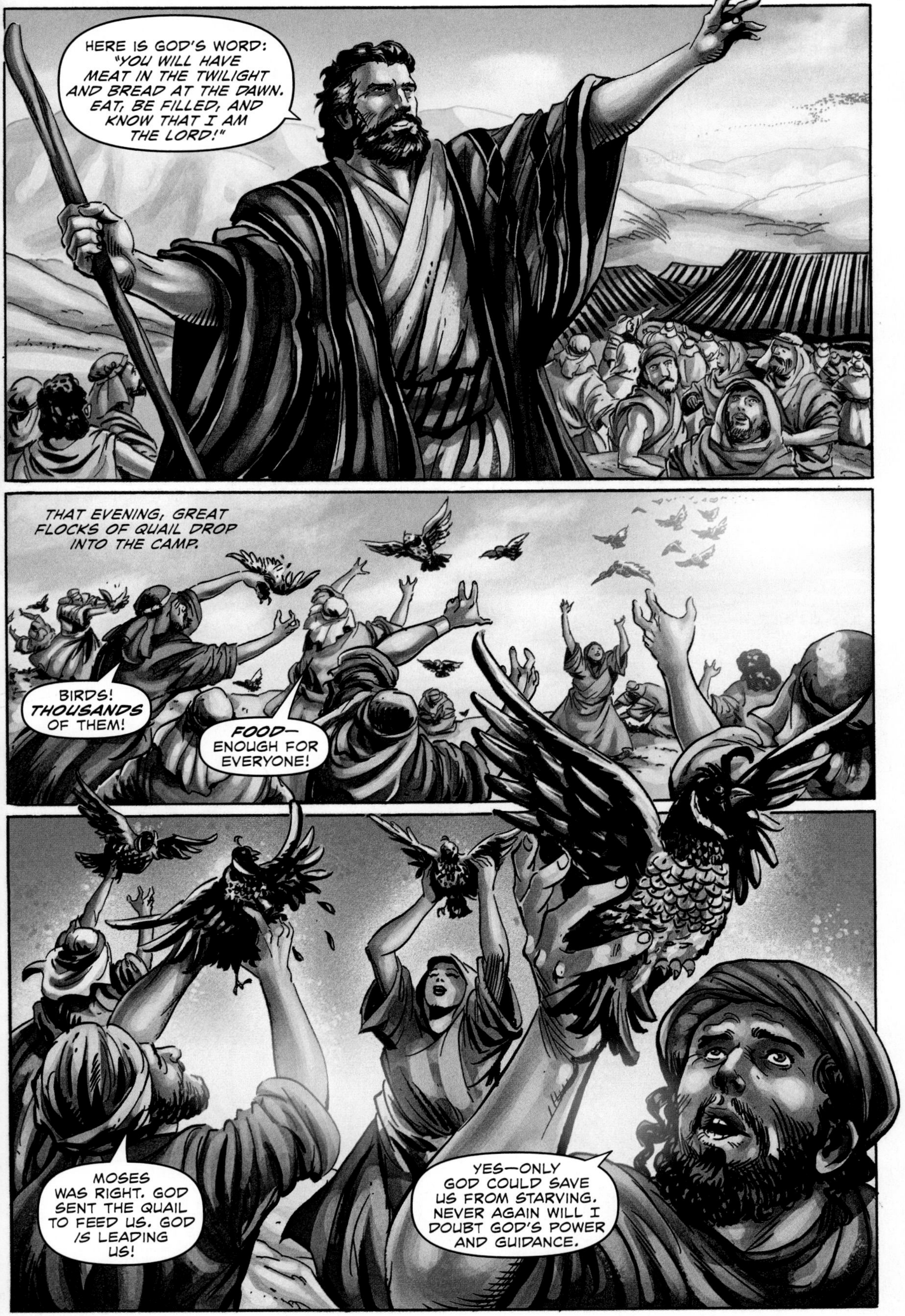
HERE IS GOD'S WORD: "YOU WILL HAVE MEAT IN THE TWILIGHT AND BREAD AT THE DAWN. EAT, BE FILLED, AND KNOW THAT I AM THE LORD!"
THAT EVENING, GREAT FLOCKS OF QUAIL DROP INTO THE CAMP.
BIRDS! THOUSANDS OF THEM!
FOOD— ENOUGH FOR EVERYONE!
MOSES WAS RIGHT. GOD SENT THE QUAIL TO FEED US. GOD IS LEADING US!
YES—ONLY GOD COULD SAVE US FROM STARVING. NEVER AGAIN WILL I DOUBT GOD'S POWER AND GUIDANCE.

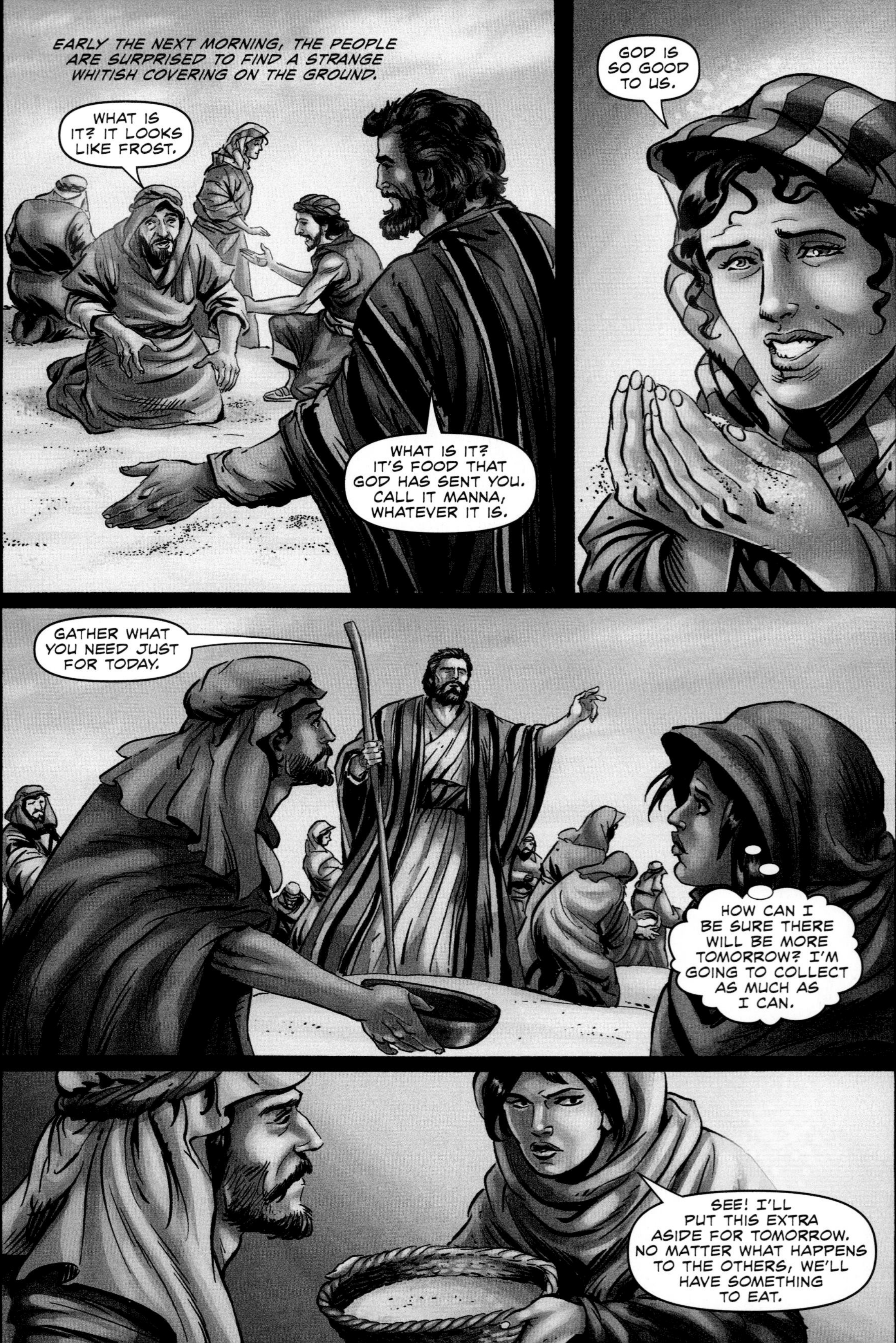
EARLY THE NEXT MORNING, THE PEOPLE ARE SURPRISED TO FIND A STRANGE WHITISH COVERING ON THE GROUND.
WHAT IS IT? IT LOOKS LIKE FROST.
WHAT IS IT? IT'S FOOD THAT GOD HAS SENT YOU. CALL IT MANNA, WHATEVER IT IS.
GOD IS SO GOOD TO US.
GATHER WHAT YOU NEED JUST FOR TODAY.
HOW CAN I BE SURE THERE WILL BE MORE TOMORROW? I'M GOING TO COLLECT AS MUCH AS I CAN.
SEE! I'LL PUT THIS EXTRA ASIDE FOR TOMORROW. NO MATTER WHAT HAPPENS TO THE OTHERS, WE'LL HAVE SOMETHING TO EAT.

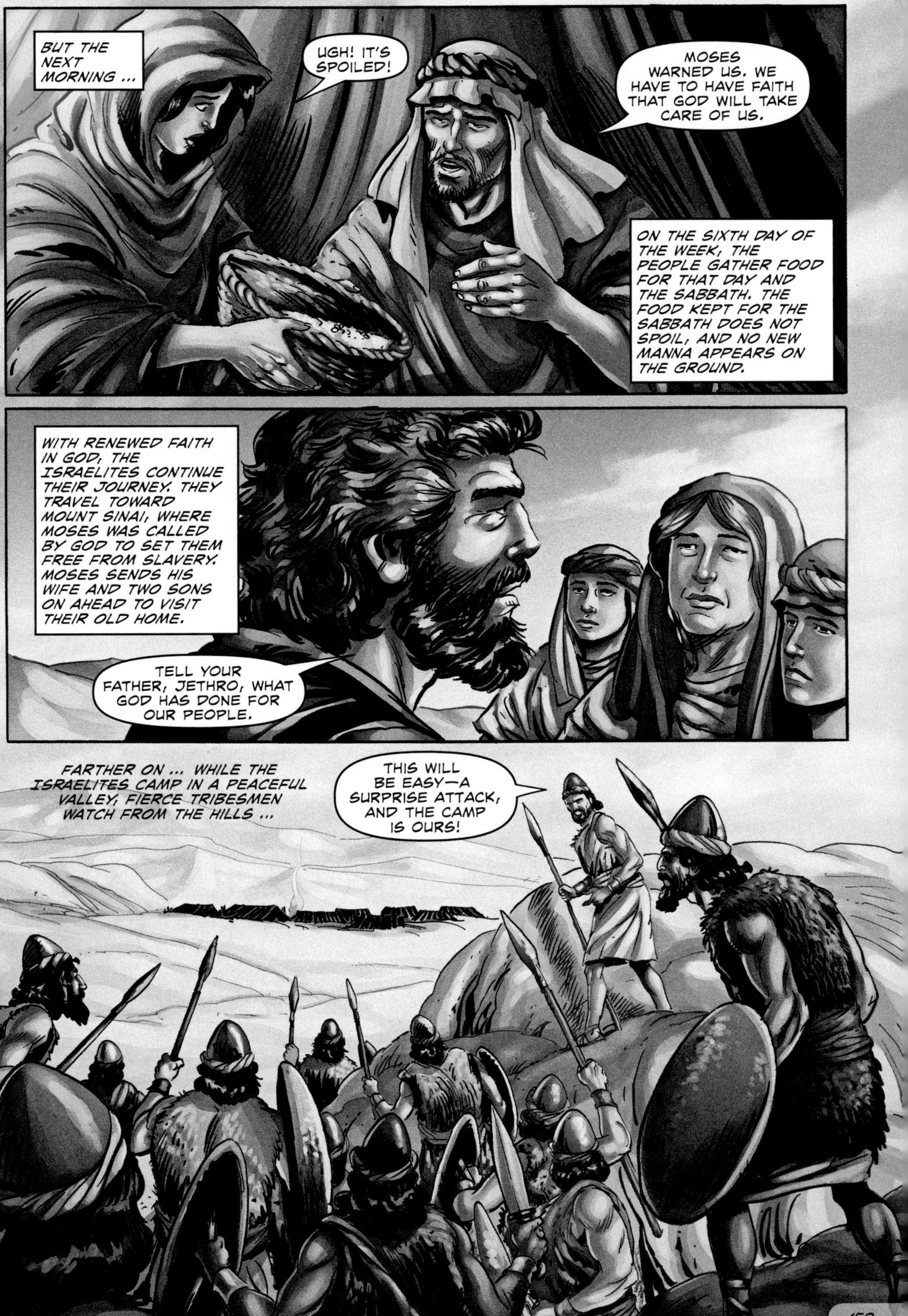
BUT THE NEXT MORNING ...
UGH! IT'S SPOILED!
MOSES WARNED US. WE HAVE TO HAVE FAITH THAT GOD WILL TAKE CARE OF US.
ON THE SIXTH DAY OF THE WEEK, THE PEOPLE GATHER FOOD FOR THAT DAY AND THE SABBATH. THE FOOD KEPT FOR THE SABBATH DOES NOT SPOIL, AND NO NEW MANNA APPEARS ON THE GROUND.
WITH RENEWED FAITH IN GOD, THE ISRAELITES CONTINUE THEIR JOURNEY. THEY TRAVEL TOWARD MOUNT SINAI, WHERE MOSES WAS CALLED BY GOD TO SET THEM FREE FROM SLAVERY. MOSES SENDS HIS WIFE AND TWO SONS ON AHEAD TO VISIT THEIR OLD HOME.
TELL YOUR FATHER, JETHRO, WHAT GOD HAS DONE FOR OUR PEOPLE.
FARTHER ON ... WHILE THE ISRAELITES CAMP IN A PEACEFUL VALLEY, FIERCE TRIBESMEN WATCH FROM THE HILLS ...
THIS WILL BE EASY—A SURPRISE ATTACK, AND THE CAMP IS OURS!

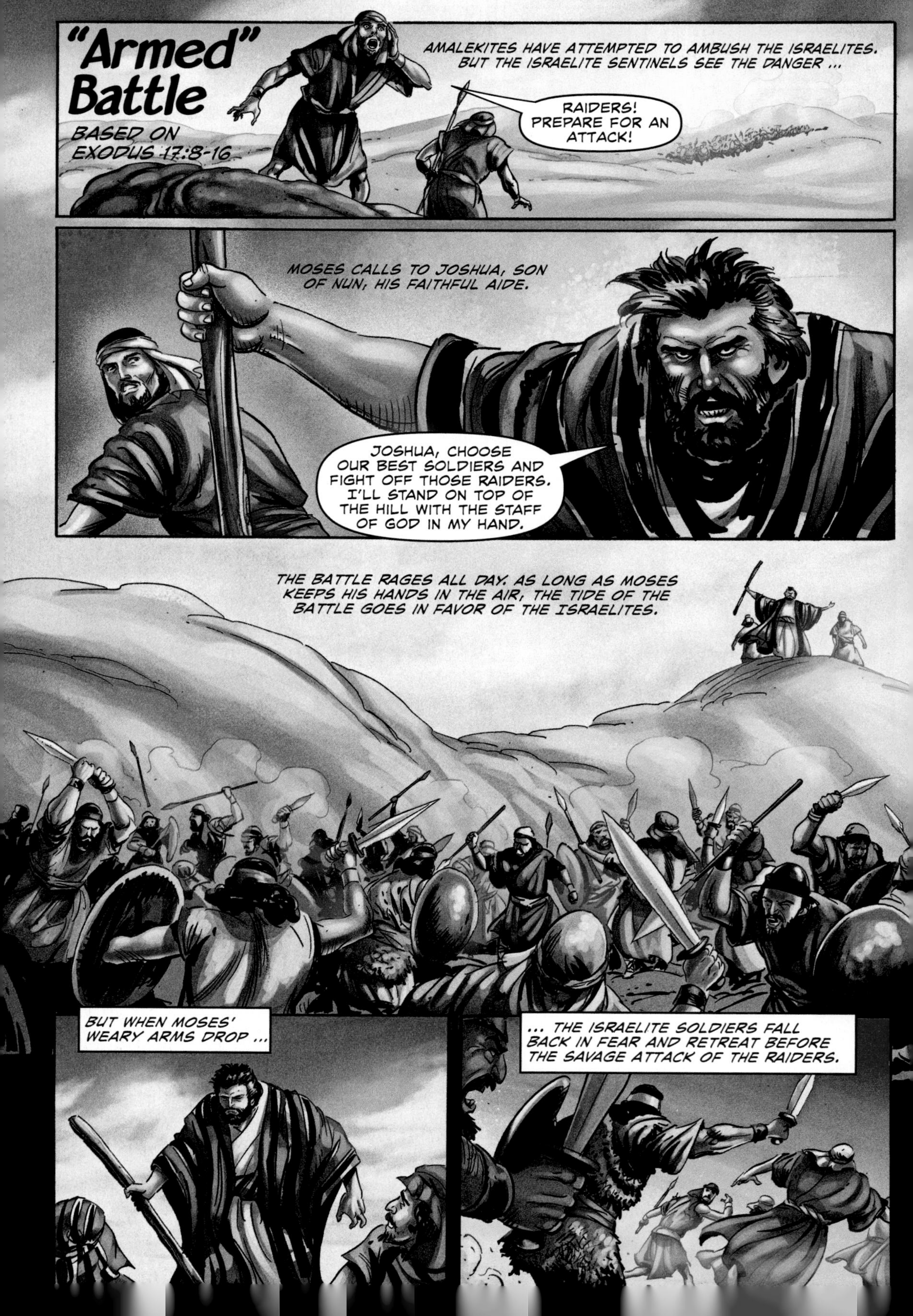

"Armed" Battle
BASED ON EXODUS 17:8-16
AMALEKITES HAVE ATTEMPTED TO AMBUSH THE ISRAELITES. BUT THE ISRAELITE SENTINELS SEE THE DANGER ...
RAIDERS! PREPARE FOR AN ATTACK!
MOSES CALLS TO JOSHUA, SON OF NUN, HIS FAITHFUL AIDE.
JOSHUA, CHOOSE OUR BEST SOLDIERS AND FIGHT OFF THOSE RAIDERS. I'LL STAND ON TOP OF THE HILL WITH THE STAFF OF GOD IN MY HAND.
THE BATTLE RAGES ALL DAY. AS LONG AS MOSES KEEPS HIS HANDS IN THE AIR, THE TIDE OF THE BATTLE GOES IN FAVOR OF THE ISRAELITES.
BUT WHEN MOSES' WEARY ARMS DROP ...
... THE ISRAELITE SOLDIERS FALL BACK IN FEAR AND RETREAT BEFORE THE SAVAGE ATTACK OF THE RAIDERS.

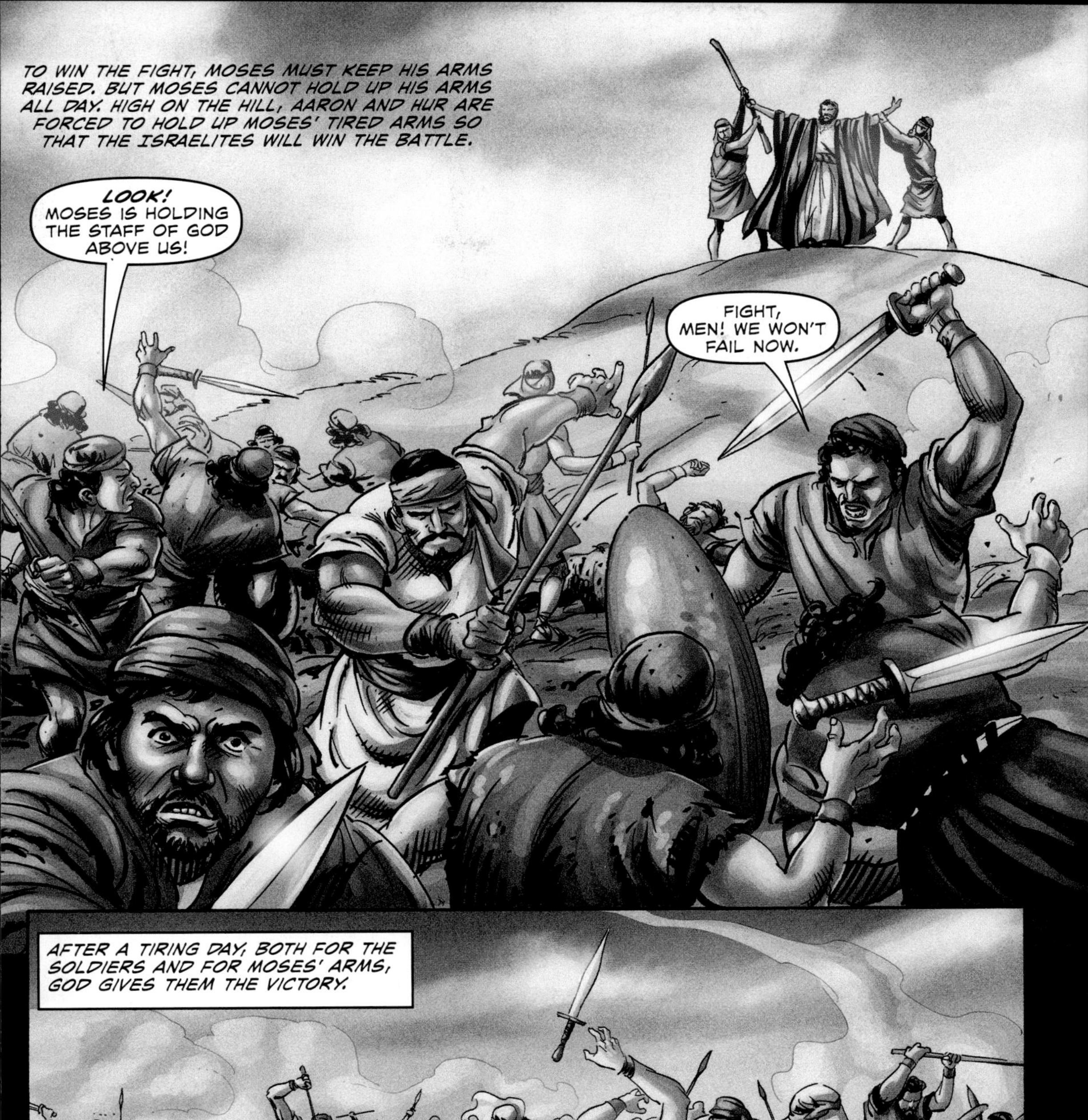
TO WIN THE FIGHT, MOSES MUST KEEP HIS ARMS RAISED. BUT MOSES CANNOT HOLD UP HIS ARMS ALL DAY. HIGH ON THE HILL, AARON AND HUR ARE FORCED TO HOLD UP MOSES' TIRED ARMS SO THAT THE ISRAELITES WILL WIN THE BATTLE.
LOOK! MOSES IS HOLDING THE STAFF OF GOD ABOVE US!
FIGHT, MEN! WE WON'T FAIL NOW.

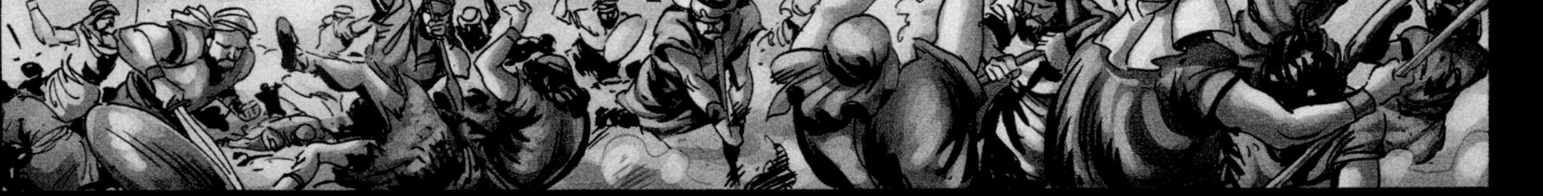
AFTER A TIRING DAY, BOTH FOR THE SOLDIERS AND FOR MOSES' ARMS, GOD GIVES THEM THE VICTORY.

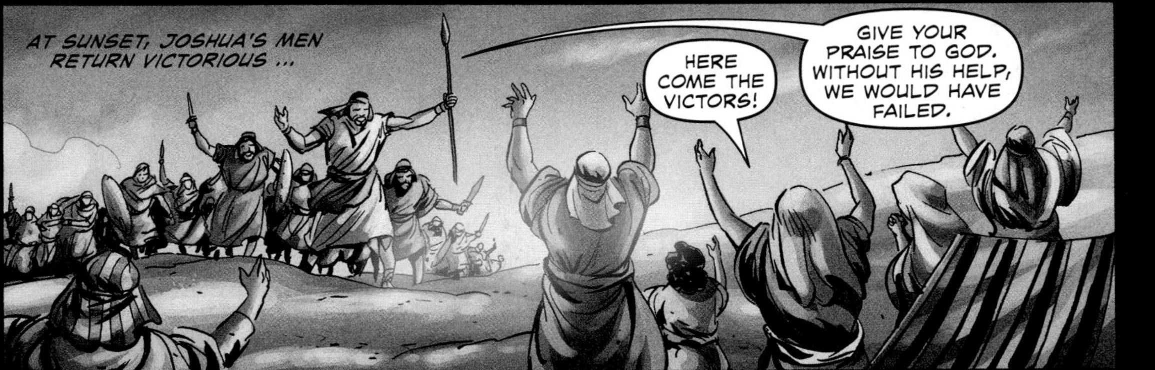
AT SUNSET, JOSHUA'S MEN RETURN VICTORIOUS ...
HERE COME THE VICTORS!
GIVE YOUR PRAISE TO GOD. WITHOUT HIS HELP, WE WOULD HAVE FAILED.

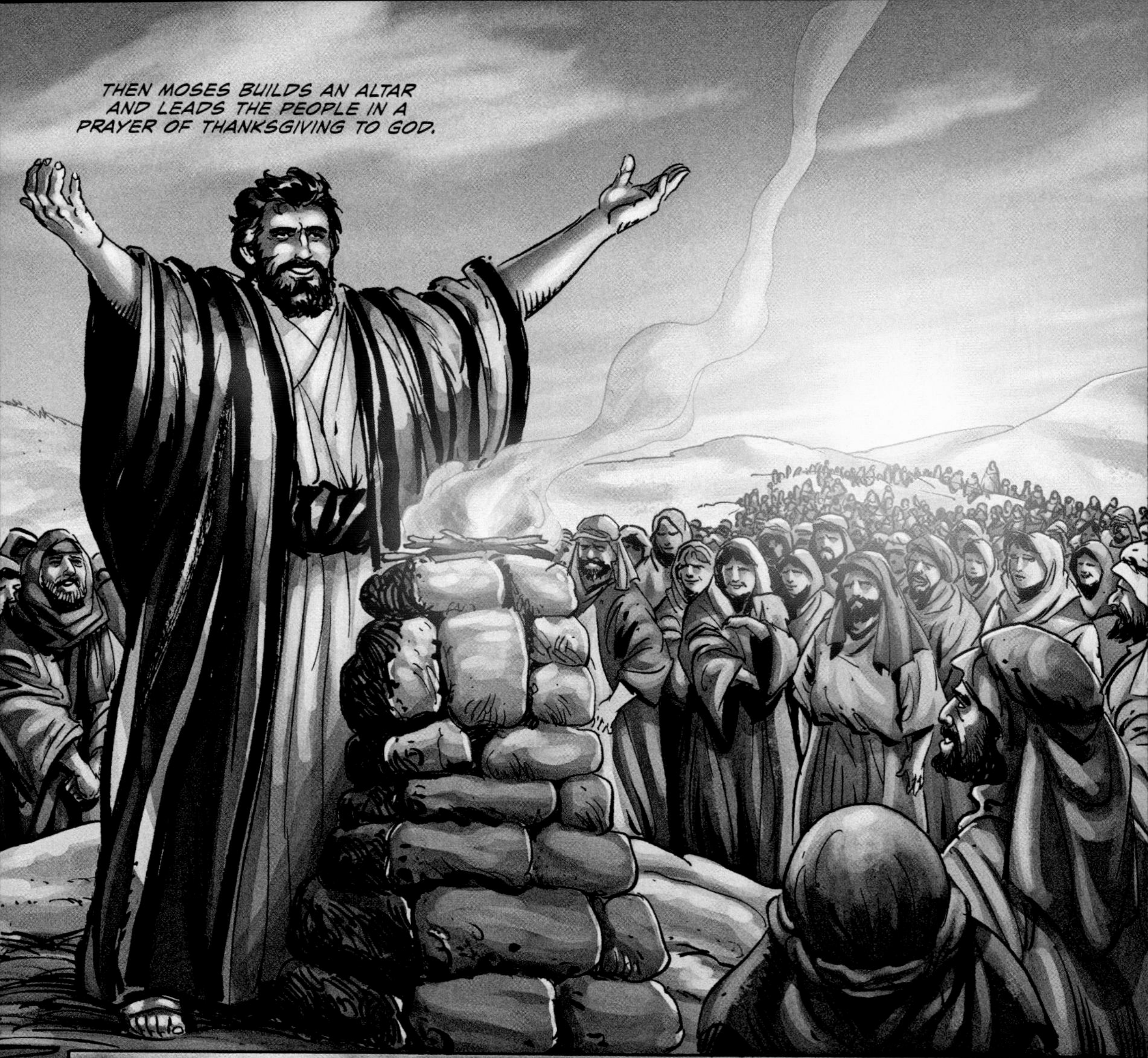
THEN MOSES BUILDS AN ALTAR AND LEADS THE PEOPLE IN A PRAYER OF THANKSGIVING TO GOD.

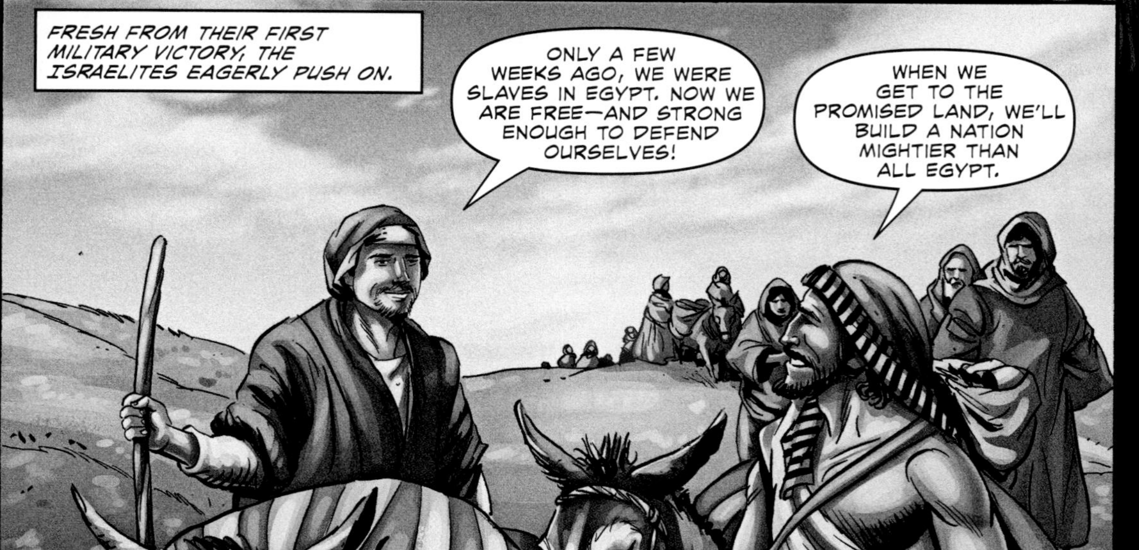
FRESH FROM THEIR FIRST MILITARY VICTORY, THE ISRAELITES EAGERLY PUSH ON.
ONLY A FEW WEEKS AGO, WE WERE SLAVES IN EGYPT. NOW WE ARE FREE—AND STRONG ENOUGH TO DEFEND OURSELVES!
WHEN WE GET TO THE PROMISED LAND, WE'LL BUILD A NATION MIGHTIER THAN ALL EGYPT.

Goo[illegible] Advice

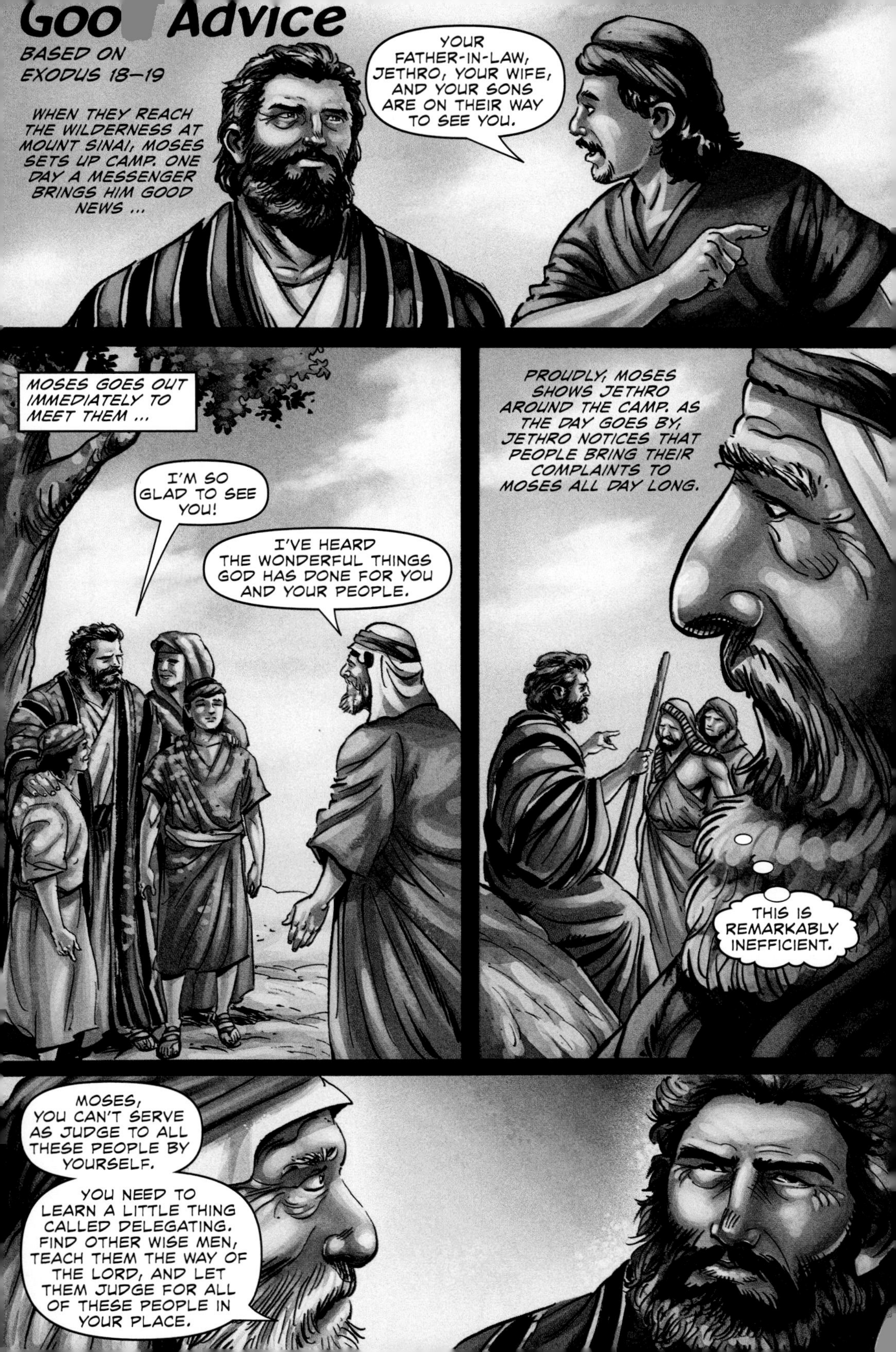
BASED ON EXODUS 18–19
WHEN THEY REACH THE WILDERNESS AT MOUNT SINAI, MOSES SETS UP CAMP. ONE DAY A MESSENGER BRINGS HIM GOOD NEWS ...
YOUR FATHER-IN-LAW, JETHRO, YOUR WIFE, AND YOUR SONS ARE ON THEIR WAY TO SEE YOU.
MOSES GOES OUT IMMEDIATELY TO MEET THEM ...
I'M SO GLAD TO SEE YOU!
I'VE HEARD THE WONDERFUL THINGS GOD HAS DONE FOR YOU AND YOUR PEOPLE.
PROUDLY, MOSES SHOWS JETHRO AROUND THE CAMP. AS THE DAY GOES BY, JETHRO NOTICES THAT PEOPLE BRING THEIR COMPLAINTS TO MOSES ALL DAY LONG.
THIS IS REMARKABLY INEFFICIENT.
MOSES, YOU CAN'T SERVE AS JUDGE TO ALL THESE PEOPLE BY YOURSELF.
YOU NEED TO LEARN A LITTLE THING CALLED DELEGATING. FIND OTHER WISE MEN, TEACH THEM THE WAY OF THE LORD, AND LET THEM JUDGE FOR ALL OF THESE PEOPLE IN YOUR PLACE.

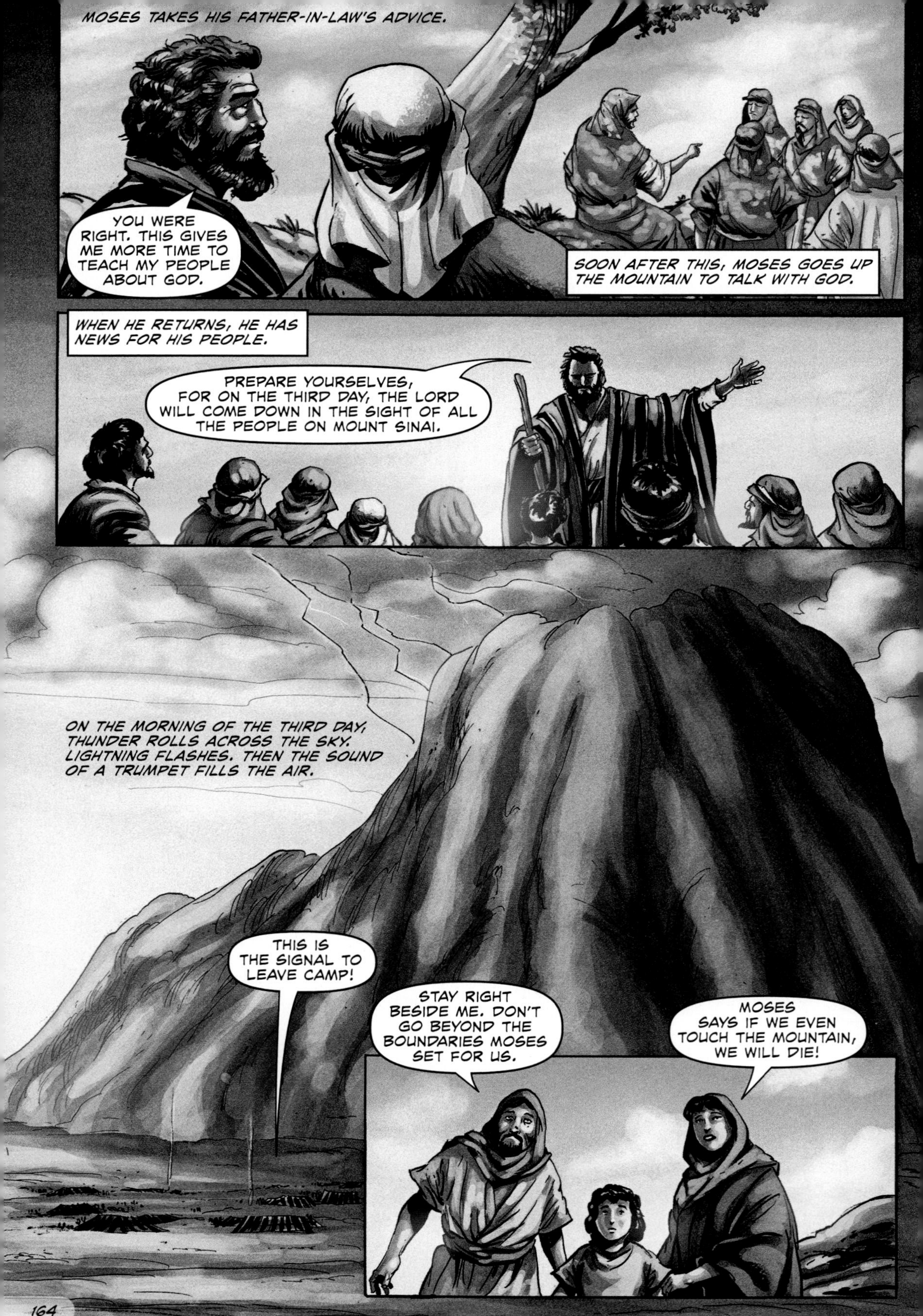
MOSES TAKES HIS FATHER-IN-LAW'S ADVICE.
YOU WERE RIGHT. THIS GIVES ME MORE TIME TO TEACH MY PEOPLE ABOUT GOD.
SOON AFTER THIS, MOSES GOES UP THE MOUNTAIN TO TALK WITH GOD.
WHEN HE RETURNS, HE HAS NEWS FOR HIS PEOPLE.
PREPARE YOURSELVES, FOR ON THE THIRD DAY, THE LORD WILL COME DOWN IN THE SIGHT OF ALL THE PEOPLE ON MOUNT SINAI.
ON THE MORNING OF THE THIRD DAY, THUNDER ROLLS ACROSS THE SKY. LIGHTNING FLASHES. THEN THE SOUND OF A TRUMPET FILLS THE AIR.
THIS IS THE SIGNAL TO LEAVE CAMP!
STAY RIGHT BESIDE ME. DON'T GO BEYOND THE BOUNDARIES MOSES SET FOR US.
MOSES SAYS IF WE EVEN TOUCH THE MOUNTAIN, WE WILL DIE!

God's Commandments

BASED ON EXODUS 20

WHILE THE PEOPLE OF ISRAEL STAND BEFORE MOUNT SINAI, GOD SPEAKS FROM THE MOUNTAIN AND GIVES THEM THE TEN COMMANDMENTS:

I am the Lord your God. You must not worship other gods.

You must not make any idols.

You must not use the name of the Lord your God wrongly.

Remember the Sabbath day and keep it holy.

Respect your father and your mother.

You must not murder.

You must not cheat on your husband or wife.

You must not steal.

You must not lie.

You must not be jealous of other people's possessions.

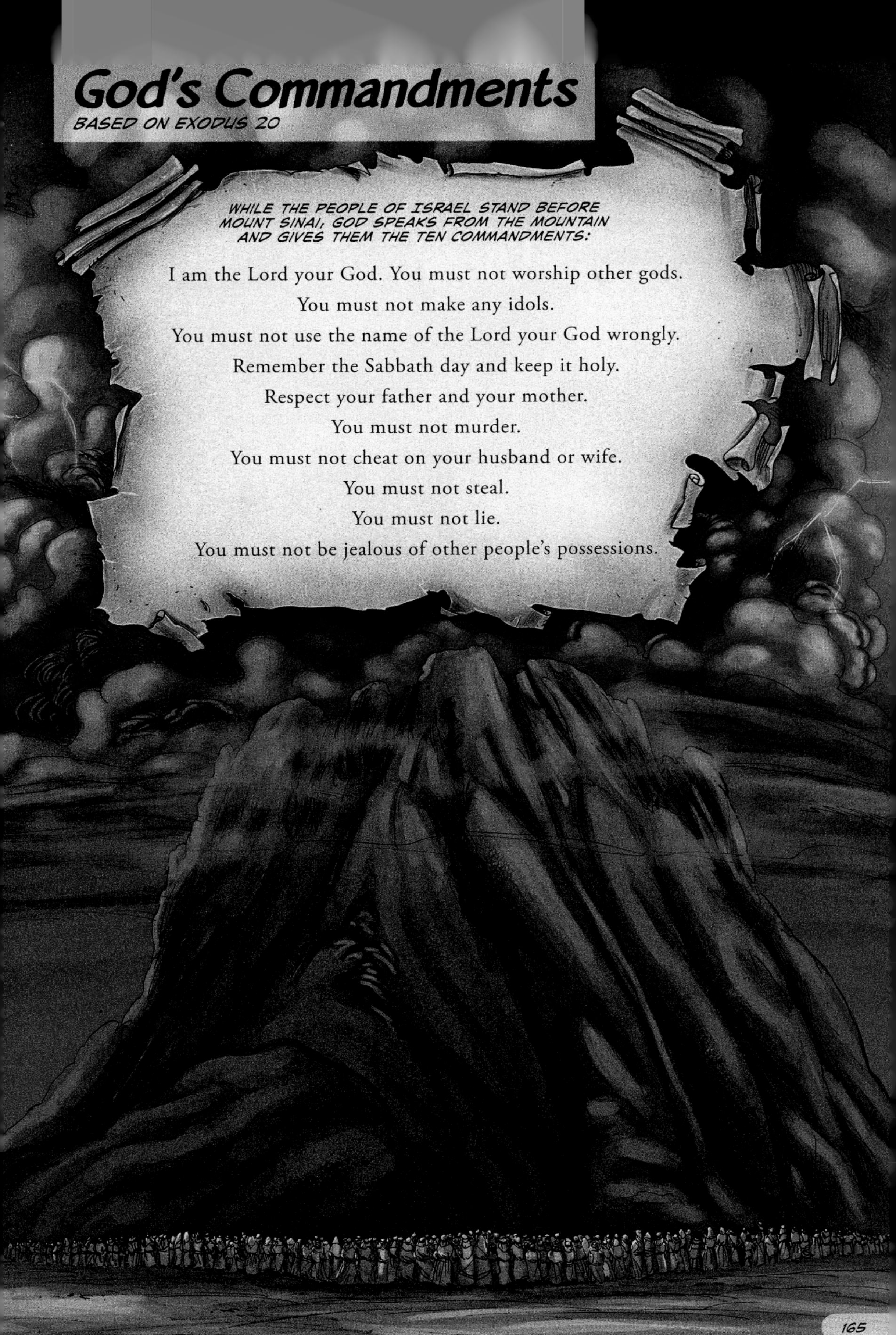

A Golden Calf

BASED ON EXODUS 32

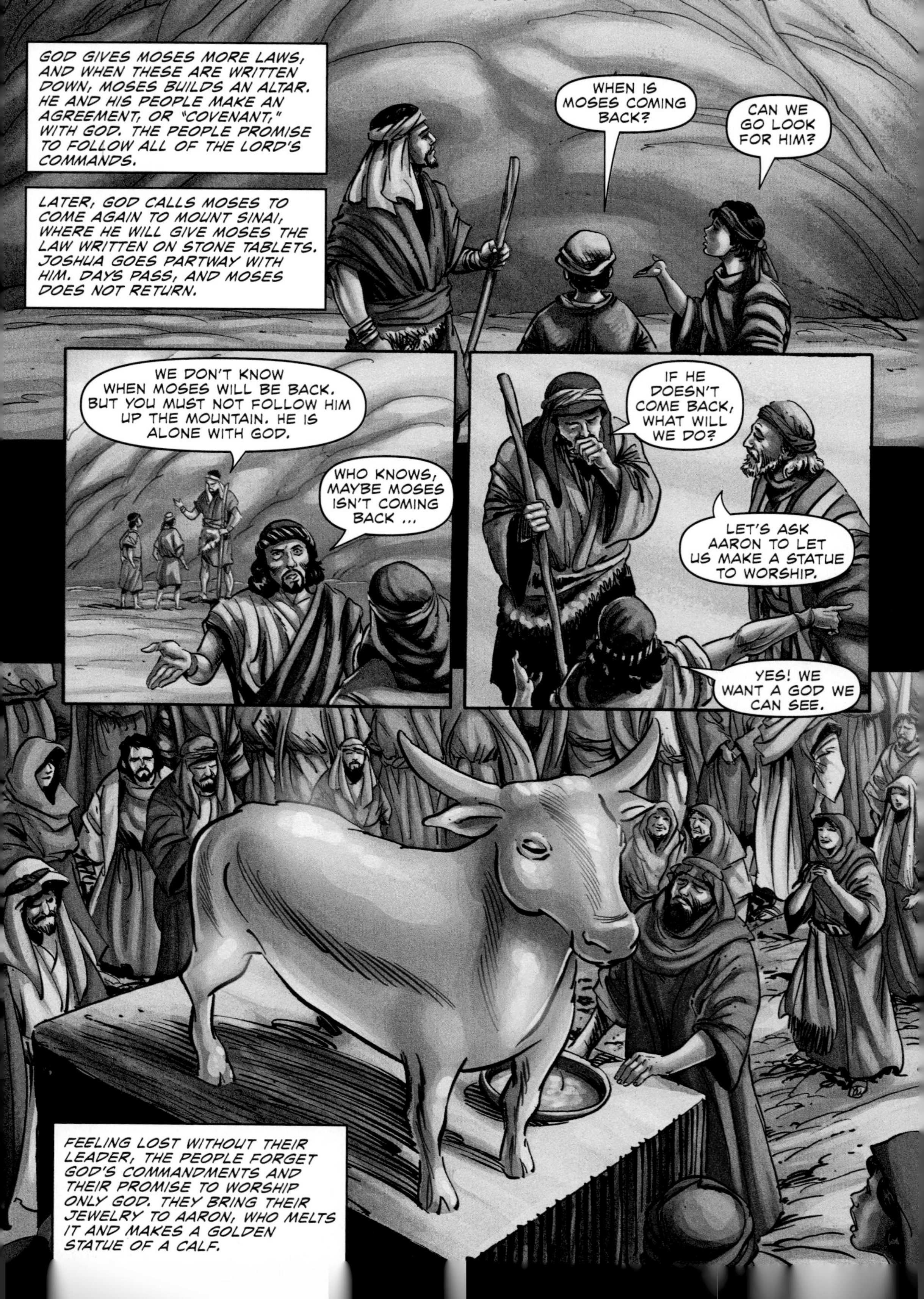

GOD GIVES MOSES MORE LAWS, AND WHEN THESE ARE WRITTEN DOWN, MOSES BUILDS AN ALTAR. HE AND HIS PEOPLE MAKE AN AGREEMENT, OR "COVENANT," WITH GOD. THE PEOPLE PROMISE TO FOLLOW ALL OF THE LORD'S COMMANDS.
LATER, GOD CALLS MOSES TO COME AGAIN TO MOUNT SINAI, WHERE HE WILL GIVE MOSES THE LAW WRITTEN ON STONE TABLETS. JOSHUA GOES PARTWAY WITH HIM. DAYS PASS, AND MOSES DOES NOT RETURN.
WHEN IS MOSES COMING BACK?
CAN WE GO LOOK FOR HIM?
WE DON'T KNOW WHEN MOSES WILL BE BACK. BUT YOU MUST NOT FOLLOW HIM UP THE MOUNTAIN. HE IS ALONE WITH GOD.
WHO KNOWS, MAYBE MOSES ISN'T COMING BACK ...
IF HE DOESN'T COME BACK, WHAT WILL WE DO?
LET'S ASK AARON TO LET US MAKE A STATUE TO WORSHIP.
YES! WE WANT A GOD WE CAN SEE.
FEELING LOST WITHOUT THEIR LEADER, THE PEOPLE FORGET GOD'S COMMANDMENTS AND THEIR PROMISE TO WORSHIP ONLY GOD. THEY BRING THEIR JEWELRY TO AARON, WHO MELTS IT AND MAKES A GOLDEN STATUE OF A CALF.

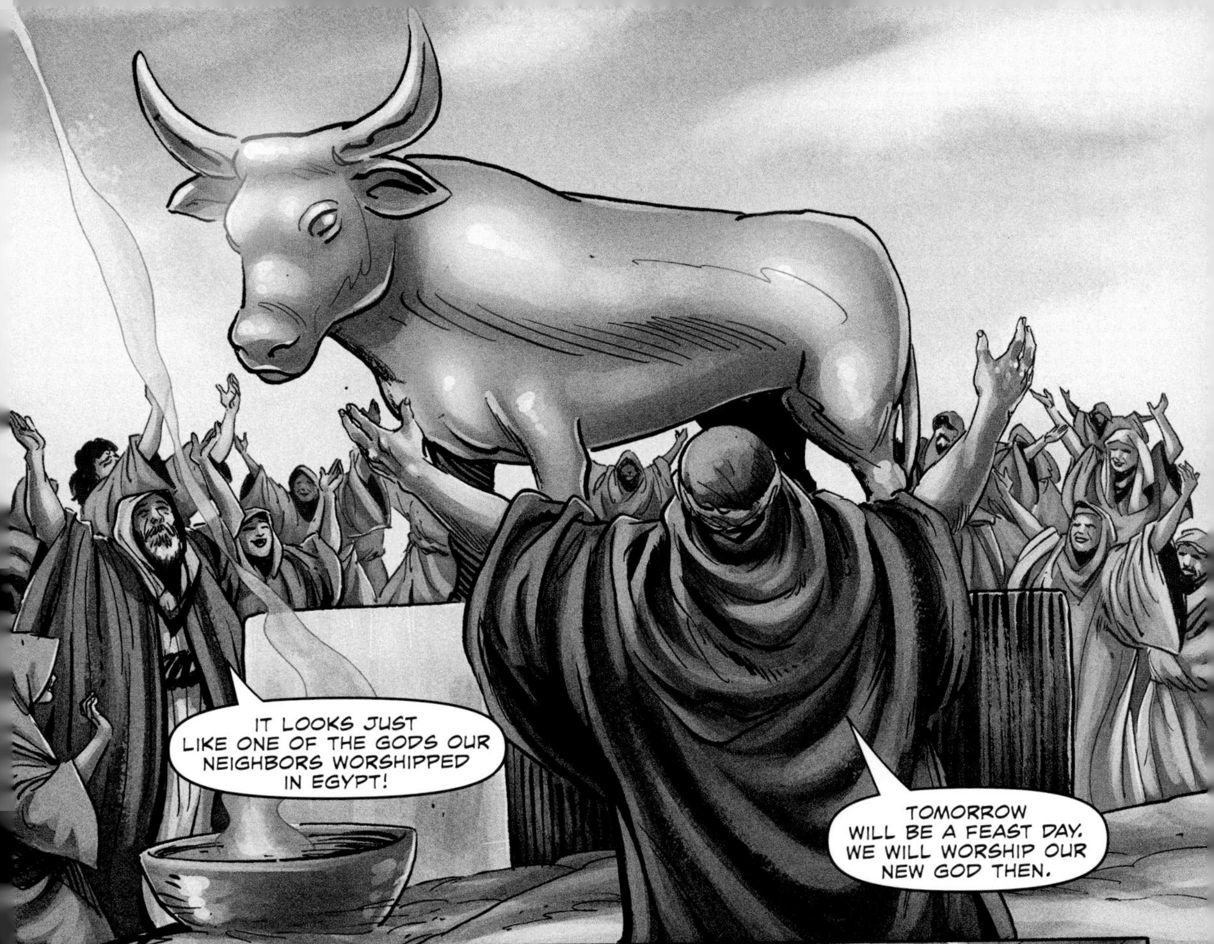
IT LOOKS JUST LIKE ONE OF THE GODS OUR NEIGHBORS WORSHIPPED IN EGYPT!
TOMORROW WILL BE A FEAST DAY. WE WILL WORSHIP OUR NEW GOD THEN.

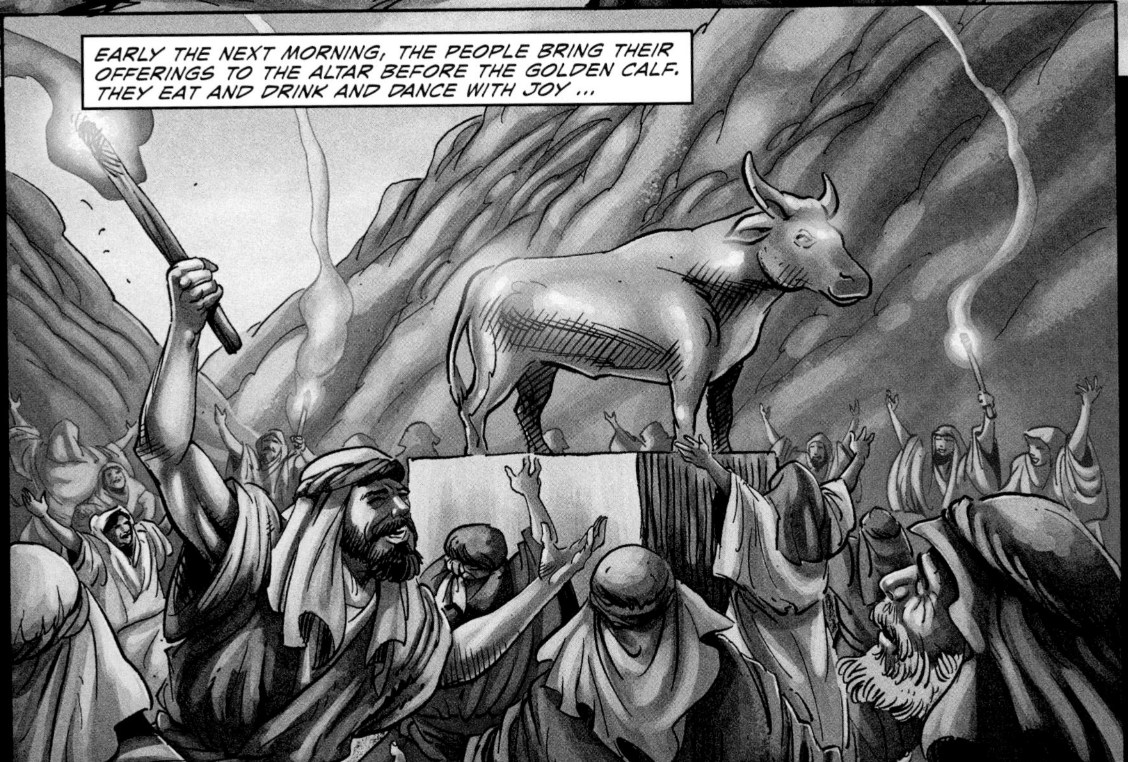
EARLY THE NEXT MORNING, THE PEOPLE BRING THEIR OFFERINGS TO THE ALTAR BEFORE THE GOLDEN CALF. THEY EAT AND DRINK AND DANCE WITH JOY ...

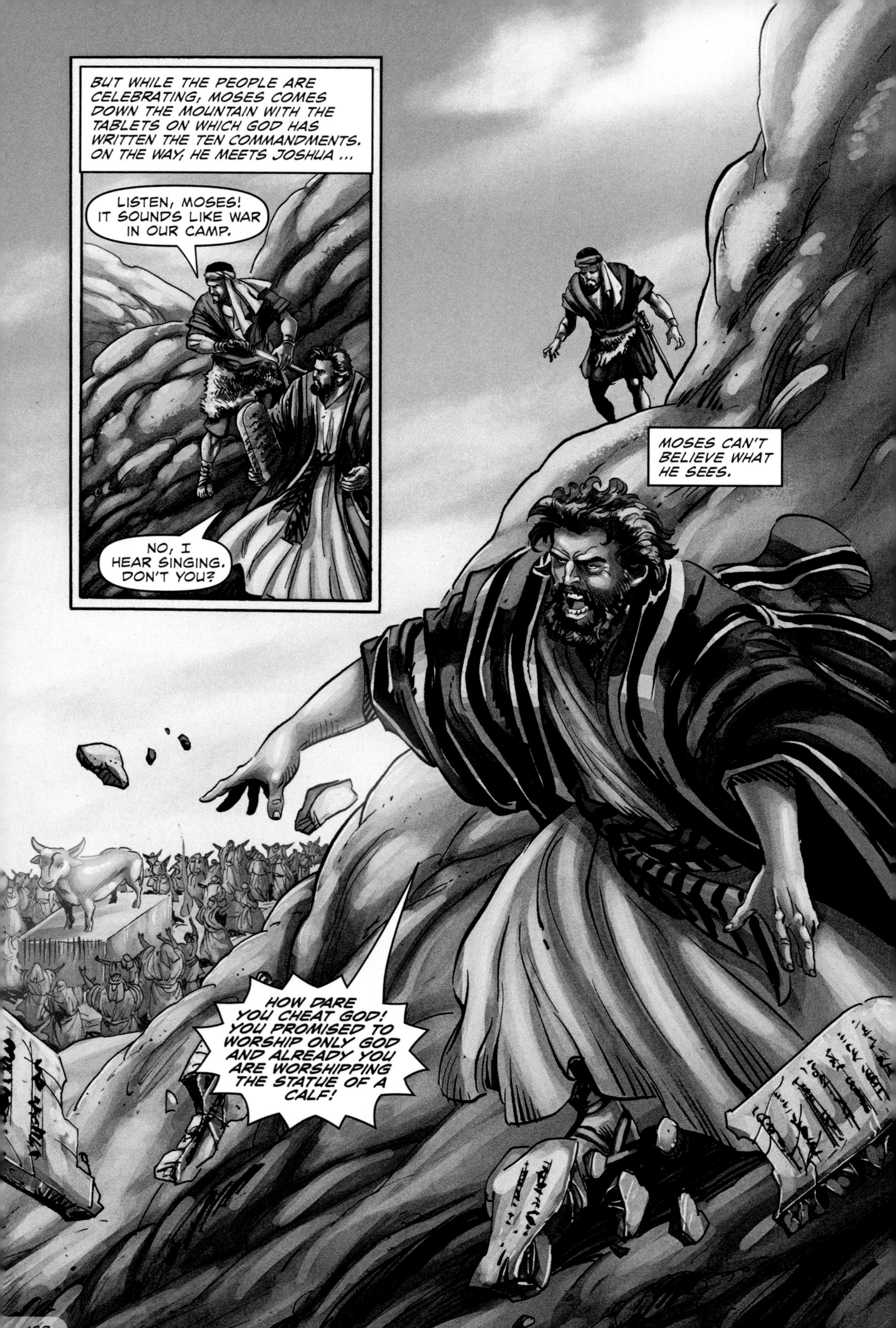
BUT WHILE THE PEOPLE ARE CELEBRATING, MOSES COMES DOWN THE MOUNTAIN WITH THE TABLETS ON WHICH GOD HAS WRITTEN THE TEN COMMANDMENTS. ON THE WAY, HE MEETS JOSHUA ...
LISTEN, MOSES! IT SOUNDS LIKE WAR IN OUR CAMP.
NO, I HEAR SINGING. DON'T YOU?
MOSES CAN'T BELIEVE WHAT HE SEES.
HOW DARE YOU CHEAT GOD! YOU PROMISED TO WORSHIP ONLY GOD AND ALREADY YOU ARE WORSHIPPING THE STATUE OF A CALF!

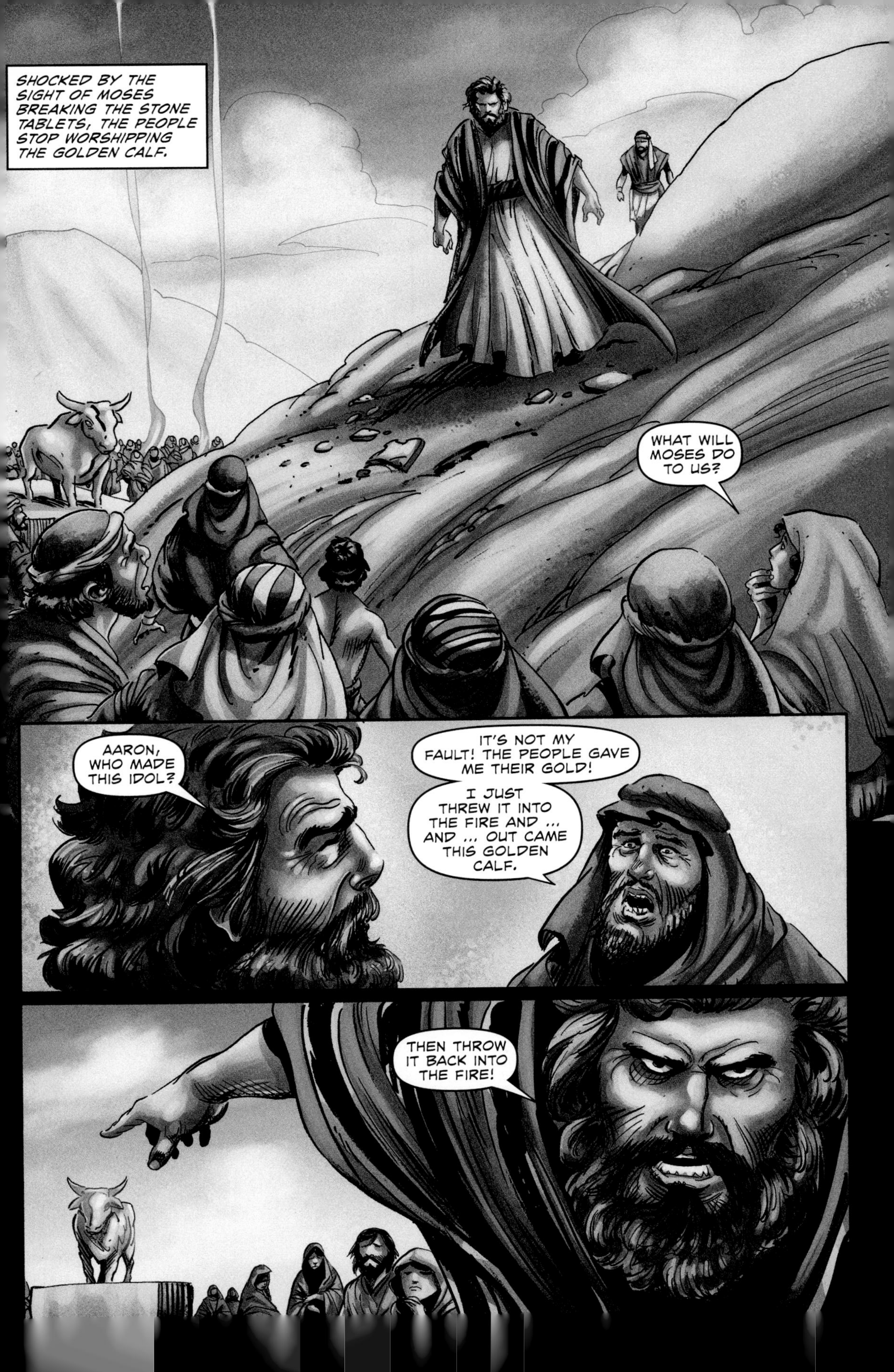
SHOCKED BY THE SIGHT OF MOSES BREAKING THE STONE TABLETS, THE PEOPLE STOP WORSHIPPING THE GOLDEN CALF.
WHAT WILL MOSES DO TO US?
AARON, WHO MADE THIS IDOL?
IT'S NOT MY FAULT! THE PEOPLE GAVE ME THEIR GOLD!
I JUST THREW IT INTO THE FIRE AND ... AND ... OUT CAME THIS GOLDEN CALF.
THEN THROW IT BACK INTO THE FIRE!

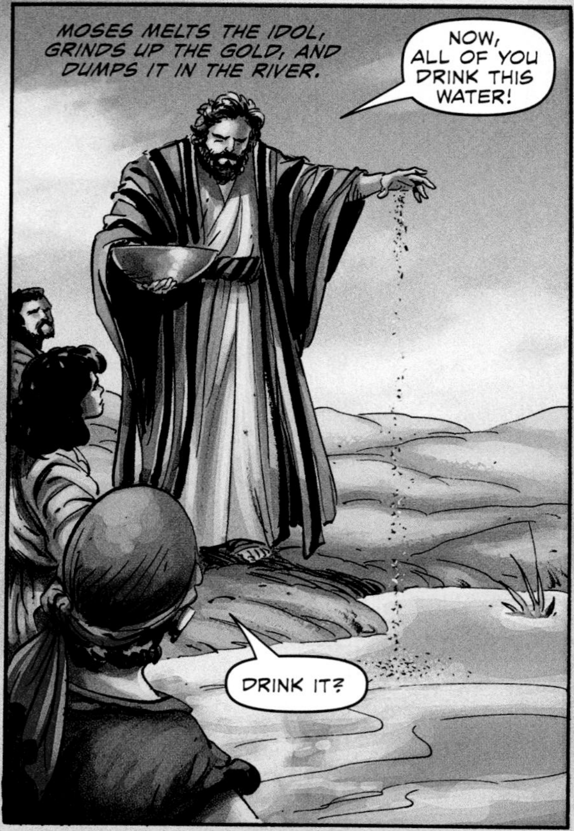
MOSES MELTS THE IDOL, GRINDS UP THE GOLD, AND DUMPS IT IN THE RIVER.
NOW, ALL OF YOU DRINK THIS WATER!
DRINK IT?

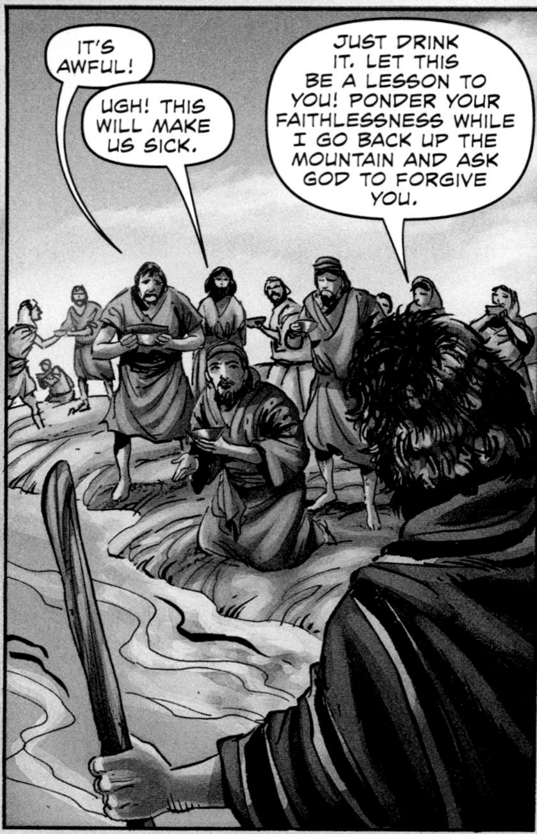
IT'S AWFUL!
UGH! THIS WILL MAKE US SICK.
JUST DRINK IT. LET THIS BE A LESSON TO YOU! PONDER YOUR FAITHLESSNESS WHILE I GO BACK UP THE MOUNTAIN AND ASK GOD TO FORGIVE YOU.

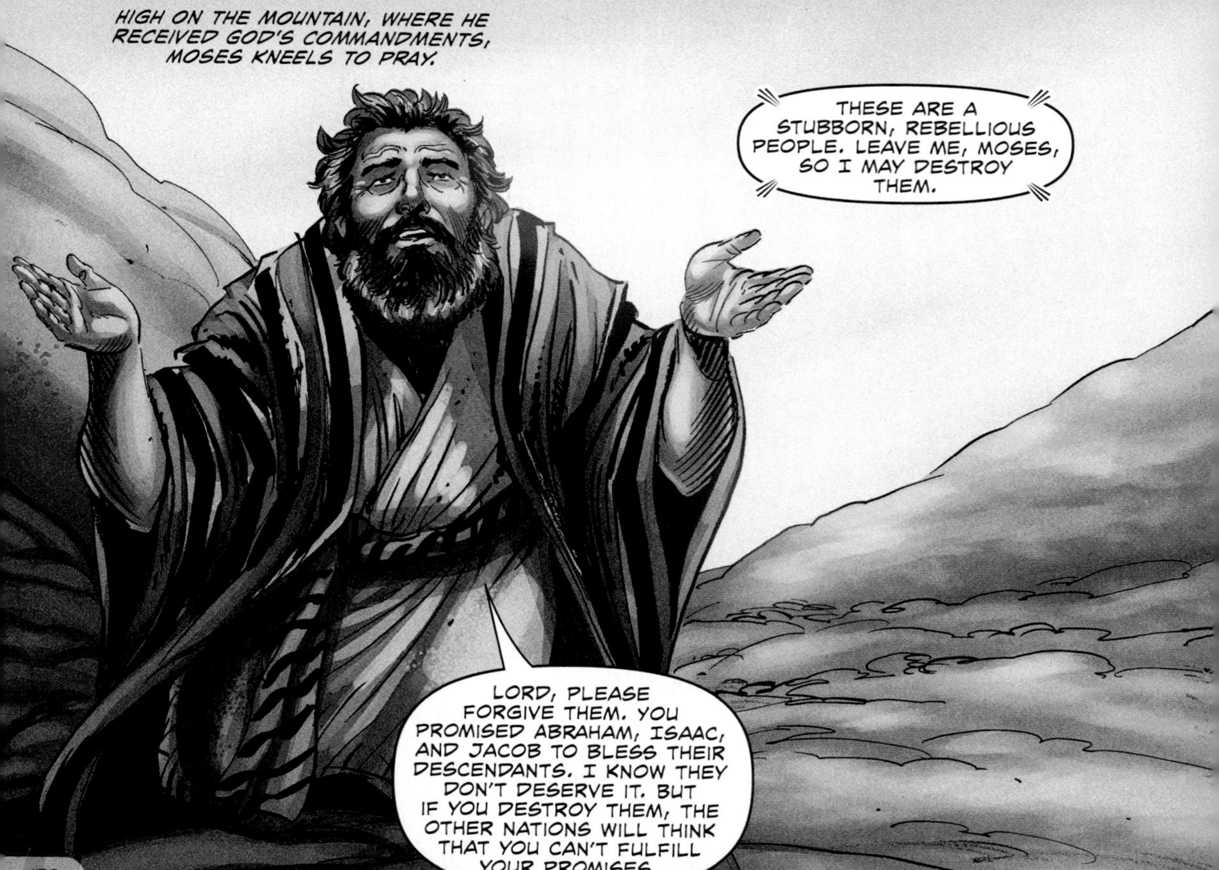
HIGH ON THE MOUNTAIN, WHERE HE RECEIVED GOD'S COMMANDMENTS, MOSES KNEELS TO PRAY.
THESE ARE A STUBBORN, REBELLIOUS PEOPLE. LEAVE ME, MOSES, SO I MAY DESTROY THEM.
LORD, PLEASE FORGIVE THEM. YOU PROMISED ABRAHAM, ISAAC, AND JACOB TO BLESS THEIR DESCENDANTS. I KNOW THEY DON'T DESERVE IT. BUT IF YOU DESTROY THEM, THE OTHER NATIONS WILL THINK THAT YOU CAN'T FULFILL YOUR PROMISES.

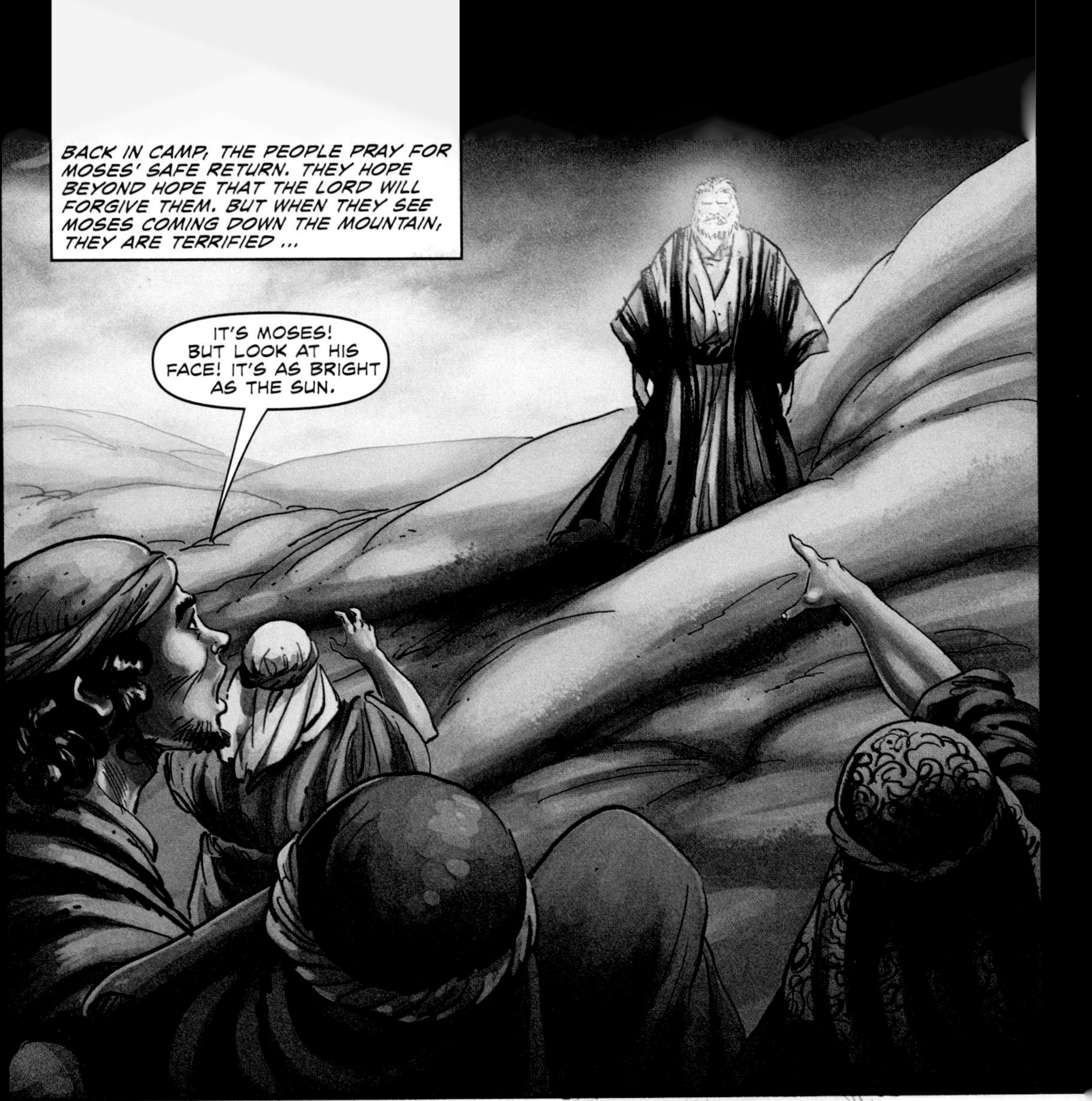
BACK IN CAMP, THE PEOPLE PRAY FOR MOSES' SAFE RETURN. THEY HOPE BEYOND HOPE THAT THE LORD WILL FORGIVE THEM. BUT WHEN THEY SEE MOSES COMING DOWN THE MOUNTAIN, THEY ARE TERRIFIED ...
IT'S MOSES! BUT LOOK AT HIS FACE! IT'S AS BRIGHT AS THE SUN.

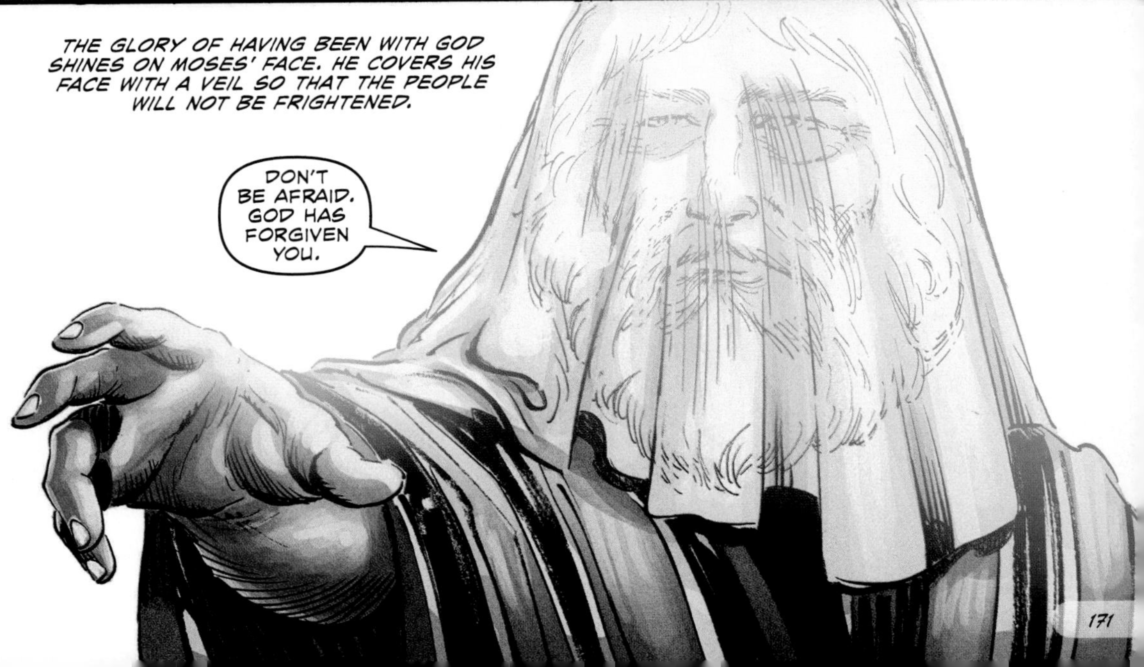
THE GLORY OF HAVING BEEN WITH GOD SHINES ON MOSES' FACE. HE COVERS HIS FACE WITH A VEIL SO THAT THE PEOPLE WILL NOT BE FRIGHTENED.
DON'T BE AFRAID. GOD HAS FORGIVEN YOU.

The Tent of Meeting

BASED ON EXODUS 35–40

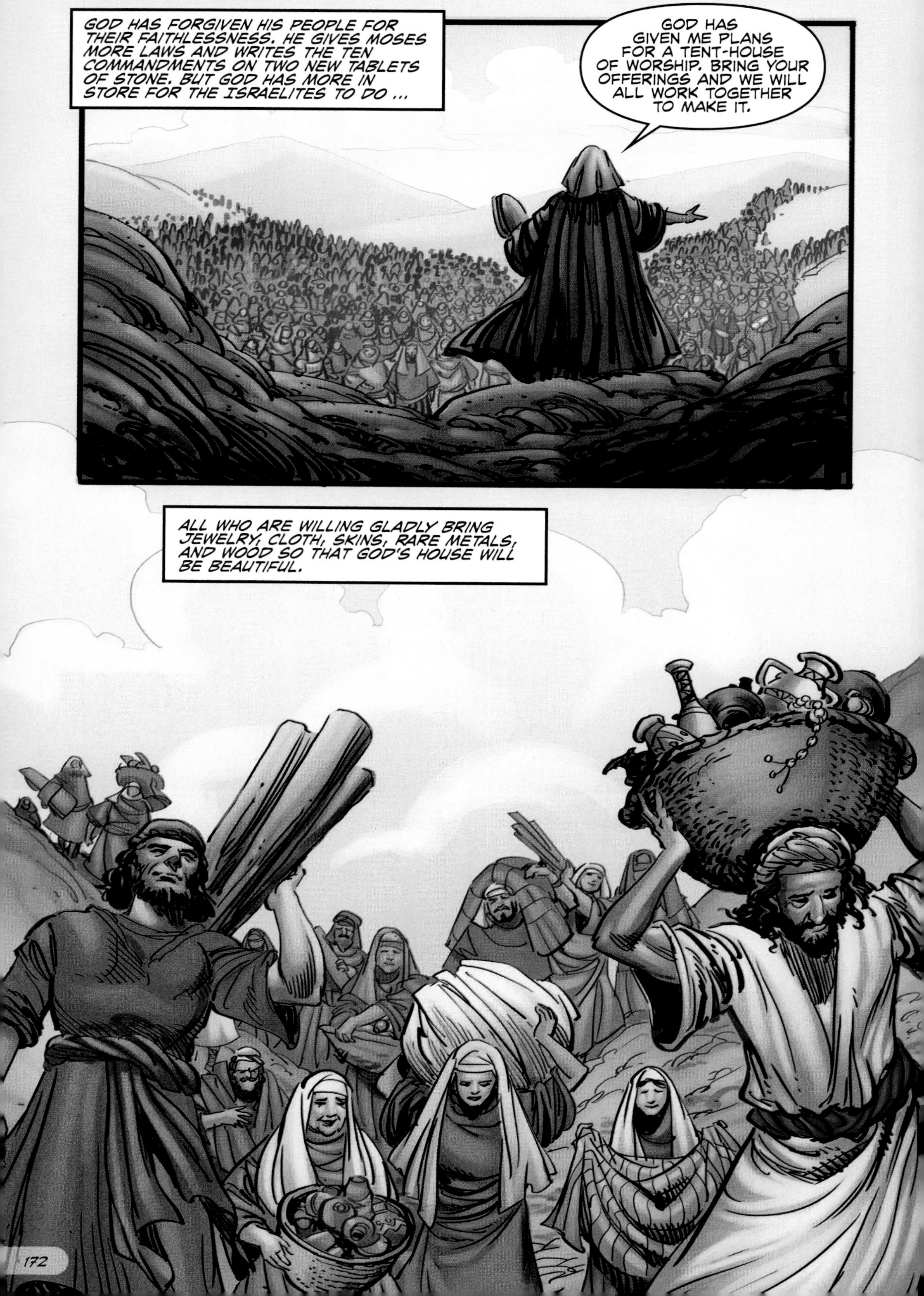
GOD HAS FORGIVEN HIS PEOPLE FOR THEIR FAITHLESSNESS. HE GIVES MOSES MORE LAWS AND WRITES THE TEN COMMANDMENTS ON TWO NEW TABLETS OF STONE. BUT GOD HAS MORE IN STORE FOR THE ISRAELITES TO DO ...
GOD HAS GIVEN ME PLANS FOR A TENT-HOUSE OF WORSHIP. BRING YOUR OFFERINGS AND WE WILL ALL WORK TOGETHER TO MAKE IT.
ALL WHO ARE WILLING GLADLY BRING JEWELRY, CLOTH, SKINS, RARE METALS, AND WOOD SO THAT GOD'S HOUSE WILL BE BEAUTIFUL.

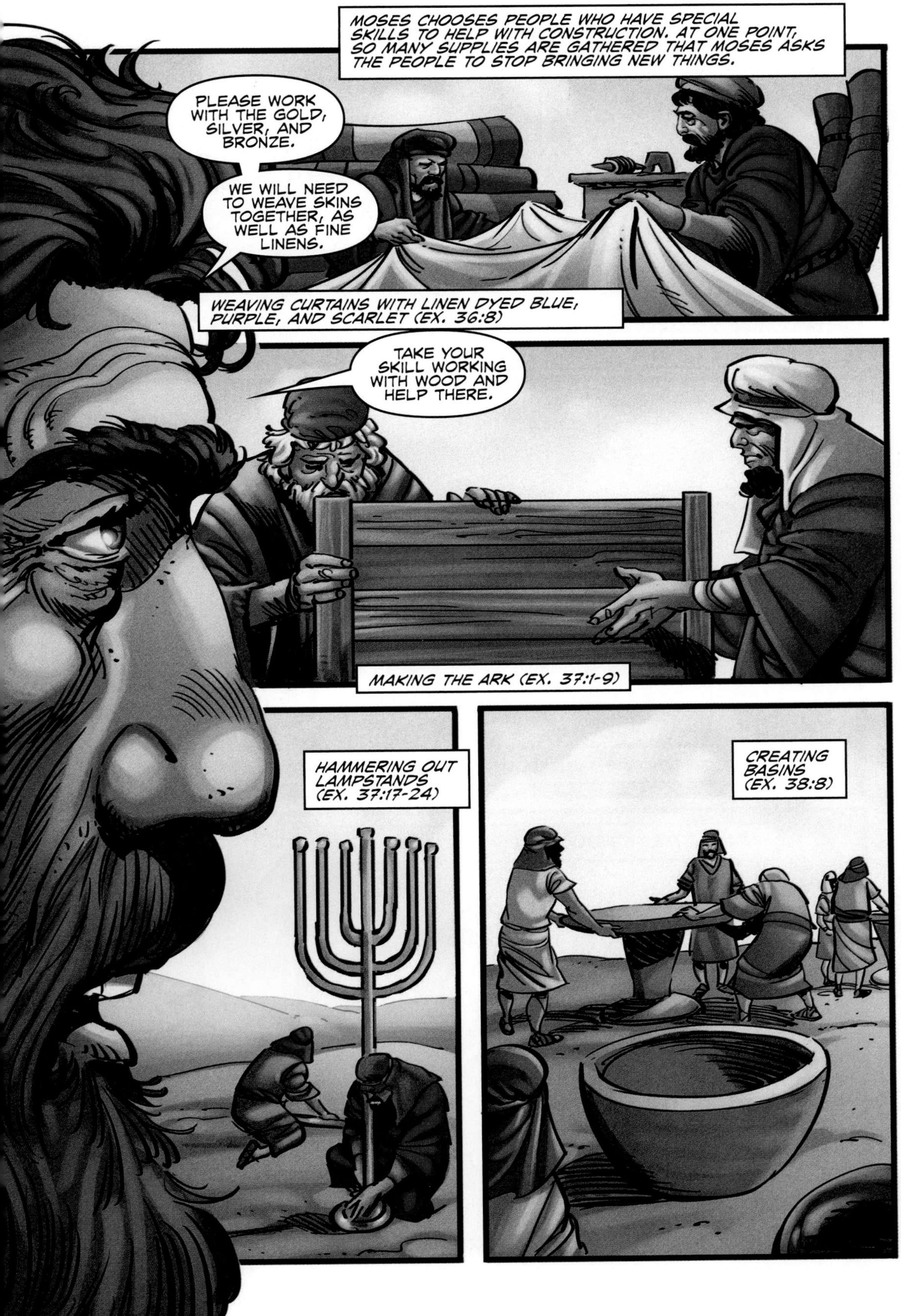

MOSES CHOOSES PEOPLE WHO HAVE SPECIAL SKILLS TO HELP WITH CONSTRUCTION. AT ONE POINT, SO MANY SUPPLIES ARE GATHERED THAT MOSES ASKS THE PEOPLE TO STOP BRINGING NEW THINGS.
PLEASE WORK WITH THE GOLD, SILVER, AND BRONZE.
WE WILL NEED TO WEAVE SKINS TOGETHER, AS WELL AS FINE LINENS.
WEAVING CURTAINS WITH LINEN DYED BLUE, PURPLE, AND SCARLET (EX. 36:8)
TAKE YOUR SKILL WORKING WITH WOOD AND HELP THERE.
MAKING THE ARK (EX. 37:1-9)
HAMMERING OUT LAMPSTANDS (EX. 37:17-24)
CREATING BASINS (EX. 38:8)

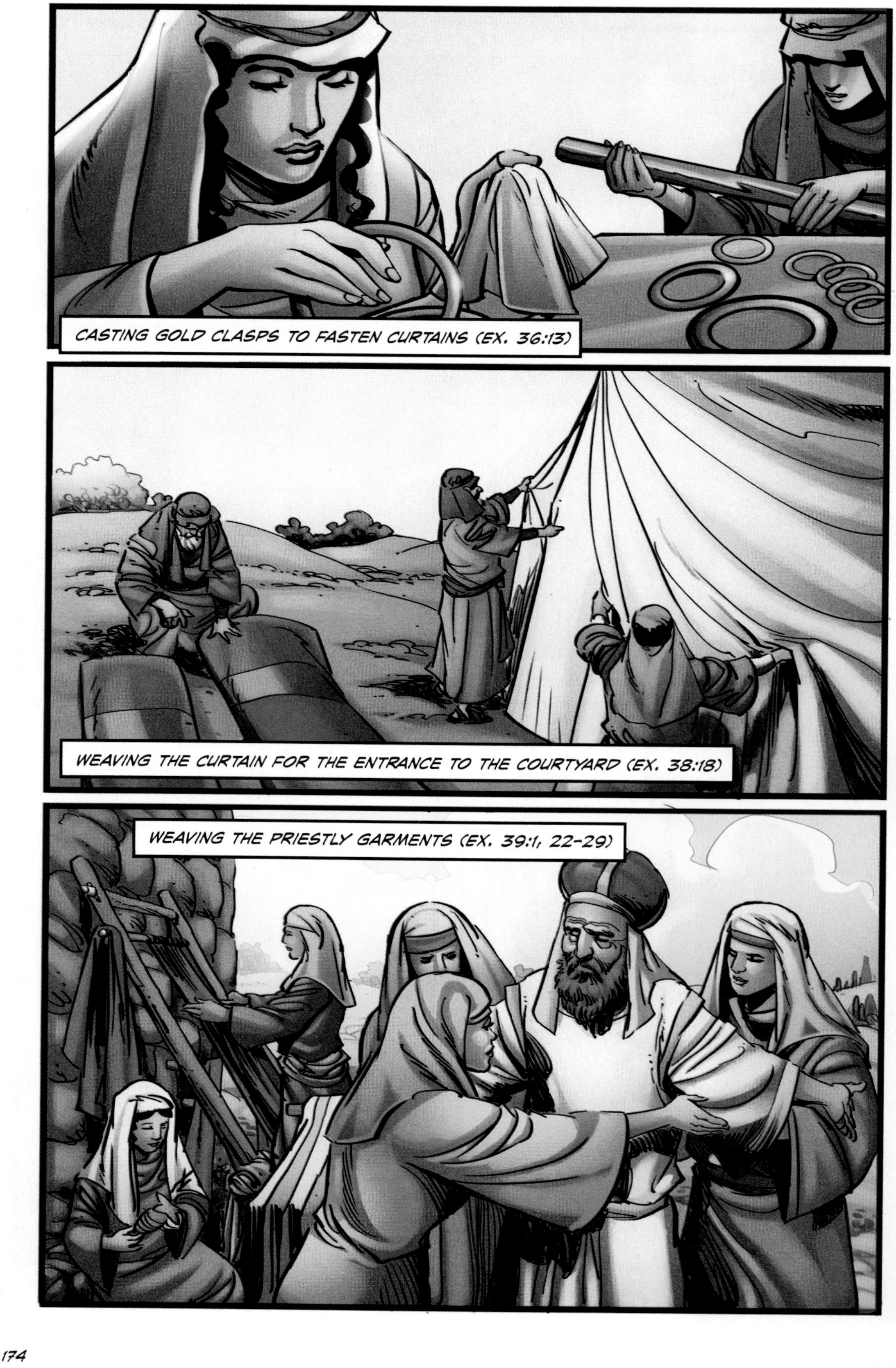
CASTING GOLD CLASPS TO FASTEN CURTAINS (EX. 36:13)
WEAVING THE CURTAIN FOR THE ENTRANCE TO THE COURTYARD (EX. 38:18)
WEAVING THE PRIESTLY GARMENTS (EX. 39:1, 22-29)

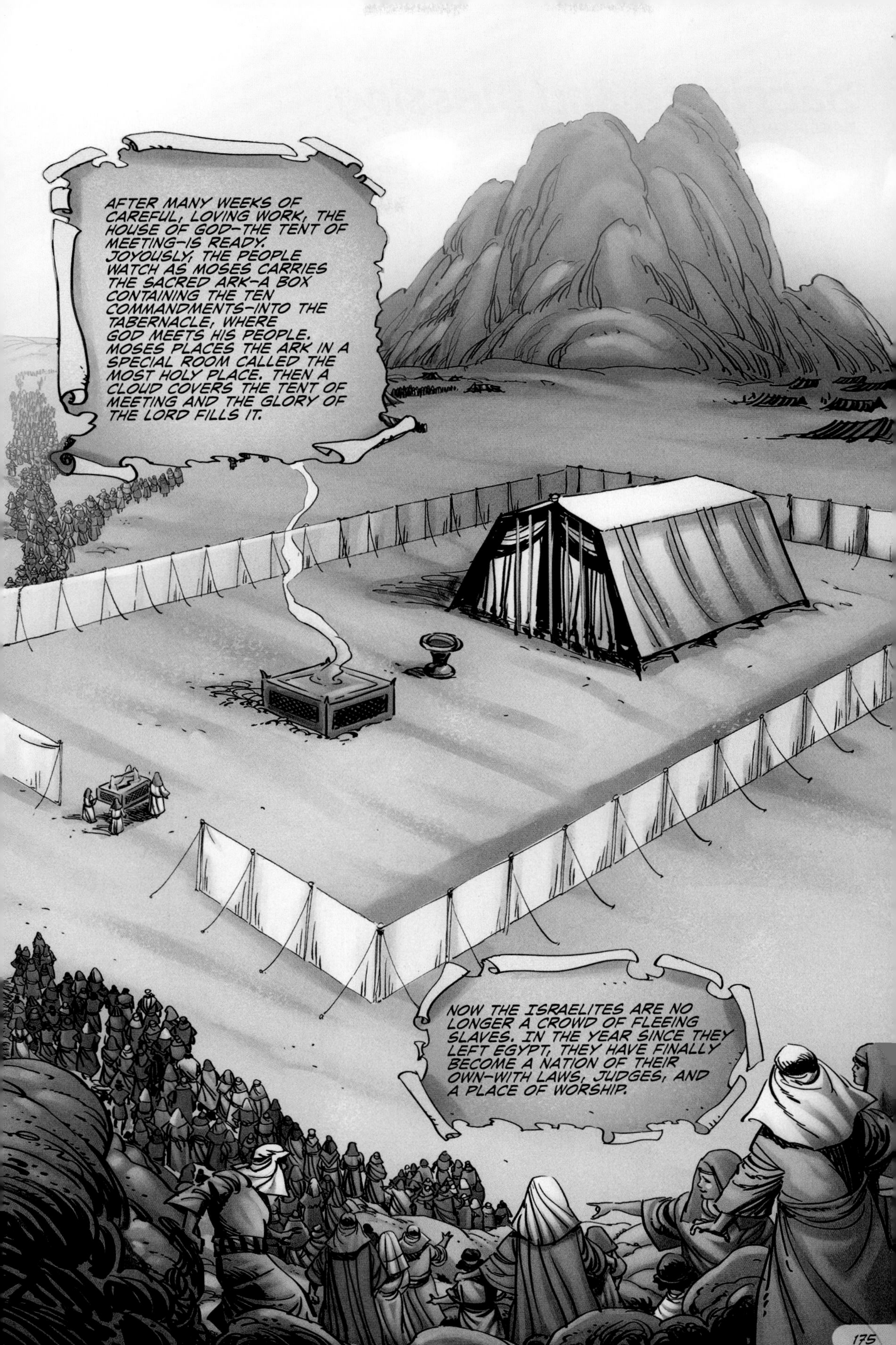
AFTER MANY WEEKS OF CAREFUL, LOVING WORK, THE HOUSE OF GOD–THE TENT OF MEETING–IS READY. JOYOUSLY, THE PEOPLE WATCH AS MOSES CARRIES THE SACRED ARK–A BOX CONTAINING THE TEN COMMANDMENTS–INTO THE TABERNACLE, WHERE GOD MEETS HIS PEOPLE. MOSES PLACES THE ARK IN A SPECIAL ROOM CALLED THE MOST HOLY PLACE. THEN A CLOUD COVERS THE TENT OF MEETING AND THE GLORY OF THE LORD FILLS IT.
NOW THE ISRAELITES ARE NO LONGER A CROWD OF FLEEING SLAVES. IN THE YEAR SINCE THEY LEFT EGYPT, THEY HAVE FINALLY BECOME A NATION OF THEIR OWN–WITH LAWS, JUDGES, AND A PLACE OF WORSHIP.

Sacrifice and Blessing

BASED ON LEVITICUS AND NUMBERS

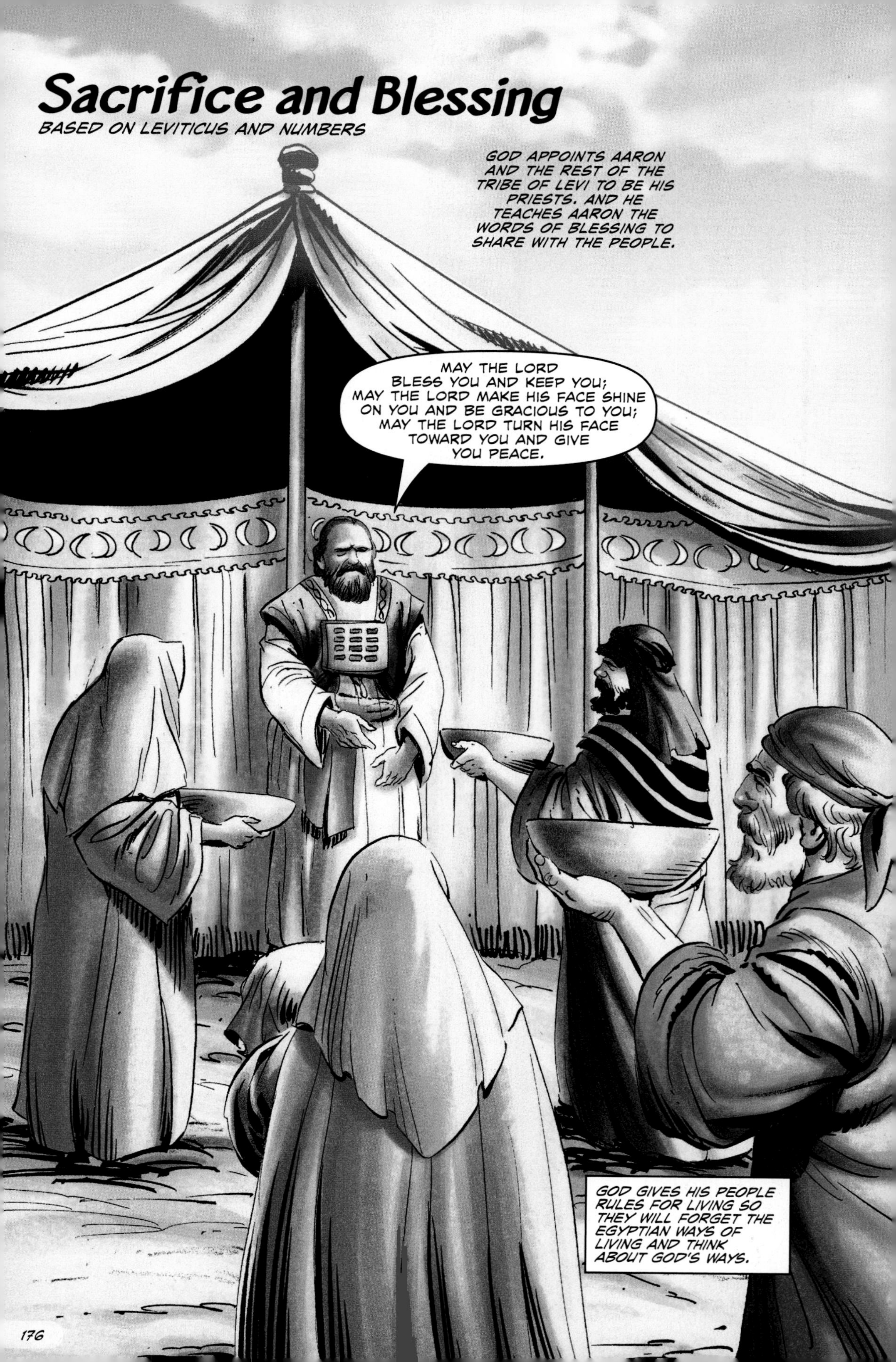
GOD APPOINTS AARON AND THE REST OF THE TRIBE OF LEVI TO BE HIS PRIESTS. AND HE TEACHES AARON THE WORDS OF BLESSING TO SHARE WITH THE PEOPLE.
MAY THE LORD BLESS YOU AND KEEP YOU; MAY THE LORD MAKE HIS FACE SHINE ON YOU AND BE GRACIOUS TO YOU; MAY THE LORD TURN HIS FACE TOWARD YOU AND GIVE YOU PEACE.
GOD GIVES HIS PEOPLE RULES FOR LIVING SO THEY WILL FORGET THE EGYPTIAN WAYS OF LIVING AND THINK ABOUT GOD'S WAYS.

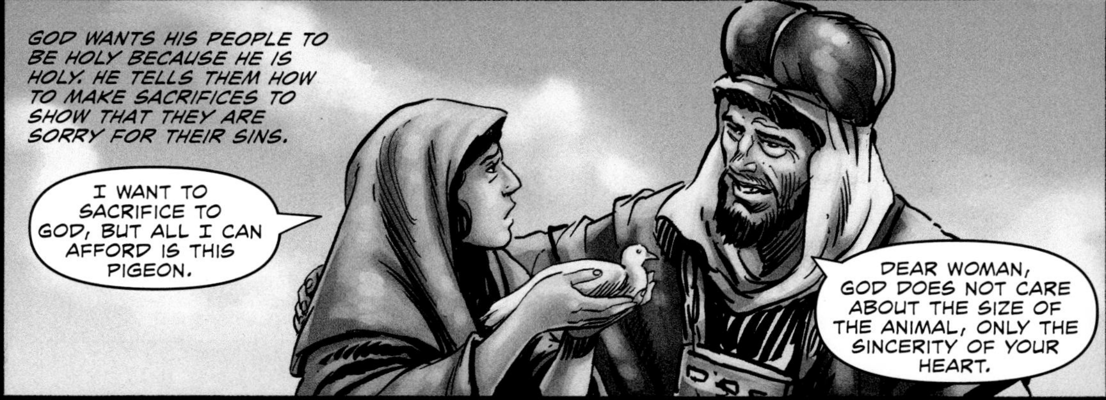
GOD WANTS HIS PEOPLE TO BE HOLY BECAUSE HE IS HOLY. HE TELLS THEM HOW TO MAKE SACRIFICES TO SHOW THAT THEY ARE SORRY FOR THEIR SINS.
I WANT TO SACRIFICE TO GOD, BUT ALL I CAN AFFORD IS THIS PIGEON.
DEAR WOMAN, GOD DOES NOT CARE ABOUT THE SIZE OF THE ANIMAL, ONLY THE SINCERITY OF YOUR HEART.

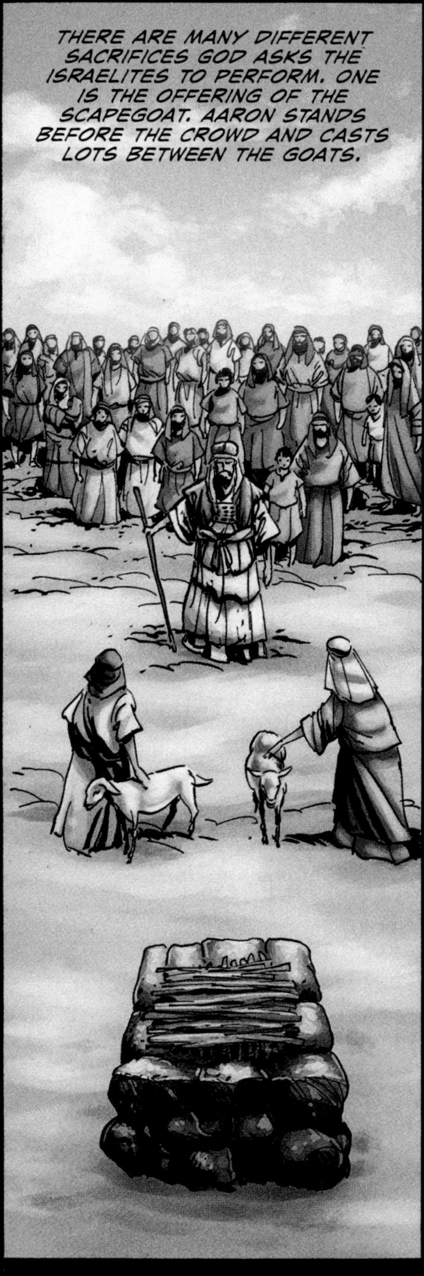
THERE ARE MANY DIFFERENT SACRIFICES GOD ASKS THE ISRAELITES TO PERFORM. ONE IS THE OFFERING OF THE SCAPEGOAT. AARON STANDS BEFORE THE CROWD AND CASTS LOTS BETWEEN THE GOATS.

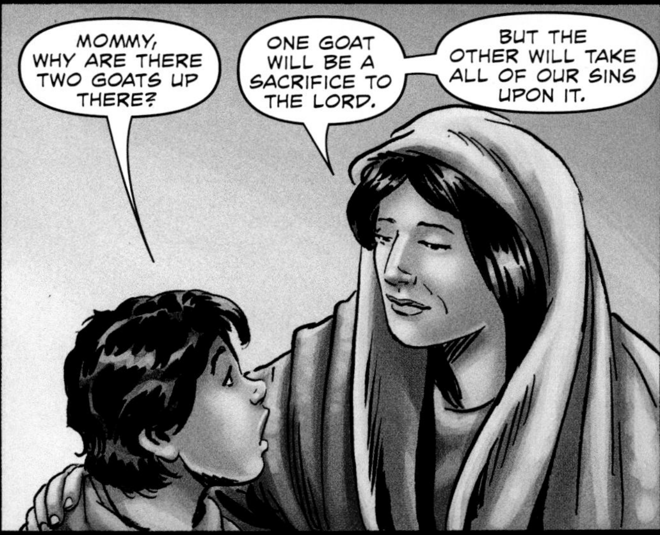
MOMMY, WHY ARE THERE TWO GOATS UP THERE?
ONE GOAT WILL BE A SACRIFICE TO THE LORD.
BUT THE OTHER WILL TAKE ALL OF OUR SINS UPON IT.

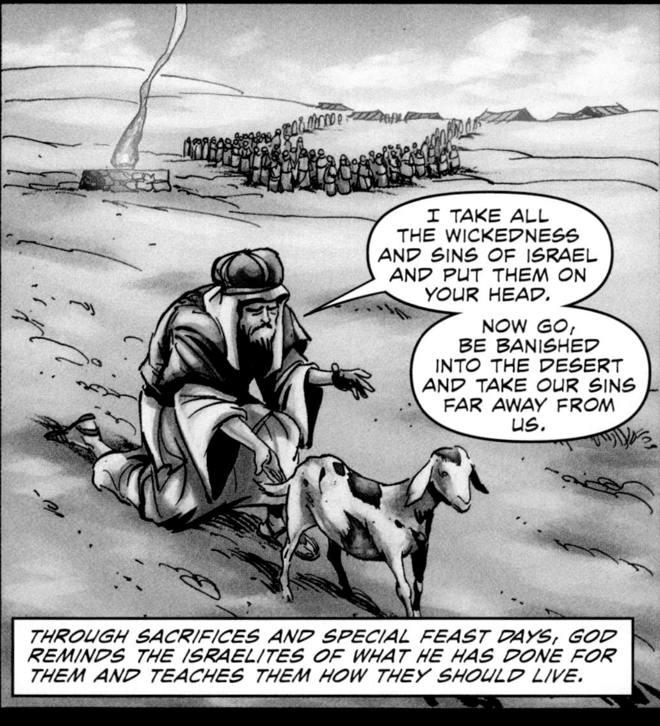
I TAKE ALL THE WICKEDNESS AND SINS OF ISRAEL AND PUT THEM ON YOUR HEAD.
NOW GO, BE BANISHED INTO THE DESERT AND TAKE OUR SINS FAR AWAY FROM US.
THROUGH SACRIFICES AND SPECIAL FEAST DAYS, GOD REMINDS THE ISRAELITES OF WHAT HE HAS DONE FOR THEM AND TEACHES THEM HOW THEY SHOULD LIVE.

Counting the Numbers
BASED ON NUMBERS 10

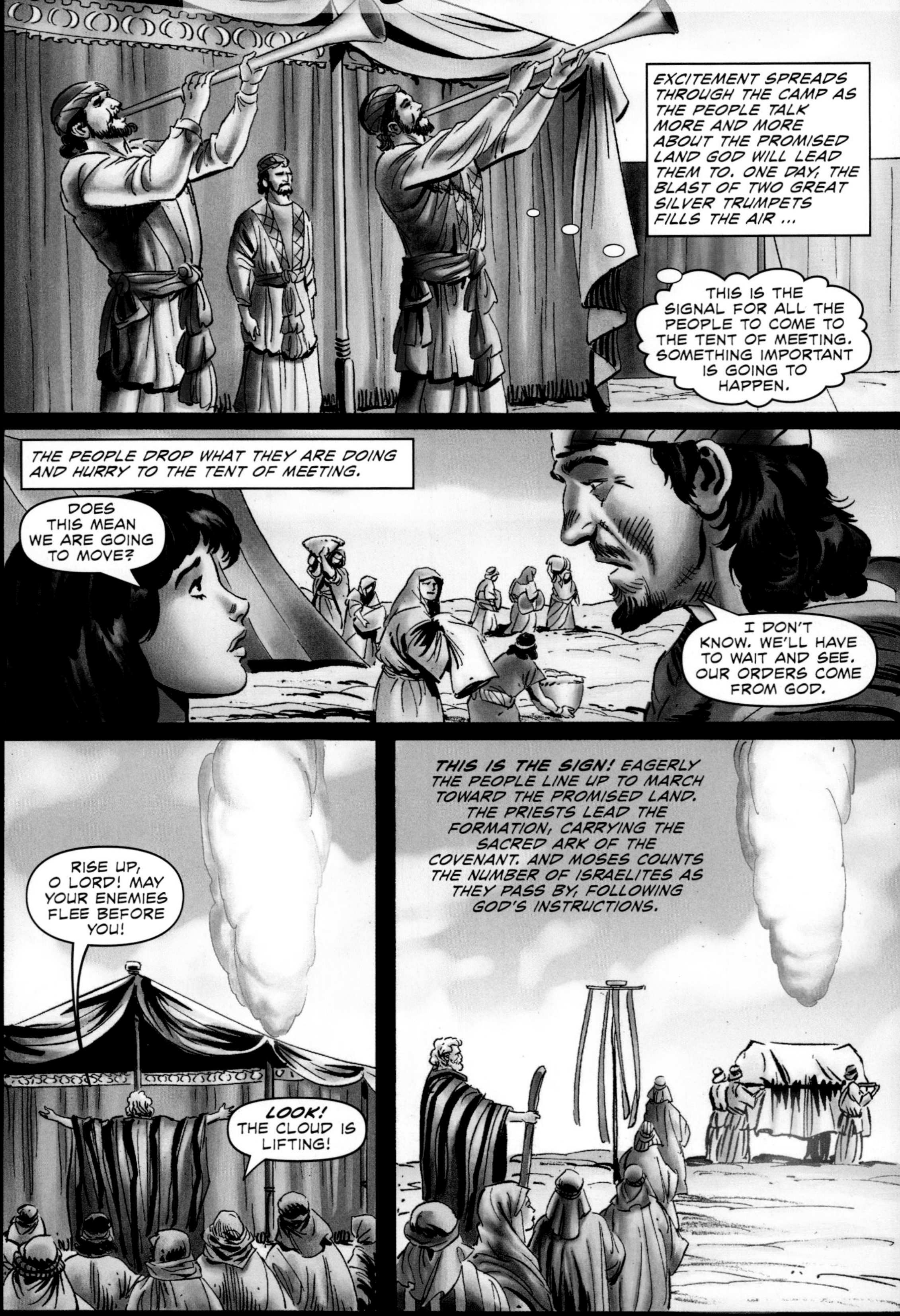

EXCITEMENT SPREADS THROUGH THE CAMP AS THE PEOPLE TALK MORE AND MORE ABOUT THE PROMISED LAND GOD WILL LEAD THEM TO. ONE DAY, THE BLAST OF TWO GREAT SILVER TRUMPETS FILLS THE AIR ...
THIS IS THE SIGNAL FOR ALL THE PEOPLE TO COME TO THE TENT OF MEETING. SOMETHING IMPORTANT IS GOING TO HAPPEN.
THE PEOPLE DROP WHAT THEY ARE DOING AND HURRY TO THE TENT OF MEETING.
DOES THIS MEAN WE ARE GOING TO MOVE?
I DON'T KNOW. WE'LL HAVE TO WAIT AND SEE. OUR ORDERS COME FROM GOD.
RISE UP, O LORD! MAY YOUR ENEMIES FLEE BEFORE YOU!
LOOK! THE CLOUD IS LIFTING!
THIS IS THE SIGN! EAGERLY THE PEOPLE LINE UP TO MARCH TOWARD THE PROMISED LAND. THE PRIESTS LEAD THE FORMATION, CARRYING THE SACRED ARK OF THE COVENANT. AND MOSES COUNTS THE NUMBER OF ISRAELITES AS THEY PASS BY, FOLLOWING GOD'S INSTRUCTIONS.

Quail Coming Out of Their Noses

BASED ON NUMBERS 11

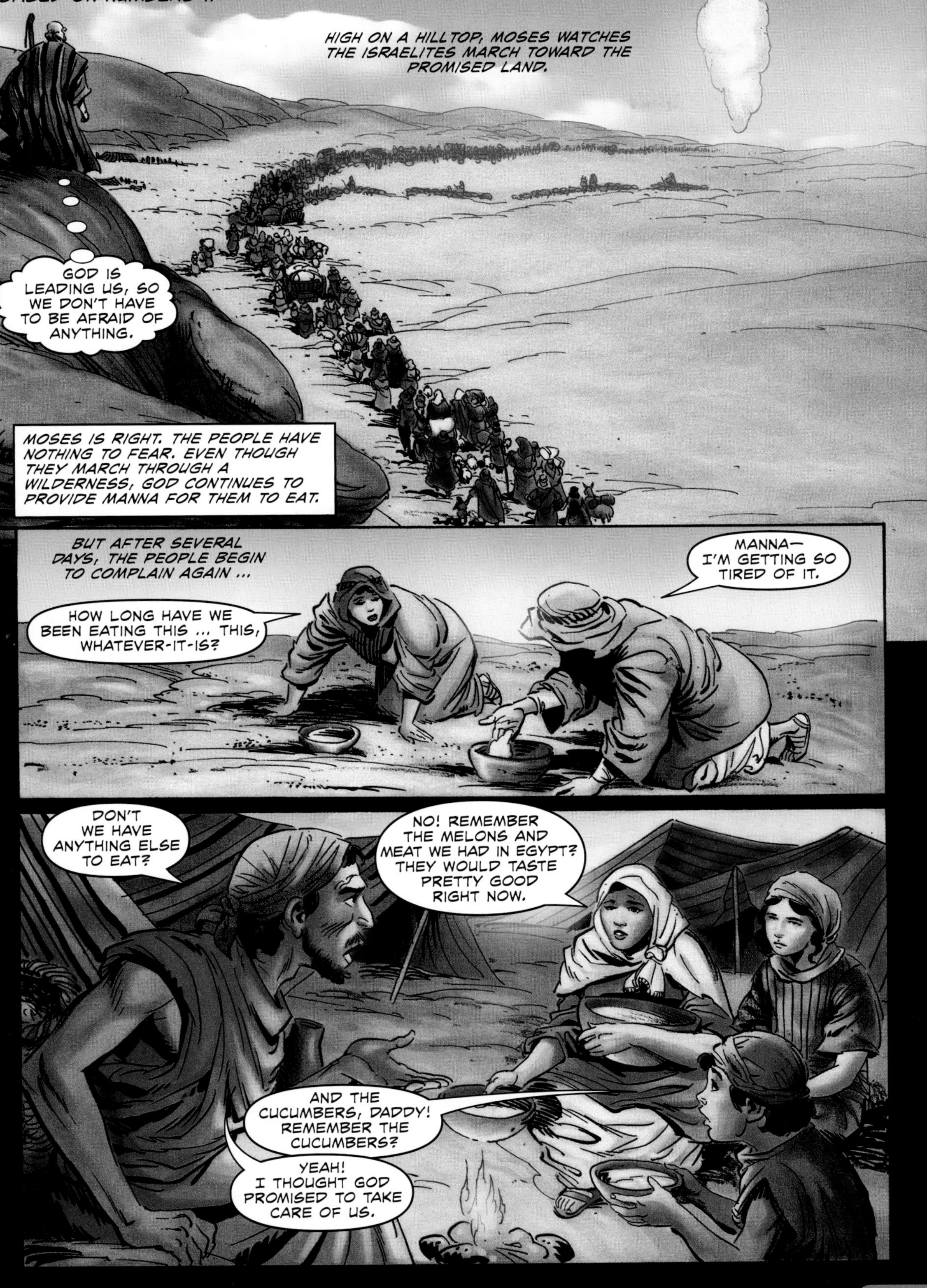
HIGH ON A HILLTOP, MOSES WATCHES THE ISRAELITES MARCH TOWARD THE PROMISED LAND.
GOD IS LEADING US, SO WE DON'T HAVE TO BE AFRAID OF ANYTHING.
MOSES IS RIGHT. THE PEOPLE HAVE NOTHING TO FEAR. EVEN THOUGH THEY MARCH THROUGH A WILDERNESS, GOD CONTINUES TO PROVIDE MANNA FOR THEM TO EAT.
BUT AFTER SEVERAL DAYS, THE PEOPLE BEGIN TO COMPLAIN AGAIN ...
HOW LONG HAVE WE BEEN EATING THIS ... THIS, WHATEVER-IT-IS?
MANNA— I'M GETTING SO TIRED OF IT.
DON'T WE HAVE ANYTHING ELSE TO EAT?
NO! REMEMBER THE MELONS AND MEAT WE HAD IN EGYPT? THEY WOULD TASTE PRETTY GOOD RIGHT NOW.
AND THE CUCUMBERS, DADDY! REMEMBER THE CUCUMBERS?
YEAH! I THOUGHT GOD PROMISED TO TAKE CARE OF US.

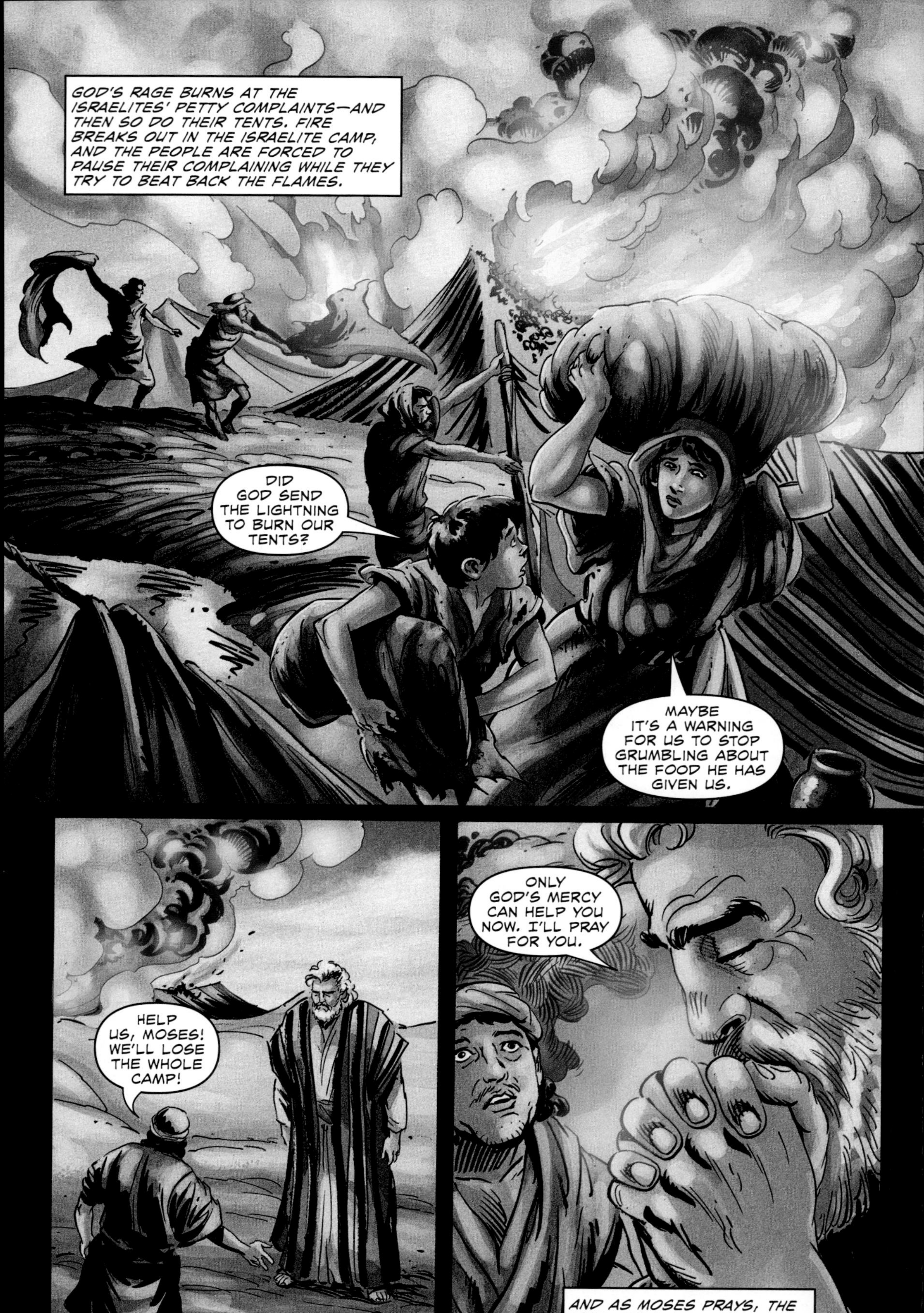
GOD'S RAGE BURNS AT THE ISRAELITES' PETTY COMPLAINTS—AND THEN SO DO THEIR TENTS. FIRE BREAKS OUT IN THE ISRAELITE CAMP, AND THE PEOPLE ARE FORCED TO PAUSE THEIR COMPLAINING WHILE THEY TRY TO BEAT BACK THE FLAMES.
DID GOD SEND THE LIGHTNING TO BURN OUR TENTS?
MAYBE IT'S A WARNING FOR US TO STOP GRUMBLING ABOUT THE FOOD HE HAS GIVEN US.
HELP US, MOSES! WE'LL LOSE THE WHOLE CAMP!
ONLY GOD'S MERCY CAN HELP YOU NOW. I'LL PRAY FOR YOU.
AND AS MOSES PRAYS, THE FIRE GOES OUT ON ITS OWN.

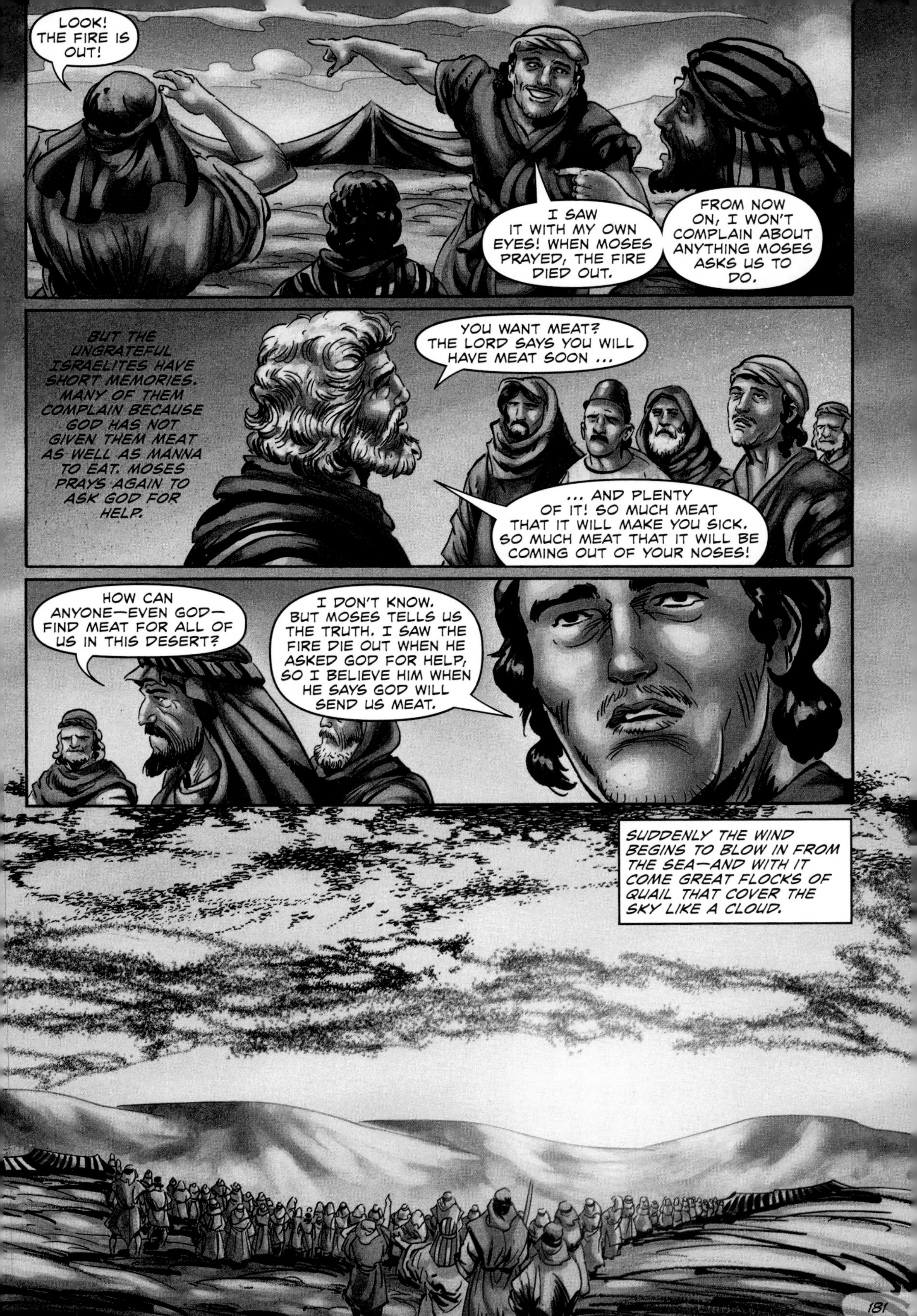
LOOK! THE FIRE IS OUT!
I SAW IT WITH MY OWN EYES! WHEN MOSES PRAYED, THE FIRE DIED OUT.
FROM NOW ON, I WON'T COMPLAIN ABOUT ANYTHING MOSES ASKS US TO DO.
BUT THE UNGRATEFUL ISRAELITES HAVE SHORT MEMORIES. MANY OF THEM COMPLAIN BECAUSE GOD HAS NOT GIVEN THEM MEAT AS WELL AS MANNA TO EAT. MOSES PRAYS AGAIN TO ASK GOD FOR HELP.
YOU WANT MEAT? THE LORD SAYS YOU WILL HAVE MEAT SOON ...
... AND PLENTY OF IT! SO MUCH MEAT THAT IT WILL MAKE YOU SICK. SO MUCH MEAT THAT IT WILL BE COMING OUT OF YOUR NOSES!
HOW CAN ANYONE—EVEN GOD—FIND MEAT FOR ALL OF US IN THIS DESERT?
I DON'T KNOW. BUT MOSES TELLS US THE TRUTH. I SAW THE FIRE DIE OUT WHEN HE ASKED GOD FOR HELP, SO I BELIEVE HIM WHEN HE SAYS GOD WILL SEND US MEAT.
SUDDENLY THE WIND BEGINS TO BLOW IN FROM THE SEA—AND WITH IT COME GREAT FLOCKS OF QUAIL THAT COVER THE SKY LIKE A CLOUD.

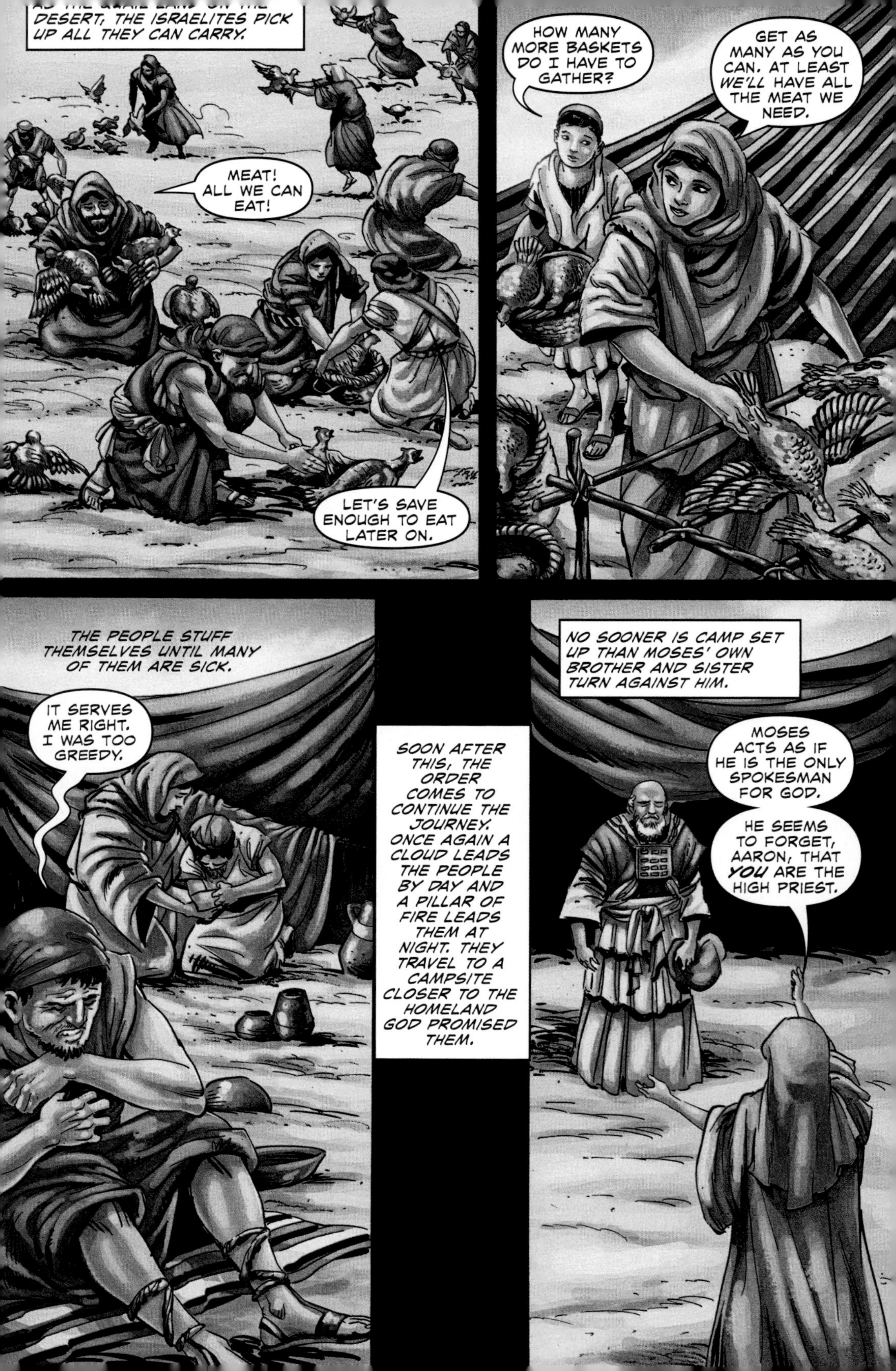
DESERT, THE ISRAELITES PICK UP ALL THEY CAN CARRY.
MEAT! ALL WE CAN EAT!
LET'S SAVE ENOUGH TO EAT LATER ON.
HOW MANY MORE BASKETS DO I HAVE TO GATHER?
GET AS MANY AS YOU CAN. AT LEAST *WE'LL* HAVE ALL THE MEAT WE NEED.
THE PEOPLE STUFF THEMSELVES UNTIL MANY OF THEM ARE SICK.
IT SERVES ME RIGHT. I WAS TOO GREEDY.
SOON AFTER THIS, THE ORDER COMES TO CONTINUE THE JOURNEY. ONCE AGAIN A CLOUD LEADS THE PEOPLE BY DAY AND A PILLAR OF FIRE LEADS THEM AT NIGHT. THEY TRAVEL TO A CAMPSITE CLOSER TO THE HOMELAND GOD PROMISED THEM.
NO SOONER IS CAMP SET UP THAN MOSES' OWN BROTHER AND SISTER TURN AGAINST HIM.
MOSES ACTS AS IF HE IS THE ONLY SPOKESMAN FOR GOD.
HE SEEMS TO FORGET, AARON, THAT ***YOU*** ARE THE HIGH PRIEST.

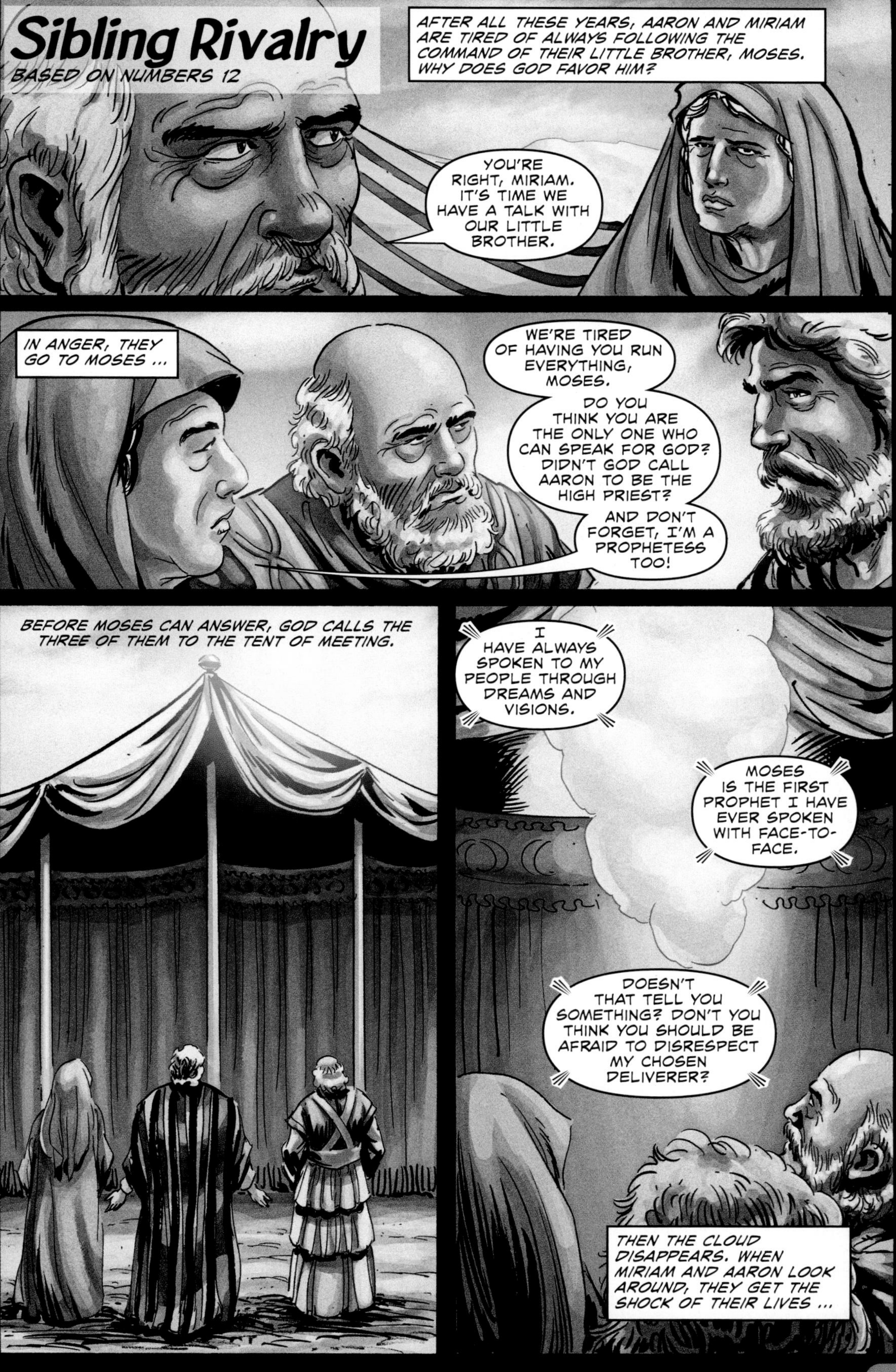
Sibling Rivalry
BASED ON NUMBERS 12
AFTER ALL THESE YEARS, AARON AND MIRIAM ARE TIRED OF ALWAYS FOLLOWING THE COMMAND OF THEIR LITTLE BROTHER, MOSES. WHY DOES GOD FAVOR HIM?
YOU'RE RIGHT, MIRIAM. IT'S TIME WE HAVE A TALK WITH OUR LITTLE BROTHER.
IN ANGER, THEY GO TO MOSES ...
WE'RE TIRED OF HAVING YOU RUN EVERYTHING, MOSES.
DO YOU THINK YOU ARE THE ONLY ONE WHO CAN SPEAK FOR GOD? DIDN'T GOD CALL AARON TO BE THE HIGH PRIEST?
AND DON'T FORGET, I'M A PROPHETESS TOO!
BEFORE MOSES CAN ANSWER, GOD CALLS THE THREE OF THEM TO THE TENT OF MEETING.
I HAVE ALWAYS SPOKEN TO MY PEOPLE THROUGH DREAMS AND VISIONS.
MOSES IS THE FIRST PROPHET I HAVE EVER SPOKEN WITH FACE-TO-FACE.
DOESN'T THAT TELL YOU SOMETHING? DON'T YOU THINK YOU SHOULD BE AFRAID TO DISRESPECT MY CHOSEN DELIVERER?
THEN THE CLOUD DISAPPEARS. WHEN MIRIAM AND AARON LOOK AROUND, THEY GET THE SHOCK OF THEIR LIVES ...

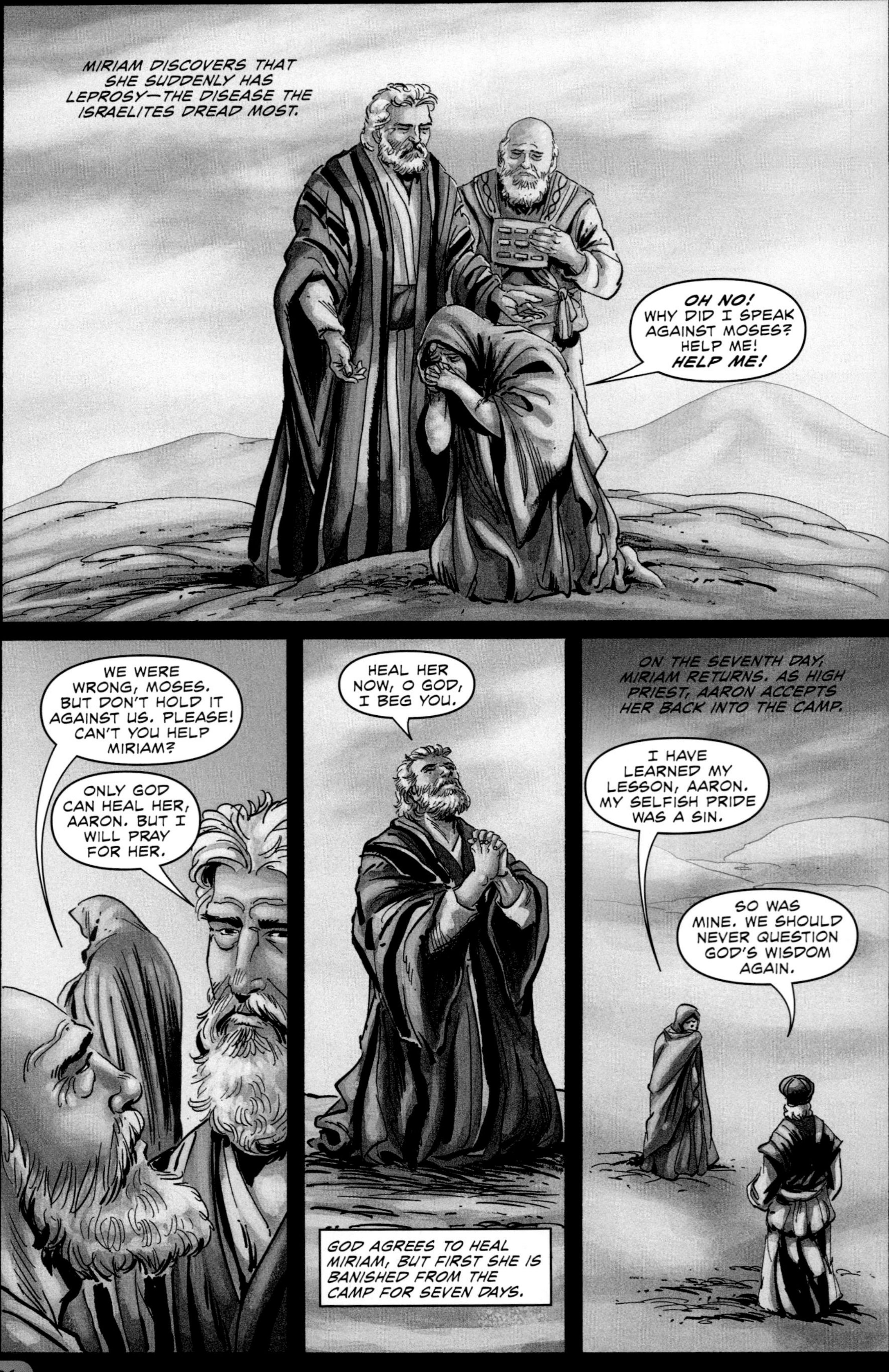
MIRIAM DISCOVERS THAT SHE SUDDENLY HAS LEPROSY—THE DISEASE THE ISRAELITES DREAD MOST.
OH NO! WHY DID I SPEAK AGAINST MOSES? HELP ME! HELP ME!
WE WERE WRONG, MOSES. BUT DON'T HOLD IT AGAINST US. PLEASE! CAN'T YOU HELP MIRIAM?
ONLY GOD CAN HEAL HER, AARON. BUT I WILL PRAY FOR HER.
HEAL HER NOW, O GOD, I BEG YOU.
GOD AGREES TO HEAL MIRIAM, BUT FIRST SHE IS BANISHED FROM THE CAMP FOR SEVEN DAYS.
ON THE SEVENTH DAY, MIRIAM RETURNS. AS HIGH PRIEST, AARON ACCEPTS HER BACK INTO THE CAMP.
I HAVE LEARNED MY LESSON, AARON. MY SELFISH PRIDE WAS A SIN.
SO WAS MINE. WE SHOULD NEVER QUESTION GOD'S WISDOM AGAIN.

Spy vs. Spy

BASED ON NUMBERS 13:1–14:10

Route of the Spies

Mediterranean Sea

EGYPT

Hebron

CANAAN

Israelite Camp

Wilderness of Paran

THE ISRAELITES CONTINUE THEIR JOURNEY UNTIL THEY REACH THE WILDERNESS OF PARAN. THERE MOSES ORDERS THEM TO SET UP CAMP.

MOSES CALLS ONE MAN FROM EACH TRIBE TO ATTEND AN IMPORTANT MEETING.

WE ARE ON THE BORDER OF CANAAN, THE LAND GOD HAS PROMISED TO US.

BUT BEFORE WE GO INTO IT, WE MUST KNOW WHAT LIES AHEAD.

WHAT ARE YOUR PLANS?

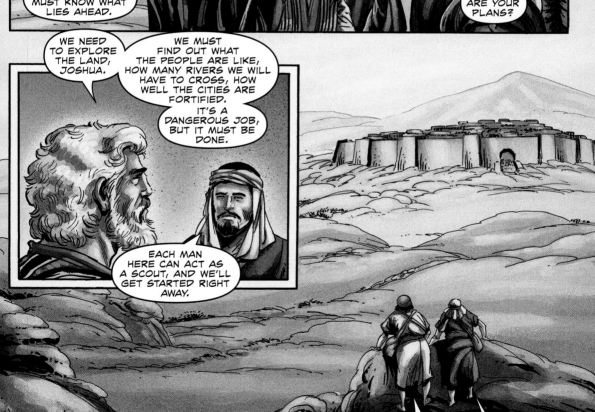

WE NEED TO EXPLORE THE LAND, JOSHUA.

WE MUST FIND OUT WHAT THE PEOPLE ARE LIKE, HOW MANY RIVERS WE WILL HAVE TO CROSS, HOW WELL THE CITIES ARE FORTIFIED.

IT'S A DANGEROUS JOB, BUT IT MUST BE DONE.

EACH MAN HERE CAN ACT AS A SCOUT, AND WE'LL GET STARTED RIGHT AWAY.

LOOK AT THAT CITY!

AND THE SIZE OF THOSE WALLS!

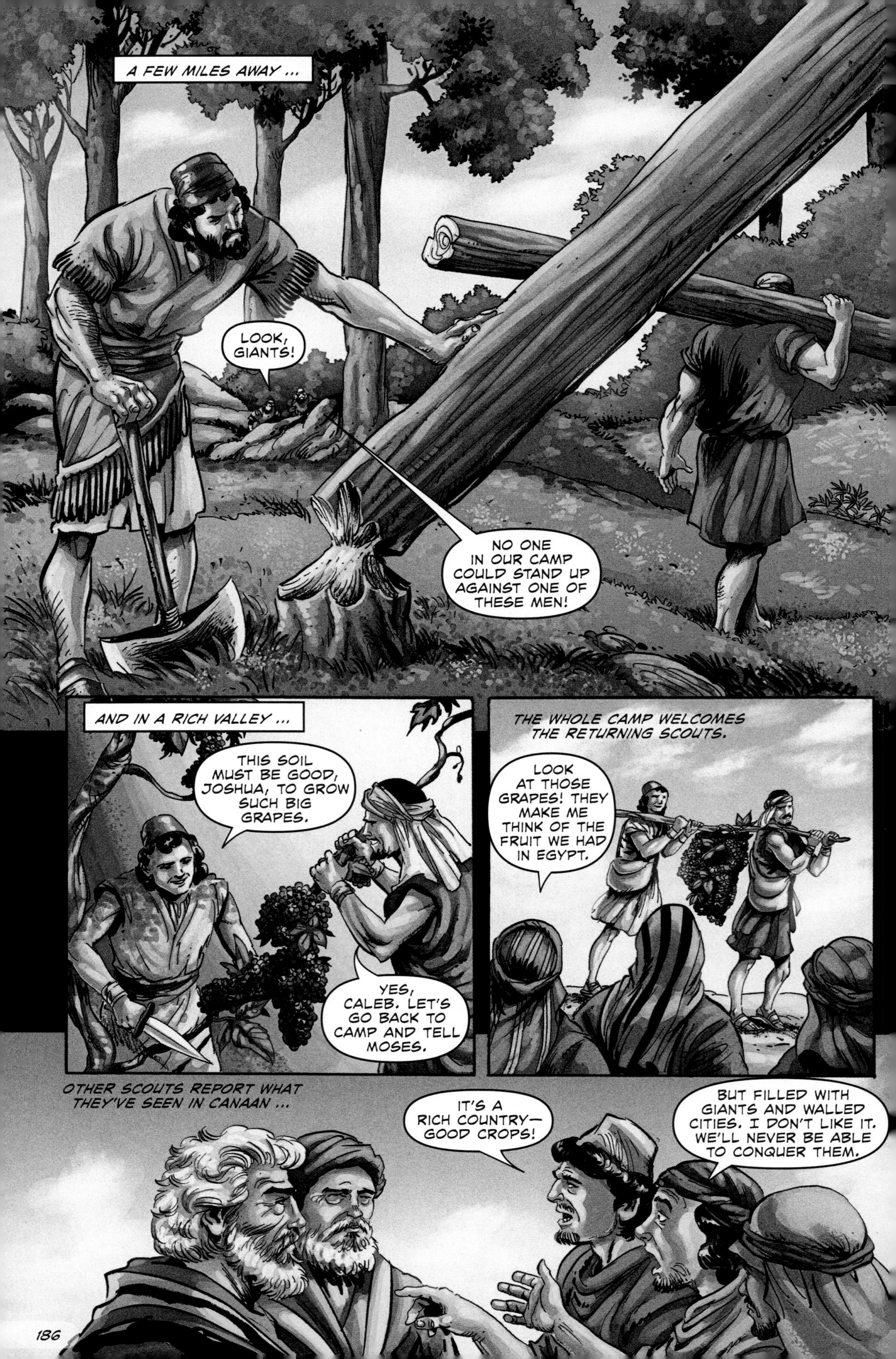
A FEW MILES AWAY ...
LOOK, GIANTS!
NO ONE IN OUR CAMP COULD STAND UP AGAINST ONE OF THESE MEN!
AND IN A RICH VALLEY ...
THIS SOIL MUST BE GOOD, JOSHUA, TO GROW SUCH BIG GRAPES.
YES, CALEB. LET'S GO BACK TO CAMP AND TELL MOSES.
THE WHOLE CAMP WELCOMES THE RETURNING SCOUTS.
LOOK AT THOSE GRAPES! THEY MAKE ME THINK OF THE FRUIT WE HAD IN EGYPT.
OTHER SCOUTS REPORT WHAT THEY'VE SEEN IN CANAAN ...
IT'S A RICH COUNTRY—GOOD CROPS!
BUT FILLED WITH GIANTS AND WALLED CITIES. I DON'T LIKE IT. WE'LL NEVER BE ABLE TO CONQUER THEM.

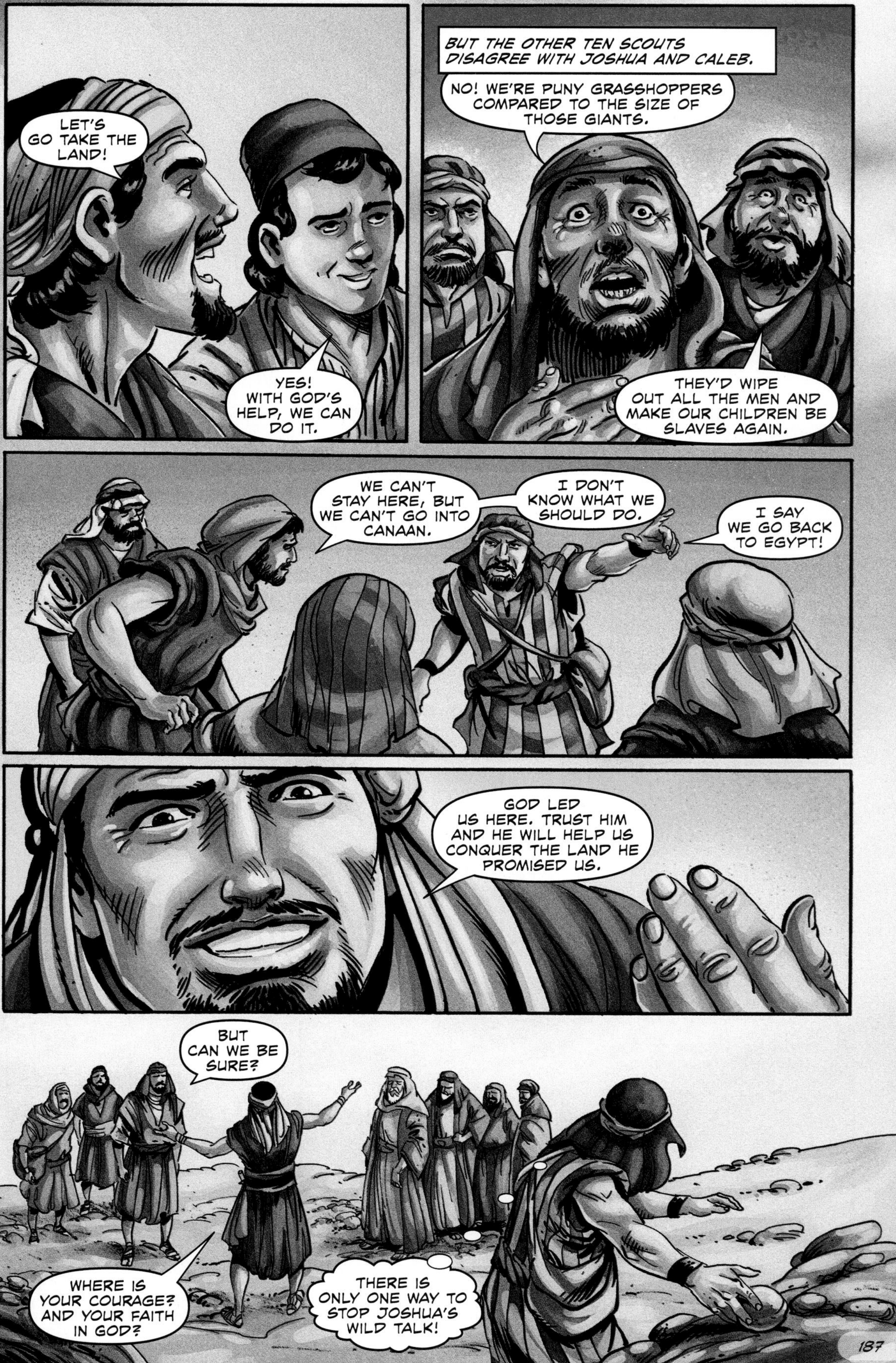
LET'S GO TAKE THE LAND!
YES! WITH GOD'S HELP, WE CAN DO IT.
BUT THE OTHER TEN SCOUTS DISAGREE WITH JOSHUA AND CALEB.
NO! WE'RE PUNY GRASSHOPPERS COMPARED TO THE SIZE OF THOSE GIANTS.
THEY'D WIPE OUT ALL THE MEN AND MAKE OUR CHILDREN BE SLAVES AGAIN.
WE CAN'T STAY HERE, BUT WE CAN'T GO INTO CANAAN.
I DON'T KNOW WHAT WE SHOULD DO.
I SAY WE GO BACK TO EGYPT!
GOD LED US HERE. TRUST HIM AND HE WILL HELP US CONQUER THE LAND HE PROMISED US.
BUT CAN WE BE SURE?
WHERE IS YOUR COURAGE? AND YOUR FAITH IN GOD?
THERE IS ONLY ONE WAY TO STOP JOSHUA'S WILD TALK!

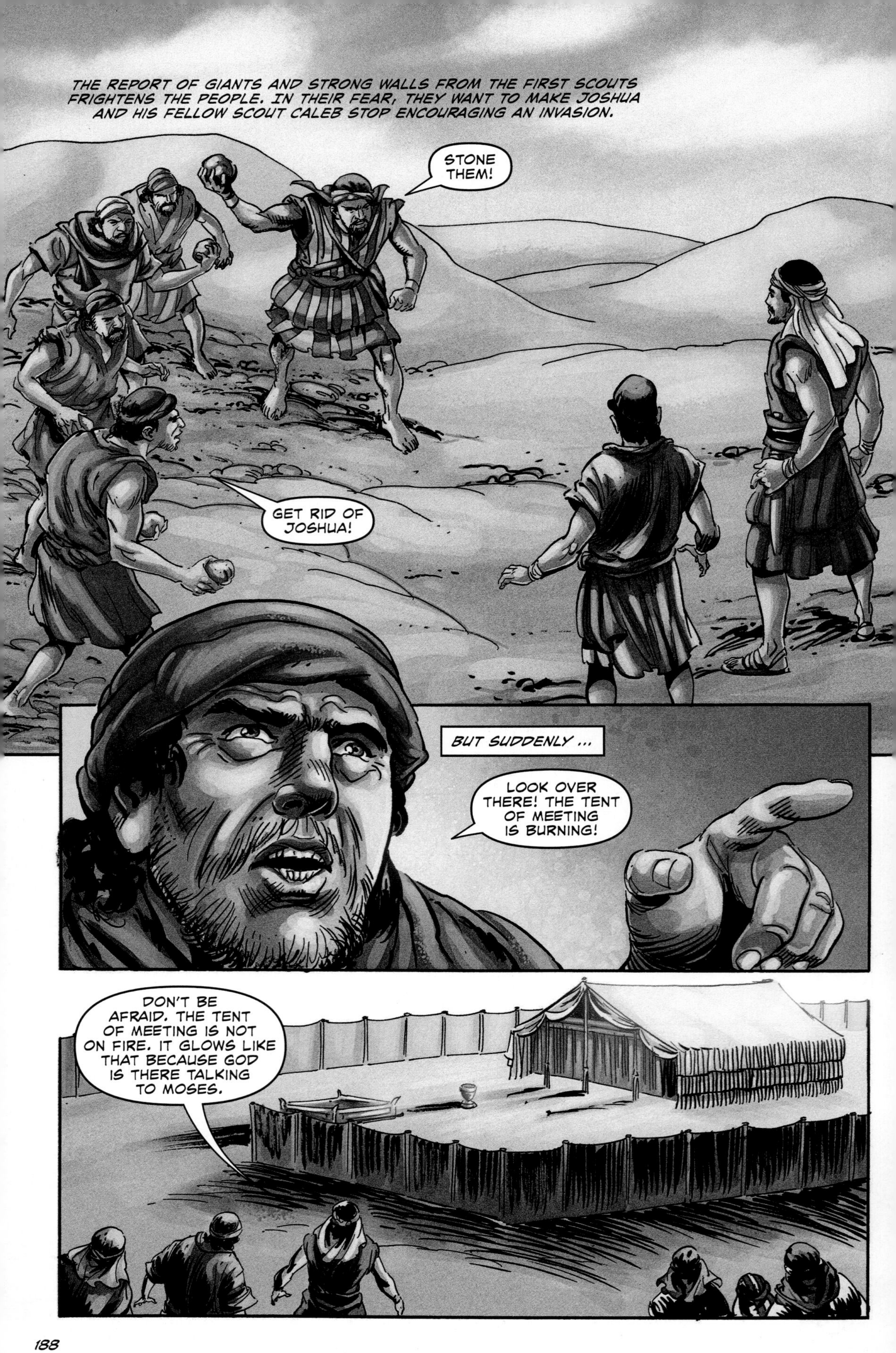
THE REPORT OF GIANTS AND STRONG WALLS FROM THE FIRST SCOUTS FRIGHTENS THE PEOPLE. IN THEIR FEAR, THEY WANT TO MAKE JOSHUA AND HIS FELLOW SCOUT CALEB STOP ENCOURAGING AN INVASION.
STONE THEM!
GET RID OF JOSHUA!
BUT SUDDENLY ...
LOOK OVER THERE! THE TENT OF MEETING IS BURNING!
DON'T BE AFRAID. THE TENT OF MEETING IS NOT ON FIRE. IT GLOWS LIKE THAT BECAUSE GOD IS THERE TALKING TO MOSES.

A Rebellious People

BASED ON NUMBERS 14:11—16:34

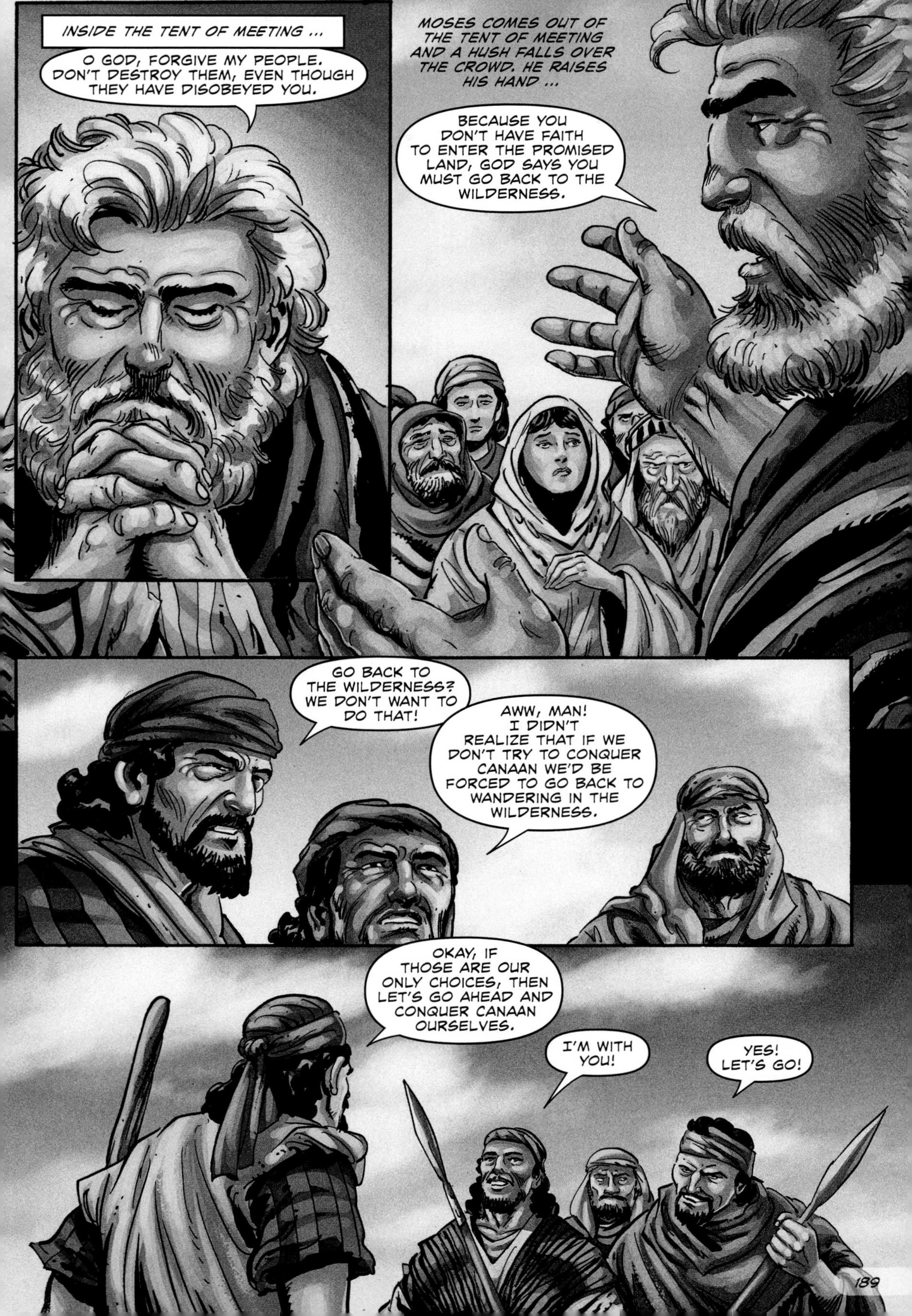

INSIDE THE TENT OF MEETING ...
O GOD, FORGIVE MY PEOPLE. DON'T DESTROY THEM, EVEN THOUGH THEY HAVE DISOBEYED YOU.
MOSES COMES OUT OF THE TENT OF MEETING AND A HUSH FALLS OVER THE CROWD. HE RAISES HIS HAND ...
BECAUSE YOU DON'T HAVE FAITH TO ENTER THE PROMISED LAND, GOD SAYS YOU MUST GO BACK TO THE WILDERNESS.
GO BACK TO THE WILDERNESS? WE DON'T WANT TO DO THAT!
AWW, MAN! I DIDN'T REALIZE THAT IF WE DON'T TRY TO CONQUER CANAAN WE'D BE FORCED TO GO BACK TO WANDERING IN THE WILDERNESS.
OKAY, IF THOSE ARE OUR ONLY CHOICES, THEN LET'S GO AHEAD AND CONQUER CANAAN OURSELVES.
I'M WITH YOU!
YES! LET'S GO!

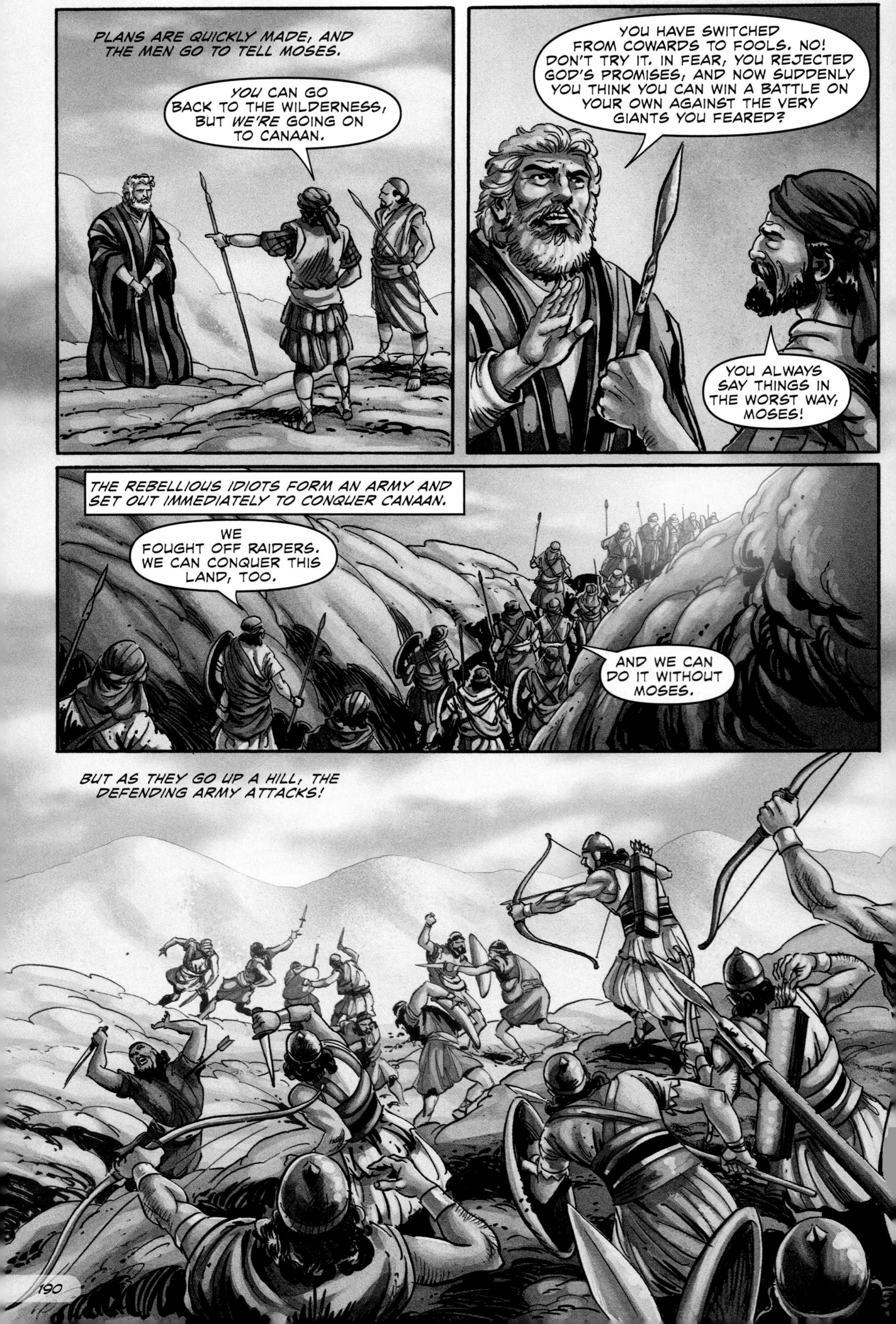
PLANS ARE QUICKLY MADE, AND THE MEN GO TO TELL MOSES.
YOU CAN GO BACK TO THE WILDERNESS, BUT WE'RE GOING ON TO CANAAN.
YOU HAVE SWITCHED FROM COWARDS TO FOOLS. NO! DON'T TRY IT. IN FEAR, YOU REJECTED GOD'S PROMISES, AND NOW SUDDENLY YOU THINK YOU CAN WIN A BATTLE ON YOUR OWN AGAINST THE VERY GIANTS YOU FEARED?
YOU ALWAYS SAY THINGS IN THE WORST WAY, MOSES!
THE REBELLIOUS IDIOTS FORM AN ARMY AND SET OUT IMMEDIATELY TO CONQUER CANAAN.
WE FOUGHT OFF RAIDERS. WE CAN CONQUER THIS LAND, TOO.
AND WE CAN DO IT WITHOUT MOSES.
BUT AS THEY GO UP A HILL, THE DEFENDING ARMY ATTACKS!

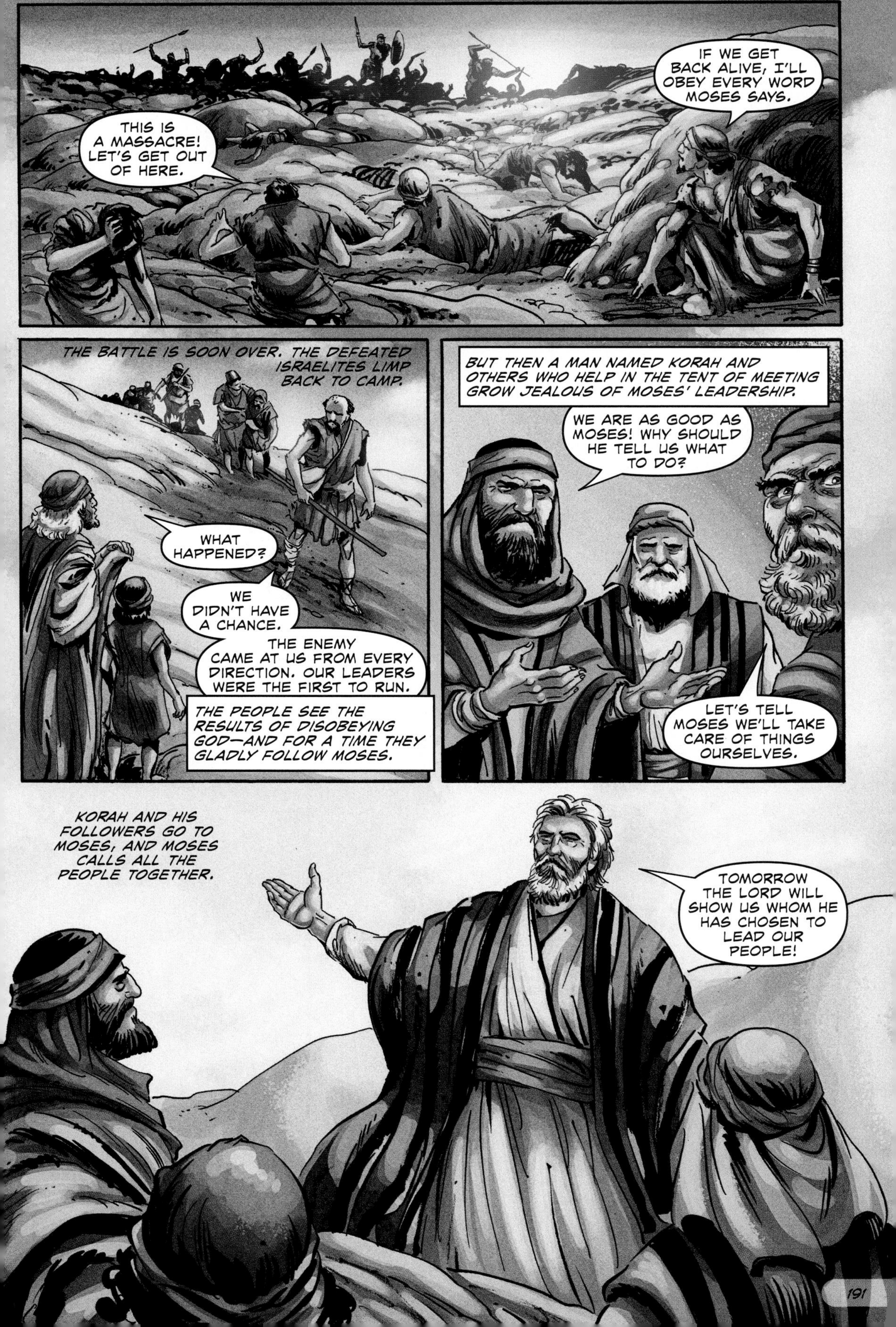
THIS IS A MASSACRE! LET'S GET OUT OF HERE.
IF WE GET BACK ALIVE, I'LL OBEY EVERY WORD MOSES SAYS.
THE BATTLE IS SOON OVER. THE DEFEATED ISRAELITES LIMP BACK TO CAMP.
WHAT HAPPENED?
WE DIDN'T HAVE A CHANCE.
THE ENEMY CAME AT US FROM EVERY DIRECTION. OUR LEADERS WERE THE FIRST TO RUN.
THE PEOPLE SEE THE RESULTS OF DISOBEYING GOD—AND FOR A TIME THEY GLADLY FOLLOW MOSES.
BUT THEN A MAN NAMED KORAH AND OTHERS WHO HELP IN THE TENT OF MEETING GROW JEALOUS OF MOSES' LEADERSHIP.
WE ARE AS GOOD AS MOSES! WHY SHOULD HE TELL US WHAT TO DO?
LET'S TELL MOSES WE'LL TAKE CARE OF THINGS OURSELVES.
KORAH AND HIS FOLLOWERS GO TO MOSES, AND MOSES CALLS ALL THE PEOPLE TOGETHER.
TOMORROW THE LORD WILL SHOW US WHOM HE HAS CHOSEN TO LEAD OUR PEOPLE!

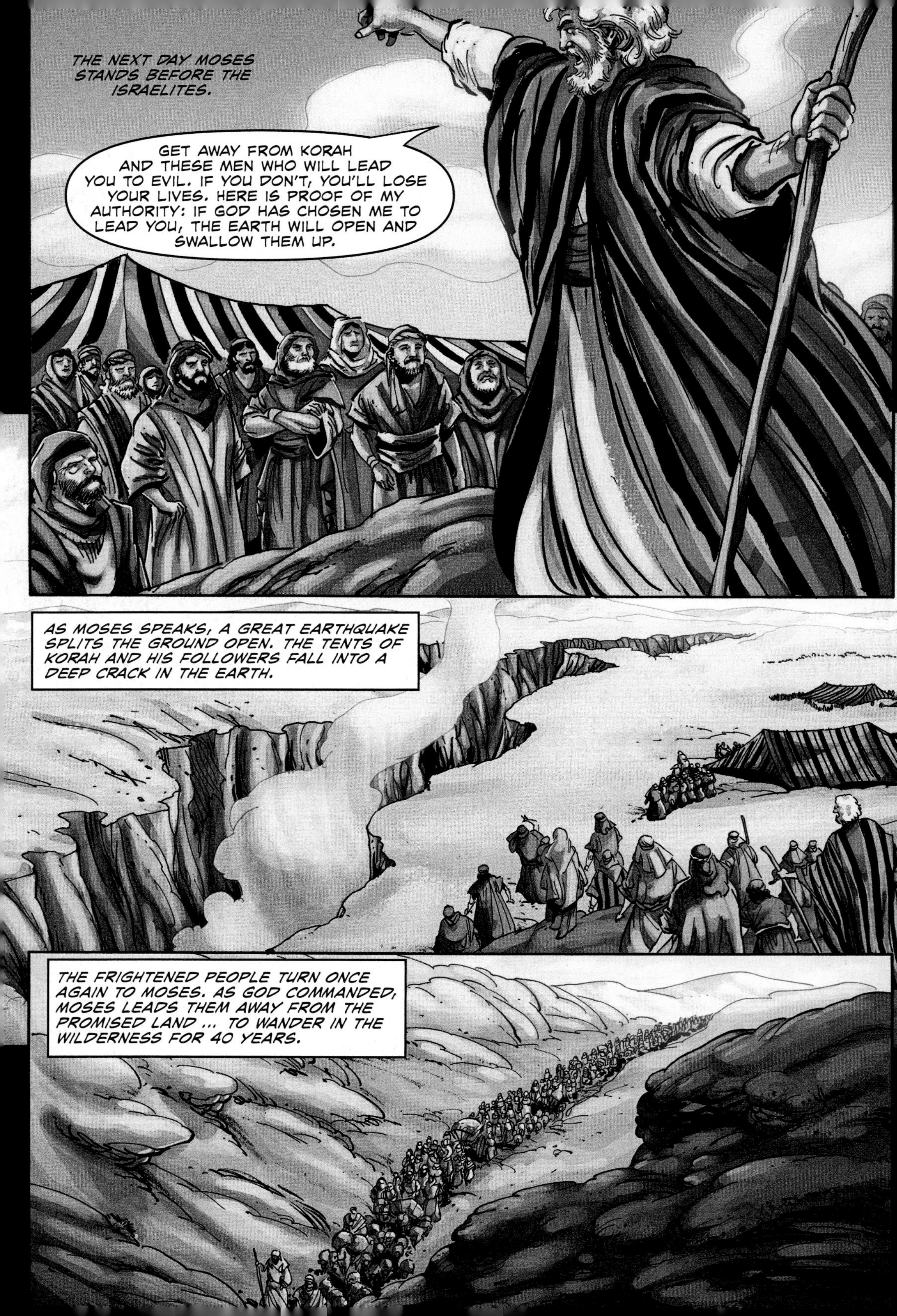
THE NEXT DAY MOSES STANDS BEFORE THE ISRAELITES.
GET AWAY FROM KORAH AND THESE MEN WHO WILL LEAD YOU TO EVIL. IF YOU DON'T, YOU'LL LOSE YOUR LIVES. HERE IS PROOF OF MY AUTHORITY: IF GOD HAS CHOSEN ME TO LEAD YOU, THE EARTH WILL OPEN AND SWALLOW THEM UP.
AS MOSES SPEAKS, A GREAT EARTHQUAKE SPLITS THE GROUND OPEN. THE TENTS OF KORAH AND HIS FOLLOWERS FALL INTO A DEEP CRACK IN THE EARTH.
THE FRIGHTENED PEOPLE TURN ONCE AGAIN TO MOSES. AS GOD COMMANDED, MOSES LEADS THEM AWAY FROM THE PROMISED LAND ... TO WANDER IN THE WILDERNESS FOR 40 YEARS.

Two Strikes— You're Out!

BASED ON NUMBERS 20:1-13

WHEN HARDSHIPS COME, THE PEOPLE FORGET THAT IT WAS THEIR FEAR THAT KEPT THEM FROM TAKING THE GOOD LAND GOD HAD PROMISED THEM. AGAIN AND AGAIN THEY COMPLAIN ...

NO WATER! NOW WHAT WILL I DO?

THE SPRING IS DRY! HOW CAN I COOK— OR WASH?

I'LL HAVE OUR TRIBAL LEADERS TAKE THIS UP WITH MOSES.

WELL, MOSES, WHERE ARE WE GOING TO GET WATER?

DID YOU LEAD US OUT HERE TO DIE OF THIRST?

WE'VE HAD ENOUGH. LET'S GO BACK TO EGYPT. AT LEAST THERE WE HAD FOOD AND WATER.

YOU WANT WATER? I'LL GIVE YOU WATER!!

IN A FIT OF ANGER, MOSES STRIKES A NEARBY ROCK WITH HIS STAFF—TWICE! WATER POURS OUT, BUT GOD IS NOT HAPPY. HOW CAN MOSES TEACH THE PEOPLE TO OBEY IF HE DOESN'T OBEY? BECAUSE OF HIS BAD EXAMPLE, GOD TELLS MOSES THAT HE WILL NOT ENTER THE PROMISED LAND.

193

The Bronze Snake

BASED ON NUMBERS 20:22–21:22

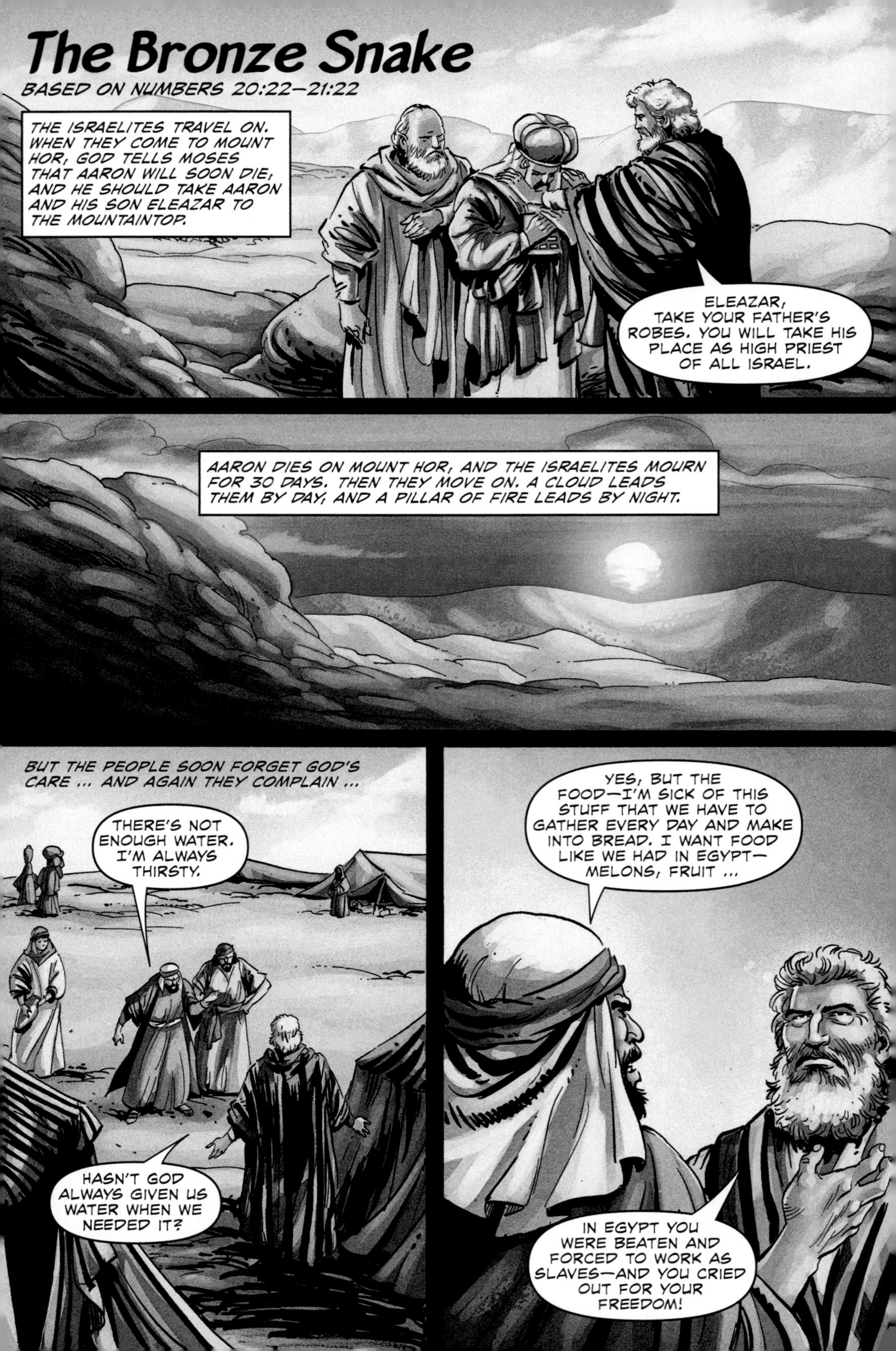
THE ISRAELITES TRAVEL ON. WHEN THEY COME TO MOUNT HOR, GOD TELLS MOSES THAT AARON WILL SOON DIE, AND HE SHOULD TAKE AARON AND HIS SON ELEAZAR TO THE MOUNTAINTOP.
ELEAZAR, TAKE YOUR FATHER'S ROBES. YOU WILL TAKE HIS PLACE AS HIGH PRIEST OF ALL ISRAEL.
AARON DIES ON MOUNT HOR, AND THE ISRAELITES MOURN FOR 30 DAYS. THEN THEY MOVE ON. A CLOUD LEADS THEM BY DAY, AND A PILLAR OF FIRE LEADS BY NIGHT.
BUT THE PEOPLE SOON FORGET GOD'S CARE ... AND AGAIN THEY COMPLAIN ...
THERE'S NOT ENOUGH WATER. I'M ALWAYS THIRSTY.
HASN'T GOD ALWAYS GIVEN US WATER WHEN WE NEEDED IT?
YES, BUT THE FOOD—I'M SICK OF THIS STUFF THAT WE HAVE TO GATHER EVERY DAY AND MAKE INTO BREAD. I WANT FOOD LIKE WE HAD IN EGYPT—MELONS, FRUIT ...
IN EGYPT YOU WERE BEATEN AND FORCED TO WORK AS SLAVES—AND YOU CRIED OUT FOR YOUR FREEDOM!

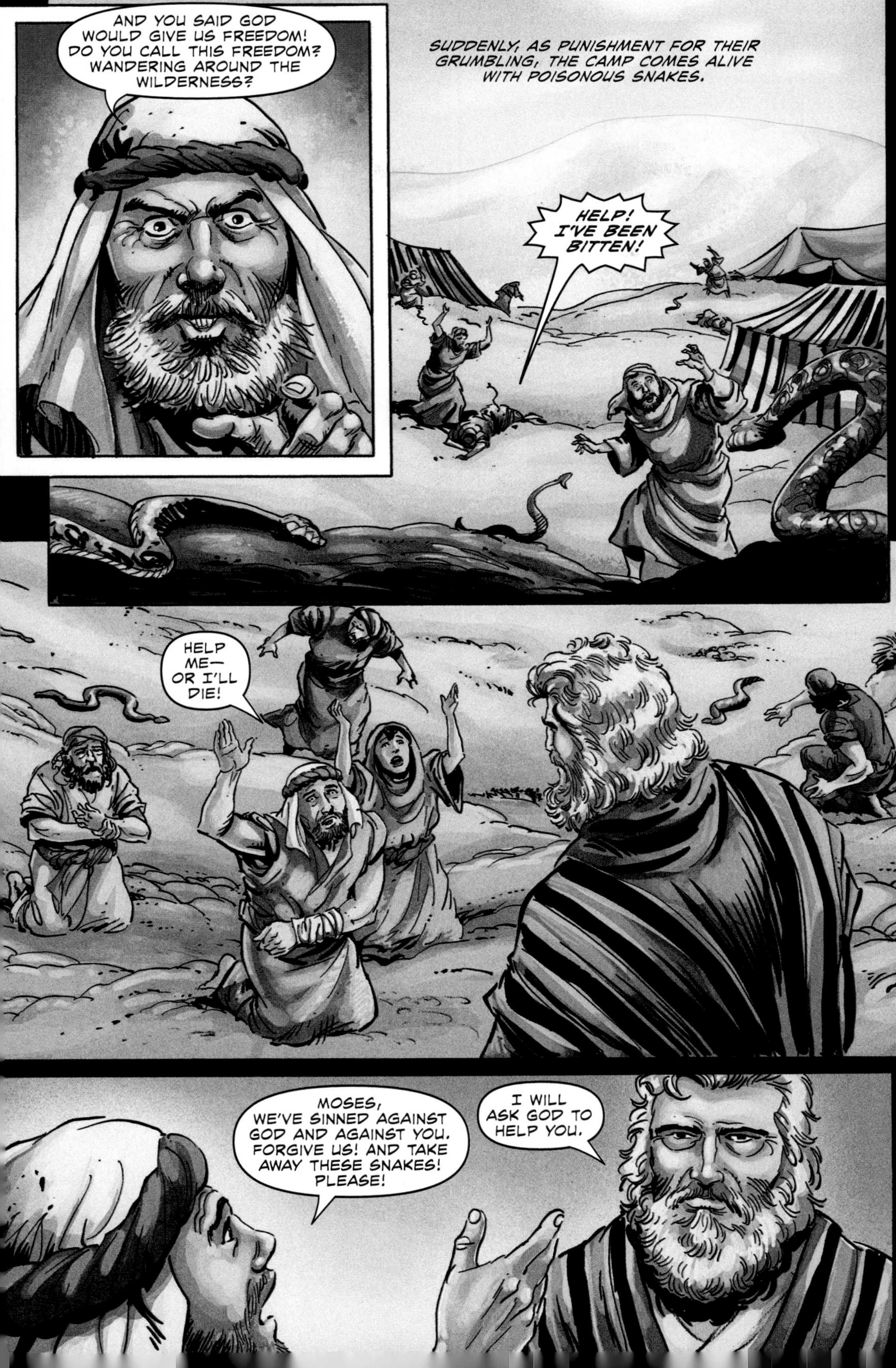
AND YOU SAID GOD WOULD GIVE US FREEDOM! DO YOU CALL THIS FREEDOM? WANDERING AROUND THE WILDERNESS?
SUDDENLY, AS PUNISHMENT FOR THEIR GRUMBLING, THE CAMP COMES ALIVE WITH POISONOUS SNAKES.
HELP! I'VE BEEN BITTEN!
HELP ME— OR I'LL DIE!
MOSES, WE'VE SINNED AGAINST GOD AND AGAINST YOU. FORGIVE US! AND TAKE AWAY THESE SNAKES! PLEASE!
I WILL ASK GOD TO HELP YOU.

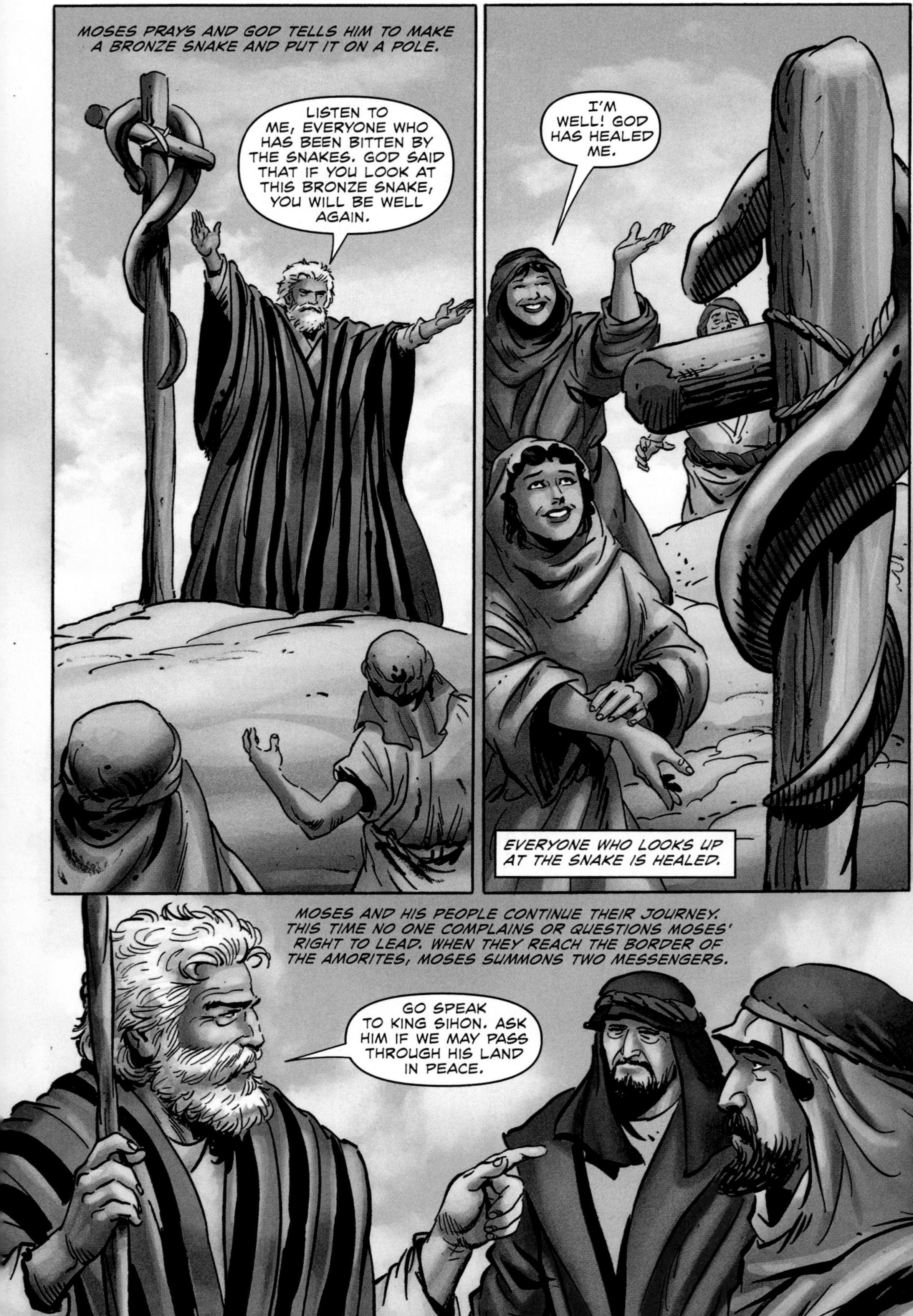
MOSES PRAYS AND GOD TELLS HIM TO MAKE A BRONZE SNAKE AND PUT IT ON A POLE.
LISTEN TO ME, EVERYONE WHO HAS BEEN BITTEN BY THE SNAKES. GOD SAID THAT IF YOU LOOK AT THIS BRONZE SNAKE, YOU WILL BE WELL AGAIN.
I'M WELL! GOD HAS HEALED ME.
EVERYONE WHO LOOKS UP AT THE SNAKE IS HEALED.
MOSES AND HIS PEOPLE CONTINUE THEIR JOURNEY. THIS TIME NO ONE COMPLAINS OR QUESTIONS MOSES' RIGHT TO LEAD. WHEN THEY REACH THE BORDER OF THE AMORITES, MOSES SUMMONS TWO MESSENGERS.
GO SPEAK TO KING SIHON. ASK HIM IF WE MAY PASS THROUGH HIS LAND IN PEACE.

The Wonderful Win Against Og

BASED ON NUMBERS 21:21–35

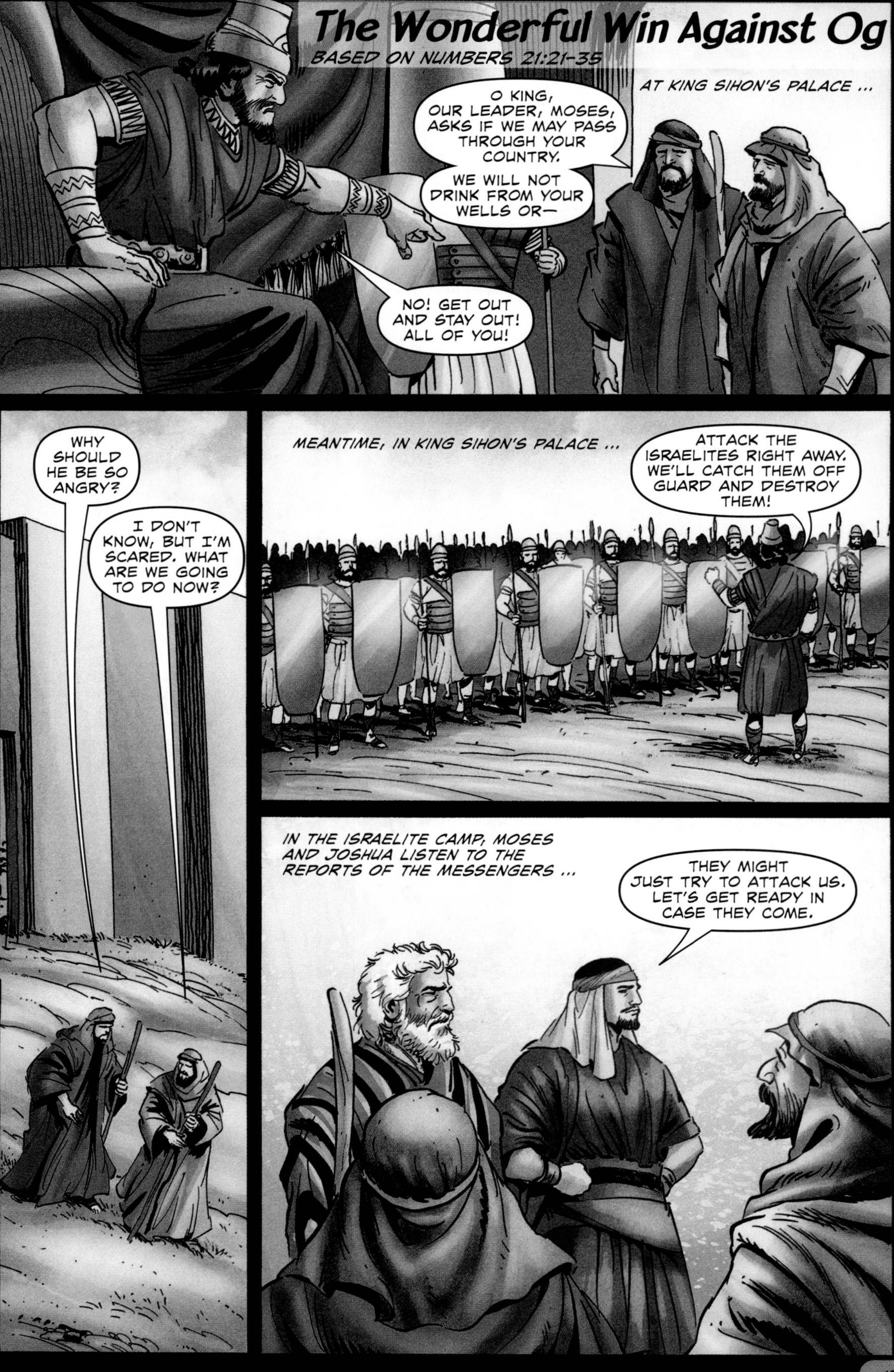

AT KING SIHON'S PALACE ...
O KING, OUR LEADER, MOSES, ASKS IF WE MAY PASS THROUGH YOUR COUNTRY.
WE WILL NOT DRINK FROM YOUR WELLS OR—
NO! GET OUT AND STAY OUT! ALL OF YOU!
WHY SHOULD HE BE SO ANGRY?
I DON'T KNOW, BUT I'M SCARED. WHAT ARE WE GOING TO DO NOW?
MEANTIME, IN KING SIHON'S PALACE ...
ATTACK THE ISRAELITES RIGHT AWAY. WE'LL CATCH THEM OFF GUARD AND DESTROY THEM!
IN THE ISRAELITE CAMP, MOSES AND JOSHUA LISTEN TO THE REPORTS OF THE MESSENGERS ...
THEY MIGHT JUST TRY TO ATTACK US. LET'S GET READY IN CASE THEY COME.

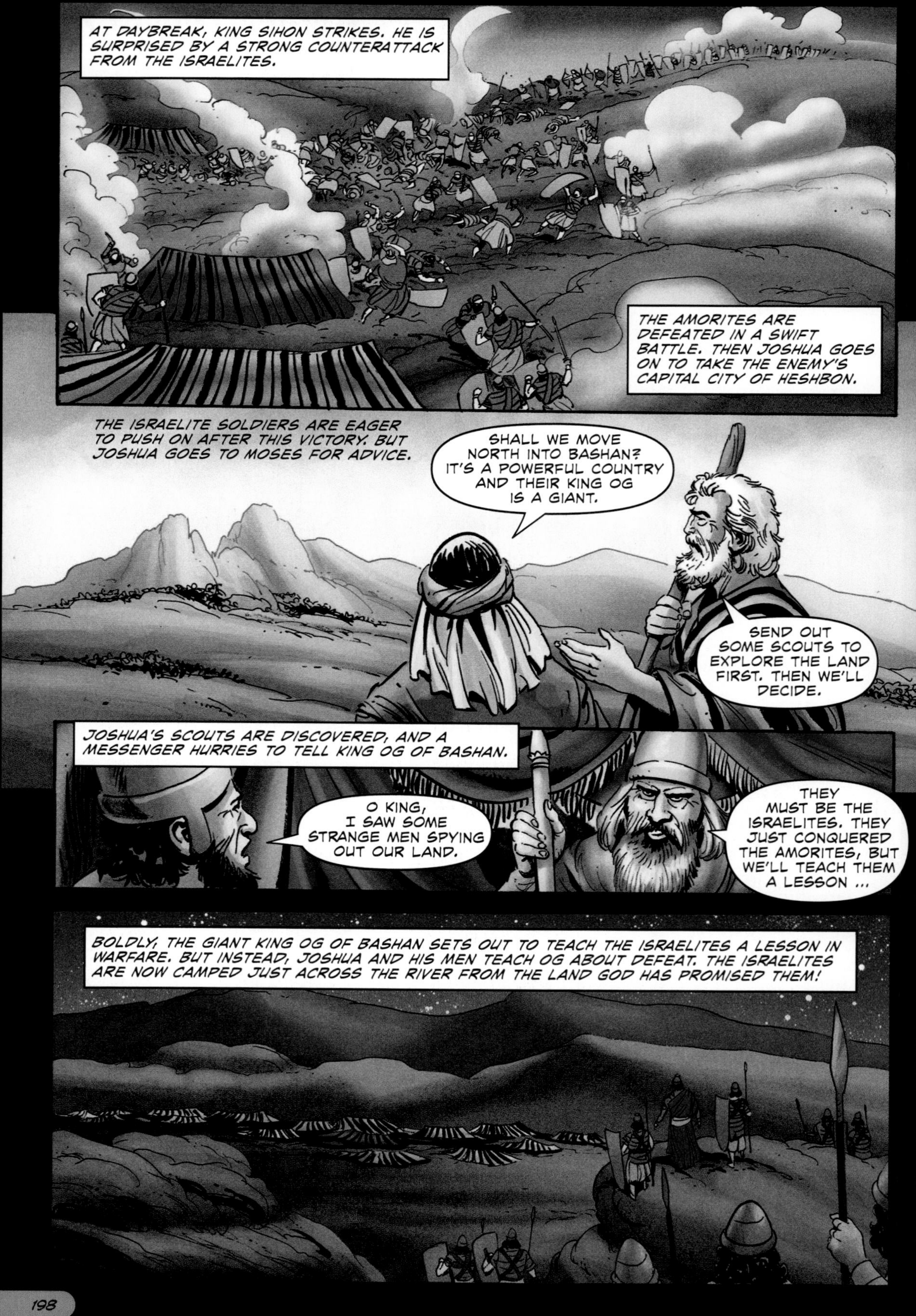
AT DAYBREAK, KING SIHON STRIKES. HE IS SURPRISED BY A STRONG COUNTERATTACK FROM THE ISRAELITES.
THE AMORITES ARE DEFEATED IN A SWIFT BATTLE. THEN JOSHUA GOES ON TO TAKE THE ENEMY'S CAPITAL CITY OF HESHBON.
THE ISRAELITE SOLDIERS ARE EAGER TO PUSH ON AFTER THIS VICTORY. BUT JOSHUA GOES TO MOSES FOR ADVICE.
SHALL WE MOVE NORTH INTO BASHAN? IT'S A POWERFUL COUNTRY AND THEIR KING OG IS A GIANT.
SEND OUT SOME SCOUTS TO EXPLORE THE LAND FIRST. THEN WE'LL DECIDE.
JOSHUA'S SCOUTS ARE DISCOVERED, AND A MESSENGER HURRIES TO TELL KING OG OF BASHAN.
O KING, I SAW SOME STRANGE MEN SPYING OUT OUR LAND.
THEY MUST BE THE ISRAELITES. THEY JUST CONQUERED THE AMORITES, BUT WE'LL TEACH THEM A LESSON ...
BOLDLY, THE GIANT KING OG OF BASHAN SETS OUT TO TEACH THE ISRAELITES A LESSON IN WARFARE. BUT INSTEAD, JOSHUA AND HIS MEN TEACH OG ABOUT DEFEAT. THE ISRAELITES ARE NOW CAMPED JUST ACROSS THE RIVER FROM THE LAND GOD HAS PROMISED THEM!

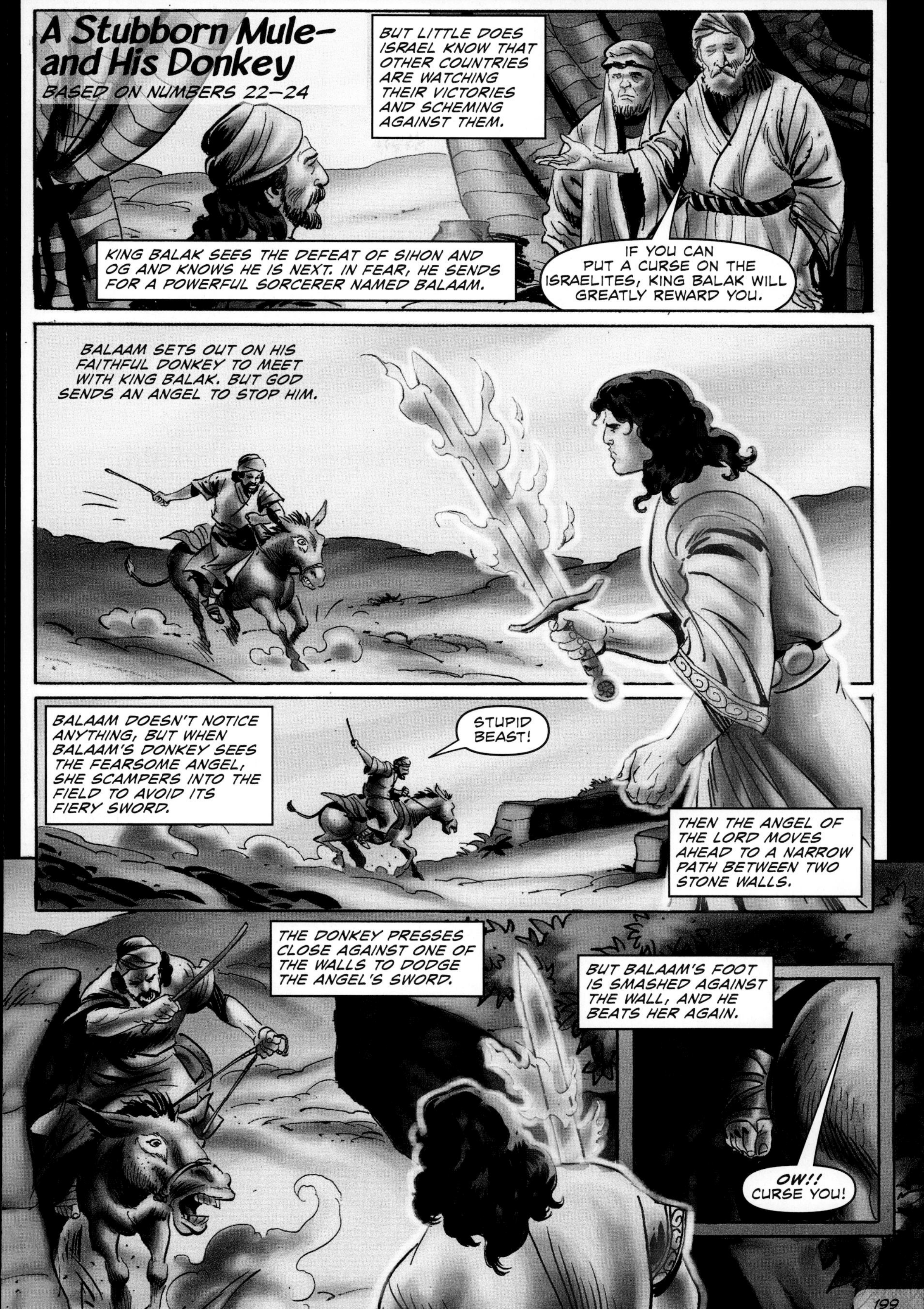
A Stubborn Mule-
and His Donkey
BASED ON NUMBERS 22–24
BUT LITTLE DOES ISRAEL KNOW THAT OTHER COUNTRIES ARE WATCHING THEIR VICTORIES AND SCHEMING AGAINST THEM.
KING BALAK SEES THE DEFEAT OF SIHON AND OG AND KNOWS HE IS NEXT. IN FEAR, HE SENDS FOR A POWERFUL SORCERER NAMED BALAAM.
IF YOU CAN PUT A CURSE ON THE ISRAELITES, KING BALAK WILL GREATLY REWARD YOU.
BALAAM SETS OUT ON HIS FAITHFUL DONKEY TO MEET WITH KING BALAK. BUT GOD SENDS AN ANGEL TO STOP HIM.
BALAAM DOESN'T NOTICE ANYTHING, BUT WHEN BALAAM'S DONKEY SEES THE FEARSOME ANGEL, SHE SCAMPERS INTO THE FIELD TO AVOID ITS FIERY SWORD.
STUPID BEAST!
THEN THE ANGEL OF THE LORD MOVES AHEAD TO A NARROW PATH BETWEEN TWO STONE WALLS.
THE DONKEY PRESSES CLOSE AGAINST ONE OF THE WALLS TO DODGE THE ANGEL'S SWORD.
BUT BALAAM'S FOOT IS SMASHED AGAINST THE WALL, AND HE BEATS HER AGAIN.
OW!! CURSE YOU!

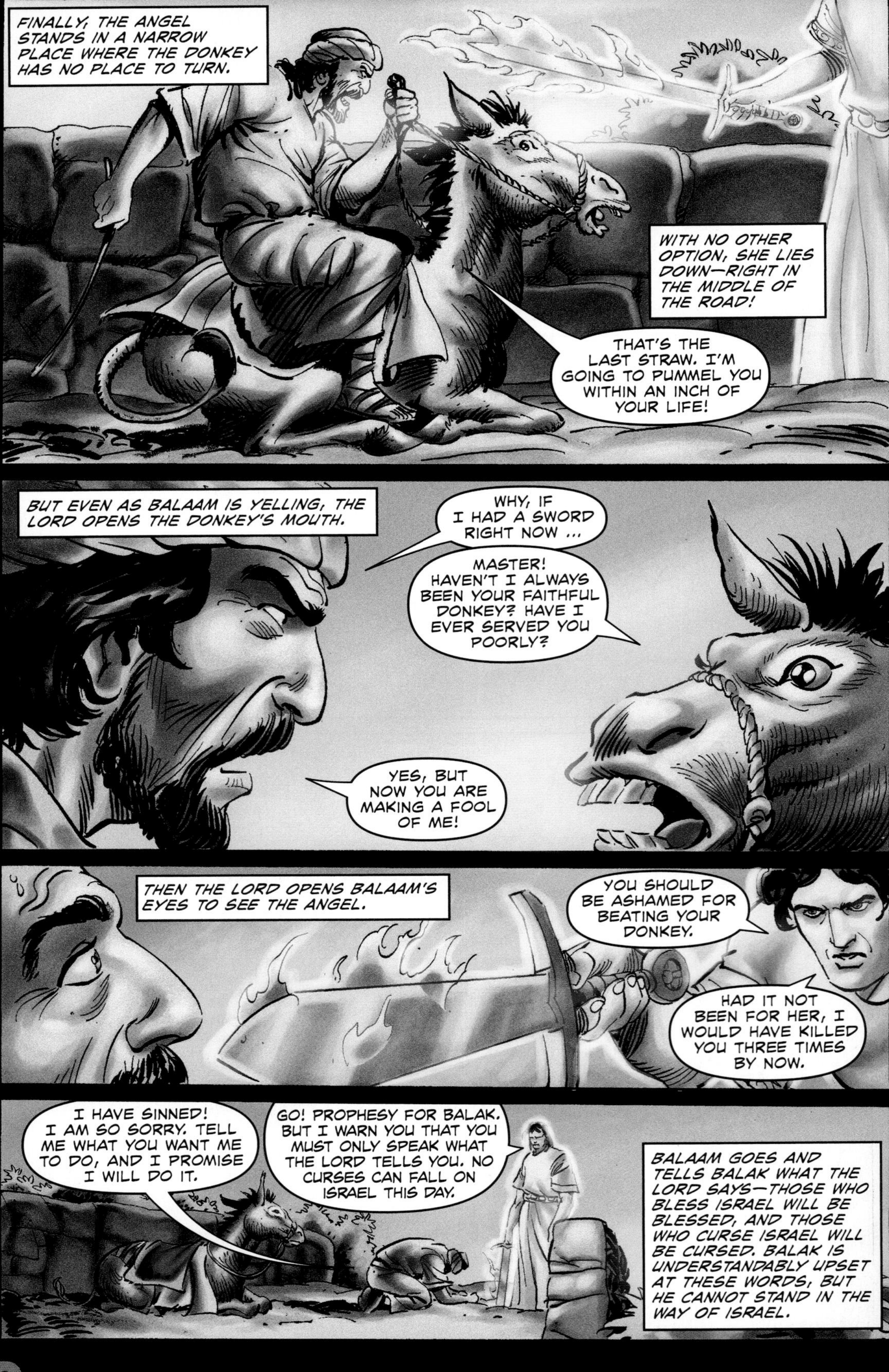
FINALLY, THE ANGEL STANDS IN A NARROW PLACE WHERE THE DONKEY HAS NO PLACE TO TURN.
WITH NO OTHER OPTION, SHE LIES DOWN—RIGHT IN THE MIDDLE OF THE ROAD!
THAT'S THE LAST STRAW. I'M GOING TO PUMMEL YOU WITHIN AN INCH OF YOUR LIFE!
BUT EVEN AS BALAAM IS YELLING, THE LORD OPENS THE DONKEY'S MOUTH.
WHY, IF I HAD A SWORD RIGHT NOW ...
MASTER! HAVEN'T I ALWAYS BEEN YOUR FAITHFUL DONKEY? HAVE I EVER SERVED YOU POORLY?
YES, BUT NOW YOU ARE MAKING A FOOL OF ME!
THEN THE LORD OPENS BALAAM'S EYES TO SEE THE ANGEL.
YOU SHOULD BE ASHAMED FOR BEATING YOUR DONKEY.
HAD IT NOT BEEN FOR HER, I WOULD HAVE KILLED YOU THREE TIMES BY NOW.
I HAVE SINNED! I AM SO SORRY. TELL ME WHAT YOU WANT ME TO DO, AND I PROMISE I WILL DO IT.
GO! PROPHESY FOR BALAK. BUT I WARN YOU THAT YOU MUST ONLY SPEAK WHAT THE LORD TELLS YOU. NO CURSES CAN FALL ON ISRAEL THIS DAY.
BALAAM GOES AND TELLS BALAK WHAT THE LORD SAYS—THOSE WHO BLESS ISRAEL WILL BE BLESSED, AND THOSE WHO CURSE ISRAEL WILL BE CURSED. BALAK IS UNDERSTANDABLY UPSET AT THESE WORDS, BUT HE CANNOT STAND IN THE WAY OF ISRAEL.

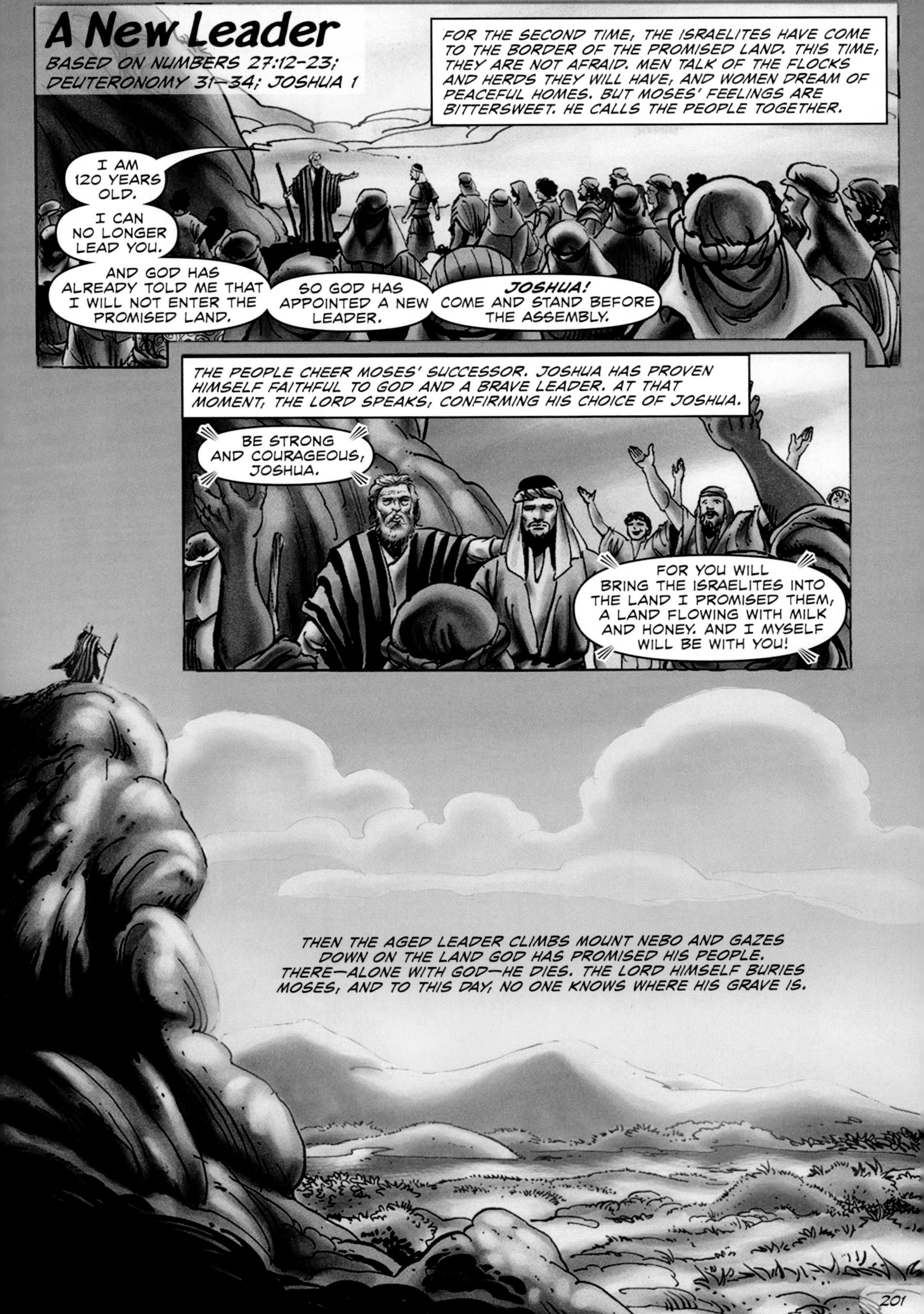
A New Leader
BASED ON NUMBERS 27:12–23; DEUTERONOMY 31–34; JOSHUA 1
FOR THE SECOND TIME, THE ISRAELITES HAVE COME TO THE BORDER OF THE PROMISED LAND. THIS TIME, THEY ARE NOT AFRAID. MEN TALK OF THE FLOCKS AND HERDS THEY WILL HAVE, AND WOMEN DREAM OF PEACEFUL HOMES. BUT MOSES' FEELINGS ARE BITTERSWEET. HE CALLS THE PEOPLE TOGETHER.
I AM 120 YEARS OLD.
I CAN NO LONGER LEAD YOU.
AND GOD HAS ALREADY TOLD ME THAT I WILL NOT ENTER THE PROMISED LAND.
SO GOD HAS APPOINTED A NEW LEADER.
JOSHUA! COME AND STAND BEFORE THE ASSEMBLY.
THE PEOPLE CHEER MOSES' SUCCESSOR. JOSHUA HAS PROVEN HIMSELF FAITHFUL TO GOD AND A BRAVE LEADER. AT THAT MOMENT, THE LORD SPEAKS, CONFIRMING HIS CHOICE OF JOSHUA.
BE STRONG AND COURAGEOUS, JOSHUA.
FOR YOU WILL BRING THE ISRAELITES INTO THE LAND I PROMISED THEM, A LAND FLOWING WITH MILK AND HONEY. AND I MYSELF WILL BE WITH YOU!
THEN THE AGED LEADER CLIMBS MOUNT NEBO AND GAZES DOWN ON THE LAND GOD HAS PROMISED HIS PEOPLE. THERE—ALONE WITH GOD—HE DIES. THE LORD HIMSELF BURIES MOSES, AND TO THIS DAY, NO ONE KNOWS WHERE HIS GRAVE IS.

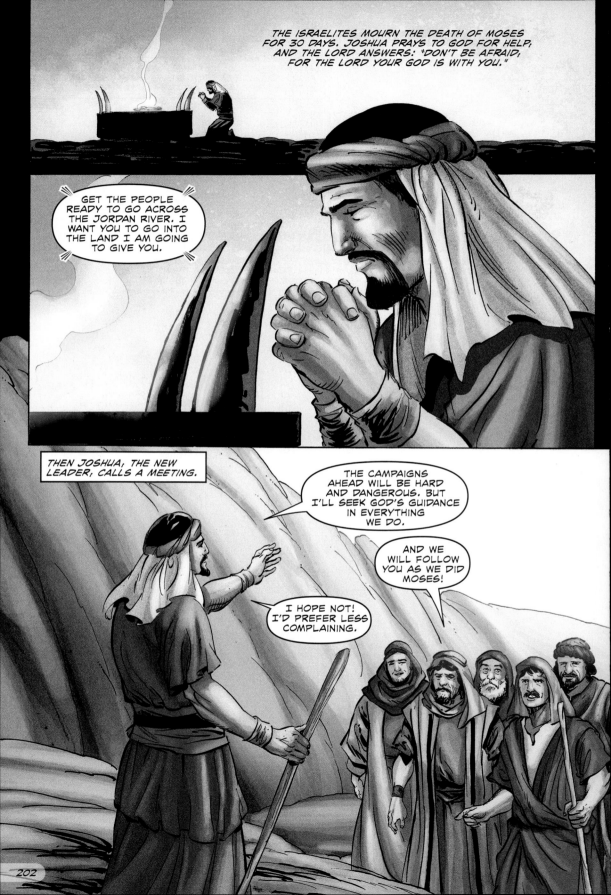

THE ISRAELITES MOURN THE DEATH OF MOSES FOR 30 DAYS. JOSHUA PRAYS TO GOD FOR HELP, AND THE LORD ANSWERS: "DON'T BE AFRAID, FOR THE LORD YOUR GOD IS WITH YOU."

GET THE PEOPLE READY TO GO ACROSS THE JORDAN RIVER. I WANT YOU TO GO INTO THE LAND I AM GOING TO GIVE YOU.

THEN JOSHUA, THE NEW LEADER, CALLS A MEETING.

THE CAMPAIGNS AHEAD WILL BE HARD AND DANGEROUS. BUT I'LL SEEK GOD'S GUIDANCE IN EVERYTHING WE DO.

AND WE WILL FOLLOW YOU AS WE DID MOSES!

I HOPE NOT! I'D PREFER LESS COMPLAINING.

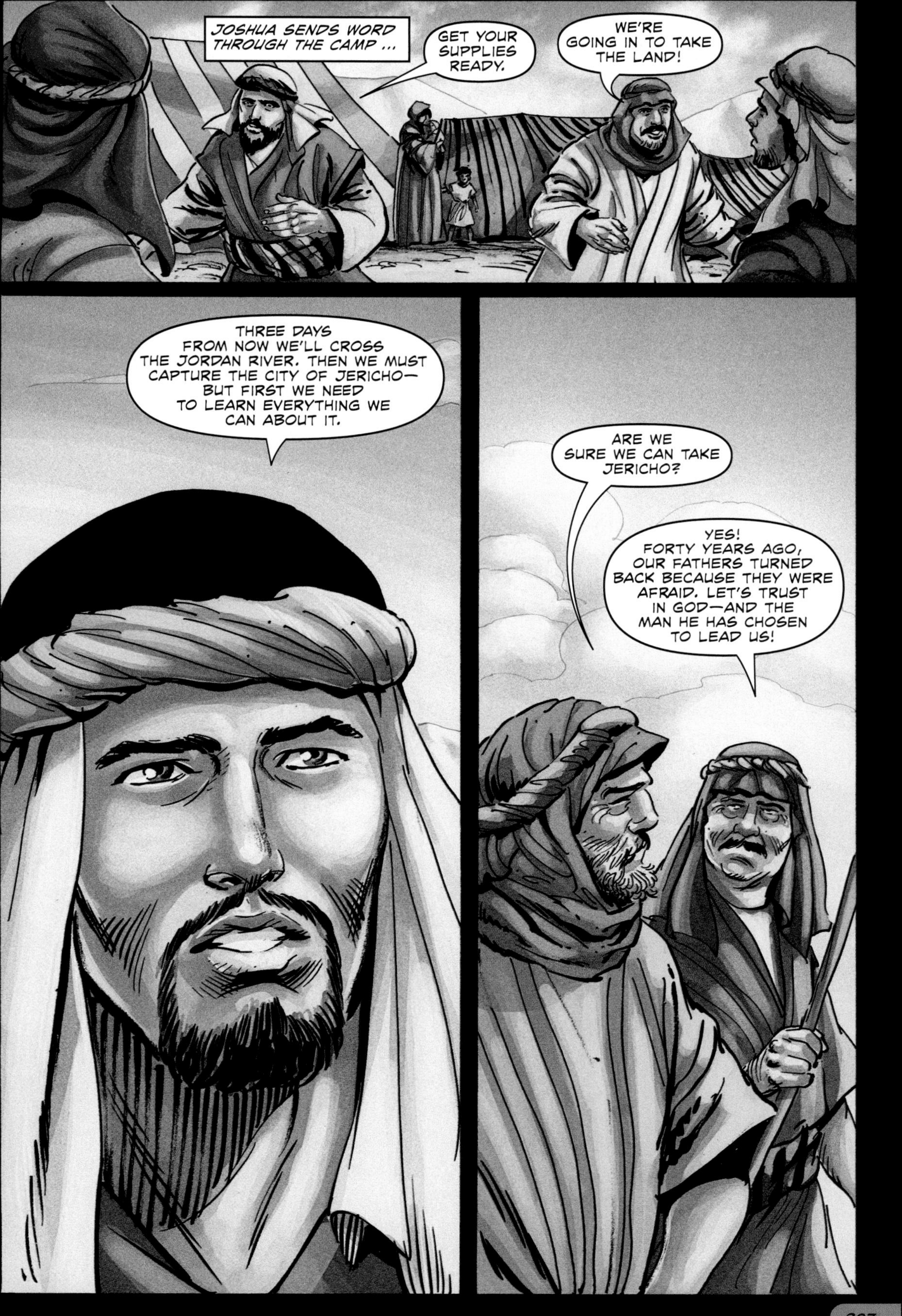
JOSHUA SENDS WORD THROUGH THE CAMP ...
GET YOUR SUPPLIES READY.
WE'RE GOING IN TO TAKE THE LAND!
THREE DAYS FROM NOW WE'LL CROSS THE JORDAN RIVER. THEN WE MUST CAPTURE THE CITY OF JERICHO—BUT FIRST WE NEED TO LEARN EVERYTHING WE CAN ABOUT IT.
ARE WE SURE WE CAN TAKE JERICHO?
YES! FORTY YEARS AGO, OUR FATHERS TURNED BACK BECAUSE THEY WERE AFRAID. LET'S TRUST IN GOD—AND THE MAN HE HAS CHOSEN TO LEAD US!

The Roof of Rahab
BASED ON JOSHUA 2

THAT NIGHT AT THE RIVER'S EDGE ...

YOU SCOUTS WILL BE IN DANGER EVERY MINUTE. BE CAREFUL. LEARN ALL YOU CAN AND COME BACK SOON!

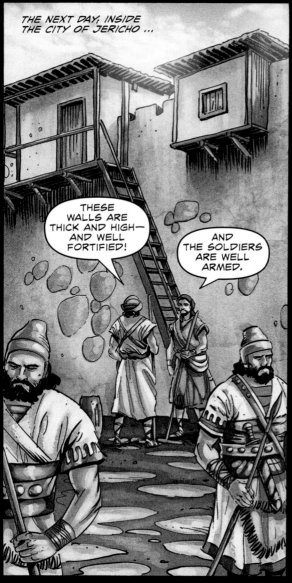

THE NEXT DAY, INSIDE THE CITY OF JERICHO ...

THESE WALLS ARE THICK AND HIGH— AND WELL FORTIFIED!

AND THE SOLDIERS ARE WELL ARMED.

LET'S SEE IF WE CAN FIND A ROOM TO STAY IN AT THIS HOUSE.

THOSE STRANGERS LOOK SUSPICIOUS. I'M GOING TO REPORT THEM TO THE CAPTAIN OF THE GUARD.

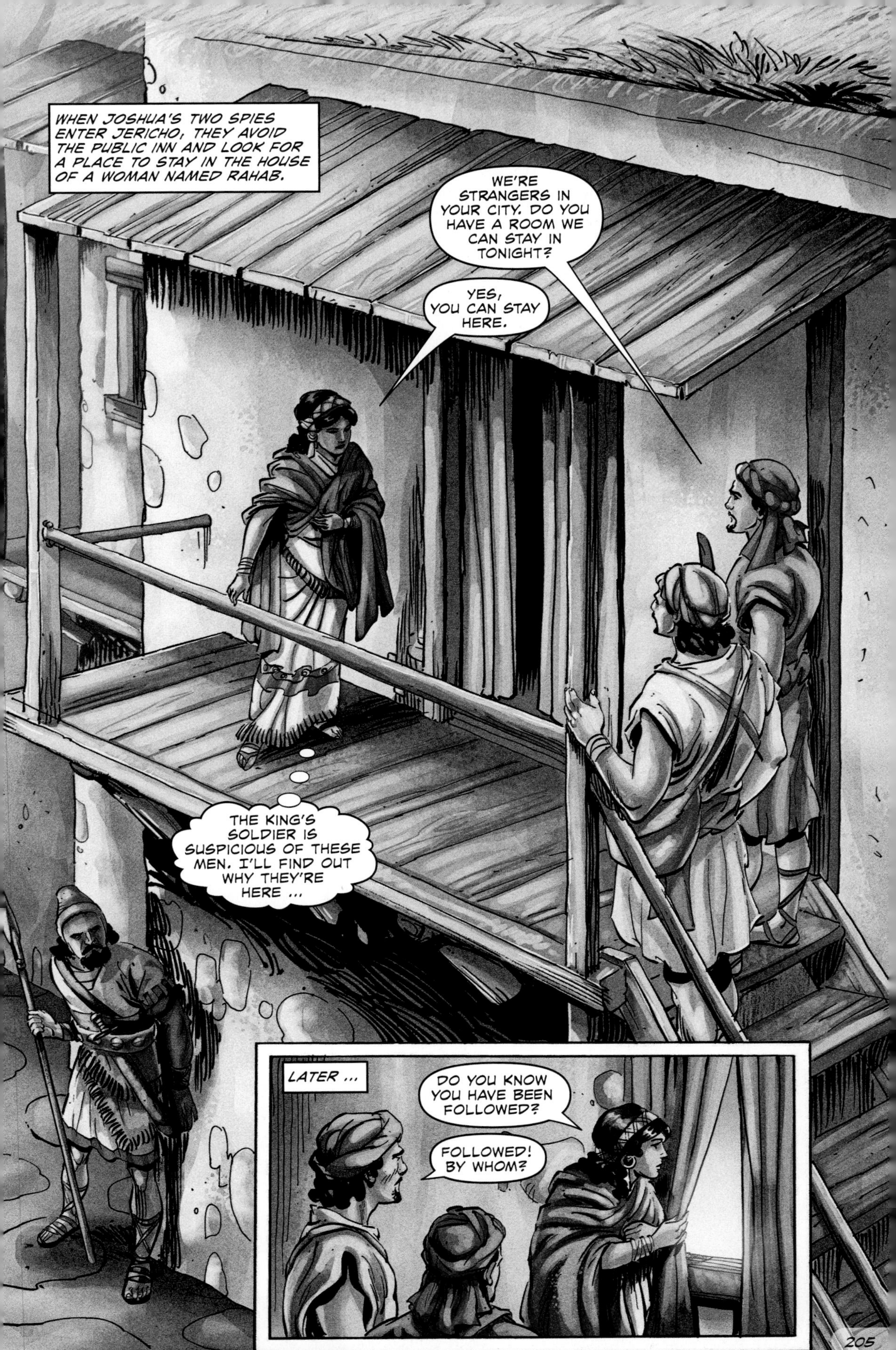
WHEN JOSHUA'S TWO SPIES ENTER JERICHO, THEY AVOID THE PUBLIC INN AND LOOK FOR A PLACE TO STAY IN THE HOUSE OF A WOMAN NAMED RAHAB.
WE'RE STRANGERS IN YOUR CITY. DO YOU HAVE A ROOM WE CAN STAY IN TONIGHT?
YES, YOU CAN STAY HERE.
THE KING'S SOLDIER IS SUSPICIOUS OF THESE MEN. I'LL FIND OUT WHY THEY'RE HERE ...
LATER ...
DO YOU KNOW YOU HAVE BEEN FOLLOWED?
FOLLOWED! BY WHOM?

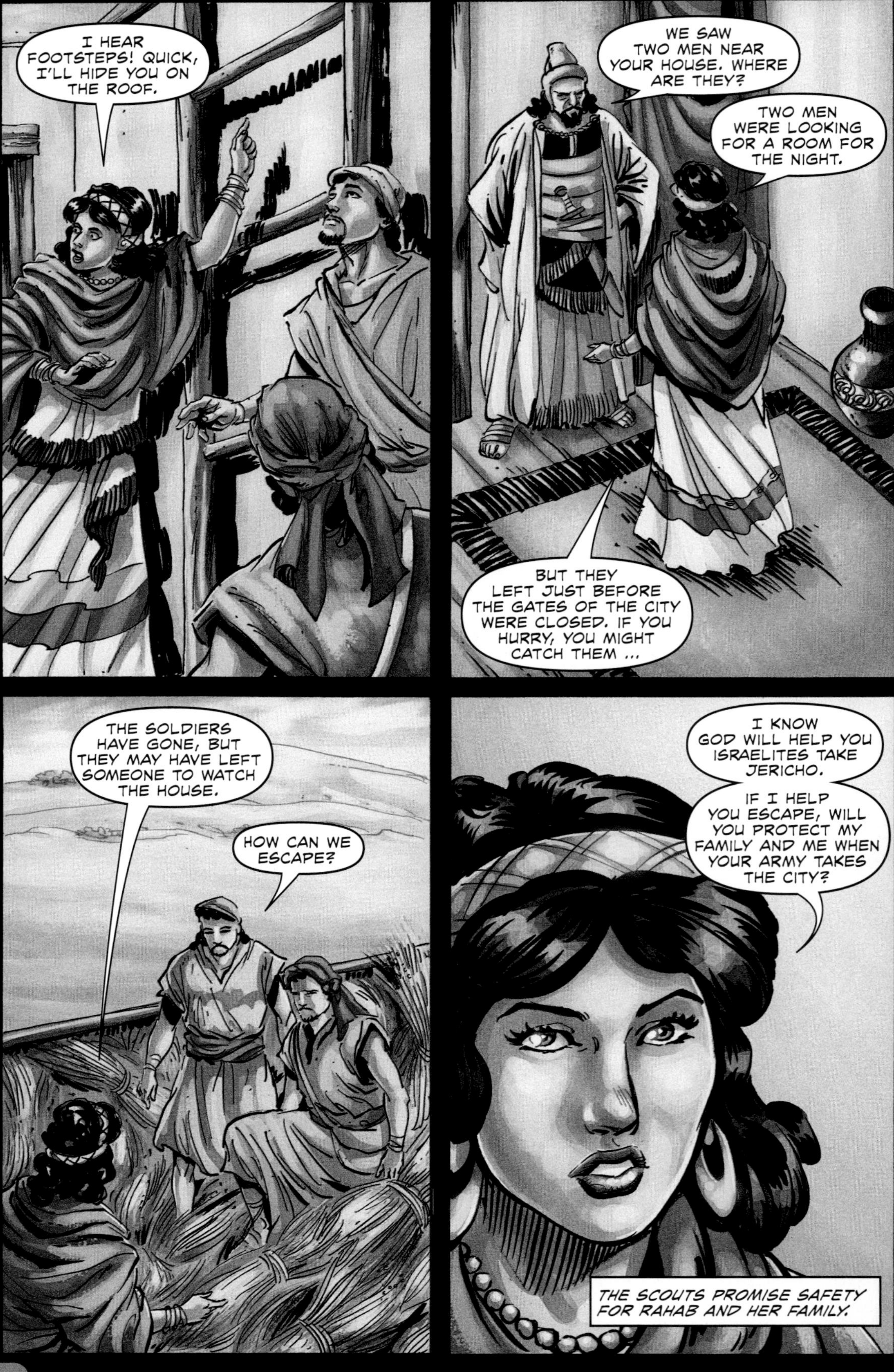
I HEAR FOOTSTEPS! QUICK, I'LL HIDE YOU ON THE ROOF.
WE SAW TWO MEN NEAR YOUR HOUSE. WHERE ARE THEY?
TWO MEN WERE LOOKING FOR A ROOM FOR THE NIGHT.
BUT THEY LEFT JUST BEFORE THE GATES OF THE CITY WERE CLOSED. IF YOU HURRY, YOU MIGHT CATCH THEM ...
THE SOLDIERS HAVE GONE, BUT THEY MAY HAVE LEFT SOMEONE TO WATCH THE HOUSE.
HOW CAN WE ESCAPE?
I KNOW GOD WILL HELP YOU ISRAELITES TAKE JERICHO.
IF I HELP YOU ESCAPE, WILL YOU PROTECT MY FAMILY AND ME WHEN YOUR ARMY TAKES THE CITY?
THE SCOUTS PROMISE SAFETY FOR RAHAB AND HER FAMILY.

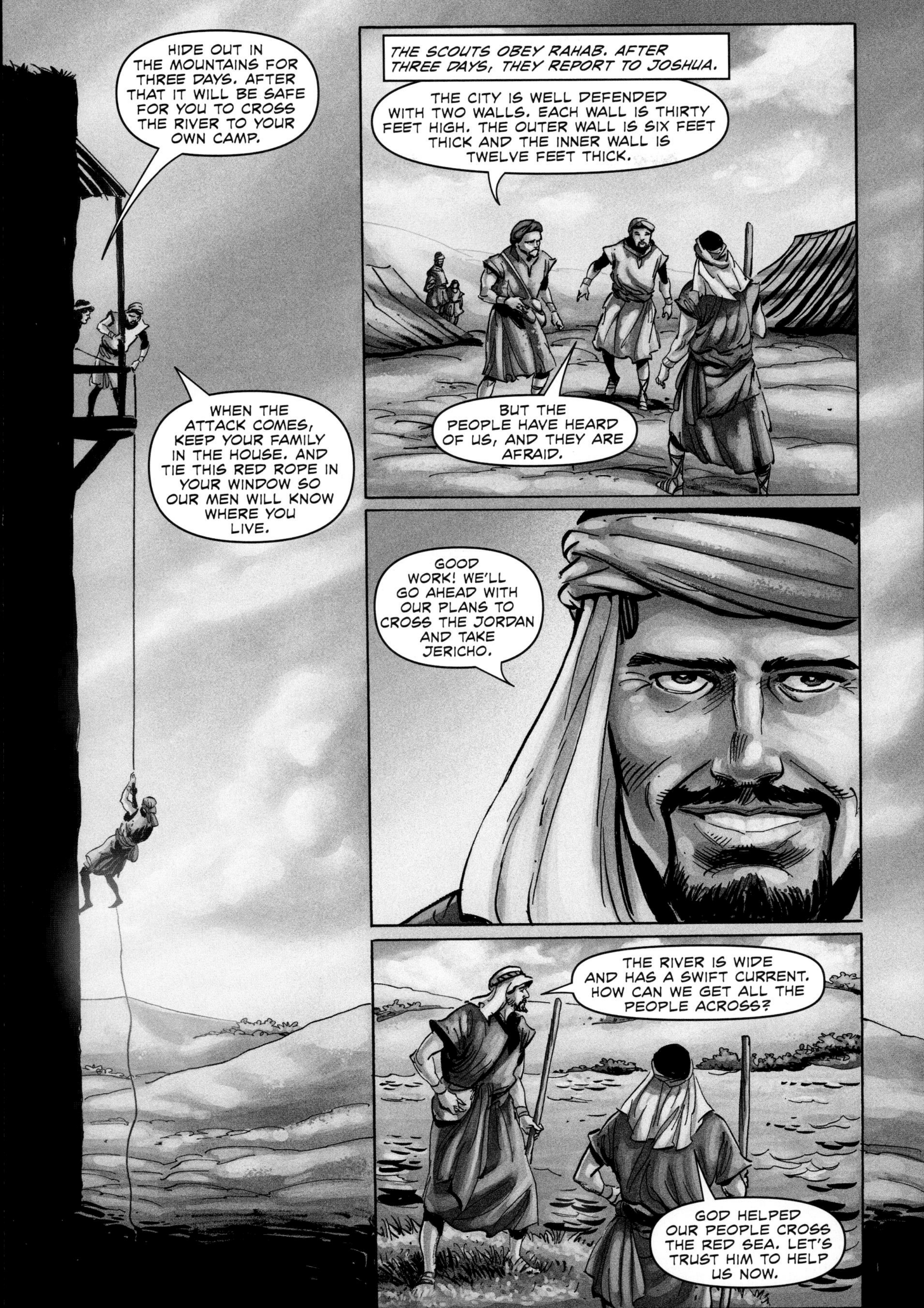
HIDE OUT IN THE MOUNTAINS FOR THREE DAYS. AFTER THAT IT WILL BE SAFE FOR YOU TO CROSS THE RIVER TO YOUR OWN CAMP.
WHEN THE ATTACK COMES, KEEP YOUR FAMILY IN THE HOUSE. AND TIE THIS RED ROPE IN YOUR WINDOW SO OUR MEN WILL KNOW WHERE YOU LIVE.
THE SCOUTS OBEY RAHAB. AFTER THREE DAYS, THEY REPORT TO JOSHUA.
THE CITY IS WELL DEFENDED WITH TWO WALLS. EACH WALL IS THIRTY FEET HIGH. THE OUTER WALL IS SIX FEET THICK AND THE INNER WALL IS TWELVE FEET THICK.
BUT THE PEOPLE HAVE HEARD OF US, AND THEY ARE AFRAID.
GOOD WORK! WE'LL GO AHEAD WITH OUR PLANS TO CROSS THE JORDAN AND TAKE JERICHO.
THE RIVER IS WIDE AND HAS A SWIFT CURRENT. HOW CAN WE GET ALL THE PEOPLE ACROSS?
GOD HELPED OUR PEOPLE CROSS THE RED SEA. LET'S TRUST HIM TO HELP US NOW.

Entering the Promised Land

BASED ON JOSHUA 3—4

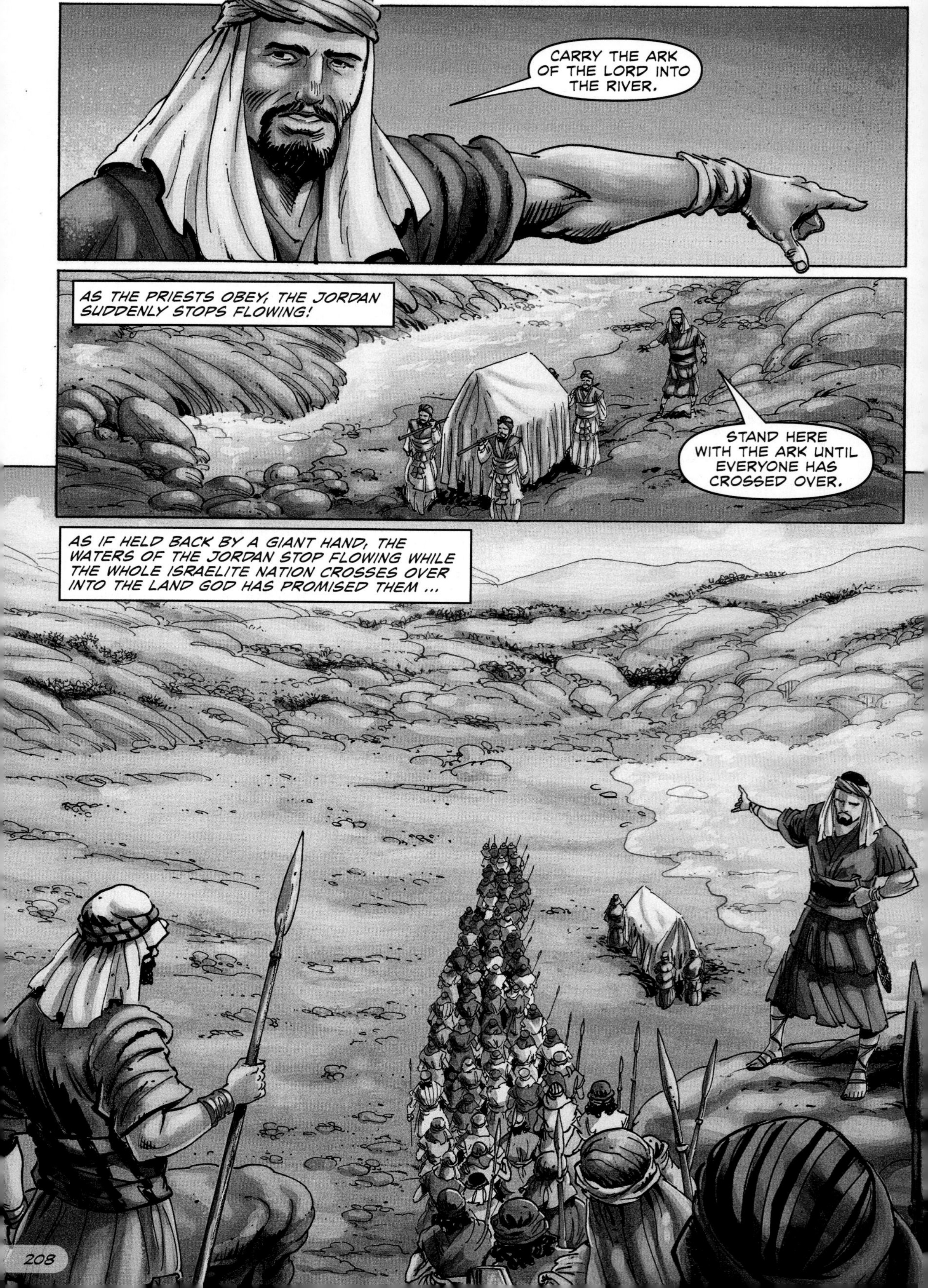

CARRY THE ARK OF THE LORD INTO THE RIVER.
AS THE PRIESTS OBEY, THE JORDAN SUDDENLY STOPS FLOWING!
STAND HERE WITH THE ARK UNTIL EVERYONE HAS CROSSED OVER.
AS IF HELD BACK BY A GIANT HAND, THE WATERS OF THE JORDAN STOP FLOWING WHILE THE WHOLE ISRAELITE NATION CROSSES OVER INTO THE LAND GOD HAS PROMISED THEM ...

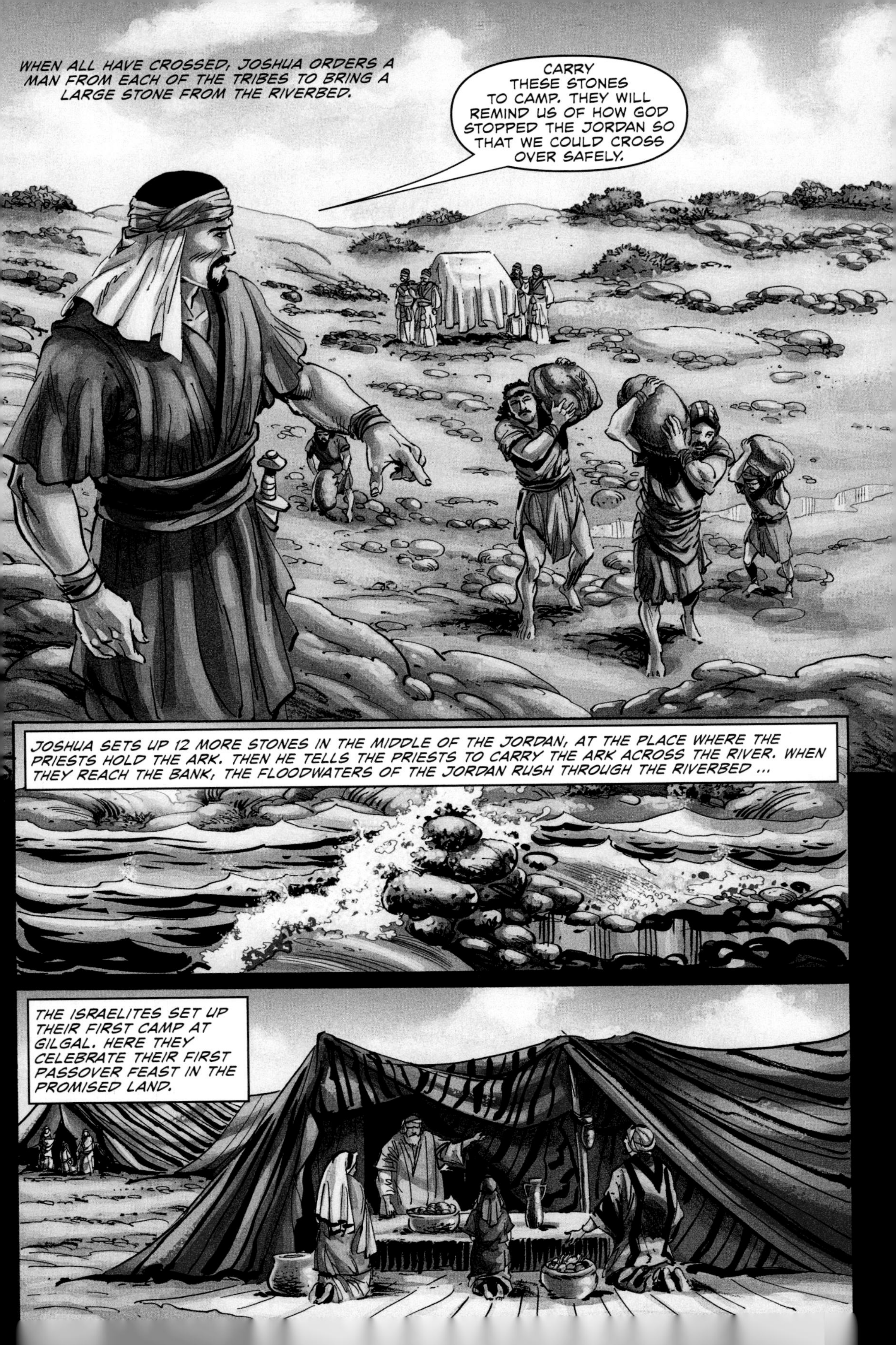
WHEN ALL HAVE CROSSED, JOSHUA ORDERS A MAN FROM EACH OF THE TRIBES TO BRING A LARGE STONE FROM THE RIVERBED.
CARRY THESE STONES TO CAMP. THEY WILL REMIND US OF HOW GOD STOPPED THE JORDAN SO THAT WE COULD CROSS OVER SAFELY.
JOSHUA SETS UP 12 MORE STONES IN THE MIDDLE OF THE JORDAN, AT THE PLACE WHERE THE PRIESTS HOLD THE ARK. THEN HE TELLS THE PRIESTS TO CARRY THE ARK ACROSS THE RIVER. WHEN THEY REACH THE BANK, THE FLOODWATERS OF THE JORDAN RUSH THROUGH THE RIVERBED ...
THE ISRAELITES SET UP THEIR FIRST CAMP AT GILGAL. HERE THEY CELEBRATE THEIR FIRST PASSOVER FEAST IN THE PROMISED LAND.

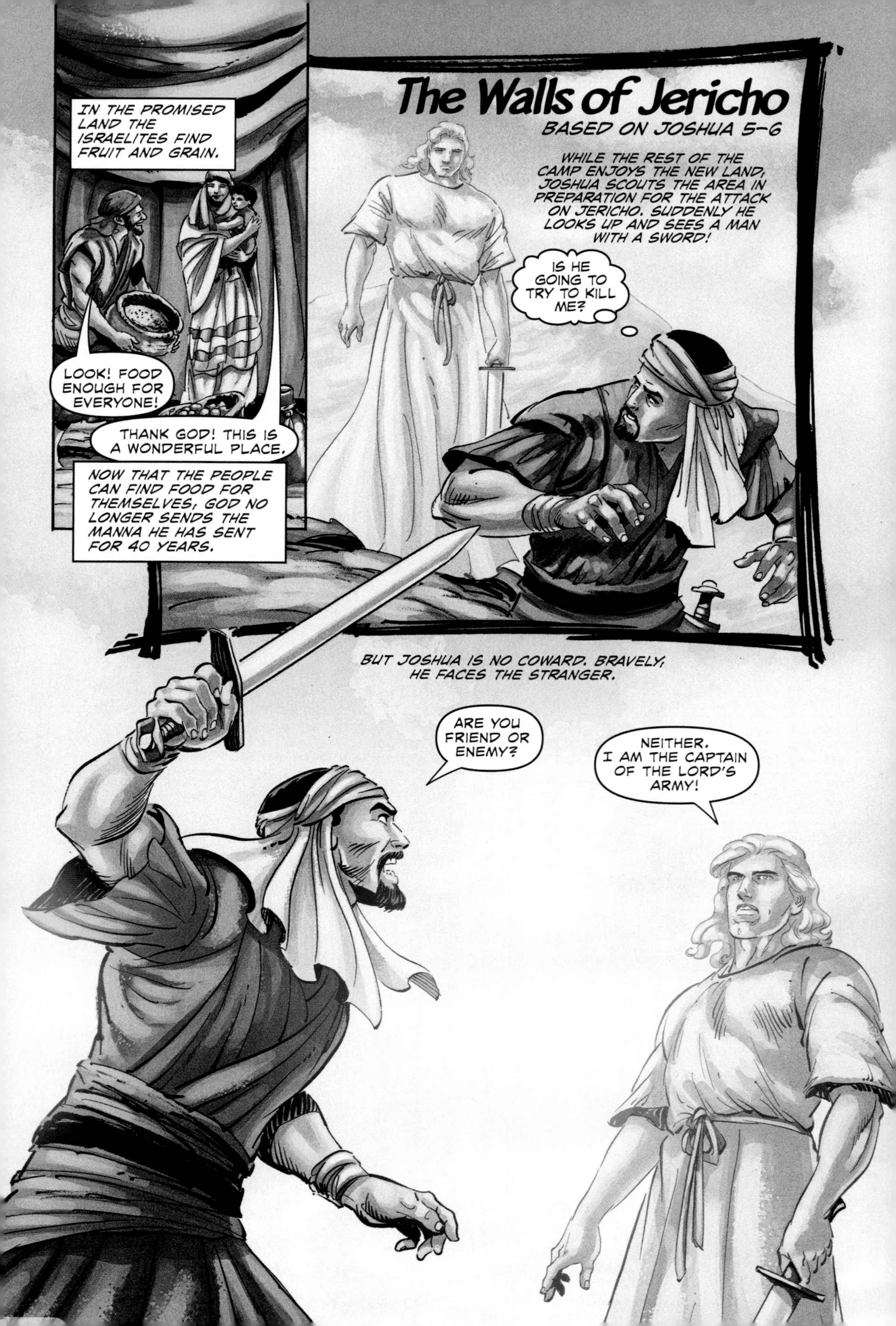
The Walls of Jericho
BASED ON JOSHUA 5–6
IN THE PROMISED LAND THE ISRAELITES FIND FRUIT AND GRAIN.
LOOK! FOOD ENOUGH FOR EVERYONE!
THANK GOD! THIS IS A WONDERFUL PLACE.
NOW THAT THE PEOPLE CAN FIND FOOD FOR THEMSELVES, GOD NO LONGER SENDS THE MANNA HE HAS SENT FOR 40 YEARS.
WHILE THE REST OF THE CAMP ENJOYS THE NEW LAND, JOSHUA SCOUTS THE AREA IN PREPARATION FOR THE ATTACK ON JERICHO. SUDDENLY HE LOOKS UP AND SEES A MAN WITH A SWORD!
IS HE GOING TO TRY TO KILL ME?
BUT JOSHUA IS NO COWARD. BRAVELY, HE FACES THE STRANGER.
ARE YOU FRIEND OR ENEMY?
NEITHER. I AM THE CAPTAIN OF THE LORD'S ARMY!

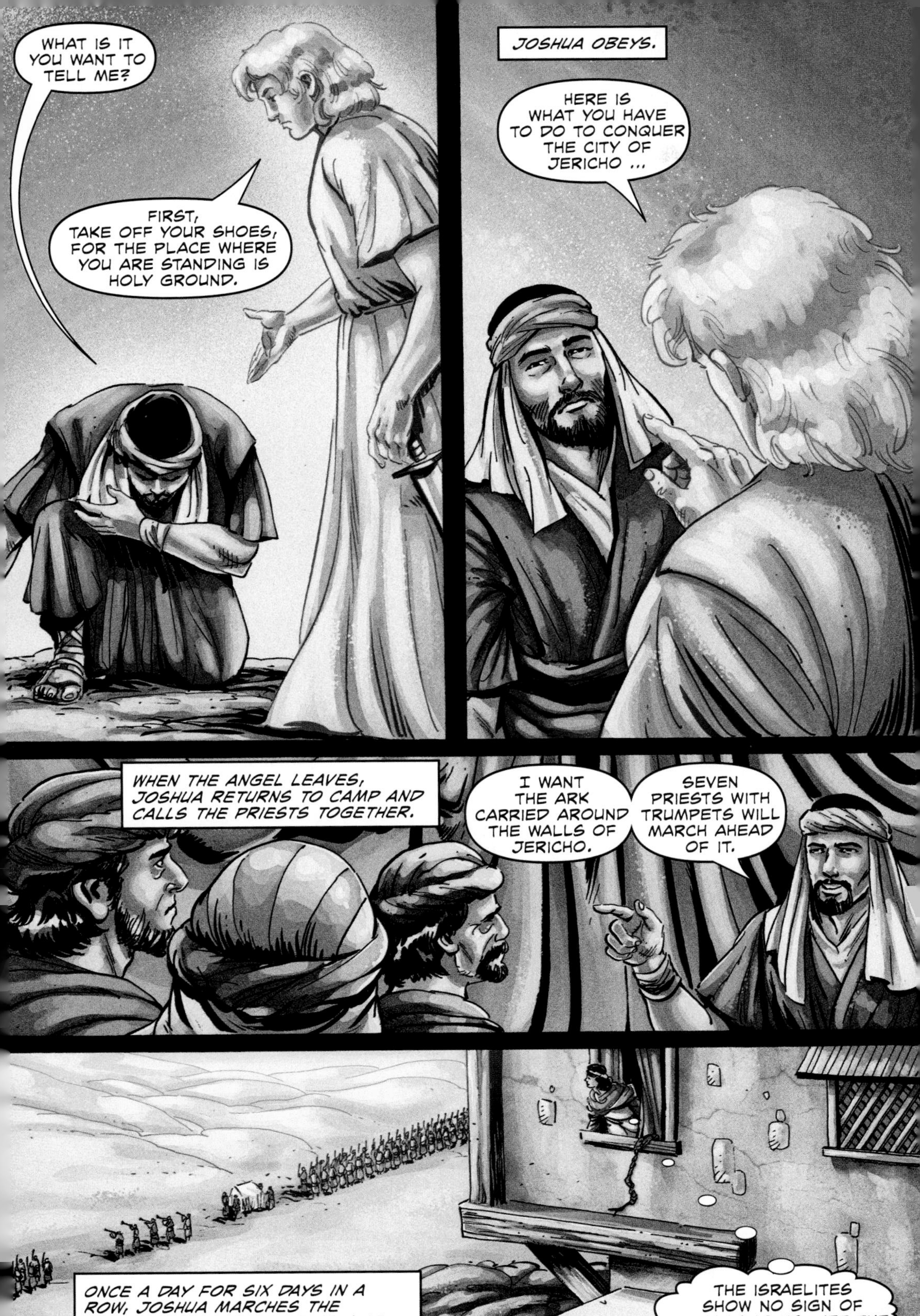
WHAT IS IT YOU WANT TO TELL ME?
FIRST, TAKE OFF YOUR SHOES, FOR THE PLACE WHERE YOU ARE STANDING IS HOLY GROUND.
JOSHUA OBEYS.
HERE IS WHAT YOU HAVE TO DO TO CONQUER THE CITY OF JERICHO ...
WHEN THE ANGEL LEAVES, JOSHUA RETURNS TO CAMP AND CALLS THE PRIESTS TOGETHER.
I WANT THE ARK CARRIED AROUND THE WALLS OF JERICHO.
SEVEN PRIESTS WITH TRUMPETS WILL MARCH AHEAD OF IT.
ONCE A DAY FOR SIX DAYS IN A ROW, JOSHUA MARCHES THE ISRAELITES AROUND THE CITY OF JERICHO. FROM HER HOUSE ON THE WALL, RAHAB WATCHES ANXIOUSLY.
THE ISRAELITES SHOW NO SIGN OF ATTACKING US. YET THE CITY IS BREATHLESS WITH FEAR.

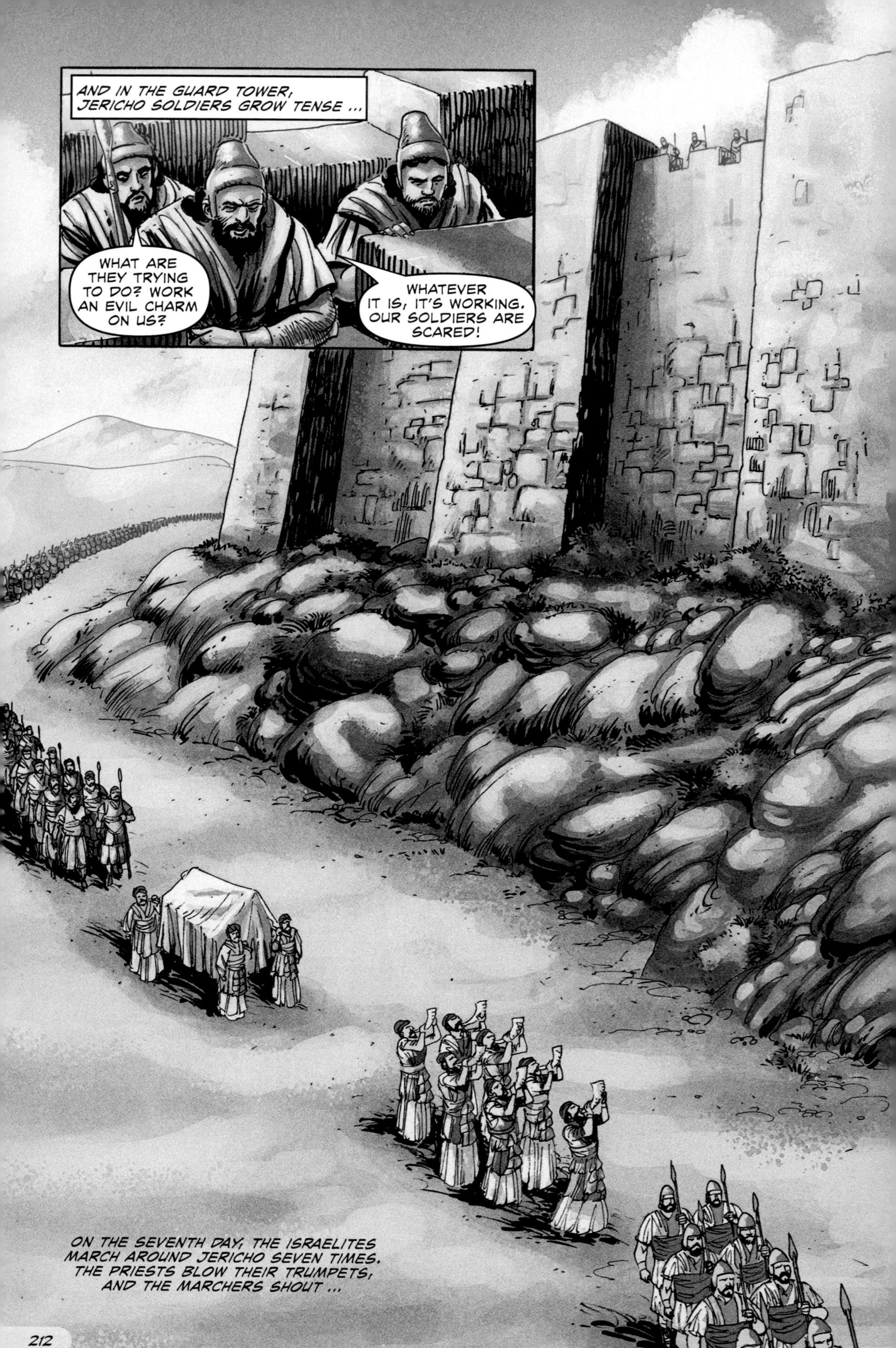
AND IN THE GUARD TOWER, JERICHO SOLDIERS GROW TENSE ...
WHAT ARE THEY TRYING TO DO? WORK AN EVIL CHARM ON US?
WHATEVER IT IS, IT'S WORKING. OUR SOLDIERS ARE SCARED!
ON THE SEVENTH DAY, THE ISRAELITES MARCH AROUND JERICHO SEVEN TIMES. THE PRIESTS BLOW THEIR TRUMPETS, AND THE MARCHERS SHOUT ...

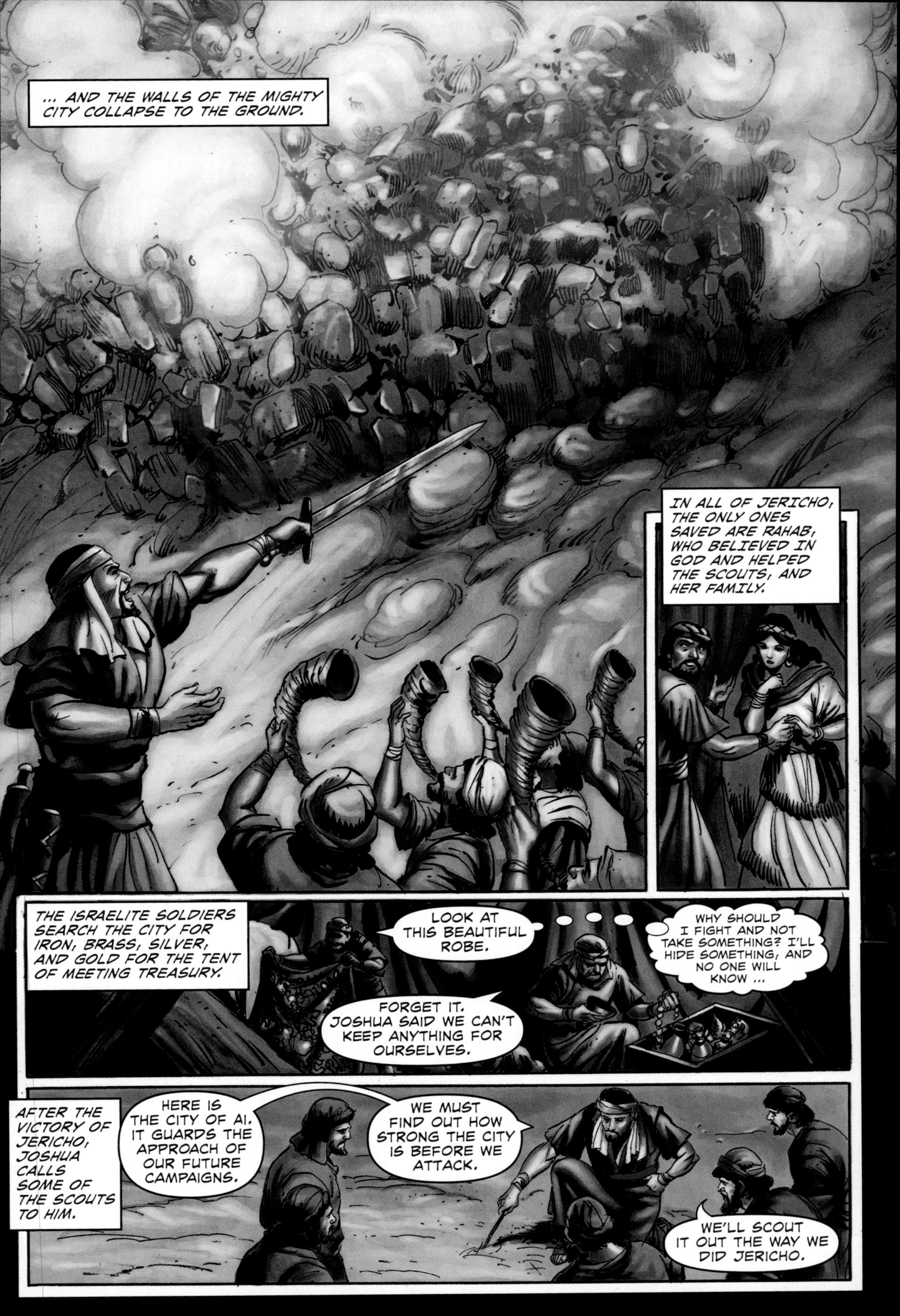
... AND THE WALLS OF THE MIGHTY CITY COLLAPSE TO THE GROUND.
IN ALL OF JERICHO, THE ONLY ONES SAVED ARE RAHAB, WHO BELIEVED IN GOD AND HELPED THE SCOUTS, AND HER FAMILY.
THE ISRAELITE SOLDIERS SEARCH THE CITY FOR IRON, BRASS, SILVER, AND GOLD FOR THE TENT OF MEETING TREASURY.
LOOK AT THIS BEAUTIFUL ROBE.
WHY SHOULD I FIGHT AND NOT TAKE SOMETHING? I'LL HIDE SOMETHING, AND NO ONE WILL KNOW ...
FORGET IT. JOSHUA SAID WE CAN'T KEEP ANYTHING FOR OURSELVES.
AFTER THE VICTORY OF JERICHO, JOSHUA CALLS SOME OF THE SCOUTS TO HIM.
HERE IS THE CITY OF AI. IT GUARDS THE APPROACH OF OUR FUTURE CAMPAIGNS.
WE MUST FIND OUT HOW STRONG THE CITY IS BEFORE WE ATTACK.
WE'LL SCOUT IT OUT THE WAY WE DID JERICHO.

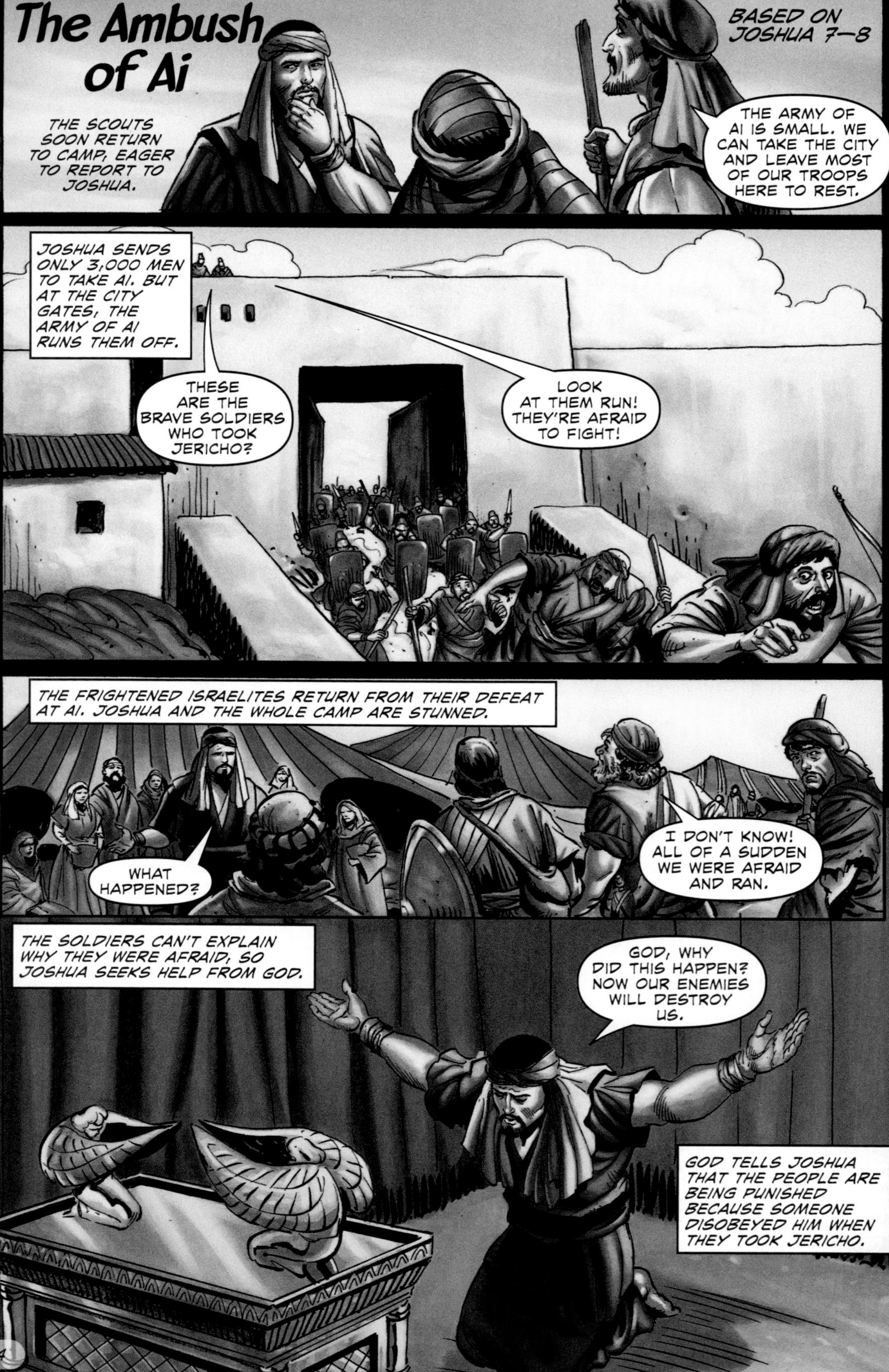
The Ambush of Ai
BASED ON JOSHUA 7—8
THE SCOUTS SOON RETURN TO CAMP, EAGER TO REPORT TO JOSHUA.
THE ARMY OF AI IS SMALL. WE CAN TAKE THE CITY AND LEAVE MOST OF OUR TROOPS HERE TO REST.
JOSHUA SENDS ONLY 3,000 MEN TO TAKE AI. BUT AT THE CITY GATES, THE ARMY OF AI RUNS THEM OFF.
THESE ARE THE BRAVE SOLDIERS WHO TOOK JERICHO?
LOOK AT THEM RUN! THEY'RE AFRAID TO FIGHT!
THE FRIGHTENED ISRAELITES RETURN FROM THEIR DEFEAT AT AI. JOSHUA AND THE WHOLE CAMP ARE STUNNED.
WHAT HAPPENED?
I DON'T KNOW! ALL OF A SUDDEN WE WERE AFRAID AND RAN.
THE SOLDIERS CAN'T EXPLAIN WHY THEY WERE AFRAID, SO JOSHUA SEEKS HELP FROM GOD.
GOD, WHY DID THIS HAPPEN? NOW OUR ENEMIES WILL DESTROY US.
GOD TELLS JOSHUA THAT THE PEOPLE ARE BEING PUNISHED BECAUSE SOMEONE DISOBEYED HIM WHEN THEY TOOK JERICHO.

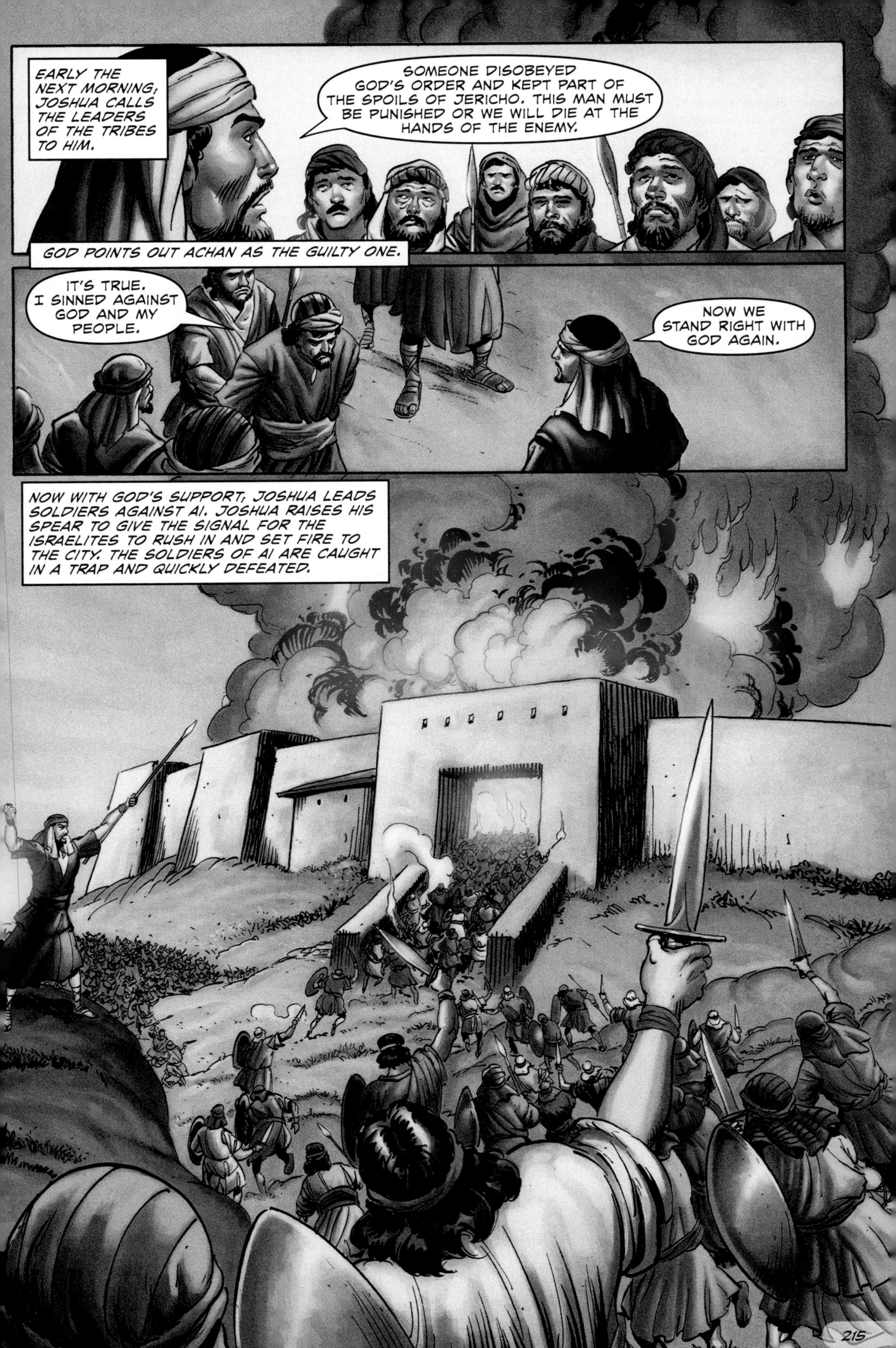
EARLY THE NEXT MORNING, JOSHUA CALLS THE LEADERS OF THE TRIBES TO HIM.
SOMEONE DISOBEYED GOD'S ORDER AND KEPT PART OF THE SPOILS OF JERICHO. THIS MAN MUST BE PUNISHED OR WE WILL DIE AT THE HANDS OF THE ENEMY.
GOD POINTS OUT ACHAN AS THE GUILTY ONE.
IT'S TRUE. I SINNED AGAINST GOD AND MY PEOPLE.
NOW WE STAND RIGHT WITH GOD AGAIN.
NOW WITH GOD'S SUPPORT, JOSHUA LEADS SOLDIERS AGAINST AI. JOSHUA RAISES HIS SPEAR TO GIVE THE SIGNAL FOR THE ISRAELITES TO RUSH IN AND SET FIRE TO THE CITY. THE SOLDIERS OF AI ARE CAUGHT IN A TRAP AND QUICKLY DEFEATED.

Stop the Sun *BASED ON JOSHUA 9—10*

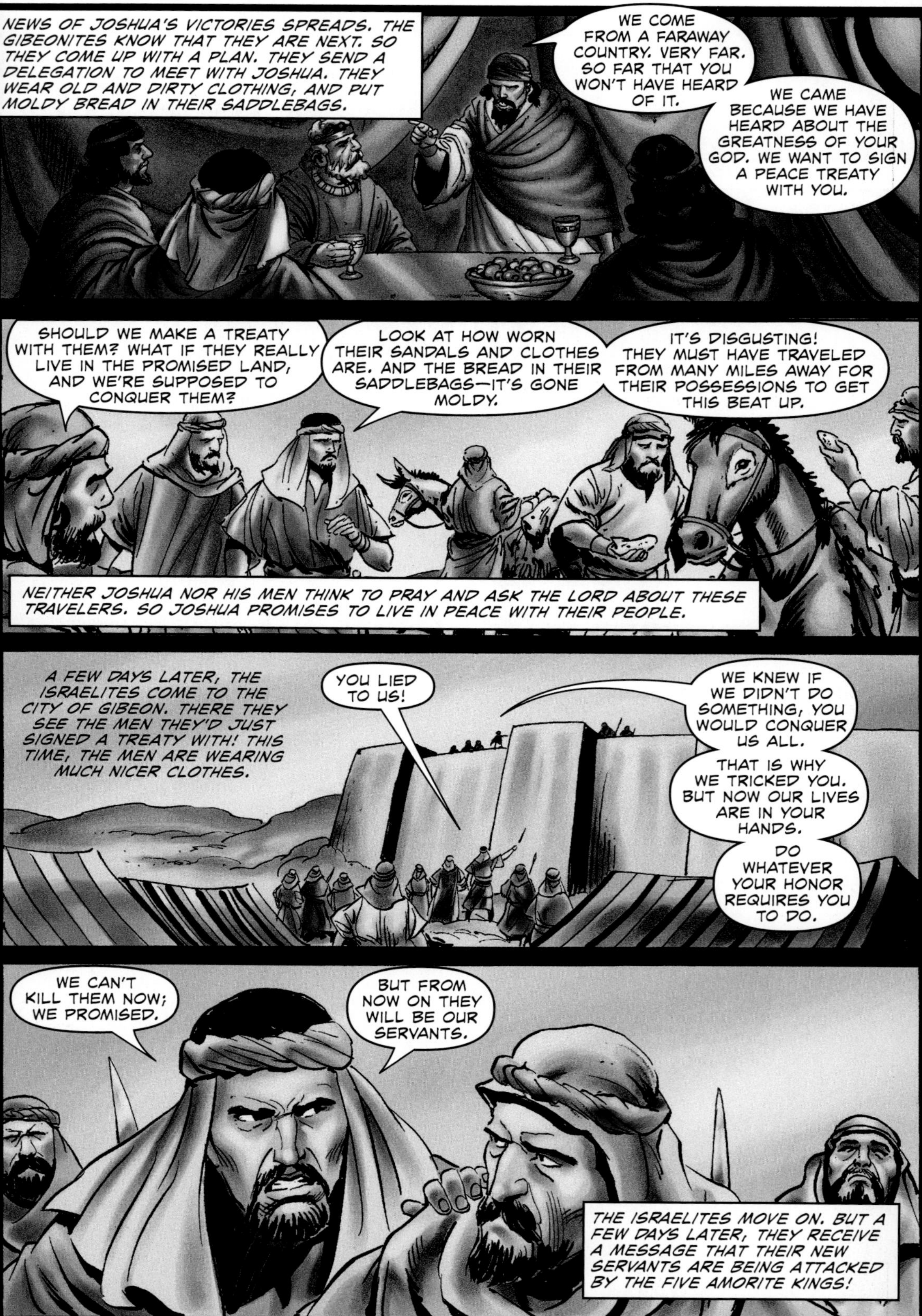

NEWS OF JOSHUA'S VICTORIES SPREADS. THE GIBEONITES KNOW THAT THEY ARE NEXT. SO THEY COME UP WITH A PLAN. THEY SEND A DELEGATION TO MEET WITH JOSHUA. THEY WEAR OLD AND DIRTY CLOTHING, AND PUT MOLDY BREAD IN THEIR SADDLEBAGS.
WE COME FROM A FARAWAY COUNTRY. VERY FAR. SO FAR THAT YOU WON'T HAVE HEARD OF IT.
WE CAME BECAUSE WE HAVE HEARD ABOUT THE GREATNESS OF YOUR GOD. WE WANT TO SIGN A PEACE TREATY WITH YOU.
SHOULD WE MAKE A TREATY WITH THEM? WHAT IF THEY REALLY LIVE IN THE PROMISED LAND, AND WE'RE SUPPOSED TO CONQUER THEM?
LOOK AT HOW WORN THEIR SANDALS AND CLOTHES ARE. AND THE BREAD IN THEIR SADDLEBAGS—IT'S GONE MOLDY.
IT'S DISGUSTING! THEY MUST HAVE TRAVELED FROM MANY MILES AWAY FOR THEIR POSSESSIONS TO GET THIS BEAT UP.
NEITHER JOSHUA NOR HIS MEN THINK TO PRAY AND ASK THE LORD ABOUT THESE TRAVELERS. SO JOSHUA PROMISES TO LIVE IN PEACE WITH THEIR PEOPLE.
A FEW DAYS LATER, THE ISRAELITES COME TO THE CITY OF GIBEON. THERE THEY SEE THE MEN THEY'D JUST SIGNED A TREATY WITH! THIS TIME, THE MEN ARE WEARING MUCH NICER CLOTHES.
YOU LIED TO US!
WE KNEW IF WE DIDN'T DO SOMETHING, YOU WOULD CONQUER US ALL.
THAT IS WHY WE TRICKED YOU. BUT NOW OUR LIVES ARE IN YOUR HANDS.
DO WHATEVER YOUR HONOR REQUIRES YOU TO DO.
WE CAN'T KILL THEM NOW; WE PROMISED.
BUT FROM NOW ON THEY WILL BE OUR SERVANTS.
THE ISRAELITES MOVE ON. BUT A FEW DAYS LATER, THEY RECEIVE A MESSAGE THAT THEIR NEW SERVANTS ARE BEING ATTACKED BY THE FIVE AMORITE KINGS!

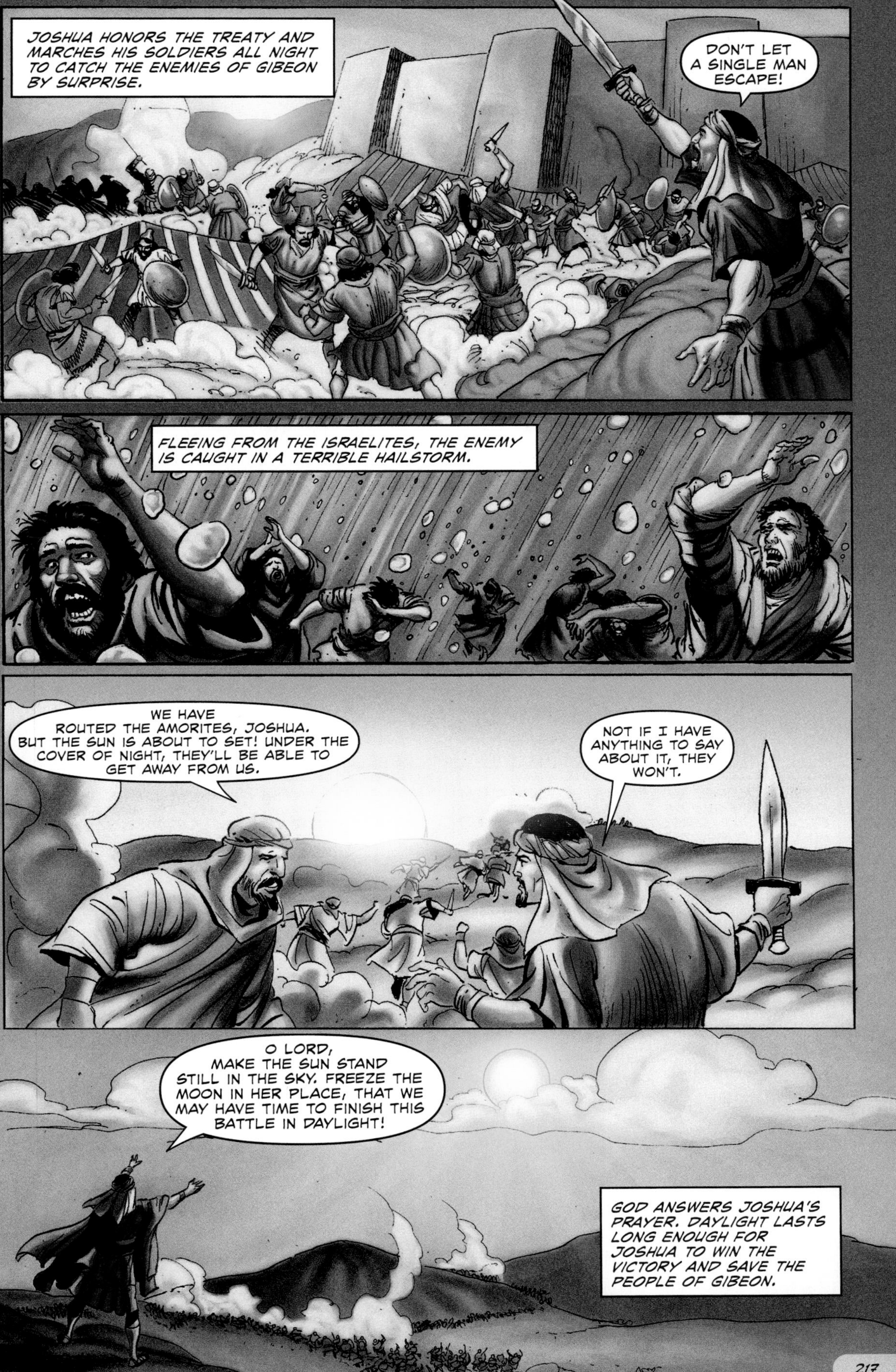
JOSHUA HONORS THE TREATY AND MARCHES HIS SOLDIERS ALL NIGHT TO CATCH THE ENEMIES OF GIBEON BY SURPRISE.
DON'T LET A SINGLE MAN ESCAPE!
FLEEING FROM THE ISRAELITES, THE ENEMY IS CAUGHT IN A TERRIBLE HAILSTORM.
WE HAVE ROUTED THE AMORITES, JOSHUA. BUT THE SUN IS ABOUT TO SET! UNDER THE COVER OF NIGHT, THEY'LL BE ABLE TO GET AWAY FROM US.
NOT IF I HAVE ANYTHING TO SAY ABOUT IT, THEY WON'T.
O LORD, MAKE THE SUN STAND STILL IN THE SKY. FREEZE THE MOON IN HER PLACE, THAT WE MAY HAVE TIME TO FINISH THIS BATTLE IN DAYLIGHT!
GOD ANSWERS JOSHUA'S PRAYER. DAYLIGHT LASTS LONG ENOUGH FOR JOSHUA TO WIN THE VICTORY AND SAVE THE PEOPLE OF GIBEON.

A Division Problem

BASED ON JOSHUA 11:1—24:18

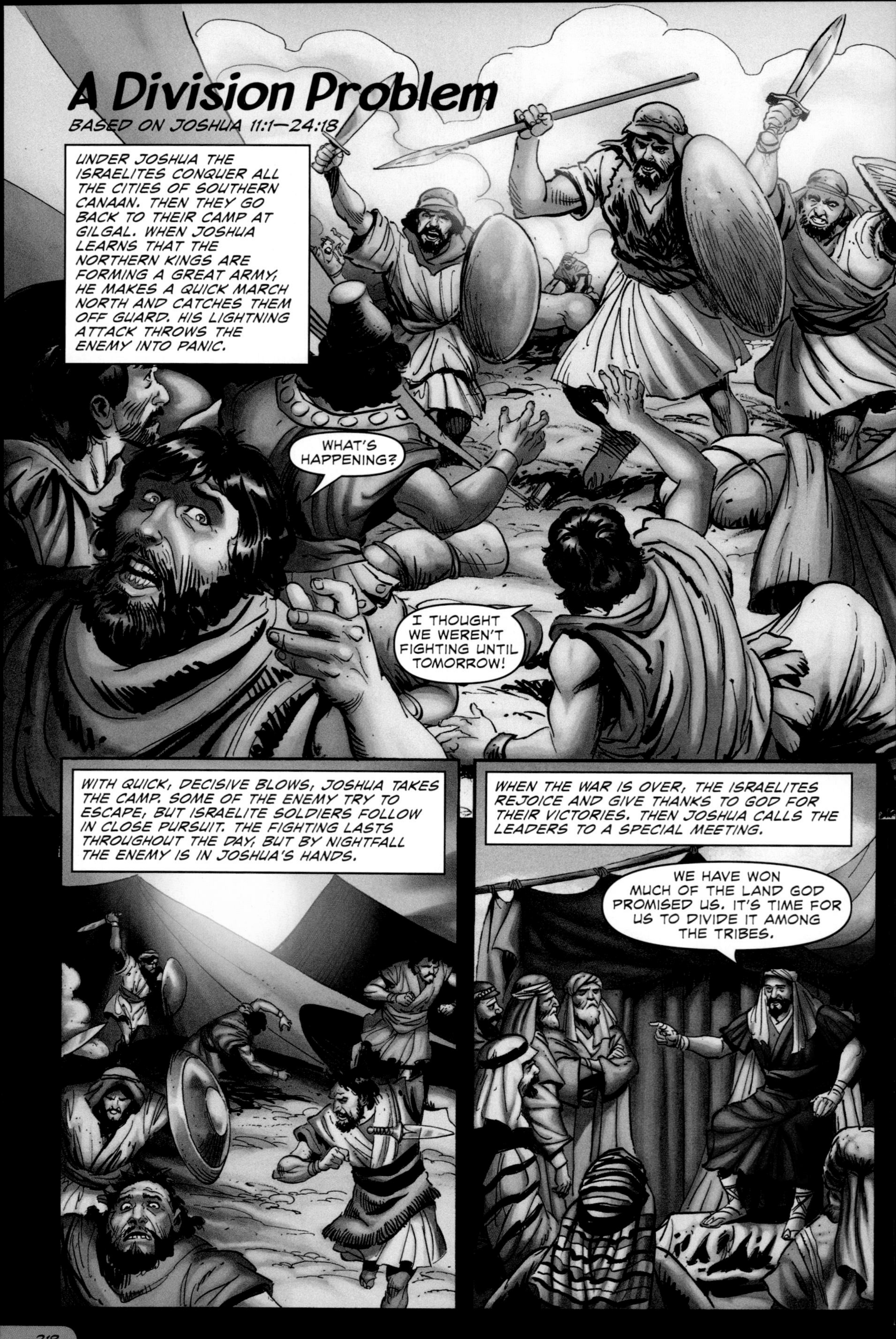
UNDER JOSHUA THE ISRAELITES CONQUER ALL THE CITIES OF SOUTHERN CANAAN. THEN THEY GO BACK TO THEIR CAMP AT GILGAL. WHEN JOSHUA LEARNS THAT THE NORTHERN KINGS ARE FORMING A GREAT ARMY, HE MAKES A QUICK MARCH NORTH AND CATCHES THEM OFF GUARD. HIS LIGHTNING ATTACK THROWS THE ENEMY INTO PANIC.
WHAT'S HAPPENING?
I THOUGHT WE WEREN'T FIGHTING UNTIL TOMORROW!
WITH QUICK, DECISIVE BLOWS, JOSHUA TAKES THE CAMP. SOME OF THE ENEMY TRY TO ESCAPE, BUT ISRAELITE SOLDIERS FOLLOW IN CLOSE PURSUIT. THE FIGHTING LASTS THROUGHOUT THE DAY, BUT BY NIGHTFALL THE ENEMY IS IN JOSHUA'S HANDS.
WHEN THE WAR IS OVER, THE ISRAELITES REJOICE AND GIVE THANKS TO GOD FOR THEIR VICTORIES. THEN JOSHUA CALLS THE LEADERS TO A SPECIAL MEETING.
WE HAVE WON MUCH OF THE LAND GOD PROMISED US. IT'S TIME FOR US TO DIVIDE IT AMONG THE TRIBES.

CALEB, JOSHUA'S FRIEND, SPEAKS FIRST.

BECAUSE I WAS ONE OF THE SCOUTS WHO WAS NOT AFRAID TO TAKE CANAAN 45 YEARS AGO, GOD PROMISED THAT SOMEDAY I COULD HAVE THE LAND I SAW.

GIVE ME THE LAND AROUND MOUNT HEBRON, AND I'LL DRIVE OFF THE GIANTS WHO LIVE THERE AND MAKE IT MY HOME.

YOUR WISH IS GRANTED, CALEB, AND MAY GOD BLESS YOU.

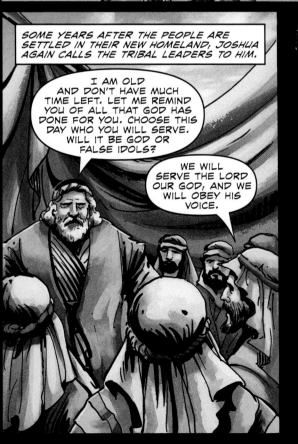

SOME YEARS AFTER THE PEOPLE ARE SETTLED IN THEIR NEW HOMELAND, JOSHUA AGAIN CALLS THE TRIBAL LEADERS TO HIM.

I AM OLD AND DON'T HAVE MUCH TIME LEFT. LET ME REMIND YOU OF ALL THAT GOD HAS DONE FOR YOU. CHOOSE THIS DAY WHO YOU WILL SERVE. WILL IT BE GOD OR FALSE IDOLS?

WE WILL SERVE THE LORD OUR GOD, AND WE WILL OBEY HIS VOICE.

"You know with all your heart and soul that not one of all the good promises the LORD your God gave you has failed. Every promise has been fulfilled; not one has failed."

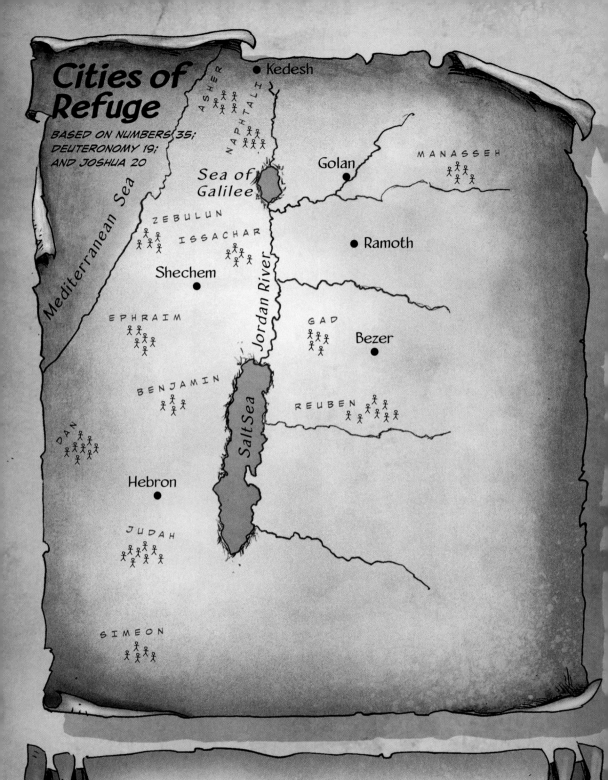

Cities of Refuge

BASED ON NUMBERS 35;
DEUTERONOMY 19;
AND JOSHUA 20

Mediterranean Sea

ASHER

NAPHTALI

Kedesh

MANASSEH

Golan

Sea of Galilee

ZEBULUN

ISSACHAR

Ramoth

Shechem

Jordan River

EPHRAIM

GAD

Bezer

BENJAMIN

Salt Sea

REUBEN

DAN

Hebron

JUDAH

SIMEON

JOSHUA DIVIDES THE LAND AMONG THE TRIBES
AND SETS UP SIX CITIES OF REFUGE WHERE
PEOPLE CAN GO TO RECEIVE MERCY—EVEN IF
THEY DO SOMETHING AS BAD AS KILLING A
PERSON.

Left-Handed Judge

BASED ON JUDGES 1–3

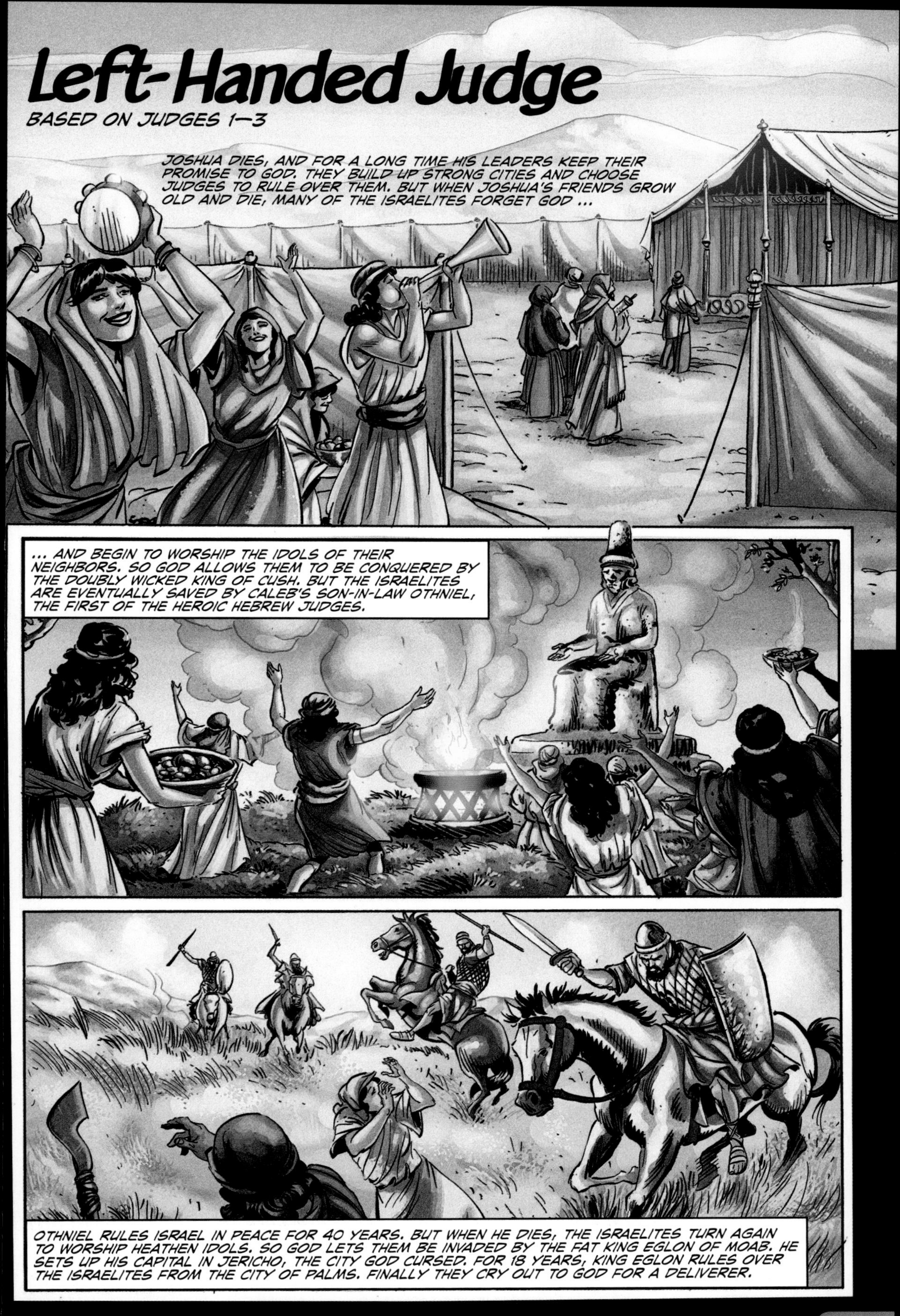
JOSHUA DIES, AND FOR A LONG TIME HIS LEADERS KEEP THEIR PROMISE TO GOD. THEY BUILD UP STRONG CITIES AND CHOOSE JUDGES TO RULE OVER THEM. BUT WHEN JOSHUA'S FRIENDS GROW OLD AND DIE, MANY OF THE ISRAELITES FORGET GOD ...
... AND BEGIN TO WORSHIP THE IDOLS OF THEIR NEIGHBORS. SO GOD ALLOWS THEM TO BE CONQUERED BY THE DOUBLY WICKED KING OF CUSH. BUT THE ISRAELITES ARE EVENTUALLY SAVED BY CALEB'S SON-IN-LAW OTHNIEL, THE FIRST OF THE HEROIC HEBREW JUDGES.
OTHNIEL RULES ISRAEL IN PEACE FOR 40 YEARS. BUT WHEN HE DIES, THE ISRAELITES TURN AGAIN TO WORSHIP HEATHEN IDOLS. SO GOD LETS THEM BE INVADED BY THE FAT KING EGLON OF MOAB. HE SETS UP HIS CAPITAL IN JERICHO, THE CITY GOD CURSED. FOR 18 YEARS, KING EGLON RULES OVER THE ISRAELITES FROM THE CITY OF PALMS. FINALLY THEY CRY OUT TO GOD FOR A DELIVERER.

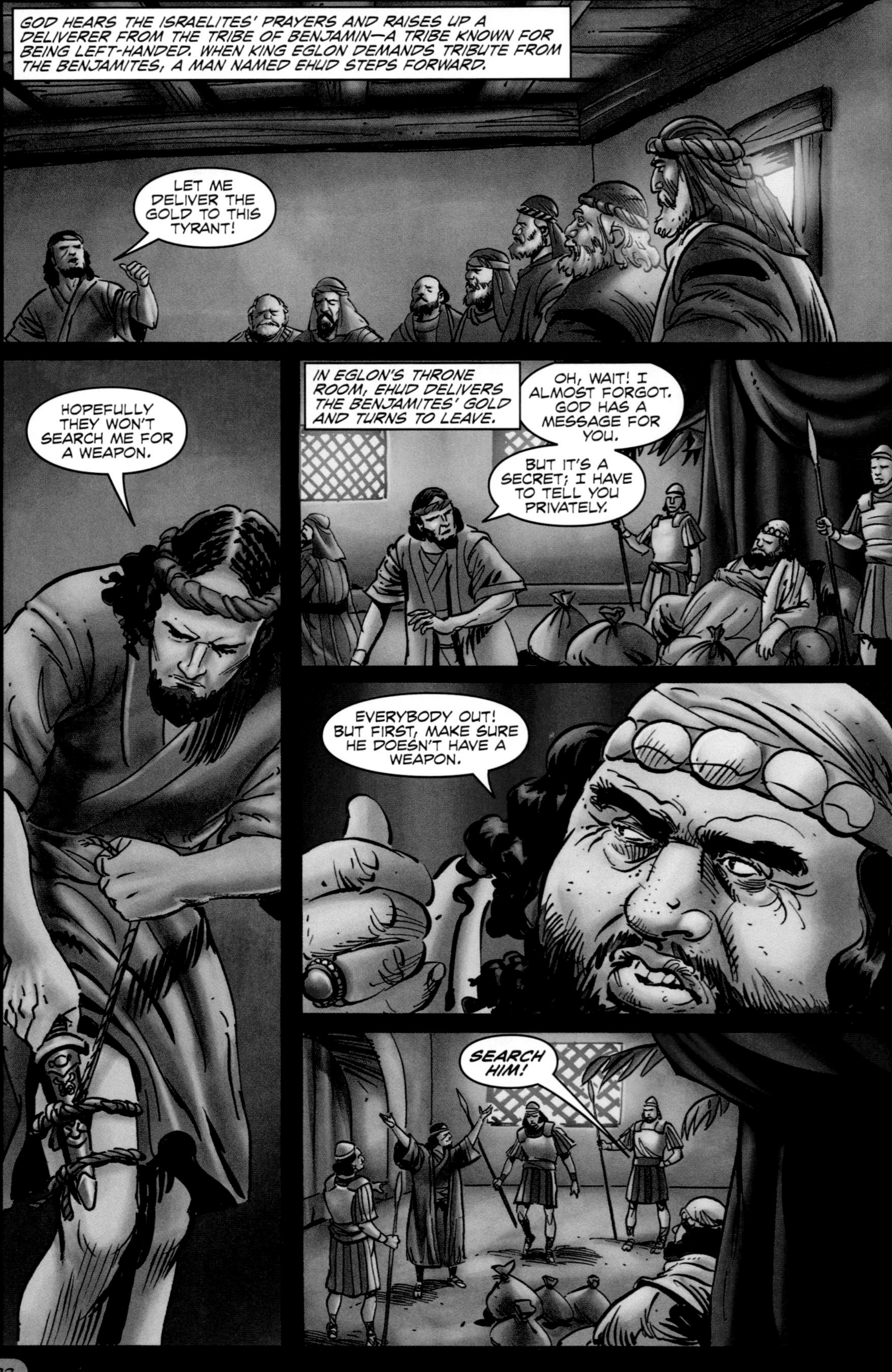
GOD HEARS THE ISRAELITES' PRAYERS AND RAISES UP A DELIVERER FROM THE TRIBE OF BENJAMIN—A TRIBE KNOWN FOR BEING LEFT-HANDED. WHEN KING EGLON DEMANDS TRIBUTE FROM THE BENJAMITES, A MAN NAMED EHUD STEPS FORWARD.
LET ME DELIVER THE GOLD TO THIS TYRANT!
HOPEFULLY THEY WON'T SEARCH ME FOR A WEAPON.
IN EGLON'S THRONE ROOM, EHUD DELIVERS THE BENJAMITES' GOLD AND TURNS TO LEAVE.
OH, WAIT! I ALMOST FORGOT. GOD HAS A MESSAGE FOR YOU.
BUT IT'S A SECRET; I HAVE TO TELL YOU PRIVATELY.
EVERYBODY OUT! BUT FIRST, MAKE SURE HE DOESN'T HAVE A WEAPON.
SEARCH HIM!

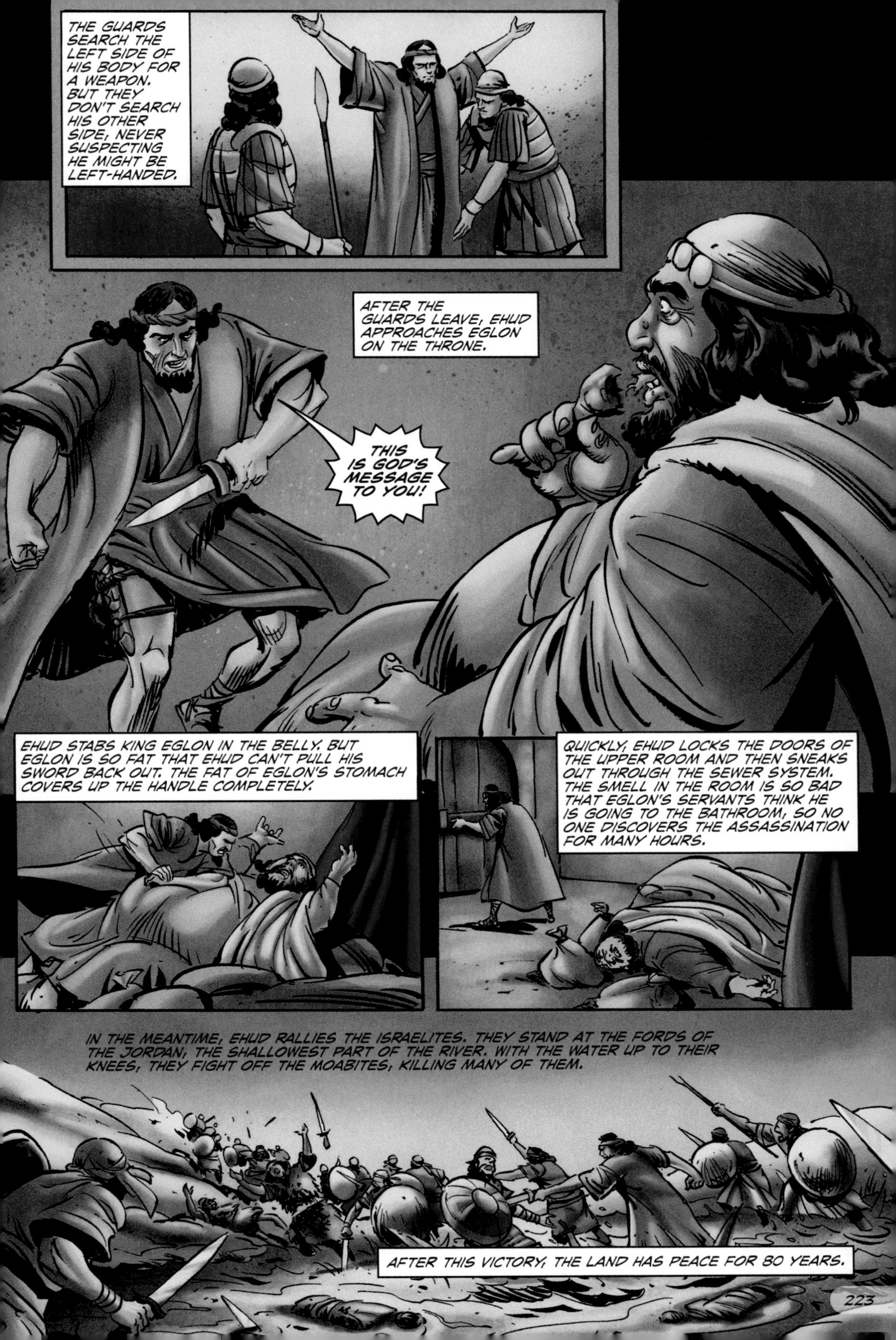

THE GUARDS SEARCH THE LEFT SIDE OF HIS BODY FOR A WEAPON. BUT THEY DON'T SEARCH HIS OTHER SIDE, NEVER SUSPECTING HE MIGHT BE LEFT-HANDED.
AFTER THE GUARDS LEAVE, EHUD APPROACHES EGLON ON THE THRONE.
THIS IS GOD'S MESSAGE TO YOU!
EHUD STABS KING EGLON IN THE BELLY. BUT EGLON IS SO FAT THAT EHUD CAN'T PULL HIS SWORD BACK OUT. THE FAT OF EGLON'S STOMACH COVERS UP THE HANDLE COMPLETELY.
QUICKLY, EHUD LOCKS THE DOORS OF THE UPPER ROOM AND THEN SNEAKS OUT THROUGH THE SEWER SYSTEM. THE SMELL IN THE ROOM IS SO BAD THAT EGLON'S SERVANTS THINK HE IS GOING TO THE BATHROOM, SO NO ONE DISCOVERS THE ASSASSINATION FOR MANY HOURS.
IN THE MEANTIME, EHUD RALLIES THE ISRAELITES. THEY STAND AT THE FORDS OF THE JORDAN, THE SHALLOWEST PART OF THE RIVER. WITH THE WATER UP TO THEIR KNEES, THEY FIGHT OFF THE MOABITES, KILLING MANY OF THEM.
AFTER THIS VICTORY, THE LAND HAS PEACE FOR 80 YEARS.

The Song of Deborah

BASED ON JUDGES 4—5

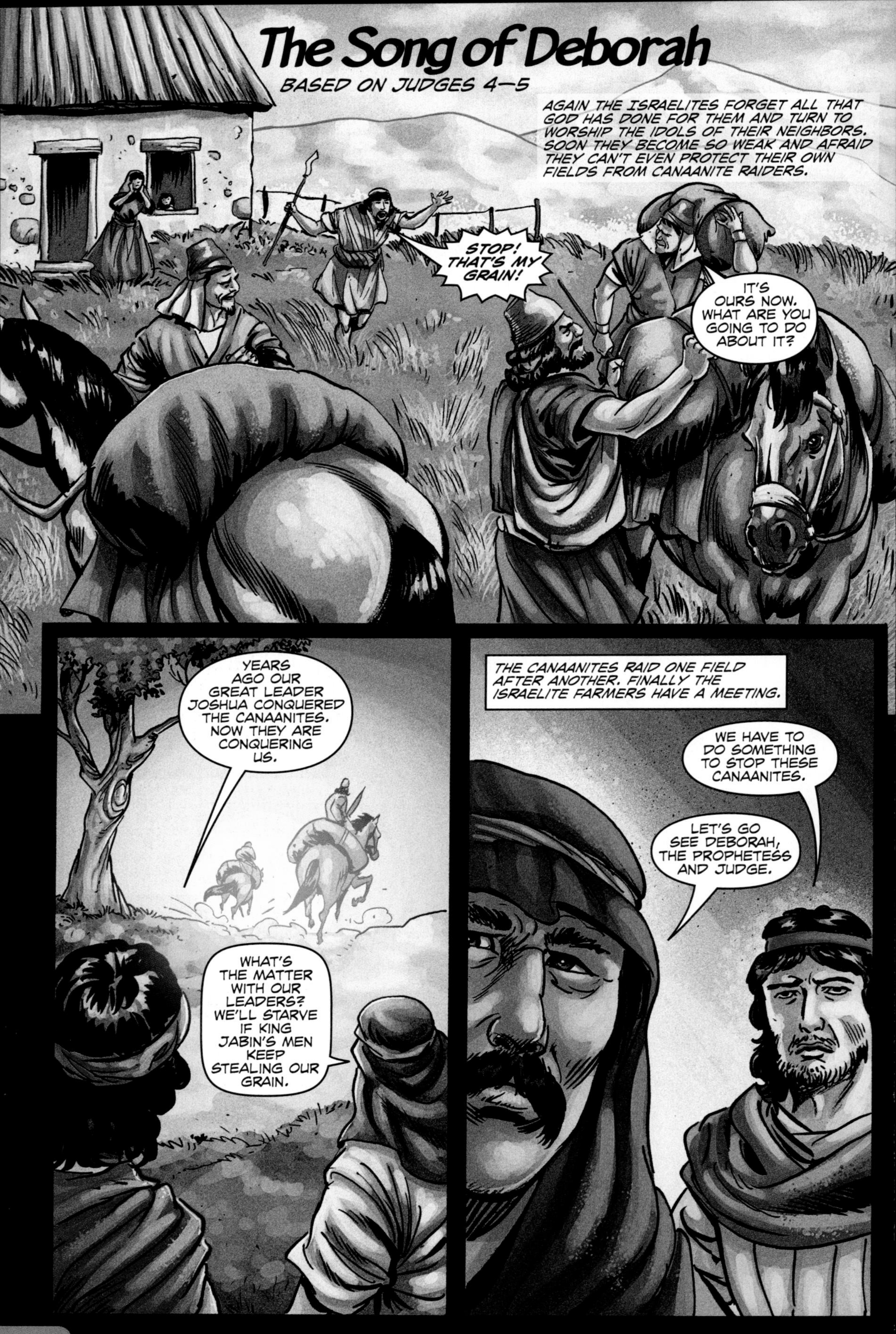

AGAIN THE ISRAELITES FORGET ALL THAT GOD HAS DONE FOR THEM AND TURN TO WORSHIP THE IDOLS OF THEIR NEIGHBORS. SOON THEY BECOME SO WEAK AND AFRAID THEY CAN'T EVEN PROTECT THEIR OWN FIELDS FROM CANAANITE RAIDERS.
STOP! THAT'S MY GRAIN!
IT'S OURS NOW. WHAT ARE YOU GOING TO DO ABOUT IT?
YEARS AGO OUR GREAT LEADER JOSHUA CONQUERED THE CANAANITES. NOW THEY ARE CONQUERING US.
WHAT'S THE MATTER WITH OUR LEADERS? WE'LL STARVE IF KING JABIN'S MEN KEEP STEALING OUR GRAIN.
THE CANAANITES RAID ONE FIELD AFTER ANOTHER. FINALLY THE ISRAELITE FARMERS HAVE A MEETING.
WE HAVE TO DO SOMETHING TO STOP THESE CANAANITES.
LET'S GO SEE DEBORAH, THE PROPHETESS AND JUDGE.

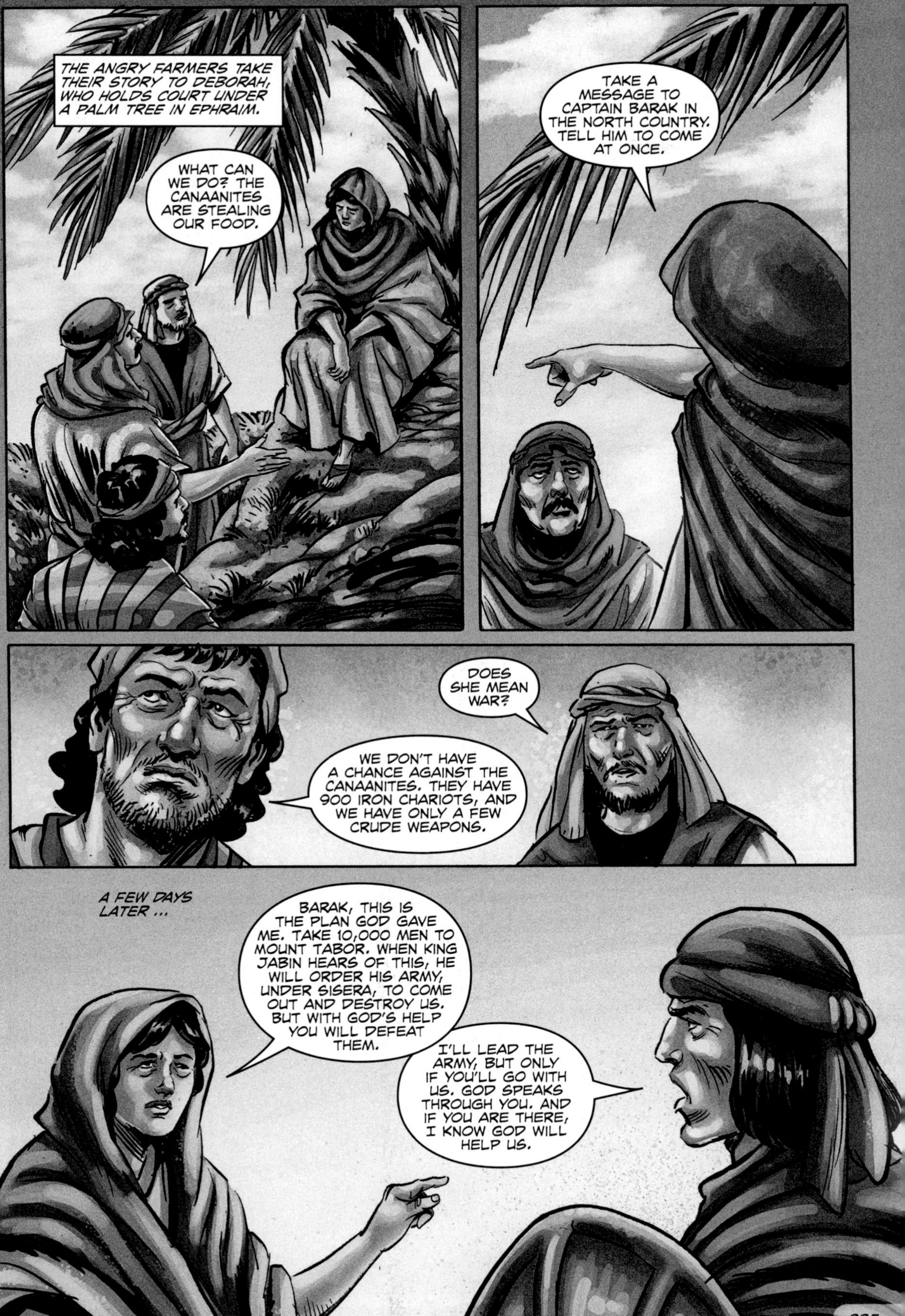
THE ANGRY FARMERS TAKE THEIR STORY TO DEBORAH, WHO HOLDS COURT UNDER A PALM TREE IN EPHRAIM.
WHAT CAN WE DO? THE CANAANITES ARE STEALING OUR FOOD.
TAKE A MESSAGE TO CAPTAIN BARAK IN THE NORTH COUNTRY. TELL HIM TO COME AT ONCE.
DOES SHE MEAN WAR?
WE DON'T HAVE A CHANCE AGAINST THE CANAANITES. THEY HAVE 900 IRON CHARIOTS, AND WE HAVE ONLY A FEW CRUDE WEAPONS.
A FEW DAYS LATER ...
BARAK, THIS IS THE PLAN GOD GAVE ME. TAKE 10,000 MEN TO MOUNT TABOR. WHEN KING JABIN HEARS OF THIS, HE WILL ORDER HIS ARMY, UNDER SISERA, TO COME OUT AND DESTROY US. BUT WITH GOD'S HELP YOU WILL DEFEAT THEM.
I'LL LEAD THE ARMY, BUT ONLY IF YOU'LL GO WITH US. GOD SPEAKS THROUGH YOU. AND IF YOU ARE THERE, I KNOW GOD WILL HELP US.

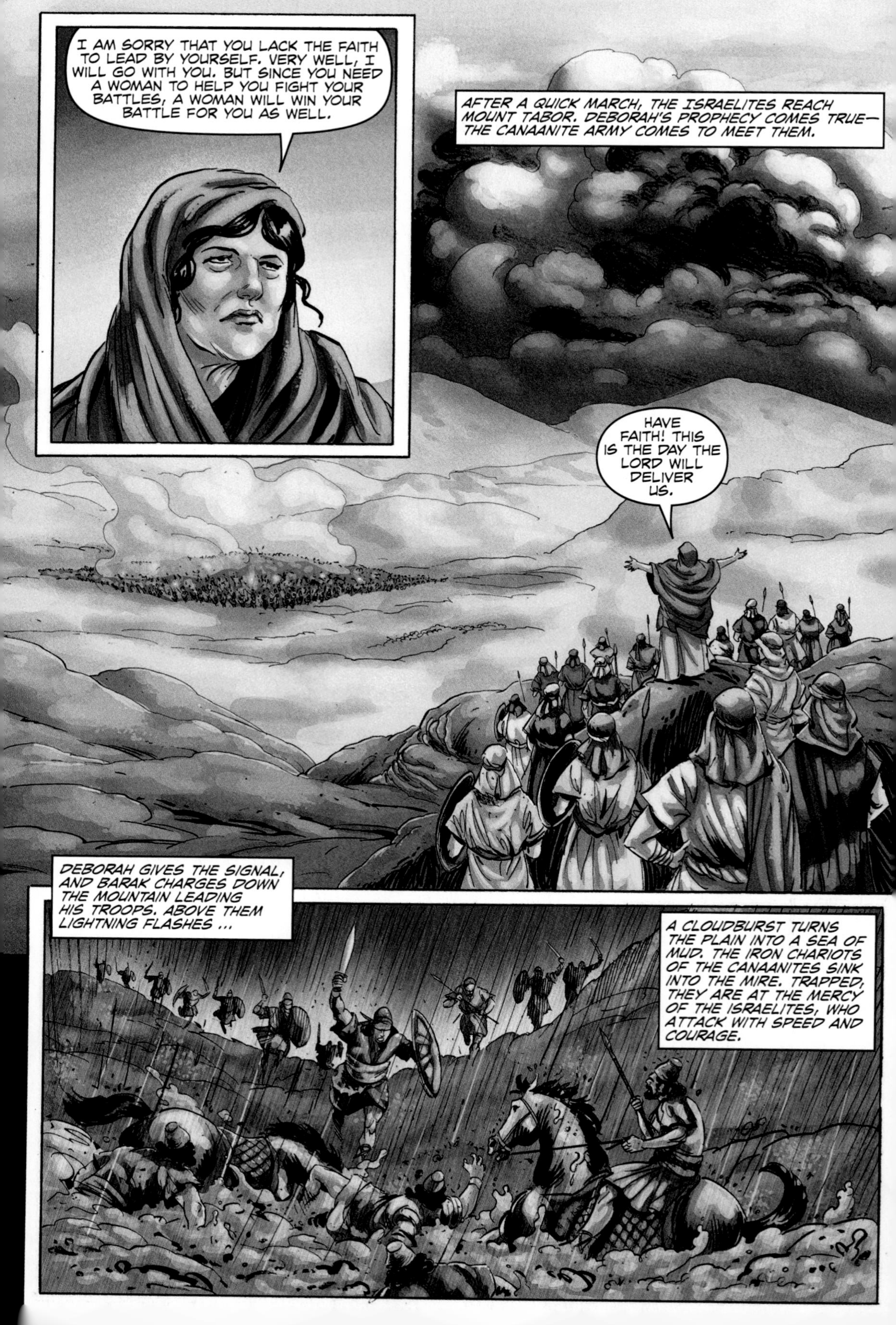
I AM SORRY THAT YOU LACK THE FAITH TO LEAD BY YOURSELF. VERY WELL, I WILL GO WITH YOU. BUT SINCE YOU NEED A WOMAN TO HELP YOU FIGHT YOUR BATTLES, A WOMAN WILL WIN YOUR BATTLE FOR YOU AS WELL.
AFTER A QUICK MARCH, THE ISRAELITES REACH MOUNT TABOR. DEBORAH'S PROPHECY COMES TRUE—THE CANAANITE ARMY COMES TO MEET THEM.
HAVE FAITH! THIS IS THE DAY THE LORD WILL DELIVER US.
DEBORAH GIVES THE SIGNAL, AND BARAK CHARGES DOWN THE MOUNTAIN LEADING HIS TROOPS. ABOVE THEM LIGHTNING FLASHES ...
A CLOUDBURST TURNS THE PLAIN INTO A SEA OF MUD. THE IRON CHARIOTS OF THE CANAANITES SINK INTO THE MIRE. TRAPPED, THEY ARE AT THE MERCY OF THE ISRAELITES, WHO ATTACK WITH SPEED AND COURAGE.

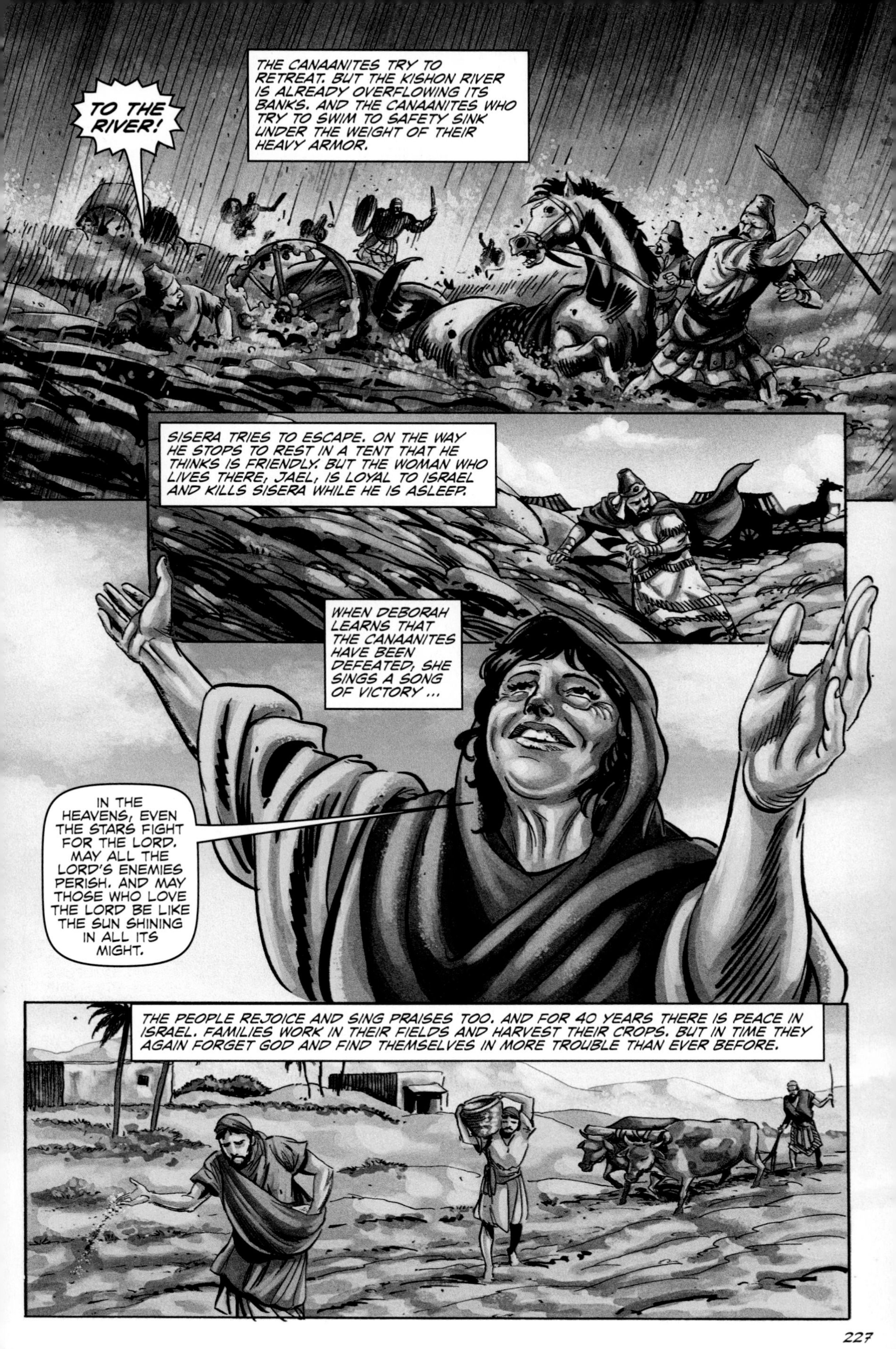
THE CANAANITES TRY TO RETREAT. BUT THE KISHON RIVER IS ALREADY OVERFLOWING ITS BANKS. AND THE CANAANITES WHO TRY TO SWIM TO SAFETY SINK UNDER THE WEIGHT OF THEIR HEAVY ARMOR.
TO THE RIVER!
SISERA TRIES TO ESCAPE. ON THE WAY HE STOPS TO REST IN A TENT THAT HE THINKS IS FRIENDLY. BUT THE WOMAN WHO LIVES THERE, JAEL, IS LOYAL TO ISRAEL AND KILLS SISERA WHILE HE IS ASLEEP.
WHEN DEBORAH LEARNS THAT THE CANAANITES HAVE BEEN DEFEATED, SHE SINGS A SONG OF VICTORY ...
IN THE HEAVENS, EVEN THE STARS FIGHT FOR THE LORD. MAY ALL THE LORD'S ENEMIES PERISH. AND MAY THOSE WHO LOVE THE LORD BE LIKE THE SUN SHINING IN ALL ITS MIGHT.
THE PEOPLE REJOICE AND SING PRAISES TOO. AND FOR 40 YEARS THERE IS PEACE IN ISRAEL. FAMILIES WORK IN THEIR FIELDS AND HARVEST THEIR CROPS. BUT IN TIME THEY AGAIN FORGET GOD AND FIND THEMSELVES IN MORE TROUBLE THAN EVER BEFORE.

Cowardly Judge

BASED ON JUDGES 6–7

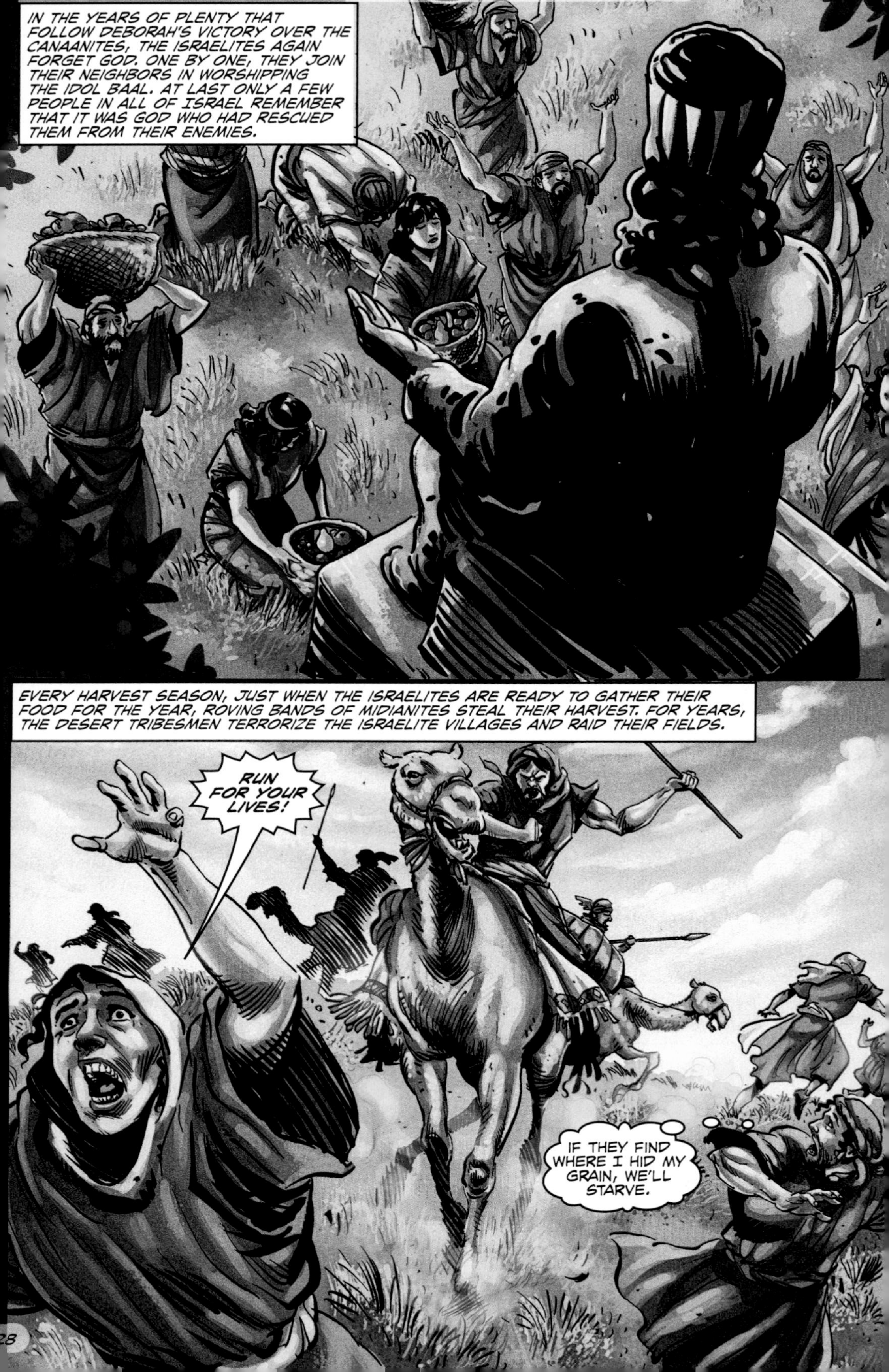
IN THE YEARS OF PLENTY THAT FOLLOW DEBORAH'S VICTORY OVER THE CANAANITES, THE ISRAELITES AGAIN FORGET GOD. ONE BY ONE, THEY JOIN THEIR NEIGHBORS IN WORSHIPPING THE IDOL BAAL. AT LAST ONLY A FEW PEOPLE IN ALL OF ISRAEL REMEMBER THAT IT WAS GOD WHO HAD RESCUED THEM FROM THEIR ENEMIES.
EVERY HARVEST SEASON, JUST WHEN THE ISRAELITES ARE READY TO GATHER THEIR FOOD FOR THE YEAR, ROVING BANDS OF MIDIANITES STEAL THEIR HARVEST. FOR YEARS, THE DESERT TRIBESMEN TERRORIZE THE ISRAELITE VILLAGES AND RAID THEIR FIELDS.
RUN FOR YOUR LIVES!
IF THEY FIND WHERE I HID MY GRAIN, WE'LL STARVE.

BUT WHEN THE RAID IS OVER ...

IT'S GONE! OUR GRAIN IS GONE!

FOR SEVEN LONG YEARS THE ISRAELITES SUFFER AT THE HANDS OF THE DESERT TRIBESMEN. THEY HIDE OUT IN CAVES AND THRESH THEIR GRAIN IN SECRET PLACES ... BUT THE RAIDERS ALWAYS RETURN.

THEN EVEN MORE FRIGHTENING NEWS COMES ...

THE MIDIANITES ARE COMING AGAIN, AND THEY'RE BRINGING GREAT ARMIES FROM THE EAST.

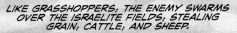

LIKE GRASSHOPPERS, THE ENEMY SWARMS OVER THE ISRAELITE FIELDS, STEALING GRAIN, CATTLE, AND SHEEP.

ONE DAY A YOUNG ISRAELITE IS SECRETLY THRESHING HIS GRAIN WHEN A STRANGER APPEARS BEFORE HIM.

WHO ARE YOU? WHAT DO YOU WANT?

YOU ARE A MIGHTY WARRIOR, GIDEON. GOD HAS CHOSEN YOU TO SAVE HIS PEOPLE.

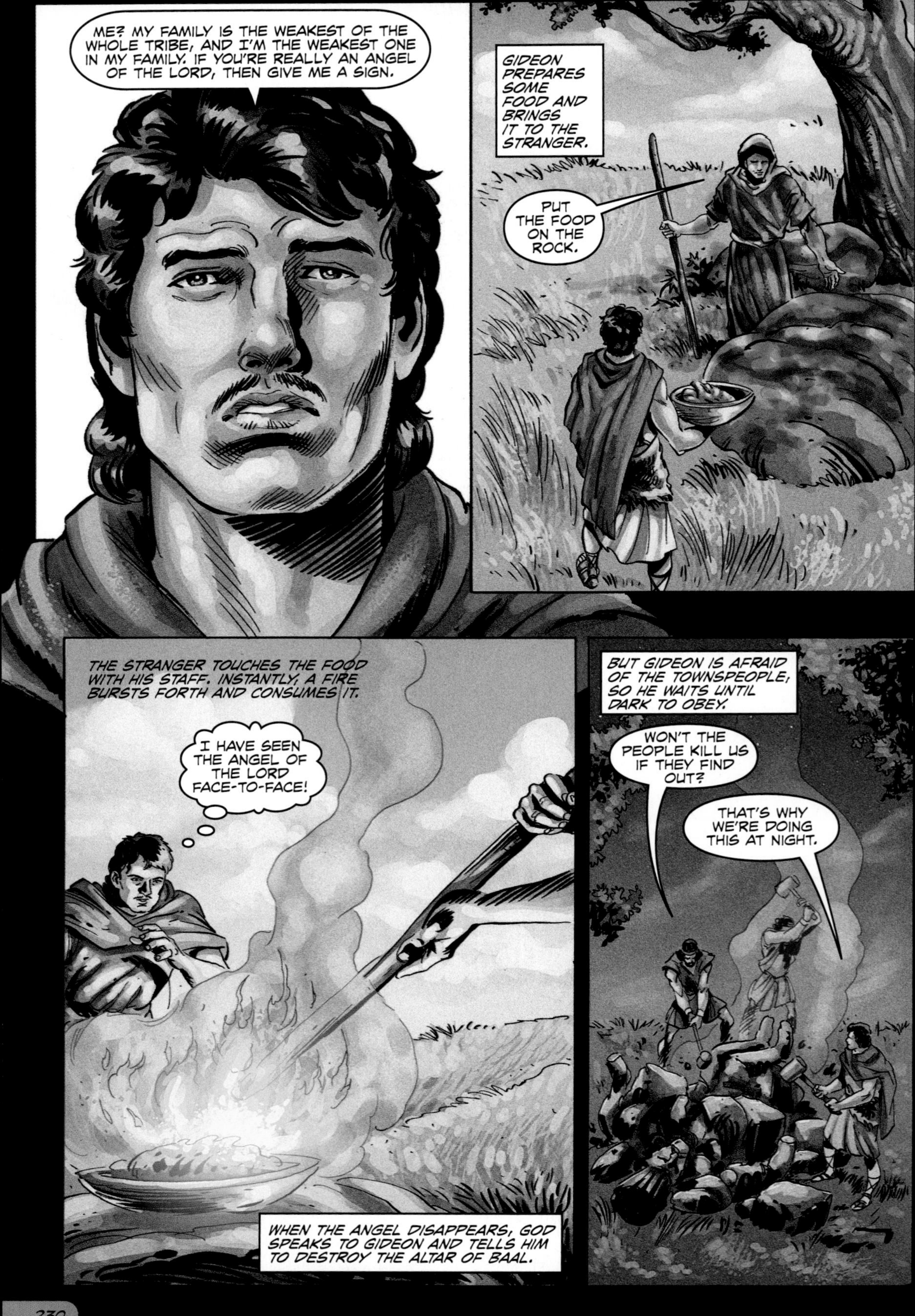

ME? MY FAMILY IS THE WEAKEST OF THE WHOLE TRIBE, AND I'M THE WEAKEST ONE IN MY FAMILY. IF YOU'RE REALLY AN ANGEL OF THE LORD, THEN GIVE ME A SIGN.
GIDEON PREPARES SOME FOOD AND BRINGS IT TO THE STRANGER.
PUT THE FOOD ON THE ROCK.
THE STRANGER TOUCHES THE FOOD WITH HIS STAFF. INSTANTLY, A FIRE BURSTS FORTH AND CONSUMES IT.
I HAVE SEEN THE ANGEL OF THE LORD FACE-TO-FACE!
WHEN THE ANGEL DISAPPEARS, GOD SPEAKS TO GIDEON AND TELLS HIM TO DESTROY THE ALTAR OF BAAL.
BUT GIDEON IS AFRAID OF THE TOWNSPEOPLE, SO HE WAITS UNTIL DARK TO OBEY.
WON'T THE PEOPLE KILL US IF THEY FIND OUT?
THAT'S WHY WE'RE DOING THIS AT NIGHT.

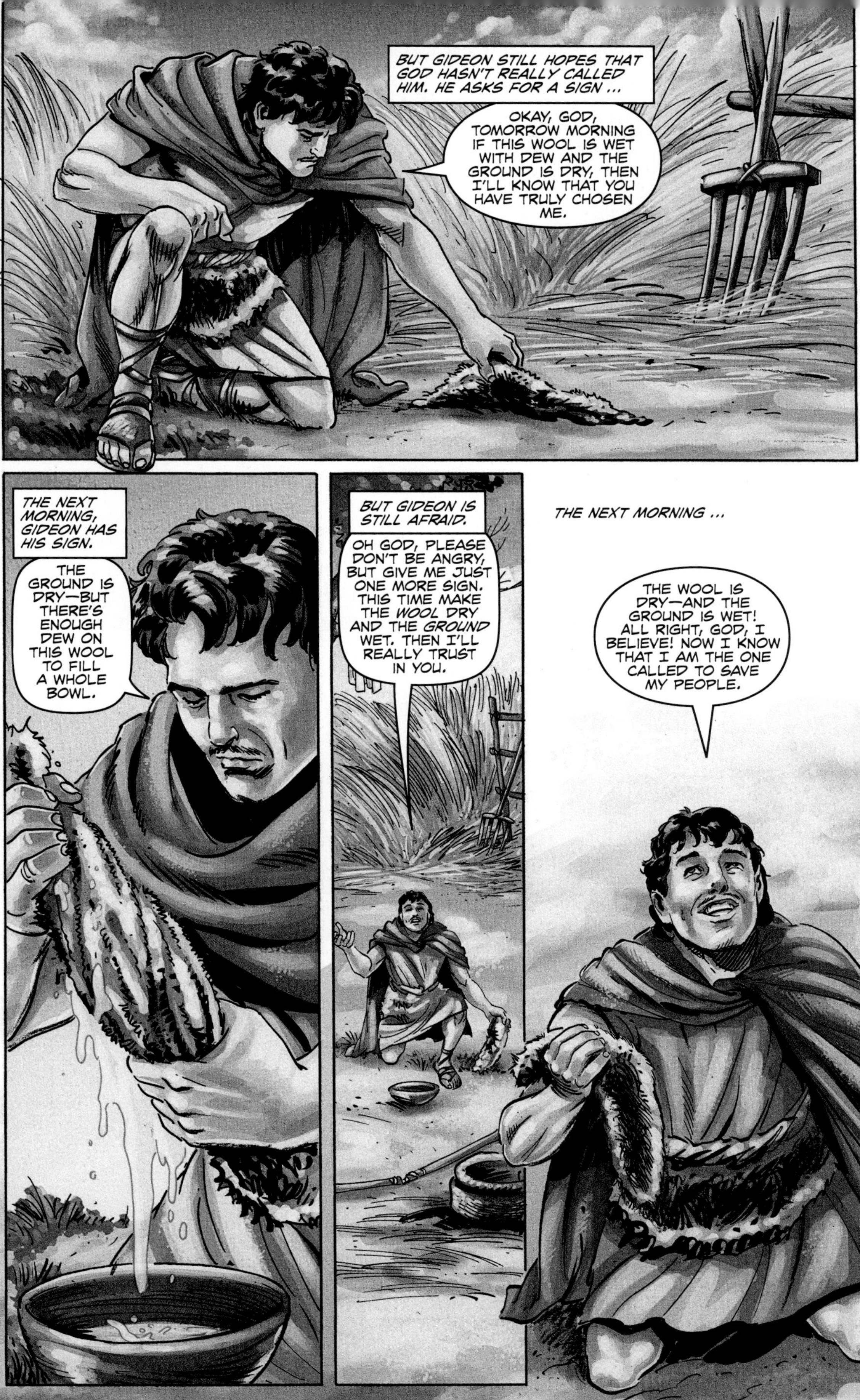
BUT GIDEON STILL HOPES THAT GOD HASN'T REALLY CALLED HIM. HE ASKS FOR A SIGN ...
OKAY, GOD, TOMORROW MORNING IF THIS WOOL IS WET WITH DEW AND THE GROUND IS DRY, THEN I'LL KNOW THAT YOU HAVE TRULY CHOSEN ME.
THE NEXT MORNING, GIDEON HAS HIS SIGN.
THE GROUND IS DRY—BUT THERE'S ENOUGH DEW ON THIS WOOL TO FILL A WHOLE BOWL.
BUT GIDEON IS STILL AFRAID.
OH GOD, PLEASE DON'T BE ANGRY, BUT GIVE ME JUST ONE MORE SIGN. THIS TIME MAKE THE *WOOL* DRY AND THE *GROUND* WET. THEN I'LL REALLY TRUST IN YOU.
THE NEXT MORNING ...
THE WOOL IS DRY—AND THE GROUND IS WET! ALL RIGHT, GOD, I BELIEVE! NOW I KNOW THAT I AM THE ONE CALLED TO SAVE MY PEOPLE.

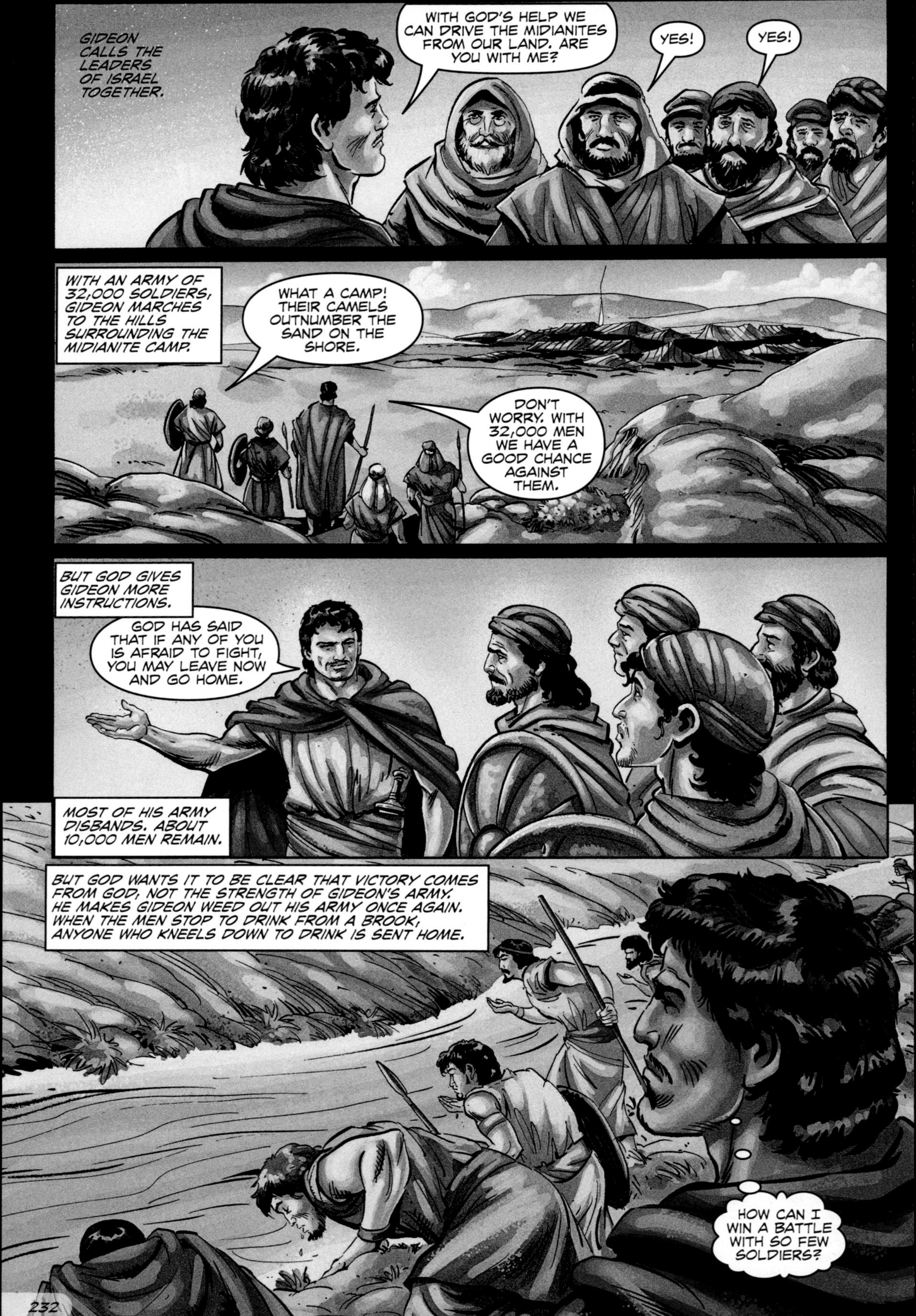
GIDEON CALLS THE LEADERS OF ISRAEL TOGETHER.
WITH GOD'S HELP WE CAN DRIVE THE MIDIANITES FROM OUR LAND. ARE YOU WITH ME?
YES!
YES!
WITH AN ARMY OF 32,000 SOLDIERS, GIDEON MARCHES TO THE HILLS SURROUNDING THE MIDIANITE CAMP.
WHAT A CAMP! THEIR CAMELS OUTNUMBER THE SAND ON THE SHORE.
DON'T WORRY. WITH 32,000 MEN WE HAVE A GOOD CHANCE AGAINST THEM.
BUT GOD GIVES GIDEON MORE INSTRUCTIONS.
GOD HAS SAID THAT IF ANY OF YOU IS AFRAID TO FIGHT, YOU MAY LEAVE NOW AND GO HOME.
MOST OF HIS ARMY DISBANDS. ABOUT 10,000 MEN REMAIN.
BUT GOD WANTS IT TO BE CLEAR THAT VICTORY COMES FROM GOD, NOT THE STRENGTH OF GIDEON'S ARMY. HE MAKES GIDEON WEED OUT HIS ARMY ONCE AGAIN. WHEN THE MEN STOP TO DRINK FROM A BROOK, ANYONE WHO KNEELS DOWN TO DRINK IS SENT HOME.
HOW CAN I WIN A BATTLE WITH SO FEW SOLDIERS?

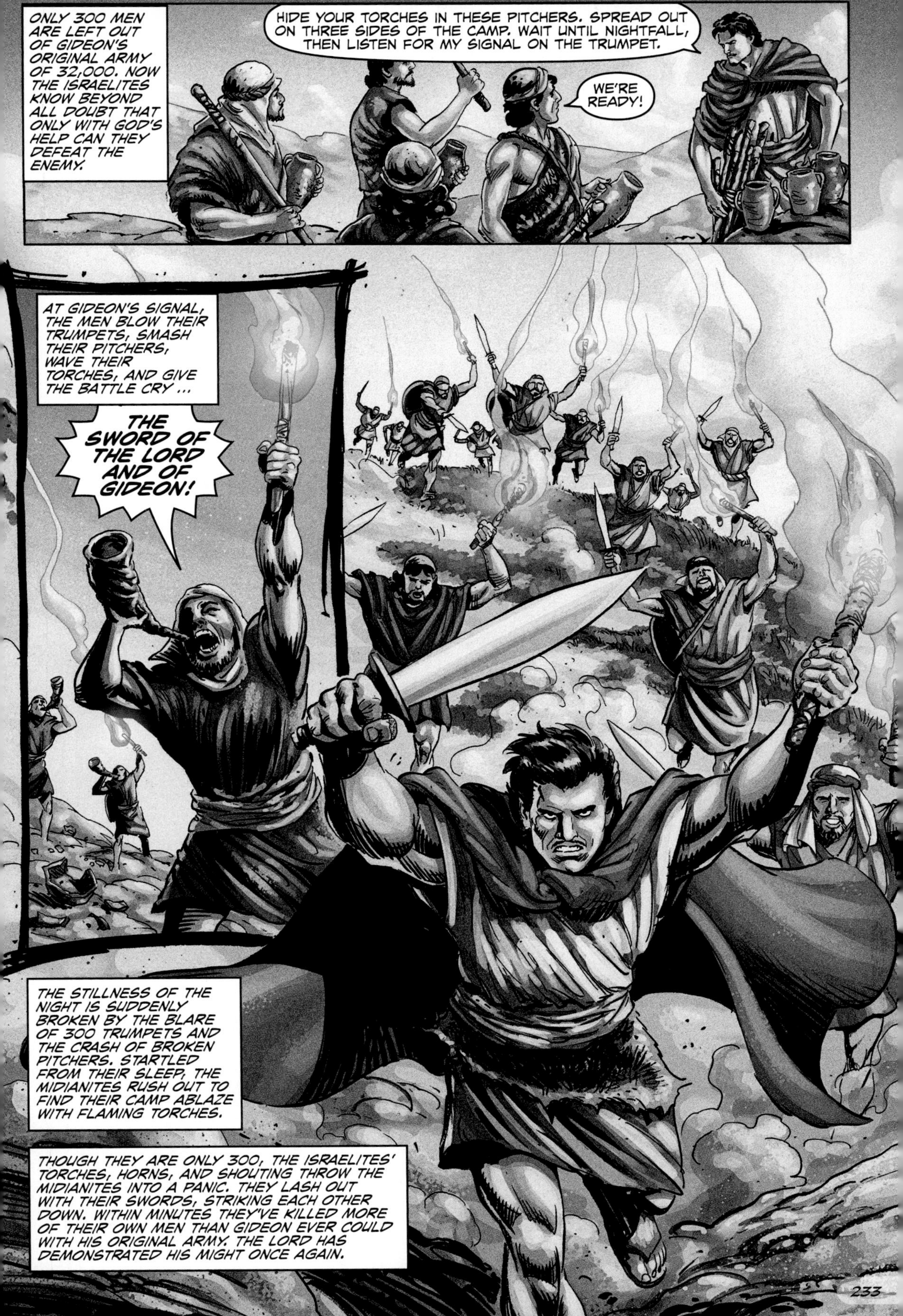
ONLY 300 MEN ARE LEFT OUT OF GIDEON'S ORIGINAL ARMY OF 32,000. NOW THE ISRAELITES KNOW BEYOND ALL DOUBT THAT ONLY WITH GOD'S HELP CAN THEY DEFEAT THE ENEMY.
HIDE YOUR TORCHES IN THESE PITCHERS. SPREAD OUT ON THREE SIDES OF THE CAMP. WAIT UNTIL NIGHTFALL, THEN LISTEN FOR MY SIGNAL ON THE TRUMPET.
WE'RE READY!
AT GIDEON'S SIGNAL, THE MEN BLOW THEIR TRUMPETS, SMASH THEIR PITCHERS, WAVE THEIR TORCHES, AND GIVE THE BATTLE CRY ...
THE SWORD OF THE LORD AND OF GIDEON!
THE STILLNESS OF THE NIGHT IS SUDDENLY BROKEN BY THE BLARE OF 300 TRUMPETS AND THE CRASH OF BROKEN PITCHERS. STARTLED FROM THEIR SLEEP, THE MIDIANITES RUSH OUT TO FIND THEIR CAMP ABLAZE WITH FLAMING TORCHES.
THOUGH THEY ARE ONLY 300, THE ISRAELITES' TORCHES, HORNS, AND SHOUTING THROW THE MIDIANITES INTO A PANIC. THEY LASH OUT WITH THEIR SWORDS, STRIKING EACH OTHER DOWN. WITHIN MINUTES THEY'VE KILLED MORE OF THEIR OWN MEN THAN GIDEON EVER COULD WITH HIS ORIGINAL ARMY. THE LORD HAS DEMONSTRATED HIS MIGHT ONCE AGAIN.

God's Enforcer

BASED ON JUDGES 13–14

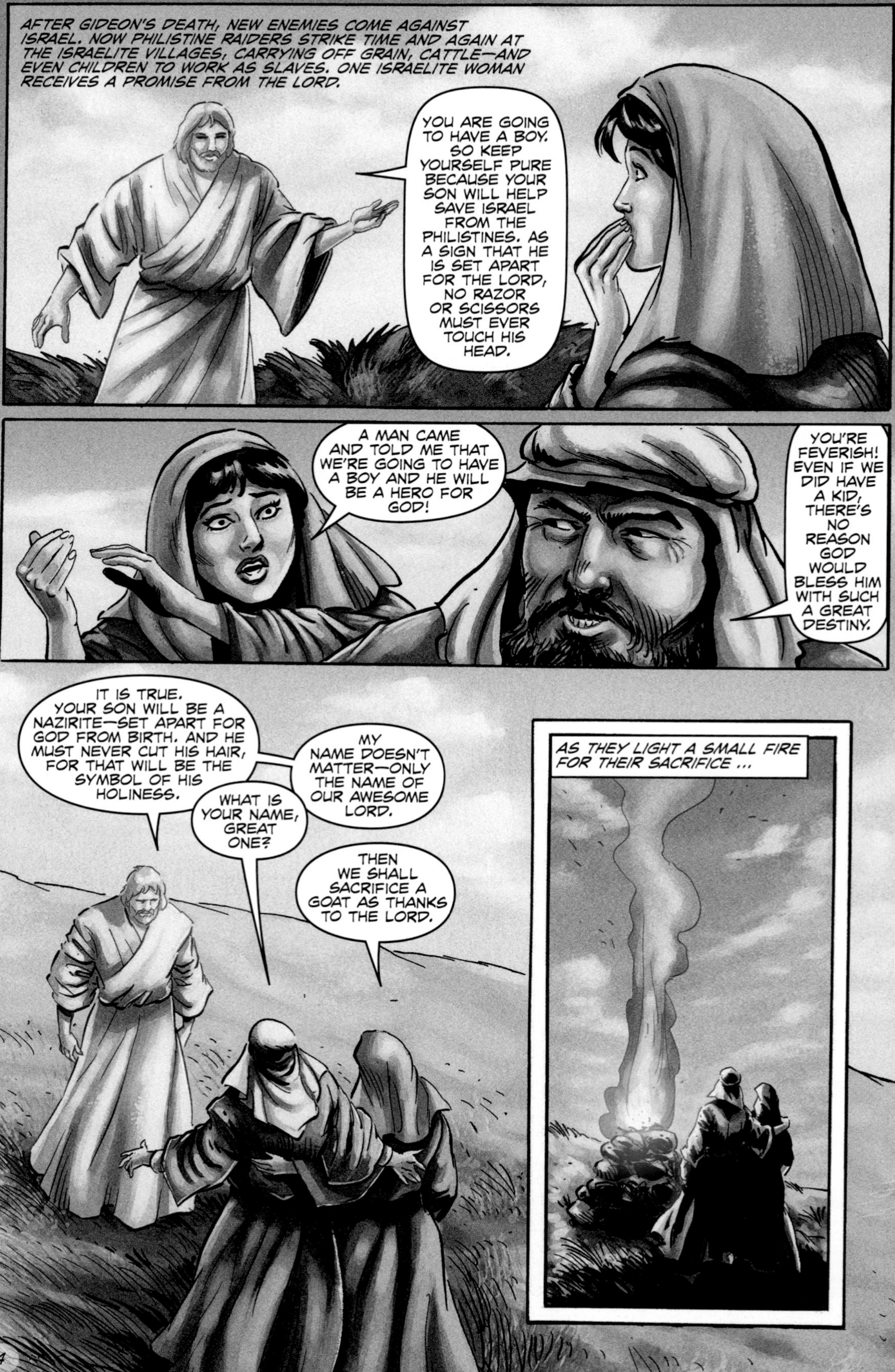

AFTER GIDEON'S DEATH, NEW ENEMIES COME AGAINST ISRAEL. NOW PHILISTINE RAIDERS STRIKE TIME AND AGAIN AT THE ISRAELITE VILLAGES, CARRYING OFF GRAIN, CATTLE—AND EVEN CHILDREN TO WORK AS SLAVES. ONE ISRAELITE WOMAN RECEIVES A PROMISE FROM THE LORD.
YOU ARE GOING TO HAVE A BOY. SO KEEP YOURSELF PURE BECAUSE YOUR SON WILL HELP SAVE ISRAEL FROM THE PHILISTINES. AS A SIGN THAT HE IS SET APART FOR THE LORD, NO RAZOR OR SCISSORS MUST EVER TOUCH HIS HEAD.
A MAN CAME AND TOLD ME THAT WE'RE GOING TO HAVE A BOY AND HE WILL BE A HERO FOR GOD!
YOU'RE FEVERISH! EVEN IF WE DID HAVE A KID, THERE'S NO REASON GOD WOULD BLESS HIM WITH SUCH A GREAT DESTINY.
IT IS TRUE. YOUR SON WILL BE A NAZIRITE—SET APART FOR GOD FROM BIRTH. AND HE MUST NEVER CUT HIS HAIR, FOR THAT WILL BE THE SYMBOL OF HIS HOLINESS.
WHAT IS YOUR NAME, GREAT ONE?
MY NAME DOESN'T MATTER—ONLY THE NAME OF OUR AWESOME LORD.
THEN WE SHALL SACRIFICE A GOAT AS THANKS TO THE LORD.
AS THEY LIGHT A SMALL FIRE FOR THEIR SACRIFICE ...

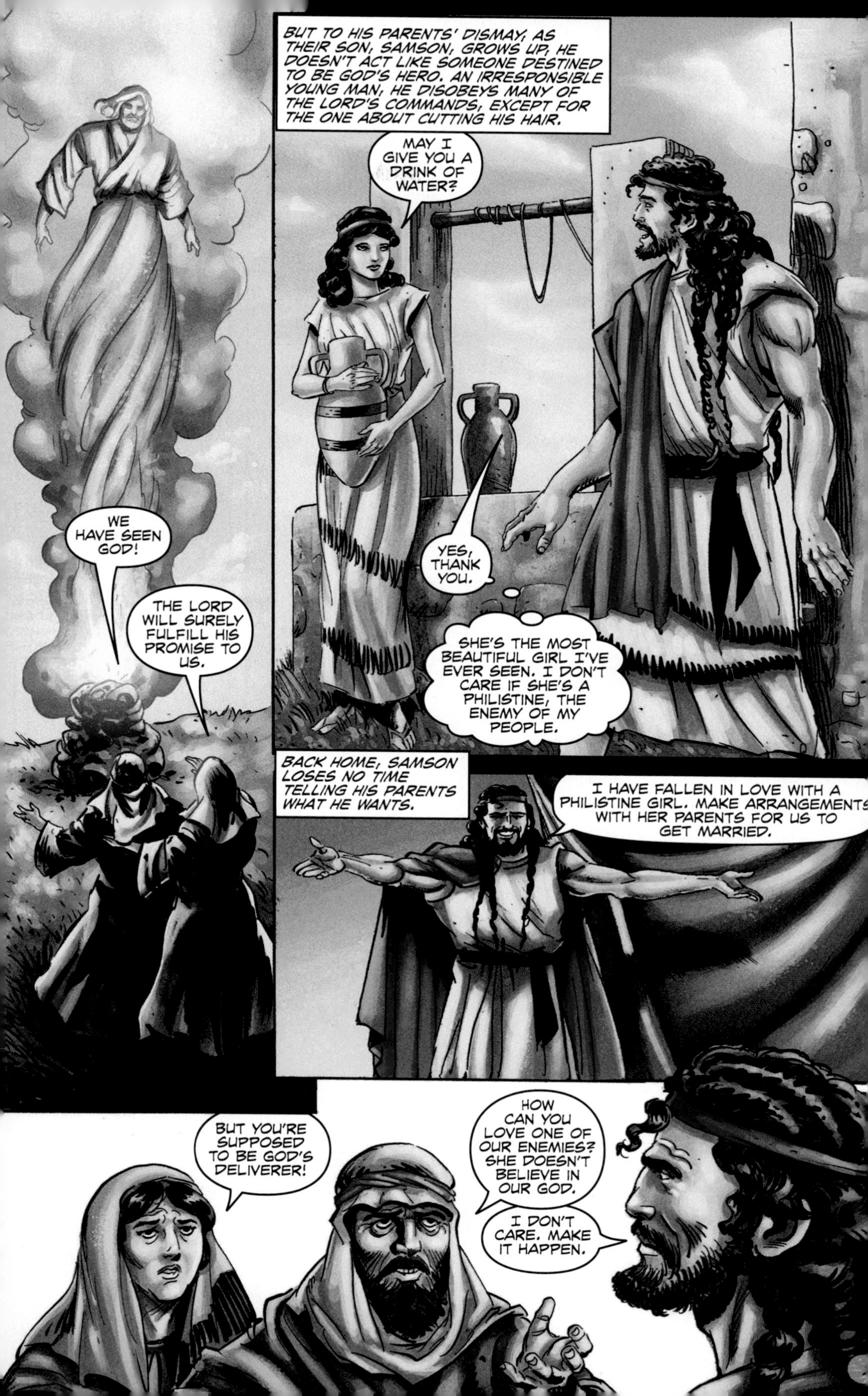
WE HAVE SEEN GOD!
THE LORD WILL SURELY FULFILL HIS PROMISE TO US.
BUT TO HIS PARENTS' DISMAY, AS THEIR SON, SAMSON, GROWS UP, HE DOESN'T ACT LIKE SOMEONE DESTINED TO BE GOD'S HERO. AN IRRESPONSIBLE YOUNG MAN, HE DISOBEYS MANY OF THE LORD'S COMMANDS, EXCEPT FOR THE ONE ABOUT CUTTING HIS HAIR.
MAY I GIVE YOU A DRINK OF WATER?
YES, THANK YOU.
SHE'S THE MOST BEAUTIFUL GIRL I'VE EVER SEEN. I DON'T CARE IF SHE'S A PHILISTINE, THE ENEMY OF MY PEOPLE.
BACK HOME, SAMSON LOSES NO TIME TELLING HIS PARENTS WHAT HE WANTS.
I HAVE FALLEN IN LOVE WITH A PHILISTINE GIRL. MAKE ARRANGEMENTS WITH HER PARENTS FOR US TO GET MARRIED.
BUT YOU'RE SUPPOSED TO BE GOD'S DELIVERER!
HOW CAN YOU LOVE ONE OF OUR ENEMIES? SHE DOESN'T BELIEVE IN OUR GOD.
I DON'T CARE. MAKE IT HAPPEN.

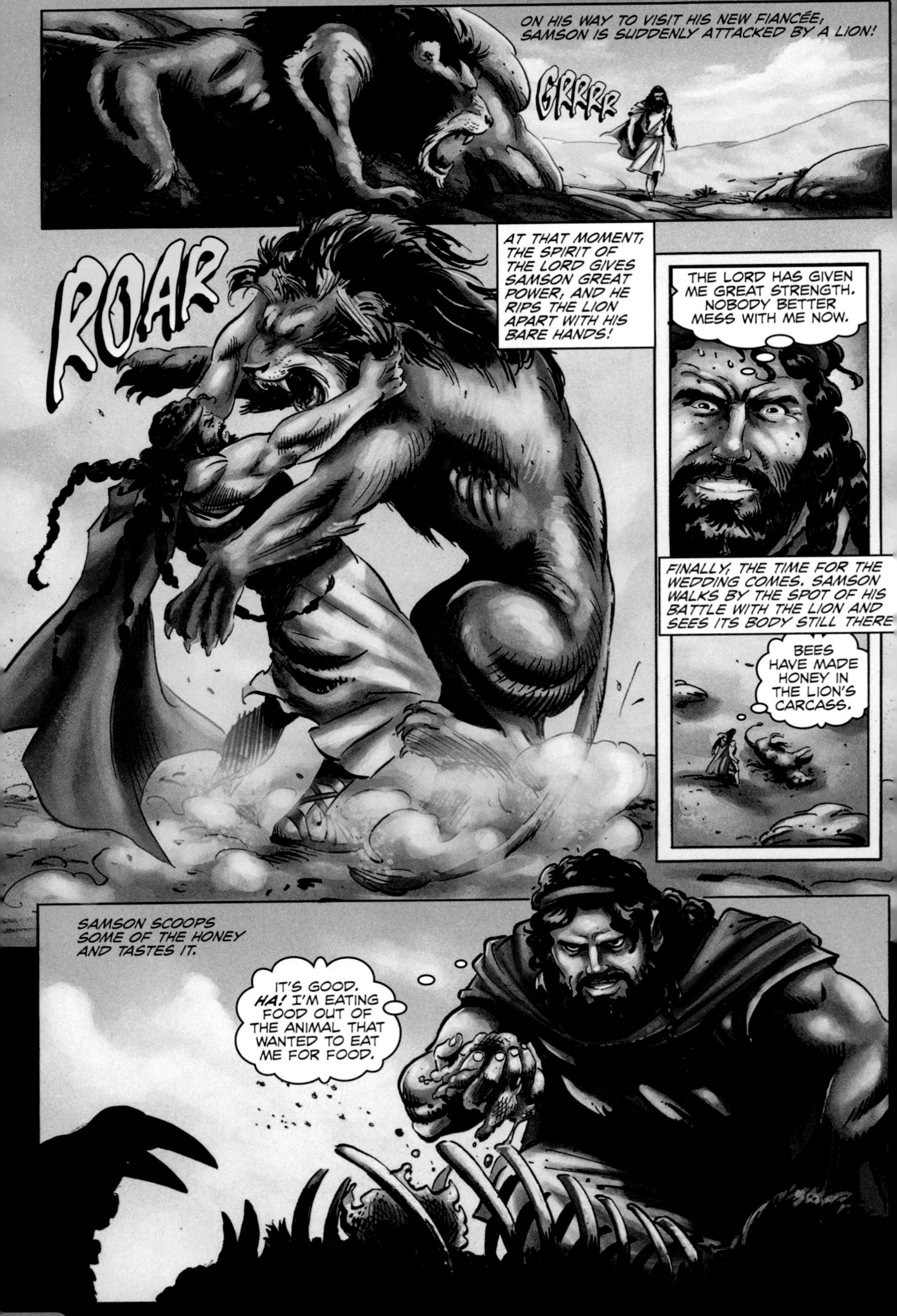
ON HIS WAY TO VISIT HIS NEW FIANCÉE, SAMSON IS SUDDENLY ATTACKED BY A LION!
GRRRR
ROAR
AT THAT MOMENT, THE SPIRIT OF THE LORD GIVES SAMSON GREAT POWER, AND HE RIPS THE LION APART WITH HIS BARE HANDS!
THE LORD HAS GIVEN ME GREAT STRENGTH. NOBODY BETTER MESS WITH ME NOW.
FINALLY, THE TIME FOR THE WEDDING COMES. SAMSON WALKS BY THE SPOT OF HIS BATTLE WITH THE LION AND SEES ITS BODY STILL THERE.
BEES HAVE MADE HONEY IN THE LION'S CARCASS.
SAMSON SCOOPS SOME OF THE HONEY AND TASTES IT.
IT'S GOOD. **HA!** I'M EATING FOOD OUT OF THE ANIMAL THAT WANTED TO EAT ME FOR FOOD.

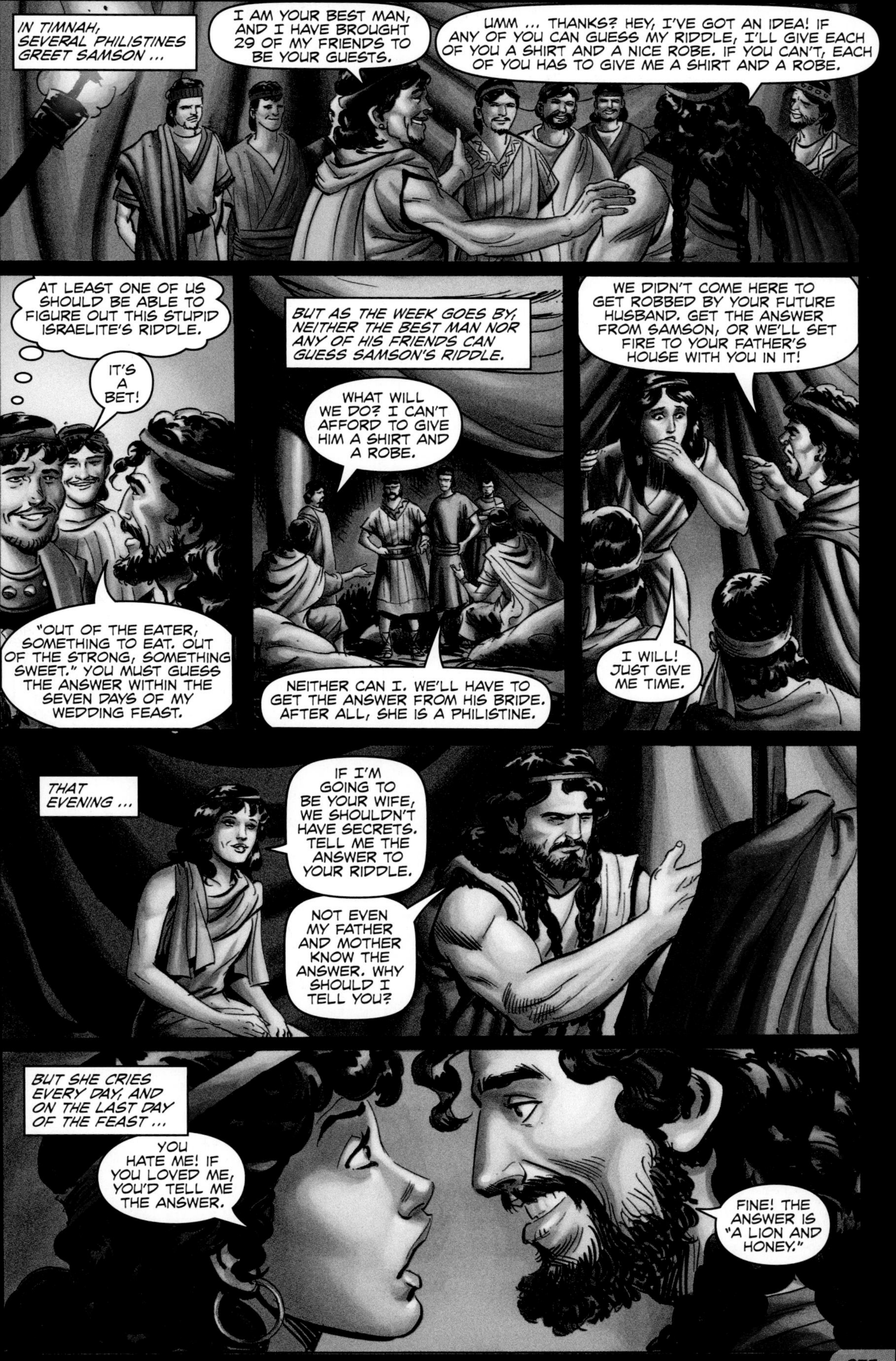
IN TIMNAH, SEVERAL PHILISTINES GREET SAMSON ...
I AM YOUR BEST MAN, AND I HAVE BROUGHT 29 OF MY FRIENDS TO BE YOUR GUESTS.
UMM ... THANKS? HEY, I'VE GOT AN IDEA! IF ANY OF YOU CAN GUESS MY RIDDLE, I'LL GIVE EACH OF YOU A SHIRT AND A NICE ROBE. IF YOU CAN'T, EACH OF YOU HAS TO GIVE ME A SHIRT AND A ROBE.
AT LEAST ONE OF US SHOULD BE ABLE TO FIGURE OUT THIS STUPID ISRAELITE'S RIDDLE.
IT'S A BET!
"OUT OF THE EATER, SOMETHING TO EAT. OUT OF THE STRONG, SOMETHING SWEET." YOU MUST GUESS THE ANSWER WITHIN THE SEVEN DAYS OF MY WEDDING FEAST.
BUT AS THE WEEK GOES BY, NEITHER THE BEST MAN NOR ANY OF HIS FRIENDS CAN GUESS SAMSON'S RIDDLE.
WHAT WILL WE DO? I CAN'T AFFORD TO GIVE HIM A SHIRT AND A ROBE.
NEITHER CAN I. WE'LL HAVE TO GET THE ANSWER FROM HIS BRIDE. AFTER ALL, SHE IS A PHILISTINE.
WE DIDN'T COME HERE TO GET ROBBED BY YOUR FUTURE HUSBAND. GET THE ANSWER FROM SAMSON, OR WE'LL SET FIRE TO YOUR FATHER'S HOUSE WITH YOU IN IT!
I WILL! JUST GIVE ME TIME.
THAT EVENING ...
IF I'M GOING TO BE YOUR WIFE, WE SHOULDN'T HAVE SECRETS. TELL ME THE ANSWER TO YOUR RIDDLE.
NOT EVEN MY FATHER AND MOTHER KNOW THE ANSWER. WHY SHOULD I TELL YOU?
BUT SHE CRIES EVERY DAY, AND ON THE LAST DAY OF THE FEAST ...
YOU HATE ME! IF YOU LOVED ME, YOU'D TELL ME THE ANSWER.
FINE! THE ANSWER IS "A LION AND HONEY."

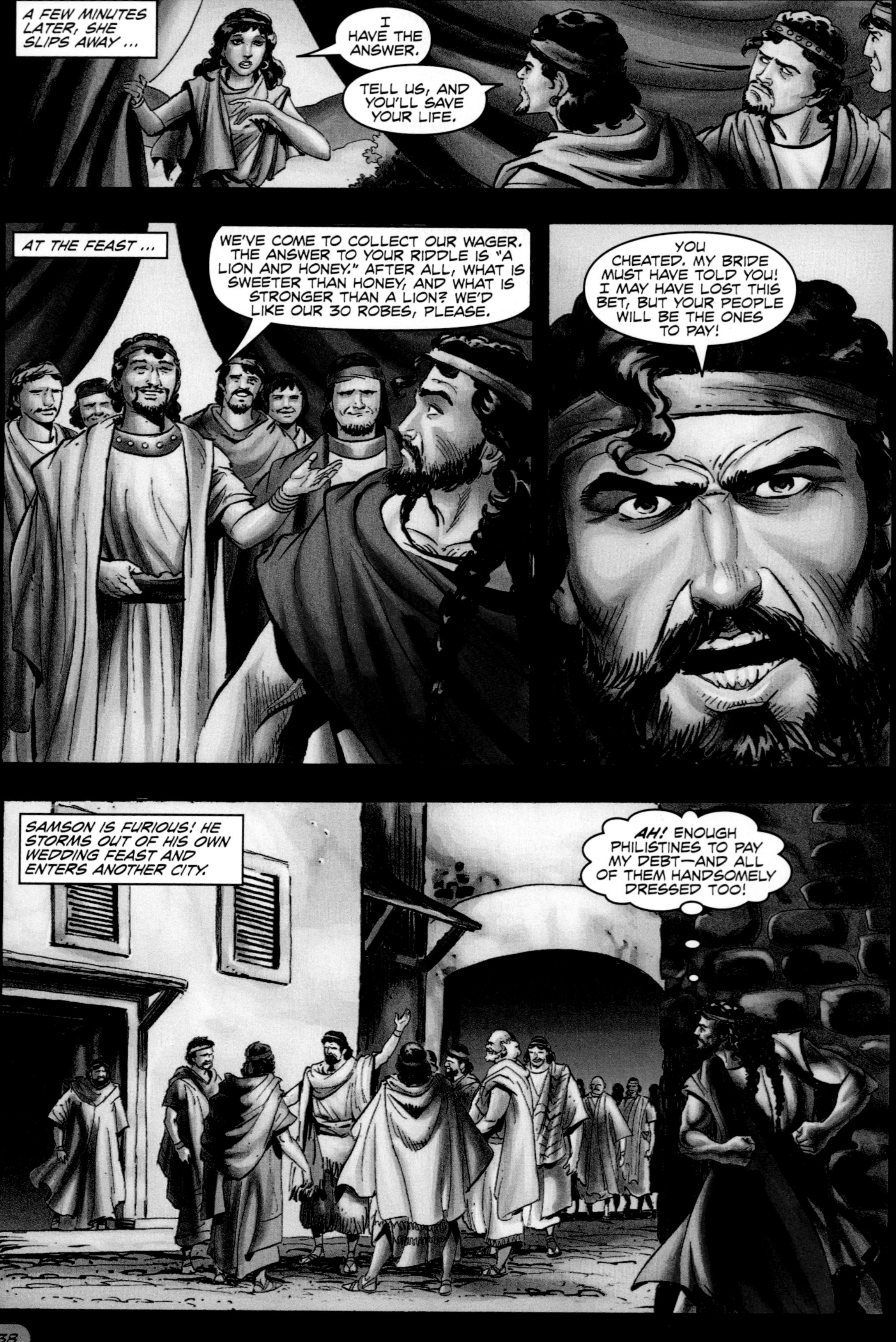
A FEW MINUTES LATER, SHE SLIPS AWAY ...
I HAVE THE ANSWER.
TELL US, AND YOU'LL SAVE YOUR LIFE.
AT THE FEAST ...
WE'VE COME TO COLLECT OUR WAGER. THE ANSWER TO YOUR RIDDLE IS "A LION AND HONEY." AFTER ALL, WHAT IS SWEETER THAN HONEY, AND WHAT IS STRONGER THAN A LION? WE'D LIKE OUR 30 ROBES, PLEASE.
YOU CHEATED. MY BRIDE MUST HAVE TOLD YOU! I MAY HAVE LOST THIS BET, BUT YOUR PEOPLE WILL BE THE ONES TO PAY!
SAMSON IS FURIOUS! HE STORMS OUT OF HIS OWN WEDDING FEAST AND ENTERS ANOTHER CITY.
AH! ENOUGH PHILISTINES TO PAY MY DEBT—AND ALL OF THEM HANDSOMELY DRESSED TOO!

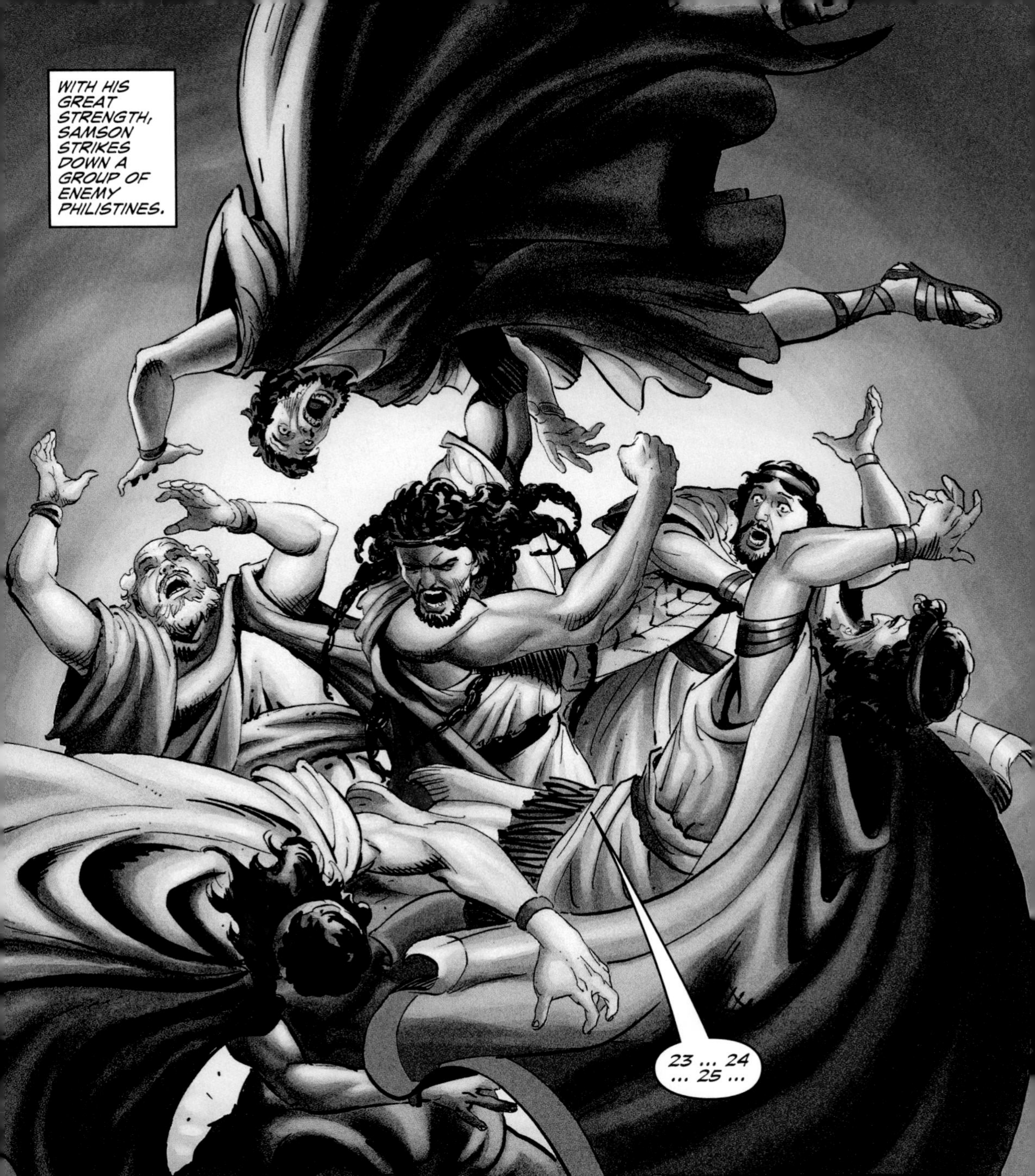
WITH HIS GREAT STRENGTH, SAMSON STRIKES DOWN A GROUP OF ENEMY PHILISTINES.
23 ... 24 ... 25 ...

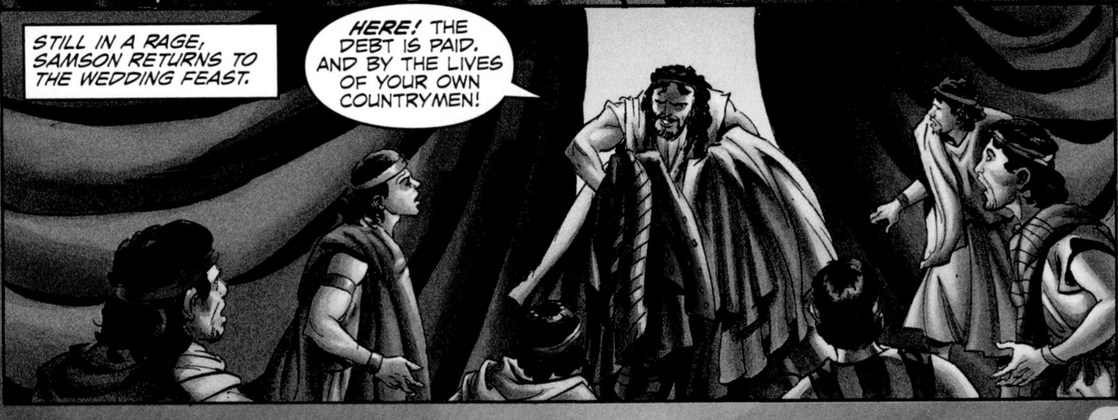
STILL IN A RAGE, SAMSON RETURNS TO THE WEDDING FEAST.
HERE! THE DEBT IS PAID. AND BY THE LIVES OF YOUR OWN COUNTRYMEN!

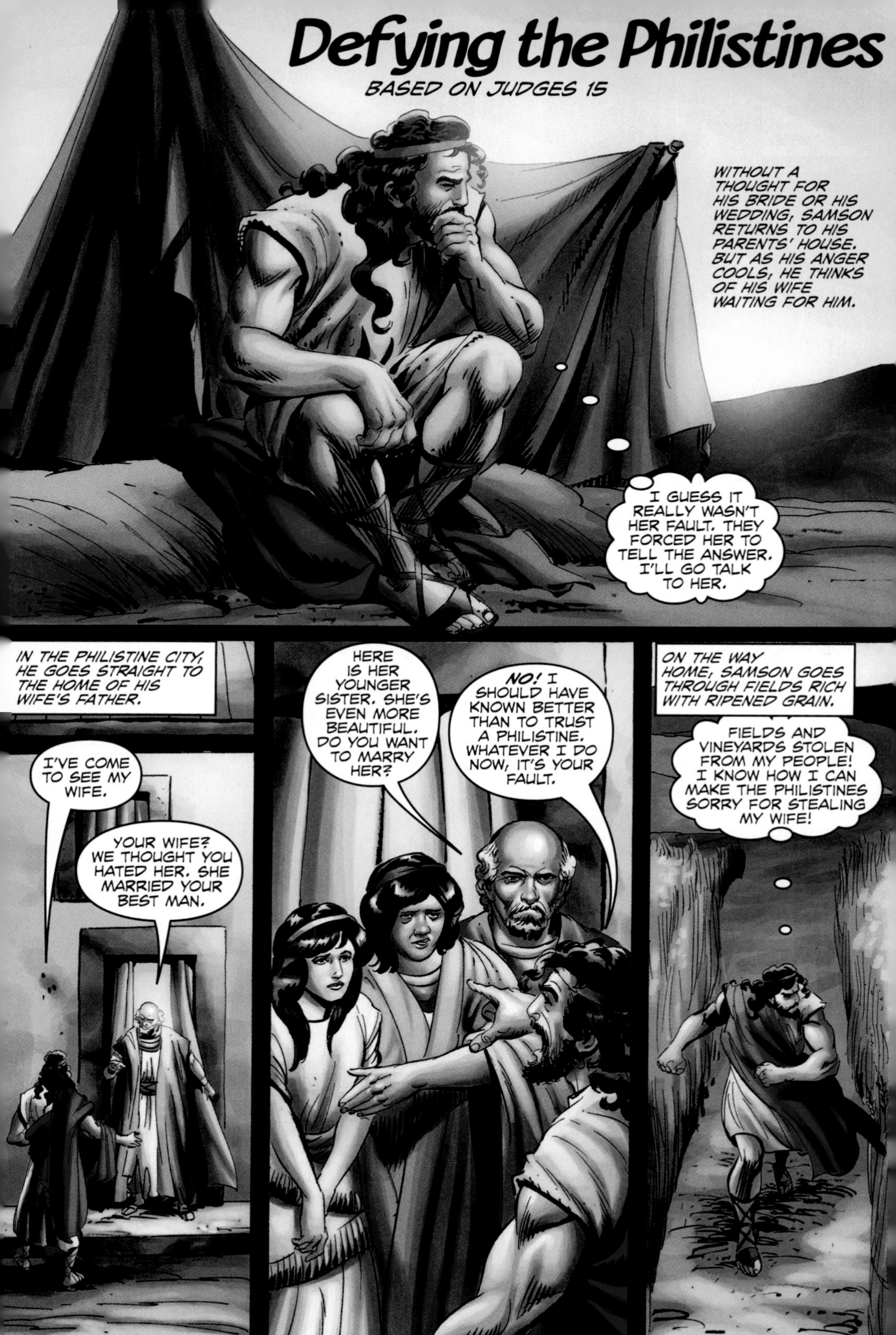
Defying the Philistines
BASED ON JUDGES 15
WITHOUT A THOUGHT FOR HIS BRIDE OR HIS WEDDING, SAMSON RETURNS TO HIS PARENTS' HOUSE. BUT AS HIS ANGER COOLS, HE THINKS OF HIS WIFE WAITING FOR HIM.
I GUESS IT REALLY WASN'T HER FAULT. THEY FORCED HER TO TELL THE ANSWER. I'LL GO TALK TO HER.
IN THE PHILISTINE CITY, HE GOES STRAIGHT TO THE HOME OF HIS WIFE'S FATHER.
I'VE COME TO SEE MY WIFE.
YOUR WIFE? WE THOUGHT YOU HATED HER. SHE MARRIED YOUR BEST MAN.
HERE IS HER YOUNGER SISTER. SHE'S EVEN MORE BEAUTIFUL. DO YOU WANT TO MARRY HER?
NO! I SHOULD HAVE KNOWN BETTER THAN TO TRUST A PHILISTINE. WHATEVER I DO NOW, IT'S YOUR FAULT.
ON THE WAY HOME, SAMSON GOES THROUGH FIELDS RICH WITH RIPENED GRAIN.
FIELDS AND VINEYARDS STOLEN FROM MY PEOPLE! I KNOW HOW I CAN MAKE THE PHILISTINES SORRY FOR STEALING MY WIFE!

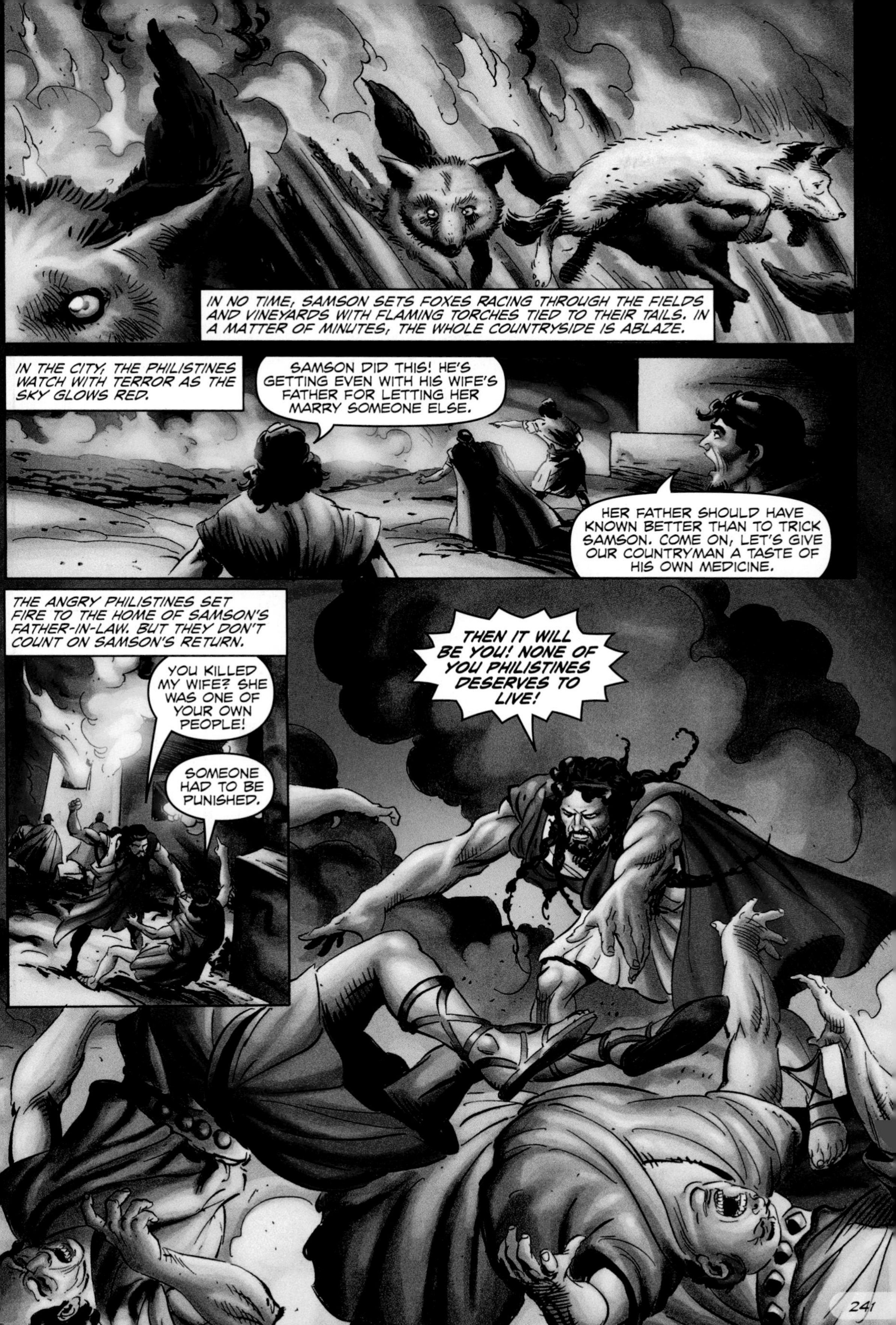
IN NO TIME, SAMSON SETS FOXES RACING THROUGH THE FIELDS AND VINEYARDS WITH FLAMING TORCHES TIED TO THEIR TAILS. IN A MATTER OF MINUTES, THE WHOLE COUNTRYSIDE IS ABLAZE.
IN THE CITY, THE PHILISTINES WATCH WITH TERROR AS THE SKY GLOWS RED.
SAMSON DID THIS! HE'S GETTING EVEN WITH HIS WIFE'S FATHER FOR LETTING HER MARRY SOMEONE ELSE.
HER FATHER SHOULD HAVE KNOWN BETTER THAN TO TRICK SAMSON. COME ON, LET'S GIVE OUR COUNTRYMAN A TASTE OF HIS OWN MEDICINE.
THE ANGRY PHILISTINES SET FIRE TO THE HOME OF SAMSON'S FATHER-IN-LAW. BUT THEY DON'T COUNT ON SAMSON'S RETURN.
YOU KILLED MY WIFE? SHE WAS ONE OF YOUR OWN PEOPLE!
SOMEONE HAD TO BE PUNISHED.
THEN IT WILL BE YOU! NONE OF YOU PHILISTINES DESERVES TO LIVE!

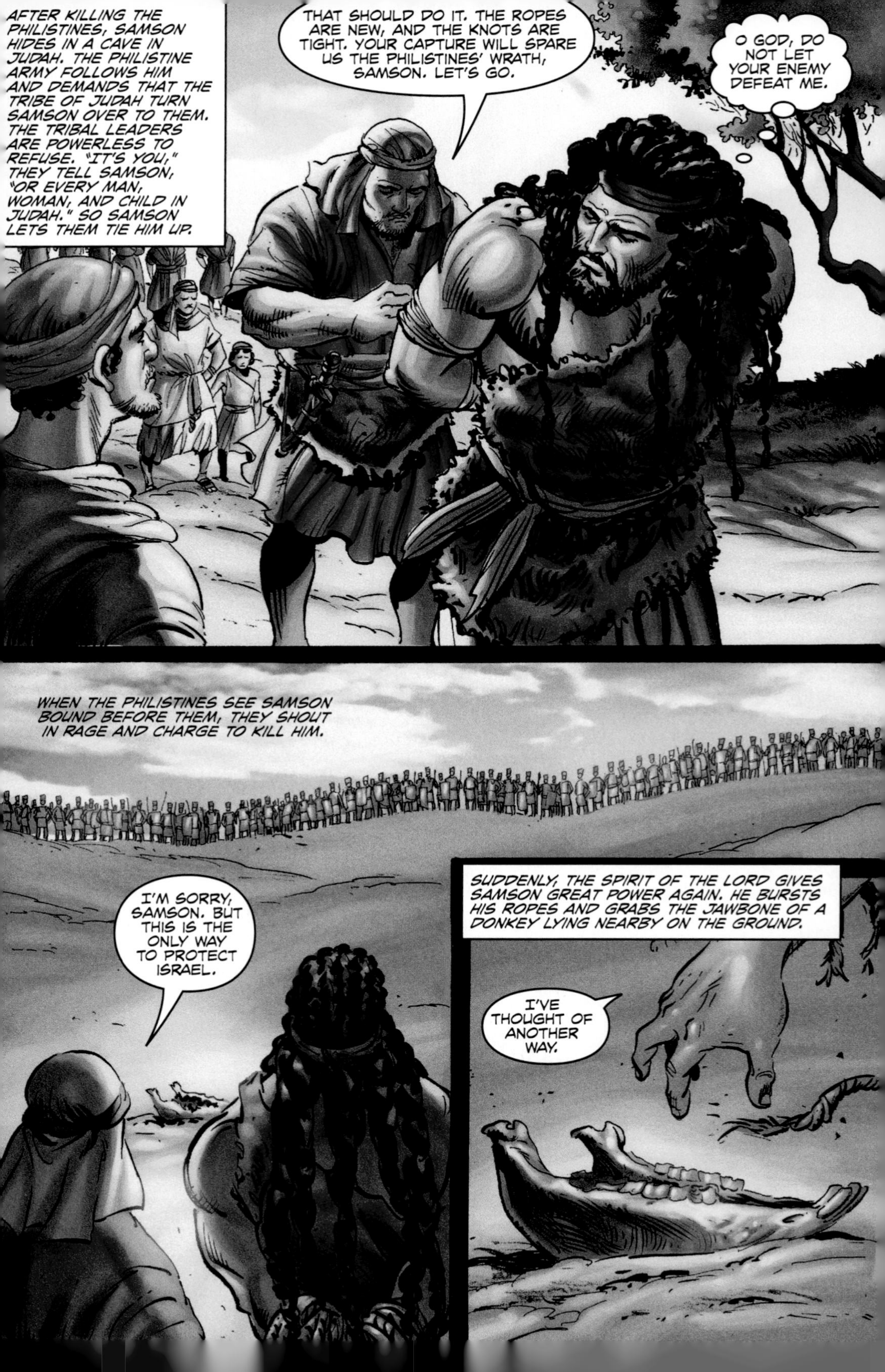
AFTER KILLING THE PHILISTINES, SAMSON HIDES IN A CAVE IN JUDAH. THE PHILISTINE ARMY FOLLOWS HIM AND DEMANDS THAT THE TRIBE OF JUDAH TURN SAMSON OVER TO THEM. THE TRIBAL LEADERS ARE POWERLESS TO REFUSE. "IT'S YOU," THEY TELL SAMSON, "OR EVERY MAN, WOMAN, AND CHILD IN JUDAH." SO SAMSON LETS THEM TIE HIM UP.
THAT SHOULD DO IT. THE ROPES ARE NEW, AND THE KNOTS ARE TIGHT. YOUR CAPTURE WILL SPARE US THE PHILISTINES' WRATH, SAMSON. LET'S GO.
O GOD, DO NOT LET YOUR ENEMY DEFEAT ME.
WHEN THE PHILISTINES SEE SAMSON BOUND BEFORE THEM, THEY SHOUT IN RAGE AND CHARGE TO KILL HIM.
I'M SORRY, SAMSON. BUT THIS IS THE ONLY WAY TO PROTECT ISRAEL.
SUDDENLY, THE SPIRIT OF THE LORD GIVES SAMSON GREAT POWER AGAIN. HE BURSTS HIS ROPES AND GRABS THE JAWBONE OF A DONKEY LYING NEARBY ON THE GROUND.
I'VE THOUGHT OF ANOTHER WAY.

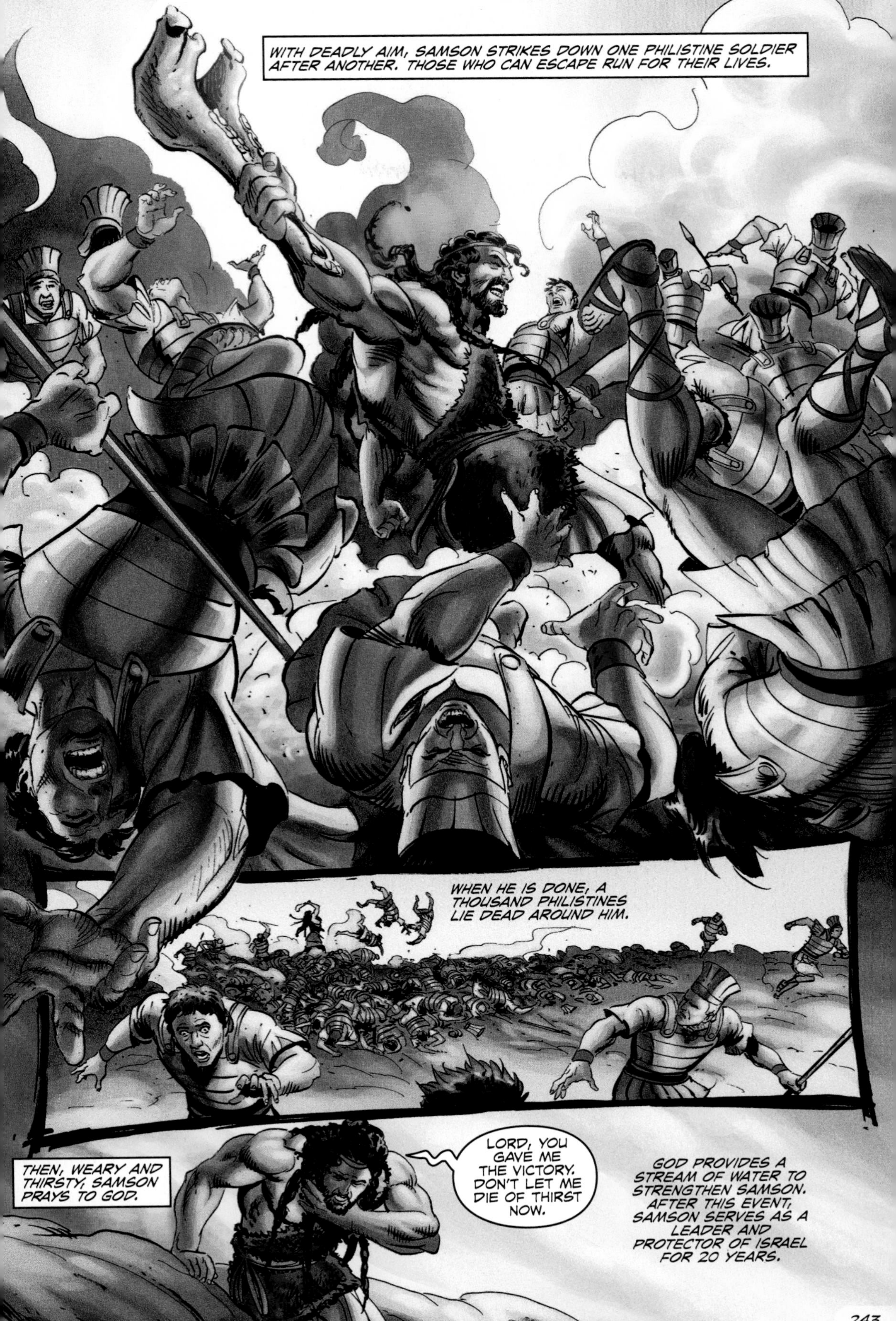
WITH DEADLY AIM, SAMSON STRIKES DOWN ONE PHILISTINE SOLDIER AFTER ANOTHER. THOSE WHO CAN ESCAPE RUN FOR THEIR LIVES.
WHEN HE IS DONE, A THOUSAND PHILISTINES LIE DEAD AROUND HIM.
THEN, WEARY AND THIRSTY, SAMSON PRAYS TO GOD.
LORD, YOU GAVE ME THE VICTORY. DON'T LET ME DIE OF THIRST NOW.
GOD PROVIDES A STREAM OF WATER TO STRENGTHEN SAMSON. AFTER THIS EVENT, SAMSON SERVES AS A LEADER AND PROTECTOR OF ISRAEL FOR 20 YEARS.

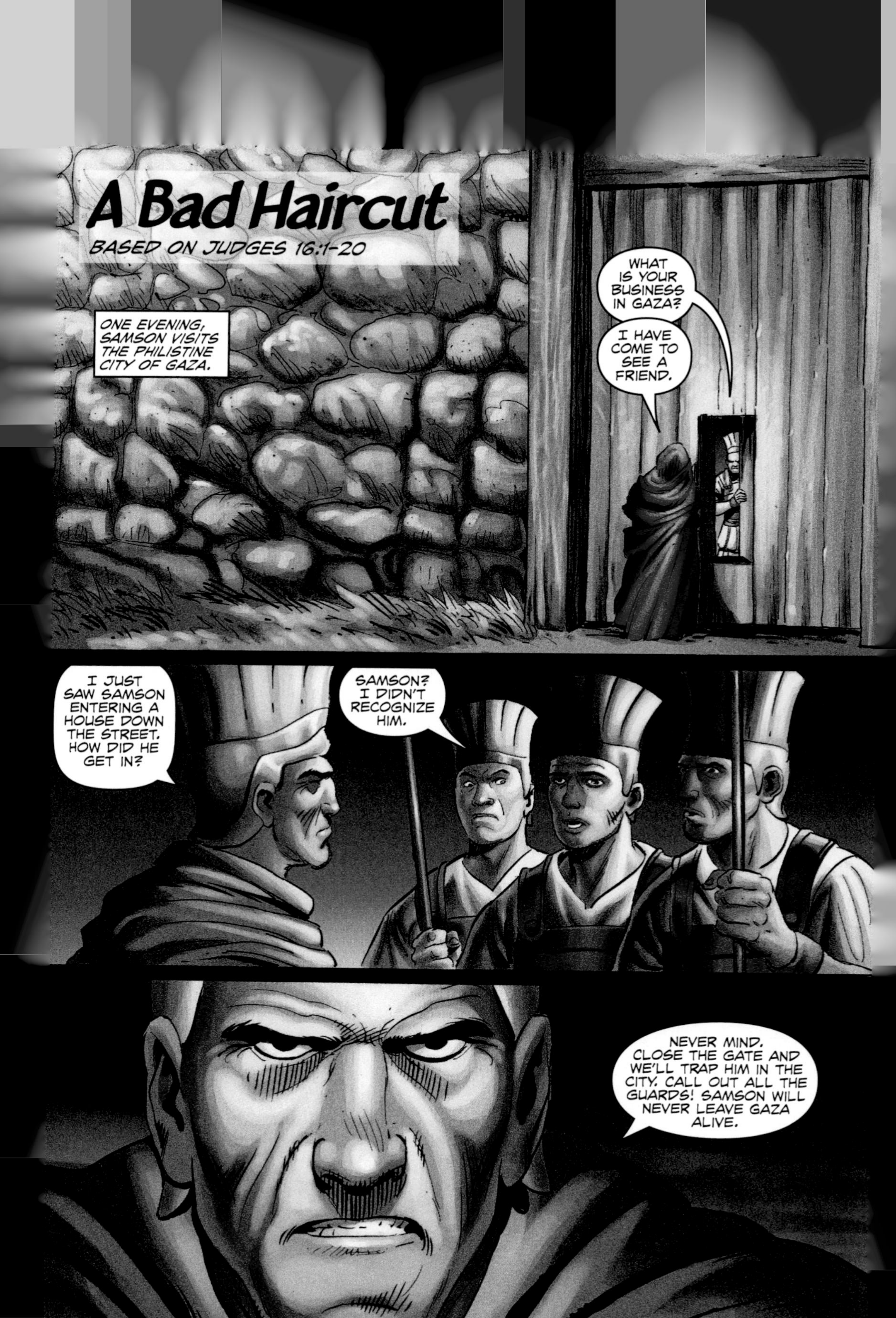
A Bad Haircut
BASED ON JUDGES 16:1-20
ONE EVENING, SAMSON VISITS THE PHILISTINE CITY OF GAZA.
WHAT IS YOUR BUSINESS IN GAZA?
I HAVE COME TO SEE A FRIEND.
I JUST SAW SAMSON ENTERING A HOUSE DOWN THE STREET. HOW DID HE GET IN?
SAMSON? I DIDN'T RECOGNIZE HIM.
NEVER MIND. CLOSE THE GATE AND WE'LL TRAP HIM IN THE CITY. CALL OUT ALL THE GUARDS! SAMSON WILL NEVER LEAVE GAZA ALIVE.

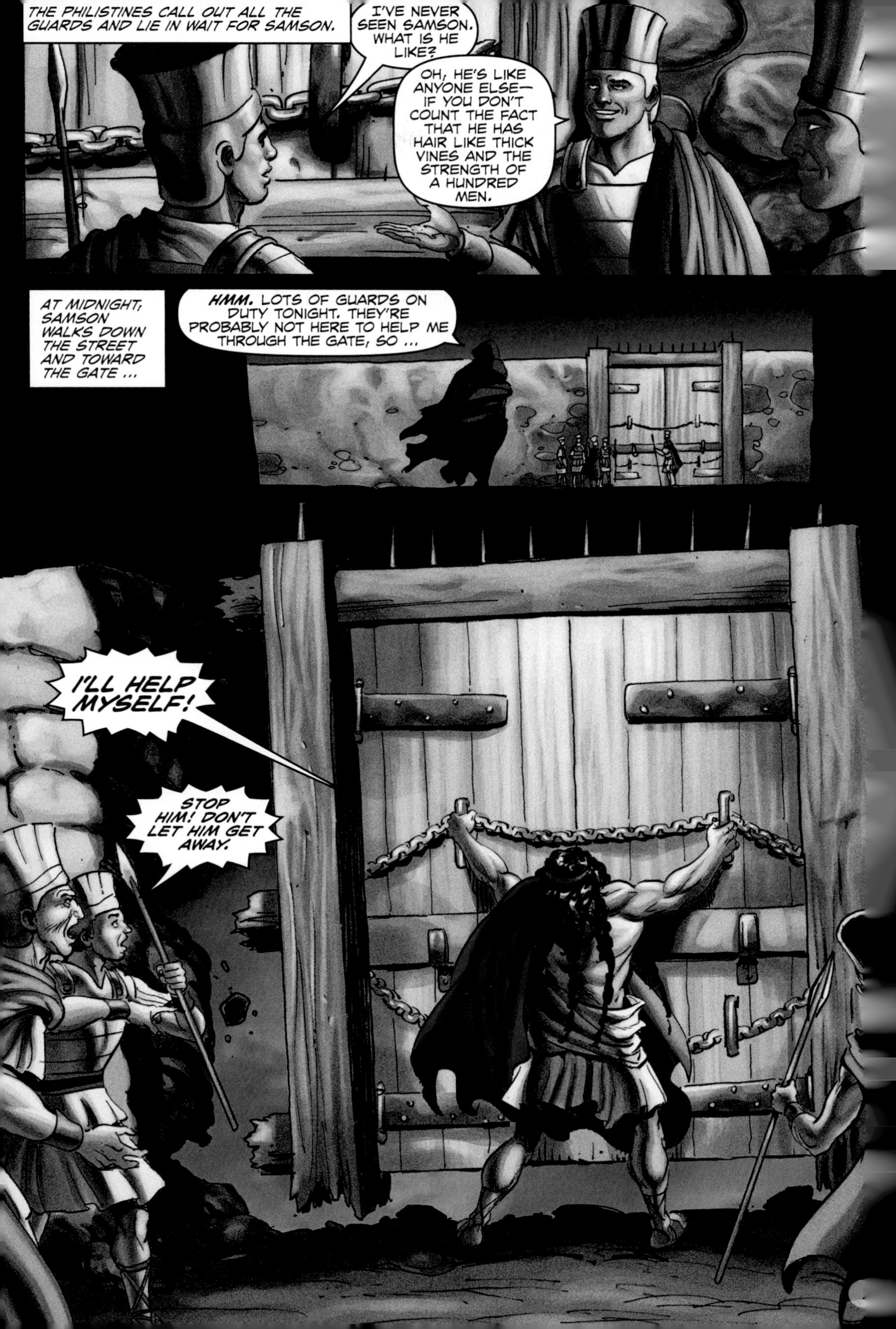
THE PHILISTINES CALL OUT ALL THE GUARDS AND LIE IN WAIT FOR SAMSON.
I'VE NEVER SEEN SAMSON. WHAT IS HE LIKE?
OH, HE'S LIKE ANYONE ELSE— IF YOU DON'T COUNT THE FACT THAT HE HAS HAIR LIKE THICK VINES AND THE STRENGTH OF A HUNDRED MEN.
AT MIDNIGHT, SAMSON WALKS DOWN THE STREET AND TOWARD THE GATE ...
HMM. LOTS OF GUARDS ON DUTY TONIGHT. THEY'RE PROBABLY NOT HERE TO HELP ME THROUGH THE GATE, SO ...
I'LL HELP MYSELF!
STOP HIM! DON'T LET HIM GET AWAY.

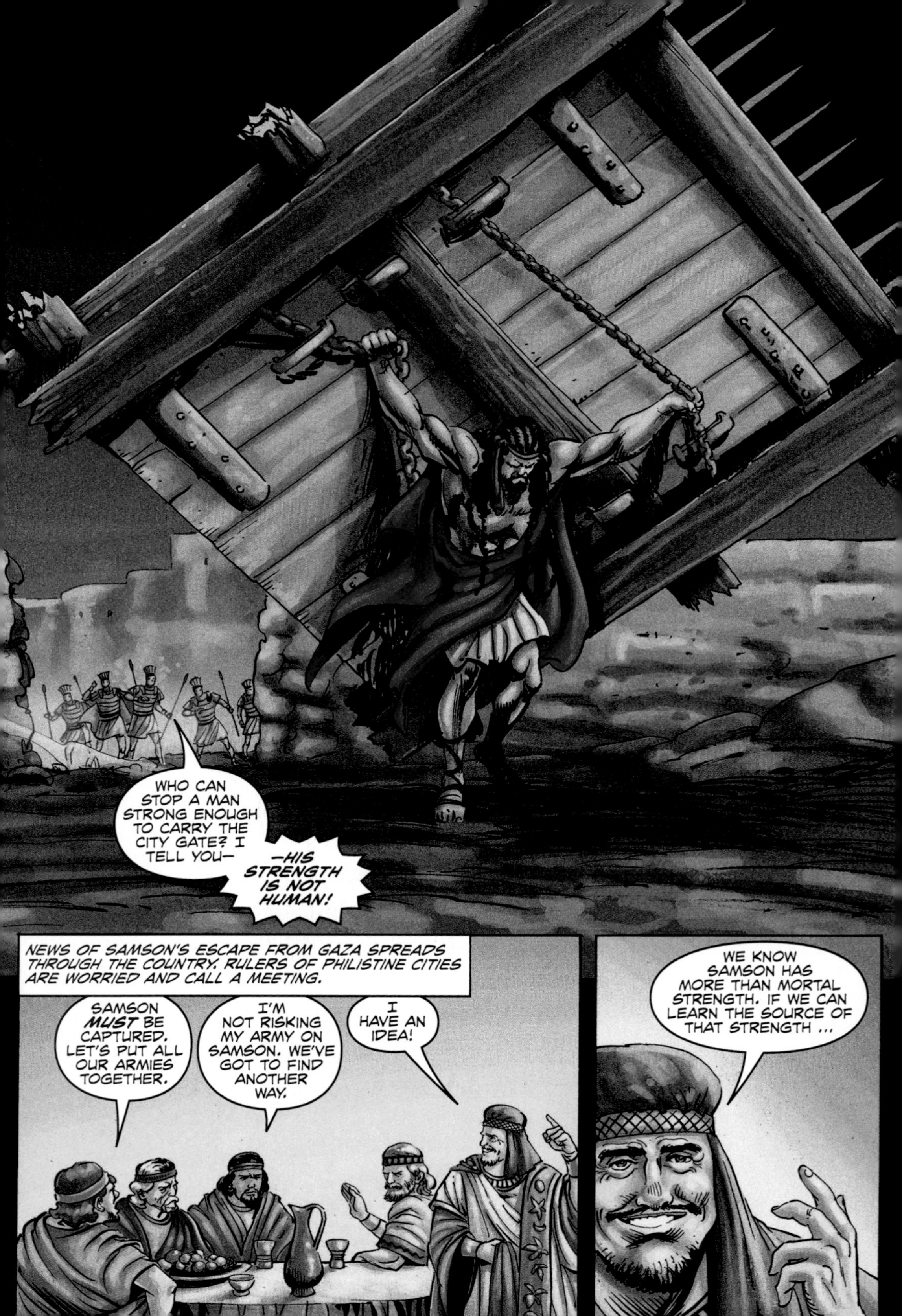
WHO CAN STOP A MAN STRONG ENOUGH TO CARRY THE CITY GATE? I TELL YOU—
—HIS STRENGTH IS NOT HUMAN!
NEWS OF SAMSON'S ESCAPE FROM GAZA SPREADS THROUGH THE COUNTRY. RULERS OF PHILISTINE CITIES ARE WORRIED AND CALL A MEETING.
SAMSON MUST BE CAPTURED. LET'S PUT ALL OUR ARMIES TOGETHER.
I'M NOT RISKING MY ARMY ON SAMSON. WE'VE GOT TO FIND ANOTHER WAY.
I HAVE AN IDEA!
WE KNOW SAMSON HAS MORE THAN MORTAL STRENGTH. IF WE CAN LEARN THE SOURCE OF THAT STRENGTH ...

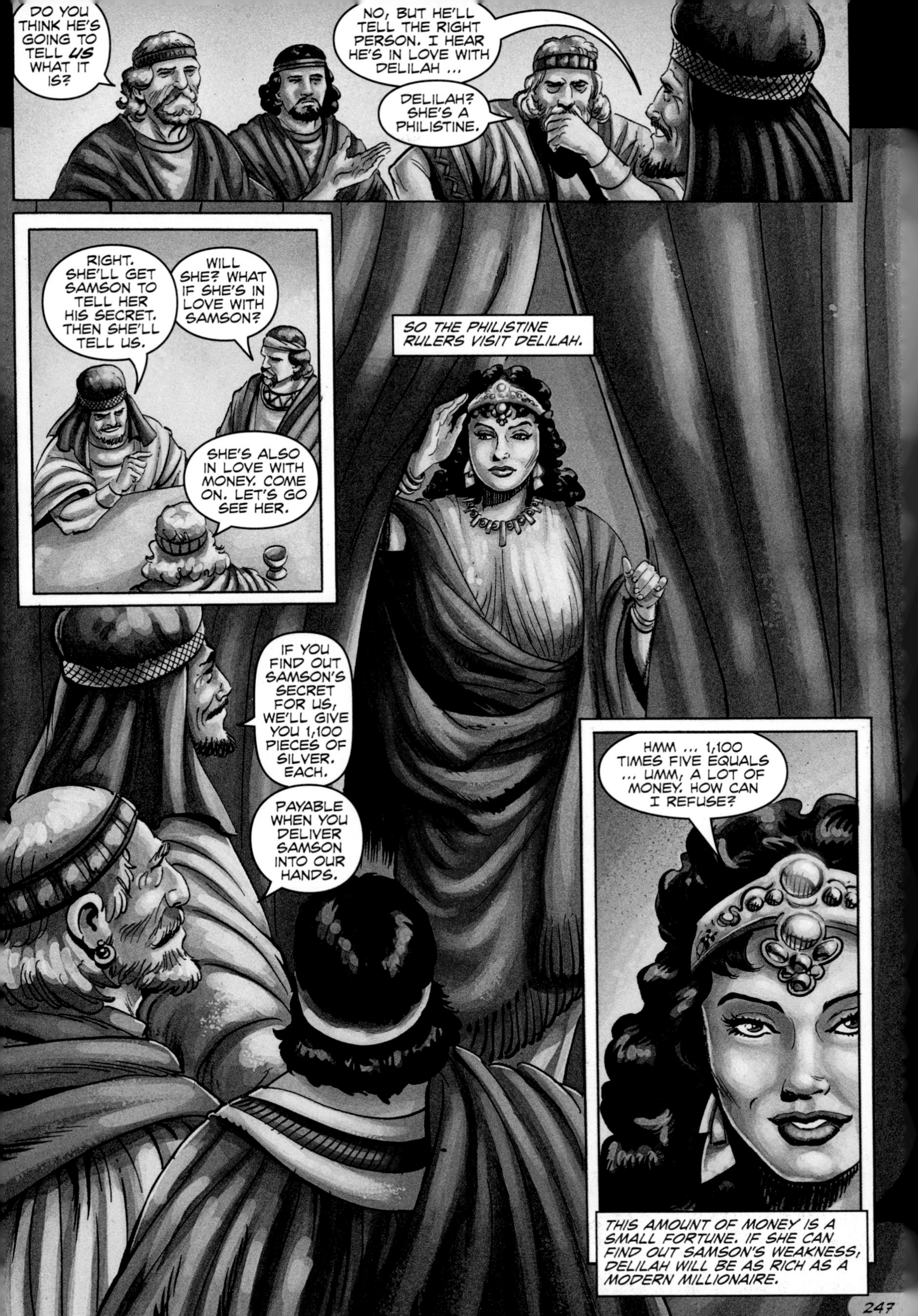
DO YOU THINK HE'S GOING TO TELL US WHAT IT IS?
NO, BUT HE'LL TELL THE RIGHT PERSON. I HEAR HE'S IN LOVE WITH DELILAH ...
DELILAH? SHE'S A PHILISTINE.
RIGHT. SHE'LL GET SAMSON TO TELL HER HIS SECRET. THEN SHE'LL TELL US.
WILL SHE? WHAT IF SHE'S IN LOVE WITH SAMSON?
SHE'S ALSO IN LOVE WITH MONEY. COME ON. LET'S GO SEE HER.
SO THE PHILISTINE RULERS VISIT DELILAH.
IF YOU FIND OUT SAMSON'S SECRET FOR US, WE'LL GIVE YOU 1,100 PIECES OF SILVER. EACH.
PAYABLE WHEN YOU DELIVER SAMSON INTO OUR HANDS.
HMM ... 1,100 TIMES FIVE EQUALS ... UMM, A LOT OF MONEY. HOW CAN I REFUSE?
THIS AMOUNT OF MONEY IS A SMALL FORTUNE. IF SHE CAN FIND OUT SAMSON'S WEAKNESS, DELILAH WILL BE AS RICH AS A MODERN MILLIONAIRE.

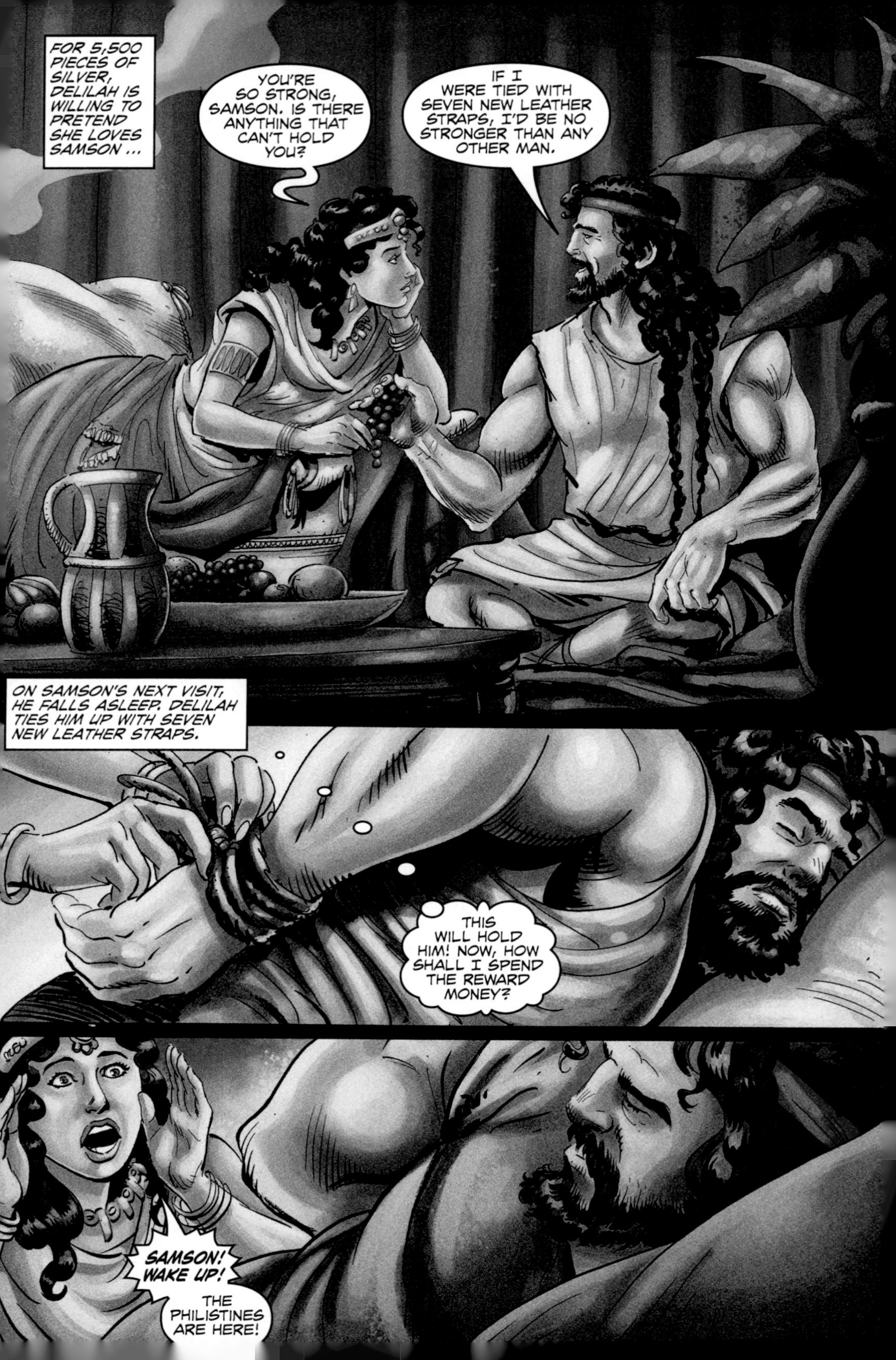
FOR 5,500 PIECES OF SILVER, DELILAH IS WILLING TO PRETEND SHE LOVES SAMSON ...
YOU'RE SO STRONG, SAMSON. IS THERE ANYTHING THAT CAN'T HOLD YOU?
IF I WERE TIED WITH SEVEN NEW LEATHER STRAPS, I'D BE NO STRONGER THAN ANY OTHER MAN.
ON SAMSON'S NEXT VISIT, HE FALLS ASLEEP. DELILAH TIES HIM UP WITH SEVEN NEW LEATHER STRAPS.
THIS WILL HOLD HIM! NOW, HOW SHALL I SPEND THE REWARD MONEY?
SAMSON! WAKE UP!
THE PHILISTINES ARE HERE!

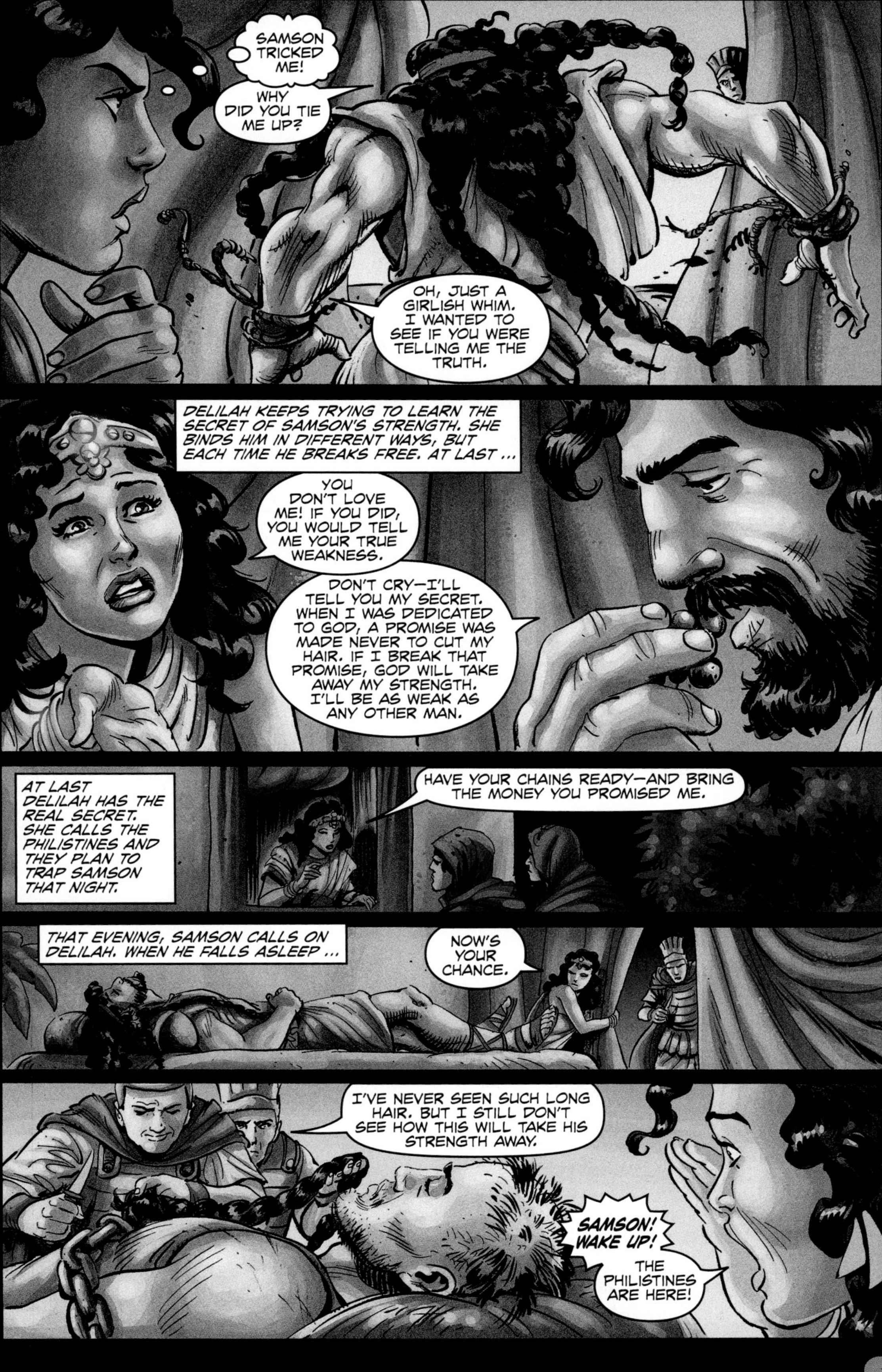
SAMSON TRICKED ME!
WHY DID YOU TIE ME UP?
OH, JUST A GIRLISH WHIM. I WANTED TO SEE IF YOU WERE TELLING ME THE TRUTH.
DELILAH KEEPS TRYING TO LEARN THE SECRET OF SAMSON'S STRENGTH. SHE BINDS HIM IN DIFFERENT WAYS, BUT EACH TIME HE BREAKS FREE. AT LAST ...
YOU DON'T LOVE ME! IF YOU DID, YOU WOULD TELL ME YOUR TRUE WEAKNESS.
DON'T CRY—I'LL TELL YOU MY SECRET. WHEN I WAS DEDICATED TO GOD, A PROMISE WAS MADE NEVER TO CUT MY HAIR. IF I BREAK THAT PROMISE, GOD WILL TAKE AWAY MY STRENGTH. I'LL BE AS WEAK AS ANY OTHER MAN.
AT LAST DELILAH HAS THE REAL SECRET. SHE CALLS THE PHILISTINES AND THEY PLAN TO TRAP SAMSON THAT NIGHT.
HAVE YOUR CHAINS READY—AND BRING THE MONEY YOU PROMISED ME.
THAT EVENING, SAMSON CALLS ON DELILAH. WHEN HE FALLS ASLEEP ...
NOW'S YOUR CHANCE.
I'VE NEVER SEEN SUCH LONG HAIR. BUT I STILL DON'T SEE HOW THIS WILL TAKE HIS STRENGTH AWAY.
SAMSON! WAKE UP!
THE PHILISTINES ARE HERE!

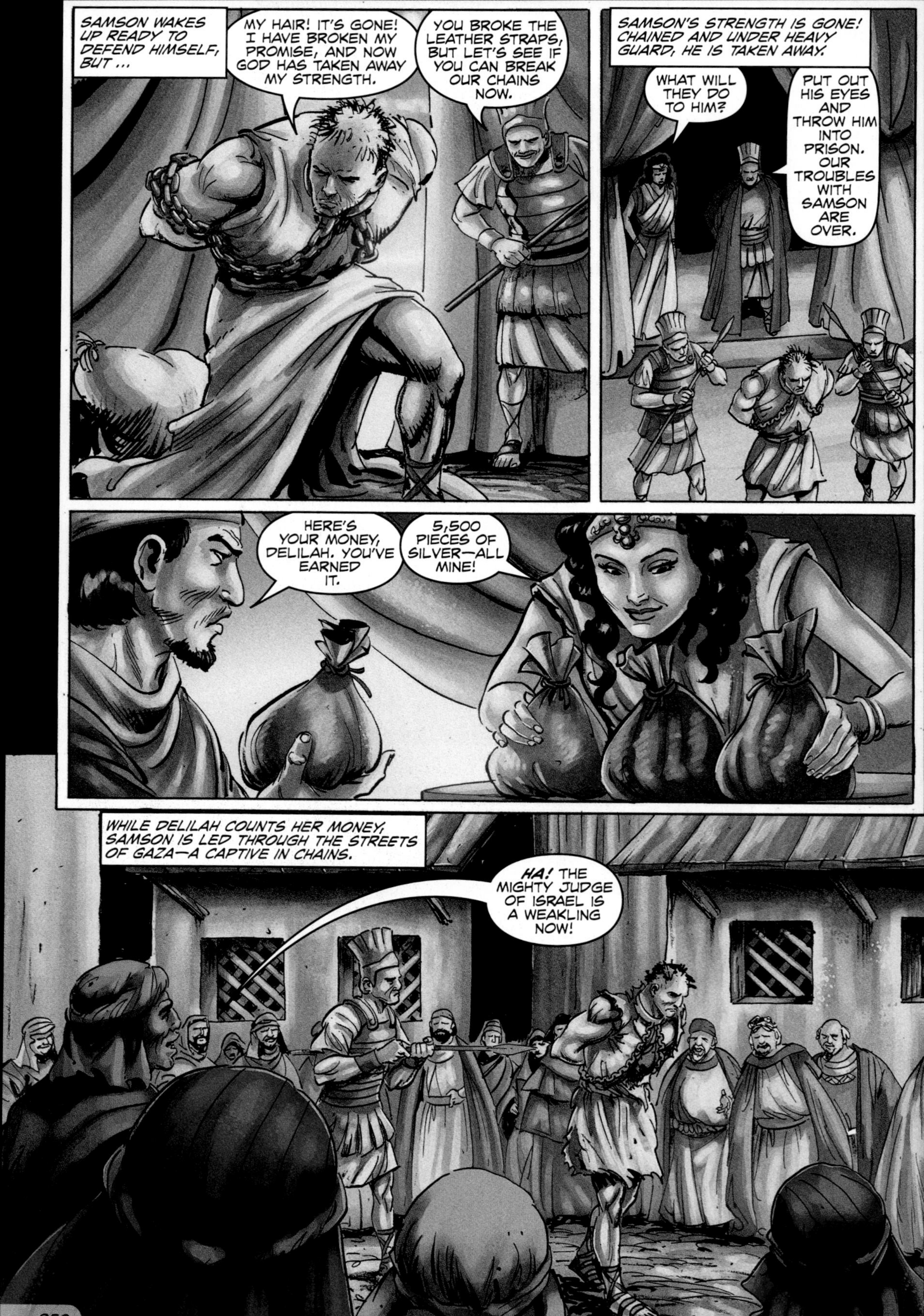
SAMSON WAKES UP READY TO DEFEND HIMSELF, BUT ...
MY HAIR! IT'S GONE! I HAVE BROKEN MY PROMISE, AND NOW GOD HAS TAKEN AWAY MY STRENGTH.
YOU BROKE THE LEATHER STRAPS, BUT LET'S SEE IF YOU CAN BREAK OUR CHAINS NOW.
SAMSON'S STRENGTH IS GONE! CHAINED AND UNDER HEAVY GUARD, HE IS TAKEN AWAY.
WHAT WILL THEY DO TO HIM?
PUT OUT HIS EYES AND THROW HIM INTO PRISON. OUR TROUBLES WITH SAMSON ARE OVER.
HERE'S YOUR MONEY, DELILAH. YOU'VE EARNED IT.
5,500 PIECES OF SILVER—ALL MINE!
WHILE DELILAH COUNTS HER MONEY, SAMSON IS LED THROUGH THE STREETS OF GAZA—A CAPTIVE IN CHAINS.
HA! THE MIGHTY JUDGE OF ISRAEL IS A WEAKLING NOW!

Bringing Down the House

BASED ON JUDGES 16:21-30

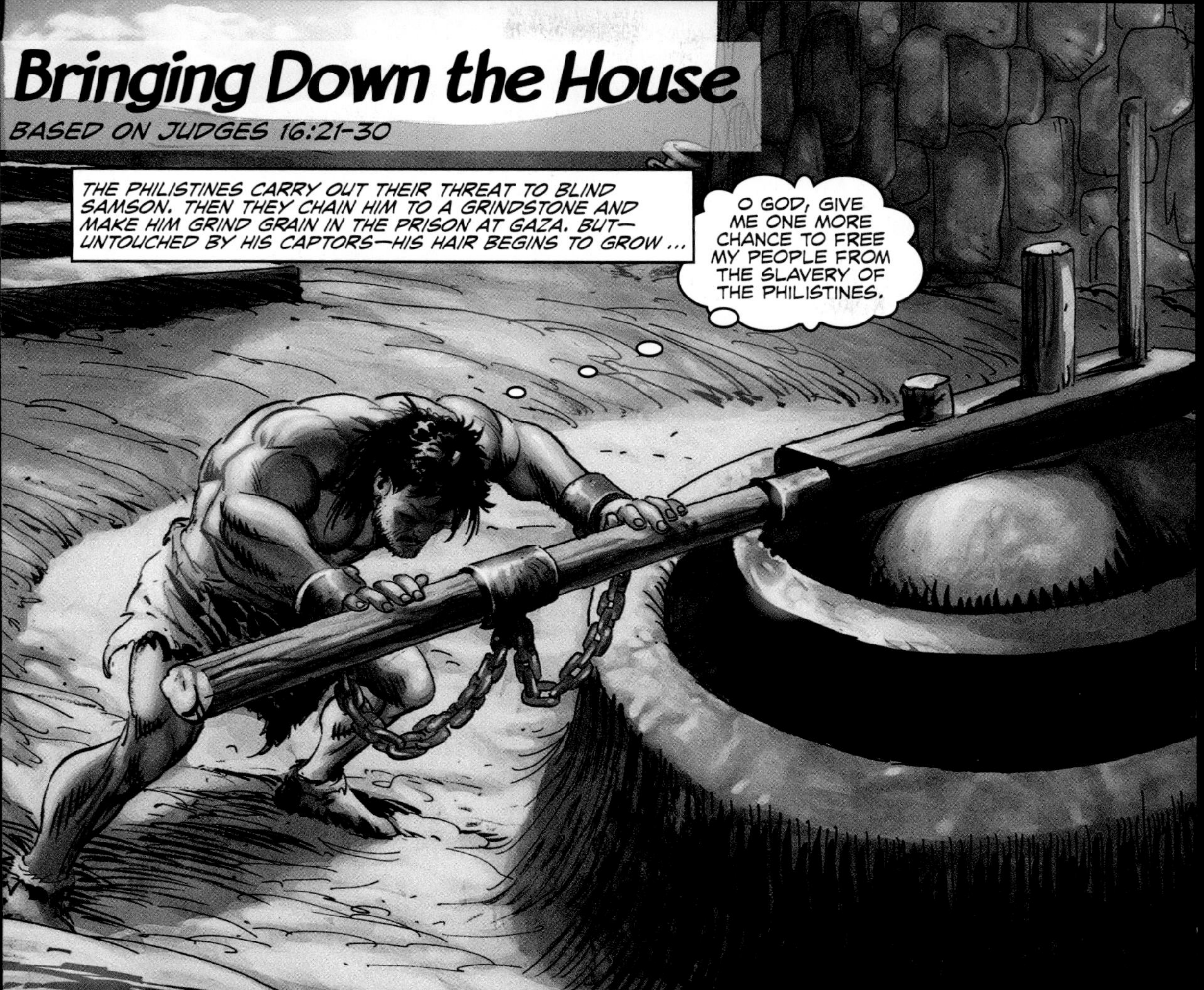
THE PHILISTINES CARRY OUT THEIR THREAT TO BLIND SAMSON. THEN THEY CHAIN HIM TO A GRINDSTONE AND MAKE HIM GRIND GRAIN IN THE PRISON AT GAZA. BUT—UNTOUCHED BY HIS CAPTORS—HIS HAIR BEGINS TO GROW ...
O GOD, GIVE ME ONE MORE CHANCE TO FREE MY PEOPLE FROM THE SLAVERY OF THE PHILISTINES.

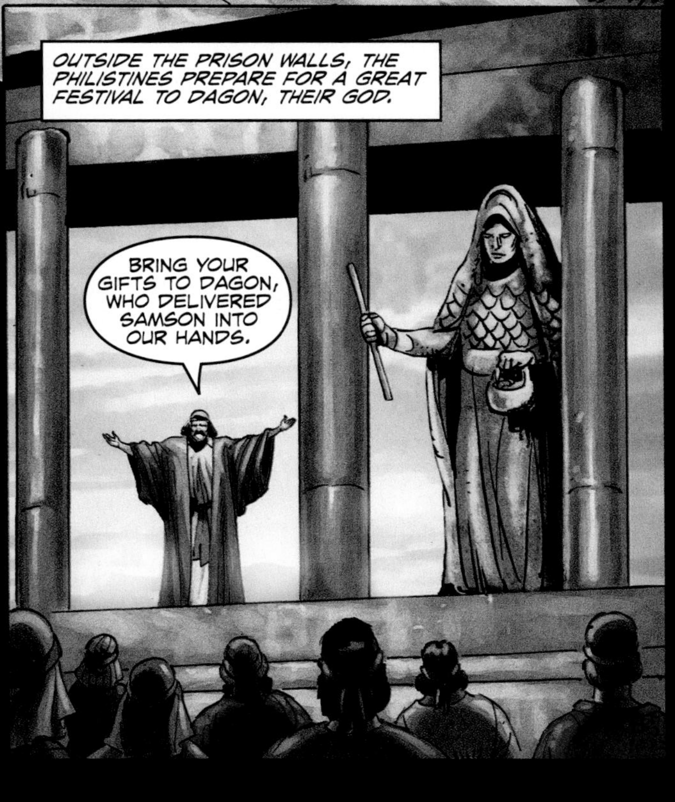
OUTSIDE THE PRISON WALLS, THE PHILISTINES PREPARE FOR A GREAT FESTIVAL TO DAGON, THEIR GOD.
BRING YOUR GIFTS TO DAGON, WHO DELIVERED SAMSON INTO OUR HANDS.

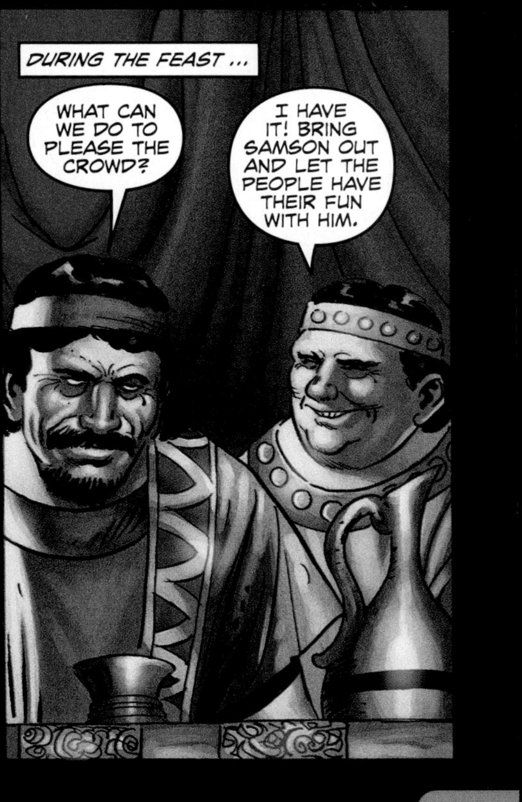
DURING THE FEAST ...
WHAT CAN WE DO TO PLEASE THE CROWD?
I HAVE IT! BRING SAMSON OUT AND LET THE PEOPLE HAVE THEIR FUN WITH HIM.

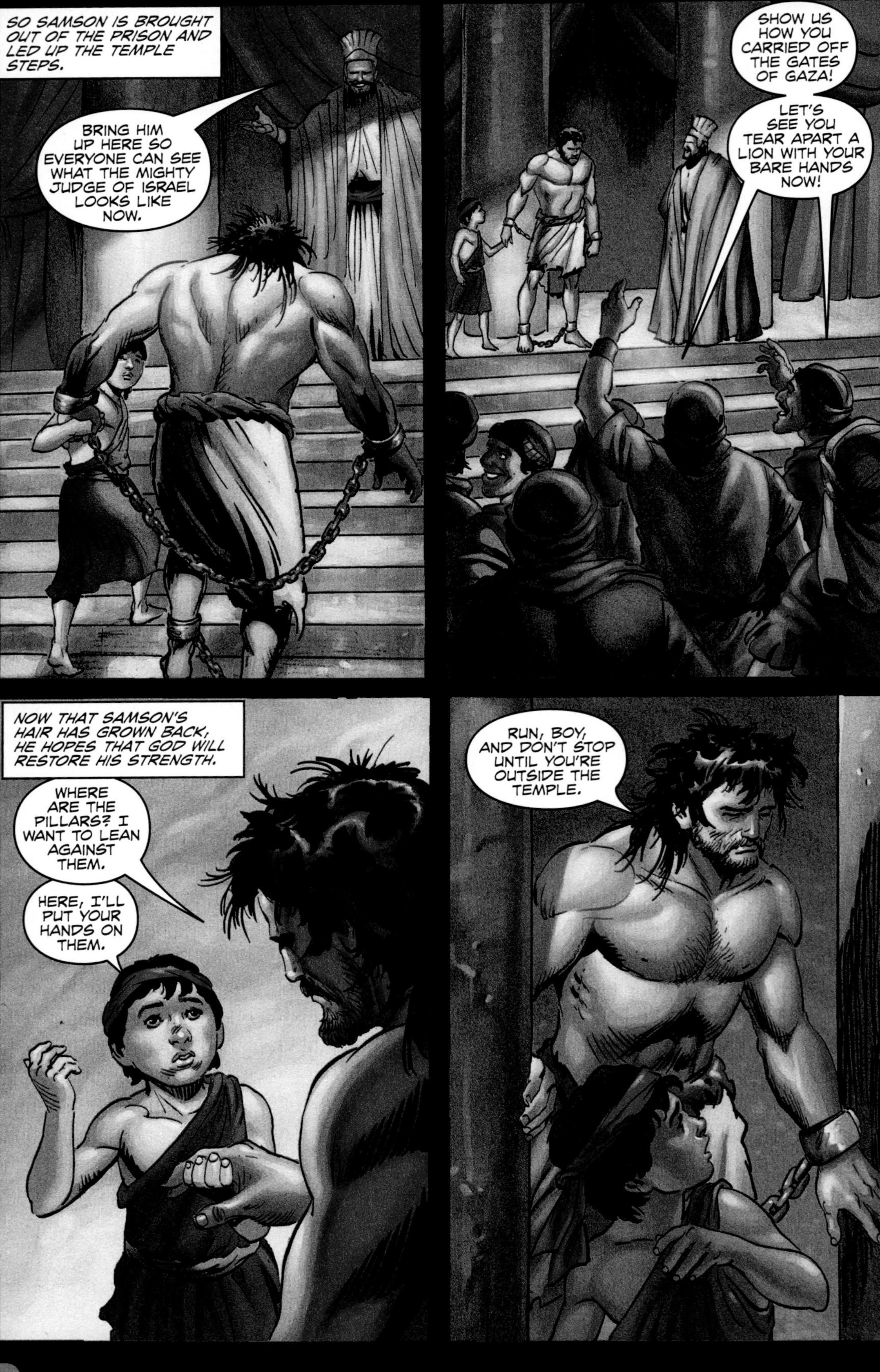
SO SAMSON IS BROUGHT OUT OF THE PRISON AND LED UP THE TEMPLE STEPS.
BRING HIM UP HERE SO EVERYONE CAN SEE WHAT THE MIGHTY JUDGE OF ISRAEL LOOKS LIKE NOW.
SHOW US HOW YOU CARRIED OFF THE GATES OF GAZA!
LET'S SEE YOU TEAR APART A LION WITH YOUR BARE HANDS NOW!
NOW THAT SAMSON'S HAIR HAS GROWN BACK, HE HOPES THAT GOD WILL RESTORE HIS STRENGTH.
WHERE ARE THE PILLARS? I WANT TO LEAN AGAINST THEM.
HERE, I'LL PUT YOUR HANDS ON THEM.
RUN, BOY, AND DON'T STOP UNTIL YOU'RE OUTSIDE THE TEMPLE.

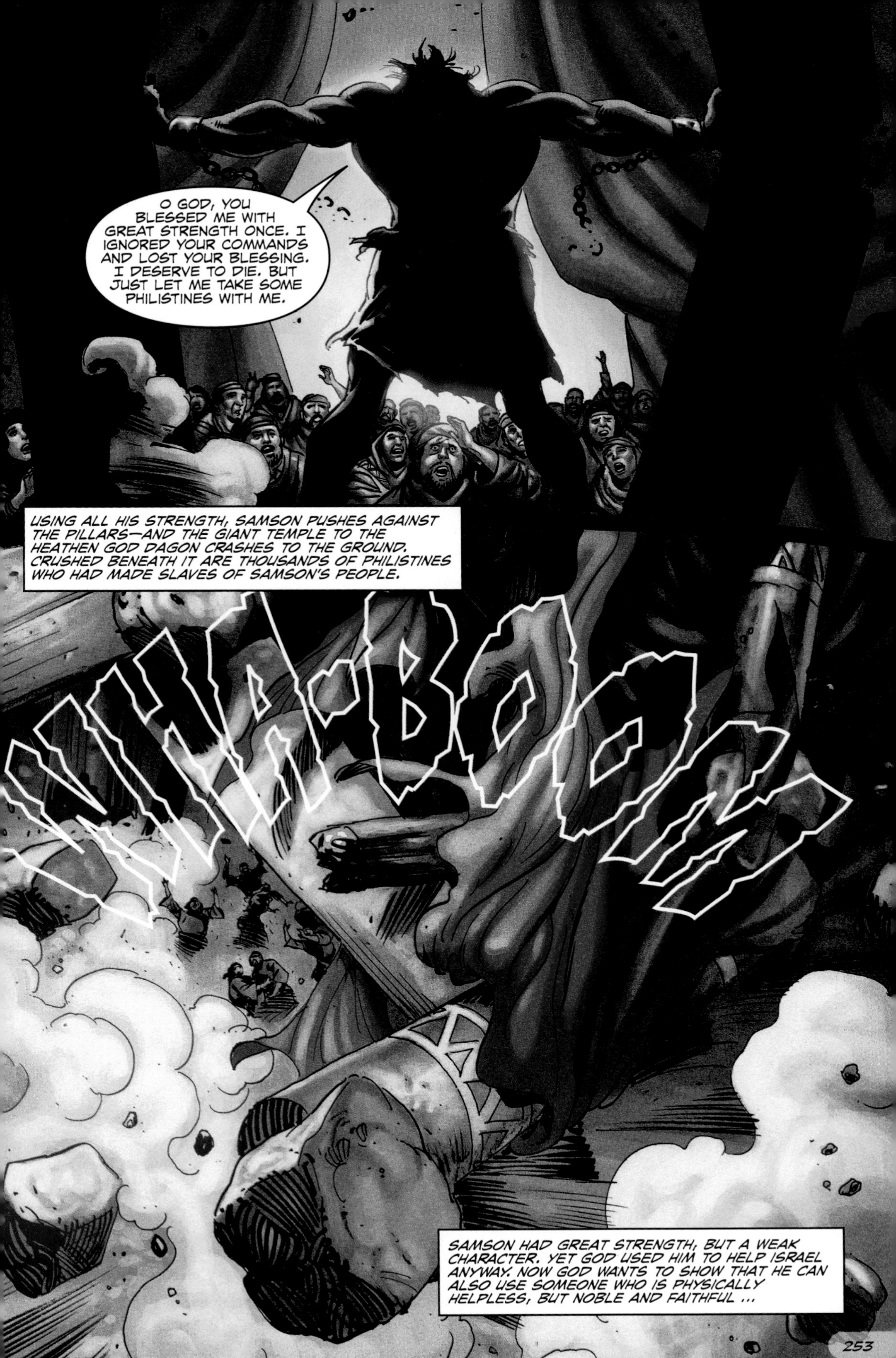
O GOD, YOU BLESSED ME WITH GREAT STRENGTH ONCE. I IGNORED YOUR COMMANDS AND LOST YOUR BLESSING. I DESERVE TO DIE. BUT JUST LET ME TAKE SOME PHILISTINES WITH ME.
USING ALL HIS STRENGTH, SAMSON PUSHES AGAINST THE PILLARS—AND THE GIANT TEMPLE TO THE HEATHEN GOD DAGON CRASHES TO THE GROUND. CRUSHED BENEATH IT ARE THOUSANDS OF PHILISTINES WHO HAD MADE SLAVES OF SAMSON'S PEOPLE.
WHA-BOOM
SAMSON HAD GREAT STRENGTH, BUT A WEAK CHARACTER. YET GOD USED HIM TO HELP ISRAEL ANYWAY. NOW GOD WANTS TO SHOW THAT HE CAN ALSO USE SOMEONE WHO IS PHYSICALLY HELPLESS, BUT NOBLE AND FAITHFUL ...

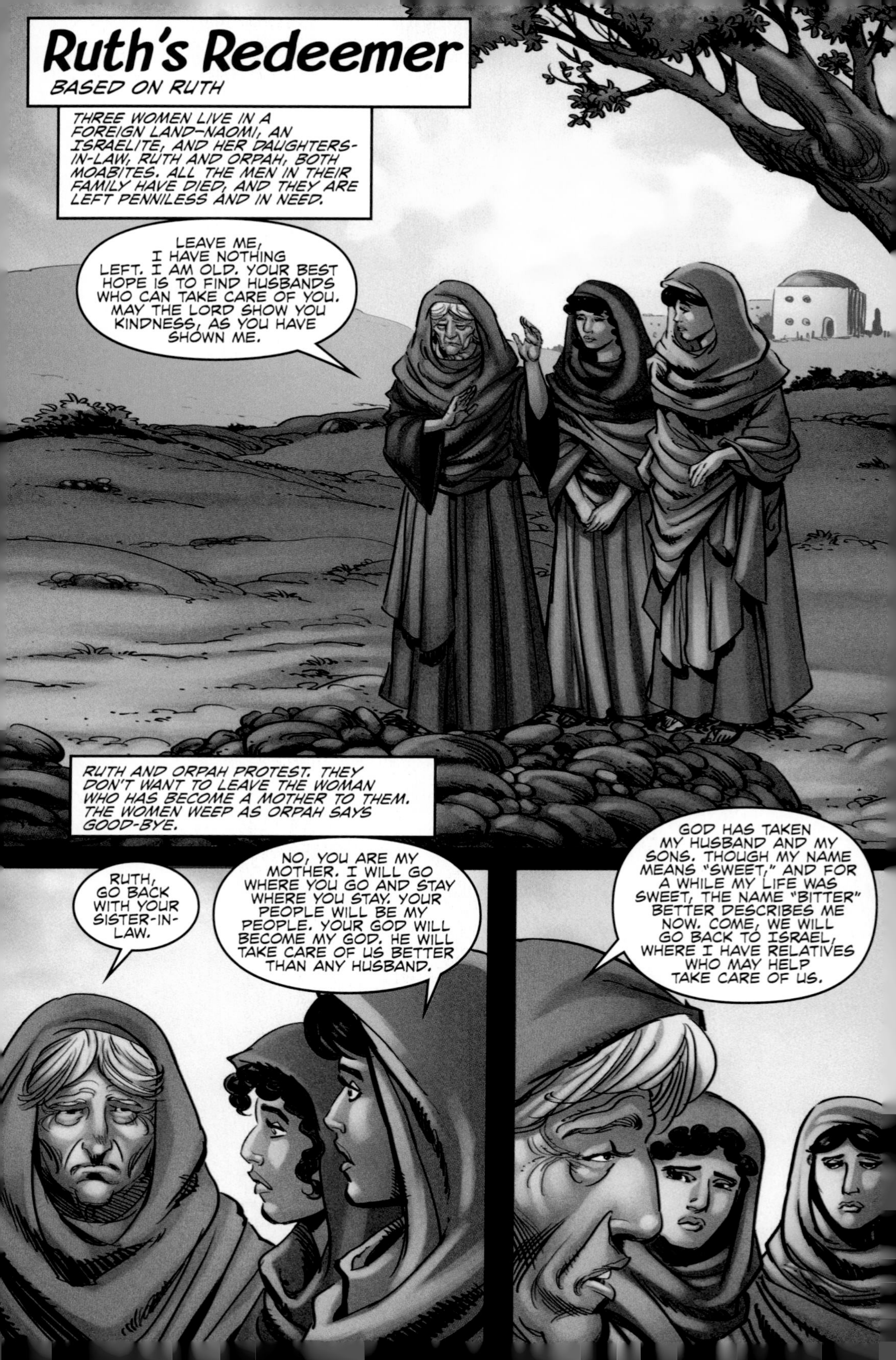
Ruth's Redeemer
BASED ON RUTH
THREE WOMEN LIVE IN A FOREIGN LAND—NAOMI, AN ISRAELITE, AND HER DAUGHTERS-IN-LAW, RUTH AND ORPAH, BOTH MOABITES. ALL THE MEN IN THEIR FAMILY HAVE DIED, AND THEY ARE LEFT PENNILESS AND IN NEED.
LEAVE ME, I HAVE NOTHING LEFT. I AM OLD. YOUR BEST HOPE IS TO FIND HUSBANDS WHO CAN TAKE CARE OF YOU. MAY THE LORD SHOW YOU KINDNESS, AS YOU HAVE SHOWN ME.
RUTH AND ORPAH PROTEST. THEY DON'T WANT TO LEAVE THE WOMAN WHO HAS BECOME A MOTHER TO THEM. THE WOMEN WEEP AS ORPAH SAYS GOOD-BYE.
RUTH, GO BACK WITH YOUR SISTER-IN-LAW.
NO, YOU ARE MY MOTHER. I WILL GO WHERE YOU GO AND STAY WHERE YOU STAY. YOUR PEOPLE WILL BE MY PEOPLE. YOUR GOD WILL BECOME MY GOD. HE WILL TAKE CARE OF US BETTER THAN ANY HUSBAND.
GOD HAS TAKEN MY HUSBAND AND MY SONS. THOUGH MY NAME MEANS "SWEET," AND FOR A WHILE MY LIFE WAS SWEET, THE NAME "BITTER" BETTER DESCRIBES ME NOW. COME, WE WILL GO BACK TO ISRAEL, WHERE I HAVE RELATIVES WHO MAY HELP TAKE CARE OF US.

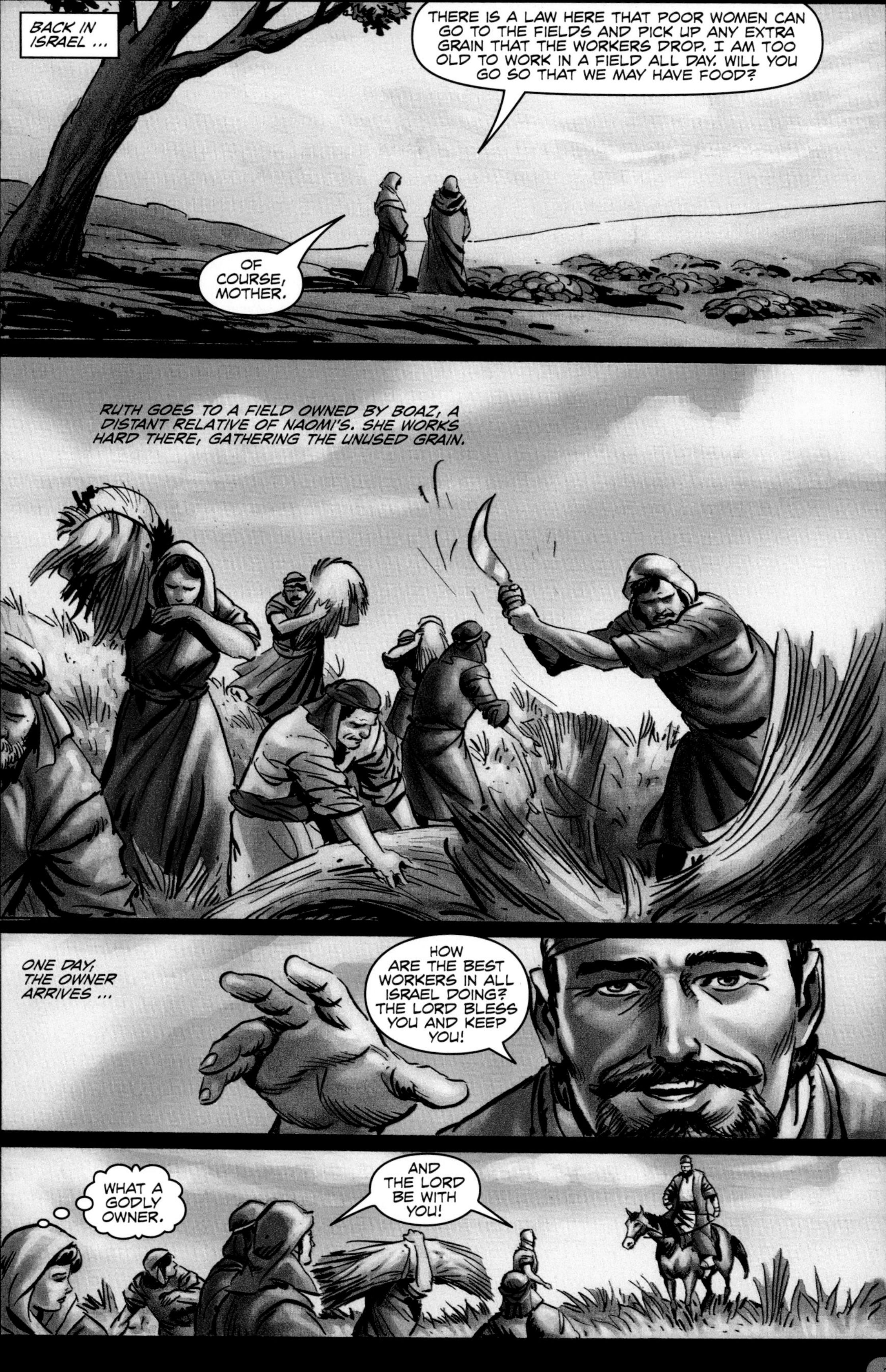
BACK IN ISRAEL ...
THERE IS A LAW HERE THAT POOR WOMEN CAN GO TO THE FIELDS AND PICK UP ANY EXTRA GRAIN THAT THE WORKERS DROP. I AM TOO OLD TO WORK IN A FIELD ALL DAY. WILL YOU GO SO THAT WE MAY HAVE FOOD?
OF COURSE, MOTHER.
RUTH GOES TO A FIELD OWNED BY BOAZ, A DISTANT RELATIVE OF NAOMI'S. SHE WORKS HARD THERE, GATHERING THE UNUSED GRAIN.
ONE DAY, THE OWNER ARRIVES ...
HOW ARE THE BEST WORKERS IN ALL ISRAEL DOING? THE LORD BLESS YOU AND KEEP YOU!
WHAT A GODLY OWNER.
AND THE LORD BE WITH YOU!

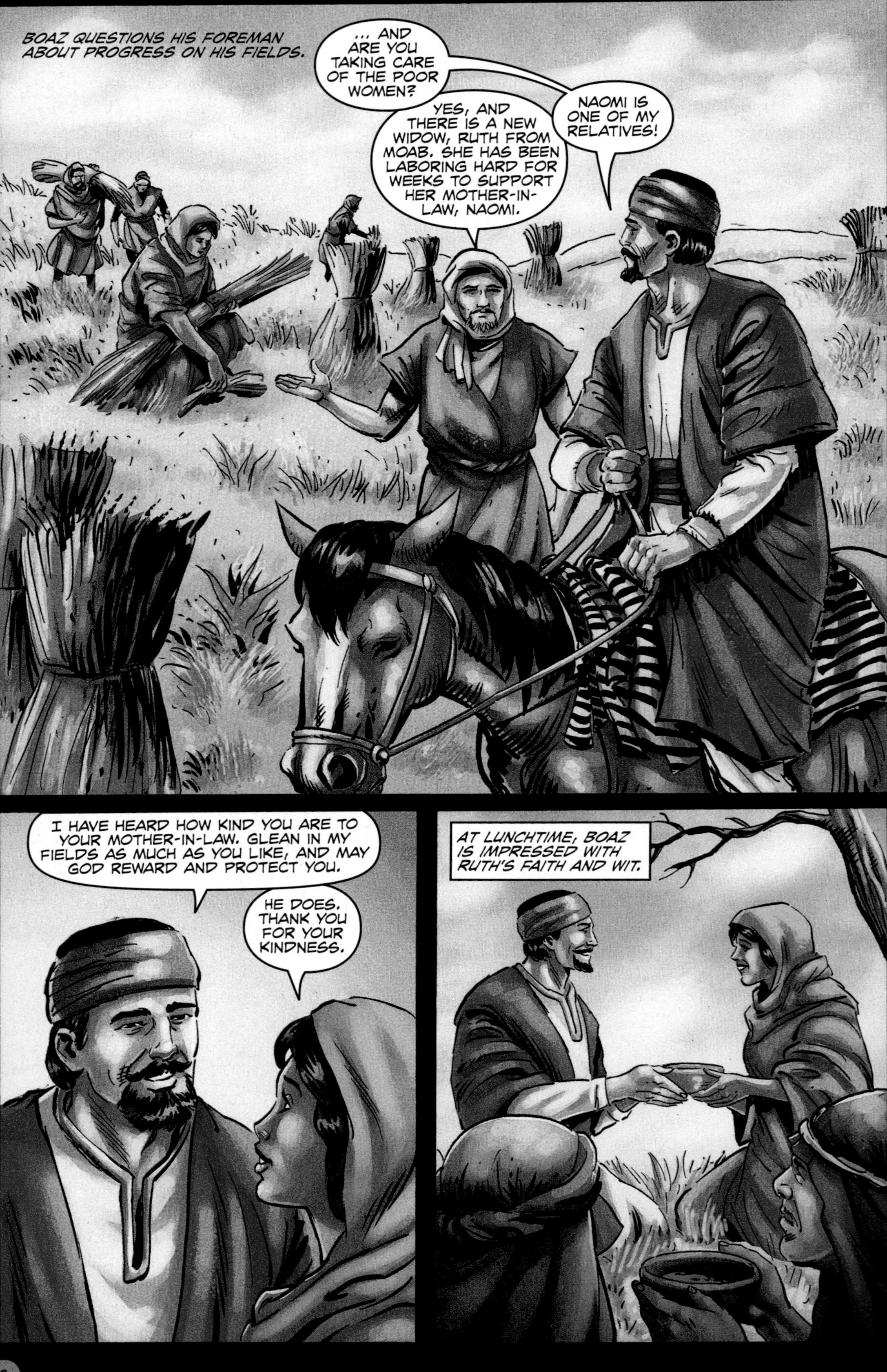
BOAZ QUESTIONS HIS FOREMAN ABOUT PROGRESS ON HIS FIELDS.
... AND ARE YOU TAKING CARE OF THE POOR WOMEN?
YES, AND THERE IS A NEW WIDOW, RUTH FROM MOAB. SHE HAS BEEN LABORING HARD FOR WEEKS TO SUPPORT HER MOTHER-IN-LAW, NAOMI.
NAOMI IS ONE OF MY RELATIVES!
I HAVE HEARD HOW KIND YOU ARE TO YOUR MOTHER-IN-LAW. GLEAN IN MY FIELDS AS MUCH AS YOU LIKE, AND MAY GOD REWARD AND PROTECT YOU.
HE DOES. THANK YOU FOR YOUR KINDNESS.
AT LUNCHTIME, BOAZ IS IMPRESSED WITH RUTH'S FAITH AND WIT.

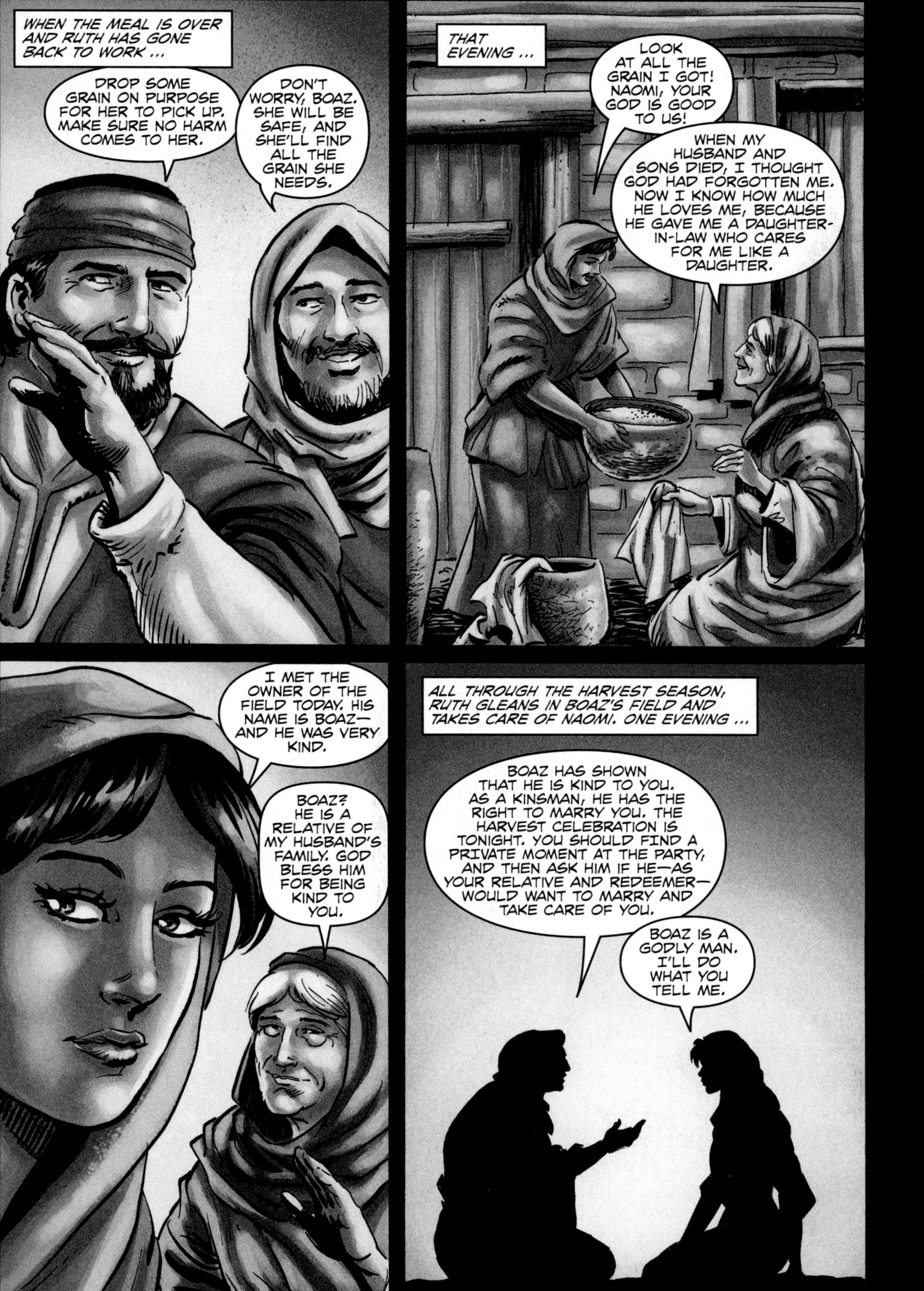
WHEN THE MEAL IS OVER AND RUTH HAS GONE BACK TO WORK ...
DROP SOME GRAIN ON PURPOSE FOR HER TO PICK UP. MAKE SURE NO HARM COMES TO HER.
DON'T WORRY, BOAZ. SHE WILL BE SAFE, AND SHE'LL FIND ALL THE GRAIN SHE NEEDS.
THAT EVENING ...
LOOK AT ALL THE GRAIN I GOT! NAOMI, YOUR GOD IS GOOD TO US!
WHEN MY HUSBAND AND SONS DIED, I THOUGHT GOD HAD FORGOTTEN ME. NOW I KNOW HOW MUCH HE LOVES ME, BECAUSE HE GAVE ME A DAUGHTER-IN-LAW WHO CARES FOR ME LIKE A DAUGHTER.
I MET THE OWNER OF THE FIELD TODAY. HIS NAME IS BOAZ—AND HE WAS VERY KIND.
BOAZ? HE IS A RELATIVE OF MY HUSBAND'S FAMILY. GOD BLESS HIM FOR BEING KIND TO YOU.
ALL THROUGH THE HARVEST SEASON, RUTH GLEANS IN BOAZ'S FIELD AND TAKES CARE OF NAOMI. ONE EVENING ...
BOAZ HAS SHOWN THAT HE IS KIND TO YOU. AS A KINSMAN, HE HAS THE RIGHT TO MARRY YOU. THE HARVEST CELEBRATION IS TONIGHT. YOU SHOULD FIND A PRIVATE MOMENT AT THE PARTY, AND THEN ASK HIM IF HE—AS YOUR RELATIVE AND REDEEMER—WOULD WANT TO MARRY AND TAKE CARE OF YOU.
BOAZ IS A GODLY MAN. I'LL DO WHAT YOU TELL ME.

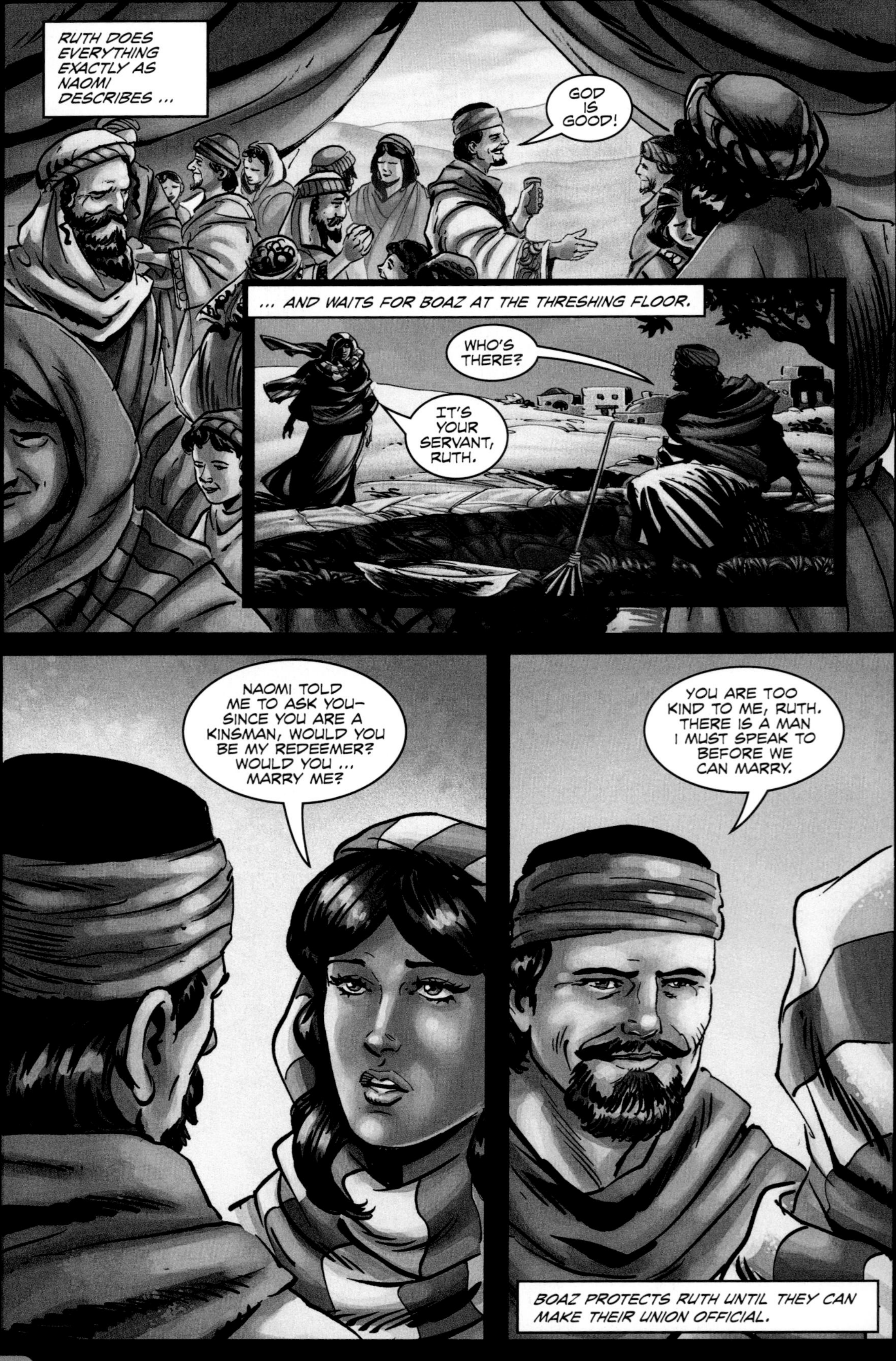
RUTH DOES EVERYTHING EXACTLY AS NAOMI DESCRIBES ...
GOD IS GOOD!
... AND WAITS FOR BOAZ AT THE THRESHING FLOOR.
WHO'S THERE?
IT'S YOUR SERVANT, RUTH.
NAOMI TOLD ME TO ASK YOU— SINCE YOU ARE A KINSMAN, WOULD YOU BE MY REDEEMER? WOULD YOU ... MARRY ME?
YOU ARE TOO KIND TO ME, RUTH. THERE IS A MAN I MUST SPEAK TO BEFORE WE CAN MARRY.
BOAZ PROTECTS RUTH UNTIL THEY CAN MAKE THEIR UNION OFFICIAL.

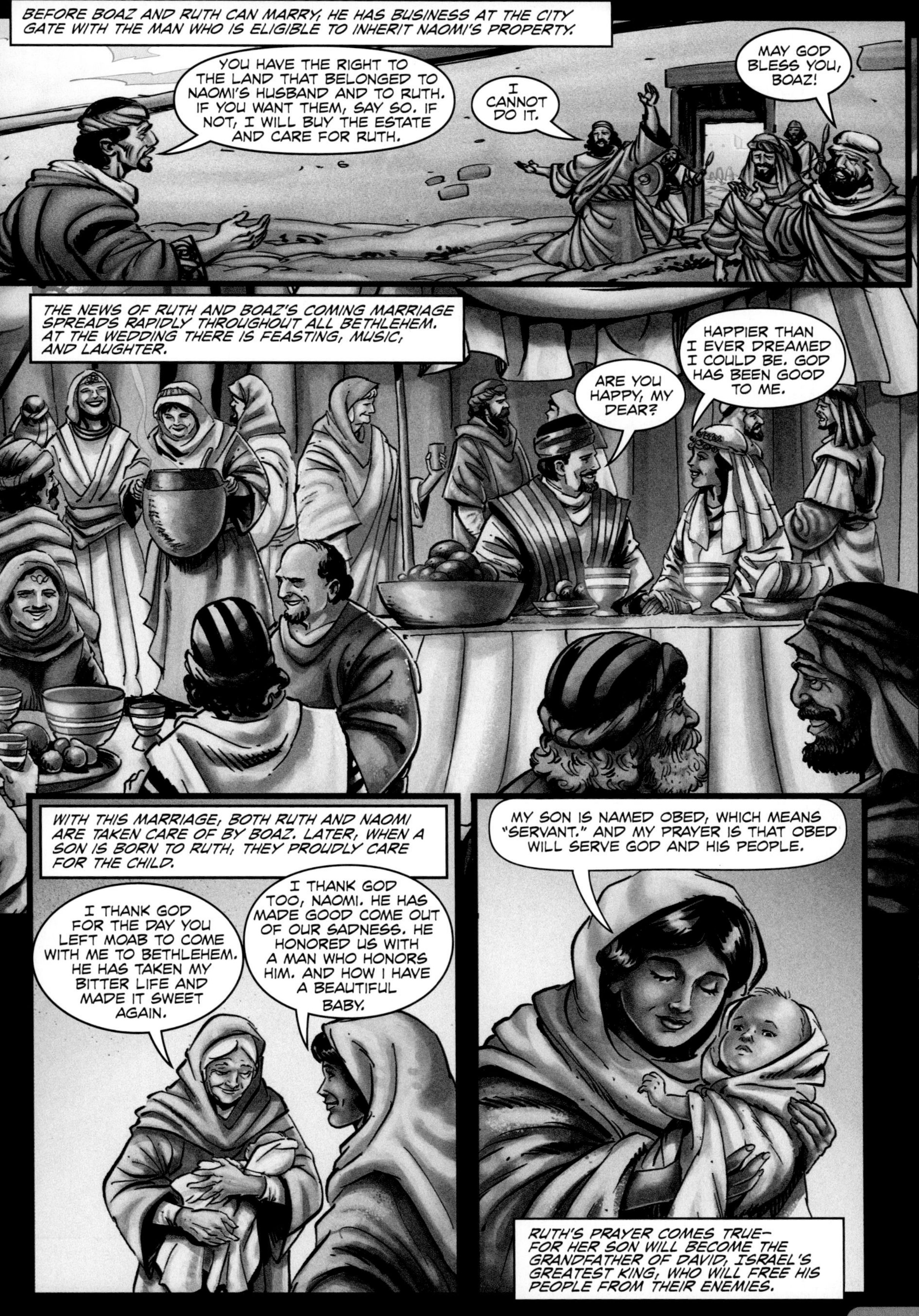
BEFORE BOAZ AND RUTH CAN MARRY, HE HAS BUSINESS AT THE CITY GATE WITH THE MAN WHO IS ELIGIBLE TO INHERIT NAOMI'S PROPERTY.
YOU HAVE THE RIGHT TO THE LAND THAT BELONGED TO NAOMI'S HUSBAND AND TO RUTH. IF YOU WANT THEM, SAY SO. IF NOT, I WILL BUY THE ESTATE AND CARE FOR RUTH.
I CANNOT DO IT.
MAY GOD BLESS YOU, BOAZ!
THE NEWS OF RUTH AND BOAZ'S COMING MARRIAGE SPREADS RAPIDLY THROUGHOUT ALL BETHLEHEM. AT THE WEDDING THERE IS FEASTING, MUSIC, AND LAUGHTER.
ARE YOU HAPPY, MY DEAR?
HAPPIER THAN I EVER DREAMED I COULD BE. GOD HAS BEEN GOOD TO ME.
WITH THIS MARRIAGE, BOTH RUTH AND NAOMI ARE TAKEN CARE OF BY BOAZ. LATER, WHEN A SON IS BORN TO RUTH, THEY PROUDLY CARE FOR THE CHILD.
I THANK GOD FOR THE DAY YOU LEFT MOAB TO COME WITH ME TO BETHLEHEM. HE HAS TAKEN MY BITTER LIFE AND MADE IT SWEET AGAIN.
I THANK GOD TOO, NAOMI. HE HAS MADE GOOD COME OUT OF OUR SADNESS. HE HONORED US WITH A MAN WHO HONORS HIM. AND HOW I HAVE A BEAUTIFUL BABY.
MY SON IS NAMED OBED, WHICH MEANS "SERVANT." AND MY PRAYER IS THAT OBED WILL SERVE GOD AND HIS PEOPLE.
RUTH'S PRAYER COMES TRUE— FOR HER SON WILL BECOME THE GRANDFATHER OF DAVID, ISRAEL'S GREATEST KING, WHO WILL FREE HIS PEOPLE FROM THEIR ENEMIES.

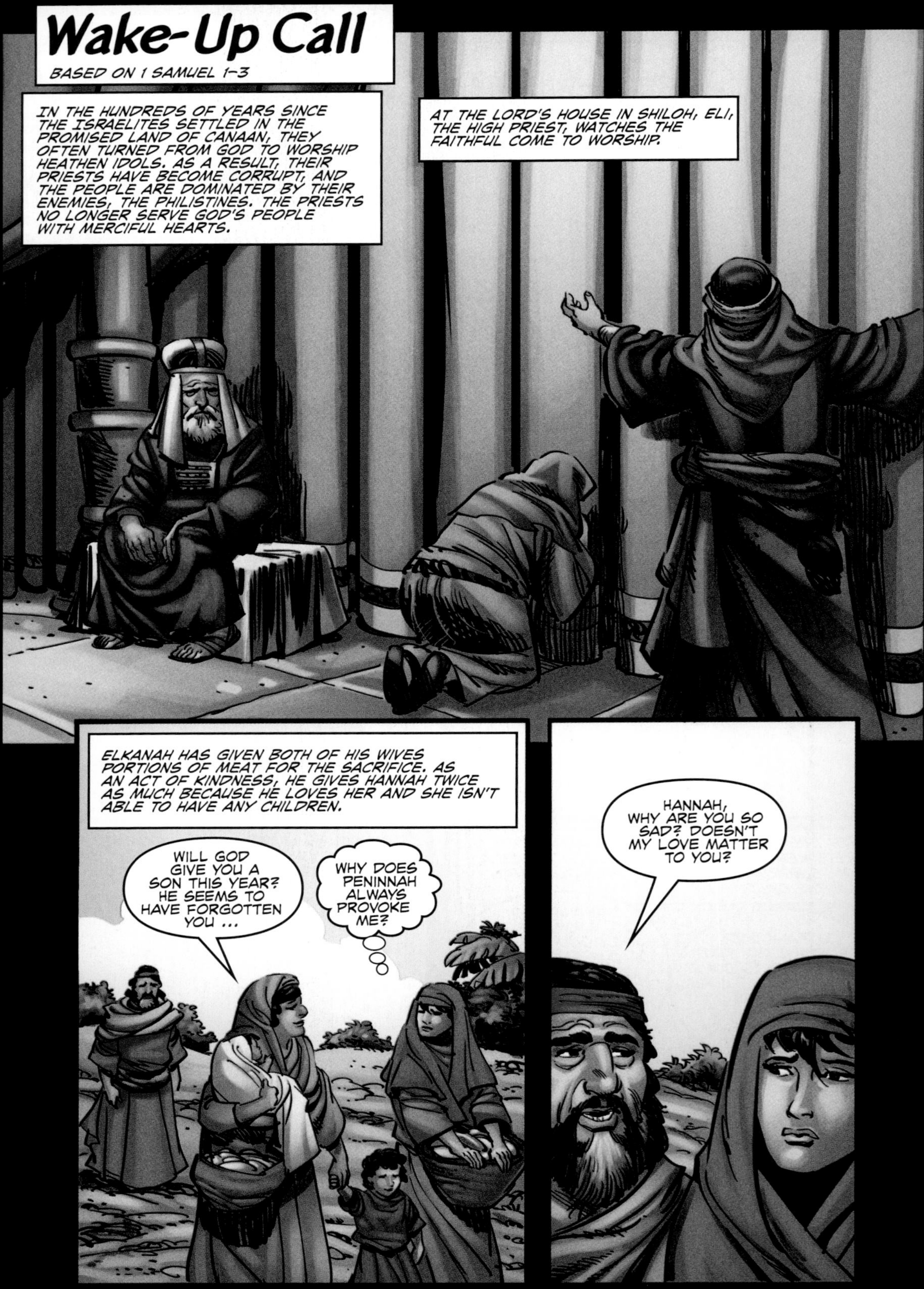
Wake-Up Call
BASED ON 1 SAMUEL 1–3
IN THE HUNDREDS OF YEARS SINCE THE ISRAELITES SETTLED IN THE PROMISED LAND OF CANAAN, THEY OFTEN TURNED FROM GOD TO WORSHIP HEATHEN IDOLS. AS A RESULT, THEIR PRIESTS HAVE BECOME CORRUPT, AND THE PEOPLE ARE DOMINATED BY THEIR ENEMIES, THE PHILISTINES. THE PRIESTS NO LONGER SERVE GOD'S PEOPLE WITH MERCIFUL HEARTS.
AT THE LORD'S HOUSE IN SHILOH, ELI, THE HIGH PRIEST, WATCHES THE FAITHFUL COME TO WORSHIP.
ELKANAH HAS GIVEN BOTH OF HIS WIVES PORTIONS OF MEAT FOR THE SACRIFICE. AS AN ACT OF KINDNESS, HE GIVES HANNAH TWICE AS MUCH BECAUSE HE LOVES HER AND SHE ISN'T ABLE TO HAVE ANY CHILDREN.
WILL GOD GIVE YOU A SON THIS YEAR? HE SEEMS TO HAVE FORGOTTEN YOU ...
WHY DOES PENINNAH ALWAYS PROVOKE ME?
HANNAH, WHY ARE YOU SO SAD? DOESN'T MY LOVE MATTER TO YOU?

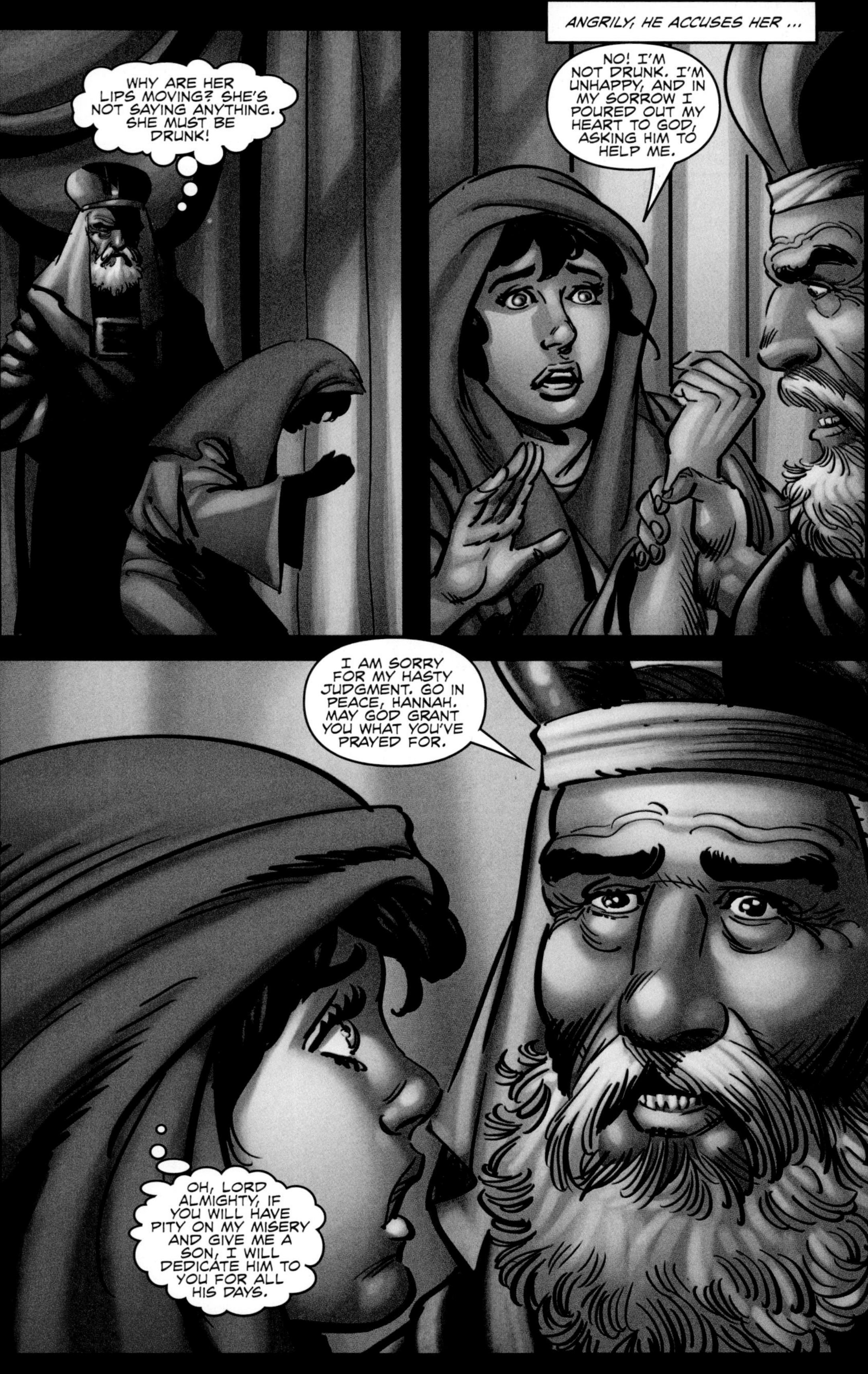
ANGRILY, HE ACCUSES HER ...
WHY ARE HER LIPS MOVING? SHE'S NOT SAYING ANYTHING. SHE MUST BE DRUNK!
NO! I'M NOT DRUNK. I'M UNHAPPY, AND IN MY SORROW I POURED OUT MY HEART TO GOD, ASKING HIM TO HELP ME.
I AM SORRY FOR MY HASTY JUDGMENT. GO IN PEACE, HANNAH. MAY GOD GRANT YOU WHAT YOU'VE PRAYED FOR.
OH, LORD ALMIGHTY, IF YOU WILL HAVE PITY ON MY MISERY AND GIVE ME A SON, I WILL DEDICATE HIM TO YOU FOR ALL HIS DAYS.

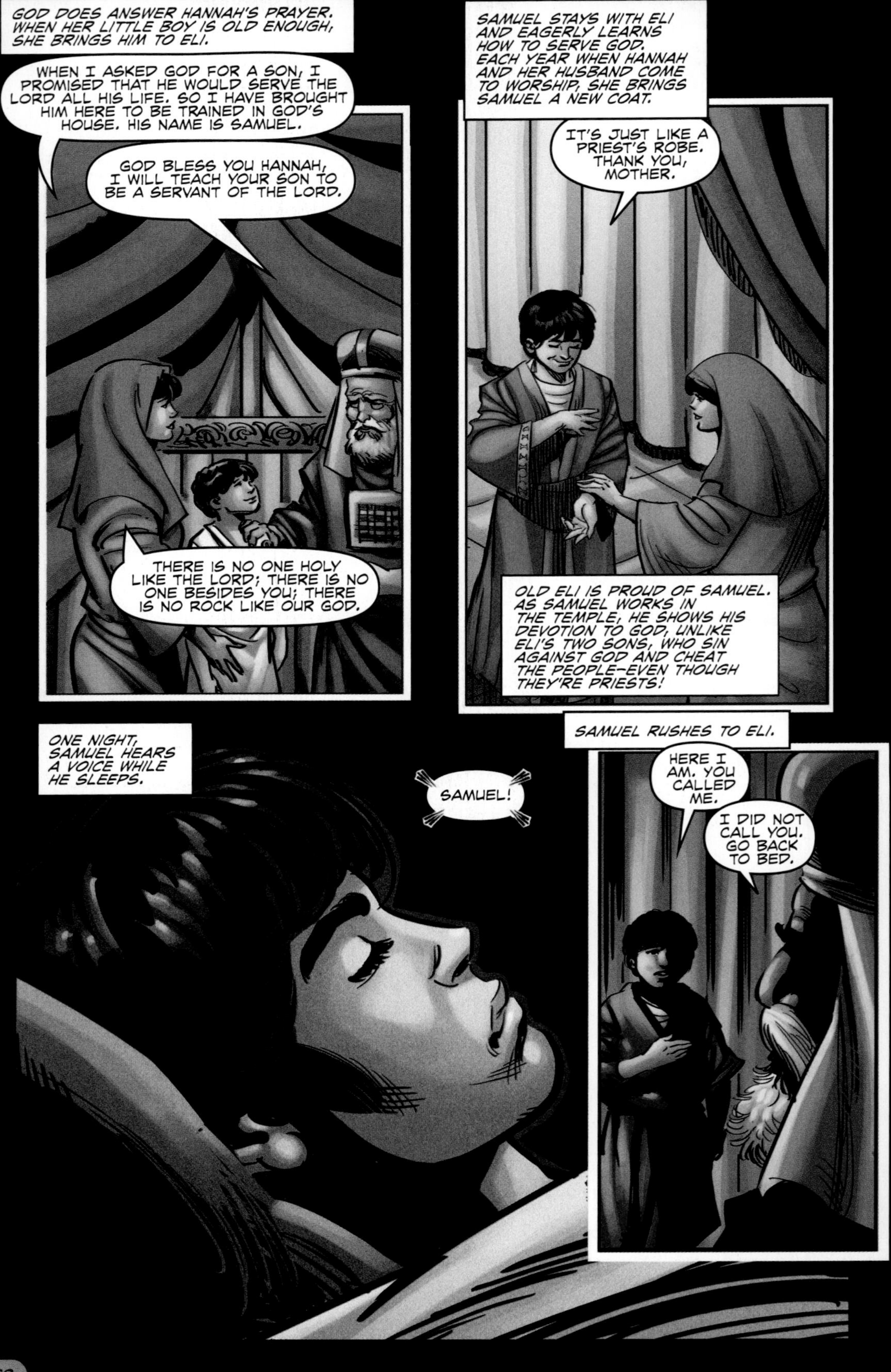
GOD DOES ANSWER HANNAH'S PRAYER. WHEN HER LITTLE BOY IS OLD ENOUGH, SHE BRINGS HIM TO ELI.
WHEN I ASKED GOD FOR A SON, I PROMISED THAT HE WOULD SERVE THE LORD ALL HIS LIFE. SO I HAVE BROUGHT HIM HERE TO BE TRAINED IN GOD'S HOUSE. HIS NAME IS SAMUEL.
GOD BLESS YOU HANNAH, I WILL TEACH YOUR SON TO BE A SERVANT OF THE LORD.
THERE IS NO ONE HOLY LIKE THE LORD; THERE IS NO ONE BESIDES YOU; THERE IS NO ROCK LIKE OUR GOD.
SAMUEL STAYS WITH ELI AND EAGERLY LEARNS HOW TO SERVE GOD. EACH YEAR WHEN HANNAH AND HER HUSBAND COME TO WORSHIP, SHE BRINGS SAMUEL A NEW COAT.
IT'S JUST LIKE A PRIEST'S ROBE. THANK YOU, MOTHER.
OLD ELI IS PROUD OF SAMUEL. AS SAMUEL WORKS IN THE TEMPLE, HE SHOWS HIS DEVOTION TO GOD, UNLIKE ELI'S TWO SONS, WHO SIN AGAINST GOD AND CHEAT THE PEOPLE—EVEN THOUGH THEY'RE PRIESTS!
ONE NIGHT, SAMUEL HEARS A VOICE WHILE HE SLEEPS.
SAMUEL!
SAMUEL RUSHES TO ELI.
HERE I AM. YOU CALLED ME.
I DID NOT CALL YOU. GO BACK TO BED.

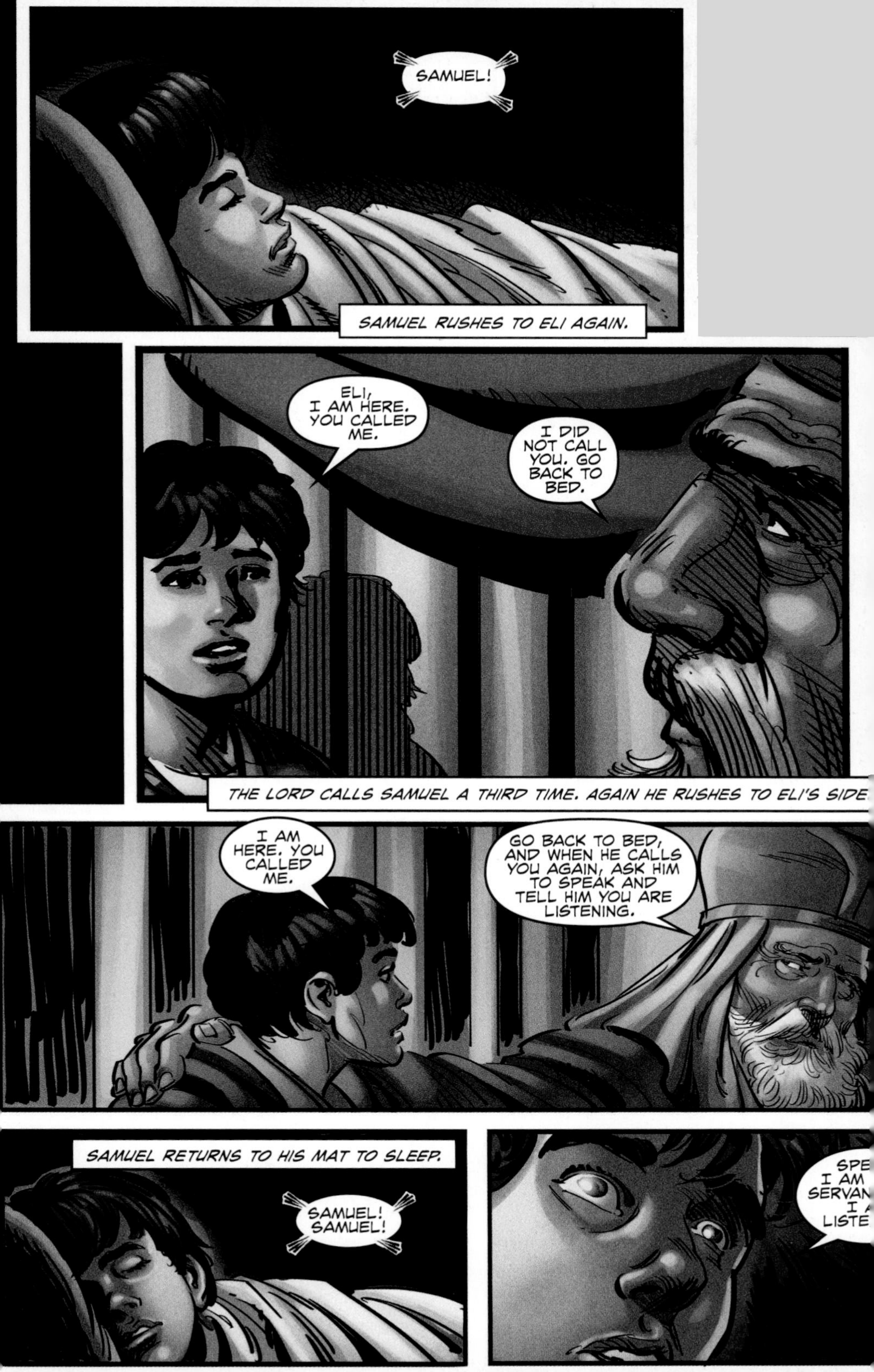
SAMUEL!
SAMUEL RUSHES TO ELI AGAIN.
ELI, I AM HERE. YOU CALLED ME.
I DID NOT CALL YOU. GO BACK TO BED.
THE LORD CALLS SAMUEL A THIRD TIME. AGAIN HE RUSHES TO ELI'S SIDE.
I AM HERE. YOU CALLED ME.
GO BACK TO BED, AND WHEN HE CALLS YOU AGAIN, ASK HIM TO SPEAK AND TELL HIM YOU ARE LISTENING.
SAMUEL RETURNS TO HIS MAT TO SLEEP.
SAMUEL! SAMUEL!

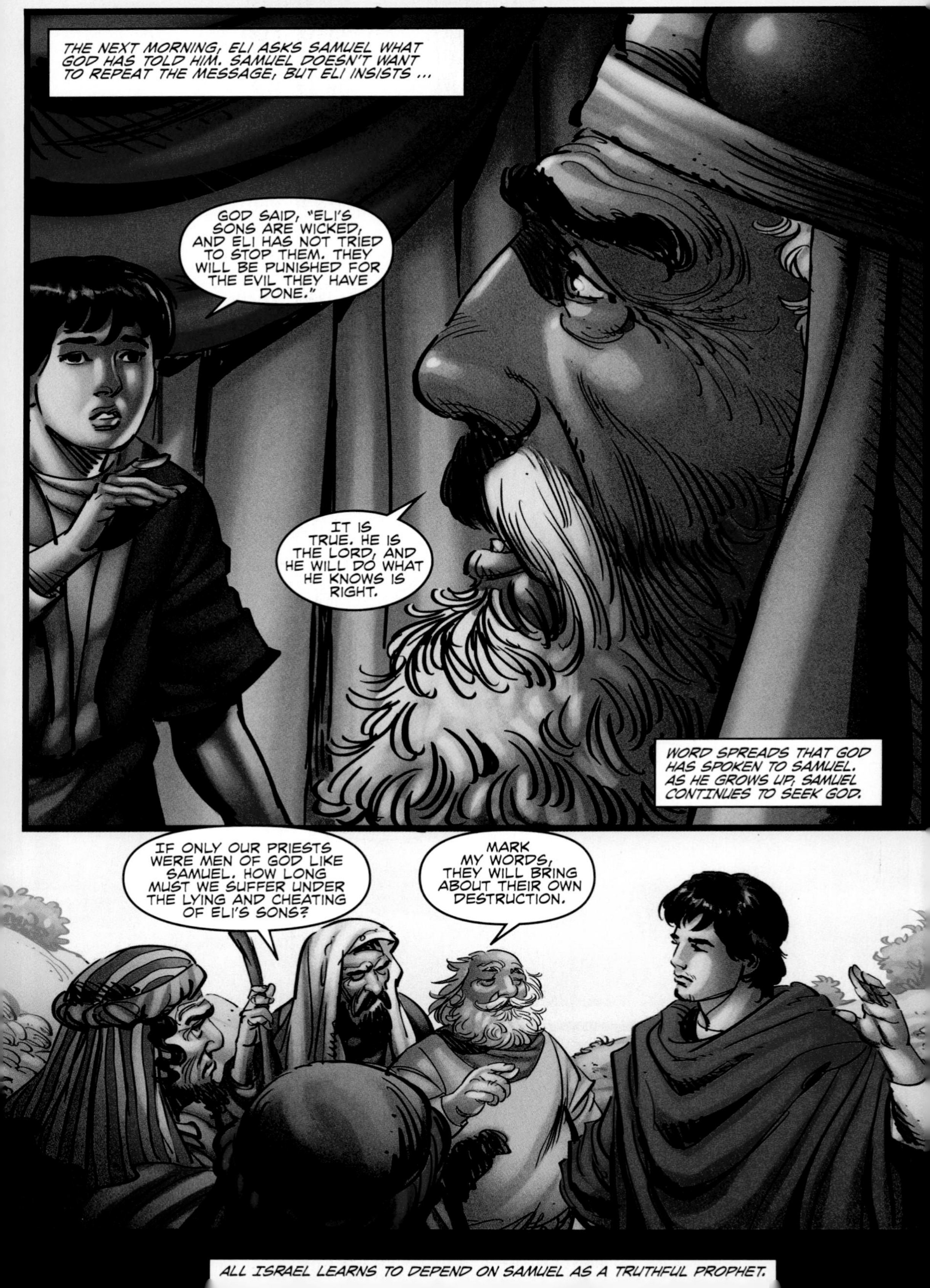
THE NEXT MORNING, ELI ASKS SAMUEL WHAT GOD HAS TOLD HIM. SAMUEL DOESN'T WANT TO REPEAT THE MESSAGE, BUT ELI INSISTS ...
GOD SAID, "ELI'S SONS ARE WICKED, AND ELI HAS NOT TRIED TO STOP THEM. THEY WILL BE PUNISHED FOR THE EVIL THEY HAVE DONE."
IT IS TRUE. HE IS THE LORD, AND HE WILL DO WHAT HE KNOWS IS RIGHT.
WORD SPREADS THAT GOD HAS SPOKEN TO SAMUEL. AS HE GROWS UP, SAMUEL CONTINUES TO SEEK GOD.
IF ONLY OUR PRIESTS WERE MEN OF GOD LIKE SAMUEL. HOW LONG MUST WE SUFFER UNDER THE LYING AND CHEATING OF ELI'S SONS?
MARK MY WORDS, THEY WILL BRING ABOUT THEIR OWN DESTRUCTION.
ALL ISRAEL LEARNS TO DEPEND ON SAMUEL AS A TRUTHFUL PROPHET.

Pass the Ark

BASED ON 1 SAMUEL 4—6

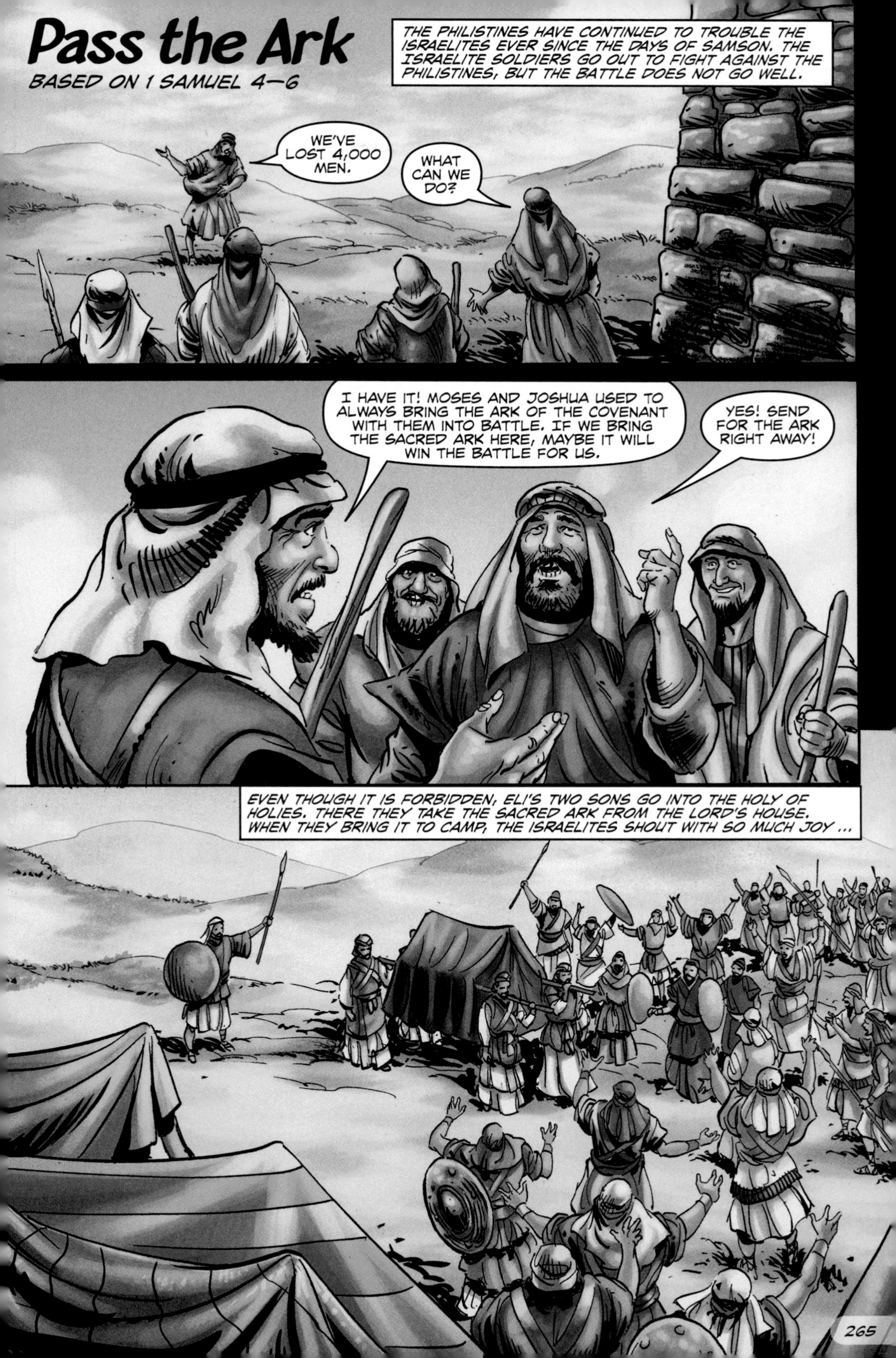

THE PHILISTINES HAVE CONTINUED TO TROUBLE THE ISRAELITES EVER SINCE THE DAYS OF SAMSON. THE ISRAELITE SOLDIERS GO OUT TO FIGHT AGAINST THE PHILISTINES, BUT THE BATTLE DOES NOT GO WELL.
WE'VE LOST 4,000 MEN.
WHAT CAN WE DO?
I HAVE IT! MOSES AND JOSHUA USED TO ALWAYS BRING THE ARK OF THE COVENANT WITH THEM INTO BATTLE. IF WE BRING THE SACRED ARK HERE, MAYBE IT WILL WIN THE BATTLE FOR US.
YES! SEND FOR THE ARK RIGHT AWAY!
EVEN THOUGH IT IS FORBIDDEN, ELI'S TWO SONS GO INTO THE HOLY OF HOLIES. THERE THEY TAKE THE SACRED ARK FROM THE LORD'S HOUSE. WHEN THEY BRING IT TO CAMP, THE ISRAELITES SHOUT WITH SO MUCH JOY ...

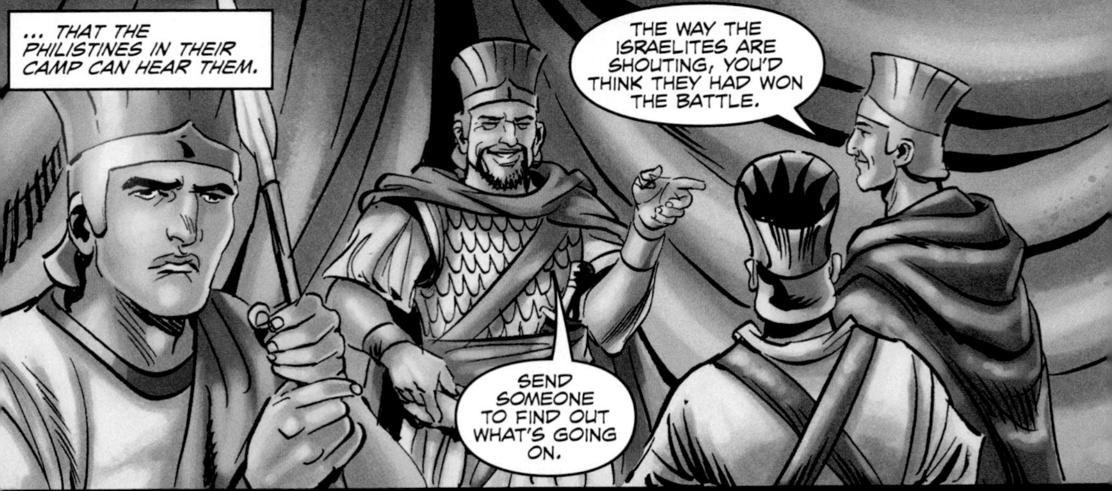
... THAT THE PHILISTINES IN THEIR CAMP CAN HEAR THEM.
THE WAY THE ISRAELITES ARE SHOUTING, YOU'D THINK THEY HAD WON THE BATTLE.
SEND SOMEONE TO FIND OUT WHAT'S GOING ON.
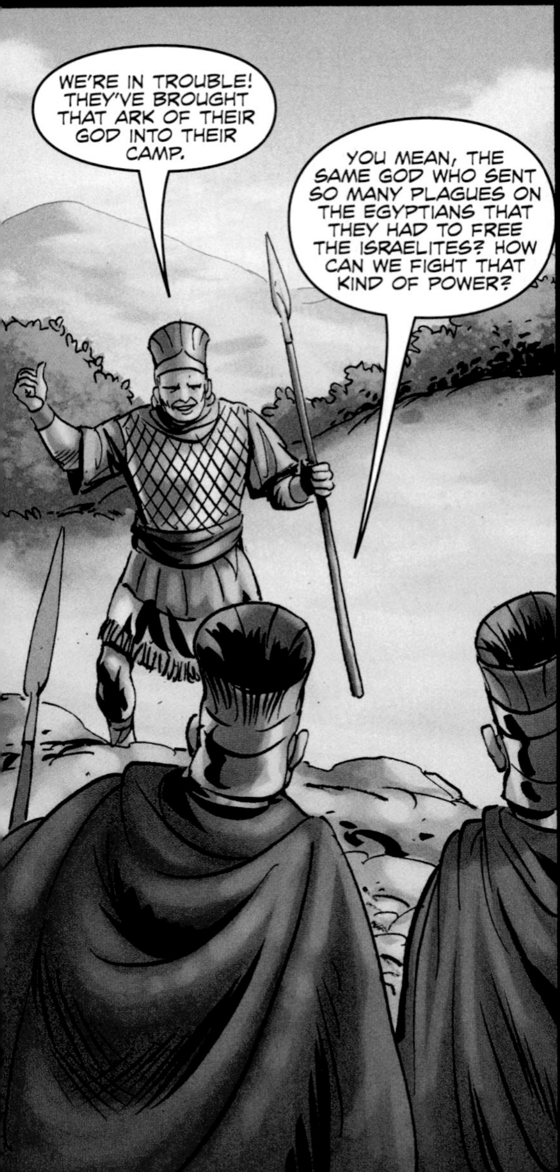
WE'RE IN TROUBLE! THEY'VE BROUGHT THAT ARK OF THEIR GOD INTO THEIR CAMP.
YOU MEAN, THE SAME GOD WHO SENT SO MANY PLAGUES ON THE EGYPTIANS THAT THEY HAD TO FREE THE ISRAELITES? HOW CAN WE FIGHT THAT KIND OF POWER?
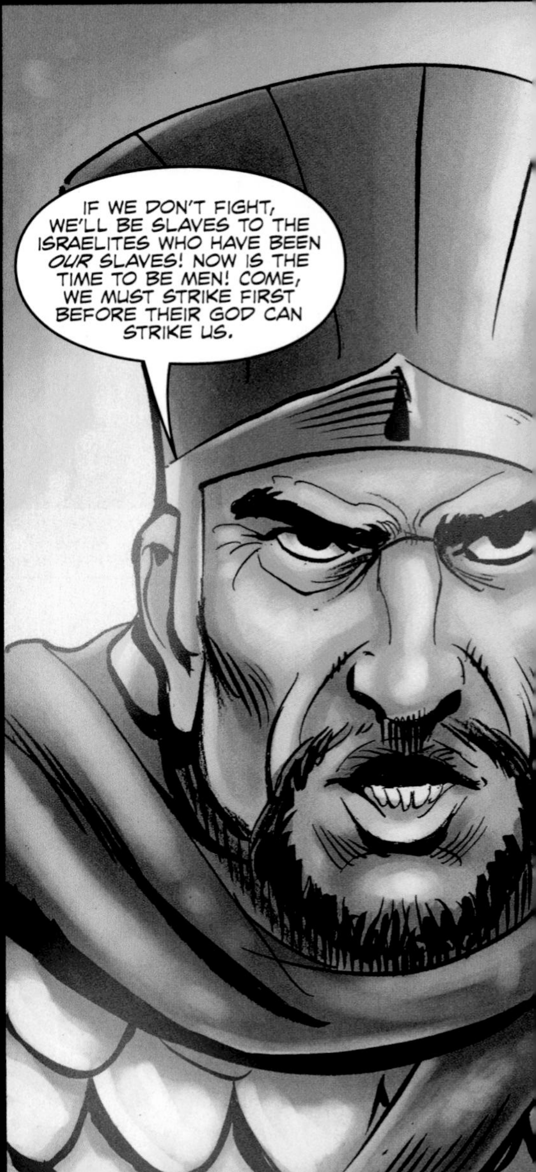
IF WE DON'T FIGHT, WE'LL BE SLAVES TO THE ISRAELITES WHO HAVE BEEN *OUR* SLAVES! NOW IS THE TIME TO BE MEN! COME, WE MUST STRIKE FIRST BEFORE THEIR GOD CAN STRIKE US.

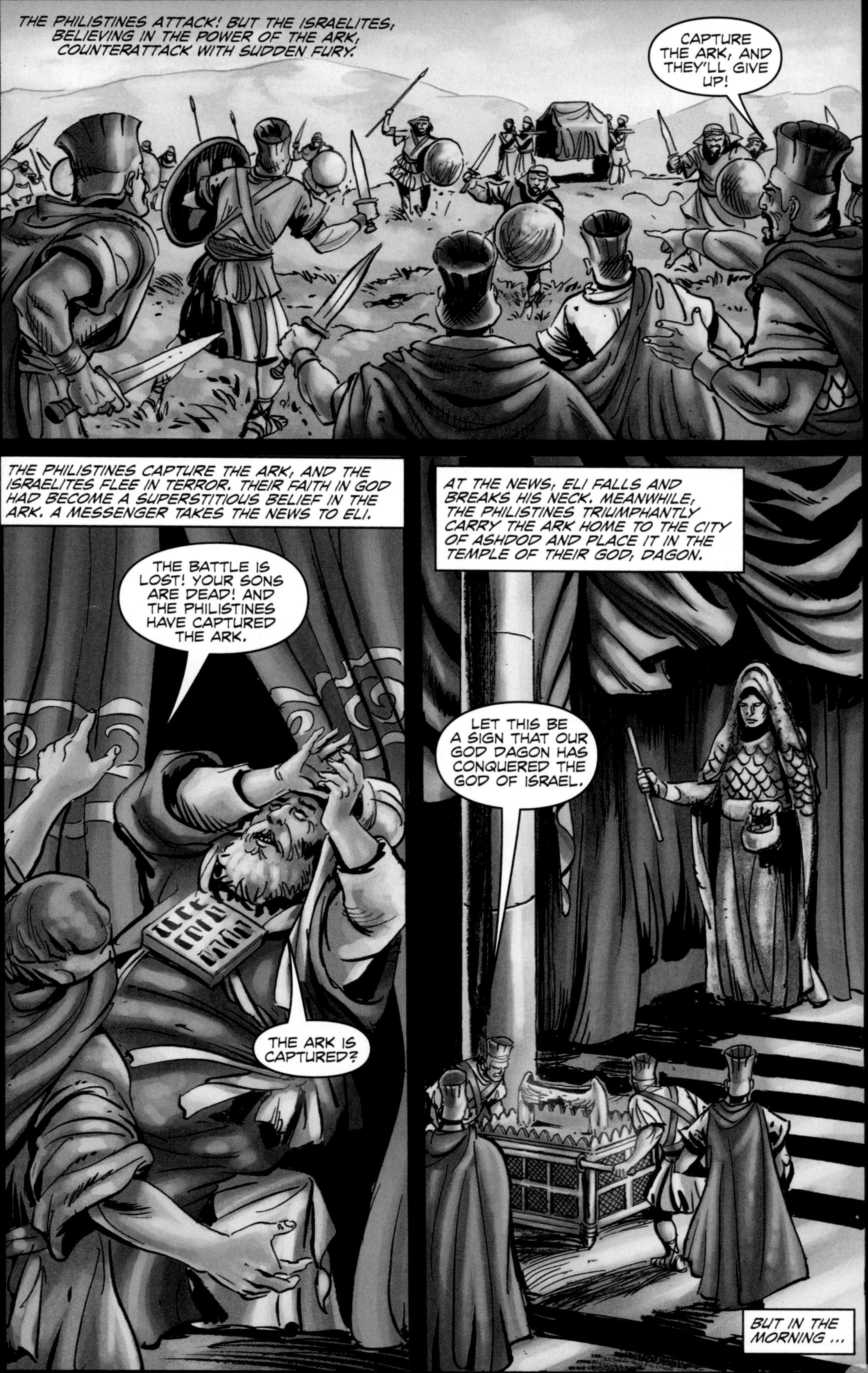
THE PHILISTINES ATTACK! BUT THE ISRAELITES, BELIEVING IN THE POWER OF THE ARK, COUNTERATTACK WITH SUDDEN FURY.
CAPTURE THE ARK, AND THEY'LL GIVE UP!
THE PHILISTINES CAPTURE THE ARK, AND THE ISRAELITES FLEE IN TERROR. THEIR FAITH IN GOD HAD BECOME A SUPERSTITIOUS BELIEF IN THE ARK. A MESSENGER TAKES THE NEWS TO ELI.
THE BATTLE IS LOST! YOUR SONS ARE DEAD! AND THE PHILISTINES HAVE CAPTURED THE ARK.
THE ARK IS CAPTURED?
AT THE NEWS, ELI FALLS AND BREAKS HIS NECK. MEANWHILE, THE PHILISTINES TRIUMPHANTLY CARRY THE ARK HOME TO THE CITY OF ASHDOD AND PLACE IT IN THE TEMPLE OF THEIR GOD, DAGON.
LET THIS BE A SIGN THAT OUR GOD DAGON HAS CONQUERED THE GOD OF ISRAEL.
BUT IN THE MORNING ...

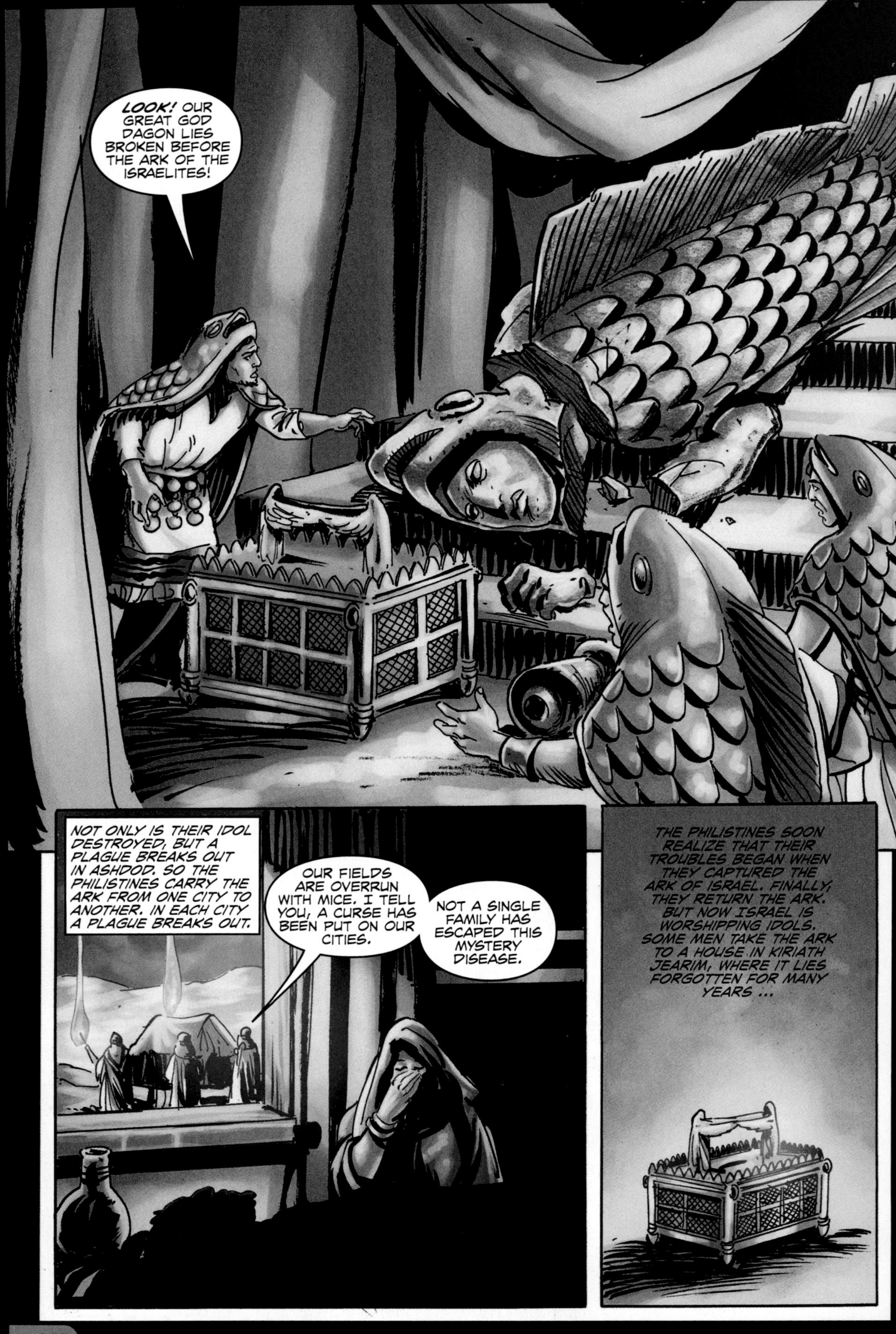
LOOK! OUR GREAT GOD DAGON LIES BROKEN BEFORE THE ARK OF THE ISRAELITES!
NOT ONLY IS THEIR IDOL DESTROYED, BUT A PLAGUE BREAKS OUT IN ASHDOD. SO THE PHILISTINES CARRY THE ARK FROM ONE CITY TO ANOTHER. IN EACH CITY A PLAGUE BREAKS OUT.
OUR FIELDS ARE OVERRUN WITH MICE. I TELL YOU, A CURSE HAS BEEN PUT ON OUR CITIES.
NOT A SINGLE FAMILY HAS ESCAPED THIS MYSTERY DISEASE.
THE PHILISTINES SOON REALIZE THAT THEIR TROUBLES BEGAN WHEN THEY CAPTURED THE ARK OF ISRAEL. FINALLY, THEY RETURN THE ARK. BUT NOW ISRAEL IS WORSHIPPING IDOLS. SOME MEN TAKE THE ARK TO A HOUSE IN KIRIATH JEARIM, WHERE IT LIES FORGOTTEN FOR MANY YEARS ...

A Miracle at Mizpah

BASED ON 1 SAMUEL 7

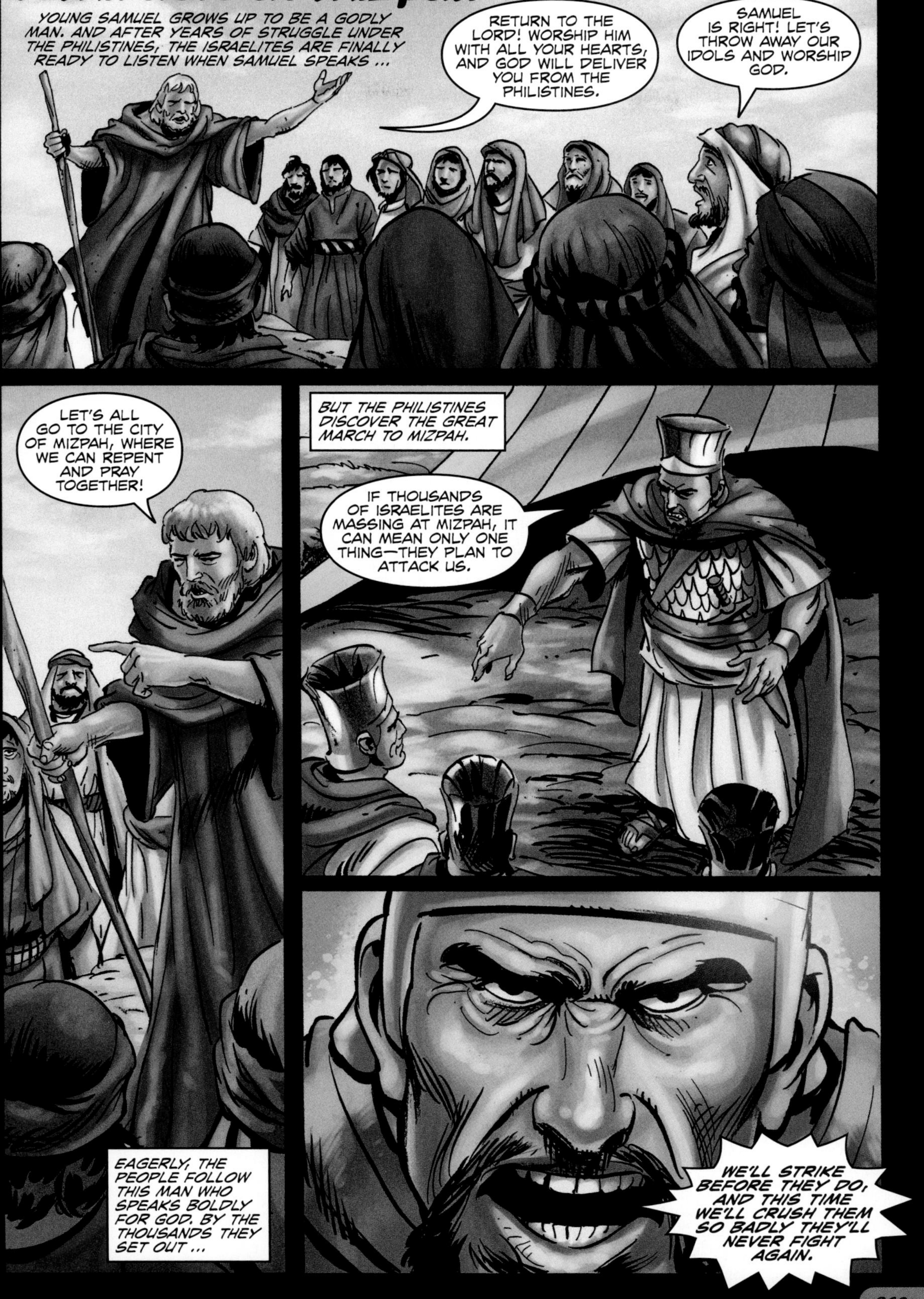
YOUNG SAMUEL GROWS UP TO BE A GODLY MAN. AND AFTER YEARS OF STRUGGLE UNDER THE PHILISTINES, THE ISRAELITES ARE FINALLY READY TO LISTEN WHEN SAMUEL SPEAKS ...
RETURN TO THE LORD! WORSHIP HIM WITH ALL YOUR HEARTS, AND GOD WILL DELIVER YOU FROM THE PHILISTINES.
SAMUEL IS RIGHT! LET'S THROW AWAY OUR IDOLS AND WORSHIP GOD.
LET'S ALL GO TO THE CITY OF MIZPAH, WHERE WE CAN REPENT AND PRAY TOGETHER!
EAGERLY, THE PEOPLE FOLLOW THIS MAN WHO SPEAKS BOLDLY FOR GOD. BY THE THOUSANDS THEY SET OUT ...
BUT THE PHILISTINES DISCOVER THE GREAT MARCH TO MIZPAH.
IF THOUSANDS OF ISRAELITES ARE MASSING AT MIZPAH, IT CAN MEAN ONLY ONE THING—THEY PLAN TO ATTACK US.
WE'LL STRIKE BEFORE THEY DO, AND THIS TIME WE'LL CRUSH THEM SO BADLY THEY'LL NEVER FIGHT AGAIN.

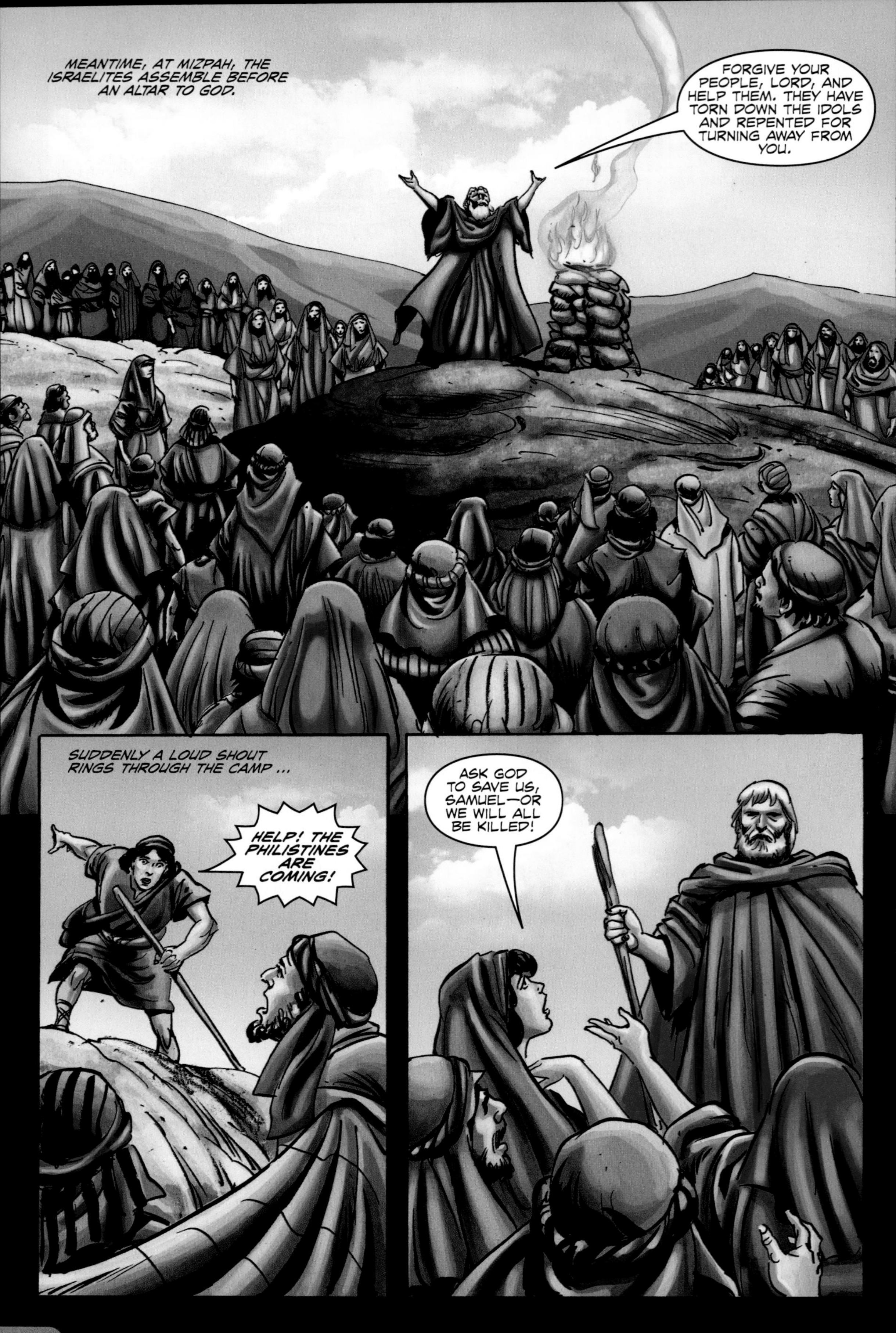
MEANTIME, AT MIZPAH, THE ISRAELITES ASSEMBLE BEFORE AN ALTAR TO GOD.
FORGIVE YOUR PEOPLE, LORD, AND HELP THEM. THEY HAVE TORN DOWN THE IDOLS AND REPENTED FOR TURNING AWAY FROM YOU.
SUDDENLY A LOUD SHOUT RINGS THROUGH THE CAMP ...
HELP! THE PHILISTINES ARE COMING!
ASK GOD TO SAVE US, SAMUEL—OR WE WILL ALL BE KILLED!

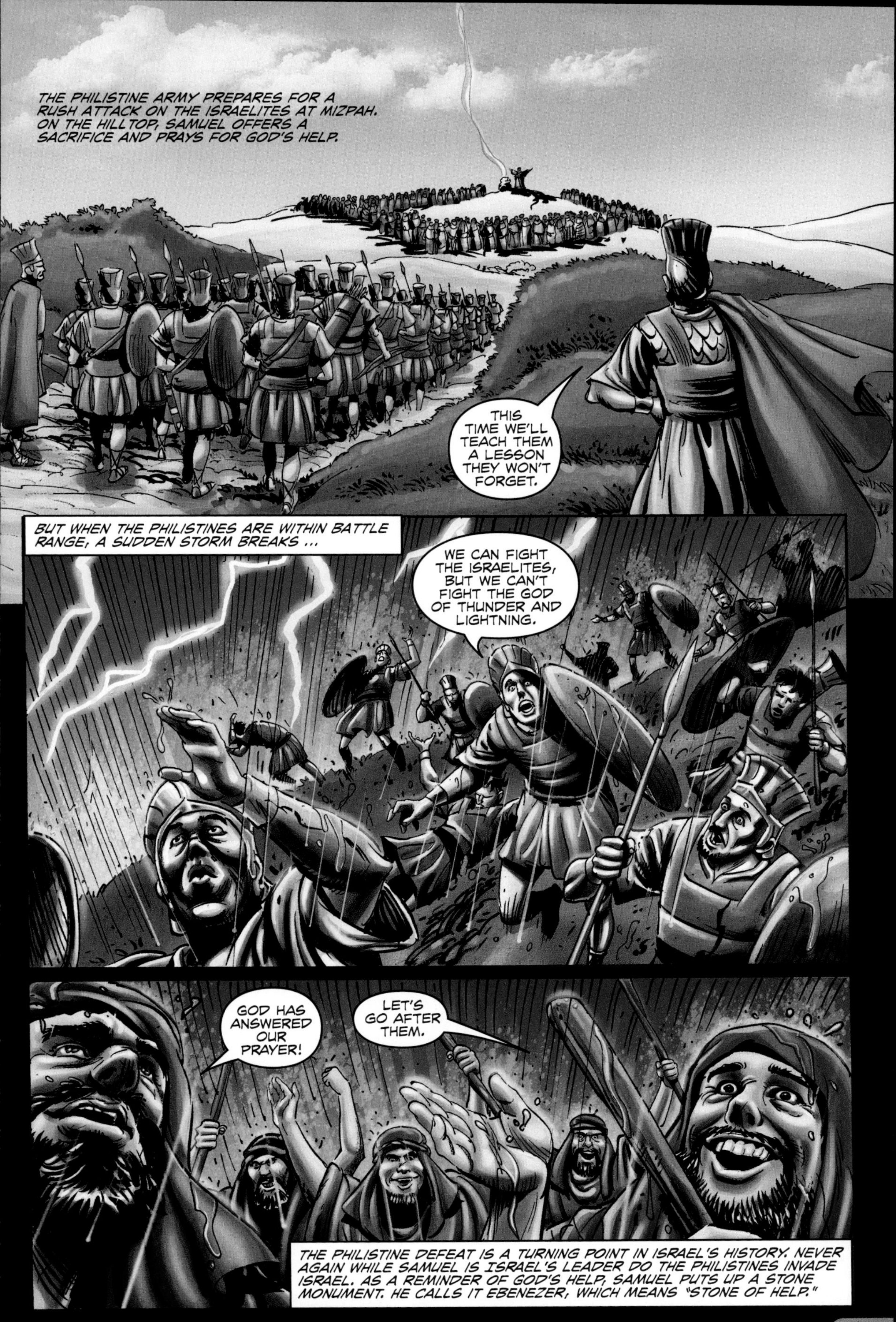
THE PHILISTINE ARMY PREPARES FOR A RUSH ATTACK ON THE ISRAELITES AT MIZPAH. ON THE HILLTOP, SAMUEL OFFERS A SACRIFICE AND PRAYS FOR GOD'S HELP.
THIS TIME WE'LL TEACH THEM A LESSON THEY WON'T FORGET.
BUT WHEN THE PHILISTINES ARE WITHIN BATTLE RANGE, A SUDDEN STORM BREAKS ...
WE CAN FIGHT THE ISRAELITES, BUT WE CAN'T FIGHT THE GOD OF THUNDER AND LIGHTNING.
GOD HAS ANSWERED OUR PRAYER!
LET'S GO AFTER THEM.
THE PHILISTINE DEFEAT IS A TURNING POINT IN ISRAEL'S HISTORY. NEVER AGAIN WHILE SAMUEL IS ISRAEL'S LEADER DO THE PHILISTINES INVADE ISRAEL. AS A REMINDER OF GOD'S HELP, SAMUEL PUTS UP A STONE MONUMENT. HE CALLS IT EBENEZER, WHICH MEANS "STONE OF HELP."

Search for a King

BASED ON 1 SAMUEL 8—10

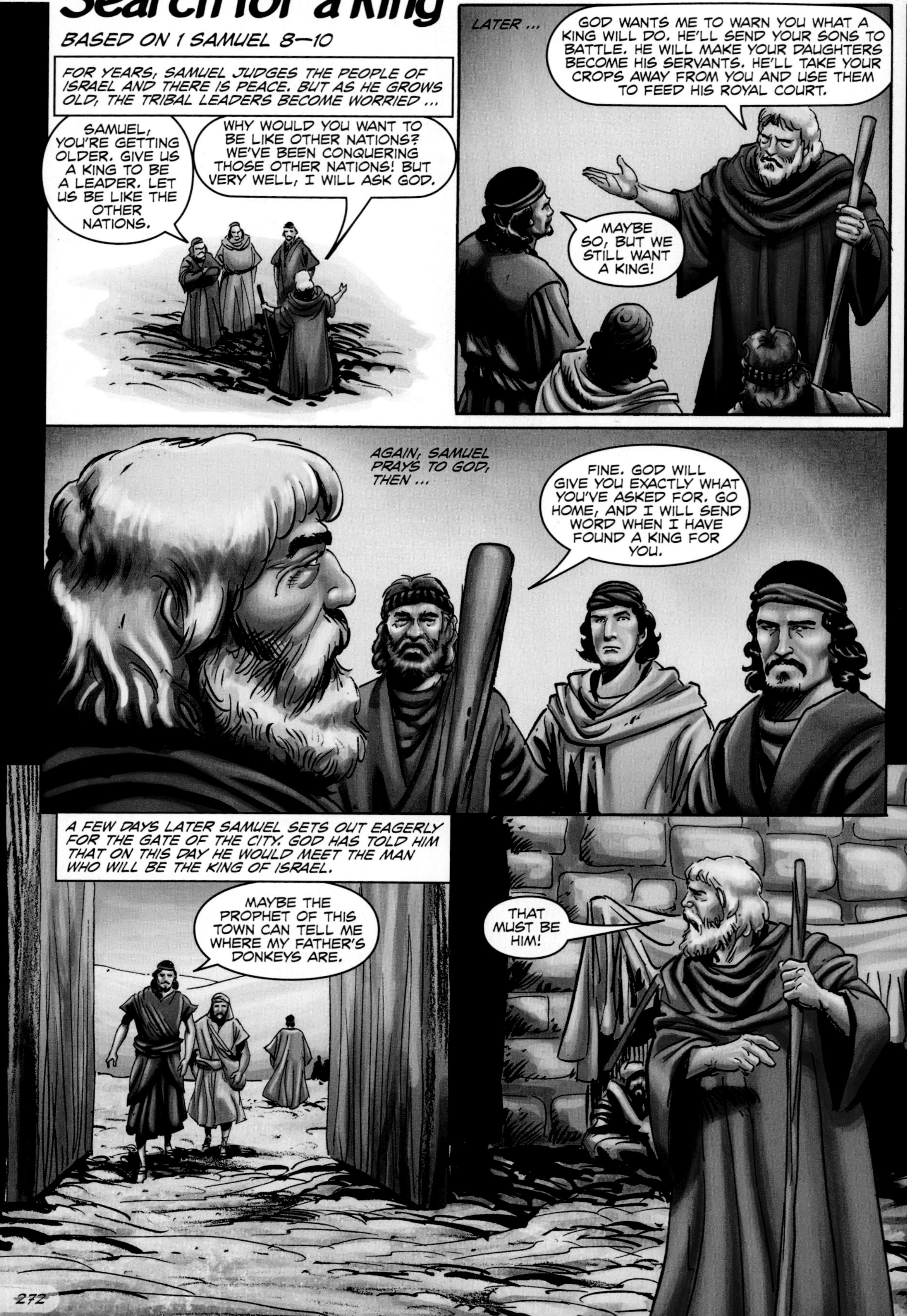
FOR YEARS, SAMUEL JUDGES THE PEOPLE OF ISRAEL AND THERE IS PEACE. BUT AS HE GROWS OLD, THE TRIBAL LEADERS BECOME WORRIED ...
SAMUEL, YOU'RE GETTING OLDER. GIVE US A KING TO BE A LEADER. LET US BE LIKE THE OTHER NATIONS.
WHY WOULD YOU WANT TO BE LIKE OTHER NATIONS? WE'VE BEEN CONQUERING THOSE OTHER NATIONS! BUT VERY WELL, I WILL ASK GOD.
LATER ...
GOD WANTS ME TO WARN YOU WHAT A KING WILL DO. HE'LL SEND YOUR SONS TO BATTLE. HE WILL MAKE YOUR DAUGHTERS BECOME HIS SERVANTS. HE'LL TAKE YOUR CROPS AWAY FROM YOU AND USE THEM TO FEED HIS ROYAL COURT.
MAYBE SO, BUT WE STILL WANT A KING!
AGAIN, SAMUEL PRAYS TO GOD, THEN ...
FINE. GOD WILL GIVE YOU EXACTLY WHAT YOU'VE ASKED FOR. GO HOME, AND I WILL SEND WORD WHEN I HAVE FOUND A KING FOR YOU.
A FEW DAYS LATER SAMUEL SETS OUT EAGERLY FOR THE GATE OF THE CITY. GOD HAS TOLD HIM THAT ON THIS DAY HE WOULD MEET THE MAN WHO WILL BE THE KING OF ISRAEL.
MAYBE THE PROPHET OF THIS TOWN CAN TELL ME WHERE MY FATHER'S DONKEYS ARE.
THAT MUST BE HIM!

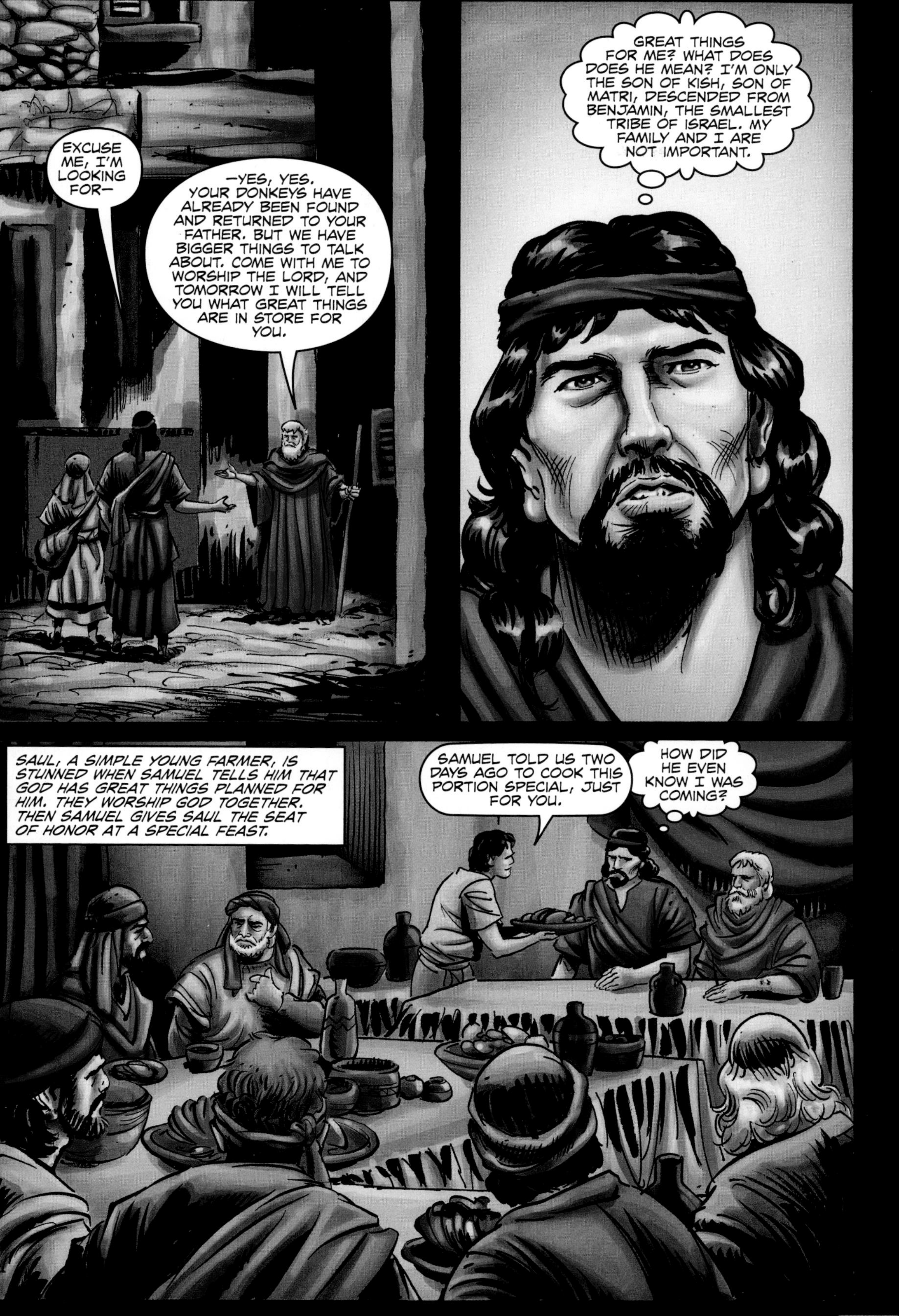
EXCUSE ME, I'M LOOKING FOR—
—YES, YES. YOUR DONKEYS HAVE ALREADY BEEN FOUND AND RETURNED TO YOUR FATHER. BUT WE HAVE BIGGER THINGS TO TALK ABOUT. COME WITH ME TO WORSHIP THE LORD, AND TOMORROW I WILL TELL YOU WHAT GREAT THINGS ARE IN STORE FOR YOU.
GREAT THINGS FOR ME? WHAT DOES DOES HE MEAN? I'M ONLY THE SON OF KISH, SON OF MATRI, DESCENDED FROM BENJAMIN, THE SMALLEST TRIBE OF ISRAEL. MY FAMILY AND I ARE NOT IMPORTANT.
SAUL, A SIMPLE YOUNG FARMER, IS STUNNED WHEN SAMUEL TELLS HIM THAT GOD HAS GREAT THINGS PLANNED FOR HIM. THEY WORSHIP GOD TOGETHER. THEN SAMUEL GIVES SAUL THE SEAT OF HONOR AT A SPECIAL FEAST.
SAMUEL TOLD US TWO DAYS AGO TO COOK THIS PORTION SPECIAL, JUST FOR YOU.
HOW DID HE EVEN KNOW I WAS COMING?

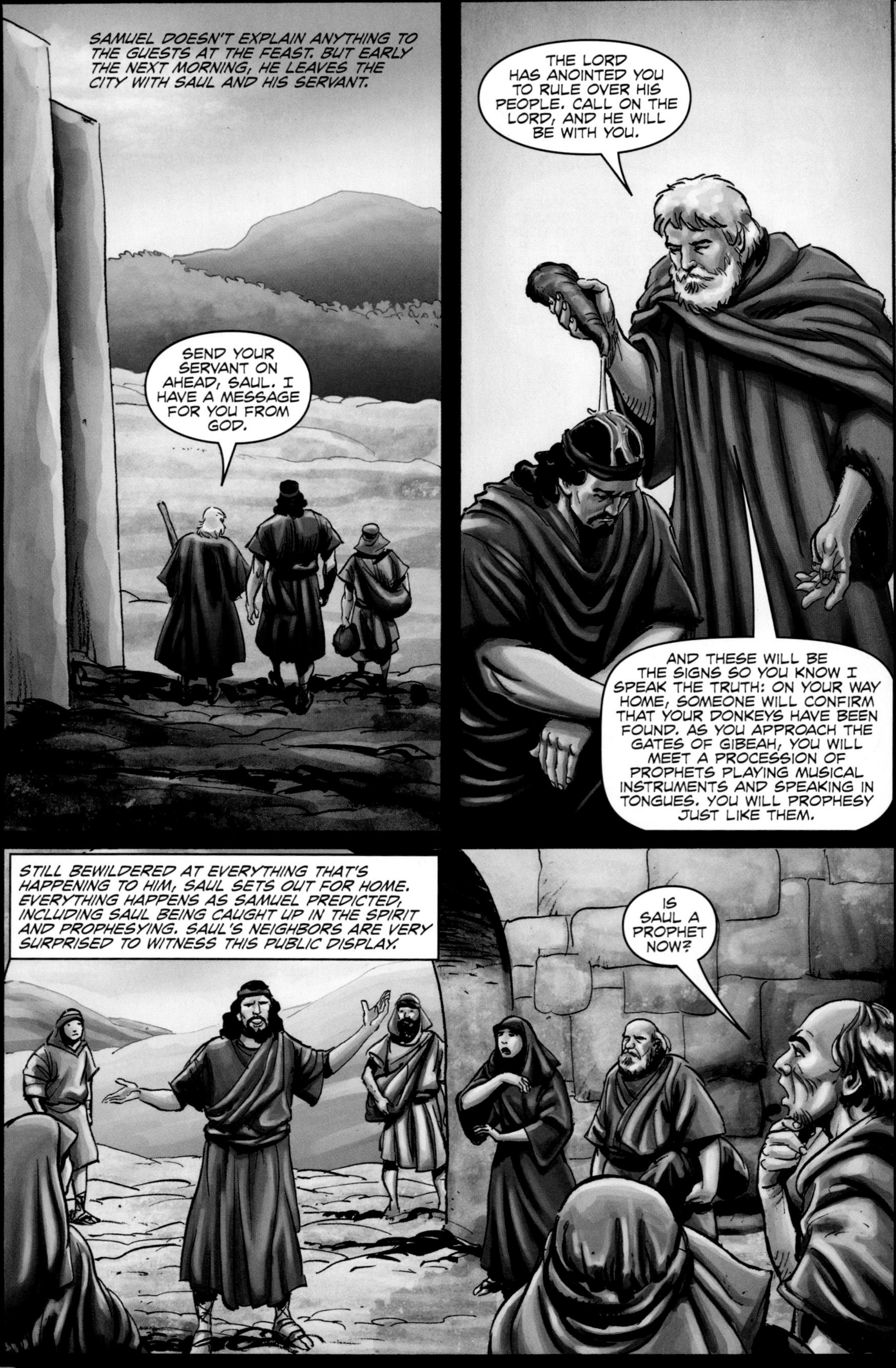
SAMUEL DOESN'T EXPLAIN ANYTHING TO THE GUESTS AT THE FEAST. BUT EARLY THE NEXT MORNING, HE LEAVES THE CITY WITH SAUL AND HIS SERVANT.
SEND YOUR SERVANT ON AHEAD, SAUL. I HAVE A MESSAGE FOR YOU FROM GOD.
THE LORD HAS ANOINTED YOU TO RULE OVER HIS PEOPLE. CALL ON THE LORD, AND HE WILL BE WITH YOU.
AND THESE WILL BE THE SIGNS SO YOU KNOW I SPEAK THE TRUTH: ON YOUR WAY HOME, SOMEONE WILL CONFIRM THAT YOUR DONKEYS HAVE BEEN FOUND. AS YOU APPROACH THE GATES OF GIBEAH, YOU WILL MEET A PROCESSION OF PROPHETS PLAYING MUSICAL INSTRUMENTS AND SPEAKING IN TONGUES. YOU WILL PROPHESY JUST LIKE THEM.
STILL BEWILDERED AT EVERYTHING THAT'S HAPPENING TO HIM, SAUL SETS OUT FOR HOME. EVERYTHING HAPPENS AS SAMUEL PREDICTED, INCLUDING SAUL BEING CAUGHT UP IN THE SPIRIT AND PROPHESYING. SAUL'S NEIGHBORS ARE VERY SURPRISED TO WITNESS THIS PUBLIC DISPLAY.
IS SAUL A PROPHET NOW?

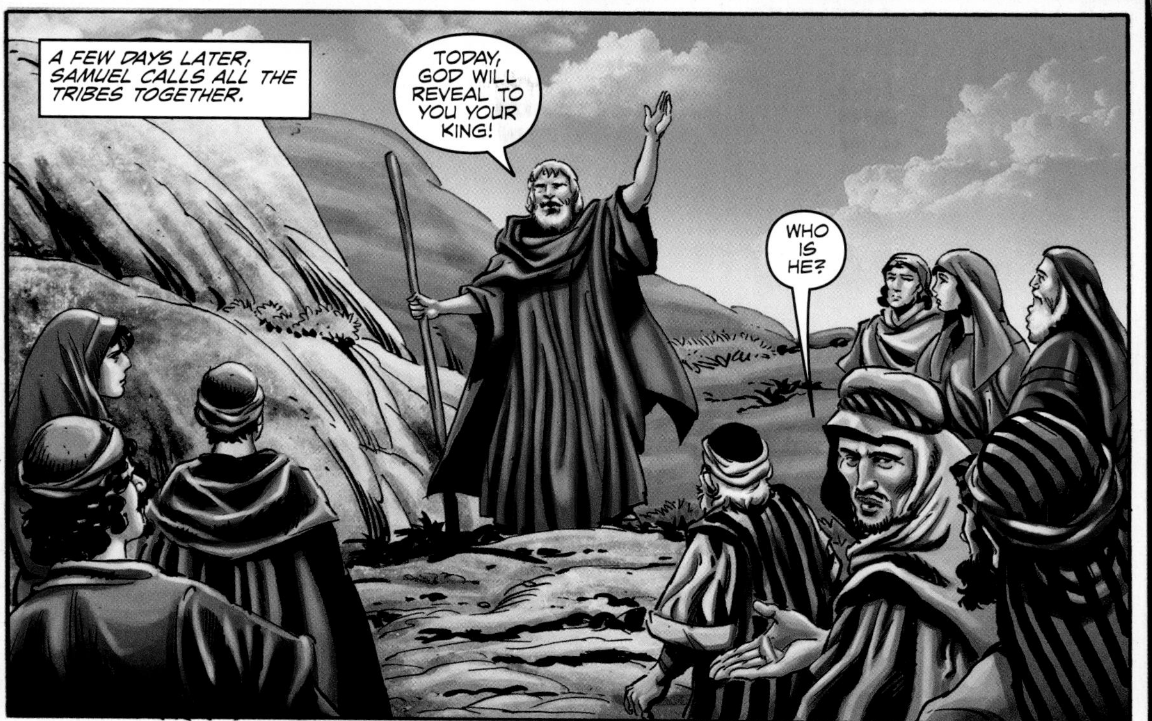
A FEW DAYS LATER, SAMUEL CALLS ALL THE TRIBES TOGETHER.
TODAY, GOD WILL REVEAL TO YOU YOUR KING!
WHO IS HE?

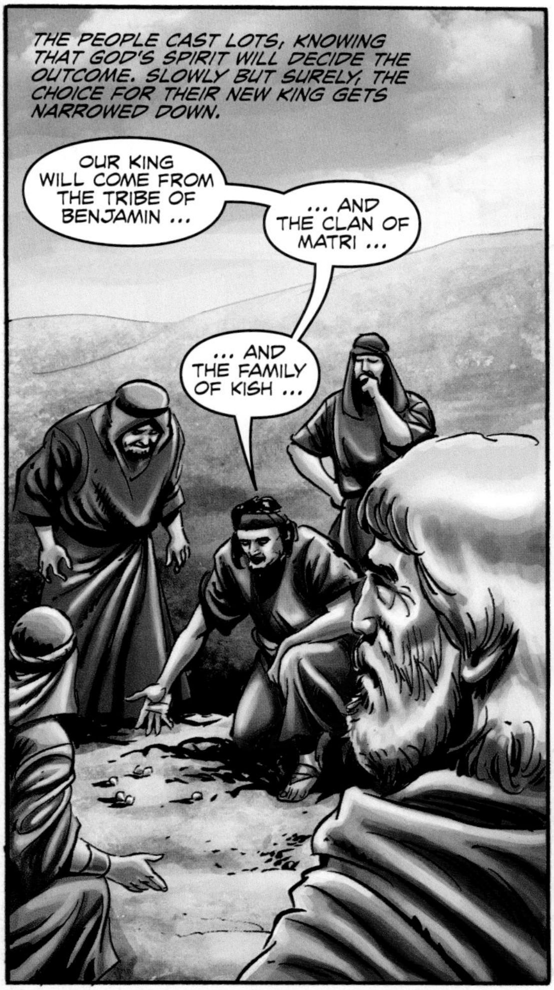
THE PEOPLE CAST LOTS, KNOWING THAT GOD'S SPIRIT WILL DECIDE THE OUTCOME. SLOWLY BUT SURELY, THE CHOICE FOR THEIR NEW KING GETS NARROWED DOWN.
OUR KING WILL COME FROM THE TRIBE OF BENJAMIN ...
... AND THE CLAN OF MATRI ...
... AND THE FAMILY OF KISH ...

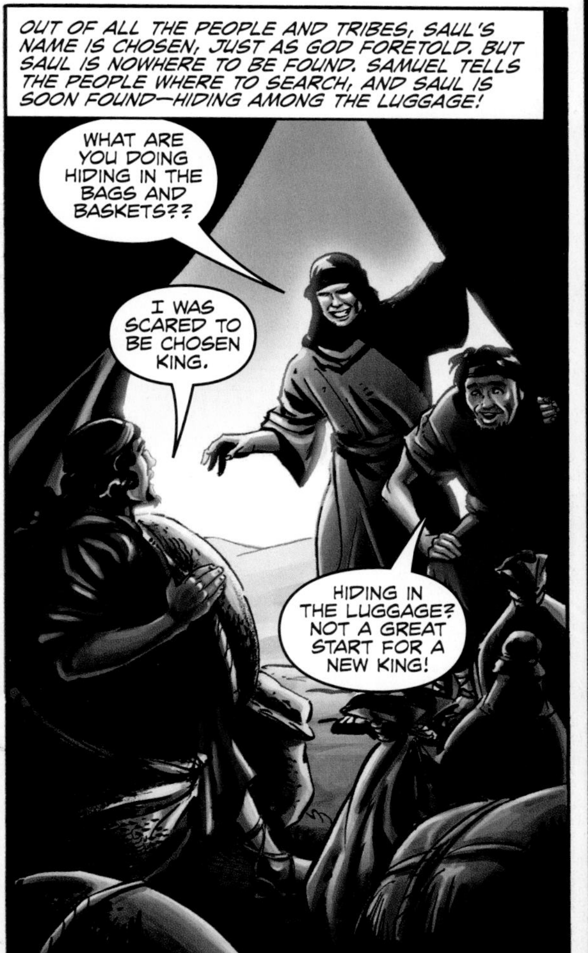
OUT OF ALL THE PEOPLE AND TRIBES, SAUL'S NAME IS CHOSEN, JUST AS GOD FORETOLD. BUT SAUL IS NOWHERE TO BE FOUND. SAMUEL TELLS THE PEOPLE WHERE TO SEARCH, AND SAUL IS SOON FOUND—HIDING AMONG THE LUGGAGE!
WHAT ARE YOU DOING HIDING IN THE BAGS AND BASKETS??
I WAS SCARED TO BE CHOSEN KING.
HIDING IN THE LUGGAGE? NOT A GREAT START FOR A NEW KING!

Saul's Bravery *BASED ON 1 SAMUEL 11–12*

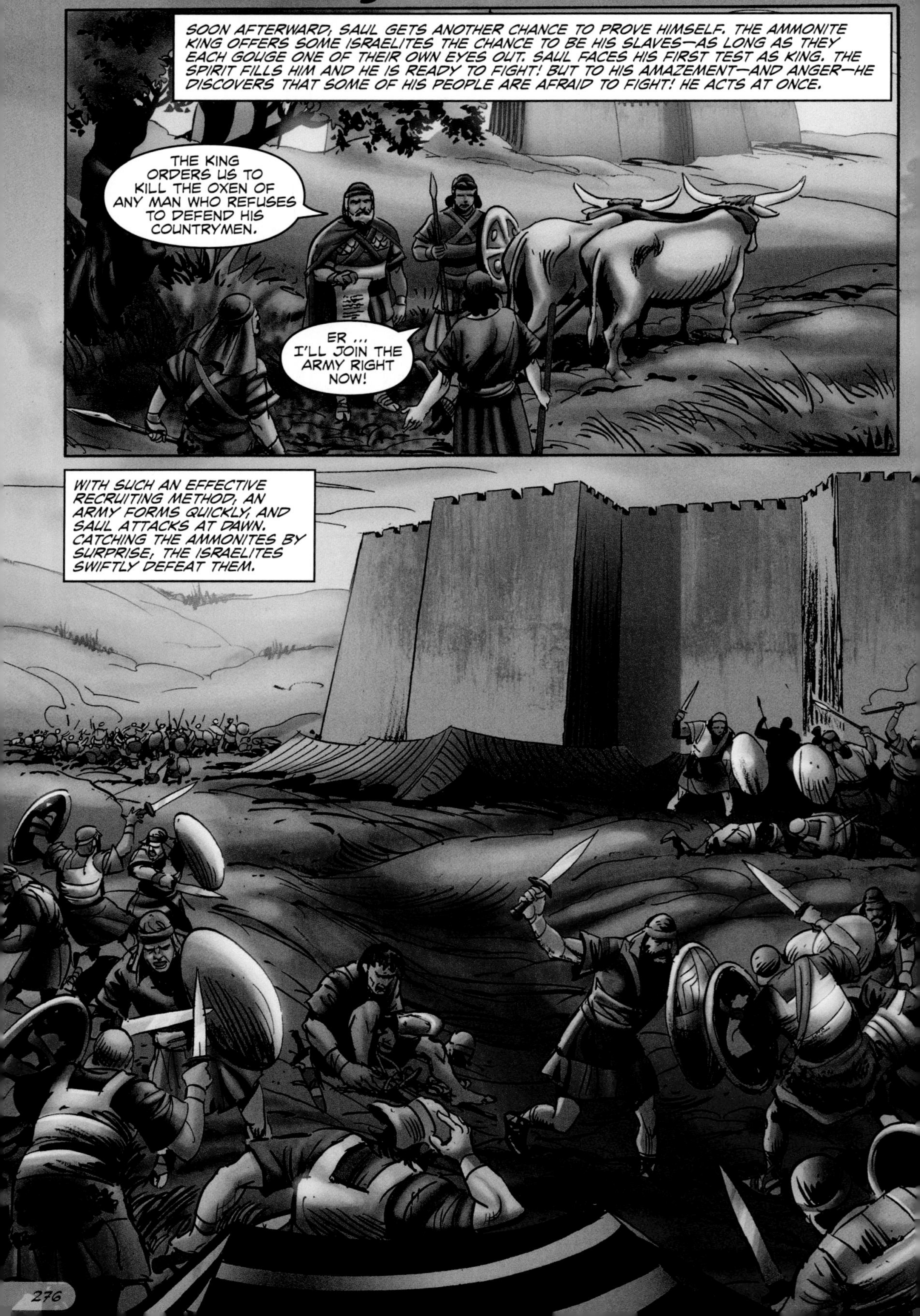
SOON AFTERWARD, SAUL GETS ANOTHER CHANCE TO PROVE HIMSELF. THE AMMONITE KING OFFERS SOME ISRAELITES THE CHANCE TO BE HIS SLAVES—AS LONG AS THEY EACH GOUGE ONE OF THEIR OWN EYES OUT. SAUL FACES HIS FIRST TEST AS KING. THE SPIRIT FILLS HIM AND HE IS READY TO FIGHT! BUT TO HIS AMAZEMENT—AND ANGER—HE DISCOVERS THAT SOME OF HIS PEOPLE ARE AFRAID TO FIGHT! HE ACTS AT ONCE.
THE KING ORDERS US TO KILL THE OXEN OF ANY MAN WHO REFUSES TO DEFEND HIS COUNTRYMEN.
ER ... I'LL JOIN THE ARMY RIGHT NOW!
WITH SUCH AN EFFECTIVE RECRUITING METHOD, AN ARMY FORMS QUICKLY, AND SAUL ATTACKS AT DAWN. CATCHING THE AMMONITES BY SURPRISE, THE ISRAELITES SWIFTLY DEFEAT THEM.

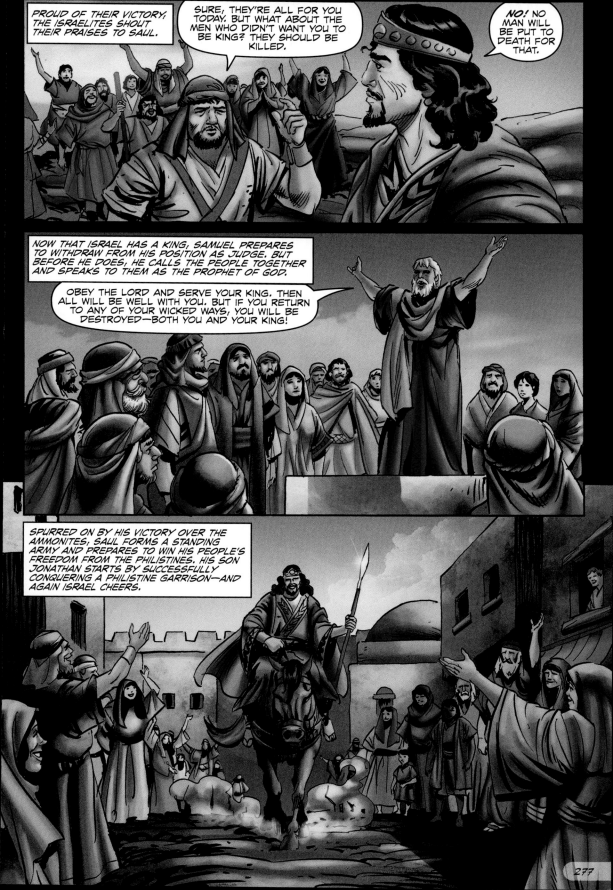

PROUD OF THEIR VICTORY, THE ISRAELITES SHOUT THEIR PRAISES TO SAUL.

SURE, THEY'RE ALL FOR YOU TODAY. BUT WHAT ABOUT THE MEN WHO DIDN'T WANT YOU TO BE KING? THEY SHOULD BE KILLED.

NO! NO MAN WILL BE PUT TO DEATH FOR THAT.

NOW THAT ISRAEL HAS A KING, SAMUEL PREPARES TO WITHDRAW FROM HIS POSITION AS JUDGE. BUT BEFORE HE DOES, HE CALLS THE PEOPLE TOGETHER AND SPEAKS TO THEM AS THE PROPHET OF GOD.

OBEY THE LORD AND SERVE YOUR KING. THEN ALL WILL BE WELL WITH YOU. BUT IF YOU RETURN TO ANY OF YOUR WICKED WAYS, YOU WILL BE DESTROYED—BOTH YOU AND YOUR KING!

SPURRED ON BY HIS VICTORY OVER THE AMMONITES, SAUL FORMS A STANDING ARMY AND PREPARES TO WIN HIS PEOPLE'S FREEDOM FROM THE PHILISTINES. HIS SON JONATHAN STARTS BY SUCCESSFULLY CONQUERING A PHILISTINE GARRISON—AND AGAIN ISRAEL CHEERS.

Honeycomb Argument
BASED ON 1 SAMUEL 13—14

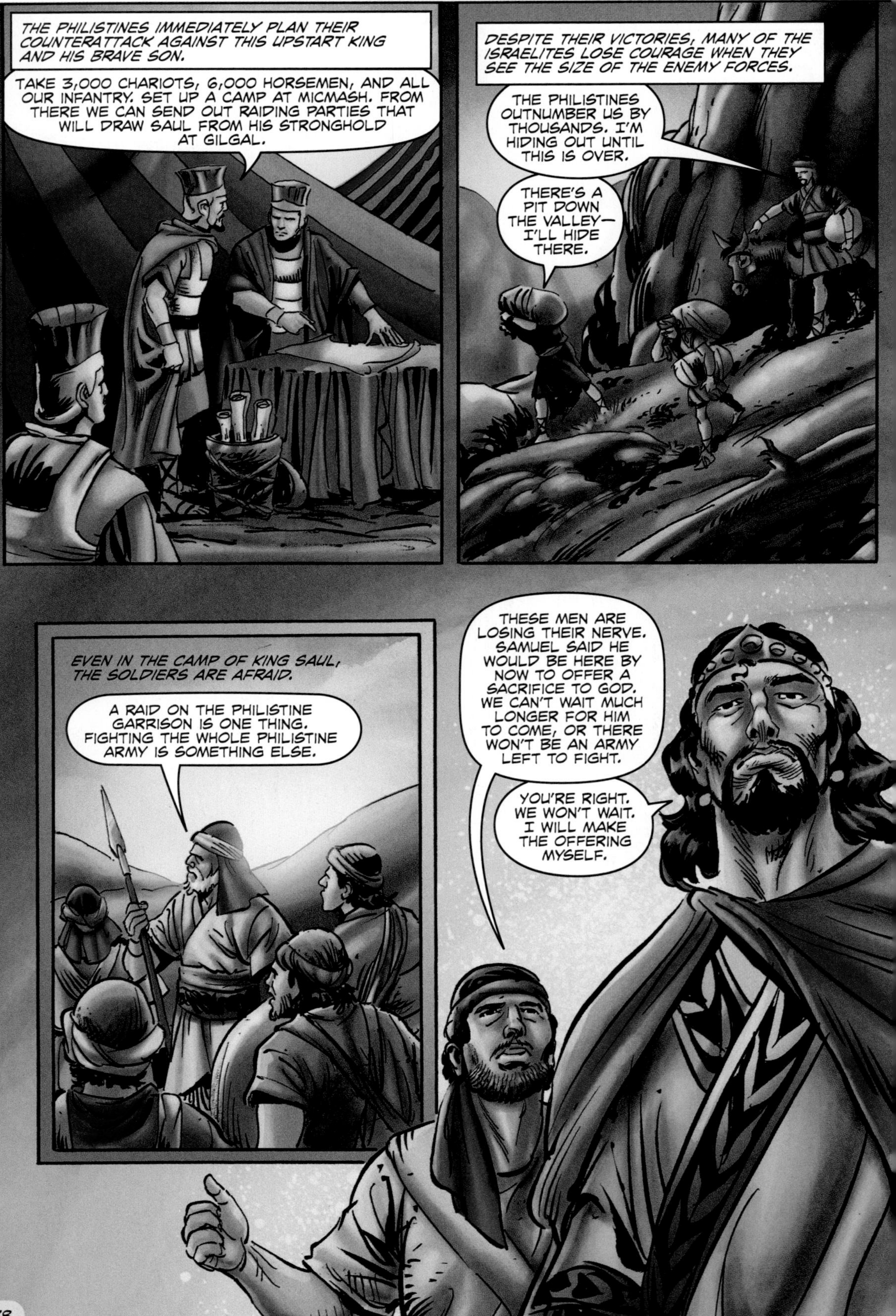
THE PHILISTINES IMMEDIATELY PLAN THEIR COUNTERATTACK AGAINST THIS UPSTART KING AND HIS BRAVE SON.
TAKE 3,000 CHARIOTS, 6,000 HORSEMEN, AND ALL OUR INFANTRY. SET UP A CAMP AT MICMASH. FROM THERE WE CAN SEND OUT RAIDING PARTIES THAT WILL DRAW SAUL FROM HIS STRONGHOLD AT GILGAL.
DESPITE THEIR VICTORIES, MANY OF THE ISRAELITES LOSE COURAGE WHEN THEY SEE THE SIZE OF THE ENEMY FORCES.
THE PHILISTINES OUTNUMBER US BY THOUSANDS. I'M HIDING OUT UNTIL THIS IS OVER.
THERE'S A PIT DOWN THE VALLEY— I'LL HIDE THERE.
EVEN IN THE CAMP OF KING SAUL, THE SOLDIERS ARE AFRAID.
A RAID ON THE PHILISTINE GARRISON IS ONE THING. FIGHTING THE WHOLE PHILISTINE ARMY IS SOMETHING ELSE.
THESE MEN ARE LOSING THEIR NERVE. SAMUEL SAID HE WOULD BE HERE BY NOW TO OFFER A SACRIFICE TO GOD. WE CAN'T WAIT MUCH LONGER FOR HIM TO COME, OR THERE WON'T BE AN ARMY LEFT TO FIGHT.
YOU'RE RIGHT. WE WON'T WAIT. I WILL MAKE THE OFFERING MYSELF.

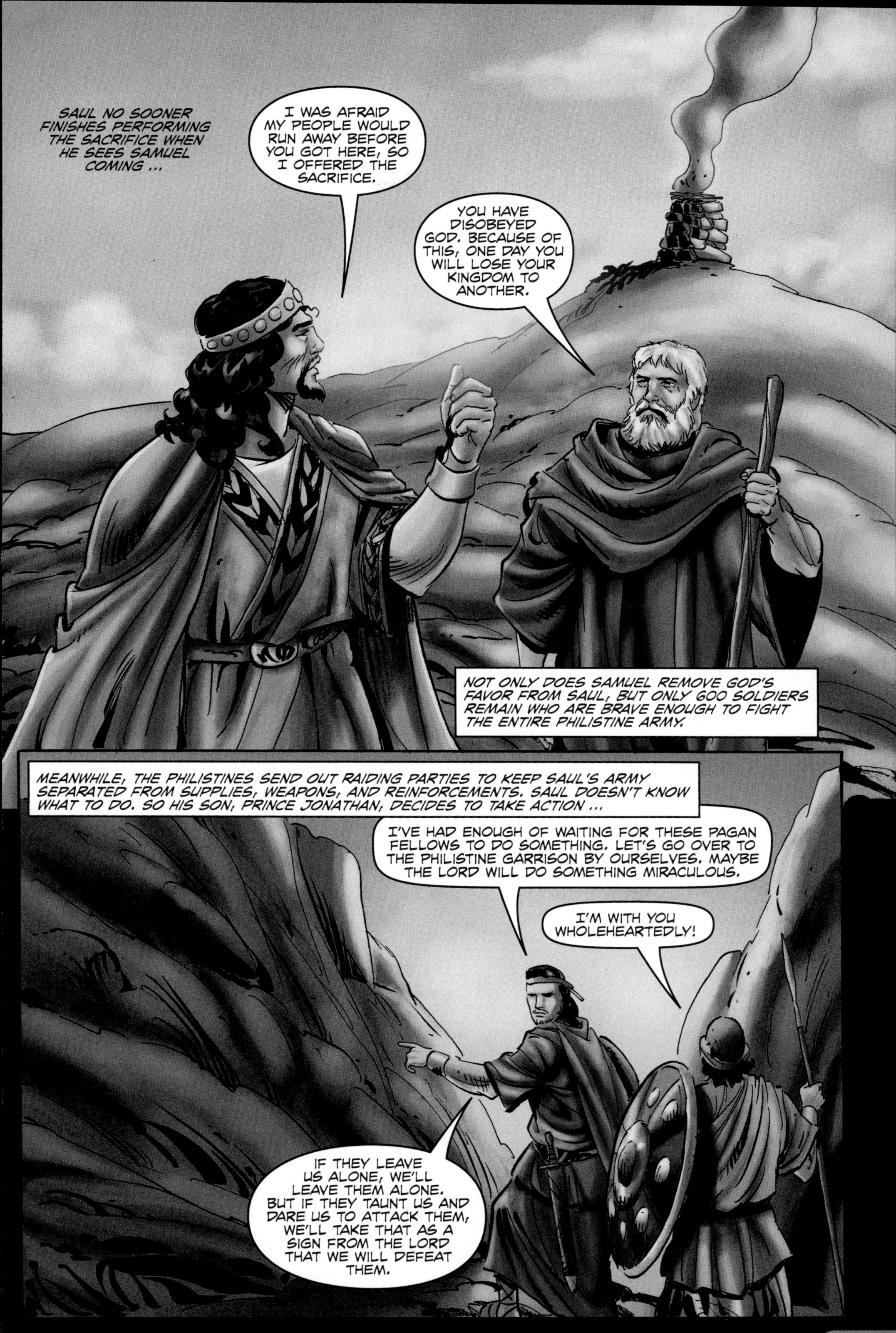
SAUL NO SOONER FINISHES PERFORMING THE SACRIFICE WHEN HE SEES SAMUEL COMING ...
I WAS AFRAID MY PEOPLE WOULD RUN AWAY BEFORE YOU GOT HERE, SO I OFFERED THE SACRIFICE.
YOU HAVE DISOBEYED GOD. BECAUSE OF THIS, ONE DAY YOU WILL LOSE YOUR KINGDOM TO ANOTHER.
NOT ONLY DOES SAMUEL REMOVE GOD'S FAVOR FROM SAUL, BUT ONLY 600 SOLDIERS REMAIN WHO ARE BRAVE ENOUGH TO FIGHT THE ENTIRE PHILISTINE ARMY.
MEANWHILE, THE PHILISTINES SEND OUT RAIDING PARTIES TO KEEP SAUL'S ARMY SEPARATED FROM SUPPLIES, WEAPONS, AND REINFORCEMENTS. SAUL DOESN'T KNOW WHAT TO DO. SO HIS SON, PRINCE JONATHAN, DECIDES TO TAKE ACTION ...
I'VE HAD ENOUGH OF WAITING FOR THESE PAGAN FELLOWS TO DO SOMETHING. LET'S GO OVER TO THE PHILISTINE GARRISON BY OURSELVES. MAYBE THE LORD WILL DO SOMETHING MIRACULOUS.
I'M WITH YOU WHOLEHEARTEDLY!
IF THEY LEAVE US ALONE, WE'LL LEAVE THEM ALONE. BUT IF THEY TAUNT US AND DARE US TO ATTACK THEM, WE'LL TAKE THAT AS A SIGN FROM THE LORD THAT WE WILL DEFEAT THEM.

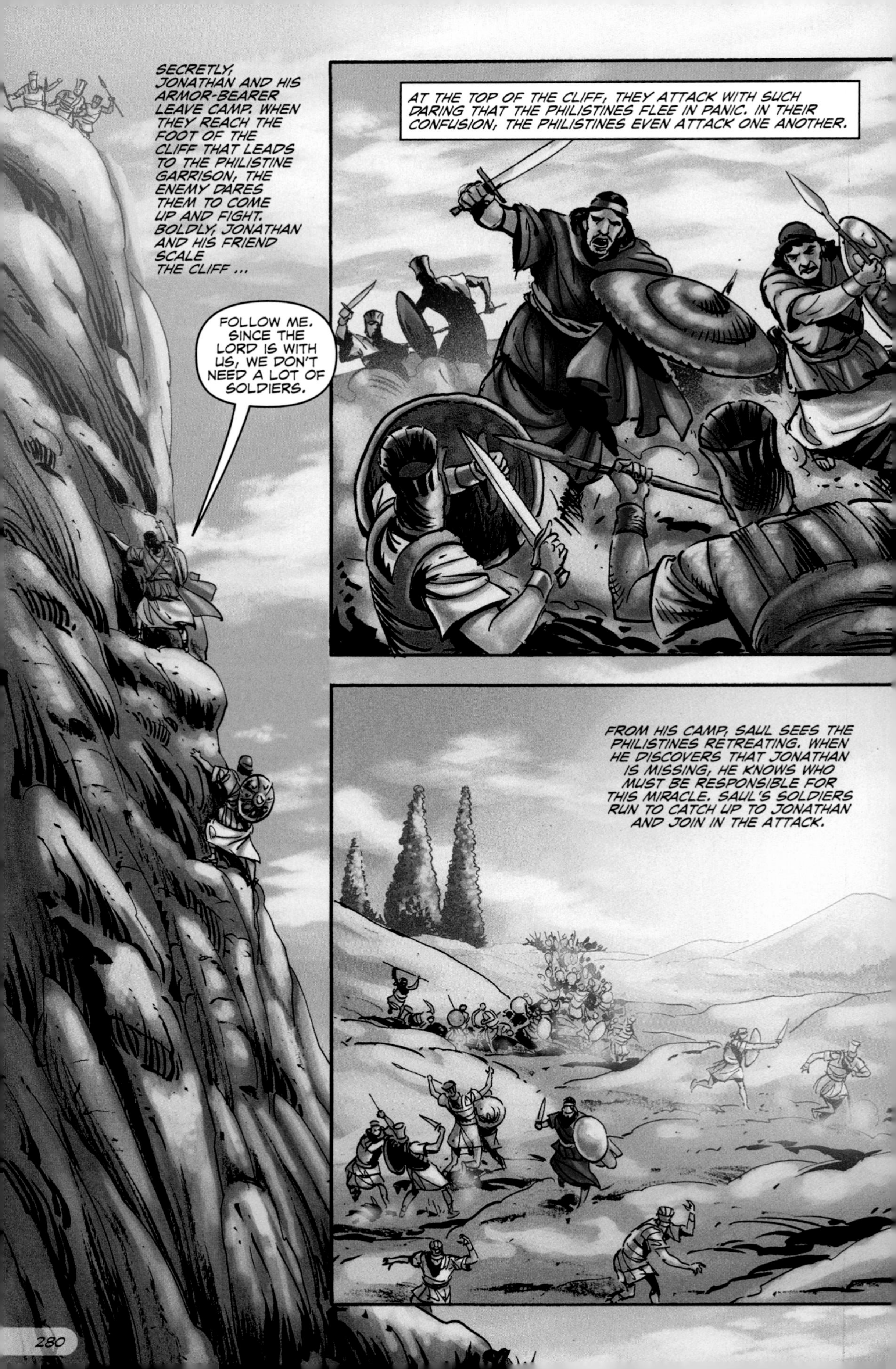
SECRETLY, JONATHAN AND HIS ARMOR-BEARER LEAVE CAMP. WHEN THEY REACH THE FOOT OF THE CLIFF THAT LEADS TO THE PHILISTINE GARRISON, THE ENEMY DARES THEM TO COME UP AND FIGHT. BOLDLY, JONATHAN AND HIS FRIEND SCALE THE CLIFF ...
FOLLOW ME. SINCE THE LORD IS WITH US, WE DON'T NEED A LOT OF SOLDIERS.
AT THE TOP OF THE CLIFF, THEY ATTACK WITH SUCH DARING THAT THE PHILISTINES FLEE IN PANIC. IN THEIR CONFUSION, THE PHILISTINES EVEN ATTACK ONE ANOTHER.
FROM HIS CAMP, SAUL SEES THE PHILISTINES RETREATING. WHEN HE DISCOVERS THAT JONATHAN IS MISSING, HE KNOWS WHO MUST BE RESPONSIBLE FOR THIS MIRACLE. SAUL'S SOLDIERS RUN TO CATCH UP TO JONATHAN AND JOIN IN THE ATTACK.

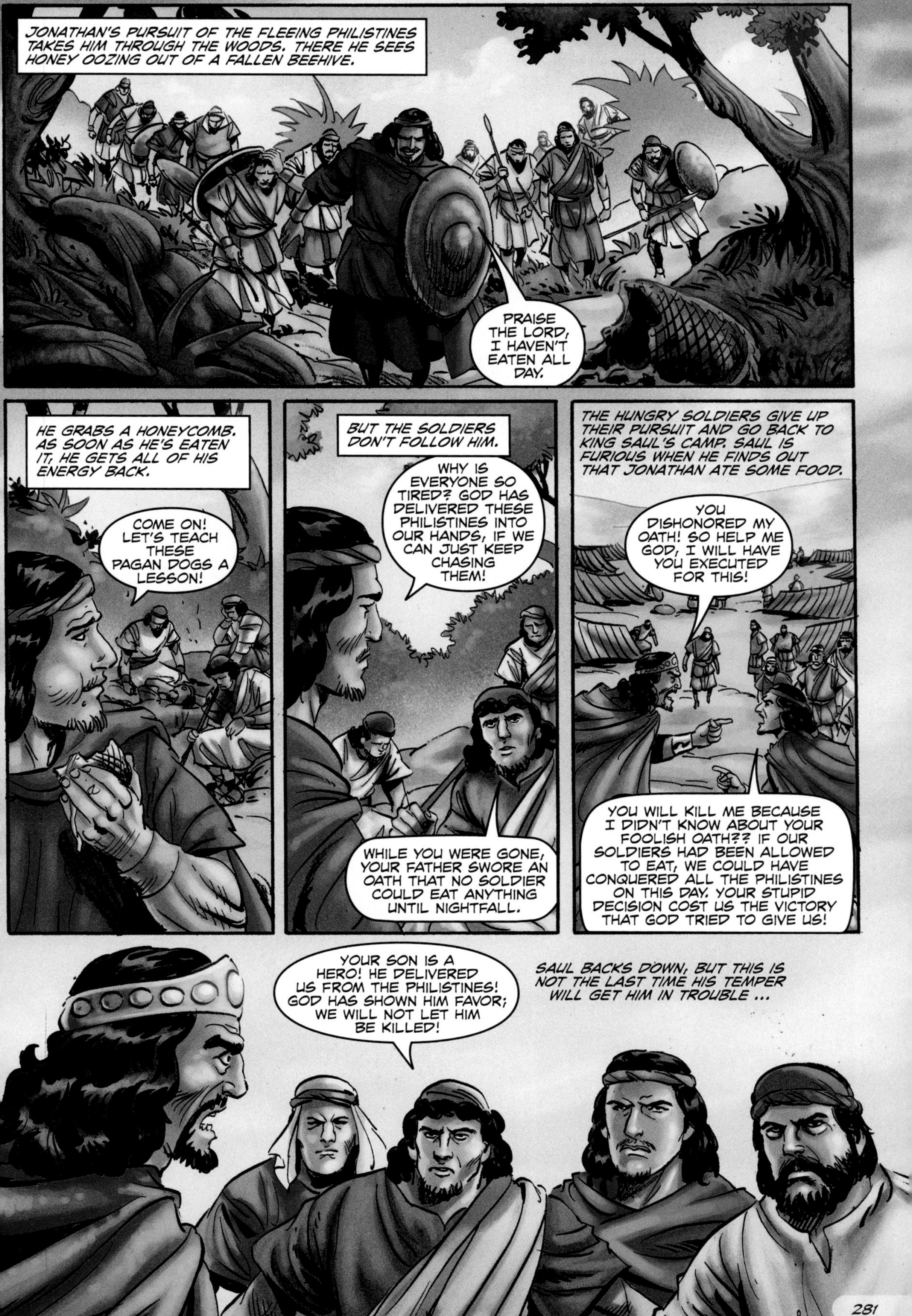
JONATHAN'S PURSUIT OF THE FLEEING PHILISTINES TAKES HIM THROUGH THE WOODS. THERE HE SEES HONEY OOZING OUT OF A FALLEN BEEHIVE.
PRAISE THE LORD, I HAVEN'T EATEN ALL DAY.
HE GRABS A HONEYCOMB. AS SOON AS HE'S EATEN IT, HE GETS ALL OF HIS ENERGY BACK.
COME ON! LET'S TEACH THESE PAGAN DOGS A LESSON!
BUT THE SOLDIERS DON'T FOLLOW HIM.
WHY IS EVERYONE SO TIRED? GOD HAS DELIVERED THESE PHILISTINES INTO OUR HANDS, IF WE CAN JUST KEEP CHASING THEM!
WHILE YOU WERE GONE, YOUR FATHER SWORE AN OATH THAT NO SOLDIER COULD EAT ANYTHING UNTIL NIGHTFALL.
THE HUNGRY SOLDIERS GIVE UP THEIR PURSUIT AND GO BACK TO KING SAUL'S CAMP. SAUL IS FURIOUS WHEN HE FINDS OUT THAT JONATHAN ATE SOME FOOD.
YOU DISHONORED MY OATH! SO HELP ME GOD, I WILL HAVE YOU EXECUTED FOR THIS!
YOU WILL KILL ME BECAUSE I DIDN'T KNOW ABOUT YOUR FOOLISH OATH?? IF OUR SOLDIERS HAD BEEN ALLOWED TO EAT, WE COULD HAVE CONQUERED ALL THE PHILISTINES ON THIS DAY. YOUR STUPID DECISION COST US THE VICTORY THAT GOD TRIED TO GIVE US!
YOUR SON IS A HERO! HE DELIVERED US FROM THE PHILISTINES! GOD HAS SHOWN HIM FAVOR; WE WILL NOT LET HIM BE KILLED!
SAUL BACKS DOWN, BUT THIS IS NOT THE LAST TIME HIS TEMPER WILL GET HIM IN TROUBLE ...

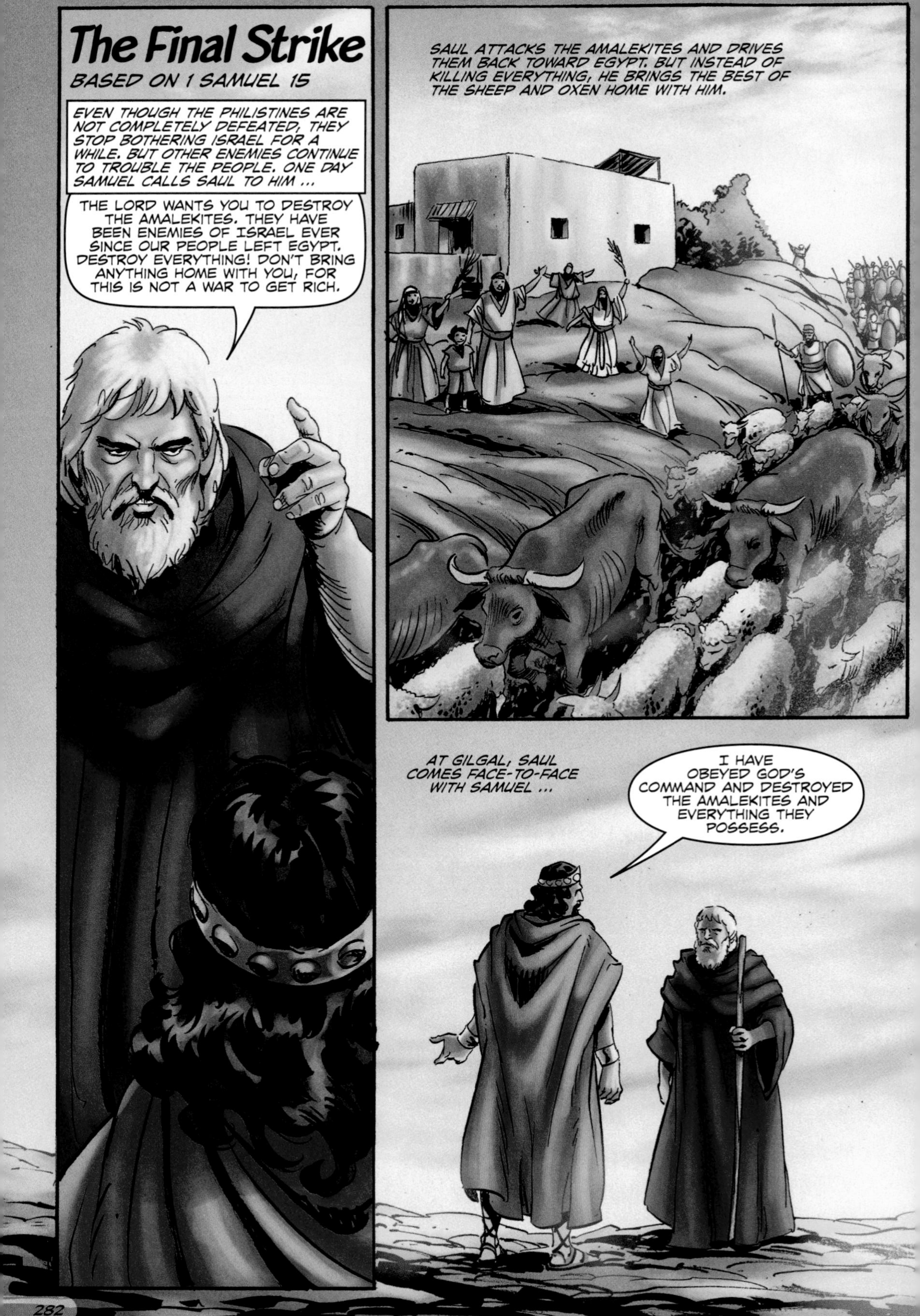
The Final Strike
BASED ON 1 SAMUEL 15
EVEN THOUGH THE PHILISTINES ARE NOT COMPLETELY DEFEATED, THEY STOP BOTHERING ISRAEL FOR A WHILE. BUT OTHER ENEMIES CONTINUE TO TROUBLE THE PEOPLE. ONE DAY SAMUEL CALLS SAUL TO HIM ...
THE LORD WANTS YOU TO DESTROY THE AMALEKITES. THEY HAVE BEEN ENEMIES OF ISRAEL EVER SINCE OUR PEOPLE LEFT EGYPT. DESTROY EVERYTHING! DON'T BRING ANYTHING HOME WITH YOU, FOR THIS IS NOT A WAR TO GET RICH.
SAUL ATTACKS THE AMALEKITES AND DRIVES THEM BACK TOWARD EGYPT. BUT INSTEAD OF KILLING EVERYTHING, HE BRINGS THE BEST OF THE SHEEP AND OXEN HOME WITH HIM.
AT GILGAL, SAUL COMES FACE-TO-FACE WITH SAMUEL ...
I HAVE OBEYED GOD'S COMMAND AND DESTROYED THE AMALEKITES AND EVERYTHING THEY POSSESS.

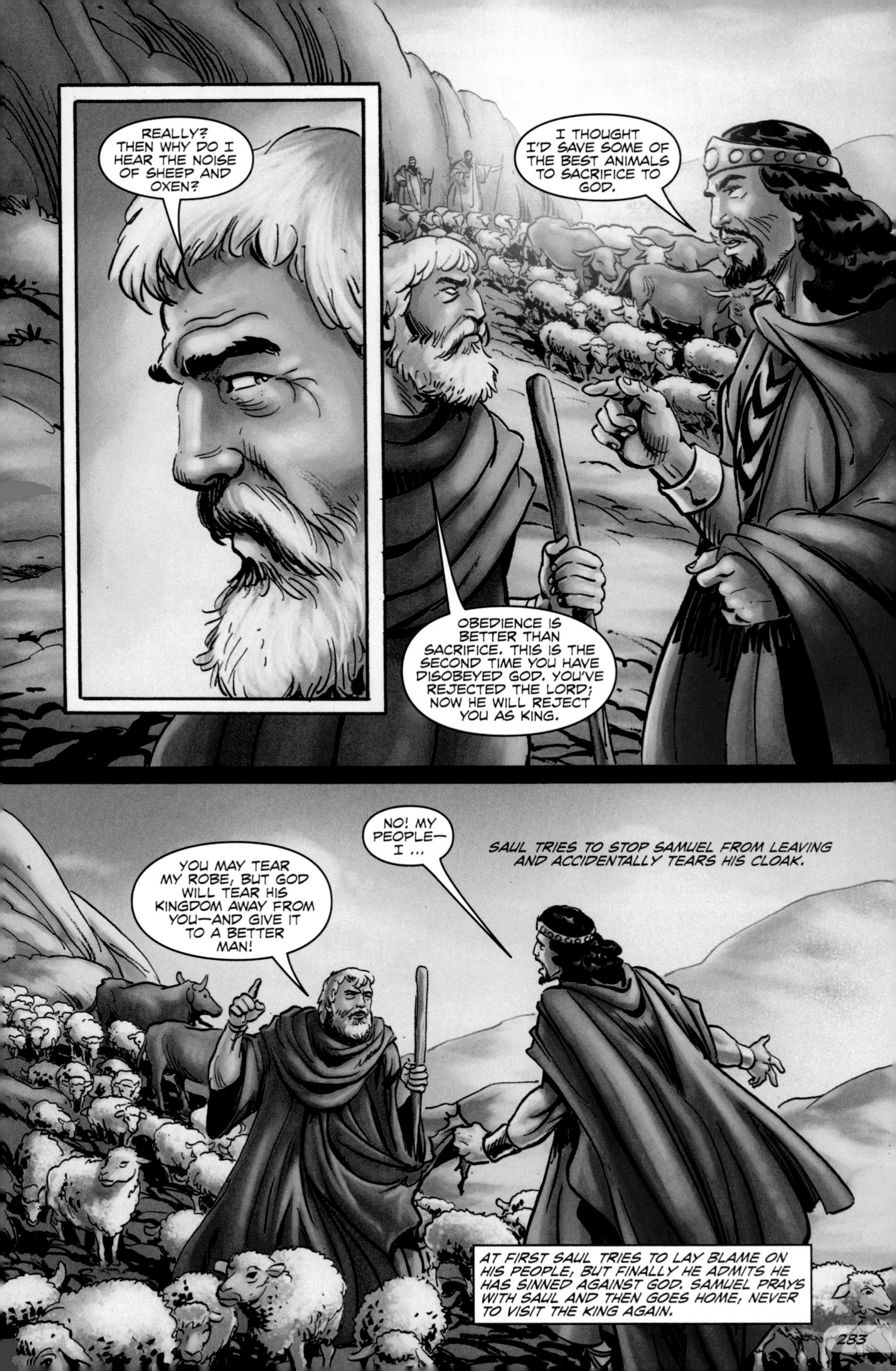
REALLY? THEN WHY DO I HEAR THE NOISE OF SHEEP AND OXEN?
I THOUGHT I'D SAVE SOME OF THE BEST ANIMALS TO SACRIFICE TO GOD.
OBEDIENCE IS BETTER THAN SACRIFICE. THIS IS THE SECOND TIME YOU HAVE DISOBEYED GOD. YOU'VE REJECTED THE LORD; NOW HE WILL REJECT YOU AS KING.
SAUL TRIES TO STOP SAMUEL FROM LEAVING AND ACCIDENTALLY TEARS HIS CLOAK.
NO! MY PEOPLE— I ...
YOU MAY TEAR MY ROBE, BUT GOD WILL TEAR HIS KINGDOM AWAY FROM YOU—AND GIVE IT TO A BETTER MAN!
AT FIRST SAUL TRIES TO LAY BLAME ON HIS PEOPLE, BUT FINALLY HE ADMITS HE HAS SINNED AGAINST GOD. SAMUEL PRAYS WITH SAUL AND THEN GOES HOME, NEVER TO VISIT THE KING AGAIN.

God's New King

BASED ON 1 SAMUEL 16:1–13

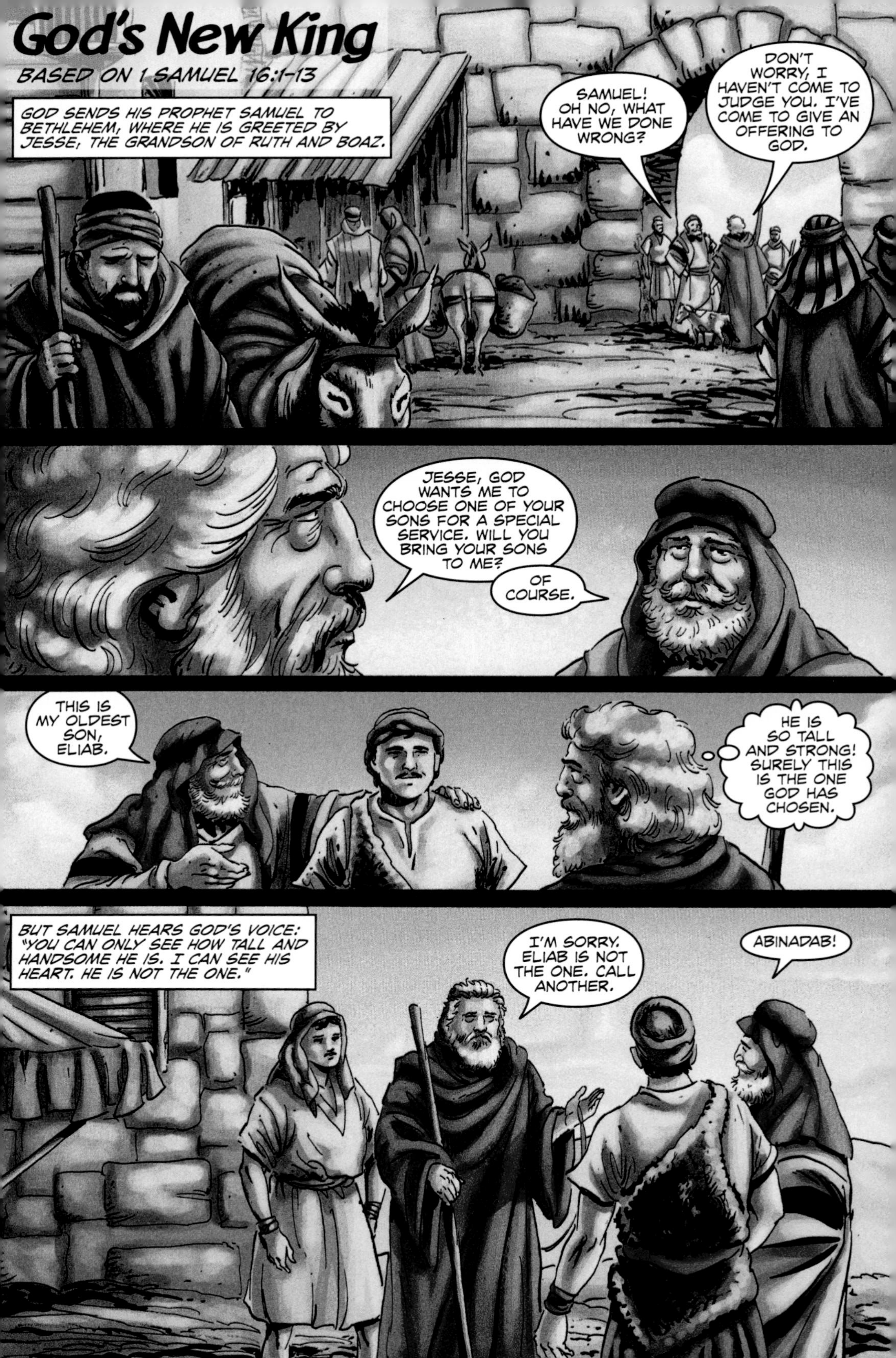
GOD SENDS HIS PROPHET SAMUEL TO BETHLEHEM, WHERE HE IS GREETED BY JESSE, THE GRANDSON OF RUTH AND BOAZ.
SAMUEL! OH NO, WHAT HAVE WE DONE WRONG?
DON'T WORRY, I HAVEN'T COME TO JUDGE YOU. I'VE COME TO GIVE AN OFFERING TO GOD.
JESSE, GOD WANTS ME TO CHOOSE ONE OF YOUR SONS FOR A SPECIAL SERVICE. WILL YOU BRING YOUR SONS TO ME?
OF COURSE.
THIS IS MY OLDEST SON, ELIAB.
HE IS SO TALL AND STRONG! SURELY THIS IS THE ONE GOD HAS CHOSEN.
BUT SAMUEL HEARS GOD'S VOICE: "YOU CAN ONLY SEE HOW TALL AND HANDSOME HE IS. I CAN SEE HIS HEART. HE IS NOT THE ONE."
I'M SORRY. ELIAB IS NOT THE ONE. CALL ANOTHER.
ABINADAB!

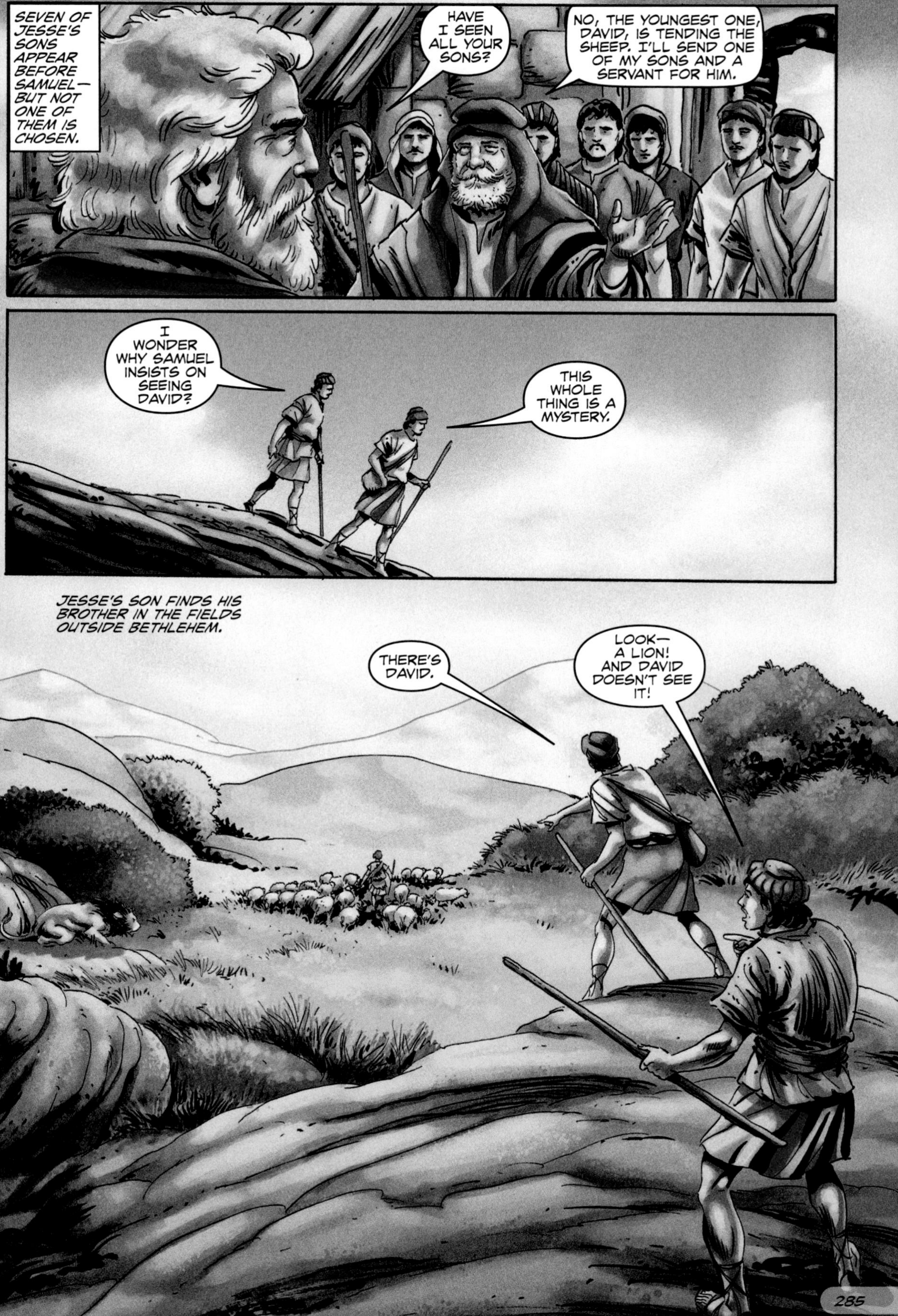
SEVEN OF JESSE'S SONS APPEAR BEFORE SAMUEL—BUT NOT ONE OF THEM IS CHOSEN.
HAVE I SEEN ALL YOUR SONS?
NO, THE YOUNGEST ONE, DAVID, IS TENDING THE SHEEP. I'LL SEND ONE OF MY SONS AND A SERVANT FOR HIM.
I WONDER WHY SAMUEL INSISTS ON SEEING DAVID?
THIS WHOLE THING IS A MYSTERY.
JESSE'S SON FINDS HIS BROTHER IN THE FIELDS OUTSIDE BETHLEHEM.
THERE'S DAVID.
LOOK—A LION! AND DAVID DOESN'T SEE IT!

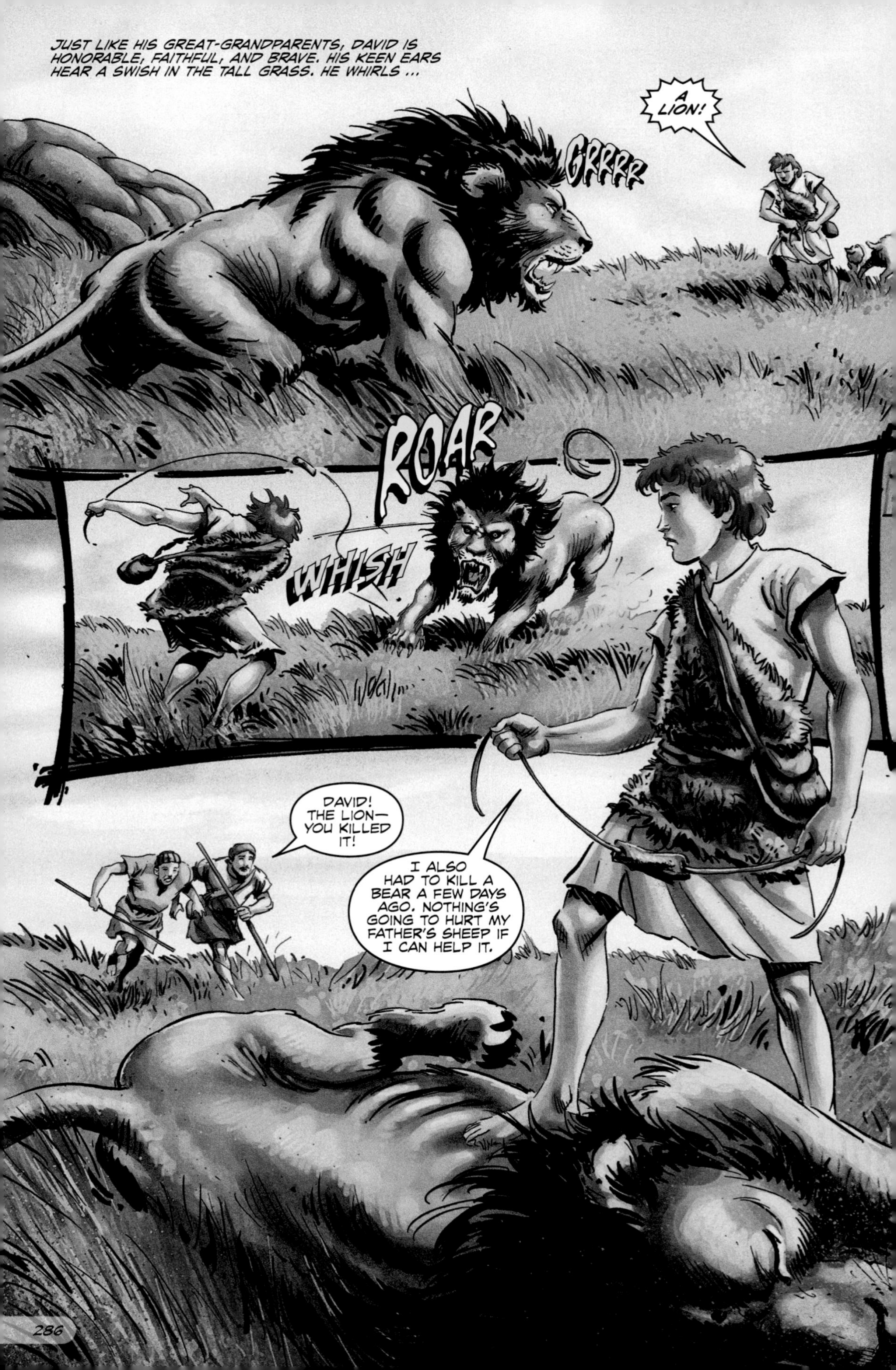
JUST LIKE HIS GREAT-GRANDPARENTS, DAVID IS HONORABLE, FAITHFUL, AND BRAVE. HIS KEEN EARS HEAR A SWISH IN THE TALL GRASS. HE WHIRLS ...
A LION!
GRRRRR
ROAR
WHISH
DAVID! THE LION— YOU KILLED IT!
I ALSO HAD TO KILL A BEAR A FEW DAYS AGO. NOTHING'S GOING TO HURT MY FATHER'S SHEEP IF I CAN HELP IT.

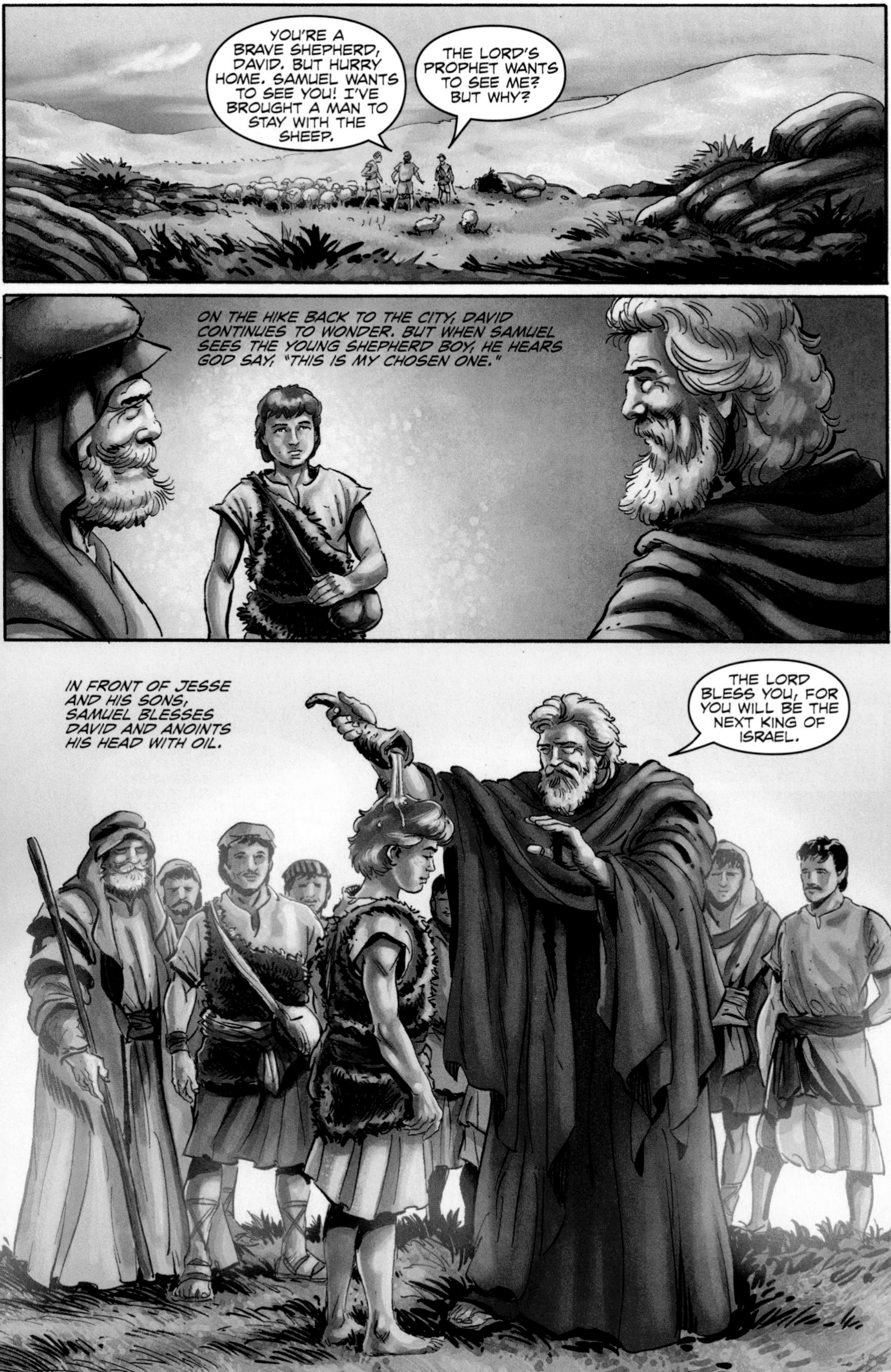
YOU'RE A BRAVE SHEPHERD, DAVID. BUT HURRY HOME. SAMUEL WANTS TO SEE YOU! I'VE BROUGHT A MAN TO STAY WITH THE SHEEP.
THE LORD'S PROPHET WANTS TO SEE ME? BUT WHY?
ON THE HIKE BACK TO THE CITY, DAVID CONTINUES TO WONDER. BUT WHEN SAMUEL SEES THE YOUNG SHEPHERD BOY, HE HEARS GOD SAY, "THIS IS MY CHOSEN ONE."
IN FRONT OF JESSE AND HIS SONS, SAMUEL BLESSES DAVID AND ANOINTS HIS HEAD WITH OIL.
THE LORD BLESS YOU, FOR YOU WILL BE THE NEXT KING OF ISRAEL.

A Psalming Influence

BASED ON 1 SAMUEL 16:14-23; PSALM 23

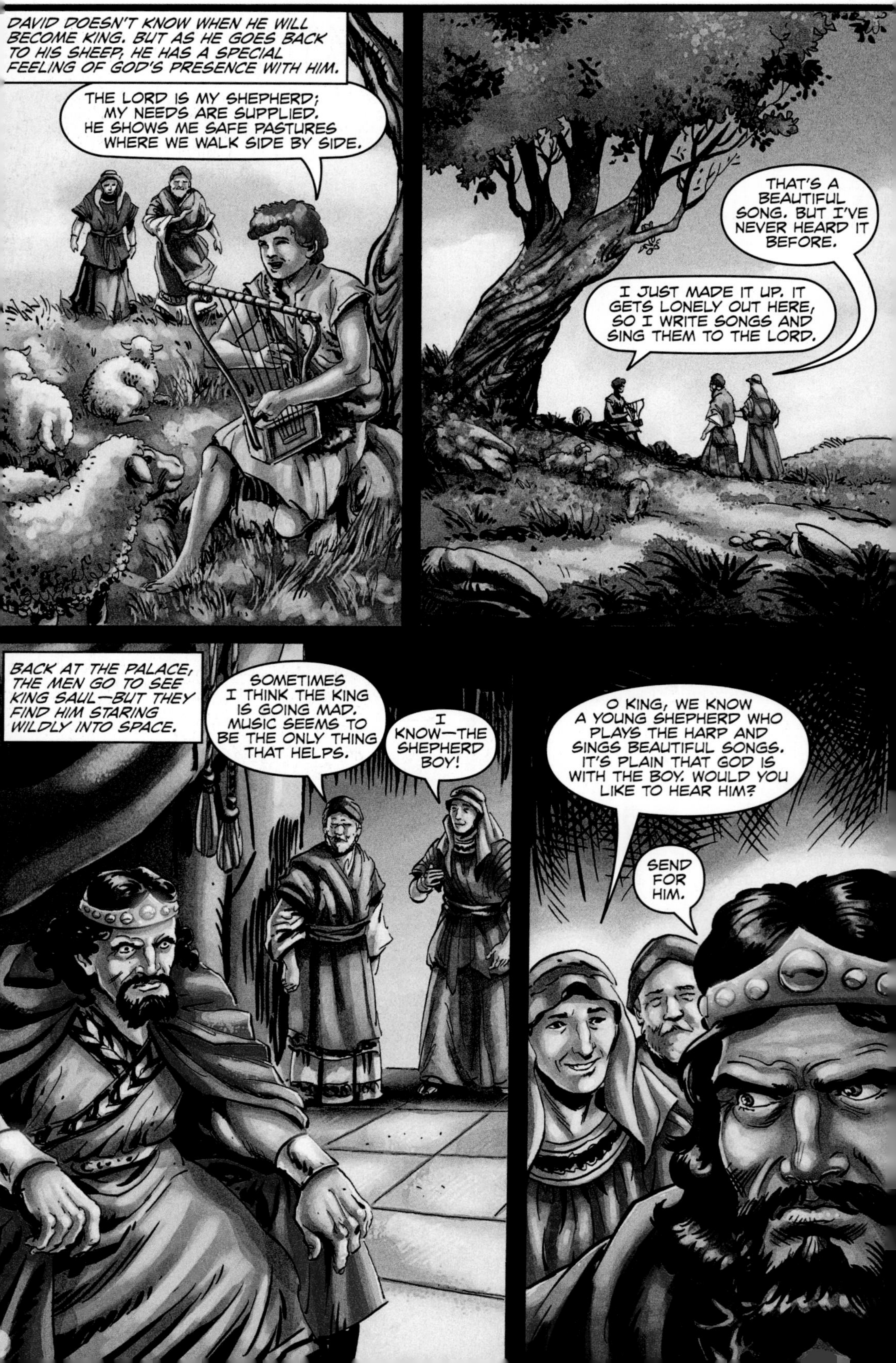

DAVID DOESN'T KNOW WHEN HE WILL BECOME KING. BUT AS HE GOES BACK TO HIS SHEEP, HE HAS A SPECIAL FEELING OF GOD'S PRESENCE WITH HIM.
THE LORD IS MY SHEPHERD; MY NEEDS ARE SUPPLIED. HE SHOWS ME SAFE PASTURES WHERE WE WALK SIDE BY SIDE.
THAT'S A BEAUTIFUL SONG. BUT I'VE NEVER HEARD IT BEFORE.
I JUST MADE IT UP. IT GETS LONELY OUT HERE, SO I WRITE SONGS AND SING THEM TO THE LORD.
BACK AT THE PALACE, THE MEN GO TO SEE KING SAUL—BUT THEY FIND HIM STARING WILDLY INTO SPACE.
SOMETIMES I THINK THE KING IS GOING MAD. MUSIC SEEMS TO BE THE ONLY THING THAT HELPS.
I KNOW—THE SHEPHERD BOY!
O KING, WE KNOW A YOUNG SHEPHERD WHO PLAYS THE HARP AND SINGS BEAUTIFUL SONGS. IT'S PLAIN THAT GOD IS WITH THE BOY. WOULD YOU LIKE TO HEAR HIM?
SEND FOR HIM.

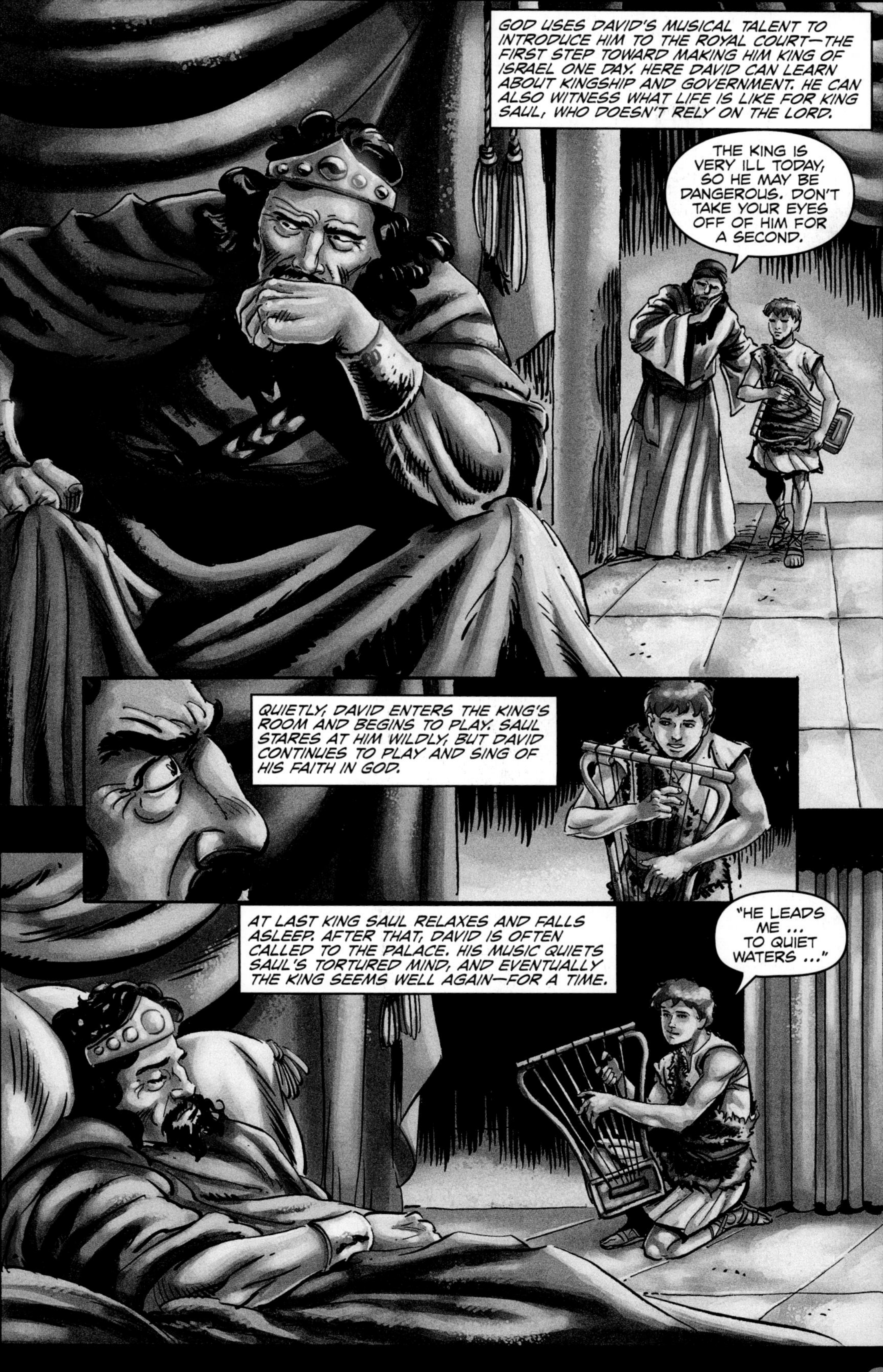
GOD USES DAVID'S MUSICAL TALENT TO INTRODUCE HIM TO THE ROYAL COURT—THE FIRST STEP TOWARD MAKING HIM KING OF ISRAEL ONE DAY. HERE DAVID CAN LEARN ABOUT KINGSHIP AND GOVERNMENT. HE CAN ALSO WITNESS WHAT LIFE IS LIKE FOR KING SAUL, WHO DOESN'T RELY ON THE LORD.
THE KING IS VERY ILL TODAY, SO HE MAY BE DANGEROUS. DON'T TAKE YOUR EYES OFF OF HIM FOR A SECOND.
QUIETLY, DAVID ENTERS THE KING'S ROOM AND BEGINS TO PLAY. SAUL STARES AT HIM WILDLY, BUT DAVID CONTINUES TO PLAY AND SING OF HIS FAITH IN GOD.
AT LAST KING SAUL RELAXES AND FALLS ASLEEP. AFTER THAT, DAVID IS OFTEN CALLED TO THE PALACE. HIS MUSIC QUIETS SAUL'S TORTURED MIND, AND EVENTUALLY THE KING SEEMS WELL AGAIN—FOR A TIME.
"HE LEADS ME ... TO QUIET WATERS ..."

A Giant Challenge

BASED ON 1 SAMUEL 17

A FEW YEARS LATER, THE PHILISTINES COLLECT THEIR FORCES FOR AN ATTACK AGAINST ISRAEL. SAUL MASSES HIS ARMY AGAINST THEM, AND DAVID'S THREE OLDEST BROTHERS JOIN THE KING'S FORCES.

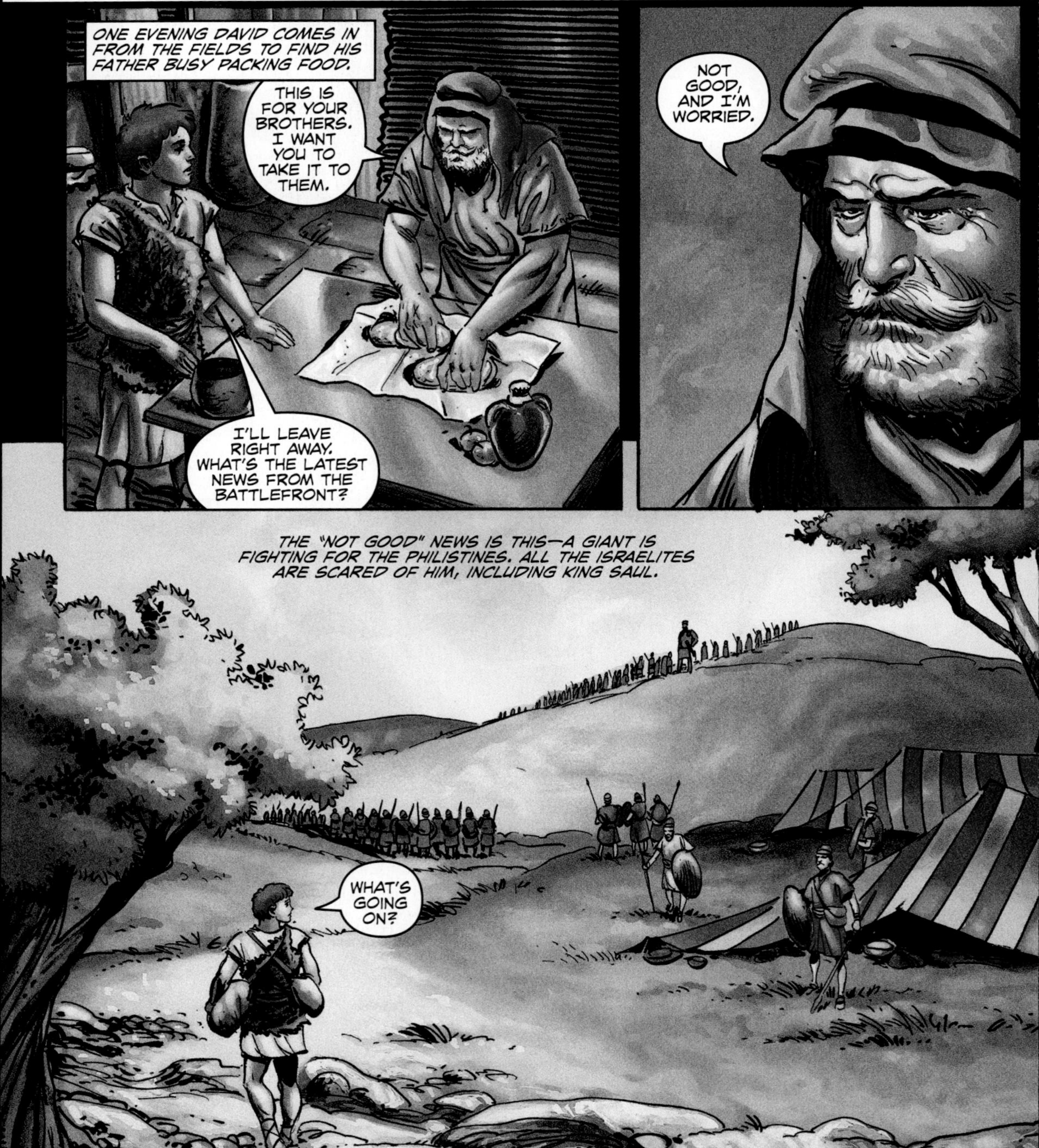

ONE EVENING DAVID COMES IN FROM THE FIELDS TO FIND HIS FATHER BUSY PACKING FOOD.
THIS IS FOR YOUR BROTHERS. I WANT YOU TO TAKE IT TO THEM.
I'LL LEAVE RIGHT AWAY. WHAT'S THE LATEST NEWS FROM THE BATTLEFRONT?
NOT GOOD, AND I'M WORRIED.
THE "NOT GOOD" NEWS IS THIS—A GIANT IS FIGHTING FOR THE PHILISTINES. ALL THE ISRAELITES ARE SCARED OF HIM, INCLUDING KING SAUL.
WHAT'S GOING ON?

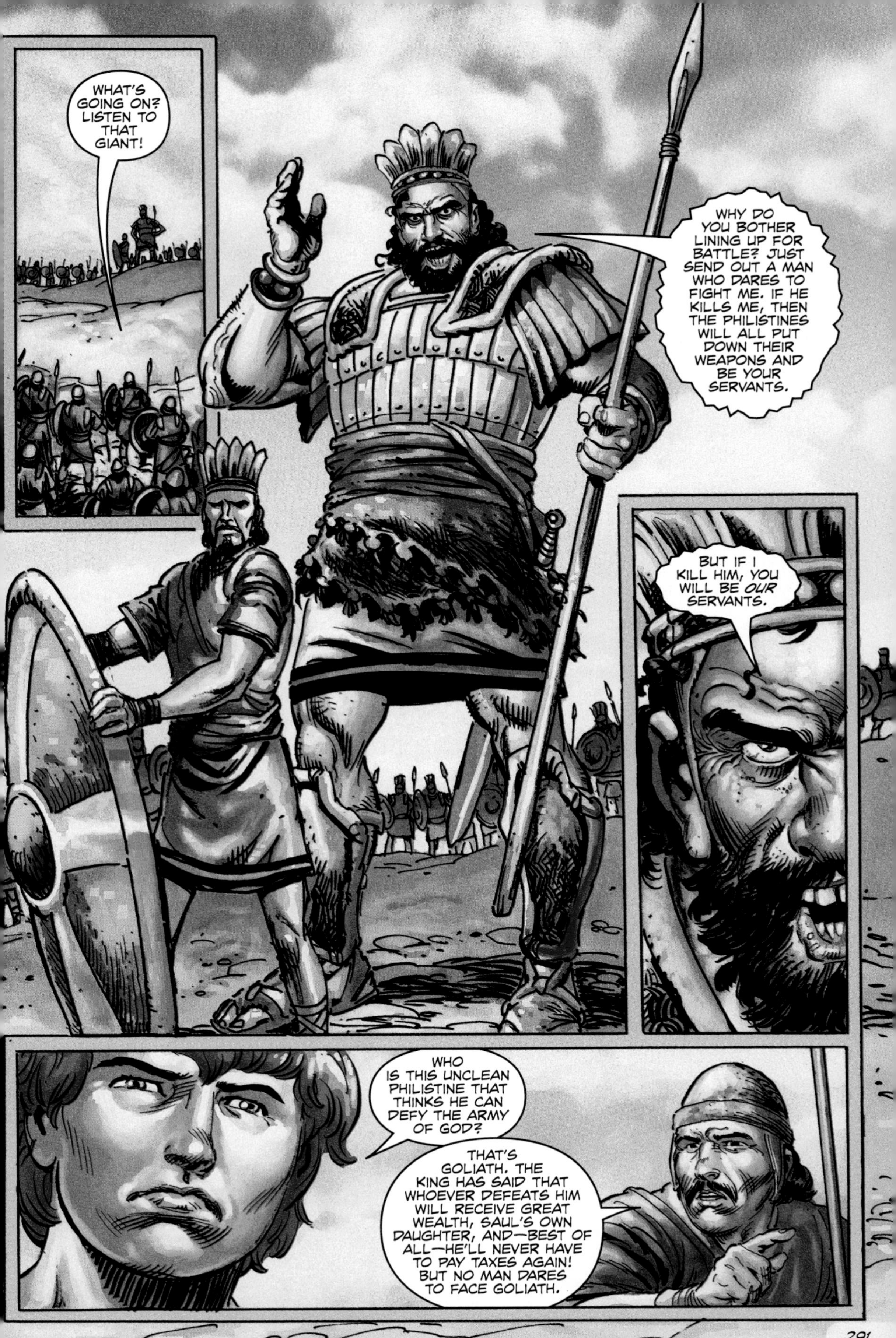
WHAT'S GOING ON? LISTEN TO THAT GIANT!
WHY DO YOU BOTHER LINING UP FOR BATTLE? JUST SEND OUT A MAN WHO DARES TO FIGHT ME. IF HE KILLS ME, THEN THE PHILISTINES WILL ALL PUT DOWN THEIR WEAPONS AND BE YOUR SERVANTS.
BUT IF I KILL HIM, YOU WILL BE *OUR* SERVANTS.
WHO IS THIS UNCLEAN PHILISTINE THAT THINKS HE CAN DEFY THE ARMY OF GOD?
THAT'S GOLIATH. THE KING HAS SAID THAT WHOEVER DEFEATS HIM WILL RECEIVE GREAT WEALTH, SAUL'S OWN DAUGHTER, AND—BEST OF ALL—HE'LL NEVER HAVE TO PAY TAXES AGAIN! BUT NO MAN DARES TO FACE GOLIATH.

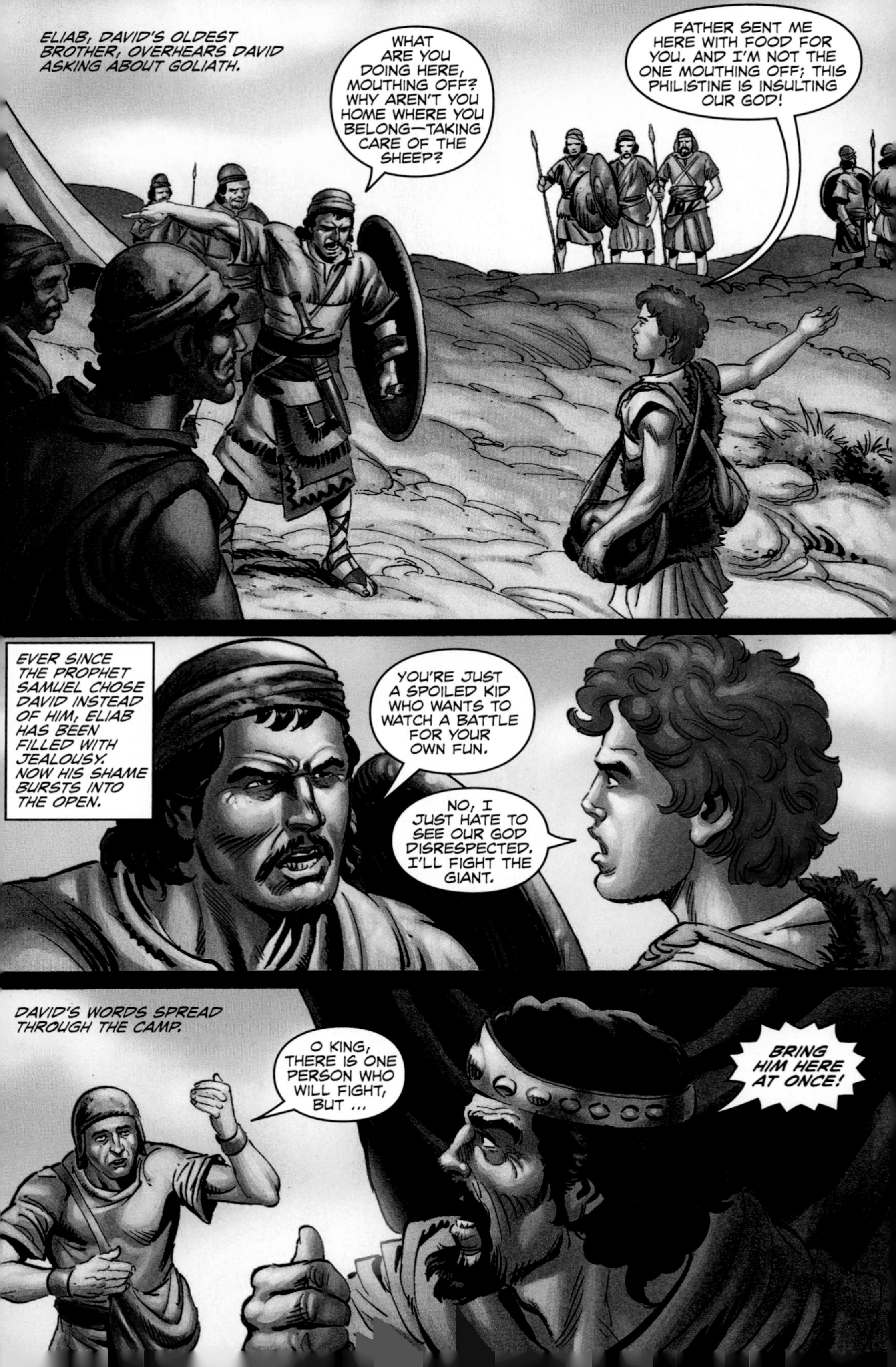
ELIAB, DAVID'S OLDEST BROTHER, OVERHEARS DAVID ASKING ABOUT GOLIATH.
WHAT ARE YOU DOING HERE, MOUTHING OFF? WHY AREN'T YOU HOME WHERE YOU BELONG—TAKING CARE OF THE SHEEP?
FATHER SENT ME HERE WITH FOOD FOR YOU. AND I'M NOT THE ONE MOUTHING OFF; THIS PHILISTINE IS INSULTING OUR GOD!
EVER SINCE THE PROPHET SAMUEL CHOSE DAVID INSTEAD OF HIM, ELIAB HAS BEEN FILLED WITH JEALOUSY. NOW HIS SHAME BURSTS INTO THE OPEN.
YOU'RE JUST A SPOILED KID WHO WANTS TO WATCH A BATTLE FOR YOUR OWN FUN.
NO, I JUST HATE TO SEE OUR GOD DISRESPECTED. I'LL FIGHT THE GIANT.
DAVID'S WORDS SPREAD THROUGH THE CAMP.
O KING, THERE IS ONE PERSON WHO WILL FIGHT, BUT ...
BRING HIM HERE AT ONCE!

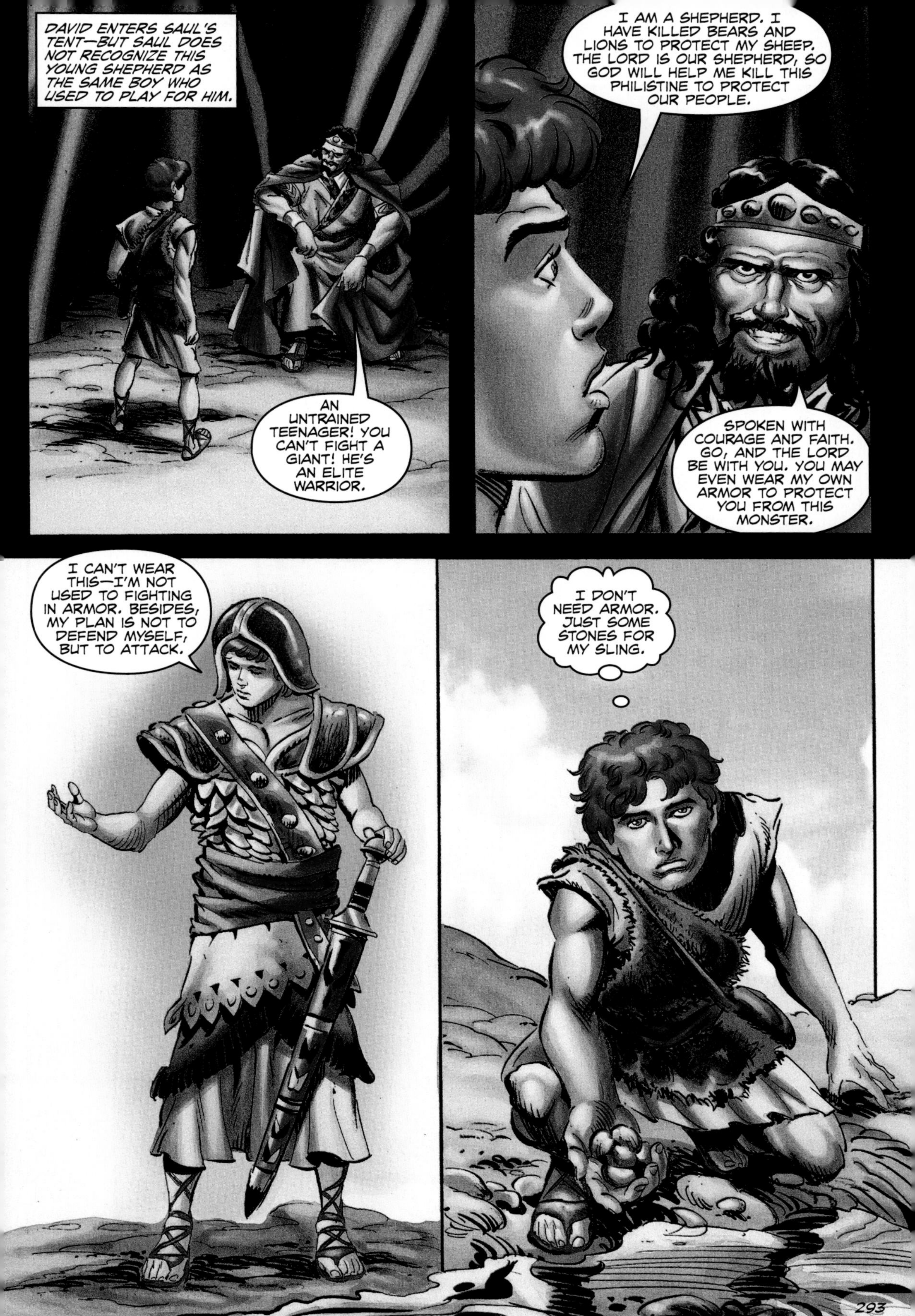
DAVID ENTERS SAUL'S TENT—BUT SAUL DOES NOT RECOGNIZE THIS YOUNG SHEPHERD AS THE SAME BOY WHO USED TO PLAY FOR HIM.
AN UNTRAINED TEENAGER! YOU CAN'T FIGHT A GIANT! HE'S AN ELITE WARRIOR.
I AM A SHEPHERD. I HAVE KILLED BEARS AND LIONS TO PROTECT MY SHEEP. THE LORD IS OUR SHEPHERD, SO GOD WILL HELP ME KILL THIS PHILISTINE TO PROTECT OUR PEOPLE.
SPOKEN WITH COURAGE AND FAITH. GO, AND THE LORD BE WITH YOU. YOU MAY EVEN WEAR MY OWN ARMOR TO PROTECT YOU FROM THIS MONSTER.
I CAN'T WEAR THIS—I'M NOT USED TO FIGHTING IN ARMOR. BESIDES, MY PLAN IS NOT TO DEFEND MYSELF, BUT TO ATTACK.
I DON'T NEED ARMOR. JUST SOME STONES FOR MY SLING.

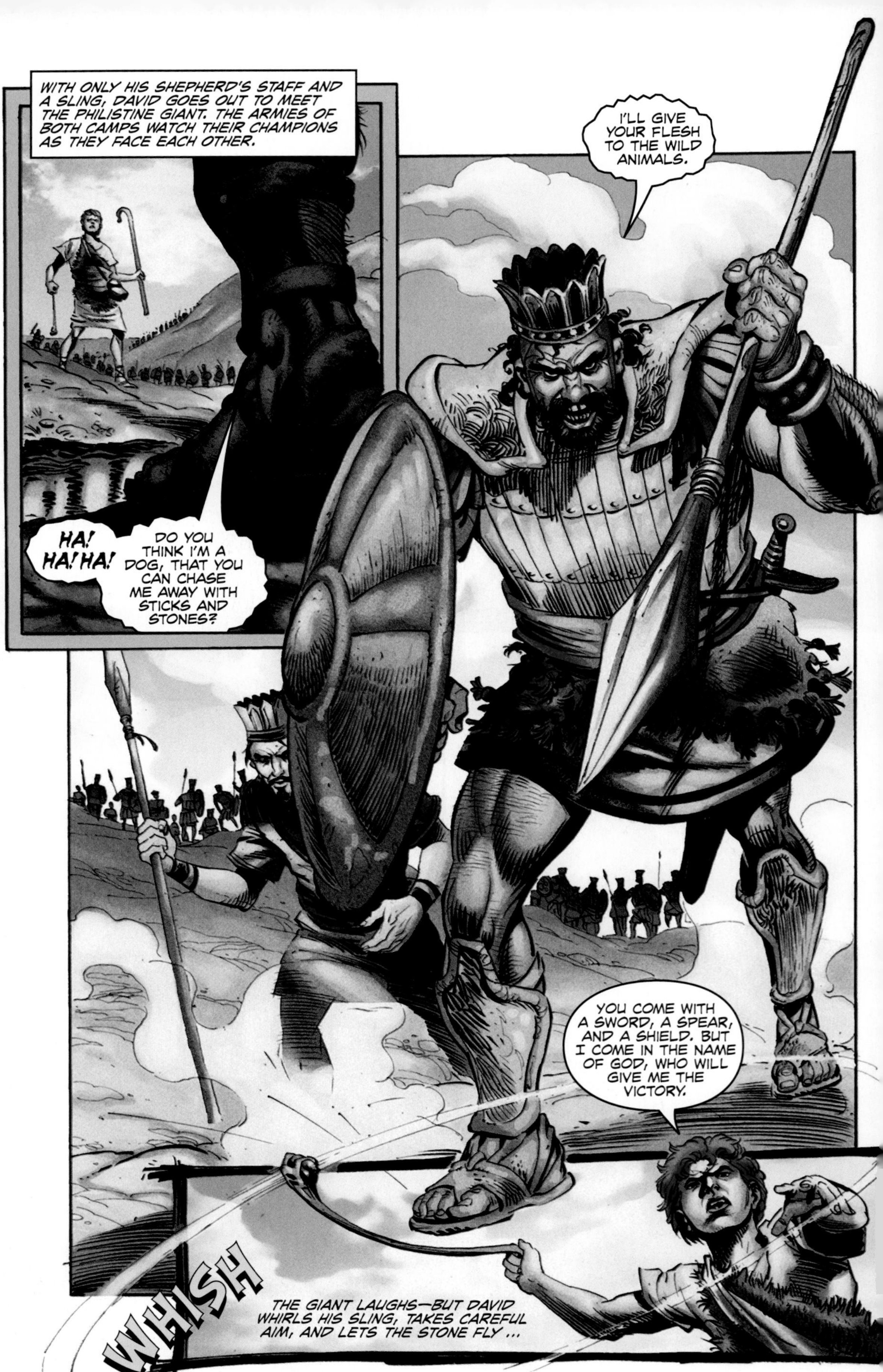
WITH ONLY HIS SHEPHERD'S STAFF AND A SLING, DAVID GOES OUT TO MEET THE PHILISTINE GIANT. THE ARMIES OF BOTH CAMPS WATCH THEIR CHAMPIONS AS THEY FACE EACH OTHER.
HA! HA! HA!
DO YOU THINK I'M A DOG, THAT YOU CAN CHASE ME AWAY WITH STICKS AND STONES?
I'LL GIVE YOUR FLESH TO THE WILD ANIMALS.
YOU COME WITH A SWORD, A SPEAR, AND A SHIELD. BUT I COME IN THE NAME OF GOD, WHO WILL GIVE ME THE VICTORY.
WHISH
THE GIANT LAUGHS—BUT DAVID WHIRLS HIS SLING, TAKES CAREFUL AIM, AND LETS THE STONE FLY ...

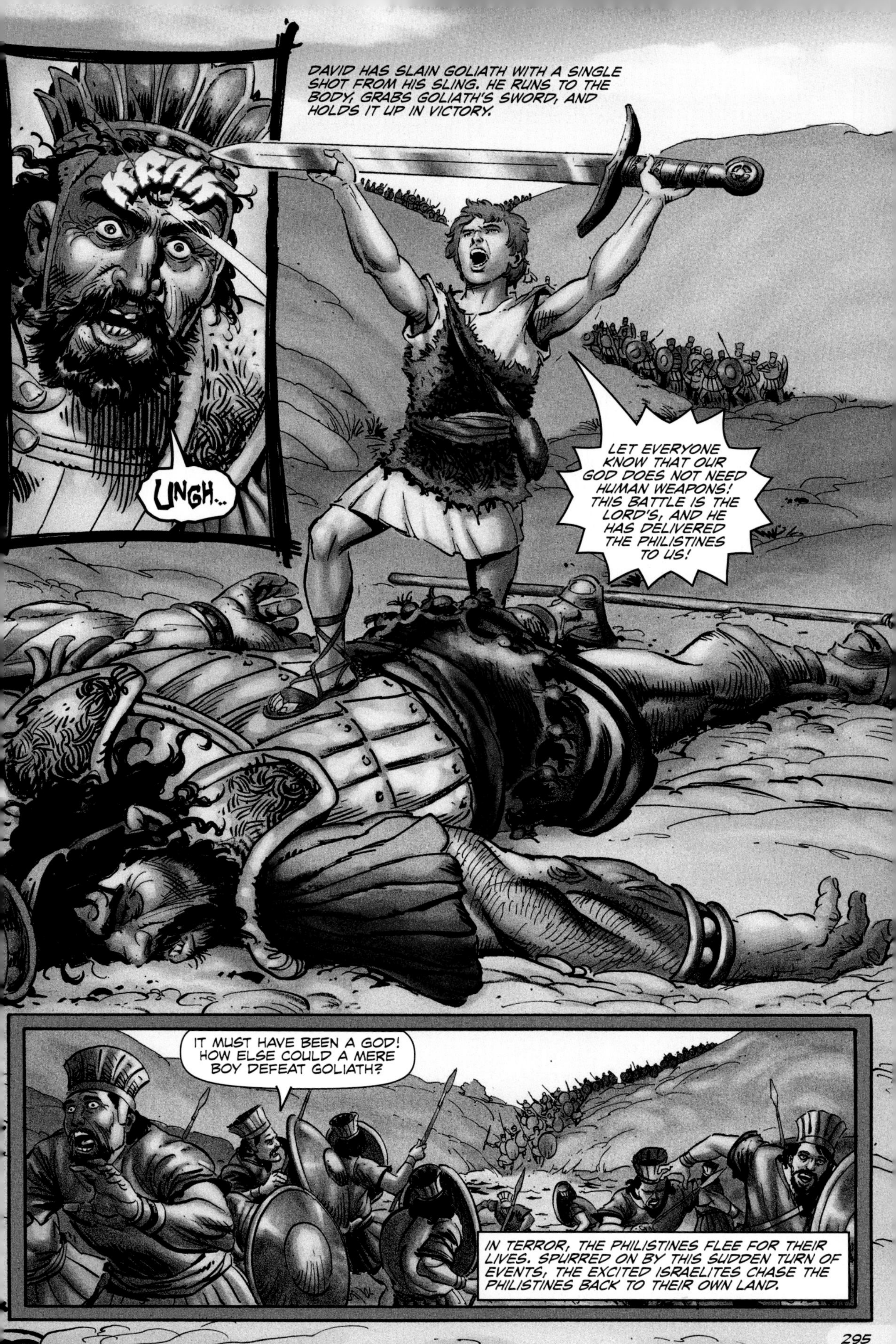
DAVID HAS SLAIN GOLIATH WITH A SINGLE SHOT FROM HIS SLING. HE RUNS TO THE BODY, GRABS GOLIATH'S SWORD, AND HOLDS IT UP IN VICTORY.
KRAK
UNGH...
LET EVERYONE KNOW THAT OUR GOD DOES NOT NEED HUMAN WEAPONS! THIS BATTLE IS THE LORD'S, AND HE HAS DELIVERED THE PHILISTINES TO US!
IT MUST HAVE BEEN A GOD! HOW ELSE COULD A MERE BOY DEFEAT GOLIATH?
IN TERROR, THE PHILISTINES FLEE FOR THEIR LIVES. SPURRED ON BY THIS SUDDEN TURN OF EVENTS, THE EXCITED ISRAELITES CHASE THE PHILISTINES BACK TO THEIR OWN LAND.

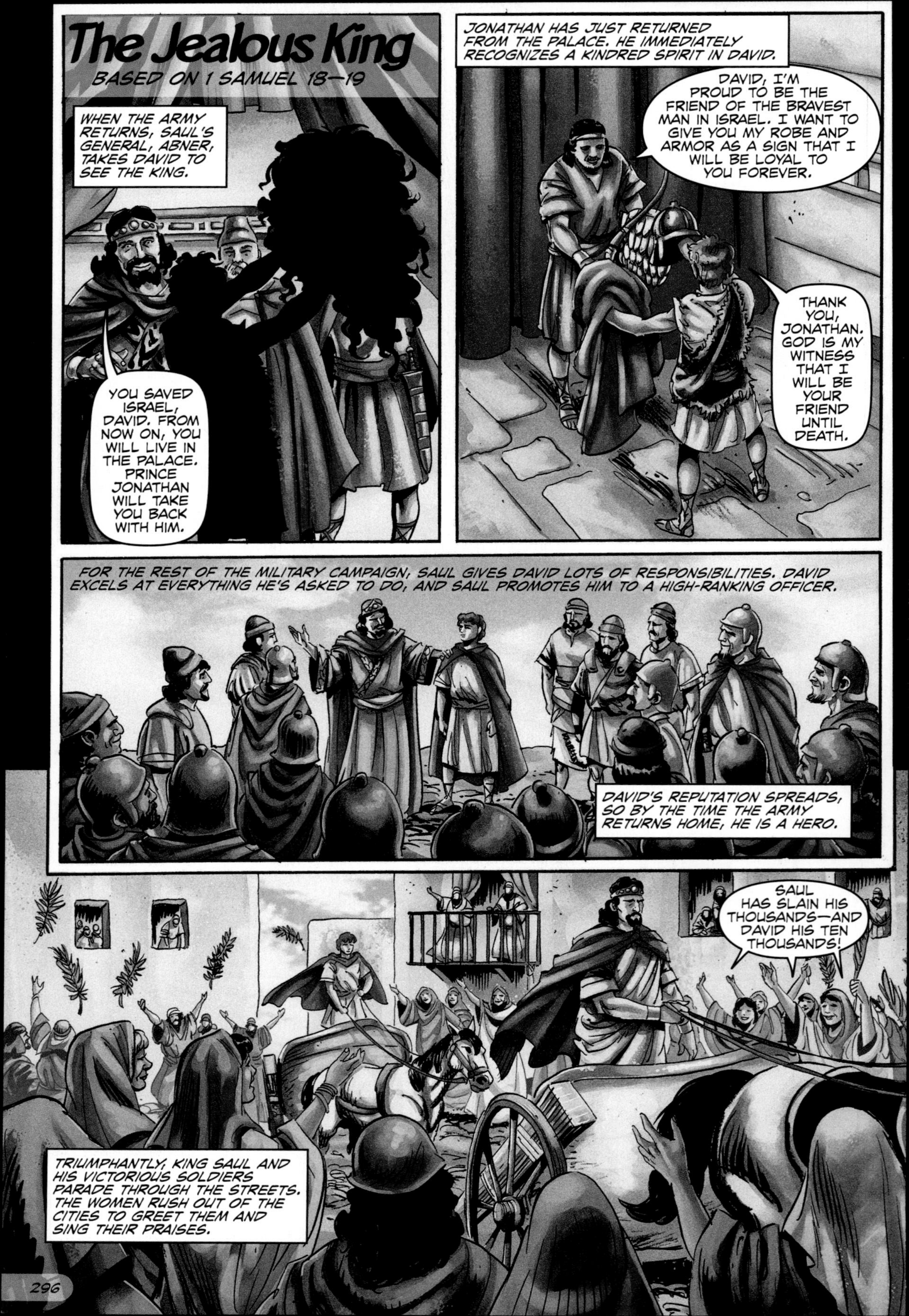
The Jealous King
BASED ON 1 SAMUEL 18—19
WHEN THE ARMY RETURNS, SAUL'S GENERAL, ABNER, TAKES DAVID TO SEE THE KING.
YOU SAVED ISRAEL, DAVID. FROM NOW ON, YOU WILL LIVE IN THE PALACE. PRINCE JONATHAN WILL TAKE YOU BACK WITH HIM.
JONATHAN HAS JUST RETURNED FROM THE PALACE. HE IMMEDIATELY RECOGNIZES A KINDRED SPIRIT IN DAVID.
DAVID, I'M PROUD TO BE THE FRIEND OF THE BRAVEST MAN IN ISRAEL. I WANT TO GIVE YOU MY ROBE AND ARMOR AS A SIGN THAT I WILL BE LOYAL TO YOU FOREVER.
THANK YOU, JONATHAN. GOD IS MY WITNESS THAT I WILL BE YOUR FRIEND UNTIL DEATH.
FOR THE REST OF THE MILITARY CAMPAIGN, SAUL GIVES DAVID LOTS OF RESPONSIBILITIES. DAVID EXCELS AT EVERYTHING HE'S ASKED TO DO, AND SAUL PROMOTES HIM TO A HIGH-RANKING OFFICER.
DAVID'S REPUTATION SPREADS, SO BY THE TIME THE ARMY RETURNS HOME, HE IS A HERO.
SAUL HAS SLAIN HIS THOUSANDS—AND DAVID HIS TEN THOUSANDS!
TRIUMPHANTLY, KING SAUL AND HIS VICTORIOUS SOLDIERS PARADE THROUGH THE STREETS. THE WOMEN RUSH OUT OF THE CITIES TO GREET THEM AND SING THEIR PRAISES.

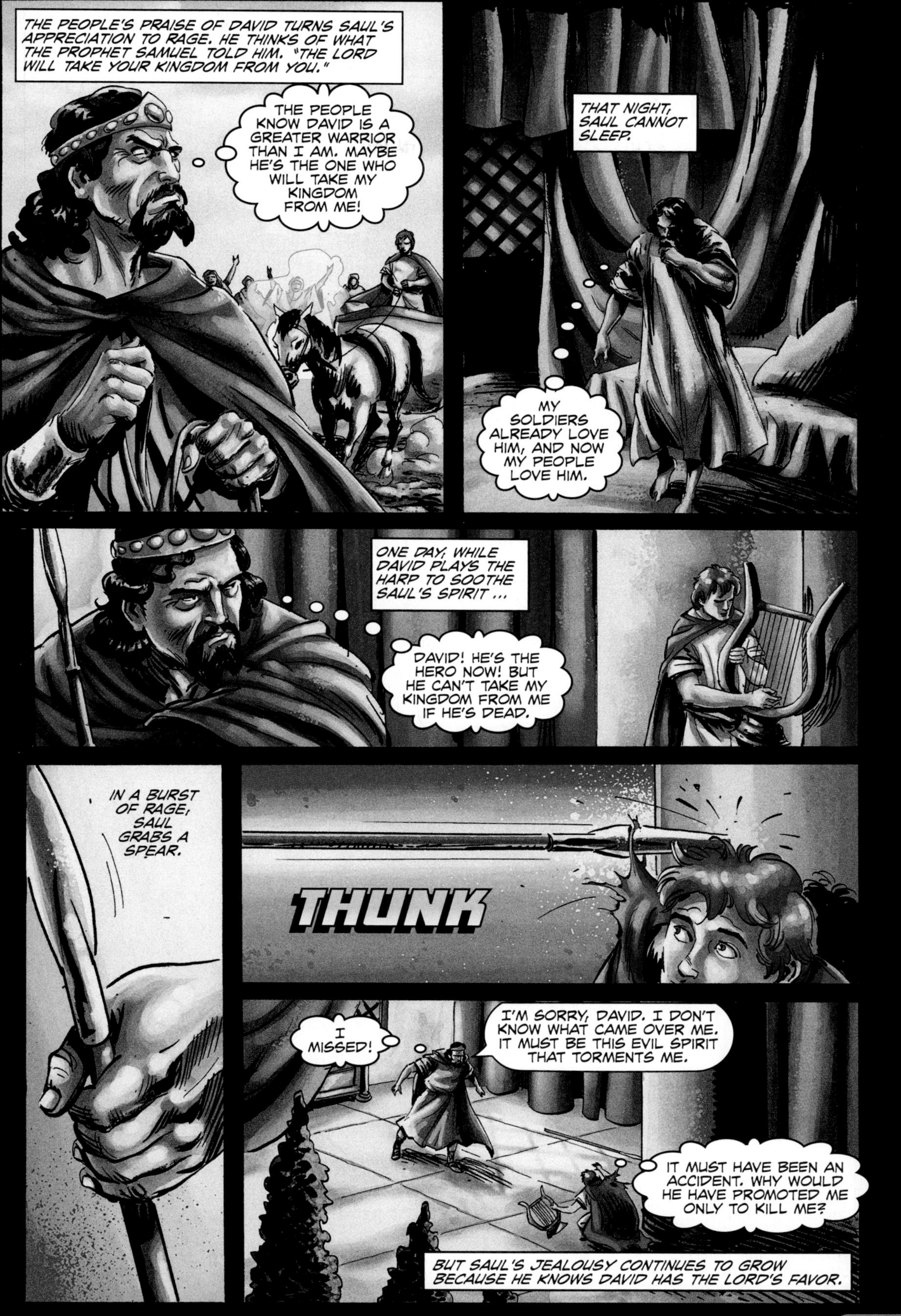
THE PEOPLE'S PRAISE OF DAVID TURNS SAUL'S APPRECIATION TO RAGE. HE THINKS OF WHAT THE PROPHET SAMUEL TOLD HIM. "THE LORD WILL TAKE YOUR KINGDOM FROM YOU."
THE PEOPLE KNOW DAVID IS A GREATER WARRIOR THAN I AM. MAYBE HE'S THE ONE WHO WILL TAKE MY KINGDOM FROM ME!
THAT NIGHT, SAUL CANNOT SLEEP.
MY SOLDIERS ALREADY LOVE HIM, AND NOW MY PEOPLE LOVE HIM.
ONE DAY, WHILE DAVID PLAYS THE HARP TO SOOTHE SAUL'S SPIRIT ...
DAVID! HE'S THE HERO NOW! BUT HE CAN'T TAKE MY KINGDOM FROM ME IF HE'S DEAD.
IN A BURST OF RAGE, SAUL GRABS A SPEAR.
THUNK
I MISSED!
I'M SORRY, DAVID. I DON'T KNOW WHAT CAME OVER ME. IT MUST BE THIS EVIL SPIRIT THAT TORMENTS ME.
IT MUST HAVE BEEN AN ACCIDENT. WHY WOULD HE HAVE PROMOTED ME ONLY TO KILL ME?
BUT SAUL'S JEALOUSY CONTINUES TO GROW BECAUSE HE KNOWS DAVID HAS THE LORD'S FAVOR.

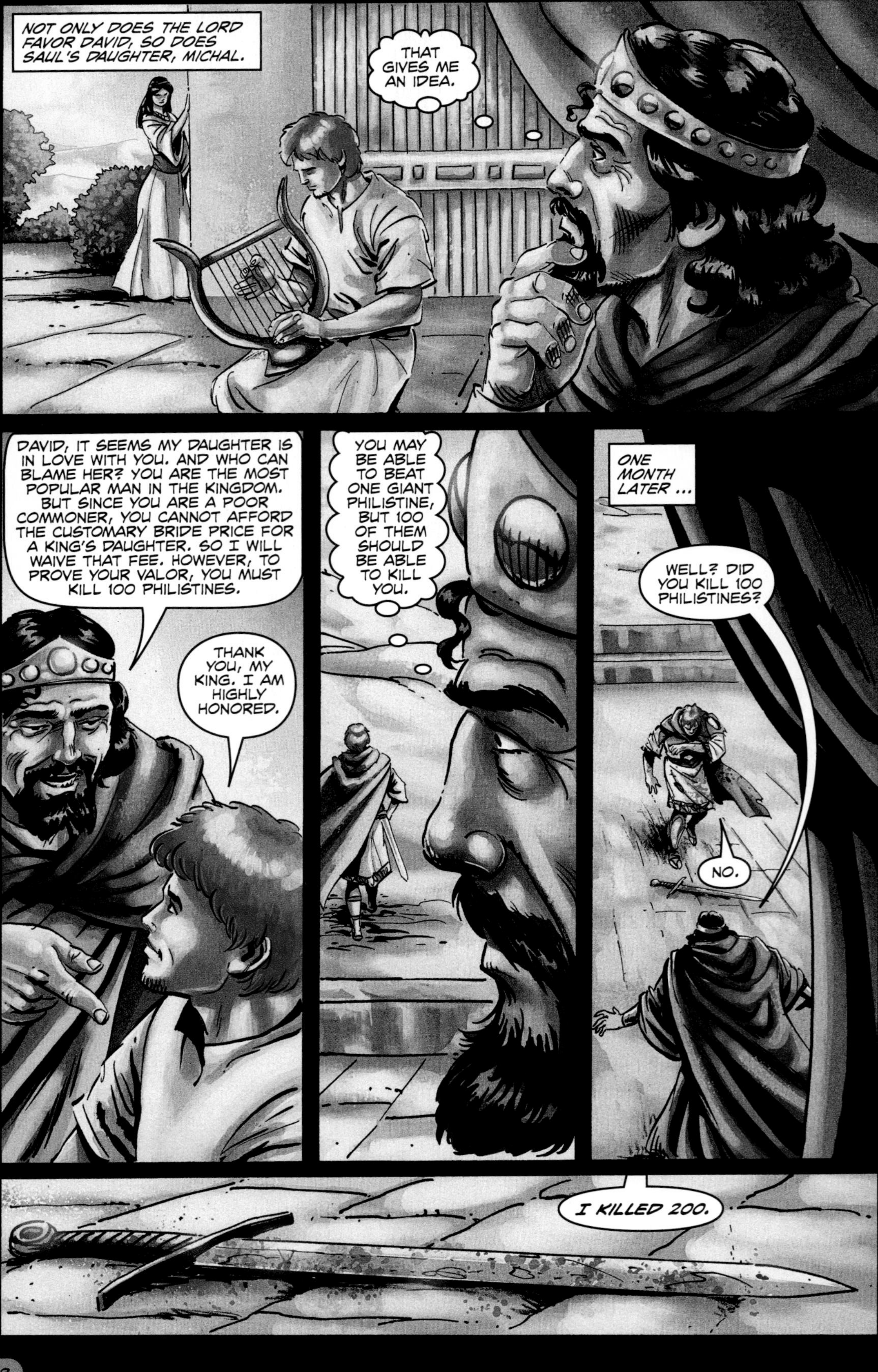
NOT ONLY DOES THE LORD FAVOR DAVID, SO DOES SAUL'S DAUGHTER, MICHAL.
THAT GIVES ME AN IDEA.
DAVID, IT SEEMS MY DAUGHTER IS IN LOVE WITH YOU. AND WHO CAN BLAME HER? YOU ARE THE MOST POPULAR MAN IN THE KINGDOM. BUT SINCE YOU ARE A POOR COMMONER, YOU CANNOT AFFORD THE CUSTOMARY BRIDE PRICE FOR A KING'S DAUGHTER. SO I WILL WAIVE THAT FEE. HOWEVER, TO PROVE YOUR VALOR, YOU MUST KILL 100 PHILISTINES.
THANK YOU, MY KING. I AM HIGHLY HONORED.
YOU MAY BE ABLE TO BEAT ONE GIANT PHILISTINE, BUT 100 OF THEM SHOULD BE ABLE TO KILL YOU.
ONE MONTH LATER ...
WELL? DID YOU KILL 100 PHILISTINES?
NO.
I KILLED 200.

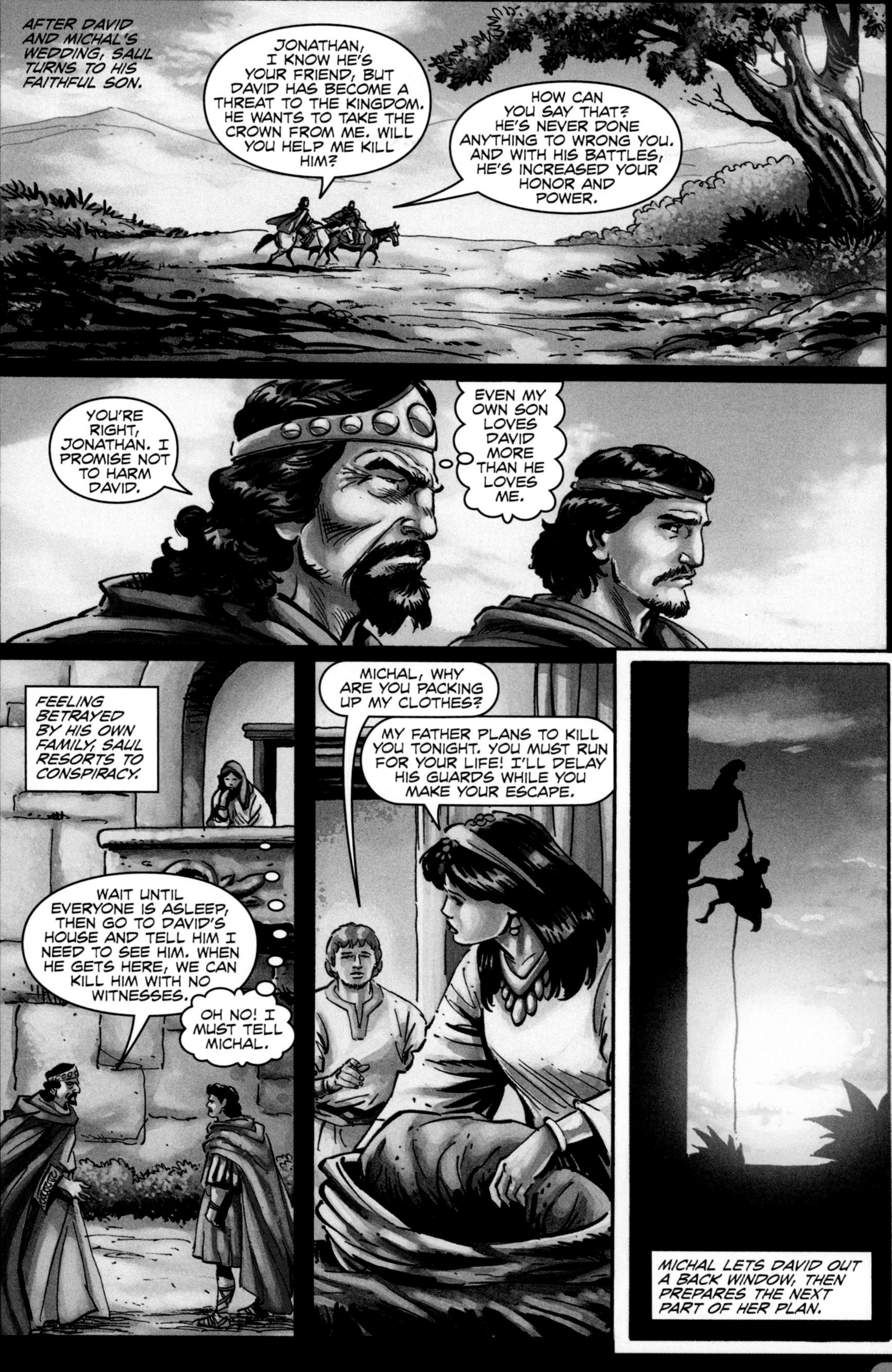
AFTER DAVID AND MICHAL'S WEDDING, SAUL TURNS TO HIS FAITHFUL SON.
JONATHAN, I KNOW HE'S YOUR FRIEND, BUT DAVID HAS BECOME A THREAT TO THE KINGDOM. HE WANTS TO TAKE THE CROWN FROM ME. WILL YOU HELP ME KILL HIM?
HOW CAN YOU SAY THAT? HE'S NEVER DONE ANYTHING TO WRONG YOU. AND WITH HIS BATTLES, HE'S INCREASED YOUR HONOR AND POWER.
YOU'RE RIGHT, JONATHAN. I PROMISE NOT TO HARM DAVID.
EVEN MY OWN SON LOVES DAVID MORE THAN HE LOVES ME.
FEELING BETRAYED BY HIS OWN FAMILY, SAUL RESORTS TO CONSPIRACY.
WAIT UNTIL EVERYONE IS ASLEEP, THEN GO TO DAVID'S HOUSE AND TELL HIM I NEED TO SEE HIM. WHEN HE GETS HERE, WE CAN KILL HIM WITH NO WITNESSES.
OH NO! I MUST TELL MICHAL.
MICHAL, WHY ARE YOU PACKING UP MY CLOTHES?
MY FATHER PLANS TO KILL YOU TONIGHT. YOU MUST RUN FOR YOUR LIFE! I'LL DELAY HIS GUARDS WHILE YOU MAKE YOUR ESCAPE.
MICHAL LETS DAVID OUT A BACK WINDOW, THEN PREPARES THE NEXT PART OF HER PLAN.

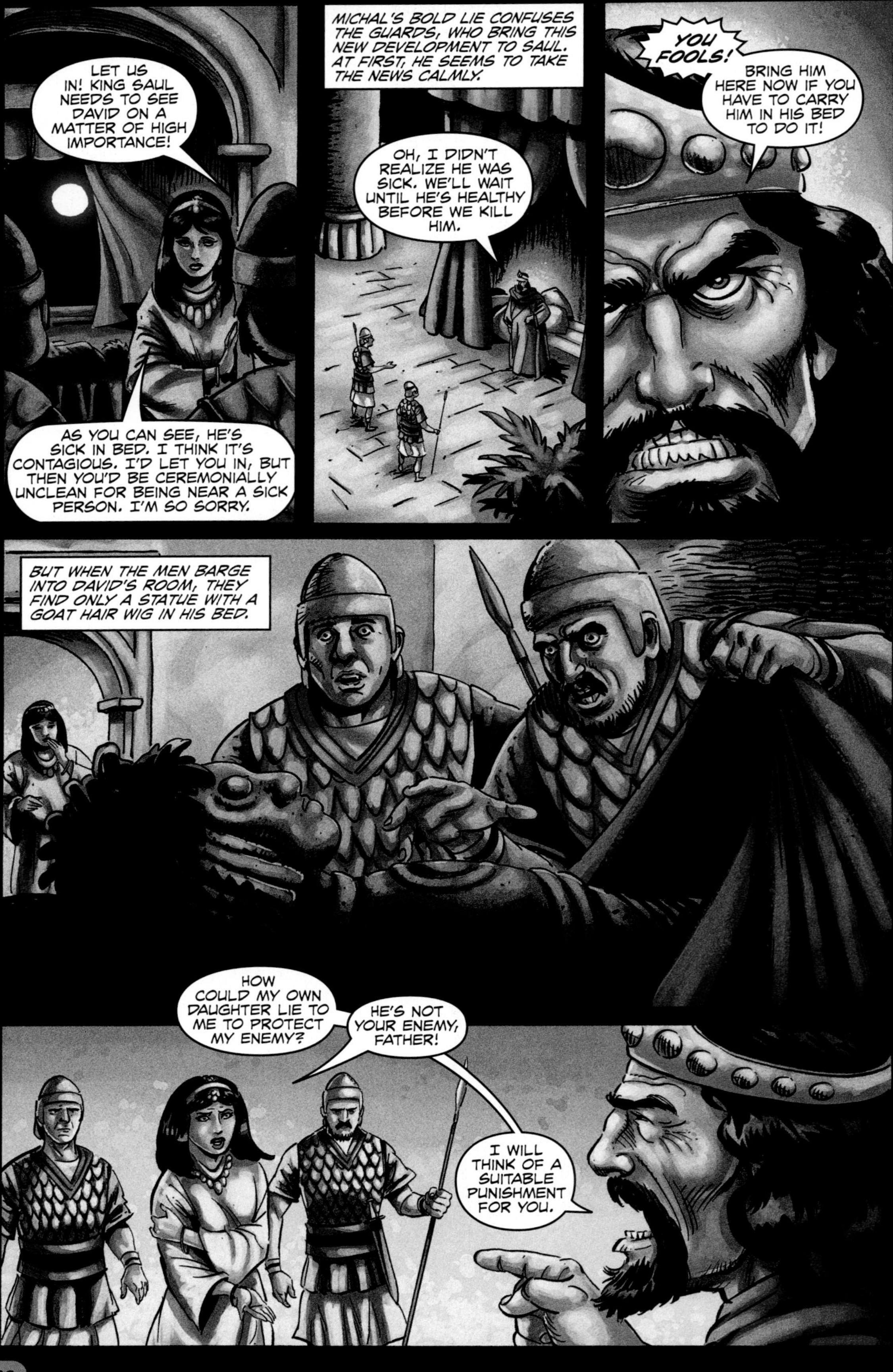
LET US IN! KING SAUL NEEDS TO SEE DAVID ON A MATTER OF HIGH IMPORTANCE!
AS YOU CAN SEE, HE'S SICK IN BED. I THINK IT'S CONTAGIOUS. I'D LET YOU IN, BUT THEN YOU'D BE CEREMONIALLY UNCLEAN FOR BEING NEAR A SICK PERSON. I'M SO SORRY.
MICHAL'S BOLD LIE CONFUSES THE GUARDS, WHO BRING THIS NEW DEVELOPMENT TO SAUL. AT FIRST, HE SEEMS TO TAKE THE NEWS CALMLY.
OH, I DIDN'T REALIZE HE WAS SICK. WE'LL WAIT UNTIL HE'S HEALTHY BEFORE WE KILL HIM.
YOU FOOLS!
BRING HIM HERE NOW IF YOU HAVE TO CARRY HIM IN HIS BED TO DO IT!
BUT WHEN THE MEN BARGE INTO DAVID'S ROOM, THEY FIND ONLY A STATUE WITH A GOAT HAIR WIG IN HIS BED.
HOW COULD MY OWN DAUGHTER LIE TO ME TO PROTECT MY ENEMY?
HE'S NOT YOUR ENEMY, FATHER!
I WILL THINK OF A SUITABLE PUNISHMENT FOR YOU.

A Prince of a Friend

BASED ON 1 SAMUEL 19:18—20:42; PSALM 19

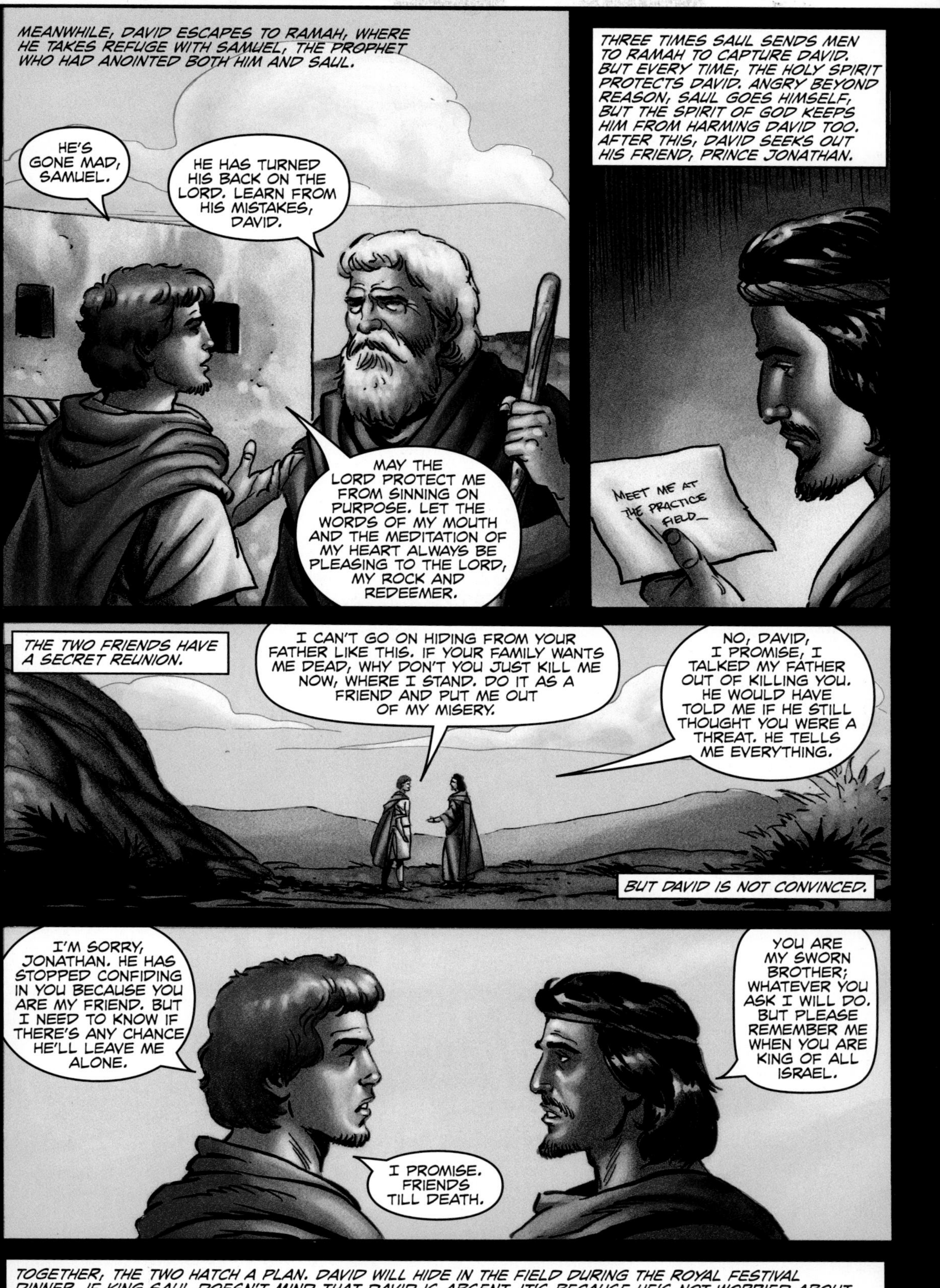
MEANWHILE, DAVID ESCAPES TO RAMAH, WHERE HE TAKES REFUGE WITH SAMUEL, THE PROPHET WHO HAD ANOINTED BOTH HIM AND SAUL.
HE'S GONE MAD, SAMUEL.
HE HAS TURNED HIS BACK ON THE LORD. LEARN FROM HIS MISTAKES, DAVID.
MAY THE LORD PROTECT ME FROM SINNING ON PURPOSE. LET THE WORDS OF MY MOUTH AND THE MEDITATION OF MY HEART ALWAYS BE PLEASING TO THE LORD, MY ROCK AND REDEEMER.
THREE TIMES SAUL SENDS MEN TO RAMAH TO CAPTURE DAVID. BUT EVERY TIME, THE HOLY SPIRIT PROTECTS DAVID. ANGRY BEYOND REASON, SAUL GOES HIMSELF, BUT THE SPIRIT OF GOD KEEPS HIM FROM HARMING DAVID TOO. AFTER THIS, DAVID SEEKS OUT HIS FRIEND, PRINCE JONATHAN.
MEET ME AT THE PRACTICE FIELD_
THE TWO FRIENDS HAVE A SECRET REUNION.
I CAN'T GO ON HIDING FROM YOUR FATHER LIKE THIS. IF YOUR FAMILY WANTS ME DEAD, WHY DON'T YOU JUST KILL ME NOW, WHERE I STAND. DO IT AS A FRIEND AND PUT ME OUT OF MY MISERY.
NO, DAVID, I PROMISE, I TALKED MY FATHER OUT OF KILLING YOU. HE WOULD HAVE TOLD ME IF HE STILL THOUGHT YOU WERE A THREAT. HE TELLS ME EVERYTHING.
BUT DAVID IS NOT CONVINCED.
I'M SORRY, JONATHAN. HE HAS STOPPED CONFIDING IN YOU BECAUSE YOU ARE MY FRIEND. BUT I NEED TO KNOW IF THERE'S ANY CHANCE HE'LL LEAVE ME ALONE.
YOU ARE MY SWORN BROTHER; WHATEVER YOU ASK I WILL DO. BUT PLEASE REMEMBER ME WHEN YOU ARE KING OF ALL ISRAEL.
I PROMISE. FRIENDS TILL DEATH.

TOGETHER, THE TWO HATCH A PLAN. DAVID WILL HIDE IN THE FIELD DURING THE ROYAL FESTIVAL DINNER. IF KING SAUL DOESN'T MIND THAT DAVID IS ABSENT, IT'S BECAUSE HE'S NOT WORRIED ABOUT DAVID. BUT IF HE BECOMES ANGRY, JONATHAN WILL KNOW THAT IT'S BECAUSE HE STILL SEEKS DAVID'S DEATH. THEN HE WILL GO BACK TO THE FIELD AND USE A CODE TO LET DAVID KNOW THE ANSWER.

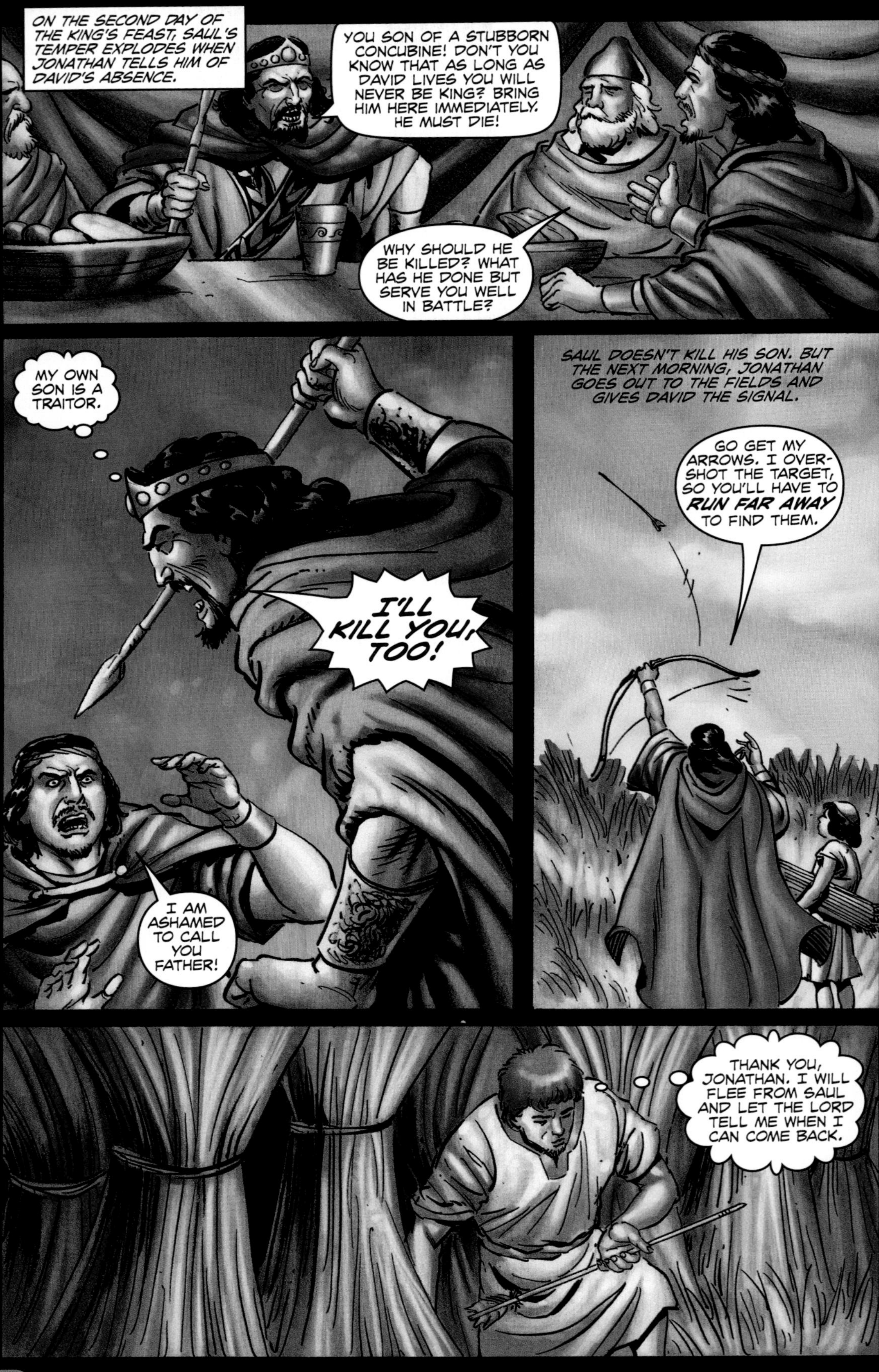

ON THE SECOND DAY OF THE KING'S FEAST, SAUL'S TEMPER EXPLODES WHEN JONATHAN TELLS HIM OF DAVID'S ABSENCE.
YOU SON OF A STUBBORN CONCUBINE! DON'T YOU KNOW THAT AS LONG AS DAVID LIVES YOU WILL NEVER BE KING? BRING HIM HERE IMMEDIATELY. HE MUST DIE!
WHY SHOULD HE BE KILLED? WHAT HAS HE DONE BUT SERVE YOU WELL IN BATTLE?
MY OWN SON IS A TRAITOR.
I'LL KILL YOU, TOO!
I AM ASHAMED TO CALL YOU FATHER!
SAUL DOESN'T KILL HIS SON. BUT THE NEXT MORNING, JONATHAN GOES OUT TO THE FIELDS AND GIVES DAVID THE SIGNAL.
GO GET MY ARROWS. I OVERSHOT THE TARGET, SO YOU'LL HAVE TO RUN FAR AWAY TO FIND THEM.
THANK YOU, JONATHAN. I WILL FLEE FROM SAUL AND LET THE LORD TELL ME WHEN I CAN COME BACK.

Psalm 22:1-2, 19-21

DAVID WROTE THE FOLLOWING WORDS TO GOD WHILE HE WAS GOING THROUGH
VERY HARD TIMES IN HIS LIFE. THIS PSALM CAN READ AS A PRAYER.

MY GOD, MY GOD, WHY HAVE YOU FORSAKEN ME?
    WHY ARE YOU SO FAR FROM SAVING ME,
    SO FAR FROM MY CRIES OF ANGUISH?
MY GOD, I CRY OUT BY DAY, BUT YOU DO NOT ANSWER,
    BY NIGHT, BUT I FIND NO REST.

BUT YOU, LORD, DO NOT BE FAR FROM ME.
    YOU ARE MY STRENGTH; COME QUICKLY TO HELP ME.
DELIVER ME FROM THE SWORD,
    MY PRECIOUS LIFE FROM THE POWER OF THE DOGS.
RESCUE ME FROM THE MOUTH OF THE LIONS;
    SAVE ME FROM THE HORNS OF THE WILD OXEN.

Psalm 22:25-31

THESE WORDS WRITTEN BY DAVID CAN BE USED FOR PRAISE.

FROM YOU COMES THE THEME OF MY PRAISE IN THE GREAT ASSEMBLY;
   BEFORE THOSE WHO FEAR YOU I WILL FULFILL MY VOWS.
THE POOR WILL EAT AND BE SATISFIED;
   THOSE WHO SEEK THE LORD WILL PRAISE HIM—
   MAY YOUR HEARTS LIVE FOREVER!
ALL THE ENDS OF THE EARTH
   WILL REMEMBER AND TURN TO THE LORD,
AND ALL THE FAMILIES OF THE NATIONS
   WILL BOW DOWN BEFORE HIM,
FOR DOMINION BELONGS TO THE LORD
   AND HE RULES OVER THE NATIONS.
ALL THE RICH OF THE EARTH WILL FEAST AND WORSHIP;
   ALL WHO GO DOWN TO THE DUST WILL KNEEL BEFORE HIM—
   THOSE WHO CANNOT KEEP THEMSELVES ALIVE.
POSTERITY WILL SERVE HIM;
   FUTURE GENERATIONS WILL BE TOLD ABOUT THE LORD.
THEY WILL PROCLAIM HIS RIGHTEOUSNESS,
   DECLARING TO A PEOPLE YET UNBORN:
   HE HAS DONE IT!

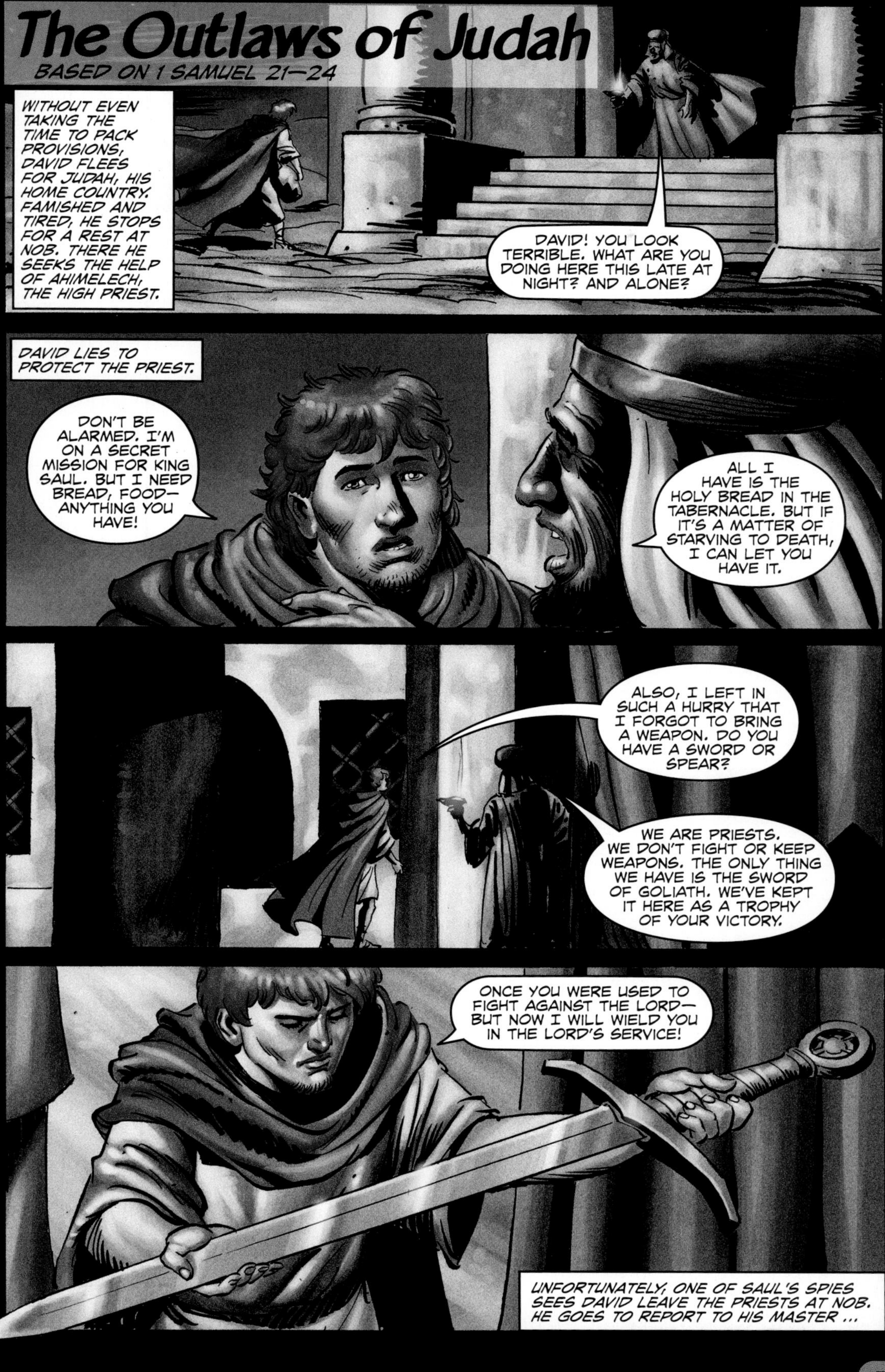
The Outlaws of Judah
BASED ON 1 SAMUEL 21—24
WITHOUT EVEN TAKING THE TIME TO PACK PROVISIONS, DAVID FLEES FOR JUDAH, HIS HOME COUNTRY. FAMISHED AND TIRED, HE STOPS FOR A REST AT NOB. THERE HE SEEKS THE HELP OF AHIMELECH, THE HIGH PRIEST.
DAVID! YOU LOOK TERRIBLE. WHAT ARE YOU DOING HERE THIS LATE AT NIGHT? AND ALONE?
DAVID LIES TO PROTECT THE PRIEST.
DON'T BE ALARMED. I'M ON A SECRET MISSION FOR KING SAUL. BUT I NEED BREAD, FOOD—ANYTHING YOU HAVE!
ALL I HAVE IS THE HOLY BREAD IN THE TABERNACLE. BUT IF IT'S A MATTER OF STARVING TO DEATH, I CAN LET YOU HAVE IT.
ALSO, I LEFT IN SUCH A HURRY THAT I FORGOT TO BRING A WEAPON. DO YOU HAVE A SWORD OR SPEAR?
WE ARE PRIESTS. WE DON'T FIGHT OR KEEP WEAPONS. THE ONLY THING WE HAVE IS THE SWORD OF GOLIATH. WE'VE KEPT IT HERE AS A TROPHY OF YOUR VICTORY.
ONCE YOU WERE USED TO FIGHT AGAINST THE LORD—BUT NOW I WILL WIELD YOU IN THE LORD'S SERVICE!
UNFORTUNATELY, ONE OF SAUL'S SPIES SEES DAVID LEAVE THE PRIESTS AT NOB. HE GOES TO REPORT TO HIS MASTER ...

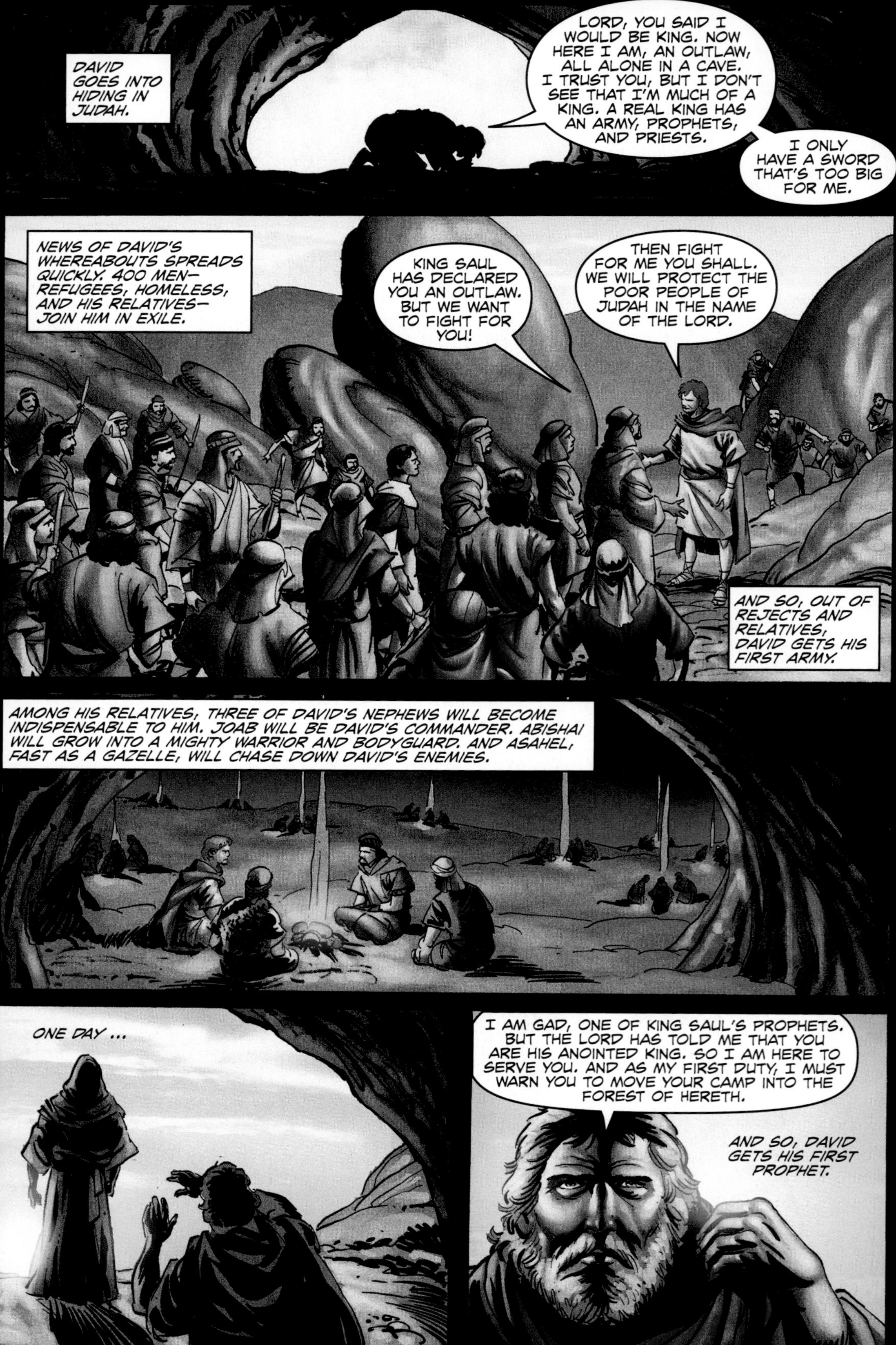
DAVID GOES INTO HIDING IN JUDAH.
LORD, YOU SAID I WOULD BE KING. NOW HERE I AM, AN OUTLAW, ALL ALONE IN A CAVE. I TRUST YOU, BUT I DON'T SEE THAT I'M MUCH OF A KING. A REAL KING HAS AN ARMY, PROPHETS, AND PRIESTS.
I ONLY HAVE A SWORD THAT'S TOO BIG FOR ME.
NEWS OF DAVID'S WHEREABOUTS SPREADS QUICKLY. 400 MEN—REFUGEES, HOMELESS, AND HIS RELATIVES—JOIN HIM IN EXILE.
KING SAUL HAS DECLARED YOU AN OUTLAW. BUT WE WANT TO FIGHT FOR YOU!
THEN FIGHT FOR ME YOU SHALL. WE WILL PROTECT THE POOR PEOPLE OF JUDAH IN THE NAME OF THE LORD.
AND SO, OUT OF REJECTS AND RELATIVES, DAVID GETS HIS FIRST ARMY.
AMONG HIS RELATIVES, THREE OF DAVID'S NEPHEWS WILL BECOME INDISPENSABLE TO HIM. JOAB WILL BE DAVID'S COMMANDER. ABISHAI WILL GROW INTO A MIGHTY WARRIOR AND BODYGUARD. AND ASAHEL, FAST AS A GAZELLE, WILL CHASE DOWN DAVID'S ENEMIES.
ONE DAY ...
I AM GAD, ONE OF KING SAUL'S PROPHETS. BUT THE LORD HAS TOLD ME THAT YOU ARE HIS ANOINTED KING. SO I AM HERE TO SERVE YOU. AND AS MY FIRST DUTY, I MUST WARN YOU TO MOVE YOUR CAMP INTO THE FOREST OF HERETH.
AND SO, DAVID GETS HIS FIRST PROPHET.

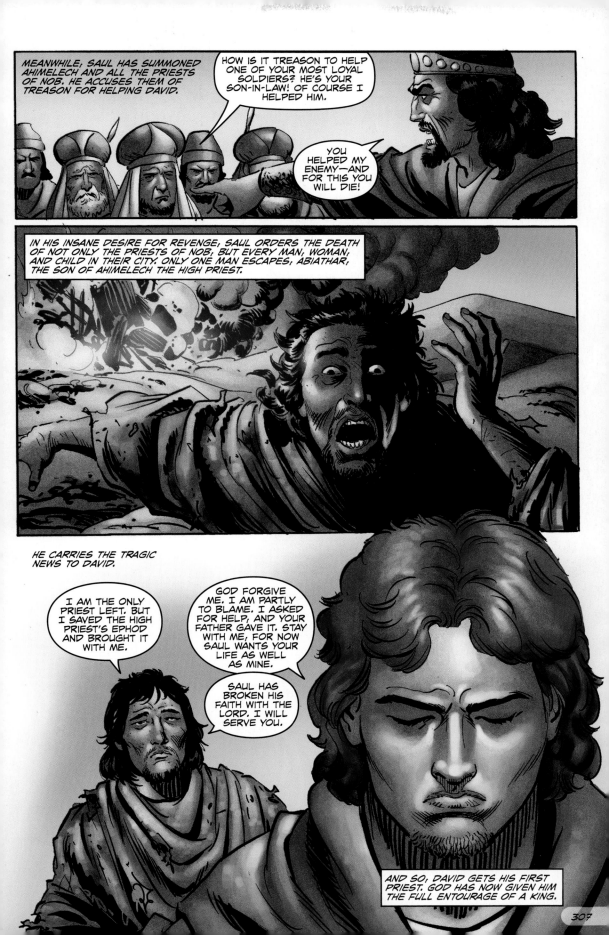

MEANWHILE, SAUL HAS SUMMONED AHIMELECH AND ALL THE PRIESTS OF NOB. HE ACCUSES THEM OF TREASON FOR HELPING DAVID.

HOW IS IT TREASON TO HELP ONE OF YOUR MOST LOYAL SOLDIERS? HE'S YOUR SON-IN-LAW! OF COURSE I HELPED HIM.

YOU HELPED MY ENEMY—AND FOR THIS YOU WILL DIE!

IN HIS INSANE DESIRE FOR REVENGE, SAUL ORDERS THE DEATH OF NOT ONLY THE PRIESTS OF NOB, BUT EVERY MAN, WOMAN, AND CHILD IN THEIR CITY. ONLY ONE MAN ESCAPES, ABIATHAR, THE SON OF AHIMELECH THE HIGH PRIEST.

HE CARRIES THE TRAGIC NEWS TO DAVID.

I AM THE ONLY PRIEST LEFT. BUT I SAVED THE HIGH PRIEST'S EPHOD AND BROUGHT IT WITH ME.

GOD FORGIVE ME. I AM PARTLY TO BLAME. I ASKED FOR HELP, AND YOUR FATHER GAVE IT. STAY WITH ME, FOR NOW SAUL WANTS YOUR LIFE AS WELL AS MINE.

SAUL HAS BROKEN HIS FAITH WITH THE LORD. I WILL SERVE YOU.

AND SO, DAVID GETS HIS FIRST PRIEST. GOD HAS NOW GIVEN HIM THE FULL ENTOURAGE OF A KING.

307

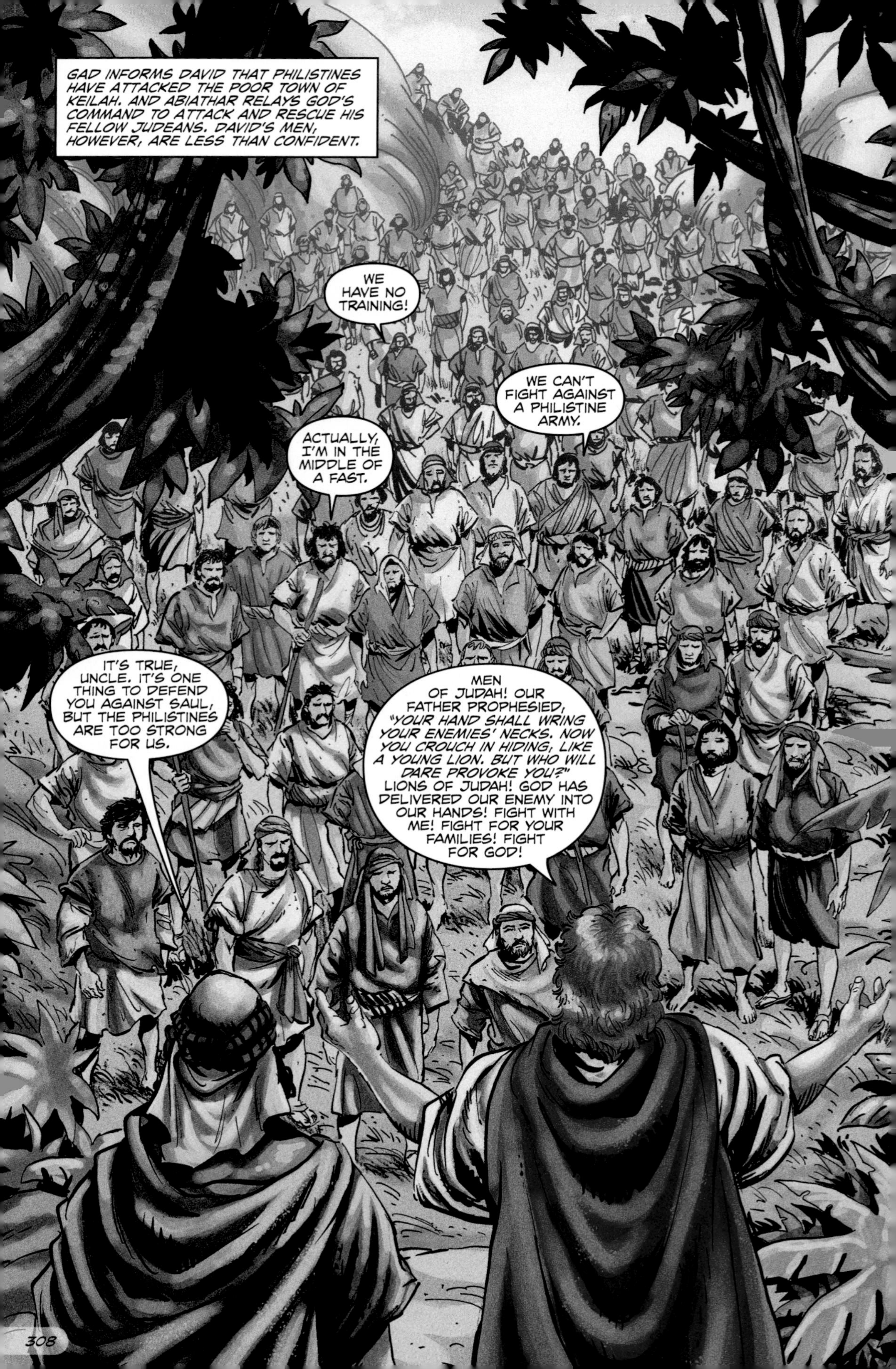

GAD INFORMS DAVID THAT PHILISTINES HAVE ATTACKED THE POOR TOWN OF KEILAH. AND ABIATHAR RELAYS GOD'S COMMAND TO ATTACK AND RESCUE HIS FELLOW JUDEANS. DAVID'S MEN, HOWEVER, ARE LESS THAN CONFIDENT.
WE HAVE NO TRAINING!
WE CAN'T FIGHT AGAINST A PHILISTINE ARMY.
ACTUALLY, I'M IN THE MIDDLE OF A FAST.
IT'S TRUE, UNCLE. IT'S ONE THING TO DEFEND YOU AGAINST SAUL, BUT THE PHILISTINES ARE TOO STRONG FOR US.
MEN OF JUDAH! OUR FATHER PROPHESIED, "YOUR HAND SHALL WRING YOUR ENEMIES' NECKS. NOW YOU CROUCH IN HIDING, LIKE A YOUNG LION. BUT WHO WILL DARE PROVOKE YOU?" LIONS OF JUDAH! GOD HAS DELIVERED OUR ENEMY INTO OUR HANDS! FIGHT WITH ME! FIGHT FOR YOUR FAMILIES! FIGHT FOR GOD!

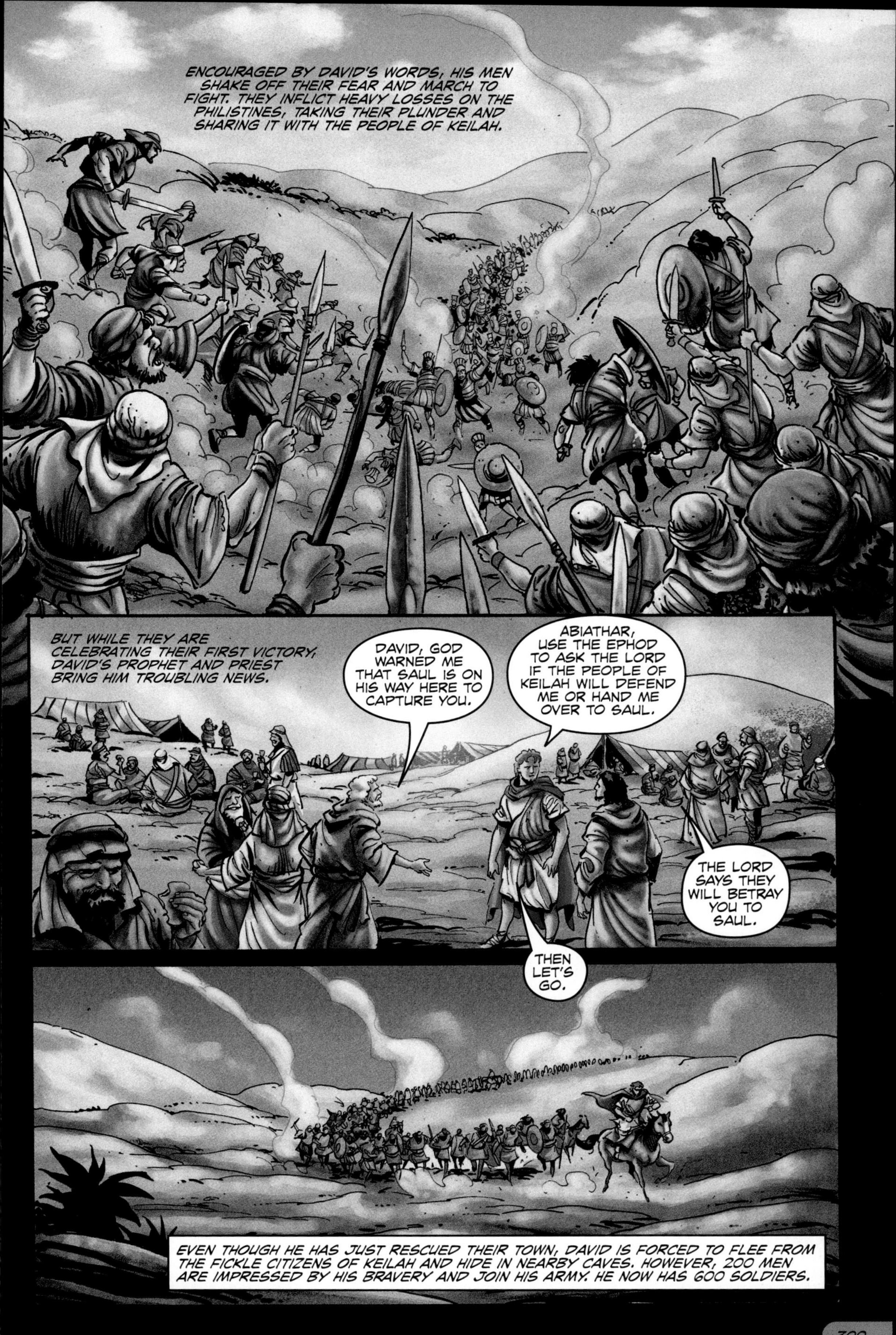
ENCOURAGED BY DAVID'S WORDS, HIS MEN SHAKE OFF THEIR FEAR AND MARCH TO FIGHT. THEY INFLICT HEAVY LOSSES ON THE PHILISTINES, TAKING THEIR PLUNDER AND SHARING IT WITH THE PEOPLE OF KEILAH.
BUT WHILE THEY ARE CELEBRATING THEIR FIRST VICTORY, DAVID'S PROPHET AND PRIEST BRING HIM TROUBLING NEWS.
DAVID, GOD WARNED ME THAT SAUL IS ON HIS WAY HERE TO CAPTURE YOU.
ABIATHAR, USE THE EPHOD TO ASK THE LORD IF THE PEOPLE OF KEILAH WILL DEFEND ME OR HAND ME OVER TO SAUL.
THE LORD SAYS THEY WILL BETRAY YOU TO SAUL.
THEN LET'S GO.
EVEN THOUGH HE HAS JUST RESCUED THEIR TOWN, DAVID IS FORCED TO FLEE FROM THE FICKLE CITIZENS OF KEILAH AND HIDE IN NEARBY CAVES. HOWEVER, 200 MEN ARE IMPRESSED BY HIS BRAVERY AND JOIN HIS ARMY. HE NOW HAS 600 SOLDIERS.

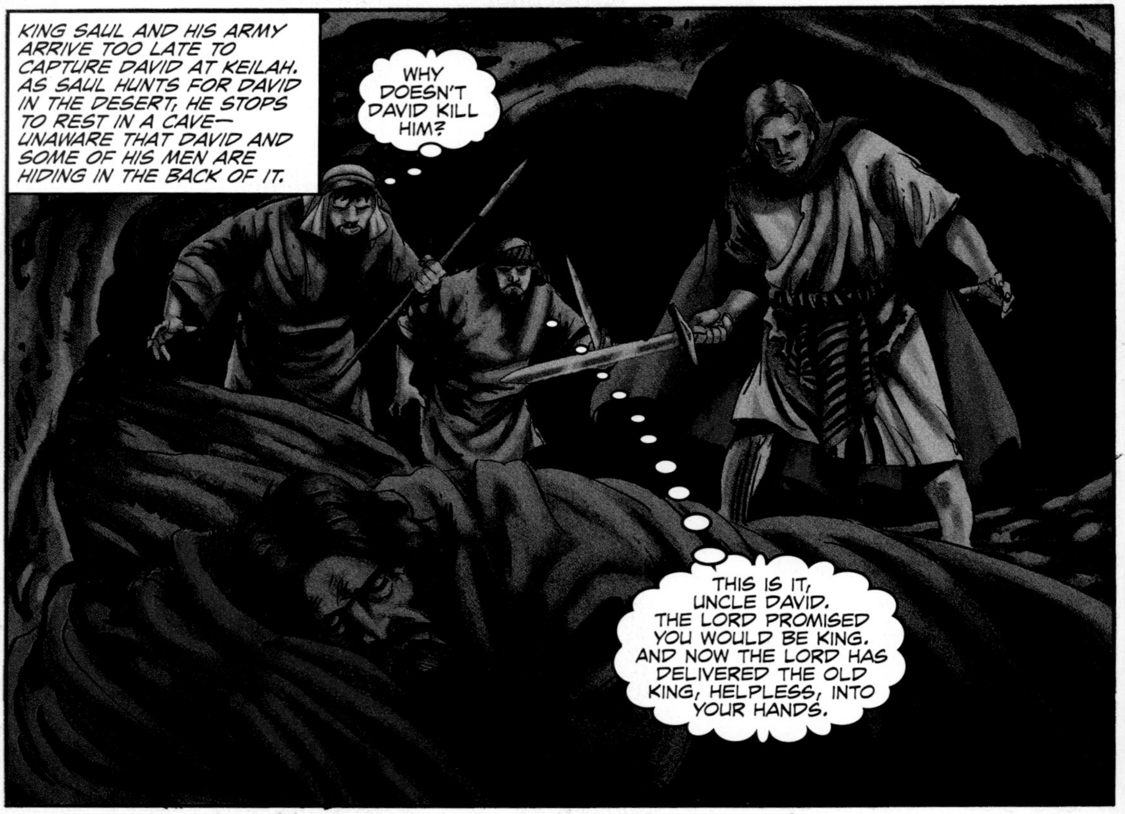
KING SAUL AND HIS ARMY ARRIVE TOO LATE TO CAPTURE DAVID AT KEILAH. AS SAUL HUNTS FOR DAVID IN THE DESERT, HE STOPS TO REST IN A CAVE—UNAWARE THAT DAVID AND SOME OF HIS MEN ARE HIDING IN THE BACK OF IT.
WHY DOESN'T DAVID KILL HIM?
THIS IS IT, UNCLE DAVID. THE LORD PROMISED YOU WOULD BE KING. AND NOW THE LORD HAS DELIVERED THE OLD KING, HELPLESS, INTO YOUR HANDS.

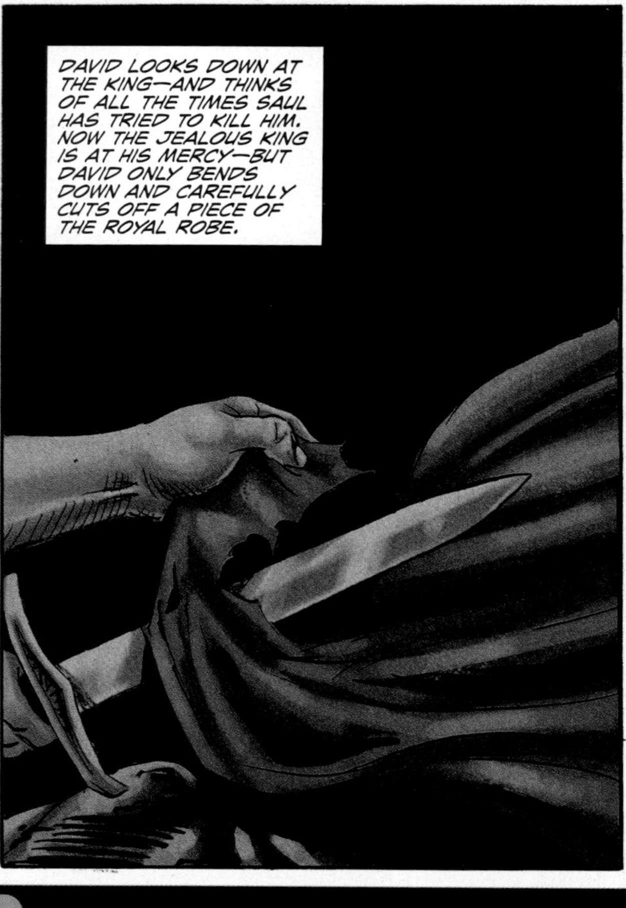
DAVID LOOKS DOWN AT THE KING—AND THINKS OF ALL THE TIMES SAUL HAS TRIED TO KILL HIM. NOW THE JEALOUS KING IS AT HIS MERCY—BUT DAVID ONLY BENDS DOWN AND CAREFULLY CUTS OFF A PIECE OF THE ROYAL ROBE.

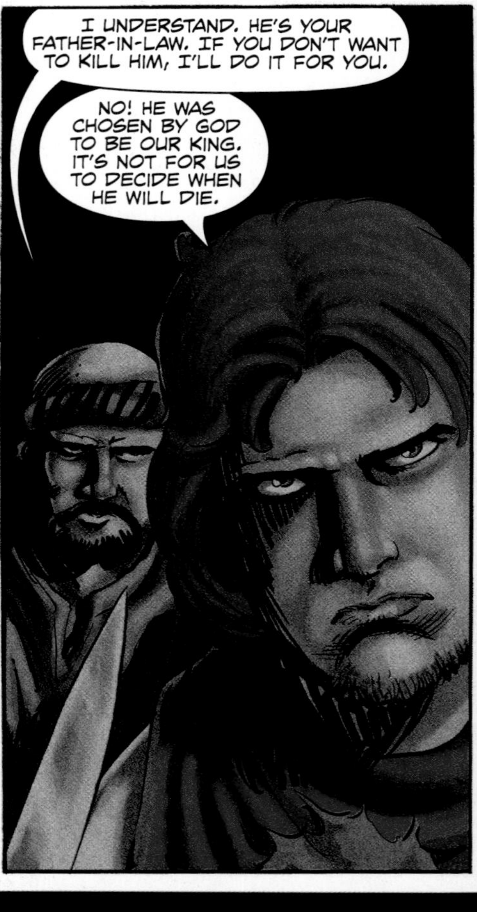
I UNDERSTAND. HE'S YOUR FATHER-IN-LAW. IF YOU DON'T WANT TO KILL HIM, I'LL DO IT FOR YOU.
NO! HE WAS CHOSEN BY GOD TO BE OUR KING. IT'S NOT FOR US TO DECIDE WHEN HE WILL DIE.

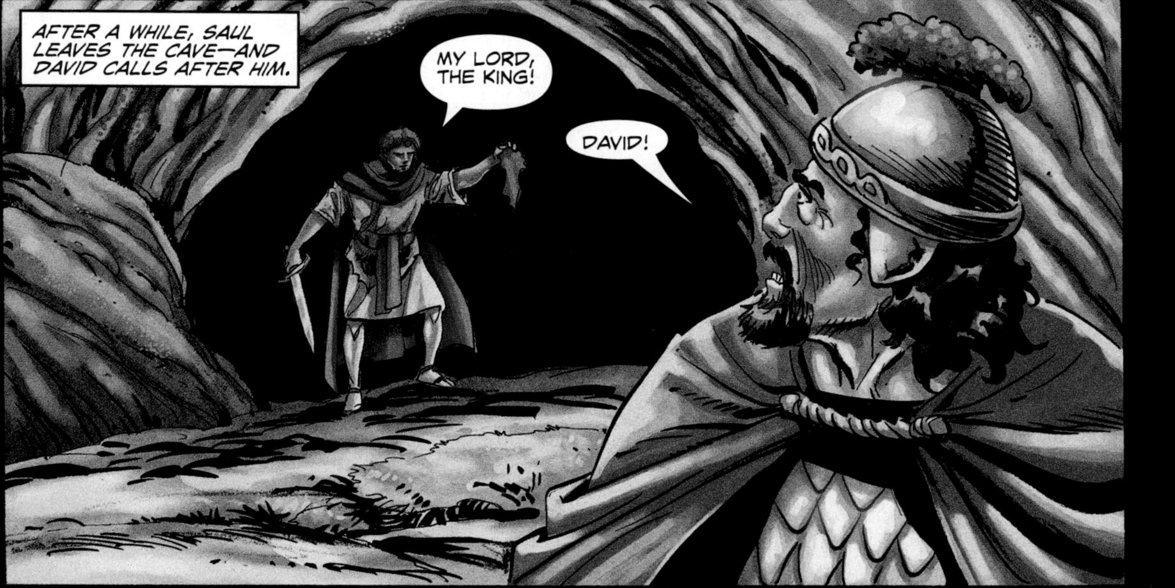
AFTER A WHILE, SAUL LEAVES THE CAVE—AND DAVID CALLS AFTER HIM.
MY LORD, THE KING!
DAVID!

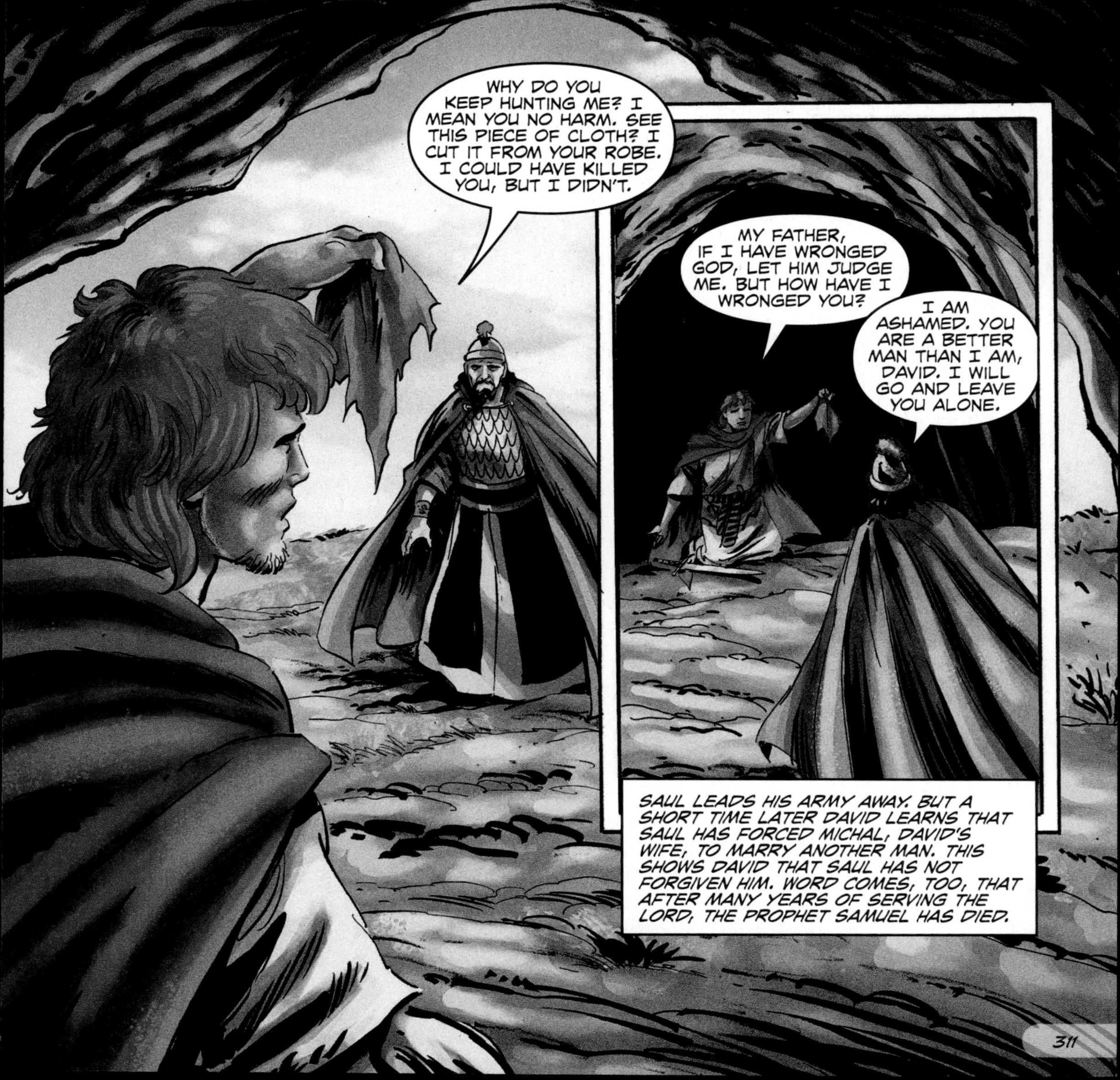
WHY DO YOU KEEP HUNTING ME? I MEAN YOU NO HARM. SEE THIS PIECE OF CLOTH? I CUT IT FROM YOUR ROBE. I COULD HAVE KILLED YOU, BUT I DIDN'T.
MY FATHER, IF I HAVE WRONGED GOD, LET HIM JUDGE ME. BUT HOW HAVE I WRONGED YOU?
I AM ASHAMED. YOU ARE A BETTER MAN THAN I AM, DAVID. I WILL GO AND LEAVE YOU ALONE.
SAUL LEADS HIS ARMY AWAY. BUT A SHORT TIME LATER DAVID LEARNS THAT SAUL HAS FORCED MICHAL, DAVID'S WIFE, TO MARRY ANOTHER MAN. THIS SHOWS DAVID THAT SAUL HAS NOT FORGIVEN HIM. WORD COMES, TOO, THAT AFTER MANY YEARS OF SERVING THE LORD, THE PROPHET SAMUEL HAS DIED.

A Fool and His Wife ... BASED ON 1 SAMUEL 25

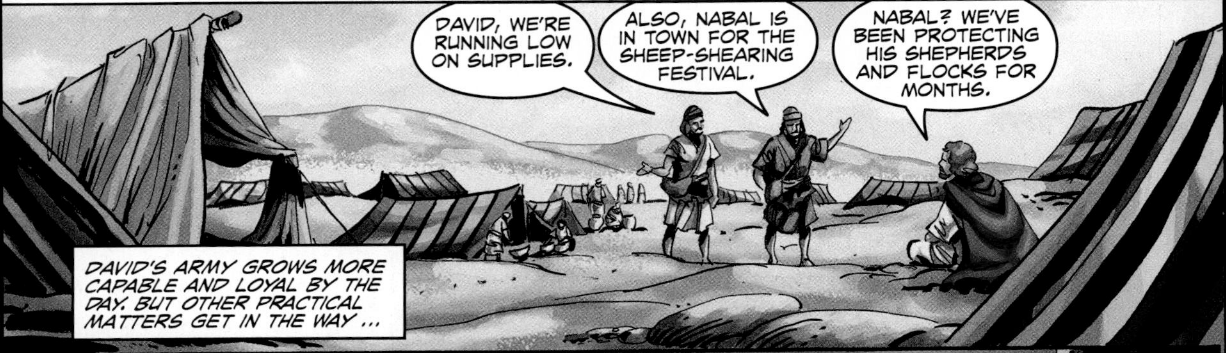
DAVID, WE'RE RUNNING LOW ON SUPPLIES.
ALSO, NABAL IS IN TOWN FOR THE SHEEP-SHEARING FESTIVAL.
NABAL? WE'VE BEEN PROTECTING HIS SHEPHERDS AND FLOCKS FOR MONTHS.
DAVID'S ARMY GROWS MORE CAPABLE AND LOYAL BY THE DAY. BUT OTHER PRACTICAL MATTERS GET IN THE WAY ...

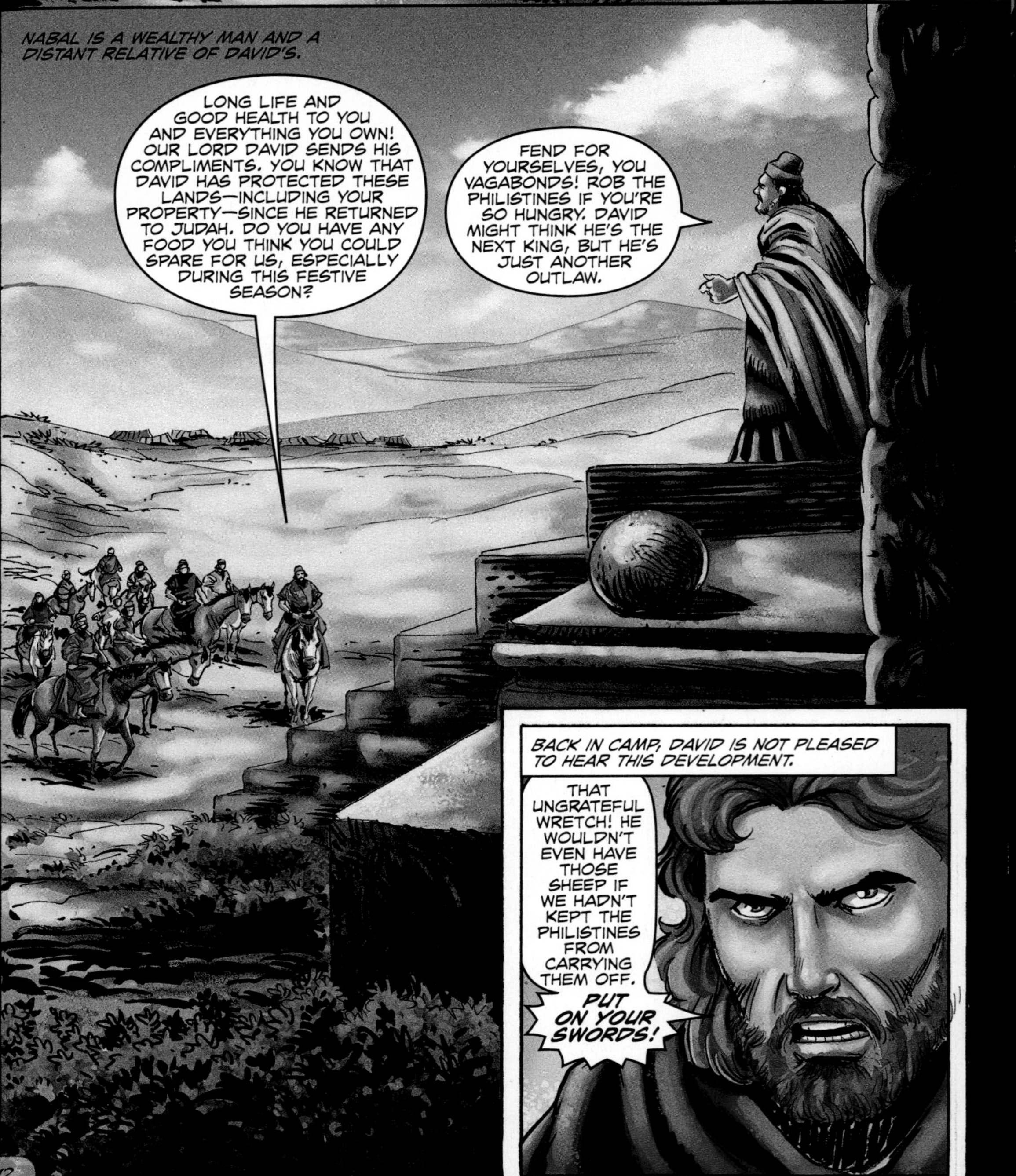
NABAL IS A WEALTHY MAN AND A DISTANT RELATIVE OF DAVID'S.
LONG LIFE AND GOOD HEALTH TO YOU AND EVERYTHING YOU OWN! OUR LORD DAVID SENDS HIS COMPLIMENTS. YOU KNOW THAT DAVID HAS PROTECTED THESE LANDS—INCLUDING YOUR PROPERTY—SINCE HE RETURNED TO JUDAH. DO YOU HAVE ANY FOOD YOU THINK YOU COULD SPARE FOR US, ESPECIALLY DURING THIS FESTIVE SEASON?
FEND FOR YOURSELVES, YOU VAGABONDS! ROB THE PHILISTINES IF YOU'RE SO HUNGRY. DAVID MIGHT THINK HE'S THE NEXT KING, BUT HE'S JUST ANOTHER OUTLAW.
BACK IN CAMP, DAVID IS NOT PLEASED TO HEAR THIS DEVELOPMENT.
THAT UNGRATEFUL WRETCH! HE WOULDN'T EVEN HAVE THOSE SHEEP IF WE HADN'T KEPT THE PHILISTINES FROM CARRYING THEM OFF. PUT ON YOUR SWORDS!

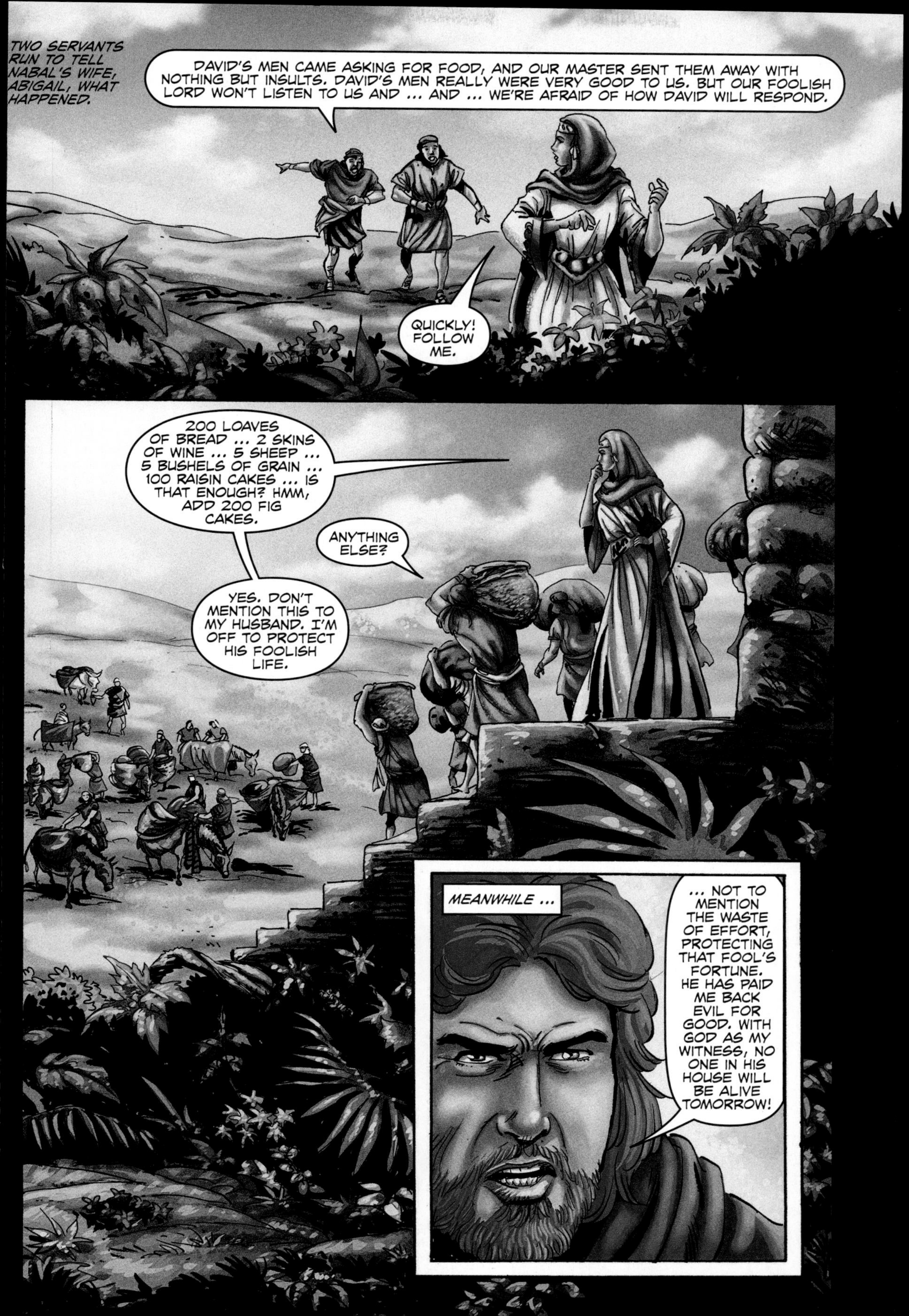
TWO SERVANTS RUN TO TELL NABAL'S WIFE, ABIGAIL, WHAT HAPPENED.
DAVID'S MEN CAME ASKING FOR FOOD, AND OUR MASTER SENT THEM AWAY WITH NOTHING BUT INSULTS. DAVID'S MEN REALLY WERE VERY GOOD TO US. BUT OUR FOOLISH LORD WON'T LISTEN TO US AND ... AND ... WE'RE AFRAID OF HOW DAVID WILL RESPOND.
QUICKLY! FOLLOW ME.
200 LOAVES OF BREAD ... 2 SKINS OF WINE ... 5 SHEEP ... 5 BUSHELS OF GRAIN ... 100 RAISIN CAKES ... IS THAT ENOUGH? HMM, ADD 200 FIG CAKES.
ANYTHING ELSE?
YES. DON'T MENTION THIS TO MY HUSBAND. I'M OFF TO PROTECT HIS FOOLISH LIFE.
MEANWHILE ...
... NOT TO MENTION THE WASTE OF EFFORT, PROTECTING THAT FOOL'S FORTUNE. HE HAS PAID ME BACK EVIL FOR GOOD. WITH GOD AS MY WITNESS, NO ONE IN HIS HOUSE WILL BE ALIVE TOMORROW!

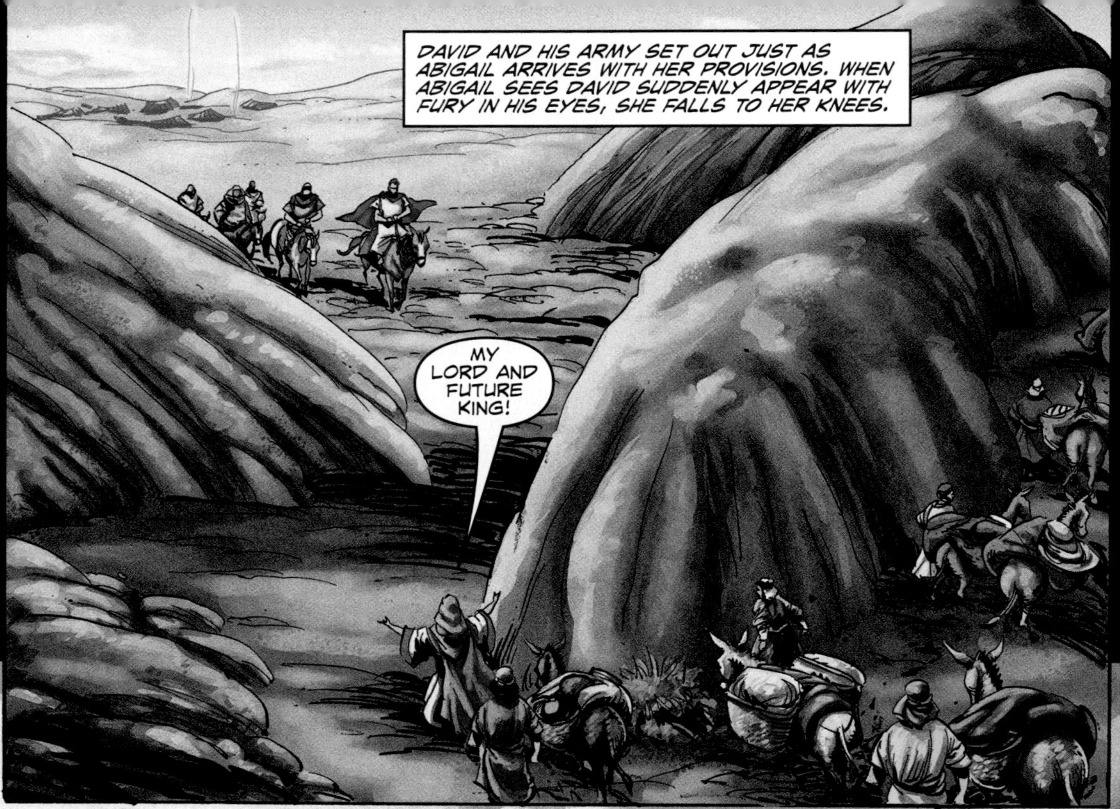
DAVID AND HIS ARMY SET OUT JUST AS ABIGAIL ARRIVES WITH HER PROVISIONS. WHEN ABIGAIL SEES DAVID SUDDENLY APPEAR WITH FURY IN HIS EYES, SHE FALLS TO HER KNEES.
MY LORD AND FUTURE KING!

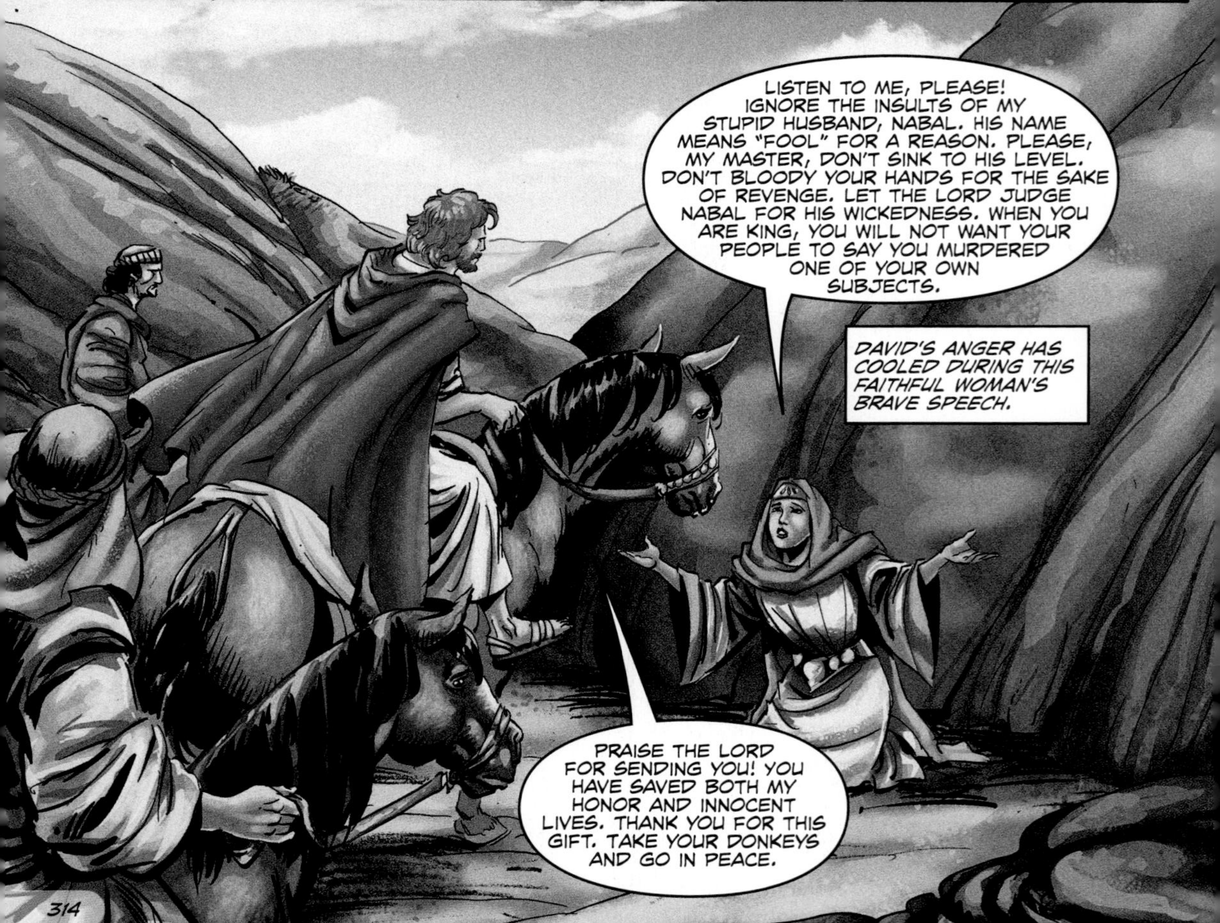
LISTEN TO ME, PLEASE! IGNORE THE INSULTS OF MY STUPID HUSBAND, NABAL. HIS NAME MEANS "FOOL" FOR A REASON. PLEASE, MY MASTER, DON'T SINK TO HIS LEVEL. DON'T BLOODY YOUR HANDS FOR THE SAKE OF REVENGE. LET THE LORD JUDGE NABAL FOR HIS WICKEDNESS. WHEN YOU ARE KING, YOU WILL NOT WANT YOUR PEOPLE TO SAY YOU MURDERED ONE OF YOUR OWN SUBJECTS.
DAVID'S ANGER HAS COOLED DURING THIS FAITHFUL WOMAN'S BRAVE SPEECH.
PRAISE THE LORD FOR SENDING YOU! YOU HAVE SAVED BOTH MY HONOR AND INNOCENT LIVES. THANK YOU FOR THIS GIFT. TAKE YOUR DONKEYS AND GO IN PEACE.

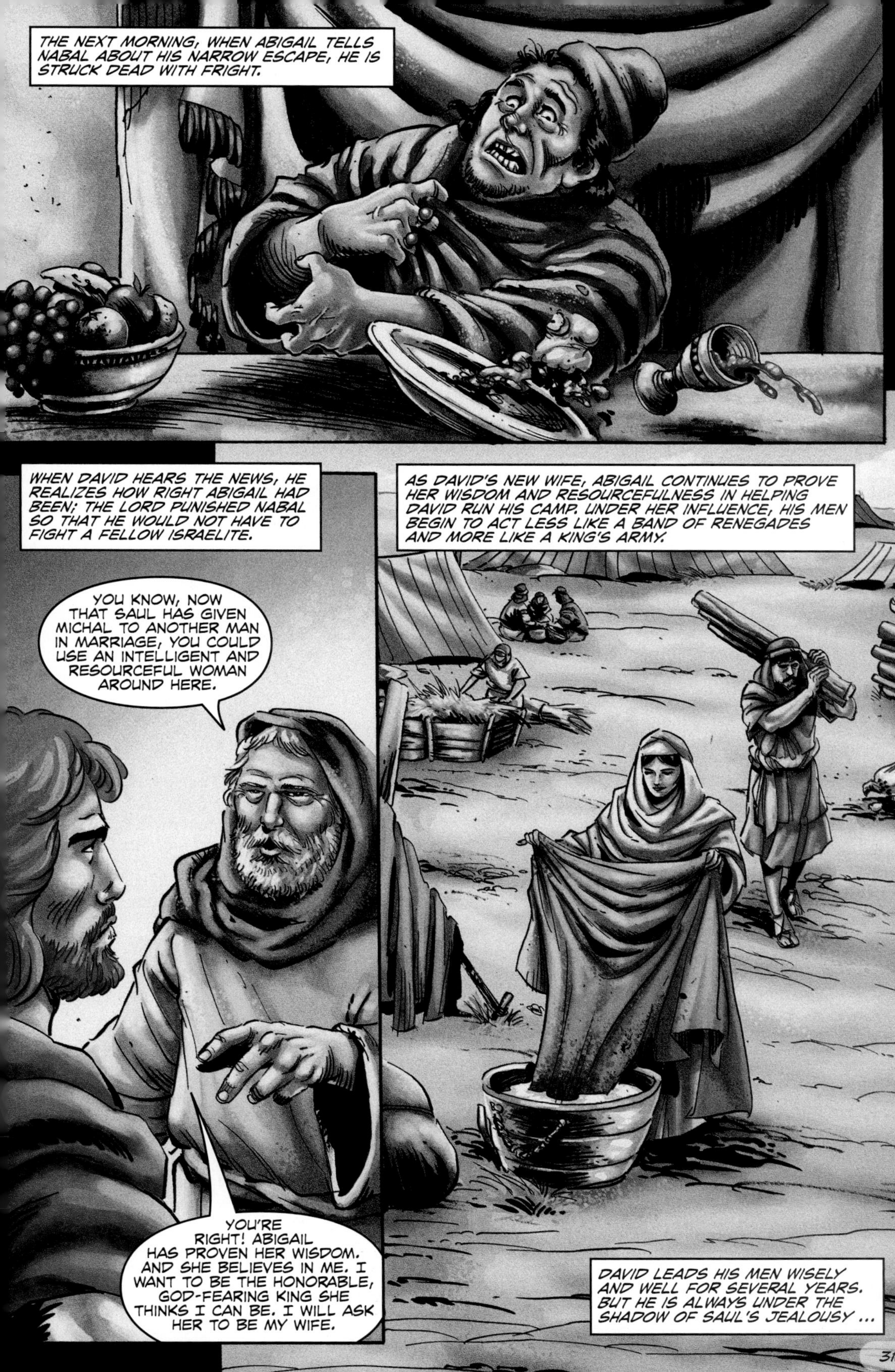
THE NEXT MORNING, WHEN ABIGAIL TELLS NABAL ABOUT HIS NARROW ESCAPE, HE IS STRUCK DEAD WITH FRIGHT.
WHEN DAVID HEARS THE NEWS, HE REALIZES HOW RIGHT ABIGAIL HAD BEEN; THE LORD PUNISHED NABAL SO THAT HE WOULD NOT HAVE TO FIGHT A FELLOW ISRAELITE.
YOU KNOW, NOW THAT SAUL HAS GIVEN MICHAL TO ANOTHER MAN IN MARRIAGE, YOU COULD USE AN INTELLIGENT AND RESOURCEFUL WOMAN AROUND HERE.
YOU'RE RIGHT! ABIGAIL HAS PROVEN HER WISDOM. AND SHE BELIEVES IN ME. I WANT TO BE THE HONORABLE, GOD-FEARING KING SHE THINKS I CAN BE. I WILL ASK HER TO BE MY WIFE.
AS DAVID'S NEW WIFE, ABIGAIL CONTINUES TO PROVE HER WISDOM AND RESOURCEFULNESS IN HELPING DAVID RUN HIS CAMP. UNDER HER INFLUENCE, HIS MEN BEGIN TO ACT LESS LIKE A BAND OF RENEGADES AND MORE LIKE A KING'S ARMY.
DAVID LEADS HIS MEN WISELY AND WELL FOR SEVERAL YEARS. BUT HE IS ALWAYS UNDER THE SHADOW OF SAUL'S JEALOUSY ...

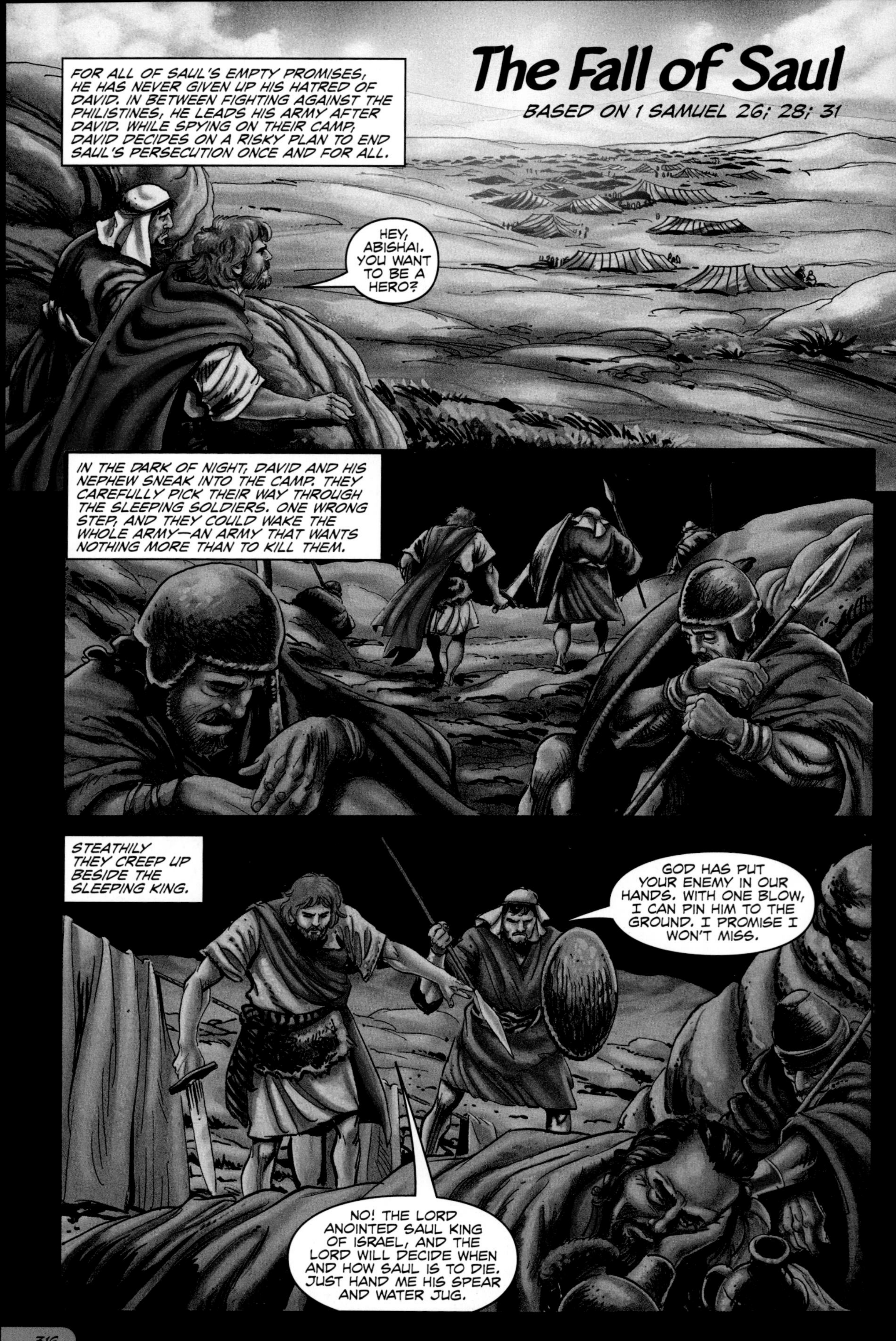
The Fall of Saul
BASED ON 1 SAMUEL 26; 28; 31
FOR ALL OF SAUL'S EMPTY PROMISES, HE HAS NEVER GIVEN UP HIS HATRED OF DAVID. IN BETWEEN FIGHTING AGAINST THE PHILISTINES, HE LEADS HIS ARMY AFTER DAVID. WHILE SPYING ON THEIR CAMP, DAVID DECIDES ON A RISKY PLAN TO END SAUL'S PERSECUTION ONCE AND FOR ALL.
HEY, ABISHAI. YOU WANT TO BE A HERO?
IN THE DARK OF NIGHT, DAVID AND HIS NEPHEW SNEAK INTO THE CAMP. THEY CAREFULLY PICK THEIR WAY THROUGH THE SLEEPING SOLDIERS. ONE WRONG STEP, AND THEY COULD WAKE THE WHOLE ARMY—AN ARMY THAT WANTS NOTHING MORE THAN TO KILL THEM.
STEATHILY THEY CREEP UP BESIDE THE SLEEPING KING.
GOD HAS PUT YOUR ENEMY IN OUR HANDS. WITH ONE BLOW, I CAN PIN HIM TO THE GROUND. I PROMISE I WON'T MISS.
NO! THE LORD ANOINTED SAUL KING OF ISRAEL, AND THE LORD WILL DECIDE WHEN AND HOW SAUL IS TO DIE. JUST HAND ME HIS SPEAR AND WATER JUG.

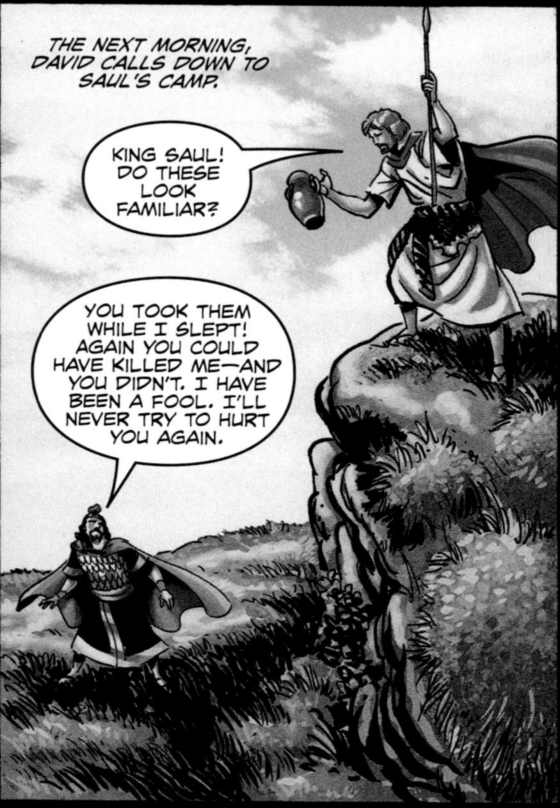
THE NEXT MORNING, DAVID CALLS DOWN TO SAUL'S CAMP.
KING SAUL! DO THESE LOOK FAMILIAR?
YOU TOOK THEM WHILE I SLEPT! AGAIN YOU COULD HAVE KILLED ME—AND YOU DIDN'T. I HAVE BEEN A FOOL. I'LL NEVER TRY TO HURT YOU AGAIN.
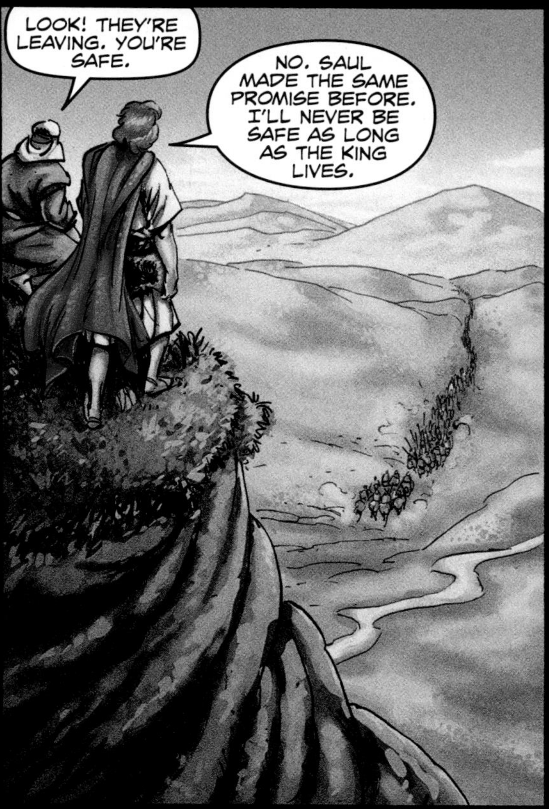
LOOK! THEY'RE LEAVING. YOU'RE SAFE.
NO. SAUL MADE THE SAME PROMISE BEFORE. I'LL NEVER BE SAFE AS LONG AS THE KING LIVES.
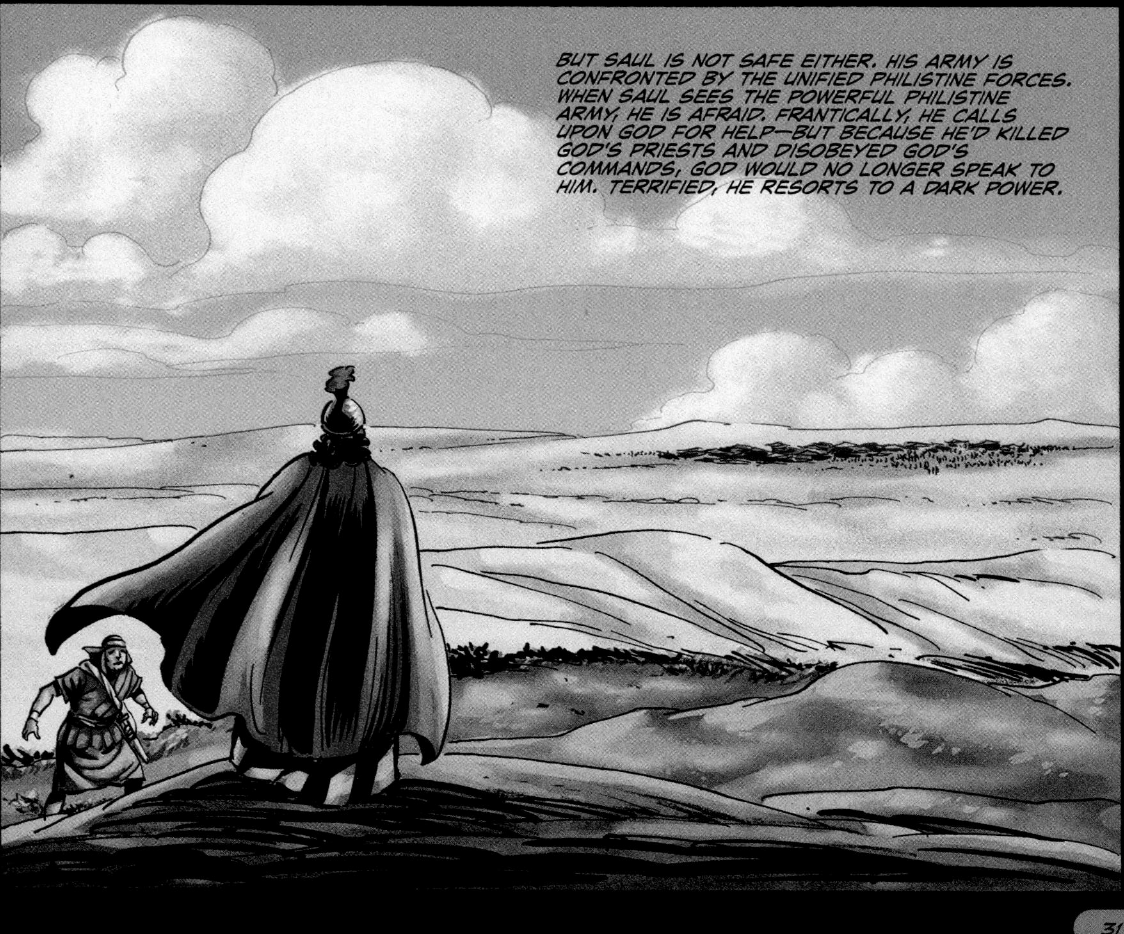
BUT SAUL IS NOT SAFE EITHER. HIS ARMY IS CONFRONTED BY THE UNIFIED PHILISTINE FORCES. WHEN SAUL SEES THE POWERFUL PHILISTINE ARMY, HE IS AFRAID. FRANTICALLY, HE CALLS UPON GOD FOR HELP—BUT BECAUSE HE'D KILLED GOD'S PRIESTS AND DISOBEYED GOD'S COMMANDS, GOD WOULD NO LONGER SPEAK TO HIM. TERRIFIED, HE RESORTS TO A DARK POWER.

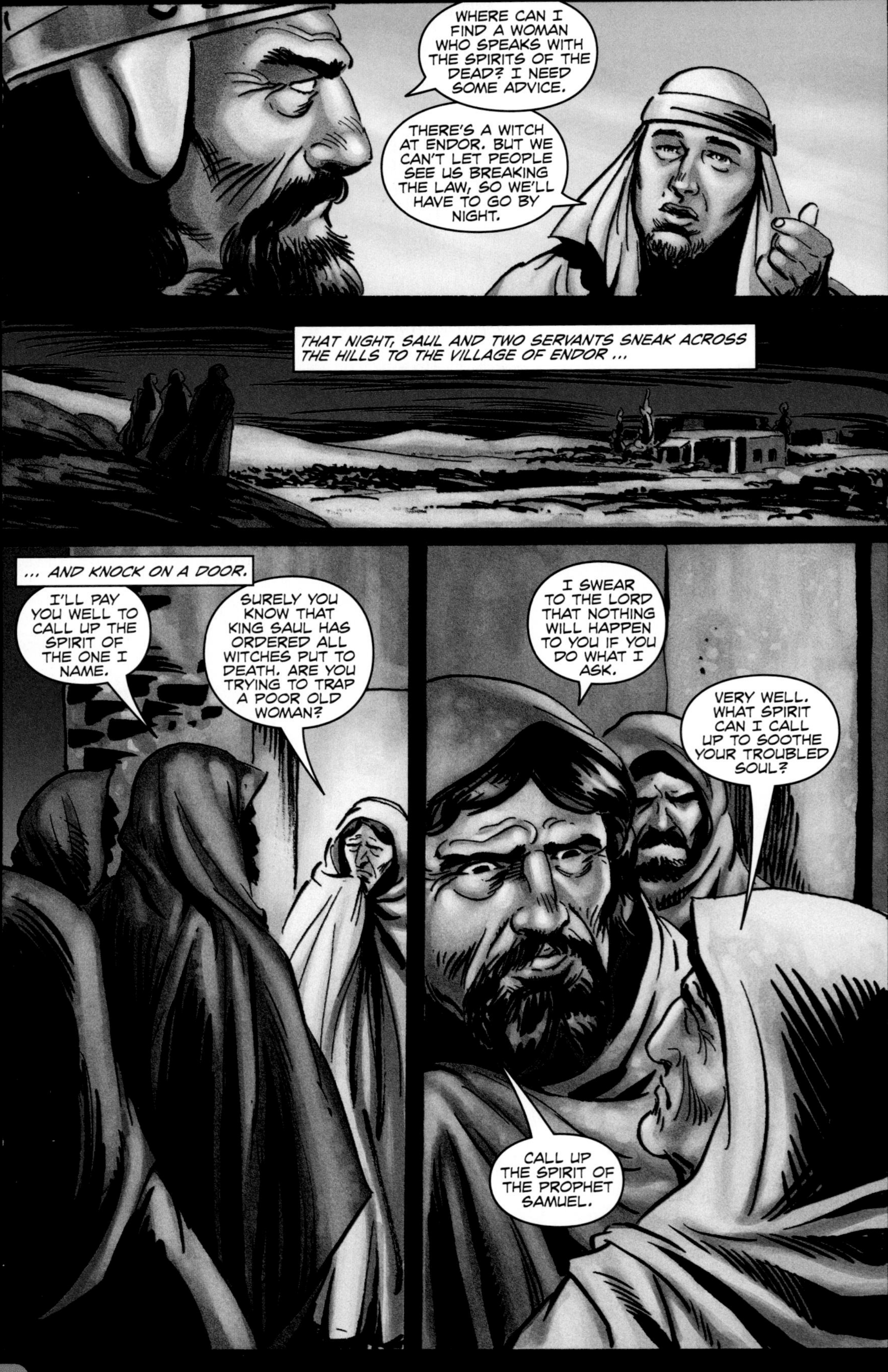
WHERE CAN I FIND A WOMAN WHO SPEAKS WITH THE SPIRITS OF THE DEAD? I NEED SOME ADVICE.
THERE'S A WITCH AT ENDOR. BUT WE CAN'T LET PEOPLE SEE US BREAKING THE LAW, SO WE'LL HAVE TO GO BY NIGHT.
THAT NIGHT, SAUL AND TWO SERVANTS SNEAK ACROSS THE HILLS TO THE VILLAGE OF ENDOR ...
... AND KNOCK ON A DOOR.
I'LL PAY YOU WELL TO CALL UP THE SPIRIT OF THE ONE I NAME.
SURELY YOU KNOW THAT KING SAUL HAS ORDERED ALL WITCHES PUT TO DEATH. ARE YOU TRYING TO TRAP A POOR OLD WOMAN?
I SWEAR TO THE LORD THAT NOTHING WILL HAPPEN TO YOU IF YOU DO WHAT I ASK.
VERY WELL. WHAT SPIRIT CAN I CALL UP TO SOOTHE YOUR TROUBLED SOUL?
CALL UP THE SPIRIT OF THE PROPHET SAMUEL.

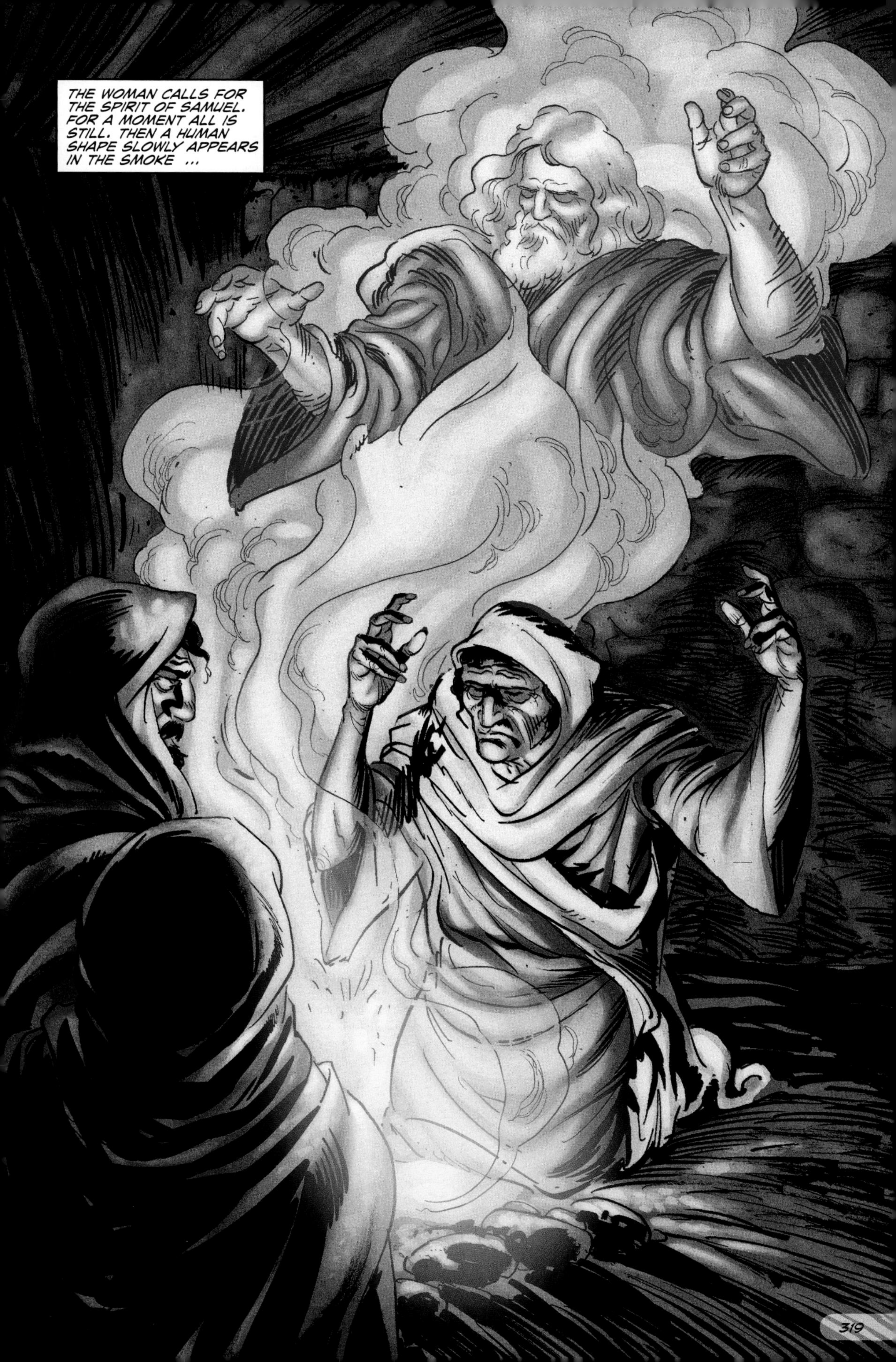
THE WOMAN CALLS FOR THE SPIRIT OF SAMUEL. FOR A MOMENT ALL IS STILL. THEN A HUMAN SHAPE SLOWLY APPEARS IN THE SMOKE ...

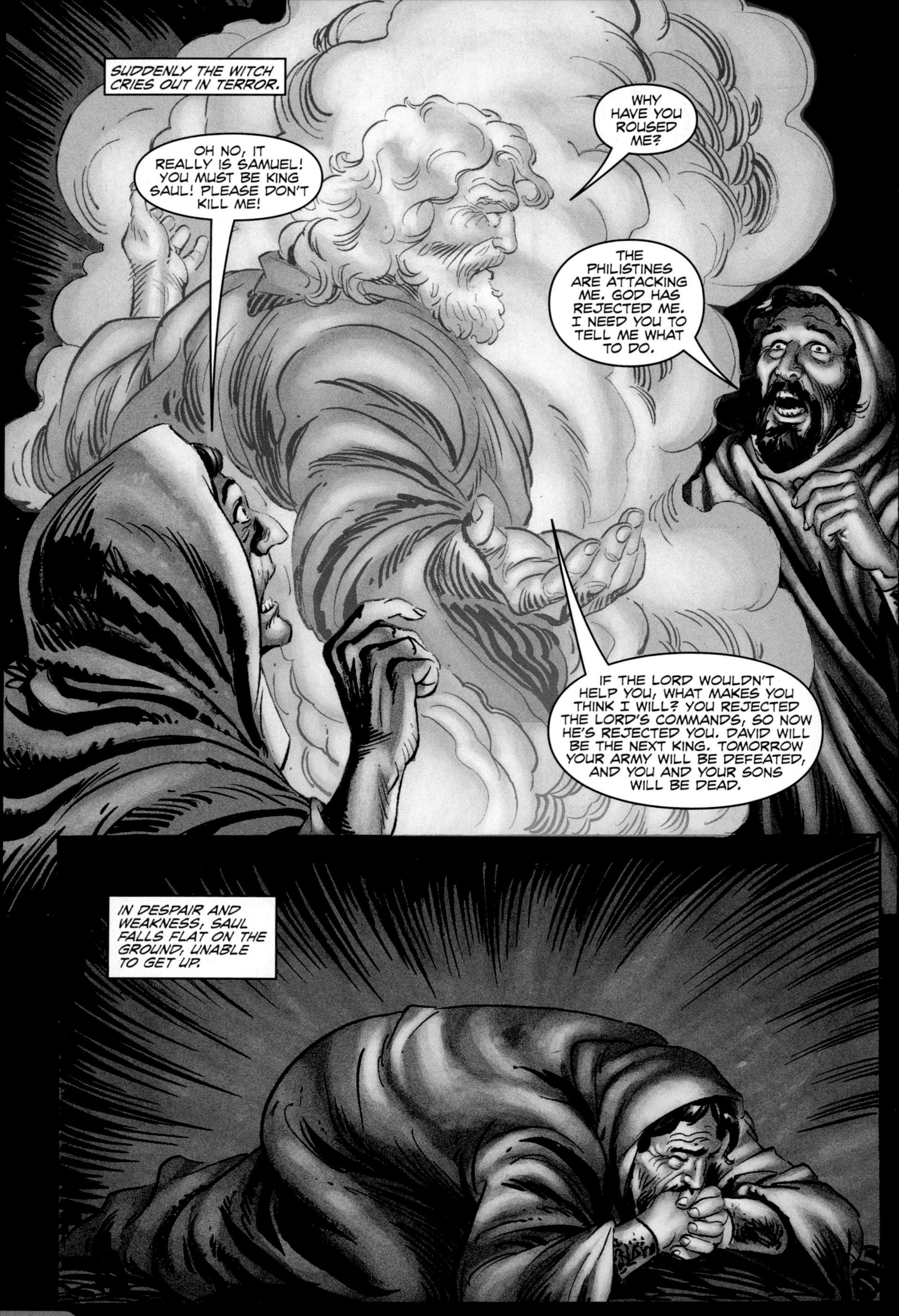
SUDDENLY THE WITCH CRIES OUT IN TERROR.
OH NO, IT REALLY IS SAMUEL! YOU MUST BE KING SAUL! PLEASE DON'T KILL ME!
WHY HAVE YOU ROUSED ME?
THE PHILISTINES ARE ATTACKING ME. GOD HAS REJECTED ME. I NEED YOU TO TELL ME WHAT TO DO.
IF THE LORD WOULDN'T HELP YOU, WHAT MAKES YOU THINK I WILL? YOU REJECTED THE LORD'S COMMANDS, SO NOW HE'S REJECTED YOU. DAVID WILL BE THE NEXT KING. TOMORROW YOUR ARMY WILL BE DEFEATED, AND YOU AND YOUR SONS WILL BE DEAD.
IN DESPAIR AND WEAKNESS, SAUL FALLS FLAT ON THE GROUND, UNABLE TO GET UP.

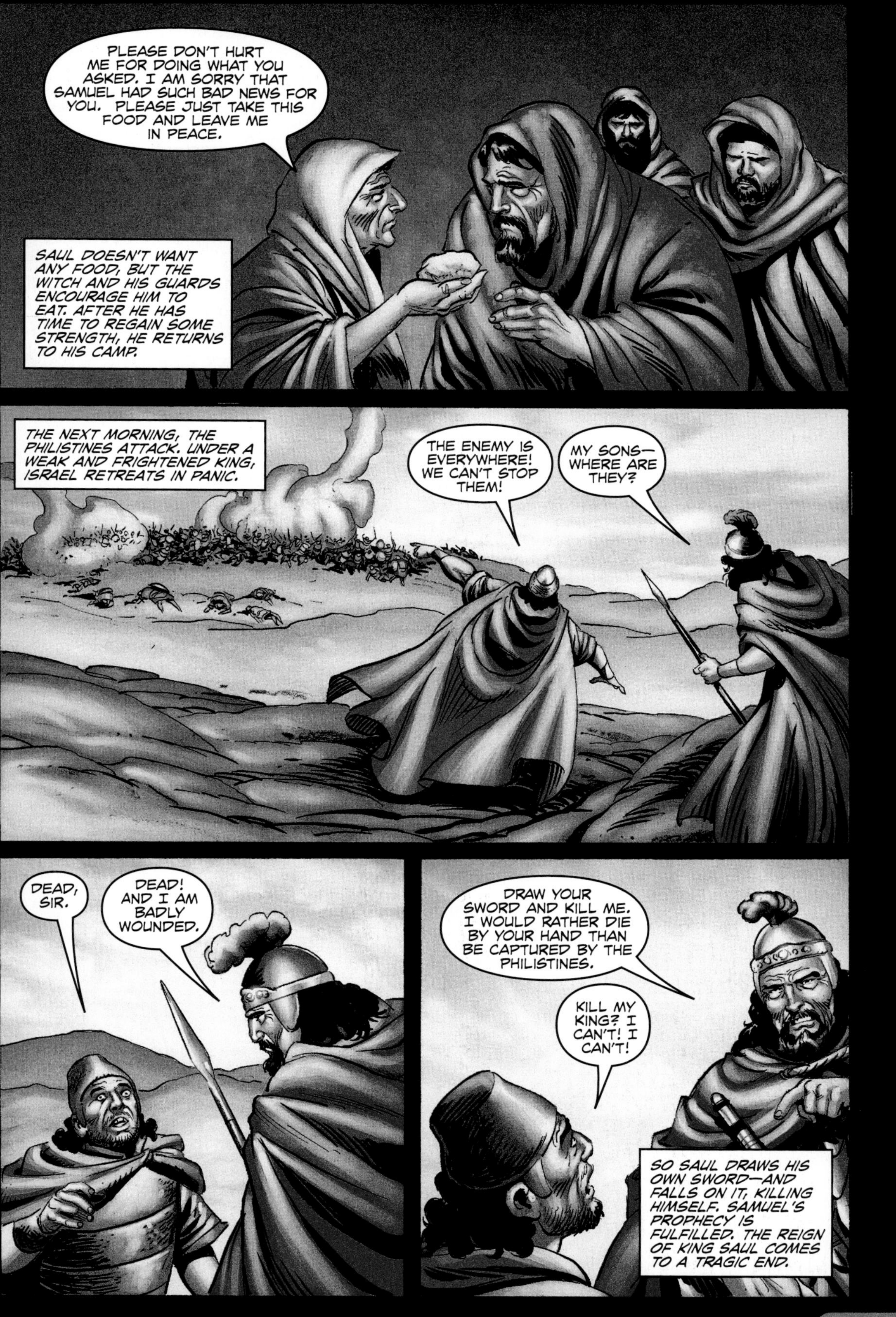
PLEASE DON'T HURT ME FOR DOING WHAT YOU ASKED. I AM SORRY THAT SAMUEL HAD SUCH BAD NEWS FOR YOU. PLEASE JUST TAKE THIS FOOD AND LEAVE ME IN PEACE.
SAUL DOESN'T WANT ANY FOOD, BUT THE WITCH AND HIS GUARDS ENCOURAGE HIM TO EAT. AFTER HE HAS TIME TO REGAIN SOME STRENGTH, HE RETURNS TO HIS CAMP.
THE NEXT MORNING, THE PHILISTINES ATTACK. UNDER A WEAK AND FRIGHTENED KING, ISRAEL RETREATS IN PANIC.
THE ENEMY IS EVERYWHERE! WE CAN'T STOP THEM!
MY SONS—WHERE ARE THEY?
DEAD, SIR.
DEAD! AND I AM BADLY WOUNDED.
DRAW YOUR SWORD AND KILL ME. I WOULD RATHER DIE BY YOUR HAND THAN BE CAPTURED BY THE PHILISTINES.
KILL MY KING? I CAN'T! I CAN'T!
SO SAUL DRAWS HIS OWN SWORD—AND FALLS ON IT, KILLING HIMSELF. SAMUEL'S PROPHECY IS FULFILLED. THE REIGN OF KING SAUL COMES TO A TRAGIC END.

Just Rewards

BASED ON 2 SAMUEL 1:1—2:7

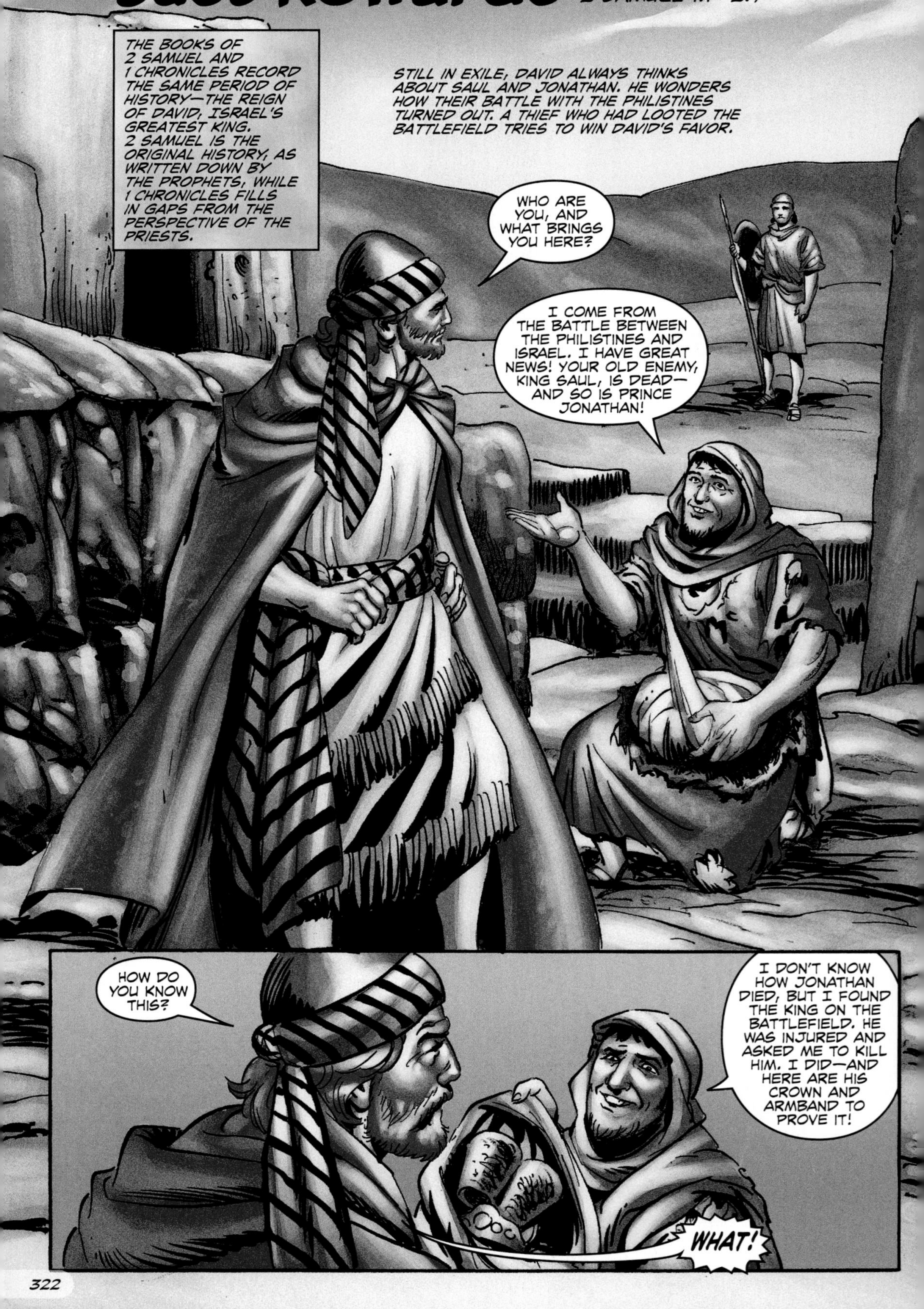
THE BOOKS OF 2 SAMUEL AND 1 CHRONICLES RECORD THE SAME PERIOD OF HISTORY—THE REIGN OF DAVID, ISRAEL'S GREATEST KING. 2 SAMUEL IS THE ORIGINAL HISTORY, AS WRITTEN DOWN BY THE PROPHETS, WHILE 1 CHRONICLES FILLS IN GAPS FROM THE PERSPECTIVE OF THE PRIESTS.
STILL IN EXILE, DAVID ALWAYS THINKS ABOUT SAUL AND JONATHAN. HE WONDERS HOW THEIR BATTLE WITH THE PHILISTINES TURNED OUT. A THIEF WHO HAD LOOTED THE BATTLEFIELD TRIES TO WIN DAVID'S FAVOR.
WHO ARE YOU, AND WHAT BRINGS YOU HERE?
I COME FROM THE BATTLE BETWEEN THE PHILISTINES AND ISRAEL. I HAVE GREAT NEWS! YOUR OLD ENEMY, KING SAUL, IS DEAD—AND SO IS PRINCE JONATHAN!
HOW DO YOU KNOW THIS?
I DON'T KNOW HOW JONATHAN DIED, BUT I FOUND THE KING ON THE BATTLEFIELD. HE WAS INJURED AND ASKED ME TO KILL HIM. I DID—AND HERE ARE HIS CROWN AND ARMBAND TO PROVE IT!
WHAT!

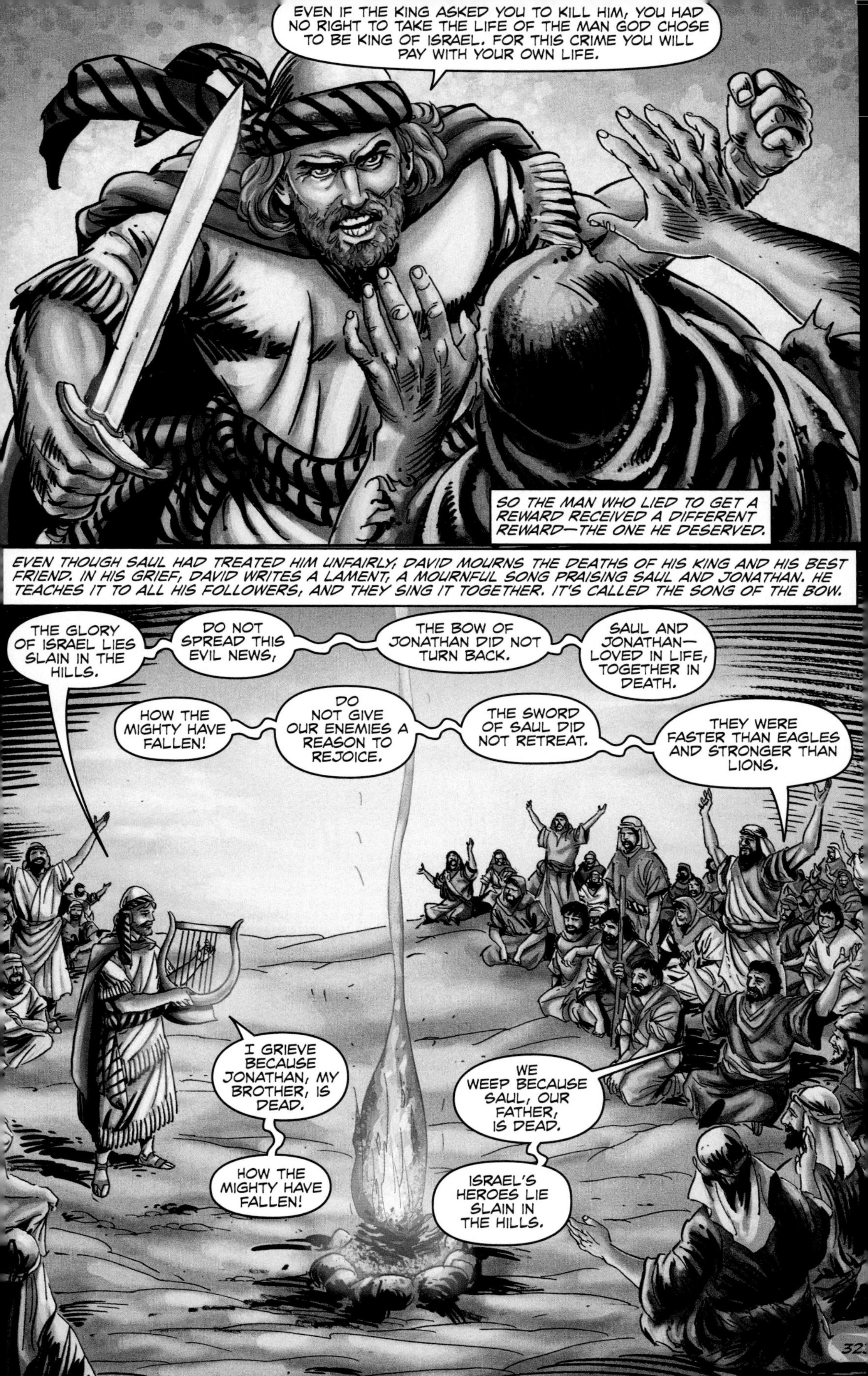

EVEN IF THE KING ASKED YOU TO KILL HIM, YOU HAD NO RIGHT TO TAKE THE LIFE OF THE MAN GOD CHOSE TO BE KING OF ISRAEL. FOR THIS CRIME YOU WILL PAY WITH YOUR OWN LIFE.
SO THE MAN WHO LIED TO GET A REWARD RECEIVED A DIFFERENT REWARD—THE ONE HE DESERVED.
EVEN THOUGH SAUL HAD TREATED HIM UNFAIRLY, DAVID MOURNS THE DEATHS OF HIS KING AND HIS BEST FRIEND. IN HIS GRIEF, DAVID WRITES A LAMENT, A MOURNFUL SONG PRAISING SAUL AND JONATHAN. HE TEACHES IT TO ALL HIS FOLLOWERS, AND THEY SING IT TOGETHER. IT'S CALLED THE SONG OF THE BOW.
THE GLORY OF ISRAEL LIES SLAIN IN THE HILLS.
DO NOT SPREAD THIS EVIL NEWS,
THE BOW OF JONATHAN DID NOT TURN BACK.
SAUL AND JONATHAN—LOVED IN LIFE, TOGETHER IN DEATH.
HOW THE MIGHTY HAVE FALLEN!
DO NOT GIVE OUR ENEMIES A REASON TO REJOICE.
THE SWORD OF SAUL DID NOT RETREAT.
THEY WERE FASTER THAN EAGLES AND STRONGER THAN LIONS.
I GRIEVE BECAUSE JONATHAN, MY BROTHER, IS DEAD.
HOW THE MIGHTY HAVE FALLEN!
WE WEEP BECAUSE SAUL, OUR FATHER, IS DEAD.
ISRAEL'S HEROES LIE SLAIN IN THE HILLS.

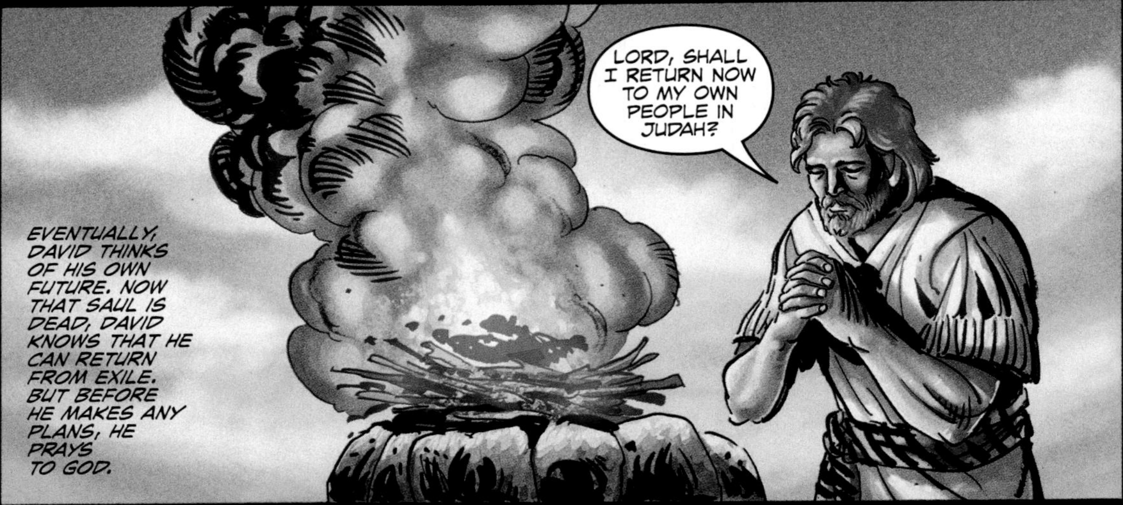
EVENTUALLY, DAVID THINKS OF HIS OWN FUTURE. NOW THAT SAUL IS DEAD, DAVID KNOWS THAT HE CAN RETURN FROM EXILE. BUT BEFORE HE MAKES ANY PLANS, HE PRAYS TO GOD.
LORD, SHALL I RETURN NOW TO MY OWN PEOPLE IN JUDAH?

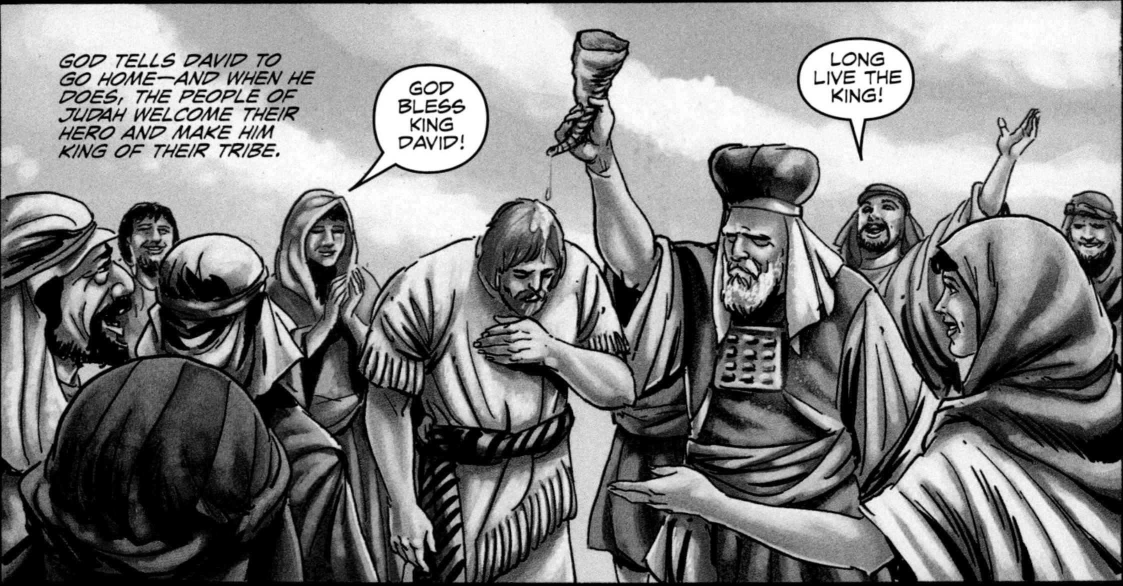
GOD TELLS DAVID TO GO HOME—AND WHEN HE DOES, THE PEOPLE OF JUDAH WELCOME THEIR HERO AND MAKE HIM KING OF THEIR TRIBE.
GOD BLESS KING DAVID!
LONG LIVE THE KING!

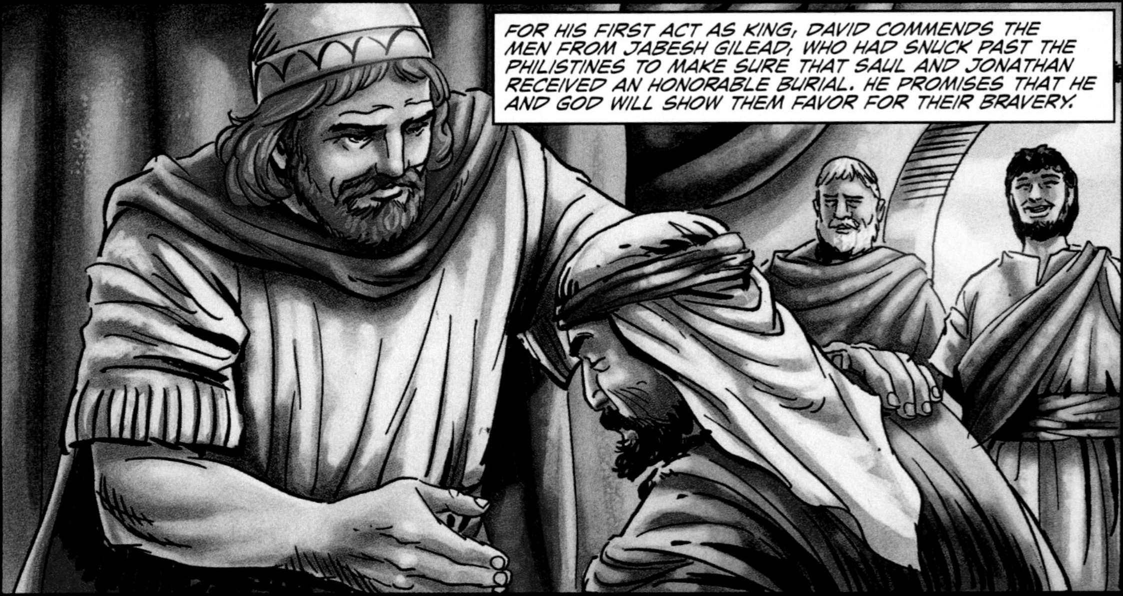
FOR HIS FIRST ACT AS KING, DAVID COMMENDS THE MEN FROM JABESH GILEAD, WHO HAD SNUCK PAST THE PHILISTINES TO MAKE SURE THAT SAUL AND JONATHAN RECEIVED AN HONORABLE BURIAL. HE PROMISES THAT HE AND GOD WILL SHOW THEM FAVOR FOR THEIR BRAVERY.

Royal Rivals
BASED ON 2 SAMUEL 2:8—3:21

NOW THAT KING SAUL IS DEAD, DAVID IS MADE KING OF HIS OWN TRIBE OF JUDAH. BUT TROUBLE BREWS ACROSS THE JORDAN RIVER. SAUL'S MOST POWERFUL GENERAL, ABNER, DECLARES THAT SAUL'S YOUNGEST SON, ISH-BOSHETH, IS KING OVER ALL THE OTHER TRIBES OF ISRAEL. BUT THE CRAFTY GENERAL KNOWS THAT ISH-BOSHETH IS SO WEAK THAT ABNER HIMSELF WILL ALWAYS BE THE REAL POWER BEHIND THE THRONE.

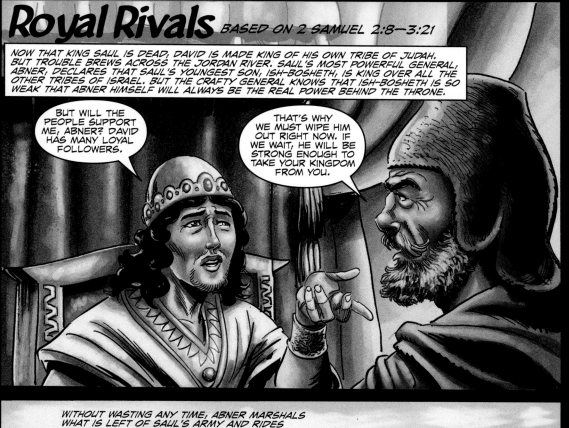

BUT WILL THE PEOPLE SUPPORT ME, ABNER? DAVID HAS MANY LOYAL FOLLOWERS.

THAT'S WHY WE MUST WIPE HIM OUT RIGHT NOW. IF WE WAIT, HE WILL BE STRONG ENOUGH TO TAKE YOUR KINGDOM FROM YOU.

WITHOUT WASTING ANY TIME, ABNER MARSHALS WHAT IS LEFT OF SAUL'S ARMY AND RIDES AGAINST JOAB AND DAVID'S FORCES.

IN TURN, JOAB RALLIES DAVID'S MEN AND MEETS ABNER'S ARMY AT THE POOL OF GIBEON. FOR A MOMENT, THE TWO ARMIES FACE EACH OTHER, UNCERTAIN WHAT TO DO AGAINST THEIR OWN COUNTRYMEN. THE FIRST BLOW IN THIS BATTLE WILL MARK THE BEGINNING OF A CIVIL WAR.

325

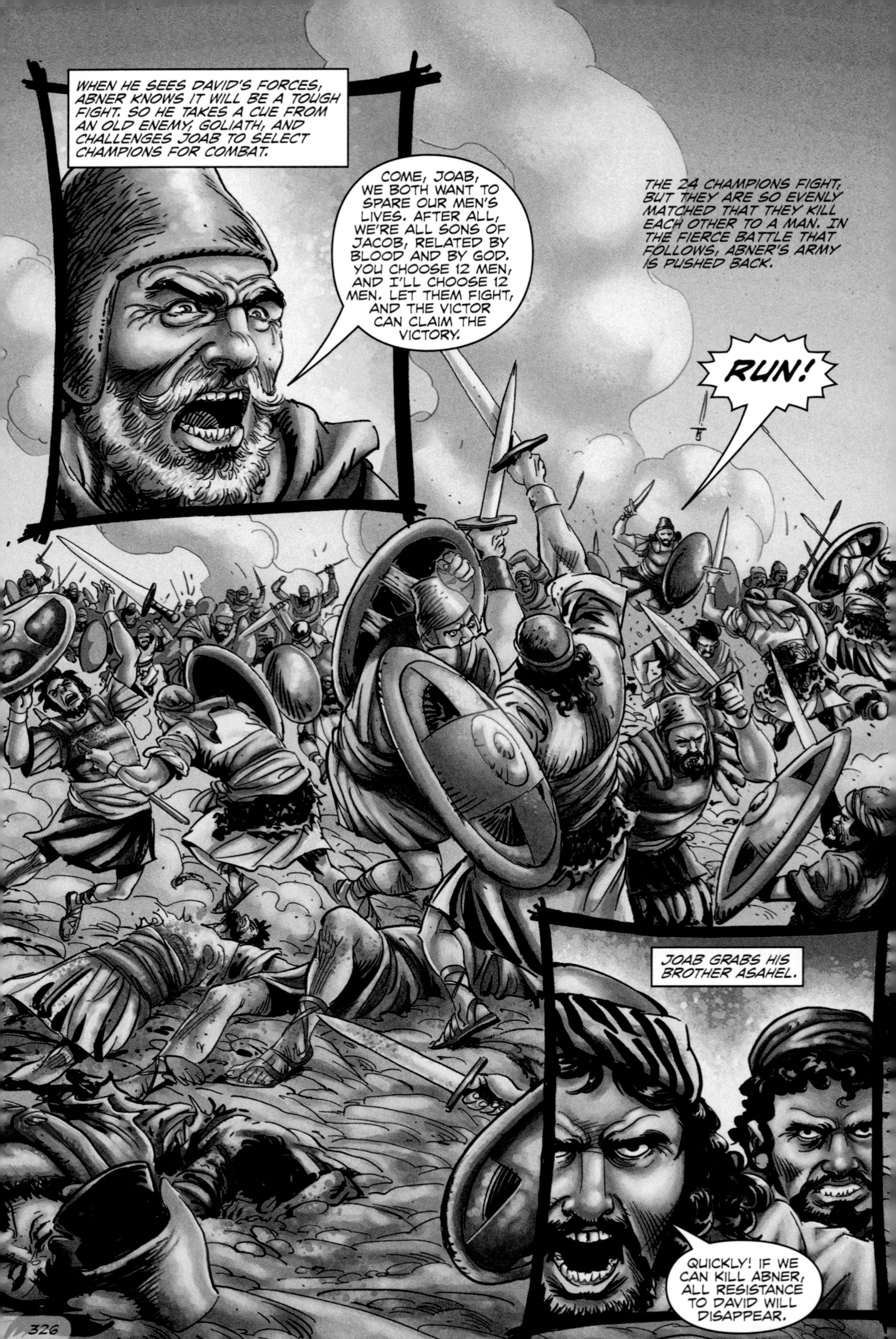
WHEN HE SEES DAVID'S FORCES, ABNER KNOWS IT WILL BE A TOUGH FIGHT. SO HE TAKES A CUE FROM AN OLD ENEMY, GOLIATH, AND CHALLENGES JOAB TO SELECT CHAMPIONS FOR COMBAT.
COME, JOAB, WE BOTH WANT TO SPARE OUR MEN'S LIVES. AFTER ALL, WE'RE ALL SONS OF JACOB, RELATED BY BLOOD AND BY GOD. YOU CHOOSE 12 MEN, AND I'LL CHOOSE 12 MEN. LET THEM FIGHT, AND THE VICTOR CAN CLAIM THE VICTORY.
THE 24 CHAMPIONS FIGHT, BUT THEY ARE SO EVENLY MATCHED THAT THEY KILL EACH OTHER TO A MAN. IN THE FIERCE BATTLE THAT FOLLOWS, ABNER'S ARMY IS PUSHED BACK.
RUN!
JOAB GRABS HIS BROTHER ASAHEL.
QUICKLY! IF WE CAN KILL ABNER, ALL RESISTANCE TO DAVID WILL DISAPPEAR.

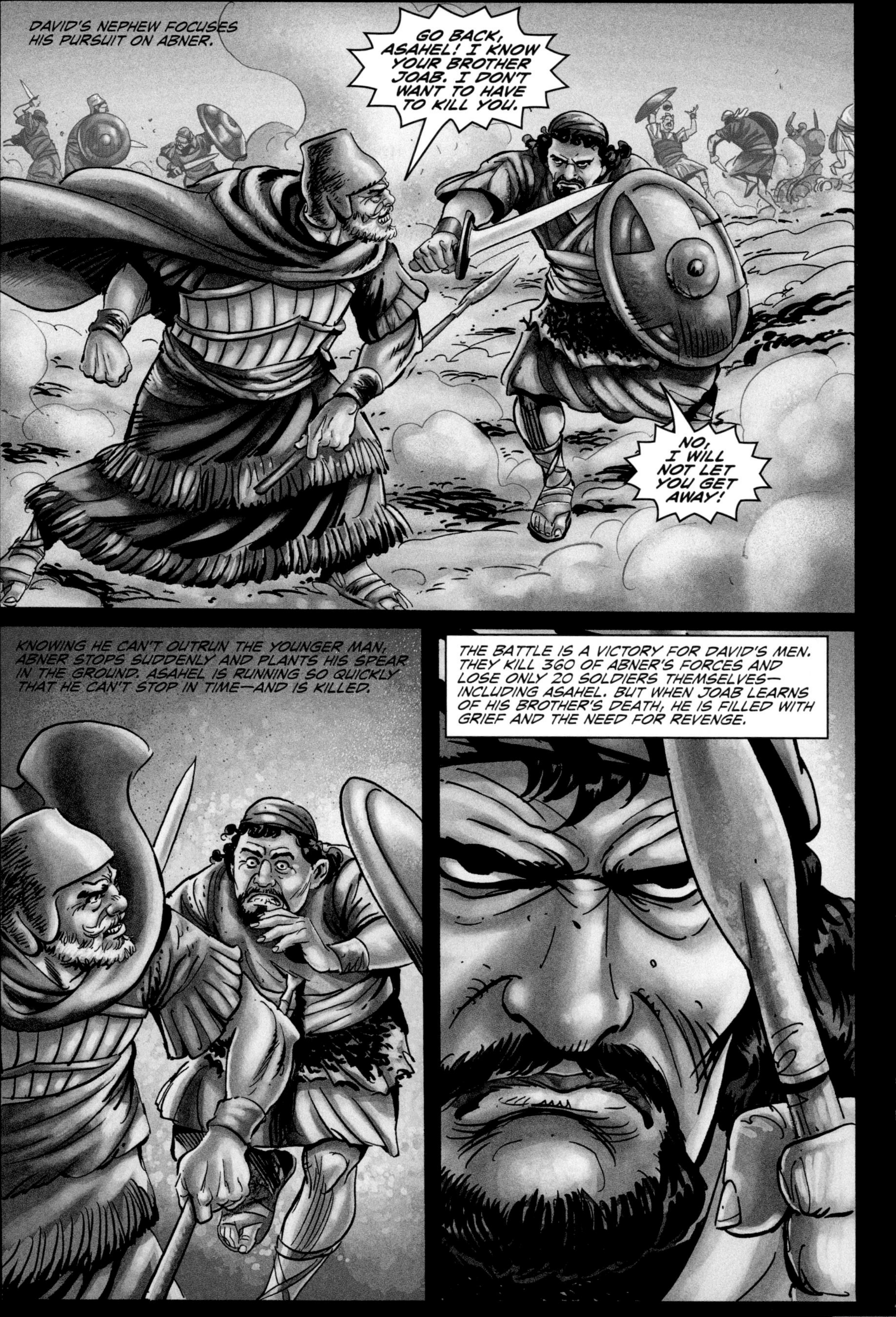
DAVID'S NEPHEW FOCUSES HIS PURSUIT ON ABNER.
GO BACK, ASAHEL! I KNOW YOUR BROTHER JOAB. I DON'T WANT TO HAVE TO KILL YOU.
NO, I WILL NOT LET YOU GET AWAY!
KNOWING HE CAN'T OUTRUN THE YOUNGER MAN, ABNER STOPS SUDDENLY AND PLANTS HIS SPEAR IN THE GROUND. ASAHEL IS RUNNING SO QUICKLY THAT HE CAN'T STOP IN TIME—AND IS KILLED.
THE BATTLE IS A VICTORY FOR DAVID'S MEN. THEY KILL 360 OF ABNER'S FORCES AND LOSE ONLY 20 SOLDIERS THEMSELVES—INCLUDING ASAHEL. BUT WHEN JOAB LEARNS OF HIS BROTHER'S DEATH, HE IS FILLED WITH GRIEF AND THE NEED FOR REVENGE.

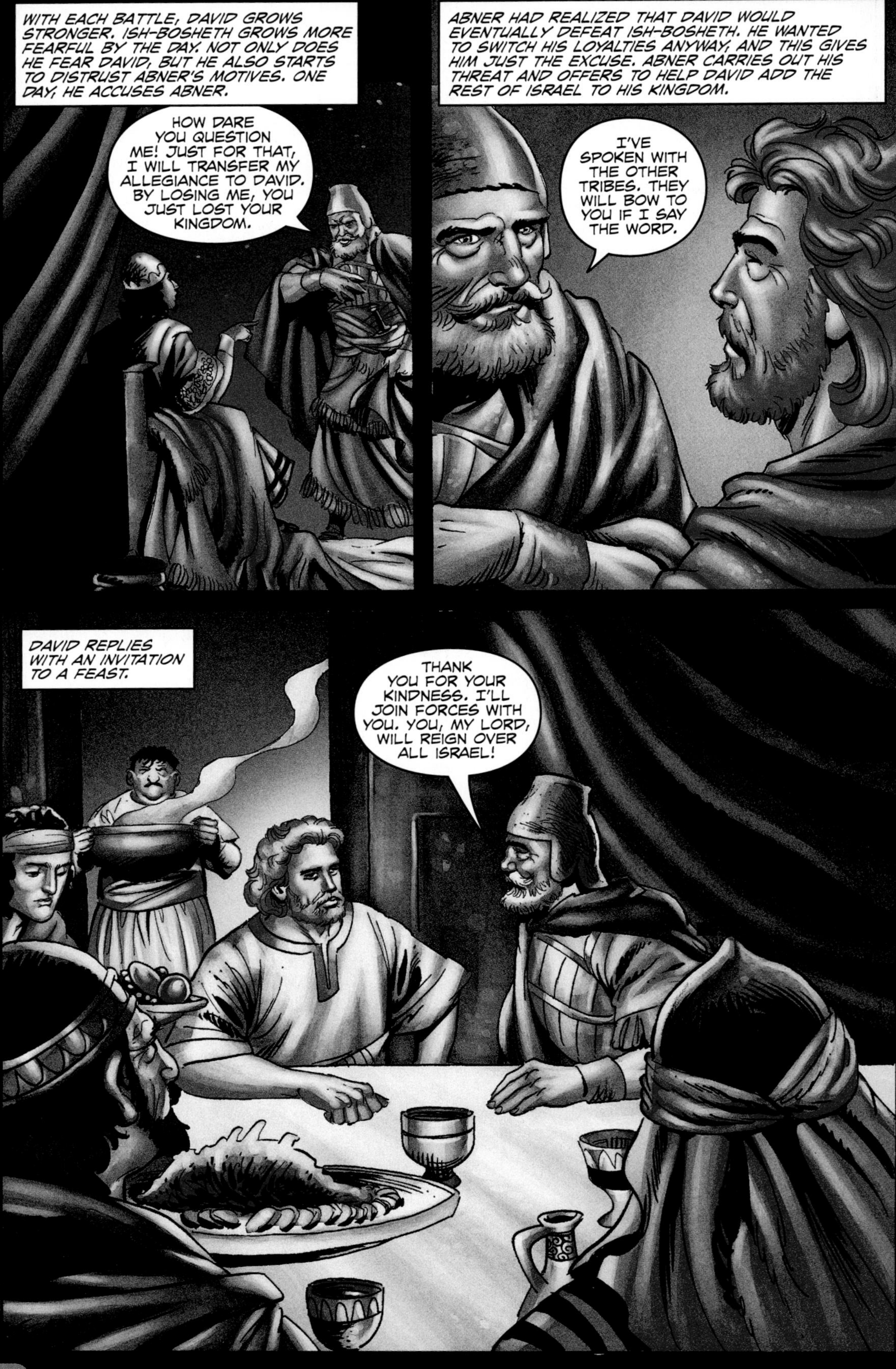
WITH EACH BATTLE, DAVID GROWS STRONGER. ISH-BOSHETH GROWS MORE FEARFUL BY THE DAY. NOT ONLY DOES HE FEAR DAVID, BUT HE ALSO STARTS TO DISTRUST ABNER'S MOTIVES. ONE DAY, HE ACCUSES ABNER.
HOW DARE YOU QUESTION ME! JUST FOR THAT, I WILL TRANSFER MY ALLEGIANCE TO DAVID. BY LOSING ME, YOU JUST LOST YOUR KINGDOM.
ABNER HAD REALIZED THAT DAVID WOULD EVENTUALLY DEFEAT ISH-BOSHETH. HE WANTED TO SWITCH HIS LOYALTIES ANYWAY, AND THIS GIVES HIM JUST THE EXCUSE. ABNER CARRIES OUT HIS THREAT AND OFFERS TO HELP DAVID ADD THE REST OF ISRAEL TO HIS KINGDOM.
I'VE SPOKEN WITH THE OTHER TRIBES. THEY WILL BOW TO YOU IF I SAY THE WORD.
DAVID REPLIES WITH AN INVITATION TO A FEAST.
THANK YOU FOR YOUR KINDNESS. I'LL JOIN FORCES WITH YOU. YOU, MY LORD, WILL REIGN OVER ALL ISRAEL!

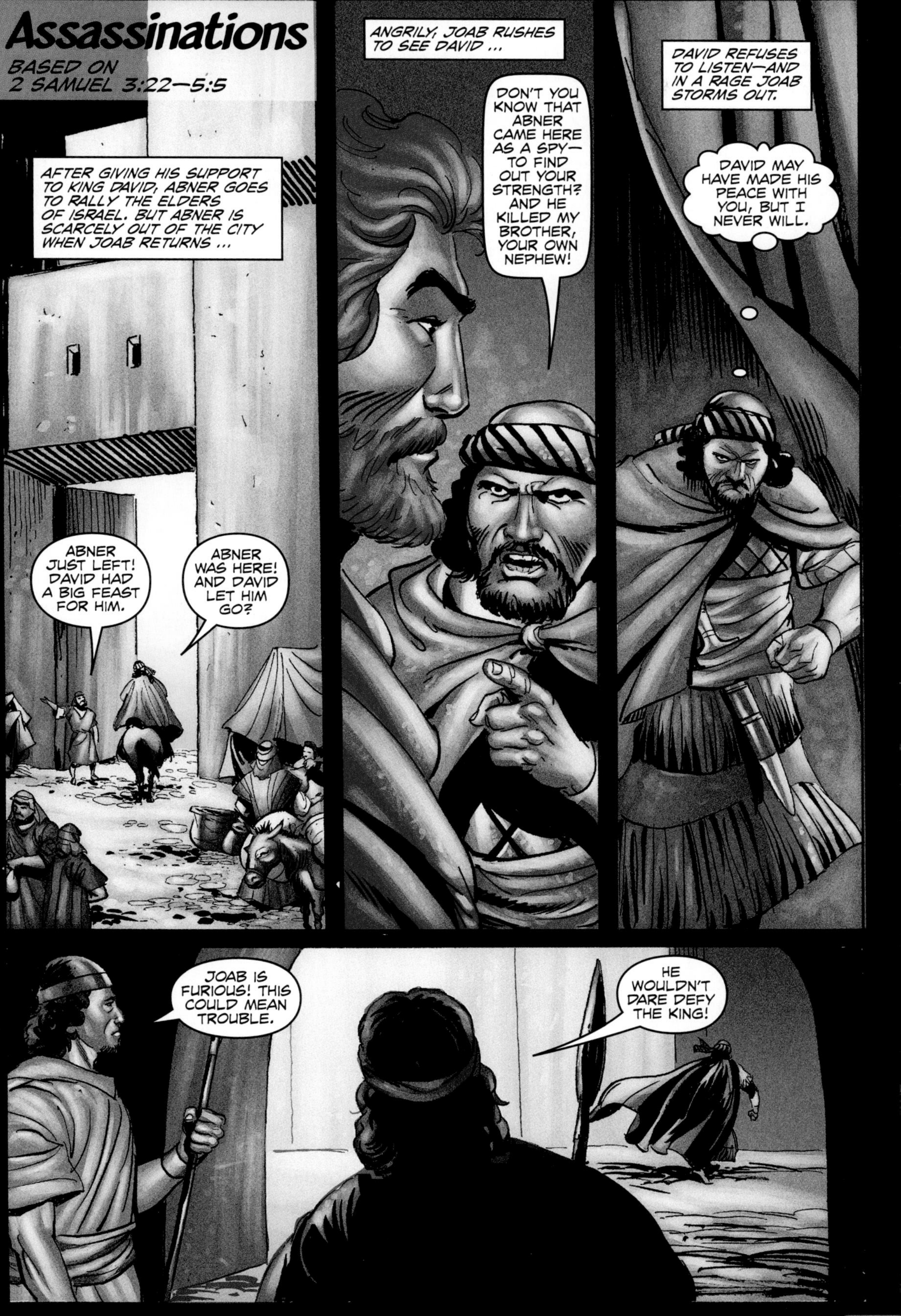
Assassinations
BASED ON 2 SAMUEL 3:22—5:5
AFTER GIVING HIS SUPPORT TO KING DAVID, ABNER GOES TO RALLY THE ELDERS OF ISRAEL. BUT ABNER IS SCARCELY OUT OF THE CITY WHEN JOAB RETURNS ...
ABNER JUST LEFT! DAVID HAD A BIG FEAST FOR HIM.
ABNER WAS HERE! AND DAVID LET HIM GO?
ANGRILY, JOAB RUSHES TO SEE DAVID ...
DON'T YOU KNOW THAT ABNER CAME HERE AS A SPY—TO FIND OUT YOUR STRENGTH? AND HE KILLED MY BROTHER, YOUR OWN NEPHEW!
DAVID REFUSES TO LISTEN—AND IN A RAGE JOAB STORMS OUT.
DAVID MAY HAVE MADE HIS PEACE WITH YOU, BUT I NEVER WILL.
JOAB IS FURIOUS! THIS COULD MEAN TROUBLE.
HE WOULDN'T DARE DEFY THE KING!

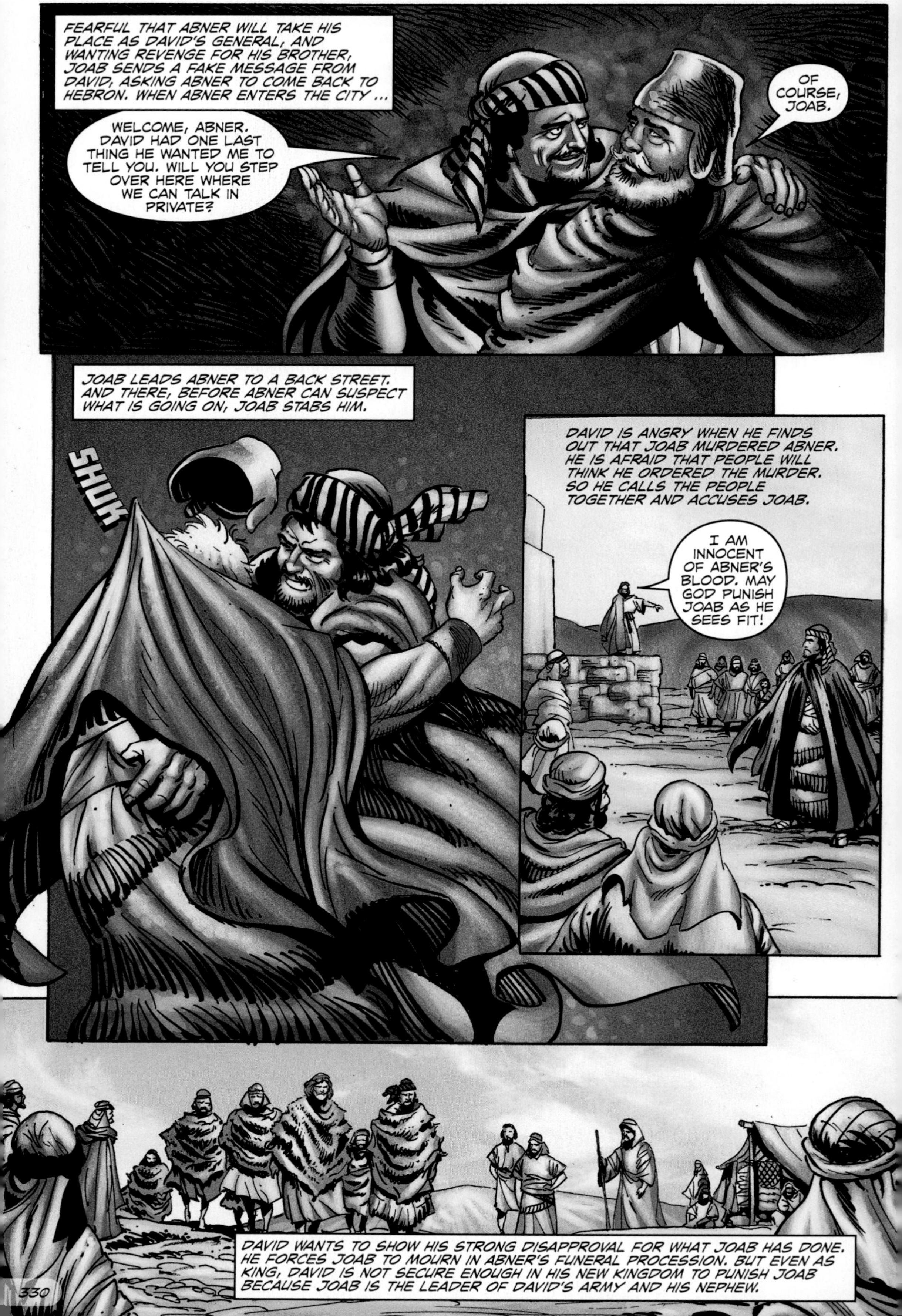

FEARFUL THAT ABNER WILL TAKE HIS PLACE AS DAVID'S GENERAL, AND WANTING REVENGE FOR HIS BROTHER, JOAB SENDS A FAKE MESSAGE FROM DAVID, ASKING ABNER TO COME BACK TO HEBRON. WHEN ABNER ENTERS THE CITY ...
WELCOME, ABNER. DAVID HAD ONE LAST THING HE WANTED ME TO TELL YOU. WILL YOU STEP OVER HERE WHERE WE CAN TALK IN PRIVATE?
OF COURSE, JOAB.
JOAB LEADS ABNER TO A BACK STREET. AND THERE, BEFORE ABNER CAN SUSPECT WHAT IS GOING ON, JOAB STABS HIM.
SHUK
DAVID IS ANGRY WHEN HE FINDS OUT THAT JOAB MURDERED ABNER. HE IS AFRAID THAT PEOPLE WILL THINK HE ORDERED THE MURDER. SO HE CALLS THE PEOPLE TOGETHER AND ACCUSES JOAB.
I AM INNOCENT OF ABNER'S BLOOD. MAY GOD PUNISH JOAB AS HE SEES FIT!
DAVID WANTS TO SHOW HIS STRONG DISAPPROVAL FOR WHAT JOAB HAS DONE. HE FORCES JOAB TO MOURN IN ABNER'S FUNERAL PROCESSION. BUT EVEN AS KING, DAVID IS NOT SECURE ENOUGH IN HIS NEW KINGDOM TO PUNISH JOAB BECAUSE JOAB IS THE LEADER OF DAVID'S ARMY AND HIS NEPHEW.

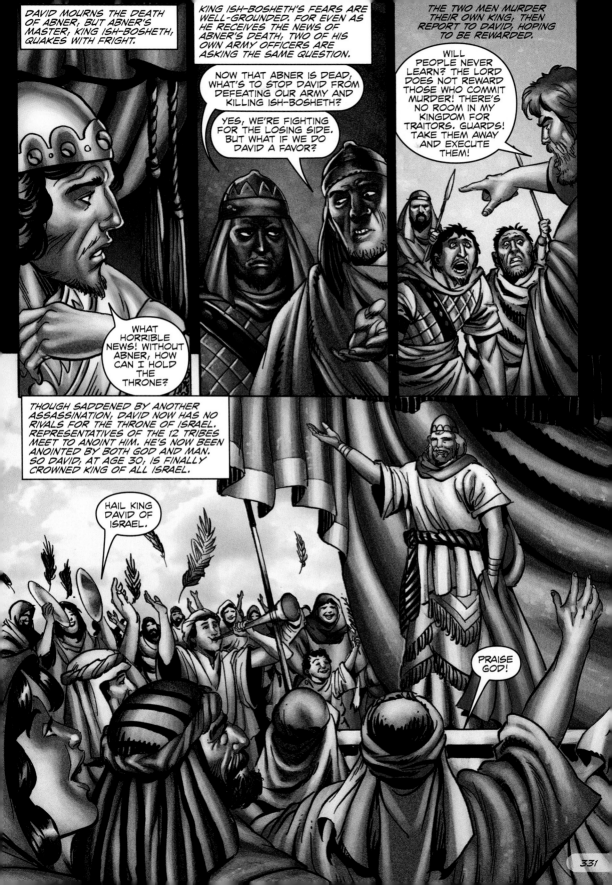

DAVID MOURNS THE DEATH OF ABNER, BUT ABNER'S MASTER, KING ISH-BOSHETH, QUAKES WITH FRIGHT.

KING ISH-BOSHETH'S FEARS ARE WELL-GROUNDED. FOR EVEN AS HE RECEIVES THE NEWS OF ABNER'S DEATH, TWO OF HIS OWN ARMY OFFICERS ARE ASKING THE SAME QUESTION.

THE TWO MEN MURDER THEIR OWN KING, THEN REPORT TO DAVID, HOPING TO BE REWARDED.

NOW THAT ABNER IS DEAD, WHAT'S TO STOP DAVID FROM DEFEATING OUR ARMY AND KILLING ISH-BOSHETH?

YES, WE'RE FIGHTING FOR THE LOSING SIDE. BUT WHAT IF WE DO DAVID A FAVOR?

WILL PEOPLE NEVER LEARN? THE LORD DOES NOT REWARD THOSE WHO COMMIT MURDER! THERE'S NO ROOM IN MY KINGDOM FOR TRAITORS. GUARDS! TAKE THEM AWAY AND EXECUTE THEM!

WHAT HORRIBLE NEWS! WITHOUT ABNER, HOW CAN I HOLD THE THRONE?

THOUGH SADDENED BY ANOTHER ASSASSINATION, DAVID NOW HAS NO RIVALS FOR THE THRONE OF ISRAEL. REPRESENTATIVES OF THE 12 TRIBES MEET TO ANOINT HIM. HE'S NOW BEEN ANOINTED BY BOTH GOD AND MAN. SO DAVID, AT AGE 30, IS FINALLY CROWNED KING OF ALL ISRAEL.

HAIL KING DAVID OF ISRAEL.

PRAISE GOD!

331

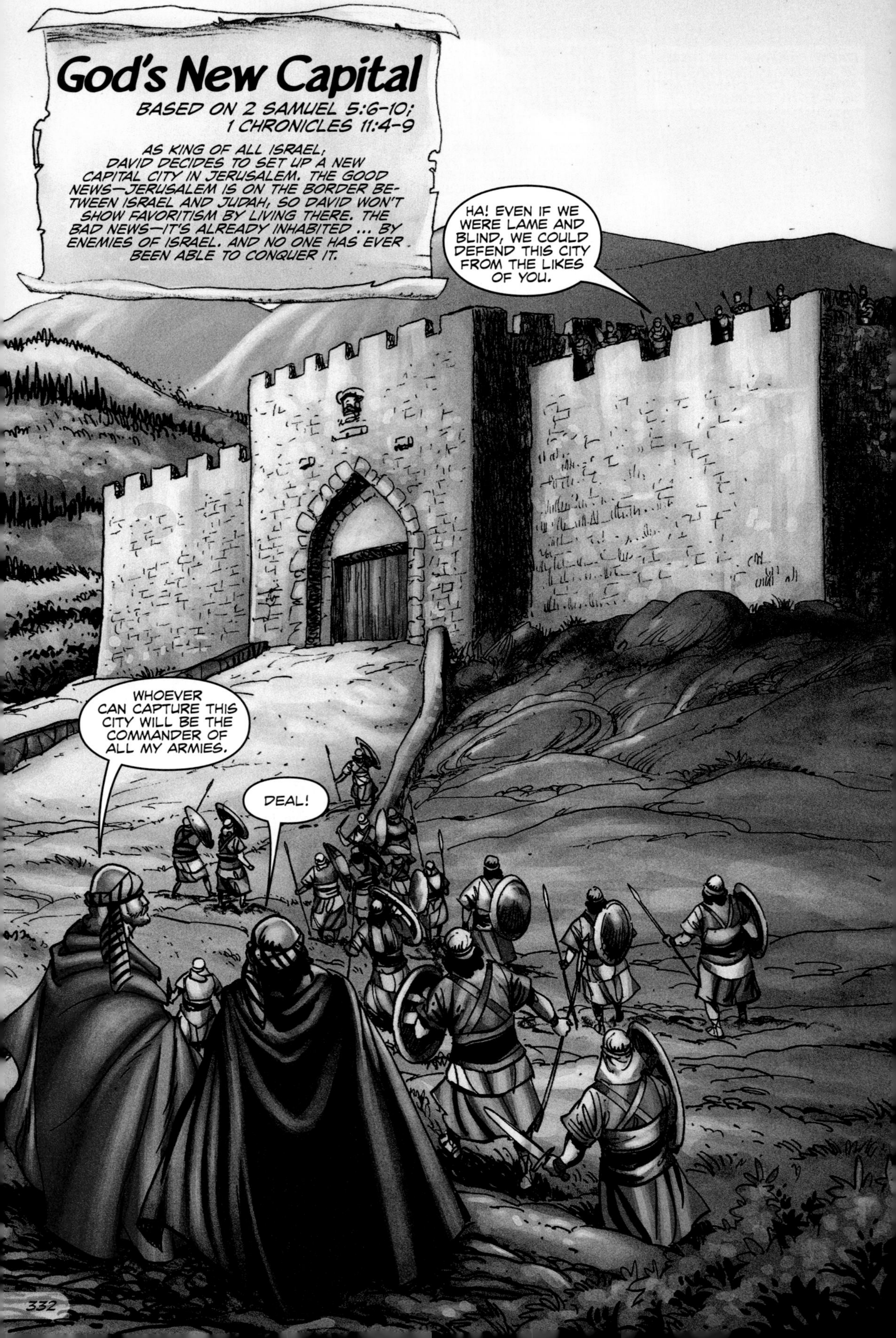
God's New Capital
BASED ON 2 SAMUEL 5:6-10; 1 CHRONICLES 11:4-9
AS KING OF ALL ISRAEL, DAVID DECIDES TO SET UP A NEW CAPITAL CITY IN JERUSALEM. THE GOOD NEWS—JERUSALEM IS ON THE BORDER BETWEEN ISRAEL AND JUDAH, SO DAVID WON'T SHOW FAVORITISM BY LIVING THERE. THE BAD NEWS—IT'S ALREADY INHABITED ... BY ENEMIES OF ISRAEL. AND NO ONE HAS EVER BEEN ABLE TO CONQUER IT.
HA! EVEN IF WE WERE LAME AND BLIND, WE COULD DEFEND THIS CITY FROM THE LIKES OF YOU.
WHOEVER CAN CAPTURE THIS CITY WILL BE THE COMMANDER OF ALL MY ARMIES.
DEAL!

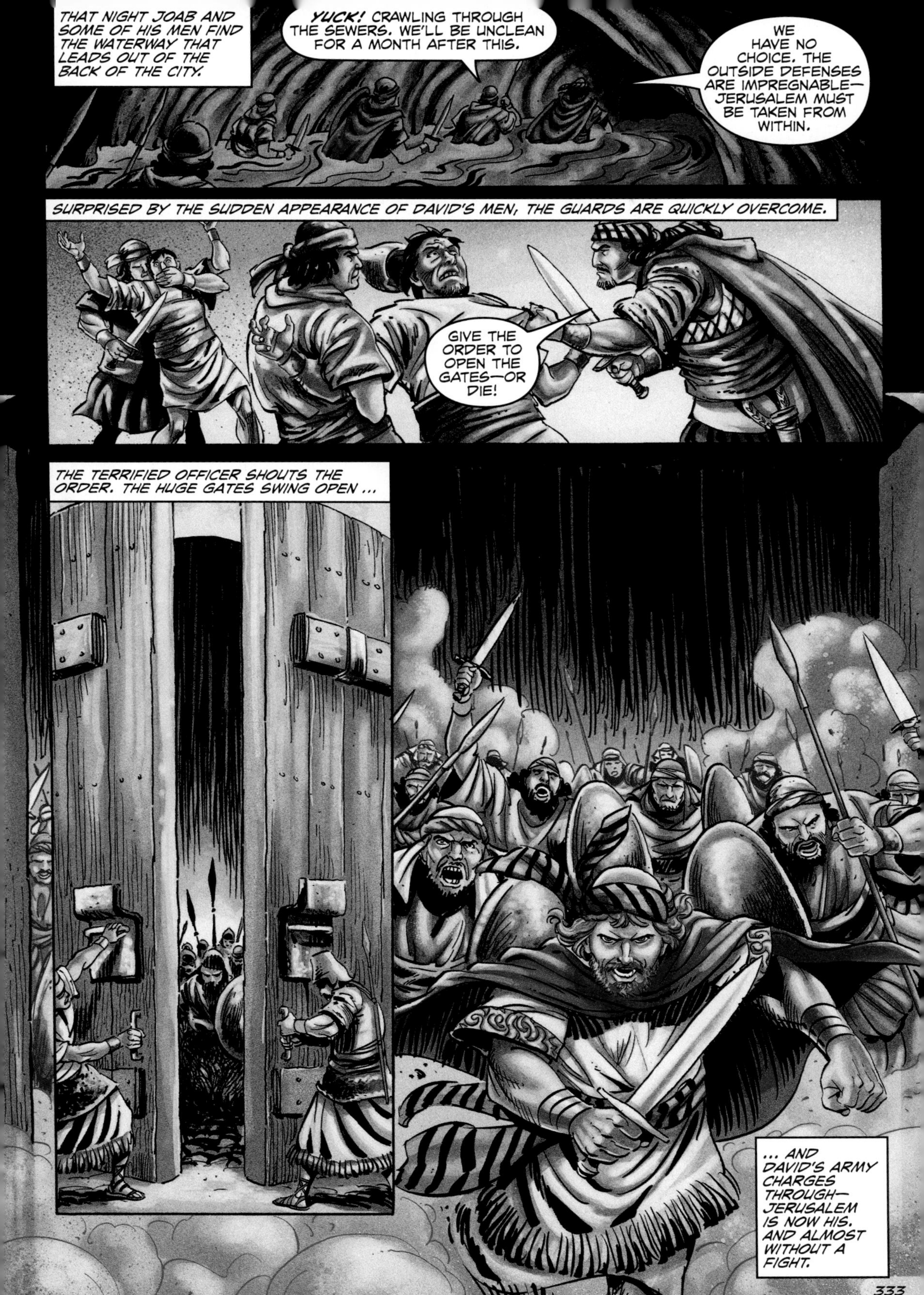
THAT NIGHT JOAB AND SOME OF HIS MEN FIND THE WATERWAY THAT LEADS OUT OF THE BACK OF THE CITY.
YUCK! CRAWLING THROUGH THE SEWERS. WE'LL BE UNCLEAN FOR A MONTH AFTER THIS.
WE HAVE NO CHOICE. THE OUTSIDE DEFENSES ARE IMPREGNABLE—JERUSALEM MUST BE TAKEN FROM WITHIN.
SURPRISED BY THE SUDDEN APPEARANCE OF DAVID'S MEN, THE GUARDS ARE QUICKLY OVERCOME.
GIVE THE ORDER TO OPEN THE GATES—OR DIE!
THE TERRIFIED OFFICER SHOUTS THE ORDER. THE HUGE GATES SWING OPEN ...
... AND DAVID'S ARMY CHARGES THROUGH—JERUSALEM IS NOW HIS. AND ALMOST WITHOUT A FIGHT.

Temple Dreams

BASED ON 2 SAMUEL 6—7;
1 CHRONICLES 13; 15—17;
PSALMS 24; 96; 105; 106

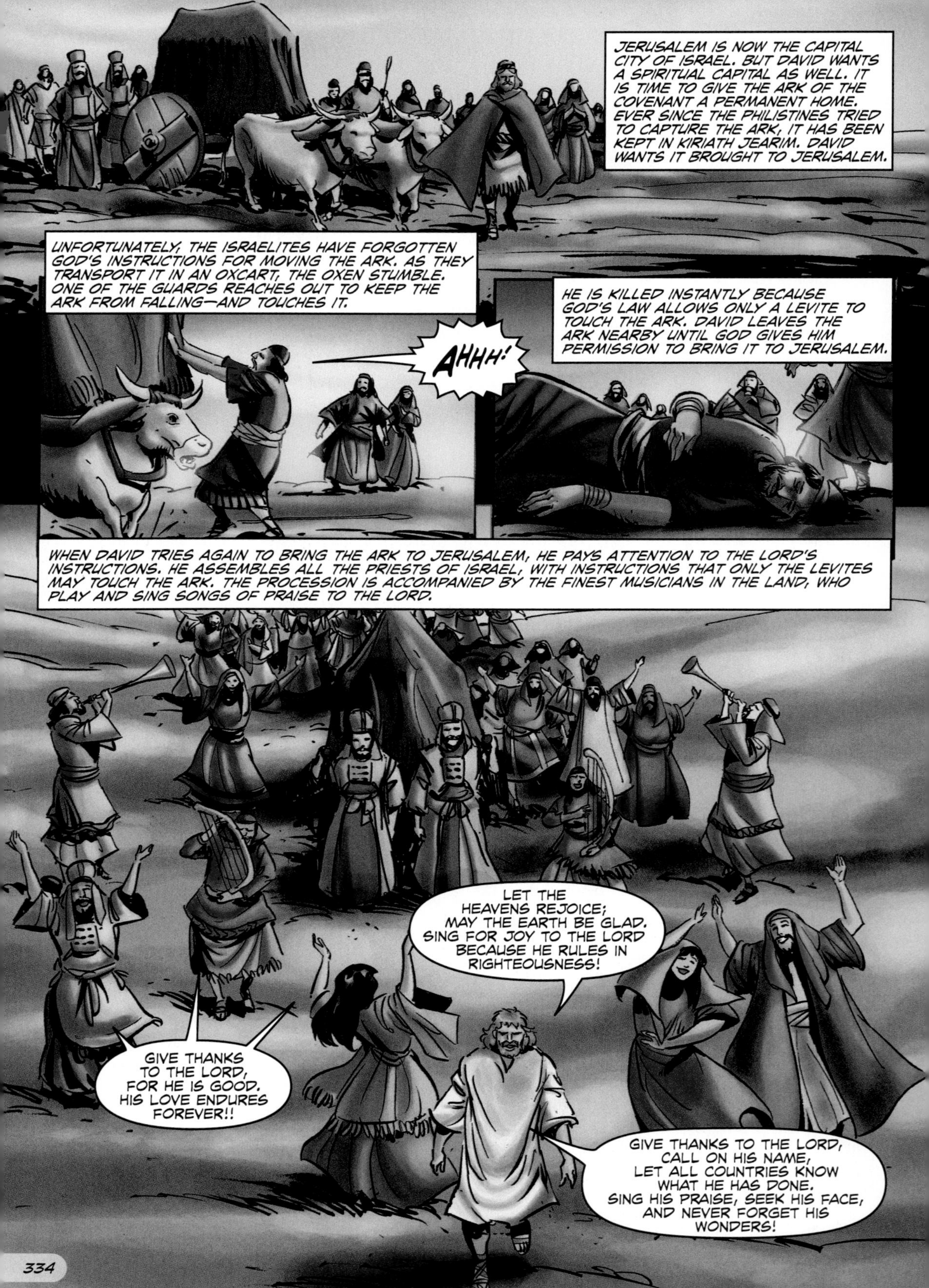

JERUSALEM IS NOW THE CAPITAL CITY OF ISRAEL. BUT DAVID WANTS A SPIRITUAL CAPITAL AS WELL. IT IS TIME TO GIVE THE ARK OF THE COVENANT A PERMANENT HOME. EVER SINCE THE PHILISTINES TRIED TO CAPTURE THE ARK, IT HAS BEEN KEPT IN KIRIATH JEARIM. DAVID WANTS IT BROUGHT TO JERUSALEM.
UNFORTUNATELY, THE ISRAELITES HAVE FORGOTTEN GOD'S INSTRUCTIONS FOR MOVING THE ARK. AS THEY TRANSPORT IT IN AN OXCART, THE OXEN STUMBLE. ONE OF THE GUARDS REACHES OUT TO KEEP THE ARK FROM FALLING—AND TOUCHES IT.
AHHH!
HE IS KILLED INSTANTLY BECAUSE GOD'S LAW ALLOWS ONLY A LEVITE TO TOUCH THE ARK. DAVID LEAVES THE ARK NEARBY UNTIL GOD GIVES HIM PERMISSION TO BRING IT TO JERUSALEM.
WHEN DAVID TRIES AGAIN TO BRING THE ARK TO JERUSALEM, HE PAYS ATTENTION TO THE LORD'S INSTRUCTIONS. HE ASSEMBLES ALL THE PRIESTS OF ISRAEL, WITH INSTRUCTIONS THAT ONLY THE LEVITES MAY TOUCH THE ARK. THE PROCESSION IS ACCOMPANIED BY THE FINEST MUSICIANS IN THE LAND, WHO PLAY AND SING SONGS OF PRAISE TO THE LORD.
LET THE HEAVENS REJOICE; MAY THE EARTH BE GLAD. SING FOR JOY TO THE LORD BECAUSE HE RULES IN RIGHTEOUSNESS!
GIVE THANKS TO THE LORD, FOR HE IS GOOD. HIS LOVE ENDURES FOREVER!!
GIVE THANKS TO THE LORD, CALL ON HIS NAME, LET ALL COUNTRIES KNOW WHAT HE HAS DONE. SING HIS PRAISE, SEEK HIS FACE, AND NEVER FORGET HIS WONDERS!

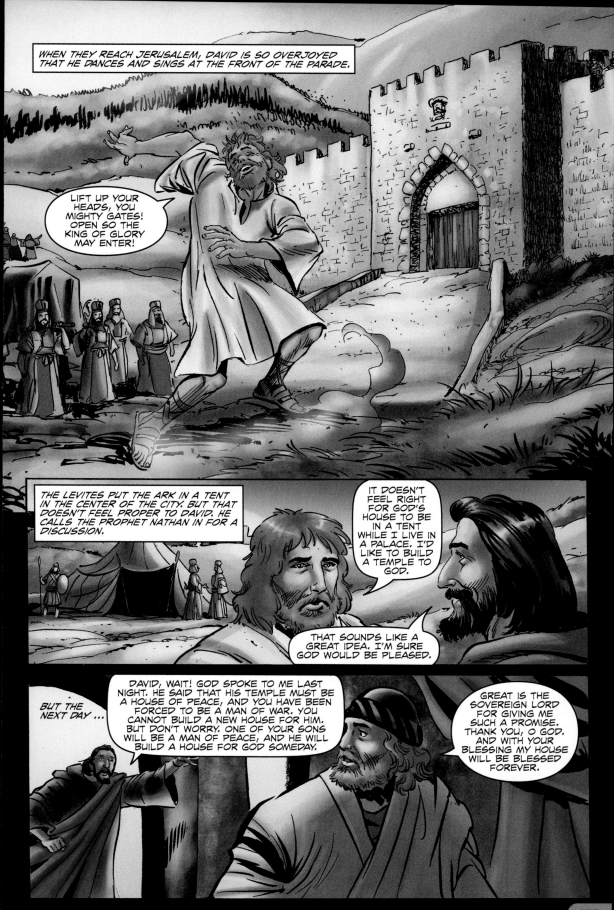

WHEN THEY REACH JERUSALEM, DAVID IS SO OVERJOYED THAT HE DANCES AND SINGS AT THE FRONT OF THE PARADE.

LIFT UP YOUR HEADS, YOU MIGHTY GATES! OPEN SO THE KING OF GLORY MAY ENTER!

THE LEVITES PUT THE ARK IN A TENT IN THE CENTER OF THE CITY. BUT THAT DOESN'T FEEL PROPER TO DAVID. HE CALLS THE PROPHET NATHAN IN FOR A DISCUSSION.

IT DOESN'T FEEL RIGHT FOR GOD'S HOUSE TO BE IN A TENT WHILE I LIVE IN A PALACE. I'D LIKE TO BUILD A TEMPLE TO GOD.

THAT SOUNDS LIKE A GREAT IDEA. I'M SURE GOD WOULD BE PLEASED.

BUT THE NEXT DAY ...

DAVID, WAIT! GOD SPOKE TO ME LAST NIGHT. HE SAID THAT HIS TEMPLE MUST BE A HOUSE OF PEACE, AND YOU HAVE BEEN FORCED TO BE A MAN OF WAR. YOU CANNOT BUILD A NEW HOUSE FOR HIM. BUT DON'T WORRY. ONE OF YOUR SONS WILL BE A MAN OF PEACE, AND HE WILL BUILD A HOUSE FOR GOD SOMEDAY.

GREAT IS THE SOVEREIGN LORD FOR GIVING ME SUCH A PROMISE. THANK YOU, O GOD. AND WITH YOUR BLESSING MY HOUSE WILL BE BLESSED FOREVER.

Psalm 96

DAVID WROTE THESE WORDS OF GRATITUDE TO GOD AFTER
HEARING FROM THE PROPHET NATHAN.

SING TO THE LORD A NEW SONG;
 SING TO THE LORD, ALL THE EARTH.
SING TO THE LORD, PRAISE HIS NAME;
 PROCLAIM HIS SALVATION DAY AFTER DAY.
DECLARE HIS GLORY AMONG THE NATIONS,
 HIS MARVELOUS DEEDS AMONG ALL PEOPLES.
FOR GREAT IS THE LORD AND MOST WORTHY OF PRAISE;
 HE IS TO BE FEARED ABOVE ALL GODS.
FOR ALL THE GODS OF THE NATIONS ARE IDOLS,
 BUT THE LORD MADE THE HEAVENS.
SPLENDOR AND MAJESTY ARE BEFORE HIM;
 STRENGTH AND GLORY ARE IN HIS SANCTUARY.

ASCRIBE TO THE LORD, ALL YOU FAMILIES OF NATIONS,
    ASCRIBE TO THE LORD GLORY AND STRENGTH.
ASCRIBE TO THE LORD THE GLORY DUE HIS NAME;
    BRING AN OFFERING AND COME INTO HIS COURTS.
WORSHIP THE LORD IN THE SPLENDOR OF HIS HOLINESS;
    TREMBLE BEFORE HIM, ALL THE EARTH.
SAY AMONG THE NATIONS, "THE LORD REIGNS."
    THE WORLD IS FIRMLY ESTABLISHED, IT CANNOT BE MOVED;
    HE WILL JUDGE THE PEOPLES WITH EQUITY.
LET THE HEAVENS REJOICE, LET THE EARTH BE GLAD;
    LET THE SEA RESOUND, AND ALL THAT IS IN IT.
LET THE FIELDS BE JUBILANT, AND EVERYTHING IN THEM;
    LET ALL THE TREES OF THE FOREST SING FOR JOY.
LET ALL CREATION REJOICE BEFORE THE LORD, FOR HE COMES,
    HE COMES TO JUDGE THE EARTH.
HE WILL JUDGE THE WORLD IN RIGHTEOUSNESS
    AND THE PEOPLES IN HIS FAITHFULNESS.

David's Sins

BASED ON 2 SAMUEL 11

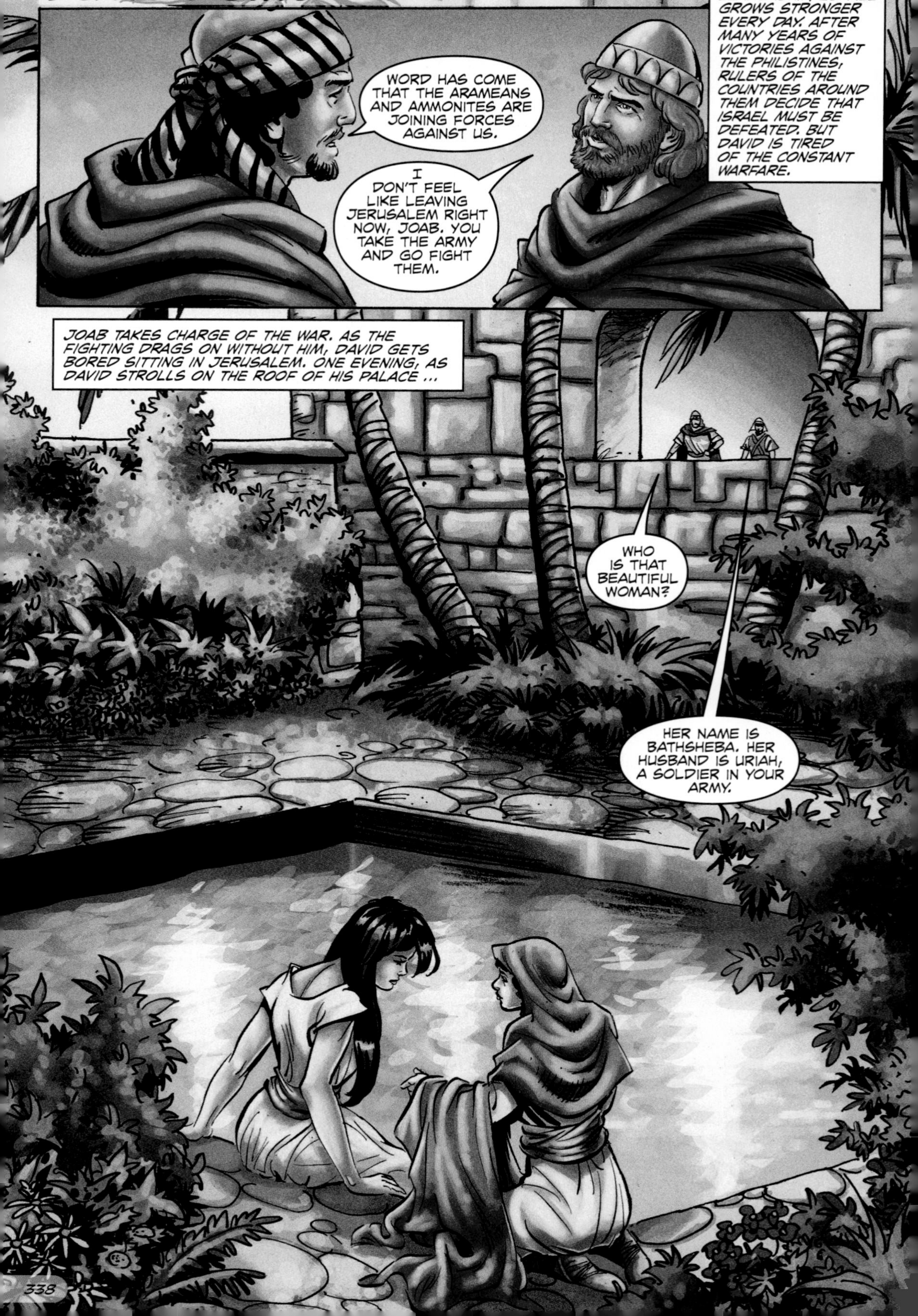
UNDER DAVID'S LEADERSHIP, ISRAEL GROWS STRONGER EVERY DAY. AFTER MANY YEARS OF VICTORIES AGAINST THE PHILISTINES, RULERS OF THE COUNTRIES AROUND THEM DECIDE THAT ISRAEL MUST BE DEFEATED. BUT DAVID IS TIRED OF THE CONSTANT WARFARE.
WORD HAS COME THAT THE ARAMEANS AND AMMONITES ARE JOINING FORCES AGAINST US.
I DON'T FEEL LIKE LEAVING JERUSALEM RIGHT NOW, JOAB. YOU TAKE THE ARMY AND GO FIGHT THEM.
JOAB TAKES CHARGE OF THE WAR. AS THE FIGHTING DRAGS ON WITHOUT HIM, DAVID GETS BORED SITTING IN JERUSALEM. ONE EVENING, AS DAVID STROLLS ON THE ROOF OF HIS PALACE ...
WHO IS THAT BEAUTIFUL WOMAN?
HER NAME IS BATHSHEBA. HER HUSBAND IS URIAH, A SOLDIER IN YOUR ARMY.

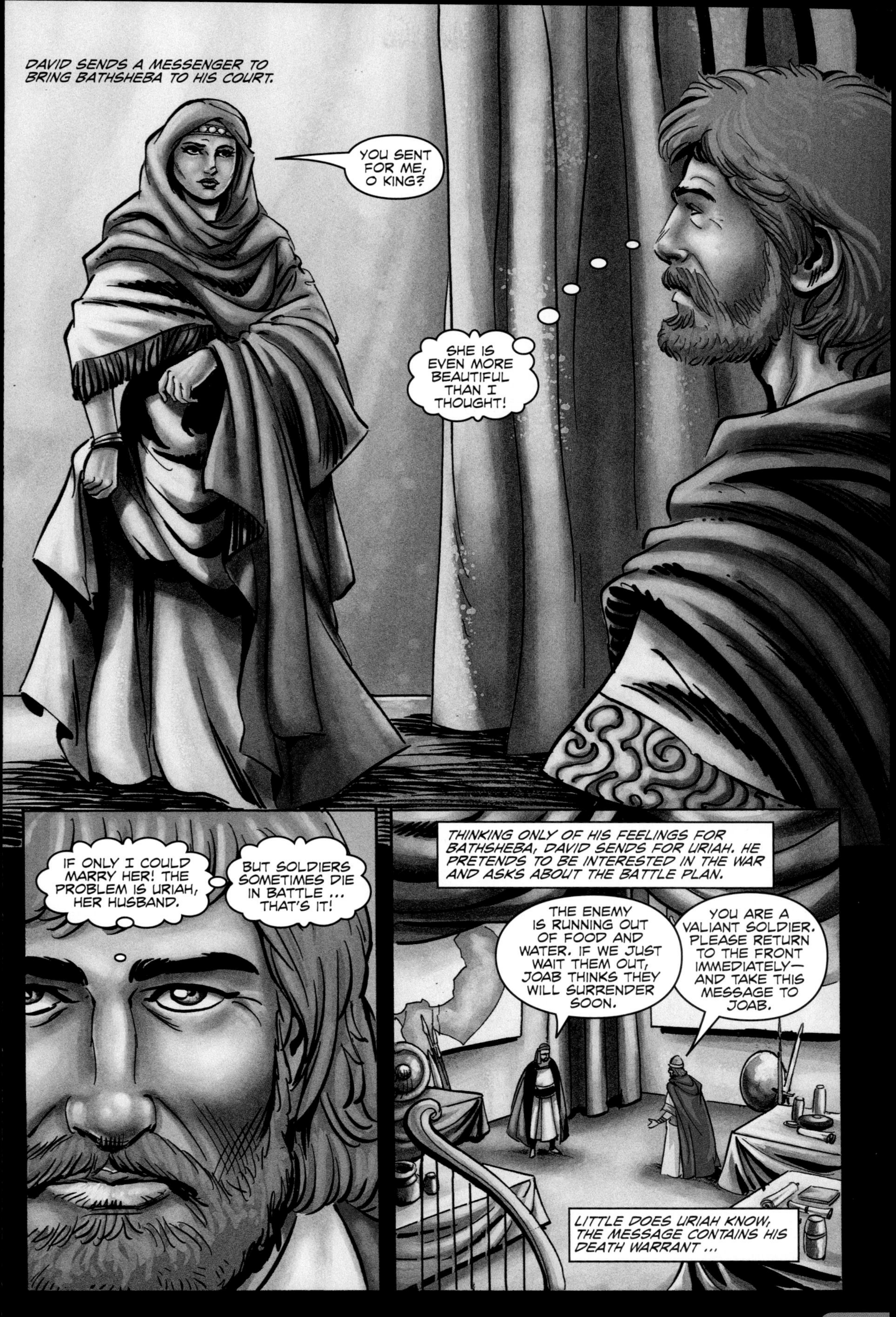
DAVID SENDS A MESSENGER TO BRING BATHSHEBA TO HIS COURT.
YOU SENT FOR ME, O KING?
SHE IS EVEN MORE BEAUTIFUL THAN I THOUGHT!
IF ONLY I COULD MARRY HER! THE PROBLEM IS URIAH, HER HUSBAND.
BUT SOLDIERS SOMETIMES DIE IN BATTLE ... THAT'S IT!
THINKING ONLY OF HIS FEELINGS FOR BATHSHEBA, DAVID SENDS FOR URIAH. HE PRETENDS TO BE INTERESTED IN THE WAR AND ASKS ABOUT THE BATTLE PLAN.
THE ENEMY IS RUNNING OUT OF FOOD AND WATER. IF WE JUST WAIT THEM OUT, JOAB THINKS THEY WILL SURRENDER SOON.
YOU ARE A VALIANT SOLDIER. PLEASE RETURN TO THE FRONT IMMEDIATELY—AND TAKE THIS MESSAGE TO JOAB.
LITTLE DOES URIAH KNOW, THE MESSAGE CONTAINS HIS DEATH WARRANT ...

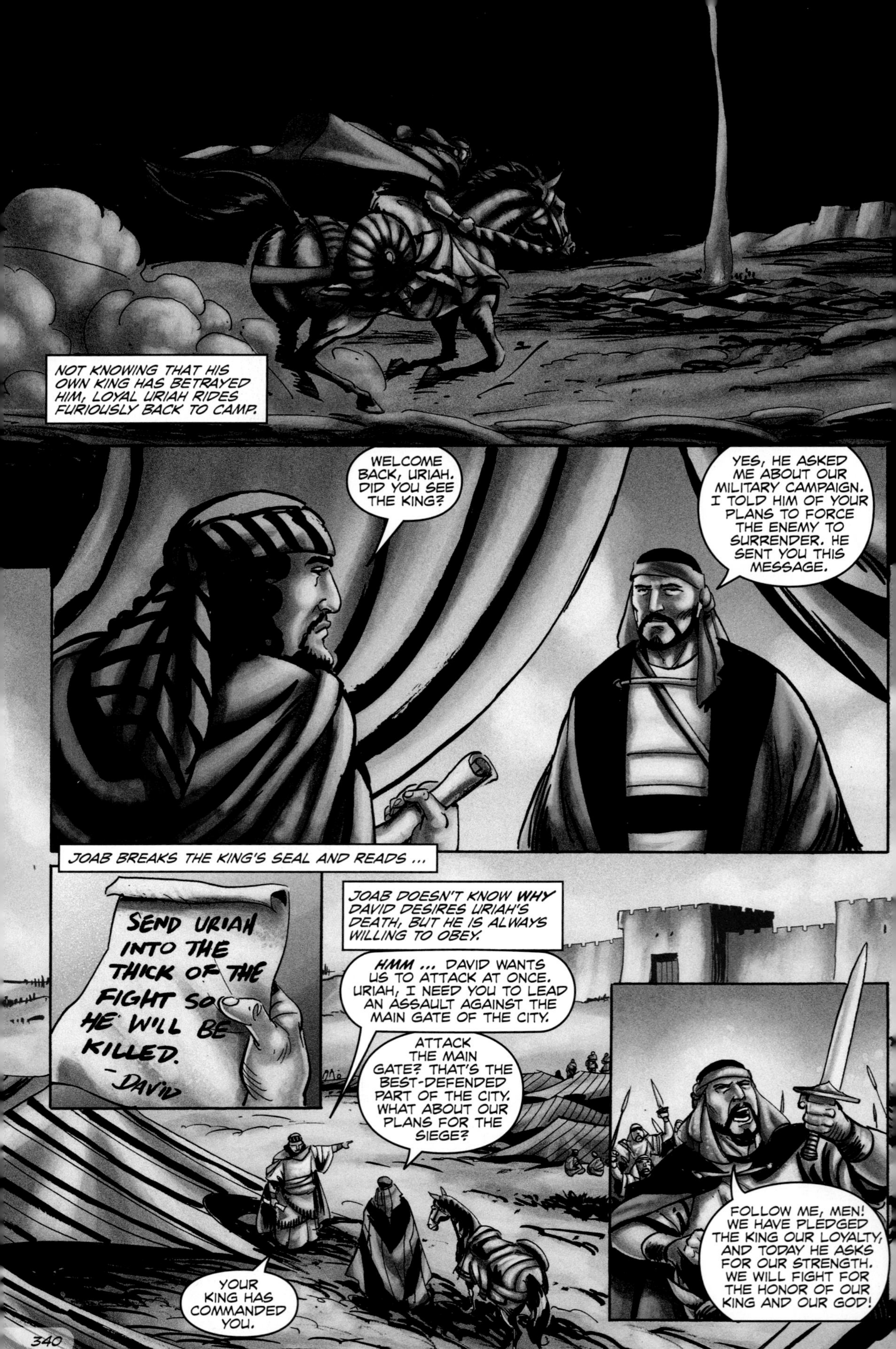

NOT KNOWING THAT HIS OWN KING HAS BETRAYED HIM, LOYAL URIAH RIDES FURIOUSLY BACK TO CAMP.
WELCOME BACK, URIAH. DID YOU SEE THE KING?
YES, HE ASKED ME ABOUT OUR MILITARY CAMPAIGN. I TOLD HIM OF YOUR PLANS TO FORCE THE ENEMY TO SURRENDER. HE SENT YOU THIS MESSAGE.
JOAB BREAKS THE KING'S SEAL AND READS ...
SEND URIAH INTO THE THICK OF THE FIGHT SO HE WILL BE KILLED. -DAVID
JOAB DOESN'T KNOW WHY DAVID DESIRES URIAH'S DEATH, BUT HE IS ALWAYS WILLING TO OBEY.
HMM ... DAVID WANTS US TO ATTACK AT ONCE. URIAH, I NEED YOU TO LEAD AN ASSAULT AGAINST THE MAIN GATE OF THE CITY.
ATTACK THE MAIN GATE? THAT'S THE BEST-DEFENDED PART OF THE CITY. WHAT ABOUT OUR PLANS FOR THE SIEGE?
YOUR KING HAS COMMANDED YOU.
FOLLOW ME, MEN! WE HAVE PLEDGED THE KING OUR LOYALTY, AND TODAY HE ASKS FOR OUR STRENGTH. WE WILL FIGHT FOR THE HONOR OF OUR KING AND OUR GOD!

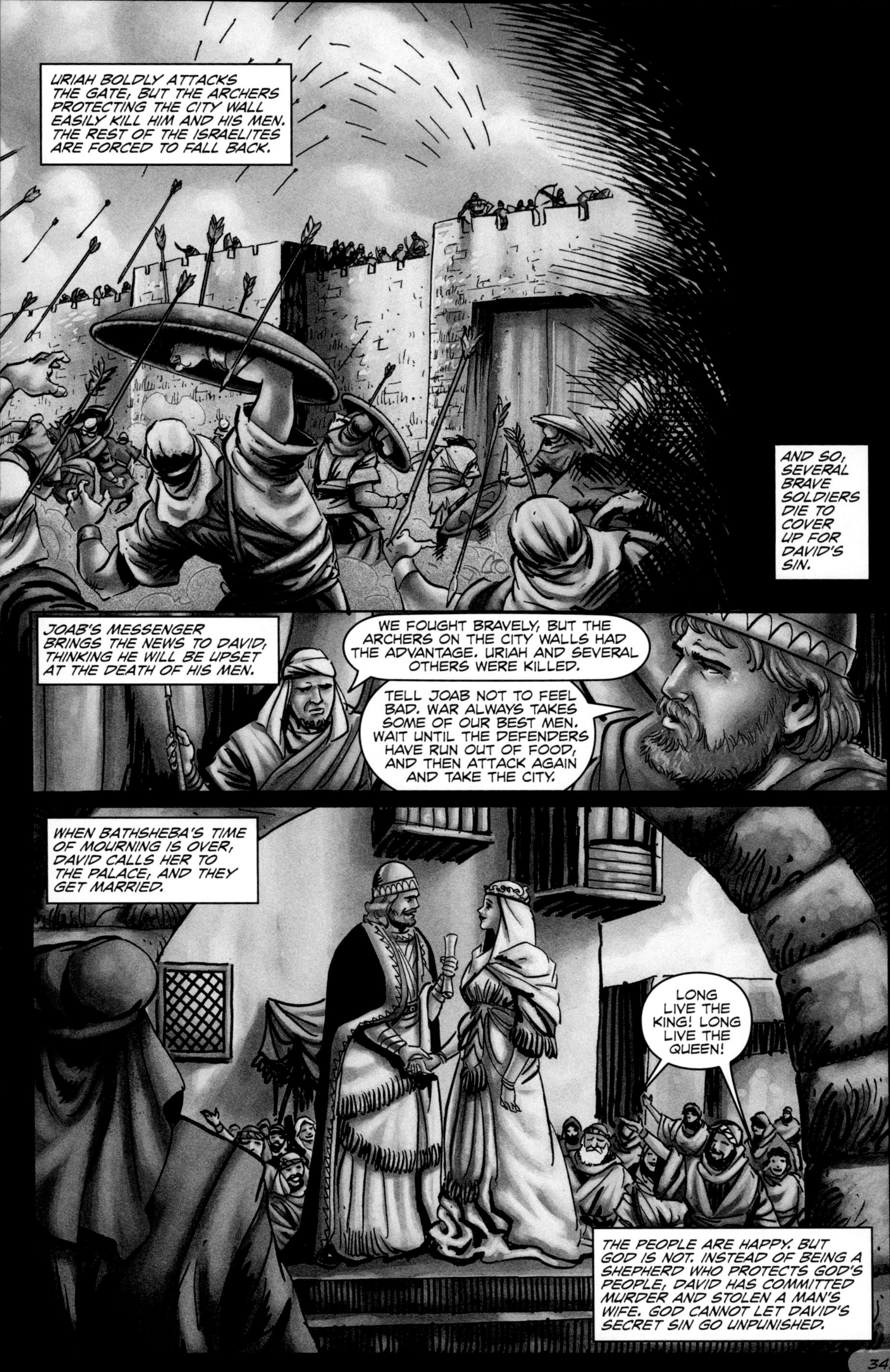
URIAH BOLDLY ATTACKS THE GATE, BUT THE ARCHERS PROTECTING THE CITY WALL EASILY KILL HIM AND HIS MEN. THE REST OF THE ISRAELITES ARE FORCED TO FALL BACK.
AND SO, SEVERAL BRAVE SOLDIERS DIE TO COVER UP FOR DAVID'S SIN.
JOAB'S MESSENGER BRINGS THE NEWS TO DAVID, THINKING HE WILL BE UPSET AT THE DEATH OF HIS MEN.
WE FOUGHT BRAVELY, BUT THE ARCHERS ON THE CITY WALLS HAD THE ADVANTAGE. URIAH AND SEVERAL OTHERS WERE KILLED.
TELL JOAB NOT TO FEEL BAD. WAR ALWAYS TAKES SOME OF OUR BEST MEN. WAIT UNTIL THE DEFENDERS HAVE RUN OUT OF FOOD, AND THEN ATTACK AGAIN AND TAKE THE CITY.
WHEN BATHSHEBA'S TIME OF MOURNING IS OVER, DAVID CALLS HER TO THE PALACE, AND THEY GET MARRIED.
LONG LIVE THE KING! LONG LIVE THE QUEEN!
THE PEOPLE ARE HAPPY. BUT GOD IS NOT. INSTEAD OF BEING A SHEPHERD WHO PROTECTS GOD'S PEOPLE, DAVID HAS COMMITTED MURDER AND STOLEN A MAN'S WIFE. GOD CANNOT LET DAVID'S SECRET SIN GO UNPUNISHED.

David's Punishment

BASED ON 2 SAMUEL 12

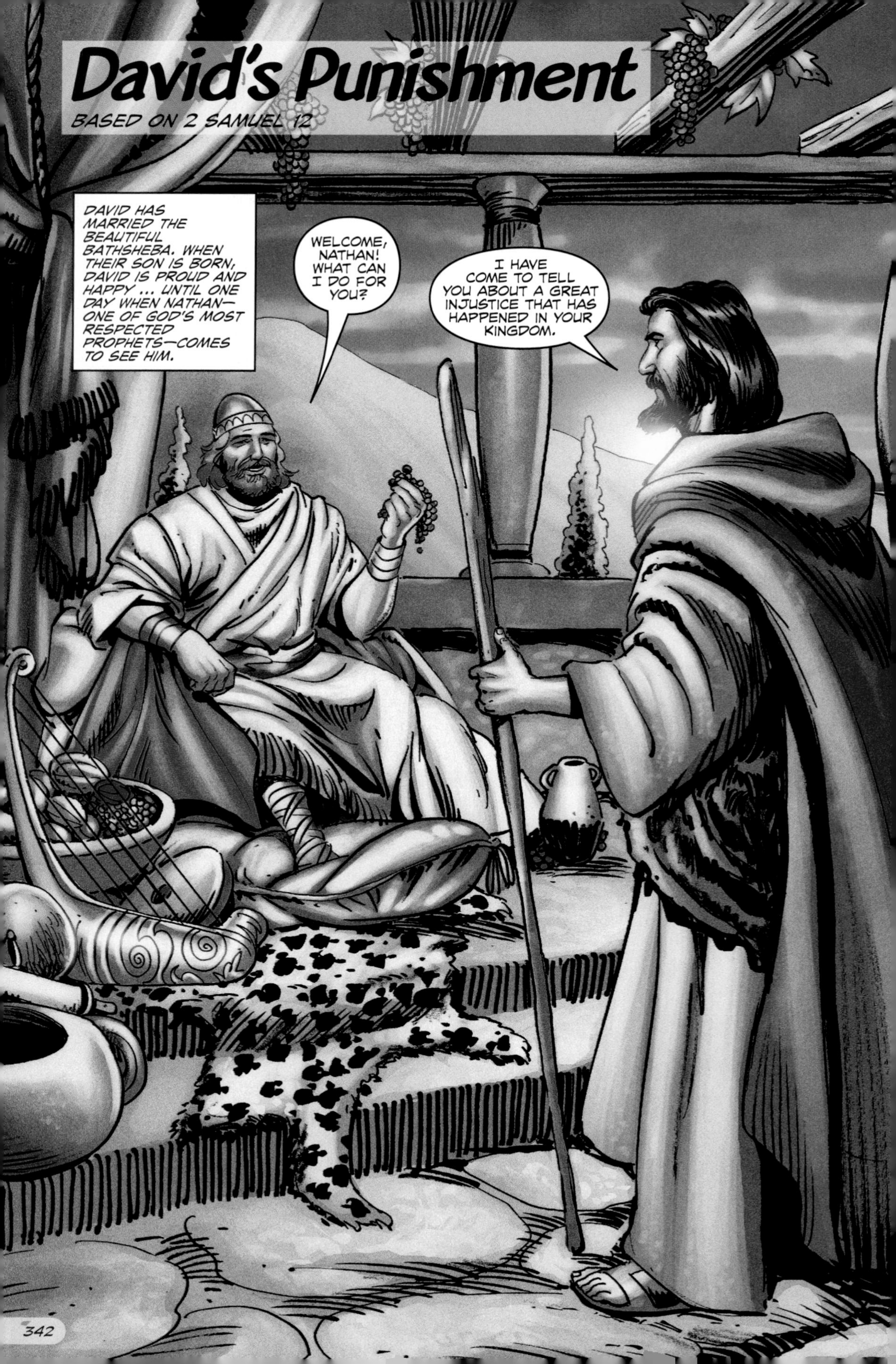

DAVID HAS MARRIED THE BEAUTIFUL BATHSHEBA. WHEN THEIR SON IS BORN, DAVID IS PROUD AND HAPPY ... UNTIL ONE DAY WHEN NATHAN—ONE OF GOD'S MOST RESPECTED PROPHETS—COMES TO SEE HIM.
WELCOME, NATHAN! WHAT CAN I DO FOR YOU?
I HAVE COME TO TELL YOU ABOUT A GREAT INJUSTICE THAT HAS HAPPENED IN YOUR KINGDOM.

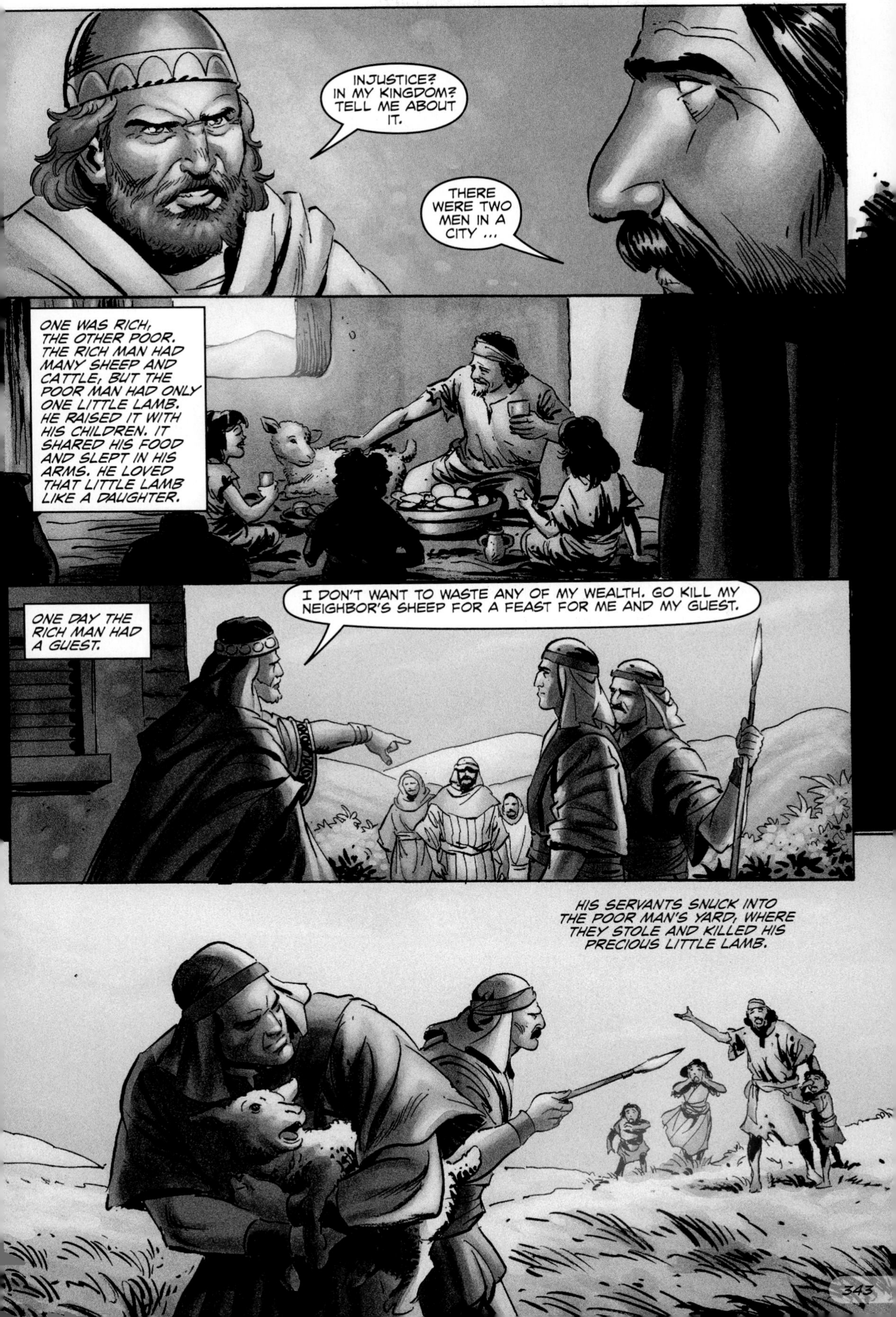
INJUSTICE? IN MY KINGDOM? TELL ME ABOUT IT.
THERE WERE TWO MEN IN A CITY ...
ONE WAS RICH, THE OTHER POOR. THE RICH MAN HAD MANY SHEEP AND CATTLE, BUT THE POOR MAN HAD ONLY ONE LITTLE LAMB. HE RAISED IT WITH HIS CHILDREN. IT SHARED HIS FOOD AND SLEPT IN HIS ARMS. HE LOVED THAT LITTLE LAMB LIKE A DAUGHTER.
ONE DAY THE RICH MAN HAD A GUEST.
I DON'T WANT TO WASTE ANY OF MY WEALTH. GO KILL MY NEIGHBOR'S SHEEP FOR A FEAST FOR ME AND MY GUEST.
HIS SERVANTS SNUCK INTO THE POOR MAN'S YARD, WHERE THEY STOLE AND KILLED HIS PRECIOUS LITTLE LAMB.

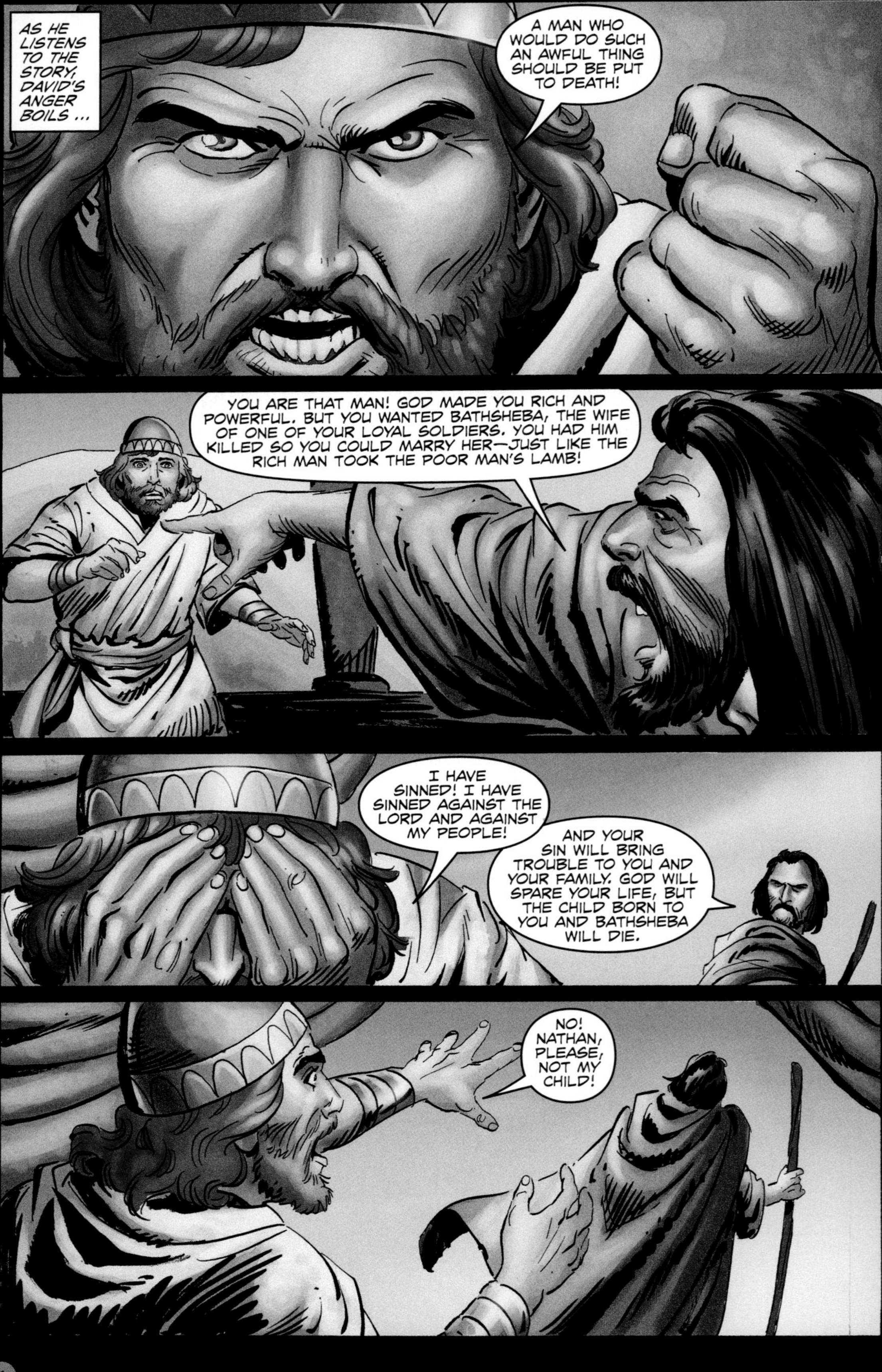
AS HE LISTENS TO THE STORY, DAVID'S ANGER BOILS ...
A MAN WHO WOULD DO SUCH AN AWFUL THING SHOULD BE PUT TO DEATH!
YOU ARE THAT MAN! GOD MADE YOU RICH AND POWERFUL. BUT YOU WANTED BATHSHEBA, THE WIFE OF ONE OF YOUR LOYAL SOLDIERS. YOU HAD HIM KILLED SO YOU COULD MARRY HER—JUST LIKE THE RICH MAN TOOK THE POOR MAN'S LAMB!
I HAVE SINNED! I HAVE SINNED AGAINST THE LORD AND AGAINST MY PEOPLE!
AND YOUR SIN WILL BRING TROUBLE TO YOU AND YOUR FAMILY. GOD WILL SPARE YOUR LIFE, BUT THE CHILD BORN TO YOU AND BATHSHEBA WILL DIE.
NO! NATHAN, PLEASE, NOT MY CHILD!

Psalm 51

DAVID PRAYED TO GOD AFTER NATHAN CONFRONTED DAVID WITH HIS SIN.

HAVE MERCY ON ME, O GOD,
 ACCORDING TO YOUR UNFAILING LOVE;
ACCORDING TO YOUR GREAT COMPASSION
 BLOT OUT MY TRANSGRESSIONS.
WASH AWAY ALL MY INIQUITY
 AND CLEANSE ME FROM MY SIN.
FOR I KNOW MY TRANSGRESSIONS,
 AND MY SIN IS ALWAYS BEFORE ME.
AGAINST YOU, YOU ONLY, HAVE I SINNED
 AND DONE WHAT IS EVIL IN YOUR SIGHT;
SO YOU ARE RIGHT IN YOUR VERDICT
 AND JUSTIFIED WHEN YOU JUDGE.
SURELY I WAS SINFUL AT BIRTH,
 SINFUL FROM THE TIME MY MOTHER CONCEIVED ME.

YET YOU DESIRED FAITHFULNESS EVEN IN THE WOMB;
    YOU TAUGHT ME WISDOM IN THAT SECRET PLACE.
CLEANSE ME WITH HYSSOP, AND I WILL BE CLEAN;
    WASH ME, AND I WILL BE WHITER THAN SNOW.
LET ME HEAR JOY AND GLADNESS;
    LET THE BONES YOU HAVE CRUSHED REJOICE.
HIDE YOUR FACE FROM MY SINS
    AND BLOT OUT ALL MY INIQUITY.
CREATE IN ME A PURE HEART, O GOD,
    AND RENEW A STEADFAST SPIRIT WITHIN ME.
DO NOT CAST ME FROM YOUR PRESENCE
    OR TAKE YOUR HOLY SPIRIT FROM ME.
RESTORE TO ME THE JOY OF YOUR SALVATION
    AND GRANT ME A WILLING SPIRIT, TO SUSTAIN ME.
THEN I WILL TEACH TRANSGRESSORS YOUR WAYS,
    SO THAT SINNERS WILL TURN BACK TO YOU.
DELIVER ME FROM THE GUILT OF BLOODSHED, O GOD,
    YOU WHO ARE GOD MY SAVIOR,
    AND MY TONGUE WILL SING OF YOUR RIGHTEOUSNESS.
OPEN MY LIPS, LORD,
    AND MY MOUTH WILL DECLARE YOUR PRAISE.
YOU DO NOT DELIGHT IN SACRIFICE, OR I WOULD BRING IT;
    YOU DO NOT TAKE PLEASURE IN BURNT OFFERINGS.
MY SACRIFICE, O GOD, IS A BROKEN SPIRIT;
    A BROKEN AND CONTRITE HEART
    YOU, GOD, WILL NOT DESPISE.
MAY IT PLEASE YOU TO PROSPER ZION,
    TO BUILD UP THE WALLS OF JERUSALEM.
THEN YOU WILL DELIGHT IN THE SACRIFICES OF THE RIGHTEOUS,
    IN BURNT OFFERINGS OFFERED WHOLE;
    THEN BULLS WILL BE OFFERED ON YOUR ALTAR.

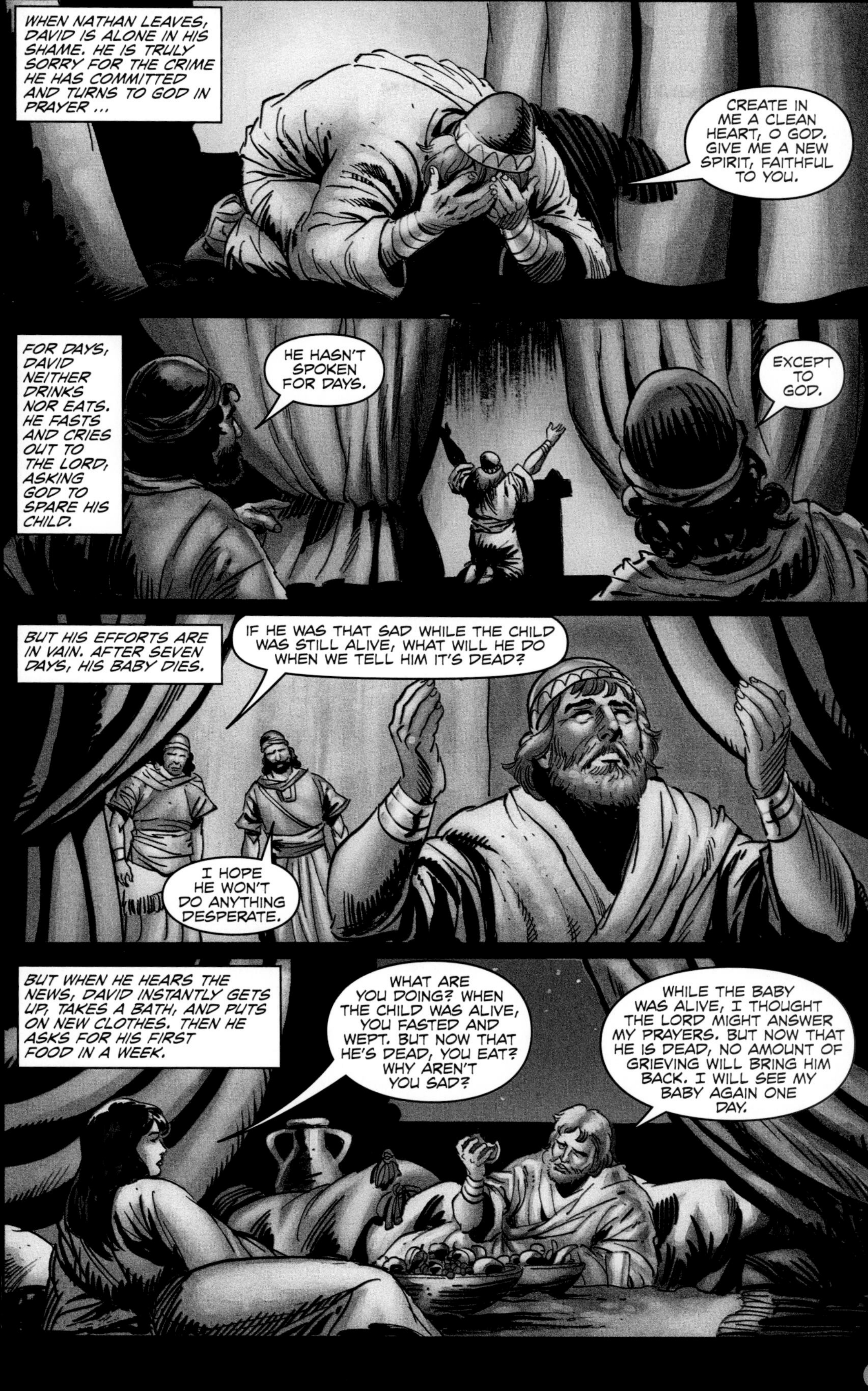
WHEN NATHAN LEAVES, DAVID IS ALONE IN HIS SHAME. HE IS TRULY SORRY FOR THE CRIME HE HAS COMMITTED AND TURNS TO GOD IN PRAYER ...
CREATE IN ME A CLEAN HEART, O GOD. GIVE ME A NEW SPIRIT, FAITHFUL TO YOU.
FOR DAYS, DAVID NEITHER DRINKS NOR EATS. HE FASTS AND CRIES OUT TO THE LORD, ASKING GOD TO SPARE HIS CHILD.
HE HASN'T SPOKEN FOR DAYS.
EXCEPT TO GOD.
BUT HIS EFFORTS ARE IN VAIN. AFTER SEVEN DAYS, HIS BABY DIES.
IF HE WAS THAT SAD WHILE THE CHILD WAS STILL ALIVE, WHAT WILL HE DO WHEN WE TELL HIM IT'S DEAD?
I HOPE HE WON'T DO ANYTHING DESPERATE.
BUT WHEN HE HEARS THE NEWS, DAVID INSTANTLY GETS UP, TAKES A BATH, AND PUTS ON NEW CLOTHES. THEN HE ASKS FOR HIS FIRST FOOD IN A WEEK.
WHAT ARE YOU DOING? WHEN THE CHILD WAS ALIVE, YOU FASTED AND WEPT. BUT NOW THAT HE'S DEAD, YOU EAT? WHY AREN'T YOU SAD?
WHILE THE BABY WAS ALIVE, I THOUGHT THE LORD MIGHT ANSWER MY PRAYERS. BUT NOW THAT HE IS DEAD, NO AMOUNT OF GRIEVING WILL BRING HIM BACK. I WILL SEE MY BABY AGAIN ONE DAY.

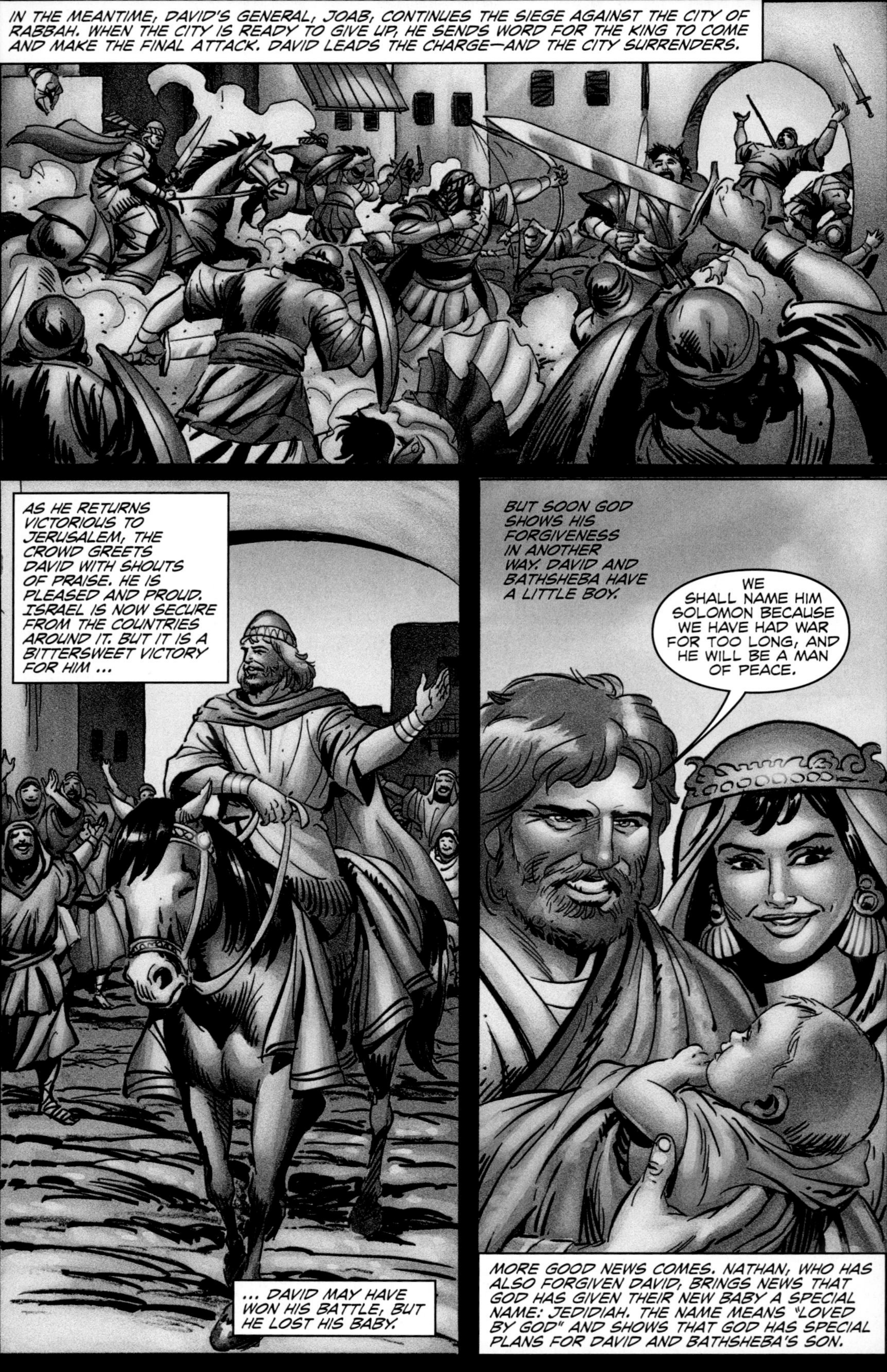
IN THE MEANTIME, DAVID'S GENERAL, JOAB, CONTINUES THE SIEGE AGAINST THE CITY OF RABBAH. WHEN THE CITY IS READY TO GIVE UP, HE SENDS WORD FOR THE KING TO COME AND MAKE THE FINAL ATTACK. DAVID LEADS THE CHARGE—AND THE CITY SURRENDERS.
AS HE RETURNS VICTORIOUS TO JERUSALEM, THE CROWD GREETS DAVID WITH SHOUTS OF PRAISE. HE IS PLEASED AND PROUD. ISRAEL IS NOW SECURE FROM THE COUNTRIES AROUND IT. BUT IT IS A BITTERSWEET VICTORY FOR HIM ...
... DAVID MAY HAVE WON HIS BATTLE, BUT HE LOST HIS BABY.
BUT SOON GOD SHOWS HIS FORGIVENESS IN ANOTHER WAY. DAVID AND BATHSHEBA HAVE A LITTLE BOY.
WE SHALL NAME HIM SOLOMON BECAUSE WE HAVE HAD WAR FOR TOO LONG, AND HE WILL BE A MAN OF PEACE.
MORE GOOD NEWS COMES. NATHAN, WHO HAS ALSO FORGIVEN DAVID, BRINGS NEWS THAT GOD HAS GIVEN THEIR NEW BABY A SPECIAL NAME: JEDIDIAH. THE NAME MEANS "LOVED BY GOD" AND SHOWS THAT GOD HAS SPECIAL PLANS FOR DAVID AND BATHSHEBA'S SON.

Battling Brothers

BASED ON 2 SAMUEL 13:23–39

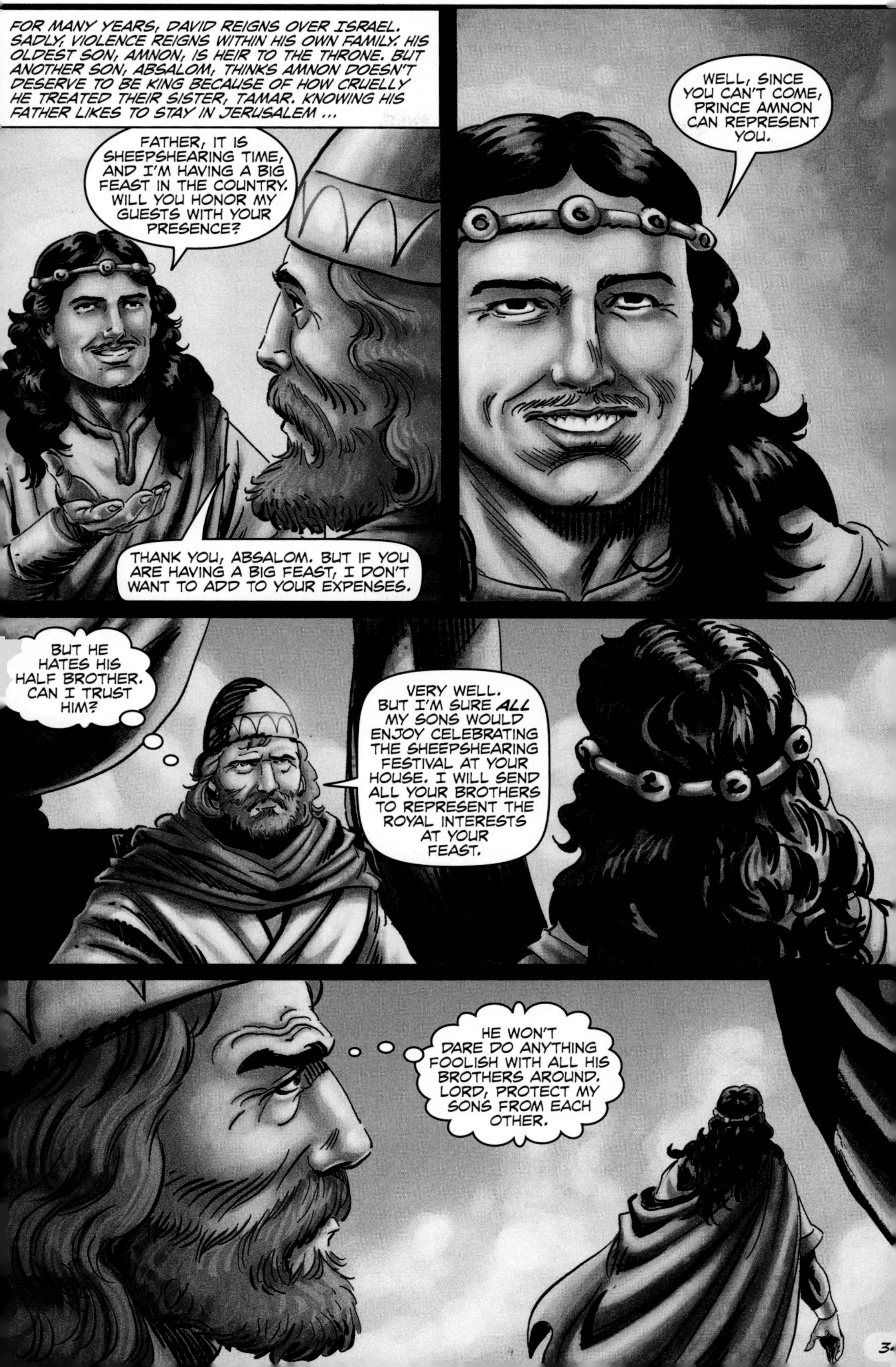
FOR MANY YEARS, DAVID REIGNS OVER ISRAEL. SADLY, VIOLENCE REIGNS WITHIN HIS OWN FAMILY. HIS OLDEST SON, AMNON, IS HEIR TO THE THRONE. BUT ANOTHER SON, ABSALOM, THINKS AMNON DOESN'T DESERVE TO BE KING BECAUSE OF HOW CRUELLY HE TREATED THEIR SISTER, TAMAR. KNOWING HIS FATHER LIKES TO STAY IN JERUSALEM ...
FATHER, IT IS SHEEPSHEARING TIME, AND I'M HAVING A BIG FEAST IN THE COUNTRY. WILL YOU HONOR MY GUESTS WITH YOUR PRESENCE?
THANK YOU, ABSALOM. BUT IF YOU ARE HAVING A BIG FEAST, I DON'T WANT TO ADD TO YOUR EXPENSES.
WELL, SINCE YOU CAN'T COME, PRINCE AMNON CAN REPRESENT YOU.
BUT HE HATES HIS HALF BROTHER. CAN I TRUST HIM?
VERY WELL. BUT I'M SURE ALL MY SONS WOULD ENJOY CELEBRATING THE SHEEPSHEARING FESTIVAL AT YOUR HOUSE. I WILL SEND ALL YOUR BROTHERS TO REPRESENT THE ROYAL INTERESTS AT YOUR FEAST.
HE WON'T DARE DO ANYTHING FOOLISH WITH ALL HIS BROTHERS AROUND. LORD, PROTECT MY SONS FROM EACH OTHER.

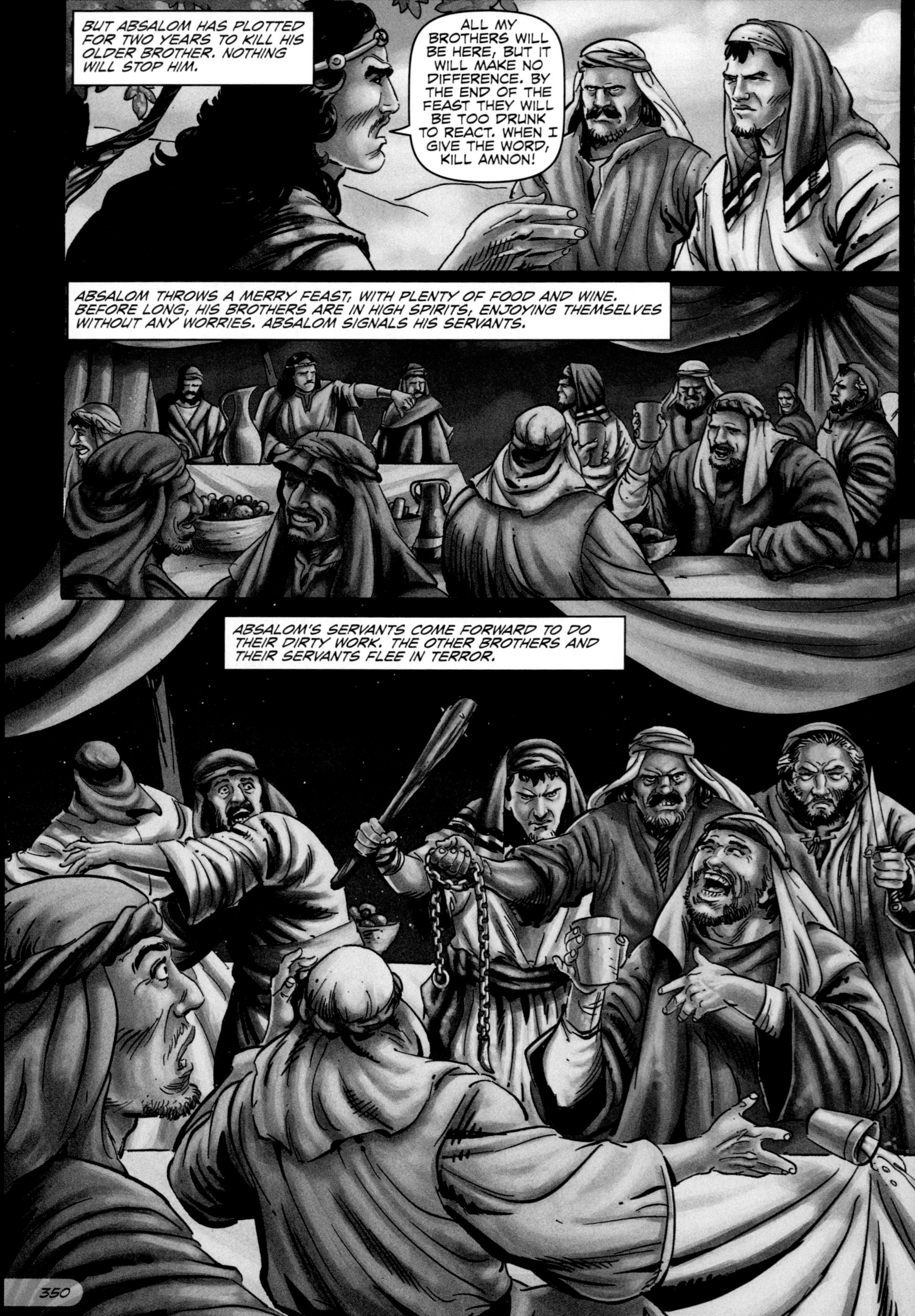
BUT ABSALOM HAS PLOTTED FOR TWO YEARS TO KILL HIS OLDER BROTHER. NOTHING WILL STOP HIM.
ALL MY BROTHERS WILL BE HERE, BUT IT WILL MAKE NO DIFFERENCE. BY THE END OF THE FEAST THEY WILL BE TOO DRUNK TO REACT. WHEN I GIVE THE WORD, KILL AMNON!
ABSALOM THROWS A MERRY FEAST, WITH PLENTY OF FOOD AND WINE. BEFORE LONG, HIS BROTHERS ARE IN HIGH SPIRITS, ENJOYING THEMSELVES WITHOUT ANY WORRIES. ABSALOM SIGNALS HIS SERVANTS.
ABSALOM'S SERVANTS COME FORWARD TO DO THEIR DIRTY WORK. THE OTHER BROTHERS AND THEIR SERVANTS FLEE IN TERROR.

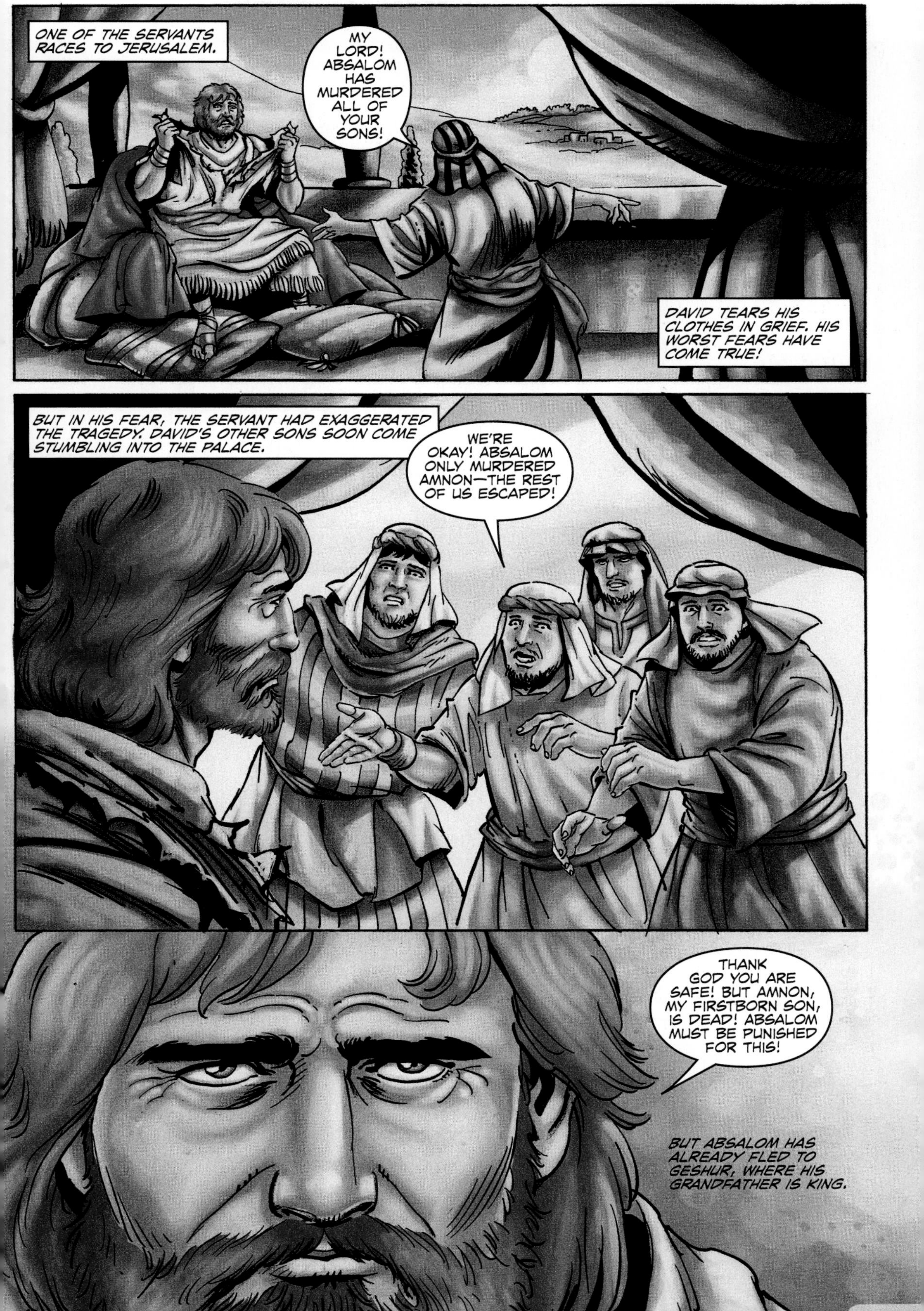
ONE OF THE SERVANTS RACES TO JERUSALEM.
MY LORD! ABSALOM HAS MURDERED ALL OF YOUR SONS!
DAVID TEARS HIS CLOTHES IN GRIEF. HIS WORST FEARS HAVE COME TRUE!
BUT IN HIS FEAR, THE SERVANT HAD EXAGGERATED THE TRAGEDY. DAVID'S OTHER SONS SOON COME STUMBLING INTO THE PALACE.
WE'RE OKAY! ABSALOM ONLY MURDERED AMNON—THE REST OF US ESCAPED!
THANK GOD YOU ARE SAFE! BUT AMNON, MY FIRSTBORN SON, IS DEAD! ABSALOM MUST BE PUNISHED FOR THIS!
BUT ABSALOM HAS ALREADY FLED TO GESHUR, WHERE HIS GRANDFATHER IS KING.

The Scheming Prince

BASED ON 2 SAMUEL 14:1—15:13

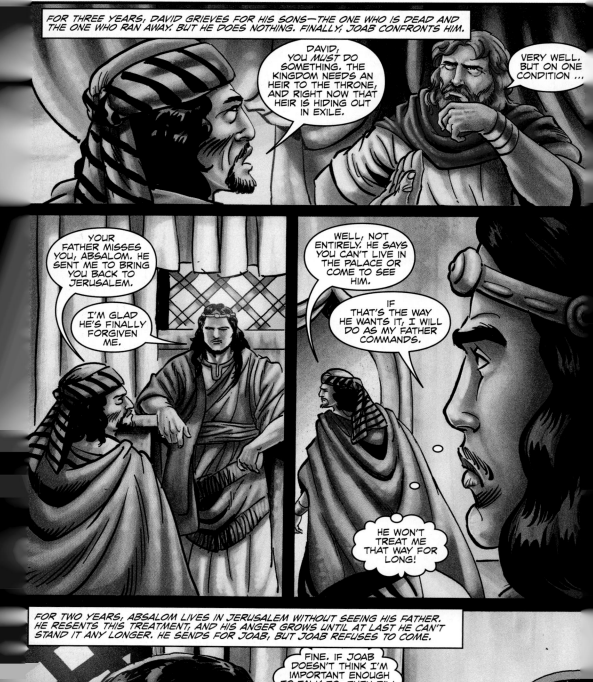

FOR THREE YEARS, DAVID GRIEVES FOR HIS SONS—THE ONE WHO IS DEAD AND THE ONE WHO RAN AWAY. BUT HE DOES NOTHING. FINALLY, JOAB CONFRONTS HIM.

DAVID, YOU MUST DO SOMETHING. THE KINGDOM NEEDS AN HEIR TO THE THRONE, AND RIGHT NOW THAT HEIR IS HIDING OUT IN EXILE.

VERY WELL. BUT ON ONE CONDITION ...

YOUR FATHER MISSES YOU, ABSALOM. HE SENT ME TO BRING YOU BACK TO JERUSALEM.

I'M GLAD HE'S FINALLY FORGIVEN ME.

WELL, NOT ENTIRELY. HE SAYS YOU CAN'T LIVE IN THE PALACE OR COME TO SEE HIM.

IF THAT'S THE WAY HE WANTS IT, I WILL DO AS MY FATHER COMMANDS.

HE WON'T TREAT ME THAT WAY FOR LONG!

FOR TWO YEARS, ABSALOM LIVES IN JERUSALEM WITHOUT SEEING HIS FATHER. HE RESENTS THIS TREATMENT, AND HIS ANGER GROWS UNTIL AT LAST HE CAN'T STAND IT ANY LONGER. HE SENDS FOR JOAB, BUT JOAB REFUSES TO COME.

FINE. IF JOAB DOESN'T THINK I'M IMPORTANT ENOUGH TO TALK TO, THEN I'LL GIVE HIM SOMETHING IMPORTANT TO DEAL WITH.

JOAB HAS A BARLEY FIELD NEXT TO MINE. SET FIRE TO IT!

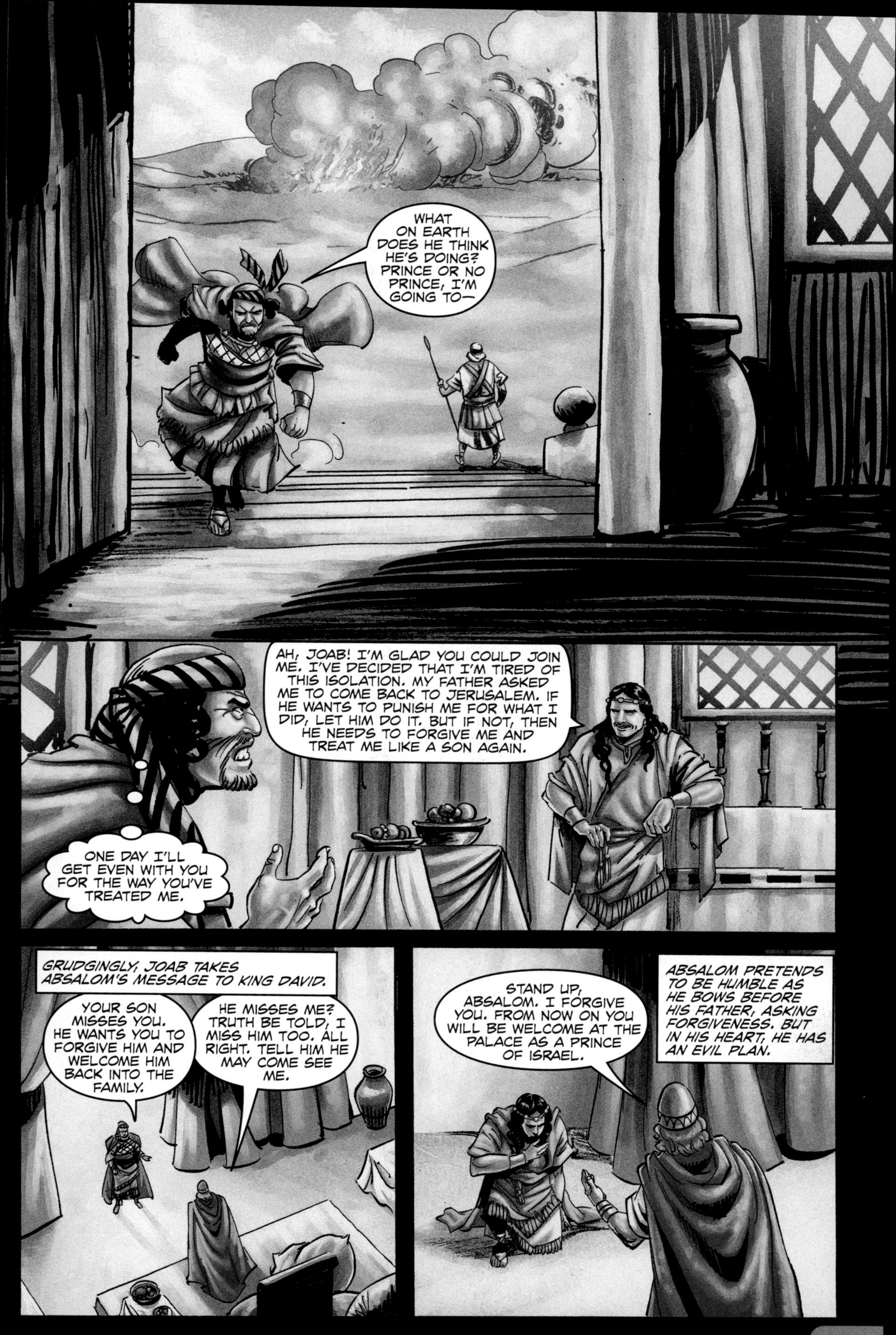
WHAT ON EARTH DOES HE THINK HE'S DOING? PRINCE OR NO PRINCE, I'M GOING TO—
AH, JOAB! I'M GLAD YOU COULD JOIN ME. I'VE DECIDED THAT I'M TIRED OF THIS ISOLATION. MY FATHER ASKED ME TO COME BACK TO JERUSALEM. IF HE WANTS TO PUNISH ME FOR WHAT I DID, LET HIM DO IT. BUT IF NOT, THEN HE NEEDS TO FORGIVE ME AND TREAT ME LIKE A SON AGAIN.
ONE DAY I'LL GET EVEN WITH YOU FOR THE WAY YOU'VE TREATED ME.
GRUDGINGLY, JOAB TAKES ABSALOM'S MESSAGE TO KING DAVID.
YOUR SON MISSES YOU. HE WANTS YOU TO FORGIVE HIM AND WELCOME HIM BACK INTO THE FAMILY.
HE MISSES ME? TRUTH BE TOLD, I MISS HIM TOO. ALL RIGHT. TELL HIM HE MAY COME SEE ME.
ABSALOM PRETENDS TO BE HUMBLE AS HE BOWS BEFORE HIS FATHER, ASKING FORGIVENESS. BUT IN HIS HEART, HE HAS AN EVIL PLAN.
STAND UP, ABSALOM. I FORGIVE YOU. FROM NOW ON YOU WILL BE WELCOME AT THE PALACE AS A PRINCE OF ISRAEL.

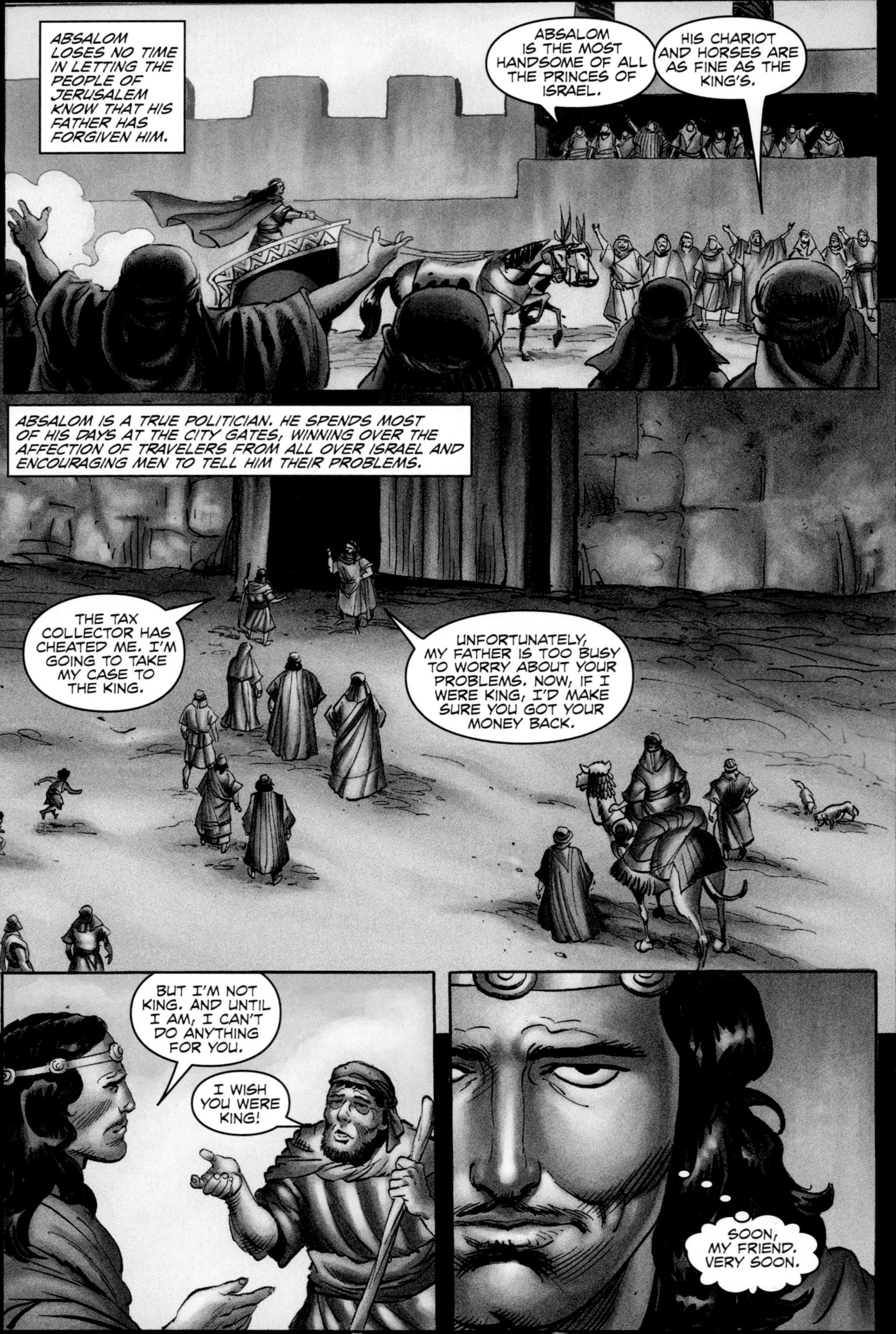

ABSALOM LOSES NO TIME IN LETTING THE PEOPLE OF JERUSALEM KNOW THAT HIS FATHER HAS FORGIVEN HIM.
ABSALOM IS THE MOST HANDSOME OF ALL THE PRINCES OF ISRAEL.
HIS CHARIOT AND HORSES ARE AS FINE AS THE KING'S.
ABSALOM IS A TRUE POLITICIAN. HE SPENDS MOST OF HIS DAYS AT THE CITY GATES, WINNING OVER THE AFFECTION OF TRAVELERS FROM ALL OVER ISRAEL AND ENCOURAGING MEN TO TELL HIM THEIR PROBLEMS.
THE TAX COLLECTOR HAS CHEATED ME. I'M GOING TO TAKE MY CASE TO THE KING.
UNFORTUNATELY, MY FATHER IS TOO BUSY TO WORRY ABOUT YOUR PROBLEMS. NOW, IF I WERE KING, I'D MAKE SURE YOU GOT YOUR MONEY BACK.
BUT I'M NOT KING. AND UNTIL I AM, I CAN'T DO ANYTHING FOR YOU.
I WISH YOU WERE KING!
SOON, MY FRIEND. VERY SOON.

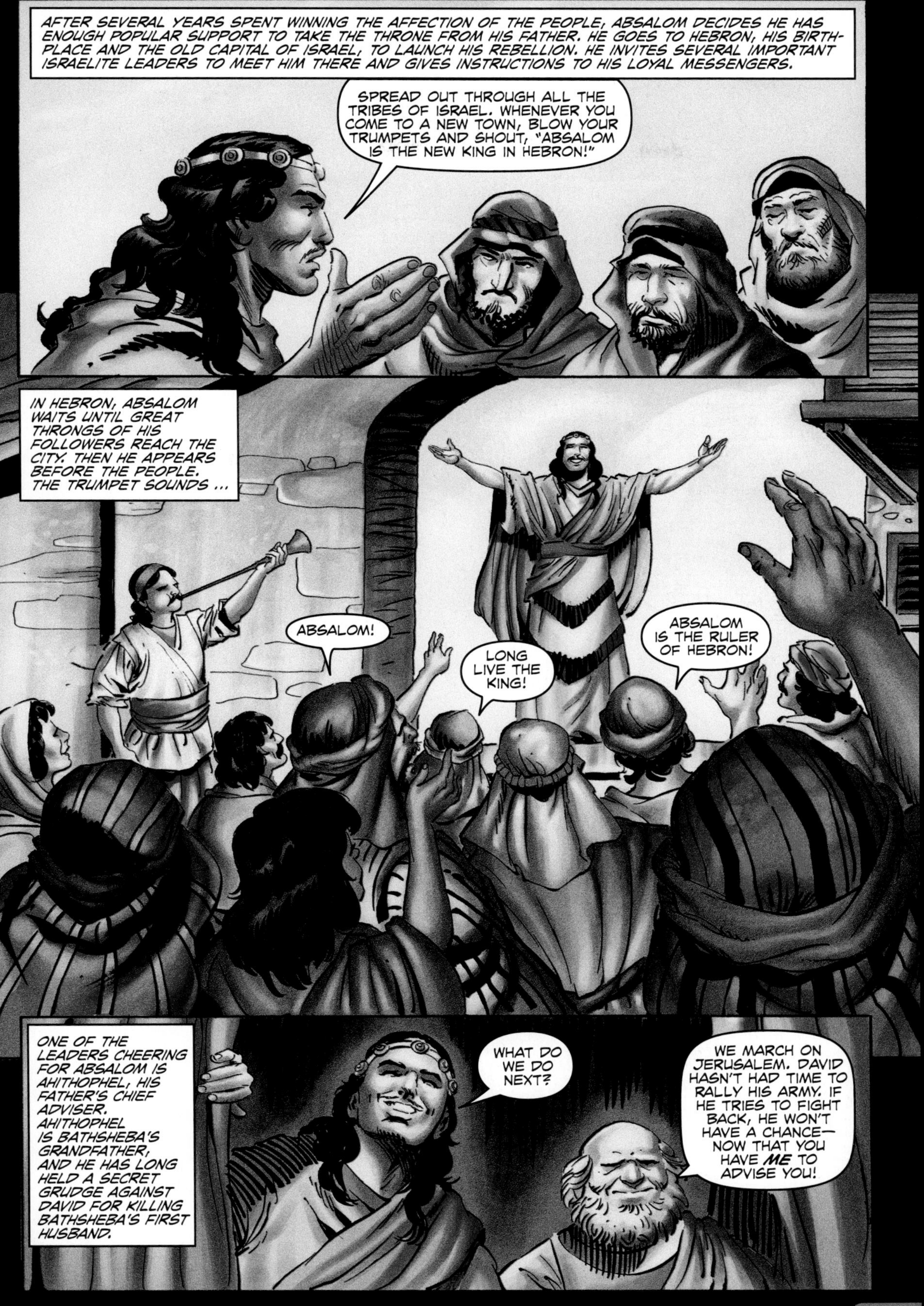
AFTER SEVERAL YEARS SPENT WINNING THE AFFECTION OF THE PEOPLE, ABSALOM DECIDES HE HAS ENOUGH POPULAR SUPPORT TO TAKE THE THRONE FROM HIS FATHER. HE GOES TO HEBRON, HIS BIRTHPLACE AND THE OLD CAPITAL OF ISRAEL, TO LAUNCH HIS REBELLION. HE INVITES SEVERAL IMPORTANT ISRAELITE LEADERS TO MEET HIM THERE AND GIVES INSTRUCTIONS TO HIS LOYAL MESSENGERS.
SPREAD OUT THROUGH ALL THE TRIBES OF ISRAEL. WHENEVER YOU COME TO A NEW TOWN, BLOW YOUR TRUMPETS AND SHOUT, "ABSALOM IS THE NEW KING IN HEBRON!"
IN HEBRON, ABSALOM WAITS UNTIL GREAT THRONGS OF HIS FOLLOWERS REACH THE CITY. THEN HE APPEARS BEFORE THE PEOPLE. THE TRUMPET SOUNDS ...
ABSALOM!
LONG LIVE THE KING!
ABSALOM IS THE RULER OF HEBRON!
ONE OF THE LEADERS CHEERING FOR ABSALOM IS AHITHOPHEL, HIS FATHER'S CHIEF ADVISER. AHITHOPHEL IS BATHSHEBA'S GRANDFATHER, AND HE HAS LONG HELD A SECRET GRUDGE AGAINST DAVID FOR KILLING BATHSHEBA'S FIRST HUSBAND.
WHAT DO WE DO NEXT?
WE MARCH ON JERUSALEM. DAVID HASN'T HAD TIME TO RALLY HIS ARMY. IF HE TRIES TO FIGHT BACK, HE WON'T HAVE A CHANCE—NOW THAT YOU HAVE ME TO ADVISE YOU!

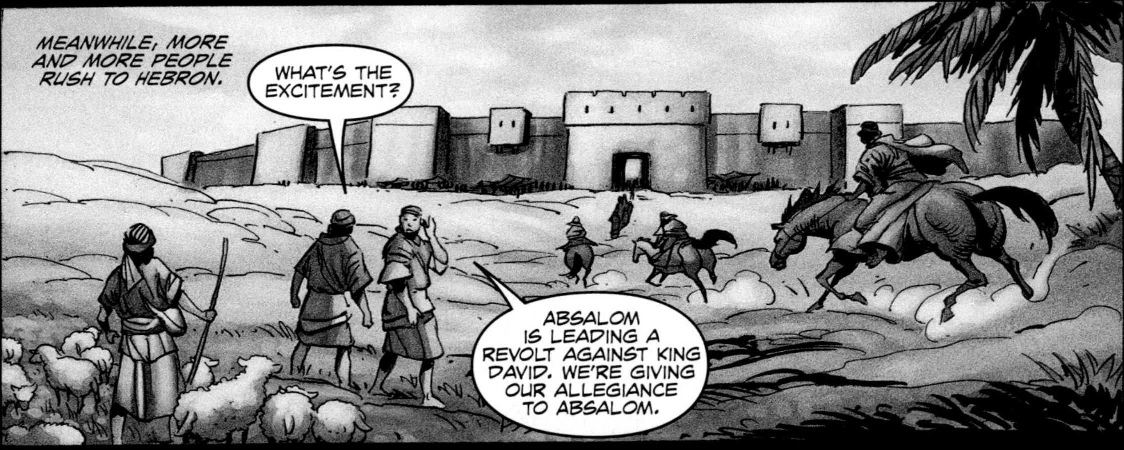
MEANWHILE, MORE AND MORE PEOPLE RUSH TO HEBRON.
WHAT'S THE EXCITEMENT?
ABSALOM IS LEADING A REVOLT AGAINST KING DAVID. WE'RE GIVING OUR ALLEGIANCE TO ABSALOM.

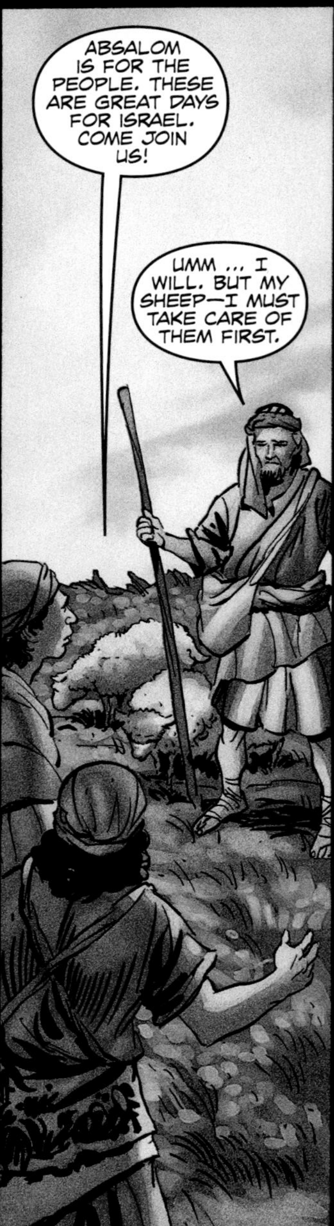
ABSALOM IS FOR THE PEOPLE. THESE ARE GREAT DAYS FOR ISRAEL. COME JOIN US!
UMM ... I WILL. BUT MY SHEEP—I MUST TAKE CARE OF THEM FIRST.

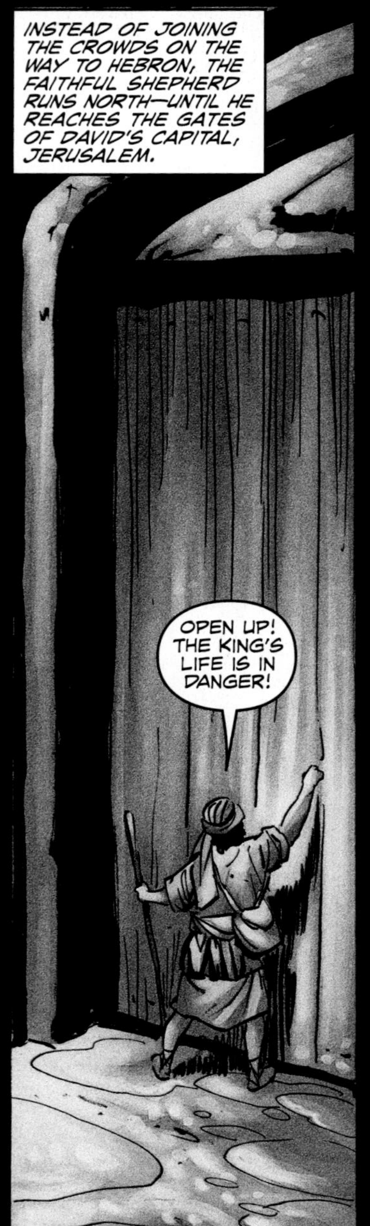
INSTEAD OF JOINING THE CROWDS ON THE WAY TO HEBRON, THE FAITHFUL SHEPHERD RUNS NORTH—UNTIL HE REACHES THE GATES OF DAVID'S CAPITAL, JERUSALEM.
OPEN UP! THE KING'S LIFE IS IN DANGER!

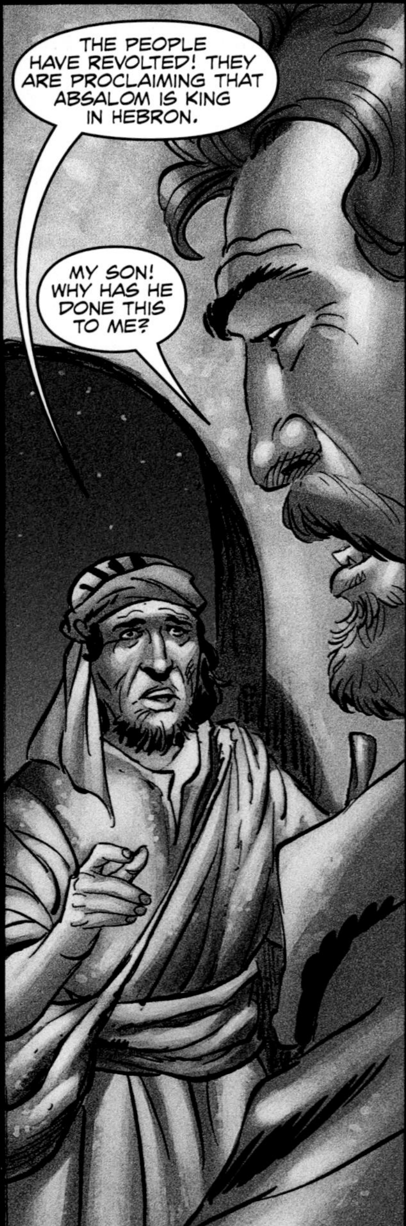
THE PEOPLE HAVE REVOLTED! THEY ARE PROCLAIMING THAT ABSALOM IS KING IN HEBRON.
MY SON! WHY HAS HE DONE THIS TO ME?

David's Spies

BASED ON 2 SAMUEL 15:13—17:29

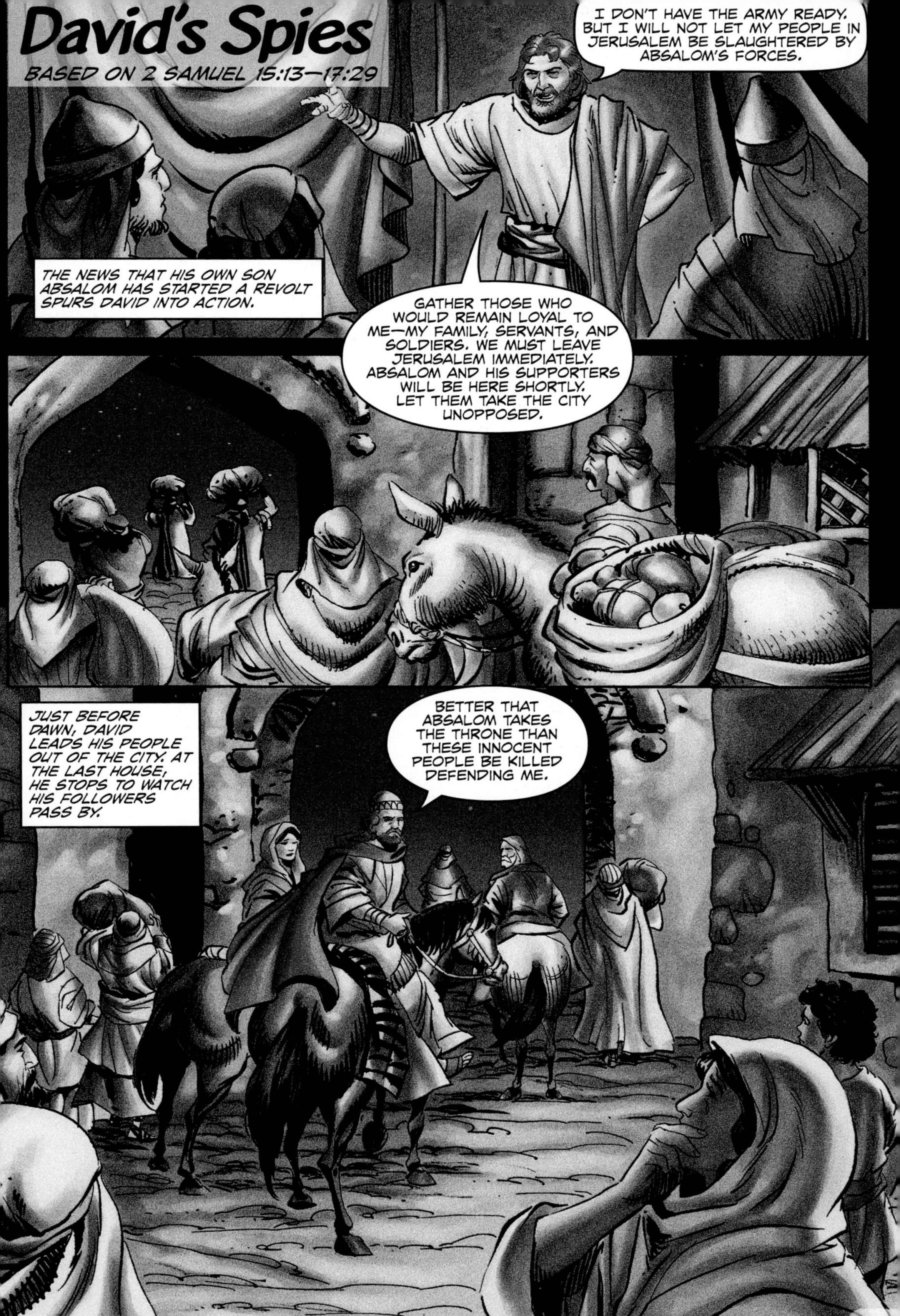

THE NEWS THAT HIS OWN SON ABSALOM HAS STARTED A REVOLT SPURS DAVID INTO ACTION.
I DON'T HAVE THE ARMY READY. BUT I WILL NOT LET MY PEOPLE IN JERUSALEM BE SLAUGHTERED BY ABSALOM'S FORCES.
GATHER THOSE WHO WOULD REMAIN LOYAL TO ME—MY FAMILY, SERVANTS, AND SOLDIERS. WE MUST LEAVE JERUSALEM IMMEDIATELY. ABSALOM AND HIS SUPPORTERS WILL BE HERE SHORTLY. LET THEM TAKE THE CITY UNOPPOSED.
JUST BEFORE DAWN, DAVID LEADS HIS PEOPLE OUT OF THE CITY. AT THE LAST HOUSE, HE STOPS TO WATCH HIS FOLLOWERS PASS BY.
BETTER THAT ABSALOM TAKES THE THRONE THAN THESE INNOCENT PEOPLE BE KILLED DEFENDING ME.

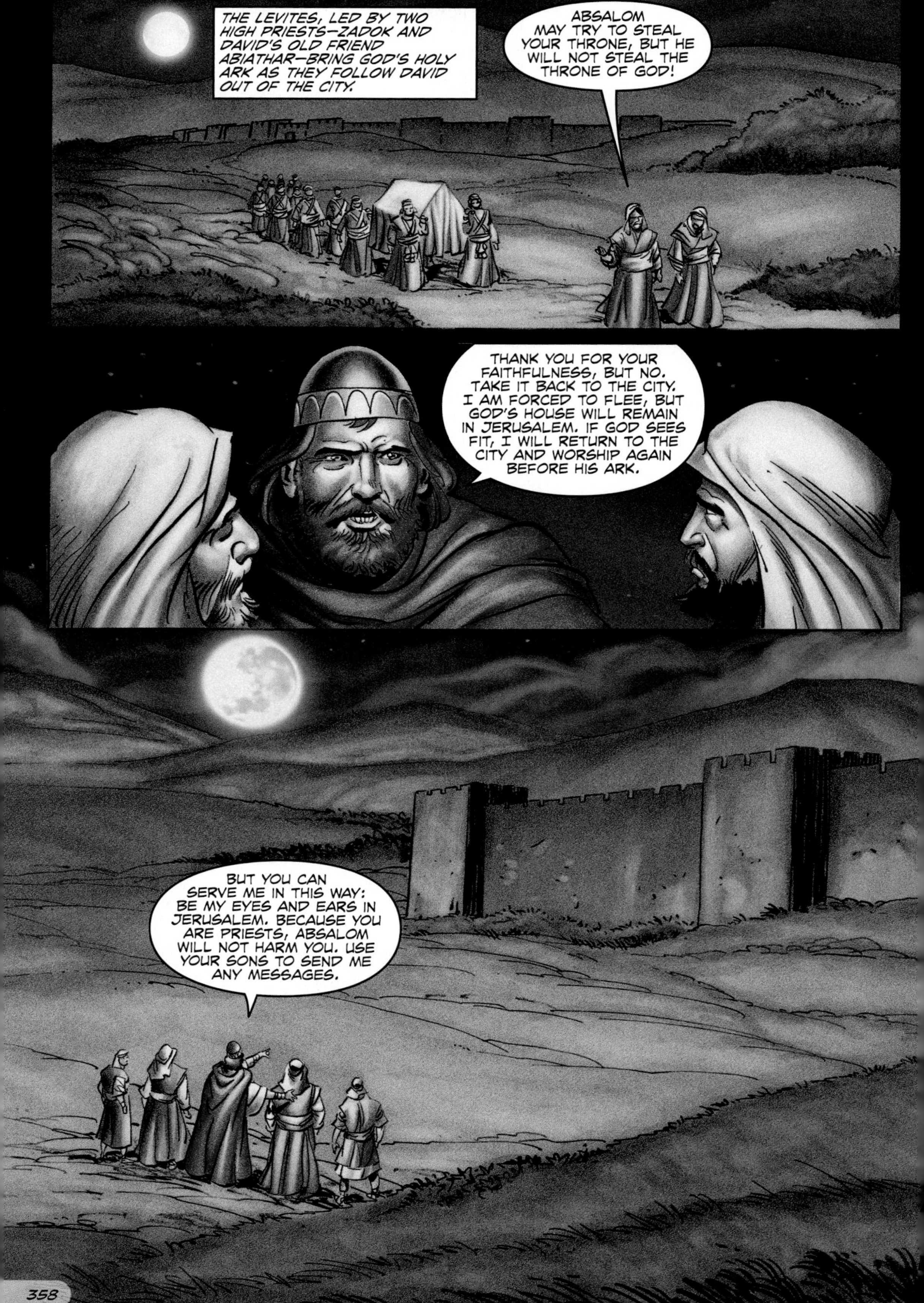
THE LEVITES, LED BY TWO HIGH PRIESTS—ZADOK AND DAVID'S OLD FRIEND ABIATHAR—BRING GOD'S HOLY ARK AS THEY FOLLOW DAVID OUT OF THE CITY.
ABSALOM MAY TRY TO STEAL YOUR THRONE, BUT HE WILL NOT STEAL THE THRONE OF GOD!
THANK YOU FOR YOUR FAITHFULNESS, BUT NO. TAKE IT BACK TO THE CITY. I AM FORCED TO FLEE, BUT GOD'S HOUSE WILL REMAIN IN JERUSALEM. IF GOD SEES FIT, I WILL RETURN TO THE CITY AND WORSHIP AGAIN BEFORE HIS ARK.
BUT YOU CAN SERVE ME IN THIS WAY: BE MY EYES AND EARS IN JERUSALEM. BECAUSE YOU ARE PRIESTS, ABSALOM WILL NOT HARM YOU. USE YOUR SONS TO SEND ME ANY MESSAGES.

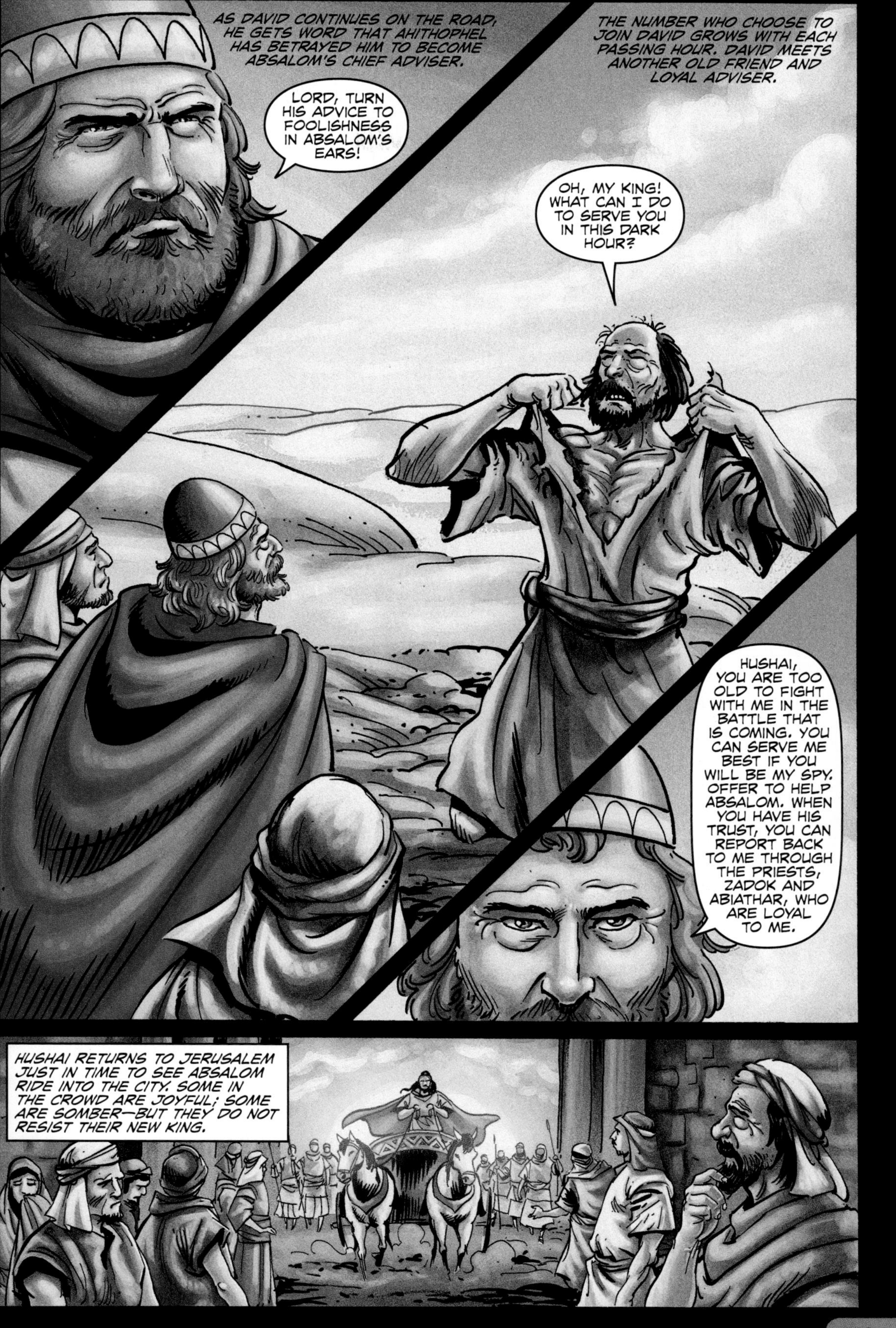
AS DAVID CONTINUES ON THE ROAD, HE GETS WORD THAT AHITHOPHEL HAS BETRAYED HIM TO BECOME ABSALOM'S CHIEF ADVISER.
LORD, TURN HIS ADVICE TO FOOLISHNESS IN ABSALOM'S EARS!
THE NUMBER WHO CHOOSE TO JOIN DAVID GROWS WITH EACH PASSING HOUR. DAVID MEETS ANOTHER OLD FRIEND AND LOYAL ADVISER.
OH, MY KING! WHAT CAN I DO TO SERVE YOU IN THIS DARK HOUR?
HUSHAI, YOU ARE TOO OLD TO FIGHT WITH ME IN THE BATTLE THAT IS COMING. YOU CAN SERVE ME BEST IF YOU WILL BE MY SPY. OFFER TO HELP ABSALOM. WHEN YOU HAVE HIS TRUST, YOU CAN REPORT BACK TO ME THROUGH THE PRIESTS, ZADOK AND ABIATHAR, WHO ARE LOYAL TO ME.
HUSHAI RETURNS TO JERUSALEM JUST IN TIME TO SEE ABSALOM RIDE INTO THE CITY. SOME IN THE CROWD ARE JOYFUL; SOME ARE SOMBER—BUT THEY DO NOT RESIST THEIR NEW KING.

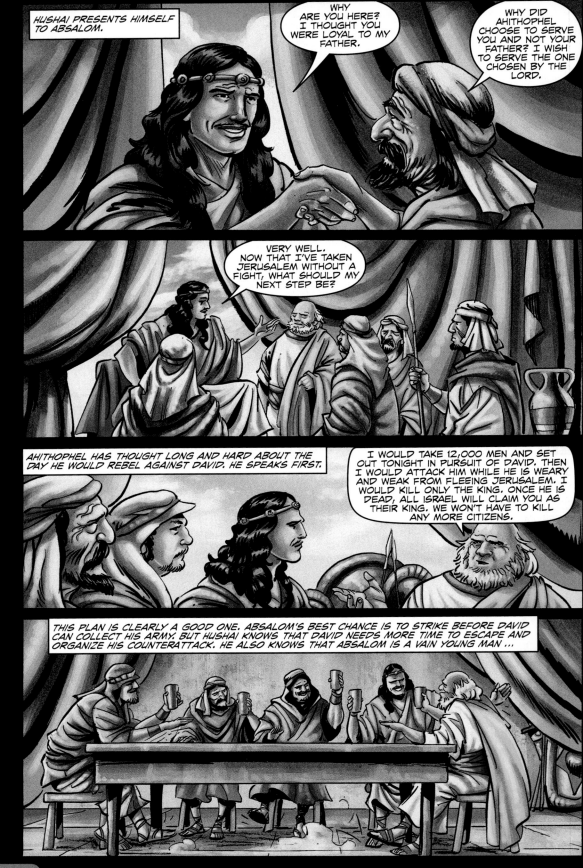

HUSHAI PRESENTS HIMSELF TO ABSALOM.

WHY ARE YOU HERE? I THOUGHT YOU WERE LOYAL TO MY FATHER.

WHY DID AHITHOPHEL CHOOSE TO SERVE YOU AND NOT YOUR FATHER? I WISH TO SERVE THE ONE CHOSEN BY THE LORD.

VERY WELL. NOW THAT I'VE TAKEN JERUSALEM WITHOUT A FIGHT, WHAT SHOULD MY NEXT STEP BE?

AHITHOPHEL HAS THOUGHT LONG AND HARD ABOUT THE DAY HE WOULD REBEL AGAINST DAVID. HE SPEAKS FIRST.

I WOULD TAKE 12,000 MEN AND SET OUT TONIGHT IN PURSUIT OF DAVID. THEN I WOULD ATTACK HIM WHILE HE IS WEARY AND WEAK FROM FLEEING JERUSALEM. I WOULD KILL ONLY THE KING. ONCE HE IS DEAD, ALL ISRAEL WILL CLAIM YOU AS THEIR KING. WE WON'T HAVE TO KILL ANY MORE CITIZENS.

THIS PLAN IS CLEARLY A GOOD ONE. ABSALOM'S BEST CHANCE IS TO STRIKE BEFORE DAVID CAN COLLECT HIS ARMY. BUT HUSHAI KNOWS THAT DAVID NEEDS MORE TIME TO ESCAPE AND ORGANIZE HIS COUNTERATTACK. HE ALSO KNOWS THAT ABSALOM IS A VAIN YOUNG MAN ...

AHITHOPHEL'S ADVICE IS GOOD—FOR AHITHOPHEL. OF COURSE HE WANTS TO TRY TO CAPTURE DAVID HIMSELF. IT'S HIS BEST CHANCE FOR GLORY. BUT HE FORGETS ONE THING: DAVID AND HIS MEN ARE ISRAEL'S BEST FIGHTERS. RIGHT NOW THEY ARE ANGRY AS BEARS WHO HAVE BEEN ROBBED OF THEIR CUBS. IF YOU ATTACK AND SUFFER ANY DEFEAT, THE PEOPLE WILL SAY THAT YOU ARE WEAK AND WILL TURN AGAINST YOU.

INSTEAD, O KING, YOU SHOULD WAIT UNTIL YOU CAN CALL ON THOUSANDS OF MEN FROM THE SURROUNDING TRIBES. THEN IF YOU, AS THEIR HEROIC LEADER, GO FORTH BEFORE YOUR ARMY, DAVID WILL NOT BE ABLE TO STAND AGAINST YOU.

YES, HUSHAI'S PLAN MAKES SURE THAT I GET ALL THE GLORY.

I HAVE CHOSEN THE WRONG MAN TO SUPPORT AS KING—A CONCEITED FOOL!

IF ABSALOM LISTENS TO ME, DAVID WILL HAVE TIME TO ESCAPE.

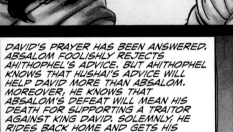

DAVID'S PRAYER HAS BEEN ANSWERED. ABSALOM FOOLISHLY REJECTS AHITHOPHEL'S ADVICE. BUT AHITHOPHEL KNOWS THAT HUSHAI'S ADVICE WILL HELP DAVID MORE THAN ABSALOM. MOREOVER, HE KNOWS THAT ABSALOM'S DEFEAT WILL MEAN HIS DEATH FOR SUPPORTING A TRAITOR AGAINST KING DAVID. SOLEMNLY, HE RIDES BACK HOME AND GETS HIS AFFAIRS IN ORDER.

ONCE HIS WILL AND BUSINESS MATTERS ARE ARRANGED, AHITHOPHEL HANGS HIMSELF. IT IS A SORRY END FOR A MAN WHO ONCE WAS ONE OF THE KING'S WISEST ADVISERS.

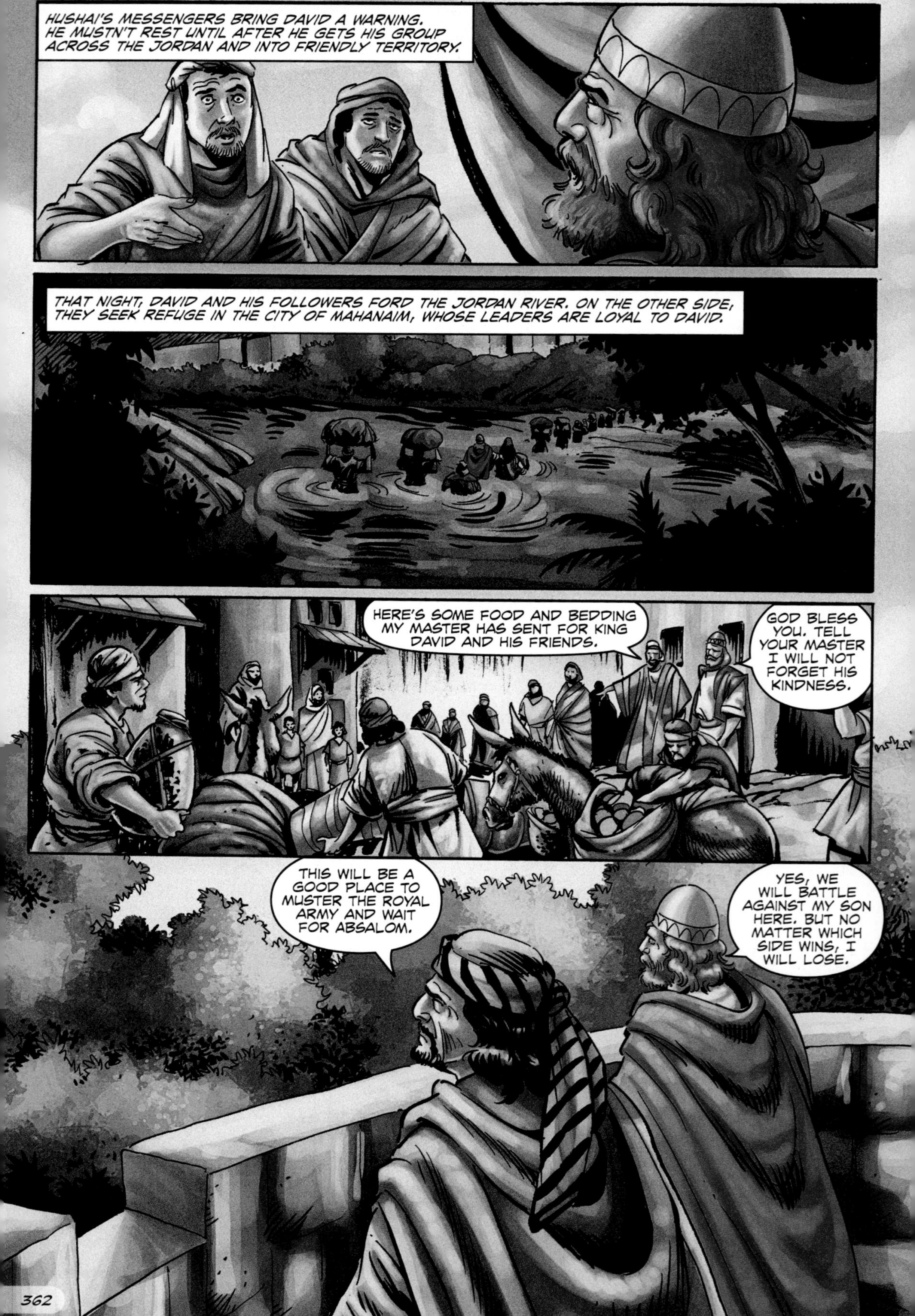
HUSHAI'S MESSENGERS BRING DAVID A WARNING. HE MUSTN'T REST UNTIL AFTER HE GETS HIS GROUP ACROSS THE JORDAN AND INTO FRIENDLY TERRITORY.
THAT NIGHT, DAVID AND HIS FOLLOWERS FORD THE JORDAN RIVER. ON THE OTHER SIDE, THEY SEEK REFUGE IN THE CITY OF MAHANAIM, WHOSE LEADERS ARE LOYAL TO DAVID.
HERE'S SOME FOOD AND BEDDING MY MASTER HAS SENT FOR KING DAVID AND HIS FRIENDS.
GOD BLESS YOU. TELL YOUR MASTER I WILL NOT FORGET HIS KINDNESS.
THIS WILL BE A GOOD PLACE TO MUSTER THE ROYAL ARMY AND WAIT FOR ABSALOM.
YES, WE WILL BATTLE AGAINST MY SON HERE. BUT NO MATTER WHICH SIDE WINS, I WILL LOSE.

O Absalom!

BASED ON 2 SAMUEL 18:1—19:15

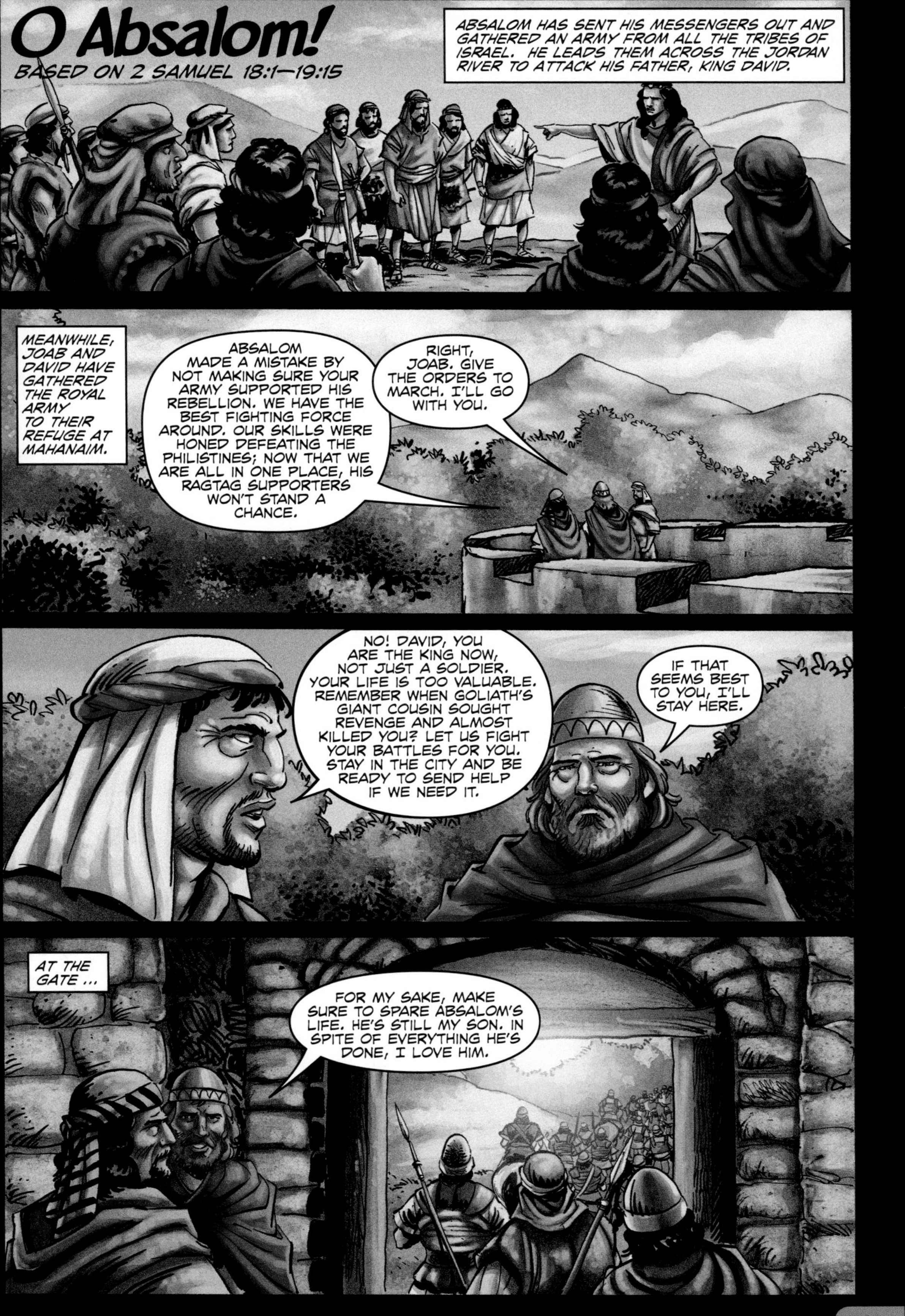

ABSALOM HAS SENT HIS MESSENGERS OUT AND GATHERED AN ARMY FROM ALL THE TRIBES OF ISRAEL. HE LEADS THEM ACROSS THE JORDAN RIVER TO ATTACK HIS FATHER, KING DAVID.
MEANWHILE, JOAB AND DAVID HAVE GATHERED THE ROYAL ARMY TO THEIR REFUGE AT MAHANAIM.
ABSALOM MADE A MISTAKE BY NOT MAKING SURE YOUR ARMY SUPPORTED HIS REBELLION. WE HAVE THE BEST FIGHTING FORCE AROUND. OUR SKILLS WERE HONED DEFEATING THE PHILISTINES; NOW THAT WE ARE ALL IN ONE PLACE, HIS RAGTAG SUPPORTERS WON'T STAND A CHANCE.
RIGHT, JOAB. GIVE THE ORDERS TO MARCH. I'LL GO WITH YOU.
NO! DAVID, YOU ARE THE KING NOW, NOT JUST A SOLDIER. YOUR LIFE IS TOO VALUABLE. REMEMBER WHEN GOLIATH'S GIANT COUSIN SOUGHT REVENGE AND ALMOST KILLED YOU? LET US FIGHT YOUR BATTLES FOR YOU. STAY IN THE CITY AND BE READY TO SEND HELP IF WE NEED IT.
IF THAT SEEMS BEST TO YOU, I'LL STAY HERE.
AT THE GATE ...
FOR MY SAKE, MAKE SURE TO SPARE ABSALOM'S LIFE. HE'S STILL MY SON. IN SPITE OF EVERYTHING HE'S DONE, I LOVE HIM.

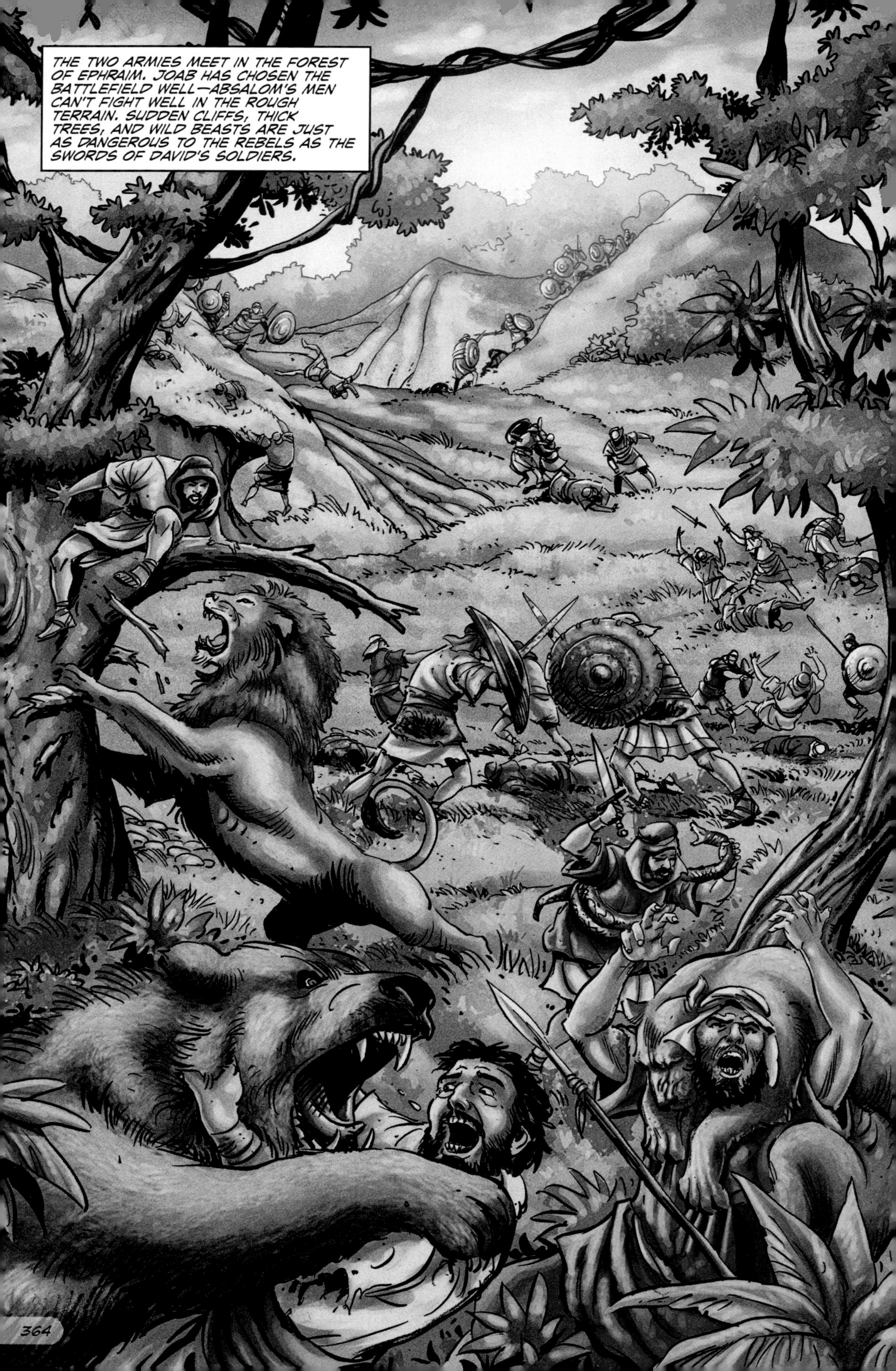
THE TWO ARMIES MEET IN THE FOREST OF EPHRAIM. JOAB HAS CHOSEN THE BATTLEFIELD WELL—ABSALOM'S MEN CAN'T FIGHT WELL IN THE ROUGH TERRAIN. SUDDEN CLIFFS, THICK TREES, AND WILD BEASTS ARE JUST AS DANGEROUS TO THE REBELS AS THE SWORDS OF DAVID'S SOLDIERS.

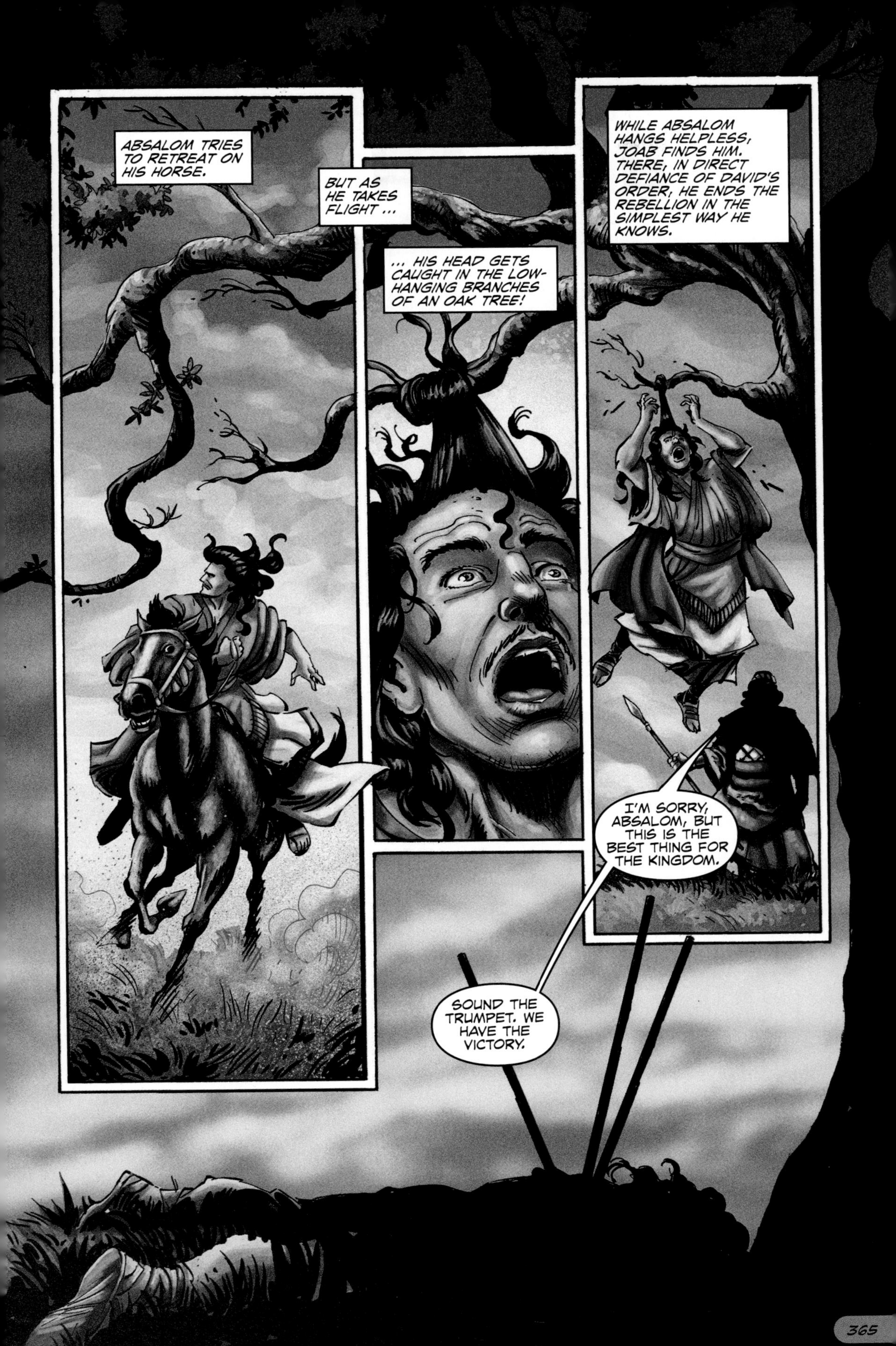
ABSALOM TRIES TO RETREAT ON HIS HORSE.
BUT AS HE TAKES FLIGHT ...
... HIS HEAD GETS CAUGHT IN THE LOW-HANGING BRANCHES OF AN OAK TREE!
WHILE ABSALOM HANGS HELPLESS, JOAB FINDS HIM. THERE, IN DIRECT DEFIANCE OF DAVID'S ORDER, HE ENDS THE REBELLION IN THE SIMPLEST WAY HE KNOWS.
I'M SORRY, ABSALOM, BUT THIS IS THE BEST THING FOR THE KINGDOM.
SOUND THE TRUMPET. WE HAVE THE VICTORY.

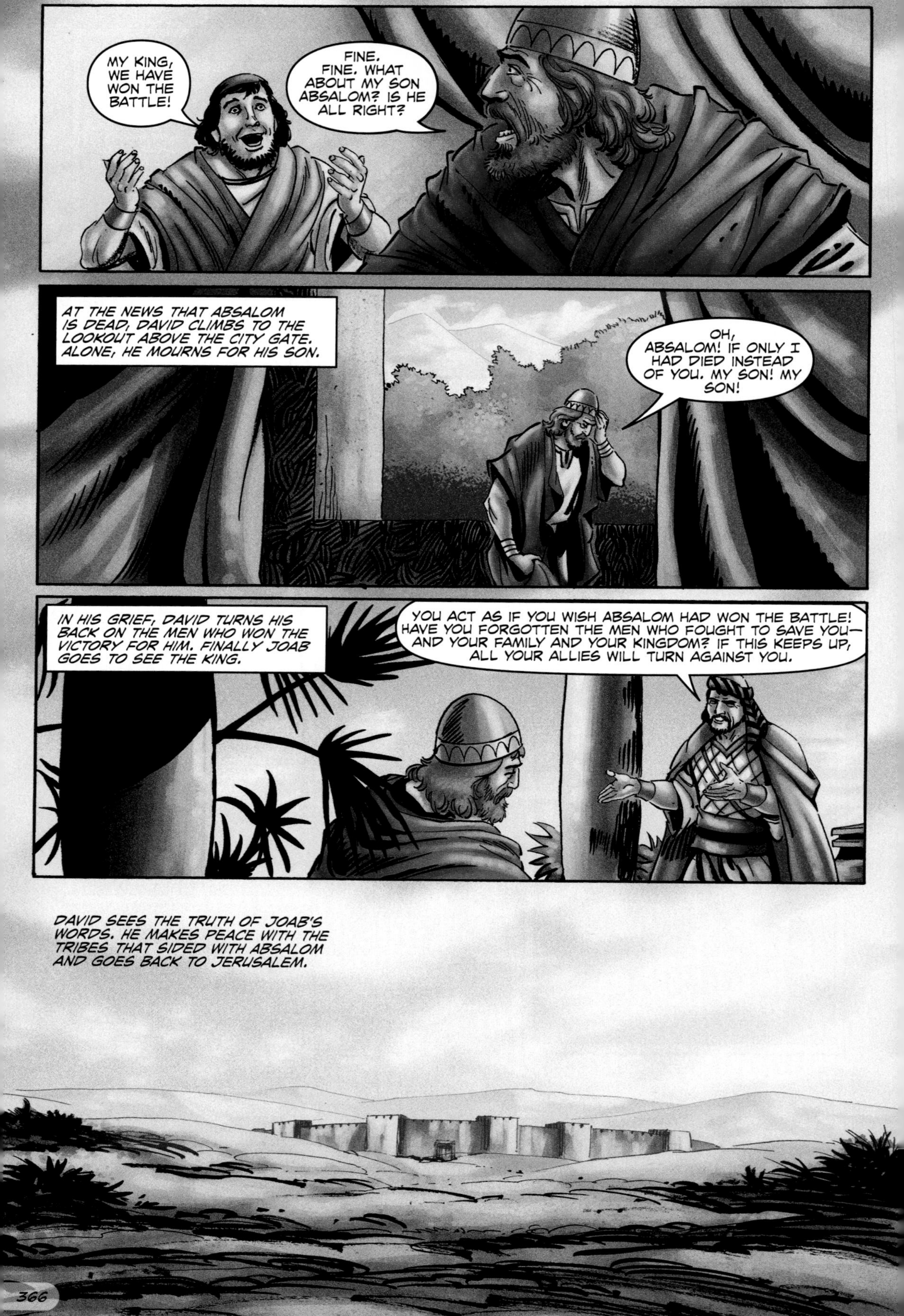
MY KING, WE HAVE WON THE BATTLE!
FINE. FINE. WHAT ABOUT MY SON ABSALOM? IS HE ALL RIGHT?
AT THE NEWS THAT ABSALOM IS DEAD, DAVID CLIMBS TO THE LOOKOUT ABOVE THE CITY GATE. ALONE, HE MOURNS FOR HIS SON.
OH, ABSALOM! IF ONLY I HAD DIED INSTEAD OF YOU. MY SON! MY SON!
IN HIS GRIEF, DAVID TURNS HIS BACK ON THE MEN WHO WON THE VICTORY FOR HIM. FINALLY JOAB GOES TO SEE THE KING.
YOU ACT AS IF YOU WISH ABSALOM HAD WON THE BATTLE! HAVE YOU FORGOTTEN THE MEN WHO FOUGHT TO SAVE YOU—AND YOUR FAMILY AND YOUR KINGDOM? IF THIS KEEPS UP, ALL YOUR ALLIES WILL TURN AGAINST YOU.
DAVID SEES THE TRUTH OF JOAB'S WORDS. HE MAKES PEACE WITH THE TRIBES THAT SIDED WITH ABSALOM AND GOES BACK TO JERUSALEM.

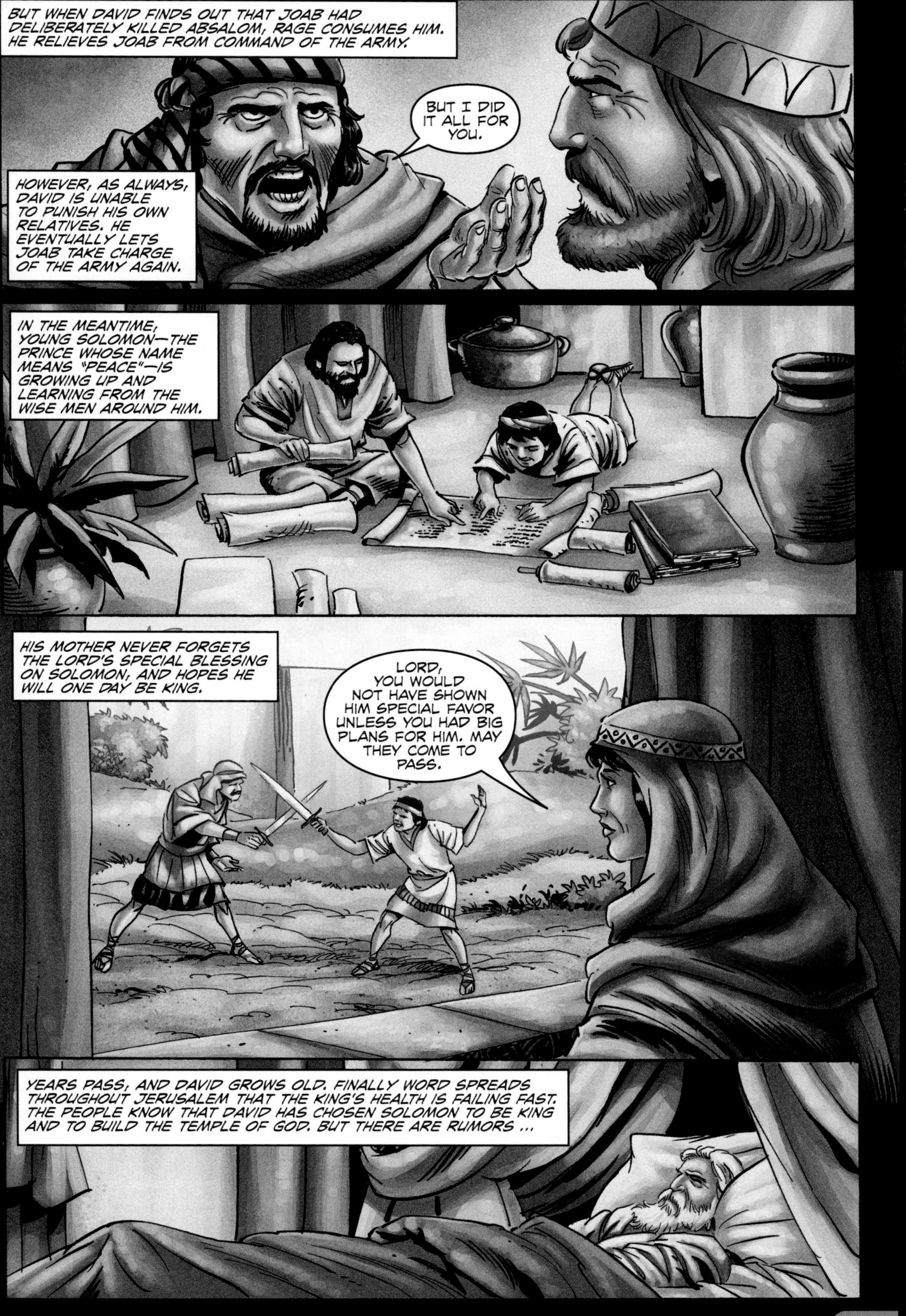
BUT WHEN DAVID FINDS OUT THAT JOAB HAD DELIBERATELY KILLED ABSALOM, RAGE CONSUMES HIM. HE RELIEVES JOAB FROM COMMAND OF THE ARMY.
BUT I DID IT ALL FOR YOU.
HOWEVER, AS ALWAYS, DAVID IS UNABLE TO PUNISH HIS OWN RELATIVES. HE EVENTUALLY LETS JOAB TAKE CHARGE OF THE ARMY AGAIN.
IN THE MEANTIME, YOUNG SOLOMON—THE PRINCE WHOSE NAME MEANS "PEACE"—IS GROWING UP AND LEARNING FROM THE WISE MEN AROUND HIM.
HIS MOTHER NEVER FORGETS THE LORD'S SPECIAL BLESSING ON SOLOMON, AND HOPES HE WILL ONE DAY BE KING.
LORD, YOU WOULD NOT HAVE SHOWN HIM SPECIAL FAVOR UNLESS YOU HAD BIG PLANS FOR HIM. MAY THEY COME TO PASS.
YEARS PASS, AND DAVID GROWS OLD. FINALLY WORD SPREADS THROUGHOUT JERUSALEM THAT THE KING'S HEALTH IS FAILING FAST. THE PEOPLE KNOW THAT DAVID HAS CHOSEN SOLOMON TO BE KING AND TO BUILD THE TEMPLE OF GOD. BUT THERE ARE RUMORS ...

Family Plots

BASED ON 1 KINGS 1

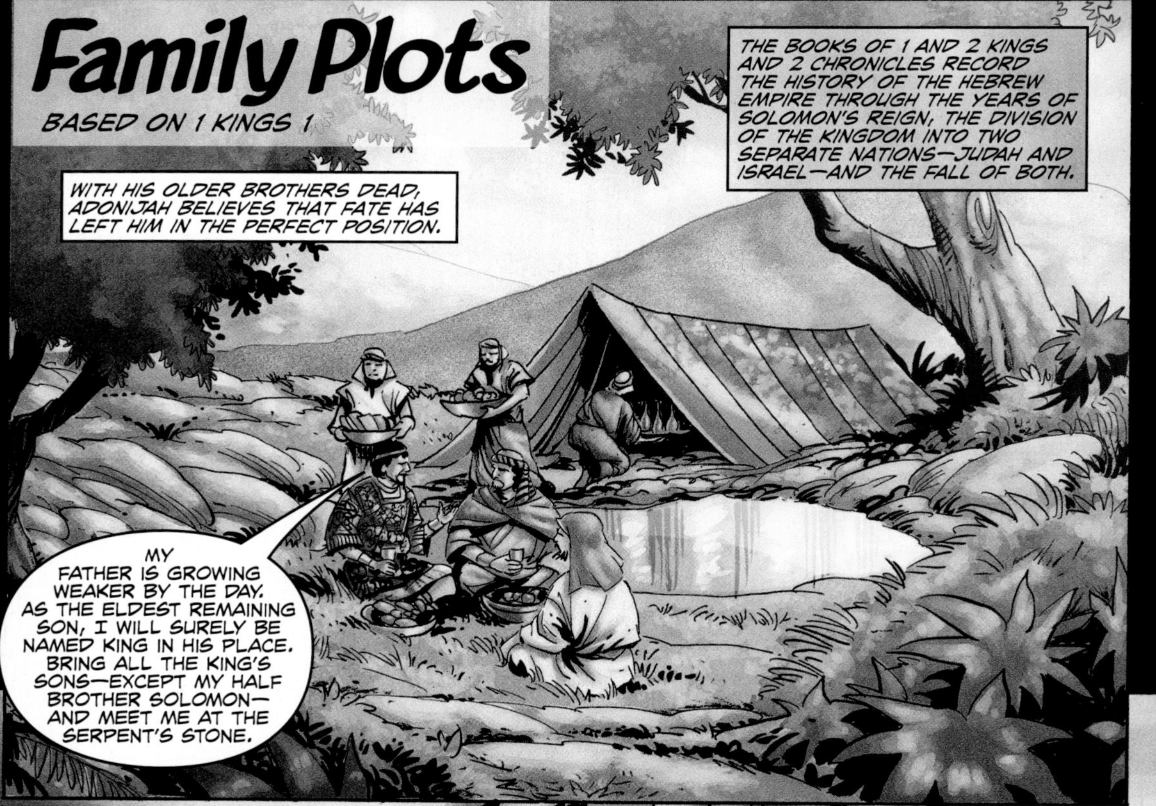
THE BOOKS OF 1 AND 2 KINGS AND 2 CHRONICLES RECORD THE HISTORY OF THE HEBREW EMPIRE THROUGH THE YEARS OF SOLOMON'S REIGN, THE DIVISION OF THE KINGDOM INTO TWO SEPARATE NATIONS—JUDAH AND ISRAEL—AND THE FALL OF BOTH.
WITH HIS OLDER BROTHERS DEAD, ADONIJAH BELIEVES THAT FATE HAS LEFT HIM IN THE PERFECT POSITION.
MY FATHER IS GROWING WEAKER BY THE DAY. AS THE ELDEST REMAINING SON, I WILL SURELY BE NAMED KING IN HIS PLACE. BRING ALL THE KING'S SONS—EXCEPT MY HALF BROTHER SOLOMON—AND MEET ME AT THE SERPENT'S STONE.

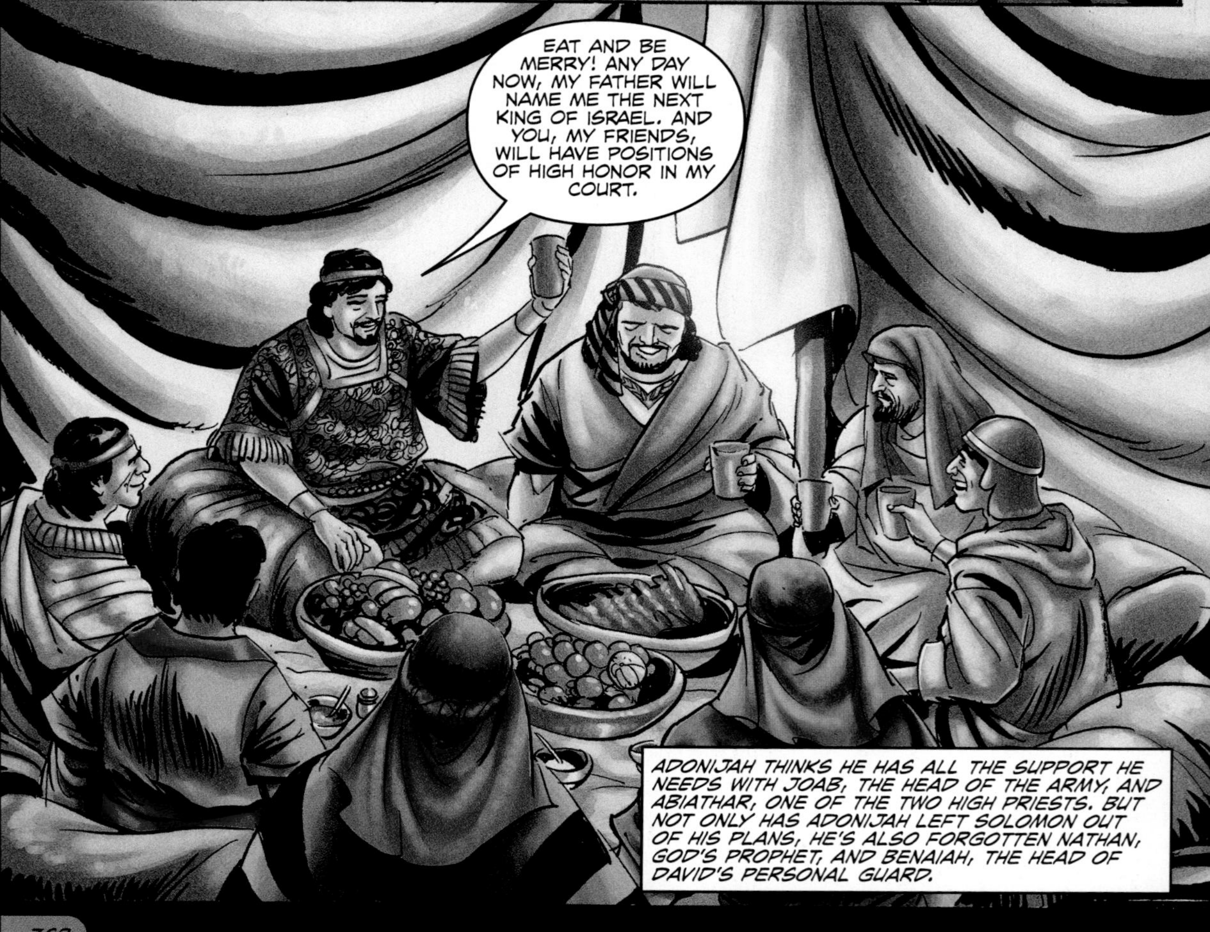
EAT AND BE MERRY! ANY DAY NOW, MY FATHER WILL NAME ME THE NEXT KING OF ISRAEL. AND YOU, MY FRIENDS, WILL HAVE POSITIONS OF HIGH HONOR IN MY COURT.
ADONIJAH THINKS HE HAS ALL THE SUPPORT HE NEEDS WITH JOAB, THE HEAD OF THE ARMY, AND ABIATHAR, ONE OF THE TWO HIGH PRIESTS. BUT NOT ONLY HAS ADONIJAH LEFT SOLOMON OUT OF HIS PLANS, HE'S ALSO FORGOTTEN NATHAN, GOD'S PROPHET, AND BENAIAH, THE HEAD OF DAVID'S PERSONAL GUARD.

AND UNFORTUNATELY FOR ADONIJAH, NATHAN ALREADY KNOWS GOD'S WILL.

THAT PRIDEFUL PEACOCK IS SO CERTAIN HE WILL BE THE NEXT KING. BUT GOD HAS CHOSEN ANOTHER.

WHILE ADONIJAH IS FEASTING, NATHAN IS TALKING WITH QUEEN BATHSHEBA.

IF ADONIJAH BECOMES KING, HE WILL CERTAINLY HAVE YOU AND SOLOMON EXILED, IF NOT EXECUTED. IF YOU WANT TO SAVE YOURSELF AND YOUR SON, DO AS I SAY.

TELL ME WHAT TO DO AND I'LL DO IT.

FOLLOWING NATHAN'S ADVICE, SHE GOES AT ONCE TO DAVID.

MY LORD, YOU PROMISED THAT MY SON, SOLOMON, WOULD RULE AFTER YOU, BUT EVEN NOW HIS HALF BROTHER ADONIJAH HAS DECLARED HIMSELF YOUR SUCCESSOR.

SEND FOR NATHAN AND ZADOK THE PRIEST.

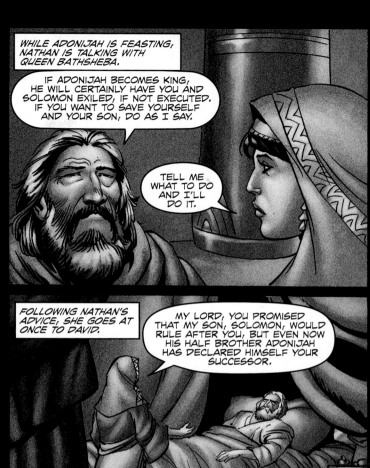

NATHAN CHOOSES THIS MOMENT TO ENTER.

IT IS TRUE WHAT SHE SAYS. ADONIJAH IS TRYING TO TAKE THE CHOICE OF THE NEXT KING AWAY FROM YOU.

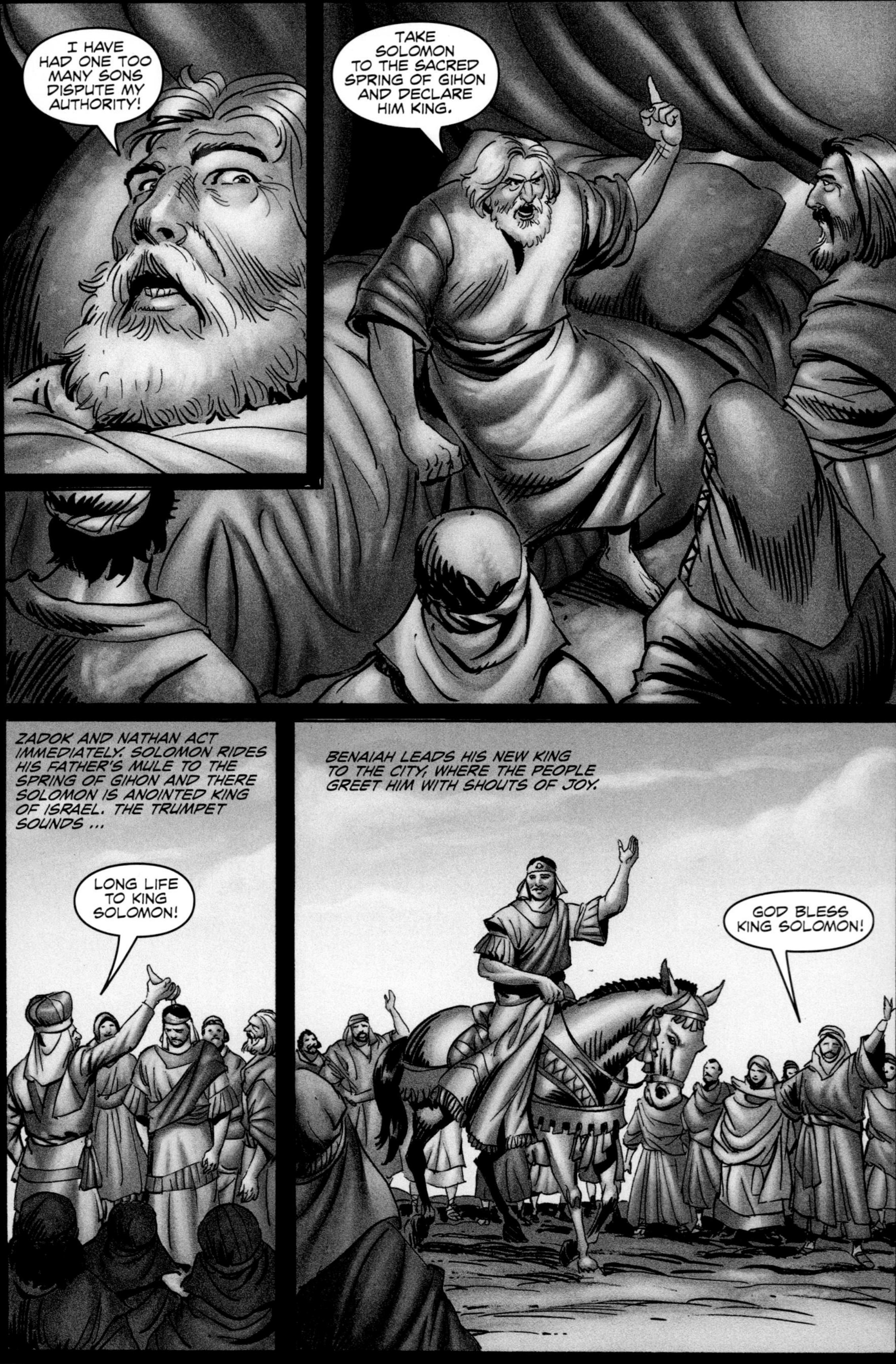
I HAVE HAD ONE TOO MANY SONS DISPUTE MY AUTHORITY!
TAKE SOLOMON TO THE SACRED SPRING OF GIHON AND DECLARE HIM KING.
ZADOK AND NATHAN ACT IMMEDIATELY. SOLOMON RIDES HIS FATHER'S MULE TO THE SPRING OF GIHON AND THERE SOLOMON IS ANOINTED KING OF ISRAEL. THE TRUMPET SOUNDS ...
LONG LIFE TO KING SOLOMON!
BENAIAH LEADS HIS NEW KING TO THE CITY, WHERE THE PEOPLE GREET HIM WITH SHOUTS OF JOY.
GOD BLESS KING SOLOMON!

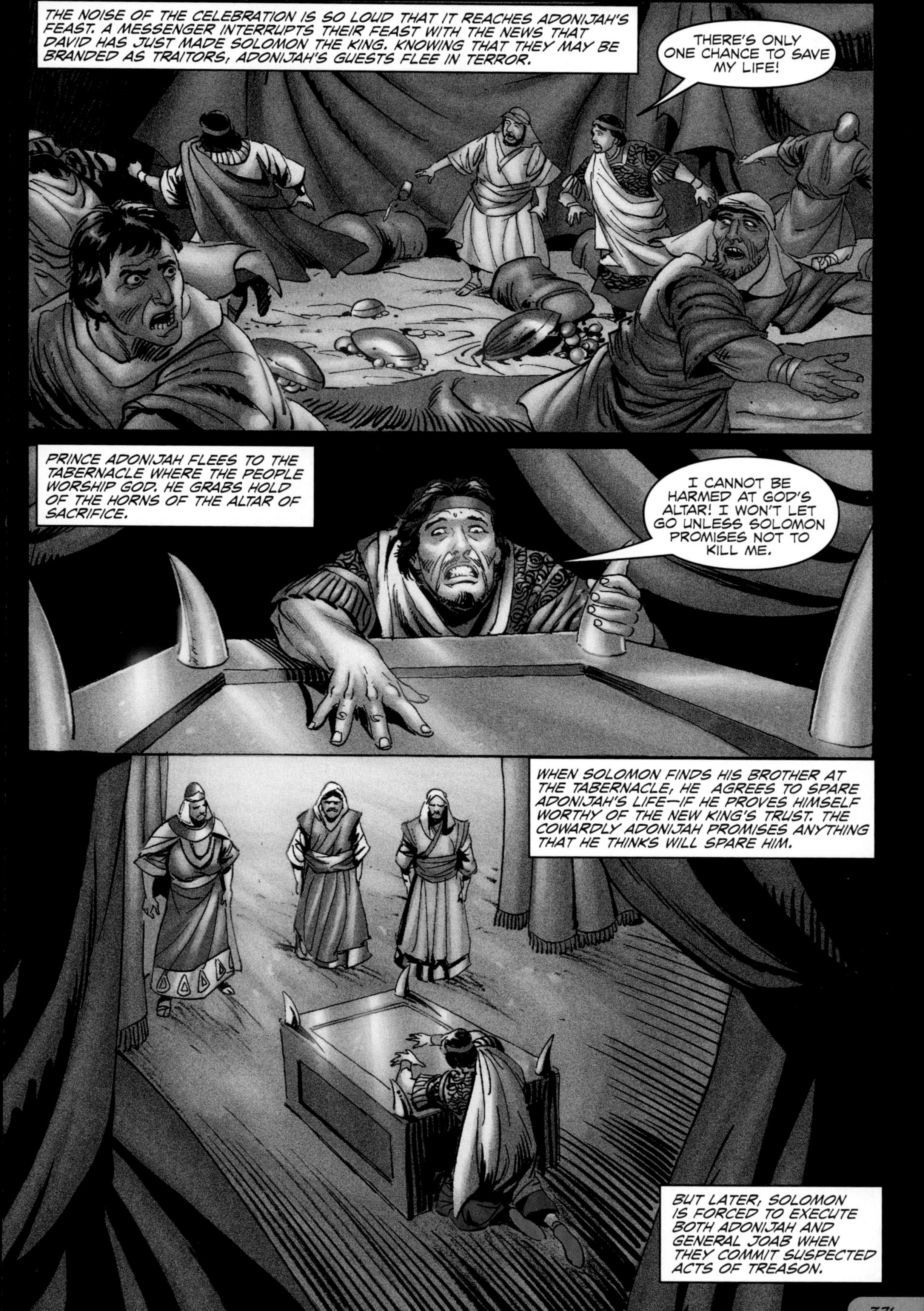
THE NOISE OF THE CELEBRATION IS SO LOUD THAT IT REACHES ADONIJAH'S FEAST. A MESSENGER INTERRUPTS THEIR FEAST WITH THE NEWS THAT DAVID HAS JUST MADE SOLOMON THE KING. KNOWING THAT THEY MAY BE BRANDED AS TRAITORS, ADONIJAH'S GUESTS FLEE IN TERROR.
THERE'S ONLY ONE CHANCE TO SAVE MY LIFE!
PRINCE ADONIJAH FLEES TO THE TABERNACLE WHERE THE PEOPLE WORSHIP GOD. HE GRABS HOLD OF THE HORNS OF THE ALTAR OF SACRIFICE.
I CANNOT BE HARMED AT GOD'S ALTAR! I WON'T LET GO UNLESS SOLOMON PROMISES NOT TO KILL ME.
WHEN SOLOMON FINDS HIS BROTHER AT THE TABERNACLE, HE AGREES TO SPARE ADONIJAH'S LIFE—IF HE PROVES HIMSELF WORTHY OF THE NEW KING'S TRUST. THE COWARDLY ADONIJAH PROMISES ANYTHING THAT HE THINKS WILL SPARE HIM.
BUT LATER, SOLOMON IS FORCED TO EXECUTE BOTH ADONIJAH AND GENERAL JOAB WHEN THEY COMMIT SUSPECTED ACTS OF TREASON.

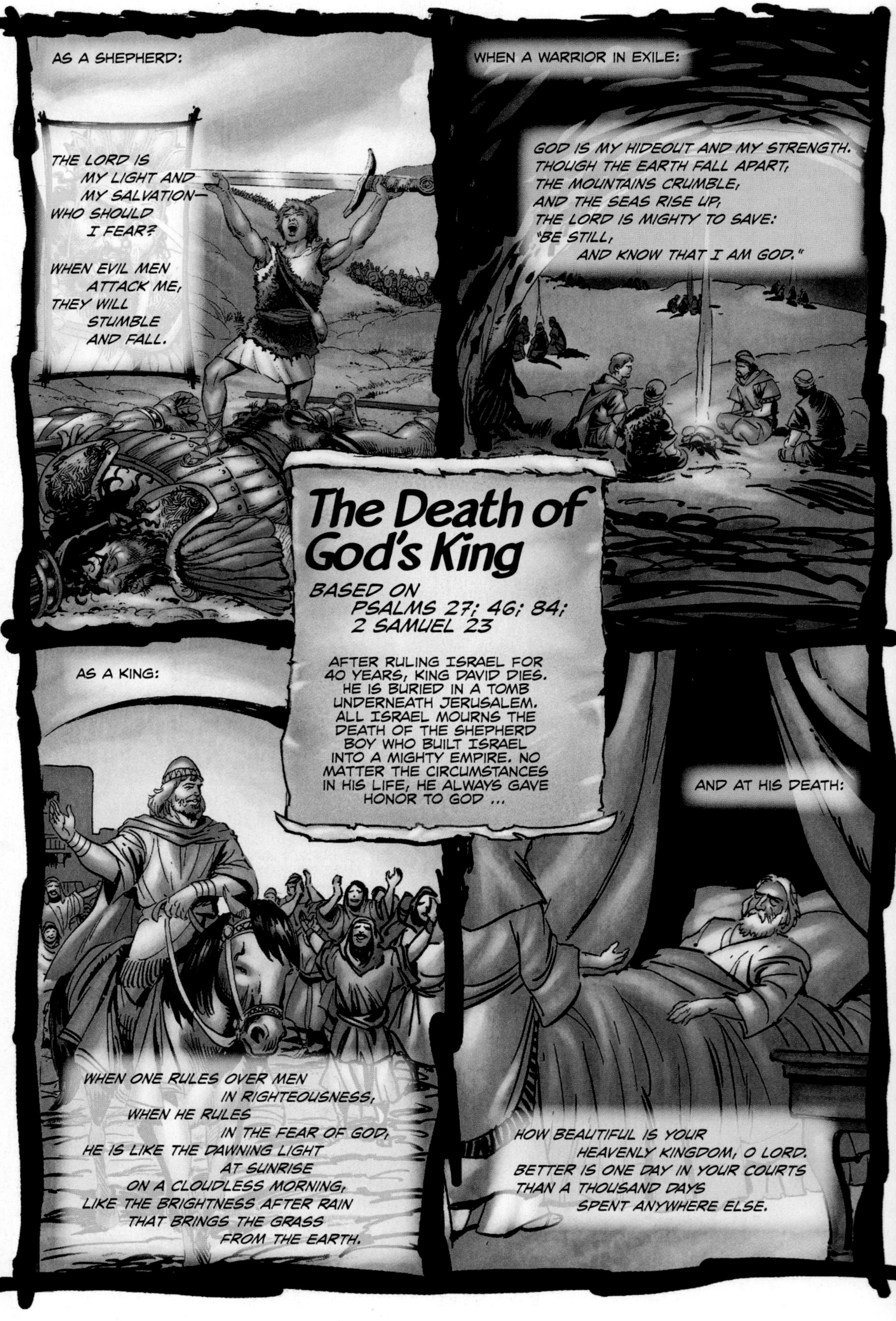
The Death of God's King
BASED ON PSALMS 27; 46; 84; 2 SAMUEL 23
AFTER RULING ISRAEL FOR 40 YEARS, KING DAVID DIES. HE IS BURIED IN A TOMB UNDERNEATH JERUSALEM. ALL ISRAEL MOURNS THE DEATH OF THE SHEPHERD BOY WHO BUILT ISRAEL INTO A MIGHTY EMPIRE. NO MATTER THE CIRCUMSTANCES IN HIS LIFE, HE ALWAYS GAVE HONOR TO GOD ...
AS A SHEPHERD:
THE LORD IS MY LIGHT AND MY SALVATION— WHO SHOULD I FEAR?
WHEN EVIL MEN ATTACK ME, THEY WILL STUMBLE AND FALL.
WHEN A WARRIOR IN EXILE:
GOD IS MY HIDEOUT AND MY STRENGTH. THOUGH THE EARTH FALL APART, THE MOUNTAINS CRUMBLE, AND THE SEAS RISE UP, THE LORD IS MIGHTY TO SAVE: "BE STILL, AND KNOW THAT I AM GOD."
AS A KING:
WHEN ONE RULES OVER MEN IN RIGHTEOUSNESS, WHEN HE RULES IN THE FEAR OF GOD, HE IS LIKE THE DAWNING LIGHT AT SUNRISE ON A CLOUDLESS MORNING, LIKE THE BRIGHTNESS AFTER RAIN THAT BRINGS THE GRASS FROM THE EARTH.
AND AT HIS DEATH:
HOW BEAUTIFUL IS YOUR HEAVENLY KINGDOM, O LORD. BETTER IS ONE DAY IN YOUR COURTS THAN A THOUSAND DAYS SPENT ANYWHERE ELSE.

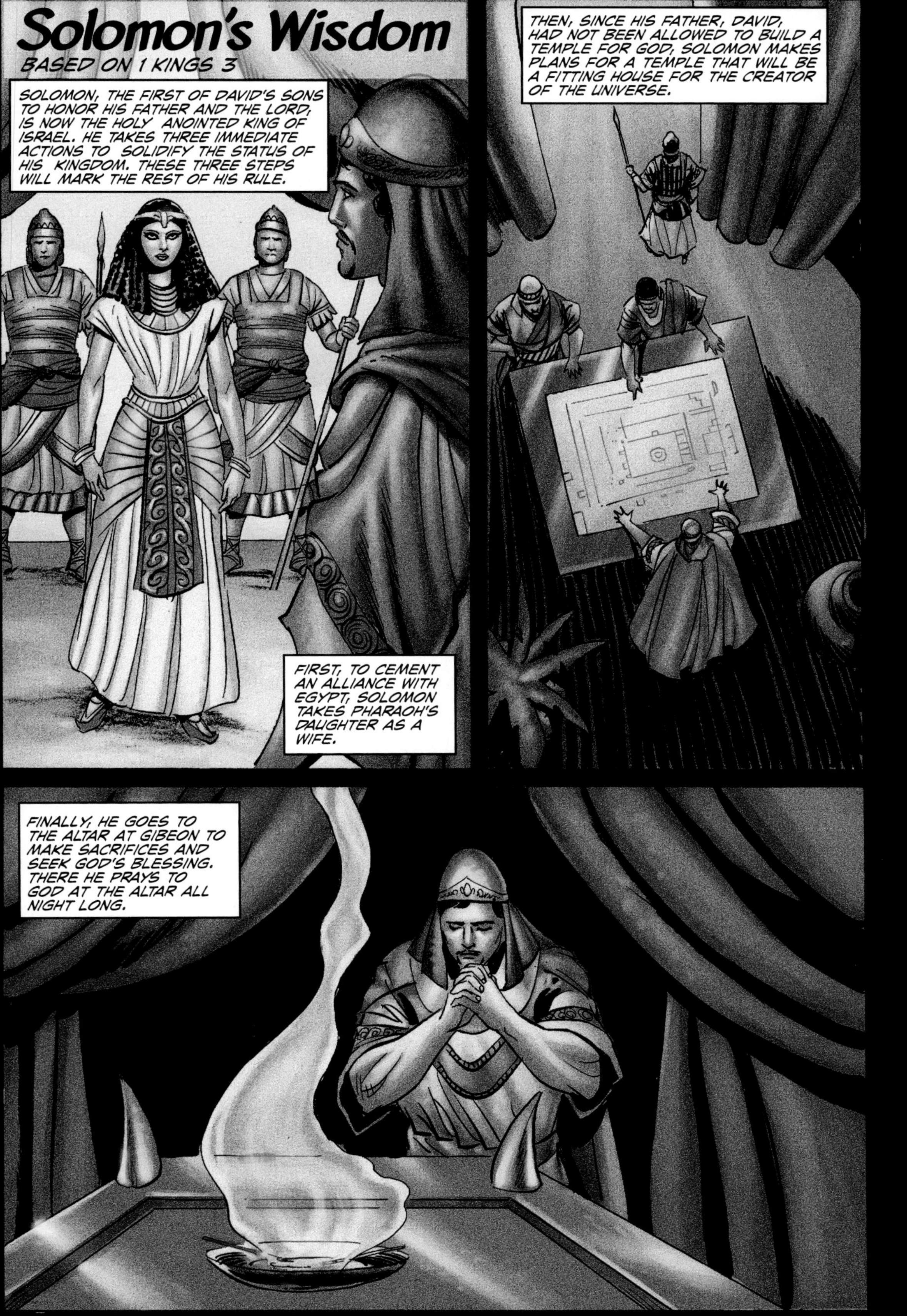
Solomon's Wisdom
BASED ON 1 KINGS 3
SOLOMON, THE FIRST OF DAVID'S SONS TO HONOR HIS FATHER AND THE LORD, IS NOW THE HOLY ANOINTED KING OF ISRAEL. HE TAKES THREE IMMEDIATE ACTIONS TO SOLIDIFY THE STATUS OF HIS KINGDOM. THESE THREE STEPS WILL MARK THE REST OF HIS RULE.
FIRST, TO CEMENT AN ALLIANCE WITH EGYPT, SOLOMON TAKES PHARAOH'S DAUGHTER AS A WIFE.
THEN, SINCE HIS FATHER, DAVID, HAD NOT BEEN ALLOWED TO BUILD A TEMPLE FOR GOD, SOLOMON MAKES PLANS FOR A TEMPLE THAT WILL BE A FITTING HOUSE FOR THE CREATOR OF THE UNIVERSE.
FINALLY, HE GOES TO THE ALTAR AT GIBEON TO MAKE SACRIFICES AND SEEK GOD'S BLESSING. THERE HE PRAYS TO GOD AT THE ALTAR ALL NIGHT LONG.

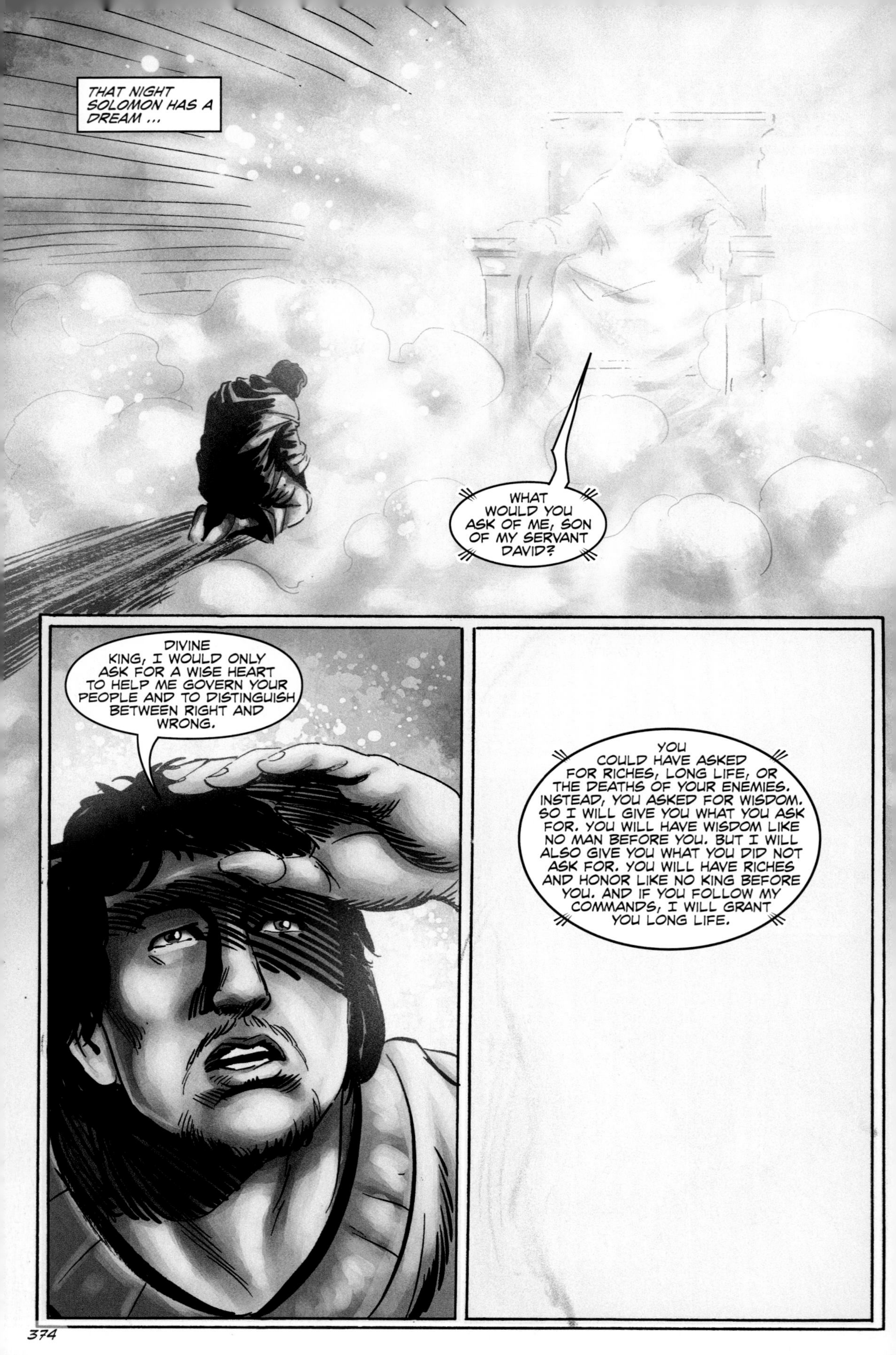

THAT NIGHT SOLOMON HAS A DREAM ...
WHAT WOULD YOU ASK OF ME, SON OF MY SERVANT DAVID?
DIVINE KING, I WOULD ONLY ASK FOR A WISE HEART TO HELP ME GOVERN YOUR PEOPLE AND TO DISTINGUISH BETWEEN RIGHT AND WRONG.
YOU COULD HAVE ASKED FOR RICHES, LONG LIFE, OR THE DEATHS OF YOUR ENEMIES. INSTEAD, YOU ASKED FOR WISDOM. SO I WILL GIVE YOU WHAT YOU ASK FOR. YOU WILL HAVE WISDOM LIKE NO MAN BEFORE YOU. BUT I WILL ALSO GIVE YOU WHAT YOU DID NOT ASK FOR. YOU WILL HAVE RICHES AND HONOR LIKE NO KING BEFORE YOU. AND IF YOU FOLLOW MY COMMANDS, I WILL GRANT YOU LONG LIFE.

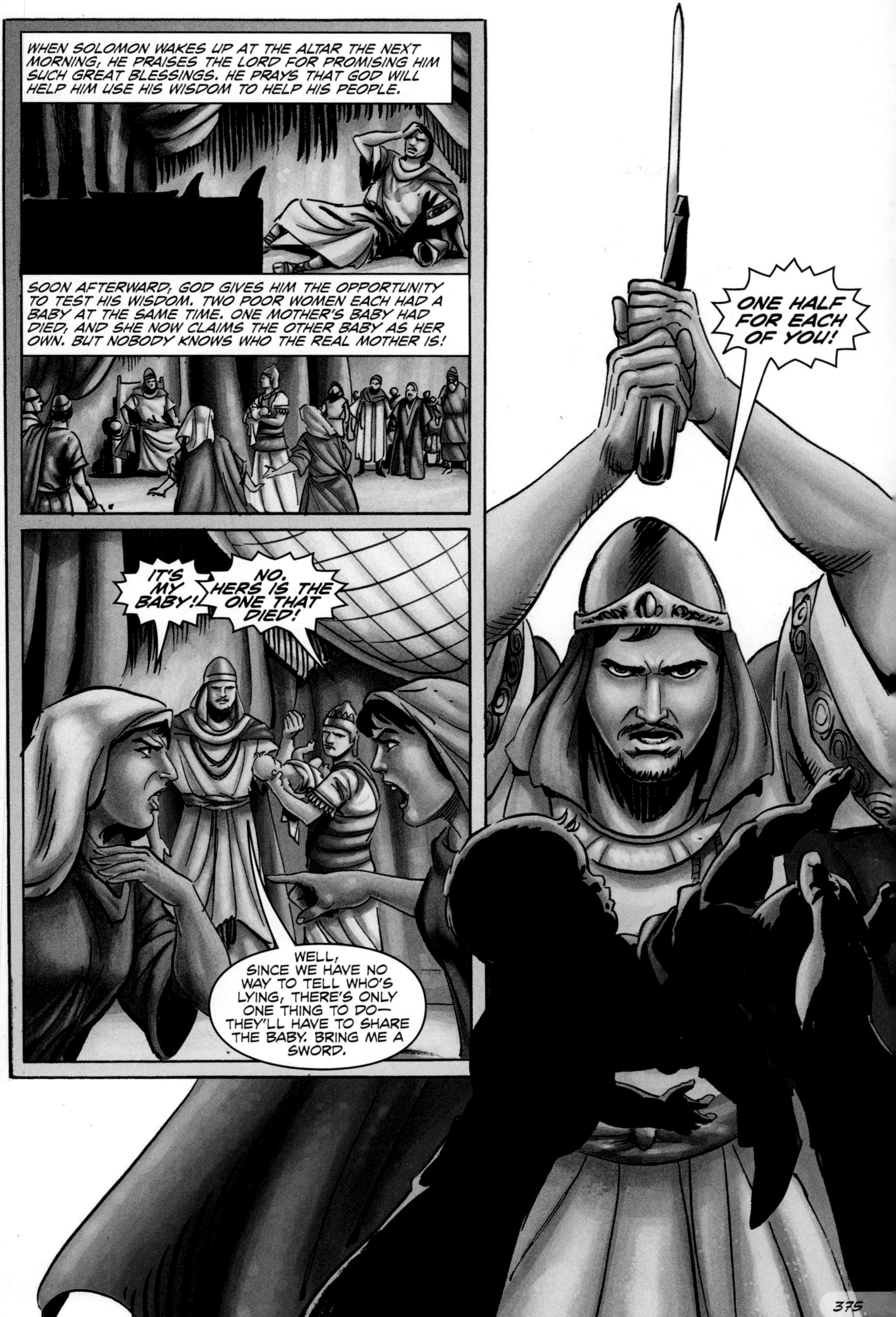
WHEN SOLOMON WAKES UP AT THE ALTAR THE NEXT MORNING, HE PRAISES THE LORD FOR PROMISING HIM SUCH GREAT BLESSINGS. HE PRAYS THAT GOD WILL HELP HIM USE HIS WISDOM TO HELP HIS PEOPLE.
SOON AFTERWARD, GOD GIVES HIM THE OPPORTUNITY TO TEST HIS WISDOM. TWO POOR WOMEN EACH HAD A BABY AT THE SAME TIME. ONE MOTHER'S BABY HAD DIED, AND SHE NOW CLAIMS THE OTHER BABY AS HER OWN. BUT NOBODY KNOWS WHO THE REAL MOTHER IS!
IT'S MY BABY!
NO. HERS IS THE ONE THAT DIED!
WELL, SINCE WE HAVE NO WAY TO TELL WHO'S LYING, THERE'S ONLY ONE THING TO DO—THEY'LL HAVE TO SHARE THE BABY. BRING ME A SWORD.
ONE HALF FOR EACH OF YOU!

NO, DON'T!

JUST GIVE THE BABY TO THE OTHER WOMAN. PLEASE DON'T KILL HIM.

THAT'S WHAT I WANTED TO KNOW. THE TRUE MOTHER WOULD RATHER LOSE HER CHILD TO ANOTHER THAN LET HIM BE KILLED. TAKE YOUR BABY BACK AND BE HAPPY.

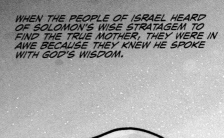

WHEN THE PEOPLE OF ISRAEL HEARD OF SOLOMON'S WISE STRATAGEM TO FIND THE TRUE MOTHER, THEY WERE IN AWE BECAUSE THEY KNEW HE SPOKE WITH GOD'S WISDOM.

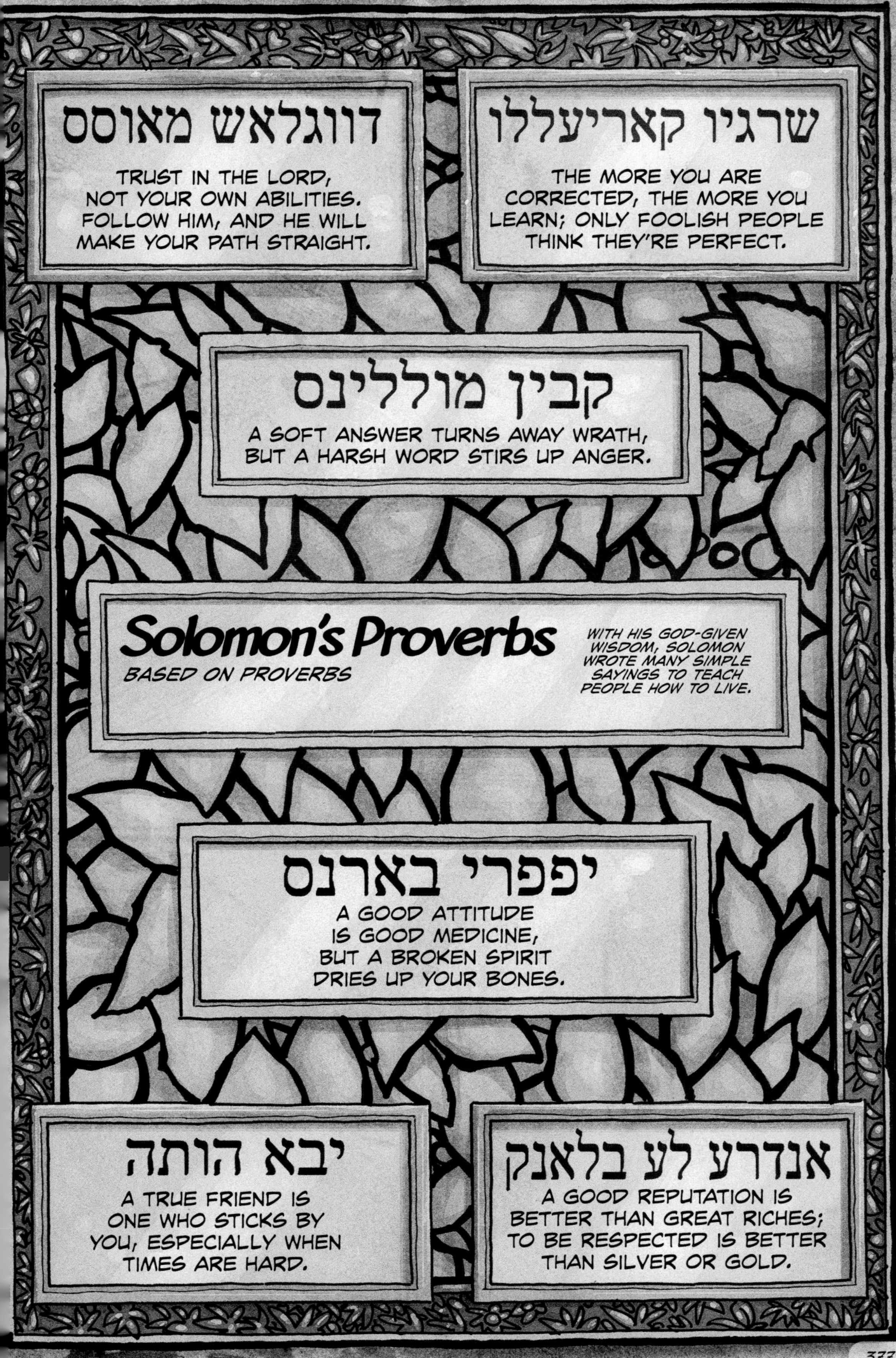
דווגלאש מאוסס
TRUST IN THE LORD, NOT YOUR OWN ABILITIES. FOLLOW HIM, AND HE WILL MAKE YOUR PATH STRAIGHT.
שרגיו קאריעללו
THE MORE YOU ARE CORRECTED, THE MORE YOU LEARN; ONLY FOOLISH PEOPLE THINK THEY'RE PERFECT.
קבין מוללינס
A SOFT ANSWER TURNS AWAY WRATH, BUT A HARSH WORD STIRS UP ANGER.
Solomon's Proverbs
BASED ON PROVERBS
WITH HIS GOD-GIVEN WISDOM, SOLOMON WROTE MANY SIMPLE SAYINGS TO TEACH PEOPLE HOW TO LIVE.
יפפרי בארנס
A GOOD ATTITUDE IS GOOD MEDICINE, BUT A BROKEN SPIRIT DRIES UP YOUR BONES.
יבא הותה
A TRUE FRIEND IS ONE WHO STICKS BY YOU, ESPECIALLY WHEN TIMES ARE HARD.
אנדרע לע בלאנק
A GOOD REPUTATION IS BETTER THAN GREAT RICHES; TO BE RESPECTED IS BETTER THAN SILVER OR GOLD.

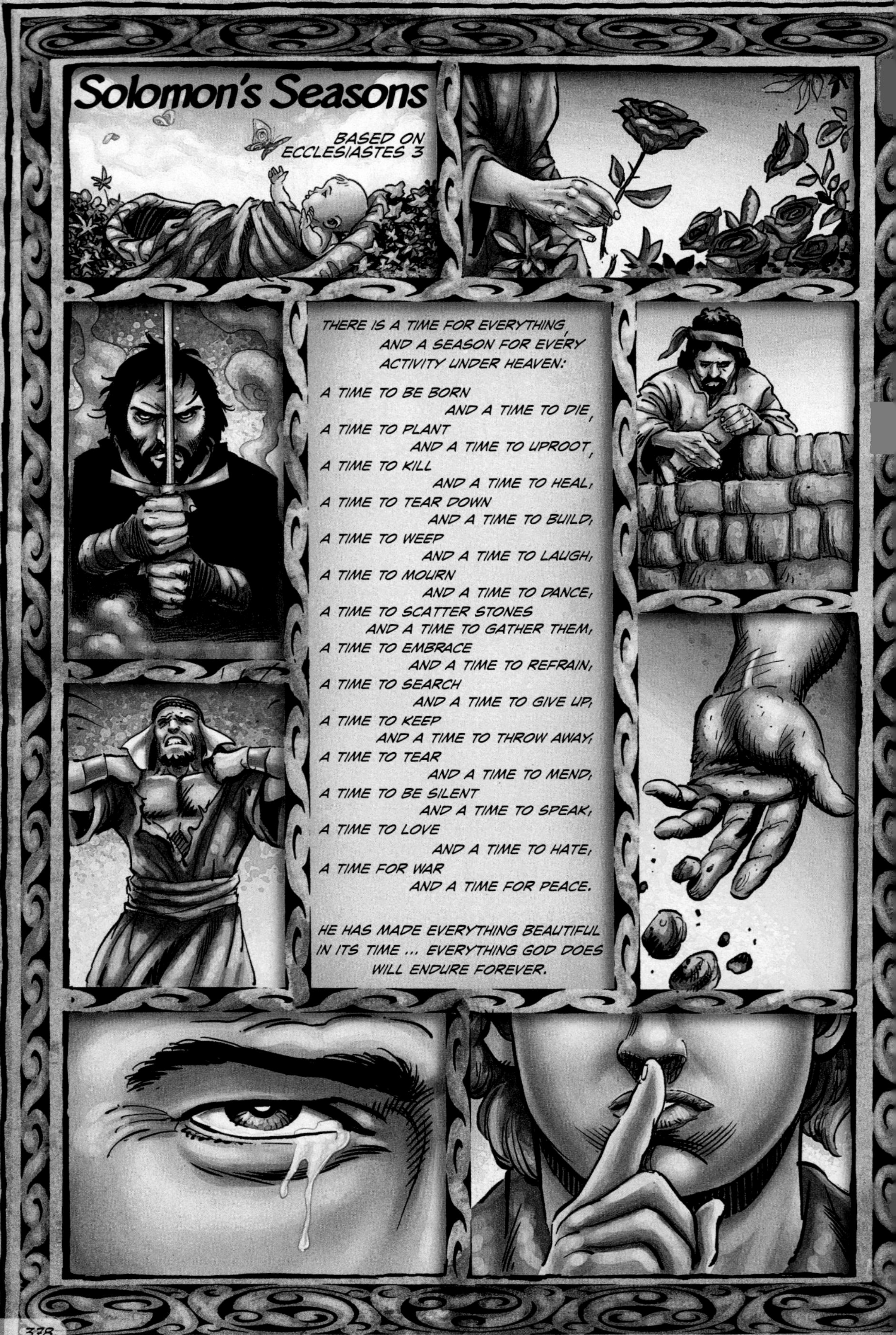
Solomon's Seasons
BASED ON ECCLESIASTES 3
THERE IS A TIME FOR EVERYTHING,
AND A SEASON FOR EVERY
ACTIVITY UNDER HEAVEN:
A TIME TO BE BORN
AND A TIME TO DIE,
A TIME TO PLANT
AND A TIME TO UPROOT,
A TIME TO KILL
AND A TIME TO HEAL,
A TIME TO TEAR DOWN
AND A TIME TO BUILD,
A TIME TO WEEP
AND A TIME TO LAUGH,
A TIME TO MOURN
AND A TIME TO DANCE,
A TIME TO SCATTER STONES
AND A TIME TO GATHER THEM,
A TIME TO EMBRACE
AND A TIME TO REFRAIN,
A TIME TO SEARCH
AND A TIME TO GIVE UP,
A TIME TO KEEP
AND A TIME TO THROW AWAY,
A TIME TO TEAR
AND A TIME TO MEND,
A TIME TO BE SILENT
AND A TIME TO SPEAK,
A TIME TO LOVE
AND A TIME TO HATE,
A TIME FOR WAR
AND A TIME FOR PEACE.
HE HAS MADE EVERYTHING BEAUTIFUL
IN ITS TIME ... EVERYTHING GOD DOES
WILL ENDURE FOREVER.

Solomon's Temple

BASED ON 1 KINGS 5–9; 2 CHRONICLES 2–8

THE PEOPLE ARE HAPPY. ISRAEL IS AT PEACE. SOLOMON HAS ESTABLISHED GOOD RELATIONSHIPS WITH MANY NEIGHBORING COUNTRIES. RULERS OF THE COUNTRIES DAVID HAD CONQUERED PAY TRIBUTE MONEY TO SOLOMON'S TREASURY. SO BEGINS THE GOLDEN AGE OF ISRAEL.

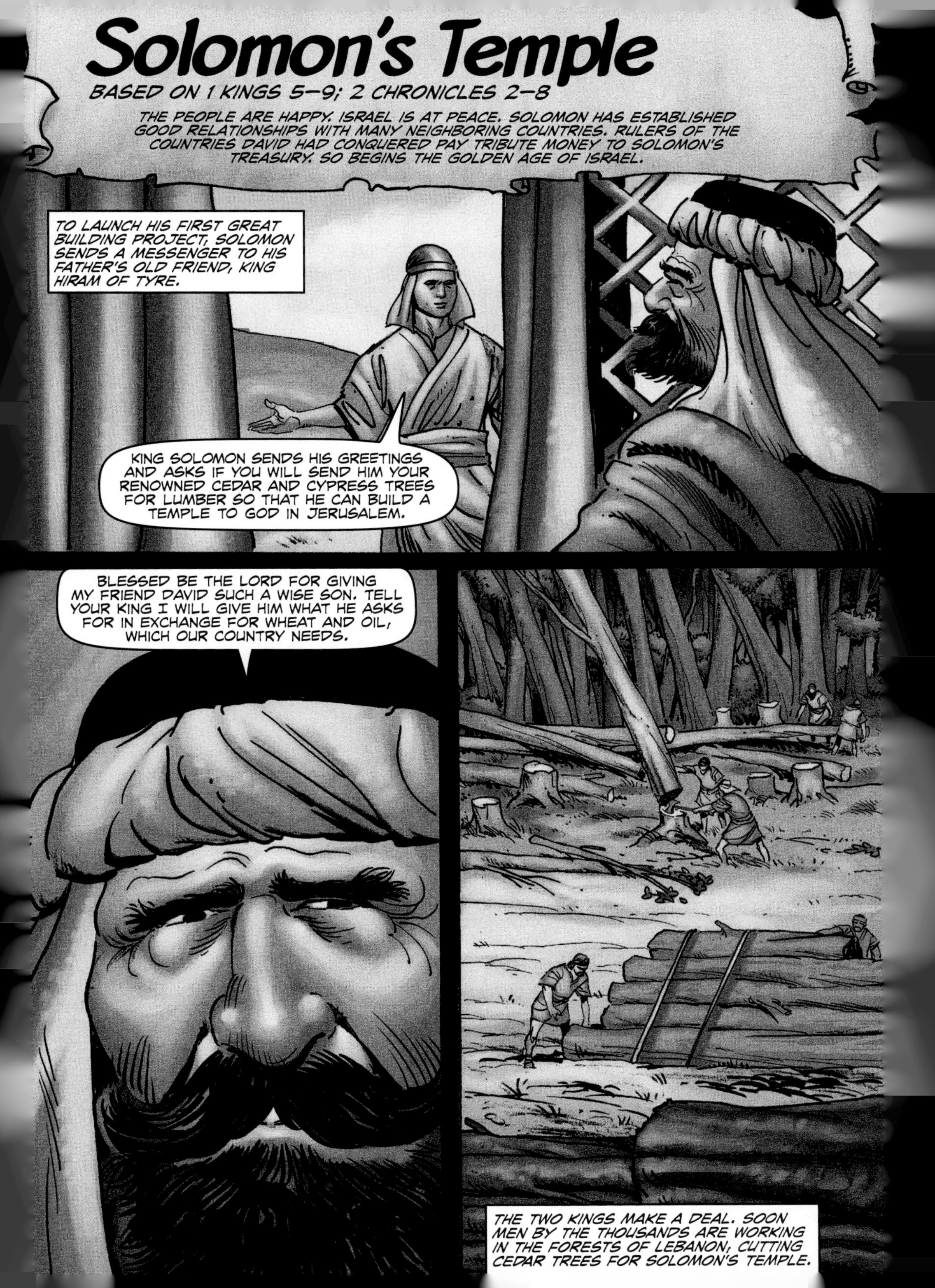
TO LAUNCH HIS FIRST GREAT BUILDING PROJECT, SOLOMON SENDS A MESSENGER TO HIS FATHER'S OLD FRIEND, KING HIRAM OF TYRE.
KING SOLOMON SENDS HIS GREETINGS AND ASKS IF YOU WILL SEND HIM YOUR RENOWNED CEDAR AND CYPRESS TREES FOR LUMBER SO THAT HE CAN BUILD A TEMPLE TO GOD IN JERUSALEM.
BLESSED BE THE LORD FOR GIVING MY FRIEND DAVID SUCH A WISE SON. TELL YOUR KING I WILL GIVE HIM WHAT HE ASKS FOR IN EXCHANGE FOR WHEAT AND OIL, WHICH OUR COUNTRY NEEDS.
THE TWO KINGS MAKE A DEAL. SOON MEN BY THE THOUSANDS ARE WORKING IN THE FORESTS OF LEBANON, CUTTING CEDAR TREES FOR SOLOMON'S TEMPLE.

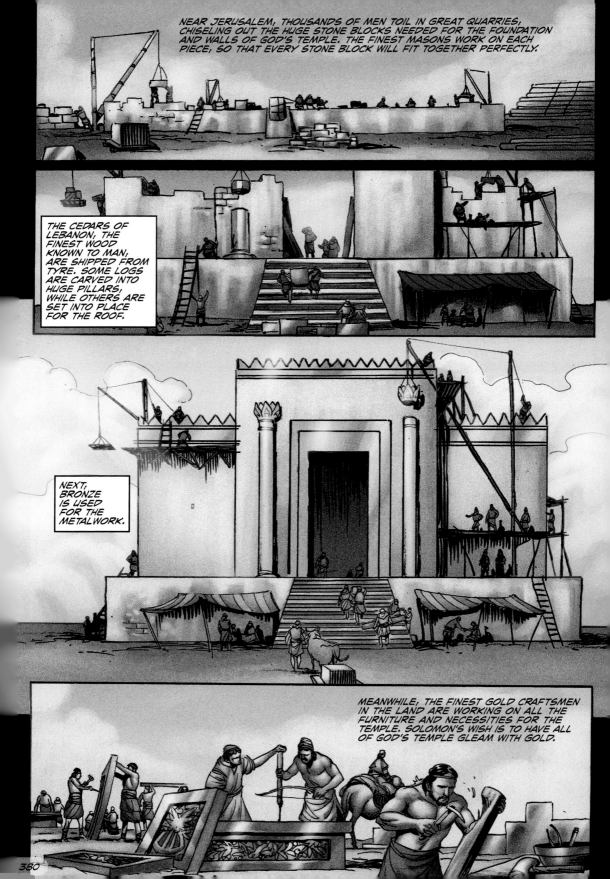

NEAR JERUSALEM, THOUSANDS OF MEN TOIL IN GREAT QUARRIES, CHISELING OUT THE HUGE STONE BLOCKS NEEDED FOR THE FOUNDATION AND WALLS OF GOD'S TEMPLE. THE FINEST MASONS WORK ON EACH PIECE, SO THAT EVERY STONE BLOCK WILL FIT TOGETHER PERFECTLY.

THE CEDARS OF LEBANON, THE FINEST WOOD KNOWN TO MAN, ARE SHIPPED FROM TYRE. SOME LOGS ARE CARVED INTO HUGE PILLARS, WHILE OTHERS ARE SET INTO PLACE FOR THE ROOF.

NEXT, BRONZE IS USED FOR THE METALWORK.

MEANWHILE, THE FINEST GOLD CRAFTSMEN IN THE LAND ARE WORKING ON ALL THE FURNITURE AND NECESSITIES FOR THE TEMPLE. SOLOMON'S WISH IS TO HAVE ALL OF GOD'S TEMPLE GLEAM WITH GOLD.

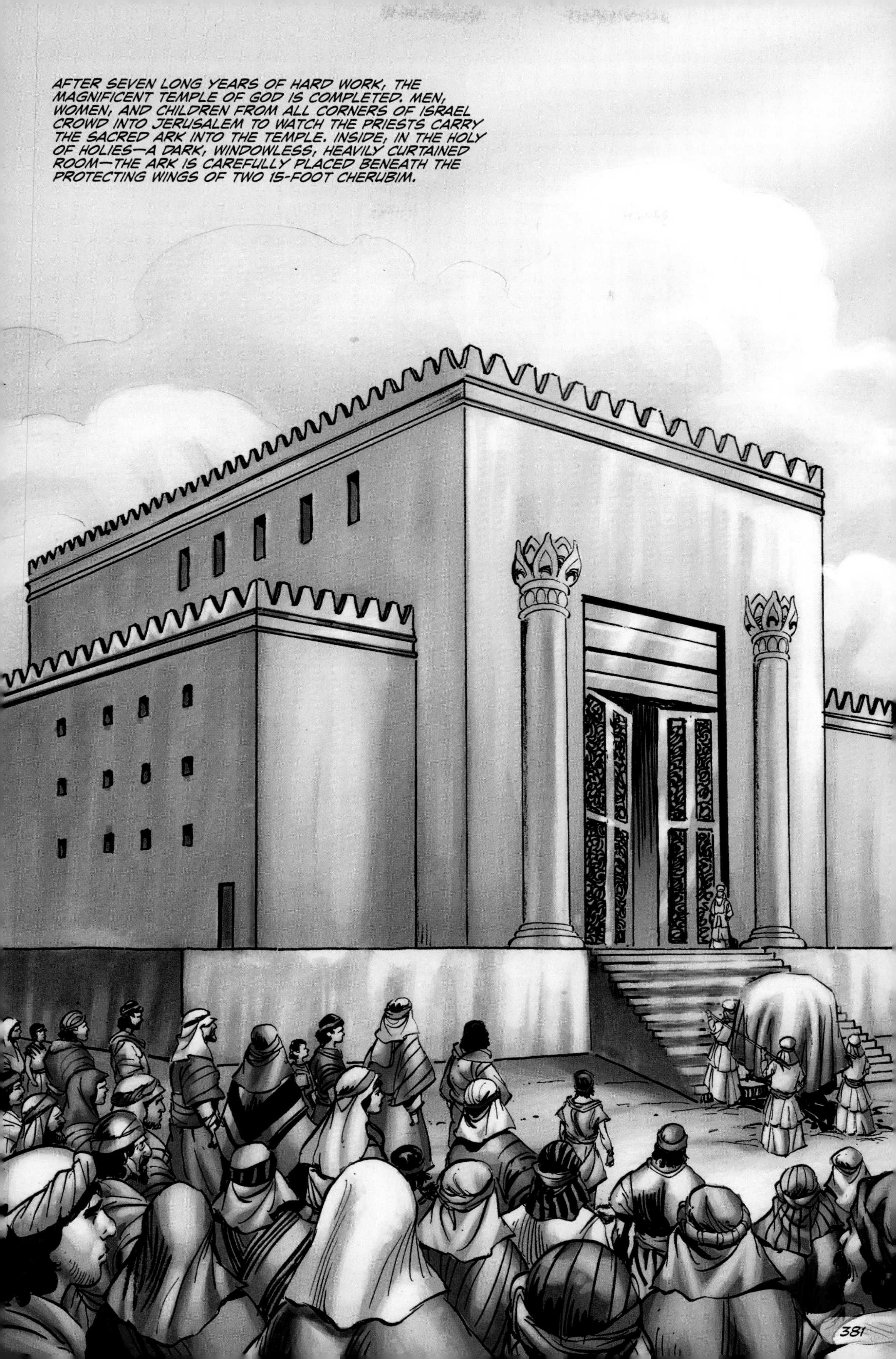
AFTER SEVEN LONG YEARS OF HARD WORK, THE MAGNIFICENT TEMPLE OF GOD IS COMPLETED. MEN, WOMEN, AND CHILDREN FROM ALL CORNERS OF ISRAEL CROWD INTO JERUSALEM TO WATCH THE PRIESTS CARRY THE SACRED ARK INTO THE TEMPLE. INSIDE, IN THE HOLY OF HOLIES—A DARK, WINDOWLESS, HEAVILY CURTAINED ROOM—THE ARK IS CAREFULLY PLACED BENEATH THE PROTECTING WINGS OF TWO 15-FOOT CHERUBIM.

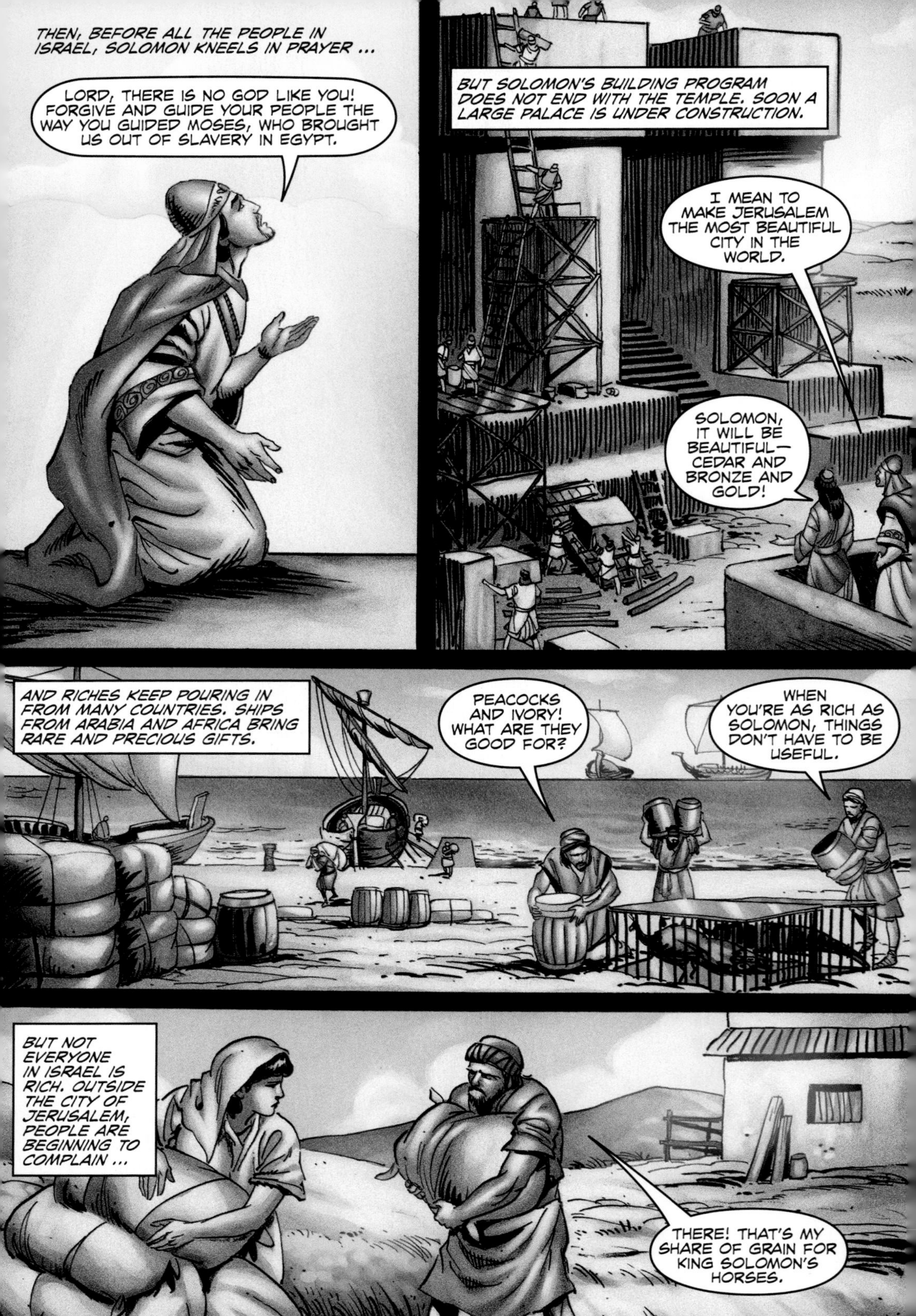
THEN, BEFORE ALL THE PEOPLE IN ISRAEL, SOLOMON KNEELS IN PRAYER ...
LORD, THERE IS NO GOD LIKE YOU! FORGIVE AND GUIDE YOUR PEOPLE THE WAY YOU GUIDED MOSES, WHO BROUGHT US OUT OF SLAVERY IN EGYPT.
BUT SOLOMON'S BUILDING PROGRAM DOES NOT END WITH THE TEMPLE. SOON A LARGE PALACE IS UNDER CONSTRUCTION.
I MEAN TO MAKE JERUSALEM THE MOST BEAUTIFUL CITY IN THE WORLD.
SOLOMON, IT WILL BE BEAUTIFUL—CEDAR AND BRONZE AND GOLD!
AND RICHES KEEP POURING IN FROM MANY COUNTRIES. SHIPS FROM ARABIA AND AFRICA BRING RARE AND PRECIOUS GIFTS.
PEACOCKS AND IVORY! WHAT ARE THEY GOOD FOR?
WHEN YOU'RE AS RICH AS SOLOMON, THINGS DON'T HAVE TO BE USEFUL.
BUT NOT EVERYONE IN ISRAEL IS RICH. OUTSIDE THE CITY OF JERUSALEM, PEOPLE ARE BEGINNING TO COMPLAIN ...
THERE! THAT'S MY SHARE OF GRAIN FOR KING SOLOMON'S HORSES.

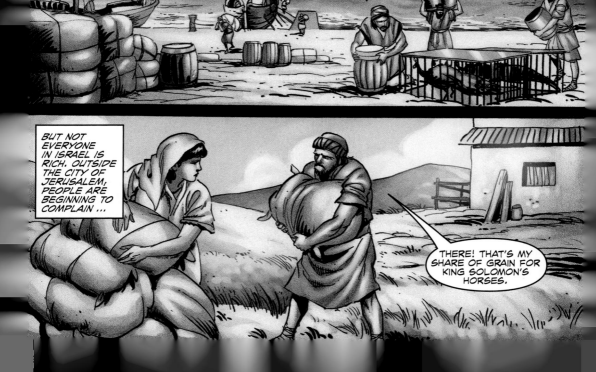

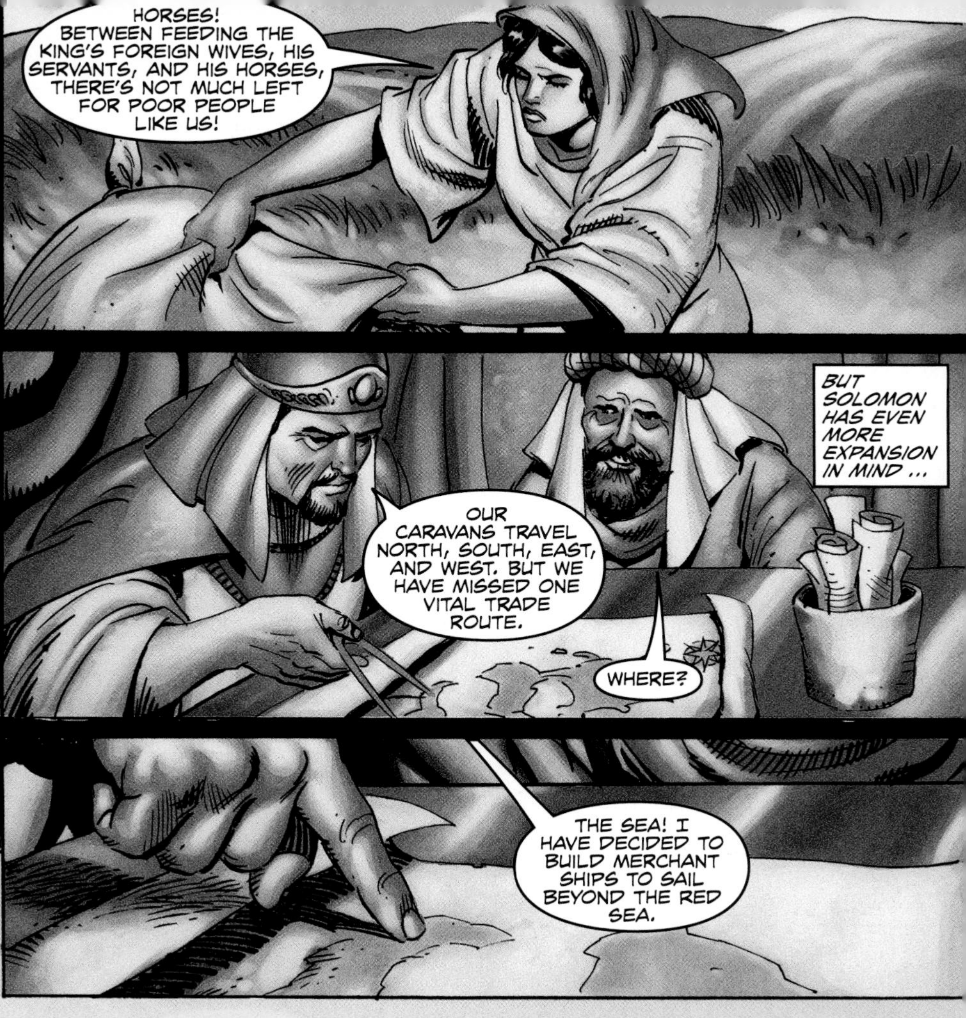
HORSES! BETWEEN FEEDING THE KING'S FOREIGN WIVES, HIS SERVANTS, AND HIS HORSES, THERE'S NOT MUCH LEFT FOR POOR PEOPLE LIKE US!
BUT SOLOMON HAS EVEN MORE EXPANSION IN MIND ...
OUR CARAVANS TRAVEL NORTH, SOUTH, EAST, AND WEST. BUT WE HAVE MISSED ONE VITAL TRADE ROUTE.
WHERE?
THE SEA! I HAVE DECIDED TO BUILD MERCHANT SHIPS TO SAIL BEYOND THE RED SEA.

THE FLEET IS BUILT. ITS SHIPS BRING TREASURES INTO JERUSALEM AND CARRY AWAY WITH THEM STORIES OF THE CITY'S BEAUTY AND THE RULER'S WISDOM. THE STORIES REACH FAR AND WIDE—EVEN TO DISTANT LANDS IN THE ARABIAN PENINSULA.

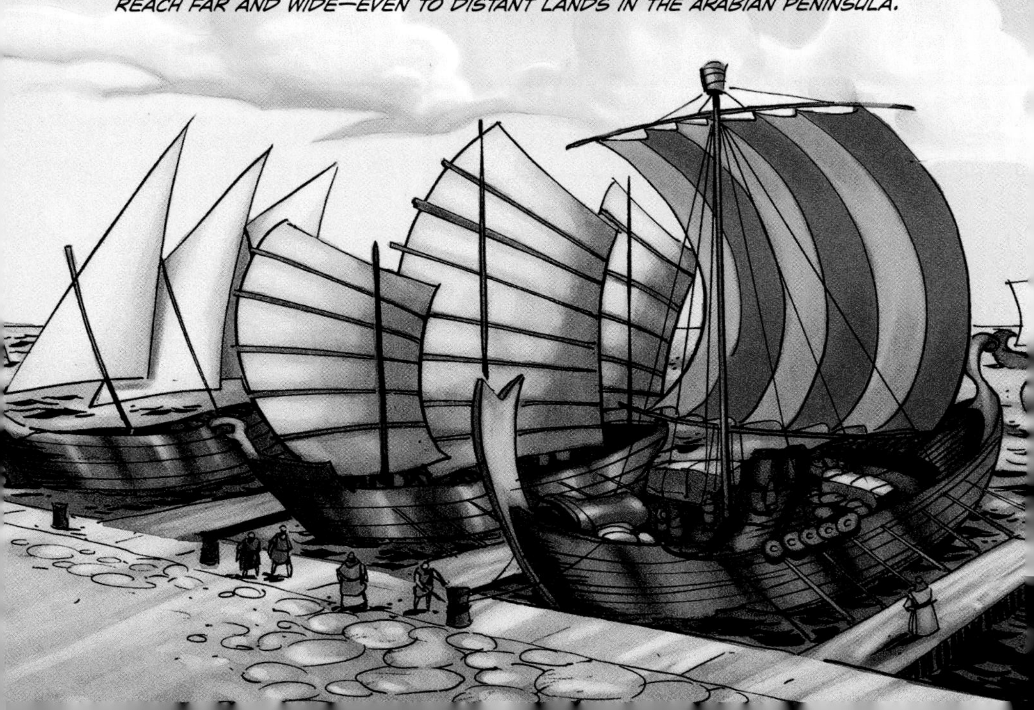

Foreign Fame

BASED ON 1 KINGS 10:1—11:8

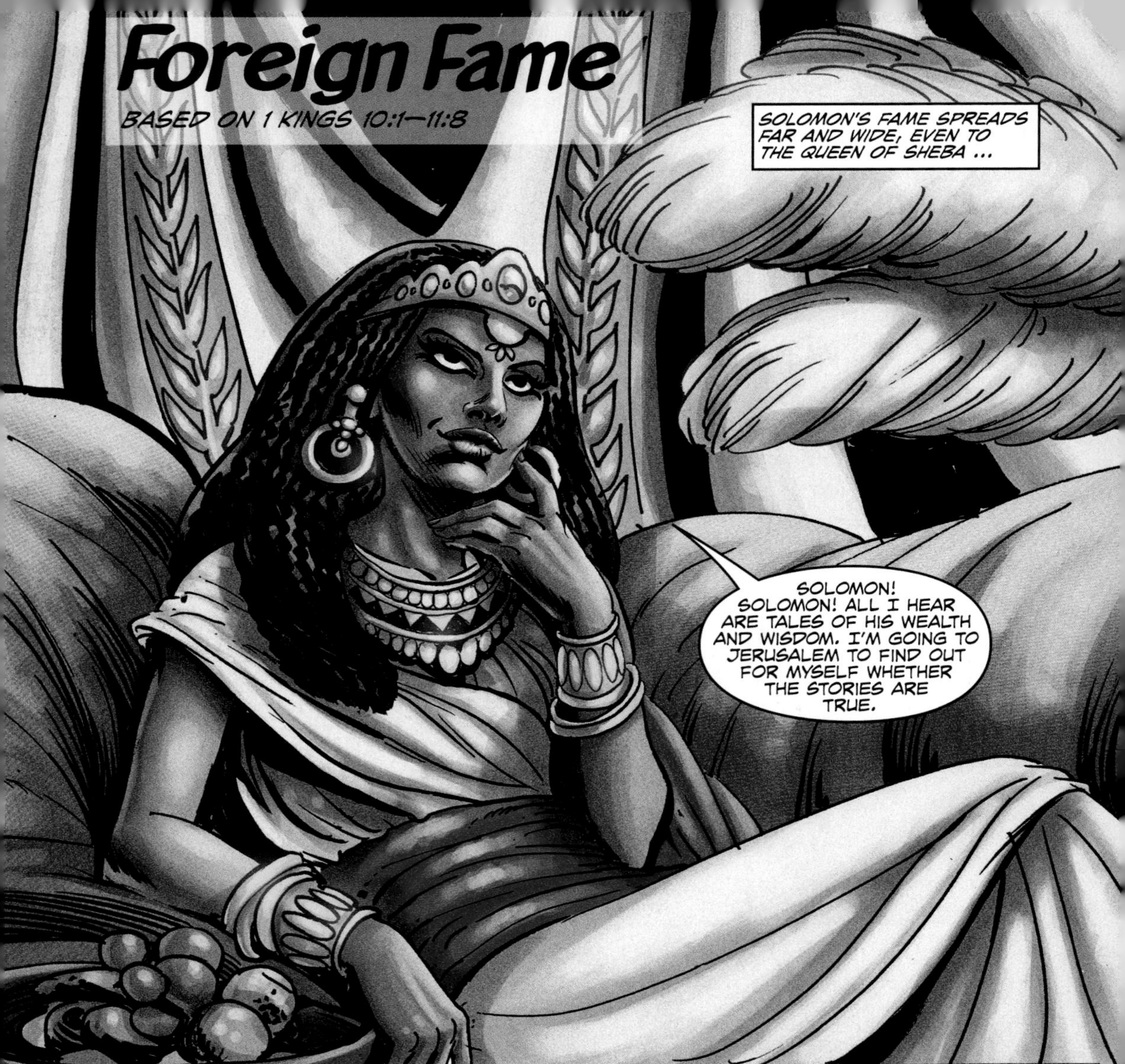
SOLOMON'S FAME SPREADS FAR AND WIDE, EVEN TO THE QUEEN OF SHEBA ...
SOLOMON! SOLOMON! ALL I HEAR ARE TALES OF HIS WEALTH AND WISDOM. I'M GOING TO JERUSALEM TO FIND OUT FOR MYSELF WHETHER THE STORIES ARE TRUE.

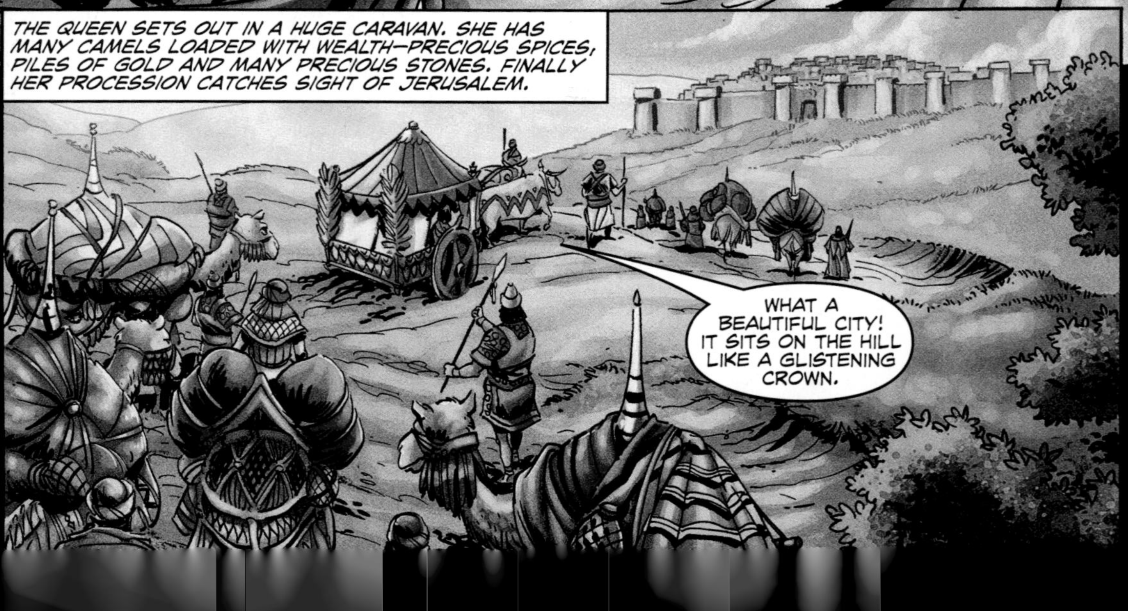
THE QUEEN SETS OUT IN A HUGE CARAVAN. SHE HAS MANY CAMELS LOADED WITH WEALTH—PRECIOUS SPICES, PILES OF GOLD AND MANY PRECIOUS STONES. FINALLY HER PROCESSION CATCHES SIGHT OF JERUSALEM.
WHAT A BEAUTIFUL CITY! IT SITS ON THE HILL LIKE A GLISTENING CROWN.

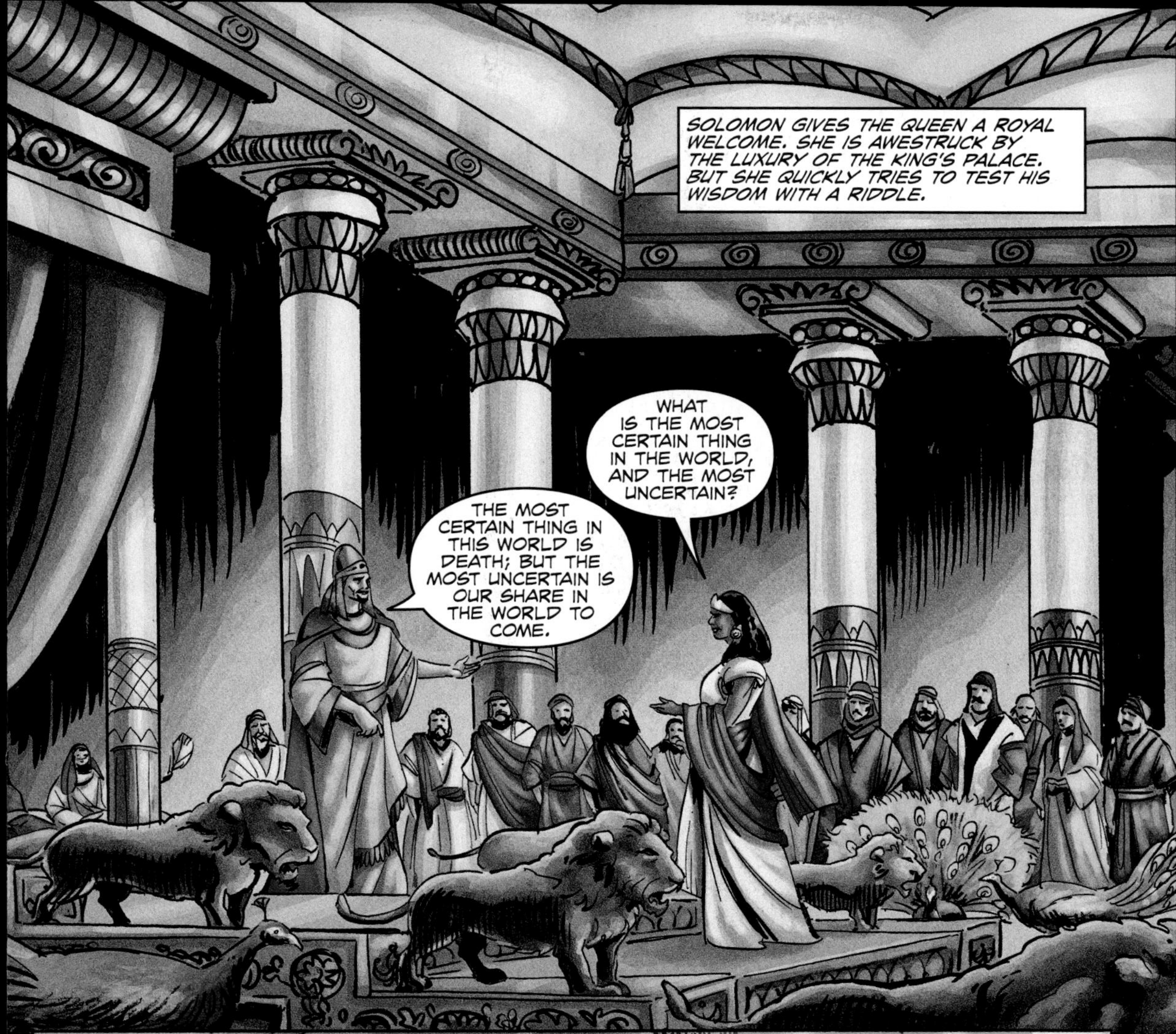
SOLOMON GIVES THE QUEEN A ROYAL WELCOME. SHE IS AWESTRUCK BY THE LUXURY OF THE KING'S PALACE. BUT SHE QUICKLY TRIES TO TEST HIS WISDOM WITH A RIDDLE.
WHAT IS THE MOST CERTAIN THING IN THE WORLD, AND THE MOST UNCERTAIN?
THE MOST CERTAIN THING IN THIS WORLD IS DEATH; BUT THE MOST UNCERTAIN IS OUR SHARE IN THE WORLD TO COME.

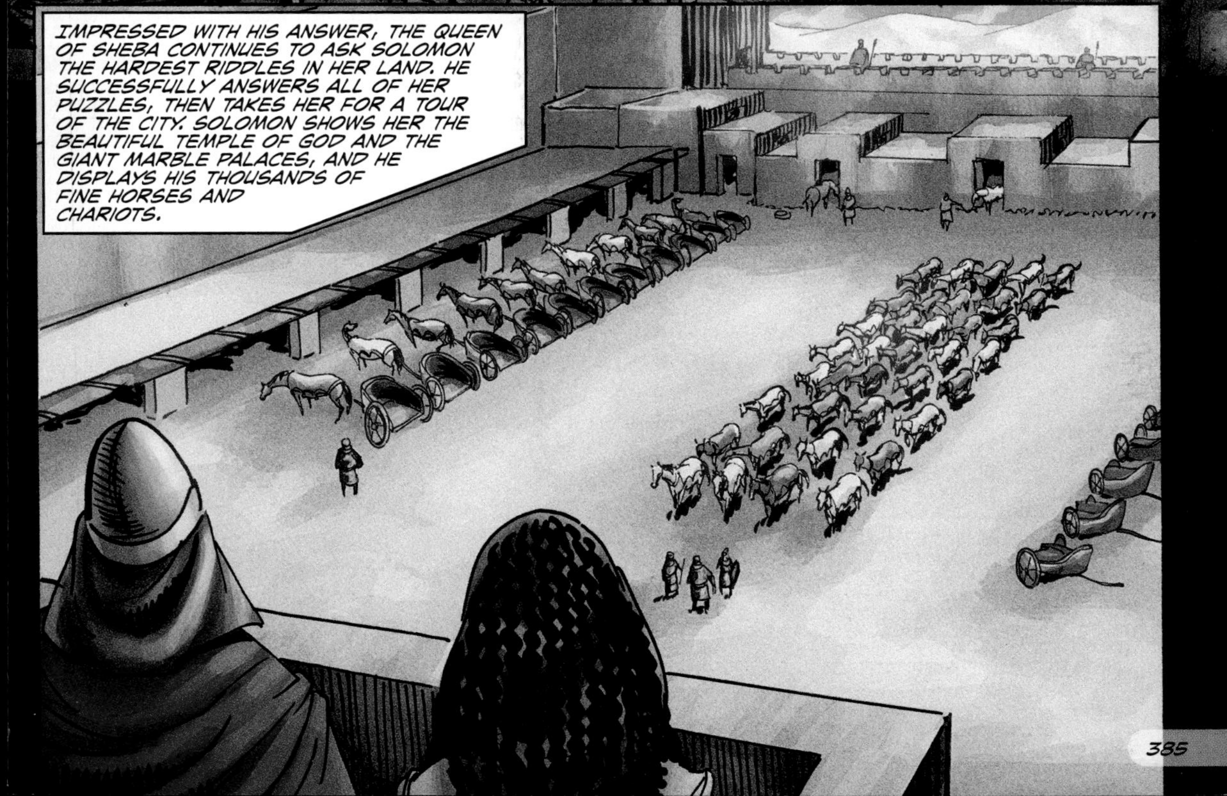
IMPRESSED WITH HIS ANSWER, THE QUEEN OF SHEBA CONTINUES TO ASK SOLOMON THE HARDEST RIDDLES IN HER LAND. HE SUCCESSFULLY ANSWERS ALL OF HER PUZZLES, THEN TAKES HER FOR A TOUR OF THE CITY. SOLOMON SHOWS HER THE BEAUTIFUL TEMPLE OF GOD AND THE GIANT MARBLE PALACES, AND HE DISPLAYS HIS THOUSANDS OF FINE HORSES AND CHARIOTS.

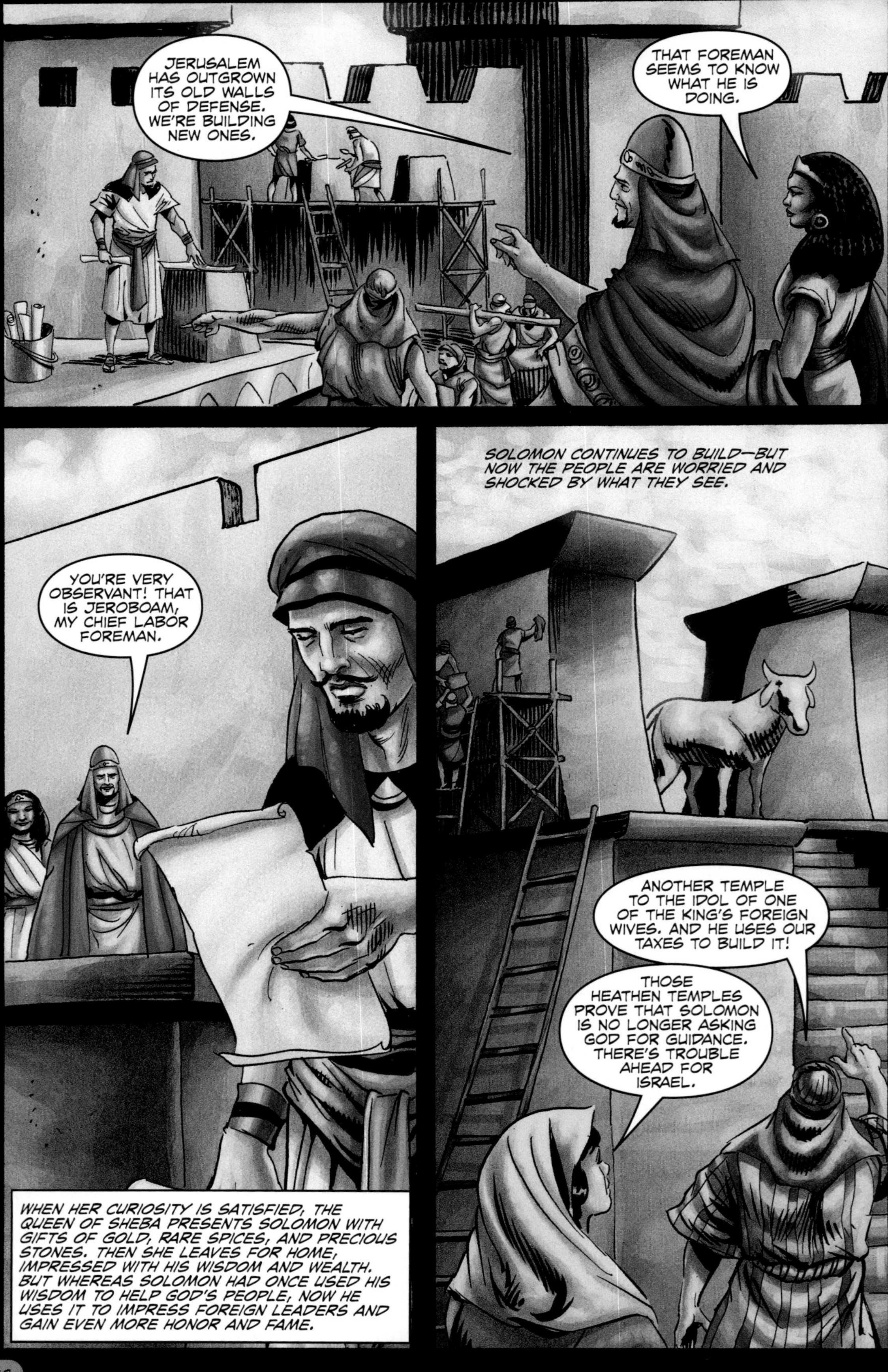
JERUSALEM HAS OUTGROWN ITS OLD WALLS OF DEFENSE. WE'RE BUILDING NEW ONES.
THAT FOREMAN SEEMS TO KNOW WHAT HE IS DOING.
YOU'RE VERY OBSERVANT! THAT IS JEROBOAM, MY CHIEF LABOR FOREMAN.
WHEN HER CURIOSITY IS SATISFIED, THE QUEEN OF SHEBA PRESENTS SOLOMON WITH GIFTS OF GOLD, RARE SPICES, AND PRECIOUS STONES. THEN SHE LEAVES FOR HOME, IMPRESSED WITH HIS WISDOM AND WEALTH. BUT WHEREAS SOLOMON HAD ONCE USED HIS WISDOM TO HELP GOD'S PEOPLE, NOW HE USES IT TO IMPRESS FOREIGN LEADERS AND GAIN EVEN MORE HONOR AND FAME.
SOLOMON CONTINUES TO BUILD—BUT NOW THE PEOPLE ARE WORRIED AND SHOCKED BY WHAT THEY SEE.
ANOTHER TEMPLE TO THE IDOL OF ONE OF THE KING'S FOREIGN WIVES. AND HE USES OUR TAXES TO BUILD IT!
THOSE HEATHEN TEMPLES PROVE THAT SOLOMON IS NO LONGER ASKING GOD FOR GUIDANCE. THERE'S TROUBLE AHEAD FOR ISRAEL.

From Wisdom to Folly

BASED ON 1 KINGS 11:29-43

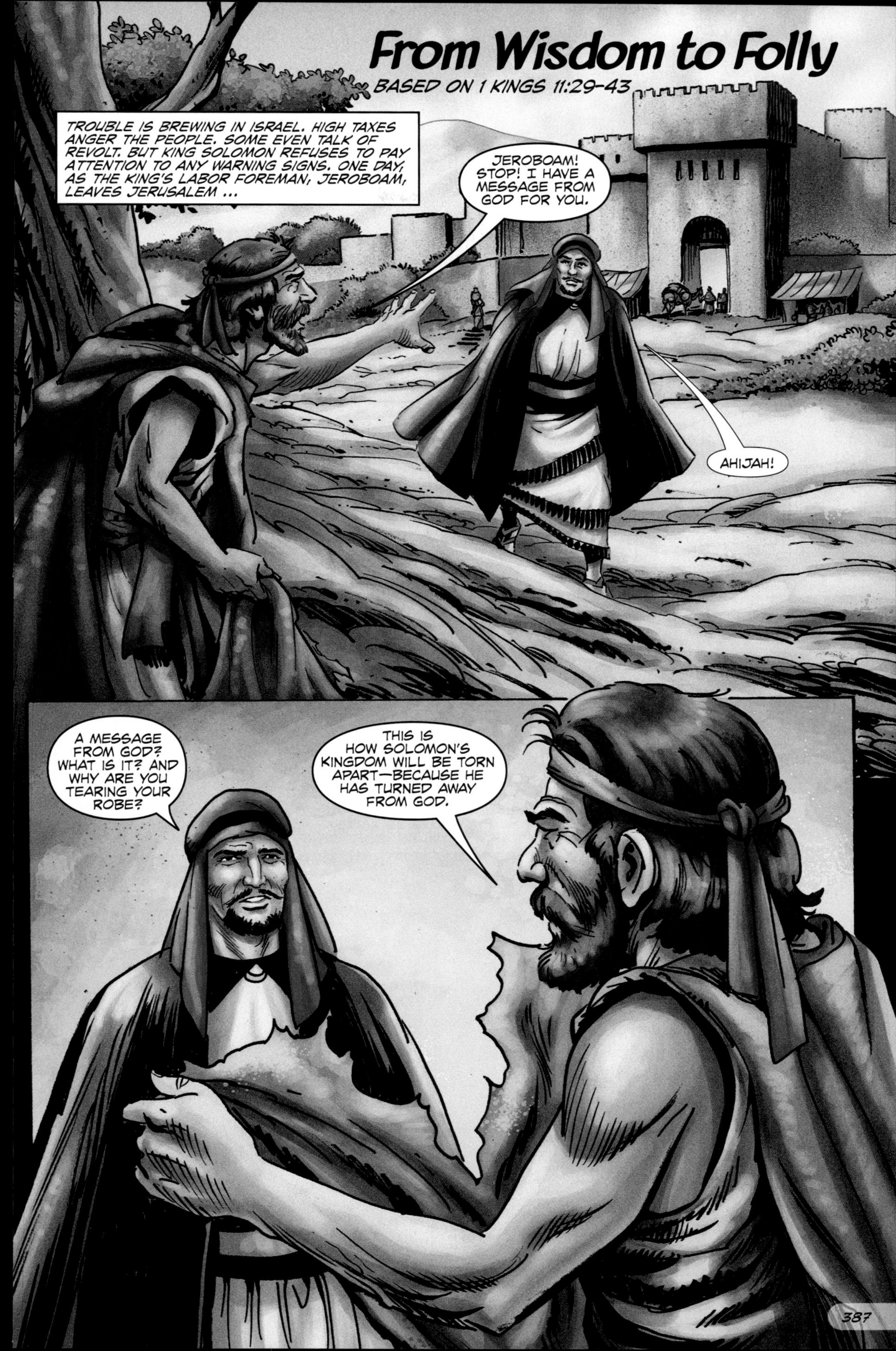
TROUBLE IS BREWING IN ISRAEL. HIGH TAXES ANGER THE PEOPLE. SOME EVEN TALK OF REVOLT. BUT KING SOLOMON REFUSES TO PAY ATTENTION TO ANY WARNING SIGNS. ONE DAY, AS THE KING'S LABOR FOREMAN, JEROBOAM, LEAVES JERUSALEM ...
JEROBOAM! STOP! I HAVE A MESSAGE FROM GOD FOR YOU.
AHIJAH!
A MESSAGE FROM GOD? WHAT IS IT? AND WHY ARE YOU TEARING YOUR ROBE?
THIS IS HOW SOLOMON'S KINGDOM WILL BE TORN APART—BECAUSE HE HAS TURNED AWAY FROM GOD.

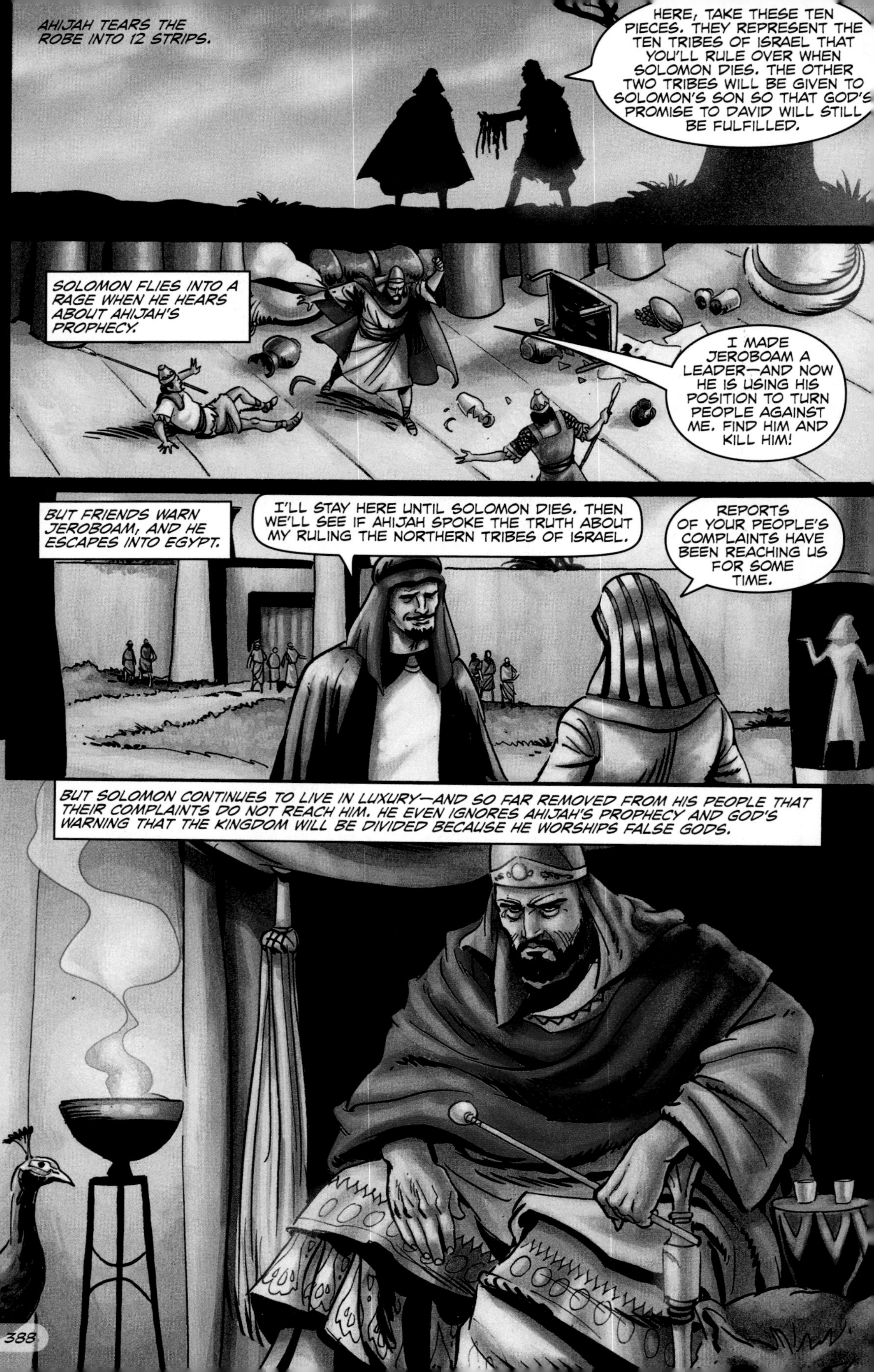
AHIJAH TEARS THE ROBE INTO 12 STRIPS.
HERE, TAKE THESE TEN PIECES. THEY REPRESENT THE TEN TRIBES OF ISRAEL THAT YOU'LL RULE OVER WHEN SOLOMON DIES. THE OTHER TWO TRIBES WILL BE GIVEN TO SOLOMON'S SON SO THAT GOD'S PROMISE TO DAVID WILL STILL BE FULFILLED.
SOLOMON FLIES INTO A RAGE WHEN HE HEARS ABOUT AHIJAH'S PROPHECY.
I MADE JEROBOAM A LEADER—AND NOW HE IS USING HIS POSITION TO TURN PEOPLE AGAINST ME. FIND HIM AND KILL HIM!
BUT FRIENDS WARN JEROBOAM, AND HE ESCAPES INTO EGYPT.
I'LL STAY HERE UNTIL SOLOMON DIES. THEN WE'LL SEE IF AHIJAH SPOKE THE TRUTH ABOUT MY RULING THE NORTHERN TRIBES OF ISRAEL.
REPORTS OF YOUR PEOPLE'S COMPLAINTS HAVE BEEN REACHING US FOR SOME TIME.
BUT SOLOMON CONTINUES TO LIVE IN LUXURY—AND SO FAR REMOVED FROM HIS PEOPLE THAT THEIR COMPLAINTS DO NOT REACH HIM. HE EVEN IGNORES AHIJAH'S PROPHECY AND GOD'S WARNING THAT THE KINGDOM WILL BE DIVIDED BECAUSE HE WORSHIPS FALSE GODS.

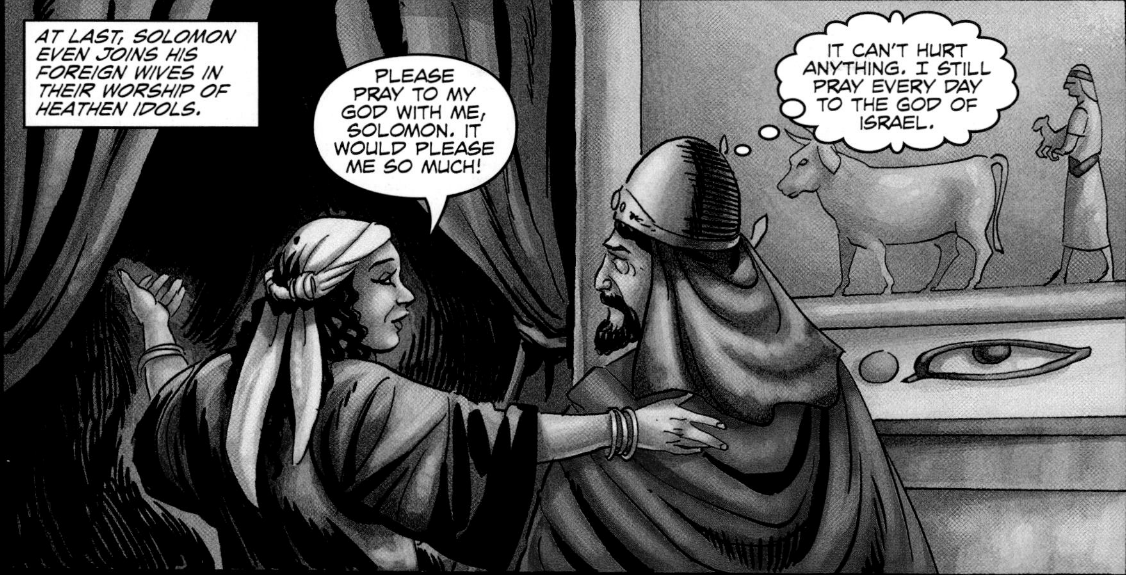
AT LAST, SOLOMON EVEN JOINS HIS FOREIGN WIVES IN THEIR WORSHIP OF HEATHEN IDOLS.
PLEASE PRAY TO MY GOD WITH ME, SOLOMON. IT WOULD PLEASE ME SO MUCH!
IT CAN'T HURT ANYTHING. I STILL PRAY EVERY DAY TO THE GOD OF ISRAEL.

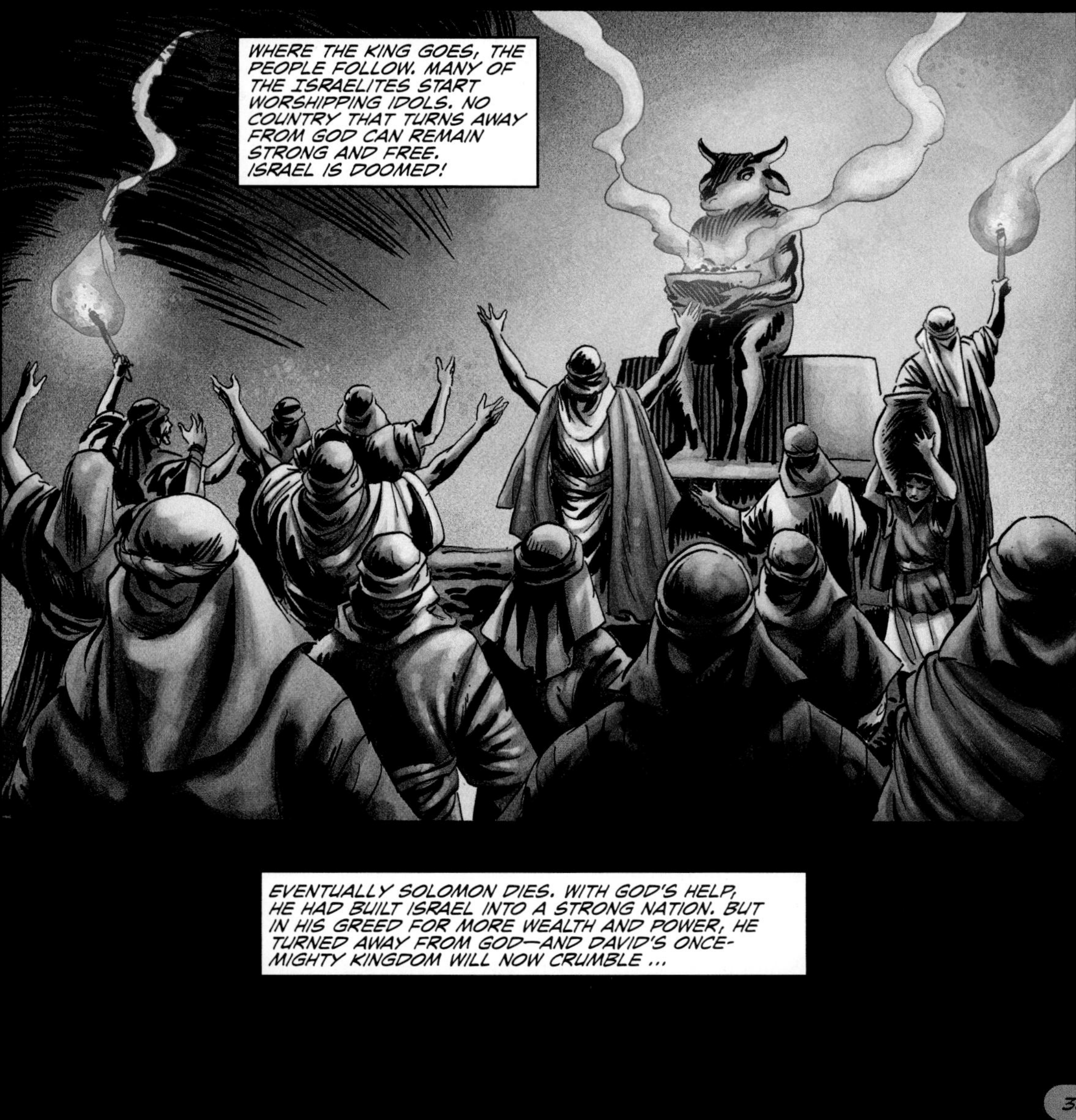
WHERE THE KING GOES, THE PEOPLE FOLLOW. MANY OF THE ISRAELITES START WORSHIPPING IDOLS. NO COUNTRY THAT TURNS AWAY FROM GOD CAN REMAIN STRONG AND FREE. ISRAEL IS DOOMED!

EVENTUALLY SOLOMON DIES. WITH GOD'S HELP, HE HAD BUILT ISRAEL INTO A STRONG NATION. BUT IN HIS GREED FOR MORE WEALTH AND POWER, HE TURNED AWAY FROM GOD—AND DAVID'S ONCE-MIGHTY KINGDOM WILL NOW CRUMBLE ...

A Kingdom Torn in Two

BASED ON 1 KINGS 12:1–24

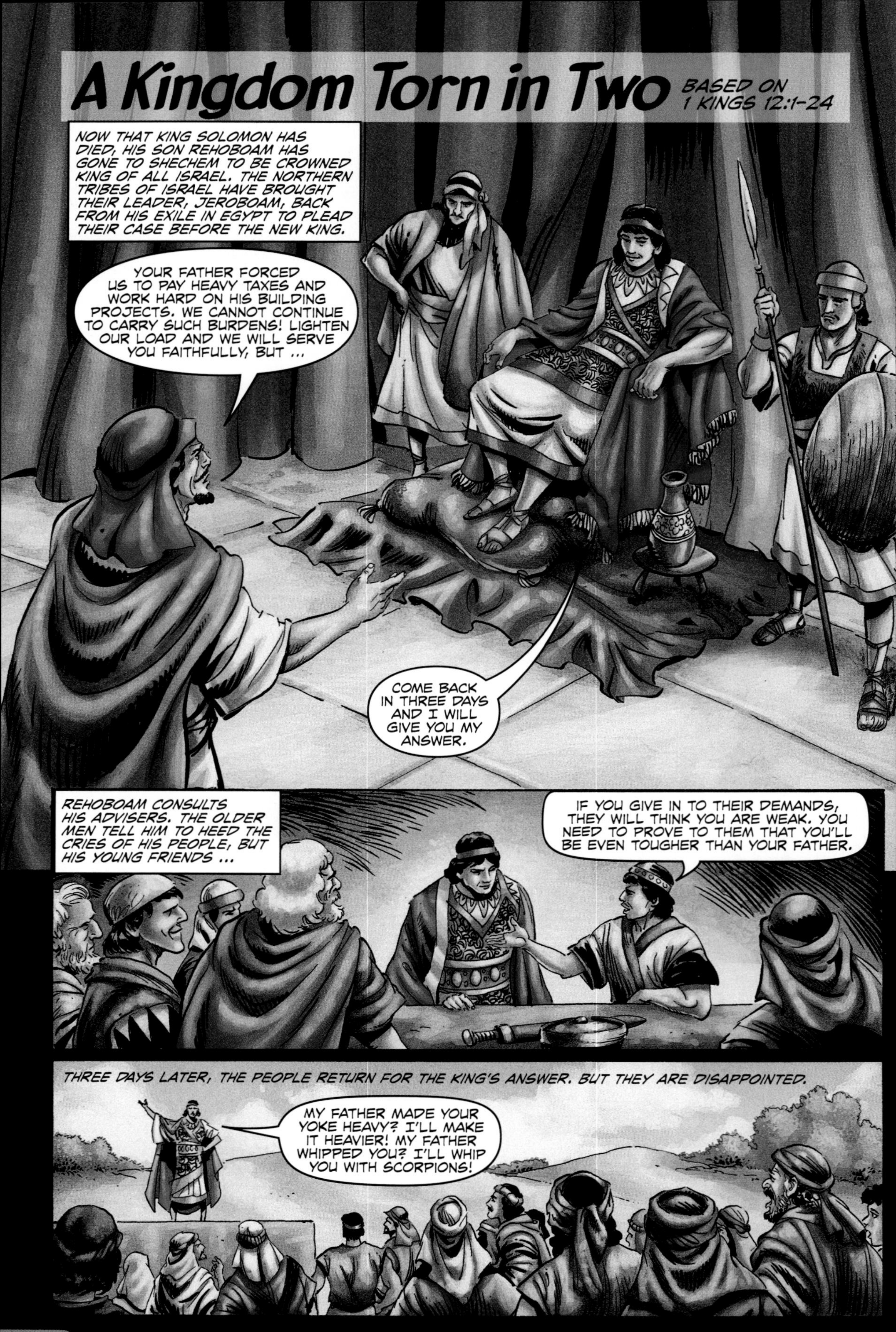
NOW THAT KING SOLOMON HAS DIED, HIS SON REHOBOAM HAS GONE TO SHECHEM TO BE CROWNED KING OF ALL ISRAEL. THE NORTHERN TRIBES OF ISRAEL HAVE BROUGHT THEIR LEADER, JEROBOAM, BACK FROM HIS EXILE IN EGYPT TO PLEAD THEIR CASE BEFORE THE NEW KING.
YOUR FATHER FORCED US TO PAY HEAVY TAXES AND WORK HARD ON HIS BUILDING PROJECTS. WE CANNOT CONTINUE TO CARRY SUCH BURDENS! LIGHTEN OUR LOAD AND WE WILL SERVE YOU FAITHFULLY, BUT ...
COME BACK IN THREE DAYS AND I WILL GIVE YOU MY ANSWER.
REHOBOAM CONSULTS HIS ADVISERS. THE OLDER MEN TELL HIM TO HEED THE CRIES OF HIS PEOPLE, BUT HIS YOUNG FRIENDS ...
IF YOU GIVE IN TO THEIR DEMANDS, THEY WILL THINK YOU ARE WEAK. YOU NEED TO PROVE TO THEM THAT YOU'LL BE EVEN TOUGHER THAN YOUR FATHER.
THREE DAYS LATER, THE PEOPLE RETURN FOR THE KING'S ANSWER. BUT THEY ARE DISAPPOINTED.
MY FATHER MADE YOUR YOKE HEAVY? I'LL MAKE IT HEAVIER! MY FATHER WHIPPED YOU? I'LL WHIP YOU WITH SCORPIONS!

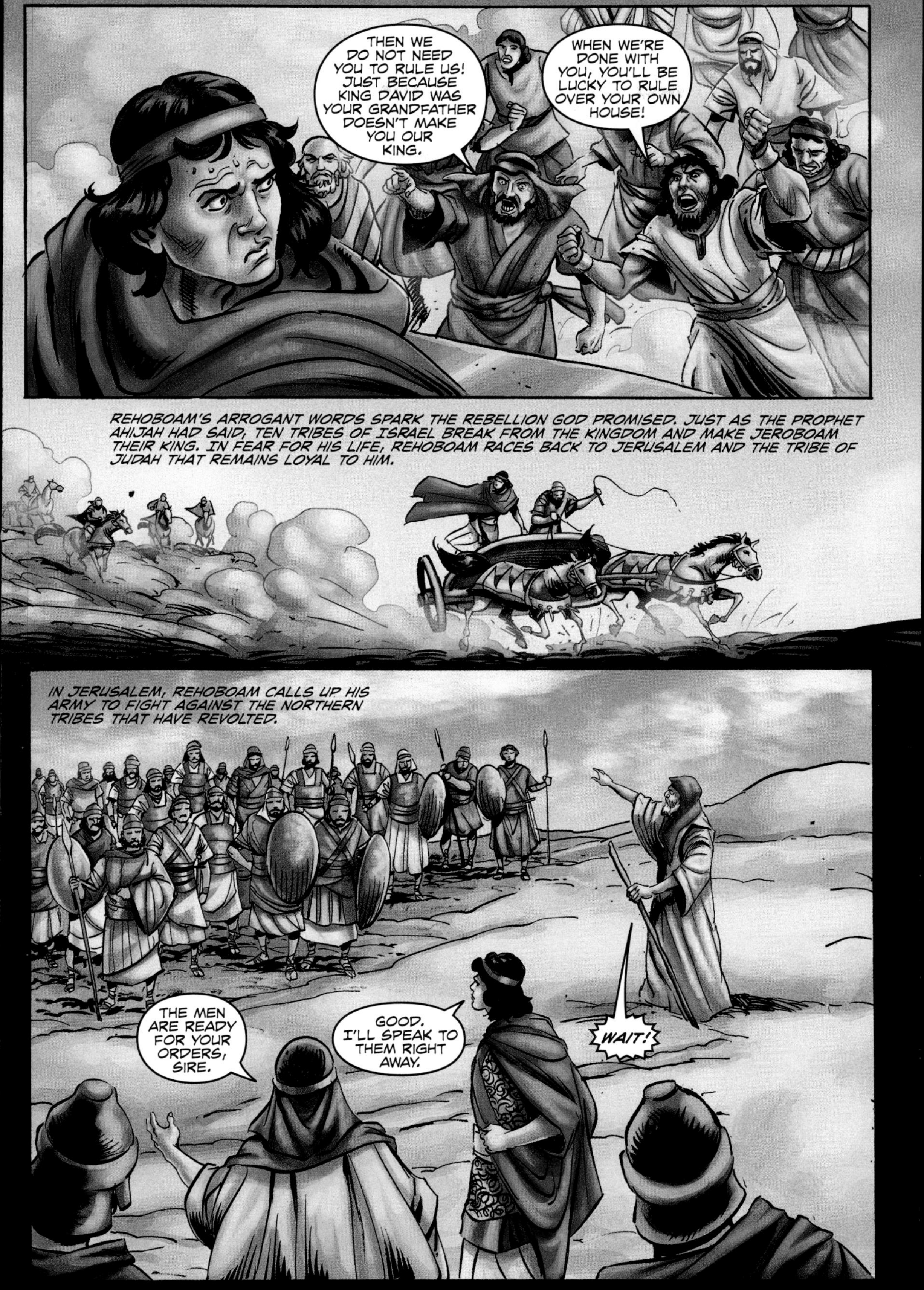
THEN WE DO NOT NEED YOU TO RULE US! JUST BECAUSE KING DAVID WAS YOUR GRANDFATHER DOESN'T MAKE YOU OUR KING.
WHEN WE'RE DONE WITH YOU, YOU'LL BE LUCKY TO RULE OVER YOUR OWN HOUSE!
REHOBOAM'S ARROGANT WORDS SPARK THE REBELLION GOD PROMISED. JUST AS THE PROPHET AHIJAH HAD SAID, TEN TRIBES OF ISRAEL BREAK FROM THE KINGDOM AND MAKE JEROBOAM THEIR KING. IN FEAR FOR HIS LIFE, REHOBOAM RACES BACK TO JERUSALEM AND THE TRIBE OF JUDAH THAT REMAINS LOYAL TO HIM.
IN JERUSALEM, REHOBOAM CALLS UP HIS ARMY TO FIGHT AGAINST THE NORTHERN TRIBES THAT HAVE REVOLTED.
THE MEN ARE READY FOR YOUR ORDERS, SIRE.
GOOD. I'LL SPEAK TO THEM RIGHT AWAY.
WAIT!

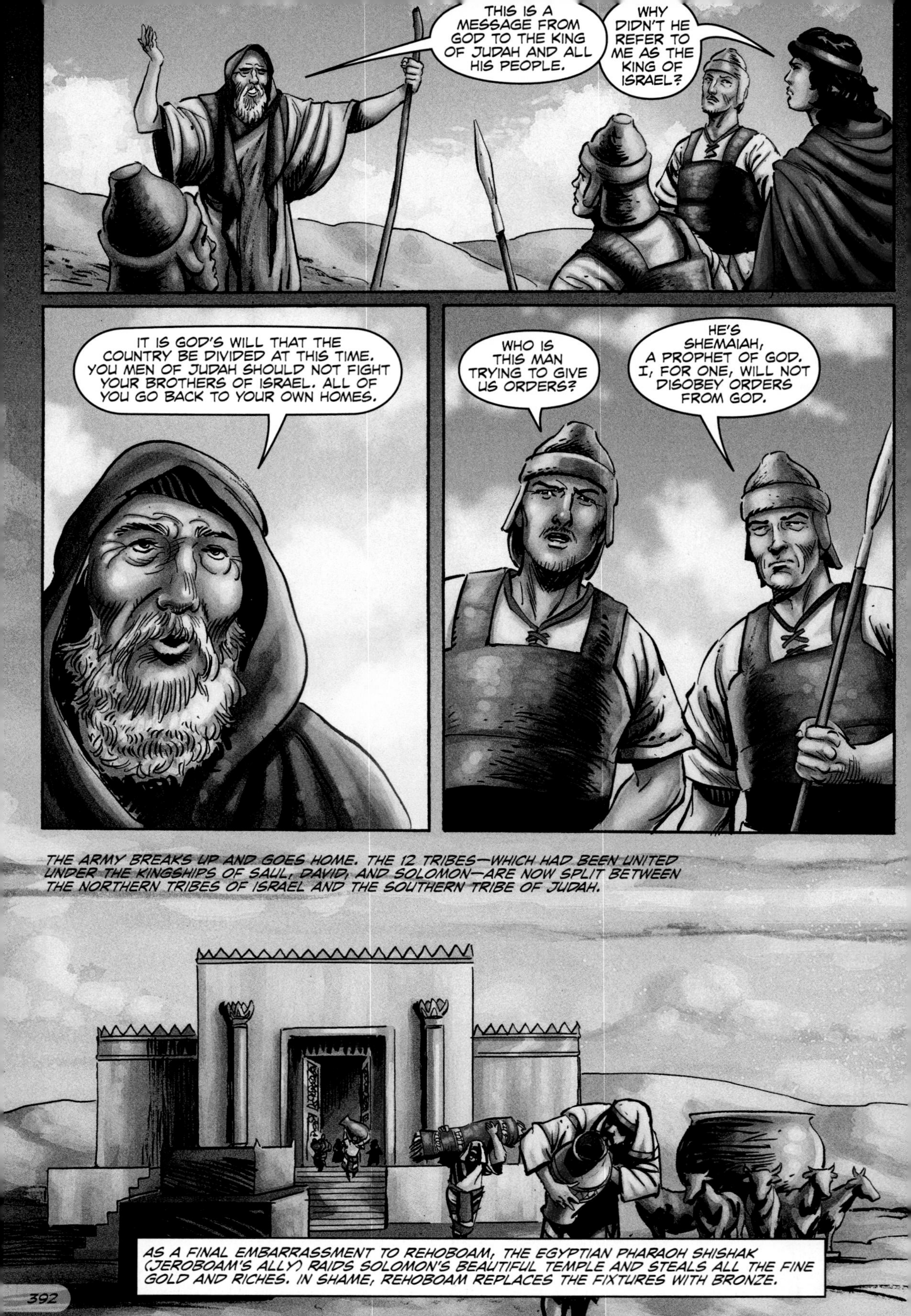
THIS IS A MESSAGE FROM GOD TO THE KING OF JUDAH AND ALL HIS PEOPLE.
WHY DIDN'T HE REFER TO ME AS THE KING OF ISRAEL?
IT IS GOD'S WILL THAT THE COUNTRY BE DIVIDED AT THIS TIME. YOU MEN OF JUDAH SHOULD NOT FIGHT YOUR BROTHERS OF ISRAEL. ALL OF YOU GO BACK TO YOUR OWN HOMES.
WHO IS THIS MAN TRYING TO GIVE US ORDERS?
HE'S SHEMAIAH, A PROPHET OF GOD. I, FOR ONE, WILL NOT DISOBEY ORDERS FROM GOD.
THE ARMY BREAKS UP AND GOES HOME. THE 12 TRIBES—WHICH HAD BEEN UNITED UNDER THE KINGSHIPS OF SAUL, DAVID, AND SOLOMON—ARE NOW SPLIT BETWEEN THE NORTHERN TRIBES OF ISRAEL AND THE SOUTHERN TRIBE OF JUDAH.
AS A FINAL EMBARRASSMENT TO REHOBOAM, THE EGYPTIAN PHARAOH SHISHAK (JEROBOAM'S ALLY) RAIDS SOLOMON'S BEAUTIFUL TEMPLE AND STEALS ALL THE FINE GOLD AND RICHES. IN SHAME, REHOBOAM REPLACES THE FIXTURES WITH BRONZE.

A Bad Start for Israel

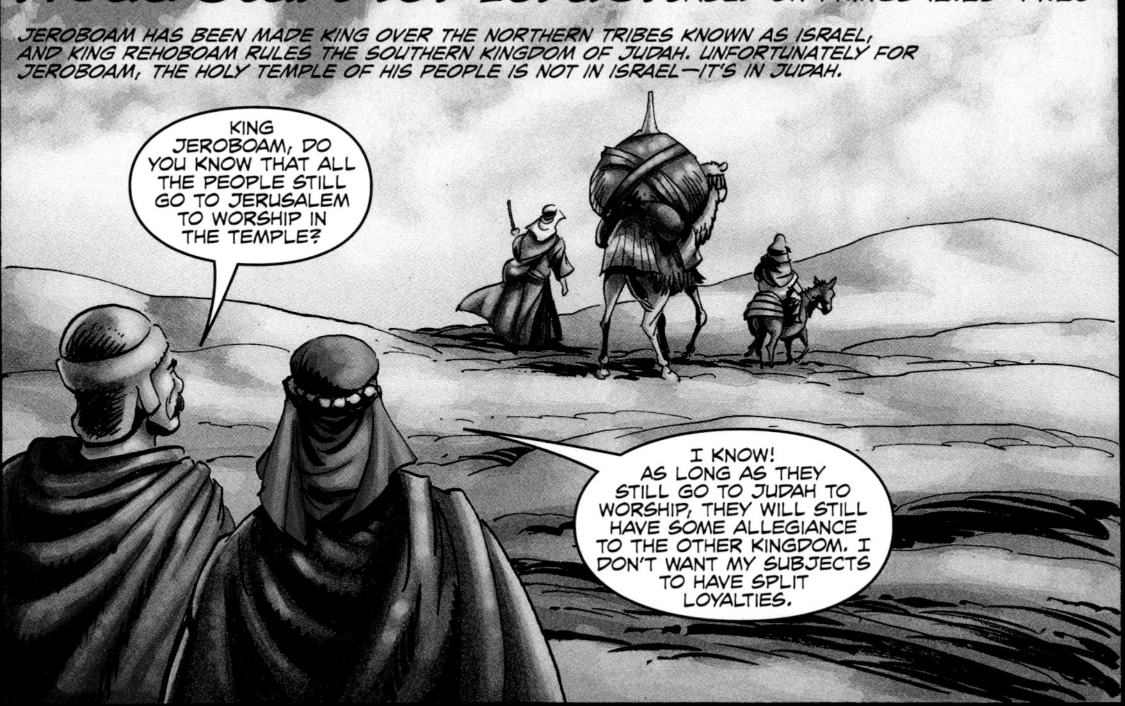
BASED ON 1 KINGS 12:25–14:20
JEROBOAM HAS BEEN MADE KING OVER THE NORTHERN TRIBES KNOWN AS ISRAEL, AND KING REHOBOAM RULES THE SOUTHERN KINGDOM OF JUDAH. UNFORTUNATELY FOR JEROBOAM, THE HOLY TEMPLE OF HIS PEOPLE IS NOT IN ISRAEL—IT'S IN JUDAH.
KING JEROBOAM, DO YOU KNOW THAT ALL THE PEOPLE STILL GO TO JERUSALEM TO WORSHIP IN THE TEMPLE?
I KNOW! AS LONG AS THEY STILL GO TO JUDAH TO WORSHIP, THEY WILL STILL HAVE SOME ALLEGIANCE TO THE OTHER KINGDOM. I DON'T WANT MY SUBJECTS TO HAVE SPLIT LOYALTIES.

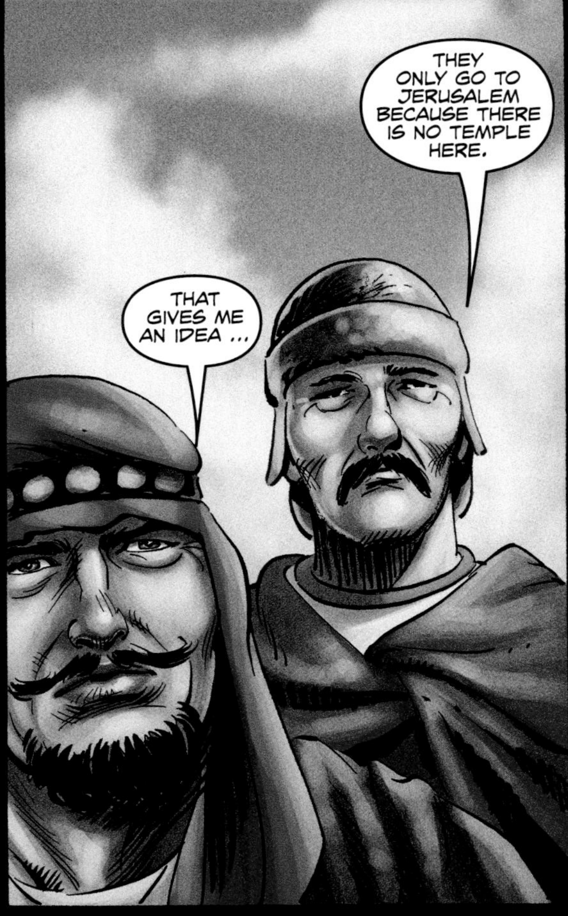
THEY ONLY GO TO JERUSALEM BECAUSE THERE IS NO TEMPLE HERE.
THAT GIVES ME AN IDEA ...

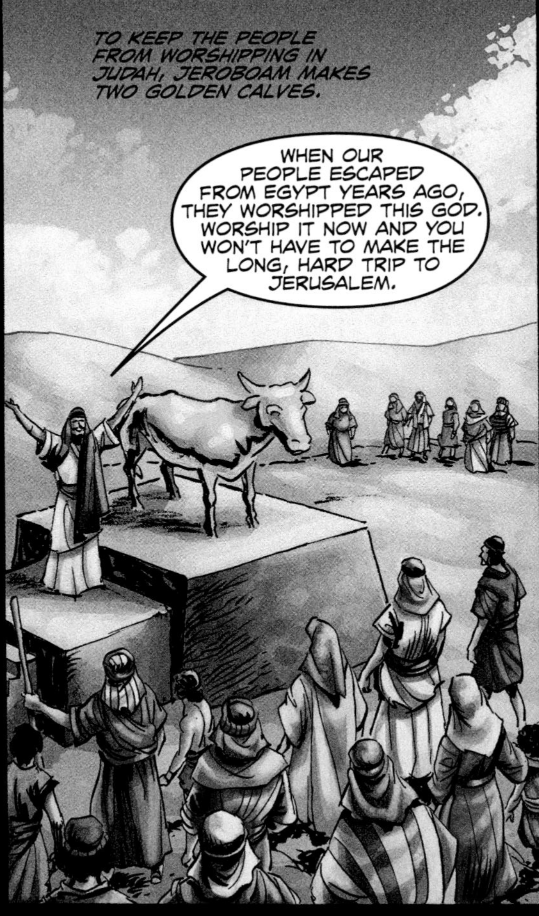
TO KEEP THE PEOPLE FROM WORSHIPPING IN JUDAH, JEROBOAM MAKES TWO GOLDEN CALVES.
WHEN OUR PEOPLE ESCAPED FROM EGYPT YEARS AGO, THEY WORSHIPPED THIS GOD. WORSHIP IT NOW AND YOU WON'T HAVE TO MAKE THE LONG, HARD TRIP TO JERUSALEM.

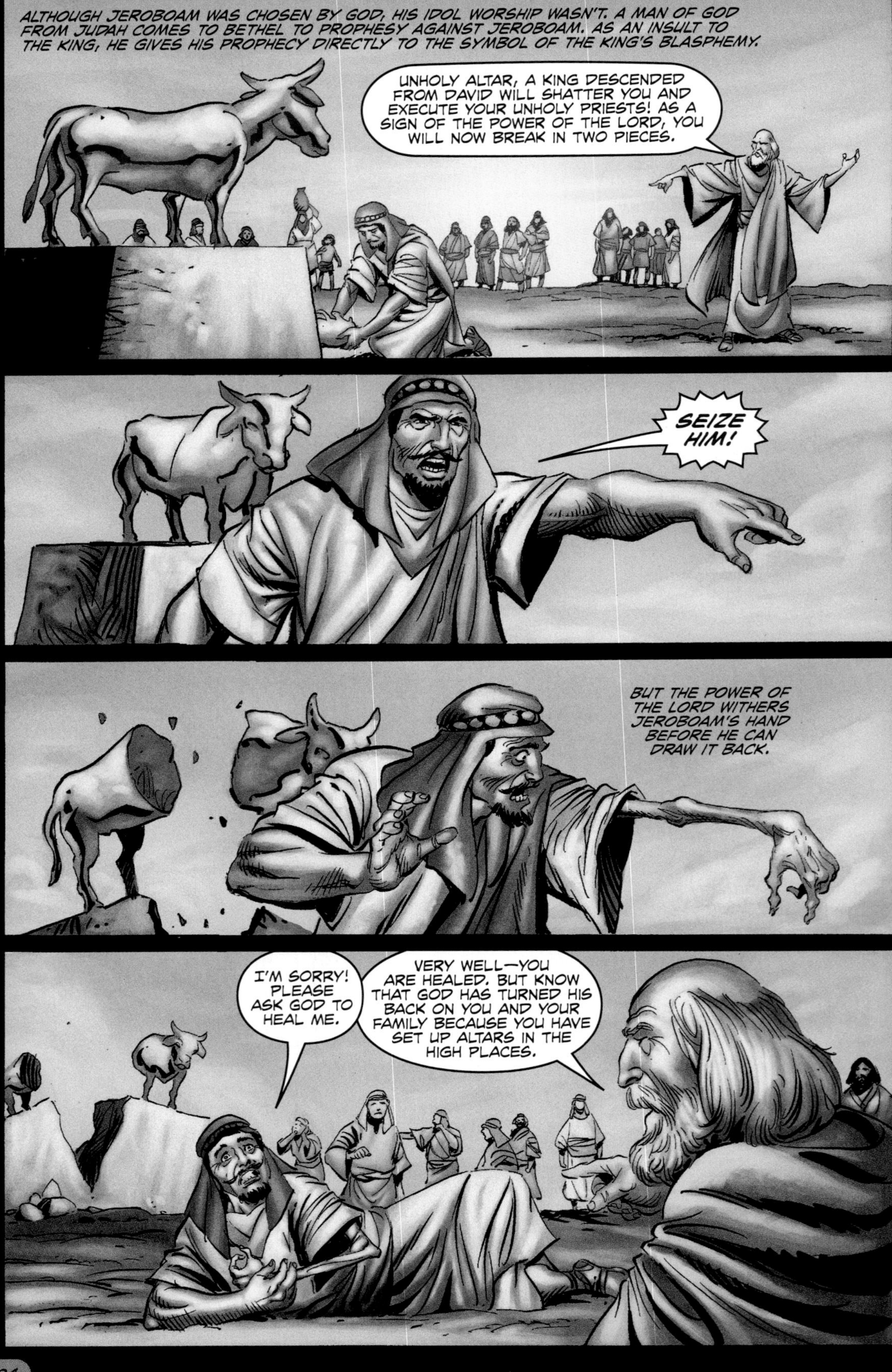
ALTHOUGH JEROBOAM WAS CHOSEN BY GOD, HIS IDOL WORSHIP WASN'T. A MAN OF GOD FROM JUDAH COMES TO BETHEL TO PROPHESY AGAINST JEROBOAM. AS AN INSULT TO THE KING, HE GIVES HIS PROPHECY DIRECTLY TO THE SYMBOL OF THE KING'S BLASPHEMY.
UNHOLY ALTAR, A KING DESCENDED FROM DAVID WILL SHATTER YOU AND EXECUTE YOUR UNHOLY PRIESTS! AS A SIGN OF THE POWER OF THE LORD, YOU WILL NOW BREAK IN TWO PIECES.
SEIZE HIM!
BUT THE POWER OF THE LORD WITHERS JEROBOAM'S HAND BEFORE HE CAN DRAW IT BACK.
I'M SORRY! PLEASE ASK GOD TO HEAL ME.
VERY WELL—YOU ARE HEALED. BUT KNOW THAT GOD HAS TURNED HIS BACK ON YOU AND YOUR FAMILY BECAUSE YOU HAVE SET UP ALTARS IN THE HIGH PLACES.

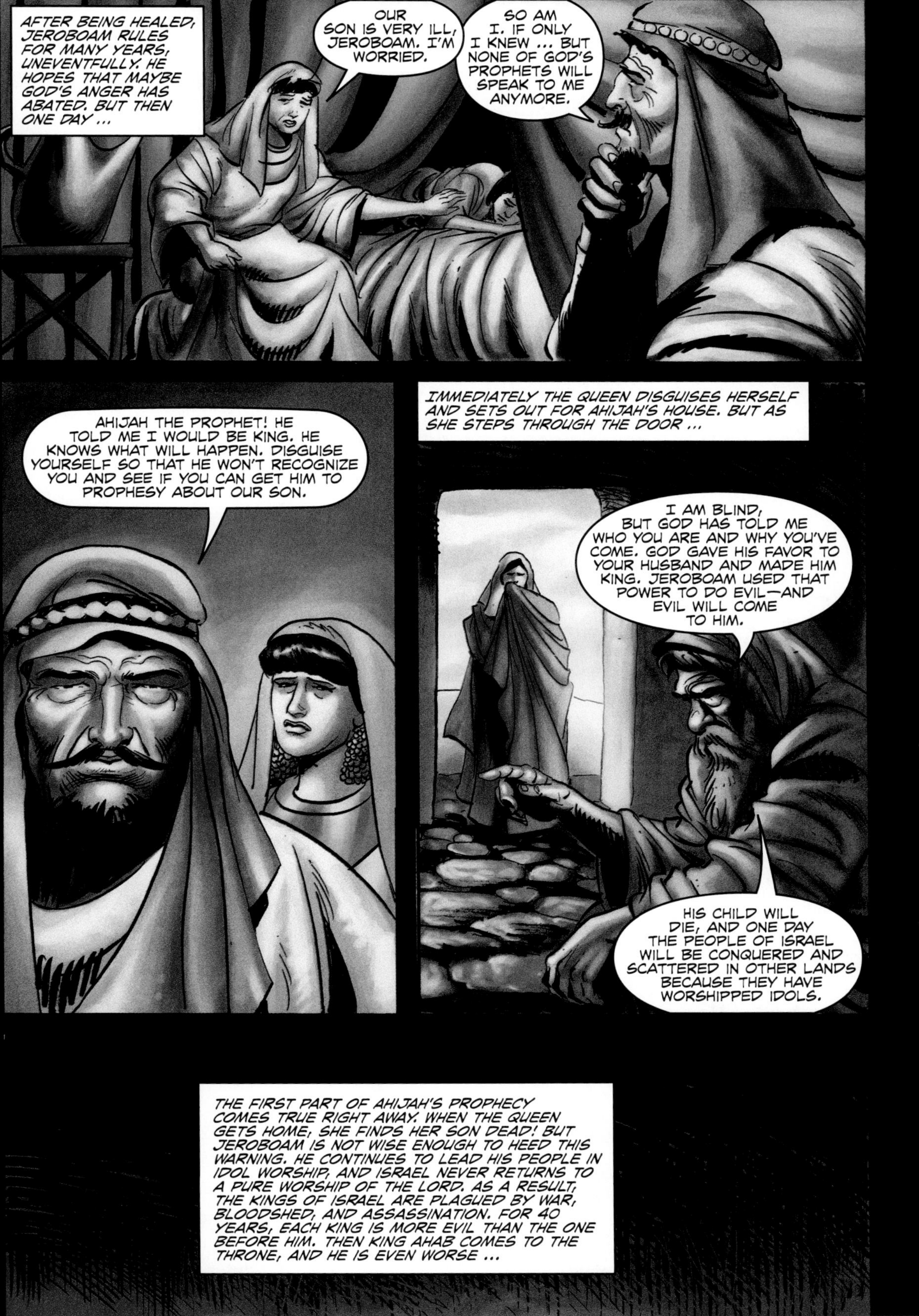
AFTER BEING HEALED, JEROBOAM RULES FOR MANY YEARS, UNEVENTFULLY. HE HOPES THAT MAYBE GOD'S ANGER HAS ABATED. BUT THEN ONE DAY ...
OUR SON IS VERY ILL, JEROBOAM. I'M WORRIED.
SO AM I. IF ONLY I KNEW ... BUT NONE OF GOD'S PROPHETS WILL SPEAK TO ME ANYMORE.
AHIJAH THE PROPHET! HE TOLD ME I WOULD BE KING. HE KNOWS WHAT WILL HAPPEN. DISGUISE YOURSELF SO THAT HE WON'T RECOGNIZE YOU AND SEE IF YOU CAN GET HIM TO PROPHESY ABOUT OUR SON.
IMMEDIATELY THE QUEEN DISGUISES HERSELF AND SETS OUT FOR AHIJAH'S HOUSE. BUT AS SHE STEPS THROUGH THE DOOR ...
I AM BLIND, BUT GOD HAS TOLD ME WHO YOU ARE AND WHY YOU'VE COME. GOD GAVE HIS FAVOR TO YOUR HUSBAND AND MADE HIM KING. JEROBOAM USED THAT POWER TO DO EVIL—AND EVIL WILL COME TO HIM.
HIS CHILD WILL DIE, AND ONE DAY THE PEOPLE OF ISRAEL WILL BE CONQUERED AND SCATTERED IN OTHER LANDS BECAUSE THEY HAVE WORSHIPPED IDOLS.
THE FIRST PART OF AHIJAH'S PROPHECY COMES TRUE RIGHT AWAY. WHEN THE QUEEN GETS HOME, SHE FINDS HER SON DEAD! BUT JEROBOAM IS NOT WISE ENOUGH TO HEED THIS WARNING. HE CONTINUES TO LEAD HIS PEOPLE IN IDOL WORSHIP, AND ISRAEL NEVER RETURNS TO A PURE WORSHIP OF THE LORD. AS A RESULT, THE KINGS OF ISRAEL ARE PLAGUED BY WAR, BLOODSHED, AND ASSASSINATION. FOR 40 YEARS, EACH KING IS MORE EVIL THAN THE ONE BEFORE HIM. THEN KING AHAB COMES TO THE THRONE, AND HE IS EVEN WORSE ...

he Wicked Queen and he Defiant Prophet

BASED ON 1 KINGS 16:29—17:6

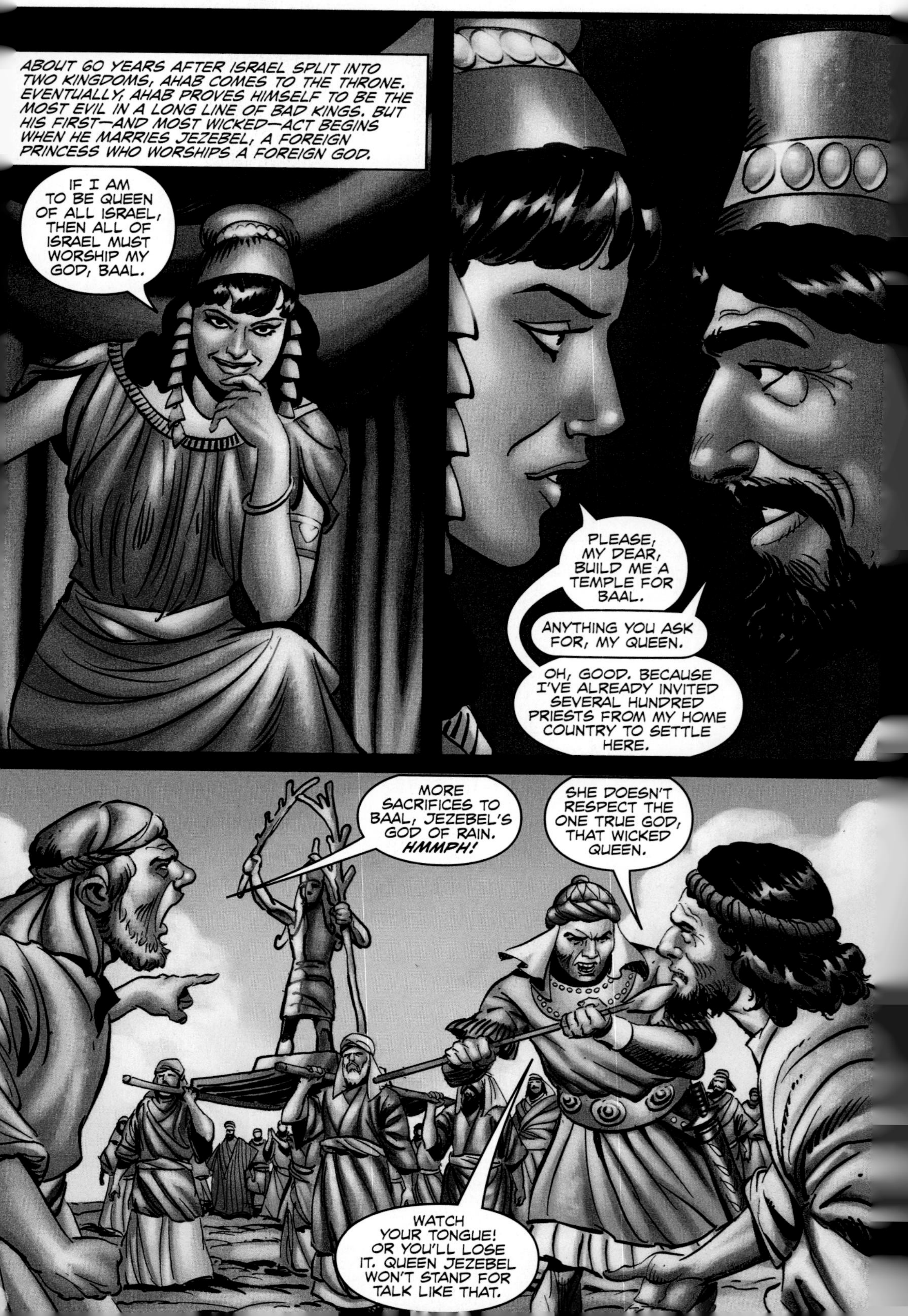

ABOUT 60 YEARS AFTER ISRAEL SPLIT INTO TWO KINGDOMS, AHAB COMES TO THE THRONE. EVENTUALLY, AHAB PROVES HIMSELF TO BE THE MOST EVIL IN A LONG LINE OF BAD KINGS. BUT HIS FIRST—AND MOST WICKED—ACT BEGINS WHEN HE MARRIES JEZEBEL, A FOREIGN PRINCESS WHO WORSHIPS A FOREIGN GOD.
IF I AM TO BE QUEEN OF ALL ISRAEL, THEN ALL OF ISRAEL MUST WORSHIP MY GOD, BAAL.
PLEASE, MY DEAR, BUILD ME A TEMPLE FOR BAAL.
ANYTHING YOU ASK FOR, MY QUEEN.
OH, GOOD. BECAUSE I'VE ALREADY INVITED SEVERAL HUNDRED PRIESTS FROM MY HOME COUNTRY TO SETTLE HERE.
MORE SACRIFICES TO BAAL, JEZEBEL'S GOD OF RAIN. HMMPH!
SHE DOESN'T RESPECT THE ONE TRUE GOD, THAT WICKED QUEEN.
WATCH YOUR TONGUE! OR YOU'LL LOSE IT. QUEEN JEZEBEL WON'T STAND FOR TALK LIKE THAT.

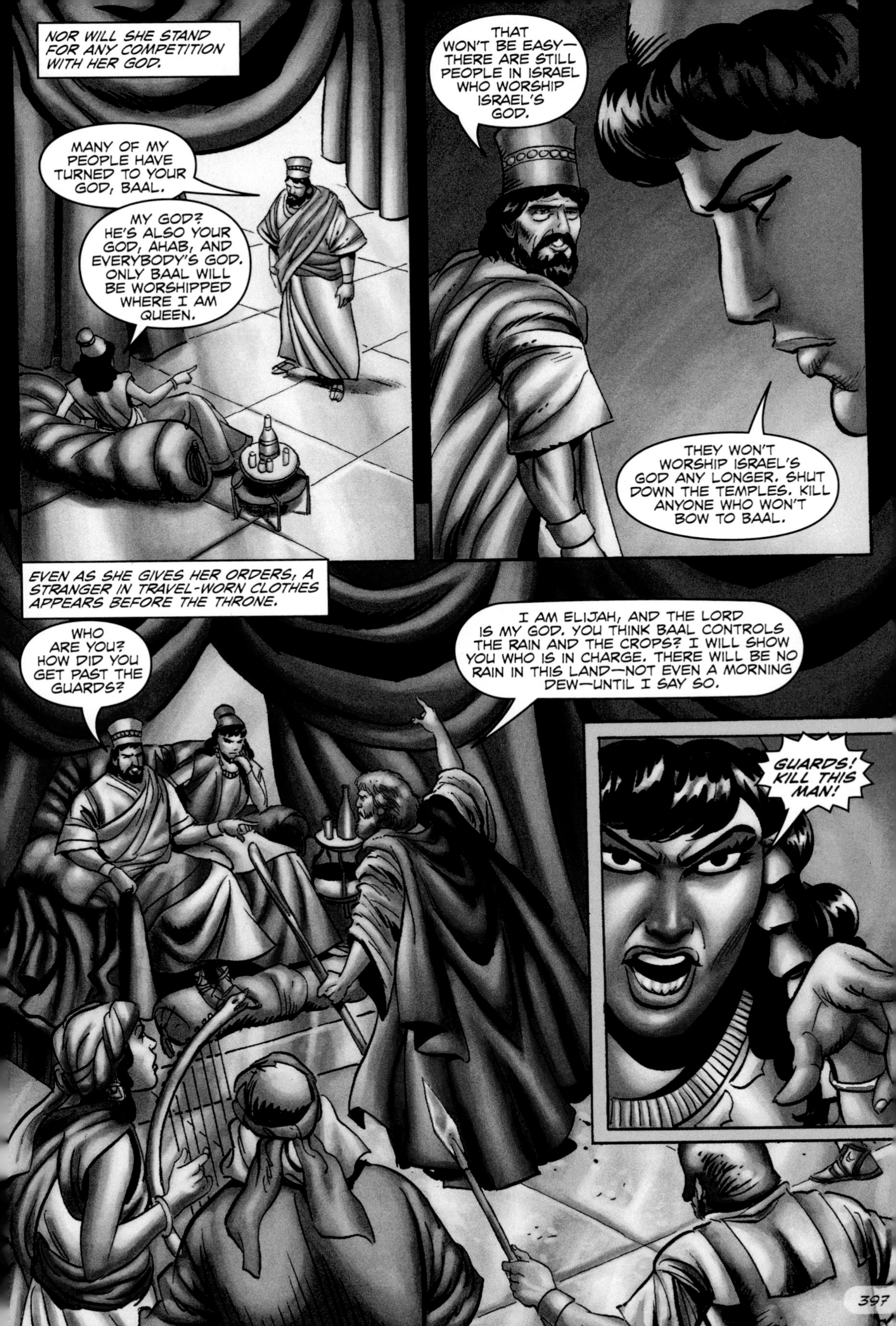
NOR WILL SHE STAND FOR ANY COMPETITION WITH HER GOD.
MANY OF MY PEOPLE HAVE TURNED TO YOUR GOD, BAAL.
MY GOD? HE'S ALSO YOUR GOD, AHAB, AND EVERYBODY'S GOD. ONLY BAAL WILL BE WORSHIPPED WHERE I AM QUEEN.
THAT WON'T BE EASY—THERE ARE STILL PEOPLE IN ISRAEL WHO WORSHIP ISRAEL'S GOD.
THEY WON'T WORSHIP ISRAEL'S GOD ANY LONGER. SHUT DOWN THE TEMPLES. KILL ANYONE WHO WON'T BOW TO BAAL.
EVEN AS SHE GIVES HER ORDERS, A STRANGER IN TRAVEL-WORN CLOTHES APPEARS BEFORE THE THRONE.
WHO ARE YOU? HOW DID YOU GET PAST THE GUARDS?
I AM ELIJAH, AND THE LORD IS MY GOD. YOU THINK BAAL CONTROLS THE RAIN AND THE CROPS? I WILL SHOW YOU WHO IS IN CHARGE. THERE WILL BE NO RAIN IN THIS LAND—NOT EVEN A MORNING DEW—UNTIL I SAY SO.
GUARDS! KILL THIS MAN!

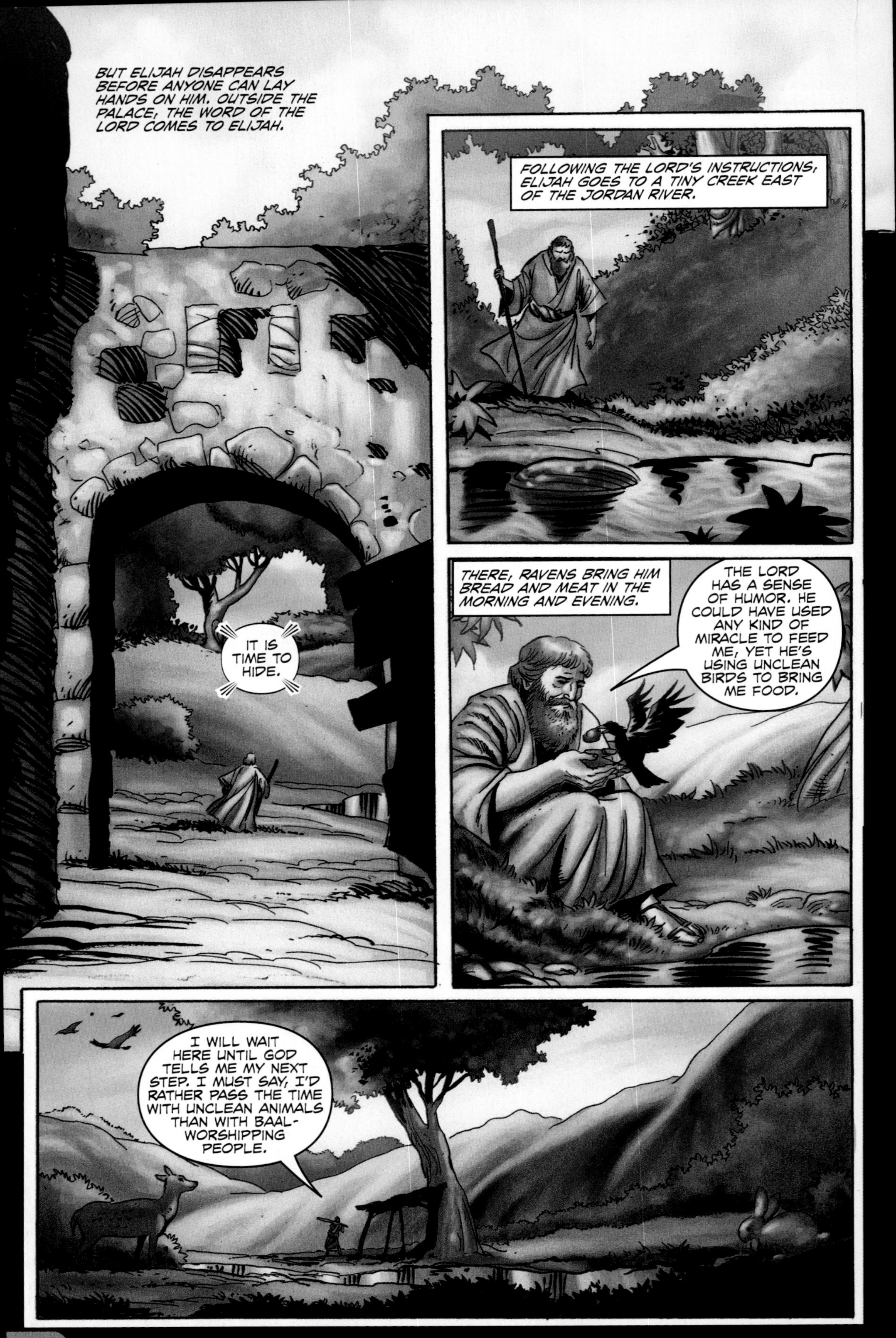
BUT ELIJAH DISAPPEARS BEFORE ANYONE CAN LAY HANDS ON HIM. OUTSIDE THE PALACE, THE WORD OF THE LORD COMES TO ELIJAH.
IT IS TIME TO HIDE.
FOLLOWING THE LORD'S INSTRUCTIONS, ELIJAH GOES TO A TINY CREEK EAST OF THE JORDAN RIVER.
THERE, RAVENS BRING HIM BREAD AND MEAT IN THE MORNING AND EVENING.
THE LORD HAS A SENSE OF HUMOR. HE COULD HAVE USED ANY KIND OF MIRACLE TO FEED ME, YET HE'S USING UNCLEAN BIRDS TO BRING ME FOOD.
I WILL WAIT HERE UNTIL GOD TELLS ME MY NEXT STEP. I MUST SAY, I'D RATHER PASS THE TIME WITH UNCLEAN ANIMALS THAN WITH BAAL-WORSHIPPING PEOPLE.

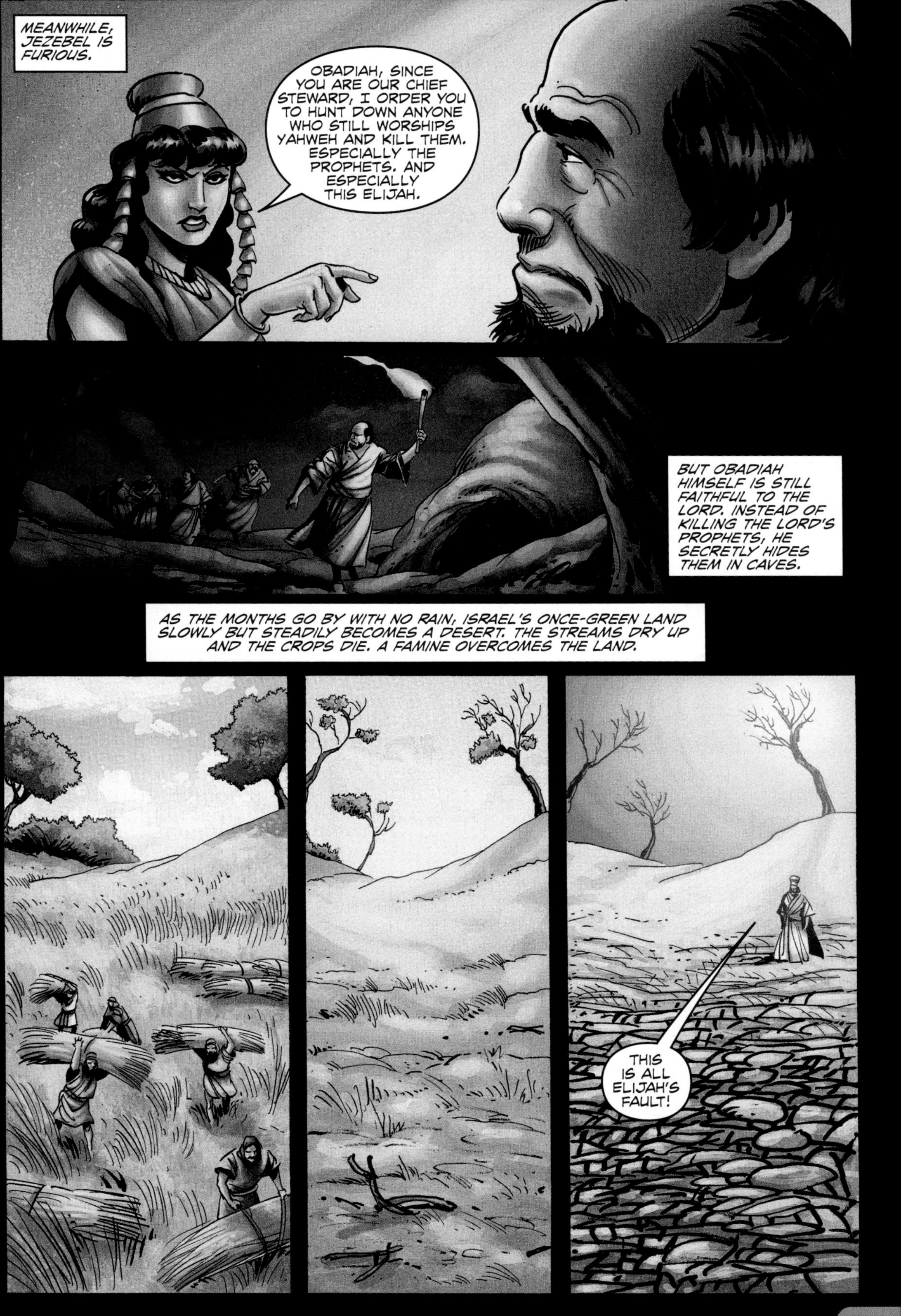
MEANWHILE, JEZEBEL IS FURIOUS.
OBADIAH, SINCE YOU ARE OUR CHIEF STEWARD, I ORDER YOU TO HUNT DOWN ANYONE WHO STILL WORSHIPS YAHWEH AND KILL THEM. ESPECIALLY THE PROPHETS. AND ESPECIALLY THIS ELIJAH.
BUT OBADIAH HIMSELF IS STILL FAITHFUL TO THE LORD. INSTEAD OF KILLING THE LORD'S PROPHETS, HE SECRETLY HIDES THEM IN CAVES.
AS THE MONTHS GO BY WITH NO RAIN, ISRAEL'S ONCE-GREEN LAND SLOWLY BUT STEADILY BECOMES A DESERT. THE STREAMS DRY UP AND THE CROPS DIE. A FAMINE OVERCOMES THE LAND.
THIS IS ALL ELIJAH'S FAULT!

Elijah's Flour Power BASED ON 1 KINGS 17:7-24

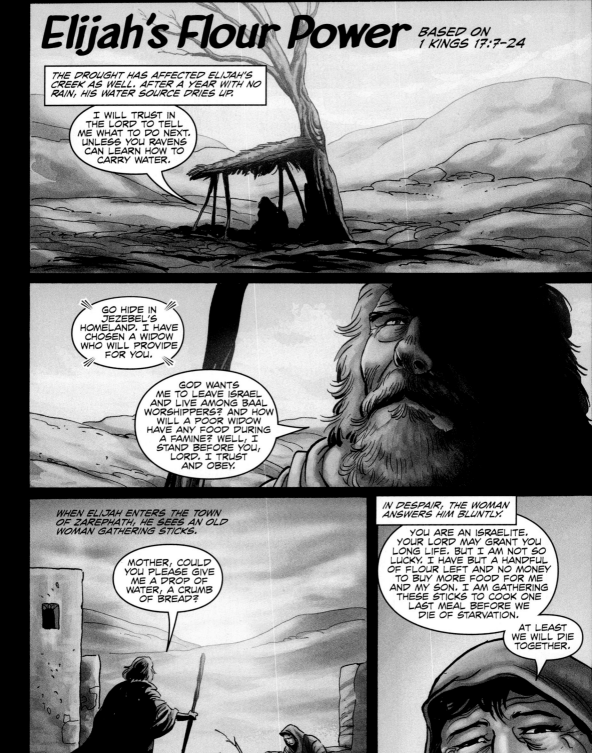

THE DROUGHT HAS AFFECTED ELIJAH'S CREEK AS WELL. AFTER A YEAR WITH NO RAIN, HIS WATER SOURCE DRIES UP.

I WILL TRUST IN THE LORD TO TELL ME WHAT TO DO NEXT. UNLESS YOU RAVENS CAN LEARN HOW TO CARRY WATER.

GO HIDE IN JEZEBEL'S HOMELAND. I HAVE CHOSEN A WIDOW WHO WILL PROVIDE FOR YOU.

GOD WANTS ME TO LEAVE ISRAEL AND LIVE AMONG BAAL WORSHIPPERS? AND HOW WILL A POOR WIDOW HAVE ANY FOOD DURING A FAMINE? WELL, I STAND BEFORE YOU, LORD. I TRUST AND OBEY.

WHEN ELIJAH ENTERS THE TOWN OF ZAREPHATH, HE SEES AN OLD WOMAN GATHERING STICKS.

MOTHER, COULD YOU PLEASE GIVE ME A DROP OF WATER, A CRUMB OF BREAD?

IN DESPAIR, THE WOMAN ANSWERS HIM BLUNTLY.

YOU ARE AN ISRAELITE. YOUR LORD MAY GRANT YOU LONG LIFE. BUT I AM NOT SO LUCKY. I HAVE BUT A HANDFUL OF FLOUR LEFT AND NO MONEY TO BUY MORE FOOD FOR ME AND MY SON. I AM GATHERING THESE STICKS TO COOK ONE LAST MEAL BEFORE WE DIE OF STARVATION.

AT LEAST WE WILL DIE TOGETHER.

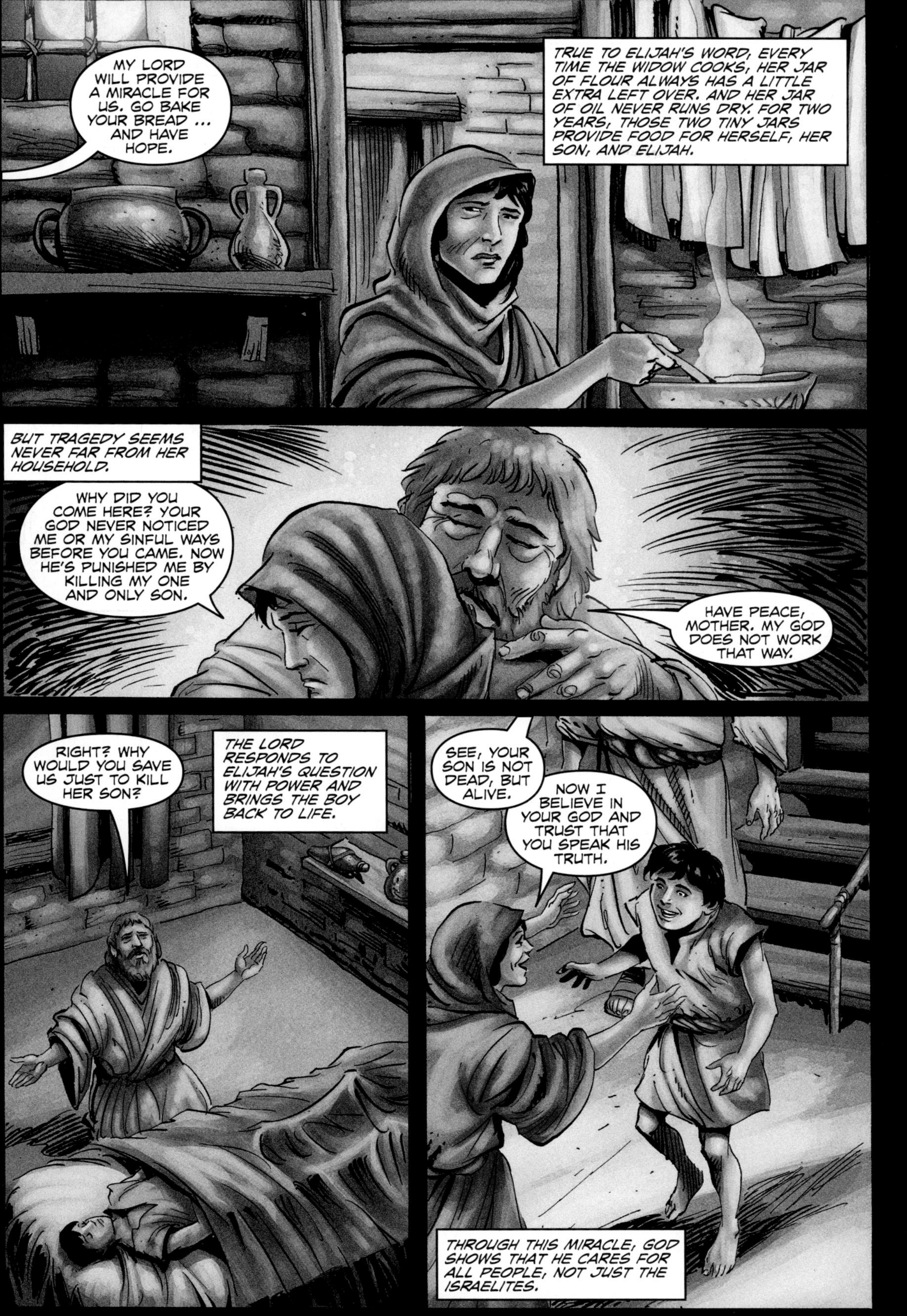

MY LORD WILL PROVIDE A MIRACLE FOR US. GO BAKE YOUR BREAD ... AND HAVE HOPE.
TRUE TO ELIJAH'S WORD, EVERY TIME THE WIDOW COOKS, HER JAR OF FLOUR ALWAYS HAS A LITTLE EXTRA LEFT OVER. AND HER JAR OF OIL NEVER RUNS DRY. FOR TWO YEARS, THOSE TWO TINY JARS PROVIDE FOOD FOR HERSELF, HER SON, AND ELIJAH.
BUT TRAGEDY SEEMS NEVER FAR FROM HER HOUSEHOLD.
WHY DID YOU COME HERE? YOUR GOD NEVER NOTICED ME OR MY SINFUL WAYS BEFORE YOU CAME. NOW HE'S PUNISHED ME BY KILLING MY ONE AND ONLY SON.
HAVE PEACE, MOTHER. MY GOD DOES NOT WORK THAT WAY.
RIGHT? WHY WOULD YOU SAVE US JUST TO KILL HER SON?
THE LORD RESPONDS TO ELIJAH'S QUESTION WITH POWER AND BRINGS THE BOY BACK TO LIFE.
SEE, YOUR SON IS NOT DEAD, BUT ALIVE.
NOW I BELIEVE IN YOUR GOD AND TRUST THAT YOU SPEAK HIS TRUTH.
THROUGH THIS MIRACLE, GOD SHOWS THAT HE CARES FOR ALL PEOPLE, NOT JUST THE ISRAELITES.

Battle of the Gods

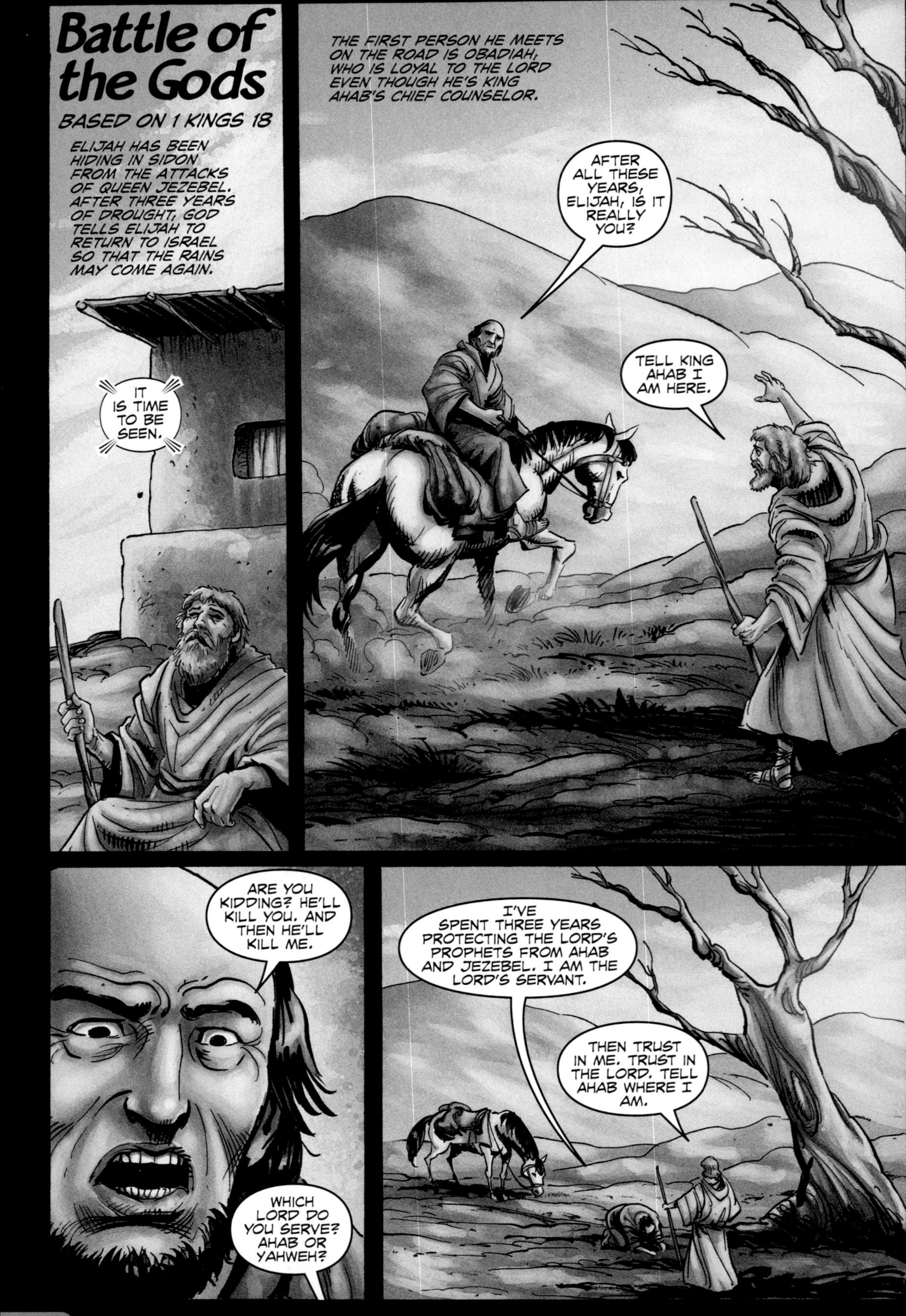
BASED ON 1 KINGS 18
ELIJAH HAS BEEN HIDING IN SIDON FROM THE ATTACKS OF QUEEN JEZEBEL. AFTER THREE YEARS OF DROUGHT, GOD TELLS ELIJAH TO RETURN TO ISRAEL SO THAT THE RAINS MAY COME AGAIN.
IT IS TIME TO BE SEEN.
THE FIRST PERSON HE MEETS ON THE ROAD IS OBADIAH, WHO IS LOYAL TO THE LORD EVEN THOUGH HE'S KING AHAB'S CHIEF COUNSELOR.
AFTER ALL THESE YEARS, ELIJAH, IS IT REALLY YOU?
TELL KING AHAB I AM HERE.
ARE YOU KIDDING? HE'LL KILL YOU. AND THEN HE'LL KILL ME.
WHICH LORD DO YOU SERVE? AHAB OR YAHWEH?
I'VE SPENT THREE YEARS PROTECTING THE LORD'S PROPHETS FROM AHAB AND JEZEBEL. I AM THE LORD'S SERVANT.
THEN TRUST IN ME. TRUST IN THE LORD. TELL AHAB WHERE I AM.

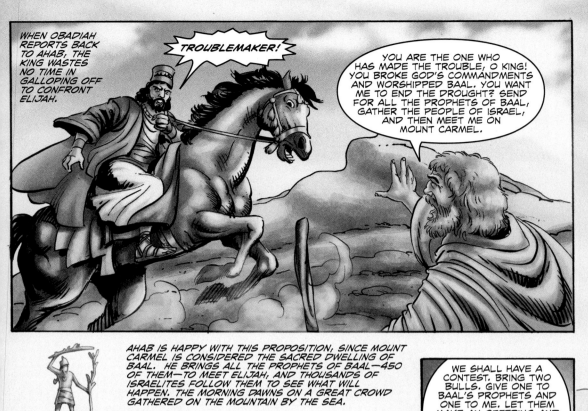

WHEN OBADIAH REPORTS BACK TO AHAB, THE KING WASTES NO TIME IN GALLOPING OFF TO CONFRONT ELIJAH.

TROUBLEMAKER!

YOU ARE THE ONE WHO HAS MADE THE TROUBLE, O KING! YOU BROKE GOD'S COMMANDMENTS AND WORSHIPPED BAAL. YOU WANT ME TO END THE DROUGHT? SEND FOR ALL THE PROPHETS OF BAAL, GATHER THE PEOPLE OF ISRAEL, AND THEN MEET ME ON MOUNT CARMEL.

AHAB IS HAPPY WITH THIS PROPOSITION, SINCE MOUNT CARMEL IS CONSIDERED THE SACRED DWELLING OF BAAL. HE BRINGS ALL THE PROPHETS OF BAAL—450 OF THEM—TO MEET ELIJAH; AND THOUSANDS OF ISRAELITES FOLLOW THEM TO SEE WHAT WILL HAPPEN. THE MORNING DAWNS ON A GREAT CROWD GATHERED ON THE MOUNTAIN BY THE SEA.

WE SHALL HAVE A CONTEST. BRING TWO BULLS. GIVE ONE TO BAAL'S PROPHETS AND ONE TO ME. LET THEM MAKE AN OFFERING AND CALL ON THE NAME OF THEIR GOD. I WILL CALL ON THE NAME OF THE LORD. THE GOD WHO ANSWERS—WITH FIRE—IS THE REAL GOD.

OH! AND I'LL LET THEM GO FIRST.

PEOPLE OF ISRAEL! HOW LONG WILL YOU LIMP BACK AND FORTH BETWEEN THE LORD AND BAAL? IF BAAL IS GOD, WORSHIP HIM. IF THE LORD IS GOD, WORSHIP HIM—AND HIM ONLY. TODAY, YOU MUST CHOOSE!

THE CROWD REACTS WITH AWE AT THIS TEST, KNOWING THAT IF ELIJAH LOSES, AHAB WILL CONDEMN HIM TO DEATH.

403

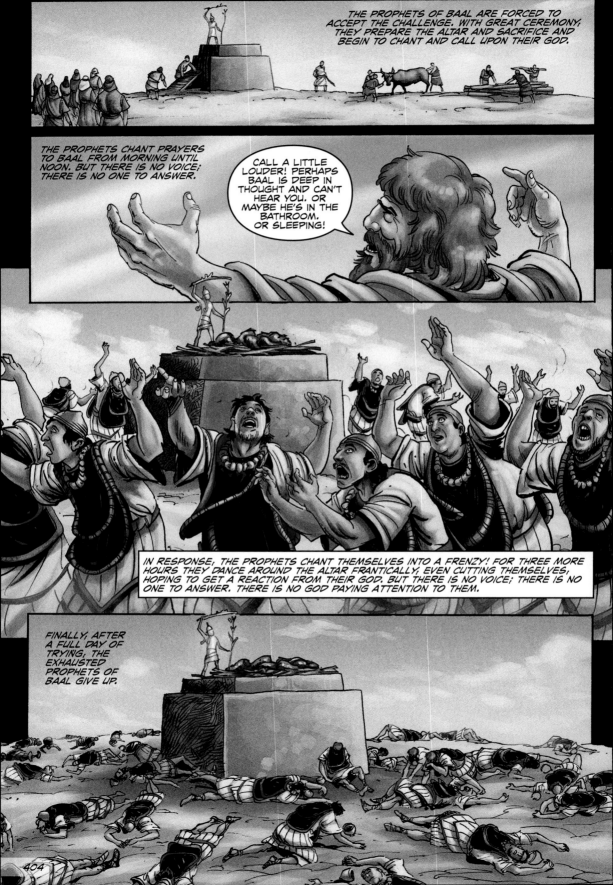

THE PROPHETS OF BAAL ARE FORCED TO ACCEPT THE CHALLENGE. WITH GREAT CEREMONY, THEY PREPARE THE ALTAR AND SACRIFICE AND BEGIN TO CHANT AND CALL UPON THEIR GOD.

THE PROPHETS CHANT PRAYERS TO BAAL FROM MORNING UNTIL NOON. BUT THERE IS NO VOICE; THERE IS NO ONE TO ANSWER.

CALL A LITTLE LOUDER! PERHAPS BAAL IS DEEP IN THOUGHT AND CAN'T HEAR YOU. OR MAYBE HE'S IN THE BATHROOM. OR SLEEPING!

IN RESPONSE, THE PROPHETS CHANT THEMSELVES INTO A FRENZY! FOR THREE MORE HOURS THEY DANCE AROUND THE ALTAR FRANTICALLY, EVEN CUTTING THEMSELVES, HOPING TO GET A REACTION FROM THEIR GOD. BUT THERE IS NO VOICE; THERE IS NO ONE TO ANSWER. THERE IS NO GOD PAYING ATTENTION TO THEM.

FINALLY, AFTER A FULL DAY OF TRYING, THE EXHAUSTED PROPHETS OF BAAL GIVE UP.

404

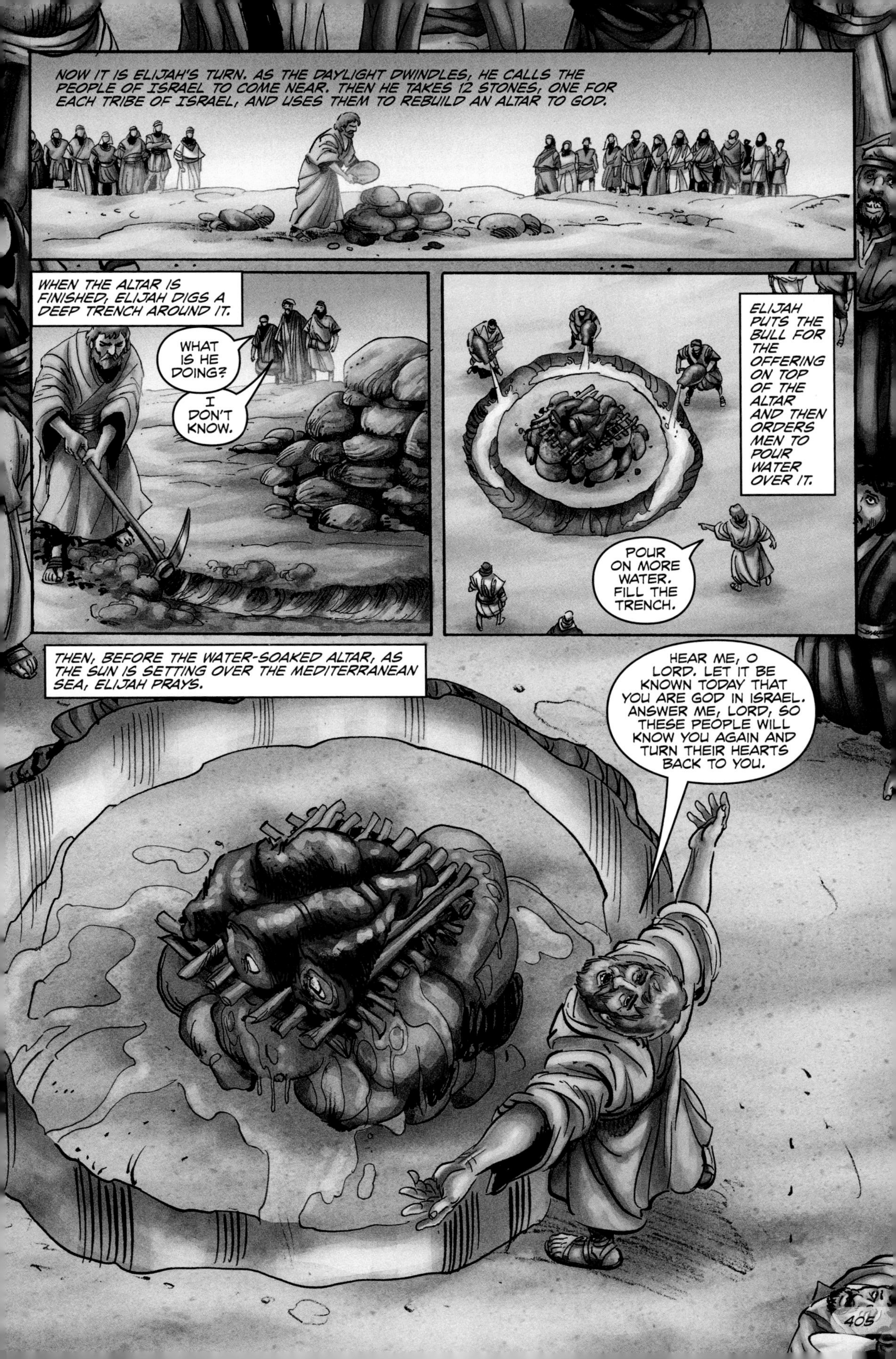

NOW IT IS ELIJAH'S TURN. AS THE DAYLIGHT DWINDLES, HE CALLS THE PEOPLE OF ISRAEL TO COME NEAR. THEN HE TAKES 12 STONES, ONE FOR EACH TRIBE OF ISRAEL, AND USES THEM TO REBUILD AN ALTAR TO GOD.
WHEN THE ALTAR IS FINISHED, ELIJAH DIGS A DEEP TRENCH AROUND IT.
WHAT IS HE DOING?
I DON'T KNOW.
ELIJAH PUTS THE BULL FOR THE OFFERING ON TOP OF THE ALTAR AND THEN ORDERS MEN TO POUR WATER OVER IT.
POUR ON MORE WATER. FILL THE TRENCH.
THEN, BEFORE THE WATER-SOAKED ALTAR, AS THE SUN IS SETTING OVER THE MEDITERRANEAN SEA, ELIJAH PRAYS.
HEAR ME, O LORD. LET IT BE KNOWN TODAY THAT YOU ARE GOD IN ISRAEL. ANSWER ME, LORD, SO THESE PEOPLE WILL KNOW YOU AGAIN AND TURN THEIR HEARTS BACK TO YOU.

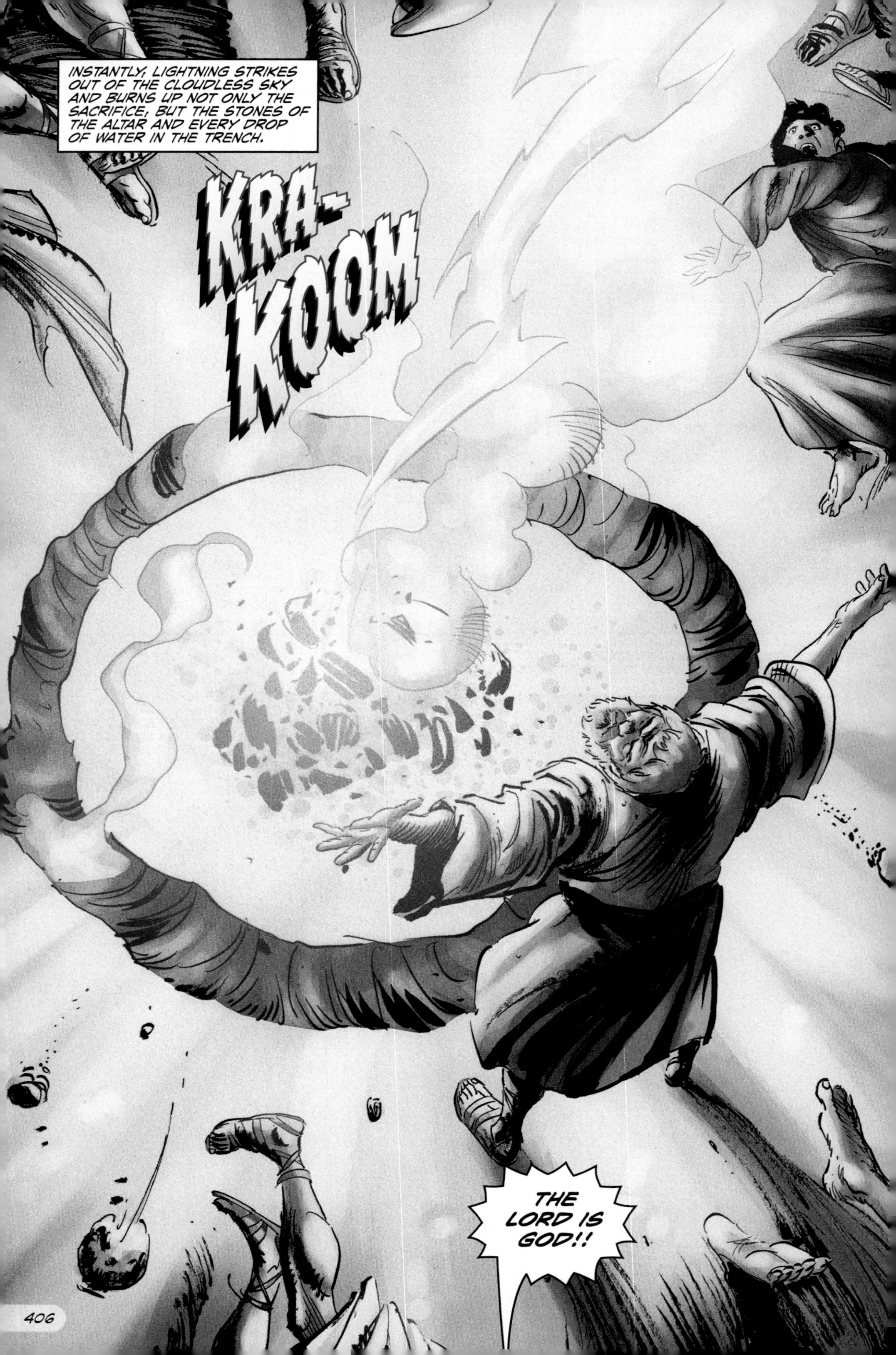
INSTANTLY, LIGHTNING STRIKES OUT OF THE CLOUDLESS SKY AND BURNS UP NOT ONLY THE SACRIFICE, BUT THE STONES OF THE ALTAR AND EVERY DROP OF WATER IN THE TRENCH.
KRA-KOOM
THE LORD IS GOD!!

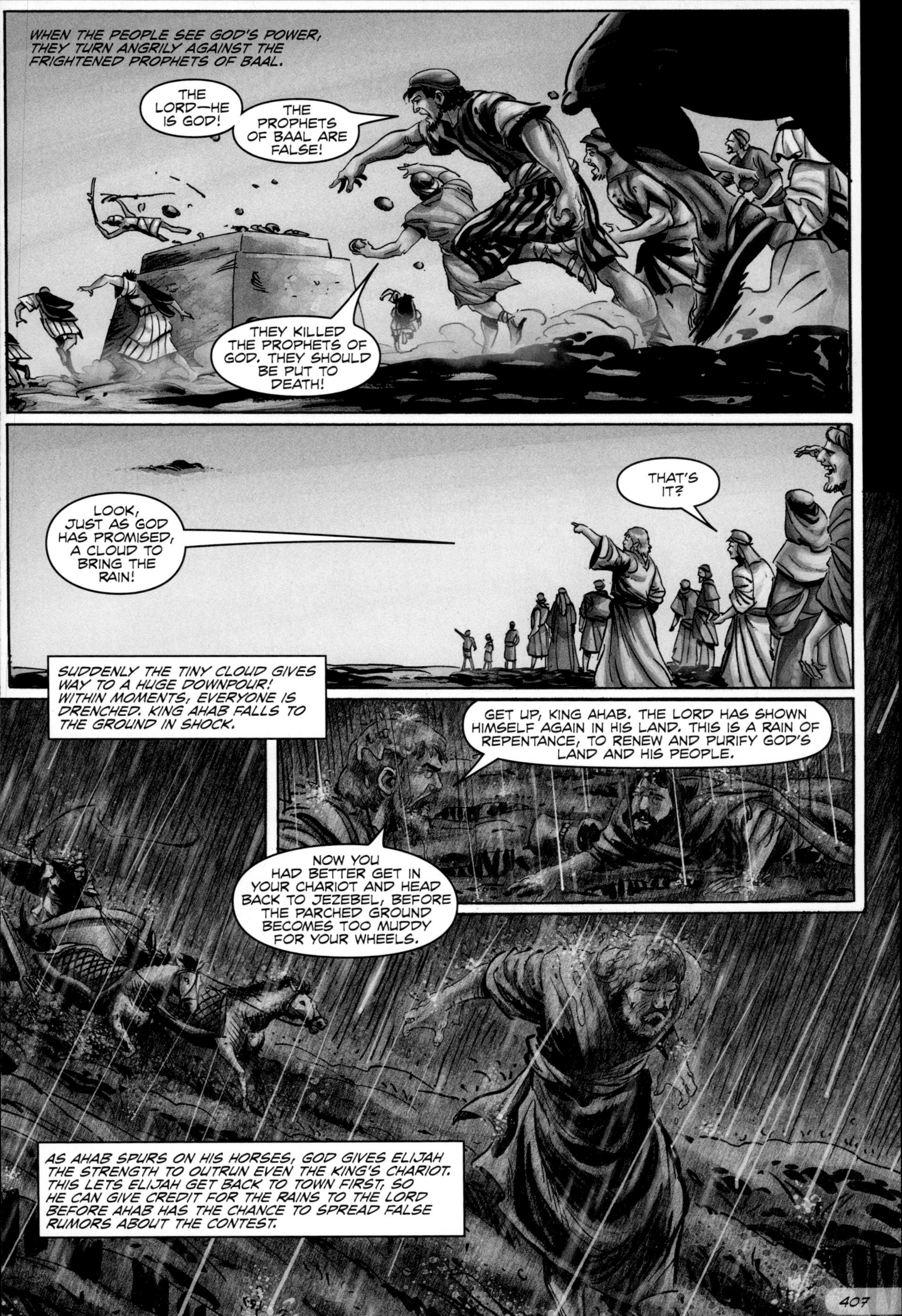

WHEN THE PEOPLE SEE GOD'S POWER, THEY TURN ANGRILY AGAINST THE FRIGHTENED PROPHETS OF BAAL.
THE LORD—HE IS GOD!
THE PROPHETS OF BAAL ARE FALSE!
THEY KILLED THE PROPHETS OF GOD. THEY SHOULD BE PUT TO DEATH!
LOOK, JUST AS GOD HAS PROMISED, A CLOUD TO BRING THE RAIN!
THAT'S IT?
SUDDENLY THE TINY CLOUD GIVES WAY TO A HUGE DOWNPOUR! WITHIN MOMENTS, EVERYONE IS DRENCHED. KING AHAB FALLS TO THE GROUND IN SHOCK.
GET UP, KING AHAB. THE LORD HAS SHOWN HIMSELF AGAIN IN HIS LAND. THIS IS A RAIN OF REPENTANCE, TO RENEW AND PURIFY GOD'S LAND AND HIS PEOPLE.
NOW YOU HAD BETTER GET IN YOUR CHARIOT AND HEAD BACK TO JEZEBEL, BEFORE THE PARCHED GROUND BECOMES TOO MUDDY FOR YOUR WHEELS.
AS AHAB SPURS ON HIS HORSES, GOD GIVES ELIJAH THE STRENGTH TO OUTRUN EVEN THE KING'S CHARIOT. THIS LETS ELIJAH GET BACK TO TOWN FIRST, SO HE CAN GIVE CREDIT FOR THE RAINS TO THE LORD BEFORE AHAB HAS THE CHANCE TO SPREAD FALSE RUMORS ABOUT THE CONTEST.

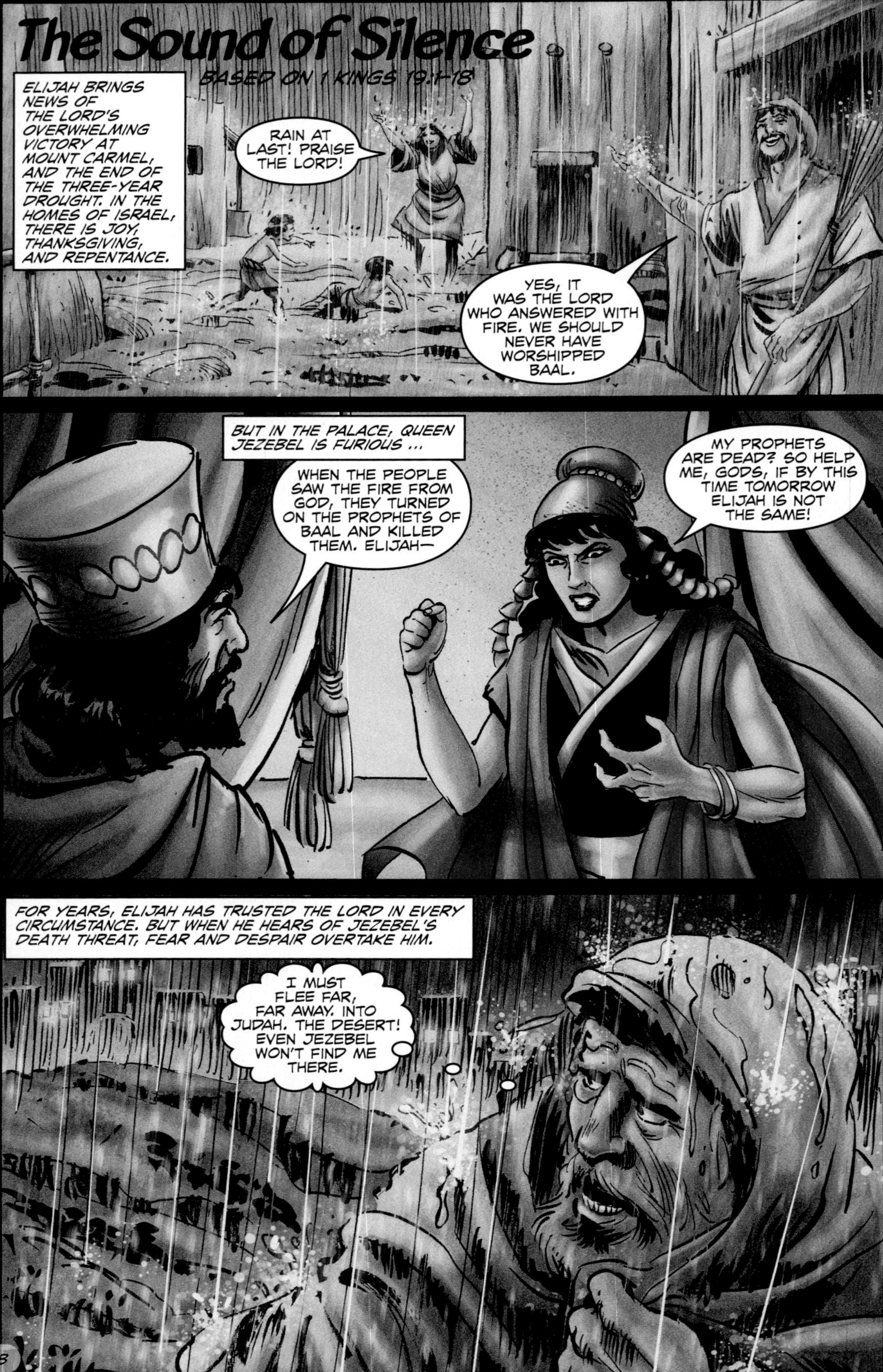
The Sound of Silence
BASED ON 1 KINGS 19:1-18
ELIJAH BRINGS NEWS OF THE LORD'S OVERWHELMING VICTORY AT MOUNT CARMEL, AND THE END OF THE THREE-YEAR DROUGHT. IN THE HOMES OF ISRAEL, THERE IS JOY, THANKSGIVING, AND REPENTANCE.
RAIN AT LAST! PRAISE THE LORD!
YES, IT WAS THE LORD WHO ANSWERED WITH FIRE. WE SHOULD NEVER HAVE WORSHIPPED BAAL.
BUT IN THE PALACE, QUEEN JEZEBEL IS FURIOUS ...
WHEN THE PEOPLE SAW THE FIRE FROM GOD, THEY TURNED ON THE PROPHETS OF BAAL AND KILLED THEM. ELIJAH—
MY PROPHETS ARE DEAD? SO HELP ME, GODS, IF BY THIS TIME TOMORROW ELIJAH IS NOT THE SAME!
FOR YEARS, ELIJAH HAS TRUSTED THE LORD IN EVERY CIRCUMSTANCE. BUT WHEN HE HEARS OF JEZEBEL'S DEATH THREAT, FEAR AND DESPAIR OVERTAKE HIM.
I MUST FLEE FAR, FAR AWAY. INTO JUDAH. THE DESERT! EVEN JEZEBEL WON'T FIND ME THERE.

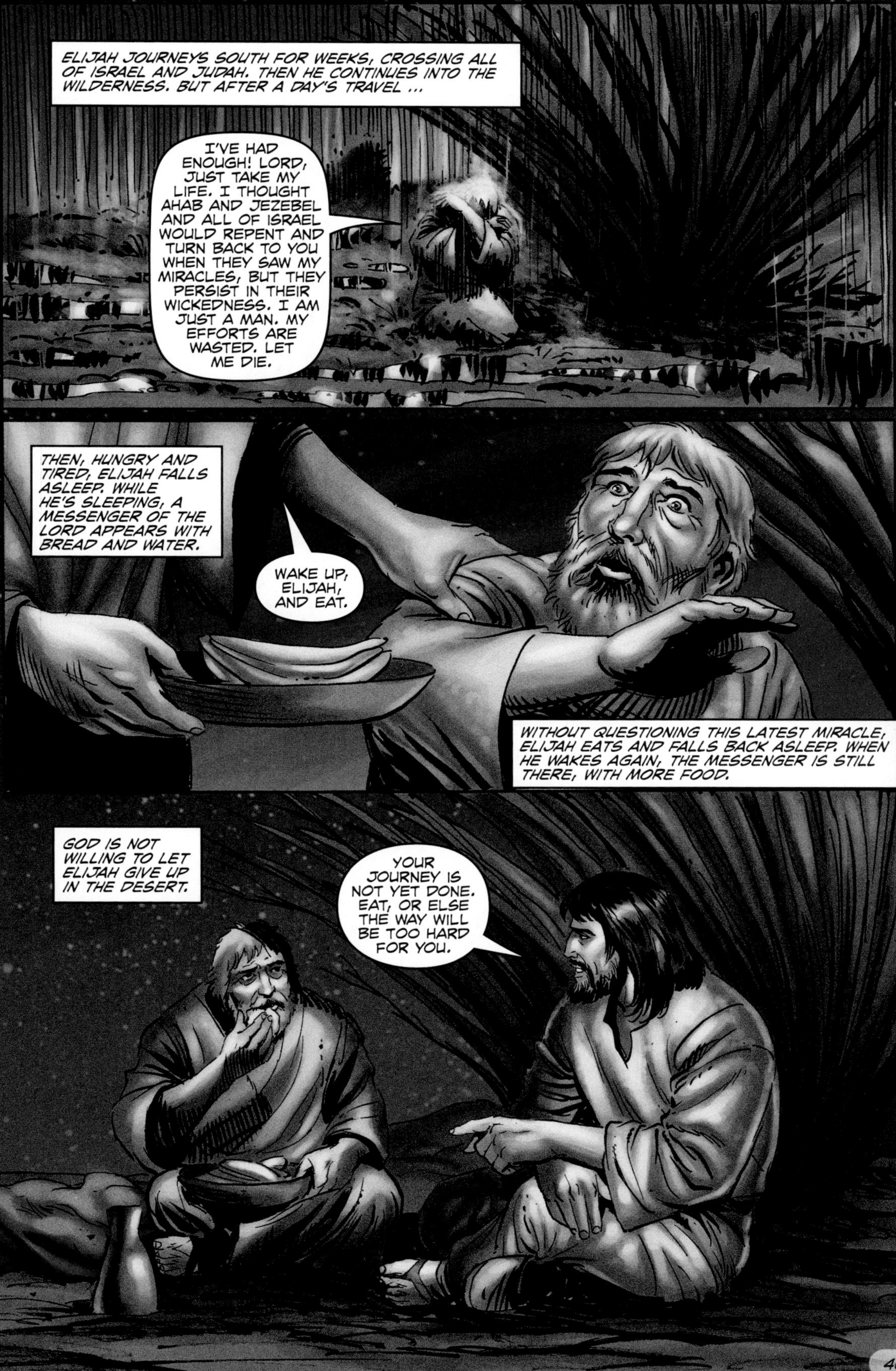
ELIJAH JOURNEYS SOUTH FOR WEEKS, CROSSING ALL OF ISRAEL AND JUDAH. THEN HE CONTINUES INTO THE WILDERNESS. BUT AFTER A DAY'S TRAVEL ...
I'VE HAD ENOUGH! LORD, JUST TAKE MY LIFE. I THOUGHT AHAB AND JEZEBEL AND ALL OF ISRAEL WOULD REPENT AND TURN BACK TO YOU WHEN THEY SAW MY MIRACLES, BUT THEY PERSIST IN THEIR WICKEDNESS. I AM JUST A MAN. MY EFFORTS ARE WASTED. LET ME DIE.
THEN, HUNGRY AND TIRED, ELIJAH FALLS ASLEEP. WHILE HE'S SLEEPING, A MESSENGER OF THE LORD APPEARS WITH BREAD AND WATER.
WAKE UP, ELIJAH, AND EAT.
WITHOUT QUESTIONING THIS LATEST MIRACLE, ELIJAH EATS AND FALLS BACK ASLEEP. WHEN HE WAKES AGAIN, THE MESSENGER IS STILL THERE, WITH MORE FOOD.
GOD IS NOT WILLING TO LET ELIJAH GIVE UP IN THE DESERT.
YOUR JOURNEY IS NOT YET DONE. EAT, OR ELSE THE WAY WILL BE TOO HARD FOR YOU.

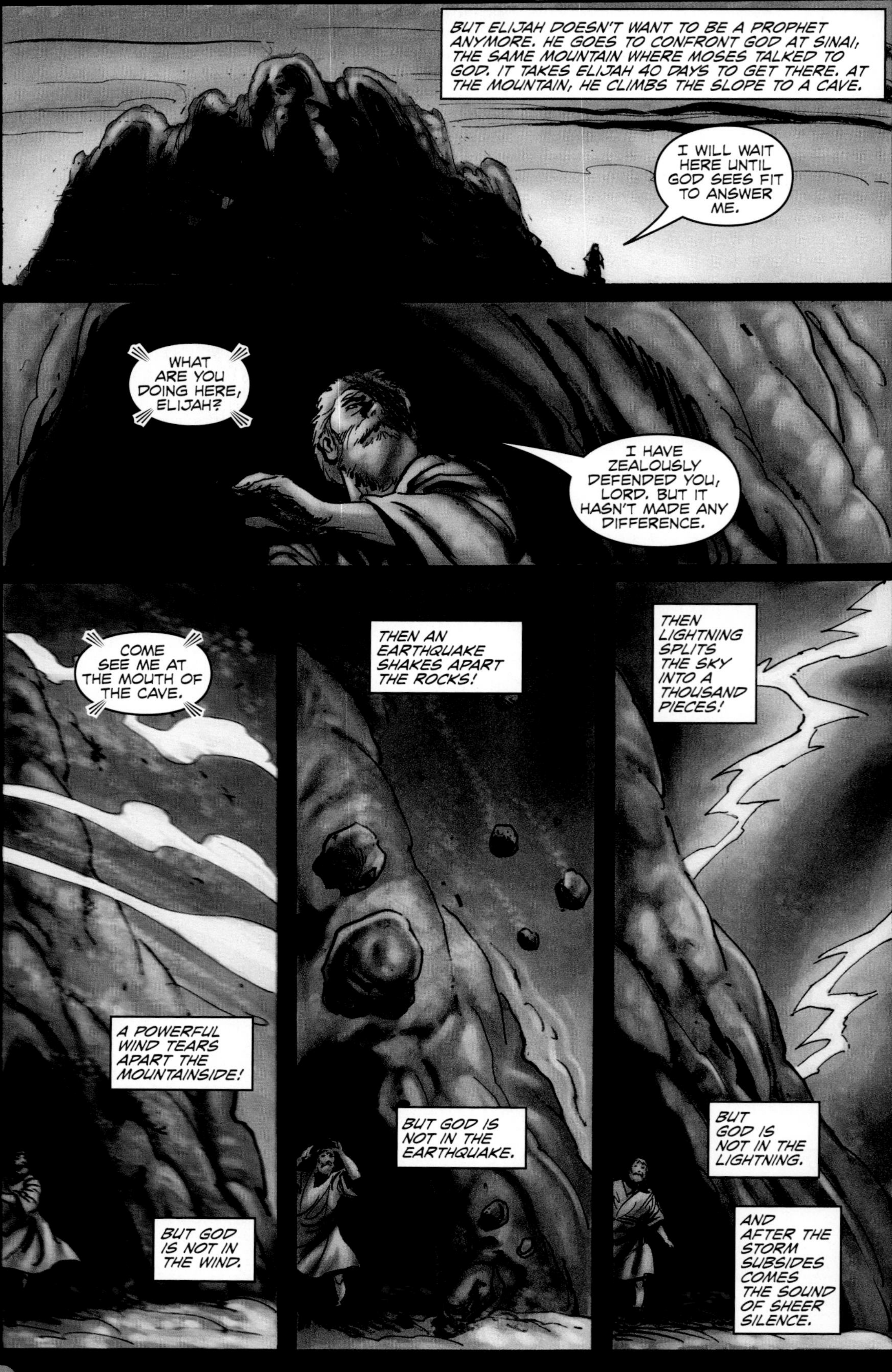
BUT ELIJAH DOESN'T WANT TO BE A PROPHET ANYMORE. HE GOES TO CONFRONT GOD AT SINAI, THE SAME MOUNTAIN WHERE MOSES TALKED TO GOD. IT TAKES ELIJAH 40 DAYS TO GET THERE. AT THE MOUNTAIN, HE CLIMBS THE SLOPE TO A CAVE.
I WILL WAIT HERE UNTIL GOD SEES FIT TO ANSWER ME.
WHAT ARE YOU DOING HERE, ELIJAH?
I HAVE ZEALOUSLY DEFENDED YOU, LORD. BUT IT HASN'T MADE ANY DIFFERENCE.
COME SEE ME AT THE MOUTH OF THE CAVE.
A POWERFUL WIND TEARS APART THE MOUNTAINSIDE!
BUT GOD IS NOT IN THE WIND.
THEN AN EARTHQUAKE SHAKES APART THE ROCKS!
BUT GOD IS NOT IN THE EARTHQUAKE.
THEN LIGHTNING SPLITS THE SKY INTO A THOUSAND PIECES!
BUT GOD IS NOT IN THE LIGHTNING.
AND AFTER THE STORM SUBSIDES COMES THE SOUND OF SHEER SILENCE.

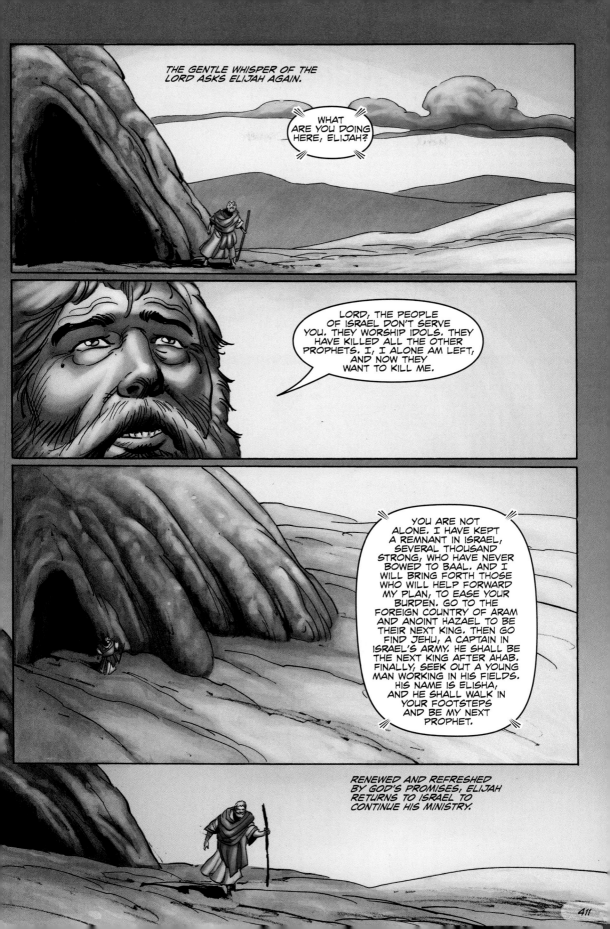

THE GENTLE WHISPER OF THE LORD ASKS ELIJAH AGAIN.

WHAT ARE YOU DOING HERE, ELIJAH?

LORD, THE PEOPLE OF ISRAEL DON'T SERVE YOU. THEY WORSHIP IDOLS. THEY HAVE KILLED ALL THE OTHER PROPHETS. I, I ALONE AM LEFT, AND NOW THEY WANT TO KILL ME.

YOU ARE NOT ALONE. I HAVE KEPT A REMNANT IN ISRAEL, SEVERAL THOUSAND STRONG, WHO HAVE NEVER BOWED TO BAAL. AND I WILL BRING FORTH THOSE WHO WILL HELP FORWARD MY PLAN, TO EASE YOUR BURDEN. GO TO THE FOREIGN COUNTRY OF ARAM AND ANOINT HAZAEL TO BE THEIR NEXT KING. THEN GO FIND JEHU, A CAPTAIN IN ISRAEL'S ARMY. HE SHALL BE THE NEXT KING AFTER AHAB. FINALLY, SEEK OUT A YOUNG MAN WORKING IN HIS FIELDS. HIS NAME IS ELISHA, AND HE SHALL WALK IN YOUR FOOTSTEPS AND BE MY NEXT PROPHET.

RENEWED AND REFRESHED BY GOD'S PROMISES, ELIJAH RETURNS TO ISRAEL TO CONTINUE HIS MINISTRY.

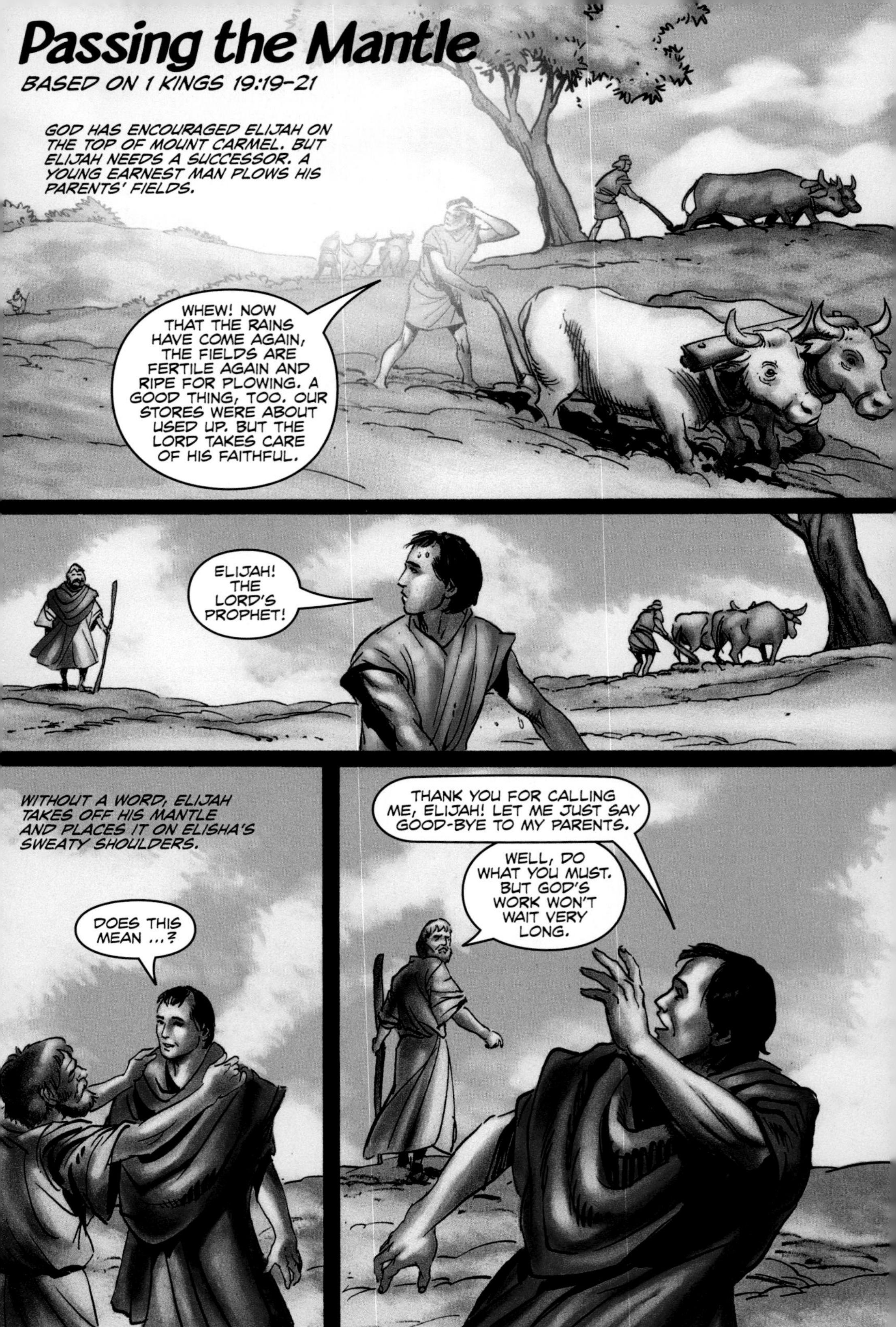
Passing the Mantle
BASED ON 1 KINGS 19:19-21
GOD HAS ENCOURAGED ELIJAH ON THE TOP OF MOUNT CARMEL. BUT ELIJAH NEEDS A SUCCESSOR. A YOUNG EARNEST MAN PLOWS HIS PARENTS' FIELDS.
WHEW! NOW THAT THE RAINS HAVE COME AGAIN, THE FIELDS ARE FERTILE AGAIN AND RIPE FOR PLOWING. A GOOD THING, TOO. OUR STORES WERE ABOUT USED UP. BUT THE LORD TAKES CARE OF HIS FAITHFUL.
ELIJAH! THE LORD'S PROPHET!
WITHOUT A WORD, ELIJAH TAKES OFF HIS MANTLE AND PLACES IT ON ELISHA'S SWEATY SHOULDERS.
DOES THIS MEAN ...?
THANK YOU FOR CALLING ME, ELIJAH! LET ME JUST SAY GOOD-BYE TO MY PARENTS.
WELL, DO WHAT YOU MUST. BUT GOD'S WORK WON'T WAIT VERY LONG.

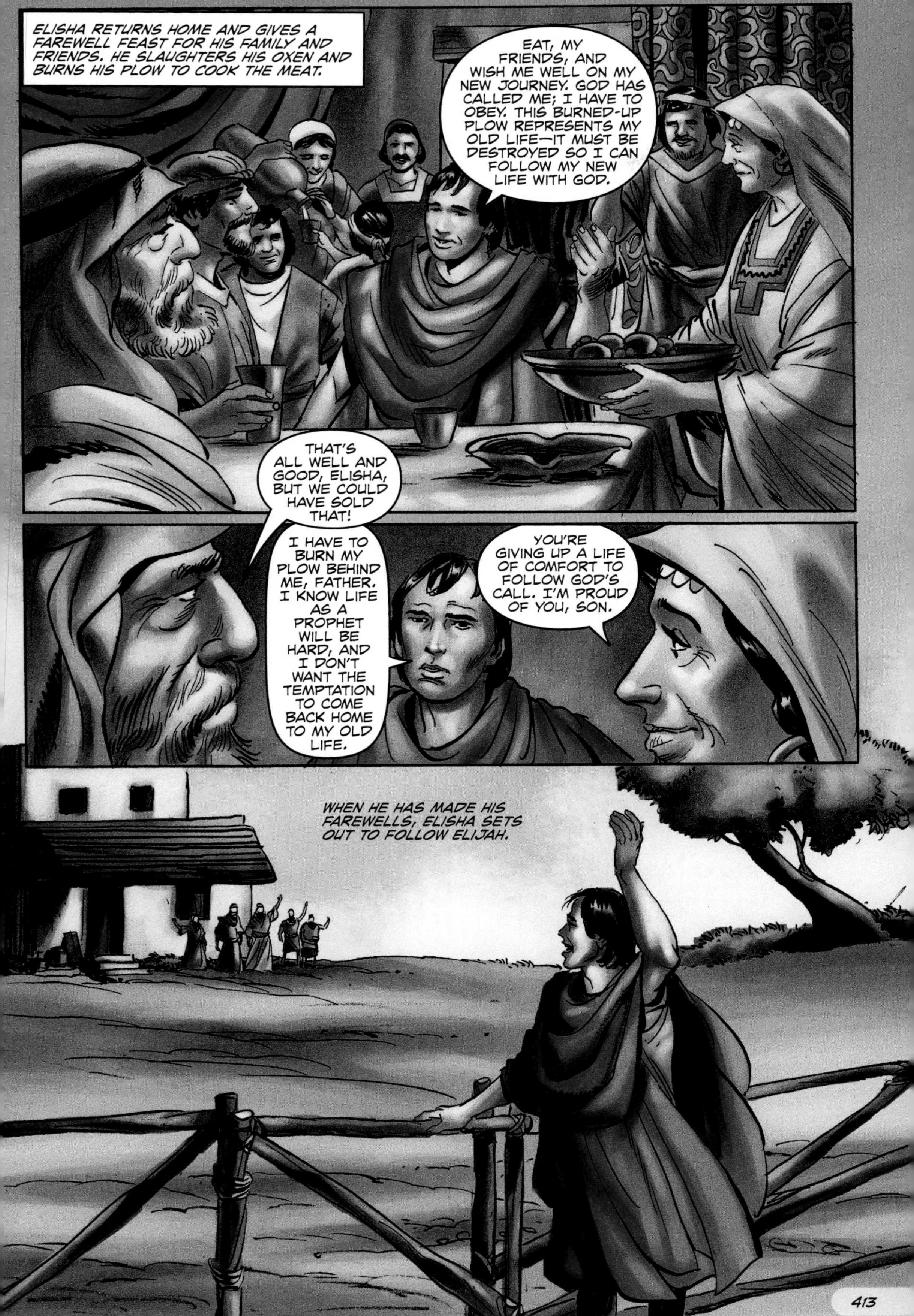
ELISHA RETURNS HOME AND GIVES A FAREWELL FEAST FOR HIS FAMILY AND FRIENDS. HE SLAUGHTERS HIS OXEN AND BURNS HIS PLOW TO COOK THE MEAT.
EAT, MY FRIENDS, AND WISH ME WELL ON MY NEW JOURNEY. GOD HAS CALLED ME; I HAVE TO OBEY. THIS BURNED-UP PLOW REPRESENTS MY OLD LIFE—IT MUST BE DESTROYED SO I CAN FOLLOW MY NEW LIFE WITH GOD.
THAT'S ALL WELL AND GOOD, ELISHA, BUT WE COULD HAVE SOLD THAT!
I HAVE TO BURN MY PLOW BEHIND ME, FATHER. I KNOW LIFE AS A PROPHET WILL BE HARD, AND I DON'T WANT THE TEMPTATION TO COME BACK HOME TO MY OLD LIFE.
YOU'RE GIVING UP A LIFE OF COMFORT TO FOLLOW GOD'S CALL. I'M PROUD OF YOU, SON.
WHEN HE HAS MADE HIS FAREWELLS, ELISHA SETS OUT TO FOLLOW ELIJAH.

The Grapes of Envy
BASED ON 1 KINGS 21

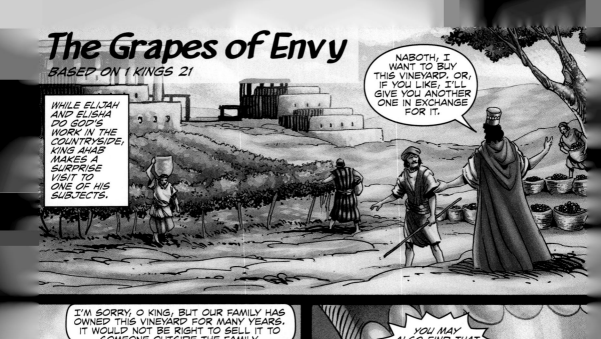

WHILE ELIJAH AND ELISHA DO GOD'S WORK IN THE COUNTRYSIDE, KING AHAB MAKES A SURPRISE VISIT TO ONE OF HIS SUBJECTS.

NABOTH, I WANT TO BUY THIS VINEYARD. OR, IF YOU LIKE, I'LL GIVE YOU ANOTHER ONE IN EXCHANGE FOR IT.

I'M SORRY, O KING, BUT OUR FAMILY HAS OWNED THIS VINEYARD FOR MANY YEARS. IT WOULD NOT BE RIGHT TO SELL IT TO SOMEONE OUTSIDE THE FAMILY.

YOU MAY ALSO FIND THAT IT IS NOT RIGHT TO DISPLEASE YOUR KING!

LIKE A SPOILED CHILD WHO CAN'T HAVE HIS OWN WAY, AHAB RETURNS TO THE PALACE.

WHAT'S THE MATTER? ARE YOU ILL?

NO. I WANT NABOTH'S VINEYARD, BUT HE WON'T SELL IT TO ME.

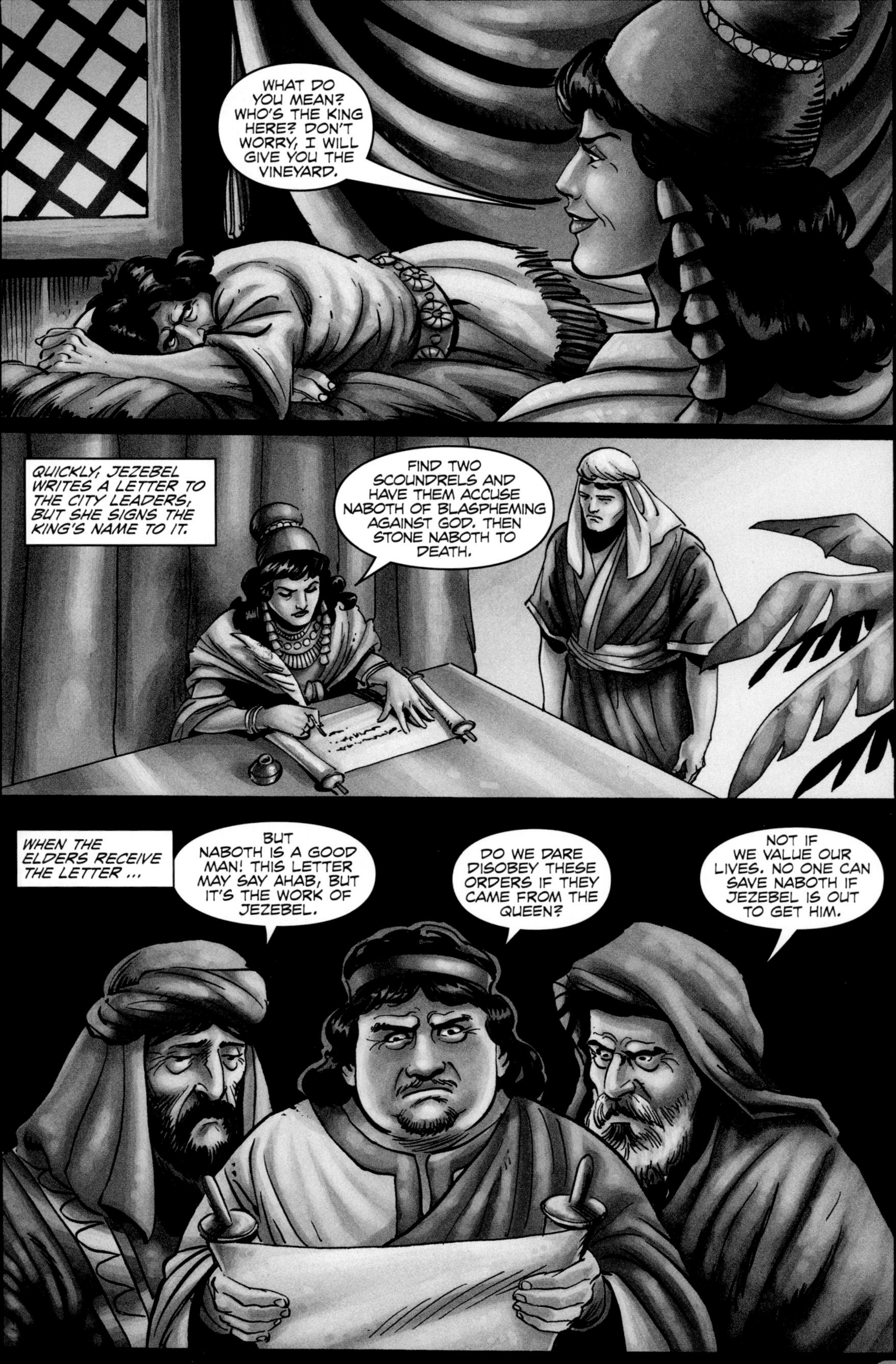
WHAT DO YOU MEAN? WHO'S THE KING HERE? DON'T WORRY, I WILL GIVE YOU THE VINEYARD.
QUICKLY, JEZEBEL WRITES A LETTER TO THE CITY LEADERS, BUT SHE SIGNS THE KING'S NAME TO IT.
FIND TWO SCOUNDRELS AND HAVE THEM ACCUSE NABOTH OF BLASPHEMING AGAINST GOD. THEN STONE NABOTH TO DEATH.
WHEN THE ELDERS RECEIVE THE LETTER ...
BUT NABOTH IS A GOOD MAN! THIS LETTER MAY SAY AHAB, BUT IT'S THE WORK OF JEZEBEL.
DO WE DARE DISOBEY THESE ORDERS IF THEY CAME FROM THE QUEEN?
NOT IF WE VALUE OUR LIVES. NO ONE CAN SAVE NABOTH IF JEZEBEL IS OUT TO GET HIM.

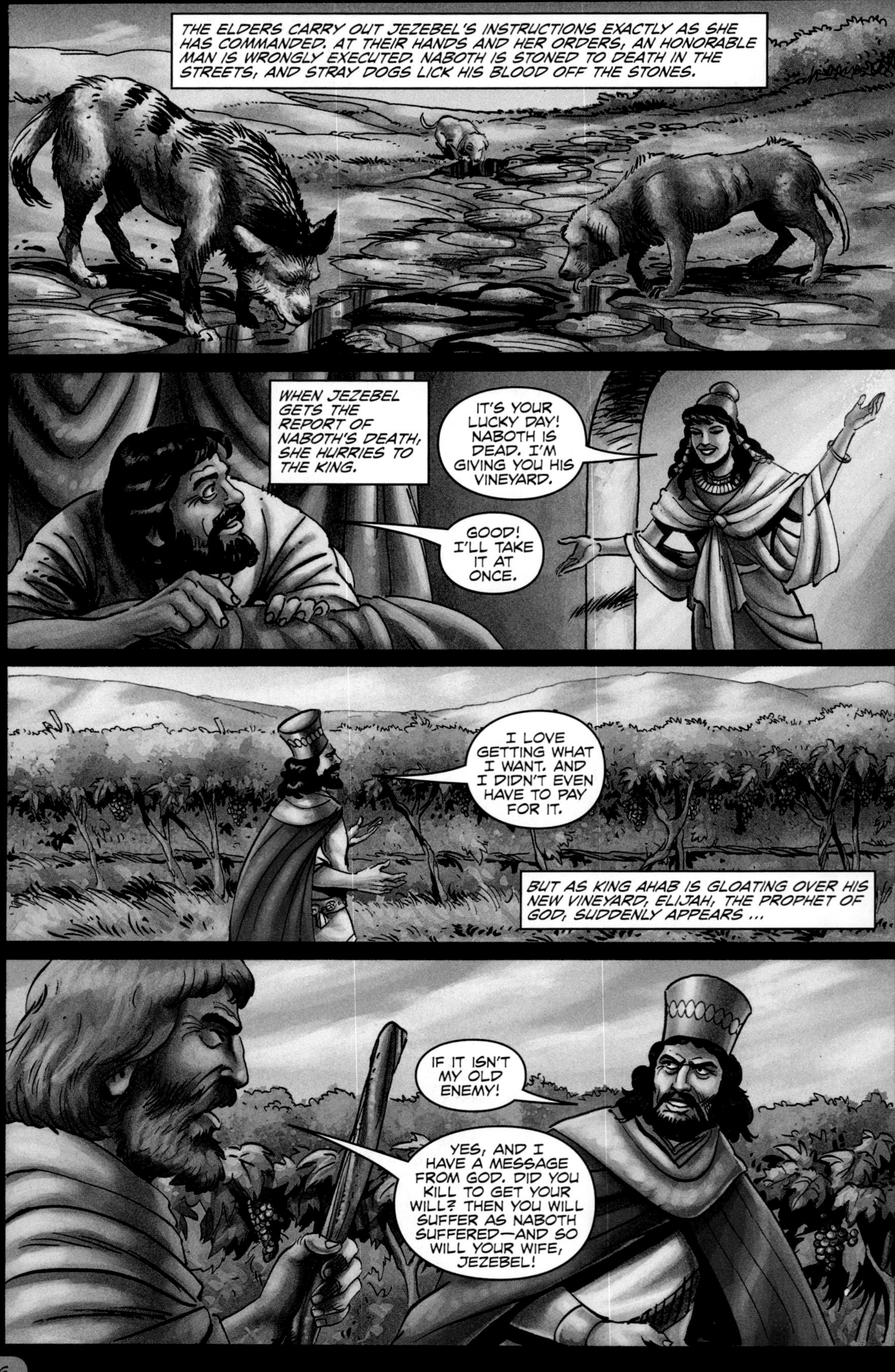
THE ELDERS CARRY OUT JEZEBEL'S INSTRUCTIONS EXACTLY AS SHE HAS COMMANDED. AT THEIR HANDS AND HER ORDERS, AN HONORABLE MAN IS WRONGLY EXECUTED. NABOTH IS STONED TO DEATH IN THE STREETS, AND STRAY DOGS LICK HIS BLOOD OFF THE STONES.
WHEN JEZEBEL GETS THE REPORT OF NABOTH'S DEATH, SHE HURRIES TO THE KING.
IT'S YOUR LUCKY DAY! NABOTH IS DEAD. I'M GIVING YOU HIS VINEYARD.
GOOD! I'LL TAKE IT AT ONCE.
I LOVE GETTING WHAT I WANT. AND I DIDN'T EVEN HAVE TO PAY FOR IT.
BUT AS KING AHAB IS GLOATING OVER HIS NEW VINEYARD, ELIJAH, THE PROPHET OF GOD, SUDDENLY APPEARS ...
IF IT ISN'T MY OLD ENEMY!
YES, AND I HAVE A MESSAGE FROM GOD. DID YOU KILL TO GET YOUR WILL? THEN YOU WILL SUFFER AS NABOTH SUFFERED—AND SO WILL YOUR WIFE, JEZEBEL!

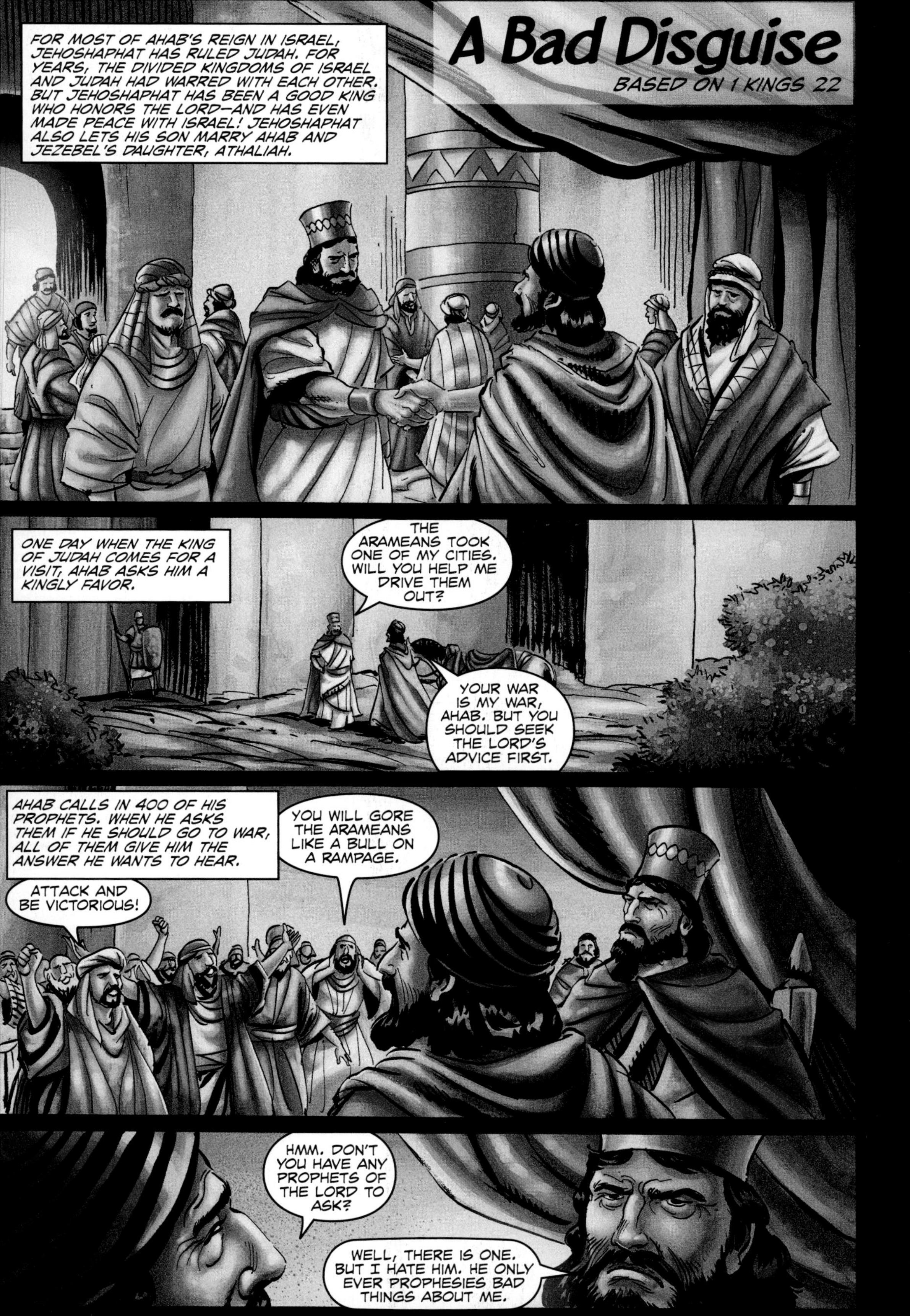
A Bad Disguise
BASED ON 1 KINGS 22
FOR MOST OF AHAB'S REIGN IN ISRAEL, JEHOSHAPHAT HAS RULED JUDAH. FOR YEARS, THE DIVIDED KINGDOMS OF ISRAEL AND JUDAH HAD WARRED WITH EACH OTHER. BUT JEHOSHAPHAT HAS BEEN A GOOD KING WHO HONORS THE LORD—AND HAS EVEN MADE PEACE WITH ISRAEL! JEHOSHAPHAT ALSO LETS HIS SON MARRY AHAB AND JEZEBEL'S DAUGHTER, ATHALIAH.
ONE DAY WHEN THE KING OF JUDAH COMES FOR A VISIT, AHAB ASKS HIM A KINGLY FAVOR.
THE ARAMEANS TOOK ONE OF MY CITIES. WILL YOU HELP ME DRIVE THEM OUT?
YOUR WAR IS MY WAR, AHAB. BUT YOU SHOULD SEEK THE LORD'S ADVICE FIRST.
AHAB CALLS IN 400 OF HIS PROPHETS. WHEN HE ASKS THEM IF HE SHOULD GO TO WAR, ALL OF THEM GIVE HIM THE ANSWER HE WANTS TO HEAR.
YOU WILL GORE THE ARAMEANS LIKE A BULL ON A RAMPAGE.
ATTACK AND BE VICTORIOUS!
HMM. DON'T YOU HAVE ANY PROPHETS OF THE LORD TO ASK?
WELL, THERE IS ONE. BUT I HATE HIM. HE ONLY EVER PROPHESIES BAD THINGS ABOUT ME.

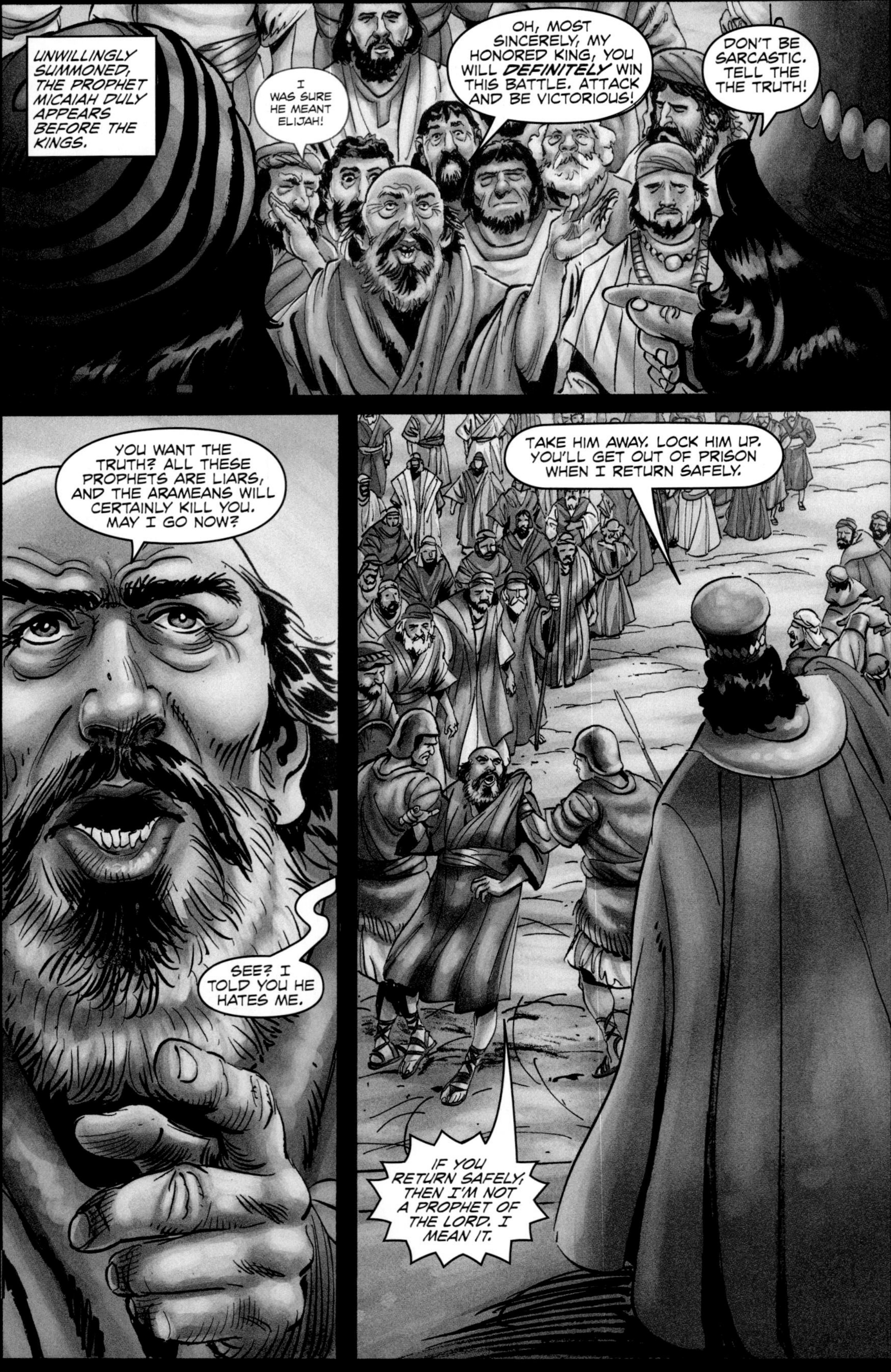
UNWILLINGLY SUMMONED, THE PROPHET MICAIAH DULY APPEARS BEFORE THE KINGS.
I WAS SURE HE MEANT ELIJAH!
OH, MOST SINCERELY, MY HONORED KING, YOU WILL *DEFINITELY* WIN THIS BATTLE. ATTACK AND BE VICTORIOUS!
DON'T BE SARCASTIC. TELL THE THE TRUTH!
YOU WANT THE TRUTH? ALL THESE PROPHETS ARE LIARS, AND THE ARAMEANS WILL CERTAINLY KILL YOU. MAY I GO NOW?
SEE? I TOLD YOU HE HATES ME.
TAKE HIM AWAY. LOCK HIM UP. YOU'LL GET OUT OF PRISON WHEN I RETURN SAFELY.
IF YOU RETURN SAFELY, THEN I'M NOT A PROPHET OF THE LORD. I MEAN IT.

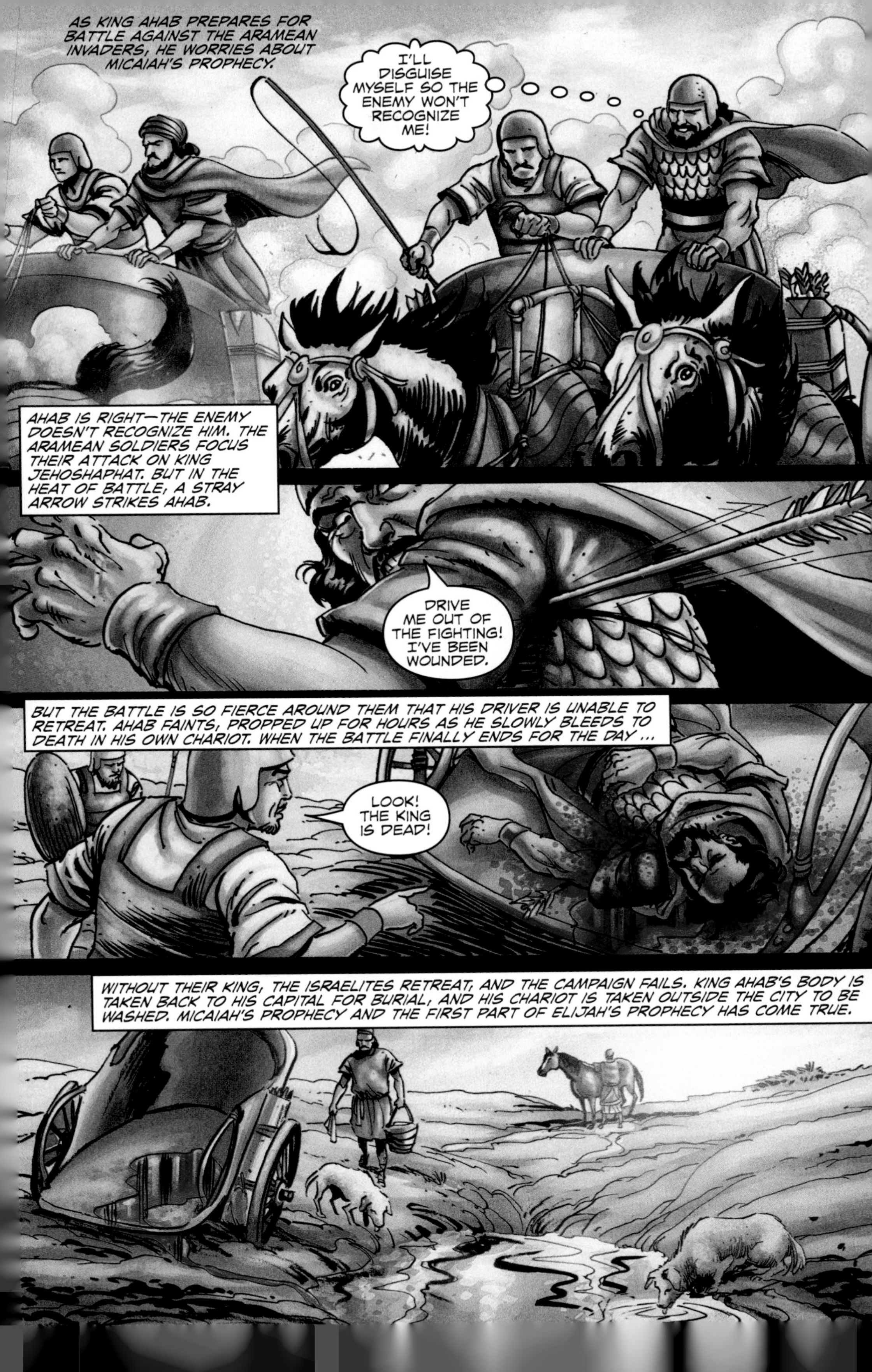
AS KING AHAB PREPARES FOR BATTLE AGAINST THE ARAMEAN INVADERS, HE WORRIES ABOUT MICAIAH'S PROPHECY.
I'LL DISGUISE MYSELF SO THE ENEMY WON'T RECOGNIZE ME!
AHAB IS RIGHT—THE ENEMY DOESN'T RECOGNIZE HIM. THE ARAMEAN SOLDIERS FOCUS THEIR ATTACK ON KING JEHOSHAPHAT. BUT IN THE HEAT OF BATTLE, A STRAY ARROW STRIKES AHAB.
DRIVE ME OUT OF THE FIGHTING! I'VE BEEN WOUNDED.
BUT THE BATTLE IS SO FIERCE AROUND THEM THAT HIS DRIVER IS UNABLE TO RETREAT. AHAB FAINTS, PROPPED UP FOR HOURS AS HE SLOWLY BLEEDS TO DEATH IN HIS OWN CHARIOT. WHEN THE BATTLE FINALLY ENDS FOR THE DAY ...
LOOK! THE KING IS DEAD!
WITHOUT THEIR KING, THE ISRAELITES RETREAT, AND THE CAMPAIGN FAILS. KING AHAB'S BODY IS TAKEN BACK TO HIS CAPITAL FOR BURIAL, AND HIS CHARIOT IS TAKEN OUTSIDE THE CITY TO BE WASHED. MICAIAH'S PROPHECY AND THE FIRST PART OF ELIJAH'S PROPHECY HAS COME TRUE.

Chariots of Fire BASED ON 2 KINGS 2:1-18

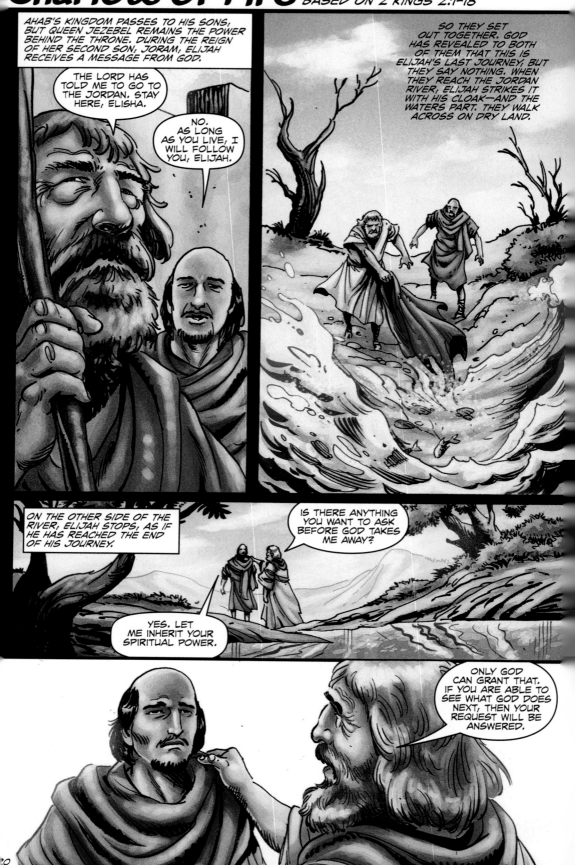

AHAB'S KINGDOM PASSES TO HIS SONS, BUT QUEEN JEZEBEL REMAINS THE POWER BEHIND THE THRONE. DURING THE REIGN OF HER SECOND SON, JORAM, ELIJAH RECEIVES A MESSAGE FROM GOD.

THE LORD HAS TOLD ME TO GO TO THE JORDAN. STAY HERE, ELISHA.

NO. AS LONG AS YOU LIVE, I WILL FOLLOW YOU, ELIJAH.

SO THEY SET OUT TOGETHER. GOD HAS REVEALED TO BOTH OF THEM THAT THIS IS ELIJAH'S LAST JOURNEY, BUT THEY SAY NOTHING. WHEN THEY REACH THE JORDAN RIVER, ELIJAH STRIKES IT WITH HIS CLOAK—AND THE WATERS PART. THEY WALK ACROSS ON DRY LAND.

ON THE OTHER SIDE OF THE RIVER, ELIJAH STOPS, AS IF HE HAS REACHED THE END OF HIS JOURNEY.

IS THERE ANYTHING YOU WANT TO ASK BEFORE GOD TAKES ME AWAY?

YES. LET ME INHERIT YOUR SPIRITUAL POWER.

ONLY GOD CAN GRANT THAT. IF YOU ARE ABLE TO SEE WHAT GOD DOES NEXT, THEN YOUR REQUEST WILL BE ANSWERED.

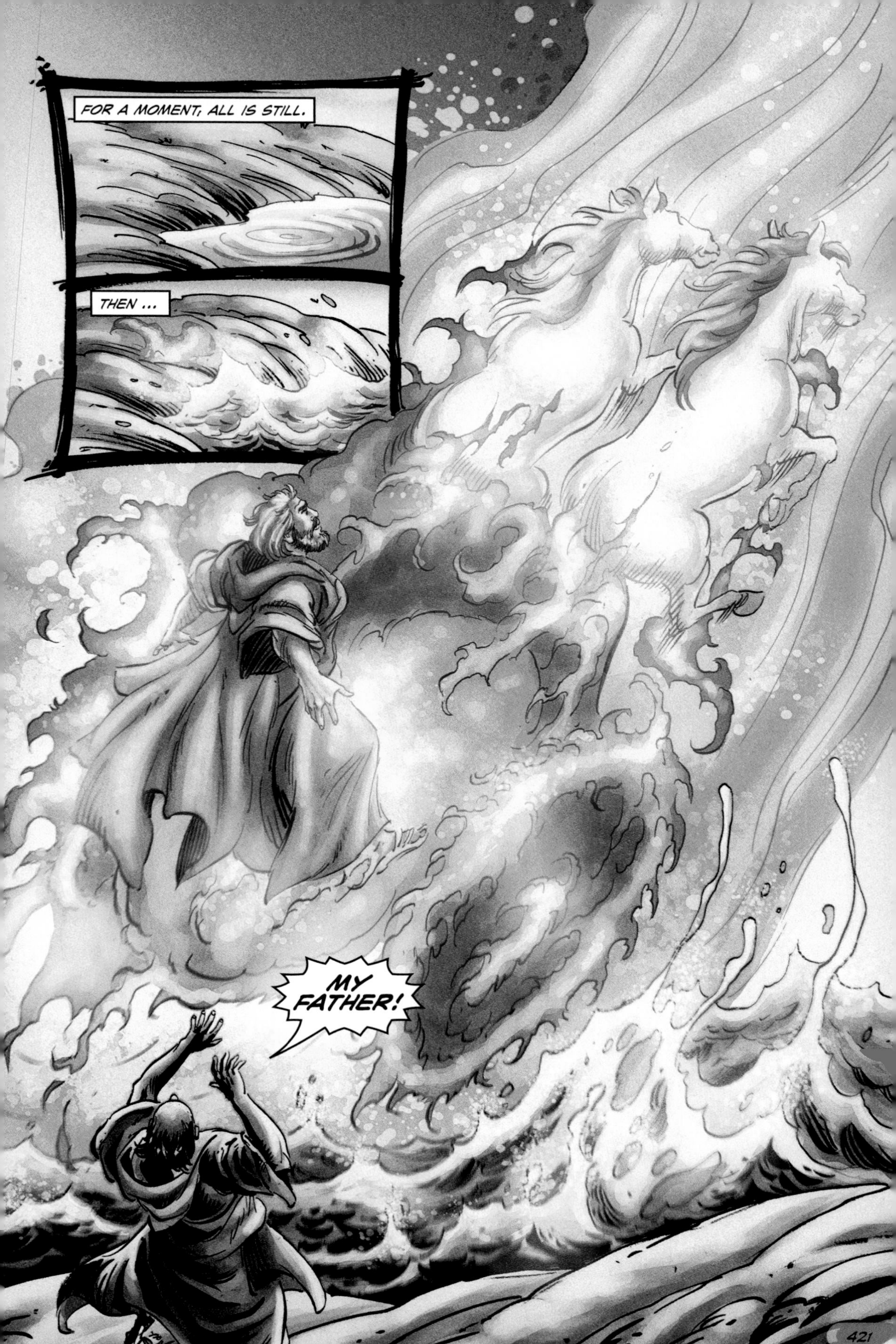
FOR A MOMENT, ALL IS STILL.
THEN ...
MY FATHER!

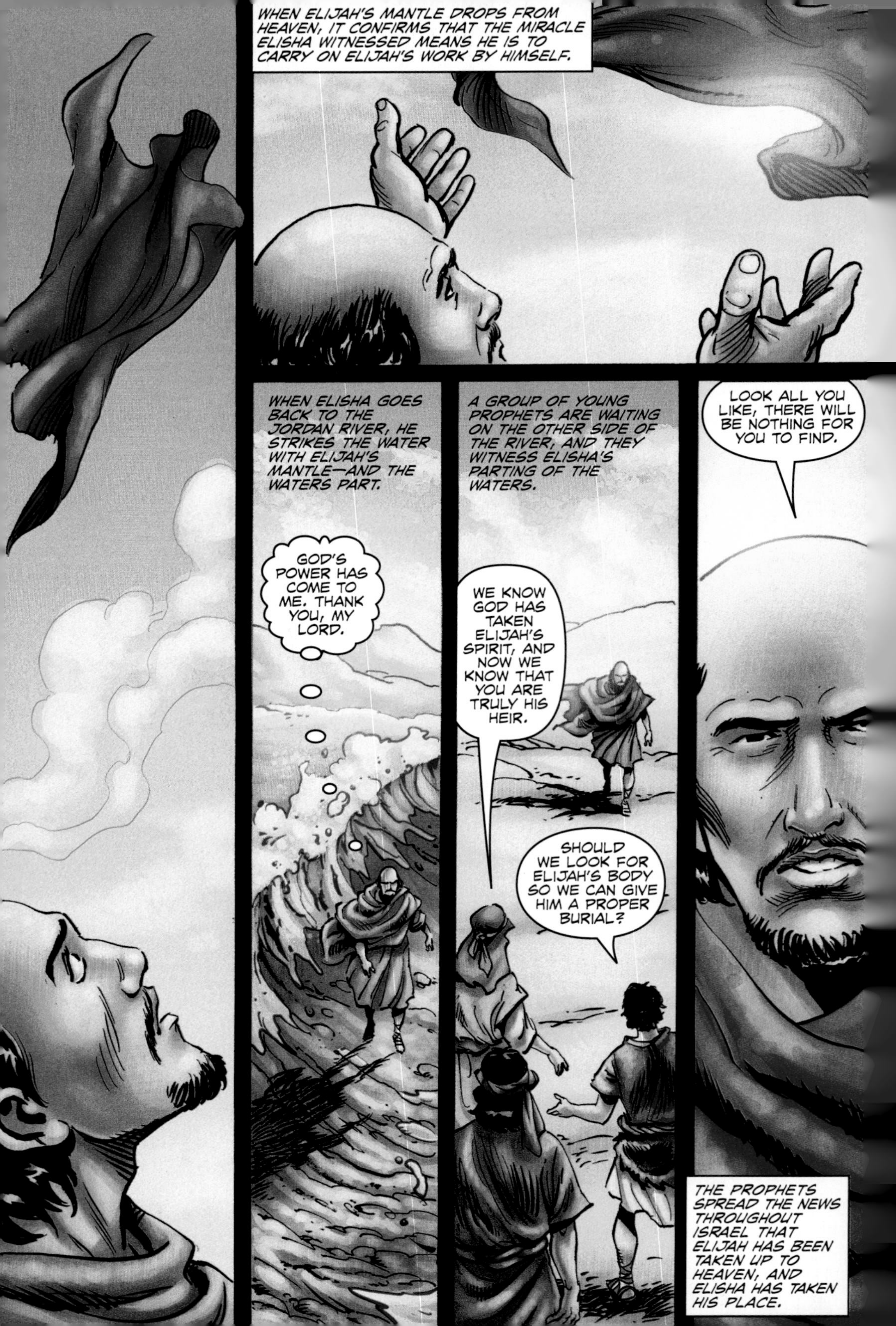
WHEN ELIJAH'S MANTLE DROPS FROM HEAVEN, IT CONFIRMS THAT THE MIRACLE ELISHA WITNESSED MEANS HE IS TO CARRY ON ELIJAH'S WORK BY HIMSELF.
WHEN ELISHA GOES BACK TO THE JORDAN RIVER, HE STRIKES THE WATER WITH ELIJAH'S MANTLE—AND THE WATERS PART.
GOD'S POWER HAS COME TO ME. THANK YOU, MY LORD.
A GROUP OF YOUNG PROPHETS ARE WAITING ON THE OTHER SIDE OF THE RIVER, AND THEY WITNESS ELISHA'S PARTING OF THE WATERS.
WE KNOW GOD HAS TAKEN ELIJAH'S SPIRIT, AND NOW WE KNOW THAT YOU ARE TRULY HIS HEIR.
SHOULD WE LOOK FOR ELIJAH'S BODY SO WE CAN GIVE HIM A PROPER BURIAL?
LOOK ALL YOU LIKE, THERE WILL BE NOTHING FOR YOU TO FIND.
THE PROPHETS SPREAD THE NEWS THROUGHOUT ISRAEL THAT ELIJAH HAS BEEN TAKEN UP TO HEAVEN, AND ELISHA HAS TAKEN HIS PLACE.

A Rash of Miracles

BASED ON 2 KINGS 2:19-24; 4; 6:1-7

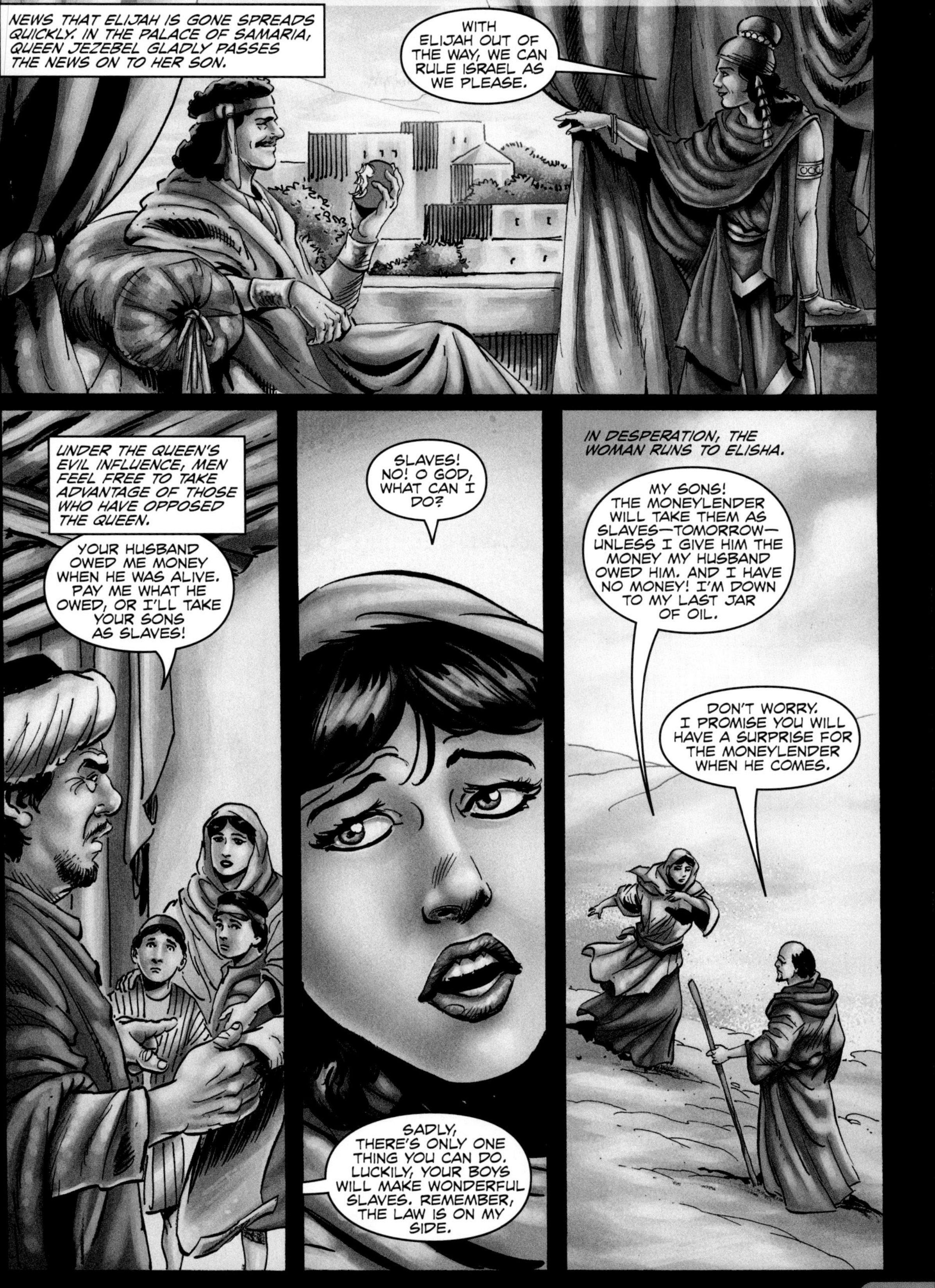
NEWS THAT ELIJAH IS GONE SPREADS QUICKLY. IN THE PALACE OF SAMARIA, QUEEN JEZEBEL GLADLY PASSES THE NEWS ON TO HER SON.
WITH ELIJAH OUT OF THE WAY, WE CAN RULE ISRAEL AS WE PLEASE.
UNDER THE QUEEN'S EVIL INFLUENCE, MEN FEEL FREE TO TAKE ADVANTAGE OF THOSE WHO HAVE OPPOSED THE QUEEN.
YOUR HUSBAND OWED ME MONEY WHEN HE WAS ALIVE. PAY ME WHAT HE OWED, OR I'LL TAKE YOUR SONS AS SLAVES!
SLAVES! NO! O GOD, WHAT CAN I DO?
SADLY, THERE'S ONLY ONE THING YOU CAN DO. LUCKILY, YOUR BOYS WILL MAKE WONDERFUL SLAVES. REMEMBER, THE LAW IS ON MY SIDE.
IN DESPERATION, THE WOMAN RUNS TO ELISHA.
MY SONS! THE MONEYLENDER WILL TAKE THEM AS SLAVES—TOMORROW—UNLESS I GIVE HIM THE MONEY MY HUSBAND OWED HIM. AND I HAVE NO MONEY! I'M DOWN TO MY LAST JAR OF OIL.
DON'T WORRY. I PROMISE YOU WILL HAVE A SURPRISE FOR THE MONEYLENDER WHEN HE COMES.

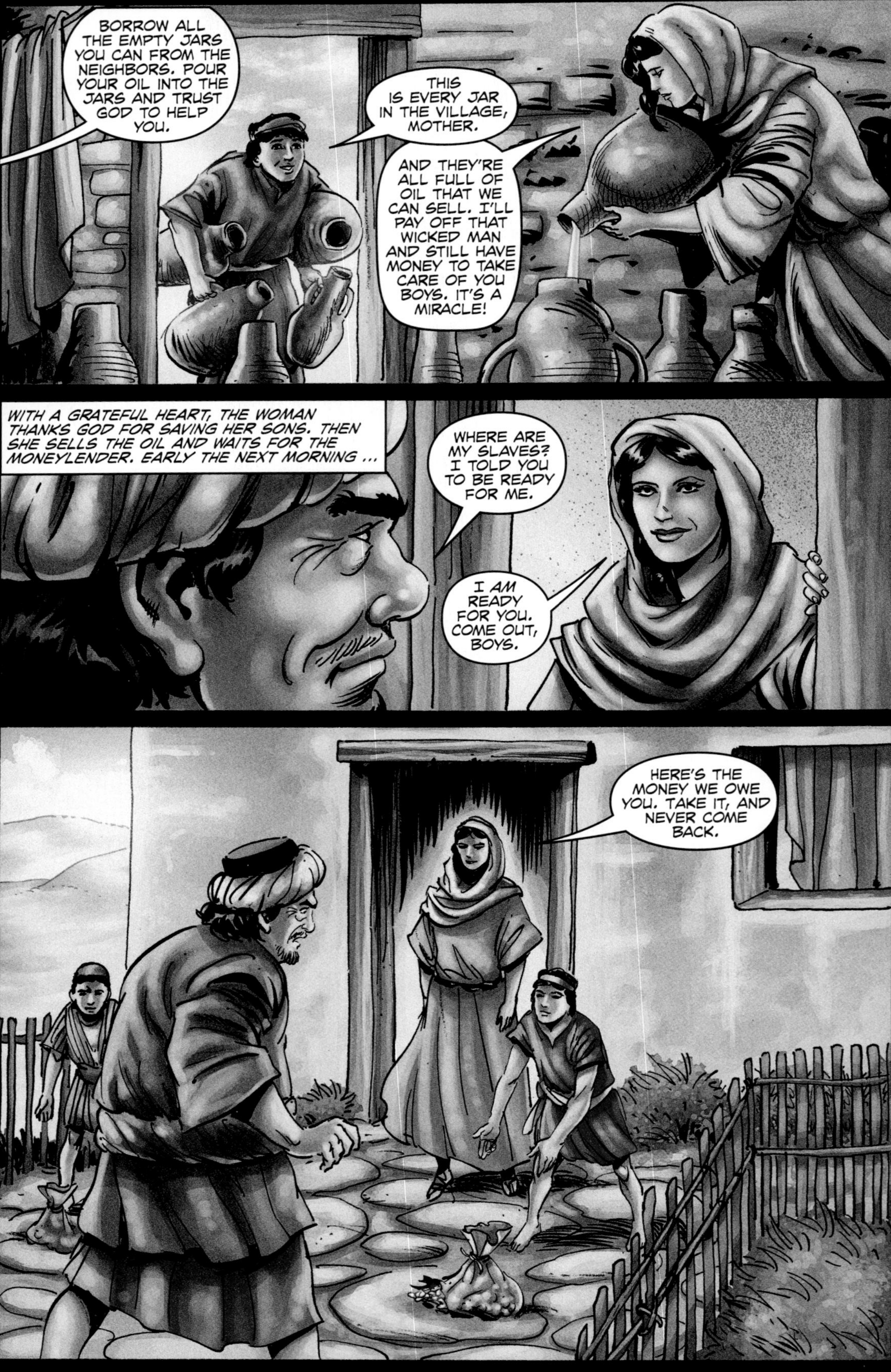
BORROW ALL THE EMPTY JARS YOU CAN FROM THE NEIGHBORS. POUR YOUR OIL INTO THE JARS AND TRUST GOD TO HELP YOU.
THIS IS EVERY JAR IN THE VILLAGE, MOTHER.
AND THEY'RE ALL FULL OF OIL THAT WE CAN SELL. I'LL PAY OFF THAT WICKED MAN AND STILL HAVE MONEY TO TAKE CARE OF YOU BOYS. IT'S A MIRACLE!
WITH A GRATEFUL HEART, THE WOMAN THANKS GOD FOR SAVING HER SONS. THEN SHE SELLS THE OIL AND WAITS FOR THE MONEYLENDER. EARLY THE NEXT MORNING ...
WHERE ARE MY SLAVES? I TOLD YOU TO BE READY FOR ME.
I AM READY FOR YOU. COME OUT, BOYS.
HERE'S THE MONEY WE OWE YOU. TAKE IT, AND NEVER COME BACK.

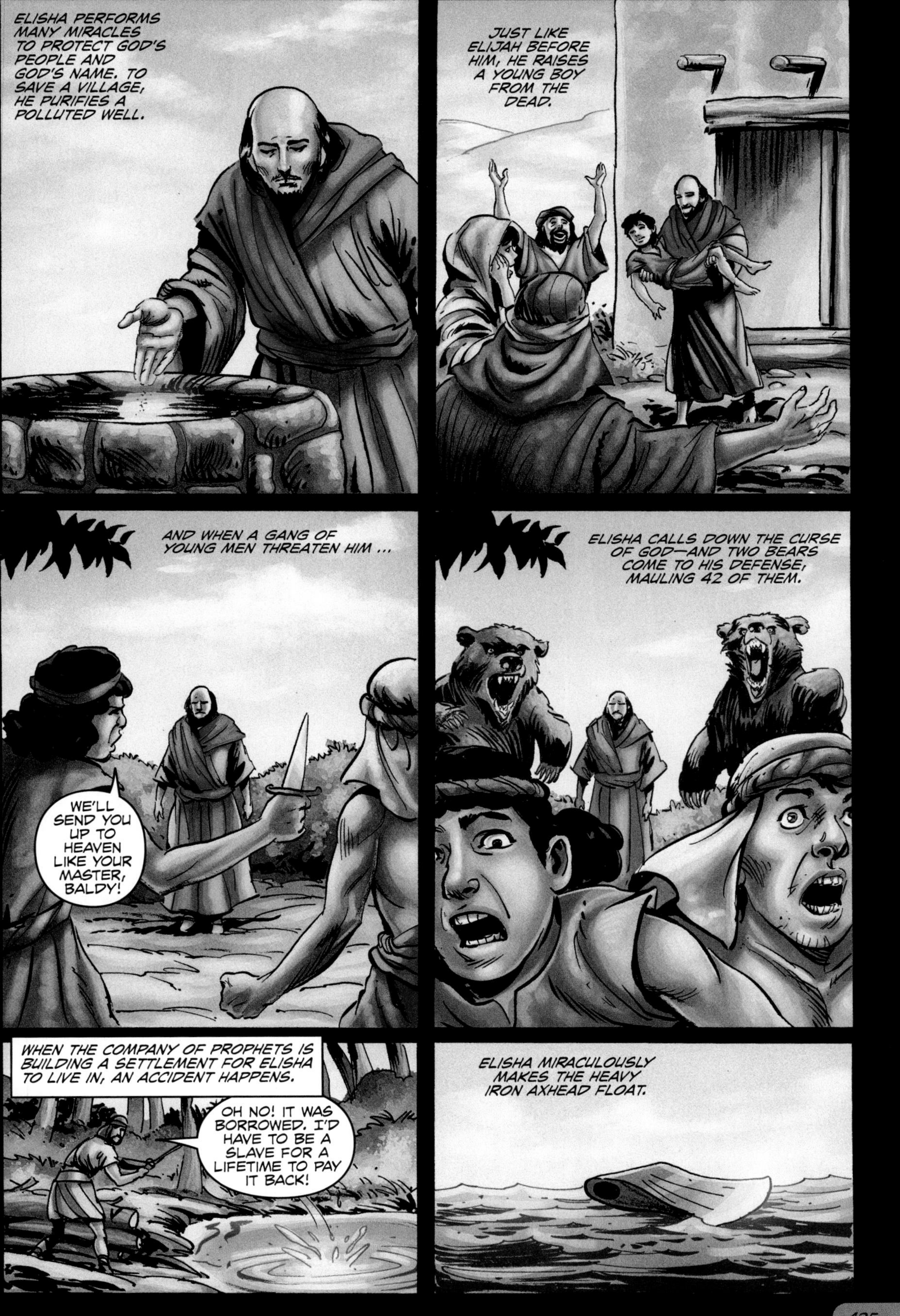
ELISHA PERFORMS MANY MIRACLES TO PROTECT GOD'S PEOPLE AND GOD'S NAME. TO SAVE A VILLAGE, HE PURIFIES A POLLUTED WELL.
JUST LIKE ELIJAH BEFORE HIM, HE RAISES A YOUNG BOY FROM THE DEAD.
AND WHEN A GANG OF YOUNG MEN THREATEN HIM ...
WE'LL SEND YOU UP TO HEAVEN LIKE YOUR MASTER, BALDY!
ELISHA CALLS DOWN THE CURSE OF GOD—AND TWO BEARS COME TO HIS DEFENSE, MAULING 42 OF THEM.
WHEN THE COMPANY OF PROPHETS IS BUILDING A SETTLEMENT FOR ELISHA TO LIVE IN, AN ACCIDENT HAPPENS.
OH NO! IT WAS BORROWED. I'D HAVE TO BE A SLAVE FOR A LIFETIME TO PAY IT BACK!
ELISHA MIRACULOUSLY MAKES THE HEAVY IRON AXHEAD FLOAT.

A Miracle for a Rash

BASED ON 2 KINGS 5

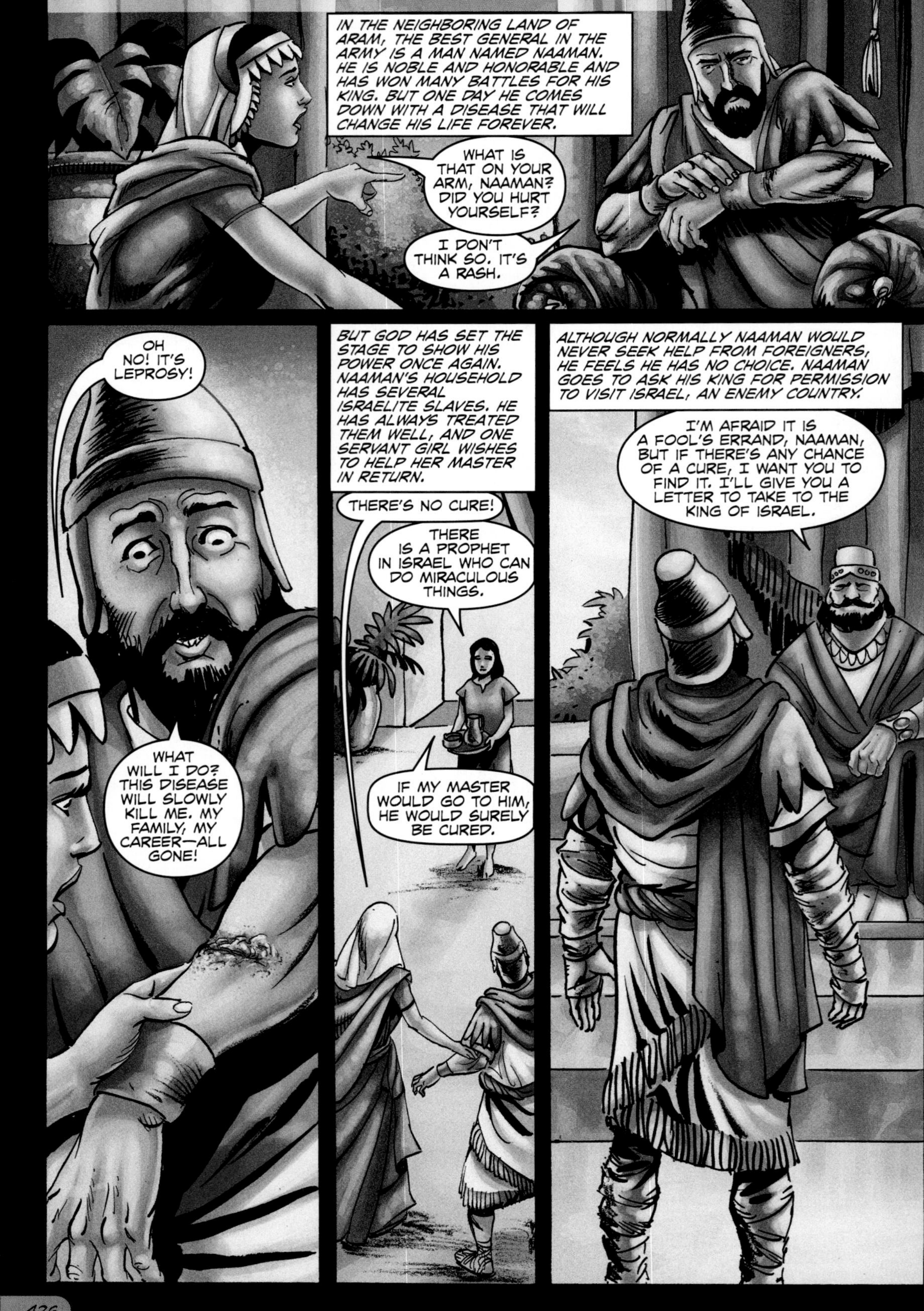
IN THE NEIGHBORING LAND OF ARAM, THE BEST GENERAL IN THE ARMY IS A MAN NAMED NAAMAN. HE IS NOBLE AND HONORABLE AND HAS WON MANY BATTLES FOR HIS KING. BUT ONE DAY HE COMES DOWN WITH A DISEASE THAT WILL CHANGE HIS LIFE FOREVER.
WHAT IS THAT ON YOUR ARM, NAAMAN? DID YOU HURT YOURSELF?
I DON'T THINK SO. IT'S A RASH.
OH NO! IT'S LEPROSY!
WHAT WILL I DO? THIS DISEASE WILL SLOWLY KILL ME. MY FAMILY, MY CAREER—ALL GONE!
BUT GOD HAS SET THE STAGE TO SHOW HIS POWER ONCE AGAIN. NAAMAN'S HOUSEHOLD HAS SEVERAL ISRAELITE SLAVES. HE HAS ALWAYS TREATED THEM WELL, AND ONE SERVANT GIRL WISHES TO HELP HER MASTER IN RETURN.
THERE'S NO CURE!
THERE IS A PROPHET IN ISRAEL WHO CAN DO MIRACULOUS THINGS.
IF MY MASTER WOULD GO TO HIM, HE WOULD SURELY BE CURED.
ALTHOUGH NORMALLY NAAMAN WOULD NEVER SEEK HELP FROM FOREIGNERS, HE FEELS HE HAS NO CHOICE. NAAMAN GOES TO ASK HIS KING FOR PERMISSION TO VISIT ISRAEL, AN ENEMY COUNTRY.
I'M AFRAID IT IS A FOOL'S ERRAND, NAAMAN, BUT IF THERE'S ANY CHANCE OF A CURE, I WANT YOU TO FIND IT. I'LL GIVE YOU A LETTER TO TAKE TO THE KING OF ISRAEL.

NAAMAN SENDS THE LETTER TO KING JORAM IN SAMARIA, THE CAPITAL OF ISRAEL. THE LETTER DOES NOT MENTION ELISHA BY NAME, SO THE KING DOESN'T UNDERSTAND IT.

WHAT'S THIS? THE KING OF ARAM IS ASKING ME TO CURE HIS GENERAL OF LEPROSY?

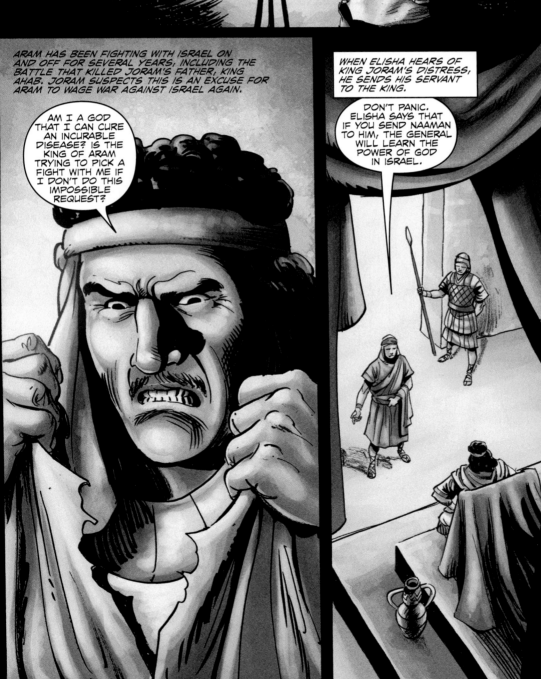

ARAM HAS BEEN FIGHTING WITH ISRAEL ON AND OFF FOR SEVERAL YEARS, INCLUDING THE BATTLE THAT KILLED JORAM'S FATHER, KING AHAB. JORAM SUSPECTS THIS IS AN EXCUSE FOR ARAM TO WAGE WAR AGAINST ISRAEL AGAIN.

AM I A GOD THAT I CAN CURE AN INCURABLE DISEASE? IS THE KING OF ARAM TRYING TO PICK A FIGHT WITH ME IF I DON'T DO THIS IMPOSSIBLE REQUEST?

WHEN ELISHA HEARS OF KING JORAM'S DISTRESS, HE SENDS HIS SERVANT TO THE KING.

DON'T PANIC. ELISHA SAYS THAT IF YOU SEND NAAMAN TO HIM, THE GENERAL WILL LEARN THE POWER OF GOD IN ISRAEL.

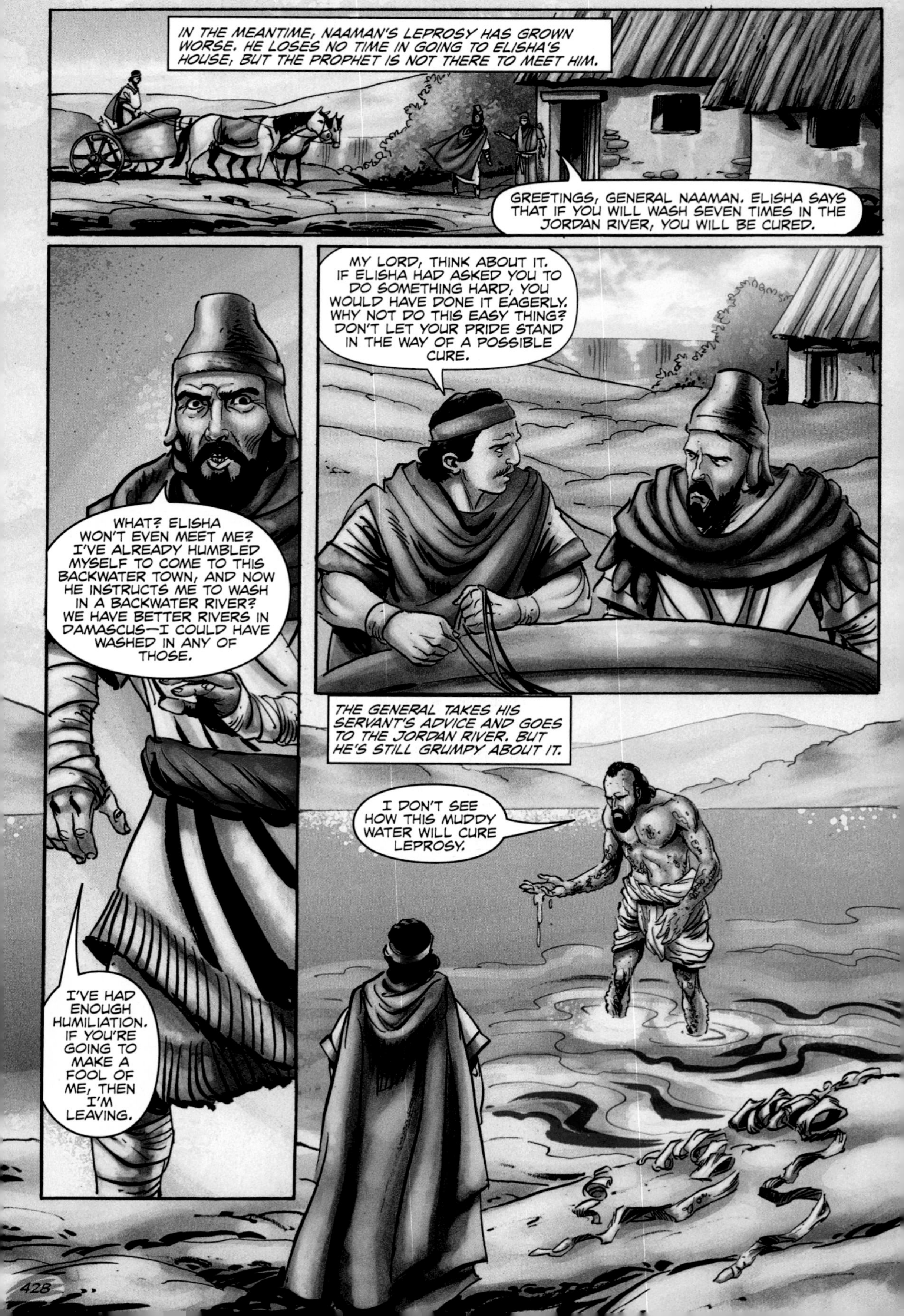
IN THE MEANTIME, NAAMAN'S LEPROSY HAS GROWN WORSE. HE LOSES NO TIME IN GOING TO ELISHA'S HOUSE; BUT THE PROPHET IS NOT THERE TO MEET HIM.
GREETINGS, GENERAL NAAMAN. ELISHA SAYS THAT IF YOU WILL WASH SEVEN TIMES IN THE JORDAN RIVER, YOU WILL BE CURED.
WHAT? ELISHA WON'T EVEN MEET ME? I'VE ALREADY HUMBLED MYSELF TO COME TO THIS BACKWATER TOWN, AND NOW HE INSTRUCTS ME TO WASH IN A BACKWATER RIVER? WE HAVE BETTER RIVERS IN DAMASCUS—I COULD HAVE WASHED IN ANY OF THOSE.
I'VE HAD ENOUGH HUMILIATION. IF YOU'RE GOING TO MAKE A FOOL OF ME, THEN I'M LEAVING.
MY LORD, THINK ABOUT IT. IF ELISHA HAD ASKED YOU TO DO SOMETHING HARD, YOU WOULD HAVE DONE IT EAGERLY. WHY NOT DO THIS EASY THING? DON'T LET YOUR PRIDE STAND IN THE WAY OF A POSSIBLE CURE.
THE GENERAL TAKES HIS SERVANT'S ADVICE AND GOES TO THE JORDAN RIVER. BUT HE'S STILL GRUMPY ABOUT IT.
I DON'T SEE HOW THIS MUDDY WATER WILL CURE LEPROSY.

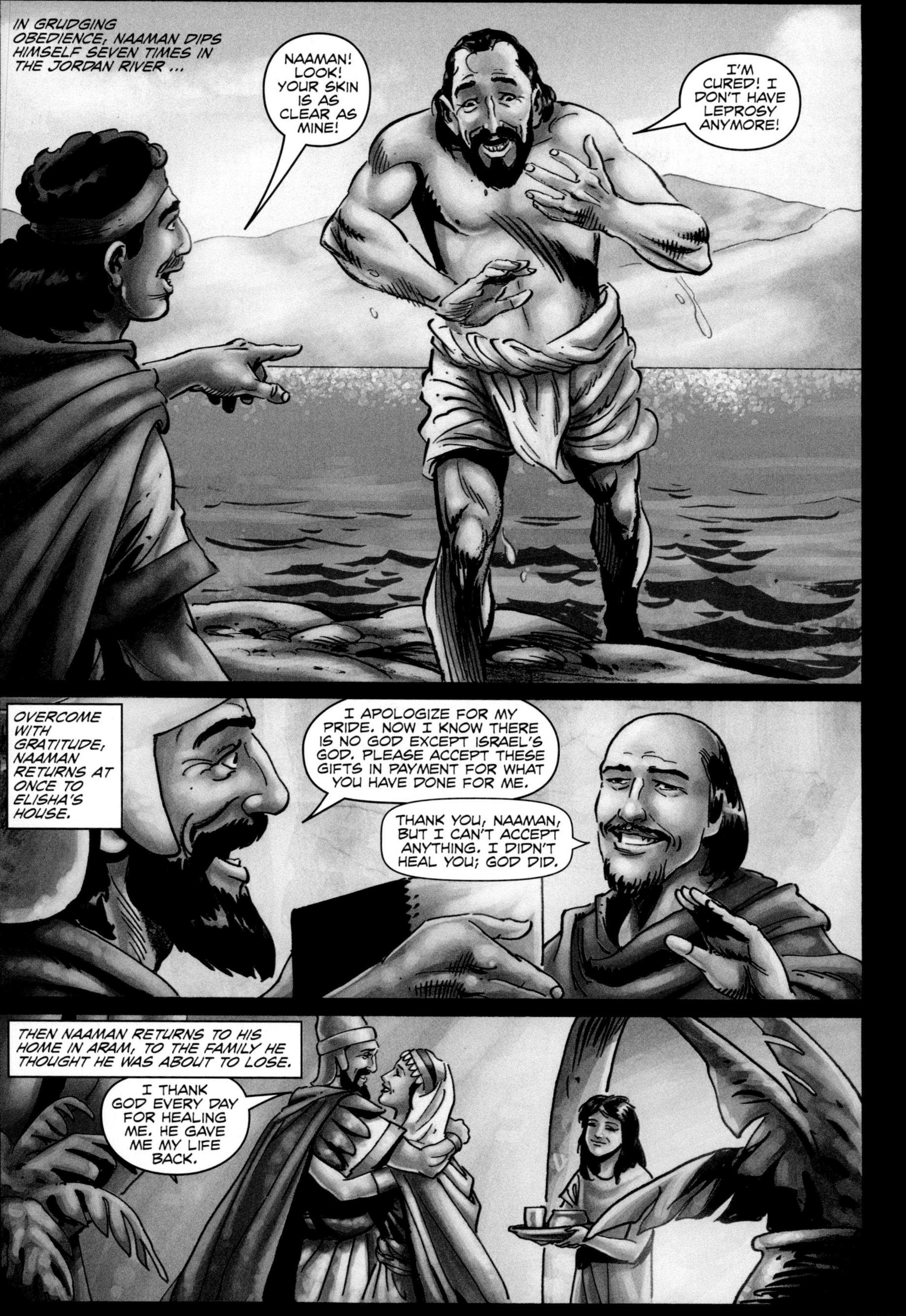
IN GRUDGING OBEDIENCE, NAAMAN DIPS HIMSELF SEVEN TIMES IN THE JORDAN RIVER ...
NAAMAN! LOOK! YOUR SKIN IS AS CLEAR AS MINE!
I'M CURED! I DON'T HAVE LEPROSY ANYMORE!
OVERCOME WITH GRATITUDE, NAAMAN RETURNS AT ONCE TO ELISHA'S HOUSE.
I APOLOGIZE FOR MY PRIDE. NOW I KNOW THERE IS NO GOD EXCEPT ISRAEL'S GOD. PLEASE ACCEPT THESE GIFTS IN PAYMENT FOR WHAT YOU HAVE DONE FOR ME.
THANK YOU, NAAMAN, BUT I CAN'T ACCEPT ANYTHING. I DIDN'T HEAL YOU; GOD DID.
THEN NAAMAN RETURNS TO HIS HOME IN ARAM, TO THE FAMILY HE THOUGHT HE WAS ABOUT TO LOSE.
I THANK GOD EVERY DAY FOR HEALING ME. HE GAVE ME MY LIFE BACK.

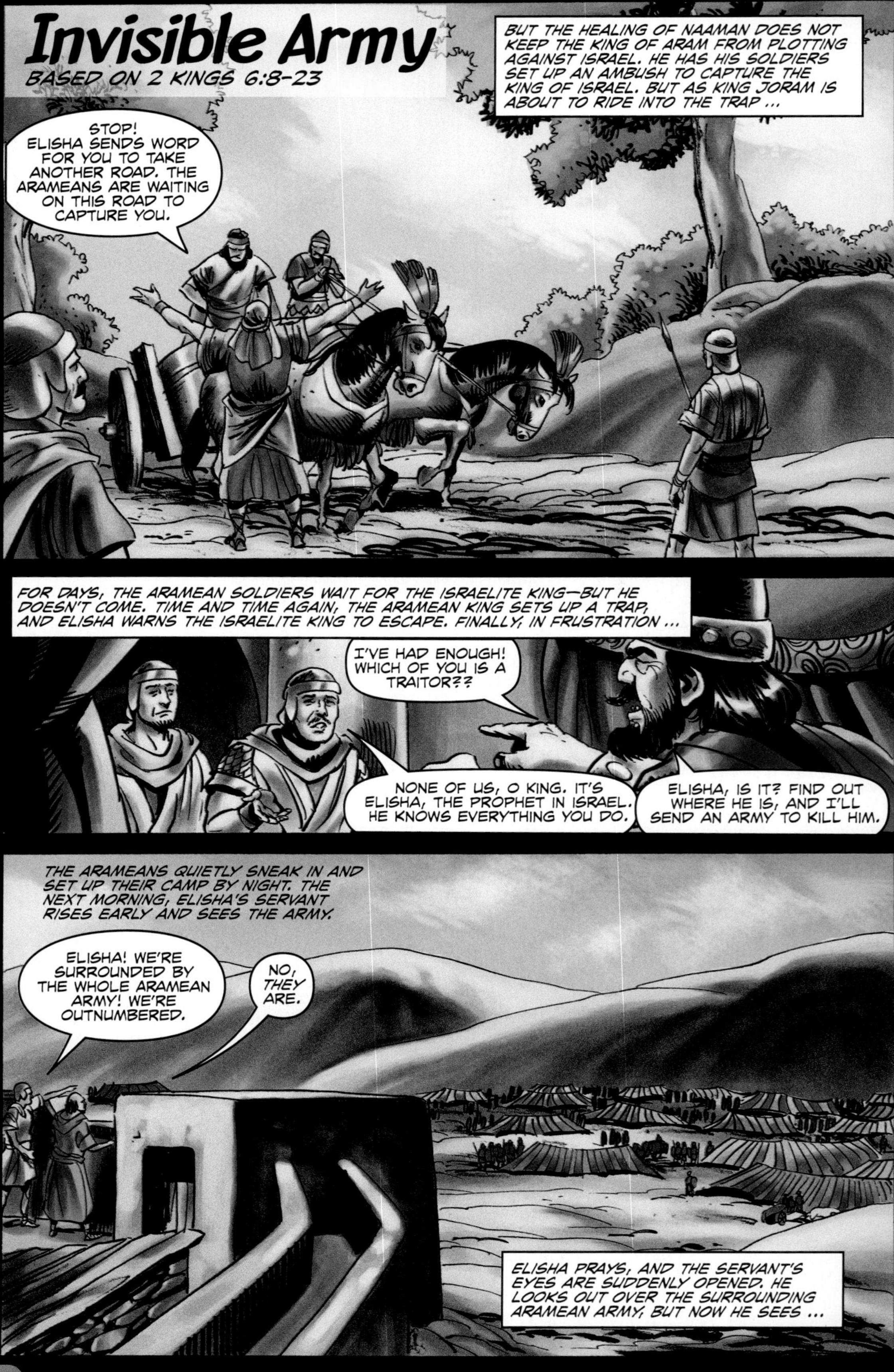

Invisible Army
BASED ON 2 KINGS 6:8-23
BUT THE HEALING OF NAAMAN DOES NOT KEEP THE KING OF ARAM FROM PLOTTING AGAINST ISRAEL. HE HAS HIS SOLDIERS SET UP AN AMBUSH TO CAPTURE THE KING OF ISRAEL. BUT AS KING JORAM IS ABOUT TO RIDE INTO THE TRAP ...
STOP! ELISHA SENDS WORD FOR YOU TO TAKE ANOTHER ROAD. THE ARAMEANS ARE WAITING ON THIS ROAD TO CAPTURE YOU.
FOR DAYS, THE ARAMEAN SOLDIERS WAIT FOR THE ISRAELITE KING—BUT HE DOESN'T COME. TIME AND TIME AGAIN, THE ARAMEAN KING SETS UP A TRAP, AND ELISHA WARNS THE ISRAELITE KING TO ESCAPE. FINALLY, IN FRUSTRATION ...
I'VE HAD ENOUGH! WHICH OF YOU IS A TRAITOR??
NONE OF US, O KING. IT'S ELISHA, THE PROPHET IN ISRAEL. HE KNOWS EVERYTHING YOU DO.
ELISHA, IS IT? FIND OUT WHERE HE IS, AND I'LL SEND AN ARMY TO KILL HIM.
THE ARAMEANS QUIETLY SNEAK IN AND SET UP THEIR CAMP BY NIGHT. THE NEXT MORNING, ELISHA'S SERVANT RISES EARLY AND SEES THE ARMY.
ELISHA! WE'RE SURROUNDED BY THE WHOLE ARAMEAN ARMY! WE'RE OUTNUMBERED.
NO, THEY ARE.
ELISHA PRAYS, AND THE SERVANT'S EYES ARE SUDDENLY OPENED. HE LOOKS OUT OVER THE SURROUNDING ARAMEAN ARMY, BUT NOW HE SEES ...

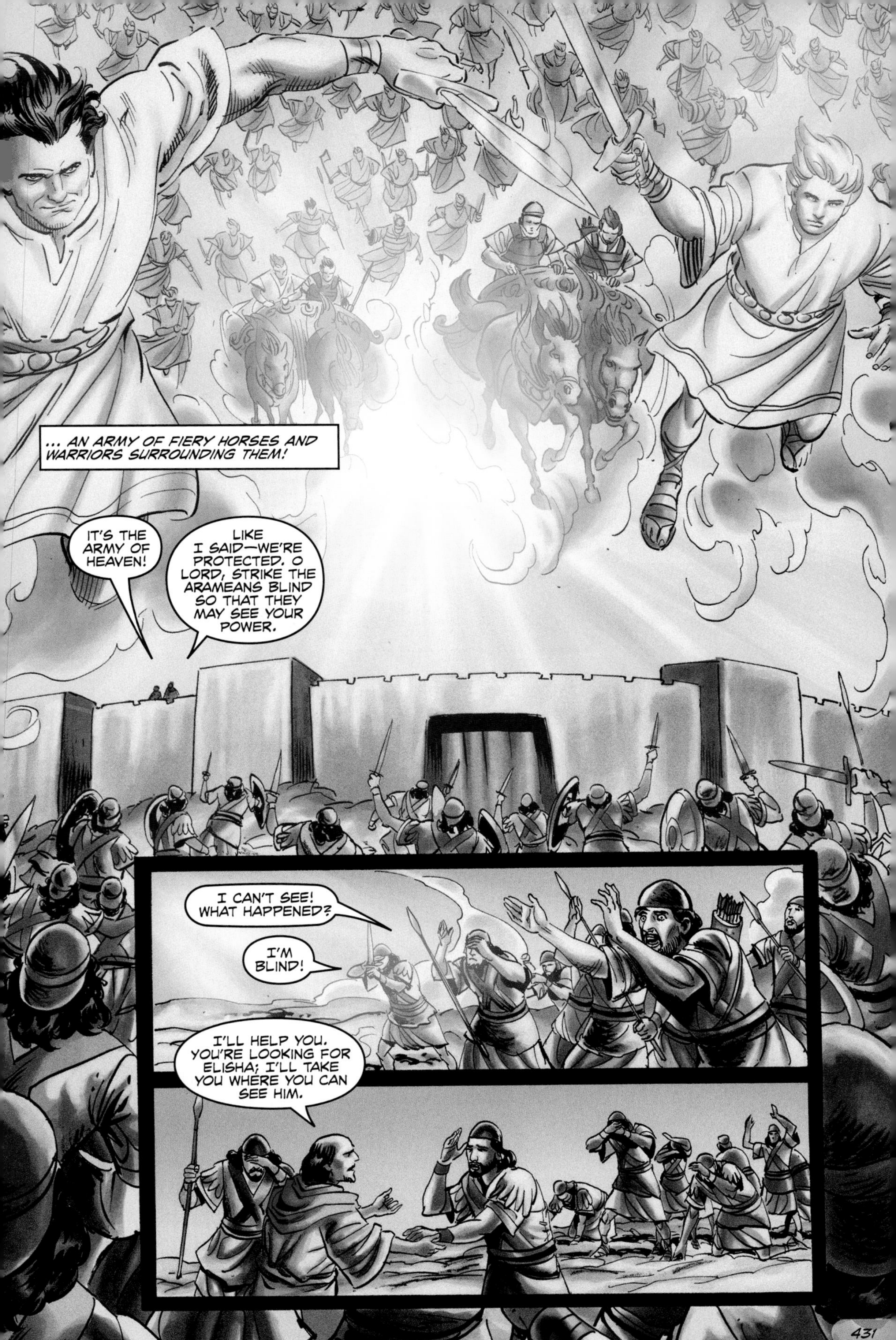
... AN ARMY OF FIERY HORSES AND WARRIORS SURROUNDING THEM!
IT'S THE ARMY OF HEAVEN!
LIKE I SAID—WE'RE PROTECTED. O LORD, STRIKE THE ARAMEANS BLIND SO THAT THEY MAY SEE YOUR POWER.
I CAN'T SEE! WHAT HAPPENED?
I'M BLIND!
I'LL HELP YOU. YOU'RE LOOKING FOR ELISHA; I'LL TAKE YOU WHERE YOU CAN SEE HIM.

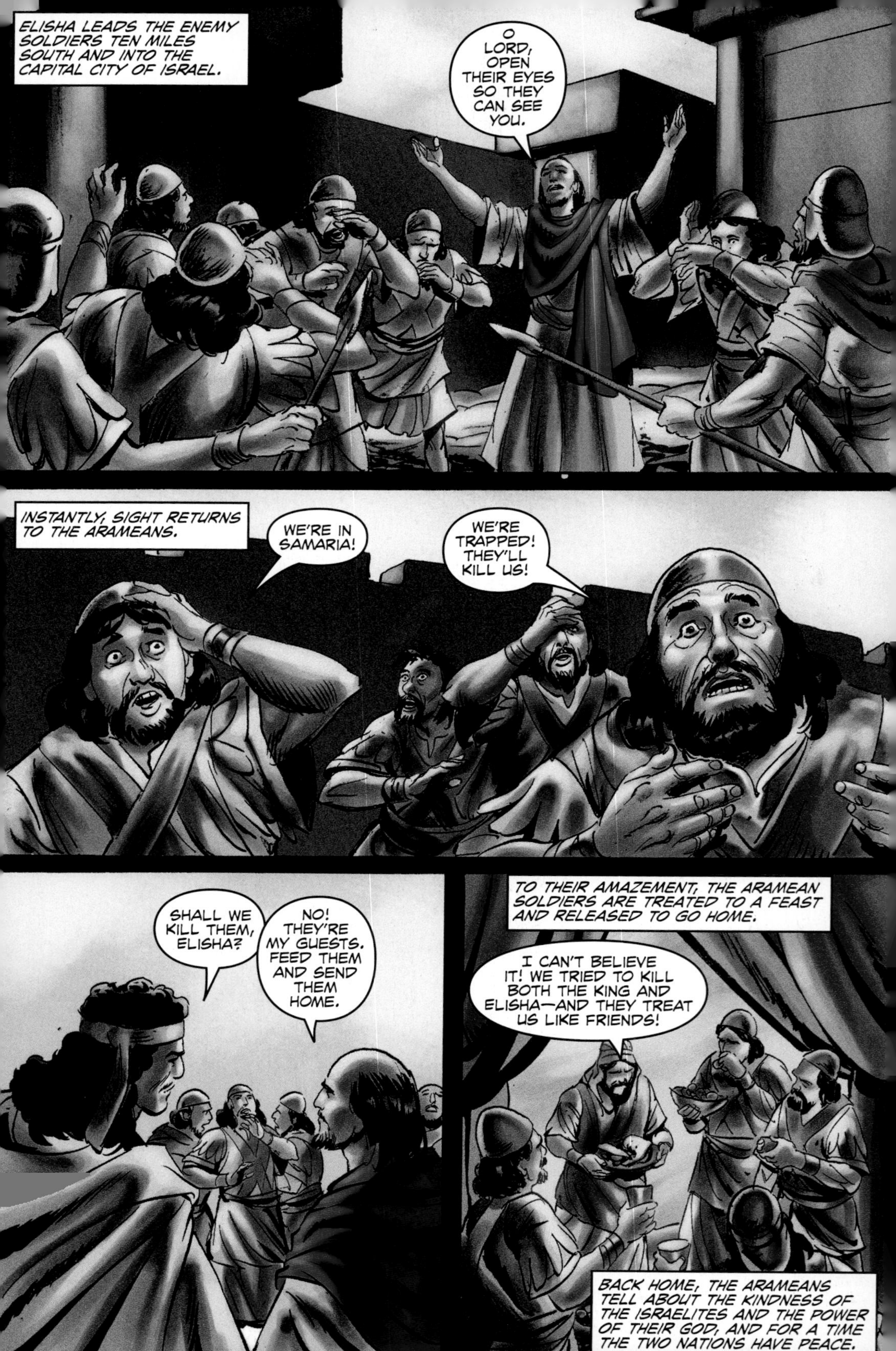

ELISHA LEADS THE ENEMY SOLDIERS TEN MILES SOUTH AND INTO THE CAPITAL CITY OF ISRAEL.
O LORD, OPEN THEIR EYES SO THEY CAN SEE YOU.
INSTANTLY, SIGHT RETURNS TO THE ARAMEANS.
WE'RE IN SAMARIA!
WE'RE TRAPPED! THEY'LL KILL US!
SHALL WE KILL THEM, ELISHA?
NO! THEY'RE MY GUESTS. FEED THEM AND SEND THEM HOME.
TO THEIR AMAZEMENT, THE ARAMEAN SOLDIERS ARE TREATED TO A FEAST AND RELEASED TO GO HOME.
I CAN'T BELIEVE IT! WE TRIED TO KILL BOTH THE KING AND ELISHA—AND THEY TREAT US LIKE FRIENDS!
BACK HOME, THE ARAMEANS TELL ABOUT THE KINDNESS OF THE ISRAELITES AND THE POWER OF THEIR GOD, AND FOR A TIME THE TWO NATIONS HAVE PEACE.

Lepers Under Siege! BASED ON 2 KINGS 6:24—7:16

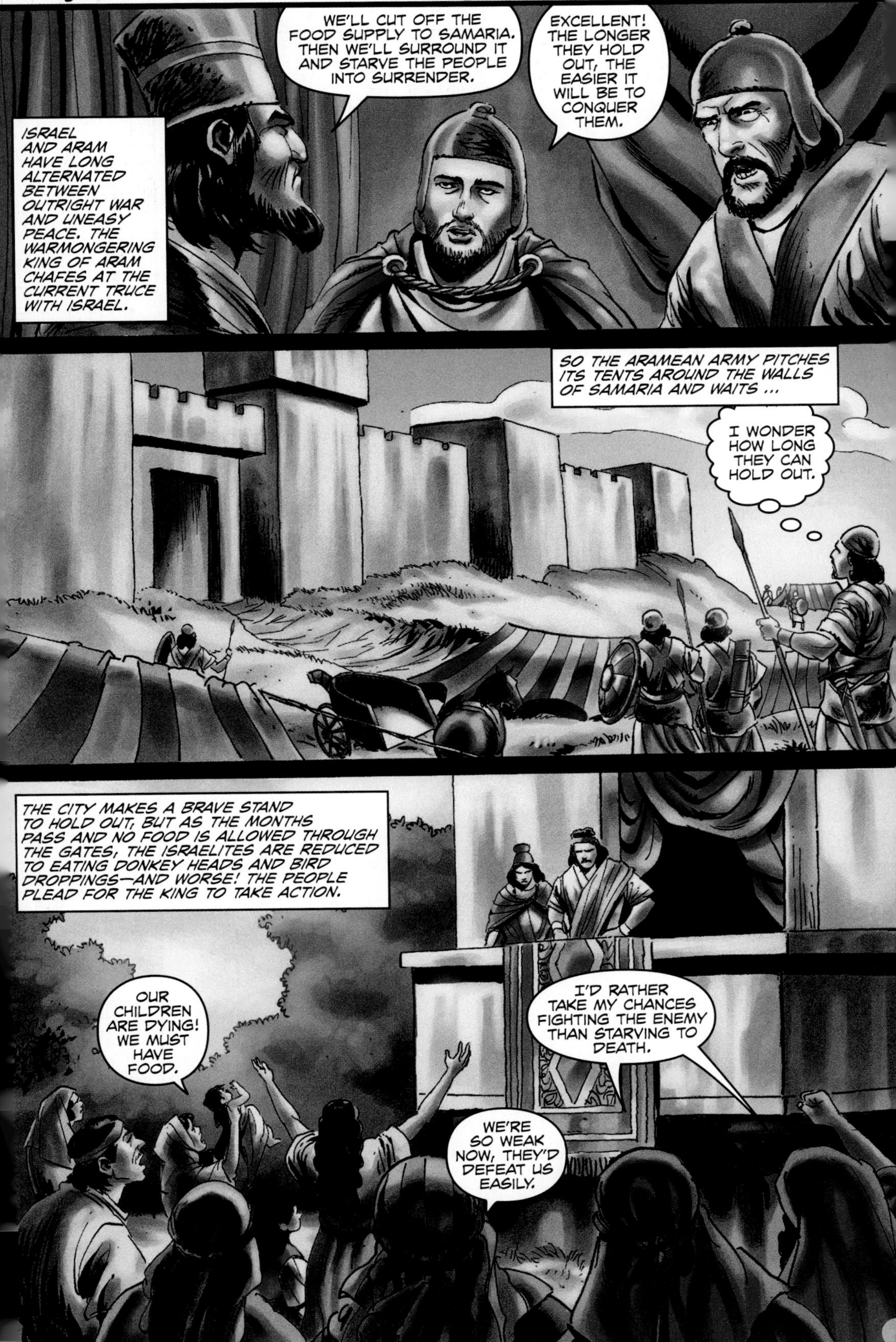
ISRAEL AND ARAM HAVE LONG ALTERNATED BETWEEN OUTRIGHT WAR AND UNEASY PEACE. THE WARMONGERING KING OF ARAM CHAFES AT THE CURRENT TRUCE WITH ISRAEL.
WE'LL CUT OFF THE FOOD SUPPLY TO SAMARIA. THEN WE'LL SURROUND IT AND STARVE THE PEOPLE INTO SURRENDER.
EXCELLENT! THE LONGER THEY HOLD OUT, THE EASIER IT WILL BE TO CONQUER THEM.
SO THE ARAMEAN ARMY PITCHES ITS TENTS AROUND THE WALLS OF SAMARIA AND WAITS ...
I WONDER HOW LONG THEY CAN HOLD OUT.
THE CITY MAKES A BRAVE STAND TO HOLD OUT, BUT AS THE MONTHS PASS AND NO FOOD IS ALLOWED THROUGH THE GATES, THE ISRAELITES ARE REDUCED TO EATING DONKEY HEADS AND BIRD DROPPINGS—AND WORSE! THE PEOPLE PLEAD FOR THE KING TO TAKE ACTION.
OUR CHILDREN ARE DYING! WE MUST HAVE FOOD.
I'D RATHER TAKE MY CHANCES FIGHTING THE ENEMY THAN STARVING TO DEATH.
WE'RE SO WEAK NOW, THEY'D DEFEAT US EASILY.

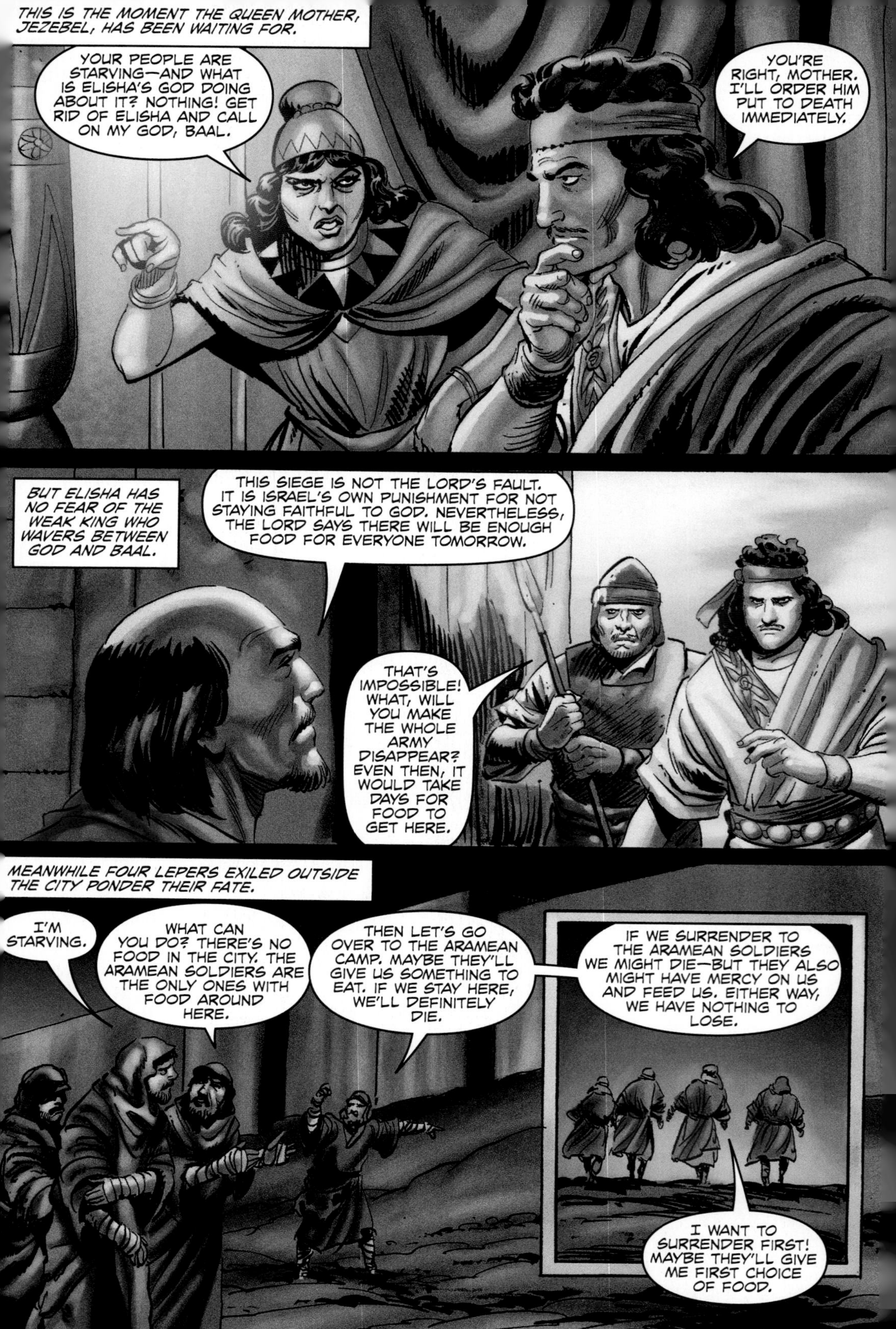
THIS IS THE MOMENT THE QUEEN MOTHER, JEZEBEL, HAS BEEN WAITING FOR.
YOUR PEOPLE ARE STARVING—AND WHAT IS ELISHA'S GOD DOING ABOUT IT? NOTHING! GET RID OF ELISHA AND CALL ON MY GOD, BAAL.
YOU'RE RIGHT, MOTHER. I'LL ORDER HIM PUT TO DEATH IMMEDIATELY.
BUT ELISHA HAS NO FEAR OF THE WEAK KING WHO WAVERS BETWEEN GOD AND BAAL.
THIS SIEGE IS NOT THE LORD'S FAULT. IT IS ISRAEL'S OWN PUNISHMENT FOR NOT STAYING FAITHFUL TO GOD. NEVERTHELESS, THE LORD SAYS THERE WILL BE ENOUGH FOOD FOR EVERYONE TOMORROW.
THAT'S IMPOSSIBLE! WHAT, WILL YOU MAKE THE WHOLE ARMY DISAPPEAR? EVEN THEN, IT WOULD TAKE DAYS FOR FOOD TO GET HERE.
MEANWHILE FOUR LEPERS EXILED OUTSIDE THE CITY PONDER THEIR FATE.
I'M STARVING.
WHAT CAN YOU DO? THERE'S NO FOOD IN THE CITY. THE ARAMEAN SOLDIERS ARE THE ONLY ONES WITH FOOD AROUND HERE.
THEN LET'S GO OVER TO THE ARAMEAN CAMP. MAYBE THEY'LL GIVE US SOMETHING TO EAT. IF WE STAY HERE, WE'LL DEFINITELY DIE.
IF WE SURRENDER TO THE ARAMEAN SOLDIERS WE MIGHT DIE—BUT THEY ALSO MIGHT HAVE MERCY ON US AND FEED US. EITHER WAY, WE HAVE NOTHING TO LOSE.
I WANT TO SURRENDER FIRST! MAYBE THEY'LL GIVE ME FIRST CHOICE OF FOOD.

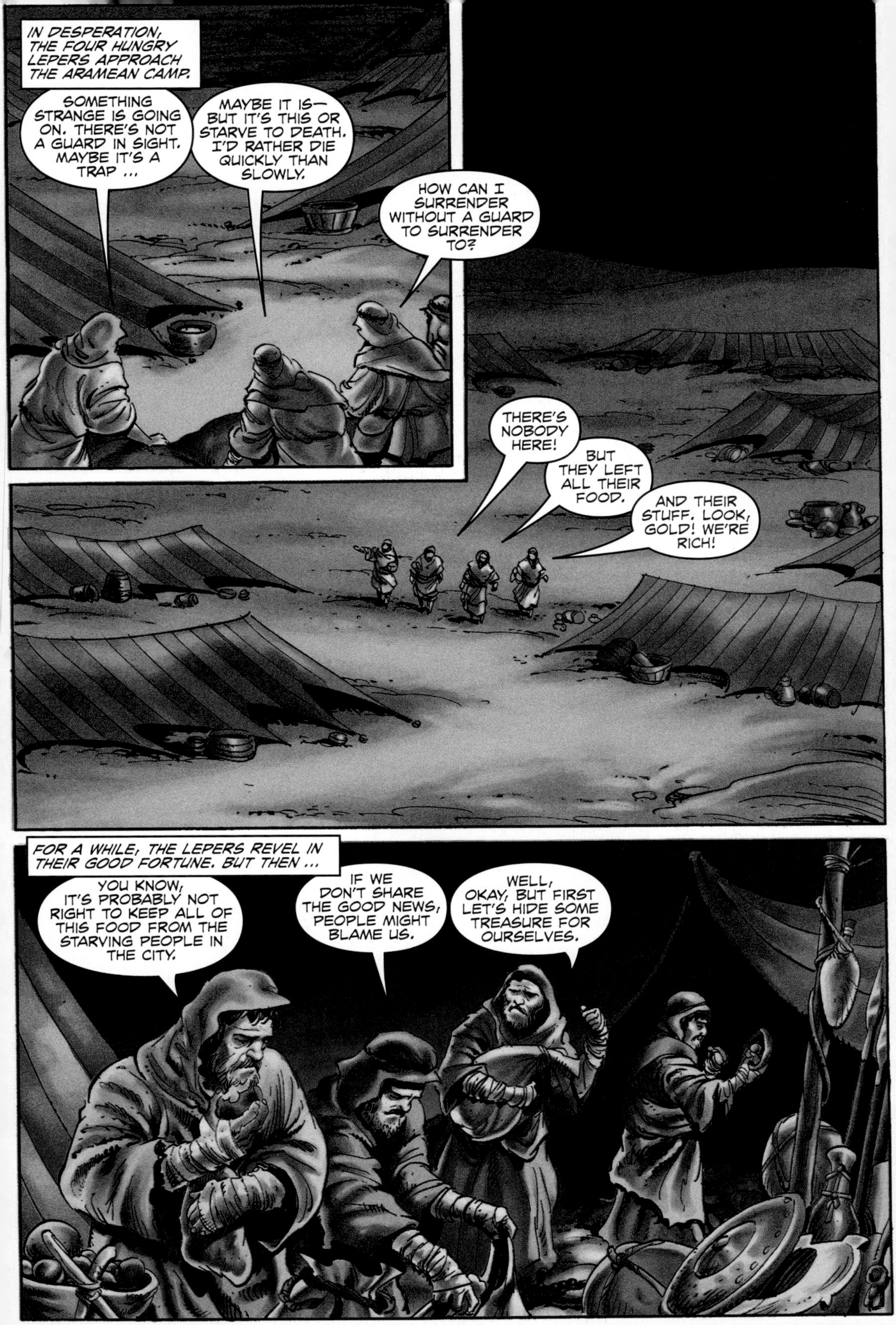
IN DESPERATION, THE FOUR HUNGRY LEPERS APPROACH THE ARAMEAN CAMP.
SOMETHING STRANGE IS GOING ON. THERE'S NOT A GUARD IN SIGHT. MAYBE IT'S A TRAP ...
MAYBE IT IS— BUT IT'S THIS OR STARVE TO DEATH. I'D RATHER DIE QUICKLY THAN SLOWLY.
HOW CAN I SURRENDER WITHOUT A GUARD TO SURRENDER TO?
THERE'S NOBODY HERE!
BUT THEY LEFT ALL THEIR FOOD.
AND THEIR STUFF. LOOK, GOLD! WE'RE RICH!
FOR A WHILE, THE LEPERS REVEL IN THEIR GOOD FORTUNE. BUT THEN ...
YOU KNOW, IT'S PROBABLY NOT RIGHT TO KEEP ALL OF THIS FOOD FROM THE STARVING PEOPLE IN THE CITY.
IF WE DON'T SHARE THE GOOD NEWS, PEOPLE MIGHT BLAME US.
WELL, OKAY, BUT FIRST LET'S HIDE SOME TREASURE FOR OURSELVES.

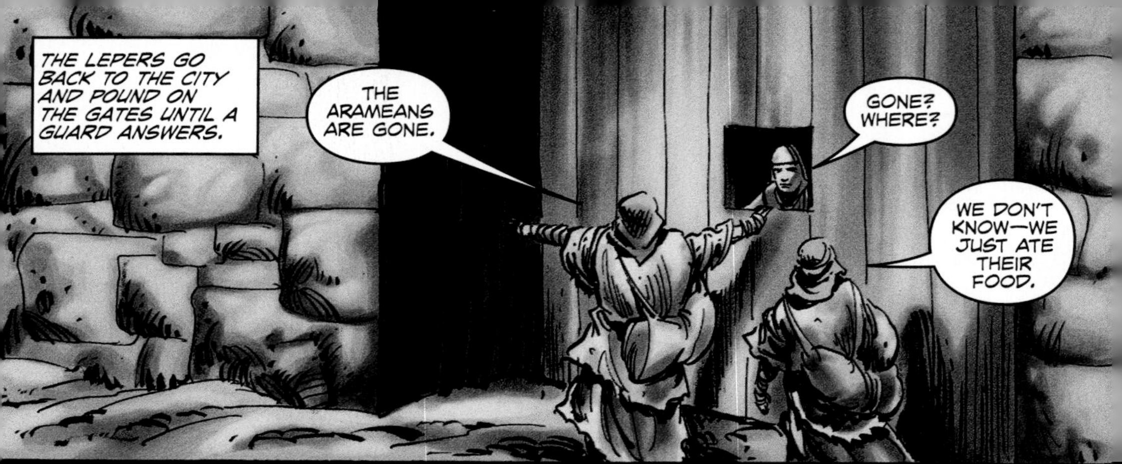
THE LEPERS GO BACK TO THE CITY AND POUND ON THE GATES UNTIL A GUARD ANSWERS.
THE ARAMEANS ARE GONE.
GONE? WHERE?
WE DON'T KNOW—WE JUST ATE THEIR FOOD.

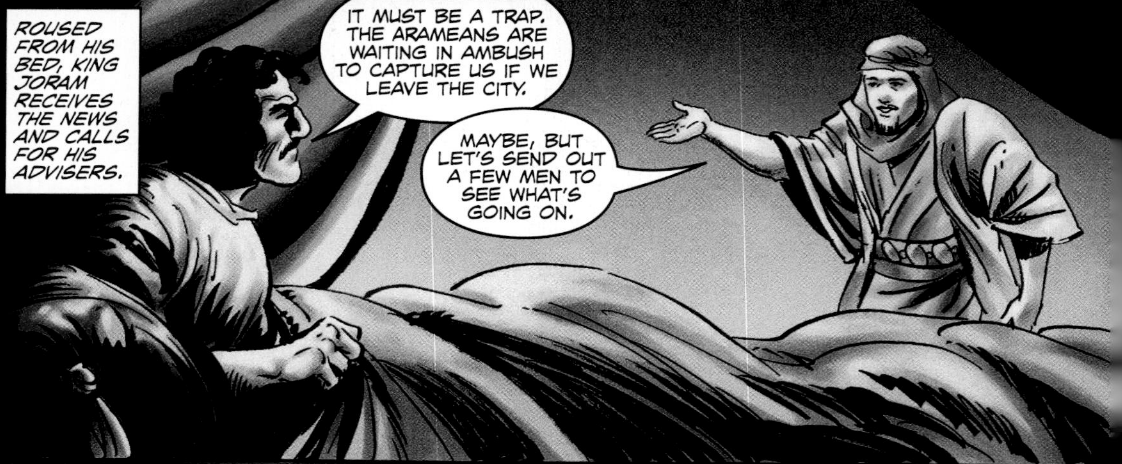
ROUSED FROM HIS BED, KING JORAM RECEIVES THE NEWS AND CALLS FOR HIS ADVISERS.
IT MUST BE A TRAP. THE ARAMEANS ARE WAITING IN AMBUSH TO CAPTURE US IF WE LEAVE THE CITY.
MAYBE, BUT LET'S SEND OUT A FEW MEN TO SEE WHAT'S GOING ON.

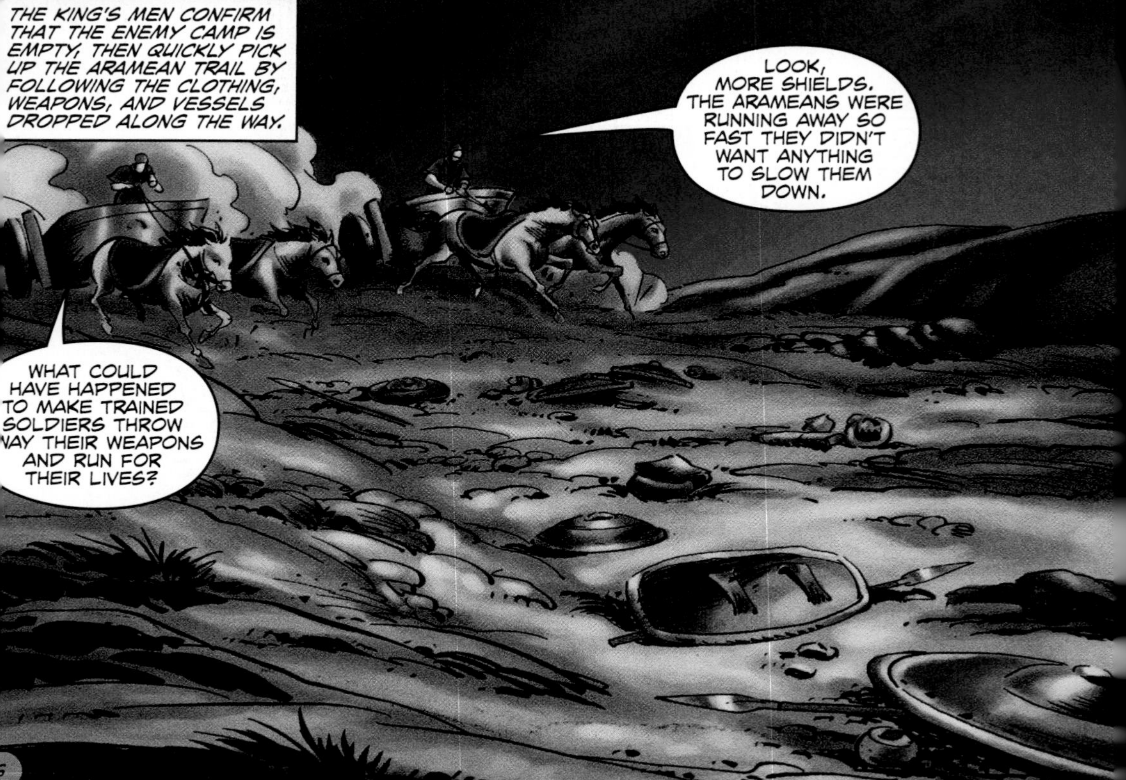
THE KING'S MEN CONFIRM THAT THE ENEMY CAMP IS EMPTY, THEN QUICKLY PICK UP THE ARAMEAN TRAIL BY FOLLOWING THE CLOTHING, WEAPONS, AND VESSELS DROPPED ALONG THE WAY.
LOOK, MORE SHIELDS. THE ARAMEANS WERE RUNNING AWAY SO FAST THEY DIDN'T WANT ANYTHING TO SLOW THEM DOWN.
WHAT COULD HAVE HAPPENED TO MAKE TRAINED SOLDIERS THROW WAY THEIR WEAPONS AND RUN FOR THEIR LIVES?

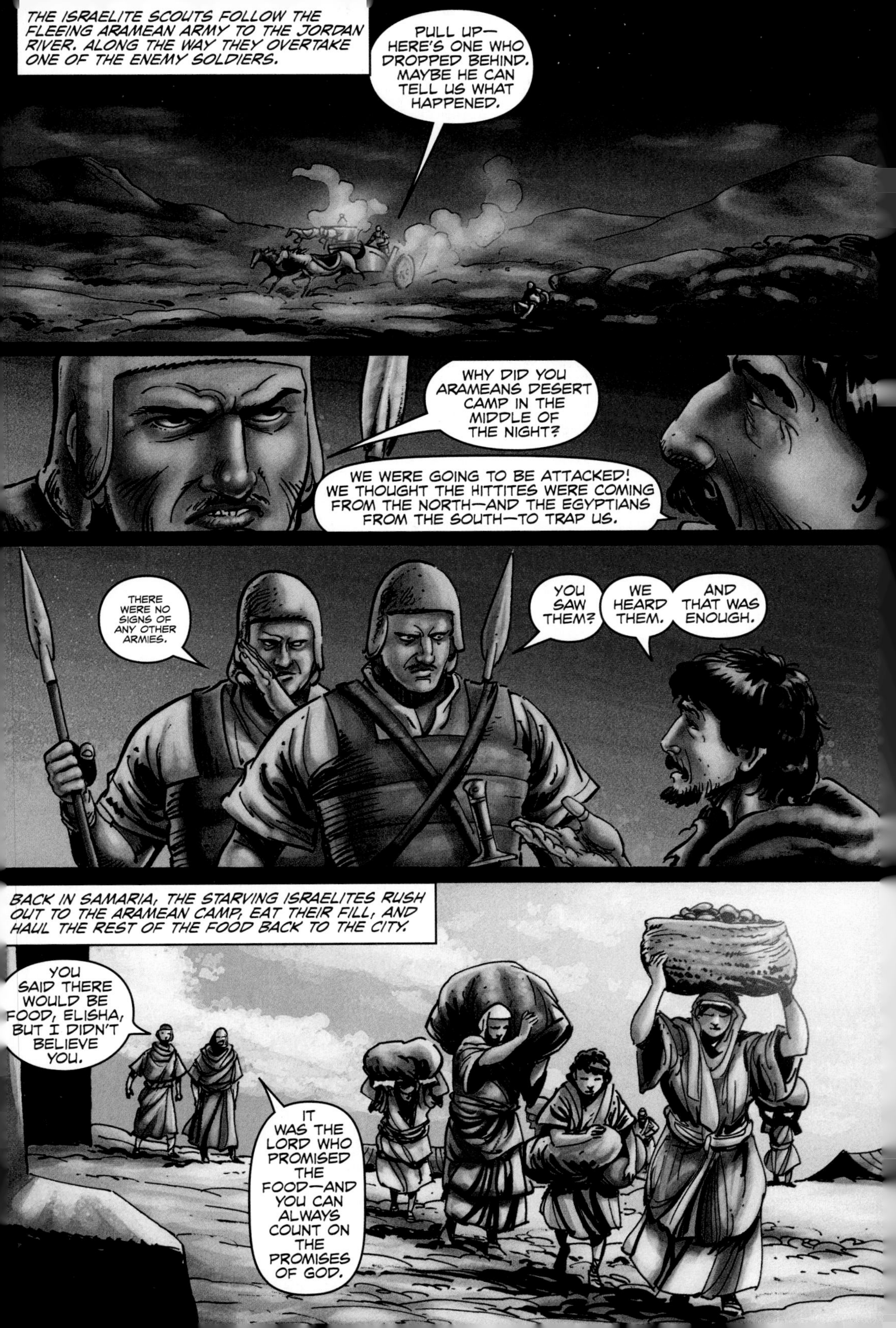

THE ISRAELITE SCOUTS FOLLOW THE FLEEING ARAMEAN ARMY TO THE JORDAN RIVER. ALONG THE WAY THEY OVERTAKE ONE OF THE ENEMY SOLDIERS.
PULL UP—HERE'S ONE WHO DROPPED BEHIND. MAYBE HE CAN TELL US WHAT HAPPENED.
WHY DID YOU ARAMEANS DESERT CAMP IN THE MIDDLE OF THE NIGHT?
WE WERE GOING TO BE ATTACKED! WE THOUGHT THE HITTITES WERE COMING FROM THE NORTH—AND THE EGYPTIANS FROM THE SOUTH—TO TRAP US.
THERE WERE NO SIGNS OF ANY OTHER ARMIES.
YOU SAW THEM?
WE HEARD THEM.
AND THAT WAS ENOUGH.
BACK IN SAMARIA, THE STARVING ISRAELITES RUSH OUT TO THE ARAMEAN CAMP, EAT THEIR FILL, AND HAUL THE REST OF THE FOOD BACK TO THE CITY.
YOU SAID THERE WOULD BE FOOD, ELISHA, BUT I DIDN'T BELIEVE YOU.
IT WAS THE LORD WHO PROMISED THE FOOD—AND YOU CAN ALWAYS COUNT ON THE PROMISES OF GOD.

Anointed Jehu, Painted Jezebel

BASED ON 2 KINGS 9

IN SPITE OF THE FACT THAT GOD HAD SAVED ISRAEL, KING JORAM AND HIS MOTHER KEEP ON WORSHIPPING BAAL. IN ANOTHER BATTLE AGAINST ARAM, JORAM IS WOUNDED. HE LEAVES CAPTAIN JEHU IN CHARGE AND RETURNS HOME TO RECUPERATE. THE TIME HAS COME FOR THE LORD'S PROPHECY TO ELIJAH TO BE FULFILLED. ELISHA CALLS FOR A YOUNG PROPHET TO MAKE A QUICK JOURNEY FOR HIM.

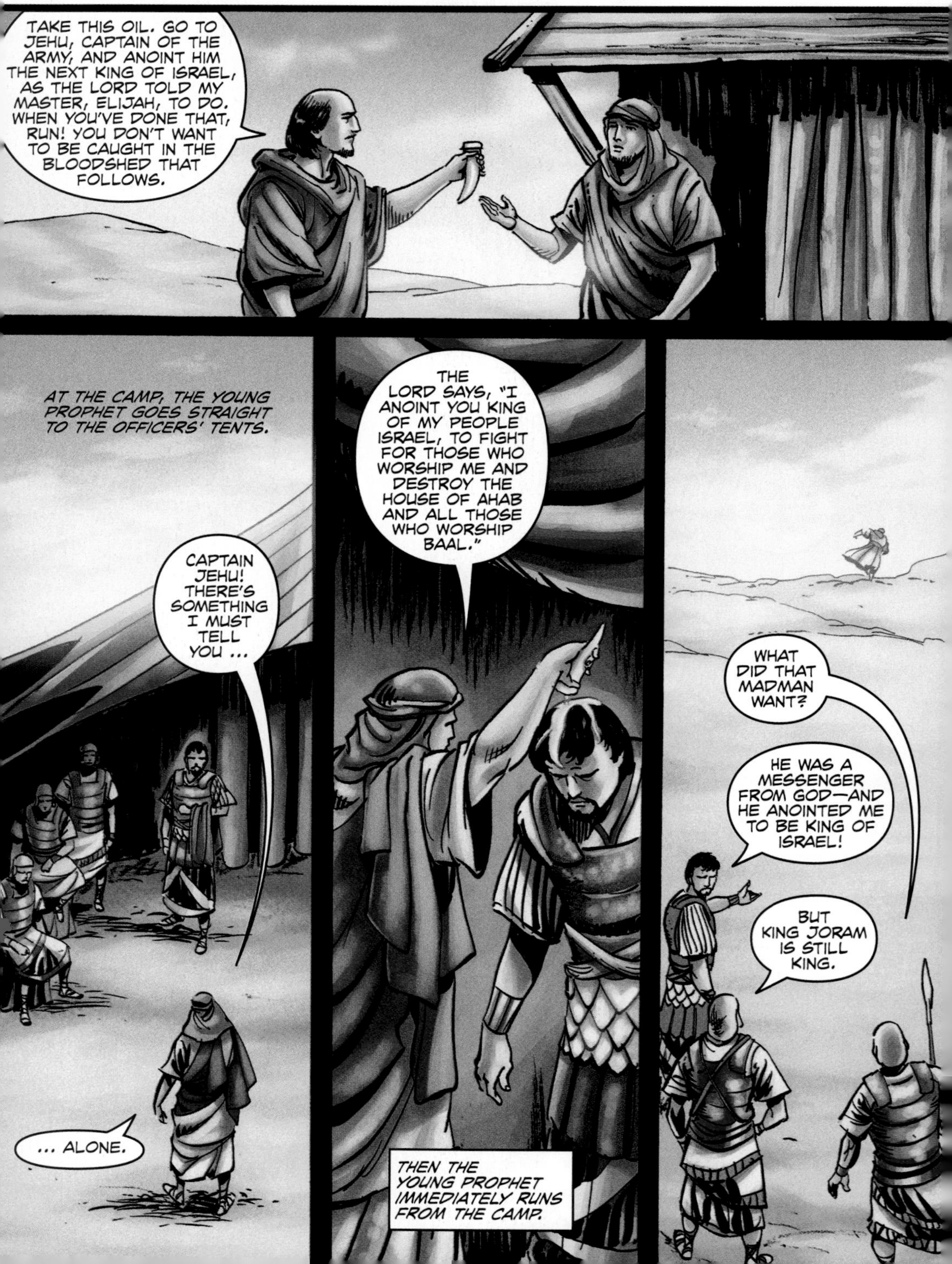

TAKE THIS OIL. GO TO JEHU, CAPTAIN OF THE ARMY, AND ANOINT HIM THE NEXT KING OF ISRAEL, AS THE LORD TOLD MY MASTER, ELIJAH, TO DO. WHEN YOU'VE DONE THAT, RUN! YOU DON'T WANT TO BE CAUGHT IN THE BLOODSHED THAT FOLLOWS.
AT THE CAMP, THE YOUNG PROPHET GOES STRAIGHT TO THE OFFICERS' TENTS.
CAPTAIN JEHU! THERE'S SOMETHING I MUST TELL YOU ...
... ALONE.
THE LORD SAYS, "I ANOINT YOU KING OF MY PEOPLE ISRAEL, TO FIGHT FOR THOSE WHO WORSHIP ME AND DESTROY THE HOUSE OF AHAB AND ALL THOSE WHO WORSHIP BAAL."
THEN THE YOUNG PROPHET IMMEDIATELY RUNS FROM THE CAMP.
WHAT DID THAT MADMAN WANT?
HE WAS A MESSENGER FROM GOD—AND HE ANOINTED ME TO BE KING OF ISRAEL!
BUT KING JORAM IS STILL KING.

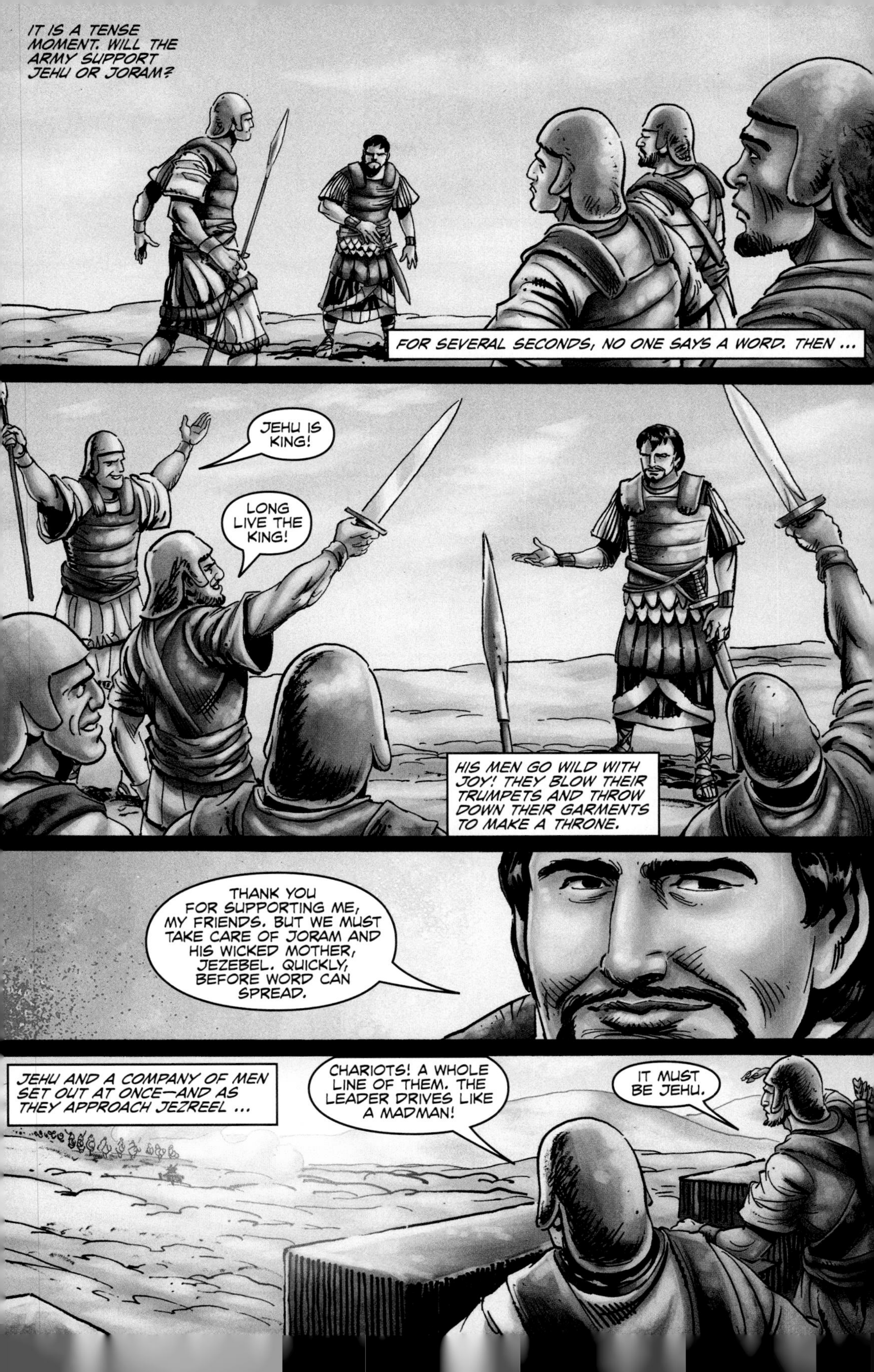
IT IS A TENSE MOMENT. WILL THE ARMY SUPPORT JEHU OR JORAM?
FOR SEVERAL SECONDS, NO ONE SAYS A WORD. THEN ...
JEHU IS KING!
LONG LIVE THE KING!
HIS MEN GO WILD WITH JOY! THEY BLOW THEIR TRUMPETS AND THROW DOWN THEIR GARMENTS TO MAKE A THRONE.
THANK YOU FOR SUPPORTING ME, MY FRIENDS. BUT WE MUST TAKE CARE OF JORAM AND HIS WICKED MOTHER, JEZEBEL. QUICKLY, BEFORE WORD CAN SPREAD.
JEHU AND A COMPANY OF MEN SET OUT AT ONCE—AND AS THEY APPROACH JEZREEL ...
CHARIOTS! A WHOLE LINE OF THEM. THE LEADER DRIVES LIKE A MADMAN!
IT MUST BE JEHU.

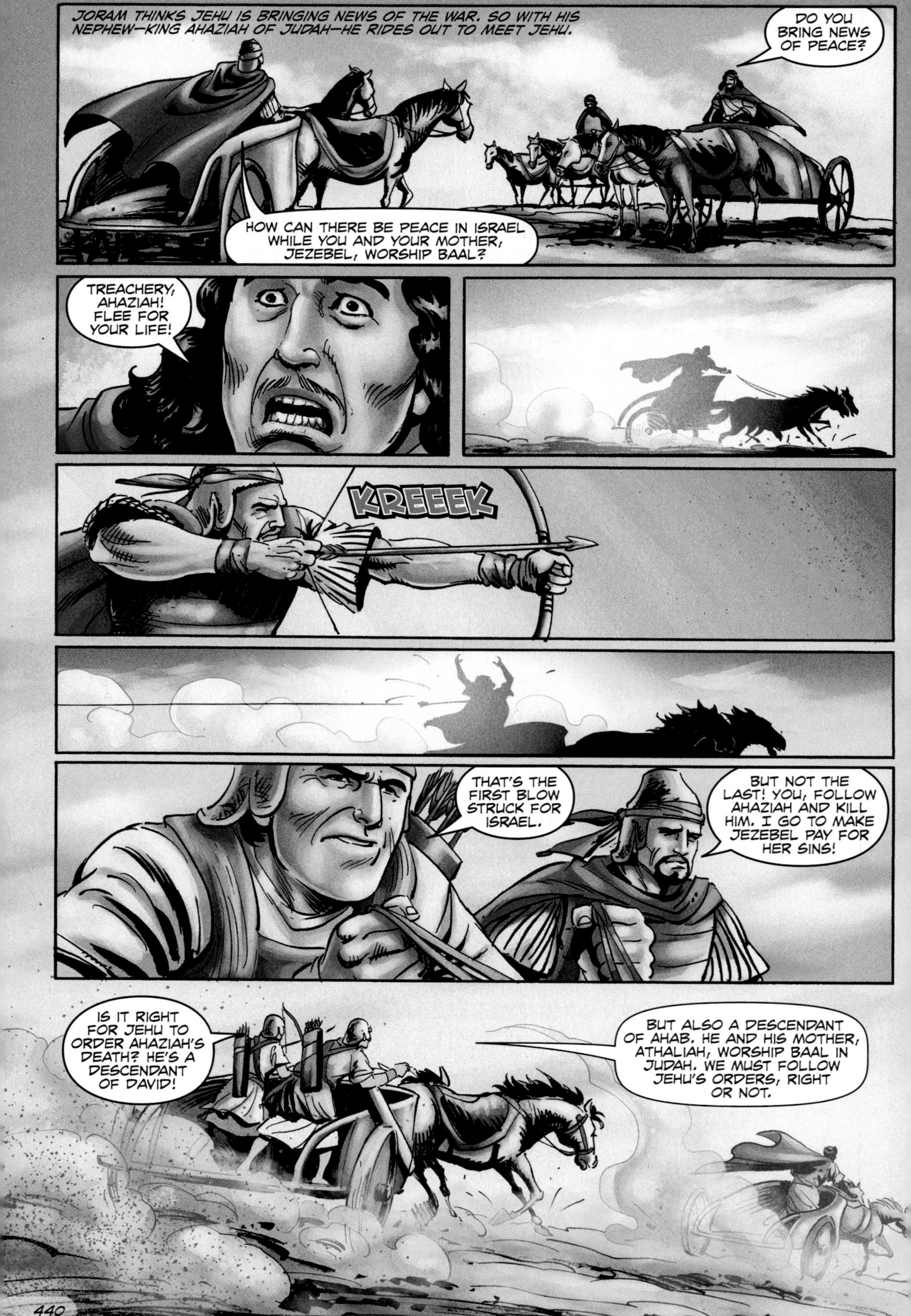
JORAM THINKS JEHU IS BRINGING NEWS OF THE WAR. SO WITH HIS NEPHEW—KING AHAZIAH OF JUDAH—HE RIDES OUT TO MEET JEHU.
DO YOU BRING NEWS OF PEACE?
HOW CAN THERE BE PEACE IN ISRAEL WHILE YOU AND YOUR MOTHER, JEZEBEL, WORSHIP BAAL?
TREACHERY, AHAZIAH! FLEE FOR YOUR LIFE!
KREEEK
THAT'S THE FIRST BLOW STRUCK FOR ISRAEL.
BUT NOT THE LAST! YOU, FOLLOW AHAZIAH AND KILL HIM. I GO TO MAKE JEZEBEL PAY FOR HER SINS!
IS IT RIGHT FOR JEHU TO ORDER AHAZIAH'S DEATH? HE'S A DESCENDANT OF DAVID!
BUT ALSO A DESCENDANT OF AHAB. HE AND HIS MOTHER, ATHALIAH, WORSHIP BAAL IN JUDAH. WE MUST FOLLOW JEHU'S ORDERS, RIGHT OR NOT.

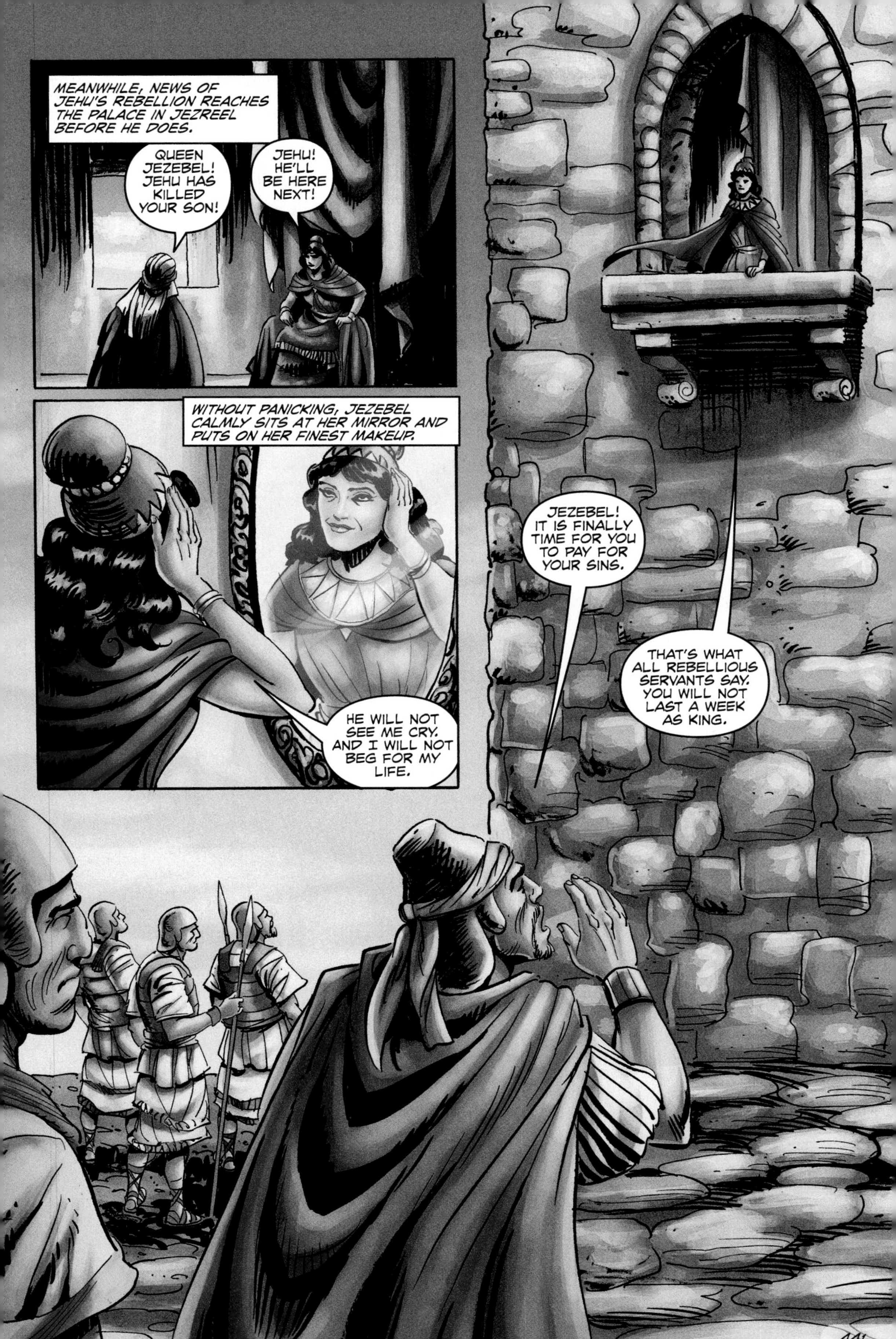
MEANWHILE, NEWS OF JEHU'S REBELLION REACHES THE PALACE IN JEZREEL BEFORE HE DOES.
QUEEN JEZEBEL! JEHU HAS KILLED YOUR SON!
JEHU! HE'LL BE HERE NEXT!
WITHOUT PANICKING, JEZEBEL CALMLY SITS AT HER MIRROR AND PUTS ON HER FINEST MAKEUP.
HE WILL NOT SEE ME CRY. AND I WILL NOT BEG FOR MY LIFE.
JEZEBEL! IT IS FINALLY TIME FOR YOU TO PAY FOR YOUR SINS.
THAT'S WHAT ALL REBELLIOUS SERVANTS SAY. YOU WILL NOT LAST A WEEK AS KING.

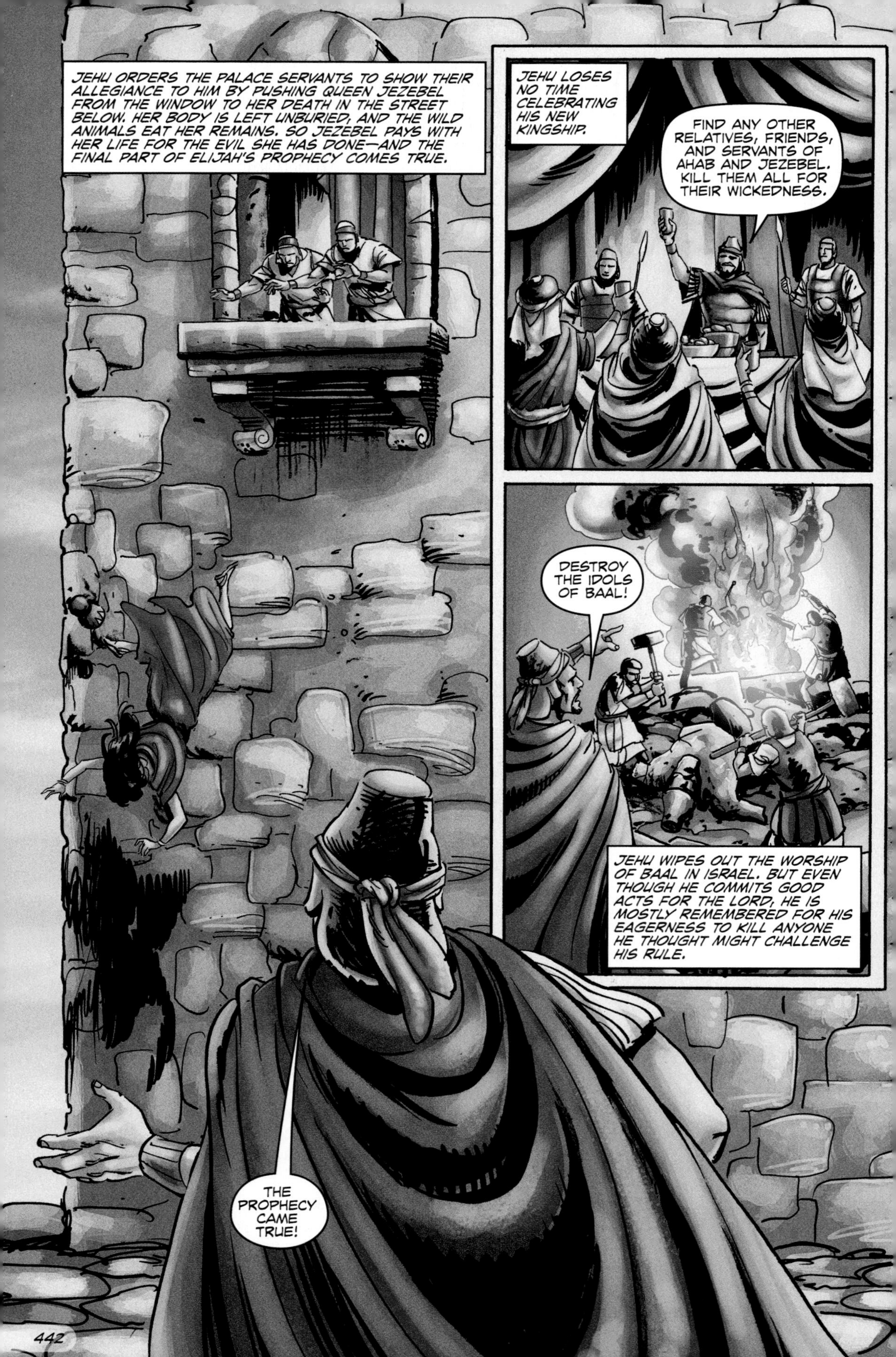
JEHU ORDERS THE PALACE SERVANTS TO SHOW THEIR ALLEGIANCE TO HIM BY PUSHING QUEEN JEZEBEL FROM THE WINDOW TO HER DEATH IN THE STREET BELOW. HER BODY IS LEFT UNBURIED, AND THE WILD ANIMALS EAT HER REMAINS. SO JEZEBEL PAYS WITH HER LIFE FOR THE EVIL SHE HAS DONE—AND THE FINAL PART OF ELIJAH'S PROPHECY COMES TRUE.
THE PROPHECY CAME TRUE!
JEHU LOSES NO TIME CELEBRATING HIS NEW KINGSHIP.
FIND ANY OTHER RELATIVES, FRIENDS, AND SERVANTS OF AHAB AND JEZEBEL. KILL THEM ALL FOR THEIR WICKEDNESS.
DESTROY THE IDOLS OF BAAL!
JEHU WIPES OUT THE WORSHIP OF BAAL IN ISRAEL. BUT EVEN THOUGH HE COMMITS GOOD ACTS FOR THE LORD, HE IS MOSTLY REMEMBERED FOR HIS EAGERNESS TO KILL ANYONE HE THOUGHT MIGHT CHALLENGE HIS RULE.

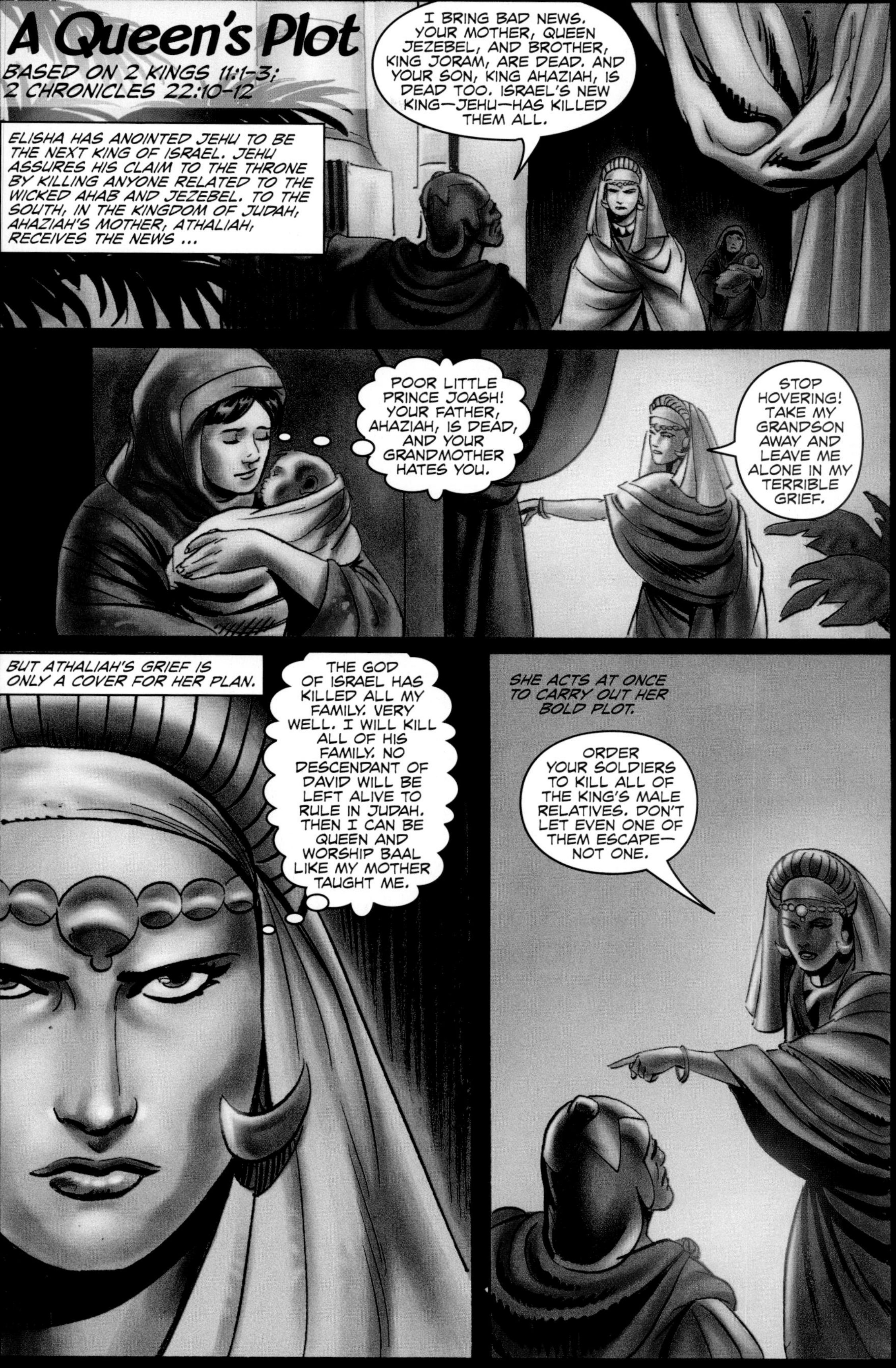
A Queen's Plot
BASED ON 2 KINGS 11:1-3; 2 CHRONICLES 22:10-12
ELISHA HAS ANOINTED JEHU TO BE THE NEXT KING OF ISRAEL. JEHU ASSURES HIS CLAIM TO THE THRONE BY KILLING ANYONE RELATED TO THE WICKED AHAB AND JEZEBEL. TO THE SOUTH, IN THE KINGDOM OF JUDAH, AHAZIAH'S MOTHER, ATHALIAH, RECEIVES THE NEWS ...
I BRING BAD NEWS. YOUR MOTHER, QUEEN JEZEBEL, AND BROTHER, KING JORAM, ARE DEAD. AND YOUR SON, KING AHAZIAH, IS DEAD TOO. ISRAEL'S NEW KING—JEHU—HAS KILLED THEM ALL.
POOR LITTLE PRINCE JOASH! YOUR FATHER, AHAZIAH, IS DEAD, AND YOUR GRANDMOTHER HATES YOU.
STOP HOVERING! TAKE MY GRANDSON AWAY AND LEAVE ME ALONE IN MY TERRIBLE GRIEF.
BUT ATHALIAH'S GRIEF IS ONLY A COVER FOR HER PLAN.
THE GOD OF ISRAEL HAS KILLED ALL MY FAMILY. VERY WELL. I WILL KILL ALL OF HIS FAMILY. NO DESCENDANT OF DAVID WILL BE LEFT ALIVE TO RULE IN JUDAH. THEN I CAN BE QUEEN AND WORSHIP BAAL LIKE MY MOTHER TAUGHT ME.
SHE ACTS AT ONCE TO CARRY OUT HER BOLD PLOT.
ORDER YOUR SOLDIERS TO KILL ALL OF THE KING'S MALE RELATIVES. DON'T LET EVEN ONE OF THEM ESCAPE—NOT ONE.

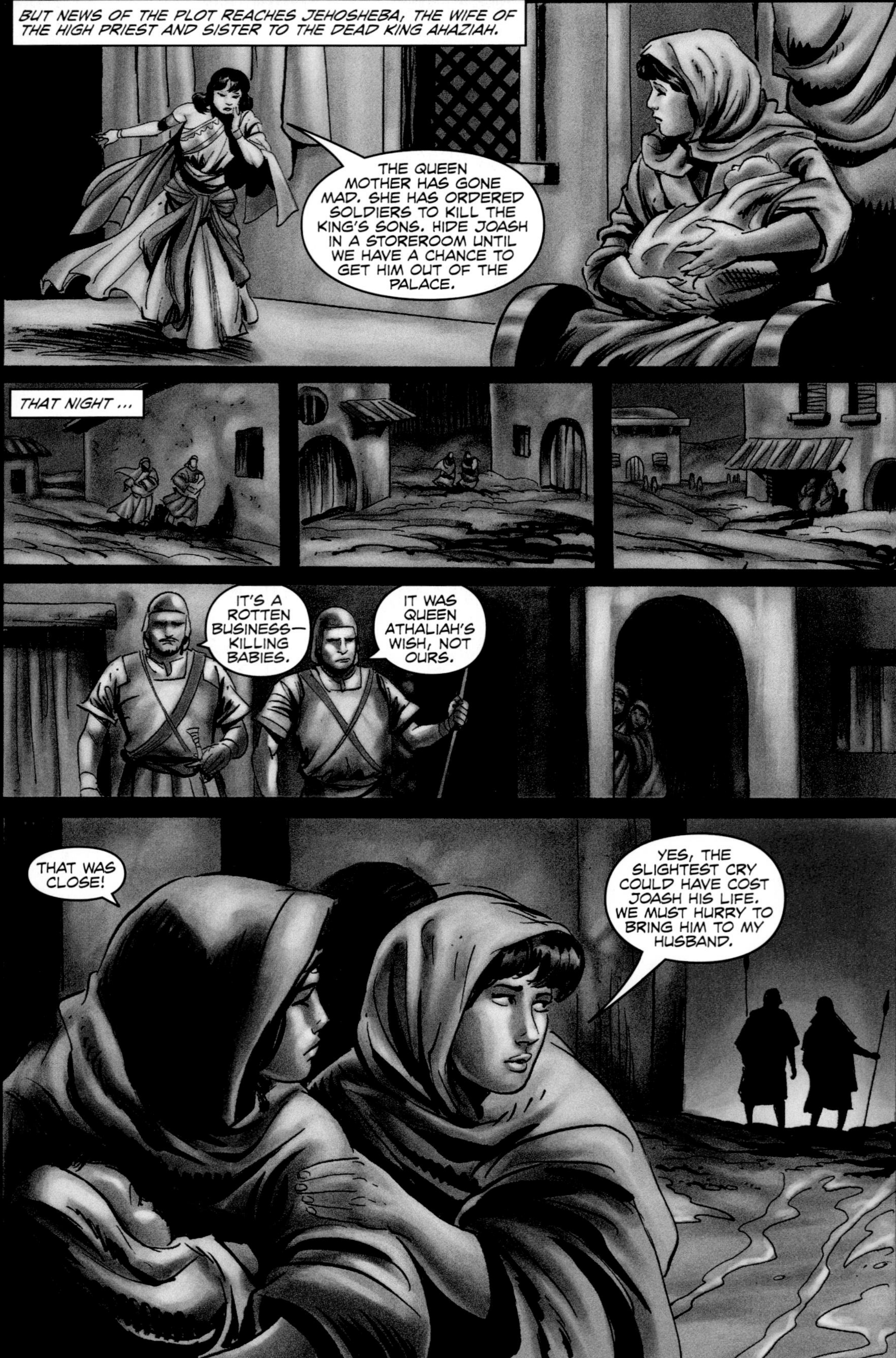

BUT NEWS OF THE PLOT REACHES JEHOSHEBA, THE WIFE OF THE HIGH PRIEST AND SISTER TO THE DEAD KING AHAZIAH.
THE QUEEN MOTHER HAS GONE MAD. SHE HAS ORDERED SOLDIERS TO KILL THE KING'S SONS. HIDE JOASH IN A STOREROOM UNTIL WE HAVE A CHANCE TO GET HIM OUT OF THE PALACE.
THAT NIGHT ...
IT'S A ROTTEN BUSINESS—KILLING BABIES.
IT WAS QUEEN ATHALIAH'S WISH, NOT OURS.
THAT WAS CLOSE!
YES, THE SLIGHTEST CRY COULD HAVE COST JOASH HIS LIFE. WE MUST HURRY TO BRING HIM TO MY HUSBAND.

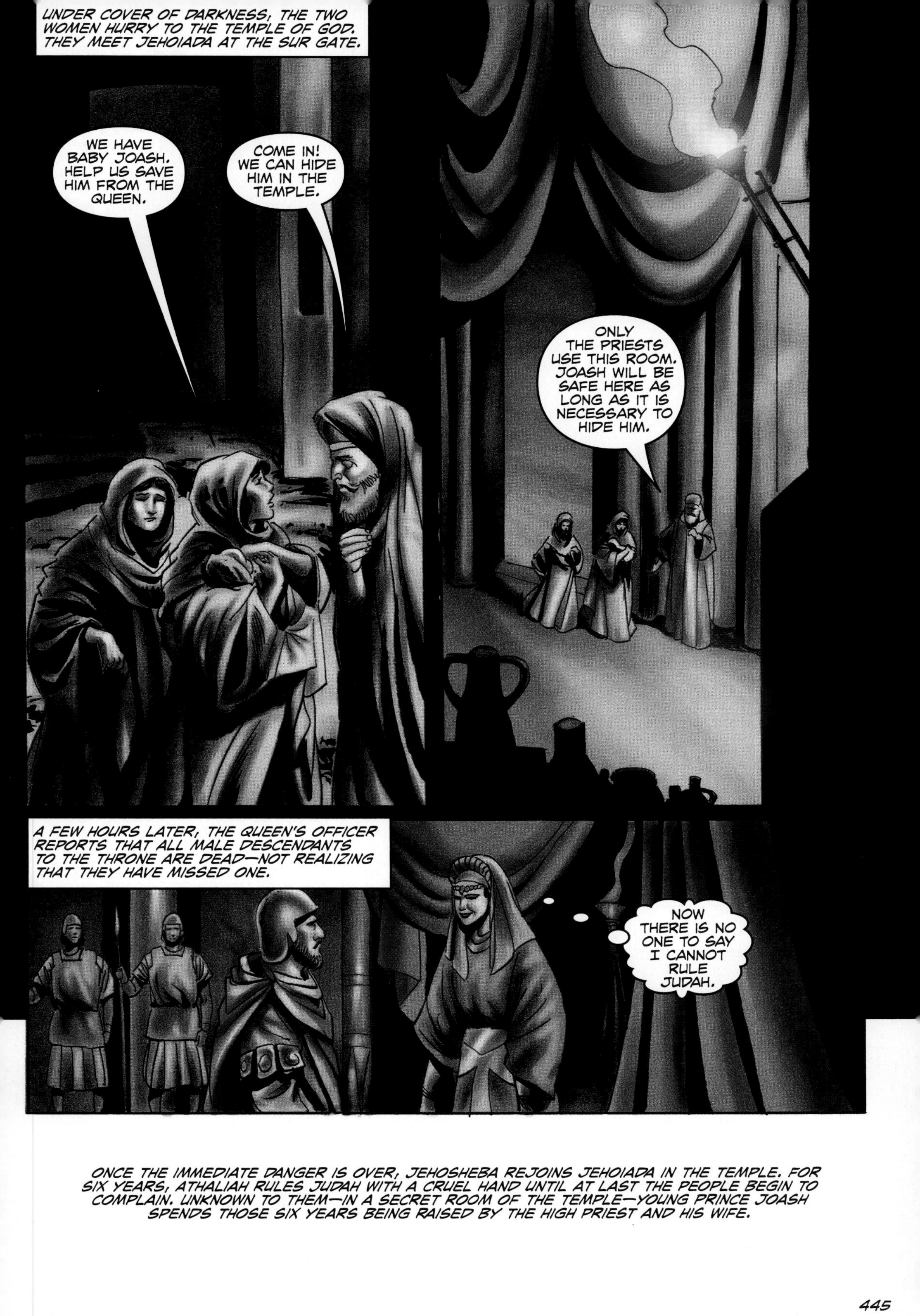
UNDER COVER OF DARKNESS, THE TWO WOMEN HURRY TO THE TEMPLE OF GOD. THEY MEET JEHOIADA AT THE SUR GATE.
WE HAVE BABY JOASH. HELP US SAVE HIM FROM THE QUEEN.
COME IN! WE CAN HIDE HIM IN THE TEMPLE.
ONLY THE PRIESTS USE THIS ROOM. JOASH WILL BE SAFE HERE AS LONG AS IT IS NECESSARY TO HIDE HIM.
A FEW HOURS LATER, THE QUEEN'S OFFICER REPORTS THAT ALL MALE DESCENDANTS TO THE THRONE ARE DEAD—NOT REALIZING THAT THEY HAVE MISSED ONE.
NOW THERE IS NO ONE TO SAY I CANNOT RULE JUDAH.

ONCE THE IMMEDIATE DANGER IS OVER, JEHOSHEBA REJOINS JEHOIADA IN THE TEMPLE. FOR SIX YEARS, ATHALIAH RULES JUDAH WITH A CRUEL HAND UNTIL AT LAST THE PEOPLE BEGIN TO COMPLAIN. UNKNOWN TO THEM—IN A SECRET ROOM OF THE TEMPLE—YOUNG PRINCE JOASH SPENDS THOSE SIX YEARS BEING RAISED BY THE HIGH PRIEST AND HIS WIFE.

The Boy King of Judah

BASED ON 2 KINGS 11:4–21; 2 CHRONICLES 23

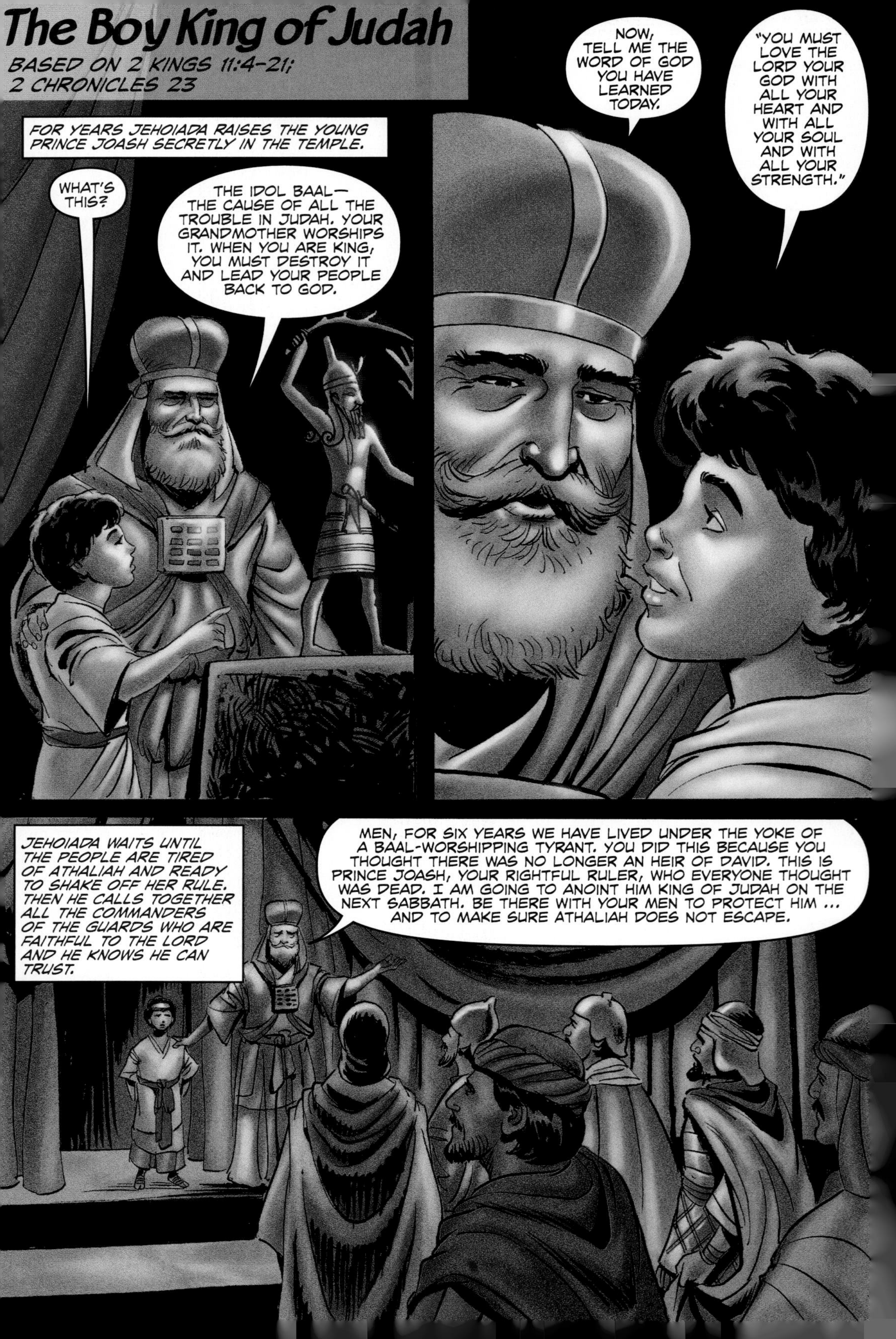
FOR YEARS JEHOIADA RAISES THE YOUNG PRINCE JOASH SECRETLY IN THE TEMPLE.
WHAT'S THIS?
THE IDOL BAAL— THE CAUSE OF ALL THE TROUBLE IN JUDAH. YOUR GRANDMOTHER WORSHIPS IT. WHEN YOU ARE KING, YOU MUST DESTROY IT AND LEAD YOUR PEOPLE BACK TO GOD.
NOW, TELL ME THE WORD OF GOD YOU HAVE LEARNED TODAY.
"YOU MUST LOVE THE LORD YOUR GOD WITH ALL YOUR HEART AND WITH ALL YOUR SOUL AND WITH ALL YOUR STRENGTH."
JEHOIADA WAITS UNTIL THE PEOPLE ARE TIRED OF ATHALIAH AND READY TO SHAKE OFF HER RULE. THEN HE CALLS TOGETHER ALL THE COMMANDERS OF THE GUARDS WHO ARE FAITHFUL TO THE LORD AND HE KNOWS HE CAN TRUST.
MEN, FOR SIX YEARS WE HAVE LIVED UNDER THE YOKE OF A BAAL-WORSHIPPING TYRANT. YOU DID THIS BECAUSE YOU THOUGHT THERE WAS NO LONGER AN HEIR OF DAVID. THIS IS PRINCE JOASH, YOUR RIGHTFUL RULER, WHO EVERYONE THOUGHT WAS DEAD. I AM GOING TO ANOINT HIM KING OF JUDAH ON THE NEXT SABBATH. BE THERE WITH YOUR MEN TO PROTECT HIM ... AND TO MAKE SURE ATHALIAH DOES NOT ESCAPE.

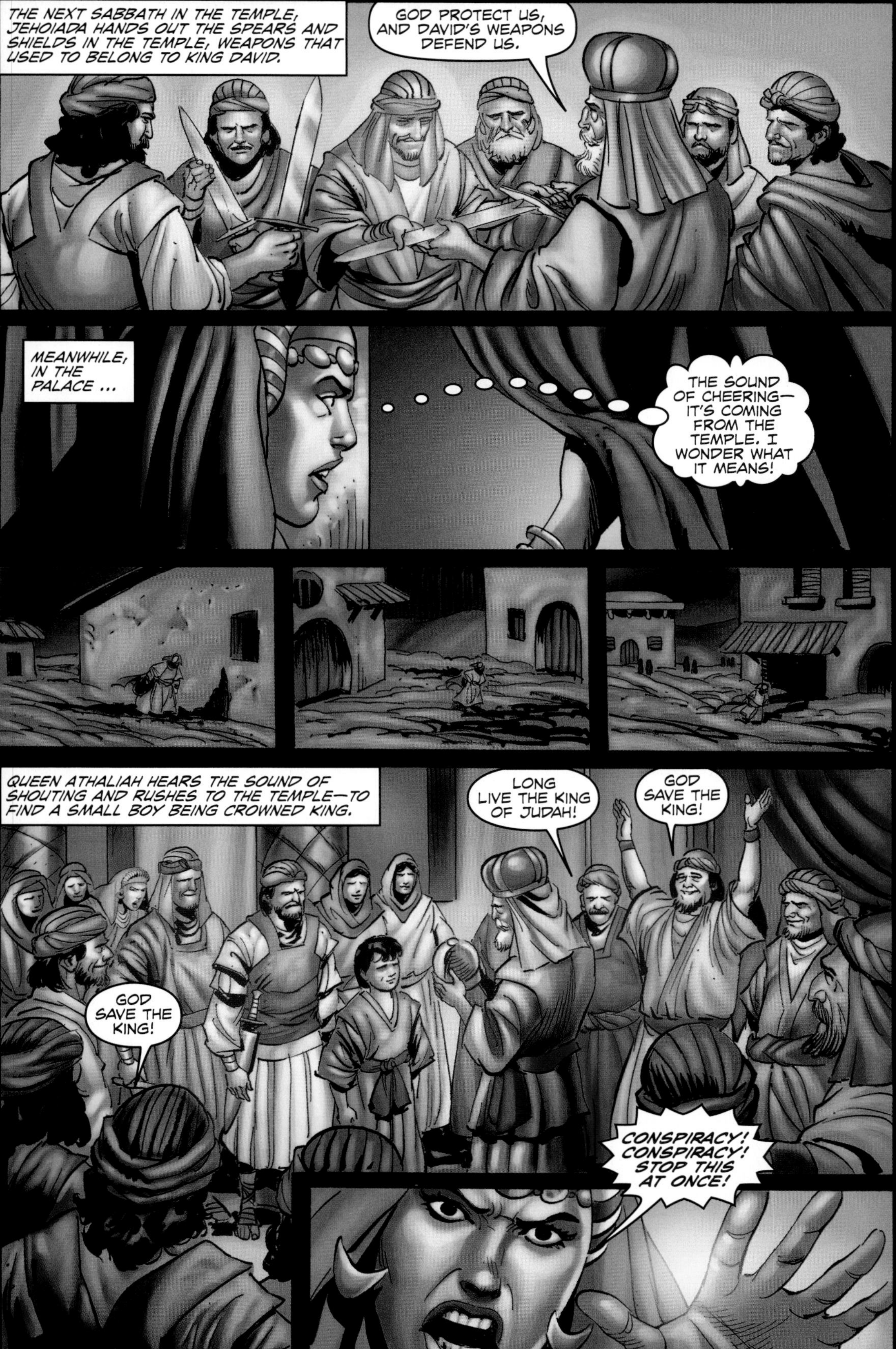
THE NEXT SABBATH IN THE TEMPLE, JEHOIADA HANDS OUT THE SPEARS AND SHIELDS IN THE TEMPLE, WEAPONS THAT USED TO BELONG TO KING DAVID.
GOD PROTECT US, AND DAVID'S WEAPONS DEFEND US.
MEANWHILE, IN THE PALACE ...
THE SOUND OF CHEERING—IT'S COMING FROM THE TEMPLE. I WONDER WHAT IT MEANS!
QUEEN ATHALIAH HEARS THE SOUND OF SHOUTING AND RUSHES TO THE TEMPLE—TO FIND A SMALL BOY BEING CROWNED KING.
LONG LIVE THE KING OF JUDAH!
GOD SAVE THE KING!
GOD SAVE THE KING!
CONSPIRACY! CONSPIRACY! STOP THIS AT ONCE!

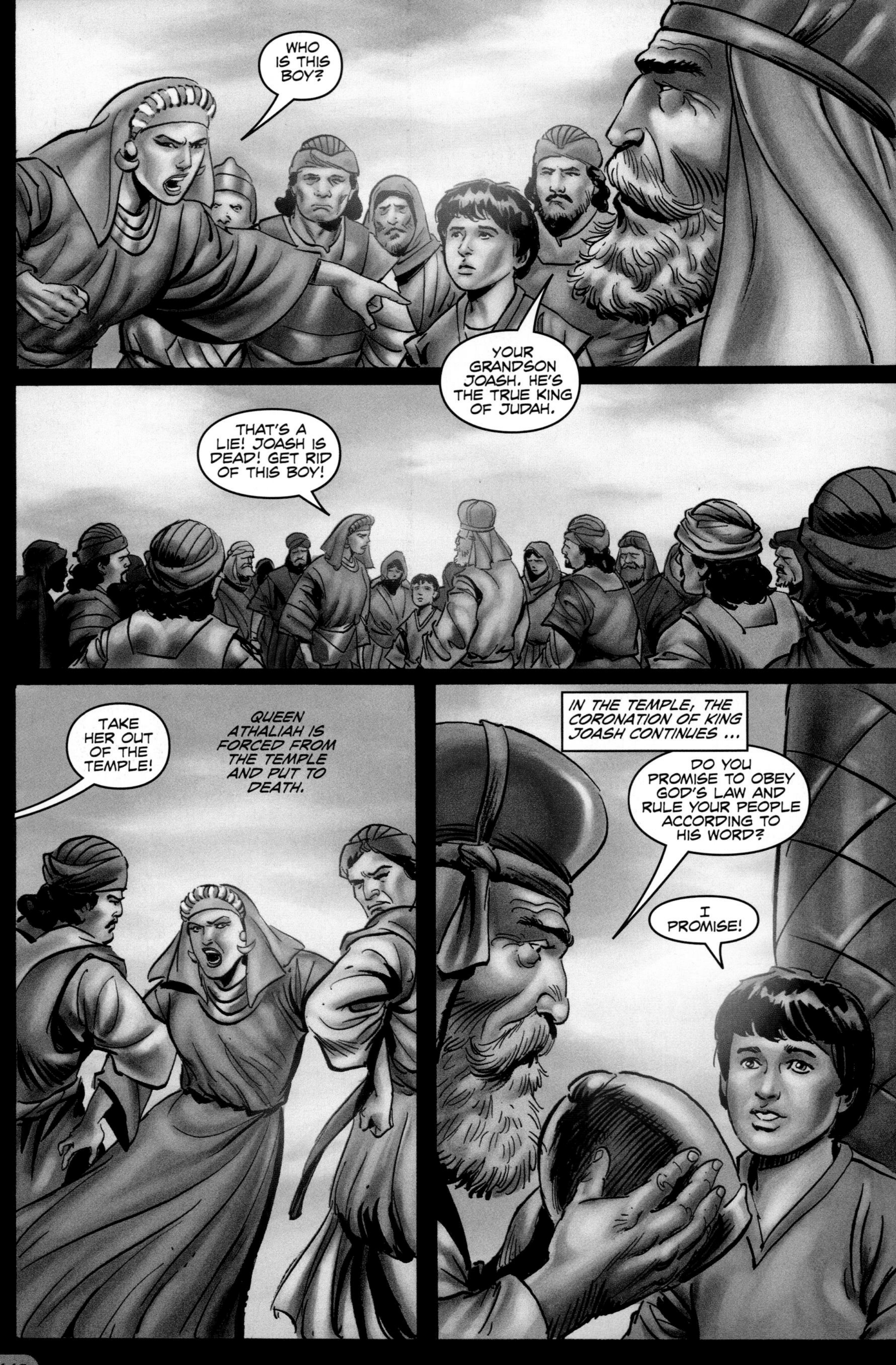
WHO IS THIS BOY?
YOUR GRANDSON JOASH. HE'S THE TRUE KING OF JUDAH.
THAT'S A LIE! JOASH IS DEAD! GET RID OF THIS BOY!
TAKE HER OUT OF THE TEMPLE!
QUEEN ATHALIAH IS FORCED FROM THE TEMPLE AND PUT TO DEATH.
IN THE TEMPLE, THE CORONATION OF KING JOASH CONTINUES ...
DO YOU PROMISE TO OBEY GOD'S LAW AND RULE YOUR PEOPLE ACCORDING TO HIS WORD?
I PROMISE!

Dagger in the Night

BASED ON 2 CHRONICLES 24:17-27; 2 KINGS 12

UNDER THE GUIDANCE OF JEHOIADA, THE HIGH PRIEST, JOASH DESTROYS THE TEMPLE OF BAAL AND LEADS HIS PEOPLE BACK TO THE WORSHIP OF GOD. THE HOUSE OF GOD IS REPAIRED, AND FOR YEARS JUDAH PROSPERS. BUT WHEN JEHOIADA DIES, JOASH IS TOO WEAK TO STAND UP UNDER THE PRESSURE OF THOSE WHO WANT TO TURN HIM AWAY FROM GOD. FINALLY, JEHOIADA'S SON, ZECHARIAH, GOES TO THE KING.

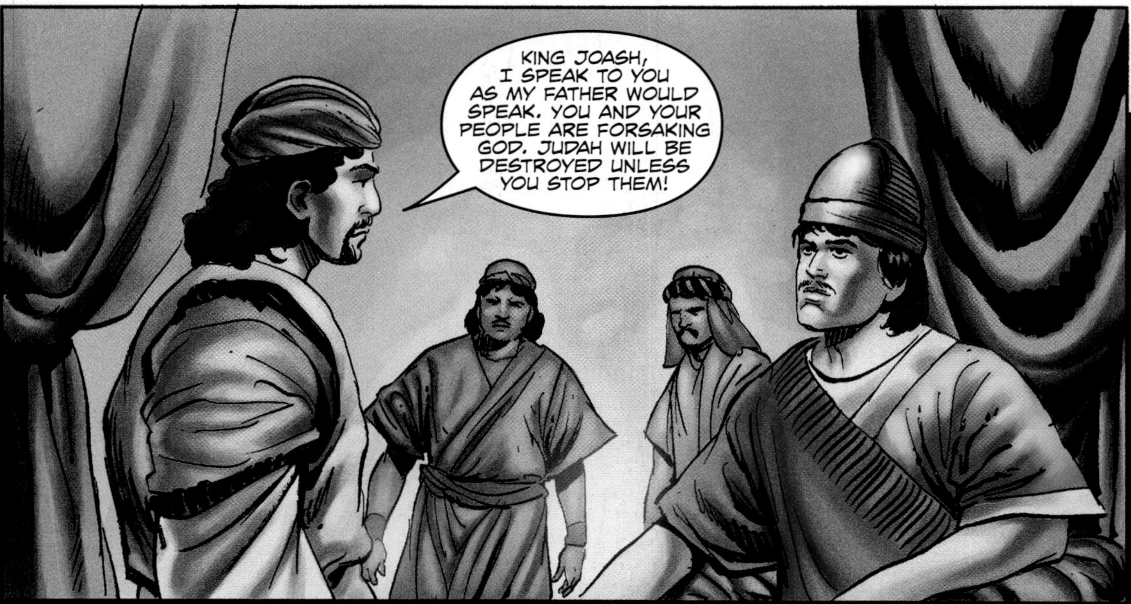
KING JOASH, I SPEAK TO YOU AS MY FATHER WOULD SPEAK. YOU AND YOUR PEOPLE ARE FORSAKING GOD. JUDAH WILL BE DESTROYED UNLESS YOU STOP THEM!

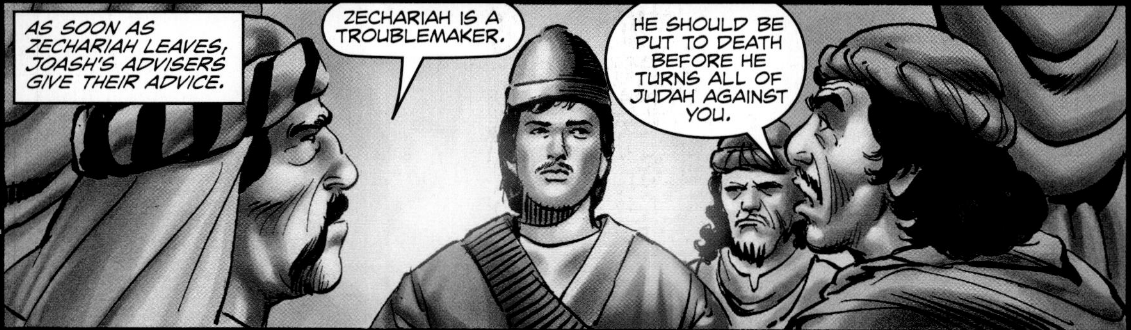
AS SOON AS ZECHARIAH LEAVES, JOASH'S ADVISERS GIVE THEIR ADVICE.
ZECHARIAH IS A TROUBLEMAKER.
HE SHOULD BE PUT TO DEATH BEFORE HE TURNS ALL OF JUDAH AGAINST YOU.

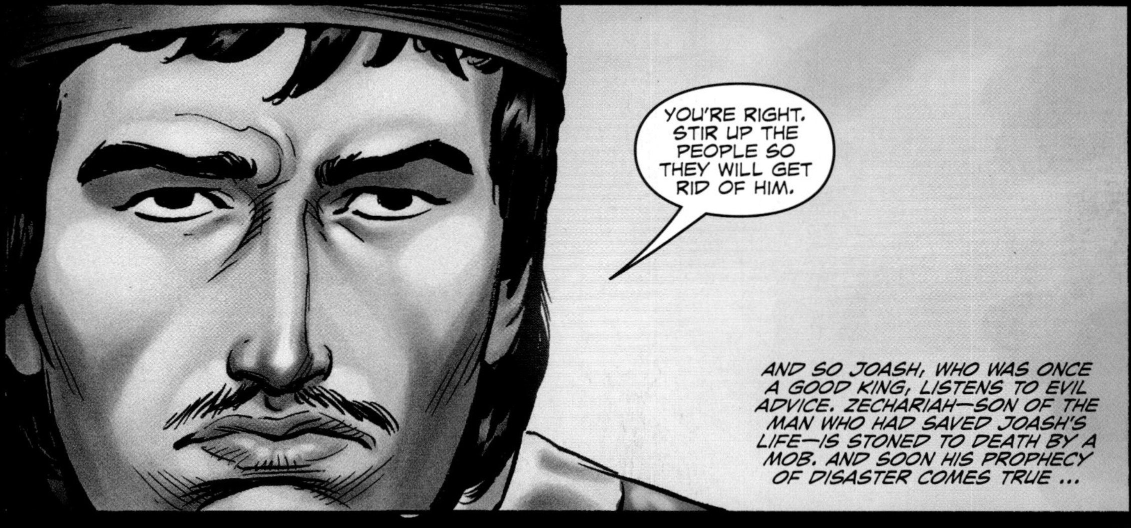
YOU'RE RIGHT. STIR UP THE PEOPLE SO THEY WILL GET RID OF HIM.
AND SO JOASH, WHO WAS ONCE A GOOD KING, LISTENS TO EVIL ADVICE. ZECHARIAH—SON OF THE MAN WHO HAD SAVED JOASH'S LIFE—IS STONED TO DEATH BY A MOB. AND SOON HIS PROPHECY OF DISASTER COMES TRUE ...

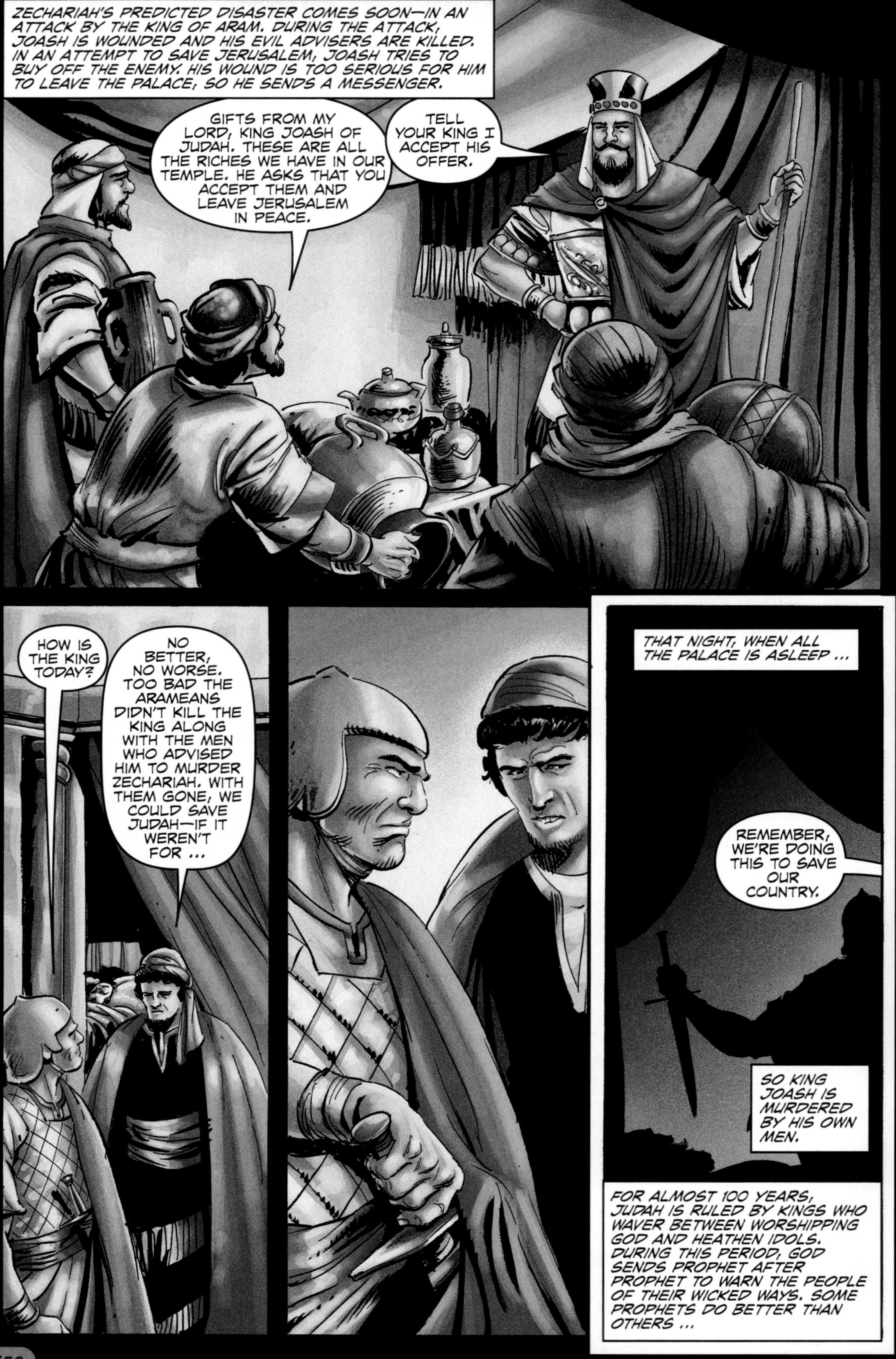
ZECHARIAH'S PREDICTED DISASTER COMES SOON—IN AN ATTACK BY THE KING OF ARAM. DURING THE ATTACK, JOASH IS WOUNDED AND HIS EVIL ADVISERS ARE KILLED. IN AN ATTEMPT TO SAVE JERUSALEM, JOASH TRIES TO BUY OFF THE ENEMY. HIS WOUND IS TOO SERIOUS FOR HIM TO LEAVE THE PALACE, SO HE SENDS A MESSENGER.
GIFTS FROM MY LORD, KING JOASH OF JUDAH. THESE ARE ALL THE RICHES WE HAVE IN OUR TEMPLE. HE ASKS THAT YOU ACCEPT THEM AND LEAVE JERUSALEM IN PEACE.
TELL YOUR KING I ACCEPT HIS OFFER.
HOW IS THE KING TODAY?
NO BETTER, NO WORSE. TOO BAD THE ARAMEANS DIDN'T KILL THE KING ALONG WITH THE MEN WHO ADVISED HIM TO MURDER ZECHARIAH. WITH THEM GONE, WE COULD SAVE JUDAH—IF IT WEREN'T FOR ...
THAT NIGHT, WHEN ALL THE PALACE IS ASLEEP ...
REMEMBER, WE'RE DOING THIS TO SAVE OUR COUNTRY.
SO KING JOASH IS MURDERED BY HIS OWN MEN.
FOR ALMOST 100 YEARS, JUDAH IS RULED BY KINGS WHO WAVER BETWEEN WORSHIPPING GOD AND HEATHEN IDOLS. DURING THIS PERIOD, GOD SENDS PROPHET AFTER PROPHET TO WARN THE PEOPLE OF THEIR WICKED WAYS. SOME PROPHETS DO BETTER THAN OTHERS ...

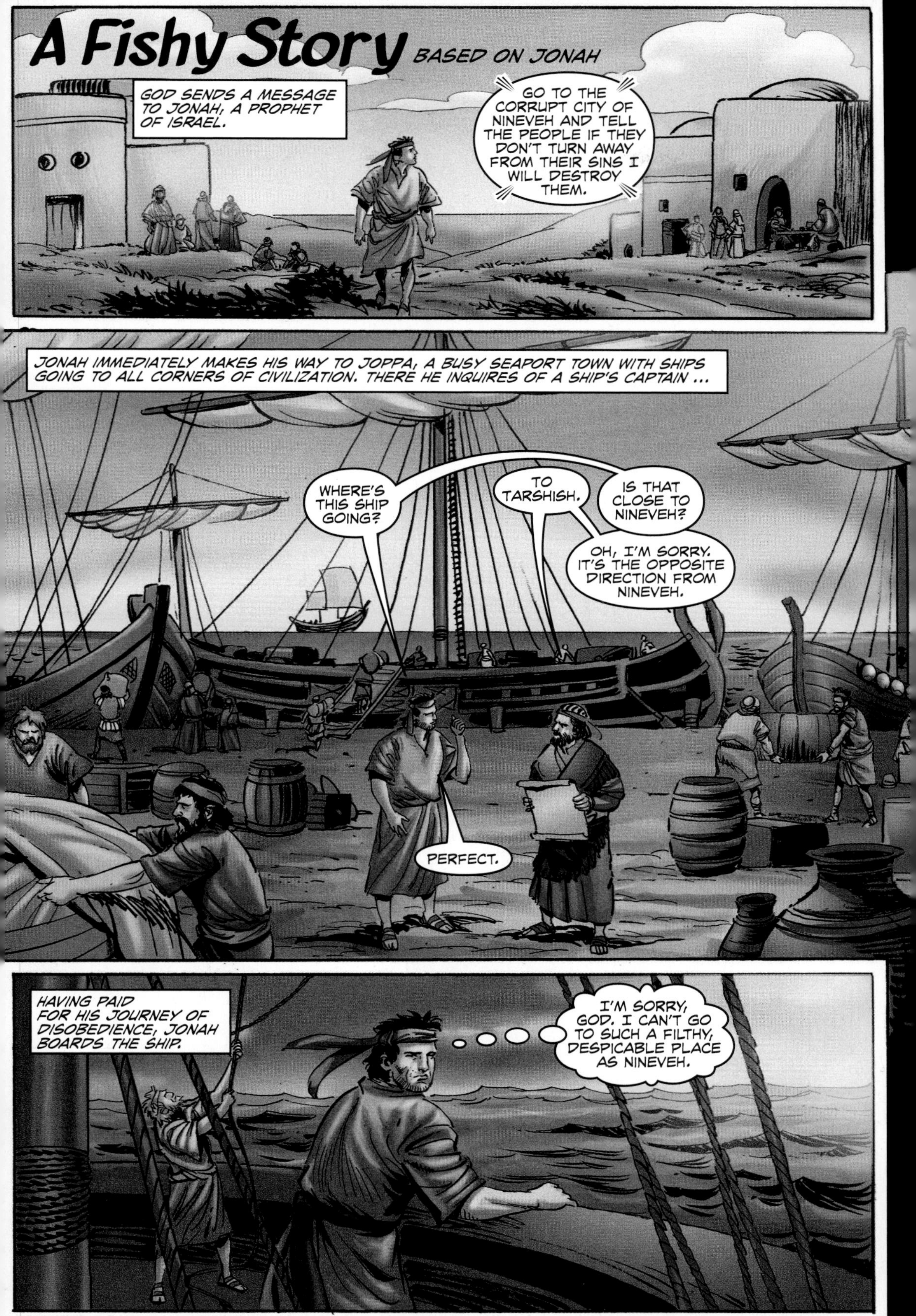
A Fishy Story
BASED ON JONAH
GOD SENDS A MESSAGE TO JONAH, A PROPHET OF ISRAEL.
GO TO THE CORRUPT CITY OF NINEVEH AND TELL THE PEOPLE IF THEY DON'T TURN AWAY FROM THEIR SINS I WILL DESTROY THEM.
JONAH IMMEDIATELY MAKES HIS WAY TO JOPPA, A BUSY SEAPORT TOWN WITH SHIPS GOING TO ALL CORNERS OF CIVILIZATION. THERE HE INQUIRES OF A SHIP'S CAPTAIN ...
WHERE'S THIS SHIP GOING?
TO TARSHISH.
IS THAT CLOSE TO NINEVEH?
OH, I'M SORRY. IT'S THE OPPOSITE DIRECTION FROM NINEVEH.
PERFECT.
HAVING PAID FOR HIS JOURNEY OF DISOBEDIENCE, JONAH BOARDS THE SHIP.
I'M SORRY, GOD. I CAN'T GO TO SUCH A FILTHY, DESPICABLE PLACE AS NINEVEH.

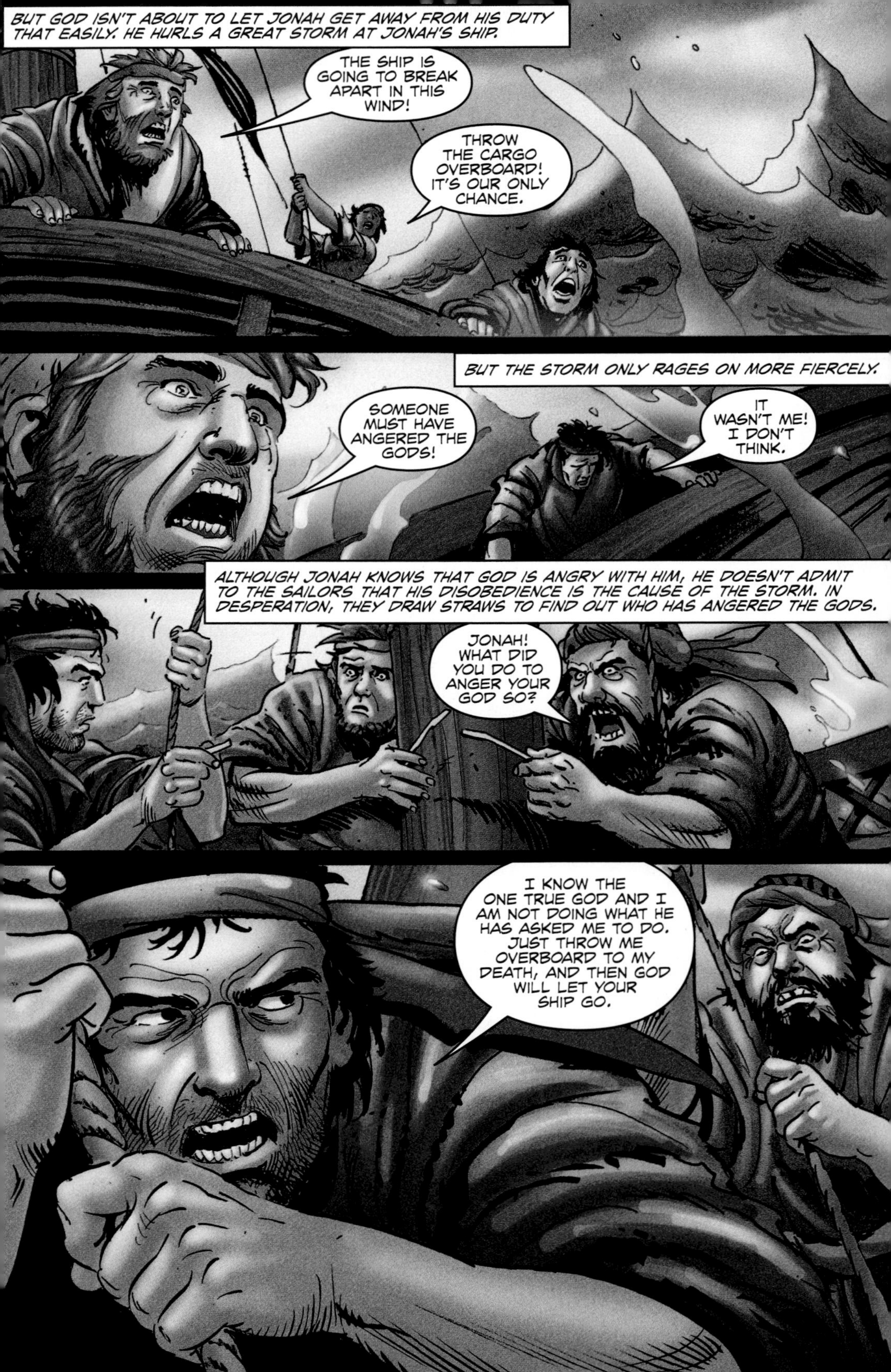
BUT GOD ISN'T ABOUT TO LET JONAH GET AWAY FROM HIS DUTY THAT EASILY. HE HURLS A GREAT STORM AT JONAH'S SHIP.
THE SHIP IS GOING TO BREAK APART IN THIS WIND!
THROW THE CARGO OVERBOARD! IT'S OUR ONLY CHANCE.
BUT THE STORM ONLY RAGES ON MORE FIERCELY.
SOMEONE MUST HAVE ANGERED THE GODS!
IT WASN'T ME! I DON'T THINK.
ALTHOUGH JONAH KNOWS THAT GOD IS ANGRY WITH HIM, HE DOESN'T ADMIT TO THE SAILORS THAT HIS DISOBEDIENCE IS THE CAUSE OF THE STORM. IN DESPERATION, THEY DRAW STRAWS TO FIND OUT WHO HAS ANGERED THE GODS.
JONAH! WHAT DID YOU DO TO ANGER YOUR GOD SO?
I KNOW THE ONE TRUE GOD AND I AM NOT DOING WHAT HE HAS ASKED ME TO DO. JUST THROW ME OVERBOARD TO MY DEATH, AND THEN GOD WILL LET YOUR SHIP GO.

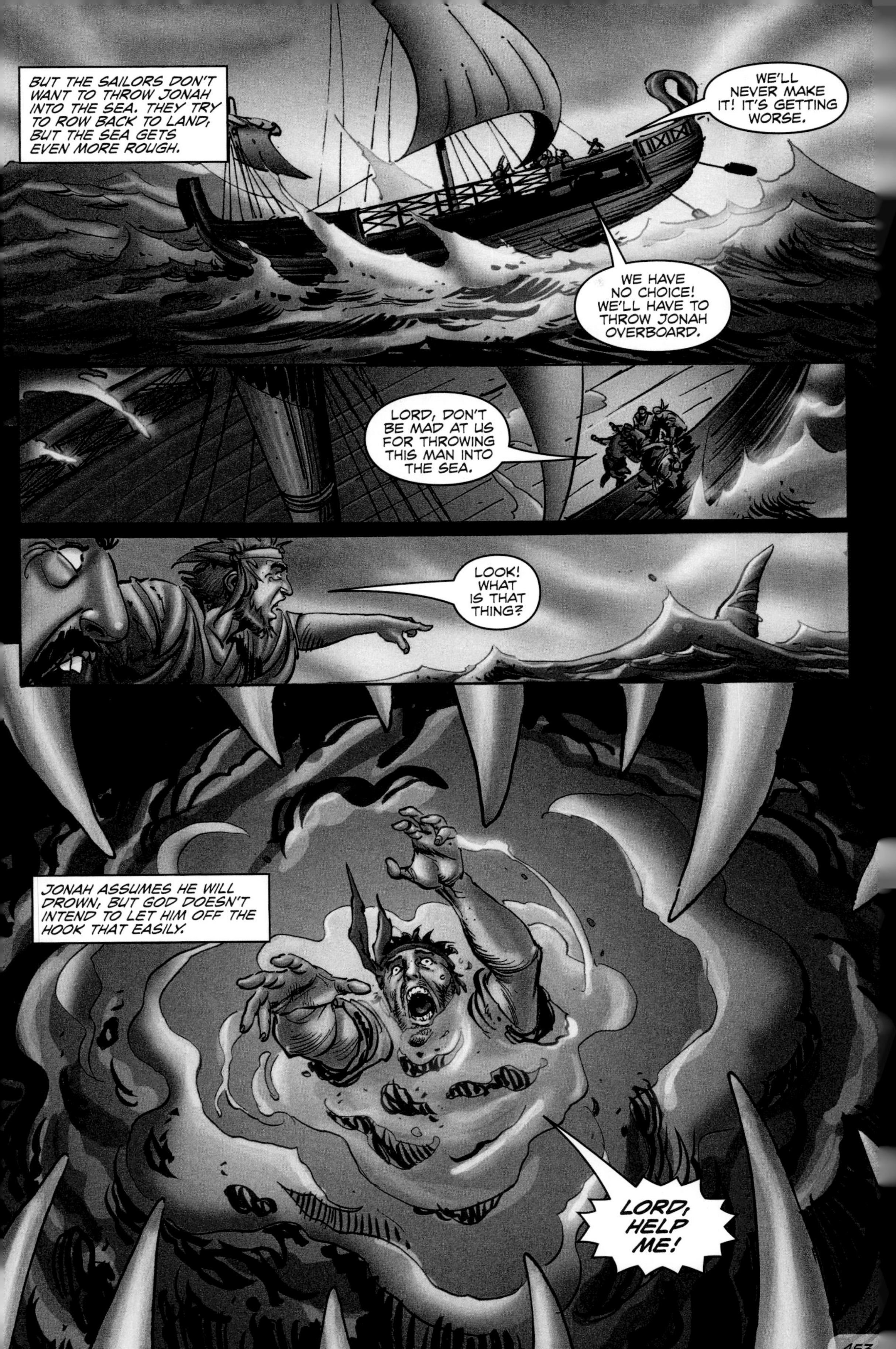
BUT THE SAILORS DON'T WANT TO THROW JONAH INTO THE SEA. THEY TRY TO ROW BACK TO LAND, BUT THE SEA GETS EVEN MORE ROUGH.
WE'LL NEVER MAKE IT! IT'S GETTING WORSE.
WE HAVE NO CHOICE! WE'LL HAVE TO THROW JONAH OVERBOARD.
LORD, DON'T BE MAD AT US FOR THROWING THIS MAN INTO THE SEA.
LOOK! WHAT IS THAT THING?
JONAH ASSUMES HE WILL DROWN, BUT GOD DOESN'T INTEND TO LET HIM OFF THE HOOK THAT EASILY.
LORD, HELP ME!

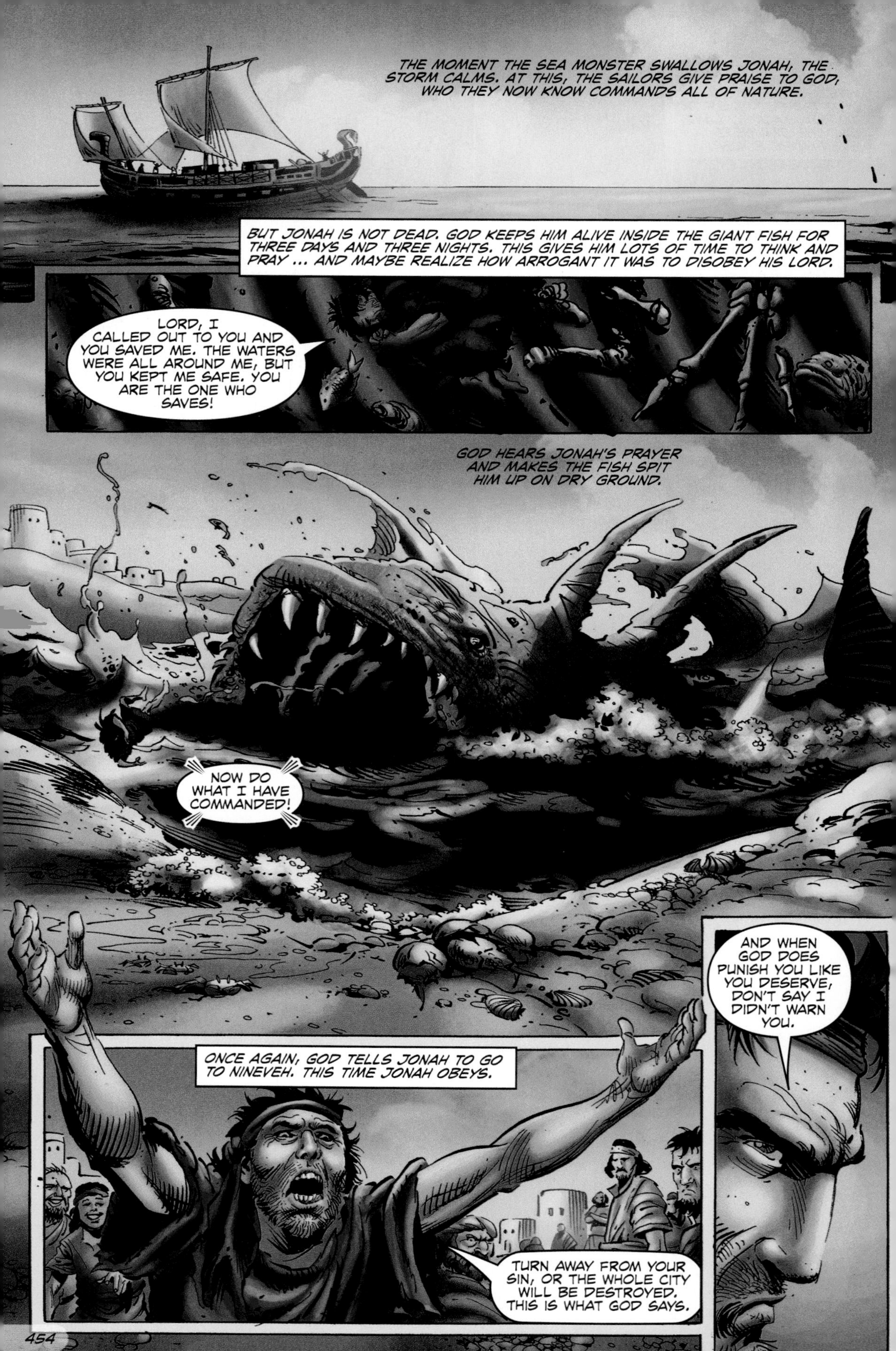
THE MOMENT THE SEA MONSTER SWALLOWS JONAH, THE STORM CALMS. AT THIS, THE SAILORS GIVE PRAISE TO GOD, WHO THEY NOW KNOW COMMANDS ALL OF NATURE.
BUT JONAH IS NOT DEAD. GOD KEEPS HIM ALIVE INSIDE THE GIANT FISH FOR THREE DAYS AND THREE NIGHTS. THIS GIVES HIM LOTS OF TIME TO THINK AND PRAY ... AND MAYBE REALIZE HOW ARROGANT IT WAS TO DISOBEY HIS LORD.
LORD, I CALLED OUT TO YOU AND YOU SAVED ME. THE WATERS WERE ALL AROUND ME, BUT YOU KEPT ME SAFE. YOU ARE THE ONE WHO SAVES!
GOD HEARS JONAH'S PRAYER AND MAKES THE FISH SPIT HIM UP ON DRY GROUND.
NOW DO WHAT I HAVE COMMANDED!
ONCE AGAIN, GOD TELLS JONAH TO GO TO NINEVEH. THIS TIME JONAH OBEYS.
TURN AWAY FROM YOUR SIN, OR THE WHOLE CITY WILL BE DESTROYED. THIS IS WHAT GOD SAYS.
AND WHEN GOD DOES PUNISH YOU LIKE YOU DESERVE, DON'T SAY I DIDN'T WARN YOU.

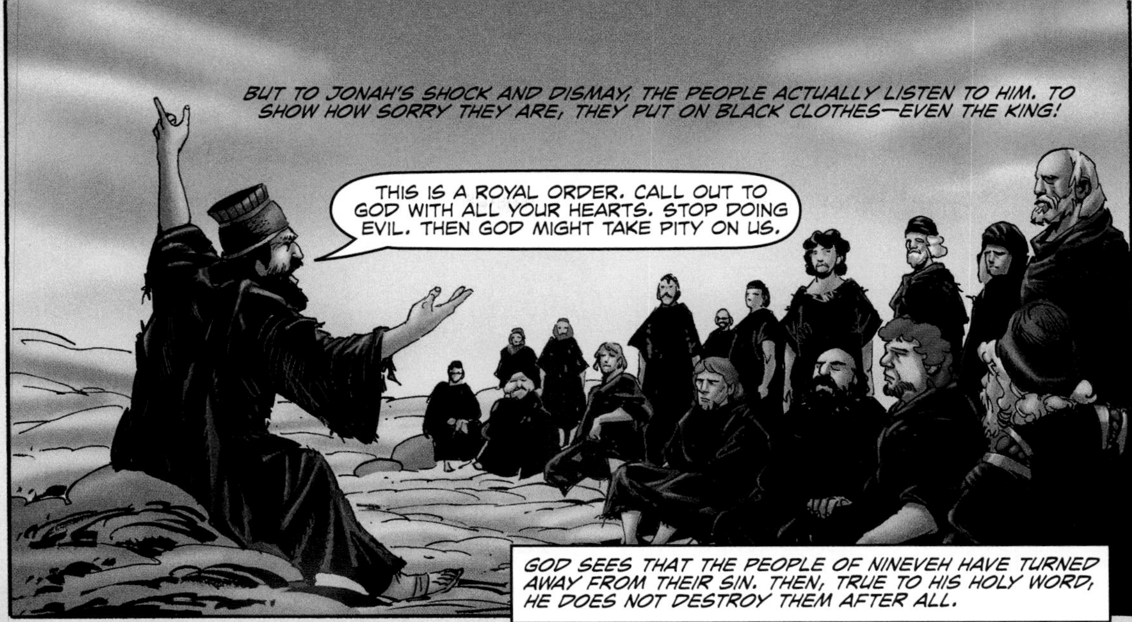
BUT TO JONAH'S SHOCK AND DISMAY, THE PEOPLE ACTUALLY LISTEN TO HIM. TO SHOW HOW SORRY THEY ARE, THEY PUT ON BLACK CLOTHES—EVEN THE KING!
THIS IS A ROYAL ORDER. CALL OUT TO GOD WITH ALL YOUR HEARTS. STOP DOING EVIL. THEN GOD MIGHT TAKE PITY ON US.
GOD SEES THAT THE PEOPLE OF NINEVEH HAVE TURNED AWAY FROM THEIR SIN. THEN, TRUE TO HIS HOLY WORD, HE DOES NOT DESTROY THEM AFTER ALL.

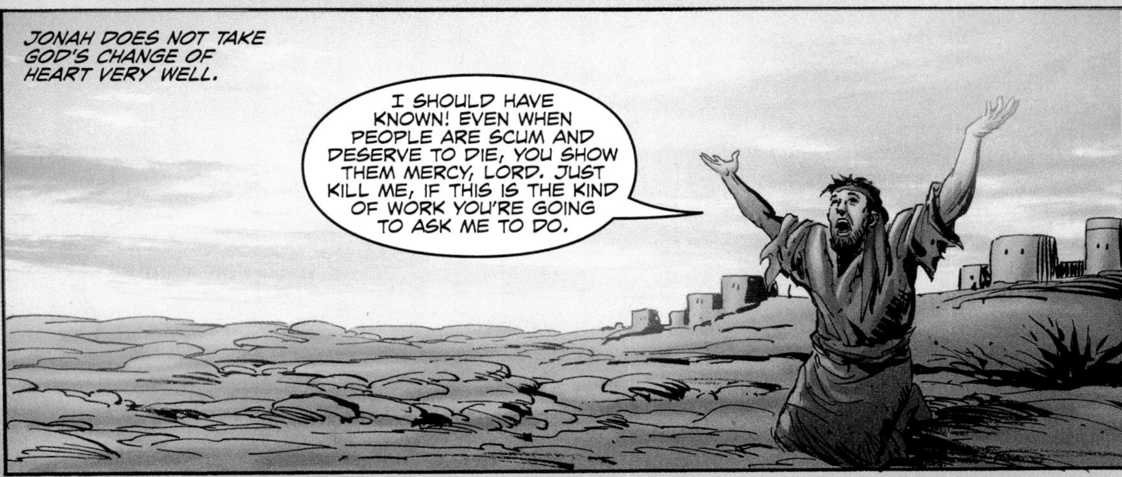
JONAH DOES NOT TAKE GOD'S CHANGE OF HEART VERY WELL.
I SHOULD HAVE KNOWN! EVEN WHEN PEOPLE ARE SCUM AND DESERVE TO DIE, YOU SHOW THEM MERCY, LORD. JUST KILL ME, IF THIS IS THE KIND OF WORK YOU'RE GOING TO ASK ME TO DO.

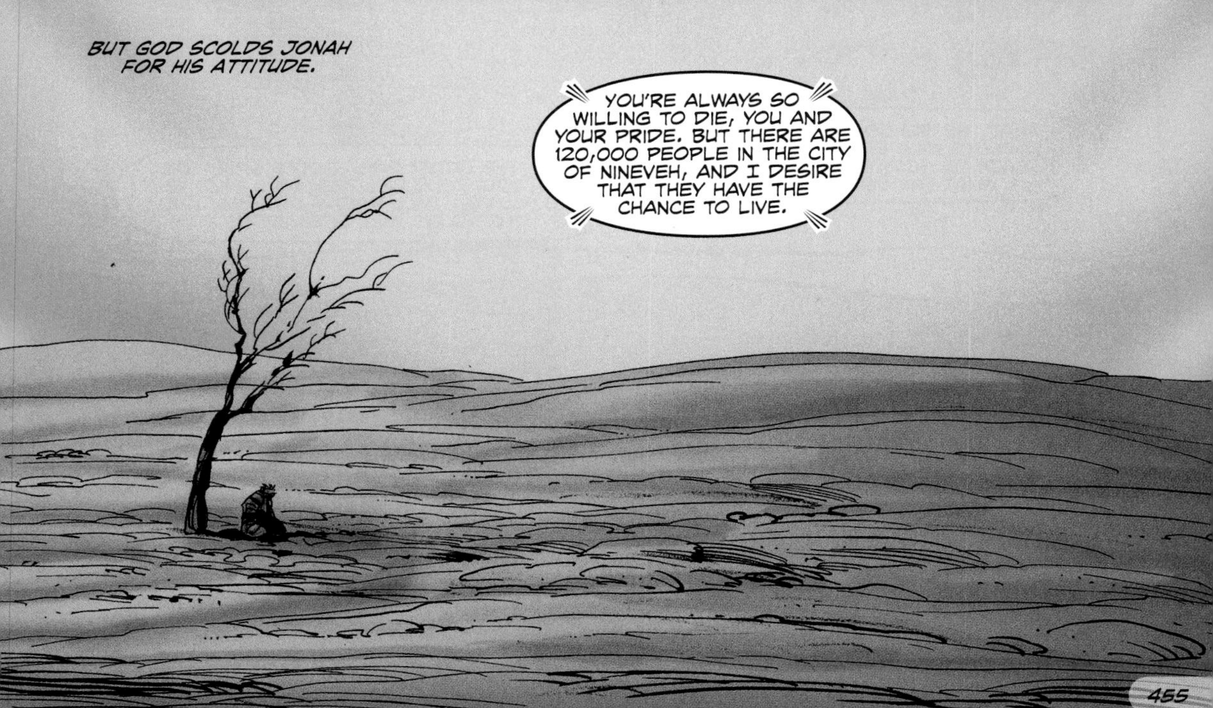
BUT GOD SCOLDS JONAH FOR HIS ATTITUDE.
YOU'RE ALWAYS SO WILLING TO DIE, YOU AND YOUR PRIDE. BUT THERE ARE 120,000 PEOPLE IN THE CITY OF NINEVEH, AND I DESIRE THAT THEY HAVE THE CHANCE TO LIVE.

Four Prophets

SPEAK TO GOD'S PEOPLE IN DIFFERENT WAYS ...

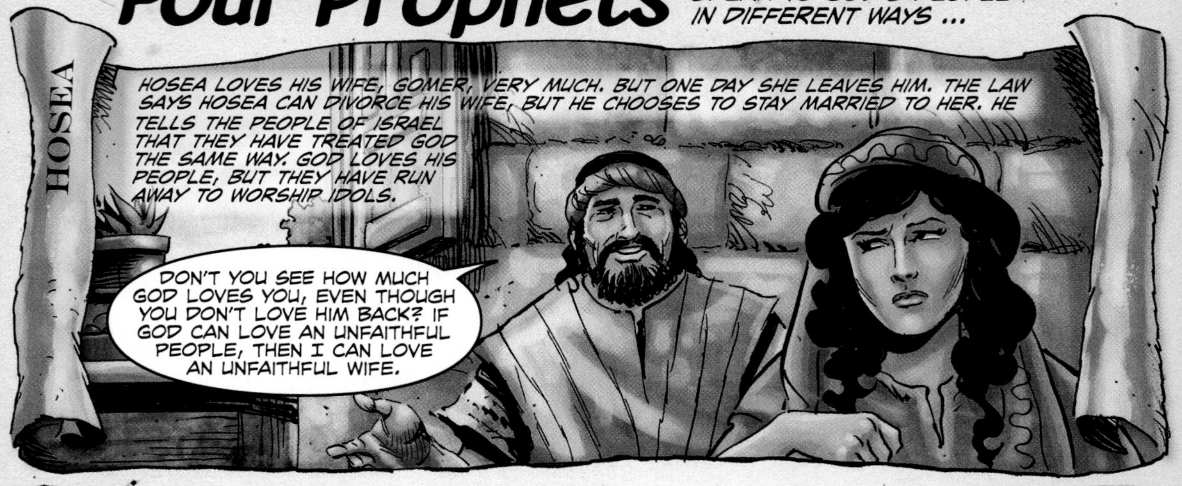
HOSEA
HOSEA LOVES HIS WIFE, GOMER, VERY MUCH. BUT ONE DAY SHE LEAVES HIM. THE LAW SAYS HOSEA CAN DIVORCE HIS WIFE, BUT HE CHOOSES TO STAY MARRIED TO HER. HE TELLS THE PEOPLE OF ISRAEL THAT THEY HAVE TREATED GOD THE SAME WAY. GOD LOVES HIS PEOPLE, BUT THEY HAVE RUN AWAY TO WORSHIP IDOLS.
DON'T YOU SEE HOW MUCH GOD LOVES YOU, EVEN THOUGH YOU DON'T LOVE HIM BACK? IF GOD CAN LOVE AN UNFAITHFUL PEOPLE, THEN I CAN LOVE AN UNFAITHFUL WIFE.

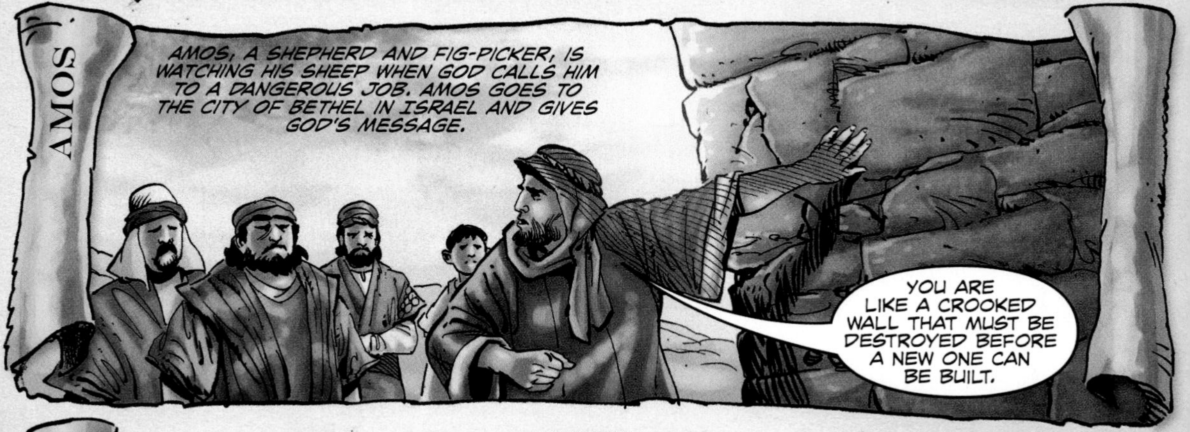
AMOS
AMOS, A SHEPHERD AND FIG-PICKER, IS WATCHING HIS SHEEP WHEN GOD CALLS HIM TO A DANGEROUS JOB. AMOS GOES TO THE CITY OF BETHEL IN ISRAEL AND GIVES GOD'S MESSAGE.
YOU ARE LIKE A CROOKED WALL THAT MUST BE DESTROYED BEFORE A NEW ONE CAN BE BUILT.

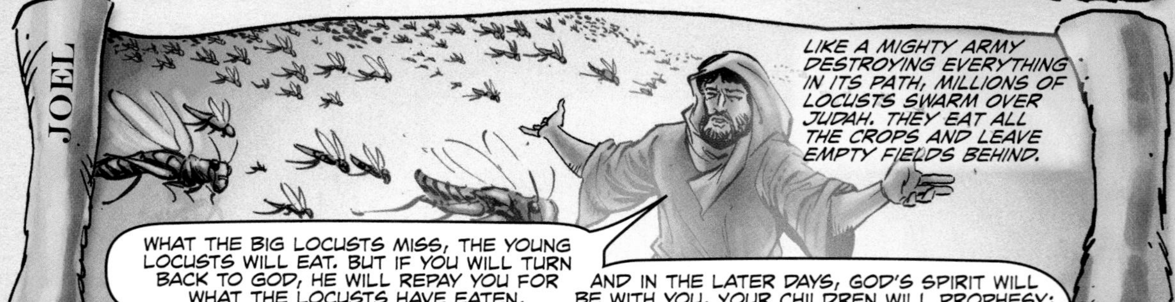
JOEL
LIKE A MIGHTY ARMY DESTROYING EVERYTHING IN ITS PATH, MILLIONS OF LOCUSTS SWARM OVER JUDAH. THEY EAT ALL THE CROPS AND LEAVE EMPTY FIELDS BEHIND.
WHAT THE BIG LOCUSTS MISS, THE YOUNG LOCUSTS WILL EAT. BUT IF YOU WILL TURN BACK TO GOD, HE WILL REPAY YOU FOR WHAT THE LOCUSTS HAVE EATEN.
AND IN THE LATER DAYS, GOD'S SPIRIT WILL BE WITH YOU. YOUR CHILDREN WILL PROPHESY; THE ELDERLY WILL DREAM DREAMS, AND THE YOUNG WILL SEE VISIONS.

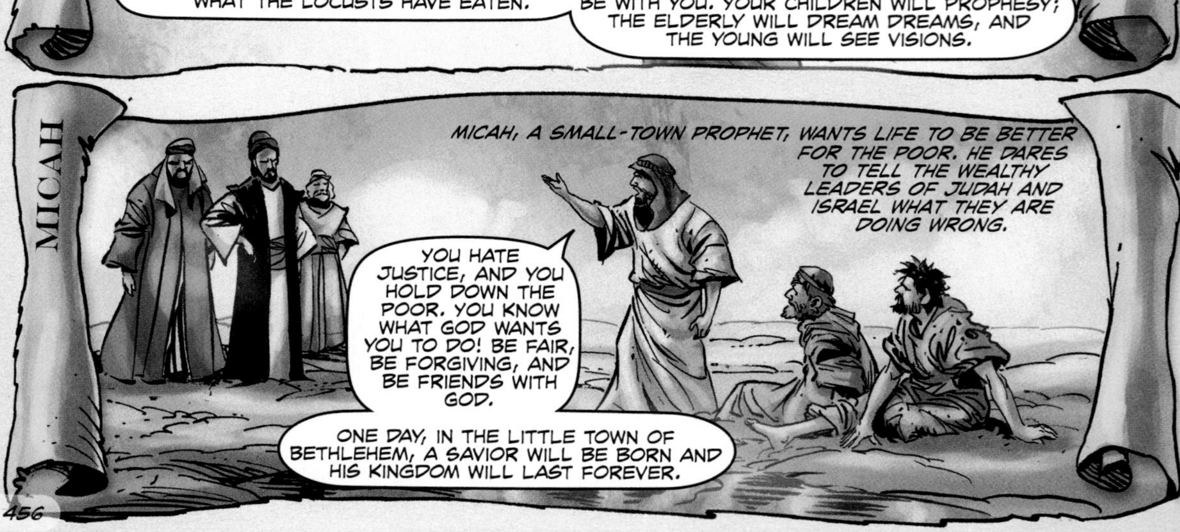
MICAH
MICAH, A SMALL-TOWN PROPHET, WANTS LIFE TO BE BETTER FOR THE POOR. HE DARES TO TELL THE WEALTHY LEADERS OF JUDAH AND ISRAEL WHAT THEY ARE DOING WRONG.
YOU HATE JUSTICE, AND YOU HOLD DOWN THE POOR. YOU KNOW WHAT GOD WANTS YOU TO DO! BE FAIR, BE FORGIVING, AND BE FRIENDS WITH GOD.
ONE DAY, IN THE LITTLE TOWN OF BETHLEHEM, A SAVIOR WILL BE BORN AND HIS KINGDOM WILL LAST FOREVER.

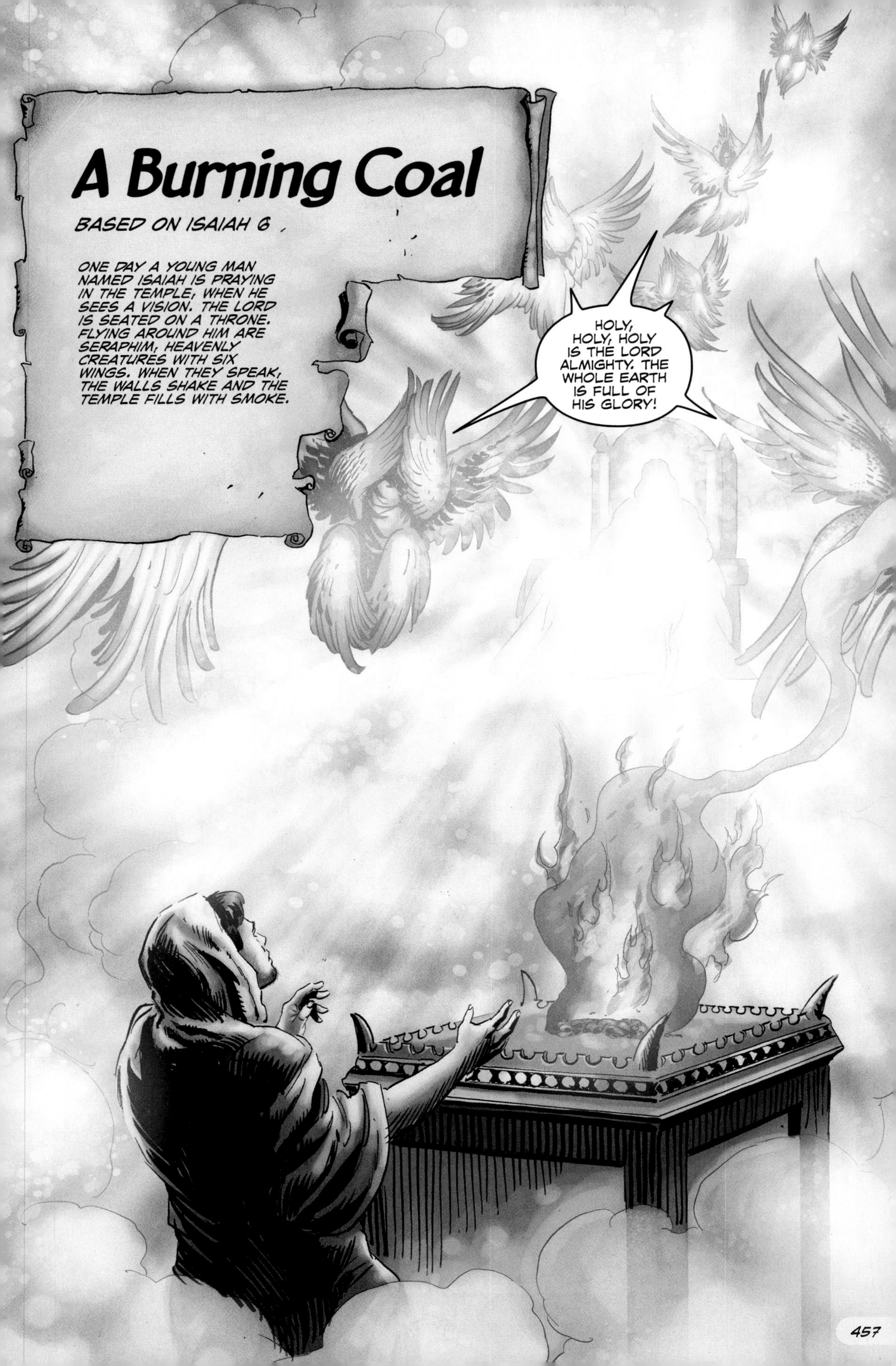
A Burning Coal
BASED ON ISAIAH 6
ONE DAY A YOUNG MAN NAMED ISAIAH IS PRAYING IN THE TEMPLE, WHEN HE SEES A VISION. THE LORD IS SEATED ON A THRONE. FLYING AROUND HIM ARE SERAPHIM, HEAVENLY CREATURES WITH SIX WINGS. WHEN THEY SPEAK, THE WALLS SHAKE AND THE TEMPLE FILLS WITH SMOKE.
HOLY, HOLY, HOLY IS THE LORD ALMIGHTY. THE WHOLE EARTH IS FULL OF HIS GLORY!

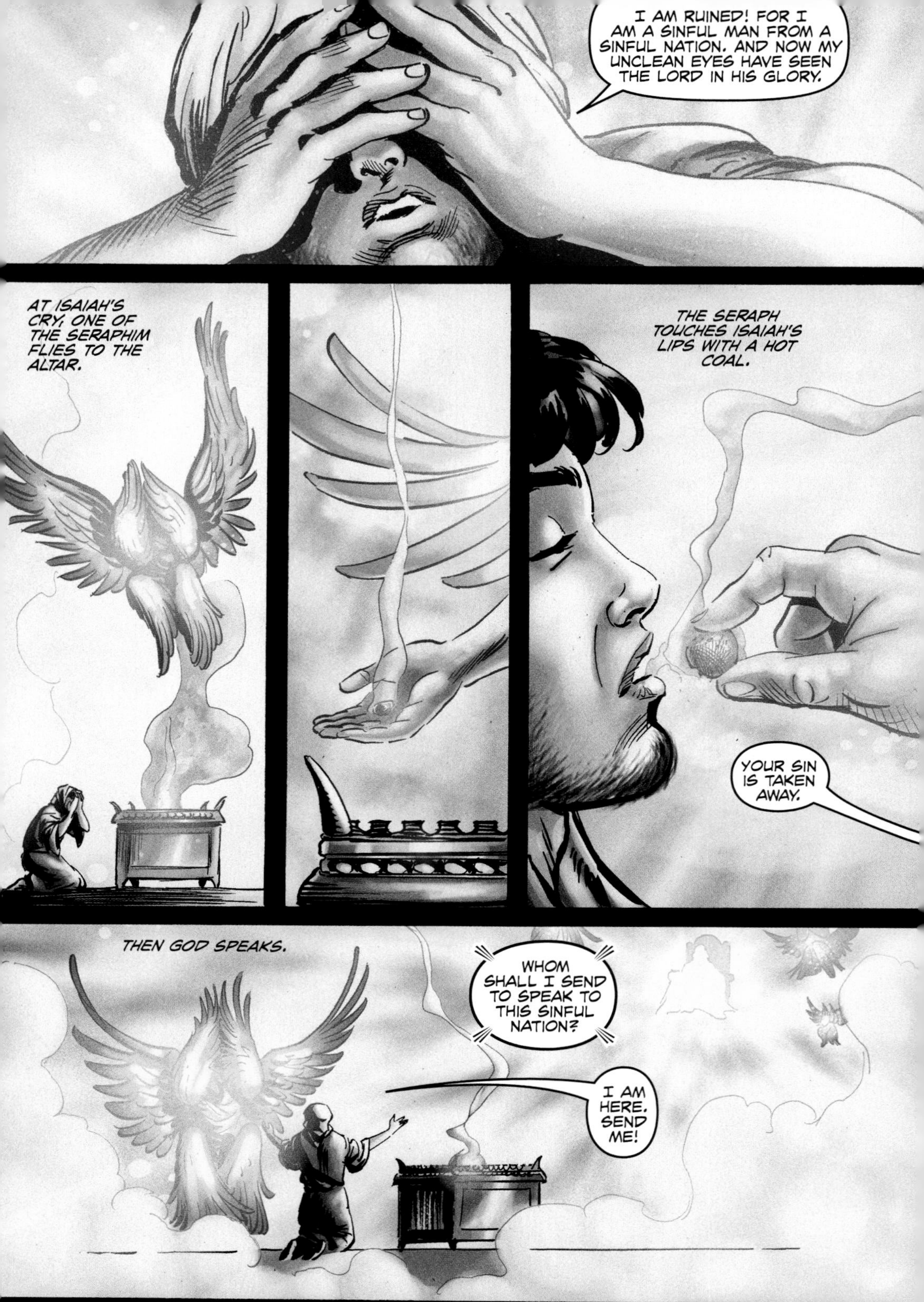
I AM RUINED! FOR I AM A SINFUL MAN FROM A SINFUL NATION. AND NOW MY UNCLEAN EYES HAVE SEEN THE LORD IN HIS GLORY.
AT ISAIAH'S CRY, ONE OF THE SERAPHIM FLIES TO THE ALTAR.
THE SERAPH TOUCHES ISAIAH'S LIPS WITH A HOT COAL.
YOUR SIN IS TAKEN AWAY.
THEN GOD SPEAKS.
WHOM SHALL I SEND TO SPEAK TO THIS SINFUL NATION?
I AM HERE. SEND ME!

WITH THIS COURAGEOUS ANSWER, ISAIAH STARTS ON HIS JOURNEY TO BECOME ONE OF THE GREATEST OF THE HEBREW PROPHETS. HE PROPHESIES MOSTLY DURING THE REIGN OF KING HEZEKIAH.

Hezekiah's Healing

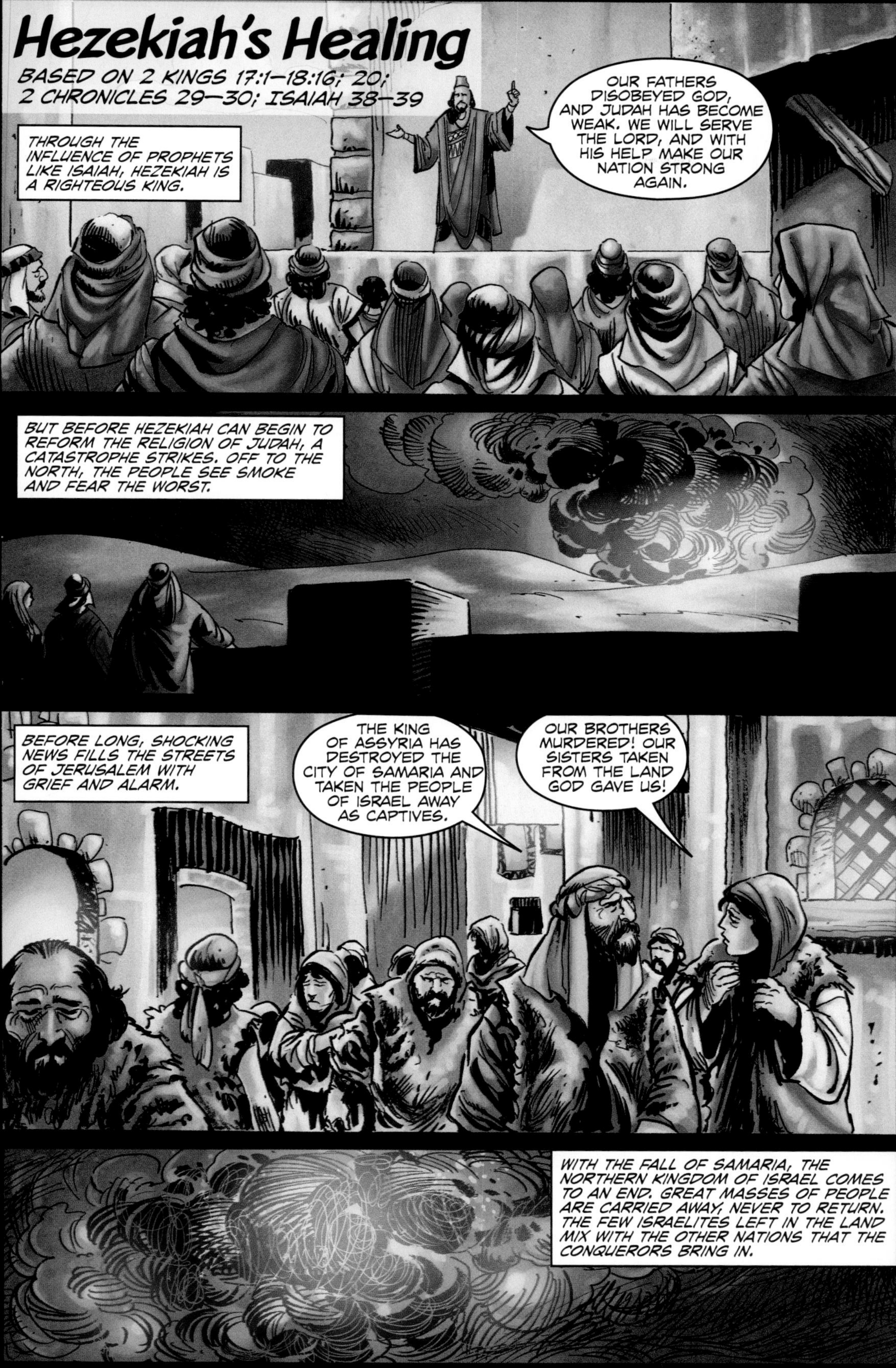
BASED ON 2 KINGS 17:1–18:16; 20; 2 CHRONICLES 29–30; ISAIAH 38–39
THROUGH THE INFLUENCE OF PROPHETS LIKE ISAIAH, HEZEKIAH IS A RIGHTEOUS KING.
OUR FATHERS DISOBEYED GOD, AND JUDAH HAS BECOME WEAK. WE WILL SERVE THE LORD, AND WITH HIS HELP MAKE OUR NATION STRONG AGAIN.
BUT BEFORE HEZEKIAH CAN BEGIN TO REFORM THE RELIGION OF JUDAH, A CATASTROPHE STRIKES. OFF TO THE NORTH, THE PEOPLE SEE SMOKE AND FEAR THE WORST.
BEFORE LONG, SHOCKING NEWS FILLS THE STREETS OF JERUSALEM WITH GRIEF AND ALARM.
THE KING OF ASSYRIA HAS DESTROYED THE CITY OF SAMARIA AND TAKEN THE PEOPLE OF ISRAEL AWAY AS CAPTIVES.
OUR BROTHERS MURDERED! OUR SISTERS TAKEN FROM THE LAND GOD GAVE US!
WITH THE FALL OF SAMARIA, THE NORTHERN KINGDOM OF ISRAEL COMES TO AN END. GREAT MASSES OF PEOPLE ARE CARRIED AWAY, NEVER TO RETURN. THE FEW ISRAELITES LEFT IN THE LAND MIX WITH THE OTHER NATIONS THAT THE CONQUERORS BRING IN.

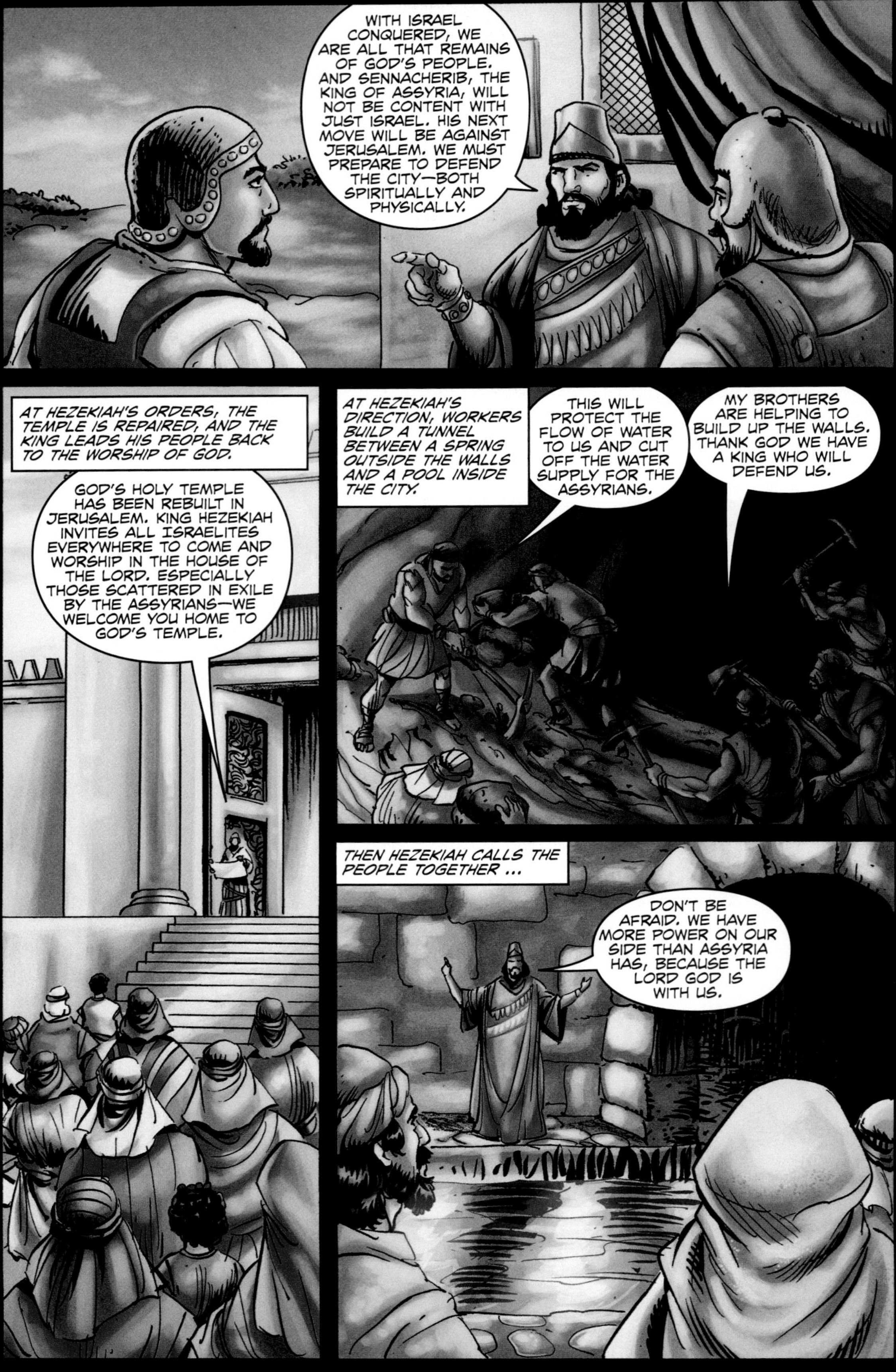
WITH ISRAEL CONQUERED, WE ARE ALL THAT REMAINS OF GOD'S PEOPLE. AND SENNACHERIB, THE KING OF ASSYRIA, WILL NOT BE CONTENT WITH JUST ISRAEL. HIS NEXT MOVE WILL BE AGAINST JERUSALEM. WE MUST PREPARE TO DEFEND THE CITY—BOTH SPIRITUALLY AND PHYSICALLY.
AT HEZEKIAH'S ORDERS, THE TEMPLE IS REPAIRED, AND THE KING LEADS HIS PEOPLE BACK TO THE WORSHIP OF GOD.
GOD'S HOLY TEMPLE HAS BEEN REBUILT IN JERUSALEM. KING HEZEKIAH INVITES ALL ISRAELITES EVERYWHERE TO COME AND WORSHIP IN THE HOUSE OF THE LORD. ESPECIALLY THOSE SCATTERED IN EXILE BY THE ASSYRIANS—WE WELCOME YOU HOME TO GOD'S TEMPLE.
AT HEZEKIAH'S DIRECTION, WORKERS BUILD A TUNNEL BETWEEN A SPRING OUTSIDE THE WALLS AND A POOL INSIDE THE CITY.
THIS WILL PROTECT THE FLOW OF WATER TO US AND CUT OFF THE WATER SUPPLY FOR THE ASSYRIANS.
MY BROTHERS ARE HELPING TO BUILD UP THE WALLS. THANK GOD WE HAVE A KING WHO WILL DEFEND US.
THEN HEZEKIAH CALLS THE PEOPLE TOGETHER ...
DON'T BE AFRAID. WE HAVE MORE POWER ON OUR SIDE THAN ASSYRIA HAS, BECAUSE THE LORD GOD IS WITH US.

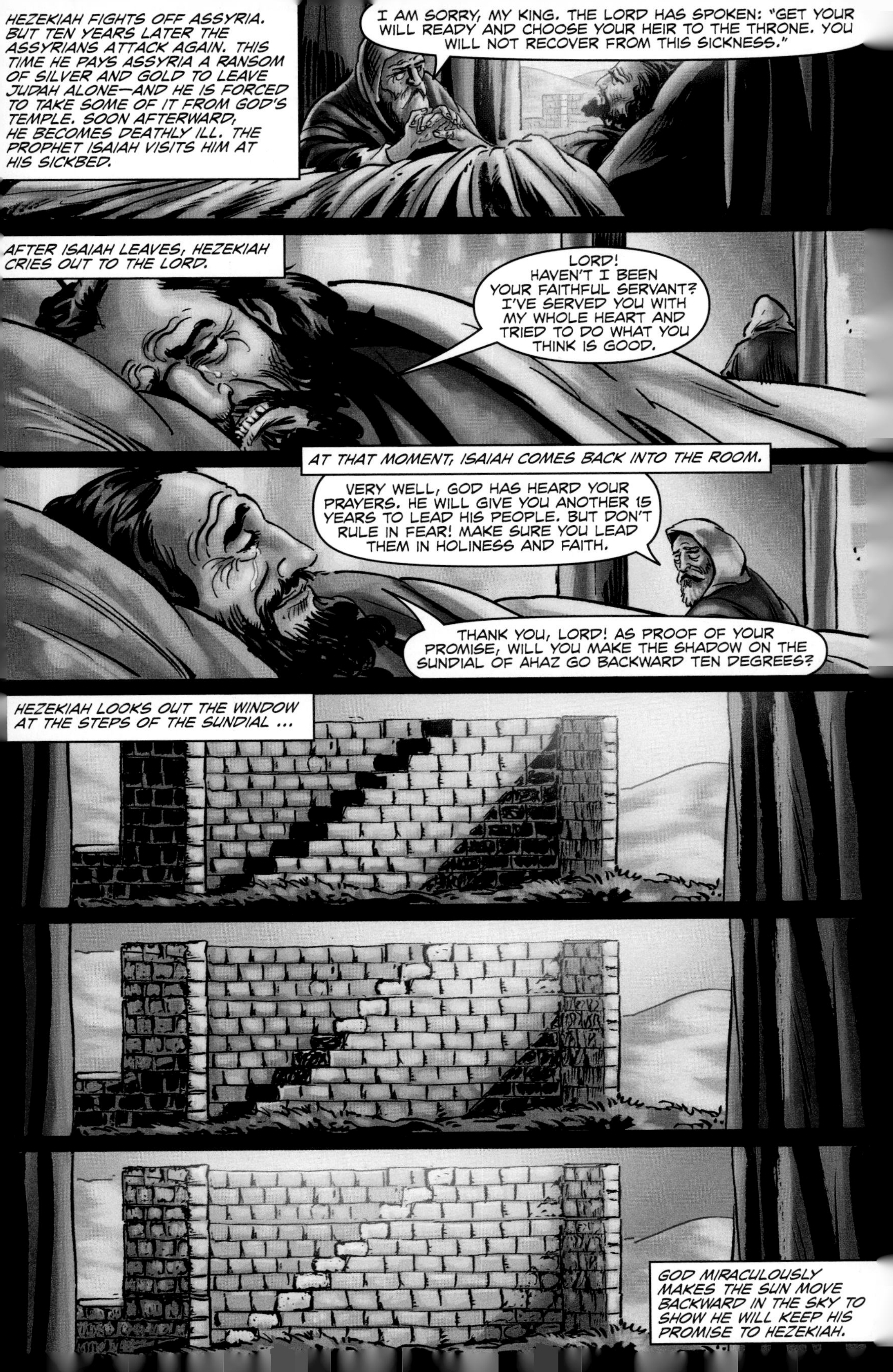
HEZEKIAH FIGHTS OFF ASSYRIA. BUT TEN YEARS LATER THE ASSYRIANS ATTACK AGAIN. THIS TIME HE PAYS ASSYRIA A RANSOM OF SILVER AND GOLD TO LEAVE JUDAH ALONE—AND HE IS FORCED TO TAKE SOME OF IT FROM GOD'S TEMPLE. SOON AFTERWARD, HE BECOMES DEATHLY ILL. THE PROPHET ISAIAH VISITS HIM AT HIS SICKBED.
I AM SORRY, MY KING. THE LORD HAS SPOKEN: "GET YOUR WILL READY AND CHOOSE YOUR HEIR TO THE THRONE. YOU WILL NOT RECOVER FROM THIS SICKNESS."
AFTER ISAIAH LEAVES, HEZEKIAH CRIES OUT TO THE LORD.
LORD! HAVEN'T I BEEN YOUR FAITHFUL SERVANT? I'VE SERVED YOU WITH MY WHOLE HEART AND TRIED TO DO WHAT YOU THINK IS GOOD.
AT THAT MOMENT, ISAIAH COMES BACK INTO THE ROOM.
VERY WELL, GOD HAS HEARD YOUR PRAYERS. HE WILL GIVE YOU ANOTHER 15 YEARS TO LEAD HIS PEOPLE. BUT DON'T RULE IN FEAR! MAKE SURE YOU LEAD THEM IN HOLINESS AND FAITH.
THANK YOU, LORD! AS PROOF OF YOUR PROMISE, WILL YOU MAKE THE SHADOW ON THE SUNDIAL OF AHAZ GO BACKWARD TEN DEGREES?
HEZEKIAH LOOKS OUT THE WINDOW AT THE STEPS OF THE SUNDIAL ...
GOD MIRACULOUSLY MAKES THE SUN MOVE BACKWARD IN THE SKY TO SHOW HE WILL KEEP HIS PROMISE TO HEZEKIAH.

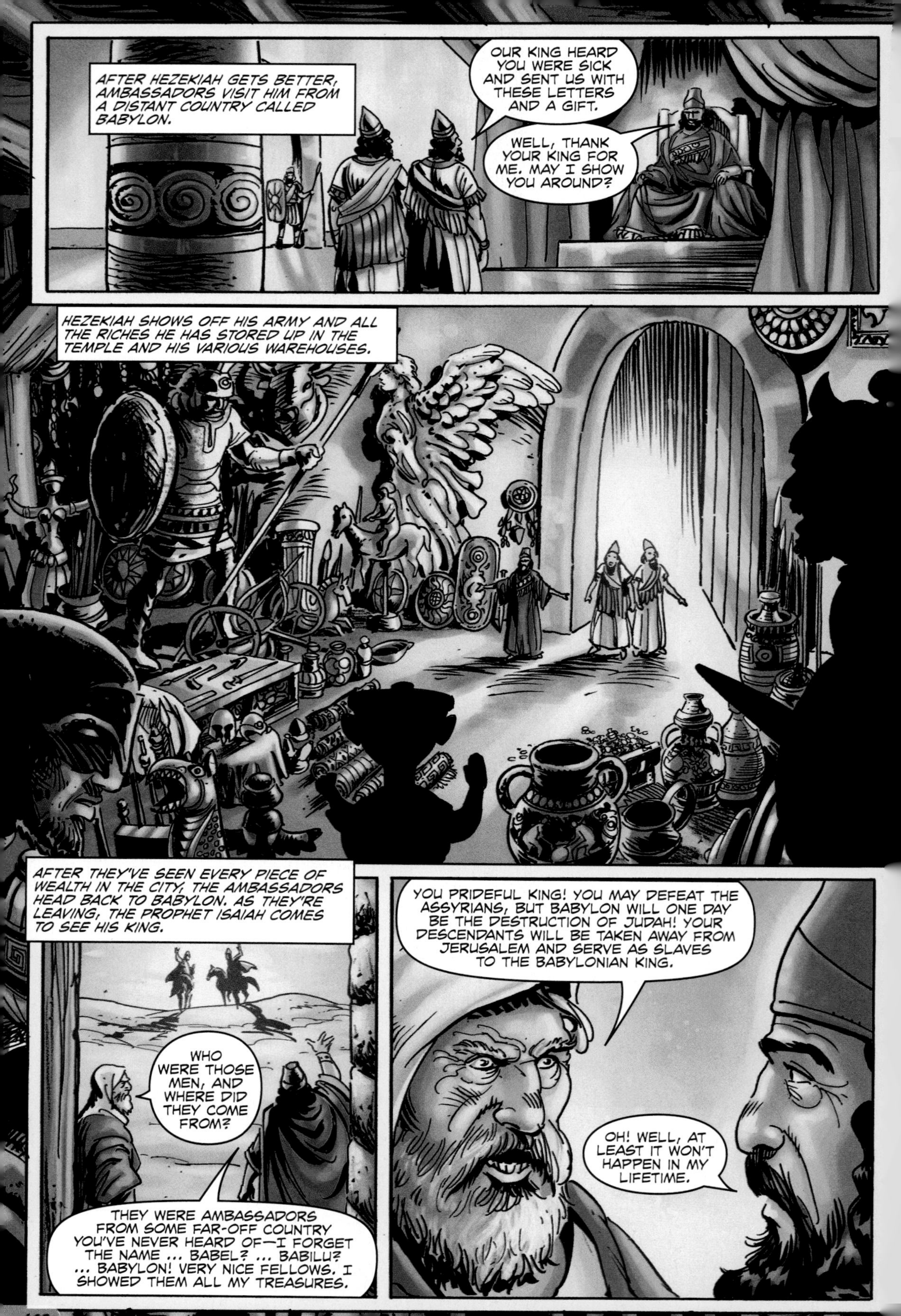

AFTER HEZEKIAH GETS BETTER, AMBASSADORS VISIT HIM FROM A DISTANT COUNTRY CALLED BABYLON.
OUR KING HEARD YOU WERE SICK AND SENT US WITH THESE LETTERS AND A GIFT.
WELL, THANK YOUR KING FOR ME. MAY I SHOW YOU AROUND?
HEZEKIAH SHOWS OFF HIS ARMY AND ALL THE RICHES HE HAS STORED UP IN THE TEMPLE AND HIS VARIOUS WAREHOUSES.
AFTER THEY'VE SEEN EVERY PIECE OF WEALTH IN THE CITY, THE AMBASSADORS HEAD BACK TO BABYLON. AS THEY'RE LEAVING, THE PROPHET ISAIAH COMES TO SEE HIS KING.
WHO WERE THOSE MEN, AND WHERE DID THEY COME FROM?
THEY WERE AMBASSADORS FROM SOME FAR-OFF COUNTRY YOU'VE NEVER HEARD OF—I FORGET THE NAME ... BABEL? ... BABILU? ... BABYLON! VERY NICE FELLOWS. I SHOWED THEM ALL MY TREASURES.
YOU PRIDEFUL KING! YOU MAY DEFEAT THE ASSYRIANS, BUT BABYLON WILL ONE DAY BE THE DESTRUCTION OF JUDAH! YOUR DESCENDANTS WILL BE TAKEN AWAY FROM JERUSALEM AND SERVE AS SLAVES TO THE BABYLONIAN KING.
OH! WELL, AT LEAST IT WON'T HAPPEN IN MY LIFETIME.

Insults and Prophecies

BASED ON 2 KINGS 18:17—19:37; 2 CHRONICLES 32; ISAIAH 9:6; 36; 52:13—53:12; NAHUM

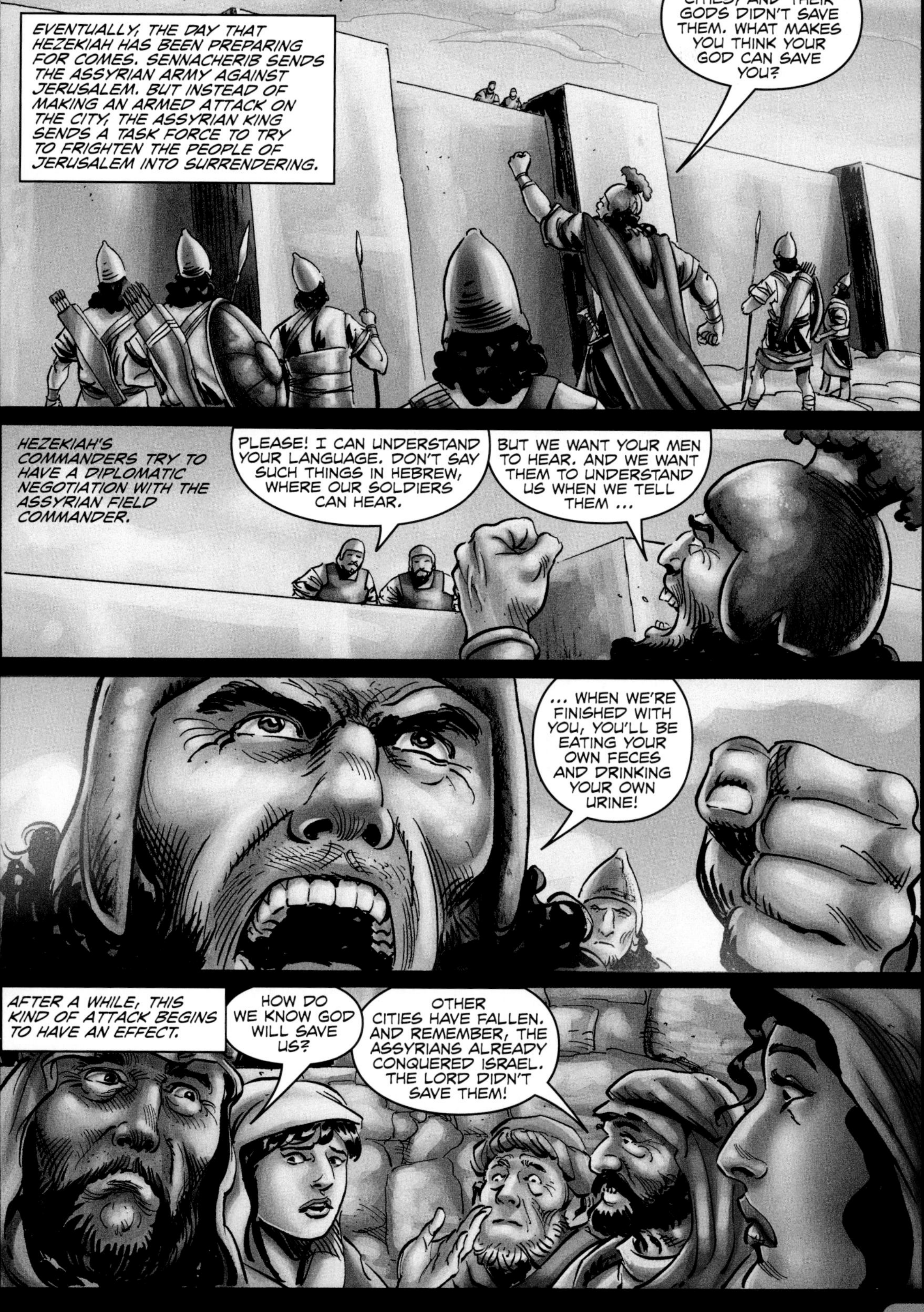
EVENTUALLY, THE DAY THAT HEZEKIAH HAS BEEN PREPARING FOR COMES. SENNACHERIB SENDS THE ASSYRIAN ARMY AGAINST JERUSALEM. BUT INSTEAD OF MAKING AN ARMED ATTACK ON THE CITY, THE ASSYRIAN KING SENDS A TASK FORCE TO TRY TO FRIGHTEN THE PEOPLE OF JERUSALEM INTO SURRENDERING.
WE HAVE CONQUERED OTHER CITIES, AND THEIR GODS DIDN'T SAVE THEM. WHAT MAKES YOU THINK YOUR GOD CAN SAVE YOU?
HEZEKIAH'S COMMANDERS TRY TO HAVE A DIPLOMATIC NEGOTIATION WITH THE ASSYRIAN FIELD COMMANDER.
PLEASE! I CAN UNDERSTAND YOUR LANGUAGE. DON'T SAY SUCH THINGS IN HEBREW, WHERE OUR SOLDIERS CAN HEAR.
BUT WE WANT YOUR MEN TO HEAR. AND WE WANT THEM TO UNDERSTAND US WHEN WE TELL THEM ...
... WHEN WE'RE FINISHED WITH YOU, YOU'LL BE EATING YOUR OWN FECES AND DRINKING YOUR OWN URINE!
AFTER A WHILE, THIS KIND OF ATTACK BEGINS TO HAVE AN EFFECT.
HOW DO WE KNOW GOD WILL SAVE US?
OTHER CITIES HAVE FALLEN. AND REMEMBER, THE ASSYRIANS ALREADY CONQUERED ISRAEL. THE LORD DIDN'T SAVE THEM!

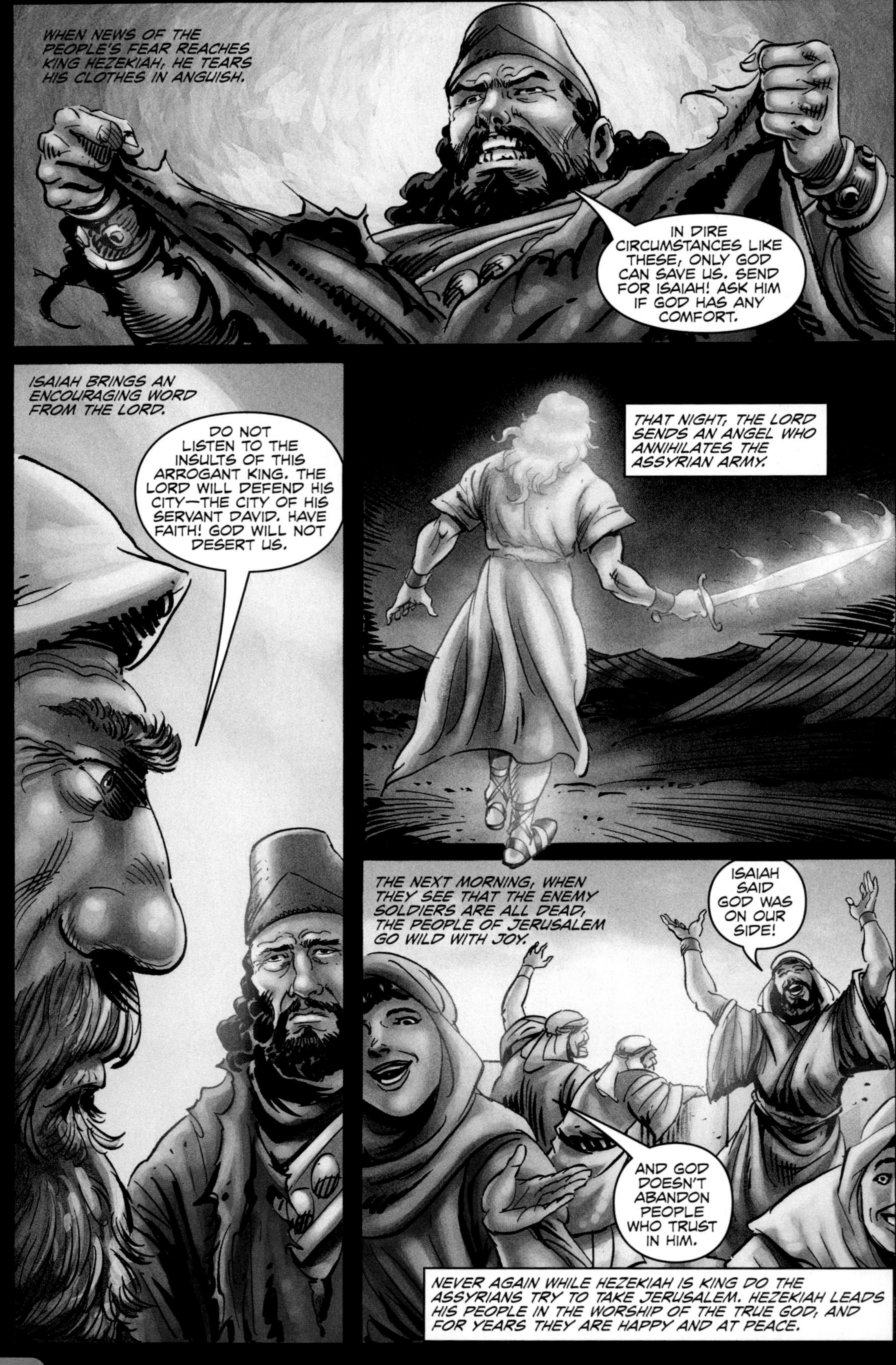
WHEN NEWS OF THE PEOPLE'S FEAR REACHES KING HEZEKIAH, HE TEARS HIS CLOTHES IN ANGUISH.
IN DIRE CIRCUMSTANCES LIKE THESE, ONLY GOD CAN SAVE US. SEND FOR ISAIAH! ASK HIM IF GOD HAS ANY COMFORT.
ISAIAH BRINGS AN ENCOURAGING WORD FROM THE LORD.
DO NOT LISTEN TO THE INSULTS OF THIS ARROGANT KING. THE LORD WILL DEFEND HIS CITY—THE CITY OF HIS SERVANT DAVID. HAVE FAITH! GOD WILL NOT DESERT US.
THAT NIGHT, THE LORD SENDS AN ANGEL WHO ANNIHILATES THE ASSYRIAN ARMY.
THE NEXT MORNING, WHEN THEY SEE THAT THE ENEMY SOLDIERS ARE ALL DEAD, THE PEOPLE OF JERUSALEM GO WILD WITH JOY.
ISAIAH SAID GOD WAS ON OUR SIDE!
AND GOD DOESN'T ABANDON PEOPLE WHO TRUST IN HIM.
NEVER AGAIN WHILE HEZEKIAH IS KING DO THE ASSYRIANS TRY TO TAKE JERUSALEM. HEZEKIAH LEADS HIS PEOPLE IN THE WORSHIP OF THE TRUE GOD, AND FOR YEARS THEY ARE HAPPY AND AT PEACE.

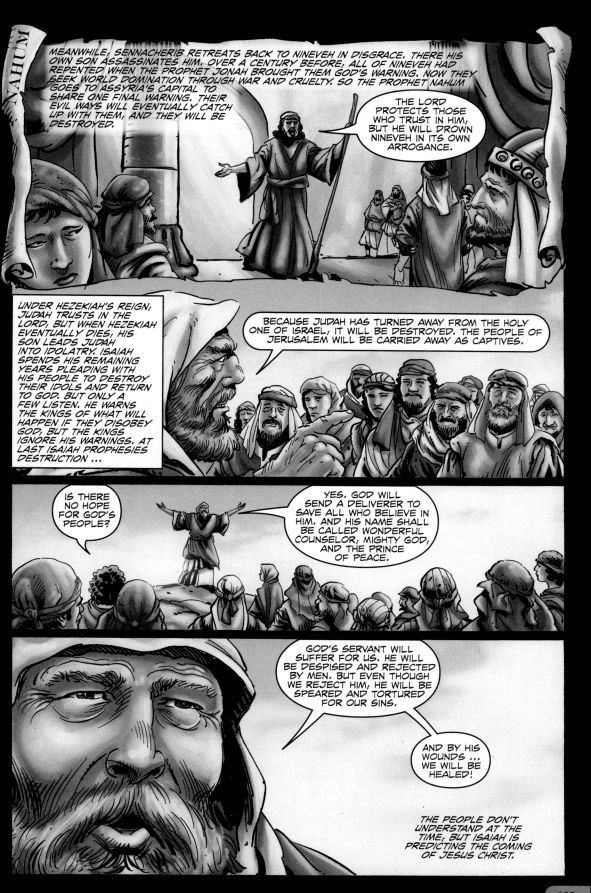

NAHUM

MEANWHILE, SENNACHERIB RETREATS BACK TO NINEVEH IN DISGRACE. THERE HIS OWN SON ASSASSINATES HIM. OVER A CENTURY BEFORE, ALL OF NINEVEH HAD REPENTED WHEN THE PROPHET JONAH BROUGHT THEM GOD'S WARNING. NOW THEY SEEK WORLD DOMINATION THROUGH WAR AND CRUELTY. SO THE PROPHET NAHUM GOES TO ASSYRIA'S CAPITAL TO SHARE ONE FINAL WARNING. THEIR EVIL WAYS WILL EVENTUALLY CATCH UP WITH THEM, AND THEY WILL BE DESTROYED.

THE LORD PROTECTS THOSE WHO TRUST IN HIM, BUT HE WILL DROWN NINEVEH IN ITS OWN ARROGANCE.

UNDER HEZEKIAH'S REIGN, JUDAH TRUSTS IN THE LORD, BUT WHEN HEZEKIAH EVENTUALLY DIES, HIS SON LEADS JUDAH INTO IDOLATRY. ISAIAH SPENDS HIS REMAINING YEARS PLEADING WITH HIS PEOPLE TO DESTROY THEIR IDOLS AND RETURN TO GOD. BUT ONLY A FEW LISTEN. HE WARNS THE KINGS OF WHAT WILL HAPPEN IF THEY DISOBEY GOD, BUT THE KINGS IGNORE HIS WARNINGS. AT LAST ISAIAH PROPHESIES DESTRUCTION ...

BECAUSE JUDAH HAS TURNED AWAY FROM THE HOLY ONE OF ISRAEL, IT WILL BE DESTROYED. THE PEOPLE OF JERUSALEM WILL BE CARRIED AWAY AS CAPTIVES.

IS THERE NO HOPE FOR GOD'S PEOPLE?

YES. GOD WILL SEND A DELIVERER TO SAVE ALL WHO BELIEVE IN HIM. AND HIS NAME SHALL BE CALLED WONDERFUL COUNSELOR, MIGHTY GOD, AND THE PRINCE OF PEACE.

GOD'S SERVANT WILL SUFFER FOR US. HE WILL BE DESPISED AND REJECTED BY MEN. BUT EVEN THOUGH WE REJECT HIM, HE WILL BE SPEARED AND TORTURED FOR OUR SINS.

AND BY HIS WOUNDS ... WE WILL BE HEALED!

THE PEOPLE DON'T UNDERSTAND AT THE TIME, BUT ISAIAH IS PREDICTING THE COMING OF JESUS CHRIST.

Isaiah 53: A Prophecy

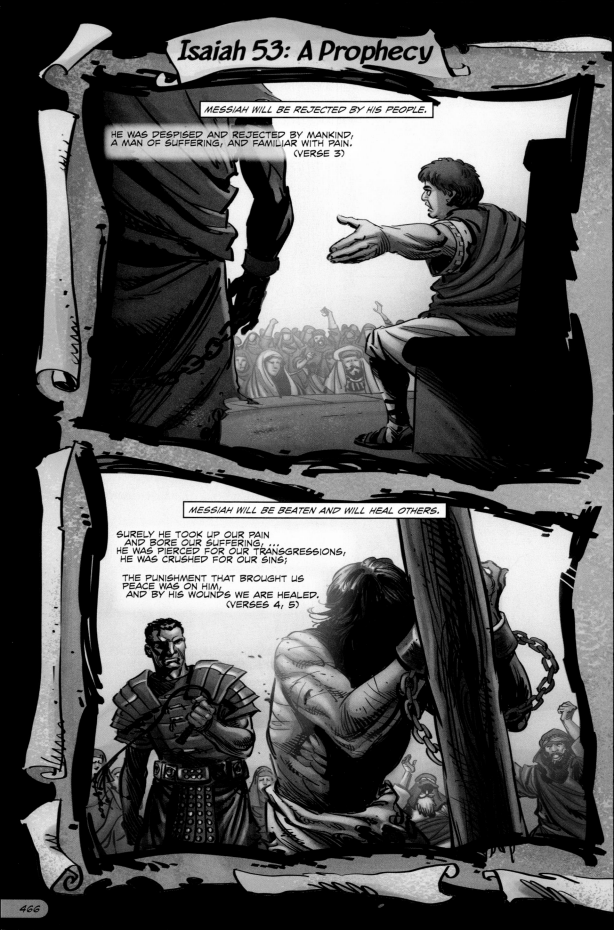

MESSIAH WILL BE REJECTED BY HIS PEOPLE.

HE WAS DESPISED AND REJECTED BY MANKIND, A MAN OF SUFFERING, AND FAMILIAR WITH PAIN.
(VERSE 3)

MESSIAH WILL BE BEATEN AND WILL HEAL OTHERS.

SURELY HE TOOK UP OUR PAIN AND BORE OUR SUFFERING, ...
HE WAS PIERCED FOR OUR TRANSGRESSIONS, HE WAS CRUSHED FOR OUR SINS;

THE PUNISHMENT THAT BROUGHT US PEACE WAS ON HIM, AND BY HIS WOUNDS WE ARE HEALED.
(VERSES 4, 5)

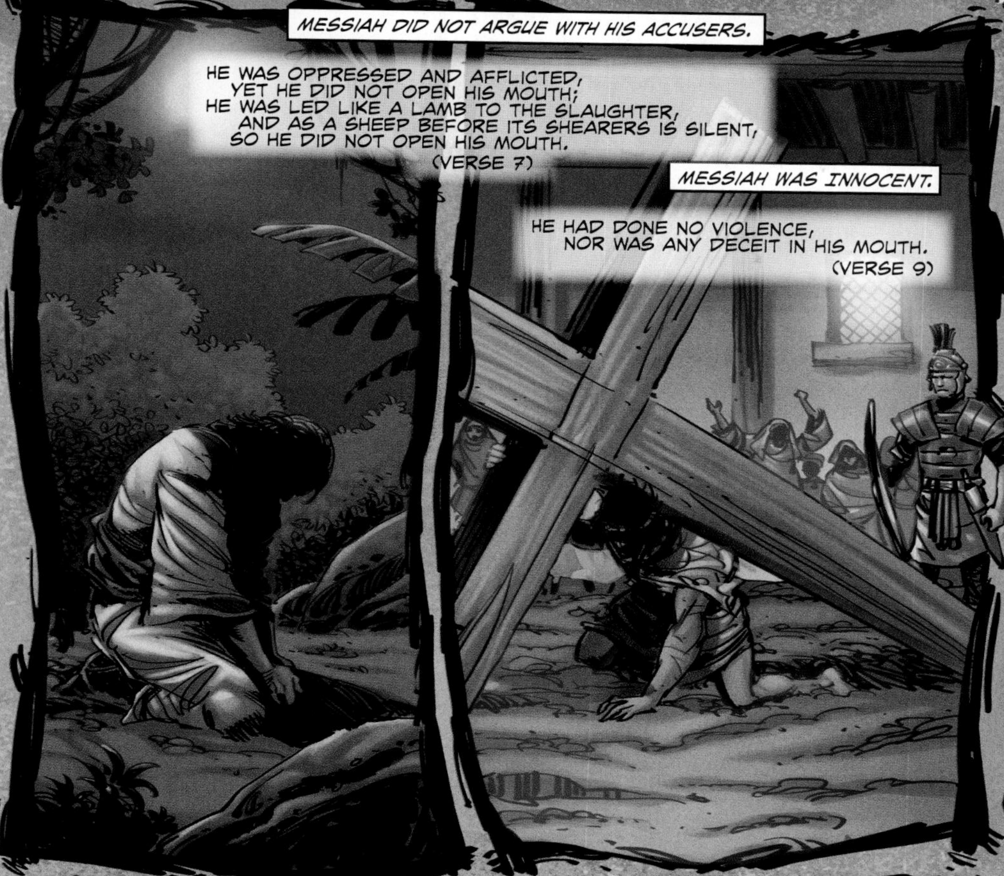
MESSIAH DID NOT ARGUE WITH HIS ACCUSERS.
HE WAS OPPRESSED AND AFFLICTED,
YET HE DID NOT OPEN HIS MOUTH;
HE WAS LED LIKE A LAMB TO THE SLAUGHTER,
AND AS A SHEEP BEFORE ITS SHEARERS IS SILENT,
SO HE DID NOT OPEN HIS MOUTH.
(VERSE 7)
MESSIAH WAS INNOCENT.
HE HAD DONE NO VIOLENCE,
NOR WAS ANY DECEIT IN HIS MOUTH.
(VERSE 9)

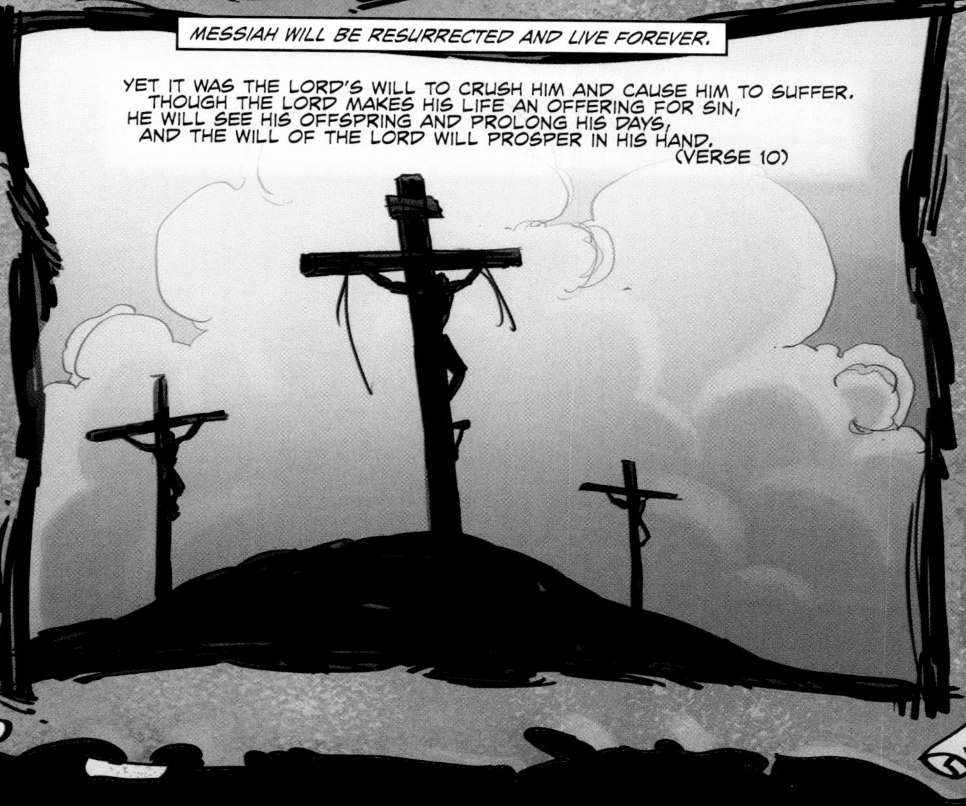
MESSIAH WILL BE RESURRECTED AND LIVE FOREVER.
YET IT WAS THE LORD'S WILL TO CRUSH HIM AND CAUSE HIM TO SUFFER.
THOUGH THE LORD MAKES HIS LIFE AN OFFERING FOR SIN,
HE WILL SEE HIS OFFSPRING AND PROLONG HIS DAYS,
AND THE WILL OF THE LORD WILL PROSPER IN HIS HAND.
(VERSE 10)

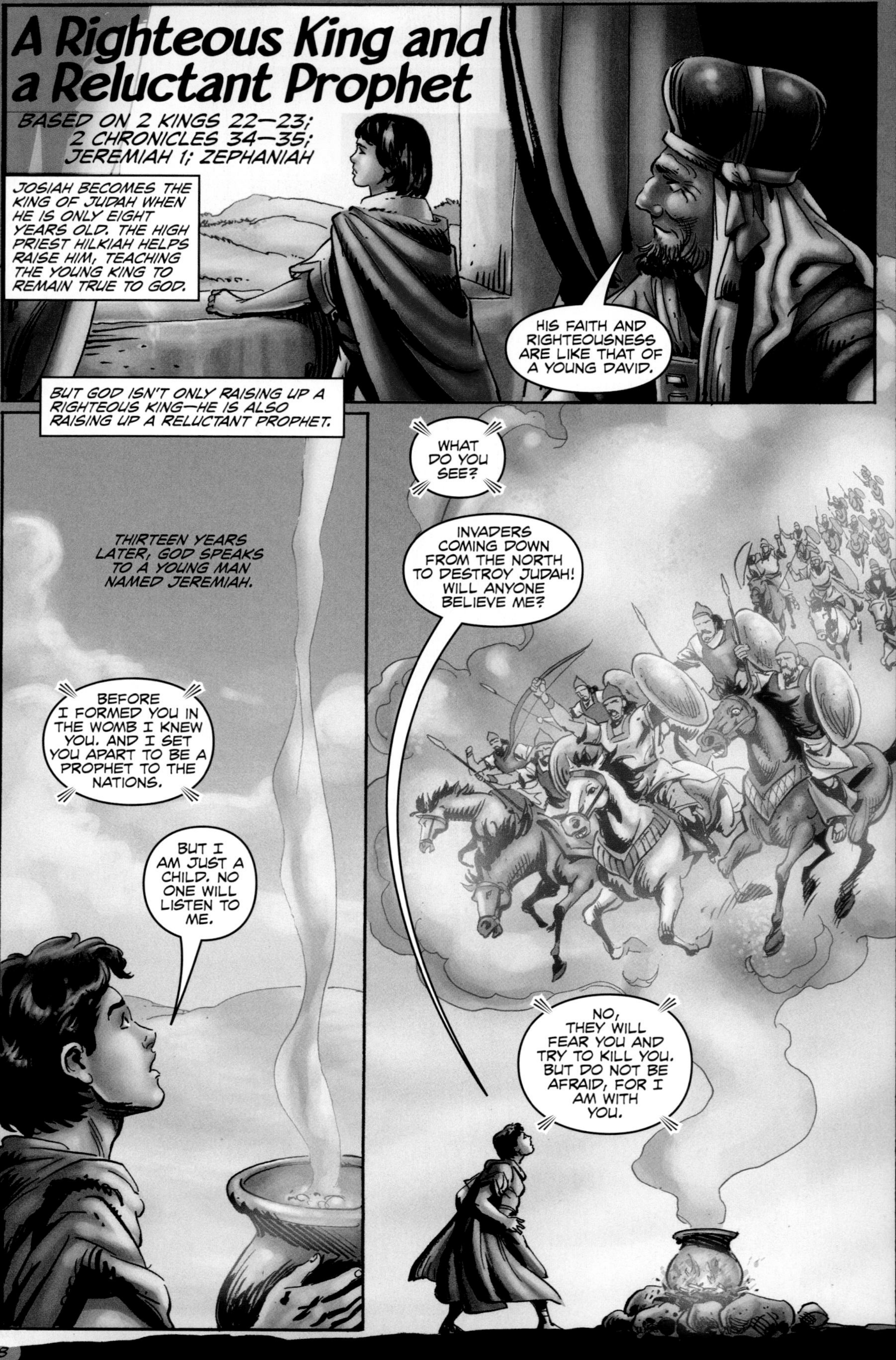
A Righteous King and a Reluctant Prophet
BASED ON 2 KINGS 22—23; 2 CHRONICLES 34—35; JEREMIAH 1; ZEPHANIAH
JOSIAH BECOMES THE KING OF JUDAH WHEN HE IS ONLY EIGHT YEARS OLD. THE HIGH PRIEST HILKIAH HELPS RAISE HIM, TEACHING THE YOUNG KING TO REMAIN TRUE TO GOD.
HIS FAITH AND RIGHTEOUSNESS ARE LIKE THAT OF A YOUNG DAVID.
BUT GOD ISN'T ONLY RAISING UP A RIGHTEOUS KING—HE IS ALSO RAISING UP A RELUCTANT PROPHET.
THIRTEEN YEARS LATER, GOD SPEAKS TO A YOUNG MAN NAMED JEREMIAH.
BEFORE I FORMED YOU IN THE WOMB I KNEW YOU. AND I SET YOU APART TO BE A PROPHET TO THE NATIONS.
BUT I AM JUST A CHILD. NO ONE WILL LISTEN TO ME.
WHAT DO YOU SEE?
INVADERS COMING DOWN FROM THE NORTH TO DESTROY JUDAH! WILL ANYONE BELIEVE ME?
NO, THEY WILL FEAR YOU AND TRY TO KILL YOU. BUT DO NOT BE AFRAID, FOR I AM WITH YOU.

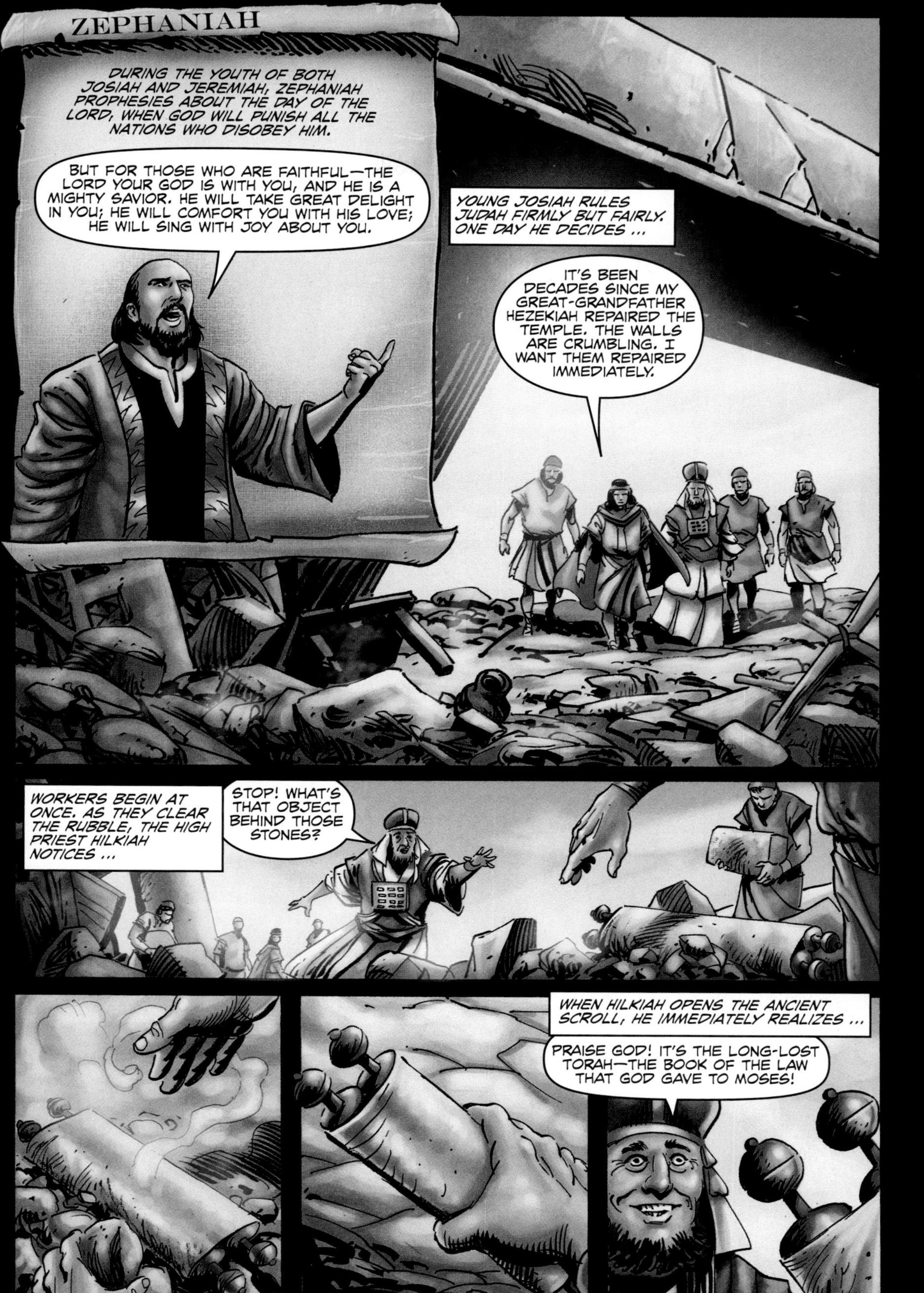
ZEPHANIAH
DURING THE YOUTH OF BOTH JOSIAH AND JEREMIAH, ZEPHANIAH PROPHESIES ABOUT THE DAY OF THE LORD, WHEN GOD WILL PUNISH ALL THE NATIONS WHO DISOBEY HIM.
BUT FOR THOSE WHO ARE FAITHFUL—THE LORD YOUR GOD IS WITH YOU, AND HE IS A MIGHTY SAVIOR. HE WILL TAKE GREAT DELIGHT IN YOU; HE WILL COMFORT YOU WITH HIS LOVE; HE WILL SING WITH JOY ABOUT YOU.
YOUNG JOSIAH RULES JUDAH FIRMLY BUT FAIRLY. ONE DAY HE DECIDES ...
IT'S BEEN DECADES SINCE MY GREAT-GRANDFATHER HEZEKIAH REPAIRED THE TEMPLE. THE WALLS ARE CRUMBLING. I WANT THEM REPAIRED IMMEDIATELY.
WORKERS BEGIN AT ONCE. AS THEY CLEAR THE RUBBLE, THE HIGH PRIEST HILKIAH NOTICES ...
STOP! WHAT'S THAT OBJECT BEHIND THOSE STONES?
WHEN HILKIAH OPENS THE ANCIENT SCROLL, HE IMMEDIATELY REALIZES ...
PRAISE GOD! IT'S THE LONG-LOST TORAH—THE BOOK OF THE LAW THAT GOD GAVE TO MOSES!

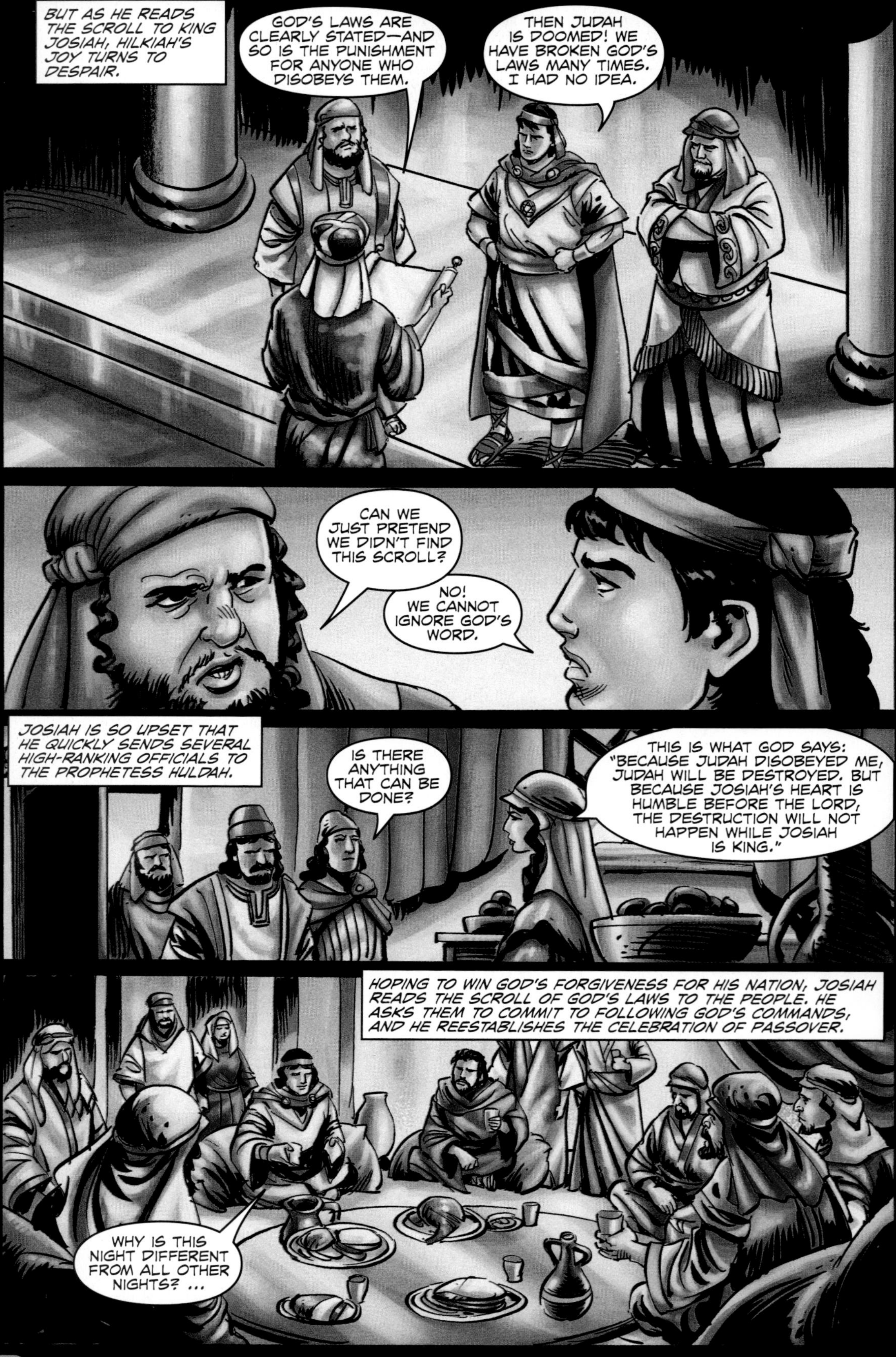
BUT AS HE READS THE SCROLL TO KING JOSIAH, HILKIAH'S JOY TURNS TO DESPAIR.
GOD'S LAWS ARE CLEARLY STATED—AND SO IS THE PUNISHMENT FOR ANYONE WHO DISOBEYS THEM.
THEN JUDAH IS DOOMED! WE HAVE BROKEN GOD'S LAWS MANY TIMES. I HAD NO IDEA.
CAN WE JUST PRETEND WE DIDN'T FIND THIS SCROLL?
NO! WE CANNOT IGNORE GOD'S WORD.
JOSIAH IS SO UPSET THAT HE QUICKLY SENDS SEVERAL HIGH-RANKING OFFICIALS TO THE PROPHETESS HULDAH.
IS THERE ANYTHING THAT CAN BE DONE?
THIS IS WHAT GOD SAYS: "BECAUSE JUDAH DISOBEYED ME, JUDAH WILL BE DESTROYED. BUT BECAUSE JOSIAH'S HEART IS HUMBLE BEFORE THE LORD, THE DESTRUCTION WILL NOT HAPPEN WHILE JOSIAH IS KING."
HOPING TO WIN GOD'S FORGIVENESS FOR HIS NATION, JOSIAH READS THE SCROLL OF GOD'S LAWS TO THE PEOPLE. HE ASKS THEM TO COMMIT TO FOLLOWING GOD'S COMMANDS, AND HE REESTABLISHES THE CELEBRATION OF PASSOVER.
WHY IS THIS NIGHT DIFFERENT FROM ALL OTHER NIGHTS? ...

Why Do Bad Things Happen to Good People?

BASED ON 2 KINGS 23:29—24:4; HABAKKUK

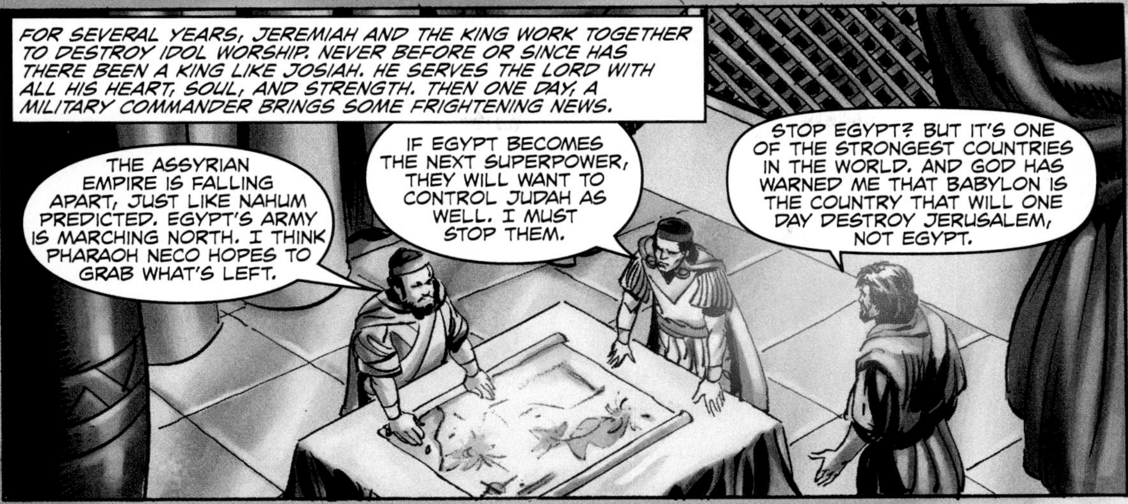
FOR SEVERAL YEARS, JEREMIAH AND THE KING WORK TOGETHER TO DESTROY IDOL WORSHIP. NEVER BEFORE OR SINCE HAS THERE BEEN A KING LIKE JOSIAH. HE SERVES THE LORD WITH ALL HIS HEART, SOUL, AND STRENGTH. THEN ONE DAY, A MILITARY COMMANDER BRINGS SOME FRIGHTENING NEWS.
THE ASSYRIAN EMPIRE IS FALLING APART, JUST LIKE NAHUM PREDICTED. EGYPT'S ARMY IS MARCHING NORTH. I THINK PHARAOH NECO HOPES TO GRAB WHAT'S LEFT.
IF EGYPT BECOMES THE NEXT SUPERPOWER, THEY WILL WANT TO CONTROL JUDAH AS WELL. I MUST STOP THEM.
STOP EGYPT? BUT IT'S ONE OF THE STRONGEST COUNTRIES IN THE WORLD. AND GOD HAS WARNED ME THAT BABYLON IS THE COUNTRY THAT WILL ONE DAY DESTROY JERUSALEM, NOT EGYPT.

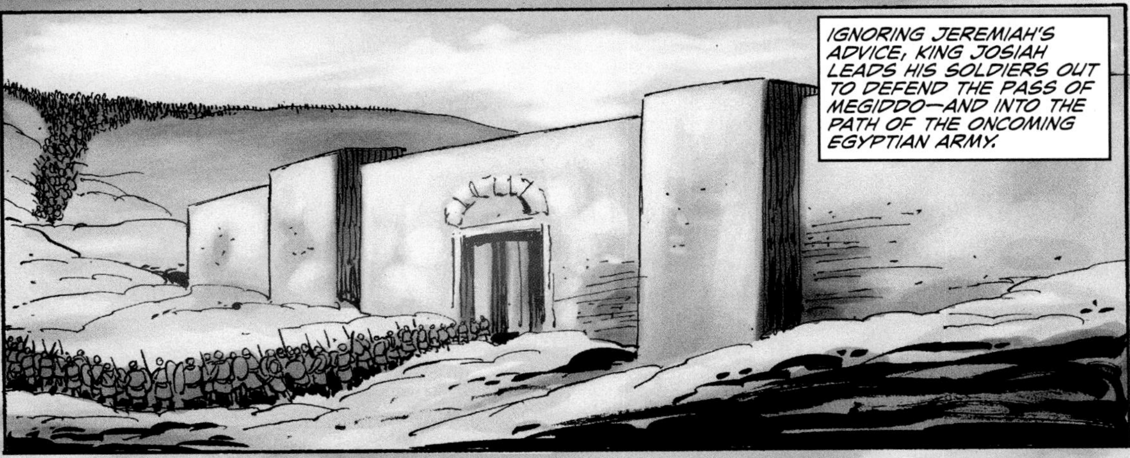
IGNORING JEREMIAH'S ADVICE, KING JOSIAH LEADS HIS SOLDIERS OUT TO DEFEND THE PASS OF MEGIDDO—AND INTO THE PATH OF THE ONCOMING EGYPTIAN ARMY.

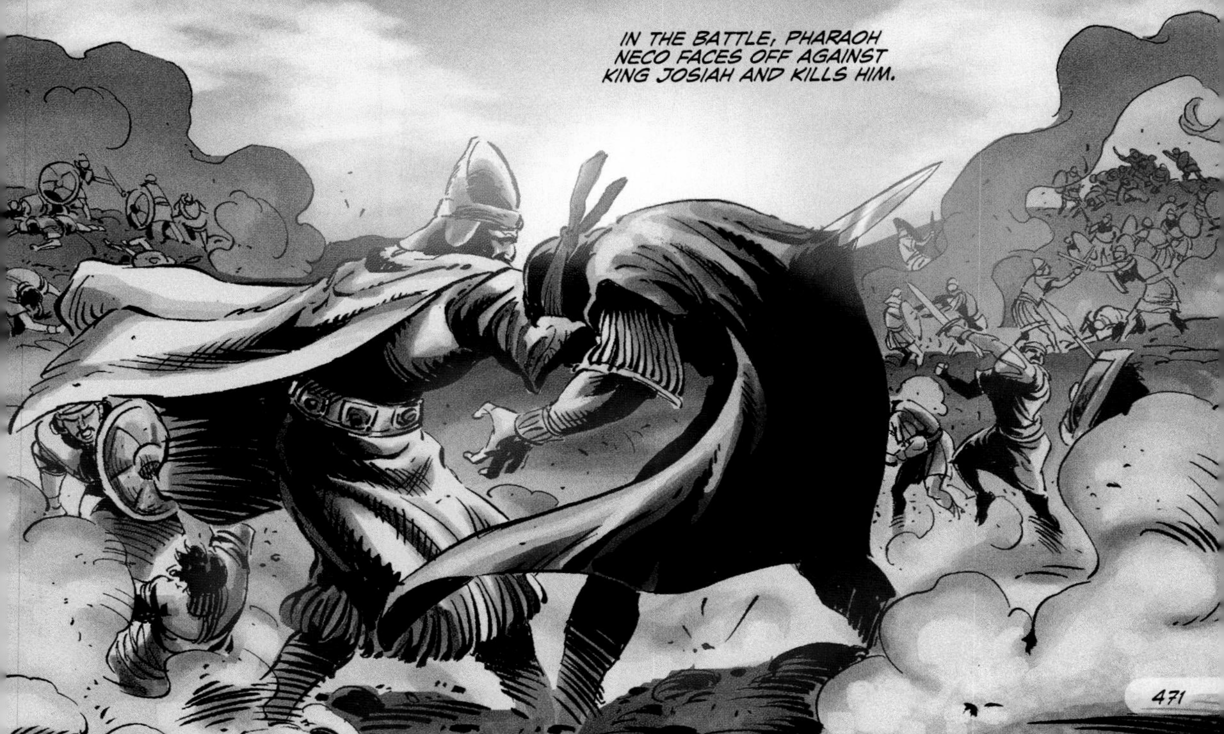
IN THE BATTLE, PHARAOH NECO FACES OFF AGAINST KING JOSIAH AND KILLS HIM.

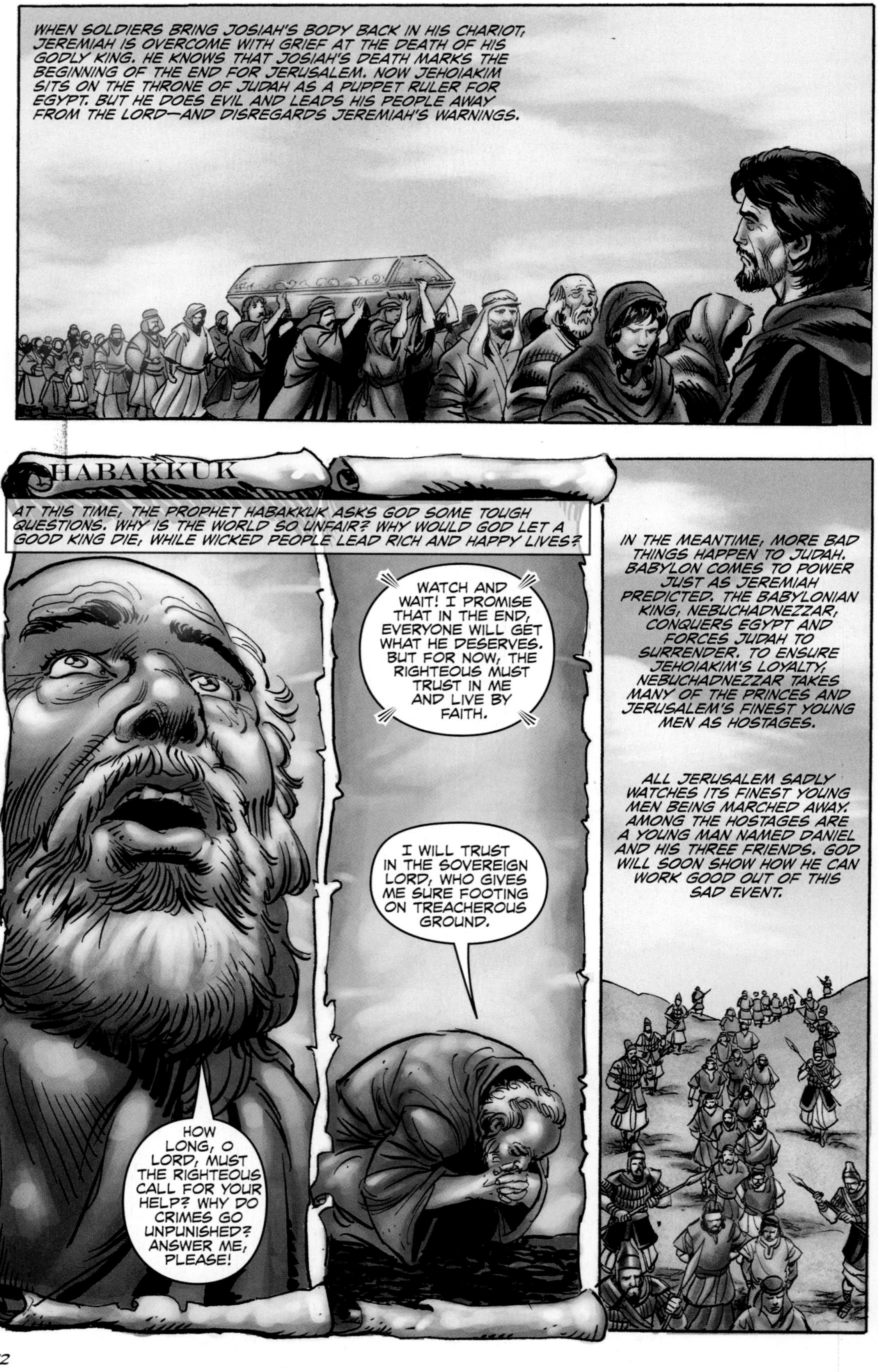
WHEN SOLDIERS BRING JOSIAH'S BODY BACK IN HIS CHARIOT, JEREMIAH IS OVERCOME WITH GRIEF AT THE DEATH OF HIS GODLY KING. HE KNOWS THAT JOSIAH'S DEATH MARKS THE BEGINNING OF THE END FOR JERUSALEM. NOW JEHOIAKIM SITS ON THE THRONE OF JUDAH AS A PUPPET RULER FOR EGYPT. BUT HE DOES EVIL AND LEADS HIS PEOPLE AWAY FROM THE LORD—AND DISREGARDS JEREMIAH'S WARNINGS.
HABAKKUK
AT THIS TIME, THE PROPHET HABAKKUK ASKS GOD SOME TOUGH QUESTIONS. WHY IS THE WORLD SO UNFAIR? WHY WOULD GOD LET A GOOD KING DIE, WHILE WICKED PEOPLE LEAD RICH AND HAPPY LIVES?
HOW LONG, O LORD, MUST THE RIGHTEOUS CALL FOR YOUR HELP? WHY DO CRIMES GO UNPUNISHED? ANSWER ME, PLEASE!
WATCH AND WAIT! I PROMISE THAT IN THE END, EVERYONE WILL GET WHAT HE DESERVES. BUT FOR NOW, THE RIGHTEOUS MUST TRUST IN ME AND LIVE BY FAITH.
I WILL TRUST IN THE SOVEREIGN LORD, WHO GIVES ME SURE FOOTING ON TREACHEROUS GROUND.
IN THE MEANTIME, MORE BAD THINGS HAPPEN TO JUDAH. BABYLON COMES TO POWER JUST AS JEREMIAH PREDICTED. THE BABYLONIAN KING, NEBUCHADNEZZAR, CONQUERS EGYPT AND FORCES JUDAH TO SURRENDER. TO ENSURE JEHOIAKIM'S LOYALTY, NEBUCHADNEZZAR TAKES MANY OF THE PRINCES AND JERUSALEM'S FINEST YOUNG MEN AS HOSTAGES.
ALL JERUSALEM SADLY WATCHES ITS FINEST YOUNG MEN BEING MARCHED AWAY. AMONG THE HOSTAGES ARE A YOUNG MAN NAMED DANIEL AND HIS THREE FRIENDS. GOD WILL SOON SHOW HOW HE CAN WORK GOOD OUT OF THIS SAD EVENT.

Unpopular Prophecies

BASED ON JEREMIAH; 2 KINGS 23:36–24:1

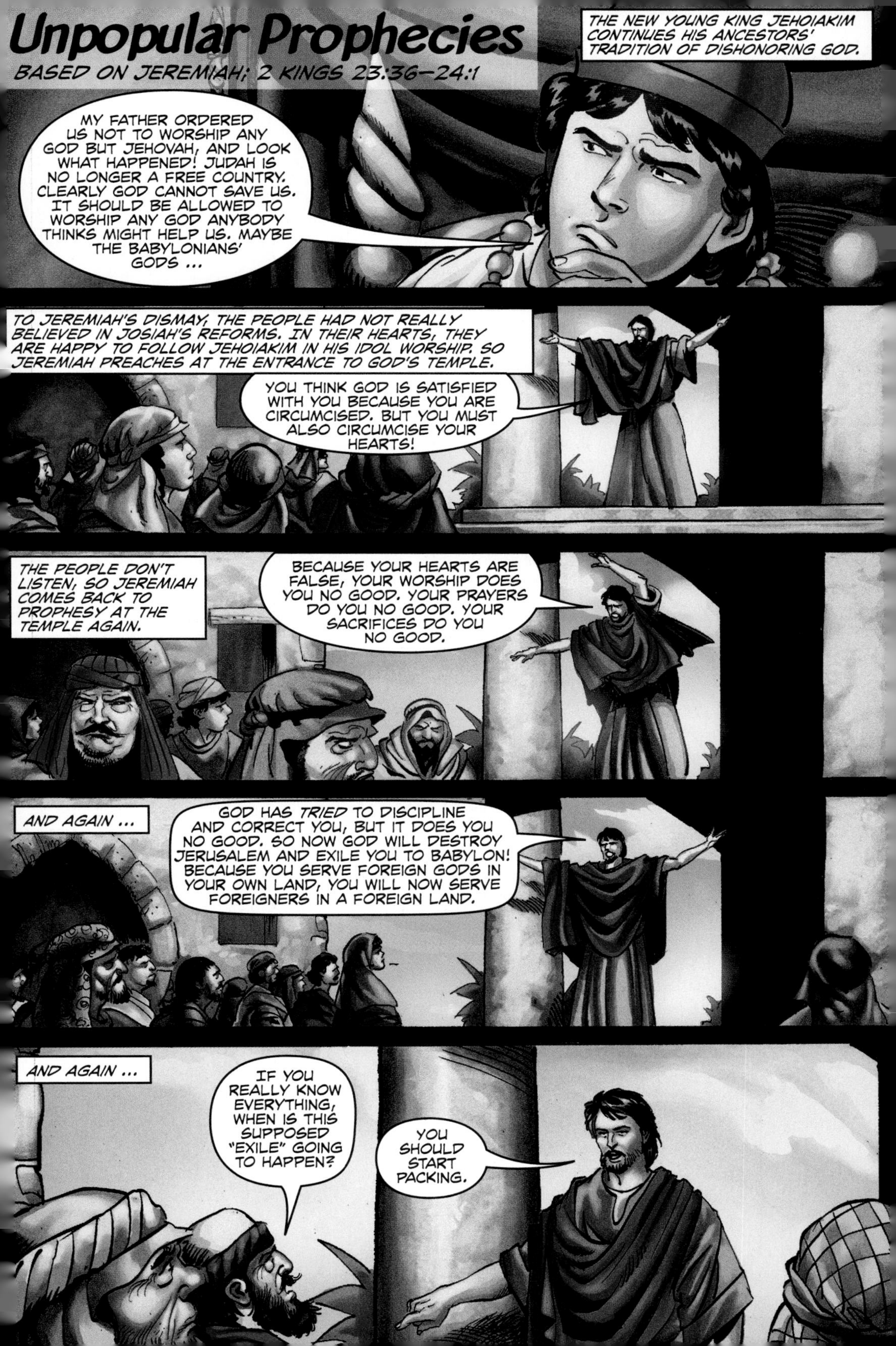

THE NEW YOUNG KING JEHOIAKIM CONTINUES HIS ANCESTORS' TRADITION OF DISHONORING GOD.
MY FATHER ORDERED US NOT TO WORSHIP ANY GOD BUT JEHOVAH, AND LOOK WHAT HAPPENED! JUDAH IS NO LONGER A FREE COUNTRY. CLEARLY GOD CANNOT SAVE US. IT SHOULD BE ALLOWED TO WORSHIP ANY GOD ANYBODY THINKS MIGHT HELP US. MAYBE THE BABYLONIANS' GODS ...
TO JEREMIAH'S DISMAY, THE PEOPLE HAD NOT REALLY BELIEVED IN JOSIAH'S REFORMS. IN THEIR HEARTS, THEY ARE HAPPY TO FOLLOW JEHOIAKIM IN HIS IDOL WORSHIP. SO JEREMIAH PREACHES AT THE ENTRANCE TO GOD'S TEMPLE.
YOU THINK GOD IS SATISFIED WITH YOU BECAUSE YOU ARE CIRCUMCISED. BUT YOU MUST ALSO CIRCUMCISE YOUR HEARTS!
THE PEOPLE DON'T LISTEN, SO JEREMIAH COMES BACK TO PROPHESY AT THE TEMPLE AGAIN.
BECAUSE YOUR HEARTS ARE FALSE, YOUR WORSHIP DOES YOU NO GOOD. YOUR PRAYERS DO YOU NO GOOD. YOUR SACRIFICES DO YOU NO GOOD.
AND AGAIN ...
GOD HAS *TRIED* TO DISCIPLINE AND CORRECT YOU, BUT IT DOES YOU NO GOOD. SO NOW GOD WILL DESTROY JERUSALEM AND EXILE YOU TO BABYLON! BECAUSE YOU SERVE FOREIGN GODS IN YOUR OWN LAND, YOU WILL NOW SERVE FOREIGNERS IN A FOREIGN LAND.
AND AGAIN ...
IF YOU REALLY KNOW EVERYTHING, WHEN IS THIS SUPPOSED "EXILE" GOING TO HAPPEN?
YOU SHOULD START PACKING.

AT THESE WORDS, THE CROWD FLIES INTO A RAGE. THEY DRAG JEREMIAH TO THE CITY OFFICIALS.

HE IS SPEAKING AGAINST US AND AGAINST GOD'S CITY OF JERUSALEM! HE SHOULD BE STONED TO DEATH.

WHAT DO YOU HAVE TO SAY FOR YOURSELF?

I AM ONLY SAYING WHAT THE LORD HIMSELF TOLD ME TO SAY. "YOUR OWN BEHAVIOR AND ACTIONS HAVE BROUGHT THIS PUNISHMENT UPON YOU." AND IF YOU KILL ME TODAY, THE LORD WILL ADD IT TO YOUR LIST OF SINS FOR SHEDDING INNOCENT BLOOD.

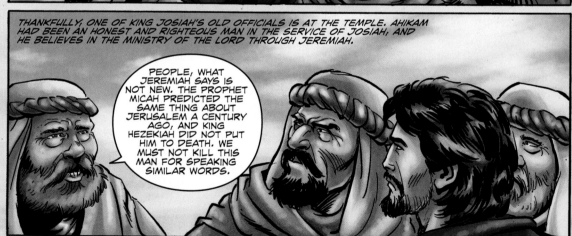

THANKFULLY, ONE OF KING JOSIAH'S OLD OFFICIALS IS AT THE TEMPLE. AHIKAM HAD BEEN AN HONEST AND RIGHTEOUS MAN IN THE SERVICE OF JOSIAH, AND HE BELIEVES IN THE MINISTRY OF THE LORD THROUGH JEREMIAH.

PEOPLE, WHAT JEREMIAH SAYS IS NOT NEW. THE PROPHET MICAH PREDICTED THE SAME THING ABOUT JERUSALEM A CENTURY AGO, AND KING HEZEKIAH DID NOT PUT HIM TO DEATH. WE MUST NOT KILL THIS MAN FOR SPEAKING SIMILAR WORDS.

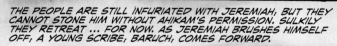

THE PEOPLE ARE STILL INFURIATED WITH JEREMIAH, BUT THEY CANNOT STONE HIM WITHOUT AHIKAM'S PERMISSION. SULKILY THEY RETREAT ... FOR NOW. AS JEREMIAH BRUSHES HIMSELF OFF, A YOUNG SCRIBE, BARUCH, COMES FORWARD.

I BELIEVE YOU, JEREMIAH! IS THERE ANYTHING I CAN DO TO HELP YOU?

I NEED SOMEONE TO WRITE DOWN MY PROPHECIES. THESE PEOPLE MAY ACTUALLY KILL ME SOMEDAY, AND GOD'S WORD MUST LIVE ON.

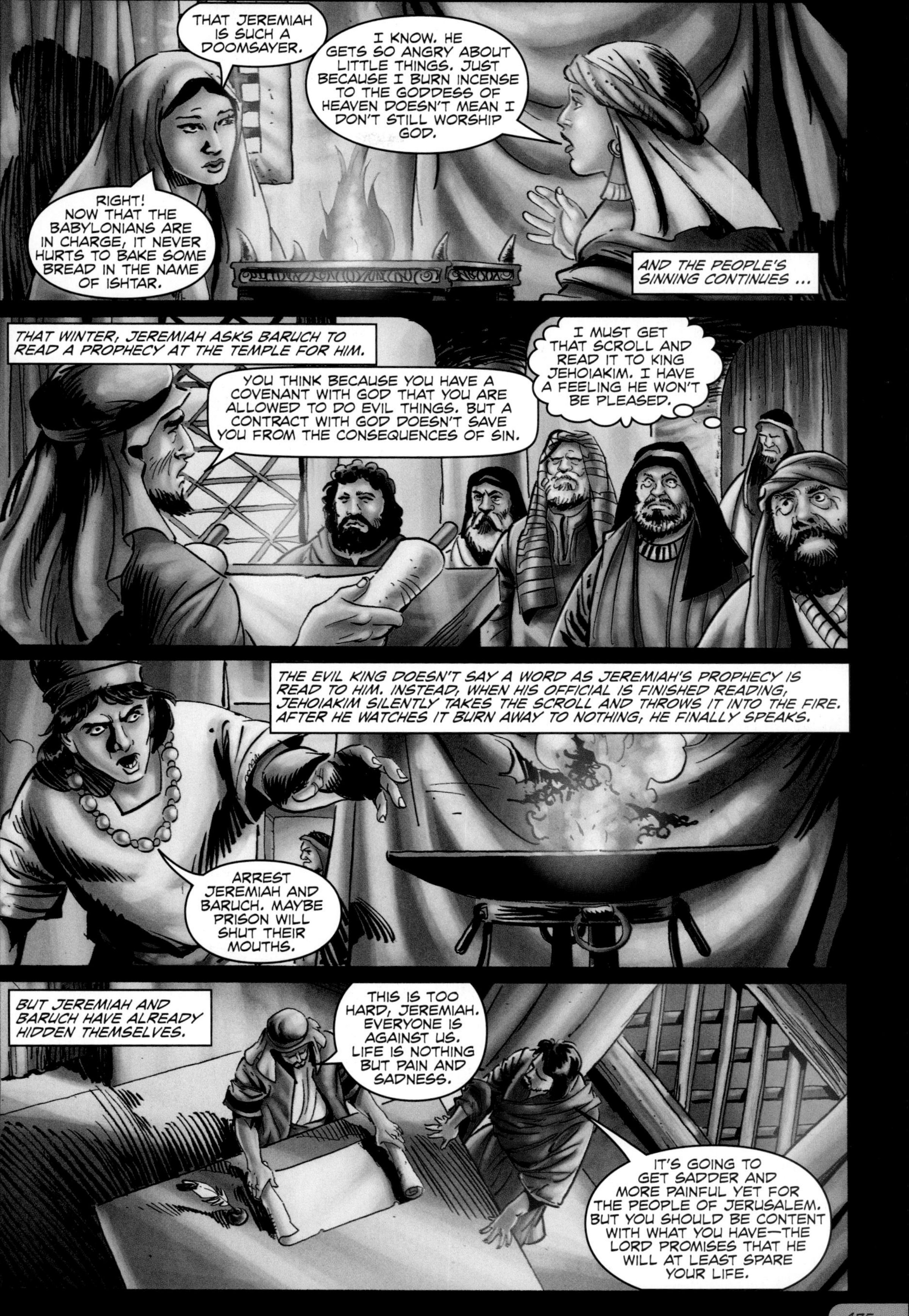
THAT JEREMIAH IS SUCH A DOOMSAYER.
I KNOW. HE GETS SO ANGRY ABOUT LITTLE THINGS. JUST BECAUSE I BURN INCENSE TO THE GODDESS OF HEAVEN DOESN'T MEAN I DON'T STILL WORSHIP GOD.
RIGHT! NOW THAT THE BABYLONIANS ARE IN CHARGE, IT NEVER HURTS TO BAKE SOME BREAD IN THE NAME OF ISHTAR.
AND THE PEOPLE'S SINNING CONTINUES ...
THAT WINTER, JEREMIAH ASKS BARUCH TO READ A PROPHECY AT THE TEMPLE FOR HIM.
YOU THINK BECAUSE YOU HAVE A COVENANT WITH GOD THAT YOU ARE ALLOWED TO DO EVIL THINGS. BUT A CONTRACT WITH GOD DOESN'T SAVE YOU FROM THE CONSEQUENCES OF SIN.
I MUST GET THAT SCROLL AND READ IT TO KING JEHOIAKIM. I HAVE A FEELING HE WON'T BE PLEASED.
THE EVIL KING DOESN'T SAY A WORD AS JEREMIAH'S PROPHECY IS READ TO HIM. INSTEAD, WHEN HIS OFFICIAL IS FINISHED READING, JEHOIAKIM SILENTLY TAKES THE SCROLL AND THROWS IT INTO THE FIRE. AFTER HE WATCHES IT BURN AWAY TO NOTHING, HE FINALLY SPEAKS.
ARREST JEREMIAH AND BARUCH. MAYBE PRISON WILL SHUT THEIR MOUTHS.
BUT JEREMIAH AND BARUCH HAVE ALREADY HIDDEN THEMSELVES.
THIS IS TOO HARD, JEREMIAH. EVERYONE IS AGAINST US. LIFE IS NOTHING BUT PAIN AND SADNESS.
IT'S GOING TO GET SADDER AND MORE PAINFUL YET FOR THE PEOPLE OF JERUSALEM. BUT YOU SHOULD BE CONTENT WITH WHAT YOU HAVE—THE LORD PROMISES THAT HE WILL AT LEAST SPARE YOUR LIFE.

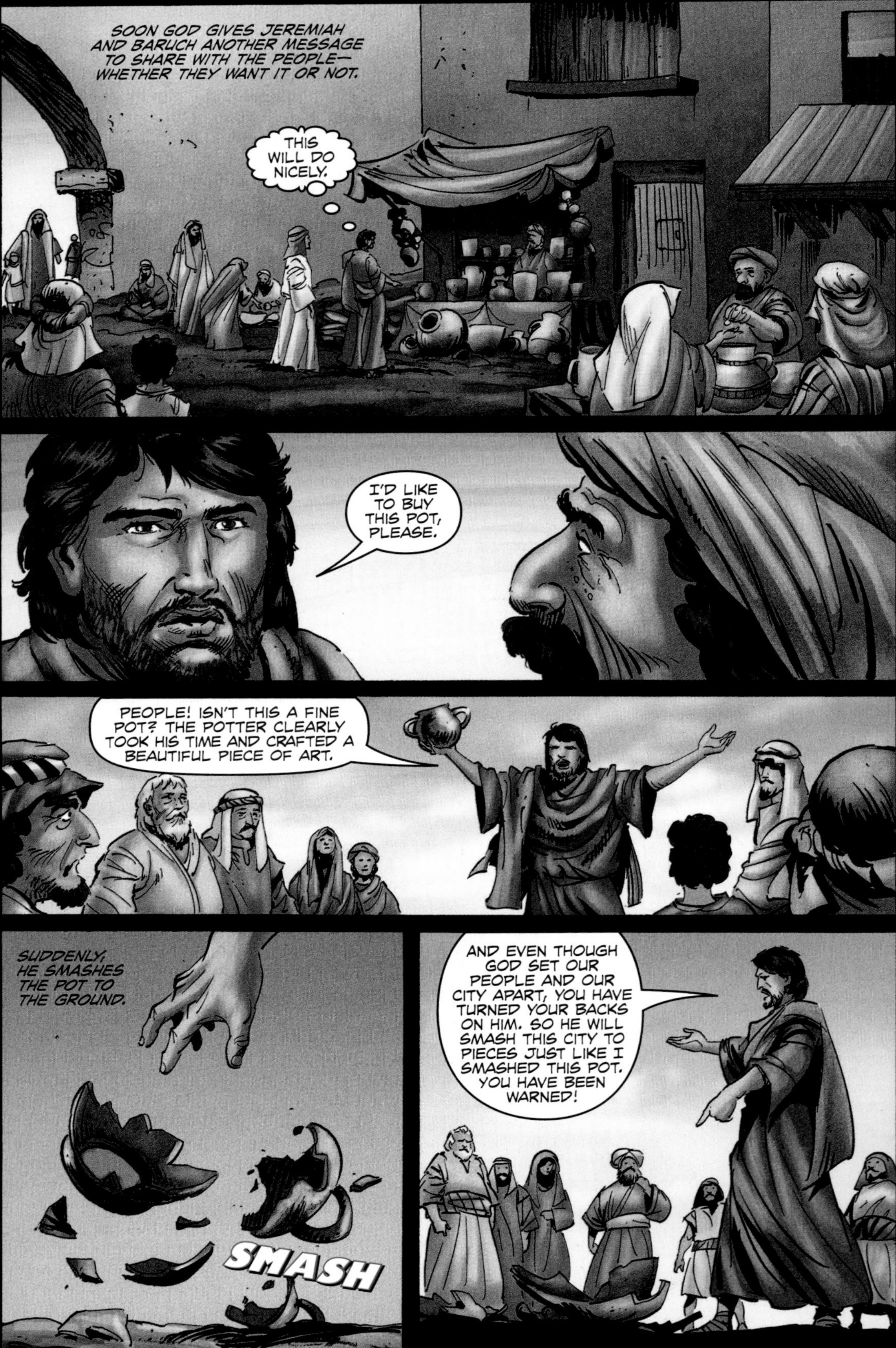
SOON GOD GIVES JEREMIAH AND BARUCH ANOTHER MESSAGE TO SHARE WITH THE PEOPLE—WHETHER THEY WANT IT OR NOT.
THIS WILL DO NICELY.
I'D LIKE TO BUY THIS POT, PLEASE.
PEOPLE! ISN'T THIS A FINE POT? THE POTTER CLEARLY TOOK HIS TIME AND CRAFTED A BEAUTIFUL PIECE OF ART.
SUDDENLY, HE SMASHES THE POT TO THE GROUND.
SMASH
AND EVEN THOUGH GOD SET OUR PEOPLE AND OUR CITY APART, YOU HAVE TURNED YOUR BACKS ON HIM. SO HE WILL SMASH THIS CITY TO PIECES JUST LIKE I SMASHED THIS POT. YOU HAVE BEEN WARNED!

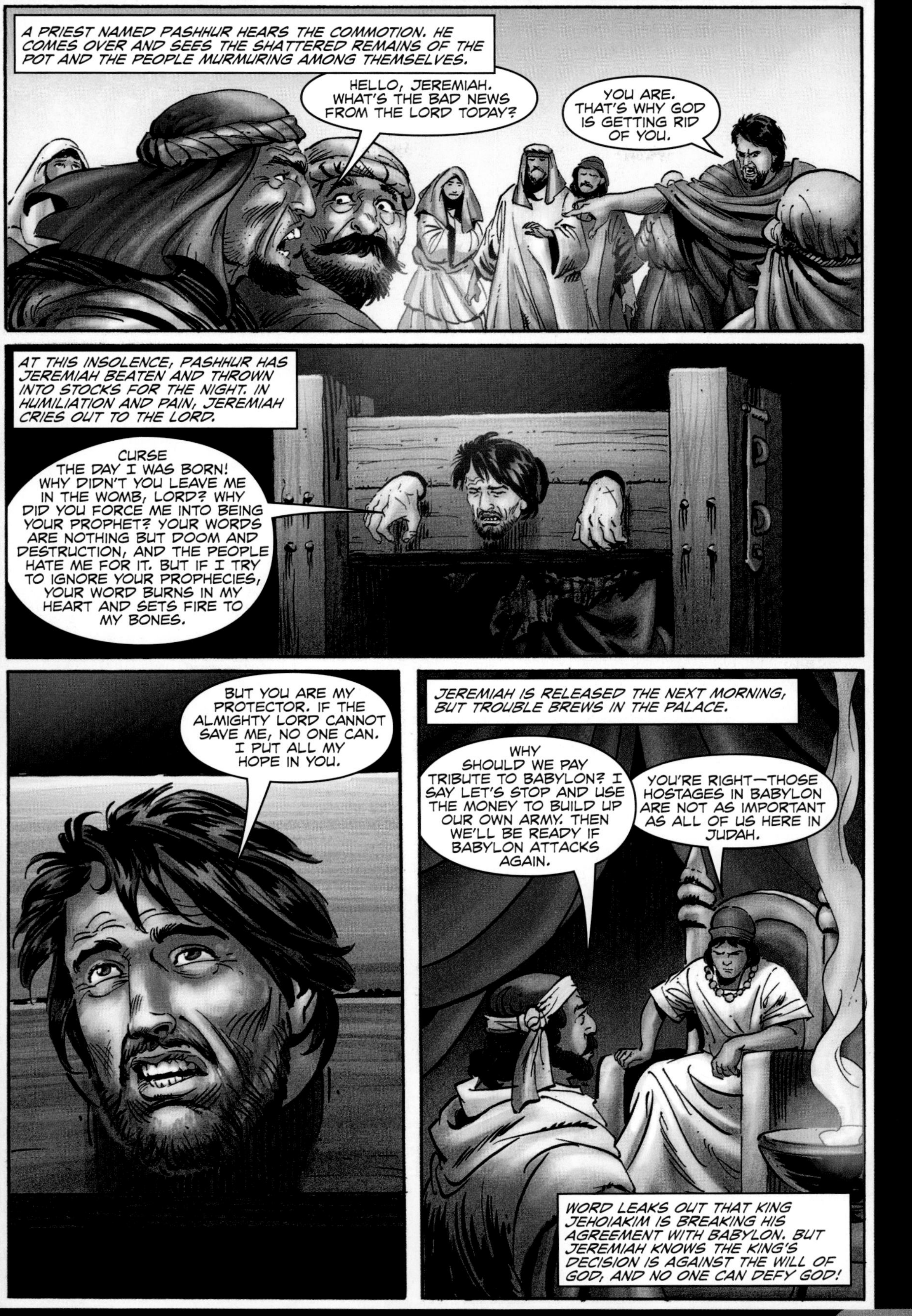
A PRIEST NAMED PASHHUR HEARS THE COMMOTION. HE COMES OVER AND SEES THE SHATTERED REMAINS OF THE POT AND THE PEOPLE MURMURING AMONG THEMSELVES.
HELLO, JEREMIAH. WHAT'S THE BAD NEWS FROM THE LORD TODAY?
YOU ARE. THAT'S WHY GOD IS GETTING RID OF YOU.
AT THIS INSOLENCE, PASHHUR HAS JEREMIAH BEATEN AND THROWN INTO STOCKS FOR THE NIGHT. IN HUMILIATION AND PAIN, JEREMIAH CRIES OUT TO THE LORD.
CURSE THE DAY I WAS BORN! WHY DIDN'T YOU LEAVE ME IN THE WOMB, LORD? WHY DID YOU FORCE ME INTO BEING YOUR PROPHET? YOUR WORDS ARE NOTHING BUT DOOM AND DESTRUCTION, AND THE PEOPLE HATE ME FOR IT. BUT IF I TRY TO IGNORE YOUR PROPHECIES, YOUR WORD BURNS IN MY HEART AND SETS FIRE TO MY BONES.
BUT YOU ARE MY PROTECTOR. IF THE ALMIGHTY LORD CANNOT SAVE ME, NO ONE CAN. I PUT ALL MY HOPE IN YOU.
JEREMIAH IS RELEASED THE NEXT MORNING, BUT TROUBLE BREWS IN THE PALACE.
WHY SHOULD WE PAY TRIBUTE TO BABYLON? I SAY LET'S STOP AND USE THE MONEY TO BUILD UP OUR OWN ARMY. THEN WE'LL BE READY IF BABYLON ATTACKS AGAIN.
YOU'RE RIGHT—THOSE HOSTAGES IN BABYLON ARE NOT AS IMPORTANT AS ALL OF US HERE IN JUDAH.
WORD LEAKS OUT THAT KING JEHOIAKIM IS BREAKING HIS AGREEMENT WITH BABYLON. BUT JEREMIAH KNOWS THE KING'S DECISION IS AGAINST THE WILL OF GOD, AND NO ONE CAN DEFY GOD!

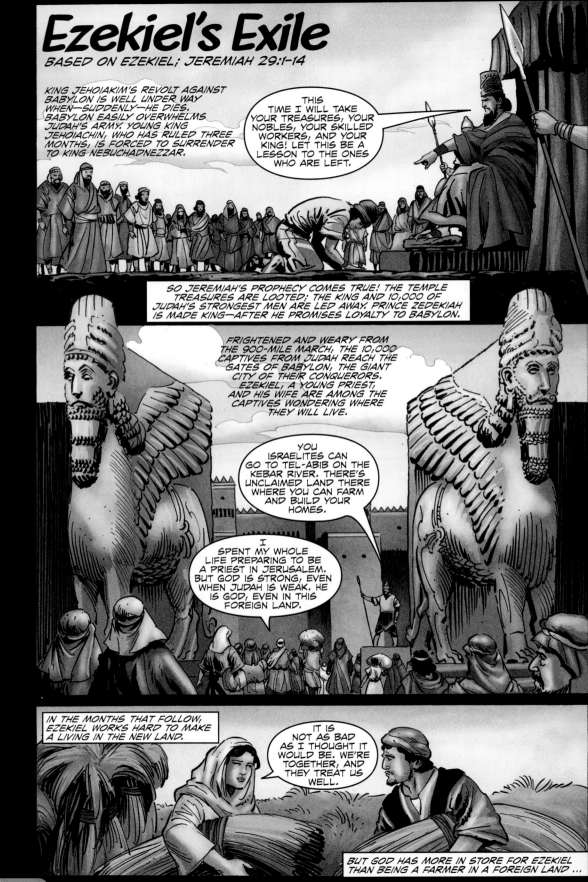

Ezekiel's Exile

BASED ON EZEKIEL; JEREMIAH 29:1-14

KING JEHOIAKIM'S REVOLT AGAINST BABYLON IS WELL UNDER WAY WHEN—SUDDENLY—HE DIES. BABYLON EASILY OVERWHELMS JUDAH'S ARMY. YOUNG KING JEHOIACHIN, WHO HAS RULED THREE MONTHS, IS FORCED TO SURRENDER TO KING NEBUCHADNEZZAR.

THIS TIME I WILL TAKE YOUR TREASURES, YOUR NOBLES, YOUR SKILLED WORKERS, AND YOUR KING! LET THIS BE A LESSON TO THE ONES WHO ARE LEFT.

SO JEREMIAH'S PROPHECY COMES TRUE! THE TEMPLE TREASURES ARE LOOTED; THE KING AND 10,000 OF JUDAH'S STRONGEST MEN ARE LED AWAY. PRINCE ZEDEKIAH IS MADE KING—AFTER HE PROMISES LOYALTY TO BABYLON.

FRIGHTENED AND WEARY FROM THE 900-MILE MARCH, THE 10,000 CAPTIVES FROM JUDAH REACH THE GATES OF BABYLON, THE GIANT CITY OF THEIR CONQUERORS. EZEKIEL, A YOUNG PRIEST, AND HIS WIFE ARE AMONG THE CAPTIVES WONDERING WHERE THEY WILL LIVE.

YOU ISRAELITES CAN GO TO TEL-ABIB ON THE KEBAR RIVER. THERE'S UNCLAIMED LAND THERE WHERE YOU CAN FARM AND BUILD YOUR HOMES.

I SPENT MY WHOLE LIFE PREPARING TO BE A PRIEST IN JERUSALEM. BUT GOD IS STRONG, EVEN WHEN JUDAH IS WEAK. HE IS GOD, EVEN IN THIS FOREIGN LAND.

IN THE MONTHS THAT FOLLOW, EZEKIEL WORKS HARD TO MAKE A LIVING IN THE NEW LAND.

IT IS NOT AS BAD AS I THOUGHT IT WOULD BE. WE'RE TOGETHER, AND THEY TREAT US WELL.

BUT GOD HAS MORE IN STORE FOR EZEKIEL THAN BEING A FARMER IN A FOREIGN LAND ...

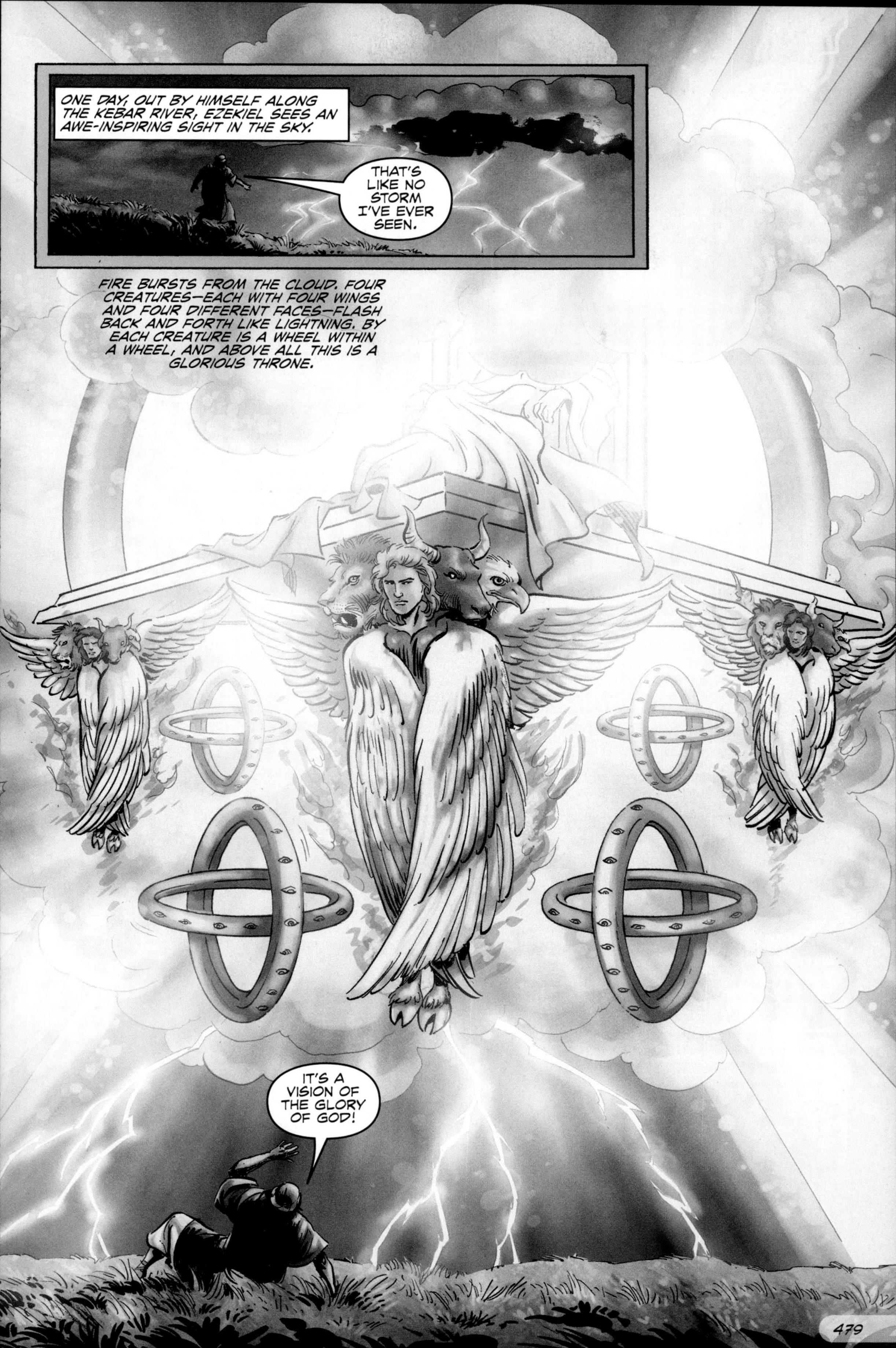
ONE DAY, OUT BY HIMSELF ALONG THE KEBAR RIVER, EZEKIEL SEES AN AWE-INSPIRING SIGHT IN THE SKY.
THAT'S LIKE NO STORM I'VE EVER SEEN.
FIRE BURSTS FROM THE CLOUD. FOUR CREATURES—EACH WITH FOUR WINGS AND FOUR DIFFERENT FACES—FLASH BACK AND FORTH LIKE LIGHTNING. BY EACH CREATURE IS A WHEEL WITHIN A WHEEL, AND ABOVE ALL THIS IS A GLORIOUS THRONE.
IT'S A VISION OF THE GLORY OF GOD!

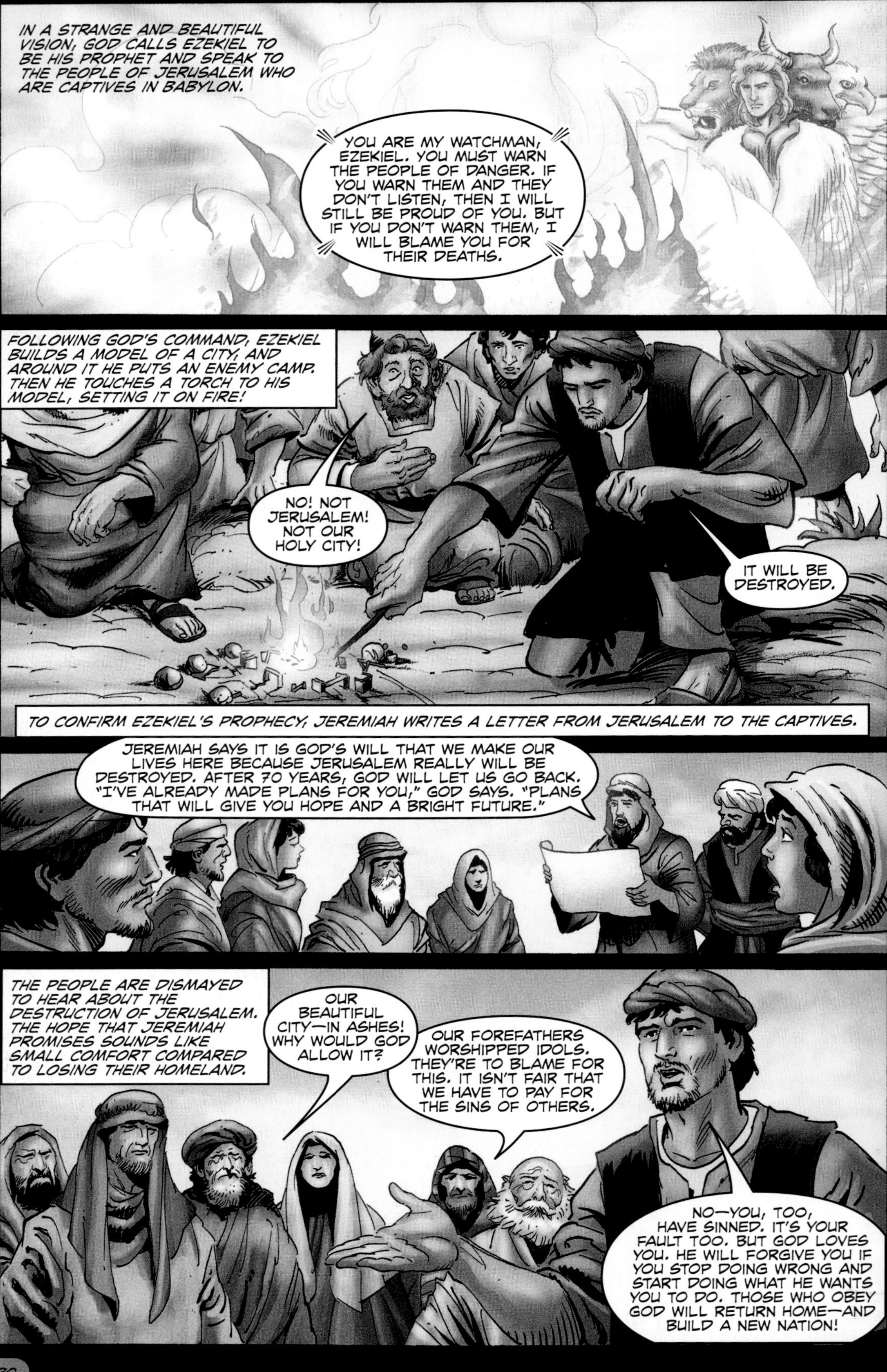
IN A STRANGE AND BEAUTIFUL VISION, GOD CALLS EZEKIEL TO BE HIS PROPHET AND SPEAK TO THE PEOPLE OF JERUSALEM WHO ARE CAPTIVES IN BABYLON.
YOU ARE MY WATCHMAN, EZEKIEL. YOU MUST WARN THE PEOPLE OF DANGER. IF YOU WARN THEM AND THEY DON'T LISTEN, THEN I WILL STILL BE PROUD OF YOU. BUT IF YOU DON'T WARN THEM, I WILL BLAME YOU FOR THEIR DEATHS.
FOLLOWING GOD'S COMMAND, EZEKIEL BUILDS A MODEL OF A CITY, AND AROUND IT HE PUTS AN ENEMY CAMP. THEN HE TOUCHES A TORCH TO HIS MODEL, SETTING IT ON FIRE!
NO! NOT JERUSALEM! NOT OUR HOLY CITY!
IT WILL BE DESTROYED.
TO CONFIRM EZEKIEL'S PROPHECY, JEREMIAH WRITES A LETTER FROM JERUSALEM TO THE CAPTIVES.
JEREMIAH SAYS IT IS GOD'S WILL THAT WE MAKE OUR LIVES HERE BECAUSE JERUSALEM REALLY WILL BE DESTROYED. AFTER 70 YEARS, GOD WILL LET US GO BACK. "I'VE ALREADY MADE PLANS FOR YOU," GOD SAYS. "PLANS THAT WILL GIVE YOU HOPE AND A BRIGHT FUTURE."
THE PEOPLE ARE DISMAYED TO HEAR ABOUT THE DESTRUCTION OF JERUSALEM. THE HOPE THAT JEREMIAH PROMISES SOUNDS LIKE SMALL COMFORT COMPARED TO LOSING THEIR HOMELAND.
OUR BEAUTIFUL CITY—IN ASHES! WHY WOULD GOD ALLOW IT?
OUR FOREFATHERS WORSHIPPED IDOLS. THEY'RE TO BLAME FOR THIS. IT ISN'T FAIR THAT WE HAVE TO PAY FOR THE SINS OF OTHERS.
NO—YOU, TOO, HAVE SINNED. IT'S YOUR FAULT TOO. BUT GOD LOVES YOU. HE WILL FORGIVE YOU IF YOU STOP DOING WRONG AND START DOING WHAT HE WANTS YOU TO DO. THOSE WHO OBEY GOD WILL RETURN HOME—AND BUILD A NEW NATION!

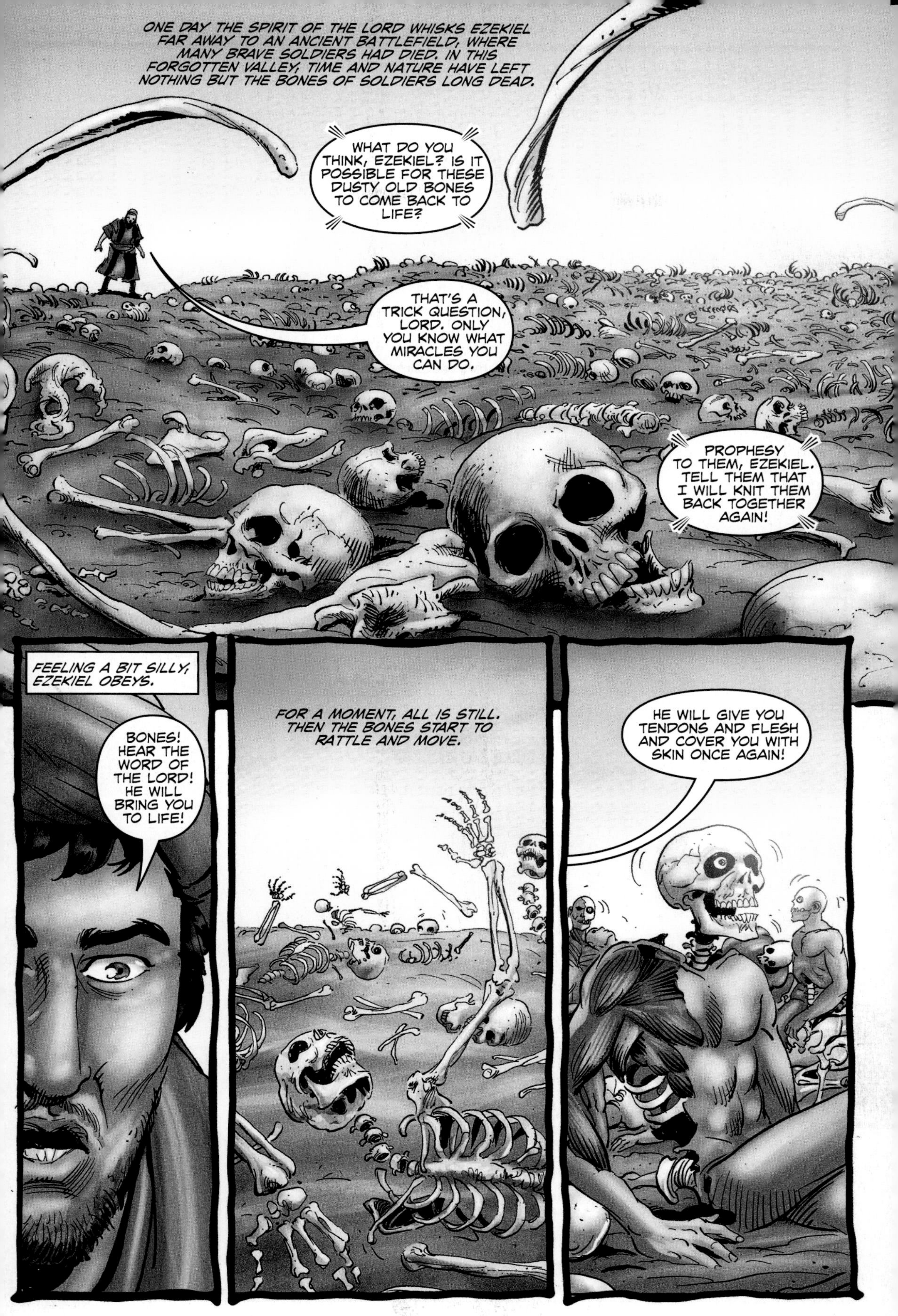

ONE DAY THE SPIRIT OF THE LORD WHISKS EZEKIEL FAR AWAY TO AN ANCIENT BATTLEFIELD, WHERE MANY BRAVE SOLDIERS HAD DIED. IN THIS FORGOTTEN VALLEY, TIME AND NATURE HAVE LEFT NOTHING BUT THE BONES OF SOLDIERS LONG DEAD.
WHAT DO YOU THINK, EZEKIEL? IS IT POSSIBLE FOR THESE DUSTY OLD BONES TO COME BACK TO LIFE?
THAT'S A TRICK QUESTION, LORD. ONLY YOU KNOW WHAT MIRACLES YOU CAN DO.
PROPHESY TO THEM, EZEKIEL. TELL THEM THAT I WILL KNIT THEM BACK TOGETHER AGAIN!
FEELING A BIT SILLY, EZEKIEL OBEYS.
BONES! HEAR THE WORD OF THE LORD! HE WILL BRING YOU TO LIFE!
FOR A MOMENT, ALL IS STILL. THEN THE BONES START TO RATTLE AND MOVE.
HE WILL GIVE YOU TENDONS AND FLESH AND COVER YOU WITH SKIN ONCE AGAIN!

AS EZEKIEL PROPHESIES, THE BONES FORM BACK INTO HUMAN BEINGS— BUT THERE IS STILL NO LIFE IN THEM.

TELL THEM I WILL FILL THEM WITH MY BREATH, MY SPIRIT.

EZEKIEL CONTINUES TO PREACH, AND THE BODIES START BREATHING AGAIN. THEY COME TO LIFE AND STAND UP, THOUSANDS OF THEM!

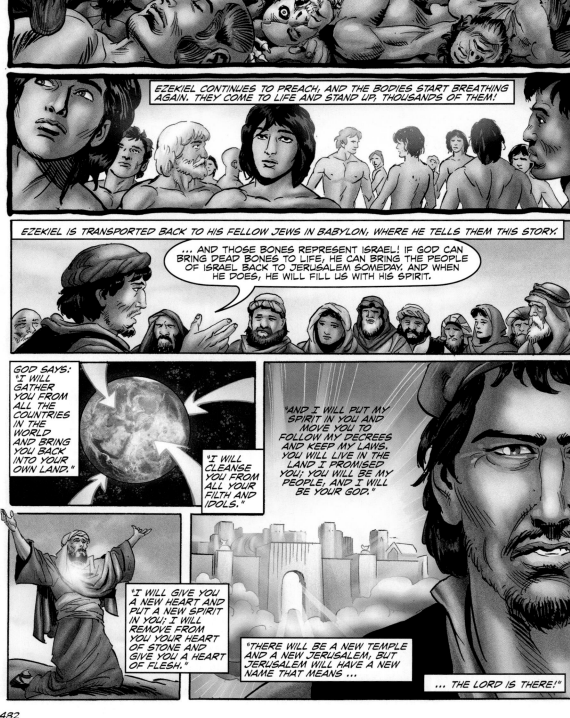

EZEKIEL IS TRANSPORTED BACK TO HIS FELLOW JEWS IN BABYLON, WHERE HE TELLS THEM THIS STORY.

... AND THOSE BONES REPRESENT ISRAEL! IF GOD CAN BRING DEAD BONES TO LIFE, HE CAN BRING THE PEOPLE OF ISRAEL BACK TO JERUSALEM SOMEDAY. AND WHEN HE DOES, HE WILL FILL US WITH HIS SPIRIT.

GOD SAYS: "I WILL GATHER YOU FROM ALL THE COUNTRIES IN THE WORLD AND BRING YOU BACK INTO YOUR OWN LAND."

"I WILL CLEANSE YOU FROM ALL YOUR FILTH AND IDOLS."

"AND I WILL PUT MY SPIRIT IN YOU AND MOVE YOU TO FOLLOW MY DECREES AND KEEP MY LAWS. YOU WILL LIVE IN THE LAND I PROMISED YOU; YOU WILL BE MY PEOPLE, AND I WILL BE YOUR GOD."

"I WILL GIVE YOU A NEW HEART AND PUT A NEW SPIRIT IN YOU; I WILL REMOVE FROM YOU YOUR HEART OF STONE AND GIVE YOU A HEART OF FLESH."

"THERE WILL BE A NEW TEMPLE AND A NEW JERUSALEM, BUT JERUSALEM WILL HAVE A NEW NAME THAT MEANS ...

... THE LORD IS THERE!"

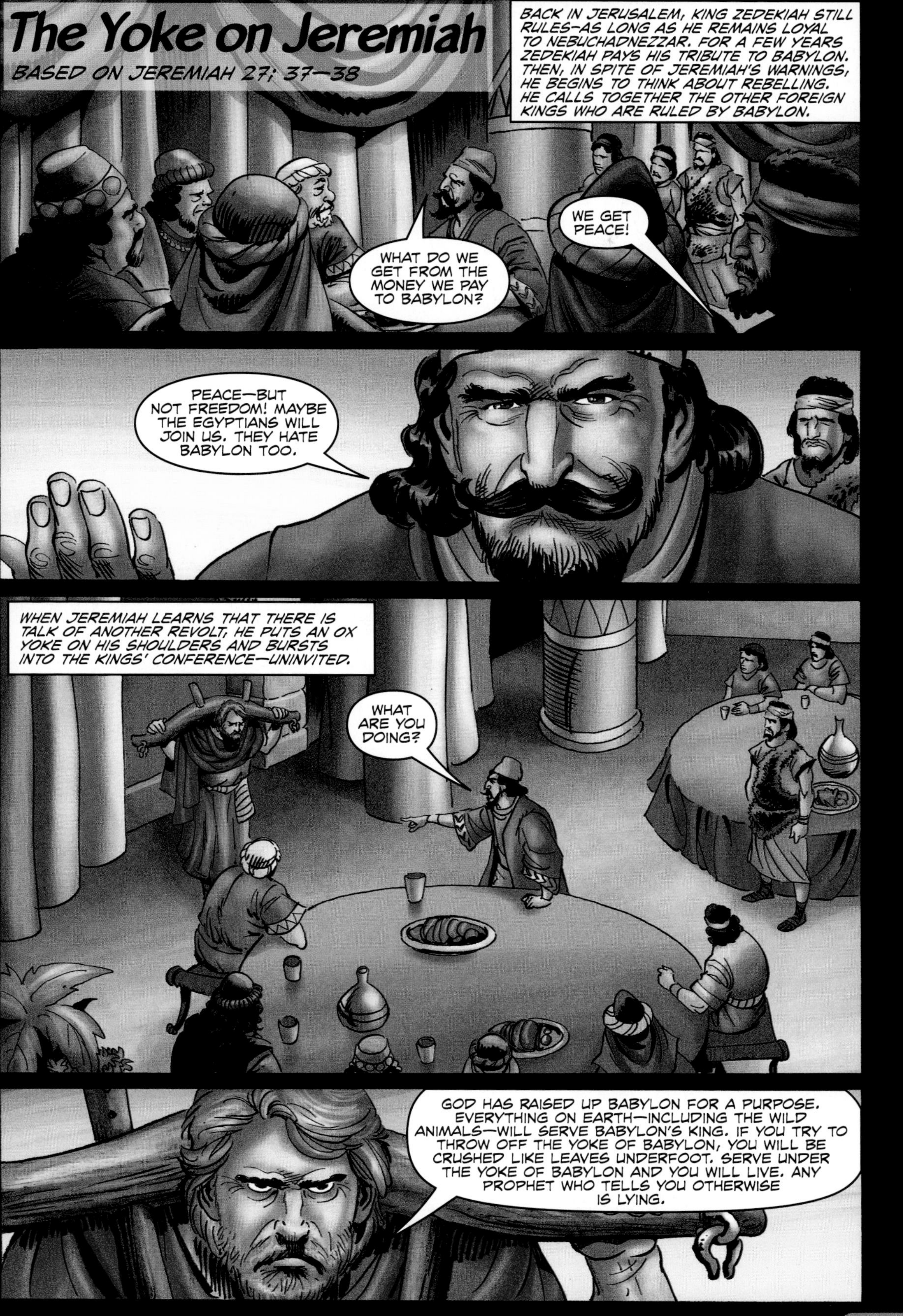
The Yoke on Jeremiah
BASED ON JEREMIAH 27; 37—38
BACK IN JERUSALEM, KING ZEDEKIAH STILL RULES—AS LONG AS HE REMAINS LOYAL TO NEBUCHADNEZZAR. FOR A FEW YEARS ZEDEKIAH PAYS HIS TRIBUTE TO BABYLON. THEN, IN SPITE OF JEREMIAH'S WARNINGS, HE BEGINS TO THINK ABOUT REBELLING. HE CALLS TOGETHER THE OTHER FOREIGN KINGS WHO ARE RULED BY BABYLON.
WHAT DO WE GET FROM THE MONEY WE PAY TO BABYLON?
WE GET PEACE!
PEACE—BUT NOT FREEDOM! MAYBE THE EGYPTIANS WILL JOIN US. THEY HATE BABYLON TOO.
WHEN JEREMIAH LEARNS THAT THERE IS TALK OF ANOTHER REVOLT; HE PUTS AN OX YOKE ON HIS SHOULDERS AND BURSTS INTO THE KINGS' CONFERENCE—UNINVITED.
WHAT ARE YOU DOING?
GOD HAS RAISED UP BABYLON FOR A PURPOSE. EVERYTHING ON EARTH—INCLUDING THE WILD ANIMALS—WILL SERVE BABYLON'S KING. IF YOU TRY TO THROW OFF THE YOKE OF BABYLON, YOU WILL BE CRUSHED LIKE LEAVES UNDERFOOT. SERVE UNDER THE YOKE OF BABYLON AND YOU WILL LIVE. ANY PROPHET WHO TELLS YOU OTHERWISE IS LYING.

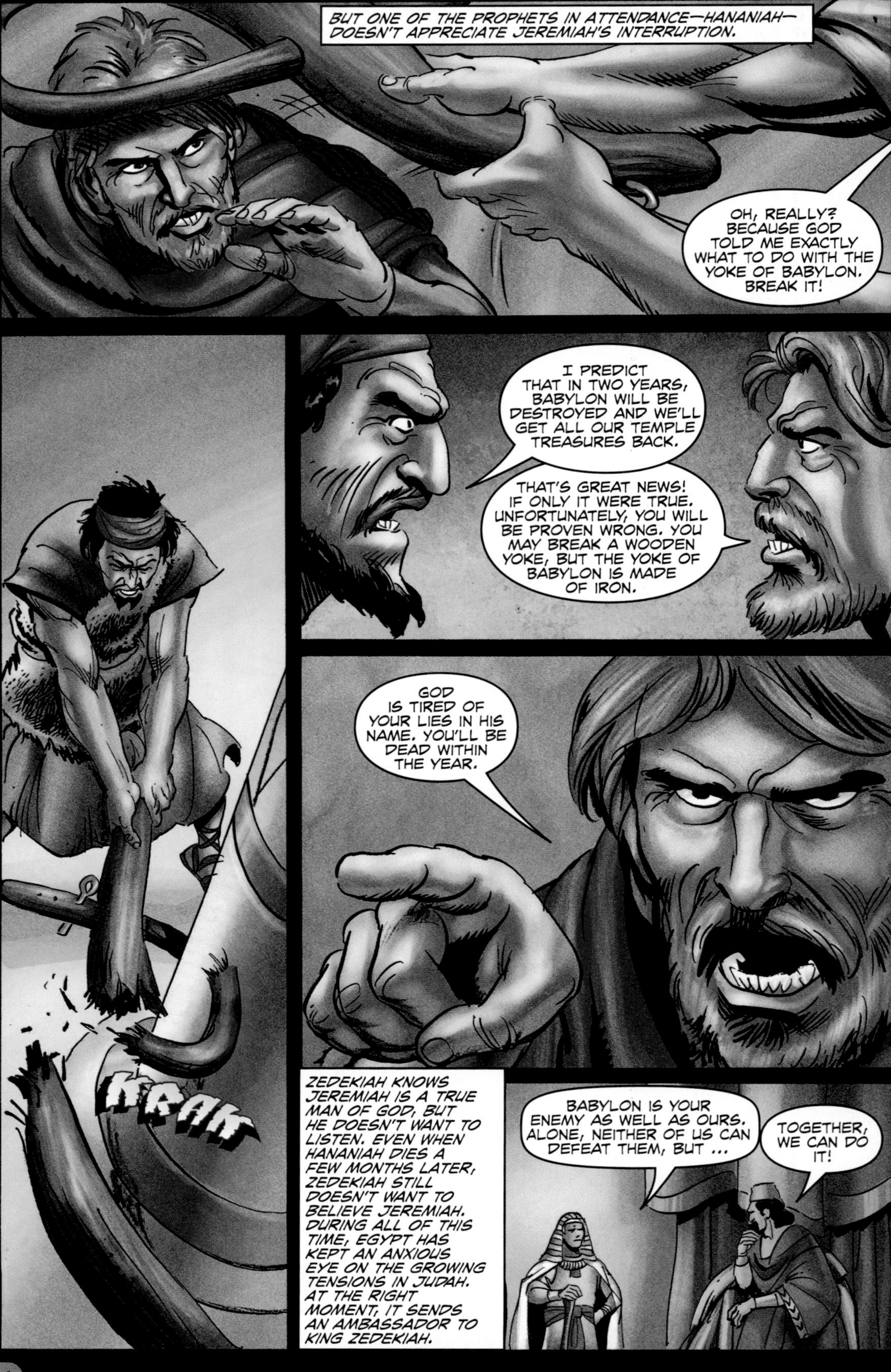

BUT ONE OF THE PROPHETS IN ATTENDANCE—HANANIAH—DOESN'T APPRECIATE JEREMIAH'S INTERRUPTION.
OH, REALLY? BECAUSE GOD TOLD ME EXACTLY WHAT TO DO WITH THE YOKE OF BABYLON. BREAK IT!
KRAK
I PREDICT THAT IN TWO YEARS, BABYLON WILL BE DESTROYED AND WE'LL GET ALL OUR TEMPLE TREASURES BACK.
THAT'S GREAT NEWS! IF ONLY IT WERE TRUE. UNFORTUNATELY, YOU WILL BE PROVEN WRONG. YOU MAY BREAK A WOODEN YOKE, BUT THE YOKE OF BABYLON IS MADE OF IRON.
GOD IS TIRED OF YOUR LIES IN HIS NAME. YOU'LL BE DEAD WITHIN THE YEAR.
ZEDEKIAH KNOWS JEREMIAH IS A TRUE MAN OF GOD, BUT HE DOESN'T WANT TO LISTEN. EVEN WHEN HANANIAH DIES A FEW MONTHS LATER, ZEDEKIAH STILL DOESN'T WANT TO BELIEVE JEREMIAH. DURING ALL OF THIS TIME, EGYPT HAS KEPT AN ANXIOUS EYE ON THE GROWING TENSIONS IN JUDAH. AT THE RIGHT MOMENT, IT SENDS AN AMBASSADOR TO KING ZEDEKIAH.
BABYLON IS YOUR ENEMY AS WELL AS OURS. ALONE, NEITHER OF US CAN DEFEAT THEM, BUT ...
TOGETHER, WE CAN DO IT!

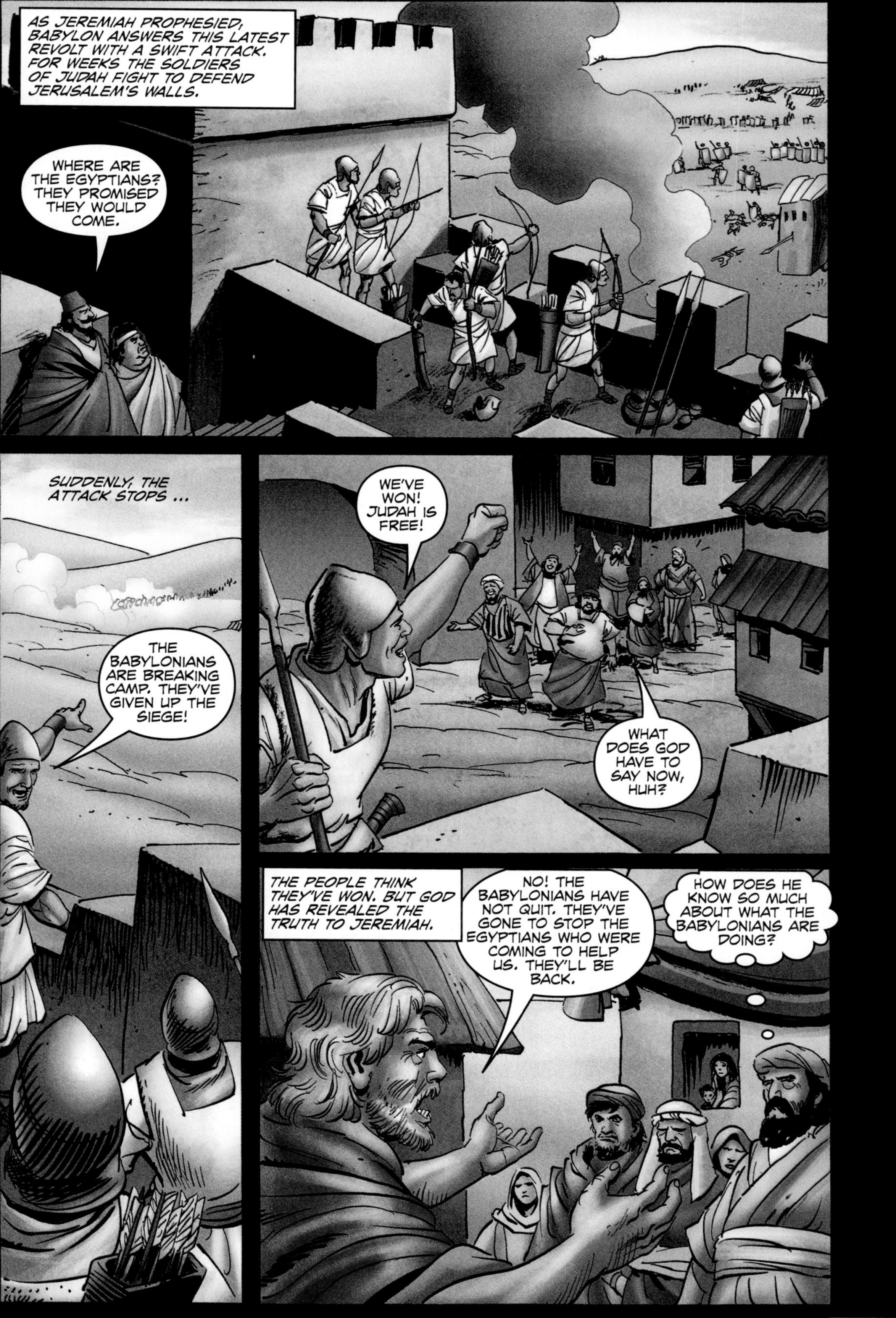
AS JEREMIAH PROPHESIED, BABYLON ANSWERS THIS LATEST REVOLT WITH A SWIFT ATTACK. FOR WEEKS THE SOLDIERS OF JUDAH FIGHT TO DEFEND JERUSALEM'S WALLS.
WHERE ARE THE EGYPTIANS? THEY PROMISED THEY WOULD COME.
SUDDENLY, THE ATTACK STOPS ...
THE BABYLONIANS ARE BREAKING CAMP. THEY'VE GIVEN UP THE SIEGE!
WE'VE WON! JUDAH IS FREE!
WHAT DOES GOD HAVE TO SAY NOW, HUH?
THE PEOPLE THINK THEY'VE WON. BUT GOD HAS REVEALED THE TRUTH TO JEREMIAH.
NO! THE BABYLONIANS HAVE NOT QUIT. THEY'VE GONE TO STOP THE EGYPTIANS WHO WERE COMING TO HELP US. THEY'LL BE BACK.
HOW DOES HE KNOW SO MUCH ABOUT WHAT THE BABYLONIANS ARE DOING?

A FEW DAYS LATER, JEREMIAH STARTS ON A TRIP TO HIS HOMETOWN A FEW MILES FROM JERUSALEM. BEFORE HE GETS OUT OF THE GATE, SOLDIERS STOP HIM.

YOU'RE THE ONE WHO PROPHESIED THAT BABYLON WOULD CONQUER US. THIS IS ALL YOUR FAULT!

SINCE YOU DON'T SUPPORT US IN THE WAR, YOU'RE A TRAITOR TO JUDAH.

WHAT? I'VE ONLY SPOKEN GOD'S TRUTH.

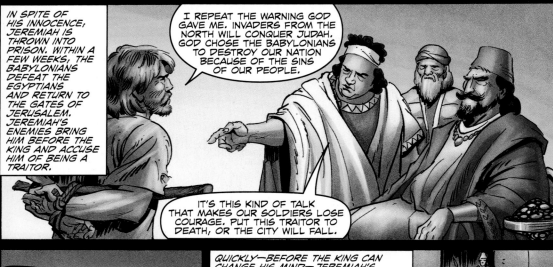

IN SPITE OF HIS INNOCENCE, JEREMIAH IS THROWN INTO PRISON. WITHIN A FEW WEEKS, THE BABYLONIANS DEFEAT THE EGYPTIANS AND RETURN TO THE GATES OF JERUSALEM. JEREMIAH'S ENEMIES BRING HIM BEFORE THE KING AND ACCUSE HIM OF BEING A TRAITOR.

I REPEAT THE WARNING GOD GAVE ME. INVADERS FROM THE NORTH WILL CONQUER JUDAH. GOD CHOSE THE BABYLONIANS TO DESTROY OUR NATION BECAUSE OF THE SINS OF OUR PEOPLE.

IT'S THIS KIND OF TALK THAT MAKES OUR SOLDIERS LOSE COURAGE. PUT THIS TRAITOR TO DEATH, OR THE CITY WILL FALL.

HE'S IN YOUR HANDS. DO WHAT YOU WANT WITH HIM.

QUICKLY—BEFORE THE KING CAN CHANGE HIS MIND—JEREMIAH'S ACCUSERS PUT HIM IN AN OLD EMPTY WELL BENEATH THE PRISON FLOOR.

LET HIM STARVE TO DEATH!

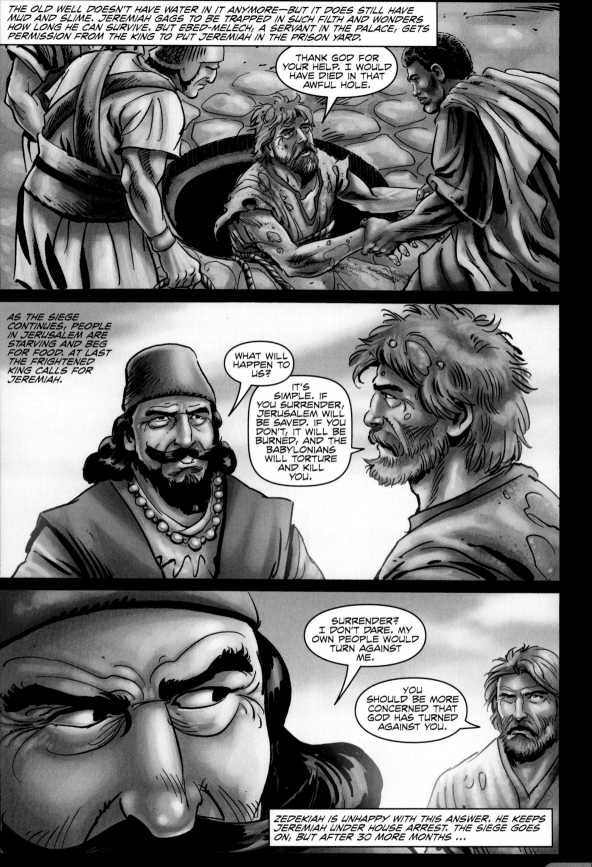

THE OLD WELL DOESN'T HAVE WATER IN IT ANYMORE—BUT IT DOES STILL HAVE MUD AND SLIME. JEREMIAH GAGS TO BE TRAPPED IN SUCH FILTH AND WONDERS HOW LONG HE CAN SURVIVE. BUT EBED-MELECH, A SERVANT IN THE PALACE, GETS PERMISSION FROM THE KING TO PUT JEREMIAH IN THE PRISON YARD.

THANK GOD FOR YOUR HELP. I WOULD HAVE DIED IN THAT AWFUL HOLE.

AS THE SIEGE CONTINUES, PEOPLE IN JERUSALEM ARE STARVING AND BEG FOR FOOD. AT LAST THE FRIGHTENED KING CALLS FOR JEREMIAH.

WHAT WILL HAPPEN TO US?

IT'S SIMPLE. IF YOU SURRENDER, JERUSALEM WILL BE SAVED. IF YOU DON'T, IT WILL BE BURNED, AND THE BABYLONIANS WILL TORTURE AND KILL YOU.

SURRENDER? I DON'T DARE. MY OWN PEOPLE WOULD TURN AGAINST ME.

YOU SHOULD BE MORE CONCERNED THAT GOD HAS TURNED AGAINST YOU.

ZEDEKIAH IS UNHAPPY WITH THIS ANSWER. HE KEEPS JEREMIAH UNDER HOUSE ARREST. THE SIEGE GOES ON; BUT AFTER 30 MORE MONTHS ...

Jerusalem Falls!

BASED ON JEREMIAH 39—44; 2 KINGS 25;
2 CHRONICLES 36:15-23;
LAMENTATIONS; OBADIAH

FOR TWO AND A HALF YEARS, FORCES FROM THE GREAT BABYLONIAN ARMY ATTACK THE CITY OF JERUSALEM. AT LAST THEY BREAK THROUGH THE WALL. AS BABYLONIAN SOLDIERS POUR THROUGH THE BROKEN WALLS, KING ZEDEKIAH TRIES TO ESCAPE WITH HIS FAMILY.

THE BABYLONIANS CAPTURE ZEDEKIAH BEFORE HE CAN REACH THE RIVER. THEY PUT OUT HIS EYES AND BRING HIM TO THE CAPTAIN OF THE GUARD.

SINCE YOU COULDN'T SEE YOUR DUTY TO KING NEBUCHADNEZZAR, NOW YOU WILL SEE NOTHING EVER AGAIN.

TAKE HIM TO BABYLON!

BUT KING NEBUCHADNEZZAR HAS HEARD OF JEREMIAH'S PROPHECIES ALL THE WAY FROM BABYLON. HIS CAPTAIN HAS SPECIAL INSTRUCTIONS.

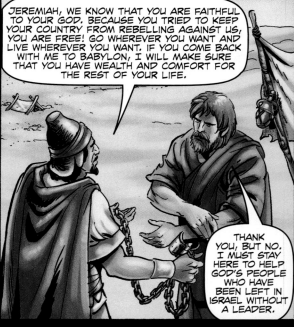

JEREMIAH, WE KNOW THAT YOU ARE FAITHFUL TO YOUR GOD. BECAUSE YOU TRIED TO KEEP YOUR COUNTRY FROM REBELLING AGAINST US, YOU ARE FREE! GO WHEREVER YOU WANT AND LIVE WHEREVER YOU WANT. IF YOU COME BACK WITH ME TO BABYLON, I WILL MAKE SURE THAT YOU HAVE WEALTH AND COMFORT FOR THE REST OF YOUR LIFE.

THANK YOU, BUT NO. I MUST STAY HERE TO HELP GOD'S PEOPLE WHO HAVE BEEN LEFT IN ISRAEL WITHOUT A LEADER.

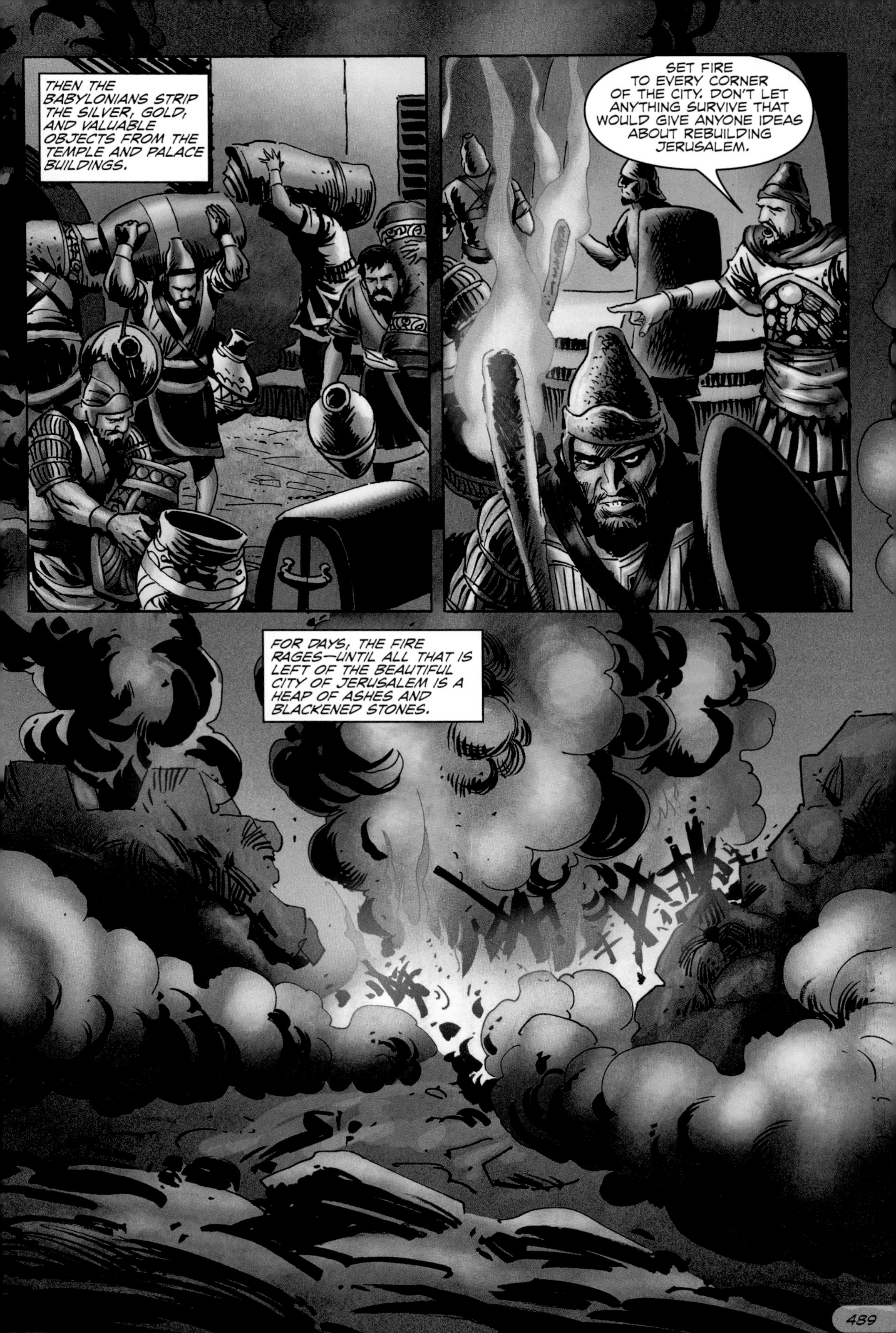
THEN THE BABYLONIANS STRIP THE SILVER, GOLD, AND VALUABLE OBJECTS FROM THE TEMPLE AND PALACE BUILDINGS.
SET FIRE TO EVERY CORNER OF THE CITY. DON'T LET ANYTHING SURVIVE THAT WOULD GIVE ANYONE IDEAS ABOUT REBUILDING JERUSALEM.
FOR DAYS, THE FIRE RAGES—UNTIL ALL THAT IS LEFT OF THE BEAUTIFUL CITY OF JERUSALEM IS A HEAP OF ASHES AND BLACKENED STONES.

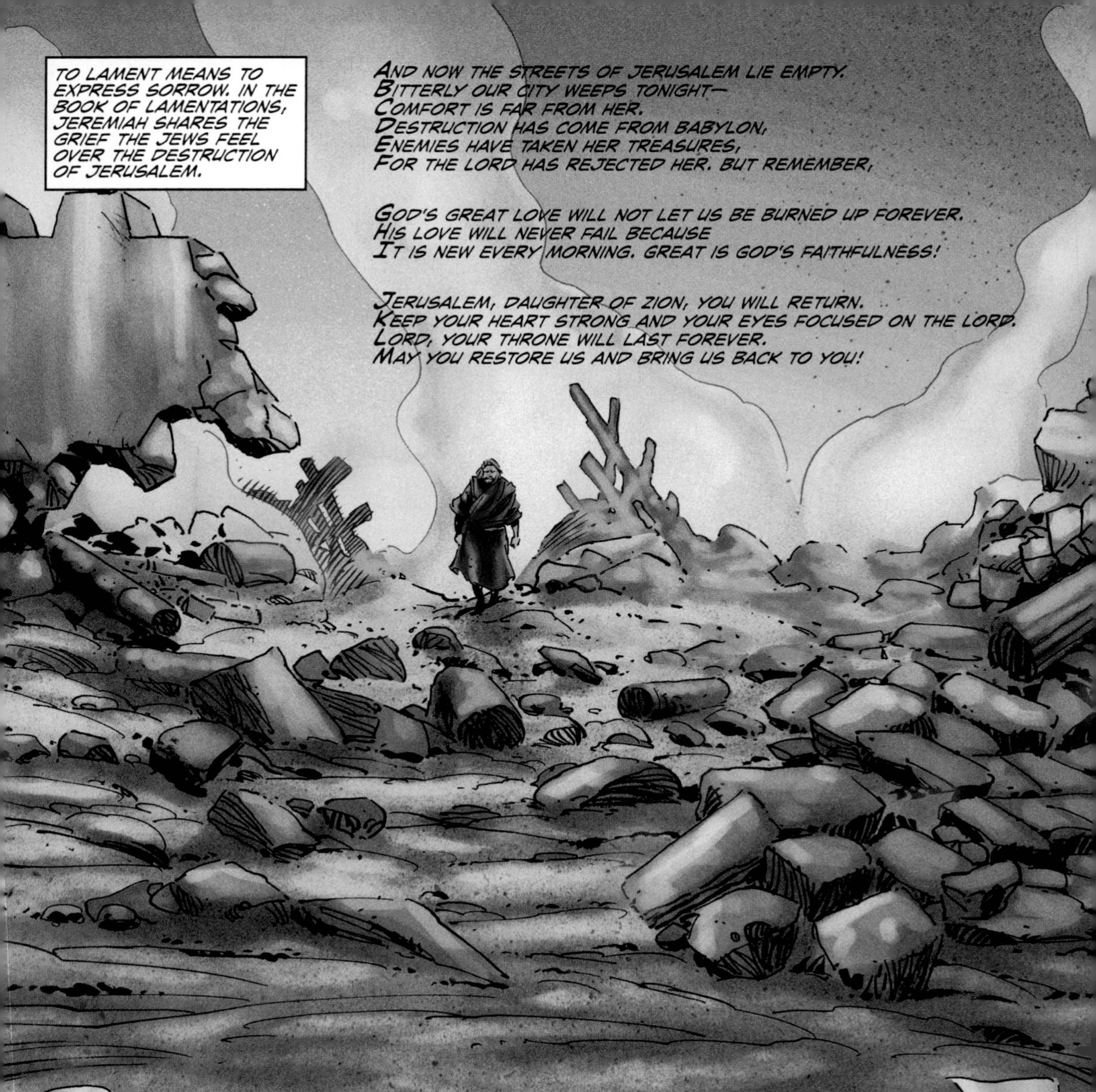
TO LAMENT MEANS TO EXPRESS SORROW. IN THE BOOK OF LAMENTATIONS, JEREMIAH SHARES THE GRIEF THE JEWS FEEL OVER THE DESTRUCTION OF JERUSALEM.
AND NOW THE STREETS OF JERUSALEM LIE EMPTY.
BITTERLY OUR CITY WEEPS TONIGHT—
COMFORT IS FAR FROM HER.
DESTRUCTION HAS COME FROM BABYLON,
ENEMIES HAVE TAKEN HER TREASURES,
FOR THE LORD HAS REJECTED HER. BUT REMEMBER,
GOD'S GREAT LOVE WILL NOT LET US BE BURNED UP FOREVER.
HIS LOVE WILL NEVER FAIL BECAUSE
IT IS NEW EVERY MORNING. GREAT IS GOD'S FAITHFULNESS!
JERUSALEM, DAUGHTER OF ZION, YOU WILL RETURN.
KEEP YOUR HEART STRONG AND YOUR EYES FOCUSED ON THE LORD.
LORD, YOUR THRONE WILL LAST FOREVER.
MAY YOU RESTORE US AND BRING US BACK TO YOU!

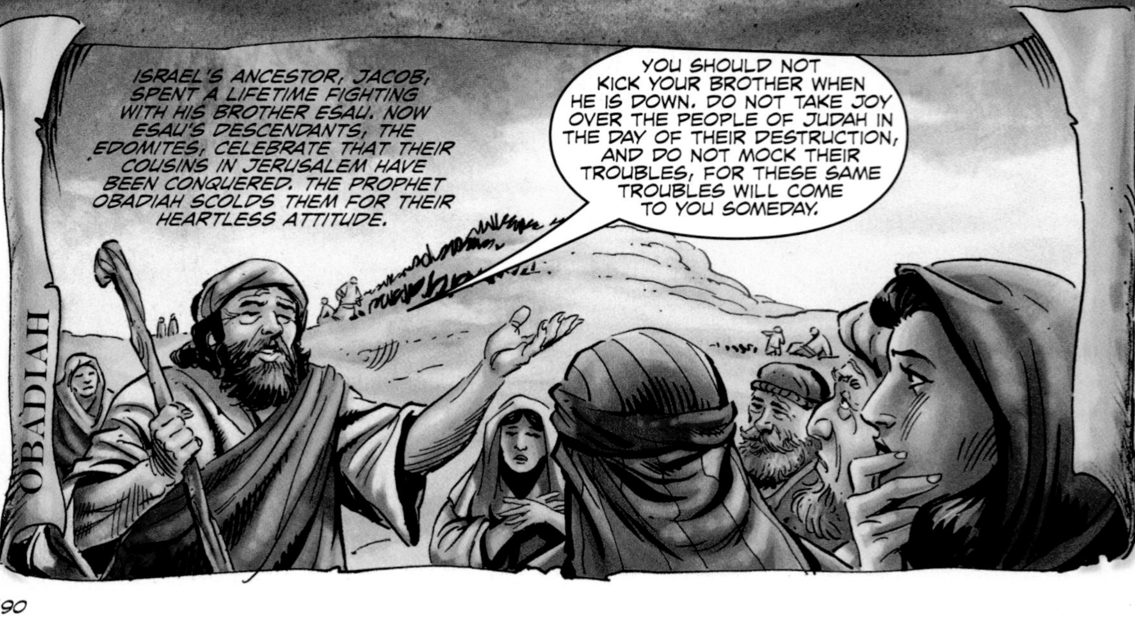
OBADIAH
ISRAEL'S ANCESTOR, JACOB, SPENT A LIFETIME FIGHTING WITH HIS BROTHER ESAU. NOW ESAU'S DESCENDANTS, THE EDOMITES, CELEBRATE THAT THEIR COUSINS IN JERUSALEM HAVE BEEN CONQUERED. THE PROPHET OBADIAH SCOLDS THEM FOR THEIR HEARTLESS ATTITUDE.
YOU SHOULD NOT KICK YOUR BROTHER WHEN HE IS DOWN. DO NOT TAKE JOY OVER THE PEOPLE OF JUDAH IN THE DAY OF THEIR DESTRUCTION, AND DO NOT MOCK THEIR TROUBLES, FOR THESE SAME TROUBLES WILL COME TO YOU SOMEDAY.

THE BABYLONIANS SET UP HEADQUARTERS AT MIZPAH AND APPOINT GEDALIAH AS GOVERNOR. GEDALIAH HAS ALWAYS BEEN FAITHFUL TO THE LORD AND BELIEVED THE WORDS OF JEREMIAH. PLEASED TO HAVE A GODLY GOVERNOR, JEREMIAH JOINS HIM AND BECOMES HIS ADVISER.

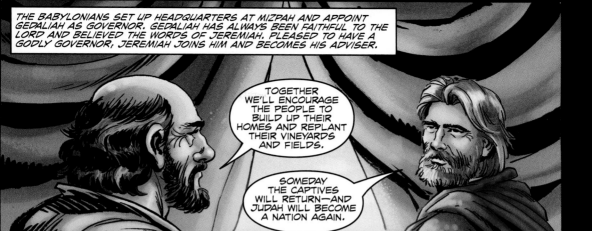

TOGETHER WE'LL ENCOURAGE THE PEOPLE TO BUILD UP THEIR HOMES AND REPLANT THEIR VINEYARDS AND FIELDS.

SOMEDAY THE CAPTIVES WILL RETURN—AND JUDAH WILL BECOME A NATION AGAIN.

BUT GOOD NEWS IS ALWAYS TEMPORARY FOR JEREMIAH. BEFORE THE GOVERNOR'S DREAM CAN COME TRUE, HE IS MURDERED. FEARFUL THAT BABYLON WILL BLAME ALL ISRAEL FOR THE MURDER, A GROUP OF PEOPLE GO TO SEE JEREMIAH ...

GOD HASN'T DONE SUCH A GOOD JOB KEEPING US SAFE IN JERUSALEM. WE'RE GOING TO EGYPT.

EVEN AFTER EVERYTHING THAT'S HAPPENED, YOU *STILL* DON'T BELIEVE IN GOD'S WORD. YOU JUST HOPED I'D GIVE YOU PERMISSION FOR WHAT YOU'D ALREADY DECIDED TO DO.

WE WANT TO GO TO EGYPT, WHERE THERE IS PEACE AND PLENTY TO EAT. WILL YOU ASK OF THE LORD IF THAT'S OKAY?

THE LORD HAS WARNED ME THAT YOU WILL FIND NEITHER PEACE NOR FOOD IN EGYPT. STAY HERE. THE BABYLONIANS WILL NOT HURT YOU.

BUT THE PEOPLE DO NOT CARE. THEY FLEE TO EGYPT, FORCING JEREMIAH TO GO WITH THEM. THEY THINK THEY WILL BE SAFE, BUT NEBUCHADNEZZAR CONQUERS EGYPT NEXT, KILLING EVERYONE WHO FLED FROM JERUSALEM. THE FUTURE HOPE FOR GOD'S PEOPLE NOW LIES WITH THE EXILES IN BABYLON ...

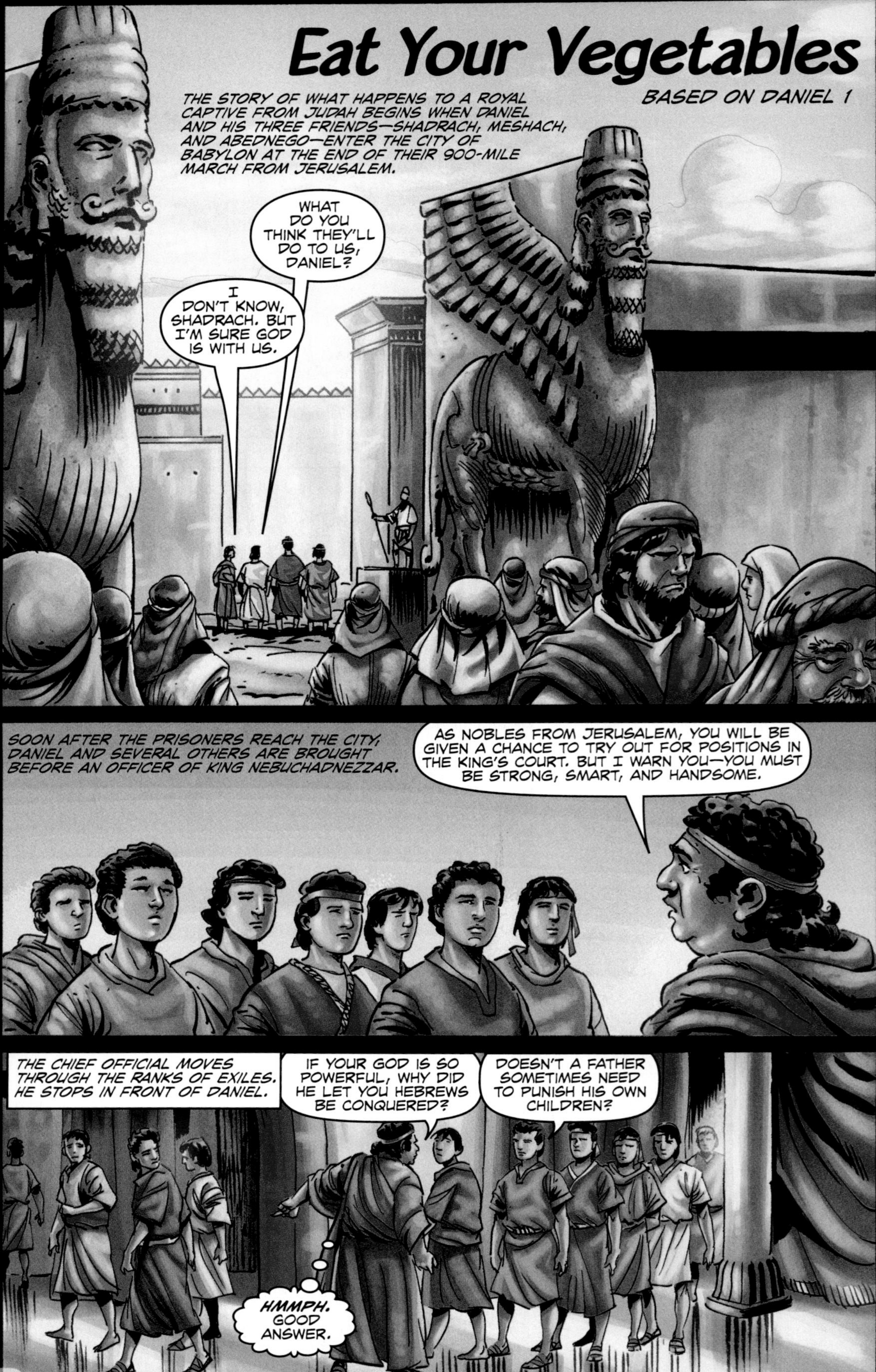
Eat Your Vegetables
BASED ON DANIEL 1
THE STORY OF WHAT HAPPENS TO A ROYAL CAPTIVE FROM JUDAH BEGINS WHEN DANIEL AND HIS THREE FRIENDS—SHADRACH, MESHACH, AND ABEDNEGO—ENTER THE CITY OF BABYLON AT THE END OF THEIR 900-MILE MARCH FROM JERUSALEM.
WHAT DO YOU THINK THEY'LL DO TO US, DANIEL?
I DON'T KNOW, SHADRACH. BUT I'M SURE GOD IS WITH US.
SOON AFTER THE PRISONERS REACH THE CITY, DANIEL AND SEVERAL OTHERS ARE BROUGHT BEFORE AN OFFICER OF KING NEBUCHADNEZZAR.
AS NOBLES FROM JERUSALEM, YOU WILL BE GIVEN A CHANCE TO TRY OUT FOR POSITIONS IN THE KING'S COURT. BUT I WARN YOU—YOU MUST BE STRONG, SMART, AND HANDSOME.
THE CHIEF OFFICIAL MOVES THROUGH THE RANKS OF EXILES. HE STOPS IN FRONT OF DANIEL.
IF YOUR GOD IS SO POWERFUL, WHY DID HE LET YOU HEBREWS BE CONQUERED?
DOESN'T A FATHER SOMETIMES NEED TO PUNISH HIS OWN CHILDREN?
HMMPH. GOOD ANSWER.

THE NEXT DAY ...

YOU HAVE BEEN CHOSEN! NOW YOU'LL BE GIVEN THREE YEARS TO STUDY UNDER OUR WISE MEN. AFTER THAT, THE KING HIMSELF WILL CHOOSE THOSE BEST QUALIFIED TO BE HIS ADVISERS. AS A BONUS, YOU WILL GET TO EAT THE EXTRA FOOD FROM THE KING'S TABLE!

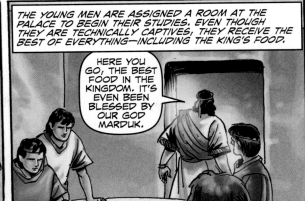

THE YOUNG MEN ARE ASSIGNED A ROOM AT THE PALACE TO BEGIN THEIR STUDIES. EVEN THOUGH THEY ARE TECHNICALLY CAPTIVES, THEY RECEIVE THE BEST OF EVERYTHING—INCLUDING THE KING'S FOOD.

HERE YOU GO, THE BEST FOOD IN THE KINGDOM. IT'S EVEN BEEN BLESSED BY OUR GOD MARDUK.

WE CAN'T EAT THIS! IT'S BEEN DEDICATED TO THE BABYLONIAN IDOLS.

THANK YOU FOR THE HONOR YOU HAVE SHOWN US, BUT OUR HEBREW LAWS FORBID US FROM EATING YOUR MEAT AND WINE. PLEASE JUST GIVE US PLAIN VEGETABLES AND WATER.

VEGETABLES AND WATER? THAT'S NOT ENOUGH FOOD FOR GROWING YOUNG MEN. I NEED YOU LOOKING STRONG AND WELL-FED, OR THE KING WILL HAVE MY HEAD.

HOW ABOUT THIS? TEST US FOR A FEW DAYS. LET US EAT OUR PLAIN FOOD AND THEN SEE HOW WE COMPARE TO THE OTHERS.

FOR TEN DAYS, THE OTHER TRAINEES EAT THEIR STEAK AND FINE WINE TAKEN FROM THE TEMPLE OF MARDUK. DANIEL AND HIS THREE FRIENDS EAT NOTHING BUT BOILED VEGETABLES AND WATER.

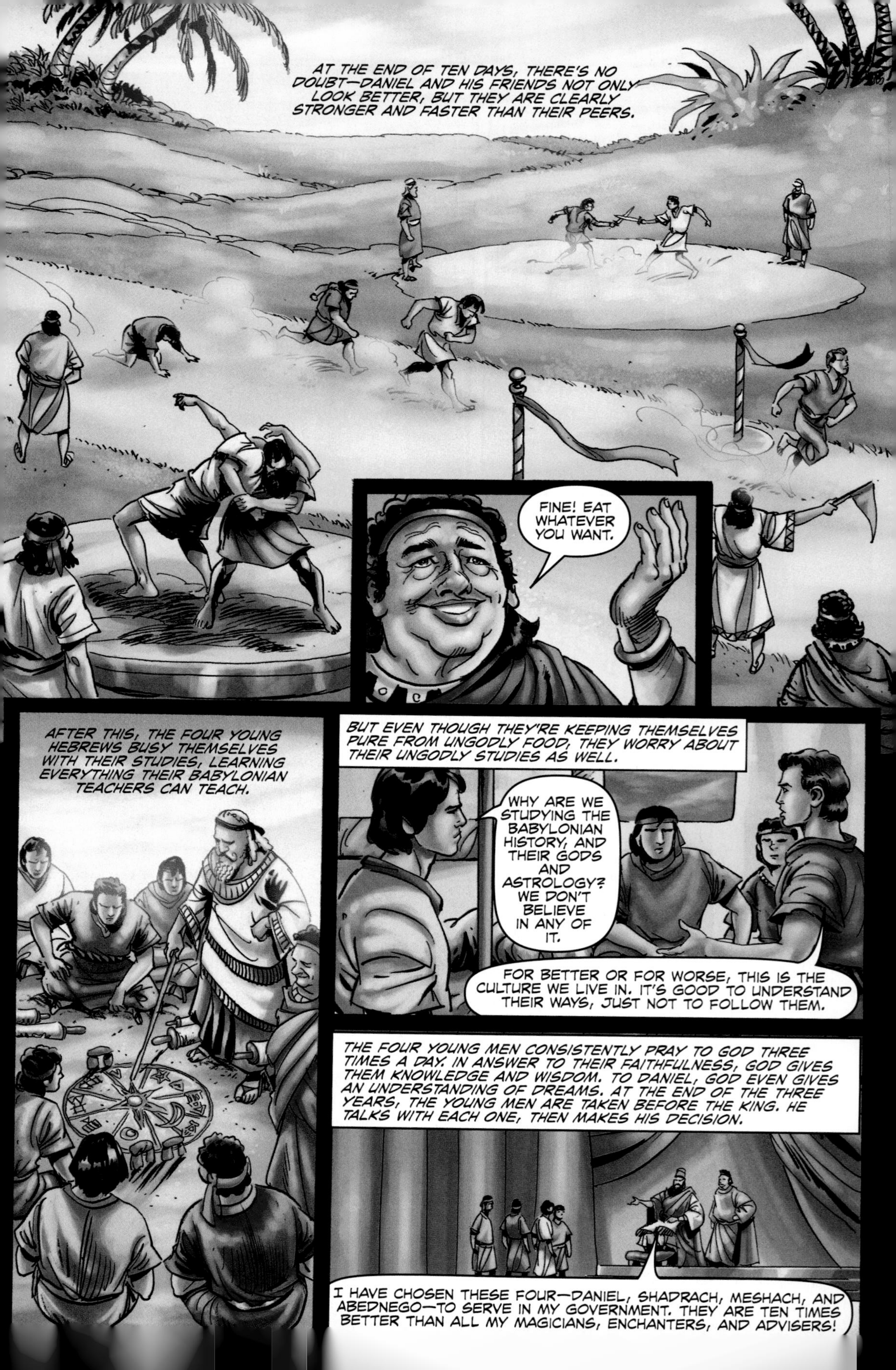
AT THE END OF TEN DAYS, THERE'S NO DOUBT—DANIEL AND HIS FRIENDS NOT ONLY LOOK BETTER, BUT THEY ARE CLEARLY STRONGER AND FASTER THAN THEIR PEERS.
FINE! EAT WHATEVER YOU WANT.
AFTER THIS, THE FOUR YOUNG HEBREWS BUSY THEMSELVES WITH THEIR STUDIES, LEARNING EVERYTHING THEIR BABYLONIAN TEACHERS CAN TEACH.
BUT EVEN THOUGH THEY'RE KEEPING THEMSELVES PURE FROM UNGODLY FOOD, THEY WORRY ABOUT THEIR UNGODLY STUDIES AS WELL.
WHY ARE WE STUDYING THE BABYLONIAN HISTORY, AND THEIR GODS AND ASTROLOGY? WE DON'T BELIEVE IN ANY OF IT.
FOR BETTER OR FOR WORSE, THIS IS THE CULTURE WE LIVE IN. IT'S GOOD TO UNDERSTAND THEIR WAYS, JUST NOT TO FOLLOW THEM.
THE FOUR YOUNG MEN CONSISTENTLY PRAY TO GOD THREE TIMES A DAY. IN ANSWER TO THEIR FAITHFULNESS, GOD GIVES THEM KNOWLEDGE AND WISDOM. TO DANIEL, GOD EVEN GIVES AN UNDERSTANDING OF DREAMS. AT THE END OF THE THREE YEARS, THE YOUNG MEN ARE TAKEN BEFORE THE KING. HE TALKS WITH EACH ONE, THEN MAKES HIS DECISION.
I HAVE CHOSEN THESE FOUR—DANIEL, SHADRACH, MESHACH, AND ABEDNEGO—TO SERVE IN MY GOVERNMENT. THEY ARE TEN TIMES BETTER THAN ALL MY MAGICIANS, ENCHANTERS, AND ADVISERS!

A Deadly Dream *BASED ON DANIEL 2*

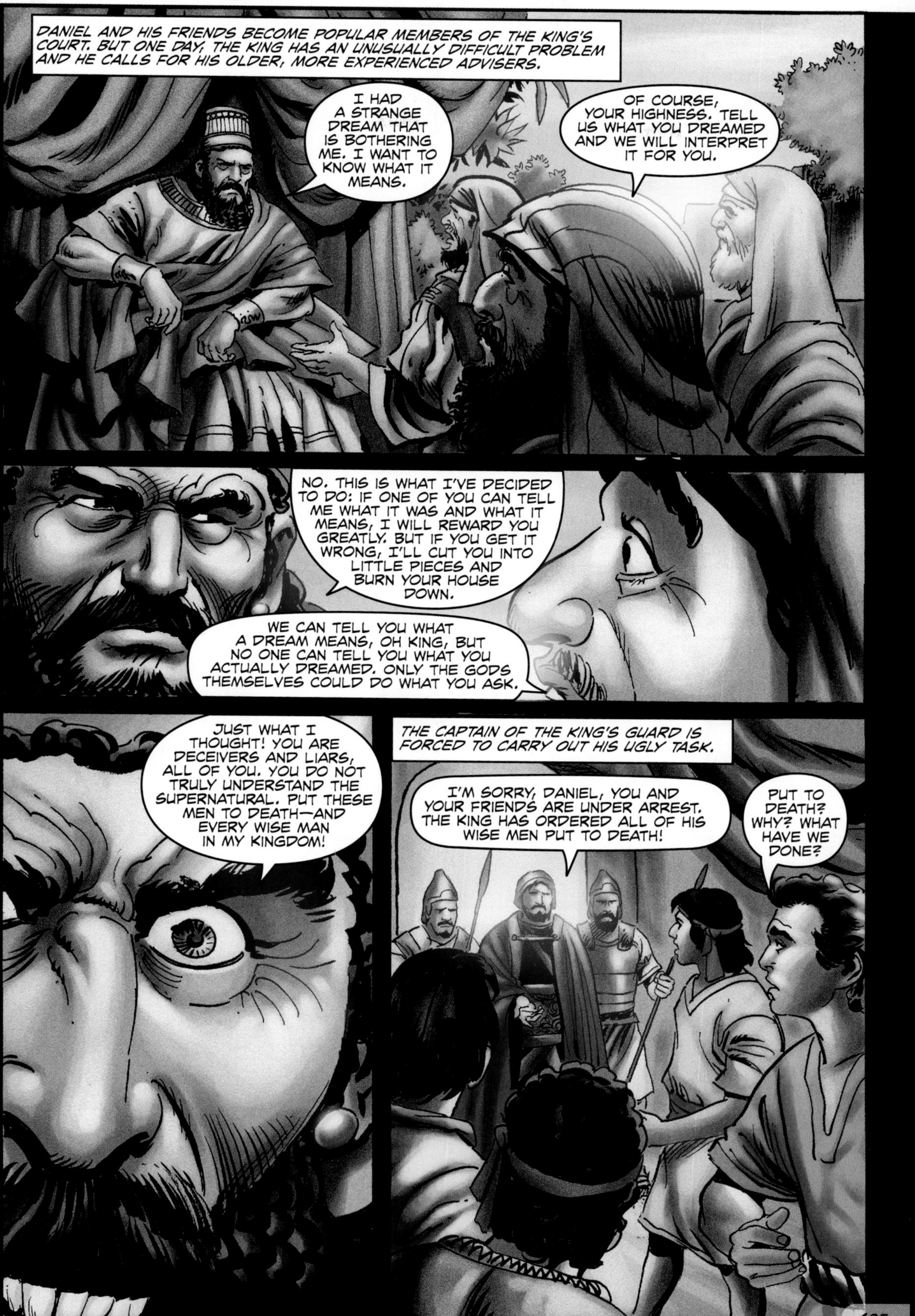
DANIEL AND HIS FRIENDS BECOME POPULAR MEMBERS OF THE KING'S COURT. BUT ONE DAY, THE KING HAS AN UNUSUALLY DIFFICULT PROBLEM AND HE CALLS FOR HIS OLDER, MORE EXPERIENCED ADVISERS.
I HAD A STRANGE DREAM THAT IS BOTHERING ME. I WANT TO KNOW WHAT IT MEANS.
OF COURSE, YOUR HIGHNESS. TELL US WHAT YOU DREAMED AND WE WILL INTERPRET IT FOR YOU.
NO. THIS IS WHAT I'VE DECIDED TO DO: IF ONE OF YOU CAN TELL ME WHAT IT WAS AND WHAT IT MEANS, I WILL REWARD YOU GREATLY. BUT IF YOU GET IT WRONG, I'LL CUT YOU INTO LITTLE PIECES AND BURN YOUR HOUSE DOWN.
WE CAN TELL YOU WHAT A DREAM MEANS, OH KING, BUT NO ONE CAN TELL YOU WHAT YOU ACTUALLY DREAMED. ONLY THE GODS THEMSELVES COULD DO WHAT YOU ASK.
JUST WHAT I THOUGHT! YOU ARE DECEIVERS AND LIARS, ALL OF YOU. YOU DO NOT TRULY UNDERSTAND THE SUPERNATURAL. PUT THESE MEN TO DEATH—AND EVERY WISE MAN IN MY KINGDOM!
THE CAPTAIN OF THE KING'S GUARD IS FORCED TO CARRY OUT HIS UGLY TASK.
I'M SORRY, DANIEL, YOU AND YOUR FRIENDS ARE UNDER ARREST. THE KING HAS ORDERED ALL OF HIS WISE MEN PUT TO DEATH!
PUT TO DEATH? WHY? WHAT HAVE WE DONE?

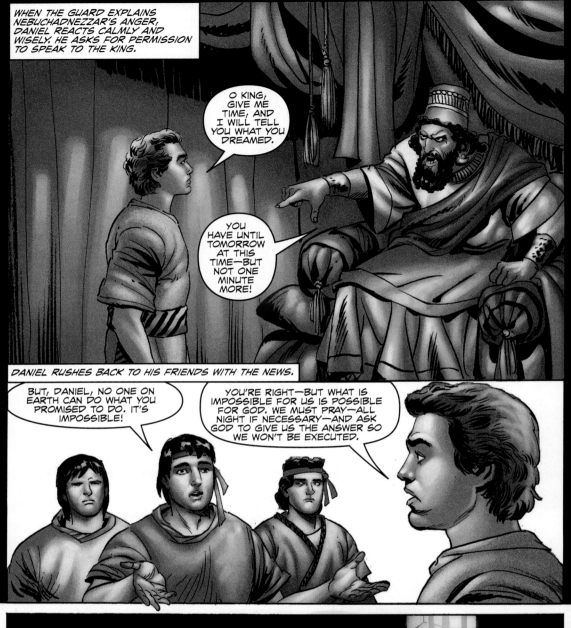

WHEN THE GUARD EXPLAINS NEBUCHADNEZZAR'S ANGER, DANIEL REACTS CALMLY AND WISELY. HE ASKS FOR PERMISSION TO SPEAK TO THE KING.

O KING, GIVE ME TIME, AND I WILL TELL YOU WHAT YOU DREAMED.

YOU HAVE UNTIL TOMORROW AT THIS TIME—BUT NOT ONE MINUTE MORE!

DANIEL RUSHES BACK TO HIS FRIENDS WITH THE NEWS.

BUT, DANIEL, NO ONE ON EARTH CAN DO WHAT YOU PROMISED TO DO. IT'S IMPOSSIBLE!

YOU'RE RIGHT—BUT WHAT IS IMPOSSIBLE FOR US IS POSSIBLE FOR GOD. WE MUST PRAY—ALL NIGHT IF NECESSARY—AND ASK GOD TO GIVE US THE ANSWER SO WE WON'T BE EXECUTED.

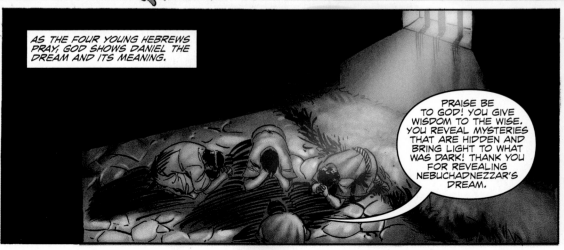

AS THE FOUR YOUNG HEBREWS PRAY, GOD SHOWS DANIEL THE DREAM AND ITS MEANING.

PRAISE BE TO GOD! YOU GIVE WISDOM TO THE WISE. YOU REVEAL MYSTERIES THAT ARE HIDDEN AND BRING LIGHT TO WHAT WAS DARK! THANK YOU FOR REVEALING NEBUCHADNEZZAR'S DREAM.

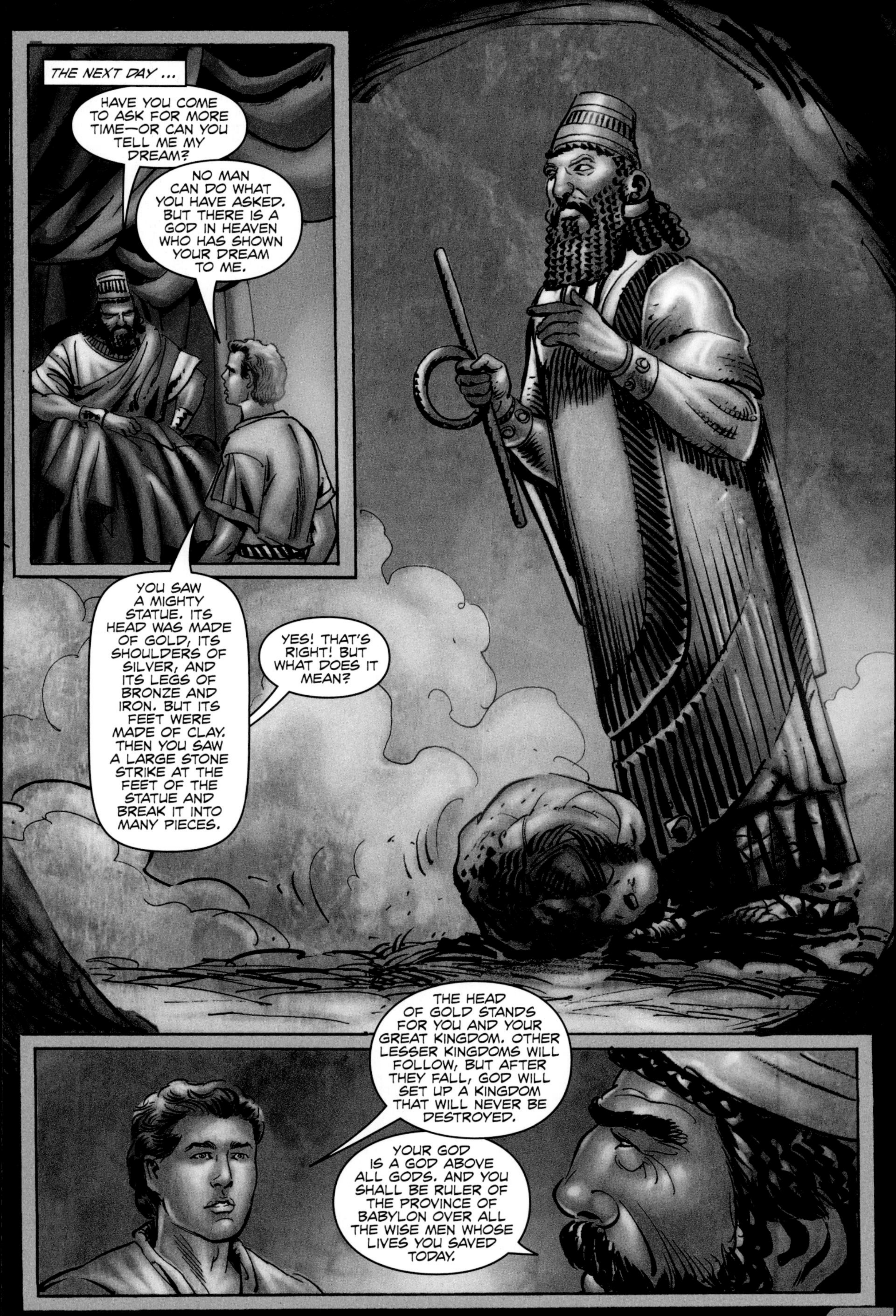

THE NEXT DAY ...
HAVE YOU COME TO ASK FOR MORE TIME—OR CAN YOU TELL ME MY DREAM?
NO MAN CAN DO WHAT YOU HAVE ASKED. BUT THERE IS A GOD IN HEAVEN WHO HAS SHOWN YOUR DREAM TO ME.
YOU SAW A MIGHTY STATUE. ITS HEAD WAS MADE OF GOLD, ITS SHOULDERS OF SILVER, AND ITS LEGS OF BRONZE AND IRON. BUT ITS FEET WERE MADE OF CLAY. THEN YOU SAW A LARGE STONE STRIKE AT THE FEET OF THE STATUE AND BREAK IT INTO MANY PIECES.
YES! THAT'S RIGHT! BUT WHAT DOES IT MEAN?
THE HEAD OF GOLD STANDS FOR YOU AND YOUR GREAT KINGDOM. OTHER LESSER KINGDOMS WILL FOLLOW, BUT AFTER THEY FALL, GOD WILL SET UP A KINGDOM THAT WILL NEVER BE DESTROYED.
YOUR GOD IS A GOD ABOVE ALL GODS. AND YOU SHALL BE RULER OF THE PROVINCE OF BABYLON OVER ALL THE WISE MEN WHOSE LIVES YOU SAVED TODAY.

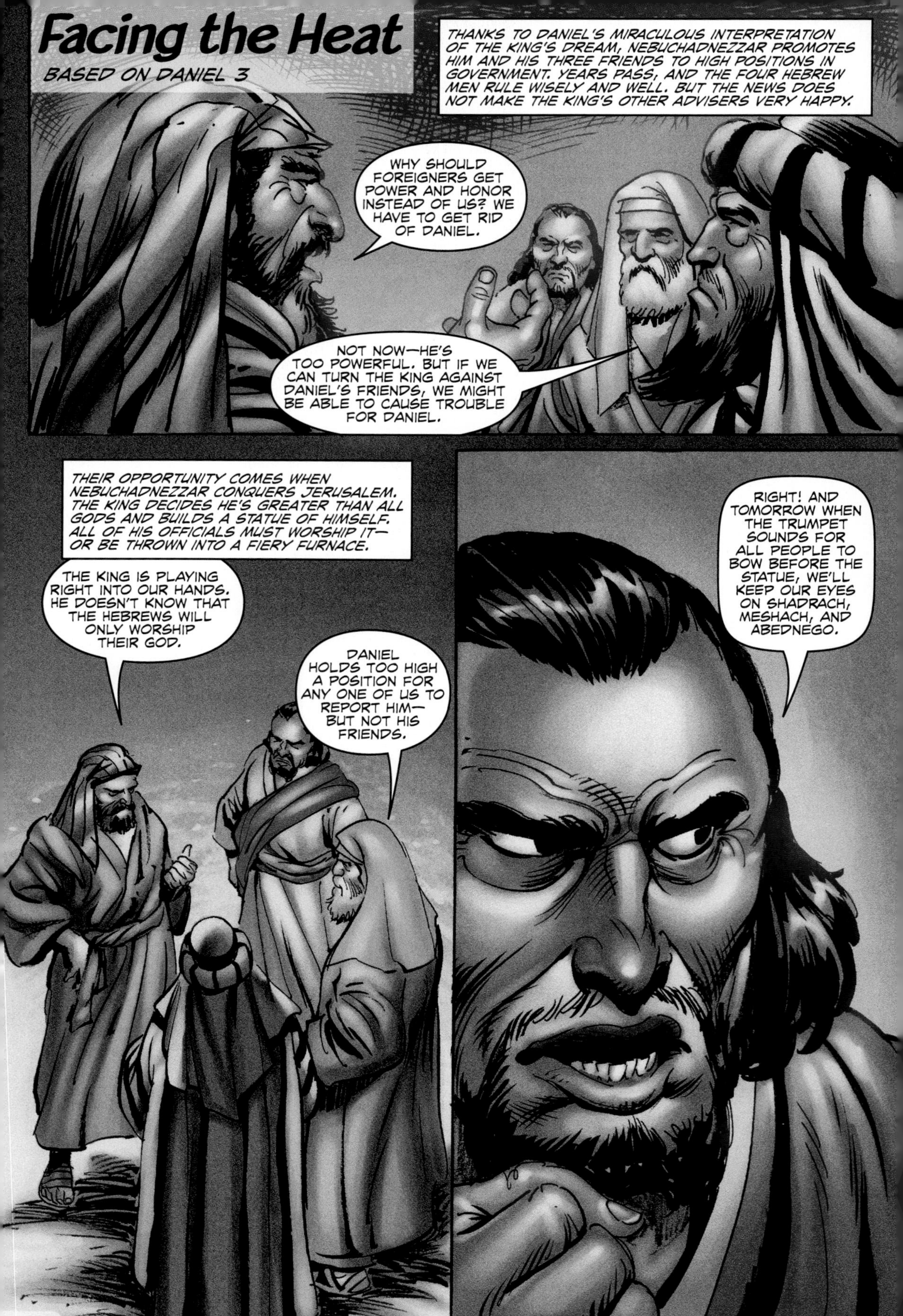
Facing the Heat
BASED ON DANIEL 3
THANKS TO DANIEL'S MIRACULOUS INTERPRETATION OF THE KING'S DREAM, NEBUCHADNEZZAR PROMOTES HIM AND HIS THREE FRIENDS TO HIGH POSITIONS IN GOVERNMENT. YEARS PASS, AND THE FOUR HEBREW MEN RULE WISELY AND WELL. BUT THE NEWS DOES NOT MAKE THE KING'S OTHER ADVISERS VERY HAPPY.
WHY SHOULD FOREIGNERS GET POWER AND HONOR INSTEAD OF US? WE HAVE TO GET RID OF DANIEL.
NOT NOW—HE'S TOO POWERFUL. BUT IF WE CAN TURN THE KING AGAINST DANIEL'S FRIENDS, WE MIGHT BE ABLE TO CAUSE TROUBLE FOR DANIEL.
THEIR OPPORTUNITY COMES WHEN NEBUCHADNEZZAR CONQUERS JERUSALEM. THE KING DECIDES HE'S GREATER THAN ALL GODS AND BUILDS A STATUE OF HIMSELF. ALL OF HIS OFFICIALS MUST WORSHIP IT—OR BE THROWN INTO A FIERY FURNACE.
THE KING IS PLAYING RIGHT INTO OUR HANDS. HE DOESN'T KNOW THAT THE HEBREWS WILL ONLY WORSHIP THEIR GOD.
DANIEL HOLDS TOO HIGH A POSITION FOR ANY ONE OF US TO REPORT HIM—BUT NOT HIS FRIENDS.
RIGHT! AND TOMORROW WHEN THE TRUMPET SOUNDS FOR ALL PEOPLE TO BOW BEFORE THE STATUE, WE'LL KEEP OUR EYES ON SHADRACH, MESHACH, AND ABEDNEGO.

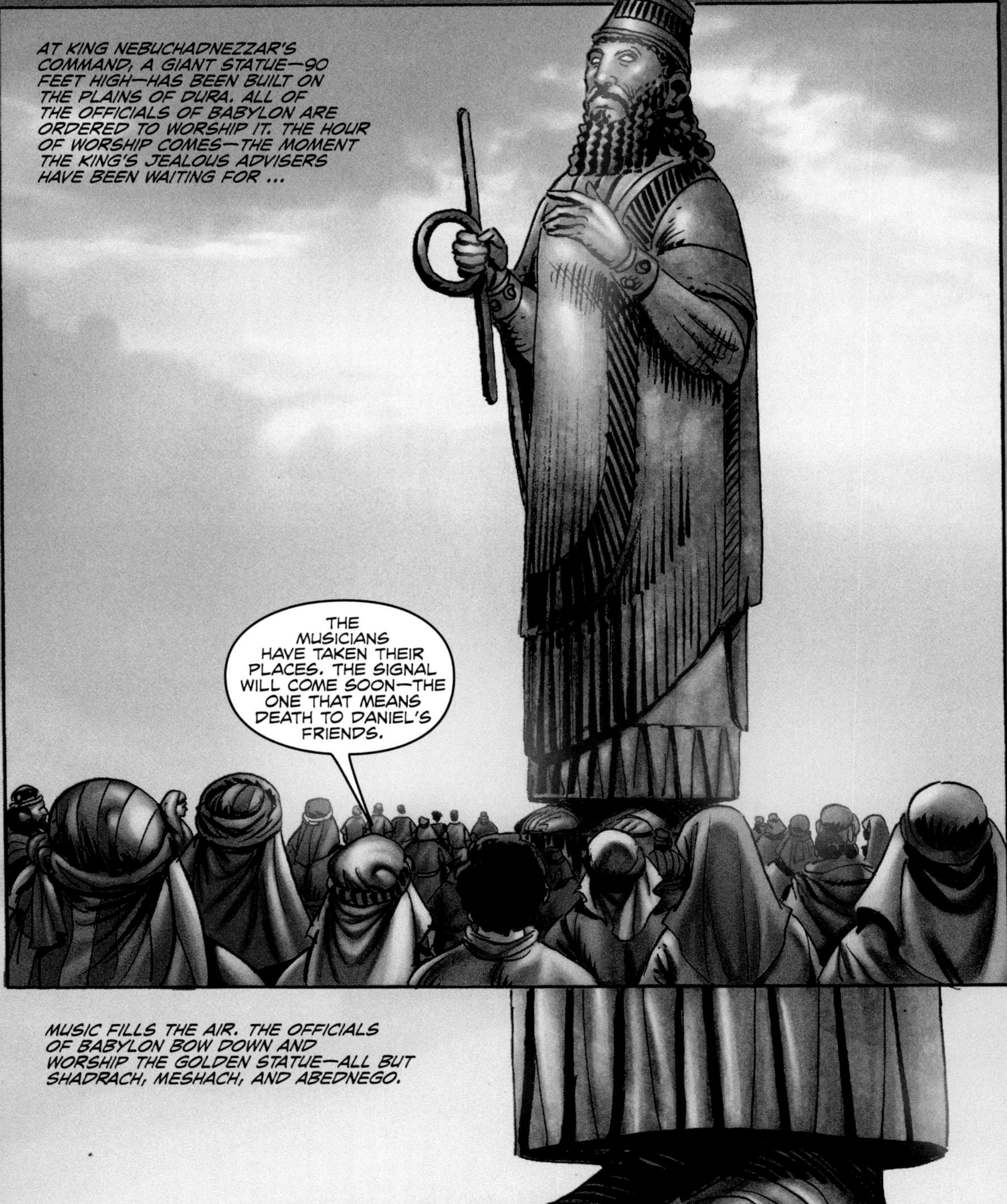
AT KING NEBUCHADNEZZAR'S COMMAND, A GIANT STATUE—90 FEET HIGH—HAS BEEN BUILT ON THE PLAINS OF DURA. ALL OF THE OFFICIALS OF BABYLON ARE ORDERED TO WORSHIP IT. THE HOUR OF WORSHIP COMES—THE MOMENT THE KING'S JEALOUS ADVISERS HAVE BEEN WAITING FOR ...
THE MUSICIANS HAVE TAKEN THEIR PLACES. THE SIGNAL WILL COME SOON—THE ONE THAT MEANS DEATH TO DANIEL'S FRIENDS.

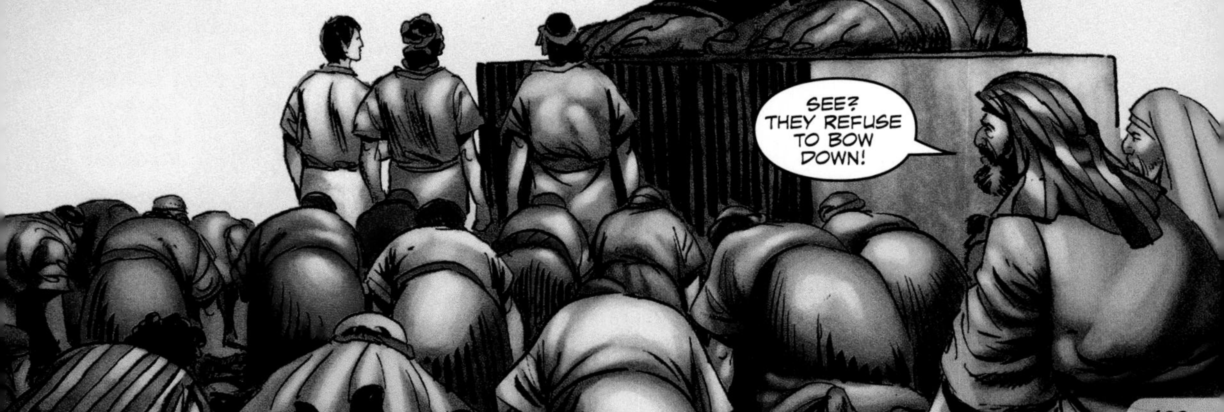
MUSIC FILLS THE AIR. THE OFFICIALS OF BABYLON BOW DOWN AND WORSHIP THE GOLDEN STATUE—ALL BUT SHADRACH, MESHACH, AND ABEDNEGO.
SEE? THEY REFUSE TO BOW DOWN!

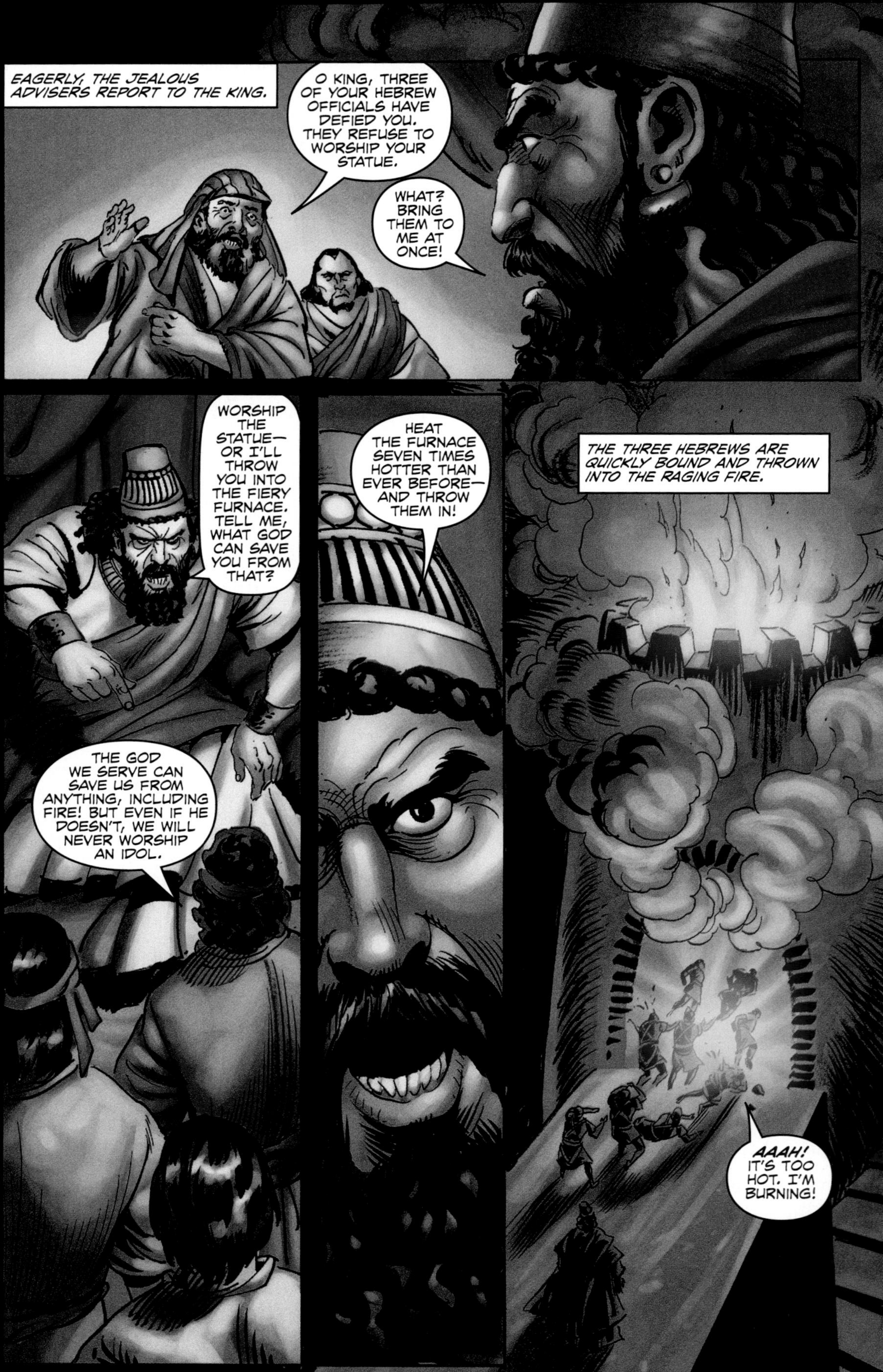
EAGERLY, THE JEALOUS ADVISERS REPORT TO THE KING.
O KING, THREE OF YOUR HEBREW OFFICIALS HAVE DEFIED YOU. THEY REFUSE TO WORSHIP YOUR STATUE.
WHAT? BRING THEM TO ME AT ONCE!
WORSHIP THE STATUE—OR I'LL THROW YOU INTO THE FIERY FURNACE. TELL ME, WHAT GOD CAN SAVE YOU FROM THAT?
THE GOD WE SERVE CAN SAVE US FROM ANYTHING, INCLUDING FIRE! BUT EVEN IF HE DOESN'T, WE WILL NEVER WORSHIP AN IDOL.
HEAT THE FURNACE SEVEN TIMES HOTTER THAN EVER BEFORE—AND THROW THEM IN!
THE THREE HEBREWS ARE QUICKLY BOUND AND THROWN INTO THE RAGING FIRE.
AAAH! IT'S TOO HOT. I'M BURNING!

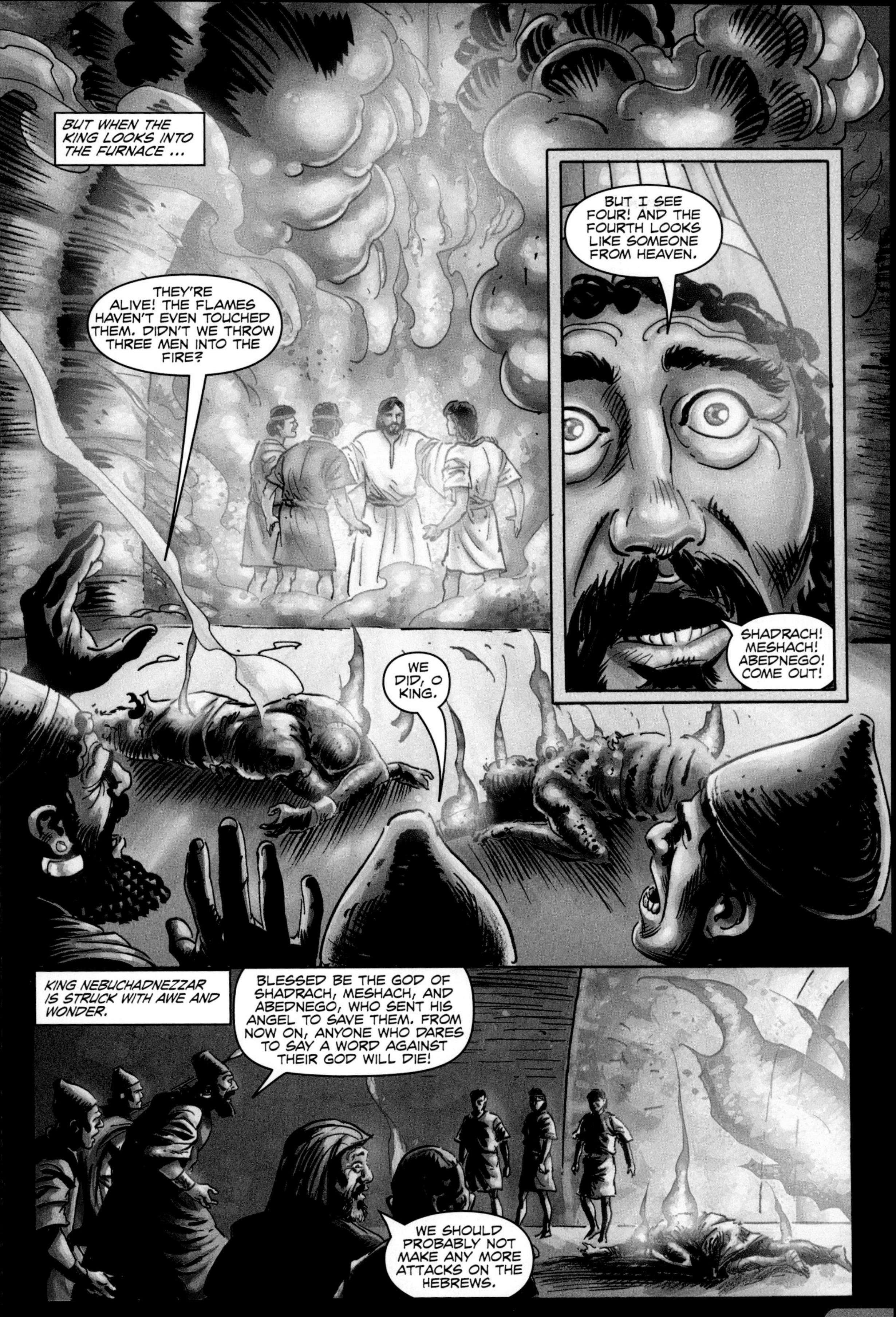

BUT WHEN THE KING LOOKS INTO THE FURNACE ...
THEY'RE ALIVE! THE FLAMES HAVEN'T EVEN TOUCHED THEM. DIDN'T WE THROW THREE MEN INTO THE FIRE?
BUT I SEE FOUR! AND THE FOURTH LOOKS LIKE SOMEONE FROM HEAVEN.
WE DID, O KING.
SHADRACH! MESHACH! ABEDNEGO! COME OUT!
KING NEBUCHADNEZZAR IS STRUCK WITH AWE AND WONDER.
BLESSED BE THE GOD OF SHADRACH, MESHACH, AND ABEDNEGO, WHO SENT HIS ANGEL TO SAVE THEM. FROM NOW ON, ANYONE WHO DARES TO SAY A WORD AGAINST THEIR GOD WILL DIE!
WE SHOULD PROBABLY NOT MAKE ANY MORE ATTACKS ON THE HEBREWS.

The Four Beasts from Below

BASED ON DANIEL 7

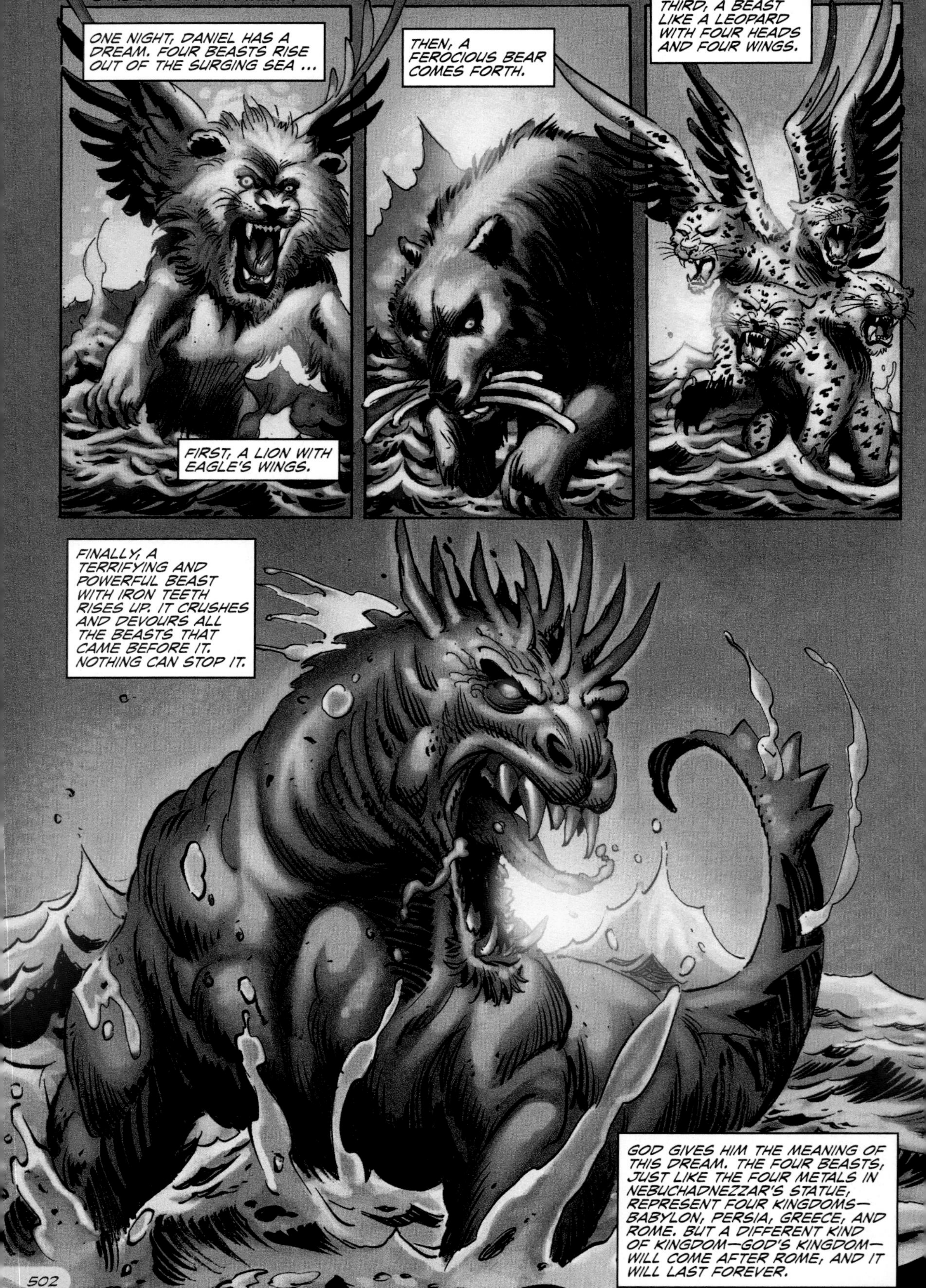

ONE NIGHT, DANIEL HAS A DREAM. FOUR BEASTS RISE OUT OF THE SURGING SEA ...
FIRST, A LION WITH EAGLE'S WINGS.
THEN, A FEROCIOUS BEAR COMES FORTH.
THIRD, A BEAST LIKE A LEOPARD WITH FOUR HEADS AND FOUR WINGS.
FINALLY, A TERRIFYING AND POWERFUL BEAST WITH IRON TEETH RISES UP. IT CRUSHES AND DEVOURS ALL THE BEASTS THAT CAME BEFORE IT. NOTHING CAN STOP IT.
GOD GIVES HIM THE MEANING OF THIS DREAM. THE FOUR BEASTS, JUST LIKE THE FOUR METALS IN NEBUCHADNEZZAR'S STATUE, REPRESENT FOUR KINGDOMS—BABYLON, PERSIA, GREECE, AND ROME. BUT A DIFFERENT KIND OF KINGDOM—GOD'S KINGDOM—WILL COME AFTER ROME, AND IT WILL LAST FOREVER.

The Writing on the Wall BASED ON DANIEL 5

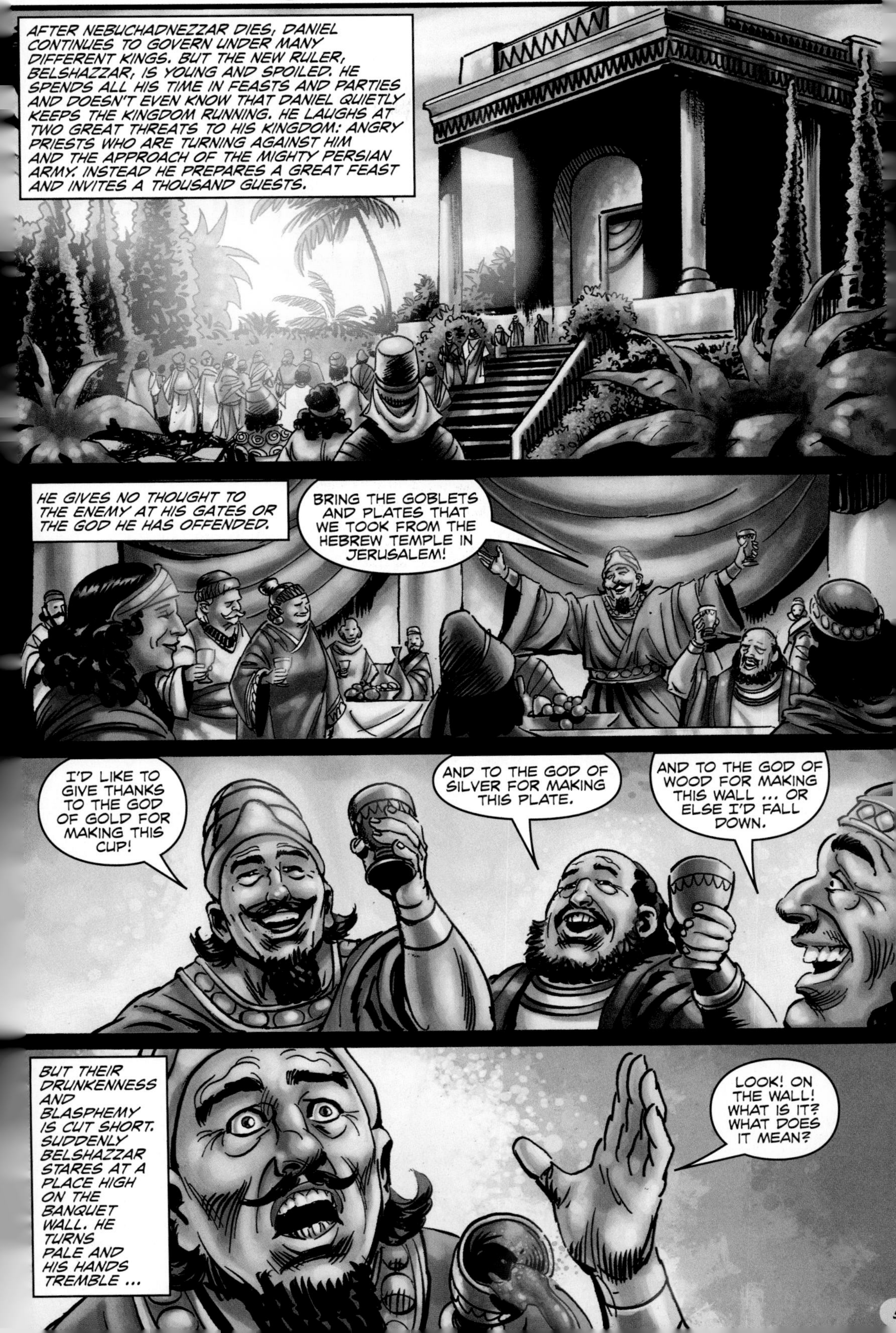

AFTER NEBUCHADNEZZAR DIES, DANIEL CONTINUES TO GOVERN UNDER MANY DIFFERENT KINGS. BUT THE NEW RULER, BELSHAZZAR, IS YOUNG AND SPOILED. HE SPENDS ALL HIS TIME IN FEASTS AND PARTIES AND DOESN'T EVEN KNOW THAT DANIEL QUIETLY KEEPS THE KINGDOM RUNNING. HE LAUGHS AT TWO GREAT THREATS TO HIS KINGDOM: ANGRY PRIESTS WHO ARE TURNING AGAINST HIM AND THE APPROACH OF THE MIGHTY PERSIAN ARMY. INSTEAD HE PREPARES A GREAT FEAST AND INVITES A THOUSAND GUESTS.
HE GIVES NO THOUGHT TO THE ENEMY AT HIS GATES OR THE GOD HE HAS OFFENDED.
BRING THE GOBLETS AND PLATES THAT WE TOOK FROM THE HEBREW TEMPLE IN JERUSALEM!
I'D LIKE TO GIVE THANKS TO THE GOD OF GOLD FOR MAKING THIS CUP!
AND TO THE GOD OF SILVER FOR MAKING THIS PLATE.
AND TO THE GOD OF WOOD FOR MAKING THIS WALL ... OR ELSE I'D FALL DOWN.
BUT THEIR DRUNKENNESS AND BLASPHEMY IS CUT SHORT. SUDDENLY BELSHAZZAR STARES AT A PLACE HIGH ON THE BANQUET WALL. HE TURNS PALE AND HIS HANDS TREMBLE ...
LOOK! ON THE WALL! WHAT IS IT? WHAT DOES IT MEAN?

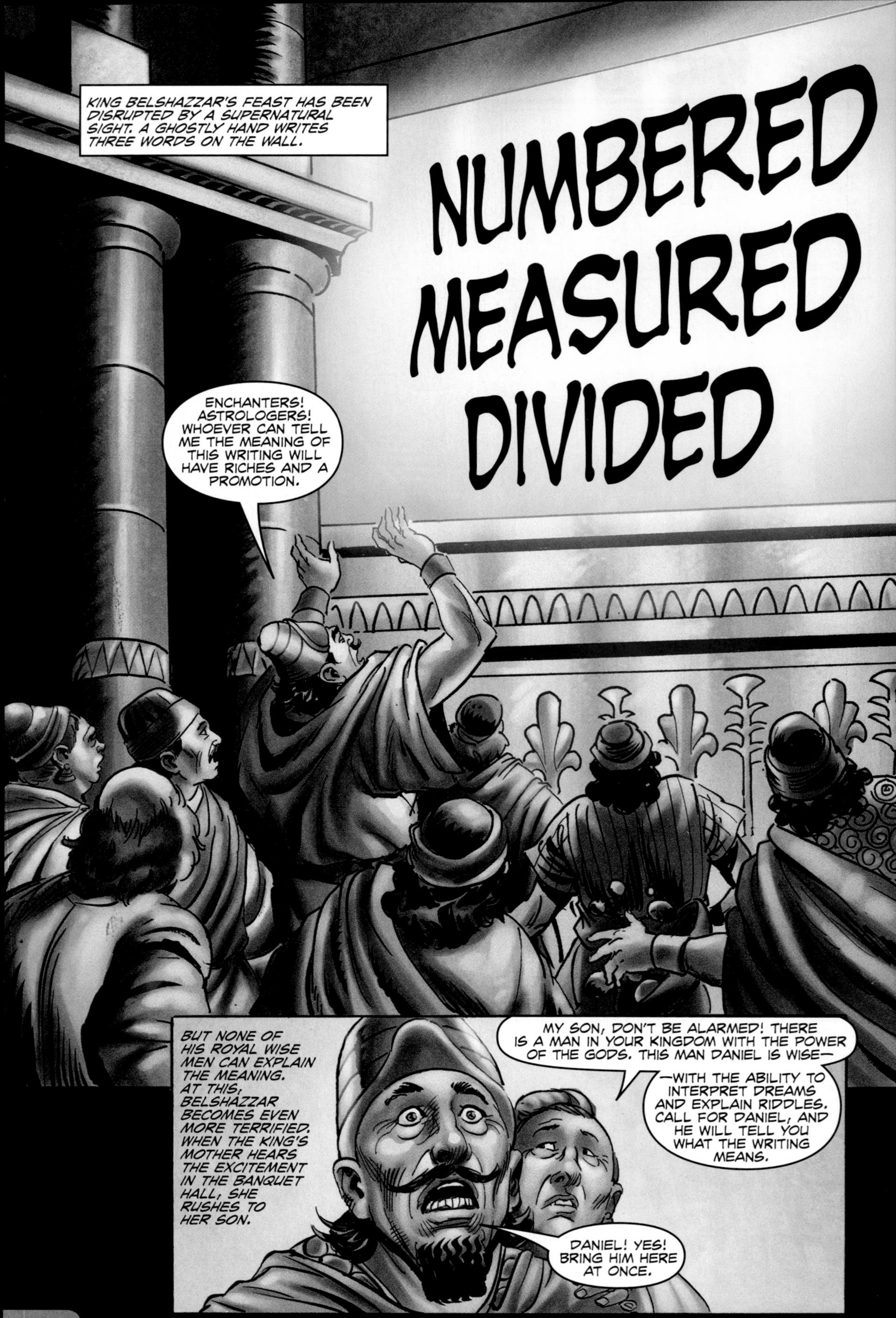
KING BELSHAZZAR'S FEAST HAS BEEN DISRUPTED BY A SUPERNATURAL SIGHT. A GHOSTLY HAND WRITES THREE WORDS ON THE WALL.
NUMBERED MEASURED DIVIDED
ENCHANTERS! ASTROLOGERS! WHOEVER CAN TELL ME THE MEANING OF THIS WRITING WILL HAVE RICHES AND A PROMOTION.
BUT NONE OF HIS ROYAL WISE MEN CAN EXPLAIN THE MEANING. AT THIS, BELSHAZZAR BECOMES EVEN MORE TERRIFIED. WHEN THE KING'S MOTHER HEARS THE EXCITEMENT IN THE BANQUET HALL, SHE RUSHES TO HER SON.
MY SON, DON'T BE ALARMED! THERE IS A MAN IN YOUR KINGDOM WITH THE POWER OF THE GODS. THIS MAN DANIEL IS WISE—
—WITH THE ABILITY TO INTERPRET DREAMS AND EXPLAIN RIDDLES. CALL FOR DANIEL, AND HE WILL TELL YOU WHAT THE WRITING MEANS.
DANIEL! YES! BRING HIM HERE AT ONCE.

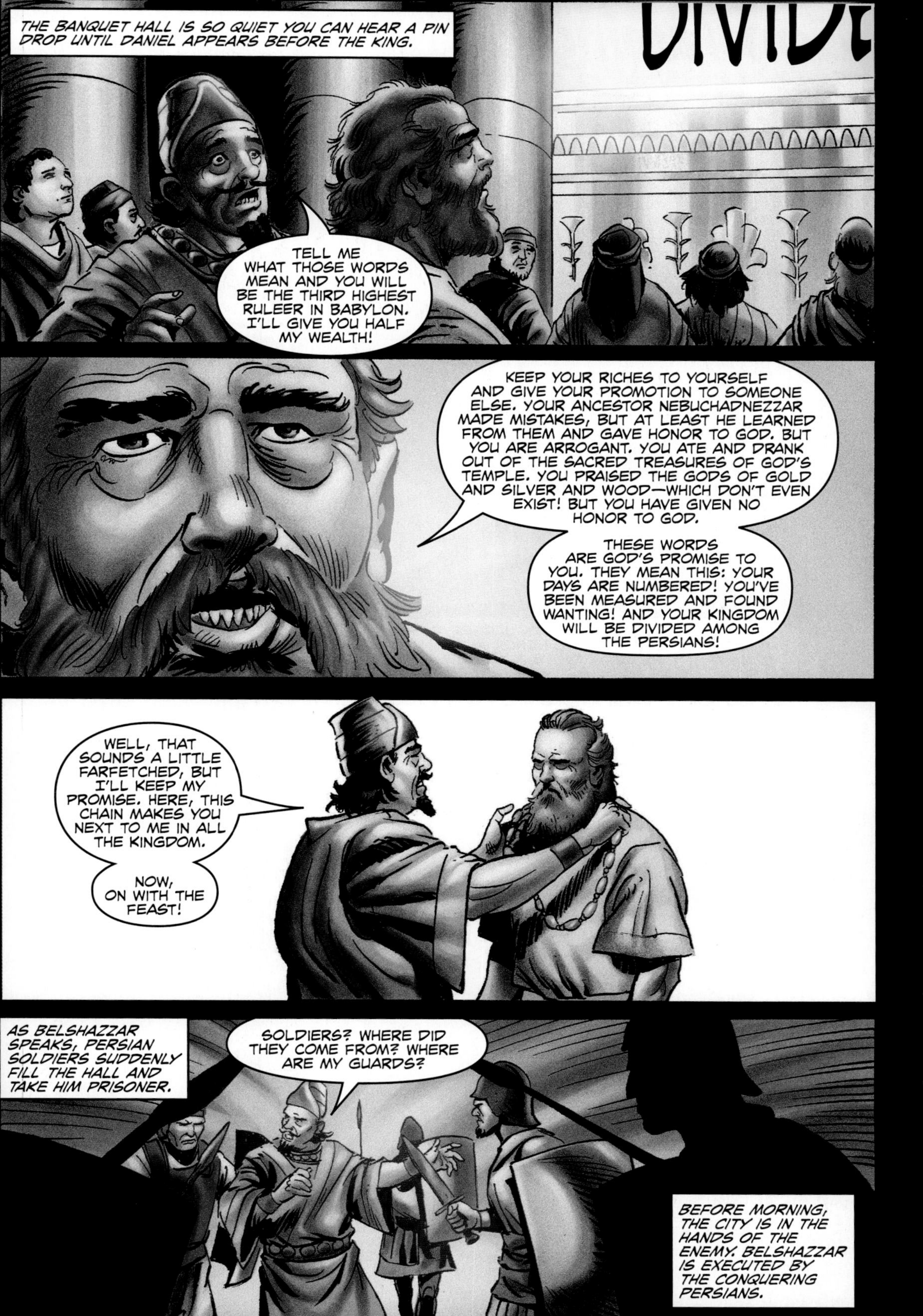

THE BANQUET HALL IS SO QUIET YOU CAN HEAR A PIN DROP UNTIL DANIEL APPEARS BEFORE THE KING.
DIVIDE
TELL ME WHAT THOSE WORDS MEAN AND YOU WILL BE THE THIRD HIGHEST RULEER IN BABYLON. I'LL GIVE YOU HALF MY WEALTH!
KEEP YOUR RICHES TO YOURSELF AND GIVE YOUR PROMOTION TO SOMEONE ELSE. YOUR ANCESTOR NEBUCHADNEZZAR MADE MISTAKES, BUT AT LEAST HE LEARNED FROM THEM AND GAVE HONOR TO GOD. BUT YOU ARE ARROGANT. YOU ATE AND DRANK OUT OF THE SACRED TREASURES OF GOD'S TEMPLE. YOU PRAISED THE GODS OF GOLD AND SILVER AND WOOD—WHICH DON'T EVEN EXIST! BUT YOU HAVE GIVEN NO HONOR TO GOD.
THESE WORDS ARE GOD'S PROMISE TO YOU. THEY MEAN THIS: YOUR DAYS ARE NUMBERED! YOU'VE BEEN MEASURED AND FOUND WANTING! AND YOUR KINGDOM WILL BE DIVIDED AMONG THE PERSIANS!
WELL, THAT SOUNDS A LITTLE FARFETCHED, BUT I'LL KEEP MY PROMISE. HERE, THIS CHAIN MAKES YOU NEXT TO ME IN ALL THE KINGDOM.
NOW, ON WITH THE FEAST!
AS BELSHAZZAR SPEAKS, PERSIAN SOLDIERS SUDDENLY FILL THE HALL AND TAKE HIM PRISONER.
SOLDIERS? WHERE DID THEY COME FROM? WHERE ARE MY GUARDS?
BEFORE MORNING, THE CITY IS IN THE HANDS OF THE ENEMY. BELSHAZZAR IS EXECUTED BY THE CONQUERING PERSIANS.

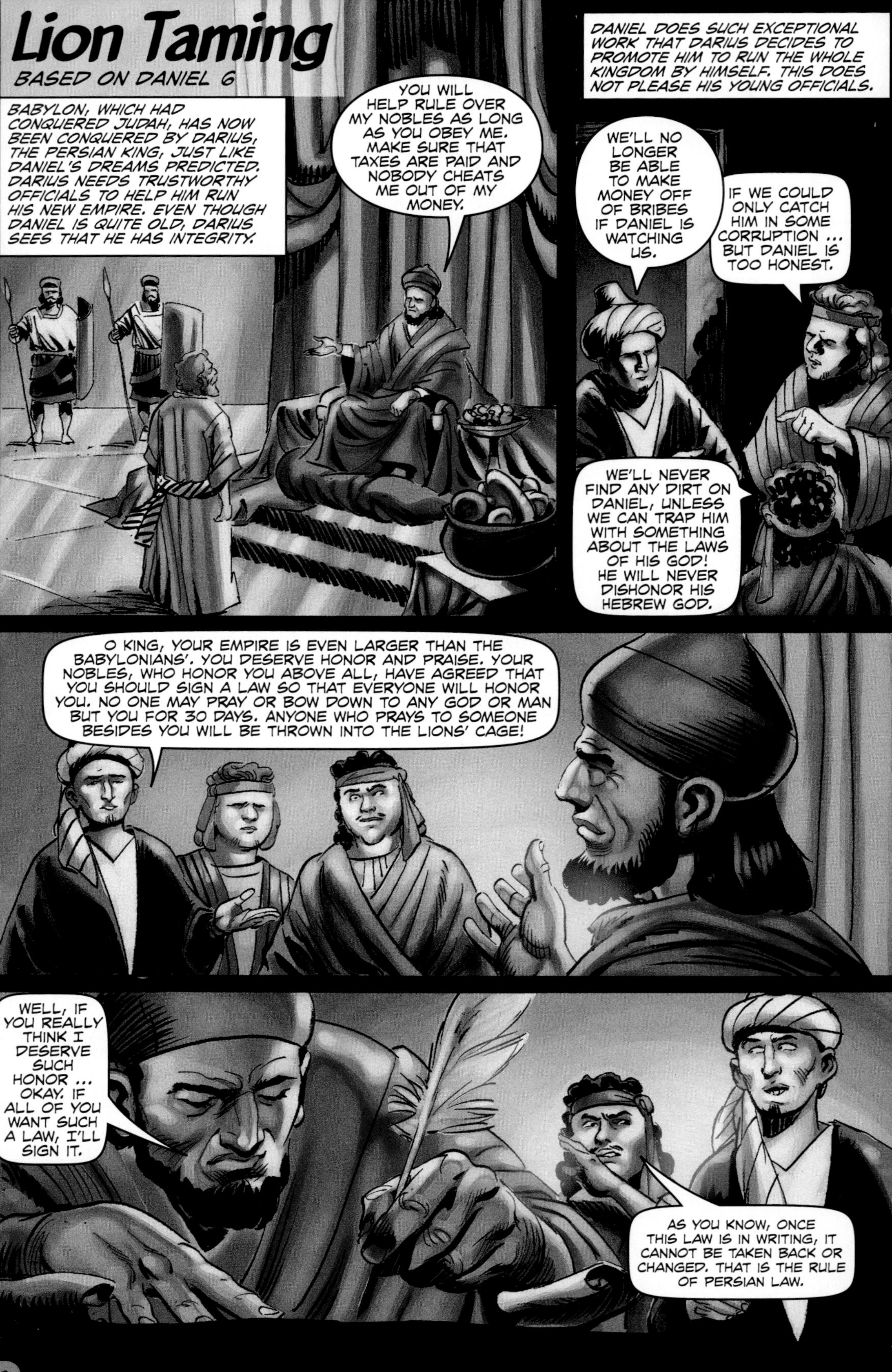
Lion Taming
BASED ON DANIEL 6
BABYLON, WHICH HAD CONQUERED JUDAH, HAS NOW BEEN CONQUERED BY DARIUS, THE PERSIAN KING, JUST LIKE DANIEL'S DREAMS PREDICTED. DARIUS NEEDS TRUSTWORTHY OFFICIALS TO HELP HIM RUN HIS NEW EMPIRE. EVEN THOUGH DANIEL IS QUITE OLD, DARIUS SEES THAT HE HAS INTEGRITY.
YOU WILL HELP RULE OVER MY NOBLES AS LONG AS YOU OBEY ME. MAKE SURE THAT TAXES ARE PAID AND NOBODY CHEATS ME OUT OF MY MONEY.
DANIEL DOES SUCH EXCEPTIONAL WORK THAT DARIUS DECIDES TO PROMOTE HIM TO RUN THE WHOLE KINGDOM BY HIMSELF. THIS DOES NOT PLEASE HIS YOUNG OFFICIALS.
WE'LL NO LONGER BE ABLE TO MAKE MONEY OFF OF BRIBES IF DANIEL IS WATCHING US.
IF WE COULD ONLY CATCH HIM IN SOME CORRUPTION ... BUT DANIEL IS TOO HONEST.
WE'LL NEVER FIND ANY DIRT ON DANIEL, UNLESS WE CAN TRAP HIM WITH SOMETHING ABOUT THE LAWS OF HIS GOD! HE WILL NEVER DISHONOR HIS HEBREW GOD.
O KING, YOUR EMPIRE IS EVEN LARGER THAN THE BABYLONIANS'. YOU DESERVE HONOR AND PRAISE. YOUR NOBLES, WHO HONOR YOU ABOVE ALL, HAVE AGREED THAT YOU SHOULD SIGN A LAW SO THAT EVERYONE WILL HONOR YOU. NO ONE MAY PRAY OR BOW DOWN TO ANY GOD OR MAN BUT YOU FOR 30 DAYS. ANYONE WHO PRAYS TO SOMEONE BESIDES YOU WILL BE THROWN INTO THE LIONS' CAGE!
WELL, IF YOU REALLY THINK I DESERVE SUCH HONOR ... OKAY. IF ALL OF YOU WANT SUCH A LAW, I'LL SIGN IT.
AS YOU KNOW, ONCE THIS LAW IS IN WRITING, IT CANNOT BE TAKEN BACK OR CHANGED. THAT IS THE RULE OF PERSIAN LAW.

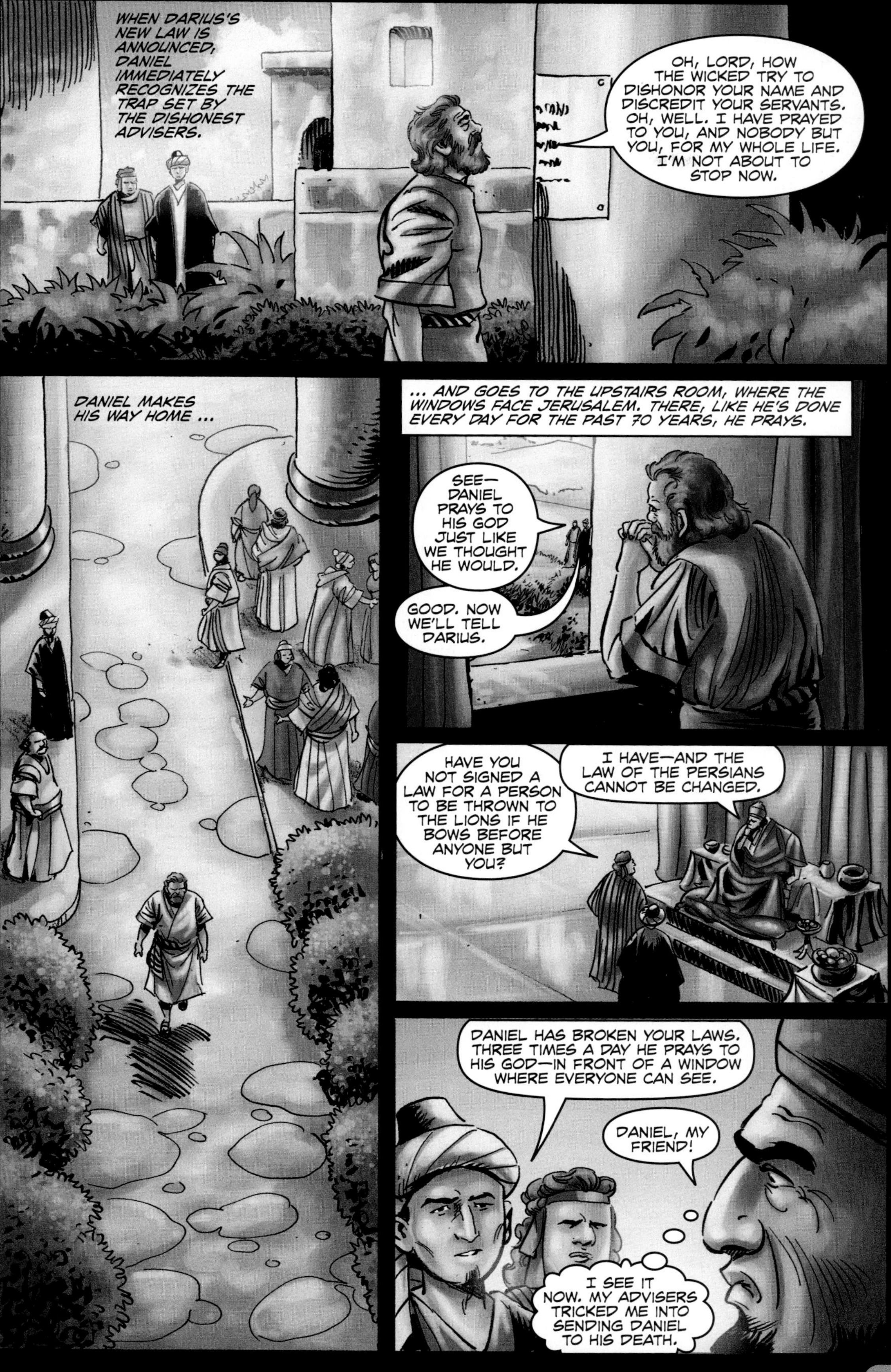
WHEN DARIUS'S NEW LAW IS ANNOUNCED, DANIEL IMMEDIATELY RECOGNIZES THE TRAP SET BY THE DISHONEST ADVISERS.
OH, LORD, HOW THE WICKED TRY TO DISHONOR YOUR NAME AND DISCREDIT YOUR SERVANTS. OH, WELL. I HAVE PRAYED TO YOU, AND NOBODY BUT YOU, FOR MY WHOLE LIFE. I'M NOT ABOUT TO STOP NOW.
DANIEL MAKES HIS WAY HOME ...
... AND GOES TO THE UPSTAIRS ROOM, WHERE THE WINDOWS FACE JERUSALEM. THERE, LIKE HE'S DONE EVERY DAY FOR THE PAST 70 YEARS, HE PRAYS.
SEE—DANIEL PRAYS TO HIS GOD JUST LIKE WE THOUGHT HE WOULD.
GOOD. NOW WE'LL TELL DARIUS.
HAVE YOU NOT SIGNED A LAW FOR A PERSON TO BE THROWN TO THE LIONS IF HE BOWS BEFORE ANYONE BUT YOU?
I HAVE—AND THE LAW OF THE PERSIANS CANNOT BE CHANGED.
DANIEL HAS BROKEN YOUR LAWS. THREE TIMES A DAY HE PRAYS TO HIS GOD—IN FRONT OF A WINDOW WHERE EVERYONE CAN SEE.
DANIEL, MY FRIEND!
I SEE IT NOW. MY ADVISERS TRICKED ME INTO SENDING DANIEL TO HIS DEATH.

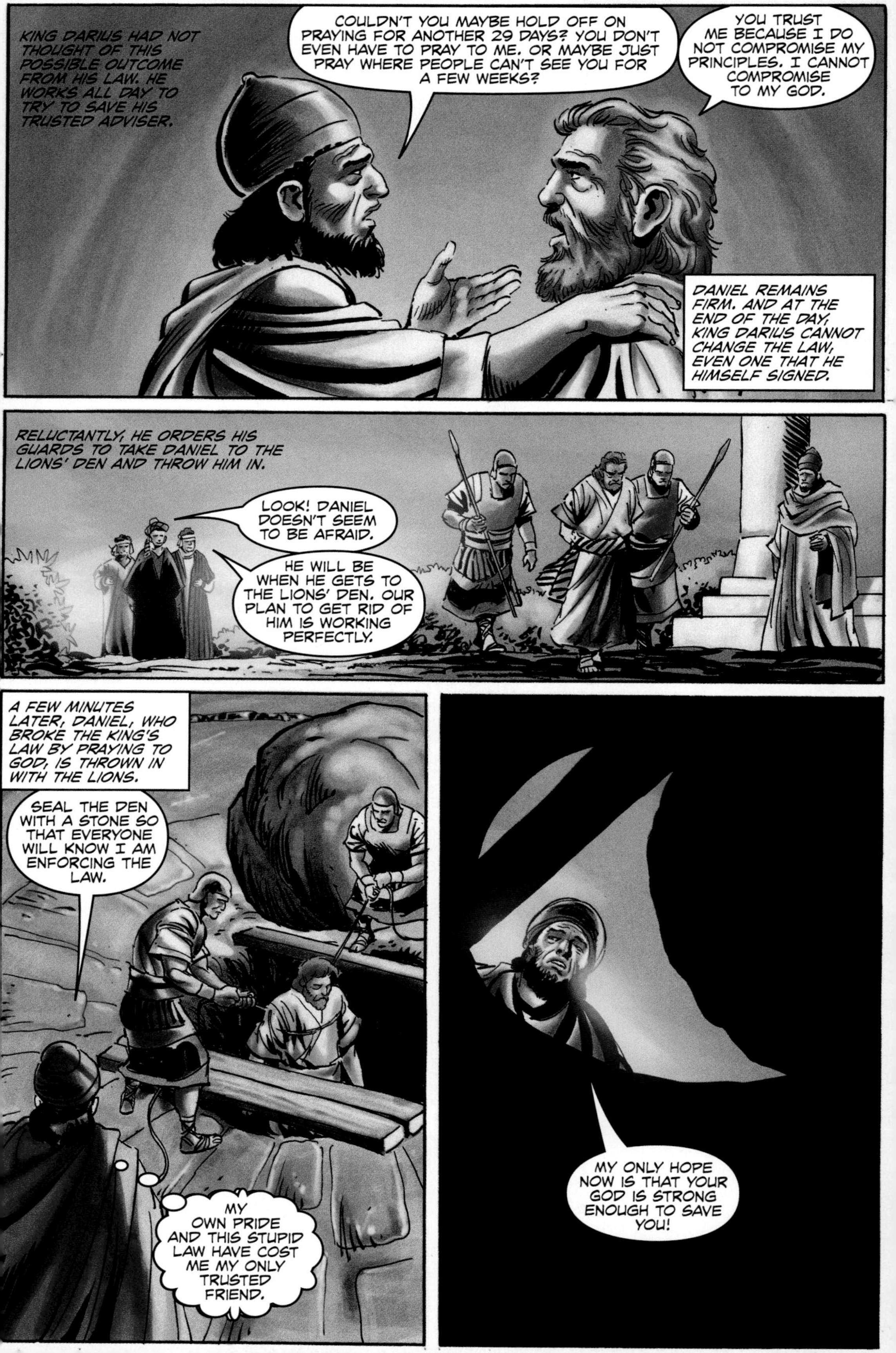

KING DARIUS HAD NOT THOUGHT OF THIS POSSIBLE OUTCOME FROM HIS LAW. HE WORKS ALL DAY TO TRY TO SAVE HIS TRUSTED ADVISER.
COULDN'T YOU MAYBE HOLD OFF ON PRAYING FOR ANOTHER 29 DAYS? YOU DON'T EVEN HAVE TO PRAY TO ME. OR MAYBE JUST PRAY WHERE PEOPLE CAN'T SEE YOU FOR A FEW WEEKS?
YOU TRUST ME BECAUSE I DO NOT COMPROMISE MY PRINCIPLES. I CANNOT COMPROMISE TO MY GOD.
DANIEL REMAINS FIRM. AND AT THE END OF THE DAY, KING DARIUS CANNOT CHANGE THE LAW, EVEN ONE THAT HE HIMSELF SIGNED.
RELUCTANTLY, HE ORDERS HIS GUARDS TO TAKE DANIEL TO THE LIONS' DEN AND THROW HIM IN.
LOOK! DANIEL DOESN'T SEEM TO BE AFRAID.
HE WILL BE WHEN HE GETS TO THE LIONS' DEN. OUR PLAN TO GET RID OF HIM IS WORKING PERFECTLY.
A FEW MINUTES LATER, DANIEL, WHO BROKE THE KING'S LAW BY PRAYING TO GOD, IS THROWN IN WITH THE LIONS.
SEAL THE DEN WITH A STONE SO THAT EVERYONE WILL KNOW I AM ENFORCING THE LAW.
MY OWN PRIDE AND THIS STUPID LAW HAVE COST ME MY ONLY TRUSTED FRIEND.
MY ONLY HOPE NOW IS THAT YOUR GOD IS STRONG ENOUGH TO SAVE YOU!

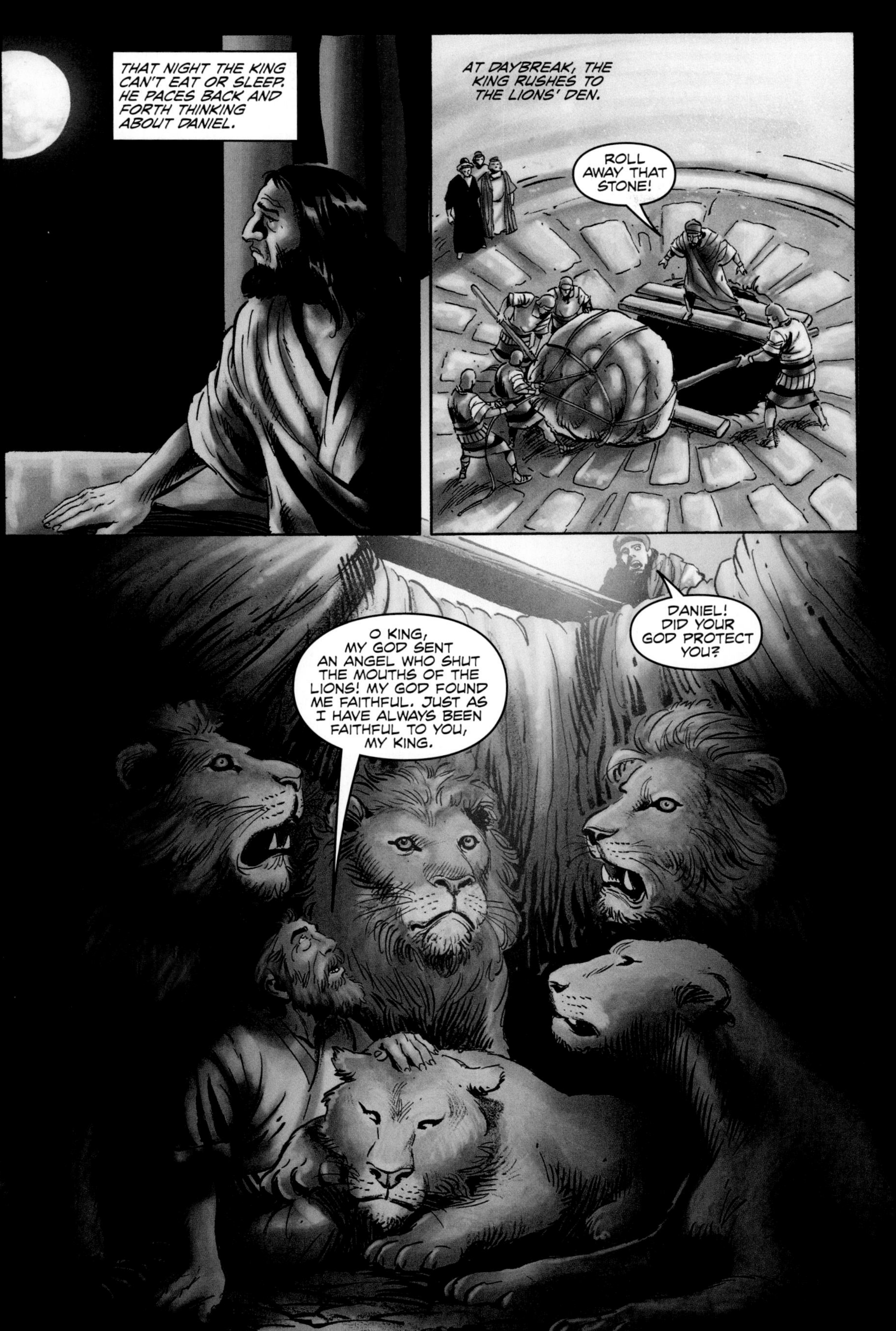
THAT NIGHT THE KING CAN'T EAT OR SLEEP. HE PACES BACK AND FORTH THINKING ABOUT DANIEL.
AT DAYBREAK, THE KING RUSHES TO THE LIONS' DEN.
ROLL AWAY THAT STONE!
DANIEL! DID YOUR GOD PROTECT YOU?
O KING, MY GOD SENT AN ANGEL WHO SHUT THE MOUTHS OF THE LIONS! MY GOD FOUND ME FAITHFUL. JUST AS I HAVE ALWAYS BEEN FAITHFUL TO YOU, MY KING.

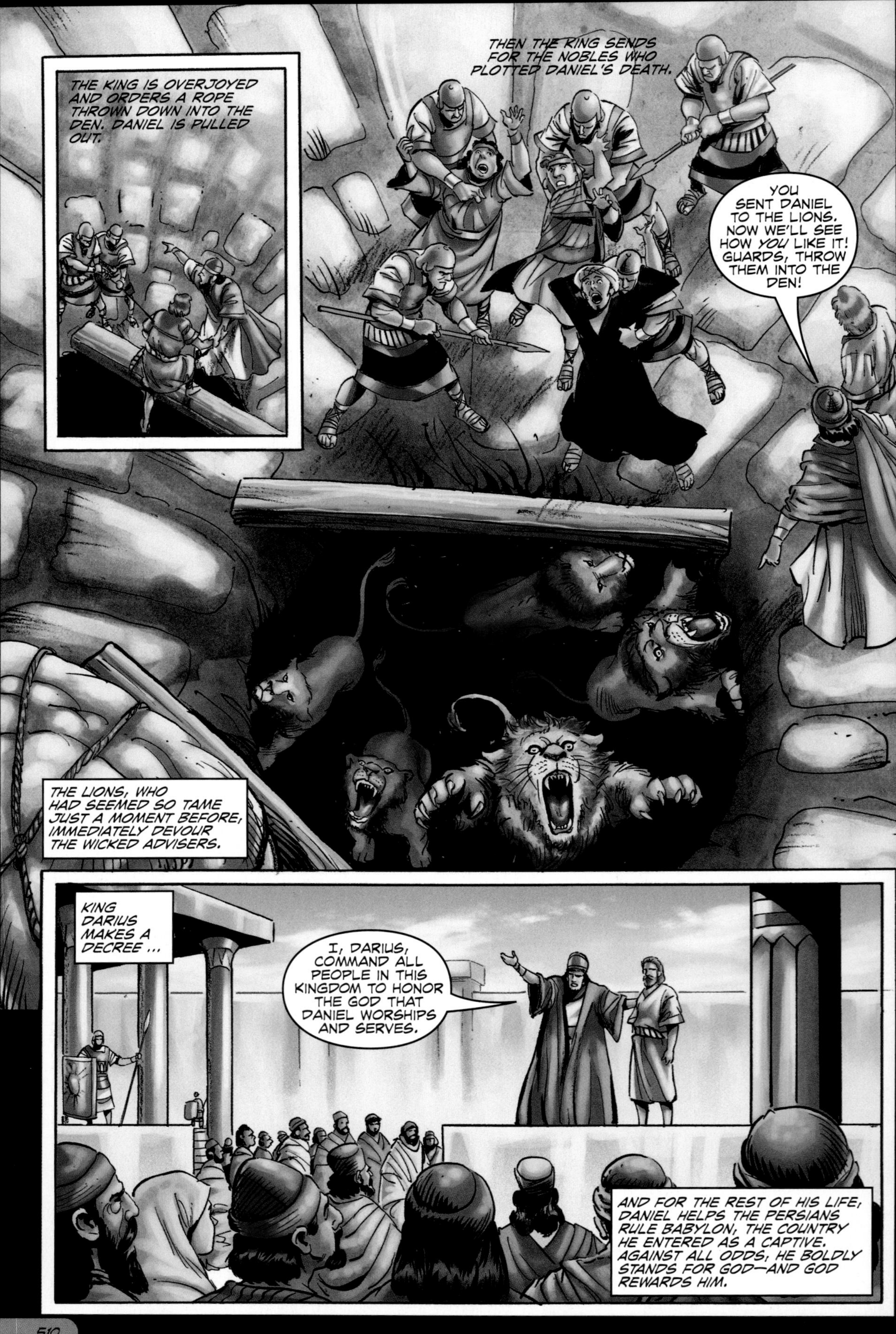
THE KING IS OVERJOYED AND ORDERS A ROPE THROWN DOWN INTO THE DEN. DANIEL IS PULLED OUT.
THEN THE KING SENDS FOR THE NOBLES WHO PLOTTED DANIEL'S DEATH.
YOU SENT DANIEL TO THE LIONS. NOW WE'LL SEE HOW *YOU* LIKE IT! GUARDS, THROW THEM INTO THE DEN!
THE LIONS, WHO HAD SEEMED SO TAME JUST A MOMENT BEFORE, IMMEDIATELY DEVOUR THE WICKED ADVISERS.
KING DARIUS MAKES A DECREE ...
I, DARIUS, COMMAND ALL PEOPLE IN THIS KINGDOM TO HONOR THE GOD THAT DANIEL WORSHIPS AND SERVES.
AND FOR THE REST OF HIS LIFE, DANIEL HELPS THE PERSIANS RULE BABYLON, THE COUNTRY HE ENTERED AS A CAPTIVE. AGAINST ALL ODDS, HE BOLDLY STANDS FOR GOD—AND GOD REWARDS HIM.

A Pair of Queens
BASED ON ESTHER 1:1—2:18

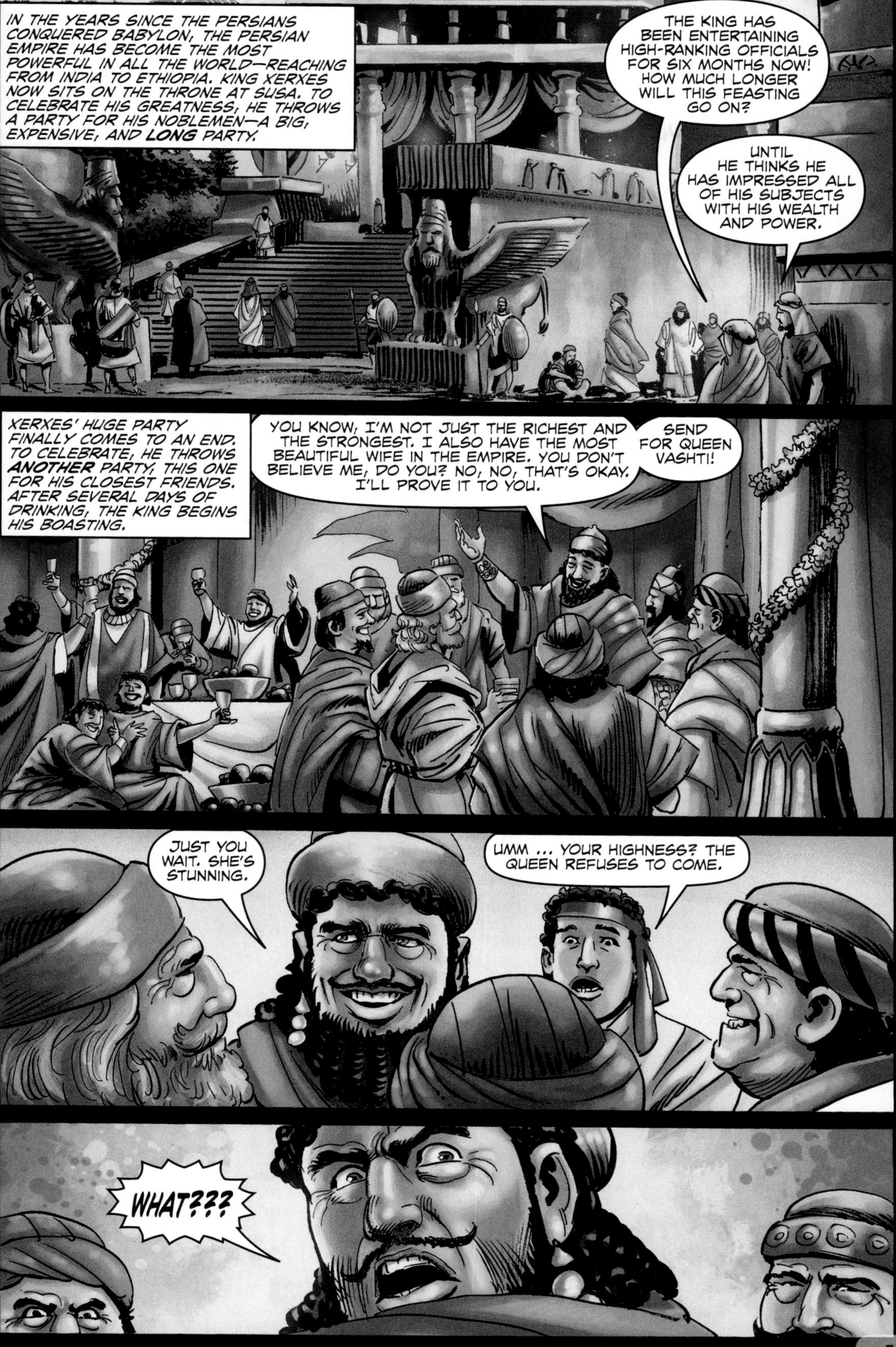
IN THE YEARS SINCE THE PERSIANS CONQUERED BABYLON, THE PERSIAN EMPIRE HAS BECOME THE MOST POWERFUL IN ALL THE WORLD—REACHING FROM INDIA TO ETHIOPIA. KING XERXES NOW SITS ON THE THRONE AT SUSA. TO CELEBRATE HIS GREATNESS, HE THROWS A PARTY FOR HIS NOBLEMEN—A BIG, EXPENSIVE, AND LONG PARTY.
THE KING HAS BEEN ENTERTAINING HIGH-RANKING OFFICIALS FOR SIX MONTHS NOW! HOW MUCH LONGER WILL THIS FEASTING GO ON?
UNTIL HE THINKS HE HAS IMPRESSED ALL OF HIS SUBJECTS WITH HIS WEALTH AND POWER.
XERXES' HUGE PARTY FINALLY COMES TO AN END. TO CELEBRATE, HE THROWS ANOTHER PARTY, THIS ONE FOR HIS CLOSEST FRIENDS. AFTER SEVERAL DAYS OF DRINKING, THE KING BEGINS HIS BOASTING.
YOU KNOW, I'M NOT JUST THE RICHEST AND THE STRONGEST. I ALSO HAVE THE MOST BEAUTIFUL WIFE IN THE EMPIRE. YOU DON'T BELIEVE ME, DO YOU? NO, NO, THAT'S OKAY. I'LL PROVE IT TO YOU.
SEND FOR QUEEN VASHTI!
JUST YOU WAIT. SHE'S STUNNING.
UMM ... YOUR HIGHNESS? THE QUEEN REFUSES TO COME.
WHAT???

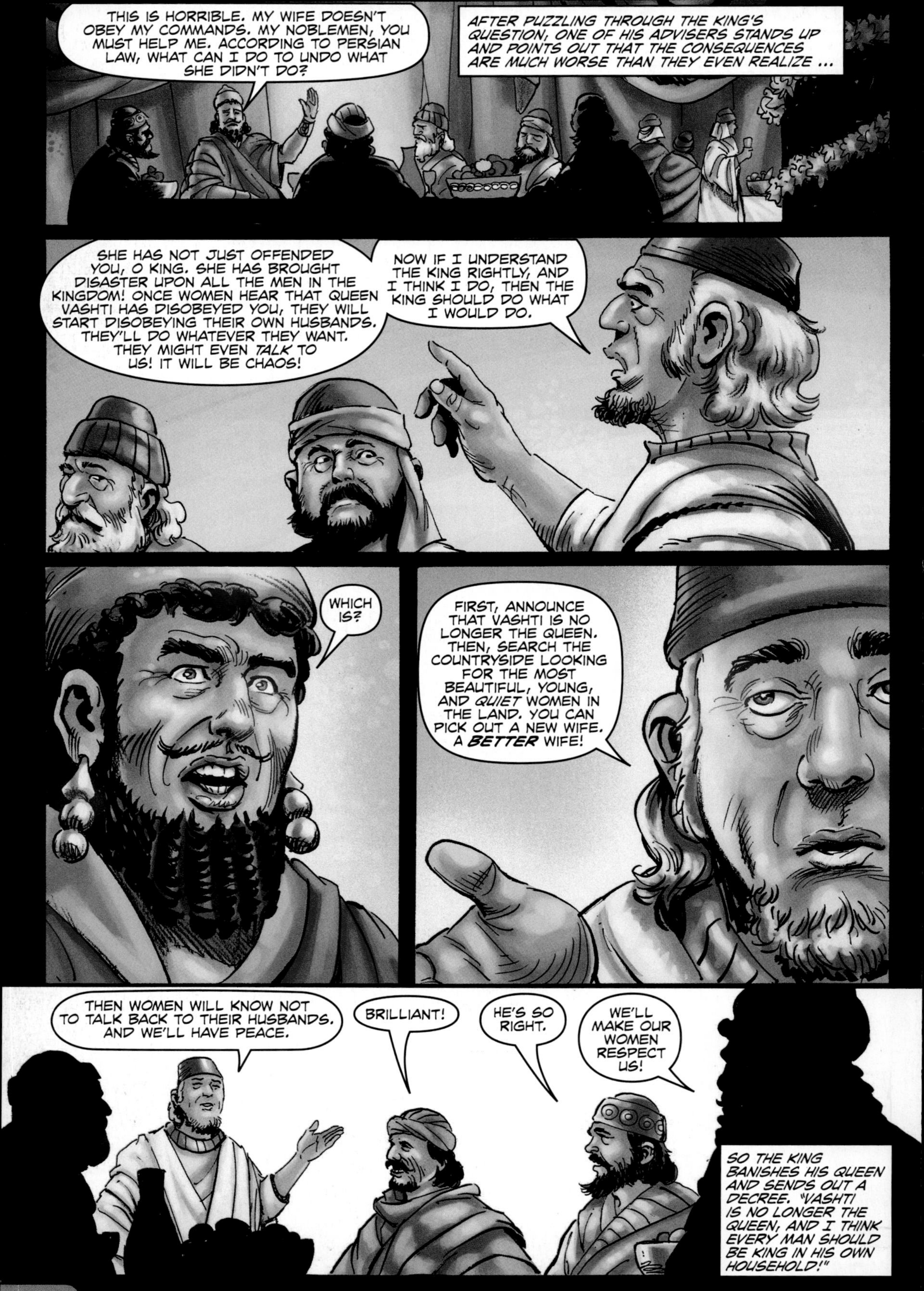
THIS IS HORRIBLE. MY WIFE DOESN'T OBEY MY COMMANDS. MY NOBLEMEN, YOU MUST HELP ME. ACCORDING TO PERSIAN LAW, WHAT CAN I DO TO UNDO WHAT SHE DIDN'T DO?
AFTER PUZZLING THROUGH THE KING'S QUESTION, ONE OF HIS ADVISERS STANDS UP AND POINTS OUT THAT THE CONSEQUENCES ARE MUCH WORSE THAN THEY EVEN REALIZE ...
SHE HAS NOT JUST OFFENDED YOU, O KING. SHE HAS BROUGHT DISASTER UPON ALL THE MEN IN THE KINGDOM! ONCE WOMEN HEAR THAT QUEEN VASHTI HAS DISOBEYED YOU, THEY WILL START DISOBEYING THEIR OWN HUSBANDS. THEY'LL DO WHATEVER THEY WANT. THEY MIGHT EVEN *TALK* TO US! IT WILL BE CHAOS!
NOW IF I UNDERSTAND THE KING RIGHTLY, AND I THINK I DO, THEN THE KING SHOULD DO WHAT I WOULD DO.
WHICH IS?
FIRST, ANNOUNCE THAT VASHTI IS NO LONGER THE QUEEN. THEN, SEARCH THE COUNTRYSIDE LOOKING FOR THE MOST BEAUTIFUL, YOUNG, AND *QUIET* WOMEN IN THE LAND. YOU CAN PICK OUT A NEW WIFE. A ***BETTER*** WIFE!
THEN WOMEN WILL KNOW NOT TO TALK BACK TO THEIR HUSBANDS. AND WE'LL HAVE PEACE.
BRILLIANT!
HE'S SO RIGHT.
WE'LL MAKE OUR WOMEN RESPECT US!
SO THE KING BANISHES HIS QUEEN AND SENDS OUT A DECREE. "VASHTI IS NO LONGER THE QUEEN, AND I THINK EVERY MAN SHOULD BE KING IN HIS OWN HOUSEHOLD!"

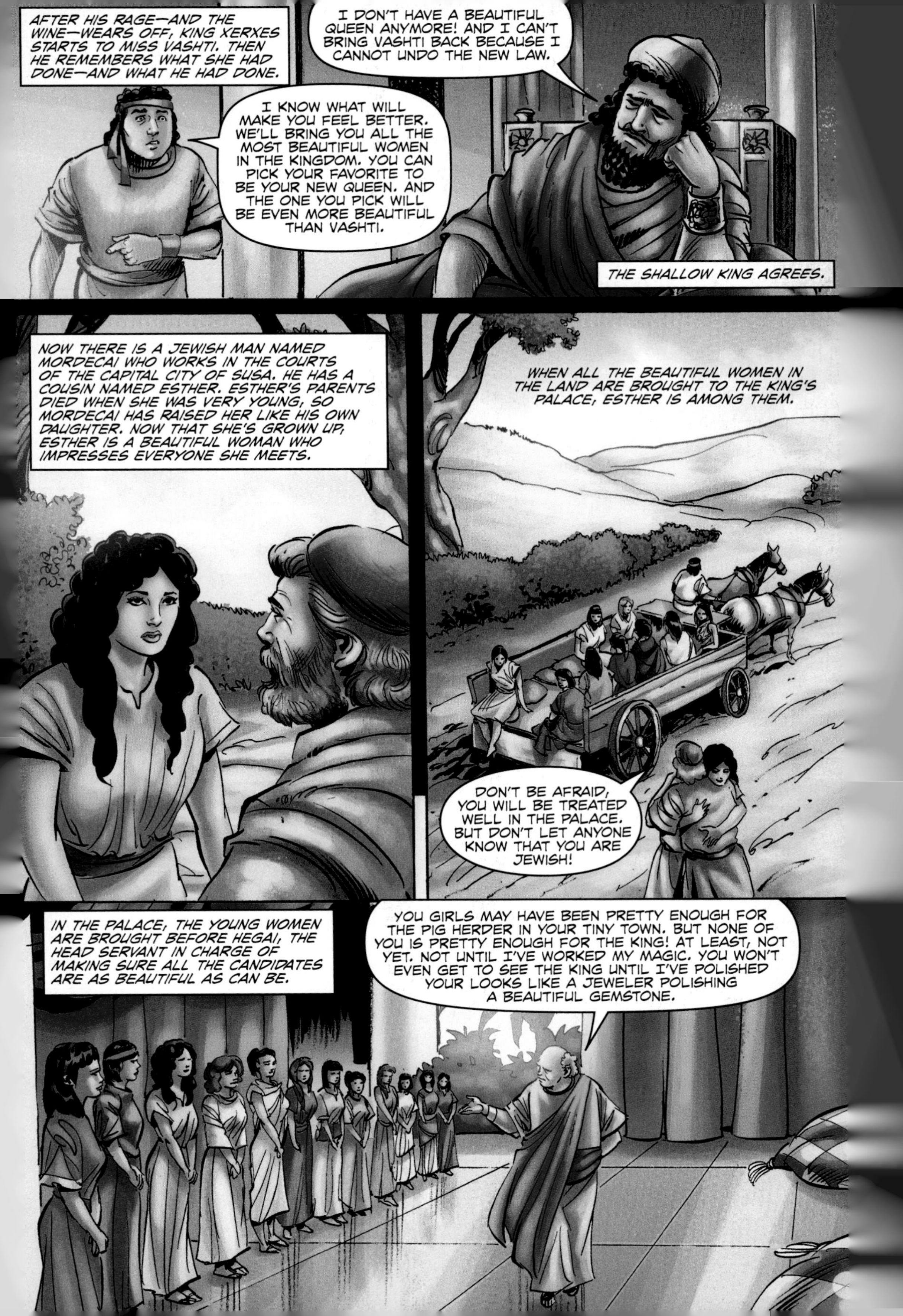
AFTER HIS RAGE—AND THE WINE—WEARS OFF, KING XERXES STARTS TO MISS VASHTI. THEN HE REMEMBERS WHAT SHE HAD DONE—AND WHAT HE HAD DONE.
I DON'T HAVE A BEAUTIFUL QUEEN ANYMORE! AND I CAN'T BRING VASHTI BACK BECAUSE I CANNOT UNDO THE NEW LAW.
I KNOW WHAT WILL MAKE YOU FEEL BETTER. WE'LL BRING YOU ALL THE MOST BEAUTIFUL WOMEN IN THE KINGDOM. YOU CAN PICK YOUR FAVORITE TO BE YOUR NEW QUEEN. AND THE ONE YOU PICK WILL BE EVEN MORE BEAUTIFUL THAN VASHTI.
THE SHALLOW KING AGREES.
NOW THERE IS A JEWISH MAN NAMED MORDECAI WHO WORKS IN THE COURTS OF THE CAPITAL CITY OF SUSA. HE HAS A COUSIN NAMED ESTHER. ESTHER'S PARENTS DIED WHEN SHE WAS VERY YOUNG, SO MORDECAI HAS RAISED HER LIKE HIS OWN DAUGHTER. NOW THAT SHE'S GROWN UP, ESTHER IS A BEAUTIFUL WOMAN WHO IMPRESSES EVERYONE SHE MEETS.
WHEN ALL THE BEAUTIFUL WOMEN IN THE LAND ARE BROUGHT TO THE KING'S PALACE, ESTHER IS AMONG THEM.
DON'T BE AFRAID, YOU WILL BE TREATED WELL IN THE PALACE. BUT DON'T LET ANYONE KNOW THAT YOU ARE JEWISH!
IN THE PALACE, THE YOUNG WOMEN ARE BROUGHT BEFORE HEGAI, THE HEAD SERVANT IN CHARGE OF MAKING SURE ALL THE CANDIDATES ARE AS BEAUTIFUL AS CAN BE.
YOU GIRLS MAY HAVE BEEN PRETTY ENOUGH FOR THE PIG HERDER IN YOUR TINY TOWN. BUT NONE OF YOU IS PRETTY ENOUGH FOR THE KING! AT LEAST, NOT YET. NOT UNTIL I'VE WORKED MY MAGIC. YOU WON'T EVEN GET TO SEE THE KING UNTIL I'VE POLISHED YOUR LOOKS LIKE A JEWELER POLISHING A BEAUTIFUL GEMSTONE.

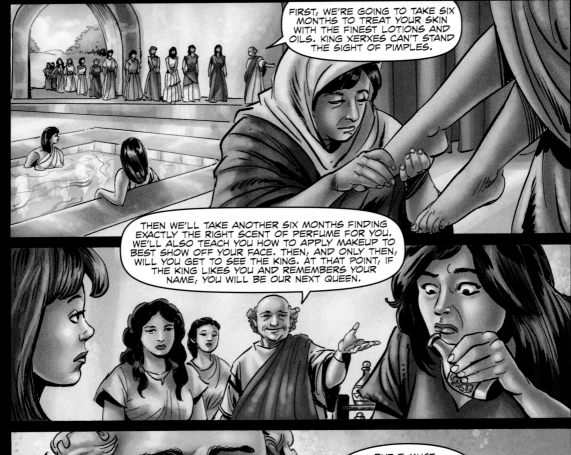

FIRST, WE'RE GOING TO TAKE SIX MONTHS TO TREAT YOUR SKIN WITH THE FINEST LOTIONS AND OILS. KING XERXES CAN'T STAND THE SIGHT OF PIMPLES.

THEN WE'LL TAKE ANOTHER SIX MONTHS FINDING EXACTLY THE RIGHT SCENT OF PERFUME FOR YOU. WE'LL ALSO TEACH YOU HOW TO APPLY MAKEUP TO BEST SHOW OFF YOUR FACE. THEN, AND ONLY THEN, WILL YOU GET TO SEE THE KING. AT THAT POINT, IF THE KING LIKES YOU AND REMEMBERS YOUR NAME, YOU WILL BE OUR NEXT QUEEN.

BUT I MUST TELL YOU—EVEN AFTER ALL MY BEAUTY TREATMENTS, THE KING HAS NEVER REMEMBERED ANY OF THE CANDIDATES' NAMES.

IN SPITE OF HIS LOW OPINION OF THE YOUNG WOMEN, HEGAI IS IMMEDIATELY CHARMED BY ESTHER.

YOU HAVE GRACE AND INTELLIGENCE LIKE NONE OF THESE OTHER GIRLS. I'M GIVING YOU SEVEN MAIDS TO ATTEND TO YOU PERSONALLY. YOU WILL HAVE THE BEST ROOM IN THE PALACE.

MEANWHILE, MORDECAI HAS BEEN WORRIED ABOUT HIS ADOPTED DAUGHTER. EVERY DAY HE HANGS AROUND THE OUTSIDE WALLS OF THE HAREM HOPING TO HEAR NEWS OF ESTHER. THERE HE MAKES FRIENDS WITH THE GUARDS, WHO LET HIM HANG OUT NEAR THE WOMEN'S SECTION OF THE PALACE.

DON'T WORRY. EVERYONE IN THE PALACE LOVES ESTHER.

YOU'RE A GOOD FATHER TO CHECK ON HER, BUT SHE IS WELL TAKEN CARE OF.

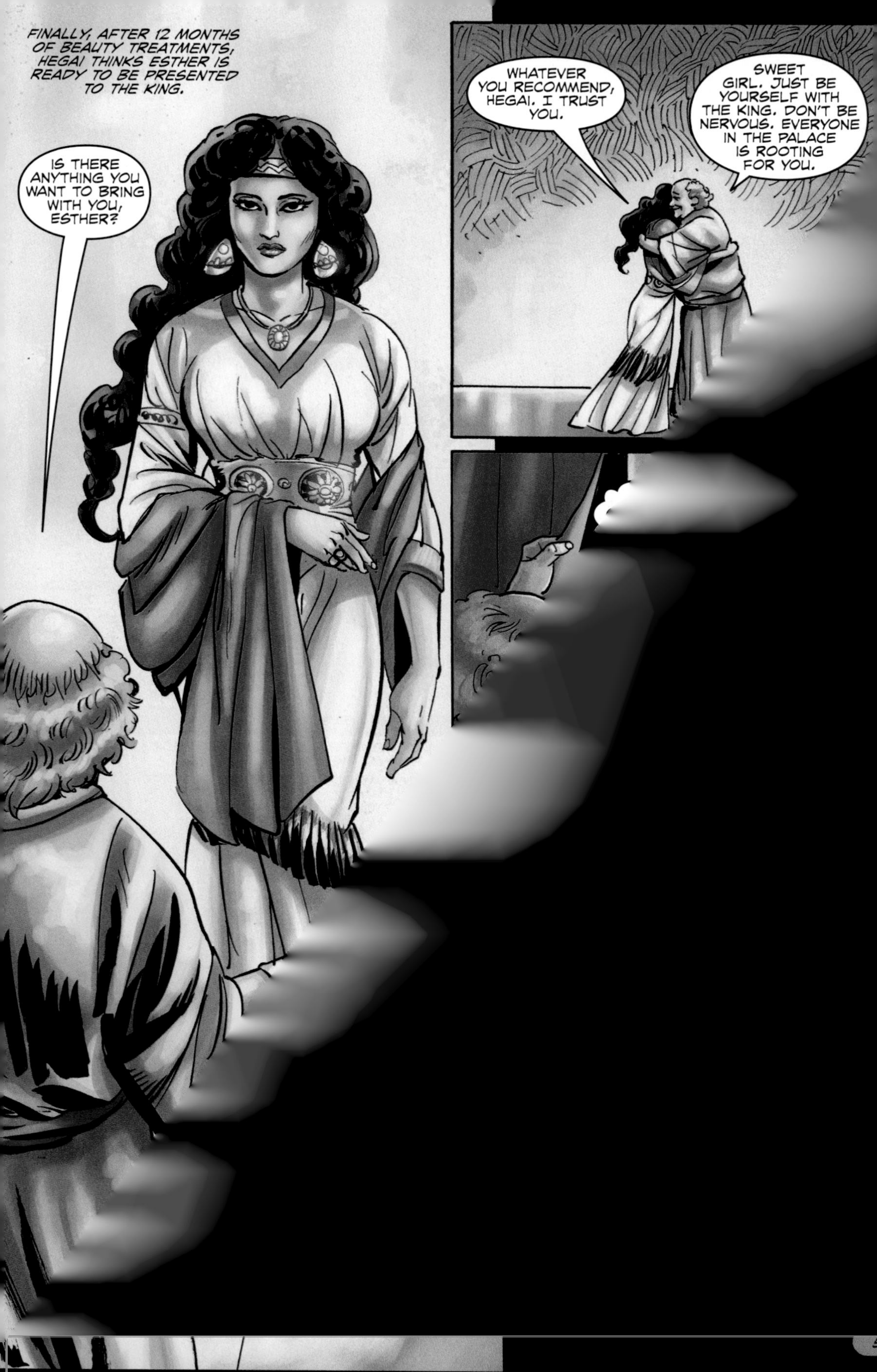
FINALLY, AFTER 12 MONTHS OF BEAUTY TREATMENTS, HEGAI THINKS ESTHER IS READY TO BE PRESENTED TO THE KING.
IS THERE ANYTHING YOU WANT TO BRING WITH YOU, ESTHER?
WHATEVER YOU RECOMMEND, HEGAI. I TRUST YOU.
SWEET GIRL. JUST BE YOURSELF WITH THE KING. DON'T BE NERVOUS. EVERYONE IN THE PALACE IS ROOTING FOR YOU.

Persian Politics

BASED ON ESTHER 2:19—3:15

FOR MONTHS, ESTHER—ALONG WITH HUNDREDS OF BEAUTIFUL WOMEN OF PERSIA—HAS LIVED IN THE PALACE WAITING FOR THE KING TO CHOOSE ONE OF THEM TO BE HIS WIFE. THE KING HAS FINALLY MADE HIS CHOICE ...

ESTHER, YOU ARE NOW MY WIFE, QUEEN OF ALL PERSIA.

I AM HONORED, MY LORD.

BUT ESTHER HAS KEPT HER FAMILY A SECRET. SHE HASN'T TOLD ANYONE ABOUT HER ADOPTED FATHER, MORDECAI, A JEWISH CITY OFFICIAL. LATE THAT NIGHT, HE GOES TO THE WALLS OF THE HAREM TO CHECK ON ESTHER, THE NEW QUEEN.

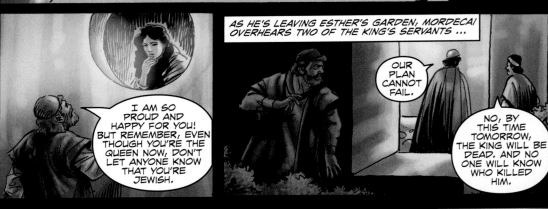

AS HE'S LEAVING ESTHER'S GARDEN, MORDECAI OVERHEARS TWO OF THE KING'S SERVANTS ...

I AM SO PROUD AND HAPPY FOR YOU! BUT REMEMBER, EVEN THOUGH YOU'RE THE QUEEN NOW, DON'T LET ANYONE KNOW THAT YOU'RE JEWISH.

OUR PLAN CANNOT FAIL.

NO, BY THIS TIME TOMORROW, THE KING WILL BE DEAD. AND NO ONE WILL KNOW WHO KILLED HIM.

MORDECAI QUICKLY SENDS WORD OF THE PLOT TO ESTHER. THAT VERY NIGHT, THE KING CALLS FOR HER.

WHY DO YOU LOOK TROUBLED, MY LOVELY? IT GIVES YOU WRINKLES.

MY KING, TWO OF YOUR SERVANTS PLAN TO ASSASSINATE YOU!

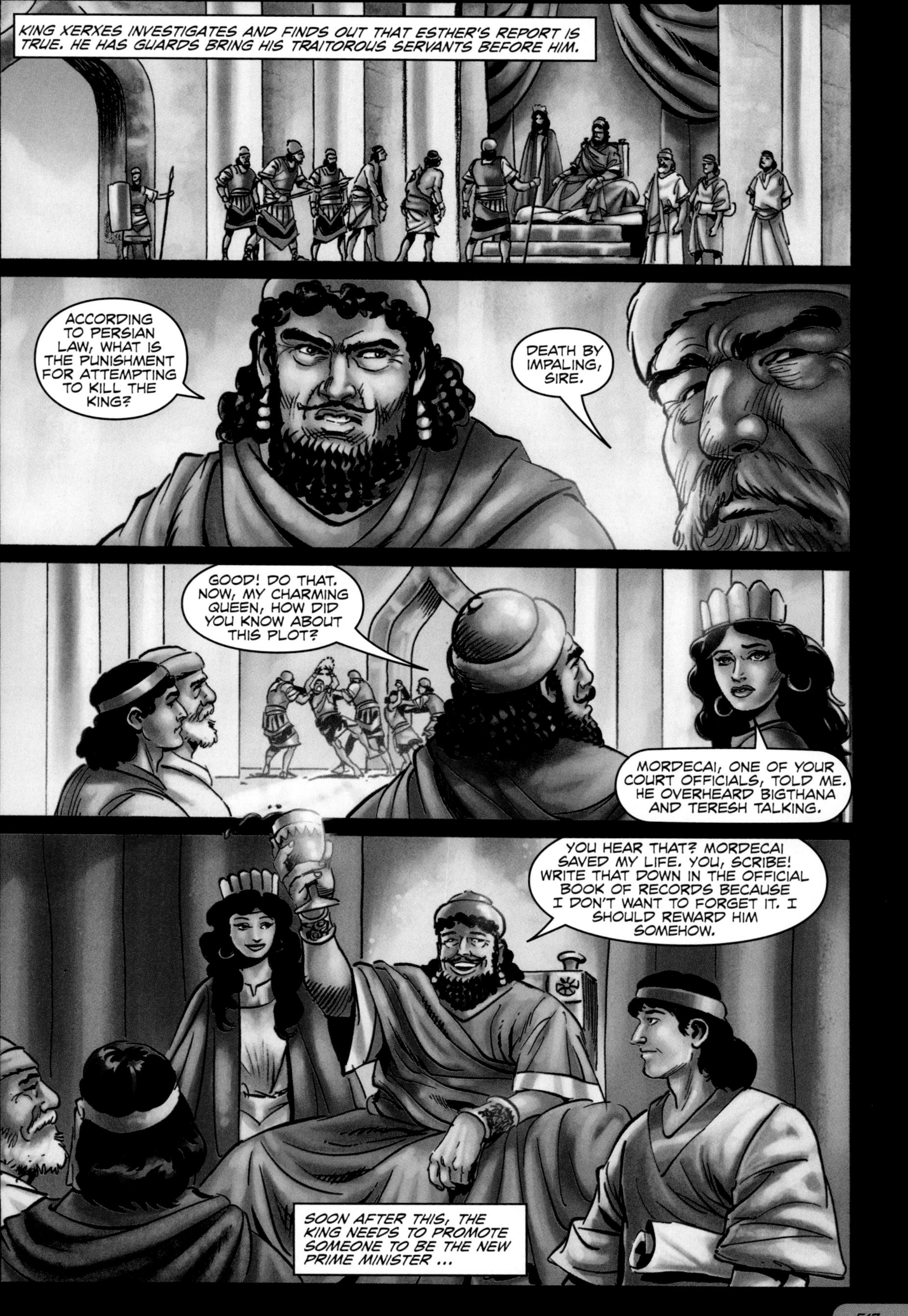
KING XERXES INVESTIGATES AND FINDS OUT THAT ESTHER'S REPORT IS TRUE. HE HAS GUARDS BRING HIS TRAITOROUS SERVANTS BEFORE HIM.
ACCORDING TO PERSIAN LAW, WHAT IS THE PUNISHMENT FOR ATTEMPTING TO KILL THE KING?
DEATH BY IMPALING, SIRE.
GOOD! DO THAT. NOW, MY CHARMING QUEEN, HOW DID YOU KNOW ABOUT THIS PLOT?
MORDECAI, ONE OF YOUR COURT OFFICIALS, TOLD ME. HE OVERHEARD BIGTHANA AND TERESH TALKING.
YOU HEAR THAT? MORDECAI SAVED MY LIFE. YOU, SCRIBE! WRITE THAT DOWN IN THE OFFICIAL BOOK OF RECORDS BECAUSE I DON'T WANT TO FORGET IT. I SHOULD REWARD HIM SOMEHOW.
SOON AFTER THIS, THE KING NEEDS TO PROMOTE SOMEONE TO BE THE NEW PRIME MINISTER ...

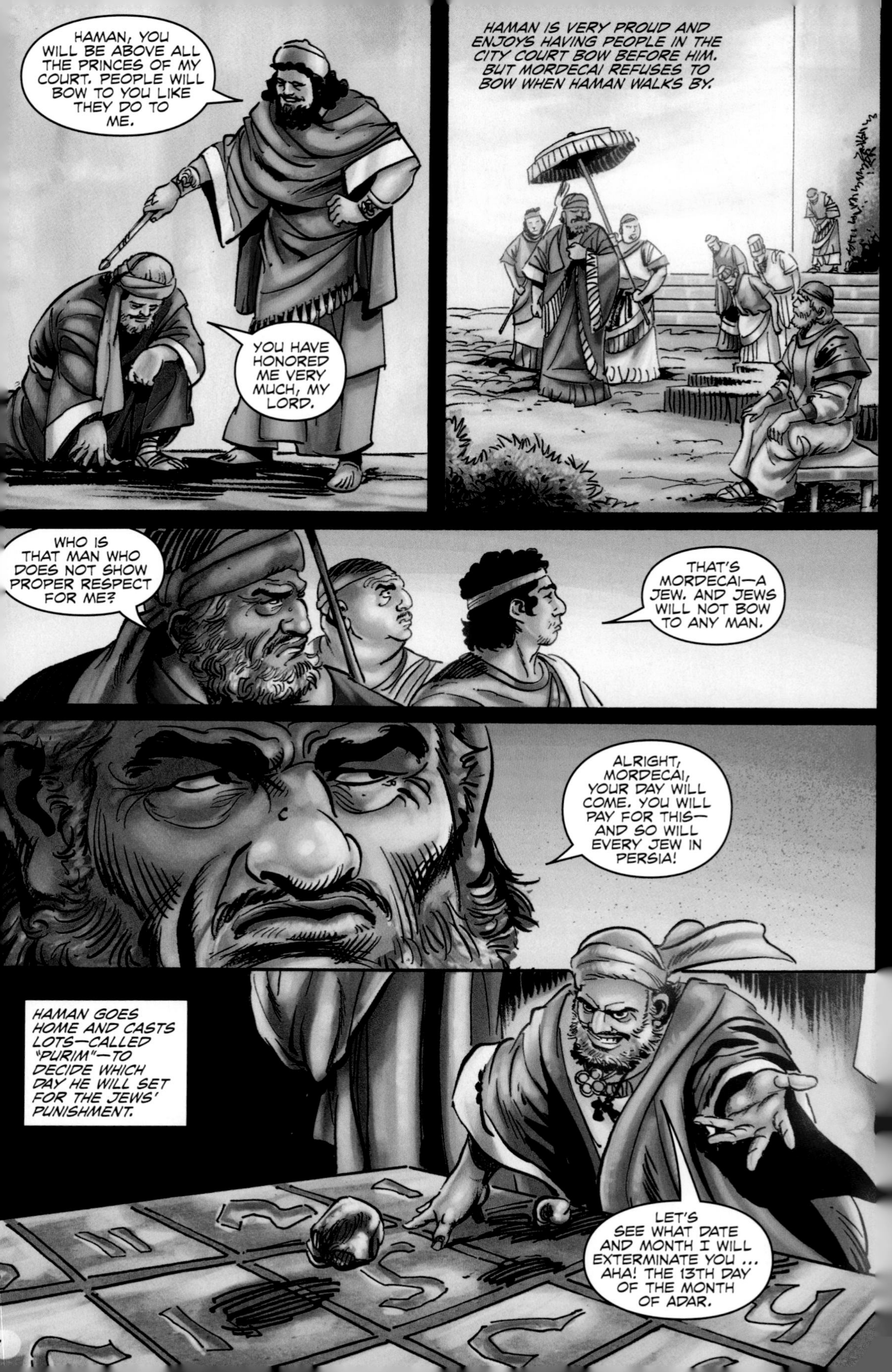
HAMAN, YOU WILL BE ABOVE ALL THE PRINCES OF MY COURT. PEOPLE WILL BOW TO YOU LIKE THEY DO TO ME.
YOU HAVE HONORED ME VERY MUCH, MY LORD.
HAMAN IS VERY PROUD AND ENJOYS HAVING PEOPLE IN THE CITY COURT BOW BEFORE HIM. BUT MORDECAI REFUSES TO BOW WHEN HAMAN WALKS BY.
WHO IS THAT MAN WHO DOES NOT SHOW PROPER RESPECT FOR ME?
THAT'S MORDECAI—A JEW. AND JEWS WILL NOT BOW TO ANY MAN.
ALRIGHT, MORDECAI, YOUR DAY WILL COME. YOU WILL PAY FOR THIS—AND SO WILL EVERY JEW IN PERSIA!
HAMAN GOES HOME AND CASTS LOTS—CALLED "PURIM"—TO DECIDE WHICH DAY HE WILL SET FOR THE JEWS' PUNISHMENT.
LET'S SEE WHAT DATE AND MONTH I WILL EXTERMINATE YOU ... AHA! THE 13TH DAY OF THE MONTH OF ADAR.

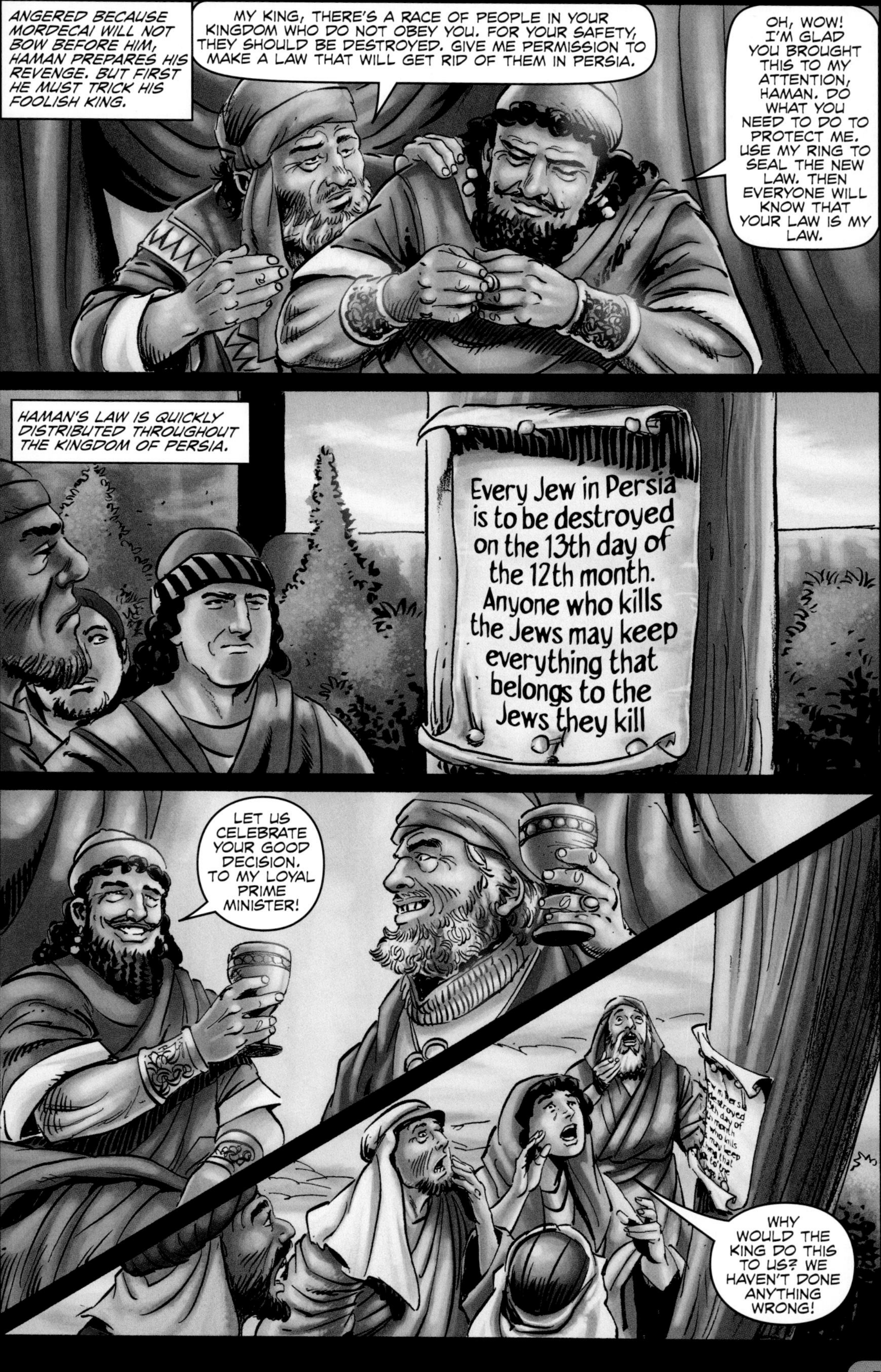
ANGERED BECAUSE MORDECAI WILL NOT BOW BEFORE HIM, HAMAN PREPARES HIS REVENGE. BUT FIRST HE MUST TRICK HIS FOOLISH KING.
MY KING, THERE'S A RACE OF PEOPLE IN YOUR KINGDOM WHO DO NOT OBEY YOU. FOR YOUR SAFETY, THEY SHOULD BE DESTROYED. GIVE ME PERMISSION TO MAKE A LAW THAT WILL GET RID OF THEM IN PERSIA.
OH, WOW! I'M GLAD YOU BROUGHT THIS TO MY ATTENTION, HAMAN. DO WHAT YOU NEED TO DO TO PROTECT ME. USE MY RING TO SEAL THE NEW LAW. THEN EVERYONE WILL KNOW THAT YOUR LAW IS MY LAW.
HAMAN'S LAW IS QUICKLY DISTRIBUTED THROUGHOUT THE KINGDOM OF PERSIA.
Every Jew in Persia is to be destroyed on the 13th day of the 12th month. Anyone who kills the Jews may keep everything that belongs to the Jews they kill
LET US CELEBRATE YOUR GOOD DECISION. TO MY LOYAL PRIME MINISTER!
WHY WOULD THE KING DO THIS TO US? WE HAVEN'T DONE ANYTHING WRONG!

If I Perish, I Perish

BASED ON ESTHER 4

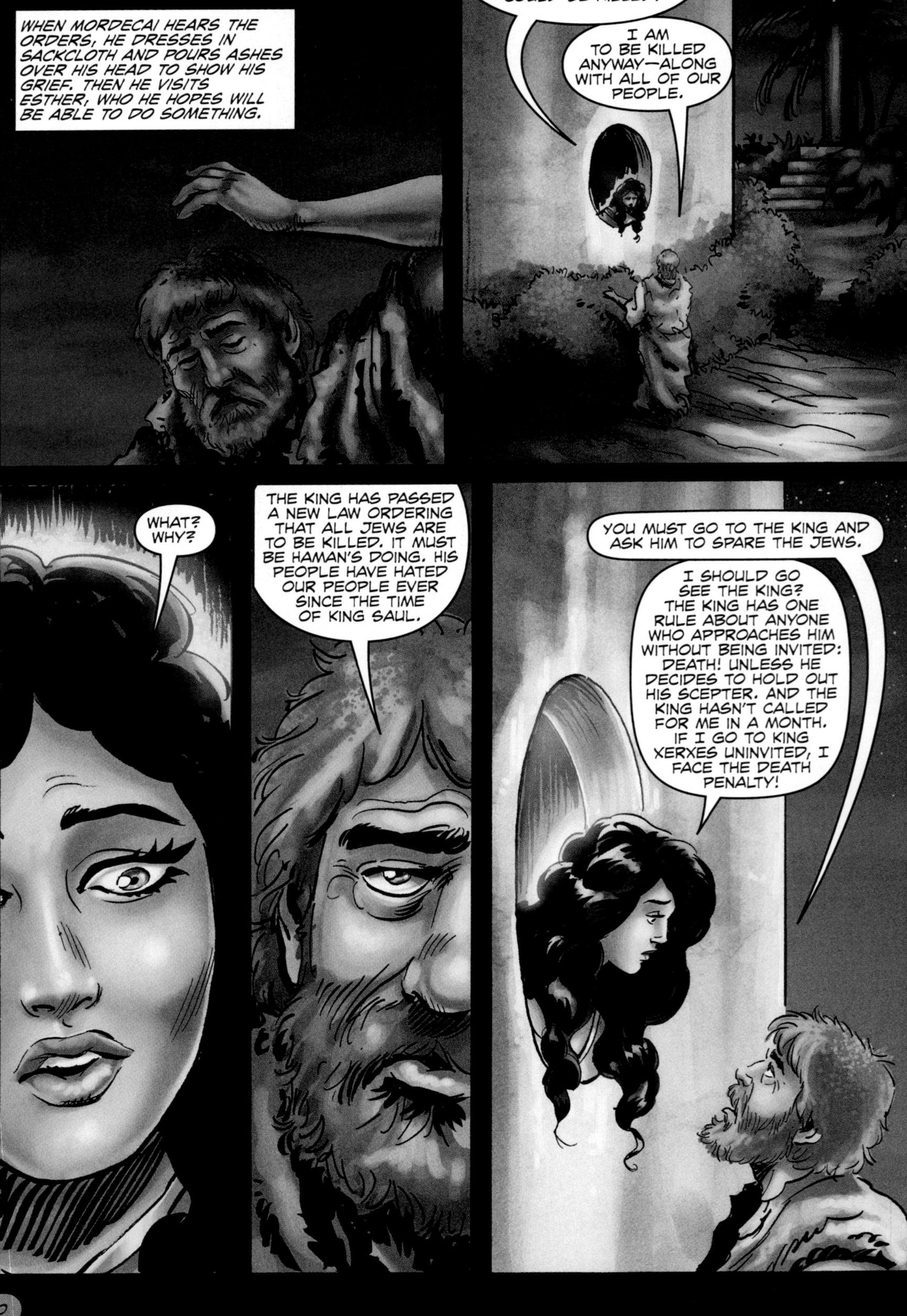

WHEN MORDECAI HEARS THE ORDERS, HE DRESSES IN SACKCLOTH AND POURS ASHES OVER HIS HEAD TO SHOW HIS GRIEF. THEN HE VISITS ESTHER, WHO HE HOPES WILL BE ABLE TO DO SOMETHING.
WHAT ARE YOU DOING HERE IN SACKCLOTH? DON'T YOU KNOW IT'S AGAINST THE LAW TO SHOW MOURNING IN THE KING'S PALACE? YOU COULD BE KILLED!
I AM TO BE KILLED ANYWAY—ALONG WITH ALL OF OUR PEOPLE.
WHAT? WHY?
THE KING HAS PASSED A NEW LAW ORDERING THAT ALL JEWS ARE TO BE KILLED. IT MUST BE HAMAN'S DOING. HIS PEOPLE HAVE HATED OUR PEOPLE EVER SINCE THE TIME OF KING SAUL.
YOU MUST GO TO THE KING AND ASK HIM TO SPARE THE JEWS.
I SHOULD GO SEE THE KING? THE KING HAS ONE RULE ABOUT ANYONE WHO APPROACHES HIM WITHOUT BEING INVITED: DEATH! UNLESS HE DECIDES TO HOLD OUT HIS SCEPTER. AND THE KING HASN'T CALLED FOR ME IN A MONTH. IF I GO TO KING XERXES UNINVITED, I FACE THE DEATH PENALTY!

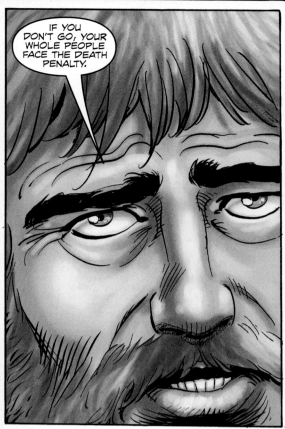

IF YOU DON'T GO, YOUR WHOLE PEOPLE FACE THE DEATH PENALTY.

WHO KNOWS? MAYBE YOU HAVE BEEN PUT INTO THIS ROYAL POSITION FOR A TIME JUST LIKE THIS.

TODAY, YOU MUST BE MORE THAN A QUEEN—YOU MUST BE A JEW. AND TO SAVE US, YOU MUST BE MORE THAN A JEW—YOU MUST BE A QUEEN.

GO, GATHER ALL THE JEWS IN THE CITY. FAST AND PRAY FOR ME. DON'T EAT OR DRINK FOR THREE DAYS. I WILL DO THE SAME. AFTER THREE DAYS, I WILL GO TO THE KING UNINVITED. AND IF I PERISH, I PERISH.

Who Will Be Hanged?

BASED ON ESTHER 5–10

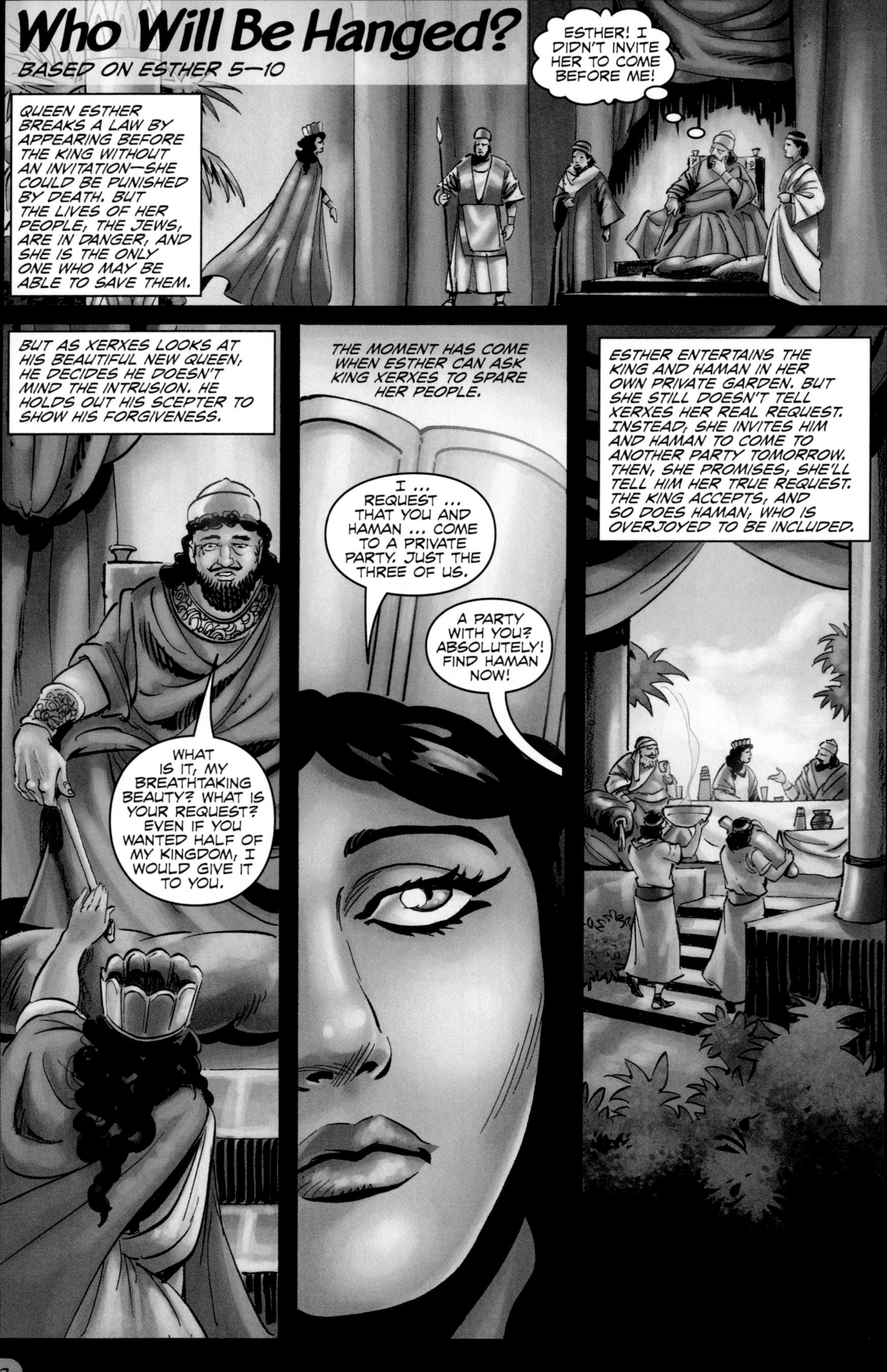

ESTHER! I DIDN'T INVITE HER TO COME BEFORE ME!
QUEEN ESTHER BREAKS A LAW BY APPEARING BEFORE THE KING WITHOUT AN INVITATION—SHE COULD BE PUNISHED BY DEATH. BUT THE LIVES OF HER PEOPLE, THE JEWS, ARE IN DANGER, AND SHE IS THE ONLY ONE WHO MAY BE ABLE TO SAVE THEM.
BUT AS XERXES LOOKS AT HIS BEAUTIFUL NEW QUEEN, HE DECIDES HE DOESN'T MIND THE INTRUSION. HE HOLDS OUT HIS SCEPTER TO SHOW HIS FORGIVENESS.
WHAT IS IT, MY BREATHTAKING BEAUTY? WHAT IS YOUR REQUEST? EVEN IF YOU WANTED HALF OF MY KINGDOM, I WOULD GIVE IT TO YOU.
THE MOMENT HAS COME WHEN ESTHER CAN ASK KING XERXES TO SPARE HER PEOPLE.
I ... REQUEST ... THAT YOU AND HAMAN ... COME TO A PRIVATE PARTY. JUST THE THREE OF US.
A PARTY WITH YOU? ABSOLUTELY! FIND HAMAN NOW!
ESTHER ENTERTAINS THE KING AND HAMAN IN HER OWN PRIVATE GARDEN. BUT SHE STILL DOESN'T TELL XERXES HER REAL REQUEST. INSTEAD, SHE INVITES HIM AND HAMAN TO COME TO ANOTHER PARTY TOMORROW. THEN, SHE PROMISES, SHE'LL TELL HIM HER TRUE REQUEST. THE KING ACCEPTS, AND SO DOES HAMAN, WHO IS OVERJOYED TO BE INCLUDED.

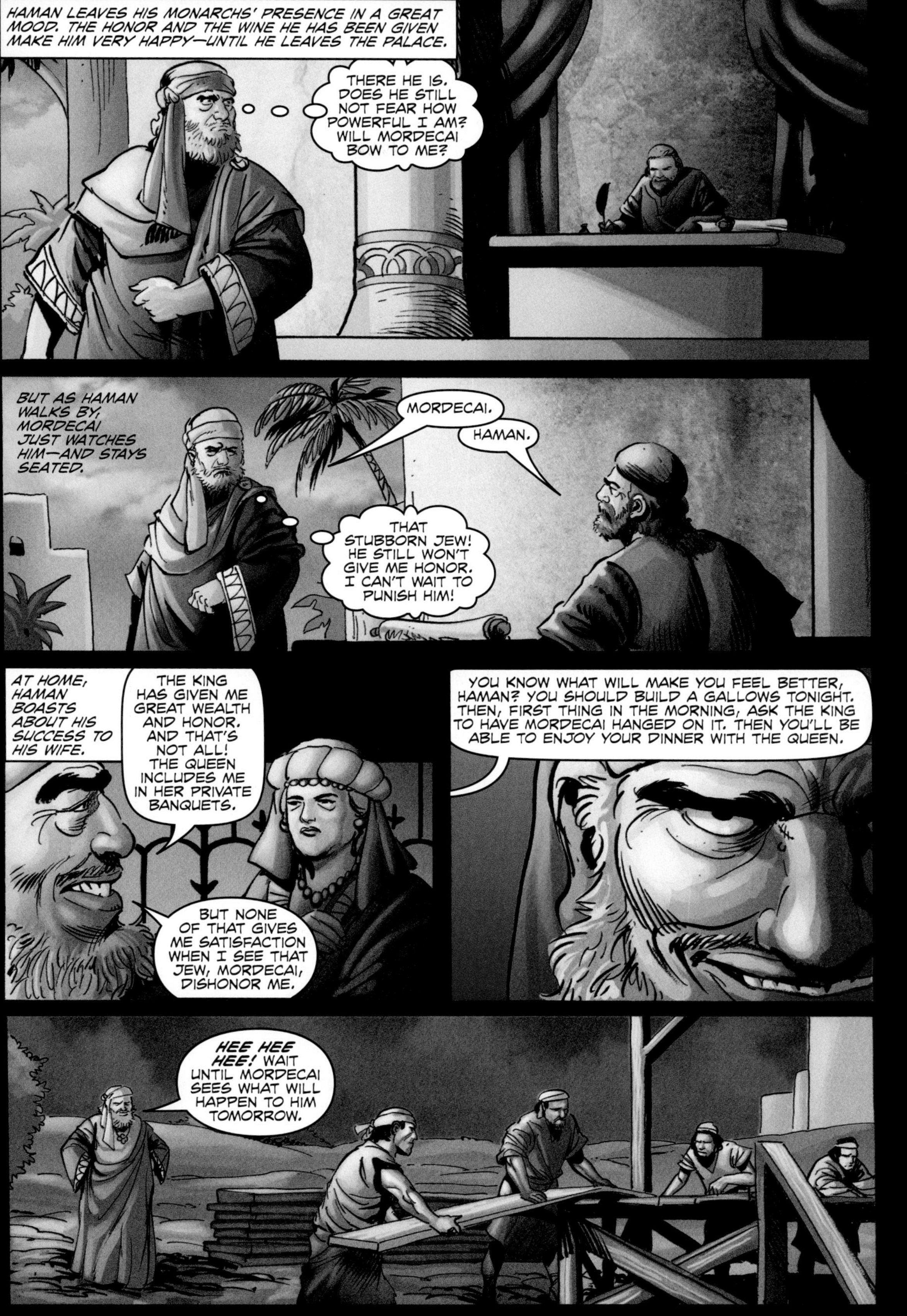
HAMAN LEAVES HIS MONARCHS' PRESENCE IN A GREAT MOOD. THE HONOR AND THE WINE HE HAS BEEN GIVEN MAKE HIM VERY HAPPY—UNTIL HE LEAVES THE PALACE.
THERE HE IS. DOES HE STILL NOT FEAR HOW POWERFUL I AM? WILL MORDECAI BOW TO ME?
BUT AS HAMAN WALKS BY, MORDECAI JUST WATCHES HIM—AND STAYS SEATED.
MORDECAI.
HAMAN.
THAT STUBBORN JEW! HE STILL WON'T GIVE ME HONOR. I CAN'T WAIT TO PUNISH HIM!
AT HOME, HAMAN BOASTS ABOUT HIS SUCCESS TO HIS WIFE.
THE KING HAS GIVEN ME GREAT WEALTH AND HONOR. AND THAT'S NOT ALL! THE QUEEN INCLUDES ME IN HER PRIVATE BANQUETS.
BUT NONE OF THAT GIVES ME SATISFACTION WHEN I SEE THAT JEW, MORDECAI, DISHONOR ME.
YOU KNOW WHAT WILL MAKE YOU FEEL BETTER, HAMAN? YOU SHOULD BUILD A GALLOWS TONIGHT. THEN, FIRST THING IN THE MORNING, ASK THE KING TO HAVE MORDECAI HANGED ON IT. THEN YOU'LL BE ABLE TO ENJOY YOUR DINNER WITH THE QUEEN.
HEE HEE HEE! WAIT UNTIL MORDECAI SEES WHAT WILL HAPPEN TO HIM TOMORROW.

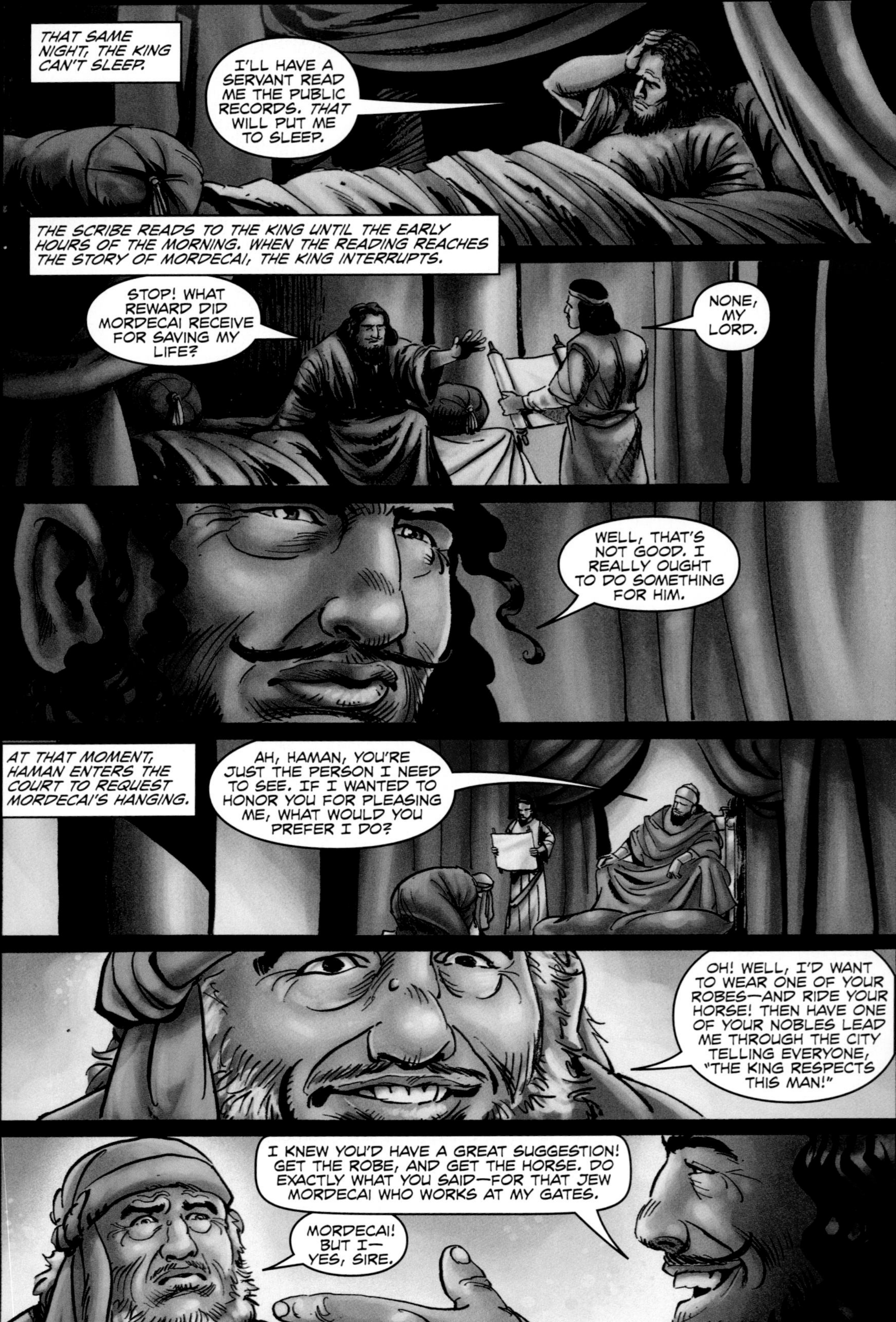
THAT SAME NIGHT, THE KING CAN'T SLEEP.
I'LL HAVE A SERVANT READ ME THE PUBLIC RECORDS. *THAT* WILL PUT ME TO SLEEP.
THE SCRIBE READS TO THE KING UNTIL THE EARLY HOURS OF THE MORNING. WHEN THE READING REACHES THE STORY OF MORDECAI, THE KING INTERRUPTS.
STOP! WHAT REWARD DID MORDECAI RECEIVE FOR SAVING MY LIFE?
NONE, MY LORD.
WELL, THAT'S NOT GOOD. I REALLY OUGHT TO DO SOMETHING FOR HIM.
AT THAT MOMENT, HAMAN ENTERS THE COURT TO REQUEST MORDECAI'S HANGING.
AH, HAMAN, YOU'RE JUST THE PERSON I NEED TO SEE. IF I WANTED TO HONOR YOU FOR PLEASING ME, WHAT WOULD YOU PREFER I DO?
OH! WELL, I'D WANT TO WEAR ONE OF YOUR ROBES—AND RIDE YOUR HORSE! THEN HAVE ONE OF YOUR NOBLES LEAD ME THROUGH THE CITY TELLING EVERYONE, "THE KING RESPECTS THIS MAN!"
I KNEW YOU'D HAVE A GREAT SUGGESTION! GET THE ROBE, AND GET THE HORSE. DO EXACTLY WHAT YOU SAID—FOR THAT JEW MORDECAI WHO WORKS AT MY GATES.
MORDECAI! BUT I— YES, SIRE.

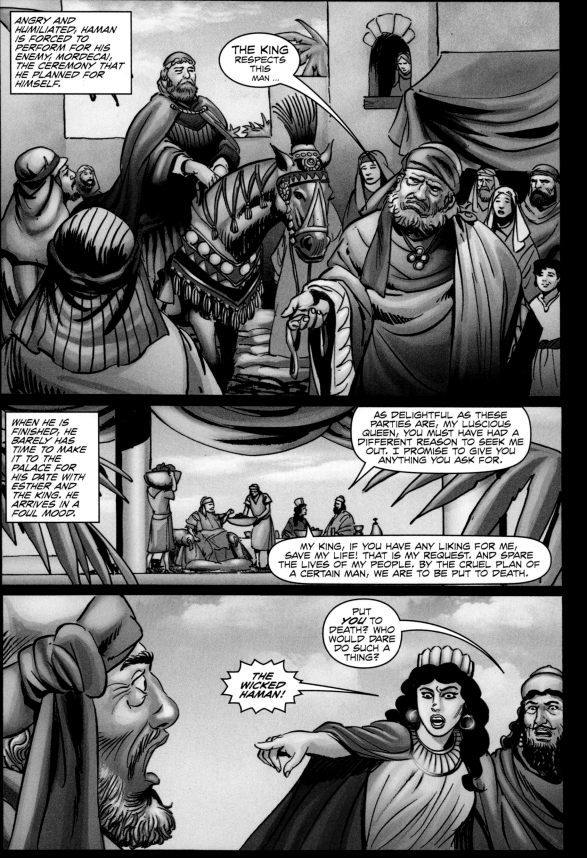

ANGRY AND HUMILIATED, HAMAN IS FORCED TO PERFORM FOR HIS ENEMY, MORDECAI, THE CEREMONY THAT HE PLANNED FOR HIMSELF.

THE KING RESPECTS THIS MAN ...

WHEN HE IS FINISHED, HE BARELY HAS TIME TO MAKE IT TO THE PALACE FOR HIS DATE WITH ESTHER AND THE KING. HE ARRIVES IN A FOUL MOOD.

AS DELIGHTFUL AS THESE PARTIES ARE, MY LUSCIOUS QUEEN, YOU MUST HAVE HAD A DIFFERENT REASON TO SEEK ME OUT. I PROMISE TO GIVE YOU ANYTHING YOU ASK FOR.

MY KING, IF YOU HAVE ANY LIKING FOR ME, SAVE MY LIFE! THAT IS MY REQUEST. AND SPARE THE LIVES OF MY PEOPLE. BY THE CRUEL PLAN OF A CERTAIN MAN, WE ARE TO BE PUT TO DEATH.

PUT YOU TO DEATH? WHO WOULD DARE DO SUCH A THING?

THE WICKED HAMAN!

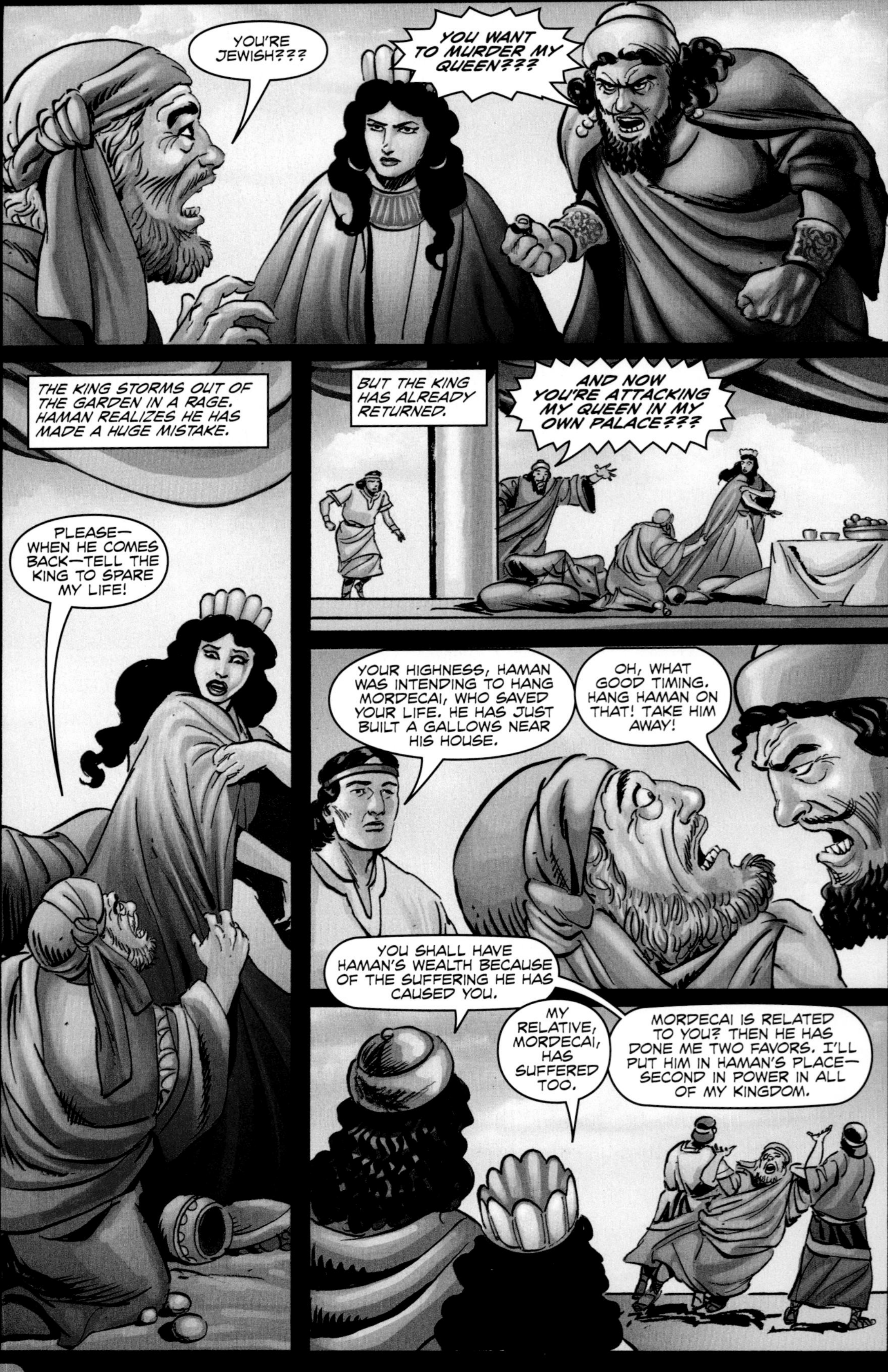
YOU'RE JEWISH???
YOU WANT TO MURDER MY QUEEN???
THE KING STORMS OUT OF THE GARDEN IN A RAGE. HAMAN REALIZES HE HAS MADE A HUGE MISTAKE.
PLEASE—WHEN HE COMES BACK—TELL THE KING TO SPARE MY LIFE!
BUT THE KING HAS ALREADY RETURNED.
AND NOW YOU'RE ATTACKING MY QUEEN IN MY OWN PALACE???
YOUR HIGHNESS, HAMAN WAS INTENDING TO HANG MORDECAI, WHO SAVED YOUR LIFE. HE HAS JUST BUILT A GALLOWS NEAR HIS HOUSE.
OH, WHAT GOOD TIMING. HANG HAMAN ON THAT! TAKE HIM AWAY!
YOU SHALL HAVE HAMAN'S WEALTH BECAUSE OF THE SUFFERING HE HAS CAUSED YOU.
MY RELATIVE, MORDECAI, HAS SUFFERED TOO.
MORDECAI IS RELATED TO YOU? THEN HE HAS DONE ME TWO FAVORS. I'LL PUT HIM IN HAMAN'S PLACE—SECOND IN POWER IN ALL OF MY KINGDOM.

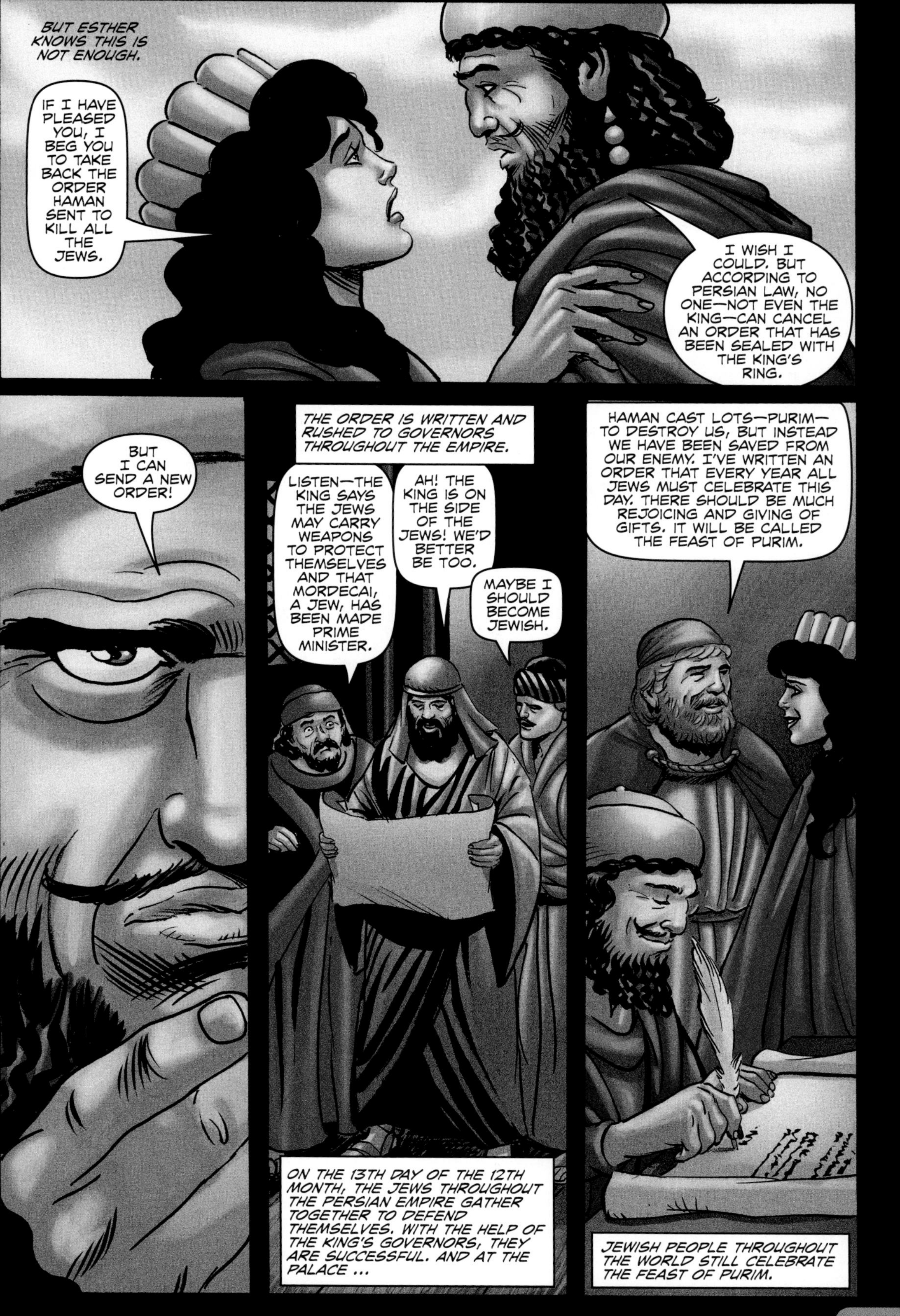
BUT ESTHER KNOWS THIS IS NOT ENOUGH.
IF I HAVE PLEASED YOU, I BEG YOU TO TAKE BACK THE ORDER HAMAN SENT TO KILL ALL THE JEWS.
I WISH I COULD. BUT ACCORDING TO PERSIAN LAW, NO ONE—NOT EVEN THE KING—CAN CANCEL AN ORDER THAT HAS BEEN SEALED WITH THE KING'S RING.
BUT I CAN SEND A NEW ORDER!
THE ORDER IS WRITTEN AND RUSHED TO GOVERNORS THROUGHOUT THE EMPIRE.
LISTEN—THE KING SAYS THE JEWS MAY CARRY WEAPONS TO PROTECT THEMSELVES AND THAT MORDECAI, A JEW, HAS BEEN MADE PRIME MINISTER.
AH! THE KING IS ON THE SIDE OF THE JEWS! WE'D BETTER BE TOO.
MAYBE I SHOULD BECOME JEWISH.
ON THE 13TH DAY OF THE 12TH MONTH, THE JEWS THROUGHOUT THE PERSIAN EMPIRE GATHER TOGETHER TO DEFEND THEMSELVES. WITH THE HELP OF THE KING'S GOVERNORS, THEY ARE SUCCESSFUL. AND AT THE PALACE ...
HAMAN CAST LOTS—PURIM—TO DESTROY US, BUT INSTEAD WE HAVE BEEN SAVED FROM OUR ENEMY. I'VE WRITTEN AN ORDER THAT EVERY YEAR ALL JEWS MUST CELEBRATE THIS DAY. THERE SHOULD BE MUCH REJOICING AND GIVING OF GIFTS. IT WILL BE CALLED THE FEAST OF PURIM.
JEWISH PEOPLE THROUGHOUT THE WORLD STILL CELEBRATE THE FEAST OF PURIM.

The Captives Return

BASED ON EZRA 1–3; ISAIAH 45

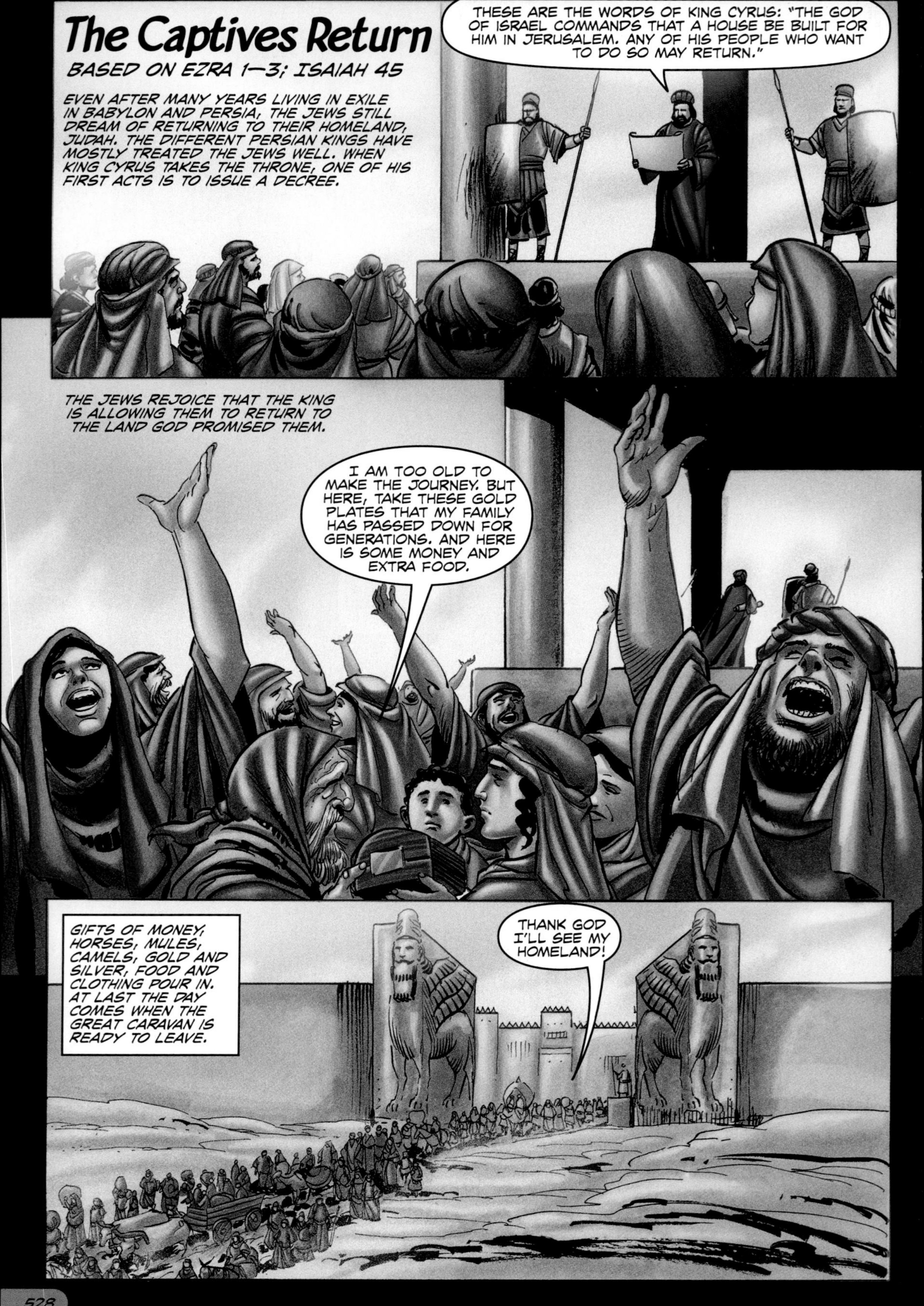
EVEN AFTER MANY YEARS LIVING IN EXILE IN BABYLON AND PERSIA, THE JEWS STILL DREAM OF RETURNING TO THEIR HOMELAND, JUDAH. THE DIFFERENT PERSIAN KINGS HAVE MOSTLY TREATED THE JEWS WELL. WHEN KING CYRUS TAKES THE THRONE, ONE OF HIS FIRST ACTS IS TO ISSUE A DECREE.
THESE ARE THE WORDS OF KING CYRUS: "THE GOD OF ISRAEL COMMANDS THAT A HOUSE BE BUILT FOR HIM IN JERUSALEM. ANY OF HIS PEOPLE WHO WANT TO DO SO MAY RETURN."
THE JEWS REJOICE THAT THE KING IS ALLOWING THEM TO RETURN TO THE LAND GOD PROMISED THEM.
I AM TOO OLD TO MAKE THE JOURNEY. BUT HERE, TAKE THESE GOLD PLATES THAT MY FAMILY HAS PASSED DOWN FOR GENERATIONS. AND HERE IS SOME MONEY AND EXTRA FOOD.
GIFTS OF MONEY, HORSES, MULES, CAMELS, GOLD AND SILVER, FOOD AND CLOTHING POUR IN. AT LAST THE DAY COMES WHEN THE GREAT CARAVAN IS READY TO LEAVE.
THANK GOD I'LL SEE MY HOMELAND!

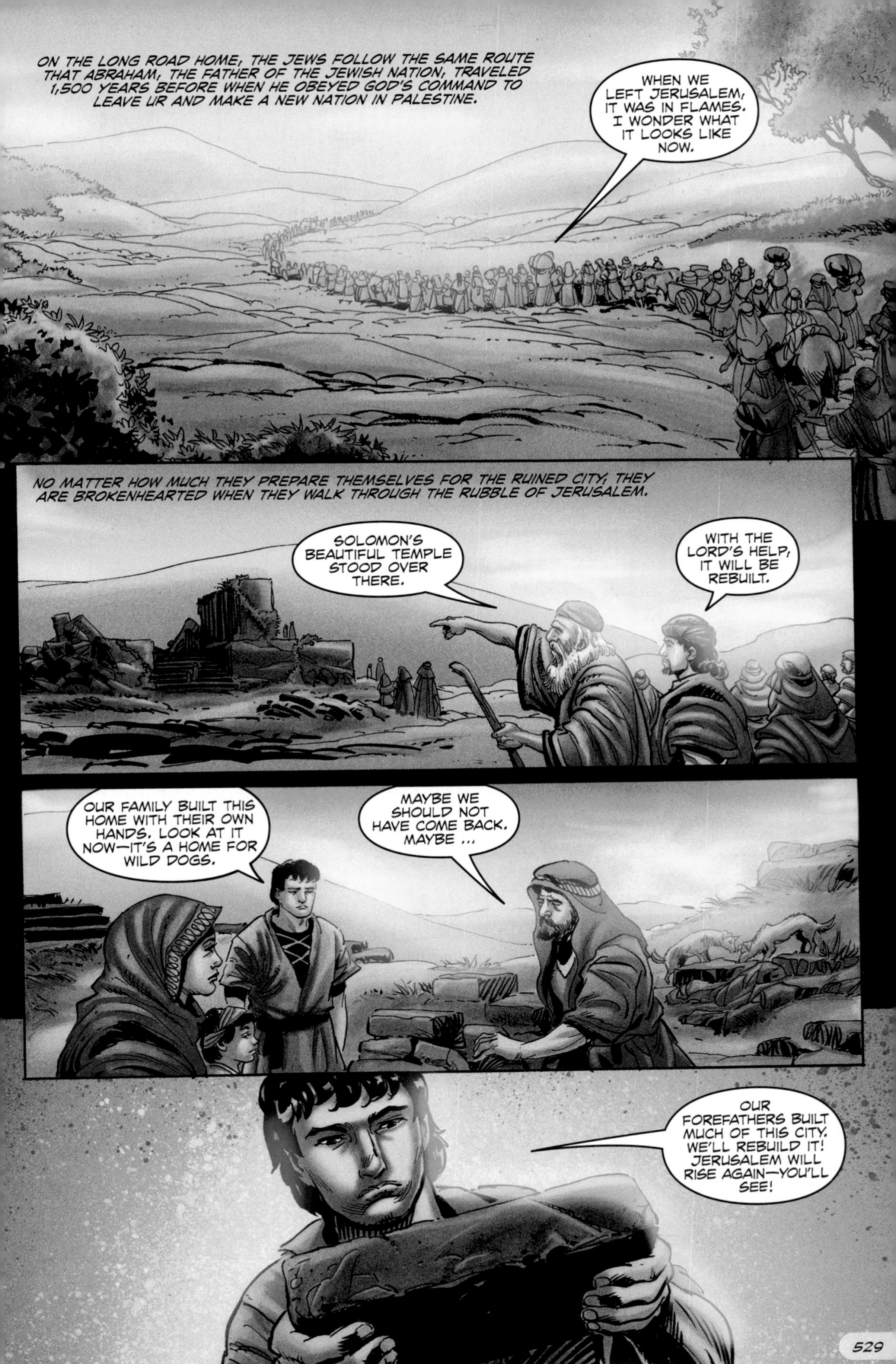
ON THE LONG ROAD HOME, THE JEWS FOLLOW THE SAME ROUTE THAT ABRAHAM, THE FATHER OF THE JEWISH NATION, TRAVELED 1,500 YEARS BEFORE WHEN HE OBEYED GOD'S COMMAND TO LEAVE UR AND MAKE A NEW NATION IN PALESTINE.
WHEN WE LEFT JERUSALEM, IT WAS IN FLAMES. I WONDER WHAT IT LOOKS LIKE NOW.
NO MATTER HOW MUCH THEY PREPARE THEMSELVES FOR THE RUINED CITY, THEY ARE BROKENHEARTED WHEN THEY WALK THROUGH THE RUBBLE OF JERUSALEM.
SOLOMON'S BEAUTIFUL TEMPLE STOOD OVER THERE.
WITH THE LORD'S HELP, IT WILL BE REBUILT.
OUR FAMILY BUILT THIS HOME WITH THEIR OWN HANDS. LOOK AT IT NOW—IT'S A HOME FOR WILD DOGS.
MAYBE WE SHOULD NOT HAVE COME BACK. MAYBE ...
OUR FOREFATHERS BUILT MUCH OF THIS CITY. WE'LL REBUILD IT! JERUSALEM WILL RISE AGAIN—YOU'LL SEE!

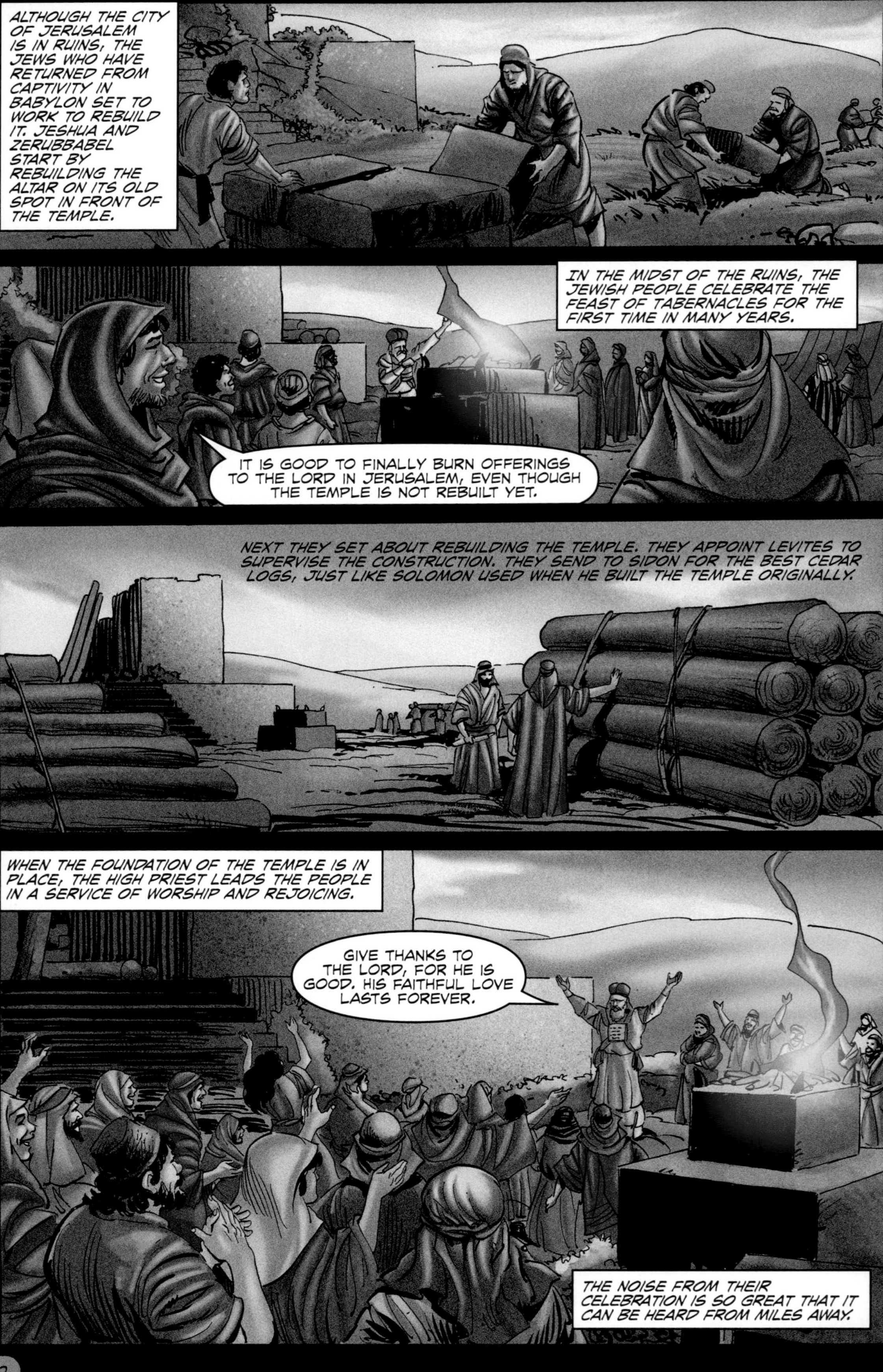
ALTHOUGH THE CITY OF JERUSALEM IS IN RUINS, THE JEWS WHO HAVE RETURNED FROM CAPTIVITY IN BABYLON SET TO WORK TO REBUILD IT. JESHUA AND ZERUBBABEL START BY REBUILDING THE ALTAR ON ITS OLD SPOT IN FRONT OF THE TEMPLE.
IN THE MIDST OF THE RUINS, THE JEWISH PEOPLE CELEBRATE THE FEAST OF TABERNACLES FOR THE FIRST TIME IN MANY YEARS.
IT IS GOOD TO FINALLY BURN OFFERINGS TO THE LORD IN JERUSALEM, EVEN THOUGH THE TEMPLE IS NOT REBUILT YET.
NEXT THEY SET ABOUT REBUILDING THE TEMPLE. THEY APPOINT LEVITES TO SUPERVISE THE CONSTRUCTION. THEY SEND TO SIDON FOR THE BEST CEDAR LOGS, JUST LIKE SOLOMON USED WHEN HE BUILT THE TEMPLE ORIGINALLY.
WHEN THE FOUNDATION OF THE TEMPLE IS IN PLACE, THE HIGH PRIEST LEADS THE PEOPLE IN A SERVICE OF WORSHIP AND REJOICING.
GIVE THANKS TO THE LORD, FOR HE IS GOOD. HIS FAITHFUL LOVE LASTS FOREVER.
THE NOISE FROM THEIR CELEBRATION IS SO GREAT THAT IT CAN BE HEARD FROM MILES AWAY.

Temple Troubles

BASED ON EZRA 4—6;
HAGGAI; ZECHARIAH

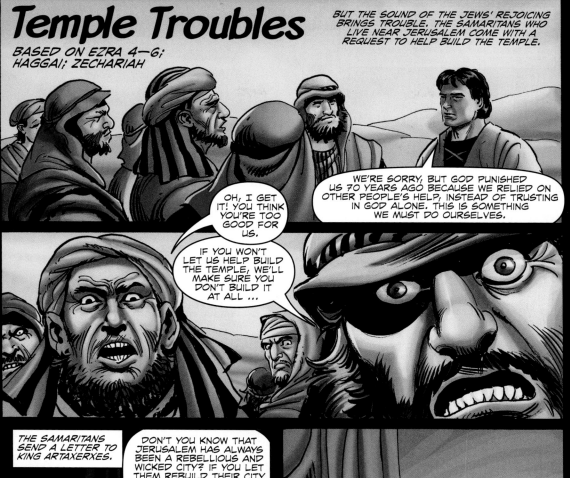

BUT THE SOUND OF THE JEWS' REJOICING BRINGS TROUBLE. THE SAMARITANS WHO LIVE NEAR JERUSALEM COME WITH A REQUEST TO HELP BUILD THE TEMPLE.

WE'RE SORRY, BUT GOD PUNISHED US 70 YEARS AGO BECAUSE WE RELIED ON OTHER PEOPLE'S HELP, INSTEAD OF TRUSTING IN GOD ALONE. THIS IS SOMETHING WE MUST DO OURSELVES.

OH, I GET IT! YOU THINK YOU'RE TOO GOOD FOR US.

IF YOU WON'T LET US HELP BUILD THE TEMPLE, WE'LL MAKE SURE YOU DON'T BUILD IT AT ALL ...

THE SAMARITANS SEND A LETTER TO KING ARTAXERXES.

DON'T YOU KNOW THAT JERUSALEM HAS ALWAYS BEEN A REBELLIOUS AND WICKED CITY? IF YOU LET THEM REBUILD THEIR CITY AND THEIR TEMPLE, THEY WILL EVENTUALLY REVOLT AGAINST YOU AND MAKE YOU LOOK WEAK.

CHECK THE HISTORY SCROLLS.

IT'S TRUE, SIRE. JERUSALEM HAS ALWAYS REBELLED AGAINST THE POWERFUL EMPIRES.

ORDER THEM TO STOP REBUILDING IMMEDIATELY! I WILL NOT LET THIS THREAT RISE FROM THE ASHES.

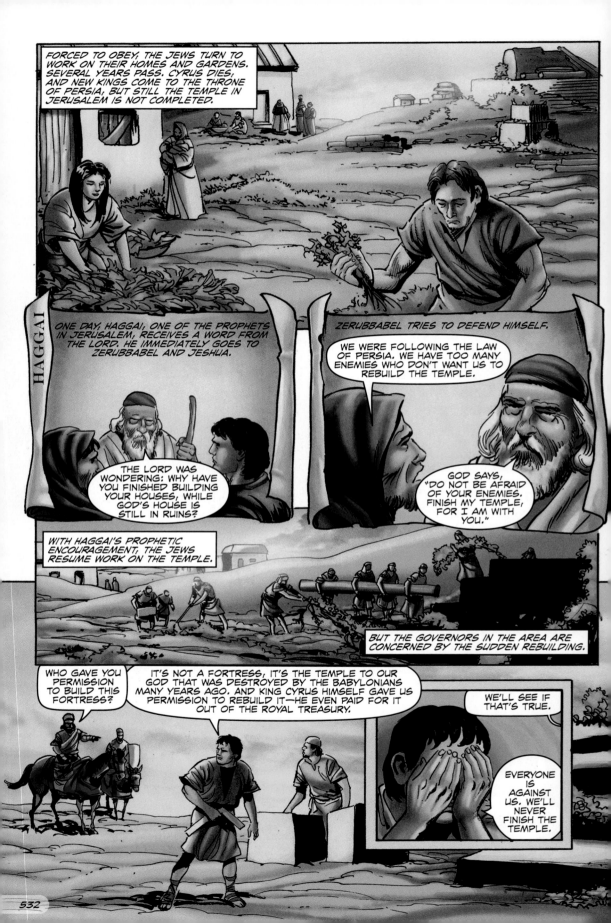

FORCED TO OBEY, THE JEWS TURN TO WORK ON THEIR HOMES AND GARDENS. SEVERAL YEARS PASS. CYRUS DIES, AND NEW KINGS COME TO THE THRONE OF PERSIA, BUT STILL THE TEMPLE IN JERUSALEM IS NOT COMPLETED.

HAGGAI

ONE DAY, HAGGAI, ONE OF THE PROPHETS IN JERUSALEM, RECEIVES A WORD FROM THE LORD. HE IMMEDIATELY GOES TO ZERUBBABEL AND JESHUA.

THE LORD WAS WONDERING: WHY HAVE YOU FINISHED BUILDING YOUR HOUSES, WHILE GOD'S HOUSE IS STILL IN RUINS?

ZERUBBABEL TRIES TO DEFEND HIMSELF.

WE WERE FOLLOWING THE LAW OF PERSIA. WE HAVE TOO MANY ENEMIES WHO DON'T WANT US TO REBUILD THE TEMPLE.

GOD SAYS, "DO NOT BE AFRAID OF YOUR ENEMIES. FINISH MY TEMPLE, FOR I AM WITH YOU."

WITH HAGGAI'S PROPHETIC ENCOURAGEMENT, THE JEWS RESUME WORK ON THE TEMPLE.

BUT THE GOVERNORS IN THE AREA ARE CONCERNED BY THE SUDDEN REBUILDING.

WHO GAVE YOU PERMISSION TO BUILD THIS FORTRESS?

IT'S NOT A FORTRESS, IT'S THE TEMPLE TO OUR GOD THAT WAS DESTROYED BY THE BABYLONIANS MANY YEARS AGO. AND KING CYRUS HIMSELF GAVE US PERMISSION TO REBUILD IT—HE EVEN PAID FOR IT OUT OF THE ROYAL TREASURY.

WE'LL SEE IF THAT'S TRUE.

EVERYONE IS AGAINST US. WE'LL NEVER FINISH THE TEMPLE.

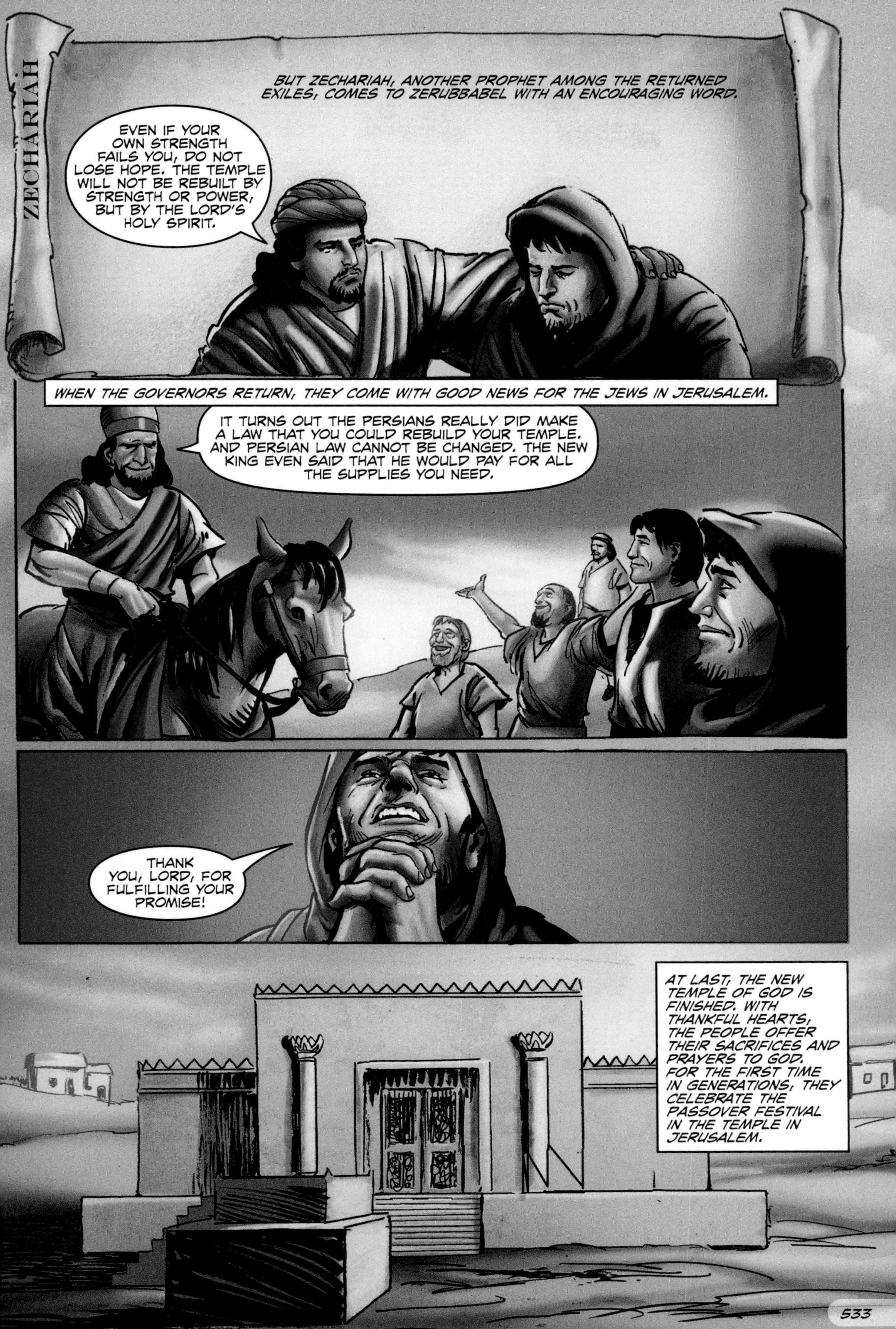
ZECHARIAH
BUT ZECHARIAH, ANOTHER PROPHET AMONG THE RETURNED EXILES, COMES TO ZERUBBABEL WITH AN ENCOURAGING WORD.
EVEN IF YOUR OWN STRENGTH FAILS YOU, DO NOT LOSE HOPE. THE TEMPLE WILL NOT BE REBUILT BY STRENGTH OR POWER, BUT BY THE LORD'S HOLY SPIRIT.
WHEN THE GOVERNORS RETURN, THEY COME WITH GOOD NEWS FOR THE JEWS IN JERUSALEM.
IT TURNS OUT THE PERSIANS REALLY DID MAKE A LAW THAT YOU COULD REBUILD YOUR TEMPLE. AND PERSIAN LAW CANNOT BE CHANGED. THE NEW KING EVEN SAID THAT HE WOULD PAY FOR ALL THE SUPPLIES YOU NEED.
THANK YOU, LORD, FOR FULFILLING YOUR PROMISE!
AT LAST, THE NEW TEMPLE OF GOD IS FINISHED. WITH THANKFUL HEARTS, THE PEOPLE OFFER THEIR SACRIFICES AND PRAYERS TO GOD. FOR THE FIRST TIME IN GENERATIONS, THEY CELEBRATE THE PASSOVER FESTIVAL IN THE TEMPLE IN JERUSALEM.

Enter Ezra

BASED ON EZRA 7—10

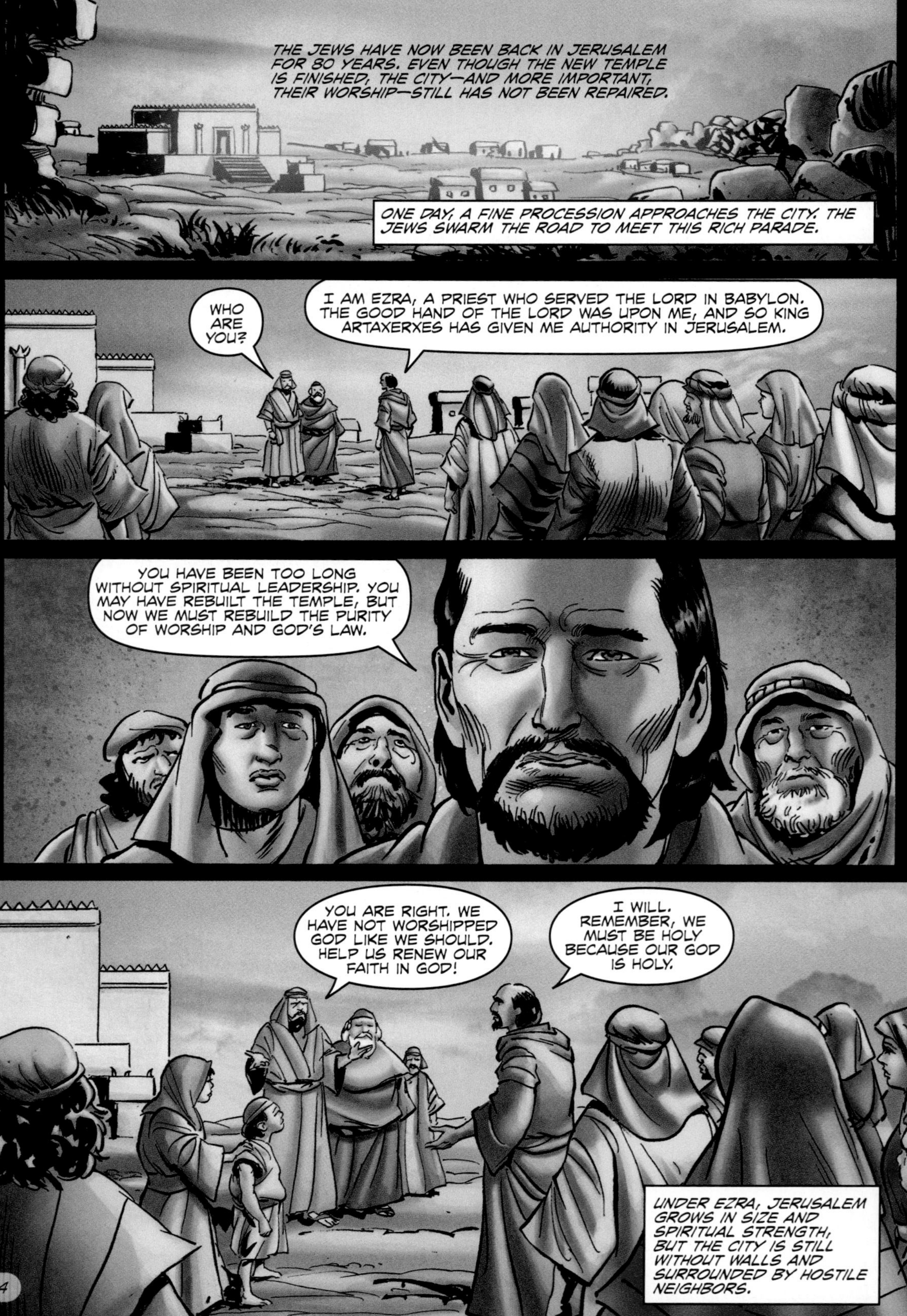
THE JEWS HAVE NOW BEEN BACK IN JERUSALEM FOR 80 YEARS. EVEN THOUGH THE NEW TEMPLE IS FINISHED, THE CITY—AND MORE IMPORTANT, THEIR WORSHIP—STILL HAS NOT BEEN REPAIRED.
ONE DAY, A FINE PROCESSION APPROACHES THE CITY. THE JEWS SWARM THE ROAD TO MEET THIS RICH PARADE.
WHO ARE YOU?
I AM EZRA, A PRIEST WHO SERVED THE LORD IN BABYLON. THE GOOD HAND OF THE LORD WAS UPON ME, AND SO KING ARTAXERXES HAS GIVEN ME AUTHORITY IN JERUSALEM.
YOU HAVE BEEN TOO LONG WITHOUT SPIRITUAL LEADERSHIP. YOU MAY HAVE REBUILT THE TEMPLE, BUT NOW WE MUST REBUILD THE PURITY OF WORSHIP AND GOD'S LAW.
YOU ARE RIGHT. WE HAVE NOT WORSHIPPED GOD LIKE WE SHOULD. HELP US RENEW OUR FAITH IN GOD!
I WILL. REMEMBER, WE MUST BE HOLY BECAUSE OUR GOD IS HOLY.
UNDER EZRA, JERUSALEM GROWS IN SIZE AND SPIRITUAL STRENGTH, BUT THE CITY IS STILL WITHOUT WALLS AND SURROUNDED BY HOSTILE NEIGHBORS.

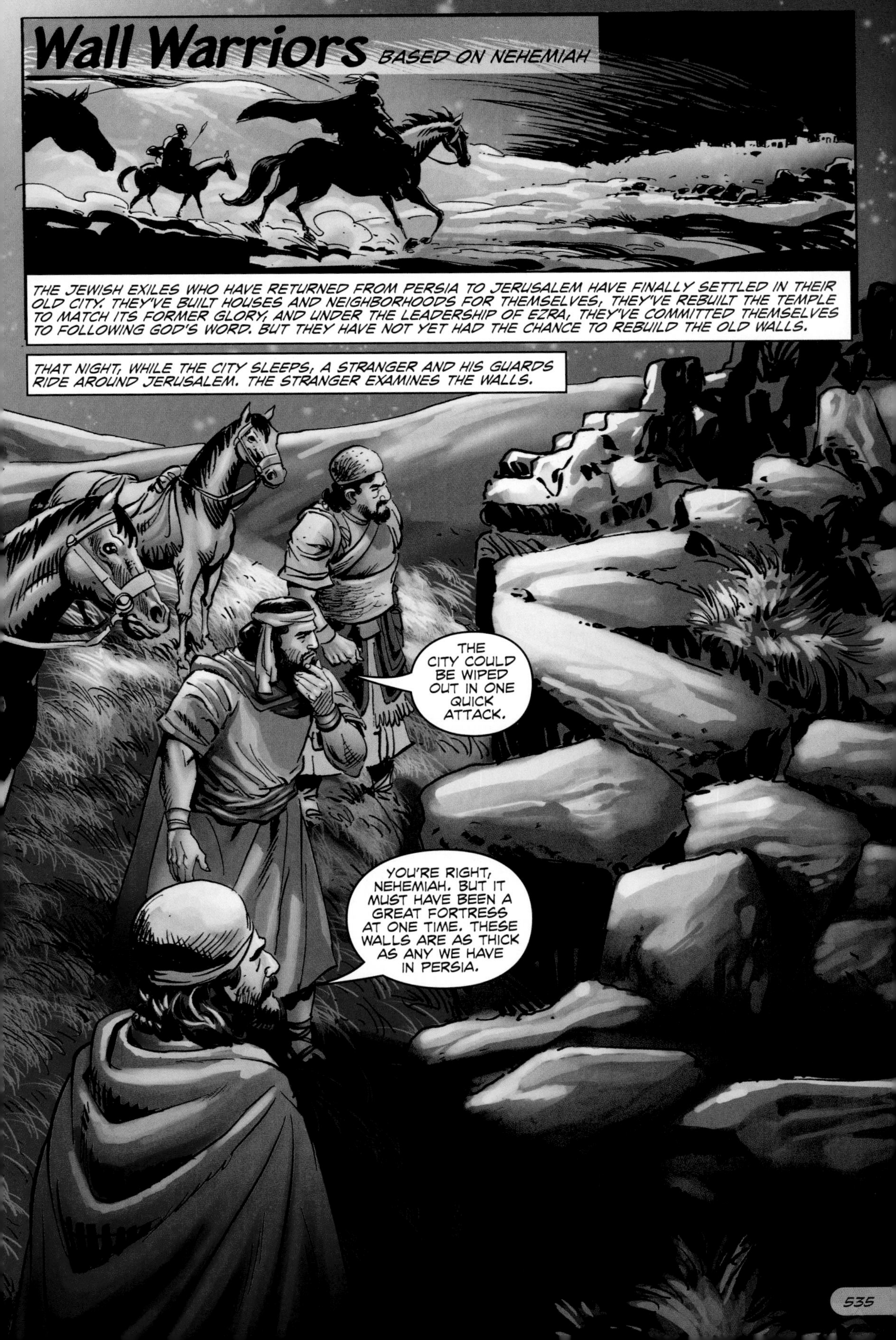
Wall Warriors BASED ON NEHEMIAH
THE JEWISH EXILES WHO HAVE RETURNED FROM PERSIA TO JERUSALEM HAVE FINALLY SETTLED IN THEIR OLD CITY. THEY'VE BUILT HOUSES AND NEIGHBORHOODS FOR THEMSELVES, THEY'VE REBUILT THE TEMPLE TO MATCH ITS FORMER GLORY, AND UNDER THE LEADERSHIP OF EZRA, THEY'VE COMMITTED THEMSELVES TO FOLLOWING GOD'S WORD. BUT THEY HAVE NOT YET HAD THE CHANCE TO REBUILD THE OLD WALLS.
THAT NIGHT, WHILE THE CITY SLEEPS, A STRANGER AND HIS GUARDS RIDE AROUND JERUSALEM. THE STRANGER EXAMINES THE WALLS.
THE CITY COULD BE WIPED OUT IN ONE QUICK ATTACK.
YOU'RE RIGHT, NEHEMIAH. BUT IT MUST HAVE BEEN A GREAT FORTRESS AT ONE TIME. THESE WALLS ARE AS THICK AS ANY WE HAVE IN PERSIA.

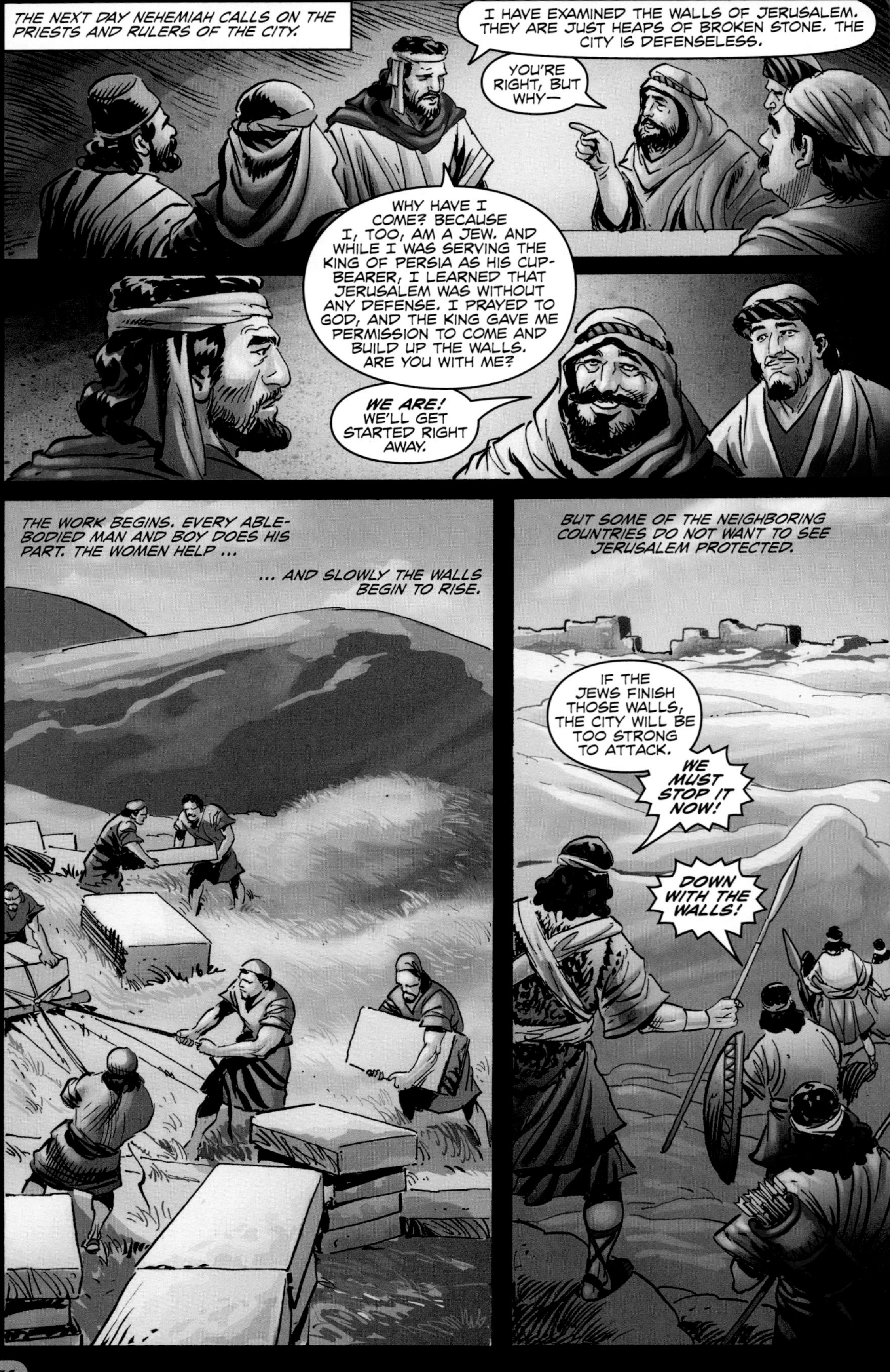
THE NEXT DAY NEHEMIAH CALLS ON THE PRIESTS AND RULERS OF THE CITY.
I HAVE EXAMINED THE WALLS OF JERUSALEM. THEY ARE JUST HEAPS OF BROKEN STONE. THE CITY IS DEFENSELESS.
YOU'RE RIGHT, BUT WHY—
WHY HAVE I COME? BECAUSE I, TOO, AM A JEW. AND WHILE I WAS SERVING THE KING OF PERSIA AS HIS CUP-BEARER, I LEARNED THAT JERUSALEM WAS WITHOUT ANY DEFENSE. I PRAYED TO GOD, AND THE KING GAVE ME PERMISSION TO COME AND BUILD UP THE WALLS. ARE YOU WITH ME?
WE ARE! WE'LL GET STARTED RIGHT AWAY.
THE WORK BEGINS. EVERY ABLE-BODIED MAN AND BOY DOES HIS PART. THE WOMEN HELP ...
... AND SLOWLY THE WALLS BEGIN TO RISE.
BUT SOME OF THE NEIGHBORING COUNTRIES DO NOT WANT TO SEE JERUSALEM PROTECTED.
IF THE JEWS FINISH THOSE WALLS, THE CITY WILL BE TOO STRONG TO ATTACK.
WE MUST STOP IT NOW!
DOWN WITH THE WALLS!

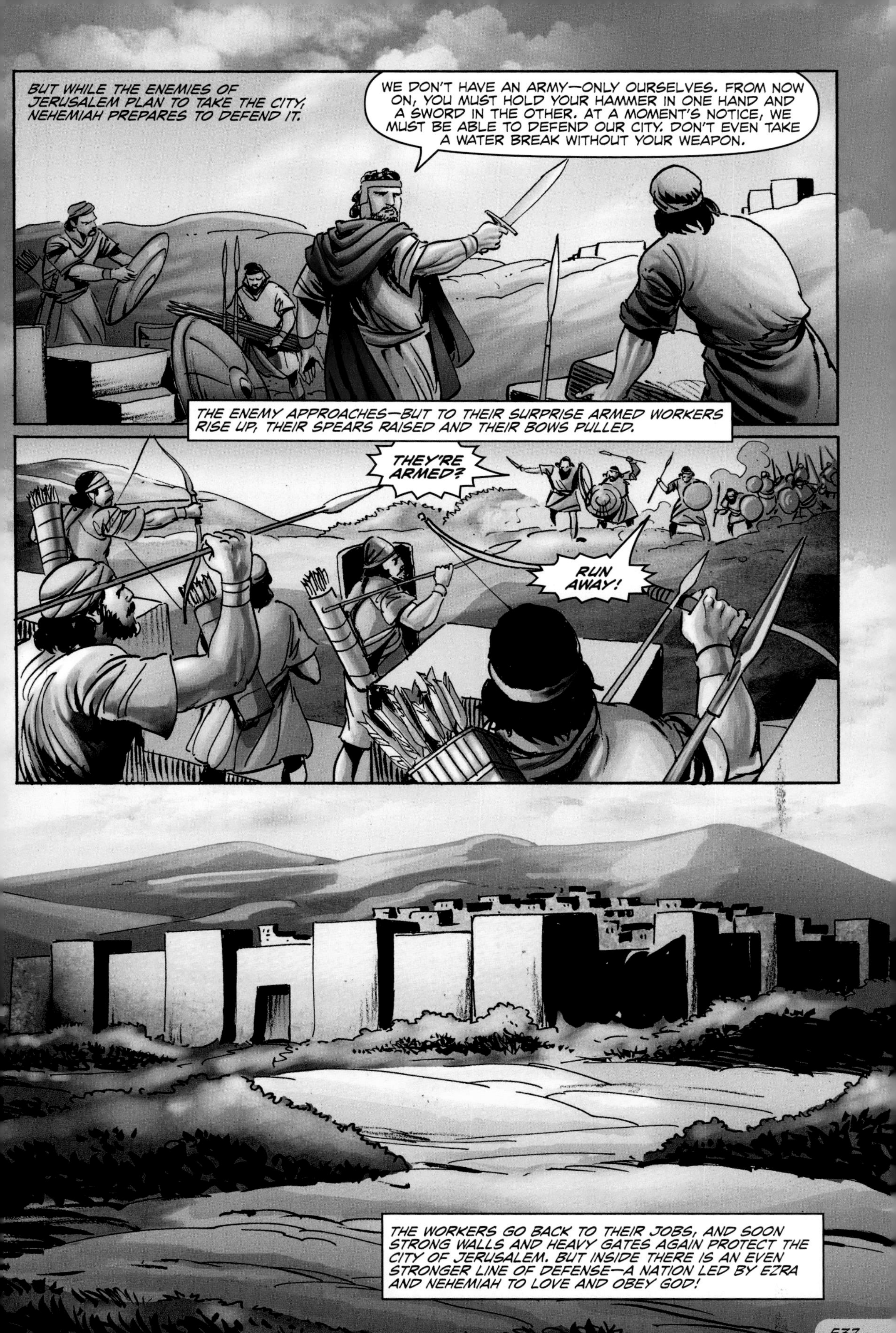
BUT WHILE THE ENEMIES OF JERUSALEM PLAN TO TAKE THE CITY, NEHEMIAH PREPARES TO DEFEND IT.
WE DON'T HAVE AN ARMY—ONLY OURSELVES. FROM NOW ON, YOU MUST HOLD YOUR HAMMER IN ONE HAND AND A SWORD IN THE OTHER. AT A MOMENT'S NOTICE, WE MUST BE ABLE TO DEFEND OUR CITY. DON'T EVEN TAKE A WATER BREAK WITHOUT YOUR WEAPON.
THE ENEMY APPROACHES—BUT TO THEIR SURPRISE ARMED WORKERS RISE UP, THEIR SPEARS RAISED AND THEIR BOWS PULLED.
THEY'RE ARMED?
RUN AWAY!
THE WORKERS GO BACK TO THEIR JOBS, AND SOON STRONG WALLS AND HEAVY GATES AGAIN PROTECT THE CITY OF JERUSALEM. BUT INSIDE THERE IS AN EVEN STRONGER LINE OF DEFENSE—A NATION LED BY EZRA AND NEHEMIAH TO LOVE AND OBEY GOD!

Women of the Old Testament

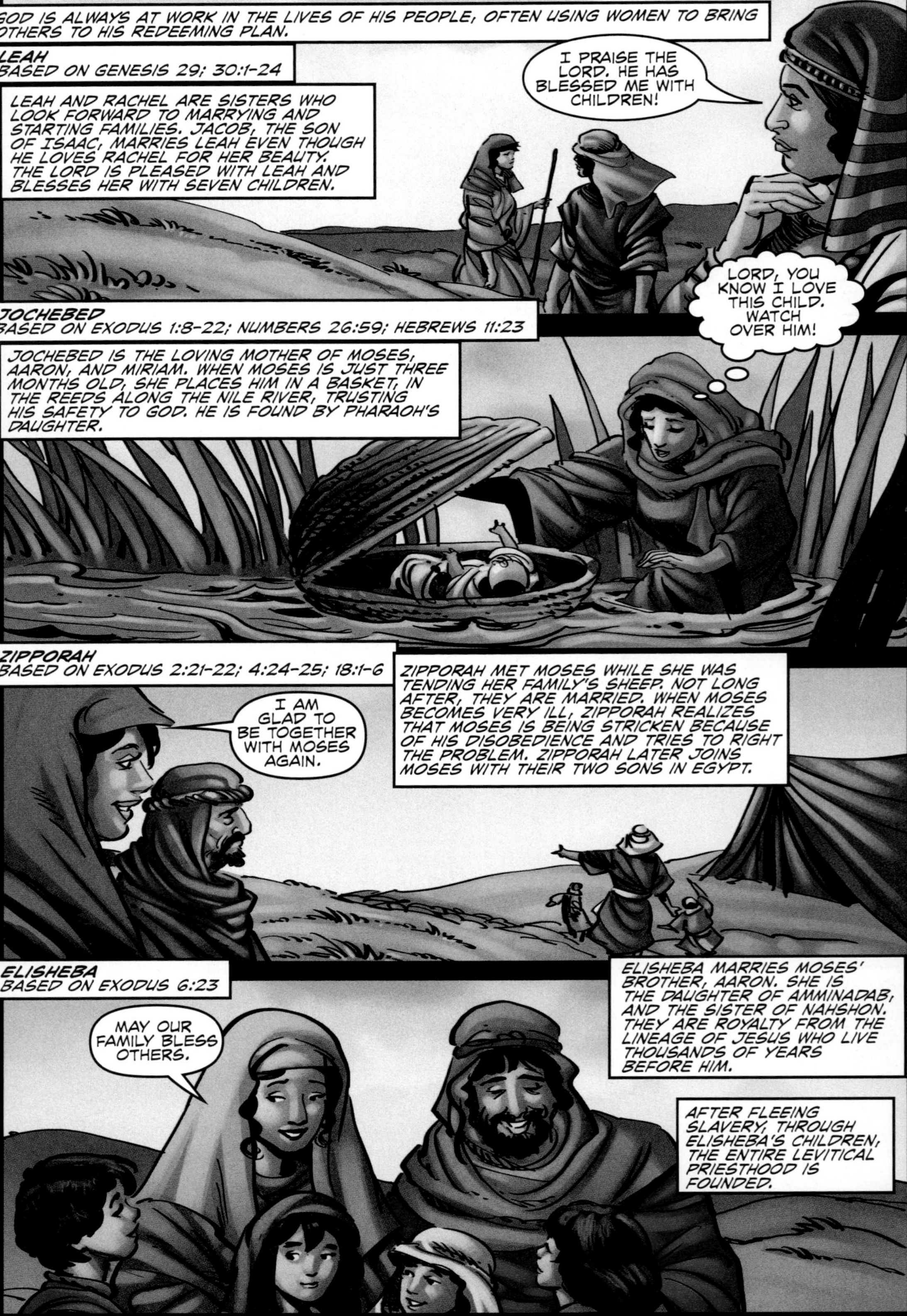

GOD IS ALWAYS AT WORK IN THE LIVES OF HIS PEOPLE, OFTEN USING WOMEN TO BRING OTHERS TO HIS REDEEMING PLAN.
LEAH
BASED ON GENESIS 29; 30:1-24
LEAH AND RACHEL ARE SISTERS WHO LOOK FORWARD TO MARRYING AND STARTING FAMILIES. JACOB, THE SON OF ISAAC, MARRIES LEAH EVEN THOUGH HE LOVES RACHEL FOR HER BEAUTY. THE LORD IS PLEASED WITH LEAH AND BLESSES HER WITH SEVEN CHILDREN.
I PRAISE THE LORD. HE HAS BLESSED ME WITH CHILDREN!
JOCHEBED
BASED ON EXODUS 1:8-22; NUMBERS 26:59; HEBREWS 11:23
JOCHEBED IS THE LOVING MOTHER OF MOSES, AARON, AND MIRIAM. WHEN MOSES IS JUST THREE MONTHS OLD, SHE PLACES HIM IN A BASKET, IN THE REEDS ALONG THE NILE RIVER, TRUSTING HIS SAFETY TO GOD. HE IS FOUND BY PHARAOH'S DAUGHTER.
LORD, YOU KNOW I LOVE THIS CHILD. WATCH OVER HIM!
ZIPPORAH
BASED ON EXODUS 2:21-22; 4:24-25; 18:1-6
ZIPPORAH MET MOSES WHILE SHE WAS TENDING HER FAMILY'S SHEEP. NOT LONG AFTER, THEY ARE MARRIED. WHEN MOSES BECOMES VERY ILL, ZIPPORAH REALIZES THAT MOSES IS BEING STRICKEN BECAUSE OF HIS DISOBEDIENCE AND TRIES TO RIGHT THE PROBLEM. ZIPPORAH LATER JOINS MOSES WITH THEIR TWO SONS IN EGYPT.
I AM GLAD TO BE TOGETHER WITH MOSES AGAIN.
ELISHEBA
BASED ON EXODUS 6:23
ELISHEBA MARRIES MOSES' BROTHER, AARON. SHE IS THE DAUGHTER OF AMMINADAB, AND THE SISTER OF NAHSHON. THEY ARE ROYALTY FROM THE LINEAGE OF JESUS WHO LIVE THOUSANDS OF YEARS BEFORE HIM.
MAY OUR FAMILY BLESS OTHERS.
AFTER FLEEING SLAVERY, THROUGH ELISHEBA'S CHILDREN, THE ENTIRE LEVITICAL PRIESTHOOD IS FOUNDED.

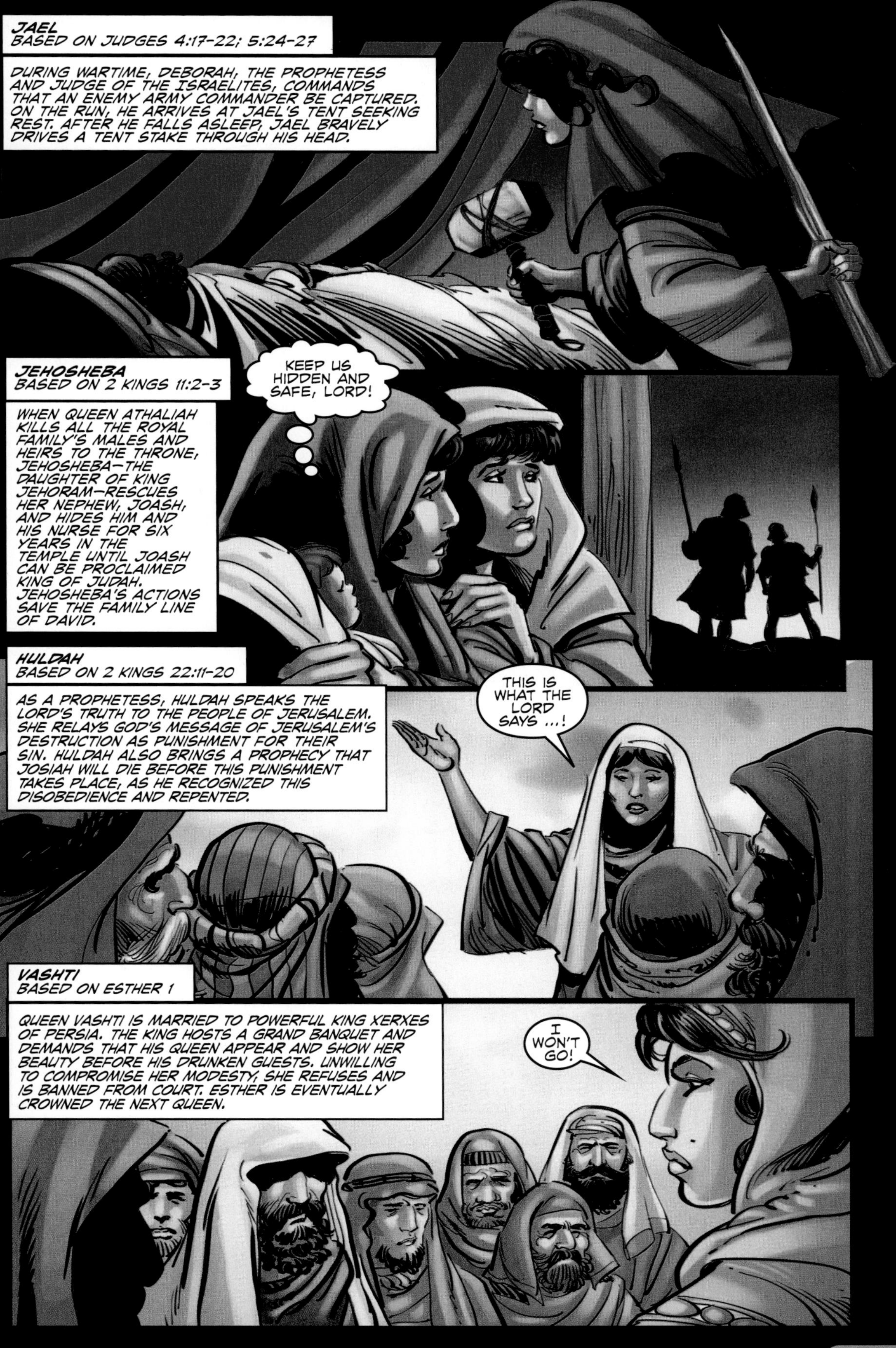
JAEL
BASED ON JUDGES 4:17-22; 5:24-27
DURING WARTIME, DEBORAH, THE PROPHETESS AND JUDGE OF THE ISRAELITES, COMMANDS THAT AN ENEMY ARMY COMMANDER BE CAPTURED. ON THE RUN, HE ARRIVES AT JAEL'S TENT SEEKING REST. AFTER HE FALLS ASLEEP, JAEL BRAVELY DRIVES A TENT STAKE THROUGH HIS HEAD.
JEHOSHEBA
BASED ON 2 KINGS 11:2-3
WHEN QUEEN ATHALIAH KILLS ALL THE ROYAL FAMILY'S MALES AND HEIRS TO THE THRONE, JEHOSHEBA—THE DAUGHTER OF KING JEHORAM—RESCUES HER NEPHEW, JOASH, AND HIDES HIM AND HIS NURSE FOR SIX YEARS IN THE TEMPLE UNTIL JOASH CAN BE PROCLAIMED KING OF JUDAH. JEHOSHEBA'S ACTIONS SAVE THE FAMILY LINE OF DAVID.
KEEP US HIDDEN AND SAFE, LORD!
HULDAH
BASED ON 2 KINGS 22:11-20
AS A PROPHETESS, HULDAH SPEAKS THE LORD'S TRUTH TO THE PEOPLE OF JERUSALEM. SHE RELAYS GOD'S MESSAGE OF JERUSALEM'S DESTRUCTION AS PUNISHMENT FOR THEIR SIN. HULDAH ALSO BRINGS A PROPHECY THAT JOSIAH WILL DIE BEFORE THIS PUNISHMENT TAKES PLACE, AS HE RECOGNIZED THIS DISOBEDIENCE AND REPENTED.
THIS IS WHAT THE LORD SAYS ...!
VASHTI
BASED ON ESTHER 1
QUEEN VASHTI IS MARRIED TO POWERFUL KING XERXES OF PERSIA. THE KING HOSTS A GRAND BANQUET AND DEMANDS THAT HIS QUEEN APPEAR AND SHOW HER BEAUTY BEFORE HIS DRUNKEN GUESTS. UNWILLING TO COMPROMISE HER MODESTY, SHE REFUSES AND IS BANNED FROM COURT. ESTHER IS EVENTUALLY CROWNED THE NEXT QUEEN.
I WON'T GO!

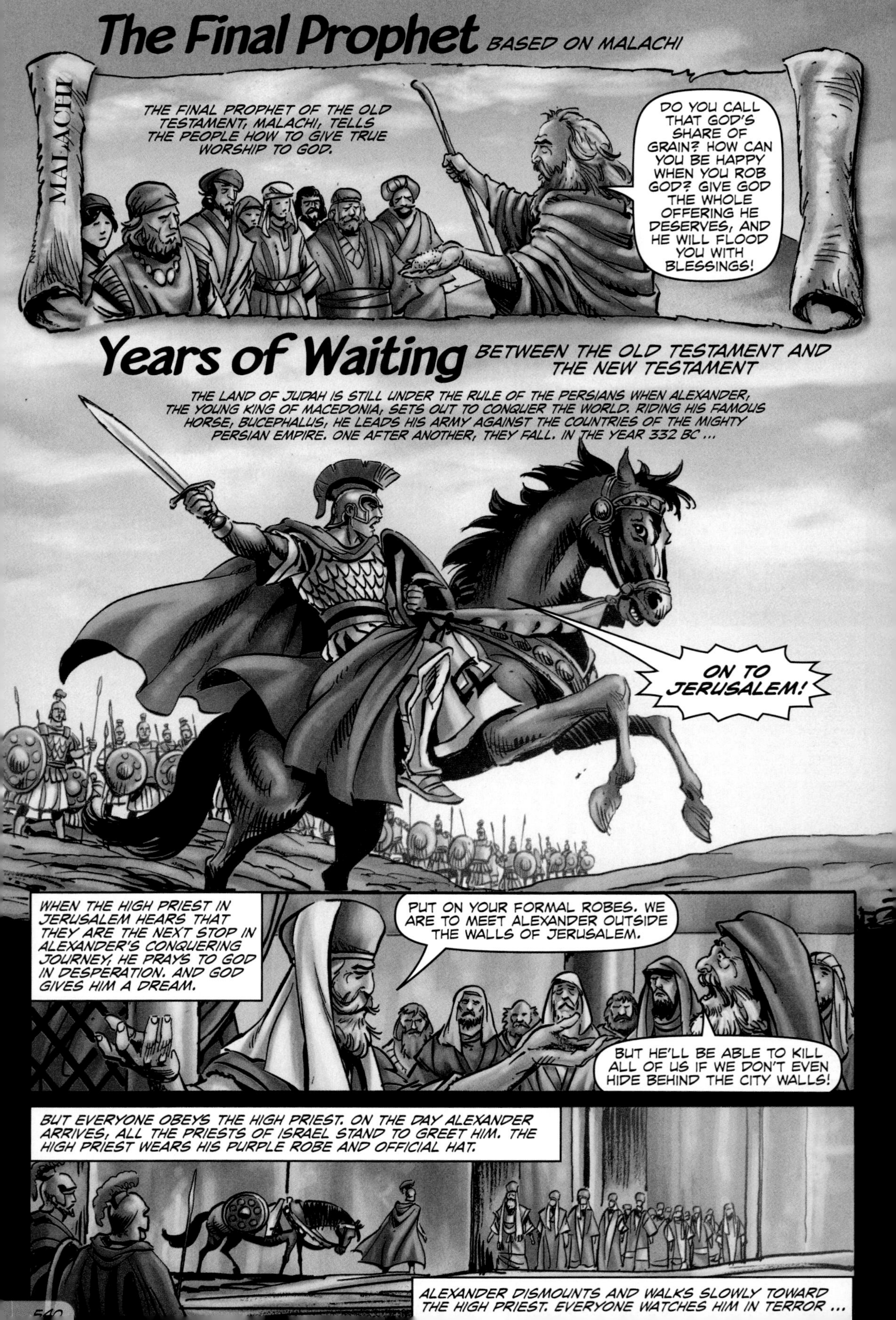

The Final Prophet
BASED ON MALACHI
MALACHI
THE FINAL PROPHET OF THE OLD TESTAMENT, MALACHI, TELLS THE PEOPLE HOW TO GIVE TRUE WORSHIP TO GOD.
DO YOU CALL THAT GOD'S SHARE OF GRAIN? HOW CAN YOU BE HAPPY WHEN YOU ROB GOD? GIVE GOD THE WHOLE OFFERING HE DESERVES, AND HE WILL FLOOD YOU WITH BLESSINGS!
Years of Waiting
BETWEEN THE OLD TESTAMENT AND THE NEW TESTAMENT
THE LAND OF JUDAH IS STILL UNDER THE RULE OF THE PERSIANS WHEN ALEXANDER, THE YOUNG KING OF MACEDONIA, SETS OUT TO CONQUER THE WORLD. RIDING HIS FAMOUS HORSE, BUCEPHALUS, HE LEADS HIS ARMY AGAINST THE COUNTRIES OF THE MIGHTY PERSIAN EMPIRE. ONE AFTER ANOTHER, THEY FALL. IN THE YEAR 332 BC ...
ON TO JERUSALEM!
WHEN THE HIGH PRIEST IN JERUSALEM HEARS THAT THEY ARE THE NEXT STOP IN ALEXANDER'S CONQUERING JOURNEY, HE PRAYS TO GOD IN DESPERATION. AND GOD GIVES HIM A DREAM.
PUT ON YOUR FORMAL ROBES. WE ARE TO MEET ALEXANDER OUTSIDE THE WALLS OF JERUSALEM.
BUT HE'LL BE ABLE TO KILL ALL OF US IF WE DON'T EVEN HIDE BEHIND THE CITY WALLS!
BUT EVERYONE OBEYS THE HIGH PRIEST. ON THE DAY ALEXANDER ARRIVES, ALL THE PRIESTS OF ISRAEL STAND TO GREET HIM. THE HIGH PRIEST WEARS HIS PURPLE ROBE AND OFFICIAL HAT.
ALEXANDER DISMOUNTS AND WALKS SLOWLY TOWARD THE HIGH PRIEST. EVERYONE WATCHES HIM IN TERROR ...

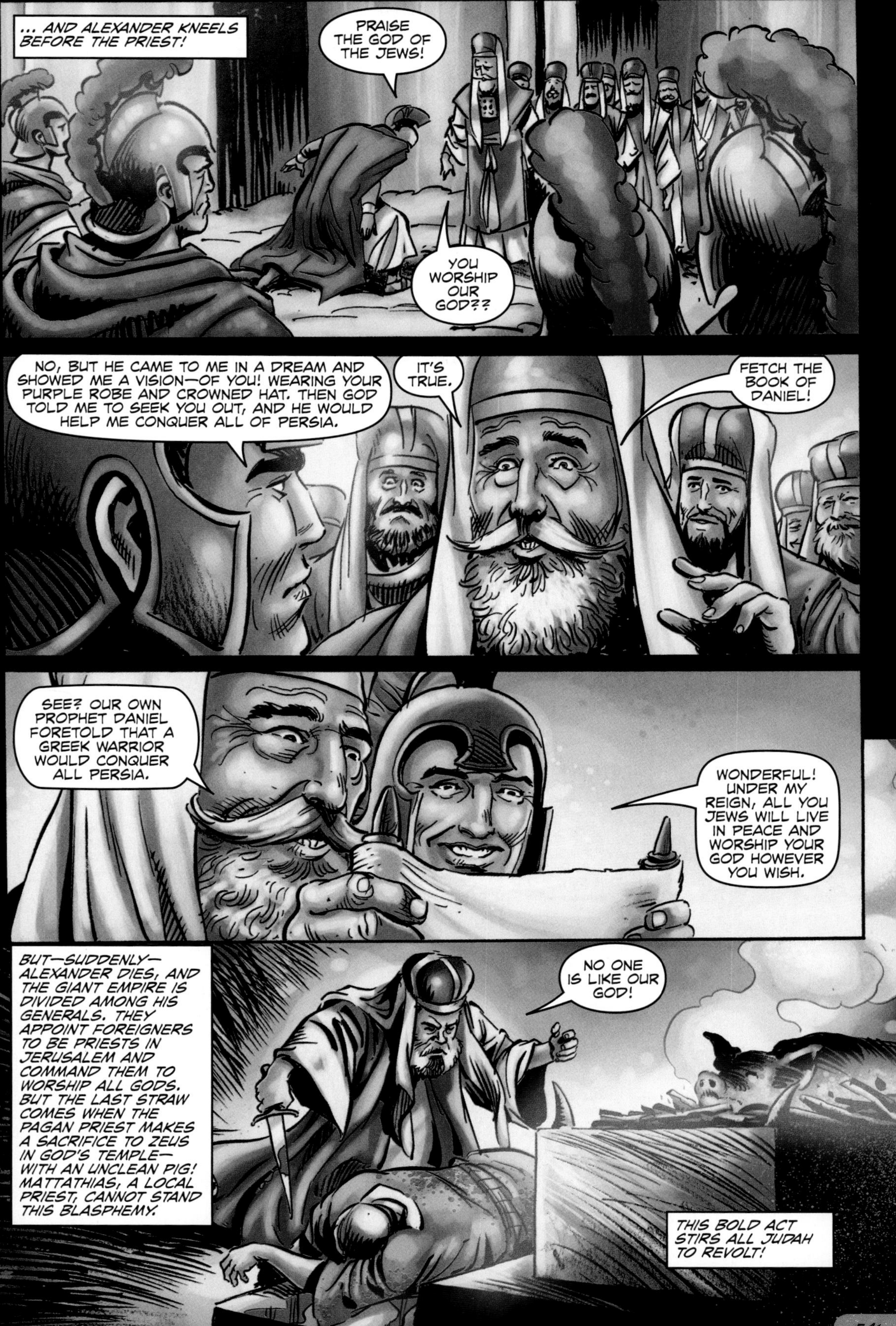
... AND ALEXANDER KNEELS BEFORE THE PRIEST!
PRAISE THE GOD OF THE JEWS!
YOU WORSHIP OUR GOD??
NO, BUT HE CAME TO ME IN A DREAM AND SHOWED ME A VISION—OF YOU! WEARING YOUR PURPLE ROBE AND CROWNED HAT. THEN GOD TOLD ME TO SEEK YOU OUT, AND HE WOULD HELP ME CONQUER ALL OF PERSIA.
IT'S TRUE.
FETCH THE BOOK OF DANIEL!
SEE? OUR OWN PROPHET DANIEL FORETOLD THAT A GREEK WARRIOR WOULD CONQUER ALL PERSIA.
WONDERFUL! UNDER MY REIGN, ALL YOU JEWS WILL LIVE IN PEACE AND WORSHIP YOUR GOD HOWEVER YOU WISH.
BUT—SUDDENLY—ALEXANDER DIES, AND THE GIANT EMPIRE IS DIVIDED AMONG HIS GENERALS. THEY APPOINT FOREIGNERS TO BE PRIESTS IN JERUSALEM AND COMMAND THEM TO WORSHIP ALL GODS. BUT THE LAST STRAW COMES WHEN THE PAGAN PRIEST MAKES A SACRIFICE TO ZEUS IN GOD'S TEMPLE—WITH AN UNCLEAN PIG! MATTATHIAS, A LOCAL PRIEST, CANNOT STAND THIS BLASPHEMY.
NO ONE IS LIKE OUR GOD!
THIS BOLD ACT STIRS ALL JUDAH TO REVOLT!

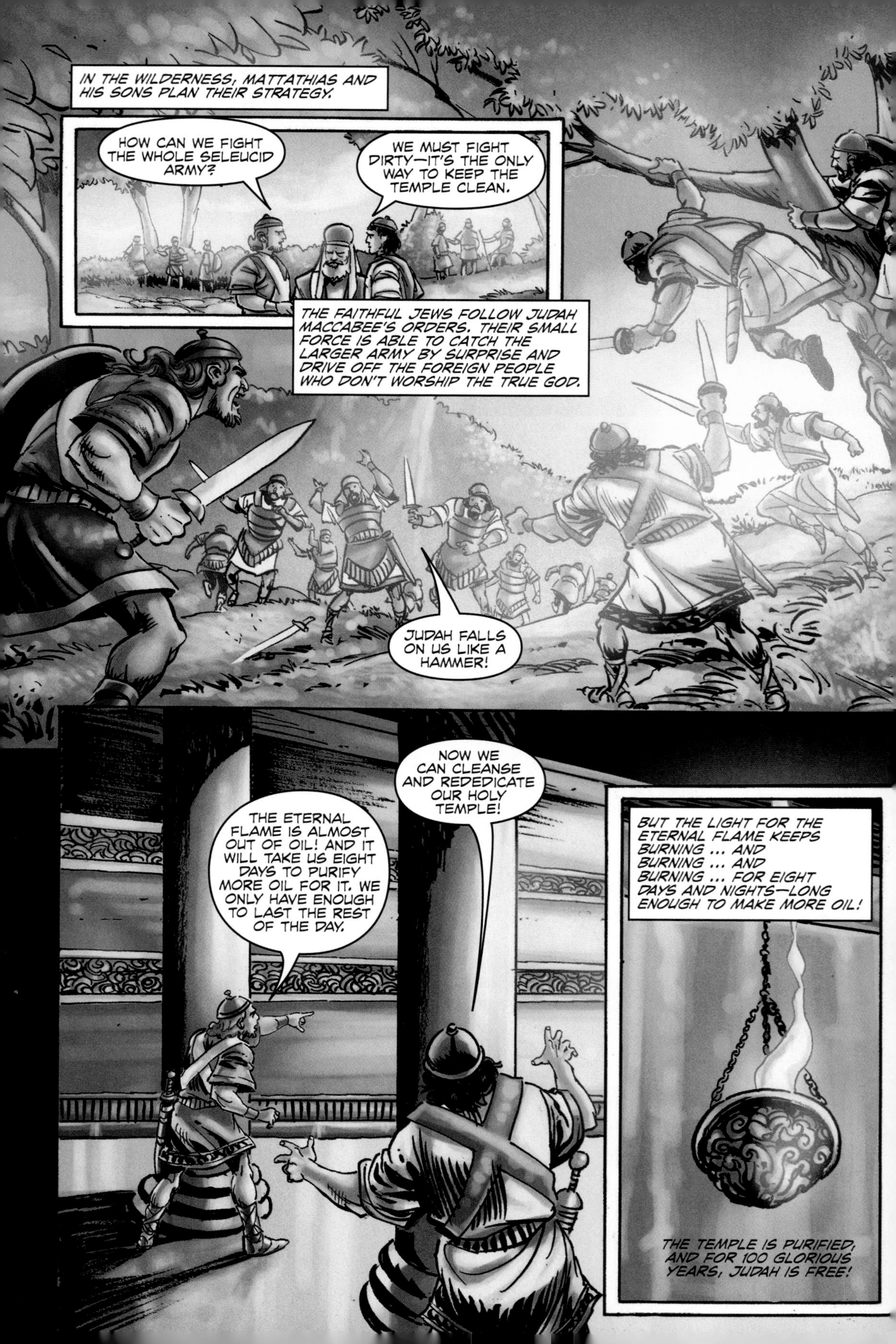
IN THE WILDERNESS, MATTATHIAS AND HIS SONS PLAN THEIR STRATEGY.
HOW CAN WE FIGHT THE WHOLE SELEUCID ARMY?
WE MUST FIGHT DIRTY—IT'S THE ONLY WAY TO KEEP THE TEMPLE CLEAN.
THE FAITHFUL JEWS FOLLOW JUDAH MACCABEE'S ORDERS. THEIR SMALL FORCE IS ABLE TO CATCH THE LARGER ARMY BY SURPRISE AND DRIVE OFF THE FOREIGN PEOPLE WHO DON'T WORSHIP THE TRUE GOD.
JUDAH FALLS ON US LIKE A HAMMER!
NOW WE CAN CLEANSE AND REDEDICATE OUR HOLY TEMPLE!
THE ETERNAL FLAME IS ALMOST OUT OF OIL! AND IT WILL TAKE US EIGHT DAYS TO PURIFY MORE OIL FOR IT. WE ONLY HAVE ENOUGH TO LAST THE REST OF THE DAY.
BUT THE LIGHT FOR THE ETERNAL FLAME KEEPS BURNING ... AND BURNING ... AND BURNING ... FOR EIGHT DAYS AND NIGHTS—LONG ENOUGH TO MAKE MORE OIL!
THE TEMPLE IS PURIFIED, AND FOR 100 GLORIOUS YEARS, JUDAH IS FREE!

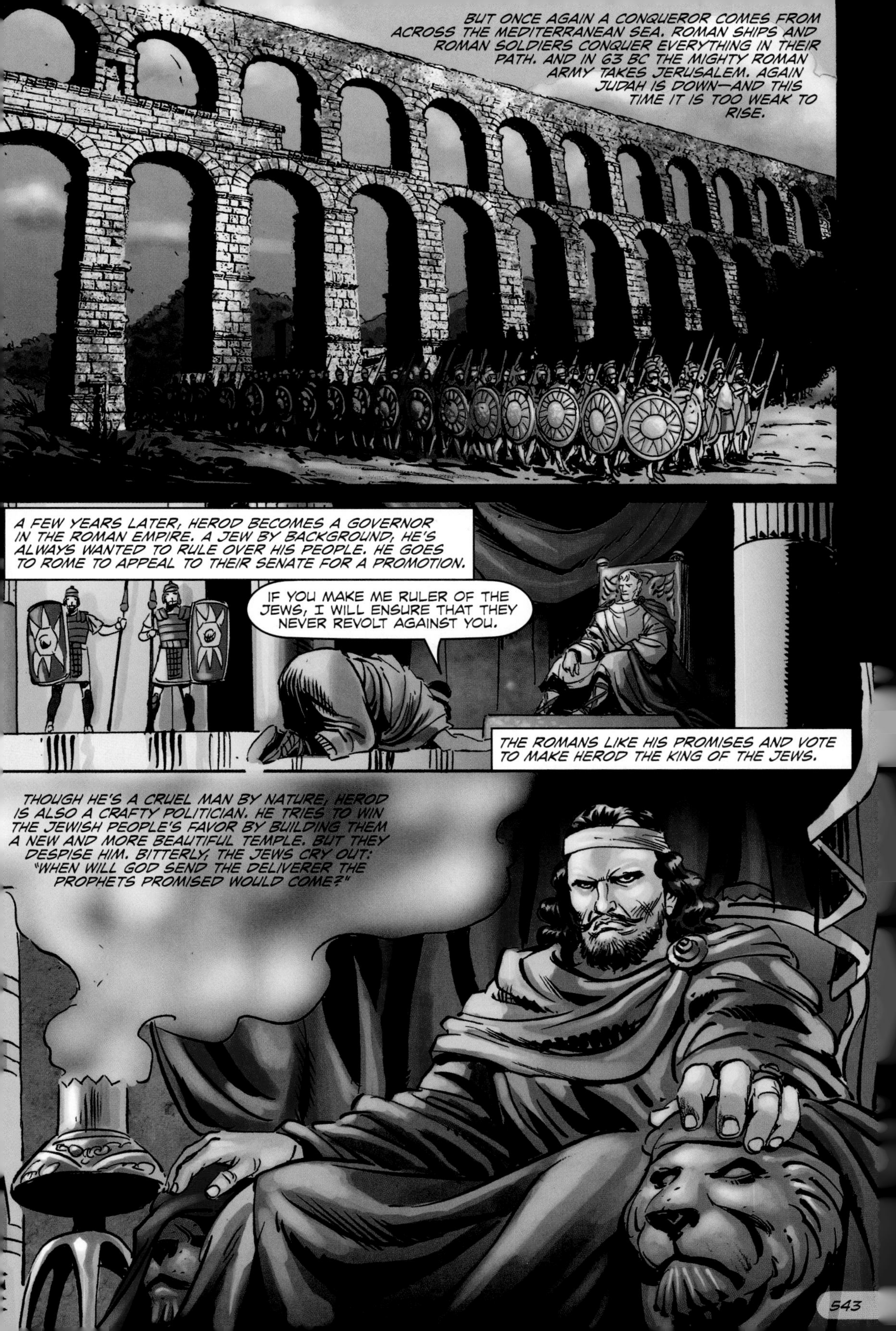

BUT ONCE AGAIN A CONQUEROR COMES FROM ACROSS THE MEDITERRANEAN SEA. ROMAN SHIPS AND ROMAN SOLDIERS CONQUER EVERYTHING IN THEIR PATH. AND IN 63 BC THE MIGHTY ROMAN ARMY TAKES JERUSALEM. AGAIN JUDAH IS DOWN—AND THIS TIME IT IS TOO WEAK TO RISE.
A FEW YEARS LATER, HEROD BECOMES A GOVERNOR IN THE ROMAN EMPIRE. A JEW BY BACKGROUND, HE'S ALWAYS WANTED TO RULE OVER HIS PEOPLE. HE GOES TO ROME TO APPEAL TO THEIR SENATE FOR A PROMOTION.
IF YOU MAKE ME RULER OF THE JEWS, I WILL ENSURE THAT THEY NEVER REVOLT AGAINST YOU.
THE ROMANS LIKE HIS PROMISES AND VOTE TO MAKE HEROD THE KING OF THE JEWS.
THOUGH HE'S A CRUEL MAN BY NATURE, HEROD IS ALSO A CRAFTY POLITICIAN. HE TRIES TO WIN THE JEWISH PEOPLE'S FAVOR BY BUILDING THEM A NEW AND MORE BEAUTIFUL TEMPLE. BUT THEY DESPISE HIM. BITTERLY, THE JEWS CRY OUT: "WHEN WILL GOD SEND THE DELIVERER THE PROPHETS PROMISED WOULD COME?"

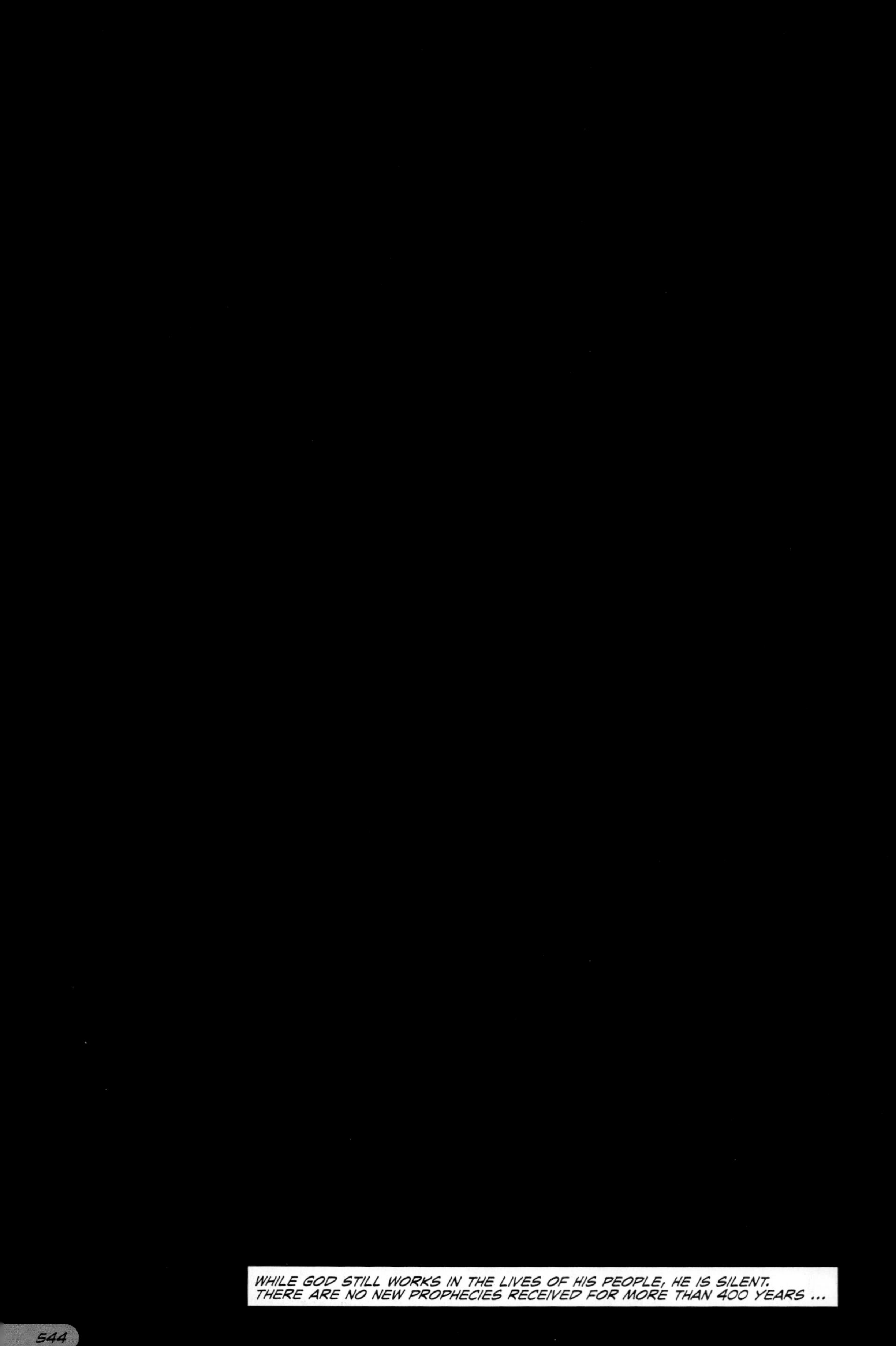
WHILE GOD STILL WORKS IN THE LIVES OF HIS PEOPLE, HE IS SILENT. THERE ARE NO NEW PROPHECIES RECEIVED FOR MORE THAN 400 YEARS ...

THE NEW TESTAMENT

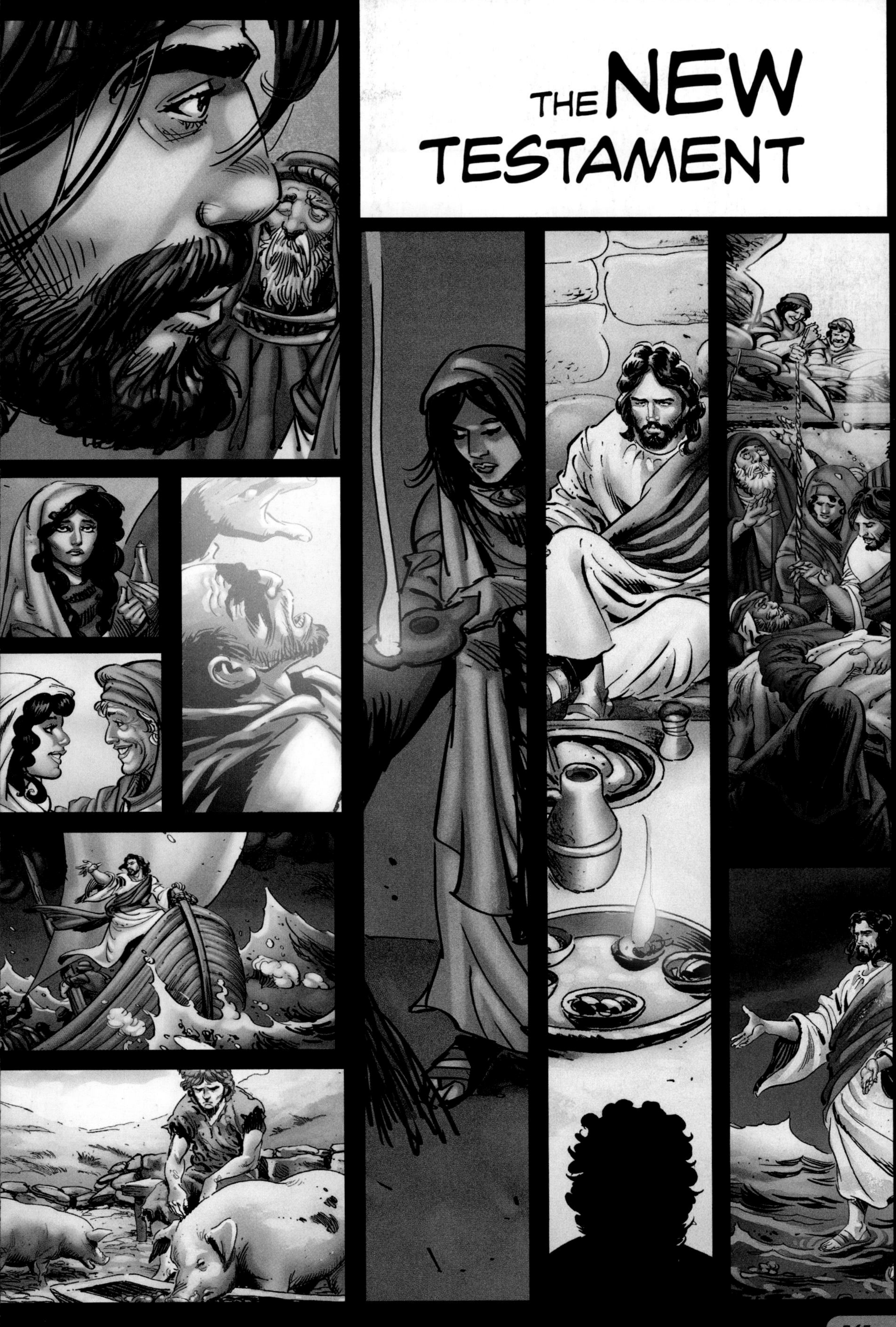

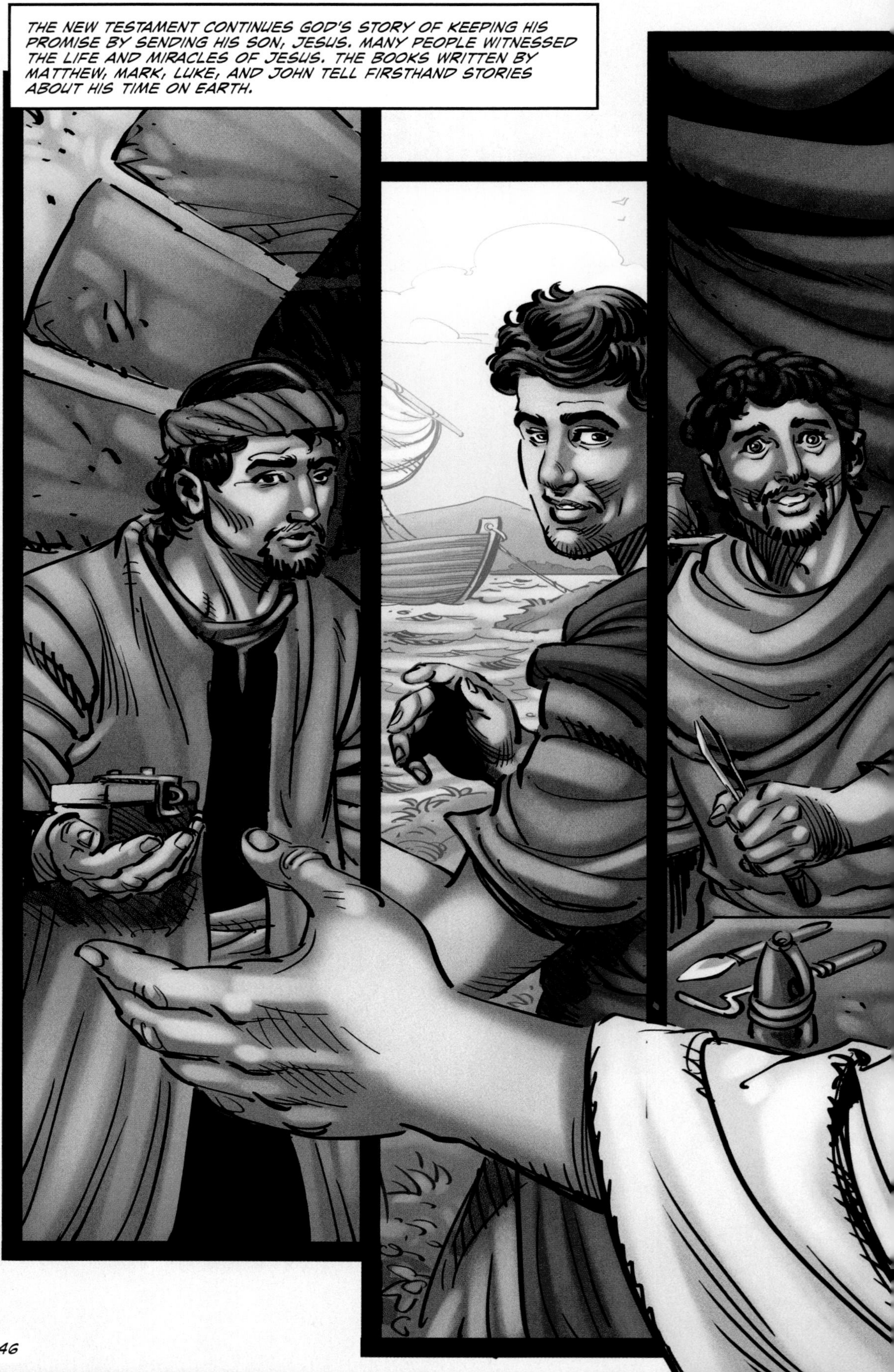
THE NEW TESTAMENT CONTINUES GOD'S STORY OF KEEPING HIS PROMISE BY SENDING HIS SON, JESUS. MANY PEOPLE WITNESSED THE LIFE AND MIRACLES OF JESUS. THE BOOKS WRITTEN BY MATTHEW, MARK, LUKE, AND JOHN TELL FIRSTHAND STORIES ABOUT HIS TIME ON EARTH.

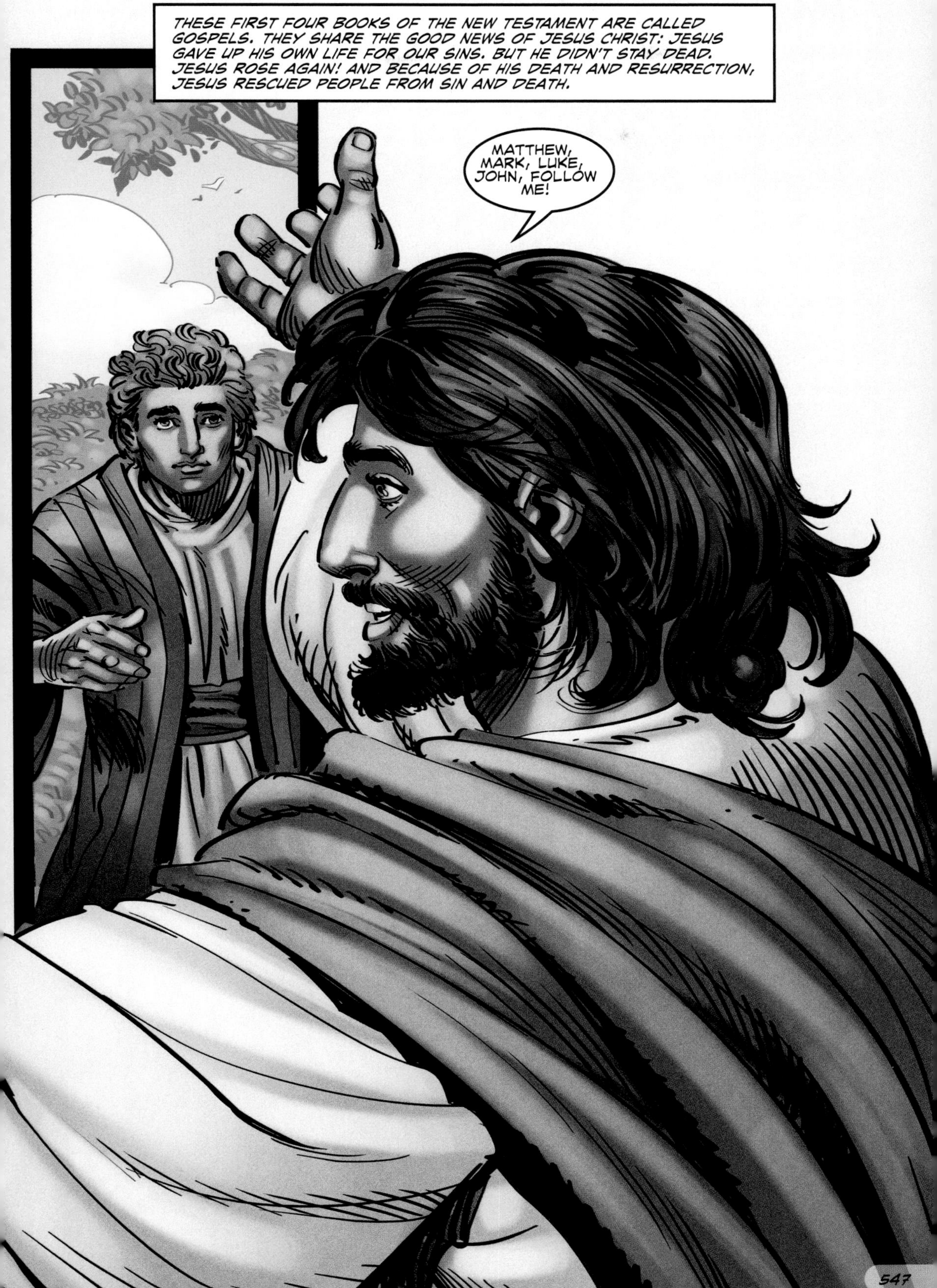
THESE FIRST FOUR BOOKS OF THE NEW TESTAMENT ARE CALLED GOSPELS. THEY SHARE THE GOOD NEWS OF JESUS CHRIST: JESUS GAVE UP HIS OWN LIFE FOR OUR SINS. BUT HE DIDN'T STAY DEAD. JESUS ROSE AGAIN! AND BECAUSE OF HIS DEATH AND RESURRECTION, JESUS RESCUED PEOPLE FROM SIN AND DEATH.
MATTHEW, MARK, LUKE, JOHN, FOLLOW ME!

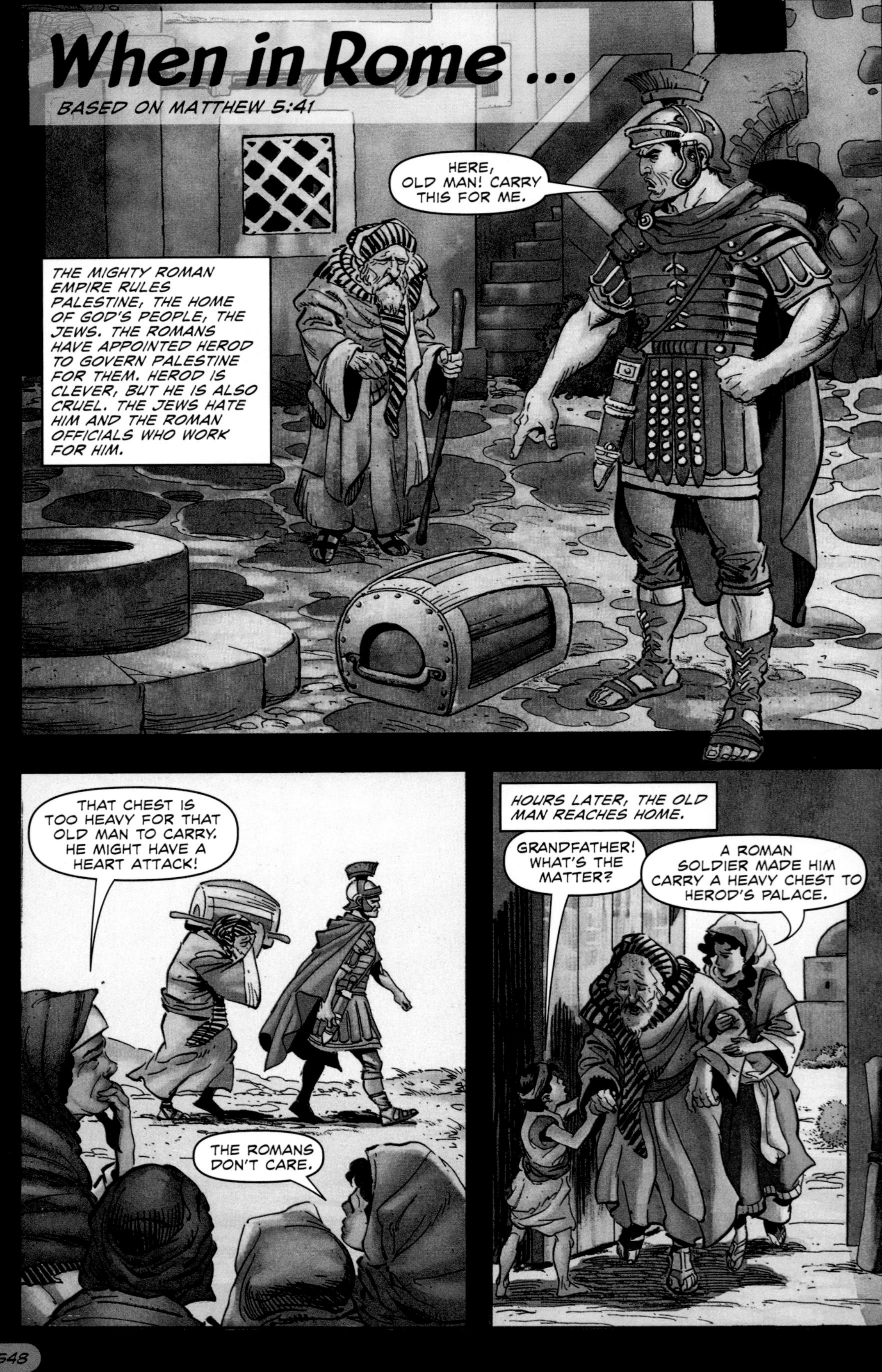
When in Rome ...
BASED ON MATTHEW 5:41
THE MIGHTY ROMAN EMPIRE RULES PALESTINE, THE HOME OF GOD'S PEOPLE, THE JEWS. THE ROMANS HAVE APPOINTED HEROD TO GOVERN PALESTINE FOR THEM. HEROD IS CLEVER, BUT HE IS ALSO CRUEL. THE JEWS HATE HIM AND THE ROMAN OFFICIALS WHO WORK FOR HIM.
HERE, OLD MAN! CARRY THIS FOR ME.
THAT CHEST IS TOO HEAVY FOR THAT OLD MAN TO CARRY. HE MIGHT HAVE A HEART ATTACK!
THE ROMANS DON'T CARE.
HOURS LATER, THE OLD MAN REACHES HOME.
GRANDFATHER! WHAT'S THE MATTER?
A ROMAN SOLDIER MADE HIM CARRY A HEAVY CHEST TO HEROD'S PALACE.

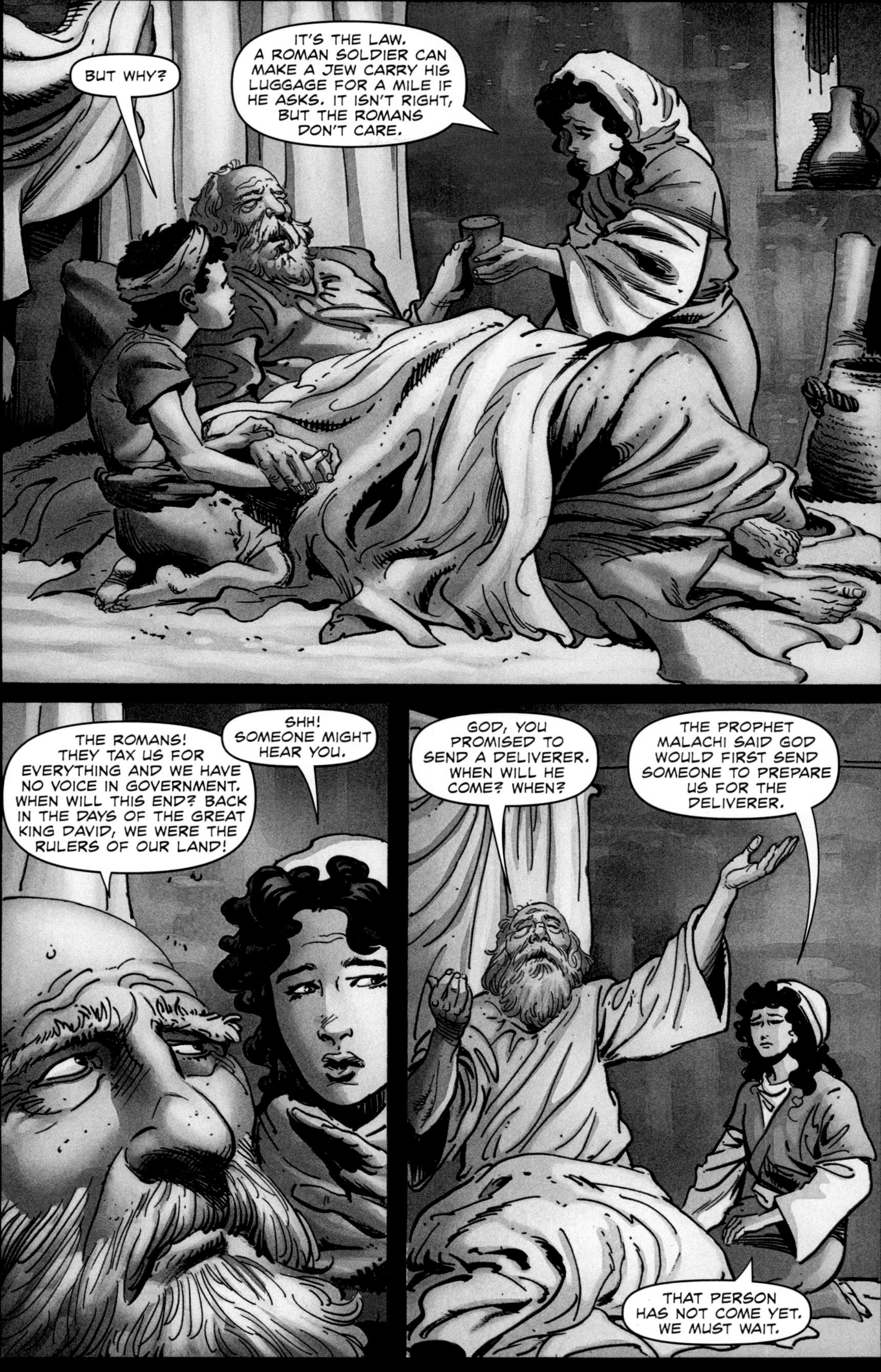
BUT WHY?
IT'S THE LAW. A ROMAN SOLDIER CAN MAKE A JEW CARRY HIS LUGGAGE FOR A MILE IF HE ASKS. IT ISN'T RIGHT, BUT THE ROMANS DON'T CARE.
THE ROMANS! THEY TAX US FOR EVERYTHING AND WE HAVE NO VOICE IN GOVERNMENT. WHEN WILL THIS END? BACK IN THE DAYS OF THE GREAT KING DAVID, WE WERE THE RULERS OF OUR LAND!
SHH! SOMEONE MIGHT HEAR YOU.
GOD, YOU PROMISED TO SEND A DELIVERER. WHEN WILL HE COME? WHEN?
THE PROPHET MALACHI SAID GOD WOULD FIRST SEND SOMEONE TO PREPARE US FOR THE DELIVERER.
THAT PERSON HAS NOT COME YET. WE MUST WAIT.

Angel Promises

BASED ON LUKE 1:5–56

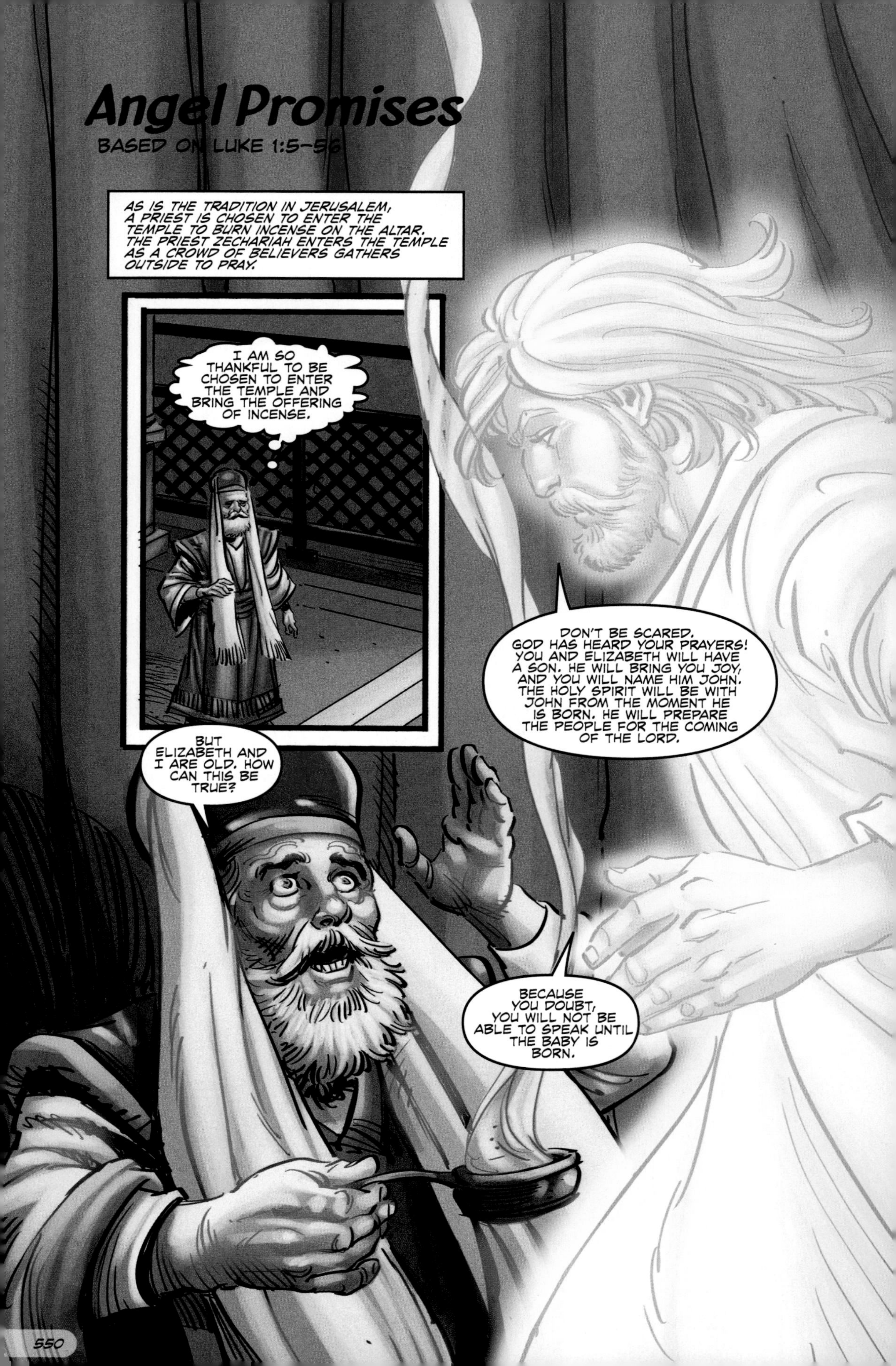
AS IS THE TRADITION IN JERUSALEM, A PRIEST IS CHOSEN TO ENTER THE TEMPLE TO BURN INCENSE ON THE ALTAR. THE PRIEST ZECHARIAH ENTERS THE TEMPLE AS A CROWD OF BELIEVERS GATHERS OUTSIDE TO PRAY.
I AM SO THANKFUL TO BE CHOSEN TO ENTER THE TEMPLE AND BRING THE OFFERING OF INCENSE.
DON'T BE SCARED. GOD HAS HEARD YOUR PRAYERS! YOU AND ELIZABETH WILL HAVE A SON. HE WILL BRING YOU JOY, AND YOU WILL NAME HIM JOHN. THE HOLY SPIRIT WILL BE WITH JOHN FROM THE MOMENT HE IS BORN. HE WILL PREPARE THE PEOPLE FOR THE COMING OF THE LORD.
BUT ELIZABETH AND I ARE OLD. HOW CAN THIS BE TRUE?
BECAUSE YOU DOUBT, YOU WILL NOT BE ABLE TO SPEAK UNTIL THE BABY IS BORN.

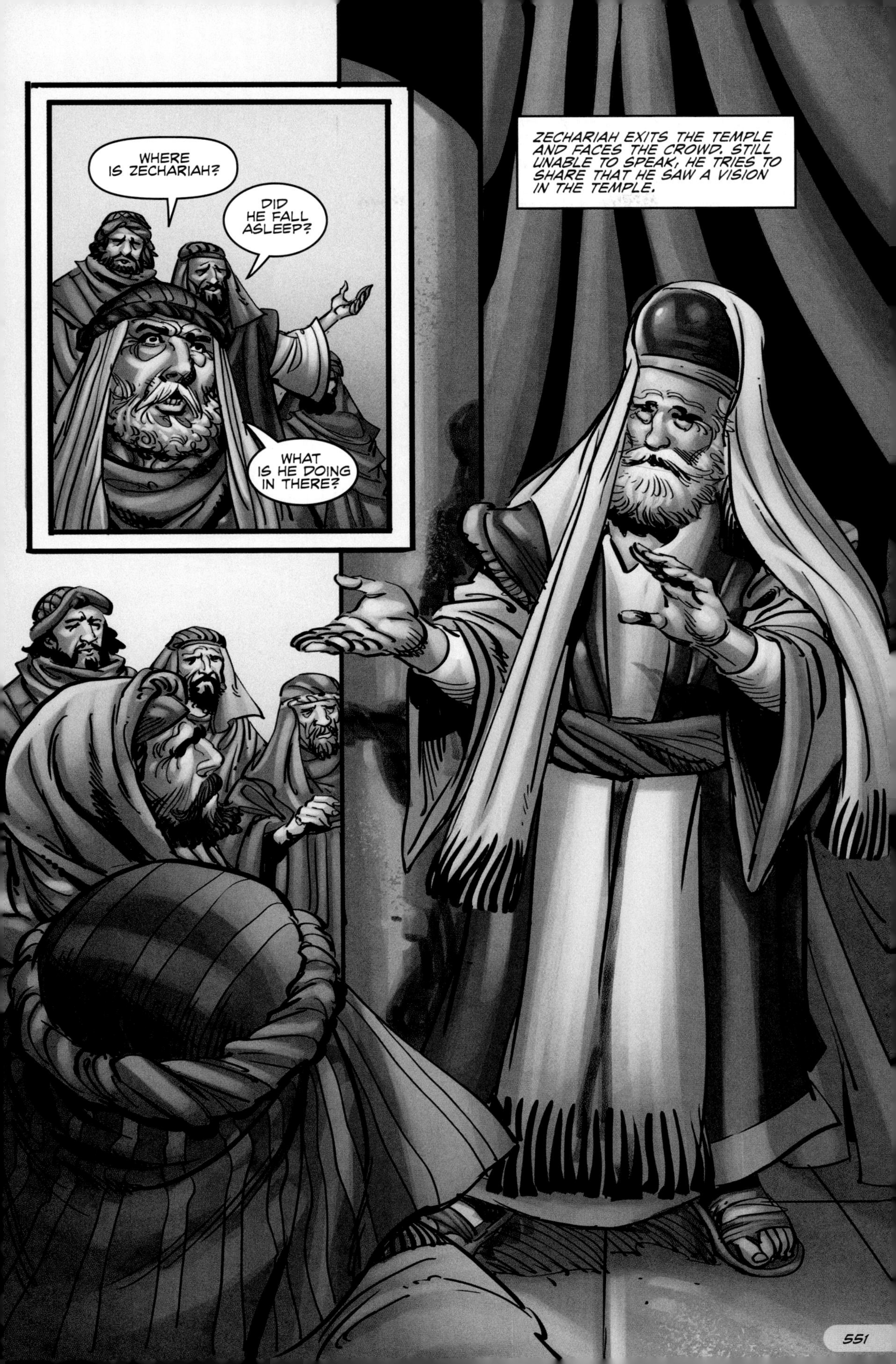
WHERE IS ZECHARIAH?
DID HE FALL ASLEEP?
WHAT IS HE DOING IN THERE?
ZECHARIAH EXITS THE TEMPLE AND FACES THE CROWD. STILL UNABLE TO SPEAK, HE TRIES TO SHARE THAT HE SAW A VISION IN THE TEMPLE.

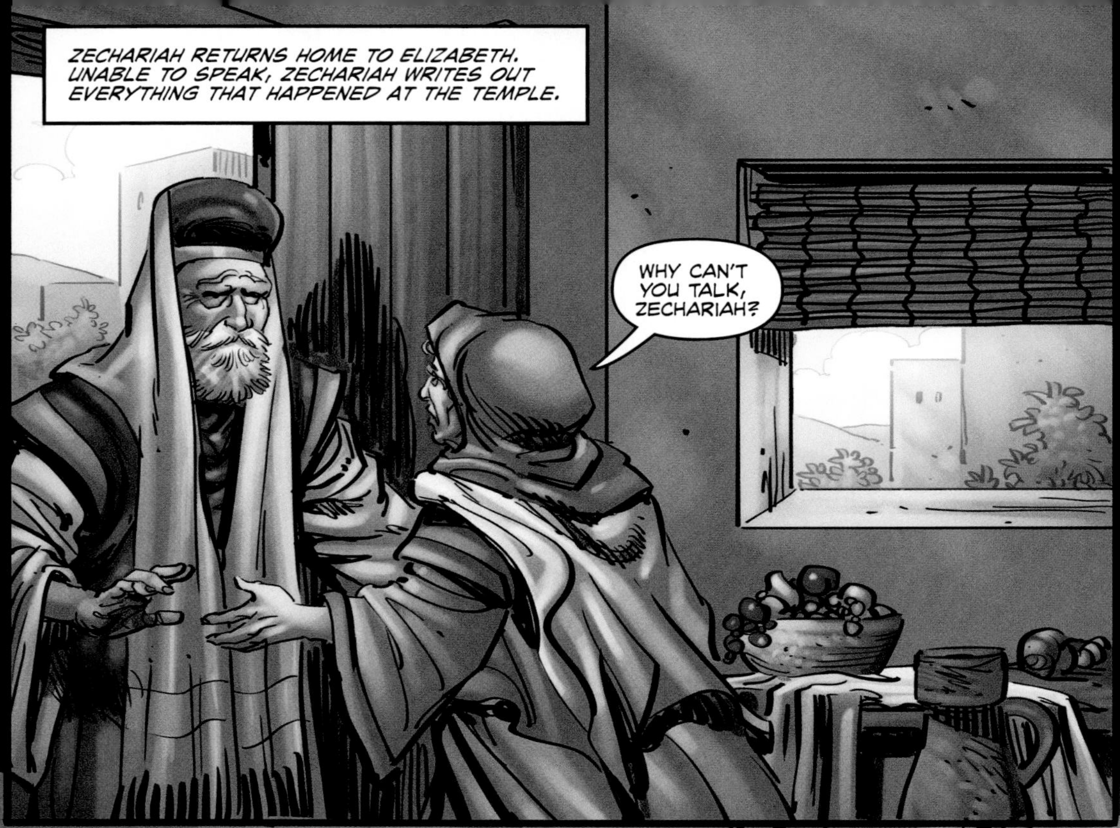
ZECHARIAH RETURNS HOME TO ELIZABETH. UNABLE TO SPEAK, ZECHARIAH WRITES OUT EVERYTHING THAT HAPPENED AT THE TEMPLE.
WHY CAN'T YOU TALK, ZECHARIAH?

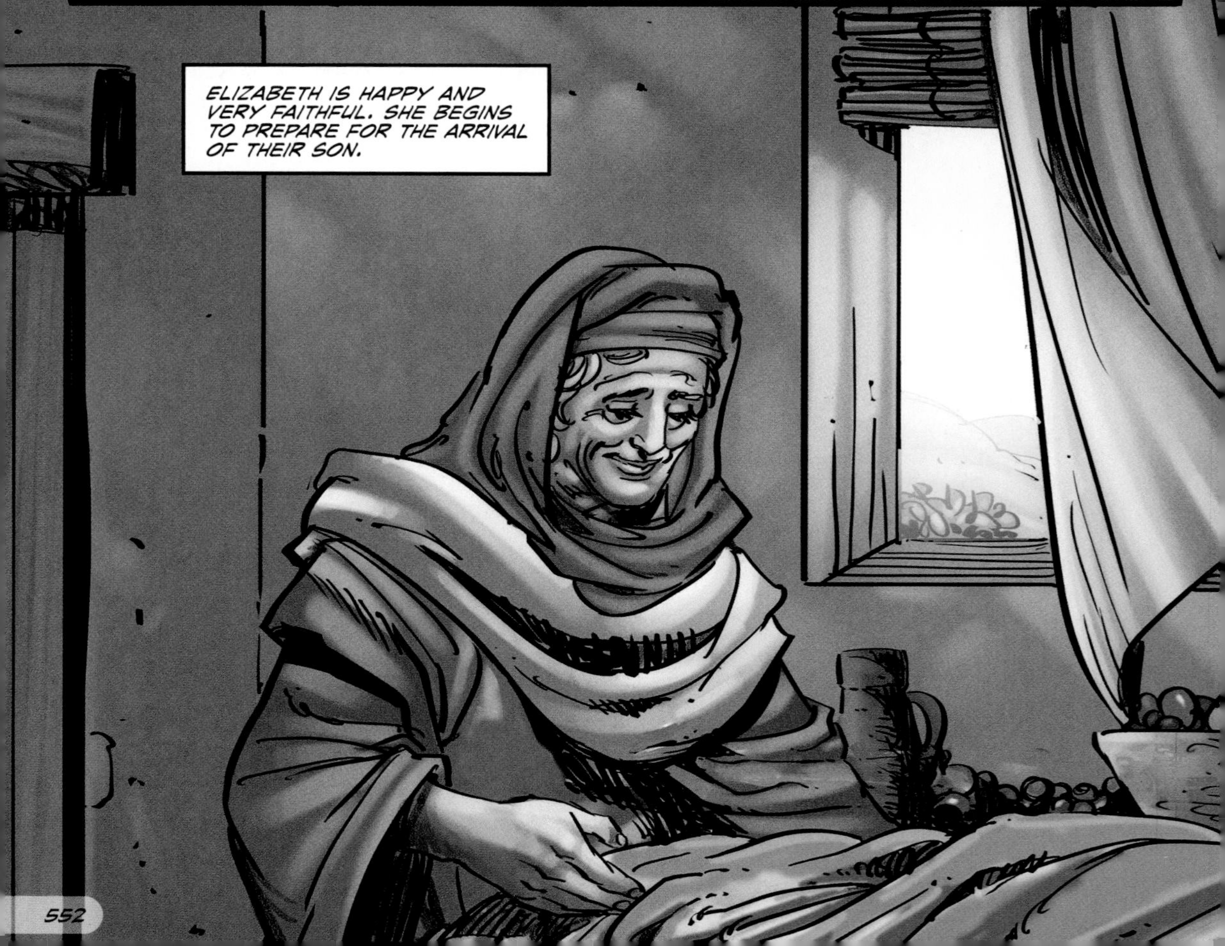
ELIZABETH IS HAPPY AND VERY FAITHFUL. SHE BEGINS TO PREPARE FOR THE ARRIVAL OF THEIR SON.

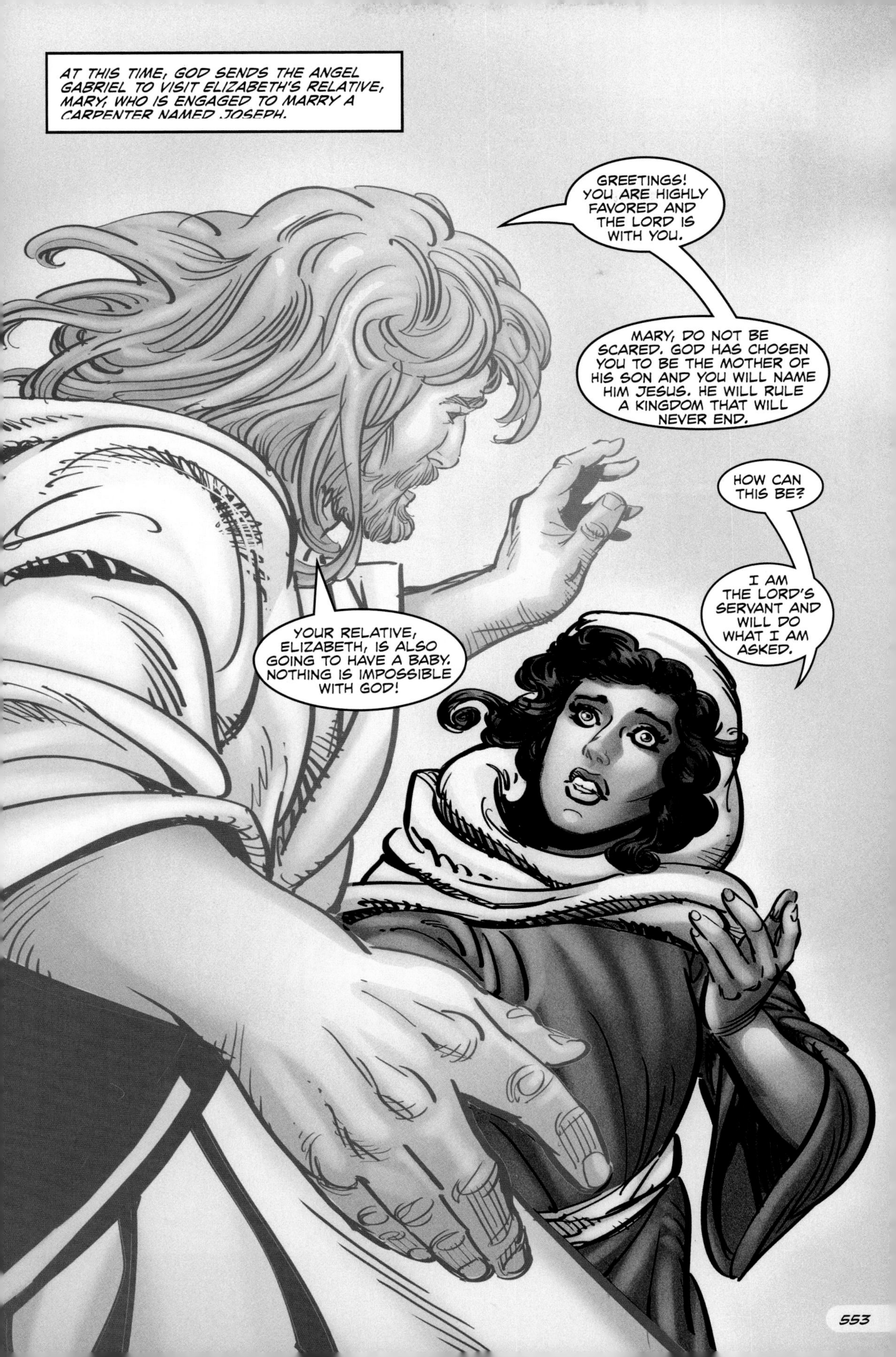
AT THIS TIME, GOD SENDS THE ANGEL GABRIEL TO VISIT ELIZABETH'S RELATIVE, MARY, WHO IS ENGAGED TO MARRY A CARPENTER NAMED JOSEPH.
GREETINGS! YOU ARE HIGHLY FAVORED AND THE LORD IS WITH YOU.
MARY, DO NOT BE SCARED. GOD HAS CHOSEN YOU TO BE THE MOTHER OF HIS SON AND YOU WILL NAME HIM JESUS. HE WILL RULE A KINGDOM THAT WILL NEVER END.
HOW CAN THIS BE?
YOUR RELATIVE, ELIZABETH, IS ALSO GOING TO HAVE A BABY. NOTHING IS IMPOSSIBLE WITH GOD!
I AM THE LORD'S SERVANT AND WILL DO WHAT I AM ASKED.

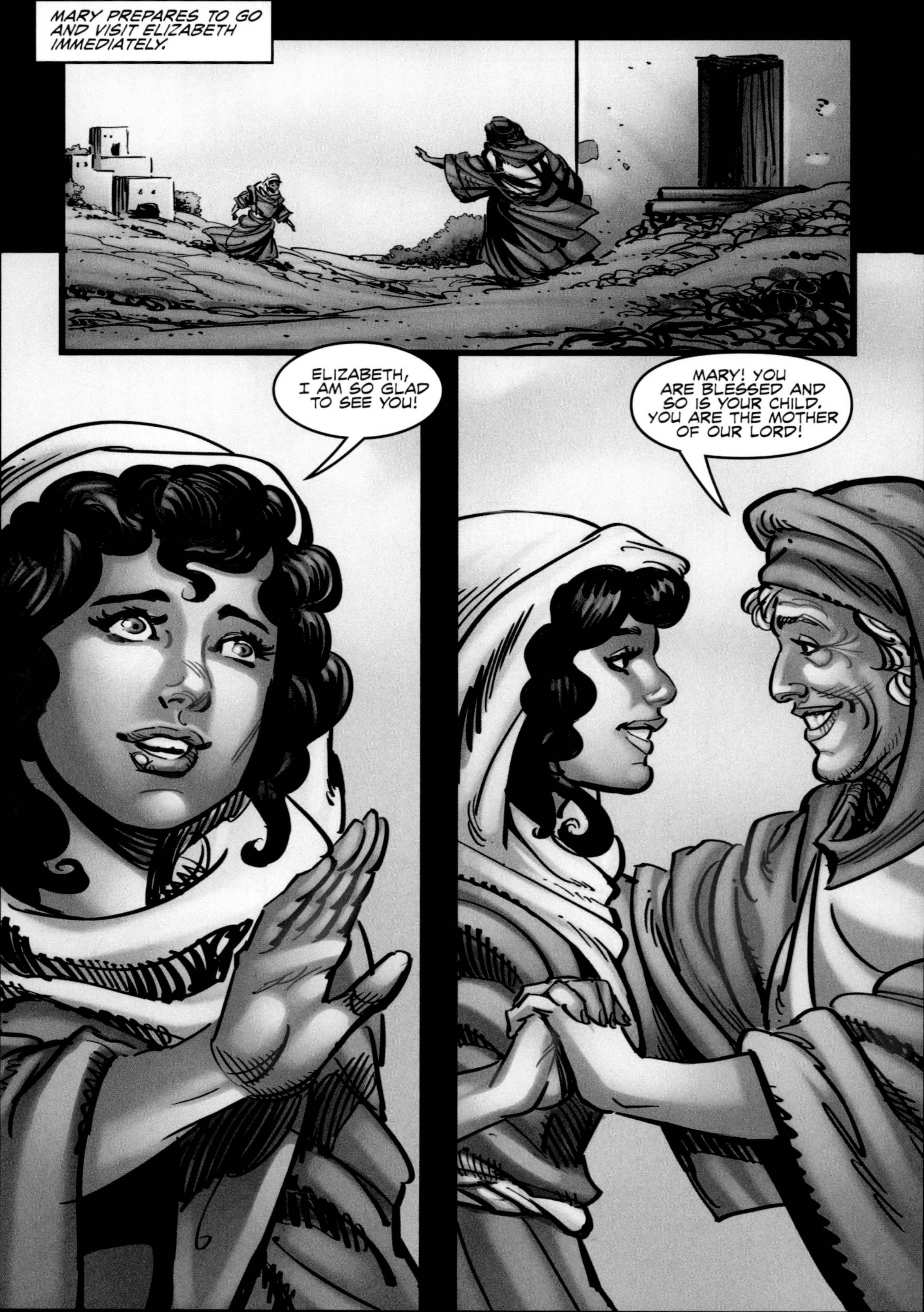
MARY PREPARES TO GO AND VISIT ELIZABETH IMMEDIATELY.
ELIZABETH, I AM SO GLAD TO SEE YOU!
MARY! YOU ARE BLESSED AND SO IS YOUR CHILD. YOU ARE THE MOTHER OF OUR LORD!

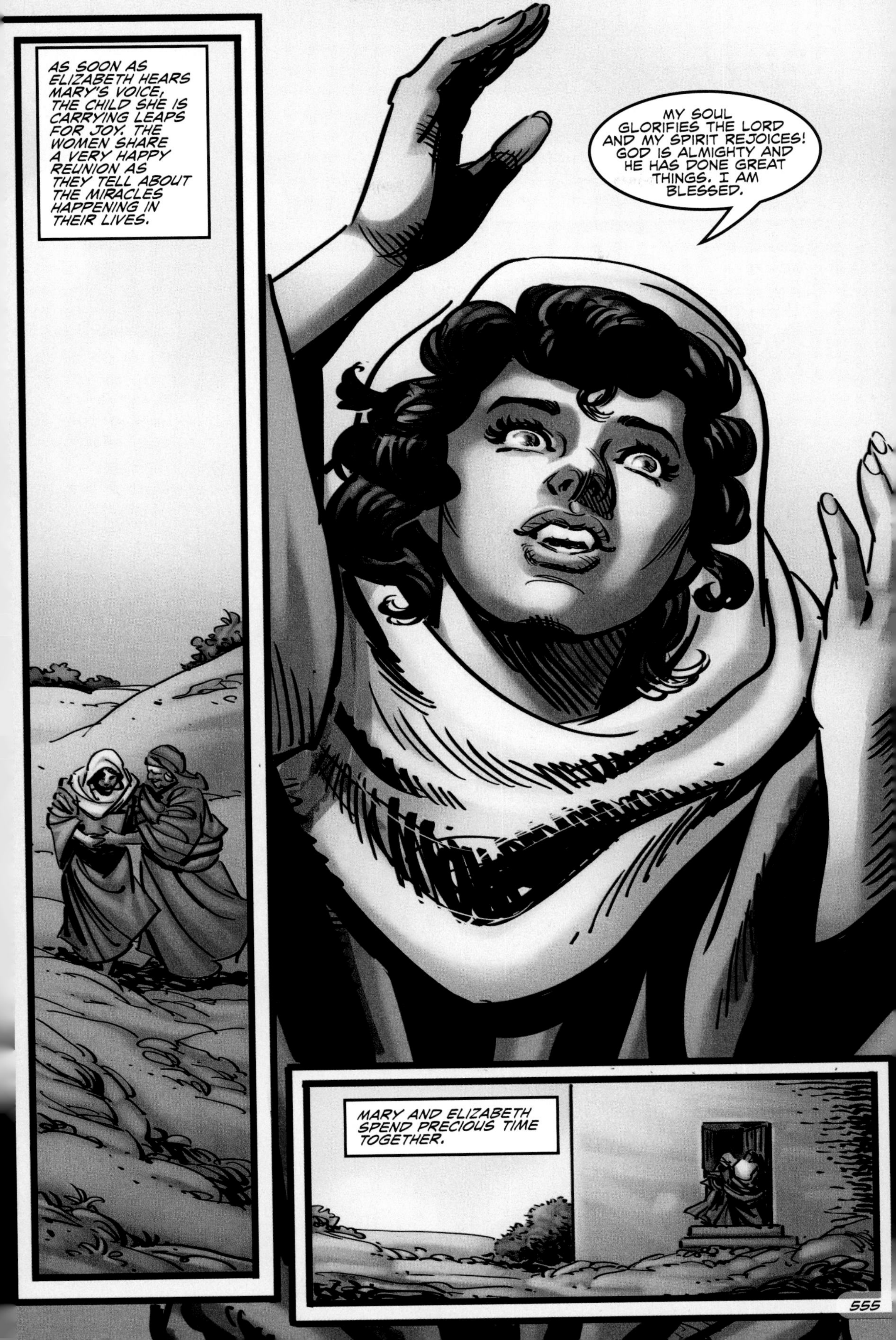
AS SOON AS ELIZABETH HEARS MARY'S VOICE, THE CHILD SHE IS CARRYING LEAPS FOR JOY. THE WOMEN SHARE A VERY HAPPY REUNION AS THEY TELL ABOUT THE MIRACLES HAPPENING IN THEIR LIVES.
MY SOUL GLORIFIES THE LORD AND MY SPIRIT REJOICES! GOD IS ALMIGHTY AND HE HAS DONE GREAT THINGS. I AM BLESSED.
MARY AND ELIZABETH SPEND PRECIOUS TIME TOGETHER.

Birth of Prophet

BASED ON LUKE 1:57–80

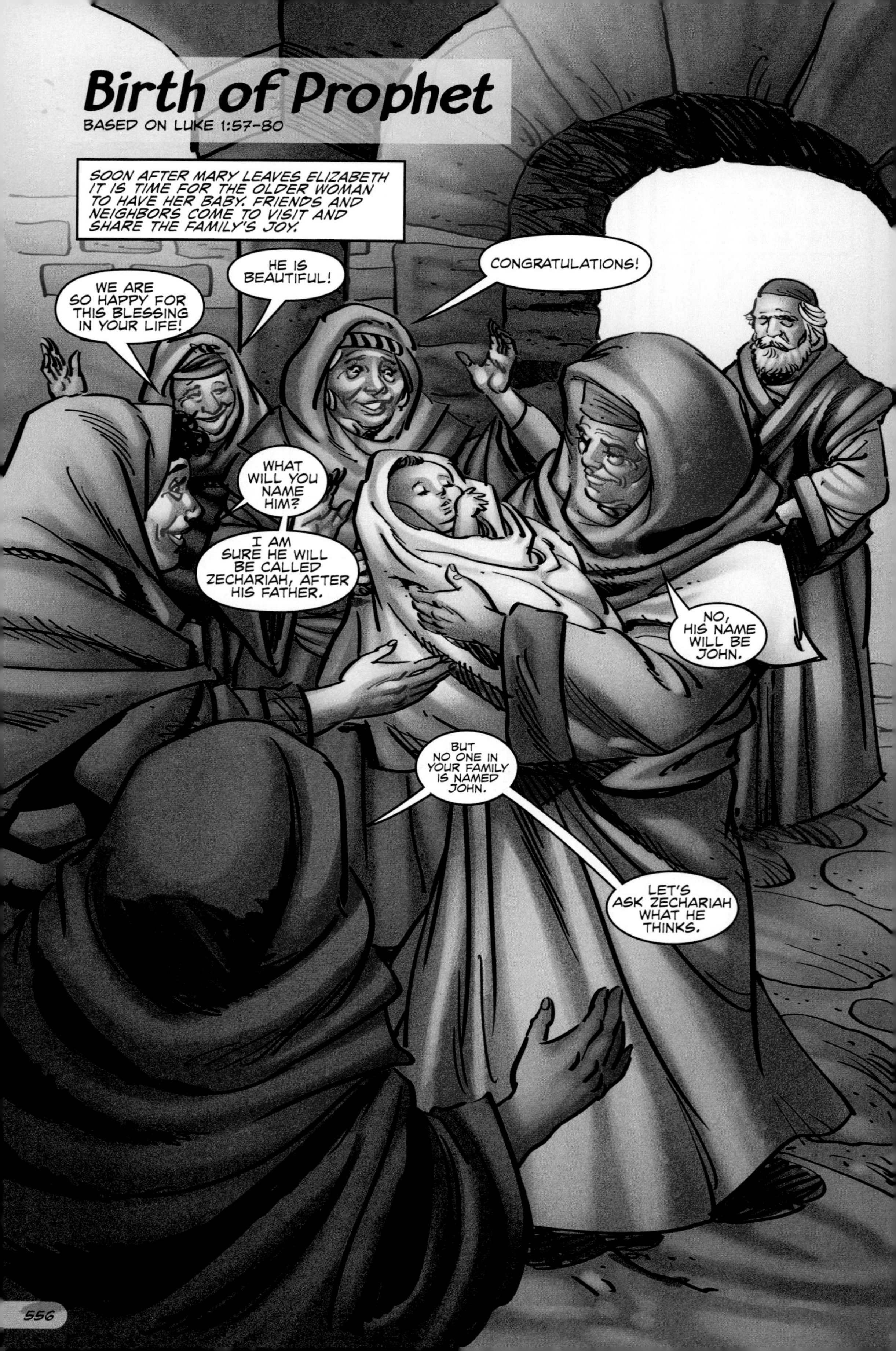
SOON AFTER MARY LEAVES ELIZABETH IT IS TIME FOR THE OLDER WOMAN TO HAVE HER BABY. FRIENDS AND NEIGHBORS COME TO VISIT AND SHARE THE FAMILY'S JOY.
WE ARE SO HAPPY FOR THIS BLESSING IN YOUR LIFE!
HE IS BEAUTIFUL!
CONGRATULATIONS!
WHAT WILL YOU NAME HIM?
I AM SURE HE WILL BE CALLED ZECHARIAH, AFTER HIS FATHER.
NO, HIS NAME WILL BE JOHN.
BUT NO ONE IN YOUR FAMILY IS NAMED JOHN.
LET'S ASK ZECHARIAH WHAT HE THINKS.

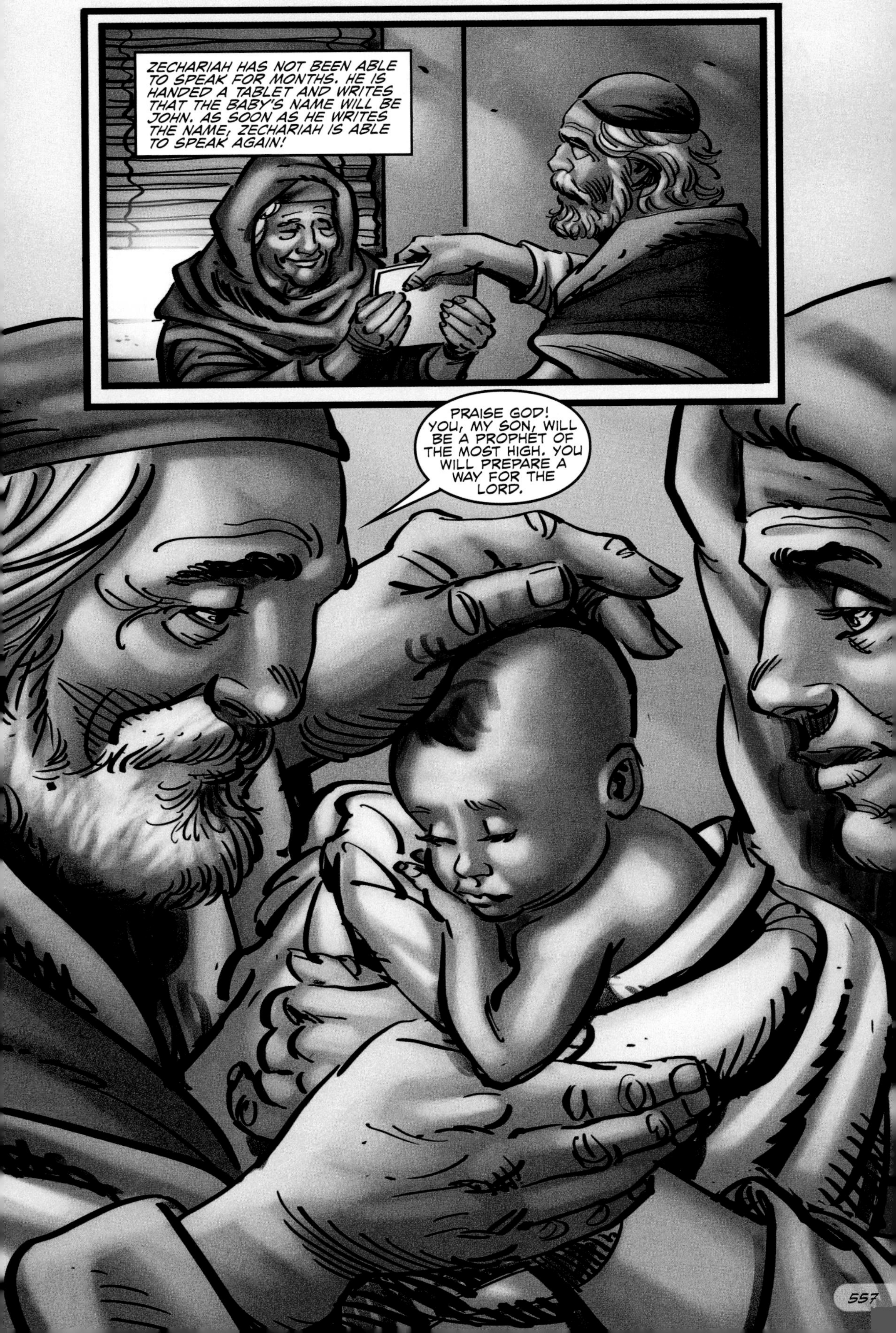
ZECHARIAH HAS NOT BEEN ABLE TO SPEAK FOR MONTHS. HE IS HANDED A TABLET AND WRITES THAT THE BABY'S NAME WILL BE JOHN. AS SOON AS HE WRITES THE NAME, ZECHARIAH IS ABLE TO SPEAK AGAIN!
PRAISE GOD! YOU, MY SON, WILL BE A PROPHET OF THE MOST HIGH. YOU WILL PREPARE A WAY FOR THE LORD.

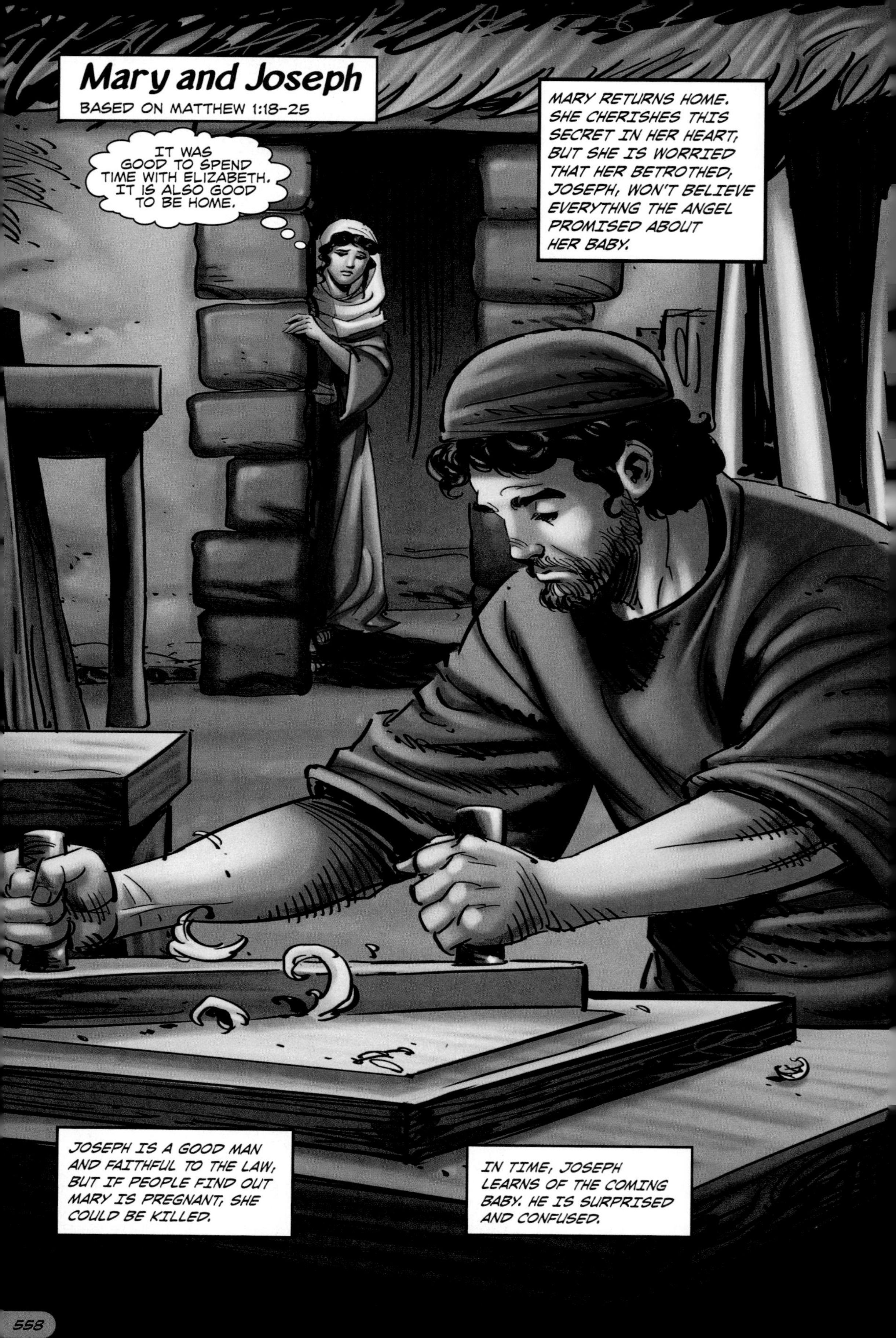
Mary and Joseph
BASED ON MATTHEW 1:18–25
MARY RETURNS HOME. SHE CHERISHES THIS SECRET IN HER HEART, BUT SHE IS WORRIED THAT HER BETROTHED, JOSEPH, WON'T BELIEVE EVERYTHNG THE ANGEL PROMISED ABOUT HER BABY.
IT WAS GOOD TO SPEND TIME WITH ELIZABETH. IT IS ALSO GOOD TO BE HOME.
JOSEPH IS A GOOD MAN AND FAITHFUL TO THE LAW, BUT IF PEOPLE FIND OUT MARY IS PREGNANT, SHE COULD BE KILLED.
IN TIME, JOSEPH LEARNS OF THE COMING BABY. HE IS SURPRISED AND CONFUSED.

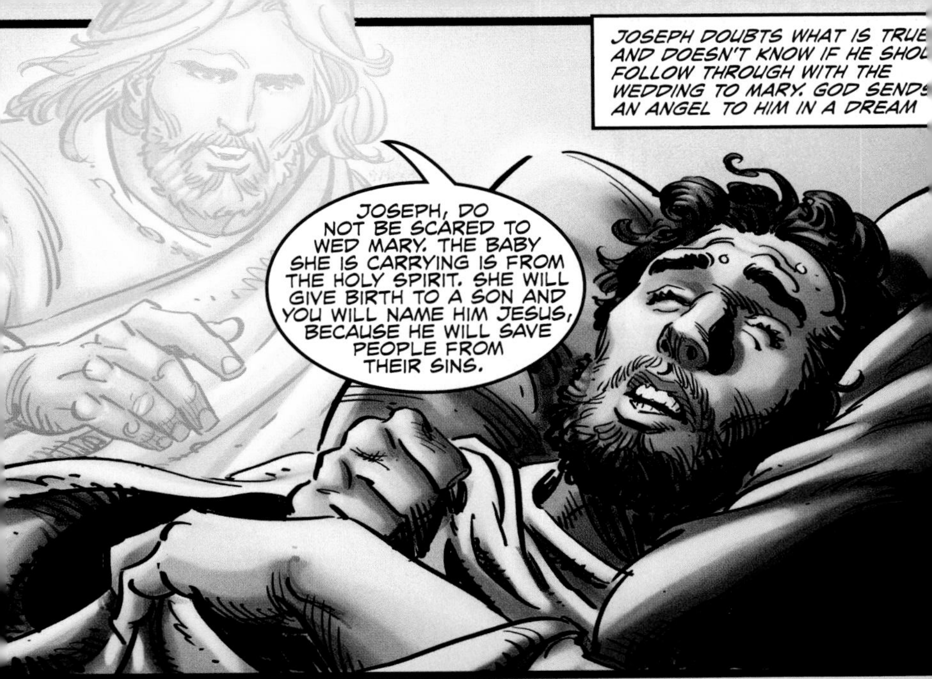
JOSEPH DOUBTS WHAT IS TRUE
AND DOESN'T KNOW IF HE SHOU
FOLLOW THROUGH WITH THE
WEDDING TO MARY. GOD SENDS
AN ANGEL TO HIM IN A DREAM
JOSEPH, DO NOT BE SCARED TO WED MARY. THE BABY SHE IS CARRYING IS FROM THE HOLY SPIRIT. SHE WILL GIVE BIRTH TO A SON AND YOU WILL NAME HIM JESUS, BECAUSE HE WILL SAVE PEOPLE FROM THEIR SINS.

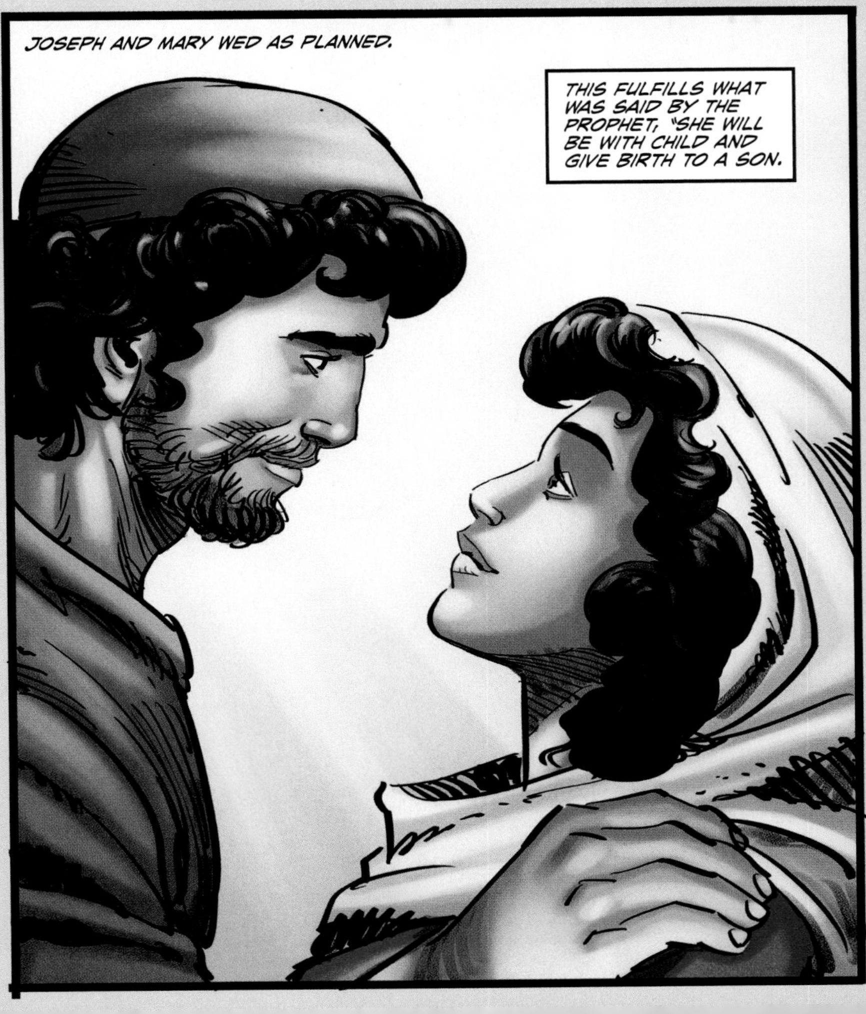
JOSEPH AND MARY WED AS PLANNED.
THIS FULFILLS WHAT WAS SAID BY THE PROPHET, "SHE WILL BE WITH CHILD AND GIVE BIRTH TO A SON.

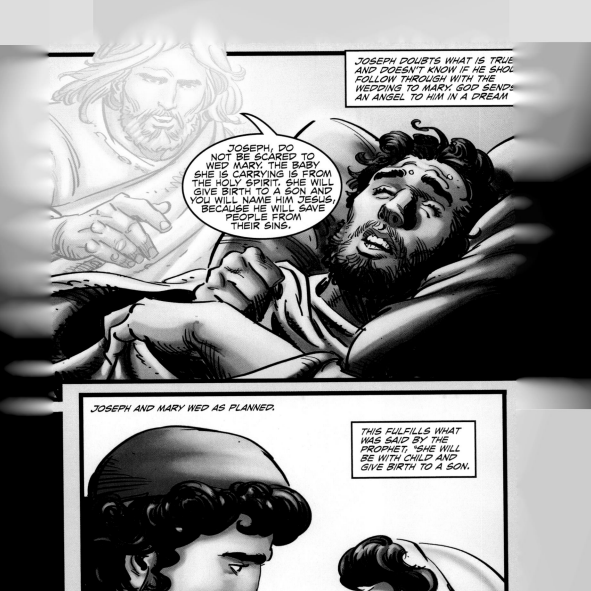

The Birth of a Savior

BASED ON LUKE 2:1–20

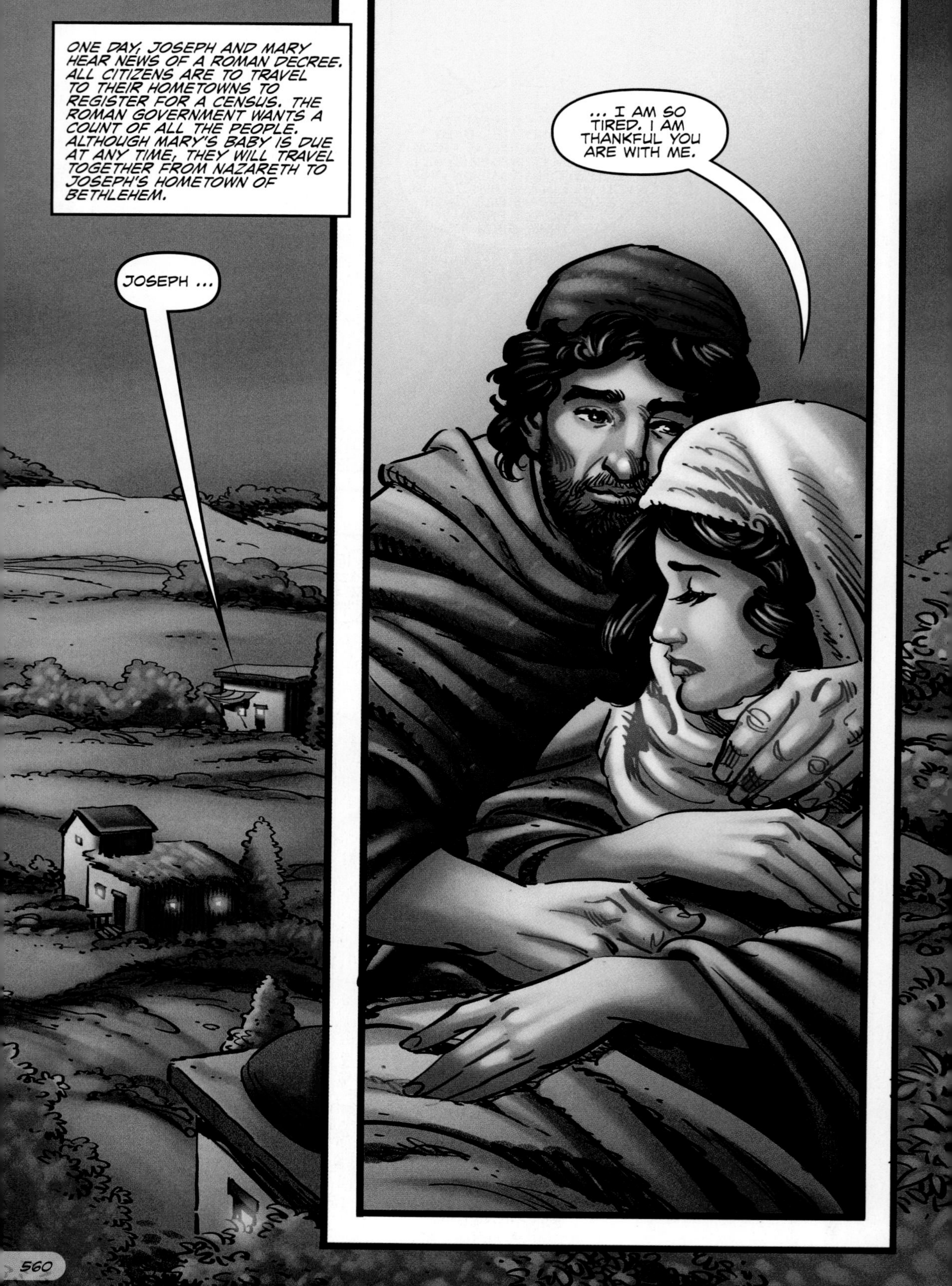
ONE DAY, JOSEPH AND MARY HEAR NEWS OF A ROMAN DECREE. ALL CITIZENS ARE TO TRAVEL TO THEIR HOMETOWNS TO REGISTER FOR A CENSUS. THE ROMAN GOVERNMENT WANTS A COUNT OF ALL THE PEOPLE. ALTHOUGH MARY'S BABY IS DUE AT ANY TIME, THEY WILL TRAVEL TOGETHER FROM NAZARETH TO JOSEPH'S HOMETOWN OF BETHLEHEM.
JOSEPH ...
... I AM SO TIRED. I AM THANKFUL YOU ARE WITH ME.

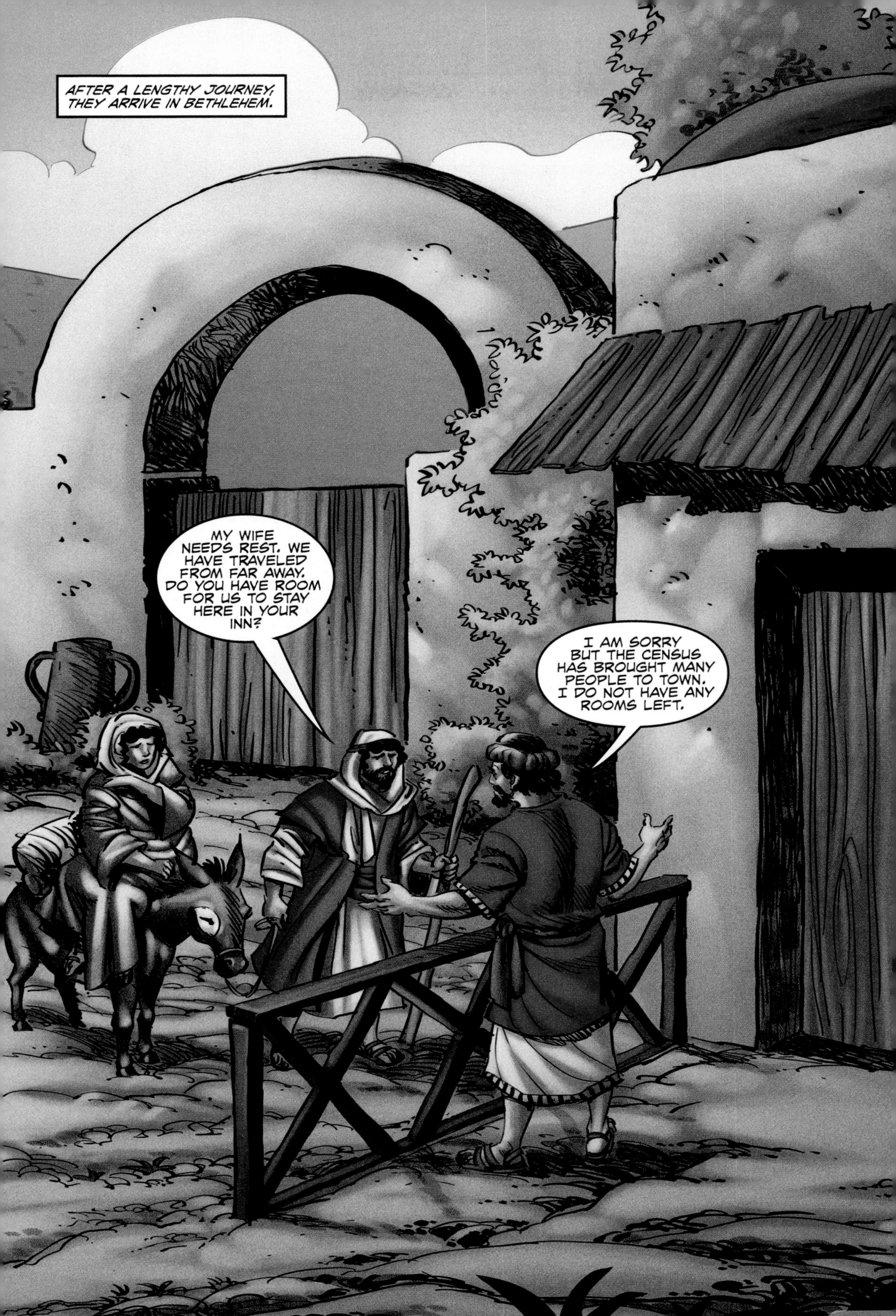
AFTER A LENGTHY JOURNEY, THEY ARRIVE IN BETHLEHEM.
MY WIFE NEEDS REST. WE HAVE TRAVELED FROM FAR AWAY. DO YOU HAVE ROOM FOR US TO STAY HERE IN YOUR INN?
I AM SORRY BUT THE CENSUS HAS BROUGHT MANY PEOPLE TO TOWN. I DO NOT HAVE ANY ROOMS LEFT.

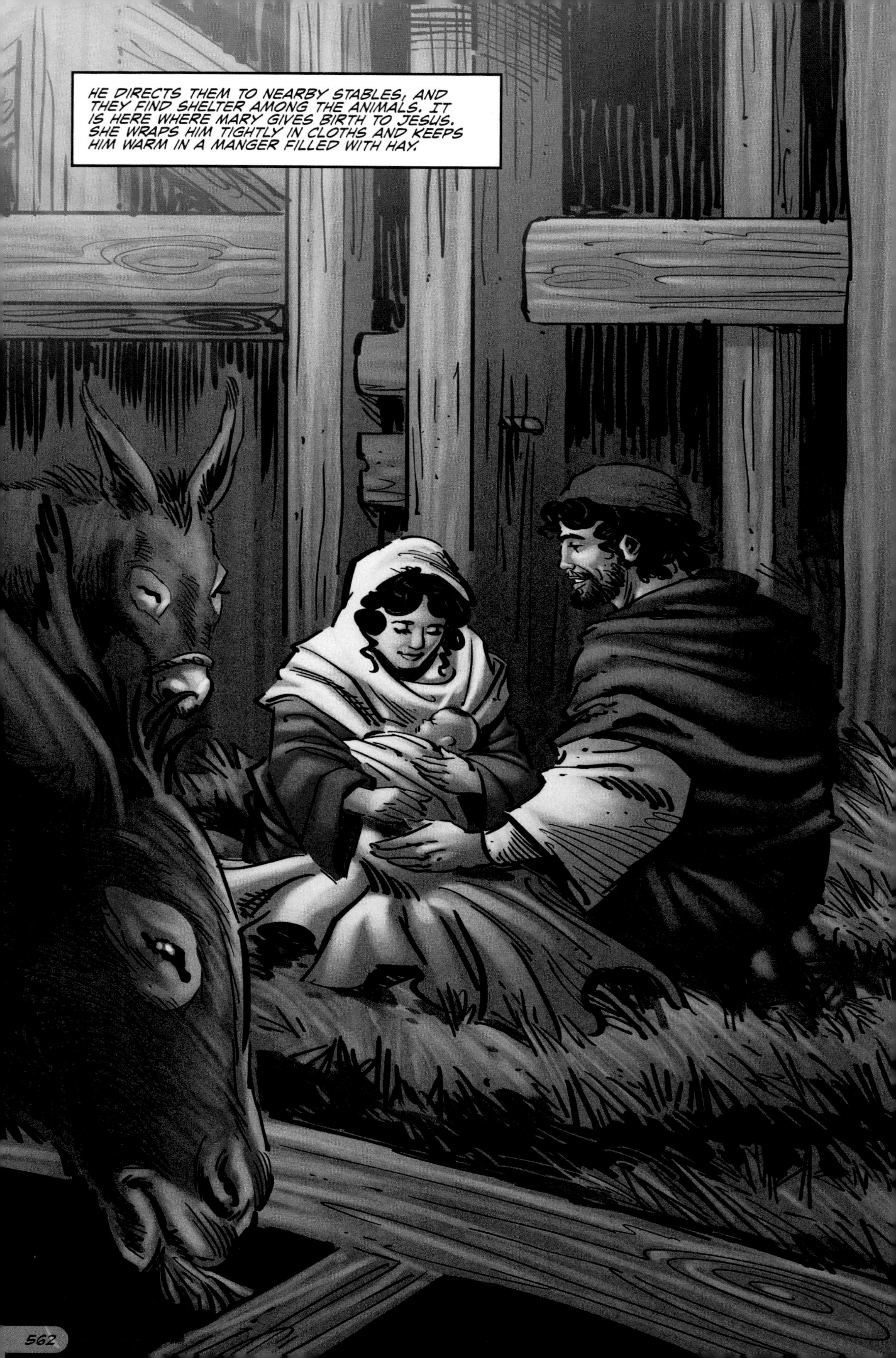
HE DIRECTS THEM TO NEARBY STABLES, AND THEY FIND SHELTER AMONG THE ANIMALS. IT IS HERE WHERE MARY GIVES BIRTH TO JESUS. SHE WRAPS HIM TIGHTLY IN CLOTHS AND KEEPS HIM WARM IN A MANGER FILLED WITH HAY.

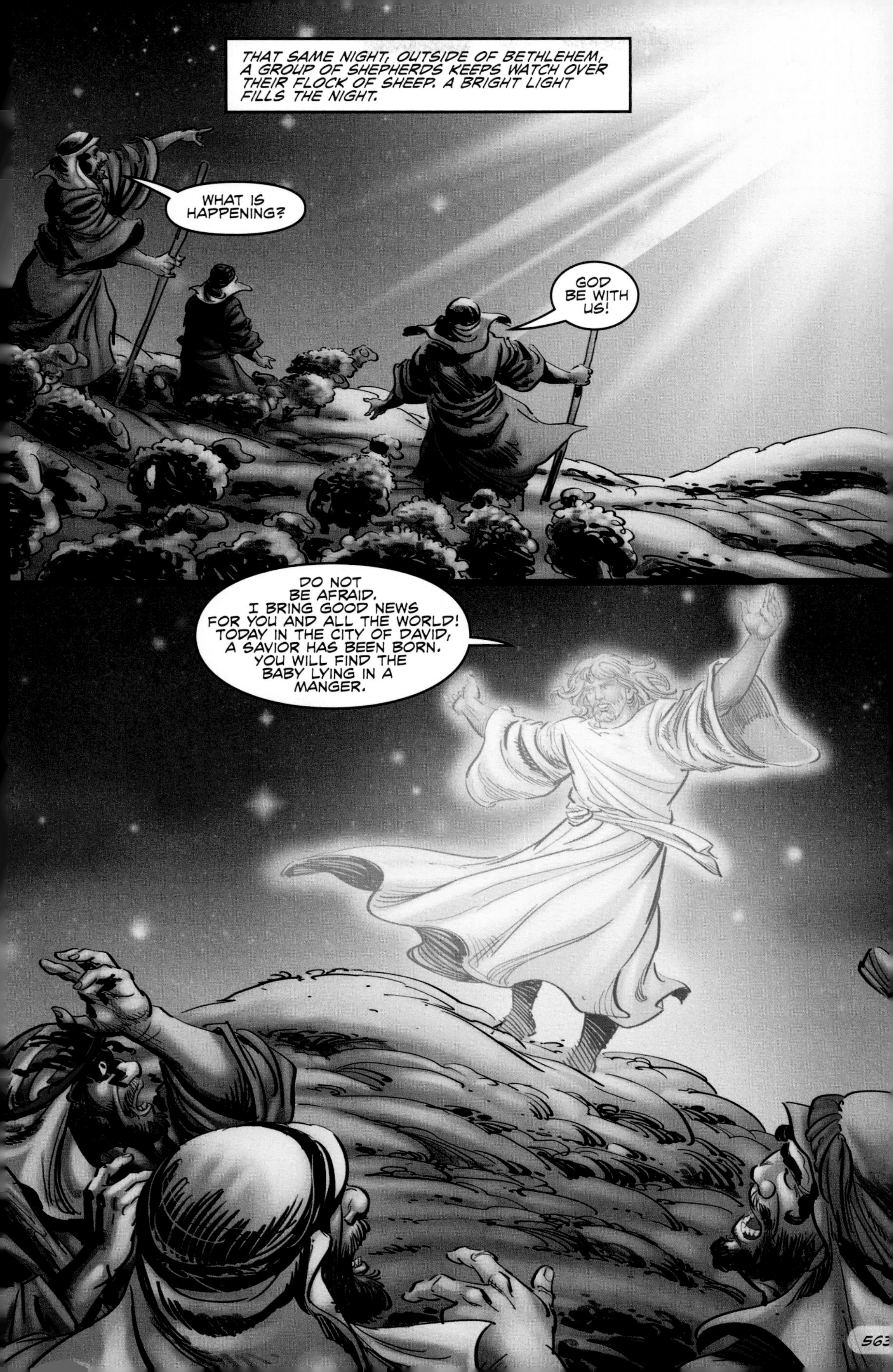
THAT SAME NIGHT, OUTSIDE OF BETHLEHEM, A GROUP OF SHEPHERDS KEEPS WATCH OVER THEIR FLOCK OF SHEEP. A BRIGHT LIGHT FILLS THE NIGHT.
WHAT IS HAPPENING?
GOD BE WITH US!
DO NOT BE AFRAID. I BRING GOOD NEWS FOR YOU AND ALL THE WORLD! TODAY IN THE CITY OF DAVID, A SAVIOR HAS BEEN BORN. YOU WILL FIND THE BABY LYING IN A MANGER.

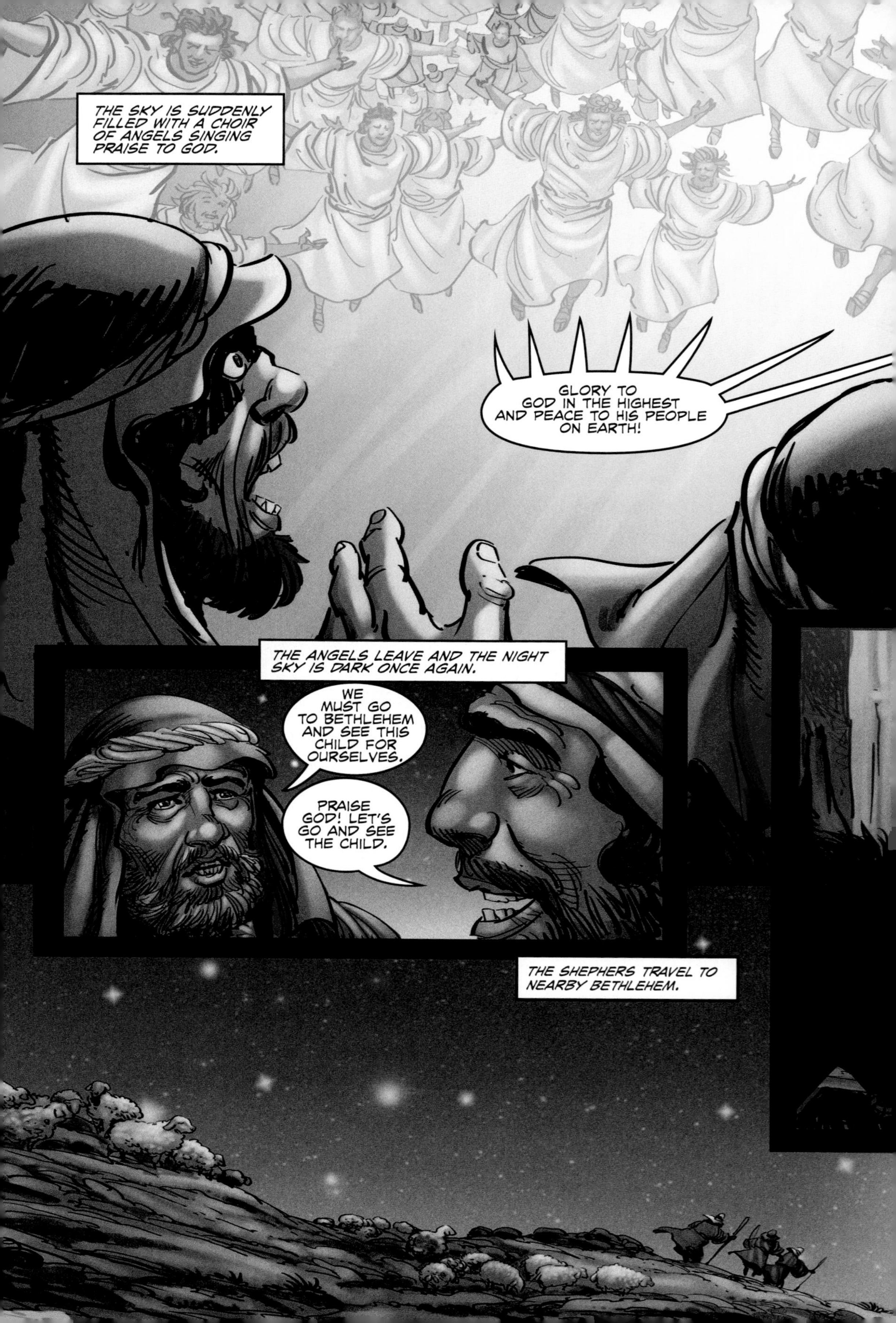
THE SKY IS SUDDENLY FILLED WITH A CHOIR OF ANGELS SINGING PRAISE TO GOD.
GLORY TO GOD IN THE HIGHEST AND PEACE TO HIS PEOPLE ON EARTH!
THE ANGELS LEAVE AND THE NIGHT SKY IS DARK ONCE AGAIN.
WE MUST GO TO BETHLEHEM AND SEE THIS CHILD FOR OURSELVES.
PRAISE GOD! LET'S GO AND SEE THE CHILD.
THE SHEPHERS TRAVEL TO NEARBY BETHLEHEM.

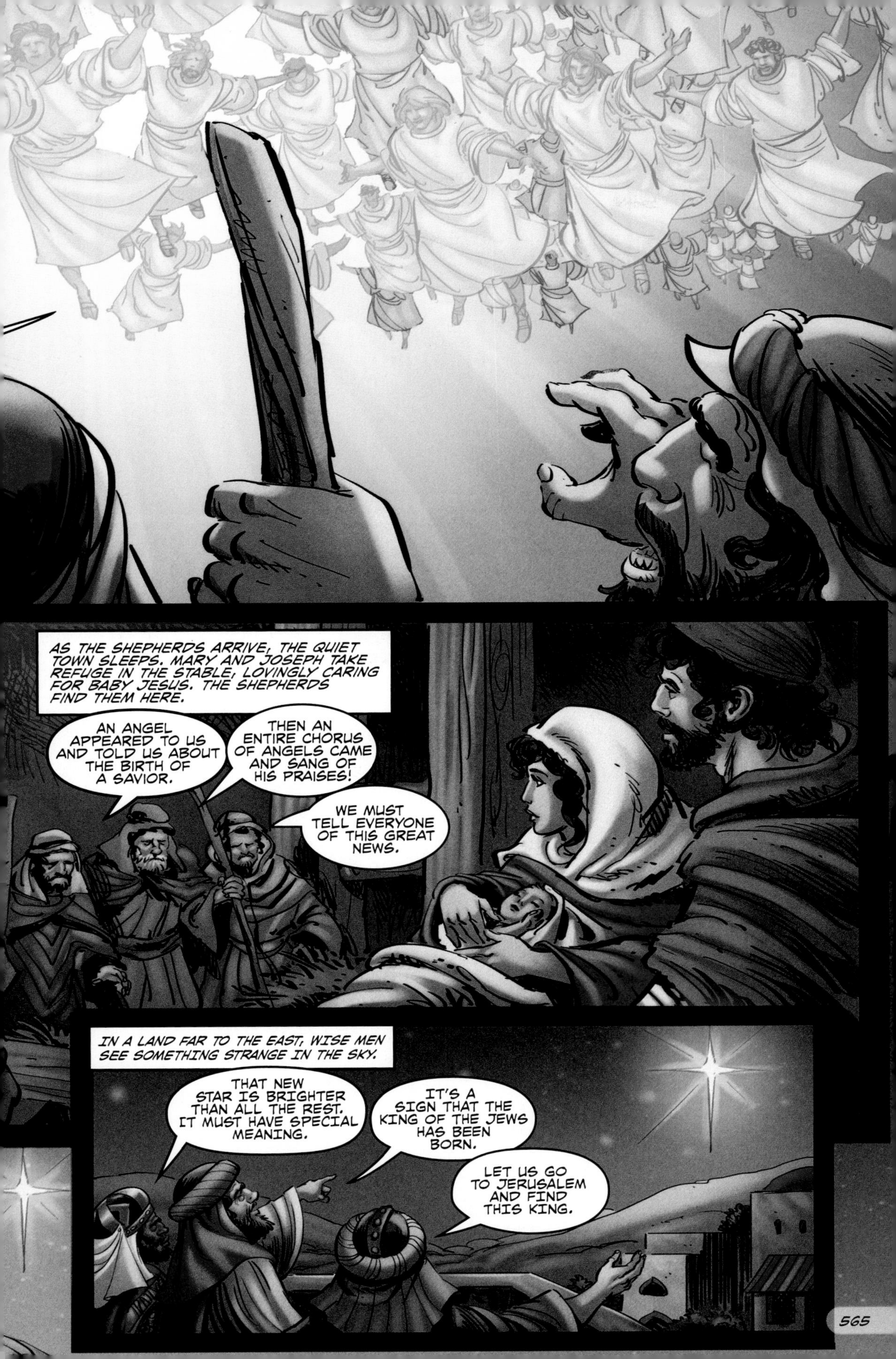
AS THE SHEPHERDS ARRIVE, THE QUIET TOWN SLEEPS. MARY AND JOSEPH TAKE REFUGE IN THE STABLE, LOVINGLY CARING FOR BABY JESUS. THE SHEPHERDS FIND THEM HERE.
AN ANGEL APPEARED TO US AND TOLD US ABOUT THE BIRTH OF A SAVIOR.
THEN AN ENTIRE CHORUS OF ANGELS CAME AND SANG OF HIS PRAISES!
WE MUST TELL EVERYONE OF THIS GREAT NEWS.
IN A LAND FAR TO THE EAST, WISE MEN SEE SOMETHING STRANGE IN THE SKY.
THAT NEW STAR IS BRIGHTER THAN ALL THE REST. IT MUST HAVE SPECIAL MEANING.
IT'S A SIGN THAT THE KING OF THE JEWS HAS BEEN BORN.
LET US GO TO JERUSALEM AND FIND THIS KING.

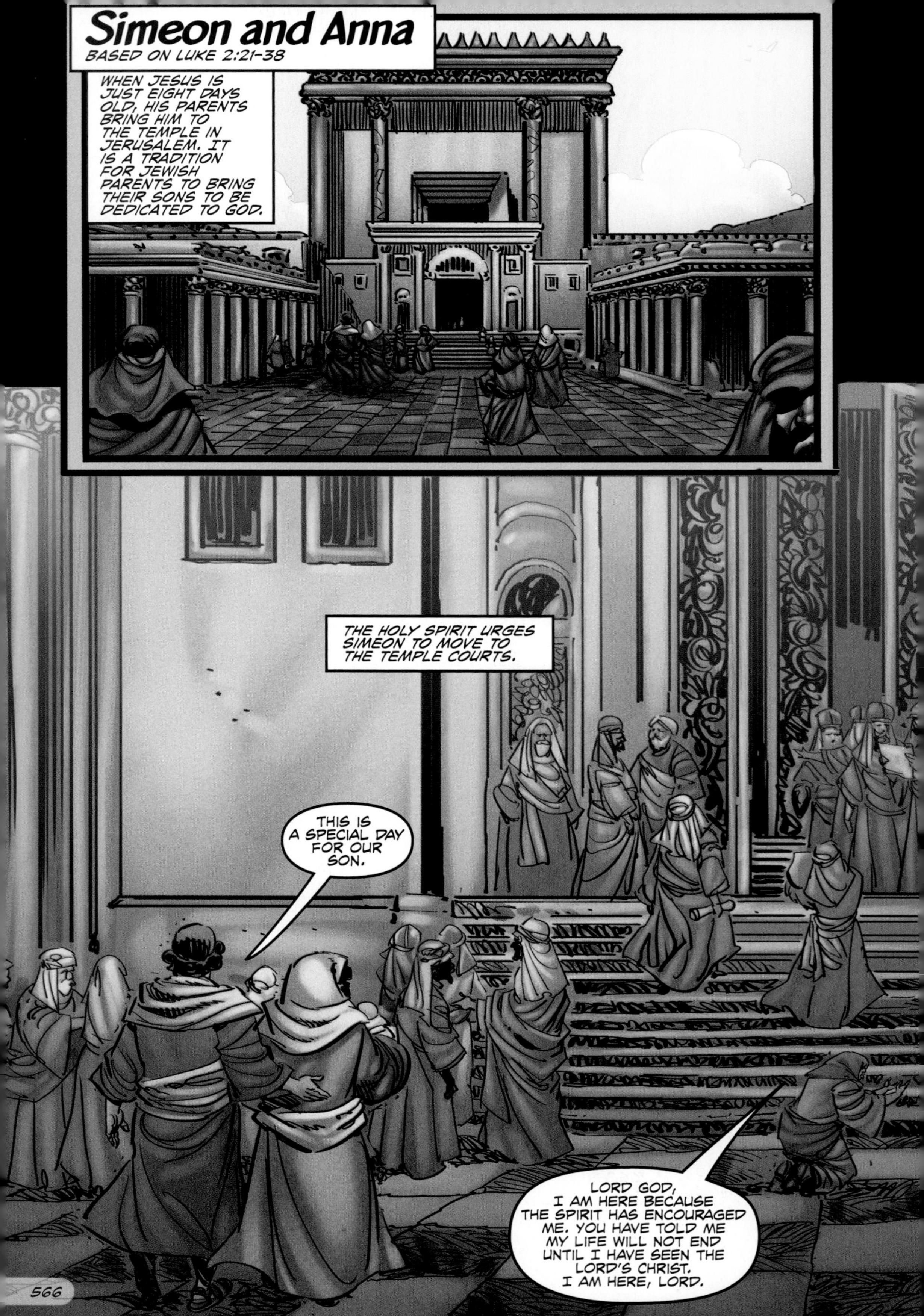
Simeon and Anna
BASED ON LUKE 2:21-38
WHEN JESUS IS JUST EIGHT DAYS OLD, HIS PARENTS BRING HIM TO THE TEMPLE IN JERUSALEM. IT IS A TRADITION FOR JEWISH PARENTS TO BRING THEIR SONS TO BE DEDICATED TO GOD.
THE HOLY SPIRIT URGES SIMEON TO MOVE TO THE TEMPLE COURTS.
THIS IS A SPECIAL DAY FOR OUR SON.
LORD GOD, I AM HERE BECAUSE THE SPIRIT HAS ENCOURAGED ME. YOU HAVE TOLD ME MY LIFE WILL NOT END UNTIL I HAVE SEEN THE LORD'S CHRIST. I AM HERE, LORD.

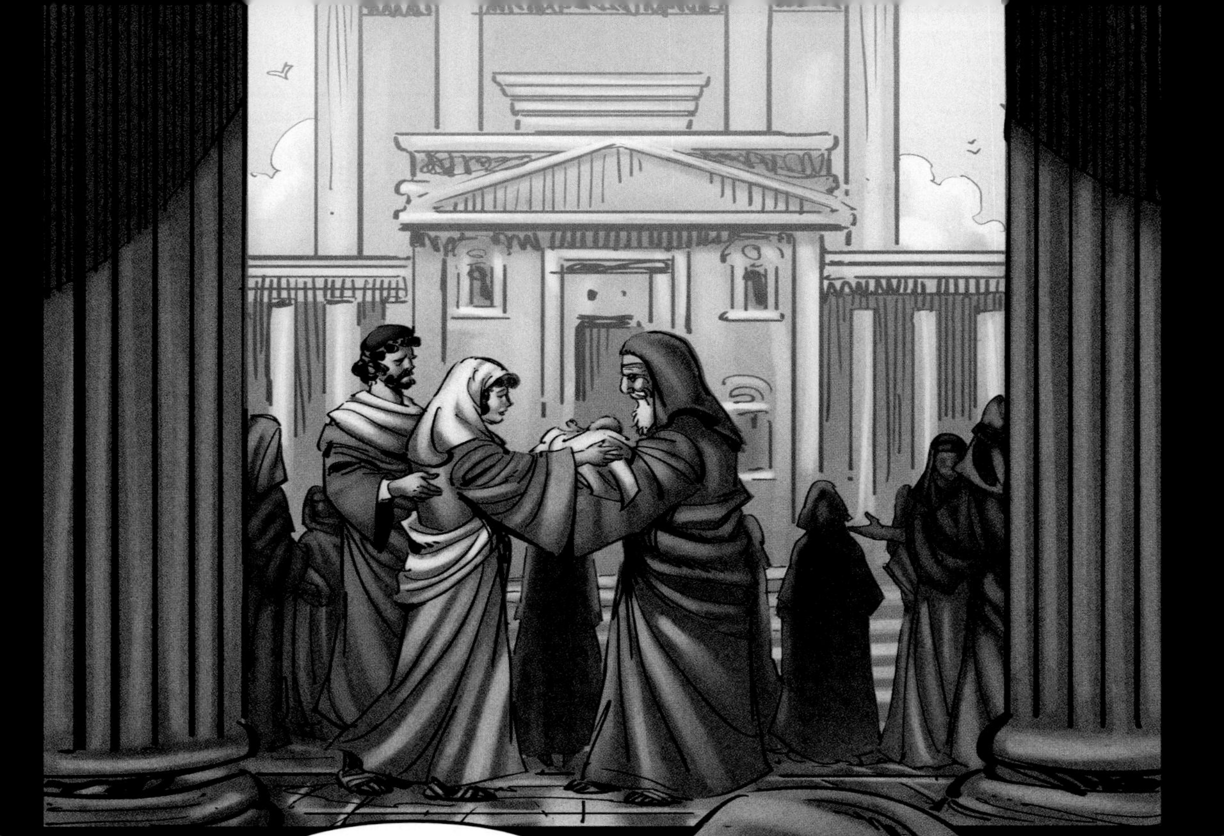

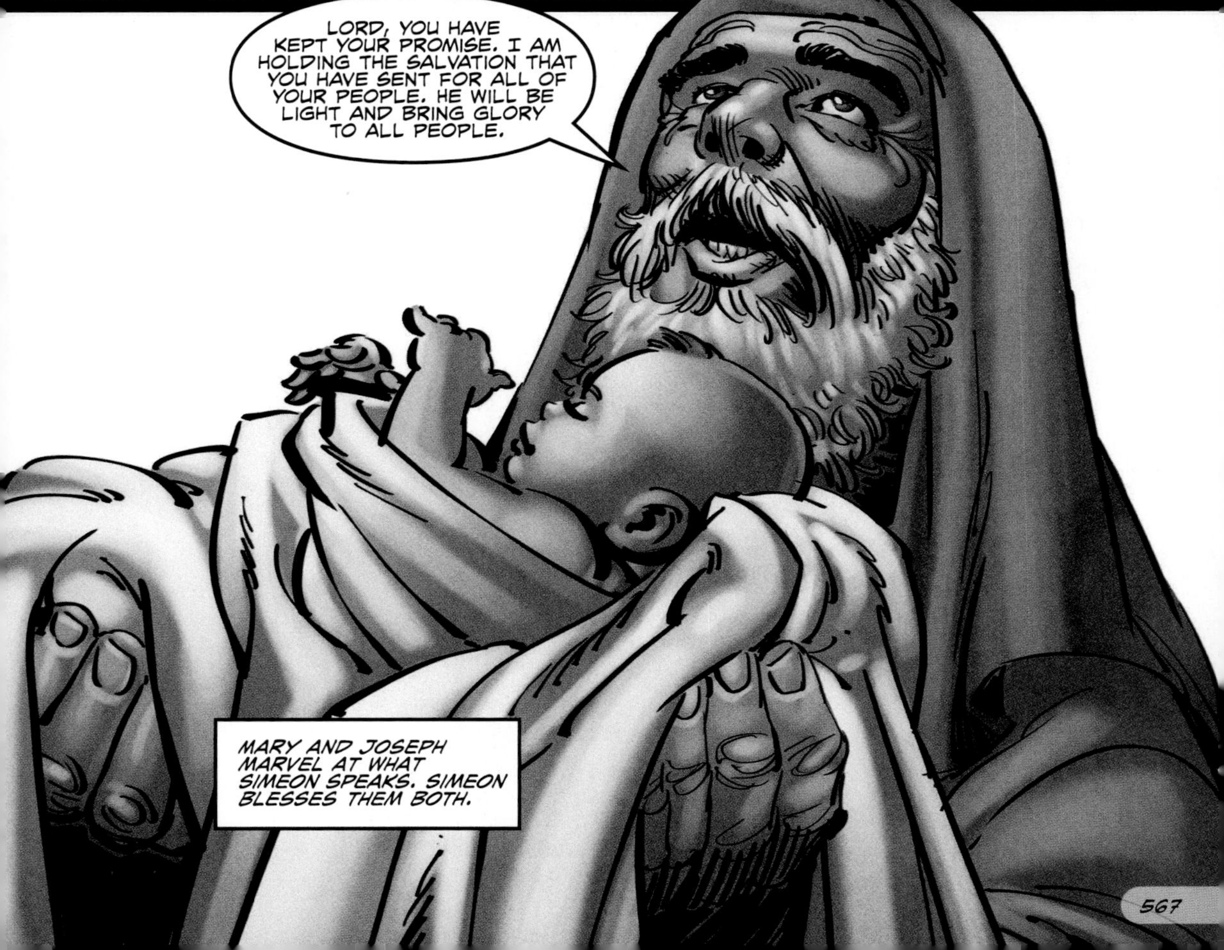
LORD, YOU HAVE KEPT YOUR PROMISE. I AM HOLDING THE SALVATION THAT YOU HAVE SENT FOR ALL OF YOUR PEOPLE. HE WILL BE LIGHT AND BRING GLORY TO ALL PEOPLE.
MARY AND JOSEPH MARVEL AT WHAT SIMEON SPEAKS. SIMEON BLESSES THEM BOTH.

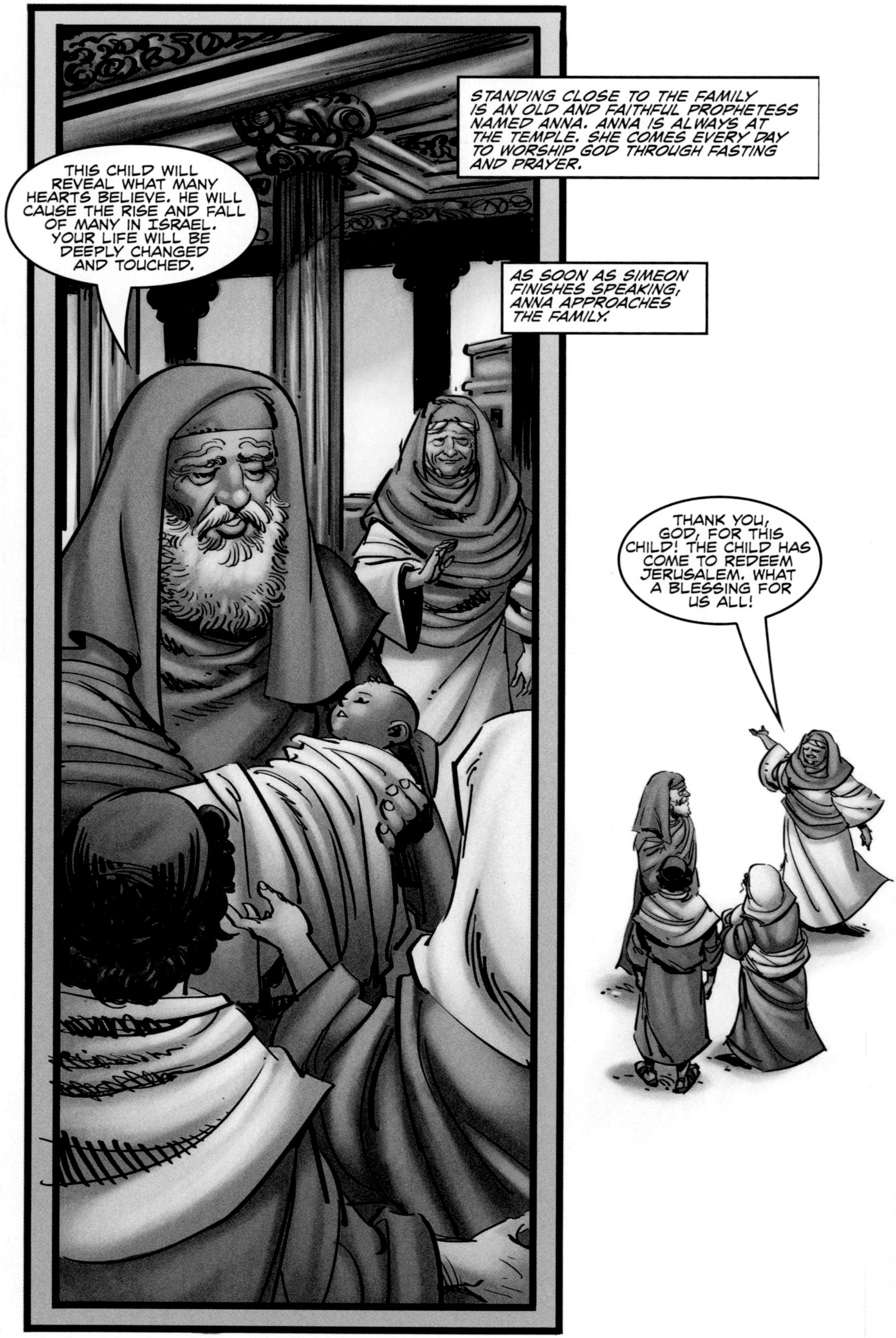
STANDING CLOSE TO THE FAMILY IS AN OLD AND FAITHFUL PROPHETESS NAMED ANNA. ANNA IS ALWAYS AT THE TEMPLE. SHE COMES EVERY DAY TO WORSHIP GOD THROUGH FASTING AND PRAYER.
THIS CHILD WILL REVEAL WHAT MANY HEARTS BELIEVE. HE WILL CAUSE THE RISE AND FALL OF MANY IN ISRAEL. YOUR LIFE WILL BE DEEPLY CHANGED AND TOUCHED.
AS SOON AS SIMEON FINISHES SPEAKING, ANNA APPROACHES THE FAMILY.
THANK YOU, GOD, FOR THIS CHILD! THE CHILD HAS COME TO REDEEM JERUSALEM. WHAT A BLESSING FOR US ALL!

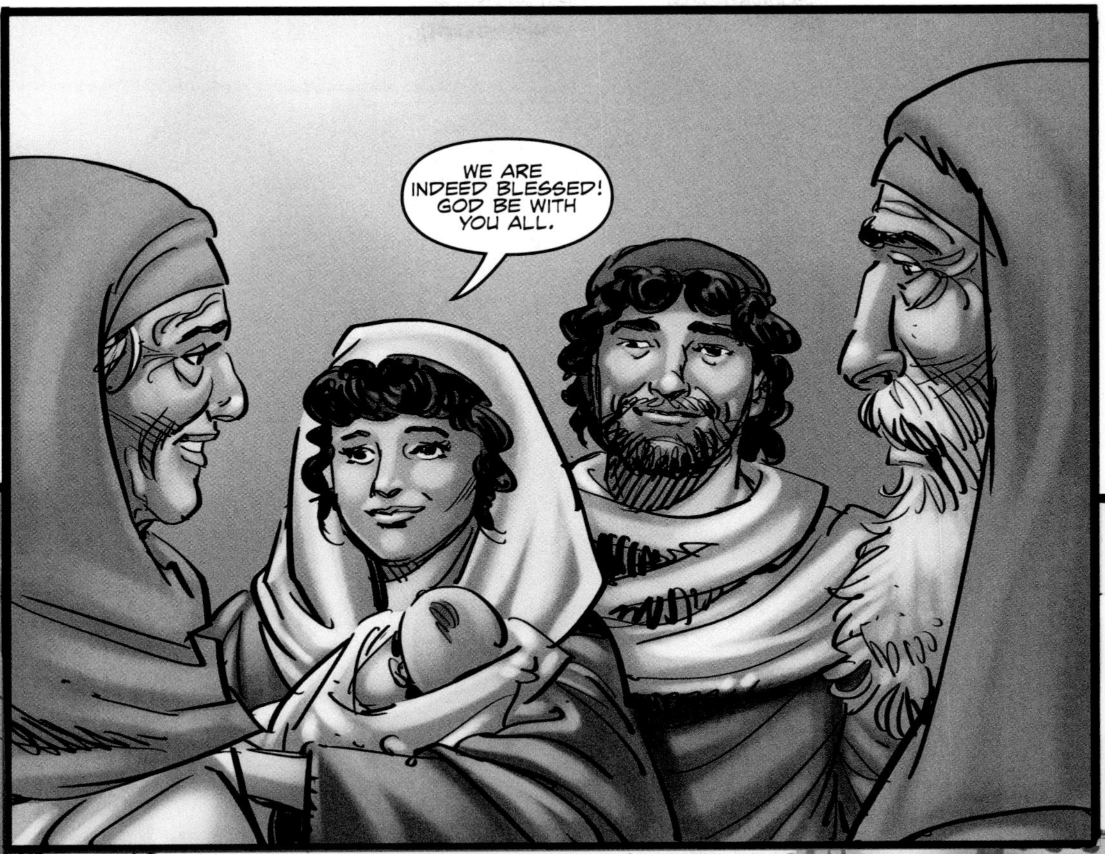
WE ARE INDEED BLESSED! GOD BE WITH YOU ALL.

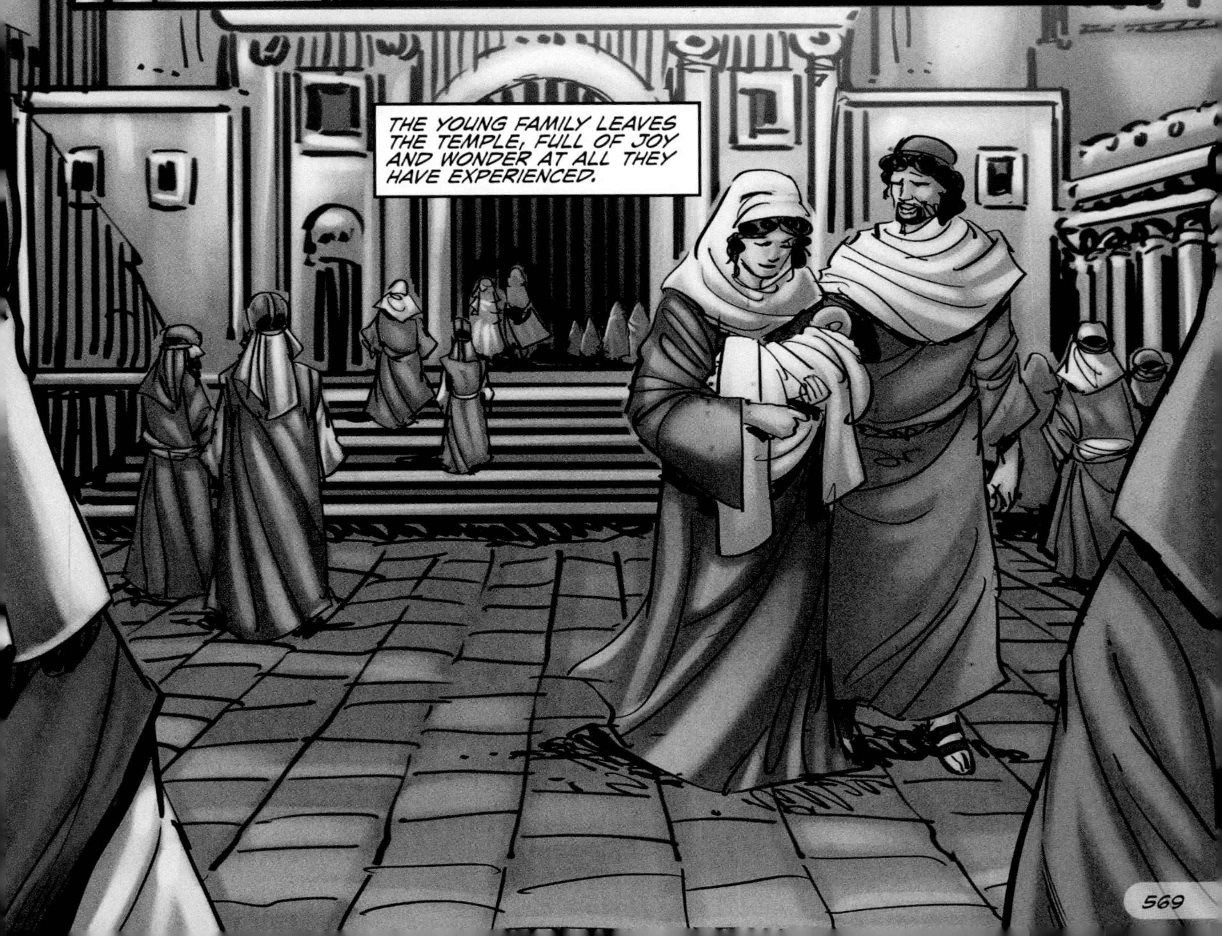
THE YOUNG FAMILY LEAVES THE TEMPLE, FULL OF JOY AND WONDER AT ALL THEY HAVE EXPERIENCED.

Magi from the East

BASED ON MATTHEW 2:1–11

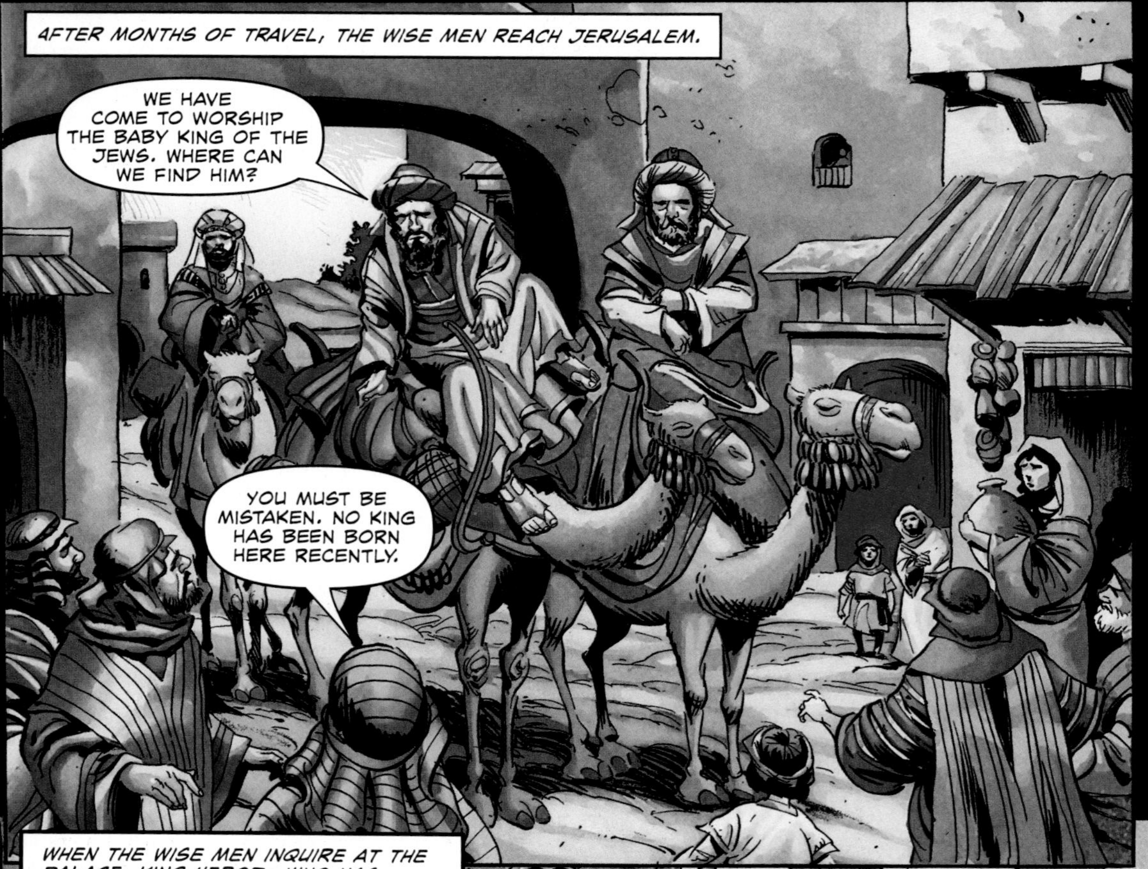
AFTER MONTHS OF TRAVEL, THE WISE MEN REACH JERUSALEM.
WE HAVE COME TO WORSHIP THE BABY KING OF THE JEWS. WHERE CAN WE FIND HIM?
YOU MUST BE MISTAKEN. NO KING HAS BEEN BORN HERE RECENTLY.

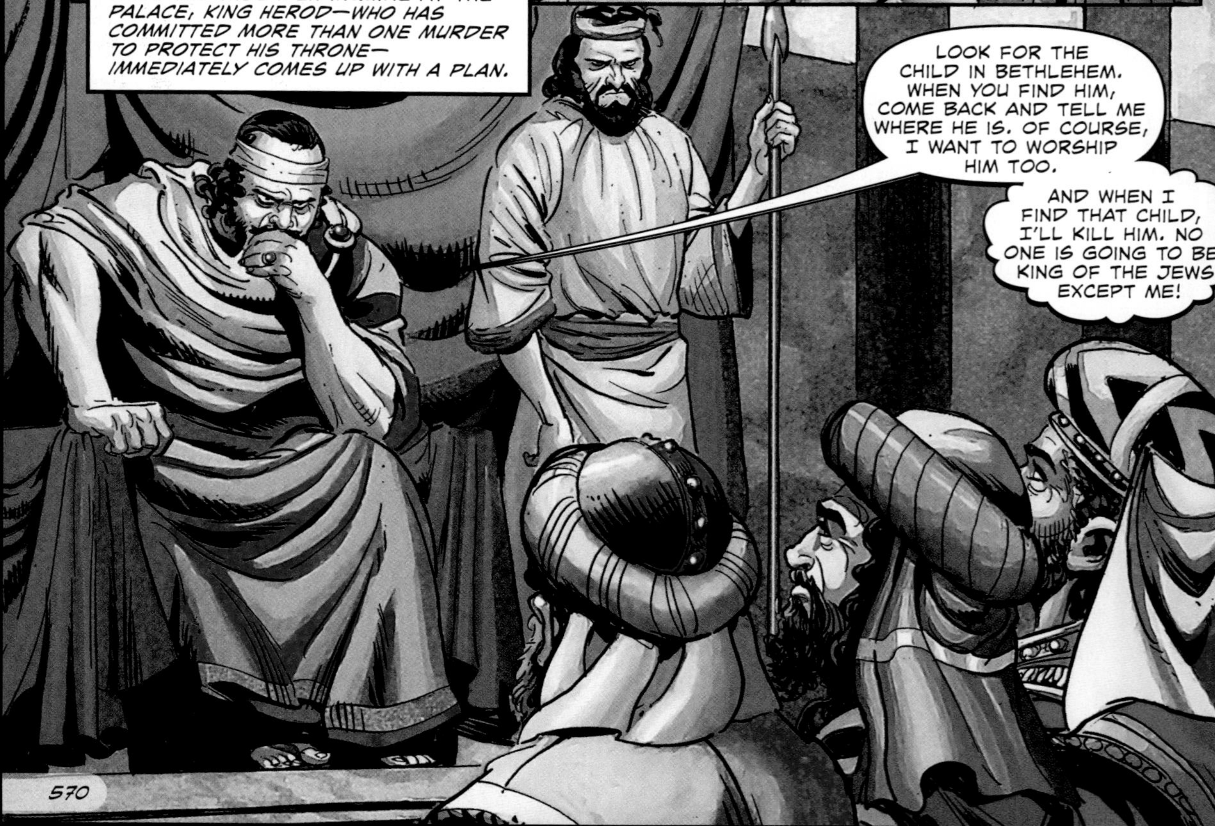
WHEN THE WISE MEN INQUIRE AT THE PALACE, KING HEROD—WHO HAS COMMITTED MORE THAN ONE MURDER TO PROTECT HIS THRONE—IMMEDIATELY COMES UP WITH A PLAN.
LOOK FOR THE CHILD IN BETHLEHEM. WHEN YOU FIND HIM, COME BACK AND TELL ME WHERE HE IS. OF COURSE, I WANT TO WORSHIP HIM TOO.
AND WHEN I FIND THAT CHILD, I'LL KILL HIM. NO ONE IS GOING TO BE KING OF THE JEWS EXCEPT ME!

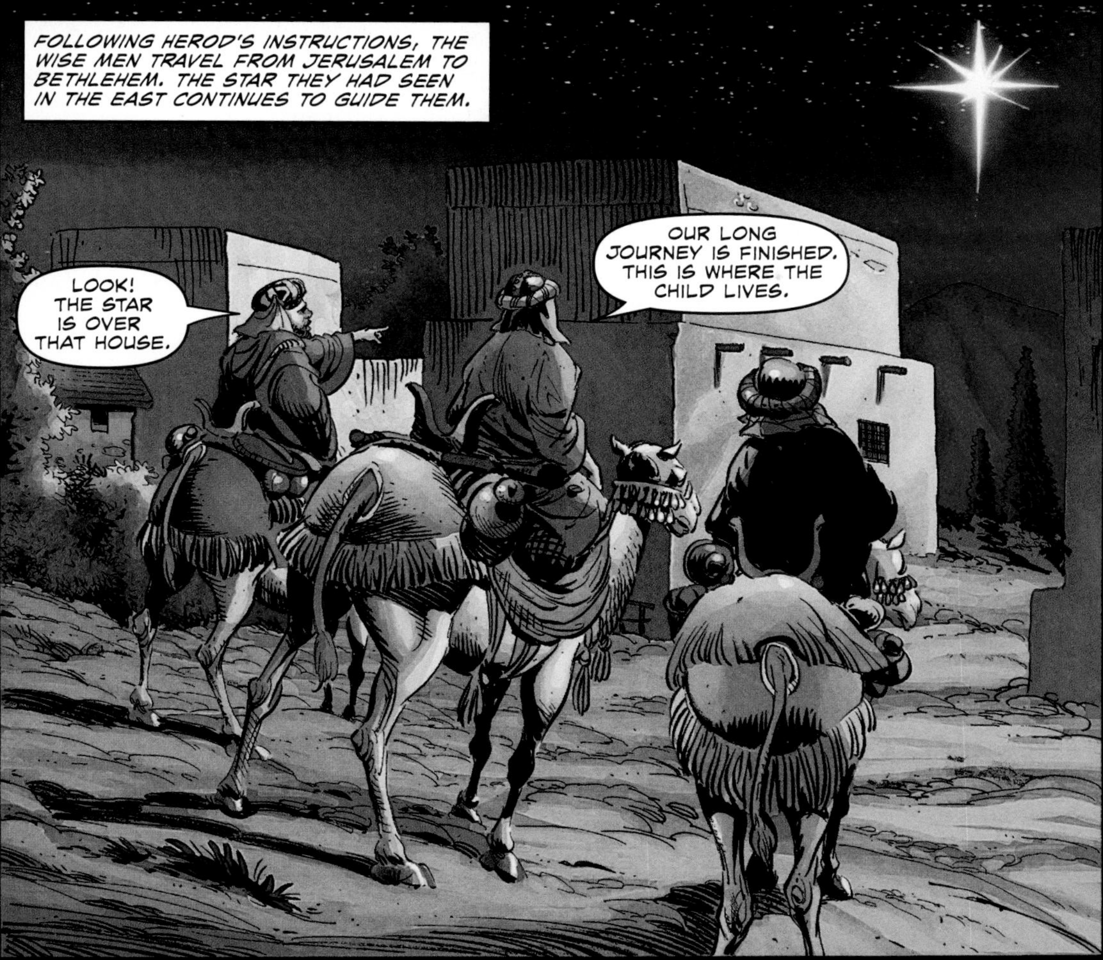
FOLLOWING HEROD'S INSTRUCTIONS, THE WISE MEN TRAVEL FROM JERUSALEM TO BETHLEHEM. THE STAR THEY HAD SEEN IN THE EAST CONTINUES TO GUIDE THEM.
LOOK! THE STAR IS OVER THAT HOUSE.
OUR LONG JOURNEY IS FINISHED. THIS IS WHERE THE CHILD LIVES.

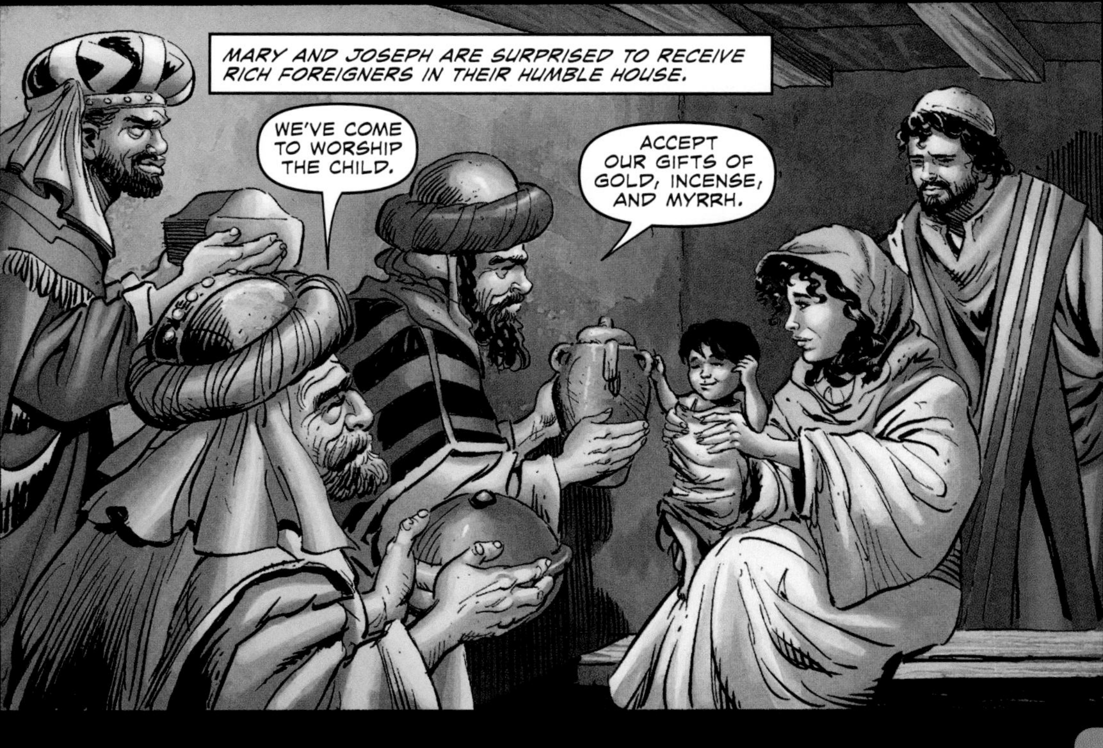
MARY AND JOSEPH ARE SURPRISED TO RECEIVE RICH FOREIGNERS IN THEIR HUMBLE HOUSE.
WE'VE COME TO WORSHIP THE CHILD.
ACCEPT OUR GIFTS OF GOLD, INCENSE, AND MYRRH.

Flight in the Night

BASED ON MATTHEW 2:12-18

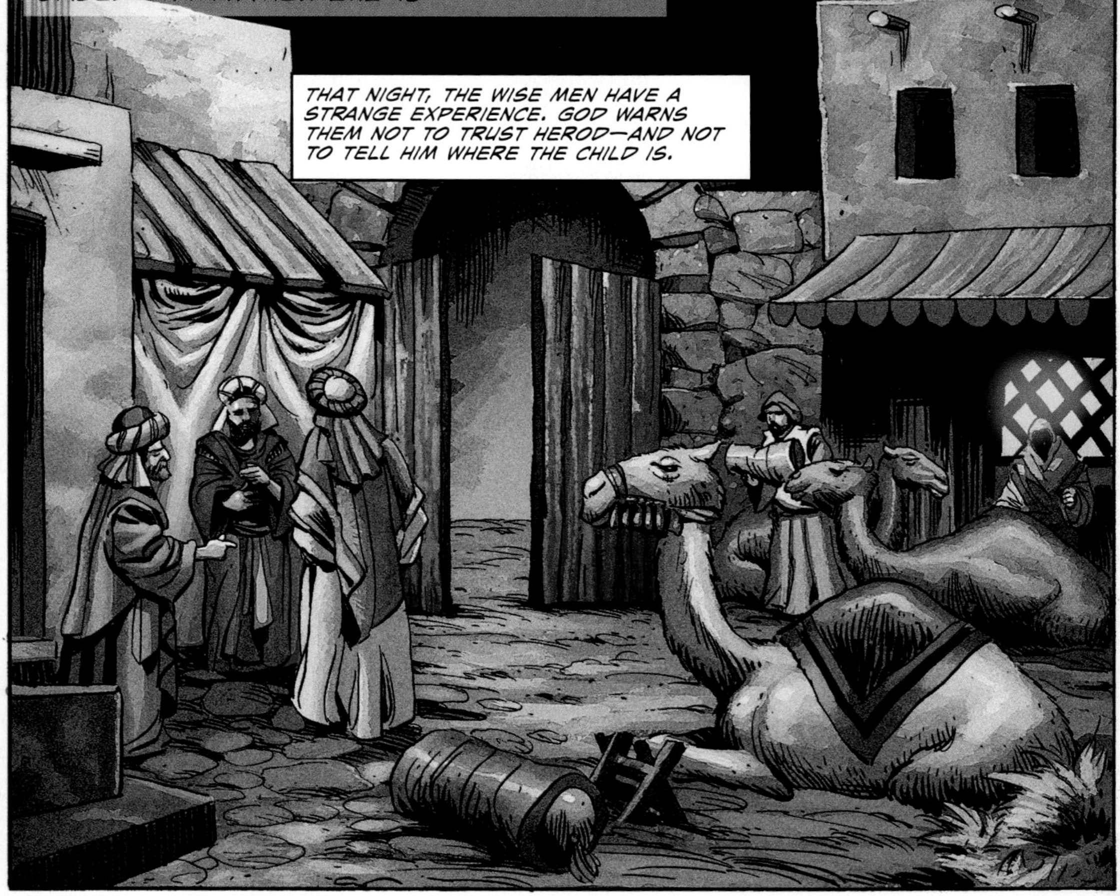
THAT NIGHT, THE WISE MEN HAVE A STRANGE EXPERIENCE. GOD WARNS THEM NOT TO TRUST HEROD—AND NOT TO TELL HIM WHERE THE CHILD IS.

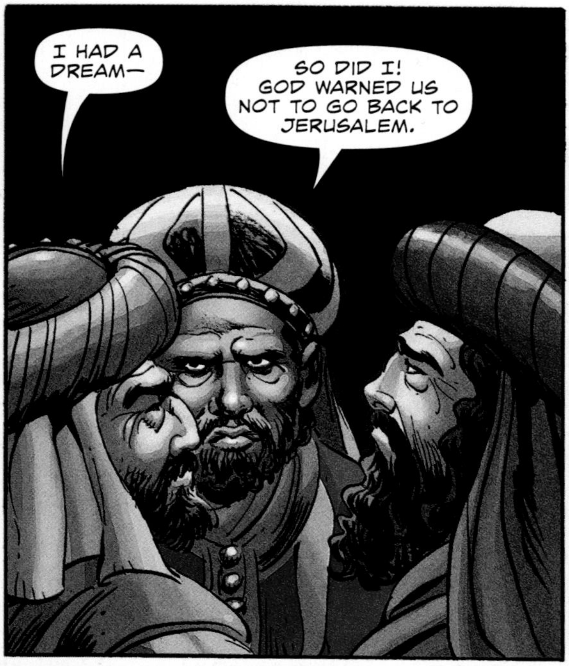
I HAD A DREAM—
SO DID I! GOD WARNED US NOT TO GO BACK TO JERUSALEM.

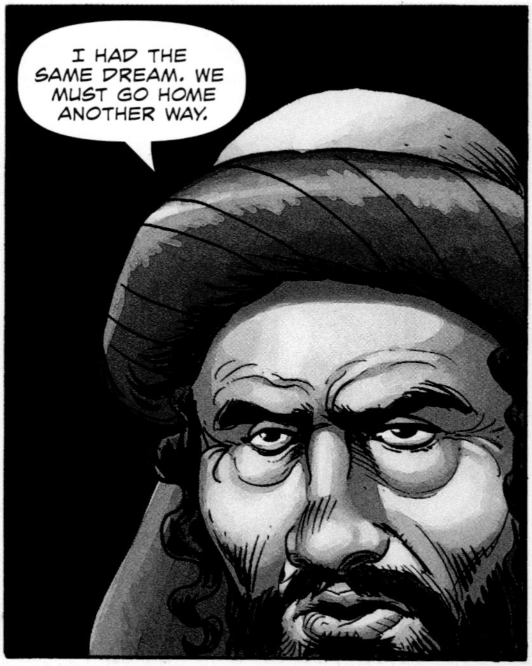
I HAD THE SAME DREAM. WE MUST GO HOME ANOTHER WAY.

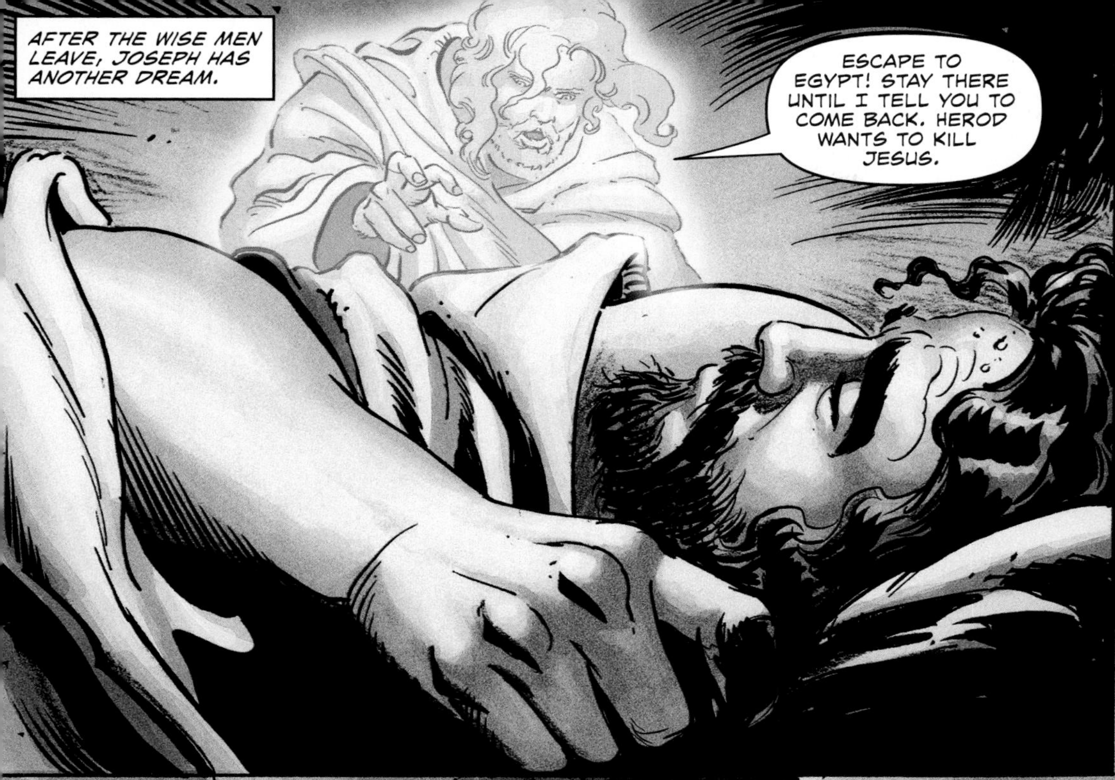
AFTER THE WISE MEN LEAVE, JOSEPH HAS ANOTHER DREAM.
ESCAPE TO EGYPT! STAY THERE UNTIL I TELL YOU TO COME BACK. HEROD WANTS TO KILL JESUS.

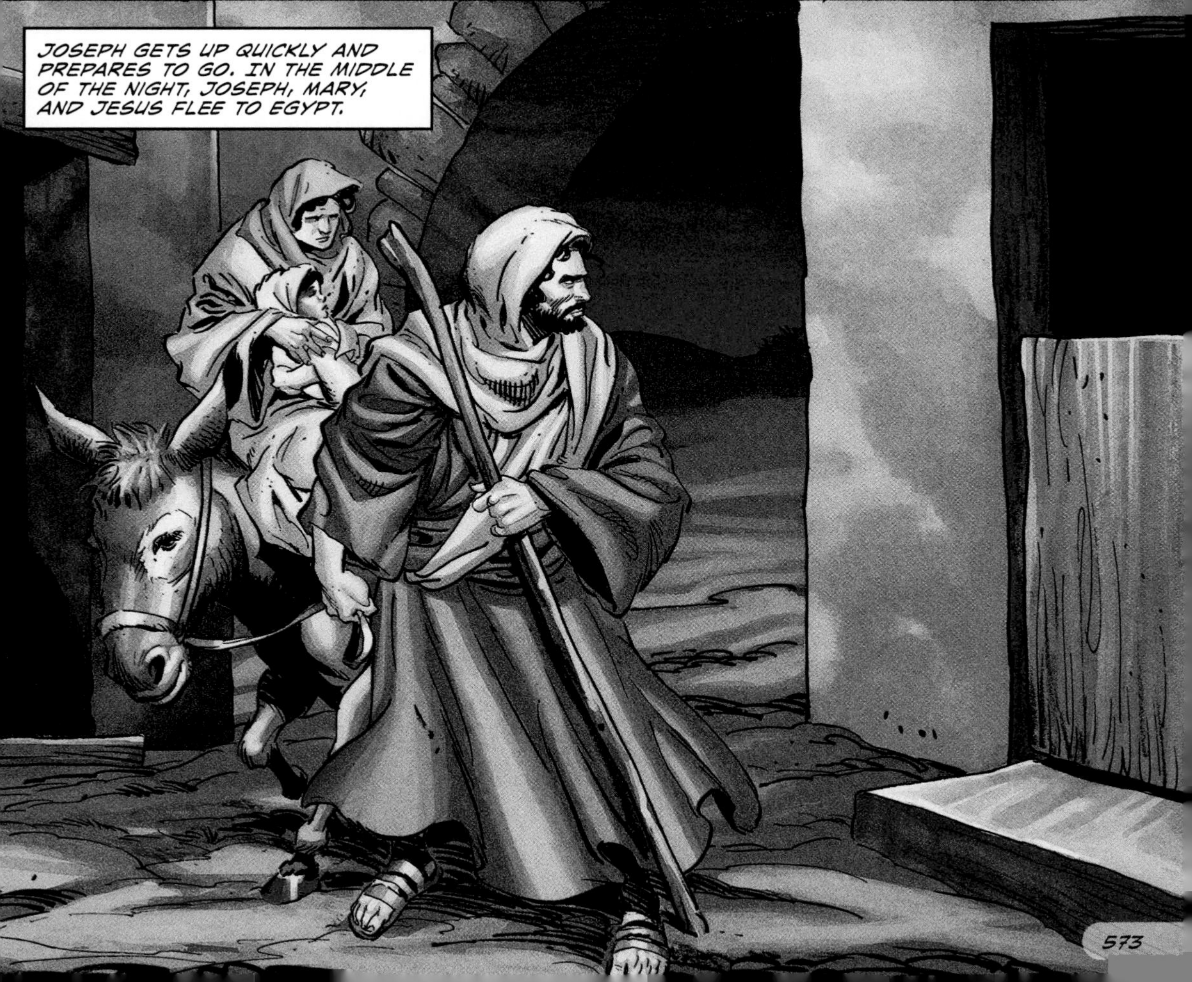
JOSEPH GETS UP QUICKLY AND PREPARES TO GO. IN THE MIDDLE OF THE NIGHT, JOSEPH, MARY, AND JESUS FLEE TO EGYPT.

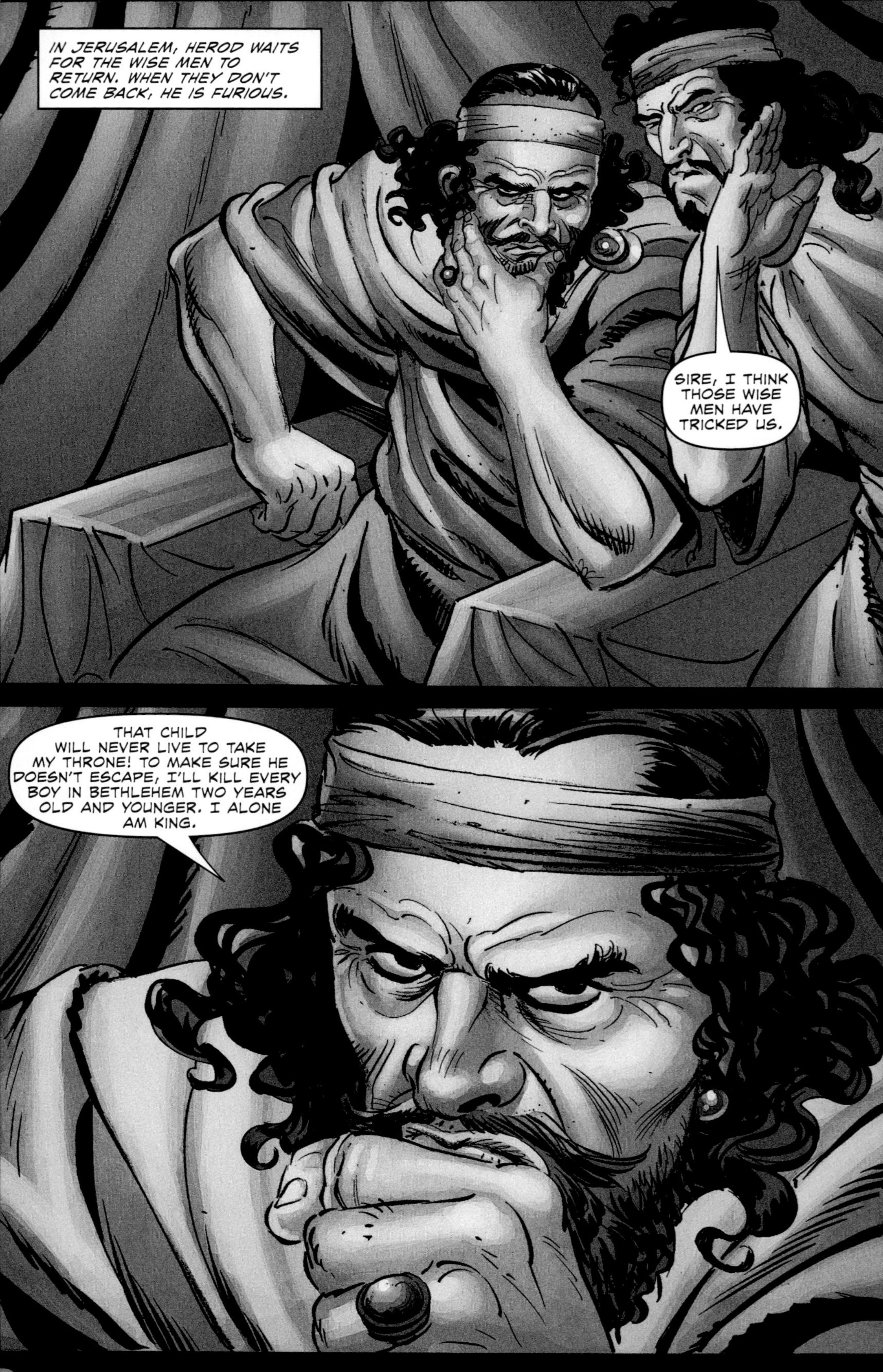
IN JERUSALEM, HEROD WAITS FOR THE WISE MEN TO RETURN. WHEN THEY DON'T COME BACK, HE IS FURIOUS.
SIRE, I THINK THOSE WISE MEN HAVE TRICKED US.
THAT CHILD WILL NEVER LIVE TO TAKE MY THRONE! TO MAKE SURE HE DOESN'T ESCAPE, I'LL KILL EVERY BOY IN BETHLEHEM TWO YEARS OLD AND YOUNGER. I ALONE AM KING.

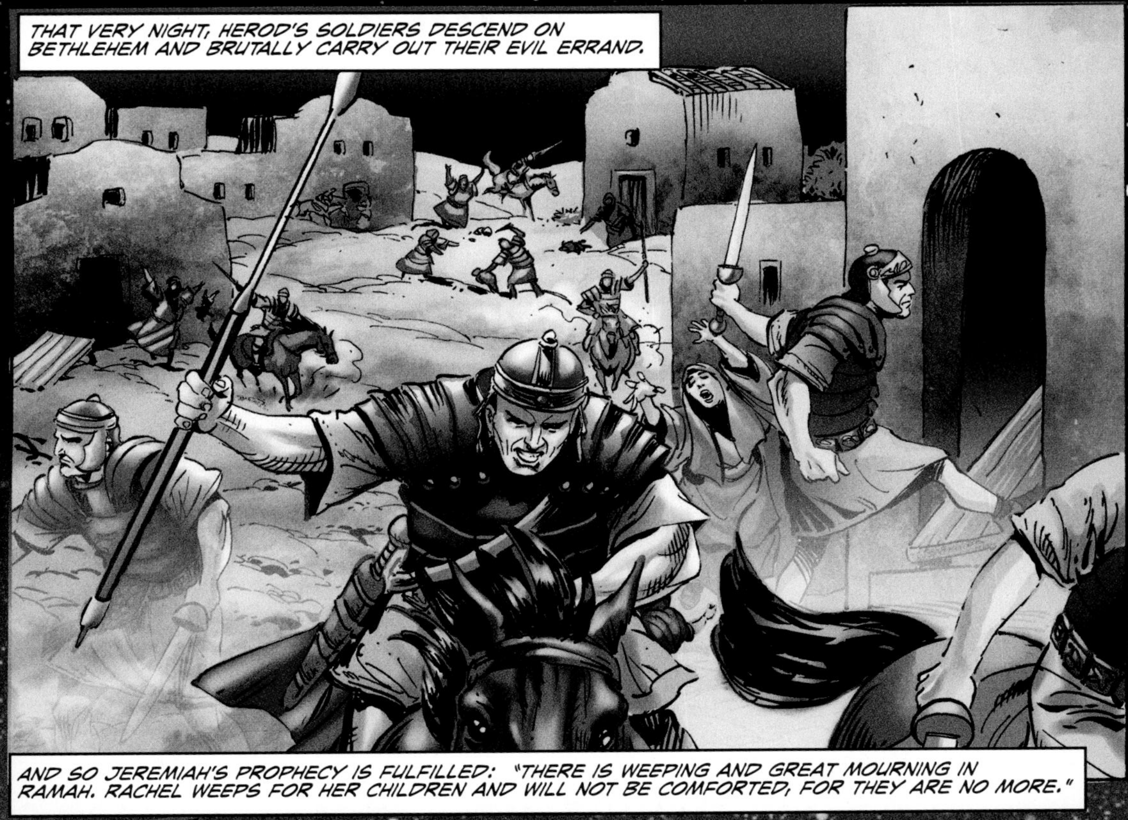

THAT VERY NIGHT, HEROD'S SOLDIERS DESCEND ON BETHLEHEM AND BRUTALLY CARRY OUT THEIR EVIL ERRAND.
AND SO JEREMIAH'S PROPHECY IS FULFILLED: "THERE IS WEEPING AND GREAT MOURNING IN RAMAH. RACHEL WEEPS FOR HER CHILDREN AND WILL NOT BE COMFORTED, FOR THEY ARE NO MORE."

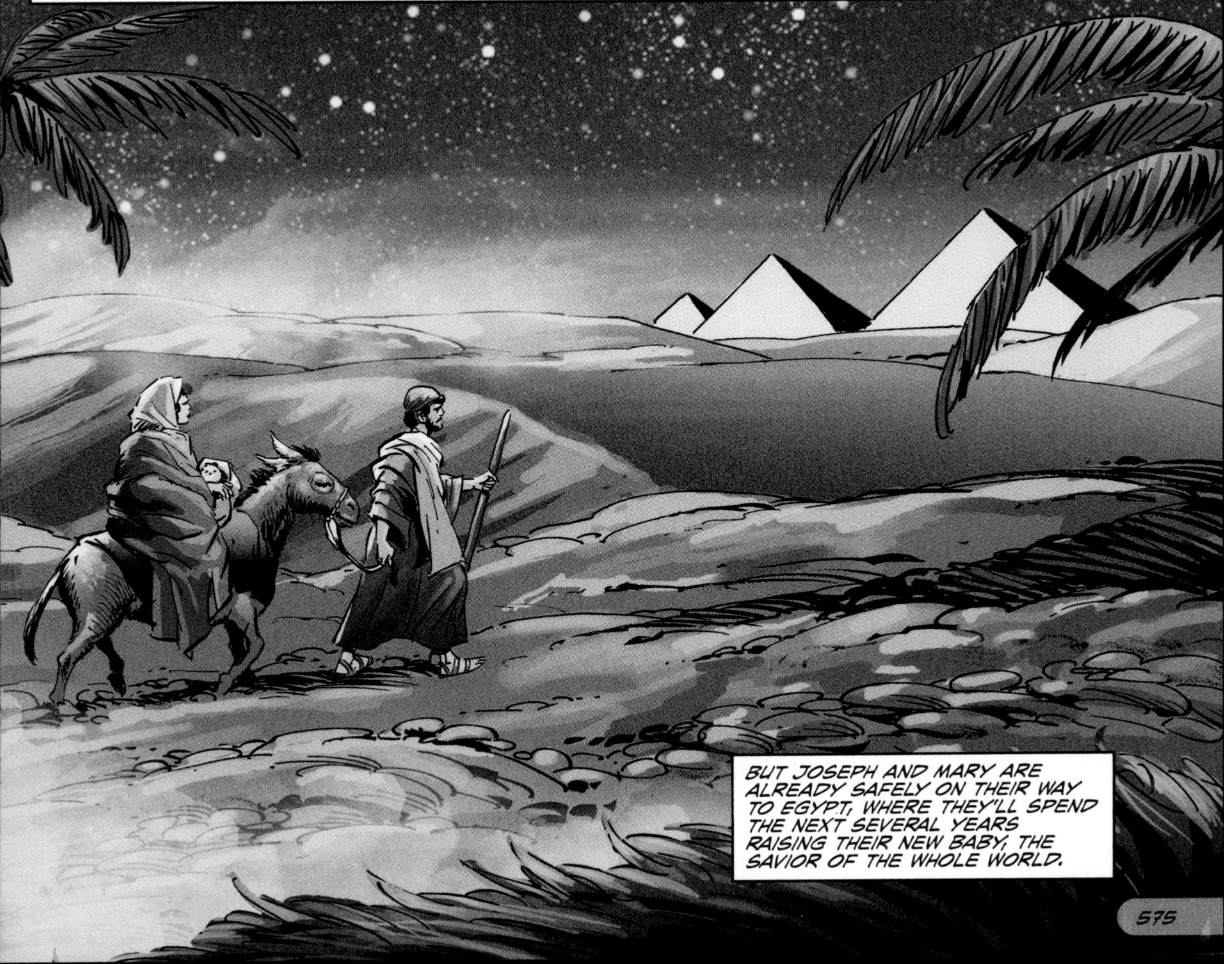

BUT JOSEPH AND MARY ARE ALREADY SAFELY ON THEIR WAY TO EGYPT, WHERE THEY'LL SPEND THE NEXT SEVERAL YEARS RAISING THEIR NEW BABY, THE SAVIOR OF THE WHOLE WORLD.

A Boy in the Temple

BASED ON MATTHEW 2:19–23; LUKE 2:39–52

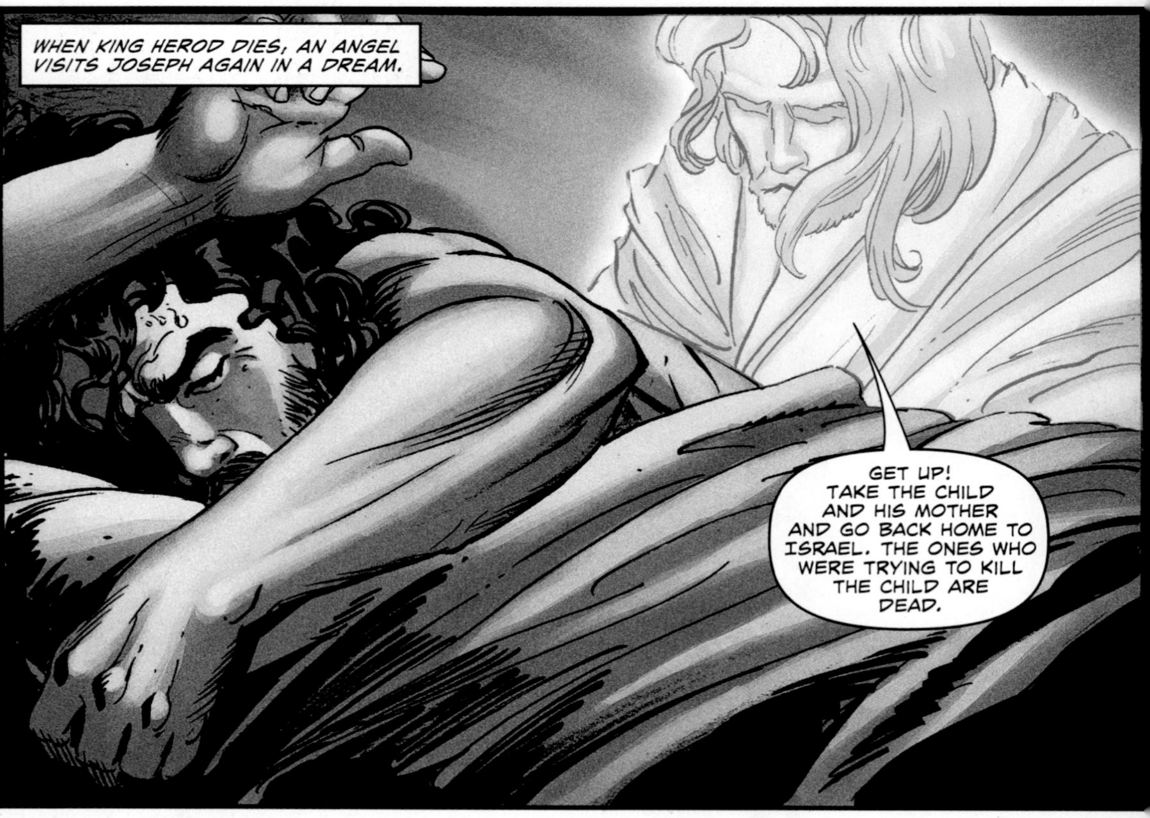
WHEN KING HEROD DIES, AN ANGEL VISITS JOSEPH AGAIN IN A DREAM.
GET UP! TAKE THE CHILD AND HIS MOTHER AND GO BACK HOME TO ISRAEL. THE ONES WHO WERE TRYING TO KILL THE CHILD ARE DEAD.

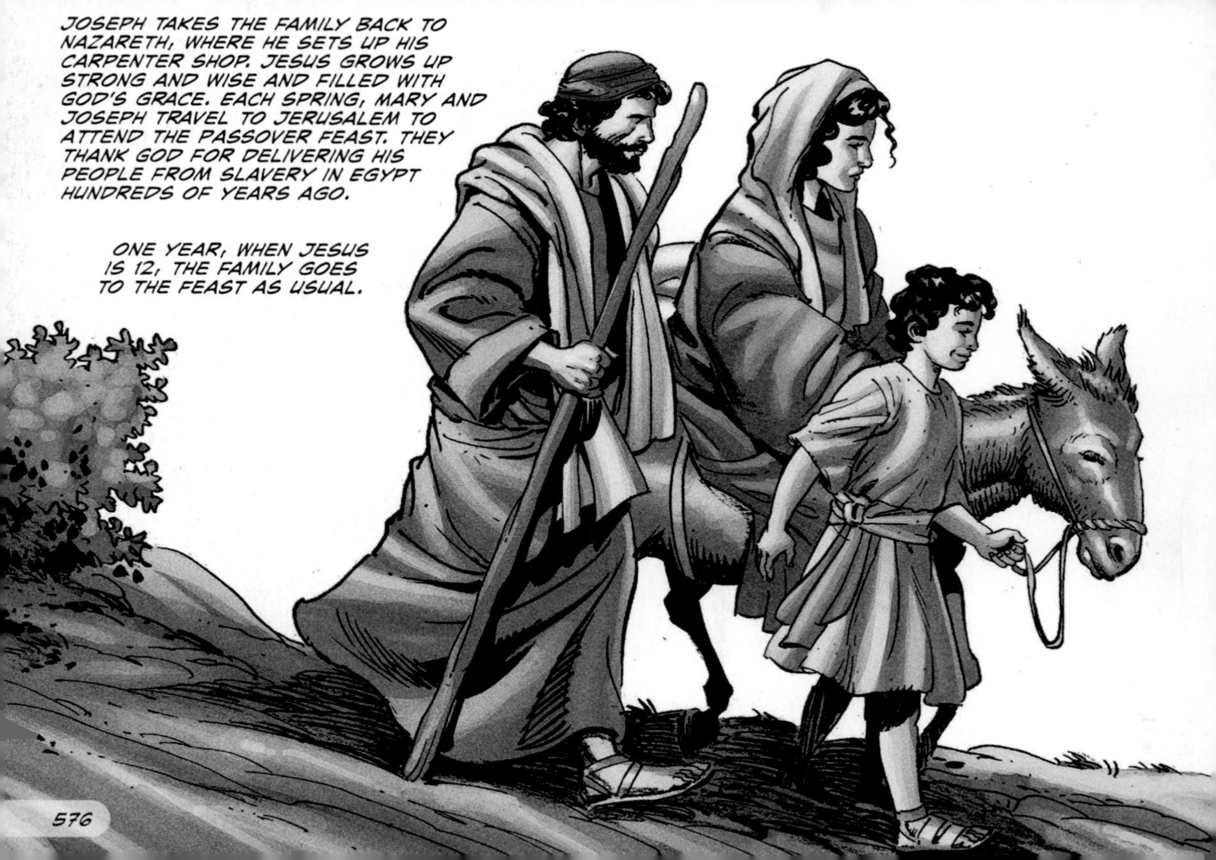
JOSEPH TAKES THE FAMILY BACK TO NAZARETH, WHERE HE SETS UP HIS CARPENTER SHOP. JESUS GROWS UP STRONG AND WISE AND FILLED WITH GOD'S GRACE. EACH SPRING, MARY AND JOSEPH TRAVEL TO JERUSALEM TO ATTEND THE PASSOVER FEAST. THEY THANK GOD FOR DELIVERING HIS PEOPLE FROM SLAVERY IN EGYPT HUNDREDS OF YEARS AGO.
ONE YEAR, WHEN JESUS IS 12, THE FAMILY GOES TO THE FEAST AS USUAL.

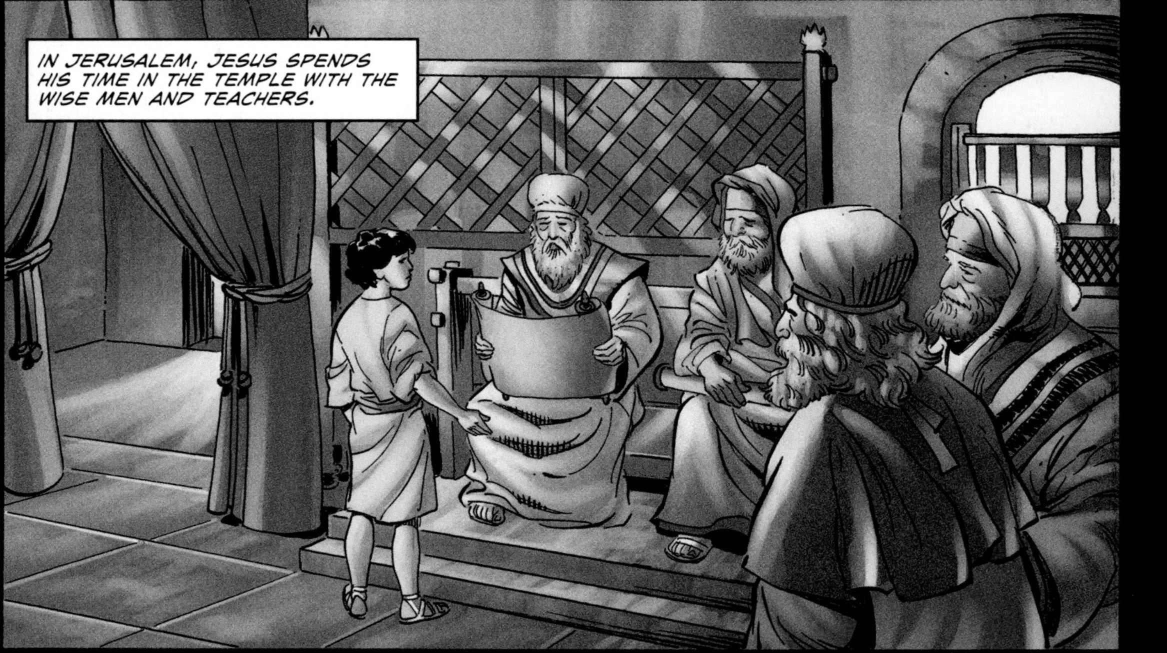
IN JERUSALEM, JESUS SPENDS HIS TIME IN THE TEMPLE WITH THE WISE MEN AND TEACHERS.

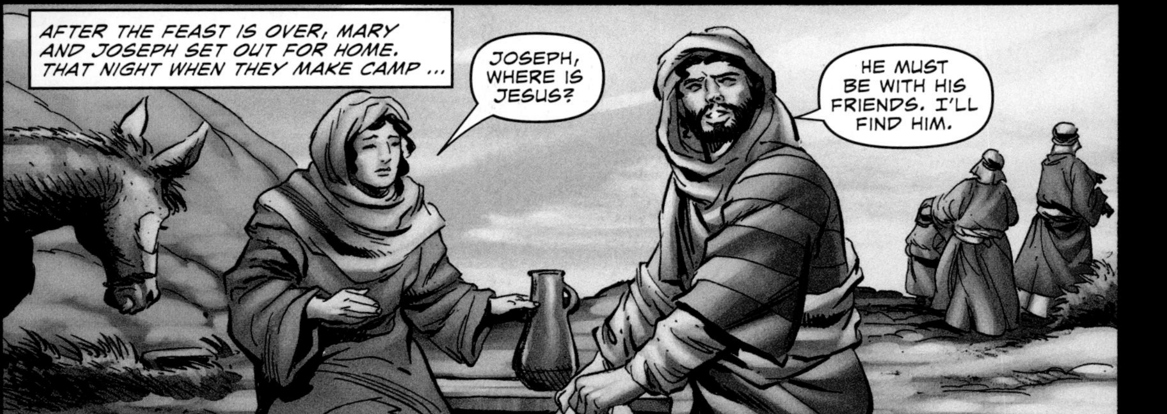
AFTER THE FEAST IS OVER, MARY AND JOSEPH SET OUT FOR HOME. THAT NIGHT WHEN THEY MAKE CAMP ...
JOSEPH, WHERE IS JESUS?
HE MUST BE WITH HIS FRIENDS. I'LL FIND HIM.

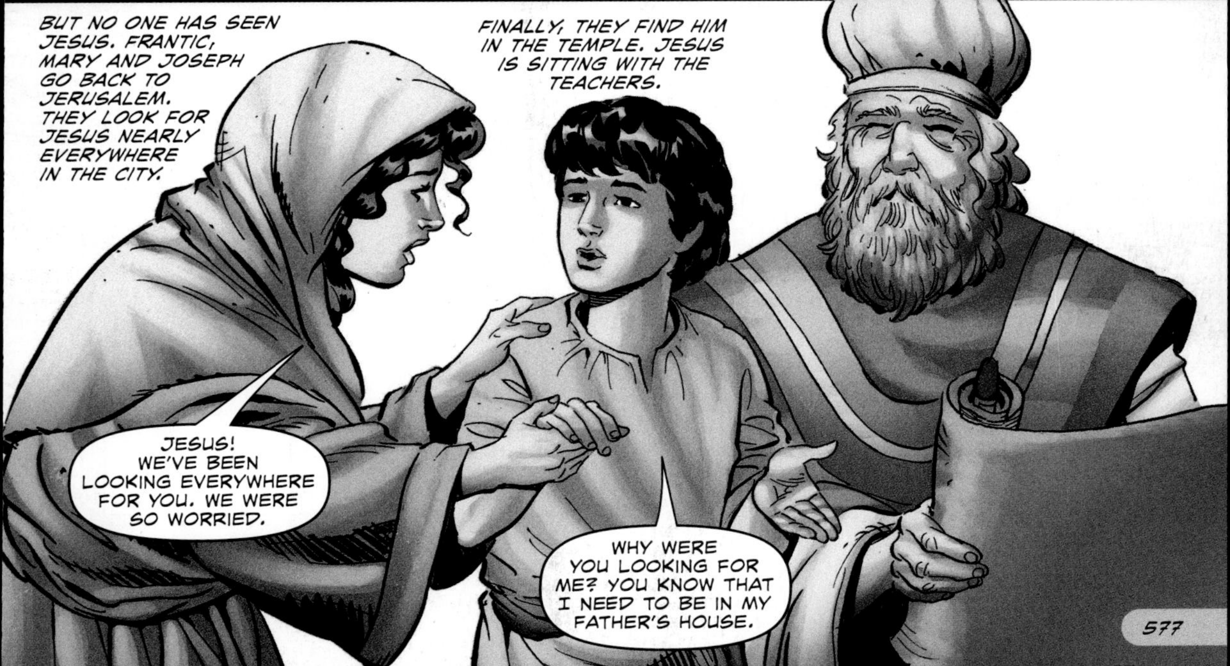
BUT NO ONE HAS SEEN JESUS. FRANTIC, MARY AND JOSEPH GO BACK TO JERUSALEM. THEY LOOK FOR JESUS NEARLY EVERYWHERE IN THE CITY.
FINALLY, THEY FIND HIM IN THE TEMPLE. JESUS IS SITTING WITH THE TEACHERS.
JESUS! WE'VE BEEN LOOKING EVERYWHERE FOR YOU. WE WERE SO WORRIED.
WHY WERE YOU LOOKING FOR ME? YOU KNOW THAT I NEED TO BE IN MY FATHER'S HOUSE.

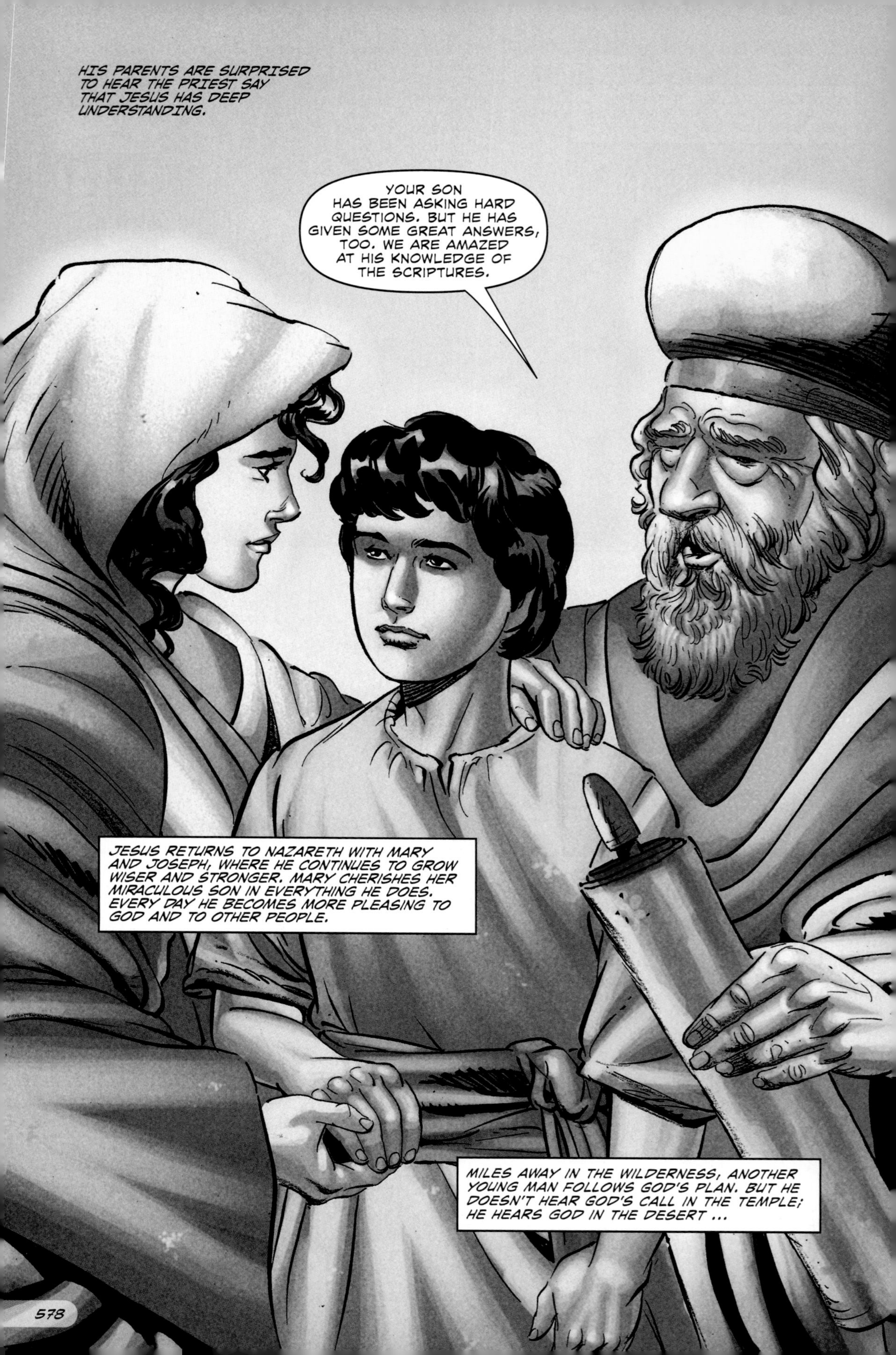
HIS PARENTS ARE SURPRISED TO HEAR THE PRIEST SAY THAT JESUS HAS DEEP UNDERSTANDING.
YOUR SON HAS BEEN ASKING HARD QUESTIONS. BUT HE HAS GIVEN SOME GREAT ANSWERS, TOO. WE ARE AMAZED AT HIS KNOWLEDGE OF THE SCRIPTURES.
JESUS RETURNS TO NAZARETH WITH MARY AND JOSEPH, WHERE HE CONTINUES TO GROW WISER AND STRONGER. MARY CHERISHES HER MIRACULOUS SON IN EVERYTHING HE DOES. EVERY DAY HE BECOMES MORE PLEASING TO GOD AND TO OTHER PEOPLE.
MILES AWAY IN THE WILDERNESS, ANOTHER YOUNG MAN FOLLOWS GOD'S PLAN. BUT HE DOESN'T HEAR GOD'S CALL IN THE TEMPLE; HE HEARS GOD IN THE DESERT ...

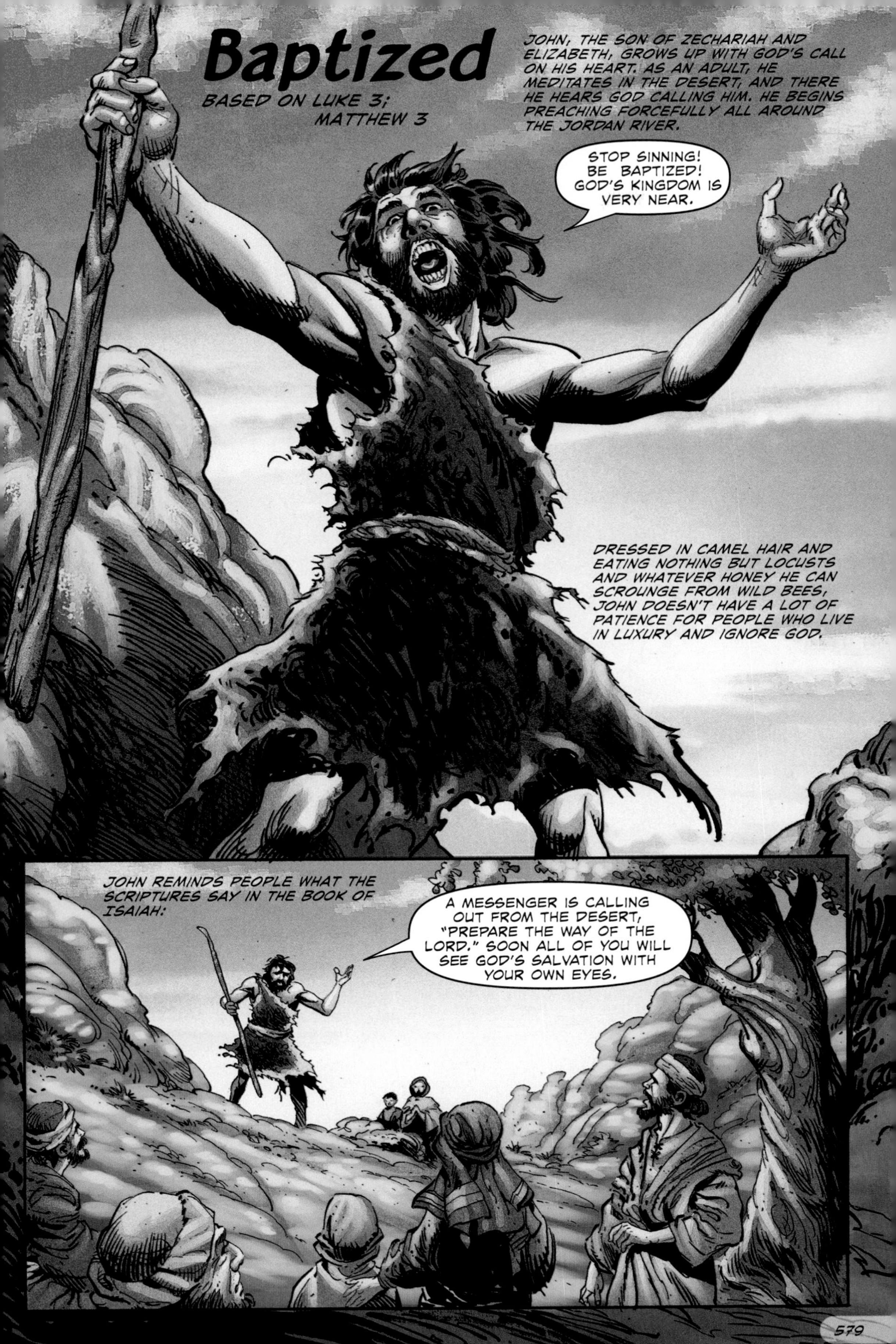
Baptized
BASED ON LUKE 3; MATTHEW 3
JOHN, THE SON OF ZECHARIAH AND ELIZABETH, GROWS UP WITH GOD'S CALL ON HIS HEART. AS AN ADULT, HE MEDITATES IN THE DESERT, AND THERE HE HEARS GOD CALLING HIM. HE BEGINS PREACHING FORCEFULLY ALL AROUND THE JORDAN RIVER.
STOP SINNING! BE BAPTIZED! GOD'S KINGDOM IS VERY NEAR.
DRESSED IN CAMEL HAIR AND EATING NOTHING BUT LOCUSTS AND WHATEVER HONEY HE CAN SCROUNGE FROM WILD BEES, JOHN DOESN'T HAVE A LOT OF PATIENCE FOR PEOPLE WHO LIVE IN LUXURY AND IGNORE GOD.
JOHN REMINDS PEOPLE WHAT THE SCRIPTURES SAY IN THE BOOK OF ISAIAH:
A MESSENGER IS CALLING OUT FROM THE DESERT, "PREPARE THE WAY OF THE LORD." SOON ALL OF YOU WILL SEE GOD'S SALVATION WITH YOUR OWN EYES.

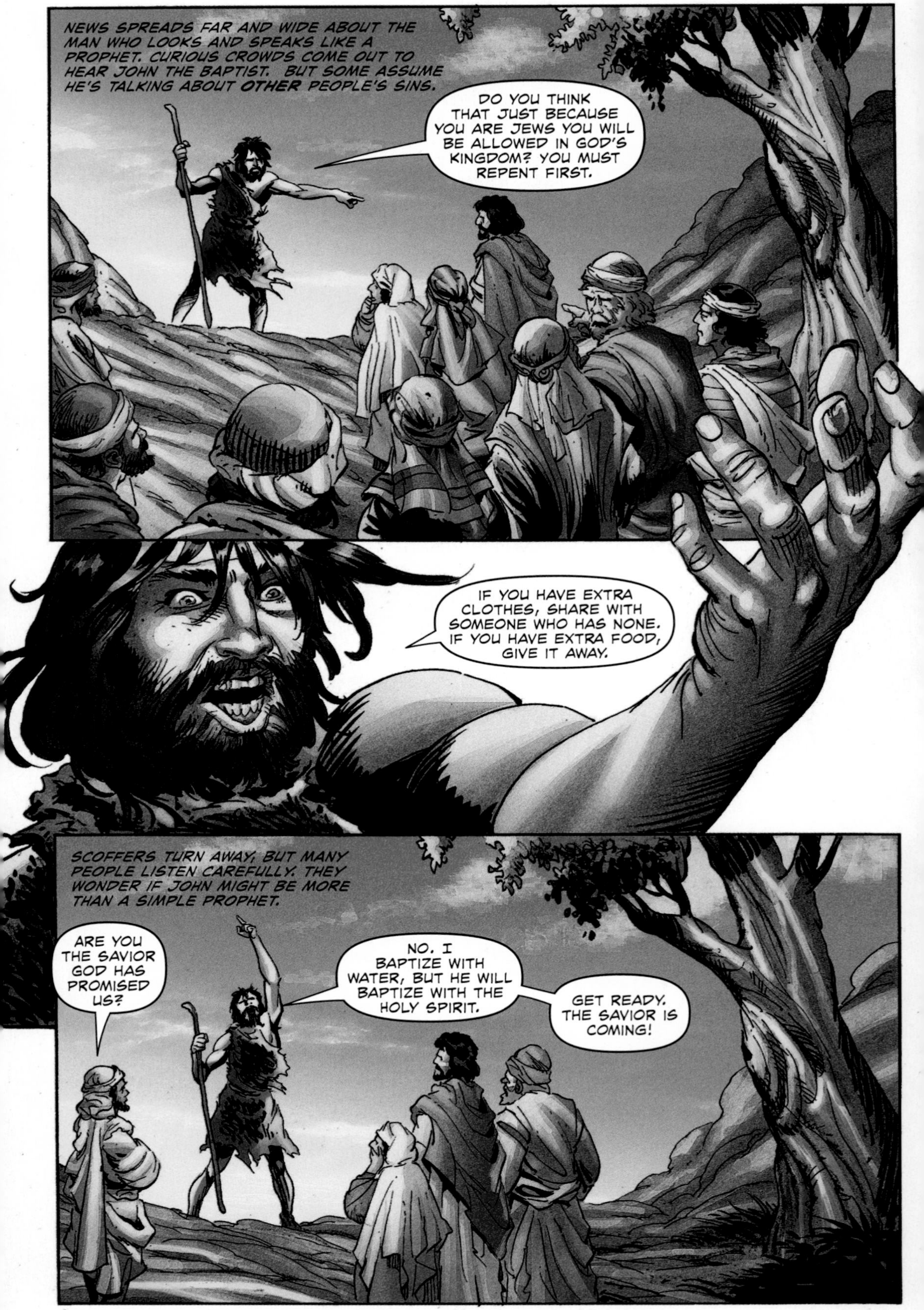
NEWS SPREADS FAR AND WIDE ABOUT THE MAN WHO LOOKS AND SPEAKS LIKE A PROPHET. CURIOUS CROWDS COME OUT TO HEAR JOHN THE BAPTIST. BUT SOME ASSUME HE'S TALKING ABOUT **OTHER** PEOPLE'S SINS.
DO YOU THINK THAT JUST BECAUSE YOU ARE JEWS YOU WILL BE ALLOWED IN GOD'S KINGDOM? YOU MUST REPENT FIRST.
IF YOU HAVE EXTRA CLOTHES, SHARE WITH SOMEONE WHO HAS NONE. IF YOU HAVE EXTRA FOOD, GIVE IT AWAY.
SCOFFERS TURN AWAY, BUT MANY PEOPLE LISTEN CAREFULLY. THEY WONDER IF JOHN MIGHT BE MORE THAN A SIMPLE PROPHET.
ARE YOU THE SAVIOR GOD HAS PROMISED US?
NO. I BAPTIZE WITH WATER, BUT HE WILL BAPTIZE WITH THE HOLY SPIRIT.
GET READY. THE SAVIOR IS COMING!

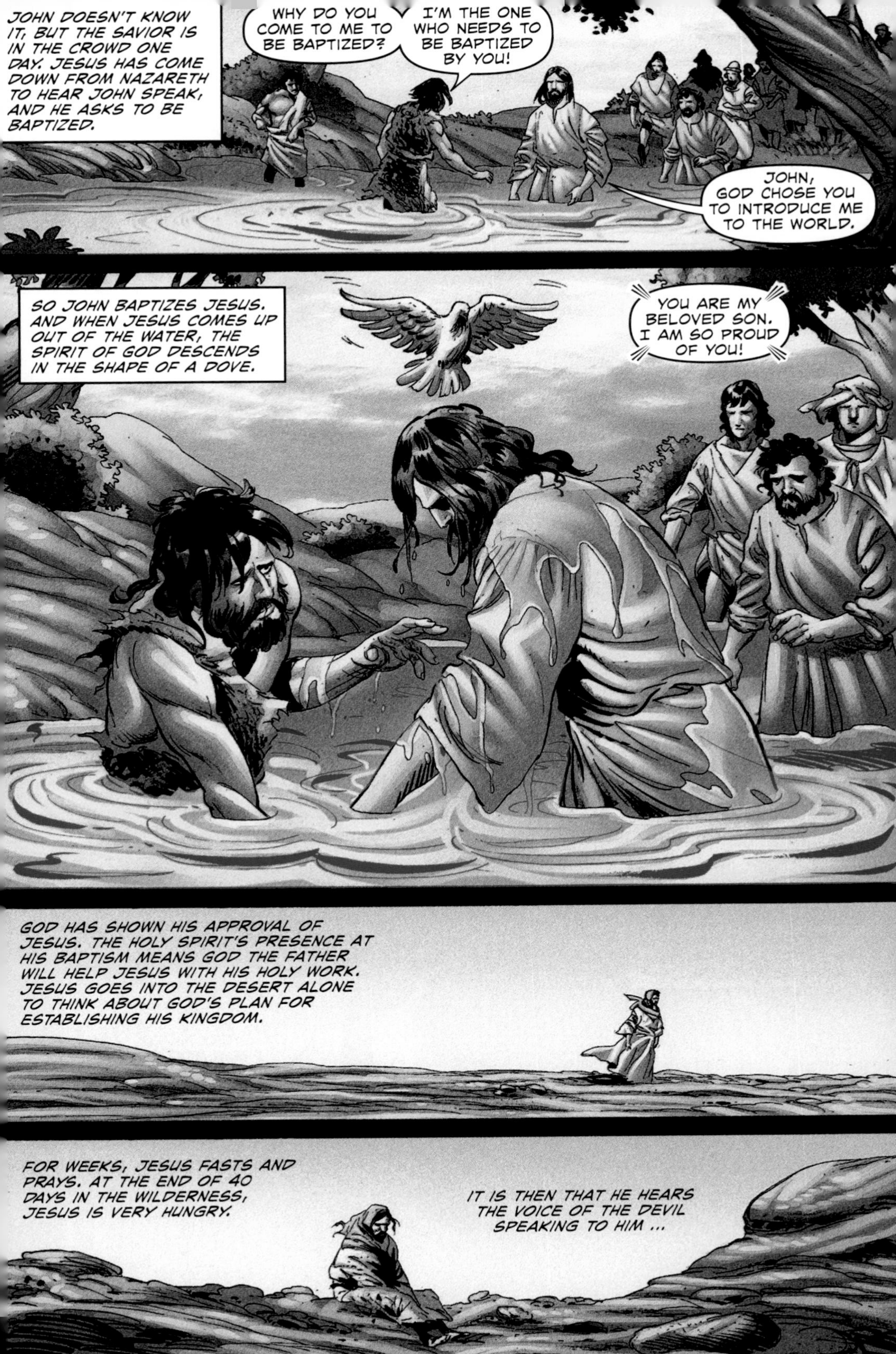
JOHN DOESN'T KNOW IT, BUT THE SAVIOR IS IN THE CROWD ONE DAY. JESUS HAS COME DOWN FROM NAZARETH TO HEAR JOHN SPEAK, AND HE ASKS TO BE BAPTIZED.
WHY DO YOU COME TO ME TO BE BAPTIZED?
I'M THE ONE WHO NEEDS TO BE BAPTIZED BY YOU!
JOHN, GOD CHOSE YOU TO INTRODUCE ME TO THE WORLD.
SO JOHN BAPTIZES JESUS. AND WHEN JESUS COMES UP OUT OF THE WATER, THE SPIRIT OF GOD DESCENDS IN THE SHAPE OF A DOVE.
YOU ARE MY BELOVED SON. I AM SO PROUD OF YOU!
GOD HAS SHOWN HIS APPROVAL OF JESUS. THE HOLY SPIRIT'S PRESENCE AT HIS BAPTISM MEANS GOD THE FATHER WILL HELP JESUS WITH HIS HOLY WORK. JESUS GOES INTO THE DESERT ALONE TO THINK ABOUT GOD'S PLAN FOR ESTABLISHING HIS KINGDOM.
FOR WEEKS, JESUS FASTS AND PRAYS. AT THE END OF 40 DAYS IN THE WILDERNESS, JESUS IS VERY HUNGRY.
IT IS THEN THAT HE HEARS THE VOICE OF THE DEVIL SPEAKING TO HIM ...

Tempted in the Desert

BASED ON LUKE 4:1–13; MATTHEW 4:1–11

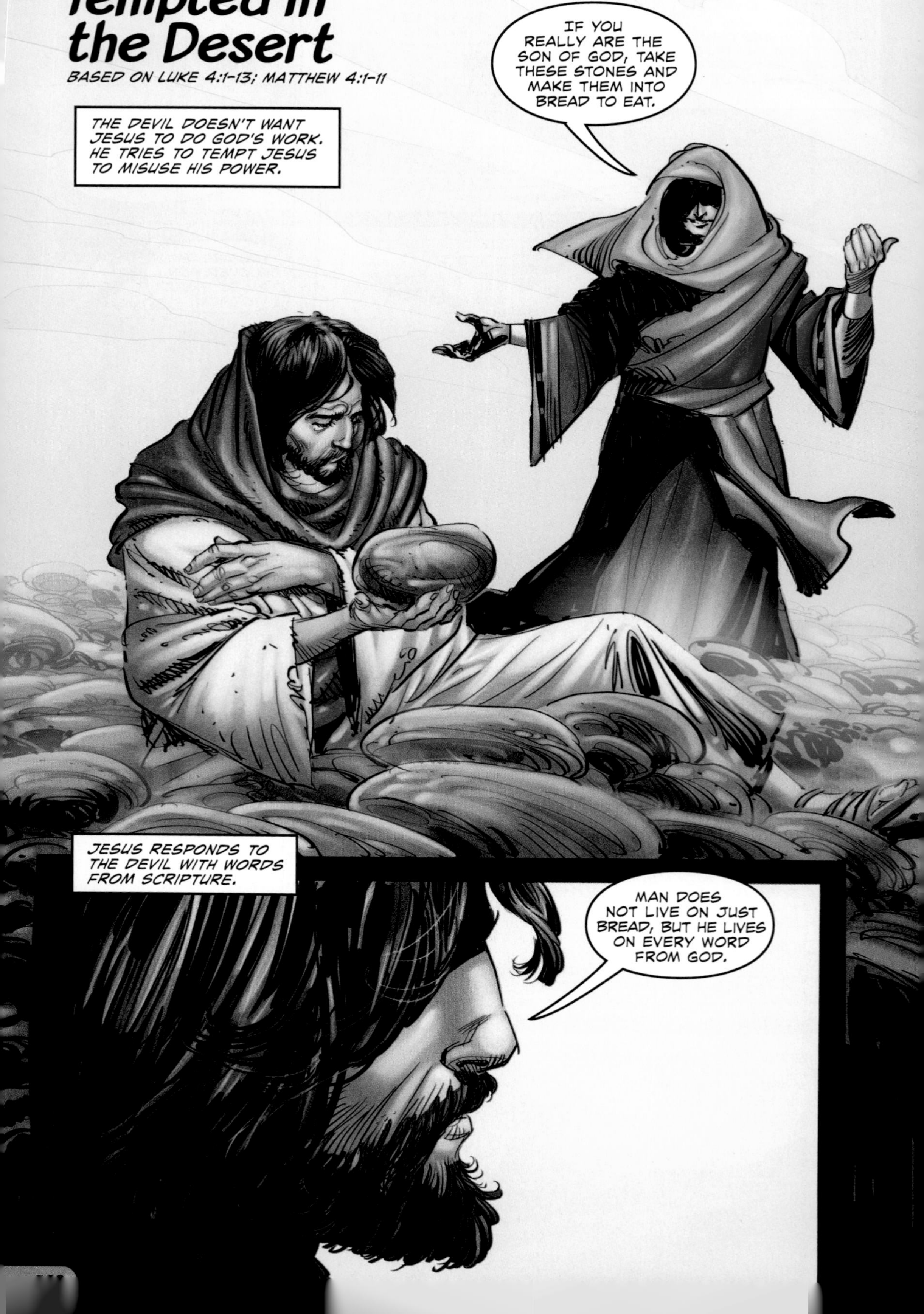
THE DEVIL DOESN'T WANT JESUS TO DO GOD'S WORK. HE TRIES TO TEMPT JESUS TO MISUSE HIS POWER.
IF YOU REALLY ARE THE SON OF GOD, TAKE THESE STONES AND MAKE THEM INTO BREAD TO EAT.
JESUS RESPONDS TO THE DEVIL WITH WORDS FROM SCRIPTURE.
MAN DOES NOT LIVE ON JUST BREAD, BUT HE LIVES ON EVERY WORD FROM GOD.

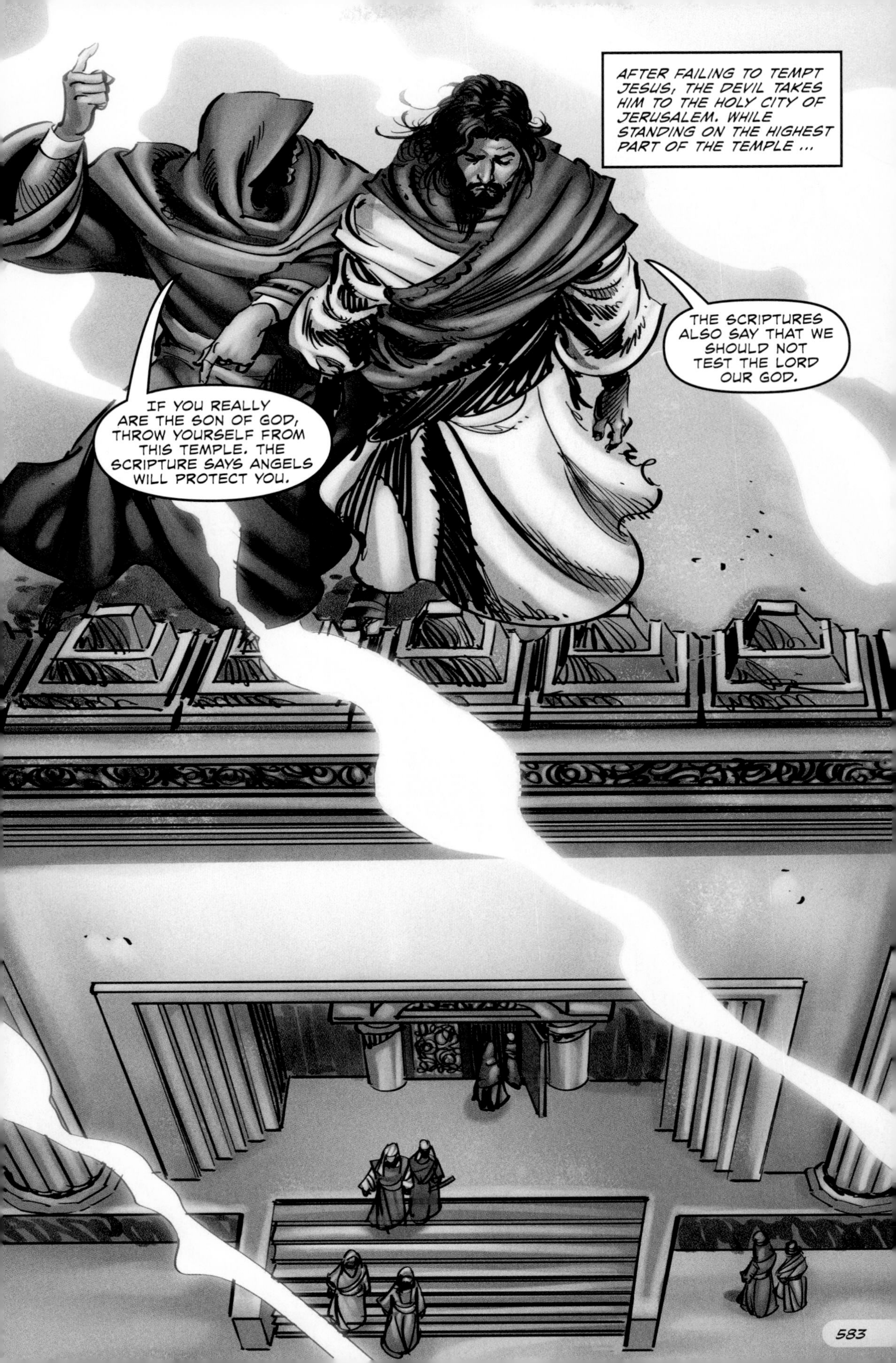
AFTER FAILING TO TEMPT JESUS, THE DEVIL TAKES HIM TO THE HOLY CITY OF JERUSALEM. WHILE STANDING ON THE HIGHEST PART OF THE TEMPLE ...
IF YOU REALLY ARE THE SON OF GOD, THROW YOURSELF FROM THIS TEMPLE. THE SCRIPTURE SAYS ANGELS WILL PROTECT YOU.
THE SCRIPTURES ALSO SAY THAT WE SHOULD NOT TEST THE LORD OUR GOD.

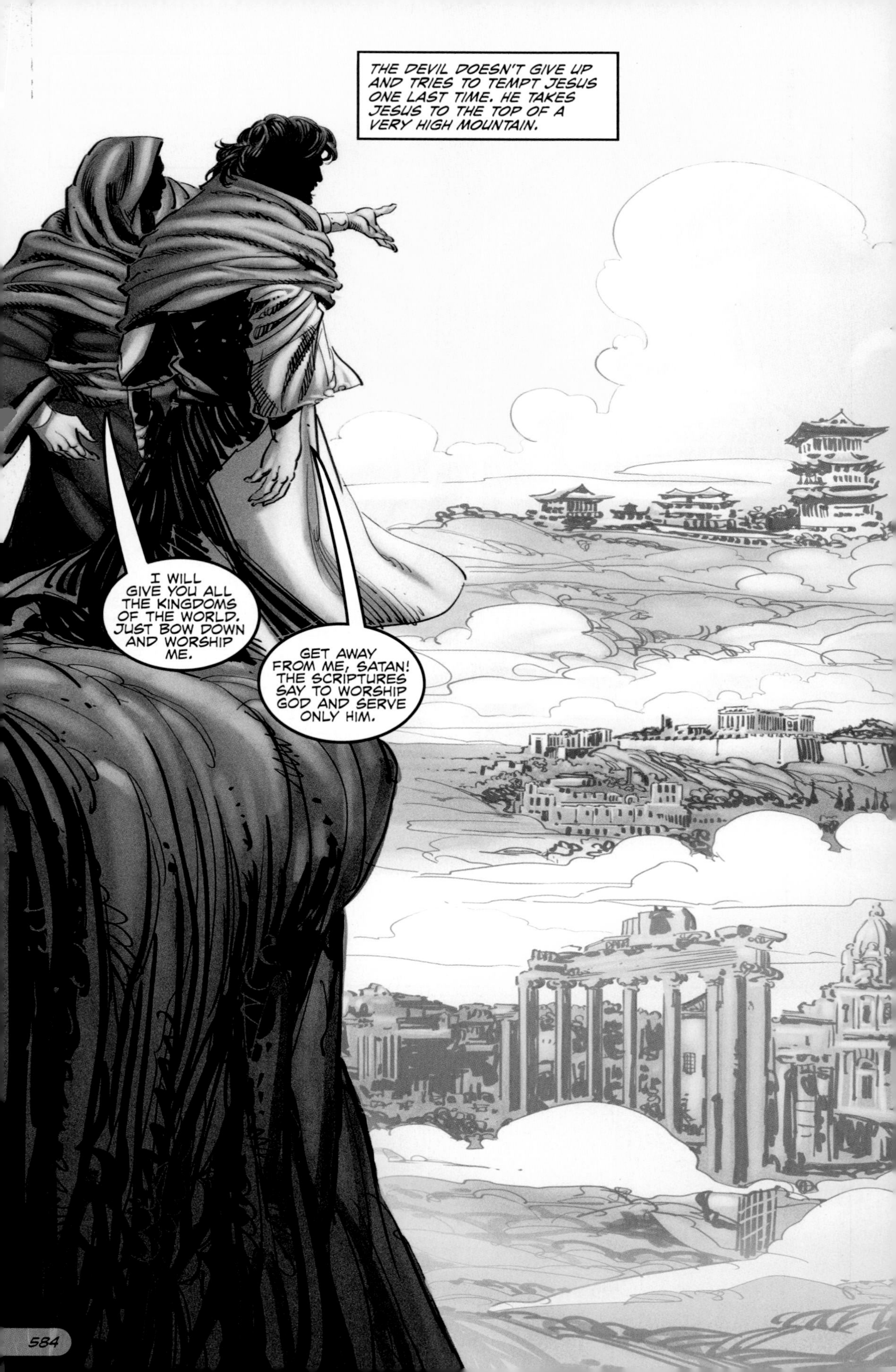
THE DEVIL DOESN'T GIVE UP AND TRIES TO TEMPT JESUS ONE LAST TIME. HE TAKES JESUS TO THE TOP OF A VERY HIGH MOUNTAIN.
I WILL GIVE YOU ALL THE KINGDOMS OF THE WORLD. JUST BOW DOWN AND WORSHIP ME.
GET AWAY FROM ME, SATAN! THE SCRIPTURES SAY TO WORSHIP GOD AND SERVE ONLY HIM.

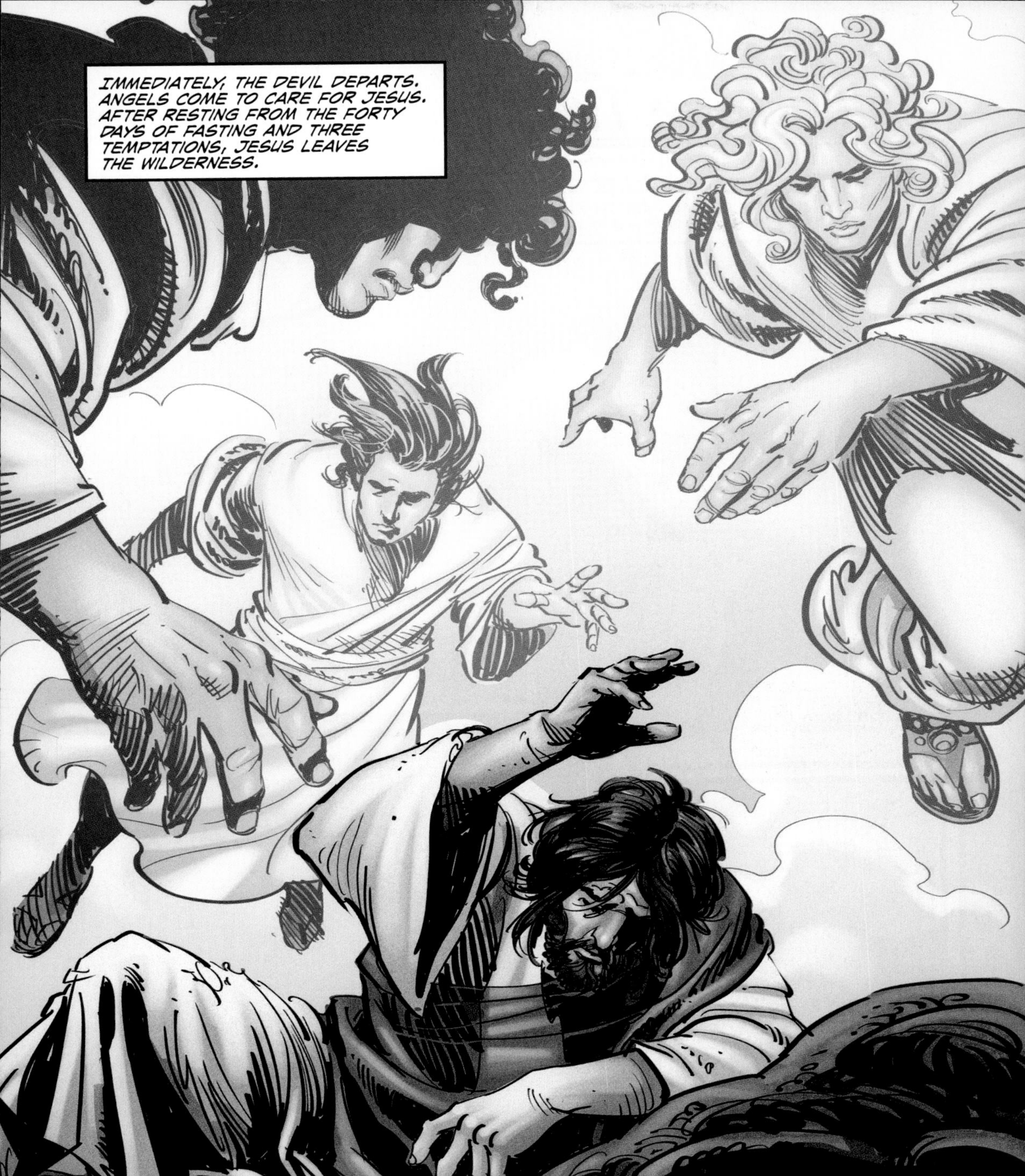
IMMEDIATELY, THE DEVIL DEPARTS. ANGELS COME TO CARE FOR JESUS. AFTER RESTING FROM THE FORTY DAYS OF FASTING AND THREE TEMPTATIONS, JESUS LEAVES THE WILDERNESS.

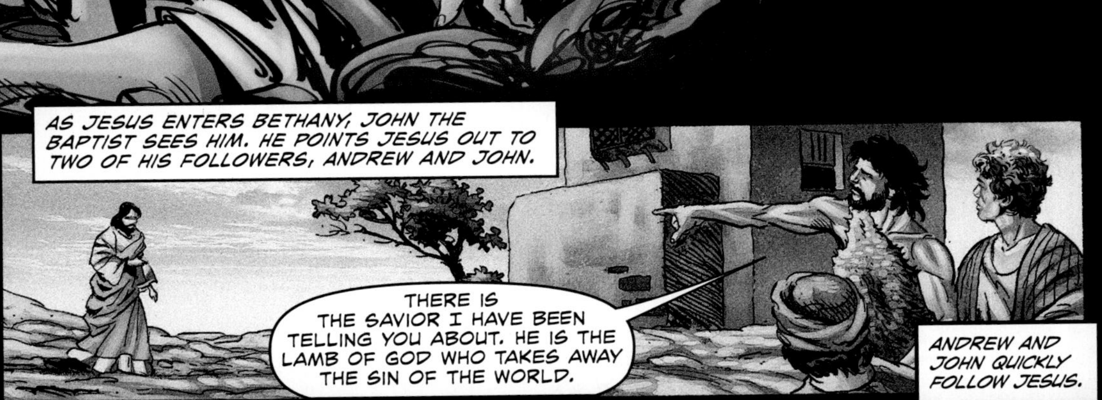
AS JESUS ENTERS BETHANY, JOHN THE BAPTIST SEES HIM. HE POINTS JESUS OUT TO TWO OF HIS FOLLOWERS, ANDREW AND JOHN.
THERE IS THE SAVIOR I HAVE BEEN TELLING YOU ABOUT. HE IS THE LAMB OF GOD WHO TAKES AWAY THE SIN OF THE WORLD.
ANDREW AND JOHN QUICKLY FOLLOW JESUS.

Calling the Twelve

BASED ON LUKE 5:1-11; JOHN 1:35-51; MATTHEW 9:9-13; 10:1-8

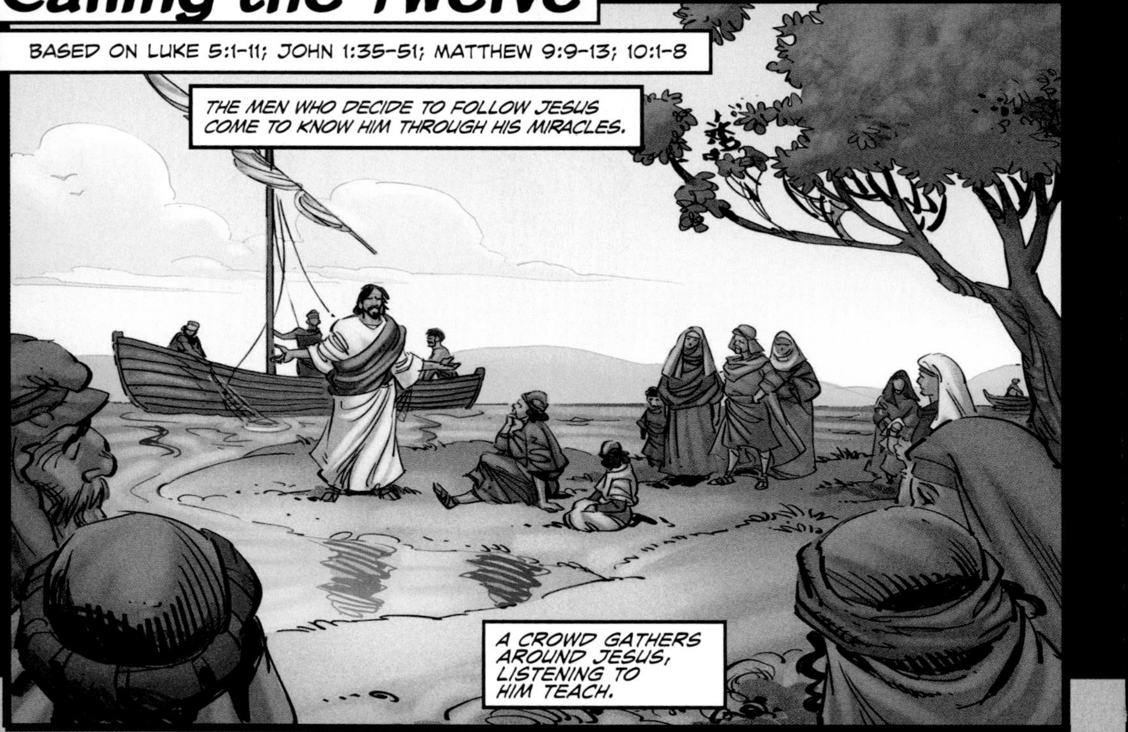
THE MEN WHO DECIDE TO FOLLOW JESUS COME TO KNOW HIM THROUGH HIS MIRACLES.
A CROWD GATHERS AROUND JESUS, LISTENING TO HIM TEACH.

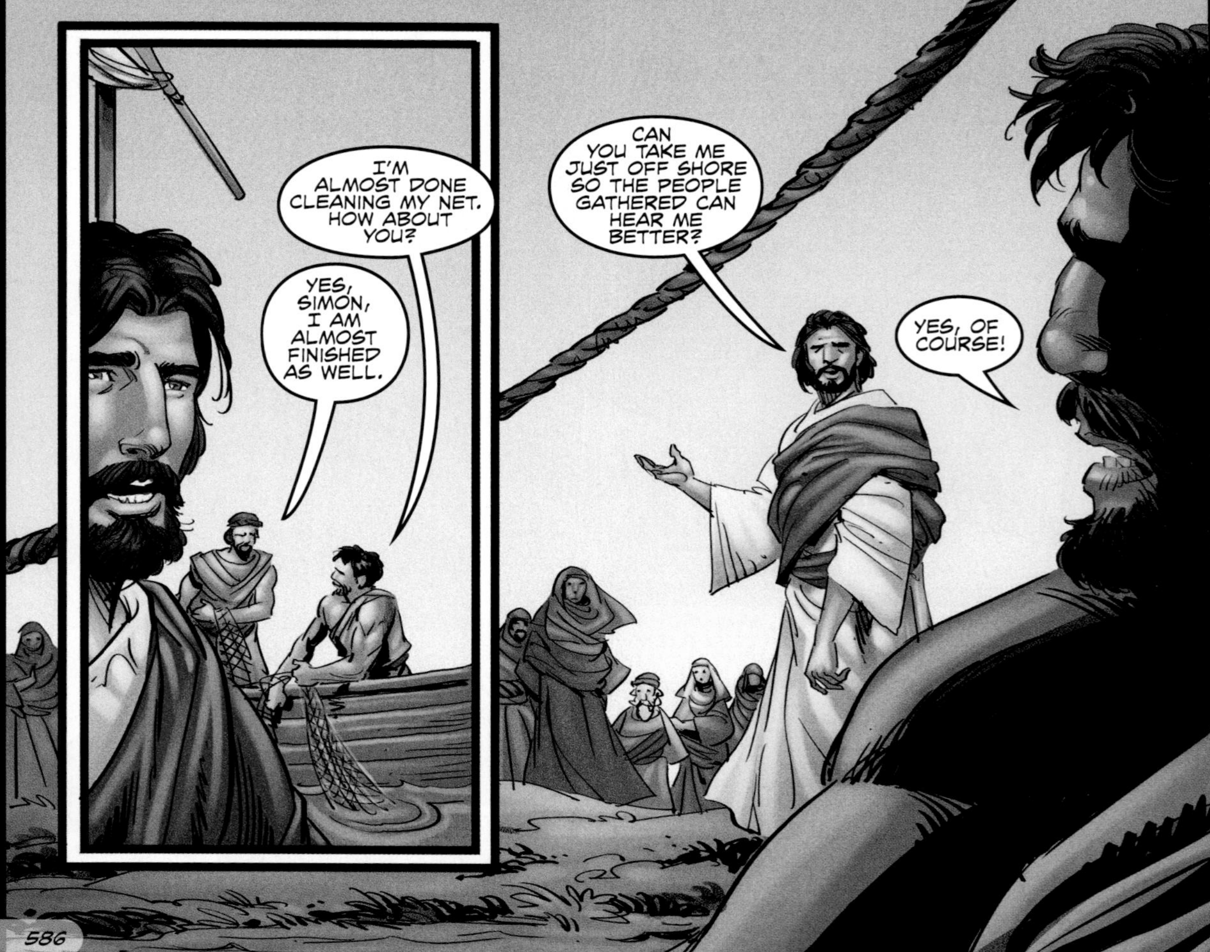
I'M ALMOST DONE CLEANING MY NET. HOW ABOUT YOU?
YES, SIMON, I AM ALMOST FINISHED AS WELL.
CAN YOU TAKE ME JUST OFF SHORE SO THE PEOPLE GATHERED CAN HEAR ME BETTER?
YES, OF COURSE!

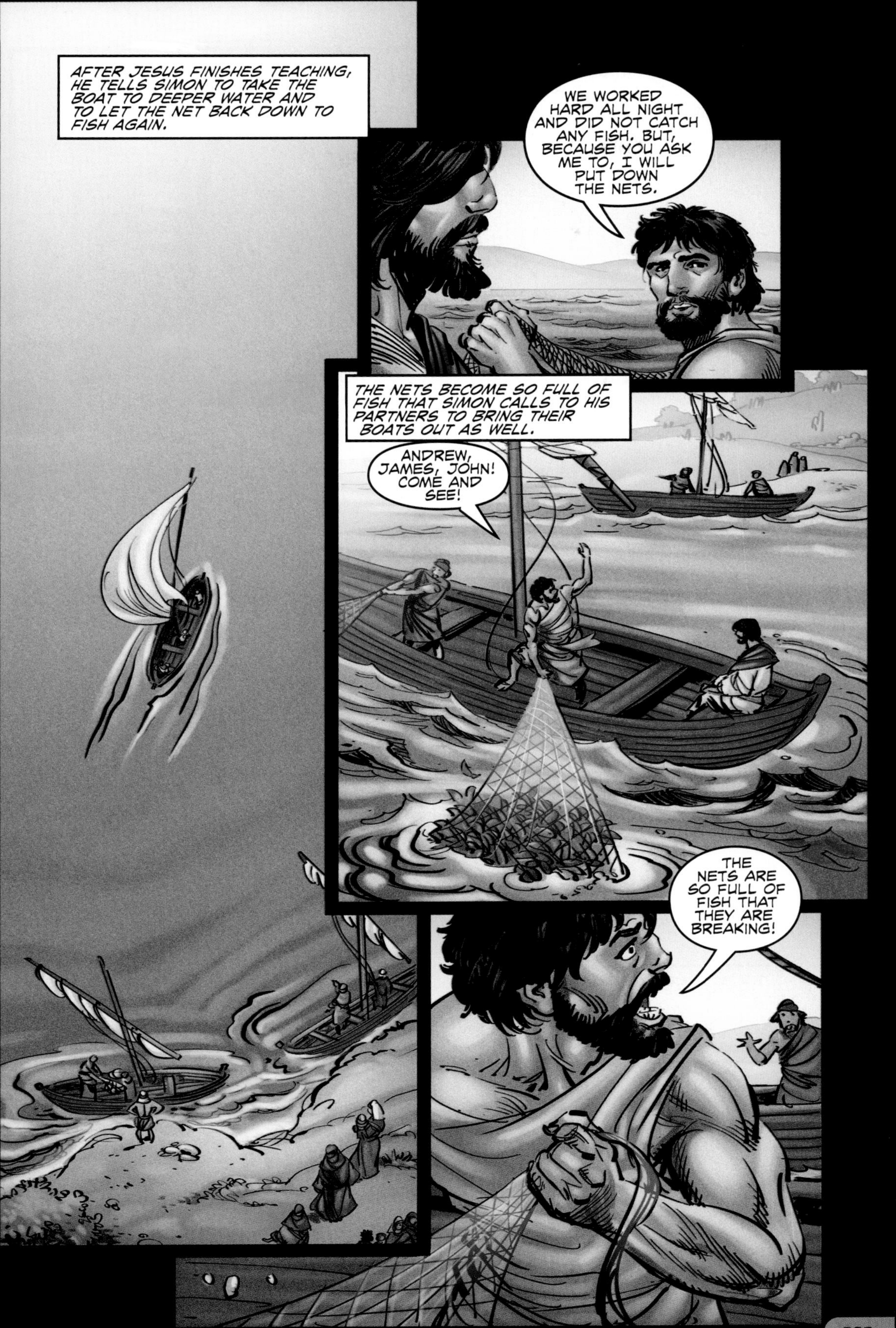
AFTER JESUS FINISHES TEACHING, HE TELLS SIMON TO TAKE THE BOAT TO DEEPER WATER AND TO LET THE NET BACK DOWN TO FISH AGAIN.
WE WORKED HARD ALL NIGHT AND DID NOT CATCH ANY FISH. BUT, BECAUSE YOU ASK ME TO, I WILL PUT DOWN THE NETS.
THE NETS BECOME SO FULL OF FISH THAT SIMON CALLS TO HIS PARTNERS TO BRING THEIR BOATS OUT AS WELL.
ANDREW, JAMES, JOHN! COME AND SEE!
THE NETS ARE SO FULL OF FISH THAT THEY ARE BREAKING!

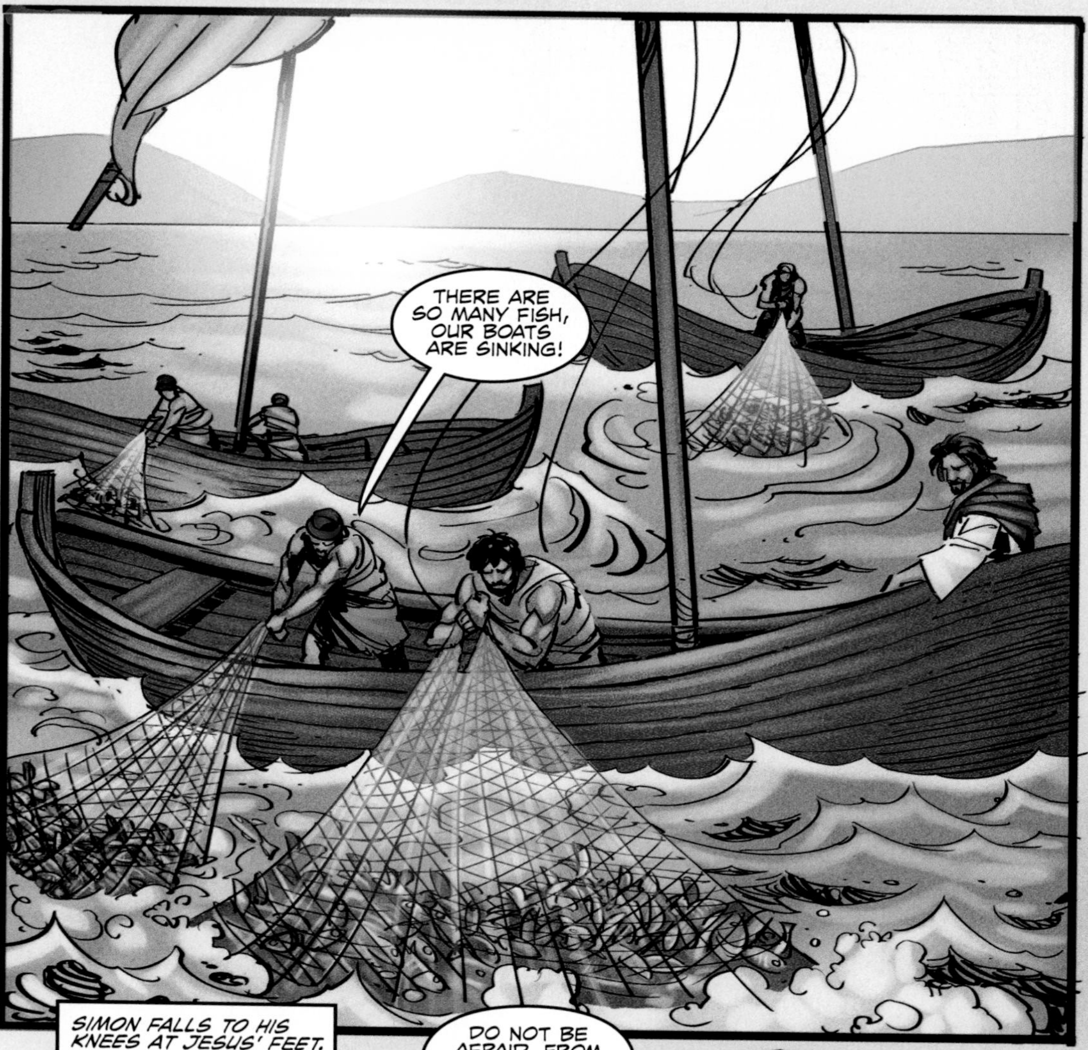
THERE ARE SO MANY FISH, OUR BOATS ARE SINKING!

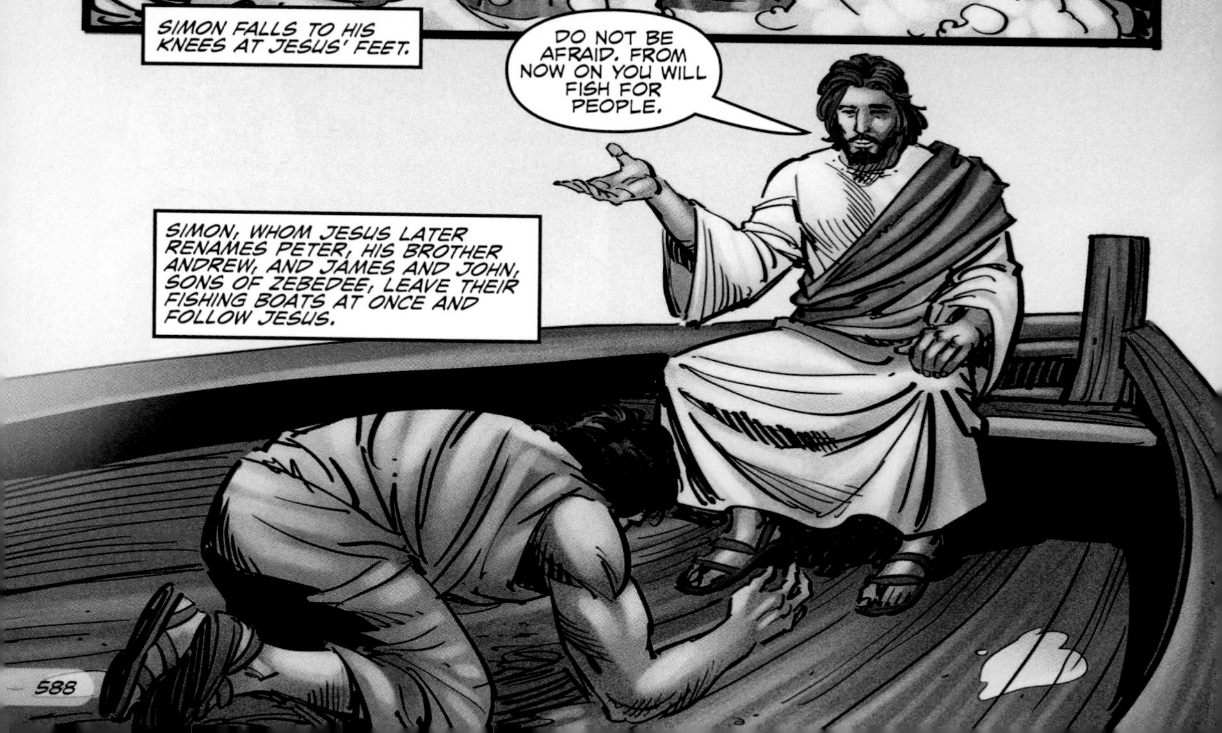
SIMON FALLS TO HIS KNEES AT JESUS' FEET.
DO NOT BE AFRAID. FROM NOW ON YOU WILL FISH FOR PEOPLE.
SIMON, WHOM JESUS LATER RENAMES PETER, HIS BROTHER ANDREW, AND JAMES AND JOHN, SONS OF ZEBEDEE, LEAVE THEIR FISHING BOATS AT ONCE AND FOLLOW JESUS.

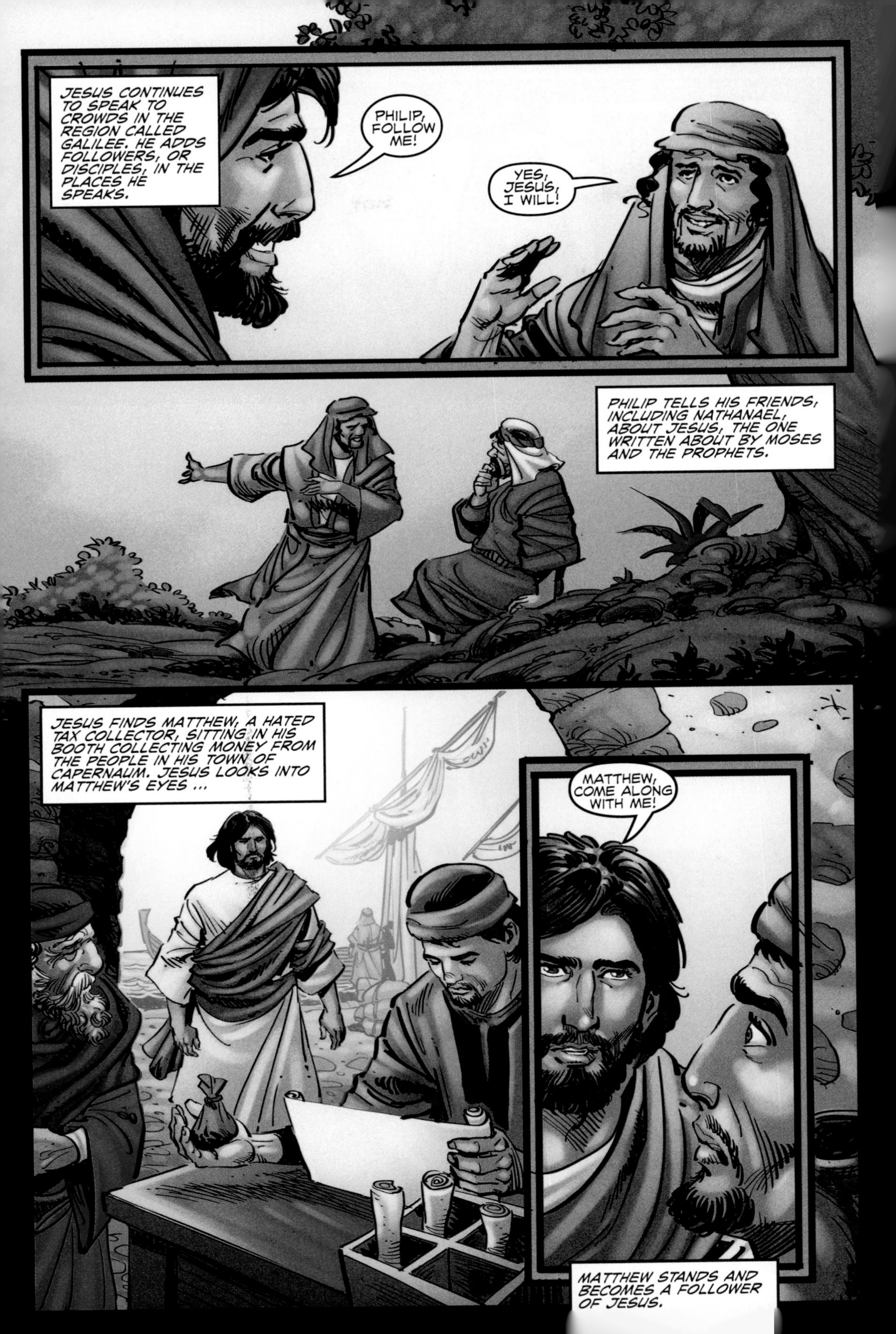
JESUS CONTINUES TO SPEAK TO CROWDS IN THE REGION CALLED GALILEE. HE ADDS FOLLOWERS, OR DISCIPLES, IN THE PLACES HE SPEAKS.
PHILIP, FOLLOW ME!
YES, JESUS, I WILL!
PHILIP TELLS HIS FRIENDS, INCLUDING NATHANAEL, ABOUT JESUS, THE ONE WRITTEN ABOUT BY MOSES AND THE PROPHETS.
JESUS FINDS MATTHEW, A HATED TAX COLLECTOR, SITTING IN HIS BOOTH COLLECTING MONEY FROM THE PEOPLE IN HIS TOWN OF CAPERNAUM. JESUS LOOKS INTO MATTHEW'S EYES ...
MATTHEW, COME ALONG WITH ME!
MATTHEW STANDS AND BECOMES A FOLLOWER OF JESUS.

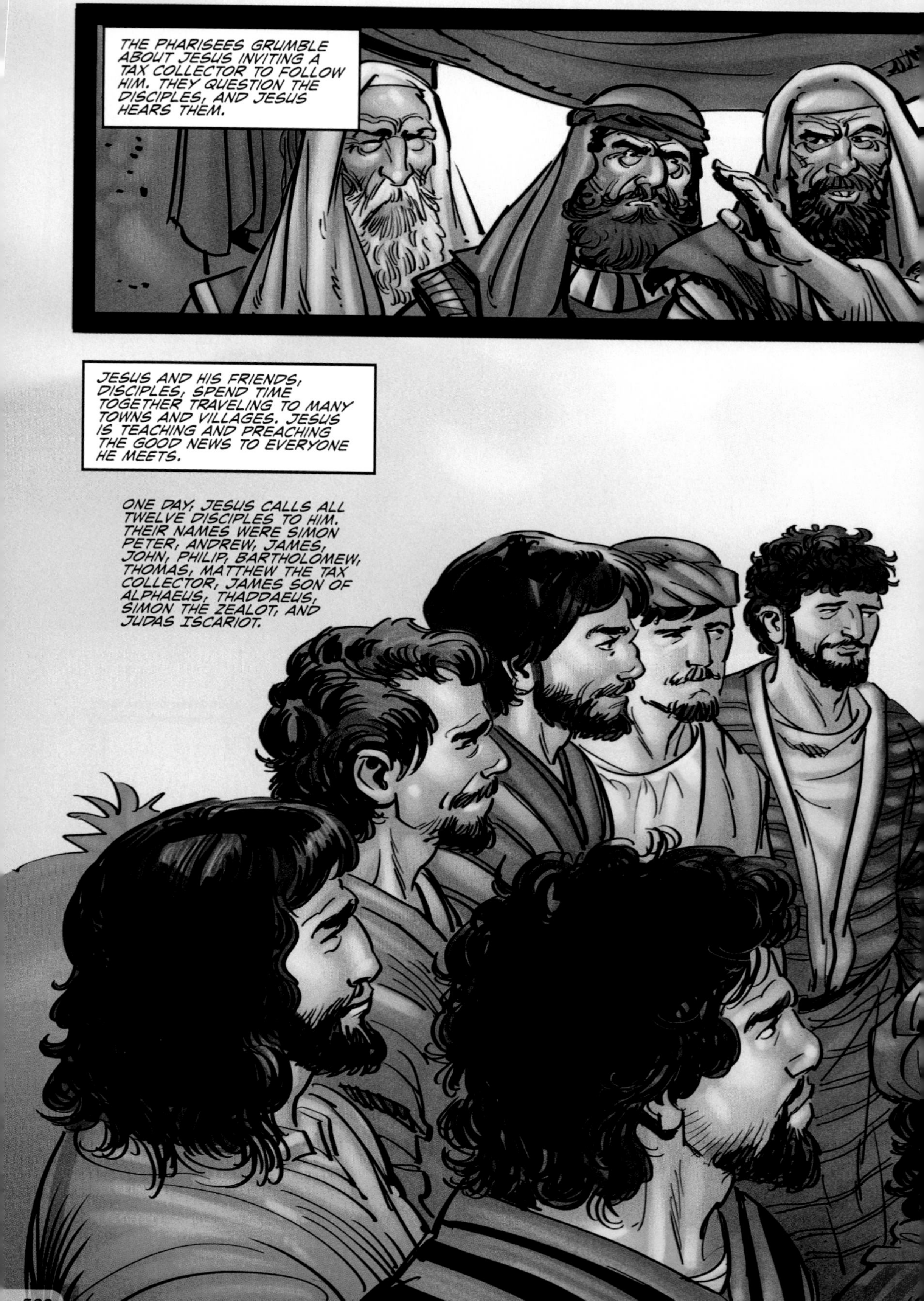
THE PHARISEES GRUMBLE ABOUT JESUS INVITING A TAX COLLECTOR TO FOLLOW HIM. THEY QUESTION THE DISCIPLES, AND JESUS HEARS THEM.
JESUS AND HIS FRIENDS, DISCIPLES, SPEND TIME TOGETHER TRAVELING TO MANY TOWNS AND VILLAGES. JESUS IS TEACHING AND PREACHING THE GOOD NEWS TO EVERYONE HE MEETS.
ONE DAY, JESUS CALLS ALL TWELVE DISCIPLES TO HIM. THEIR NAMES WERE SIMON PETER, ANDREW, JAMES, JOHN, PHILIP, BARTHOLOMEW, THOMAS, MATTHEW THE TAX COLLECTOR, JAMES SON OF ALPHAEUS, THADDAEUS, SIMON THE ZEALOT, AND JUDAS ISCARIOT.

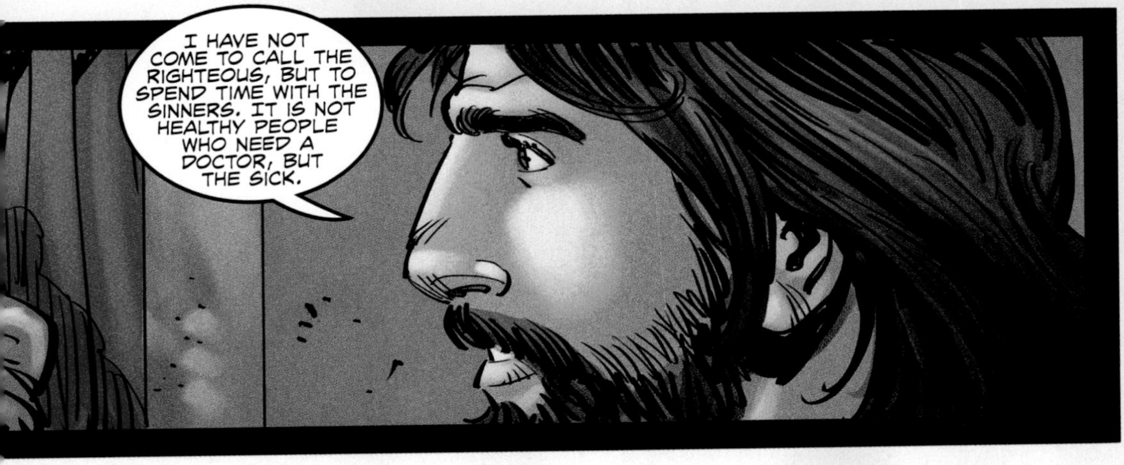
I HAVE NOT COME TO CALL THE RIGHTEOUS, BUT TO SPEND TIME WITH THE SINNERS. IT IS NOT HEALTHY PEOPLE WHO NEED A DOCTOR, BUT THE SICK.

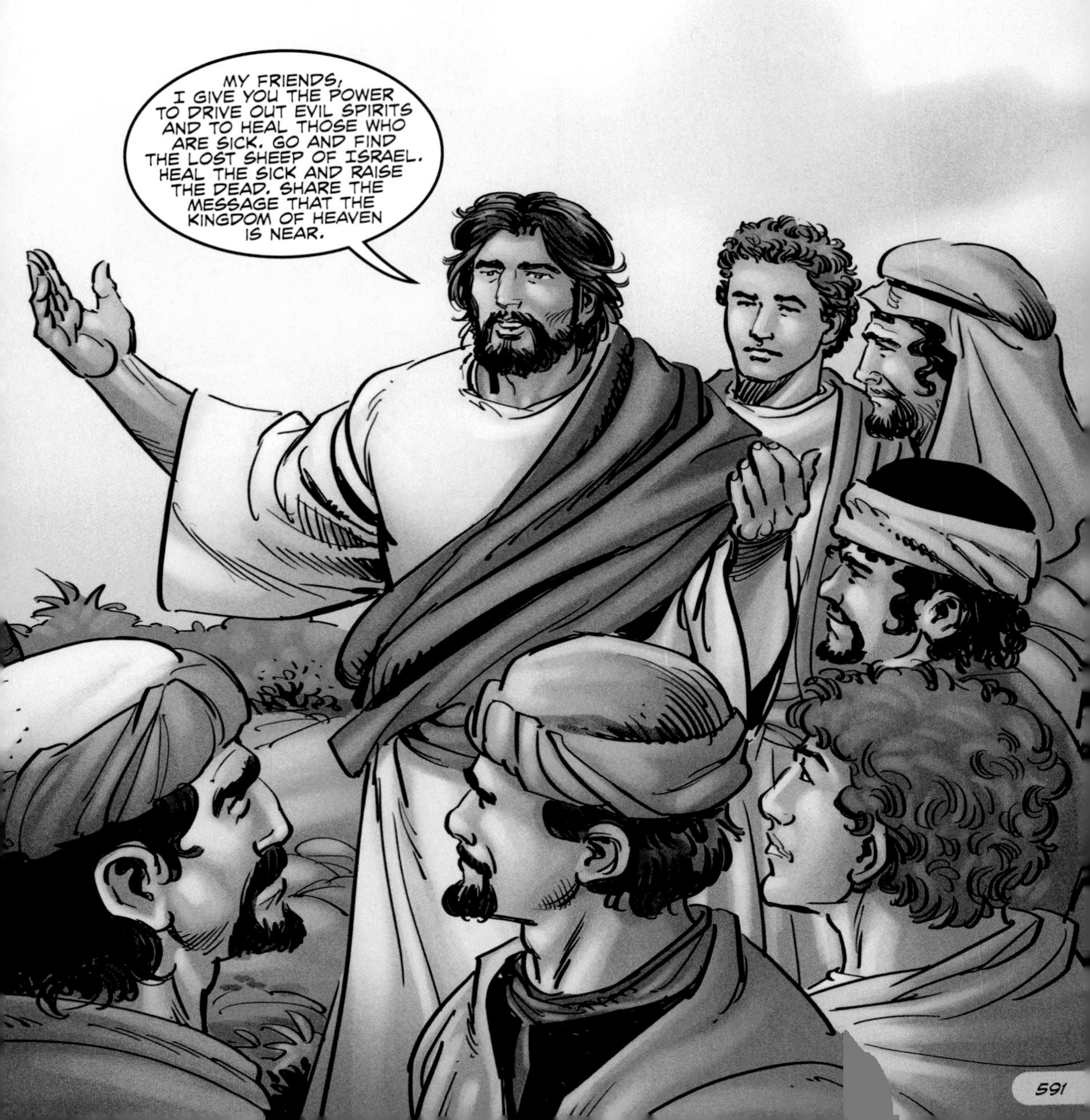
MY FRIENDS, I GIVE YOU THE POWER TO DRIVE OUT EVIL SPIRITS AND TO HEAL THOSE WHO ARE SICK. GO AND FIND THE LOST SHEEP OF ISRAEL. HEAL THE SICK AND RAISE THE DEAD. SHARE THE MESSAGE THAT THE KINGDOM OF HEAVEN IS NEAR.

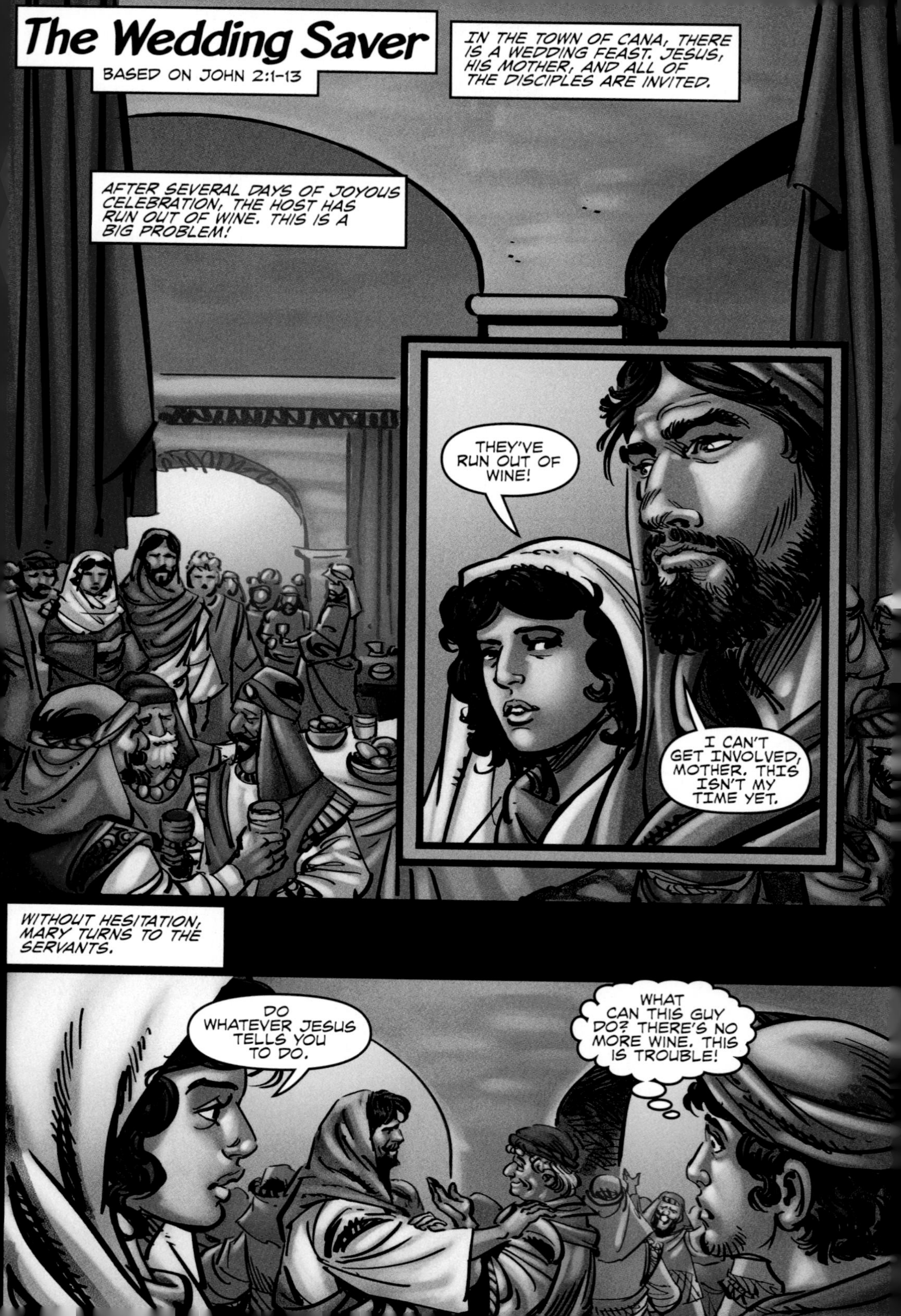
The Wedding Saver
BASED ON JOHN 2:1–13
IN THE TOWN OF CANA, THERE IS A WEDDING FEAST. JESUS, HIS MOTHER, AND ALL OF THE DISCIPLES ARE INVITED.
AFTER SEVERAL DAYS OF JOYOUS CELEBRATION, THE HOST HAS RUN OUT OF WINE. THIS IS A BIG PROBLEM!
THEY'VE RUN OUT OF WINE!
I CAN'T GET INVOLVED, MOTHER. THIS ISN'T MY TIME YET.
WITHOUT HESITATION, MARY TURNS TO THE SERVANTS.
DO WHATEVER JESUS TELLS YOU TO DO.
WHAT CAN THIS GUY DO? THERE'S NO MORE WINE. THIS IS TROUBLE!

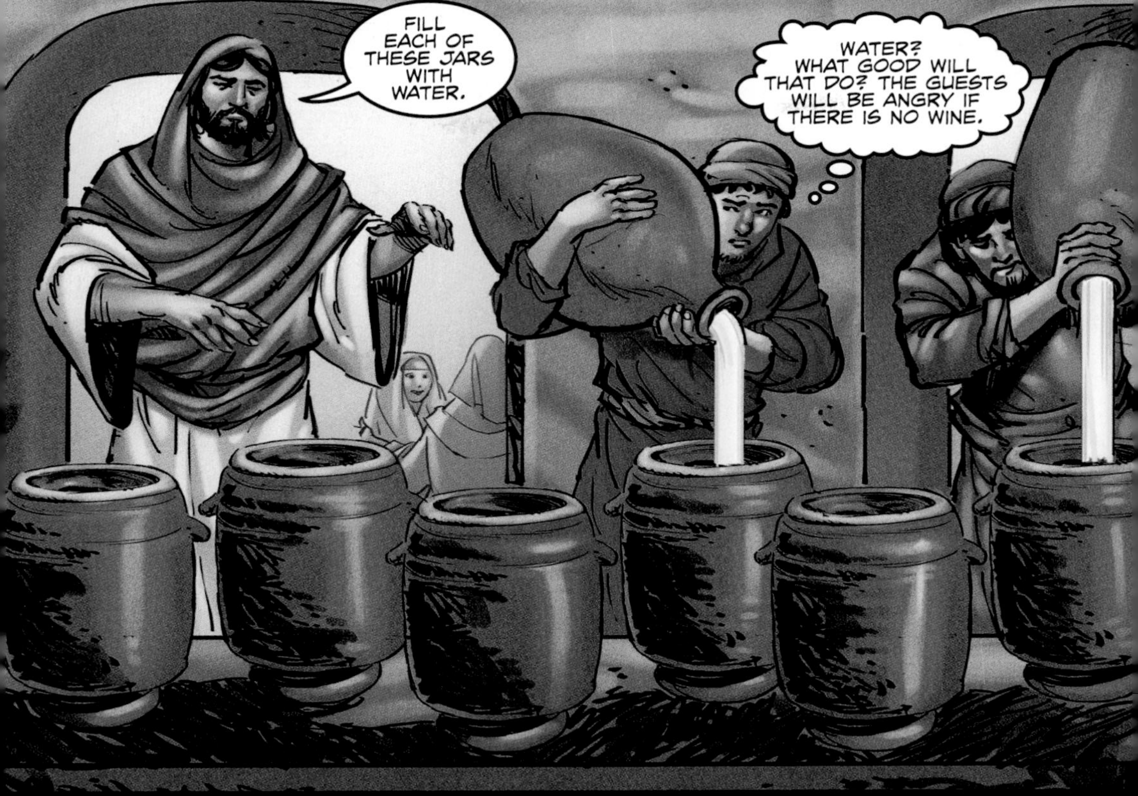
FILL EACH OF THESE JARS WITH WATER.
WATER? WHAT GOOD WILL THAT DO? THE GUESTS WILL BE ANGRY IF THERE IS NO WINE.

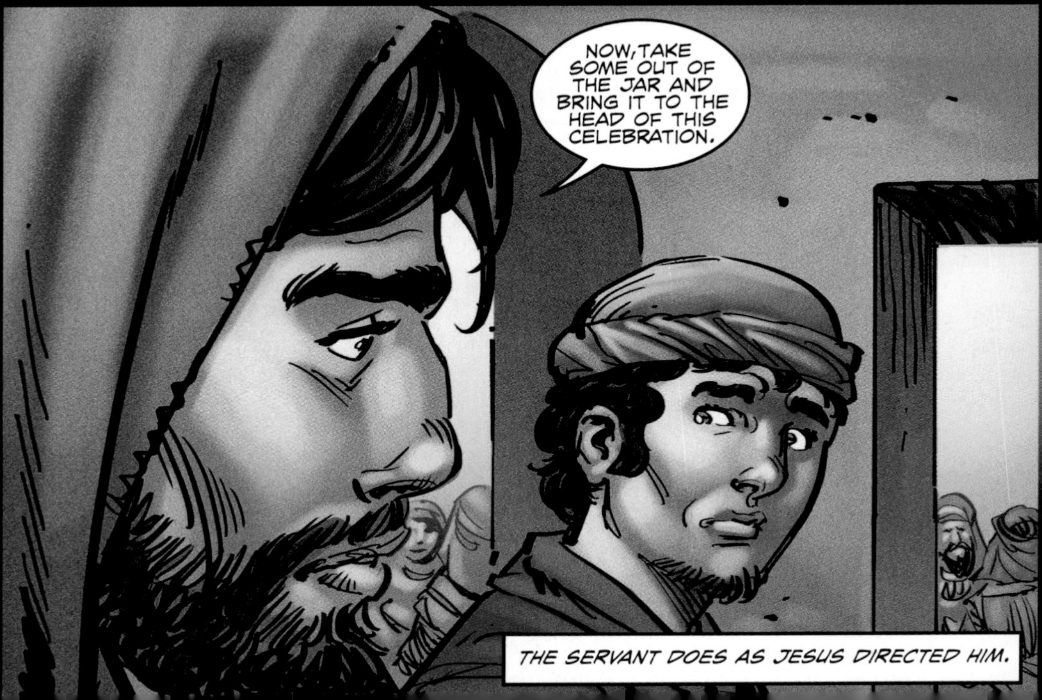
NOW, TAKE SOME OUT OF THE JAR AND BRING IT TO THE HEAD OF THIS CELEBRATION.
THE SERVANT DOES AS JESUS DIRECTED HIM.

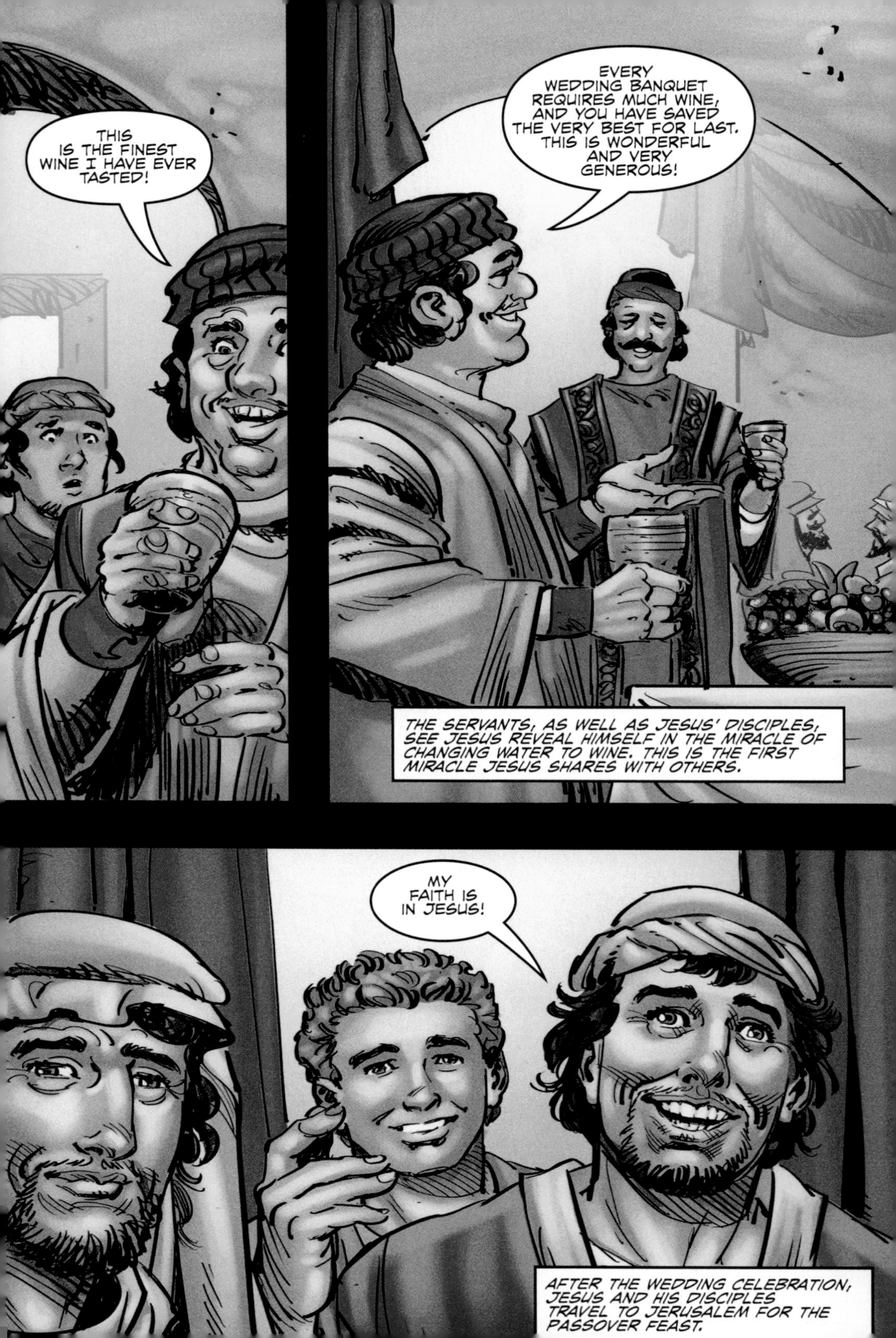
THIS IS THE FINEST WINE I HAVE EVER TASTED!
EVERY WEDDING BANQUET REQUIRES MUCH WINE, AND YOU HAVE SAVED THE VERY BEST FOR LAST. THIS IS WONDERFUL AND VERY GENEROUS!
THE SERVANTS, AS WELL AS JESUS' DISCIPLES, SEE JESUS REVEAL HIMSELF IN THE MIRACLE OF CHANGING WATER TO WINE. THIS IS THE FIRST MIRACLE JESUS SHARES WITH OTHERS.
MY FAITH IS IN JESUS!
AFTER THE WEDDING CELEBRATION, JESUS AND HIS DISCIPLES TRAVEL TO JERUSALEM FOR THE PASSOVER FEAST.

Miracles for New Beginnings

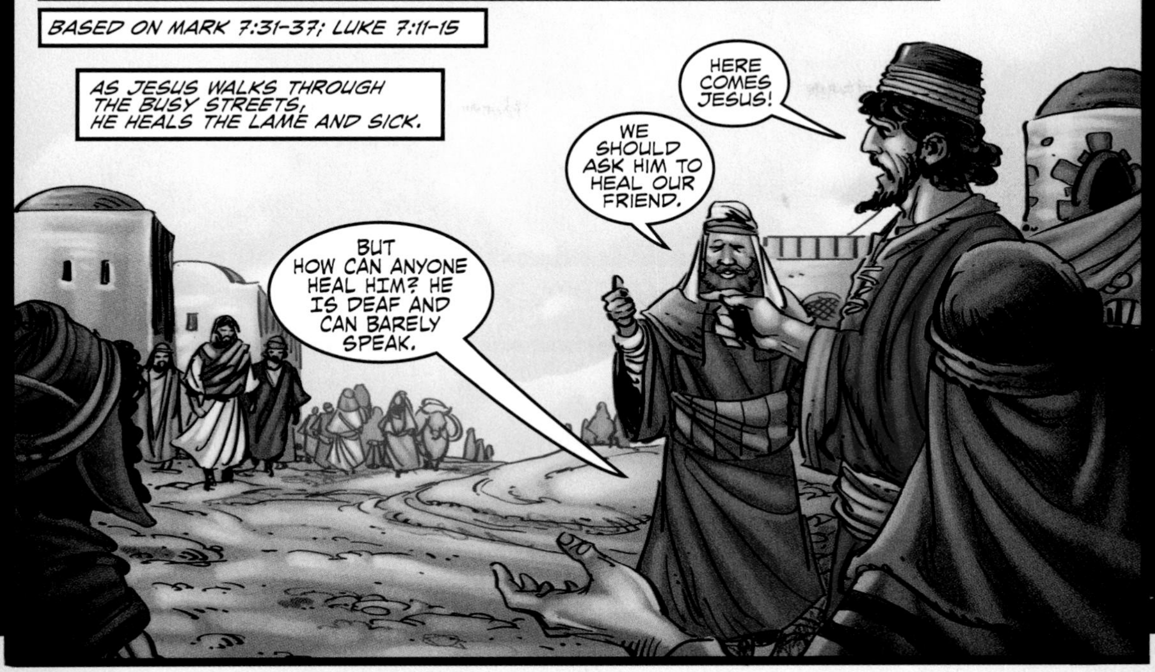
BASED ON MARK 7:31–37; LUKE 7:11–15
AS JESUS WALKS THROUGH THE BUSY STREETS, HE HEALS THE LAME AND SICK.
HERE COMES JESUS!
WE SHOULD ASK HIM TO HEAL OUR FRIEND.
BUT HOW CAN ANYONE HEAL HIM? HE IS DEAF AND CAN BARELY SPEAK.

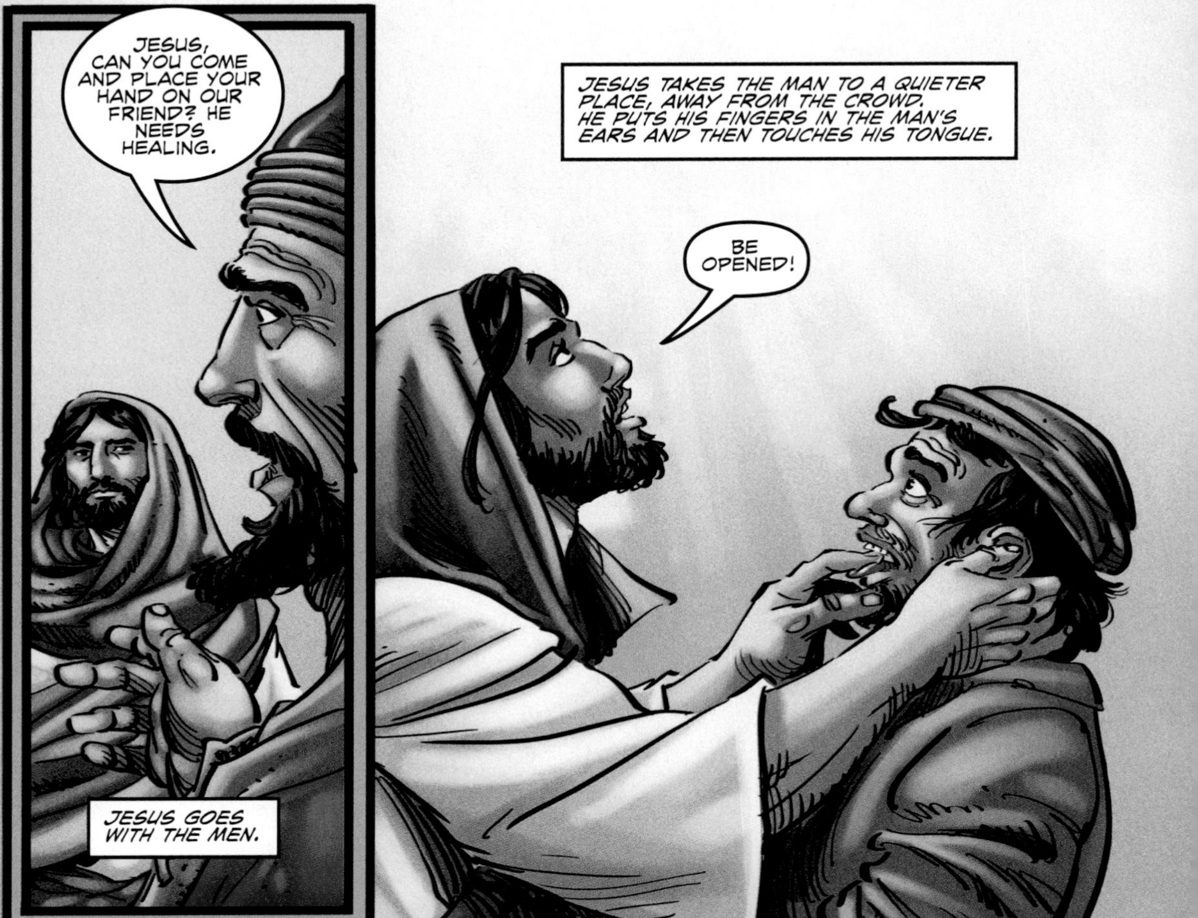
JESUS, CAN YOU COME AND PLACE YOUR HAND ON OUR FRIEND? HE NEEDS HEALING.
JESUS GOES WITH THE MEN.
JESUS TAKES THE MAN TO A QUIETER PLACE, AWAY FROM THE CROWD. HE PUTS HIS FINGERS IN THE MAN'S EARS AND THEN TOUCHES HIS TONGUE.
BE OPENED!

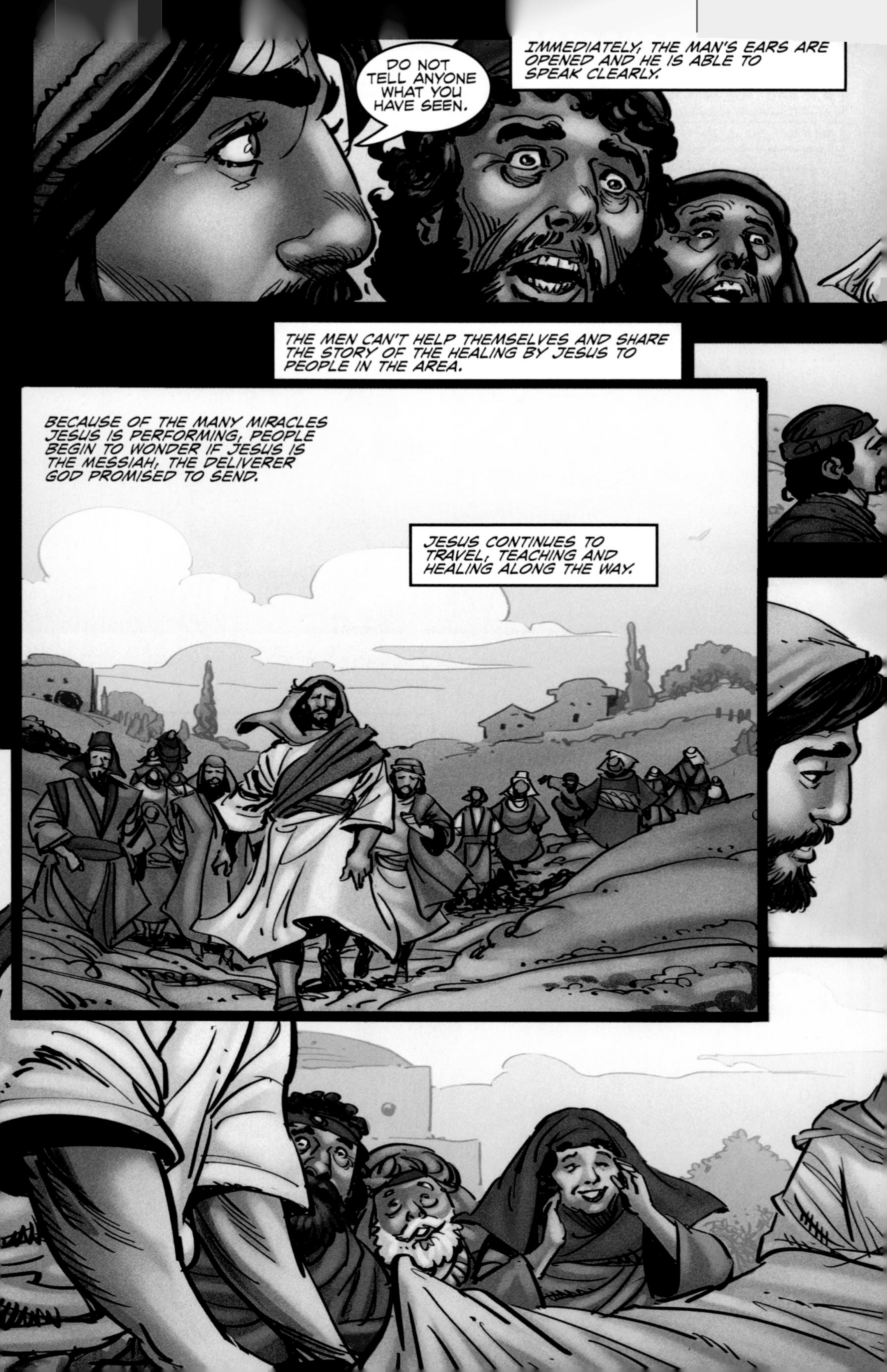

DO NOT TELL ANYONE WHAT YOU HAVE SEEN.
IMMEDIATELY, THE MAN'S EARS ARE OPENED AND HE IS ABLE TO SPEAK CLEARLY.
THE MEN CAN'T HELP THEMSELVES AND SHARE THE STORY OF THE HEALING BY JESUS TO PEOPLE IN THE AREA.
BECAUSE OF THE MANY MIRACLES JESUS IS PERFORMING, PEOPLE BEGIN TO WONDER IF JESUS IS THE MESSIAH, THE DELIVERER GOD PROMISED TO SEND.
JESUS CONTINUES TO TRAVEL, TEACHING AND HEALING ALONG THE WAY.

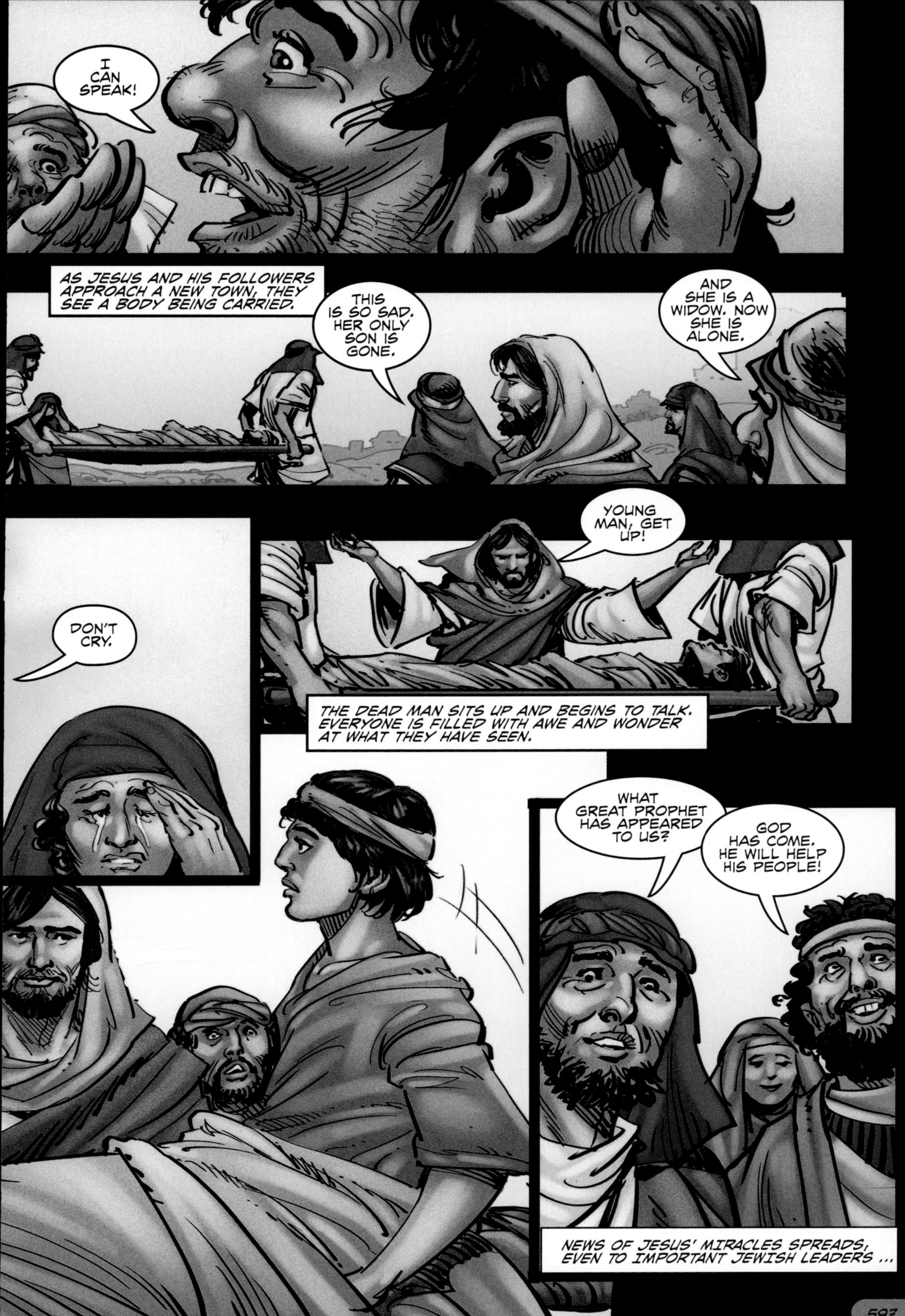
I CAN SPEAK!
AS JESUS AND HIS FOLLOWERS APPROACH A NEW TOWN, THEY SEE A BODY BEING CARRIED.
THIS IS SO SAD. HER ONLY SON IS GONE.
AND SHE IS A WIDOW. NOW SHE IS ALONE.
DON'T CRY.
YOUNG MAN, GET UP!
THE DEAD MAN SITS UP AND BEGINS TO TALK. EVERYONE IS FILLED WITH AWE AND WONDER AT WHAT THEY HAVE SEEN.
WHAT GREAT PROPHET HAS APPEARED TO US?
GOD HAS COME. HE WILL HELP HIS PEOPLE!
NEWS OF JESUS' MIRACLES SPREADS, EVEN TO IMPORTANT JEWISH LEADERS ...

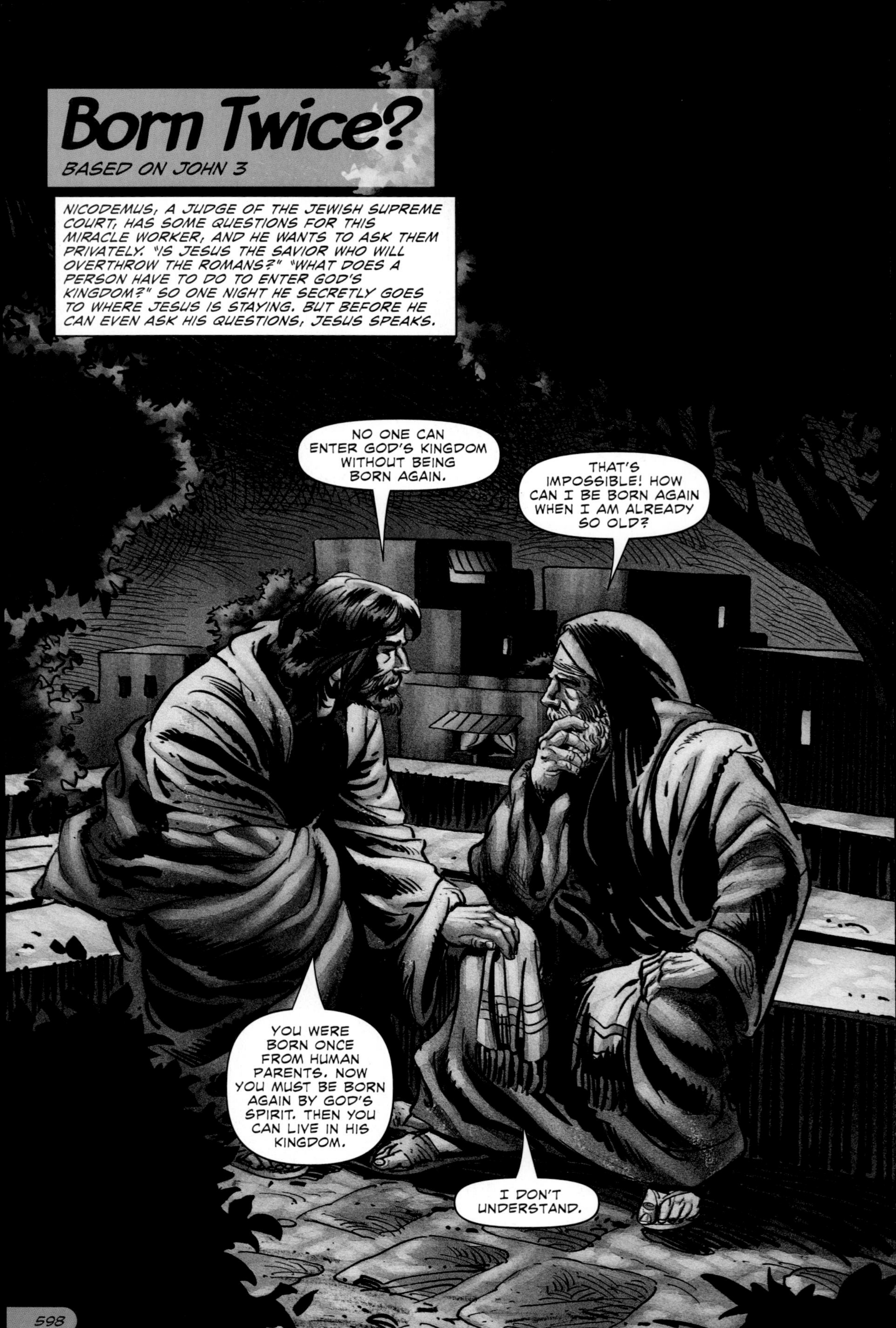
Born Twice?
BASED ON JOHN 3
NICODEMUS, A JUDGE OF THE JEWISH SUPREME COURT, HAS SOME QUESTIONS FOR THIS MIRACLE WORKER, AND HE WANTS TO ASK THEM PRIVATELY. "IS JESUS THE SAVIOR WHO WILL OVERTHROW THE ROMANS?" "WHAT DOES A PERSON HAVE TO DO TO ENTER GOD'S KINGDOM?" SO ONE NIGHT HE SECRETLY GOES TO WHERE JESUS IS STAYING. BUT BEFORE HE CAN EVEN ASK HIS QUESTIONS, JESUS SPEAKS.
NO ONE CAN ENTER GOD'S KINGDOM WITHOUT BEING BORN AGAIN.
THAT'S IMPOSSIBLE! HOW CAN I BE BORN AGAIN WHEN I AM ALREADY SO OLD?
YOU WERE BORN ONCE FROM HUMAN PARENTS. NOW YOU MUST BE BORN AGAIN BY GOD'S SPIRIT. THEN YOU CAN LIVE IN HIS KINGDOM.
I DON'T UNDERSTAND.

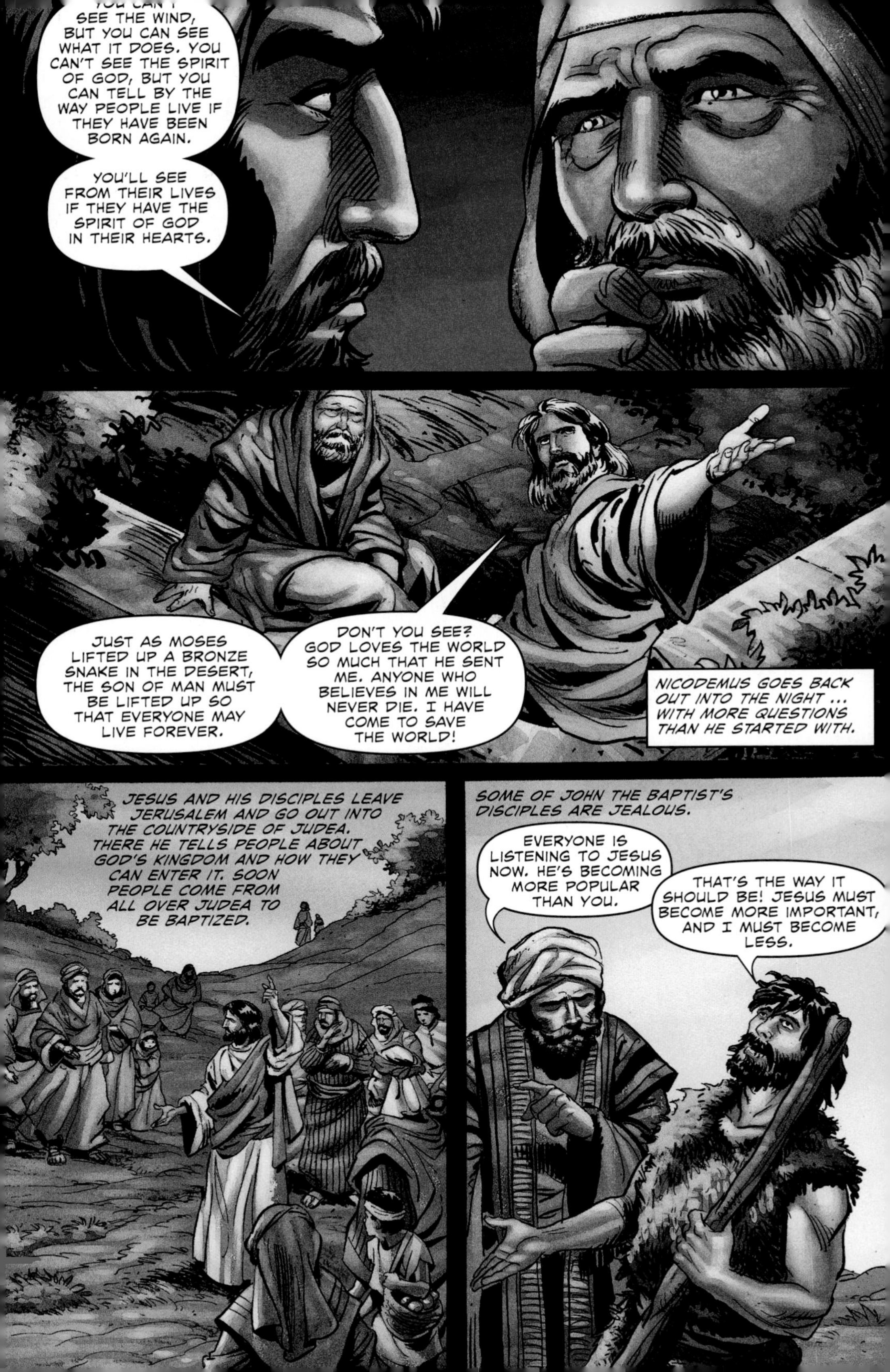

SEE THE WIND, BUT YOU CAN SEE WHAT IT DOES. YOU CAN'T SEE THE SPIRIT OF GOD, BUT YOU CAN TELL BY THE WAY PEOPLE LIVE IF THEY HAVE BEEN BORN AGAIN.
YOU'LL SEE FROM THEIR LIVES IF THEY HAVE THE SPIRIT OF GOD IN THEIR HEARTS.
JUST AS MOSES LIFTED UP A BRONZE SNAKE IN THE DESERT, THE SON OF MAN MUST BE LIFTED UP SO THAT EVERYONE MAY LIVE FOREVER.
DON'T YOU SEE? GOD LOVES THE WORLD SO MUCH THAT HE SENT ME. ANYONE WHO BELIEVES IN ME WILL NEVER DIE. I HAVE COME TO SAVE THE WORLD!
NICODEMUS GOES BACK OUT INTO THE NIGHT ... WITH MORE QUESTIONS THAN HE STARTED WITH.
JESUS AND HIS DISCIPLES LEAVE JERUSALEM AND GO OUT INTO THE COUNTRYSIDE OF JUDEA. THERE HE TELLS PEOPLE ABOUT GOD'S KINGDOM AND HOW THEY CAN ENTER IT. SOON PEOPLE COME FROM ALL OVER JUDEA TO BE BAPTIZED.
SOME OF JOHN THE BAPTIST'S DISCIPLES ARE JEALOUS.
EVERYONE IS LISTENING TO JESUS NOW. HE'S BECOMING MORE POPULAR THAN YOU.
THAT'S THE WAY IT SHOULD BE! JESUS MUST BECOME MORE IMPORTANT, AND I MUST BECOME LESS.

Living Water

BASED ON JOHN 4

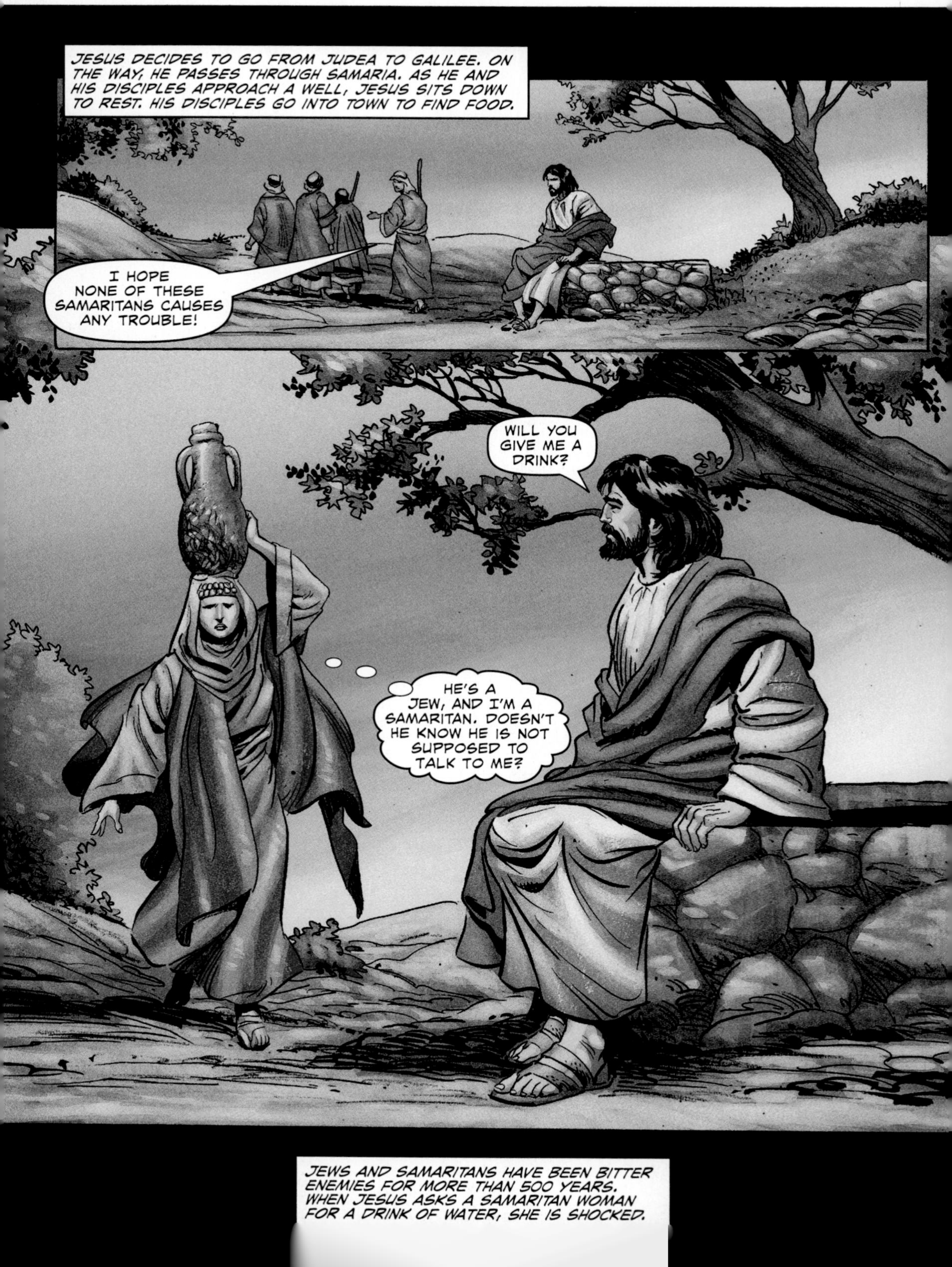

JESUS DECIDES TO GO FROM JUDEA TO GALILEE. ON THE WAY, HE PASSES THROUGH SAMARIA. AS HE AND HIS DISCIPLES APPROACH A WELL, JESUS SITS DOWN TO REST. HIS DISCIPLES GO INTO TOWN TO FIND FOOD.
I HOPE NONE OF THESE SAMARITANS CAUSES ANY TROUBLE!
WILL YOU GIVE ME A DRINK?
HE'S A JEW, AND I'M A SAMARITAN. DOESN'T HE KNOW HE IS NOT SUPPOSED TO TALK TO ME?
JEWS AND SAMARITANS HAVE BEEN BITTER ENEMIES FOR MORE THAN 500 YEARS. WHEN JESUS ASKS A SAMARITAN WOMAN FOR A DRINK OF WATER, SHE IS SHOCKED.

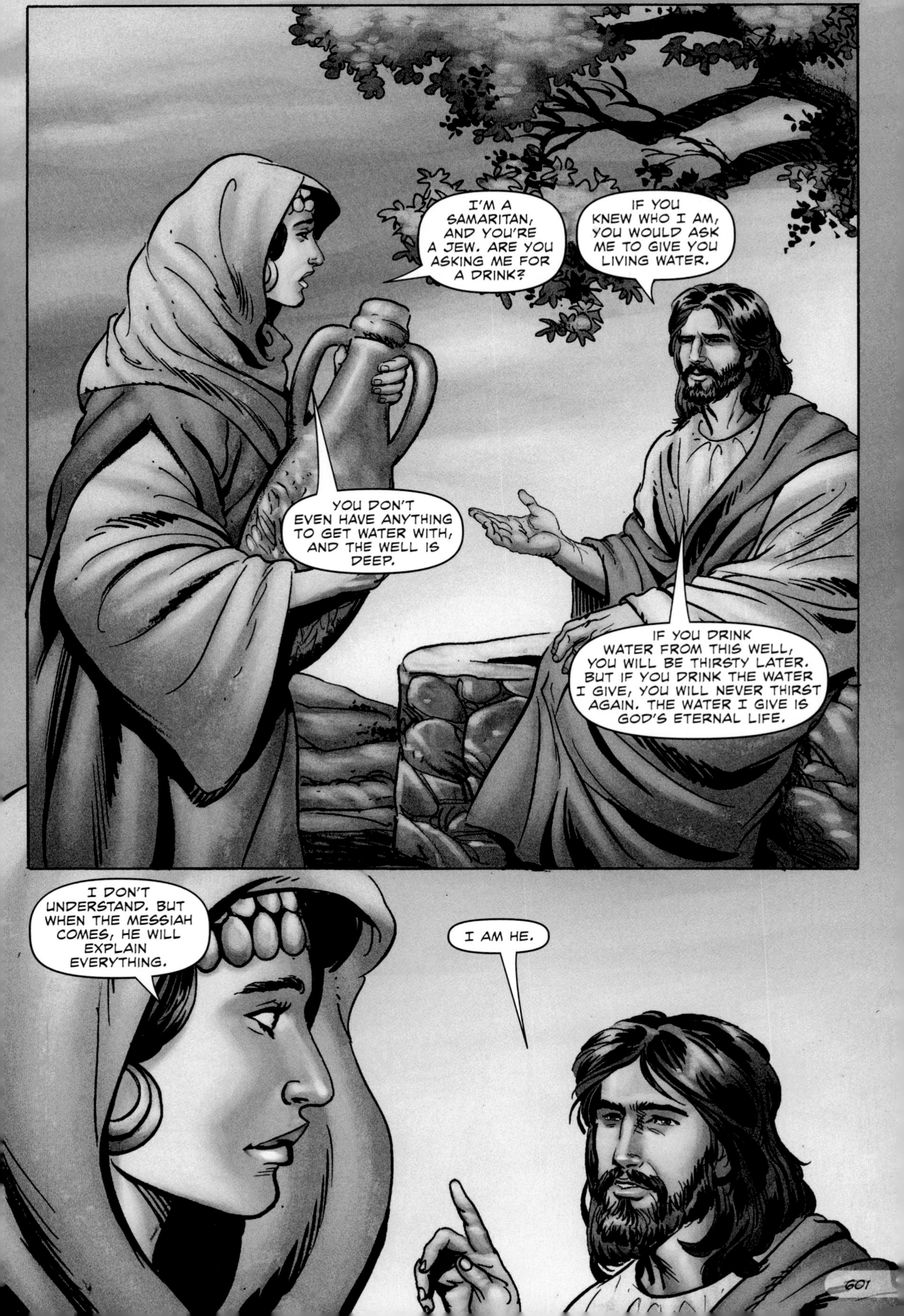
I'M A SAMARITAN, AND YOU'RE A JEW. ARE YOU ASKING ME FOR A DRINK?
IF YOU KNEW WHO I AM, YOU WOULD ASK ME TO GIVE YOU LIVING WATER.
YOU DON'T EVEN HAVE ANYTHING TO GET WATER WITH, AND THE WELL IS DEEP.
IF YOU DRINK WATER FROM THIS WELL, YOU WILL BE THIRSTY LATER. BUT IF YOU DRINK THE WATER I GIVE, YOU WILL NEVER THIRST AGAIN. THE WATER I GIVE IS GOD'S ETERNAL LIFE.
I DON'T UNDERSTAND. BUT WHEN THE MESSIAH COMES, HE WILL EXPLAIN EVERYTHING.
I AM HE.

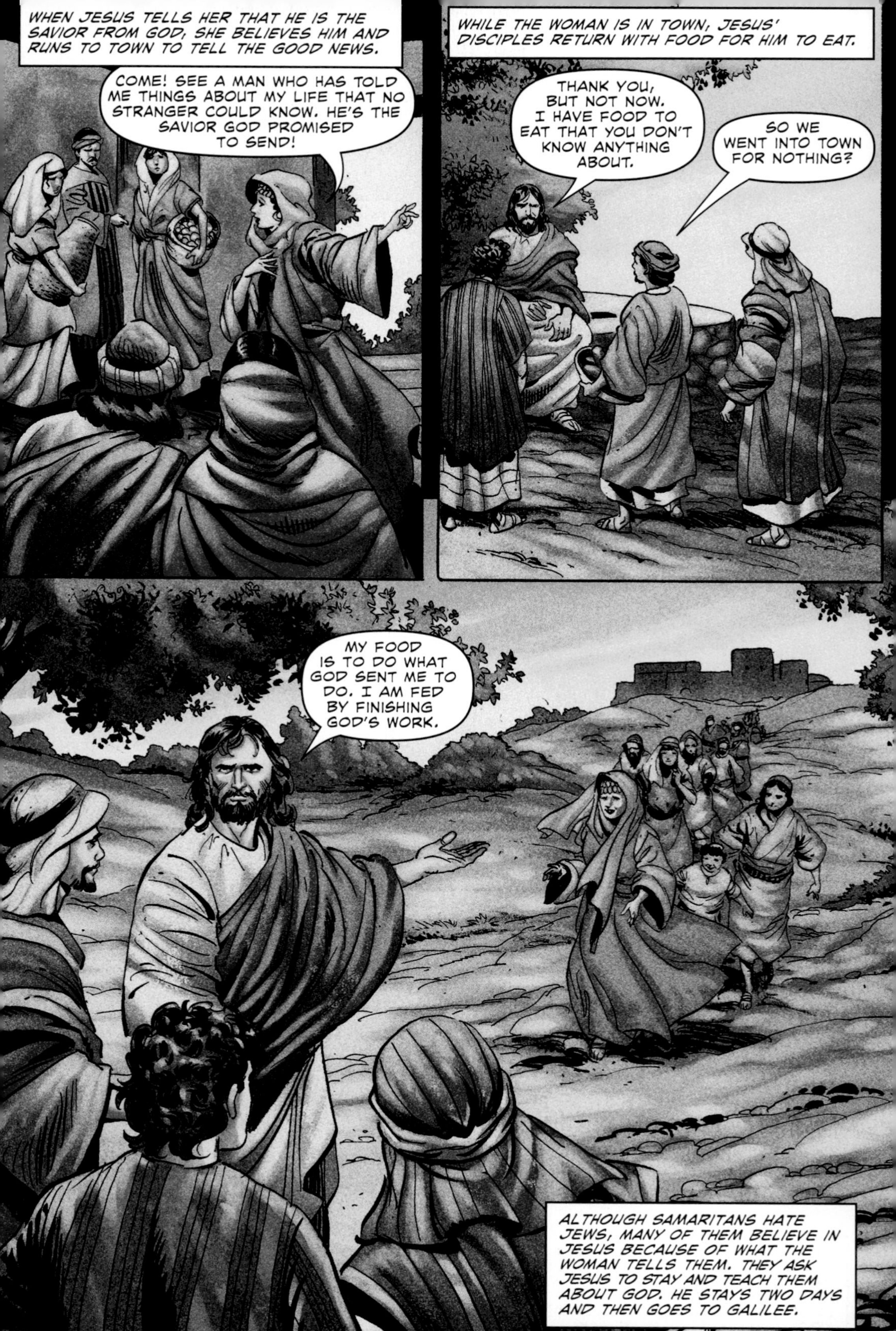
WHEN JESUS TELLS HER THAT HE IS THE SAVIOR FROM GOD, SHE BELIEVES HIM AND RUNS TO TOWN TO TELL THE GOOD NEWS.
COME! SEE A MAN WHO HAS TOLD ME THINGS ABOUT MY LIFE THAT NO STRANGER COULD KNOW. HE'S THE SAVIOR GOD PROMISED TO SEND!
WHILE THE WOMAN IS IN TOWN, JESUS' DISCIPLES RETURN WITH FOOD FOR HIM TO EAT.
THANK YOU, BUT NOT NOW. I HAVE FOOD TO EAT THAT YOU DON'T KNOW ANYTHING ABOUT.
SO WE WENT INTO TOWN FOR NOTHING?
MY FOOD IS TO DO WHAT GOD SENT ME TO DO. I AM FED BY FINISHING GOD'S WORK.
ALTHOUGH SAMARITANS HATE JEWS, MANY OF THEM BELIEVE IN JESUS BECAUSE OF WHAT THE WOMAN TELLS THEM. THEY ASK JESUS TO STAY AND TEACH THEM ABOUT GOD. HE STAYS TWO DAYS AND THEN GOES TO GALILEE.

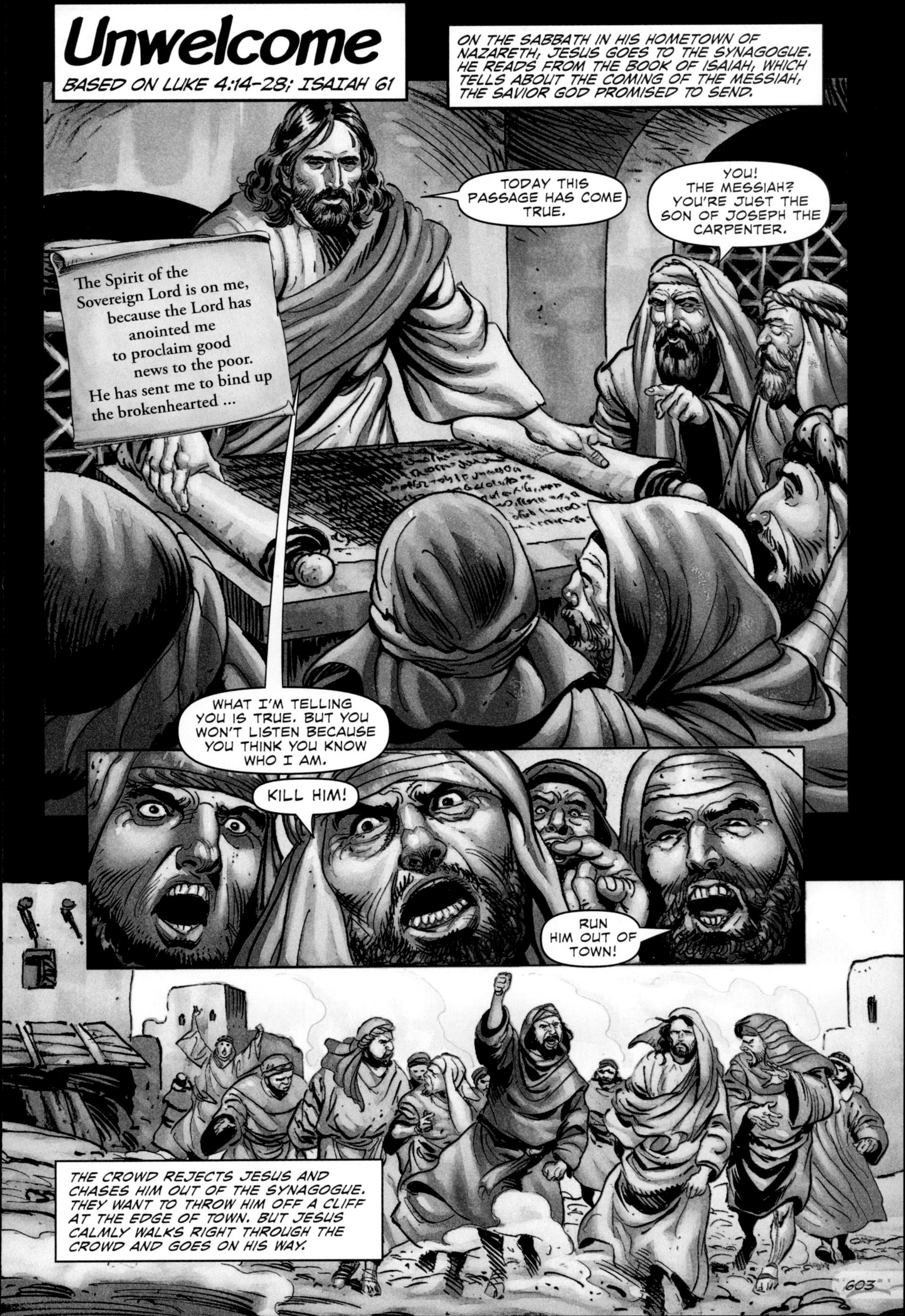

Unwelcome
BASED ON LUKE 4:14-28; ISAIAH 61
ON THE SABBATH IN HIS HOMETOWN OF NAZARETH, JESUS GOES TO THE SYNAGOGUE. HE READS FROM THE BOOK OF ISAIAH, WHICH TELLS ABOUT THE COMING OF THE MESSIAH, THE SAVIOR GOD PROMISED TO SEND.
The Spirit of the Sovereign Lord is on me, because the Lord has anointed me to proclaim good news to the poor. He has sent me to bind up the brokenhearted ...
TODAY THIS PASSAGE HAS COME TRUE.
YOU! THE MESSIAH? YOU'RE JUST THE SON OF JOSEPH THE CARPENTER.
WHAT I'M TELLING YOU IS TRUE. BUT YOU WON'T LISTEN BECAUSE YOU THINK YOU KNOW WHO I AM.
KILL HIM!
RUN HIM OUT OF TOWN!
THE CROWD REJECTS JESUS AND CHASES HIM OUT OF THE SYNAGOGUE. THEY WANT TO THROW HIM OFF A CLIFF AT THE EDGE OF TOWN. BUT JESUS CALMLY WALKS RIGHT THROUGH THE CROWD AND GOES ON HIS WAY.

Up on the Roof

BASED ON MARK 2:1-12; JOHN 5:1-9

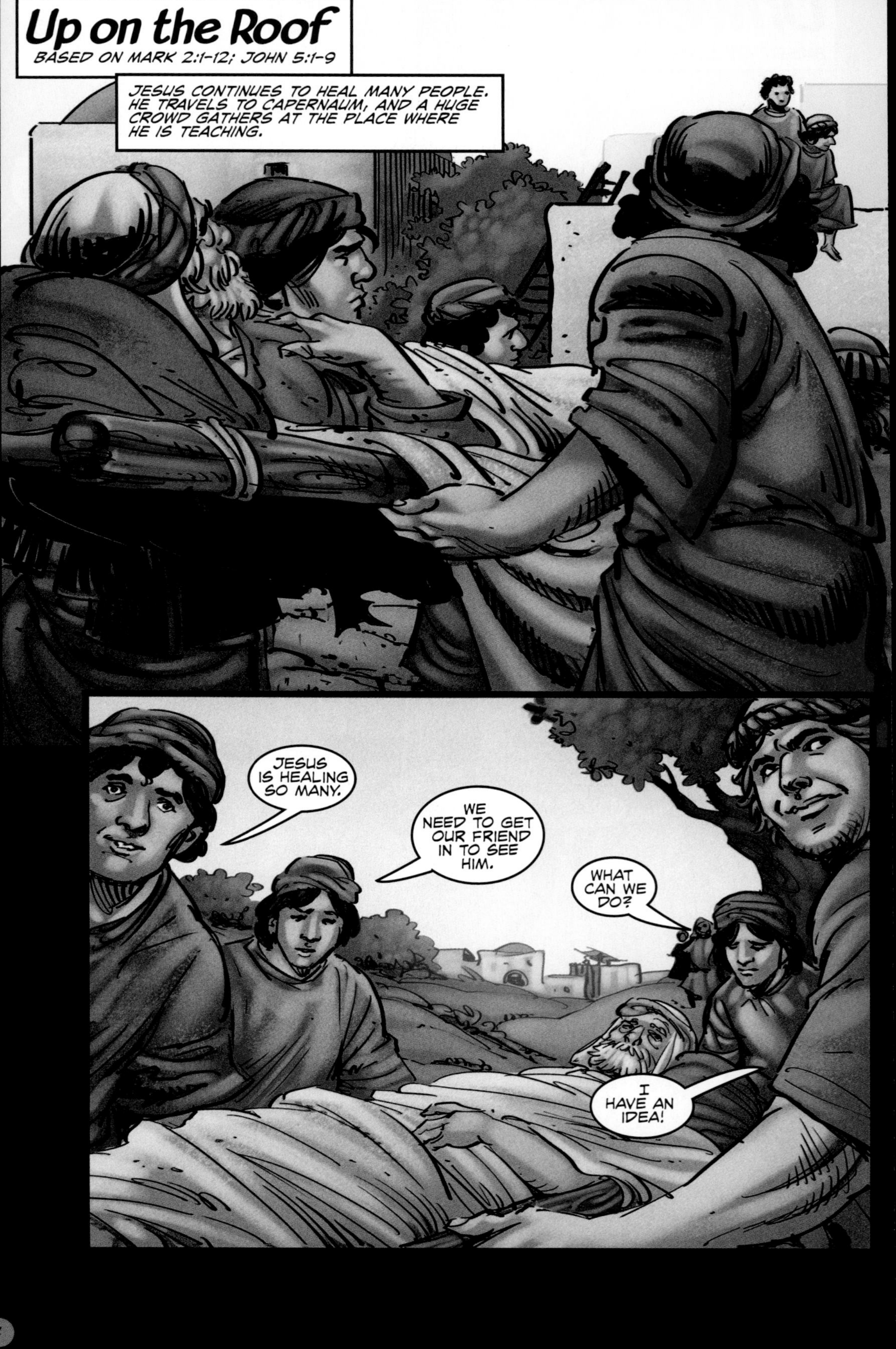
JESUS CONTINUES TO HEAL MANY PEOPLE. HE TRAVELS TO CAPERNAUM, AND A HUGE CROWD GATHERS AT THE PLACE WHERE HE IS TEACHING.
JESUS IS HEALING SO MANY.
WE NEED TO GET OUR FRIEND IN TO SEE HIM.
WHAT CAN WE DO?
I HAVE AN IDEA!

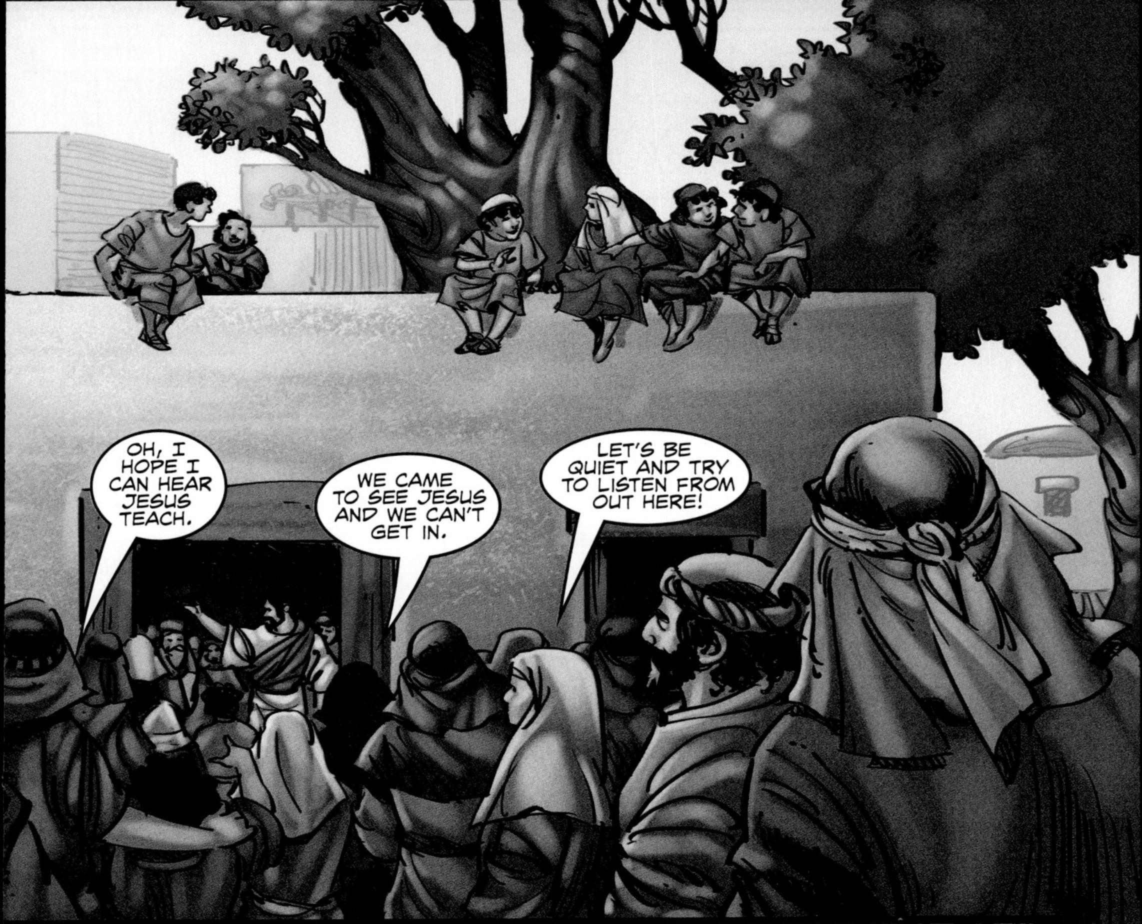
OH, I HOPE I CAN HEAR JESUS TEACH.
WE CAME TO SEE JESUS AND WE CAN'T GET IN.
LET'S BE QUIET AND TRY TO LISTEN FROM OUT HERE!

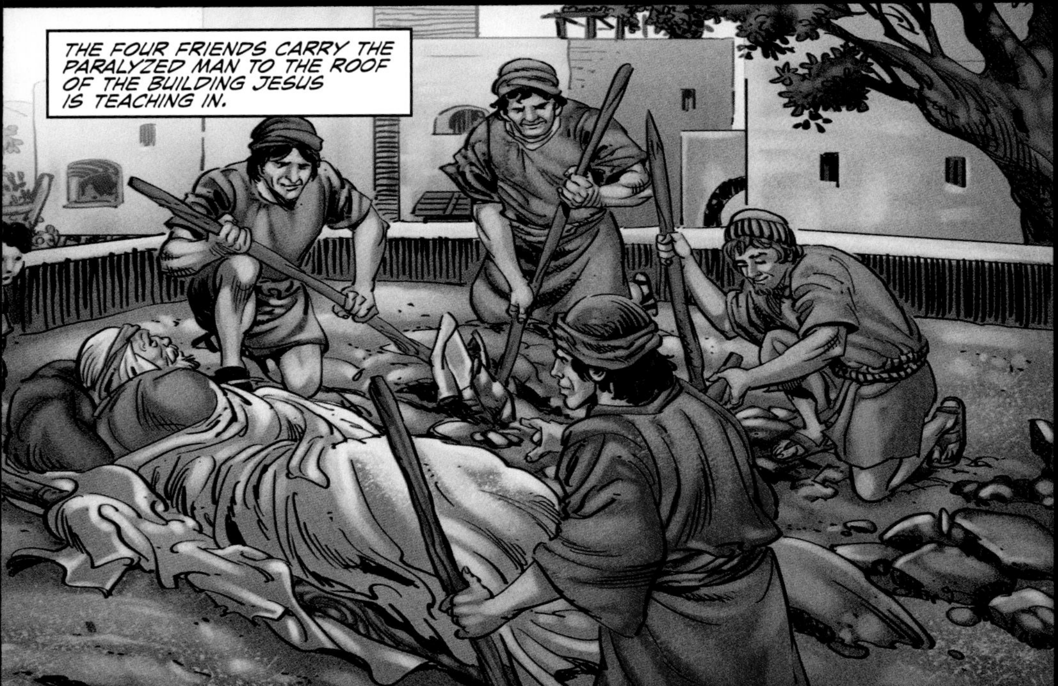
THE FOUR FRIENDS CARRY THE PARALYZED MAN TO THE ROOF OF THE BUILDING JESUS IS TEACHING IN.

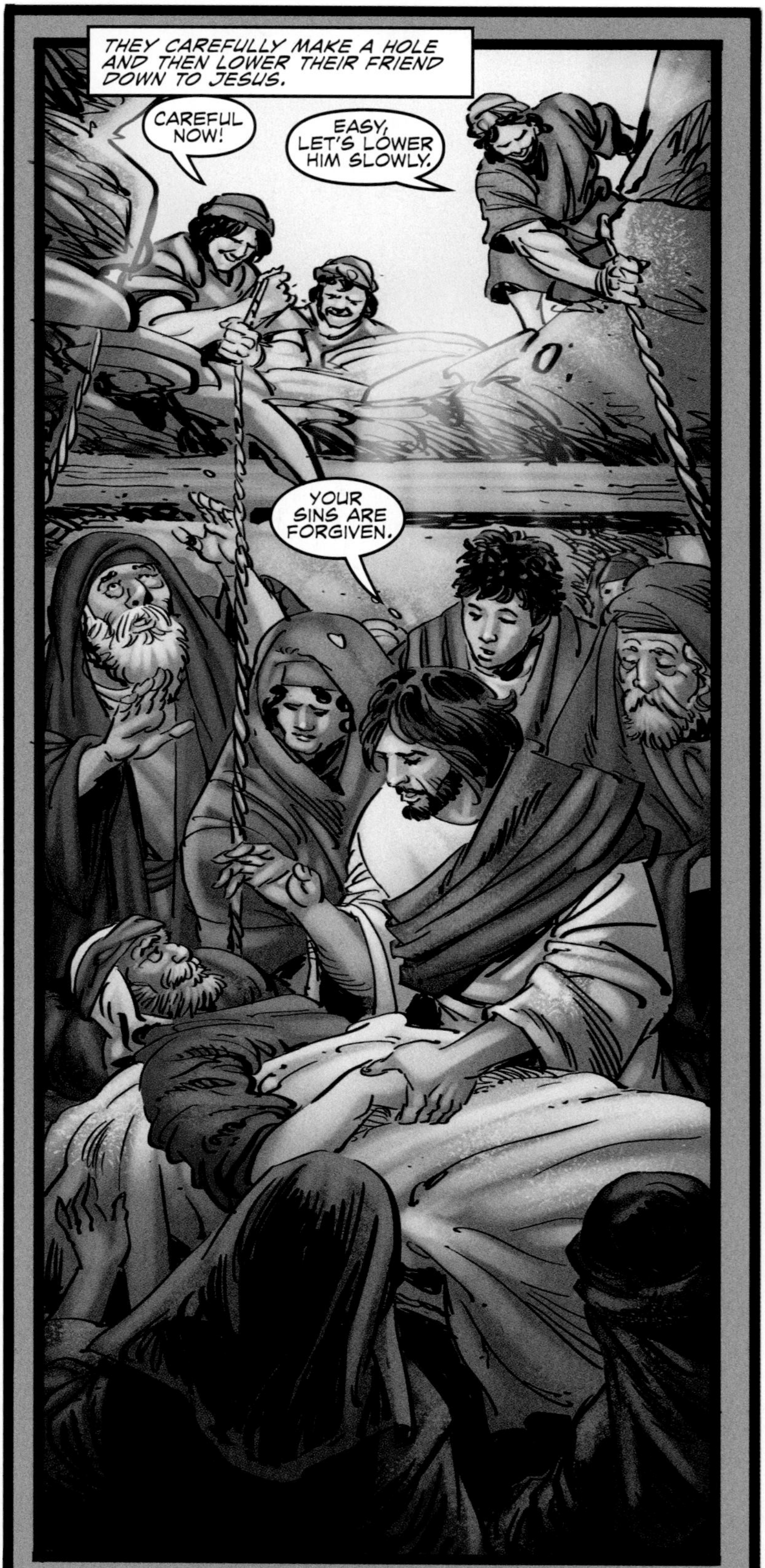
THEY CAREFULLY MAKE A HOLE AND THEN LOWER THEIR FRIEND DOWN TO JESUS.
CAREFUL NOW!
EASY, LET'S LOWER HIM SLOWLY.
YOUR SINS ARE FORGIVEN.
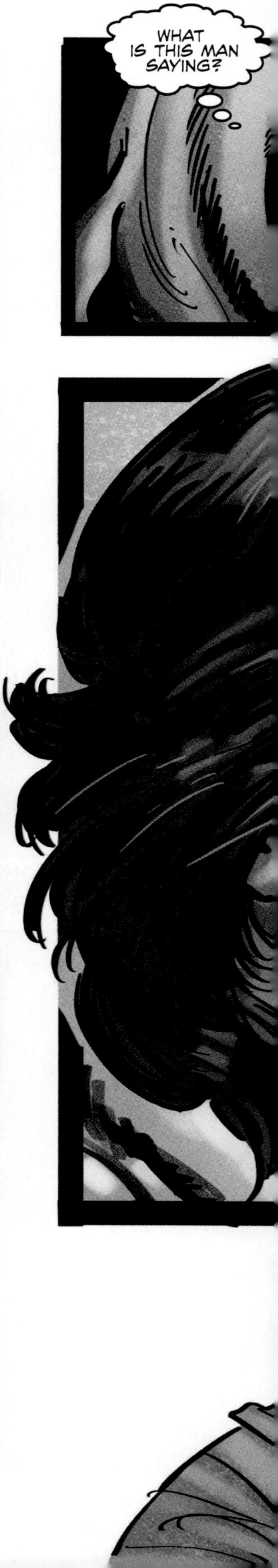
WHAT IS THIS MAN SAYING?

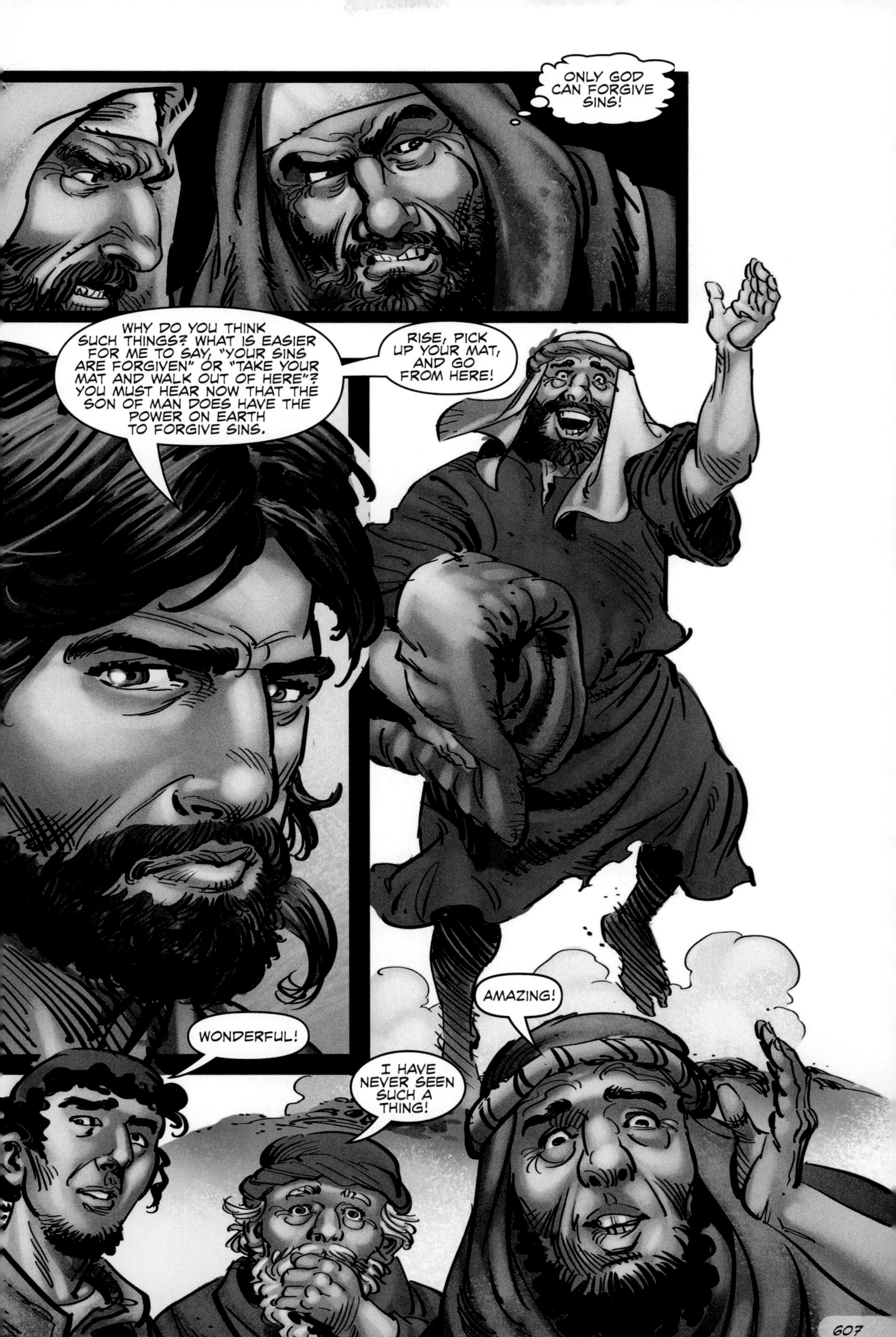
ONLY GOD CAN FORGIVE SINS!
WHY DO YOU THINK SUCH THINGS? WHAT IS EASIER FOR ME TO SAY, "YOUR SINS ARE FORGIVEN" OR "TAKE YOUR MAT AND WALK OUT OF HERE"? YOU MUST HEAR NOW THAT THE SON OF MAN DOES HAVE THE POWER ON EARTH TO FORGIVE SINS.
RISE, PICK UP YOUR MAT, AND GO FROM HERE!
WONDERFUL!
I HAVE NEVER SEEN SUCH A THING!
AMAZING!

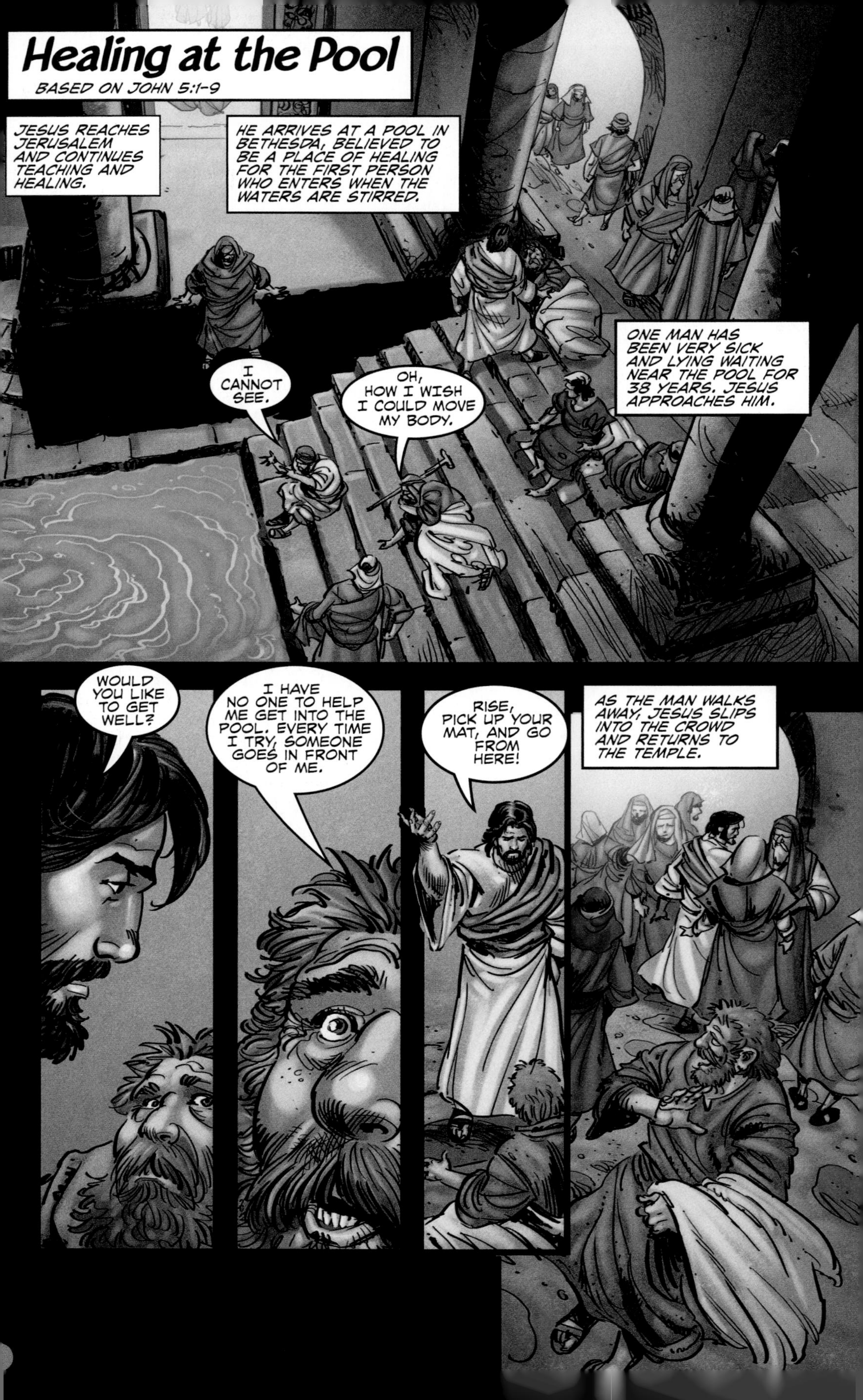
Healing at the Pool
BASED ON JOHN 5:1-9
JESUS REACHES JERUSALEM AND CONTINUES TEACHING AND HEALING.
HE ARRIVES AT A POOL IN BETHESDA, BELIEVED TO BE A PLACE OF HEALING FOR THE FIRST PERSON WHO ENTERS WHEN THE WATERS ARE STIRRED.
I CANNOT SEE.
OH, HOW I WISH I COULD MOVE MY BODY.
ONE MAN HAS BEEN VERY SICK AND LYING WAITING NEAR THE POOL FOR 38 YEARS. JESUS APPROACHES HIM.
WOULD YOU LIKE TO GET WELL?
I HAVE NO ONE TO HELP ME GET INTO THE POOL. EVERY TIME I TRY, SOMEONE GOES IN FRONT OF ME.
RISE, PICK UP YOUR MAT, AND GO FROM HERE!
AS THE MAN WALKS AWAY, JESUS SLIPS INTO THE CROWD AND RETURNS TO THE TEMPLE.

Dinner with Sinners

BASED ON MATTHEW 9:9–13; 12:9–14

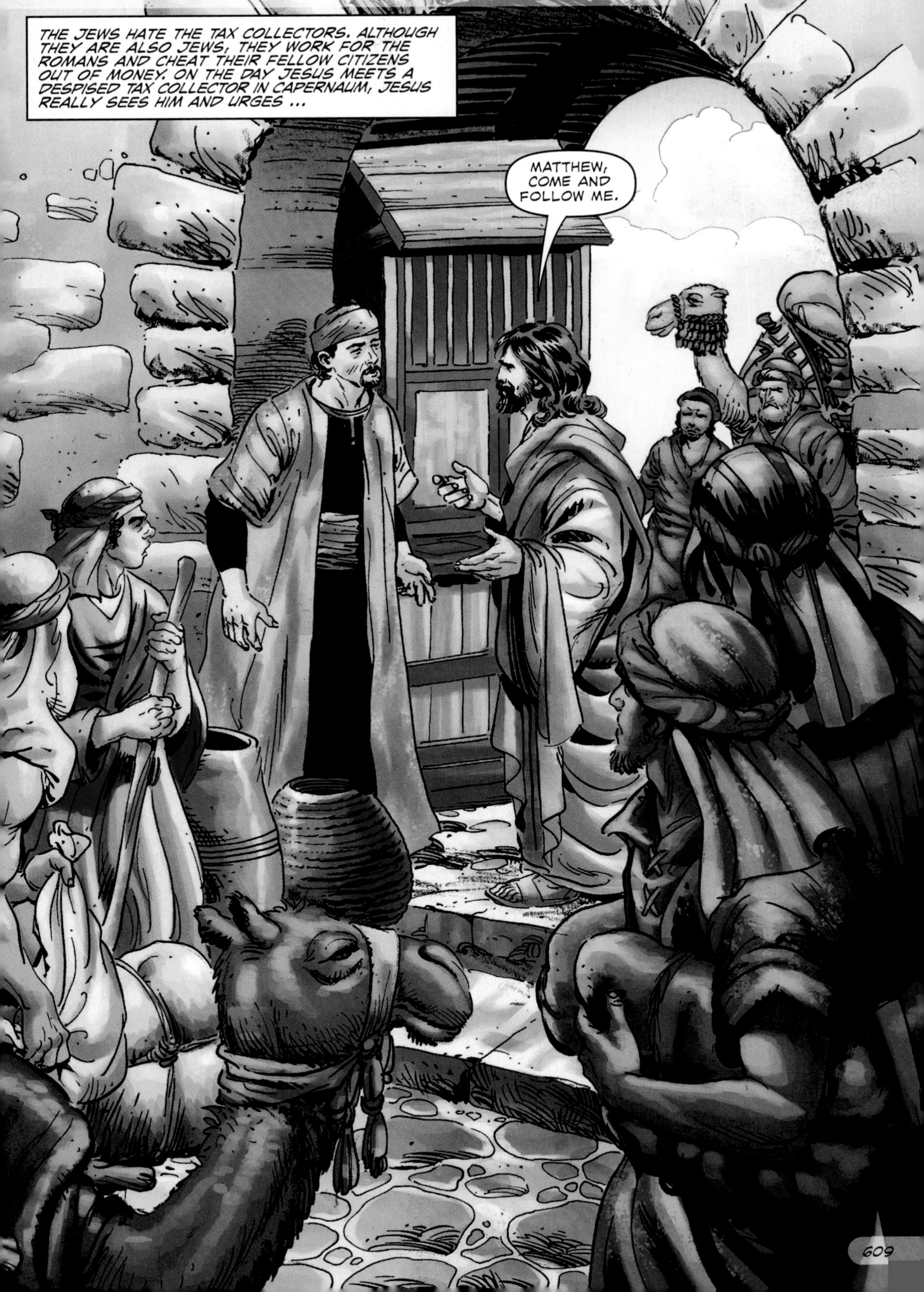
THE JEWS HATE THE TAX COLLECTORS. ALTHOUGH THEY ARE ALSO JEWS, THEY WORK FOR THE ROMANS AND CHEAT THEIR FELLOW CITIZENS OUT OF MONEY. ON THE DAY JESUS MEETS A DESPISED TAX COLLECTOR IN CAPERNAUM, JESUS REALLY SEES HIM AND URGES ...
MATTHEW, COME AND FOLLOW ME.

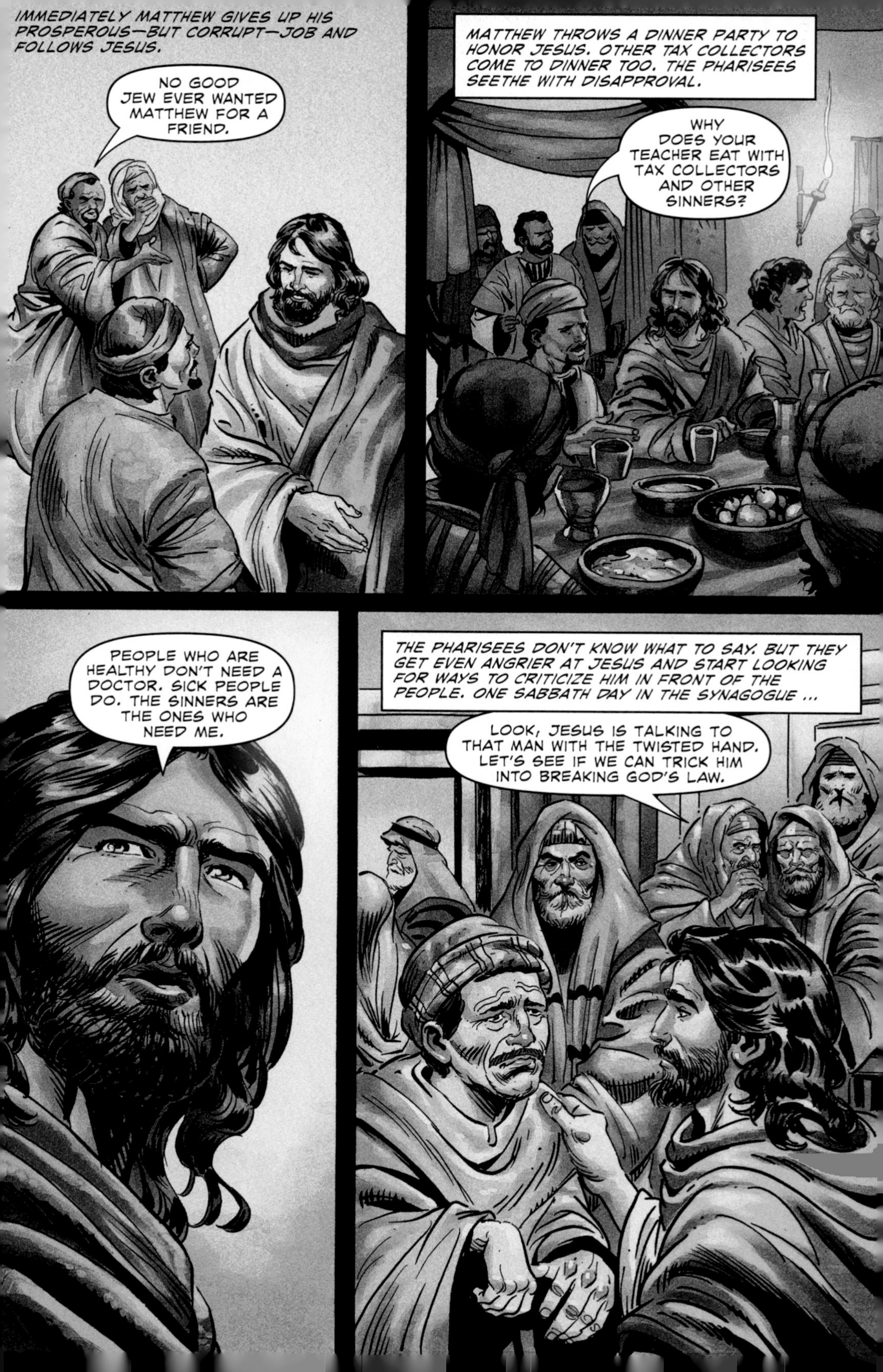
IMMEDIATELY MATTHEW GIVES UP HIS PROSPEROUS—BUT CORRUPT—JOB AND FOLLOWS JESUS.
NO GOOD JEW EVER WANTED MATTHEW FOR A FRIEND.
MATTHEW THROWS A DINNER PARTY TO HONOR JESUS. OTHER TAX COLLECTORS COME TO DINNER TOO. THE PHARISEES SEETHE WITH DISAPPROVAL.
WHY DOES YOUR TEACHER EAT WITH TAX COLLECTORS AND OTHER SINNERS?
PEOPLE WHO ARE HEALTHY DON'T NEED A DOCTOR. SICK PEOPLE DO. THE SINNERS ARE THE ONES WHO NEED ME.
THE PHARISEES DON'T KNOW WHAT TO SAY. BUT THEY GET EVEN ANGRIER AT JESUS AND START LOOKING FOR WAYS TO CRITICIZE HIM IN FRONT OF THE PEOPLE. ONE SABBATH DAY IN THE SYNAGOGUE ...
LOOK, JESUS IS TALKING TO THAT MAN WITH THE TWISTED HAND. LET'S SEE IF WE CAN TRICK HIM INTO BREAKING GOD'S LAW.

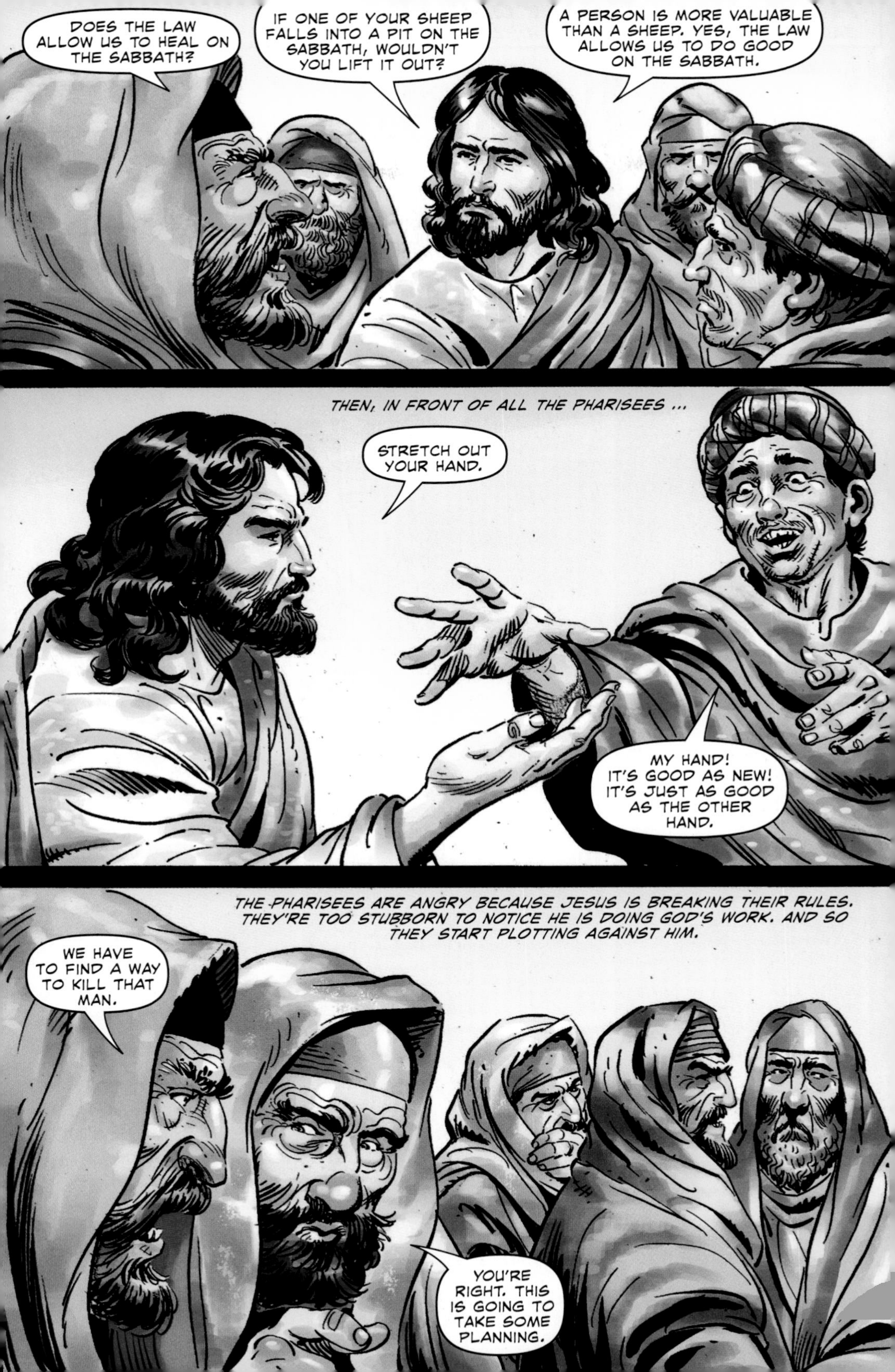
DOES THE LAW ALLOW US TO HEAL ON THE SABBATH?
IF ONE OF YOUR SHEEP FALLS INTO A PIT ON THE SABBATH, WOULDN'T YOU LIFT IT OUT?
A PERSON IS MORE VALUABLE THAN A SHEEP. YES, THE LAW ALLOWS US TO DO GOOD ON THE SABBATH.
THEN, IN FRONT OF ALL THE PHARISEES ...
STRETCH OUT YOUR HAND.
MY HAND! IT'S GOOD AS NEW! IT'S JUST AS GOOD AS THE OTHER HAND.
THE PHARISEES ARE ANGRY BECAUSE JESUS IS BREAKING THEIR RULES. THEY'RE TOO STUBBORN TO NOTICE HE IS DOING GOD'S WORK. AND SO THEY START PLOTTING AGAINST HIM.
WE HAVE TO FIND A WAY TO KILL THAT MAN.
YOU'RE RIGHT. THIS IS GOING TO TAKE SOME PLANNING.

A Sermon with Parables

BASED ON MATTHEW 5–8, 13; MARK 4:1–20; LUKE 6:12, 17–26, 46–49

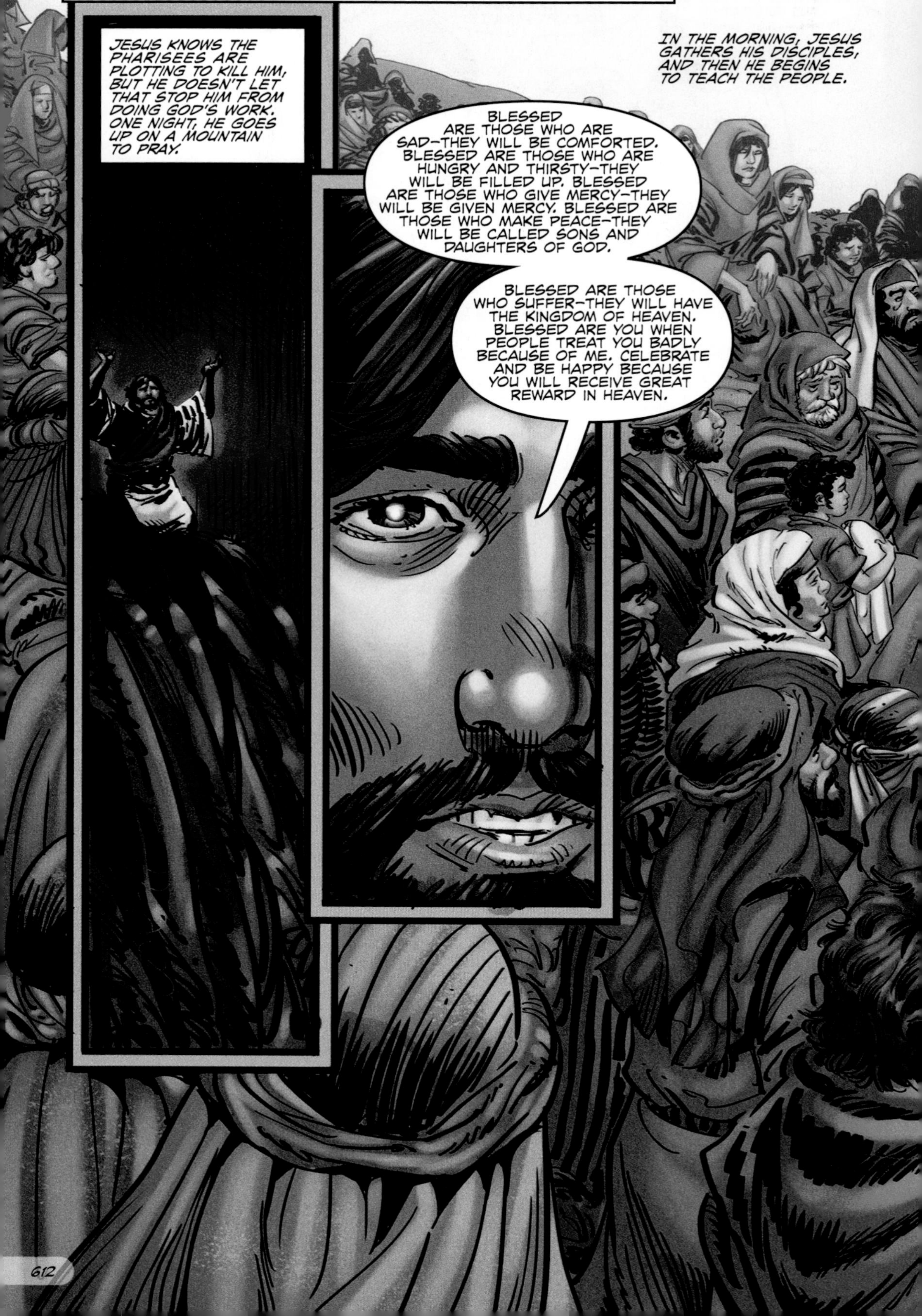
JESUS KNOWS THE PHARISEES ARE PLOTTING TO KILL HIM, BUT HE DOESN'T LET THAT STOP HIM FROM DOING GOD'S WORK. ONE NIGHT, HE GOES UP ON A MOUNTAIN TO PRAY.
IN THE MORNING, JESUS GATHERS HIS DISCIPLES, AND THEN HE BEGINS TO TEACH THE PEOPLE.
BLESSED ARE THOSE WHO ARE SAD—THEY WILL BE COMFORTED. BLESSED ARE THOSE WHO ARE HUNGRY AND THIRSTY—THEY WILL BE FILLED UP. BLESSED ARE THOSE WHO GIVE MERCY—THEY WILL BE GIVEN MERCY. BLESSED ARE THOSE WHO MAKE PEACE—THEY WILL BE CALLED SONS AND DAUGHTERS OF GOD.
BLESSED ARE THOSE WHO SUFFER—THEY WILL HAVE THE KINGDOM OF HEAVEN. BLESSED ARE YOU WHEN PEOPLE TREAT YOU BADLY BECAUSE OF ME. CELEBRATE AND BE HAPPY BECAUSE YOU WILL RECEIVE GREAT REWARD IN HEAVEN.

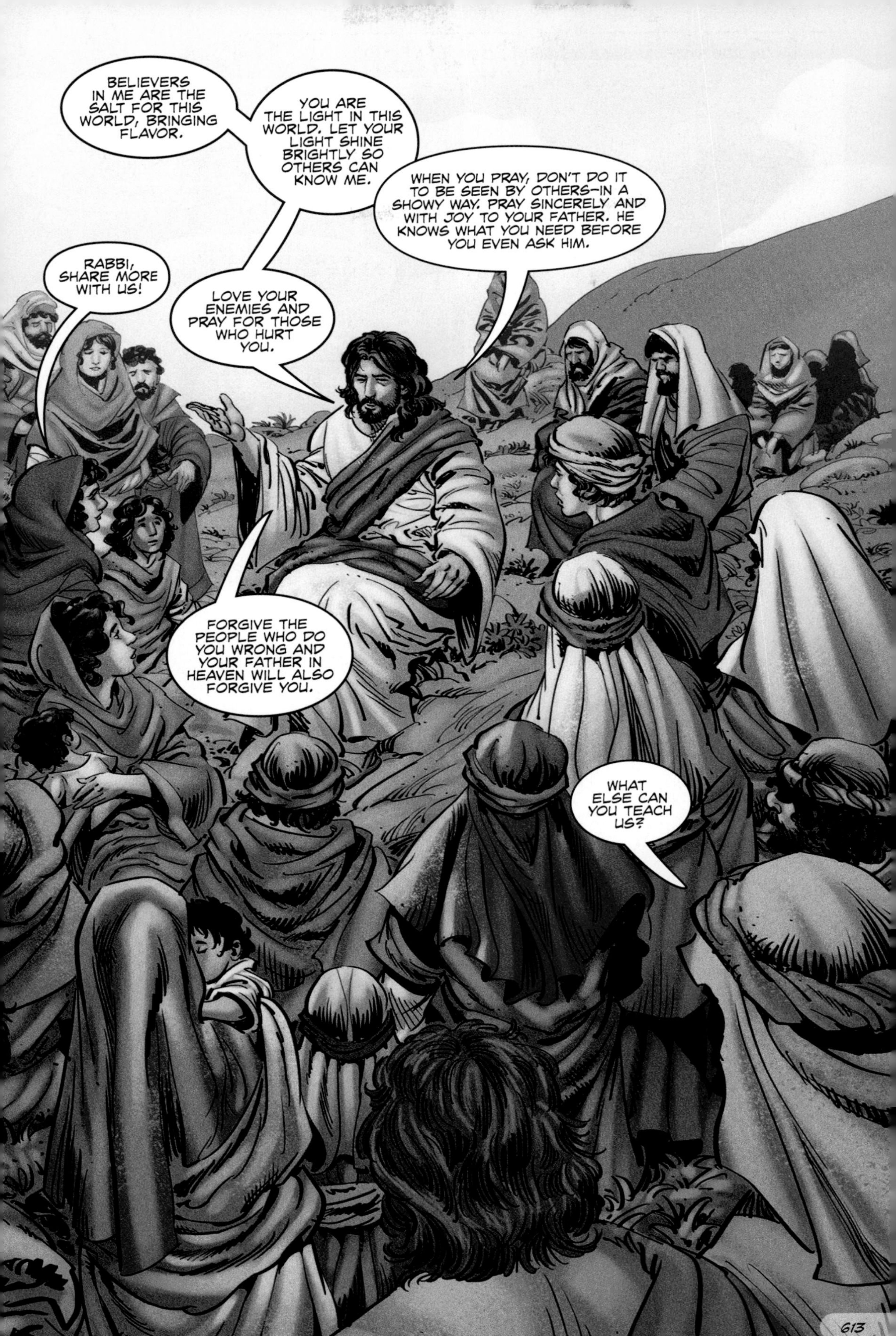
BELIEVERS IN ME ARE THE SALT FOR THIS WORLD, BRINGING FLAVOR.
YOU ARE THE LIGHT IN THIS WORLD. LET YOUR LIGHT SHINE BRIGHTLY SO OTHERS CAN KNOW ME.
WHEN YOU PRAY, DON'T DO IT TO BE SEEN BY OTHERS—IN A SHOWY WAY. PRAY SINCERELY AND WITH JOY TO YOUR FATHER. HE KNOWS WHAT YOU NEED BEFORE YOU EVEN ASK HIM.
RABBI, SHARE MORE WITH US!
LOVE YOUR ENEMIES AND PRAY FOR THOSE WHO HURT YOU.
FORGIVE THE PEOPLE WHO DO YOU WRONG AND YOUR FATHER IN HEAVEN WILL ALSO FORGIVE YOU.
WHAT ELSE CAN YOU TEACH US?

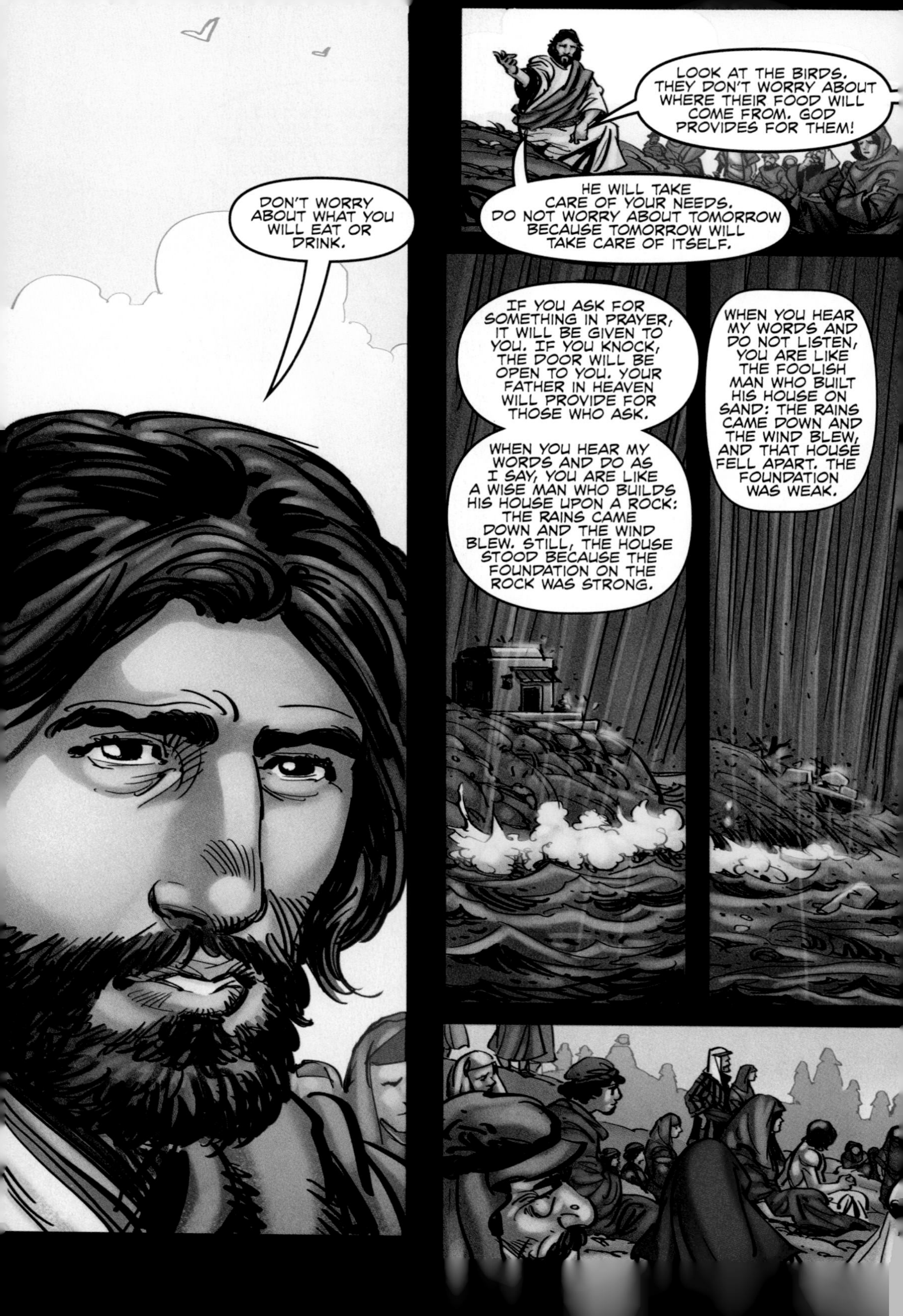
DON'T WORRY ABOUT WHAT YOU WILL EAT OR DRINK.
LOOK AT THE BIRDS. THEY DON'T WORRY ABOUT WHERE THEIR FOOD WILL COME FROM. GOD PROVIDES FOR THEM!
HE WILL TAKE CARE OF YOUR NEEDS. DO NOT WORRY ABOUT TOMORROW BECAUSE TOMORROW WILL TAKE CARE OF ITSELF.
IF YOU ASK FOR SOMETHING IN PRAYER, IT WILL BE GIVEN TO YOU. IF YOU KNOCK, THE DOOR WILL BE OPEN TO YOU. YOUR FATHER IN HEAVEN WILL PROVIDE FOR THOSE WHO ASK.
WHEN YOU HEAR MY WORDS AND DO AS I SAY, YOU ARE LIKE A WISE MAN WHO BUILDS HIS HOUSE UPON A ROCK: THE RAINS CAME DOWN AND THE WIND BLEW. STILL, THE HOUSE STOOD BECAUSE THE FOUNDATION ON THE ROCK WAS STRONG.
WHEN YOU HEAR MY WORDS AND DO NOT LISTEN, YOU ARE LIKE THE FOOLISH MAN WHO BUILT HIS HOUSE ON SAND: THE RAINS CAME DOWN AND THE WIND BLEW, AND THAT HOUSE FELL APART. THE FOUNDATION WAS WEAK.

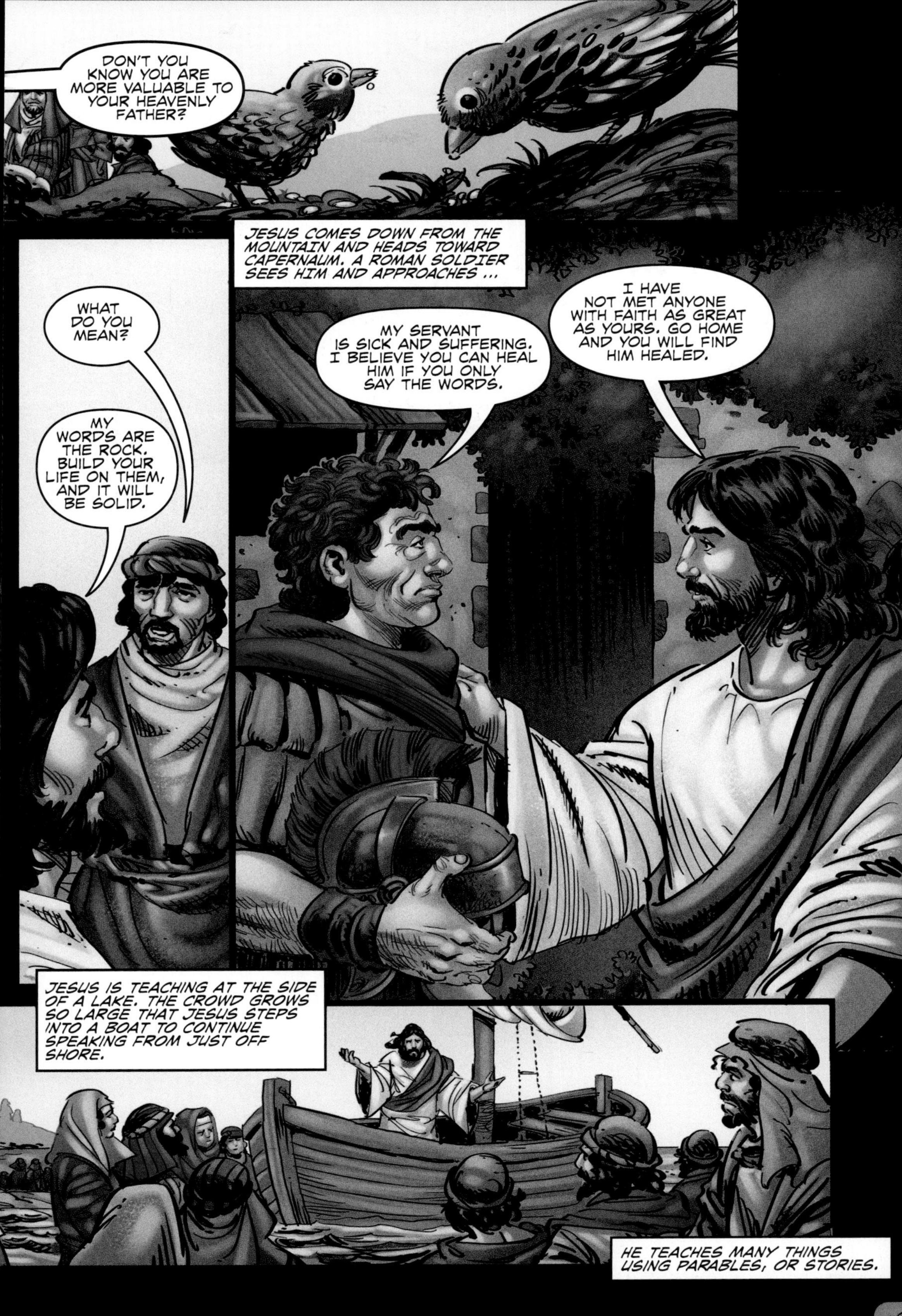
DON'T YOU KNOW YOU ARE MORE VALUABLE TO YOUR HEAVENLY FATHER?
WHAT DO YOU MEAN?
MY WORDS ARE THE ROCK. BUILD YOUR LIFE ON THEM, AND IT WILL BE SOLID.
JESUS COMES DOWN FROM THE MOUNTAIN AND HEADS TOWARD CAPERNAUM. A ROMAN SOLDIER SEES HIM AND APPROACHES ...
MY SERVANT IS SICK AND SUFFERING. I BELIEVE YOU CAN HEAL HIM IF YOU ONLY SAY THE WORDS.
I HAVE NOT MET ANYONE WITH FAITH AS GREAT AS YOURS. GO HOME AND YOU WILL FIND HIM HEALED.
JESUS IS TEACHING AT THE SIDE OF A LAKE. THE CROWD GROWS SO LARGE THAT JESUS STEPS INTO A BOAT TO CONTINUE SPEAKING FROM JUST OFF SHORE.
HE TEACHES MANY THINGS USING PARABLES, OR STORIES.

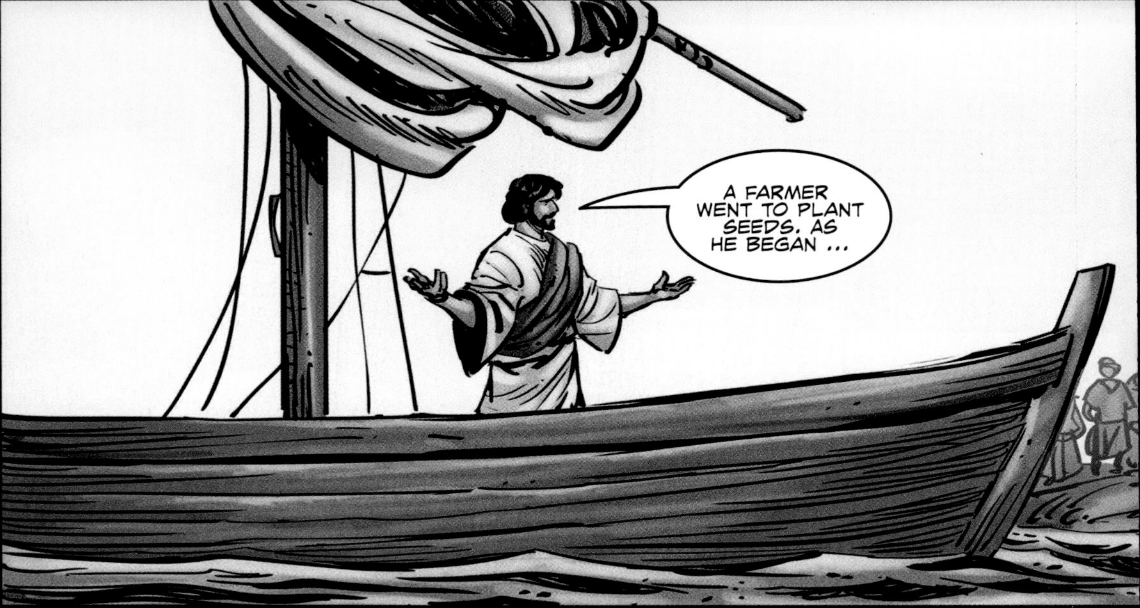
A FARMER WENT TO PLANT SEEDS. AS HE BEGAN ...

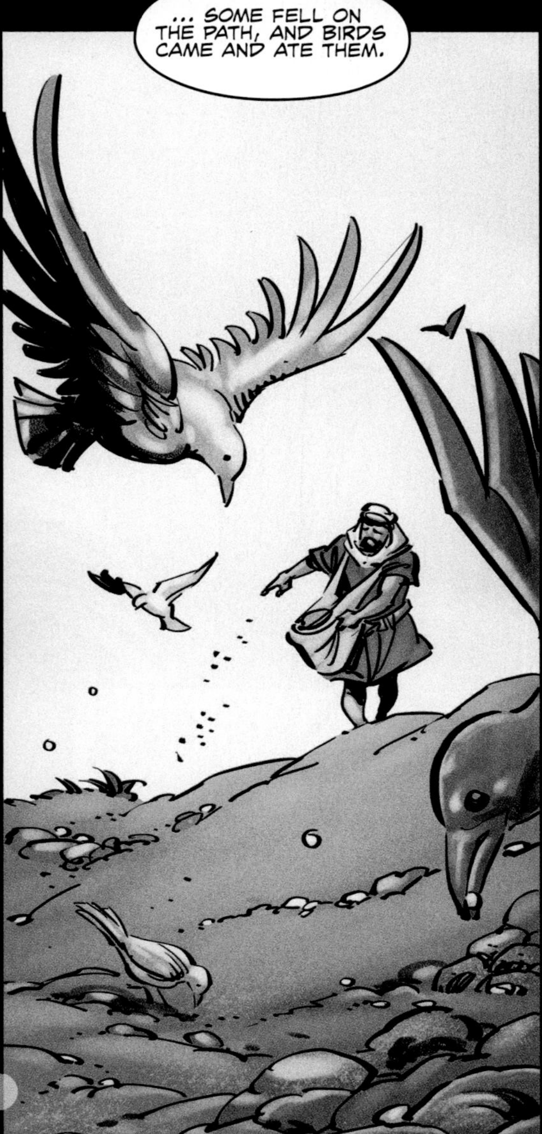
... SOME FELL ON THE PATH, AND BIRDS CAME AND ATE THEM.

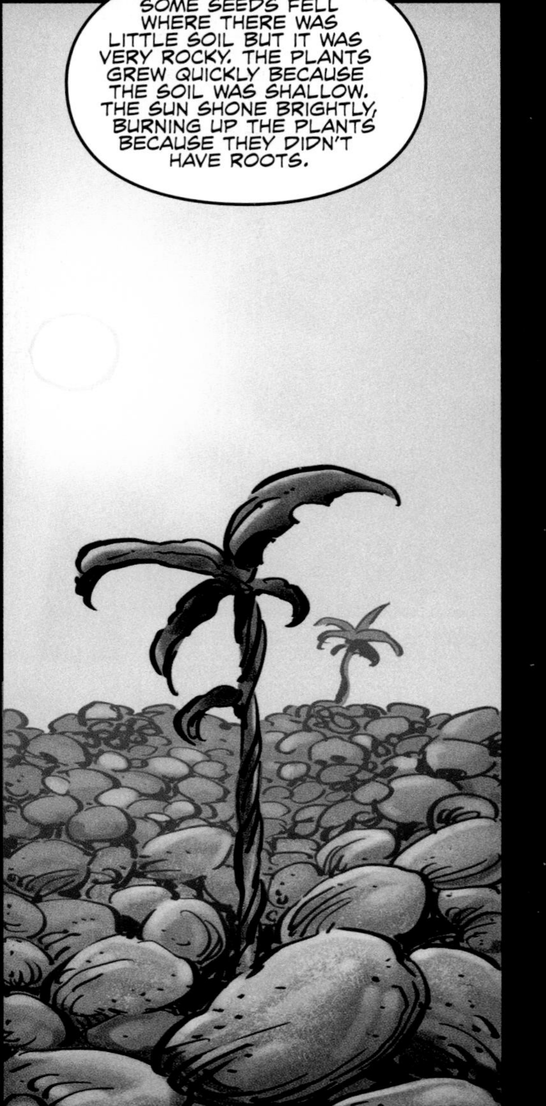
SOME SEEDS FELL WHERE THERE WAS LITTLE SOIL BUT IT WAS VERY ROCKY. THE PLANTS GREW QUICKLY BECAUSE THE SOIL WAS SHALLOW. THE SUN SHONE BRIGHTLY, BURNING UP THE PLANTS BECAUSE THEY DIDN'T HAVE ROOTS.

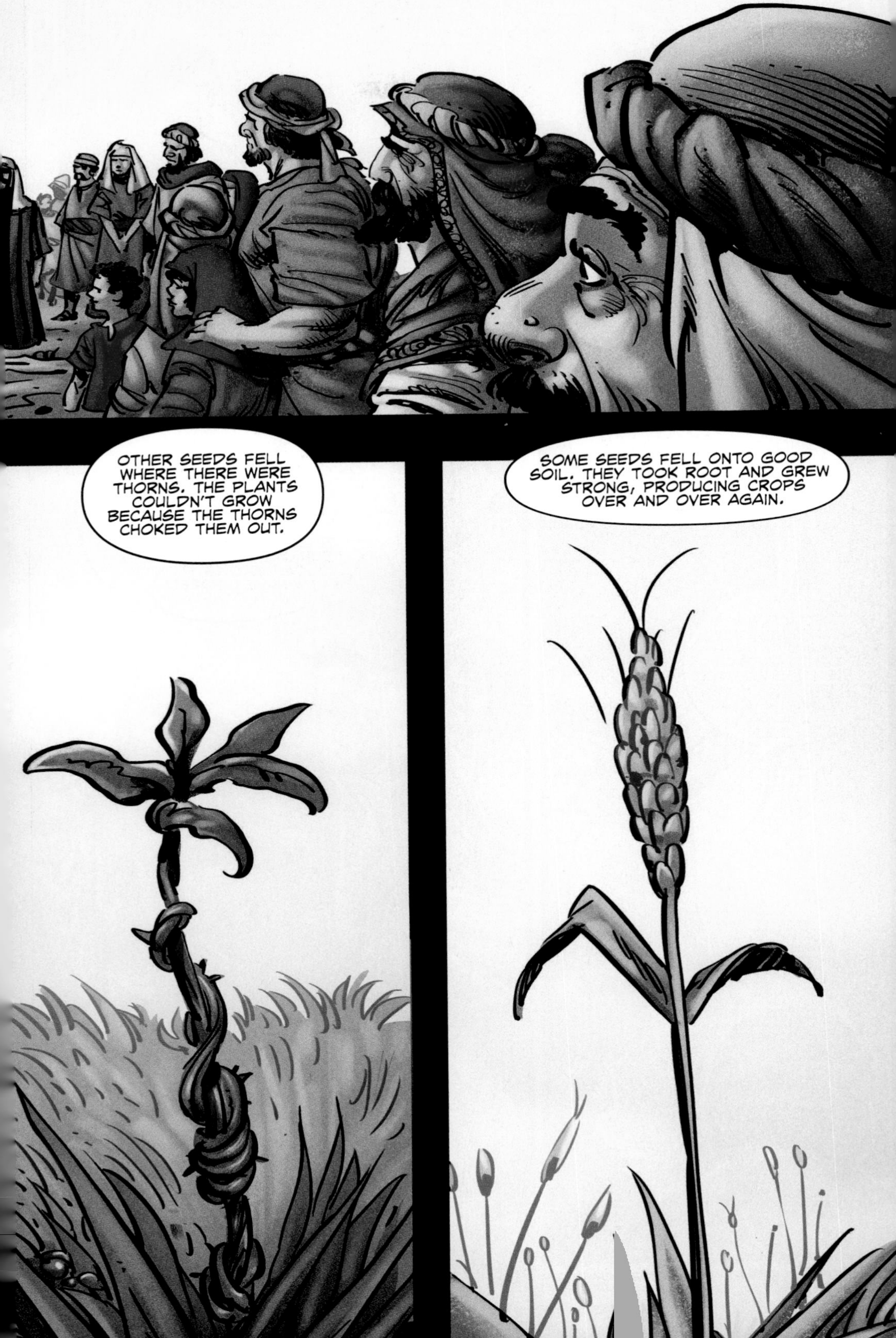
OTHER SEEDS FELL WHERE THERE WERE THORNS. THE PLANTS COULDN'T GROW BECAUSE THE THORNS CHOKED THEM OUT.
SOME SEEDS FELL ONTO GOOD SOIL. THEY TOOK ROOT AND GREW STRONG, PRODUCING CROPS OVER AND OVER AGAIN.

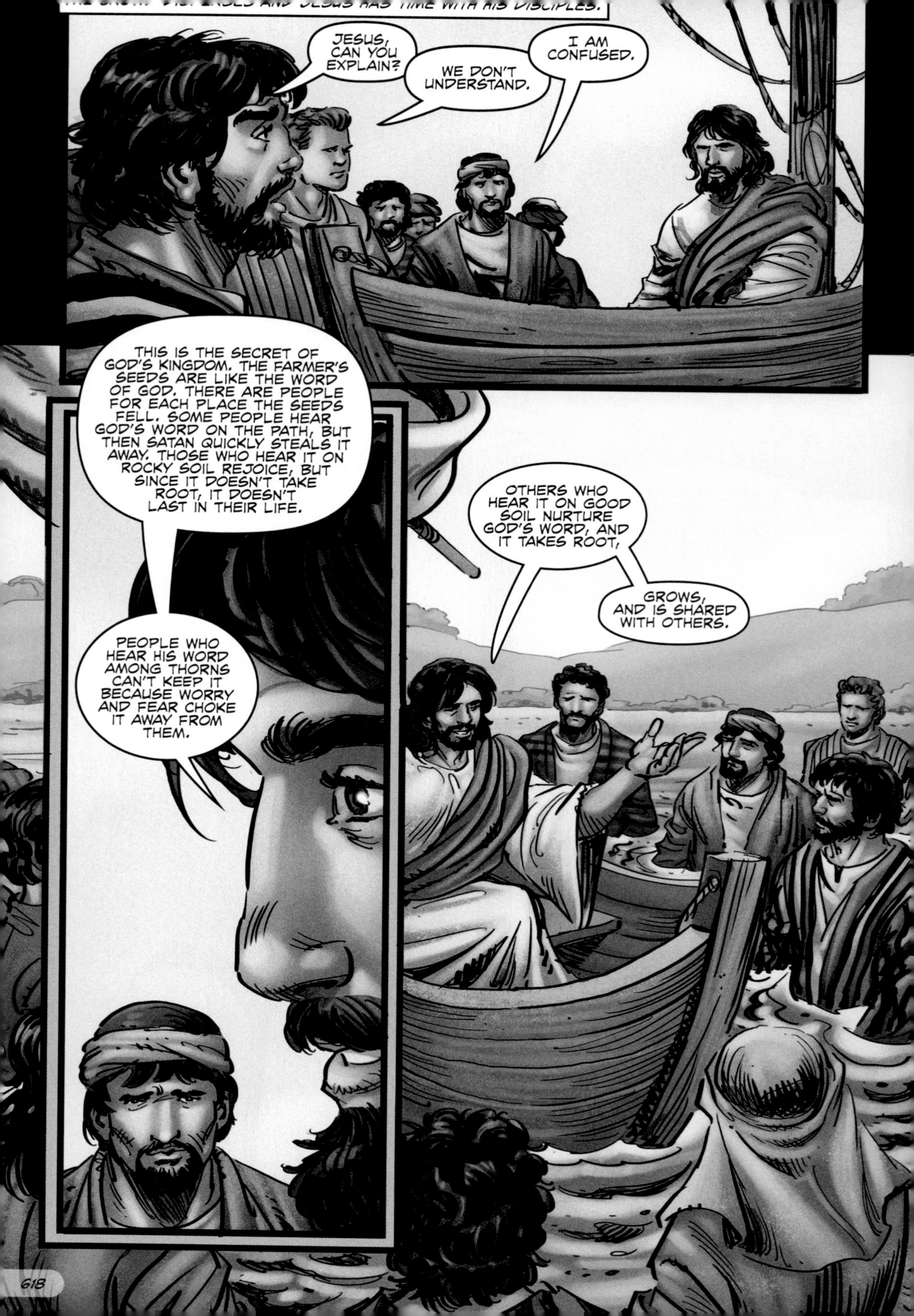
AND JESUS HAS TIME WITH HIS DISCIPLES.
JESUS, CAN YOU EXPLAIN?
WE DON'T UNDERSTAND.
I AM CONFUSED.
THIS IS THE SECRET OF GOD'S KINGDOM. THE FARMER'S SEEDS ARE LIKE THE WORD OF GOD. THERE ARE PEOPLE FOR EACH PLACE THE SEEDS FELL. SOME PEOPLE HEAR GOD'S WORD ON THE PATH, BUT THEN SATAN QUICKLY STEALS IT AWAY. THOSE WHO HEAR IT ON ROCKY SOIL REJOICE, BUT SINCE IT DOESN'T TAKE ROOT, IT DOESN'T LAST IN THEIR LIFE.
PEOPLE WHO HEAR HIS WORD AMONG THORNS CAN'T KEEP IT BECAUSE WORRY AND FEAR CHOKE IT AWAY FROM THEM.
OTHERS WHO HEAR IT ON GOOD SOIL NURTURE GOD'S WORD, AND IT TAKES ROOT,
GROWS, AND IS SHARED WITH OTHERS.

Storm at Sea

BASED ON MARK 4:35–5:34

AFTER A DAY OF TEACHING, JESUS TELLS HIS DISCIPLES THEY SHOULD CROSS TO THE OTHER SIDE OF THE SEA OF GALILEE. JESUS FALLS ASLEEP IN THE BACK OF THE BOAT. THE WEATHER IS CALM AS THE GROUP SETS OFF.

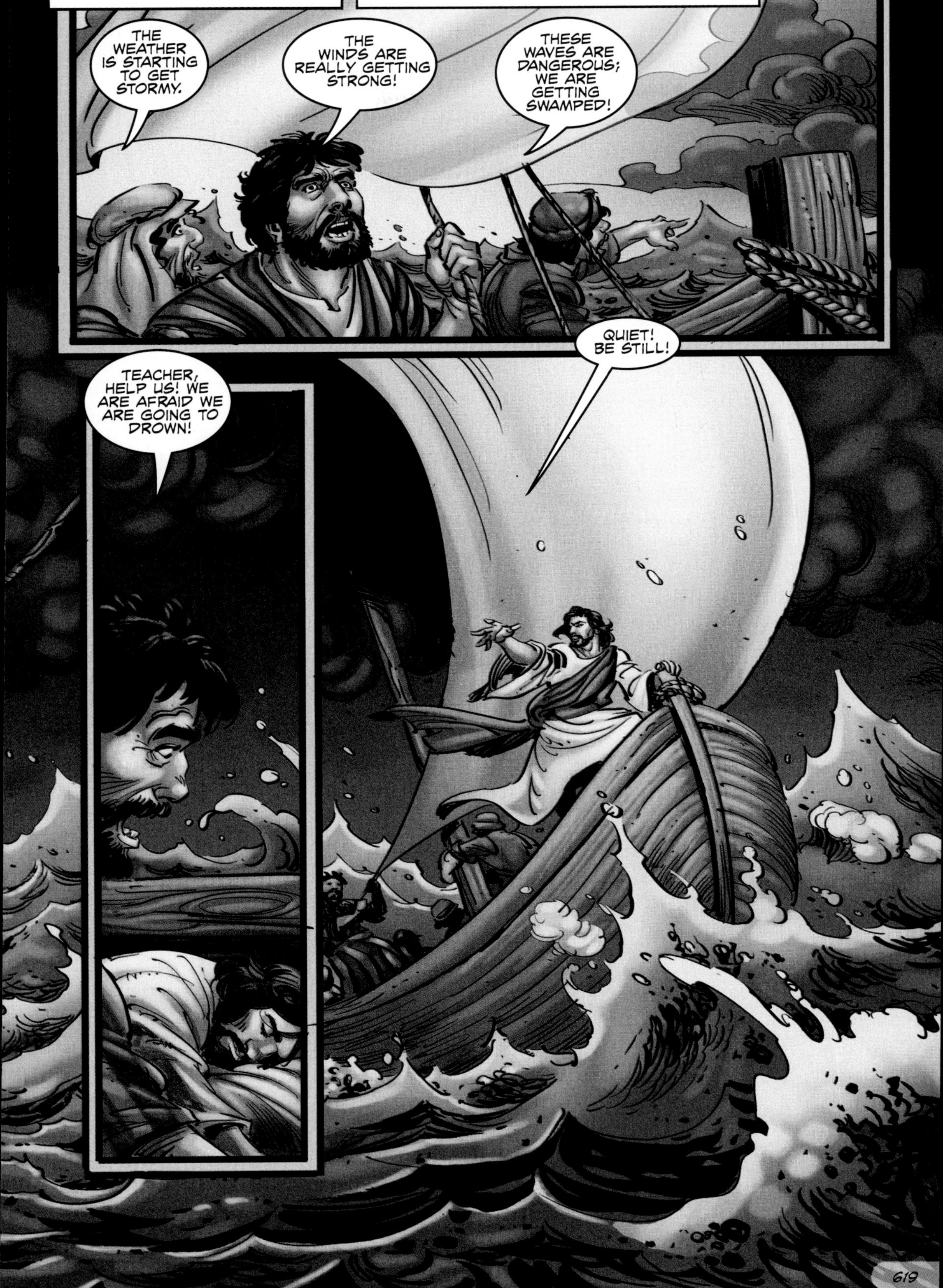
THE WEATHER IS STARTING TO GET STORMY.
THE WINDS ARE REALLY GETTING STRONG!
THESE WAVES ARE DANGEROUS; WE ARE GETTING SWAMPED!
TEACHER, HELP US! WE ARE AFRAID WE ARE GOING TO DROWN!
QUIET! BE STILL!

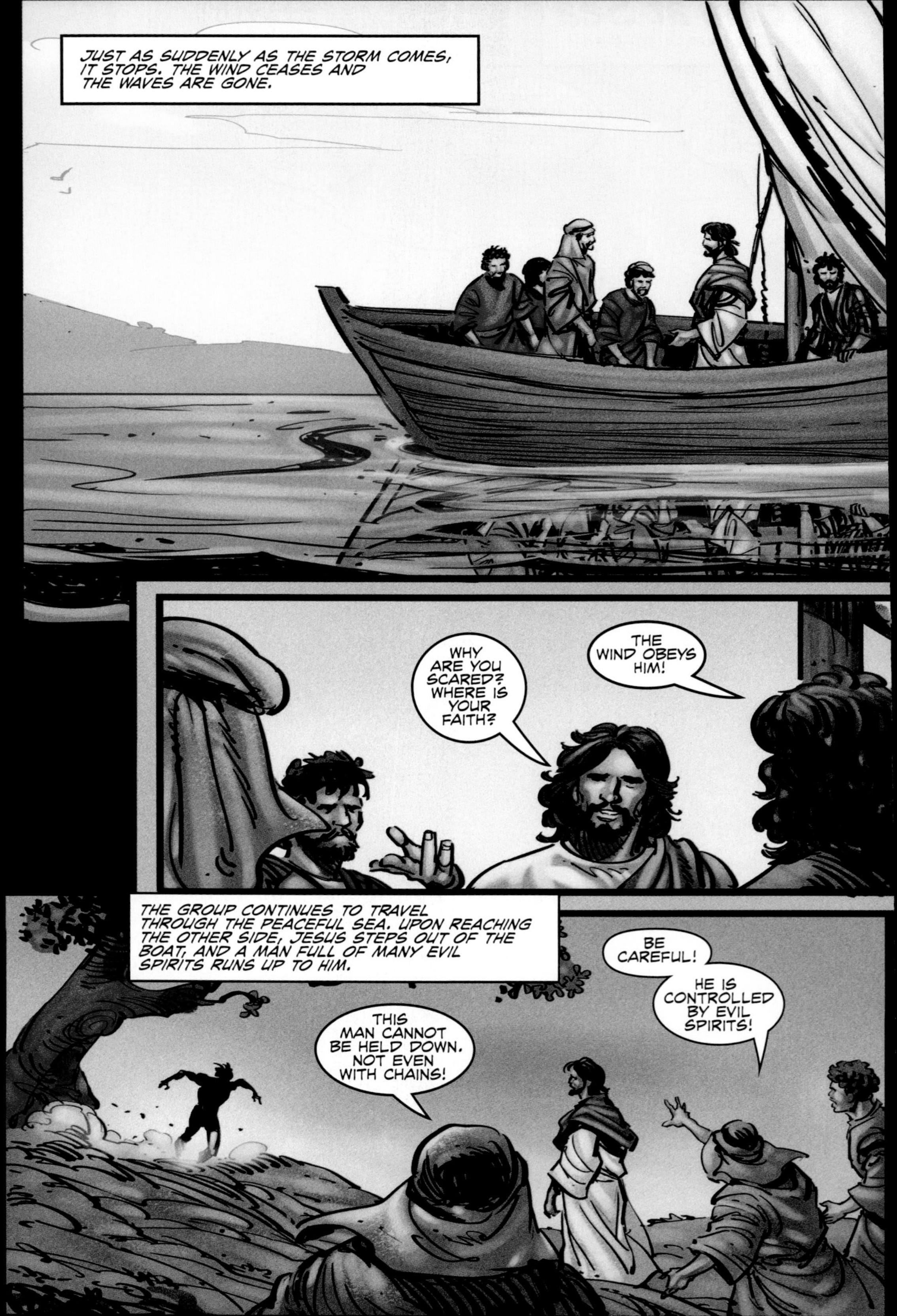
JUST AS SUDDENLY AS THE STORM COMES, IT STOPS. THE WIND CEASES AND THE WAVES ARE GONE.
WHY ARE YOU SCARED? WHERE IS YOUR FAITH?
THE WIND OBEYS HIM!
THE GROUP CONTINUES TO TRAVEL THROUGH THE PEACEFUL SEA. UPON REACHING THE OTHER SIDE, JESUS STEPS OUT OF THE BOAT, AND A MAN FULL OF MANY EVIL SPIRITS RUNS UP TO HIM.
BE CAREFUL!
HE IS CONTROLLED BY EVIL SPIRITS!
THIS MAN CANNOT BE HELD DOWN. NOT EVEN WITH CHAINS!

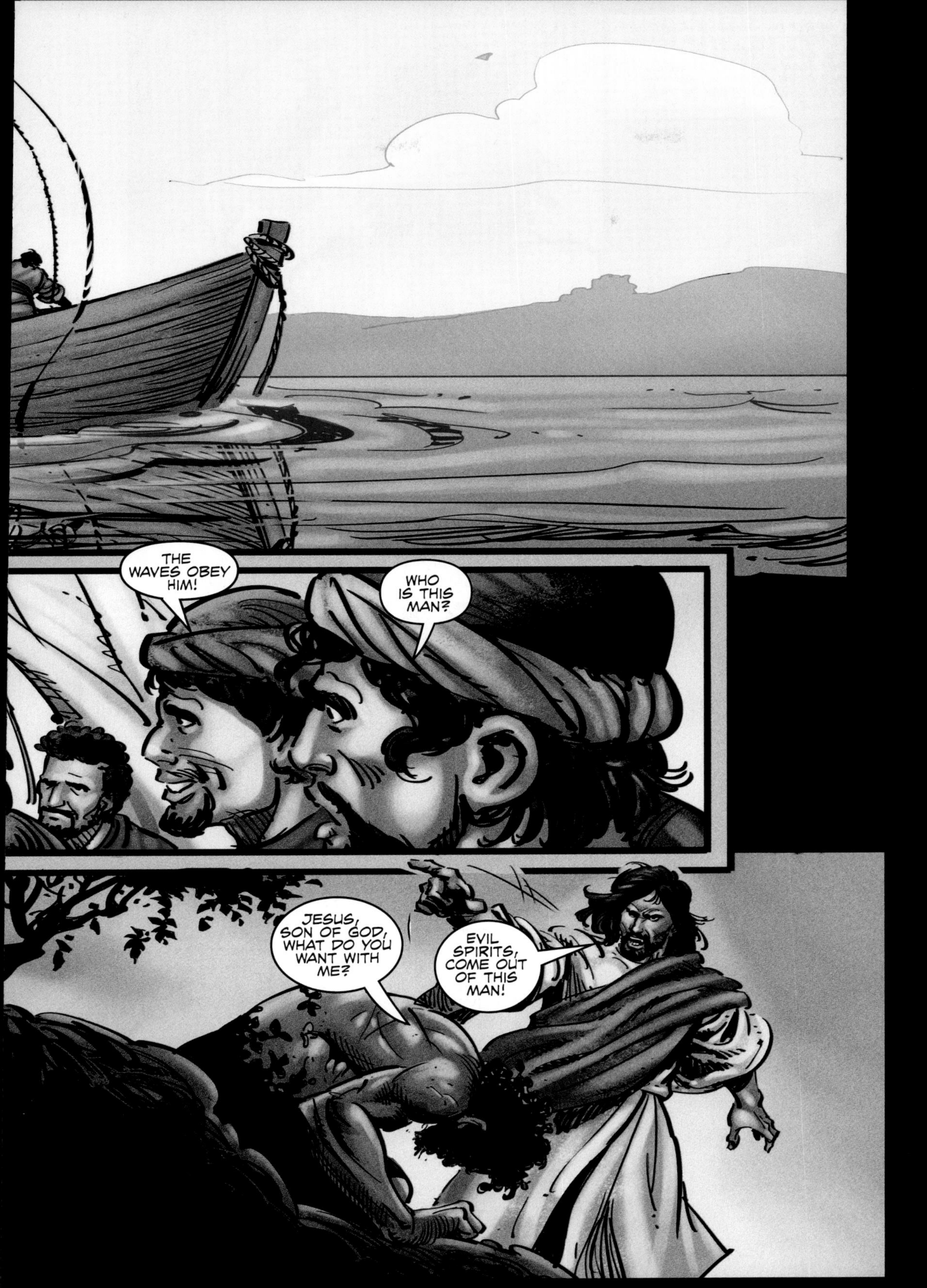
THE WAVES OBEY HIM!
WHO IS THIS MAN?
JESUS, SON OF GOD, WHAT DO YOU WANT WITH ME?
EVIL SPIRITS, COME OUT OF THIS MAN!

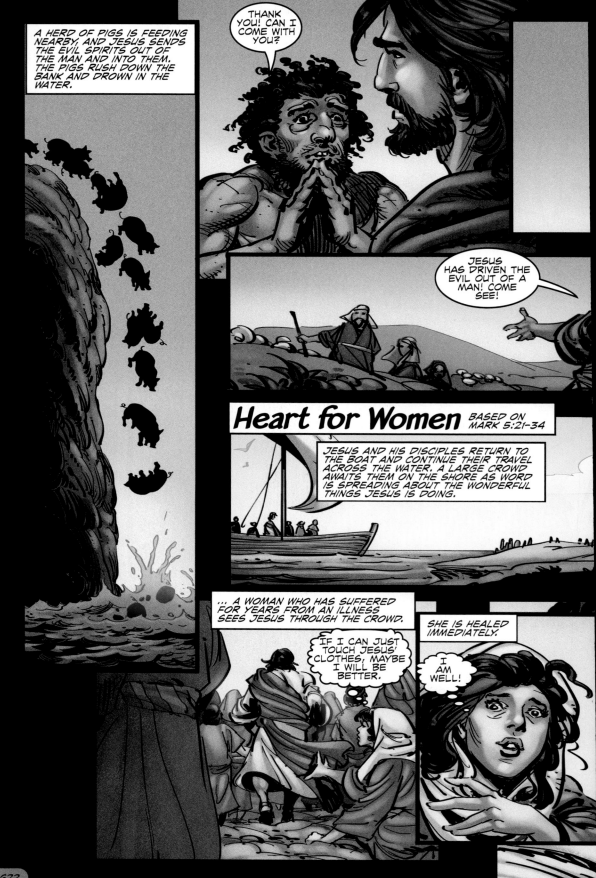

A HERD OF PIGS IS FEEDING NEARBY, AND JESUS SENDS THE EVIL SPIRITS OUT OF THE MAN AND INTO THEM. THE PIGS RUSH DOWN THE BANK AND DROWN IN THE WATER.

THANK YOU! CAN I COME WITH YOU?

JESUS HAS DRIVEN THE EVIL OUT OF A MAN! COME SEE!

Heart for Women
BASED ON MARK 5:21-34

JESUS AND HIS DISCIPLES RETURN TO THE BOAT AND CONTINUE THEIR TRAVEL ACROSS THE WATER. A LARGE CROWD AWAITS THEM ON THE SHORE AS WORD IS SPREADING ABOUT THE WONDERFUL THINGS JESUS IS DOING.

... A WOMAN WHO HAS SUFFERED FOR YEARS FROM AN ILLNESS SEES JESUS THROUGH THE CROWD.

IF I CAN JUST TOUCH JESUS' CLOTHES, MAYBE I WILL BE BETTER.

SHE IS HEALED IMMEDIATELY.

I AM WELL!

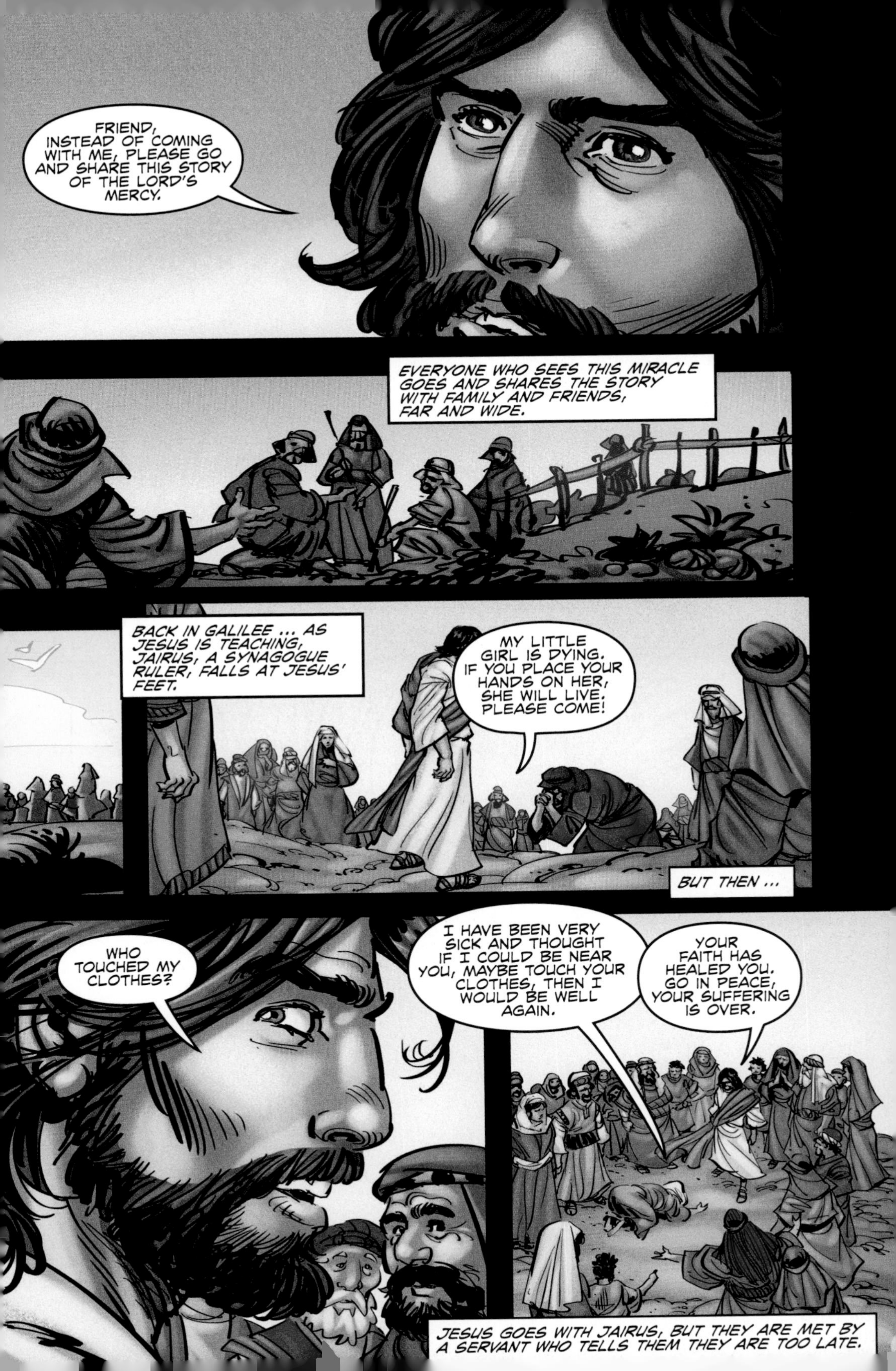
FRIEND, INSTEAD OF COMING WITH ME, PLEASE GO AND SHARE THIS STORY OF THE LORD'S MERCY.
EVERYONE WHO SEES THIS MIRACLE GOES AND SHARES THE STORY WITH FAMILY AND FRIENDS, FAR AND WIDE.
BACK IN GALILEE ... AS JESUS IS TEACHING, JAIRUS, A SYNAGOGUE RULER, FALLS AT JESUS' FEET.
MY LITTLE GIRL IS DYING. IF YOU PLACE YOUR HANDS ON HER, SHE WILL LIVE. PLEASE COME!
BUT THEN ...
WHO TOUCHED MY CLOTHES?
I HAVE BEEN VERY SICK AND THOUGHT IF I COULD BE NEAR YOU, MAYBE TOUCH YOUR CLOTHES, THEN I WOULD BE WELL AGAIN.
YOUR FAITH HAS HEALED YOU. GO IN PEACE, YOUR SUFFERING IS OVER.
JESUS GOES WITH JAIRUS, BUT THEY ARE MET BY A SERVANT WHO TELLS THEM THEY ARE TOO LATE.

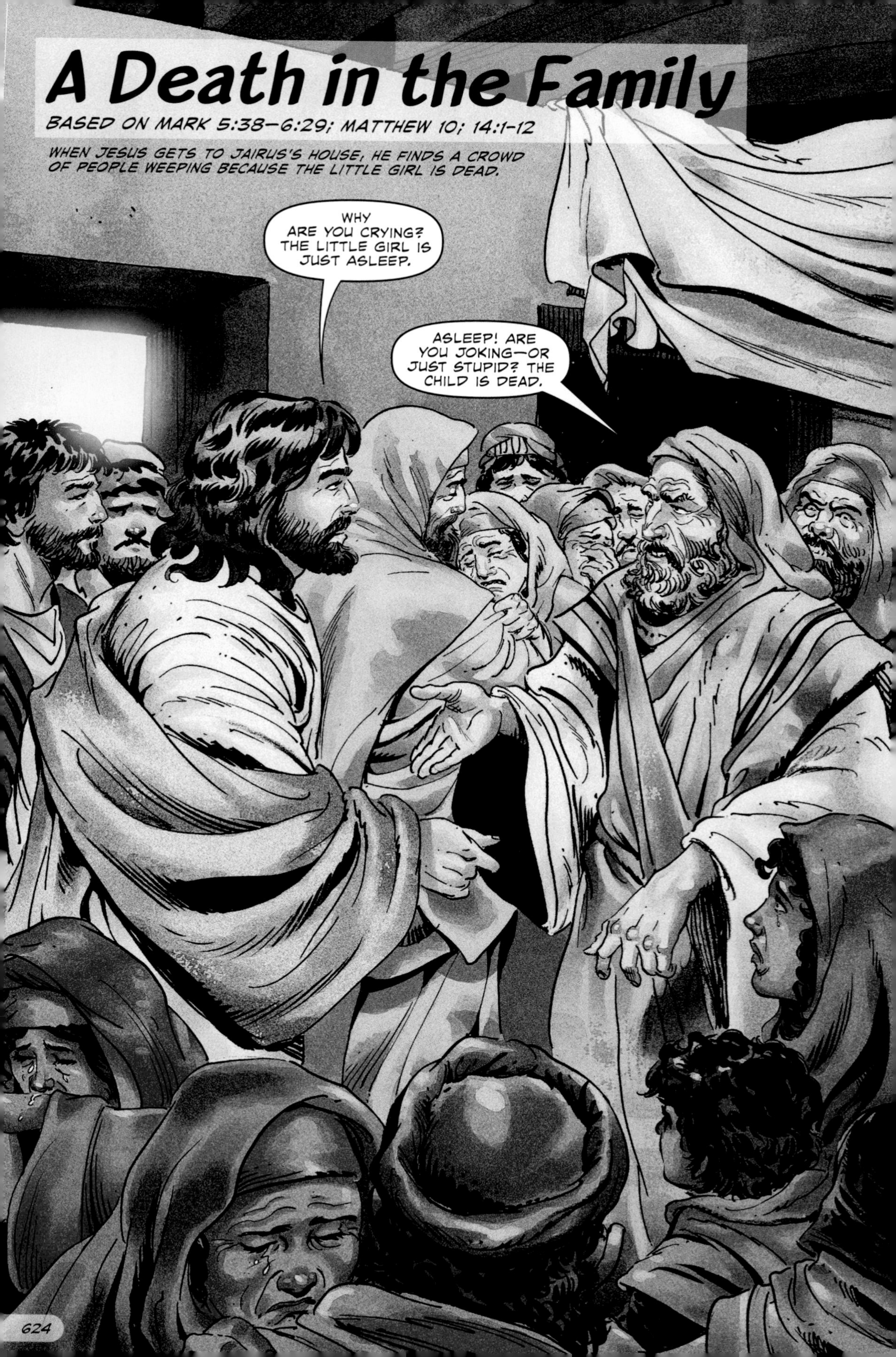
A Death in the Family
BASED ON MARK 5:38–6:29; MATTHEW 10; 14:1–12
WHEN JESUS GETS TO JAIRUS'S HOUSE, HE FINDS A CROWD OF PEOPLE WEEPING BECAUSE THE LITTLE GIRL IS DEAD.
WHY ARE YOU CRYING? THE LITTLE GIRL IS JUST ASLEEP.
ASLEEP! ARE YOU JOKING—OR JUST STUPID? THE CHILD IS DEAD.

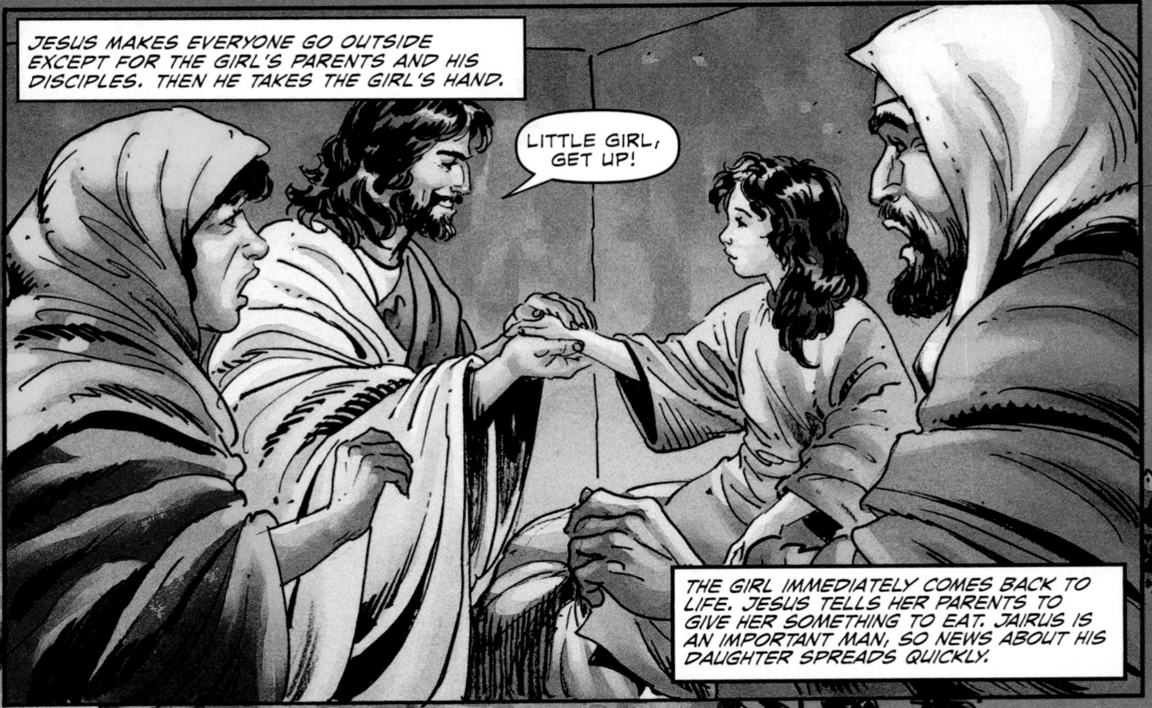
JESUS MAKES EVERYONE GO OUTSIDE EXCEPT FOR THE GIRL'S PARENTS AND HIS DISCIPLES. THEN HE TAKES THE GIRL'S HAND.
LITTLE GIRL, GET UP!
THE GIRL IMMEDIATELY COMES BACK TO LIFE. JESUS TELLS HER PARENTS TO GIVE HER SOMETHING TO EAT. JAIRUS IS AN IMPORTANT MAN, SO NEWS ABOUT HIS DAUGHTER SPREADS QUICKLY.

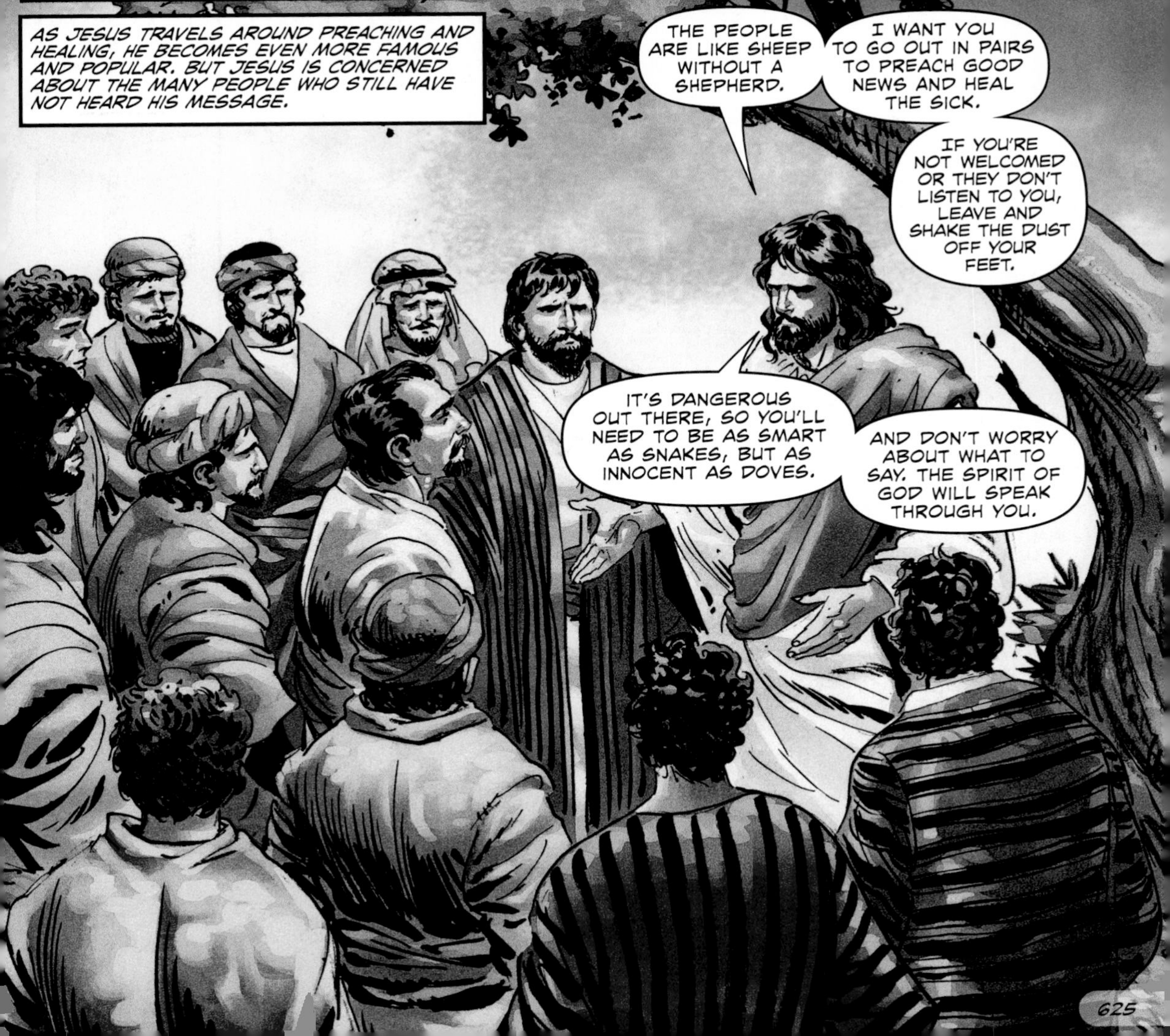
AS JESUS TRAVELS AROUND PREACHING AND HEALING, HE BECOMES EVEN MORE FAMOUS AND POPULAR. BUT JESUS IS CONCERNED ABOUT THE MANY PEOPLE WHO STILL HAVE NOT HEARD HIS MESSAGE.
THE PEOPLE ARE LIKE SHEEP WITHOUT A SHEPHERD.
I WANT YOU TO GO OUT IN PAIRS TO PREACH GOOD NEWS AND HEAL THE SICK.
IF YOU'RE NOT WELCOMED OR THEY DON'T LISTEN TO YOU, LEAVE AND SHAKE THE DUST OFF YOUR FEET.
IT'S DANGEROUS OUT THERE, SO YOU'LL NEED TO BE AS SMART AS SNAKES, BUT AS INNOCENT AS DOVES.
AND DON'T WORRY ABOUT WHAT TO SAY. THE SPIRIT OF GOD WILL SPEAK THROUGH YOU.

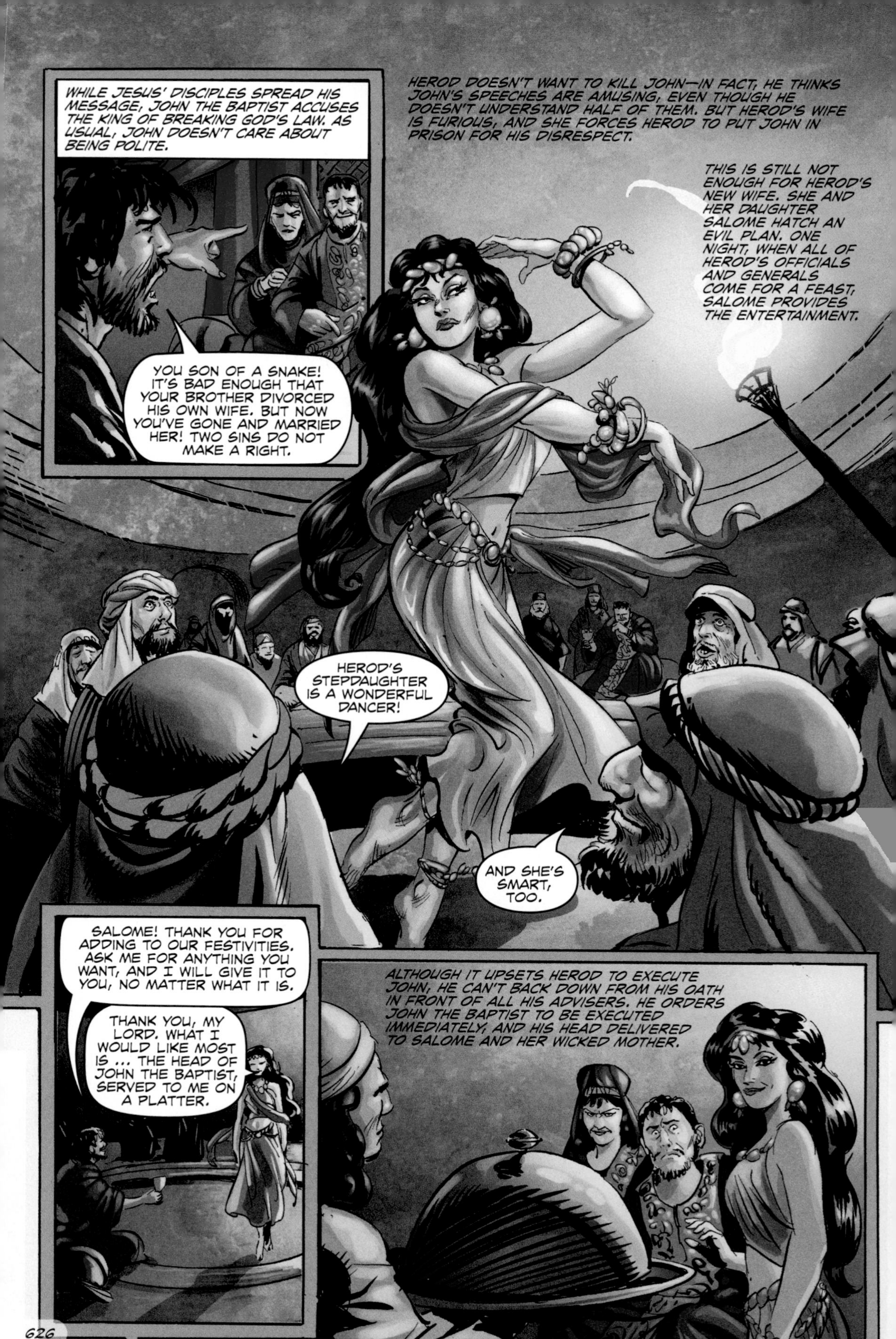
WHILE JESUS' DISCIPLES SPREAD HIS MESSAGE, JOHN THE BAPTIST ACCUSES THE KING OF BREAKING GOD'S LAW. AS USUAL, JOHN DOESN'T CARE ABOUT BEING POLITE.
YOU SON OF A SNAKE! IT'S BAD ENOUGH THAT YOUR BROTHER DIVORCED HIS OWN WIFE. BUT NOW YOU'VE GONE AND MARRIED HER! TWO SINS DO NOT MAKE A RIGHT.
HEROD DOESN'T WANT TO KILL JOHN—IN FACT, HE THINKS JOHN'S SPEECHES ARE AMUSING, EVEN THOUGH HE DOESN'T UNDERSTAND HALF OF THEM. BUT HEROD'S WIFE IS FURIOUS, AND SHE FORCES HEROD TO PUT JOHN IN PRISON FOR HIS DISRESPECT.
THIS IS STILL NOT ENOUGH FOR HEROD'S NEW WIFE. SHE AND HER DAUGHTER SALOME HATCH AN EVIL PLAN. ONE NIGHT, WHEN ALL OF HEROD'S OFFICIALS AND GENERALS COME FOR A FEAST, SALOME PROVIDES THE ENTERTAINMENT.
HEROD'S STEPDAUGHTER IS A WONDERFUL DANCER!
AND SHE'S SMART, TOO.
SALOME! THANK YOU FOR ADDING TO OUR FESTIVITIES. ASK ME FOR ANYTHING YOU WANT, AND I WILL GIVE IT TO YOU, NO MATTER WHAT IT IS.
THANK YOU, MY LORD. WHAT I WOULD LIKE MOST IS ... THE HEAD OF JOHN THE BAPTIST, SERVED TO ME ON A PLATTER.
ALTHOUGH IT UPSETS HEROD TO EXECUTE JOHN, HE CAN'T BACK DOWN FROM HIS OATH IN FRONT OF ALL HIS ADVISERS. HE ORDERS JOHN THE BAPTIST TO BE EXECUTED IMMEDIATELY, AND HIS HEAD DELIVERED TO SALOME AND HER WICKED MOTHER.

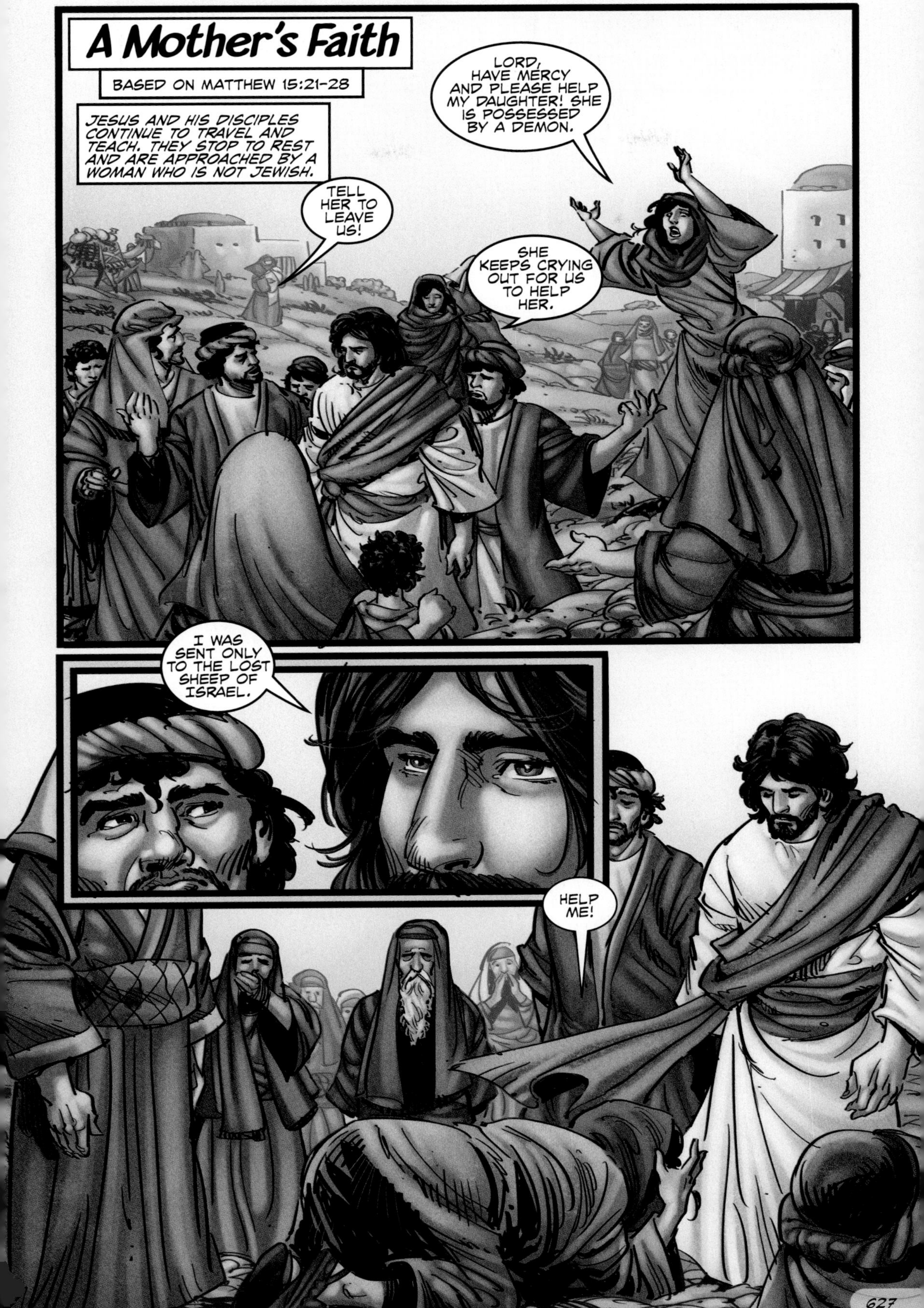
A Mother's Faith
BASED ON MATTHEW 15:21-28
JESUS AND HIS DISCIPLES CONTINUE TO TRAVEL AND TEACH. THEY STOP TO REST AND ARE APPROACHED BY A WOMAN WHO IS NOT JEWISH.
LORD, HAVE MERCY AND PLEASE HELP MY DAUGHTER! SHE IS POSSESSED BY A DEMON.
TELL HER TO LEAVE US!
SHE KEEPS CRYING OUT FOR US TO HELP HER.
I WAS SENT ONLY TO THE LOST SHEEP OF ISRAEL.
HELP ME!

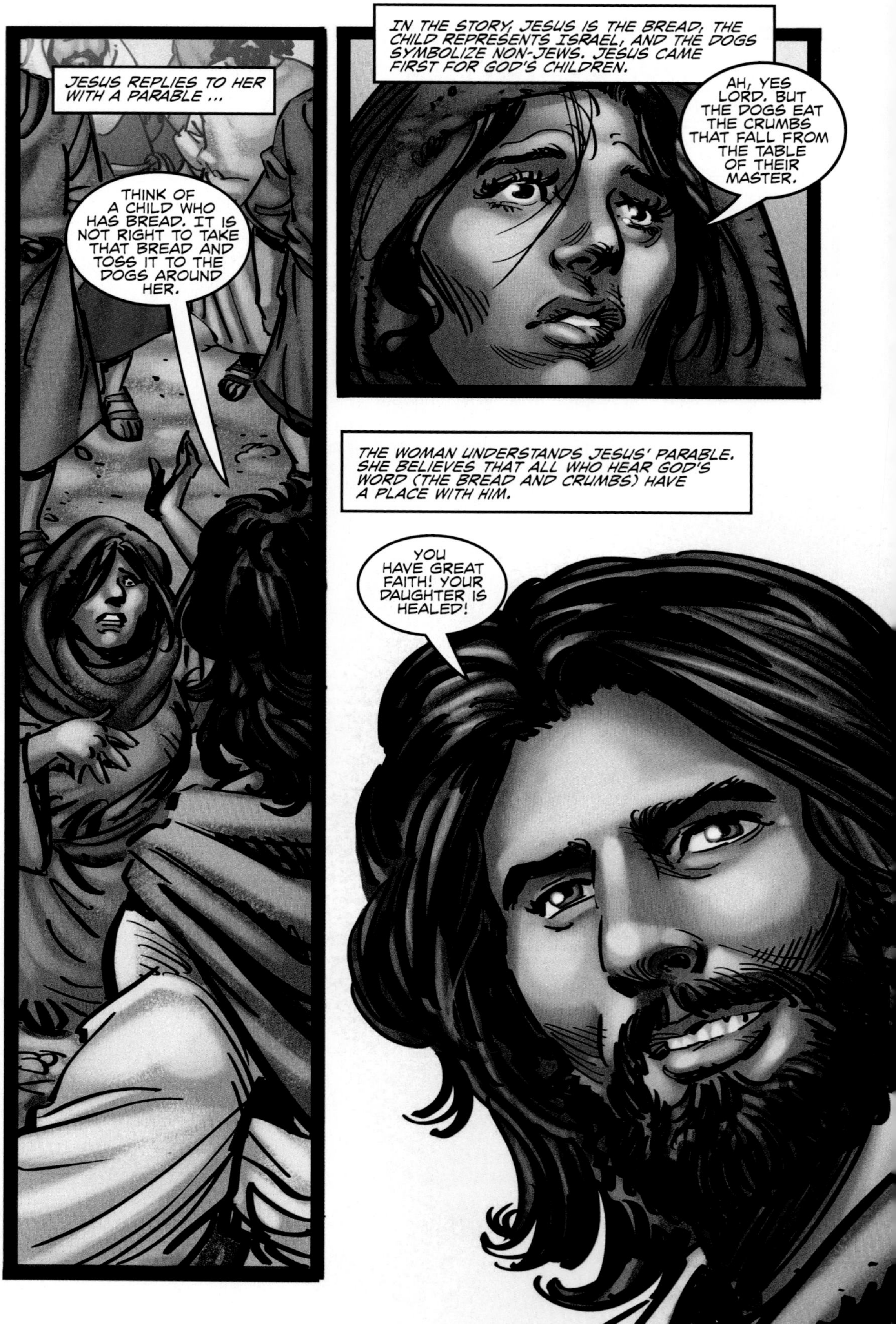
JESUS REPLIES TO HER WITH A PARABLE ...
THINK OF A CHILD WHO HAS BREAD. IT IS NOT RIGHT TO TAKE THAT BREAD AND TOSS IT TO THE DOGS AROUND HER.
IN THE STORY, JESUS IS THE BREAD, THE CHILD REPRESENTS ISRAEL, AND THE DOGS SYMBOLIZE NON-JEWS. JESUS CAME FIRST FOR GOD'S CHILDREN.
AH, YES LORD. BUT THE DOGS EAT THE CRUMBS THAT FALL FROM THE TABLE OF THEIR MASTER.
THE WOMAN UNDERSTANDS JESUS' PARABLE. SHE BELIEVES THAT ALL WHO HEAR GOD'S WORD (THE BREAD AND CRUMBS) HAVE A PLACE WITH HIM.
YOU HAVE GREAT FAITH! YOUR DAUGHTER IS HEALED!

A Hungry Crowd

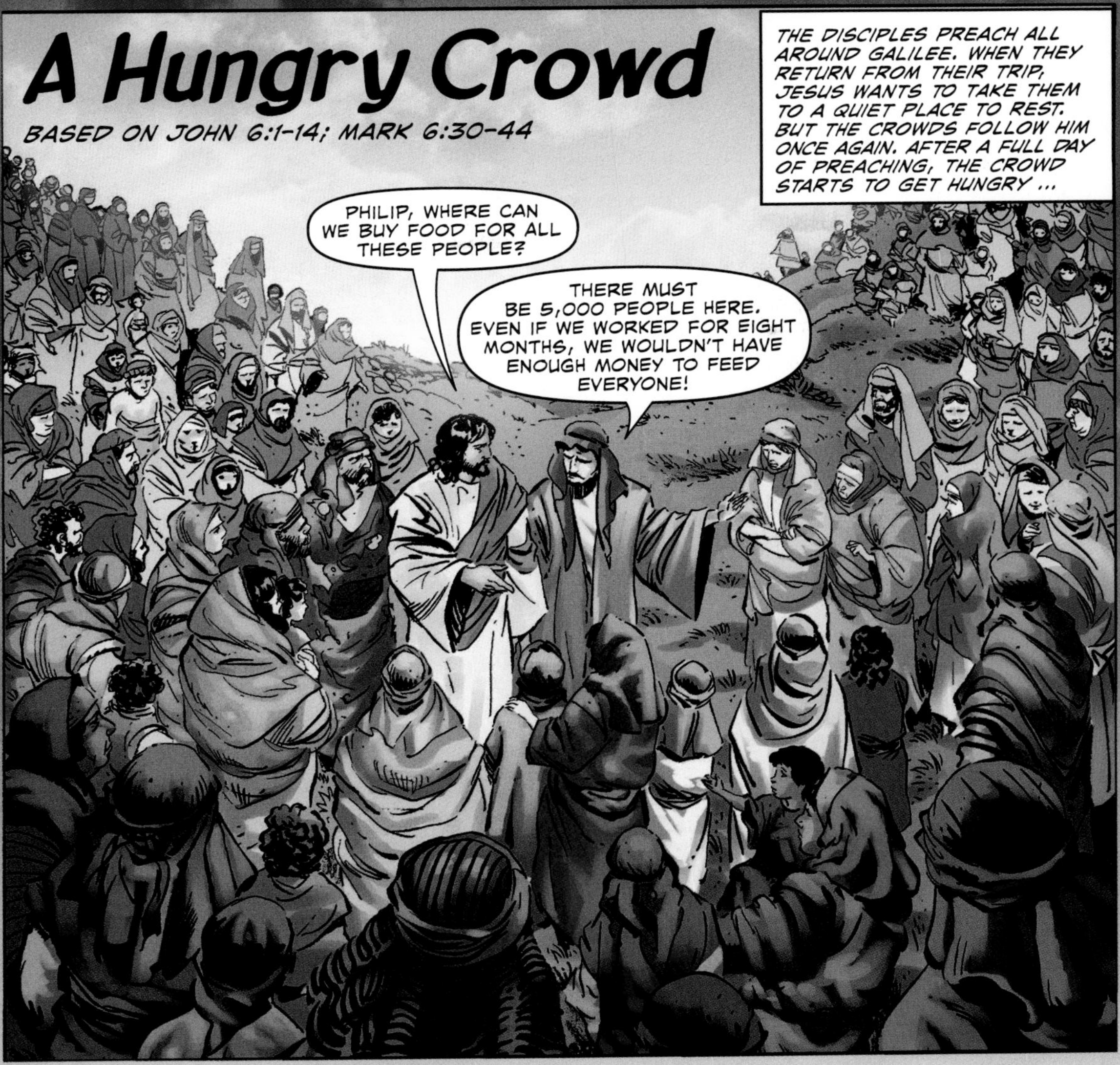
BASED ON JOHN 6:1-14; MARK 6:30-44
THE DISCIPLES PREACH ALL AROUND GALILEE. WHEN THEY RETURN FROM THEIR TRIP, JESUS WANTS TO TAKE THEM TO A QUIET PLACE TO REST. BUT THE CROWDS FOLLOW HIM ONCE AGAIN. AFTER A FULL DAY OF PREACHING, THE CROWD STARTS TO GET HUNGRY ...
PHILIP, WHERE CAN WE BUY FOOD FOR ALL THESE PEOPLE?
THERE MUST BE 5,000 PEOPLE HERE. EVEN IF WE WORKED FOR EIGHT MONTHS, WE WOULDN'T HAVE ENOUGH MONEY TO FEED EVERYONE!

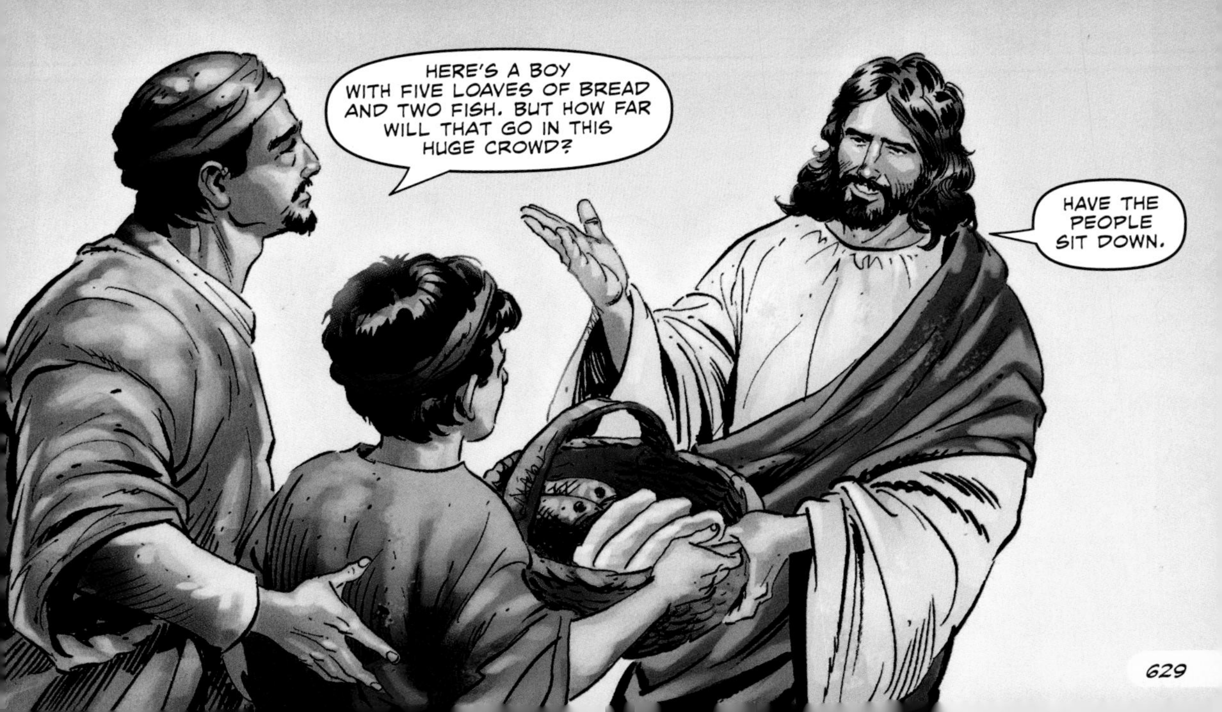
HERE'S A BOY WITH FIVE LOAVES OF BREAD AND TWO FISH. BUT HOW FAR WILL THAT GO IN THIS HUGE CROWD?
HAVE THE PEOPLE SIT DOWN.

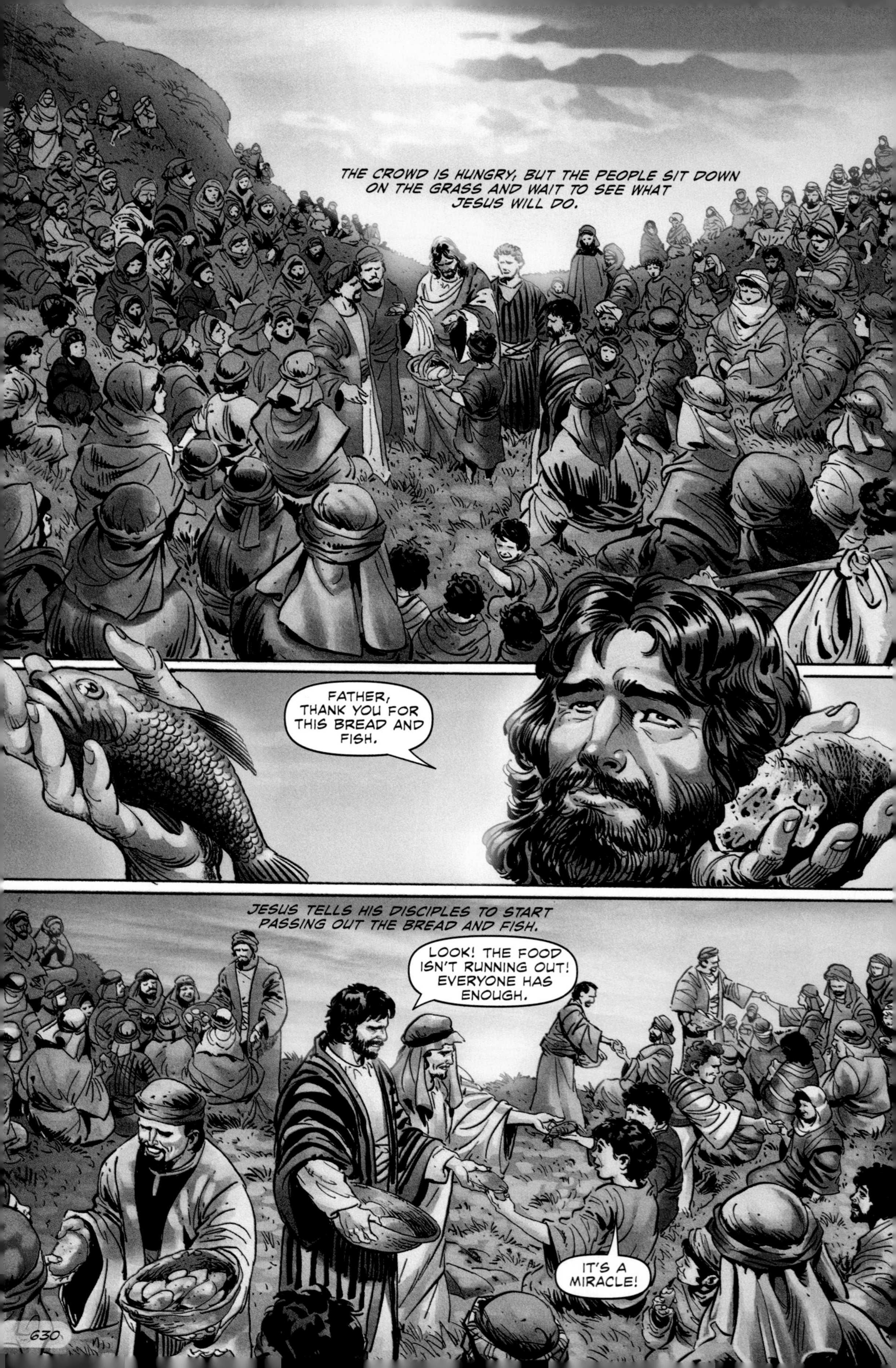
THE CROWD IS HUNGRY, BUT THE PEOPLE SIT DOWN ON THE GRASS AND WAIT TO SEE WHAT JESUS WILL DO.
FATHER, THANK YOU FOR THIS BREAD AND FISH.
JESUS TELLS HIS DISCIPLES TO START PASSING OUT THE BREAD AND FISH.
LOOK! THE FOOD ISN'T RUNNING OUT! EVERYONE HAS ENOUGH.
IT'S A MIRACLE!

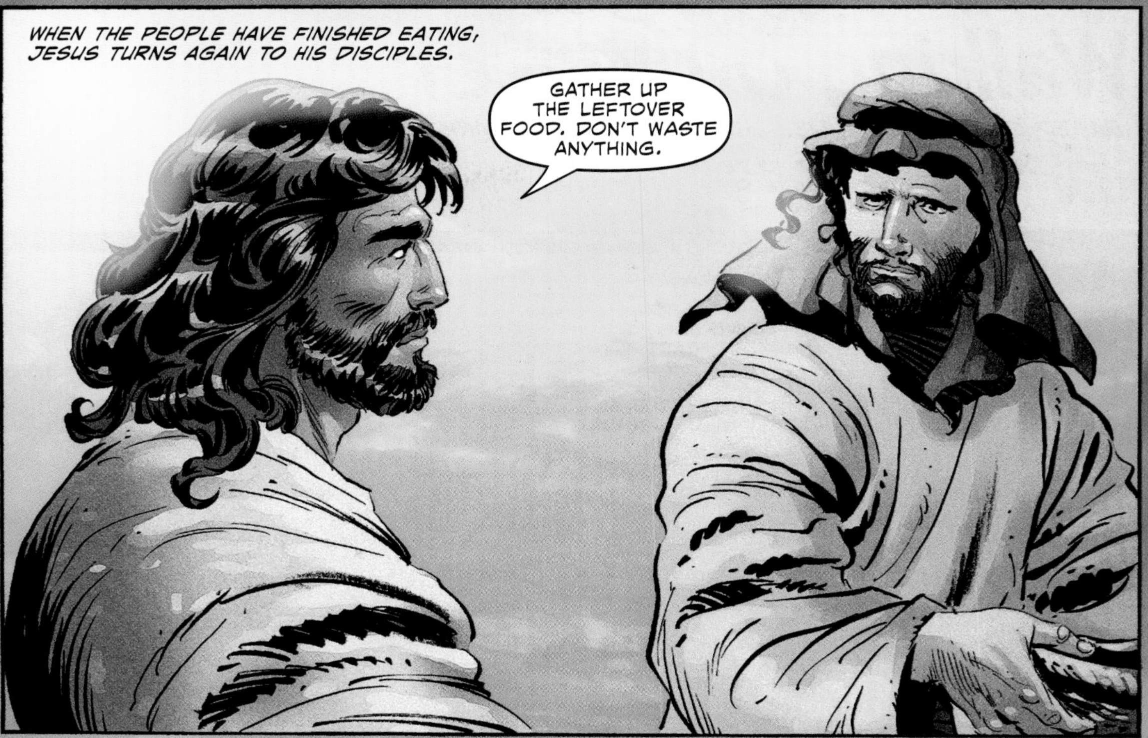
WHEN THE PEOPLE HAVE FINISHED EATING, JESUS TURNS AGAIN TO HIS DISCIPLES.
GATHER UP THE LEFTOVER FOOD. DON'T WASTE ANYTHING.

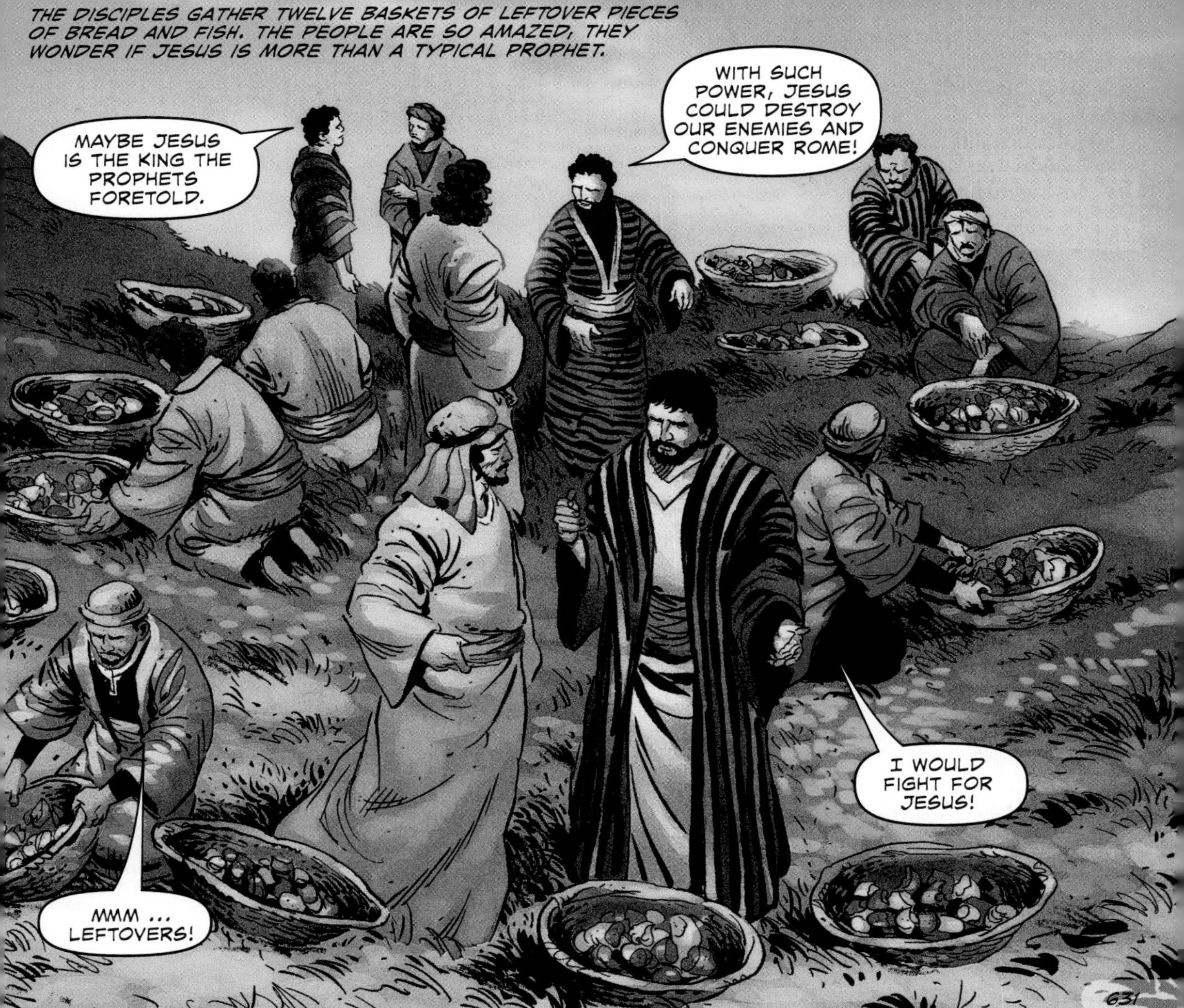
THE DISCIPLES GATHER TWELVE BASKETS OF LEFTOVER PIECES OF BREAD AND FISH. THE PEOPLE ARE SO AMAZED, THEY WONDER IF JESUS IS MORE THAN A TYPICAL PROPHET.
MAYBE JESUS IS THE KING THE PROPHETS FORETOLD.
WITH SUCH POWER, JESUS COULD DESTROY OUR ENEMIES AND CONQUER ROME!
I WOULD FIGHT FOR JESUS!
MMM ... LEFTOVERS!

Walking on Water

BASED ON MATTHEW 14:22-33; JOHN 6:15-21; MARK 6:45-52

BUT GOD SENT JESUS TO BE THE SAVIOR OF THE WORLD—NOT THE CONQUEROR OF ARMIES. WHEN JESUS SEES THAT THE CROWD WANTS TO FORCE HIM TO BE A KING, HE QUICKLY CALLS HIS DISCIPLES AWAY FROM THE PEOPLE.

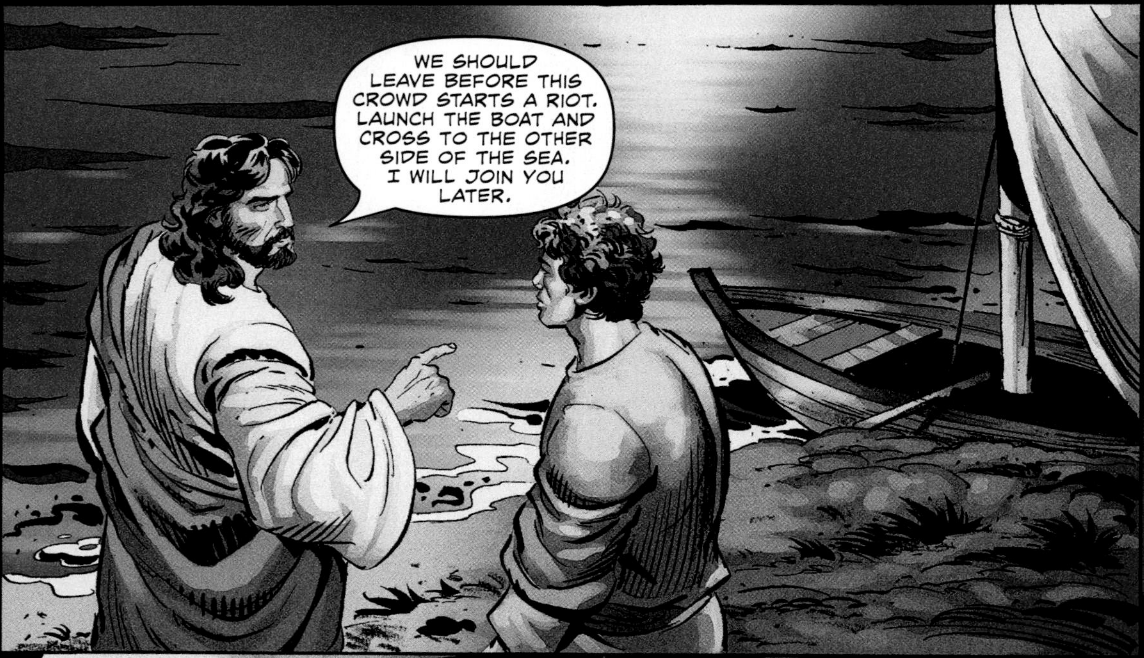
WE SHOULD LEAVE BEFORE THIS CROWD STARTS A RIOT. LAUNCH THE BOAT AND CROSS TO THE OTHER SIDE OF THE SEA. I WILL JOIN YOU LATER.

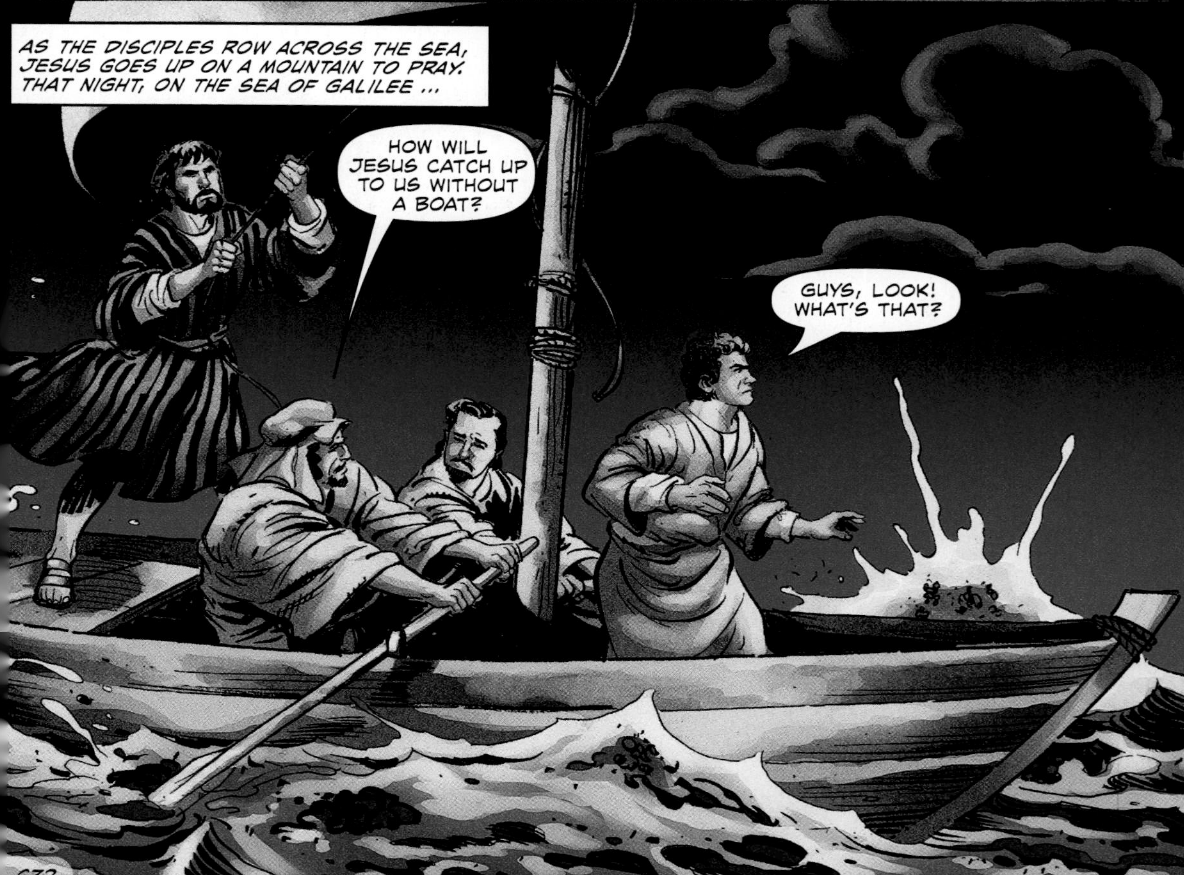
AS THE DISCIPLES ROW ACROSS THE SEA, JESUS GOES UP ON A MOUNTAIN TO PRAY. THAT NIGHT, ON THE SEA OF GALILEE ...
HOW WILL JESUS CATCH UP TO US WITHOUT A BOAT?
GUYS, LOOK! WHAT'S THAT?

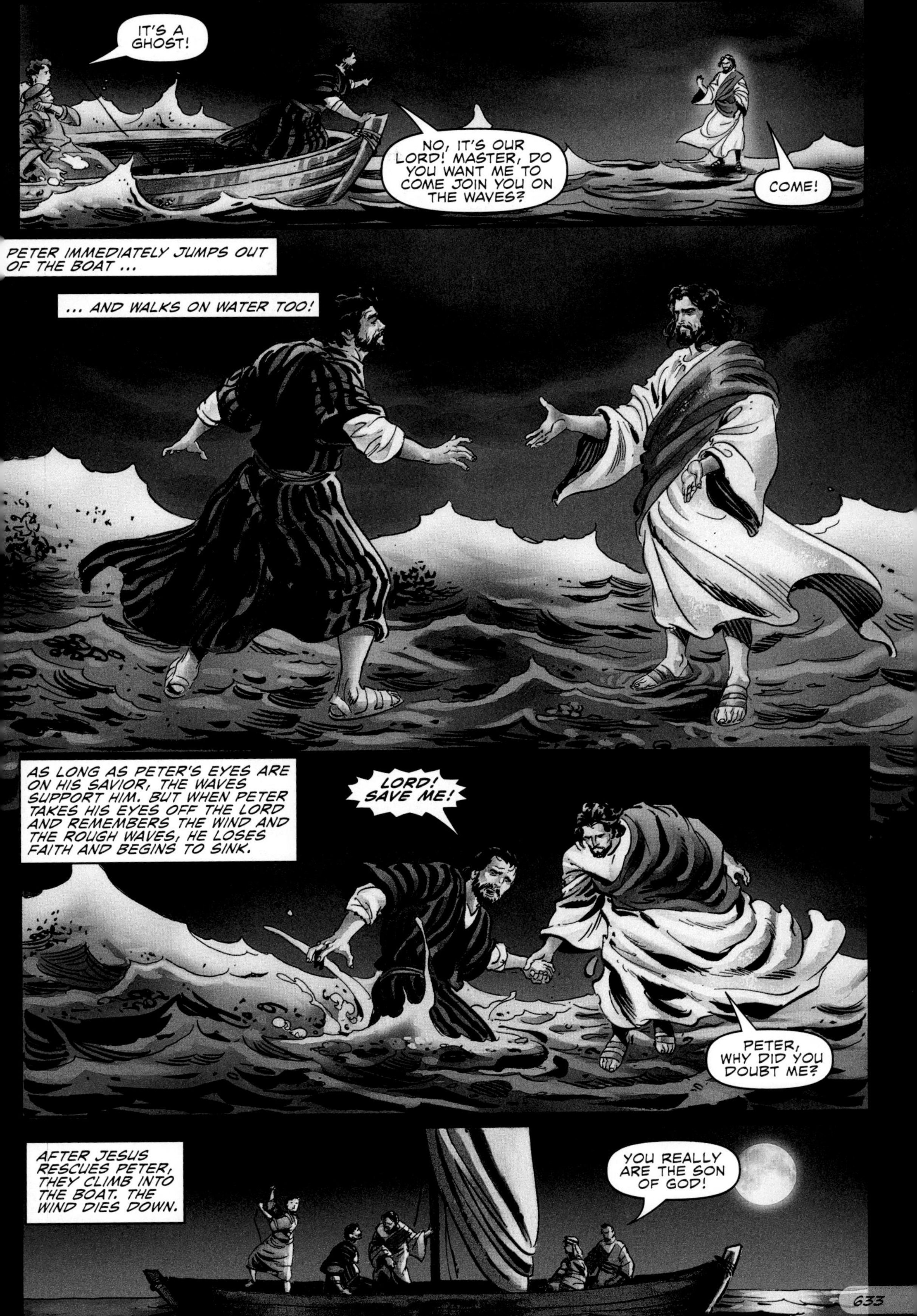

IT'S A GHOST!
NO, IT'S OUR LORD! MASTER, DO YOU WANT ME TO COME JOIN YOU ON THE WAVES?
COME!
PETER IMMEDIATELY JUMPS OUT OF THE BOAT ...
... AND WALKS ON WATER TOO!
AS LONG AS PETER'S EYES ARE ON HIS SAVIOR, THE WAVES SUPPORT HIM. BUT WHEN PETER TAKES HIS EYES OFF THE LORD AND REMEMBERS THE WIND AND THE ROUGH WAVES, HE LOSES FAITH AND BEGINS TO SINK.
LORD! SAVE ME!
PETER, WHY DID YOU DOUBT ME?
AFTER JESUS RESCUES PETER, THEY CLIMB INTO THE BOAT. THE WIND DIES DOWN.
YOU REALLY ARE THE SON OF GOD!

Who Am I?

BASED ON MARK 6:53–7:23; MATTHEW 14:34–15:20; 16:13–28

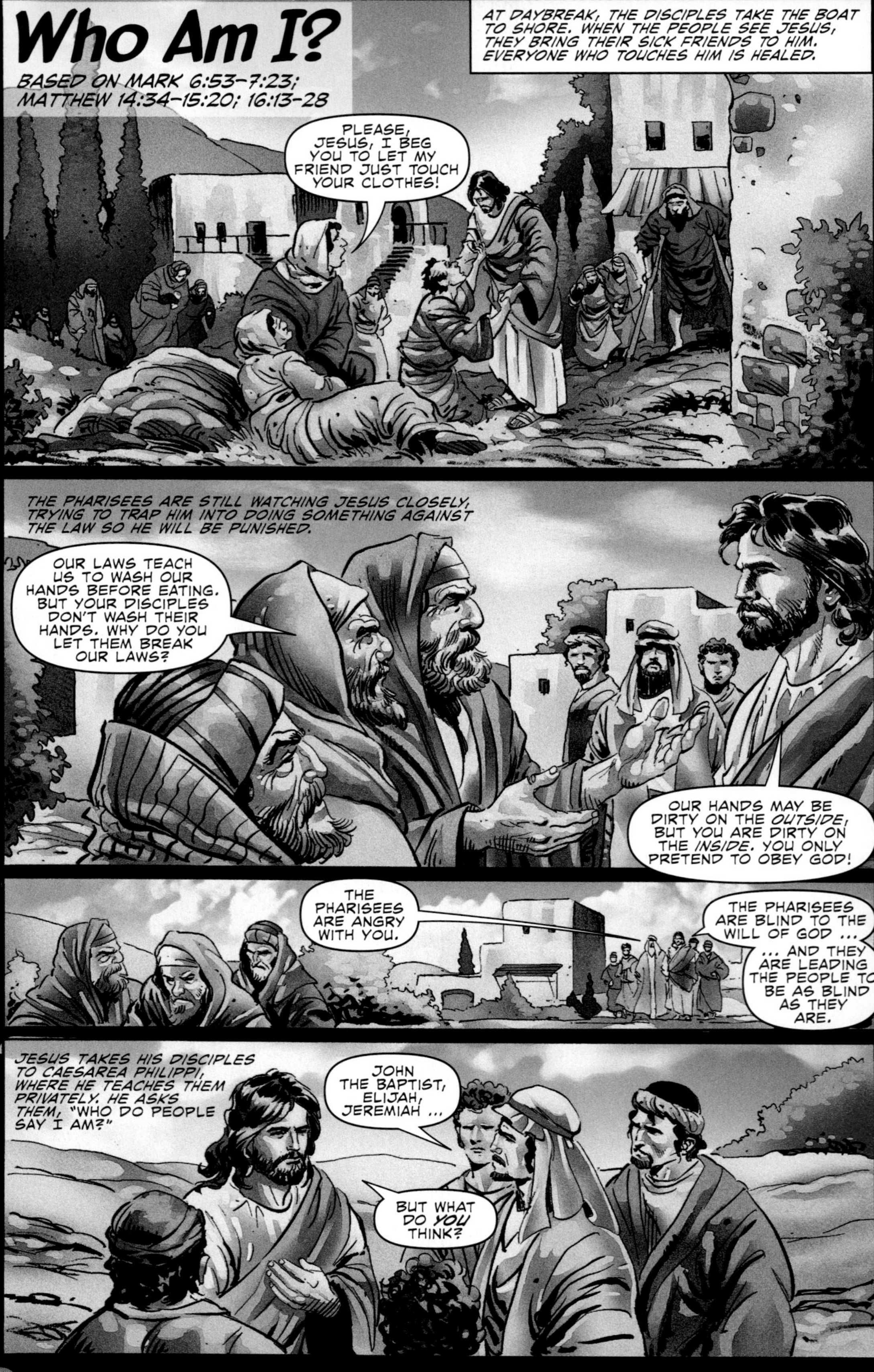
AT DAYBREAK, THE DISCIPLES TAKE THE BOAT TO SHORE. WHEN THE PEOPLE SEE JESUS, THEY BRING THEIR SICK FRIENDS TO HIM. EVERYONE WHO TOUCHES HIM IS HEALED.
PLEASE, JESUS, I BEG YOU TO LET MY FRIEND JUST TOUCH YOUR CLOTHES!
THE PHARISEES ARE STILL WATCHING JESUS CLOSELY, TRYING TO TRAP HIM INTO DOING SOMETHING AGAINST THE LAW SO HE WILL BE PUNISHED.
OUR LAWS TEACH US TO WASH OUR HANDS BEFORE EATING. BUT YOUR DISCIPLES DON'T WASH THEIR HANDS. WHY DO YOU LET THEM BREAK OUR LAWS?
OUR HANDS MAY BE DIRTY ON THE *OUTSIDE*, BUT YOU ARE DIRTY ON THE *INSIDE*. YOU ONLY PRETEND TO OBEY GOD!
THE PHARISEES ARE ANGRY WITH YOU.
THE PHARISEES ARE BLIND TO THE WILL OF GOD ...
... AND THEY ARE LEADING THE PEOPLE TO BE AS BLIND AS THEY ARE.
JESUS TAKES HIS DISCIPLES TO CAESAREA PHILIPPI, WHERE HE TEACHES THEM PRIVATELY. HE ASKS THEM, "WHO DO PEOPLE SAY I AM?"
JOHN THE BAPTIST, ELIJAH, JEREMIAH ...
BUT WHAT DO ***YOU*** THINK?

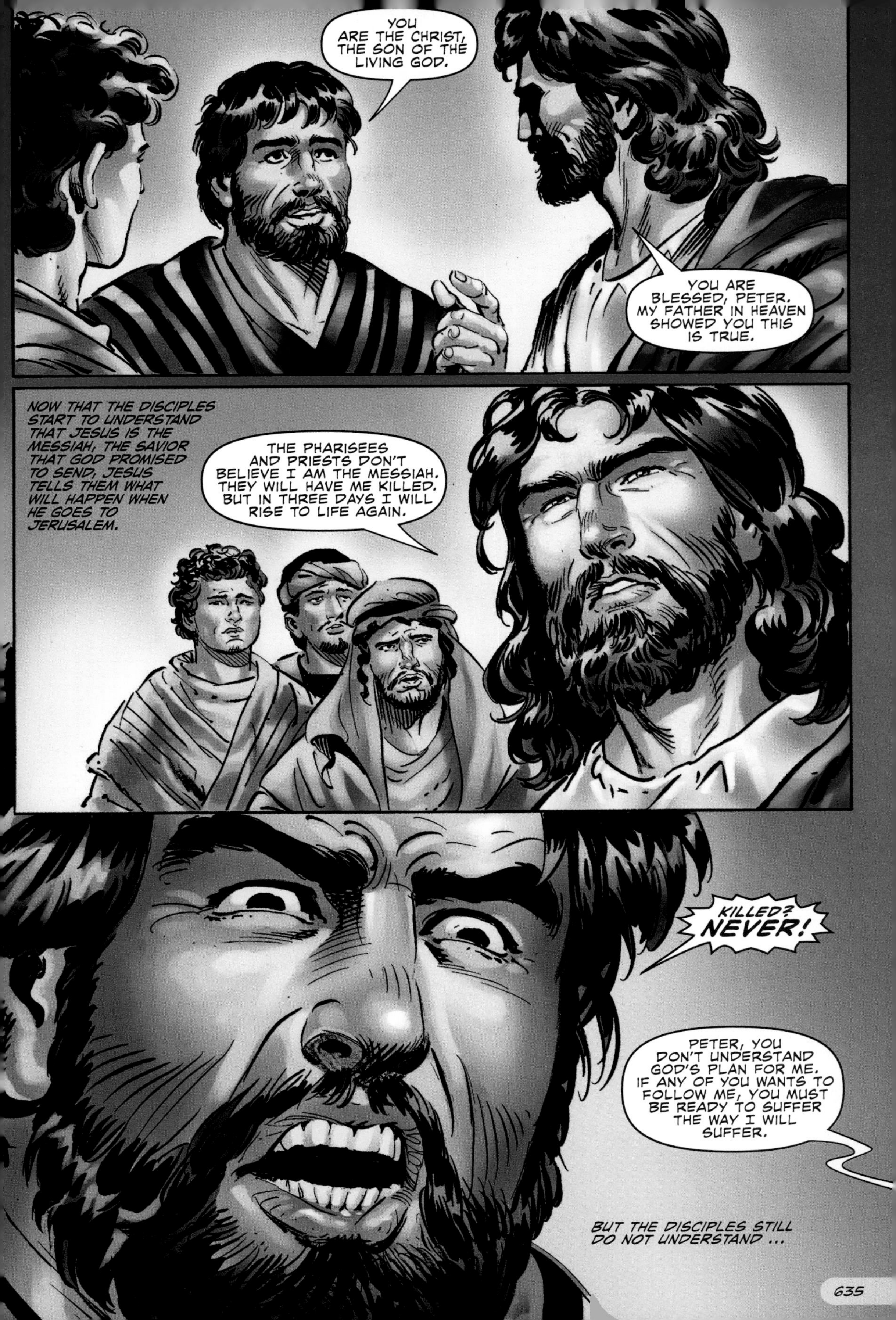
YOU ARE THE CHRIST, THE SON OF THE LIVING GOD.
YOU ARE BLESSED, PETER. MY FATHER IN HEAVEN SHOWED YOU THIS IS TRUE.
NOW THAT THE DISCIPLES START TO UNDERSTAND THAT JESUS IS THE MESSIAH, THE SAVIOR THAT GOD PROMISED TO SEND, JESUS TELLS THEM WHAT WILL HAPPEN WHEN HE GOES TO JERUSALEM.
THE PHARISEES AND PRIESTS DON'T BELIEVE I AM THE MESSIAH. THEY WILL HAVE ME KILLED. BUT IN THREE DAYS I WILL RISE TO LIFE AGAIN.
KILLED? NEVER!
PETER, YOU DON'T UNDERSTAND GOD'S PLAN FOR ME. IF ANY OF YOU WANTS TO FOLLOW ME, YOU MUST BE READY TO SUFFER THE WAY I WILL SUFFER.
BUT THE DISCIPLES STILL DO NOT UNDERSTAND ...

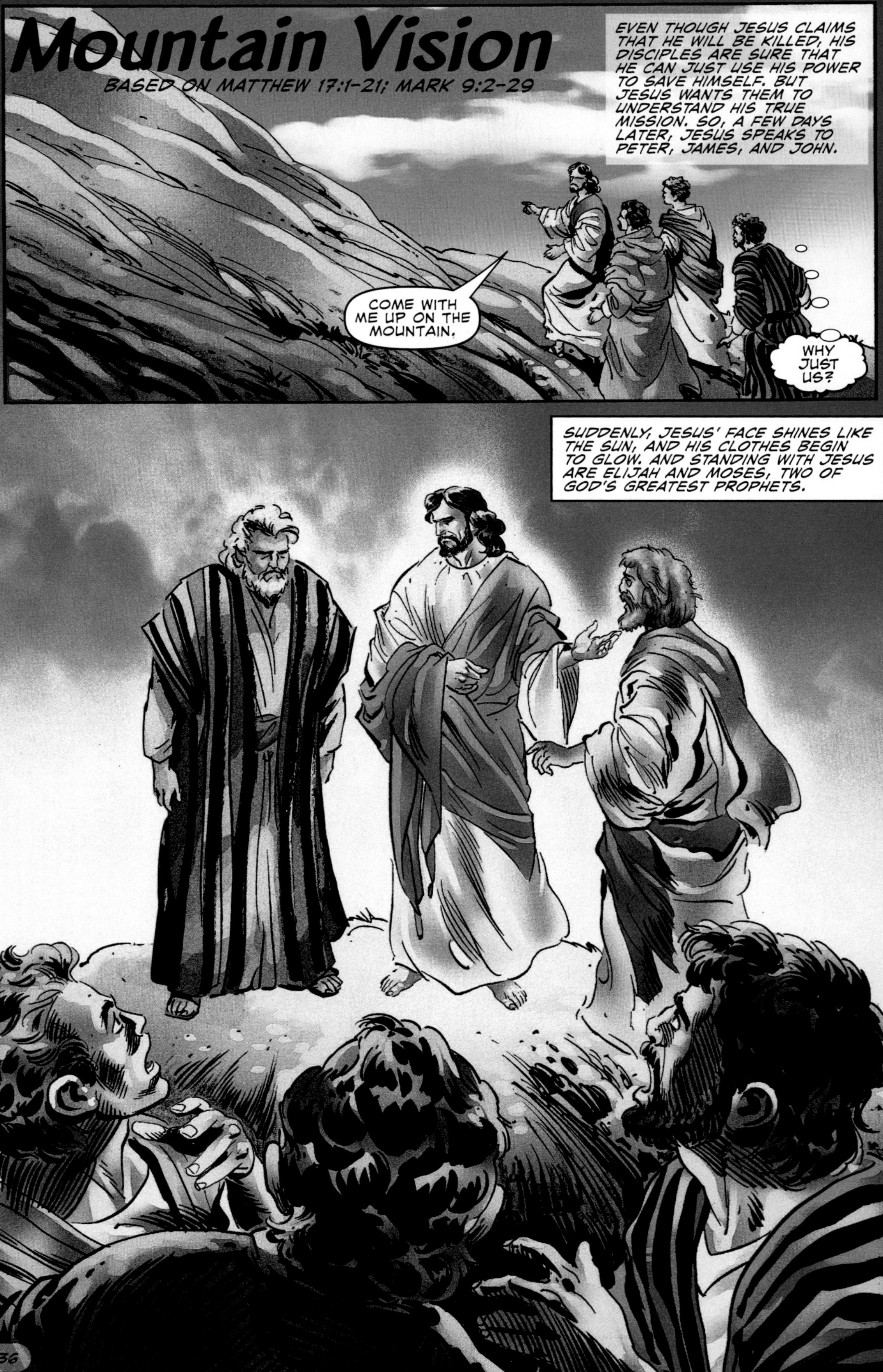
Mountain Vision
BASED ON MATTHEW 17:1–21; MARK 9:2–29
EVEN THOUGH JESUS CLAIMS THAT HE WILL BE KILLED, HIS DISCIPLES ARE SURE THAT HE CAN JUST USE HIS POWER TO SAVE HIMSELF. BUT JESUS WANTS THEM TO UNDERSTAND HIS TRUE MISSION. SO, A FEW DAYS LATER, JESUS SPEAKS TO PETER, JAMES, AND JOHN.
COME WITH ME UP ON THE MOUNTAIN.
WHY JUST US?
SUDDENLY, JESUS' FACE SHINES LIKE THE SUN, AND HIS CLOTHES BEGIN TO GLOW. AND STANDING WITH JESUS ARE ELIJAH AND MOSES, TWO OF GOD'S GREATEST PROPHETS.

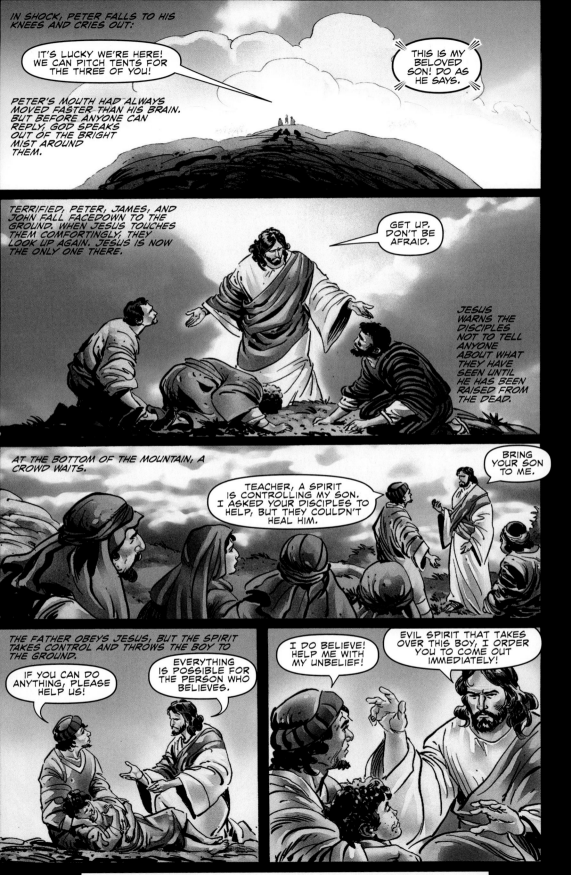

IN SHOCK, PETER FALLS TO HIS KNEES AND CRIES OUT:

IT'S LUCKY WE'RE HERE! WE CAN PITCH TENTS FOR THE THREE OF YOU!

THIS IS MY BELOVED SON! DO AS HE SAYS.

PETER'S MOUTH HAD ALWAYS MOVED FASTER THAN HIS BRAIN. BUT BEFORE ANYONE CAN REPLY, GOD SPEAKS OUT OF THE BRIGHT MIST AROUND THEM.

TERRIFIED, PETER, JAMES, AND JOHN FALL FACEDOWN TO THE GROUND. WHEN JESUS TOUCHES THEM COMFORTINGLY; THEY LOOK UP AGAIN. JESUS IS NOW THE ONLY ONE THERE.

GET UP. DON'T BE AFRAID.

JESUS WARNS THE DISCIPLES NOT TO TELL ANYONE ABOUT WHAT THEY HAVE SEEN UNTIL HE HAS BEEN RAISED FROM THE DEAD.

AT THE BOTTOM OF THE MOUNTAIN, A CROWD WAITS.

BRING YOUR SON TO ME.

TEACHER, A SPIRIT IS CONTROLLING MY SON. I ASKED YOUR DISCIPLES TO HELP, BUT THEY COULDN'T HEAL HIM.

THE FATHER OBEYS JESUS, BUT THE SPIRIT TAKES CONTROL AND THROWS THE BOY TO THE GROUND.

EVERYTHING IS POSSIBLE FOR THE PERSON WHO BELIEVES.

IF YOU CAN DO ANYTHING, PLEASE HELP US!

I DO BELIEVE! HELP ME WITH MY UNBELIEF!

EVIL SPIRIT THAT TAKES OVER THIS BOY, I ORDER YOU TO COME OUT IMMEDIATELY!

THE SPIRIT SCREAMS AND SHAKES THE BOY. THEN IT LEAVES HIM. THE BOY IS SO STILL THAT PEOPLE THINK HE IS DEAD. BUT JESUS HELPS HIM UP.

637

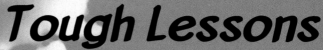

Tough Lessons

BASED ON MATTHEW 18; JOHN 7:11—8:59

WHEN THEY ARE ALONE, THE DISCIPLES HAVE SOME QUESTIONS FOR JESUS.

WHY COULDN'T WE HEAL THAT BOY?

YOU DIDN'T HAVE ENOUGH FAITH. IF YOU HAVE FAITH EVEN AS SMALL AS A MUSTARD SEED, NOTHING IS IMPOSSIBLE.

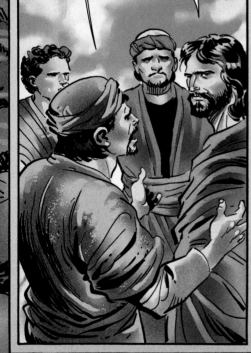

LATER, ON THEIR WAY TO CAPERNAUM, THE DISCIPLES ARGUE ABOUT WHICH OF THEM IS THE MOST IMPORTANT ...

I HOPE I GET TO BE THE ONE WHO SITS NEXT TO JESUS IN HEAVEN ...

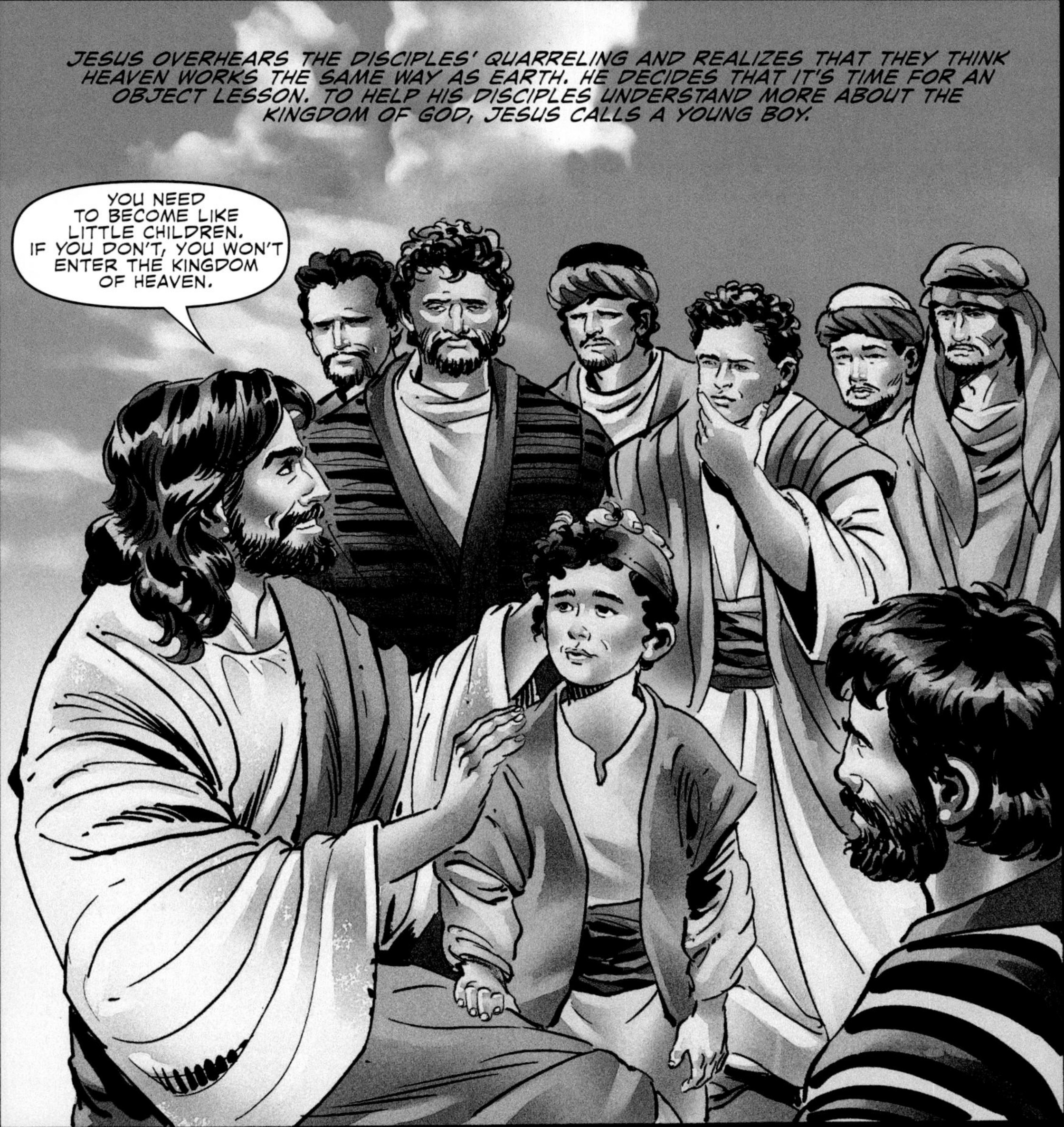
JESUS OVERHEARS THE DISCIPLES' QUARRELING AND REALIZES THAT THEY THINK HEAVEN WORKS THE SAME WAY AS EARTH. HE DECIDES THAT IT'S TIME FOR AN OBJECT LESSON. TO HELP HIS DISCIPLES UNDERSTAND MORE ABOUT THE KINGDOM OF GOD, JESUS CALLS A YOUNG BOY.
YOU NEED TO BECOME LIKE LITTLE CHILDREN. IF YOU DON'T, YOU WON'T ENTER THE KINGDOM OF HEAVEN.

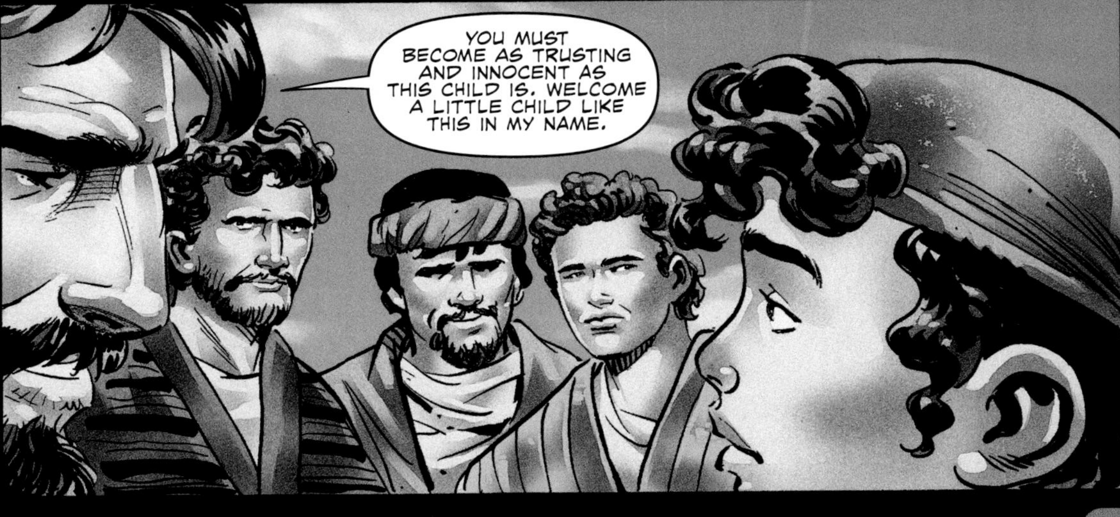
YOU MUST BECOME AS TRUSTING AND INNOCENT AS THIS CHILD IS. WELCOME A LITTLE CHILD LIKE THIS IN MY NAME.

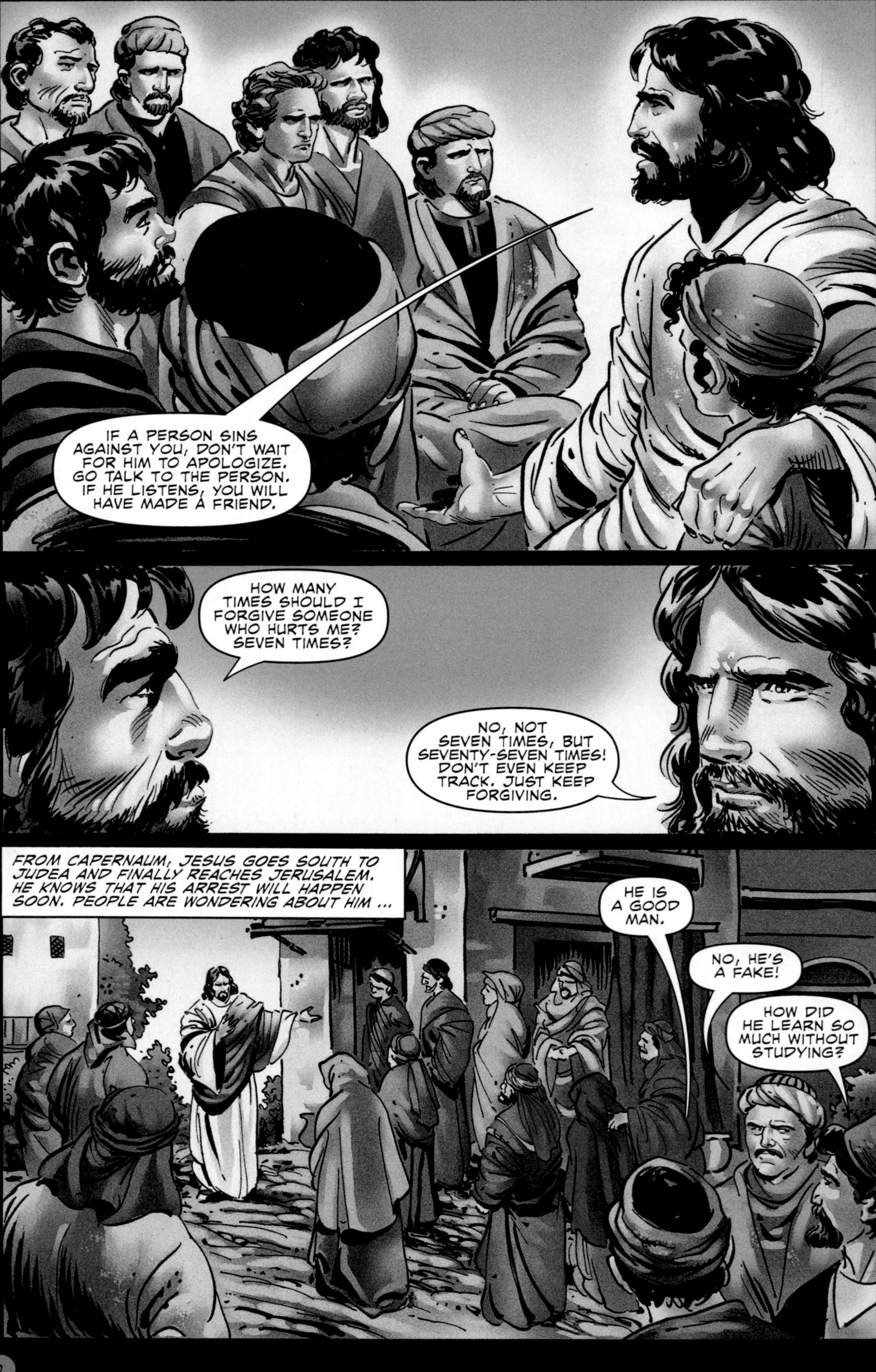
IF A PERSON SINS AGAINST YOU, DON'T WAIT FOR HIM TO APOLOGIZE. GO TALK TO THE PERSON. IF HE LISTENS, YOU WILL HAVE MADE A FRIEND.
HOW MANY TIMES SHOULD I FORGIVE SOMEONE WHO HURTS ME? SEVEN TIMES?
NO, NOT SEVEN TIMES, BUT SEVENTY-SEVEN TIMES! DON'T EVEN KEEP TRACK. JUST KEEP FORGIVING.
FROM CAPERNAUM, JESUS GOES SOUTH TO JUDEA AND FINALLY REACHES JERUSALEM. HE KNOWS THAT HIS ARREST WILL HAPPEN SOON. PEOPLE ARE WONDERING ABOUT HIM ...
HE IS A GOOD MAN.
NO, HE'S A FAKE!
HOW DID HE LEARN SO MUCH WITHOUT STUDYING?

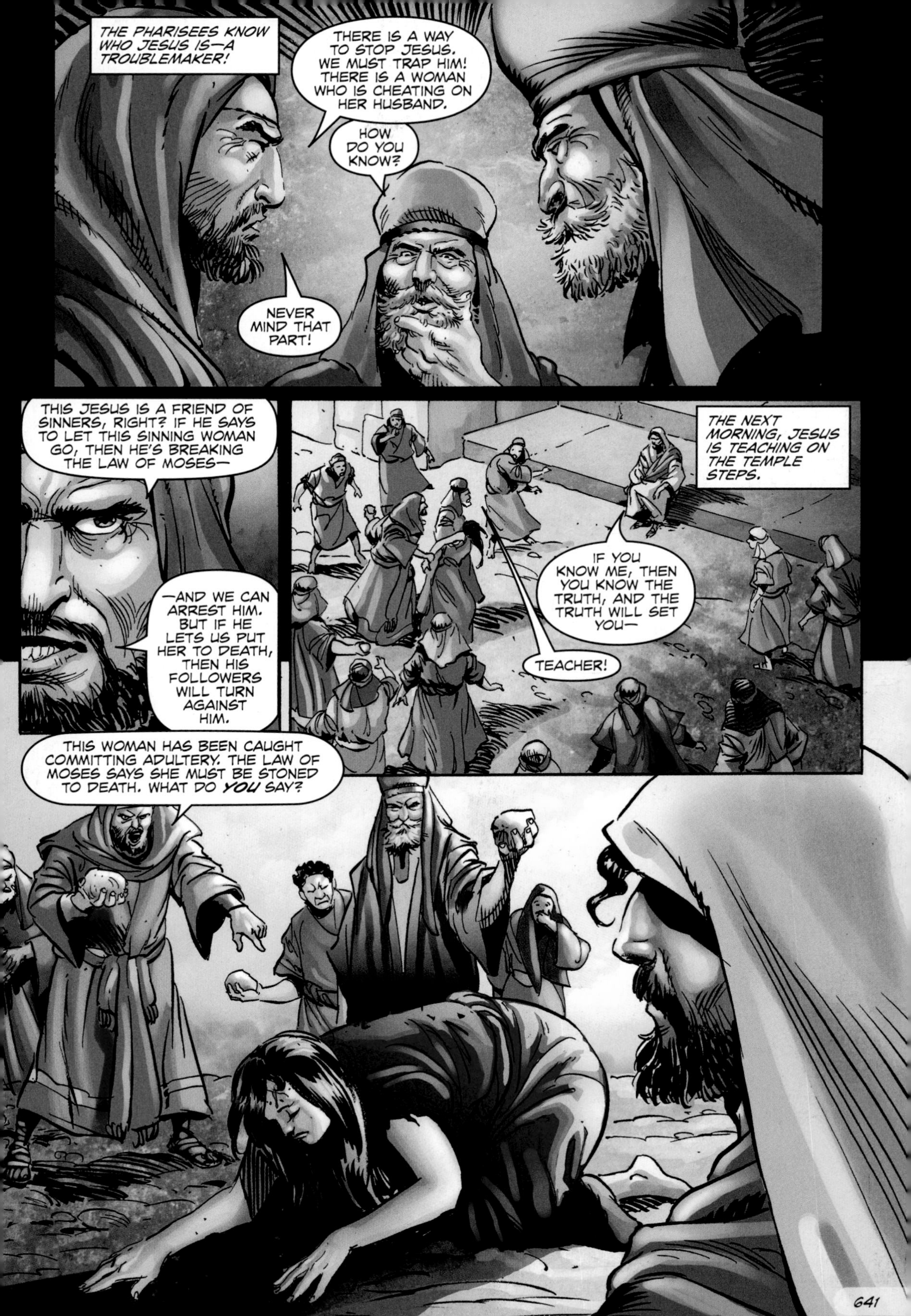

THE PHARISEES KNOW WHO JESUS IS—A TROUBLEMAKER!
THERE IS A WAY TO STOP JESUS. WE MUST TRAP HIM! THERE IS A WOMAN WHO IS CHEATING ON HER HUSBAND.
HOW DO YOU KNOW?
NEVER MIND THAT PART!
THIS JESUS IS A FRIEND OF SINNERS, RIGHT? IF HE SAYS TO LET THIS SINNING WOMAN GO, THEN HE'S BREAKING THE LAW OF MOSES—
—AND WE CAN ARREST HIM. BUT IF HE LETS US PUT HER TO DEATH, THEN HIS FOLLOWERS WILL TURN AGAINST HIM.
THE NEXT MORNING, JESUS IS TEACHING ON THE TEMPLE STEPS.
IF YOU KNOW ME, THEN YOU KNOW THE TRUTH, AND THE TRUTH WILL SET YOU—
TEACHER!
THIS WOMAN HAS BEEN CAUGHT COMMITTING ADULTERY. THE LAW OF MOSES SAYS SHE MUST BE STONED TO DEATH. WHAT DO *YOU* SAY?

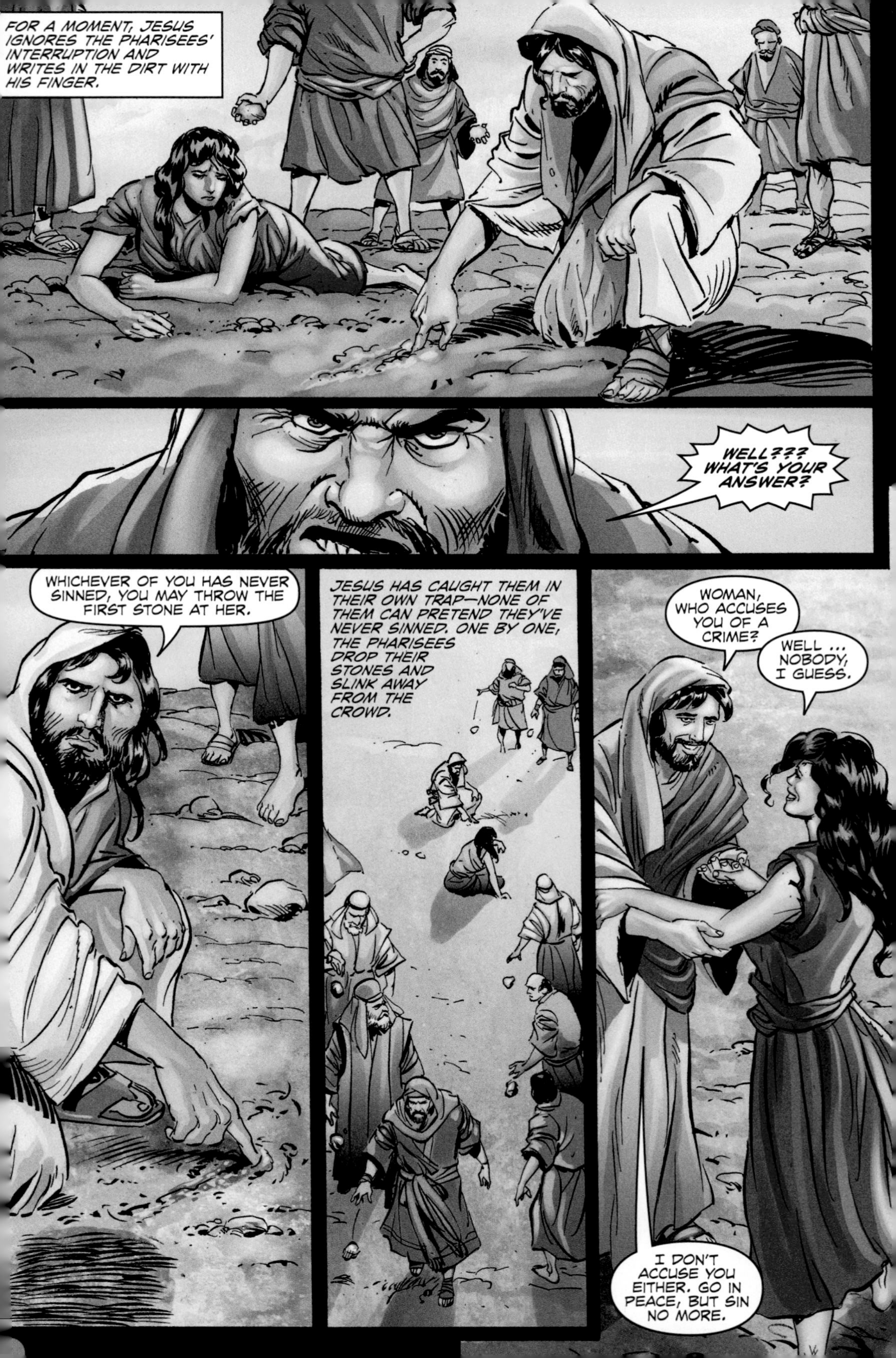
FOR A MOMENT, JESUS IGNORES THE PHARISEES' INTERRUPTION AND WRITES IN THE DIRT WITH HIS FINGER.
WELL??? WHAT'S YOUR ANSWER?
WHICHEVER OF YOU HAS NEVER SINNED, YOU MAY THROW THE FIRST STONE AT HER.
JESUS HAS CAUGHT THEM IN THEIR OWN TRAP—NONE OF THEM CAN PRETEND THEY'VE NEVER SINNED. ONE BY ONE, THE PHARISEES DROP THEIR STONES AND SLINK AWAY FROM THE CROWD.
WOMAN, WHO ACCUSES YOU OF A CRIME?
WELL ... NOBODY, I GUESS.
I DON'T ACCUSE YOU EITHER. GO IN PEACE, BUT SIN NO MORE.

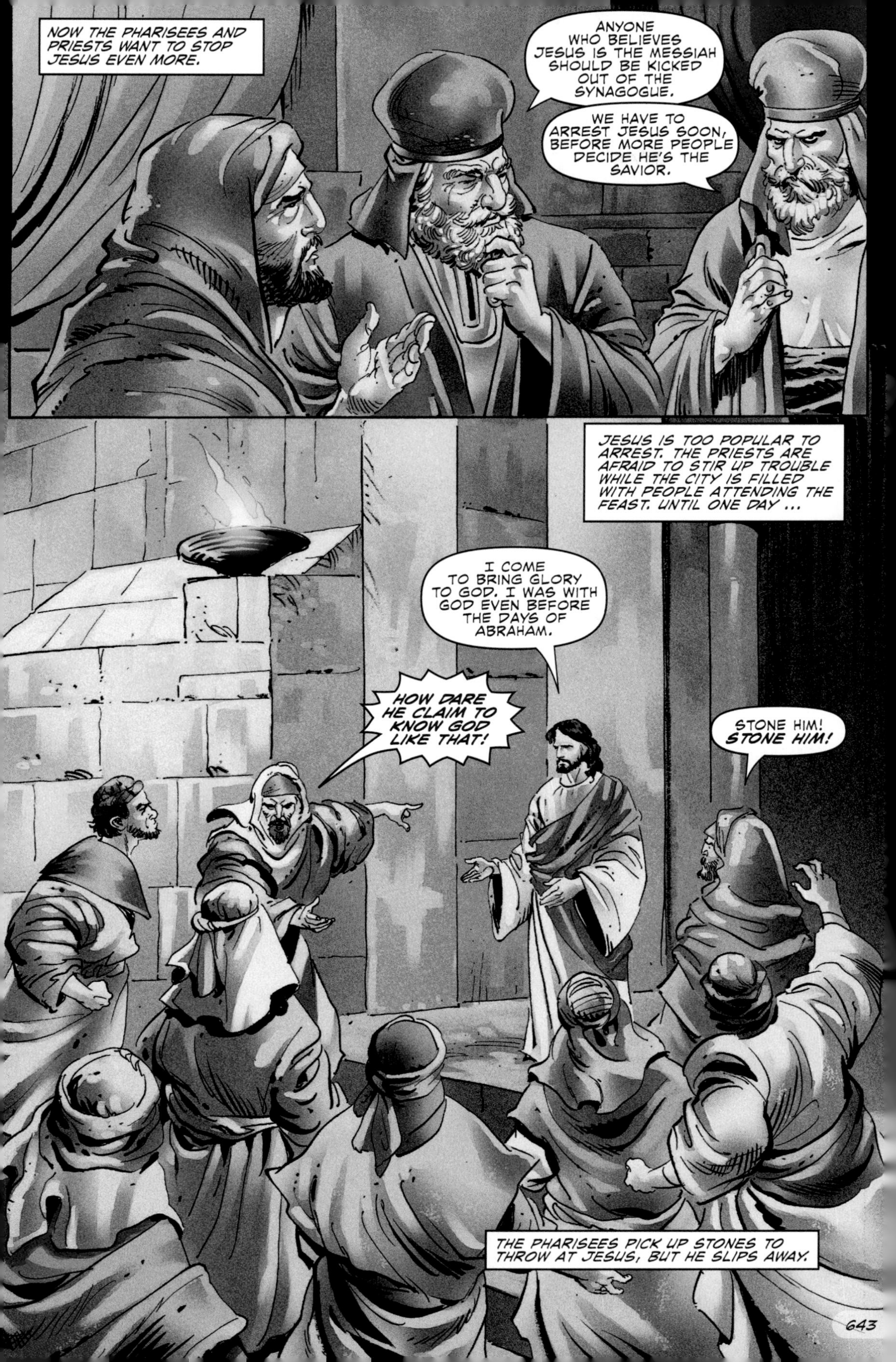
NOW THE PHARISEES AND PRIESTS WANT TO STOP JESUS EVEN MORE.
ANYONE WHO BELIEVES JESUS IS THE MESSIAH SHOULD BE KICKED OUT OF THE SYNAGOGUE.
WE HAVE TO ARREST JESUS SOON, BEFORE MORE PEOPLE DECIDE HE'S THE SAVIOR.
JESUS IS TOO POPULAR TO ARREST. THE PRIESTS ARE AFRAID TO STIR UP TROUBLE WHILE THE CITY IS FILLED WITH PEOPLE ATTENDING THE FEAST. UNTIL ONE DAY ...
I COME TO BRING GLORY TO GOD. I WAS WITH GOD EVEN BEFORE THE DAYS OF ABRAHAM.
HOW DARE HE CLAIM TO KNOW GOD LIKE THAT!
STONE HIM! STONE HIM!
THE PHARISEES PICK UP STONES TO THROW AT JESUS, BUT HE SLIPS AWAY.

Faith at First Sight

BASED ON JOHN 9:1—10:21

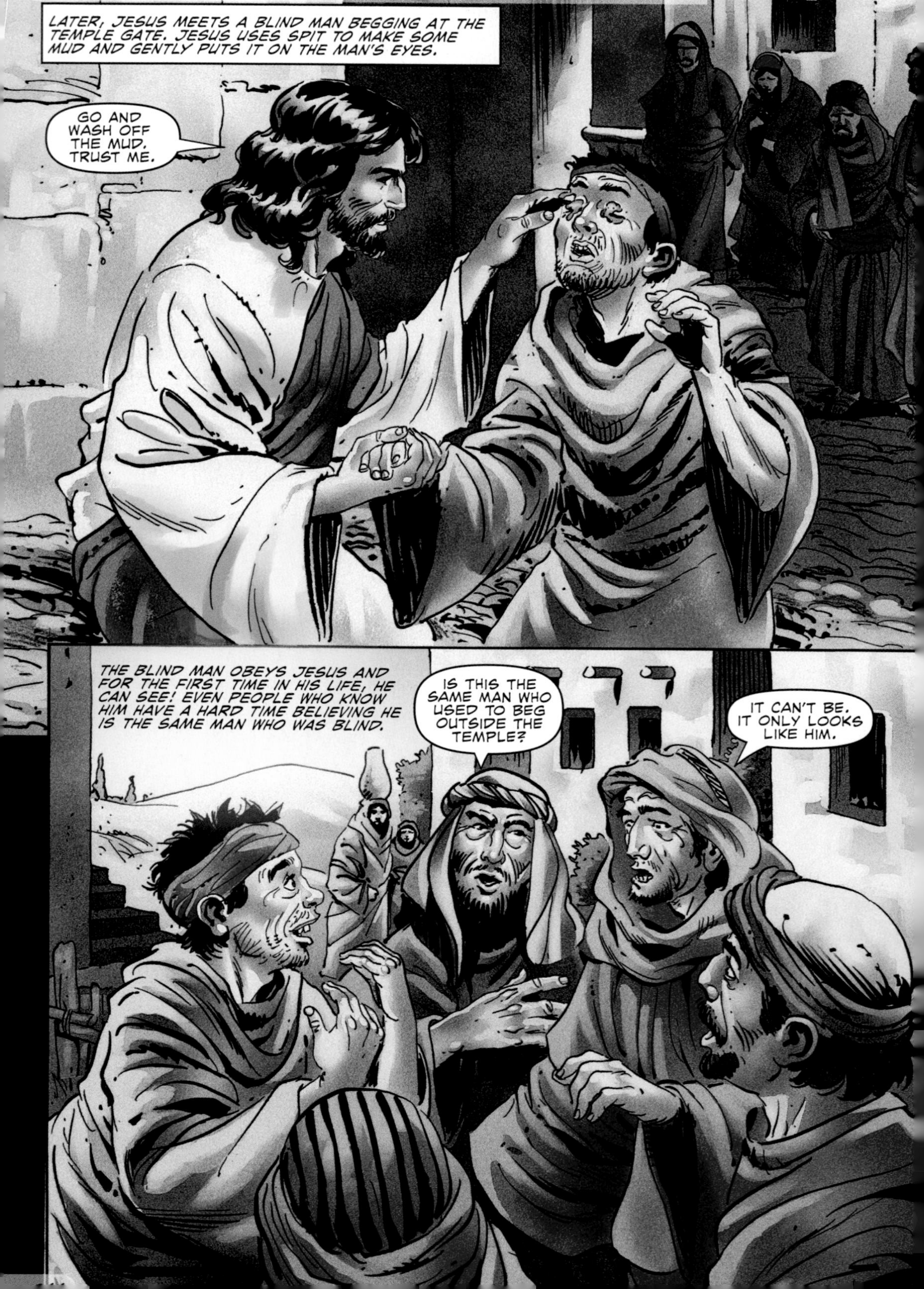
LATER, JESUS MEETS A BLIND MAN BEGGING AT THE TEMPLE GATE. JESUS USES SPIT TO MAKE SOME MUD AND GENTLY PUTS IT ON THE MAN'S EYES.
GO AND WASH OFF THE MUD. TRUST ME.
THE BLIND MAN OBEYS JESUS AND FOR THE FIRST TIME IN HIS LIFE, HE CAN SEE! EVEN PEOPLE WHO KNOW HIM HAVE A HARD TIME BELIEVING HE IS THE SAME MAN WHO WAS BLIND.
IS THIS THE SAME MAN WHO USED TO BEG OUTSIDE THE TEMPLE?
IT CAN'T BE. IT ONLY LOOKS LIKE HIM.

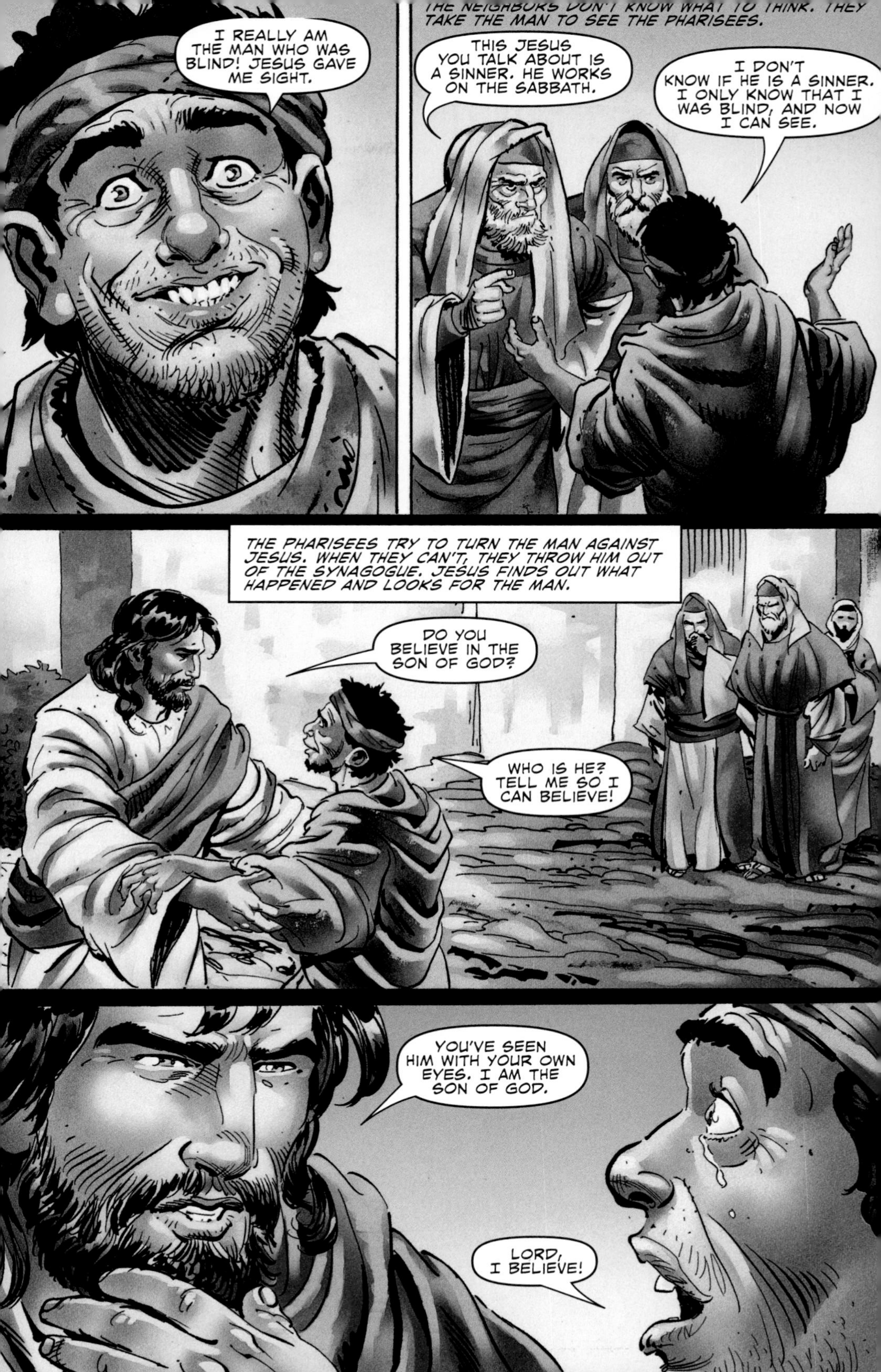
I REALLY AM THE MAN WHO WAS BLIND! JESUS GAVE ME SIGHT.
THE NEIGHBORS DON'T KNOW WHAT TO THINK. THEY TAKE THE MAN TO SEE THE PHARISEES.
THIS JESUS YOU TALK ABOUT IS A SINNER. HE WORKS ON THE SABBATH.
I DON'T KNOW IF HE IS A SINNER. I ONLY KNOW THAT I WAS BLIND, AND NOW I CAN SEE.
THE PHARISEES TRY TO TURN THE MAN AGAINST JESUS. WHEN THEY CAN'T, THEY THROW HIM OUT OF THE SYNAGOGUE. JESUS FINDS OUT WHAT HAPPENED AND LOOKS FOR THE MAN.
DO YOU BELIEVE IN THE SON OF GOD?
WHO IS HE? TELL ME SO I CAN BELIEVE!
YOU'VE SEEN HIM WITH YOUR OWN EYES. I AM THE SON OF GOD.
LORD, I BELIEVE!

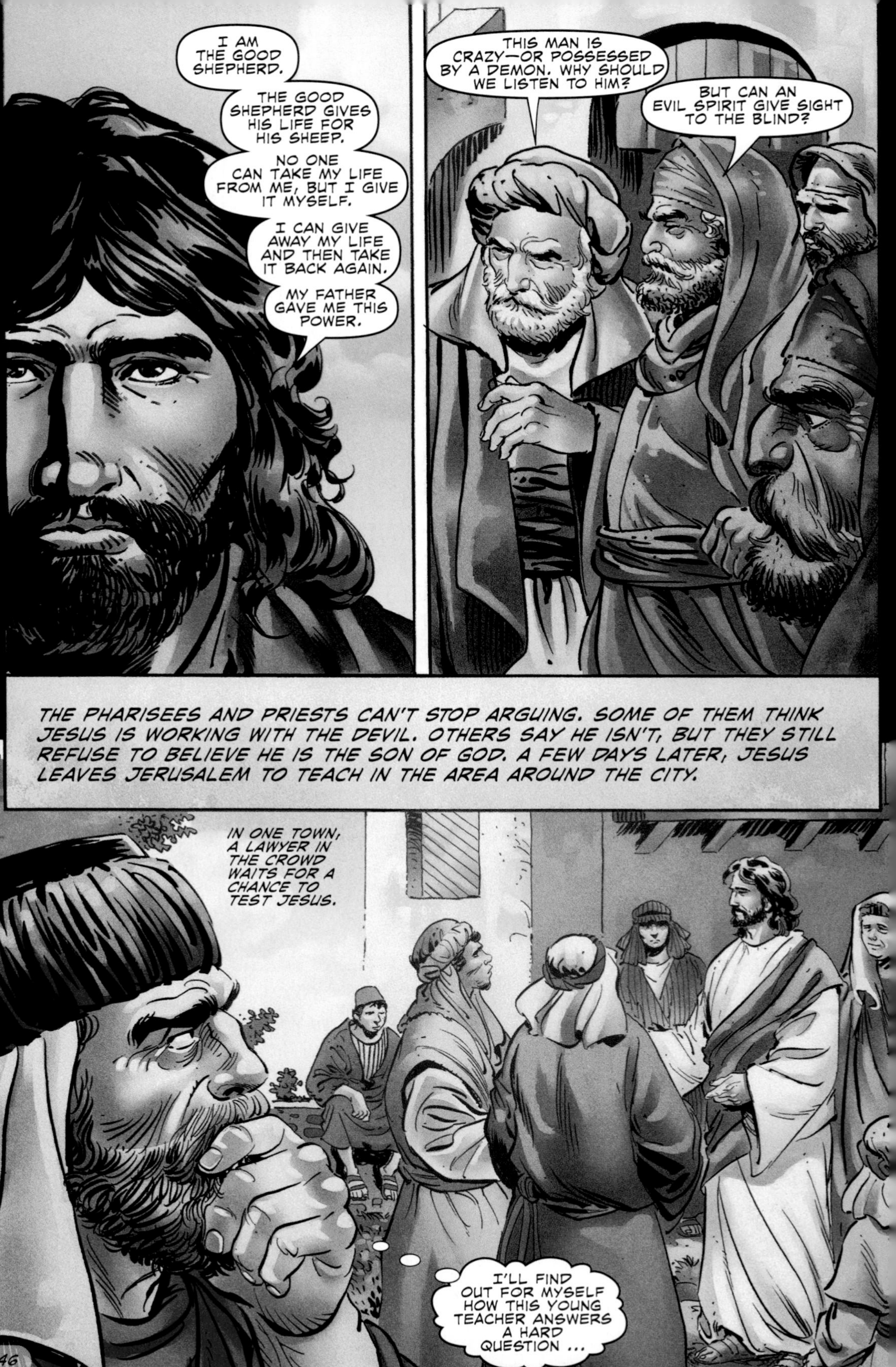
I AM THE GOOD SHEPHERD.
THE GOOD SHEPHERD GIVES HIS LIFE FOR HIS SHEEP.
NO ONE CAN TAKE MY LIFE FROM ME, BUT I GIVE IT MYSELF.
I CAN GIVE AWAY MY LIFE AND THEN TAKE IT BACK AGAIN.
MY FATHER GAVE ME THIS POWER.
THIS MAN IS CRAZY—OR POSSESSED BY A DEMON. WHY SHOULD WE LISTEN TO HIM?
BUT CAN AN EVIL SPIRIT GIVE SIGHT TO THE BLIND?
THE PHARISEES AND PRIESTS CAN'T STOP ARGUING. SOME OF THEM THINK JESUS IS WORKING WITH THE DEVIL. OTHERS SAY HE ISN'T, BUT THEY STILL REFUSE TO BELIEVE HE IS THE SON OF GOD. A FEW DAYS LATER, JESUS LEAVES JERUSALEM TO TEACH IN THE AREA AROUND THE CITY.
IN ONE TOWN, A LAWYER IN THE CROWD WAITS FOR A CHANCE TO TEST JESUS.
I'LL FIND OUT FOR MYSELF HOW THIS YOUNG TEACHER ANSWERS A HARD QUESTION ...

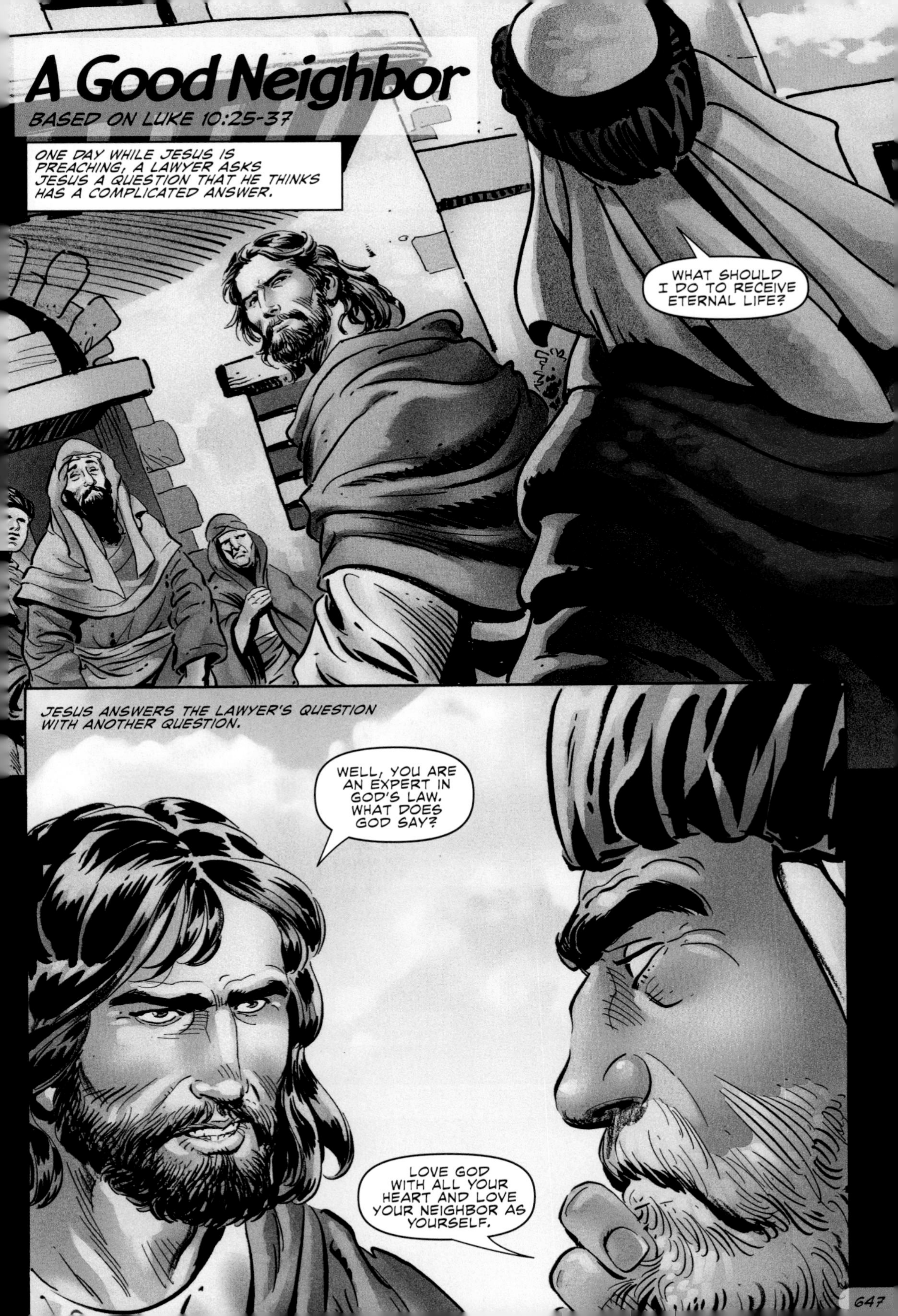
A Good Neighbor
BASED ON LUKE 10:25-37
ONE DAY WHILE JESUS IS PREACHING, A LAWYER ASKS JESUS A QUESTION THAT HE THINKS HAS A COMPLICATED ANSWER.
WHAT SHOULD I DO TO RECEIVE ETERNAL LIFE?
JESUS ANSWERS THE LAWYER'S QUESTION WITH ANOTHER QUESTION.
WELL, YOU ARE AN EXPERT IN GOD'S LAW. WHAT DOES GOD SAY?
LOVE GOD WITH ALL YOUR HEART AND LOVE YOUR NEIGHBOR AS YOURSELF.

YOU'RE RIGHT. DO THAT AND YOU WILL HAVE ETERNAL LIFE.

THAT'S EASY FOR YOU TO SAY. BUT WHO IS MY NEIGHBOR?

JESUS ANSWERS WITH A STORY ...

A MAN IS TRAVELING FROM JERUSALEM TO JERICHO. ON THE WAY, ROBBERS ATTACK HIM. THEY BEAT HIM UP AND LEAVE HIM FOR DEAD.

A PRIEST COMES DOWN THE ROAD. HE SEES THE WOUNDED MAN AND FEARS THAT THE ROBBERS MIGHT STILL BE NEARBY ...

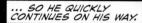

... SO HE QUICKLY CONTINUES ON HIS WAY.

A LITTLE LATER A LEVITE, AN ASSISTANT TO THE PRIESTS, COMES ALONG. BUT HE HAS IMPORTANT THINGS TO DO IN JERICHO ...

... SO HE, TOO, HURRIES BY.

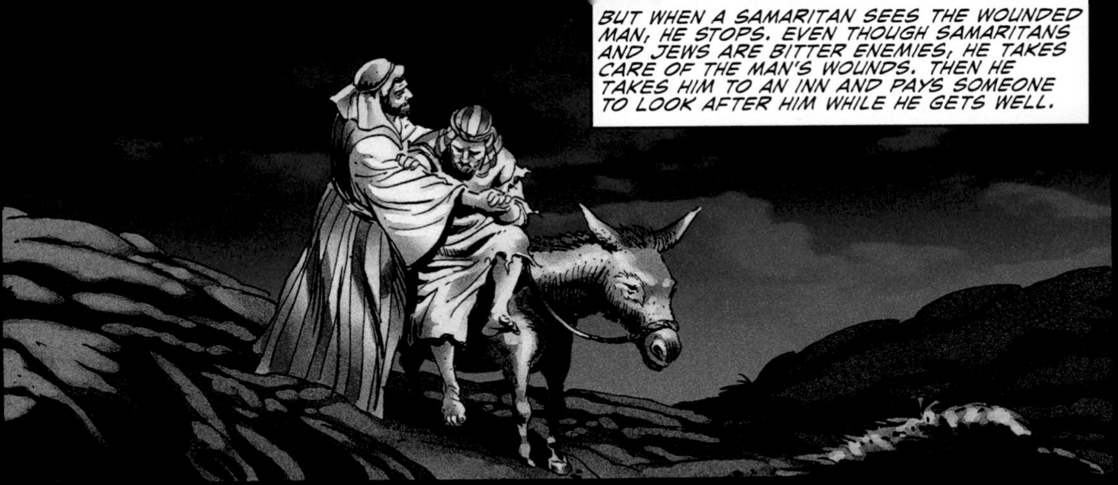
BUT WHEN A SAMARITAN SEES THE WOUNDED MAN, HE STOPS. EVEN THOUGH SAMARITANS AND JEWS ARE BITTER ENEMIES, HE TAKES CARE OF THE MAN'S WOUNDS. THEN HE TAKES HIM TO AN INN AND PAYS SOMEONE TO LOOK AFTER HIM WHILE HE GETS WELL.

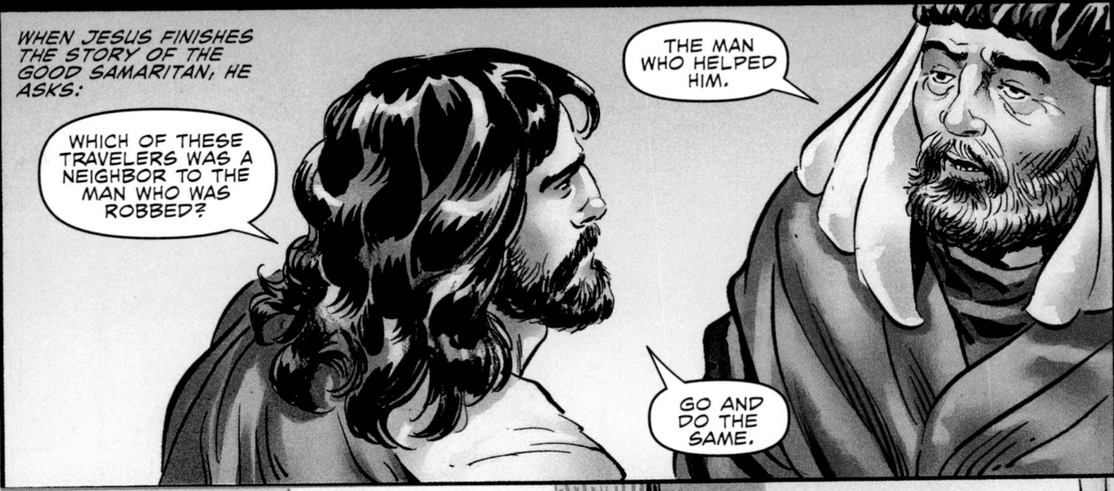
WHEN JESUS FINISHES THE STORY OF THE GOOD SAMARITAN, HE ASKS:
WHICH OF THESE TRAVELERS WAS A NEIGHBOR TO THE MAN WHO WAS ROBBED?
THE MAN WHO HELPED HIM.
GO AND DO THE SAME.

Help for Martha

BASED ON LUKE 10:38–11:4; JOHN 10:22-39

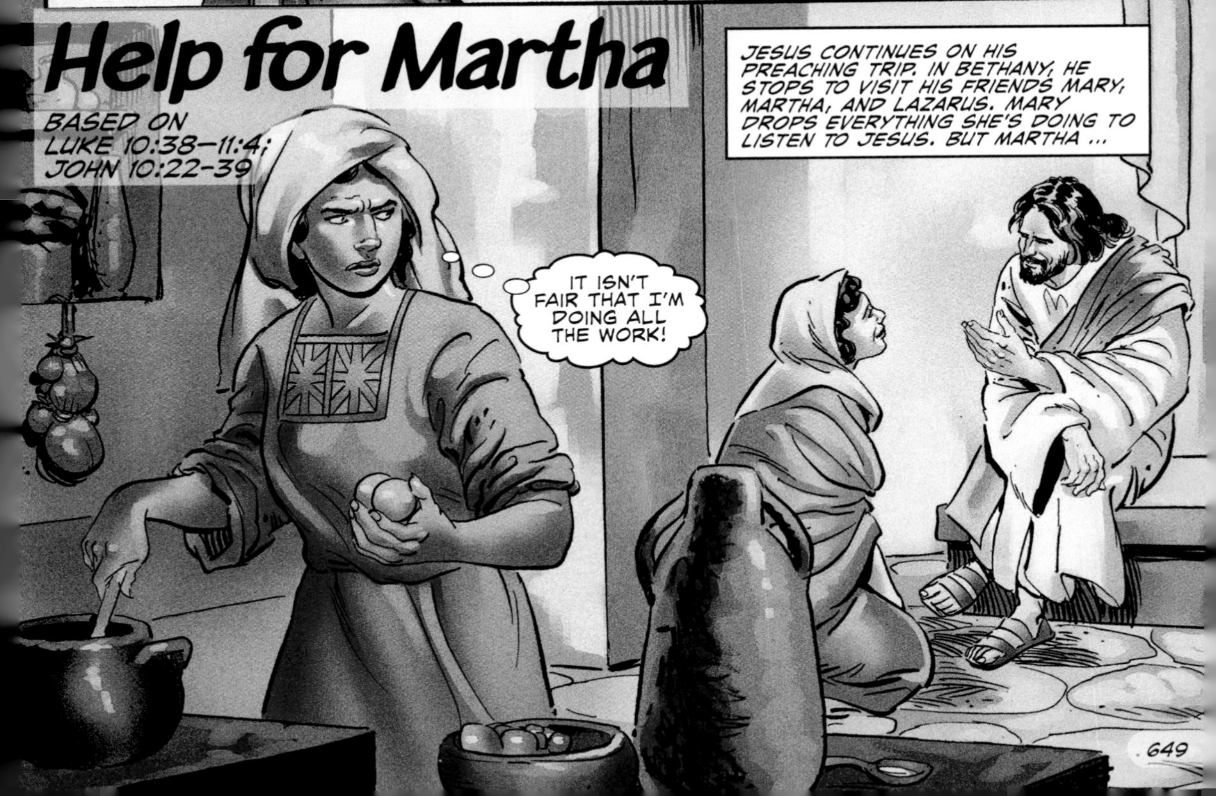
JESUS CONTINUES ON HIS PREACHING TRIP. IN BETHANY, HE STOPS TO VISIT HIS FRIENDS MARY, MARTHA, AND LAZARUS. MARY DROPS EVERYTHING SHE'S DOING TO LISTEN TO JESUS. BUT MARTHA ...
IT ISN'T FAIR THAT I'M DOING ALL THE WORK!

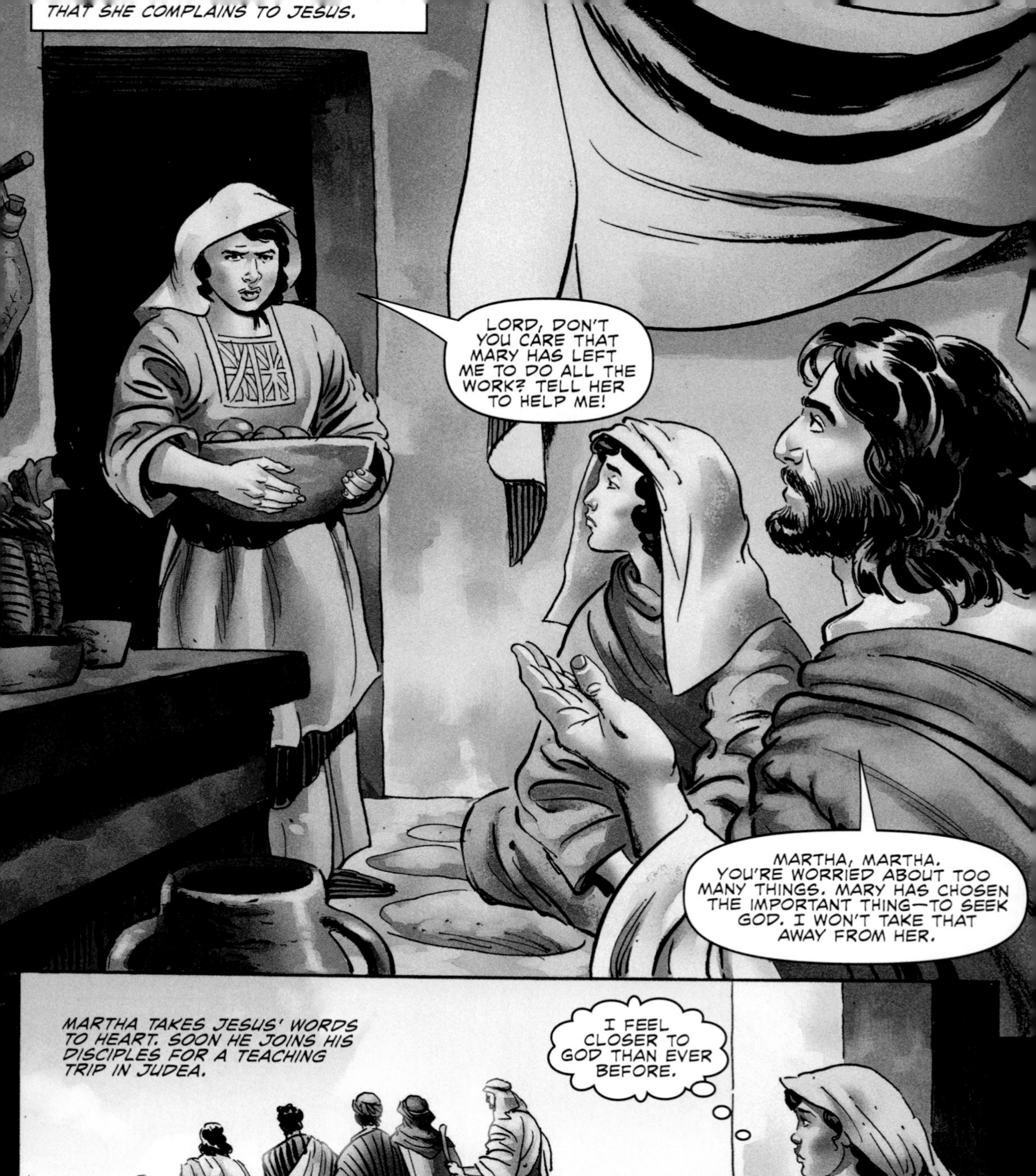
THAT SHE COMPLAINS TO JESUS.
LORD, DON'T YOU CARE THAT MARY HAS LEFT ME TO DO ALL THE WORK? TELL HER TO HELP ME!
MARTHA, MARTHA. YOU'RE WORRIED ABOUT TOO MANY THINGS. MARY HAS CHOSEN THE IMPORTANT THING—TO SEEK GOD. I WON'T TAKE THAT AWAY FROM HER.

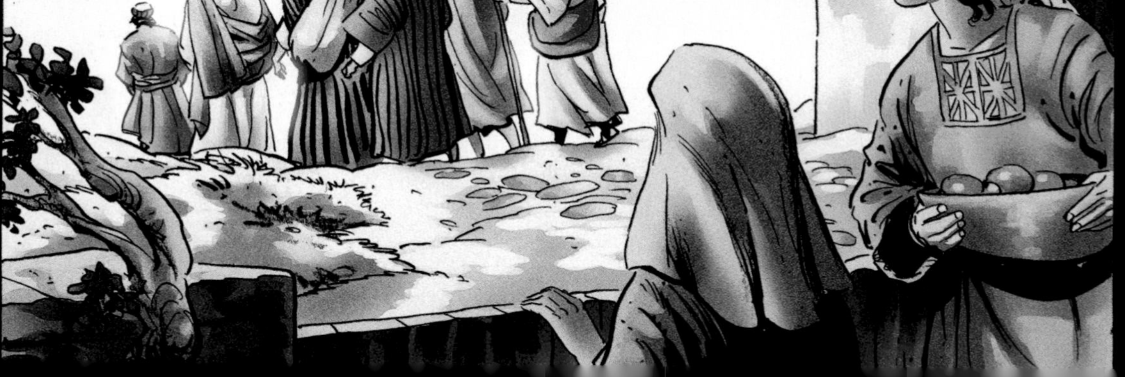
MARTHA TAKES JESUS' WORDS TO HEART. SOON HE JOINS HIS DISCIPLES FOR A TEACHING TRIP IN JUDEA.
I FEEL CLOSER TO GOD THAN EVER BEFORE.

The Lord's Prayer

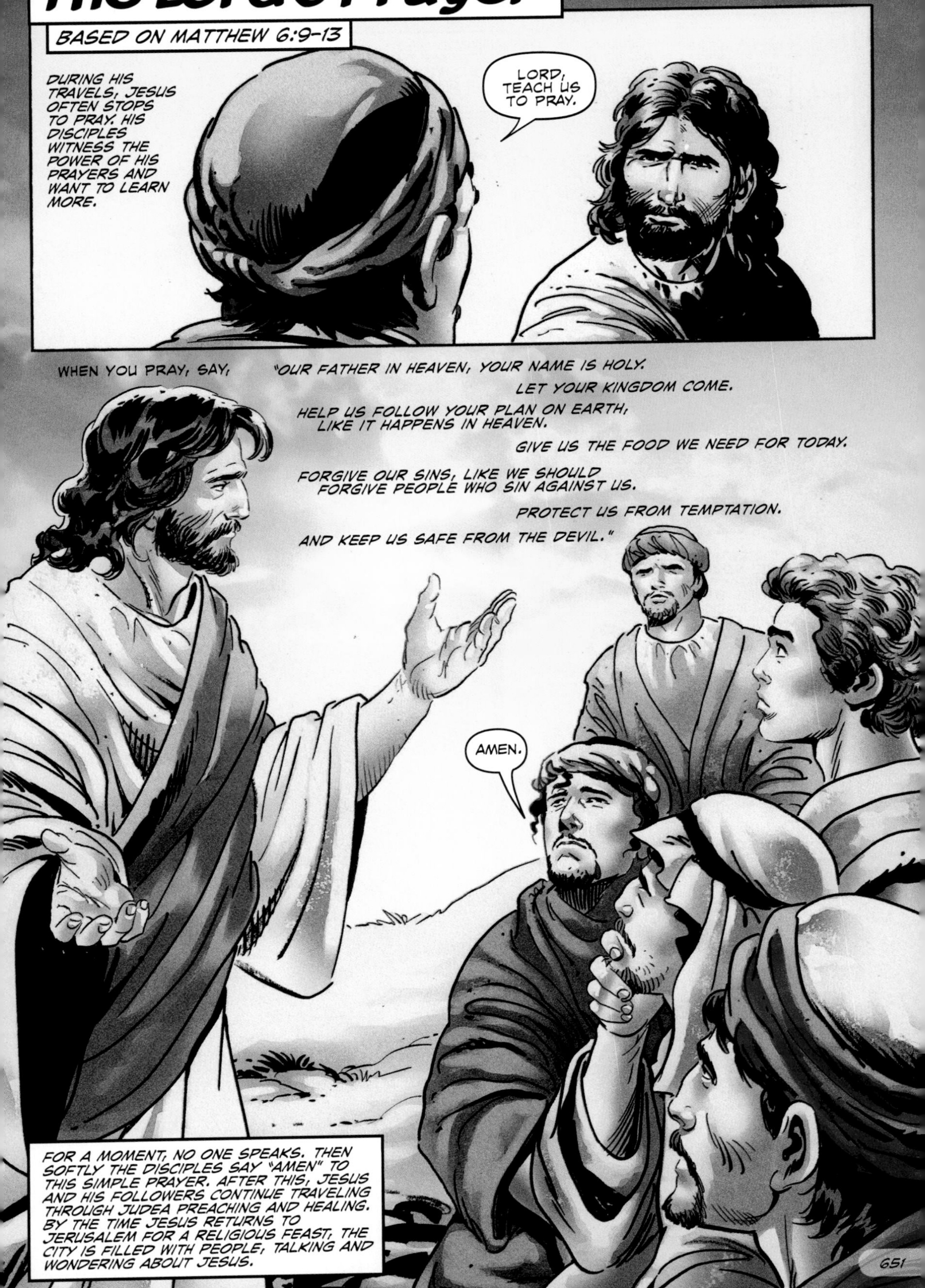
BASED ON MATTHEW 6:9–13
DURING HIS TRAVELS, JESUS OFTEN STOPS TO PRAY. HIS DISCIPLES WITNESS THE POWER OF HIS PRAYERS AND WANT TO LEARN MORE.
LORD, TEACH US TO PRAY.
WHEN YOU PRAY, SAY,
"OUR FATHER IN HEAVEN, YOUR NAME IS HOLY.
LET YOUR KINGDOM COME.
HELP US FOLLOW YOUR PLAN ON EARTH, LIKE IT HAPPENS IN HEAVEN.
GIVE US THE FOOD WE NEED FOR TODAY.
FORGIVE OUR SINS, LIKE WE SHOULD FORGIVE PEOPLE WHO SIN AGAINST US.
PROTECT US FROM TEMPTATION.
AND KEEP US SAFE FROM THE DEVIL."
AMEN.
FOR A MOMENT, NO ONE SPEAKS. THEN SOFTLY THE DISCIPLES SAY "AMEN" TO THIS SIMPLE PRAYER. AFTER THIS, JESUS AND HIS FOLLOWERS CONTINUE TRAVELING THROUGH JUDEA PREACHING AND HEALING. BY THE TIME JESUS RETURNS TO JERUSALEM FOR A RELIGIOUS FEAST, THE CITY IS FILLED WITH PEOPLE, TALKING AND WONDERING ABOUT JESUS.

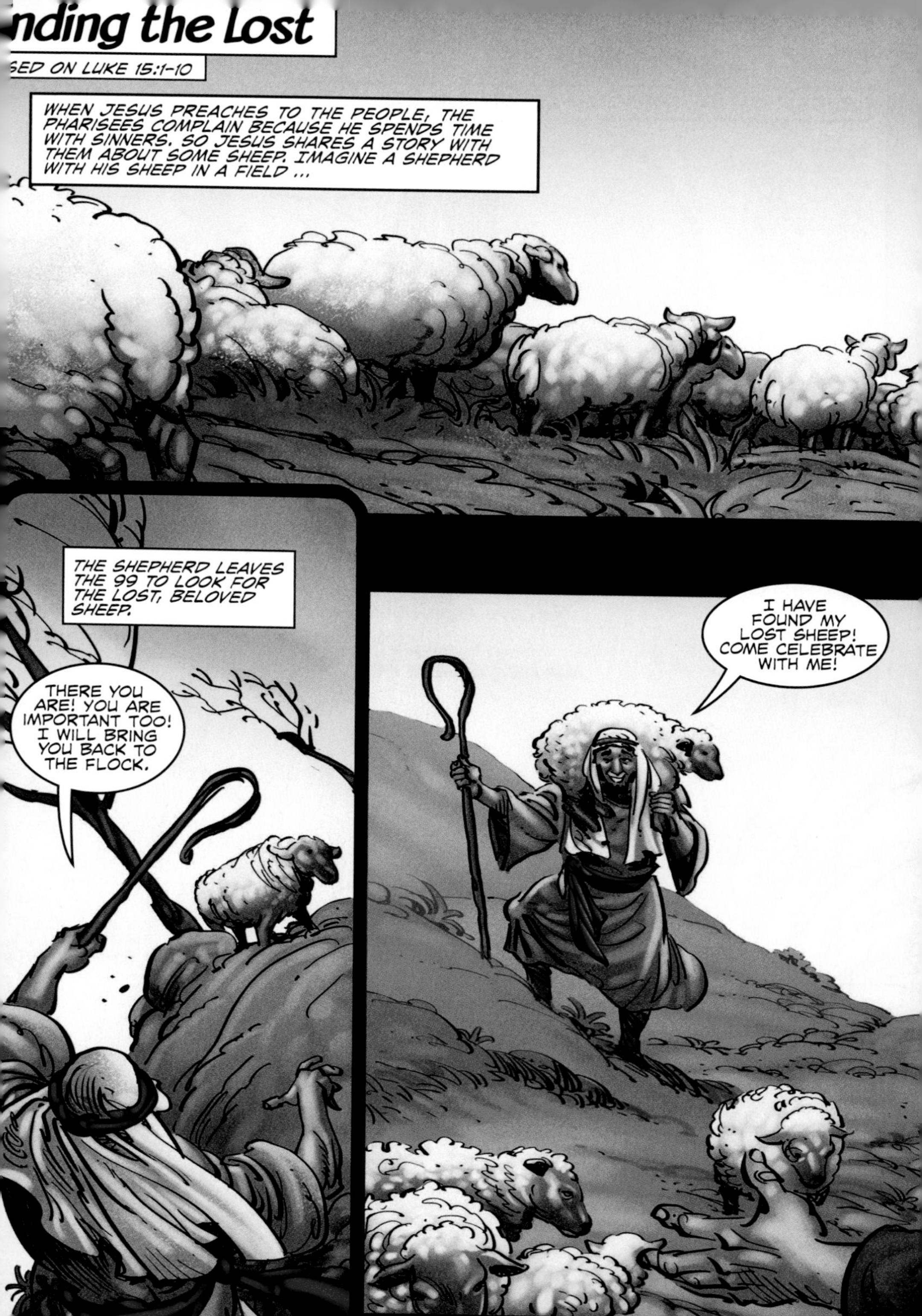

nding the Lost
SED ON LUKE 15:1–10
WHEN JESUS PREACHES TO THE PEOPLE, THE PHARISEES COMPLAIN BECAUSE HE SPENDS TIME WITH SINNERS. SO JESUS SHARES A STORY WITH THEM ABOUT SOME SHEEP. IMAGINE A SHEPHERD WITH HIS SHEEP IN A FIELD ...
THE SHEPHERD LEAVES THE 99 TO LOOK FOR THE LOST, BELOVED SHEEP.
THERE YOU ARE! YOU ARE IMPORTANT TOO! I WILL BRING YOU BACK TO THE FLOCK.
I HAVE FOUND MY LOST SHEEP! COME CELEBRATE WITH ME!

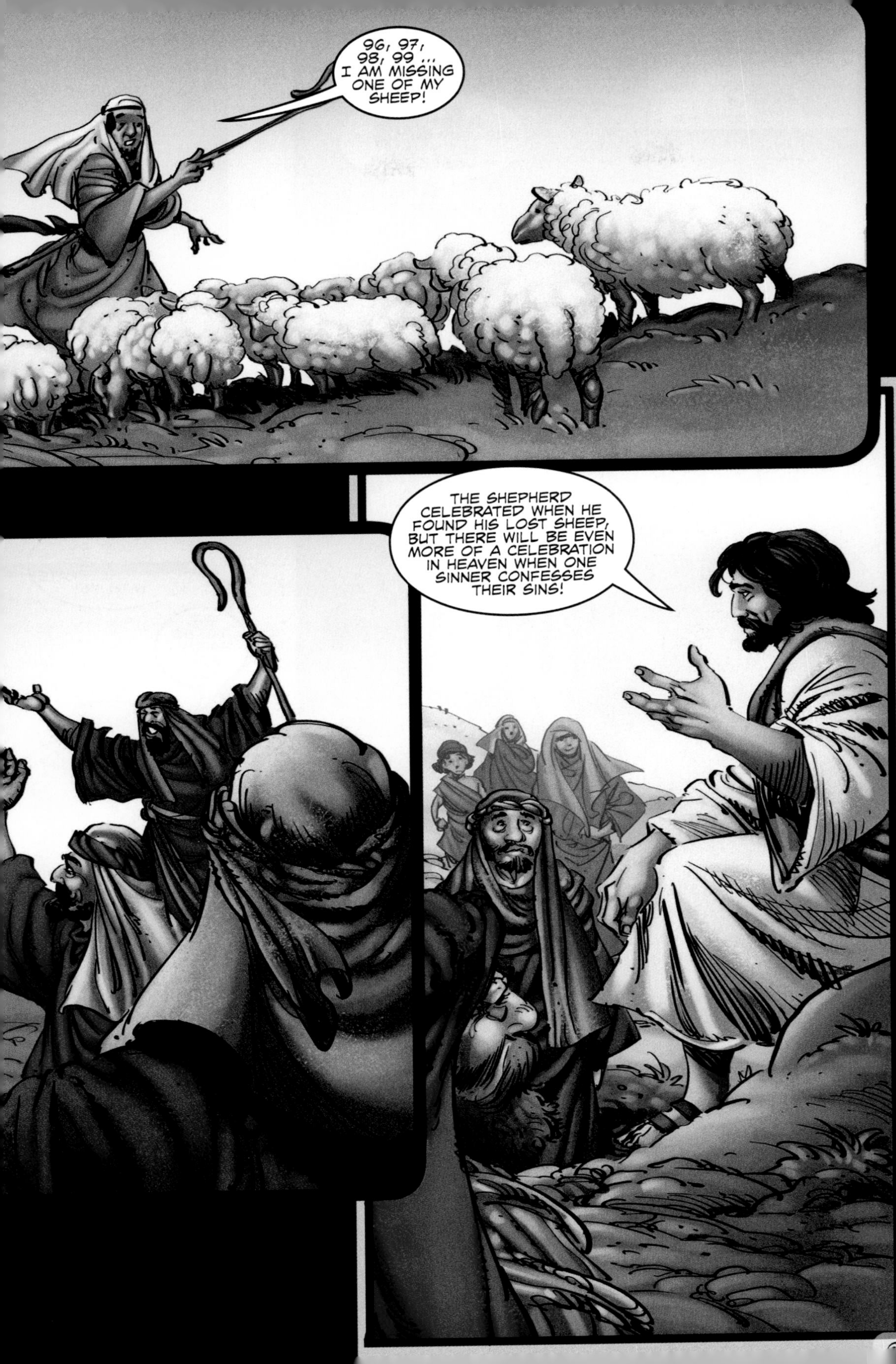
96, 97, 98, 99 ... I AM MISSING ONE OF MY SHEEP!
THE SHEPHERD CELEBRATED WHEN HE FOUND HIS LOST SHEEP, BUT THERE WILL BE EVEN MORE OF A CELEBRATION IN HEAVEN WHEN ONE SINNER CONFESSES THEIR SINS!

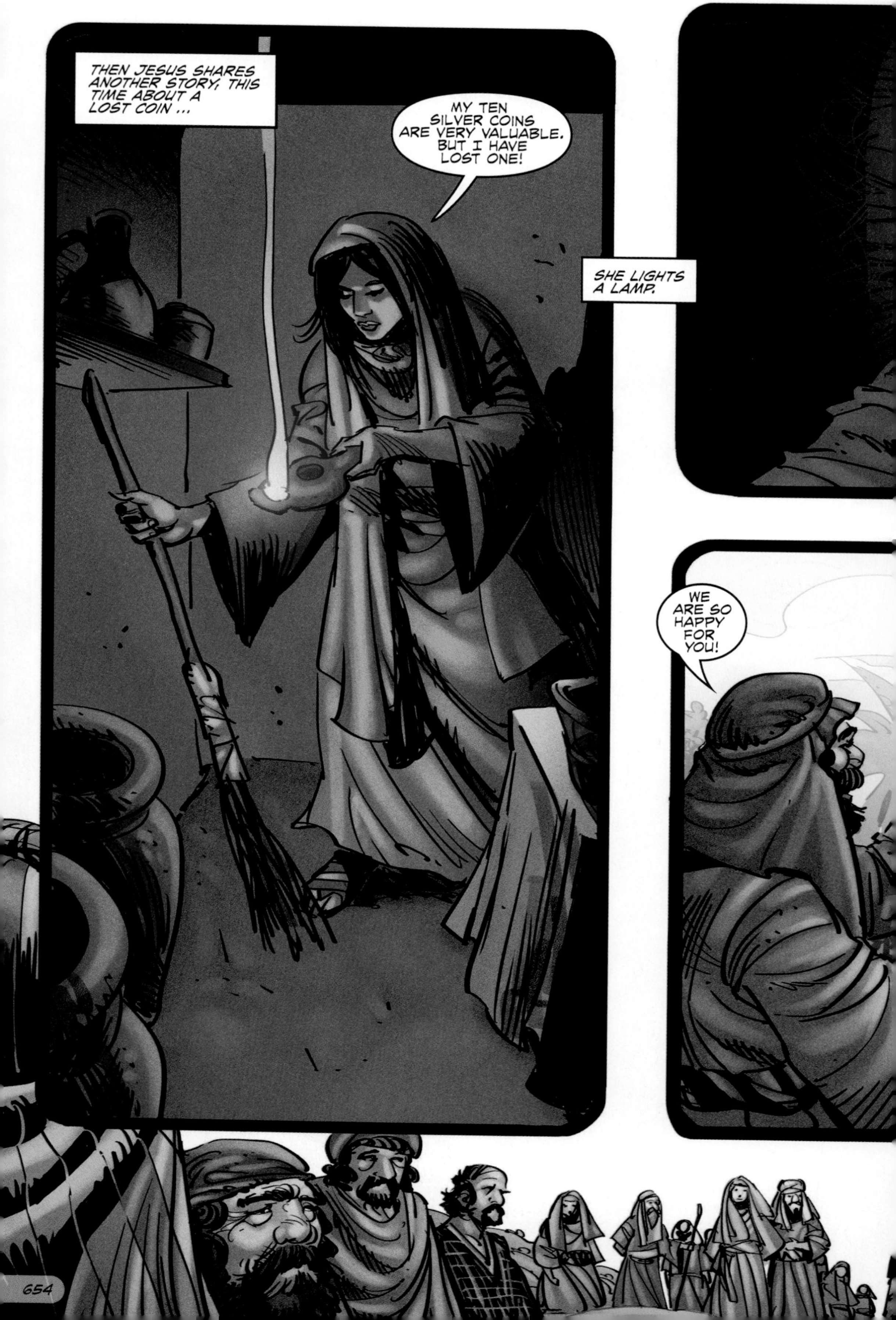
THEN JESUS SHARES ANOTHER STORY; THIS TIME ABOUT A LOST COIN ...
MY TEN SILVER COINS ARE VERY VALUABLE. BUT I HAVE LOST ONE!
SHE LIGHTS A LAMP.
WE ARE SO HAPPY FOR YOU!

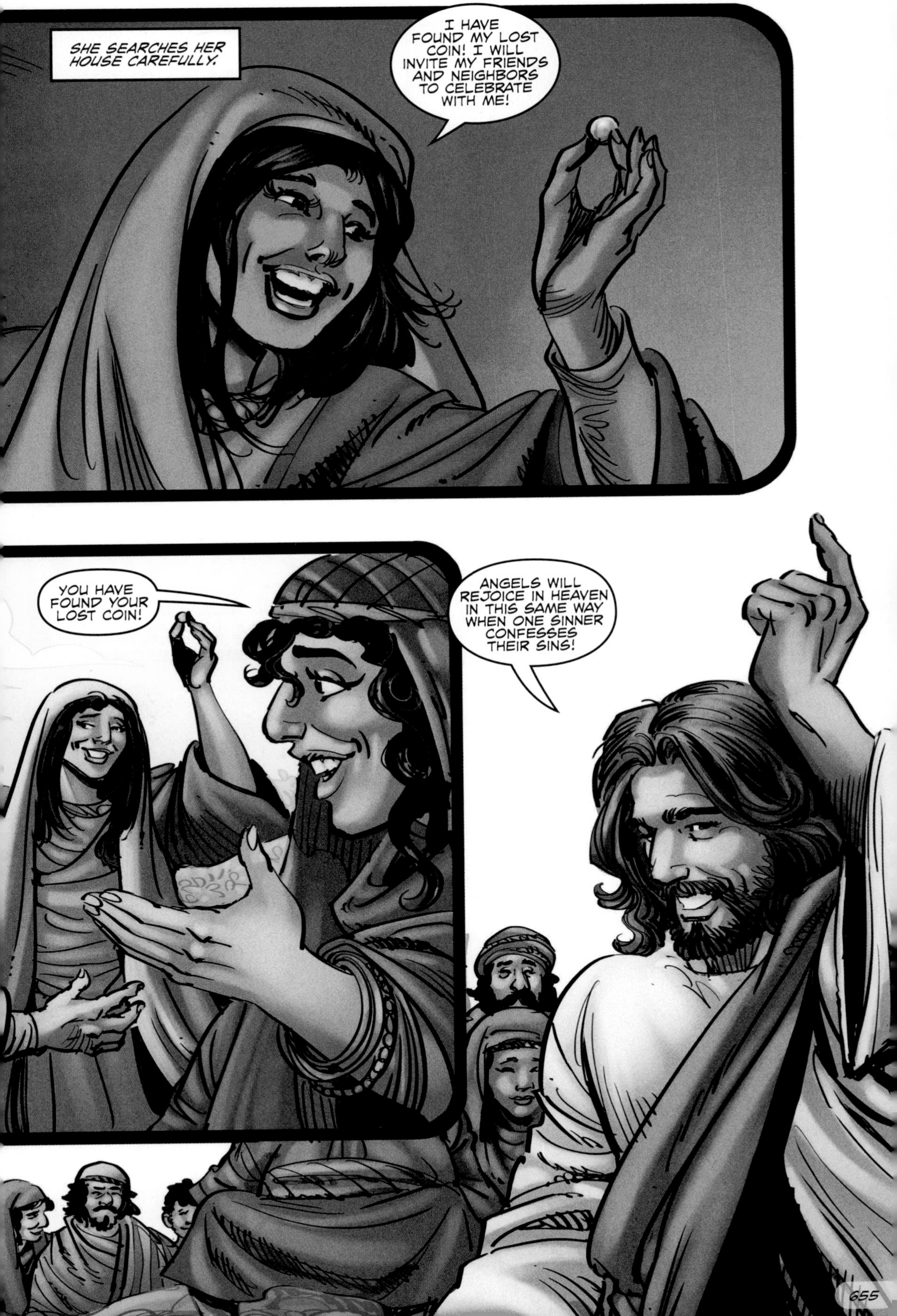
SHE SEARCHES HER HOUSE CAREFULLY.
I HAVE FOUND MY LOST COIN! I WILL INVITE MY FRIENDS AND NEIGHBORS TO CELEBRATE WITH ME!
YOU HAVE FOUND YOUR LOST COIN!
ANGELS WILL REJOICE IN HEAVEN IN THIS SAME WAY WHEN ONE SINNER CONFESSES THEIR SINS!

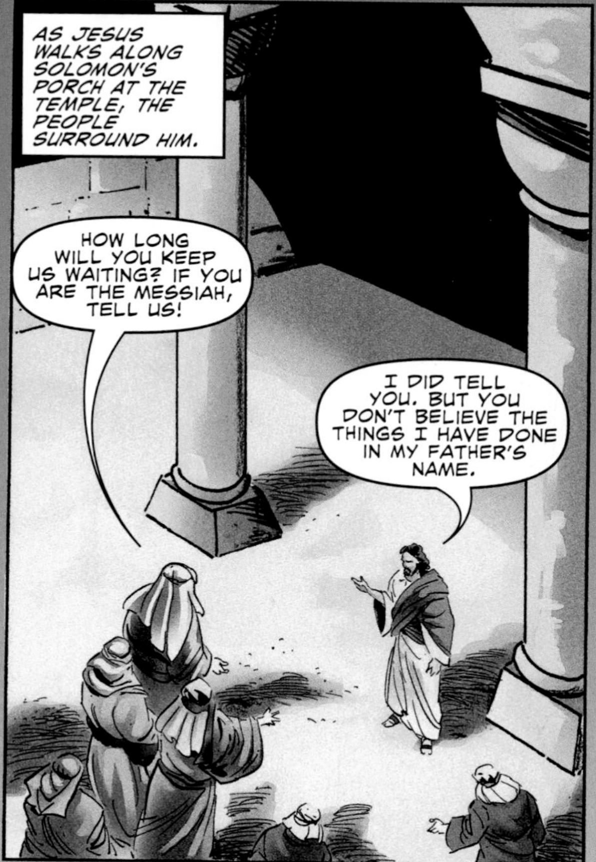
AS JESUS WALKS ALONG SOLOMON'S PORCH AT THE TEMPLE, THE PEOPLE SURROUND HIM.
HOW LONG WILL YOU KEEP US WAITING? IF YOU ARE THE MESSIAH, TELL US!
I DID TELL YOU. BUT YOU DON'T BELIEVE THE THINGS I HAVE DONE IN MY FATHER'S NAME.

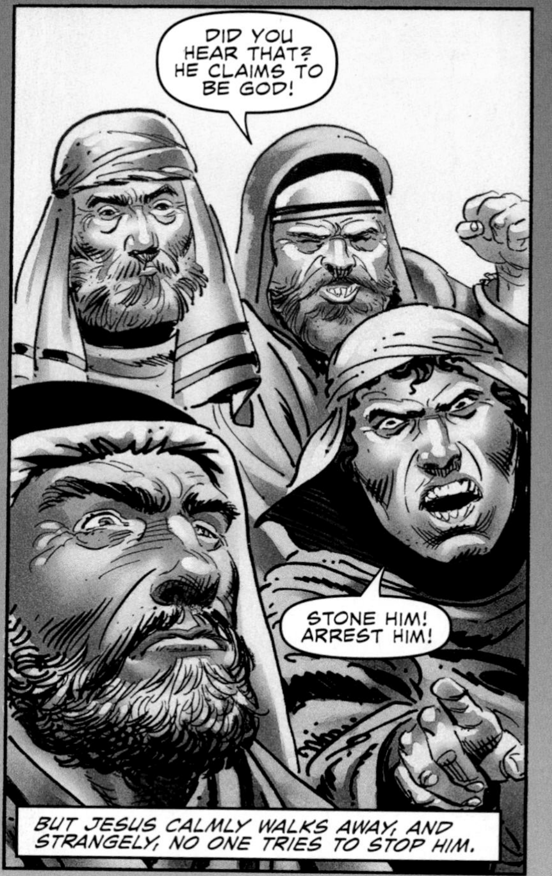
DID YOU HEAR THAT? HE CLAIMS TO BE GOD!
STONE HIM! ARREST HIM!
BUT JESUS CALMLY WALKS AWAY, AND STRANGELY, NO ONE TRIES TO STOP HIM.

A Loving Father

BASED ON LUKE 15:11–32

JESUS LEAVES JERUSALEM AND CONTINUES TO PREACH. THE PHARISEES COMPLAIN AGAIN BECAUSE HE SPENDS TIME WITH SINNERS. SO JESUS TELLS THEM A STORY ABOUT A MAN WITH TWO SONS. ONE DAY THE YOUNGER SON COMES TO THE FATHER ...

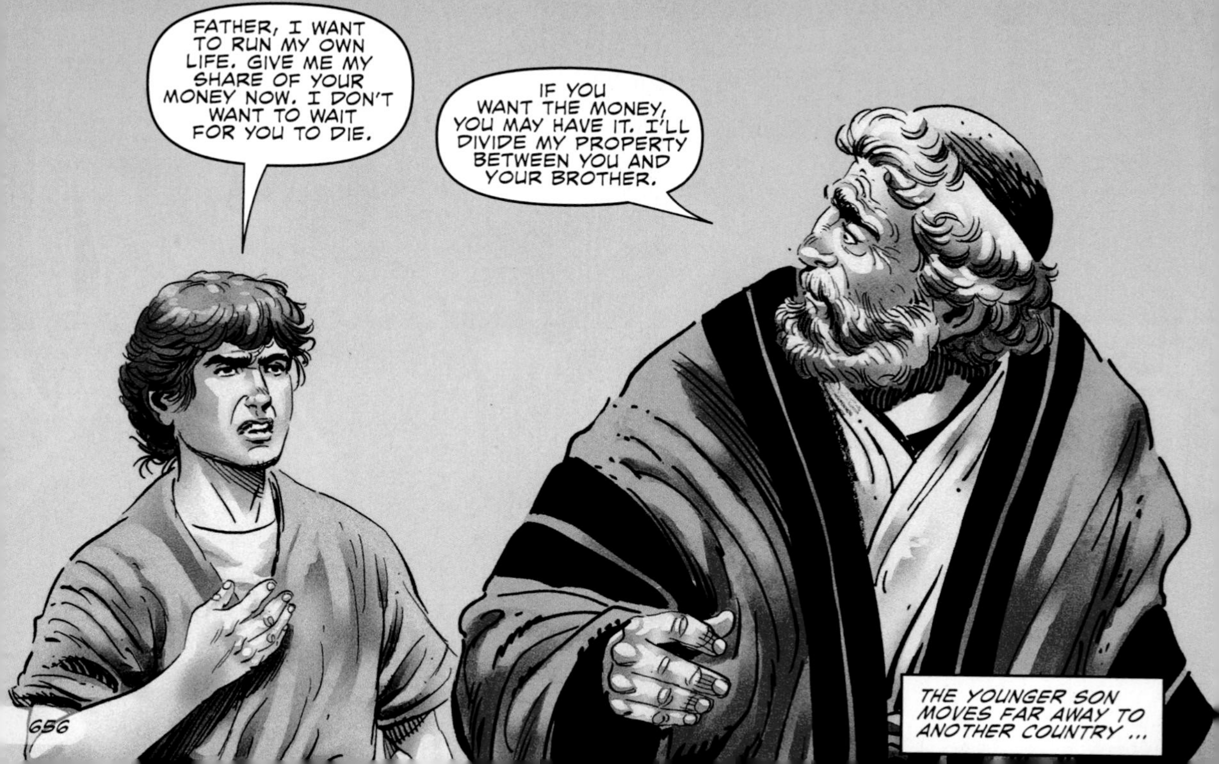
FATHER, I WANT TO RUN MY OWN LIFE. GIVE ME MY SHARE OF YOUR MONEY NOW. I DON'T WANT TO WAIT FOR YOU TO DIE.
IF YOU WANT THE MONEY, YOU MAY HAVE IT. I'LL DIVIDE MY PROPERTY BETWEEN YOU AND YOUR BROTHER.
THE YOUNGER SON MOVES FAR AWAY TO ANOTHER COUNTRY ...

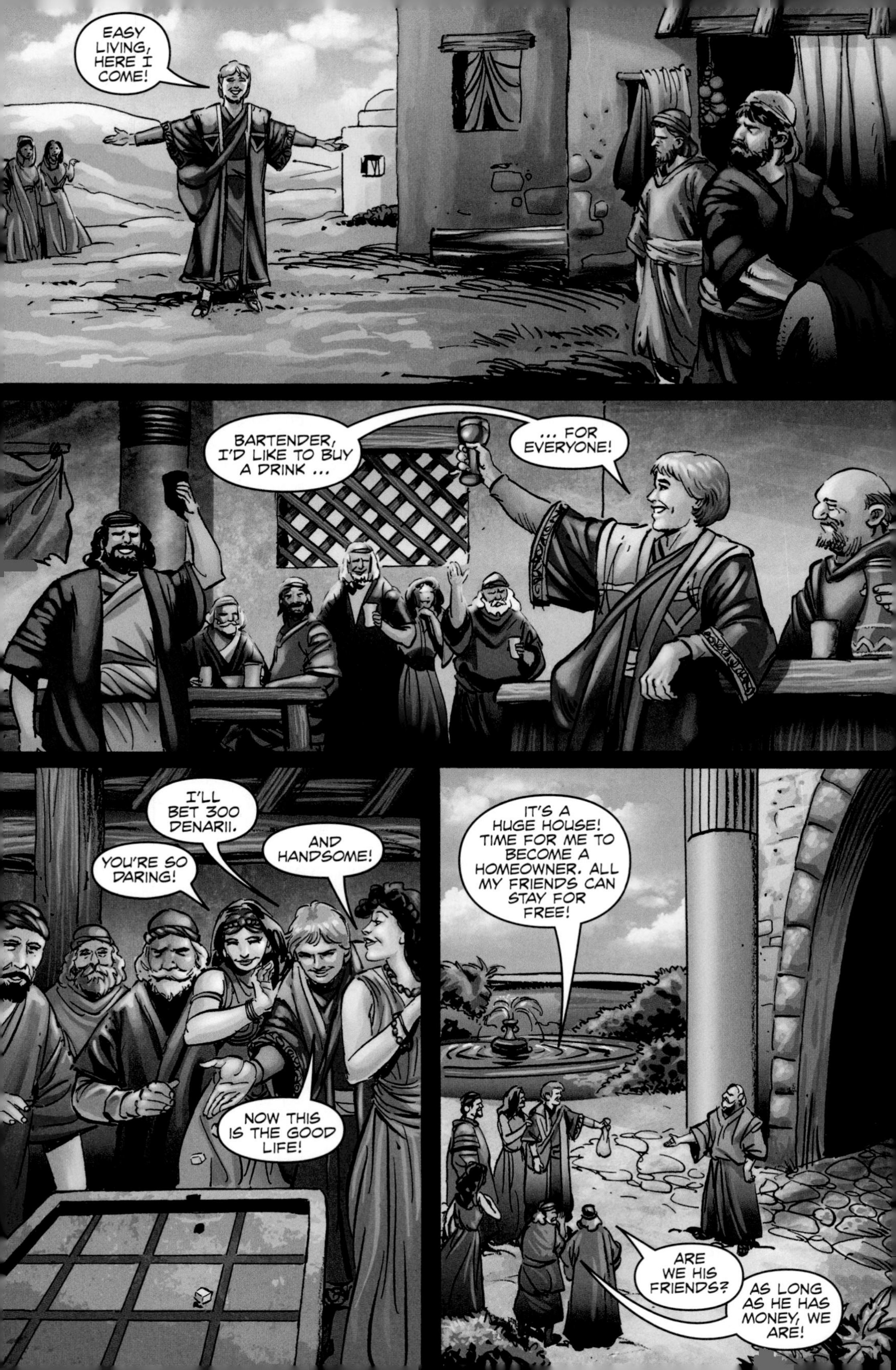
EASY LIVING, HERE I COME!
BARTENDER, I'D LIKE TO BUY A DRINK ...
... FOR EVERYONE!
I'LL BET 300 DENARII.
YOU'RE SO DARING!
AND HANDSOME!
NOW THIS IS THE GOOD LIFE!
IT'S A HUGE HOUSE! TIME FOR ME TO BECOME A HOMEOWNER. ALL MY FRIENDS CAN STAY FOR FREE!
ARE WE HIS FRIENDS?
AS LONG AS HE HAS MONEY, WE ARE!

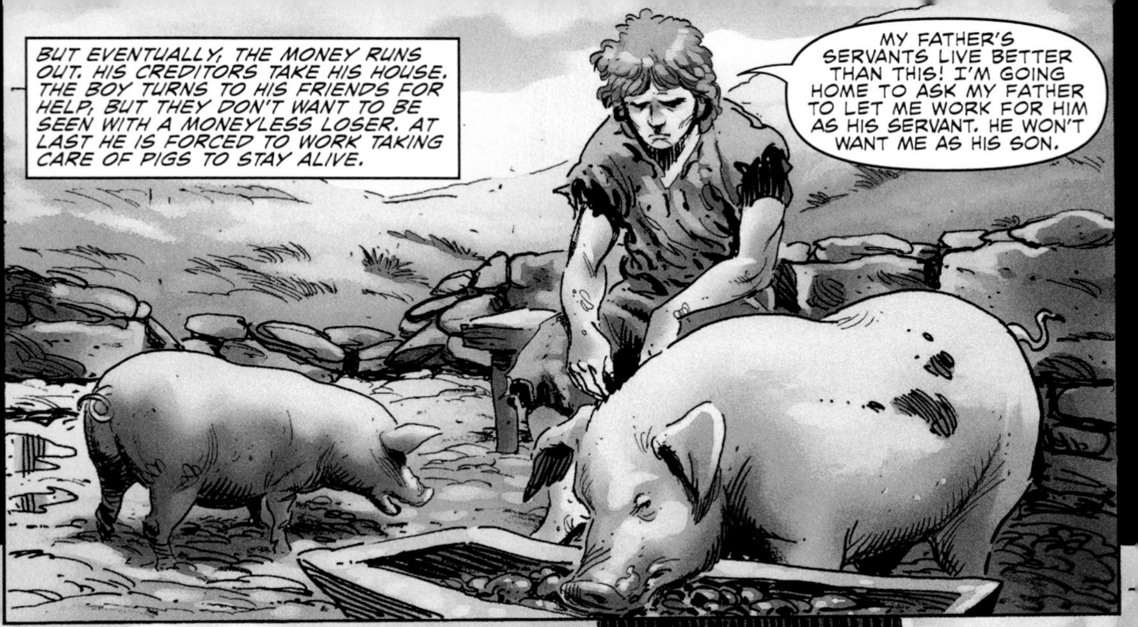
BUT EVENTUALLY, THE MONEY RUNS OUT. HIS CREDITORS TAKE HIS HOUSE. THE BOY TURNS TO HIS FRIENDS FOR HELP, BUT THEY DON'T WANT TO BE SEEN WITH A MONEYLESS LOSER. AT LAST HE IS FORCED TO WORK TAKING CARE OF PIGS TO STAY ALIVE.
MY FATHER'S SERVANTS LIVE BETTER THAN THIS! I'M GOING HOME TO ASK MY FATHER TO LET ME WORK FOR HIM AS HIS SERVANT. HE WON'T WANT ME AS HIS SON.

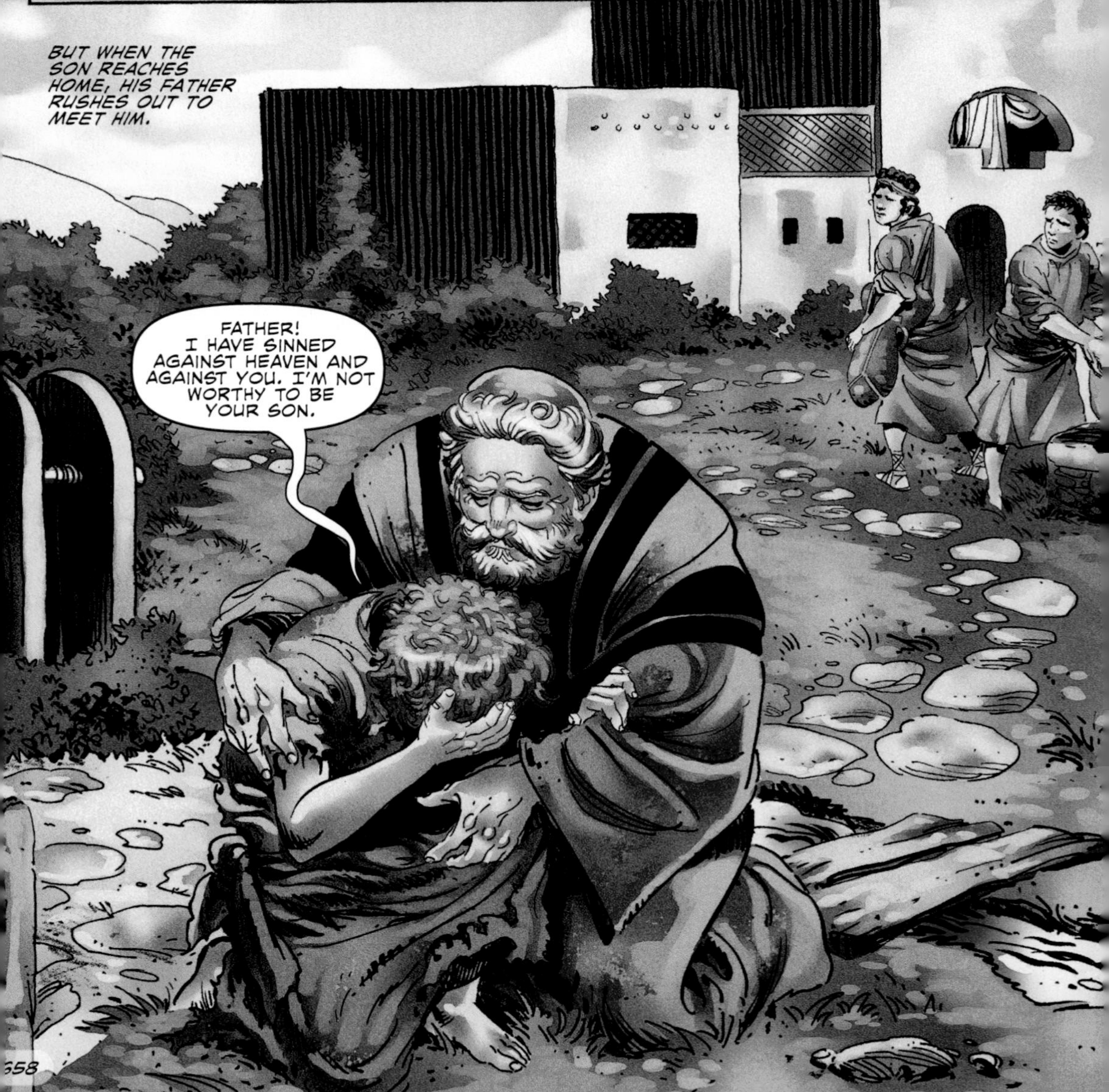
BUT WHEN THE SON REACHES HOME, HIS FATHER RUSHES OUT TO MEET HIM.
FATHER! I HAVE SINNED AGAINST HEAVEN AND AGAINST YOU. I'M NOT WORTHY TO BE YOUR SON.

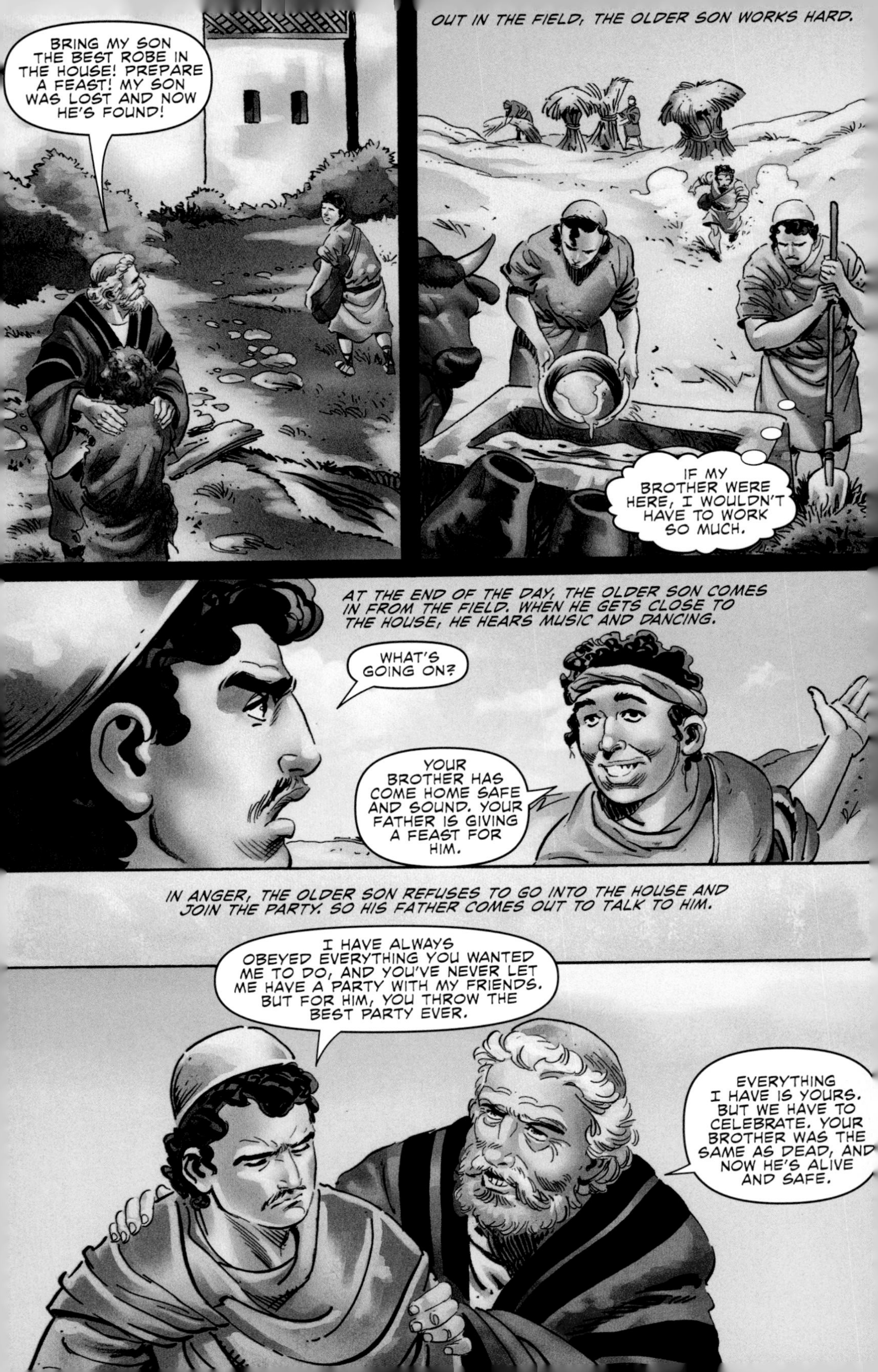
BRING MY SON THE BEST ROBE IN THE HOUSE! PREPARE A FEAST! MY SON WAS LOST AND NOW HE'S FOUND!
OUT IN THE FIELD, THE OLDER SON WORKS HARD.
IF MY BROTHER WERE HERE, I WOULDN'T HAVE TO WORK SO MUCH.
AT THE END OF THE DAY, THE OLDER SON COMES IN FROM THE FIELD. WHEN HE GETS CLOSE TO THE HOUSE, HE HEARS MUSIC AND DANCING.
WHAT'S GOING ON?
YOUR BROTHER HAS COME HOME SAFE AND SOUND. YOUR FATHER IS GIVING A FEAST FOR HIM.
IN ANGER, THE OLDER SON REFUSES TO GO INTO THE HOUSE AND JOIN THE PARTY. SO HIS FATHER COMES OUT TO TALK TO HIM.
I HAVE ALWAYS OBEYED EVERYTHING YOU WANTED ME TO DO, AND YOU'VE NEVER LET ME HAVE A PARTY WITH MY FRIENDS. BUT FOR HIM, YOU THROW THE BEST PARTY EVER.
EVERYTHING I HAVE IS YOURS. BUT WE HAVE TO CELEBRATE. YOUR BROTHER WAS THE SAME AS DEAD, AND NOW HE'S ALIVE AND SAFE.

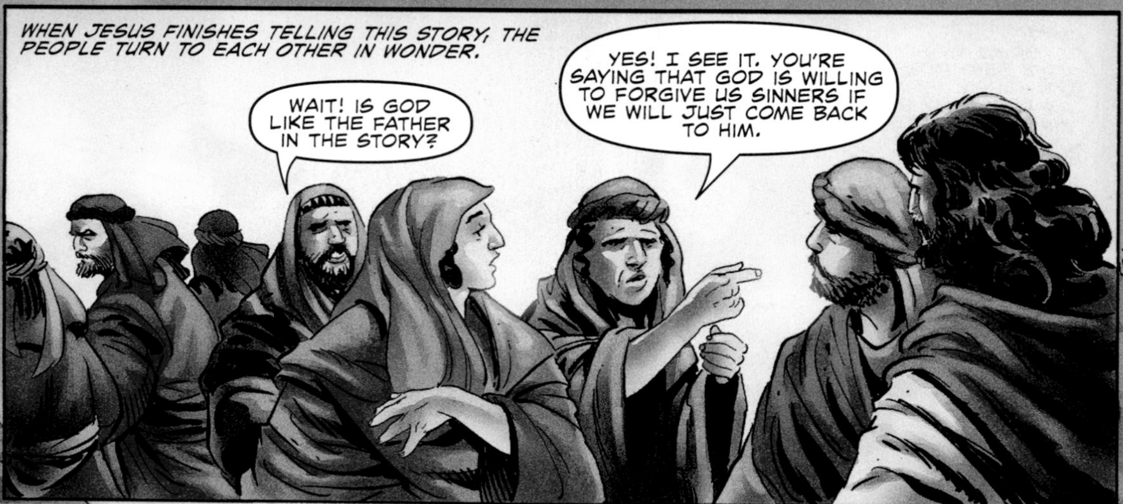
WHEN JESUS FINISHES TELLING THIS STORY, THE PEOPLE TURN TO EACH OTHER IN WONDER.
WAIT! IS GOD LIKE THE FATHER IN THE STORY?
YES! I SEE IT. YOU'RE SAYING THAT GOD IS WILLING TO FORGIVE US SINNERS IF WE WILL JUST COME BACK TO HIM.

Jesus Wept

BASED ON JOHN 11

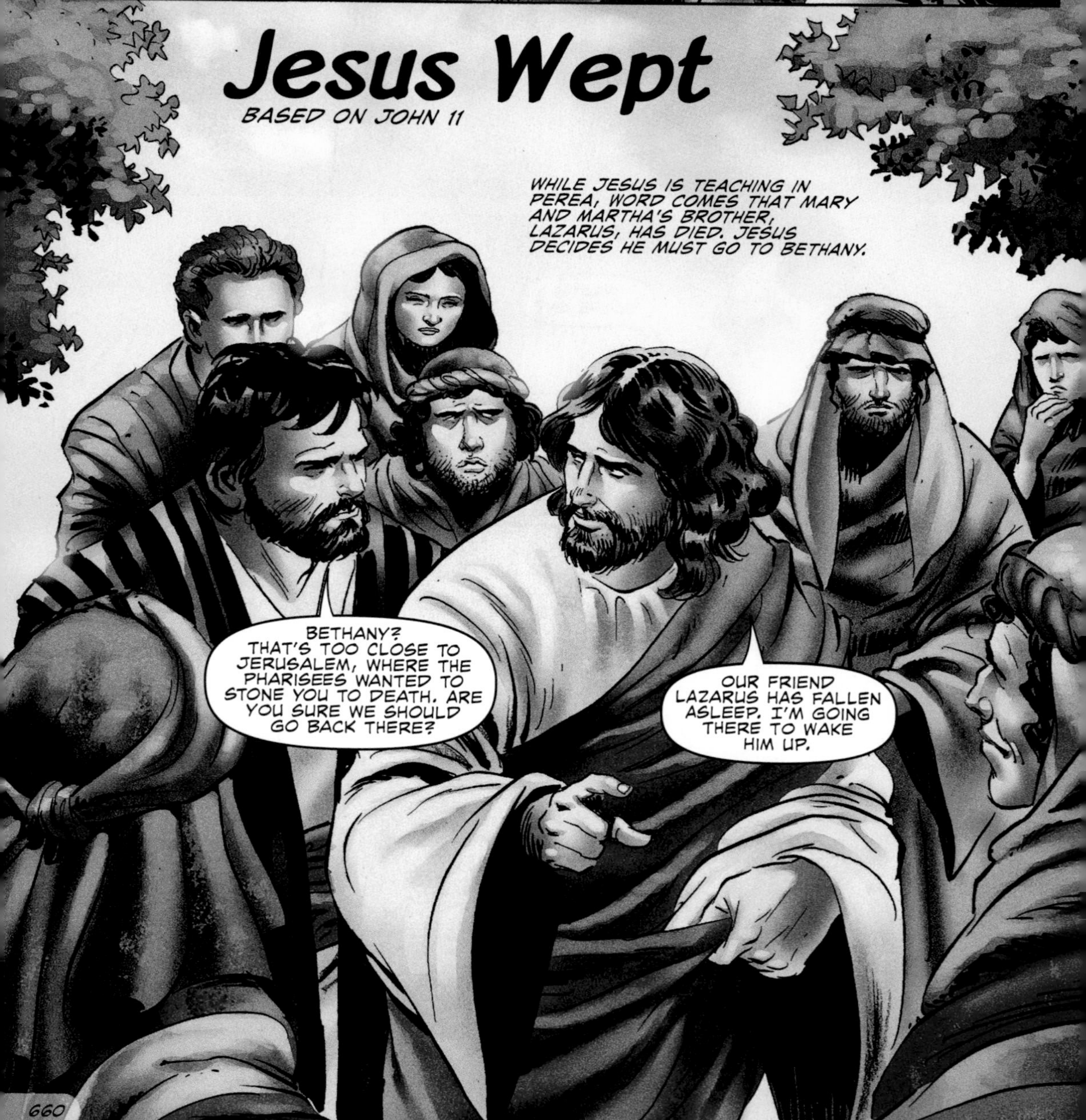
WHILE JESUS IS TEACHING IN PEREA, WORD COMES THAT MARY AND MARTHA'S BROTHER, LAZARUS, HAS DIED. JESUS DECIDES HE MUST GO TO BETHANY.
BETHANY? THAT'S TOO CLOSE TO JERUSALEM, WHERE THE PHARISEES WANTED TO STONE YOU TO DEATH. ARE YOU SURE WE SHOULD GO BACK THERE?
OUR FRIEND LAZARUS HAS FALLEN ASLEEP. I'M GOING THERE TO WAKE HIM UP.

BY THE TIME JESUS AND HIS DISCIPLES GET TO BETHANY, LAZARUS HAS BEEN DEAD FOR FOUR DAYS. MARTHA COMES OUT TO MEET JESUS, GRIEVING FOR HER BROTHER.

LORD, IF YOU HAD BEEN HERE, YOU COULD HAVE HEALED MY BROTHER.

YOUR BROTHER WILL LIVE AGAIN.

I KNOW HE WILL, ON THE RESURRECTION DAY.

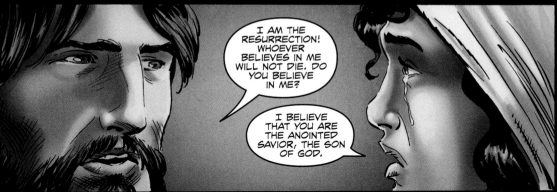

I AM THE RESURRECTION! WHOEVER BELIEVES IN ME WILL NOT DIE. DO YOU BELIEVE IN ME?

I BELIEVE THAT YOU ARE THE ANOINTED SAVIOR, THE SON OF GOD.

THEN MARY RUNS OUT AND THROWS HERSELF AT JESUS' FEET, WEEPING.

LORD, IF YOU HAD BEEN HERE, OUR BROTHER WOULD NOT HAVE DIED!

I KNOW!

JESUS WEEPS ALONG WITH HER.

WOW, HE REALLY CARED ABOUT LAZARUS.

THEN WHY DID HE TAKE SO LONG TO GET HERE?

MARY AND MARTHA TAKE JESUS TO WHERE THEY BURIED LAZARUS. A HUGE CROWD FOLLOWS THEM. THERE JESUS ASKS THEM TO ROLL AWAY THE STONE.

OH NO, LORD. HE'S BEEN DEAD FOR DAYS. THE SMELL WILL BE HORRIBLE.

BELIEVE IN ME.

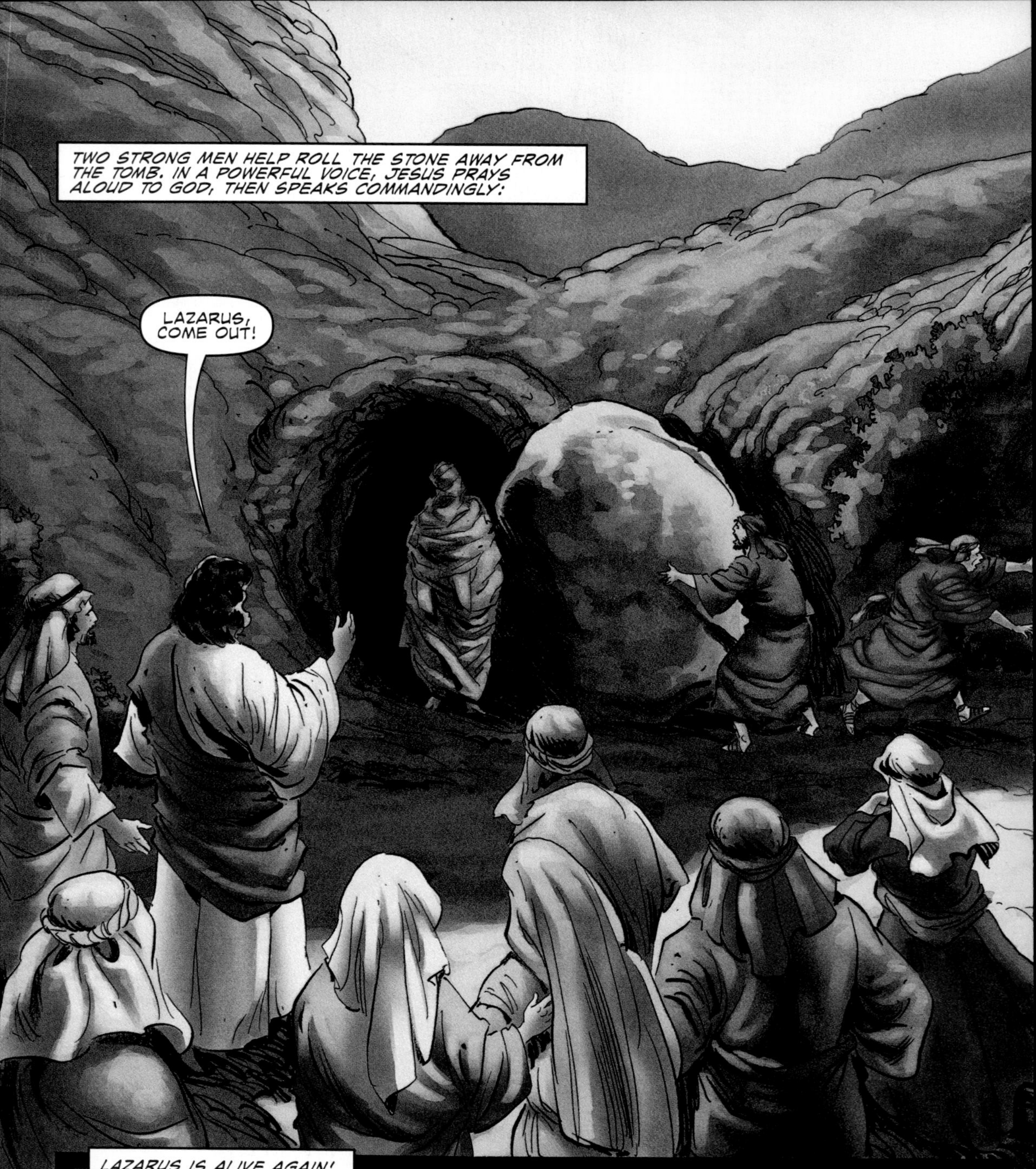
TWO STRONG MEN HELP ROLL THE STONE AWAY FROM THE TOMB. IN A POWERFUL VOICE, JESUS PRAYS ALOUD TO GOD, THEN SPEAKS COMMANDINGLY:
LAZARUS, COME OUT!

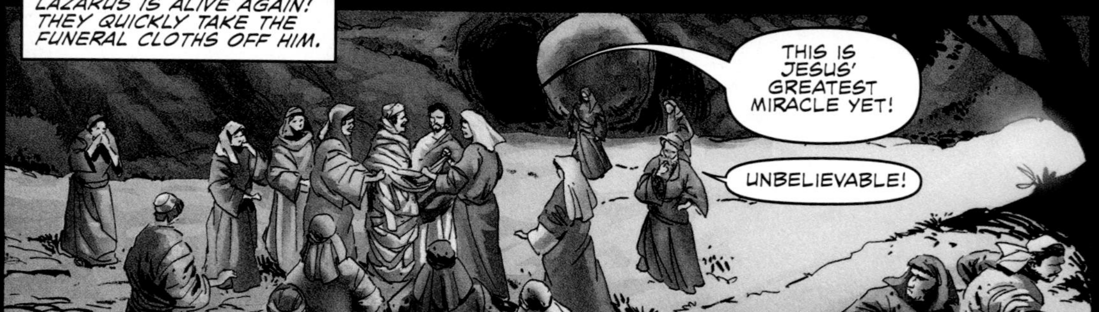
LAZARUS IS ALIVE AGAIN! THEY QUICKLY TAKE THE FUNERAL CLOTHS OFF HIM.
THIS IS JESUS' GREATEST MIRACLE YET!
UNBELIEVABLE!

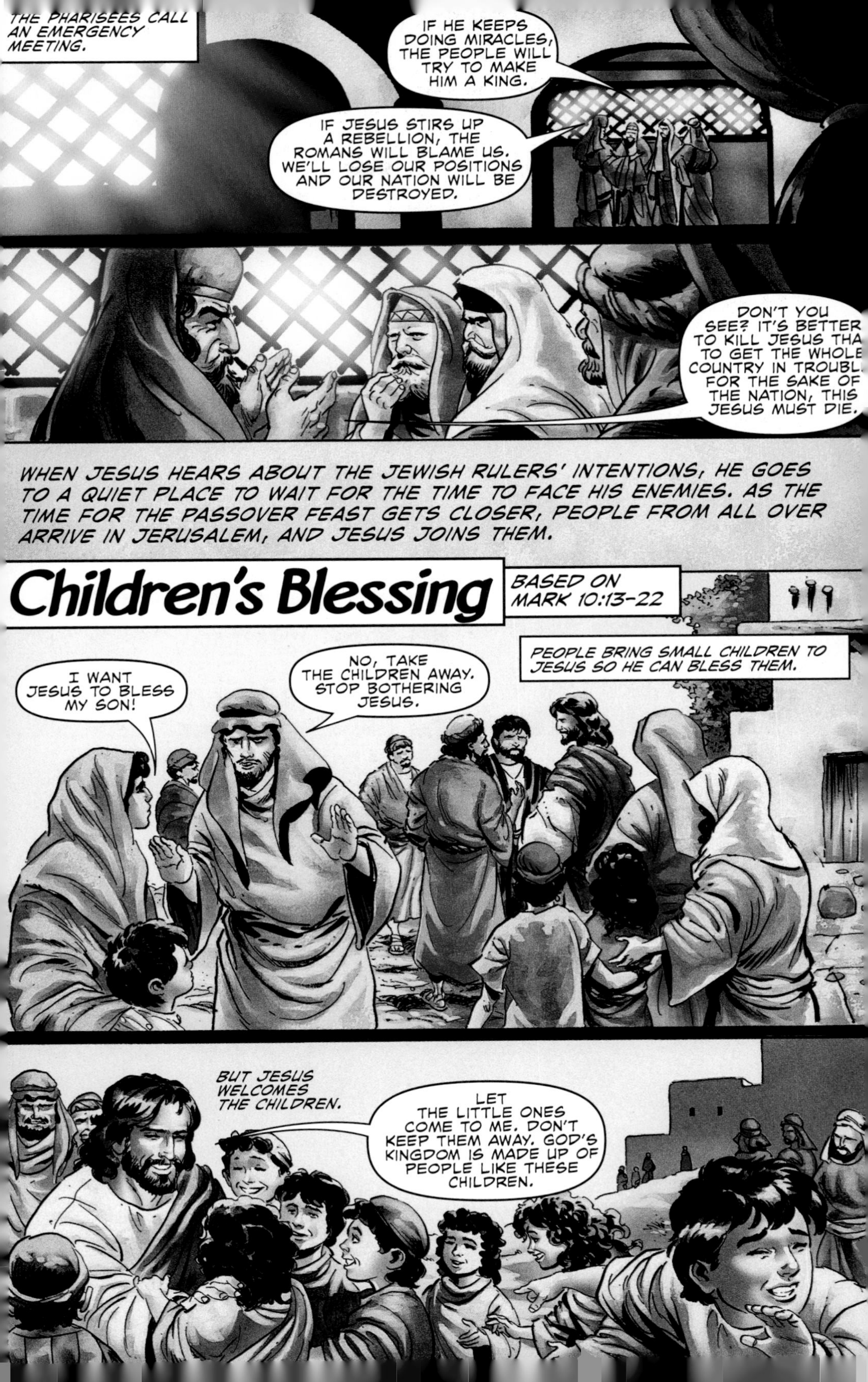
THE PHARISEES CALL AN EMERGENCY MEETING.
IF HE KEEPS DOING MIRACLES, THE PEOPLE WILL TRY TO MAKE HIM A KING.
IF JESUS STIRS UP A REBELLION, THE ROMANS WILL BLAME US. WE'LL LOSE OUR POSITIONS AND OUR NATION WILL BE DESTROYED.
DON'T YOU SEE? IT'S BETTER TO KILL JESUS THA TO GET THE WHOLE COUNTRY IN TROUBL. FOR THE SAKE OF THE NATION, THIS JESUS MUST DIE.
WHEN JESUS HEARS ABOUT THE JEWISH RULERS' INTENTIONS, HE GOES TO A QUIET PLACE TO WAIT FOR THE TIME TO FACE HIS ENEMIES. AS THE TIME FOR THE PASSOVER FEAST GETS CLOSER, PEOPLE FROM ALL OVER ARRIVE IN JERUSALEM, AND JESUS JOINS THEM.
Children's Blessing
BASED ON MARK 10:13-22
PEOPLE BRING SMALL CHILDREN TO JESUS SO HE CAN BLESS THEM.
I WANT JESUS TO BLESS MY SON!
NO, TAKE THE CHILDREN AWAY. STOP BOTHERING JESUS.
BUT JESUS WELCOMES THE CHILDREN.
LET THE LITTLE ONES COME TO ME. DON'T KEEP THEM AWAY. GOD'S KINGDOM IS MADE UP OF PEOPLE LIKE THESE CHILDREN.

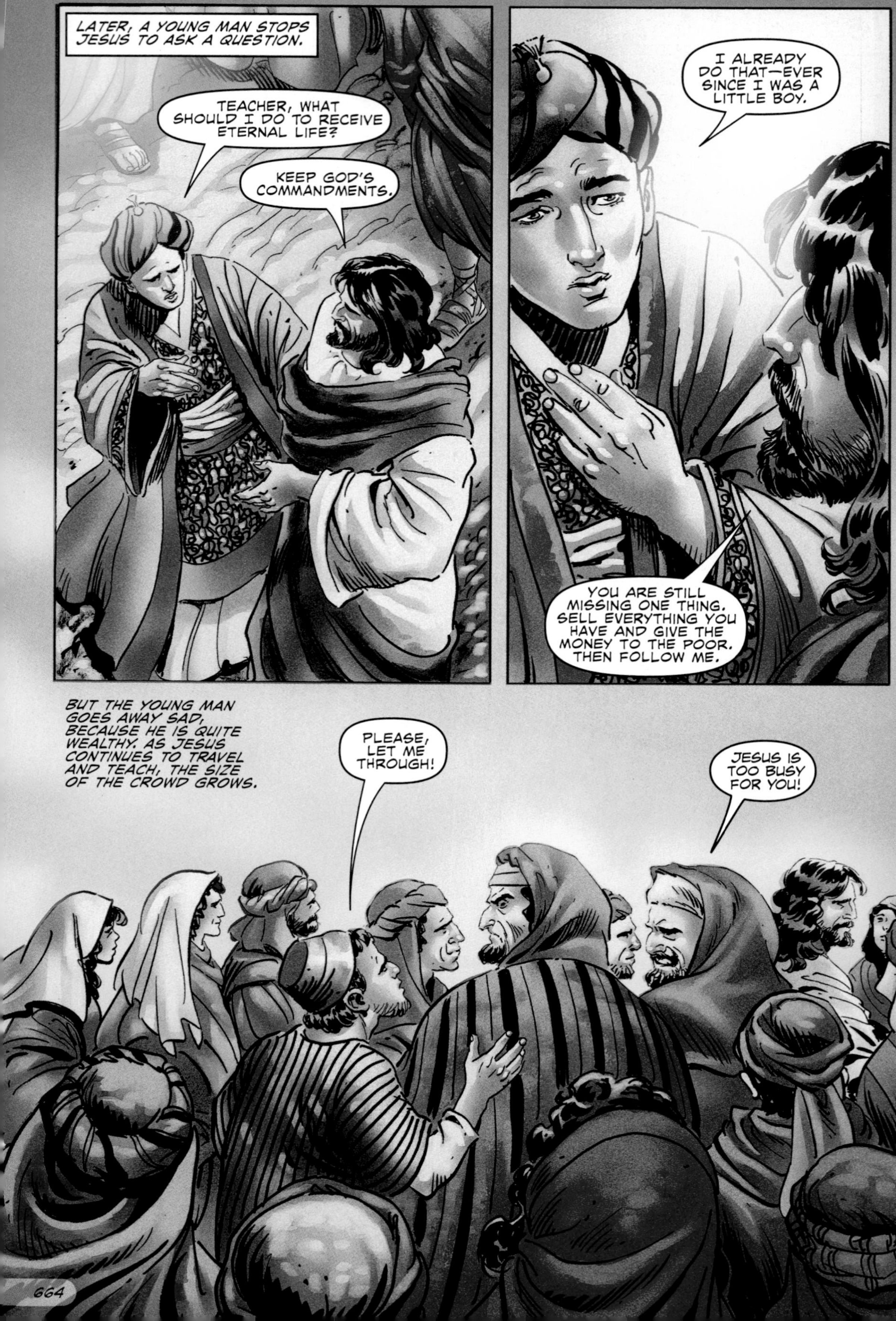
LATER, A YOUNG MAN STOPS JESUS TO ASK A QUESTION.
TEACHER, WHAT SHOULD I DO TO RECEIVE ETERNAL LIFE?
KEEP GOD'S COMMANDMENTS.
I ALREADY DO THAT—EVER SINCE I WAS A LITTLE BOY.
YOU ARE STILL MISSING ONE THING. SELL EVERYTHING YOU HAVE AND GIVE THE MONEY TO THE POOR. THEN FOLLOW ME.
BUT THE YOUNG MAN GOES AWAY SAD, BECAUSE HE IS QUITE WEALTHY. AS JESUS CONTINUES TO TRAVEL AND TEACH, THE SIZE OF THE CROWD GROWS.
PLEASE, LET ME THROUGH!
JESUS IS TOO BUSY FOR YOU!

en Sick Men

BASED ON LUKE 17:11–17

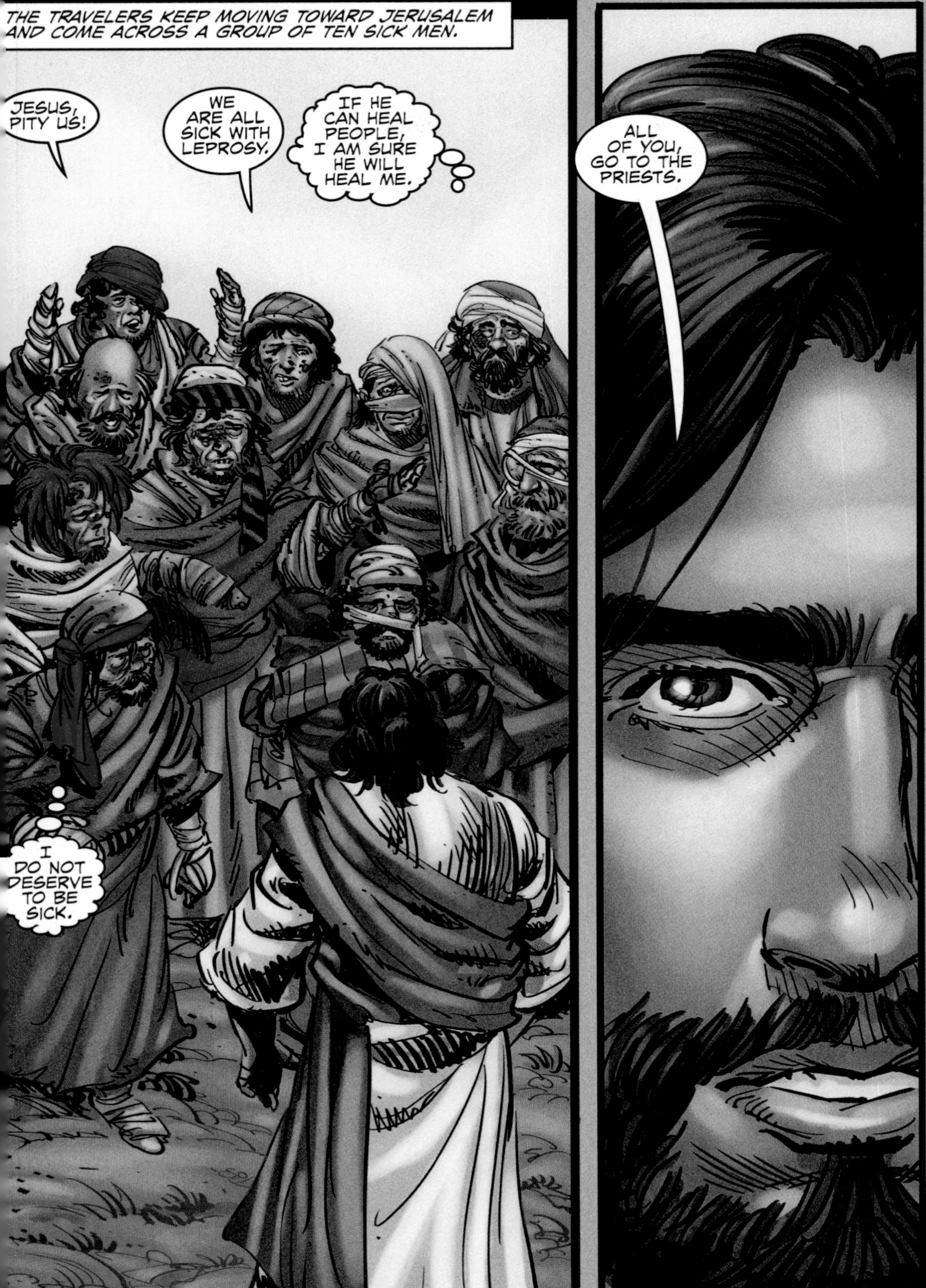
THE TRAVELERS KEEP MOVING TOWARD JERUSALEM AND COME ACROSS A GROUP OF TEN SICK MEN.
JESUS, PITY US!
WE ARE ALL SICK WITH LEPROSY.
IF HE CAN HEAL PEOPLE, I AM SURE HE WILL HEAL ME.
I DO NOT DESERVE TO BE SICK.
ALL OF YOU, GO TO THE PRIESTS.

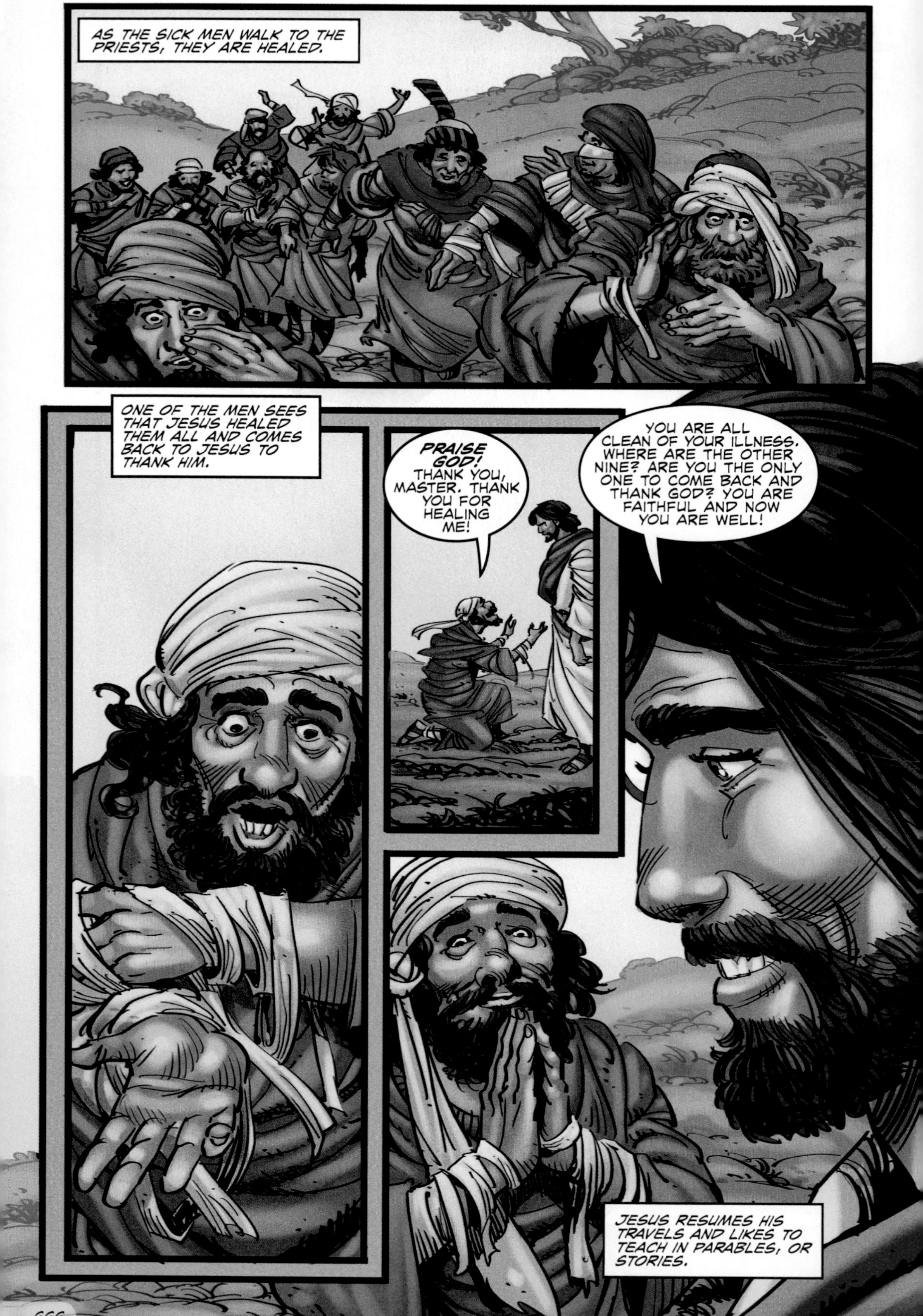

AS THE SICK MEN WALK TO THE PRIESTS, THEY ARE HEALED.
ONE OF THE MEN SEES THAT JESUS HEALED THEM ALL AND COMES BACK TO JESUS TO THANK HIM.
PRAISE GOD! THANK YOU, MASTER. THANK YOU FOR HEALING ME!
YOU ARE ALL CLEAN OF YOUR ILLNESS. WHERE ARE THE OTHER NINE? ARE YOU THE ONLY ONE TO COME BACK AND THANK GOD? YOU ARE FAITHFUL AND NOW YOU ARE WELL!
JESUS RESUMES HIS TRAVELS AND LIKES TO TEACH IN PARABLES, OR STORIES.

The Widow's Plea

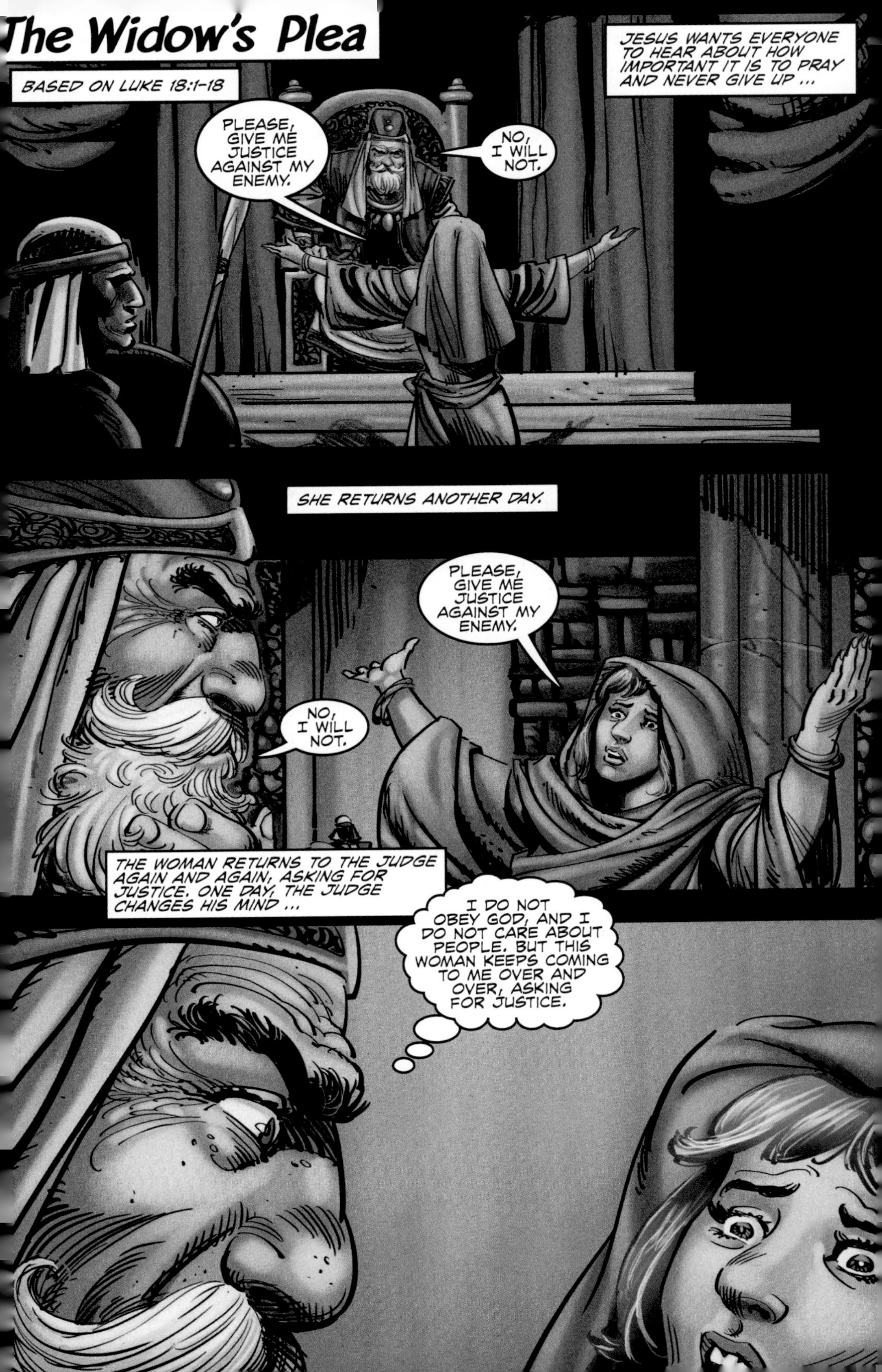
BASED ON LUKE 18:1–18
JESUS WANTS EVERYONE TO HEAR ABOUT HOW IMPORTANT IT IS TO PRAY AND NEVER GIVE UP ...
PLEASE, GIVE ME JUSTICE AGAINST MY ENEMY.
NO, I WILL NOT.
SHE RETURNS ANOTHER DAY.
PLEASE, GIVE ME JUSTICE AGAINST MY ENEMY.
NO, I WILL NOT.
THE WOMAN RETURNS TO THE JUDGE AGAIN AND AGAIN, ASKING FOR JUSTICE. ONE DAY, THE JUDGE CHANGES HIS MIND ...
I DO NOT OBEY GOD, AND I DO NOT CARE ABOUT PEOPLE. BUT THIS WOMAN KEEPS COMING TO ME OVER AND OVER, ASKING FOR JUSTICE.

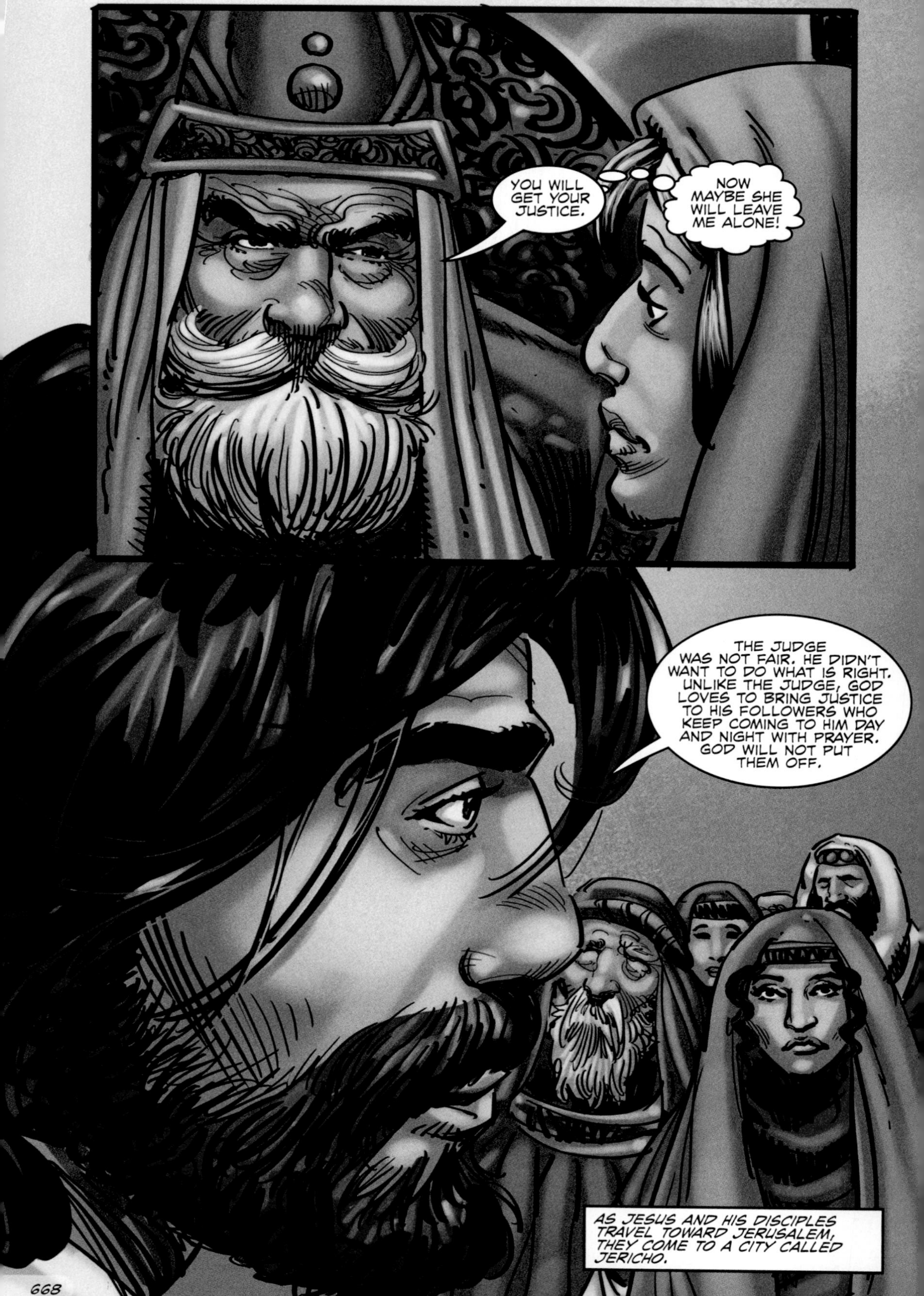
YOU WILL GET YOUR JUSTICE.
NOW MAYBE SHE WILL LEAVE ME ALONE!
THE JUDGE WAS NOT FAIR. HE DIDN'T WANT TO DO WHAT IS RIGHT. UNLIKE THE JUDGE, GOD LOVES TO BRING JUSTICE TO HIS FOLLOWERS WHO KEEP COMING TO HIM DAY AND NIGHT WITH PRAYER. GOD WILL NOT PUT THEM OFF.
AS JESUS AND HIS DISCIPLES TRAVEL TOWARD JERUSALEM, THEY COME TO A CITY CALLED JERICHO.

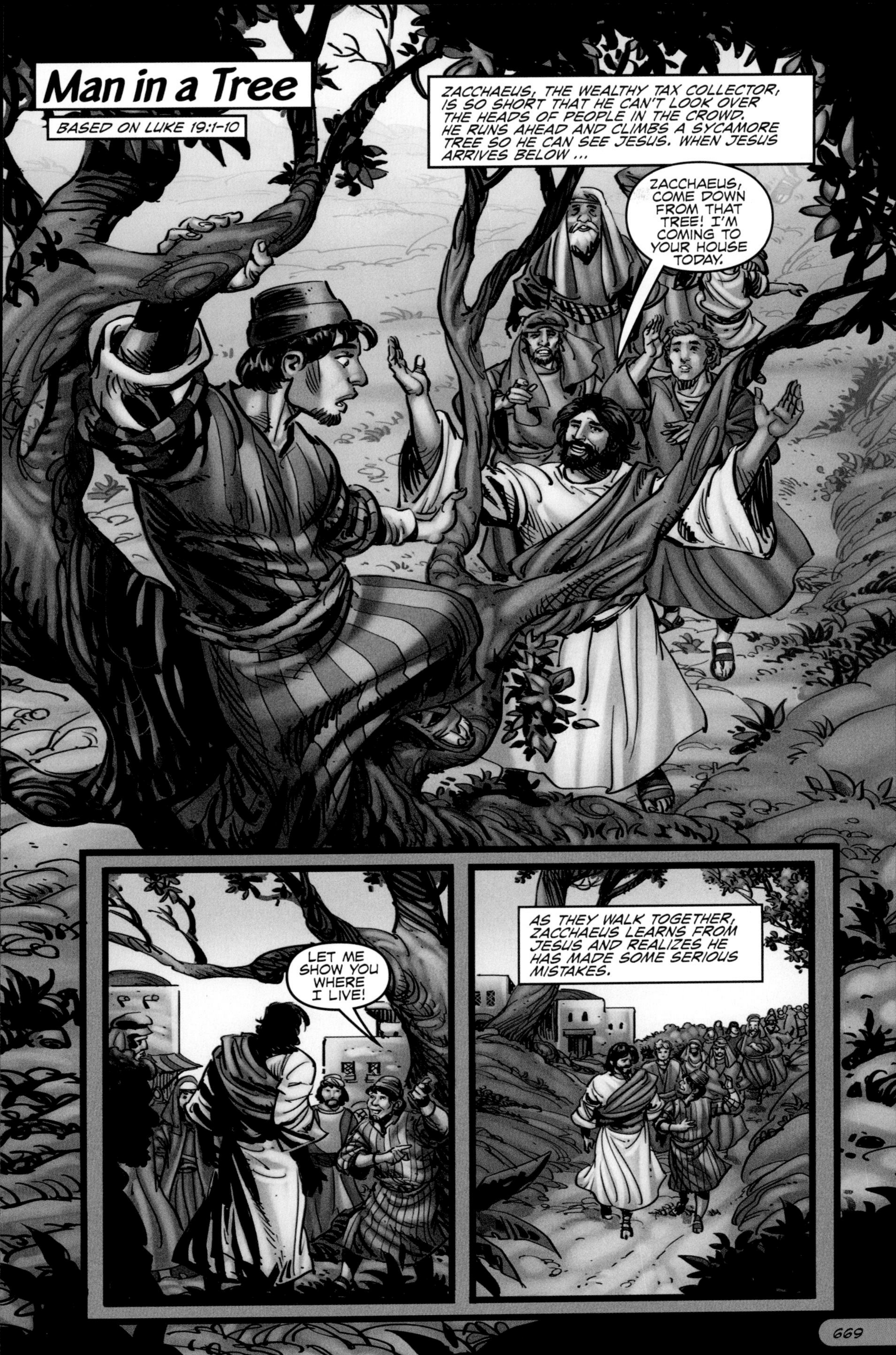
Man in a Tree
BASED ON LUKE 19:1–10
ZACCHAEUS, THE WEALTHY TAX COLLECTOR, IS SO SHORT THAT HE CAN'T LOOK OVER THE HEADS OF PEOPLE IN THE CROWD. HE RUNS AHEAD AND CLIMBS A SYCAMORE TREE SO HE CAN SEE JESUS. WHEN JESUS ARRIVES BELOW ...
ZACCHAEUS, COME DOWN FROM THAT TREE! I'M COMING TO YOUR HOUSE TODAY.
LET ME SHOW YOU WHERE I LIVE!
AS THEY WALK TOGETHER, ZACCHAEUS LEARNS FROM JESUS AND REALIZES HE HAS MADE SOME SERIOUS MISTAKES.

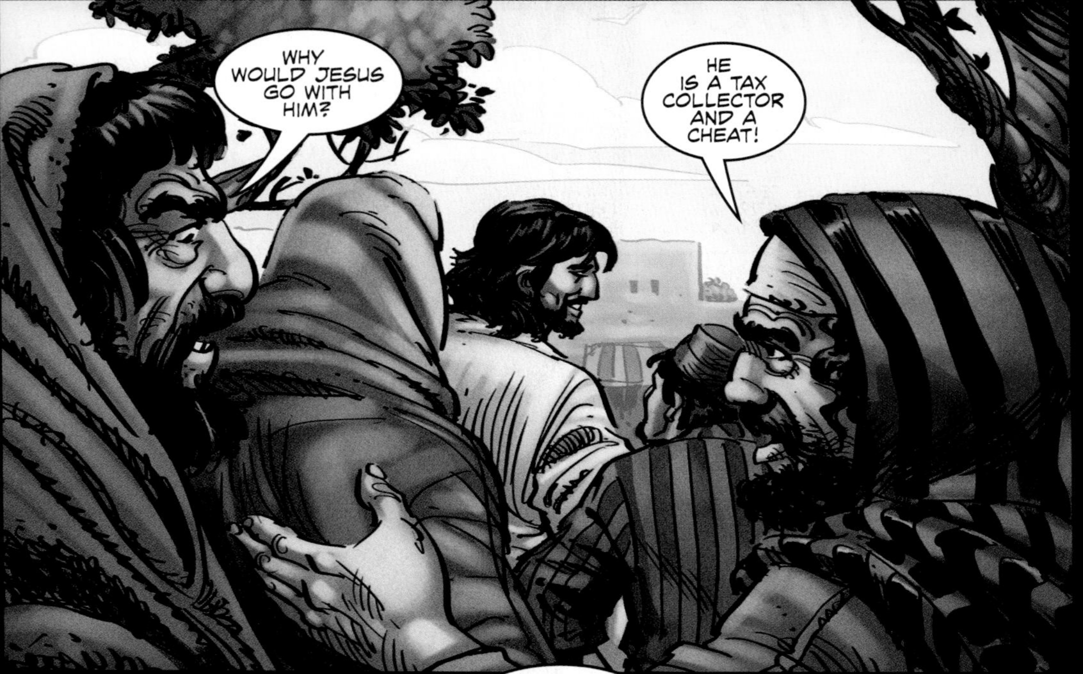
WHY WOULD JESUS GO WITH HIM?
HE IS A TAX COLLECTOR AND A CHEAT!

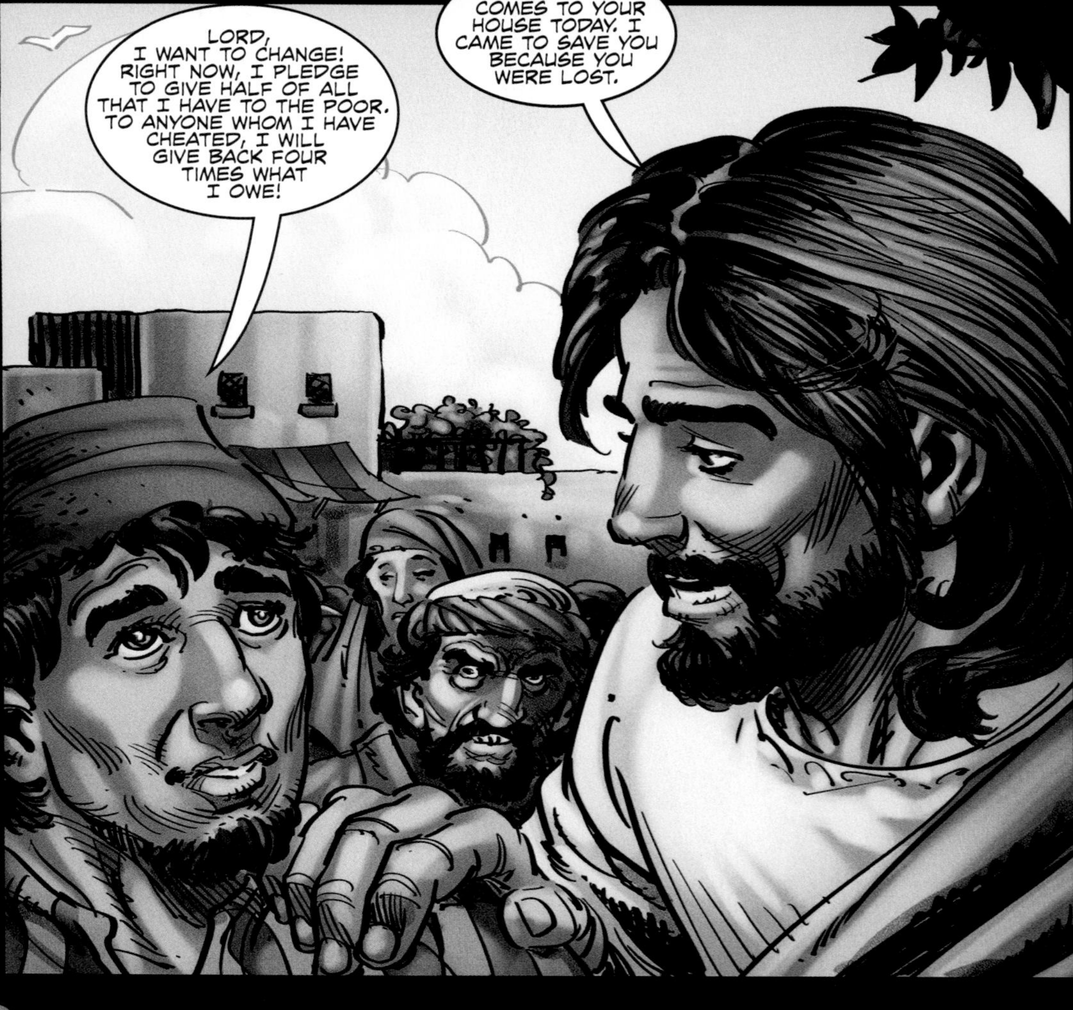
LORD, I WANT TO CHANGE! RIGHT NOW, I PLEDGE TO GIVE HALF OF ALL THAT I HAVE TO THE POOR. TO ANYONE WHOM I HAVE CHEATED, I WILL GIVE BACK FOUR TIMES WHAT I OWE!
SALVATION COMES TO YOUR HOUSE TODAY. I CAME TO SAVE YOU BECAUSE YOU WERE LOST.

Woman with Oils

BASED ON JOHN 12:1–8

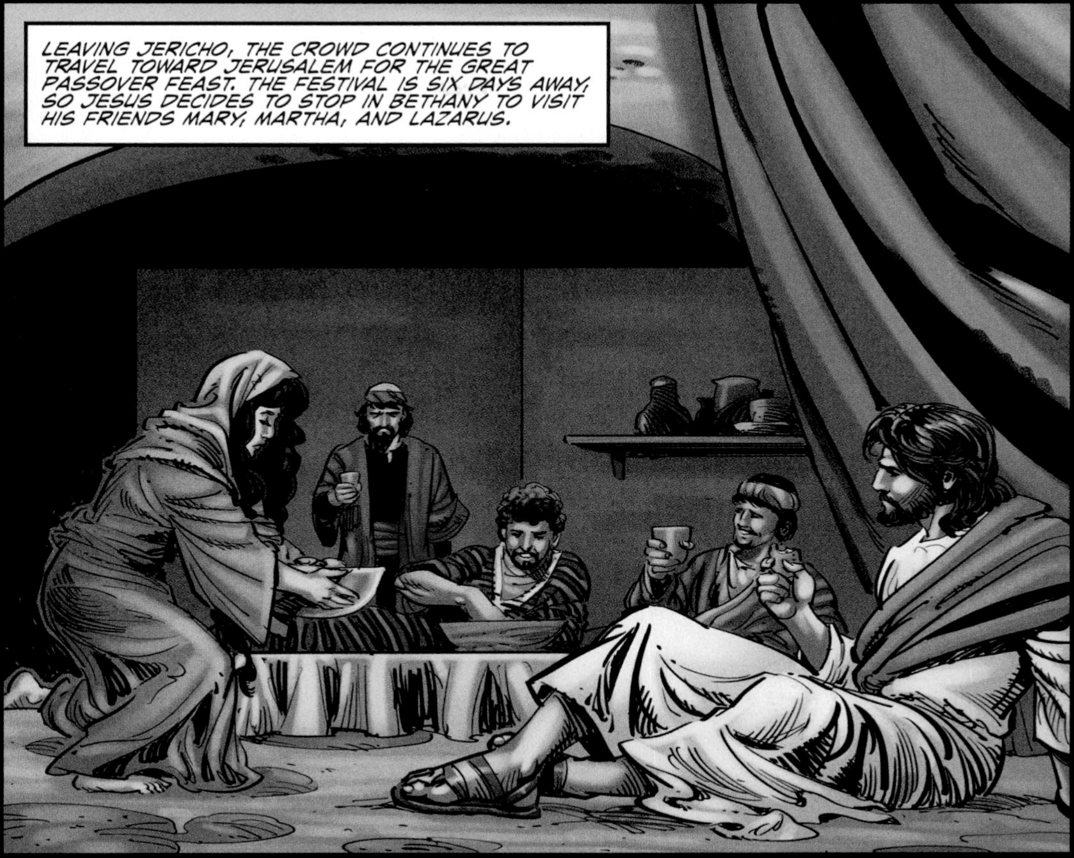

LEAVING JERICHO, THE CROWD CONTINUES TO TRAVEL TOWARD JERUSALEM FOR THE GREAT PASSOVER FEAST. THE FESTIVAL IS SIX DAYS AWAY, SO JESUS DECIDES TO STOP IN BETHANY TO VISIT HIS FRIENDS MARY, MARTHA, AND LAZARUS.

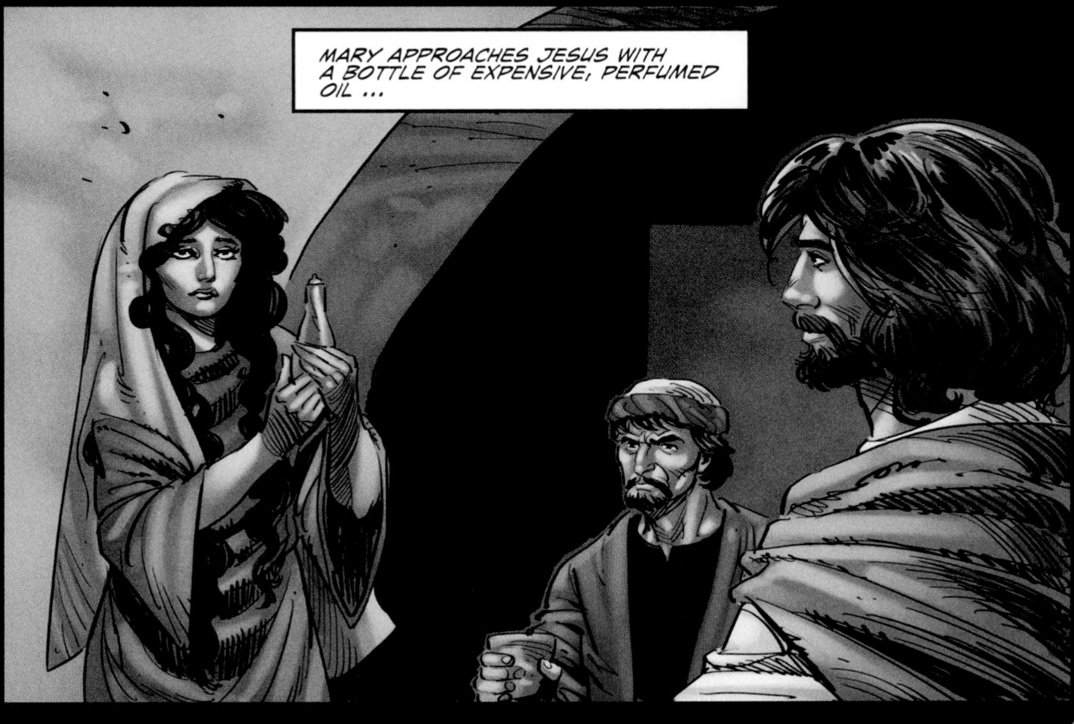

MARY APPROACHES JESUS WITH A BOTTLE OF EXPENSIVE, PERFUMED OIL ...

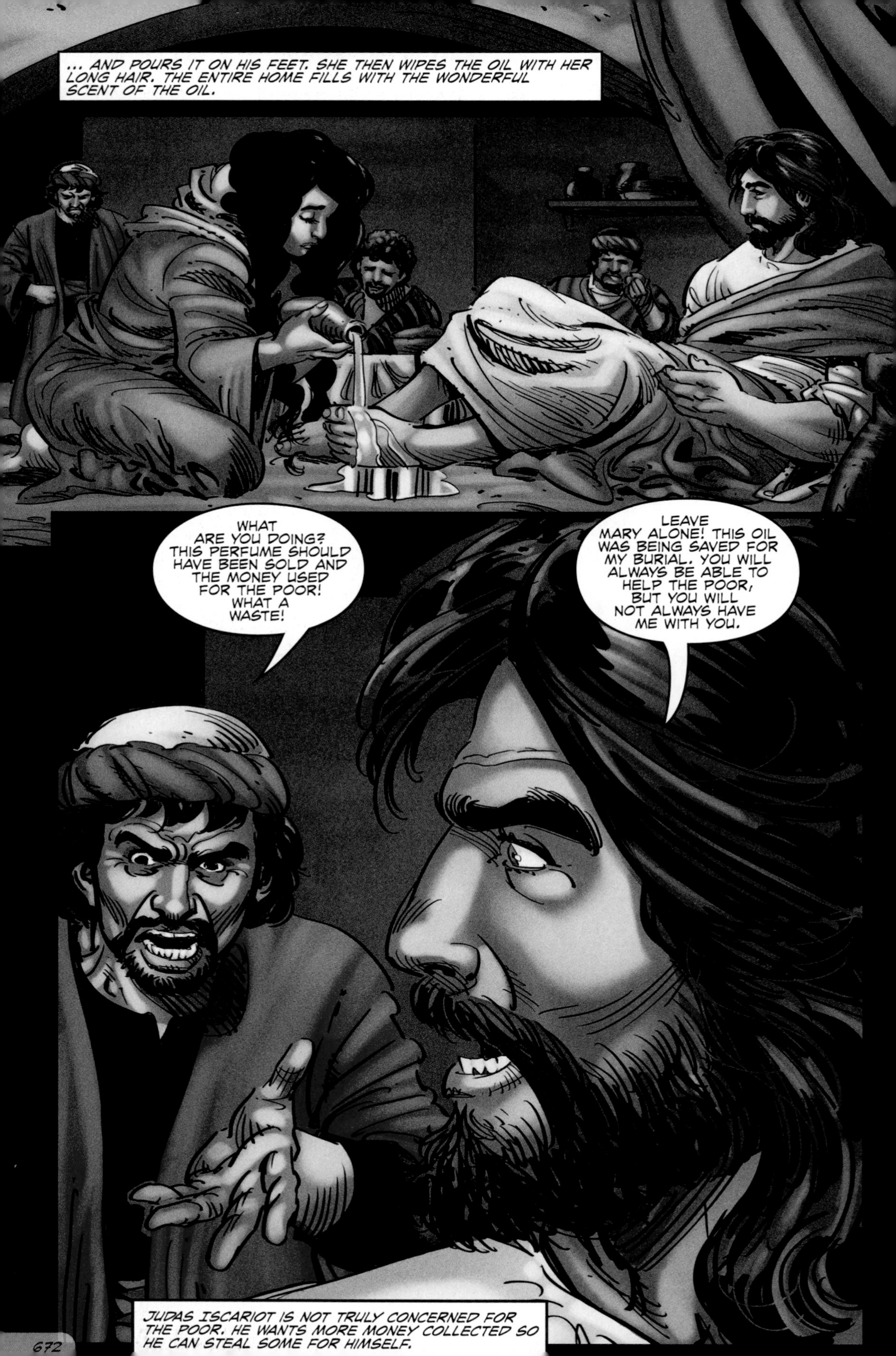
... AND POURS IT ON HIS FEET. SHE THEN WIPES THE OIL WITH HER LONG HAIR. THE ENTIRE HOME FILLS WITH THE WONDERFUL SCENT OF THE OIL.
WHAT ARE YOU DOING? THIS PERFUME SHOULD HAVE BEEN SOLD AND THE MONEY USED FOR THE POOR! WHAT A WASTE!
LEAVE MARY ALONE! THIS OIL WAS BEING SAVED FOR MY BURIAL. YOU WILL ALWAYS BE ABLE TO HELP THE POOR, BUT YOU WILL NOT ALWAYS HAVE ME WITH YOU.
JUDAS ISCARIOT IS NOT TRULY CONCERNED FOR THE POOR. HE WANTS MORE MONEY COLLECTED SO HE CAN STEAL SOME FOR HIMSELF.

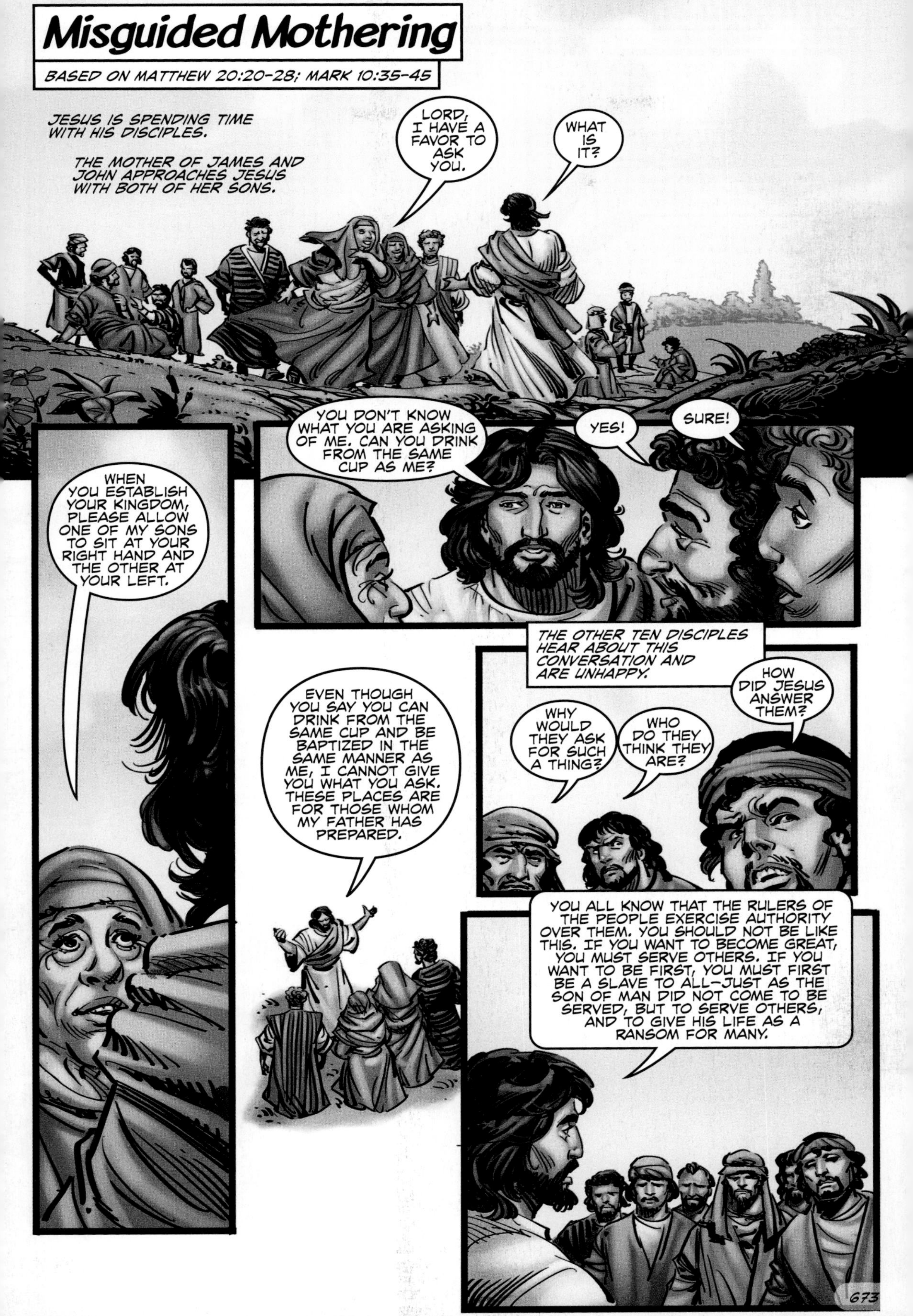
Misguided Mothering
BASED ON MATTHEW 20:20-28; MARK 10:35-45
JESUS IS SPENDING TIME WITH HIS DISCIPLES.
THE MOTHER OF JAMES AND JOHN APPROACHES JESUS WITH BOTH OF HER SONS.
LORD, I HAVE A FAVOR TO ASK YOU.
WHAT IS IT?
WHEN YOU ESTABLISH YOUR KINGDOM, PLEASE ALLOW ONE OF MY SONS TO SIT AT YOUR RIGHT HAND AND THE OTHER AT YOUR LEFT.
YOU DON'T KNOW WHAT YOU ARE ASKING OF ME. CAN YOU DRINK FROM THE SAME CUP AS ME?
YES!
SURE!
EVEN THOUGH YOU SAY YOU CAN DRINK FROM THE SAME CUP AND BE BAPTIZED IN THE SAME MANNER AS ME, I CANNOT GIVE YOU WHAT YOU ASK. THESE PLACES ARE FOR THOSE WHOM MY FATHER HAS PREPARED.
THE OTHER TEN DISCIPLES HEAR ABOUT THIS CONVERSATION AND ARE UNHAPPY.
WHY WOULD THEY ASK FOR SUCH A THING?
WHO DO THEY THINK THEY ARE?
HOW DID JESUS ANSWER THEM?
YOU ALL KNOW THAT THE RULERS OF THE PEOPLE EXERCISE AUTHORITY OVER THEM. YOU SHOULD NOT BE LIKE THIS. IF YOU WANT TO BECOME GREAT, YOU MUST SERVE OTHERS. IF YOU WANT TO BE FIRST, YOU MUST FIRST BE A SLAVE TO ALL—JUST AS THE SON OF MAN DID NOT COME TO BE SERVED, BUT TO SERVE OTHERS, AND TO GIVE HIS LIFE AS A RANSOM FOR MANY.

Blind Bartimaeus

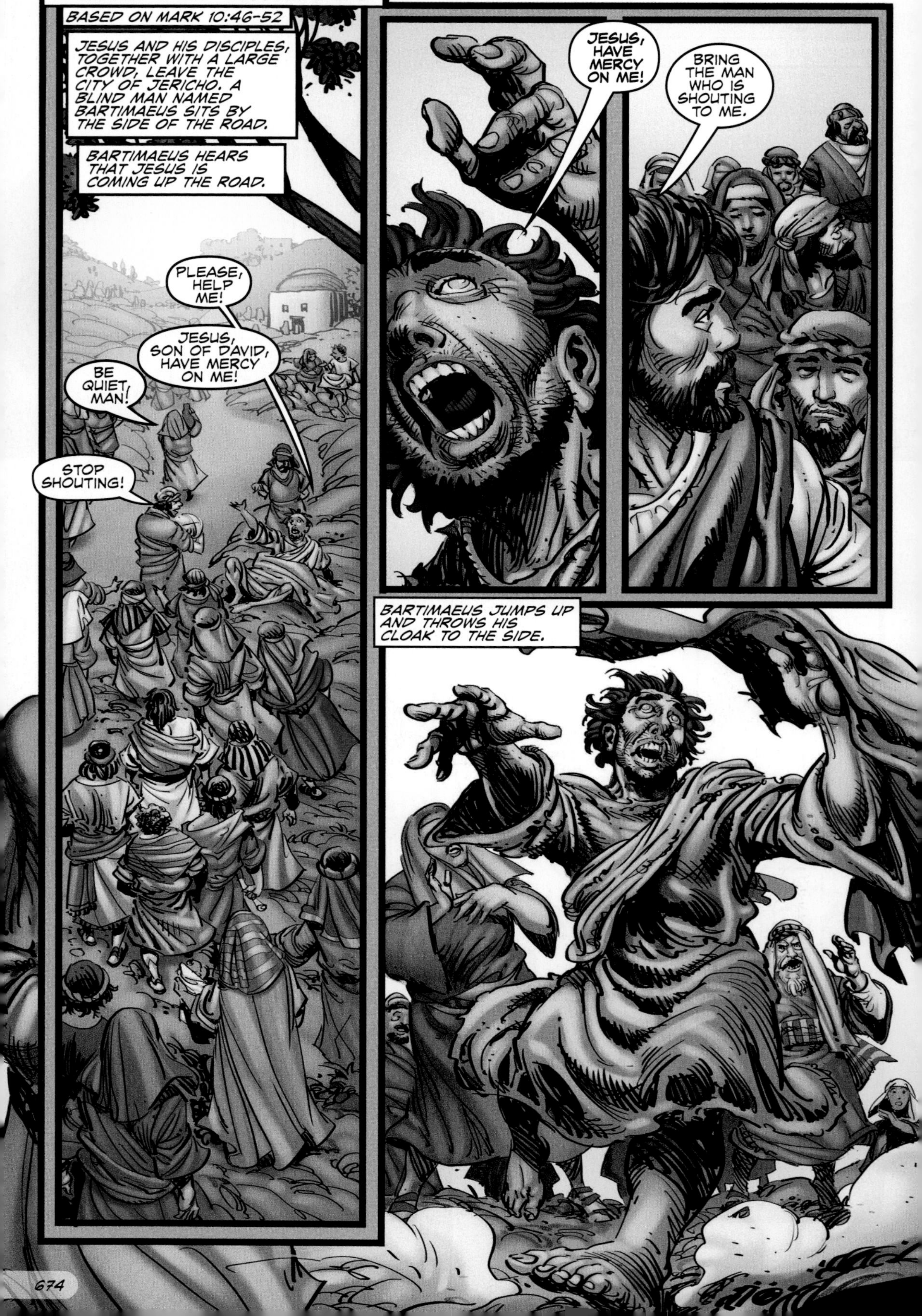
BASED ON MARK 10:46-52
JESUS AND HIS DISCIPLES, TOGETHER WITH A LARGE CROWD, LEAVE THE CITY OF JERICHO. A BLIND MAN NAMED BARTIMAEUS SITS BY THE SIDE OF THE ROAD.
BARTIMAEUS HEARS THAT JESUS IS COMING UP THE ROAD.
PLEASE, HELP ME!
JESUS, SON OF DAVID, HAVE MERCY ON ME!
BE QUIET MAN!
STOP SHOUTING!
JESUS, HAVE MERCY ON ME!
BRING THE MAN WHO IS SHOUTING TO ME.
BARTIMAEUS JUMPS UP AND THROWS HIS CLOAK TO THE SIDE.

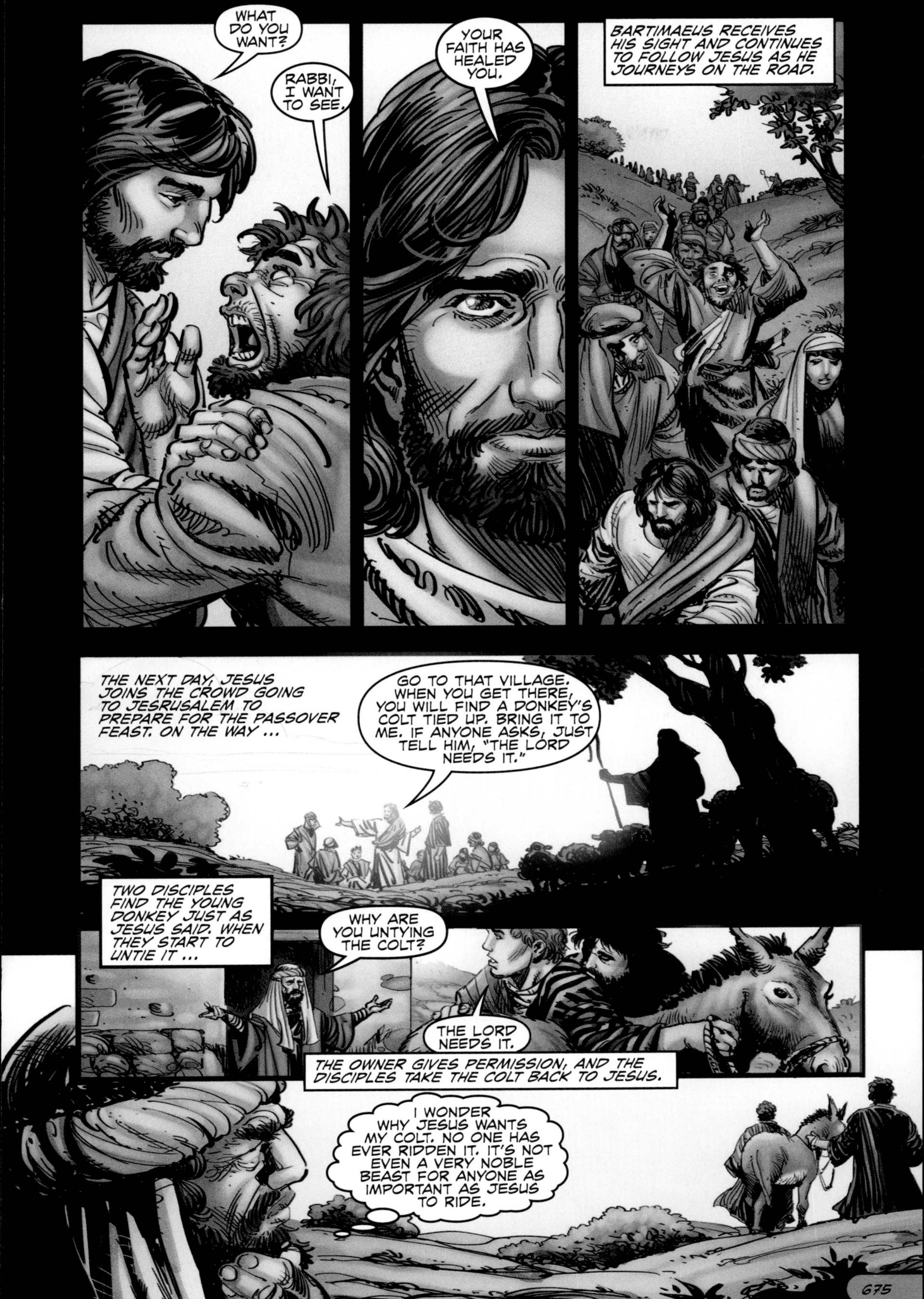
WHAT DO YOU WANT?
RABBI, I WANT TO SEE.
YOUR FAITH HAS HEALED YOU.
BARTIMAEUS RECEIVES HIS SIGHT AND CONTINUES TO FOLLOW JESUS AS HE JOURNEYS ON THE ROAD.
THE NEXT DAY, JESUS JOINS THE CROWD GOING TO JESRUSALEM TO PREPARE FOR THE PASSOVER FEAST. ON THE WAY ...
GO TO THAT VILLAGE. WHEN YOU GET THERE, YOU WILL FIND A DONKEY'S COLT TIED UP. BRING IT TO ME. IF ANYONE ASKS, JUST TELL HIM, "THE LORD NEEDS IT."
TWO DISCIPLES FIND THE YOUNG DONKEY JUST AS JESUS SAID. WHEN THEY START TO UNTIE IT ...
WHY ARE YOU UNTYING THE COLT?
THE LORD NEEDS IT.
THE OWNER GIVES PERMISSION, AND THE DISCIPLES TAKE THE COLT BACK TO JESUS.
I WONDER WHY JESUS WANTS MY COLT. NO ONE HAS EVER RIDDEN IT. IT'S NOT EVEN A VERY NOBLE BEAST FOR ANYONE AS IMPORTANT AS JESUS TO RIDE.

Palm Sunday

BASED ON LUKE 19:36-46;
MATTHEW 21:8-17

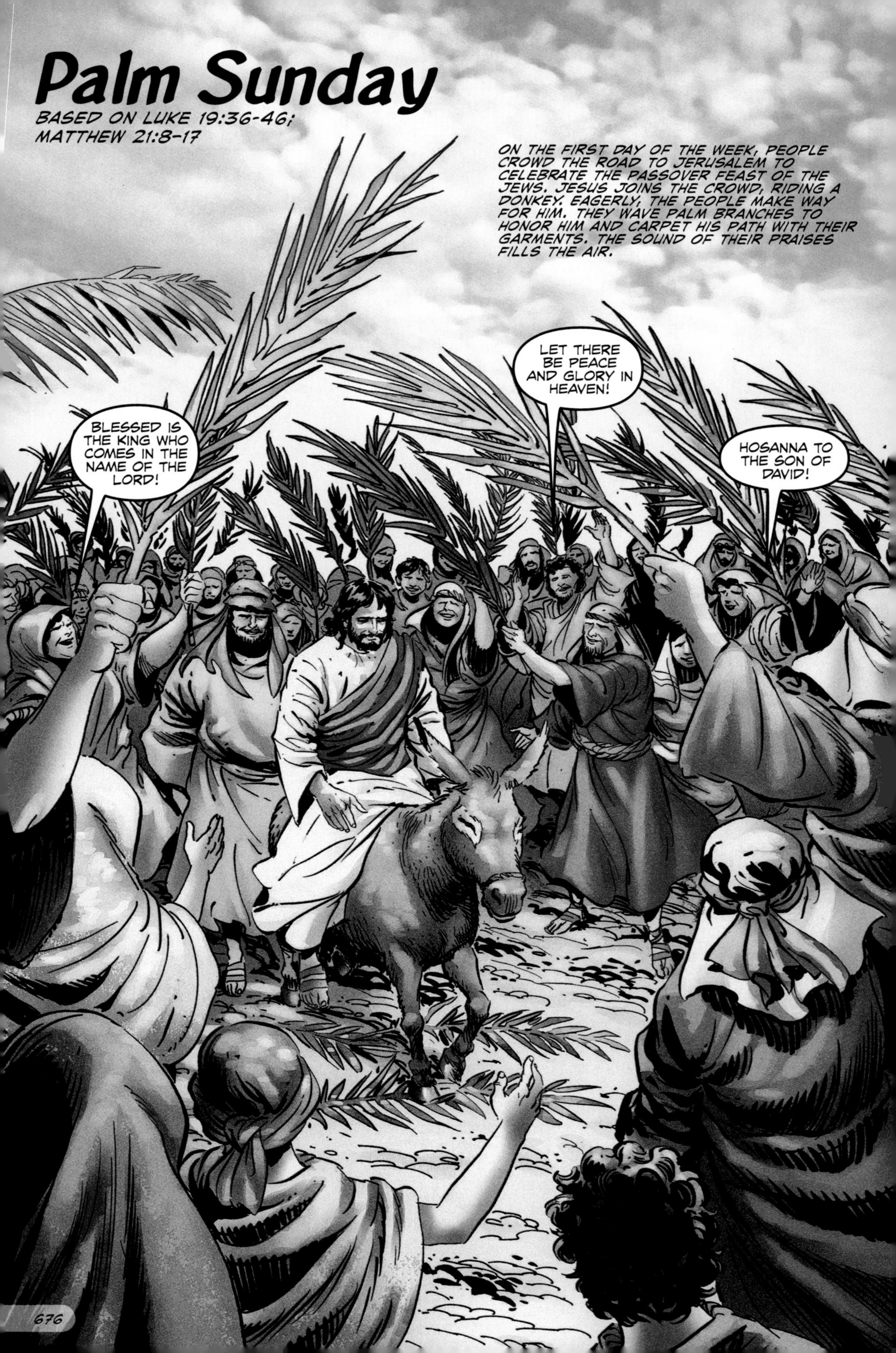
ON THE FIRST DAY OF THE WEEK, PEOPLE CROWD THE ROAD TO JERUSALEM TO CELEBRATE THE PASSOVER FEAST OF THE JEWS. JESUS JOINS THE CROWD, RIDING A DONKEY. EAGERLY, THE PEOPLE MAKE WAY FOR HIM. THEY WAVE PALM BRANCHES TO HONOR HIM AND CARPET HIS PATH WITH THEIR GARMENTS. THE SOUND OF THEIR PRAISES FILLS THE AIR.
BLESSED IS THE KING WHO COMES IN THE NAME OF THE LORD!
LET THERE BE PEACE AND GLORY IN HEAVEN!
HOSANNA TO THE SON OF DAVID!

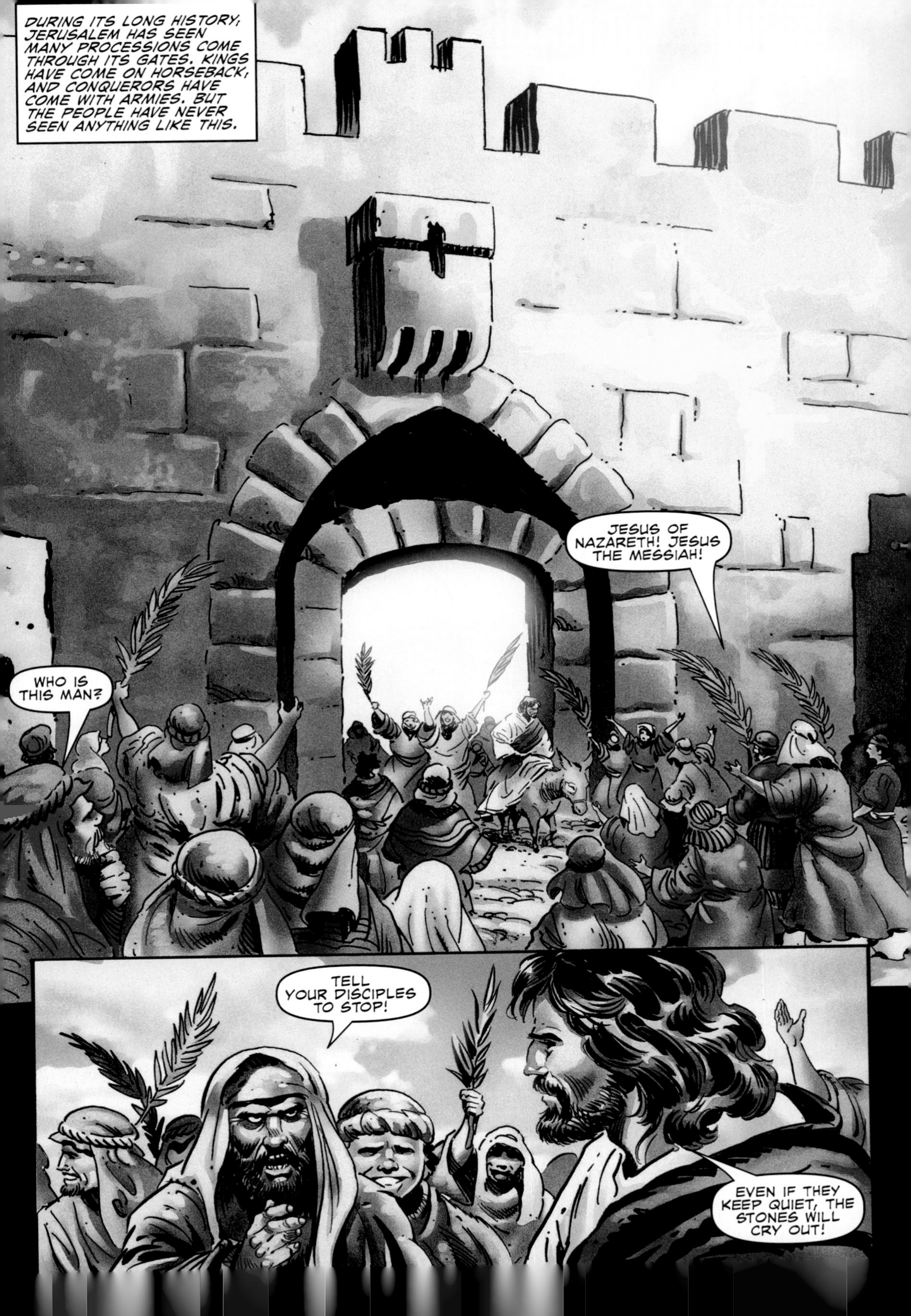
DURING ITS LONG HISTORY, JERUSALEM HAS SEEN MANY PROCESSIONS COME THROUGH ITS GATES. KINGS HAVE COME ON HORSEBACK, AND CONQUERORS HAVE COME WITH ARMIES. BUT THE PEOPLE HAVE NEVER SEEN ANYTHING LIKE THIS.
JESUS OF NAZARETH! JESUS THE MESSIAH!
WHO IS THIS MAN?
TELL YOUR DISCIPLES TO STOP!
EVEN IF THEY KEEP QUIET, THE STONES WILL CRY OUT!

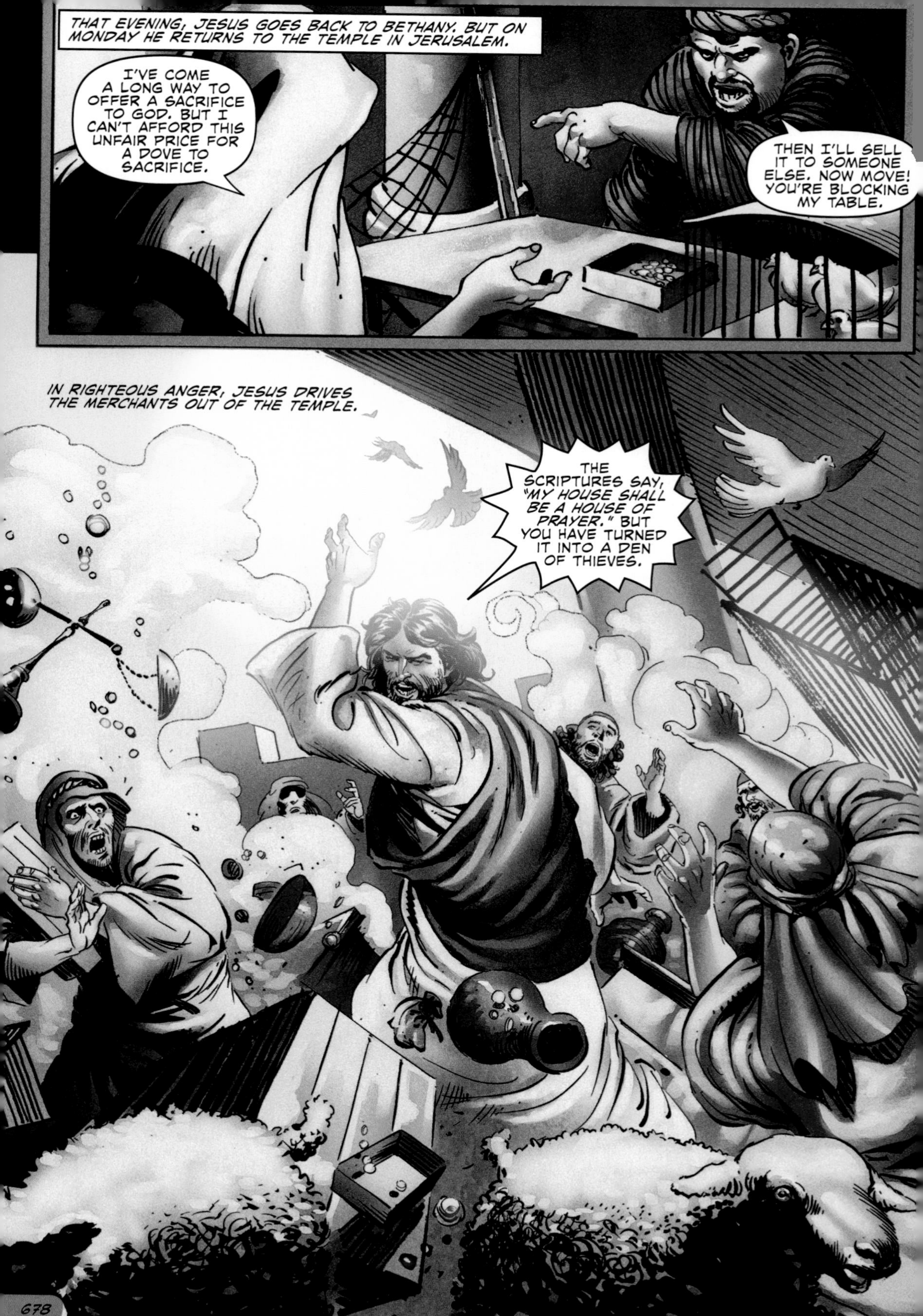

THAT EVENING, JESUS GOES BACK TO BETHANY. BUT ON MONDAY HE RETURNS TO THE TEMPLE IN JERUSALEM.
I'VE COME A LONG WAY TO OFFER A SACRIFICE TO GOD. BUT I CAN'T AFFORD THIS UNFAIR PRICE FOR A DOVE TO SACRIFICE.
THEN I'LL SELL IT TO SOMEONE ELSE. NOW MOVE! YOU'RE BLOCKING MY TABLE.
IN RIGHTEOUS ANGER, JESUS DRIVES THE MERCHANTS OUT OF THE TEMPLE.
THE SCRIPTURES SAY, "MY HOUSE SHALL BE A HOUSE OF PRAYER." BUT YOU HAVE TURNED IT INTO A DEN OF THIEVES.

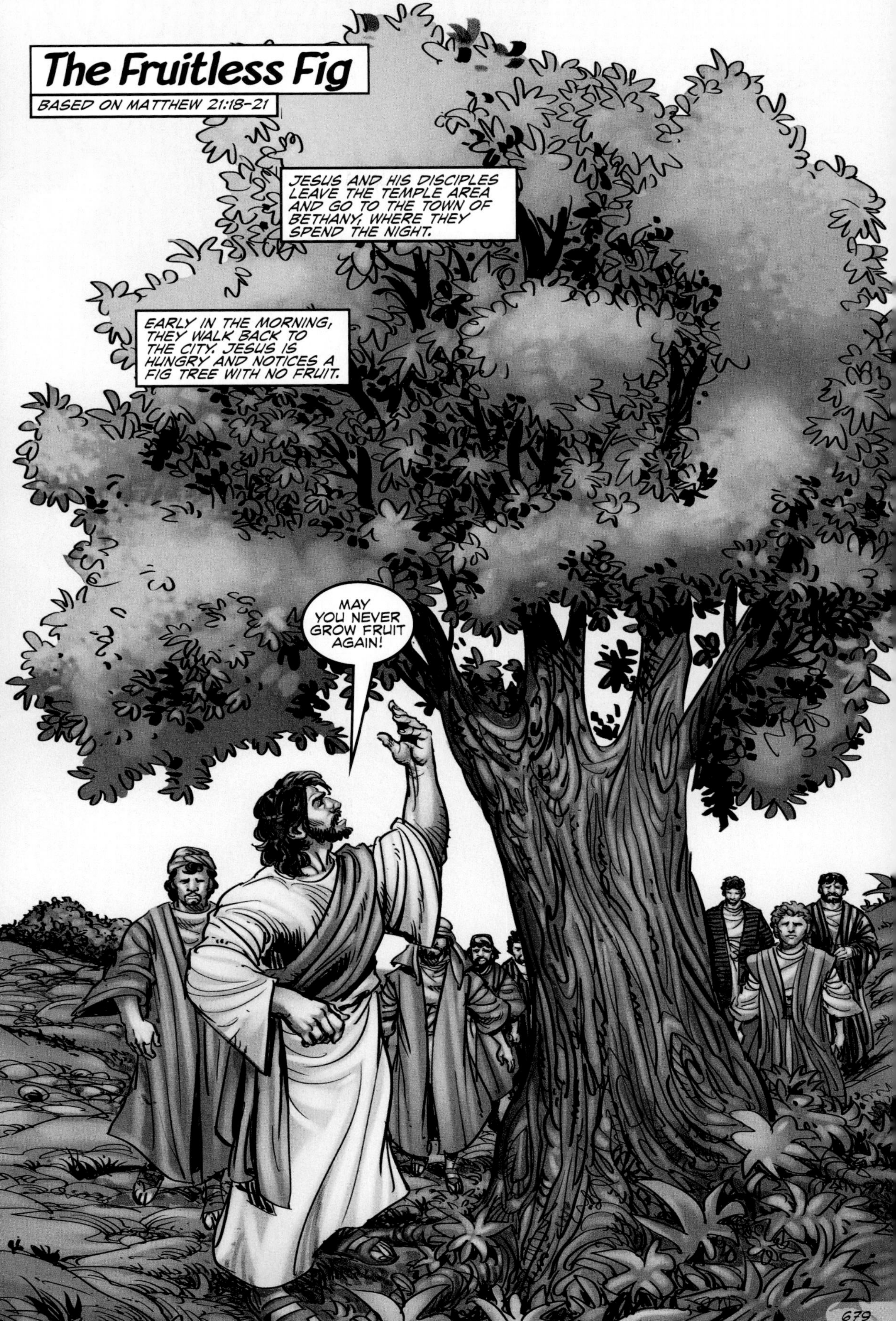
The Fruitless Fig
BASED ON MATTHEW 21:18–21
JESUS AND HIS DISCIPLES LEAVE THE TEMPLE AREA AND GO TO THE TOWN OF BETHANY, WHERE THEY SPEND THE NIGHT.
EARLY IN THE MORNING, THEY WALK BACK TO THE CITY. JESUS IS HUNGRY AND NOTICES A FIG TREE WITH NO FRUIT.
MAY YOU NEVER GROW FRUIT AGAIN!

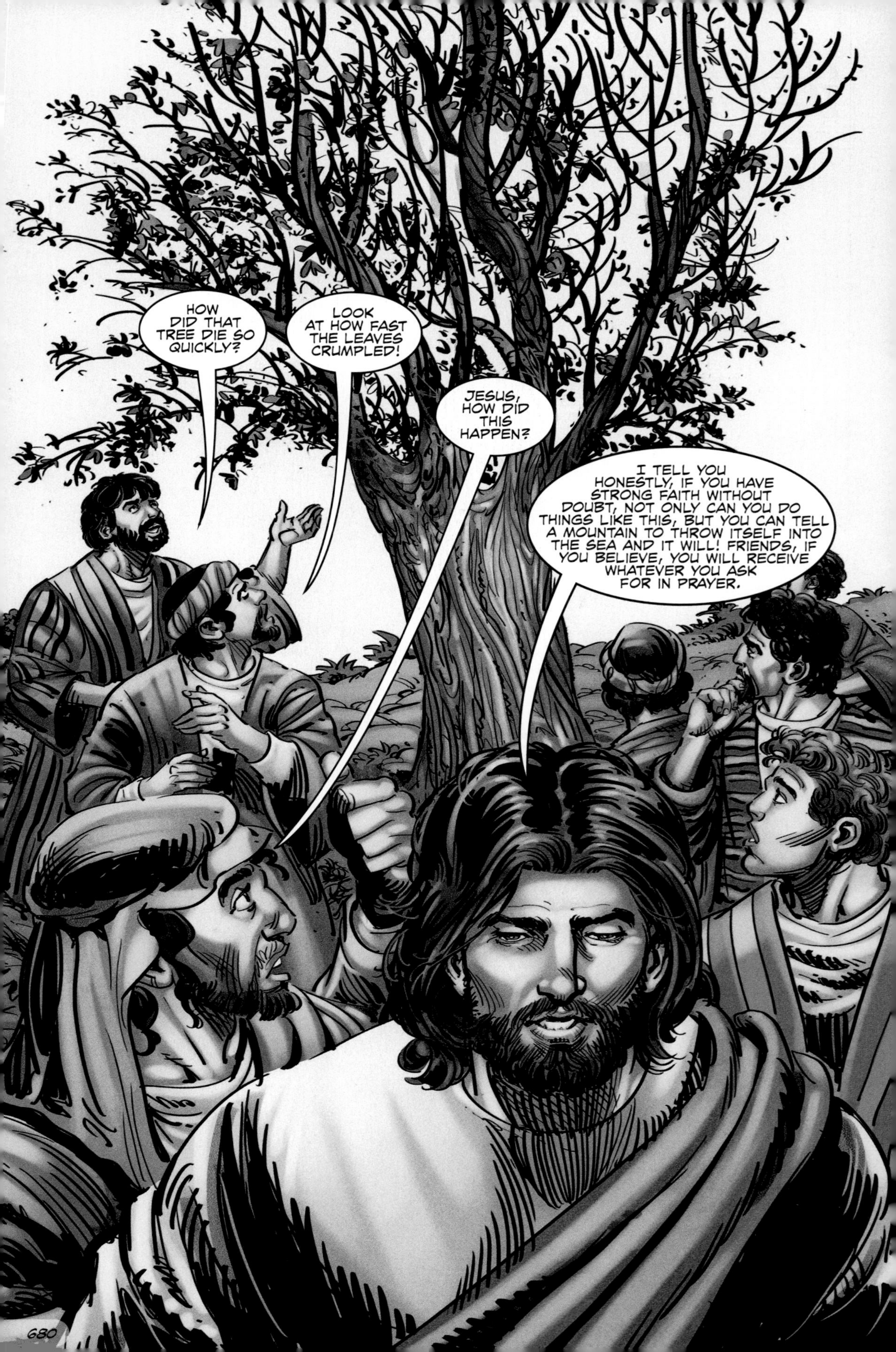
HOW DID THAT TREE DIE SO QUICKLY?
LOOK AT HOW FAST THE LEAVES CRUMPLED!
JESUS, HOW DID THIS HAPPEN?
I TELL YOU HONESTLY, IF YOU HAVE STRONG FAITH WITHOUT DOUBT, NOT ONLY CAN YOU DO THINGS LIKE THIS, BUT YOU CAN TELL A MOUNTAIN TO THROW ITSELF INTO THE SEA AND IT WILL! FRIENDS, IF YOU BELIEVE, YOU WILL RECEIVE WHATEVER YOU ASK FOR IN PRAYER.

Money Troubles

BASED ON LUKE 20:20-26; MARK 12:12-44; MATTHEW 22:15-22

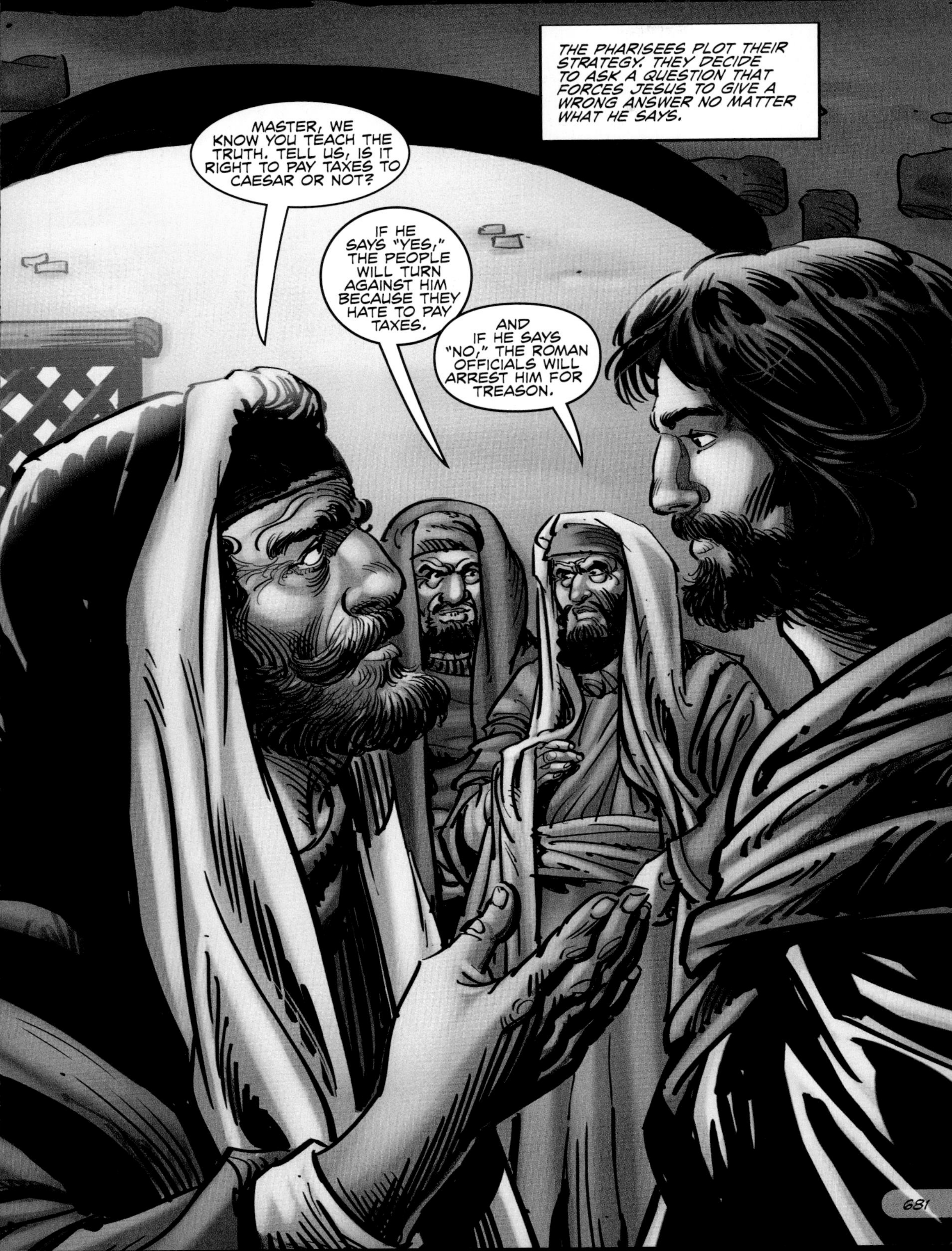

THE PHARISEES PLOT THEIR STRATEGY. THEY DECIDE TO ASK A QUESTION THAT FORCES JESUS TO GIVE A WRONG ANSWER NO MATTER WHAT HE SAYS.
MASTER, WE KNOW YOU TEACH THE TRUTH. TELL US, IS IT RIGHT TO PAY TAXES TO CAESAR OR NOT?
IF HE SAYS "YES," THE PEOPLE WILL TURN AGAINST HIM BECAUSE THEY HATE TO PAY TAXES.
AND IF HE SAYS "NO," THE ROMAN OFFICIALS WILL ARREST HIM FOR TREASON.

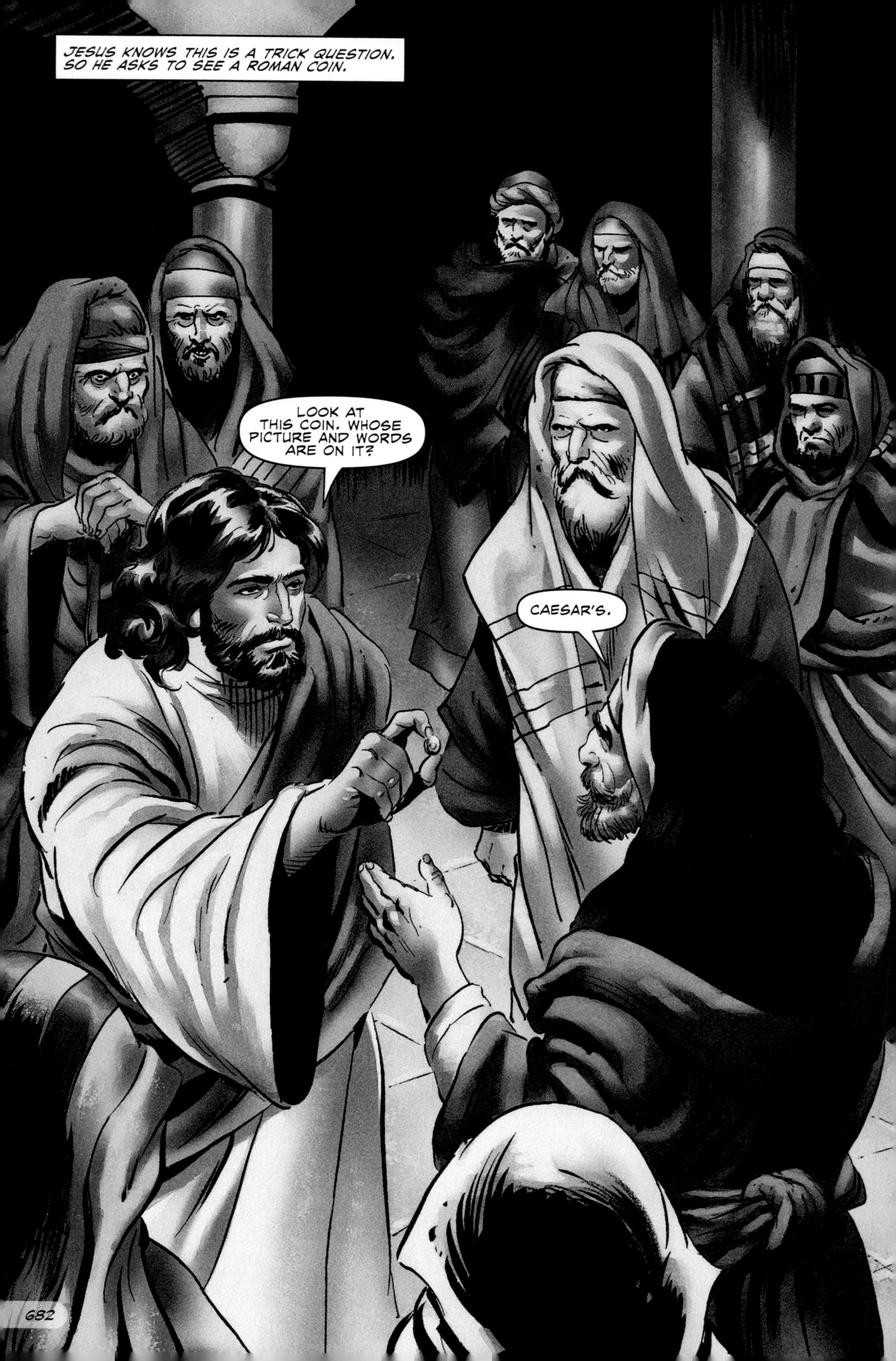
JESUS KNOWS THIS IS A TRICK QUESTION. SO HE ASKS TO SEE A ROMAN COIN.
LOOK AT THIS COIN. WHOSE PICTURE AND WORDS ARE ON IT?
CAESAR'S.

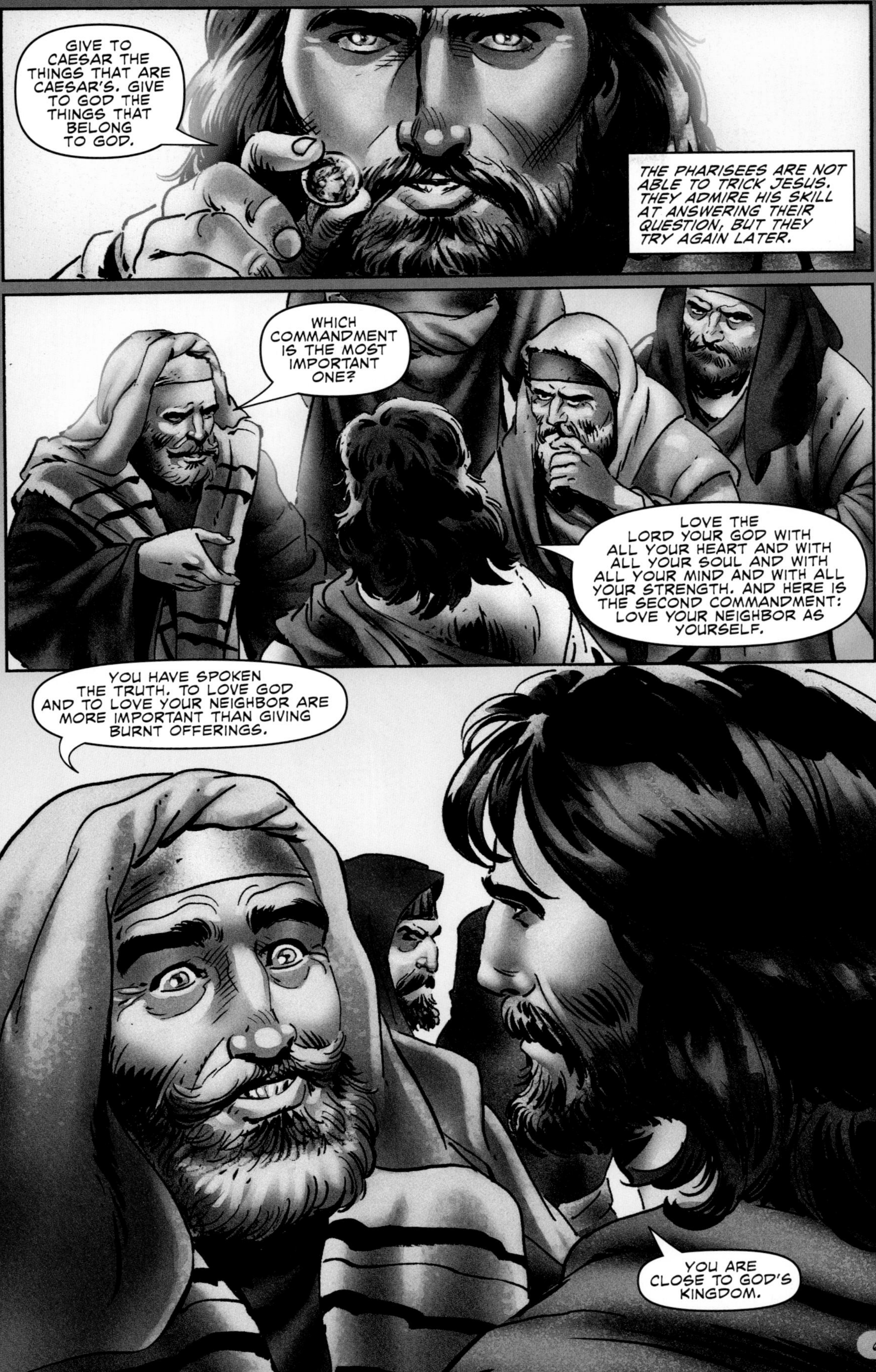
GIVE TO CAESAR THE THINGS THAT ARE CAESAR'S. GIVE TO GOD THE THINGS THAT BELONG TO GOD.
THE PHARISEES ARE NOT ABLE TO TRICK JESUS. THEY ADMIRE HIS SKILL AT ANSWERING THEIR QUESTION, BUT THEY TRY AGAIN LATER.
WHICH COMMANDMENT IS THE MOST IMPORTANT ONE?
LOVE THE LORD YOUR GOD WITH ALL YOUR HEART AND WITH ALL YOUR SOUL AND WITH ALL YOUR MIND AND WITH ALL YOUR STRENGTH. AND HERE IS THE SECOND COMMANDMENT: LOVE YOUR NEIGHBOR AS YOURSELF.
YOU HAVE SPOKEN THE TRUTH. TO LOVE GOD AND TO LOVE YOUR NEIGHBOR ARE MORE IMPORTANT THAN GIVING BURNT OFFERINGS.
YOU ARE CLOSE TO GOD'S KINGDOM.

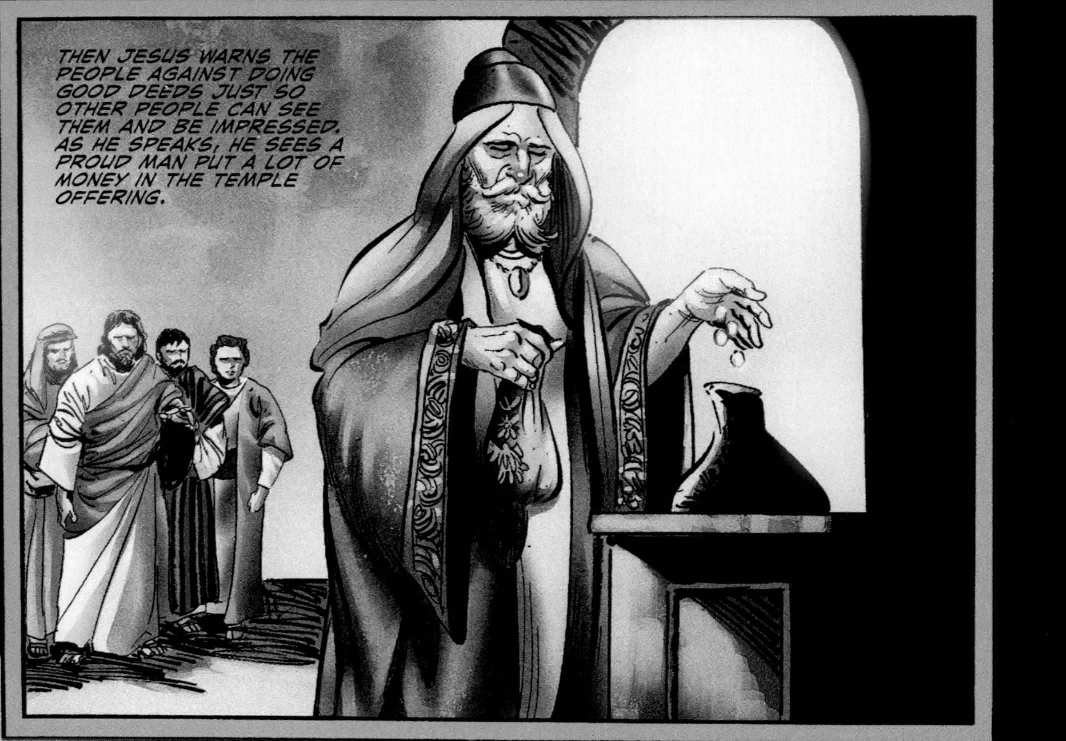
THEN JESUS WARNS THE PEOPLE AGAINST DOING GOOD DEEDS JUST SO OTHER PEOPLE CAN SEE THEM AND BE IMPRESSED. AS HE SPEAKS, HE SEES A PROUD MAN PUT A LOT OF MONEY IN THE TEMPLE OFFERING.

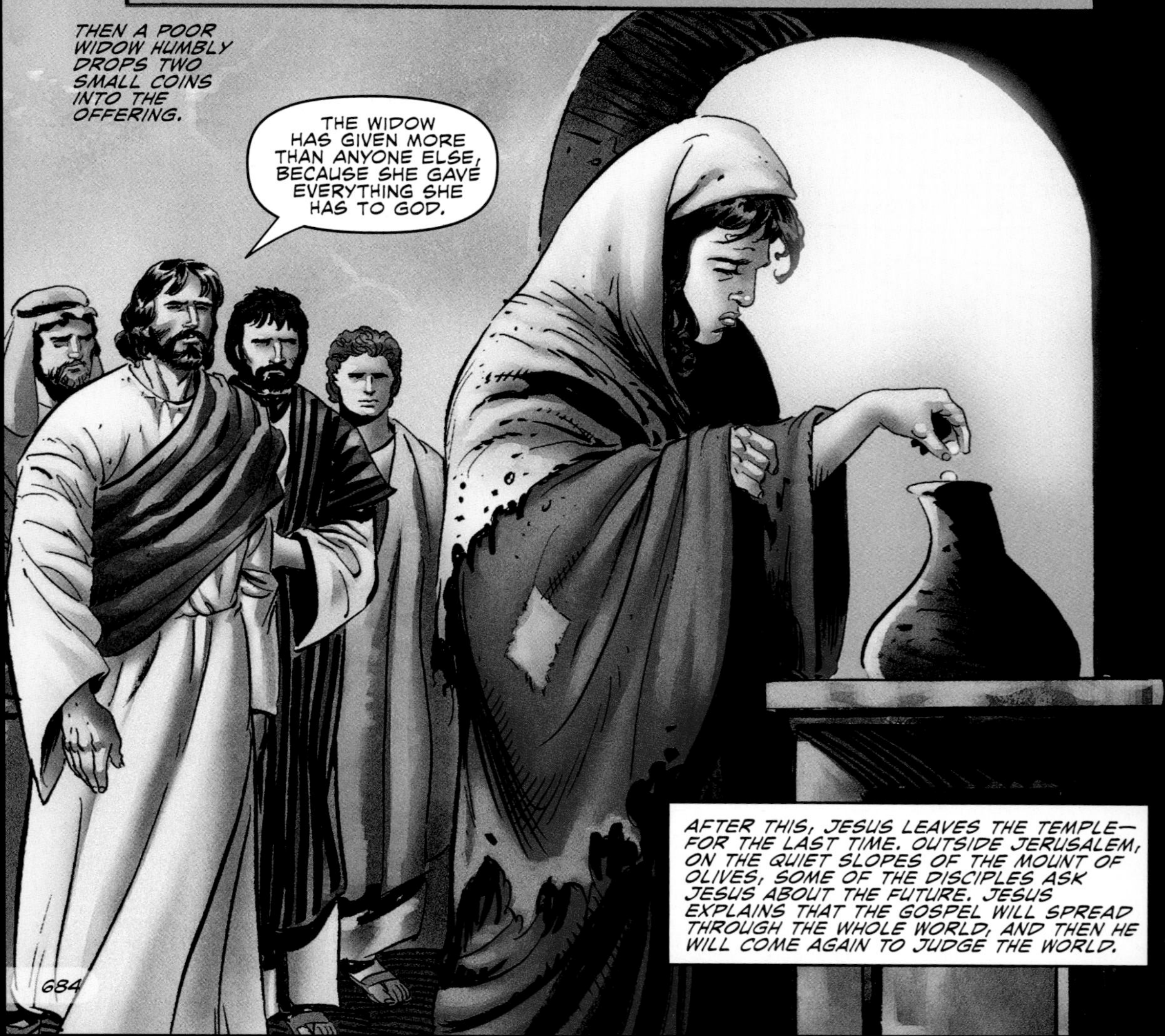
THEN A POOR WIDOW HUMBLY DROPS TWO SMALL COINS INTO THE OFFERING.
THE WIDOW HAS GIVEN MORE THAN ANYONE ELSE, BECAUSE SHE GAVE EVERYTHING SHE HAS TO GOD.
AFTER THIS, JESUS LEAVES THE TEMPLE—FOR THE LAST TIME. OUTSIDE JERUSALEM, ON THE QUIET SLOPES OF THE MOUNT OF OLIVES, SOME OF THE DISCIPLES ASK JESUS ABOUT THE FUTURE. JESUS EXPLAINS THAT THE GOSPEL WILL SPREAD THROUGH THE WHOLE WORLD, AND THEN HE WILL COME AGAIN TO JUDGE THE WORLD.

Sheep and Goats

BASED ON MATTHEW 25:31–46

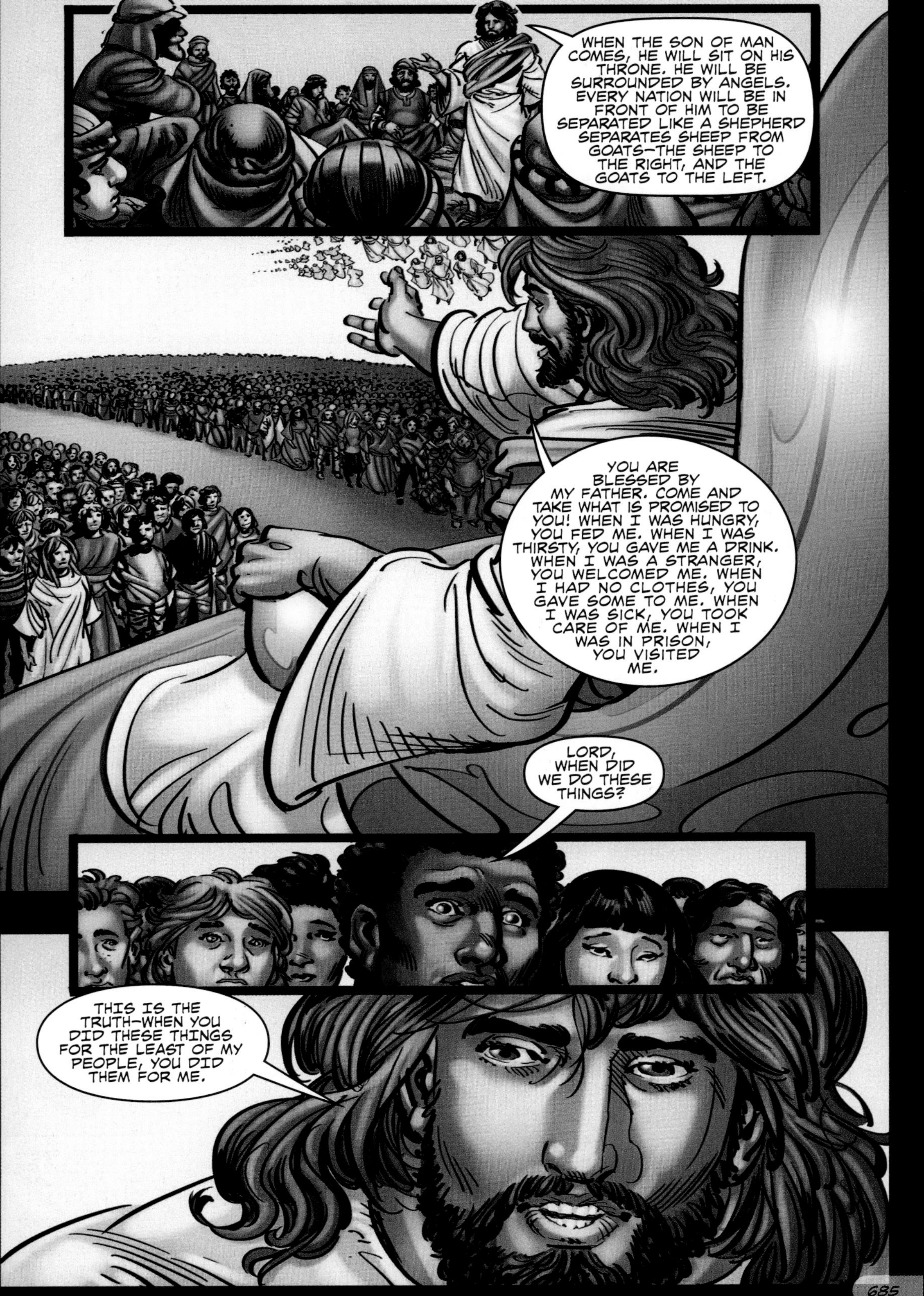

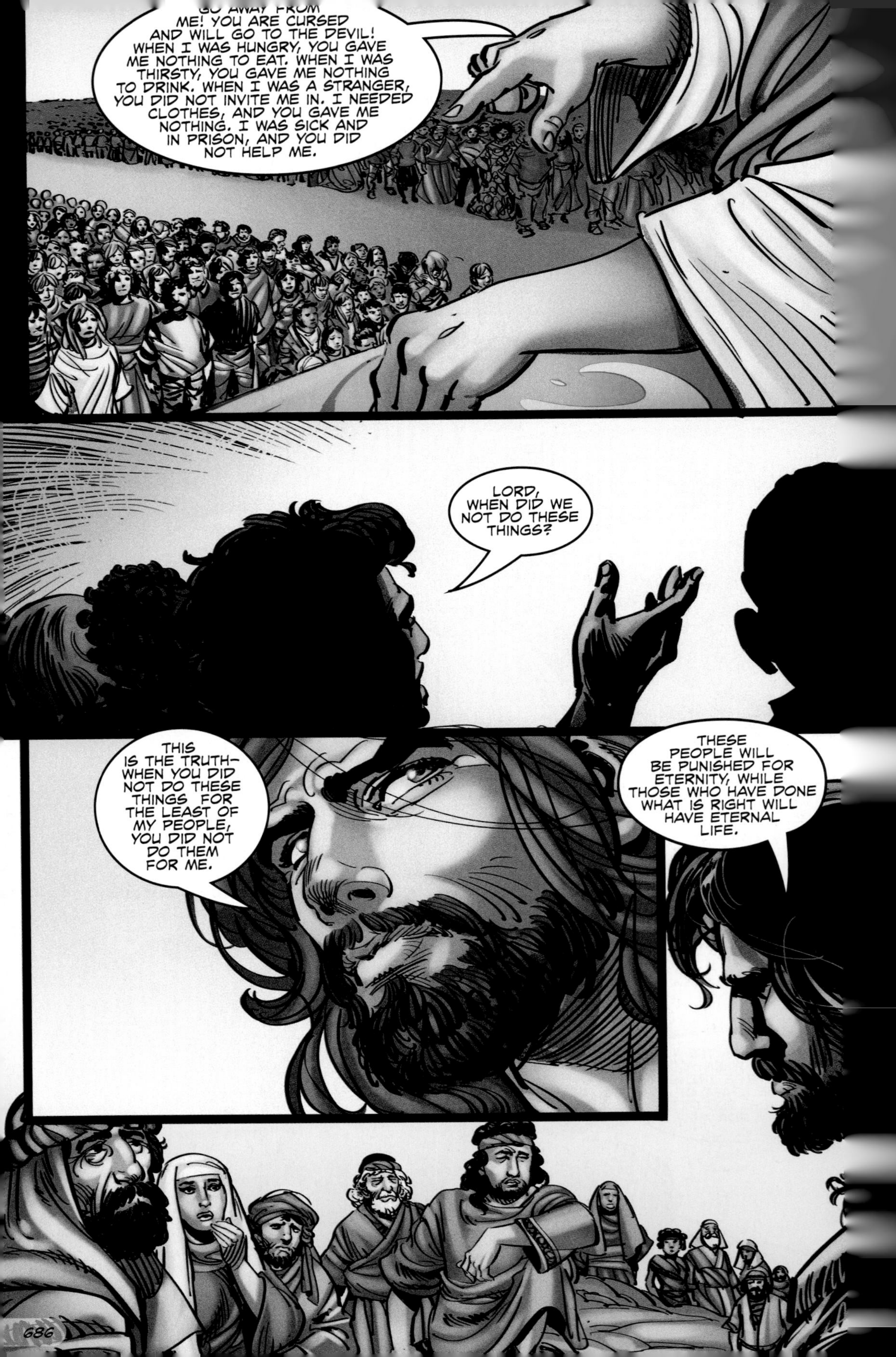
GO AWAY FROM ME! YOU ARE CURSED AND WILL GO TO THE DEVIL! WHEN I WAS HUNGRY, YOU GAVE ME NOTHING TO EAT. WHEN I WAS THIRSTY, YOU GAVE ME NOTHING TO DRINK. WHEN I WAS A STRANGER, YOU DID NOT INVITE ME IN. I NEEDED CLOTHES, AND YOU GAVE ME NOTHING. I WAS SICK AND IN PRISON, AND YOU DID NOT HELP ME.
LORD, WHEN DID WE NOT DO THESE THINGS?
THIS IS THE TRUTH—WHEN YOU DID NOT DO THESE THINGS FOR THE LEAST OF MY PEOPLE, YOU DID NOT DO THEM FOR ME.
THESE PEOPLE WILL BE PUNISHED FOR ETERNITY, WHILE THOSE WHO HAVE DONE WHAT IS RIGHT WILL HAVE ETERNAL LIFE.

Passover Problems

BASED ON MATTHEW 26:14-25; LUKE 22:1-13; JOHN 13:1-30

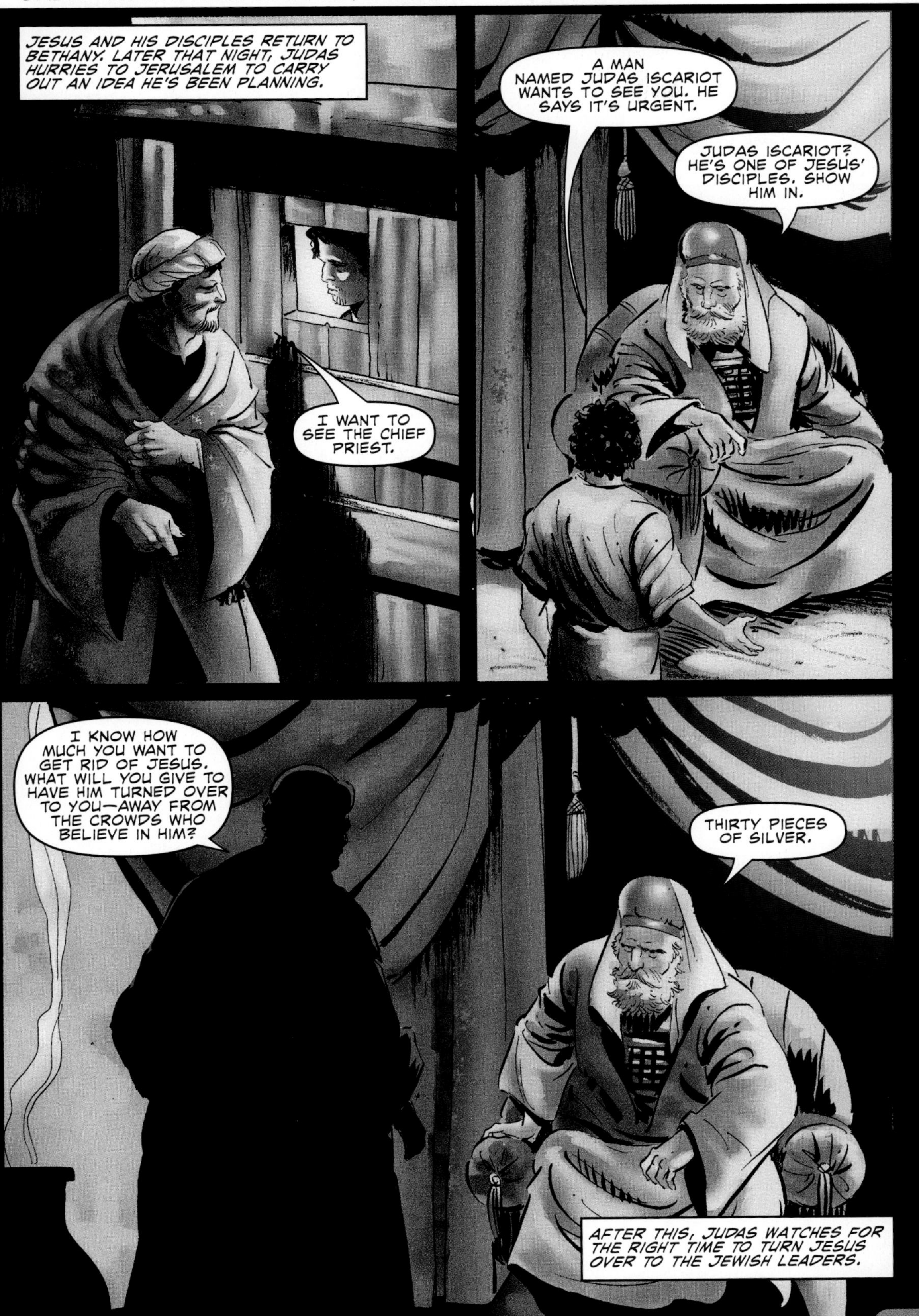
JESUS AND HIS DISCIPLES RETURN TO BETHANY. LATER THAT NIGHT, JUDAS HURRIES TO JERUSALEM TO CARRY OUT AN IDEA HE'S BEEN PLANNING.
I WANT TO SEE THE CHIEF PRIEST.
A MAN NAMED JUDAS ISCARIOT WANTS TO SEE YOU. HE SAYS IT'S URGENT.
JUDAS ISCARIOT? HE'S ONE OF JESUS' DISCIPLES. SHOW HIM IN.
I KNOW HOW MUCH YOU WANT TO GET RID OF JESUS. WHAT WILL YOU GIVE TO HAVE HIM TURNED OVER TO YOU—AWAY FROM THE CROWDS WHO BELIEVE IN HIM?
THIRTY PIECES OF SILVER.
AFTER THIS, JUDAS WATCHES FOR THE RIGHT TIME TO TURN JESUS OVER TO THE JEWISH LEADERS.

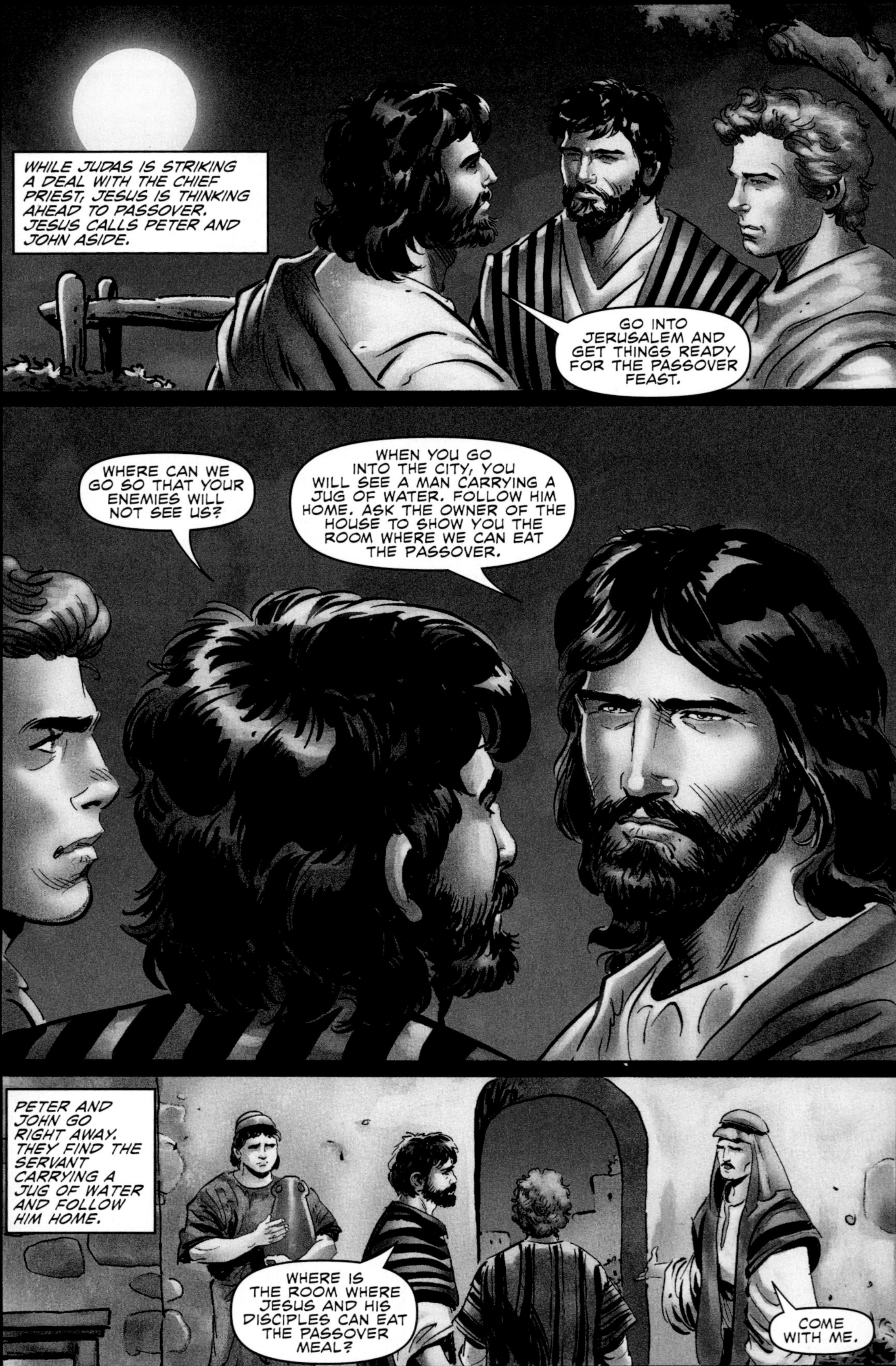
WHILE JUDAS IS STRIKING A DEAL WITH THE CHIEF PRIEST, JESUS IS THINKING AHEAD TO PASSOVER. JESUS CALLS PETER AND JOHN ASIDE.
GO INTO JERUSALEM AND GET THINGS READY FOR THE PASSOVER FEAST.
WHERE CAN WE GO SO THAT YOUR ENEMIES WILL NOT SEE US?
WHEN YOU GO INTO THE CITY, YOU WILL SEE A MAN CARRYING A JUG OF WATER. FOLLOW HIM HOME. ASK THE OWNER OF THE HOUSE TO SHOW YOU THE ROOM WHERE WE CAN EAT THE PASSOVER.
PETER AND JOHN GO RIGHT AWAY. THEY FIND THE SERVANT CARRYING A JUG OF WATER AND FOLLOW HIM HOME.
WHERE IS THE ROOM WHERE JESUS AND HIS DISCIPLES CAN EAT THE PASSOVER MEAL?
COME WITH ME.

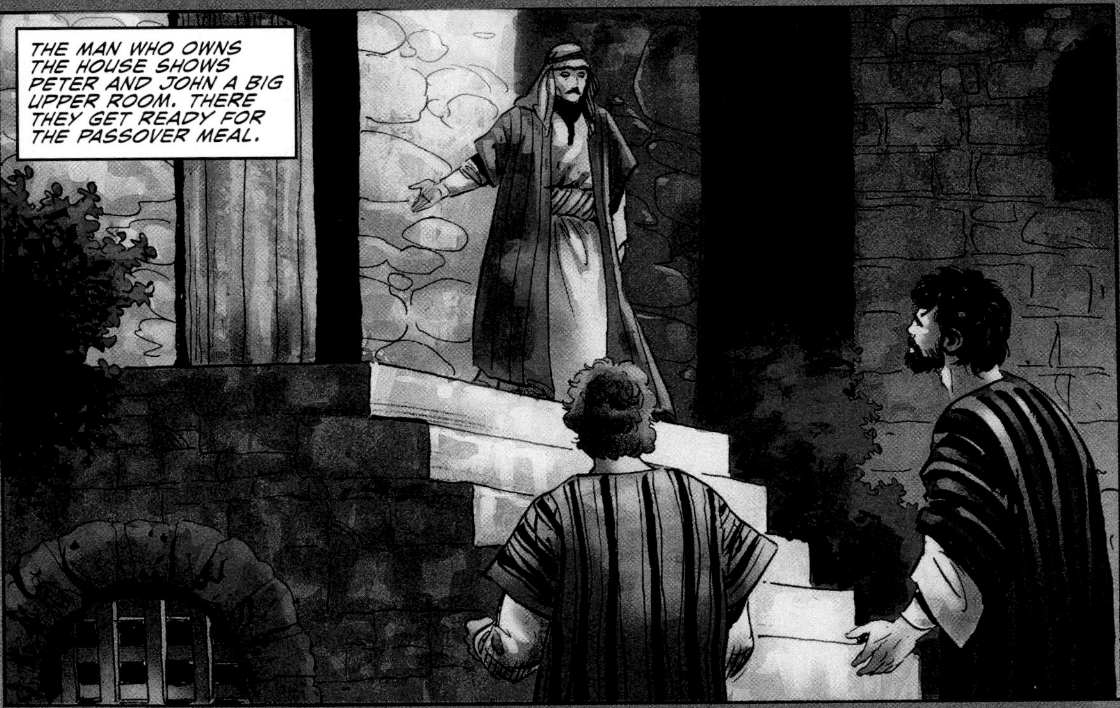
THE MAN WHO OWNS THE HOUSE SHOWS PETER AND JOHN A BIG UPPER ROOM. THERE THEY GET READY FOR THE PASSOVER MEAL.

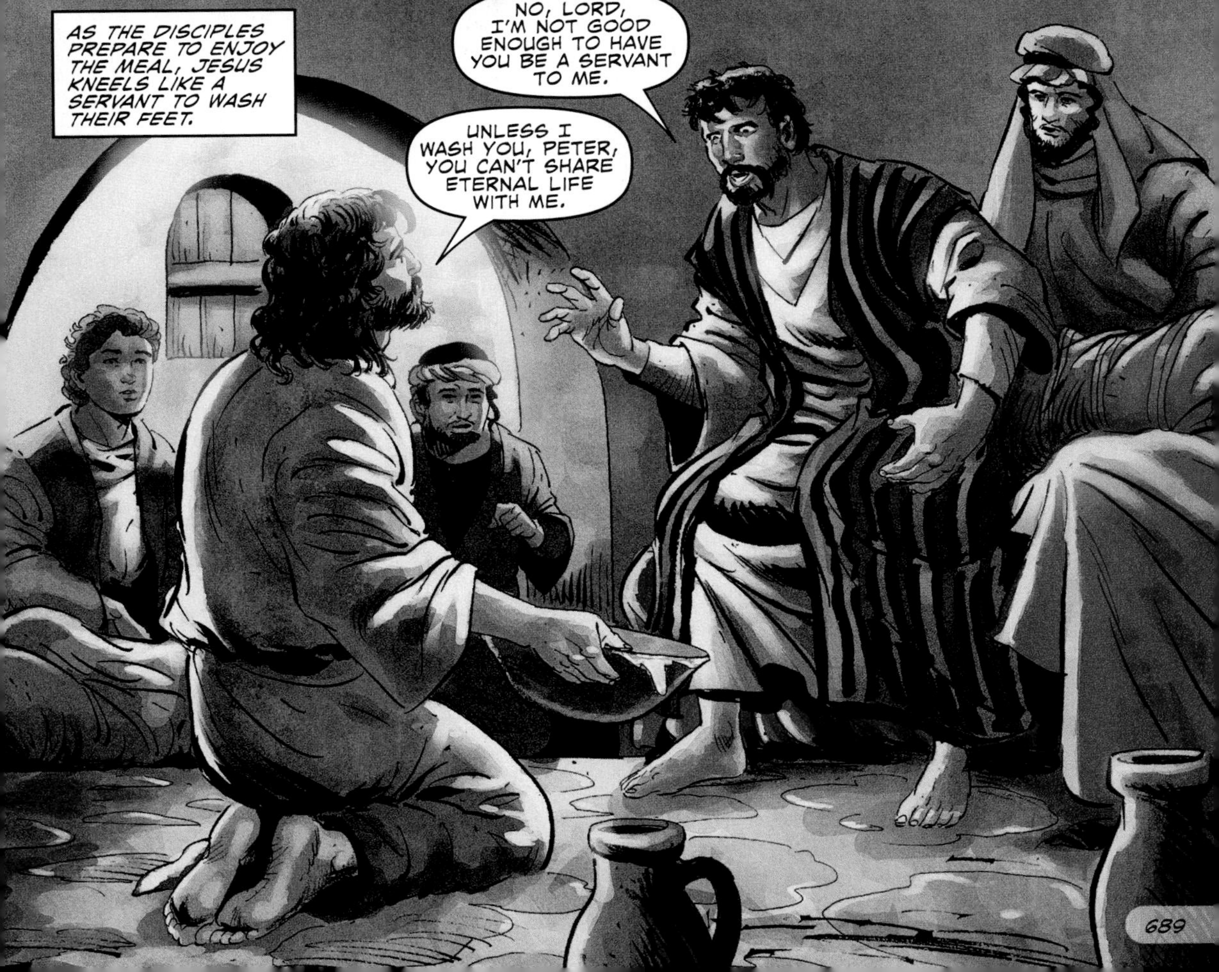
AS THE DISCIPLES PREPARE TO ENJOY THE MEAL, JESUS KNEELS LIKE A SERVANT TO WASH THEIR FEET.
NO, LORD, I'M NOT GOOD ENOUGH TO HAVE YOU BE A SERVANT TO ME.
UNLESS I WASH YOU, PETER, YOU CAN'T SHARE ETERNAL LIFE WITH ME.

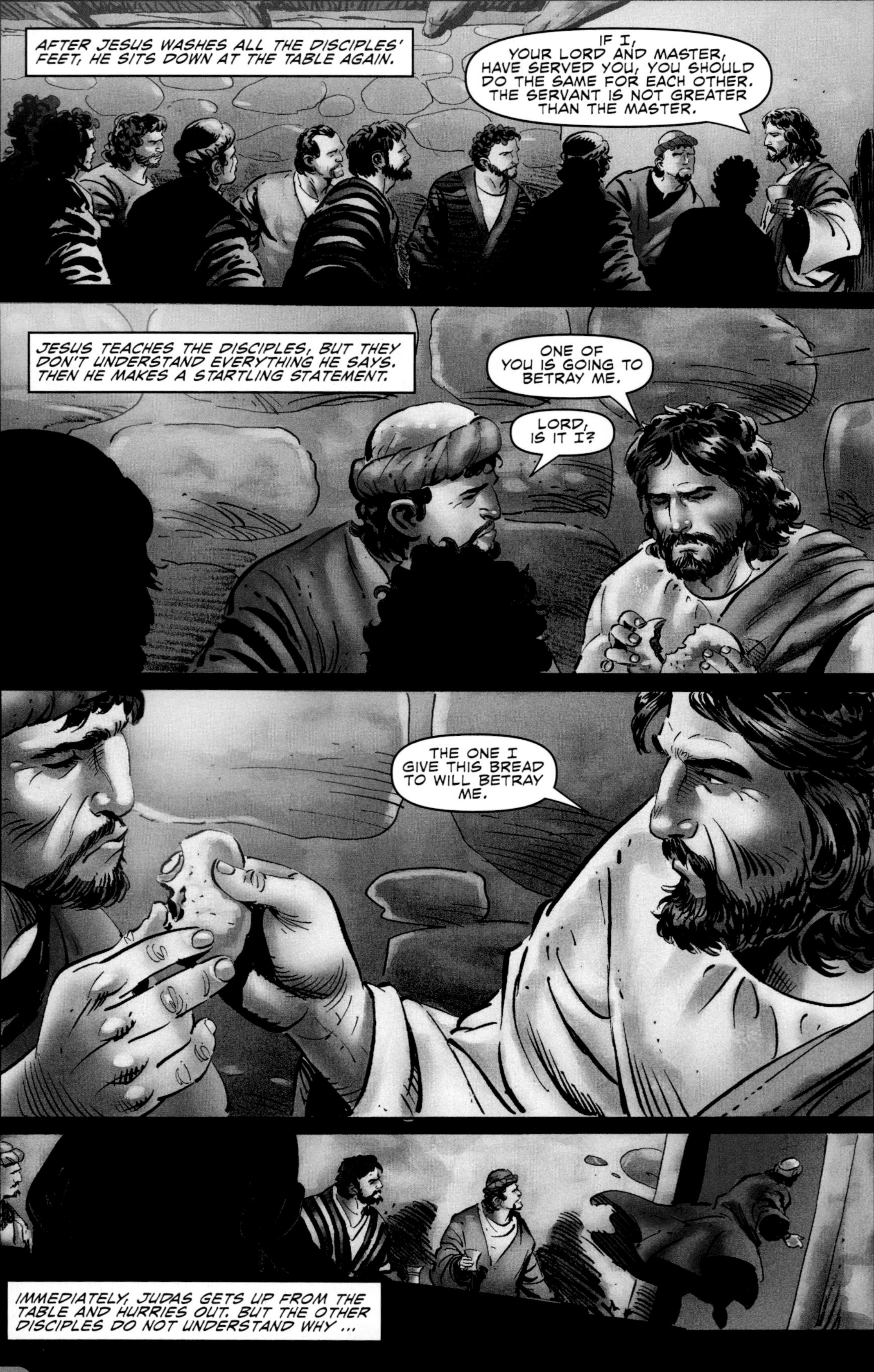
AFTER JESUS WASHES ALL THE DISCIPLES' FEET, HE SITS DOWN AT THE TABLE AGAIN.
IF I, YOUR LORD AND MASTER, HAVE SERVED YOU, YOU SHOULD DO THE SAME FOR EACH OTHER. THE SERVANT IS NOT GREATER THAN THE MASTER.
JESUS TEACHES THE DISCIPLES, BUT THEY DON'T UNDERSTAND EVERYTHING HE SAYS. THEN HE MAKES A STARTLING STATEMENT.
ONE OF YOU IS GOING TO BETRAY ME.
LORD, IS IT I?
THE ONE I GIVE THIS BREAD TO WILL BETRAY ME.
IMMEDIATELY, JUDAS GETS UP FROM THE TABLE AND HURRIES OUT. BUT THE OTHER DISCIPLES DO NOT UNDERSTAND WHY ...

The Lord's Supper

BASED ON JOHN 13:31–14:31; MATTHEW 26:26–56; LUKE 22:14–53

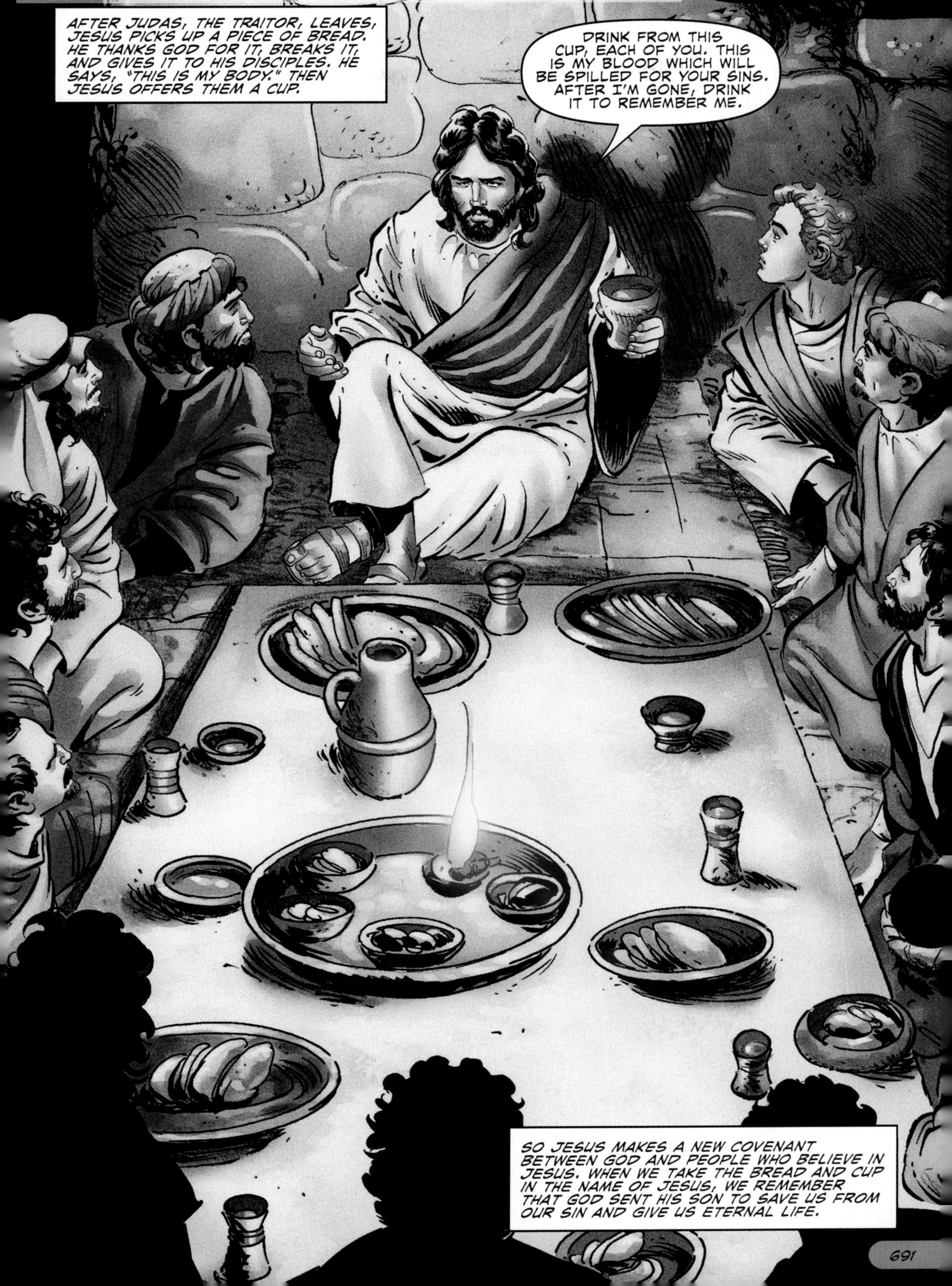
AFTER JUDAS, THE TRAITOR, LEAVES, JESUS PICKS UP A PIECE OF BREAD. HE THANKS GOD FOR IT, BREAKS IT, AND GIVES IT TO HIS DISCIPLES. HE SAYS, "THIS IS MY BODY." THEN JESUS OFFERS THEM A CUP.
DRINK FROM THIS CUP, EACH OF YOU. THIS IS MY BLOOD WHICH WILL BE SPILLED FOR YOUR SINS. AFTER I'M GONE, DRINK IT TO REMEMBER ME.
SO JESUS MAKES A NEW COVENANT BETWEEN GOD AND PEOPLE WHO BELIEVE IN JESUS. WHEN WE TAKE THE BREAD AND CUP IN THE NAME OF JESUS, WE REMEMBER THAT GOD SENT HIS SON TO SAVE US FROM OUR SIN AND GIVE US ETERNAL LIFE.

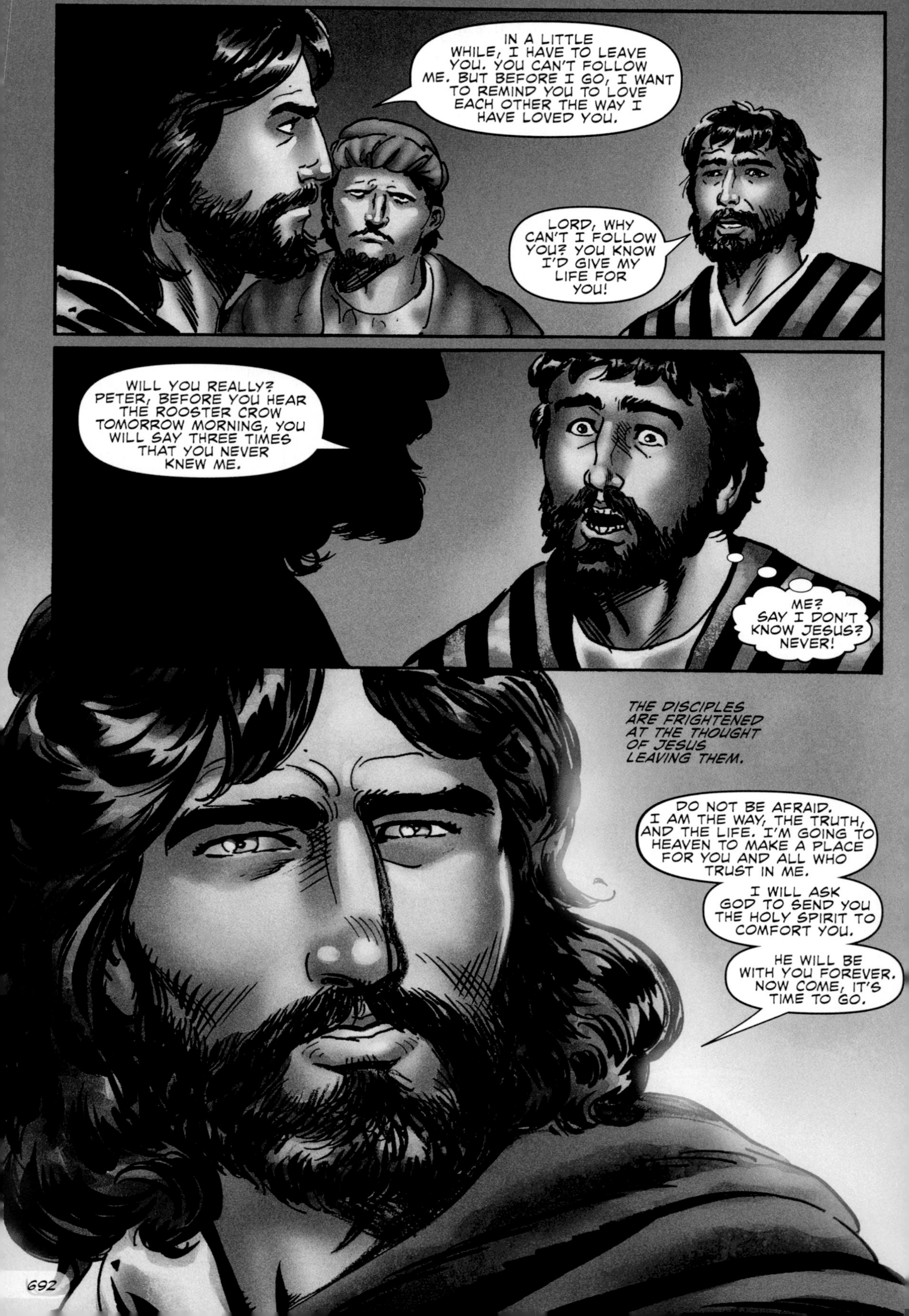
IN A LITTLE WHILE, I HAVE TO LEAVE YOU. YOU CAN'T FOLLOW ME. BUT BEFORE I GO, I WANT TO REMIND YOU TO LOVE EACH OTHER THE WAY I HAVE LOVED YOU.
LORD, WHY CAN'T I FOLLOW YOU? YOU KNOW I'D GIVE MY LIFE FOR YOU!
WILL YOU REALLY? PETER, BEFORE YOU HEAR THE ROOSTER CROW TOMORROW MORNING, YOU WILL SAY THREE TIMES THAT YOU NEVER KNEW ME.
ME? SAY I DON'T KNOW JESUS? NEVER!
THE DISCIPLES ARE FRIGHTENED AT THE THOUGHT OF JESUS LEAVING THEM.
DO NOT BE AFRAID. I AM THE WAY, THE TRUTH, AND THE LIFE. I'M GOING TO HEAVEN TO MAKE A PLACE FOR YOU AND ALL WHO TRUST IN ME.
I WILL ASK GOD TO SEND YOU THE HOLY SPIRIT TO COMFORT YOU.
HE WILL BE WITH YOU FOREVER. NOW COME, IT'S TIME TO GO.

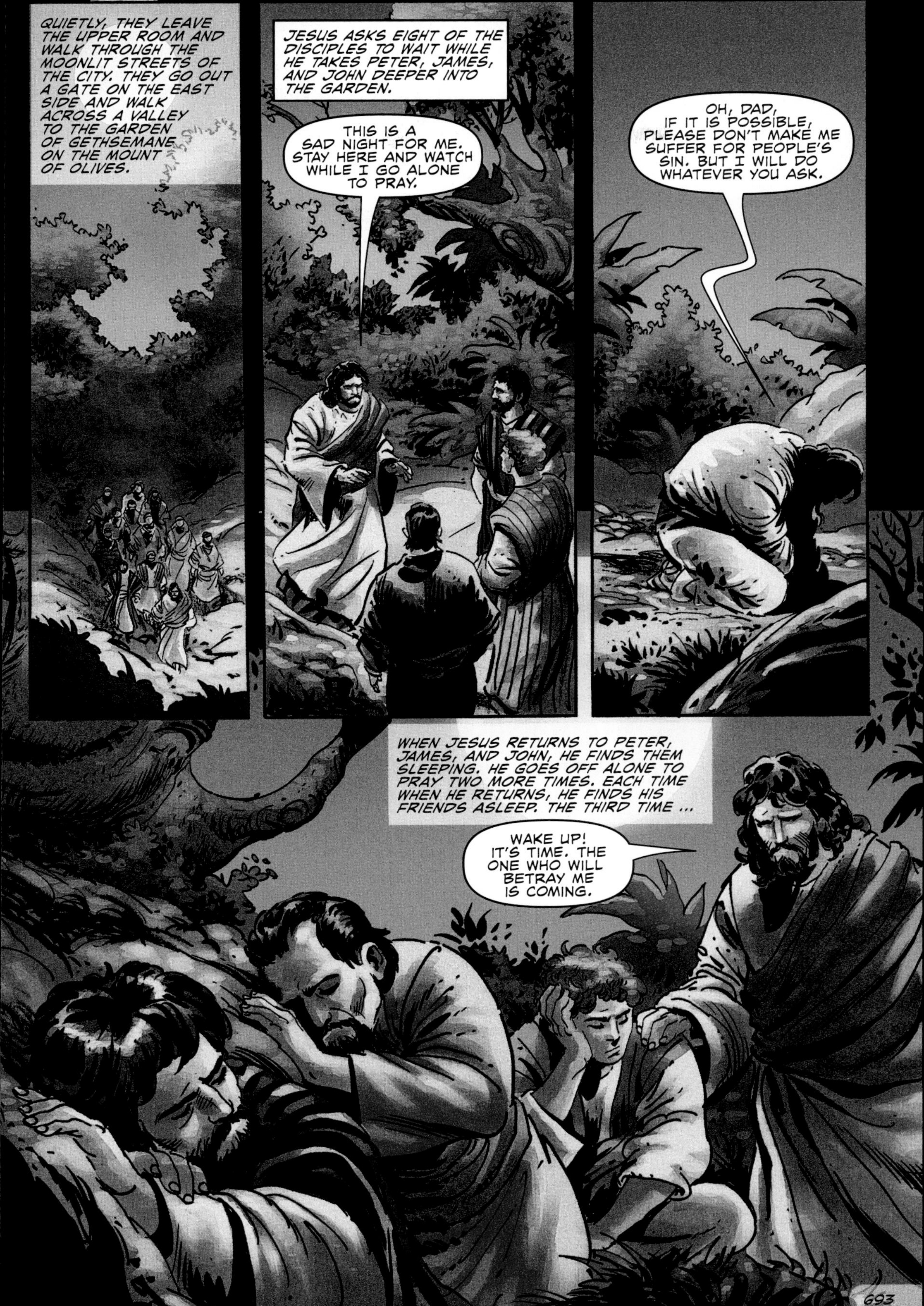
QUIETLY, THEY LEAVE THE UPPER ROOM AND WALK THROUGH THE MOONLIT STREETS OF THE CITY. THEY GO OUT A GATE ON THE EAST SIDE AND WALK ACROSS A VALLEY TO THE GARDEN OF GETHSEMANE ON THE MOUNT OF OLIVES.
JESUS ASKS EIGHT OF THE DISCIPLES TO WAIT WHILE HE TAKES PETER, JAMES, AND JOHN DEEPER INTO THE GARDEN.
THIS IS A SAD NIGHT FOR ME. STAY HERE AND WATCH WHILE I GO ALONE TO PRAY.
OH, DAD, IF IT IS POSSIBLE, PLEASE DON'T MAKE ME SUFFER FOR PEOPLE'S SIN. BUT I WILL DO WHATEVER YOU ASK.
WHEN JESUS RETURNS TO PETER, JAMES, AND JOHN, HE FINDS THEM SLEEPING. HE GOES OFF ALONE TO PRAY TWO MORE TIMES. EACH TIME WHEN HE RETURNS, HE FINDS HIS FRIENDS ASLEEP. THE THIRD TIME ...
WAKE UP! IT'S TIME. THE ONE WHO WILL BETRAY ME IS COMING.

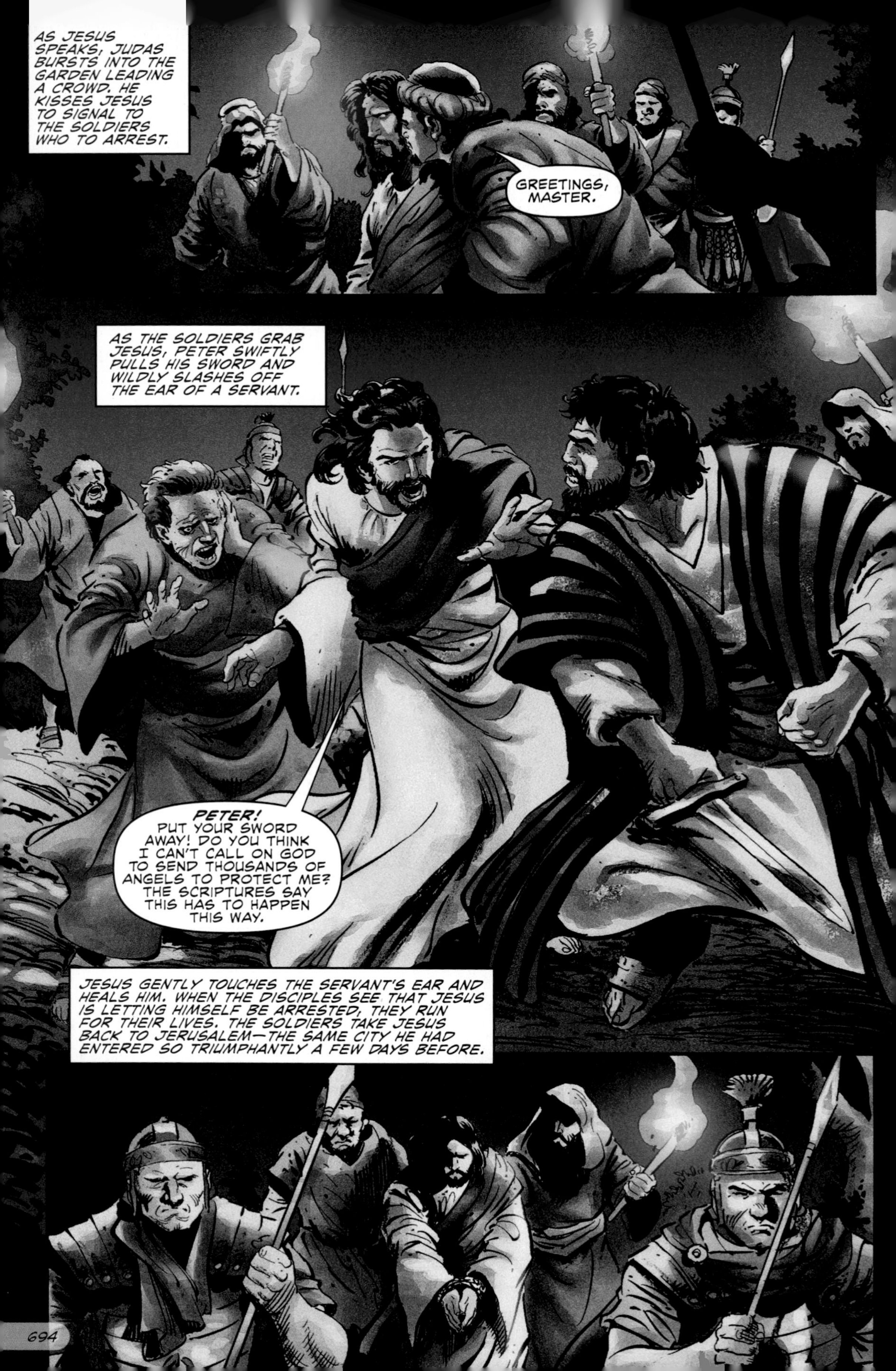

AS JESUS SPEAKS, JUDAS BURSTS INTO THE GARDEN LEADING A CROWD. HE KISSES JESUS TO SIGNAL TO THE SOLDIERS WHO TO ARREST.
GREETINGS, MASTER.
AS THE SOLDIERS GRAB JESUS, PETER SWIFTLY PULLS HIS SWORD AND WILDLY SLASHES OFF THE EAR OF A SERVANT.
PETER! PUT YOUR SWORD AWAY! DO YOU THINK I CAN'T CALL ON GOD TO SEND THOUSANDS OF ANGELS TO PROTECT ME? THE SCRIPTURES SAY THIS HAS TO HAPPEN THIS WAY.
JESUS GENTLY TOUCHES THE SERVANT'S EAR AND HEALS HIM. WHEN THE DISCIPLES SEE THAT JESUS IS LETTING HIMSELF BE ARRESTED, THEY RUN FOR THEIR LIVES. THE SOLDIERS TAKE JESUS BACK TO JERUSALEM—THE SAME CITY HE HAD ENTERED SO TRIUMPHANTLY A FEW DAYS BEFORE.

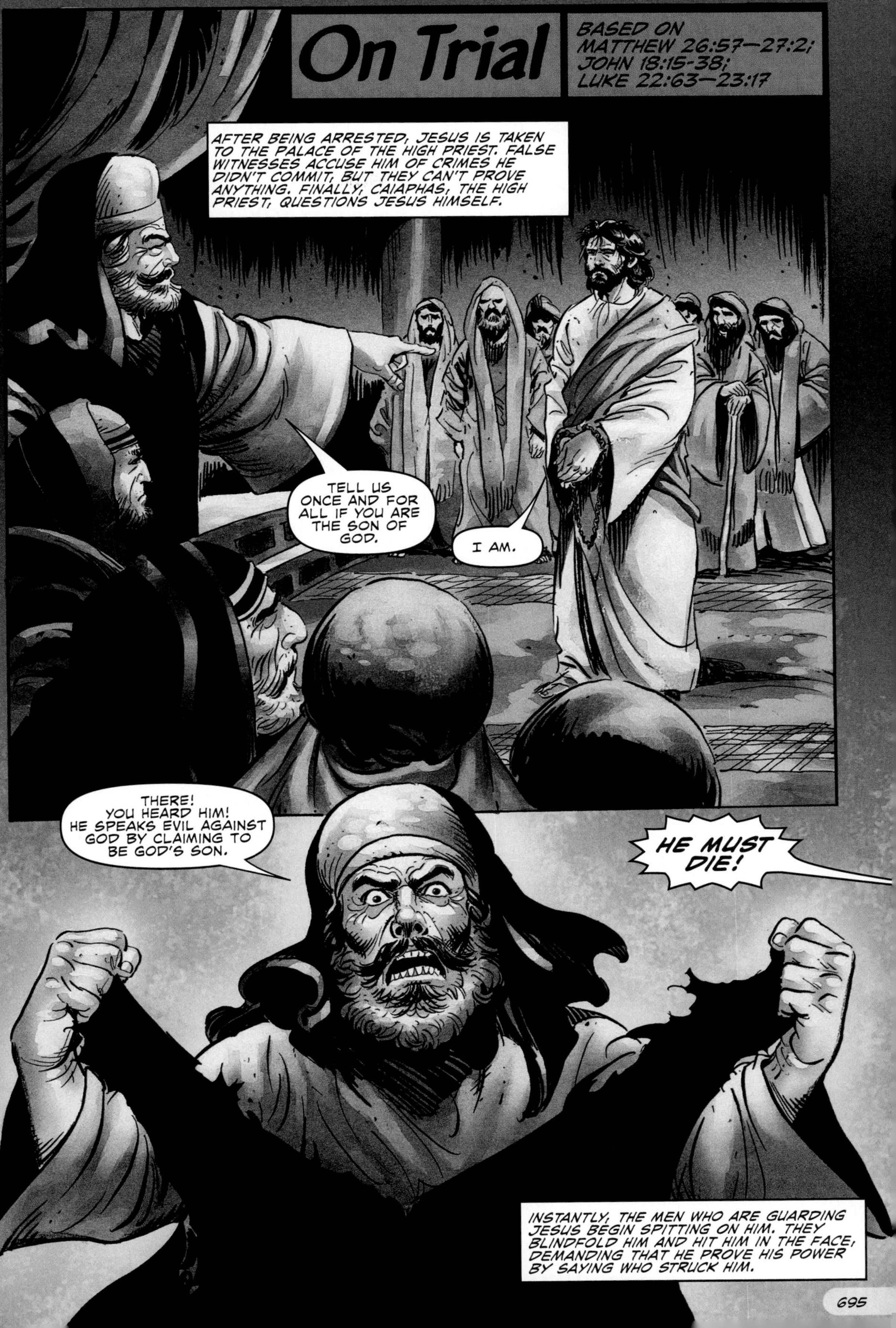
On Trial
BASED ON MATTHEW 26:57—27:2; JOHN 18:15-38; LUKE 22:63—23:17
AFTER BEING ARRESTED, JESUS IS TAKEN TO THE PALACE OF THE HIGH PRIEST. FALSE WITNESSES ACCUSE HIM OF CRIMES HE DIDN'T COMMIT, BUT THEY CAN'T PROVE ANYTHING. FINALLY, CAIAPHAS, THE HIGH PRIEST, QUESTIONS JESUS HIMSELF.
TELL US ONCE AND FOR ALL IF YOU ARE THE SON OF GOD.
I AM.
THERE! YOU HEARD HIM! HE SPEAKS EVIL AGAINST GOD BY CLAIMING TO BE GOD'S SON.
HE MUST DIE!
INSTANTLY, THE MEN WHO ARE GUARDING JESUS BEGIN SPITTING ON HIM. THEY BLINDFOLD HIM AND HIT HIM IN THE FACE, DEMANDING THAT HE PROVE HIS POWER BY SAYING WHO STRUCK HIM.

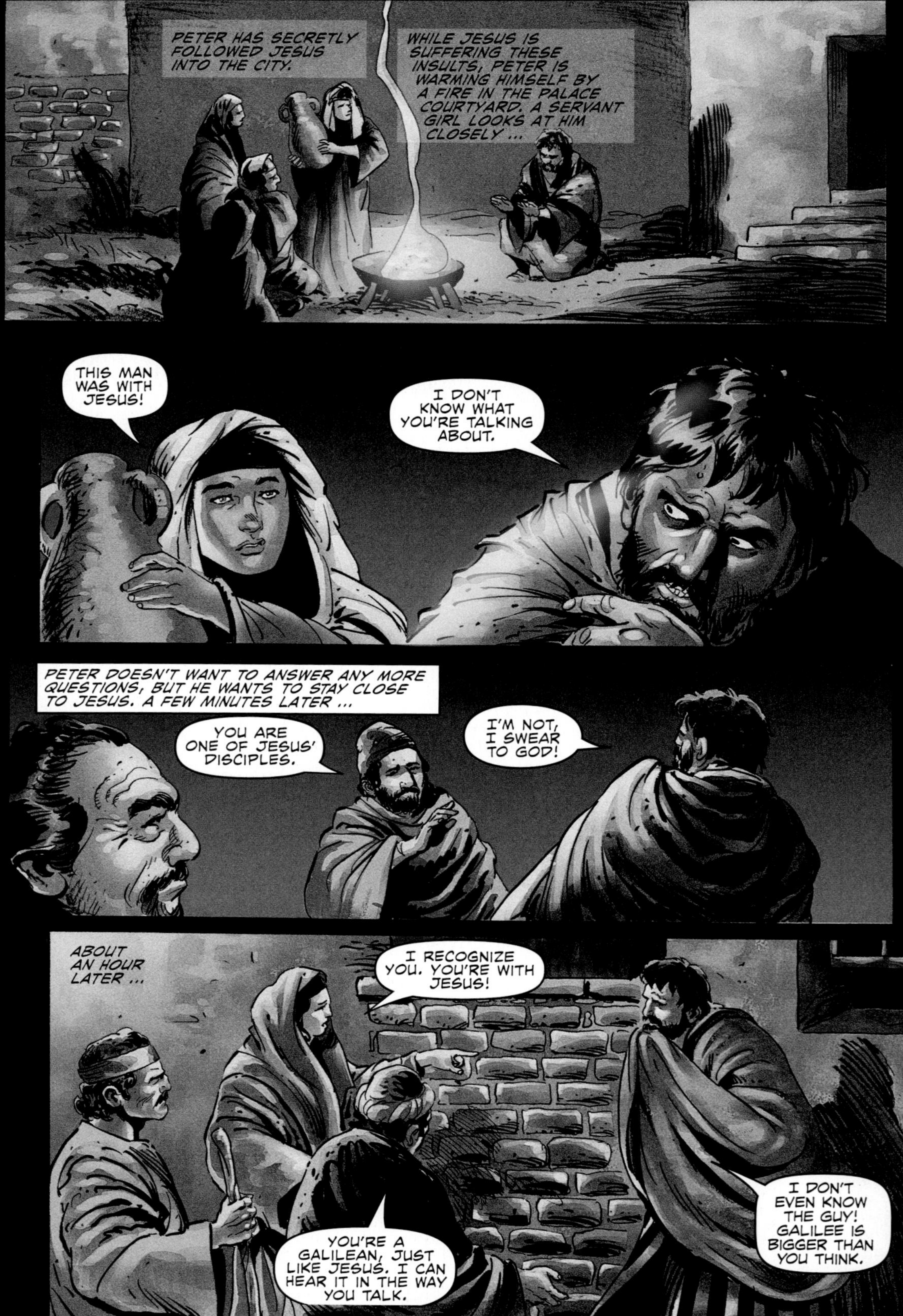
PETER HAS SECRETLY FOLLOWED JESUS INTO THE CITY.
WHILE JESUS IS SUFFERING THESE INSULTS, PETER IS WARMING HIMSELF BY A FIRE IN THE PALACE COURTYARD. A SERVANT GIRL LOOKS AT HIM CLOSELY ...
THIS MAN WAS WITH JESUS!
I DON'T KNOW WHAT YOU'RE TALKING ABOUT.
PETER DOESN'T WANT TO ANSWER ANY MORE QUESTIONS, BUT HE WANTS TO STAY CLOSE TO JESUS. A FEW MINUTES LATER ...
YOU ARE ONE OF JESUS' DISCIPLES.
I'M NOT, I SWEAR TO GOD!
ABOUT AN HOUR LATER ...
I RECOGNIZE YOU. YOU'RE WITH JESUS!
YOU'RE A GALILEAN, JUST LIKE JESUS. I CAN HEAR IT IN THE WAY YOU TALK.
I DON'T EVEN KNOW THE GUY! GALILEE IS BIGGER THAN YOU THINK.

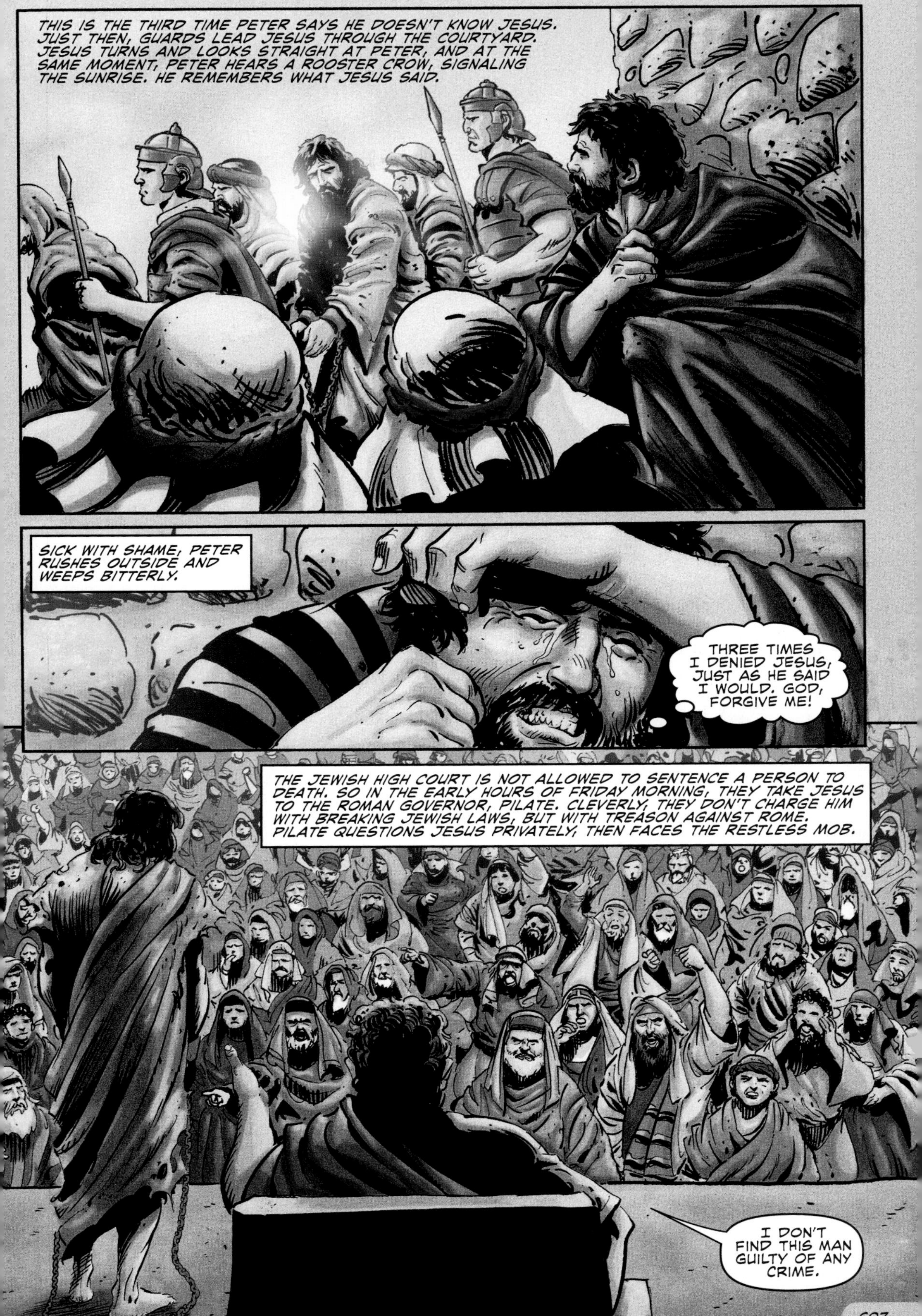
THIS IS THE THIRD TIME PETER SAYS HE DOESN'T KNOW JESUS. JUST THEN, GUARDS LEAD JESUS THROUGH THE COURTYARD. JESUS TURNS AND LOOKS STRAIGHT AT PETER, AND AT THE SAME MOMENT, PETER HEARS A ROOSTER CROW, SIGNALING THE SUNRISE. HE REMEMBERS WHAT JESUS SAID.
SICK WITH SHAME, PETER RUSHES OUTSIDE AND WEEPS BITTERLY.
THREE TIMES I DENIED JESUS, JUST AS HE SAID I WOULD. GOD, FORGIVE ME!
THE JEWISH HIGH COURT IS NOT ALLOWED TO SENTENCE A PERSON TO DEATH. SO IN THE EARLY HOURS OF FRIDAY MORNING, THEY TAKE JESUS TO THE ROMAN GOVERNOR, PILATE. CLEVERLY, THEY DON'T CHARGE HIM WITH BREAKING JEWISH LAWS, BUT WITH TREASON AGAINST ROME. PILATE QUESTIONS JESUS PRIVATELY, THEN FACES THE RESTLESS MOB.
I DON'T FIND THIS MAN GUILTY OF ANY CRIME.

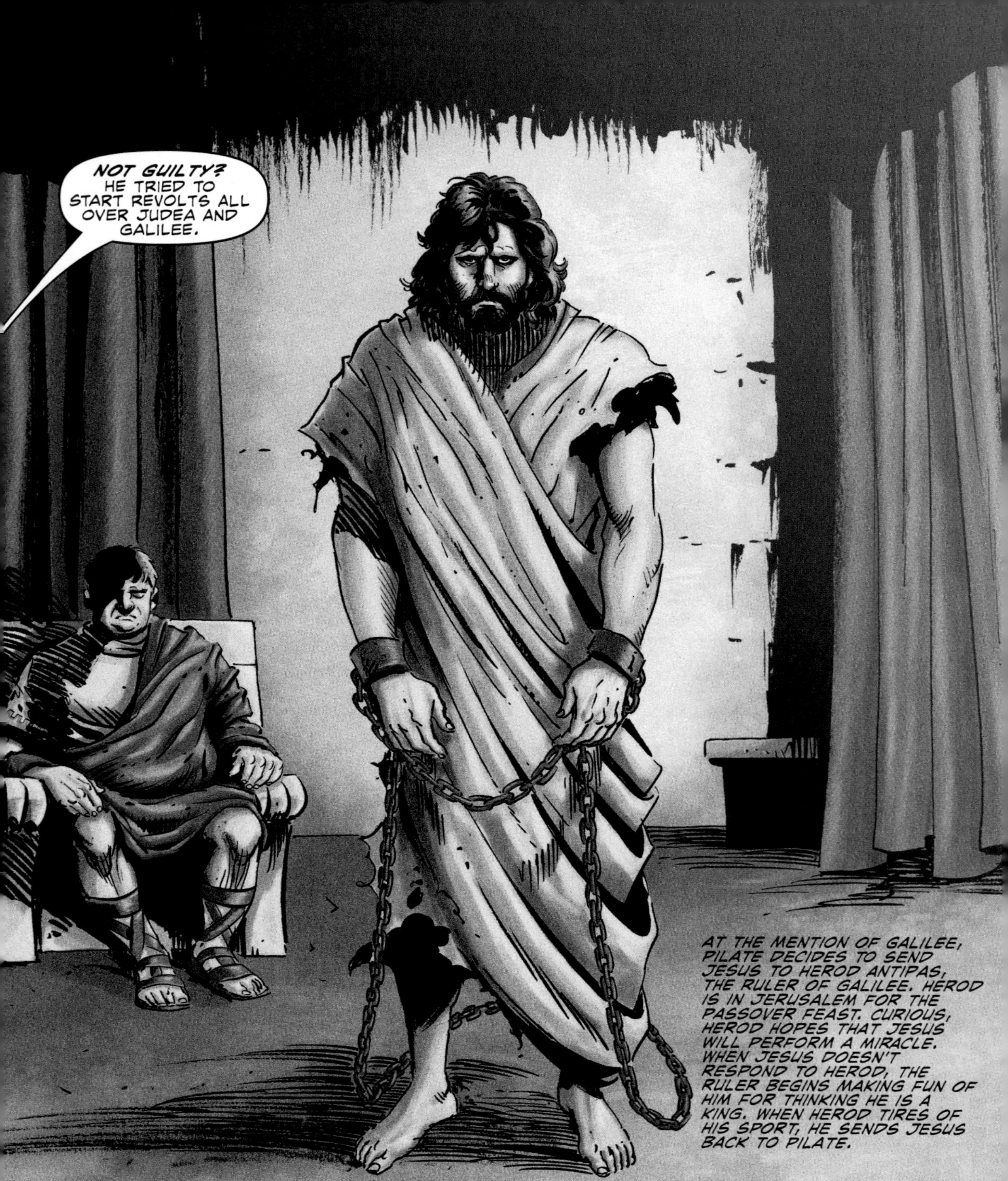
NOT GUILTY? HE TRIED TO START REVOLTS ALL OVER JUDEA AND GALILEE.
AT THE MENTION OF GALILEE, PILATE DECIDES TO SEND JESUS TO HEROD ANTIPAS, THE RULER OF GALILEE. HEROD IS IN JERUSALEM FOR THE PASSOVER FEAST. CURIOUS, HEROD HOPES THAT JESUS WILL PERFORM A MIRACLE. WHEN JESUS DOESN'T RESPOND TO HEROD, THE RULER BEGINS MAKING FUN OF HIM FOR THINKING HE IS A KING. WHEN HEROD TIRES OF HIS SPORT, HE SENDS JESUS BACK TO PILATE.

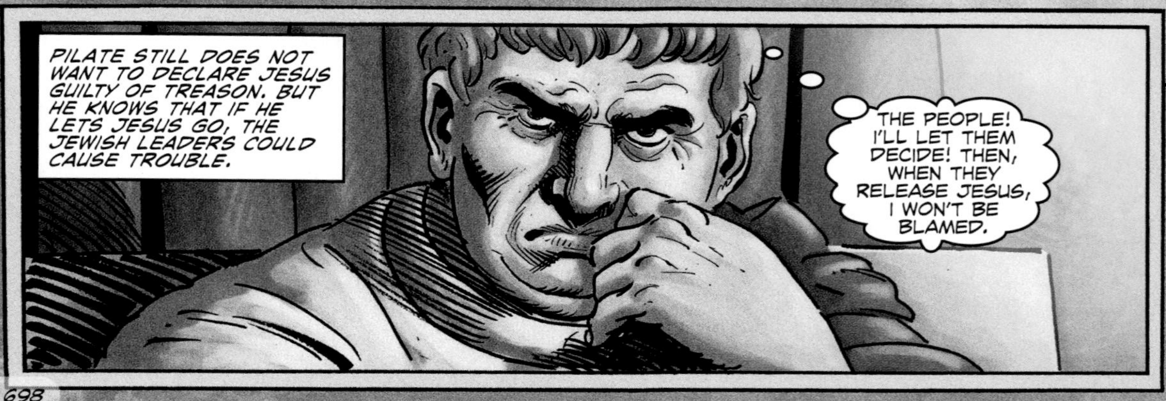
PILATE STILL DOES NOT WANT TO DECLARE JESUS GUILTY OF TREASON. BUT HE KNOWS THAT IF HE LETS JESUS GO, THE JEWISH LEADERS COULD CAUSE TROUBLE.
THE PEOPLE! I'LL LET THEM DECIDE! THEN, WHEN THEY RELEASE JESUS, I WON'T BE BLAMED.

Death Sentence

BASED ON JOHN 18:39—19:22; MATTHEW 27:3-10

PILATE IS AFRAID TO MAKE THE JEWS ANGRY BECAUSE HE DOES NOT WANT REPORTS OF TROUBLE TO REACH THE EMPEROR IN ROME. PILATE IS DESPERATE FOR AN IDEA THAT WILL MAKE THE JEWS HAPPY AND NOT MAKE HIM RESPONSIBLE FOR WHAT HAPPENS TO JESUS.

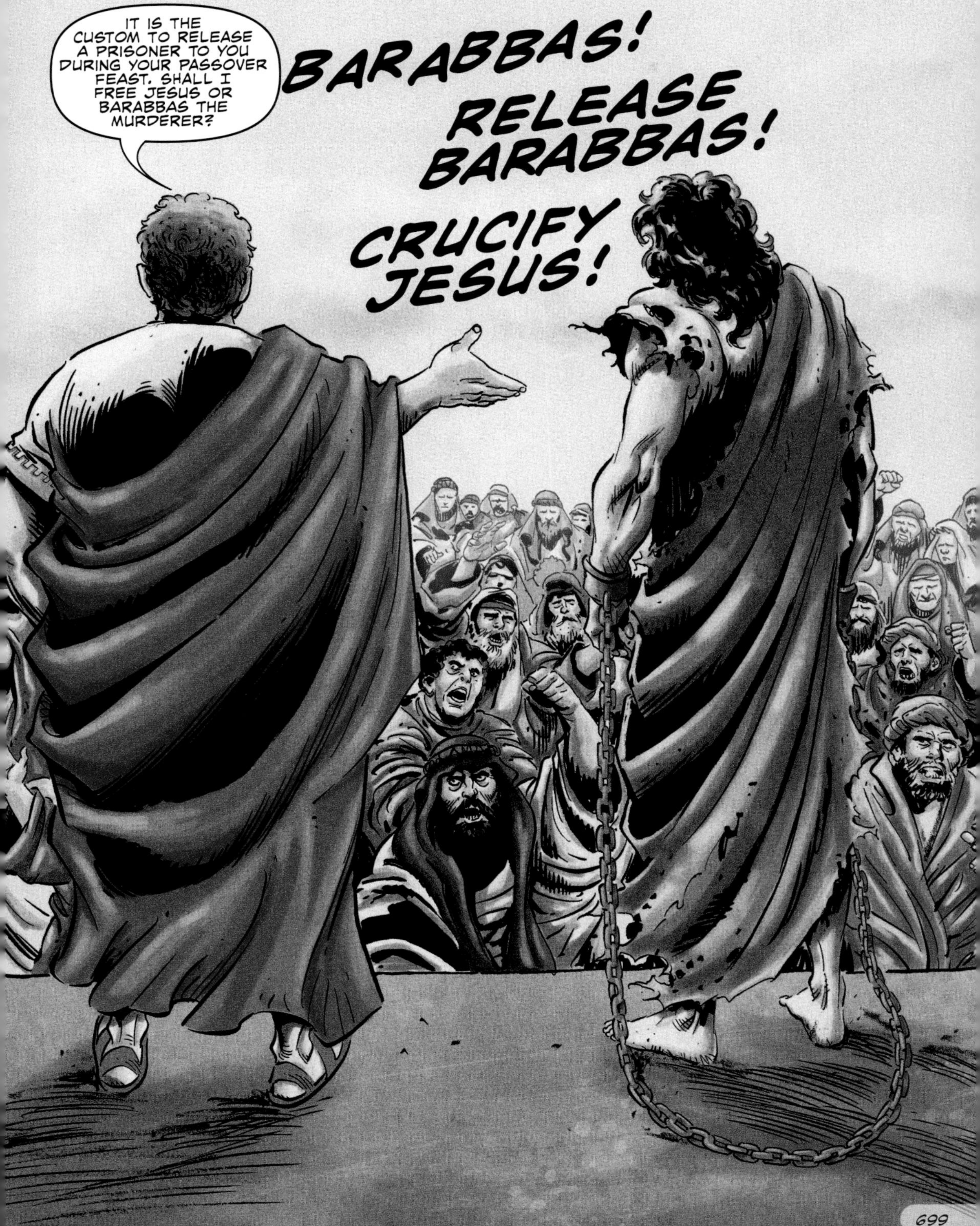
IT IS THE CUSTOM TO RELEASE A PRISONER TO YOU DURING YOUR PASSOVER FEAST. SHALL I FREE JESUS OR BARABBAS THE MURDERER?
BARABBAS!
RELEASE BARABBAS!
CRUCIFY JESUS!

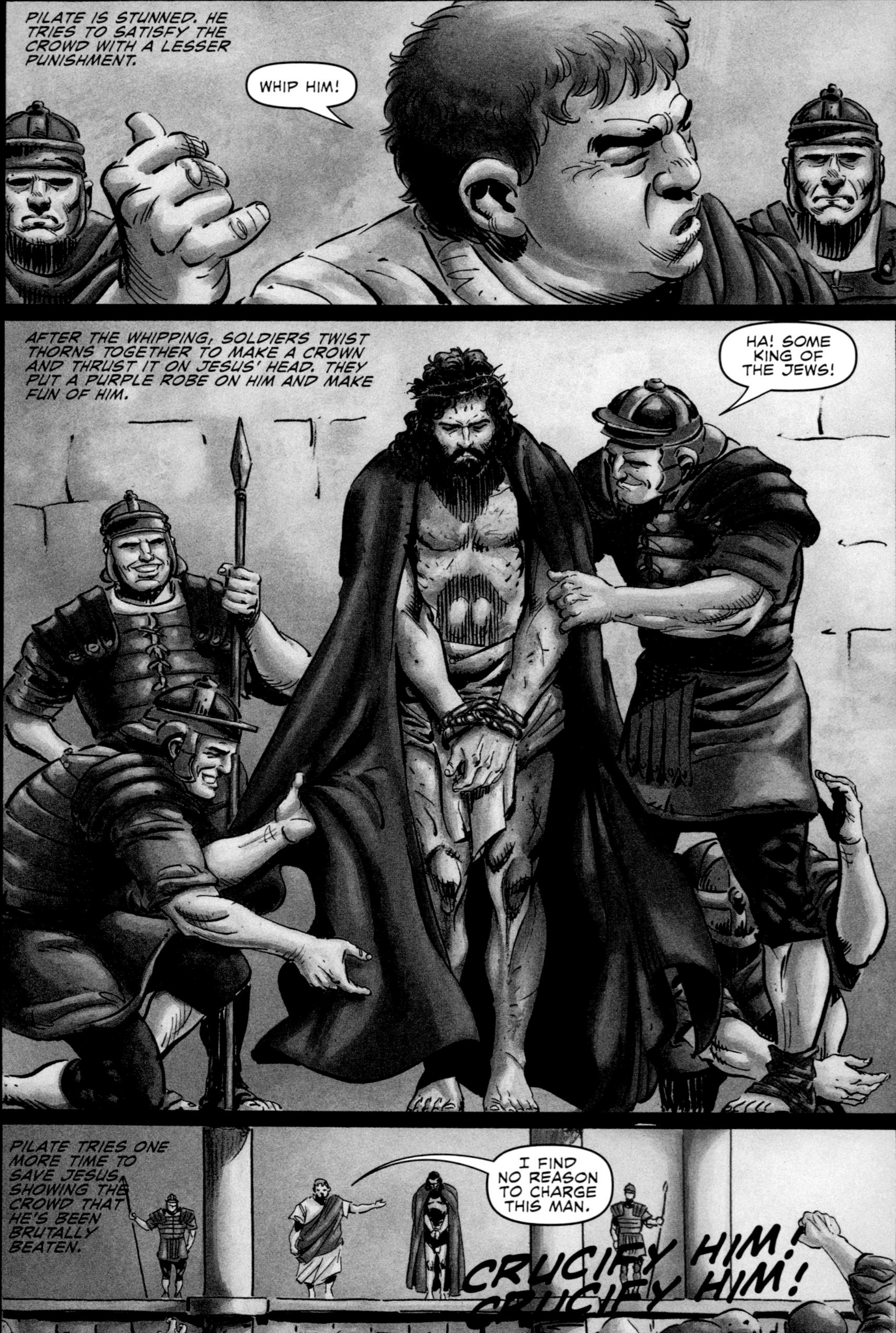
PILATE IS STUNNED. HE TRIES TO SATISFY THE CROWD WITH A LESSER PUNISHMENT.
WHIP HIM!
AFTER THE WHIPPING, SOLDIERS TWIST THORNS TOGETHER TO MAKE A CROWN AND THRUST IT ON JESUS' HEAD. THEY PUT A PURPLE ROBE ON HIM AND MAKE FUN OF HIM.
HA! SOME KING OF THE JEWS!
PILATE TRIES ONE MORE TIME TO SAVE JESUS, SHOWING THE CROWD THAT HE'S BEEN BRUTALLY BEATEN.
I FIND NO REASON TO CHARGE THIS MAN.
CRUCIFY HIM! CRUCIFY HIM!

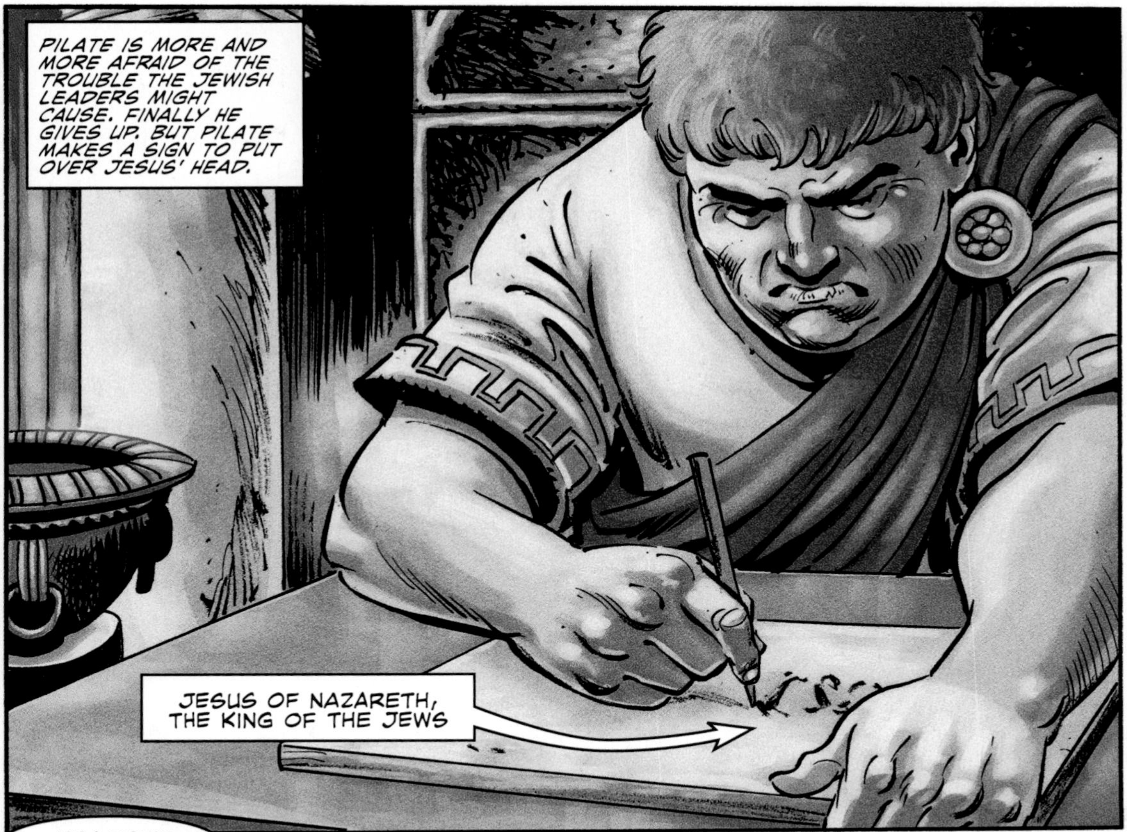
PILATE IS MORE AND MORE AFRAID OF THE TROUBLE THE JEWISH LEADERS MIGHT CAUSE. FINALLY HE GIVES UP. BUT PILATE MAKES A SIGN TO PUT OVER JESUS' HEAD.
JESUS OF NAZARETH, THE KING OF THE JEWS

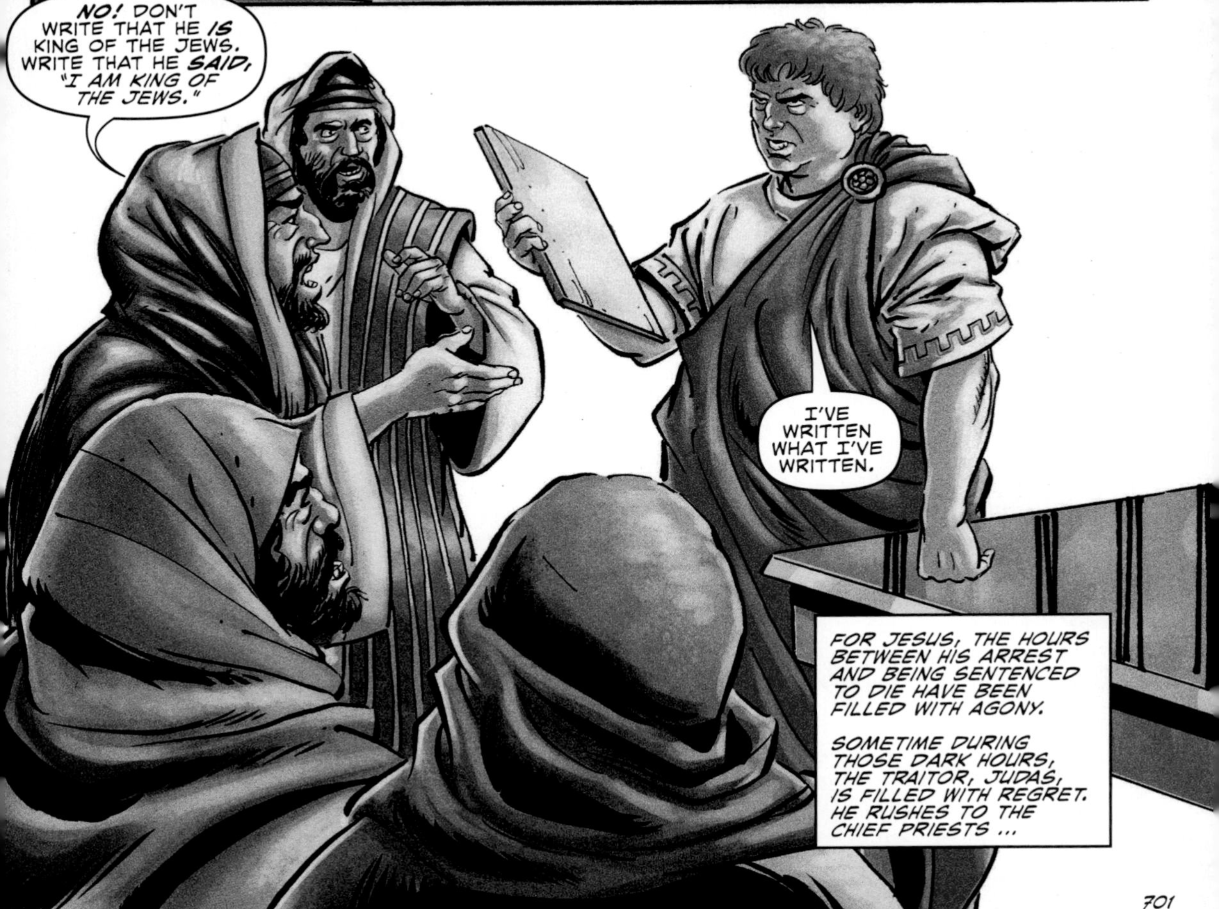
NO! DON'T WRITE THAT HE IS KING OF THE JEWS. WRITE THAT HE SAID, "I AM KING OF THE JEWS."
I'VE WRITTEN WHAT I'VE WRITTEN.
FOR JESUS, THE HOURS BETWEEN HIS ARREST AND BEING SENTENCED TO DIE HAVE BEEN FILLED WITH AGONY.
SOMETIME DURING THOSE DARK HOURS, THE TRAITOR, JUDAS, IS FILLED WITH REGRET. HE RUSHES TO THE CHIEF PRIESTS ...

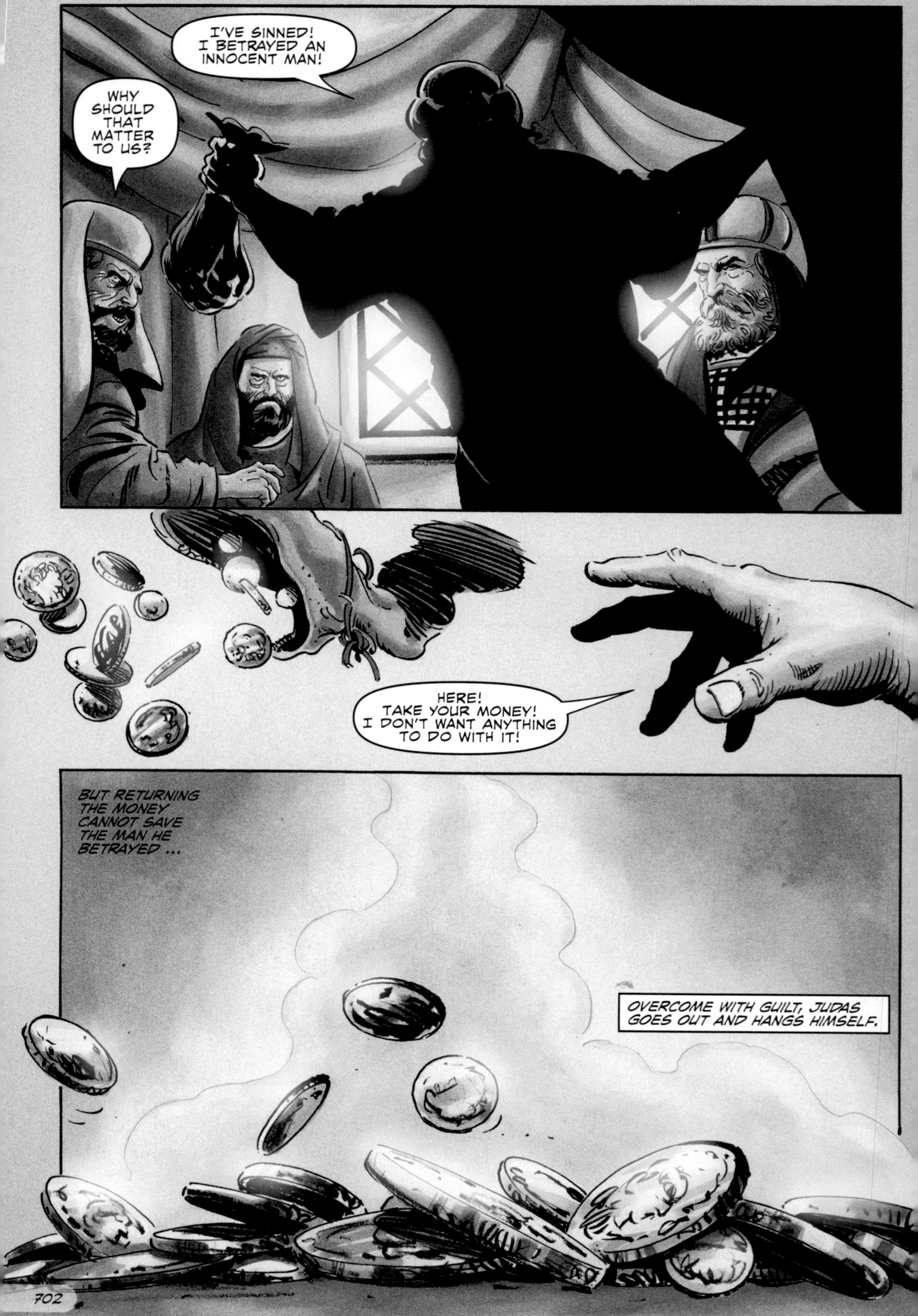
I'VE SINNED! I BETRAYED AN INNOCENT MAN!
WHY SHOULD THAT MATTER TO US?
HERE! TAKE YOUR MONEY! I DON'T WANT ANYTHING TO DO WITH IT!
BUT RETURNING THE MONEY CANNOT SAVE THE MAN HE BETRAYED ...
OVERCOME WITH GUILT, JUDAS GOES OUT AND HANGS HIMSELF.

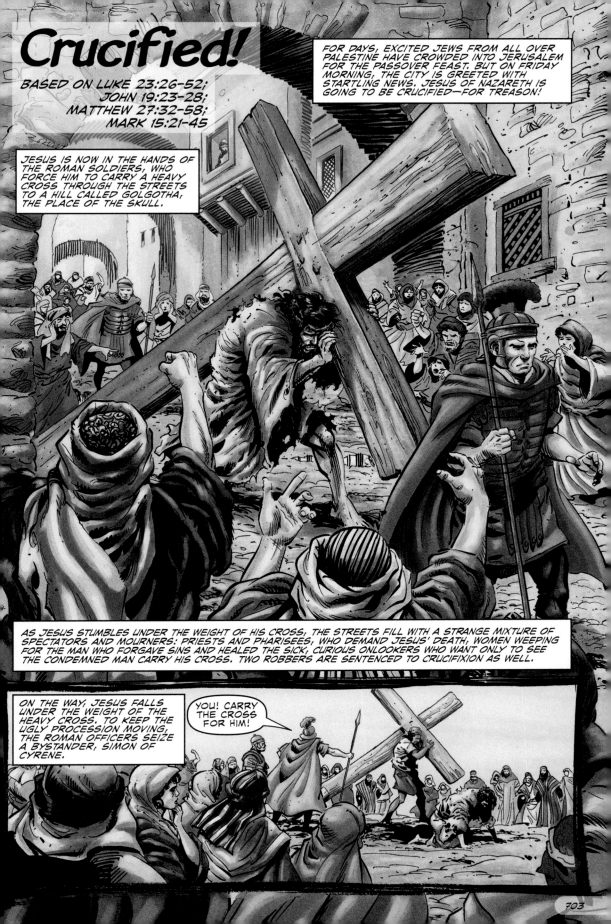

Crucified!

BASED ON LUKE 23:26-52;
JOHN 19:23-28;
MATTHEW 27:32-58;
MARK 15:21-45

FOR DAYS, EXCITED JEWS FROM ALL OVER PALESTINE HAVE CROWDED INTO JERUSALEM FOR THE PASSOVER FEAST. BUT ON FRIDAY MORNING, THE CITY IS GREETED WITH STARTLING NEWS. JESUS OF NAZARETH IS GOING TO BE CRUCIFIED—FOR TREASON!

JESUS IS NOW IN THE HANDS OF THE ROMAN SOLDIERS, WHO FORCE HIM TO CARRY A HEAVY CROSS THROUGH THE STREETS TO A HILL CALLED GOLGOTHA, THE PLACE OF THE SKULL.

AS JESUS STUMBLES UNDER THE WEIGHT OF HIS CROSS, THE STREETS FILL WITH A STRANGE MIXTURE OF SPECTATORS AND MOURNERS: PRIESTS AND PHARISEES, WHO DEMAND JESUS' DEATH, WOMEN WEEPING FOR THE MAN WHO FORGAVE SINS AND HEALED THE SICK, CURIOUS ONLOOKERS WHO WANT ONLY TO SEE THE CONDEMNED MAN CARRY HIS CROSS. TWO ROBBERS ARE SENTENCED TO CRUCIFIXION AS WELL.

ON THE WAY, JESUS FALLS UNDER THE WEIGHT OF THE HEAVY CROSS. TO KEEP THE UGLY PROCESSION MOVING, THE ROMAN OFFICERS SEIZE A BYSTANDER, SIMON OF CYRENE.

YOU! CARRY THE CROSS FOR HIM!

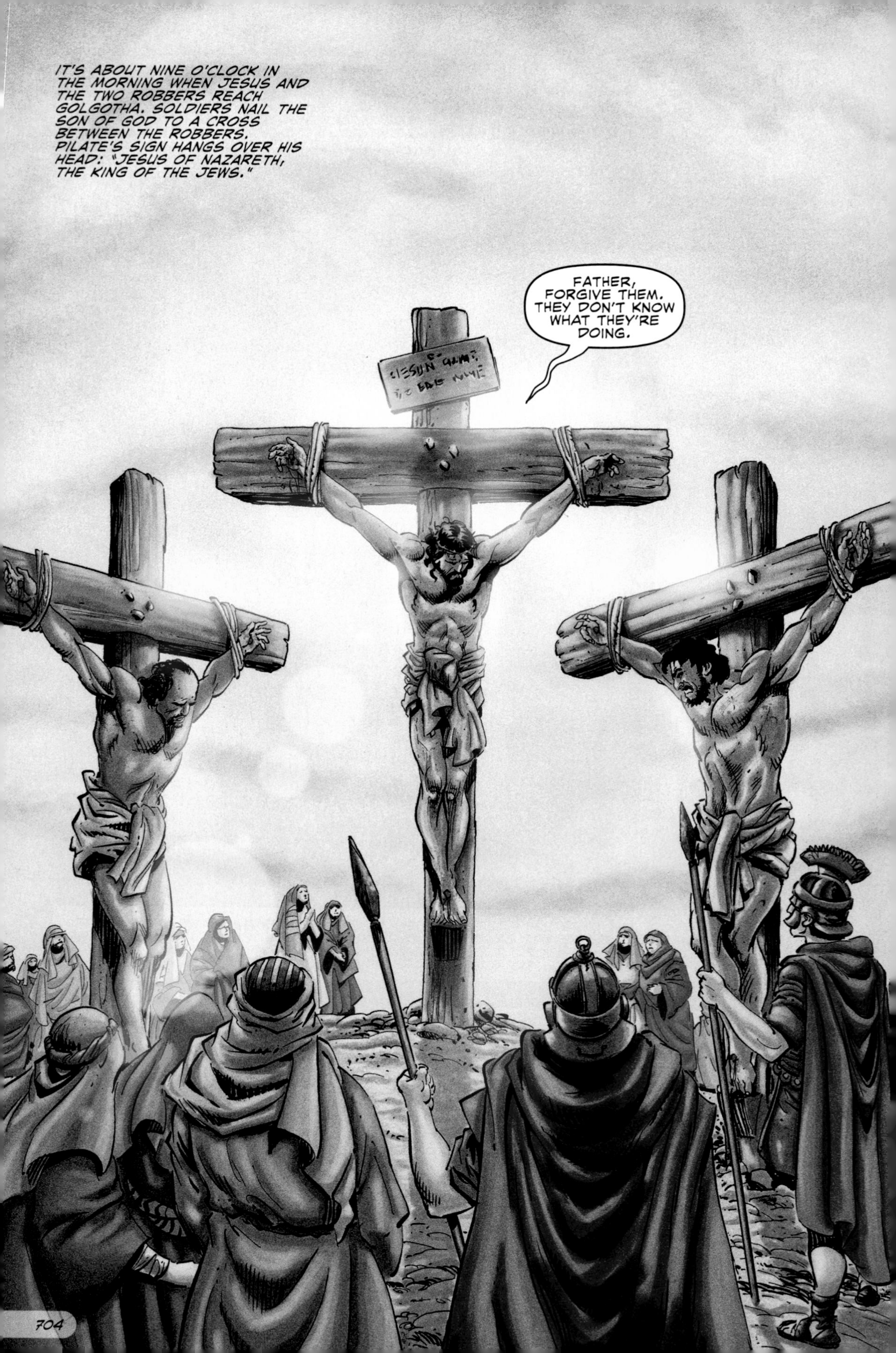
IT'S ABOUT NINE O'CLOCK IN THE MORNING WHEN JESUS AND THE TWO ROBBERS REACH GOLGOTHA. SOLDIERS NAIL THE SON OF GOD TO A CROSS BETWEEN THE ROBBERS. PILATE'S SIGN HANGS OVER HIS HEAD: "JESUS OF NAZARETH, THE KING OF THE JEWS."
FATHER, FORGIVE THEM. THEY DON'T KNOW WHAT THEY'RE DOING.

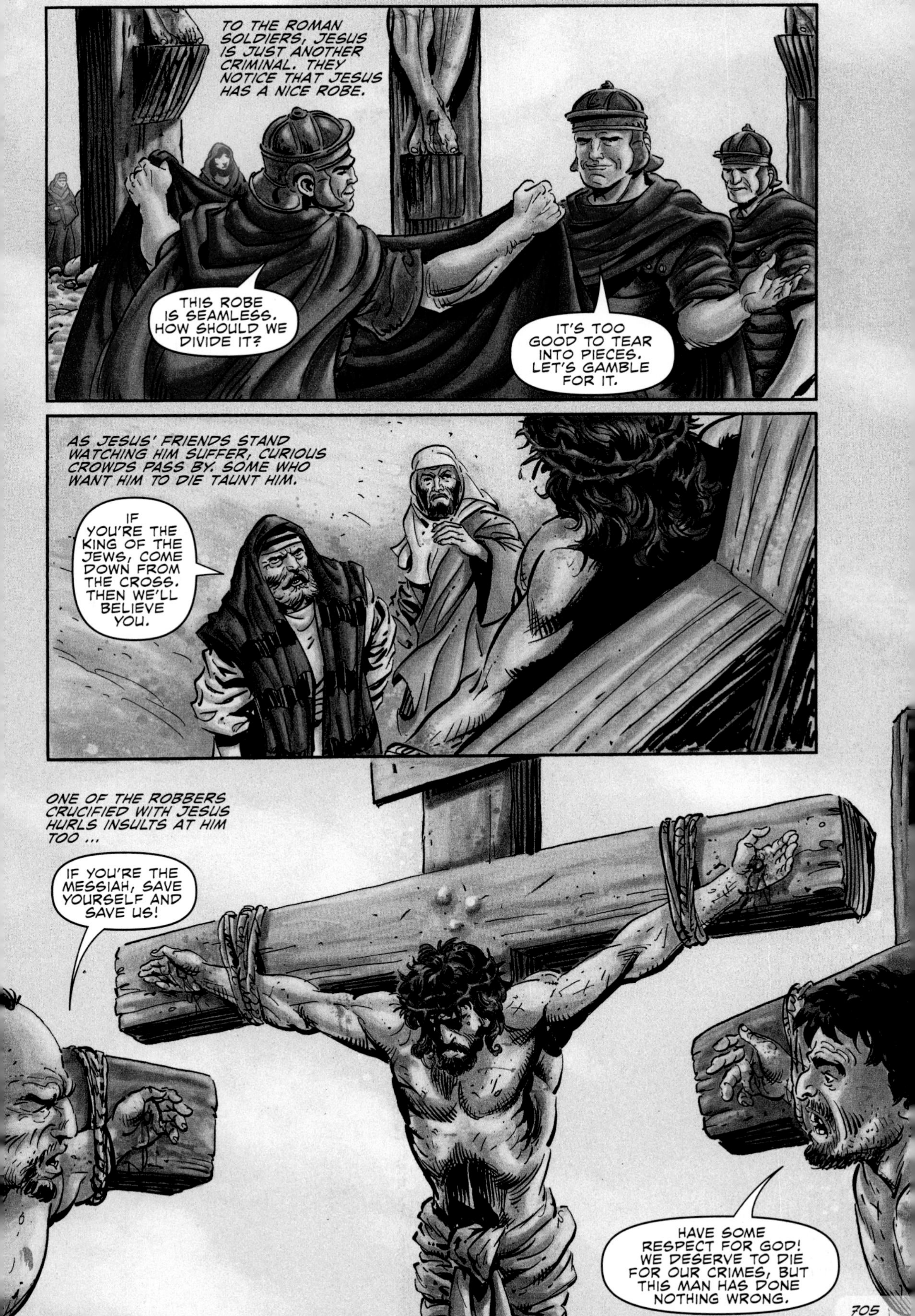
TO THE ROMAN SOLDIERS, JESUS IS JUST ANOTHER CRIMINAL. THEY NOTICE THAT JESUS HAS A NICE ROBE.
THIS ROBE IS SEAMLESS. HOW SHOULD WE DIVIDE IT?
IT'S TOO GOOD TO TEAR INTO PIECES. LET'S GAMBLE FOR IT.
AS JESUS' FRIENDS STAND WATCHING HIM SUFFER, CURIOUS CROWDS PASS BY. SOME WHO WANT HIM TO DIE TAUNT HIM.
IF YOU'RE THE KING OF THE JEWS, COME DOWN FROM THE CROSS. THEN WE'LL BELIEVE YOU.
ONE OF THE ROBBERS CRUCIFIED WITH JESUS HURLS INSULTS AT HIM TOO ...
IF YOU'RE THE MESSIAH, SAVE YOURSELF AND SAVE US!
HAVE SOME RESPECT FOR GOD! WE DESERVE TO DIE FOR OUR CRIMES, BUT THIS MAN HAS DONE NOTHING WRONG.

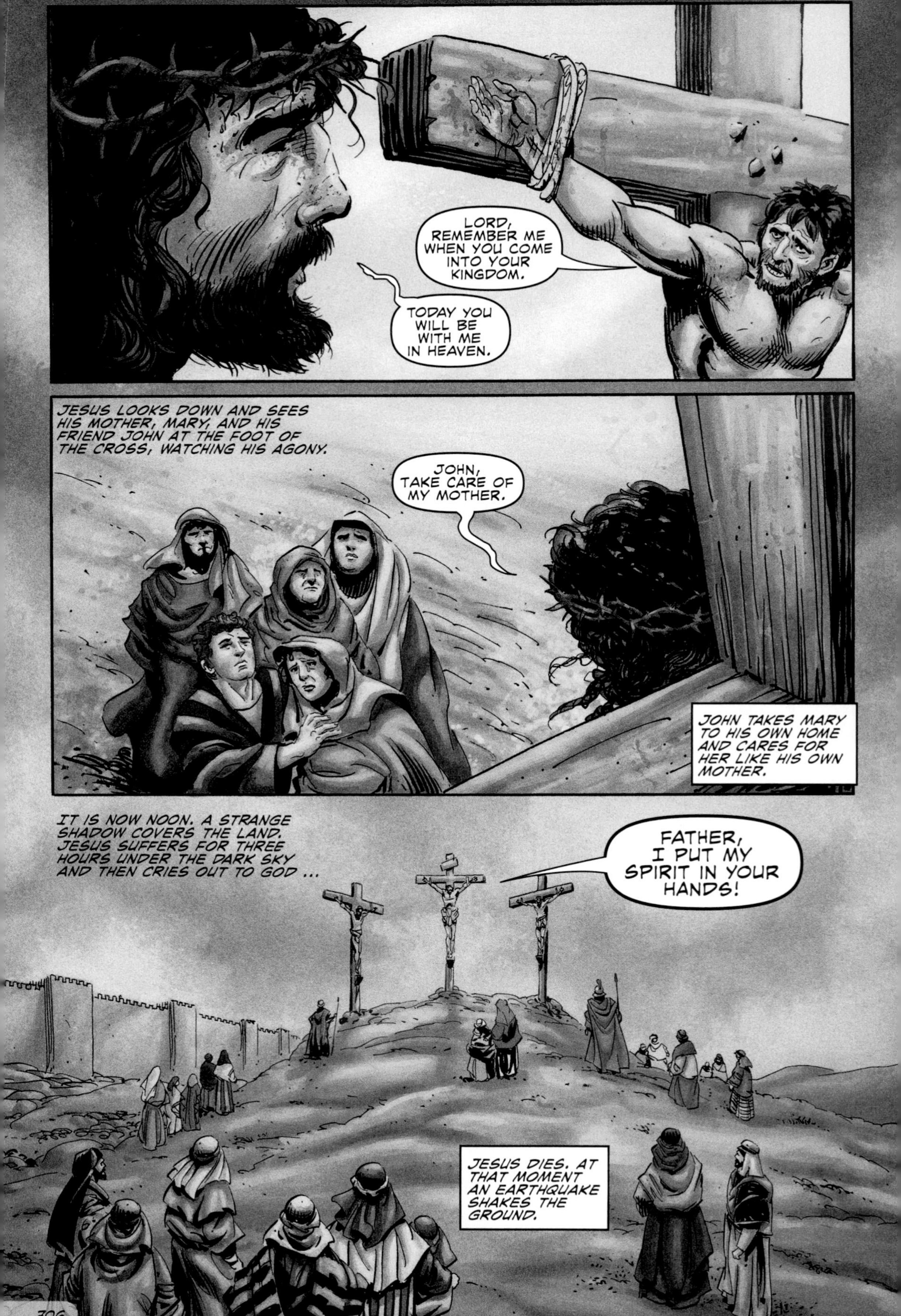
LORD, REMEMBER ME WHEN YOU COME INTO YOUR KINGDOM.
TODAY YOU WILL BE WITH ME IN HEAVEN.
JESUS LOOKS DOWN AND SEES HIS MOTHER, MARY, AND HIS FRIEND JOHN AT THE FOOT OF THE CROSS, WATCHING HIS AGONY.
JOHN, TAKE CARE OF MY MOTHER.
JOHN TAKES MARY TO HIS OWN HOME AND CARES FOR HER LIKE HIS OWN MOTHER.
IT IS NOW NOON. A STRANGE SHADOW COVERS THE LAND. JESUS SUFFERS FOR THREE HOURS UNDER THE DARK SKY AND THEN CRIES OUT TO GOD ...
FATHER, I PUT MY SPIRIT IN YOUR HANDS!
JESUS DIES. AT THAT MOMENT AN EARTHQUAKE SHAKES THE GROUND.

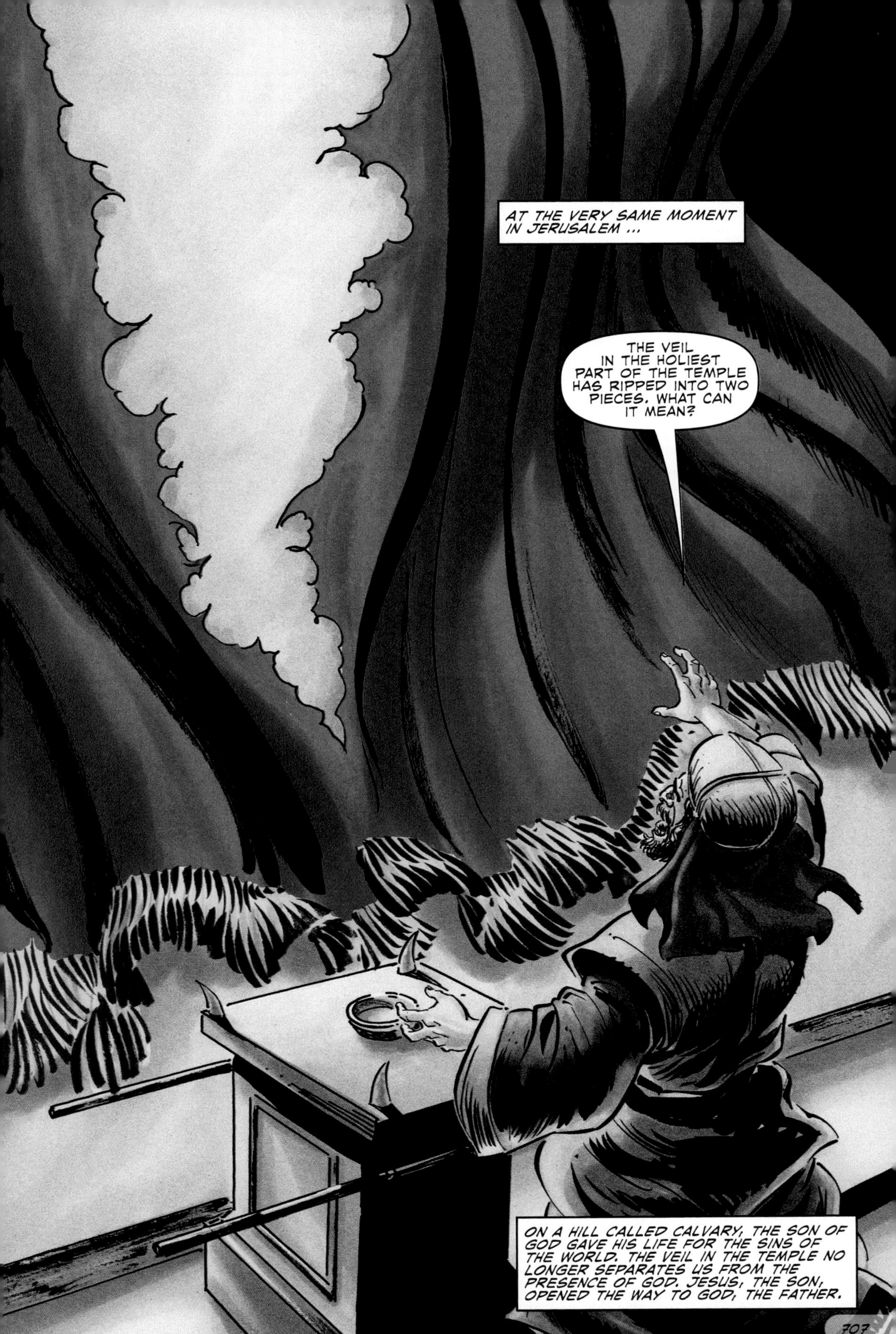
AT THE VERY SAME MOMENT IN JERUSALEM ...
THE VEIL IN THE HOLIEST PART OF THE TEMPLE HAS RIPPED INTO TWO PIECES. WHAT CAN IT MEAN?
ON A HILL CALLED CALVARY, THE SON OF GOD GAVE HIS LIFE FOR THE SINS OF THE WORLD. THE VEIL IN THE TEMPLE NO LONGER SEPARATES US FROM THE PRESENCE OF GOD. JESUS, THE SON, OPENED THE WAY TO GOD, THE FATHER.

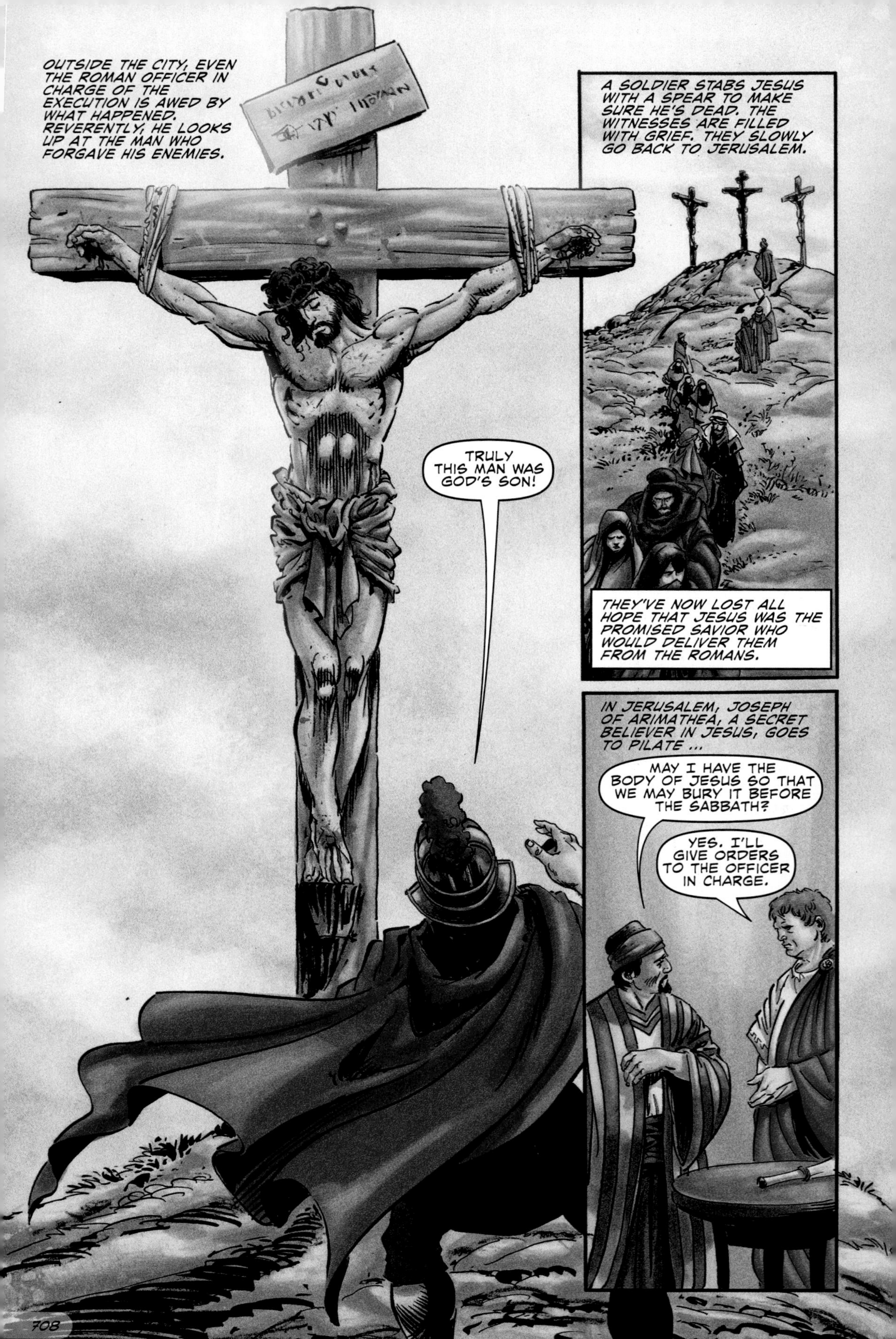
OUTSIDE THE CITY, EVEN THE ROMAN OFFICER IN CHARGE OF THE EXECUTION IS AWED BY WHAT HAPPENED. REVERENTLY, HE LOOKS UP AT THE MAN WHO FORGAVE HIS ENEMIES.
TRULY THIS MAN WAS GOD'S SON!
A SOLDIER STABS JESUS WITH A SPEAR TO MAKE SURE HE'S DEAD. THE WITNESSES ARE FILLED WITH GRIEF. THEY SLOWLY GO BACK TO JERUSALEM.
THEY'VE NOW LOST ALL HOPE THAT JESUS WAS THE PROMISED SAVIOR WHO WOULD DELIVER THEM FROM THE ROMANS.
IN JERUSALEM, JOSEPH OF ARIMATHEA, A SECRET BELIEVER IN JESUS, GOES TO PILATE ...
MAY I HAVE THE BODY OF JESUS SO THAT WE MAY BURY IT BEFORE THE SABBATH?
YES. I'LL GIVE ORDERS TO THE OFFICER IN CHARGE.

The Sealed Tomb

BASED ON MATTHEW 27:59–28:15; JOHN 19:38–20:18; LUKE 24:13–32

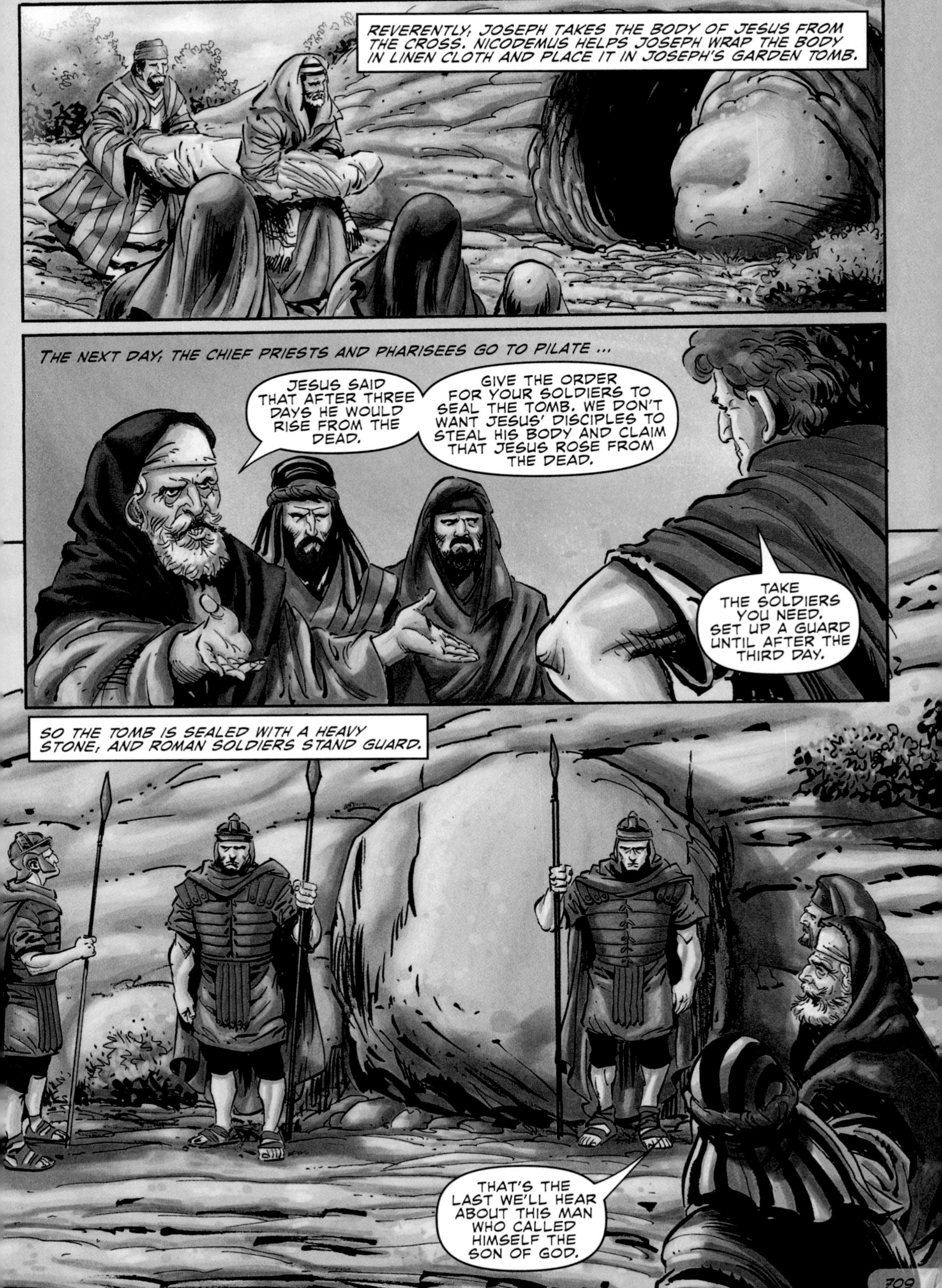

REVERENTLY, JOSEPH TAKES THE BODY OF JESUS FROM THE CROSS. NICODEMUS HELPS JOSEPH WRAP THE BODY IN LINEN CLOTH AND PLACE IT IN JOSEPH'S GARDEN TOMB.
THE NEXT DAY, THE CHIEF PRIESTS AND PHARISEES GO TO PILATE ...
JESUS SAID THAT AFTER THREE DAYS HE WOULD RISE FROM THE DEAD.
GIVE THE ORDER FOR YOUR SOLDIERS TO SEAL THE TOMB. WE DON'T WANT JESUS' DISCIPLES TO STEAL HIS BODY AND CLAIM THAT JESUS ROSE FROM THE DEAD.
TAKE THE SOLDIERS YOU NEED. SET UP A GUARD UNTIL AFTER THE THIRD DAY.
SO THE TOMB IS SEALED WITH A HEAVY STONE, AND ROMAN SOLDIERS STAND GUARD.
THAT'S THE LAST WE'LL HEAR ABOUT THIS MAN WHO CALLED HIMSELF THE SON OF GOD.

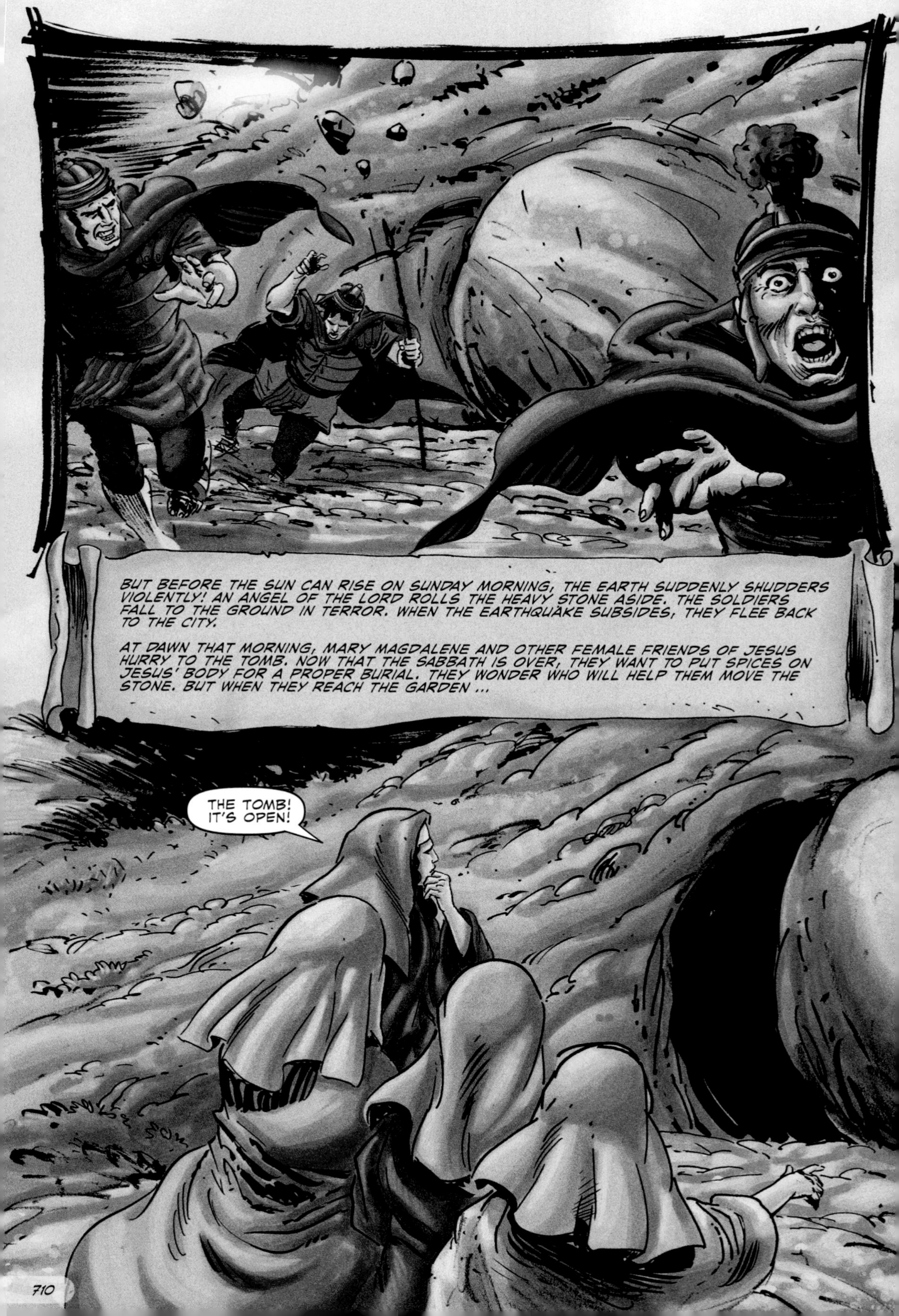

BUT BEFORE THE SUN CAN RISE ON SUNDAY MORNING, THE EARTH SUDDENLY SHUDDERS VIOLENTLY! AN ANGEL OF THE LORD ROLLS THE HEAVY STONE ASIDE. THE SOLDIERS FALL TO THE GROUND IN TERROR. WHEN THE EARTHQUAKE SUBSIDES, THEY FLEE BACK TO THE CITY.
AT DAWN THAT MORNING, MARY MAGDALENE AND OTHER FEMALE FRIENDS OF JESUS HURRY TO THE TOMB. NOW THAT THE SABBATH IS OVER, THEY WANT TO PUT SPICES ON JESUS' BODY FOR A PROPER BURIAL. THEY WONDER WHO WILL HELP THEM MOVE THE STONE. BUT WHEN THEY REACH THE GARDEN ...
THE TOMB! IT'S OPEN!

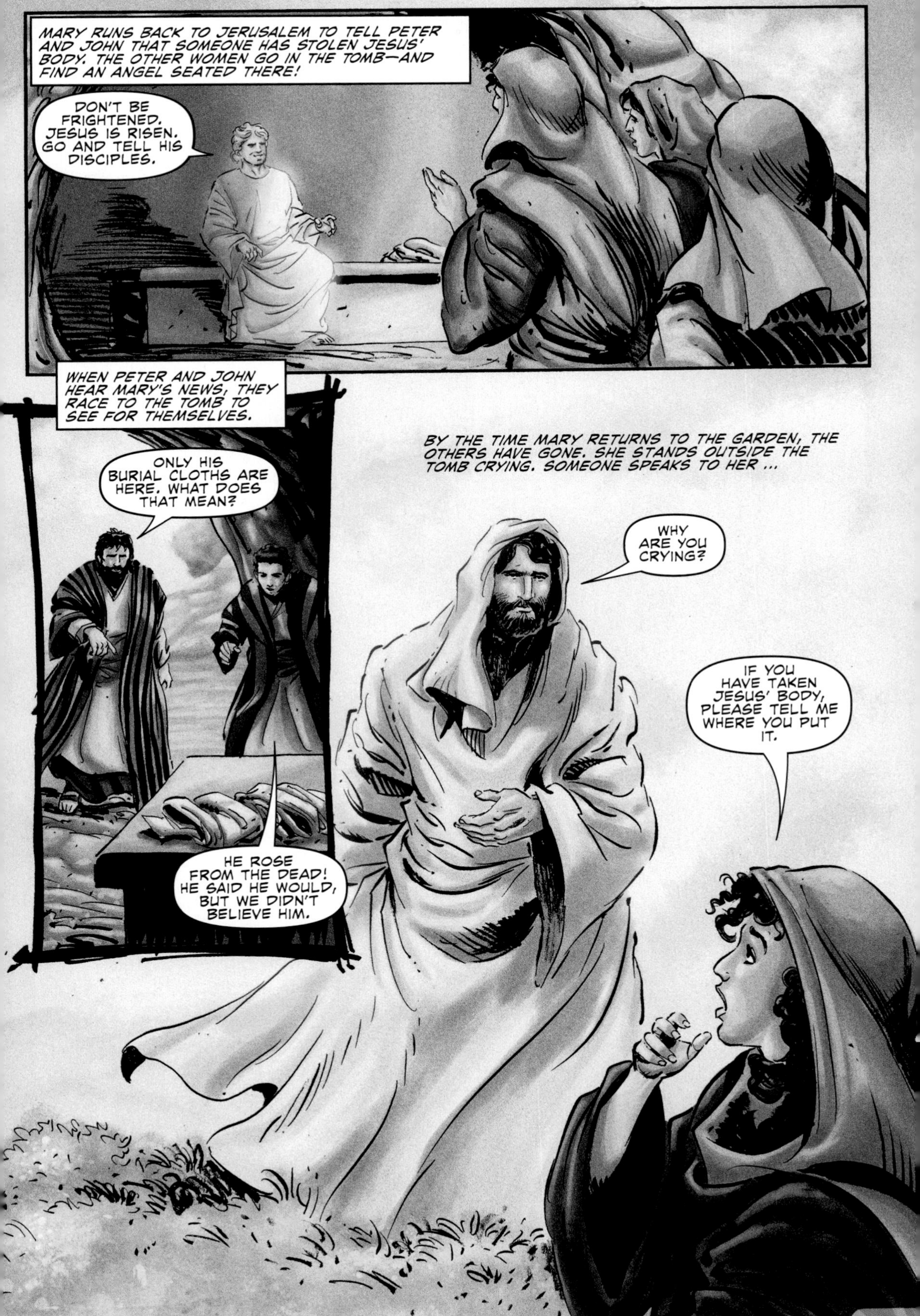
MARY RUNS BACK TO JERUSALEM TO TELL PETER AND JOHN THAT SOMEONE HAS STOLEN JESUS' BODY. THE OTHER WOMEN GO IN THE TOMB—AND FIND AN ANGEL SEATED THERE!
DON'T BE FRIGHTENED. JESUS IS RISEN. GO AND TELL HIS DISCIPLES.
WHEN PETER AND JOHN HEAR MARY'S NEWS, THEY RACE TO THE TOMB TO SEE FOR THEMSELVES.
ONLY HIS BURIAL CLOTHS ARE HERE. WHAT DOES THAT MEAN?
HE ROSE FROM THE DEAD! HE SAID HE WOULD, BUT WE DIDN'T BELIEVE HIM.
BY THE TIME MARY RETURNS TO THE GARDEN, THE OTHERS HAVE GONE. SHE STANDS OUTSIDE THE TOMB CRYING. SOMEONE SPEAKS TO HER ...
WHY ARE YOU CRYING?
IF YOU HAVE TAKEN JESUS' BODY, PLEASE TELL ME WHERE YOU PUT IT.

TENDERLY, JESUS SPEAKS MARY'S NAME. SHE RECOGNIZES HIS VOICE NOW ...

MASTER!

JESUS' FRIENDS ARE NOT THE ONLY ONES TO HEAR THE NEWS. THE GUARDS FROM THE TOMB GO STRAIGHT TO THE PRIESTS TO TELL THEM WHAT HAPPENED. ALARMED, THE PRIESTS DON'T WANT ANYONE TO HEAR THE TRUTH, SO THEY COME UP WITH A DEVIOUS PLAN ...

HERE, TAKE THIS MONEY. TELL PEOPLE THAT JESUS' DISCIPLES STOLE HIS BODY WHILE ALL OF YOU WERE ASLEEP.

WHILE THE SOLDIERS SPREAD THIS LIE, JESUS JOINS TWO OF HIS FOLLOWERS AS THEY ARE TRAVELING. HE KEEPS THEM FROM RECOGNIZING HIM, AND HE EXPLAINS TO THEM WHAT THE SCRIPTURES SAY ABOUT HIS OWN DEATH.

THE PROPHETS *SAID* THAT THE CHRIST WOULD HAVE TO SUFFER BEFORE HE COULD BE THE SAVIOR OF THE WORLD.

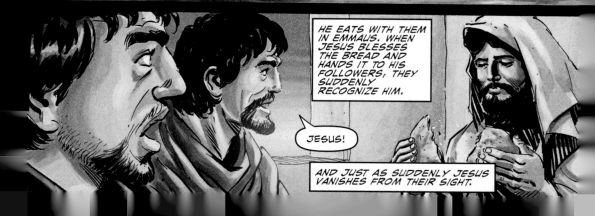

HE EATS WITH THEM IN EMMAUS. WHEN JESUS BLESSES THE BREAD AND HANDS IT TO HIS FOLLOWERS, THEY SUDDENLY RECOGNIZE HIM.

JESUS!

AND JUST AS SUDDENLY JESUS VANISHES FROM THEIR SIGHT.

Seeing Jesus Again

BASED ON LUKE 24:33-53; JOHN 20:19—21:17; MATTHEW 28:16-20

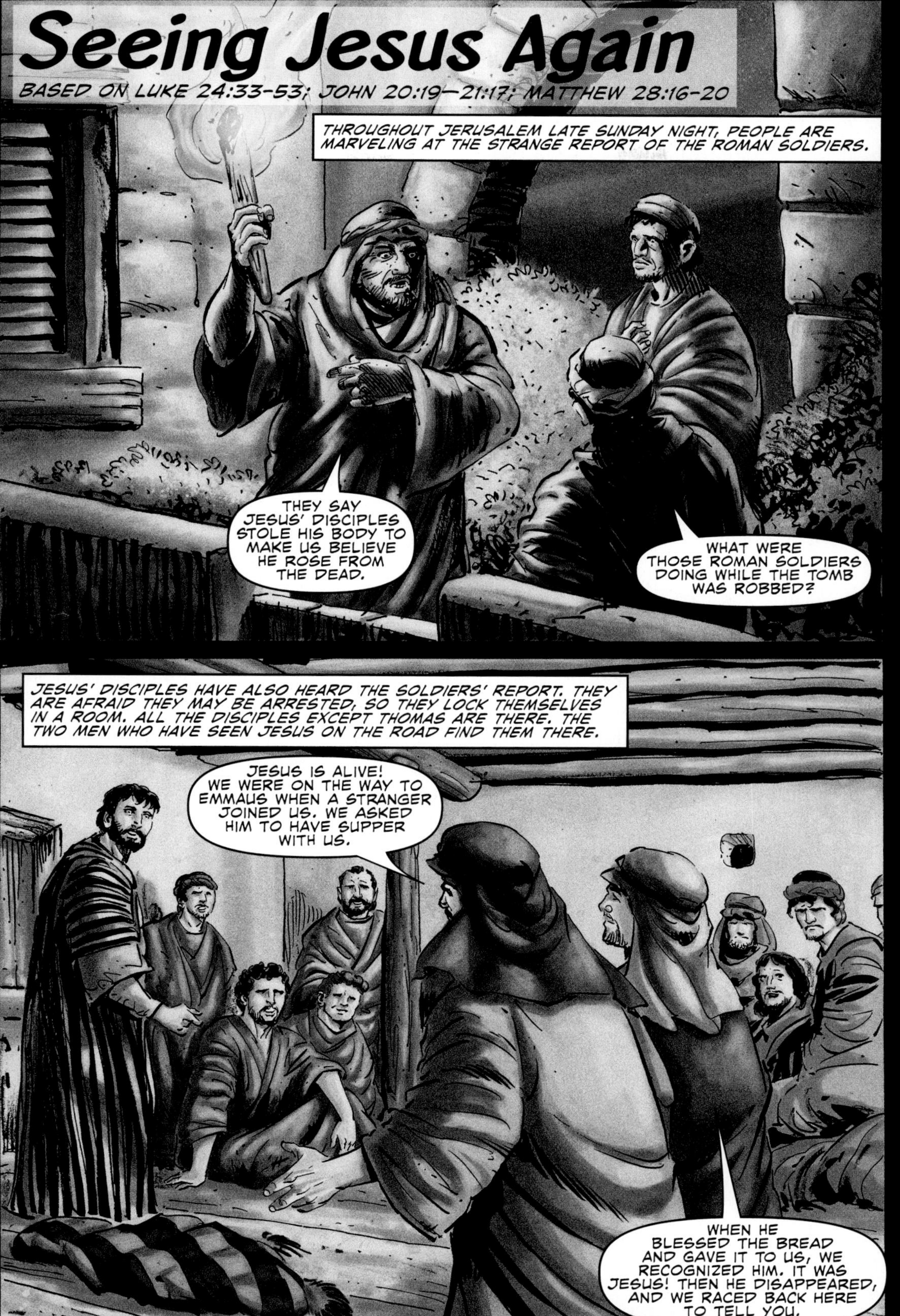

THROUGHOUT JERUSALEM LATE SUNDAY NIGHT, PEOPLE ARE MARVELING AT THE STRANGE REPORT OF THE ROMAN SOLDIERS.
THEY SAY JESUS' DISCIPLES STOLE HIS BODY TO MAKE US BELIEVE HE ROSE FROM THE DEAD.
WHAT WERE THOSE ROMAN SOLDIERS DOING WHILE THE TOMB WAS ROBBED?
JESUS' DISCIPLES HAVE ALSO HEARD THE SOLDIERS' REPORT. THEY ARE AFRAID THEY MAY BE ARRESTED, SO THEY LOCK THEMSELVES IN A ROOM. ALL THE DISCIPLES EXCEPT THOMAS ARE THERE. THE TWO MEN WHO HAVE SEEN JESUS ON THE ROAD FIND THEM THERE.
JESUS IS ALIVE! WE WERE ON THE WAY TO EMMAUS WHEN A STRANGER JOINED US. WE ASKED HIM TO HAVE SUPPER WITH US.
WHEN HE BLESSED THE BREAD AND GAVE IT TO US, WE RECOGNIZED HIM. IT WAS JESUS! THEN HE DISAPPEARED, AND WE RACED BACK HERE TO TELL YOU.

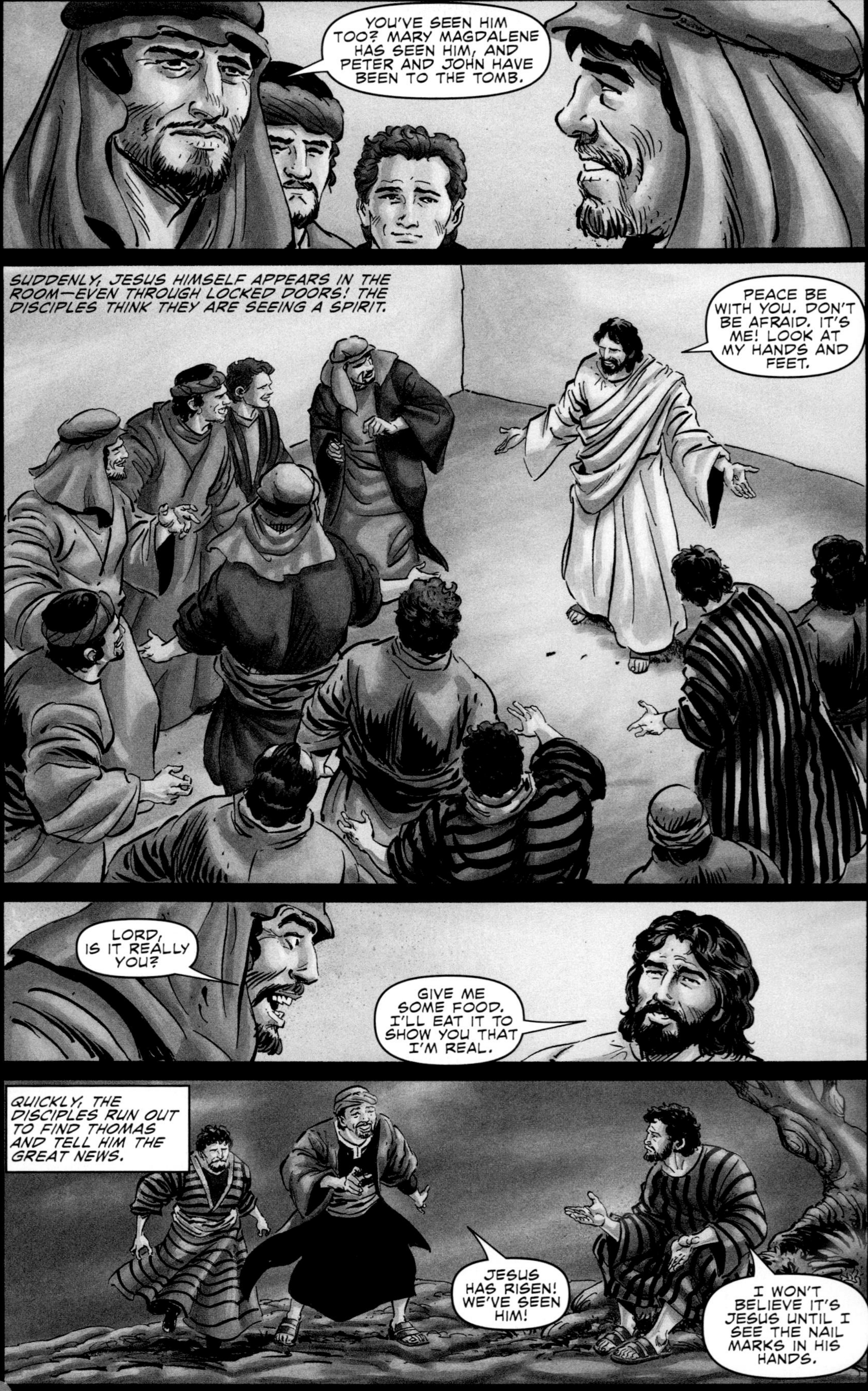
YOU'VE SEEN HIM TOO? MARY MAGDALENE HAS SEEN HIM, AND PETER AND JOHN HAVE BEEN TO THE TOMB.
SUDDENLY, JESUS HIMSELF APPEARS IN THE ROOM—EVEN THROUGH LOCKED DOORS! THE DISCIPLES THINK THEY ARE SEEING A SPIRIT.
PEACE BE WITH YOU. DON'T BE AFRAID. IT'S ME! LOOK AT MY HANDS AND FEET.
LORD, IS IT REALLY YOU?
GIVE ME SOME FOOD. I'LL EAT IT TO SHOW YOU THAT I'M REAL.
QUICKLY, THE DISCIPLES RUN OUT TO FIND THOMAS AND TELL HIM THE GREAT NEWS.
JESUS HAS RISEN! WE'VE SEEN HIM!
I WON'T BELIEVE IT'S JESUS UNTIL I SEE THE NAIL MARKS IN HIS HANDS.

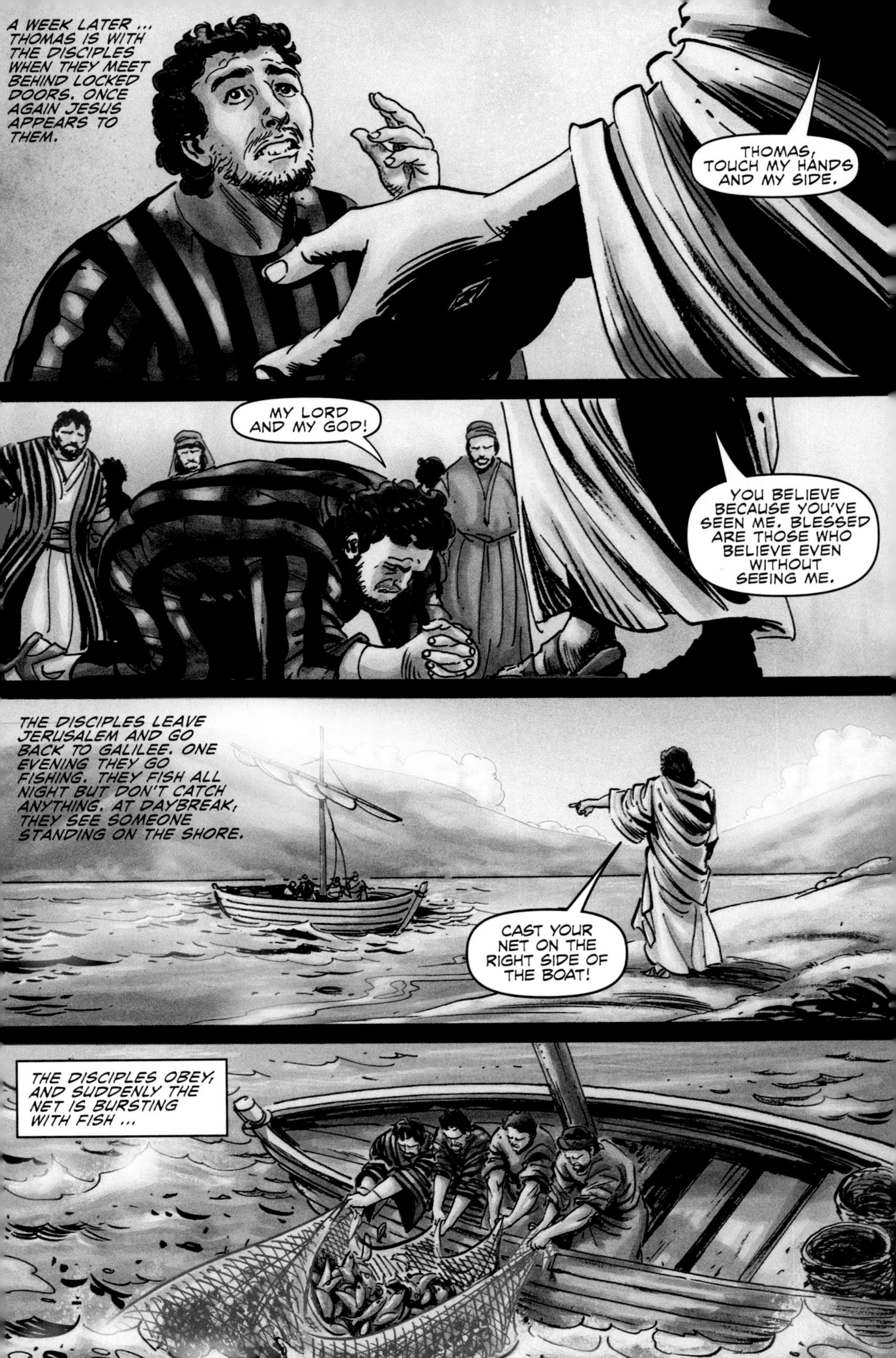
A WEEK LATER ... THOMAS IS WITH THE DISCIPLES WHEN THEY MEET BEHIND LOCKED DOORS. ONCE AGAIN JESUS APPEARS TO THEM.
THOMAS, TOUCH MY HANDS AND MY SIDE.
MY LORD AND MY GOD!
YOU BELIEVE BECAUSE YOU'VE SEEN ME. BLESSED ARE THOSE WHO BELIEVE EVEN WITHOUT SEEING ME.
THE DISCIPLES LEAVE JERUSALEM AND GO BACK TO GALILEE. ONE EVENING THEY GO FISHING. THEY FISH ALL NIGHT BUT DON'T CATCH ANYTHING. AT DAYBREAK, THEY SEE SOMEONE STANDING ON THE SHORE.
CAST YOUR NET ON THE RIGHT SIDE OF THE BOAT!
THE DISCIPLES OBEY, AND SUDDENLY THE NET IS BURSTING WITH FISH ...

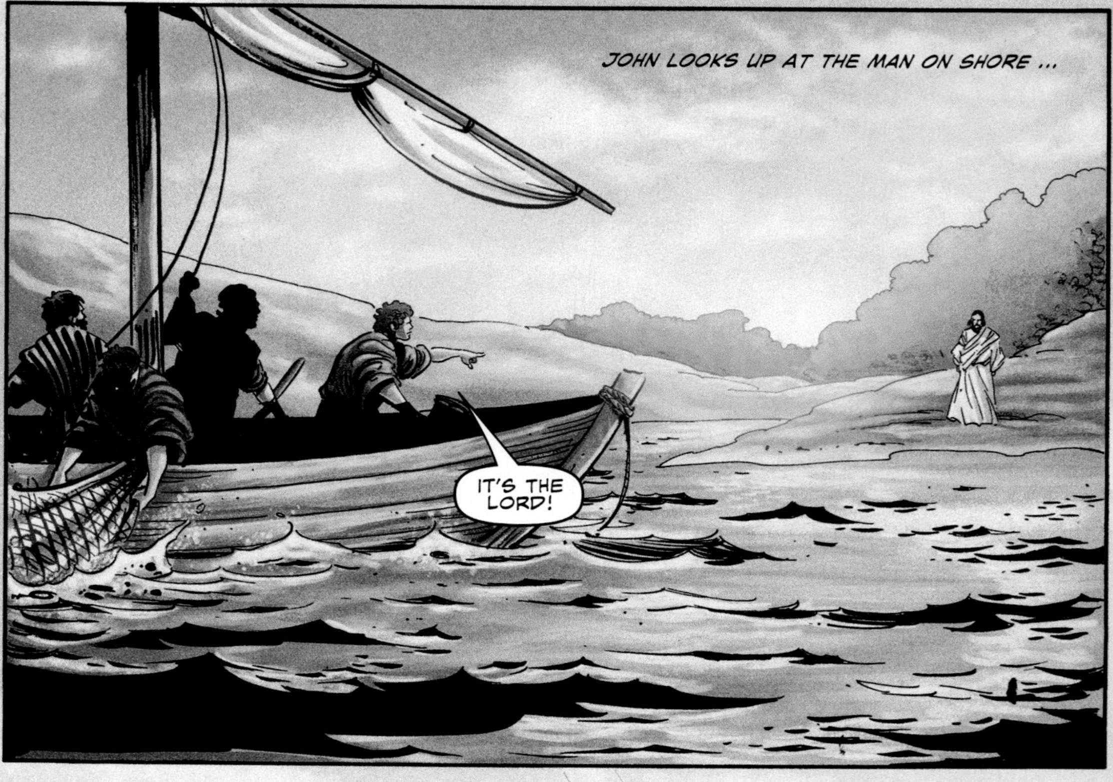
JOHN LOOKS UP AT THE MAN ON SHORE ...
IT'S THE LORD!

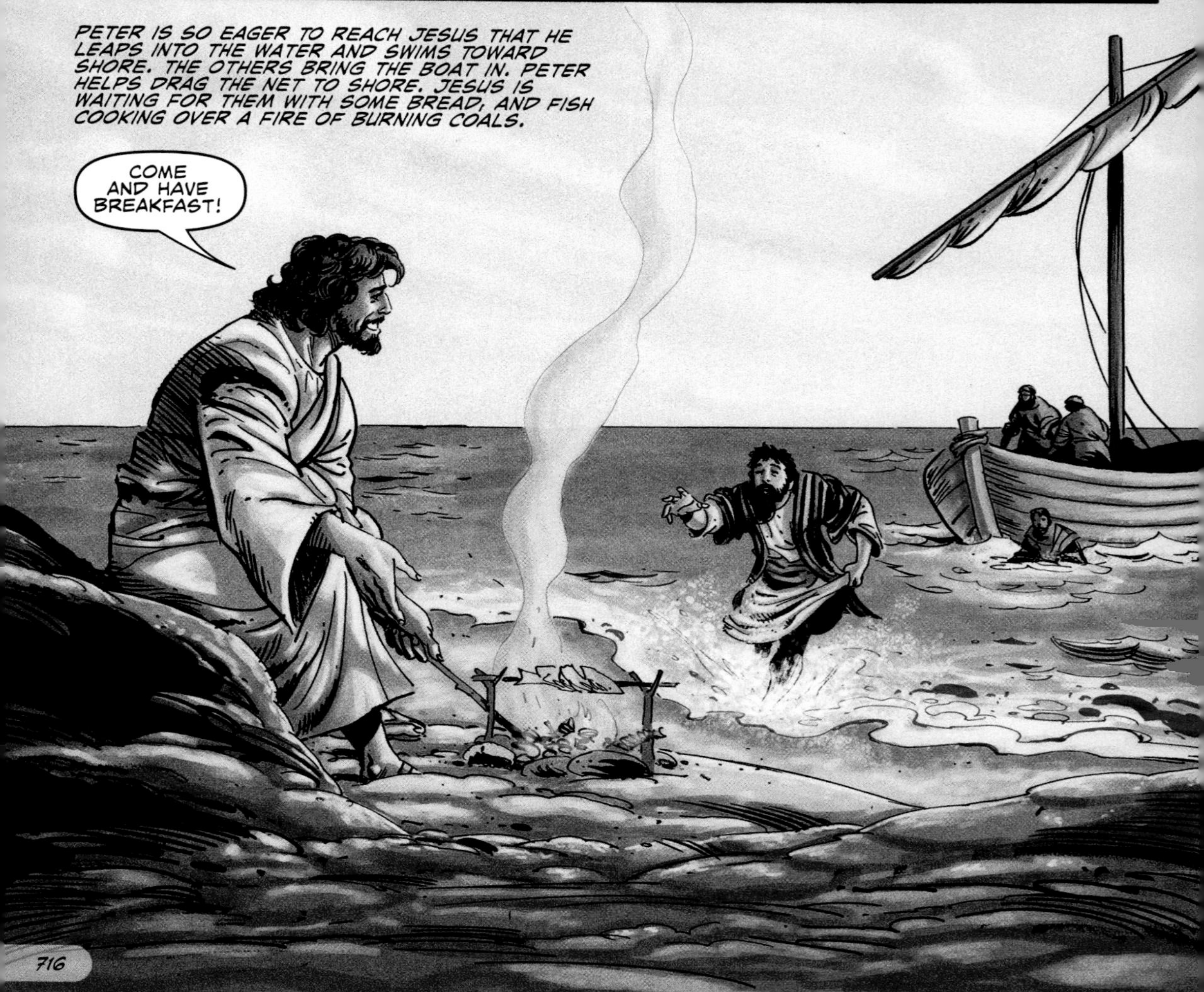
PETER IS SO EAGER TO REACH JESUS THAT HE LEAPS INTO THE WATER AND SWIMS TOWARD SHORE. THE OTHERS BRING THE BOAT IN. PETER HELPS DRAG THE NET TO SHORE. JESUS IS WAITING FOR THEM WITH SOME BREAD, AND FISH COOKING OVER A FIRE OF BURNING COALS.
COME AND HAVE BREAKFAST!

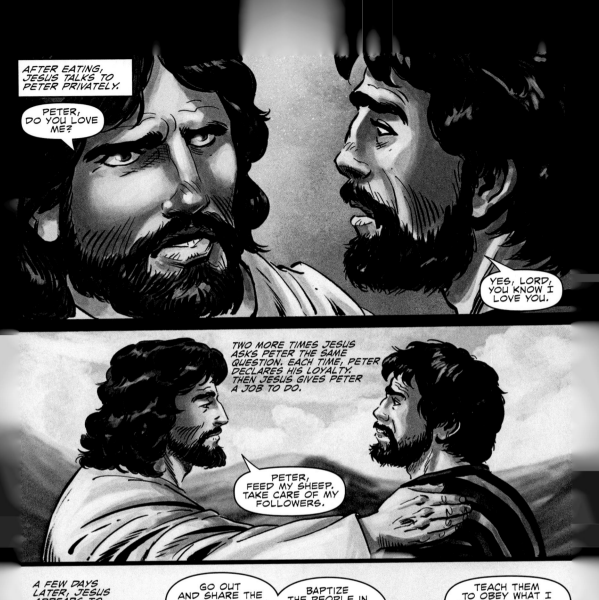

AFTER EATING, JESUS TALKS TO PETER PRIVATELY.

PETER, DO YOU LOVE ME?

YES, LORD, YOU KNOW I LOVE YOU.

TWO MORE TIMES JESUS ASKS PETER THE SAME QUESTION. EACH TIME, PETER DECLARES HIS LOYALTY. THEN JESUS GIVES PETER A JOB TO DO.

PETER, FEED MY SHEEP. TAKE CARE OF MY FOLLOWERS.

A FEW DAYS LATER, JESUS APPEARS TO 500 OF HIS FOLLOWERS GATHERED ON A MOUNTAIN NEAR THE SEA OF GALILEE. HE GIVES THEM ONE LAST COMMAND.

GO OUT AND SHARE THE GOOD NEWS WITH THE WHOLE WORLD.

BAPTIZE THE PEOPLE IN THE NAME OF THE FATHER AND OF THE SON AND OF THE HOLY SPIRIT.

TEACH THEM TO OBEY WHAT I HAVE COMMANDED. AND I WILL ALWAYS BE WITH YOU.

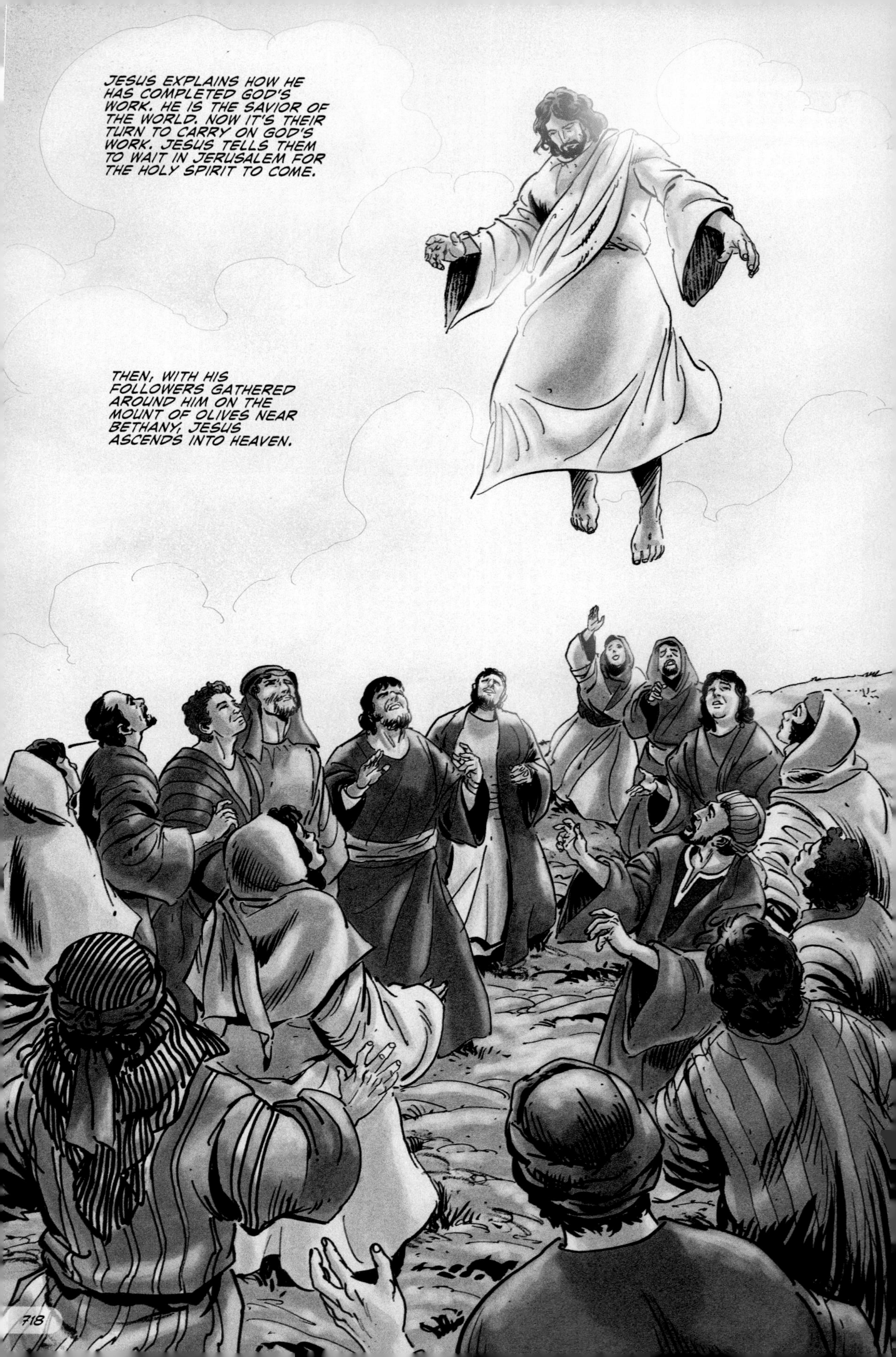
JESUS EXPLAINS HOW HE HAS COMPLETED GOD'S WORK. HE IS THE SAVIOR OF THE WORLD. NOW IT'S THEIR TURN TO CARRY ON GOD'S WORK. JESUS TELLS THEM TO WAIT IN JERUSALEM FOR THE HOLY SPIRIT TO COME.
THEN, WITH HIS FOLLOWERS GATHERED AROUND HIM ON THE MOUNT OF OLIVES NEAR BETHANY, JESUS ASCENDS INTO HEAVEN.

Waiting for the Spirit

BASED ON ACTS 1

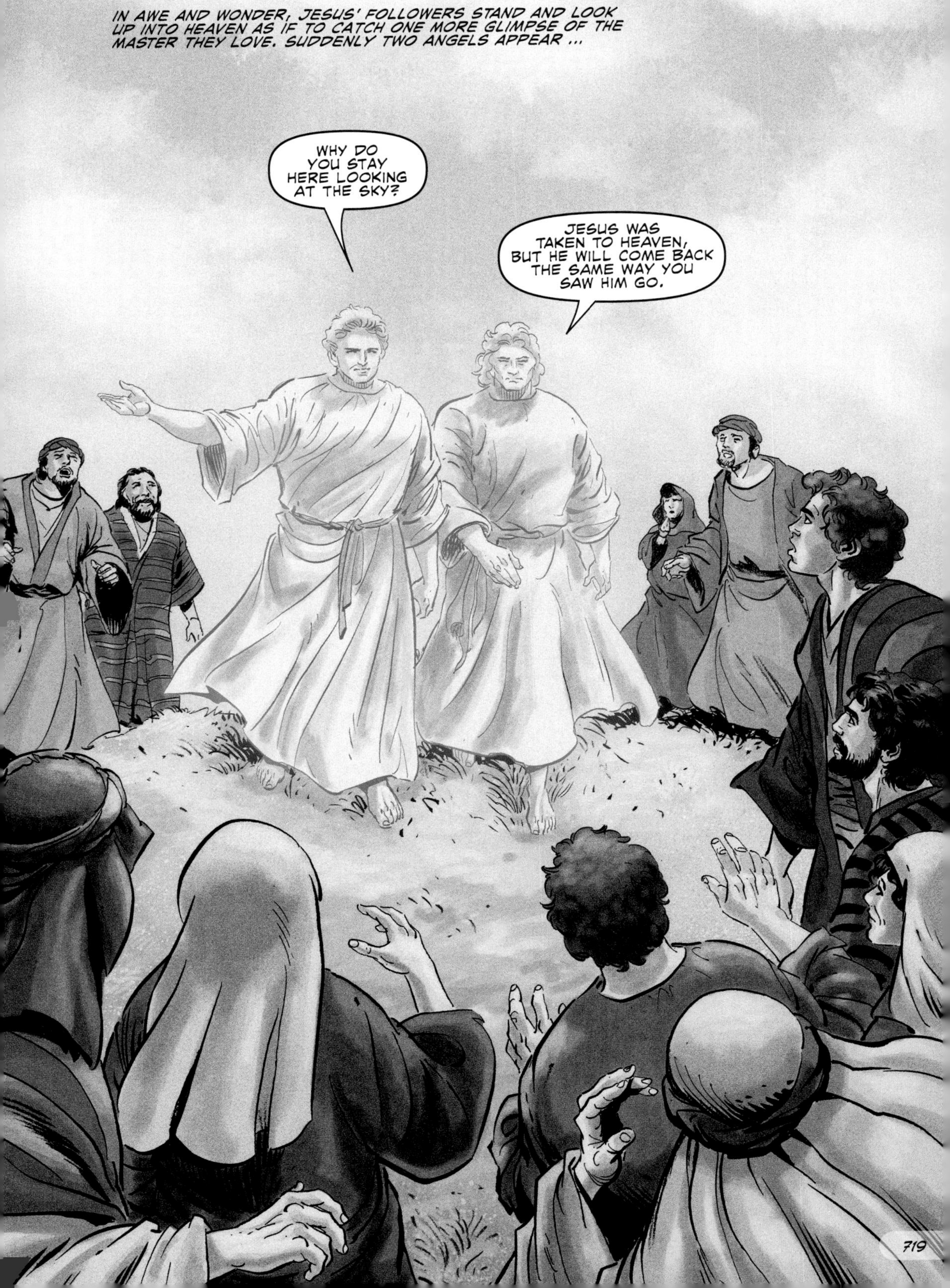
IN AWE AND WONDER, JESUS' FOLLOWERS STAND AND LOOK UP INTO HEAVEN AS IF TO CATCH ONE MORE GLIMPSE OF THE MASTER THEY LOVE. SUDDENLY TWO ANGELS APPEAR ...
WHY DO YOU STAY HERE LOOKING AT THE SKY?
JESUS WAS TAKEN TO HEAVEN, BUT HE WILL COME BACK THE SAME WAY YOU SAW HIM GO.

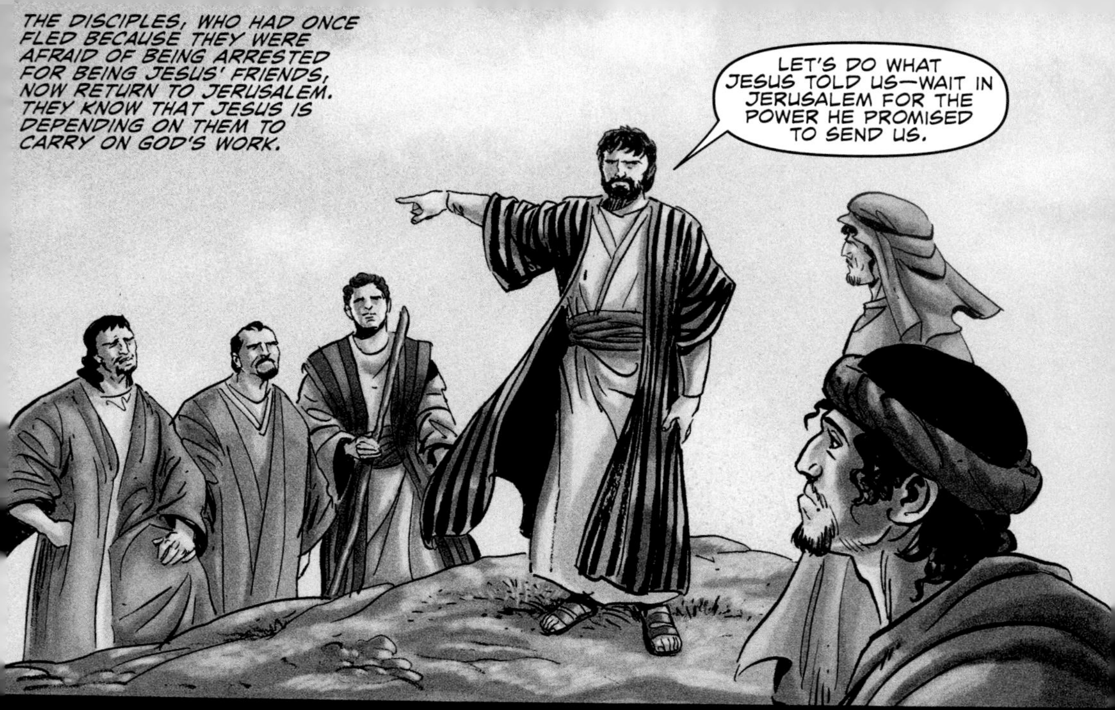
THE DISCIPLES, WHO HAD ONCE FLED BECAUSE THEY WERE AFRAID OF BEING ARRESTED FOR BEING JESUS' FRIENDS, NOW RETURN TO JERUSALEM. THEY KNOW THAT JESUS IS DEPENDING ON THEM TO CARRY ON GOD'S WORK.
LET'S DO WHAT JESUS TOLD US—WAIT IN JERUSALEM FOR THE POWER HE PROMISED TO SEND US.

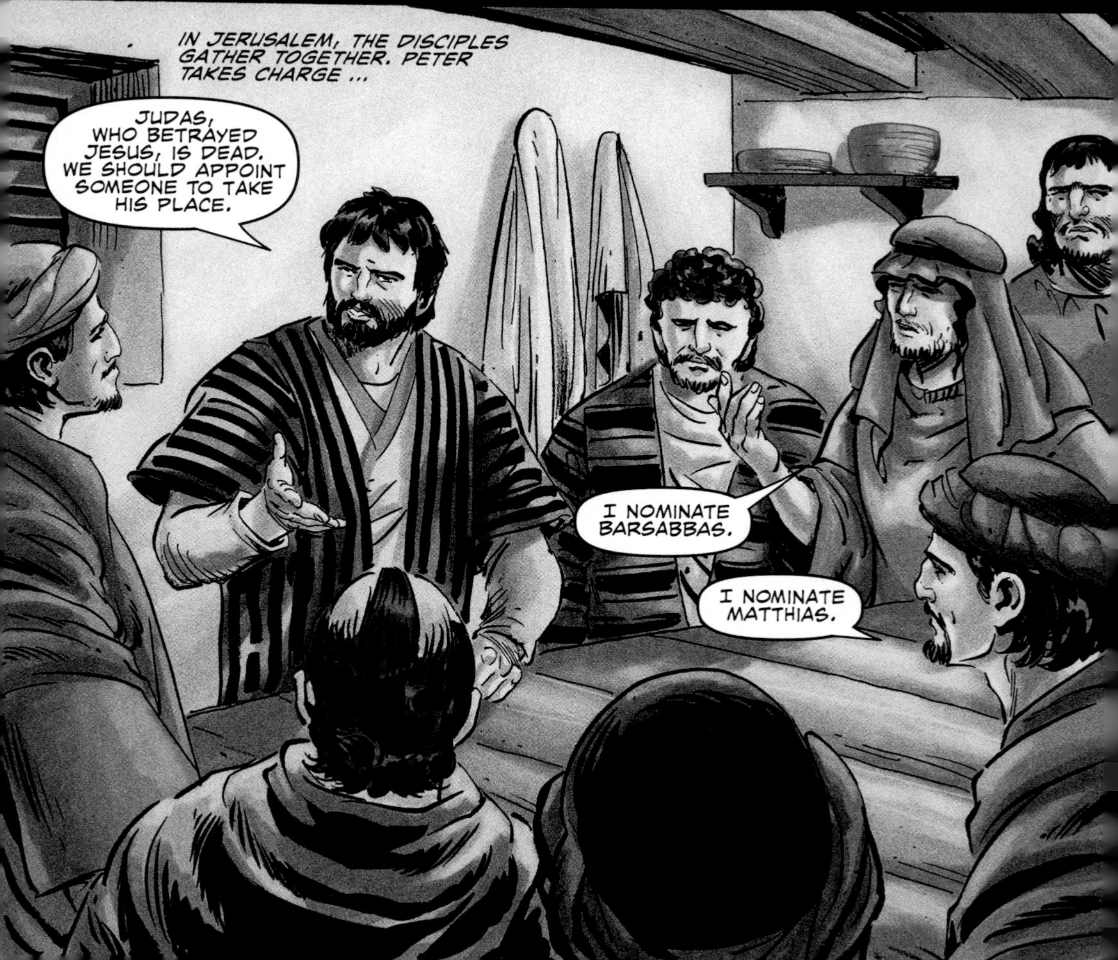
IN JERUSALEM, THE DISCIPLES GATHER TOGETHER. PETER TAKES CHARGE ...
JUDAS, WHO BETRAYED JESUS, IS DEAD. WE SHOULD APPOINT SOMEONE TO TAKE HIS PLACE.
I NOMINATE BARSABBAS.
I NOMINATE MATTHIAS.

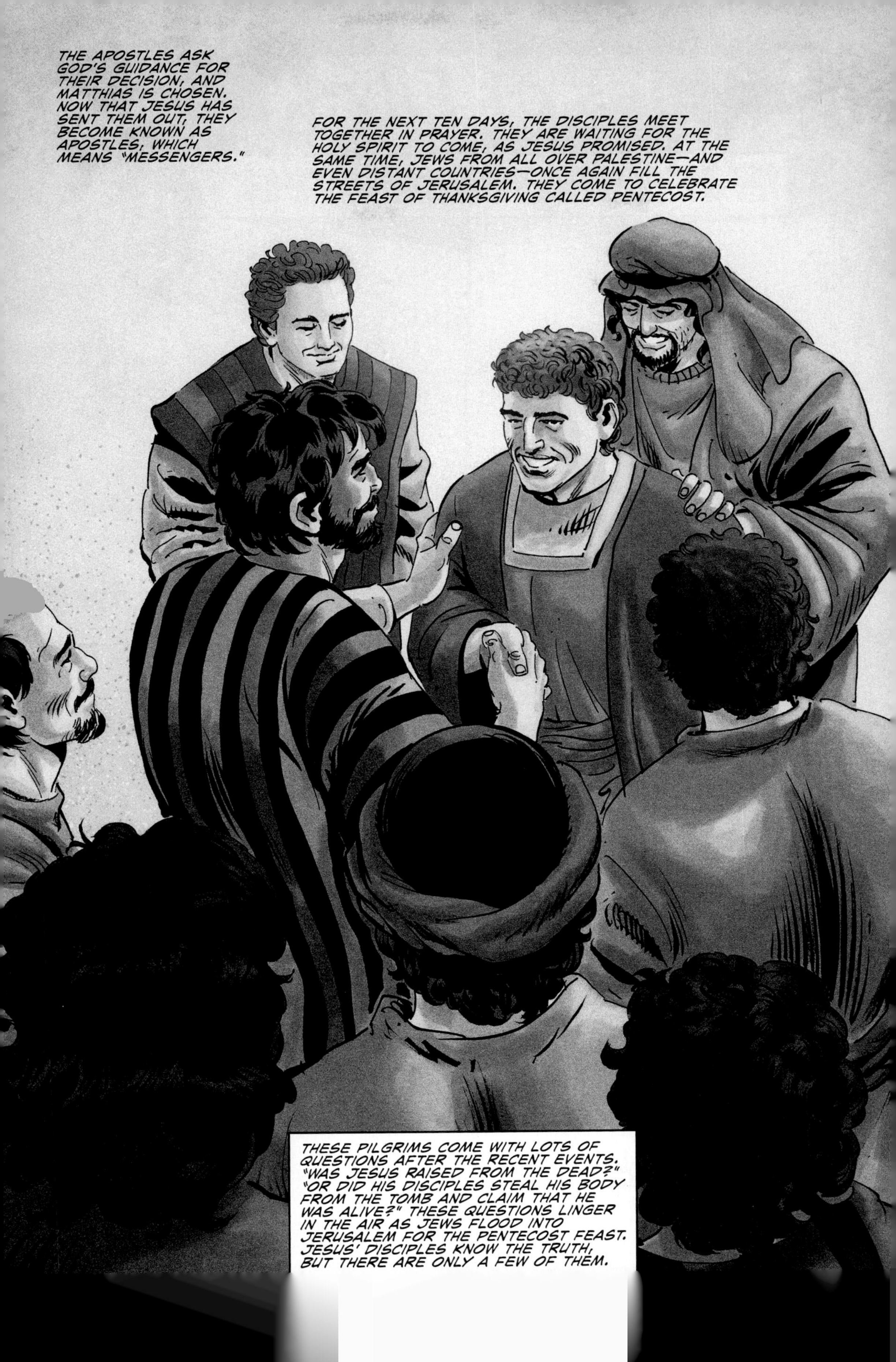
THE APOSTLES ASK GOD'S GUIDANCE FOR THEIR DECISION, AND MATTHIAS IS CHOSEN. NOW THAT JESUS HAS SENT THEM OUT, THEY BECOME KNOWN AS APOSTLES, WHICH MEANS "MESSENGERS."
FOR THE NEXT TEN DAYS, THE DISCIPLES MEET TOGETHER IN PRAYER. THEY ARE WAITING FOR THE HOLY SPIRIT TO COME, AS JESUS PROMISED. AT THE SAME TIME, JEWS FROM ALL OVER PALESTINE—AND EVEN DISTANT COUNTRIES—ONCE AGAIN FILL THE STREETS OF JERUSALEM. THEY COME TO CELEBRATE THE FEAST OF THANKSGIVING CALLED PENTECOST.
THESE PILGRIMS COME WITH LOTS OF QUESTIONS AFTER THE RECENT EVENTS. "WAS JESUS RAISED FROM THE DEAD?" "OR DID HIS DISCIPLES STEAL HIS BODY FROM THE TOMB AND CLAIM THAT HE WAS ALIVE?" THESE QUESTIONS LINGER IN THE AIR AS JEWS FLOOD INTO JERUSALEM FOR THE PENTECOST FEAST. JESUS' DISCIPLES KNOW THE TRUTH, BUT THERE ARE ONLY A FEW OF THEM.

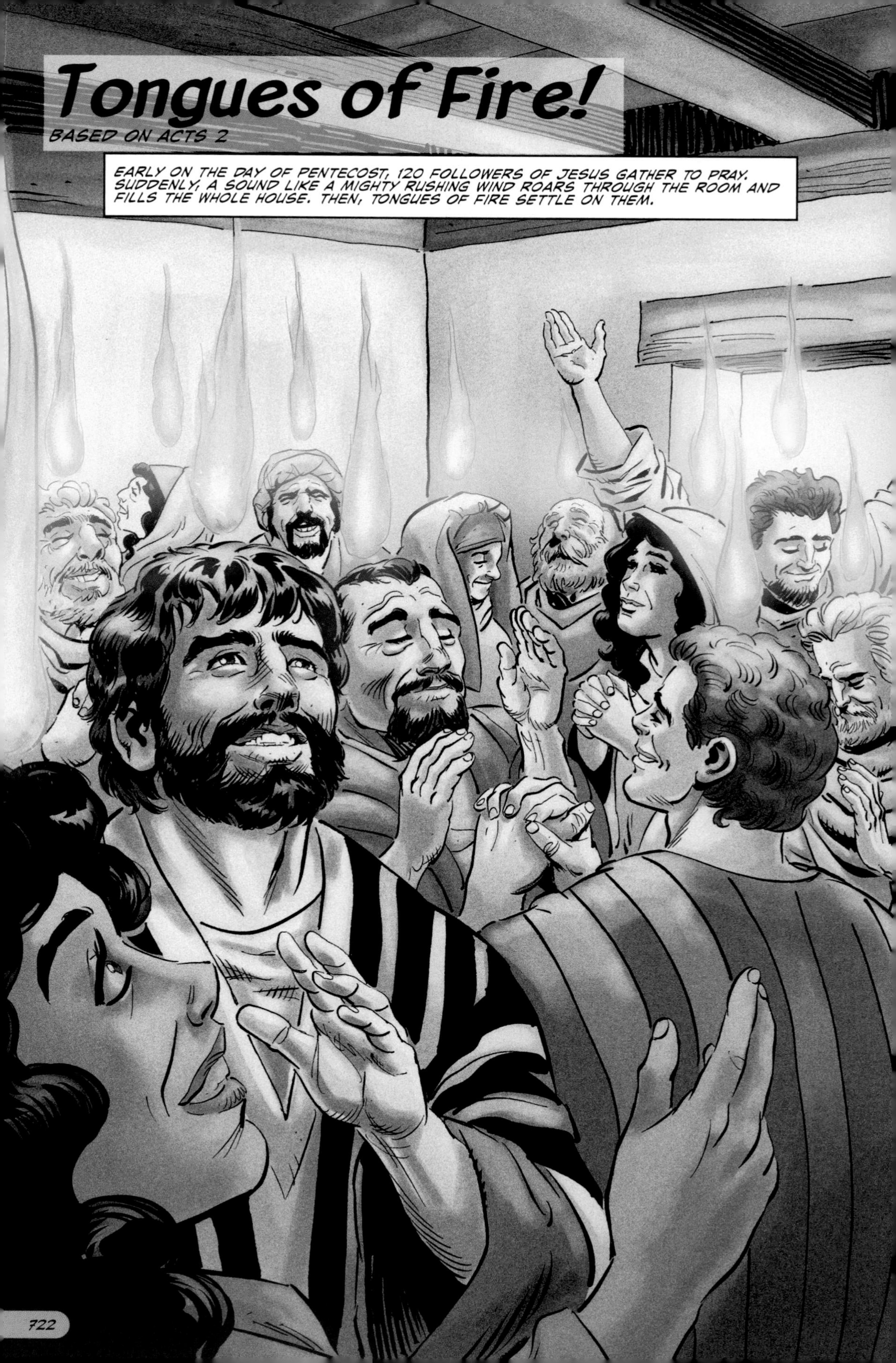
Tongues of Fire!
BASED ON ACTS 2
EARLY ON THE DAY OF PENTECOST, 120 FOLLOWERS OF JESUS GATHER TO PRAY. SUDDENLY, A SOUND LIKE A MIGHTY RUSHING WIND ROARS THROUGH THE ROOM AND FILLS THE WHOLE HOUSE. THEN, TONGUES OF FIRE SETTLE ON THEM.

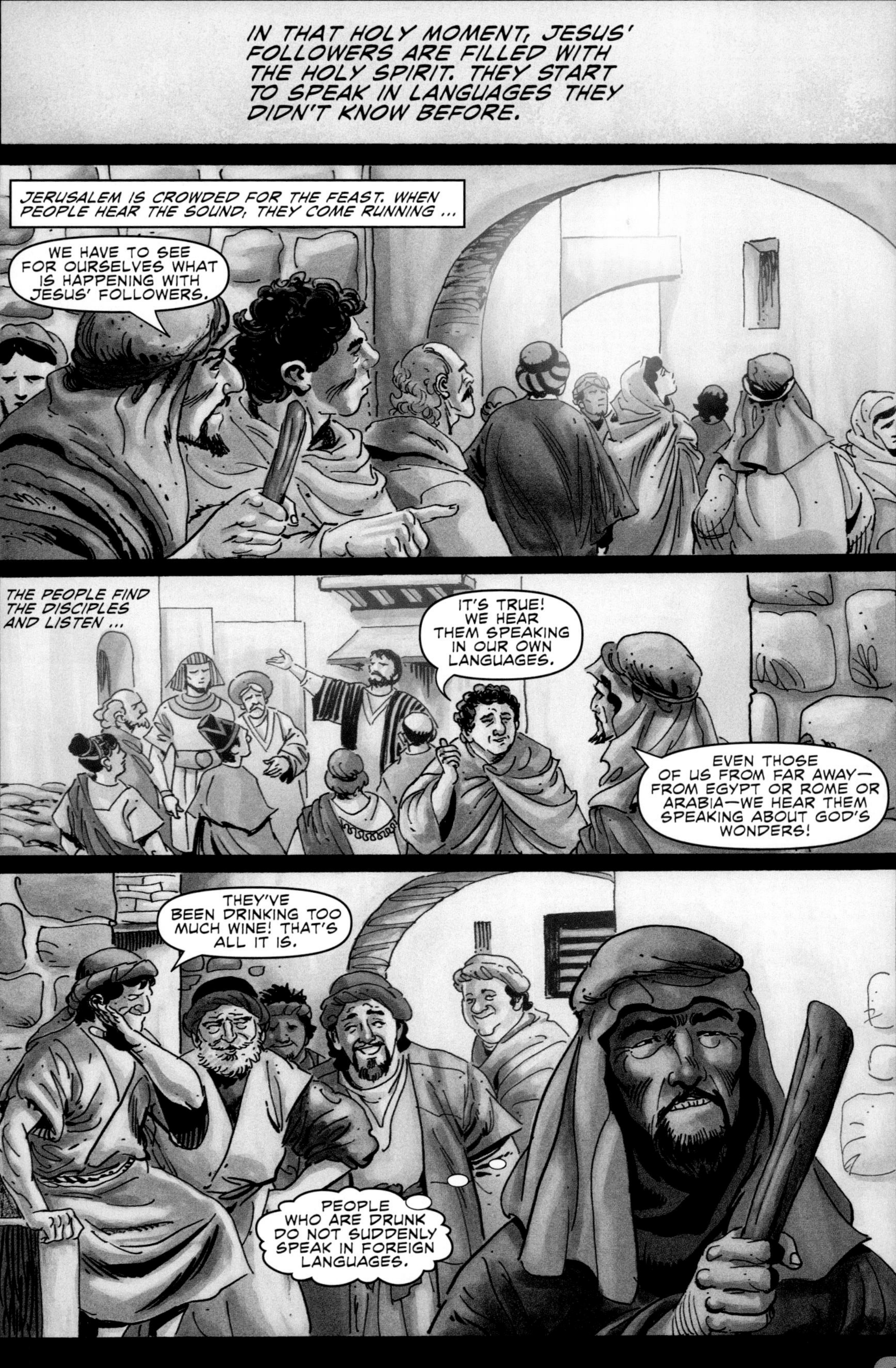
IN THAT HOLY MOMENT, JESUS' FOLLOWERS ARE FILLED WITH THE HOLY SPIRIT. THEY START TO SPEAK IN LANGUAGES THEY DIDN'T KNOW BEFORE.
JERUSALEM IS CROWDED FOR THE FEAST. WHEN PEOPLE HEAR THE SOUND, THEY COME RUNNING ...
WE HAVE TO SEE FOR OURSELVES WHAT IS HAPPENING WITH JESUS' FOLLOWERS.
THE PEOPLE FIND THE DISCIPLES AND LISTEN ...
IT'S TRUE! WE HEAR THEM SPEAKING IN OUR OWN LANGUAGES.
EVEN THOSE OF US FROM FAR AWAY—FROM EGYPT OR ROME OR ARABIA—WE HEAR THEM SPEAKING ABOUT GOD'S WONDERS!
THEY'VE BEEN DRINKING TOO MUCH WINE! THAT'S ALL IT IS.
PEOPLE WHO ARE DRUNK DO NOT SUDDENLY SPEAK IN FOREIGN LANGUAGES.

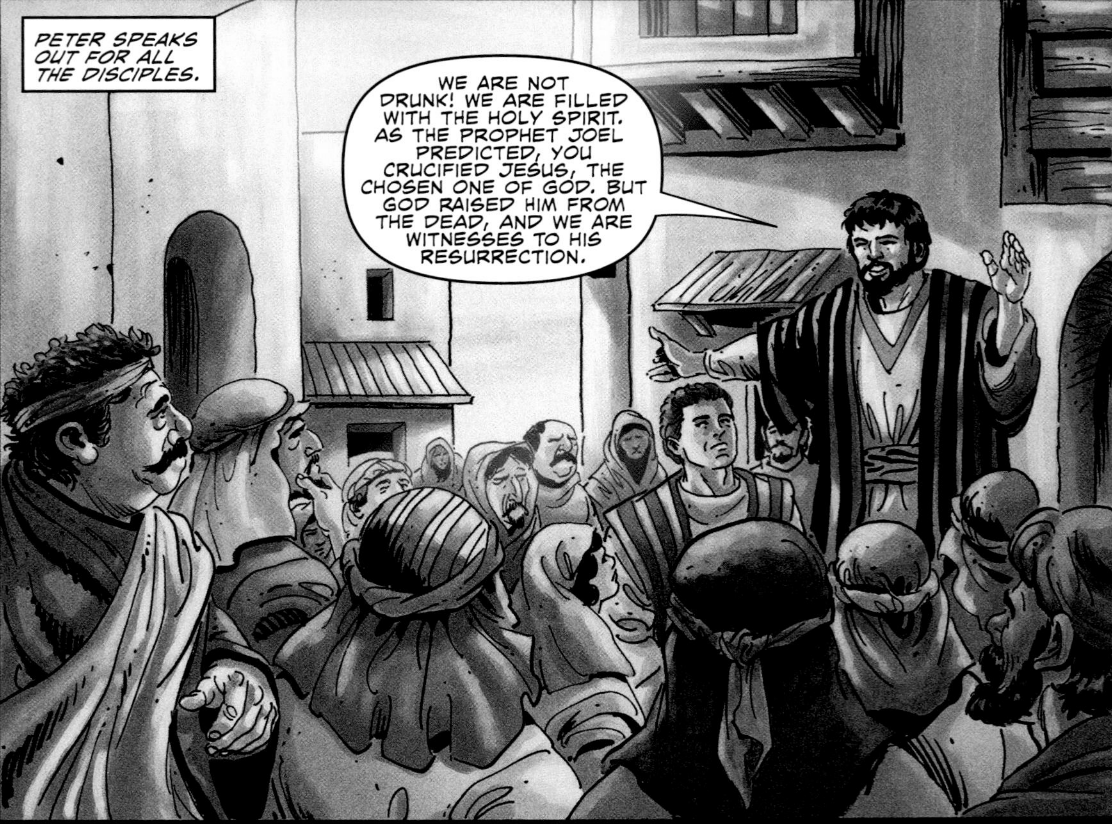
PETER SPEAKS OUT FOR ALL THE DISCIPLES.
WE ARE NOT DRUNK! WE ARE FILLED WITH THE HOLY SPIRIT. AS THE PROPHET JOEL PREDICTED, YOU CRUCIFIED JESUS, THE CHOSEN ONE OF GOD. BUT GOD RAISED HIM FROM THE DEAD, AND WE ARE WITNESSES TO HIS RESURRECTION.

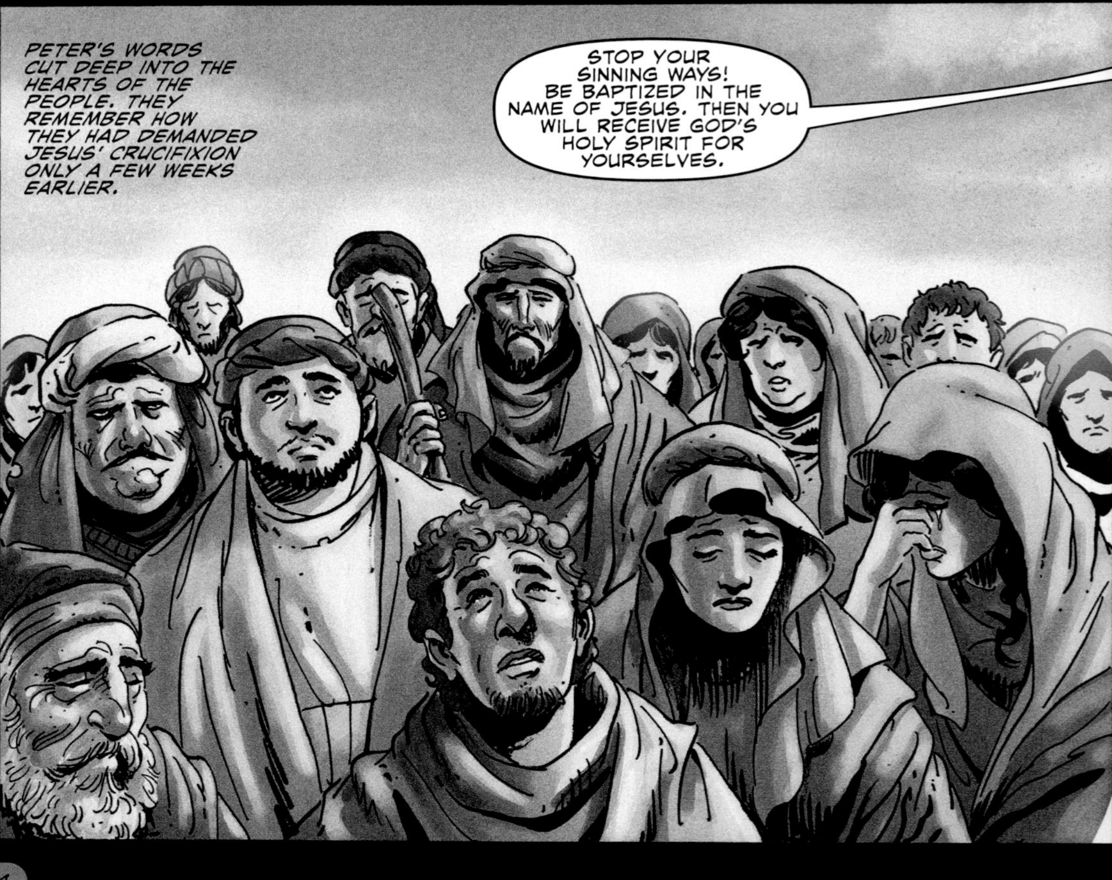
PETER'S WORDS CUT DEEP INTO THE HEARTS OF THE PEOPLE. THEY REMEMBER HOW THEY HAD DEMANDED JESUS' CRUCIFIXION ONLY A FEW WEEKS EARLIER.
STOP YOUR SINNING WAYS! BE BAPTIZED IN THE NAME OF JESUS. THEN YOU WILL RECEIVE GOD'S HOLY SPIRIT FOR YOURSELVES.

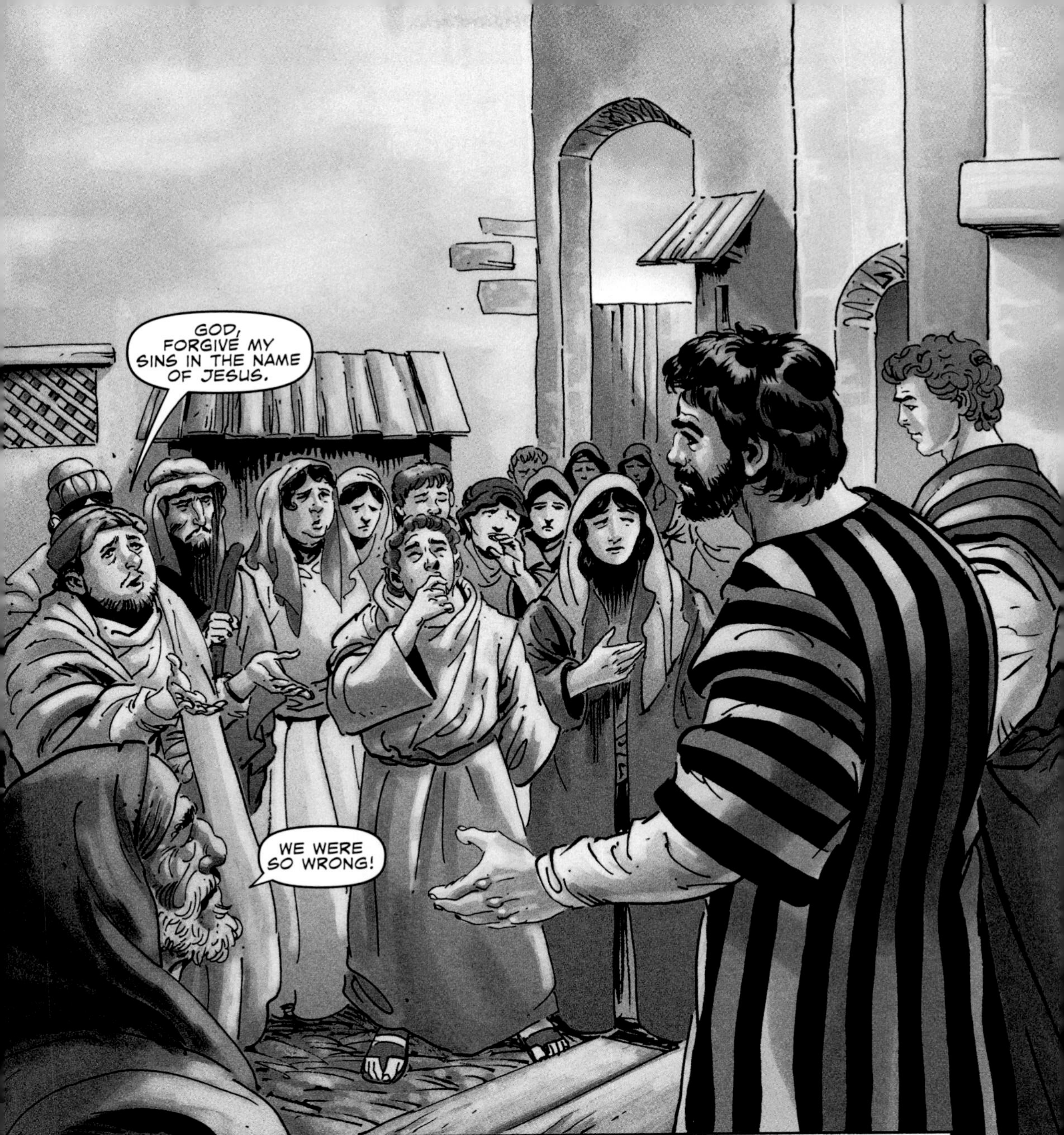
GOD, FORGIVE MY SINS IN THE NAME OF JESUS.
WE WERE SO WRONG!

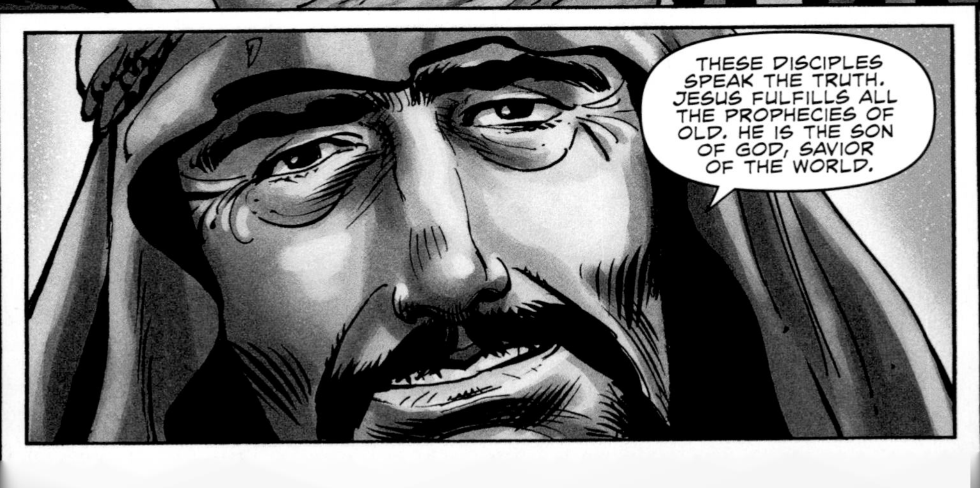
THESE DISCIPLES SPEAK THE TRUTH. JESUS FULFILLS ALL THE PROPHECIES OF OLD. HE IS THE SON OF GOD, SAVIOR OF THE WORLD.

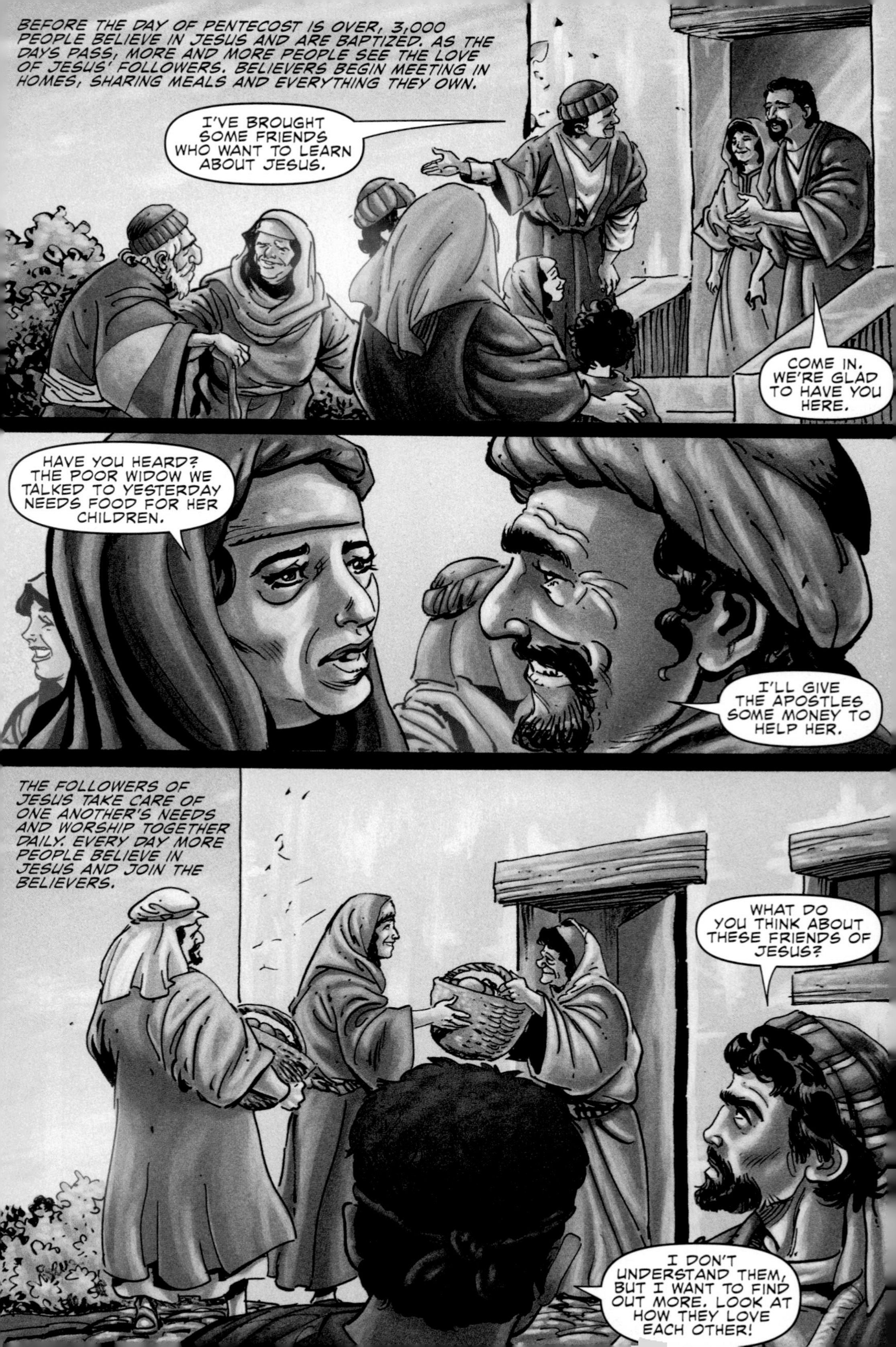
BEFORE THE DAY OF PENTECOST IS OVER, 3,000 PEOPLE BELIEVE IN JESUS AND ARE BAPTIZED. AS THE DAYS PASS, MORE AND MORE PEOPLE SEE THE LOVE OF JESUS' FOLLOWERS. BELIEVERS BEGIN MEETING IN HOMES, SHARING MEALS AND EVERYTHING THEY OWN.
I'VE BROUGHT SOME FRIENDS WHO WANT TO LEARN ABOUT JESUS.
COME IN. WE'RE GLAD TO HAVE YOU HERE.
HAVE YOU HEARD? THE POOR WIDOW WE TALKED TO YESTERDAY NEEDS FOOD FOR HER CHILDREN.
I'LL GIVE THE APOSTLES SOME MONEY TO HELP HER.
THE FOLLOWERS OF JESUS TAKE CARE OF ONE ANOTHER'S NEEDS AND WORSHIP TOGETHER DAILY. EVERY DAY MORE PEOPLE BELIEVE IN JESUS AND JOIN THE BELIEVERS.
WHAT DO YOU THINK ABOUT THESE FRIENDS OF JESUS?
I DON'T UNDERSTAND THEM, BUT I WANT TO FIND OUT MORE. LOOK AT HOW THEY LOVE EACH OTHER!

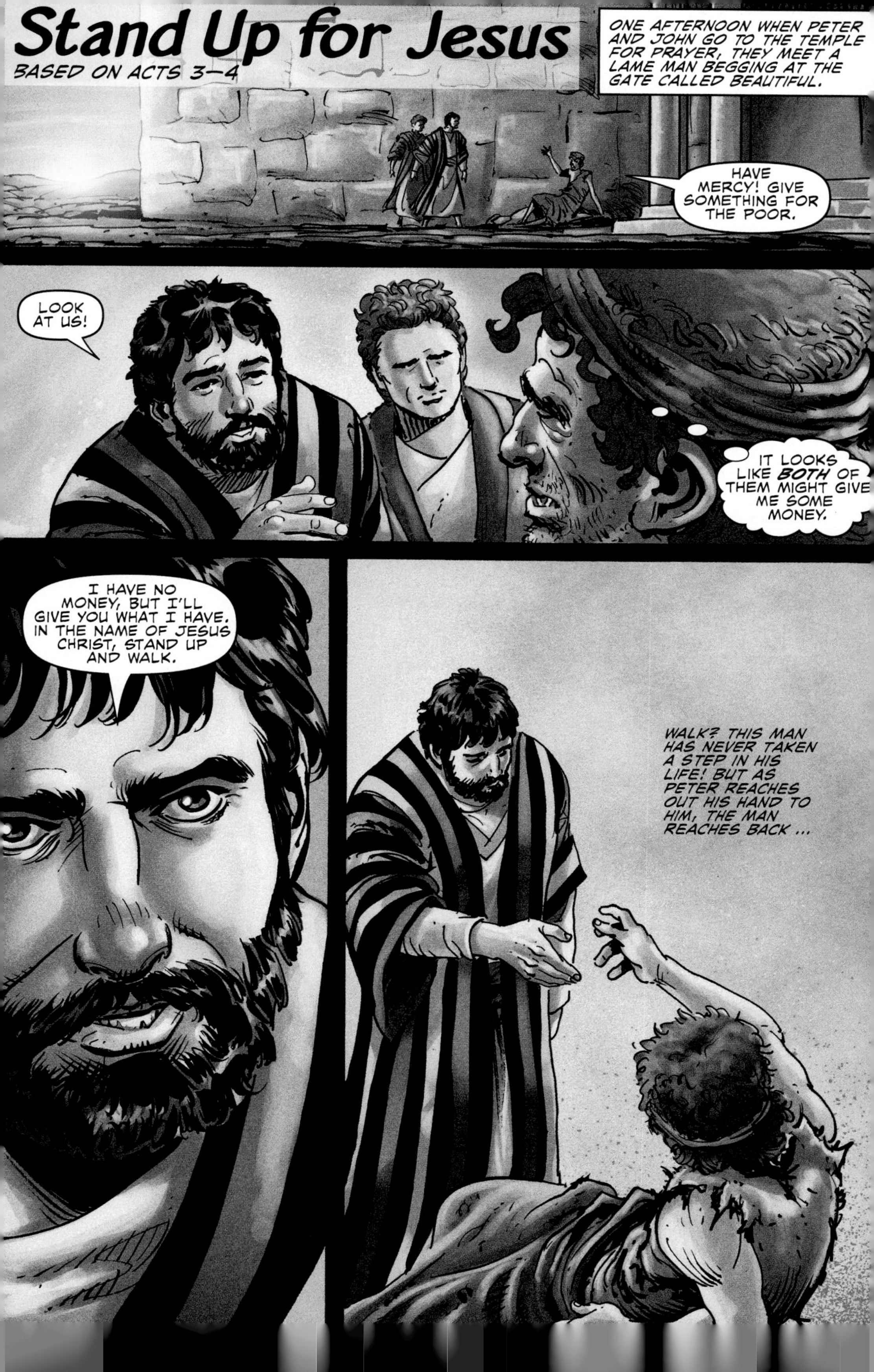
Stand Up for Jesus
BASED ON ACTS 3—4
ONE AFTERNOON WHEN PETER AND JOHN GO TO THE TEMPLE FOR PRAYER, THEY MEET A LAME MAN BEGGING AT THE GATE CALLED BEAUTIFUL.
HAVE MERCY! GIVE SOMETHING FOR THE POOR.
LOOK AT US!
IT LOOKS LIKE BOTH OF THEM MIGHT GIVE ME SOME MONEY.
I HAVE NO MONEY, BUT I'LL GIVE YOU WHAT I HAVE. IN THE NAME OF JESUS CHRIST, STAND UP AND WALK.
WALK? THIS MAN HAS NEVER TAKEN A STEP IN HIS LIFE! BUT AS PETER REACHES OUT HIS HAND TO HIM, THE MAN REACHES BACK ...

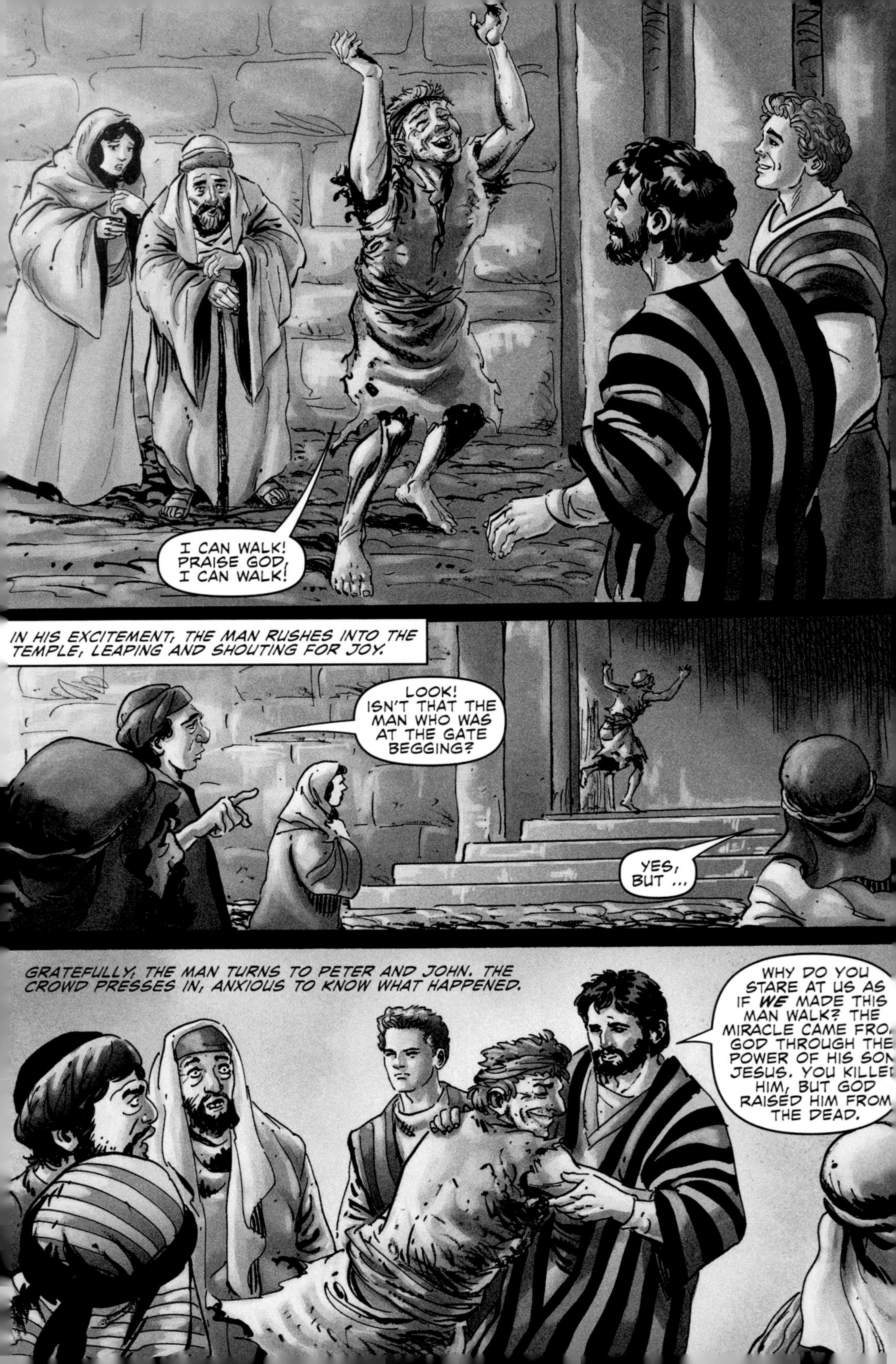
I CAN WALK! PRAISE GOD, I CAN WALK!
IN HIS EXCITEMENT, THE MAN RUSHES INTO THE TEMPLE, LEAPING AND SHOUTING FOR JOY.
LOOK! ISN'T THAT THE MAN WHO WAS AT THE GATE BEGGING?
YES, BUT ...
GRATEFULLY, THE MAN TURNS TO PETER AND JOHN. THE CROWD PRESSES IN, ANXIOUS TO KNOW WHAT HAPPENED.
WHY DO YOU STARE AT US AS IF WE MADE THIS MAN WALK? THE MIRACLE CAME FRO GOD THROUGH THE POWER OF HIS SON JESUS. YOU KILLE HIM, BUT GOD RAISED HIM FROM THE DEAD.

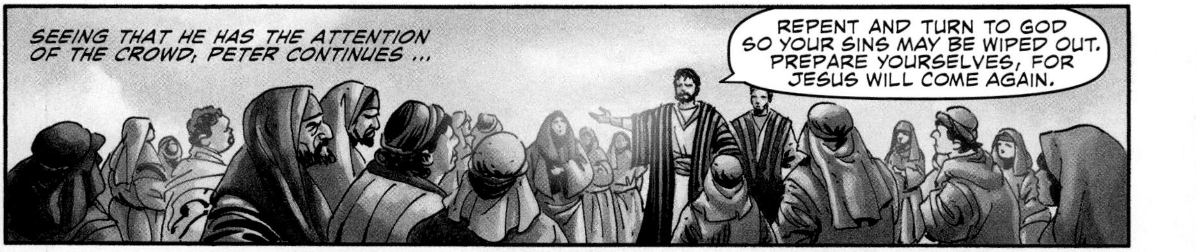
SEEING THAT HE HAS THE ATTENTION OF THE CROWD, PETER CONTINUES ...
REPENT AND TURN TO GOD SO YOUR SINS MAY BE WIPED OUT. PREPARE YOURSELVES, FOR JESUS WILL COME AGAIN.

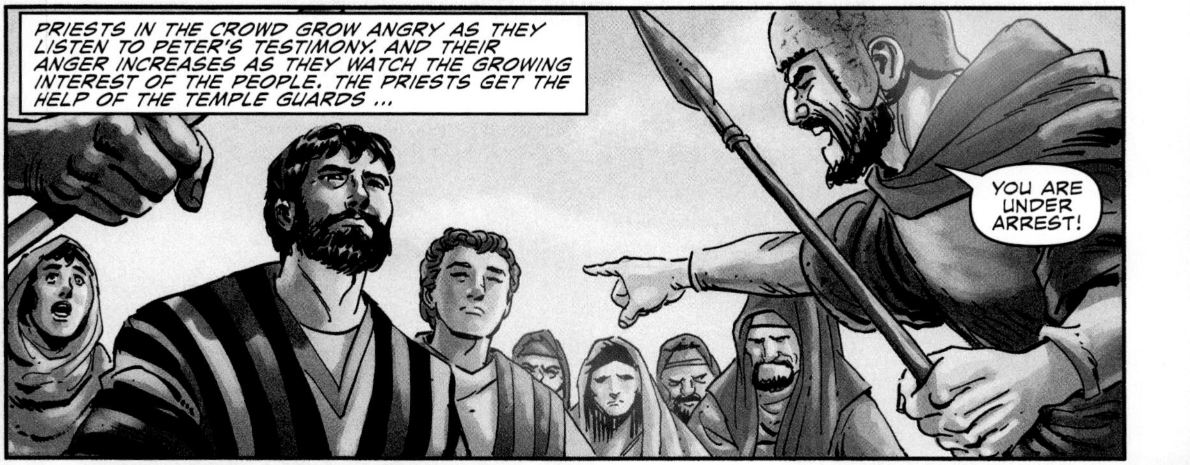
PRIESTS IN THE CROWD GROW ANGRY AS THEY LISTEN TO PETER'S TESTIMONY. AND THEIR ANGER INCREASES AS THEY WATCH THE GROWING INTEREST OF THE PEOPLE. THE PRIESTS GET THE HELP OF THE TEMPLE GUARDS ...
YOU ARE UNDER ARREST!

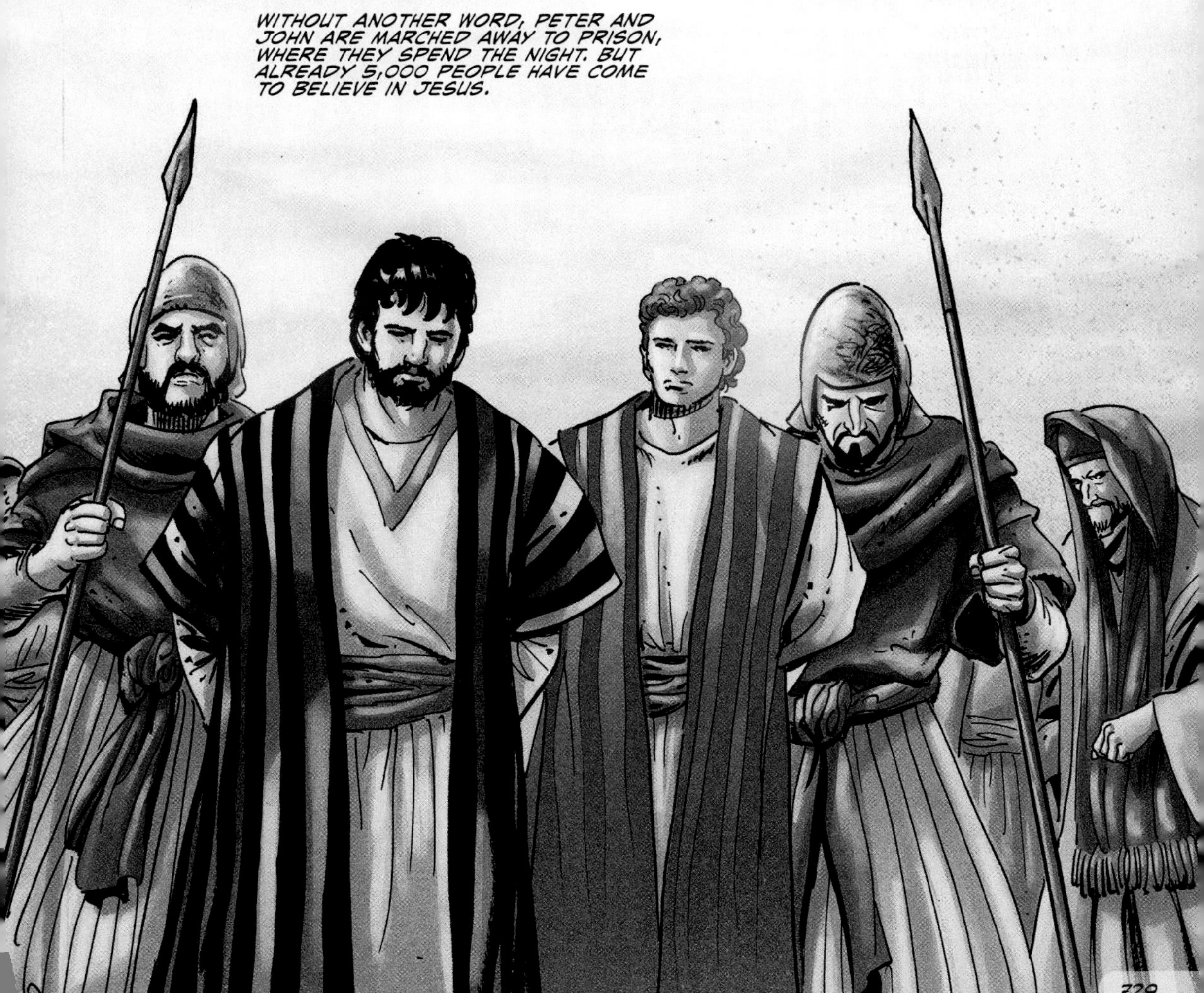
WITHOUT ANOTHER WORD, PETER AND JOHN ARE MARCHED AWAY TO PRISON, WHERE THEY SPEND THE NIGHT. BUT ALREADY 5,000 PEOPLE HAVE COME TO BELIEVE IN JESUS.

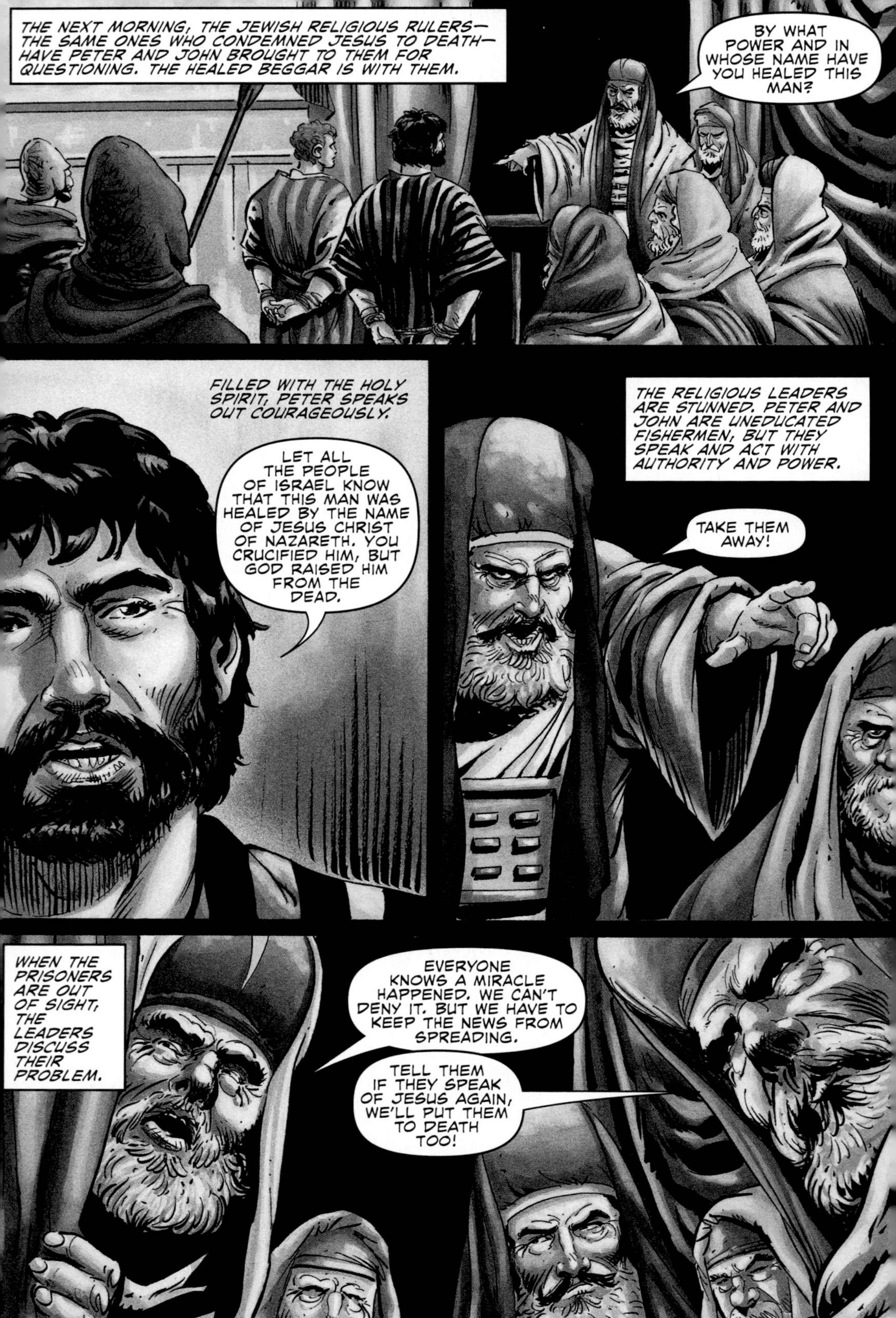
THE NEXT MORNING, THE JEWISH RELIGIOUS RULERS—THE SAME ONES WHO CONDEMNED JESUS TO DEATH—HAVE PETER AND JOHN BROUGHT TO THEM FOR QUESTIONING. THE HEALED BEGGAR IS WITH THEM.
BY WHAT POWER AND IN WHOSE NAME HAVE YOU HEALED THIS MAN?
FILLED WITH THE HOLY SPIRIT, PETER SPEAKS OUT COURAGEOUSLY.
LET ALL THE PEOPLE OF ISRAEL KNOW THAT THIS MAN WAS HEALED BY THE NAME OF JESUS CHRIST OF NAZARETH. YOU CRUCIFIED HIM, BUT GOD RAISED HIM FROM THE DEAD.
THE RELIGIOUS LEADERS ARE STUNNED. PETER AND JOHN ARE UNEDUCATED FISHERMEN, BUT THEY SPEAK AND ACT WITH AUTHORITY AND POWER.
TAKE THEM AWAY!
WHEN THE PRISONERS ARE OUT OF SIGHT, THE LEADERS DISCUSS THEIR PROBLEM.
EVERYONE KNOWS A MIRACLE HAPPENED. WE CAN'T DENY IT. BUT WE HAVE TO KEEP THE NEWS FROM SPREADING.
TELL THEM IF THEY SPEAK OF JESUS AGAIN, WE'LL PUT THEM TO DEATH TOO!

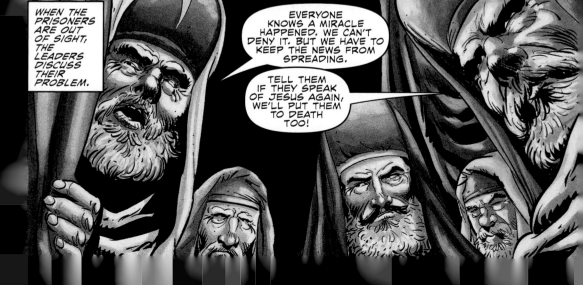

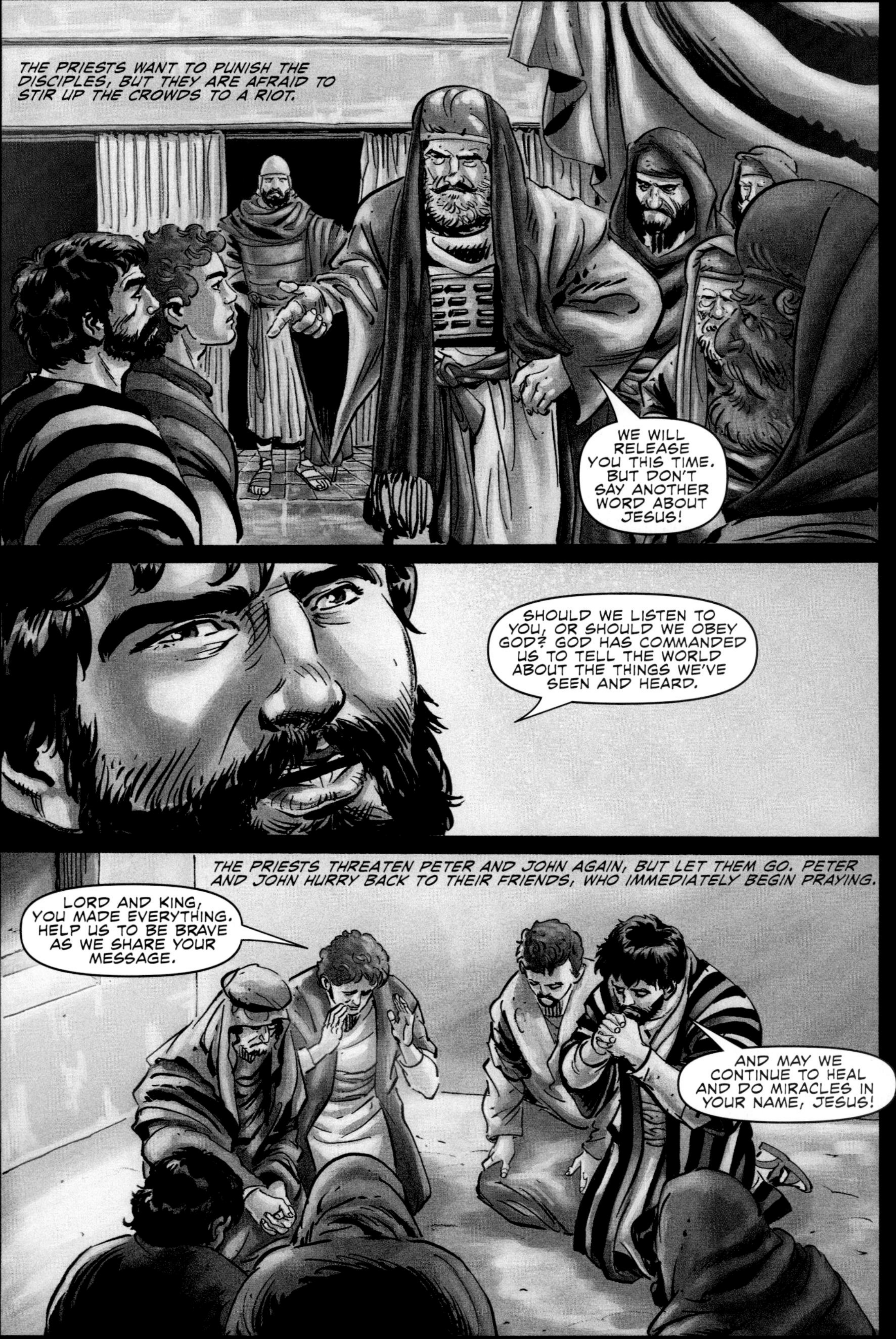
THE PRIESTS WANT TO PUNISH THE DISCIPLES, BUT THEY ARE AFRAID TO STIR UP THE CROWDS TO A RIOT.
WE WILL RELEASE YOU THIS TIME. BUT DON'T SAY ANOTHER WORD ABOUT JESUS!
SHOULD WE LISTEN TO YOU, OR SHOULD WE OBEY GOD? GOD HAS COMMANDED US TO TELL THE WORLD ABOUT THE THINGS WE'VE SEEN AND HEARD.
THE PRIESTS THREATEN PETER AND JOHN AGAIN, BUT LET THEM GO. PETER AND JOHN HURRY BACK TO THEIR FRIENDS, WHO IMMEDIATELY BEGIN PRAYING.
LORD AND KING, YOU MADE EVERYTHING. HELP US TO BE BRAVE AS WE SHARE YOUR MESSAGE.
AND MAY WE CONTINUE TO HEAL AND DO MIRACLES IN YOUR NAME, JESUS!

A Grave Lie — BASED ON ACTS 4:32–5:11

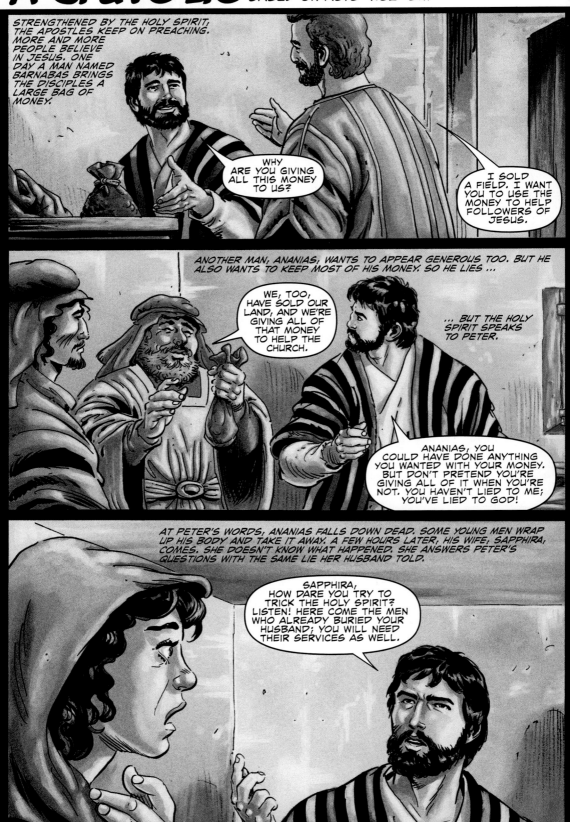

STRENGTHENED BY THE HOLY SPIRIT, THE APOSTLES KEEP ON PREACHING. MORE AND MORE PEOPLE BELIEVE IN JESUS. ONE DAY A MAN NAMED BARNABAS BRINGS THE DISCIPLES A LARGE BAG OF MONEY.

WHY ARE YOU GIVING ALL THIS MONEY TO US?

I SOLD A FIELD. I WANT YOU TO USE THE MONEY TO HELP FOLLOWERS OF JESUS.

ANOTHER MAN, ANANIAS, WANTS TO APPEAR GENEROUS TOO. BUT HE ALSO WANTS TO KEEP MOST OF HIS MONEY. SO HE LIES ...

WE, TOO, HAVE SOLD OUR LAND, AND WE'RE GIVING ALL OF THAT MONEY TO HELP THE CHURCH.

... BUT THE HOLY SPIRIT SPEAKS TO PETER.

ANANIAS, YOU COULD HAVE DONE ANYTHING YOU WANTED WITH YOUR MONEY. BUT DON'T PRETEND YOU'RE GIVING ALL OF IT WHEN YOU'RE NOT. YOU HAVEN'T LIED TO ME; YOU'VE LIED TO GOD!

AT PETER'S WORDS, ANANIAS FALLS DOWN DEAD. SOME YOUNG MEN WRAP UP HIS BODY AND TAKE IT AWAY. A FEW HOURS LATER, HIS WIFE, SAPPHIRA, COMES. SHE DOESN'T KNOW WHAT HAPPENED. SHE ANSWERS PETER'S QUESTIONS WITH THE SAME LIE HER HUSBAND TOLD.

SAPPHIRA, HOW DARE YOU TRY TO TRICK THE HOLY SPIRIT? LISTEN! HERE COME THE MEN WHO ALREADY BURIED YOUR HUSBAND; YOU WILL NEED THEIR SERVICES AS WELL.

INSTANTLY, SAPPHIRA FALLS DEAD ON THE FLOOR. THE FOLLOWERS OF JESUS SEE THIS AS A WARNING TO ANYONE WHO TRIES TO DECEIVE GOD OR THE CHURCH.

Prison Break

BASED ON ACTS 5:12—6:11

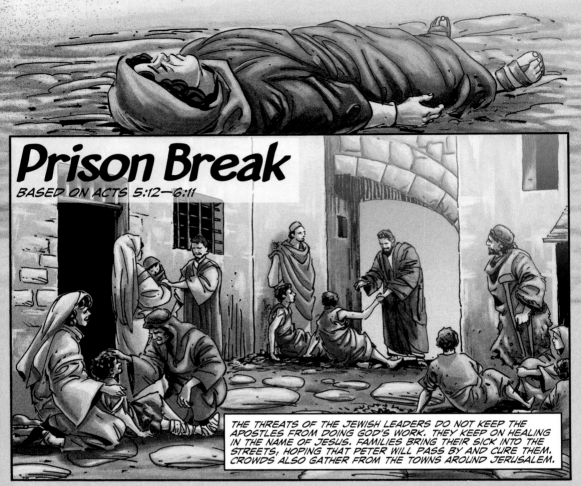

THE THREATS OF THE JEWISH LEADERS DO NOT KEEP THE APOSTLES FROM DOING GOD'S WORK. THEY KEEP ON HEALING IN THE NAME OF JESUS. FAMILIES BRING THEIR SICK INTO THE STREETS, HOPING THAT PETER WILL PASS BY AND CURE THEM. CROWDS ALSO GATHER FROM THE TOWNS AROUND JERUSALEM.

HE CAN'T WALK. PLEASE MAKE HIM STRONG SO HE CAN RUN AND PLAY WITH THE OTHER CHILDREN.

I CANNOT HEAL HIM, BUT JESUS, THE SON OF GOD, CAN. IN JESUS' NAME, I TELL YOU YOUR SON IS HEALED.

EVERYONE WHO COMES IS HEALED. THE HIGH PRIEST AND THE ONES WHO WORK WITH HIM ARE SO JEALOUS THEY CAN'T STAND IT. THEY HATE SEEING THE PEOPLE COME INTO TOWN TO BE HEALED. IN A FIT OF RAGE, THEY HAVE THE DISCIPLES ARRESTED AND THROWN INTO JAIL.

THIS TIME THEY'RE NOT GETTING OUT. WE'LL PUT AN END TO THIS NONSENSE!

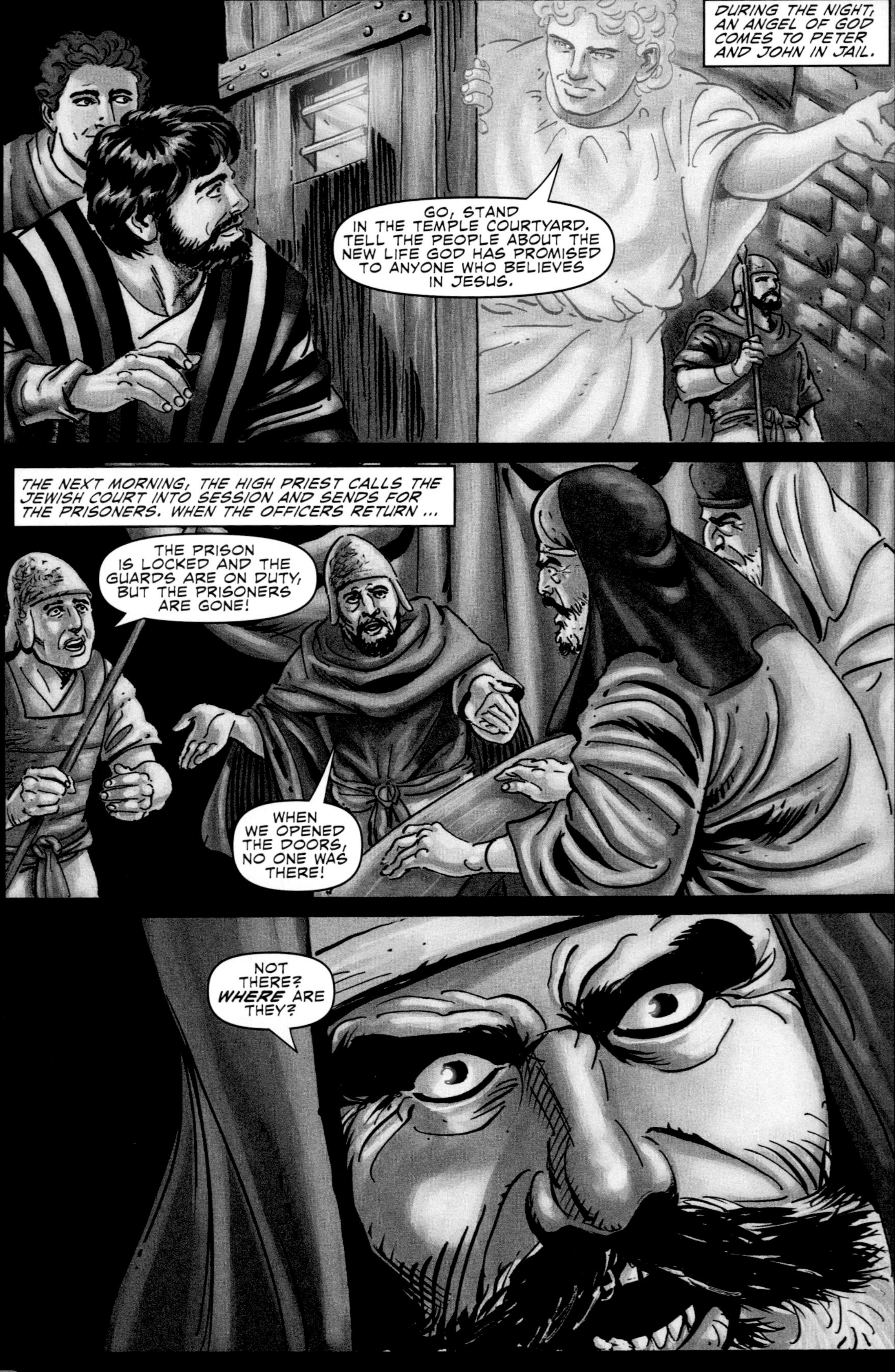
DURING THE NIGHT, AN ANGEL OF GOD COMES TO PETER AND JOHN IN JAIL.
GO, STAND IN THE TEMPLE COURTYARD. TELL THE PEOPLE ABOUT THE NEW LIFE GOD HAS PROMISED TO ANYONE WHO BELIEVES IN JESUS.
THE NEXT MORNING, THE HIGH PRIEST CALLS THE JEWISH COURT INTO SESSION AND SENDS FOR THE PRISONERS. WHEN THE OFFICERS RETURN ...
THE PRISON IS LOCKED AND THE GUARDS ARE ON DUTY, BUT THE PRISONERS ARE GONE!
WHEN WE OPENED THE DOORS, NO ONE WAS THERE!
NOT THERE? *WHERE* ARE THEY?

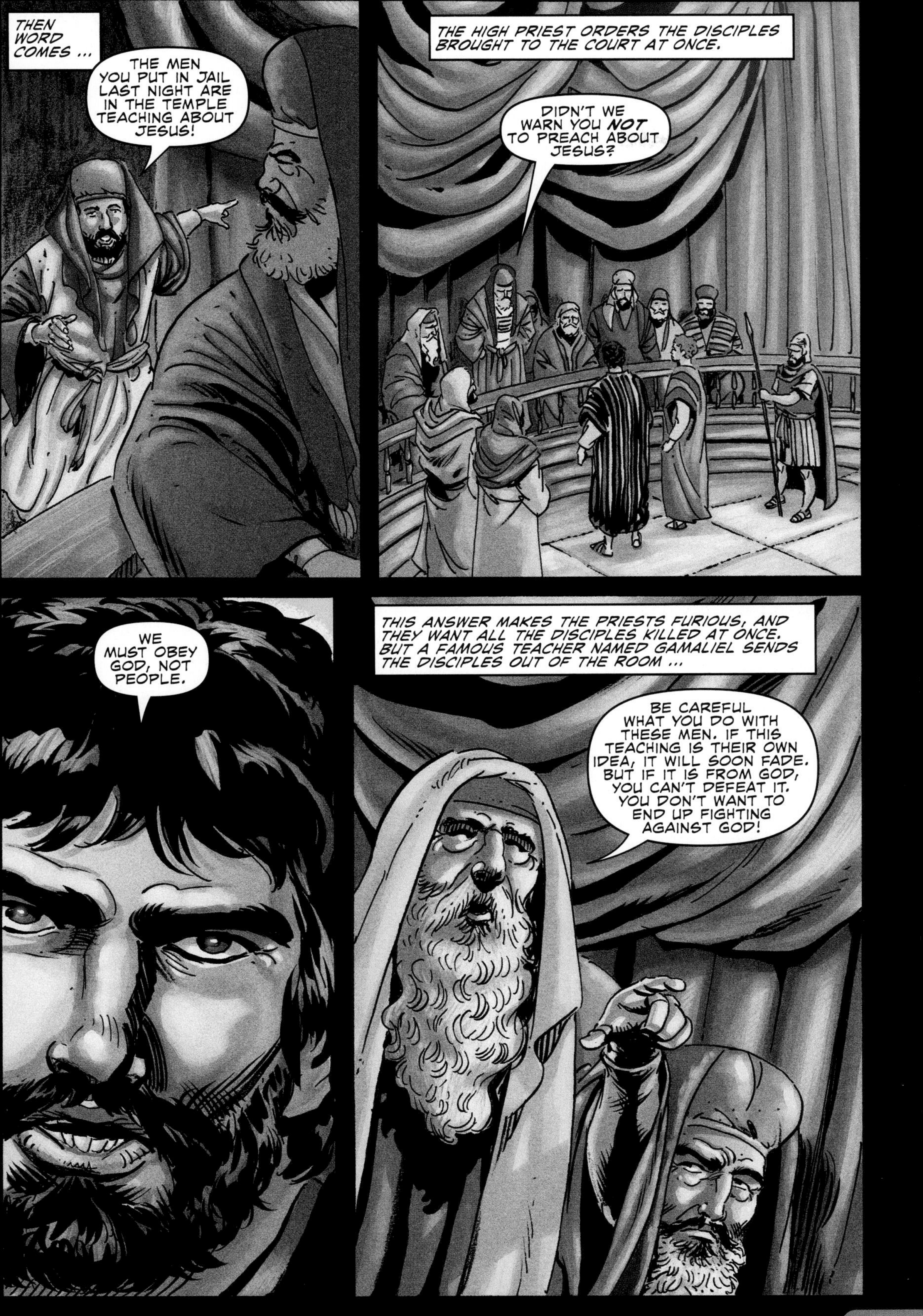
THEN WORD COMES ...
THE MEN YOU PUT IN JAIL LAST NIGHT ARE IN THE TEMPLE TEACHING ABOUT JESUS!
THE HIGH PRIEST ORDERS THE DISCIPLES BROUGHT TO THE COURT AT ONCE.
DIDN'T WE WARN YOU NOT TO PREACH ABOUT JESUS?
WE MUST OBEY GOD, NOT PEOPLE.
THIS ANSWER MAKES THE PRIESTS FURIOUS, AND THEY WANT ALL THE DISCIPLES KILLED AT ONCE. BUT A FAMOUS TEACHER NAMED GAMALIEL SENDS THE DISCIPLES OUT OF THE ROOM ...
BE CAREFUL WHAT YOU DO WITH THESE MEN. IF THIS TEACHING IS THEIR OWN IDEA, IT WILL SOON FADE. BUT IF IT IS FROM GOD, YOU CAN'T DEFEAT IT. YOU DON'T WANT TO END UP FIGHTING AGAINST GOD!

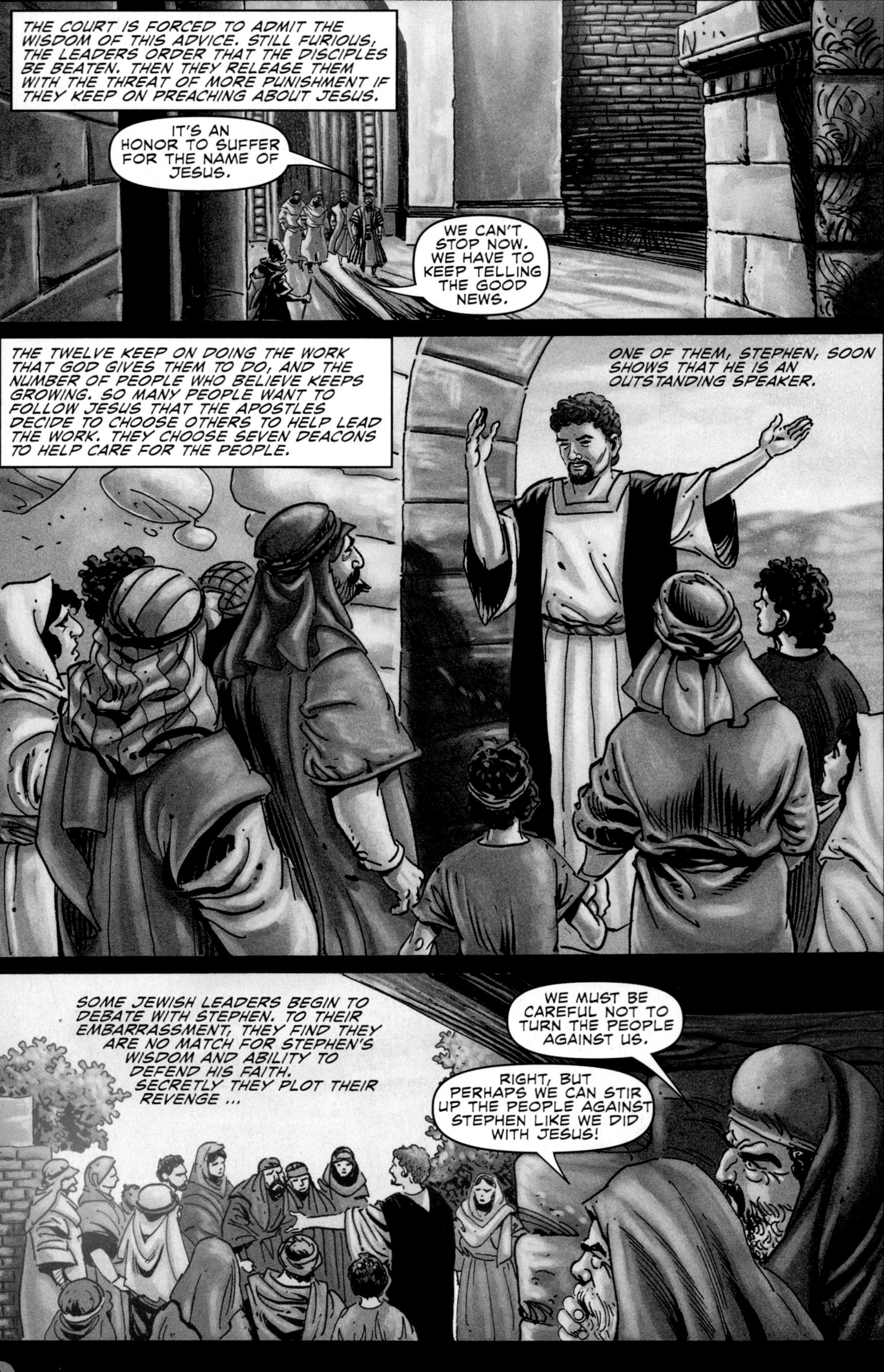
THE COURT IS FORCED TO ADMIT THE WISDOM OF THIS ADVICE. STILL FURIOUS, THE LEADERS ORDER THAT THE DISCIPLES BE BEATEN. THEN THEY RELEASE THEM WITH THE THREAT OF MORE PUNISHMENT IF THEY KEEP ON PREACHING ABOUT JESUS.
IT'S AN HONOR TO SUFFER FOR THE NAME OF JESUS.
WE CAN'T STOP NOW. WE HAVE TO KEEP TELLING THE GOOD NEWS.
THE TWELVE KEEP ON DOING THE WORK THAT GOD GIVES THEM TO DO, AND THE NUMBER OF PEOPLE WHO BELIEVE KEEPS GROWING. SO MANY PEOPLE WANT TO FOLLOW JESUS THAT THE APOSTLES DECIDE TO CHOOSE OTHERS TO HELP LEAD THE WORK. THEY CHOOSE SEVEN DEACONS TO HELP CARE FOR THE PEOPLE.
ONE OF THEM, STEPHEN, SOON SHOWS THAT HE IS AN OUTSTANDING SPEAKER.
SOME JEWISH LEADERS BEGIN TO DEBATE WITH STEPHEN. TO THEIR EMBARRASSMENT, THEY FIND THEY ARE NO MATCH FOR STEPHEN'S WISDOM AND ABILITY TO DEFEND HIS FAITH. SECRETLY THEY PLOT THEIR REVENGE ...
WE MUST BE CAREFUL NOT TO TURN THE PEOPLE AGAINST US.
RIGHT, BUT PERHAPS WE CAN STIR UP THE PEOPLE AGAINST STEPHEN LIKE WE DID WITH JESUS!

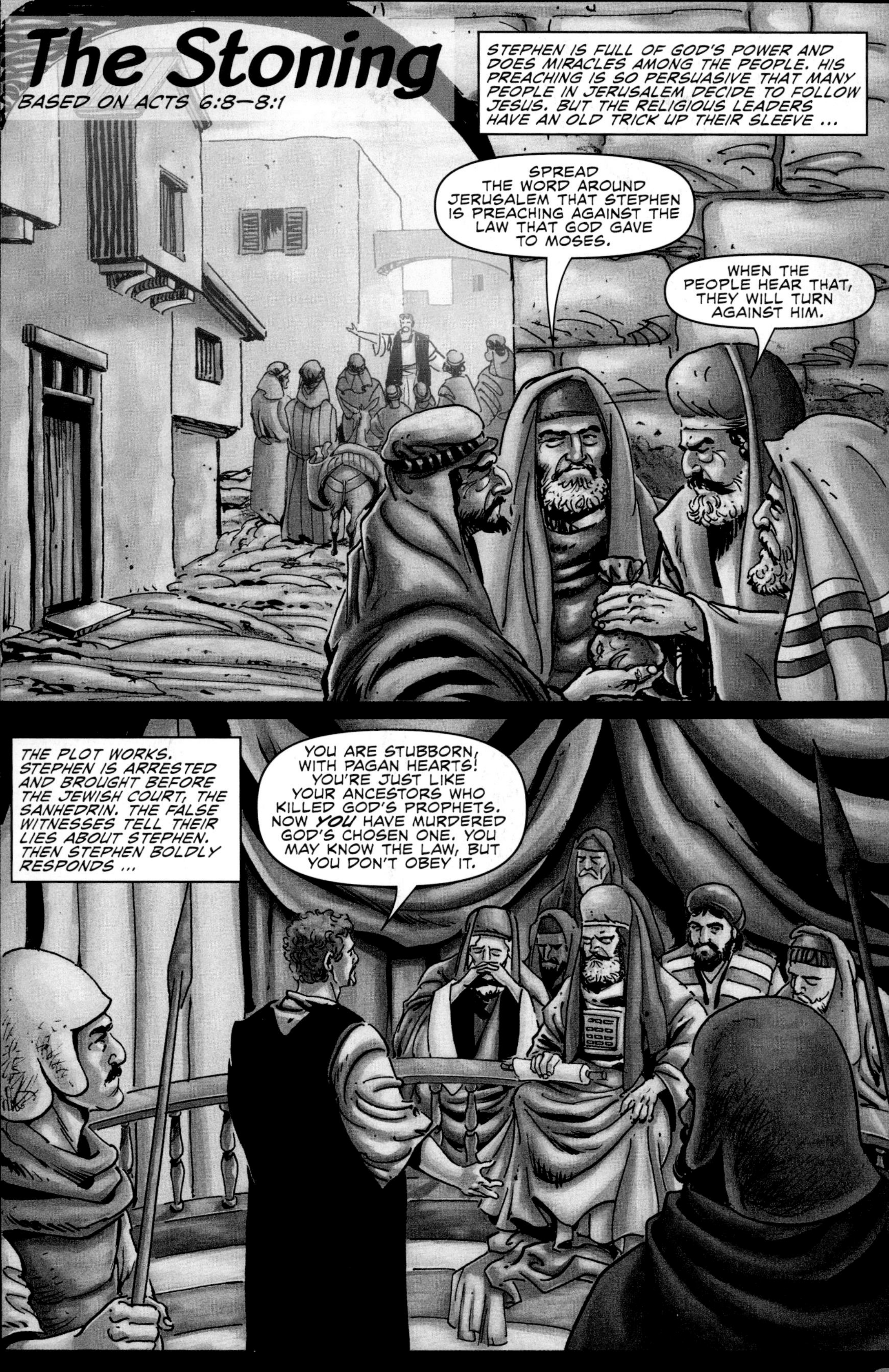
The Stoning
BASED ON ACTS 6:8—8:1
STEPHEN IS FULL OF GOD'S POWER AND DOES MIRACLES AMONG THE PEOPLE. HIS PREACHING IS SO PERSUASIVE THAT MANY PEOPLE IN JERUSALEM DECIDE TO FOLLOW JESUS. BUT THE RELIGIOUS LEADERS HAVE AN OLD TRICK UP THEIR SLEEVE ...
SPREAD THE WORD AROUND JERUSALEM THAT STEPHEN IS PREACHING AGAINST THE LAW THAT GOD GAVE TO MOSES.
WHEN THE PEOPLE HEAR THAT, THEY WILL TURN AGAINST HIM.
THE PLOT WORKS. STEPHEN IS ARRESTED AND BROUGHT BEFORE THE JEWISH COURT, THE SANHEDRIN. THE FALSE WITNESSES TELL THEIR LIES ABOUT STEPHEN. THEN STEPHEN BOLDLY RESPONDS ...
YOU ARE STUBBORN, WITH PAGAN HEARTS! YOU'RE JUST LIKE YOUR ANCESTORS WHO KILLED GOD'S PROPHETS. NOW YOU HAVE MURDERED GOD'S CHOSEN ONE. YOU MAY KNOW THE LAW, BUT YOU DON'T OBEY IT.

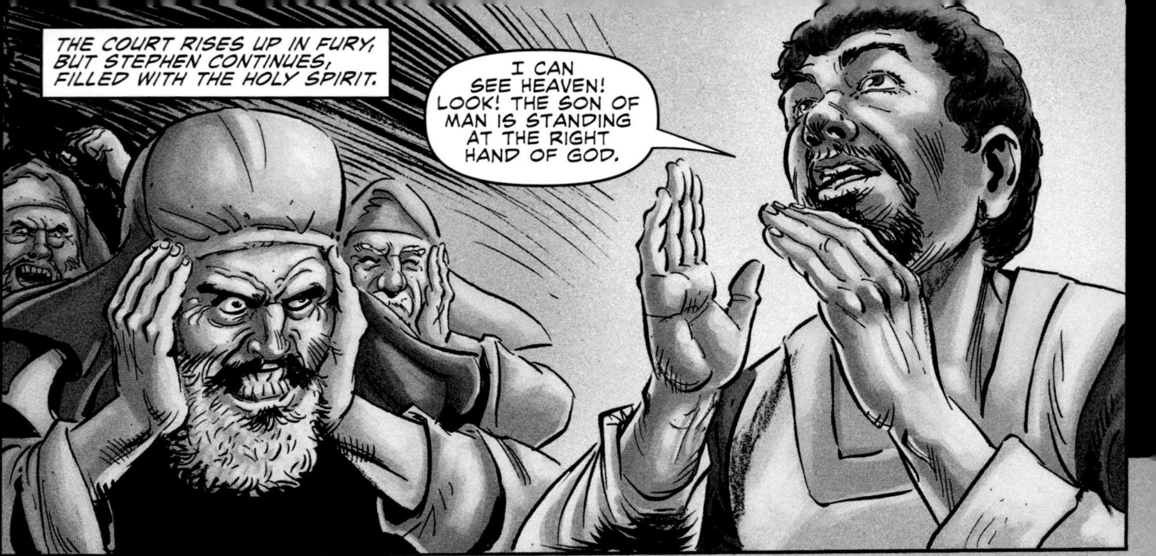
THE COURT RISES UP IN FURY, BUT STEPHEN CONTINUES, FILLED WITH THE HOLY SPIRIT.
I CAN SEE HEAVEN! LOOK! THE SON OF MAN IS STANDING AT THE RIGHT HAND OF GOD.

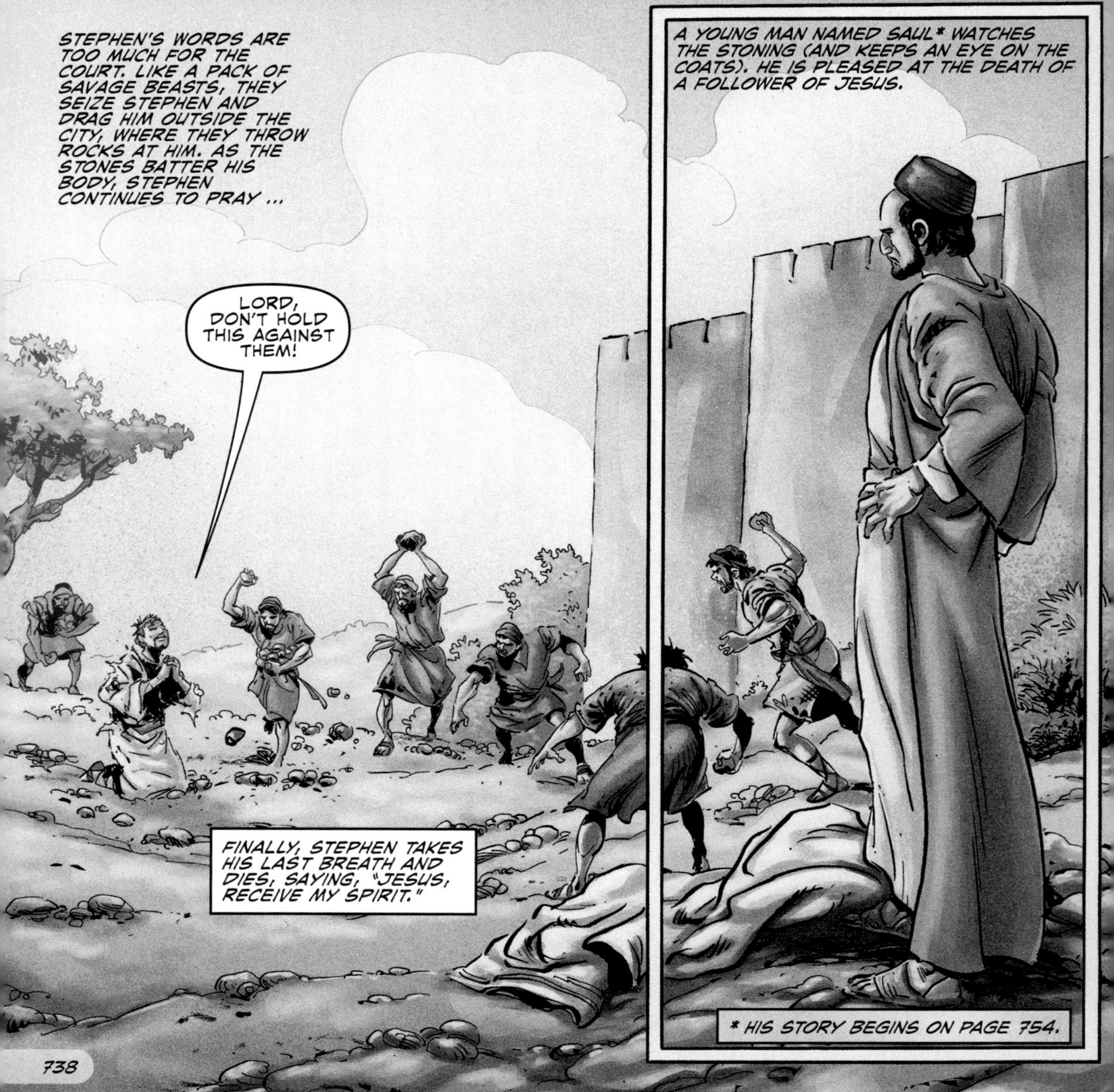
STEPHEN'S WORDS ARE TOO MUCH FOR THE COURT. LIKE A PACK OF SAVAGE BEASTS, THEY SEIZE STEPHEN AND DRAG HIM OUTSIDE THE CITY, WHERE THEY THROW ROCKS AT HIM. AS THE STONES BATTER HIS BODY, STEPHEN CONTINUES TO PRAY ...
LORD, DON'T HOLD THIS AGAINST THEM!
FINALLY, STEPHEN TAKES HIS LAST BREATH AND DIES, SAYING, "JESUS, RECEIVE MY SPIRIT."
A YOUNG MAN NAMED SAUL* WATCHES THE STONING (AND KEEPS AN EYE ON THE COATS). HE IS PLEASED AT THE DEATH OF A FOLLOWER OF JESUS.
* HIS STORY BEGINS ON PAGE 754.

Stranger on the Gaza Road

BASED ON ACTS 8:1-4, 26-40

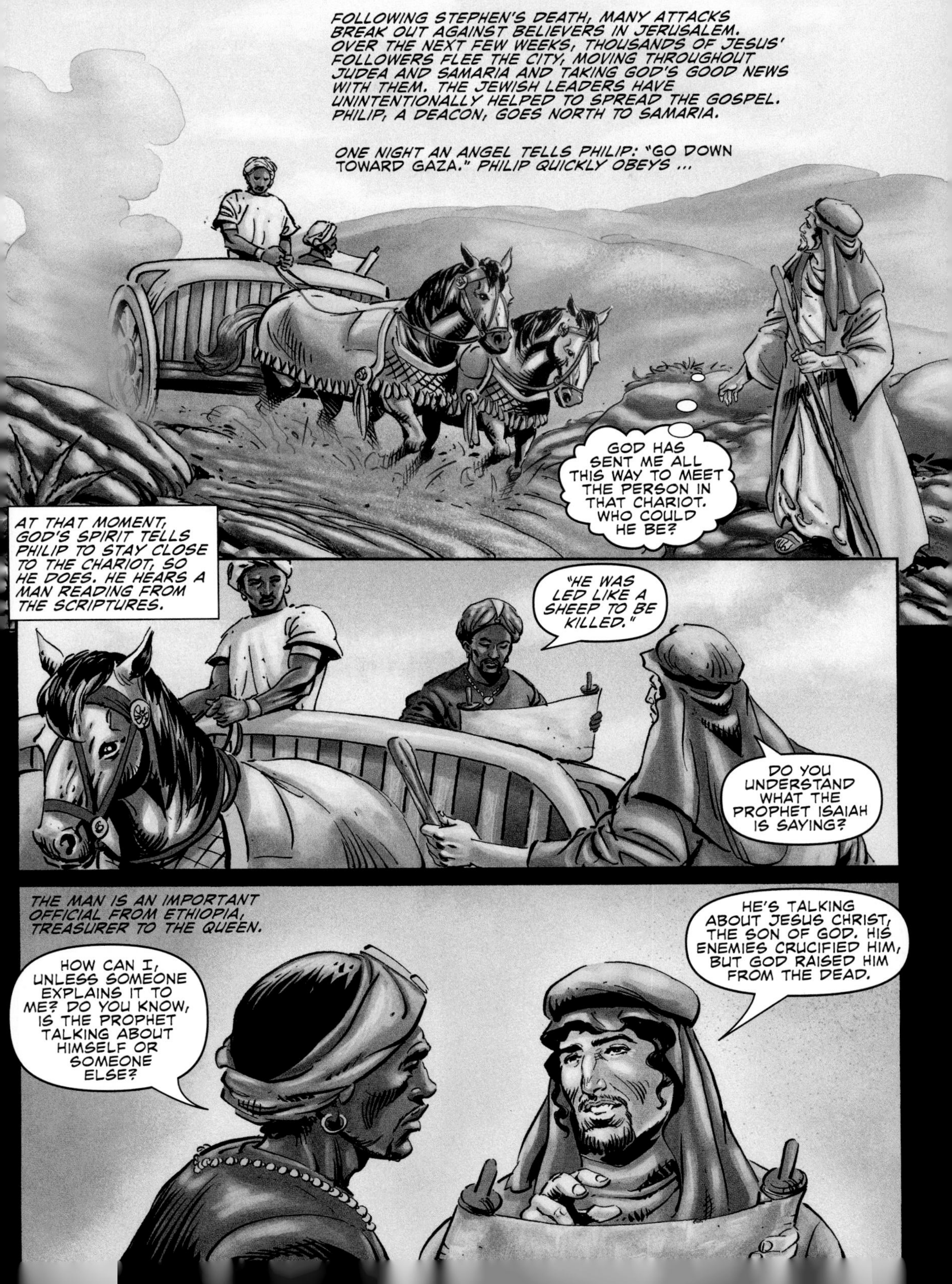

FOLLOWING STEPHEN'S DEATH, MANY ATTACKS BREAK OUT AGAINST BELIEVERS IN JERUSALEM. OVER THE NEXT FEW WEEKS, THOUSANDS OF JESUS' FOLLOWERS FLEE THE CITY, MOVING THROUGHOUT JUDEA AND SAMARIA AND TAKING GOD'S GOOD NEWS WITH THEM. THE JEWISH LEADERS HAVE UNINTENTIONALLY HELPED TO SPREAD THE GOSPEL. PHILIP, A DEACON, GOES NORTH TO SAMARIA.
ONE NIGHT AN ANGEL TELLS PHILIP: "GO DOWN TOWARD GAZA." PHILIP QUICKLY OBEYS ...
GOD HAS SENT ME ALL THIS WAY TO MEET THE PERSON IN THAT CHARIOT. WHO COULD HE BE?
AT THAT MOMENT, GOD'S SPIRIT TELLS PHILIP TO STAY CLOSE TO THE CHARIOT, SO HE DOES. HE HEARS A MAN READING FROM THE SCRIPTURES.
"HE WAS LED LIKE A SHEEP TO BE KILLED."
DO YOU UNDERSTAND WHAT THE PROPHET ISAIAH IS SAYING?
THE MAN IS AN IMPORTANT OFFICIAL FROM ETHIOPIA, TREASURER TO THE QUEEN.
HOW CAN I, UNLESS SOMEONE EXPLAINS IT TO ME? DO YOU KNOW, IS THE PROPHET TALKING ABOUT HIMSELF OR SOMEONE ELSE?
HE'S TALKING ABOUT JESUS CHRIST, THE SON OF GOD. HIS ENEMIES CRUCIFIED HIM, BUT GOD RAISED HIM FROM THE DEAD.

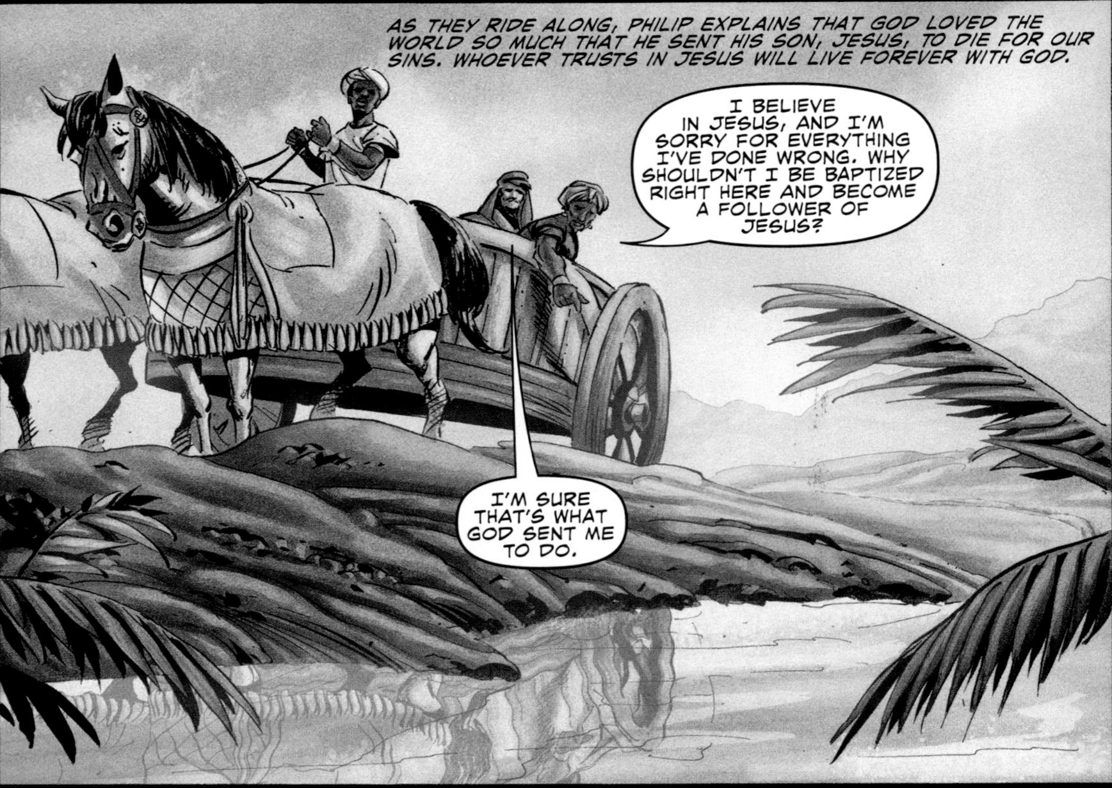
AS THEY RIDE ALONG, PHILIP EXPLAINS THAT GOD LOVED THE WORLD SO MUCH THAT HE SENT HIS SON, JESUS, TO DIE FOR OUR SINS. WHOEVER TRUSTS IN JESUS WILL LIVE FOREVER WITH GOD.
I BELIEVE IN JESUS, AND I'M SORRY FOR EVERYTHING I'VE DONE WRONG. WHY SHOULDN'T I BE BAPTIZED RIGHT HERE AND BECOME A FOLLOWER OF JESUS?
I'M SURE THAT'S WHAT GOD SENT ME TO DO.

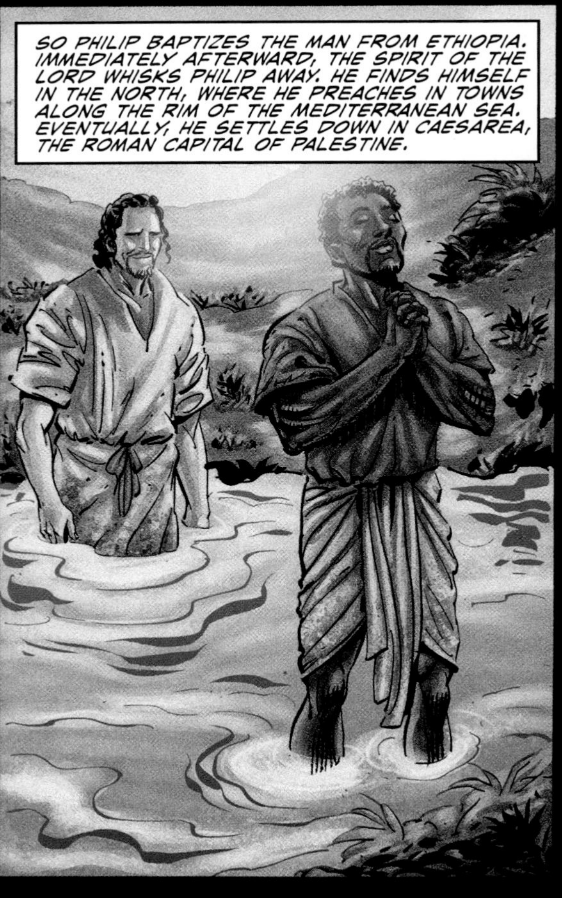
SO PHILIP BAPTIZES THE MAN FROM ETHIOPIA. IMMEDIATELY AFTERWARD, THE SPIRIT OF THE LORD WHISKS PHILIP AWAY. HE FINDS HIMSELF IN THE NORTH, WHERE HE PREACHES IN TOWNS ALONG THE RIM OF THE MEDITERRANEAN SEA. EVENTUALLY, HE SETTLES DOWN IN CAESAREA, THE ROMAN CAPITAL OF PALESTINE.

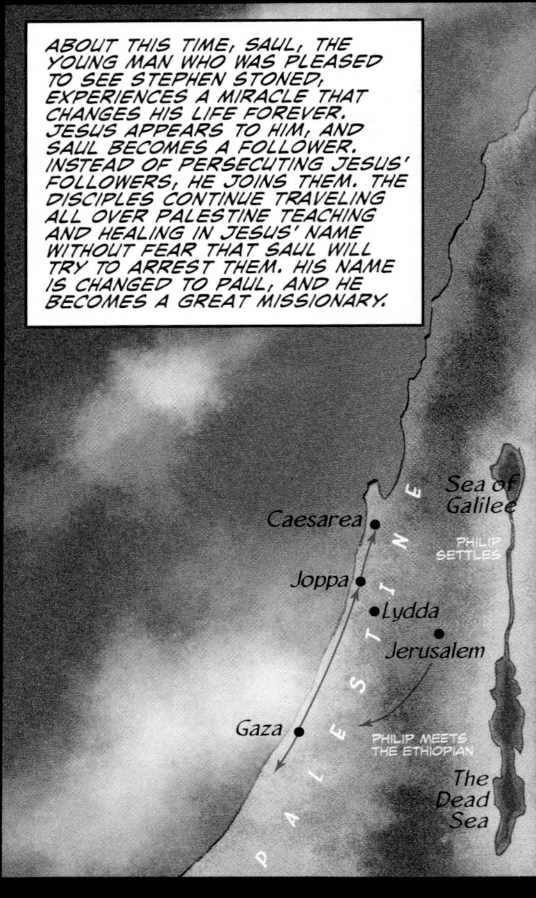
ABOUT THIS TIME, SAUL, THE YOUNG MAN WHO WAS PLEASED TO SEE STEPHEN STONED, EXPERIENCES A MIRACLE THAT CHANGES HIS LIFE FOREVER. JESUS APPEARS TO HIM, AND SAUL BECOMES A FOLLOWER. INSTEAD OF PERSECUTING JESUS' FOLLOWERS, HE JOINS THEM. THE DISCIPLES CONTINUE TRAVELING ALL OVER PALESTINE TEACHING AND HEALING IN JESUS' NAME WITHOUT FEAR THAT SAUL WILL TRY TO ARREST THEM. HIS NAME IS CHANGED TO PAUL, AND HE BECOMES A GREAT MISSIONARY.
Sea of Galilee
Caesarea
PHILIP SETTLES
Joppa
Lydda
Jerusalem
Gaza
PHILIP MEETS THE ETHIOPIAN
The Dead Sea
PALESTINE

Peter as the Rock

BASED ON ACTS 9:32—10:2

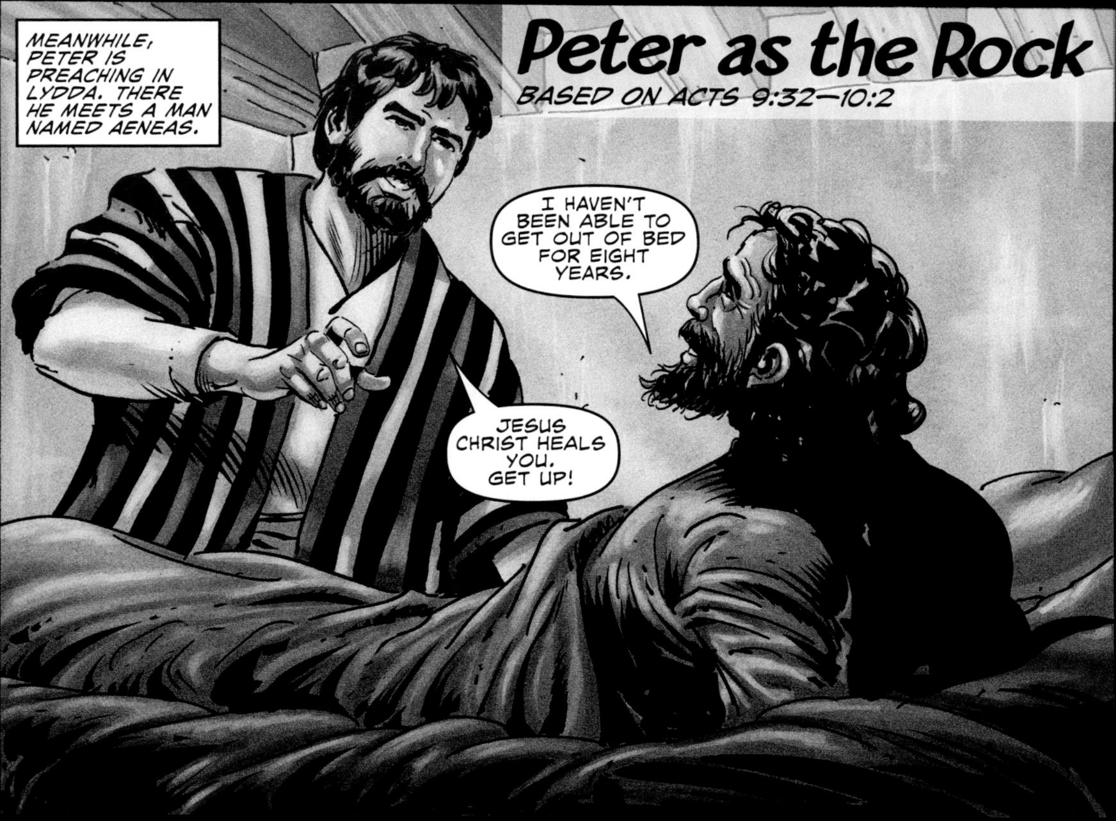
MEANWHILE, PETER IS PREACHING IN LYDDA. THERE HE MEETS A MAN NAMED AENEAS.
I HAVEN'T BEEN ABLE TO GET OUT OF BED FOR EIGHT YEARS.
JESUS CHRIST HEALS YOU. GET UP!

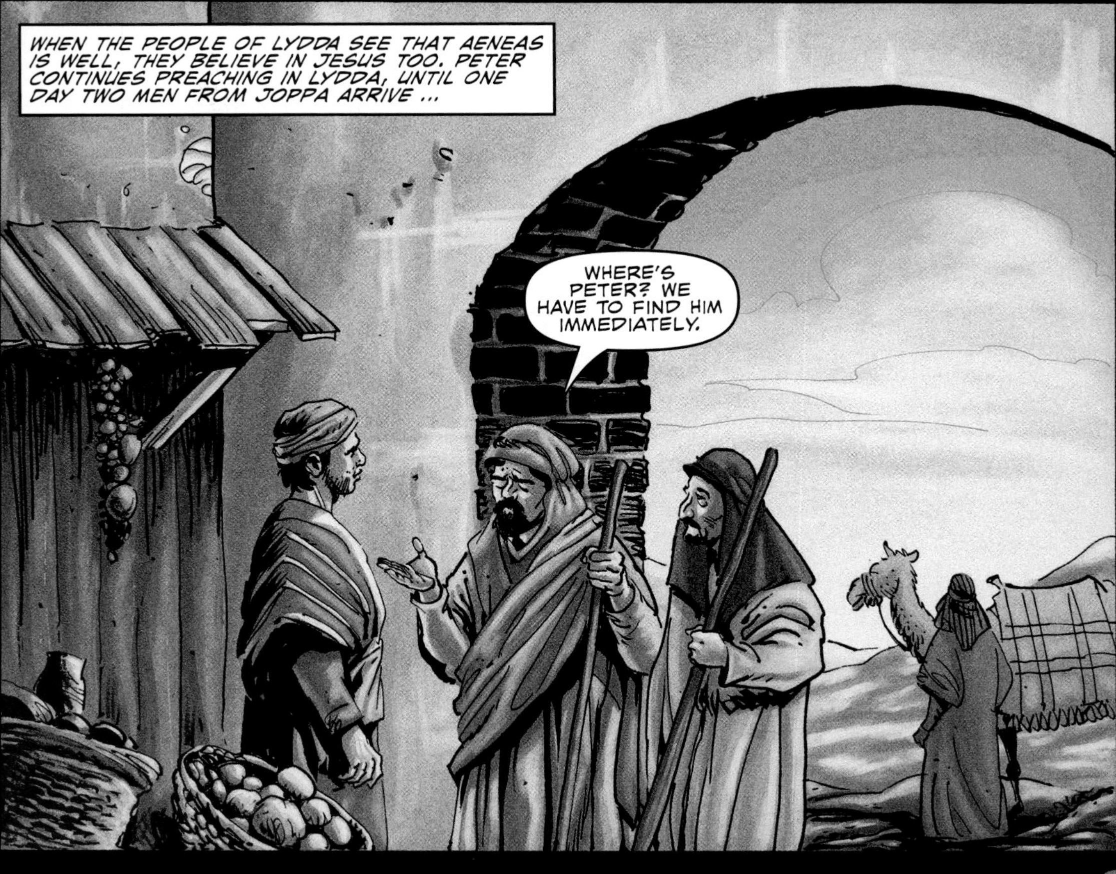
WHEN THE PEOPLE OF LYDDA SEE THAT AENEAS IS WELL, THEY BELIEVE IN JESUS TOO. PETER CONTINUES PREACHING IN LYDDA, UNTIL ONE DAY TWO MEN FROM JOPPA ARRIVE ...
WHERE'S PETER? WE HAVE TO FIND HIM IMMEDIATELY.

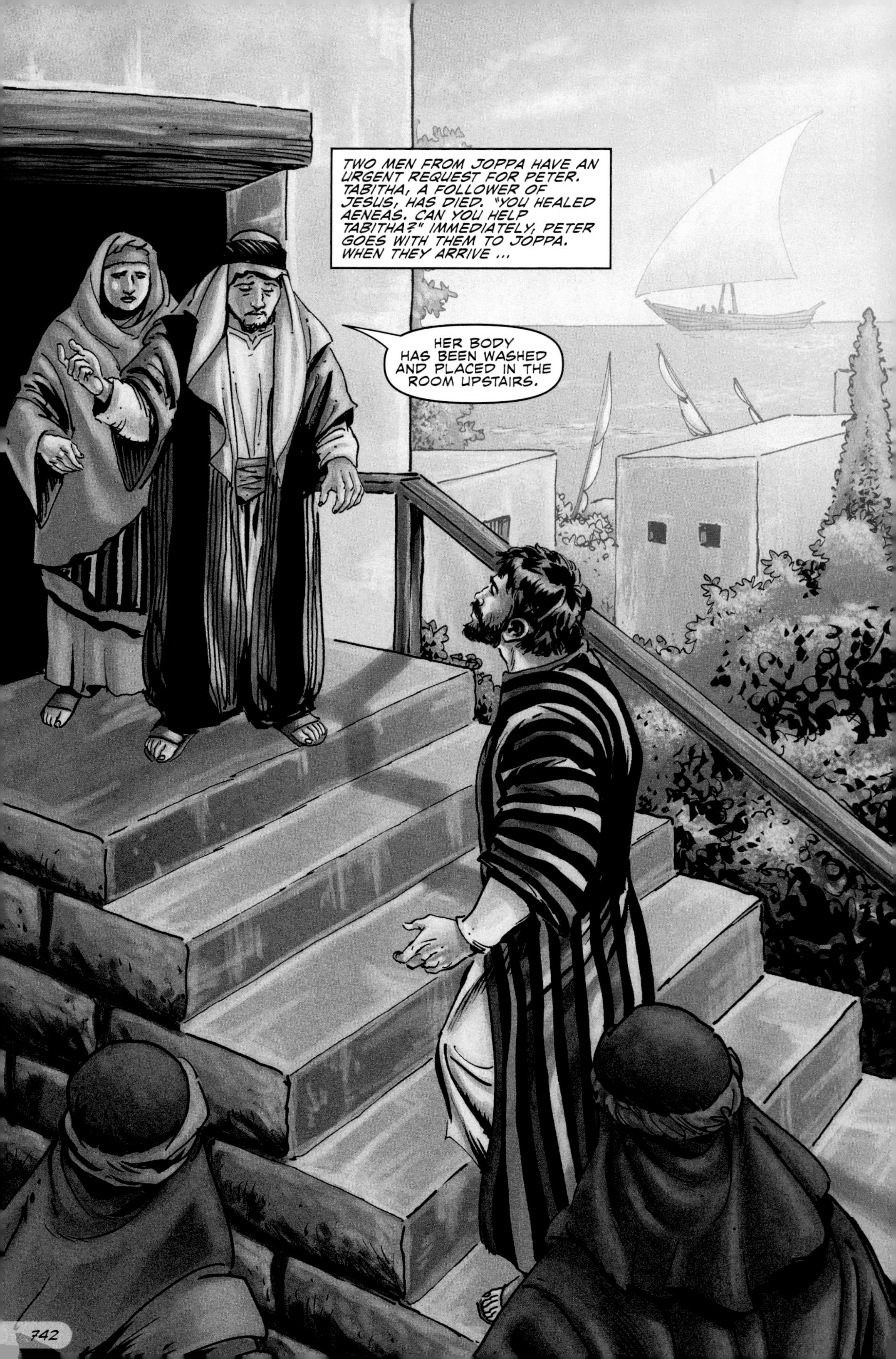
TWO MEN FROM JOPPA HAVE AN URGENT REQUEST FOR PETER. TABITHA, A FOLLOWER OF JESUS, HAS DIED. "YOU HEALED AENEAS. CAN YOU HELP TABITHA?" IMMEDIATELY, PETER GOES WITH THEM TO JOPPA. WHEN THEY ARRIVE ...
HER BODY HAS BEEN WASHED AND PLACED IN THE ROOM UPSTAIRS.

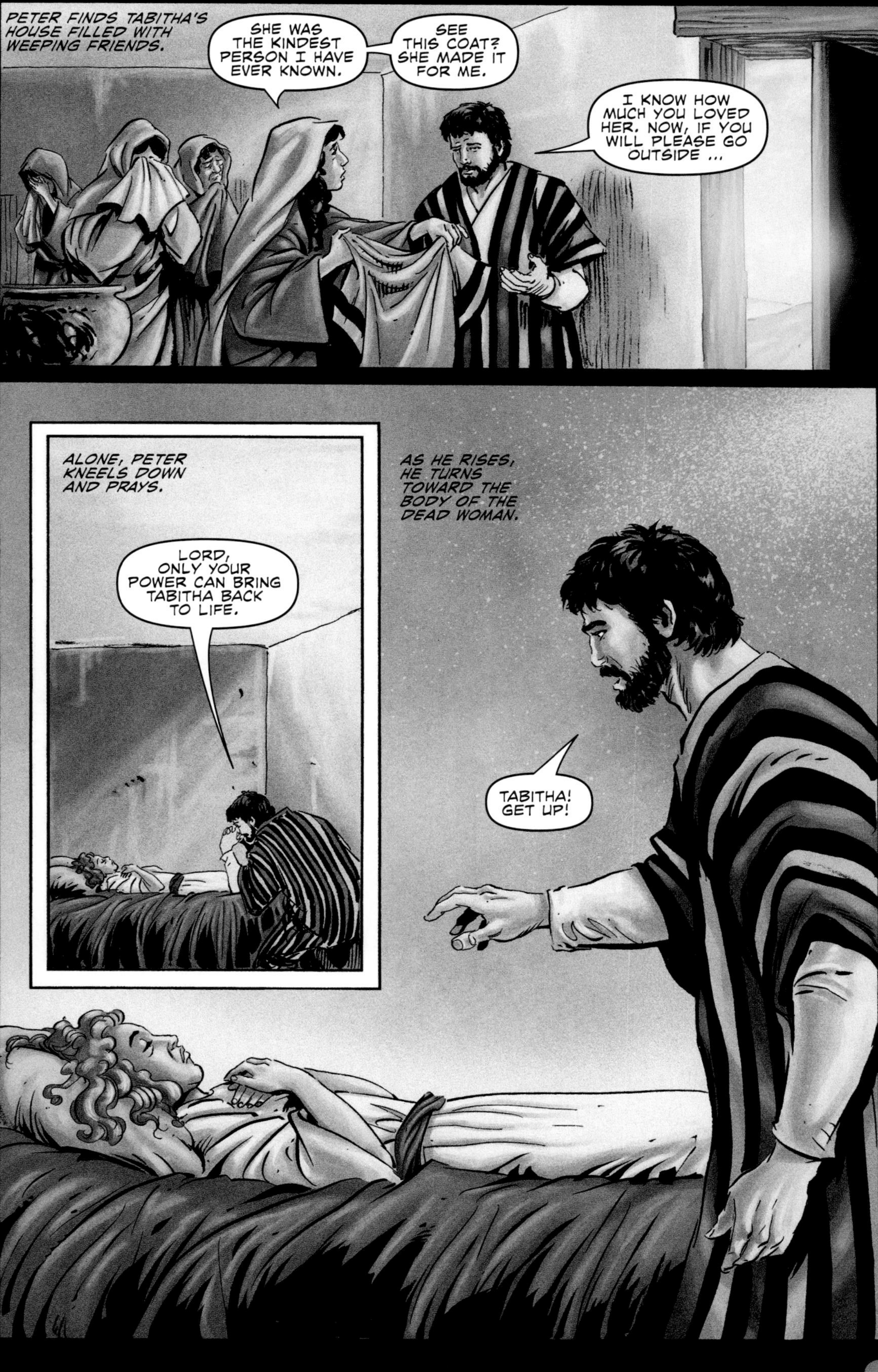
PETER FINDS TABITHA'S HOUSE FILLED WITH WEEPING FRIENDS.
SHE WAS THE KINDEST PERSON I HAVE EVER KNOWN.
SEE THIS COAT? SHE MADE IT FOR ME.
I KNOW HOW MUCH YOU LOVED HER. NOW, IF YOU WILL PLEASE GO OUTSIDE ...
ALONE, PETER KNEELS DOWN AND PRAYS.
LORD, ONLY YOUR POWER CAN BRING TABITHA BACK TO LIFE.
AS HE RISES, HE TURNS TOWARD THE BODY OF THE DEAD WOMAN.
TABITHA! GET UP!

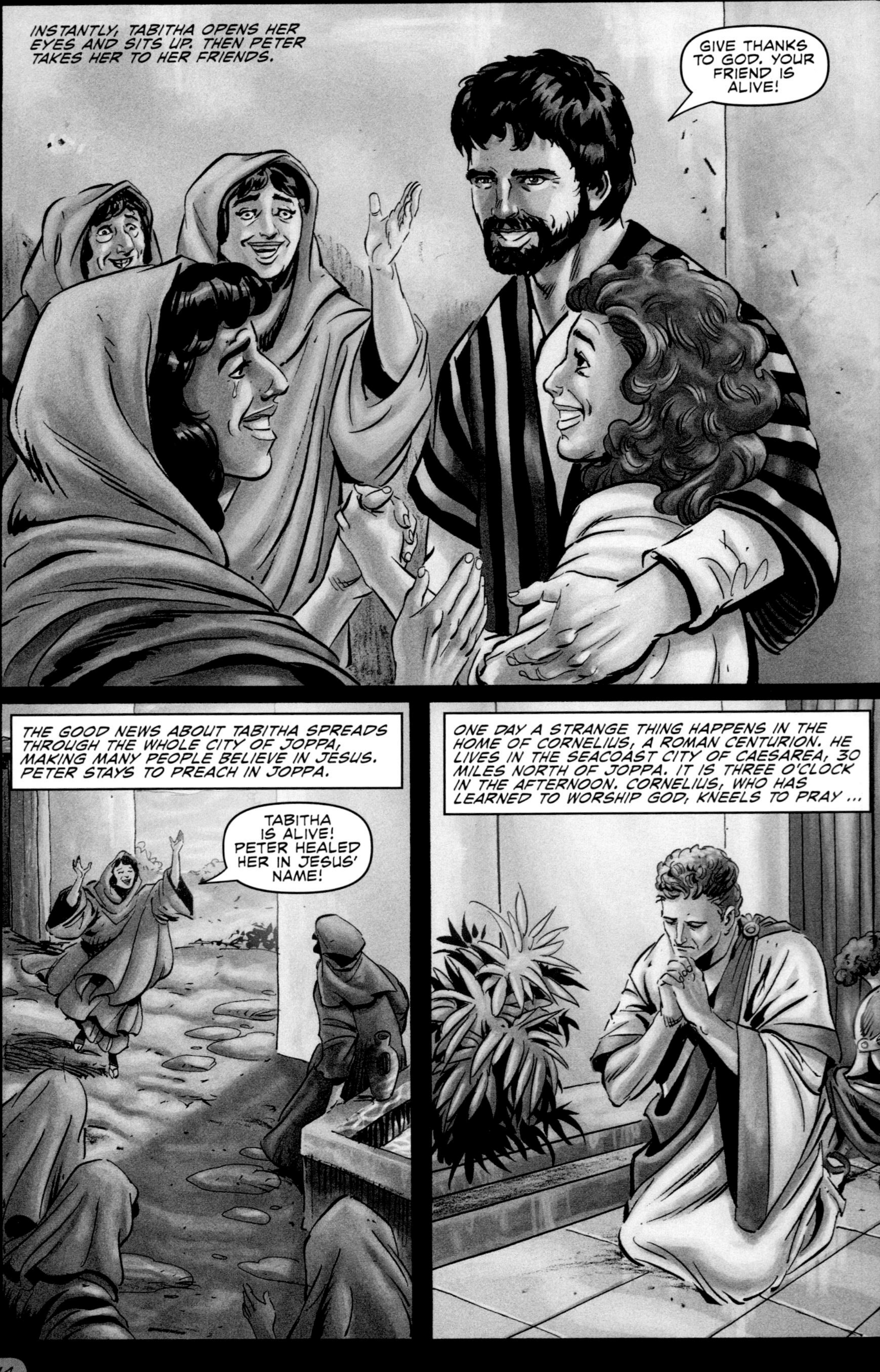
INSTANTLY, TABITHA OPENS HER EYES AND SITS UP. THEN PETER TAKES HER TO HER FRIENDS.
GIVE THANKS TO GOD. YOUR FRIEND IS ALIVE!
THE GOOD NEWS ABOUT TABITHA SPREADS THROUGH THE WHOLE CITY OF JOPPA, MAKING MANY PEOPLE BELIEVE IN JESUS. PETER STAYS TO PREACH IN JOPPA.
TABITHA IS ALIVE! PETER HEALED HER IN JESUS' NAME!
ONE DAY A STRANGE THING HAPPENS IN THE HOME OF CORNELIUS, A ROMAN CENTURION. HE LIVES IN THE SEACOAST CITY OF CAESAREA, 30 MILES NORTH OF JOPPA. IT IS THREE O'CLOCK IN THE AFTERNOON. CORNELIUS, WHO HAS LEARNED TO WORSHIP GOD, KNEELS TO PRAY ...

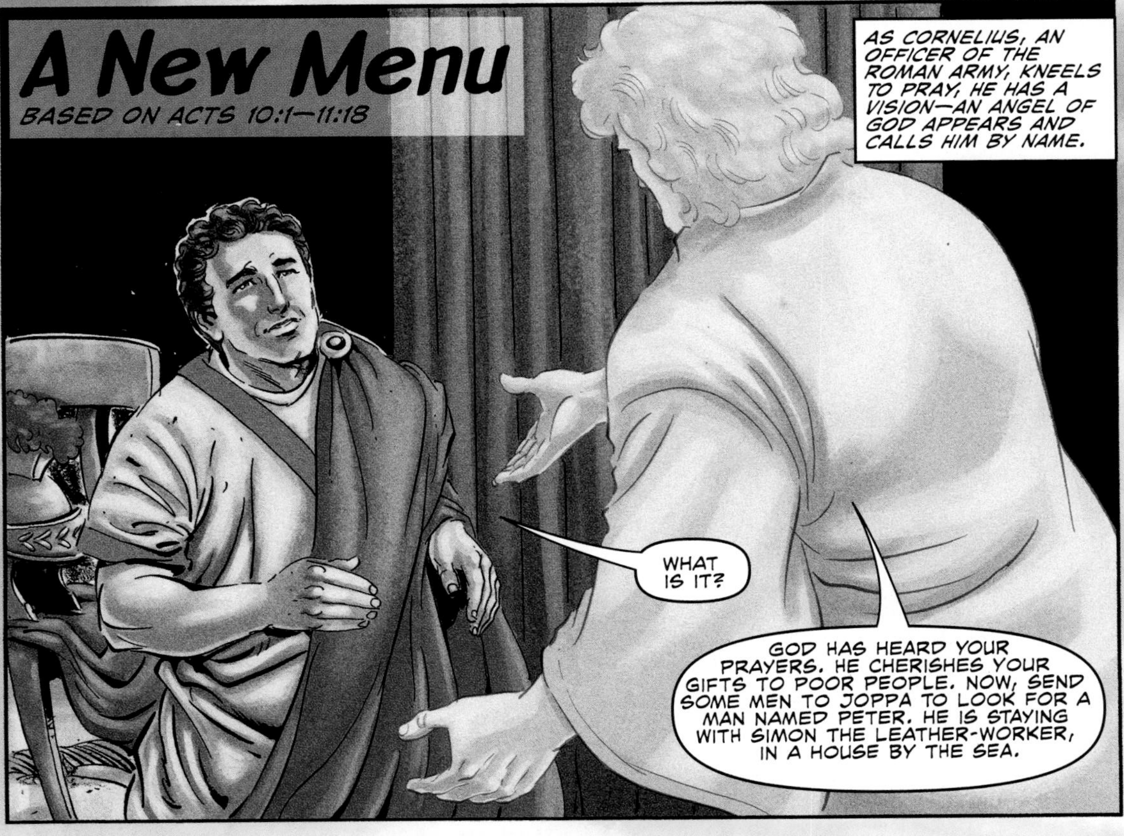
A New Menu
BASED ON ACTS 10:1—11:18
AS CORNELIUS, AN OFFICER OF THE ROMAN ARMY, KNEELS TO PRAY, HE HAS A VISION—AN ANGEL OF GOD APPEARS AND CALLS HIM BY NAME.
WHAT IS IT?
GOD HAS HEARD YOUR PRAYERS. HE CHERISHES YOUR GIFTS TO POOR PEOPLE. NOW, SEND SOME MEN TO JOPPA TO LOOK FOR A MAN NAMED PETER. HE IS STAYING WITH SIMON THE LEATHER-WORKER, IN A HOUSE BY THE SEA.

AFTER THE ANGEL LEAVES, CORNELIUS SENDS THREE OF HIS MOST TRUSTED MEN TO JOPPA. AS THEY APPROACH THE CITY, THE MAN THEY'RE LOOKING FOR GOES UP ON A ROOFTOP TO PRAY ...

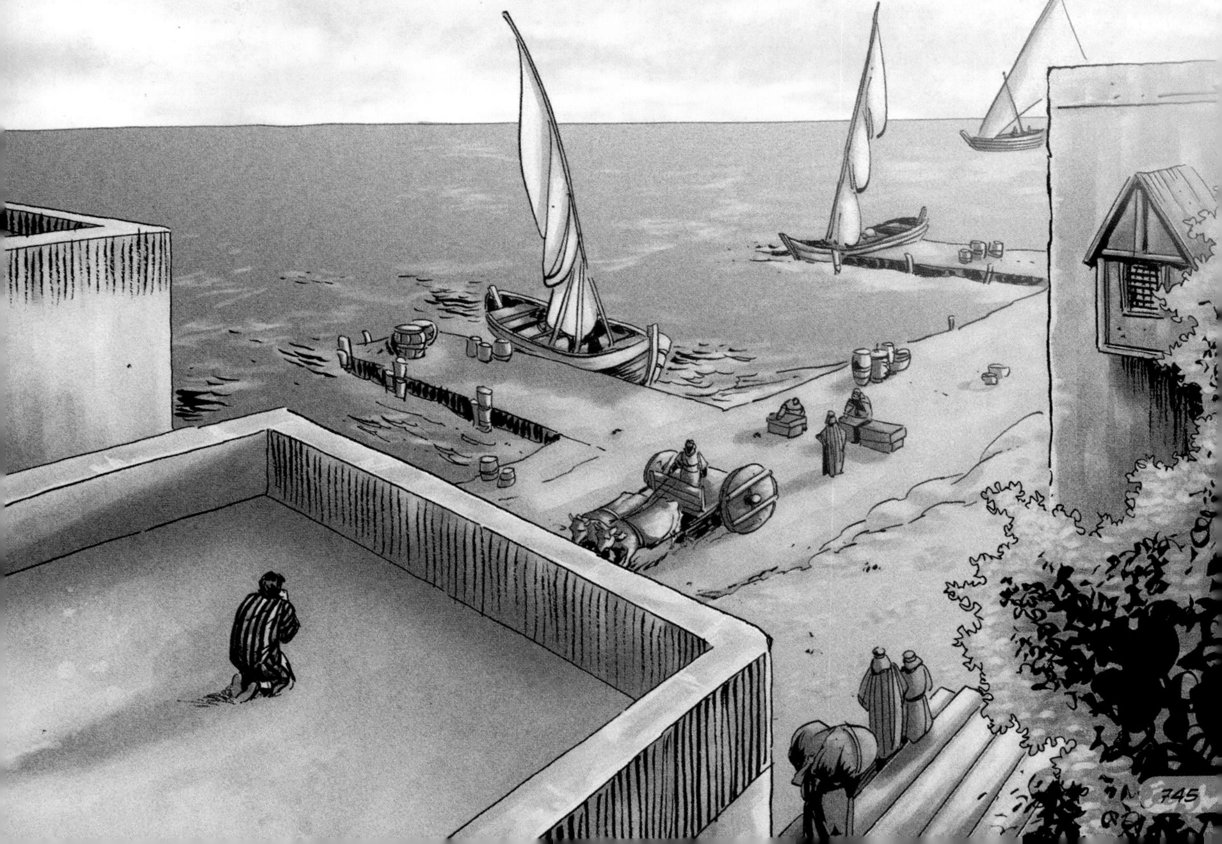

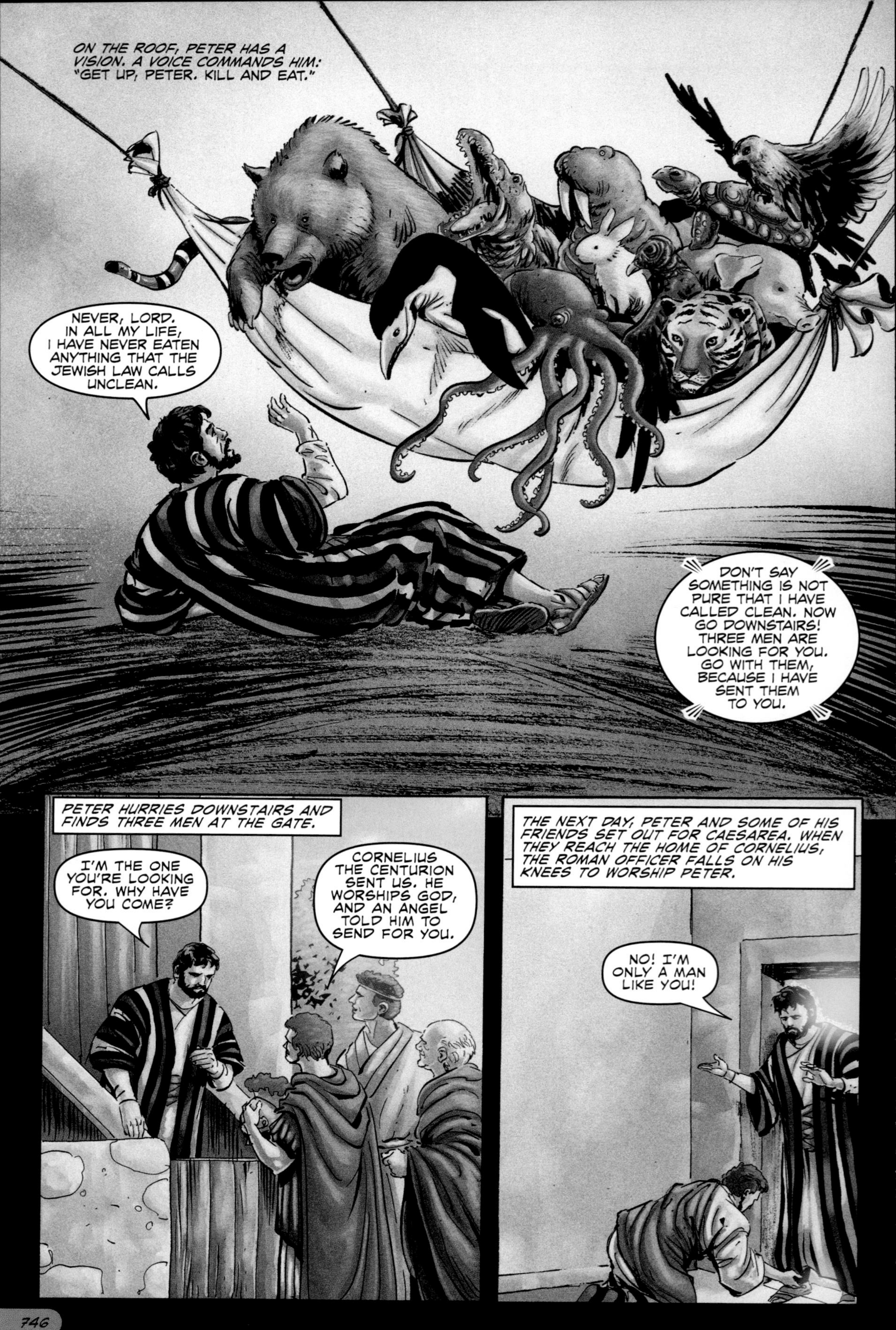
ON THE ROOF, PETER HAS A VISION. A VOICE COMMANDS HIM: "GET UP, PETER. KILL AND EAT."
NEVER, LORD. IN ALL MY LIFE, I HAVE NEVER EATEN ANYTHING THAT THE JEWISH LAW CALLS UNCLEAN.
DON'T SAY SOMETHING IS NOT PURE THAT I HAVE CALLED CLEAN. NOW GO DOWNSTAIRS! THREE MEN ARE LOOKING FOR YOU. GO WITH THEM, BECAUSE I HAVE SENT THEM TO YOU.
PETER HURRIES DOWNSTAIRS AND FINDS THREE MEN AT THE GATE.
I'M THE ONE YOU'RE LOOKING FOR. WHY HAVE YOU COME?
CORNELIUS THE CENTURION SENT US. HE WORSHIPS GOD, AND AN ANGEL TOLD HIM TO SEND FOR YOU.
THE NEXT DAY, PETER AND SOME OF HIS FRIENDS SET OUT FOR CAESAREA. WHEN THEY REACH THE HOME OF CORNELIUS, THE ROMAN OFFICER FALLS ON HIS KNEES TO WORSHIP PETER.
NO! I'M ONLY A MAN LIKE YOU!

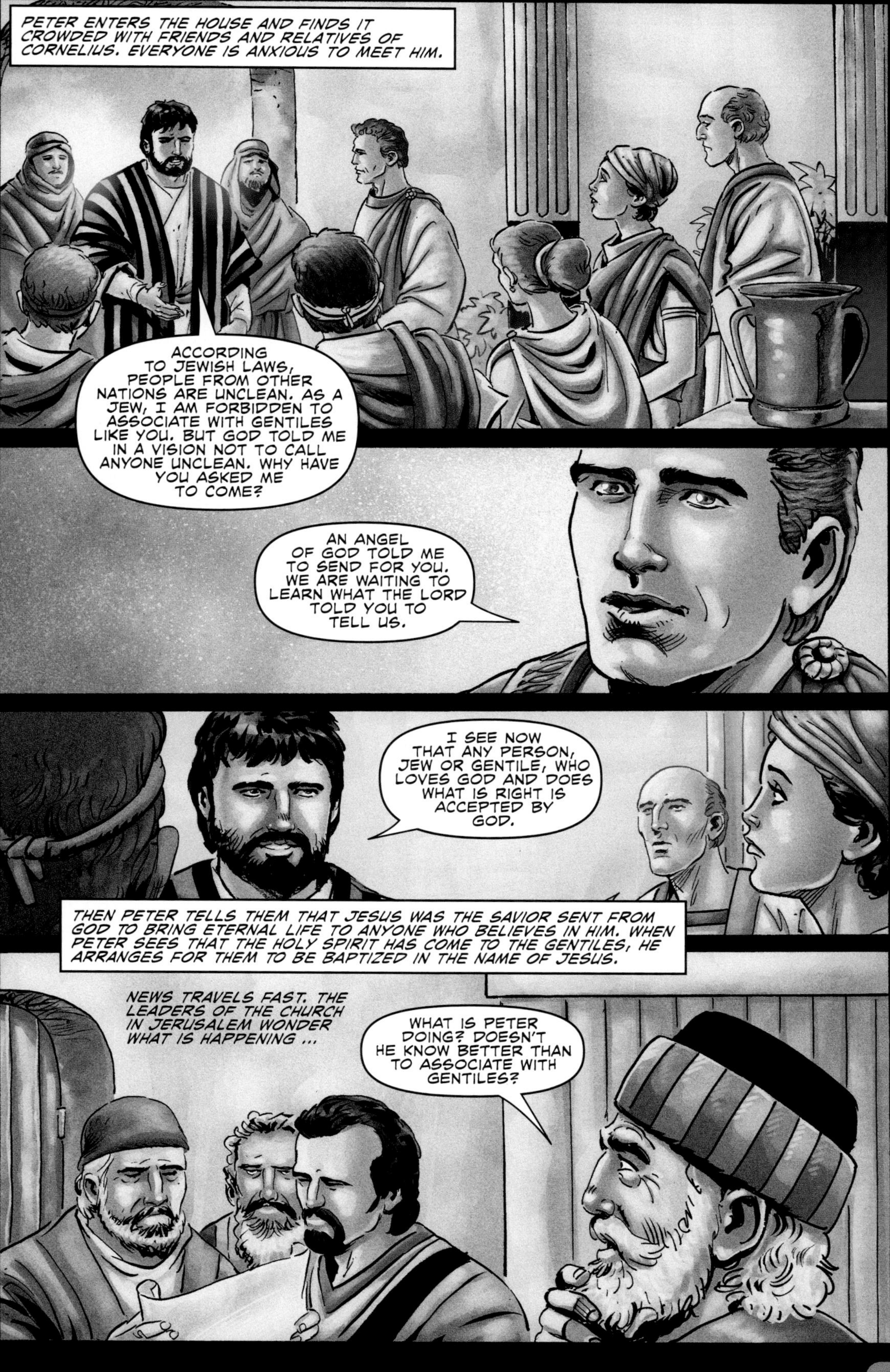

PETER ENTERS THE HOUSE AND FINDS IT CROWDED WITH FRIENDS AND RELATIVES OF CORNELIUS. EVERYONE IS ANXIOUS TO MEET HIM.
ACCORDING TO JEWISH LAWS, PEOPLE FROM OTHER NATIONS ARE UNCLEAN. AS A JEW, I AM FORBIDDEN TO ASSOCIATE WITH GENTILES LIKE YOU. BUT GOD TOLD ME IN A VISION NOT TO CALL ANYONE UNCLEAN. WHY HAVE YOU ASKED ME TO COME?
AN ANGEL OF GOD TOLD ME TO SEND FOR YOU. WE ARE WAITING TO LEARN WHAT THE LORD TOLD YOU TO TELL US.
I SEE NOW THAT ANY PERSON, JEW OR GENTILE, WHO LOVES GOD AND DOES WHAT IS RIGHT IS ACCEPTED BY GOD.
THEN PETER TELLS THEM THAT JESUS WAS THE SAVIOR SENT FROM GOD TO BRING ETERNAL LIFE TO ANYONE WHO BELIEVES IN HIM. WHEN PETER SEES THAT THE HOLY SPIRIT HAS COME TO THE GENTILES, HE ARRANGES FOR THEM TO BE BAPTIZED IN THE NAME OF JESUS.
NEWS TRAVELS FAST. THE LEADERS OF THE CHURCH IN JERUSALEM WONDER WHAT IS HAPPENING ...
WHAT IS PETER DOING? DOESN'T HE KNOW BETTER THAN TO ASSOCIATE WITH GENTILES?

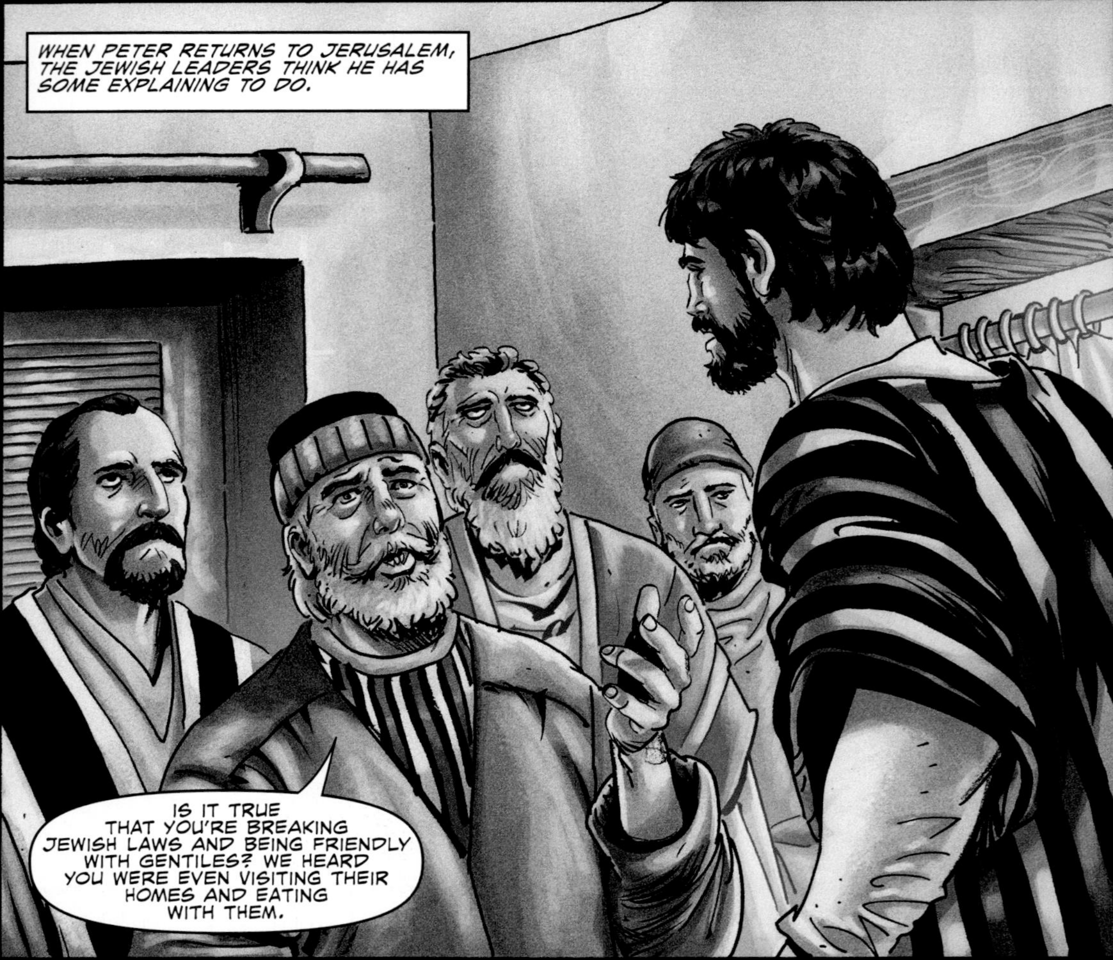
WHEN PETER RETURNS TO JERUSALEM, THE JEWISH LEADERS THINK HE HAS SOME EXPLAINING TO DO.
IS IT TRUE THAT YOU'RE BREAKING JEWISH LAWS AND BEING FRIENDLY WITH GENTILES? WE HEARD YOU WERE EVEN VISITING THEIR HOMES AND EATING WITH THEM.

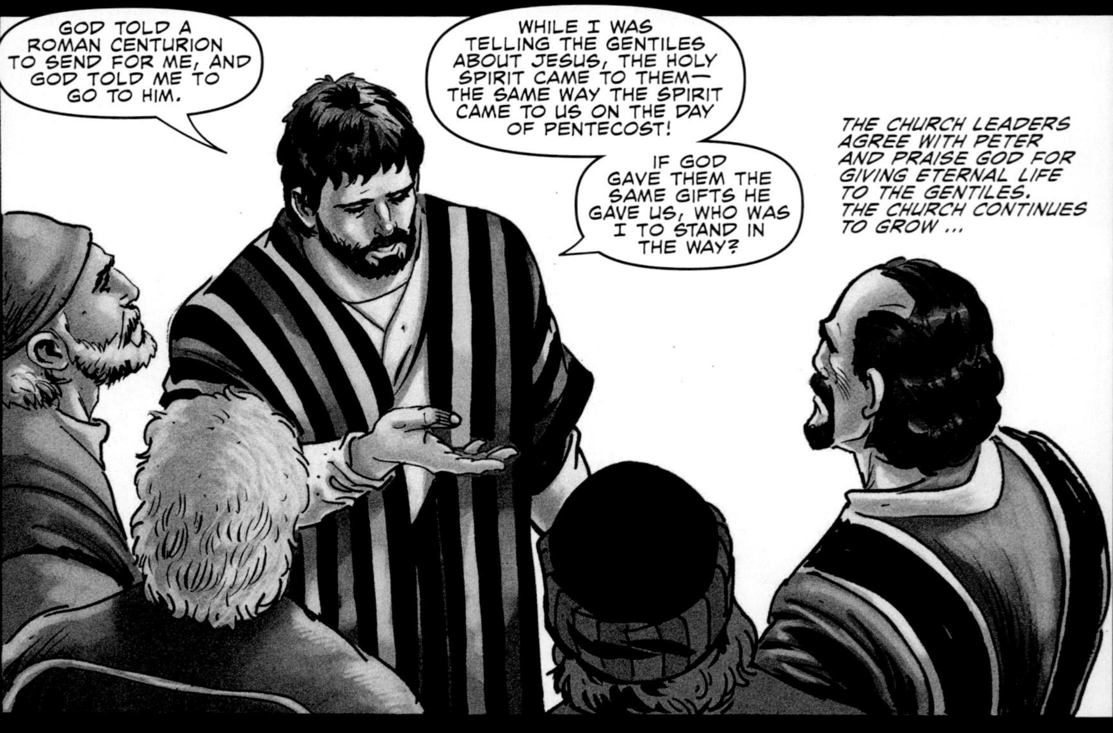
GOD TOLD A ROMAN CENTURION TO SEND FOR ME, AND GOD TOLD ME TO GO TO HIM.
WHILE I WAS TELLING THE GENTILES ABOUT JESUS, THE HOLY SPIRIT CAME TO THEM—THE SAME WAY THE SPIRIT CAME TO US ON THE DAY OF PENTECOST!
IF GOD GAVE THEM THE SAME GIFTS HE GAVE US, WHO WAS I TO STAND IN THE WAY?
THE CHURCH LEADERS AGREE WITH PETER AND PRAISE GOD FOR GIVING ETERNAL LIFE TO THE GENTILES. THE CHURCH CONTINUES TO GROW ...

Death to the Tyrant

BASED ON ACTS 12

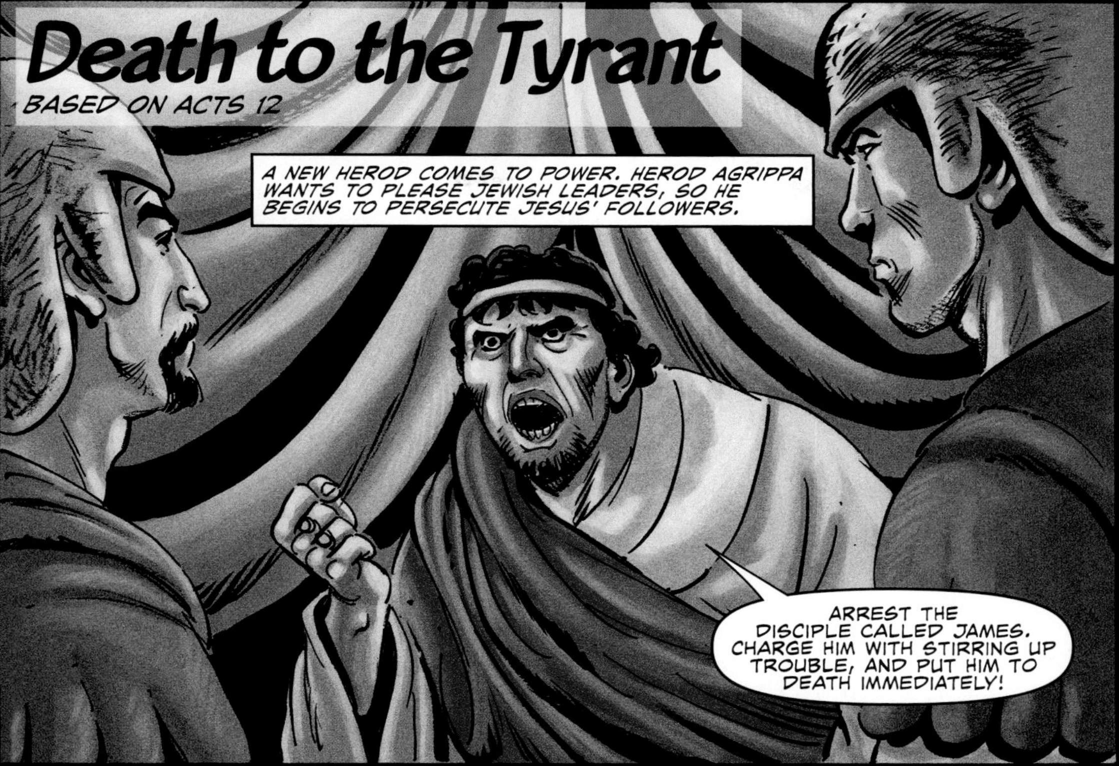
A NEW HEROD COMES TO POWER. HEROD AGRIPPA WANTS TO PLEASE JEWISH LEADERS, SO HE BEGINS TO PERSECUTE JESUS' FOLLOWERS.
ARREST THE DISCIPLE CALLED JAMES. CHARGE HIM WITH STIRRING UP TROUBLE, AND PUT HIM TO DEATH IMMEDIATELY!

SO JAMES, ONE OF THE FOUR FISHERMEN WHO LEFT HIS NETS TO FOLLOW JESUS, IS KILLED TO SATISFY A WICKED KING'S STRUGGLE FOR POWER.

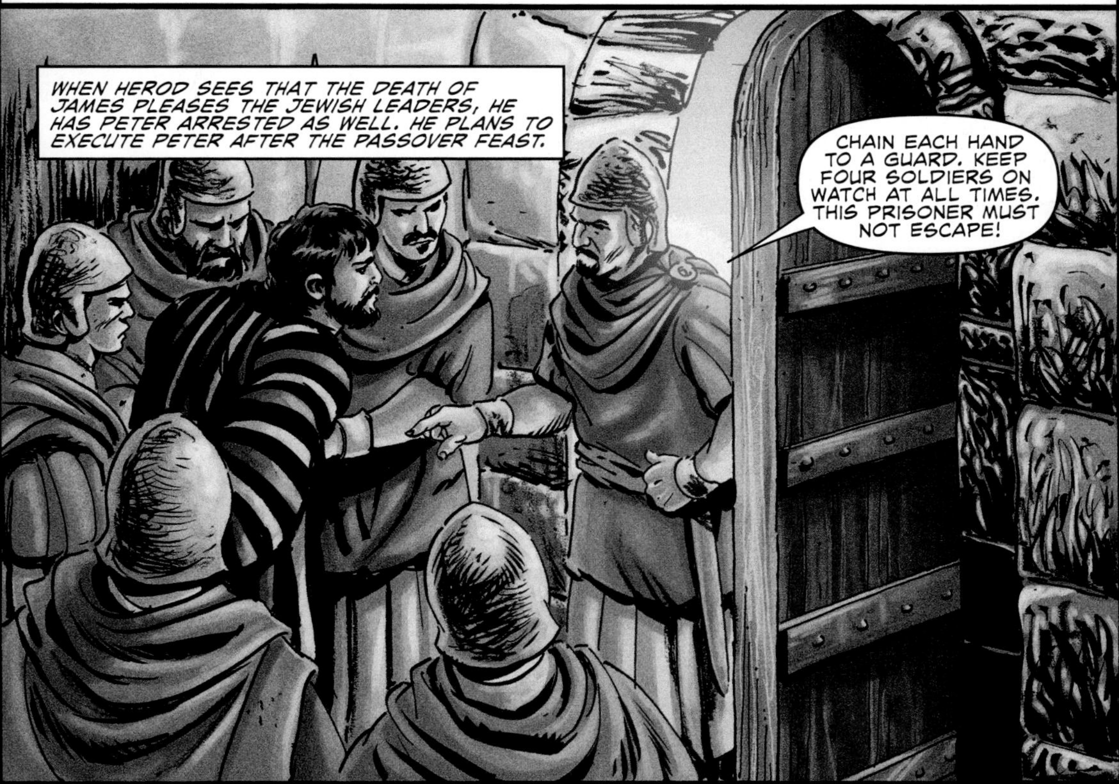
WHEN HEROD SEES THAT THE DEATH OF JAMES PLEASES THE JEWISH LEADERS, HE HAS PETER ARRESTED AS WELL. HE PLANS TO EXECUTE PETER AFTER THE PASSOVER FEAST.
CHAIN EACH HAND TO A GUARD. KEEP FOUR SOLDIERS ON WATCH AT ALL TIMES. THIS PRISONER MUST NOT ESCAPE!

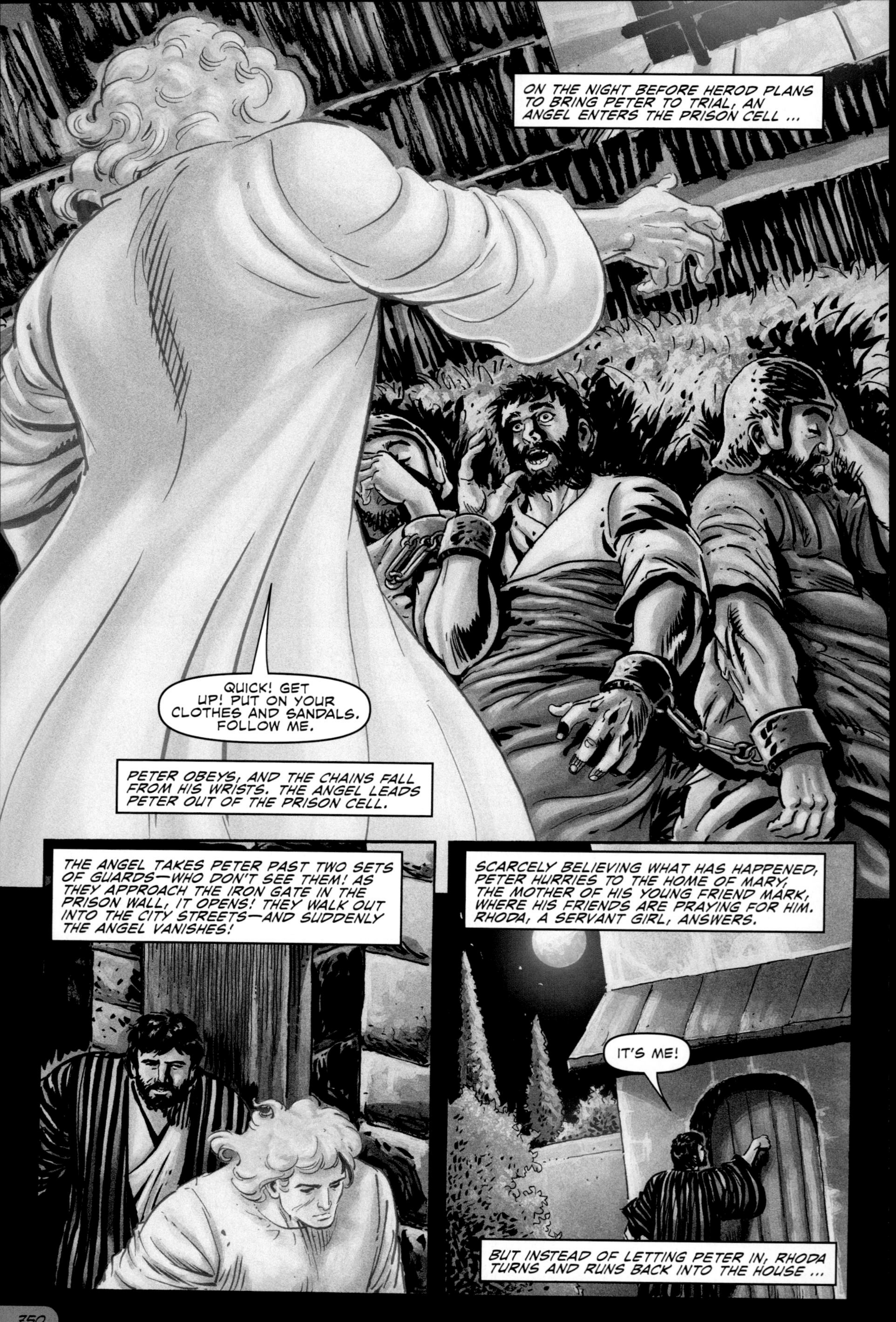
ON THE NIGHT BEFORE HEROD PLANS TO BRING PETER TO TRIAL, AN ANGEL ENTERS THE PRISON CELL ...
QUICK! GET UP! PUT ON YOUR CLOTHES AND SANDALS. FOLLOW ME.
PETER OBEYS, AND THE CHAINS FALL FROM HIS WRISTS. THE ANGEL LEADS PETER OUT OF THE PRISON CELL.
THE ANGEL TAKES PETER PAST TWO SETS OF GUARDS—WHO DON'T SEE THEM! AS THEY APPROACH THE IRON GATE IN THE PRISON WALL, IT OPENS! THEY WALK OUT INTO THE CITY STREETS—AND SUDDENLY THE ANGEL VANISHES!
SCARCELY BELIEVING WHAT HAS HAPPENED, PETER HURRIES TO THE HOME OF MARY, THE MOTHER OF HIS YOUNG FRIEND MARK, WHERE HIS FRIENDS ARE PRAYING FOR HIM. RHODA, A SERVANT GIRL, ANSWERS.
IT'S ME!
BUT INSTEAD OF LETTING PETER IN, RHODA TURNS AND RUNS BACK INTO THE HOUSE ...

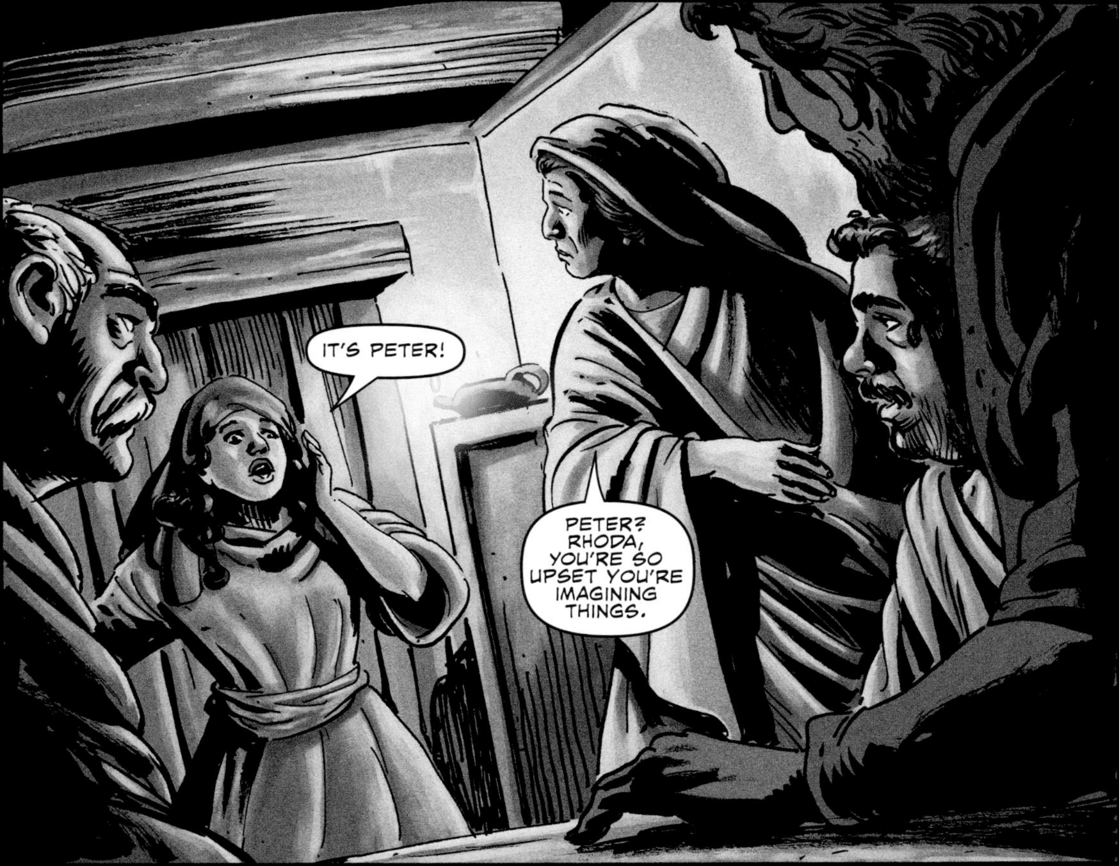
IT'S PETER!
PETER? RHODA, YOU'RE SO UPSET YOU'RE IMAGINING THINGS.

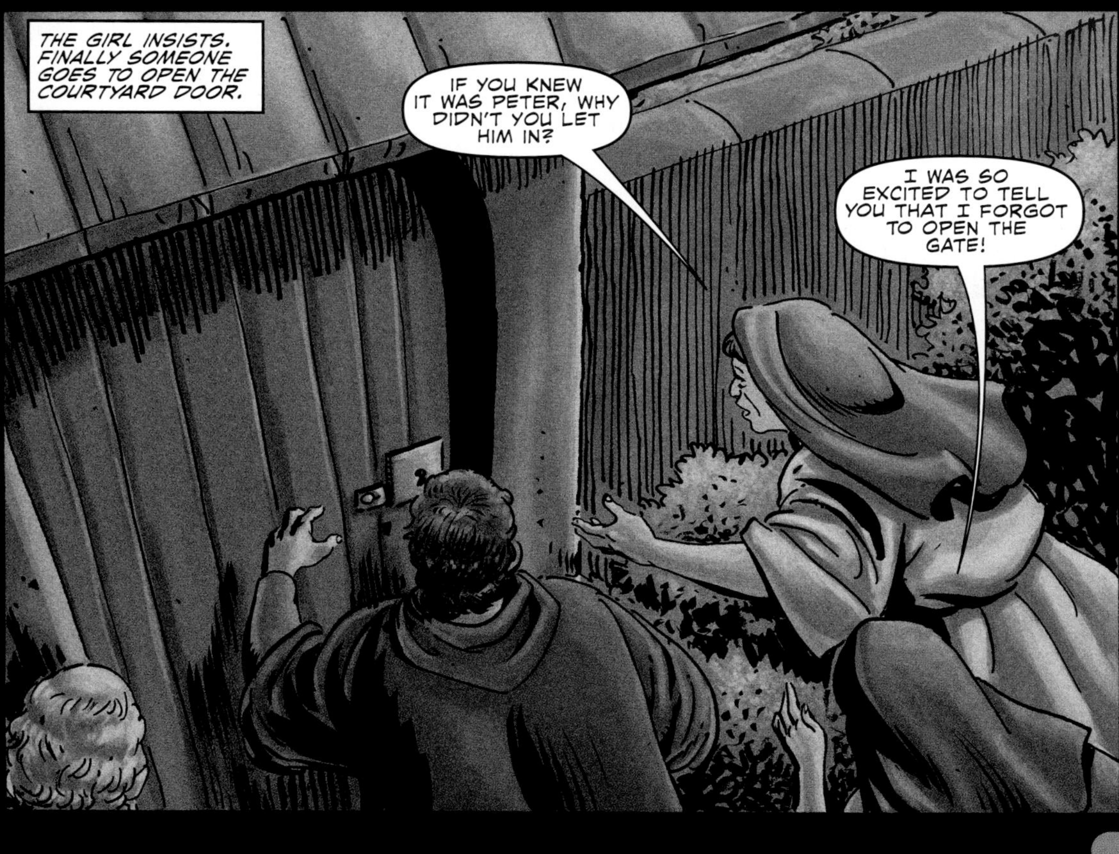
THE GIRL INSISTS. FINALLY SOMEONE GOES TO OPEN THE COURTYARD DOOR.
IF YOU KNEW IT WAS PETER, WHY DIDN'T YOU LET HIM IN?
I WAS SO EXCITED TO TELL YOU THAT I FORGOT TO OPEN THE GATE!

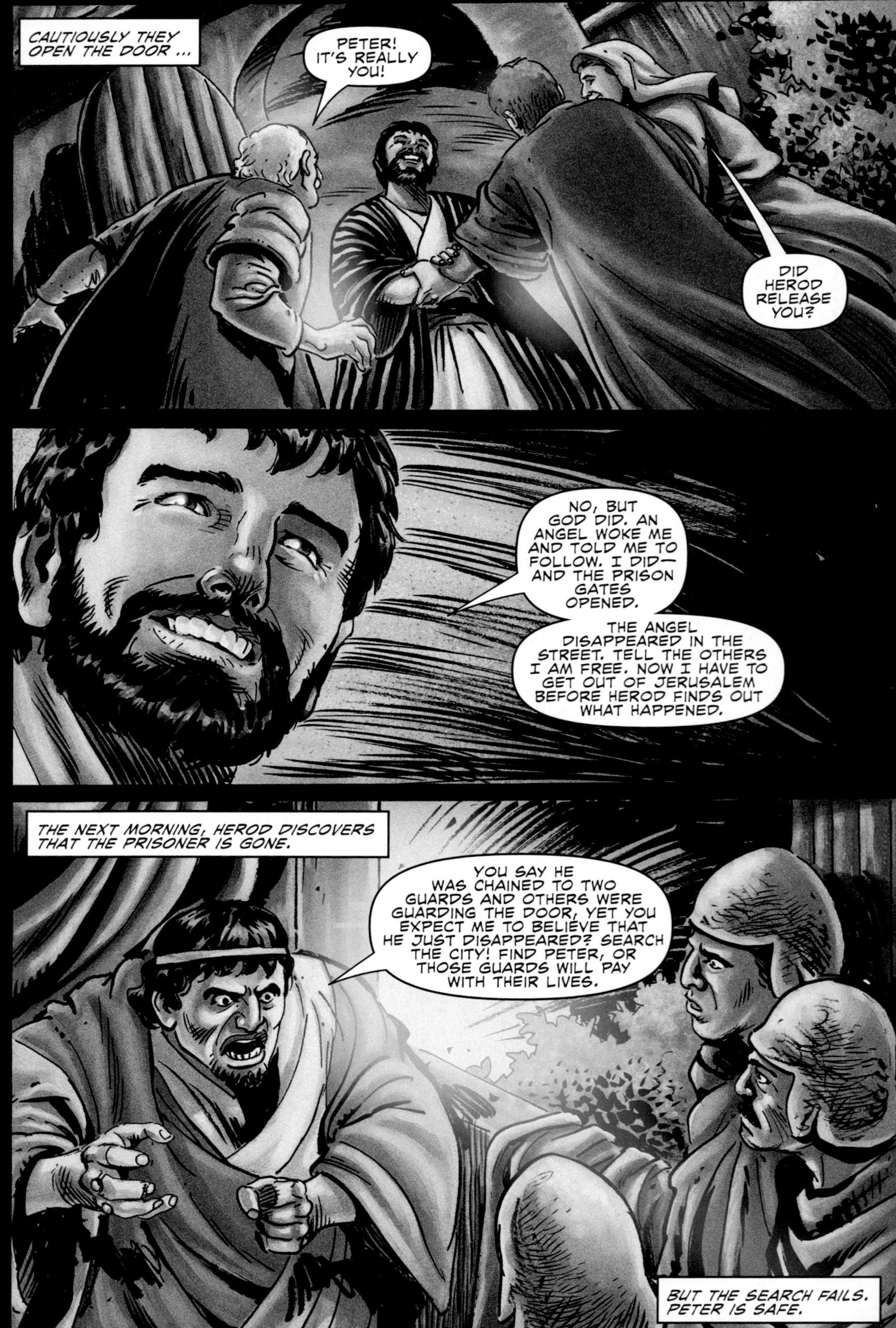

CAUTIOUSLY THEY OPEN THE DOOR ...
PETER! IT'S REALLY YOU!
DID HEROD RELEASE YOU?
NO, BUT GOD DID. AN ANGEL WOKE ME AND TOLD ME TO FOLLOW. I DID—AND THE PRISON GATES OPENED.
THE ANGEL DISAPPEARED IN THE STREET. TELL THE OTHERS I AM FREE. NOW I HAVE TO GET OUT OF JERUSALEM BEFORE HEROD FINDS OUT WHAT HAPPENED.
THE NEXT MORNING, HEROD DISCOVERS THAT THE PRISONER IS GONE.
YOU SAY HE WAS CHAINED TO TWO GUARDS AND OTHERS WERE GUARDING THE DOOR, YET YOU EXPECT ME TO BELIEVE THAT HE JUST DISAPPEARED? SEARCH THE CITY! FIND PETER, OR THOSE GUARDS WILL PAY WITH THEIR LIVES.
BUT THE SEARCH FAILS. PETER IS SAFE.

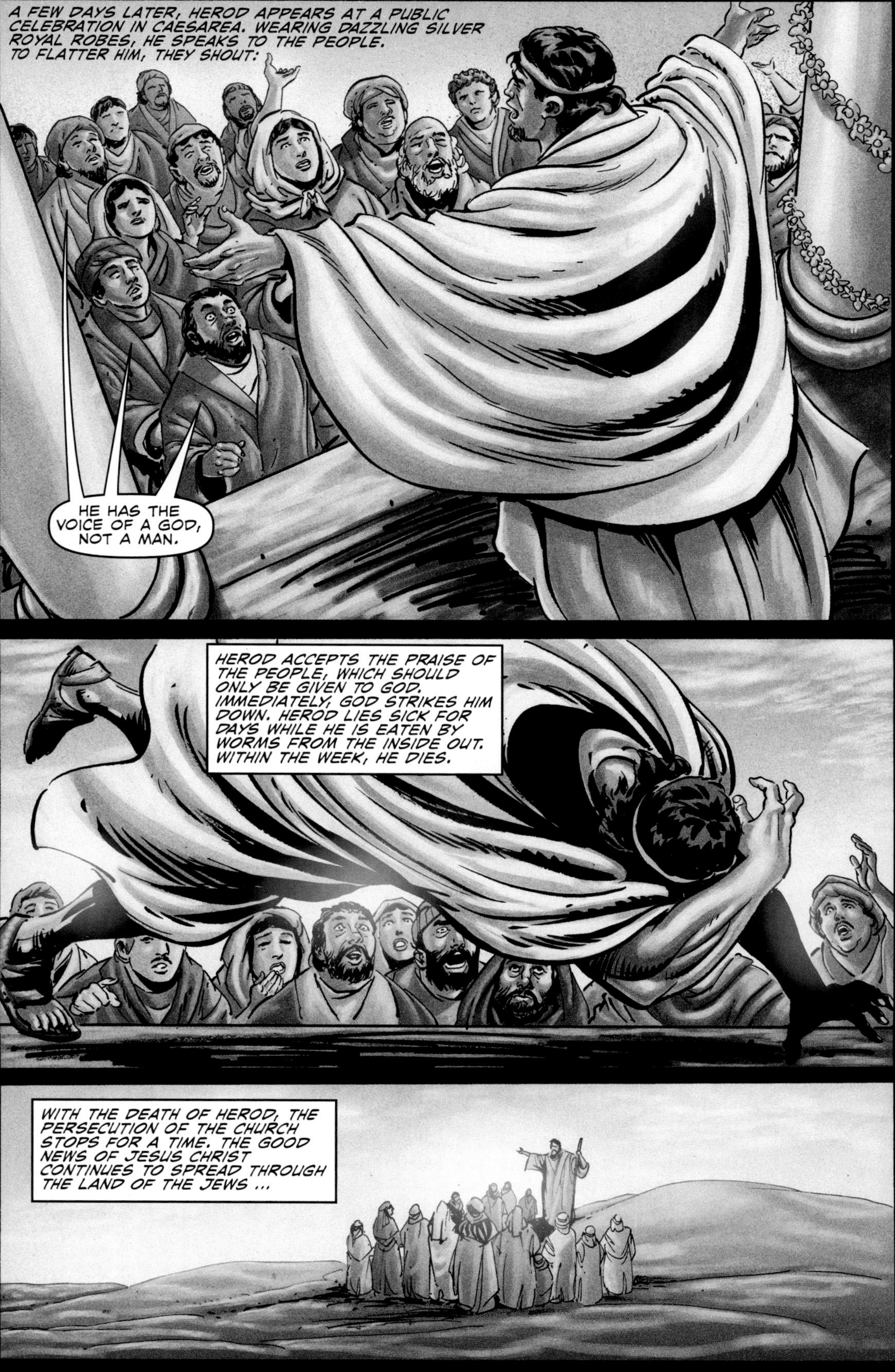
A FEW DAYS LATER, HEROD APPEARS AT A PUBLIC CELEBRATION IN CAESAREA. WEARING DAZZLING SILVER ROYAL ROBES, HE SPEAKS TO THE PEOPLE. TO FLATTER HIM, THEY SHOUT:
HE HAS THE VOICE OF A GOD, NOT A MAN.
HEROD ACCEPTS THE PRAISE OF THE PEOPLE, WHICH SHOULD ONLY BE GIVEN TO GOD. IMMEDIATELY, GOD STRIKES HIM DOWN. HEROD LIES SICK FOR DAYS WHILE HE IS EATEN BY WORMS FROM THE INSIDE OUT. WITHIN THE WEEK, HE DIES.
WITH THE DEATH OF HEROD, THE PERSECUTION OF THE CHURCH STOPS FOR A TIME. THE GOOD NEWS OF JESUS CHRIST CONTINUES TO SPREAD THROUGH THE LAND OF THE JEWS ...

A Blinding Light

BASED ON ACTS 9:1-18

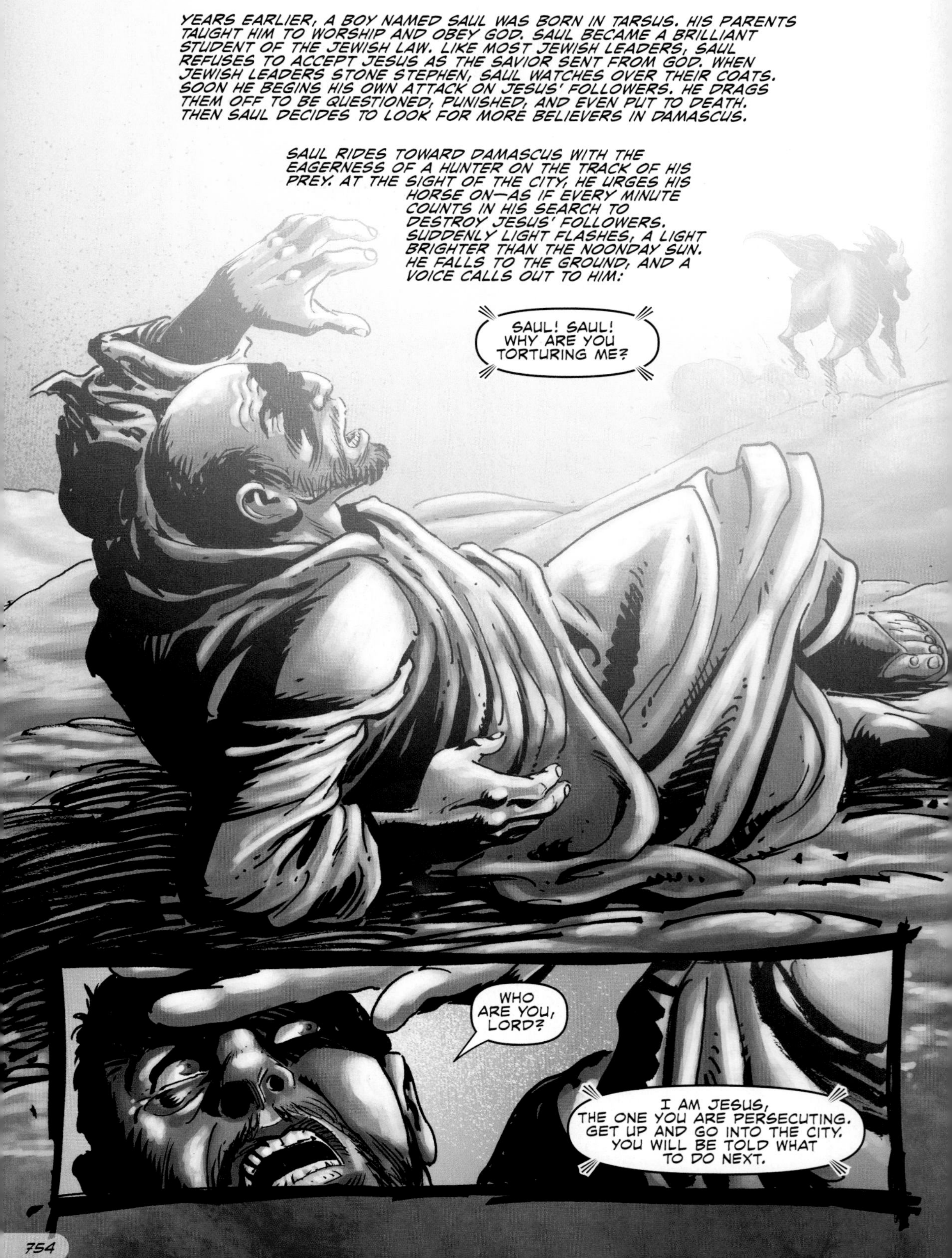
YEARS EARLIER, A BOY NAMED SAUL WAS BORN IN TARSUS. HIS PARENTS TAUGHT HIM TO WORSHIP AND OBEY GOD. SAUL BECAME A BRILLIANT STUDENT OF THE JEWISH LAW. LIKE MOST JEWISH LEADERS, SAUL REFUSES TO ACCEPT JESUS AS THE SAVIOR SENT FROM GOD. WHEN JEWISH LEADERS STONE STEPHEN, SAUL WATCHES OVER THEIR COATS. SOON HE BEGINS HIS OWN ATTACK ON JESUS' FOLLOWERS. HE DRAGS THEM OFF TO BE QUESTIONED, PUNISHED, AND EVEN PUT TO DEATH. THEN SAUL DECIDES TO LOOK FOR MORE BELIEVERS IN DAMASCUS.
SAUL RIDES TOWARD DAMASCUS WITH THE EAGERNESS OF A HUNTER ON THE TRACK OF HIS PREY. AT THE SIGHT OF THE CITY, HE URGES HIS HORSE ON—AS IF EVERY MINUTE COUNTS IN HIS SEARCH TO DESTROY JESUS' FOLLOWERS. SUDDENLY LIGHT FLASHES, A LIGHT BRIGHTER THAN THE NOONDAY SUN. HE FALLS TO THE GROUND, AND A VOICE CALLS OUT TO HIM:
SAUL! SAUL! WHY ARE YOU TORTURING ME?
WHO ARE YOU, LORD?
I AM JESUS, THE ONE YOU ARE PERSECUTING. GET UP AND GO INTO THE CITY. YOU WILL BE TOLD WHAT TO DO NEXT.

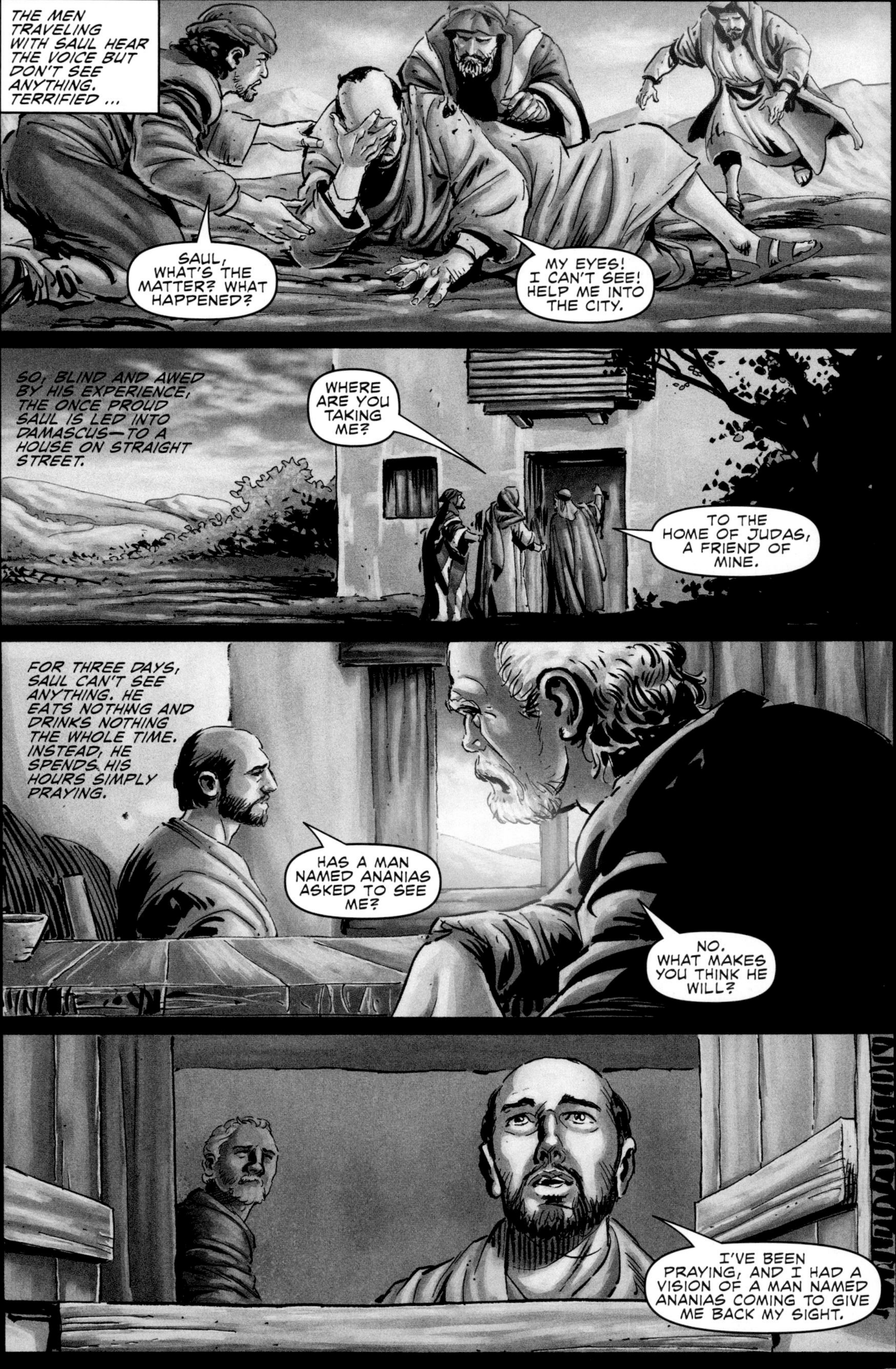
THE MEN TRAVELING WITH SAUL HEAR THE VOICE BUT DON'T SEE ANYTHING. TERRIFIED ...
SAUL, WHAT'S THE MATTER? WHAT HAPPENED?
MY EYES! I CAN'T SEE! HELP ME INTO THE CITY.
SO, BLIND AND AWED BY HIS EXPERIENCE, THE ONCE PROUD SAUL IS LED INTO DAMASCUS—TO A HOUSE ON STRAIGHT STREET.
WHERE ARE YOU TAKING ME?
TO THE HOME OF JUDAS, A FRIEND OF MINE.
FOR THREE DAYS, SAUL CAN'T SEE ANYTHING. HE EATS NOTHING AND DRINKS NOTHING THE WHOLE TIME. INSTEAD, HE SPENDS HIS HOURS SIMPLY PRAYING.
HAS A MAN NAMED ANANIAS ASKED TO SEE ME?
NO. WHAT MAKES YOU THINK HE WILL?
I'VE BEEN PRAYING, AND I HAD A VISION OF A MAN NAMED ANANIAS COMING TO GIVE ME BACK MY SIGHT.

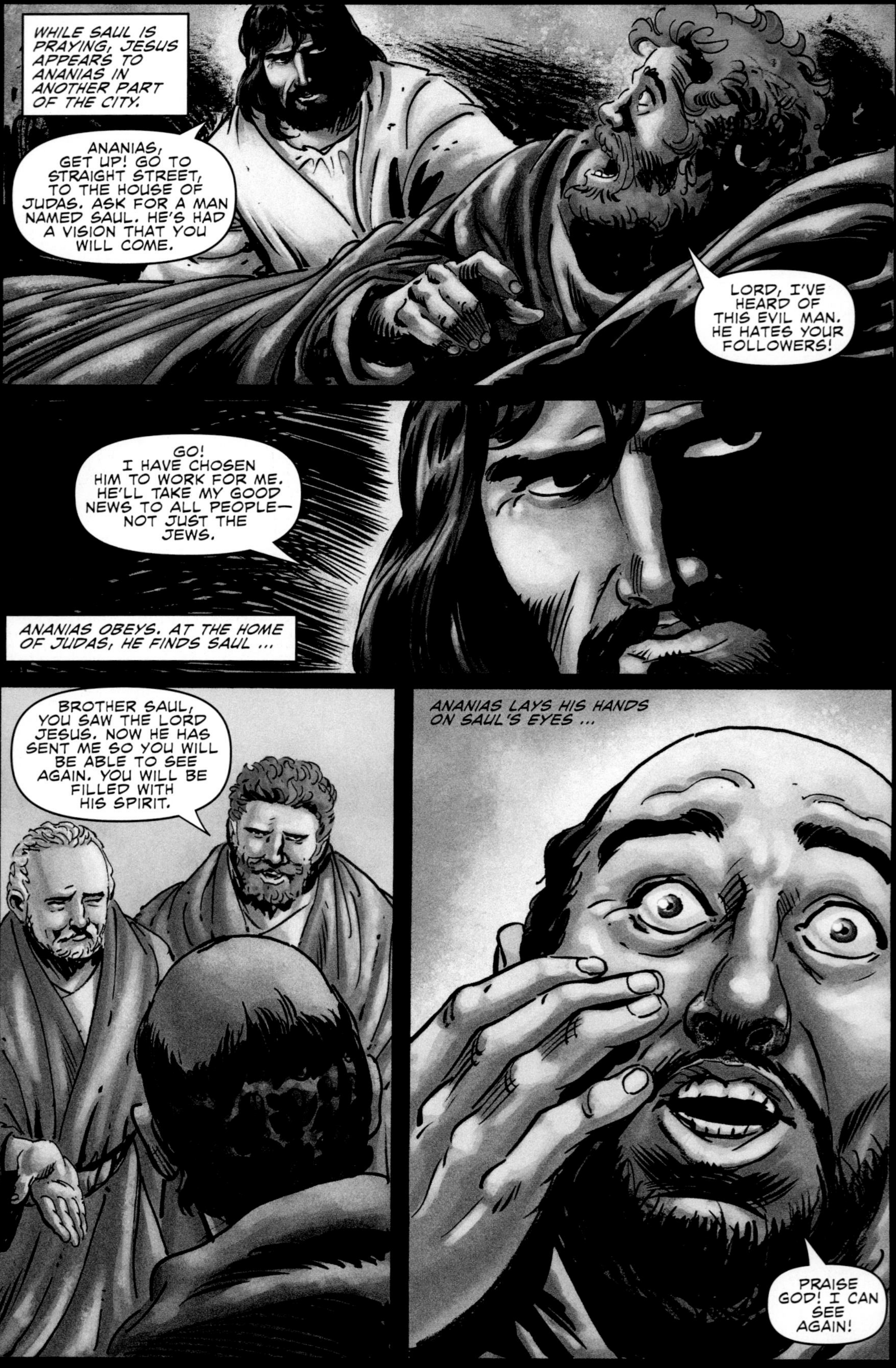
WHILE SAUL IS PRAYING, JESUS APPEARS TO ANANIAS IN ANOTHER PART OF THE CITY.
ANANIAS, GET UP! GO TO STRAIGHT STREET, TO THE HOUSE OF JUDAS. ASK FOR A MAN NAMED SAUL. HE'S HAD A VISION THAT YOU WILL COME.
LORD, I'VE HEARD OF THIS EVIL MAN. HE HATES YOUR FOLLOWERS!
GO! I HAVE CHOSEN HIM TO WORK FOR ME. HE'LL TAKE MY GOOD NEWS TO ALL PEOPLE— NOT JUST THE JEWS.
ANANIAS OBEYS. AT THE HOME OF JUDAS, HE FINDS SAUL ...
BROTHER SAUL, YOU SAW THE LORD JESUS. NOW HE HAS SENT ME SO YOU WILL BE ABLE TO SEE AGAIN. YOU WILL BE FILLED WITH HIS SPIRIT.
ANANIAS LAYS HIS HANDS ON SAUL'S EYES ...
PRAISE GOD! I CAN SEE AGAIN!

The New Paul

BASED ON ACTS 9:26-31

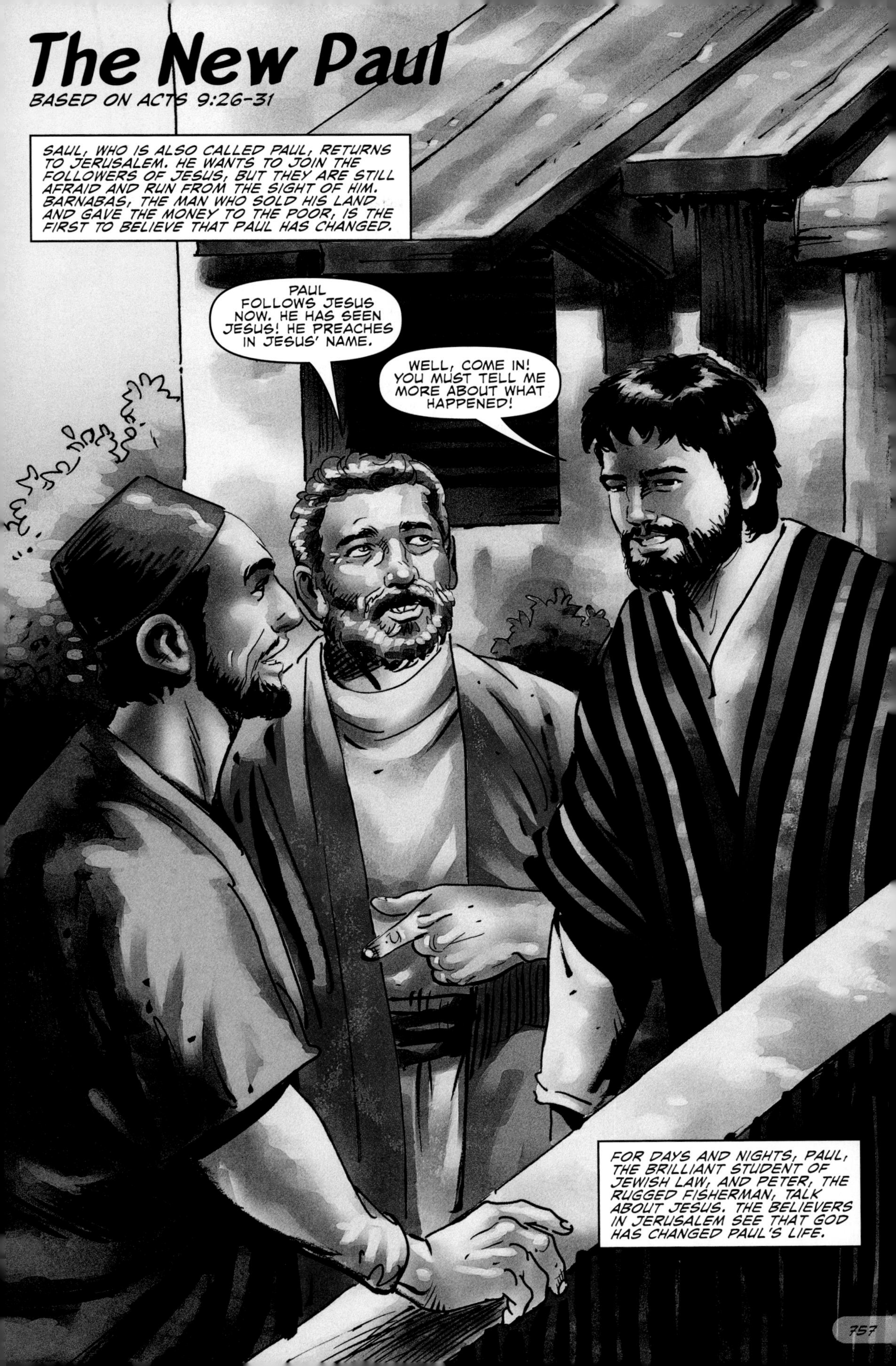
SAUL, WHO IS ALSO CALLED PAUL, RETURNS TO JERUSALEM. HE WANTS TO JOIN THE FOLLOWERS OF JESUS, BUT THEY ARE STILL AFRAID AND RUN FROM THE SIGHT OF HIM. BARNABAS, THE MAN WHO SOLD HIS LAND AND GAVE THE MONEY TO THE POOR, IS THE FIRST TO BELIEVE THAT PAUL HAS CHANGED.
PAUL FOLLOWS JESUS NOW. HE HAS SEEN JESUS! HE PREACHES IN JESUS' NAME.
WELL, COME IN! YOU MUST TELL ME MORE ABOUT WHAT HAPPENED!
FOR DAYS AND NIGHTS, PAUL, THE BRILLIANT STUDENT OF JEWISH LAW, AND PETER, THE RUGGED FISHERMAN, TALK ABOUT JESUS. THE BELIEVERS IN JERUSALEM SEE THAT GOD HAS CHANGED PAUL'S LIFE.

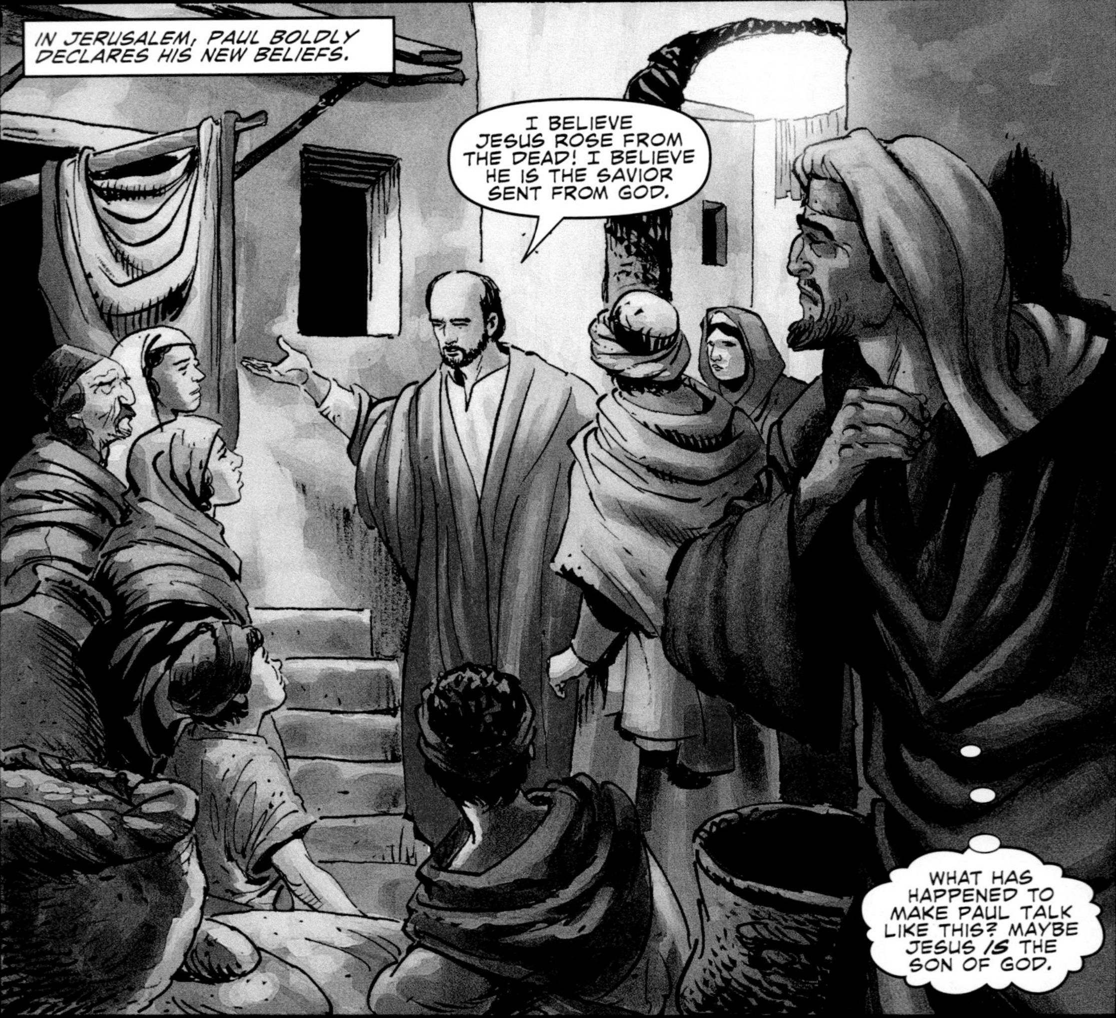
IN JERUSALEM, PAUL BOLDLY DECLARES HIS NEW BELIEFS.
I BELIEVE JESUS ROSE FROM THE DEAD! I BELIEVE HE IS THE SAVIOR SENT FROM GOD.
WHAT HAS HAPPENED TO MAKE PAUL TALK LIKE THIS? MAYBE JESUS *IS* THE SON OF GOD.

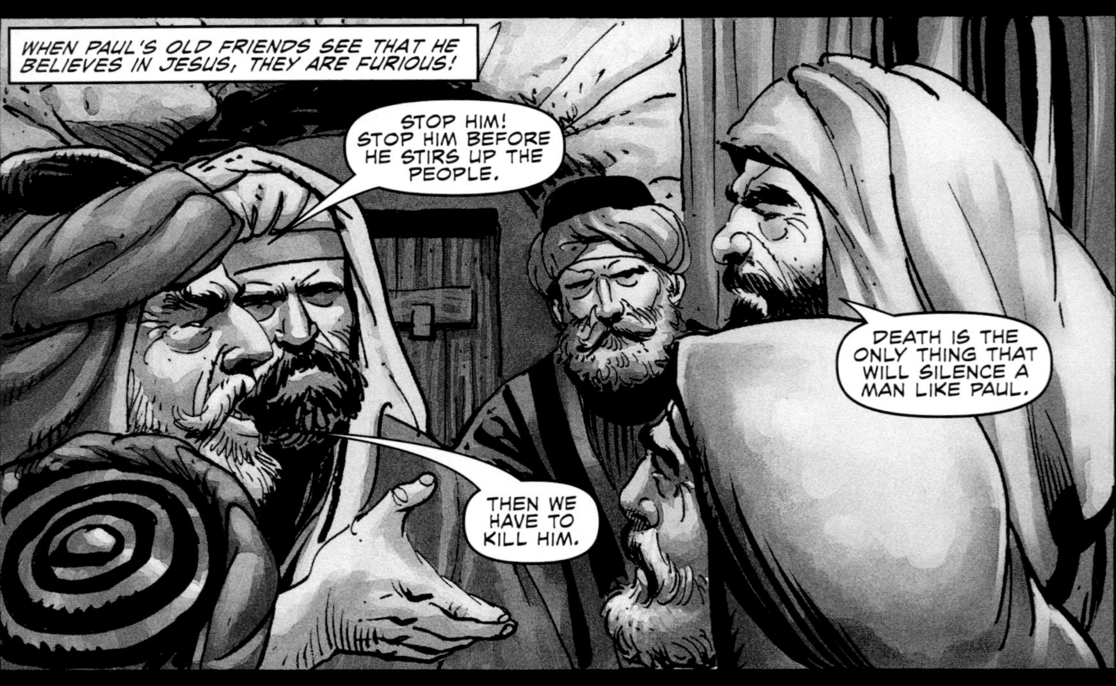
WHEN PAUL'S OLD FRIENDS SEE THAT HE BELIEVES IN JESUS, THEY ARE FURIOUS!
STOP HIM! STOP HIM BEFORE HE STIRS UP THE PEOPLE.
THEN WE HAVE TO KILL HIM.
DEATH IS THE ONLY THING THAT WILL SILENCE A MAN LIKE PAUL.

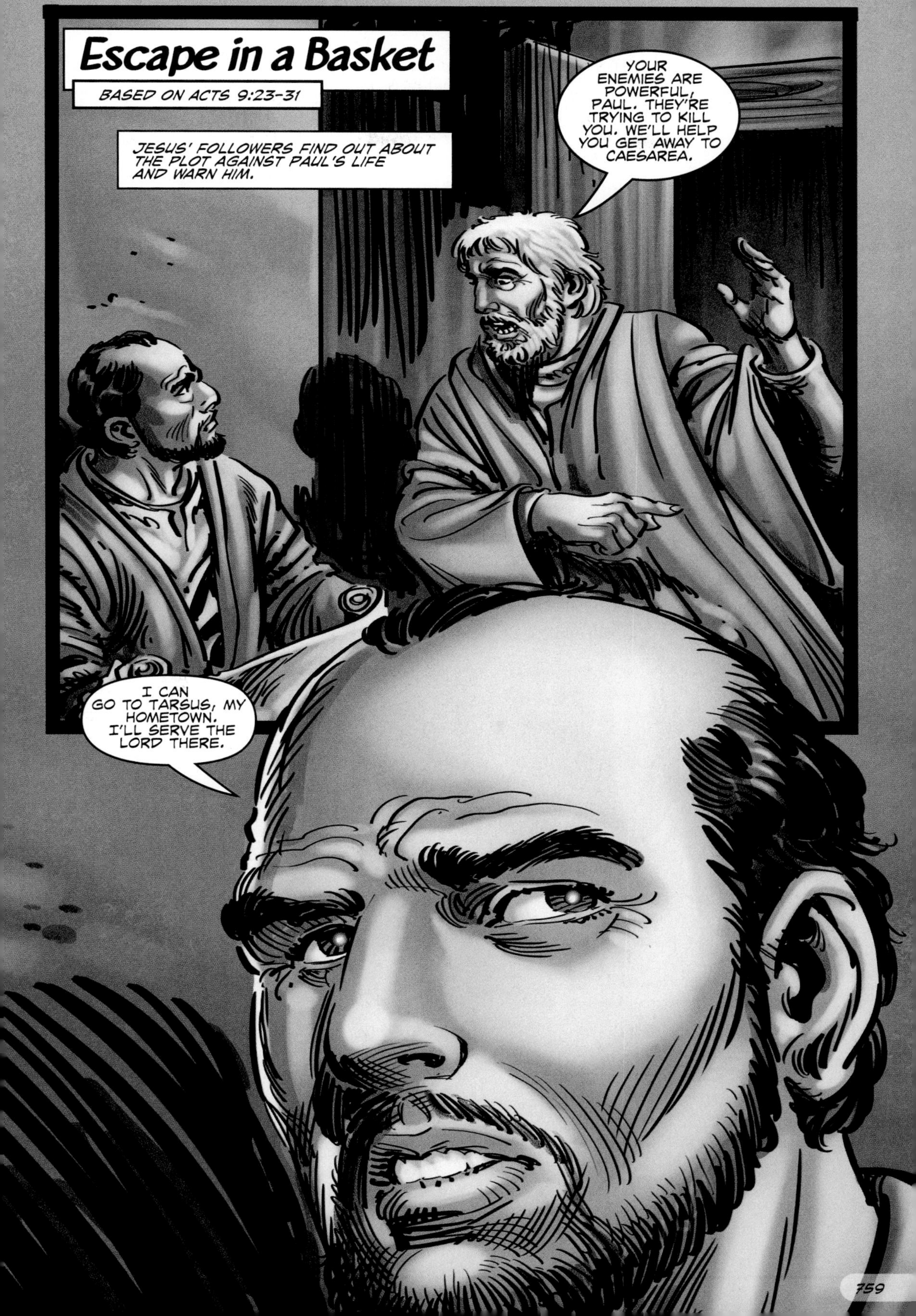
Escape in a Basket
BASED ON ACTS 9:23-31
JESUS' FOLLOWERS FIND OUT ABOUT THE PLOT AGAINST PAUL'S LIFE AND WARN HIM.
YOUR ENEMIES ARE POWERFUL, PAUL. THEY'RE TRYING TO KILL YOU. WE'LL HELP YOU GET AWAY TO CAESAREA.
I CAN GO TO TARSUS, MY HOMETOWN. I'LL SERVE THE LORD THERE.

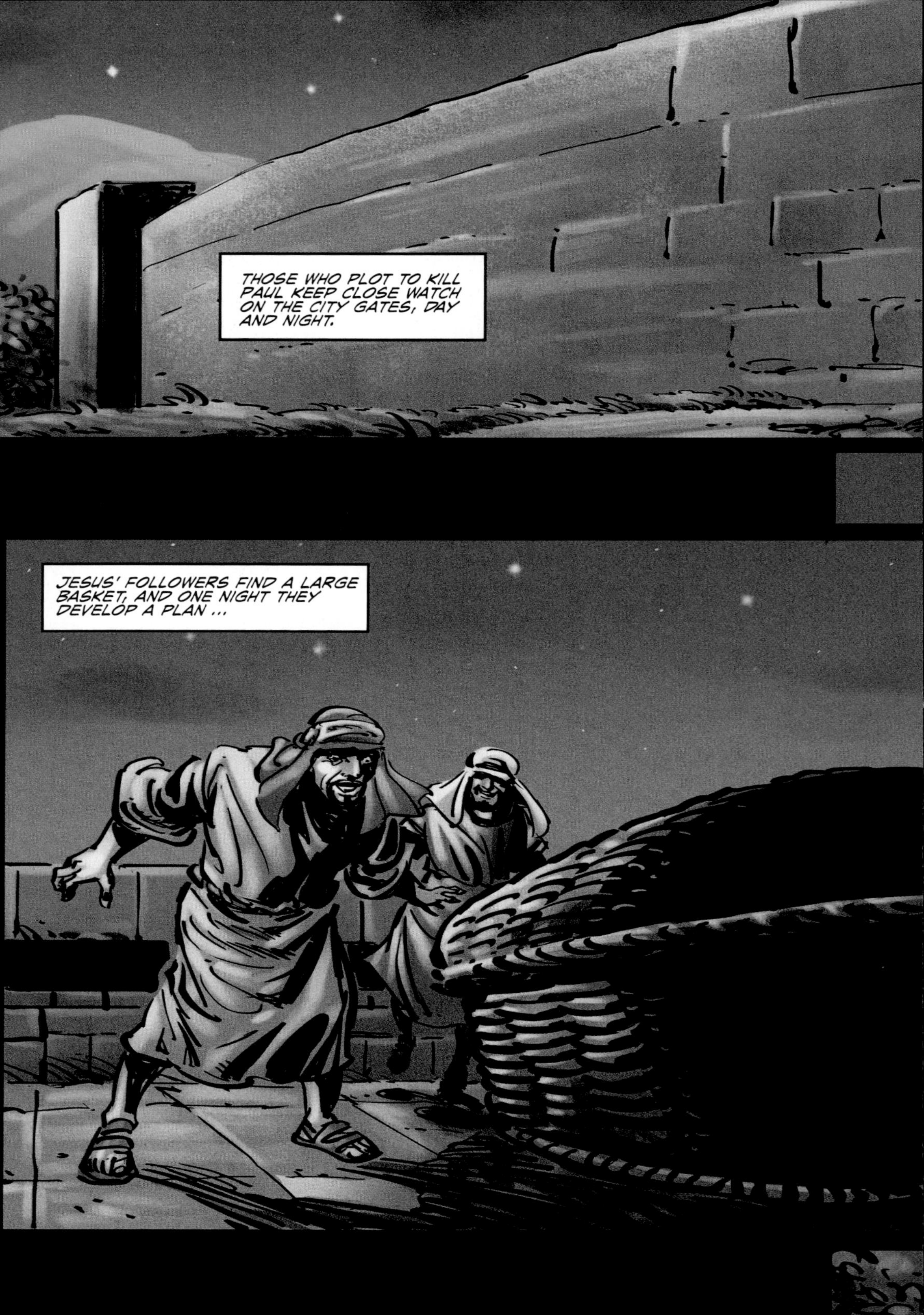

THOSE WHO PLOT TO KILL PAUL KEEP CLOSE WATCH ON THE CITY GATES, DAY AND NIGHT.
JESUS' FOLLOWERS FIND A LARGE BASKET, AND ONE NIGHT THEY DEVELOP A PLAN ...

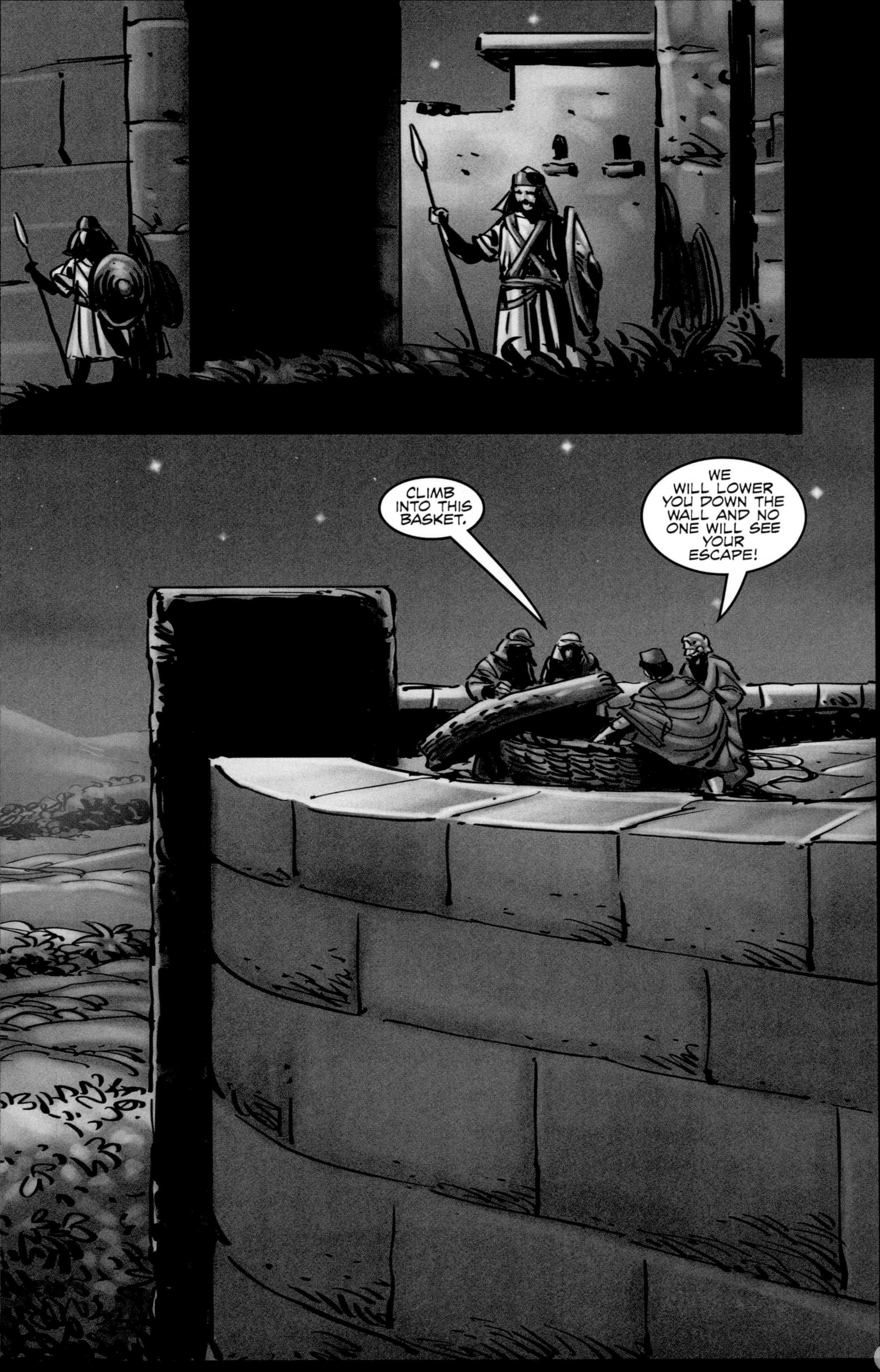
CLIMB INTO THIS BASKET.
WE WILL LOWER YOU DOWN THE WALL AND NO ONE WILL SEE YOUR ESCAPE!

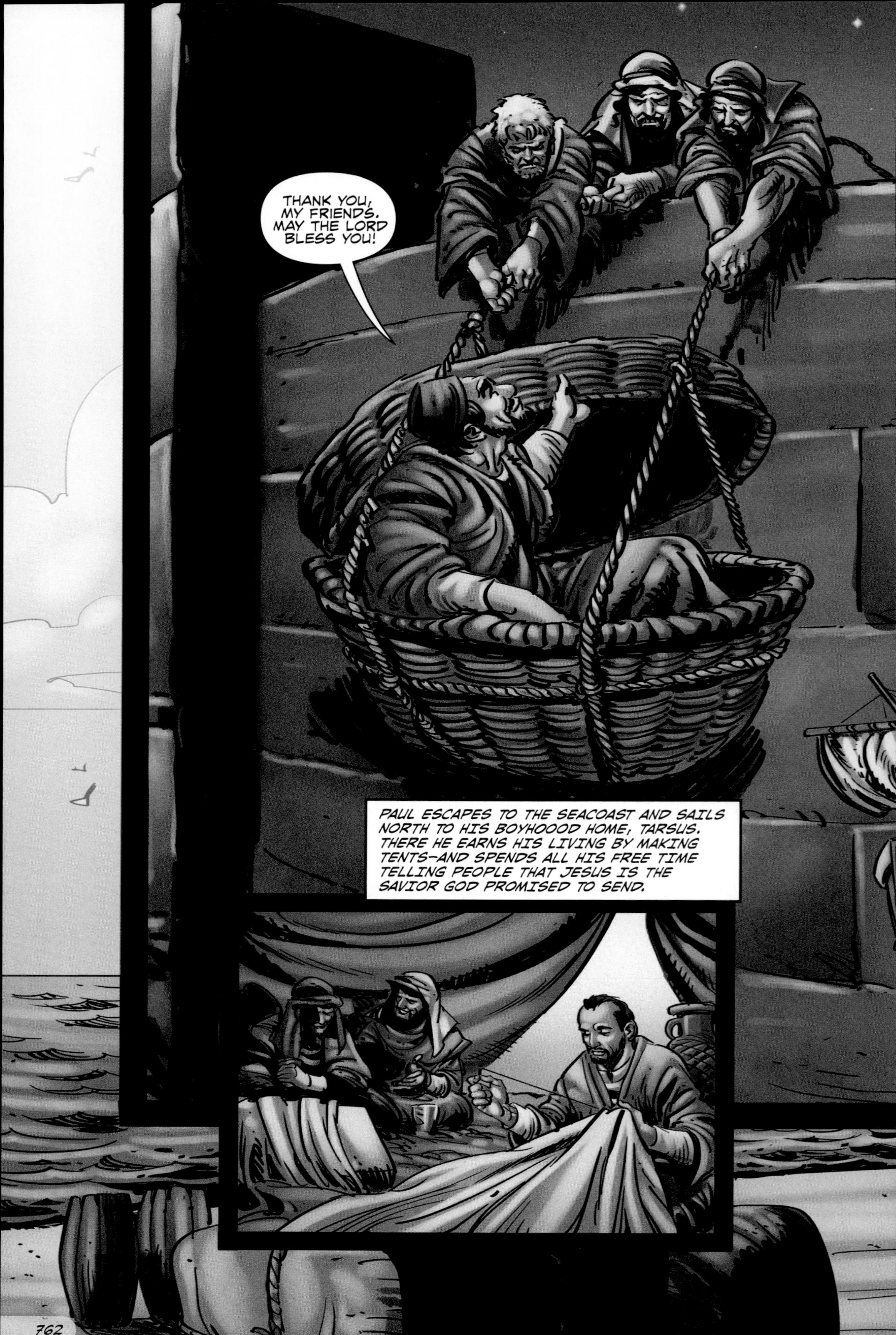
THANK YOU, MY FRIENDS. MAY THE LORD BLESS YOU!
PAUL ESCAPES TO THE SEACOAST AND SAILS NORTH TO HIS BOYHOOOD HOME; TARSUS. THERE HE EARNS HIS LIVING BY MAKING TENTS—AND SPENDS ALL HIS FREE TIME TELLING PEOPLE THAT JESUS IS THE SAVIOR GOD PROMISED TO SEND.

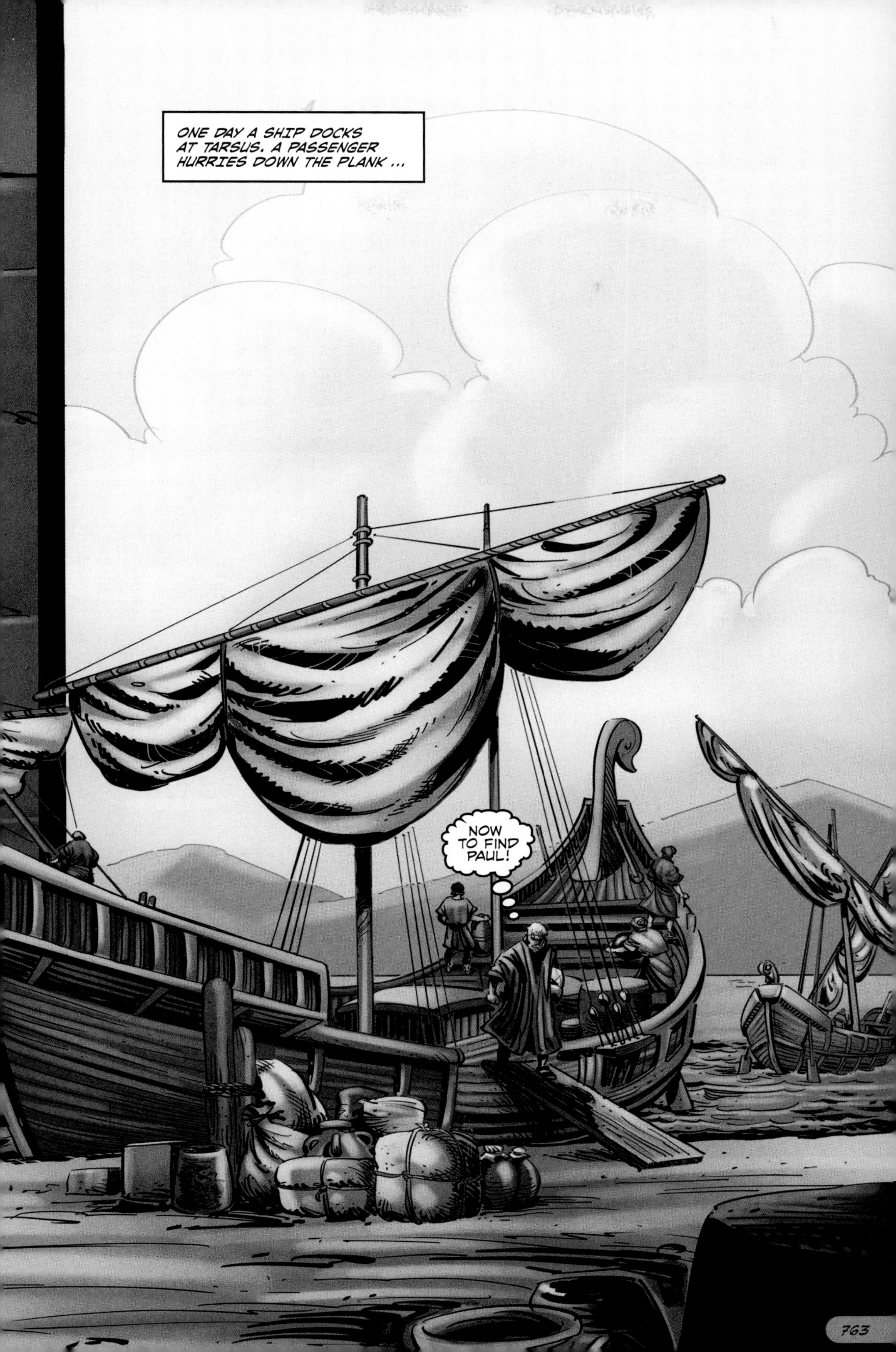
ONE DAY A SHIP DOCKS AT TARSUS. A PASSENGER HURRIES DOWN THE PLANK ...
NOW TO FIND PAUL!

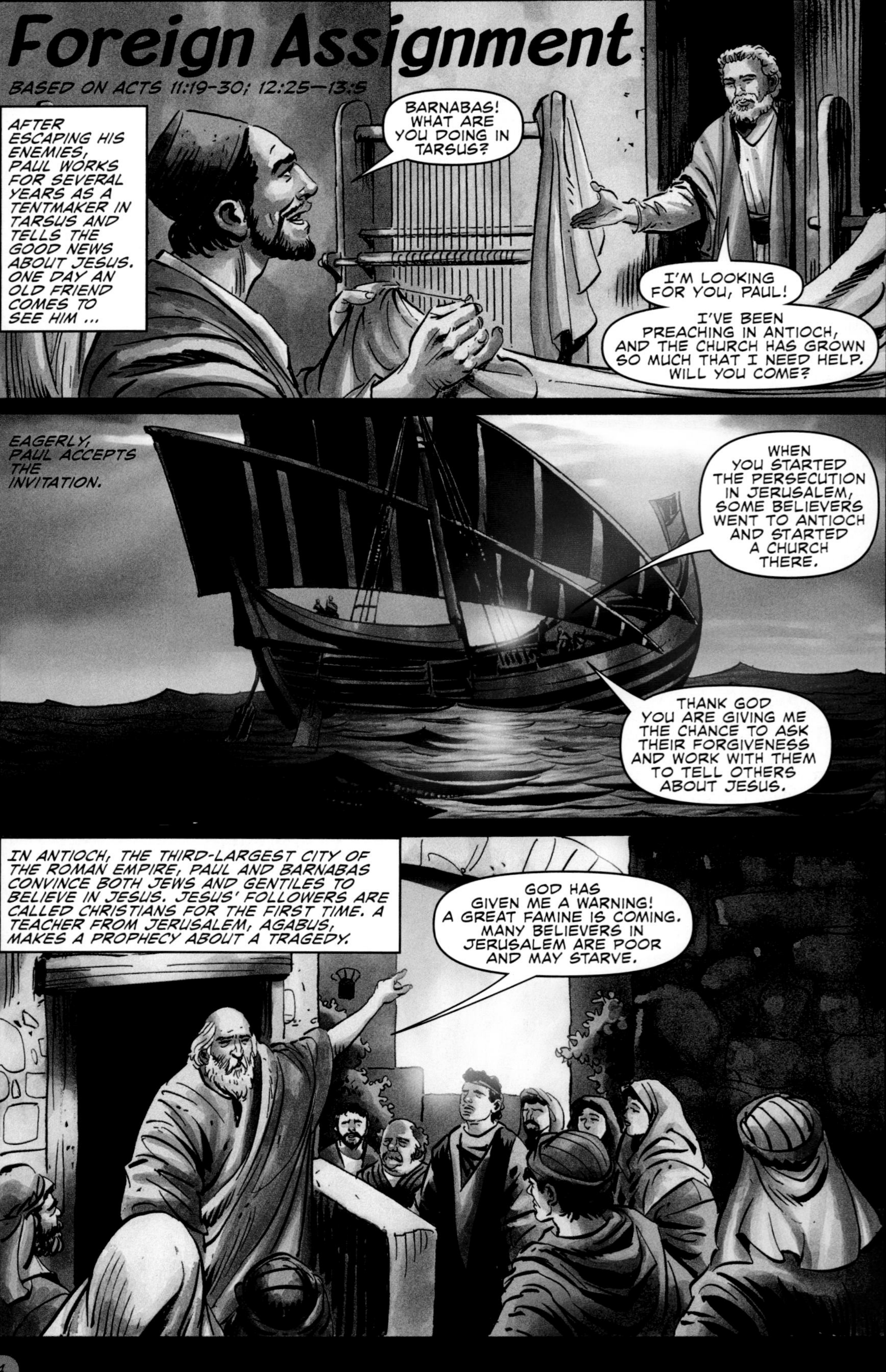
Foreign Assignment
BASED ON ACTS 11:19-30; 12:25—13:5
AFTER ESCAPING HIS ENEMIES, PAUL WORKS FOR SEVERAL YEARS AS A TENTMAKER IN TARSUS AND TELLS THE GOOD NEWS ABOUT JESUS. ONE DAY AN OLD FRIEND COMES TO SEE HIM ...
BARNABAS! WHAT ARE YOU DOING IN TARSUS?
I'M LOOKING FOR YOU, PAUL!
I'VE BEEN PREACHING IN ANTIOCH, AND THE CHURCH HAS GROWN SO MUCH THAT I NEED HELP. WILL YOU COME?
EAGERLY, PAUL ACCEPTS THE INVITATION.
WHEN YOU STARTED THE PERSECUTION IN JERUSALEM, SOME BELIEVERS WENT TO ANTIOCH AND STARTED A CHURCH THERE.
THANK GOD YOU ARE GIVING ME THE CHANCE TO ASK THEIR FORGIVENESS AND WORK WITH THEM TO TELL OTHERS ABOUT JESUS.
IN ANTIOCH, THE THIRD-LARGEST CITY OF THE ROMAN EMPIRE, PAUL AND BARNABAS CONVINCE BOTH JEWS AND GENTILES TO BELIEVE IN JESUS. JESUS' FOLLOWERS ARE CALLED CHRISTIANS FOR THE FIRST TIME. A TEACHER FROM JERUSALEM, AGABUS, MAKES A PROPHECY ABOUT A TRAGEDY.
GOD HAS GIVEN ME A WARNING! A GREAT FAMINE IS COMING. MANY BELIEVERS IN JERUSALEM ARE POOR AND MAY STARVE.

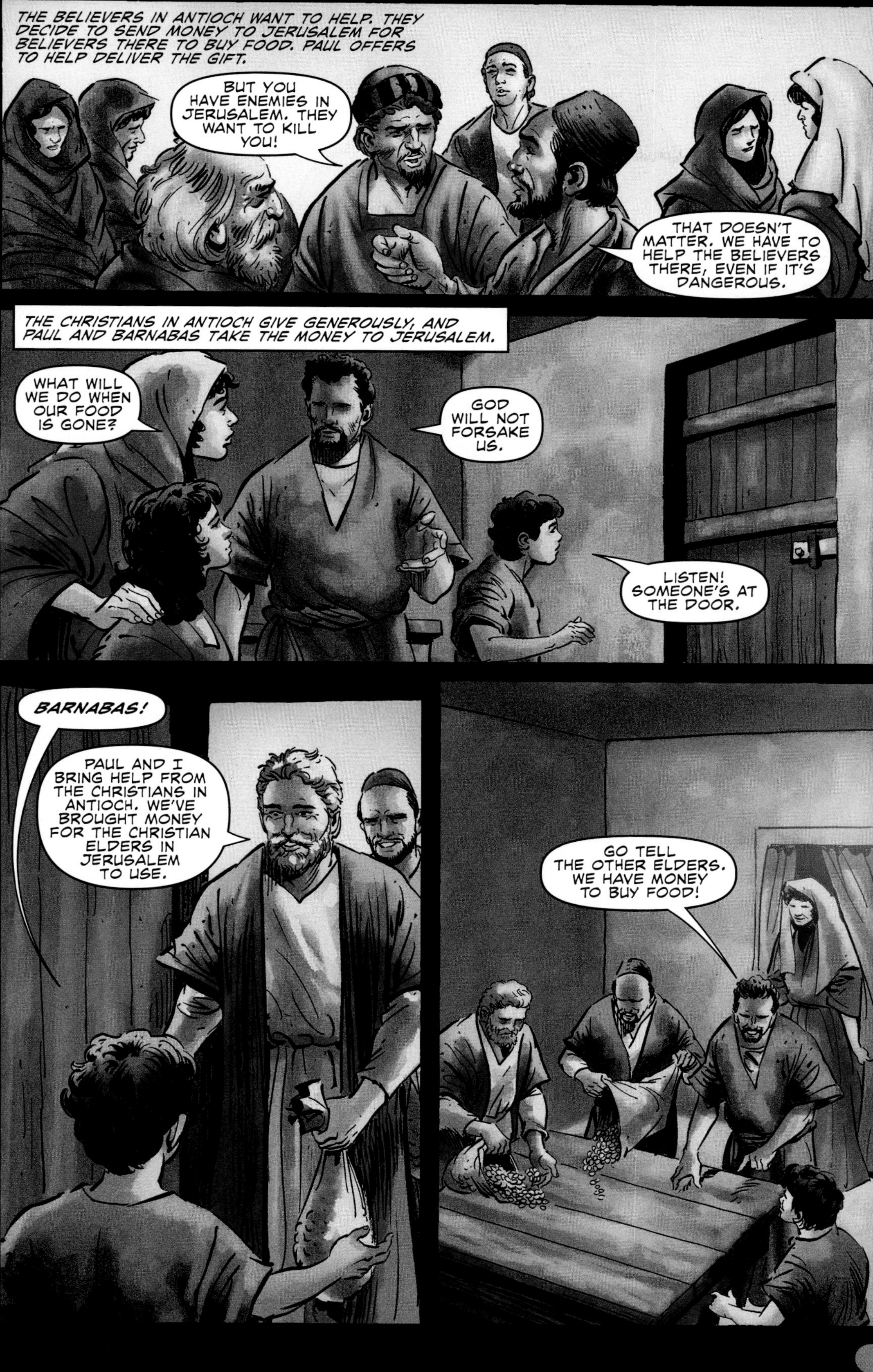
THE BELIEVERS IN ANTIOCH WANT TO HELP. THEY DECIDE TO SEND MONEY TO JERUSALEM FOR BELIEVERS THERE TO BUY FOOD. PAUL OFFERS TO HELP DELIVER THE GIFT.
BUT YOU HAVE ENEMIES IN JERUSALEM. THEY WANT TO KILL YOU!
THAT DOESN'T MATTER. WE HAVE TO HELP THE BELIEVERS THERE, EVEN IF IT'S DANGEROUS.
THE CHRISTIANS IN ANTIOCH GIVE GENEROUSLY, AND PAUL AND BARNABAS TAKE THE MONEY TO JERUSALEM.
WHAT WILL WE DO WHEN OUR FOOD IS GONE?
GOD WILL NOT FORSAKE US.
LISTEN! SOMEONE'S AT THE DOOR.
BARNABAS!
PAUL AND I BRING HELP FROM THE CHRISTIANS IN ANTIOCH. WE'VE BROUGHT MONEY FOR THE CHRISTIAN ELDERS IN JERUSALEM TO USE.
GO TELL THE OTHER ELDERS. WE HAVE MONEY TO BUY FOOD!

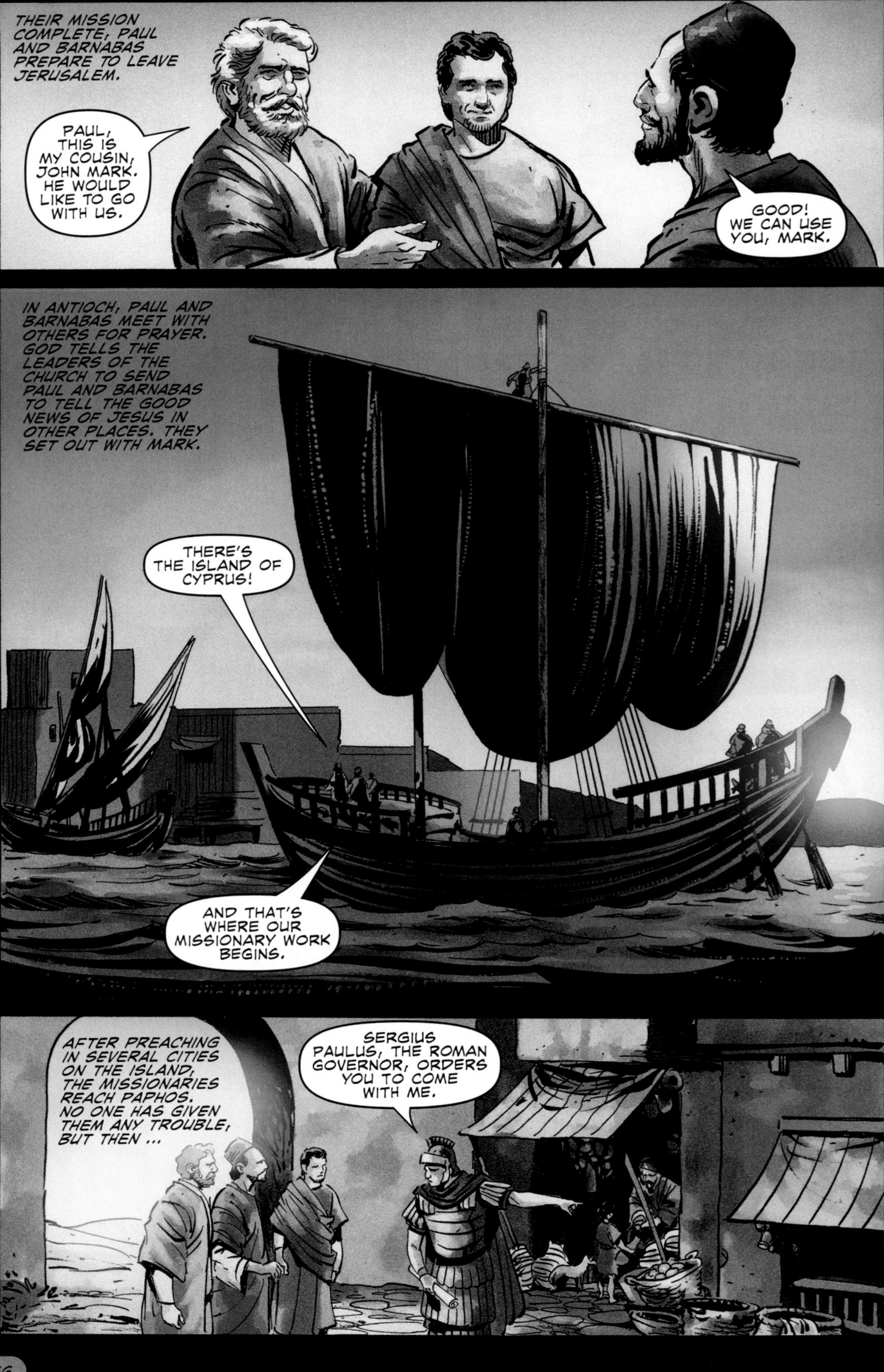
THEIR MISSION COMPLETE, PAUL AND BARNABAS PREPARE TO LEAVE JERUSALEM.
PAUL, THIS IS MY COUSIN, JOHN MARK. HE WOULD LIKE TO GO WITH US.
GOOD! WE CAN USE YOU, MARK.
IN ANTIOCH, PAUL AND BARNABAS MEET WITH OTHERS FOR PRAYER. GOD TELLS THE LEADERS OF THE CHURCH TO SEND PAUL AND BARNABAS TO TELL THE GOOD NEWS OF JESUS IN OTHER PLACES. THEY SET OUT WITH MARK.
THERE'S THE ISLAND OF CYPRUS!
AND THAT'S WHERE OUR MISSIONARY WORK BEGINS.
AFTER PREACHING IN SEVERAL CITIES ON THE ISLAND, THE MISSIONARIES REACH PAPHOS. NO ONE HAS GIVEN THEM ANY TROUBLE, BUT THEN ...
SERGIUS PAULUS, THE ROMAN GOVERNOR, ORDERS YOU TO COME WITH ME.

Silence, Sorcerer!

BASED ON ACTS 13:6–14:7

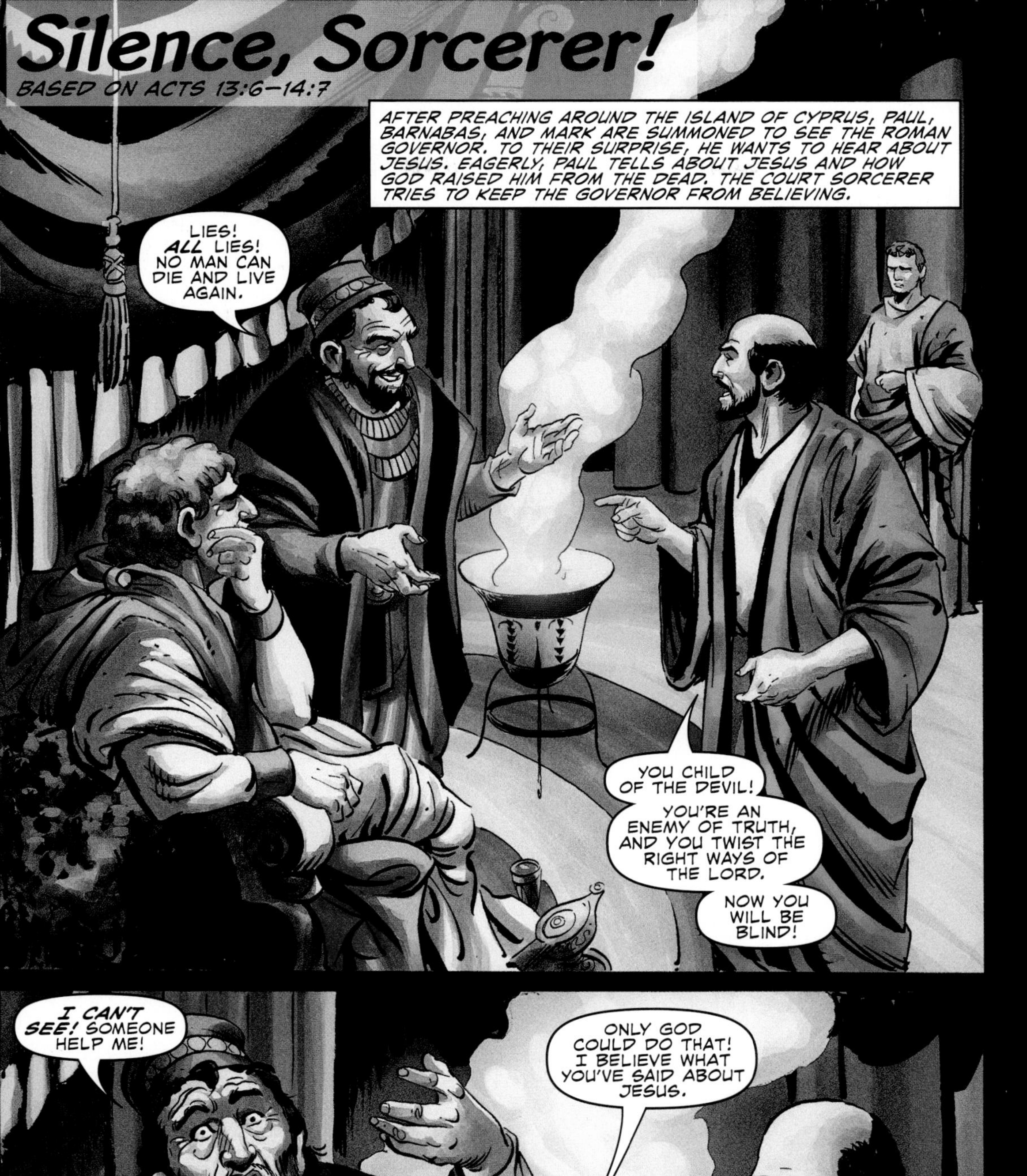
AFTER PREACHING AROUND THE ISLAND OF CYPRUS, PAUL, BARNABAS, AND MARK ARE SUMMONED TO SEE THE ROMAN GOVERNOR. TO THEIR SURPRISE, HE WANTS TO HEAR ABOUT JESUS. EAGERLY, PAUL TELLS ABOUT JESUS AND HOW GOD RAISED HIM FROM THE DEAD. THE COURT SORCERER TRIES TO KEEP THE GOVERNOR FROM BELIEVING.
LIES! **ALL** LIES! NO MAN CAN DIE AND LIVE AGAIN.
YOU CHILD OF THE DEVIL!
YOU'RE AN ENEMY OF TRUTH, AND YOU TWIST THE RIGHT WAYS OF THE LORD.
NOW YOU WILL BE BLIND!

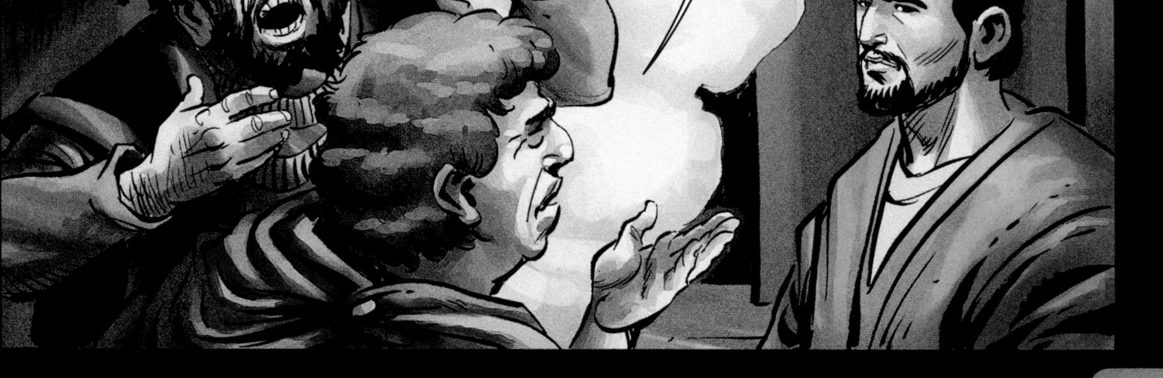
I CAN'T SEE! SOMEONE HELP ME!
ONLY GOD COULD DO THAT! I BELIEVE WHAT YOU'VE SAID ABOUT JESUS.

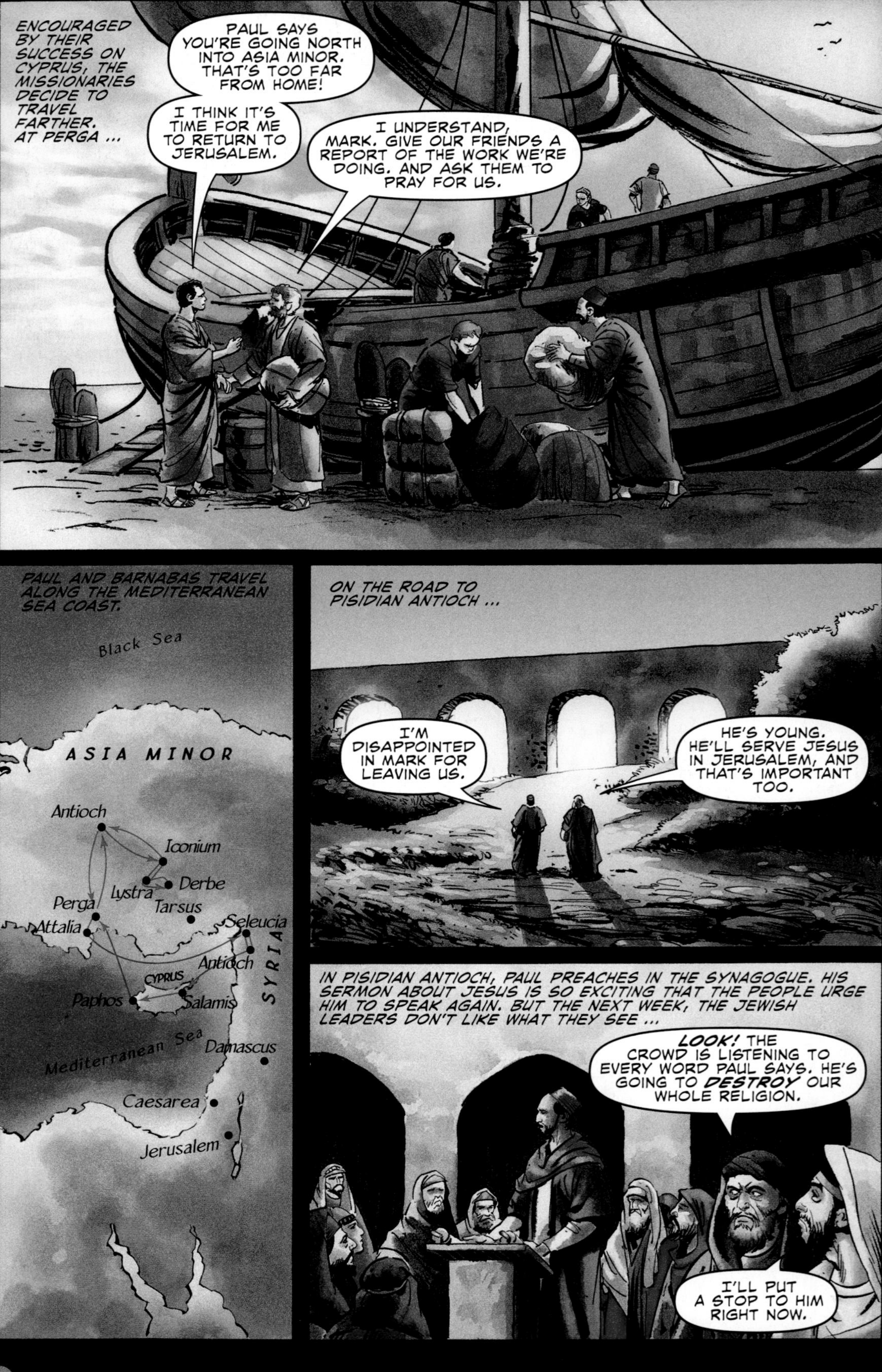
ENCOURAGED BY THEIR SUCCESS ON CYPRUS, THE MISSIONARIES DECIDE TO TRAVEL FARTHER. AT PERGA ...
PAUL SAYS YOU'RE GOING NORTH INTO ASIA MINOR. THAT'S TOO FAR FROM HOME!
I THINK IT'S TIME FOR ME TO RETURN TO JERUSALEM.
I UNDERSTAND, MARK. GIVE OUR FRIENDS A REPORT OF THE WORK WE'RE DOING. AND ASK THEM TO PRAY FOR US.
PAUL AND BARNABAS TRAVEL ALONG THE MEDITERRANEAN SEA COAST.
Black Sea
ASIA MINOR
Antioch
Iconium
Lystra
Derbe
Perga
Tarsus
Attalia
Seleucia
Antioch
SYRIA
CYPRUS
Paphos
Salamis
Mediterranean Sea
Damascus
Caesarea
Jerusalem
ON THE ROAD TO PISIDIAN ANTIOCH ...
I'M DISAPPOINTED IN MARK FOR LEAVING US.
HE'S YOUNG. HE'LL SERVE JESUS IN JERUSALEM, AND THAT'S IMPORTANT TOO.
IN PISIDIAN ANTIOCH, PAUL PREACHES IN THE SYNAGOGUE. HIS SERMON ABOUT JESUS IS SO EXCITING THAT THE PEOPLE URGE HIM TO SPEAK AGAIN. BUT THE NEXT WEEK, THE JEWISH LEADERS DON'T LIKE WHAT THEY SEE ...
LOOK! THE CROWD IS LISTENING TO EVERY WORD PAUL SAYS. HE'S GOING TO DESTROY OUR WHOLE RELIGION.
I'LL PUT A STOP TO HIM RIGHT NOW.

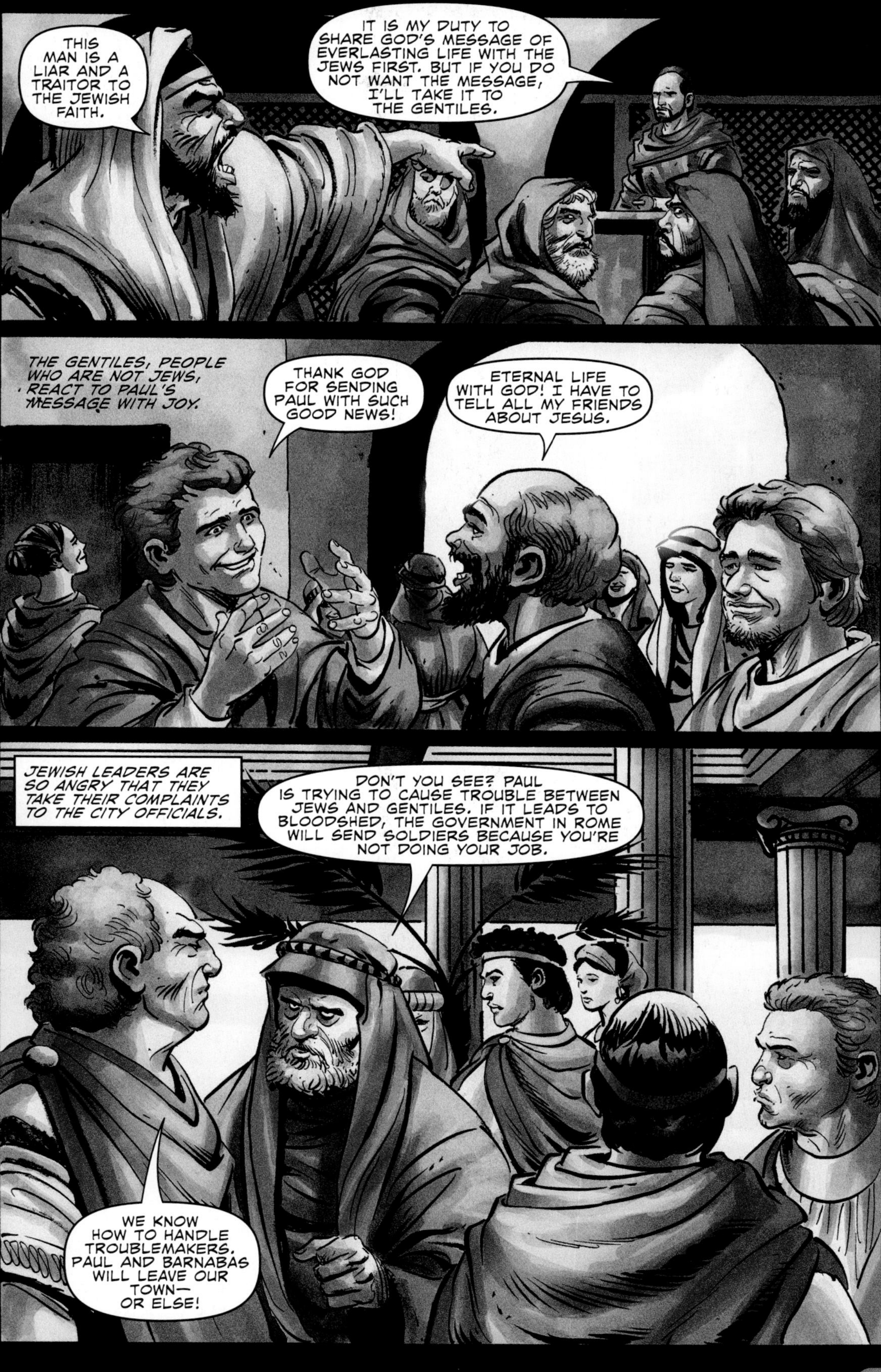
THIS MAN IS A LIAR AND A TRAITOR TO THE JEWISH FAITH.
IT IS MY DUTY TO SHARE GOD'S MESSAGE OF EVERLASTING LIFE WITH THE JEWS FIRST. BUT IF YOU DO NOT WANT THE MESSAGE, I'LL TAKE IT TO THE GENTILES.
THE GENTILES, PEOPLE WHO ARE NOT JEWS, REACT TO PAUL'S MESSAGE WITH JOY.
THANK GOD FOR SENDING PAUL WITH SUCH GOOD NEWS!
ETERNAL LIFE WITH GOD! I HAVE TO TELL ALL MY FRIENDS ABOUT JESUS.
JEWISH LEADERS ARE SO ANGRY THAT THEY TAKE THEIR COMPLAINTS TO THE CITY OFFICIALS.
DON'T YOU SEE? PAUL IS TRYING TO CAUSE TROUBLE BETWEEN JEWS AND GENTILES. IF IT LEADS TO BLOODSHED, THE GOVERNMENT IN ROME WILL SEND SOLDIERS BECAUSE YOU'RE NOT DOING YOUR JOB.
WE KNOW HOW TO HANDLE TROUBLEMAKERS. PAUL AND BARNABAS WILL LEAVE OUR TOWN— OR ELSE!

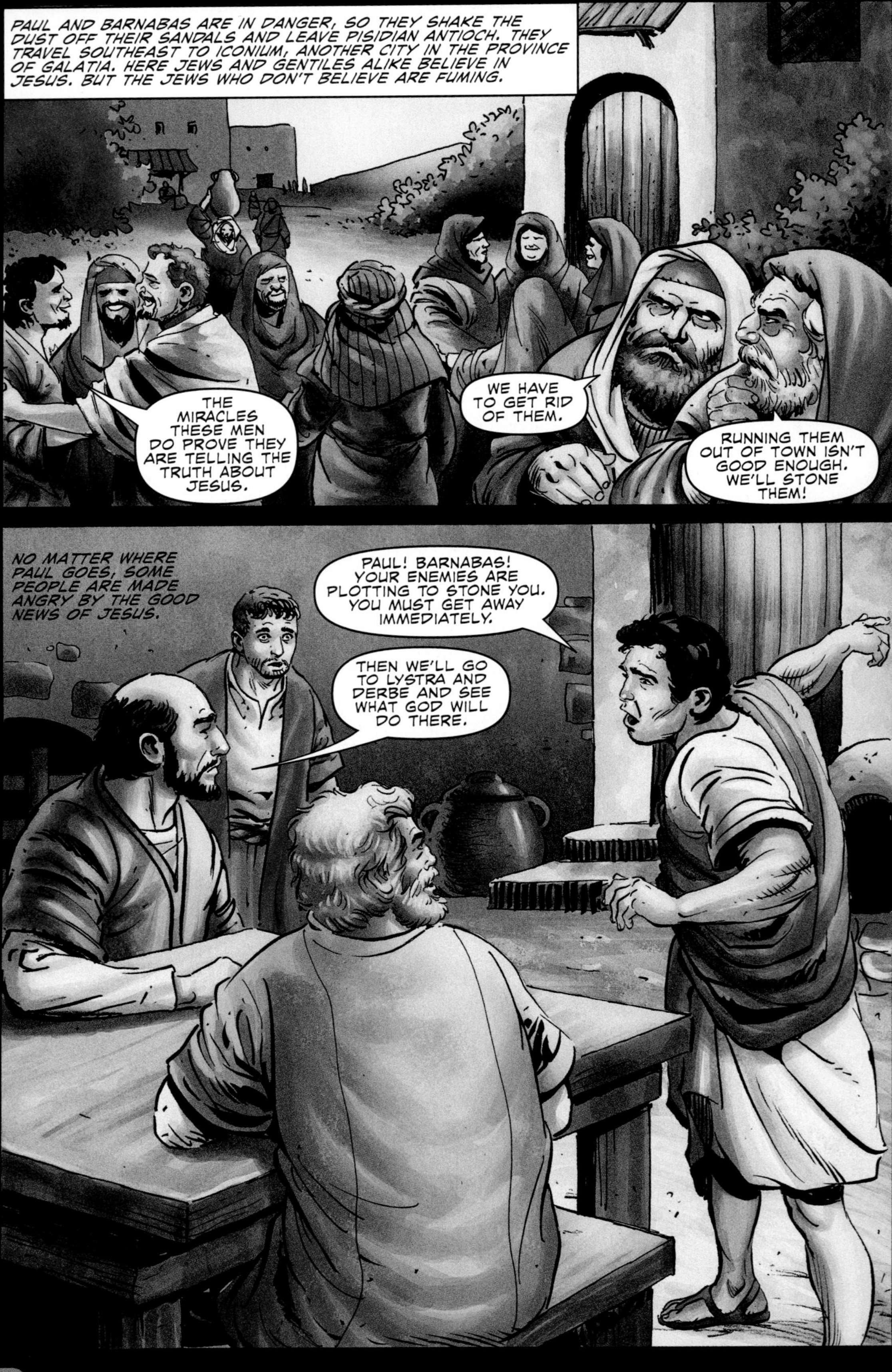
PAUL AND BARNABAS ARE IN DANGER, SO THEY SHAKE THE DUST OFF THEIR SANDALS AND LEAVE PISIDIAN ANTIOCH. THEY TRAVEL SOUTHEAST TO ICONIUM, ANOTHER CITY IN THE PROVINCE OF GALATIA. HERE JEWS AND GENTILES ALIKE BELIEVE IN JESUS. BUT THE JEWS WHO DON'T BELIEVE ARE FUMING.
THE MIRACLES THESE MEN DO PROVE THEY ARE TELLING THE TRUTH ABOUT JESUS.
WE HAVE TO GET RID OF THEM.
RUNNING THEM OUT OF TOWN ISN'T GOOD ENOUGH. WE'LL STONE THEM!
NO MATTER WHERE PAUL GOES, SOME PEOPLE ARE MADE ANGRY BY THE GOOD NEWS OF JESUS.
PAUL! BARNABAS! YOUR ENEMIES ARE PLOTTING TO STONE YOU. YOU MUST GET AWAY IMMEDIATELY.
THEN WE'LL GO TO LYSTRA AND DERBE AND SEE WHAT GOD WILL DO THERE.

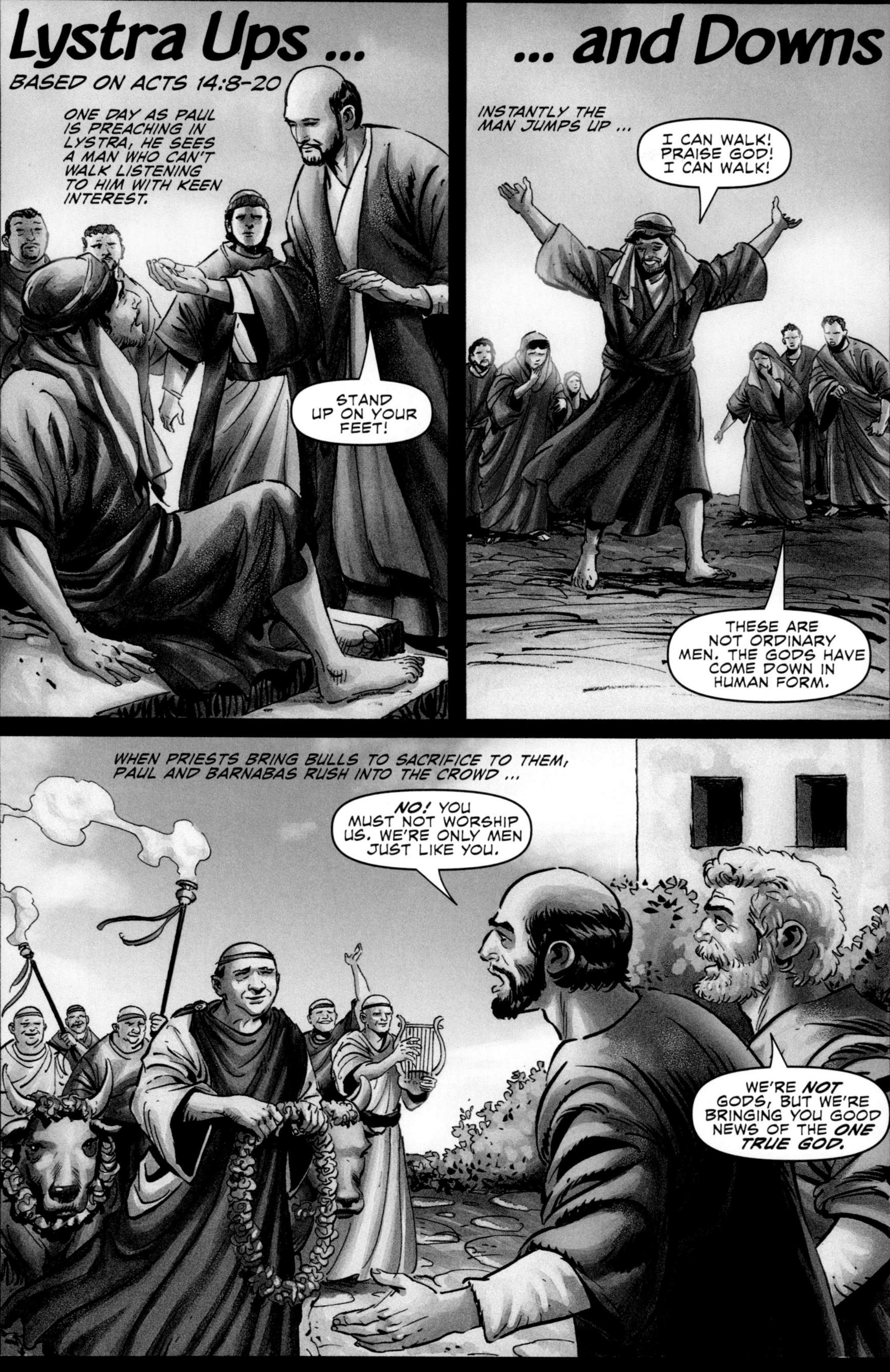
Lystra Ups ...
... and Downs
BASED ON ACTS 14:8-20
ONE DAY AS PAUL IS PREACHING IN LYSTRA, HE SEES A MAN WHO CAN'T WALK LISTENING TO HIM WITH KEEN INTEREST.
STAND UP ON YOUR FEET!
INSTANTLY THE MAN JUMPS UP ...
I CAN WALK! PRAISE GOD! I CAN WALK!
THESE ARE NOT ORDINARY MEN. THE GODS HAVE COME DOWN IN HUMAN FORM.
WHEN PRIESTS BRING BULLS TO SACRIFICE TO THEM, PAUL AND BARNABAS RUSH INTO THE CROWD ...
NO! YOU MUST NOT WORSHIP US. WE'RE ONLY MEN JUST LIKE YOU.
WE'RE NOT GODS, BUT WE'RE BRINGING YOU GOOD NEWS OF THE ONE TRUE GOD.

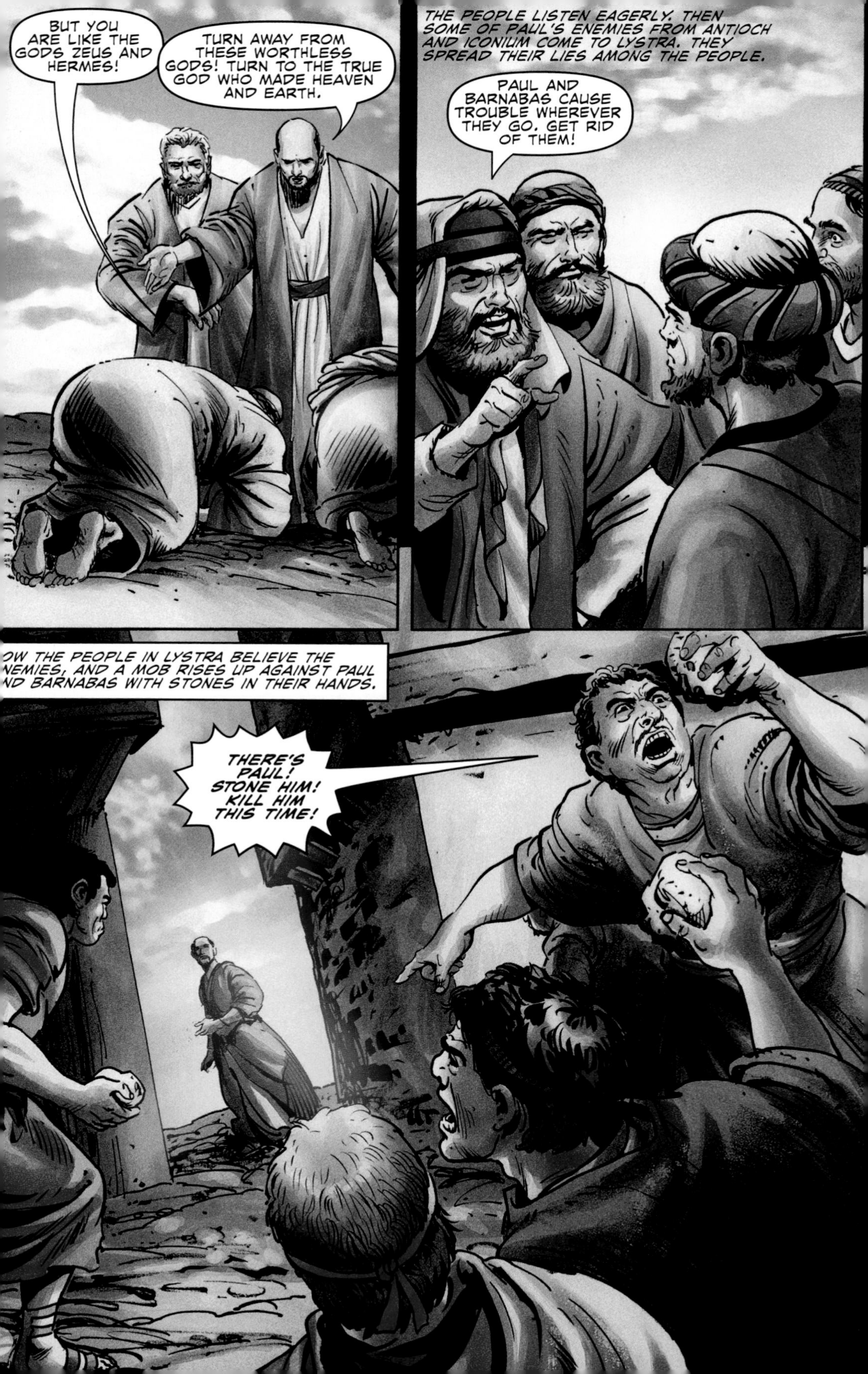
BUT YOU ARE LIKE THE GODS ZEUS AND HERMES!
TURN AWAY FROM THESE WORTHLESS GODS! TURN TO THE TRUE GOD WHO MADE HEAVEN AND EARTH.
THE PEOPLE LISTEN EAGERLY. THEN SOME OF PAUL'S ENEMIES FROM ANTIOCH AND ICONIUM COME TO LYSTRA. THEY SPREAD THEIR LIES AMONG THE PEOPLE.
PAUL AND BARNABAS CAUSE TROUBLE WHEREVER THEY GO. GET RID OF THEM!
OW THE PEOPLE IN LYSTRA BELIEVE THE NEMIES, AND A MOB RISES UP AGAINST PAUL ND BARNABAS WITH STONES IN THEIR HANDS.
THERE'S PAUL! STONE HIM! KILL HIM THIS TIME!

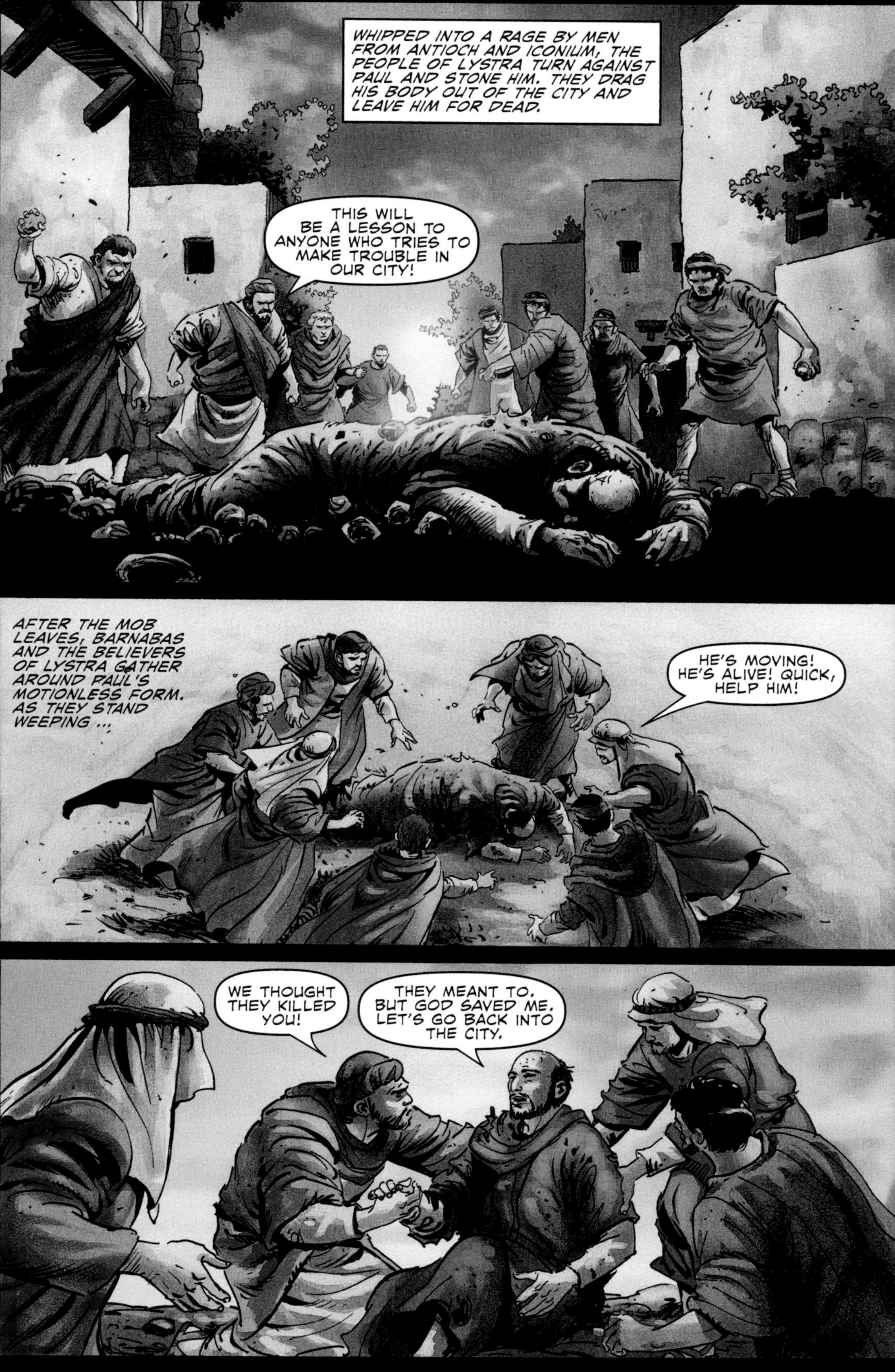

WHIPPED INTO A RAGE BY MEN FROM ANTIOCH AND ICONIUM, THE PEOPLE OF LYSTRA TURN AGAINST PAUL AND STONE HIM. THEY DRAG HIS BODY OUT OF THE CITY AND LEAVE HIM FOR DEAD.
THIS WILL BE A LESSON TO ANYONE WHO TRIES TO MAKE TROUBLE IN OUR CITY!
AFTER THE MOB LEAVES, BARNABAS AND THE BELIEVERS OF LYSTRA GATHER AROUND PAUL'S MOTIONLESS FORM. AS THEY STAND WEEPING ...
HE'S MOVING! HE'S ALIVE! QUICK, HELP HIM!
WE THOUGHT THEY KILLED YOU!
THEY MEANT TO. BUT GOD SAVED ME. LET'S GO BACK INTO THE CITY.

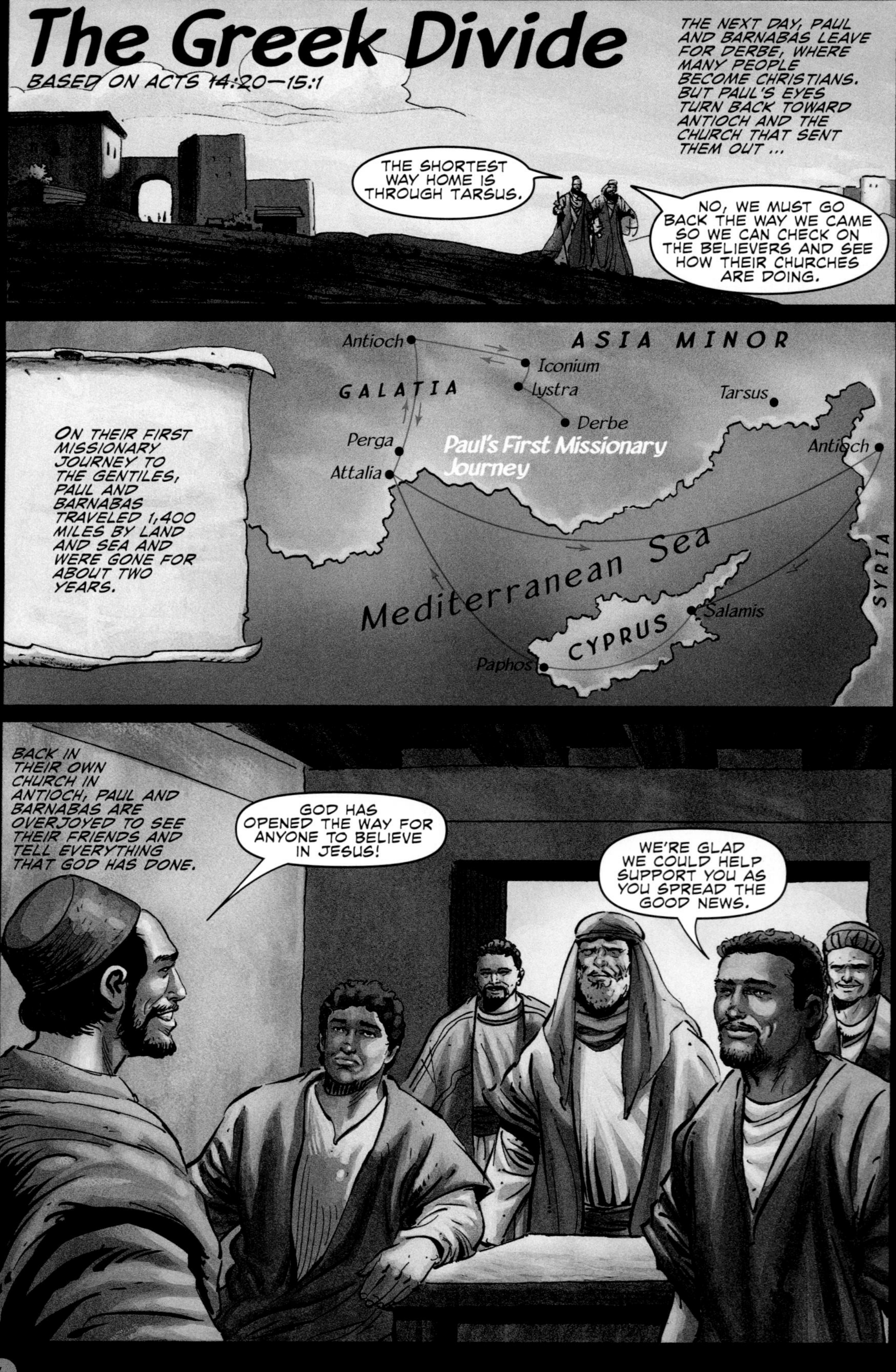
The Greek Divide
BASED ON ACTS 14:20—15:1
THE NEXT DAY, PAUL AND BARNABAS LEAVE FOR DERBE, WHERE MANY PEOPLE BECOME CHRISTIANS. BUT PAUL'S EYES TURN BACK TOWARD ANTIOCH AND THE CHURCH THAT SENT THEM OUT ...
THE SHORTEST WAY HOME IS THROUGH TARSUS.
NO, WE MUST GO BACK THE WAY WE CAME SO WE CAN CHECK ON THE BELIEVERS AND SEE HOW THEIR CHURCHES ARE DOING.
ON THEIR FIRST MISSIONARY JOURNEY TO THE GENTILES, PAUL AND BARNABAS TRAVELED 1,400 MILES BY LAND AND SEA AND WERE GONE FOR ABOUT TWO YEARS.
ASIA MINOR
Antioch
Iconium
Lystra
GALATIA
Tarsus
Derbe
Perga
Attalia
Paul's First Missionary Journey
Antioch
Mediterranean Sea
SYRIA
Salamis
CYPRUS
Paphos
BACK IN THEIR OWN CHURCH IN ANTIOCH, PAUL AND BARNABAS ARE OVERJOYED TO SEE THEIR FRIENDS AND TELL EVERYTHING THAT GOD HAS DONE.
GOD HAS OPENED THE WAY FOR ANYONE TO BELIEVE IN JESUS!
WE'RE GLAD WE COULD HELP SUPPORT YOU AS YOU SPREAD THE GOOD NEWS.

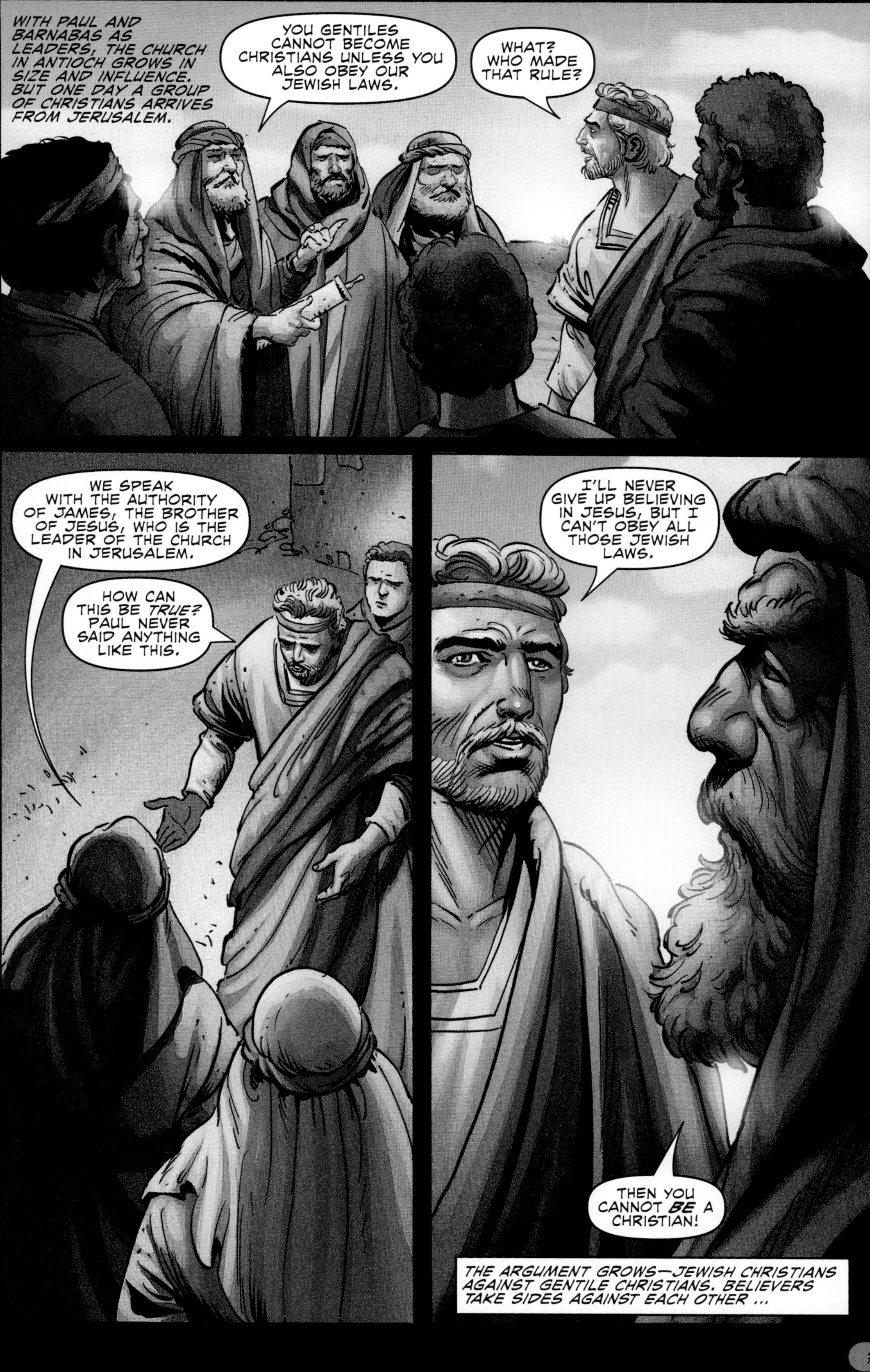
WITH PAUL AND BARNABAS AS LEADERS, THE CHURCH IN ANTIOCH GROWS IN SIZE AND INFLUENCE. BUT ONE DAY A GROUP OF CHRISTIANS ARRIVES FROM JERUSALEM.
YOU GENTILES CANNOT BECOME CHRISTIANS UNLESS YOU ALSO OBEY OUR JEWISH LAWS.
WHAT? WHO MADE THAT RULE?
WE SPEAK WITH THE AUTHORITY OF JAMES, THE BROTHER OF JESUS, WHO IS THE LEADER OF THE CHURCH IN JERUSALEM.
HOW CAN THIS BE TRUE? PAUL NEVER SAID ANYTHING LIKE THIS.
I'LL NEVER GIVE UP BELIEVING IN JESUS, BUT I CAN'T OBEY ALL THOSE JEWISH LAWS.
THEN YOU CANNOT BE A CHRISTIAN!
THE ARGUMENT GROWS—JEWISH CHRISTIANS AGAINST GENTILE CHRISTIANS. BELIEVERS TAKE SIDES AGAINST EACH OTHER ...

Jerusalem Council

BASED ON ACTS 15:1–35; GALATIANS

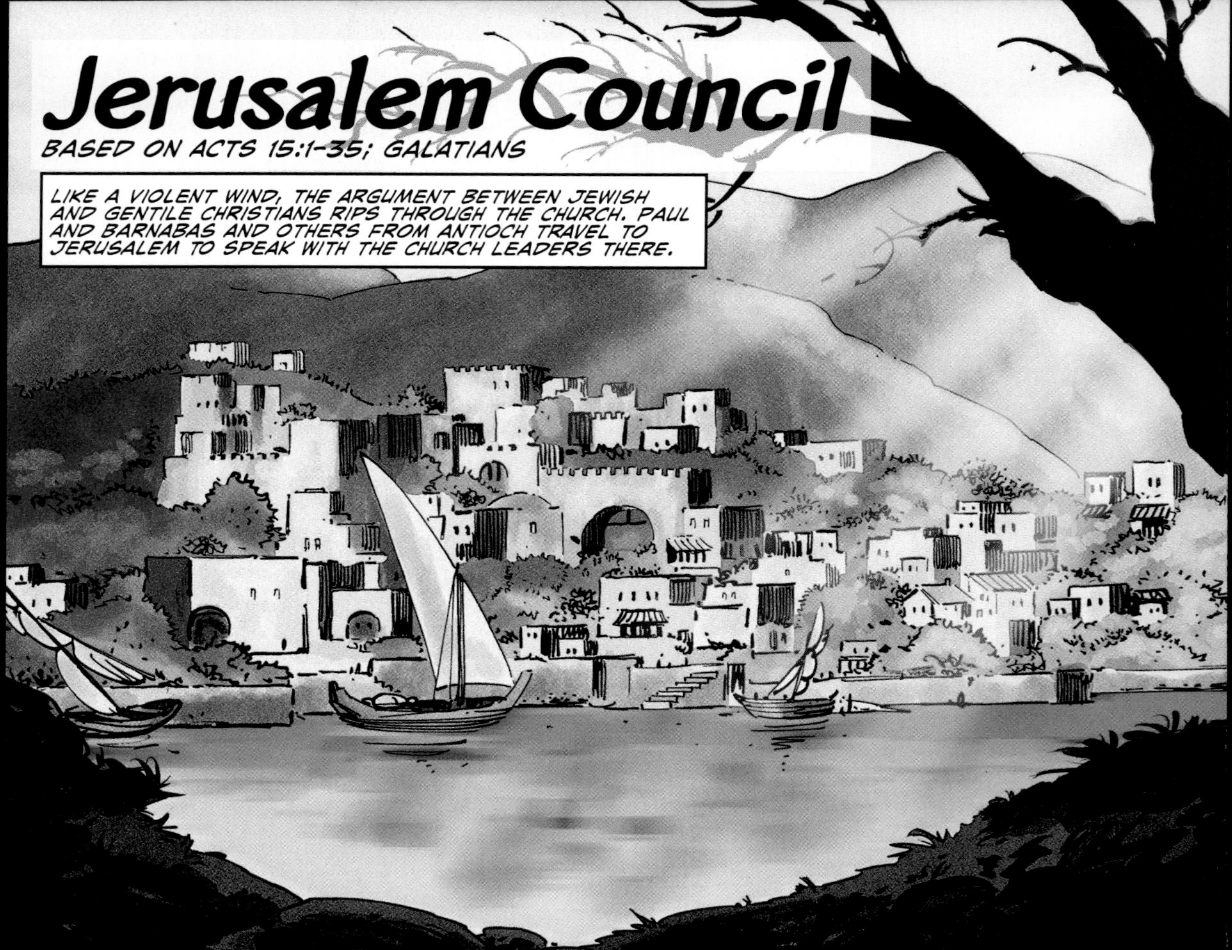
LIKE A VIOLENT WIND, THE ARGUMENT BETWEEN JEWISH AND GENTILE CHRISTIANS RIPS THROUGH THE CHURCH. PAUL AND BARNABAS AND OTHERS FROM ANTIOCH TRAVEL TO JERUSALEM TO SPEAK WITH THE CHURCH LEADERS THERE.

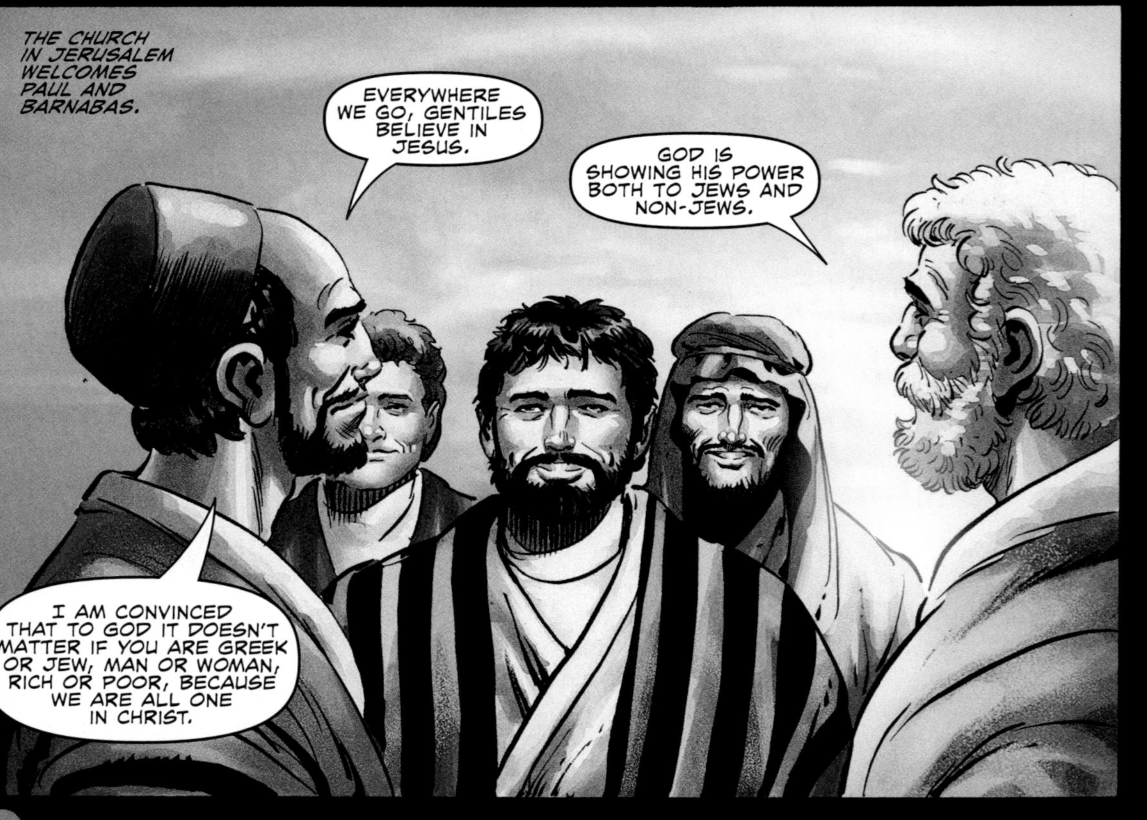
THE CHURCH IN JERUSALEM WELCOMES PAUL AND BARNABAS.
EVERYWHERE WE GO, GENTILES BELIEVE IN JESUS.
GOD IS SHOWING HIS POWER BOTH TO JEWS AND NON-JEWS.
I AM CONVINCED THAT TO GOD IT DOESN'T MATTER IF YOU ARE GREEK OR JEW, MAN OR WOMAN, RICH OR POOR, BECAUSE WE ARE ALL ONE IN CHRIST.

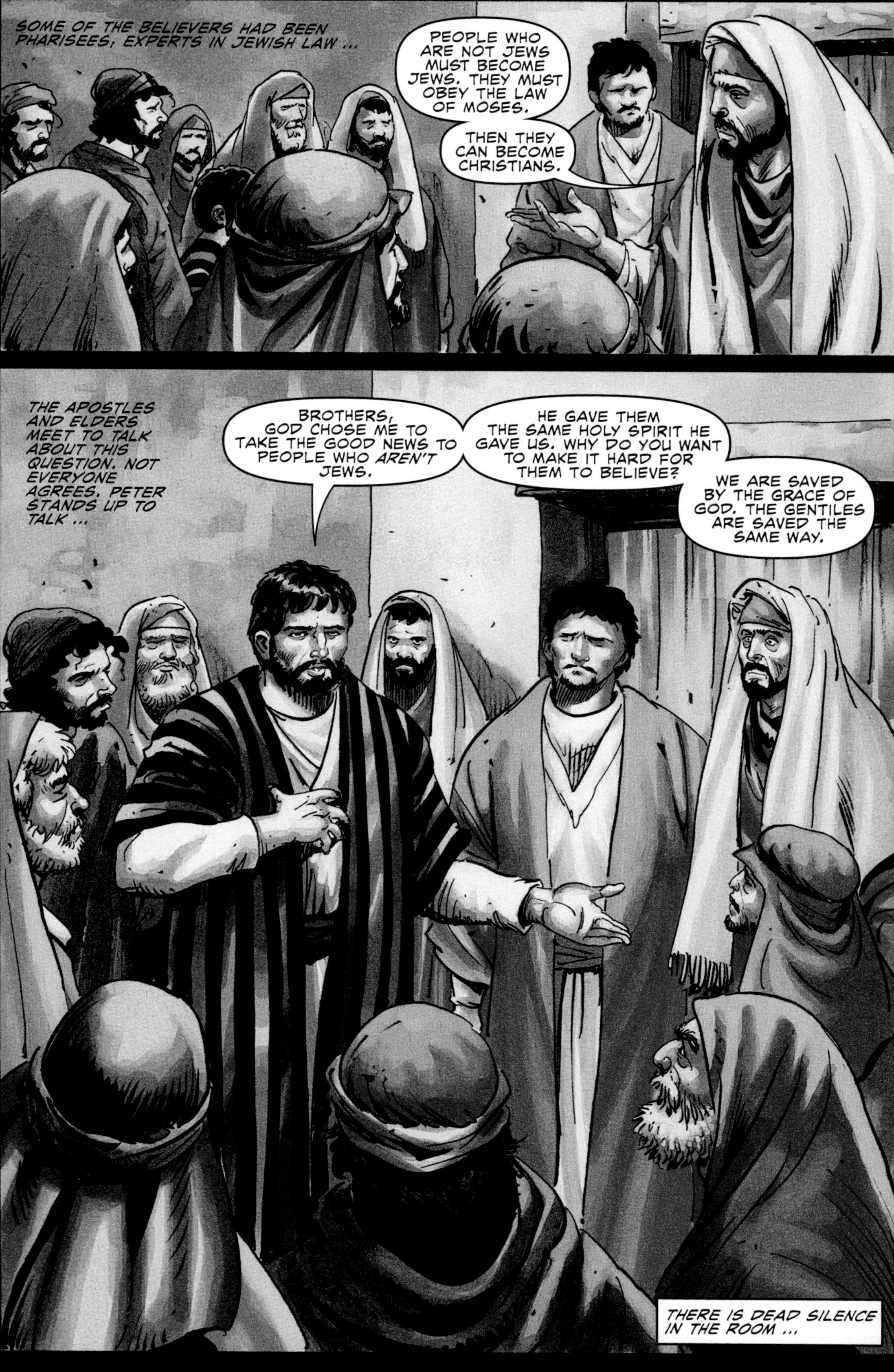
SOME OF THE BELIEVERS HAD BEEN PHARISEES, EXPERTS IN JEWISH LAW ...
PEOPLE WHO ARE NOT JEWS MUST BECOME JEWS. THEY MUST OBEY THE LAW OF MOSES.
THEN THEY CAN BECOME CHRISTIANS.
THE APOSTLES AND ELDERS MEET TO TALK ABOUT THIS QUESTION. NOT EVERYONE AGREES. PETER STANDS UP TO TALK ...
BROTHERS, GOD CHOSE ME TO TAKE THE GOOD NEWS TO PEOPLE WHO *AREN'T* JEWS.
HE GAVE THEM THE SAME HOLY SPIRIT HE GAVE US. WHY DO YOU WANT TO MAKE IT HARD FOR THEM TO BELIEVE?
WE ARE SAVED BY THE GRACE OF GOD. THE GENTILES ARE SAVED THE SAME WAY.
THERE IS DEAD SILENCE IN THE ROOM ...

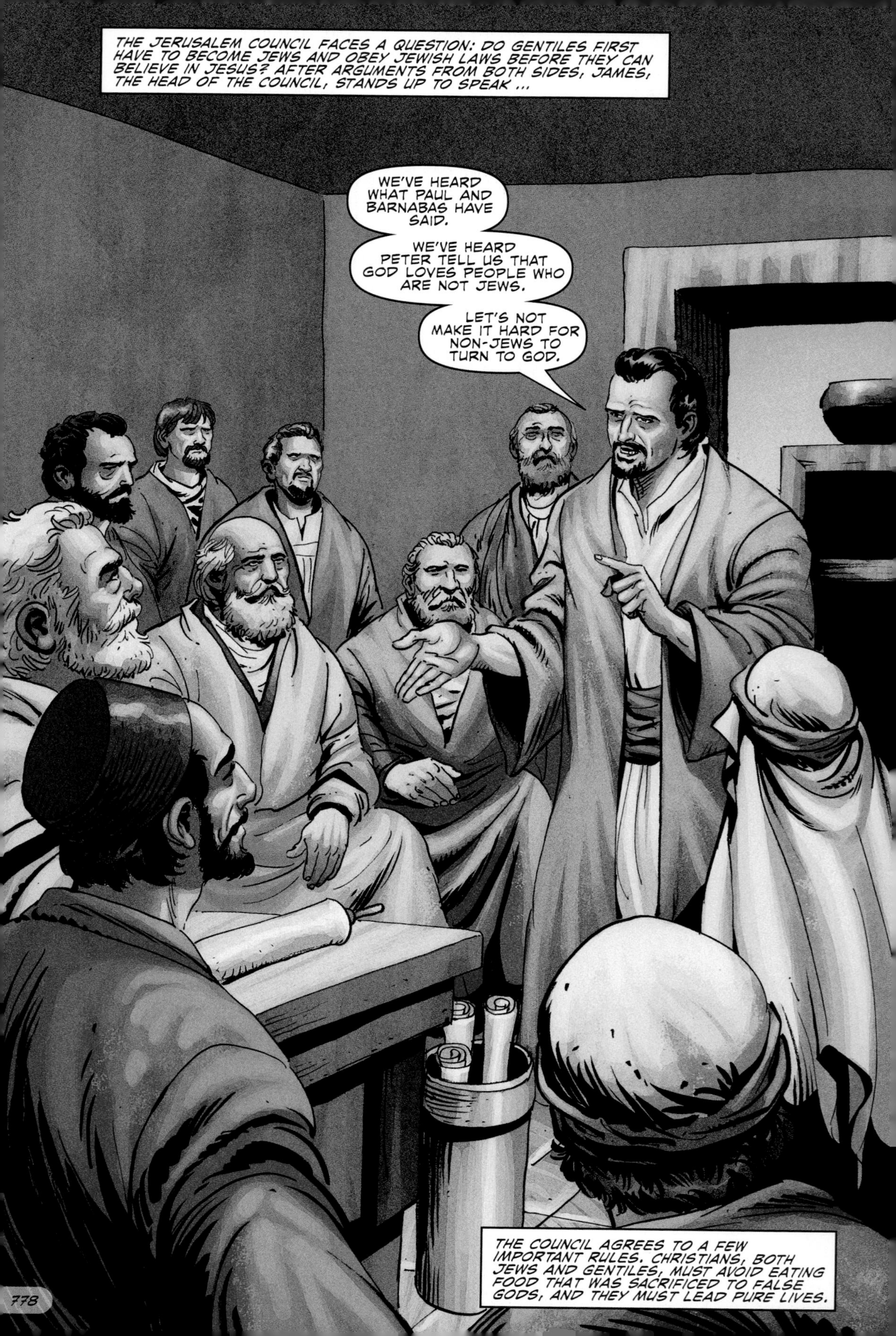
THE JERUSALEM COUNCIL FACES A QUESTION: DO GENTILES FIRST HAVE TO BECOME JEWS AND OBEY JEWISH LAWS BEFORE THEY CAN BELIEVE IN JESUS? AFTER ARGUMENTS FROM BOTH SIDES, JAMES, THE HEAD OF THE COUNCIL, STANDS UP TO SPEAK ...
WE'VE HEARD WHAT PAUL AND BARNABAS HAVE SAID.
WE'VE HEARD PETER TELL US THAT GOD LOVES PEOPLE WHO ARE NOT JEWS.
LET'S NOT MAKE IT HARD FOR NON-JEWS TO TURN TO GOD.
THE COUNCIL AGREES TO A FEW IMPORTANT RULES. CHRISTIANS, BOTH JEWS AND GENTILES, MUST AVOID EATING FOOD THAT WAS SACRIFICED TO FALSE GODS, AND THEY MUST LEAD PURE LIVES.

The Next Journey
BASED ON ACTS 15:36—16:19

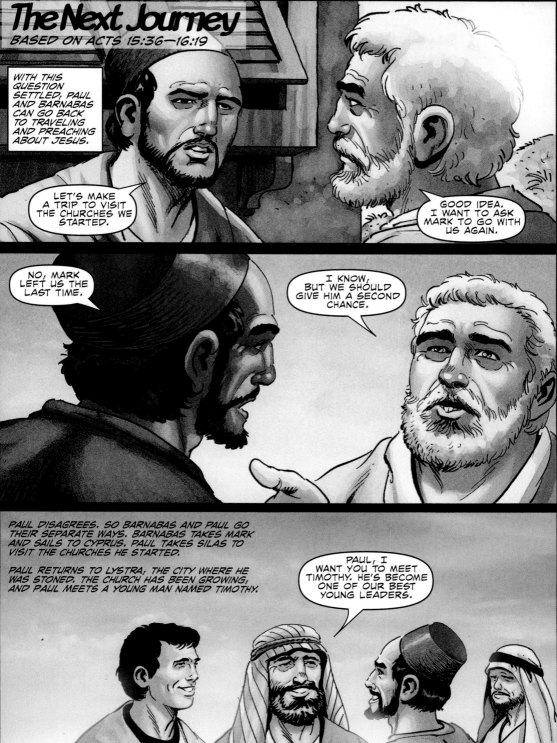

WITH THIS QUESTION SETTLED, PAUL AND BARNABAS CAN GO BACK TO TRAVELING AND PREACHING ABOUT JESUS.

LET'S MAKE A TRIP TO VISIT THE CHURCHES WE STARTED.

GOOD IDEA. I WANT TO ASK MARK TO GO WITH US AGAIN.

NO, MARK LEFT US THE LAST TIME.

I KNOW, BUT WE SHOULD GIVE HIM A SECOND CHANCE.

PAUL DISAGREES. SO BARNABAS AND PAUL GO THEIR SEPARATE WAYS. BARNABAS TAKES MARK AND SAILS TO CYPRUS. PAUL TAKES SILAS TO VISIT THE CHURCHES HE STARTED.

PAUL RETURNS TO LYSTRA, THE CITY WHERE HE WAS STONED. THE CHURCH HAS BEEN GROWING, AND PAUL MEETS A YOUNG MAN NAMED TIMOTHY.

PAUL, I WANT YOU TO MEET TIMOTHY. HE'S BECOME ONE OF OUR BEST YOUNG LEADERS.

TIMOTHY, NEVER LET ANYONE LOOK DOWN ON YOU BECAUSE YOU ARE YOUNG. YOU CAN SET A GOOD EXAMPLE FOR OTHER BELIEVERS.

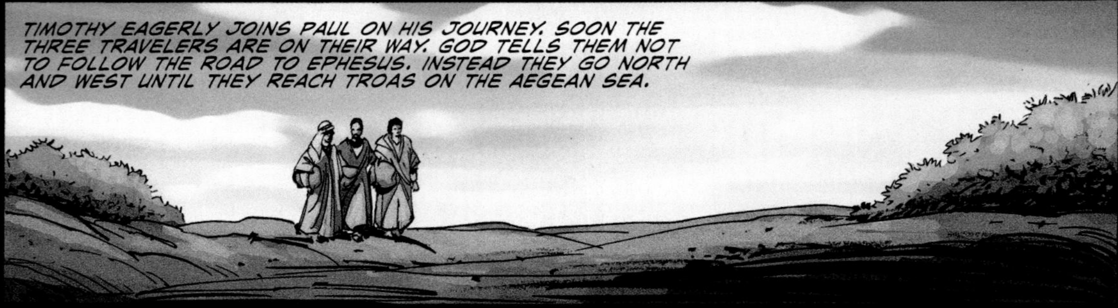
TIMOTHY EAGERLY JOINS PAUL ON HIS JOURNEY. SOON THE THREE TRAVELERS ARE ON THEIR WAY. GOD TELLS THEM NOT TO FOLLOW THE ROAD TO EPHESUS. INSTEAD THEY GO NORTH AND WEST UNTIL THEY REACH TROAS ON THE AEGEAN SEA.

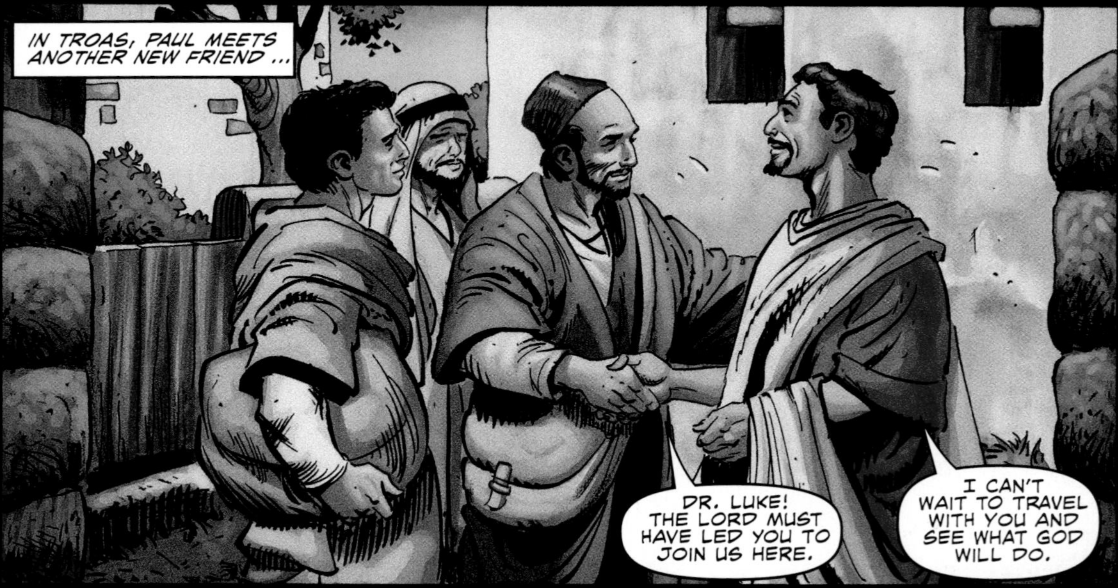
IN TROAS, PAUL MEETS ANOTHER NEW FRIEND ...
DR. LUKE! THE LORD MUST HAVE LED YOU TO JOIN US HERE.
I CAN'T WAIT TO TRAVEL WITH YOU AND SEE WHAT GOD WILL DO.

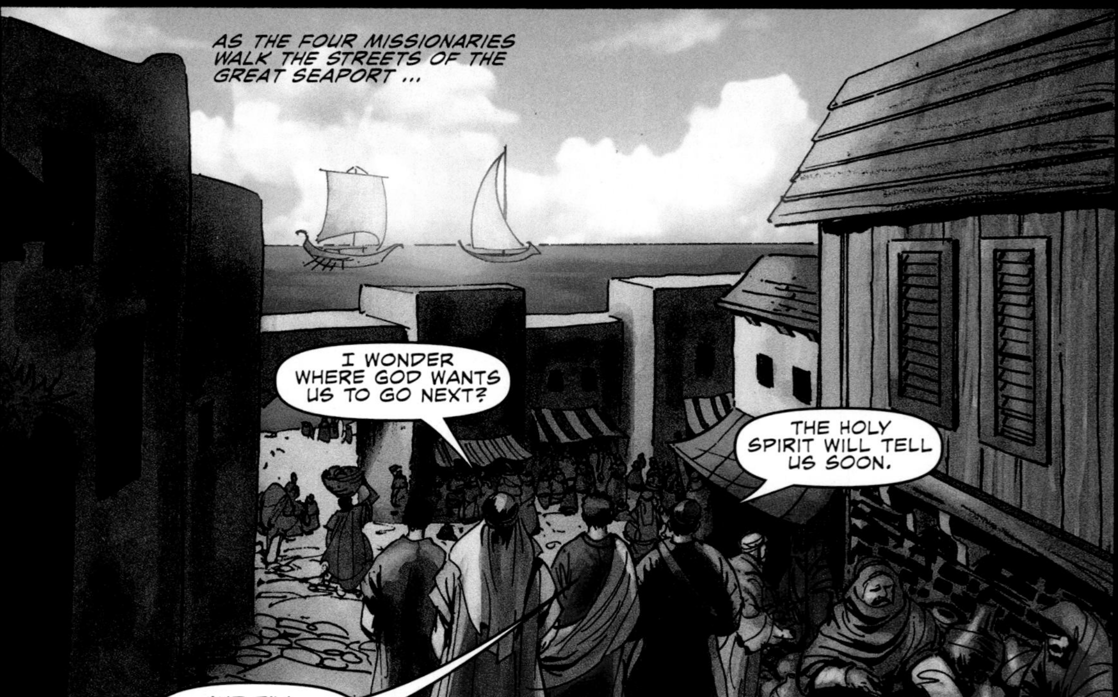
AS THE FOUR MISSIONARIES WALK THE STREETS OF THE GREAT SEAPORT ...
I WONDER WHERE GOD WANTS US TO GO NEXT?
THE HOLY SPIRIT WILL TELL US SOON.
AND I'LL RECORD ALL OUR ADVENTURES IN MY JOURNAL!

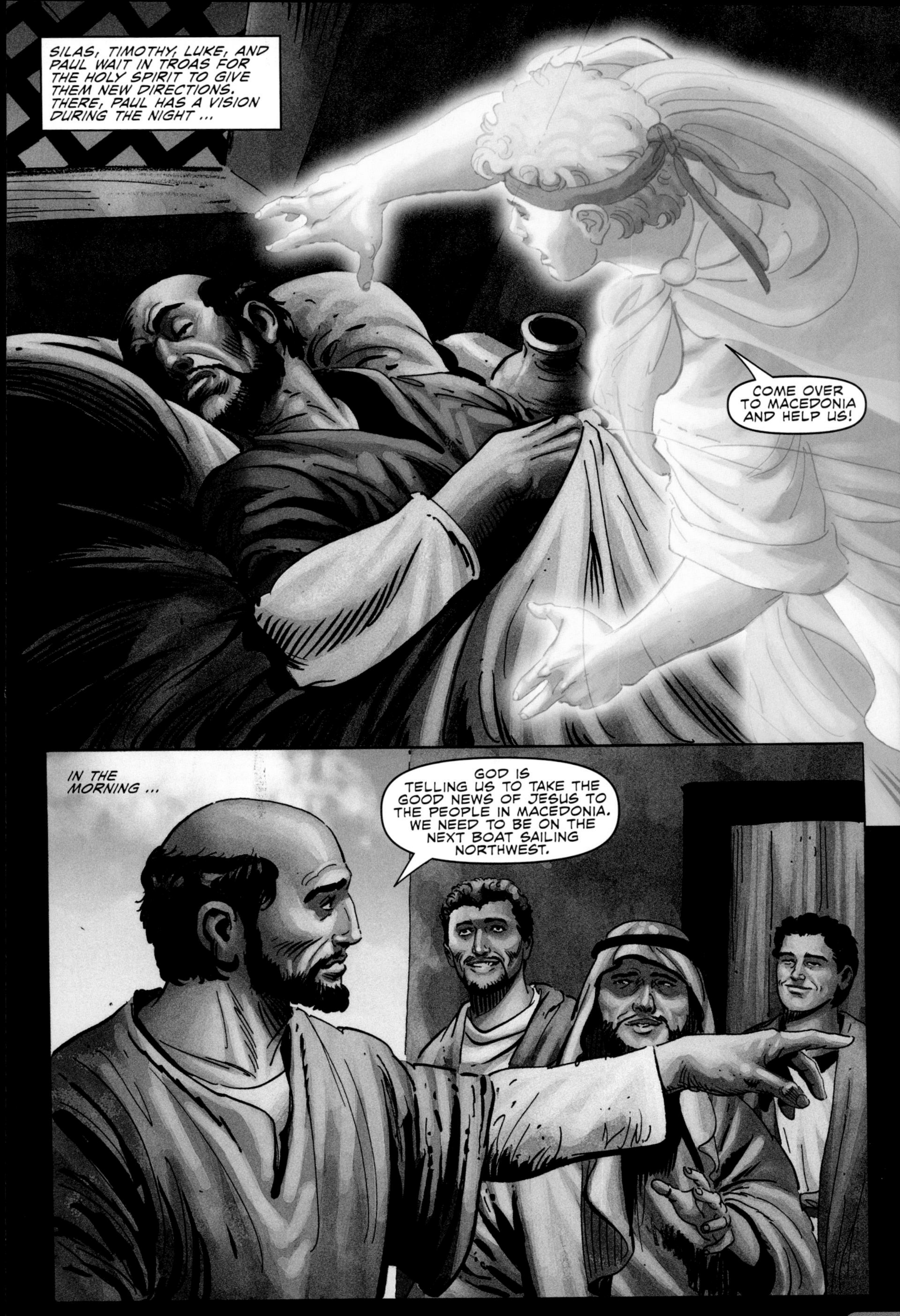
SILAS, TIMOTHY, LUKE, AND PAUL WAIT IN TROAS FOR THE HOLY SPIRIT TO GIVE THEM NEW DIRECTIONS. THERE, PAUL HAS A VISION DURING THE NIGHT ...
COME OVER TO MACEDONIA AND HELP US!
IN THE MORNING ...
GOD IS TELLING US TO TAKE THE GOOD NEWS OF JESUS TO THE PEOPLE IN MACEDONIA. WE NEED TO BE ON THE NEXT BOAT SAILING NORTHWEST.

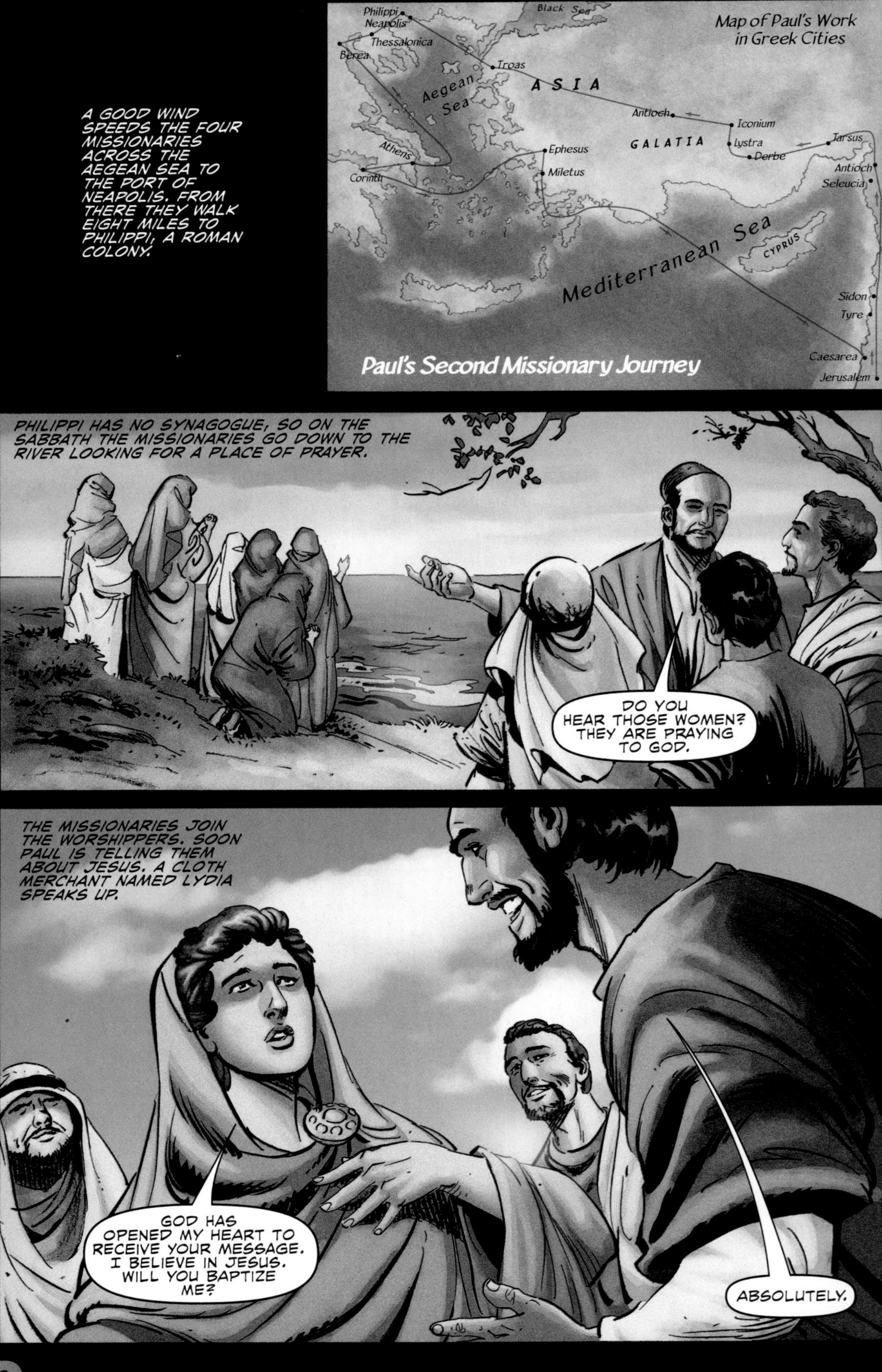
A GOOD WIND SPEEDS THE FOUR MISSIONARIES ACROSS THE AEGEAN SEA TO THE PORT OF NEAPOLIS. FROM THERE THEY WALK EIGHT MILES TO PHILIPPI, A ROMAN COLONY.
Map of Paul's Work in Greek Cities
Black Sea
Philippi
Neapolis
Thessalonica
Berea
Troas
Aegean Sea
ASIA
Antioch
Iconium
GALATIA
Lystra
Derbe
Tarsus
Antioch
Seleucia
Athens
Corinth
Ephesus
Miletus
Mediterranean Sea
CYPRUS
Sidon
Tyre
Caesarea
Jerusalem
Paul's Second Missionary Journey
PHILIPPI HAS NO SYNAGOGUE, SO ON THE SABBATH THE MISSIONARIES GO DOWN TO THE RIVER LOOKING FOR A PLACE OF PRAYER.
DO YOU HEAR THOSE WOMEN? THEY ARE PRAYING TO GOD.
THE MISSIONARIES JOIN THE WORSHIPPERS. SOON PAUL IS TELLING THEM ABOUT JESUS. A CLOTH MERCHANT NAMED LYDIA SPEAKS UP.
GOD HAS OPENED MY HEART TO RECEIVE YOUR MESSAGE. I BELIEVE IN JESUS. WILL YOU BAPTIZE ME?
ABSOLUTELY.

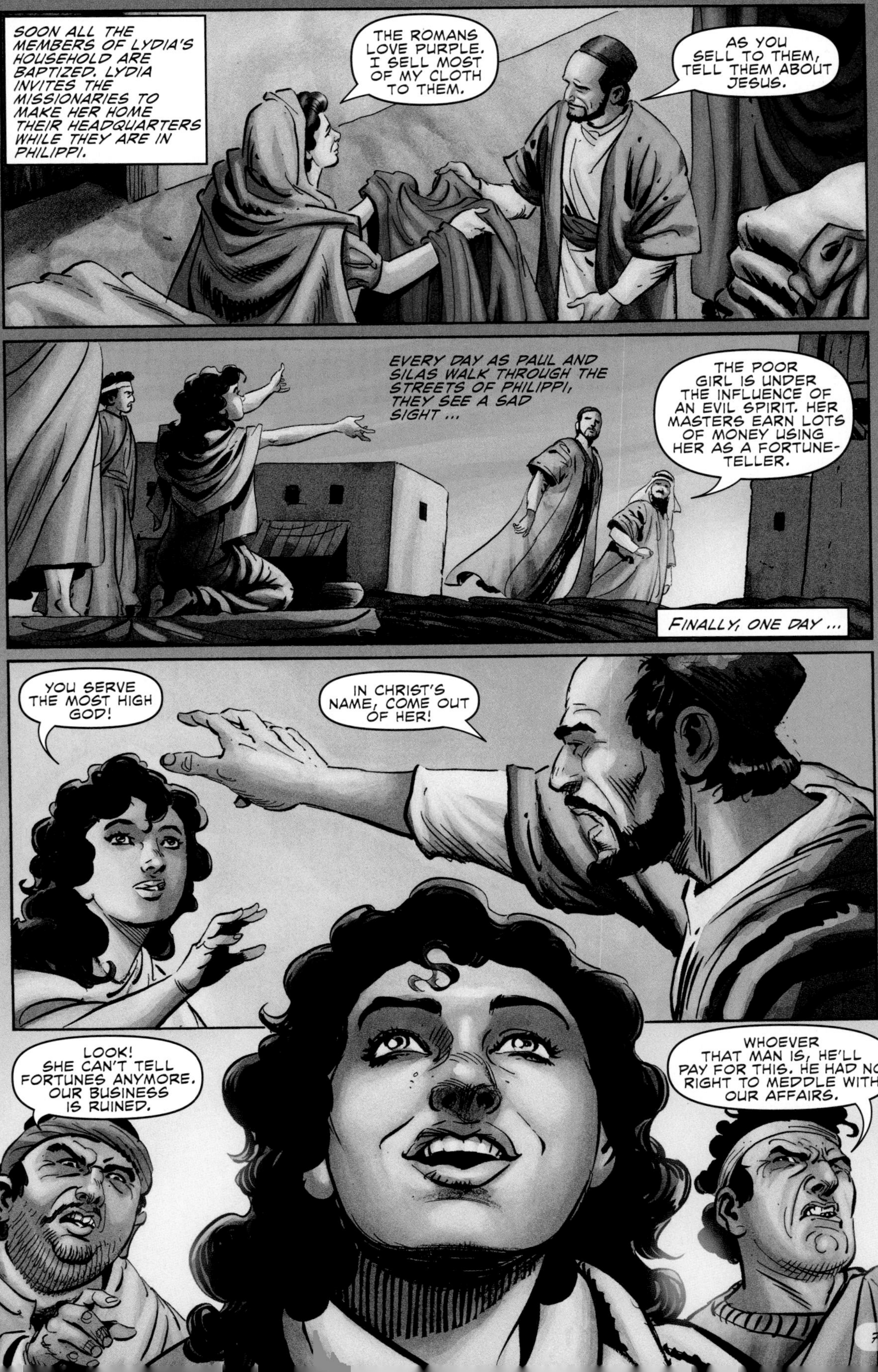
SOON ALL THE MEMBERS OF LYDIA'S HOUSEHOLD ARE BAPTIZED. LYDIA INVITES THE MISSIONARIES TO MAKE HER HOME THEIR HEADQUARTERS WHILE THEY ARE IN PHILIPPI.
THE ROMANS LOVE PURPLE. I SELL MOST OF MY CLOTH TO THEM.
AS YOU SELL TO THEM, TELL THEM ABOUT JESUS.
EVERY DAY AS PAUL AND SILAS WALK THROUGH THE STREETS OF PHILIPPI, THEY SEE A SAD SIGHT ...
THE POOR GIRL IS UNDER THE INFLUENCE OF AN EVIL SPIRIT. HER MASTERS EARN LOTS OF MONEY USING HER AS A FORTUNE-TELLER.
FINALLY, ONE DAY ...
YOU SERVE THE MOST HIGH GOD!
IN CHRIST'S NAME, COME OUT OF HER!
LOOK! SHE CAN'T TELL FORTUNES ANYMORE. OUR BUSINESS IS RUINED.
WHOEVER THAT MAN IS, HE'LL PAY FOR THIS. HE HAD NO RIGHT TO MEDDLE WITH OUR AFFAIRS.

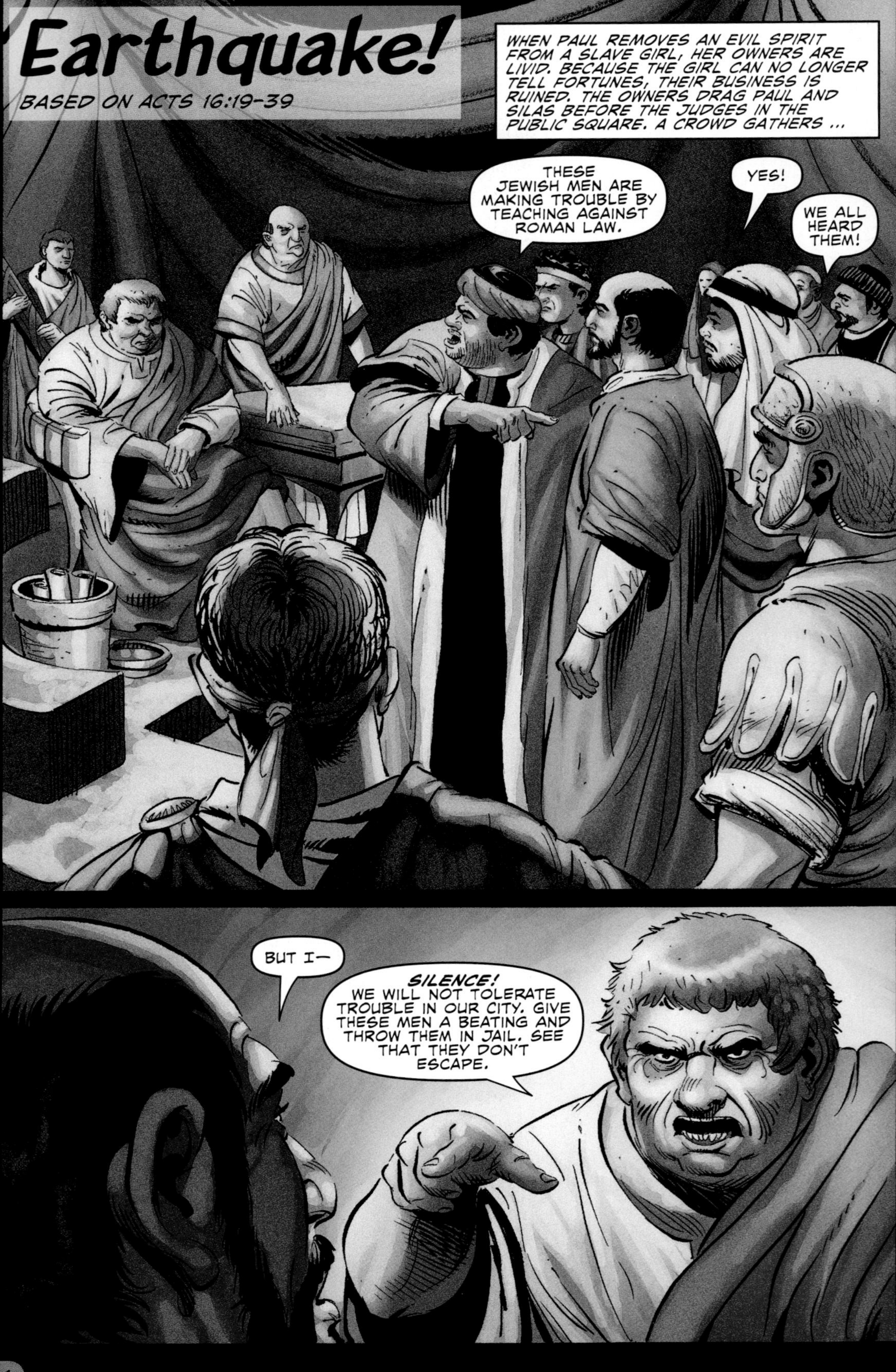
Earthquake!
BASED ON ACTS 16:19-39
WHEN PAUL REMOVES AN EVIL SPIRIT FROM A SLAVE GIRL, HER OWNERS ARE LIVID. BECAUSE THE GIRL CAN NO LONGER TELL FORTUNES, THEIR BUSINESS IS RUINED. THE OWNERS DRAG PAUL AND SILAS BEFORE THE JUDGES IN THE PUBLIC SQUARE. A CROWD GATHERS ...
THESE JEWISH MEN ARE MAKING TROUBLE BY TEACHING AGAINST ROMAN LAW.
YES!
WE ALL HEARD THEM!
BUT I—
SILENCE! WE WILL NOT TOLERATE TROUBLE IN OUR CITY. GIVE THESE MEN A BEATING AND THROW THEM IN JAIL. SEE THAT THEY DON'T ESCAPE.

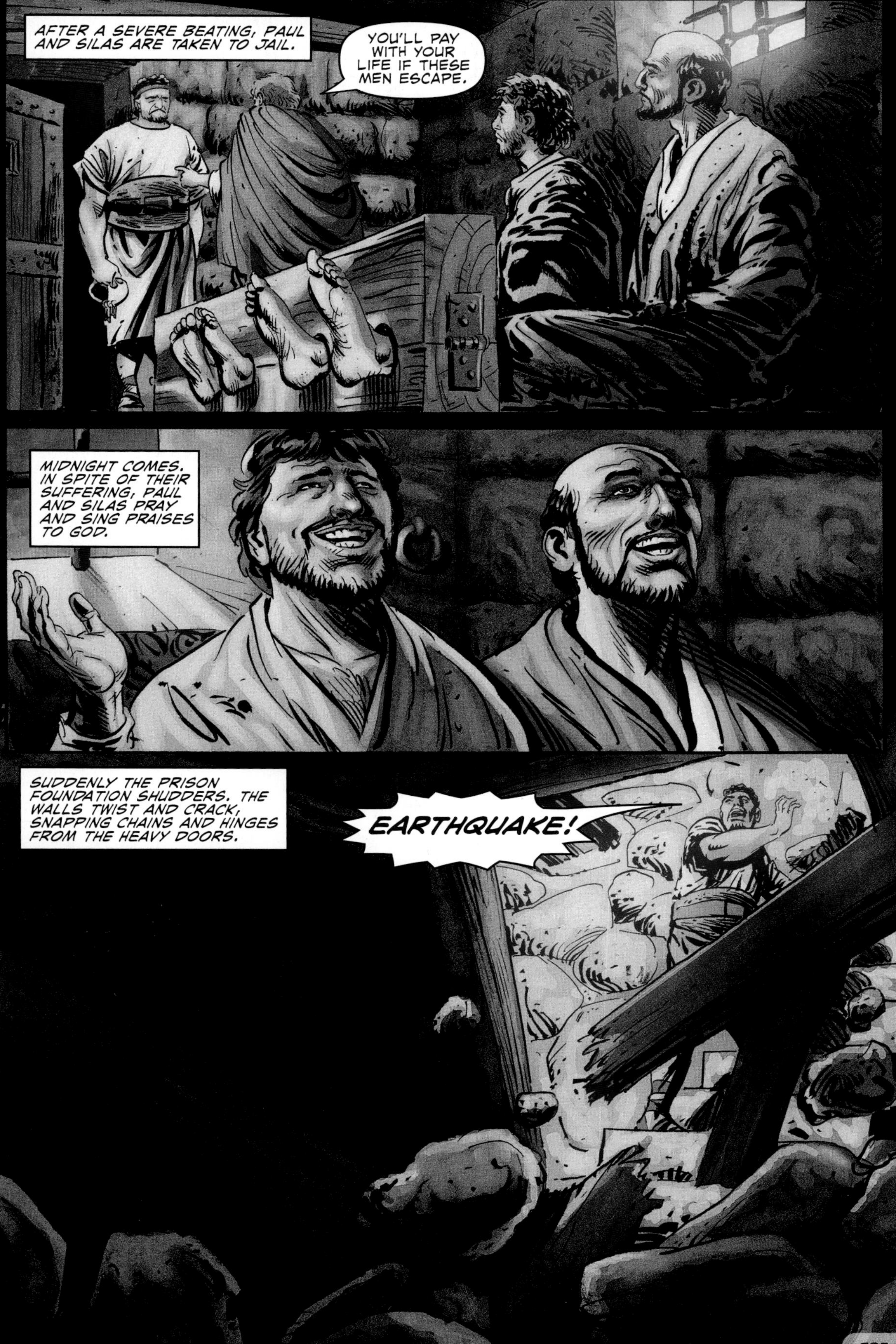
AFTER A SEVERE BEATING, PAUL AND SILAS ARE TAKEN TO JAIL.
YOU'LL PAY WITH YOUR LIFE IF THESE MEN ESCAPE.
MIDNIGHT COMES. IN SPITE OF THEIR SUFFERING, PAUL AND SILAS PRAY AND SING PRAISES TO GOD.
SUDDENLY THE PRISON FOUNDATION SHUDDERS. THE WALLS TWIST AND CRACK, SNAPPING CHAINS AND HINGES FROM THE HEAVY DOORS.
EARTHQUAKE!

THE JAILER RUSHES DOWN INTO THE DUNGEON, SURE THAT HIS PRISONERS HAVE ESCAPED.

THEY'RE GONE! I MIGHT AS WELL KILL MYSELF.

NO! NO! WE'RE ALL HERE! DON'T HURT YOURSELF.

BELIEVING PAUL AND SILAS CAUSED THE EARTHQUAKE, THE JAILER FALLS DOWN IN FRONT OF THEM.

WHAT MUST I DO TO BE SAVED?

BELIEVE IN THE LORD JESUS CHRIST.

IN THE MIDDLE OF THE NIGHT, THE JAILER TAKES PAUL AND SILAS TO HIS HOUSE AND CARES FOR THEM. HE AND HIS FAMILY LISTEN AS PAUL TELLS THEM ABOUT JESUS. THEN THEY ARE ALL BAPTIZED!

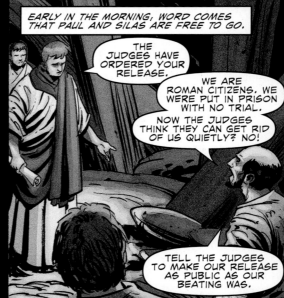

EARLY IN THE MORNING, WORD COMES THAT PAUL AND SILAS ARE FREE TO GO.

THE JUDGES HAVE ORDERED YOUR RELEASE.

WE ARE ROMAN CITIZENS. WE WERE PUT IN PRISON WITH NO TRIAL. NOW THE JUDGES THINK THEY CAN GET RID OF US QUIETLY? NO!

TELL THE JUDGES TO MAKE OUR RELEASE AS PUBLIC AS OUR BEATING WAS.

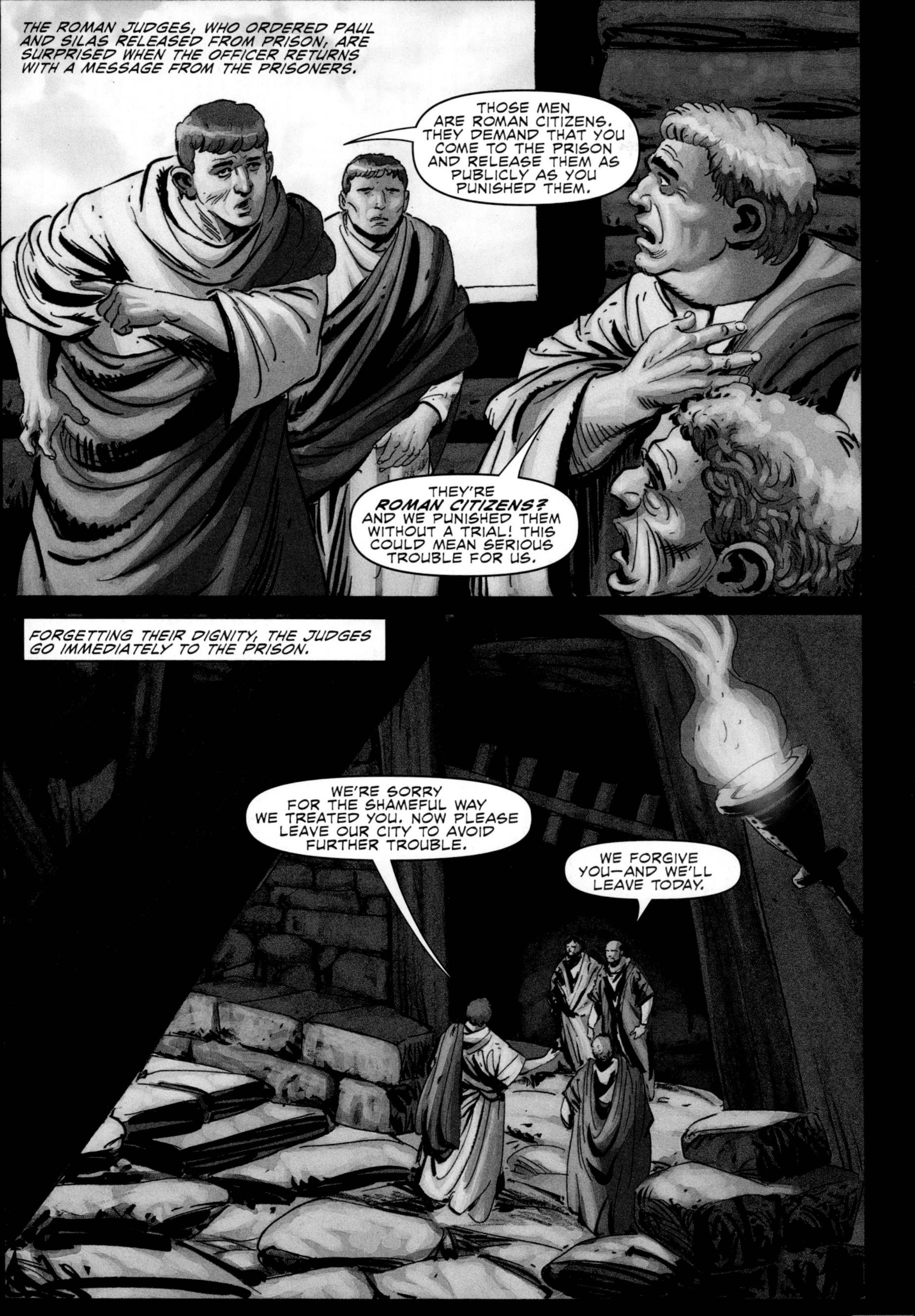
THE ROMAN JUDGES, WHO ORDERED PAUL AND SILAS RELEASED FROM PRISON, ARE SURPRISED WHEN THE OFFICER RETURNS WITH A MESSAGE FROM THE PRISONERS.
THOSE MEN ARE ROMAN CITIZENS. THEY DEMAND THAT YOU COME TO THE PRISON AND RELEASE THEM AS PUBLICLY AS YOU PUNISHED THEM.
THEY'RE *ROMAN CITIZENS?* AND WE PUNISHED THEM WITHOUT A TRIAL! THIS COULD MEAN SERIOUS TROUBLE FOR US.
FORGETTING THEIR DIGNITY, THE JUDGES GO IMMEDIATELY TO THE PRISON.
WE'RE SORRY FOR THE SHAMEFUL WAY WE TREATED YOU. NOW PLEASE LEAVE OUR CITY TO AVOID FURTHER TROUBLE.
WE FORGIVE YOU—AND WE'LL LEAVE TODAY.

Trouble in Thessalonica

BASED ON ACTS 16:40—18:11; 1 AND 2 THESSALONIANS

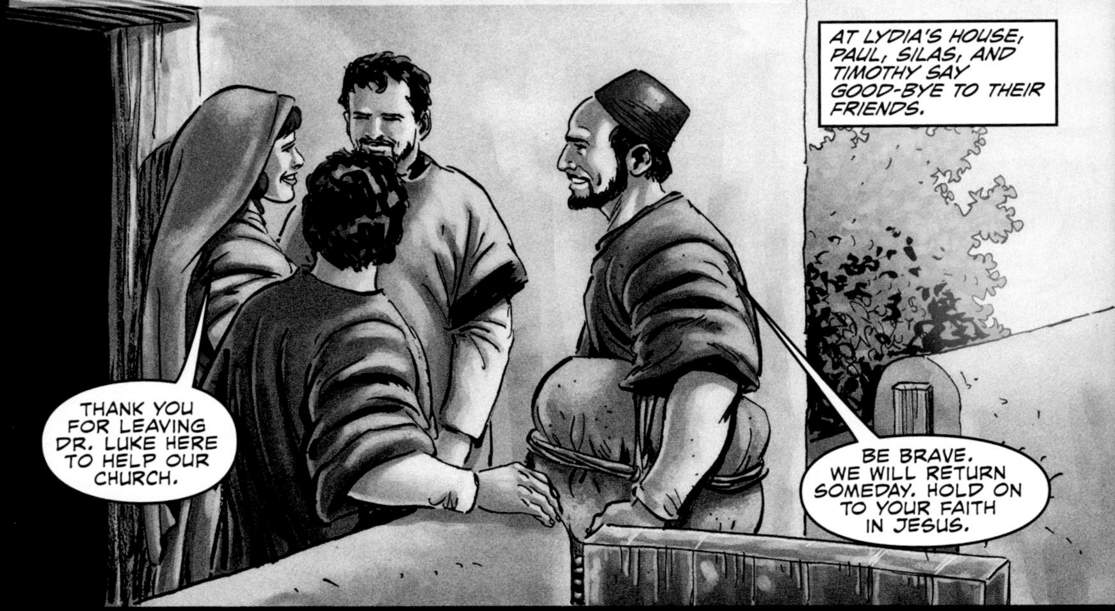
AT LYDIA'S HOUSE, PAUL, SILAS, AND TIMOTHY SAY GOOD-BYE TO THEIR FRIENDS.
THANK YOU FOR LEAVING DR. LUKE HERE TO HELP OUR CHURCH.
BE BRAVE. WE WILL RETURN SOMEDAY. HOLD ON TO YOUR FAITH IN JESUS.

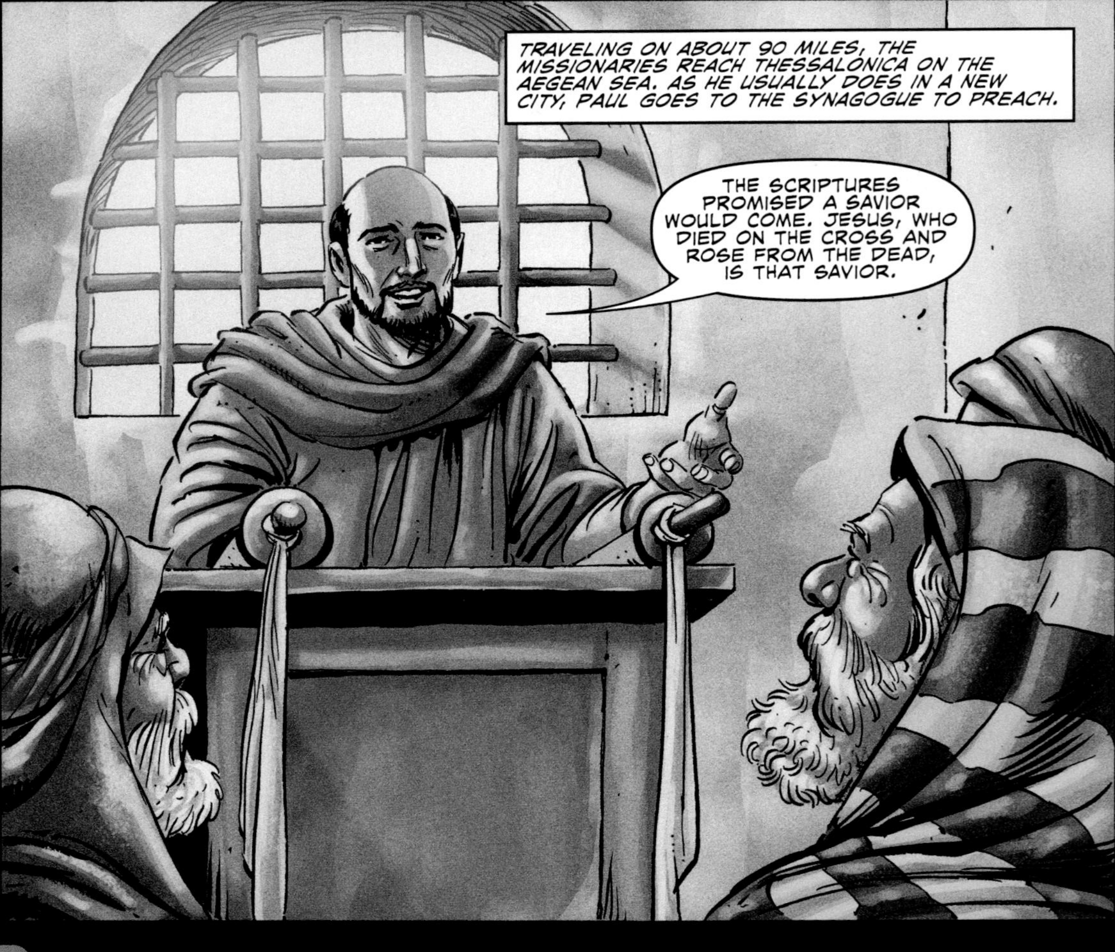
TRAVELING ON ABOUT 90 MILES, THE MISSIONARIES REACH THESSALONICA ON THE AEGEAN SEA. AS HE USUALLY DOES IN A NEW CITY, PAUL GOES TO THE SYNAGOGUE TO PREACH.
THE SCRIPTURES PROMISED A SAVIOR WOULD COME. JESUS, WHO DIED ON THE CROSS AND ROSE FROM THE DEAD, IS THAT SAVIOR.

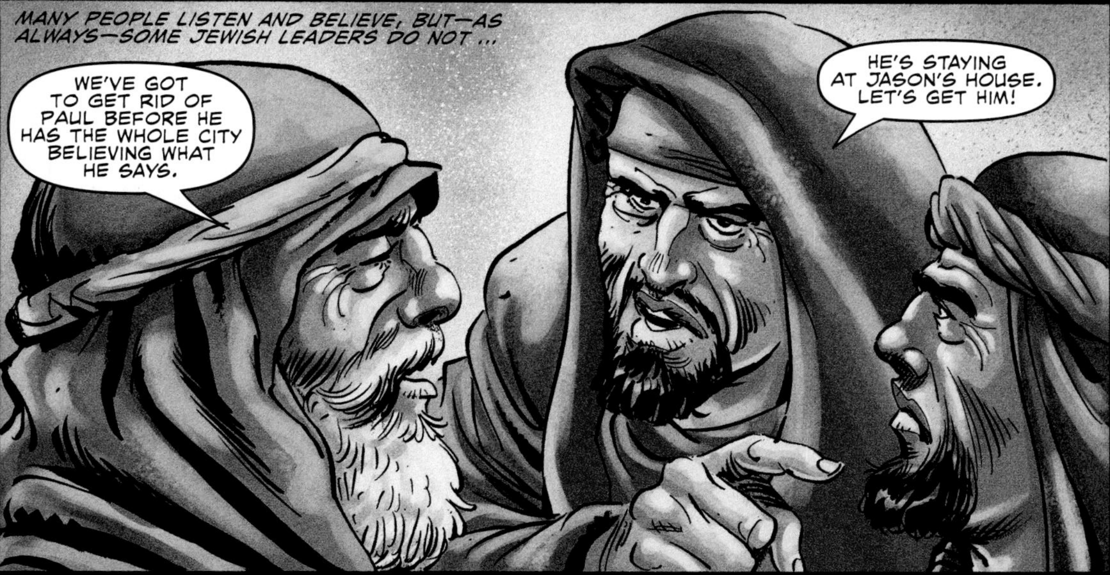
MANY PEOPLE LISTEN AND BELIEVE, BUT—AS ALWAYS—SOME JEWISH LEADERS DO NOT ...
WE'VE GOT TO GET RID OF PAUL BEFORE HE HAS THE WHOLE CITY BELIEVING WHAT HE SAYS.
HE'S STAYING AT JASON'S HOUSE. LET'S GET HIM!

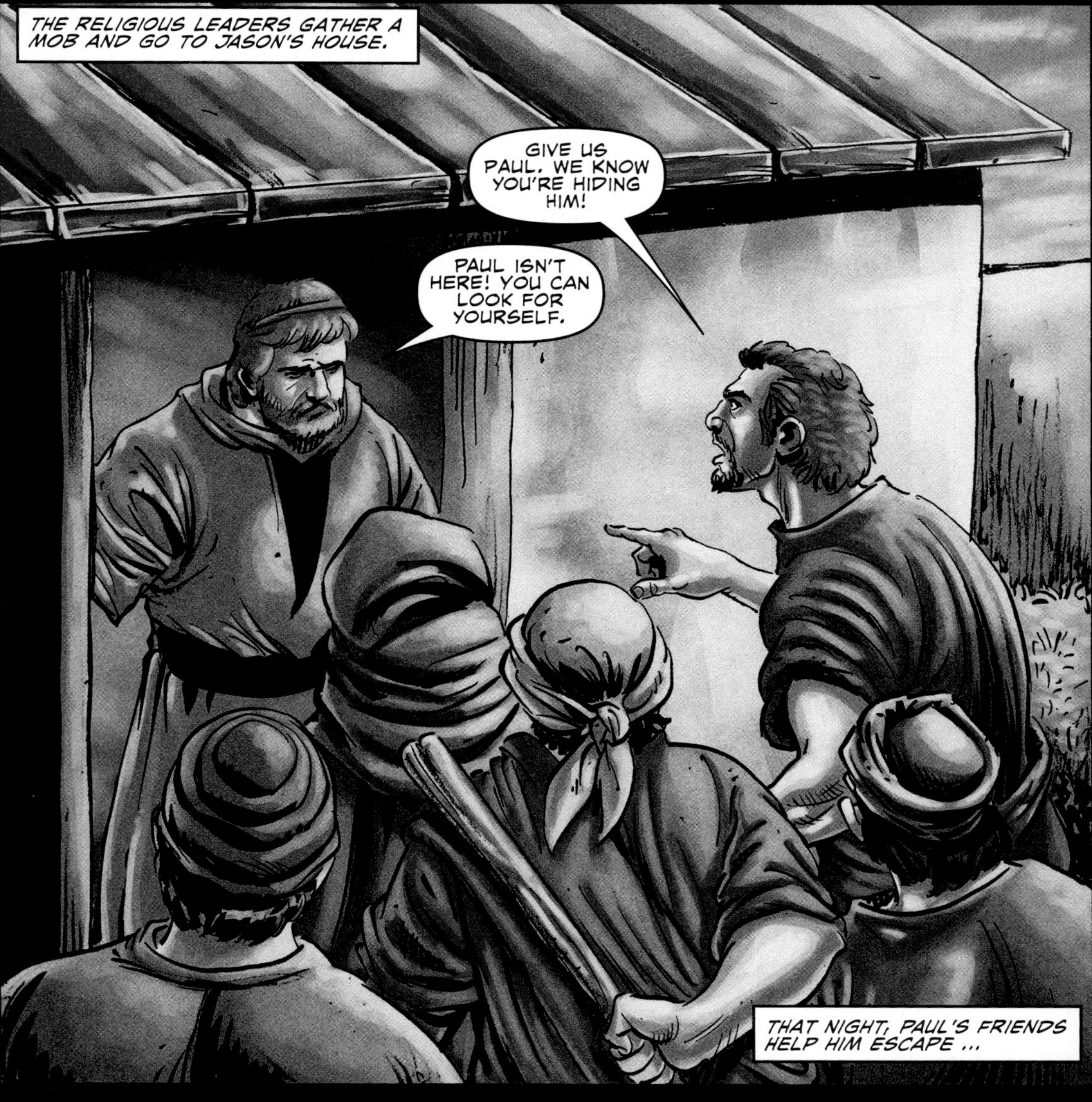
THE RELIGIOUS LEADERS GATHER A MOB AND GO TO JASON'S HOUSE.
GIVE US PAUL. WE KNOW YOU'RE HIDING HIM!
PAUL ISN'T HERE! YOU CAN LOOK FOR YOURSELF.
THAT NIGHT, PAUL'S FRIENDS HELP HIM ESCAPE ...

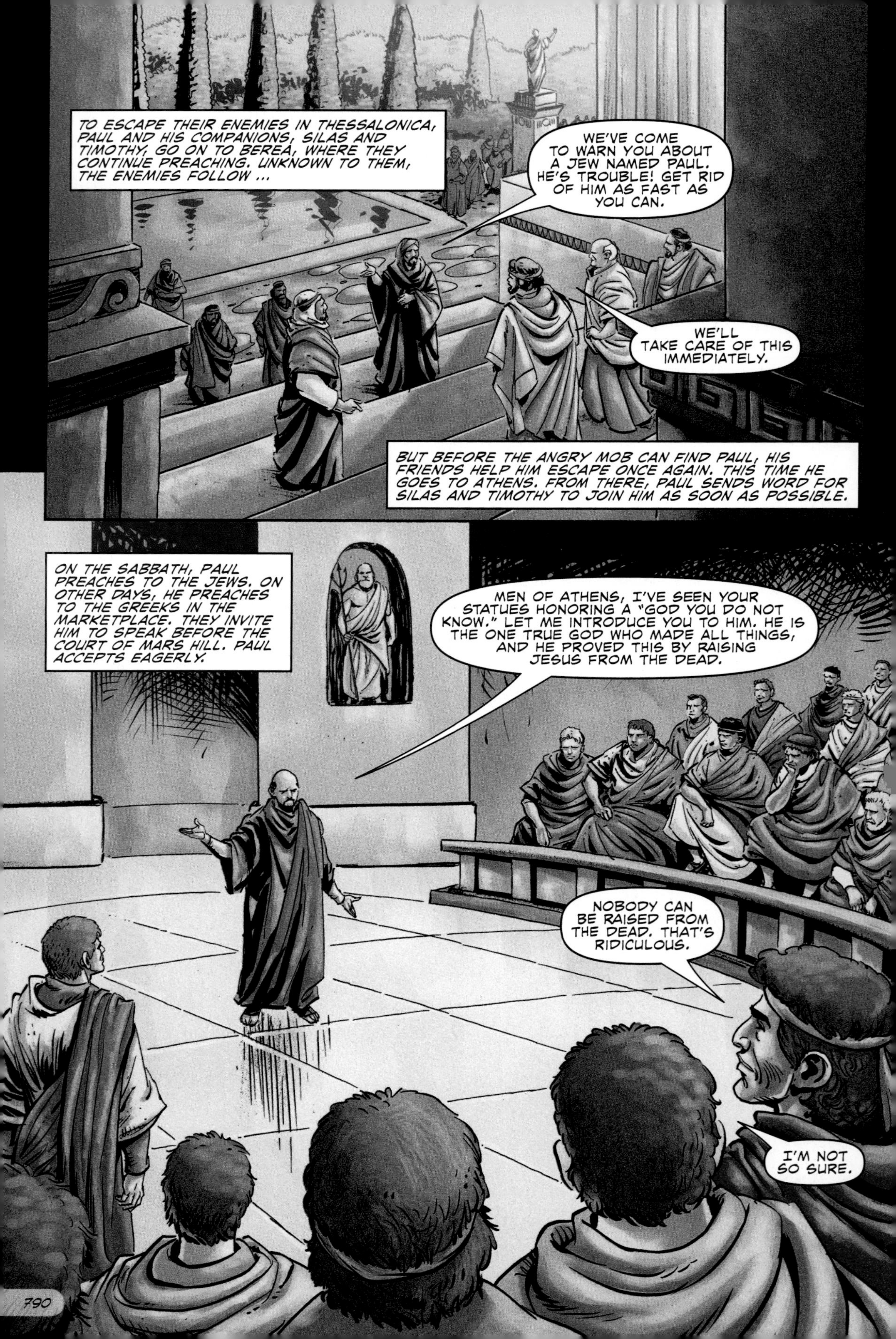
TO ESCAPE THEIR ENEMIES IN THESSALONICA, PAUL AND HIS COMPANIONS, SILAS AND TIMOTHY, GO ON TO BEREA, WHERE THEY CONTINUE PREACHING. UNKNOWN TO THEM, THE ENEMIES FOLLOW ...
WE'VE COME TO WARN YOU ABOUT A JEW NAMED PAUL. HE'S TROUBLE! GET RID OF HIM AS FAST AS YOU CAN.
WE'LL TAKE CARE OF THIS IMMEDIATELY.
BUT BEFORE THE ANGRY MOB CAN FIND PAUL, HIS FRIENDS HELP HIM ESCAPE ONCE AGAIN. THIS TIME HE GOES TO ATHENS. FROM THERE, PAUL SENDS WORD FOR SILAS AND TIMOTHY TO JOIN HIM AS SOON AS POSSIBLE.
ON THE SABBATH, PAUL PREACHES TO THE JEWS. ON OTHER DAYS, HE PREACHES TO THE GREEKS IN THE MARKETPLACE. THEY INVITE HIM TO SPEAK BEFORE THE COURT OF MARS HILL. PAUL ACCEPTS EAGERLY.
MEN OF ATHENS, I'VE SEEN YOUR STATUES HONORING A "GOD YOU DO NOT KNOW." LET ME INTRODUCE YOU TO HIM. HE IS THE ONE TRUE GOD WHO MADE ALL THINGS, AND HE PROVED THIS BY RAISING JESUS FROM THE DEAD.
NOBODY CAN BE RAISED FROM THE DEAD. THAT'S RIDICULOUS.
I'M NOT SO SURE.

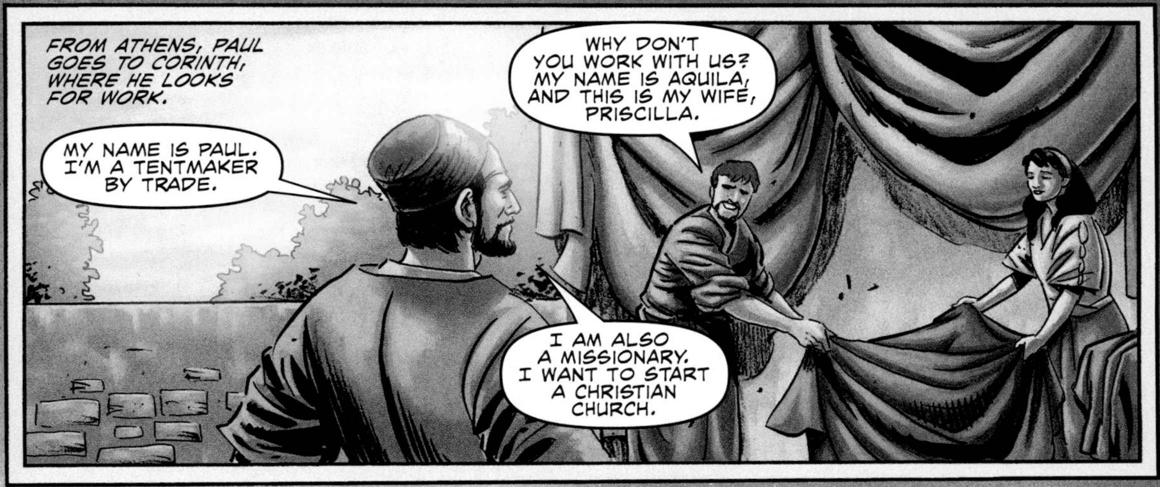
FROM ATHENS, PAUL GOES TO CORINTH, WHERE HE LOOKS FOR WORK.
MY NAME IS PAUL. I'M A TENTMAKER BY TRADE.
WHY DON'T YOU WORK WITH US? MY NAME IS AQUILA, AND THIS IS MY WIFE, PRISCILLA.
I AM ALSO A MISSIONARY. I WANT TO START A CHRISTIAN CHURCH.

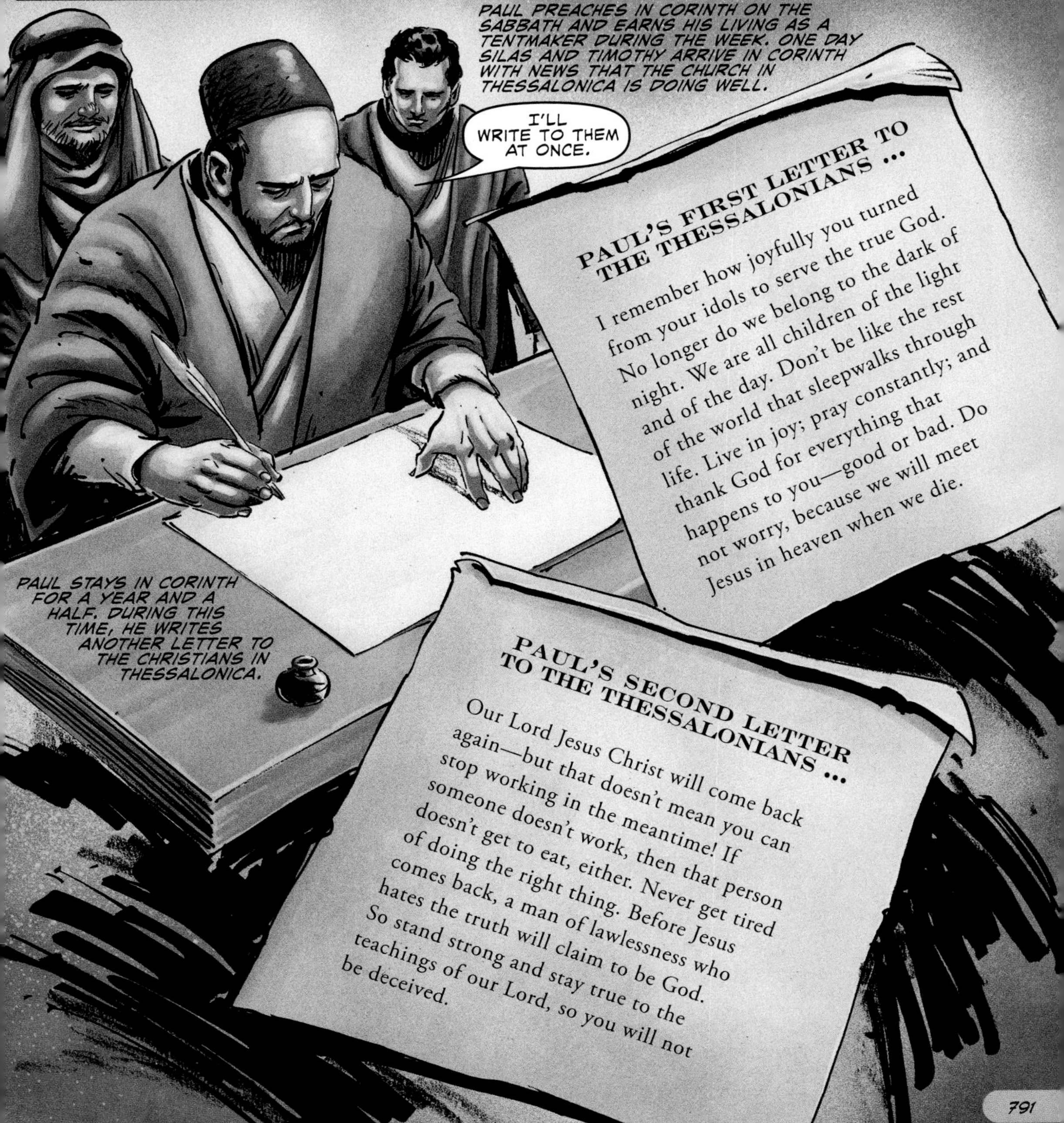
PAUL PREACHES IN CORINTH ON THE SABBATH AND EARNS HIS LIVING AS A TENTMAKER DURING THE WEEK. ONE DAY SILAS AND TIMOTHY ARRIVE IN CORINTH WITH NEWS THAT THE CHURCH IN THESSALONICA IS DOING WELL.
I'LL WRITE TO THEM AT ONCE.
PAUL'S FIRST LETTER TO THE THESSALONIANS ...
I remember how joyfully you turned from your idols to serve the true God. No longer do we belong to the dark of night. We are all children of the light and of the day. Don't be like the rest of the world that sleepwalks through life. Live in joy; pray constantly; and thank God for everything that happens to you—good or bad. Do not worry, because we will meet Jesus in heaven when we die.
PAUL STAYS IN CORINTH FOR A YEAR AND A HALF. DURING THIS TIME, HE WRITES ANOTHER LETTER TO THE CHRISTIANS IN THESSALONICA.
PAUL'S SECOND LETTER TO THE THESSALONIANS ...
Our Lord Jesus Christ will come back again—but that doesn't mean you can stop working in the meantime! If someone doesn't work, then that person doesn't get to eat, either. Never get tired of doing the right thing. Before Jesus comes back, a man of lawlessness who hates the truth will claim to be God. So stand strong and stay true to the teachings of our Lord, so you will not be deceived.

Corinthian Court

BASED ON ACTS 18:12–19:22;
ROMANS; 1 CORINTHIANS

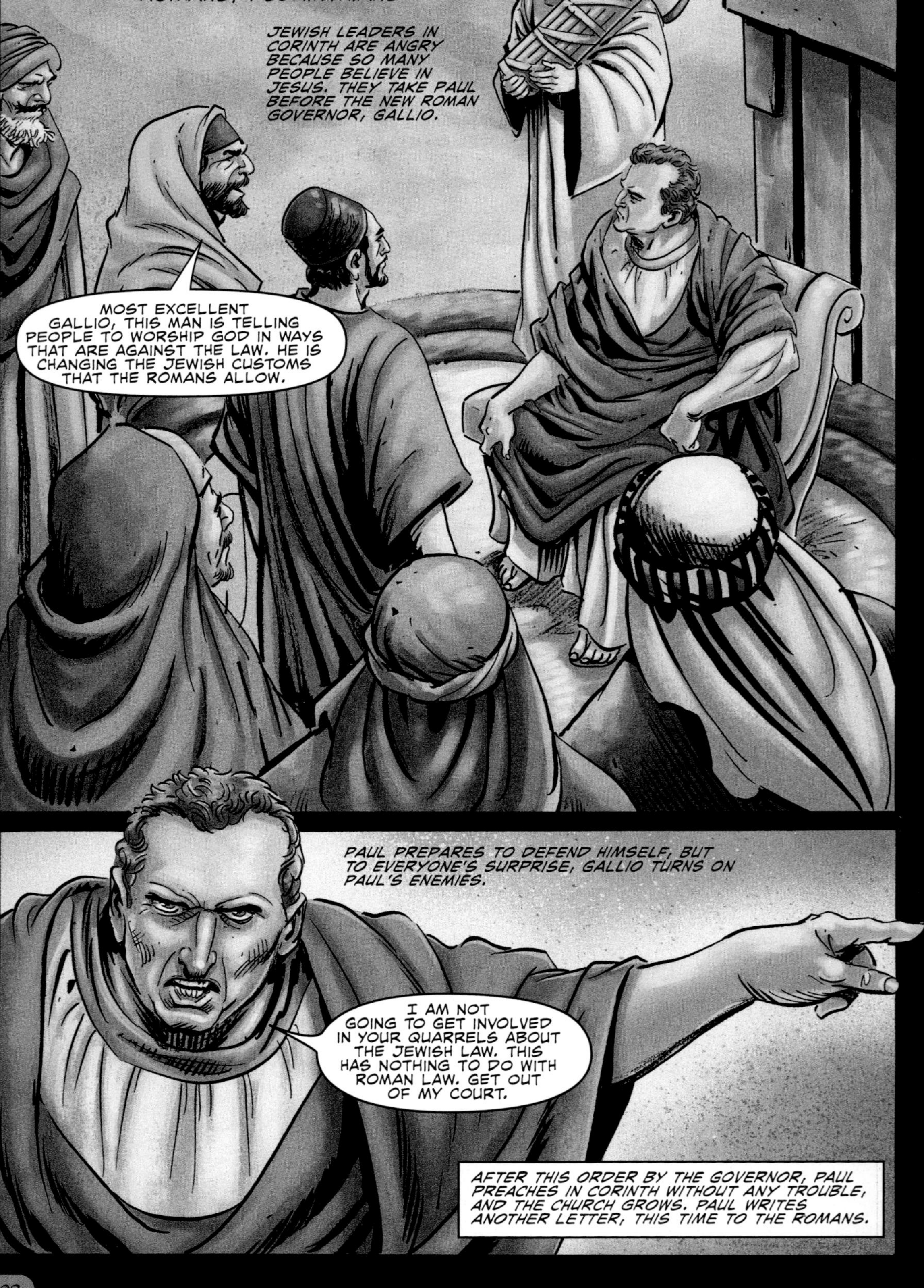
JEWISH LEADERS IN CORINTH ARE ANGRY BECAUSE SO MANY PEOPLE BELIEVE IN JESUS. THEY TAKE PAUL BEFORE THE NEW ROMAN GOVERNOR, GALLIO.
MOST EXCELLENT GALLIO, THIS MAN IS TELLING PEOPLE TO WORSHIP GOD IN WAYS THAT ARE AGAINST THE LAW. HE IS CHANGING THE JEWISH CUSTOMS THAT THE ROMANS ALLOW.
PAUL PREPARES TO DEFEND HIMSELF; BUT TO EVERYONE'S SURPRISE, GALLIO TURNS ON PAUL'S ENEMIES.
I AM NOT GOING TO GET INVOLVED IN YOUR QUARRELS ABOUT THE JEWISH LAW. THIS HAS NOTHING TO DO WITH ROMAN LAW. GET OUT OF MY COURT.
AFTER THIS ORDER BY THE GOVERNOR, PAUL PREACHES IN CORINTH WITHOUT ANY TROUBLE, AND THE CHURCH GROWS. PAUL WRITES ANOTHER LETTER, THIS TIME TO THE ROMANS.

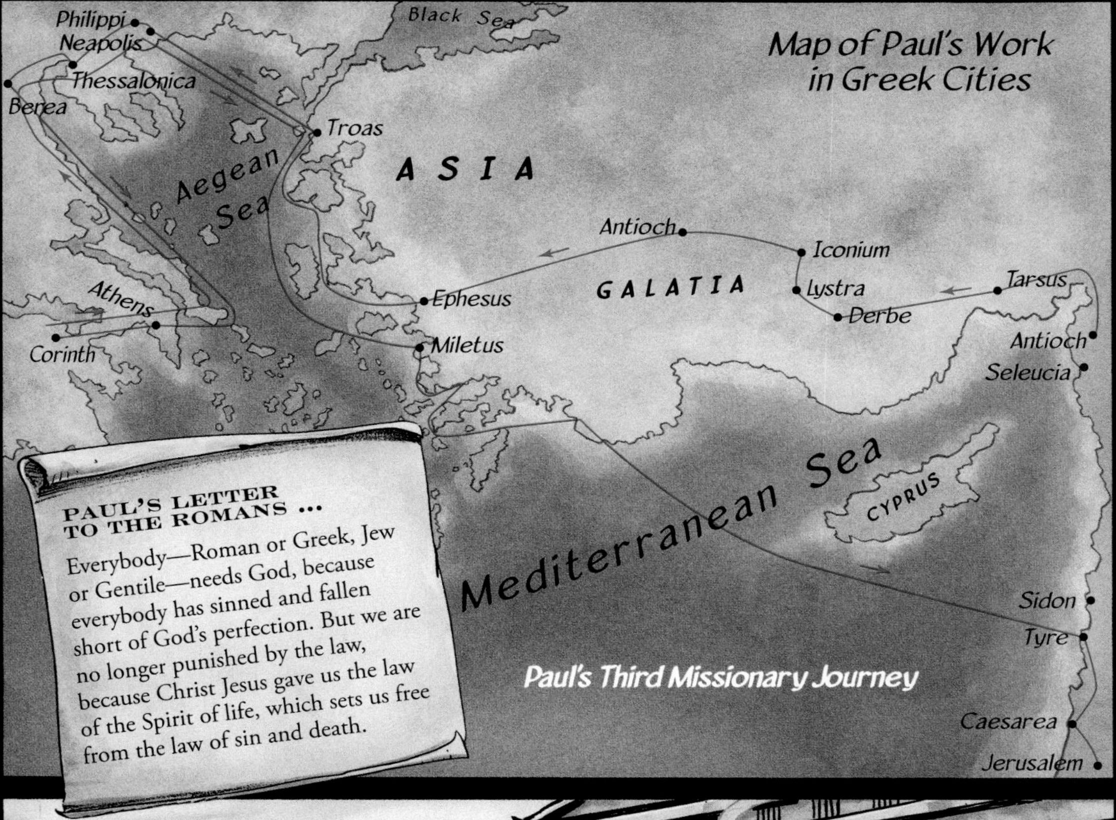

Map of Paul's Work in Greek Cities
Philippi
Neapolis
Black Sea
Thessalonica
Berea
Troas
Aegean Sea
ASIA
Antioch
Iconium
Athens
GALATIA
Lystra
Tarsus
Ephesus
Derbe
Corinth
Miletus
Antioch
Seleucia
Mediterranean Sea
CYPRUS
Sidon
Tyre
Paul's Third Missionary Journey
Caesarea
Jerusalem
PAUL'S LETTER TO THE ROMANS ...
Everybody—Roman or Greek, Jew or Gentile—needs God, because everybody has sinned and fallen short of God's perfection. But we are no longer punished by the law, because Christ Jesus gave us the law of the Spirit of life, which sets us free from the law of sin and death.

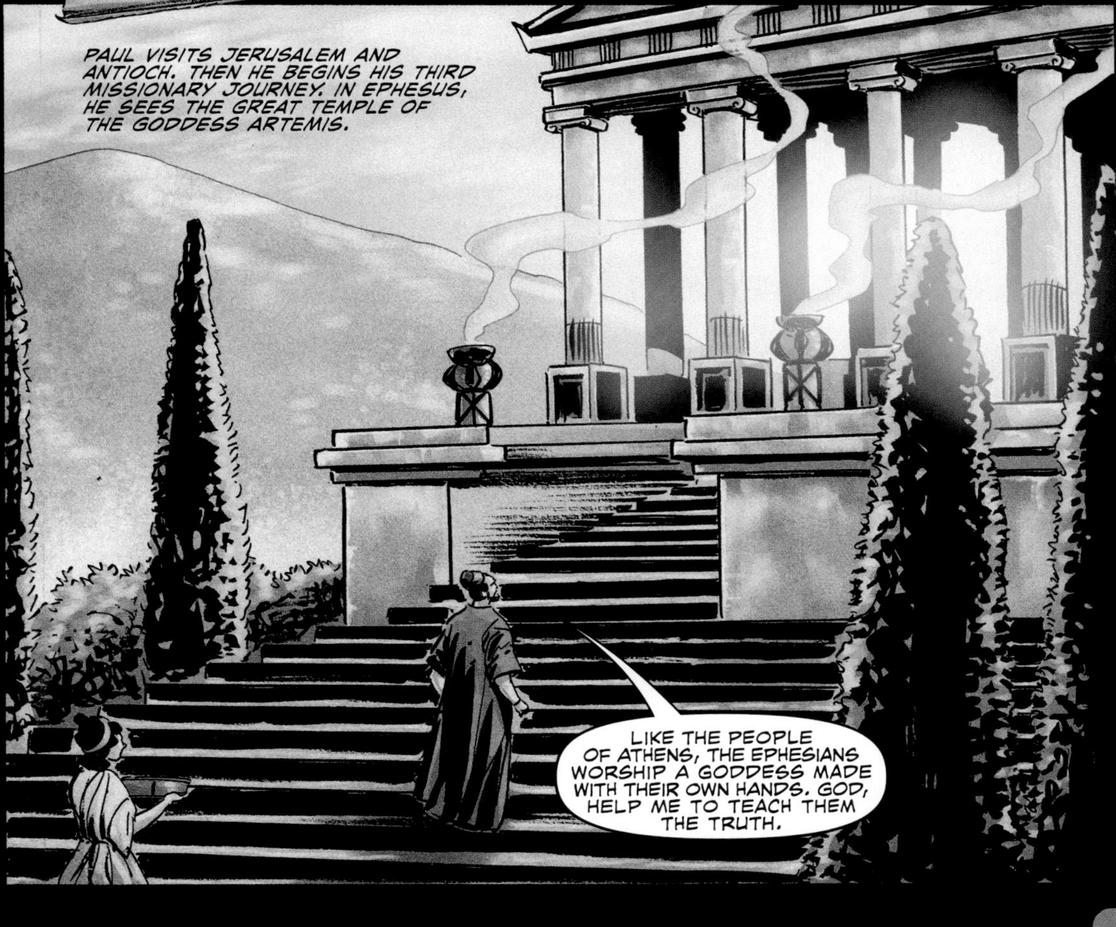

PAUL VISITS JERUSALEM AND ANTIOCH. THEN HE BEGINS HIS THIRD MISSIONARY JOURNEY. IN EPHESUS, HE SEES THE GREAT TEMPLE OF THE GODDESS ARTEMIS.
LIKE THE PEOPLE OF ATHENS, THE EPHESIANS WORSHIP A GODDESS MADE WITH THEIR OWN HANDS. GOD, HELP ME TO TEACH THEM THE TRUTH.

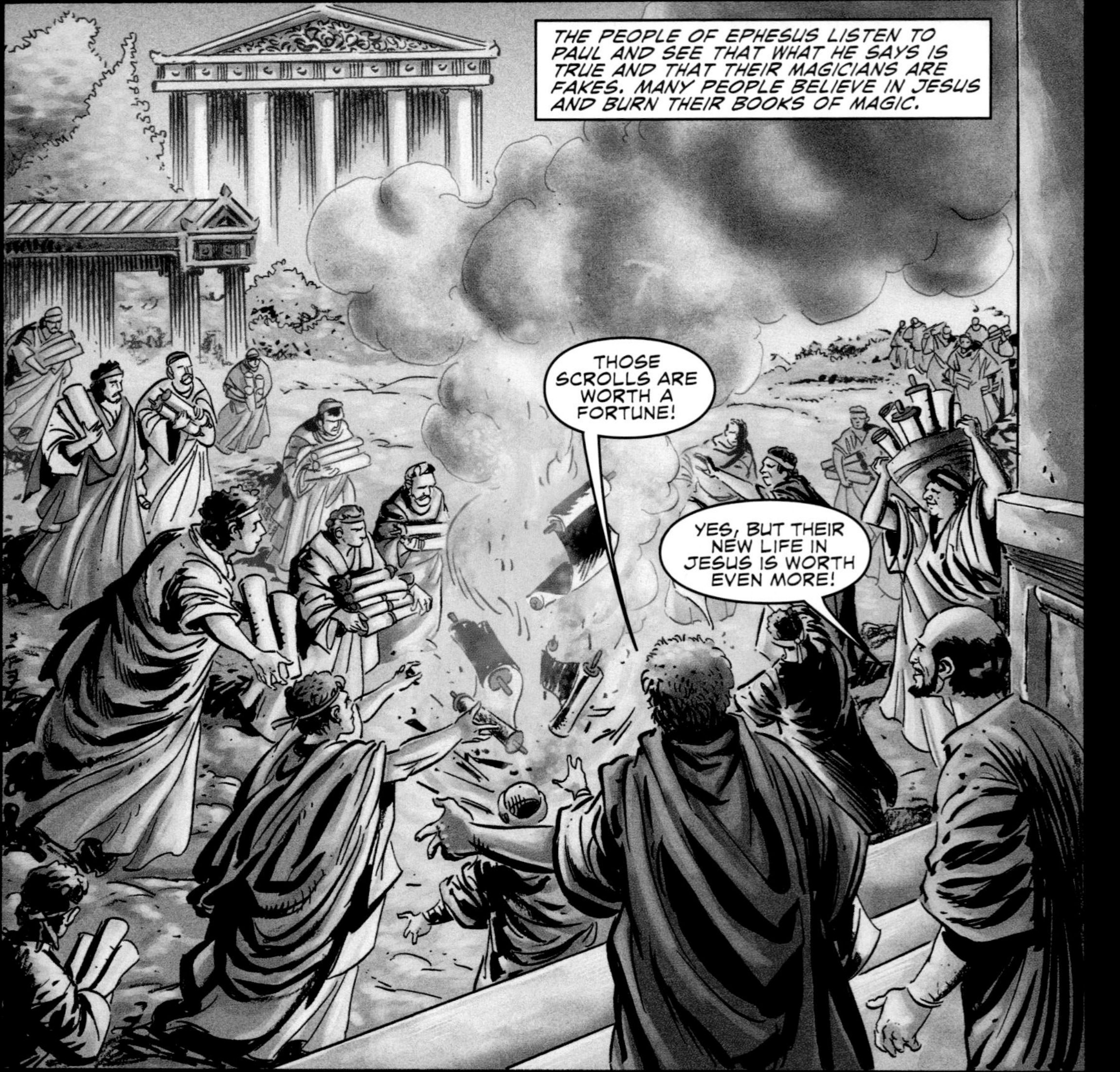
THE PEOPLE OF EPHESUS LISTEN TO PAUL AND SEE THAT WHAT HE SAYS IS TRUE AND THAT THEIR MAGICIANS ARE FAKES. MANY PEOPLE BELIEVE IN JESUS AND BURN THEIR BOOKS OF MAGIC.
THOSE SCROLLS ARE WORTH A FORTUNE!
YES, BUT THEIR NEW LIFE IN JESUS IS WORTH EVEN MORE!

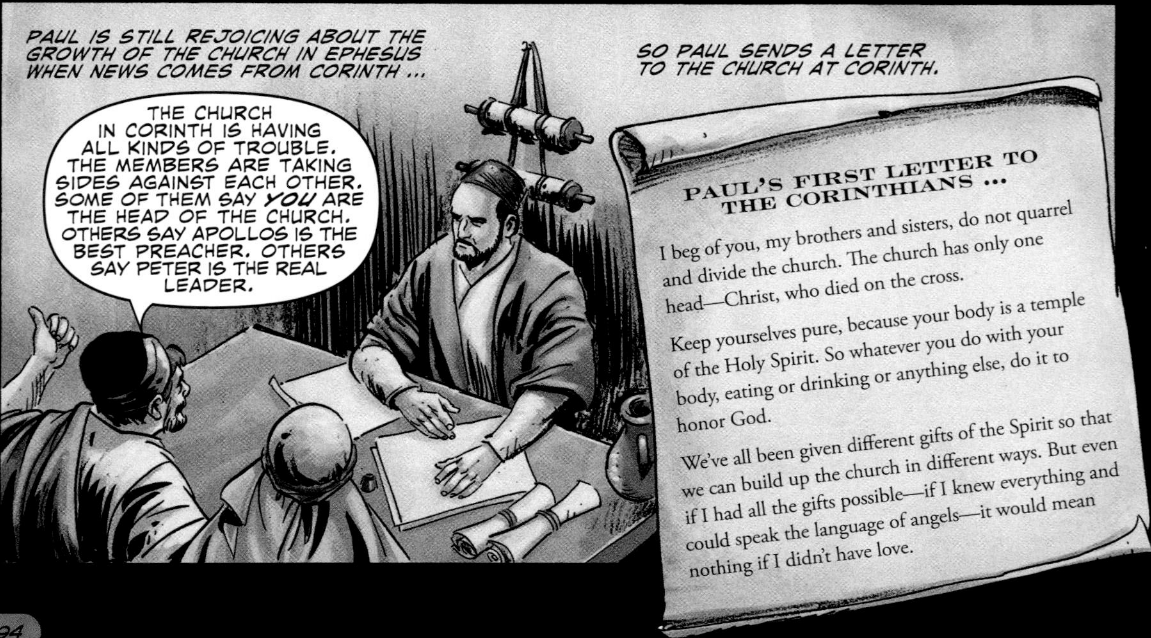
PAUL IS STILL REJOICING ABOUT THE GROWTH OF THE CHURCH IN EPHESUS WHEN NEWS COMES FROM CORINTH ...
THE CHURCH IN CORINTH IS HAVING ALL KINDS OF TROUBLE. THE MEMBERS ARE TAKING SIDES AGAINST EACH OTHER. SOME OF THEM SAY *YOU* ARE THE HEAD OF THE CHURCH. OTHERS SAY APOLLOS IS THE BEST PREACHER. OTHERS SAY PETER IS THE REAL LEADER.
SO PAUL SENDS A LETTER TO THE CHURCH AT CORINTH.
PAUL'S FIRST LETTER TO THE CORINTHIANS ...
I beg of you, my brothers and sisters, do not quarrel and divide the church. The church has only one head—Christ, who died on the cross.
Keep yourselves pure, because your body is a temple of the Holy Spirit. So whatever you do with your body, eating or drinking or anything else, do it to honor God.
We've all been given different gifts of the Spirit so that we can build up the church in different ways. But even if I had all the gifts possible—if I knew everything and could speak the language of angels—it would mean nothing if I didn't have love.

Ephesian Mob

BASED ON ACTS 19:23—20:5; 2 CORINTHIANS

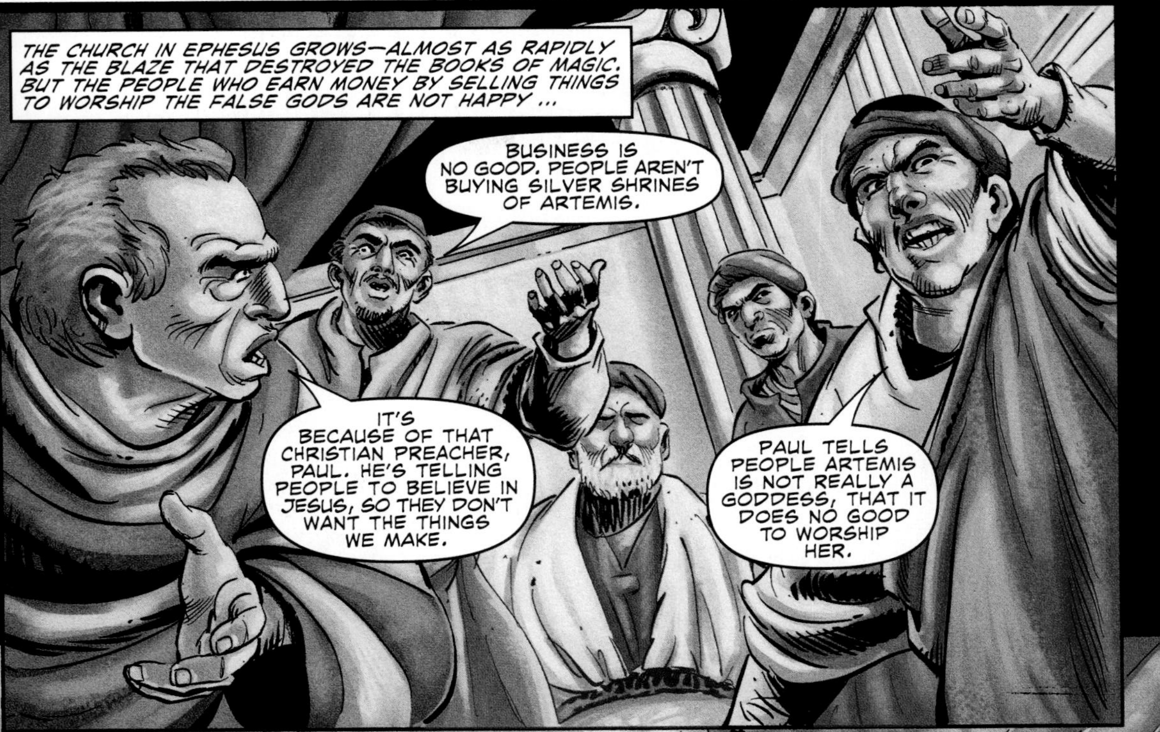
THE CHURCH IN EPHESUS GROWS—ALMOST AS RAPIDLY AS THE BLAZE THAT DESTROYED THE BOOKS OF MAGIC. BUT THE PEOPLE WHO EARN MONEY BY SELLING THINGS TO WORSHIP THE FALSE GODS ARE NOT HAPPY ...
BUSINESS IS NO GOOD. PEOPLE AREN'T BUYING SILVER SHRINES OF ARTEMIS.
IT'S BECAUSE OF THAT CHRISTIAN PREACHER, PAUL. HE'S TELLING PEOPLE TO BELIEVE IN JESUS, SO THEY DON'T WANT THE THINGS WE MAKE.
PAUL TELLS PEOPLE ARTEMIS IS NOT REALLY A GODDESS, THAT IT DOES NO GOOD TO WORSHIP HER.

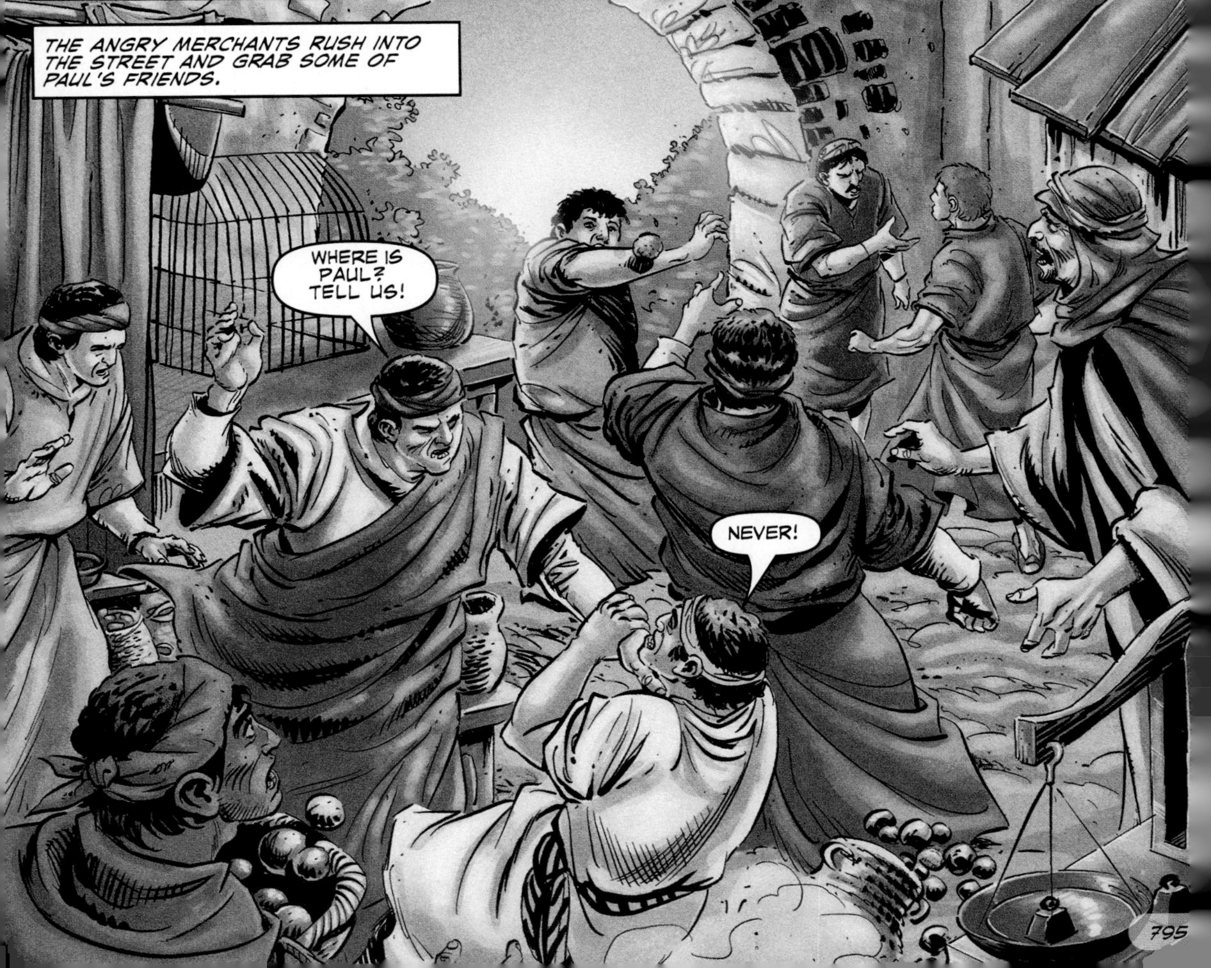
THE ANGRY MERCHANTS RUSH INTO THE STREET AND GRAB SOME OF PAUL'S FRIENDS.
WHERE IS PAUL? TELL US!
NEVER!

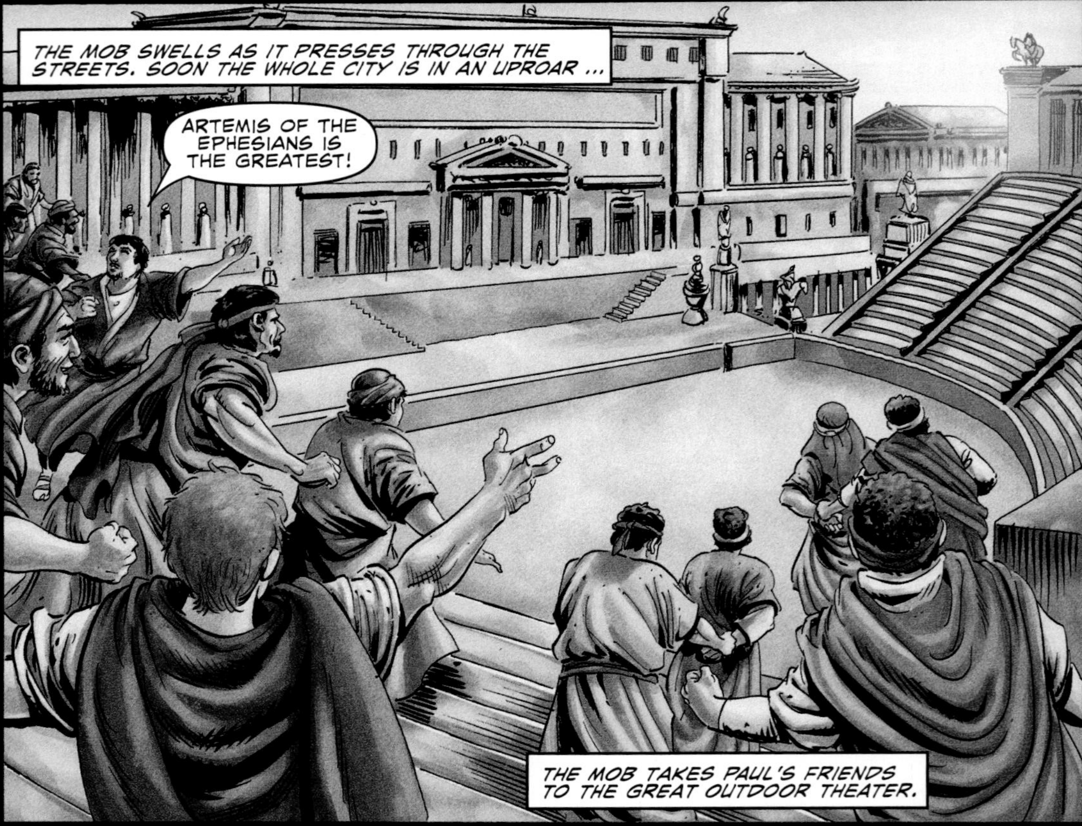
THE MOB SWELLS AS IT PRESSES THROUGH THE STREETS. SOON THE WHOLE CITY IS IN AN UPROAR ...
ARTEMIS OF THE EPHESIANS IS THE GREATEST!
THE MOB TAKES PAUL'S FRIENDS TO THE GREAT OUTDOOR THEATER.

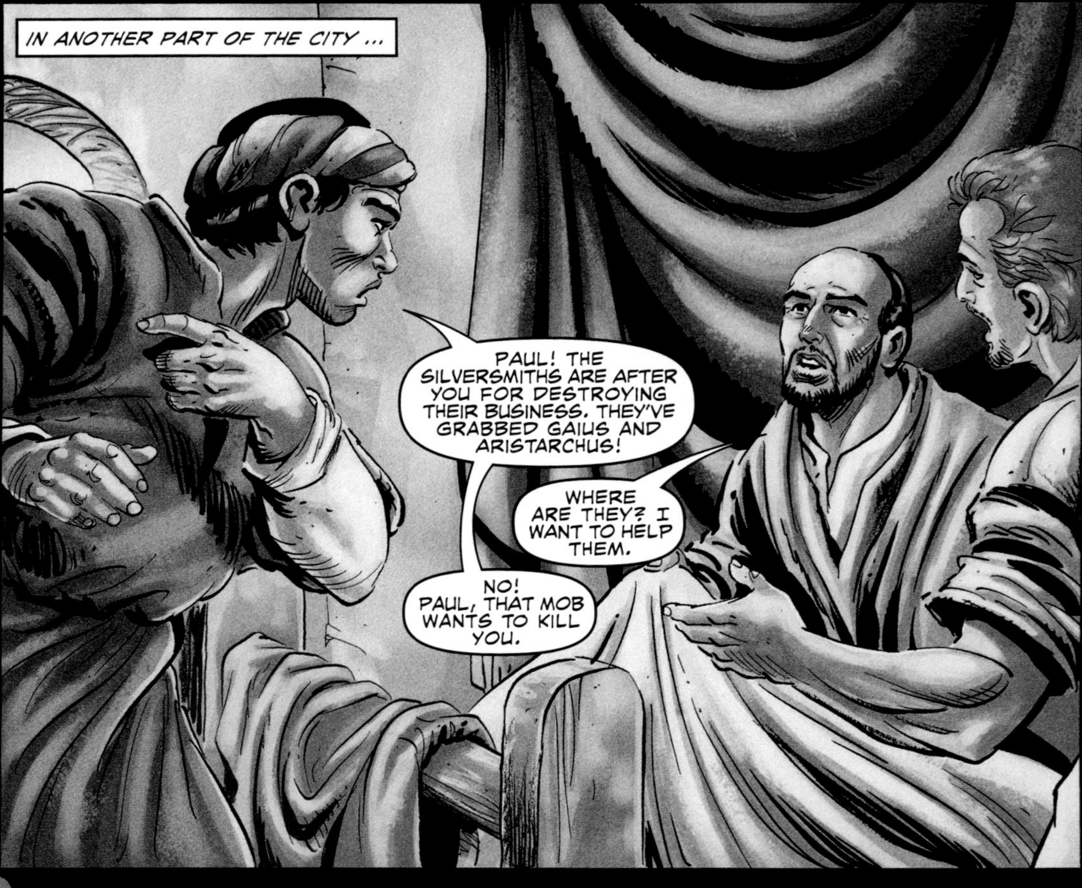
IN ANOTHER PART OF THE CITY ...
PAUL! THE SILVERSMITHS ARE AFTER YOU FOR DESTROYING THEIR BUSINESS. THEY'VE GRABBED GAIUS AND ARISTARCHUS!
WHERE ARE THEY? I WANT TO HELP THEM.
NO! PAUL, THAT MOB WANTS TO KILL YOU.

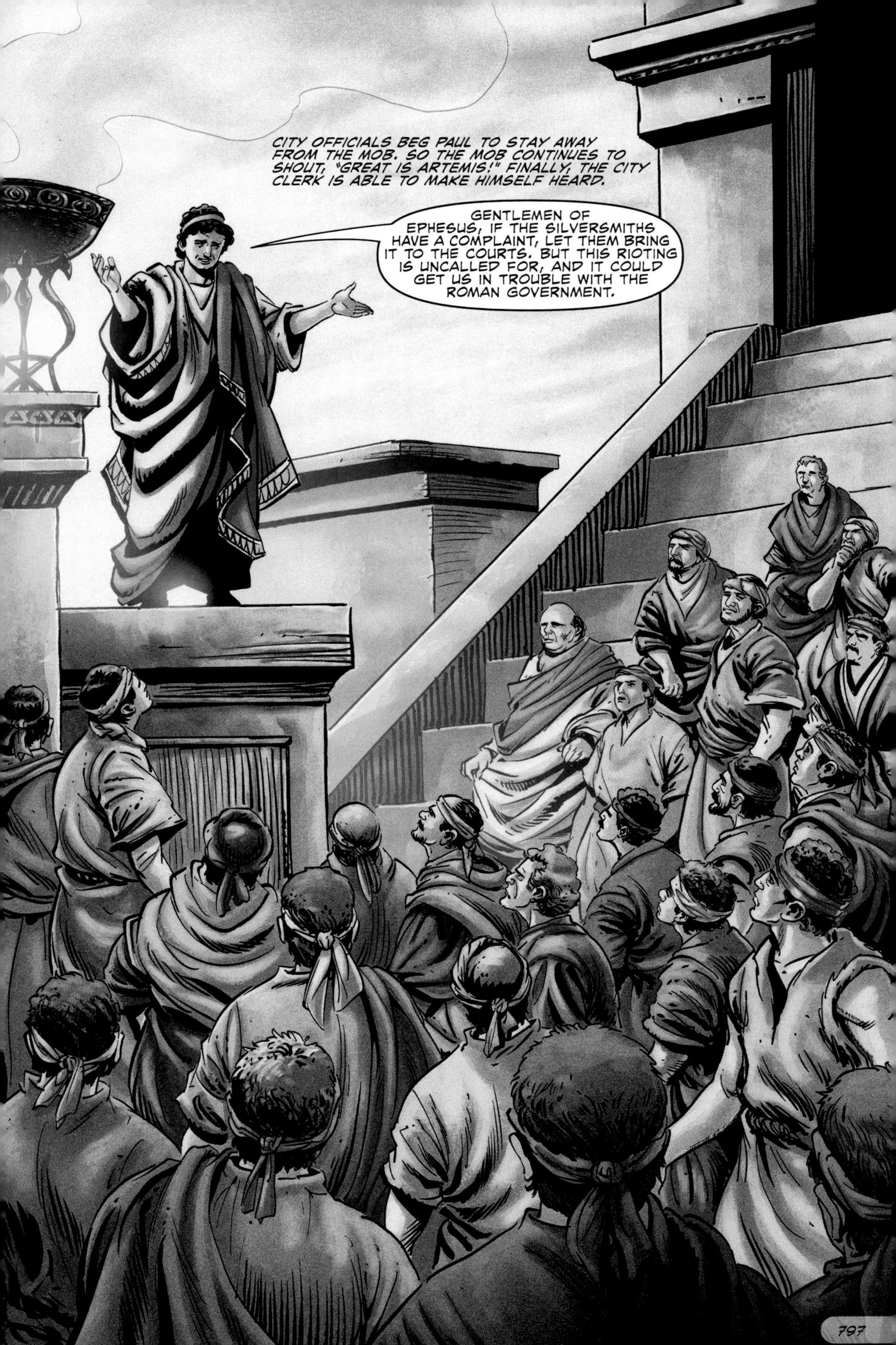
CITY OFFICIALS BEG PAUL TO STAY AWAY FROM THE MOB. SO THE MOB CONTINUES TO SHOUT, "GREAT IS ARTEMIS!" FINALLY, THE CITY CLERK IS ABLE TO MAKE HIMSELF HEARD.
GENTLEMEN OF EPHESUS, IF THE SILVERSMITHS HAVE A COMPLAINT, LET THEM BRING IT TO THE COURTS. BUT THIS RIOTING IS UNCALLED FOR, AND IT COULD GET US IN TROUBLE WITH THE ROMAN GOVERNMENT.

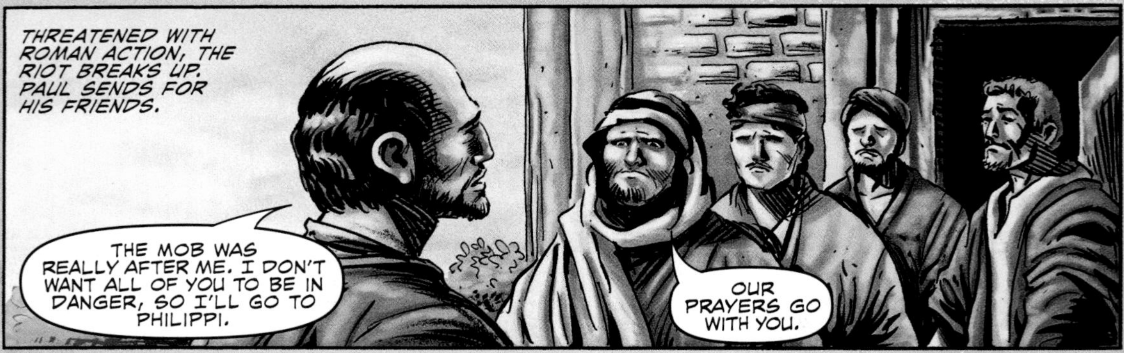
THREATENED WITH ROMAN ACTION, THE RIOT BREAKS UP. PAUL SENDS FOR HIS FRIENDS.
THE MOB WAS REALLY AFTER ME. I DON'T WANT ALL OF YOU TO BE IN DANGER, SO I'LL GO TO PHILIPPI.
OUR PRAYERS GO WITH YOU.

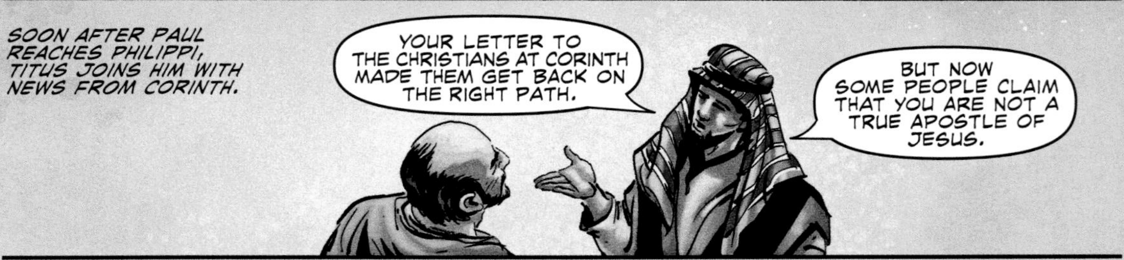
SOON AFTER PAUL REACHES PHILIPPI, TITUS JOINS HIM WITH NEWS FROM CORINTH.
YOUR LETTER TO THE CHRISTIANS AT CORINTH MADE THEM GET BACK ON THE RIGHT PATH.
BUT NOW SOME PEOPLE CLAIM THAT YOU ARE NOT A TRUE APOSTLE OF JESUS.

ONCE AGAIN PAUL WRITES TO THE CHURCH IN CORINTH ...

PAUL'S SECOND LETTER TO THE CORINTHIANS ...

I can see that my first letter upset you, but I am glad I sent it. I don't want to hurt you but to help you grow in your faith. I know that many of you are suffering, but take comfort: though we share Christ's pain, He also floods us with his comfort.

So don't lose heart! Our troubles only last for a moment, but they earn us eternal life. And life in heaven will quickly make us forget our earthly hardships. So don't focus on the things you can see—those things are temporary. It is the unseen things that are eternal.

For those who question my authority, remember this: I have been imprisoned and beaten; I have faced down death; I've been stoned and shipwrecked. And I've endured all that to carry out the work of Christ.

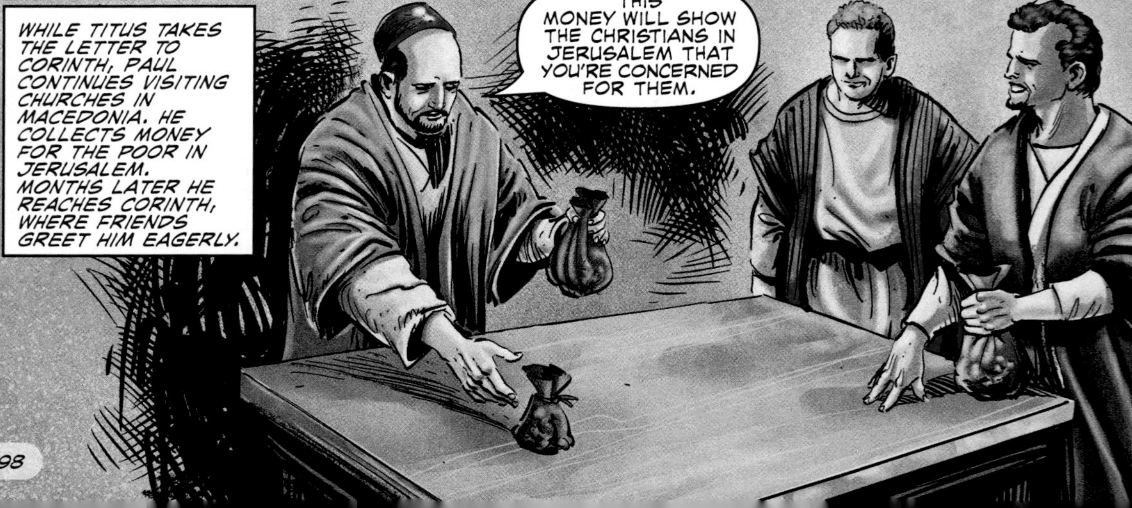
WHILE TITUS TAKES THE LETTER TO CORINTH, PAUL CONTINUES VISITING CHURCHES IN MACEDONIA. HE COLLECTS MONEY FOR THE POOR IN JERUSALEM. MONTHS LATER HE REACHES CORINTH, WHERE FRIENDS GREET HIM EAGERLY.
THIS MONEY WILL SHOW THE CHRISTIANS IN JERUSALEM THAT YOU'RE CONCERNED FOR THEM.

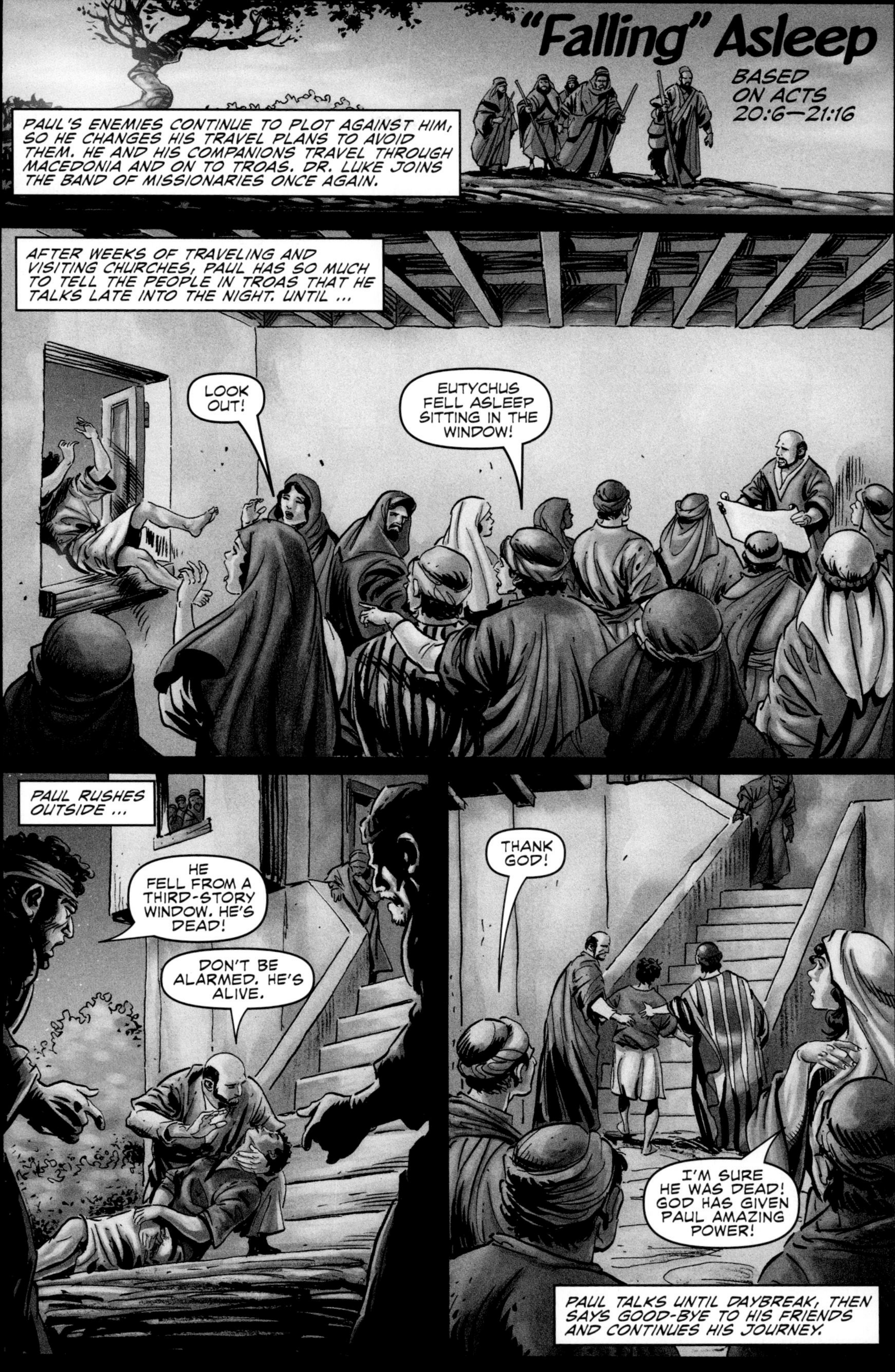
"Falling" Asleep
BASED ON ACTS 20:6—21:16
PAUL'S ENEMIES CONTINUE TO PLOT AGAINST HIM, SO HE CHANGES HIS TRAVEL PLANS TO AVOID THEM. HE AND HIS COMPANIONS TRAVEL THROUGH MACEDONIA AND ON TO TROAS. DR. LUKE JOINS THE BAND OF MISSIONARIES ONCE AGAIN.
AFTER WEEKS OF TRAVELING AND VISITING CHURCHES, PAUL HAS SO MUCH TO TELL THE PEOPLE IN TROAS THAT HE TALKS LATE INTO THE NIGHT. UNTIL ...
LOOK OUT!
EUTYCHUS FELL ASLEEP SITTING IN THE WINDOW!
PAUL RUSHES OUTSIDE ...
HE FELL FROM A THIRD-STORY WINDOW. HE'S DEAD!
DON'T BE ALARMED. HE'S ALIVE.
THANK GOD!
I'M SURE HE WAS DEAD! GOD HAS GIVEN PAUL AMAZING POWER!
PAUL TALKS UNTIL DAYBREAK, THEN SAYS GOOD-BYE TO HIS FRIENDS AND CONTINUES HIS JOURNEY.

AT MILETUS, PAUL SENDS WORD FOR THE ELDERS OF EPHESUS TO MEET WITH HIM. EAGERLY, THEY TRAVEL THE 35 MILES TO SEE PAUL AGAIN.

I AM GOING TO JERUSALEM, EVEN THOUGH IT IS DANGEROUS. MY LIFE MEANS NOTHING TO ME, SO LONG AS I FINISH THE WORK JESUS GAVE ME TO DO. SINCE I WON'T SEE ANY OF YOU AGAIN, REMEMBER WHAT I'VE SHOWN YOU: WORK HARD AND HELP THE WEAK. AS JESUS SAID, "IT IS BETTER TO GIVE THAN TO RECEIVE."

PAUL GOES ON TO TYRE, WHERE HE PREACHES FOR A WEEK. WHEN HE LEAVES, THE CHRISTIANS FOLLOW HIM TO THE BEACH FOR A PRAYERFUL GOOD-BYE.

DON'T GO TO JERUSALEM! IT'S TOO DANGEROUS. YOUR ENEMIES ARE WAITING TO KILL YOU BECAUSE YOU SAY JESUS IS THE SON OF GOD.

I MUST GO. I HAVE MONEY THAT THE GENTILE CHRISTIANS HAVE GIVEN FOR THE POOR IN JERUSALEM. I'M NOT AFRAID.

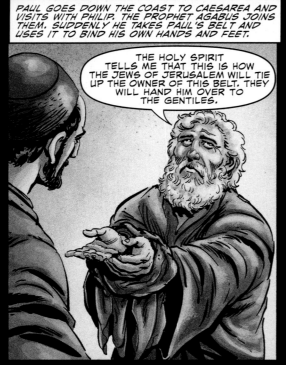

PAUL GOES DOWN THE COAST TO CAESAREA AND VISITS WITH PHILIP. THE PROPHET AGABUS JOINS THEM. SUDDENLY HE TAKES PAUL'S BELT AND USES IT TO BIND HIS OWN HANDS AND FEET.

THE HOLY SPIRIT TELLS ME THAT THIS IS HOW THE JEWS OF JERUSALEM WILL TIE UP THE OWNER OF THIS BELT. THEY WILL HAND HIM OVER TO THE GENTILES.

PAUL, CHANGE YOUR PLANS! DON'T GO TO JERUSALEM.

WHY ARE YOU CRYING? I'M READY TO GO TO PRISON. I'M EVEN READY TO DIE FOR JESUS.

Under Arrest

BASED ON ACTS 21:15—23:24

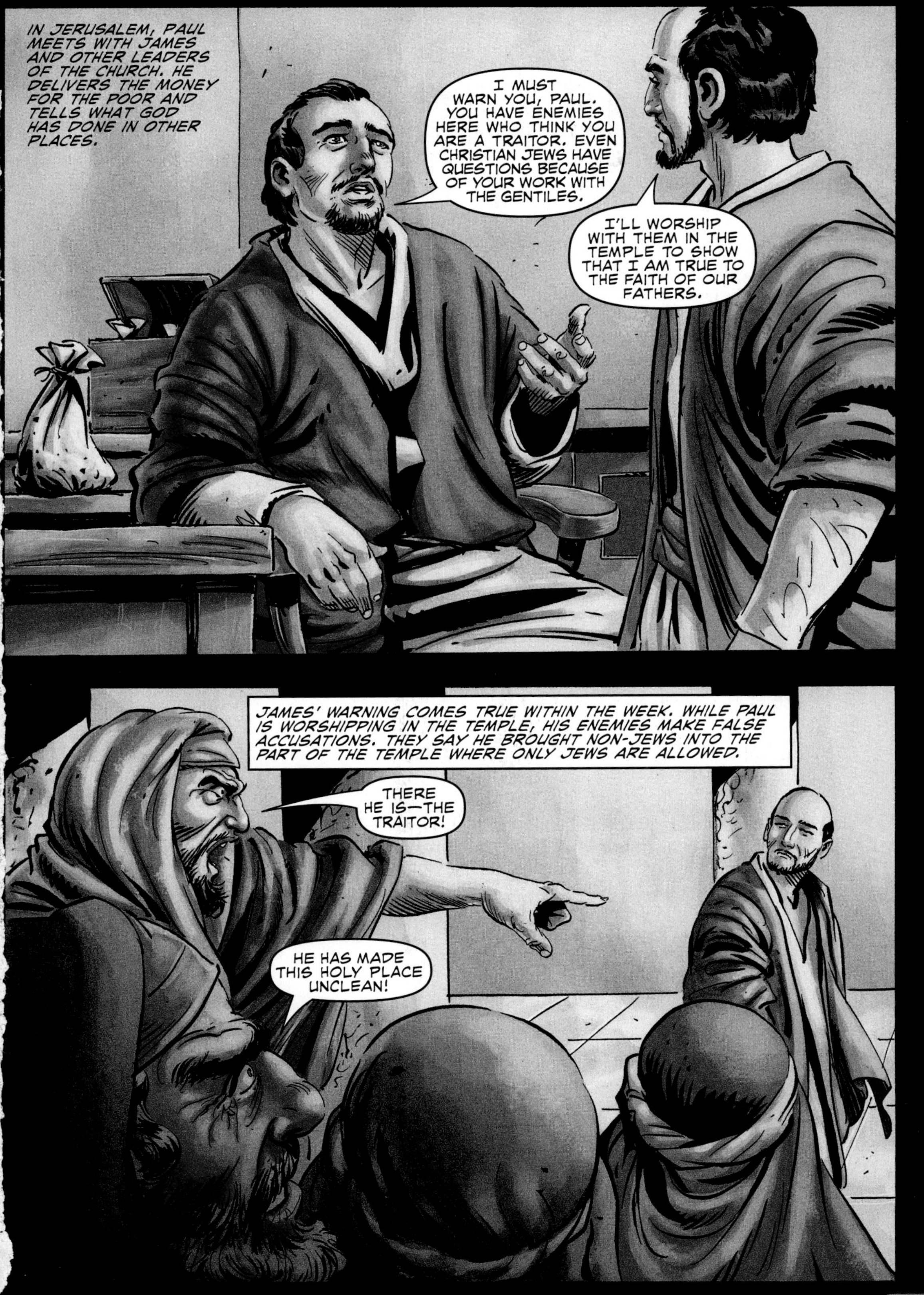

IN JERUSALEM, PAUL MEETS WITH JAMES AND OTHER LEADERS OF THE CHURCH. HE DELIVERS THE MONEY FOR THE POOR AND TELLS WHAT GOD HAS DONE IN OTHER PLACES.
I MUST WARN YOU, PAUL. YOU HAVE ENEMIES HERE WHO THINK YOU ARE A TRAITOR. EVEN CHRISTIAN JEWS HAVE QUESTIONS BECAUSE OF YOUR WORK WITH THE GENTILES.
I'LL WORSHIP WITH THEM IN THE TEMPLE TO SHOW THAT I AM TRUE TO THE FAITH OF OUR FATHERS.
JAMES' WARNING COMES TRUE WITHIN THE WEEK. WHILE PAUL IS WORSHIPPING IN THE TEMPLE, HIS ENEMIES MAKE FALSE ACCUSATIONS. THEY SAY HE BROUGHT NON-JEWS INTO THE PART OF THE TEMPLE WHERE ONLY JEWS ARE ALLOWED.
THERE HE IS—THE TRAITOR!
HE HAS MADE THIS HOLY PLACE UNCLEAN!

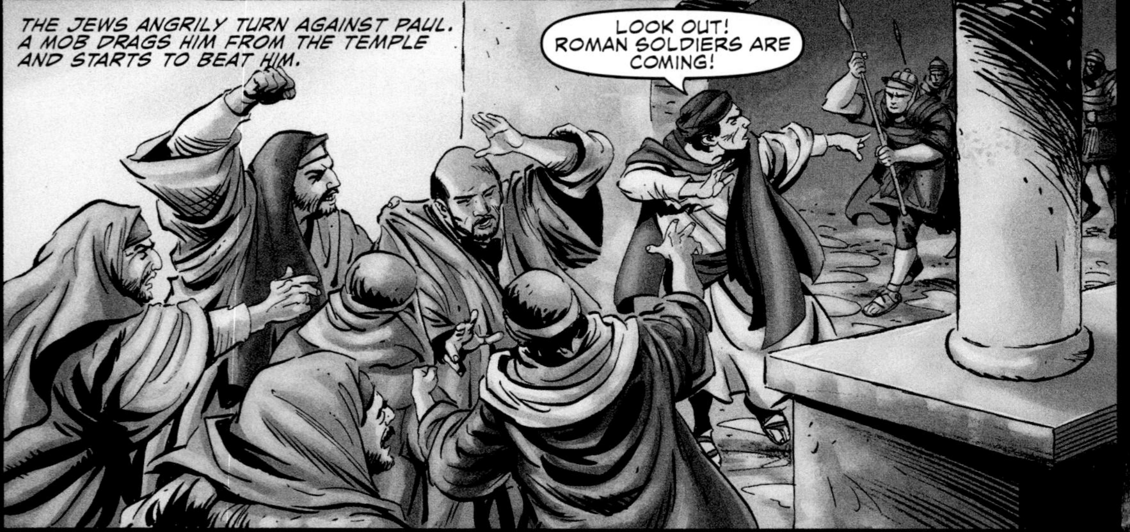
THE JEWS ANGRILY TURN AGAINST PAUL. A MOB DRAGS HIM FROM THE TEMPLE AND STARTS TO BEAT HIM.
LOOK OUT! ROMAN SOLDIERS ARE COMING!

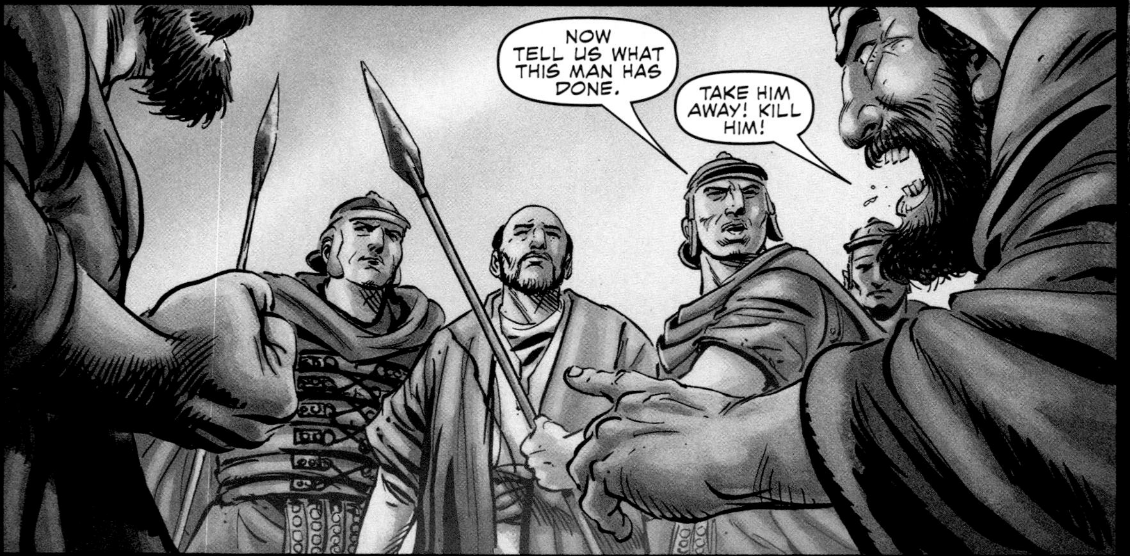
NOW TELL US WHAT THIS MAN HAS DONE.
TAKE HIM AWAY! KILL HIM!

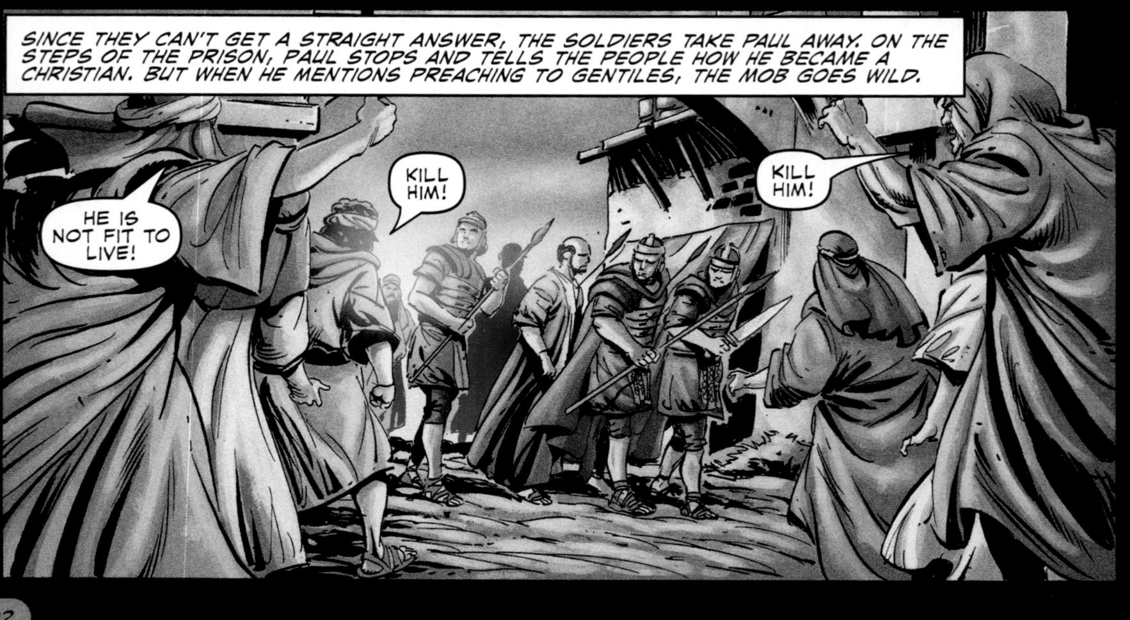
SINCE THEY CAN'T GET A STRAIGHT ANSWER, THE SOLDIERS TAKE PAUL AWAY. ON THE STEPS OF THE PRISON, PAUL STOPS AND TELLS THE PEOPLE HOW HE BECAME A CHRISTIAN. BUT WHEN HE MENTIONS PREACHING TO GENTILES, THE MOB GOES WILD.
HE IS NOT FIT TO LIVE!
KILL HIM!
KILL HIM!

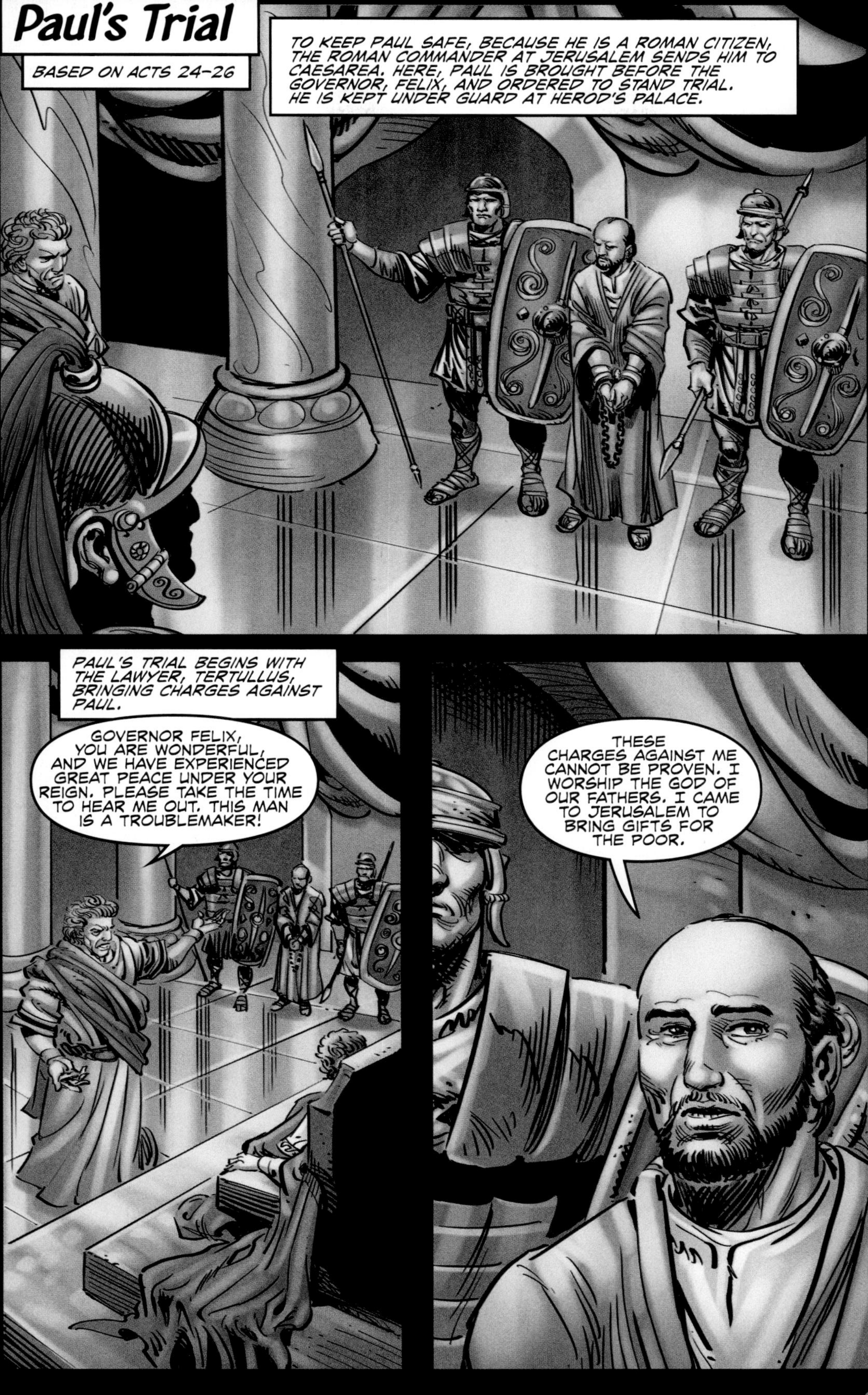
Paul's Trial
BASED ON ACTS 24–26
TO KEEP PAUL SAFE, BECAUSE HE IS A ROMAN CITIZEN, THE ROMAN COMMANDER AT JERUSALEM SENDS HIM TO CAESAREA. HERE, PAUL IS BROUGHT BEFORE THE GOVERNOR, FELIX, AND ORDERED TO STAND TRIAL. HE IS KEPT UNDER GUARD AT HEROD'S PALACE.
PAUL'S TRIAL BEGINS WITH THE LAWYER, TERTULLUS, BRINGING CHARGES AGAINST PAUL.
GOVERNOR FELIX, YOU ARE WONDERFUL, AND WE HAVE EXPERIENCED GREAT PEACE UNDER YOUR REIGN. PLEASE TAKE THE TIME TO HEAR ME OUT. THIS MAN IS A TROUBLEMAKER!
THESE CHARGES AGAINST ME CANNOT BE PROVEN. I WORSHIP THE GOD OF OUR FATHERS. I CAME TO JERUSALEM TO BRING GIFTS FOR THE POOR.

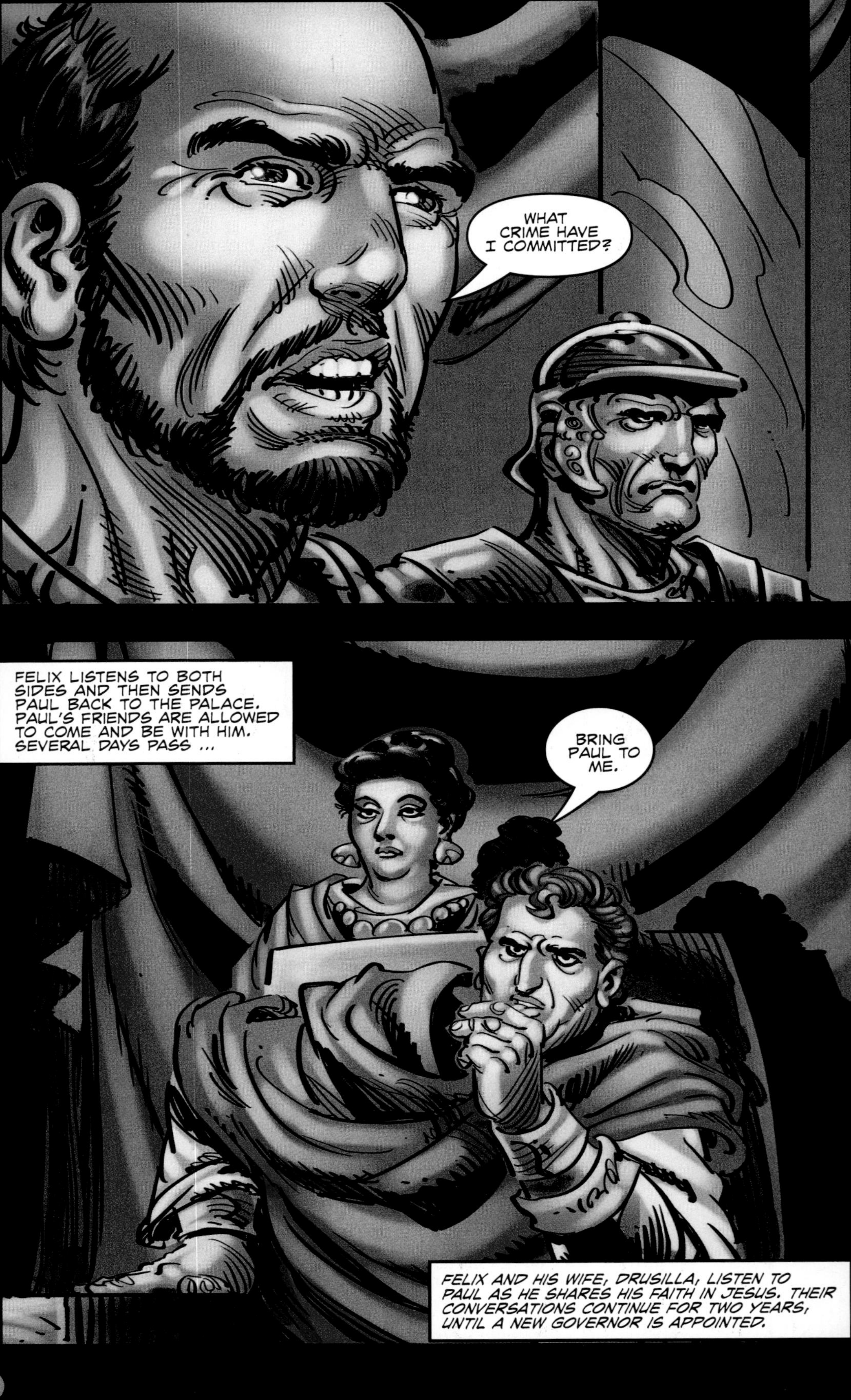
WHAT CRIME HAVE I COMMITTED?
FELIX LISTENS TO BOTH SIDES AND THEN SENDS PAUL BACK TO THE PALACE. PAUL'S FRIENDS ARE ALLOWED TO COME AND BE WITH HIM. SEVERAL DAYS PASS ...
BRING PAUL TO ME.
FELIX AND HIS WIFE, DRUSILLA, LISTEN TO PAUL AS HE SHARES HIS FAITH IN JESUS. THEIR CONVERSATIONS CONTINUE FOR TWO YEARS, UNTIL A NEW GOVERNOR IS APPOINTED.

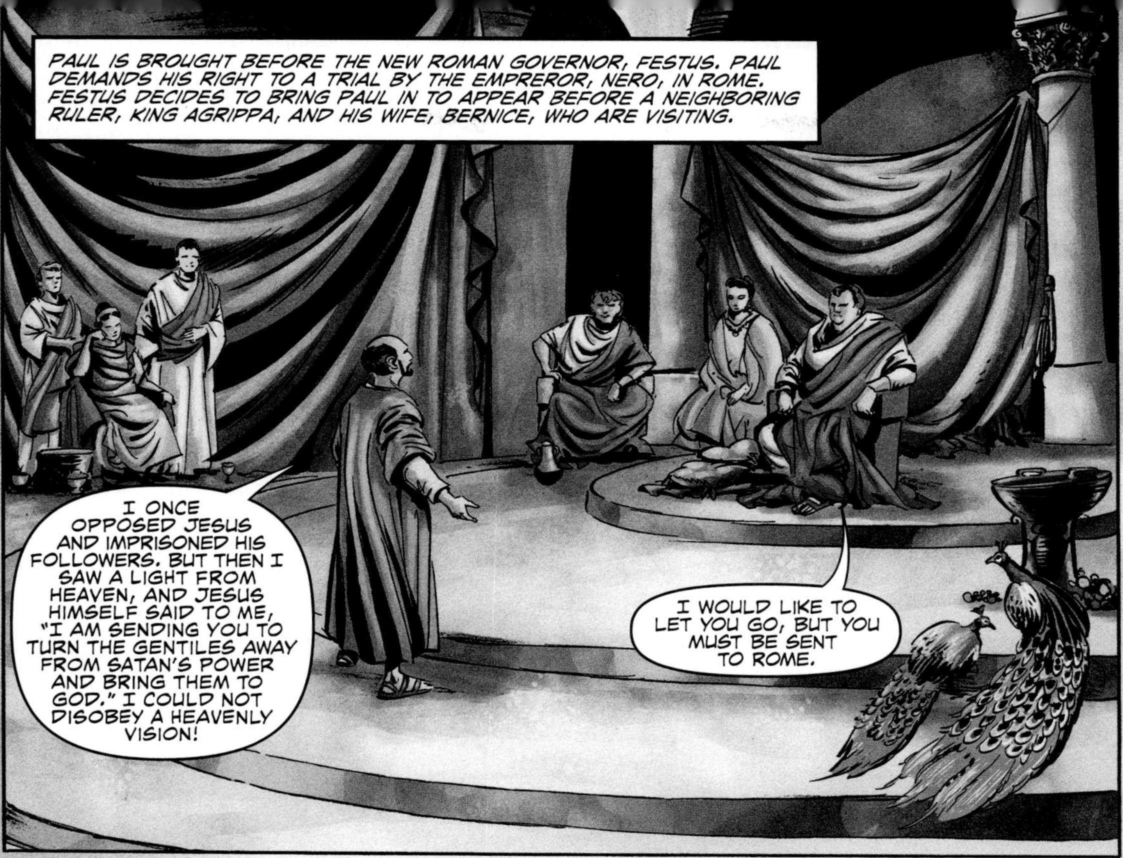
PAUL IS BROUGHT BEFORE THE NEW ROMAN GOVERNOR, FESTUS. PAUL DEMANDS HIS RIGHT TO A TRIAL BY THE EMPREROR, NERO, IN ROME. FESTUS DECIDES TO BRING PAUL IN TO APPEAR BEFORE A NEIGHBORING RULER, KING AGRIPPA, AND HIS WIFE, BERNICE, WHO ARE VISITING.
I ONCE OPPOSED JESUS AND IMPRISONED HIS FOLLOWERS. BUT THEN I SAW A LIGHT FROM HEAVEN, AND JESUS HIMSELF SAID TO ME, "I AM SENDING YOU TO TURN THE GENTILES AWAY FROM SATAN'S POWER AND BRING THEM TO GOD." I COULD NOT DISOBEY A HEAVENLY VISION!
I WOULD LIKE TO LET YOU GO, BUT YOU MUST BE SENT TO ROME.

Bound for Rome

BASED ON ACTS 27:1—28:16

UNDER ROMAN GUARD, PAUL BOARDS A SHIP HEADED TO ROME FOR HIS TRIAL. DR. LUKE GOES WITH HIM. THE SHIP SETS SAIL, ONLY TO BE STRUCK BY A VIOLENT GALE.

THE STORM RAGES DAY AFTER DAY. AFTER TWO WEEKS, THE SAILORS TRY TO DESERT THE SHIP.

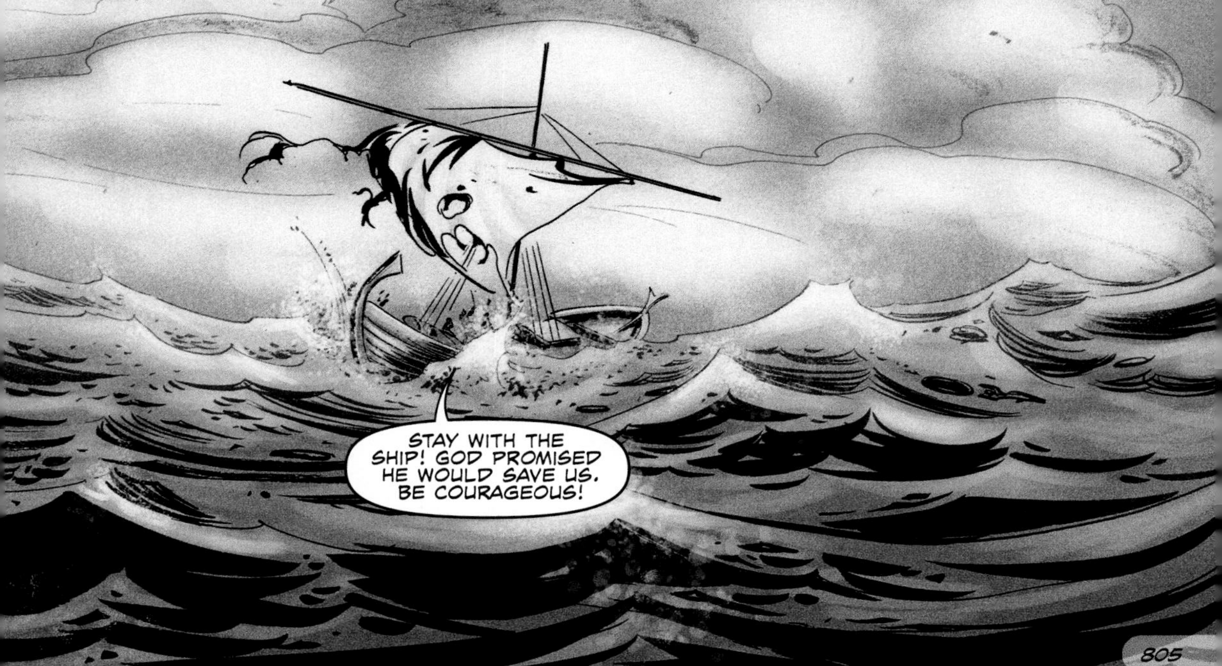
STAY WITH THE SHIP! GOD PROMISED HE WOULD SAVE US. BE COURAGEOUS!

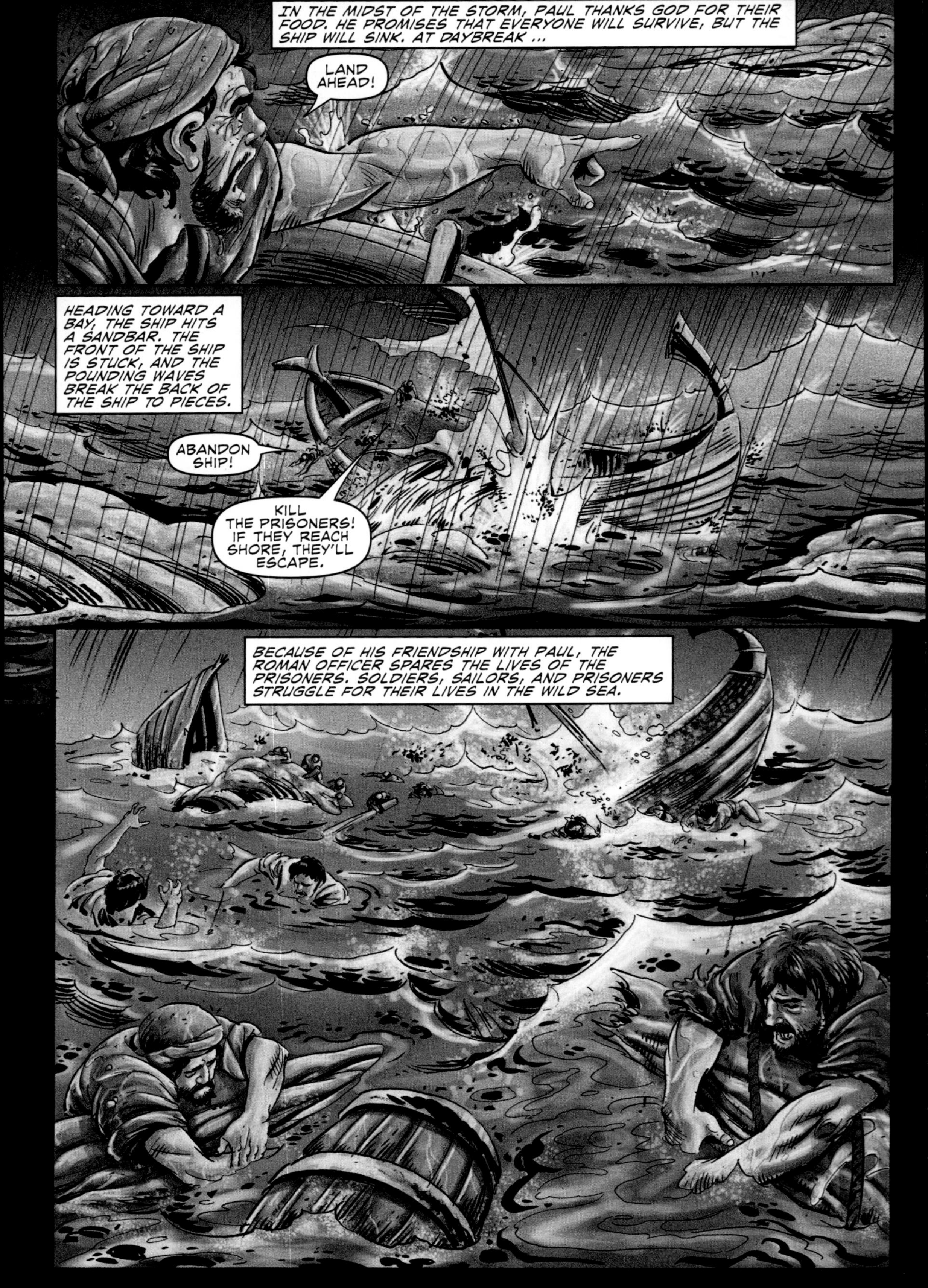
IN THE MIDST OF THE STORM, PAUL THANKS GOD FOR THEIR FOOD. HE PROMISES THAT EVERYONE WILL SURVIVE, BUT THE SHIP WILL SINK. AT DAYBREAK ...
LAND AHEAD!
HEADING TOWARD A BAY, THE SHIP HITS A SANDBAR. THE FRONT OF THE SHIP IS STUCK, AND THE POUNDING WAVES BREAK THE BACK OF THE SHIP TO PIECES.
ABANDON SHIP!
KILL THE PRISONERS! IF THEY REACH SHORE, THEY'LL ESCAPE.
BECAUSE OF HIS FRIENDSHIP WITH PAUL, THE ROMAN OFFICER SPARES THE LIVES OF THE PRISONERS. SOLDIERS, SAILORS, AND PRISONERS STRUGGLE FOR THEIR LIVES IN THE WILD SEA.

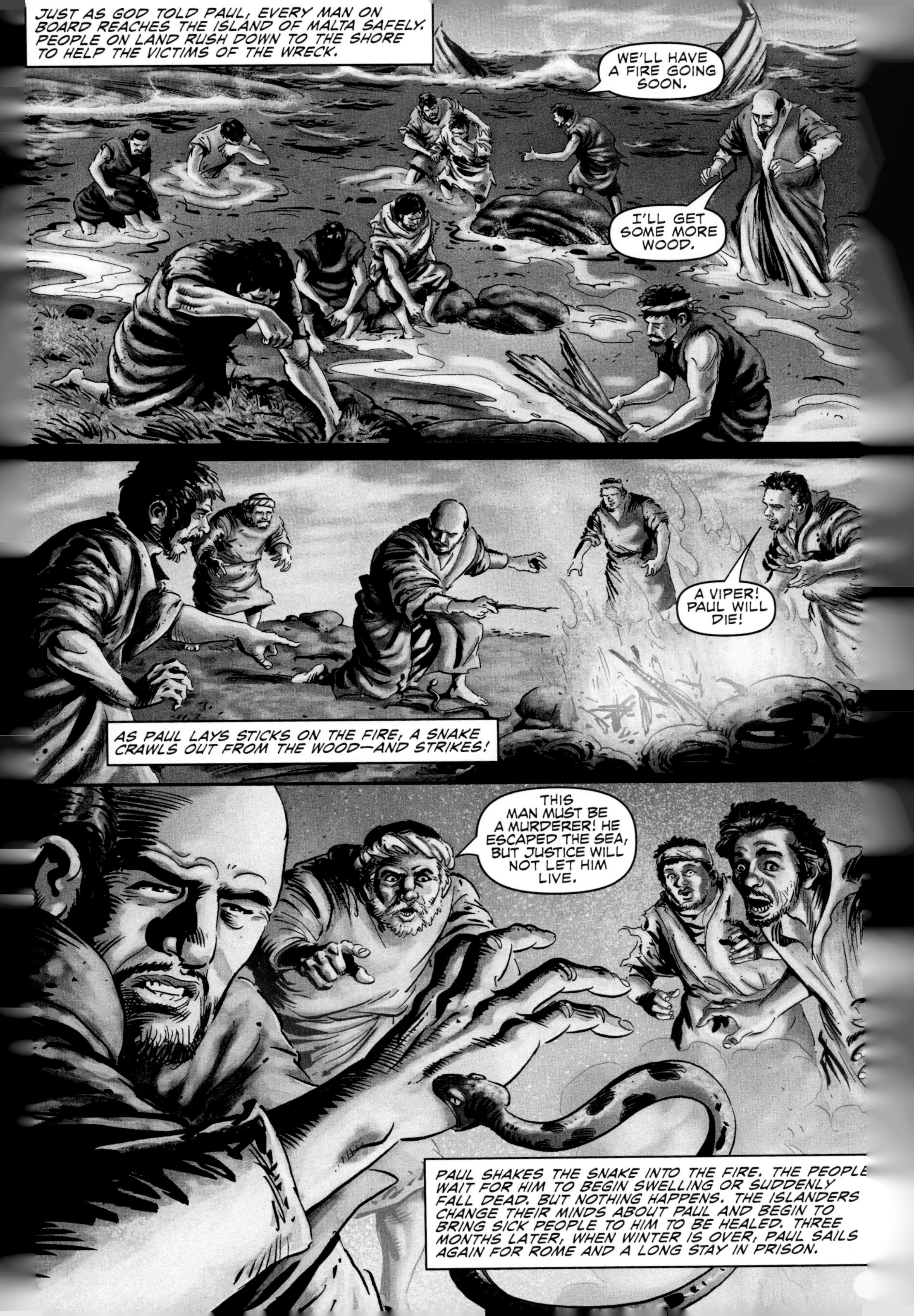
JUST AS GOD TOLD PAUL, EVERY MAN ON BOARD REACHES THE ISLAND OF MALTA SAFELY. PEOPLE ON LAND RUSH DOWN TO THE SHORE TO HELP THE VICTIMS OF THE WRECK.
WE'LL HAVE A FIRE GOING SOON.
I'LL GET SOME MORE WOOD.
A VIPER! PAUL WILL DIE!
AS PAUL LAYS STICKS ON THE FIRE, A SNAKE CRAWLS OUT FROM THE WOOD—AND STRIKES!
THIS MAN MUST BE A MURDERER! HE ESCAPED THE SEA, BUT JUSTICE WILL NOT LET HIM LIVE.
PAUL SHAKES THE SNAKE INTO THE FIRE. THE PEOPLE WAIT FOR HIM TO BEGIN SWELLING OR SUDDENLY FALL DEAD. BUT NOTHING HAPPENS. THE ISLANDERS CHANGE THEIR MINDS ABOUT PAUL AND BEGIN TO BRING SICK PEOPLE TO HIM TO BE HEALED. THREE MONTHS LATER, WHEN WINTER IS OVER, PAUL SAILS AGAIN FOR ROME AND A LONG STAY IN PRISON.

Prison Pen Pals

BASED ON EPHESIANS; PHILIPPIANS; COLOSSIANS; PHILEMON

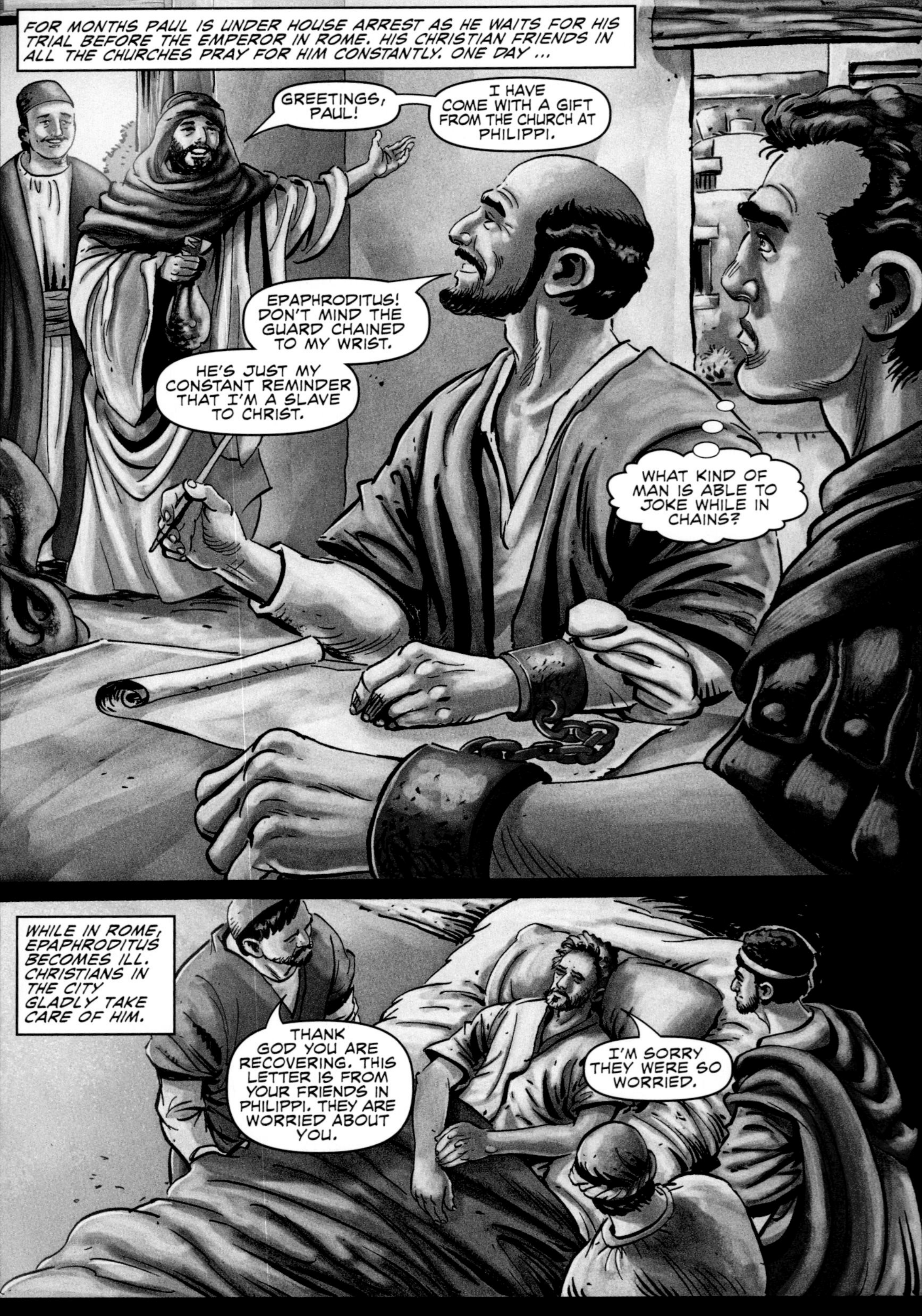
FOR MONTHS PAUL IS UNDER HOUSE ARREST AS HE WAITS FOR HIS TRIAL BEFORE THE EMPEROR IN ROME. HIS CHRISTIAN FRIENDS IN ALL THE CHURCHES PRAY FOR HIM CONSTANTLY. ONE DAY ...
GREETINGS, PAUL!
I HAVE COME WITH A GIFT FROM THE CHURCH AT PHILIPPI.
EPAPHRODITUS! DON'T MIND THE GUARD CHAINED TO MY WRIST.
HE'S JUST MY CONSTANT REMINDER THAT I'M A SLAVE TO CHRIST.
WHAT KIND OF MAN IS ABLE TO JOKE WHILE IN CHAINS?
WHILE IN ROME, EPAPHRODITUS BECOMES ILL. CHRISTIANS IN THE CITY GLADLY TAKE CARE OF HIM.
THANK GOD YOU ARE RECOVERING. THIS LETTER IS FROM YOUR FRIENDS IN PHILIPPI. THEY ARE WORRIED ABOUT YOU.
I'M SORRY THEY WERE SO WORRIED.

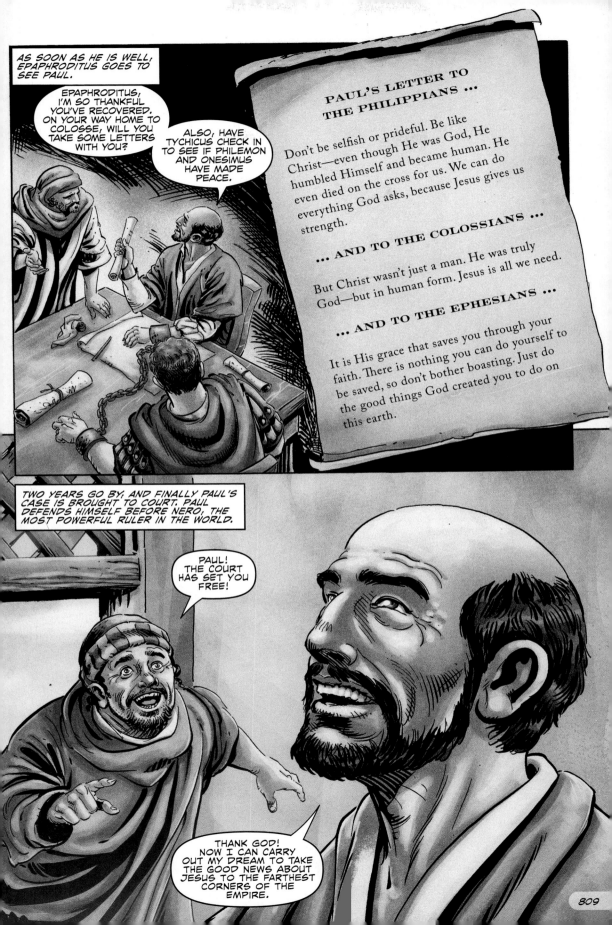

AS SOON AS HE IS WELL, EPAPHRODITUS GOES TO SEE PAUL.

EPAPHRODITUS, I'M SO THANKFUL YOU'VE RECOVERED. ON YOUR WAY HOME TO COLOSSE, WILL YOU TAKE SOME LETTERS WITH YOU?

ALSO, HAVE TYCHICUS CHECK IN TO SEE IF PHILEMON AND ONESIMUS HAVE MADE PEACE.

PAUL'S LETTER TO THE PHILIPPIANS ...

Don't be selfish or prideful. Be like Christ—even though He was God, He humbled Himself and became human. He even died on the cross for us. We can do everything God asks, because Jesus gives us strength.

... AND TO THE COLOSSIANS ...

But Christ wasn't just a man. He was truly God—but in human form. Jesus is all we need.

... AND TO THE EPHESIANS ...

It is His grace that saves you through your faith. There is nothing you can do yourself to be saved, so don't bother boasting. Just do the good things God created you to do on this earth.

TWO YEARS GO BY, AND FINALLY PAUL'S CASE IS BROUGHT TO COURT. PAUL DEFENDS HIMSELF BEFORE NERO, THE MOST POWERFUL RULER IN THE WORLD.

PAUL! THE COURT HAS SET YOU FREE!

THANK GOD! NOW I CAN CARRY OUT MY DREAM TO TAKE THE GOOD NEWS ABOUT JESUS TO THE FARTHEST CORNERS OF THE EMPIRE.

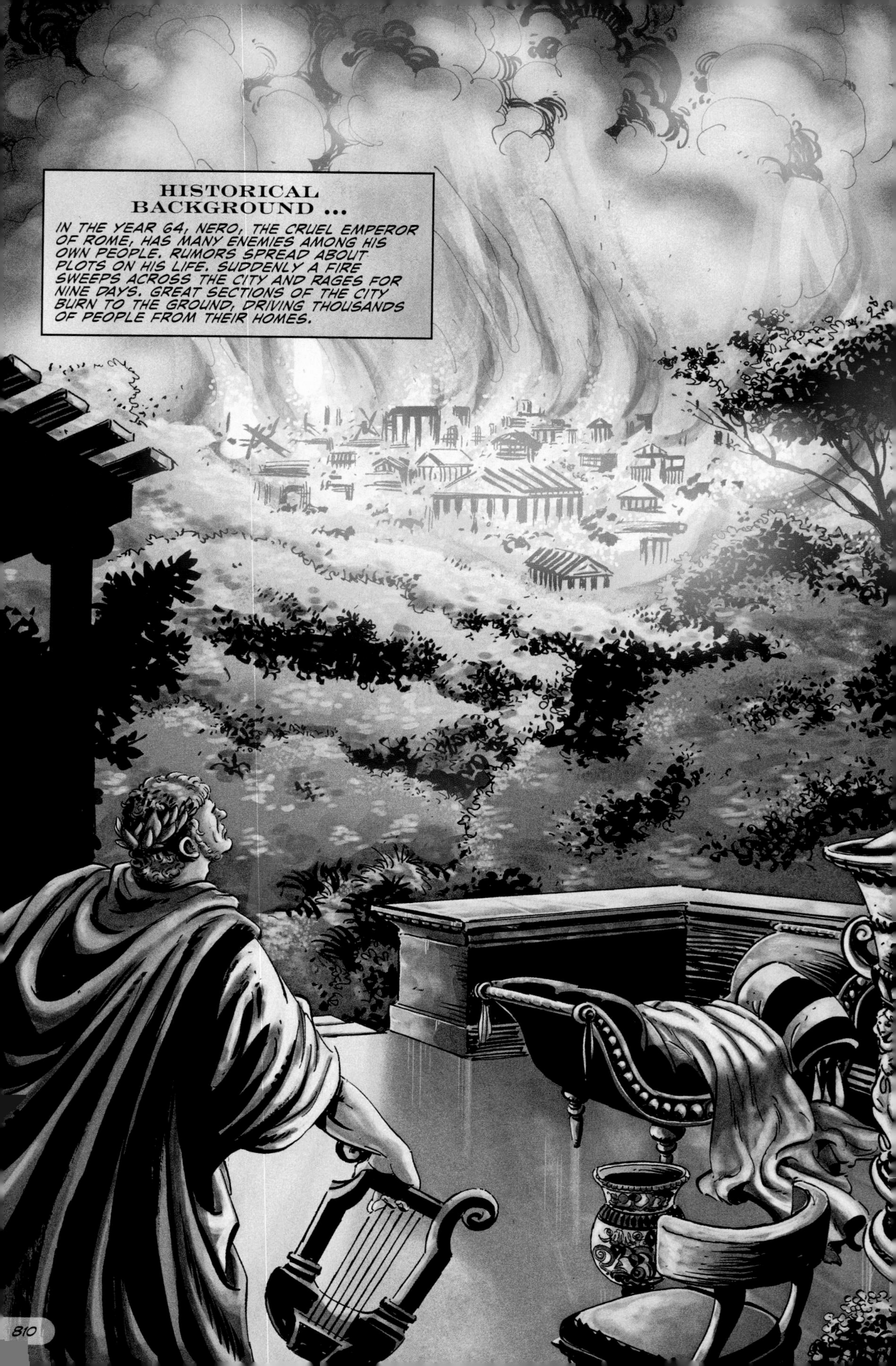
HISTORICAL BACKGROUND ...
IN THE YEAR 64, NERO, THE CRUEL EMPEROR OF ROME, HAS MANY ENEMIES AMONG HIS OWN PEOPLE. RUMORS SPREAD ABOUT PLOTS ON HIS LIFE. SUDDENLY A FIRE SWEEPS ACROSS THE CITY AND RAGES FOR NINE DAYS. GREAT SECTIONS OF THE CITY BURN TO THE GROUND, DRIVING THOUSANDS OF PEOPLE FROM THEIR HOMES.

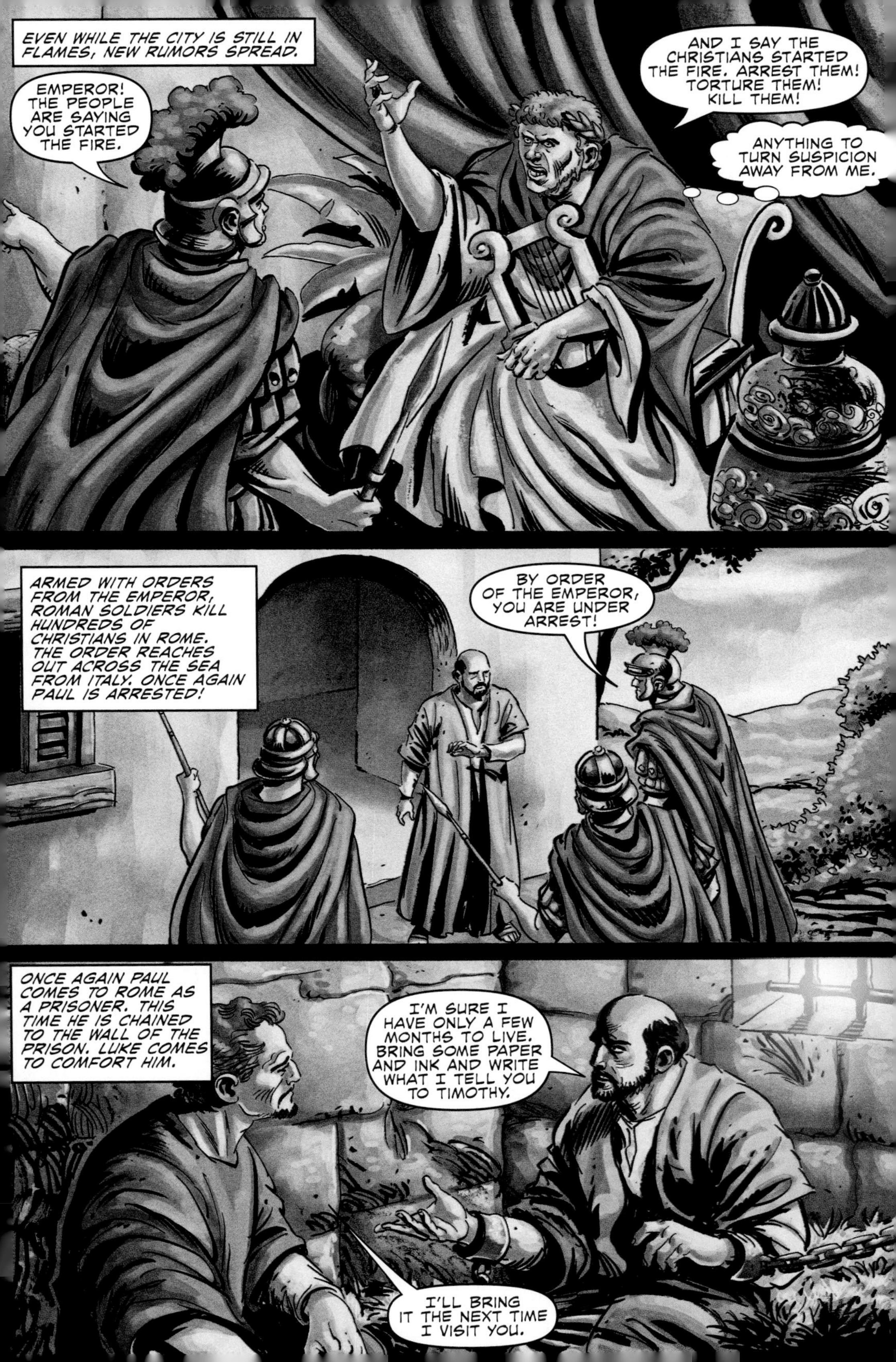
EVEN WHILE THE CITY IS STILL IN FLAMES, NEW RUMORS SPREAD.
EMPEROR! THE PEOPLE ARE SAYING YOU STARTED THE FIRE.
AND I SAY THE CHRISTIANS STARTED THE FIRE. ARREST THEM! TORTURE THEM! KILL THEM!
ANYTHING TO TURN SUSPICION AWAY FROM ME.
ARMED WITH ORDERS FROM THE EMPEROR, ROMAN SOLDIERS KILL HUNDREDS OF CHRISTIANS IN ROME. THE ORDER REACHES OUT ACROSS THE SEA FROM ITALY. ONCE AGAIN PAUL IS ARRESTED!
BY ORDER OF THE EMPEROR, YOU ARE UNDER ARREST!
ONCE AGAIN PAUL COMES TO ROME AS A PRISONER. THIS TIME HE IS CHAINED TO THE WALL OF THE PRISON. LUKE COMES TO COMFORT HIM.
I'M SURE I HAVE ONLY A FEW MONTHS TO LIVE. BRING SOME PAPER AND INK AND WRITE WHAT I TELL YOU TO TIMOTHY.
I'LL BRING IT THE NEXT TIME I VISIT YOU.

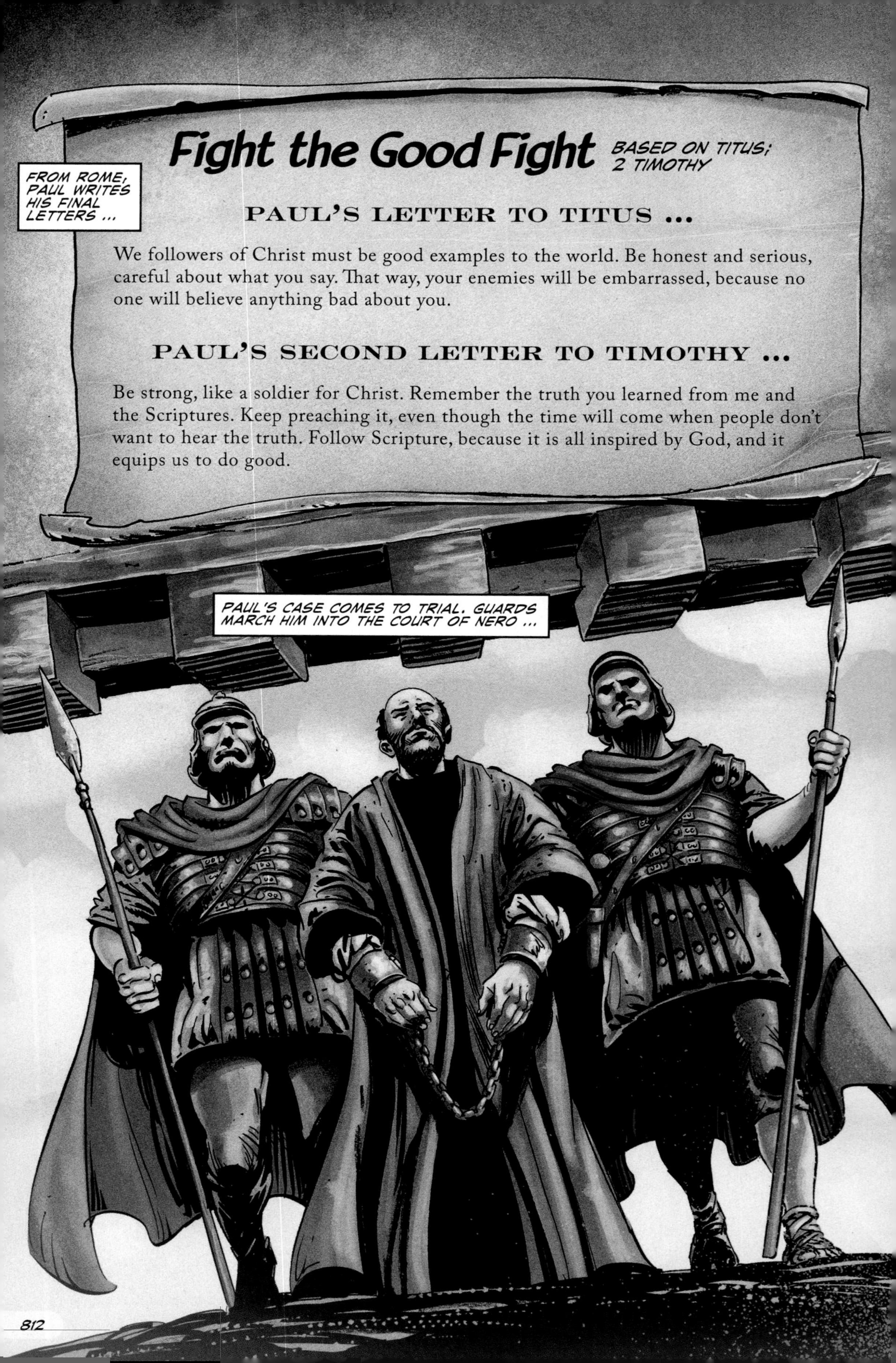
Fight the Good Fight
BASED ON TITUS; 2 TIMOTHY
FROM ROME, PAUL WRITES HIS FINAL LETTERS ...
PAUL'S LETTER TO TITUS ...
We followers of Christ must be good examples to the world. Be honest and serious, careful about what you say. That way, your enemies will be embarrassed, because no one will believe anything bad about you.
PAUL'S SECOND LETTER TO TIMOTHY ...
Be strong, like a soldier for Christ. Remember the truth you learned from me and the Scriptures. Keep preaching it, even though the time will come when people don't want to hear the truth. Follow Scripture, because it is all inspired by God, and it equips us to do good.
PAUL'S CASE COMES TO TRIAL. GUARDS MARCH HIM INTO THE COURT OF NERO ...

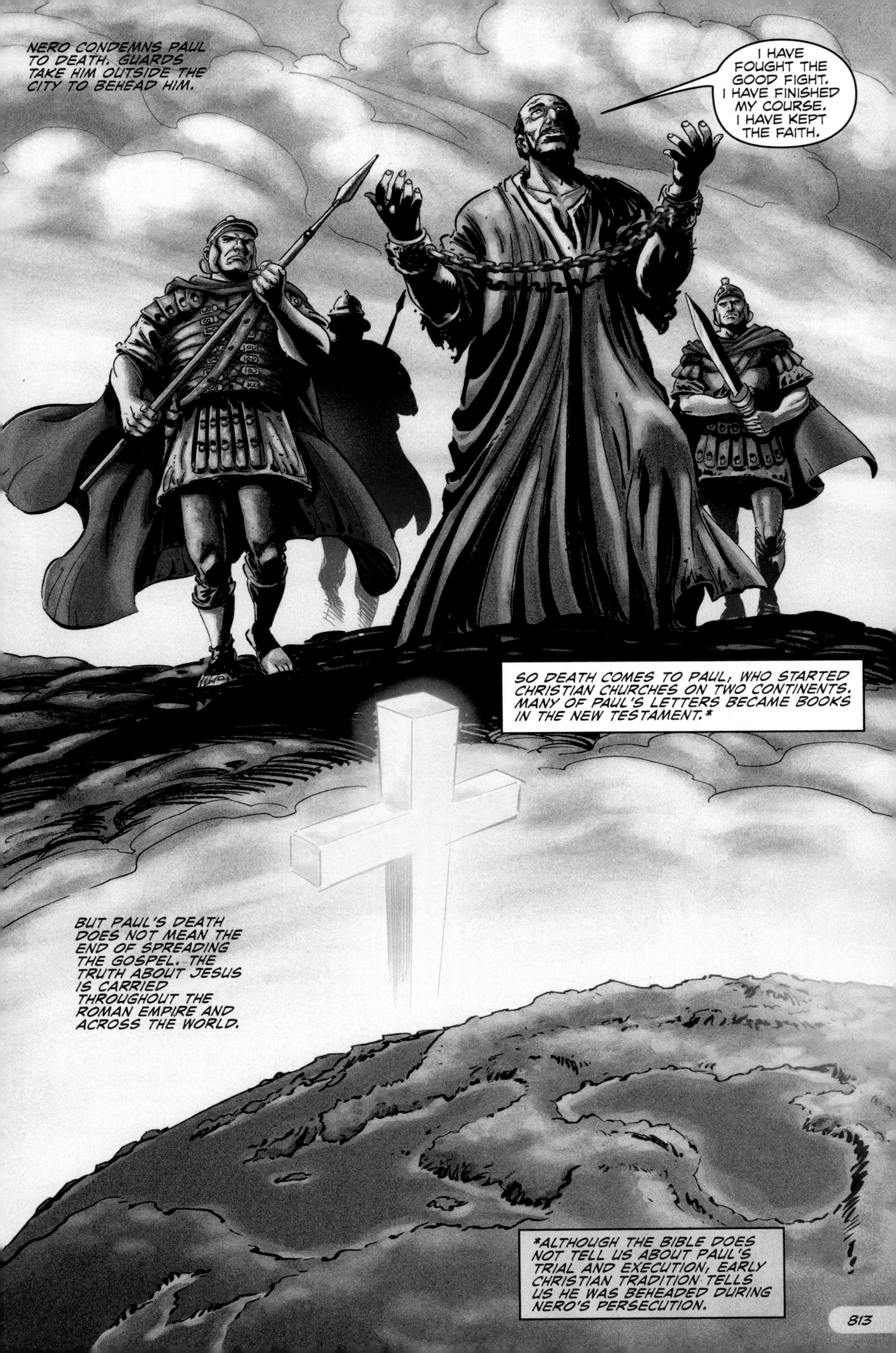
NERO CONDEMNS PAUL TO DEATH. GUARDS TAKE HIM OUTSIDE THE CITY TO BEHEAD HIM.
I HAVE FOUGHT THE GOOD FIGHT. I HAVE FINISHED MY COURSE. I HAVE KEPT THE FAITH.
SO DEATH COMES TO PAUL, WHO STARTED CHRISTIAN CHURCHES ON TWO CONTINENTS. MANY OF PAUL'S LETTERS BECAME BOOKS IN THE NEW TESTAMENT.*
BUT PAUL'S DEATH DOES NOT MEAN THE END OF SPREADING THE GOSPEL. THE TRUTH ABOUT JESUS IS CARRIED THROUGHOUT THE ROMAN EMPIRE AND ACROSS THE WORLD.
*ALTHOUGH THE BIBLE DOES NOT TELL US ABOUT PAUL'S TRIAL AND EXECUTION, EARLY CHRISTIAN TRADITION TELLS US HE WAS BEHEADED DURING NERO'S PERSECUTION.

The Final Letters

BASED ON HEBREWS—JUDE

THE LAST EIGHT LETTERS OF THE NEW TESTAMENT, HEBREWS THROUGH JUDE, ARE MESSAGES THAT JESUS' DISCIPLES WROTE TO GIVE ADVICE, COURAGE, AND COMFORT TO THE EARLY CHRISTIANS.

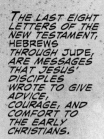

THE BOOK OF HEBREWS
THE LETTER TO THE HEBREWS WAS WRITTEN WHEN JEWISH CHRISTIANS WERE BEING PRESSURED TO GIVE UP THEIR FAITH IN JESUS AND RETURN TO THEIR JEWISH TRADITIONS. THEY ASKED THEMSELVES, WHICH IS RIGHT: FAITH IN JESUS OR FAITH IN THE RELIGION OF ABRAHAM, MOSES, AND DAVID?

In the past, God spoke to our people through the prophets. But in these last days, He has spoken to us through His Son. All the faith heroes of the past looked forward to Jesus, even though He didn't come during their lifetimes. Now that Jesus has come, throw away your sin and run the good race, because Jesus is waiting for us at the finish line. While you're running, remember what God said to us: "I will never leave you."

THE BOOK OF JAMES
THE LEADER OF THE CHURCH IN JERUSALEM, JAMES THE BROTHER OF JESUS, WROTE A LETTER TO ENCOURAGE CHRISTIANS TO LIVE IN WAYS THAT SHOW THEIR FAITH.

Faith is meaningless unless you do something with it. Take care of the helpless. Ask God for wisdom, and keep your lives pure from the muck that surrounds you. Then your prayers will be powerful and change the world.

THE BOOK OF 1 PETER
PETER WROTE TO ENCOURAGE THE CHRISTIANS WHO WERE BEING PERSECUTED. LIKE PAUL, HE WAS ALSO EXECUTED BY THE ROMANS.

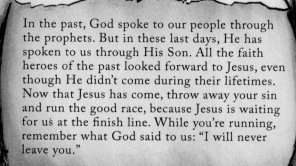

Face your hardships bravely. God chose you to be His royal priesthood and His holy nation. Even though the devil prowls like a lion to destroy you, stand firm.

THE BOOK OF 2 PETER

Don't be deceived by those who spread lies to mislead you. They'll get what they deserve when Christ returns. Don't be impatient waiting for Christ; God is taking His time so that people have a chance to repent.

JOHN, CALLED THE APOSTLE JESUS LOVED, WAS THE ONLY DISCIPLE WHO WAS NOT EXECUTED FOR HIS FAITH. HE LIVED TO AN OLD AGE, EXILED TO A GREEK ISLAND IN THE AEGEAN SEA. HE WROTE THREE LETTERS ABOUT GOD'S NATURE AND HOW CHRISTIANS SHOULD TREAT EACH OTHER.

THE BOOK OF 1 JOHN

God is pure light. Anyone who denies the truth of Jesus walks in darkness. If we pretend we've never sinned, then we're only lying to ourselves. But if we admit our sins, God forgives us and cleans us. My friends, make sure you show love to each other. Why? Because love comes from God, and by loving others we know God even better.

THE BOOK OF 2 JOHN

I am glad to hear that you are obeying God's commands and loving one another. Beware of enemies of the truth. These people say that Christ was just a man. Don't let them hang around you and do not invite them home!

I have much to say, but not with pen and ink—I cannot wait to talk with all of you face to face.

THE BOOK OF 3 JOHN

You are doing right by receiving Christians into your home, especially traveling preachers. Your kindness helps in their work. Don't copy evil. Imitate what is good. Never let anyone stop you from doing good things.

Peace to you.

JUDE WAS ANOTHER BROTHER OF JESUS WHO WROTE TO DEFEND TRUTH AGAINST FALSE TEACHERS.

THE BOOK OF JUDE

Dear friends, you must defend our Christian truth. Build up your faith, and pray with the help of the Holy Spirit. Have mercy for those who doubt, so you can save them from the fire of fear.

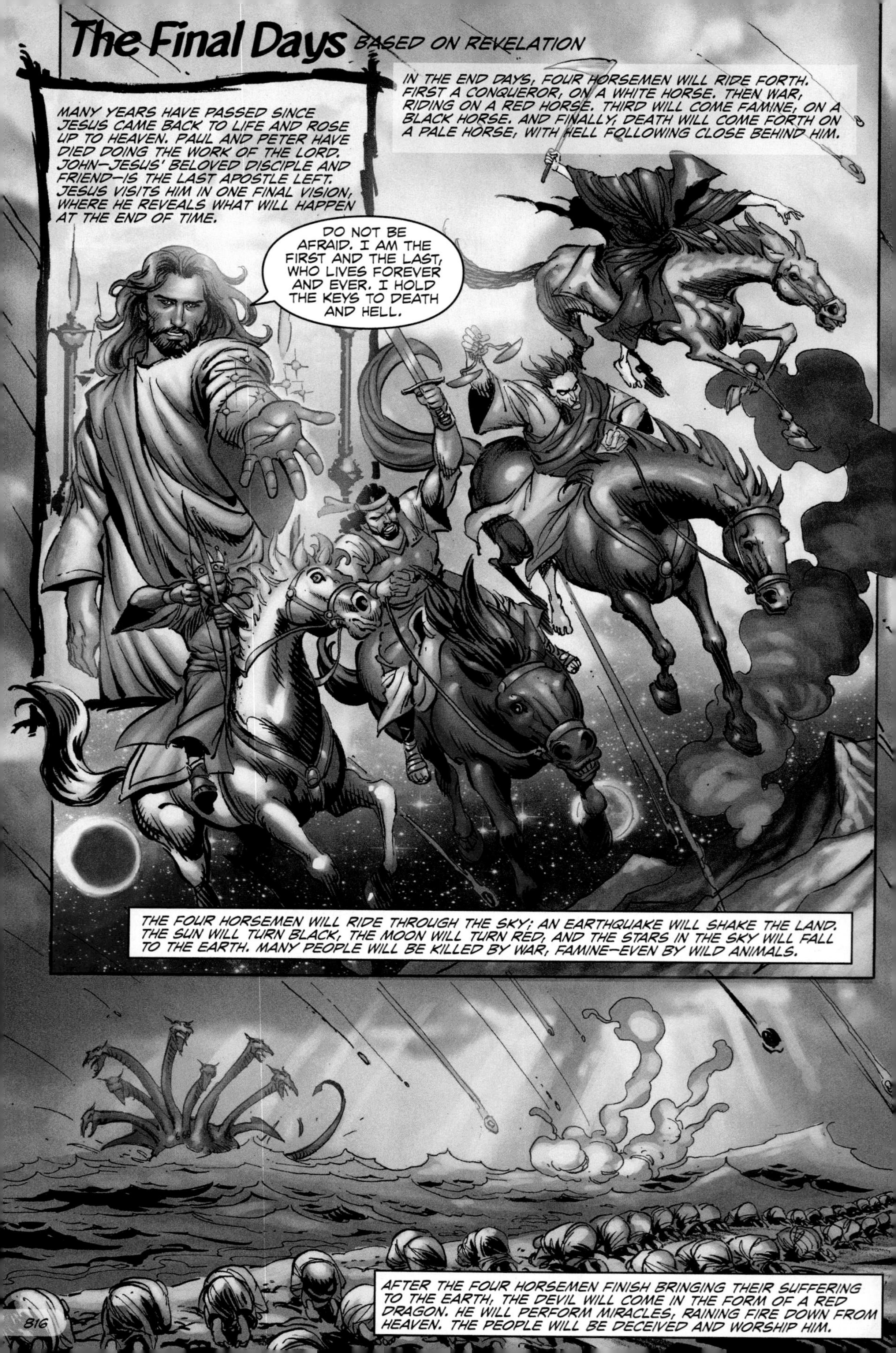
The Final Days BASED ON REVELATION
MANY YEARS HAVE PASSED SINCE JESUS CAME BACK TO LIFE AND ROSE UP TO HEAVEN. PAUL AND PETER HAVE DIED DOING THE WORK OF THE LORD. JOHN—JESUS' BELOVED DISCIPLE AND FRIEND—IS THE LAST APOSTLE LEFT. JESUS VISITS HIM IN ONE FINAL VISION, WHERE HE REVEALS WHAT WILL HAPPEN AT THE END OF TIME.
IN THE END DAYS, FOUR HORSEMEN WILL RIDE FORTH. FIRST A CONQUEROR, ON A WHITE HORSE. THEN WAR, RIDING ON A RED HORSE. THIRD WILL COME FAMINE, ON A BLACK HORSE. AND FINALLY, DEATH WILL COME FORTH ON A PALE HORSE, WITH HELL FOLLOWING CLOSE BEHIND HIM.
DO NOT BE AFRAID. I AM THE FIRST AND THE LAST, WHO LIVES FOREVER AND EVER. I HOLD THE KEYS TO DEATH AND HELL.
THE FOUR HORSEMEN WILL RIDE THROUGH THE SKY; AN EARTHQUAKE WILL SHAKE THE LAND. THE SUN WILL TURN BLACK, THE MOON WILL TURN RED, AND THE STARS IN THE SKY WILL FALL TO THE EARTH. MANY PEOPLE WILL BE KILLED BY WAR, FAMINE—EVEN BY WILD ANIMALS.
AFTER THE FOUR HORSEMEN FINISH BRINGING THEIR SUFFERING TO THE EARTH, THE DEVIL WILL COME IN THE FORM OF A RED DRAGON. HE WILL PERFORM MIRACLES, RAINING FIRE DOWN FROM HEAVEN. THE PEOPLE WILL BE DECEIVED AND WORSHIP HIM.

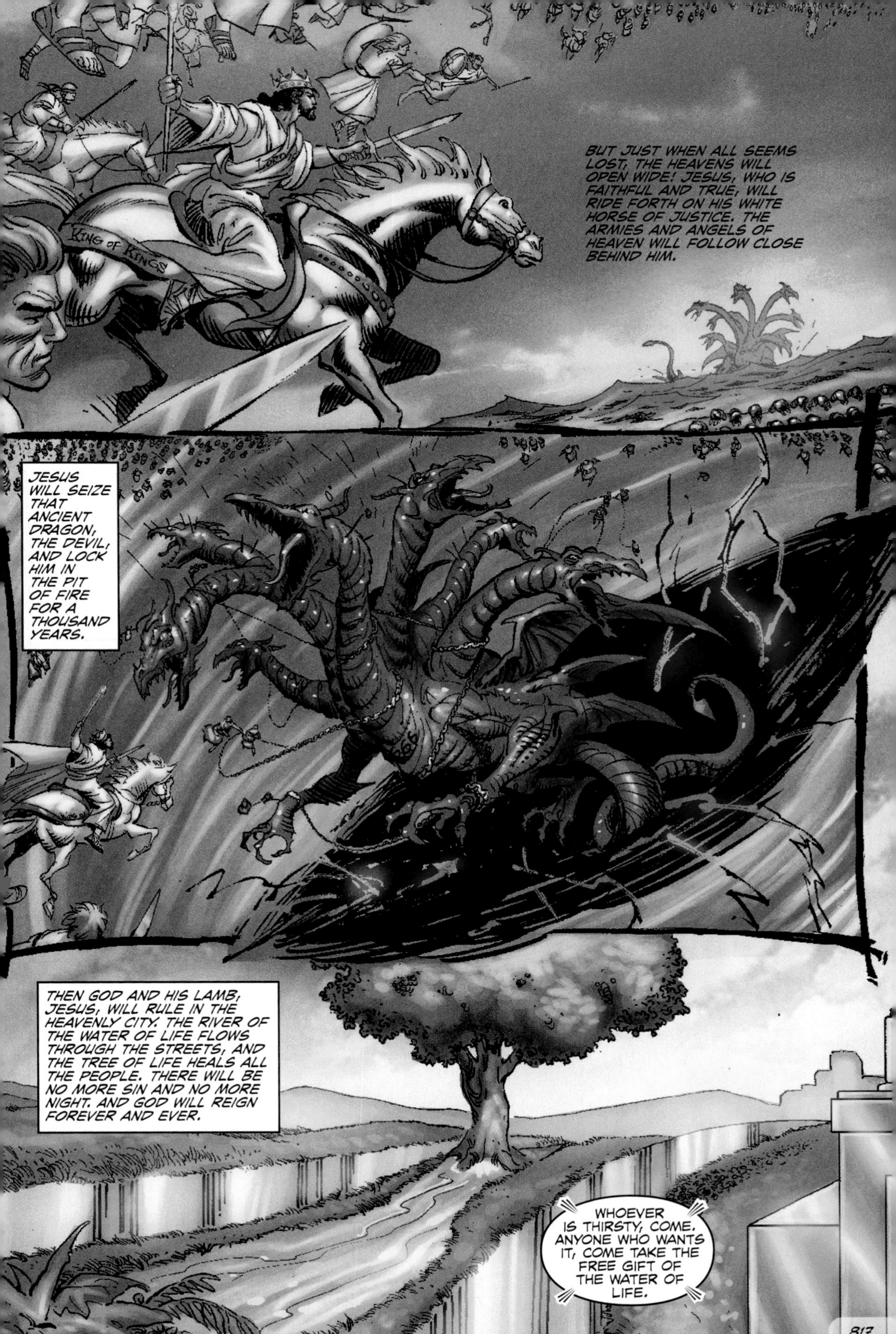
KING OF KINGS
BUT JUST WHEN ALL SEEMS LOST, THE HEAVENS WILL OPEN WIDE! JESUS, WHO IS FAITHFUL AND TRUE, WILL RIDE FORTH ON HIS WHITE HORSE OF JUSTICE. THE ARMIES AND ANGELS OF HEAVEN WILL FOLLOW CLOSE BEHIND HIM.
JESUS WILL SEIZE THAT ANCIENT DRAGON, THE DEVIL, AND LOCK HIM IN THE PIT OF FIRE FOR A THOUSAND YEARS.
THEN GOD AND HIS LAMB, JESUS, WILL RULE IN THE HEAVENLY CITY. THE RIVER OF THE WATER OF LIFE FLOWS THROUGH THE STREETS, AND THE TREE OF LIFE HEALS ALL THE PEOPLE. THERE WILL BE NO MORE SIN AND NO MORE NIGHT. AND GOD WILL REIGN FOREVER AND EVER.
WHOEVER IS THIRSTY, COME. ANYONE WHO WANTS IT, COME TAKE THE FREE GIFT OF THE WATER OF LIFE.

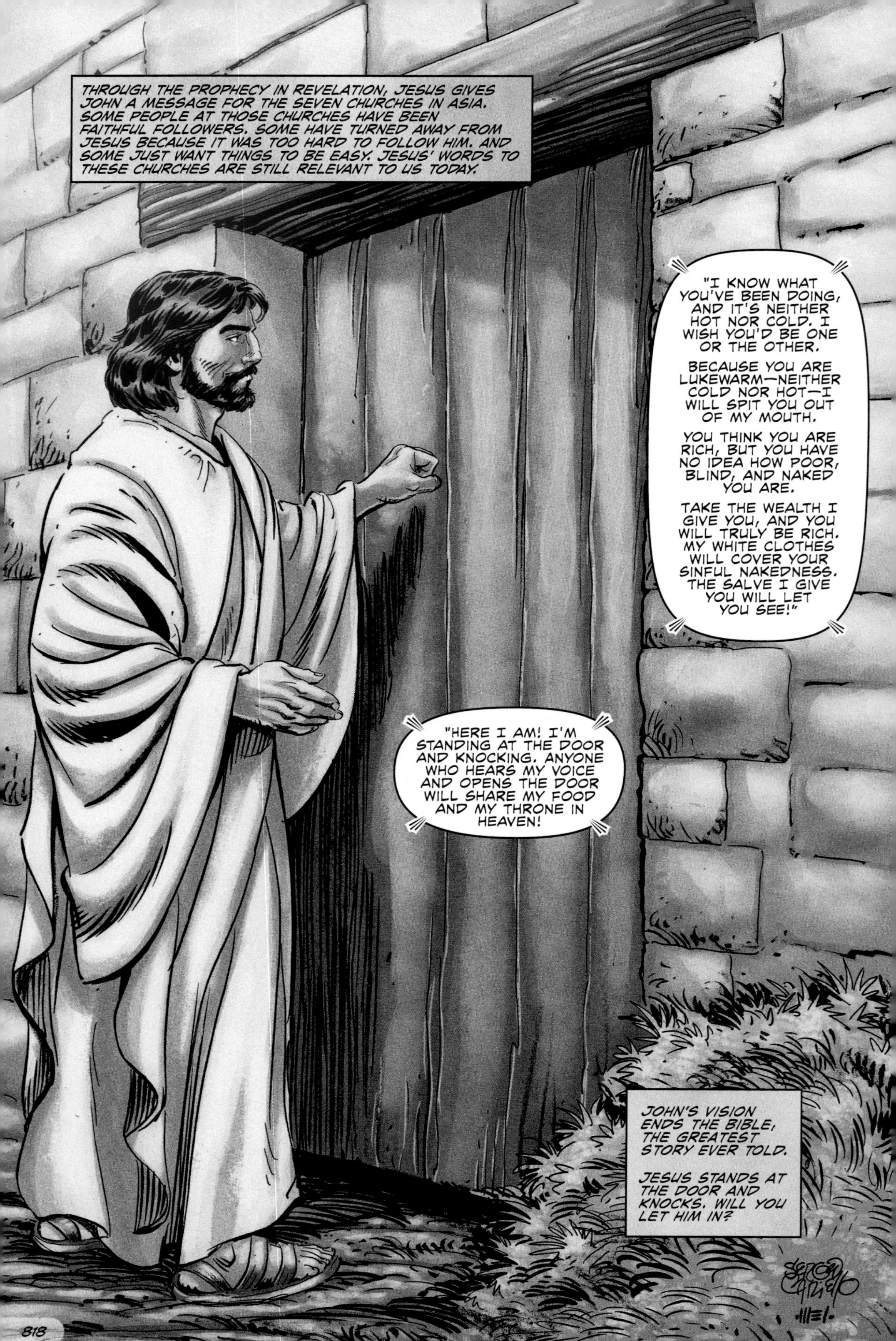
THROUGH THE PROPHECY IN REVELATION, JESUS GIVES JOHN A MESSAGE FOR THE SEVEN CHURCHES IN ASIA. SOME PEOPLE AT THOSE CHURCHES HAVE BEEN FAITHFUL FOLLOWERS. SOME HAVE TURNED AWAY FROM JESUS BECAUSE IT WAS TOO HARD TO FOLLOW HIM. AND SOME JUST WANT THINGS TO BE EASY. JESUS' WORDS TO THESE CHURCHES ARE STILL RELEVANT TO US TODAY.
"I KNOW WHAT YOU'VE BEEN DOING, AND IT'S NEITHER HOT NOR COLD. I WISH YOU'D BE ONE OR THE OTHER. BECAUSE YOU ARE LUKEWARM—NEITHER COLD NOR HOT—I WILL SPIT YOU OUT OF MY MOUTH. YOU THINK YOU ARE RICH, BUT YOU HAVE NO IDEA HOW POOR, BLIND, AND NAKED YOU ARE. TAKE THE WEALTH I GIVE YOU, AND YOU WILL TRULY BE RICH. MY WHITE CLOTHES WILL COVER YOUR SINFUL NAKEDNESS. THE SALVE I GIVE YOU WILL LET YOU SEE!"
"HERE I AM! I'M STANDING AT THE DOOR AND KNOCKING. ANYONE WHO HEARS MY VOICE AND OPENS THE DOOR WILL SHARE MY FOOD AND MY THRONE IN HEAVEN!
JOHN'S VISION ENDS THE BIBLE, THE GREATEST STORY EVER TOLD. JESUS STANDS AT THE DOOR AND KNOCKS. WILL YOU LET HIM IN?

BIBLE BOOK INDEX

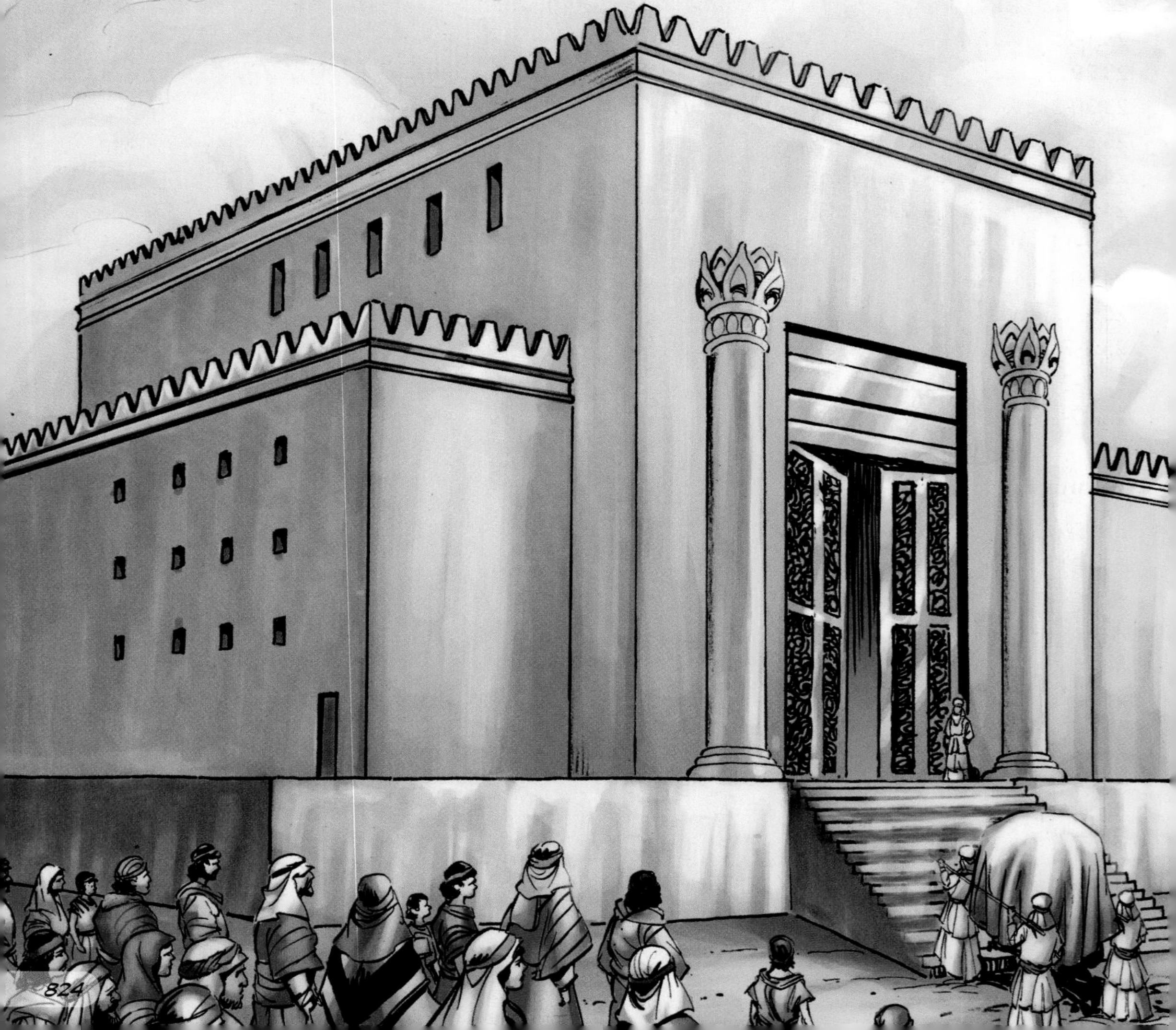

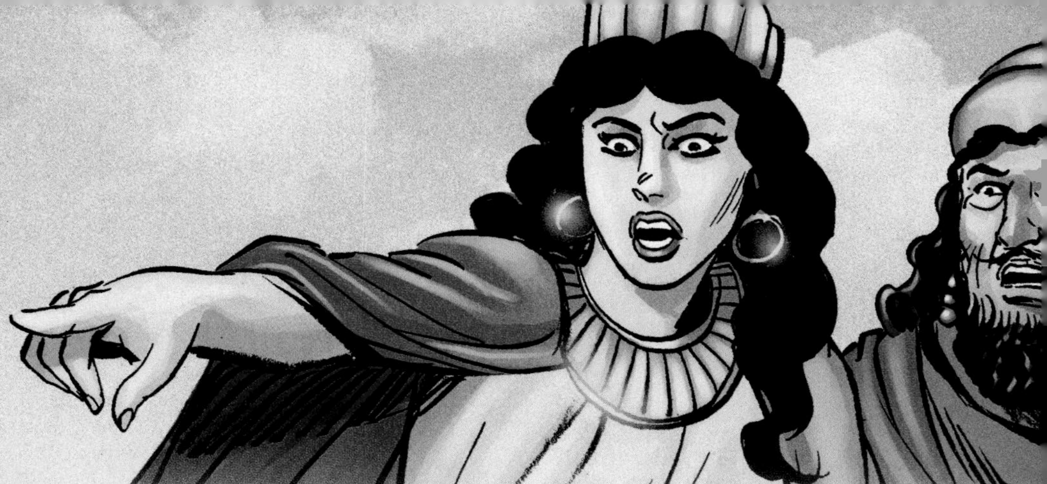

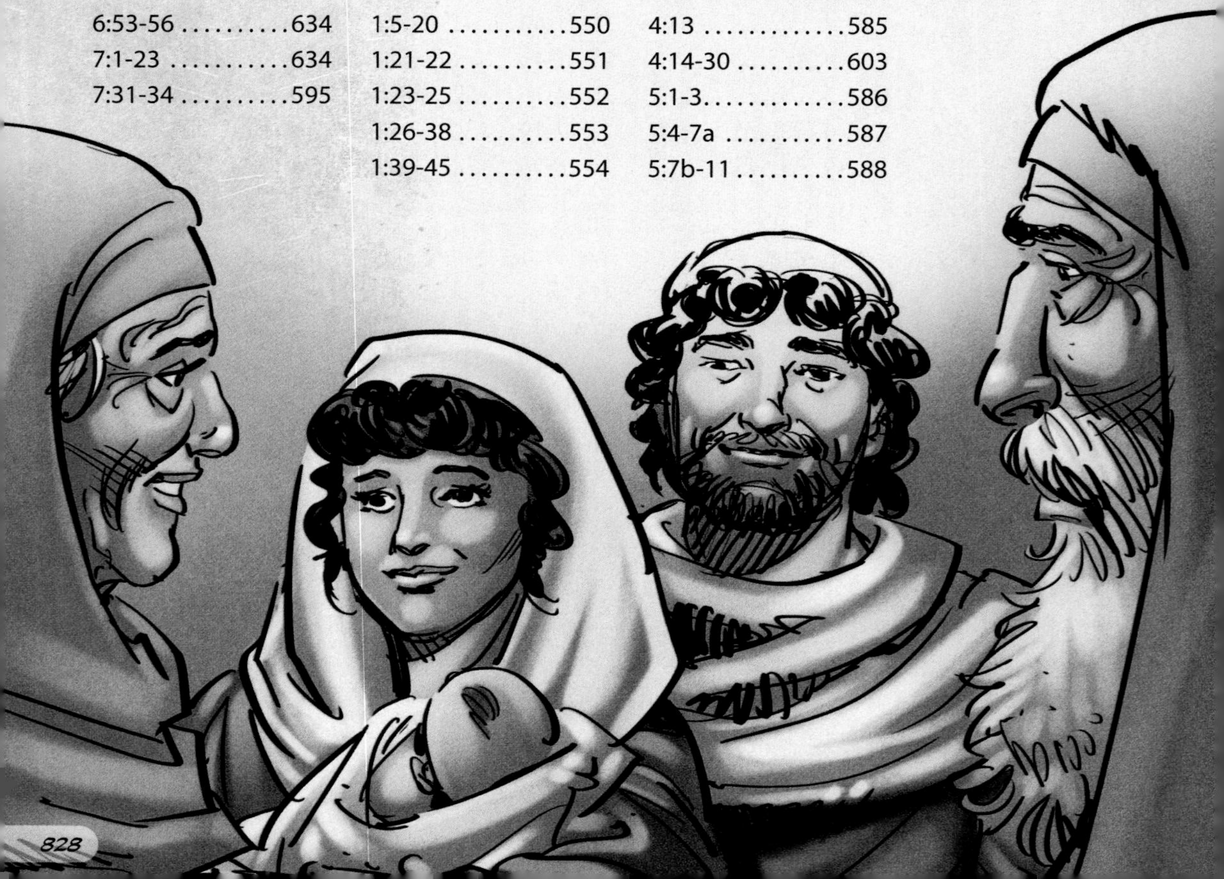

Pages 540–543 and 810–813 are based on non-biblical historical documents.

Index of Maps

Old Testament

New Testament

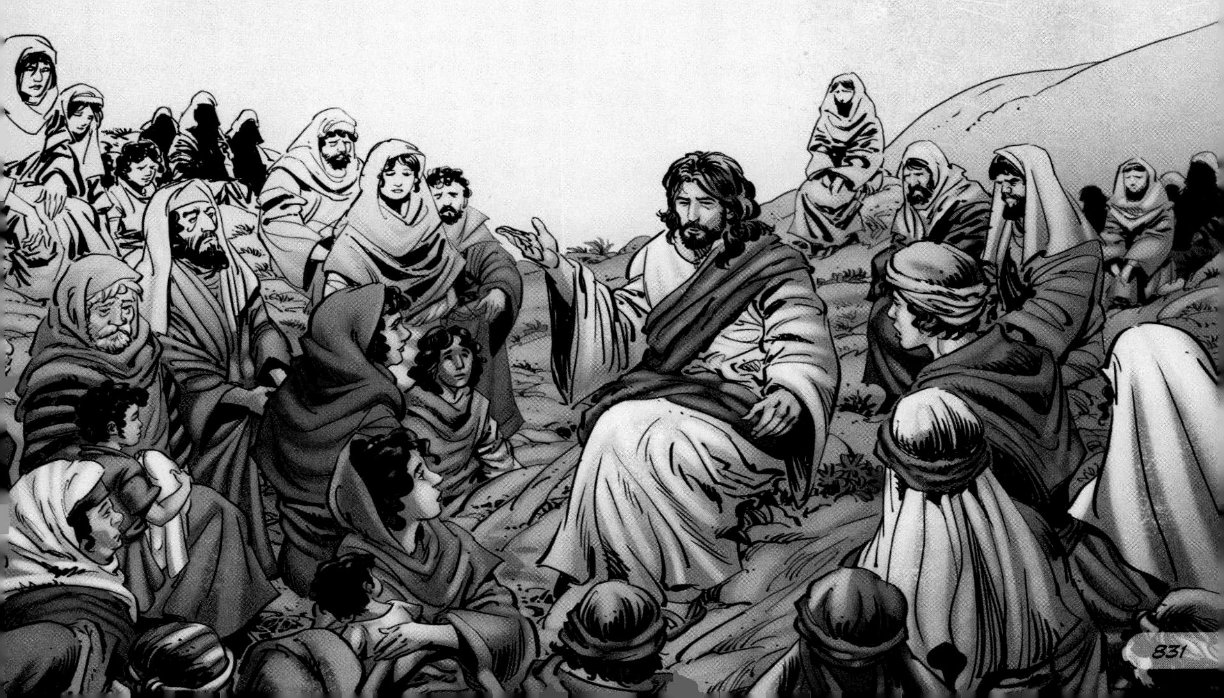

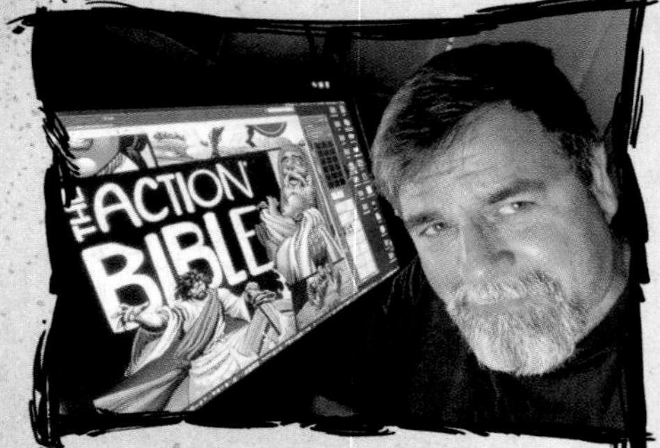
THE ACTION BIBLE

SERGIO CARIELLO WAS BORN IN BRAZIL IN 1964 AND STARTED DRAWING AS SOON AS HE COULD HOLD A PENCIL. AT THE AGE OF 5, HE ALREADY KNEW THAT HE WANTED TO BE A CARTOONIST—AND SO DID EVERYONE ELSE. HE DREW ON CHURCH BULLETINS, NAPKINS, AND EVERY SURFACE WITHIN HIS REACH.

IN FEBRUARY 2006 DAVID C COOK PUBLISHING CONTACTED HIM TO GAUGE HIS INTEREST IN A NEW PROJECT: COMPLETELY RE-ILLUSTRATING COOK'S CLASSIC *PICTURE BIBLE*. WHAT THE CHRISTIAN PUBLISHER COULDN'T KNOW IS THAT SERGIO HAD GROWN UP IN BRAZIL WITH A PORTUGUESE TRANSLATION OF THAT VERY SAME BIBLE. HE WAS READING *THE PICTURE BIBLE* BEFORE HE EVEN LEARNED HOW TO RIDE A BIKE! EVEN THOUGH HE KNEW AS A KID THAT HE WANTED TO BE A COMIC ARTIST, HE NEVER WOULD HAVE DREAMED HE WOULD ONE DAY GET TO WORK ON THIS BIBLE!

AS THE TENTH ANNIVERSARY OF *THE ACTION BIBLE* RELEASE APPROACHED, SERGIO ENTHUSIASTICALLY AGREED TO JOIN THE CELEBRATION BY PROVIDING FRESH ILLUSTRATIONS FOR NEW STORIES! FOR MORE ON SERGIO'S STORY AS WELL AS BEHIND THE SCENES FOOTAGE, VISIT THEACTIONBIBLE.COM.

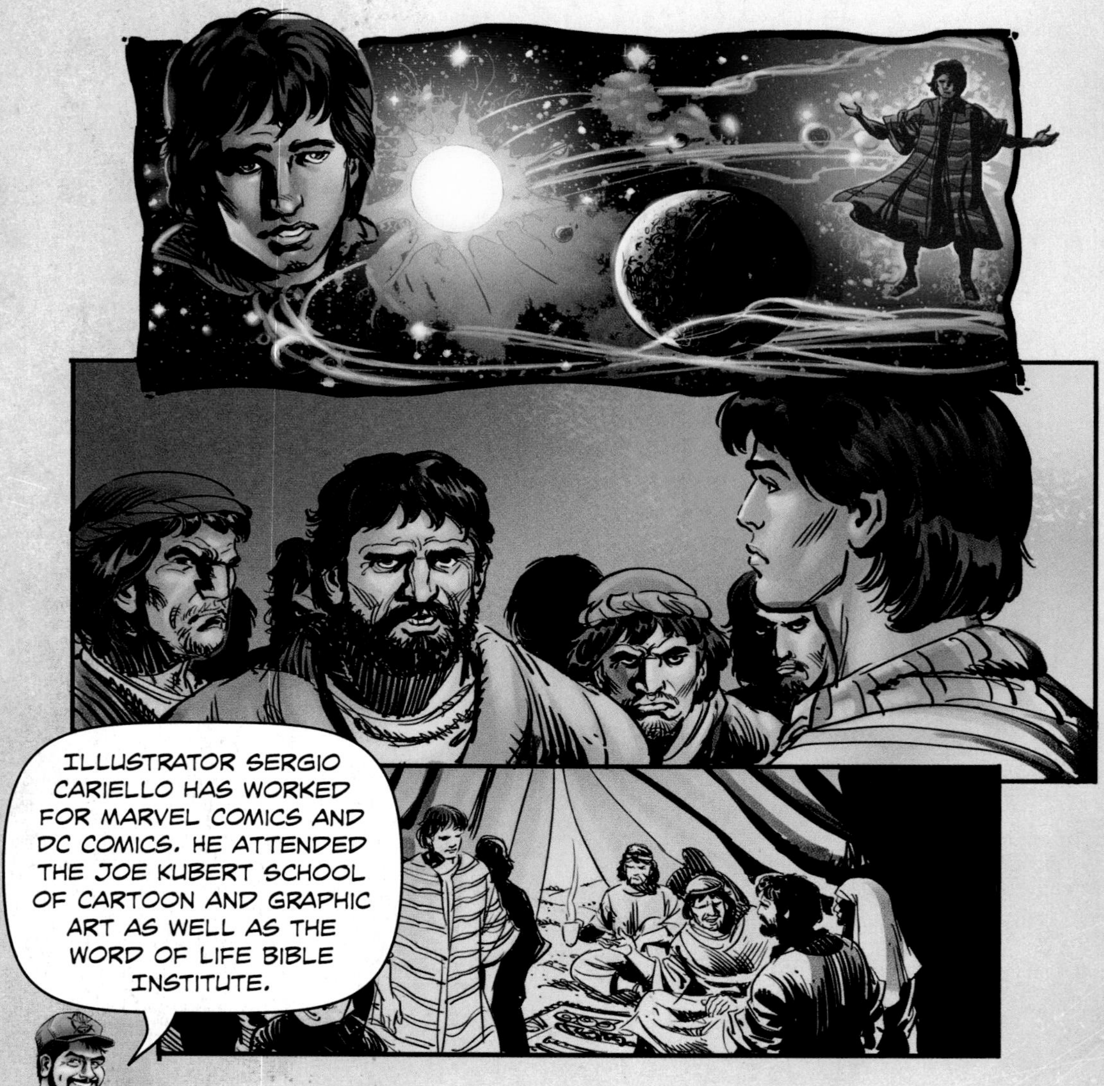
ILLUSTRATOR SERGIO CARIELLO HAS WORKED FOR MARVEL COMICS AND DC COMICS. HE ATTENDED THE JOE KUBERT SCHOOL OF CARTOON AND GRAPHIC ART AS WELL AS THE WORD OF LIFE BIBLE INSTITUTE.